Arrangement of *The Foundation Directory*

The Foundation Directory provides information on the finances, governance, and giving interests of the nation's largest grantmaking foundations—those with assets of $1 million or more or which have annual giving of at least $100,000. The information in the *Directory* is based on reports received from foundations or the most current public records available as of June 1, 1985. Grantseekers using the *Directory* to identify potential funding sources should be sure to note any limitations or restrictions on a foundation's giving program which would make his or her organization ineligible for a grant. More information on approaching foundations for funding is provided in the section on "How to Use *The Directory*."

The *Directory* is arranged alphabetically by state and, within states, by foundation name. Each entry includes the foundation's name and address, financial data for the latest year of record available, a description of funding interests, a list of officers and trustees, and its IRS Employer Identification Number. Where applicable, additional information is also provided on the types of grants and other forms of support awarded, restrictions on the giving program by geographic or subject area, publications available from the foundation, application procedures and deadlines, and the number of staff employed by the foundation.

Five indexes to the descriptive entries are provided to assist grantseekers and other users of this volume:

- The **Index of Donors, Officers, and Trustees** is an alphabetical list of individual and corporate donors, officers, and members of governing boards whose names appear in *Directory* entries.

- The **Geographic Index** lists foundations alphabetically by the states and cities in which they are located, with cross-references to foundations located elsewhere that have made substantial grants in a particular state.

- The **Types of Support Index** provides access to foundation entries by the specific types of support the

foundation awards. A glossary of types of grants and other types of support included appears at the beginning of this index. Under each type of support term, entry numbers are listed by the state location and abbreviated name of the foundation.

- The **Subject Index** provides access to the giving interests of foundations, based on the "Purpose and activities" section of the descriptive entries. A list of subject terms used is provided at the beginning of this index. Under each subject term, entry numbers are listed by the state location and abbreviated name of the foundation.

- The **Foundation Name Index** lists all foundations described in the *Directory* with the foundation's state location (using the Post Office two-letter state codes) and entry number.

In the Geographic Index, Types of Support Index, and Subject Index, foundations which award grants on a national or regional basis are listed in bold-face type. The other foundations generally limit their giving to the state or city where they are located.

In addition to the descriptive entries and indexes, the *Directory* includes three appendices. Appendix A provides descriptions of a few foundations new to the *Directory* universe for which information was received after our press deadline. Appendix B lists 192 foundations described in Edition 9 of the *Directory* that are not included in Edition 10 because they have terminated operations, changed their legal status, or no longer meet the financial criteria for inclusion. Appendix C lists 475 private foundations that hold assets of $1 million or more but do not qualify for inclusion in the *Directory* because they do not maintain ongoing grantmaking programs or their grants are restricted to specific institutions by charter. For further information, see the Introduction and the section on "How to Use *The Directory*" at the beginning of this volume.

Symbols

▼ Identifies foundations for which in-depth descriptions have been prepared for inclusion in The Foundation Center's *Source Book Profiles*.

¤ Indicates entries prepared or updated by Center staff from public records.

† Indicates individual is deceased.
(L) Ledger value of assets.
(M) Market value of assets.
* Officer is also a trustee or director.

CONTENTS

TABLES

FIGURES

THE FOUNDATION DIRECTORY

10TH EDITION

Compiled by
THE FOUNDATION CENTER

Loren Renz, Editor
Patricia Read, Editor-in-Chief

The Foundation Center
New York ● 1985

CONTRIBUTING STAFF

Director of Information Systems	Martha David
Production Editor	Rick Schoff
Assistant Editors	Susan Holt Stanley Olson
Editorial Associates	Ellen Abrams Susan Andrews Kevin Baker Gretchen Crews Michael Garland Francine Jones Diane Keitt Julia Mathews Jeffrey Sweetland Leah Weintraub
Editorial Assistants	Stephen Buscher Deborah Daniels Steven Grossmann Perry Perez
Computer Search Analysis	Phyllis Andrews Robert Chandler Sarah Johnson

The editors gratefully acknowledge the many other Foundation Center staff who contributed support, encouragement, and information which was indispensable to the preparation of this volume. Special mention should be made of the staff members of the New York and Washington, D.C. libraries who assisted in tracking changes in foundation information. We would also like to express our appreciation to the many foundations which cooperated fully in updating information prior to the compilation of this *Directory*.

Introduction

This is the tenth *Foundation Directory* issued by the Center, marking our twenty-fifth year of reference book publishing in this field. The new edition is completely revised and updated using the latest information from the foundations listed or from the most recent public records available as of June 1985.

The transformation in effective data flow to the public over the years, and the important work of our predecessors with whom the Center and its founders were associated in various ways prior to 1960 deserves mention as Edition 10 goes to press.

Seventy years ago Russell Sage Foundation published *American Foundations,* the first of 14 directories appearing between 1915 and 1955 under the imprints of Russell Sage, Twentieth Century Fund, Raymond Rich Associates, and American Foundations Information Service (AFIS). The 1915 directory consisted of only 10 pages and listed 27 foundations, and its successors through 1948 extended coverage to 899 foundations. The AFIS volume *American Foundations and Their Fields VIII* (1955), edited by Wilmer Shields Rich, the last of these pioneering directories and the first to use Treasury data under disclosure provisions of the Revenue Act of 1950, was far more comprehensive than its predecessors. Soon after the Center was established in 1956, it acquired photographic copies of records for about 7,000 organizations of the foundation type from AFIS and announced that work would begin on a new directory in mid-1957. This volume, *The Foundation Directory,* Edition 1, was three years in preparation, and documented unprecedented growth in the field in the 1950s.

Although public access to certain foundation data was mandated in the 1950 law, obstacles remained: decentralization of federal tax records, a ban on photocopying of those records by Presidential Order in 1957 (even though the records were legally open to public inspection), and the reluctance of local IRS officials to permit public examination. Marianna O. Lewis, editor of six editions of *The Foundation Directory,* and her colleagues were obliged to travel to local offices of the Internal Revenue Service in 48 of the 50 states in the late 1950s to gather information, laboriously transcribing it by hand. Officials were sometimes cooperative but more often were unhelpful, and in one notable case in California, the District Director denied access to all information except foundation names and addresses when the existence of a "foundation" set up to pay college athletes was discovered by the press.

Foundation officials, too, were reluctant to provide information. Published reports from a quarter of a century ago recite the same concerns expressed today, although infrequently, that foundations with little or no staff would be flooded with appeals, and that in any case, the privacy of private organizations ought to be respected. The answers given then are still valid: anonymity is impossible when public records exist; clear and precise published statements of a program reduce the number of inappropriate requests; and foundations are public trusts (although created from private funds) and as such should be accountable to the public and should not shield themselves from the marketplace of ideas. To quote F. Emerson Andrews in his introduction to Edition 2: "Grant applications are the lifeblood of foundations, whose sole purpose is to find good recipients for their money. To supply a bridge for two-way traffic between capable and creative persons who need support and foundations that desire to translate money into advances in knowledge and human welfare is perhaps the most useful service this *Directory* can perform."

The service this book performs has not changed, but the methods of acquiring data and the willingness of those who supply it have. There were breakthroughs in the 1960s. The Internal Revenue Service revised the old Form 990-A for calendar year 1962 requiring additional information including, for the first time, a list of grants paid. IRS files were centralized in Washington, D.C. in the early years of the decade, and the Center's Washington office, opening in 1964, began the work of copying thousands of pages for editorial use. Following the Tax Reform Act of 1969, the IRS began supplying copies of returns on film reels for all 1970 returns and then on aperture cards beginning with 1971 returns. Today more foundations supply information directly to the Center than ever before.

Editorial information-handling within the Center evolved from an environment of sharpened pencils, green visors, and mechanical hot-type setting to electronic keyboards, computer screens, and photocomposition. For Edition 10, improved database design eliminated duplicative tasks in the editorial process and released file space permitting the several new data elements found in the entries in this book.

The coverage of foundation entities today within the definition we use is virtually complete, we believe, because of federal reporting requirements and the basic structure these provide. The last Rich directory, published in 1955 using incomplete IRS data and less rigorous rules for inclusion, contained 4,162 foundations including many public charities, even the National Science Foundation. If foundations then unknown to the editors had been added, Rich estimated the number listed in her directory would have been increased to 7,800. In the improved information environment today the Center recorded in its 1985 *National Data Book* 23,578 private grantmaking foundations, 201 community foundations, and 1,309 private non-grantmaking operating foundations; in all 25,088 foundations.

WHAT'S IN THE TENTH EDITION?

Edition 10 includes entries for 4,402 foundations accounting for $63.1 billion in assets and $4.1 billion in annual giving. Although this group comprises only 18.7 percent of all active grantmaking foundations in this country, it represents approximately 97 percent of the total assets and 85 percent of the total grant dollars awarded by private foundations in 1983.

The *Directory* includes only those organizations which meet The Foundation Center's definition of a community or private grantmaking foundation and which held assets of $1 million or more or gave $100,000 or more in the latest year of record. The Center defines a foundation as a nongovernmental, nonprofit organization with its own funds (usually from a single source, either an individual, family, or corporation) and program managed by its own trustees and directors, which was established to maintain or aid educational, social, charitable, religious, or other activities serving the common welfare primarily by making grants to other nonprofit organizations.

The *Directory* does not include organizations whose giving is restricted by charter to one or more specified organizations; foundations which function as endowments for special purposes within and under the governance of a parent institution, such as a college or church; operating foundations which do not maintain active grantmaking programs; organizations which act as associations for industrial or other special groups; and organizations which make general appeals to the public for funds. A list of private foundations which meet the asset size criteria for the *Directory* but which are excluded from this volume for the reasons cited above is provided in Appendix C.

Types of Foundations

Foundations included in this *Directory*, in addition to meeting the Center's definition, fall into one of four categories:

Independent Foundation: a fund or endowment designated by the Internal Revenue Service as a private foundation under the law whose primary function is the making of grants. The assets of most independent foundations are derived from the gift of an individual or family. Some function under the voluntary direction of family members and are known as "family foundations." Depending on the range of their giving, independent foundations may also be known as "general purpose" or "special purpose" foundations.

Company-Sponsored Foundation: a private foundation under the tax law deriving its funds from a profit-making company or corporation but independently constituted, the purpose of which is to make grants, usually on a broad basis although not without regard for the business interests of the corporation. Company-sponsored foundations are legally distinct from corporate contributions programs administered within the corporation directly from corporate funds. This *Directory* does not include direct giving programs.

Operating Foundation: a fund or endowment designated under the tax law by the Internal Revenue Service as a private foundation whose primary purpose is to operate research, social welfare, or other programs determined by its governing body or charter. Most operating foundations award few or no grants to outside organizations, and therefore do not appear in the *Directory*.

Community Foundation: In its general charitable purpose, a community foundation is much like many private foundations; however, its funds are derived from many donors rather than a single source as is usually the case with private foundations. Further, community foundations are usually classified under the tax law as public charities and are therefore subject to different rules and regulations under the tax law than those which govern private foundations.

Sources of Information

To identify organizations for inclusion in this edition, Foundation Center staff researched the 5,153 foundations listed as meeting the fiscal criteria set for the *Directory* (assets of $1 million or more or annual giving of at least $100,000) in the 1983 IRS computer file of organizations filing private foundation information returns (Form 990-PF). Of these 5,153 organizations, over 750 were excluded from this volume because they had terminated, they did not meet the Center's definition of a private grantmaking foundation, or they no longer met the size criteria according to their most recent fiscal statements.

TABLE 1.　AGGREGATE FISCAL DATA BY FOUNDATION TYPE (All dollar figures expressed in thousands)

Foundation Type	Number of Foundations	Percent	Assets	Percent	Gifts Received	Percent	Total Giving*	Percent	Loans	Payout**
Independent Foundations	3,466	78.7	$52,711,992	83.6	$1,252,181	59.9	$2,898,432	71.0	$35,079	5.5
Company-Sponsored Foundations	723	16.4	2,995,589	4.7	615,239	29.4	803,580	19.7	9,958	26.8
Community Foundations	134	3.1	2,773,260	4.4	182,758	8.7	241,636	5.9	6,170	8.7
Operating Foundations	79	1.8	4,593,765	7.3	42,441	2.0	137,102	3.4	400	3.0
Total	4,402	100.0	$63,074,606	100.0	$2,092,619	100.0	$4,080,750	100.0	$51,607	6.5

*Throughout this Introduction, "Total Giving" figures include grants, scholarships, matching gifts, and program amounts paid or authorized by the foundation in the year of record. Loan amounts are indicated separately.
**Payout represents the percentage of assets paid out in total giving, not including loans.

Foundation Center staff also monitor journal and newspaper articles, press releases, and other news services related to foundation activities to identify newly-created foundations and foundations which recently received large gifts to their endowments. Entries for these foundations are prepared from the most recent IRS information returns filed and sent to the individual foundations for verification.

Requests for information were sent to each of the foundations listed in this volume, and 2,425 foundations (over 55 percent) responded fully. Entries for foundations not responding to our mailings were prepared from the most recent IRS information returns available. Entries prepared by Center staff from public records are indicated by a symbol (¤) following the foundation name.

All entries have been updated since the publication of Edition 9 and include the latest information available from government or foundation sources at the time of our press deadline. Thirteen foundations (0.3 percent) provided 1985 fiscal information; 1,051 foundations (23.9 percent) provided 1984 fiscal information; 2,407 foundations (54.7 percent) are represented by 1983 fiscal information; 872 foundations (19.8 percent) are represented by 1982 fiscal information; and 59 foundations (1.3 percent) are represented by 1981 fiscal data. Addresses, program information, and ap-plication procedures are based on the most current reports and questionnaires received by The Foundation Center, even when current fiscal data was not available.

Regulation of Foundations

Special rules for foundations, especially the first three types above, were added to the Internal Revenue Code in 1969. While these rules were modified in various ways generally favorable to the health and growth of the field in the years that followed, the basic 1969 regulatory pattern still remains.

Organizations classified as "private foundations" by federal tax law (including private operating foundations) are subject to a 2 percent excise tax on net investment income (originally 4 percent and, beginning in 1985, reduced under certain circumstances to 1 percent). With some modifications for operating foundations, they are also subject to complex rules and regulations regarding administration and grantmaking, including an annual minimum payout requirement of 5 percent of the market value of investment assets. Other rules restrict dealings between foundations and those who establish or manage them, foundation ownership of business, certain program activities of foundations, and the amounts foundations may spend on

FIGURE A.   GENERAL CHARACTERISTICS OF FOUR TYPES OF FOUNDATIONS

Foundation Type	Description	Source of Funds	Decision-Making Body	Grantmaking Activity	Reporting Requirements
Independent Foundation	An independent grant-making organization established to aid social, educational, religious, or other charitable activities	Endowment generally derived from a single source such as an individual, a family, or a group of individuals. Contributions to endowment limited as to tax deductibility	Decisions may be made by donor or members of donor's family; by an independent board of directors or trustees; or by a bank or trust officer acting on donor's behalf	Broad discretionary giving allowed but may have specific guidelines and give only in a few specific fields. About 70% limit their giving to local area	Annual information returns 990-PF filed with IRS must be made available to public. A small percentage issue separately printed annual reports
Company-sponsored Foundation	Legally an independent grantmaking organization with close ties to the corporation providing funds	Endowment and annual contributions from a profit-making corporation. May maintain small endowment and pay out most of contributions received annually in grants, or may maintain endowment to cover contributions in years when corporate profits are down	Decisions made by board of directors often composed of corporate officials, but which may include individuals with no corporate affiliation. Decisions may also be made by local company officials	Giving tends to be in fields related to corporate activities or in communities where corporation operates. Usually give more grants but in smaller dollar amounts than independent foundations	Same as above
Operating Foundation	An organization which uses its resources to conduct research or provide a direct service	Endowment usually provided from a single source, but eligible for maximum tax deductible contributions from public	Decisions generally made by independent board of directors	Makes few, if any, grants. Grants generally related directly to the foundation's program	Same as above
Community Foundation	A publicly-supported organization which makes grants for social, educational, religious, or other charitable purposes in a specific community or region	Contributions received from many donors. Usually eligible for maximum tax deductible contributions from public	Decisions made by board of directors representing the diversity of the community	Grants generally limited to charitable organizations in local community	IRS 990 return available to public. Many publish full guidelines or annual reports

administration. Federal law also requires private foundations to file a special annual information return (Form 990-PF) that is publicly available.

Recent tax law changes generally effective after January 1, 1985 increased income tax deductions for gifts to private nonoperating foundations. Such gifts are now generally deductible up to 30 percent (formerly 20 percent and still 20 percent in the case of appreciated property) of a donor's adjusted gross income. In general, gifts of appreciated property consisting of regularly marketable securities can be deducted at fair market value, and contributions in excess of the percentage limitations can be carried forward for five years.

Contributions to private operating foundations and other charities qualify for somewhat more favorable income tax deduction rules (a 50 percent of adjusted gross income limit, with a 30 percent limit for all gifts of appreciated property which are deducted at fair market value).

Community foundations are usually classified by federal tax law as "public charities" and not "private foundations." Public charities qualify for maximum income tax deductions and are generally free of the private foundation restrictions. All charitable gifts are deductible without limit for federal estate tax purposes.

Federal tax law also has implications for state regulation. The restrictions affecting private foundations are in effect incorporated into state law, and cross filing and cross-communication provisions in the law mean that federal tax rules can become a major element of state regulation of foundations. Some states, such as California, Illinois, Massachusetts, New York, and Pennsylvania, also have strong regulatory programs for charities within their borders that preceded and have now been augmented by the federal rules.

Establishment of Private Foundations

The concept of private philanthropy dates back to ancient times, but the more current understanding of foundations and philanthropy tends to be dated from the early 17th century and particularly 1601, the forty-third year of the reign of Elizabeth, when the Statute of Charitable Uses was enacted in England. While that law protected and provided what was then a new means of enforcement for charitable estates and trusts, its greater significance in history lies in the Statute's preamble where, perhaps for the first time, an effort was made to enumerate and list examples of purposes that would be (and still are) considered charitable.[1] The Statute amplified the meaning of the word. Since then, legal doctrines in the common law countries have generally preserved the favorable status of all types of charitable organizations, including foundations, churches, hospitals and colleges, ensuring their right to tax exemption and to existence in perpetuity as long as they serve a charitable function.

Most early foundations were established for the benefit of particular institutions or to answer specific social problems, such as feeding or housing the poor. In the late nineteenth and early twentieth centuries, a different approach to foundation philanthropy was introduced in the United States. These new foundations, including Russell Sage Foundation (1907), Carnegie Corporation of New York (1911), and The Rockefeller Foundation (1915), were given broad charters enabling their directors to address the causes of and seek solutions to problems affecting the world. These "general purpose" foundations have had a profound influence on the development of foundations in the United States.

---

[1] See especially *Scott on Trusts*, §§348.2, 368.1. A copy of that preamble can be seen at the Center's Gladys Brooks Library in New York City.

TABLE 2. PERIOD OF ESTABLISHMENT FOR *DIRECTORY* FOUNDATIONS BY ASSET CATEGORIES

Decade Established	Total Foundations		$100 million or more		$25 million— under $100 million		$10 million— under $25 million		$5 million— under $10 million		$1 million— under $5 million		Under $1 million	
	No.	%	No.	%	No.	%	No.	%	No.	%	No.	%	No.	%
Before 1900	38	0.9	0	—	0	—	1	0.2	6	1.0	31	1.3	0	—
1900–1909	20	0.5	0	—	6	2.3	1	0.2	3	0.5	10	0.4	0	—
1910–1919	68	1.5	8	8.3	14	5.3	9	2.0	11	1.9	25	1.2	1	0.1
1920–1929	141	3.2	7	7.3	19	7.2	16	3.5	27	4.6	69	2.9	3	0.4
1930–1939	183	4.2	19	19.8	19	7.2	39	8.6	30	5.1	67	2.9	9	1.3
1940–1949	678	15.4	28	29.2	61	23.0	103	23.0	95	15.1	327	14.1	64	9.4
1950–1959	1,510	34.3	21	21.9	77	29.0	149	33.0	195	33.1	816	35.2	252	37.0
1960–1969	973	22.1	5	5.2	39	14.7	72	16.0	139	24.5	530	22.9	188	27.6
1970–1979	516	11.7	5	5.2	24	9.0	43	9.5	59	10.0	283	12.2	102	15.0
1980–1984	169	3.8	2	2.1	6	2.3	14	3.1	16	2.7	88	3.8	43	6.3
Data not available	106	2.4	1	1.0	0	—	4	0.9	9	1.5	72	3.1	20	2.9
Total	4,402	100.0	96	100.0	265	100.0	451	100.0	590	100.0	2,318	100.0	682	100.0

The early decades of the twentieth century also marked the beginning of two other movements within the philanthropic community. The first community foundation, The Cleveland Foundation, was established in 1914 by Frederick H. Goff who believed that "better results and greater efficiency could be secured if the management and control of the property dedicated to charitable use in each community could be centralized in one or at most a few governing bodies." According to F. Emerson Andrews in *Philanthropic Giving* (Russell Sage, 1950), "the idea of the community trust was accepted enthusiastically especially by officers of trust companies, and organizations were set up at the initiative of banks in many towns and cities." Over 40 community foundations now qualifying for inclusion in the *Directory* were established within 15 years after The Cleveland Foundation began operation.

Corporations responded as well to the philanthropic spirit that pervaded the early 1900s. Although corporations were not allowed tax deductions for charitable contributions until 1936, a few corporations established their own charitable foundations long before that tax benefit took effect. The Dayton Corporation established The Dayton Foundation in Minnesota in 1918 "to promote the welfare of humankind." After the merger of the Dayton Corporation and The J.L. Hudson Company in 1969, the name was changed to Dayton Hudson Foundation, and the foundation remains a leader in the corporate philanthropic community. Other early company-sponsored foundations which still qualify for inclusion in the *Directory* include The Sears Roebuck Foundation, incorporated in 1923 in Illinois as Sears Agricultural Foundation; Bausch & Lomb Foundation, incorporated in 1927 in New York; The Belk Foundation established in 1928 in North Carolina by the Belk mercantile corporations; and The Lincoln National Life Foundation, established in 1928 and incorporated in 1962 in Indiana.

The number of foundations has grown significantly since those early days. In the decade following World War II, there was a large increase in the number of foundations established which has been attributed to the enormous societal needs that surfaced in the wake of that war, the emergence of company–sponsored foundations, a new emphasis on family foundations with living donors, and the very high tax rates then in effect. Since the 1950s, there has been a decline in the number of new foundations established—a fact which some have attributed to increased regulation of foundations. This trend was especially marked in the years immediately following the Tax Reform Act of 1969, when, as we have seen, a substantial body of special rules for private foundations was first enacted. Now, with the benefit of substantial experience and understanding of these rules and with a more hospitable regulatory climate for foundations, it is not unreasonable to expect this decline to be arrested and perhaps for a new and reasonable growth-rate period to be fostered.

Geographic Distribution of Foundations

Table 4 shows the distribution of *Directory* foundations by state and region with corresponding aggregate fiscal data. Nearly half of the nation's largest foundations are located in the Middle Atlantic states (New Jersey, New York, and Pennsylvania) and East North Central states (Illinois, Indiana, Michigan, Ohio, and Wisconsin). Foundations in these eight states account for 56.5 percent of *Directory* foundation assets and are responsible for 55.3 percent of the total dollars given by *Directory* foundations.

The relatively unequal distribution of foundation assets is rooted in past economic and industrial developments and in the personal preferences of the founders.

TABLE 3. PERIOD OF ESTABLISHMENT FOR DIRECTORY FOUNDATIONS BY FOUNDATION TYPE WITH AGGREGATE ASSETS
(All dollar figures expressed in thousands)

Decade Established	Total Foundations		Independent Foundations		Company- Sponsored Foundations		Community Foundations		Operating Foundations	
	No.	Assets	No.	Assets	No.	Assets	No.	Assets	No.	Assets
Before 1900	38	$ 109,747	35	$ 95,097	0	$ 0	0	$ 0	3	$ 14,650
1900–1909	20	298,678	15	114,350	0	0	0	0	5	184,328
1910–1919	68	3,604,465	44	2,393,027	1	9,112	19	882,579	4	319,747
1920–1929	141	4,166,437	106	3,370,774	4	15,812	23	655,386	8	124,465
1930–1939	183	11,741,492	166	11,612,643	8	58,584	5	14,404	4	55,861
1940–1949	678	13,499,945	575	12,220,603	73	348,871	16	728,108	14	202,363
1950–1959	1,510	16,383,438	1,120	11,081,982	351	1,590,724	19	230,015	20	3,480,717
1960–1969	973	6,258,631	767	5,574,035	169	336,415	22	152,294	15	195,887
1970–1979	516	5,440,934	400	4,838,620	87	491,470	24	96,458	5	14,386
1980–1984	169	1,155,235	139	1,005,752	25	136,932	5	12,551	0	0
Data not available	106	415,604	99	405,107	5	7,669	1	1,465	1	1,361
Total	4,402	$63,074,606	3,466	$52,711,992	723	$2,995,589	134	$2,773,260	79	$4,593,765

TABLE 4. FISCAL DATA OF FOUNDATIONS BY REGION AND STATE (All dollar figures expressed in thousands)

	No. of Foundations	Percent	Assets	Percent	Gifts Received	Percent	Expenditures	Percent	Total Giving	Percent
Middle Atlantic	1,226	27.9	$23,532,081	37.3	$743,438	35.5	$1,753,398	36.7	$1,484,327	36.4
New Jersey	108		2,168,900		26,098		157,485		139,966	
New York	857		16,232,459		488,538		1,257,419		1,041,259	
Pennsylvania	261		5,130,722		228,802		338,494		303,102	
East North Central	862	19.6	12,127,829	19.2	404,918	19.4	878,721	18.4	772,751	18.9
Illinois	278		4,090,261		189,179		276,706		237,849	
Indiana	64		1,403,216		27,522		77,291		67,014	
Michigan	143		3,869,976		57,562		269,405		244,592	
Ohio	273		2,121,890		103,141		193,548		169,527	
Wisconsin	104		642,486		27,514		61,771		53,769	
Pacific	488	11.1	9,328,746	14.8	235,723	11.3	621,722	13.0	536,615	13.2
Alaska	2		2,468		1,178		359		271	
California	371		8,385,377		198,550		541,590		468,551	
Hawaii	23		139,698		953		11,604		9,817	
Oregon	33		345,918		14,516		25,426		19,964	
Washington	59		455,285		20,526		42,743		38,012	
West South Central	371	8.4	5,785,322	9.2	136,686	6.5	447,769	9.4	359,244	8.8
Arkansas	12		91,210		4,215		6,709		5,379	
Louisiana	37		196,593		5,192		16,946		13,124	
Oklahoma	58		1,164,643		21,575		82,524		70,906	
Texas	264		4,332,876		105,704		341,590		269,835	
South Atlantic	539	12.2	4,961,190	7.9	141,027	6.7	383,354	8.0	322,951	7.9
Delaware	38		447,484		1,824		29,345		26,676	
District of Columbia	55		699,799		11,791		52,884		39,522	
Florida	112		773,913		50,317		67,630		58,281	
Georgia	87		755,262		23,195		53,594		43,317	
Maryland	67		363,063		17,597		36,621		30,130	
North Carolina	68		1,282,024		18,713		90,235		79,520	
South Carolina	32		179,483		7,041		11,641		9,827	
Virginia	66		419,428		9,069		38,160		32,735	
West Virginia	14		40,734		1,480		3,244		2,943	
West North Central	333	7.6	3,237,931	5.1	233,304	11.1	322,507	6.7	282,695	6.9
Iowa	32		150,630		4,645		16,708		15,172	
Kansas	40		183,683		5,812		14,460		12,253	
Minnesota	125		1,871,718		139,479		188,628		161,384	
Missouri	103		842,409		73,129		80,447		74,679	
Nebraska	27		172,090		9,719		20,421		18,118	
North Dakota	5		13,997		508		1,650		953	
South Dakota	1		3,404		12		193		136	
New England	357	8.1	2,297,955	3.6	98,262	4.7	226,496	4.7	202,382	5.0
Connecticut	108		810,775		45,075		107,866		99,839	
Maine	8		14,846		3,278		2,325		2,166	
Massachusetts	196		1,134,833		40,651		89,724		78,389	
New Hampshire	16		58,360		4,527		4,934		3,919	
Rhode Island	24		242,976		4,611		19,210		16,722	
Vermont	5		36,165		120		2,437		1,347	
Mountain	129	2.9	1,032,189	1.6	66,264	3.2	94,670	2.0	74,281	1.8
Arizona	24		232,602		38,047		26,286		15,191	
Colorado	54		549,771		16,244		48,707		42,047	
Idaho	6		19,931		3		2,026		1,892	
Montana	6		24,881		325		1,305		1,197	
Nevada	6		58,903		350		3,601		3,122	
New Mexico	8		49,145		7,073		3,524		2,741	
Utah	17		68,394		4,157		7,280		6,621	
Wyoming	8		28,562		65		1,941		1,470	
East South Central	96	2.2	770,255	1.2	32,997	1.6	52,284	1.1	45,420	1.1
Alabama	24		107,251		3,554		8,421		7,401	
Kentucky	23		203,070		12,227		15,804		13,802	
Mississippi	10		33,249		2,023		2,760		1,860	
Tennessee	39		426,685		15,193		25,299		22,357	
Puerto Rico	1	—	1,108	—	0	—	100	—	84	—
Total	4,402	100.0	$63,074,606	100.0	$2,092,619	100.0	$4,781,021	100.0	$4,080,750	100.0

These patterns have been offset to a large extent by the funding policies of the large national foundations which give substantial amounts outside the states in which they are located.

Changing demographic patterns and relatively rapid economic and industrial growth in the South, Southwest, and Pacific regions have had a strong impact on the national economy, as well as on the philanthropic world. Although foundations located in the Middle Atlantic states still represent the largest portion of foundation assets and giving, they have experienced much slower growth than foundations in other regions. In 1975 (*Foundation Directory*, Sixth Edition), foundations in the Middle Atlantic states accounted for 47.2 percent of the assets and 46 percent of the total giving of *Directory* foundations. By 1983, the portion of *Directory* foundation assets and giving represented by foundations in these three states had dropped to 37.3 percent and 36.4 percent, respectively.

Foundations in the Pacific, West South Central, and South Atlantic regions have experienced the greatest growth. Foundations in the Pacific states accounted for only 6.8 percent of the assets and 7.6 percent of the grant dollars awarded by *Directory* foundations in 1975, but by 1983 they represented 14.8 percent of the assets and 13.2 percent of the giving of *Directory* foundations. The portion of foundation assets held by foundations in the West South Central states rose from 6.5 percent in 1975 to 9.2 percent in 1983. The significant growth in these regions is also partially attributable to a few recently created or recently endowed foundations, including the J. Paul Getty Trust in California which received a major bequest of $1.2 billion in 1982, the substantial donation by the Leonard and Beryl Buck Foundation to the San Francisco Foundation in 1979, and the Fred Meyer Charitable Trust incorporated in 1982 in Oregon.

Public Accountability of Foundations

Under the requirements of the 1969 Tax Reform Act, every foundation must make its annual IRS information return (Form 990-PF) available to the public at the foundation's principal office for at least 180 days after filing. These returns are also available to the public through the IRS and The Foundation Center. This means that for every foundation there is a public record available which provides basic facts about the foundation's operations, finances, and grants. Long before the passage of the 1969 Act, however, a number of larger foundations, and even many smaller ones, had established voluntary reporting patterns that went beyond the minimum requirements set forth in that legislation.

The number of foundations that have made a commitment to providing broad information to the public about the nature of their programs, application requirements, and grant activities has grown substantially in the last decade. In 1984 and 1985, a record number of foundations responded to The Foundation Center's questionnaire mailings requesting information for the *Directory*, and over 55 percent of the entries in this edition have been verified by the foundations included.

Over 30 percent (1,332) of the foundations included in the Tenth Edition publish brochures, reports, newsletters, or other documents to inform the public about their operations. The specific nature of these publications and the number of foundations issuing them vary with the size and type of foundation and, to a lesser extent, with the geographic focus of the foundation's activities (Table 5).

The largest foundations are most likely to publish a complete annual report describing their activities. Over 70 percent of foundations with assets of $100

TABLE 5. FOUNDATIONS ISSUING ANNUAL REPORTS AND OTHER PUBLICATIONS

	Total No. of Foundations	No. Issuing Publications	Percent	No. Issuing Annual Reports	Percent	No. Issuing Brochures	Percent
All *Directory* Foundations	4,402	1,332	30.3	625	14.2	617	14.0
Geographic Orientation:							
Local	2,968	863	29.1	392	13.2	411	13.8
National or Regional	1,434	469	32.7	233	16.2	206	14.4
Foundation Type							
Independent	3,466	911	26.3	395	11.4	440	12.7
Company-Sponsored	723	265	36.7	105	14.5	150	20.7
Community	134	120	89.6	104	77.6	16	11.9
Operating	79	36	45.6	21	26.6	11	13.9
Asset Category							
$100 million and over	96	82	85.4	68	70.8	13	13.5
$50 million–under $100 m.	94	72	76.6	56	59.6	12	12.8
$25 million–under $50 m.	171	104	60.8	86	50.3	18	10.5
$10 million–under $25 m.	451	206	45.7	107	23.7	88	19.5
$5 million–under $10 m.	590	225	38.1	80	13.6	125	21.2
$1 million–under $5 m.	2,318	487	21.0	170	7.3	274	11.8
Under $1 million	682	156	22.9	58	8.5	87	12.8

TABLE 6. STAFF POSITIONS BY TYPE OF FOUNDATION

	All Foundations	Independent Foundations	Company-Sponsored Foundations	Community Foundations	Operating Foundations
Total Foundations in *Directory*	4,402	3,466	723	134	79
Foundations Responding to Survey	2,425	1,776	466	125	58
Percent Responding to Survey	55.1%	51.2%	64.5%	93.3%	73.4%
Foundations Reporting Staff	1,163	786	235	103	39
Percent of Respondents Reporting Staff	48.0%	44.3%	50.4%	82.4%	67.2%
Total Staff Positions Reported	5,724	3,874	788	514	548
Full-time Professional Positions	1,831	1,162	262	203	204
Part-time Professional Positions	712	465	117	68	62
Full-time Support Positions	1,431	916	174	162	179
Part-time Support Positions	760	479	136	75	70
Unspecified	990	852	99	6	33

million or more publish separate annual or biennial reports, and 13.5 percent of foundations in that asset category issue a separate brochure describing their program interests and application procedures instead of an annual report. Foundations in the smaller asset sizes (below $10 million) are less likely to publish separate materials about their programs, in part because of more limited staff and financial resources, and the materials they do publish are more likely to be in the form of brochures or single-page program descriptions.

Staffing Patterns of Foundations

The Foundation Center conducted separate surveys of the staffing patterns of *Directory* foundations in 1979 and 1982. In early 1985, a request for information on staff size and composition was sent with a copy of the *Directory* entry to each of the 4,402 foundations listed in this volume. Over 55 percent or 2,425 foundations responded to our request.

Of the 2,425 responding foundations, 48 percent reported employing full-time or part-time staff (Table 6). These 1,163 foundations together employ 5,724 staff members, including 1,831 full-time and 712 part-time professional staff; 1,431 full-time and 760 part-

time support staff; and 990 staff members for which the foundation did not specify position level. Information on staff shared by two or more foundations was not included as part of this survey.

Foundation staffing patterns vary considerably by the type of foundation and the size of its assets. Most community foundations (over 82 percent of those responding) employ staff to work with current and prospective donors and to administer their grantmaking programs. A high percentage of operating foundations (67.2 percent) also reported employing staff. Operating foundations also tend to have a greater number of full-time and part-time professional staff; although operating foundations represent less than 10 percent of the staffed foundations, they account for 14.3 percent of the full-time and 16.4 percent of the part-time professional positions reported.

The greater the foundation's assets, the more likely it is to employ staff. Foundations with assets of $50 million or more represent only 6.4 percent of the staffed foundations, but they account for nearly 44 percent of the total staff positions reported and over half of the full-time professional positions reported (Table 7).

Information on staff positions reported by foundations is included in their descriptive entries in this *Directory*.

TABLE 7. FOUNDATION STAFF POSITIONS BY ASSET CATEGORIES

	$100 million or more	$50 million— under $100 million	$25 million— under $50 million	$10 million— under $25 million	$5 million— under $10 million	$1 million— under $5 million	Under $1 mill.
Total Foundations in *Directory*	96	94	171	451	590	2,318	682
Foundations Responding to Survey	90	85	141	329	387	1,103	290
Percent Responding to Survey	93.8%	90.4%	82.5%	72.9%	65.6%	47.6%	42.5%
Foundations Reporting Staff	82	74	117	235	181	361	113
Percent of Respondents Reporting Staff	91.1%	87.1%	83.0%	71.4%	46.8%	32.7%	39.0%
Total Staff Positions Reported	1,899	607	620	941	507	807	343
Full-time Professional	634	279	213	292	123	179	111
Part-time Professional	84	73	78	132	98	194	53
Full-time Support	585	179	168	257	72	105	65
Part-time Support	69	45	74	199	101	202	70
Unspecified	527	31	87	61	113	127	44

TABLE 8. 50 LARGEST FOUNDATIONS BY ASSETS

Name	Assets	Total Giving	Fiscal Date
Ford Foundation	$3,497,800,000	$122,083,061	9/30/84
J. Paul Getty Trust	2,684,185,155	45,948,959	9/30/84
John T. and Catherine T. MacArthur Foundation	1,920,260,560	38,197,518	12/31/83
W. K. Kellogg Foundation	1,291,843,298	60,835,879	8/31/84
Robert Wood Johnson Foundation	1,173,836,335	57,742,282	12/31/84
Pew Memorial Trust	1,171,419,665	45,617,847	12/31/83
Rockefeller Foundation	1,101,856,013	37,889,957	12/31/84
Andrew W. Mellon Foundation	1,016,625,922	61,066,230	12/31/84
Lilly Endowment	889,437,000	24,271,000	12/31/84
Kresge Foundation	813,648,263	43,145,000	12/31/84
Charles Stewart Mott Foundation	569,037,725	26,653,627	12/31/84
Duke Endowment	551,459,647	32,999,108	12/31/84
McKnight Foundation	509,422,638	15,464,457	12/31/84
Carnegie Corporation of New York	503,942,991	19,535,239	9/30/84
W. M. Keck Foundation	500,000,000	20,000,000	12/31/84
William and Flora Hewlett Foundation	475,419,603	28,138,936	12/30/84
Richard King Mellon Foundation	465,952,000	24,520,772	12/31/84
San Francisco Foundation	461,040,287	37,753,057	6/30/84
Gannett Foundation	386,416,619	13,808,375	12/31/84
Alfred P. Sloan Foundation	371,148,237	19,855,070	12/31/84
New York Community Trust	369,988,918	37,239,322	12/31/83
J. E. and L. E. Mabee Foundation	341,450,443	18,182,834	8/31/84
Meadows Foundation	324,123,001	7,500,859	12/31/83
James Irvine Foundation	306,187,000	15,023,000	12/31/84
Cleveland Foundation	305,000,000	17,100,149	12/31/84
Houston Endowment	303,416,058	18,164,325	12/31/83
Samuel Roberts Noble Foundation	301,315,971	15,016,785	10/31/84
William Penn Foundation	278,836,985	12,047,040	12/31/84
Norton Simon Foundation	275,184,024	42,828	12/31/82
Edna McConnell Clark Foundation	274,305,565	14,065,132	9/30/84
Moody Foundation	270,000,000	13,689,894	12/31/83
Bush Foundation	261,919,051	12,365,667	11/30/84
J. Howard Pew Freedom Trust	259,978,450	7,296,000	12/31/83
Starr Foundation	258,384,711	13,955,897	12/31/83
Henry J. Kaiser Family Foundation	250,311,121	9,920,178	12/31/84
Surdna Foundation	243,073,565	14,724,555	6/30/83
Brown Foundation	241,534,223	14,833,302	6/30/84
Weingart Foundation	230,297,517	13,247,828	6/30/84
Ahmanson Foundation	211,855,538	9,433,897	10/31/84
Joyce Foundation	200,037,646	6,314,147	12/31/83
Anne Burnett and Charles D. Tandy Foundation	196,634,794	8,437,454	12/31/83
Howard Heinz Endowment	191,404,941	4,637,323	12/31/83
DeRance, Inc.	185,151,134	9,204,105	12/31/83
Henry Luce Foundation	181,681,509	4,860,042	12/31/83
Robert A. Welch Foundation	180,571,000	9,693,907	8/31/84
Chicago Community Trust	176,071,827	17,310,895	9/30/84
Amherst H. Wilder Foundation	173,516,712	21,410,781	6/30/84
Fred Meyer Charitable Trust	171,639,900	6,657,583	3/31/85
Alcoa Foundation	168,000,000	9,408,627	12/31/84
Longwood Foundation	167,901,502	7,382,296	9/30/83

TABLE 9. 50 LARGEST FOUNDATIONS BY TOTAL GIVING

Name	Total Giving	Assets	Fiscal Date
Ford Foundation	$122,083,061	$3,497,800,000	9/30/84
Andrew W. Mellon Foundation	61,066,230	1,016,625,922	12/31/84
W. K. Kellogg Foundation	60,835,879	1,291,843,298	8/31/84
Robert Wood Johnson Foundation	57,742,282	1,173,836,335	12/31/84
J. Paul Getty Trust	45,948,959	2,684,185,155	9/30/84
Pew Memorial Trust	45,617,847	1,171,419,665	12/31/83
Kresge Foundation	43,145,000	813,648,263	12/31/84
John D. and Catherine T. MacArthur Foundation	38,197,518	1,920,260,560	12/31/83
Rockefeller Foundation	37,889,957	1,101,856,013	12/31/84
San Francisco Foundation	37,753,057	461,040,287	6/30/84
New York Community Trust	37,239,322	369,988,918	12/31/83
Atlantic Richfield Foundation	35,838,831	11,895,758	12/31/84
Duke Endowment	32,999,108	551,459,647	12/31/84
General Motors Foundation	31,441,533	123,278,321	12/31/84
William and Flora Hewlett Foundation	28,138,936	475,419,603	12/30/84
Exxon Education Foundation	27,361,424	60,014,000	12/31/83
Charles Stewart Mott Foundation	26,653,627	569,037,725	12/31/84
Rockefeller Brothers Fund	26,208,888	160,055,365	12/31/83
Richard King Mellon Foundation	24,520,772	465,952,000	12/31/84
Lilly Endowment	24,271,000	889,437,000	12/31/84
Amherst H. Wilder Foundation	21,410,781	173,516,712	6/30/84
W. M. Keck Foundation	20,000,000	500,000,000	12/31/84
Arthur S. DeMoss Foundation	19,918,379	144,467,042	12/31/84
Alfred P. Sloan Foundation	19,855,070	371,148,237	12/31/84
Carnegie Corporation of New York	19,535,239	503,942,991	9/30/84
System Development Foundation	19,402,421	47,000,000	6/30/84
Amoco Foundation	19,379,851	75,804,476	12/31/84
J. E. and L. E. Mabee Foundation	18,182,834	341,450,443	8/31/84
Houston Endowment	18,164,325	303,416,058	12/31/83
High Winds Fund	17,909,307	6,634,350	12/31/82
Chicago Community Trust	17,310,895	176,071,827	9/30/84
Cleveland Foundation	17,100,149	305,000,000	12/31/84
AT&T Foundation	16,132,399	86,336,346	12/31/84
McKnight Foundation	15,464,457	509,422,638	12/31/84
James Irvine Foundation	15,023,000	306,187,000	12/31/84
Samuel Roberts Noble Foundation	15,016,785	301,315,971	10/31/84
Brown Foundation	14,833,302	241,534,223	6/30/84
Surdna Foundation	14,724,555	243,073,565	6/30/83
Mobil Foundation	14,484,000	19,736,302	12/31/84
General Electric Foundation	14,226,412	53,578,000	12/31/83
Saint Paul Foundation	14,121,091	73,859,367	12/31/84
Edna McConnell Clark Foundation	14,065,132	274,305,565	9/30/84
Starr Foundation	13,955,897	258,384,711	12/31/83
Shell Companies Foundation	13,894,959	47,609,735	12/31/83
Gannett Foundation	13,808,375	386,416,619	12/31/84
Moody Foundation	13,689,894	270,000,000	12/31/83
Weingart Foundation	13,247,828	230,297,517	6/30/84
Bush Foundation	12,365,667	261,919,051	11/30/84
Sherman Fairchild Foundation	12,075,530	148,282,112	12/31/82
William Penn Foundation	12,047,040	278,836,985	12/31/84

FOUNDATIONS IN 1983

The Foundation Center's analysis of the private foundation extract from the IRS Exempt Organization Master File shows that there are approximately 23,600 active grantmaking private foundations in the United States. In 1983, these foundations held an estimated $64.5 billion in assets and awarded approximately $4.8 billion in grants.

Most of the total foundation assets and grant dollars are attributable to the 4,402 foundations qualifying for inclusion in this volume. These 4,402 represent 18.7 percent of the total number of private foundations, but account for approximately 97 percent of the total assets held and 85 percent of the grant dollars awarded by all foundations in 1983. It is this group of foundations that is examined in the following paragraphs. Generalizations based on this aggregate data must be used with caution because of the diversity of individual private foundations and the varied conditions affecting their financial profiles.

An Increasing Number of *Directory* Foundations

The total number of foundations included in the *Directory* has grown steadily since 1977 when the present financial criteria ($1 million or more in assets or annual giving of at least $100,000) were adopted. From 1977 to 1984, 2,384 foundations have been added to the *Directory* and 700 have been dropped because they fell below the financial criteria (441 foundations), terminated operations (158), or experienced a change in status (101). During the same period the total number of active, grantmaking private foundations has remained fairly constant, ranging from 22,000 to 23,600.

The overall increase in the number of *Directory* foundations is partially attributable to the 685 foundations established during the 1970s and early 1980s and to foundations established earlier that have received substantial additions to endowment during the last decade. Market conditions over the last decade have also contributed to the increasing number of *Directory* foundations. Inflation and other economic conditions have produced appreciated foundation assets in current dollars that are sharply depreciated

when converted to constant dollars. Further, the declining value of the dollar (from $.551 in 1977 to $.335 in 1981 based on 1967 dollars) has, in effect, lowered the financial criteria for inclusion in the *Directory*.

There are 531 foundations in the Tenth Edition of the *Directory* that were not covered in the Ninth Edition, including 36 community foundations, 62 company-sponsored foundations, 6 operating foundations with major grantmaking programs, and 427 independent foundations. Eleven of these foundations hold assets of $25 million or more and were established or received major endowments during the last three years (Table 11). The most prominent of these is the J. Paul Getty Trust, an operating foundation established in 1953 which received $1.2 billion from the estate of J. Paul Getty in 1982 and now ranks as the nation's second largest private foundation.

Large and Small Foundations

Table 10 presents the number and aggregate fiscal data of *Directory* foundations in seven asset categories. There are 96 foundations (2.2 percent of the *Directory* universe) that hold assets of $100 million or more. As a group these foundations account for over half of the total assets and 35.8 percent of the total giving of all *Directory* foundations.

Over half of the foundations (2,318) in the *Directory* hold assets between $1 and $5 million, and 15.5 percent (682 foundations) hold assets under $1 million. These smaller foundations account for only 9.2 percent of *Directory* foundation assets, but they award over 21 percent of the total dollars given.

Most of the foundations which maintain assets under $1 million are company-sponsored foundations which maintain small endowments and award grants based on the contributions they receive from their parent companies.

Real Assets Rise for First Time Since 1972

The current dollar value of *Directory* foundation assets has doubled since 1972, with the largest increase in current dollar asset value (32.7 percent) occurring from 1981 to 1983. The value of *Directory* foundation

TABLE 10. FOUNDATIONS BY ASSET CATEGORIES (All dollar figures expressed in thousands)

	Number of Foundations	Percent	Assets	Percent	Gifts Received	Percent	Total Giving	Percent	Grants	Percent
$100 million and over	96	2.2	$33,643,975	53.3	$363,750	17.4	$1,459,651	35.8	$1,308,484	35.0
$50 million—under $100 million	94	2.1	6,612,602	10.5	373,696	17.8	398,472	9.8	361,389	9.7
$25 million—under $50 million	171	3.9	6,004,934	9.5	216,771	10.4	425,867	10.4	396,728	10.6
$10 million—under $25 million	451	10.2	6,861,186	10.9	334,661	16.0	532,700	13.1	497,582	13.3
$5 million—under $10 million	590	13.4	4,154,672	6.6	230,521	11.0	399,426	9.8	377,284	10.1
$1 million—under $5 million	2,318	52.7	5,538,268	8.8	367,469	17.6	578,458	14.1	535,898	14.4
Under $1 million	682	15.5	258,969	0.4	205,751	9.8	286,175	7.0	259,249	6.9
Total	4,402	100.0	$63,074,606	100.0	$2,092,619	100.0	$4,080,749	100.0	$3,736,614	100.0

TABLE 11. FOUNDATIONS NEW TO THE *DIRECTORY* WITH ASSETS OVER $25 MILLION (All dollar figures expressed in thousands)

Name	State	Establishment Date	Type of Foundation*	Fiscal Date	Assets	Gifts Received	Total Giving
J. Paul Getty Trust	CA	1953	O	9/30/84	$2,684,185	$ 459	$45,949
Horace W. Goldsmith Foundation	NY	1955	I	12/31/82	110,267	33,087	2,140
The Medical Trust	PA	1982	I	12/31/83	87,784	4,830	4,216
AT&T Foundation	NY	1984	CS	12/31/84	86,336	—	16,132
G. Harold & Leila Mathers Charitable Foundation	NY	1975	I	12/31/83	58,850	53,156	231
Jessie B. Cox Charitable Trust	MA	1982	I	10/31/83	48,352	—	4,173
Penzance Foundation	DE	1981	I	4/30/83	35,471	—	2,485
Lloyd A. Fry Foundation	IL	1959	I	2/29/84	33,286	12,595	396
Three Swallows Foundation	VA	1981	I	10/31/82	32,652	—	232
The Kettering Fund	OH	1958	I	6/30/84	32,589	—	2,125
Federated Department Stores Foundation	OH	1980**	CS	7/31/84	30,343	15,000	2,763

*Type of foundation codes: O = operating foundation; I = independent foundation; CS = company-sponsored foundation.
**Originally established in 1952, dissolved in early 1970s, and reestablished in 1980.

assets in constant dollars (based on the Consumer Price Index) increased significantly (from $17.4 billion to $21.1 billion) during the two-year period 1981–1983 despite an overall decline of 16.1 percent or $4 billion in constant dollars since 1972. That increase in constant dollar assets from 1981 to 1983 comes after a sharp drop in asset value from 1972 to 1975 and a steady plateau from 1975 to 1981 (Table 12 and Figure B).

Total giving by *Directory* foundations has risen 163.6 percent or $2.5 billion in current dollars since 1972, although in constant dollars the value of foundation giving has only increased 10.5 percent since 1972. Foundation giving rose sharply in both constant and current dollars from 1979 to 1981 when bond yields rose dramatically and federal law required foundations to pay out in grants or other charitable disbursements the greater of adjusted net income or 5 percent of the market value of assets. This payout requirement was modified by the Economic Recovery Tax Act of 1981 and set at 5 percent of the market value of assets, without regard to income. *Directory*

foundations as a group continue to make charitable awards in excess of the required 5 percent of their assets, but the 1981 legislation appears to have modified the rapid increases in foundation giving.

Total gifts received by *Directory* foundations (i.e., additions to endowment) have been increasing steadily since 1972 in both constant and current dollars. Generally the greatest portion of the total gifts received are attributable to a relatively small number of foundations. In 1983, 38 foundations (less than 1 percent of the *Directory* universe) received gifts in excess of $10 million each and as a group accounted for 45 percent of the total gifts received by *Directory* foundations.

Measuring growth in gifts received by foundations in two-year intervals is further complicated by the fact that major donations in intervening years do not appear in the aggregate totals. For example, the $1.2 billions bequest to the J. Paul Getty Trust and the $50 million bequest from the estate of Mary Ethel Pew to The Medical Trust in 1982 are not included in the 1983 aggregate totals.

TABLE 12. AGGREGATE FISCAL DATA FOR *DIRECTORY* FOUNDATIONS ADJUSTED FOR INFLATION 1972–1983
(All dollar figures expressed in thousands)

Constant Dollars based on 1967 = $1.00; 1972 = $.799; 1975 = $.62; 1977 = $.551; 1979 = $.46; 1981 = $.367; 1983 = $.335

Year of Data	No. of Foundations	Percent Increase	Assets	Percent Increase (Decrease)	Gifts Received	Percent Increase (Decrease)	Total Giving	Percent Increase (Decrease)
1972*	2,533		$31,509,711		$ 733,802		$1,548,193	
			25,176,259		586,308		1,237,006	
1975*	2,818	11.3%	28,635,339	(9.1%)	945,726	28.9%	1,807,736	16.5%
			17,753,910	(29.5%)	586,350	0.0%	1,120,796	(9.4%)
1977*	3,138	11.4%	32,358,973	13.0%	1,338,723	41.6%	2,061,784	14.1%
			17,829,794	0.4%	737,636	25.8%	1,136,043	1.4%
1979*	3,363	7.2%	38,553,328	19.1%	1,355,649	1.3%	2,483,200	20.4%
			17,734,530	(0.5%)	623,599	15.5%	1,142,272	0.5%
1981*	4,063	20.8%	47,541,276	23.3%	1,741,920	28.5%	3,479,900	40.1%
			17,447,648	(1.6%)	639,285	2.5%	1,277,123	11.8%
1983*	4,402	8.3%	63,074,606	32.7%	2,092,619	20.1%	4,080,749	17.3%
			21,129,993	21.1%	701,027	9.7%	1,367,051	7.0%

*Data drawn respectively from Editions 5, 6, 7, 8, 9, and 10 of The Foundation Directory.

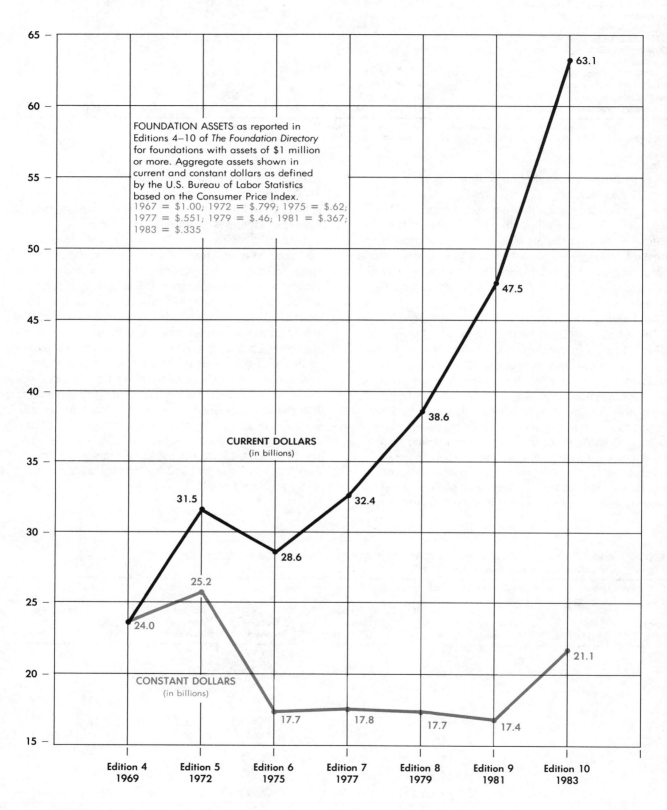

FOUNDATION ASSETS as reported in Editions 4–10 of *The Foundation Directory* for foundations with assets of $1 million or more. Aggregate assets shown in current and constant dollars as defined by the U.S. Bureau of Labor Statistics based on the Consumer Price Index. 1967 = $1.00; 1972 = $.799; 1975 = $.62; 1977 = $.551; 1979 = $.46; 1981 = $.367; 1983 = $.335

CURRENT DOLLARS
(in billions)

CONSTANT DOLLARS
(in billions)

63.1

47.5

38.6

32.4

31.5

28.6

25.2

24.0

21.1

17.7 17.8 17.7 17.4

Edition 4	Edition 5	Edition 6	Edition 7	Edition 8	Edition 9	Edition 10
1969	1972	1975	1977	1979	1981	1983

SOURCE: The Foundation Center © 1985

TABLE 13. AGGREGATE FISCAL DATA FOR INDEPENDENT FOUNDATIONS ADJUSTED FOR INFLATION 1975–1983
(All dollar figures expressed in thousands)

Constant Dollars based on 1967 = $1.00; 1975 = $.62; 1977 = $.551; 1979 = $.46; 1981 = $.367; 1983 = $.335

Year of Data	No. of Foundations	Percent Increase	Assets	Percent Increase (Decrease)	Gifts Received	Percent Increase (Decrease)	Total Grants	Percent Increase (Decrease)
1975*	2,284		$25,564,642 15,850,078		$ 685,929 425,276		$1,472,426 912,904	
1977*	2,470	8.1	28,748,812 15,840,595	12.5% (0.1%)	824,557 454,331	20.2% 6.8%	1,634,903 900,832	11.0% (1.3%)
1979*	2,618	6.0	33,828,907 15,561,297	17.7% (1.8%)	478,318 220,026	(42.0%) (51.6%)	1,910,053 878,624	16.8% (2.5%)
1981*	3,208	22.5	41,529,141 15,241,195	22.8% (2.1%)	1,057,202 387,993	121.0% 76.3%	2,583,247 948,051	35.2% 7.9%
1983*	3,466	8.0	52,711,992 17,658,917	26.9% 15.9%	1,252,181 419,481	18.4% 8.1%	2,898,432 970,974	12.2% 2.4%

* Data drawn respectively from Editions 6, 7, 8, 9, and 10 of *The Foundation Directory*.

Independent Foundations

There are 3,466 independent foundations in the Tenth Edition of the *Directory*, an increase of 9 percent (258 foundations) over the Ninth Edition. Independent foundations comprise nearly 80 percent of the total *Directory* universe. They account for 83.6 percent of the total assets and 71 percent of the total giving of *Directory* foundations.

Independent foundations fared less well than other types of foundations in the inflationary economy and regulatory environment of the 1970s. Although their combined assets in current dollars grew by $16 billion dollars from 1975 to 1981, the constant dollar value of those assets declined by over $609 million in the same six-year period. This gradual decline reversed sharply from 1981 to 1983 when assets increased by nearly 27 percent ($11.2 billion) in current dollars and the constant dollar value increased by nearly 16 percent ($2.4 billion). This was the first increase in constant dollar value of independent foundation assets since 1975 and represents an overall increase of 11.4 percent in constant dollars over 1975 levels.

Total giving by independent foundations rose sharply in 1981 in both current and constant dollars, when independent foundations paid out the equivalent of 6.2 percent of their total asset value. The high payout rate in 1981 reflected the pre-1982 payout requirements and high market rate of return on investments. With the modification of the payout requirement under the Economic Recovery Tax Act of 1981, 1983 giving by independent foundations equalled 5.5 percent of their asset value. Notwithstanding this percentage reduction, overall giving by independent foundations increased by over $315 million (12.2 percent) in current dollars and nearly $23 million in constant dollars between 1981 and 1983.

Independent foundations received gifts or additions to endowment of $1.3 billion in 1983. Over half of those gifts are attributed to 23 foundations which each

TABLE 14. 25 LARGEST INDEPENDENT FOUNDATIONS BY GIFTS RECEIVED (All dollar figures expressed in thousands)

Name	State	Gifts Received	Assets	Fiscal Date
McCune Foundation	PA	$90,608	$165,568	9/30/84
Harry Winston Research Foundation	NY	71,129	73,387	12/31/82
McKnight Foundation	MN	60,566	509,423	12/31/84
G. Harold & Leila Mathers Charitable Foundation	NY	53,157	58,850	12/31/83
The David and Lucile Packard Foundation	CA	46,582	96,288	12/31/83
Arthur S. DeMoss Foundation	PA	44,053	144,467	12/31/84
Hall Family Foundations	MO	35,748	117,877	12/31/83
Flinn Foundation	AZ	34,634	69,423	12/31/84
Horace W. Goldsmith Foundation	NY	33,087	110,267	12/31/82
Lucille P. Markey Charitable Trust	FL	23,028	17,372	6/30/84
Robert J. Kleberg, Jr. and Helen C. Kleberg Foundation	TX	18,542	51,773	12/31/83
The Fan Fox and Leslie R. Samuels Foundation	NY	17,549	19,455	7/31/84
Dillon Foundation	IL	15,486	20,618	10/31/83
J. Roderick MacArthur Foundation	IL	15,357	22,627	1/31/85
Henry P. Crowell and Susan C. Crowell Trust	IL	13,196	25,059	12/31/83
Wilbur D. May Foundation	CA	13,027	14,956	5/31/83
Ball Brothers Foundation	IN	12,653	57,049	12/31/84
Lloyd A. Fry Foundation	IL	12,595	33,286	2/29/84
M. R. Bauer Foundation	IL	12,215	29,147	12/31/83
Kresge Foundation	MI	11,774	813,648	12/31/84
Rice Foundation	IL	11,308	14,293	12/31/83
United States-Japan Foundation	NY	10,778	38,854	2/28/83
The Helen Clay Frick Foundation	PA	10,430	23,496	12/31/84
Piton Foundation	CO	9,649	3,705	11/30/83
Forchheimer Foundation	NY	9,623	3,136	12/31/82

received over $10 million in gifts (Table 14). This group includes six independent foundations that are new to the *Directory*: G. Harold and Leila Mathers Charitable Foundation established in 1975; Horace W. Goldsmith Foundation which was established in 1955

but received the major portion of its endowment during the past five years; Lucille P. Markey Charitable Trust established in 1983; J. Roderick MacArthur Foundation which was established in 1975 and received its major endowment from Mr. MacArthur's estate in 1984; Wilbur D. May Foundation established in 1951; and Lloyd A. Fry Foundation established in 1959.

Other major independent foundations that have been recently established and appear in the *Directory* for the first time include The Medical Trust, established in 1982 with a bequest from the estate of Mary Ethel Pew and which held assets of $87.8 million in 1983, and the Jessie B. Cox Charitable Trust, a split-interest trust established in 1982 in Boston which held assets of $48.4 million in 1983.

Company-Sponsored Foundations

Company-sponsored foundations are classified under current tax law as private foundations and are subject to the same rules and regulations as independent foundations. In practice, however, company-sponsored foundations generally maintain very close ties with the profit-making corporations from which they derive their funding. Their giving tends to be in fields related to corporate activities or in communities where the parent company operates, and their governing boards are frequently composed of officials of the parent company.

Company-sponsored foundations should be distinguished from direct corporate giving or company contributions programs which are administered within the corporation. Direct giving programs are based solely on corporate funds (although they can, and frequently do, include non-cash contributions such as space, equipment, staff time, or products) and tend to rise and fall with corporate profits. Company-sponsored

foundations are less subject to the ups and downs of the profit cycle. Corporations may use their foundations to set aside funds in years of heavy profits that can be used to sustain their charitable giving in years when corporate earnings are lower. Although the foundation's grantmaking program and the corporation's direct giving program are often coordinated under the same general policy and may even be administered by the same staff, they are legally separate and are subject to different regulations and reporting requirements. Company-sponsored foundations are included in the *Directory*. Direct giving programs are not.

There are now 723 company-sponsored foundations that qualify for inclusion in the *Directory*, an increase of 261 or 56.5 percent since 1975. They represent only 16.4 percent of the *Directory* foundations, but account for 19.7 percent of the total giving and 29.4 percent of the total gifts received by *Directory* foundations. Most company-sponsored foundations maintain relatively small endowments (nearly 45 percent hold assets under $1 million) and as a group they account for only 4.7 percent of the total assets held by *Directory* foundations.

Company-sponsored foundations generally fared much better than independent foundations during the inflationary economy of the 1970s. From 1975 to 1979, their total giving increased nearly 80 percent in current dollar value and over 33 percent in constant dollars, and the value of their assets rose by 23 percent in constant dollars during the same four-year period. Contributions from parent corporations to their foundations also increased dramatically during this period, rising over $330 million or 191.7 percent in current dollars from 1975 to 1979.

The rapid growth of company-sponsored foundations has slowed considerably since 1979. Corporate pre-tax income dropped 12.5 percent or $31.5 billion from the 1979 high of $252.7 billion to $221.2 billion

TABLE 15. AGGREGATE FISCAL DATA FOR COMPANY-SPONSORED FOUNDATIONS ADJUSTED FOR INFLATION 1975–1983
(All dollar figures expressed in thousands)

Constant Dollars based on 1967 = $1.00; 1975 = $.62; 1977 = $.551; 1979 = $.46; 1981 = $.367; 1983 = $.335

Year of Data	No. of Foundations	Percent Increase	Assets	Percent Increase (Decrease)	Gifts Received	Percent Increase (Decrease)	Total Grants	Percent Increase (Decrease)
1975*	462		$1,210,665		$174,368		$244,126	
			780,612		108,108		151,358	
1977*	545	18.0%	1,625,617	34.3%	425,959	144.3%	316,382	29.6%
			895,715	19.3%	234,703	117.1%	174,326	15.2%
1979*	602	10.5%	2,007,572	23.5%	508,684	19.4%	438,153	38.5%
			923,483	3.1%	233,995	(0.3%)	201,550	15.6%
1981*	701	16.4%	2,491,363	24.1%	469,115	(7.8%)	669,361	52.8%
			914,330	(1.0%)	172,165	(35.9%)	245,655	21.9%
1983*	723	3.0%	2,995,589	20.2%	615,239	31.1%	803,580	20.1%
			1,003,522	9.8%	206,105	19.7%	269,199	9.6%

*Data drawn respectively from Editions 6, 7, 8, 9, and 10 of *The Foundation Directory*.

TABLE 16. COMPANY-SPONSORED FOUNDATIONS BY ASSET CATEGORIES (All dollar figures expressed in thousands)

Asset Category	No. of Foundations	Percent	Total Assets	Percent	Gifts Received	Percent	Total Giving	Percent	Grants	Percent
$100 million and over	2	0.3	$ 291,278	9.7	$ 30	—	$ 40,850	5.1	$ 39,412	5.5
$50 million—under $100 million	5	0.7	349,059	11.7	80,303	13.1	83,060	10.3	72,570	10.1
$25 million—under $50 million	11	1.5	395,440	13.2	80,779	13.1	72,676	9.0	66,400	9.2
$10 million—under $25 million	45	6.2	644,429	21.5	103,517	16.8	159,386	19.8	141,693	19.6
$5 million—under $10 million	75	10.4	540,045	18.0	106,050	17.2	115,476	14.4	104,469	14.5
$1 million—under $5 million	260	36.0	663,255	22.1	124,580	20.3	169,289	21.1	151,145	21.0
Under $1 million	325	44.9	112,083	3.8	119,980	19.5	162,843	20.3	145,340	20.1
Total	723	100.0	$2,995,589	100.0	$615,239	100.0	$803,580	100.0	$721,029	100.0

in 1981. Corporate contributions to their foundations dropped nearly 8 percent or $39.5 million in current dollars during the same two-year period.

Based on estimates from The Conference Board and the Council for Financial Aid to Education, corporate pre-tax income dropped in 1982 to $165.5 billion, its lowest level since 1975, but climbed back up to $203.2 billion in 1983. Overall, corporate pre-tax income dropped by $18 billion or 8.9 percent from 1981 to 1983. Contributions from corporations to their foundations, however, rose over 30 percent (146.1 million) from 1981 to 1983, representing a significant increase in the percentage of pre-tax income corporations contributed to charity.[2]

Total giving by company-sponsored foundations has continued to grow throughout this period of declining corporate profits (Table 15). From 1979 to 1981, giving by these foundations rose by nearly 53 percent ($231 million) in current dollars. Company-sponsored foundation giving continued to grow from 1981 to 1983, although the increase (20.1 percent or $134 million) was less dramatic. In both 1981 and 1983, grants made by corporate foundations exceeded the

total contributions the foundations received from their parent companies. The disparity between the dollars received by company-sponsored foundations and the dollars they pay out in grants is narrowing.

There are 62 company-sponsored foundations that appear in this *Directory* for the first time, but 40 company-sponsored foundations have been dropped from the book because their assets or giving now fall below financial criteria or they have suspended operations. The 62 new foundations include the AT&T Foundation, established in 1984 in New York, which is currently the fifth largest company-sponsored foundation by total giving (Table 17). Three other company-sponsored foundations that are new to the *Directory* have annual giving over $1 million, including Caterpillar Foundation, which was established in 1952 and received contributions of $2.2 million in 1983; Warner Communications Foundation, established in 1959; and Federated Department Stores Foundation, which was originally incorporated in 1952 in Ohio, dissolved in the early 1970s, and reestablished in 1980.

[2] A fuller discussion of corporate philanthropic trends is provided in *Giving USA Annual Report 1985* (American Association of Fund-raising Counsel, 1985) and the *Annual Survey of Corporate Contributions* (The Conference Board).

TABLE 17. 15 LARGEST COMPANY-SPONSORED FOUNDATIONS BY TOTAL GIVING (All dollar figures expressed in thousands)

Name	State	Total Giving	Gifts Received	Assets	Fiscal Date
Atlantic Richfield Foundation	CA	$35,839	$32,184	$ 11,896	12/31/84
General Motors Foundation	MI	31,442	30	123,278	12/31/84
Exxon Education Foundation	NY	27,361	32,484	60,014	12/31/83
Amoco Foundation	IL	19,380	26,109	75,804	12/31/84
AT&T Foundation	NY	16,132	0	86,336	12/31/84
Mobil Foundation	NY	14,484	18,022	19,736	12/31/84
General Electric Foundation	CT	14,226	21,710	53,578	12/31/83
Shell Companies Foundation	TX	13,895	10,089	47,610	12/31/83
Proctor & Gamble Fund	OH	11,559	16,000	14,935	6/30/83
Dayton Hudson Foundation	MN	11,019	12,381	9,112	1/31/85
Ford Motor Foundation	MI	9,931	20,028	47,579	12/31/84
Alcoa Foundation	PA	9,409	0	168,000	12/31/84
Xerox Foundation	CT	9,400	0	9,100	12/31/84
BankAmerica Foundation	CA	9,185	0	10,537	12/31/84
Ætna Life & Casualty Foundation	CT	9,127	20,000	17,983	12/31/83

TABLE 18. AGGREGATE FISCAL DATA FOR COMMUNITY FOUNDATIONS ADJUSTED FOR INFLATION 1975–1983 (All dollar figures expressed in thousands)

Constant Dollars based on 1967 = $1.00; 1975 = $.62; 1977 = $.551; 1979 = $.46; 1981 = $.367; 1983 = $.335

Year of Data	No. of Foundations	Percent Increase	Assets	Percent Increase (Decrease)	Gifts Received	Percent Increase (Decrease)	Total Grants	Percent Increase (Decrease)
1975*	72		$1,154,267 715,646		$ 75,905 47,061		$ 69,097 42,840	
1977*	81	12.5%	1,299,369 715,952	12.6% .0%	70,191 38,675	(7.5%) (17.8%)	88,911 48,990	28.7% 14.4%
1979*	95	17.3%	1,655,430 761,498	27.4% 6.4%	344,550[1] 158,493	390.9%[1] 307.8%	102,201 47,012	14.9% 4.0%
1981*	98	3.2%	2,084,344 764,954	25.9% 0.5%	173,222 63,572	(49.7%) (59.9%)	175,106 64,263	71.3% 36.7%
1983*	134	36.7%	2,773,260 929,042	33.1% 21.5%	182,758 61,224	5.5% (3.7%)	241,636 80,948	38.0% 26.0%

*Data drawn respectively from Editions 6, 7, 8, 9, and 10 of *The Foundation Directory*.
[1]Includes Leonard and Beryl Buck Foundation gift of $264.6 million to The San Francisco Foundation.

Community Foundations

Community foundations are the fastest growing segment of the grantmaking foundation community, although they still represent a relatively small portion of the total foundation universe. There are 134 community foundations in the Tenth Edition, including 36 which appear in the *Directory* for the first time. Although they account for only 3.1 percent of all *Directory* foundations, they hold 4.4 percent of the total assets ($2.773 billion) and are responsible for 5.9 percent ($242 million) of the total giving of *Directory* foundations.

The total number of community foundations qualifying for inclusion in the *Directory* has grown by 86 percent (62 foundations) since 1975 (Table 18). Their combined assets increased by over 140 percent ($1.6 billion) in current dollars between 1975 and 1983; when assets are calculated in constant dollars, there was still an increase of $213 million or nearly 30 percent over the eight-year period. Total giving by community foundations rose by nearly 250 percent ($172.5 million) in current dollars between 1975 and 1983, and the increase in constant dollars was a significant 84 percent.

The IRS generally classifies community foundations as "public charities," and therefore donors receive maximum tax deductions for their contributions. Further, as "public charities," community foundations actively work with individuals and corporations within their communities in seeking major bequests and contributions. These factors, combined with the impact of the $264.6 million gift in 1981 from the Leonard and Beryl Buck Foundation to The San Francisco Community Foundation, have contributed significantly to the growth in community foundations. From 1975 to 1983, total gifts received by community foundations increased 140.8 percent in current dollars and over 30 percent in constant dollars. The appearance of a decline in gifts received over the last four years is due to the unusually large Buck Foundation gift in 1981.

Over half of the community foundations in the *Directory* (including most of the 38 newly qualifying foundations) hold assets under $5 million (Table 19). Only 11 community foundations (8.2 percent) hold assets over $50 million, but this group accounts for 67 percent of the assets and 66.8 percent of the total giving by community foundations.

TABLE 19. COMMUNITY FOUNDATIONS BY ASSET CATEGORIES (All dollar figures expressed in thousands)

	Number of Foundations	Percent	Total Assets	Percent	Gifts Received	Percent	Total Giving	Percent	Grants	Percent
$100 million and over	5	3.7	$1,427,393	51.5	$ 38,953	21.3	$118,053	48.9	$118,053	49.6
$50 million–under $100 million	6	4.5	429,929	15.5	38,775	21.2	43,180	17.9	42,093	17.7
$25 million–under $50 million	11	8.2	367,898	13.2	33,288	18.2	29,926	12.4	29,925	12.6
$10 million–under $25 million	13	9.7	208,110	7.5	17,527	9.6	15,319	6.3	14,387	6.0
$5 million–under $10 million	22	16.4	161,424	5.8	25,813	14.1	16,001	6.6	15,729	6.6
$1 million–under $5 million	72	53.8	176,768	6.4	26,677	14.6	17,436	7.2	16,314	6.8
Under $1 million	5	3.7	1,738	0.1	1,725	1.0	1,721	0.7	1,721	0.7
Total	134	100.0	$2,773,260	100.0	$182,758	100.0	$241,636	100.0	$238,222	100.0

TABLE 20.   15 LARGEST COMMUNITY FOUNDATIONS BY ASSETS
(All dollar figures expressed in thousands)

Name	State	Assets	Total Giving	Fiscal Date
San Francisco Foundation	CA	$461,040	$37,753	6/30/84
New York Community Trust	NY	369,989	37,239	12/31/83
Cleveland Foundation	OH	305,000	17,100	12/31/84
Chicago Community Trust	IL	176,072	17,311	9/30/84
Boston Foundation	MA	115,292	8,650	6/30/84
Communities Foundation of Texas	TX	89,521	11,311	6/30/84
Hartford Foundation for Public Giving	CT	78,130	4,513	9/30/84
Saint Paul Foundation	MN	73,859	14,121	12/31/84
Pittsburgh Foundation	PA	70,021	4,289	12/31/84
Columbus Foundation	OH	64,328	5,854	12/31/83
New Haven Foundation	CT	54,070	3,091	12/31/84
Kalamazoo Foundation	MI	44,002	3,945	12/31/84
Philadelphia Foundation	PA	43,000	3,266	4/30/84
California Community Foundation	CA	38,130	3,721	6/30/84
Metropolitan Atlanta Community Foundation	GA	37,688	3,546	6/30/84

Operating Foundations

Operating foundations are designated under the tax law as private foundations which spend or use a substantial portion of their adjusted net income for the direct conduct of the educational, charitable, or religious purposes for which they were established, rather than making grants to other organizations for these purposes. Many of the restrictions and requirements that apply to private grantmaking foundations also apply to operating foundations, but because of the special nature of their activities and the direct services they provide to the public, they receive some benefits under the tax code. These include higher charitable contribution deduction limits for donors, lower minimum payout requirements, and favored grantee status as compared with rules applicable to private grantmaking foundations.

Of the 2,126 currently active private operating foundations identified from current IRS records, only 420 held assets of $1 million or more and only 73 of these qualified for inclusion in *The Foundation Directory* because they maintain some level of outside grantmaking activity. Six operating foundations with assets under $1 million are also included in the *Directory* because they have ongoing grantmaking programs (Table 22). Each of these six receives substantial annual contributions and distributes a major portion of those contributions in grants to outside organizations or individuals.

The 79 operating foundations included in the *Directory* represent less than 4 percent of the total number of active operating foundations in the country. They account for over 65 percent of the estimated assets and roughly 30 percent of the estimated expenditures of operating foundations nationally. Drawing conclusions about the nature of all operating foundations on the basis of the relatively small number included in the *Directory* is further complicated by the unique grantmaking activities of the *Directory* operating foundations.

Nonetheless, certain distinctive characteristics of operating foundations can be seen when this small group is compared with other types of foundations in the *Directory*. Operating foundations account for less than 2 percent of the *Directory* universe, but they hold 7.3 percent of the assets and account for 3.4 percent of the total giving of *Directory* foundations (Table 1). Operating foundations pay out the equivalent of 3 percent of their assets for charitable purposes, as compared to 5.5 percent for independent, 26.5 percent for company-sponsored, and 8.6 percent for community foundations.

Nearly 80 percent ($108 million) of the total giving of operating foundations is expended for programs conducted directly by the foundation (Table 21). Of the $28.6 million spent for grants to outside organizations or individuals, $10.9 million (38.1 percent) is awarded by the five operating foundations with assets of $100 million or more and $8 million (27.9 percent) is awarded by the six operating foundations with assets under $1 million.

The Tenth Edition includes six operating foundations which appear in the *Directory* for the first time, including the nation's largest operating foundation, The

TABLE 21.   DIRECTORY OPERATING FOUNDATIONS BY ASSET CATEGORIES (All dollar figures expressed in thousands)

Asset Category	No. of Foundations	Percent	Total Assets	Percent	Total Giving	Percent	Program Amount	Other Giving
$100 million or more	5	6.3	$3,472,733	75.6	$ 77,450	56.5	$ 66,547	10,903
$50 million—under $100 million	6	7.6	444,576	9.7	20,458	14.9	18,764	1,694
$25 million—under $50 million	9	11.4	314,237	6.9	7,956	5.8	6,282	1,674
$10 million—under $25 million	12	15.2	174,657	3.8	7,731	5.7	6,053	1,678
$5 million—under $10 million	13	16.5	97,697	2.1	8,139	5.9	4,604	3,535
$1 million—under $5 million	28	35.4	84,543	1.8	4,512	3.3	2,970	1,542
Under $1 million	6	7.6	5,322	0.1	10,856	7.9	2,855	8,001
Total	79	100.0	$4,593,765	100.0	$137,102	100.0	$108,075	29,027

J. Paul Getty Trust. The Getty Trust was established in 1953 with the primary purpose of operating an art museum and received a $1.2 billion gift from the estate of J. Paul Getty in 1982. The Trust's publications explain that as an operating foundation it is required to spend 4.25 percent of the market value of its endowment on activities it develops and operates. These activities include the J. Paul Getty Museum, the Getty Center for the History of Art and the Humanities, the Getty Art History Information Program, the Getty Conservation Institute, the Getty Center for Education in the Arts, the Museum Management Institute, and the Program for Art on Film, a joint program with the Metropolitan Museum of Art. In addition, the Trust may spend a fraction of one percent of the endowment's market value on grants, and in 1984, the Trust awarded over $1 million in grants to outside organizations and individuals.

FUTURE OUTLOOK

As the Tenth Edition of the Directory goes to press, there is considerable cause for optimism about the future of private grantmaking foundations and the charitable and educational organizations that rely on them for support. A more favorable regulatory environment and an improved economy have allowed foundations to maintain and, in many cases, increase their giving power in recent years. The growing number of foundations publishing reports and information brochures about their giving programs and responding to inquiries from The Foundation Center, a trend we expect will continue, has helped nonprofit organizations cope more effectively with today's competitive grants market.

Although the number of new foundations established has dropped considerably since the 1950s, we find cause for optimism in the steady growth of community foundations across the country and in the number of major grantmaking foundations established or endowed during the last decade. There appears to be continued interest and support for the private foundation model as a flexible and effective channel for philanthropic dollars. Recent news reports indicate that the trustees of the Howard Hughes Medical Institute, a private medical research organization whose assets climbed to an estimated $5 billion with the sale of the Hughes Aircraft Company earlier this year, are considering applying for private foundation status for the Institute. This tax status would subject the Institute to the same rules and regulations that apply to all private foundations, but would increase the Institute's ability to support biomedical research through grants to other nonprofit organizations. The Center will continue to monitor and report on these and other changes in the foundation field through its Foundation Grants Index Bimonthly newsletter and in the Supplement to The Foundation Directory which will be published in the fall of 1986.

Thomas R. Buckman
President

Patricia Read
Vice-President and
    Director, Publications

TABLE 22. DIRECTORY OPERATING FOUNDATIONS WITH ASSETS UNDER $1 MILLION

Name	State	Assets	Gifts Received	Total Giving
Fund for the City of New York	NY	$998,472	$2,295,027	$1,979,002
JDR 3rd Fund	NY	960,276	5,000,000	6,789,782
Institute of Current World Affairs	NH	952,079	354,063	152,064
National Institute for the Food Service Industry	IL	861,660	644,850	172,500
Police Foundation	DC	825,488	1,745,175	1,501,922
American Conservation Association	NY	724,455	358,000	260,315

TABLE 23. 10 LARGEST DIRECTORY OPERATING FOUNDATIONS BY ASSETS

Name	State	Assets	Gifts Received	Total Giving
J. Paul Getty Trust	CA	$2,384,185,155	$ 459,334	$45,948,959
Norton Simon Foundation	CA	275,184,024	2,425,000	42,828
Robert A. Welch Foundation	TX	180,571,000	0	9,693,907
Amherst H. Wilder Foundation	MN	173,516,712	1,144,246	21,410,781
Norton Simon Art Foundation	CA	159,275,933	6,767,500	353,863
Menil Foundation	TX	92,540,521	528,036	1,853,653
Charles F. Kettering Foundation	OH	87,039,040	887,798	7,668,888
Annie E. Casey Foundation	CT	68,891,512	1,257,610	2,525,012
Russell Sage Foundation	NY	67,203,498	0	2,322,932
Liberty Fund	IN	66,671,363	0	2,080,200

Trends in Foundation Giving

The problems involved in collecting reliable trend data on patterns in philanthropic giving have been apparent for many years. In the Introduction to the first edition of *The Foundation Directory* published in 1960, F. Emerson Andrews outlined the three major obstacles to obtaining accurate data on the distribution of foundation funds: 1) the difficulty in obtaining complete information on the grants of smaller foundations; 2) the reliance on subjective judgment in assigning a single category to a grant which serves a variety of purposes (e.g., a grant which enables a British scholar to pursue scientific research at an American university); and 3) the nearly impossible task of establishing a classification system which divides the broad spectrum of human activities into a logical series of non-overlapping categories.

These obstacles have yet to be overcome, but a great deal of progress has been made. The current sampling base for The Foundation Center's grants analysis covers 460 foundations, including the 100 largest foundations by total giving. These 460 grantmakers represent less than 2 percent of the total number of active, grantmaking foundations, but they account for almost 40 percent of the total foundation grant dollars awarded annually. This analysis provides some insight into the grantmaking activities of smaller foundations based on a limited sample, as well as a reliable overview of the grantmaking patterns of the nation's largest foundations.

In addressing Andrews' second and third concerns, the Center introduced a new grant classification system in 1980 which enables us to categorize each grant by five areas: the subject focus, the type of organization receiving the grant, the special population groups served (if any), the type of support awarded, and the scope of the activity (domestic, foreign, or international). Although subjective judgments are still required to decide the primary subject focus of a grant, multiple codes are used to capture all aspects of the recipient organization, the population group served, and the type of support awarded. For example, a grant to a university library is coded under both "university" and "library," while a grant to an organization which serves minority children is coded under both "children" and "minorities." Therefore, giving trends in specific areas can be tracked over time.

Sampling Base

The sampling base for this grants analysis includes all grants of $5,000 or more awarded by 460 foundations which were reported to The Foundation Center between October 1983 and October 1984. Most of the grants were awarded in 1983 or early 1984.

The sample is heavily weighted towards large foundations. Comparing foundations represented in the sample with the national statistics presented in The Foundation Center's *National Data Book,* 9th Edition, 40 percent of foundations holding assets of $10 million or more are included in the sample, while only 9 percent of those foundations holding between $5 and $10 million in assets are included and less than 3 percent of foundations holding between $1 and $5 million are included. Nationally, foundations holding over $100 million in assets account for 28 percent of annual foundation giving, but foundations in this asset category account for 59 percent of the grant dollars reported in the sample. Table 24 details the distribution of foundations included in the sample by asset size.

The *Grants Index* includes grants reported by four types of foundations: independent foundations, company-sponsored foundations, operating foundations, and community foundations. The general characteristics of each of these types of foundations are outlined in Figure A.

Table 25 details the number of foundations and the number and dollar value of the grants they reported by foundation type. Independent foundations account

TABLE 24. FOUNDATIONS BY ASSET CATEGORY WITH AGGREGATE GRANTS DATA

Asset Category	Number of Foundations	Percent	Number of Grants	Percent	Dollar Value of Grants	Percent
$100 million and over	78	17.0	10,387	30.5	$ 975,229,138	59.2
$25 million—under $100 million	127	27.6	11,749	34.5	424,005,410	25.8
$10 million—under $25 million	86	18.7	7,156	21.0	156,821,883	9.5
$5 million—under $10 million	52	11.3	2,119	6.2	41,527,568	2.5
$1 million—under $5 million	83	18.0	1,795	5.3	37,353,244	2.3
Under $1 million	34	7.4	834	2.5	11,773,434	0.7
Total	460	100.0	34,040	100.0	$1,646,710,677	100.0

TABLE 25. DISTRIBUTION OF REPORTED GRANTS BY FOUNDATION TYPE

Foundation Type	Number of Foundations No.	Number of Foundations %	Dollar Value of Grants Amount	Dollar Value of Grants %	Number of Grants No.	Number of Grants %
Independent Foundations	320	69.5	$ 1,263,331,707	76.7	19,220	56.5
Company-Sponsored Foundations	69	15.0	273,309,785	16.6	11,607	34.1
Community Foundations	67	14.6	108,530,135	6.6	3,141	9.2
Operating Foundations	4	0.9	1,539,050	0.1	72	0.2
TOTAL	460	100.0	$1,646,710,677	100.0	34,040	100.0

for the largest portion of both the number and dollar value of grants in the sample (56.5 percent and 76.7 percent, respectively), while operating foundations whose giving is primarily limited to programs administered directly by the foundations themselves account for the smallest portion of grants in the sample.

Community foundations are heavily weighted in the sample in comparison to their overall numbers. Community foundations represented only 2.4 percent of the total number of foundations covered in the Foundation Center's *Foundation Directory*, Edition 9, and they awarded only 5 percent of the total annual

giving of foundations in that volume. In this grant analysis, community foundations represent 14.6 percent of the foundations included in the sample and 6.6 percent of the total grant dollars reported.

The number of grants reported in the 1984 Index volume increased 6 percent over the 1983 volume, but the total grant dollars reported decreased 8 percent from the 1983 level. This marginal decrease in the total dollars reported is due both to variations in the reporting patterns of participating foundations and to several large multi-year grant appropriations reported in the 1983 volume. Due to these variations in the sample, our analysis of funding trends is based on the percentage allocations of the total grants and grant dollars reported as opposed to variations in specific dollar amounts.

Geographic Distribution

Table 26 details the distribution of grants reported in the *Index* by foundation and recipient locations. Foundations located in California, Illinois, Michigan, New York, Pennsylvania, and Texas account for 71 percent of the total grant dollars reported, reflecting the relatively high concentration of large, national foundations located in these six states.

The distribution of grant dollars by the state locations of recipient organizations follows a somewhat different pattern. Organizations located in the District of Columbia, California, New York, Pennsylvania, and Texas received about 50 percent of the total grant dollars reported. Organizations in nine states (Alabama, Alaska, Idaho, Iowa, Mississippi, Montana, North Dakota, South Dakota, and Wyoming) received grants totalling over $22 million, even though no foundations located in those states are included in this year's sample.

Most foundation grants are awarded to organizations located in the United States for projects with a domestic focus. Grants to U.S. organizations to conduct international activities or to sponsor programs in foreign countries account for 2.4 percent of the grant dollars reported (Table 27), while grants to organizations outside the U.S. account for 3.5 percent of the total dollars reported. This general distribution pattern has remained fairly constant over the last five years.

TABLE 26. STATE DISTRIBUTION OF GRANTS AND GRANT MONEY REPORTED

	Grants Received		Grants Awarded	
	Dollar Value	Number	Dollar Value	Number
Alabama	$ 4,660,604	127	$	
Alaska	2,020,575	47		
Arizona	5,886,170	167	2,038,649	174
Arkansas	2,948,247	80	728,450	18
California	214,241,318	4,231	220,683,164	4,747
Colorado	24,991,317	618	14,088,970	336
Connecticut	24,877,748	704	33,910,990	1,375
Delaware	8,628,266	119	8,780,810	208
Dist. of Columbia	116,198,370	2,143	13,237,569	479
Florida	14,541,581	398	15,284,906	343
Georgia	28,673,183	337	8,475,971	62
Hawaii	3,982,932	200	2,456,943	155
Idaho	1,244,220	35		
Illinois	69,755,781	1,684	78,271,917	1,946
Indiana	32,660,908	488	31,733,720	285
Iowa	4,155,530	152		
Kansas	3,024,191	95	1,151,379	50
Kentucky	11,643,314	184	7,308,100	44
Louisiana	5,110,291	208	657,011	19
Maine	3,782,253	59	5,000	1
Maryland	17,941,424	336	1,842,503	90
Massachusetts	73,350,167	1,334	10,255,665	397
Michigan	92,383,504	1,030	186,147,771	1,688
Minnesota	56,292,338	1,464	63,567,205	2,070
Mississippi	4,836,604	71		
Missouri	23,737,293	400	20,257,030	364
Montana	1,008,986	52		
Nebraska	1,978,968	61	37,500	3
Nevada	1,470,421	43	422,000	14
New Hampshire	4,230,804	157	765,874	96
New Jersey	37,314,959	1,031	84,272,778	1,569
New Mexico	2,987,711	103	81,427	8
New York	241,068,364	5,527	442,839,418	9,045
North Carolina	40,079,140	823	27,005,891	632
North Dakota	1,988,351	50		
Ohio	39,066,013	1,201	39,200,657	1,416
Oklahoma	16,086,188	299	27,326,947	240
Oregon	18,528,146	414	11,350,173	273
Pennsylvania	121,009,903	2,357	141,943,083	2,833
Rhode Island	10,605,968	223	7,338,815	169
South Carolina	6,505,680	207	923,179	41
South Dakota	1,529,307	52		
Tennessee	18,704,896	288	3,869,234	36
Texas	121,077,226	2,035	104,136,125	1,811
Utah	2,462,936	60	847,588	16
Vermont	2,612,488	100	195,584	16
Virginia	20,868,264	495	11,304,129	132
Washington	12,725,564	294	7,314,291	271
West Virginia	1,167,882	67	115,452	12
Wisconsin	12,309,531	500	14,536,809	556
Wyoming	654,748	23		
TOTAL	**$1,589,610,573**	**33,172**	**$1,646,710,677**	**34,040**

TABLE 27. DOMESTIC AND FOREIGN GRANTS REPORTED

Type of Recipient	No. of Grants	% of Total Grants	Dollar Value of Grants	% of Total Value
Domestic	32,361	95.1	$ 1,549,876,140	94.1
Foreign	868	2.5	57,113,743	3.5
International—Domestic Recipients	811	2.4	39,720,794	2.4
Total	34,040	100.0	$ 1,646,710,677	100.0

TABLE 28. DISTRIBUTION OF GRANTS BY SUBJECT CATEGORIES REPORTED IN 1982, 1983 AND 1984

Subject	Dollar Value of Grants						Number of Grants					
	1982		1983		1984		1982		1983		1984	
	Amount	%	Amount	%	Amount	%	No.	%	No.	%	No.	%
Cultural Activities												
General	37,171,417	2.5	69,046,584	3.9	44,899,090	2.7	778	2.9	1,075	3.3	1,181	3.5
Art & Architecture	57,375,743	3.9	48,833,377	2.7	50,481,250	3.1	683	2.5	745	2.3	761	2.2
History	17,495,696	1.2	22,500,034	1.3	21,262,265	1.3	401	1.5	461	1.4	496	1.5
Language & Literature	12,373,622	0.8	20,486,702	1.1	14,610,019	0.9	347	1.3	405	1.3	487	1.4
Media & Communications	28,295,963	1.9	40,153,676	2.2	24,557,385	1.5	563	2.1	591	1.8	577	1.7
Music	35,675,627	2.4	47,451,305	2.6	44,101,153	2.7	892	3.3	1,012	3.2	1,082	3.2
Theater & Dance	20,329,342	1.4	28,835,059	1.6	29,109,165	1.8	771	2.8	862	2.7	958	2.8
TOTAL CULTURAL ACTIVITIES	208,717,410	14.1	277,306,737	15.4	229,020,327	14.0	4,435	16.4	5,151	16.0	5,542	16.3
Education												
General	20,026,578	1.3	13,971,580	0.8	18,386,648	1.1	490	1.8	422	1.3	489	1.4
Adult & Continuing	10,878,823	0.7	8,240,345	0.5	17,963,540	1.1	149	0.5	99	0.3	227	0.7
Elementary & Secondary	58,788,501	4.0	56,378,800	3.1	43,934,532	2.7	1,193	4.4	1,234	3.8	1,197	3.5
Higher (General)	258,771,164	17.4	200,108,854	11.2	195,759,421	11.9	3,122	11.5	3,808	11.8	3,937	11.6
Vocational	7,165,538	0.5	7,306,362	0.4	9,542,919	0.6	191	0.7	212	0.7	249	0.7
TOTAL EDUCATION	355,630,604	23.9	286,005,941	16.0	285,587,060	17.4	5,145	18.9	5,775	17.9	6,099	17.9
Health												
General	6,641,197	0.4	22,932,617	1.3	23,009,383	1.4	202	0.7	307	1.0	396	1.2
Medical & Health Education	76,692,261	5.1	65,167,373	3.6	56,268,951	3.4	637	2.4	627	1.9	548	1.6
Medical Care & Treatment	146,509,509	9.8	138,492,281	7.7	125,049,672	7.6	1,995	7.4	2,130	6.6	2,017	5.9
Medical Research	49,434,572	3.3	92,575,793	5.2	95,253,371	5.8	798	2.9	757	2.4	920	2.7
Mental Health	16,493,486	1.1	25,162,308	1.4	27,515,824	1.7	503	1.9	559	1.7	635	1.9
Public Health	16,297,736	1.1	45,190,199	2.5	63,348,284	3.8	449	1.7	967	3.0	1,395	4.1
TOTAL HEALTH	312,068,761	20.8	389,520,571	21.7	390,445,485	23.7	4,584	17.0	5,347	16.6	5,911	17.4
Religion												
General	18,182,170	1.2	24,928,597	1.4	27,899,720	1.7	448	1.7	466	1.5	589	1.7
Religious Education	9,725,195	0.7	12,574,978	0.7	10,451,266	0.6	147	0.5	198	0.6	223	0.7
TOTAL RELIGION	27,907,365	1.9	37,503,575	2.1	38,350,986	2.3	595	2.2	664	2.1	812	2.4
Science												
General	26,706,751	1.8	25,256,599	1.4	21,170,553	1.3	279	1.0	313	1.0	282	0.8
Life Sciences	32,017,382	2.2	44,595,830	2.5	29,381,380	1.8	450	1.7	486	1.5	349	1.0
Physical Sciences	19,769,417	1.3	23,361,182	1.3	19,209,230	1.2	490	1.8	497	1.6	508	1.5
Technology	17,787,355	1.2	67,703,768	3.8	53,118,908	3.2	425	1.6	747	2.3	1,009	3.0
TOTAL SCIENCE	96,280,905	6.5	160,917,379	9.0	122,880,071	7.5	1,644	6.1	2,043	6.4	2,148	6.3
Social Science												
General	25,784,944	1.7	34,693,880	1.9	22,089,746	1.3	323	1.2	310	1.0	336	1.0
Anthropology	1,094,074	0.1	6,491,069	0.4	6,893,233	0.4	30	0.1	85	0.3	79	0.2
Economics	12,964,509	0.9	18,912,147	1.1	12,577,129	0.8	316	1.2	394	1.2	311	0.9
Law & Legal Education	12,484,662	0.8	13,021,894	0.7	12,037,877	0.7	273	1.0	275	0.8	293	0.9
Political Science	50,034,744	3.4	58,943,320	3.3	72,727,572	4.4	762	2.8	1,161	3.6	1,335	3.9
TOTAL SOCIAL SCIENCE	102,362,933	6.9	132,062,310	7.4	126,325,557	7.6	1,704	6.3	2,225	6.9	2,354	6.9
Welfare												
General	94,349,790	6.3	114,965,578	6.4	109,826,087	6.7	3,019	11.1	3,317	10.3	3,682	10.8
Business &/Employment	44,857,620	3.0	56,472,201	3.2	51,791,648	3.1	1,066	3.9	1,485	4.6	1,464	4.3
Community Affairs	95,983,953	6.4	110,261,434	6.1	90,360,380	5.5	1,934	7.1	2,237	7.0	1,838	5.4
Consumer Interests	770,894	0.1	845,118	0.0	651,724	0.0	35	0.1	31	0.1	33	0.1
Crime & Law Enforcement	12,078,111	0.8	12,255,146	0.7	13,579,438	0.8	303	1.1	319	1.0	379	1.1
Environment & Energy	49,139,127	3.3	91,726,191	5.1	49,975,527	3.0	780	2.9	964	3.0	983	2.9
Equal Rights & Legal Services	20,037,518	1.3	23,200,303	1.3	23,755,528	1.4	452	1.7	594	1.8	599	1.8
Recreation	44,252,310	3.0	47,555,635	2.7	43,810,243	2.7	934	3.4	1,097	3.4	1,104	3.2
Rural Development	6,323,660	0.4	9,332,066	0.5	19,017,335	1.2	112	0.4	149	0.5	244	0.7
Urban Development	19,485,294	1.3	42,589,128	2.4	51,333,281	3.1	388	1.4	767	2.4	848	2.5
TOTAL WELFARE	387,278,277	25.9	509,202,800	28.4	454,101,191	27.5	9,014	33.1	10,960	34.1	11,174	32.8
TOTAL GRANTS	1,490,246,255	100.0	1,792,519,313	100.0	1,646,710,677	100.0	27,121	100.0	32,165	100.0	34,040	100.0

Subject Focus

For five years, The Foundation Center has been tracking general foundation giving trends within seven broad categories and 39 sub-categories. Table 28 provides a comparative analysis of the distribution of grants and grant dollars by all sub-categories as reported in the 1982, 1983, and 1984 *Grants Index* volumes. Table 29 shows general funding trends in the seven broad categories for the five-year period from 1980 to 1984.

Following a general pattern which began in 1980, foundations continue to place a strong emphasis on funding within the general welfare category; this category now accounts for 27.5 percent of the total dollars and 32.8 percent of the total number of grants reported. Within this category, the areas of rural and urban development show a gradual three-year increase in both the total dollar value and total number of grants reported. These two sub-categories include grants for economic and general community development, with urban development encompassing urban housing and transportation and rural development including both rural areas and developing countries. Grants for environment and energy programs have returned to the 3 percent level of the early 1980s; the slight jump to 5 percent in 1983 was largely attributable to two major awards from the Richard King Mellon Foundation and the John D. and Catherine T. MacArthur Foundation reported that year.

Despite slight increases in 1982, giving to education has been declining as a portion of foundation giving since 1979. In 1984, education grants accounted for only 17.4 percent of the total dollars reported, up very slightly over the 1983 figure but still below the 1980 and 1981 levels. In 1984 there was an increase in the percentage of dollars allocated for adult and continuing education programs, due in large part to a major award from the W.K. Kellogg Foundation to the University of Georgia for the development of a national center for adult continuing education.

Giving to health programs has remained fairly constant over the last five years. Despite a relatively high allocation in 1980, health programs have generally received between 21 and 23 percent of the foundation dollars reported. Within this category, there has been a slight decrease in the percentage of dollars allocated over the last three years for medical care and treatment and for medical education, but there were increases in the portion of funds awarded for medical research, mental health, and public health programs.

Social science allocations have been gradually increasing over five years, rising from 5.7 percent of foundation dollars reported in 1980 to 7.6 percent in 1984. Allocations for cultural programs have remained fairly constant over the last five years, accounting for roughly 14 to 15 percent of the total dollars reported.

Science programs accounted for 7.5 percent of the total foundation dollars reported in 1984, representing a slight increase over the five-year period. Despite a slight decrease in the current year, the sub-category of technology, which includes engineering and computer science programs, has received an increasing portion of foundation dollars in recent years. This increase is partly attributable to the creation of the System Development Foundation, one of the nation's 100 largest grantmakers, whose giving is focused primarily on computer science research.

Types of Recipient Organizations

An analysis of the types of organizations receiving grants (Table 30) reveals many of the same patterns as the subject analysis. Giving to direct service agencies, including a wide variety of social service agencies as well as other organizations that provide direct services such as scouting groups, recreational agencies, and employment services, has risen from 9.9 percent of dollars reported in 1980 to over 20 percent in 1984. Associations and professional societies have been receiving a steadily increasing proportion of foundation dollars, rising from 5.3 percent in 1980 to 9.0 percent

TABLE 29. GENERAL FOUNDATION FUNDING TRENDS, 1980—1984

Category	1980 Amount	Percent	1981 Amount	Percent	1982 Amount	Percent	1983 Amount	Percent	1984 Amount	Percent
Cultural Activities	160,793,884	13.5	192,559,945	15.3	208,717,410	14.0	277,306,737	15.4	229,020,327	14.0
Education	266,431,412	22.4	265,851,305	21.1	355,630,604	23.9	286,005,941	16.0	285,587,060	17.4
Health	298,918,710	25.1	282,531,602	22.5	312,068,761	20.9	389,520,571	21.7	390,445,485	23.7
Religion	28,718,935	2.4	24,678,672	2.0	27,907,365	1.9	37,503,575	2.1	38,350,986	2.3
Science	75,466,392	6.4	86,727,544	6.9	96,280,905	6.5	160,917,379	9.0	122,880,071	7.5
Social Science	67,977,493	5.7	75,431,276	6.0	102,362,933	6.9	132,062,310	7.4	126,325,557	7.6
Welfare	292,492,972	24.5	329,275,755	26.2	387,278,277	25.9	509,202,800	28.4	454,101,191	27.5
TOTAL	1,190,799,798	100.0	1,257,056,099	100.0	1,490,246,255	100.0	1,792,519,313	100.0	1,646,710,677	100.0

in 1984. This group includes a number of organizations active in social science research and education as well as health associations active in the public health area. The proportion of grant dollars awarded to hospitals and medical care facilities has been decreasing gradually, a point concurrent with the slight decrease in the field of medical care noted in the subject analysis.

Educational institutions continue to be the primary recipients of foundation dollars, receiving 35.1 percent of dollars reported in 1984. Although this percentage represents a slight increase over the 1983 figure, it is still under the levels reported in the early 1980s. Private universities and colleges show the largest decline in the percentage of dollars reported, but allocations for public universities and colleges have shown a slight increase.

Types of Support Awarded

The Grants Index System currently tracks foundation giving in eight type of support categories:

- Capital support, including grants for buildings, purchase of land or equipment, and capital fund drives;
- Continuing support, i.e., renewal grants to the same organization or program;
- Endowments;
- Fellowships and scholarships, including general student aid programs (excluding grants paid directly to individuals);
- General or operating support, including grants for ongoing programs, services, or staff positions;
- Matching or challenge grants, including grants to match funds provided by another organization as well as

provisional grants awarded on the condition that the recipient will raise additional support from other sources;
- Program development, including special projects, seed money or startup funds, program expansion, and new staff or faculty positions;
- Research, including studies, experiments, and demonstration projects.

Table 31 shows the total number and dollar value of grants awarded for each type of support category. Because some grants fall under more than one category (e.g., a challenge grant for building construction), each category is analyzed as a percentage of the total grant dollars and number of grants represented in this volume. A total of 28 percent of the grants included in this volume were designated as continuing support for a particular organization or program, as compared to 24.2 percent of the total number of grants reported in the 1983 volume.

The largest portion of grant dollars was allocated for program development, followed by capital support grants. Grants in the endowment category represent a relatively small proportion of the grants reported, but they tend to be comparatively large grants made on a one-time basis to specific institutions. The percentage of matching and challenge grants increased from 2 percent of the number of grants reported in 1980 to 3.8 percent in the current reporting year, reflecting the growing interest among grantmakers and grantseekers in using foundation dollars as leverage for building their financial support base.

TABLE 30. DISTRIBUTION OF REPORTED GRANTS BY RECIPIENT ORGANIZATION TYPE IN 1982, 1983, and 1984

	Dollar Value of Grants						Number of Grants					
	1982		1983		1984		1982		1983		1984	
	Amount	%	Amount	%	Amount	%	No.	%	No.	%	No.	%
Educational Institutions	634,449,836	42.5	608,239,491	33.9	578,088,524	35.1	8,316	30.6	9,454	29.4	9,887	29.1
Private Universities & Colleges	345,366,282	23.1	322,680,560	18.0	278,918,556	16.9	3,919	14.4	4,484	13.9	4,210	12.4
Public Universities & Colleges	127,045,203	8.5	107,300,608	6.0	138,943,125	8.4	1,724	6.4	2,172	6.8	2,492	7.3
Graduate Schools	84,740,767	5.7	119,747,672	6.6	106,281,454	6.5	1,114	4.1	1,229	3.8	1,585	4.7
Junior/Community Colleges	4,388,085	0.3	5,395,142	0.3	7,082,120	0.4	91	0.3	139	0.4	186	0.5
Schools	72,909,499	4.9	53,115,509	3.0	46,863,269	2.9	1,468	5.4	1,430	4.5	1,414	4.2
Direct Services Agencies	276,505,434	18.5	403,070,955	22.5	353,693,629	21.5	7,981	29.4	9,600	29.8	9,673	28.4
Hospitals & Medical Care Facilities	120,452,426	8.1	130,261,394	7.3	114,161,422	6.9	1,660	6.1	1,896	5.9	1,903	5.6
Research Institutes	77,373,178	5.2	165,034,808	9.2	147,311,240	8.9	1,101	4.1	1,357	4.2	1,453	4.3
Associations & Professional Societies	94,834,012	6.3	133,740,765	7.5	148,211,517	9.0	2,600	9.6	3,589	11.2	3,904	11.5
Museums & Historical Societies	88,175,431	5.9	88,120,853	4.9	90,908,369	5.5	1,134	4.2	1,258	3.9	1,300	3.8
Performing Arts Groups	60,610,977	4.1	82,162,693	4.6	75,597,995	4.6	1,668	6.1	1,910	5.9	2,031	6.0
Government Agencies	47,394,184	3.2	46,104,391	2.6	51,959,527	3.2	669	2.5	835	2.6	947	2.8
Community Funds	42,982,909	2.9	60,387,239	3.4	64,977,984	3.9	718	2.7	993	3.1	1,079	3.2
Libraries	26,511,466	1.8	36,939,705	2.1	24,621,096	1.5	370	1.4	378	1.2	421	1.2
Churches & Temples	24,800,332	1.7	24,341,632	1.4	22,938,957	1.4	572	2.1	539	1.7	745	2.2

TABLE 31. TYPE OF SUPPORT AWARDED

Type of Support	Dollar Value of Grants Amount	%	No. of Grants No.	%	Average Size of Grant
Capital Support	$ 331,705,015	20.1	4,743	13.9	$ 69,936
Continuing Support	434,650,337	26.4	9,540	28.0	45,561
Endowments	62,960,499	3.8	414	1.2	152,078
Fellowships & Scholarships	68,554,624	4.2	1,906	5.6	35,968
Matching/Challenge Grants	91,538,767	5.6	1,284	3.8	71,292
Program Development	580,970,994	35.3	10,447	30.7	55,611
General/Operating Funds	269,906,546	16.4	7,098	20.8	38,026
Research	230,538,247	14.0	2,820	8.3	81,751
TOTAL GRANTS REPORTED	$1,646,710,677		34,040		$ 48,376

Special Population Groups

Since 1980, The Foundation Center has gathered statistics on grants designated for the support of specific population groups when the intended audience is noted in the grant description or when the beneficiary is clear from the name and purpose of the recipient organization. If the intended beneficiary covers more than one population group, e.g., minority youth, elderly women, etc., the grant is included in the statistical totals for each applicable category.

Grants for general support of institutions or programs which serve broad public interests are not included as support for special population groups, although these target audiences also derive indirect benefit from the foundation support. Additionally, the category of "Children and Youth" does not include grants for general support of elementary and secondary schools, college scholarships, and general recreational agencies such as YMCAs and YWCAs since these grants serve a broader audience than children and youth.

Table 32 shows the actual dollars and the percentage of total grant dollars reported over the past four years within the 12 population categories. The percentage of grant dollars designated for special populations has increased steadily since 1981 in almost every category. This is partially due to improvement in the reporting of grants data and the amount of information available to the Center on intended audiences, but also reflects an emerging trend in foundation funding patterns. The percentage of grant dollars specified for the benefit of children and youth has risen from 7.3 percent in 1980 to 10.8 percent in 1984. Funding for programs benefitting women and girls has grown from 1.7 percent to 3.6 percent of the foundation dollars reported. There has also been a relatively substantial increase since 1980 in funding programs benefitting the aged.

Large and Small Foundations

Since 1980, The Foundation Center has included in the *Grants Index Annual* the nation's 100 largest foundations by total giving, thereby providing a more consistent statistical base for giving trend analysis. Over the past five years there have been slight variations both in the actual number and in the specific top 100 foundations included from year to year, based on the availability of information from qualifying foundations.

In this *Index*, the 100 largest givers reported 18,104 grants (53 percent of the total grants included) with a total dollar value of $1,180,576,032 (72 percent of the total dollars reported). The top 100 grantmakers included 67 independent foundations, 8 community foundations, and 25 company-sponsored foundations.

The inclusion of community foundations, whose giving programs are focused almost exclusively on local community needs, tends to lessen the differences in the grantmaking patterns of the largest foundations and the 360 smaller foundations reporting to the Index. Nonetheless, comparisons of the distribution of grants and grant dollars by subect (Table 33) and by types of grant recipients (Table 34) continue to support previous

TABLE 32. REPORTED GRANTS DESIGNATED FOR SPECIAL POPULATION GROUPS

Group	1981 Dollar Amount	%	1982 Dollar Amount	%	1983 Dollar Amount	%	1984 Dollar Amount	%
Aged	18,010,803	1.4	31,196,858	2.1	38,958,611	2.2	53,582,763	3.3
Alcohol & Drug Abusers	3,159,280	0.3	8,076,642	0.5	9,413,252	0.5	8,124,441	0.5
Children & Youth	123,552,714	9.8	132,380,864	8.9	181,303,293	10.1	177,473,802	10.8
Criminal & Ex-Offenders	8,435,017	0.7	8,762,553	0.6	9,347,404	0.5	9,355,096	0.6
Handicapped	22,062,891	1.8	30,233,873	2.0	35,456,271	2.0	39,059,611	2.4
Men & Boys	12,154,657	1.0	13,222,630	0.9	22,413,400	1.3	16,283,728	1.0
Minorities								
General	23,360,983	1.9	33,675,798	2.3	29,002,670	1.6	27,416,376	1.7
Asian-Americans	1,470,530	0.1	2,155,817	0.1	1,931,565	0.1	4,041,158	0.2
Blacks	35,696,678	2.8	32,376,809	2.2	46,275,988	2.6	49,178,707	3.0
Hispanics	10,182,753	0.8	14,782,287	1.0	17,333,475	1.0	15,663,488	1.0
Native Americans	4,913,173	0.4	4,043,327	0.3	5,743,278	0.3	5,994,792	0.4
Women & Girls	36,670,100	2.9	37,528,002	2.5	49,884,209	2.8	59,736,157	3.6

TABLE 33. SUBJECT FOCUS OF GRANTS AWARDED BY SIZE OF FOUNDATION

Subject	Dollar Value of Grants				Number of Grants			
	100 Largest Foundations		Other Foundations		100 Largest Foundations		Other Foundations	
	Amount	%	Amount	%	Number	%	Number	%
Cultural Activities								
General	29,301,011	2.5	15,598,079	3.3	644	3.5	537	3.4
Art & Architecture	37,511,625	3.2	12,969,625	2.8	353	1.9	408	2.5
History	14,342,600	1.2	6,919,665	1.5	269	1.5	227	1.4
Language & Literature	9,235,508	0.8	5,374,511	1.1	222	1.3	265	1.7
Media & Communications	13,836,188	1.2	10,721,197	2.3	285	1.6	292	1.8
Music	28,821,896	2.4	15,279,257	3.3	496	2.7	586	3.7
Theater & Dance	19,859,365	1.7	9,249,800	2.0	470	2.6	488	3.1
TOTAL CULTURAL ACTIVITIES	152,908,193	13.0	76,112,134	16.3	2,739	15.1	2,803	17.6
Education								
General	12,716,131	1.1	5,670,517	1.2	270	1.5	219	1.4
Adult & Continuing	15,791,880	1.3	2,171,660	0.5	123	0.7	104	0.7
Elementary & Secondary	26,846,020	2.3	17,088,512	3.7	460	2.5	737	4.6
Higher (General)	153,996,321	13.0	41,763,100	8.9	2,615	14.4	1,322	8.3
Vocational	6,876,909	0.6	2,666,010	0.6	120	0.7	129	0.8
TOTAL EDUCATION	216,227,261	18.3	69,359,799	14.9	3,588	19.8	2,511	15.8
Health								
General	18,034,172	1.5	4,975,211	1.1	227	1.3	169	1.0
Medical & Health Education	41,651,167	3.5	14,617,784	3.1	285	1.6	263	1.7
Medical Care & Treatment	90,172,365	7.7	34,877,307	7.5	1,071	5.9	946	5.9
Medical Research	62,687,554	5.3	32,565,817	7.0	337	1.8	583	3.7
Mental Health	19,351,562	1.7	8,164,262	1.7	283	1.6	352	2.2
Public Health	48,492,703	4.1	14,855,581	3.2	686	3.8	709	4.4
TOTAL HEALTH	280,389,523	23.8	110,055,962	23.6	2,889	16.0	3,022	18.9
Religion								
General	19,435,224	1.6	8,464,496	1.8	301	1.7	288	1.8
Religious Education	7,074,405	0.6	3,376,861	0.7	99	0.5	124	0.8
TOTAL RELIGION	26,509,629	2.2	11,841,357	2.5	400	2.2	412	2.6
Science								
General	15,402,392	1.3	5,768,161	1.2	150	0.8	132	0.8
Life Sciences	23,789,325	2.0	5,592,055	1.2	179	1.0	170	1.1
Physical Sciences	15,693,698	1.3	3,515,532	0.8	439	2.4	69	0.4
Technology	45,800,587	3.9	7,318,321	1.6	748	4.2	261	1.6
TOTAL SCIENCE	100,686,002	8.5	22,194,069	4.8	1,516	8.4	632	3.9
Social Science								
General	14,200,565	1.2	7,889,181	1.7	173	1.0	163	1.0
Anthropology	6,062,832	0.5	830,401	0.2	56	0.3	23	0.1
Economics	10,016,669	0.9	2,560,460	0.5	218	1.2	93	0.6
Law & Legal Education	7,438,538	0.6	4,599,339	1.0	171	0.9	122	0.8
Political Science	53,263,683	4.5	19,463,889	4.2	753	4.2	582	3.7
TOTAL SOCIAL SCIENCE	90,982,287	7.7	35,343,270	7.6	1,371	7.6	983	6.2
Welfare								
General	69,026,786	5.9	40,799,301	8.8	1,613	8.9	2,069	13.0
Business & Employment	39,195,133	3.3	12,596,515	2.7	864	4.8	600	3.8
Community Affairs	64,206,137	5.4	26,154,243	5.6	1,047	5.8	791	5.0
Consumer Interests	282,540	0.0	369,184	0.1	12	0.1	21	0.1
Crime & Law Enforcement	10,689,795	0.9	2,889,643	0.6	176	1.0	203	1.3
Environment & Energy	31,606,028	2.7	18,369,499	3.9	443	2.4	540	3.4
Equal Rights & Legal Services	16,677,018	1.4	7,078,510	1.5	281	1.5	318	2.0
Recreation	23,113,119	2.0	20,697,124	4.5	479	2.6	625	3.9
Rural Development	17,538,616	1.5	1,478,719	0.3	181	1.0	63	0.4
Urban Development	40,537,965	3.4	10,795,316	2.3	505	2.8	343	2.1
TOTAL WELFARE	312,873,137	26.5	141,228,054	30.3	5,601	30.9	5,573	35.0
TOTAL GRANTS	1,180,576,032	100.0	466,134,645	100.0	18,104	100.0	15,936	100.0

TABLE 34. DISTRIBUTION OF REPORTED GRANTS BY RECIPIENT ORGANIZATION TYPE AND SIZE OF FOUNDATION

	Dollar Value of Grants				Number of Grants			
	100 Largest Foundations		360 Other Foundations		100 Largest Foundations		360 Other Foundations	
	Amount	%	Amount	%	Number	%	Number	%
Educational Institutions	434,538,012	36.8	143,550,512	30.8	5,842	32.3	4,045	25.4
Private Universities & Colleges	215,733,782	18.3	63,184,774	13.5	2,648	14.6	1,562	9.8
Public Universities & Colleges	112,935,756	9.6	26,007,369	5.6	1,691	9.4	801	5.0
Graduate Schools	73,827,353	6.2	32,454,101	7.0	891	4.9	694	4.4
Junior/Community Colleges	5,479,966	0.5	1,602,154	0.3	119	0.7	67	0.4
Schools	26,561,155	2.2	20,302,114	4.4	493	2.7	921	5.8
Direct Service Agencies	239,911,273	20.3	113,782,356	24.4	4,360	24.1	5,313	33.3
Hospitals & Medical Care Facilities	74,266,960	6.3	39,894,462	8.6	956	5.3	947	5.9
Research Institutes	118,916,975	10.1	28,394,265	6.1	844	4.7	609	3.8
Associations & Professional Societies	111,696,464	9.5	36,515,053	7.8	2,246	12.4	1,658	10.4
Museums & Historical Societies	62,844,532	5.3	28,063,837	6.0	636	3.5	664	4.2
Performing Arts Groups	50,992,623	4.3	24,605,372	5.3	1,019	5.6	1,012	6.3
Government Agencies	38,423,921	3.3	13,535,606	2.9	499	2.8	448	2.8
Community Funds	49,026,681	4.2	15,951,303	3.4	685	3.8	394	2.5
Libraries	17,287,720	1.5	7,333,376	1.6	197	1.1	224	1.4
Churches & Temples	13,958,706	1.2	8,980,251	1.9	360	2.0	385	2.4

assumptions about the giving tendencies of large and small foundations.

In general, the larger foundations place a stronger emphasis on academic and research fields (i.e., science, social science, higher education, etc.). The smaller foundations tend to have a more local focus and put a larger percentage of their grant dollars into program areas which address specific community needs, such as general welfare programs, community affairs, medical care and treatment, and cultural programs.

As The Foundation Center continues to track giving patterns among these groups in future years, it will be necessary to look at differences in giving patterns by type of foundation as well as by the size of the giving program to form a clearer picture of grantmaking trends.

Elan Garonzik
Assistant Director, Publications

How To Use *The Foundation Directory*

The Foundation Directory is one of the first tools grantseekers should use to identify foundations that might be interested in funding their project or organization. It provides basic descriptions of the giving interests and current fiscal data for the nation's largest foundations—those with assets of $1 million or more or annual giving of at least $100,000. Indexes help grantseekers to quickly identify foundations which have expressed an interest in a particular subject field or geographic area or which provide the specific type of support needed.

Researchers, journalists, grantmakers, and others interested in philanthropic activities will also find the *Directory* useful to get a broad overview of current foundation activities nationally or within a particular geographic region or to gather basic facts about one or more specific foundations.

In using the *Directory* to identify potential funding sources, be sure to note the limitation statements many foundations have provided to see whether your project falls within the general scope of the foundation's giving program. Some foundations restrict their giving to a particular subject field or geographic area; others are not able to provide certain types of support, such as funds for buildings and equipment or for general operating funds.

ARRANGEMENT

The Directory is arranged alphabetically by state, and foundation descriptions are arranged alphabetically by name within the state in which the foundation maintains its primary offices. Each entry is assigned a sequence number, and references in the indexes which follow the main listings are to entry sequence numbers.

There are 25 basic data elements which could be included in a *Directory* entry. The completeness of an entry varies widely due to the differences in the size and nature of a foundation's program and the availability of information from the foundation. Entries which have been prepared by Foundation Center staff from public records are indicated by the symbol ¤. The specific data elements which could be included are:

1. The full legal **name of the foundation,** often inverted to provide proper alphabetical order.
2. The **former name** of the foundation, if the name has changed since the last *Directory* listing.
3. **Street address, city, and zip code** of the foundation's principal office. (Entries are arranged alphabetically within state sections.)
4. **Telephone number** supplied by the foundation.

5. Any **additional address** supplied by the foundation for correspondence or grant applications.
6. **Establishment data,** including the legal form (usually a trust or corporation) and the year and state in which the foundation was established.
7. The **donor(s)** or principal contributor(s) to the foundation, including individuals, families, and corporations. If a donor is deceased, the symbol † follows the name.
8. **The year-end date** of the foundation's accounting period for which financial data is supplied.
9. **Assets:** the total value of the foundation's investments at the end of the accounting period. In a few instances, foundations that act as "pass-throughs" for annual corporate or individual gifts report zero assets.
10. **Asset Type:** generally, assets are reported at market value (M) or ledger value (L). Occasionally, the foundation will have liabilities (such as mortgages or accounts payable) that exceed their assets by more than ten percent and will indicate their net worth at market (WM) or ledger (WL) value.
11. **Gifts Received:** the total amount of new capital received by the foundation in the year of record.
12. **Expenditures:** total disbursements of the foundation, including overhead expenses (salaries; investment, legal, and other professional fees; interest; rent; etc.) and federal excise taxes, as well as the total amount paid for grants, scholarships, matching gifts, loans, and scholarships.
13. The dollar value and number of **grants paid** during the year, with the largest grant paid (**High**) and smallest grant paid (**Low**). When supplied by the foundation, the average range of grant payments is also indicated. Grant figures do not include commitments for future payment or amounts spent for grants to individuals, employee-matching gifts, loans, or foundation-administered programs.
14. The total amount and number of **grants made directly to or on behalf of an individual,** including scholarships, fellowships, awards, or medical payments.
15. The dollar amount and number of **employee-matching gifts** awarded, generally by company-sponsored foundations.
16. The total dollars expended for **programs administered by the foundation** and the number of foundation-administered programs. These programs can include museums or other institutions supported exclusively by the foundation, research programs administered by the foundation and conducted either by foundation staff or at other institutions, etc.

17. The number of **loans** and the total dollars loaned to nonprofit organizations or individuals by the foundation. These can include program-related investments, educational loans to students, emergency loans to help nonprofits that are waiting for grants or other income payments, etc.

18. The **purpose and activities,** in general terms, of the foundation. This statement reflects funding interests as expressed by the foundation or, if no foundation statement is available, an analysis of the actual grants awarded by the foundation during the most recent two-year period for which public records exist.

19. The **types of support** (such as endowment funds, support for buildings and equipment, fellowships, etc.) offered by the foundation. Definitions of the terms used to describe the forms of support available are provided at the beginning of the Index of Types of Support at the back of this volume.

20. Any stated **limitations** on the foundation's giving program, including geographic preferences, restrictions by subject focus or type of recipient, or specific types of support the foundation cannot provide.

21. **Publications** or other printed materials distributed by the foundation which describe its activities and giving program. These can include annual or multi-year reports, newsletters, corporate giving reports, informational brochures, grant lists, etc. Program policy statements and application guidelines are noted separately, even though they are sometimes issued as part of a foundation's annual report. It is also noted if a foundation will send copies of its IRS information return (Form 990-PF) on request.

22. **Application information,** including the name of the contact person, the preferred form of application, the number of copies of proposals requested, frequency and dates of board meetings, and the general amount of time the foundation requires to notify applicants of the board's decision. Some foundations have also indicated that applications are not accepted or that their funds are currently committed to ongoing projects.

23. The names and titles of **officers, principal administrators, trustees or directors,** and members of other governing bodies. An asterisk following the individual's name indicates an officer who is also a trustee or director.

24. The number of professional and support **staff** employed by the foundation, and an indication of part-time or full-time status of these employees, as reported by the foundation.

25. **Employer Identification Number:** the number assigned to the foundation by the Internal Revenue Service for tax purposes. This number can be useful in ordering microfilm or paper copies of the foundation's annual information return, Form 990-PF.

Indexes

Five indexes to the descriptive entries are provided at the back of the book.

1. **The Index of Donors, Officers, and Trustees** is an alphabetical listing of individuals and corporations that have made substantial contributions to *Directory* foundations or who serve as officers or members of the governing boards of foundations. Many grantseekers find this index helpful to learn whether current or prospective members of their own governing boards, alumnae of their school, or current contributors are affiliated with any foundations.

2. **The Geographic Index** references foundation entries by the state and city in which the foundation maintains principal offices and includes cross-references to indicate foundations located elsewhere that have made substantial grants to a particular state. Foundations that award grants on a national or regional level are indicated in bold type. The other foundations generally limit their giving to the state or city in which they are located.

3. **The Types of Support Index** indicates entry numbers for foundations that offer specific types of grants and other forms of support, such as consulting services or program-related investments. Definitions of the terms used to describe the types of support offered are provided at the beginning of the index. Under each type of support term, entry references are arranged by the state in which the foundation is located, and foundations that award grants on a national or regional basis are again indicated in bold type. In using this index, grantseekers should focus on foundations located in their own state which offer the specific type of support needed or, if their project has national impact, on foundations listed in bold type that are located in other states.

4. **The Subject Index** allows users to identify foundations by the broad giving interests expressed in the "Purpose and Activities" section of their descriptive entry. A list of subject terms used is provided at the beginning of the index. Like the Types of Support Index, entry references are arranged under each term by the state in which the foundation is located, and foundations that

award grants on a national or regional basis are indicated in bold type. Again, grantseekers should focus on foundations located in their own state that have indicated an interest in their subject field, as well as foundations listed in bold type that are located in other states.

5. **The Foundation Name Index** is an alphabetical list of all foundations appearing in the descriptive directory. If a foundation has changed its name since the last *Directory*, the former name also appears in this index. If the name of a particular foundation does not appear in this index, users should consult the foundation listings in the appendices to determine if the foundation has terminated operations or is otherwise ineligible for inclusion in the *Directory*.

RESEARCHING FOUNDATIONS

Foundations receive many thousands of worthy requests each year. Most of these requests are declined because there are never enough funds to go around or because the applications clearly fall outside the foundation's fields of interest. Some of the applications denied are poorly prepared and do not reflect a careful analysis of the applicant organization's needs, its credibility, or its capacity to carry out the proposed project. Sometimes the qualifications of staff are not well established. The budget or the means of evaluating the project may not be presented convincingly. The organization may not have asked itself if it is especially suited to make a contribution to the solution of the problem or to provide the service proposed or if others are not already effectively engaged in the same activity.

The first step in researching foundation funding support, then, is to analyze your own program and organization to determine the need you plan to address, the audience you will serve, and the amount and type of support you need. Become familiar with the basic facts about foundations in general and how they operate. Consider other sources of funding, such as individual contributors, government grants, earned income possibilities, and so on. Although foundations are an important source of support for nonprofit organizations, their total giving represents a relatively small percentage of the total private philanthropic dollars contributed annually, and an even smaller percentage of the total support of nonprofit activities when government grants and earned income are included.

Once you have clearly in mind the amount and type of support you need and the reasons why you are seeking foundation support, *The Foundation Directory*

can help you to develop an initial list of foundations that might be interested in funding your project. In determining whether or not it is appropriate to approach a particular foundation with a grant request, keep in mind the following questions:

1. Has the foundation demonstrated a real commitment to funding in your subject area?
2. Does it seem likely that the foundation will make a grant in your geographic area?
3. Does the amount of money you are requesting fit within the foundation's grant range?
4. Does the foundation have any policy prohibiting grants for the type of support you are requesting?
5. Does the foundation prefer to make grants to cover the full cost of a project or do they favor projects where other foundations or funding sources share the cost?
6. What types of organizations does the foundation tend to support?
7. Does the foundation have specific application deadlines and procedures or does it review proposals continuously?

Some of these questions can be answered from the information provided in the *Directory*, but grantseekers will almost always want to consult a few additional resources before submitting a request for funding. If the foundation issues an annual report, application guidelines, or other printed materials describing its program, it is advisable to obtain copies and study them carefully before preparing your proposal. The foundation's annual information return (Form 990-PF) includes a list of all grants paid by the foundation, as well as basic data about its finances, officers, and giving policies. Copies of these returns are available for free examination at most of the Foundation Center's cooperating libraries listed later in this volume.

The Foundation Center's quarterly publication, *Source Book Profiles*, describes in detail the 1,000 largest U.S. foundations and, with the exception of publications issued directly by the foundations, is the most complete source of information available on this group. *Directory* foundations which are described more fully in *Source Book Profiles* are indicated by the symbol ▼ next to their entry. The Center also publishes a number of other reference tools which provide information on private foundations, as well as a guidebook on researching foundation funding sources, *Foundation Fundamentals*. Copies of all Center publications, as well as other relevant state and local foundation directories, are available for free examination at The Foundation Center libraries and cooperating collections listed in this volume. Ordering information for these publications is also provided at the end of this introduction.

Glossary

The following list includes important terms used by grantmakers and grantseekers. A number of sources have been consulted in compiling this glossary, including *The Handbook on Private Foundations,* by David F. Freeman (Washington, D.C.: Seven Locks Press, 1981); *The Law of Tax-Exempt Organizations,* 3rd Edition, by Bruce R. Hopkins (New York: John Wiley & Sons, 1979); *Corporate Philanthropy: Philosophy, Management, Trends, Future, Background* (Washington, D.C.: Council on Foundations, 1982); and a glossary prepared by Caroline McGilvray, former Director of The Foundation Center San Francisco Office, with The Northern California Foundation Group.

Annual Report: A *voluntary* report issued by a foundation or corporate giving program which provides financial data and descriptions of grantmaking activities. Annual reports vary in format from simple typewritten documents listing the year's grants to detailed publications which provide substantial information about the grantmaking program. Perhaps 10 to 15 percent of all foundations issue such reports (as distinguished from the publicly available FORM 990-PF, below, the annual information return *required* of all private foundations). A current listing of reports issued by private foundations and corporate grantmakers is provided in The Foundation Center's *Foundation Grants Index Bimonthly. Foundation Directory* entries also indicate if an annual report is published.

Assets: The amount of capital or principal—money, stocks, bonds, real estate, or other resources of the foundation. Generally, assets are invested and the income is used to make grants.

Beneficiary: In philanthropic terms, the donee or grantee receiving funds from a foundation is the beneficiary, though society benefits as well. Foundations whose legal terms of establishment restrict their giving to one or more named beneficiaries are not included in this *Directory.*

Bricks and Mortar: An informal term for grants for buildings or construction projects.

Capital Support: Funds provided for endowment purposes, buildings, construction, or equipment and including, for example, grants for "bricks and mortar."

Challenge Grant: A grant award that will be paid only if the donee organization is able to raise additional funds from another source(s). Challenge grants are often used to stimulate giving from other foundations or donors. (*See also* **Matching Grant**)

Community Fund: An organized community program which makes annual appeals to the general public for funds which are usually not retained in an endowment but are used for the ongoing operational support of local social and health service agencies. (*See also* **Federated Giving Program**)

Community Foundation: A 501(c)(3) organization which makes grants for charitable purposes in a specific community or region. Funds are usually derived from many donors and held in an endowment independently administered; income earned by the endowment is then used to make grants. Although a few community foundations may be classified by the IRS as private foundations, most are classified as public charities eligible for maximum income tax-deductible contributions from the general public. (*See also* **501(c)(3); Public Charity**)

Company-Sponsored Foundation (also referred to as Corporate Foundation):   A private foundation whose grant funds are derived primarily from the contributions of a profit-making business organization. The company-sponsored foundation may maintain close ties with the donor company, but it is an independent organization with its own endowment and is subject to the same rules and regulations as other private foundations. (*See also* **Private Foundation**)

Cooperative Venture: A joint effort between or among two or more grantmakers (including foundations, corporations, and government agencies). Partners may share in funding responsibilities or contribute information and technical resources.

Corporate Contributions: A broad term which generally encompasses all of a corporation's charitable contributions whether they are made through a company-sponsored foundation or through a direct giving program.

Corporate Giving Program: A grantmaking program established and administered within a profit-making company. Corporate giving programs do not have a separate endowment and their annual grant totals are generally more directly related to current profits. They are not subject to the same reporting requirements as private foundations. Some companies make charitable contributions through both a corporate giving program and a company-sponsored foundation. Company-sponsored foundations are included in this *Directory;* corporate giving programs are not.

Distribution Committee: The board responsible for making grant decisions for community foundations. It is intended to be broadly representative of the community served by the foundation.

Donee: The recipient of a grant. (Also known as the grantee or the beneficiary.)

Donor: The individual or organization which makes a grant or contribution. (Also known as the grantor.)

Employee Matching Gift: A contribution to a charitable organization by a corporate employee which is matched by a similar contribution from the employer. Many corporations have employee matching gift programs in higher education that stimulate their employees to give to the college or university of their choice.

Endowment: Funds intended to be kept permanently and invested to provide income for continued support of an organization.

Expenditure Responsibility: In general, when a private foundation makes a grant to an organization which is not classified by the IRS as a "public charity," the foundation is required by law to provide some assurance that the funds will be used for the intended charitable purposes. Special reports on such grants must be filed with the IRS. Most grantee organizations are public charities and many foundations do not make "expenditure responsibility" grants.

Family Foundation: An independent private foundation whose funds are derived from members of a single family. Family members often serve as officers or board members of the foundation and have a significant role in grantmaking decisions. (*See also* **Private Foundation**)

Federated Giving Program: A joint fundraising effort usually administered by a nonprofit "umbrella" organization which in turn distributes contributed funds to several nonprofit agencies. United Way and community chests or funds, United Jewish Appeal and other religious appeals, the United Negro College Fund, and joint arts councils are examples of federated giving programs. (*See also* **Community Fund**)

Financial Report: A report detailing how grant funds were used by an organization. Many foundations require this kind of report from grantees. A financial report generally includes a listing of all expenditures from grant funds as well as an overall organizational financial report covering revenue and expenses, assets and liabilities.

501(c)(3): The section of the Internal Revenue Code which defines nonprofit, charitable (as broadly defined), tax-exempt organizations. 501(c)(3) organizations are further defined as public charities, private operating foundations, and private non-operating foundations. (*See also* **Community Foundation, Operating Foundation, Private Foundation, Public Charity**)

Form 990-PF: The annual information return that all private foundations must submit to the IRS each year and which is also filed with appropriate state officials. The form requires information on the foundation's assets, income, operating expenses, contributions and grants, paid staff and salaries, program funding areas, grantmaking guidelines and restrictions, and grant application procedures. Foundation Center libraries maintain files of 990-PFs for public inspection.

General Purpose Foundation: An independent private foundation which awards grants in many different fields of interest. (*See also* **Special Purpose Foundation**)

General Purpose Grant: A grant made to further the general purpose or work of an organization, rather than for a specific purpose or project. (*See also* **Operating Support Grant**)

Grassroots Fundraising: Efforts to raise money from individuals or groups from the local community on a broad basis. Usually an organization does grassroots fundraising within its own constituency—people who live in the neighborhood served or clients of the agency's services. Grassroots fundraising activities include membership drives, raffles, bake sales, auctions, benefits, dances, and a range of other activities. Foundations often feel that successful grassroots fundraising indicates that an organization has substantial community support.

Independent Foundation: A grantmaking organization usually classified by the IRS as a private foundation. Independent foundations may also be known as family foundations, general purpose foundations, special purpose foundations, or private non-operating foundations. The *Directory* defines independent foundations and company-sponsored foundations separately; however, federal law normally classifies both as private, non-operating foundations subject to the same rules and requirements. (*See also* **Private Foundation**)

In-Kind Contribution: A contribution of equipment, supplies, or other property as distinguished from a monetary grant. Some organizations may also donate space or staff time as an in-kind contribution.

Matching Grant: A grant which is made to match funds provided by another donor. (*See also* **Challenge Grant; Employee Matching Gift**)

Operating Foundation: A 501(c)(3) organization classified by the IRS as a private foundation whose primary purpose is to conduct research, social welfare, or other programs determined by its governing body or establishment charter. Some grants may be made, but the sum is generally small relative to the funds used for the foundation's own programs. (*See also* **501(c)(3)**)

Operating Support Grant: A grant to cover the regular personnel, administrative, and other expenses for an existing program or project. (*See also* **General Purpose Grant**)

Payout Requirement: The minimum amount that private foundations are required to expend for charitable purposes (includes grants and, within certain limits, the administrative cost of making grants). In general, foundations are required to pay out the equivalent of at least 5 percent of the average market value of their assets for the year.

Private Foundation: A nongovernmental, nonprofit organization with funds (usually from a single source, such as an individual, family, or corporation) and program managed by its own trustees or directors which was established to maintain or aid social, educational, religious or other charitable

activities serving the common welfare, primarily through the making of grants. "Private foundation" also means an organization that is tax-exempt under Code section 501(c)(3) and is classified by IRS as a private foundation as defined in the Code. The Code definition usually, but not always, identifies a foundation with the characteristics first described. (See also 501(c)(3); Public Charity)

Program Amount: Funds which are expended to support a particular program. In the *Directory,* this term refers to the total dollars spent to operate programs administered internally by the foundation.

Program Officer: A staff member of a foundation who reviews grant proposals and processes applications for the board of trustees. Only a small percentage of foundations have program officers.

Program-Related Investment (PRI): A loan or other investment (as distinguished from a grant) made by a foundation to another organization (including a business enterprise) for a project related to the foundation's stated purpose and interests. Program-related investments are often made from a revolving fund; the foundation generally expects to receive its money back with interest or some other form of return at less than current market rates, which becomes available for further program-related investments. These investments are currently made by relatively few foundations.

Proposal: A written application often with supporting documents submitted to a foundation in requesting a grant. Preferred procedures and formats vary. Consult published guidelines.

Public Charity: In general, an organization which is tax-exempt under Code section 501(c)(3) and is classified by IRS as a public charity and not a private foundation. Public charities generally derive their funding or support primarily from the general public in carrying out their social, educational, religious, or other charitable activities serving the common welfare. Some public charities engage in grantmaking activities, though most engage in direct service or other tax-exempt activities. Public charities are eligible for maximum income tax-deductible contributions from the public

and are not subject to the same rules and restrictions as private foundations. Some are also referred to as "public foundations" or "publicly supported organizations" and may use the term "foundation" in their names. With few exceptions, notably community foundations, public charities are outside the scope of the *Directory.* (See also **Community Foundation; 501(c)(3); Private Foundation**)

Query Letter: A brief letter outlining an organization's activities and its request for funding sent to a foundation to determine whether it would be appropriate to submit a full grant proposal. Many foundations prefer to be contacted in this way before receiving a full proposal.

RFP: Request For Proposal. When the government issues a new contract or grant program, it sends out RFPs to agencies that might be qualified to participate. The RFP lists project specifications and application procedures. A few foundations occasionally use RFPs in specific fields, but most prefer to consider proposals that are initiated by applicants.

Seed Money: A grant or contribution used to start a new project or organization. Seed grants may cover salaries and other operating expenses of a new project.

Special Purpose Foundation: A private foundation which focuses its grantmaking activities in one or a few special areas of interest. For example, a foundation may only award grants in the area of cancer research or child development. (See also **General Purpose Foundation**)

Technical Assistance: Operational or management assistance given to nonprofit organizations. It can include fundraising assistance, budgeting and financial planning, program planning, legal advice, marketing, and other aids to management. Assistance may be offered directly by a foundation or corporate staff member or in the form of a grant to pay for the services of an outside consultant. (See also **In-Kind Contribution**)

Trustee: A member of a governing board. A foundation's board of trustees meets to review grant proposals and make decisions. Often also referred to as "director" or "board member."

Foundation Center Publications

Publications of The Foundation Center are the primary working tools of every serious grantseeker. They are also used by grantmakers, scholars, journalists, regulators, and legislators: in short, by everyone seeking any type of factual information on foundation philanthropy. Copies of all publications are available for examination free of charge at any of the regional collections listed elsewhere in this introduction. Publications may be ordered from The Foundation Center, 79 Fifth Avenue, New York, NY 10003; please include prepayment and complete shipping address. For additional information or to place credit card orders, call toll-free 800-424-9836.

SOURCE BOOK PROFILES

Source Book Profiles is an annual subscription service offering a detailed description of the 1,000 largest foundations, analyzing giving patterns by subject area, type of support, and type of recipient. The service operates on a two-year publishing cycle, with each one-year series covering 500 foundations. Each quarterly installment includes 125 new profiles as well as information on changes in address, telephone, personnel, or program, and a revised, cumulative set of indexes to all 1,000 foundations covered in the two-year cycle by name, subject interest, type of grants awarded, and city and state location or concentration of giving.

> 1985 Series—$265 annual subscription—ISBN 0-87954-128-8
>
> 1984 Cumulative Volume (500 Profiles)—$250—ISBN 0-87954-096-0

NATIONAL DATA BOOK, 9TH EDITION

Lists the 24,000 currently active grantmaking foundations in the U.S. in one easy-to-use volume arranged by state in descending order by their annual grant totals. A separate alphabetical index to foundation names is also included. Foundation entries include name, address, and principal officer, plus full fiscal data (market value of assets, grants paid, gifts received, and fiscal period) and an indication of which foundations publish annual reports. The *National Data Book* will help you find the address of any active U.S. foundation, locate all foundations in a particular city or state, identify all foundations in a particular city or state, identify all foundations that issue annual reports, and profile foundation assets or giving levels by state or region.

> 2 vols. Annually in January. ISBN 0-87954-126-1. $55

CORPORATE FOUNDATION PROFILES, 4TH EDITION

Includes comprehensive analyses of approximately 250 of the nation's largest company-sponsored foundations, with full subject, type of support, and geographic indexes. Summary financial data is provided for 473 additional corporate foundations. Entries are drawn from *Source Book Profiles* and include address and telephone number, complete information about the parent company, financial data, an analysis of the foundation's giving program, and information regarding the foundation's policies, guidelines, and application procedures.

> Nov. 1985. ISBN 0-87954-135-0. $55

FOUNDATION GRANTS TO INDIVIDUALS, 4TH EDITION

The only publication devoted entirely to specialized foundation grant opportunities for qualified individual applicants. The 4th Edition provides full descriptions of the programs for individuals of about 950 foundations. Entries also include foundation addresses and telephone numbers, names of trustees and staff, financial data, and sample grants. This volume can save individuals seeking grants countless hours of research. The fully revised 4th Edition is scheduled for publication in spring 1986.

> 4th Edition, 1986. 243 pages. ISBN 0-87954-097-4. $18

THE FOUNDATION GRANTS INDEX ANNUAL

Lists the grants of $5,000 or more awarded to nonprofit organizations by about 460 major U.S. foundations. The 14th Edition is the largest *Index* ever, listing over 34,000 grants and including an expanded analytical introduction. The volume is arranged alphabetically by state and foundation name. Each entry notes the amount and date of the grant, name and location of the recipient, and a brief description of the grant. Also provided are indexes to grant recipients and subject keywords and phrases, a combined subject and geographic category index, and a new combined index by type of recipient and type of support awarded. Published annually in May.

> 14th Edition, 1985. 848 pages. ISBN 0-87954-127-X. $44

COMSEARCH PRINTOUTS

This popular series of computer-produced guides to foundation giving derived from The Foundation Grants Index Database is now issued in four separate categories:

COMSEARCH: Broad Topics indexes and analyzes recent foundation grants in 20 broad subject categories. Each listing includes all grants in the particular subject area reported to The Foundation Center during the preceding year, along with an index listing name and geographic location of organizations which have received grants, a geographic index arranged by state of the organization which received grants, and a key word index listing descriptive words and phrases which link a foundation's giving interests with your organization's field. *COMSEARCH: Broad Topics* includes grants for:

- Arts & Cultural Programs
- Business & Employment
- Children & Youth

- Higher Education
- Hospitals & Medical Care Programs
- Museums
- Science Programs
- Social Science Programs
- Women & Girls
- International & Foreign Programs
- Minorities
- Religion & Religious Education
- Public Health
- Public Policy & Political Science
- Recreation
- Community & Urban Development
- Elementary & Secondary Education (Public & Private Schools)
- The Aged
- Matching & Challenge Support
- Film, Media, & Communications

Series published annually in June. $32 each

COMSEARCH: Subjects includes 59 specially focused subject listings of grants reported to The Foundation Center during the preceding year. Listings are arranged by the state where the foundation is located and then by foundation name, and include complete information on the name and location of the grant recipient, the amount awarded, and the purpose of the grant. *COMSEARCH: Subjects* may be purchased as a complete set on microfiche or individually by particular subject area of interest in paper or microfiche form. A full list of categories is available on request.

Series published annually in June. $225 microfiche set; $17.50 per subject on paper; $6 per subject on microfiche.

COMSEARCH: Geographics provides customized listings of grants received by organizations in two cities, eleven states, and four regions. These listings make it easy to see which major foundations have awarded grants in your area, to which nonprofit organizations, and what each grant was intended to accomplish. Listings are available for Washington D.C., New York City, California, Illinois, Massachusetts, Michigan, Minnesota, New Jersey, New York State (excluding New York City), North Carolina, Ohio, Pennsylvania, Texas, the Northeast (Maine, New Hampshire, Rhode Island, Vermont, Connecticut), Southeast (Florida, Georgia, Alabama, Mississippi, Louisiana, South Carolina), Northwest (Washington and Oregon), and the Rocky Mountains (Arizona, New Mexico, Colorado, Utah, Nevada, Idaho, Montana, Wyoming).

Series published annually in June. $28 each

COMSEARCH: Special Topics includes three of the most frequently requested special listings from the Center's computer databases. The three special listings are:
- The 1,000 Largest U.S. Foundations by Asset Size
- The 1,000 Largest U.S. Foundations by Annual Grants Total
- The nearly 1,400 Operating Foundations that Administer Their Own Projects or Programs

Series published annually in June. $17.50 each

FOUNDATION FUNDAMENTALS: A RESOURCE GUIDE FOR GRANTSEEKERS

This comprehensive, easy-to-read guidebook written by Patricia Read presents the facts you need to understand the world of foundations and to identify foundation funding sources for your organization. Over 45 illustrations take you step-by-step through the funding research process. Worksheets and checklists are provided to help you get started in your search for

funding. Comprehensive bibliographies and detailed research examples are also supplied.

Revised edition, Sept. 1985. ISBN 0-87954-100-8. $9.95

AMERICA'S VOLUNTARY SPIRIT: A BOOK OF READINGS

In this thoughtful collection, Brian O'Connell, President of INDEPENDENT SECTOR, brings together 45 selections which celebrate and examine the richness and variety of America's unique voluntary sector. O'Connell researched nearly 1,000 selections spanning over 300 years of writing to identify those speeches, articles, chapters, and papers which best define and characterize the role that philanthropy and voluntary action play in our society. Contributors as diverse as de Tocqueville and John D. Rockefeller, Thoreau and Max Lerner, Erma Bombeck and Vernon Jordan are unified in a common examination of this unique dimension of American life. The anthology includes a bibliography of over 500 important writings and a detailed subject index.

October 1983. ISBN 0-87954-079-6 (hardcover). $19.95
ISBN 0-87954-081-8 (softcover). $14.95

PHILANTHROPY IN AN AGE OF TRANSITION
The Essays of Alan Pifer

A collection of essays by one of the most respected and well-known individuals in philanthropy. In these essays, Alan Pifer analyzes issues of great concern to all Americans; the responsibilities of higher education, charitable tax deductions, women in the work force, the financial straits of the nonprofit sector, the changing age composition of the American population, bilingual education, the progress of blacks, and more. The essays have been collected from the annual reports of Carnegie Corporation, from 1966-82, some of the most turbulent years in America.

Alan Pifer is President Emeritus of Carnegie Corporation of New York where he was President for over seventeen years.

270 pages. April 1984. ISBN 0-87954-104-0. $12.50.

THE BOARD MEMBER'S BOOK
by Brian O'Connell, President, INDEPENDENT SECTOR

Based on his extensive experience working with and on the boards of voluntary organizations, Brian O'Connell has developed this practical guide to the essential functions of voluntary boards. O'Connell offers practical advice on how to be a more effective board member and how board members can help their organizations make a difference. This is an invaluable instructional and inspirational tool for anyone who works on or with a voluntary board. Includes an extensive reading list.

208 pages. May 1985. ISBN 0-87954-133-4. $16.95

WORKING IN FOUNDATIONS: Career Patterns of Women and Men
by Teresa Jean Odendahl, Elizabeth Trocolli Boris, and Arlene Kaplan Daniels

This publication is the result of a groundbreaking study of foundation career paths of women and men undertaken by Women and Foundations/Corporate Philanthropy with major funding from the Russell Sage Foundation. This book offers a detailed picture of the roles and responsibilities of foundation staff members, employment opportunities in philanthropy, and the management styles and grantmaking processes within foundations.

115 pages. April 1985. ISBN 0-87954-134-2. $12.95

The Foundation Center

The Foundation Center is an independent national service organization established by foundations to provide an authoritative source of information on private philanthropic giving. In fulfilling its mission, The Center disseminates information on private giving through public service programs, publications, and a national network of library reference collections for free public use. The New York, Washington, D.C., Cleveland, and San Francisco reference collections operated by The Foundation Center offer a wide variety of services and comprehensive collections of information on foundations and grants. The Cooperating Collections are libraries, community foundations, and other nonprofit agencies that provide a core collection of Foundation Center publications and a variety of supplementary materials and services in subject areas useful to grantseekers.

Over 100 of the network members have sets of private foundation information returns (IRS Form 990-PF) for their states or regions which are available for public use. These collections are indicated by a • next to their names. A complete set of U.S. foundation returns can be found at the New York and Washington, D.C. collections. The Cleveland and San Francisco offices contain IRS returns for those foundations in the midwestern and western states respectively.

Because the collections vary in their hours, materials and services, it is recommended that you call each collection in advance. To check on new locations or current information, call toll-free 1-800-424-9836.

Where to Go for Information on Foundation Funding

Reference Collections Operated by The Foundation Center

• The Foundation Center
79 Fifth Avenue
New York, New York 10003
212-620-4230

• The Foundation Center
1001 Connecticut Avenue, NW
Washington, D.C. 20036
202-331-1400

• The Foundation Center
Kent H. Smith Library
1442 Hanna Building
1422 Euclid Avenue
Cleveland, Ohio 44115
216-861-1933

• The Foundation Center
312 Sutter Street
San Francisco, California 94108
415-397-0902

Cooperating Collections

ALABAMA

• Birmingham Public Library
2020 Park Place
Birmingham 35203
205-226-3600

Huntsville-Madison County
Public Library
108 Fountain Circle
P.O. Box 443
Huntsville 35804
205-536-0021

• Auburn University at
Montgomery Library
Montgomery 36193-0401
205-271-9649

ALASKA

• University of Alaska,
Anchorage Library
3211 Providence Drive
Anchorage 99504
907-786-1848

ARIZONA

• Phoenix Public Library
Business and Sciences
Department
12 East McDowell Road
Phoenix 85004
602-262-4782

• Tucson Public Library
Main Library
200 South Sixth Avenue
Tucson 85701
602-791-4393

ARKANSAS

• Westark Community College
Library
Grand Avenue at Waldron Road
Fort Smith 72913
501-785-4241

• Little Rock Public Library
Reference Department
700 Louisiana Street
Little Rock 72201
501-370-5950

CALIFORNIA

Inyo County
Library—Bishop Branch
210 Academy Street
Bishop 93514
619-872-8091

• California Community
Foundation
Funding Information Center
3580 Wilshire Blvd., Suite 1660
Los Angeles 90010
213-413-4719

• Community Foundation for
Monterey County
420 Pacific Street
Monterey 93942
408-375-9712

California Community Foundation
4050 Metropolitan Drive
Orange 92668
714-937-9077

Riverside Public Library
3581 7th Street
Riverside 92501
714-787-7201

California State Library
Reference Services, Rm. 309
914 Capital Mall
Sacramento 95814
916-322-0369

• San Diego Community
Foundation
625 Broadway, Suite 1015
San Diego 92101
619-239-8815

• The Foundation Center
312 Sutter Street
San Francisco 94108
415-397-0902

Orange County Community
Development Council
1440 East First Street, 4th Floor
Santa Ana 92701
714-547-6801

Peninsula Community Foundation
1204 Burlingame Avenue
Burlingame, 94011-0627
415-342-2505

• Santa Barbara Public Library
Reference Section
40 East Anapamu
P.O. Box 1019
Santa Barbara 93102
805-962-7653

Santa Monica Public Library
1343 Sixth Street
Santa Monica 90401-1603
213-458-8603

Central Sierra Arts Council
229 South Shepherd Street
Sonora 95370
209-532-2787

North Coast Opportunities, Inc.
101 West Church Street
Ukiah 95482
707-462-1954

COLORADO

Pikes Peak Library District
20 North Cascade Avenue
Colorado Springs 80901
303-473-2080

• Denver Public Library
Sociology Division
1357 Broadway
Denver 80203
303-571-2190

CONNECTICUT

• Hartford Public Library
Reference Department
500 Main Street
Hartford 06103
203-525-9121

D.A.T.A.
880 Asylum Avenue
Hartford 06105
203-278-2477

D.A.T.A.
81 Saltonstall Avenue
New Haven 06513
203-776-0797

DELAWARE

● Hugh Morris Library
University of Delaware
Newark 19717-5267
302-451-2965

FLORIDA

● Volusia County Public
Library
City Island
Daytona Beach 32014
904-252-8374

● Jacksonville Public Library
Business, Science, and Industry
Department
122 North Ocean Street
Jacksonville 32202
904-633-3926

● Miami-Dade Public Library
Florida Collection
One Biscayne Boulevard
Miami 33132
305-579-5001

● Orlando Public Library
10 North Rosalind
Orlando 32801
305-425-4694

● University of West Florida
John C. Pace Library
Pensacola 32514
904-474-2412

Selby Public Library
1001 Boulevard of the Arts
Sarasota 33577
813-366-7303

● Leon County Public Library
Community Funding
Resources Center
1940 North Monroe Street
Tallahassee 32303
904-478-2665

Palm Beach County
Community Foundation
324 Datura Street, Suite 311
West Palm Beach 33401
305-659-6800

GEORGIA

● Atlanta-Fulton Public
Library
Ivan Allen Department
1 Margaret Mitchell Square
Atlanta 30303
404-688-4636

HAWAII

● Thomas Hale Hamilton Library
General Reference
University of Hawaii
2550 The Mall
Honolulu 96822
808-948-7214

Community Resource Center
The Hawaiian Foundation
Financial Plaza of the Pacific
111 South King Street
Honolulu 96813
808-525-8548

IDAHO

● Caldwell Public Library
1010 Dearborn Street
Caldwell 83605
208-459-3242

ILLINOIS

● Belleville Public Library
121 East Washington Street
Belleville 62220
618-234-0441

DuPage Township
300 Briarcliff Road
Bolingbrook 60439
312-759-1317

● Donors Forum of Chicago
208 South LaSalle Street
Chicago 60604
312-726-4882

● Evanston Public Library
1703 Orrington Avenue
Evanston 60201
312-866-0305

● Sangamon State University
Library
Shepherd Road
Springfield 62708
217-786-6633

INDIANA

Allen County Public Library
900 Webster Street
Fort Wayne 46802
219-424-7241

Indiana University Northwest
Library
3400 Broadway
Gary 46408
219-980-6580

● Indianapolis-Marion County
Public Library
40 East St. Clair Street
Indianapolis 46204
317-269-1733

IOWA

● Public Library of Des Moines
100 Locust Street
Des Moines 50308
515-283-4259

KANSAS

● Topeka Public Library
Adult Services Department
1515 West Tenth Street
Topeka 66604
913-233-2040

● Wichita Public Library
223 South Main
Wichita 67202
316-262-0611

KENTUCKY

Western Kentucky University
Division of Library Services
Helm-Cravens Library
Bowling Green 42101
502-745-3951

● Louisville Free Public Library
Fourth and York Streets
Louisville 40203
502-584-4154

LOUISIANA

● East Baton Rouge Parish Library
Centroplex Library
120 St. Louis Street
Baton Rouge 70821
504-389-4960

● New Orleans Public Library
Business and Science Division
219 Loyola Avenue
New Orleans 70140
504-596-2583

● Shreve Memorial Library
424 Texas Street
Shreveport 71101
318-226-5894

MAINE

● University of Southern Maine
Center for Research and
Advanced Study
246 Deering Avenue
Portland 04102
207-780-4411

MARYLAND

● Enoch Pratt Free Library
Social Science and History
Department
400 Cathedral Street
Baltimore 21201
301-396-5320

MASSACHUSETTS

● Associated Grantmakers of
Massachusetts
294 Washington Street
Suite 501
Boston 02108
617-426-2608

● Boston Public Library
Copley Square
Boston 02117
617-536-5400

Walpole Public Library
Common Street
Walpole 02081
617-668-5497 ext. 340

Western Massachusetts
Funding Resource Center
Campaign for Human
Development
Chancery Annex
73 Chestnut Street
Springfield 01103
413-732-3175 ext. 67

● Grants Resource Center
Worcester Public Library
Salem Square
Worcester 01608
617-799-1655

MICHIGAN

● Alpena County Library
211 North First Avenue
Alpena 49707
517-356-6188

University of Michigan—Ann Arbor
Reference Department
209 Hatcher Graduate Library
Ann Arbor 48109-1205
313-764-1149

● Henry Ford Centennial Library
16301 Michigan Avenue
Dearborn 48126
313-943-2337

● Purdy Library
Wayne State University
Detroit 48202
313-577-4040

● Michigan State University
Libraries
Reference Library
East Lansing 48824
517-353-9184

● Farmington Community Library
32737 West 12 Mile Road
Farmington Hills 48018
313-553-0300

● University of Michigan—
Flint Library
Reference Department
Flint 48503
313-762-3408

● Grand Rapids Public Library
Sociology and Education Dept.
Library Plaza
Grand Rapids 49502
616-456-4411

● Michigan Technological
University Library
Highway U.S. 41
Houghton 49931
906-487-2507

MINNESOTA

● Duluth Public Library
520 Superior Street
Duluth 55802
218-723-3802

● Southwest State University Library
Marshall 56258
507-537-7278

● Minneapolis Public Library
Sociology Department
300 Nicollet Mall
Minneapolis 55401
612-372-6555

Rochester Public Library
Broadway at First Street, SE
Rochester 55901
507-285-8002

Saint Paul Public Library
90 West Fourth Street
Saint Paul 55102
612-292-6311

MISSISSIPPI

Jackson Metropolitan Library
301 North State Street
Jackson 39201
601-944-1120

MISSOURI

● Clearinghouse for Midcontinent
Foundations
Univ. of Missouri, Kansas City
Law School, Suite 1-300
52nd Street and Oak
Kansas City 64113
816-276-1176

- Kansas City Public Library
  311 East 12th Street
  Kansas City 64106
  816-221-2685

- Metropolitan Association for
  Philanthropy, Inc.
  5585 Pershing Avenue
  Suite 150
  St. Louis 63112
  314-361-3900

- Springfield-Greene County
  Library
  397 East Central Street
  Springfield 65801
  417-866-4636

MONTANA

- Eastern Montana College
  Library
  Reference Department
  1500 N. 30th Street
  Billings 59101-0298
  406-657-2262

- Montana State Library
  Reference Department
  1515 E. 6th Avenue
  Helena 59620
  406-444-3004

NEBRASKA

University of Nebraska, Lincoln
106 Love Library
Lincoln 68588-0410
402-472-2526

- W. Dale Clark Library
  Social Sciences Department
  215 South 15th Street
  Omaha 68102
  402-444-4826

NEVADA

- Las Vegas–Clark County
  Library District
  1401 East Flamingo Road
  Las Vegas 89109
  702-733-7810

- Washoe County Library
  301 South Center Street
  Reno 89505
  702-785-4190

NEW HAMPSHIRE

- The New Hampshire
  Charitable Fund
  One South Street
  Concord 03301
  603-225-6641

Littleton Public Library
109 Main Street
Littleton 03561
603-444-5741

NEW JERSEY

Cumberland County Library
800 E. Commerce Street
Bridgeton 08302
609-455-0080

The Support Center
17 Academy Street, Suite 1101
Newark 07102
201-643-5774

County College of Morris
Masten Learning
  Resource Center
Route 10 and Center Grove Road
Randolph 07869
201-361-5000 ext. 470

- New Jersey State Library
  Governmental Reference
  185 West State Street
  Trenton 08625
  609-292-6220

NEW MEXICO

Albuquerque Community
  Foundation
6400 Uptown Boulevard N.E.
Suite 500-W
Albuquerque 87110
505-883-6240

- New Mexico State Library
  325 Don Gaspar Street
  Santa Fe 87503
  505-827-3824

NEW YORK

- New York State Library
  Cultural Education Center
  Humanities Section
  Empire State Plaza
  Albany 12230
  518-474-7645

Bronx Reference Center
New York Public Library
2556 Bainbridge Avenue
Bronx 10458
212-220-6575

Brooklyn in Touch
101 Willoughby Street
Room 1508
Brooklyn 11201
718-237-9300

- Buffalo and Erie County
  Public Library
  Lafayette Square
  Buffalo 14203
  716-856-7525

Huntington Public Library
338 Main Street
Huntington 11743
516-427-5165

- Levittown Public Library
  Reference Department
  One Bluegrass Lane
  Levittown 11756
  516-731-5728

SUNY/College at Old
  Westbury Library
223 Store Hill Road
Old Westbury 11568
516-876-3201

- Plattsburgh Public Library
  Reference Department
  15 Oak Street
  Plattsburgh 12901
  518-563-0921

Adriance Memorial Library
93 Market Street
Poughkeepsie 12601
914-485-4790

Queens Borough Public Library
89-11 Merrick Boulevard
Jamaica 11432
718-990-0700

- Rochester Public Library
  Business and Social Sciences
  Division
  115 South Avenue
  Rochester 14604
  716-428-7328

- Onondaga County Public Library
  335 Montgomery Street
  Syracuse 13202
  315-473-4491

- White Plains Public Library
  100 Martine Avenue
  White Plains 10601
  914-682-4488

NORTH CAROLINA

- The Duke Endowment
  200 S. Tryon Street, Ste. 1100
  Charlotte 28202
  704-376-0291

Durham County Library
300 N. Roxboro Street
Durham 27701
919-683-2626

- North Carolina State Library
  109-East Jones Street
  Raleigh 27611
  919-733-3270

- The Winston-Salem Foundation
  229 First Union National Bank
  Building
  Winston-Salem 27101
  919-725-2382

NORTH DAKOTA

Western Dakota Grants
  Resource Center
Bismarck Junior College Library
Bismarck 58501
701-224-5450

- The Library
  North Dakota State University
  Fargo 58105
  701-237-8876

OHIO

- Public Library of Cincinnati
  and Hamilton County
  Education Department
  800 Vine Street
  Cincinnati 45202
  513-369-6940

- The Foundation Center
  1442 Hanna Building
  1422 Euclid Avenue
  Cleveland 44115
  216-861-1933

CALLVAC Services, Inc.
370 South Fifth Street
Suite 1
Columbus 43215
614-221-6766

Lima-Allen County
Regional Planning Commission
212 N. Elizabeth Street
Lima 45801
419-228-1836

- Toledo-Lucas County Public
  Library
  Social Science Department
  325 Michigan Street
  Toledo 43624
  419-255-7055 ext. 221

Ohio University-Zanesville
Community Education and
  Development
1425 Newark Road
Zanesville 43701
614-453-0762

OKLAHOMA

- Oklahoma City University
  Library
  NW 23rd at North Blackwelder
  Oklahoma City 73106
  405-521-5072

- The Support Center
  525 NW Thirteenth Street
  Oklahoma City 73103
  405-236-8133

- Tulsa City-County Library
  System
  400 Civic Center
  Tulsa 74103
  918-592-7944

OREGON

- Library Association of Portland
  Government Documents Room
  801 S.W. Tenth Avenue
  Portland 97205
  503-223-7201

PENNSYLVANIA

Northampton County Area
  Community College
Learning Resources Center
3835 Green Pond Road
Bethlehem 18017
215-865-5358

- Erie County Public Library
  3 South Perry Square
  Erie 16501
  814-452-2333 ext. 54

- Dauphin County Library System
  Central Library
  101 Walnut Street
  Harrisburg 17101
  717-234-4961

Lancaster County Public Library
125 North Duke Street
Lancaster 17602
717-394-2651

- The Free Library of Philadelphia
  Logan Square
  Philadelphia 19103
  215-686-5423

- Hillman Library
  University of Pittsburgh
  Pittsburgh 15260
  412-624-4423

- Economic Development Council of
  Northeastern Pennsylvania
  1151 Oak Street
  Pittston 18640
  717-655-5581

James V. Brown Library
12 E. 4th Street
Williamsport 17701
717-326-0536

RHODE ISLAND

- Providence Public Library
  Reference Department
  150 Empire Street
  Providence 02903
  401-521-7722

SOUTH CAROLINA

- Charleston County Public
  Library
  404 King Street
  Charleston 29403
  803-723-1645

- South Carolina State Library
  Reader Services Department
  1500 Senate Street
  Columbia 29201
  803-758-3138

SOUTH DAKOTA

- South Dakota State Library
  State Library Building
  800 North Illinois Street
  Pierre 57501
  605-773-3131

  Sioux Falls Area Foundation
  404 Boyce Greeley Building
  321 South Phillips Avenue
  Sioux Falls 57102-0781
  605-336-7055

TENNESSEE

- Knoxville–Knox County Public
  Library
  500 West Church Avenue
  Knoxville 37902
  615-523-0781

- Memphis Shelby County
  Public Library
  1850 Peabody Avenue
  Memphis 38104
  901-725-8876

- Public Library of Nashville
  and Davidson County
  8th Avenue, North and
  Union Street
  Nashville 37203
  615-244-4700

TEXAS

Amarillo Area Foundation
1000 Polk
P.O. Box 25569
Amarillo 79105-269
806-376-4521

- The Hogg Foundation for
  Mental Health
  The University of Texas
  Austin 78712
  512-471-5041

- Corpus Christi State
  University Library
  6300 Ocean Drive
  Corpus Christi 78412
  512-991-6810

- Dallas Public Library
  Grants Information Service
  1515 Young Street
  Dallas 75201
  214-749-4100

- Pan American University
  Learning Resource Center
  1201 W. University Drive
  Edinburg 78539
  512-381-3304

- El Paso Community Foundation
  El Paso National Bank Building
  Suite 1616
  El Paso 79901
  915-533-4020

- Funding Information Center
  Texas Christian University
  Library
  Ft. Worth 76129
  817-921-7000 ext. 6130

- Houston Public Library
  Bibliographic & Information Center
  500 McKinney Avenue
  Houston 77002
  713-224-5441 ext. 265

- Funding Information Library
  507 Brooklyn
  San Antonio 78215
  512-227-4333

UTAH

- Salt Lake City Public Library
  Business and Science Department
  209 East Fifth South
  Salt Lake City 84111
  801-363-5733

VERMONT

- State of Vermont Department
  of Libraries
  Reference Services Unit
  111 State Street
  Montpelier 05602
  802-828-3261

VIRGINIA

- Grants Resources Library
  Hampton City Hall
  22 Lincoln Street, Ninth Floor
  Hampton 23669
  804-727-6496

- Richmond Public Library
  Business, Science, &
  Technology Department
  101 East Franklin Street
  Richmond 23219
  804-780-8223

WASHINGTON

- Seattle Public Library
  1000 Fourth Avenue
  Seattle 98104
  206-625-4881

- Spokane Public Library
  Funding Information Center
  West 906 Main Avenue
  Spokane 99201
  509-838-3361

WEST VIRGINIA

- Kanawha County Public
  Library
  123 Capital Street
  Charleston 25301
  304-343-4646

WISCONSIN

- Marquette University
  Memorial Library
  1415 West Wisconsin Avenue
  Milwaukee 53233
  414-224-1515

- University of Wisconsin–
  Madison
  Memorial Library
  728 State Street
  Madison 53706
  608-262-3647

Society for Nonprofit
  Organizations
6314 Odana Road
Suite One
Madison 53719
608-274-9777

WYOMING

- Laramie County Community
  College Library
  1400 East College Drive
  Cheyenne 82007
  307-634-5853

CANADA

Canadian Center for
  Philanthropy
185 Bay Street, Suite 504
Toronto, Ontario M5J1K6
416-364-4875

ENGLAND

Charities Aid Foundation
12 Crane Court
Fleet Street
London EC4A 2JJ
1-583-7772

MARIANA ISLANDS

Northern Marianas College
P.O. Box 1250 CK
Saipan, GM 96950

MEXICO

Biblioteca Benjamin Franklin
Londres 16
Mexico City 6, D.F.
525-591-0244

PUERTO RICO

Universidad Del Sagrado
  Corazon
M.M.T. Guevarra Library
Correo Calle Loiza
Santurce 00914
809-728-1515 ext. 274

VIRGIN ISLANDS

College of the Virgin Islands
  Library
Saint Thomas
U.S. Virgin Islands 00801
809-774-9200 ext. 487

DESCRIPTIVE DIRECTORY

ALABAMA

1
Avondale Educational & Charitable Foundation, Inc., The ¤
Avondale Mills
225 Franklin St.
Sylacauga 35150   (205) 245-5221

Incorporated in 1945 in Alabama.
Donor(s): Avondale Mills, Comer-Avondale Mills, Inc., Cowikee Mills.
Financial data: (yr. ended 12/31/83): Assets, $6,869,890 (M); gifts received, $15,000; expenditures, $419,353, including $371,550 for 124 grants (high: $45,872; low: $50).
Purpose and activities: Primarily local giving, with emphasis on higher education, health, recreation, community funds, and cultural programs.
Limitations: Giving primarily in AL.
Application information:
  Initial approach: Letter
  Deadline(s): None
  Write: Donald Comer, Jr., Chairman
Officers: Donald Comer, Jr.,* Chairman; Richard J. Comer,* Vice-Chairman; Douglas R. Bess, Secretary and Treasurer.
Trustees:* Harold D. Kingsmore.
Employer Identification Number: 636004424

2
Bedsole (J. L.) Public Welfare Trust ¤
c/o The First Nat'l Bank of Mobile
P.O. Box 1467
Mobile 36621

Established in 1972.
Financial data: (yr. ended 12/31/83): Assets, $1,578,093 (M); expenditures, $99,428, including $79,000 for 10 grants (high: $10,000; low: $500).
Purpose and activities: Primarily local giving for higher education and social services.
Limitations: Giving primarily in AL.
Trustees: Boyd Adams, James G. Bedsole, Jr., Palmer Bedsole, Jr., T. Massey Bedsole, First National Bank of Mobile.
Employer Identification Number: 237225708

3
Birmingham Foundation, The Greater ¤
P.O. Box 9096
Birmingham 35213   (205) 326-5396

Community foundation established in 1959 in Alabama by resolution and declaration of trust.
Financial data: (yr. ended 12/31/81): Assets, $5,428,799 (M); gifts received, $639,474; expenditures, $637,426, including $603,074 for 54 grants (high: $80,000; low: $100).
Purpose and activities: To promote the health, welfare, cultural, educational, and social needs of the Birmingham area only.
Limitations: Giving limited to the Birmingham, AL, area. No grants to individuals, or for endowment funds or operating budgets.
Application information:
  Initial approach: Letter
  Board meeting date(s): Quarterly
  Write: Mrs. William C. McDonald, Jr., Executive Director
Officer: Mrs. William C. McDonald, Jr., Executive Director.
Distribution Committee: Jack D. McSpadden, Chairman; Douglas Arant, Donald Brabston, Robert W. Block, Ben B. Brown, Frank Dominick, Crawford Johnson, III, William M. Spencer, III, Robert Yoe, M.D.
Trustees: Central Bank of the South, Colonial Bank of Birmingham, First Alabama Bank, First National Bank of Birmingham, South Trust Bank.
Employer Identification Number: 636019864

4
Blount Foundation, Inc., The
4520 Executive Park Dr.
P.O. Box 949
Montgomery 36192   (205) 272-8020

Incorporated in 1970 in Alabama.
Donor(s): W. Houston Blount, Blount, Inc.
Financial data: (yr. ended 2/28/83): Assets, $630,652 (M); gifts received, $15,000; expenditures, $457,679, including $439,772 for 139 grants (high: $54,956; low: $100; average: $250-$500) and $14,700 for 41 employee matching gifts.
Purpose and activities: Charitable purposes; primarily local giving for culture and the arts, higher and secondary education, including a matching gifts program, civic affairs, youth agencies, and hospitals and health.

Types of support awarded: General purposes, building funds, equipment, land acquisition, endowment funds, scholarship funds, matching funds, research, publications.
Limitations: Giving primarily in AL. No support for in-kind grants, certain religious or sectarian groups, governmental or quasi-governmental agencies, or courtesy advertising. No grants to individuals, or for demonstration projects, conferences, or seminars; no loans.
Publications: Informational brochure.
Application information:
  Initial approach: Letter or proposal
  Copies of proposal: 1
  Deadline(s): None
  Board meeting date(s): As needed
  Final notification: 12 weeks after board meets
  Write: D. Joseph McInnes, President
Officers and Directors: D. Joseph McInnes, President; W. Houston Blount, Vice-President and Treasurer; Winton M. Blount III, Secretary; Winton M. Blount.
Number of staff: 1 full-time professional; 1 full-time support.
Employer Identification Number: 636050260

5
Chandler Foundation, The ¤
304 Government St.
Mobile 36602

Established in 1963 in Alabama.
Donor(s): Ralph B. Chandler.†
Financial data: (yr. ended 12/31/83): Assets, $4,506,105 (M); expenditures, $206,210, including $157,254 for 5 grants (high: $76,073; low: $10,000).
Purpose and activities: Primarily local giving, with emphasis on civic affairs and social agencies.
Limitations: Giving primarily in AL.
Application information:
  Write: William J. Hearin, Trustee
Trustee: William J. Hearin.
Employer Identification Number: 636075470

6

Christian Workers Foundation, The ♯
3577 Bankhead Ave.
Montgomery 36111

Trust established about 1939 in Illinois.
Donor(s): Herbert J. Taylor, Stanley S. Kresge, Thesaurus Foundation.
Financial data: (yr. ended 6/30/83): Assets, $2,370,714 (M); expenditures, $149,480, including $135,658 for 17 grants (high: $94,733; low: $1,000).
Purpose and activities: To train Christian workers who are planning to enter evangelistic or mission fields of work and to assist in the support of Christian institutions which are evangelical in their nature and efforts.
Limitations: No grants to individuals.
Trustees: G. Robert Lockwood, Mrs. G. Robert Lockwood, Allen W. Mathis, Jr., Beverly T. Mathis, Mrs. H.J. Taylor.
Employer Identification Number: 362181979

7

Daniel Foundation of Alabama, The ♯
200 Office Park Dr., Suite 100
Birmingham 35223

Established in 1978 in Alabama as partial successor to the Daniel Foundation.
Donor(s): Charles W. Daniel, R. Hugh Daniel.
Financial data: (yr. ended 12/31/83): Assets, $12,594,034 (M); expenditures, $577,935, including $508,650 for 22 grants (high: $110,000; low: $1,000).
Purpose and activities: Broad purposes; primarily local giving, with emphasis on health and higher education; support also for cultural programs, social agencies, and youth.
Limitations: Giving primarily in AL.
Officers: M.C. Daniel, Chairman; Harry B. Brock, Jr., President; Charles W. Daniel, Vice-President; S. Garry Smith, Secretary and Treasurer.
Employer Identification Number: 630755676

8

Flack (J. Hunter) Foundation, Inc. ♯
625 Bell Bldg.
Montgomery 36104

Established in 1979.
Donor(s): J. Hunter Flack.
Financial data: (yr. ended 1/31/84): Assets, $595,043 (M); gifts received, $254,575; expenditures, $132,777, including $131,645 for 21 grants (high: $68,225; low: $14).
Purpose and activities: Primarily local giving for Protestant churches and religious or educational organizations.
Limitations: Giving primarily in AL.
Officer and Directors: J. Hunter Flack, President; Eleanor Flack, Alexander Green.
Employer Identification Number: 636009500

9

Gibson (E. L.) Foundation ♯
201 S. Edwards
Enterprise 36330

Established in 1944.
Financial data: (yr. ended 12/31/83): Assets, $1,781,357 (M); expenditures, $96,390, including $75,123 for 30 grants (high: $20,000; low: $73) and $4,088 for 11 grants to individuals.
Purpose and activities: Local giving for higher education and scholarships; support also for health agencies and civic affairs.
Limitations: Giving limited to Coffee County, AL, and contiguous counties.
Application information:
  Initial approach: Letter
  Deadline(s): None
  Write: J.B. Brunson, Manager
Officers and Directors: Wendell Vickers, President and Chairman; E.T. Brunson, Vice-Chairman; J.B. Brunson, Manager; Joe Bynum, J.S. DuBois, E.L. Gibson, H.D. Gibson, J.W. Herod, Homer Moates, A.R. Pappas, J.E. Pittman, Ferrell Reeves.
Employer Identification Number: 630383929

10

Linn-Henley Charitable Trust ♯
SouthTrust Bank of Alabama
P.O. Box 2554
Birmingham 35290   (205) 254-5285

Trust established in 1965 in Alabama.
Donor(s): Walter E. Henley.†
Financial data: (yr. ended 3/31/84): Assets, $3,726,978 (M); expenditures, $97,343, including $61,620 for 15 grants (high: $20,000; low: $1,000).
Purpose and activities: Local giving, with emphasis on cultural programs and higher education.
Limitations: Giving limited to Jefferson County, AL.
Application information:
  Initial approach: Letter
  Deadline(s): None
  Write: Douglas C. Bell
Trustees: John C. Henley III, SouthTrust Bank of Alabama.
Employer Identification Number: 636051833

11

Malbis Memorial Foundation ♯
c/o Antigone Papageorge
P.O. Box 639
Daphne 36526

Incorporated in 1945 in Alabama.
Donor(s): P.E. Frankos, Tom Kokenes, Angelo Mathews,† James Papas, Philip Papas,† and others.
Financial data: (yr. ended 12/31/83): Assets, $1,919,410 (M); gifts received, $10,317; expenditures, $120,393, including $61,040 for 108 grants (high: $4,200; low: $50).
Purpose and activities: Primarily religious purposes; maintains a local Greek Orthodox church; emphasis on church support.

Limitations: Giving primarily in the Southeast, particularly in AL.
Officers and Trustees: Nafseka Mallars, President; E. Vrahatis, Vice-President; Antigone Papageorge, Secretary; Perry Kontopoulos, C.D. Papadeas, Sam Papas, Nick Stavrakis.
Employer Identification Number: 636044881

12

McMillan (D. W.) Foundation
P.O. Box 867
Brewton 36427   (205) 867-4881

Trust established in 1956 in Alabama.
Donor(s): D.W. McMillan Trust.
Financial data: (yr. ended 12/31/83): Assets, $5,469,453 (M); expenditures, $350,818, including $312,000 for 20 grants (high: $80,000; low: $2,000).
Purpose and activities: Limited to aid to poor and needy people of Escambia County, Alabama and Escambia County, Florida, including welfare and medical aid, through grants to local health and welfare organizations; limited to programs giving direct aid.
Limitations: Giving limited to Escambia County, AL and Escambia County, FL. No support for education or medical research.
Application information:
  Initial approach: Letter
  Copies of proposal: 1
  Deadline(s): December 1
  Board meeting date(s): December 1
  Final notification: December 31
  Write: Ed Leigh McMillan, II, Managing Trustee
Trustees: Ed Leigh McMillan II, Managing Trustee; John David Finlay, Jr., M.N. Hoke, Jr., Allison R. Sinrod.
Employer Identification Number: 636044830

13

McWane Foundation ♯
P.O. Box 43327
Birmingham 35243

Established in 1961.
Financial data: (yr. ended 12/31/83): Assets, $1,882,386 (M); gifts received, $208,865; expenditures, $290,465, including $287,000 for 19 grants (high: $100,000; low: $500).
Purpose and activities: Primarily local giving, with emphasis on higher and secondary education and social services.
Limitations: Giving primarily in AL.
Trustees: John McMahon, J.R. McWane.
Employer Identification Number: 636044384

14

Meyer (Robert R.) Foundation ▼
c/o AmSouth Bank, Trust Dept.
P.O. Box 11426
Birmingham 35202   (205) 326-5396

Trust established in 1942 in Alabama.
Donor(s): Robert R. Meyer,† John E. Meyer.†

Financial data: (yr. ended 12/31/82): Assets, $10,639,329 (M); expenditures, $643,469, including $594,250 for 32 grants (high: $80,000; low: $1,800; average: $2,000-$25,000).

Purpose and activities: Aid largely to local health and welfare organizations, educational institutions, and cultural organizations selected by an advisory committee.

Types of support awarded: Building funds, equipment, land acquisition, research, scholarship funds.

Limitations: Giving primarily in Birmingham, AL, metropolitan area. No grants to individuals, or for endowment funds or operating budgets.

Publications: Application guidelines.

Application information:
  Initial approach: Full proposal
  Copies of proposal: 5
  Deadline(s): April 15
  Board meeting date(s): June
  Final notification: 4 weeks
  Write: Virginia C. Ramsey, Vice-President

Grants Committee: Henry S. Lynn, Seybourn H. Lynn, William J. Rushton, III, William M. Spencer, III.

Trustee: AmSouth Bank (Virginia C. Ramsey, Vice President and Trust Officer).

Number of staff: None.

Employer Identification Number: 636019645

15

Middleton (Kate Kinloch) Fund ¤
P.O. Drawer 2527
Mobile 36601

Established in 1957 in Alabama.

Financial data: (yr. ended 1/31/84): Assets, $1,721,659 (M); gifts received, $1,494; expenditures, $220,446, including $156,151 for 111 grants to individuals and $26,295 for 12 loans.

Purpose and activities: Grants and loans to individuals for medical expenses limited to local residents.

Types of support awarded: Grants to individuals.

Limitations: Giving limited to Mobile County, AL.

Application information:
  Write: Joan Sapp

Trustee: Merchants National Bank.

Employer Identification Number: 630417309

16

Mitchell Foundation, The
P.O. Box 1126
2405 First National Bank Bldg.
Mobile 36601   (205) 432-1711

Incorporated in 1957 in Alabama.

Donor(s): A.S. Mitchell,† Mrs. A.S. Mitchell.

Financial data: (yr. ended 1/31/84): Assets, $7,592,825 (M); expenditures, $448,657, including $326,126 for 30 grants (high: $85,000; low: $100).

Purpose and activities: Primarily local giving, with emphasis on secondary and higher education; support also for social service programs including religious welfare agencies, aid to the handicapped, and youth agencies; hospitals and health associations; and Protestant church support.

Limitations: Giving primarily in AL. No grants to individuals.

Application information:
  Initial approach: Letter
  Deadline(s): None
  Board meeting date(s): Quarterly
  Write: M.L. Screven, Jr., Secretary

Officers and Directors: Augustine Meaher, Jr., President; Frank B. Vinson, Jr., Vice-President; M.L. Screven, Jr., Secretary-Treasurer; W. Brevard Hand, Augustine Meaher III, Frank Vinson.

Employer Identification Number: 630368954

17

Mobile Community Foundation, The
2310 First National Bank Bldg.
Mobile 36602   (205) 438-5591

Community foundation incorporated in 1976 in Alabama.

Financial data: (yr. ended 12/31/84): Assets, $3,280,979 (M); gifts received, $531,000; expenditures, $362,528, including $298,015 for 121 grants (high: $11,638; low: $100).

Purpose and activities: Primarily local giving, in the fields of health and human services, education, civic affairs, culture, and the arts.

Limitations: Giving primarily in the Mobile, AL, metropolitan area. No grants to individuals.

Publications: Annual report, application guidelines, program policy statement, informational brochure.

Application information:
  Initial approach: Letter
  Copies of proposal: 1
  Deadline(s): October 1
  Board meeting date(s): Quarterly
  Write: William Kaufman, Executive Director

Officers and Directors: Vivian G. Johnston, Jr.,* President; Melvin Stein,* Mrs. Mayer Mitchell,* Vice-Presidents; Darrel L. Miller, Secretary; Ogden Shropshire,* Treasurer; William Kaufman, Executive Director; and 8 additional directors.

Number of staff: 1 full-time professional; 1 part-time professional; 1 part-time support.

Employer Identification Number: 630695166

18

Russell (Benjamin and Roberta) Educational and Charitable Foundation, Incorporated ¤
Alexander City 35010

Incorporated in 1944 in Alabama.

Donor(s): Benjamin Russell.†

Financial data: (yr. ended 12/31/83): Assets, $12,882,346 (M); expenditures, $535,762, including $428,841 for 23 grants (high: $110,000).

Purpose and activities: Primarily local giving, with emphasis on higher and public education, health agencies, youth programs and a hospital.

Limitations: Giving primarily in AL.

Officers and Directors: Nancy R. Gwaltney, President; Benjamin Russell, Vice-President; James D. Nabors, Secretary-Treasurer; Roberta A. Baumgardner, James W. Brown, Jr., Ann R. Caceres, Edith L. Russell, Julia W. Russell, Julia G. Shockley.

Employer Identification Number: 630393126

19

Shook (Barbara Ingalls) Foundation ¤
P.O. Box 7332A
Mountain Brook 35253

Established in 1980.

Financial data: (yr. ended 8/31/83): Assets, $4,104,117 (M); expenditures, $174,824, including $91,002 for 27 grants (high: $25,475; low: $25).

Purpose and activities: Primarily local giving, with emphasis on higher education, hospitals, medical research, and cultural programs.

Limitations: Giving primarily in AL.

Officers and Trustees: Barbara I. Shook, Chairman and Treasurer; Robert P. Shook, Vice-Chairman and Secretary; W. Bew White, Jr.

Employer Identification Number: 630792812

20

Smith (M. W.), Jr. Foundation
P.O. Box 691
Daphne 36526   (205) 626-5436

Trust established in 1960 in Alabama.

Donor(s): M.W. Smith, Jr.†

Financial data: (yr. ended 12/31/83): Assets, $1,314,587 (M); expenditures, $116,998, including $84,400 for 20 grants (high: $20,000; low: $360).

Purpose and activities: Broad purposes; primarily local giving, with emphasis on Protestant religious welfare programs and churches, and education.

Types of support awarded: Operating budgets, general purposes, continuing support, annual campaigns, seed money, emergency funds, deficit financing, building funds, equipment, land acquisition, endowment funds, special projects, research, publications, conferences and seminars, scholarship funds, matching funds.

Limitations: Giving primarily in southwest AL. No grants to individuals; no loans.

Application information:
  Initial approach: Letter
  Copies of proposal: 1
  Deadline(s): Submit proposal preferably in March or August; deadline middle of months prior to board meetings
  Board meeting date(s): May and November
  Final notification: 1 month
  Write: Mary M. Riser, Secretary

Distribution Committee: Maida Pearson, Chairman; Mary M. Riser, Secretary; Louis C. Crim, Louis M. Finlay, Jr., Sybil H. Lebherz.

Trustee: First National Bank of Mobile.

Number of staff: None.

Employer Identification Number: 636018078

21
Sonat Foundation, Inc., The ⌷
1900 Fifth Ave. North
P.O. Box 2563
Birmingham 35203   (205) 325-7133

Established in 1982 in Alabama.
Donor(s): Sonat Inc.
Financial data: (yr. ended 12/31/83): Assets,
$3,711,452 (M); gifts received, $1,500,000;
expenditures, $1,079,238, including
$1,039,968 for 127 grants (high: $130,000)
and $20,000 for 10 grants to individuals.
Purpose and activities: Giving mainly for
higher education, including company employee
scholarships, and community funds; some
support also for youth agencies, cultural
programs, and hospitals.
Types of support awarded: Matching funds,
employee related scholarships, general
purposes, operating budgets, building funds,
research.
Publications: Application guidelines.
Application information:
   Deadline(s): February 1
   Write: John C. Griffin, Secretary
Officers: Peter G. Smith, President; J. Robert
Doody, Vice-President and Treasurer; Sarrah
W. Rankin, Vice-President; John C. Griffin,
Secretary.
Employer Identification Number: 630830299

22
Stockham (The William H. and Kate F.)
   Foundation, Inc. ⌷
c/o Stockham Valves & Fittings, Inc.
4000 North Tenth Ave., P.O. Box 10326
Birmingham 35202

Incorporated in 1948 in Alabama.
Donor(s): Stockham Valves and Fittings, Inc.
Financial data: (yr. ended 12/31/83): Assets,
$3,625,985 (M); expenditures, $340,610,
including $330,780 for 54 grants (high:
$70,000; low: $200) and $22,530 for 26 grants
to individuals.
Purpose and activities: Charitable giving to
causes of interest to the founders, generally
limited to Alabama, with emphasis on
educational purposes including higher
education; community funds and hospitals;
Christian religious education and church
support; and assistance to employees and
former employees of the donor, including
scholarships and fellowships.
Types of support awarded: Employee related
scholarships.
Limitations: Giving primarily in AL and the
Southeast. No grants to individuals (except
scholarships for employees and their
dependents).
Application information:
   Initial approach: Letter
   Deadline(s): None
   Write: Herbert Stockham, Vice-Chairman
Officers and Trustees: Herbert Stockman,
Vice-Chairman and President; Sam Perry
Given, Secretary; J.R. Davis, Richard J.
Stockham, Jr.
Employer Identification Number: 636049787

23
Warner (David) Foundation Trust ⌷
c/o The First National Bank of Tuscaloosa,
P.O. Box 2028
2330 University Blvd.
Tuscaloosa 35401   (205) 345-5000

Trust established in 1936 in Alabama.
Donor(s): Mildred W. Warner, Herbert D.
Warner, Gulf States Paper Corporation, The
First National Bank of Tuscaloosa.
Financial data: (yr. ended 5/31/83): Assets,
$2,905,423 (M); gifts received, $371,618;
expenditures, $337,388, including $277,500
for 7 grants (high: $200,000; low: $2,500).
Purpose and activities: Primarily local giving
with emphasis on higher education; some
support for other educational, religious or
character building organizations including
hospitals and youth agencies.
Limitations: Giving primarily in AL.
Officer: Scott H. Black, Secretary.
Trustees: Frank M. Moody, Jonathan W.
Warner, Ernest G. Williams.
Employer Identification Number: 630782745

24
Webb (Susan Mott) Charitable Trust
c/o AmSouth Bank
P.O. Box 11426
Birmingham 35202   (205) 326-5396

Established in 1978 in Alabama.
Donor(s): Susan Mott Webb.†
Financial data: (yr. ended 12/31/83): Assets,
$6,119,484 (M); gifts received, $6,386;
expenditures, $525,643, including $489,740
for 15 grants (high: $250,000; low: $990).
Purpose and activities: Local giving, with
emphasis on a university and social services.
Types of support awarded: Building funds,
equipment, special projects.
Limitations: Giving primarily in the greater
Birmingham, AL, area. No grants to
individuals, or for scholarships or fellowships;
no loans.
Application information:
   Initial approach: Letter or proposal
   Copies of proposal: 6
   Deadline(s): Submit proposal preferably in
      April and October; deadline April 15 and
      October 15
   Board meeting date(s): June and December
   Final notification: 2 months
   Write: Mrs. Virginia Ramsey, Vice-President
Trustees: Susan D. Bird, Stewart Dansby,
Charles B. Webb, Jr., William Bew White, Jr.,
AmSouth Bank (Virginia Ramsey, Vice-President
and Trust Officer).
Number of staff: None.
Employer Identification Number: 626112593

ALASKA

25
Alaska Conservation Foundation
308 Y St., Rm. 301
Anchorage 99501   (907) 276-1917

Community foundation incorporated in 1980 in
Alaska.
Financial data: (yr. ended 12/31/83): Assets,
$261,725 (M); gifts received, $249,537;
expenditures, $260,046, including $178,246
for 50 grants.
Purpose and activities: Giving limited to
research and education projects for
environmental protection in Alaska.
Types of support awarded: General purposes,
continuing support, seed money, emergency
funds, equipment, matching funds, consulting
services, technical assistance, internships,
research, special projects, conferences and
seminars, publications.
Limitations: Giving limited to AK. No grants
for annual campaigns, deficit financing, building
funds, land acquisition, renovation projects,
general or special endowments, scholarships,
fellowships, professorships, exchange programs,
student loans, or program-related investments.
Publications: Annual report, program policy
statement, application guidelines.
Application information: Application form
required.
   Write: Denny Wilcher, President
Officer: Denny Wilcher, President.
Number of staff: 2 full-time professional; 1 full-
time support.
Employer Identification Number: 920061466

26
Atwood Foundation Incorporated ⌷
P.O. Box 40
Anchorage 99510

Foundation established in 1965 in Alaska.
Donor(s): Robert B. Atwood, Anchorage Times
Publishing Company.
Financial data: (yr. ended 12/31/82): Assets,
$2,206,178 (M); gifts received, $929,000;
expenditures, $99,087, including $92,400 for 6
grants (high: $80,000; low: $100).
Purpose and activities: Primarily local giving;
support largely for educational, cultural, and
civic affairs organizations.
Limitations: Giving primarily in AK.
Officer and Trustee: Robert B. Atwood,
President.
Employer Identification Number: 976002571

ARIZONA

27
Amerind Foundation, Inc., The
P.O. Box 248
Dragoon 85609   (602) 586-3003

Incorporated in 1937 in Connecticut.
Donor(s): William Shirley Fulton,† Rose H. Fulton.†
Financial data: (yr. ended 12/31/82): Assets, $10,473,458 (M); gifts received, $28,372; expenditures, $242,354, including $197,205 for 1 foundation-administered program.
Purpose and activities: A private operating foundation which supports archaeological field work and ethnohistorical studies in the United States and Mexico, publication of results, and the housing and display of recovered materials in the Foundation's museum.
Limitations: No grants to individuals, or for building or endowment funds, operating budgets, or special projects.
Publications: 990-PF, program policy statement.
Application information: Grant applications not invited.
  Board meeting date(s): May and November
Officers and Directors: William Duncan Fulton, President; Peter L. Formo, Vice-President; Elizabeth F. Husband, Secretary; Michael Hard, Treasurer; Anne I. Woosley, Foundation Director; Emil W. Haury, Peter Johnson, Clay Lockett, Frank M. Votaw.
Number of staff: 3 full-time professional; 6 full-time support; 12 part-time support.
Employer Identification Number: 860122680

28
Arizona Bank Charitable Foundation ⌑
P.O. Box 2511
Phoenix 85002

Established in 1977.
Donor(s): Arizona Bank.
Financial data: (yr. ended 12/31/83): Assets, $104,525 (M); gifts received, $432,168; expenditures, $377,402, including $377,402 for 260 grants (high: $122,117; low: $10).
Purpose and activities: Primarily local giving, with emphasis on a community fund, cultural programs, hospitals and health services, higher education, and economic development.
Limitations: Giving primarily in AZ.
Officers and Trustees: Richard C. Houseworth, Chairman; Leon O. Chase, Secretary; Robert L. Matthews, Don B. Tostenrud.
Employer Identification Number: 860337807

29
Arizona Community Foundation
4350 E. Camelback Rd., Suite 216C
Phoenix 85018   (602) 952-9954

Community foundation incorporated in 1978 in Arizona.
Financial data: (yr. ended 3/31/84): Assets, $2,719,370 (M); gifts received, $691,203; expenditures, $178,371, including $100,454 for 66 grants (high: $7,590; low: $100; average: $500-$10,000).
Purpose and activities: Primarily local giving, with emphasis on the performing arts, cultural programs, youth agencies, health agencies, organizations for the handicapped, and other human services programs.
Types of support awarded: Seed money, emergency funds, equipment, technical assistance, special projects, operating budgets, continuing support, annual campaigns, building funds, land acquisition, matching funds, scholarship funds, special projects.
Limitations: Giving primarily in AZ. No grants to individuals, or for deficit financing, endowment funds, employee matching gifts, consulting services, publications, research, conferences and seminars, or program-related investments; no loans.
Publications: Annual report, program policy statement, application guidelines, newsletter, financial statement, informational brochure.
Application information: Application form required.
  Initial approach: Letter or proposal
  Copies of proposal: 6
  Deadline(s): February 1 and October 1
  Board meeting date(s): Quarterly
  Final notification: 60 days
  Write: Stephen D. Mittenthal, President
Executive Committee: Bert A. Getz, Chairman; Stephen D. Mittenthal, President and Executive Director; Joan C. Nastro, Secretary; James D. Bruner, Treasurer; Edward M. Carson, Richard Whitney.
Directors: Kathy Chase, Tom Chauncey II, G.R. Herberger, Allen L. Rosenberg, Donald N. Soldwedel.
Number of staff: 1 full-time professional; 1 full-time support.
Employer Identification Number: 860348306

30
Butz Foundation, The
RFD No. 5, Box 831
Prescott 86301   (602) 445-4384

Incorporated in 1951 in Illinois.
Donor(s): Theodore C. Butz,† Jean Butz James.
Financial data: (yr. ended 1/18/85): Assets, $1,677,398 (M); expenditures, $137,740, including $113,500 for 13 grants (high: $25,000; low: $1,000; average: $10,000-$15,000).
Purpose and activities: General giving, primarily in Illinois, with emphasis on medical research; support also for higher and secondary education, aid to the handicapped, religious associations, and child welfare.
Types of support awarded: Operating budgets, continuing support, equipment, research.

Limitations: Giving primarily in IL. No grants to individuals; no loans.
Application information:
  Initial approach: Letter
  Copies of proposal: 1
  Deadline(s): Submit proposal preferably in first six months of calendar year; deadline October 1
  Board meeting date(s): Quarterly
  Final notification: 6 months
  Write: Jean Butz James, President
Officers and Directors: Jean Butz James, President; Barbara T. Butz, Secretary; Raymond E. George, Jr., Treasurer; Theodore H. Butz.
Number of staff: 2 part-time support.
Employer Identification Number: 366008818

31
Circle K/Sun World Foundation
4500 South 40th St.
Phoenix 85040   (602) 437-0600

Established in 1980 in Arizona.
Donor(s): Hervey Foundation, Circle K Corporation.
Financial data: (yr. ended 8/31/84): Assets, $158,199 (L); gifts received, $309,000; expenditures, $336,571, including $335,450 for 87 grants (high: $40,000; low: $25).
Purpose and activities: Broad purposes; giving limited to Arizona and Texas, with support for youth agencies, children's dental care programs, hospitals and health associations, and educational programs and schools.
Types of support awarded: Operating budgets, continuing support, annual campaigns, seed money, general purposes, building funds, equipment, special projects.
Limitations: Giving limited to AZ and TX. No grants to individuals, or for endowment funds, scholarships, fellowships, or matching gifts; no loans.
Application information:
  Initial approach: Letter
  Copies of proposal: 1
  Deadline(s): None
  Board meeting date(s): Monthly
  Final notification: 2 months
  Write: Bill J. Farmer, Secretary-Treasurer
Officers and Trustees: Robert E. Hutchinson, President; Millard Orick, Vice-President; Bill J. Farmer, Secretary-Treasurer; H.R. Fenstermacher, Fred Hervey, Jill Moline.
Number of staff: 1 part-time professional.
Employer Identification Number: 742137873

32
Dougherty Foundation, Inc.
3336 North 32nd St., Suite 115
Phoenix 85018   (602) 956-3980

Incorporated in 1954 in Arizona.
Donor(s): M.J. Dougherty,† Mrs. M.J. Dougherty.†
Financial data: (yr. ended 12/31/83): Assets, $5,809,093 (M); expenditures, $583,867, including $233,650 for grants to individuals and $231,200 for loans.

Purpose and activities: Student loans and scholarships to needy college students of high academic ability; restricted to Arizona residents only.
Types of support awarded: Student aid.
Limitations: Giving limited to residents of AZ who are U.S. citizens.
Publications: Program policy statement, application guidelines.
Application information: Application form required.
  Initial approach: Letter or telephone
  Copies of proposal: 1
  Deadline(s): Submit proposal between July and September; no set deadline
  Board meeting date(s): Monthly and as required
  Write: Mary J. Maffeo, Secretary
Officers and Directors: John F. Prince, President; Bruce E. Babbitt, William J. Eden, William P. Mahoney, Jr., Vice-Presidents; Mary J. Maffeo, Secretary; Ann Steinberg, Treasurer.
Employer Identification Number: 866051637

33
du Bois (E. Blois) Foundation, Inc. ⌐
3620 North Third St.
Phoenix 85012   (602) 264-3751
Grant application address: P.O. Box 33426, Phoenix, AZ 85067; Scholarship inquiries: Director of Financial Aid at University of Arizona, Arizona State University, or any one of the Arizona community colleges

Incorporated in 1960 in Arizona.
Donor(s): E. Blois du Bois.†
Financial data: (yr. ended 5/31/83): Assets, $8,901,384 (M); expenditures, $701,741, including $457,315 for 10 grants (high: $136,700; low: $500).
Purpose and activities: Grants generally limited to humane societies in Arizona and to scholarship funds for students recommended by financial aid officers of colleges, universities, and junior colleges operated by the state of Arizona or a subdivision thereof.
Types of support awarded: Scholarship funds, operating budgets.
Limitations: Giving primarily in AZ. No grants to individuals, or for endowment funds.
Application information: Application forms for scholarships avilable at various directors of financial aid offices; no form necessary for other grant requests.
  Initial approach: Letter
  Copies of proposal: 2
  Board meeting date(s): As required
  Write: Alan du Bois, President
Officers and Directors: Alan du Bois, President; Gail B. Horne, Secretary-Treasurer; Robert C. Horne.
Employer Identification Number: 866052886

34
First Interstate Bank of Arizona, N.A. Charitable Foundation ▼
(formerly First National Bank of Arizona Charitable Foundation)
P.O. Box 20551, Dept. 919
Phoenix 85036   (602) 271-1429

Established in 1976 in Arizona.
Donor(s): First Interstate Bank of Arizona.
Financial data: (yr. ended 12/31/84): Assets, $5,287,555 (M); gifts received, $1,015,994; expenditures, $1,021,079, including $1,010,329 for 328 grants (high: $122,475; low: $100; average: $3,000).
Purpose and activities: General purposes; support for community funds and higher education, community development, hospitals, social agencies, cultural programs, and youth agencies. Support restricted to Arizona-based organizations or national organizations which fund programs within the state.
Types of support awarded: Annual campaigns, building funds, continuing support, emergency funds, equipment, general purposes, land acquisition, matching funds, research, scholarship funds, seed money.
Limitations: Giving limited to AZ based organizations or national organizations which fund programs in Arizona. No support for solely religious purposes. No grants to individuals, or for endowment funds or travel; no loans.
Publications: Application guidelines.
Application information: Application form required.
  Initial approach: Letter
  Copies of proposal: 1
  Deadline(s): Submit proposals January through June and September and October
  Board meeting date(s): Twice a month
  Final notification: 2 months
  Write: Charles W. Hemann, Chairman, Corporate Contributions Committee
Trustees: Charles W. Hemann, Chairman; Mark A. Dinunzio, William T. Rauch, Dianne Stephens.
Number of staff: 1 part-time professional; 1 part-time support.
Employer Identification Number: 510204372

35
Flinn Foundation, The ▼
3300 North Central Ave., Suite 1730
Phoenix 85012   (602) 274-9000

Trust established in 1965 in Arizona.
Donor(s): Mrs. Irene Flinn,† Robert S. Flinn, M.D.†
Financial data: (yr. ended 12/31/84): Assets, $69,422,815 (M); gifts received, $34,634,074; expenditures, $2,820,272, including $1,484,343 for 54 grants (high: $285,000; low: $2,915; average: $65,000).
Purpose and activities: Giving primarily in Arizona and New Mexico, to improve the quality and cost-effectiveness of health care services through support of research and development projects which offer promise of improving the capacity of the health care system to reduce the burden of avoidable illness and premature death.
Types of support awarded: Special projects, research, conferences and seminars.

Limitations: Giving primarily in AZ and NM. No support for films. No grants to individuals, or for matching gifts, emergency funds, land acquisition, renovation projects, annual campaigns, capital or endowment funds, or operating or deficit costs; or for equipment, publications, or workshops and conferences that are not an integral part of a larger project.
Publications: Program policy statement, application guidelines.
Application information:
  Initial approach: Letter or telephone
  Copies of proposal: 2
  Deadline(s): None
  Board meeting date(s): 6 times a year
  Final notification: 6 weeks
  Write: John W. Murphy, Executive Director
Officers: Donald K. Buffmire, M.D.,* President; David R. Frazer,* Vice-President and Treasurer; Jay S. Ruffner,* Secretary; John W. Murphy, Executive Director.
Directors:* Robert A. Brooks, M.D., Merlin W. Kampfer, M.D., Edward V. O'Malley, Jr.
Number of staff: 2 full-time professional; 2 full-time support.
Employer Identification Number: 866053715

36
Fry (Erwin) Foundation ⌐
P.O. Box 610
Sierra Vista 85636   (602) 886-1263

Financial data: (yr. ended 12/31/82): Assets, $1,674,343 (M); expenditures, $71,368, including $35,000 for 1 grant.
Purpose and activities: Local giving for scholarships administered by the Cochise College Foundation, Douglas, Arizona.
Types of support awarded: Student aid.
Limitations: Giving limited to Cochise County, AZ.
Publications: Application guidelines.
Application information: Application form required.
  Deadline(s): Submit applications between January 1 and February 15; deadline February 15
  Final notification: May 1
  Write: A. Jay Busby, Trustee
Trustees: Gaytha L. Bradley, A. Jay Busby, Grace E. Pomeroy.
Employer Identification Number: 860400719

37
Goppert Foundation, The ⌐
8336 Calle de Alegria
Scottsdale 85255

Incorporated in 1958 in Missouri.
Donor(s): Clarence H. Goppert.
Financial data: (yr. ended 10/31/83): Assets, $3,162,280 (M); gifts received, $2,000; expenditures, $174,594, including $160,000 for 9 grants (high: $60,000; low: $1,000).
Purpose and activities: Broad purposes; giving primarily in western Missouri, eastern Kansas, and Maricopa County, Arizona, with emphasis on higher education, hospitals, and church support.

Limitations: Giving primarily in western MO, eastern KS, and Maricopa County, AZ. No grants to individuals.
Application information:
Write: Howard E. Bunton, Vice-President
Officers: Vita M. Goppert,* President; Howard E. Bunton, Vice-President; Thomas A. Goppert, Secretary; M. Charles Kellogg, Treasurer.
Directors:* Clarence H. Goppert, Chairman; Richard D. Goppert, Vice-Chairman; Porter C. Jeffries, Leon G. Kusnetzky, Earl Lash, James P. Regan.
Employer Identification Number: 446013933

38
Hervey Foundation
P.O. Box 20230
Phoenix 85036   (602) 437-0600

Trust established in 1957 in Texas.
Financial data: (yr. ended 1/31/84): Assets, $4,319,230 (M); expenditures, $303,471, including $243,954 for 35 grants (high: $50,000; low: $40).
Purpose and activities: Broad purposes; primarily local giving, with emphasis on community funds, youth agencies, and hospitals.
Types of support awarded: Operating budgets, continuing support, annual campaigns, building funds, equipment, special projects, research, scholarship funds.
Limitations: Giving primarily in AZ. No grants to individuals, or for endowment funds, or matching gifts; no loans.
Application information:
Initial approach: Letter
Copies of proposal: 1
Deadline(s): None
Board meeting date(s): Monthly
Final notification: 2 months
Write: Bill J. Farmer, Administrator/Trustee
Trustees: Bill J. Farmer, Fred Hervey, Robert E. Hutchinson, Rick Orick.
Number of staff: 1 part-time professional.
Employer Identification Number: 746068038

39
Kieckhefer (J. W.) Foundation ▼
116 East Gurley St.
P.O. Box 750
Prescott 86302   (602) 445-4010

Trust established in 1953 in Arizona.
Donor(s): John W. Kieckhefer.†
Financial data: (yr. ended 12/31/84): Assets, $9,559,727 (M); expenditures, $560,074, including $525,499 for 48 grants (high: $40,000; low: $1,000; average: $1,000-$10,000).
Purpose and activities: General giving, with emphasis on medical research and health agencies, social services, education, youth and child welfare agencies, and conservation.
Types of support awarded: Operating budgets, continuing support, annual campaigns, emergency funds, building funds, equipment, land acquisition, endowment funds, matching funds, research, publications, conferences and seminars, special projects.

Limitations: No grants to individuals, or for seed money, deficit financing, scholarships, fellowships, or demonstration projects; no loans.
Publications: 990-PF.
Application information:
Initial approach: Letter, proposal, or telephone
Copies of proposal: 1
Deadline(s): Submit proposal preferably between May and November
Board meeting date(s): November, December, and as required
Final notification: 6 months
Write: Eugene P. Polk, Administrative Officer
Officer: Eugene P. Polk, Administrative Officer.
Trustees: John I. Kieckhefer, Robert H. Kieckhefer, Virginia O. Kieckhefer.
Number of staff: None.
Employer Identification Number: 866022877

40
Marshall Foundation
P.O. Box 3306
Tucson 85722   (602) 622-8613

Incorporated in 1930 in Arizona.
Donor(s): Louise F. Marshall.†
Financial data: (yr. ended 12/31/82): Assets, $4,750,982 (M); expenditures, $652,988, including $188,450 for 22 grants (high: $40,950; low: $2,000).
Purpose and activities: Broad purposes; local giving, with emphasis on education, youth agencies, and social agencies.
Limitations: Giving limited to the Tuscon, AZ, area. No grants to individuals.
Publications: 990-PF.
Application information:
Initial approach: Letter
Board meeting date(s): Monthly
Officers and Directors: John F. Molloy, President; Ella L. Rimel, Secretary and Treasurer; Michael Williams.
Number of staff: 2 full-time professional.
Employer Identification Number: 860102198

41
Morris (Margaret T.) Foundation
P.O. Box 592
Prescott 86302   (602) 445-4010

Established in 1967.
Donor(s): Margaret T. Morris Trust.
Financial data: (yr. ended 12/31/84): Assets, $14,569,366 (M); gifts received, $320,000; expenditures, $643,284, including $611,700 for 50 grants (high: $50,000; low: $1,000).
Purpose and activities: Giving primarily in Arizona for the performing arts, conservation, and assistance for the handicapped.
Types of support awarded: Land acquisition, general purposes, building funds, scholarship funds, deficit financing, endowment funds, operating budgets.
Limitations: Giving primarily in AZ. No support for religious organizations or their agencies. No grants to individuals; no loans.
Publications: 990-PF.
Application information:
Initial approach: Proposal

Deadline(s): Submit proposal preferably in May through November
Write: Eugene P. Polk, Trustee
Trustees: Richard L. Menschel, Eugene P. Polk.
Employer Identification Number: 866057798

42
Mulcahy Foundation, The
80 West Franklin St.
Tucson 85701   (602) 623-6416

Incorporated in 1957 in Arizona.
Donor(s): John A. Mulcahy,† Mulcahy Lumber Co.
Financial data: (yr. ended 6/30/84): Assets, $1,455,947 (M); expenditures, $148,739, including $120,720 for 37 grants (high: $36,295; low: $100; average: $1,000).
Purpose and activities: Primarily local giving for higher education, including medical education, youth agencies, and hospitals.
Types of support awarded: General purposes, operating budgets, continuing support, annual campaigns, seed money, emergency funds, deficit financing, building funds, equipment, endowment funds, matching funds, scholarship funds, professorships, internships, exchange programs, fellowships, loans, research, conferences and seminars, special projects.
Limitations: Giving primarily in AZ, with emphasis on the Tucson area. No grants to individuals, or for land acquisition, demonstration projects or publications.
Application information:
Initial approach: Letter or telephone
Deadline(s): None
Board meeting date(s): Monthly and as required
Final notification: 1 to 2 months
Write: Janet Talaski, Program Officer
Officers: Cliffton E. Bloom, President; Ashby I. Lohse, Secretary and Treasurer.
Trustee: Florence W. Lohse.
Number of staff: 1 full-time support; 1 part-time support.
Employer Identification Number: 866053461

43
Raymond Educational Foundation, Inc. ¤
P.O. Box 1423
Flagstaff 86001   (602) 774-8081

Incorporated in 1951 in Arizona.
Donor(s): R.O. Raymond.†
Financial data: (yr. ended 4/30/83): Assets, $1,508,149 (M); expenditures, $169,528, including $150,675 for 14 grants (high: $64,700; low: $500).
Purpose and activities: Grants limited to institutions within Coconino County, Arizona, principally for scholarship funds; some support for cultural programs and health services.
Types of support awarded: Scholarship funds.
Limitations: Giving limited to Coconino County, AZ.
Publications: Program policy statement.
Application information:
Initial approach: Proposal
Copies of proposal: 2
Deadline(s): March 31

Board meeting date(s): As required
Write: Henry L. Giclas, President
Officers: Henry L. Giclas,* President; John
Stilley,* Executive Vice-President and
Treasurer; Catherine Adel,* Vice-President;
Charles B. Wilson, Secretary.
Directors:* Platt C. Kline, M.G. Fronske,
Wilfred Killip, Joyce Leamon, Lewis McDonald,
John H. Webster.
Employer Identification Number: 866050920

44
Research Corporation ▼
6840 East Broadway Blvd.
Tucson 85710 (602) 296-6400
Regional office: c/o R. Scott Pyron, Regional
Director (Grants Program), 44 S. Bayles Ave.,
Port Washington, NY 11050-3709; Tel.: (516)
944-5120

Incorporated in 1912 in New York.
Donor(s): Frederick Gardner Cottrell,† and
others.
Financial data: (yr. ended 10/31/84): Assets,
$47,103,533 (L); gifts received, $465,000;
expenditures, $14,279,772, including
$3,192,585 for 212 grants (high: $25,000; low:
$1,500; average: $11,000) and $3,306,947 for
2 foundation-administered programs.
Purpose and activities: To advance science
and technology. Through its Technology
Transfer Program (TTP), an operating program,
the Corporation furthers the transfer of useful
inventions from universities and other nonprofit
research institutions to industry. The Grants
Program, which is open to U.S. and Canadian
colleges and universities, has two subdivisions:
the Cottrell Research Program which supports
basic work in the physical sciences at private
graduate and all public academic institutions,
and the Cottrell College Science Program
which assists academic research projects in the
natural sciences at private, predominantly
undergraduate institutions.
Types of support awarded: Research.
Limitations: Giving primarily in the U.S. and
Canada. No grants to individuals, or for
building or endowment funds, special projects,
indirect costs, common supplies and services,
faculty academic year salaries, secretarial
assistance, general support, scholarships and
fellowships, publications, or matching gifts; no
loans.
Publications: Annual report, program policy
statement, application guidelines.
Application information: Application form
required.
Initial approach: Letter describing proposed
research
Deadline(s): None
Board meeting date(s): January, May, and
October
Final notification: 6 months
Write: Hal H. Ramsay, Regional Director
(Grants Program), Tucson; W. Stevenson
Bacon, Director of Communications; New
York Office: R. Scott Pyron, Regional
Director (Grants Program)

Officers: John P. Schaefer,* President; George
M. Stadler, Executive Vice-President; Gary M.
Munsinger, Vice-President for Finance; Robert
Goldsmith, Corporate Secretary; Burt N.
Dorsett,* Treasurer.
Directors:* Frederick Adler, R. Palmer Baker,
Jr., Paul J. Collins, William G. Hendrickson,
Colin B. Mackay, Robert W. Morse, L. Donald
Shields, George L. Shinn, Calvin A.
VanderWerf, G. King Walters, Theodore M.
Welp.
Number of staff: 50.
Employer Identification Number: 131963407

45
Tell Foundation, The
4020 N. 38th Ave.
Phoenix 85019

Incorporated in 1952 in Arizona.
Donor(s): Andrew P. Tell,† Mary J. Tell.
Financial data: (yr. ended 6/30/84): Assets,
$2,058,137 (M); gifts received, $22,830;
expenditures, $161,996, including $138,624
for 72 grants (high: $64,000; low: $25).
Purpose and activities: To support Protestant
churches and church-related institutions
including theological education.
Officers and Trustees: Esther T. Rhodes,
President; Lydia C. Lewis, Vice-President; Mary
J. Tell, Secretary; Marilyn P. Hamman,
Treasurer.
Employer Identification Number: 866050214

46
Van Schaik (Nellie) ¤
c/o Valley National Bank of Arizona Trust Dept.
P.O. Box 71
Phoenix 85001
Application Address: Trust Dept., Valley
National Bank of Arizona, P.O. Box 311,
Tucson, AZ 85702; Tel.: (602) 792-7160

Established in 1975.
Financial data: (yr. ended 5/31/83): Assets,
$2,352,060 (M); expenditures, $197,472,
including $175,000 for 7 grants (high: $50,000;
low: $5,000).
Purpose and activities: Grants limited to
undergraduate and graduate scholarship
programs in medicine and public health at
nonprofit dental and hospital institutions,
primarily in the Phillipines and other
developing East Asian and Western Pacific
countries, and for local students there.
Types of support awarded: Scholarship funds.
Limitations: Giving primarily in the Philippines
and other developing East Asian and Western
Pacific countries.
Application information:
Initial approach: Proposal
Copies of proposal: 1
Deadline(s): May 1
Write: Ed Handy, Trustee
Trustees: Louis W. Barassi, Ed Handy.
Employer Identification Number: 866090500

47
VNB Foundation, Inc. ¤
c/o Neil H. Christensen
P.O. Box 71-8633
Phoenix 85001

Incorporated in 1978 in Arizona.
Donor(s): Valley National Bank of Arizona.
Financial data: (yr. ended 12/31/83): Assets,
$3,781,245 (M); expenditures, $803,688,
including $788,680 for 106 grants (high:
$39,250; low: $300).
Purpose and activities: Primarily local giving,
with emphasis on community funds, cultural
programs, hospitals, higher education,
museums, performing arts, and youth agencies.
Limitations: Giving primarily in AZ.
Officers and Directors: J. Wilson Barrett,
President; Howard C. McCrady, Vice-President;
Neil H. Christensen, Secretary-Treasurer;
Timothy Creedon, Leonard W. Huck, J. Robert
White.
Employer Identification Number: 953330232

48
Waddell (Donald Ware) Foundation
110 Mountain Shadows West
Paradise Valley 85253 (602) 948-6741

Established in 1962 in Arizona.
Financial data: (yr. ended 6/30/84): Assets,
$2,884,821 (M); expenditures, $266,266,
including $126,240 for 57 grants (high:
$20,000; low: $50; average: $1,000).
Purpose and activities: Primarily local giving,
with emphasis on cultural programs, including
museums, and hospitals and medical research.
Limitations: Giving primarily in AZ. No grants
to individuals.
Application information:
Initial approach: Letter
Copies of proposal: 1
Deadline(s): None
Write: Mrs. Scott L. Libby, Jr., President
Officers and Directors: Eleanor W. Libby,
President and Treasurer; John C. Pritzlaff, Jr.,
Don B. Tostenrud, Vice-Presidents; Robert W.
McGee, Secretary; Bert A. Getz, James W.
Johnston.
Employer Identification Number: 866051227

49
Webb (Del E.) Foundation ▼ ¤
3800 North Central Ave., Suite A-6
Phoenix 85012 (602) 241-1076

Incorporated in 1960 in Arizona.
Donor(s): Del E. Webb.†
Financial data: (yr. ended 12/31/83): Assets,
$28,494,245 (M); expenditures, $1,173,730,
including $916,876 for 29 grants (high:
$100,000; low: $1,800; average: $10,000-
$50,000).
Purpose and activities: Giving primarily for
medical research in Arizona, Nevada, and
Southern California; support also for social
services and higher education.
Limitations: Giving primarily in AZ, NV, and
CA. No grants to individuals.
Application information:
Initial approach: Letter

Deadline(s): June 15 and November 15
Board meeting date(s): July and December
Final notification: Following each meeting
Write: Maxine Newman
Officers and Directors: Robert H. Johnson, President; Robert R. Alcorn, Vice-President; Owen F. Childress, Secretary-Treasurer.
Number of staff: 1.
Employer Identification Number: 866052737

50
Wilson (Robert T.) Foundation
Route 4 Box 712
Flagstaff 86001   (602) 774-5457

Trust established in 1954 in Texas; incorporated in 1963.
Donor(s): Richard F. Wilson, Jean H. Wilson, and other family members.
Financial data: (yr. ended 12/31/83): Assets, $373,776 (M); gifts received, $125,900; expenditures, $279,437, including $200,161 for 32 grants (high: $39,500; low: $130).
Purpose and activities: Broad purposes; primarily local giving, with emphasis on environmental protection, child welfare, higher education, including scholarship funds, and international relief.
Types of support awarded: Seed money, emergency funds, special projects, matching funds, scholarship funds.
Limitations: Giving primarily in AZ. No grants to individuals, or for building or endowment funds, or operating budgets; no loans.
Publications: Application guidelines.
Application information:
Initial approach: Letter
Copies of proposal: 1
Deadline(s): Submit proposal preferably in April; deadline May 1
Board meeting date(s): July and as required
Write: Robert W. Koons, Executive Director
Officers and Directors: Richard F. Wilson, President; Suzanne Horst, Vice-President; Jean H. Wilson, Secretary-Treasurer; Robert W. Koons, Executive Director; Winifred W. Hanseth, Amanda Wilson, Robert Wilson, Soonya Wilson.
Number of staff: 1 full-time professional; 1 full-time support.
Employer Identification Number: 860264036

ARKANSAS

51
Inglewood Foundation, The ▼
c/o 1950 Union National Plaza
P.O. Box 906
Little Rock 72203   (501) 376-0766

Incorporated in 1961 in Arkansas.

Donor(s): Christoph Keller, Jr., Caroline M. Keller, Christoph Keller III, Robertson L. Gilliland, Cynthia K. Davis, Caroline K. Gilliland, R. Randall Timmons, Kathryn K. Timmons, James F. Stutts, and others.
Financial data: (yr. ended 1/31/84): Assets, $1,958,474 (M); gifts received, $151,504; expenditures, $712,448, including $680,280 for 36 grants (high: $312,375; low: $800; average: $500).
Purpose and activities: Grants largely for "innovative or creative projects in public education and social services which particularly address people's need to feel a part of a community," including support for higher education and social service and youth agencies.
Types of support awarded: Seed money, emergency funds, matching funds, special projects.
Limitations: Giving primarily in the southcentral and eastern U.S. No grants to individuals, or for annual campaigns, deficit financing, capital or endowment funds, scholarships and fellowships, or continuing support; no loans.
Application information: Proposals should not exceed 1 page.
Initial approach: Letter
Copies of proposal: 1
Deadline(s): March 31 and September 30
Board meeting date(s): May and October
Write: B. Frank Mackey, Jr., Secretary
Officers and Directors: Christoph Keller III, President; Corwith Davis, Jr., Vice-President; B. Frank Mackey, Jr., Secretary; Caroline M. Keller, Treasurer; Cornelia K. Biddle, Craig Biddle, Elisabeth K. Bonsey, Steven Keller Bonsey, Cynthia K. Davis, Christoph Keller, Jr., Julie H. Keller, Caroline G. Theus, James G. Theus, Kathryn K. Timmons, R. Randall Timmons.
Number of staff: 1 part-time professional.
Employer Identification Number: 716050419

52
Jones (The Harvey and Bernice) Foundation ⌀
c/o Jones Truck Lines, Inc.
P.O. Box 233
Springdale 72765   (501) 751-2730

Trust established in 1956 in Arkansas.
Donor(s): Jones Truck Lines, Inc., Jones Investment Company, Neylon Freight Lines, Inc.
Financial data: (yr. ended 11/30/83): Assets, $3,557,492 (M); gifts received, $2,400; expenditures, $543,072, including $523,147 for 57 grants (high: $150,000; low: $12) and $8,075 for 27 grants to individuals.
Purpose and activities: Primarily local giving, with emphasis on Protestant church support, hospitals, education, and scholarships.
Limitations: Giving primarily in AR.
Application information:
Initial approach: Letter
Deadline(s): None
Write: Mary Sellers
Directors: H.G. Frost, Bernice Jones, Harvey Jones, Mary Sellers.
Employer Identification Number: 716057141

53
Lyon Foundation, Inc. ⌀
65th and Scott Hamilton Dr.
Little Rock 72204
Mailing address: P.O. Box 4408, Little Rock, AR 72214

Incorporated in 1946 in Arkansas.
Donor(s): Frank Lyon Company, Inc., members of the Lyon family, and others.
Financial data: (yr. ended 12/31/83): Assets, $671,048 (M); gifts received, $397,691; expenditures, $249,537, including $230,768 for grants and $15,765 for grants to individuals.
Purpose and activities: Broad purposes; general giving, with emphasis on higher education, welfare agencies, and Protestant churches and church-related organizations; some assistance for students and individuals in need.
Limitations: Giving primarily in AR.
Application information:
Initial approach: Letter or full proposal
Deadline(s): None
Write: Ralph Cotham, Secretary-Treasurer
Officers and Directors: Frank Lyon, President; C.W. Abrams, Marion Lyon, Vice-Presidents; Ralph Cotham, Secretary-Treasurer.
Employer Identification Number: 716052168

54
Murphy Foundation, The ▼
Murphy Bldg.
El Dorado 71730   (501) 862-6411

Incorporated in 1958 in Arkansas.
Donor(s): Members of the Murphy family.
Financial data: (yr. ended 4/30/84): Assets, $10,700,000 (M); expenditures, $430,850, including $347,238 for 39 grants (high: $120,000; low: $50) and $28,300 for 14 grants to individuals.
Purpose and activities: General purposes; giving primarily locally and in northern Louisiana, with emphasis on higher education, including scholarships; grants also for Protestant church support and youth agencies.
Types of support awarded: Student aid, operating budgets, grants to individuals.
Limitations: Giving primarily in AR and LA.
Application information: Application form required for educational grants to individuals.
Initial approach: Letter
Copies of proposal: 1
Board meeting date(s): Semiannually
Write: Lucy A. Ring, Secretary
Officers and Directors: Johnie W. Murphy, President; Bertie Murphy Deming, Vice-President; Lucy A. Ring, Secretary and Treasurer; John W. Deming, C.H. Murphy, Jr.
Employer Identification Number: 716049826

55
Rebsamen Fund ⌀
P.O. Box 3198
Little Rock 72203

Incorporated in 1944 in Arkansas.
Donor(s): Rebsamen Companies, Inc.

Financial data: (yr. ended 11/30/83): Assets, $1,168,277 (M); expenditures, $141,004, including $131,322 for 64 grants (high: $22,250; low: $25).
Purpose and activities: Educational and religious purposes; primarily local giving, with emphasis on higher education, community funds, health services, and cultural programs.
Limitations: Giving primarily in AR.
Officers and Directors: Kenneth Pat Wilson, President; H. Maurice Mitchell, Sam C. Sowell, Vice-Presidents; Doris C. Bowling, Treasurer.
Employer Identification Number: 716053911

56
Reynolds (The Donald W.) Foundation, Inc. ⋈
920 Rogers Ave.
Fort Smith 72901

Incorporated in 1954 in Nevada.
Donor(s): Donald W. Reynolds, Southwestern Publishing Company, Southwestern Operating Company, and others.
Financial data: (yr. ended 6/30/83): Assets, $6,525,901 (M); expenditures, $776,670, including $732,414 for 120 grants (high: $125,000; low: $20).
Purpose and activities: Grants largely for higher education, community funds, youth agencies, cultural programs, health and social welfare agencies and civic affairs.
Limitations: Giving primarily in AR.
Officers and Directors: Donald W. Reynolds, President; Fred W. Smith, Executive Vice-President; E.H. Patterson, Treasurer; George O. Kleier, Don E. Pray.
Employer Identification Number: 716053383

57
Riggs Benevolent Fund ⋈
c/o Worthen Bank and Trust Company
P.O. Box 1681
Little Rock 72203

Trust established in 1959 in Arkansas.
Donor(s): Members of the Riggs family, Robert G. Cress, J.A. Riggs Tractor Company, Inc.
Financial data: (yr. ended 12/31/82): Assets, $2,258,528 (M); gifts received, $177,710; expenditures, $139,990, including $127,050 for 36 grants (high: $27,000; low: $200).
Purpose and activities: Broad purposes; primarily local giving, with emphasis on higher education and Protestant church support and church-related organizations; support also for youth agencies, hospitals, and a community fund.
Limitations: Giving primarily in AR.
Trustee: Worthen Bank and Trust Company.
Employer Identification Number: 716050130

58
Rockefeller (Winthrop) Foundation ▼
308 East Eighth St.
Little Rock 72202   (501) 376-6854

Incorporated in 1956 in Arkansas as Rockwin Fund, Inc.; renamed in 1974.
Donor(s): Winthrop Rockefeller.†

Financial data: (yr. ended 12/31/83): Assets, $30,734,040 (M); gifts received, $1,500,000; expenditures, $1,927,614, including $1,294,884 for 54 grants (high: $222,695; low: $450; average: $10,000-$40,000).
Purpose and activities: Broad purposes; emphasis on economic development and education; support for local projects which (a) improve the delivery of services of administrative capacity of institutions; (b) increase the participation of people in the decision-making process; or (c) achieve more productive development and use of human, physical and fiscal resources. The foundation will fund innovative demonstration projects which improve people's living standards and the institutions which serve the community; projects which have economic development potential; and community-based projects concerned with organizational planning and fundraising.
Types of support awarded: Special projects, seed money, conferences and seminars, matching funds, technical assistance, consulting services.
Limitations: Giving primarily in AR, or projects that benefit AR. No grants to individuals, or for building funds, equipment, annual fund drives, general support, emergency funds, most types of research, trips by community organizations, scholarships, or fellowships; no loans.
Publications: Annual report, program policy statement, application guidelines.
Application information: Application form required.
 Initial approach: Telephone or letter
 Copies of proposal: 2
 Deadline(s): Submit proposal preferably eight weeks prior to meeting
 Board meeting date(s): On the first weekend in March, June, September, and December
 Final notification: 2 weeks after board meeting dates
 Write: Thomas C. McRae, President
Officers: Thomas C. McRae, President; Leland P. Gordon, Jr., Vice-President; Sandra Boatright, Secretary-Treasurer.
Directors: Marion Burton, Chairman; Henry Jones, Vice-Chairman; Richard A. Baer, Jr., Anne Bartley, James D. Bernstein, Wiley A. Branton, Ray Marshall, Winthrop Paul Rockefeller, Charlotte T. Schexnayder, Robert Shults.
Number of staff: 3 full-time professional; 1 full-time support; 1 part-time support.
Employer Identification Number: 710285871

59
Ross Foundation, The
1039 Henderson St.
Arkadelphia 71923   (501) 246-9881
Application address: P.O. Box 335, Arkadelphia, AR 71923

Established in 1966 in Arkansas.
Donor(s): Esther C. Ross,† Jane Ross.
Financial data: (yr. ended 12/31/83): Assets, $14,456,047 (M); expenditures, $526,162, including $257,798 for 44 grants (high: $60,000; low: $100; average: $5,000).

Purpose and activities: To promote the economic and cultural interests of Arkadelphia and Clark County; support for higher and public education, youth agencies, mental retardation, conservation of natural resources, and community improvement programs.
Types of support awarded: Seed money, emergency funds, building funds, equipment, endowment funds, matching funds, research, publications, general purposes, special projects.
Limitations: Giving limited to Arkadelphia and Clark County, AR. No grants to individuals, or for scholarships or fellowships; no loans.
Publications: 990-PF, program policy statement, application guidelines.
Application information: Application form required.
 Initial approach: Letter or telephone
 Copies of proposal: 4
 Deadline(s): October 15
 Board meeting date(s): Monthly
 Final notification: 30 days
 Write: Ross M. Whipple, Executive Director
Officers and Trustees: Jane Ross, Chairman; Ross M. Whipple, Executive Director; Peggy Clark, H.W. McMillan, Robert Rhodes.
Number of staff: 5.
Employer Identification Number: 716060574

60
Sturgis (The Roy and Christine) Charitable and Educational Trust ▼ ⋈
P.O. Box 92
Malvern 72104

Trust established about 1979.
Donor(s): Roy Sturgis,† Christine Sturgis.
Financial data: (yr. ended 12/31/83): Assets, $10,483,754 (M); expenditures, $485,108, including $391,465 for grants.
Purpose and activities: Primarily local giving for hospitals, youth and social agencies, education, and church support.
Limitations: Giving primarily in AR.
Trustees: Barry Findley, Katie Speer.
Employer Identification Number: 710495345

61
Trinity Foundation
P.O. Box 7008
Pine Bluff 71611   (501) 534-7120

Incorporated about 1952 in Arkansas.
Donor(s): Pine Bluff Sand & Gravel Company, McGeorge Contracting Company, Cornerstone Farm & Gin Company, Standard Investment Company, Harvey W. McGeorge.
Financial data: (yr. ended 9/30/83): Assets, $4,079,078 (M); gifts received, $336,685; expenditures, $191,867, including $144,500 for 5 grants (high: $120,000; low: $1,000) and $25,300 for 22 grants to individuals.
Purpose and activities: Primarily local giving, with emphasis on higher education, including scholarships.
Types of support awarded: Student aid.
Limitations: Giving primarily in AR.

Application information: Scholarship application information available only at guidance offices of high schools where scholarships are awarded.

Deadline(s): Deadline for scholarships April 10 of senior year in high school

Write: W.K. Atkinson, Secretary-Treasurer

Officers: H. Tyndall Dickinson, President; Wallace P. McGeorge, Jr., W. Scott McGeorge, Vice-Presidents; W.K. Atkinson, Secretary-Treasurer.

Employer Identification Number: 716050288

62
Wrape Family Charitable Trust, The ⌑
P.O. Box 412
Little Rock 72203

Trust established in 1953 in Arkansas.
Donor(s): Regina Sellmeyer,† A.M. Wrape,† and members of the Wrape family.
Financial data: (yr. ended 12/31/83): Assets, $4,617,065 (M); gifts received, $1,648,881; expenditures, $585,122, including $440,330 for 54 grants (high: $35,000; low: $100).
Purpose and activities: Support primarily for Roman Catholic educational and religious organizations.
Trustee: A.J. Wrape, Jr.
Employer Identification Number: 716050323

CALIFORNIA

63
Abelard Foundation, Inc., The
222 Agriculture Bldg.
101 The Embarcadero
San Francisco 94105   (415) 989-0450
East Coast grant application office: Joint Foundation Support, Inc., 122 East 42nd St., Suite 922, New York, NY 10017; Tel.: (212) 616-4080

Incorporated in 1958 in New York as successor to Albert B. Wells Charitable Trust established in 1950 in Massachusetts.
Donor(s): Members of the Wells family.
Financial data: (yr. ended 12/31/84): Assets, $1,100,000 (M); expenditures, $220,000, including $220,000 for 46 grants (high: $7,000; low: $4,000; average: $5,000-$7,000).
Purpose and activities: General purposes; general giving, especially for seed money to new organizations and model projects, largely in the West, New York City, and the South, with emphasis on protection of civil rights and civil liberties; support for programs designed to achieve social, political, and economic equality for urban and rural poor, including giving them a voice in decisions about their environment.

Types of support awarded: Operating budgets, seed money, matching funds, technical assistance, special projects, publications.
Limitations: Giving limited to Western states, New York City, NY, and Southern states, including Appalachia. No support for medical, educational, or cultural institutions. No grants to individuals, or for building or endowment funds, continuing support, annual campaigns, emergency funds, scholarships, fellowships, or research; no loans.
Publications: Informational brochure, program policy statement, application guidelines.
Application information:
Initial approach: Letter, telephone, or full proposal
Copies of proposal: 1
Deadline(s): None
Board meeting date(s): February, May, August, and November
Final notification: Immediately following board meeting
Write: Leah Brumer, Executive Director (West Coast); Patricia Hewitt, Executive Director, Joint Foundation Support, Inc. (East Coast)
Officers and Directors: Albert B. Wells, II, President; Kristen Wells Buck, Frances W. Magee, Adele Neufeld, Joel Schreck, Susan Wells, Vice-Presidents; Malcolm J. Edgerton, Jr., Secretary; Charles R. Schreck, Treasurer; Michael Bernhard, Nancy Bernhard, Sheryl Bernhard, Steven Bernhard, Randal Buck, Lewis H. Butler, Donald Collins, Susan Collins, Andrew D. Heineman, David B. Magee, Peter Neufeld, Albert Schreck, Christine Schreck, Daniel W. Schreck, Jean Schreck, Thomas A. Schreck, George B. Wells, II, Melissa R. Wells, Ruth D. Wells.
Number of staff: 1 full-time professional; 1 part-time support.
Employer Identification Number: 136064580

64
Adolph's Foundation, The ⌑
P.O. Box 828
Burbank 91503

Incorporated in 1953 in California.
Donor(s): Lloyd Rigler, Adolph's Ltd., Adolph's Food Products Mfg. Co., and their stockholders.
Financial data: (yr. ended 2/28/83): Assets, $2,114,556 (M); gifts received, $292,250; expenditures, $169,807, including $134,156 for 25 grants (high: $50,000; low: $200).
Purpose and activities: Charitable purposes; general giving in the field of arts and humanities, with emphasis on performing and visual arts.
Types of support awarded: Seed money, endowment funds, matching funds, special projects, building funds, equipment, land acquisition, loans, consulting services, technical assistance.
Limitations: Giving primarily in southern CA. No grants to individuals, or for scholarships or fellowships.
Application information:
Initial approach: Letter
Copies of proposal: 1
Deadline(s): None

Board meeting date(s): December
Final notification: 30 days
Write: Lloyd E. Rigler, President
Officers and Directors: Lloyd E. Rigler, President; Simon Miller, Vice-President; Don Rigler, Secretary and Treasurer.
Number of staff: 1.
Employer Identification Number: 956038247

65
Ahmanson Foundation, The ▼
3731 Wilshire Blvd.
Los Angeles 90010   (213) 383-1381

Incorporated in 1952 in California.
Donor(s): Howard F. Ahmanson,† Dorothy G. Sullivan.†
Financial data: (yr. ended 10/31/84): Assets, $211,855,588 (M); expenditures, $11,547,365, including $9,433,897 for 342 grants (high: $650,000; low: $500; average: $5,000-$15,000).
Purpose and activities: Broad purposes; primarily local giving, with emphasis on education, the arts and humanities, medicine, and health; support also for religious organizations and a broad range of social welfare programs.
Types of support awarded: Operating budgets, seed money, building funds, equipment, land acquisition, endowment funds, matching funds, scholarship funds, special projects.
Limitations: Giving primarily in Southern CA, with emphasis on the Los Angeles area. No grants to individuals; no loans.
Publications: Program policy statement, application guidelines.
Application information:
Initial approach: Full proposal or letter
Copies of proposal: 1
Deadline(s): None
Board meeting date(s): Quarterly
Final notification: 60 to 90 days
Write: Kathleen A. Gilcrest, Vice-President
Officers: Robert H. Ahmanson,* President; William H. Ahmanson,* Vice-President; Kathleen A. Gilcrest, Vice-President and Secretary; George B. Fearn, Treasurer.
Trustees:* Howard F. Ahmanson, Jr., Daniel N. Belin, Robert M. DeKruif, Franklin D. Murphy, M.D.
Number of staff: 2 full-time professional; 1 part-time professional; 4 full-time support; 1 part-time support.
Employer Identification Number: 956089998

66
A.I.D. Foundation ▼ ⌑
2010A Mission Dr.
Solvang 93463

Established in 1974 in California.
Donor(s): Lindavista, S.A., Members of the Gildred family.
Financial data: (yr. ended 5/31/83): Assets, $8,140,360 (M); expenditures, $710,326, including $602,880 for 16 grants (high: $161,480; low: $1,000).

Purpose and activities: Local giving, with emphasis on medical research and hospitals, including buildings and equipment; support also for higher education, social welfare, and cultural programs.
Types of support awarded: Annual campaigns, seed money, building funds, equipment, research, general purposes, matching funds, continuing support, special projects.
Limitations: Giving primarily in San Diego County, CA. No grants to individuals, or for endowment funds or operating budgets.
Application information: Applications for grants presently not invited.
 Initial approach: Full proposal
 Copies of proposal: 1
 Deadline(s): None
 Board meeting date(s): October and April
 Final notification: Up to 7 months
 Write: William P. Shannahan, Administrator
Officers and Director:* Stuart C. Gildred,* President; William P. Shannahan, Vice-President and Secretary.
Number of staff: 1.
Employer Identification Number: 237364942

67
Albertson Foundation, The
3600 Wilshire Blvd., Rm. 2114
Los Angeles 90010   (213) 386-1196

Incorporated in 1964 in California.
Donor(s): Hazel H. Albertson.†
Financial data: (yr. ended 12/31/82): Assets, $1,163,654 (M); expenditures, $111,558, including $96,750 for 15 grants (high: $20,000; low: $250; average: $5,000-$10,000).
Purpose and activities: Broad purposes; local giving, with emphasis on private secondary education, hospitals, and ear and cancer research.
Types of support awarded: Continuing support, annual campaigns, building funds, equipment, research.
Limitations: Giving primarily in Southern CA. No grants to individuals, or for operating budgets, seed money, emergency funds, deficit financing, endowment funds, matching gifts, scholarships, fellowships, special projects, publications, or conferences; no loans.
Application information:
 Initial approach: Letter
 Copies of proposal: 3
 Deadline(s): Submit proposal preferably in September or October; deadline October 31
 Board meeting date(s): November
 Final notification: 4 weeks
 Write: Robert F. O'Neill, President
Officers: Robert F. O'Neill, President; Kay S. Onderdonk, Vice-President and Secretary; Jean A. Peck, Vice-President and Treasurer.
Number of staff: 1 part-time professional; 1 part-time support.
Employer Identification Number: 956100378

68
Amado (Maurice) Foundation ♉
1800 Century Park East, Suite 200
Los Angeles 90067

Incorporated in 1961 in California.
Donor(s): Maurice Amado.†
Financial data: (yr. ended 11/30/83): Assets, $9,318,839 (M); expenditures, $332,127, including $264,600 for 16 grants (high: $110,000; low: $500).
Purpose and activities: Grants primarily for Sephardic Jewish organizations.
Officers: Richard J. Amado, President; Milton S. Amado, Secretary-Treasurer.
Employer Identification Number: 956041700

69
American Honda Foundation
19603 S. Vermont Ave.
Torrance 90502   (213) 327-8280

Established in 1984 in California.
Donor(s): American Honda Motor Co., Inc.
Financial data: (yr. ended 6/30/85): Assets, $5,000,000 (M); gifts received, $27,690; expenditures, $525,000, including $300,000 for 8 grants (high: $65,000; low: $25,000).
Purpose and activities: Initial year of operations 1984; support for national organizations working in the areas of youth and scientific education, including private secondary schools, public and private colleges and universities, adult education programs, scholarship and fellowship programs, and scientific and educational organizations.
Types of support awarded: Scholarship funds, fellowships, special projects, operating budgets, continuing support, research, building funds, equipment, seed money, annual campaigns, professorships, internships, matching funds.
Limitations: No support for religious, veterans', fraternal, or political organizations, or labor groups. No grants to individuals, or for operating funds for hospitals, trips, or beauty and talent contests.
Publications: Newsletter, program policy statement, application guidelines, annual report.
Application information: First annual report available July, 1985. Application form required.
 Initial approach: Letter or telephone
 Deadline(s): November 1, February 1, May 1, and August 1
 Board meeting date(s): January, April, July, and October
 Final notification: 2 months
 Write: Kathryn A. Carey, Manager
Officers and Directors: Tetsuo Chino, President; Cliff Schmillen, Vice-President; Mike Nitz, Secretary; Tak Ageno, Treasurer; John Petas.
Manager: Kathryn A. Carey.
Number of staff: 2 full-time professional.
Employer Identification Number: 953924667

70
Arakelian (K.) Foundation ♉
56372 Rd. 200
North Fork 93643

Incorporated in 1943 in California.
Donor(s): Krikor Arakelian.†
Financial data: (yr. ended 12/31/83): Assets, $1,403,535 (M); expenditures, $122,458, including $68,357 for 58 grants (high: $10,000; low: $20).
Purpose and activities: Primarily local giving for charitable and educational purposes; student loan funds established at five higher educational institutions which administer them; charitable giving largely for health agencies, education, the aged, and youth agencies.
Types of support awarded: General purposes.
Limitations: Giving primarily in CA, particularly in Fresno and Madera counties. No grants to individuals.
Application information:
 Write: Aram Arakelian, President
Officers and Directors: Aram Arakelian, President; Freddie Markarian, Vice-President; Queenie Nishkian, Secretary-Treasurer; Mike Garabedian, L. Krikorian.
Employer Identification Number: 941095610

71
Arata Brothers Trust ♉
P.O. Box 430
Sacramento 95802

Trust established in 1976 in California.
Financial data: (yr. ended 12/31/83): Assets, $2,670,086 (M); expenditures, $136,566, including $105,042 for 18 grants (high: $50,000; low: $100).
Purpose and activities: Primarily local giving, with emphasis on hospitals, higher education, and religion.
Limitations: Giving primarily in CA.
Trustees: Francis B. Dillon, Janette Lavezzo, Nellie Lavezzo, Renato R. Parenti.
Employer Identification Number: 237204615

72
Arkelian (Ben H. and Gladys)
Foundation ♉
1107 Truxtun Ave.
P.O. Box 1825
Bakersfield 93303   (805) 324-5029

Established in 1959 in California.
Financial data: (yr. ended 12/31/83): Assets, $1,778,206 (M); expenditures, $138,181, including $104,837 for 14 grants (high: $25,000; low: $100).
Purpose and activities: Primarily local giving, with emphasis on higher education, youth agencies, and hospitals.
Limitations: Giving limited to Kern County, CA.
Application information:
 Initial approach: Letter and request for appearance before Board of Directors
 Deadline(s): None
 Write: Frank I. Ford, Jr., Secretary

Officers and Directors: Henry C. Mack, President; Henry C. Mack, Jr., Vice-President; Frank I. Ford, Jr., Secretary-Treasurer; D. Bianco, Harvey H. Means.
Employer Identification Number: 956103223

73
Arrillaga (John) Foundation ⌷
2560 Mission College Blvd., Rm. 101
Santa Clara 95050

Established around 1978 in California.
Donor(s): John Arrillaga.
Financial data: (yr. ended 9/30/83): Assets, $2,062,078 (M); expenditures, $151,530, including $146,350 for 33 grants (high: $25,000; low: $50).
Purpose and activities: Primarily local giving for higher and secondary education, and social services.
Limitations: Giving primarily in CA.
Directors: Frances C. Arrillaga, John Arrillaga, Richard T. Peery.
Employer Identification Number: 942460896

74
Artevel Foundation ⌷
c/o Security Pacific Plaza
333 South Hope St., Suite 3710
Los Angeles 90071

Incorporated in 1966 in California.
Donor(s): Harm te Velde, Zwaantina te Velde.
Financial data: (yr. ended 12/31/83): Assets, $1,811,421 (M); gifts received, $2,000; expenditures, $148,615, including $137,636 for 44 grants (high: $26,685; low: $200).
Purpose and activities: Grants largely for Protestant evangelistic and missionary programs.
Types of support awarded: Building funds, general purposes.
Officers and Trustees: Harm te Velde, President; Zwaantina te Velde, Vice-President; George R. Phillips, Secretary-Treasurer; Shirley A. DeGroot, Harriet Hill, Margaret E. Houtsma, Grace Kreulen, Betty Meyer, John te Velde, Marvin te Velde, Ralph te Velde.
Employer Identification Number: 956136405

75
Associated Foundations Incorporated
600 South Commonwealth Ave., Suite 1300
Los Angeles 90005   (213) 480-0821

Incorporated in 1973 in California.
Financial data: (yr. ended 8/31/84): Assets, $3,238,997 (M); expenditures, $203,814, including $151,167 for 32 grants (high: $20,000; low: $1,000).
Purpose and activities: Primarily local giving for higher education, including achievement scholarships awarded by institutions to undergraduates majoring in business management, engineering, nursing, and agribusiness.
Types of support awarded: Scholarship funds, operating budgets, general purposes, equipment.
Limitations: Giving primarily in CA. No grants to individuals, or for building or endowment funds, research, or matching gifts; no loans.

Application information: Grant applications not invited.
    Board meeting date(s): October and as required
Officers: F. George Herlihy,* Chairman and President; Brenda K. Oddou, Secretary and Treasurer.
Trustees:* Katharine S. Burns, Florence P. Hamilton.
Employer Identification Number: 237324126

76
Atkinson Foundation ▼
Ten West Orange Ave.
South San Francisco 94080   (415) 876-1559

Incorporated in 1939 in California.
Donor(s): Geo. H. Atkinson,† Mildred M. Atkinson,† and others.
Financial data: (yr. ended 12/31/84): Assets, $15,243,393 (M); gifts received, $1,497; expenditures, $834,997, including $805,876 for 167 grants (high: $100,000; low: $500; average: $1,000-$15,000).
Purpose and activities: Giving primarily to agencies, organizations, schools and colleges serving the residents of San Mateo County. Other major beneficiaries are Willamette University and the United Methodist Church and its divisions in Northern California. Overseas grants are made in the areas of technical assistance and relief.
Types of support awarded: Seed money, operating budgets, emergency funds, building funds, scholarship funds.
Limitations: Giving primarily in OR, for a university; organizations in San Mateo County, CA; United Methodist churches and church activities in northern CA; and missions, relief efforts, and technical assistance projects overseas. No support for doctoral study, or elementary schools. No grants to individuals, or for research; no loans.
Publications: Annual report, program policy statement, application guidelines.
Application information:
    Initial approach: Telephone, full proposal, or letter
    Copies of proposal: 1
    Deadline(s): None
    Board meeting date(s): February or March, May or June, September, and December
    Final notification: 3 months
    Write: Donald K. Grant, Treasurer
Officers and Directors: Duane E. Atkinson, President; Ray N. Atkinson, First Vice-President; Bryant K. Zimmerman, Secretary; Donald K. Grant, Treasurer; Earl H. Atkinson, Lavina M. Atkinson, Elizabeth H. Curtis, James C. Ingwersen, Thomas J. Henderson.
Number of staff: 1 full-time professional.
Employer Identification Number: 946075613

77
Atkinson (Myrtle L.) Foundation ▼
P.O. Box 688
La Canada 91011

Incorporated in 1940 in California.

Donor(s): Guy F. Atkinson,† Rachel C. Atkinson, Elizabeth A. Whitsett, George H. Atkinson.
Financial data: (yr. ended 12/31/83): Assets, $19,688,079 (M); expenditures, $987,376, including $956,720 for 261 grants (high: $106,485; low: $50; average: $200-$10,000).
Purpose and activities: "To teach, promulgate and disseminate the gospel of Jesus Christ throughout the world and also to unite in Christian Fellowship the large number of consecrated Christians in the various evangelical churches...; to encourage and promote religious, scientific, technical and all other kinds of education, enlightenment and research." Giving mainly for capital funds for Christian churches and evangelism with emphasis on West Coast agencies, particularly in Southern California; support also for local and international relief and welfare agencies.
Types of support awarded: Scholarship funds, fellowships, endowment funds, building funds.
Limitations: Giving primarily in southern CA and the West Coast. No support for education, outside of foundation's primary area of interest. No grants to individuals, or for research, non-theological scholarships and fellowships, doctoral studies, or continuing programs.
Application information:
    Initial approach: Letter
    Copies of proposal: 1
    Deadline(s): Submit proposal preferably in February, early May, August, or November; no set deadline
    Board meeting date(s): January, May, September, and December
    Final notification: 2 months
    Write: Elizabeth A. Whitsett, President
Officers and Directors: Elizabeth A. Whitsett, President; Rachel C. Atkinson, Vice-President and Treasurer; Myrtle W. Harris, Secretary; Virginia L. Hutchinson, Stanley D. Ryals, John F. Whitsett, Bryant K. Zimmerman.
Number of staff: None.
Employer Identification Number: 956047161

78
Atlantic Richfield Foundation, The ▼
515 South Flower St.
Los Angeles 90071   (213) 486-3342

Incorporated in 1963 in New York.
Donor(s): Atlantic Richfield Company.
Financial data: (yr. ended 12/31/84): Assets, $11,895,758 (M); gifts received, $32,184,022; expenditures, $35,900,899, including $31,452,711 for 1,073 grants (high: $904,000; low: $500) and $4,386,120 for 16,219 employee matching gifts.
Purpose and activities: General purposes; giving primarily in areas of company operations, with support largely for higher education; community programs, including social service and youth agencies; humanities and the arts; community funds; selected health education and medical services; public information organizations; and environmental programs.

Types of support awarded: Operating budgets, seed money, building funds, equipment, land acquisition, matching funds, employee matching gifts, scholarship funds, employee related scholarships, fellowships, special projects.
Limitations: Giving primarily in areas of company operations. No support for sectarian religious organizations, professional associations, specialized health organizations, or military organizations. No grants to individuals, or for endowment funds, annual campaigns, deficit financing, hospital or university operating funds, research, publications or conferences; no loans.
Publications: Annual report, application guidelines.
Application information:
Initial approach: Full proposal limited to 2 pages
Copies of proposal: 1
Deadline(s): None
Board meeting date(s): June and December
Final notification: 4 to 6 months
Write: Eugene R. Wilson, President
Officers: Eugene R. Wilson, President; J.D. Henry, W.M. Marcussen,* D.W. McPhail, G.A. Narcavage, E.M. Pringle, G.W. Rapp, Jr., W.C. Rusnack, Vice-Presidents; R.S. Young, Treasurer.
Directors:* R.O. Anderson, Chairman; R. Stanton Avery, E.M. Benson, Jr., T.F. Bradshaw, L.M. Cook, R.F. Cox, J.P. Downer, W.F. Kieschnick, Jr., W.A. Nielsen, R.R. Van Horne, R.E. Wycoff.
Number of staff: 7 full-time professional; 6 full-time support; 1 part-time support.
Employer Identification Number: 136141996

79
Babcock (William) Memorial Endowment
1601 Second St., Suite 106
San Rafael 94901   (415) 453-0901

Trust established in 1954 in California; incorporated in 1959.
Donor(s): Julia May Babcock.†
Financial data: (yr. ended 2/28/84): Assets, $3,140,230 (M); gifts received, $274,427; expenditures, $606,395, including $458,678 for 335 grants to individuals (high: $5,000; low: $100; average: $1,000).
Purpose and activities: To meet through grants or loans the exceptional medical, surgical, and hospital expenses of residents of Marin County; project grants to institutions suspended.
Types of support awarded: Grants to individuals, loans.
Limitations: Giving limited to Marin County, CA. No support for organizations.
Publications: Application guidelines, informational brochure.
Application information:
Initial approach: Telephone
Board meeting date(s): Monthly
Write: Alelia Gillin, Executive Director
Officers: Irving Chapman,* President; Mrs. Robert Berry,* 1st Vice-President; Mrs. Harris C. Kirk,* 2nd Vice-President; J. Galen Foster,* Secretary; Edward Boero, Treasurer; Alelia Gillin, Executive Director.

Directors:* Fred Enemark, Harry P. Graves, A. Crawford Greene, Jr., Russel R. Klein, M.D., Rex Silvernale.
Number of staff: 1 full-time professional; 2 part-time support.
Employer Identification Number: 941367170

80
Bacon (The Francis) Foundation, Inc.
655 North Dartmouth Ave.
Claremont 91711-3979   (714) 624-6305

Incorporated in 1938 in California.
Donor(s): Walter Conrad Arensberg,† Louise Stevens Arensberg.†
Financial data: (yr. ended 12/31/84): Assets, $1,604,670 (M); expenditures, $93,405, including $1,130 for 4 grants (high: $600; low: $50) and $79,441 for 1 foundation-administered program.
Purpose and activities: To promote study in science, literature, religion, history, and philosophy with special reference to the works of Francis Bacon, his character and life, and his influence on his own and succeeding times; maintenance of a rare-book library for research and reference; grants to various educational institutions generally for visiting professors and lecturers. Grants restricted to privately operated colleges and universities in California, particularly the 6 Claremont colleges and their affiliates.
Types of support awarded: Publications, conferences and seminars, professorships, matching funds.
Limitations: Giving limited to CA. No grants to individuals, or for building or endowment funds, or operating budgets; no loans.
Publications: Informational brochure.
Application information:
Initial approach: Letter
Copies of proposal: 1
Deadline(s): Submit proposal preferably between January and March; no set deadline
Board meeting date(s): Bimonthly beginning in January, on third Wednesday of the month
Write: Elizabeth S. Wrigley, President
Officers and Trustees: Elizabeth S. Wrigley, President and Director of Library; W. John Niven, Vice-President; Emrys J. Ross, Secretary and Treasurer; Jack T. Ryburn, John E. Stevens.
Number of staff: 2 full-time professional; 1 part-time professional; 1 full-time support.
Employer Identification Number: 951921362

81
Baker (The R. C.) Foundation ▼
P.O. Box 6150
Orange 92667

Trust established in 1952 in California.
Donor(s): R.C. Baker, Sr.†
Financial data: (yr. ended 12/31/83): Assets, $21,098,173 (M); gifts received, $500,000; expenditures, $1,970,429, including $1,855,750 for 297 grants (high: $50,000; low: $500).

Purpose and activities: Broad purposes; emphasis on higher education, including scholarships administered by selected colleges and universities; some support for youth agencies, hospitals, health agencies, community funds, and welfare.
Types of support awarded: Seed money, emergency funds, deficit financing, building funds, equipment, research, publications, scholarship funds, fellowships, exchange programs, general purposes, continuing support.
Limitations: No grants to individuals, or for endowment funds; no loans.
Application information:
Initial approach: Cover letter with full proposal
Copies of proposal: 1
Deadline(s): Submit proposal preferably in April or September; deadline May 1 and October 1
Board meeting date(s): June and November
Write: Frank L. Scott, Trustee
Officers and Trustees: George M. Anderson, Chairman; K. Dale, Alfred Grace, L. Milan Green, Frank L. Scott, Robert N. Waters, Security Pacific National Bank, Corporate Trustee.
Number of staff: 2.
Employer Identification Number: 951742283

82
Baker (The Solomon R. and Rebecca D.) Foundation, Inc. ⌗
1901 Ave. of the Stars, Suite 1625
Los Angeles 90067   (213) 552-9822

Incorporated in 1952 in Delaware.
Donor(s): Solomon R. Baker.
Financial data: (yr. ended 4/30/83): Assets, $2,173,743 (M); expenditures, $149,940, including $145,975 for 30 grants (high: $100,000; low: $100).
Purpose and activities: Broad purposes; primarily local giving, with emphasis on medical research in autism and related fields and the care and therapy of autistic individuals; support also for education of the disadvantaged, Jewish welfare agencies, and animal welfare.
Limitations: Giving primarily in CA. No grants to individuals or for scholarships.
Application information:
Initial approach: Letter
Write: Solomon R. Baker, President
Officers and Trustees: Solomon R. Baker, President; Rebecca D. Baker, Vice-President, Secretary, and Treasurer; A. Richard Kimbrough, Robert J. Plourde.
Employer Identification Number: 237152503

83
Bank of America - Giannini Foundation
Bank of America Center
Box 37000
San Francisco 94137   (415) 953-0932

Incorporated in 1945 in California.
Donor(s): A.P. Giannini.†

Financial data: (yr. ended 12/31/83): Assets, $6,194,569 (M); gifts received, $16,182; expenditures, $380,509, including $163,039 for 13 grants (high: $37,740; low: $150) and $183,750 for 15 grants to individuals.
Purpose and activities: Medical research fellowships for advanced applicants sponsored by accredited medical schools in California. Limited number of grants made to support charitable or other educational endeavors, or those pertaining to the advancement of human health and the eradication of disease, within California.
Types of support awarded: Fellowships, research.
Limitations: Giving limited to CA. No grants to individuals (except for research fellowships), or for endowment funds or matching gifts; no loans.
Publications: Application guidelines.
Application information: Application form required.
Initial approach: Letter, telephone, or full proposal
Copies of proposal: 1
Deadline(s): August 1 for grants; December 1 for fellowships
Board meeting date(s): April and November
Write: Caroline O. Boitano, Administrator
Officers: Alfred A. Olbrycht, Secretary; Joan I. Bolin, Treasurer.
Directors: C.J. Medberry, Chairman; Claire Giannini Hoffman, Vice-Chairman; C.H. Baumhefner, J.A. Carrera, Thomas C. Fitzpatrick, Kyhl S. Smeby, Arthur V. Toupin.
Number of staff: 2.
Employer Identification Number: 946089512

84
BankAmerica Foundation ▼
Bank of America Center
Dept. 3246, P.O. Box 37000
San Francisco 94137 (415) 953-3175

Incorporated in 1968 in California.
Donor(s): BankAmerica Corporation, and subsidiaries.
Financial data: (yr. ended 12/31/84): Assets, $10,536,727 (M); expenditures, $17,676,060, including $8,425,436 for 530 grants (high: $1,100,000; low: $500; average: $1,000-$25,000), $759,072 for 3,500 employee matching gifts and $8,491,552 for 30 loans.
Purpose and activities: To fund private, non-profit, tax-exempt organizations providing services to communities locally, nationally, and internationally in areas where the company operates. Support both through grants and loans in 5 major funding areas: health, human resources, community and economic development, education, and culture and the arts; support also for special programs developed by the foundation to use its resources most effectively.
Types of support awarded: Annual campaigns, building funds, special projects, scholarship funds, employee related scholarships, employee matching gifts, matching funds, general purposes, continuing support.
Limitations: Giving limited to areas of major company operations, including communities in California, metropolitan areas nationwide, and foreign countries. No support for religious organizations for sectarian purposes, or government-funded programs. No grants to individuals or for fund-raising events, organizations where funding would primarily benefit membership, memorial campaigns, or endowment funds. Generally no support for research, conferences or seminars, publications or operating support.
Publications: Annual report, program policy statement, application guidelines.
Application information:
Initial approach: Letter
Copies of proposal: 1
Deadline(s): For capital/major campaigns, July 31; all others, none
Board meeting date(s): Semiannually; distribution committee meets quarterly
Final notification: Varies
Write: E.F. Truschke, Executive Director
Officers and Trustees: Arthur V. Toupin, Chairman; Samuel H. Armacost,* President; J.S. Stephan,* Rosemary Mans, Vice-Presidents; James Wagele, Secretary; Linda Butterfield, Treasurer; E.F. Truschke, Executive Director.
Trustees:* Robert N. Beck, Robert W. Frick, Harvey Gillis, James P. Miscoll, L.S. Prussia.
Distribution Committee: Arthur V. Toupin, Chairman; M. Freccero, W. LaRue, Rosemary Mans, Arthur Reimers, R.E. Rhody, Kyhl Smeby, E.F. Truschke.
Number of staff: 7 full-time professional; 1 part-time professional; 3 part-time support.
Employer Identification Number: 941670382

85
Battistone Foundation
1021 Tremonto Rd.
P.O. Box 3858
Santa Barbara 93105 (805) 965-2250

Trust established in 1968 in California.
Donor(s): Sam Battistone, Sr.
Financial data: (yr. ended 12/31/82): Assets, $4,692,172 (M); expenditures, $290,102, including $3,167 for 12 grants (high: $1,000).
Purpose and activities: A private operating foundation; giving to finance low-income housing for economically disadvantaged persons; grants also to local charitable organizations.
Limitations: Giving primarily in CA.
Publications: 990-PF.
Trustees: Sam Battistone, Sr., Chairman; J. Roger Battistone, Sam D. Battistone.
Employer Identification Number: 956225967

86
Baxter (The Donald E.) Foundation ⌑
611 West 6th St., Suite 777
Los Angeles 90017 (213) 626-7722

Incorporated in 1959 in California.
Donor(s): Delia B. Baxter.
Financial data: (yr. ended 12/31/83): Assets, $11,007,483 (M); expenditures, $647,144, including $634,216 for 4 grants (high: $175,000; low: $150,000).
Purpose and activities: Support for educational and scientific institutions for research and development of medicine, instruments, and fluids for alleviating pain and protecting and prolonging human life; grants primarily to higher educational institutions in California.
Types of support awarded: Research, building funds, professorships.
Limitations: Giving primarily in CA.
Application information: Grants usually initiated by the foundation's board.
Write: Richard N. Mackay, President
Officers and Directors: Richard N. Mackay, President; Richard H. Haake, Vice-President; Adam Y. Bennion, Secretary and Treasurer; Donald B. Haake.
Employer Identification Number: 956029555

87
Bechtel Foundation ▼
50 Beale St.
San Francisco 94105 (415) 768-5974

Incorporated in 1953 in California.
Donor(s): Bechtel Power Corporation.
Financial data: (yr. ended 12/31/83): Assets, $11,797,911 (M); gifts received, $1,822,000; expenditures, $2,685,879, including $2,342,355 for 406 grants (high: $400,000; low: $50) and $268,056 for employee matching gifts.
Purpose and activities: Broad purposes, with emphasis on grants to higher education and community funds, and to organizations related to some aspect of the engineering business and construction. Support also for cultural programs, health organizations, and social services.
Limitations: No grants to individuals, or for endowment funds or special projects.
Application information: Applications not invited.
Board meeting date(s): Annually
Write: Paul W. Cane, Vice-President
Officers: C.W. Hull,* President; Paul W. Cane, J.W. Weiser,* Vice-Presidents; A.R. Escola, Secretary; J.C. Stromberg, Treasurer.
Directors:* S.D. Bechtel, Jr., Chairman; A.P. Yates, Vice-Chairman.
Number of staff: 1 full-time professional; 1 part-time professional; 1 full-time support; 1 part-time support.
Employer Identification Number: 946078120

88
Bechtel (S. D.), Jr. Foundation ⌑
c/o Charles J. Spevak
50 Beale St.
San Francisco 94105 (415) 768-7620
Mailing address: P.O. Box 3809, San Francisco, CA 94119

Incorporated in 1957 in California.
Donor(s): S.D. Bechtel, Jr., Mrs. S.D. Bechtel, Jr.
Financial data: (yr. ended 12/31/83): Assets, $5,126,325 (M); gifts received, $750,000; expenditures, $57,627, including $46,000 for 24 grants (high: $5,000; low: $1,000).

Purpose and activities: Broad purposes; grants restricted to institutions in which the directors have personal involvement, primarily educational institutions and cultural programs in the San Francisco Bay Area.
Limitations: Giving primarily in the San Francisco Bay Area, CA. No grants to individuals.
Application information: Applications not accepted.
> *Board meeting date(s):* As required
> *Write:* Charles J. Spevak, Vice-President

Officers and Directors:* S.D. Bechtel, Jr.,* President; A. Barlow Ferguson,* Vice-President and Secretary; Charles J. Spevak, Vice-President and Treasurer; Elizabeth Hogan Bechtel,* Paul W. Cane, Vice-Presidents.
Employer Identification Number: 946066138

89
Beckman (Arnold and Mabel) Foundation ▼
107 Shorecliff Rd.
Corona del Mar 92625

Incorporated in 1977 in California.
Donor(s): Arnold O. Beckman, Mabel M. Beckman.
Financial data: (yr. ended 8/31/83): Assets, $17,547,679 (M); gifts received, $5,143,785; expenditures, $4,628,755, including $4,550,000 for 1 grant.
Purpose and activities: Primarily local giving, with emphasis on higher education and medical research.
Types of support awarded: Annual campaigns, conferences and seminars, emergency funds, endowment funds, equipment, matching funds, professorships, research, seed money, building funds.
Limitations: Giving primarily in CA. No grants to individuals; no loans.
Application information:
> *Initial approach:* Letter
> *Copies of proposal:* 1
> *Deadline(s):* None
> *Board meeting date(s):* November and July
> *Final notification:* 2 to 3 months
> *Write:* Arnold O. Beckman, President

Officers and Directors: Arnold O. Beckman, President; Donald A. Strauss, Vice-President; Mabel M. Beckman, Secretary and Treasurer; Maurice H. Stans.
Number of staff: None.
Employer Identification Number: 953169713

90
Bekins (Milo W.) Foundation
1335 South Figueroa St.
Los Angeles 90015

Trust established in 1953 in California.
Donor(s): Milo W. Bekins, The Bekins Company.
Financial data: (yr. ended 12/31/82): Assets, $1,787,067 (M); expenditures, $117,794, including $96,047 for 99 grants (high: $38,000; low: $100).

Purpose and activities: To assist various charitable and educational institutions, with emphasis on higher education; support also for hospitals, youth agencies, social services, and community funds.
Application information:
> *Write:* Milo W. Bekins, Jr., Trustee

Trustees: Martin B. Holt, Chairman; Mary Louise Bekins, Milo W. Bekins, Jr., Virginia Daum, John Gaines.
Employer Identification Number: 956039745

91
Berger (H. N. and Frances C.) Foundation
P.O. Box 3064
Arcadia 91006

Incorporated in 1961 in California.
Donor(s): Frances C. Berger, H.N. Berger.
Financial data: (yr. ended 12/31/83): Assets, $2,202,731 (M); gifts received, $330,938; expenditures, $72,095, including $67,200 for 40 grants (high: $27,050).
Purpose and activities: Broad purposes; primarily local giving, with emphasis on higher education and cultural programs. Committed to long-term support of present donees.
Limitations: Giving primarily in CA. No grants to individuals.
Application information: Grants initiated by foundation; applications not accepted.
> *Board meeting date(s):* Semiannually and as required

Officers and Directors: H.N. Berger, President; John N. Berger, Vice-President; Frances C. Berger, Secretary; Harry F. Booth, Jr.
Employer Identification Number: 956048939

92
Berkey (Peter) Foundation ⌑
1260 Coast Village Circle
Santa Barbara 93108

Incorporated in 1947 in Illinois.
Donor(s): Peter Berkey.†
Financial data: (yr. ended 12/31/83): Assets, $1,379,973 (M); expenditures, $146,594, including $133,630 for 59 grants (high: $30,900; low: $50).
Purpose and activities: Broad purposes; emphasis on health agencies, hospitals, youth agencies, and higher education.
Officers and Directors: Andrew D. Berkey II, President; Anne S. Berkey, Secretary; June B. D'Arcy.
Employer Identification Number: 362447326

93
Berry (The Lowell) Foundation ▼
One Kaiser Plaza, Suite 995
Oakland 94612   (415) 452-0433

Incorporated in 1950 in California.
Donor(s): Lowell W. Berry,† Farm Service Company, The Best Fertilizer Company of Texas.

Financial data: (yr. ended 8/31/84): Assets, $13,792,310 (M); expenditures, $1,160,709, including $932,300 for 175 grants (high: $136,000; low: $60; average: $1,000-$10,000).
Purpose and activities: Support only to Alameda/Contra Costa County area for evangelical Protestant church-related religious programs and institutions; grants also for youth agencies, hospitals, health agencies, community services, and cultural programs.
Limitations: Giving limited to Contra Costa and northern Alameda counties, CA. No grants to individuals, or for building and capital funds, equipment, seed money, or land acquisition.
Publications: Application guidelines, program policy statement.
Application information:
> *Initial approach:* Letter
> *Copies of proposal:* 1
> *Deadline(s):* Submit proposal between September and May
> *Board meeting date(s):* Bimonthly
> *Final notification:* 1 to 2 months for religious grants; 2 to 4 months for secular grants
> *Write:* Susan L. Shira, Administrator; John C. Branagh, President (for religious grants); Barbara Berry Corneille, Director (for secular grants)

Officers and Directors: John C. Branagh, President; Herbert Funk, Vice-President; Barbara Berry Corneille, Secretary; Robert Wiley, Treasurer; Patricia Berry Felix, William Stoddard, Eugene Wilson.
Number of staff: 1 full-time professional.
Employer Identification Number: 946108391

94
Beynon (The Kathryne) Foundation ⌑
611 West Sixth St., Suite 3320
Los Angeles 90017

Established in 1967 in California.
Donor(s): Kathryne Beynon.†
Financial data: (yr. ended 10/31/83): Assets, $4,443,048 (M); expenditures, $313,042, including $267,500 for 22 grants (high: $37,000; low: $1,000).
Purpose and activities: Broad purposes; primarily local giving, with emphasis on hospitals, youth agencies, child welfare, Catholic church support, and higher education.
Types of support awarded: Building funds, general purposes.
Limitations: Giving primarily in CA.
Application information:
> *Write:* Robert D. Bannon, Trustee

Trustees: Earl J. Bannon, Robert D. Bannon.
Employer Identification Number: 956197328

95
Bing Fund ⌑
9700 West Pico Blvd.
Los Angeles 90035

Trust established in 1958 in California.
Donor(s): Mrs. Anna Bing Arnold, Peter S. Bing.
Financial data: (yr. ended 2/28/83): Assets, $2,309,641 (M); gifts received, $15,378; expenditures, $163,812, including $158,750 for 94 grants (high: $50,000; low: $100).

Purpose and activities: Charitable purposes; primarily local giving, with emphasis on cultural programs, child welfare, and population control.
Types of support awarded: General purposes.
Limitations: Giving primarily in CA. No grants to individuals.
Application information:
 Initial approach: Letter
 Copies of proposal: 1
 Board meeting date(s): Quarterly
Trustees: Anna Bing Arnold, Peter S. Bing, Robert D. Burch.
Employer Identification Number: 956031105

96
Bireley Foundation, The
144 N. Brand Blvd.
Glendale 91203   (213) 245-3131

Incorporated in 1960 in California.
Donor(s): Frank W. Bireley.†
Financial data: (yr. ended 12/31/83): Assets, $4,813,141 (M); expenditures, $457,402, including $406,873 for 44 grants (high: $80,000; low: $500).
Purpose and activities: Grants mainly to a local medical school and children's hospital for research and treatment of adolescent skin diseases. Support also for local higher education, hospitals, and health agencies.
Limitations: Giving primarily in CA. No grants to individuals.
Application information:
 Initial approach: Letter or proposal
 Copies of proposal: 2
 Deadline(s): Submit proposal preferably between January and June; no set deadline
 Write: Christine Harriet Bireley, President
Officers and Directors: Christine Harriet Bireley, President; Ernest R. Baldwin, Vice-President and Secretary; Frank W. Bireley, William Robert Bireley, Christine Bireley Oliver, Vice-Presidents; Leroy M. Gire, Treasurer.
Number of staff: None.
Employer Identification Number: 956029475

97
Borun (Anna) and Harry Borun Foundation ¤
c/o Bank of America
555 South Flower St., 16th Fl.
Los Angeles 90071

Trust established in 1957 in California.
Donor(s): Anna Borun, Harry Borun.
Financial data: (yr. ended 12/31/82): Assets, $1,987,099 (M); expenditures, $147,303, including $135,500 for 13 grants (high: $100,000; low: $200).
Purpose and activities: Primarily local giving, with emphasis on Jewish welfare funds and education.
Limitations: Giving primarily in CA.
Trustee: Bank of America.
Employer Identification Number: 956150362

98
Boswell (The James G.) Foundation ▼
4600 Security Pacific Plaza
333 South Hope St.
Los Angeles 90071   (213) 485-1717

Incorporated in 1947 in California.
Donor(s): James G. Boswell.†
Financial data: (yr. ended 12/31/82): Assets, $49,008,391 (M); expenditures, $2,336,017, including $2,167,900 for 46 grants (high: $500,000; low: $100).
Purpose and activities: Broad purposes; general giving, locally and in Arizona, for hospitals, health, higher and secondary education, and environmental organizations.
Limitations: Giving primarily in CA and AZ.
Application information:
 Board meeting date(s): February and as required
 Write: Mrs. G.S. MacLean, Executive Secretary
Officers and Trustees: Ruth C. Crocker, President; James G. Boswell II, Secretary-Treasurer; Rosalind M. Boswell.
Employer Identification Number: 956047326

99
Bothin Foundation, The ▼
(formerly The Bothin Helping Fund)
873 Sutter St., Suite B
San Francisco 94109   (415) 771-4300

Incorporated in 1917 in California.
Donor(s): Henry E. Bothin,† Ellen Chabot Bothin,† Genevieve Bothin de Limur.†
Financial data: (yr. ended 12/31/83): Assets, $13,242,204 (M); expenditures, $865,411, including $595,383 for 81 grants (high: $25,000; low: $600; average: $1,000-$15,000).
Purpose and activities: Primarily local giving, with emphasis on community activities, cultural programs, health, the handicapped, social services, and youth.
Types of support awarded: Building funds, equipment, matching funds, emergency funds, technical assistance.
Limitations: Giving primarily in CA, with emphasis on San Francisco, Marin, and San Mateo counties. No support for religious organizations, or educational institutions (except those directly aiding the developmentally disabled), or for production or distribution of films or other documentary presentations. No grants to individuals, or for general operating funds, endowment funds, scholarships, or fellowships; no loans.
Publications: Biennial report, program policy statement, application guidelines.
Application information:
 Initial approach: Letter containing a brief and comprehensive outline of the project
 Copies of proposal: 1
 Deadline(s): 8 weeks prior to meeting
 Board meeting date(s): Mid- to late February, May, August, and November
 Final notification: 2 to 3 months
 Write: Lyman H. Casey, Executive Director
Officers: Genevieve Lyman di San Faustino,* President; Edmona Lyman Mansell,* Vice-President; Sophia P. Liss, Secretary; Lyman H. Casey,* Treasurer and Executive Director.

Directors:* William W. Budge, A. Michael Casey, William F. Geisler, Allan V. Giannini, Benjamin J. Henley, Jr.
Number of staff: 1 full-time professional; 1 full-time support.
Employer Identification Number: 941196182

100
Bowles (The Ethel Wilson) and Robert Bowles Memorial Fund ¤
c/o Adams, Duque and Hazeltine
523 West Sixth St.
Los Angeles 90014

Trust established in 1974 in California.
Donor(s): Ethel W. Bowles.†
Financial data: (yr. ended 12/31/83): Assets, $6,752,516 (M); expenditures, $396,879, including $330,000 for 7 grants (high: $47,500; low: $45,000).
Purpose and activities: Grants to tax-exempt institutions in the fields of medicine and medical research in California.
Limitations: Giving primarily in CA. No grants to individuals or for building or endowment funds.
Application information: Grant applications not accepted.
 Board meeting date(s): As required
 Write: Emrys J. Ross, Trustee
Trustees: Emrys J. Ross, Sally A. Terry.
Employer Identification Number: 956481575

101
Braun (Carl F.) Trust ▼
c/o Donald R. Spuehler
400 South Hope St.
Los Angeles 90071-2899   (818) 577 7000

Trust established in 1955 in California.
Donor(s): Carl F. Braun.†
Financial data: (yr. ended 12/31/83): Assets, $16,625,022 (M); expenditures, $1,588,792, including $1,520,000 for 9 grants (high: $448,000; low: $10,000).
Purpose and activities: Contributions to colleges and universities in California.
Limitations: Giving limited to CA.
Trustee: John G. Braun.
Number of staff: None.
Employer Identification Number: 956016828

102
Braun Foundation ▼ ¤
c/o Donald R. Spuehler
400 South Hope St.
Los Angeles 90071-2899   (213) 577-7000

Incorporated in 1953 in California.
Donor(s): Members of the Braun family.
Financial data: (yr. ended 12/31/83): Assets, $2,491,081 (M); gifts received, $591,704; expenditures, $1,468,517, including $1,295,500 for 98 grants (high: $75,000; low: $500).
Purpose and activities: Charitable purposes; primarily local giving, with emphasis on hospitals, medical research, elementary and secondary schools, museums, cultural programs, and social agencies.

Limitations: Giving primarily in CA.
Officers and Directors: Henry A. Braun,
President; John G. Braun, Secretary-Treasurer;
C. Allan Braun.
Employer Identification Number: 956016820

103
Breech Foundation, The ⊠
10889 Wilshire Blvd., Suite 750
Los Angeles 90024   (213) 879-1010

Incorporated in 1950 in Michigan.
Donor(s): Ernest R. Breech,† Thelma K. Breech.
Financial data: (yr. ended 12/31/83): Assets,
$3,281,295 (M); expenditures, $164,561,
including $151,250 for 36 grants (high:
$50,000; low: $50).
Purpose and activities: Broad purposes; grants
largely for hospitals, higher and secondary
education, church support, health agencies,
and community funds.
Limitations: No grants to individuals.
Application information:
    Deadline(s): None
Officers and Trustees: Thelma K. Breech,
President and Treasurer; William H. Breech,
Vice-President; Walter P. Feehily, Secretary; E.
Robert Breech, Jr., Austin G. Conrad.
Employer Identification Number: 386060181

104
Brenner (The Mervyn L.) Foundation, Inc. ⊠
c/o John F. Forbes & Co.
4 Embarcadero Center, Suite 400
San Francisco 94111

Incorporated in 1961 in California.
Donor(s): Mervyn L. Brenner.†
Financial data: (yr. ended 8/31/82): Assets,
$1,172,465 (M); expenditures, $99,766,
including $85,000 for 35 grants (high: $10,000;
low: $1,000).
Purpose and activities: General purposes;
primarily local giving, with emphasis on
hospitals, Jewish welfare funds, health and
youth agencies, cultural organizations, and
higher education.
Limitations: Giving primarily in CA.
Officers and Directors: John R. Gentry,
President; William D. Crawford, Marvin T.
Tepperman, Vice-Presidents; Marc H.
Monheimer, Secretary; John T. Seigle, Treasurer.
Employer Identification Number: 946088679

105
Bridges (Robert and Alice) Foundation
c/o Robert L. Bridges
Two Embarcadero Center, No. 2140
San Francisco 94111

Foundation established in 1957 in California.
Financial data: (yr. ended 12/31/82): Assets,
$1,135,860 (M); expenditures, $123,574,
including $116,200 for 77 grants (high:
$18,000; low: $25).
Purpose and activities: Primarily local giving;
support largely for higher education; grants also
for youth agencies, hospitals and health
associations, and the performing arts.

Limitations: Giving primarily in the San
Francisco Bay Area, CA.
Officers: Robert L. Bridges, President; Alice M.
Bridges, David M. Bridges, James R. Bridges,
Linda Bridges Ingham, Vice-Presidents; Michael
L. Mellor, Secretary.
Employer Identification Number: 946066355

106
Brody (Frances and Sidney) Charitable Fund, Inc. ⊠
10203 Santa Monica Blvd.
Los Angeles 90067

Established in 1944 in Illinois.
Donor(s): Frances L. Brody, Sidney F. Brody.
Financial data: (yr. ended 12/31/83): Assets,
$148,095 (M); gifts received, $100,000;
expenditures, $159,201, including $158,276
for 40 grants (high: $52,000; low: $25).
Purpose and activities: Support primarily for
education, cultural programs, particularly a
local museum, hospitals, and Jewish welfare
funds.
Officers and Directors:* Frances L. Brody,*
President; Christopher W. Brody, Vice-
President and Treasurer; Susan L. Brody, Vice-
President; James M. Cowley,* Secretary.
Employer Identification Number: 956029499

107
Brotman Foundation of California ⊠
c/o Robert D. Hartford
433 North Camden Dr., No. 600
Beverly Hills 90210

Established in 1964.
Financial data: (yr. ended 12/31/82): Assets,
$5,233,498 (M); expenditures, $326,669,
including $180,575 for 13 grants (high:
$100,000; low: $75).
Purpose and activities: Primarily local giving
for education, particularly higher education.
Limitations: Giving primarily in CA.
Officers and Directors: Michael B. Sherman,
President; Lowell Marks, Secretary; Robert D.
Hartford, Treasurer; Toni Wald.
Employer Identification Number: 956094639

108
Buchalter, Nemer, Fields, Chrystie & Younger Charitable Foundation
700 South Flower St., Suite 700
Los Angeles 90017   (213) 626-6700

Trust established in 1965 in California.
Donor(s): Buchalter, Nemer, Fields, Chrystie &
Younger.
Financial data: (yr. ended 12/31/83): Assets,
$47,694 (M); gifts received, $161,370;
expenditures, $168,202, including $166,765
for 147 grants (high: $59,368; low: $15).
Purpose and activities: Broad purposes;
primarily local giving, with emphasis on Jewish
welfare funds and hospitals.
Limitations: Giving primarily in CA. No grants
to individuals, or for endowment funds,
research, or scholarships or fellowships; no
loans.
Application information:

Initial approach: Letter, telephone, or full
    proposal
Copies of proposal: 1
Deadline(s): Submit proposal preferably in
    November or December; deadline
    December 31
Board meeting date(s): As required
Write: Elihu M. Berle, Trustee
Trustees: Irwin R. Buchalter, Arthur Chinski,
Murray M. Fields, Evelle J. Younger, Clifford J.
Meyer.
Employer Identification Number: 956112980

109
Bull (The Henry W.) Foundation ⊠
c/o Wells Fargo Bank
420 Montgomery No. 954
San Francisco 94163   (213) 550-2468
Additional address: P.O. Box 711, Beverly
Hills, CA 90213

Trust established in 1960 in California.
Donor(s): Maud L. Bull.†
Financial data: (yr. ended 12/31/83): Assets,
$3,753,590 (M); gifts received, $3,000;
expenditures, $203,900, including $169,500
for 61 grants (high: $20,000; low: $1,000).
Purpose and activities: Grants primarily for
higher education, handicapped, health, and
church support.
Limitations: No grants to individuals, or for
building or endowment funds.
Application information:
    Initial approach: Full proposal
    Copies of proposal: 1
    Board meeting date(s): Monthly
Trustees: James W.Z. Taylor, Administrator;
Fred Astaire, Jr., Peter N. Potter, Wells Fargo
Bank.
Employer Identification Number: 956062058

110
Burnand (The Alphonse A.) Medical and Educational Foundation ⊠
503 The Mall
P.O. Box B
Borrego Springs 92004   (714) 767-5314

Incorporated in 1957 in California.
Financial data: (yr. ended 12/31/83): Assets,
$1,402,676 (M); expenditures, $45,593,
including $34,856 for grants.
Purpose and activities: Primarily local giving,
with emphasis on higher education, hospitals,
youth agencies, and the handicapped.
Limitations: Giving primarily in CA. No grants
to individuals or for endowment funds.
Application information:
    Initial approach: Letter
    Copies of proposal: 1
    Deadline(s): Submit proposal in October
    Board meeting date(s): As required, at least
        semiannually
    Write: A.A. Burnand III, President
Officers: A.A. Burnand III, President; G.J.
Kuhrts III, Treasurer.
Employer Identification Number: 956083677

111
Burns (Fritz B.) Foundation ▼ ⌧
4001 West Alameda Ave., Suite 203
Los Angeles 91505   (818) 840-8802

Incorporated in 1955 in California.
Donor(s): Fritz B. Burns.†
Financial data: (yr. ended 9/30/83): Assets, $27,926,490 (M); gifts received, $8,000,000; expenditures, $3,019,636, including $2,933,000 for 34 grants (high: $1,000,000; low: $50).
Purpose and activities: Broad purposes; primarily local giving, with emphasis on a university, hospitals and medical research organizations, and Roman Catholic religious associations, social welfare agencies, and church support.
Limitations: Giving primarily in the Los Angeles, CA, area.
Application information:
  Initial approach: Letter
  Deadline(s): None
  Write: Joseph E. Rawlinson, President
Officers and Directors: W. Herbert Hannon, Chairman; Joseph E. Rawlinson, President; W.K. Skinner, Executive Vice-President and Secretary-Treasurer; Charles S. Casassa, C.W. Getchell, Edmund F. Schneiders.
Employer Identification Number: 956064403

112
Burns-Dunphy Foundation ⌧
c/o Walter M. Gleason
Hearst Bldg., Third & Market Sts., Suite 1200
San Francisco 94103

Foundation established in 1969 in California.
Donor(s): Walter M. Gleason.
Financial data: (yr. ended 12/31/83): Assets, $1,199,098 (M); gifts received, $85,000; expenditures, $82,653, including $81,700 for 43 grants (high: $10,000; low: $500).
Purpose and activities: Grants primarily for Roman Catholic welfare, educational, and missionary services.
Officers and Directors: Walter M. Gleason, President; William J. Gleason, Vice-President and Treasurer; Cressey H. Nakagawa, Secretary.
Employer Identification Number: 237043565

113
Caddock Foundation, Inc.
1793 Chicago Ave.
Riverside 92507

Incorporated in 1968 in California.
Donor(s): Richard E. Caddock.
Financial data: (yr. ended 12/31/83): Assets, $1,262,773 (M); expenditures, $310,167, including $293,500 for 33 grants (high: $34,000; low: $1,000).
Purpose and activities: Grants largely to Protestant religious associations and activities, including Bible studies.
Officers: Richard E. Caddock, President; Anne M. Caddock, Vice-President; Sue E. Brinkman, Secretary; Richard E. Caddock, Jr., Treasurer.
Employer Identification Number: 952559728

114
California Community Foundation ▼
3580 Wilshire Blvd., Suite 1680
Los Angeles 90010   (213) 413-4042
Orange County office: 4050 Metropolitan Dr., Suite 300, Orange, CA 92268; Tel.: (714) 937-9077

Community foundation established in 1915 in California by bank resolution.
Financial data: (yr. ended 6/30/84): Assets, $38,129,997 (M); gifts received, $5,316,195; expenditures, $4,602,170, including $3,719,458 for 226 grants (high: $64,540; low: $100; average: $5,000-$20,000) and $1,261 for 24 employee matching gifts.
Purpose and activities: Local support only for arts, humanities, education, the environment, health, human services, particularly youth programs, and community development.
Types of support awarded: Matching funds, technical assistance, special projects, employee matching gifts.
Limitations: Giving limited to Los Angeles, Orange, Riverside, San Bernadino, and Ventura counties, CA. No support for films, dinners or special events, or for sectarian purposes. No grants to individuals, or for building funds, annual campaigns, equipment, endowment funds, operating budgets, scholarships, or fellowships; no loans.
Publications: Annual report, application guidelines, informational brochure.
Application information:
  Initial approach: Full proposal
  Copies of proposal: 1
  Deadline(s): None
  Board meeting date(s): Quarterly
  Final notification: 3 months after board meets
  Write: Jack Shakely, Executive Director
Officer: Jack Shakely, Executive Director.
Board of Governors: Walter B. Gerken, Chairman; Caroline L. Ahmanson, Arnold O. Beckman, Camela Frost, Philip M. Hawley, Ignacio E. Lozano, Jr., Sister Marie Madeleine, S.C.L., Paul A. Miller, George F. Moody, Henry T. Mudd, Daniel H. Ridder, William French Smith.
Trustees: Bank of America, City National Bank, Crocker National Bank, First Interstate Bank, Security Pacific National Bank, Trust Services of America, Wells Fargo Bank.
Number of staff: 5 full-time professional; 2 part-time professional; 3 full-time support.
Employer Identification Number: 956013179

115
California Educational Initiatives Fund
c/o Bank of America, Tax Dept. No. 3246
555 California St., P.O. Box 37000
San Francisco 94137   (415) 953-3175

Established in 1979 in California.
Donor(s): BankAmerica Foundation, Chevron USA, Wells Fargo Foundation, First Interstate Bank of California Foundation, Del Monte Foods, Security Pacific, McKesson Corporation.
Financial data: (yr. ended 12/31/83): Assets, $351,127 (M); gifts received, $852,500; expenditures, $601,373, including $588,419 for 71 grants (high: $18,000; low: $1,500; average: $9,000).

Purpose and activities: Giving in California to public school districts that are winners of statewide competition; seeks proposals for innovative programs which address student needs and broaden support for public education; support to improve basic learning skills in the areas of language arts, mathematics, science, and the fine arts, and to encourage effective schools.
Types of support awarded: Special projects.
Limitations: Giving limited to CA. No support for public school foundations, private schools, or university schools of education. No grants to individuals.
Publications: Application guidelines, program policy statement, informational brochure.
Application information: Send original copy of proposal. Application form required.
  Initial approach: Telephone
  Deadline(s): Mid-October; funding available in January and February
  Board meeting date(s): May and November
  Final notification: December
  Write: Caroline Boitano, Administrator
Number of staff: 1 part-time professional; 1 part-time support.
Employer Identification Number: 953830359

116
California Foundation for Biochemical Research
10901 North Torrey Pines Rd.
La Jolla 92037

Incorporated in 1952 in California.
Financial data: (yr. ended 4/30/82): Assets, $5,174,870 (M); expenditures, $243,494, including $186,000 for 20 grants (high: $51,000; low: $1,000).
Purpose and activities: To support biochemical research fellowships, primarily at institutions in southern California.
Types of support awarded: Fellowships, research.
Limitations: Giving primarily in Southern CA. No grants to individuals.
Application information:
  Initial approach: Letter
  Board meeting date(s): Semiannually
  Write: William Drell, Vice-President
Officers: Eugene Roberts,* President; William Drell, Vice-President; James Bonner,* Secretary and Treasurer.
Trustees:* Emil L. Smith, Donald W. Visser.
Employer Identification Number: 956092628

117
California Masonic Foundation
1111 California St.
San Francisco 94108   (415) 776-7000

Incorporated in 1969 in California.
Donor(s): Grand Lodge F & AM of California.
Financial data: (yr. ended 6/30/84): Assets, $1,121,000 (M); gifts received, $30,600; expenditures, $85,500, including $85,500 for 174 grants to individuals (average: $500).
Purpose and activities: Scholarships for full-time undergraduate students in California and Hawaii.
Types of support awarded: Student aid.

Limitations: Giving limited to CA and HI.
Application information: Application form required.
  Initial approach: Letter
  Deadline(s): None
  Board meeting date(s): 5 times yearly
  Final notification: 6 months
Officers and Trustees: Larry C. Basker, President; J. Glen Gladson, Vice-President; Guy E. Reynolds, Secretary; James B. Bouick III, Donald C. Briggs, Robert N. Deter, Edgar L. Friedman, Bernard P. Gray, Robert W. Laversin, Thomas J. May, Andrew I. Nocas, Arthur A. Perry, Robert J. Valdisera, Glen A. Worrell, Edward B.H. Yee.
Number of staff: None.
Employer Identification Number: 237013074

118
Callison Foundation, The ⊭
c/o Feeney, Sparks & Rudy
Hearst Bldg., Suite 1100
San Francisco 94103

Established in 1965 in California.
Donor(s): Fred W. Callison.
Financial data: (yr. ended 12/31/83): Assets, $3,775,100 (M); expenditures, $427,931, including $372,190 for 26 grants (high: $59,190; low: $5,000).
Purpose and activities: Primarily local giving, with emphasis on Roman Catholic religious organizations, youth agencies, social welfare, cultural programs, hospitals, aid to the handicapped, and higher education.
Limitations: Giving primarily in San Francisco, CA.
Officers and Directors: Ward Ingersoll, President; Russell Gowans, Vice-President; Dorothy Sola, Secretary; Frances M. Smith, Treasurer; Thomas E. Feeney.
Employer Identification Number: 946127962

119
Carnation Company Foundation
5045 Wilshire Blvd.
Los Angeles 90036   (213) 932-6259

Incorporated in 1952 in California.
Donor(s): Carnation Company.
Financial data: (yr. ended 12/31/83): Assets, $4,828,805 (M); expenditures, $355,361, including $300,000 for 200 grants (high: $10,000; low: $1,000).
Purpose and activities: Sustained support for four-year private colleges and universities.
Types of support awarded: Continuing support, operating budgets.
Application information: Unsolicited proposals not encouraged.
  Initial approach: Proposal
  Copies of proposal: 1
  Deadline(s): October 15
  Board meeting date(s): December
  Final notification: January 31
  Write: Jonell Hart
Officers: J.N. Kvamme,* President and Treasurer; N.P. Devereaux, D.N. Dickson,* A. Pate, Vice-Presidents; W.N. Brakensiek, Secretary.

Directors:* T.F. Crull, R.D. Kummel, C.A. Nelson.
Number of staff: 1 full-time professional.
Employer Identification Number: 956027479

120
Carnation Company Scholarship
Foundation ⊭
c/o Board of Advisors
5045 Wilshire Blvd.
Los Angeles 90036   (213) 932-6000

Established in 1952 in California.
Donor(s): Carnation Company.
Financial data: (yr. ended 12/31/83): Assets, $2,435,099 (M); expenditures, $235,409, including $206,500 for 134 grants to individuals.
Purpose and activities: Giving to relatives of company employees for higher education scholarships.
Types of support awarded: Employee related scholarships.
Application information: Application form required.
  Initial approach: Application form
  Deadline(s): February 15
Advisors: T.F. Crull, R.D. Kummel, J.N. Kvamme.
Trustee: Seattle First-National Bank.
Employer Identification Number: 956118622

121
Center (Hugh Stuart) Charitable Trust ⊭
c/o Rankin, Oneal, Center
2 West Santa Clara St., 3rd Fl.
Santa Clara 95113

Trust established in 1977 in California.
Donor(s): Hugh Stuart Center.†
Financial data: (yr. ended 12/31/83): Assets, $4,804,461 (M); expenditures, $329,728, including $274,685 for 42 grants (high: $50,000; low: $100).
Purpose and activities: Primarily local giving; support largely for higher and secondary education, hospitals, and cultural programs.
Limitations: Giving primarily in San Jose, CA.
Trustees: Arthur K. Lund, Louis Oneal.
Employer Identification Number: 942455308

122
CFS Foundation
655 Beach St., 2nd Fl.
San Francisco 94109

Established in 1980 in California.
Donor(s): Alan J. Andreini, Tyler B. Glenn, Charles M. Hobson III, Vincent L. Ricci, Dean T. Riskas, Raymond F. Sebastian, Basil R. Twist.
Financial data: (yr. ended 9/30/82): Assets, $59,284 (M); gifts received, $275,733; expenditures, $258,806, including $252,350 for 37 grants (high: $35,000; low: $500).
Purpose and activities: Broad purposes; grants largely for social services, education, and cultural programs.
Application information: Applications not accepted.

Officers: Basil R. Twist, President; Charles M. Hobson III, Secretary; Raymond F. Sebastian, Treasurer.
Employer Identification Number: 942702212

123
Charis Fund ⊭
c/o Raymond L. Hanson, Fiduciary
2465 E. Bayshore Blvd., Embarcadero Suite 301
Palo Alto 94303

Trust established in 1938 in California.
Donor(s): Hugh Trowbridge Dobbins,† Roberta Lloyd Dobbins,† and others.
Financial data: (yr. ended 12/31/83): Assets, $1,643,702 (M); expenditures, $300,834, including $223,500 for 36 grants (high: $13,500; low: $1,000).
Purpose and activities: Giving primarily in the San Francisco Bay area and in Washington and Oregon, with emphasis on Protestant church-related organizations, higher education, and social agencies.
Limitations: Giving primarily in the San Francisco, CA, bay area, WA and OR.
Application information: Funds largely committed; new requests not encouraged.
  Initial approach: Letter
  Deadline(s): None
  Board meeting date(s): Spring and fall
  Write: Leslie E. Dobbins, Secretary
Officers: Paul D'Anneo, President; Elizabeth Dobbins Simmonds, Vice-President; Leslie E. Dobbins, Secretary-Treasurer.
Employer Identification Number: 946077619

124
Christensen Fund, The ⊭
780 Welch Rd., Suite 100
Palo Alto 94304

Incorporated in 1957 in California.
Donor(s): Allen D. Christensen, Carmen M. Christensen.
Financial data: (yr. ended 11/30/82): Assets, $6,669,359 (M); gifts received, $1,594,531; expenditures, $392,794, including $313,708 for 9 grants (high: $295,932; low: $20).
Purpose and activities: A private operating foundation to display art objects in museums and support higher educational institutions, including Oxford University in England.
Officers and Directors: Allen D. Christensen, President; Carmen M. Christensen, Vice-President; Joseph K. Allen, Secretary-Treasurer and Manager.
Employer Identification Number: 946055879

125
City Investing Company Foundation ⊭
9100 Wilshire Blvd.
Beverly Hills 90212
Scholarship application address: Bob Wood Endowment Fund, 1658 Cole Blvd., Golden, CO 80401

Incorporated in 1963 in Missouri.
Donor(s): World Color Press, Inc., City Investing Company, and related companies.

Financial data: (yr. ended 12/31/82): Assets, $1,768,552 (M); gifts received, $594,700; expenditures, $656,386, including $638,350 for 191 grants (high: $57,000; low: $200) and $2,000 for 2 grants to individuals.
Purpose and activities: Broad purposes; support primarily for community funds, higher education, hospitals, youth and civic agencies, and cultural programs.
Types of support awarded: Employee related scholarships.
Application information:
  Initial approach: Letter
  Deadline(s): May
Officers and Directors: Eben W. Pyne, President; John J. McHugh, Vice-President and Secretary; Lester J. Mantell, Vice-President and Treasurer; Roswell Messing, Jr.
Employer Identification Number: 953308551

126
Civitas Fund ¤
10880 Wilshire Blvd., Suite 2003
Los Angeles 90024

Incorporated in 1975 in California.
Donor(s): Elsie B. Ballantyne.
Financial data: (yr. ended 12/31/83): Assets, $4,037,437 (M); expenditures, $115,374, including $76,000 for 3 grants (high: $48,000; low: $3,000).
Purpose and activities: Primarily local giving for higher education and a senior center.
Limitations: Giving primarily in CA.
Officers and Trustees: Robert B. Ballantyne, President; Havourneen O'Connor, Vice-President; Yvonne Dean, Secretary-Treasurer; Norman C. Obrow.
Employer Identification Number: 952994948

127
Clorox Company Foundation, The ▼
1221 Broadway
Oakland 94612   (415) 271-7747

Incorporated in 1980 in California.
Donor(s): Clorox Company.
Financial data: (yr. ended 6/30/83): Assets, $1,901,898 (M); gifts received, $800,000; expenditures, $744,289, including $650,922 for 232 grants (high: $140,000; low: $10; average: $500-$5,000).
Purpose and activities: Primarily local giving and in areas of company operations for youth, community development, social services, education (including employee matching gifts for colleges and universities), civic affairs, and cultural programs.
Types of support awarded: Building funds, endowment funds, operating budgets, general purposes, employee matching gifts.
Limitations: Giving primarily in areas of company operations, with special emphasis on Oakland, CA. No support for sectarian religious purposes. No grants for goodwill advertising.
Publications: Annual report.
Application information: Application form required.
  Deadline(s): Furnished upon request

Board meeting date(s): Aproximately 10 times a year
Final notification: Varies
Write: Carmella Johnson, Contributions Admin.
Trustees: David S. Way, President; J.J. Calderini, R.A. Glazar, D.L. Goodman, C.S. Harder, P.F. Larned, P.J. Marino, P.M. Meehan, R.C. Soublet.
Number of staff: 1 full-time professional; 1 part-time professional; 1 full-time support.
Employer Identification Number: 942674980

128
Coburn (The Maurine Church) Charitable Trust ▼
P.O. Box 530
Pebble Beach 93953

Trust established in California.
Donor(s): Maurine Church Coburn.†
Financial data: (yr. ended 9/30/83): Assets, $5,022,958 (M); expenditures, $3,677,994, including $3,539,124 for 23 grants (high: $698,973; low: $1,000; average: $50,000-$125,000).
Purpose and activities: In 1982, the Trust committed all funds for new grants to support of The Maurine Church School of Nursing with no other grant applications considered for an indefinite period of time.
Types of support awarded: Building funds, special projects.
Limitations: Giving limited to Monterey Bay, CA, area. No support for organizations that receive a substantial portion of support from tax sources. No grants to individuals or for annual or nationwide campaigns, publication projects, or media programs.
Publications: Annual report.
Application information: Funds presently committed.
Trustees: Milton C. Coburn, Peter C. Wright, Wells Fargo Bank (Shirley A. Snyder, Vice-President and Trust Officer).
Number of staff: 4 part-time support.
Employer Identification Number: 946464628

129
Coleman (Sylvan C.) Foundation ¤
c/o C.B. Coleman
2401 Merced St.
San Leandro 94577

Established about 1956.
Donor(s): Sylvan C. Coleman.
Financial data: (yr. ended 11/30/82): Assets, $1,197,650 (M); expenditures, $46,042, including $43,950 for 26 grants (high: $10,000; low: $250).
Purpose and activities: Giving primarily for higher education, cultural programs, health, social services and Jewish welfare funds.
Trustees: Clarence B. Coleman, Henry M. Marx.
Employer Identification Number: 136091160

130
Columbia Foundation ▼
1090 Sansome St.
San Francisco 94111   (415) 986-5179

Incorporated in 1940 in California.
Donor(s): Mrs. Madeleine H. Russell.
Financial data: (yr. ended 5/31/84): Assets, $16,178,359 (M); gifts received, $76,932; expenditures, $1,374,686, including $912,990 for 62 grants (high: $100,000; low: $1,000; average: $1,000-$50,000).
Purpose and activities: General purposes; local giving, with emphasis on the arts, environment, human rights and the disadvantaged, community development, neighborhood revitalization, and world peace.
Types of support awarded: Seed money, special projects, research, publications, conferences and seminars.
Limitations: Giving primarily in northern CA, with emphasis on the San Francisco Bay Area. No support for health, specialized scientific research or religion; or for "private foundations," institutions supported by federated campaigns, or those heavily subsidized by government funds. No grants to individuals, or for building or endowment funds, matching gifts, scholarships and fellowships, or operating budgets; no loans.
Publications: Application guidelines, program policy statement.
Application information:
  Initial approach: Letter or telephone
  Copies of proposal: 1
  Deadline(s): None
  Board meeting date(s): Quarterly
  Final notification: 3 months
  Write: Susan Clark Silk, Executive Director
Officers and Directors:* Madeleine H. Russell,* President; Alice C. Russell,* Christine H. Russell,* Vice-Presidents; Willard L. Ellis, Secretary; Charles P. Russell,* Treasurer; Susan Clark Silk, Executive Director.
Number of staff: 1 part-time professional; 1 part-time support.
Employer Identification Number: 941196186

131
Connell (Michael J.) Foundation ▼
201 South Lake Ave., Suite 303
Pasadena 91101   (213) 681-8085

Incorporated in 1931 in California.
Donor(s): Michael J. Connell.†
Financial data: (yr. ended 6/30/84): Assets, $7,350,970 (M); expenditures, $698,736, including $566,000 for 26 grants (high: $100,000; low: $500; average: $5,000-$50,000).
Purpose and activities: Primarily local giving, generally restricted to programs initiated by the foundation in social, cultural, educational, and medical fields.
Types of support awarded: Internships, conferences and seminars, fellowships, operating budgets, special projects.
Limitations: Giving primarily in southern CA, with emphasis on Los Angeles. No grants to individuals, or for building funds; no loans.
Publications: Financial statement.

Application information: Giving generally to programs initiated by the foundation.
> *Initial approach:* Letter
> *Copies of proposal:* 1
> *Deadline(s):* None
> *Board meeting date(s):* Quarterly
> *Final notification:* 3 months
> *Write:* John Connell, President

Officers: John Connell,* President and Treasurer; Richard A. Wilson,* Vice-President; Kay M. Staub, Secretary.
Directors: Mary C. Bayless, Michael J. Connell.
Number of staff: 1 full-time professional; 2 part-time professional.
Employer Identification Number: 956000904

132
Cook Brothers Educational Fund ⌑
700 S. Flower St., Suite 1600
Los Angeles 90017

Established about 1980 in California.
Donor(s): Howard F. Cook.†
Financial data: (yr. ended 12/31/82): Assets, $3,004,066 (M); expenditures, $45,677.
Purpose and activities: Charitable purposes; no grants awarded in 1982.
Officers and Trustees: Franklin C. Cook, President; William H. Cook, Secretary; Kathleen M. Cook, Susan V. Cook.
Employer Identification Number: 237306457

133
Copley (James S.) Foundation ▼
7776 Ivanhoe Ave.
P.O. Box 1530
La Jolla 92038-1530   (619) 454-0411

Incorporated in 1953 in California.
Donor(s): The Copley Press Inc.
Financial data: (yr. ended 12/31/84): Assets, $9,453,545 (M); gifts received, $2,738,929; expenditures, $1,664,830, including $1,623,578 for 216 grants (high: $302,600; low: $10; average: $10-$10,000) and $24,019 for 113 employee matching gifts.
Purpose and activities: Broad purposes; giving primarily to agencies within the circulation area of Copley newspapers, with emphasis on hospitals, community funds, higher education, and cultural programs.
Types of support awarded: Annual campaigns, seed money, emergency funds, building funds, equipment, land acquisition, scholarship funds, employee matching gifts, continuing support.
Limitations: Giving primarily in circulation areas of company newspapers, particularly San Diego and La Jolla, CA. No grants to individuals, or for endowment funds, research, publications, conferences, unrestricted purposes, operating budgets or large campaigns; no loans.
Publications: Application guidelines, program policy statement.
Application information:
> *Initial approach:* Letter
> *Copies of proposal:* 1
> *Deadline(s):* September 1 for consideration for the following year's budget

Board meeting date(s): February, May, August, and November
Final notification: 2 to 3 weeks
Write: Anita A. Baumgardner, Administrative Secretary

Officers: Helen K. Copley, Chair; David C. Copley, President; Alex De Bakcsy, Hubert L. Kaltenbach, Vice-Presidents; Charles F. Patrick, Secretary and Treasurer; Anita A. Baumgardner, Administrative Secretary.
Number of staff: None.
Employer Identification Number: 956051770

134
Corcoran Community Foundation, The
P.O. Box 655
Corcoran 93212   (209) 992-5551

Community foundation incorporated in 1965 in California.
Donor(s): W.W. Boswell, Mrs. W.W. Boswell.
Financial data: (yr. ended 7/31/84): Assets, $1,023,453 (M); gifts received, $55,000; expenditures, $190,000, including $104,000 for 26 grants (high: $32,500; low: $233) and $12,000 for 2 loans.
Purpose and activities: Broad purposes; to support organizations benefiting the inhabitants of Corcoran and its surrounding area.
Types of support awarded: Operating budgets, continuing support, annual campaigns, seed money, emergency funds, building funds, equipment, land acquisition, endowment funds, matching funds, consulting services, technical assistance, program-related investments, scholarship funds, loans, special projects, research, publications, conferences and seminars.
Limitations: Giving primarily in the Corcoran, CA area. No grants to individuals or for deficit financing.
Publications: Annual report, application guidelines.
Application information: Application form required.
> *Initial approach:* Letter
> *Copies of proposal:* 1
> *Deadline(s):* Submit proposal preferably in the month preceding board meetings
> *Board meeting date(s):* October, December, February, April, June, and August
> *Final notification:* After board meeting
> *Write:* Mike Graville, Executive Director

Officers and Trustees: Mrs. W.W. Boswell, Sr., President; James B. Hansen, Vice-President; Charles Gilkey, Secretary; Robert A. Lyman, Treasurer; Barrie Boyett, Mrs. Leslie S. Corcoran, Glenda Doan, Leslie J. Doan, George M. Fuller, Jr.,Ross F. Hall, Robert Hansen, Morris Proctor, Fred Salyer, Gayle E. Tamm.
Trustee Banks: Lloyds Bank, Security Pacific National Bank.
Number of staff: 1 full-time professional.
Employer Identification Number: 941608857

135
Corti Family Agricultural Fund ⌑
c/o Bank of America N.T. & S.A. Trust Dept.
1011 Van Ness Ave., P.O. Box 1672
Fresno 93721   (805) 395-0880

Additional scholarship application address:
c/o Theresa Corti Scholarship Committee, Kern County Superintendent of Schools, 5801 Sundale Ave., Bakersfield, CA 93309

Established in 1950.
Financial data: (yr. ended 3/31/83): Assets, $1,545,128 (M); expenditures, $96,956, including $73,363 for 136 grants to individuals.
Purpose and activities: Giving to graduates of high schools in Kern County, California for agricultural scholarships.
Types of support awarded: Student aid.
Limitations: Giving limited to Kern County, CA.
Trustee: Bank of America.
Employer Identification Number: 956053041

136
Cowell (S. H.) Foundation ▼
260 California, Suite 501
San Francisco 94111   (415) 397-0285

Trust established in 1955 in California.
Donor(s): S.H. Cowell.†
Financial data: (yr. ended 9/30/84): Assets, $48,598,080 (M); expenditures, $5,215,793, including $4,416,814 for 175 grants (high: $160,000; low: $1,000; average: $25,000-$50,000).
Purpose and activities: General purposes; local giving, with emphasis on programs aiding the handicapped, primary and secondary private schools, other educational programs, community organizations, family planning projects, youth agencies, including training and employment programs; cultural programs, and social rehabilitation services.
Types of support awarded: Seed money, emergency funds, building funds, equipment, land acquisition, matching funds, scholarship funds, endowment funds.
Limitations: Giving limited to northern CA. No support for hospitals or sectarian religious purposes. No grants to individuals, or for operating budgets, media programs, continuing support, annual campaigns, routine program administration, workshops, symposia, deficit financing, fellowships, special projects, medical research, publications, or conferences; no loans.
Publications: Annual report, program policy statement, application guidelines.
Application information:
> *Initial approach:* Letter
> *Copies of proposal:* 1
> *Deadline(s):* December for primary and secondary schools, and June for colleges and universities
> *Board meeting date(s):* Monthly
> *Final notification:* 3 to 4 months
> *Write:* Stephanie R. Spivey, Administrator

Officers: Max Thelen, Jr.,* President; William P. Murray, Jr.,* Vice-President; George A. Hopiak, Secretary-Treasurer.
Trustees: J.D. Erickson, Wells Fargo Bank.
Number of staff: 3 full-time professional; 1 full-time support.
Employer Identification Number: 941392803

137
Crocker (The Mary A.) Trust
233 Post St., Suite 600
San Francisco 94108   (415) 362-3180

Trust established in 1889 in California.
Donor(s): Mary A. Crocker.†
Financial data: (yr. ended 12/31/83): Assets, $9,200,933 (M); expenditures, $301,575, including $246,995 for 28 grants (high: $15,000; low: $500; average: $5,000-$20,000).
Purpose and activities: Primarily local support for creative and innovative programs.
Types of support awarded: Seed money, emergency funds, equipment, matching funds, publications, special projects.
Limitations: Giving primarily in the San Francisco Bay Area, CA. No support for conduit agencies or tax-supported projects. No grants to individuals, or for operating budgets, continuing support, annual campaigns, deficit financing, building or endowment funds, land acquisition, scholarships and fellowships, research, demonstration projects, or conferences; no loans.
Publications: Application guidelines, program policy statement.
Application information: Application form required.
Initial approach: Letter
Copies of proposal: 1
Board meeting date(s): 2 to 3 times a year
Final notification: 3 months
Write: Carol Dugger Lerer, Administrator
Officers: Lloyd H. Skjerdal, Treasurer; Carol Dugger Lerer, Administrator.
Trustees: Frederick C. Whitman, Chairman; Charles Crocker, William H. Crocker, Tania W. Stepanian, Frederick W. Whitridge.
Number of staff: 1 full-time professional.
Employer Identification Number: 946051917

138
Crocker National Bank Foundation ▼
333 South Grand Ave., Suite 1280
Los Angeles 90071   (213) 253-3098

Established in 1978 in California.
Donor(s): Crocker National Bank.
Financial data: (yr. ended 12/31/84): Assets, $362,544 (M); expenditures, $1,388,320, including $1,280,449 for 150 grants (high: $345,000; low: $250) and $107,871 for 246 employee matching gifts.
Purpose and activities: Broad purposes; primarily local giving, largely for higher education and for cultural programs, civic affairs, community funds, and hospitals; support also for an employee matching gifts program.
Types of support awarded: Annual campaigns, seed money, emergency funds, building funds, land acquisition, research, publications, scholarship funds, employee related scholarships, fellowships, matching funds, general purposes, continuing support, employee matching gifts.

Limitations: Giving primarily in CA. No support for public or private elementary or secondary schools (except through matching gifts), public interest legal activities, religious or political organizations, professional associations, health education or medical research agencies, aid to hospitals and clinics for capital fund drives. No grants to individuals or for endowment funds, tutorial programs, or conferences; no loans.
Publications: Annual report.
Application information:
Initial approach: Full proposal
Copies of proposal: 1
Deadline(s): None
Board meeting date(s): Semiannually
Final notification: 6 to 8 weeks
Write: Iris Clark, Contributions Representative
Officers: Owen H. Harper,* President; James E. Roberts, Vice-President.
Directors:* David A. Brooks, Carl C. Gregory, Peter E. Haas, Charles M. Stockholm.
Number of staff: 1 full-time professional; 1 full-time support.
Employer Identification Number: 953169707

139
Crown Zellerbach Foundation ▼
235 Montgomery St., Suite 1527
San Francisco 94104   (415) 398-0600

Incorporated in 1952 in California.
Donor(s): Crown Zellerbach Corporation.
Financial data: (yr. ended 12/31/82): Assets, $15,150,916 (M); expenditures, $1,470,415, including $1,250,650 for 259 grants (high: $145,000; low: $1,000).
Purpose and activities: Grants made selectively to qualified organizations, primarily in the fields of higher education, international understanding, community welfare, health, rehabilitation, and related areas.
Limitations: No grants to individuals or for endowments; no loans.
Application information:
Initial approach: Letter
Copies of proposal: 1
Board meeting date(s): As required
Write: Carol K. Elliott, Secretary-Treasurer
Officers: Charles E. Stine,* President; Carol K. Elliott, Secretary-Treasurer.
Directors:* C.S. Cullenbine, C.R. Dahl, Richard G. Shephard.
Number of staff: 2.
Employer Identification Number: 941270335

140
Crummer (Roy E.) Foundation ⌑
145 S. Rodeo Dr.
Beverly Hills 90212

Established in 1964 in Nevada.
Financial data: (yr. ended 12/31/82): Assets, $5,119,688 (M); expenditures, $62,279, including $49,100 for 22 grants (high: $5,000; low: $100).
Purpose and activities: Primarily local giving with emphasis on education and social services, including animal welfare.

Officers: Jean Crummer, President; Brian Crummer, Vice-President; Kevin Crummer, Secretary-Treasurer.
Employer Identification Number: 886004422

141
Crummey (Vivan G.) Benevolent Trust
1441 University Ave.
San Jose 95126   (408) 296-6585

Trust established in 1948 in California.
Donor(s): Vivan G. Crummey, George Hunter, and members of the Crummey family.
Financial data: (yr. ended 6/30/83): Assets, $788,104 (M); gifts received, $35,761; expenditures, $540,228, including $536,542 for 160 grants (high: $100,000; low: $25).
Purpose and activities: Charitable and educational purposes; primarily local giving, with emphasis on United Methodist churches, theological education, and missionary programs; support also for social agencies, higher education, and cultural programs.
Limitations: Giving primarily in Santa Clara County, CA.
Application information:
Initial approach: Letter
Copies of proposal: 1
Deadline(s): None
Board meeting date(s): Monthly
Final notification: Usually within 2 months
Write: Caroline H. Crummey, Trustee
Trustees: Caroline H. Crummey, D. Clifford Crummey.
Number of staff: None.
Employer Identification Number: 946104563

142
Damien Foundation ⌑
c/o Cooley, Godward, Castro et al.
One Maritime Plaza, Suite 2000
San Francisco 94111

Established in 1979.
Donor(s): Kristina Tara Fondaras Charitable Lead Trust.
Financial data: (yr. ended 12/31/82): Assets, $316,546 (M); gifts received, $250,715; expenditures, $259,852, including $222,327 for 17 grants (high: $108,702; low: $1,000).
Purpose and activities: Primarily local giving for civil rights, public policy organizations, including those concerned with arms control, peace, and environmental issues, social services, and cultural programs.
Types of support awarded: General purposes, land acquisition, special projects.
Limitations: Giving primarily in the San Francisco Bay Area, CA.
Application information:
Initial approach: Letter and proposal
Deadline(s): None
Write: Michael Traynor, Secretary-Treasurer
Officers and Directors: Tara Lamont, President; Michael Traynor, Secretary-Treasurer.
Employer Identification Number: 133006359

143
Davies Charitable Trust
c/o Donald D. Crawford, Jr.
P.O. Box 45000
San Francisco 94145   (415) 765-0400

Trust established in 1974 in California.
Donor(s): Ralph K. Davies.†
Financial data: (yr. ended 9/30/83): Assets,
$2,882,725 (M); expenditures, $106,960,
including $92,250 for 33 grants (high: $10,000;
low: $500).
Purpose and activities: Giving primarily in
California and Hawaii, with emphasis on the
performing arts, cultural programs, and higher
and secondary education.
Limitations: Giving primarily in CA and HI.
Trustees: Alicia C. Davies, Maryon Davies
Lewis, Bank of California.
Employer Identification Number: 237417287

144
Day (Willametta K.) Foundation ¤
800 West Sixth St., Suite 420
Los Angeles 90017

Trust established in 1954 in California.
Donor(s): Willametta K. Day.
Financial data: (yr. ended 12/31/82): Assets,
$2,692,856 (M); expenditures, $161,814,
including $138,000 for 17 grants (high:
$30,000; low: $1,500).
Purpose and activities: Charitable purposes;
primarily local support for higher and
secondary education, hospitals, religion, and
cultural programs.
Limitations: Giving primarily in CA. No grants
to individuals.
Application information:
  Initial approach: Letter
  Copies of proposal: 1
  Deadline(s): 4th quarter
  Board meeting date(s): Annually
  Write: Willametta K. Day, Chairman
Officers: Willametta K. Day,* Chairman;
Maynard J. Toll,* Vice-Chairman; Jerry W.
Carlton,* Secretary; Fred D. Murray, Treasurer.
Trustees:* Howard M. Day, Laurence H. Day,
Robert A. Day, Jr., Tammis M. Day, Theodore
J. Day.
Employer Identification Number: 956092476

145
**de Guigne (Christian) Memorial
  Foundation**
c/o O'Donnell, Waiss, Wall and Meschke
100 Broadway, Third Fl.
San Francisco 94111   (415) 434-3323

Established in 1960 in California.
Financial data: (yr. ended 12/31/83): Assets,
$2,979,411 (M); expenditures, $223,298,
including $205,024 for 10 grants (high:
$40,000; low: $10,000).
Purpose and activities: Broad purposes; local
giving, with emphasis on higher and secondary
education, hospitals, and health agencies;
support also for a French medical institution.

Limitations: Giving limited to the San
Francisco Bay Area, CA. No grants to
individuals, or for building or endowment
funds, scholarships, fellowships, matching gifts,
or special projects; no loans.
Application information:
  Initial approach: Letter
  Copies of proposal: 3
  Deadline(s): Submit proposal anytime except
    November or December; deadline
    October 31
  Board meeting date(s): November or
    December
  Final notification: 1 month
  Write: John A. Meschke, Secretary-Treasurer
Officers and Directors: France de Sugny Bark,
President; Fredrik S. Waiss, Vice-President;
John A. Meschke, Secretary-Treasurer.
Employer Identification Number: 946076503

146
DeMille (Cecil B.) Trust ¤
2010 DeMille Dr.
Los Angeles 90027

Trust established in 1952 in California.
Financial data: (yr. ended 12/31/83): Assets,
$1,850,091 (M); expenditures, $63,002,
including $48,646 for 31 grants (high: $10,000;
low: $21).
Purpose and activities: Broad purposes;
primarily local giving, with emphasis on social
services, education, cultural programs, and
child welfare.
Limitations: Giving primarily in CA.
Trustees: Peter DeMille Calvin, Cecilia DeMille
Harper, Cecilia DeMille Presley.
Employer Identification Number: 951882931

147
Deutsch Foundation, The ¤
7001 West Imperial Hwy.
P.O. Box 92395, Airport Station
Los Angeles 90009

Incorporated in 1947 in California.
Donor(s): The Deutsch Company.
Financial data: (yr. ended 8/31/83): Assets,
$4,057,836 (M); gifts received, $380,000;
expenditures, $478,124, including $469,350
for 114 grants (high: $125,000; low: $35).
Purpose and activities: Broad purposes;
primarily local giving, with emphasis on Jewish
welfare funds; support also for hospitals, higher
education, the performing arts, and social
welfare.
Limitations: Giving primarily in CA.
Officers and Directors: Alex Deutsch,
President; Carl Deutsch, Vice-President; Lester
Deutsch, Secretary-Treasurer.
Employer Identification Number: 956027369

148
Disney Foundation ▼ ¤
500 South Buena Vista St.
Burbank 91521   (213) 840-1006

Incorporated in 1951 in California.
Donor(s): Walt Disney Productions, and its
associated companies.

Financial data: (yr. ended 9/30/82): Assets,
$24,044 (M); gifts received, $100,000;
expenditures, $902,498, including $783,936
for 160 grants (high: $100,000; low: $25;
average: $1,000-$20,000) and $106,154 for 49
grants to individuals.
Purpose and activities: General purposes;
giving primarily locally and in central Florida,
with emphasis on youth and child welfare
agencies, health, higher education, cultural
programs, and community funds in areas where
the company's businesses are located.
Types of support awarded: Annual
campaigns, continuing support, operating
budgets, special projects, scholarship funds,
employee related scholarships.
Limitations: Giving primarily in central FL, and
to Los Angeles and Orange County, CA. No
grants to individuals (except for scholarships to
children of company employees) or for
endowment funds.
Publications: Application guidelines.
Application information:
  Initial approach: Letter, full proposal or
    telephone
  Copies of proposal: 1
  Deadline(s): None
  Board meeting date(s): Annually between
    January and May
  Final notification: 20-30 days
  Write: Doris A. Smith, Secretary
Officers and Trustees:* Donn B. Tatum,*
President; E. Cardon Walker,* Vice-President;
Doris A. Smith, Secretary; Leland L. Kirk,
Treasurer.
Number of staff: None.
Employer Identification Number: 956037079

149
Disney (The Lillian B.) Foundation ¤
P.O. Box 2039
Burbank 91507-2039

Established in 1974 in California.
Donor(s): Lillian D. Truyens.
Financial data: (yr. ended 12/31/83): Assets,
$6,077,598 (M); expenditures, $351,050,
including $347,959 for 3 grants (high:
$250,000; low: $1,000).
Purpose and activities: Primarily local giving,
largely for the arts and a learning disabilities
foundation.
Limitations: Giving primarily in CA.
Officers: Lillian B. Disney, President; Diane D.
Miller, Sharon D. Lund, Vice-Presidents; Royal
Clark, Secretary and Treasurer.
Employer Identification Number: 237425637

150
Disney (Roy) Family Foundation ¤
c/o Shamrock Holding, Inc., P.O. Box 7774
4421 Riverside Dr., Suite 207
Burbank 91510

Incorporated in 1969 in California.
Donor(s): Roy E. Disney, Roy O. Disney,†
Edna F. Disney, Redna Incorporated.
Financial data: (yr. ended 5/31/82): Assets,
$2,968,511 (M); gifts received, $240,380;
expenditures, $501,619, including $488,353
for 10 grants (high: $247,853; low: $3,000).

Purpose and activities: Broad purposes; primarily local giving to an arts institute and a college.
Limitations: Giving primarily in CA. No grants to individuals, or for building or endowment funds.
Application information:
Initial approach: Letter
Copies of proposal: 1
Board meeting date(s): Annually and as required
Officers: Patricia Ann Disney,* President; Roy E. Disney,* Roy Patrick Disney,* Vice-Presidents; Abigail E. Disney,* Secretary; Denise J. Greskoviak, Treasurer.
Directors:* Timothy J. Disney, Susan M. LaRue, Richard T. Morrow.
Employer Identification Number: 237028399

151
Distribution Fund, The
247 La Cuesta Dr.
Menlo Park 94025   (415) 854-4172

Incorporated in 1965 in California.
Donor(s): Nora R. Klein, Robert H. Klein.†
Financial data: (yr. ended 8/31/84): Assets, $1,146,095 (M); expenditures, $150,759, including $146,315 for 37 grants (high: $52,500; low: $200; average: $200-$1,000).
Purpose and activities: Grants largely designated for San Francisco Bay Area agencies, primarily serving youth-oriented programs; grants also for hospitals and health agencies, welfare, and religious welfare agencies.
Types of support awarded: Continuing support, annual campaigns, seed money, equipment, matching funds, research, special projects.
Limitations: Giving primarily in CA, with emphasis on Menlo Park and the San Francisco Bay Area. No grants to individuals, or for endowment funds, or scholarships and fellowships; no loans.
Application information:
Initial approach: Letter
Copies of proposal: 1
Deadline(s): None
Board meeting date(s): Quarterly
Final notification: 2 months
Write: Nora R. Klein, President
Officers: Nora R. Klein, President; Paul R. Klein, Vice-President; Henry D. Klein, Secretary-Treasurer.
Number of staff: None.
Employer Identification Number: 946117979

152
Doe (The Marguerite) Foundation ⊭
308 East Carillo St.
Santa Barbara 93101

Established in 1968 in California.
Donor(s): Marguerite Doe Ravenscroft.†
Financial data: (yr. ended 12/31/83): Assets, $364,317 (M); gifts received, $156,347; expenditures, $237,521, including $231,500 for 11 grants (high: $50,000; low: $5,000).

Purpose and activities: To aid organizations operated for the prevention of cruelty to animals, specifically canines. Grants to humane societies, primarily in California and the Northwest.
Types of support awarded: Building funds.
Limitations: Giving primarily in CA and the Northwest.
Application information:
Initial approach: Letter
Deadline(s): None
Directors: Raymond A. Buelow, Anthony Gunterman, Antonio R. Romasanta.
Employer Identification Number: 956226536

153
Doelger Charitable Trust
950 John Daly Blvd., Suite 300
Daly City 94015

Trust established in 1978 in California.
Donor(s): Henry Doelger.†
Financial data: (yr. ended 6/30/83): Assets, $5,622,023 (M); expenditures, $762,140, including $699,647 for 8 grants (high: $166,549; low: $40,000).
Purpose and activities: Primarily local giving, with emphasis on higher education, hospitals and medical research, animal welfare, and secondary education.
Limitations: Giving primarily in CA.
Trustees: Edward M. King, Chester W. Lebsack, Frank P. McCann.
Employer Identification Number: 946468716

154
Doheny (Carrie Estelle) Foundation ▼
1010 South Flower St., Suite 400
Los Angeles 90015   (213) 748-5111

Trust established in 1949 in California.
Donor(s): Mrs. Edward L. Doheny.†
Financial data: (yr. ended 12/31/83): Assets, $55,344,512 (M); expenditures, $3,844,940, including $3,239,237 for 72 grants (high: $1,465,333; low: $250; average: $500-$10,000).
Purpose and activities: Broad purposes; primarily local giving, with emphasis on hospitals, Roman Catholic churches and church-related organizations, ophthalmological research, child welfare, higher education, and a community fund.
Types of support awarded: General purposes.
Limitations: Giving primarily in in the Los Angeles, CA, area. No support for tax-supported organizations, radio or television programs. No grants to individuals or for endowment funds, publications, travel, advertising, or scholarships.
Publications: Annual report, application guidelines.
Application information:
Initial approach: Letter
Copies of proposal: 1
Deadline(s): None
Board meeting date(s): Monthly
Final notification: 1 to 2 months
Write: Very Rev. W.G. Ward, C.M., Chairman

Trustee: Carrie Estelle Doheny Foundation Corporation.
Corporation Officers: Cleve B. Bonner,* President; Edmund F. Schnieders,* Vice-President; Arthur E. Thunell, Secretary and Treasurer.
Corporation Directors:* Very Rev. W.G. Ward, C.M., Chairman; Robert Erburu, Austin F. Gavin, Rev. Francis D. Pansini, C.M., Robert Smith.
Number of staff: 3 full-time professional; 2 full-time support.
Employer Identification Number: 952051633

155
Domino Foundation ⊭
343 East Jefferson Blvd.
Los Angeles 90011

Established in 1974 in California.
Donor(s): Domino of California, Incorporated.
Financial data: (yr. ended 6/30/83): Assets, $31,093 (M); gifts received, $213,500; expenditures, $229,830, including $228,521 for 108 grants (high: $160,650; low: $20).
Purpose and activities: Giving primarily in California and New York, with emphasis on Jewish welfare funds; support also for hospitals, higher education, and social and health agencies.
Limitations: Giving primarily in CA and NY.
Application information:
Board meeting date(s): Monthly
Write: Saul Brandman
Directors: Saul Brandman, Steven C. Gordon.
Employer Identification Number: 237406360

156
Drum Foundation, The
c/o Wells Fargo Bank
P.O. Box 44002
San Francisco 94144
Street address: 2505 Divisadero St., San Francisco, CA 94115

Incorporated in 1956 in California.
Donor(s): Frank G. Drum.†
Financial data: (yr. ended 12/31/83): Assets, $3,086,000 (M); expenditures, $249,000, including $240,000 for 20 grants (high: $50,000; low: $1,000; average: $1,000-$50,000).
Purpose and activities: To aid Roman Catholic church-related educational and charitable organizations, usually limited to the Archdiocese of San Francisco, including those supported by the donor during his lifetime.
Types of support awarded: General purposes, operating budgets, continuing support, annual campaigns, seed money, emergency funds, deficit financing, building funds, equipment, land acquisition, scholarship funds, professorships, internships, exchange programs, fellowships, special projects, research, publications, conferences and seminars, matching funds.
Limitations: Giving primarily in the San Francisco, CA area. No grants to individuals, or for endowment funds or matching gifts.
Application information:
Initial approach: Letter or full proposal

Copies of proposal: 1
Deadline(s): None
Board meeting date(s): As required
Final notification: 6 months
Write: Richard K. Miller, President
Officers and Directors: Richard K. Miller, President; Edmund J. Morrissey, M.D., Vice-President; Philip Hudner, Secretary-Treasurer; Elena Eyre Madison.
Number of staff: None.
Employer Identification Number: 946069469

157
Durfee Foundation, The
401 Wilshire Blvd., Suite 1100
Santa Monica 90401   (213) 395-9382

Incorporated in 1960 in California.
Donor(s): Ray Stanton Avery, Dorothy D. Avery.†
Financial data: (yr. ended 12/31/84): Assets, $9,067,612 (M); gifts received, $160,500; expenditures, $313,323, including $285,035 for 24 grants (high: $50,000; low: $100).
Purpose and activities: Broad purposes; primarily local giving for cultural programs and education. Biannual cash awards of up to $25,000 are made to individuals who have enhanced human dignity through the law.
Types of support awarded: Grants to individuals.
Limitations: Giving primarily in CA. No grants for endowment funds or operating budgets.
Application information: Submit grant application at request of foundation only; Foundation solicits proposals in areas of interest.
Write: Robert S. Macfarlane, Managing Director
Officers and Directors: Ray Stanton Avery, Chairman; Dennis S. Avery, President; Judith A. Newkirk, Vice-President; Russell D. Avery, Secretary-Treasurer; Robert S. Macfarlane, Managing Director.
Number of staff: 1 part-time professional; 1 part-time support.
Employer Identification Number: 952223738

158
Early (Margaret E.) Medical Research Trust ⌘
c/o Harrington, Foxx, Dubrow, Canter & Keene
611 W. Sixth St., 9th Fl.
Los Angeles 90017

Established in 1982.
Financial data: (yr. ended 12/31/83): Assets, $3,627,589 (M); gifts received, $768,619; expenditures, $293,837, including $283,168 for 5 grants (high: $63,012; low: $48,000).
Purpose and activities: Local giving for cancer research.
Types of support awarded: Research.
Limitations: Giving limited to southern CA.
Application information:
Initial approach: Proposal
Deadline(s): Established annually
Write: Eli B. Dubrow, Trustee
Trustee: Eli B. Dubrow.
Employer Identification Number: 953740506

159
East Bay Community Foundation, The
6230 Claremont Ave.
Oakland 94618   (415) 658-5441

Community foundation established in 1928 in California by resolution and declaration of trust; revised in 1972.
Financial data: (yr. ended 12/31/82): Assets, $3,524,085 (M); gifts received, $225,500; expenditures, $403,616, including $325,211 for 86 grants (high: $25,000; low: $500).
Purpose and activities: Charitable, educational, and medical purposes; grants locally for community welfare, youth, the aged, women's programs, health care, arts and culture, and educational programs.
Types of support awarded: Operating budgets, seed money, equipment, special projects, scholarship funds, matching funds.
Limitations: Giving limited to Alameda and Contra Costa Counties, CA. No grants to individuals, or for building and endowment funds, annual fund drives, or matching gifts; no loans.
Publications: Annual report, program policy statement, application guidelines.
Application information:
Initial approach: Letter or full proposal
Copies of proposal: 1
Deadline(s): March 1, June 1, September 1, and December 1
Board meeting date(s): Third Wednesday of January, April, July, and October
Final notification: 10 to 12 weeks
Write: Sandra L. Pyer, Executive Director
Officer: Sandra L. Pyer, Executive Director.
Governing Board: Barbara Donald, Chairman; Gregory L. McCoy, Vice-Chairman; Hon Chew, Penny Deleray, Salvatore V. Giuffre, Virginia H. Hooper, Margaret W. Kovar, Gordon M. Riddick, Linda C. Roodhouse.
Trustees: Crocker National Bank, First Interstate Bank, Wells Fargo Bank.
Number of staff: 3.
Employer Identification Number: 946070996

160
Eichenbaum (J. K. and Inez) Foundation ⌘
8500 Wilshire Blvd., No. 704
Beverly Hills 90211

Established in 1971.
Donor(s): J.K. Eichenbaum, Inez Eichenbaum.
Financial data: (yr. ended 11/30/83): Assets, $18,590 (M); gifts received, $125,000; expenditures, $114,425, including $114,205 for 71 grants (high: $30,000; low: $25).
Purpose and activities: Grants primarily for Jewish welfare funds and higher education in Israel.
Officers: J.K. Eichenbaum, President; Anson I. Driesen, Secretary; Sidney C. Eichenbaum, Treasurer.
Employer Identification Number: 956101264

161
Essick Foundation, Inc., The ⌘
609 South Grand Ave., Suite 1217
Los Angeles 90017

Incorporated in 1947 in California.
Donor(s): Jeanette Marie Essick,† Bryant Essick, Essick Investment Company.
Financial data: (yr. ended 12/31/83): Assets, $2,103,445 (M); expenditures, $111,039, including $98,415 for 79 grants (high: $12,000; low: $25).
Purpose and activities: General giving, mainly to local organizations in which the donors are interested, with emphasis on higher education, hospitals, and a community fund.
Limitations: Giving primarily in southern CA.
Application information: Applications for grants not invited.
Write: Bryant Essick, President
Officers and Directors:* Bryant Essick,* President; James H. Essick,* Vice-President; Lillian M. Ringe, Secretary; Robert N. Essick,* Treasurer.
Employer Identification Number: 956048985

162
Factor (Max) Family Foundation ▼
9777 Wilshire Blvd., Suite 1015
Beverly Hills 90212   (213) 274-8193

Trust established in 1941 in California.
Donor(s): Members of the Factor family.
Financial data: (yr. ended 12/31/83): Assets, $9,811,380 (M); expenditures, $941,521, including $853,364 for 65 grants (high: $250,000; low: $100; average: $100-$10,000).
Purpose and activities: General purposes; primarily local giving, with emphasis on Jewish welfare funds, hospitals, medical research, education, care of the aged, and aid to the handicapped.
Types of support awarded: Research, scholarship funds, general purposes, continuing support.
Limitations: Giving primarily in CA. No grants to individuals.
Application information:
Write: Barbara Factor Bentley, Trustee
Trustees: Barbara Factor Bentley, David Jack Factor, Jr., Freda F. Friedman.
Number of staff: None.
Employer Identification Number: 956030779

163
Fairfield (Freeman E.) Foundation ⌘
3610 Long Beach Blvd.
P.O. Box 7798
Long Beach 90807   (213) 427-7219

Established in 1969 in California.
Donor(s): Freeman E. Fairfield.†
Financial data: (yr. ended 12/31/83): Assets, $4,376,334 (M); expenditures, $401,949, including $320,724 for 25 grants (high: $122,500; low: $1,000).
Purpose and activities: Giving only in Long Beach and Signal Hill, with emphasis on youth agencies, hospitals and clinics, and aid to the handicapped.

Limitations: Giving limited to Long Beach and Signal Hill, CA. No support for religious purposes. No grants to individuals, or for endowment funds, unrestricted operating costs, deficit financing, intermediary funding agencies, or general fundraising drives.
Publications: Program policy statement, application guidelines.
Application information:
  Initial approach: Proposal
  Copies of proposal: 3
  Deadline(s): April 1
  Board meeting date(s): As required
  Write: Edna E. Sellers, Trustee
Trustees: K.R. Davis, C.F. Liebenguth, Edna E. Sellers.
Employer Identification Number: 237055338

164
Familian (Isadore and Sunny) Family Foundation
9595 Wilshire Blvd., Suite 707
Beverly Hills 90212

Incorporated in 1947 in California.
Donor(s): The Familian family and others.
Financial data: (yr. ended 12/31/82): Assets, $1,515,338 (M); gifts received, $40,016; expenditures, $125,064, including $109,143 for 68 grants (high: $27,035).
Purpose and activities: Broad purposes; primarily local giving, with emphasis on Jewish welfare funds and religious organizations, higher education, hospitals, and cultural programs.
Limitations: Giving primarily in CA.
Application information:
  Write: Isadore Familian, President
Officers and Directors: Isadore Familian, President; Sondra Smalley, Vice-President; Gary Familian, Secretary; Marvin Smalley, Treasurer; Elizabeth Familian.
Employer Identification Number: 956027950

165
Familian (Zalec) Foundation ¤
10375 Wilshire Blvd., Suite 2A
Los Angeles 90024
Mailing address: 9025 Wilshire Blvd., Suite 409, Beverly Hills, CA 90211

Established in 1958 in California.
Donor(s): Zalec Familian,† and others.
Financial data: (yr. ended 3/31/83): Assets, $1,186,758 (M); expenditures, $181,412, including $175,000 for 21 grants (high: $50,000; low: $1,000).
Purpose and activities: Primarily local giving, with emphasis on higher education, social services, and cultural programs.
Limitations: Giving primarily in CA.
Application information: Budget for grants considered late in the calendar year.
  Initial approach: Proposal
  Write: Mann Judd Landau
Officers: Victor Carter, President; Lilian Levinson, Vice-President; Albert Levinson, Secretary-Treasurer.
Employer Identification Number: 956099164

166
Faude (C. Frederick) Foundation ¤
P.O. Box 586
Sausalito 94965

Established in 1966.
Donor(s): C. Frederick Faude.
Financial data: (yr. ended 12/31/83): Assets, $80,736 (M); expenditures, $179,391, including $178,254 for 3 grants (high: $125,000; low: $18,254).
Purpose and activities: Primarily local giving for social services and a wildlife center.
Limitations: Giving primarily in Marin County, CA.
Officers and Directors: C. Frederick Faude, President; C. Kenneth Rankin, Robert P. Praetrel, Secretary-Treasurer; Rudy Geitner, James Wong.
Employer Identification Number: 946139644

167
Feitelson (Lorser and Helen Lundeberg) Arts Foundation ¤
8307 West Third St.
Los Angeles 90048

Established in 1979.
Donor(s): Lorser Feitelson.
Financial data: (yr. ended 11/30/83): Assets, $1,116,760 (M); expenditures, $29,894, including $12,500 for 1 grant.
Purpose and activities: Primarily local giving in form of art works by Lorser Feitelson, to major universities with prominent art museums and art history departments.
Limitations: Giving primarily in CA.
Officers and Directors: Helen L. Feitelson, President; Josine Ianco-Starrels, Secretary; Monroe Price, Treasurer.
Employer Identification Number: 953451355

168
Fire Fund Endowment ¤
777 San Marin Dr.
Novato 94998

Established in 1973.
Financial data: (yr. ended 12/31/83): Assets, $1,056,218 (M); expenditures, $101,782, including $100,000 for 1 grant.
Purpose and activities: Support for cultural programs and a conservation agency.
Officers: Edwin F. Cutler,* President; Francis W. Benedict,* Secretary; Michael Djordjevich, Treasurer.
Directors:* James Meenaghan, Richard K. Sears.
Employer Identification Number: 237358947

169
Fireman's Fund Insurance Company Foundation ▼
777 San Marin Dr.
P.O. Box 777
Novato 94998   (415) 899-2757

Incorporated in 1953 in California.
Donor(s): Fireman's Fund Insurance Company, and subsidiaries.

Financial data: (yr. ended 12/31/83): Assets, $576,856 (M); gifts received, $1,686,125; expenditures, $1,476,900, including $1,066,781 for 224 grants (high: $265,000; low: $100; average: $500-$5,000) and $301,344 for 635 employee matching gifts.
Purpose and activities: Primarily local giving, to assist higher education, health and welfare agencies, youth groups, and civic and cultural activities; grants also for United Way campaigns nationwide in cities where principal company offices are located.
Types of support awarded: Operating budgets, annual campaigns, building funds, equipment, endowment funds, scholarship funds, employee related scholarships, exchange programs, technical assistance, continuing support, employee matching gifts.
Limitations: Giving primarily in CA, with emphasis on the San Francisco Bay Area. No support for religious or national organizations, or other grant-making bodies. No grants to individuals, or for travel, benefit events, or operating expenses of organizations that receive federated-campaign support; no loans.
Publications: Program policy statement, application guidelines.
Application information: Application form required.
  Initial approach: Letter
  Copies of proposal: 1
  Deadline(s): December 15, February 15, May 15, and August 15
  Board meeting date(s): January, March, June, and September
  Final notification: 6 weeks
  Write: Mary K. Anderson, Manager
Officers: Edwin F. Cutler,* President; Francis W. Benedict,* Secretary; Robert Marto, Treasurer.
Directors:* William W. McCormick, Chairman; David Kalis, James Meenaghan, Richard K. Sears.
Number of staff: 1 full-time professional.
Employer Identification Number: 946078025

170
First Interstate Bank of California Foundation ▼
c/o Office of Public Affairs
707 Wilshire Blvd., 15th Fl.
Los Angeles 90017   (213) 614-3360

Established in 1978 in California.
Donor(s): First Interstate Bank of California.
Financial data: (yr. ended 12/31/84): Assets, $18,427,000 (M); expenditures, $2,250,697, including $2,107,277 for 265 grants (high: $585,000; low: $150; average: $7,900), $40,475 for 33 grants to individuals and $96,795 for 280 employee matching gifts.
Purpose and activities: Broad purposes; primarily local giving, with emphasis on education, performing arts and cultural programs, hospitals, urban and civic affairs, and youth agencies.

Types of support awarded: General purposes, building funds, land acquisition, endowment funds, matching funds, consulting services, technical assistance, internships, scholarship funds, employee related scholarships, fellowships, special projects, publications, employee matching gifts.
Limitations: Giving primarily in CA. No grants to individuals (except for company-employee scholarships), or for equipment, research or conferences; no loans.
Publications: Annual report, informational brochure, program policy statement, application guidelines.
Application information: Application form required.
  Initial approach: Letter, telephone, or proposal
  Copies of proposal: 1
  Deadline(s): None
  Board meeting date(s): Quarterly
  Final notification: 6 weeks to 3 months after board meeting
  Write: Ruth Jones-Saxey, Secretary
Officers: Lloyd B. Dennis,* President; Ruth Jones-Saxey, Secretary-Treasurer.
Directors:* Norman Barker, Jr., Chairman; Albert F. Blaylock, John F. Futcher, John F. King, Alton H. Kingman, Jr.
Number of staff: 1 full-time professional; 2 full-time support.
Employer Identification Number: 953288932

171
Fleishhacker (Janet and Mortimer) Foundation
2600 Pacific Ave.
San Francisco 94115   (415) 931-3633

Established in 1977 in California.
Donor(s): Mortimer Fleishhacker, Jr.†
Financial data: (yr. ended 12/31/83): Assets, $2,018,920 (M); expenditures, $108,805, including $91,474 for 114 grants (high: $5,000; low: $50; average: $50-$5,000).
Purpose and activities: Largely local giving, with emphasis on higher and secondary education, the arts, cultural programs, and Jewish welfare funds.
Types of support awarded: Operating budgets, continuing support, annual campaigns, emergency funds, deficit financing, building funds, equipment, endowment funds, research, special projects.
Limitations: Giving primarily in northern CA. No grants to individuals, or for seed money, land acquisition, scholarships, fellowships, publications, conferences, or matching gifts; no loans.
Application information:
  Initial approach: Full proposal
  Copies of proposal: 1
  Deadline(s): None
  Board meeting date(s): May, and as required
  Final notification: 4 months
  Write: Janet C. Fleishhacker, President
Officers: Janet C. Fleishhacker, President; David Fleishhacker, Vice-President; Jack Olive, Secretary.
Number of staff: None.
Employer Identification Number: 942732639

172
Fleishhacker (Mortimer) Foundation
The Alcoa Bldg., Suite 1150
San Francisco 94111   (415) 788-2909

Incorporated in 1947 in California.
Donor(s): Mortimer Fleishhacker, Sr.†
Financial data: (yr. ended 4/30/84): Assets, $2,410,502 (M); expenditures, $181,525, including $136,500 for 25 grants (high: $50,000; low: $1,000; average: $5,000).
Purpose and activities: The Foundation supports arts and cultural organizations in northern California in the disciplines of visual arts, theater, and literature.
Types of support awarded: Operating budgets, continuing support, seed money, building funds, equipment, special projects, publications, conferences and seminars.
Limitations: Giving limited to northern CA. No grants for annual campaigns, emergency or endowment funds, deficit financing, matching gifts, or scholarships; no loans.
Publications: Application guidelines, program policy statement.
Application information: Major guideline revisions implemented in June 1985; contact the foundation for current information.
  Initial approach: Letter, telephone, or full proposal
  Copies of proposal: 1
  Deadline(s): None
  Board meeting date(s): Quarterly
  Final notification: 2 to 5 months
  Write: Sarah Lutman, Executive Director
Officers: Delia F. Ehrlich,* President; Leon Sloss,* Vice-President; Lois Gordon,* Secretary; Mortimer Fleishhacker, III,* Treasurer; Sarah Lutman, Executive Director.
Directors:* John Stephen Ehrlich, Jr., Leslie Fleishhacker.
Number of staff: 1 part-time professional.
Employer Identification Number: 946051048

173
Fluor Foundation, The ▼
3333 Michelson Dr.
Irvine 92730   (714) 975-6326

Incorporated in 1952 in California.
Donor(s): Fluor Corporation.
Financial data: (yr. ended 10/31/83): Assets, $5,995,360 (M); gifts received, $4,064,050; expenditures, $5,073,907, including $5,030,876 for 760 grants (high: $1,379,105; low: $10) and $20,127 for grants to individuals.
Purpose and activities: Broad purposes; general giving, with emphasis on higher education, including scholarships for children of company employees, community service organizations, including medical, social, and cultural programs, in areas where the Corporation has permanent offices.
Types of support awarded: Annual campaigns, building funds, consulting services, continuing support, emergency funds, employee matching gifts, operating budgets, seed money, technical assistance, employee related scholarships, student aid.

Limitations: Giving primarily in areas where the corporation has permanent offices, with some emphasis on CA. No grants to individuals (except for company-employee scholarships), or for deficit financing, equipment and materials, land acquisition, renovation projects, endowment funds, or matching grants.
Publications: Program policy statement, application guidelines.
Application information: Application form required.
  Initial approach: Letter
  Copies of proposal: 1
  Deadline(s): 6 weeks prior to meetings
  Board meeting date(s): March, June, September, and December; committee meets in February, May, August, and November
  Final notification: 2 months
  Write: Cindy Linneberger, Director of Community Affairs
Officers: J.R. Fluor II,* President; L.N. Fisher, Secretary; V.L. Prechtl, Treasurer.
Trustees:* D.S. Tappan, Jr., Chairman; D.K. Allen, C.N. Cannon, G.W. Mefferd, B. Mickel, T.A. Murphy, N.A. Peterson, J.A. Wright.
Number of staff: 2 full-time professional; 2 full-time support.
Employer Identification Number: 510196032

174
Forest Lawn Foundation ⌑
1712 South Glendale Ave.
Glendale 91205

Incorporated in 1951 in California.
Donor(s): Forest Lawn Co., Hubert Eaton Estate Trust.
Financial data: (yr. ended 12/31/83): Assets, $3,557,759 (M); gifts received, $279,112; expenditures, $174,580, including $143,250 for 70 grants (high: $15,000; low: $250).
Purpose and activities: Broad purposes, primarily local giving; grants for higher education, welfare, health, youth agencies, hospitals, and religious institutions.
Limitations: Giving primarily in CA. No grants to individuals, or for endowment funds or special projects.
Application information:
  Board meeting date(s): Quarterly
  Write: John Llewellyn, Vice-President
Officers and Trustees: Frederick Llewellyn, President; John Llewellyn, Vice-President and Secretary-Treasurer; Jane Llewellyn, Myron Smith, Arlene Winn.
Employer Identification Number: 956030792

175
Friedman Brothers Foundation ⌑
801 East Commercial St.
Los Angeles 90012

Trust established about 1944 in California.
Donor(s): Members of the Friedman family, Friedman Bag Co.
Financial data: (yr. ended 12/31/83): Assets, $2,126,282 (M); expenditures, $226,354, including $183,750 for 27 grants (high: $40,000; low: $250).

Purpose and activities: Broad purposes; primarily local giving, with emphasis on education, including religious education, and Jewish welfare funds.
Trustees: William Bernstein, Annette Friedman Bothmen, Sam Frank, Albert Friedman, Harvey Friedman, Rudy Lowy, Leslie Mendelsohn, William S. Stein.
Employer Identification Number: 956072294

176
Fusenot (Georges and Germaine) Charity Foundation
501 North Wilcox Ave.
Los Angeles 90004   (213) 462-7702

Trust established in 1967 in California.
Donor(s): Germaine Fusenot.†
Financial data: (yr. ended 7/31/83): Assets, $3,102,185 (L); expenditures, $303,793, including $226,000 for 166 grants (high: $15,000; low: $1,000).
Purpose and activities: Primarily local giving, with emphasis on hospitals, aid to the handicapped, and child welfare.
Types of support awarded: Operating budgets, continuing support, annual campaigns, seed money, building funds, equipment, land acquisition, research.
Limitations: Giving primarily in CA. No grants to individuals, or for emergency or endowment funds, deficit financing, matching gifts, demonstration projects, publications, conferences, or scholarships or fellowships; no loans.
Application information:
   Initial approach: Full proposal
   Copies of proposal: 1
   Deadline(s): Submit proposal preferably in December through September; deadline October 1
   Board meeting date(s): November
   Final notification: January
   Write: Richard G. Herlihy, Manager
Manager: Richard G. Herlihy.
Trustees: Esta J. Hall, Howard Hall, Sr., E. Herbert Herlihy, Elizabeth Herlihy, Fred W. Hoar, Virginia Markel, Troy E. Stone.
Number of staff: 1 full-time professional.
Employer Identification Number: 956207831

177
G.A.G. Charitable Corporation ☒
50300 Highway 245
P.O. Box 42
Badger 93603   (209) 337-2885

Incorporated in 1968 in California.
Donor(s): Dorothy Salant Garrett, George A. Griesbach.
Financial data: (yr. ended 12/31/83): Assets, $1,580,308 (M); expenditures, $119,270, including $96,160 for 65 grants (high: $30,000; low: $60).
Purpose and activities: Charitable purposes; grants for religious organizations, drug addiction rehabilitation, community funds, and Jewish welfare funds, largely in New York and California.

Limitations: Giving primarily in NY and CA. No grants to individuals, or for building or endowment funds, research, scholarships, fellowships, or matching gifts; no loans.
Publications: 990-PF.
Application information:
   Initial approach: Letter
   Copies of proposal: 1
   Board meeting date(s): May
   Write: Dorothy Salant Garrett, President
Officers and Directors:* Dorothy Salant Garrett,* President; George A. Griesbach,* Vice-President; William Rybnick, Secretary; David W. Ross, Treasurer.
Employer Identification Number: 952568756

178
Gallo (The Ernest) Foundation ☒
P.O. Box 1130
Modesto 95353   (209) 521-3091

Incorporated in 1955 in California.
Donor(s): Members of the Gallo family, E. & J. Gallo Winery.
Financial data: (yr. ended 10/31/83): Assets, $3,071,327 (M); gifts received, $350,000; expenditures, $235,128, including $225,700 for 12 grants (high: $160,000; low: $300) and $4,785 for employee matching gifts.
Purpose and activities: Broad purposes; grants largely for higher education.
Types of support awarded: Matching funds.
Limitations: Giving primarily in CA. No grants to individuals.
Application information:
   Initial approach: Letter
   Copies of proposal: 1
   Board meeting date(s): As required
Officers and Directors:* Ernest Gallo,* President; David E. Gallo,* Joseph E. Gallo,* Vice-Presidents; Jack L. Dickman, Secretary; Dick Beal, Treasurer.
Employer Identification Number: 946061537

179
Gallo Foundation ☒
P.O. Box 1130
Modesto 95353

Incorporated in 1955 in California.
Financial data: (yr. ended 10/31/83): Assets, $3,071,327 (M); gifts received, $350,000; expenditures, $235,128, including $230,485 for 13 grants (high: $160,000; low: $300).
Purpose and activities: Broad purposes; primarily local giving with emphasis on education, particularly higher education; some grants also for church support.
Limitations: Giving primarily in CA.
Officers and Directors: Ernest Gallo, President; David E. Gallo, Joseph E. Gallo, Vice-Presidents; Jack L. Dickman, Secretary; Dick Beal, Treasurer.
Employer Identification Number: 946061538

180
Gallo (The Julio R.) Foundation
P.O. Box 1130
Modesto 95353   (209) 521-3091

Incorporated in 1955 in California.
Donor(s): Julio R. Gallo, Robert J. Gallo.
Financial data: (yr. ended 10/31/83): Assets, $3,008,360 (M); gifts received, $400,000; expenditures, $258,952, including $254,000 for 32 grants (high: $50,000; low: $500).
Purpose and activities: Broad purposes; primarily local giving, emphasis on education and Roman Catholic church support and religious associations.
Limitations: Giving primarily in CA. No grants to individuals.
Application information:
   Initial approach: Letter
   Write: Jon B. Shastid, Treasurer
Officers and Directors:* Julio R. Gallo,* President; Robert J. Gallo,* Vice-President; James E. Coleman,* Secretary; Jon B. Shastid, Treasurer.
Employer Identification Number: 946061539

181
Galster Foundation, The
109 East Badillo St.
P.O. Box 4126
Covina 91723   (213) 332-6278

Established in 1963 in California.
Donor(s): E.S. Galster.†
Financial data: (yr. ended 12/31/82): Assets, $2,300,033 (M); expenditures, $228,432, including $205,250 for 19 grants (high: $50,000; low: $500).
Purpose and activities: Primarily local giving, with emphasis on higher education, including scholarship funds, secondary education, health and youth agencies.
Limitations: Giving primarily in southern CA.
Application information:
   Initial approach: Letter or full proposal
   Copies of proposal: 2
   Deadline(s): July 1
   Board meeting date(s): July and December
   Write: A.M. Rulofson, Secretary-Treasurer
Officers: Harry C. Cogen, President; A.M. Rulofson, Secretary-Treasurer.
Trustees: R.J. Arguthnot, Lillian Tomlinson, Marion J. Wilhite.
Employer Identification Number: 956102189

182
Garland (John Jewett & H. Chandler) Foundation
P.O. Box 550
Pasadena 91102-0550

Trust established in 1959 in California.
Donor(s): Members of the Garland family.
Financial data: (yr. ended 12/31/82): Assets, $215,792 (M); gifts received, $658,972; expenditures, $663,803, including $643,000 for 33 grants (high: $200,000; low: $1,000).
Purpose and activities: Primarily local giving, with emphasis on cultural programs, secondary education, youth agencies, hospitals, and the aged.

Limitations: Giving primarily in CA.
Trustees: Gwendolyn Garland Babcock, Louise Grant Garland, G.E. Morrow.
Employer Identification Number: 956023587

183
Gellert (The Carl) Foundation ▼
2222 Nineteenth Ave.
San Francisco 94116   (415) 566-4420

Incorporated in 1958 in California.
Donor(s): Carl Gellert,† Atlas Realty Company, Pacific Coast Construction Company, Gertrude E. Gellert.†
Financial data: (yr. ended 11/30/84): Assets, $7,556,320 (M); expenditures, $793,757, including $771,924 for 130 grants (high: $100,000; low: $500; average: $1,000-$10,000).
Purpose and activities: Broad purposes; primarily local giving, with emphasis on the aged and hospitals; grants also for Roman Catholic church support and higher and secondary education, including scholarship funds; and to community development programs and social agencies.
Types of support awarded: Operating budgets, continuing support, annual campaigns, deficit financing, building funds, equipment, endowment funds, scholarship funds, research, publications, special projects.
Limitations: Giving primarily in the San Francisco Bay Area, CA. No grants to individuals, or for seed money, emergency funds, land acquisition, matching gifts, demonstration projects, or conferences; no loans.
Publications: 990-PF, program policy statement, application guidelines.
Application information:
 Initial approach: Proposal
 Copies of proposal: 5
 Deadline(s): Submit proposal preferably in August and September; deadline October 15
 Board meeting date(s): April and November
 Final notification: November 30, for recipients only
 Write: Peter J. Brusati, Secretary
Officers and Directors: Fred R. Bahrt, President; Robert L. Pauly, Vice-President; Peter J. Brusati, Secretary; Marie Simpson, Treasurer; Celia Berta Gellert.
Number of staff: None.
Employer Identification Number: 946062858

184
Gellert (The Fred) Foundation ▼
1655 Southgate Ave., No. 203
Daly City 94015   (415) 991-1855

Established in 1958 in California.
Donor(s): Fred Gellert, Sr.†
Financial data: (yr. ended 11/30/84): Assets, $9,084,799 (M); expenditures, $687,588, including $671,378 for 59 grants (high: $100,000; low: $1,000; average: $1,000-$5,000).

Purpose and activities: Primarily local giving; grants for cultural programs, with emphasis on the performing arts, secondary education, hospitals, ophthalmology education, and social agencies.
Types of support awarded: Operating budgets, continuing support, building funds, equipment, research, special projects.
Limitations: Giving primarily in San Francisco and San Mateo counties, CA. No grants to individuals, or for annual campaigns; no loans.
Publications: Application guidelines.
Application information:
 Initial approach: Letter
 Copies of proposal: 5
 Deadline(s): Submit proposal preferably in May through August; deadline October 1
 Board meeting date(s): November
 Final notification: 1st week in December
 Write: Fred Gellert, Jr., Chairman
Officers and Directors: Fred Gellert, Jr., Chairman; Gisela Gellert, Vice-Chairman; John D. Howard, Secretary-Treasurer; Annette Gellert, Joan Sargen.
Number of staff: 1 part-time professional.
Employer Identification Number: 946062859

185
Gemco Charitable and Scholarship Fund ⌘
6565 Knott Ave.
Buena Park 90620   (714) 739-6351

Incorporated in 1959 in California.
Donor(s): Membership Department Stores, Lucky Stores, Inc.
Financial data: (yr. ended 1/29/84): Assets, $37,750 (M); gifts received, $163,834; expenditures, $163,834, including $62,109 for 229 grants (high: $200; low: $100) and $101,725 for 96 grants to individuals.
Purpose and activities: Charitable purposes; scholarships to high school graduates residing in areas of store locations; support also for youth agencies and social services.
Types of support awarded: Student aid.
Application information: Schools select scholarship entrants, and send out application forms. Application form required.
 Initial approach: Letter
 Deadline(s): September 30 for non-profit organizations
 Write: Jim Barnett
Officers: A.E. Arnold, President; Fred J. Koch, Vice-President; Mary Enlow, Secretary; Brian Donnan, Treasurer.
Directors: B. Beekman, F. Droz, M. Jones, B. Mulholland, F. Murphy.
Employer Identification Number: 952497896

186
Gerbode (Wallace Alexander) Foundation ▼
470 Columbus Ave., Suite 201
San Francisco 94133   (415) 391-0911

Incorporated in 1953 in California.
Donor(s): Members of the Gerbode family.

Financial data: (yr. ended 12/31/83): Assets, $20,176,606 (M); expenditures, $1,156,965, including $994,529 for 96 grants (high: $60,000; low: $300).
Purpose and activities: Support for innovative positive programs and projects with a direct impact on residents of the five San Francisco Bay Area counties or Hawaii. Interests include arts, education, environment, health and urban affairs.
Types of support awarded: Consulting services, technical assistance, program-related investments, loans, special projects.
Limitations: Giving limited to programs directly affecting residents of Alameda, Contra Costa, Marin, San Francisco, and San Mateo Counties in CA, and HI. No support for religious purposes. No grants to individuals, or for general or continuing support, operating budgets, capital or endowment funds, fund-raising or annual campaigns, emergency funds, matching gifts, scholarships, fellowships, publications, deficit financing, building funds, equipment or materials, land acquisition, or renovation projects.
Publications: Annual report, application guidelines.
Application information:
 Initial approach: Letter
 Copies of proposal: 1
 Deadline(s): None
 Board meeting date(s): 6 times a year
 Final notification: 2 to 3 months
 Write: Thomas C. Layton, Executive Director
Officers and Trustees:* Frank L.A. Gerbode, M.D.,* President; Frank A. Gerbode, M.D.,* Maryanna G. Shaw,* Vice-Presidents; Charles M. Stockholm,* Secretary-Treasurer; Thomas C. Layton, Executive Director.
Number of staff: 1 full-time professional; 1 full-time support.
Employer Identification Number: 946065226

187
Getty (J. Paul) Trust
(formerly J. Paul Getty Museum)
1875 Century Park East, Suite 2300
Los Angeles 90067   (213) 277-9188

Operating trust established in 1953 in California as J. Paul Getty Museum.
Donor(s): J. Paul Getty.†
Financial data: (yr. ended 9/30/84): Assets, $2,684,185,155 (M); gifts received, $459,334; expenditures, $45,989,192, including $1,089,172 for grants and $44,859,787 for foundation-administered programs.

Purpose and activities: A private operating foundation with seven operating programs: the J. Paul Getty Museum (a public museum), the Getty Center for the History of Art and the Humanities, the Getty Center for Education in the Arts, the Getty Conservation Institute, the Getty Art History Information Program, the Museum Management Institute, and the Program for Art on Film (a joint venture with the Metropolitan Museum of Art). Limited support through a modest Grant Program, begun in 1984, for scholarship in the history of art and the humanities, centers for advanced research in art history, cataloguing of art museum collections, publications, art conservation training and treatment, museum programs, public school art education, museum education, related service organizations, and postdoctoral fellowships (administered by the Woodrow Wilson National Fellowship on behalf of the Trust).

Types of support awarded: Special projects, fellowships, internships, publications, matching funds, special projects.

Limitations: No grants to individuals except for post-doctoral fellowships in the History of Art and the Humanities (administered by Woodrow Wilson National Fellowship Foundation).

Publications: Informational brochure.

Application information: Application information refers to grant program only; application form available for publications grant requests; for information regarding postdoctoral fellowships, contact: Woodrow Wilson National Fellowship Foundation, P.O. Box 642, Princeton, NJ 08542.

  Initial approach: Letter
  Deadline(s): For publications grants, 4 to 6 months before book goes into production; otherwise, no deadline
  Board meeting date(s): As necessary
  Final notification: 6 months
  Write: Grant Program

Officers: Harold M. Williams,* President; Joseph J. Kearns, Treasurer.

Trustees:* Harold E. Berg, Chairman; Norris Bramlett, Otto Wittmann, John T. Fey, Gordon P. Getty, Ronald Getty, Jon B. Lovelace, Franklin D. Murphy, Stuart T. Peeler, Rocco C. Siciliano, Jennifer Jones Simon, J. Patrick Whaley, Frederico Zeri.

Employer Identification Number: 951790021

188
Getty Oil Company Foundation
3810 Wilshire Blvd., Rm. 1300
Los Angeles 90010   (213) 739-2254

Incorporated in 1969 in Oklahoma.
Donor(s): Skelly Oil Company.
Financial data: (yr. ended 12/31/83): Assets, $399,634 (M); expenditures, $362,725, including $250,000 for 1 grant.
Purpose and activities: Getty Oil Company awards grants mainly through its Charitable Contributions Program of which the foundation is only a very small component. Awards from the company and foundation are in the areas of higher education, health and welfare, public policy and analysis, economic education, culture and the arts, and youth activities.
Limitations: No grants to individuals.

Application information:
  Initial approach: Letter addressed to Getty Oil Company Contributions Program
  Copies of proposal: 1
  Deadline(s): Submit proposal preferably in August
  Board meeting date(s): November and as required
  Write: Pamela L. Phillips, Contributions Coordinator
Officers and Directors: S.R. Petersen, President; R.N. Miller, Vice-President; R.D. Copley, Jr., Secretary; D.A. Bland, Treasurer; P.E. Carlton, Moody Covey, S.W. Evey, H.C. Londean, E.H. Shuler, B.E. Williams.
Employer Identification Number: 237063751

189
Gildred Foundation ▼
7855 Ivanhoe
La Jolla 92037-4510

Incorporated in 1965 in California.
Donor(s): Members of the Gildred family.
Financial data: (yr. ended 5/31/83): Assets, $7,873,523 (M); expenditures, $953,587, including $804,923 for 13 grants (high: $300,000; low: $250; average: $1,000-$150,000).
Purpose and activities: Broad purposes; primarily local giving within San Diego County, with emphasis on education, medical research, youth programs, minority development, initiating projects, and international relations.
Types of support awarded: Annual campaigns, building funds, continuing support, equipment, general purposes, matching funds, research, seed money, special projects.
Limitations: Giving primarily in San Diego County, CA. No grants to individuals, or for operating budgets.
Application information:
  Initial approach: Letter with purpose statement
  Deadline(s): None
  Board meeting date(s): October and April
  Final notification: Up to 7 months
  Write: William P. Shannahan, Vice-President
Officers and Directors:* Theodore E. Gildred,* President; William P. Shannahan, Vice-President and Secretary.
Employer Identification Number: 956135592

190
Gilmore (Earl B.) Foundation ¤
6301 West Third St.
Los Angeles 90036

Incorporated in 1958 in California.
Donor(s): A.F. Gilmore Co., Marie Dent Gilmore.†
Financial data: (yr. ended 12/31/83): Assets, $2,361,368 (M); expenditures, $198,223, including $144,965 for 83 grants (high: $25,000; low: $100).
Purpose and activities: Broad purposes; primarily local giving, with emphasis on social agencies; grants also for higher and secondary education, health agencies, hospitals, youth agencies, and Protestant church support.
Limitations: Giving primarily in CA.

Officers and Directors:* John B. Gostovich,* President; Frank W. Clark, Jr.,* Vice-President and Secretary; Frances Gilmore Hilen,* Karl Samuelian,* Robert Sibert,* Vice-Presidents; M.B. Hartman, Treasurer.
Employer Identification Number: 956029602

191
Gilmore (The William G.) Foundation
120 Montgomery St., Suite 1880
San Francisco 94104   (415) 546-1400

Incorporated in 1953 in California.
Donor(s): William G. Gilmore,† Mrs. William G. Gilmore.
Financial data: (yr. ended 12/31/82): Assets, $6,089,444 (M); expenditures, $459,172, including $408,554 for 59 grants (high: $207,279; low: $100; average: $150-$2,500).
Purpose and activities: Broad purposes; giving primarily locally and in Oregon and Washington; grants largely for community funds; support also for higher and secondary education, hospitals, and youth and child welfare agencies.
Types of support awarded: Operating budgets, continuing support, annual campaigns, emergency funds.
Limitations: Giving primarily in northern CA, OR, and WA. No grants to individuals, or for seed money, deficit financing, capital or endowment funds, scholarships, fellowships, matching gifts, special projects, research, publications, or conferences; no loans.
Application information:
  Initial approach: Full proposal
  Copies of proposal: 1
  Deadline(s): November 30
  Board meeting date(s): December
  Final notification: 2 months
  Write: Miss Faye Wilson, Assistant Secretary
Officers and Trustees: Robert C. Harris, President; Lee Emerson, Vice-President, Secretary, and Treasurer; William R. Mackey.
Number of staff: 1 part-time support.
Employer Identification Number: 946079493

192
Gleason (James) Foundation ¤
Hearst Bldg., Suite 1200
Third and Market Sts.
San Francisco 94103

Established in 1978.
Donor(s): Ruth M. Gleason, Walter M. Gleason.
Financial data: (yr. ended 12/31/83): Assets, $1,220,288 (M); gifts received, $30,000; expenditures, $81,407, including $80,000 for 18 grants (high: $50,000; low: $500).
Purpose and activities: Giving primarily for a university, Roman Catholic welfare funds, and church support.
Officers and Directors: Walter M. Gleason, President and Manager; William J. Gleason, Vice-President and Treasurer; Cressey H. Nakagawa, Secretary.
Employer Identification Number: 942471399

193
Gleason (Katherine) Foundation ¤
Hearst Bldg., Suite 1200
Third and Market Sts.
San Francisco 94103

Incorporated in 1969 in California.
Donor(s): Walter M. Gleason.
Financial data: (yr. ended 12/31/83): Assets,
$2,280,754 (M); gifts received, $145,000;
expenditures, $130,268, including $129,200
for 53 grants (high: $50,000; low: $200).
Purpose and activities: General giving to
Roman Catholic religious and welfare
associations, and secondary schools; support
also for a college.
Officers and Directors: Walter M. Gleason,
President; William J. Gleason, Vice-President
and Treasurer; Cressey H. Nakagawa, Secretary.
Employer Identification Number: 237043569

194
Golden (Robert M.) Foundation ¤
123 Camino de la Reina
San Diego 92108

Established in 1960.
Donor(s): Robert M. Golden, Silvergate
Corporation.
Financial data: (yr. ended 12/31/83): Assets,
$245,740 (M); gifts received, $160,000;
expenditures, $110,449, including $109,292
for 44 grants (high: $21,000; low: $75).
Purpose and activities: Primarily local giving
for cultural programs, higher education, and
hospitals.
Limitations: Giving primarily in San Diego, CA.
Officers: Robert M. Golden, President; Morley
R. Golden, Vice-President and Treasurer;
Thomas C. Ackerman, Jr., Secretary.
Employer Identification Number: 956099985

195
Goldman (Richard and Rhoda) Fund
1090 Sansome St.
San Francisco 94111   (415) 956-4954

Incorporated in 1951 in California.
Donor(s): Rhoda H. Goldman, Richard N.
Goldman.
Financial data: (yr. ended 10/31/83): Assets,
$2,631,291 (M); gifts received, $600,000;
expenditures, $237,779, including $161,625
for 25 grants (high: $25,000).
Purpose and activities: Giving locally with
emphasis on the elderly, the environment, civic
affairs, education, and health.
Types of support awarded: Seed money,
special projects.
Limitations: Giving primarily in the San
Francisco Bay Area, CA. No grants to
individuals, or for building or endowment
funds, general fundraising campaigns,
conferences, research, scholarships and
fellowships, or matching gifts; no loans.
Publications: Program policy statement,
application guidelines.
Application information:
    Initial approach: Letter or telephone
    Deadline(s): None

Board meeting date(s): January, April, July,
    and October
    Write: Duane Silverstein, Executive Director
Officers: Richard N. Goldman, President;
Richard W. Goldman, Vice-President; Rhoda
H. Goldman, Secretary and Treasurer.
Number of staff: 1.
Employer Identification Number: 946064502

196
Goldwyn (The Samuel) Foundation ▼
10203 Santa Monica Blvd.
Los Angeles 90067   (213) 552-2255

Incorporated in 1947 in California.
Donor(s): Samuel Goldwyn,† Frances H.
Goldwyn.†
Financial data: (yr. ended 12/31/84): Assets,
$20,400,000 (M); expenditures, $2,106,268,
including $712,889 for 71 grants (high:
$457,000; low: $25; average: $1,000-$10,000).
Purpose and activities: To promote Southern
California community-related activities; grants
primarily for secondary and higher education,
cultural programs, youth, medical, and
innovative social programs.
Types of support awarded: Annual
campaigns, seed money, scholarship funds,
operating budgets, research, equipment, special
projects.
Limitations: Giving limited to the Los Angeles,
CA, metropolitan area. No grants to
individuals or for building funds.
Application information:
    Initial approach: Full proposal
    Write: Priscilla J. Mick, Executive Secretary
Officers and Directors: Samuel Goldwyn, Jr.,
President; Peggy E. Goldwyn, Vice-President;
Priscilla J. Mick, Executive Secretary; Meyer
Gottlieb, Treasurer; Francis Goldwyn, John
Goldwyn, George Slaff.
Employer Identification Number: 956006859

197
Gospel Foundation of California ▼ ¤
1462 North Stanley Ave.
Hollywood 90046   (213) 876-2172

Incorporated in 1946 in California.
Donor(s): Albert M. Johnson.
Financial data: (yr. ended 12/31/82): Assets,
$2,542,955 (M); expenditures, $435,825,
including $401,724 for 64 grants (high:
$25,000; low: $115).
Purpose and activities: "To foster, promote
and operate Christian, religious, charitable,
educational, home and foreign missions,
evangelistic and mission enterprises." Grants
primarily to institutions in California concerned
with aiding handicapped, underprivileged, or
troubled youth, Christian secondary and higher
educational institutions for scholarships, and
Christian churches and church-related programs.
Limitations: Giving primarily in CA.
Application information: Funds indefinitely
committed; no grant applications accepted.
Officers and Directors: Mary E. Liddecoat,
President; Selma C. Abnot, Secretary.
Employer Identification Number: 951556645

198
Grancell (I. H. and Anna) Foundation ¤
c/o Olincy & Olincy
10960 Wilshire Blvd., Suite 820
Los Angeles 90024

Incorporated in 1957 in California.
Donor(s): Anna Grancell, Anna Grancell
Charitable Trust.
Financial data: (yr. ended 7/31/83): Assets,
$1,222,915 (M); gifts received,
$287,833; expenditures, $391,719, including
$382,850 for 10 grants (high: $118,325; low:
$1,000).
Purpose and activities: Grants locally and
largely for three designated recipients; some
giving for hospitals and temple support.
Limitations: Giving primarily in CA.
Officers: Paul Grancell, President; Morton
Bauman, Vice-President; Sherman Grancell,
Treasurer.
Employer Identification Number: 956027429

199
Green (Burton E.) Foundation ¤
9777 Wilshire Blvd., Suite 618
Beverly Hills 90212

Incorporated in 1960 in California.
Donor(s): Burton E. Green.†
Financial data: (yr. ended 12/31/83): Assets,
$2,030,935 (M); expenditures, $59,538,
including $59,499 for 31 grants (high: $19,000;
low: $500).
Purpose and activities: Primarily local giving,
with emphasis on child welfare, animal care,
higher education, hospitals, and a community
fund.
Limitations: Giving primarily in CA.
Application information:
    Initial approach: Letter
    Deadline(s): November 30
    Write: Hugh M. Mullen, Treasurer
Officers and Trustees:* Burton G. Bettingen,*
Dorothy Green,* Liliore G. Rains,* Gyte Van
Zyl,* Vice-Presidents; Elinor F. Logan,*
Secretary; Hugh M. Mullen,* Treasurer.
Employer Identification Number: 956026935

200
Greenville Foundation, The ¤
P.O. Box 885
Pacific Palisades 90272   (602) 946-6644

Trust established in 1949 in California.
Donor(s): William Miles.
Financial data: (yr. ended 12/31/83): Assets,
$1,608,857 (M); expenditures, $96,865,
including $87,100 for 8 grants (high: $38,500;
low: $100).
Purpose and activities: Broad purposes; grants
primarily for Protestant religious programs and
higher education, including world peace studies
and experimental or pilot projects.
Limitations: Giving primarily in CA. No grants
to individuals or for operating budgets.
Application information:
    Initial approach: Full proposal
    Copies of proposal: 4

Deadline(s): Submit proposal in March or September upon foundation request; deadline October 15
Board meeting date(s): Semiannually
Write: William Miles, Jr., Chairman
Officer and Trustees: William Miles, Jr., Chairman; Herbert A. Crew, Jr., L.M. Fish, Jean H. Miles.
Employer Identification Number: 956043258

201
Gross (Stella B.) Charitable Trust
c/o Bank of the West
P.O. Box 1121
San Jose 95108   (408) 998-6856

Trust established in 1966 in California.
Donor(s): Stella B. Gross.†
Financial data: (yr. ended 6/30/83): Assets, $3,267,698 (M); expenditures, $334,296, including $272,444 for 55 grants (high: $30,000; low: $981).
Purpose and activities: Local giving to youth agencies, higher education, a hospital, aid to the handicapped, and a health agency.
Limitations: Giving limited to Santa Clara County, CA. No grants to individuals.
Application information:
Initial approach: Letter
Copies of proposal: 1
Deadline(s): Submit proposal in May or November; deadlines June 1 and December 1
Board meeting date(s): June and December
Write: Rachelle Coder, Trust Officer
Trustee: Bank of the West.
Number of staff: None.
Employer Identification Number: 237142181

202
Haas (Evelyn and Walter), Jr. Fund ▼
1090 Sansome St., Third Fl.
San Francisco 94111   (415) 544-6575

Incorporated in 1953 in California.
Donor(s): Walter A. Haas, Jr., Evelyn D. Haas.
Financial data: (yr. ended 12/31/83): Assets, $14,421,119 (M); expenditures, $1,438,349, including $1,165,246 for 95 grants (high: $225,000; average: $5,000-$50,000).
Purpose and activities: Broad purposes; primarily local giving, with emphasis on self-help programs for the elderly, corporate social responsibility and business ethics, and community development; grants also for the arts and humanities, education, and health.
Types of support awarded: Seed money, equipment, special projects, technical assistance, general purposes.
Limitations: Giving primarily in the San Francisco Bay Area, CA. No support for private foundations. No grants to individuals, or for endowment funds, workshops, conferences, scholarships, fellowships, matching gifts, or research; no loans.
Publications: Annual report, program policy statement, application guidelines.
Application information:
Initial approach: Letter
Copies of proposal: 1
Deadline(s): None

Board meeting date(s): March, June, September, and December
Final notification: Within 90 days
Write: Ira Hirschfield, Executive Director
Officers: Walter A. Haas, Jr.,* President; Evelyn D. Haas,* Vice-President; Willard L. Ellis, Secretary-Treasurer; Ira Hirschfield, Executive Director.
Trustees:* Walter J. Haas.
Advisory Trustees: Dyke Brown, Elizabeth Haas Eisenhardt, James C. Gaither, Robert D. Haas, Cecil F. Poole.
Number of staff: 1 full-time professional; 1 full-time support; 2 part-time support.
Employer Identification Number: 946068932

203
Haas (Miriam and Peter) Fund
Levi Plaza, LS/7, 1155 Battery St.
San Francisco 94111   (415) 544-6143

Incorporated in 1953 in California.
Donor(s): Peter E. Haas.
Financial data: (yr. ended 8/31/83): Assets, $3,985,538 (M); expenditures, $226,822, including $200,137 for 148 grants (high: $20,000; low: $25; average: $250-$1,000).
Purpose and activities: Broad purposes; primarily local giving, with emphasis on higher education; support also for community funds and cultural programs.
Types of support awarded: Operating budgets, continuing support, deficit financing, building funds, equipment, special projects.
Limitations: Giving primarily in northern CA. No grants to individuals, or for annual campaigns, seed money, emergency funds, land acquisition, matching gifts, scholarships or fellowships, research, demonstration projects, publications, or conferences; no loans.
Application information:
Initial approach: Letter
Copies of proposal: 1
Deadline(s): None
Board meeting date(s): As required
Final notification: 1 month
Write: Peter E. Haas, President, or Sanford M. Treguhoft
Officers: Peter E. Haas, President; Miriam L. Haas, Vice-President; Willard L. Ellis, Secretary-Treasurer.
Number of staff: None.
Employer Identification Number: 946064551

204
Haas (Walter and Elise) Fund ▼
1090 Sansome St., Third Fl.
San Francisco 94111   (415) 398-4474

Incorporated in 1952 in California.
Donor(s): Walter A. Haas,† Elise Haas.
Financial data: (yr. ended 12/31/83): Assets, $48,253,595 (M); expenditures, $2,491,675, including $2,339,510 for 104 grants (high: $250,000; low: $500; average: $1,000-$15,000).

Purpose and activities: Broad purposes; primarily local giving; interests include arts and humanities, medical research, higher education, specific hospital projects, institutions which further the public interest by the encouragement of individual initiative and the strengthening of the productive economy, and preservation of the environment.
Types of support awarded: Operating budgets, continuing support, annual campaigns, seed money, emergency funds, building funds, equipment, endowment funds, matching funds, scholarship funds, professorships, fellowships, special projects, research, conferences and seminars.
Limitations: Giving primarily in CA. No grants to individuals, or for publications, deficit financing, land acquisition, or general endowment funds; no loans.
Publications: Annual report, program policy statement, application guidelines.
Application information:
Initial approach: Letter
Copies of proposal: 1
Deadline(s): None
Board meeting date(s): As required
Final notification: 2 to 4 months
Write: Bruce R. Sievers, Executive Director
Officers and Directors:* Rhoda H. Goldman,* President; Elise S. Haas,* Peter E. Haas,* Walter A. Haas, Jr.,* Vice-Presidents; Willard L. Ellis, Secretary-Treasurer; Bruce R. Sievers, Executive Director.
Number of staff: 1 full-time professional; 1 full-time support.
Employer Identification Number: 946068564

205
Hahn (Ernest W. and Jean E.) Foundation ¤
c/o Ernest W. Hahn
3666 Kearny Villa Rd.
San Diego 92123

Established in 1981 in California.
Donor(s): Ernest W. Hahn, Jean E. Hahn.
Financial data: (yr. ended 12/31/82): Assets, $3,528,071 (M); expenditures, $517,453, including $473,604 for 71 grants (high: $207,025; low: $15).
Purpose and activities: Initial grants made in 1982; primarily local giving for a community development agency, social services, youth agencies, and hospitals and health services.
Limitations: Giving primarily in CA.
Officers: Ernest W. Hahn, President; Jean E. Hahn, Vice-President; Lois M. Stockert, Treasurer.
Employer Identification Number: 953643330

206
Hahn (Philip Y.) Foundation
c/o Home Federal Savings & Loan
P.O. Box 2070
San Diego 92112

Trust established in 1964 in New York.
Donor(s): Philip Y. Hahn.†

Financial data: (yr. ended 12/31/82): Assets, $1,224,317 (M); gifts received, $1,154,421; expenditures, $517,672, including $477,500 for 2 grants (high: $307,500; low: $170,000).
Purpose and activities: Broad purposes; aid for needy American Indian children in the Southwest; support also for a nursing program.
Limitations: No grants to individuals.
Application information: No grants to new applicants at the present time.
Initial approach: Letter
Copies of proposal: 1
Board meeting date(s): Quarterly
Write: Gilbert L. Brown, Jr., Manager
Managers: Dennis Brokaw, Gilbert L. Brown, Jr., Ralph R. Carskadden, Douglas Manchester, June Marsh, Peter Marsh, William C. Smith.
Employer Identification Number: 166058154

207
Hale (The Crescent Porter) Foundation
c/o Consultants in Philanthropy
220 Bush St., Suite 1069
San Francisco 94104 (415) 986-5177
Grant application address: Consultants in Philanthropy, 220 Bush St., Suite 1065, San Francisco, CA 94104

Incorporated in 1961 in California.
Donor(s): Elywn C. Hale, M. Eugenie Hale.†
Financial data: (yr. ended 12/31/83): Assets, $2,373,072 (M); gifts received, $1,800,000; expenditures, $90,808, including $70,000 for 10 grants (high: $17,500; low: $2,500).
Purpose and activities: Broad purposes; emphasis on Roman Catholic organizations, and for higher education, including art and music education, and specific hospital projects.
Limitations: Giving primarily in San Francisco, CA, Bay area. No grants to individuals.
Application information:
Initial approach: Letter
Deadline(s): None
Officers: Melvin M. Swig, President; L.E. Alford, Vice-President; Eugene E. Bleck, M.D., Secretary-Treasurer.
Trustees: Rev. Charles Dullea, S.J., Ephraim P. Engleman, M.D., Elfreda Hale, Daniel V. Ryan.
Employer Identification Number: 946093385

208
Halsell (O. L.) Foundation ⌑
c/o Helsley & Company
P.O. Box 6300
Santa Ana 92706

Trust established in 1948 in California.
Donor(s): Oliver L. Halsell.†
Financial data: (yr. ended 12/31/83): Assets, $1,470,431 (M); gifts received, $11,210; expenditures, $92,679, including $46,500 for 9 grants (high: $5,500; low: $5,000).
Purpose and activities: Giving primarily to youth agencies; support also for hospitals, education, and a social agency.
Officers: George V. Barr, President; Walter K. Kelley, Vice-President; Phillip R. Johnson, Secretary.
Employer Identification Number: 956027266

209
Hancock (The Luke B.) Foundation ▼
360 Bryant St.
Palo Alto 94301 (415) 321-5536

Incorporated in 1948 in Nevada.
Donor(s): Luke B. Hancock.†
Financial data: (yr. ended 4/30/84): Assets, $15,069,486 (M); expenditures, $1,057,678, including $828,728 for grants.
Purpose and activities: Broad purposes; local giving primarily for job training and employment for youth. Special project grants include: consortium with other foundations in areas where there is unmet need; some support for technical assistance, emergency funding, music and the arts in education.
Types of support awarded: Operating budgets, continuing support, seed money, emergency funds, matching funds, consulting services, technical assistance, program-related investments, conferences and seminars.
Limitations: Giving limited to CA, particularly the six counties of the San Francisco Bay Area. No support for films. No grants to individuals, or for deficit financing, capital or building funds, acquisitions, endowment funds, scholarships, fellowships, personal research, or publications.
Publications: Annual report.
Application information:
Initial approach: Letter
Copies of proposal: 1
Deadline(s): None
Board meeting date(s): January, March, June and September
Final notification: 3 to 4 months
Write: Joan H. Wylie, Executive Director
Officers and Directors: Marsha H. Adams, Chairman; Lorraine A. Hancock, President; Marian Hancock, Vice-President; Jane Hancock, Secretary; Linda Catron, Carol E. Hancock, Denise J. Hancock, Wesley Hancock, Noble Hancock, William Hancock, Susan Hillstrom-Masi, Joseph L. Masi.
Number of staff: 1 full-time professional; 1 part-time support.
Employer Identification Number: 886002013

210
Harney Foundation, The ⌑
923 Folsom St.
San Francisco 94107

Incorporated in 1951 in California.
Donor(s): Charles L. Harney,† Mrs. P.E. Harney, Charles L. Harney, Inc., Consumers Rock and Cement Company.
Financial data: (yr. ended 12/31/83): Assets, $763,322 (M); expenditures, $445,503, including $397,200 for 24 grants (high: $50,000; low: $500).
Purpose and activities: Broad purposes; primarily local giving, with emphasis on education, including religious education, hospitals, and Roman Catholic church support and religious associations.
Limitations: Giving primarily in CA.
Officers and Directors: Mrs. P.E. Harney, President; F.S. Roberts, Secretary-Treasurer; Donald C. Carroll, George T. Cronin.
Employer Identification Number: 946065590

211
Haynes (The John Randolph) and Dora Haynes Foundation ▼
727 West Seventh St., Suite 618
Los Angeles 90017 (213) 623-9151

Trust established in 1926 in California.
Donor(s): Dr. John Randolph Haynes,† Mrs. John Randolph Haynes.†
Financial data: (yr. ended 8/31/84): Assets, $23,352,144 (M); expenditures, $1,559,723, including $1,345,911 for grants (high: $100,000; low: $1,000; average: $50,000-$75,000).
Purpose and activities: "... promoting the well-being of mankind" by making grants for study and research in the social sciences - economics, history, government, and sociology - with specific application to the greater Los Angeles area; provides undergraduate scholarships, graduate fellowships, and summer fellowships for faculty members in the social sciences in selected colleges and universities. Grants made only through local colleges and universities or other nonprofit institutions.
Types of support awarded: Fellowships, research, scholarship funds, internships.
Limitations: Giving limited to the greater Los Angeles, CA, area. No grants to individuals, or for building or endowment funds, or operating budgets.
Publications: Informational brochure, program policy statement, application guidelines.
Application information:
Initial approach: Letter
Copies of proposal: 15
Deadline(s): Several weeks before board meetings
Board meeting date(s): Usually in October, December, February, and May
Final notification: 1 to 2 weeks
Write: Maynard J. Toll, President
Officers and Trustees: Francis H. Lindley, Chairman; Maynard J. Toll, President; Robert R. Dockson, 1st Vice-President; F. Haynes Lindley, Jr., 2nd Vice-President, Paul A. Albrecht, R. Stanton Avery, Philip M. Hawley, Jack K. Horton.
Number of staff: 1 full-time professional; 1 full-time support.
Employer Identification Number: 951644020

212
Hedco Foundation
1330 Broadway, Suite 1730
Oakland 94612

Incorporated in 1972 in California.
Donor(s): Herrick Corporation, Catalina Associates.
Financial data: (yr. ended 11/30/84): Assets, $5,457,952 (M); gifts received, $530,000; expenditures, $885,278, including $873,568 for 24 grants (high: $125,000; low: $500; average: $20,000-$100,000).
Purpose and activities: Primarily local giving to qualified educational and health service institutions for projects significantly aiding in the betterment of man; support mainly for capital funds.
Types of support awarded: Building funds, equipment, land acquisition, matching funds.

Limitations: Giving primarily in CA. No grants to individuals, or for general support, operating budgets, endowment funds, scholarships or fellowships, special projects, research, publications, or conferences; no loans.
Application information:
  Initial approach: Full proposal
  Copies of proposal: 1
  Deadline(s): None
  Board meeting date(s): November
  Final notification: 3 to 4 months
  Write: Mary A. Goriup, Foundation Manager
Officers and Directors: Ester M. Dornsife, President; David Dornsife, Vice-President; Dorothy Jernstedt, Secretary; Laine Ainsworth, H.W. Dornsife, S.G. Herrick, James S. Little, William Picard, J.G. Ross.
Number of staff: None.
Employer Identification Number: 237259742

213
Heller Charitable and Educational Fund ¤
244 California St., Suite 508
San Francisco 94111

Established in California.
Donor(s): Members of the Heller family.
Financial data: (yr. ended 12/31/83): Assets, $1,037,127 (M); gifts received, $20,000; expenditures, $153,964, including $150,123 for 12 grants (high: $25,000; low: $212).
Purpose and activities: Primarily local giving, with emphasis on environmental protection; support also for education, cultural programs, and social services.
Limitations: Giving primarily in CA.
Officers: Clarence E. Heller,* President and Treasurer; Alfred E. Heller,* Elinor R. Heller,* Ruth B. Heller,* Vice-Presidents; John G. Sherwood, Secretary.
Trustees:* Anne E. Heller, Janet F. Heller, Katherine Heller, Alan Mandell, Elizabeth H. Mandell, F. Jerome Tone IV, Miranda H. Tone.
Employer Identification Number: 946066671

214
Helms Foundation, Inc. ¤
P.O. Box 312
Redwood Valley 95470   (707) 485-7997

Incorporated in 1946 in California.
Donor(s): The Helms family, Helms Bakeries.
Financial data: (yr. ended 6/30/83): Assets, $3,450,596 (M); expenditures, $368,074, including $325,901 for 98 grants (high: $40,100; low: $350).
Purpose and activities: Broad purposes; largely local giving with support primarily for higher education, including scholarship funds, and Protestant church support and religious education; support also for civic organizations, health agencies, and youth.
Limitations: Giving primarily in CA.
Application information:
  Write: William D. Manuel, Assistant Secretary
Officers and Trustees: Peggy Helms Hurtig, President and Treasurer; Elizabeth Helms Adams, Vice-President and Secretary; John B. Gostovich, Frank J. Kanne, Jr.
Employer Identification Number: 956091335

215
Herbst Foundation, Inc., The ▼
Two Embarcadero Center, Suite 2300
San Francisco 94111   (415) 627-8384

Incorporated in 1961 in California.
Donor(s): Herman H. Herbst,† Maurice H. Herbst.†
Financial data: (yr. ended 7/31/84): Assets, $20,307,577 (M); expenditures, $2,931,461, including $1,546,586 for 76 grants (high: $451,050; low: $500; average: $1,000-$20,000).
Purpose and activities: Primarily local giving for capital fund projects in areas of educational facilities, recreation for the handicapped, and civic improvement of existing city structures owned by public tax-exempt entities; small budget per year for broad purposes.
Types of support awarded: Building funds.
Limitations: Giving primarily in the San Francisco, CA, area. No grants to individuals, or for endowment funds, scholarships, fellowships, general purposes, research, or matching gifts; no loans.
Application information:
  Initial approach: Letter
  Copies of proposal: 1
  Deadline(s): None
  Board meeting date(s): Usually in September, November, February, and May
  Final notification: 30 days after board meeting
  Write: John T. Seigle, President
Officers and Directors: John T. Seigle, President; William D. Crawford, George D. Hart, Dennis B. King, Melvyn I. Mark, Ralph L. Preston, Haskell Titchell.
Number of staff: 1.
Employer Identification Number: 946061680

216
Hertz (Fannie and John) Foundation ▼
P.O. Box 2230
Livermore 94550-0130   (415) 449-0855

Incorporated in 1945 in Illinois.
Donor(s): John D. Hertz,† Fannie K. Hertz.†
Financial data: (yr. ended 6/30/82): Assets, $11,224,106 (M); expenditures, $1,946,201, including $24,674 for 2 grants (average: $14,000) and $1,585,419 for 120 grants to individuals.
Purpose and activities: To promote education and the defense of the United States through support of fellowships for graduate education for students with outstanding potential in the fields constituting the applied physical sciences at specified nationwide institutions; also provides scholarships to high school graduates from the San Francisco Bay Area (U.S. citizens only).
Types of support awarded: Fellowships, student aid.
Limitations: Giving limited to San Francisco Bay Area, CA, high school graduates for scholarship program; competition for fellowship program is nationwide. No grants for general support, or for capital or endowment funds, matching gifts, program support, research, demonstration projects, publications, or conferences; no loans.

Publications: Application guidelines, program policy statement, informational brochure.
Application information: Application form required.
  Initial approach: Full proposal
  Copies of proposal: 2
  Deadline(s): Submit proposal in September or October; deadline November 1
  Board meeting date(s): March, June, and October
  Final notification: 4 months
  Write: Dr. Wilson K. Talley, President
Officers and Directors: Allan B. Hunter, Chairman and Treasurer; Wilson K. Talley, President; Jerome L. Ettelson, Paul L. Hexter, Peter Strauss, Vice-Presidents; Robert M. Pennoyer, Secretary; John W. Boyd, Gregory H. Canavan, C. Stark Draper, Robert A. Duffy, Lawrence Goldmuntz, John T. Hayward, Arthur R. Kantrowitz, Hans Mark, Edward Teller, Thomas A. Weaver, Lowell L. Wood.
Number of staff: 1 part-time professional; 2 part-time support.
Employer Identification Number: 362411723

217
Hewlett (The William and Flora) Foundation ▼
525 Middlefield Rd., Suite 200
Menlo Park 94025   (415) 329-1070

Incorporated in 1966 in California.
Donor(s): William R. Hewlett, Mrs. William R. Hewlett.†
Financial data: (yr. ended 12/30/84): Assets, $475,419,603 (M); expenditures, $30,314,674, including $28,138,936 for 354 grants (high: $2,500,000; low: $2,000; average: $5,000-$500,000).
Purpose and activities: Emphasis on conflict resolution, the environment, performing arts, education, especially at the college-university level; population, and regional grants program.
Types of support awarded: General purposes, operating budgets, continuing support, seed money, emergency funds, land acquisition, special projects, matching funds.
Limitations: Giving limited to the San Francisco Bay Area, CA, for regional grants program; other programs limited to the area in part. No support for medicine and health-related projects, law, criminal justice, and related fields; juvenile delinquency, drug and alcohol addiction, problems of the elderly and the handicapped, or television or radio projects. No grants to individuals, or for building funds, basic research, equipment, or scholarships and fellowships; no loans.
Publications: Annual report, program policy statement, application guidelines, informational brochure.
Application information:
  Initial approach: Letter
  Copies of proposal: 1
  Deadline(s): January 1, music; April 1, theatre; July 1, dance, film, and video service organizations; no deadlines for other programs
  Board meeting date(s): January, April, July, and October
  Final notification: 1 to 2 months
  Write: Roger W. Heyns, President

Officers: Roger W. Heyns,* President; Marianne Pallotti, Vice-President and Corporate Secretary; C. Ted Perry, Treasurer.
Directors:* William R. Hewlett, Chairman; Walter B. Hewlett, Vice-Chairman; Robert M. Brown, Robert Erburu, Eleanor H. Gimon, Arjay Miller, Lyle M. Nelson.
Number of staff: 9 full-time professional; 4 full-time support; 2 part-time support.
Employer Identification Number: 941655673

218
Hewlett-Packard Company Foundation
3000 Hanover St., 20AH
Palo Alto 94304   (415) 857-3053
Mailing address: P.O. Box 10301, Palo Alto, CA 94303-0890

Established in 1979.
Donor(s): Hewlett-Packard Company.
Financial data: (yr. ended 10/31/83): Assets, $1,163,248 (M); gifts received, $489,700; expenditures, $174,448, including $169,500 for 36 grants (high: $50,000; low: $300).
Purpose and activities: Support primarily for higher education and cultural programs.
Application information:
  Write: Emery H. Rogers, Director
Directors: Emery H. Rogers, Executive Director; Jack Brigham, Dean Morton, John Young.
Employer Identification Number: 942618409

219
Hills (The Edward E.) Fund ⌘
c/o Pillsbury, Madison and Sutro
225 Bush St.
San Francisco 94104

Incorporated in 1953 in California.
Donor(s): Edward E. Hills.†
Financial data: (yr. ended 12/31/83): Assets, $7,113,874 (M); expenditures, $346,057, including $295,000 for 10 grants (high: $50,000; low: $25,000).
Purpose and activities: Broad purposes; grants primarily to local higher and secondary educational institutions.
Limitations: Giving primarily in CA.
Officers: Reuben W. Hills III, President; John B. Bates,* Secretary-Treasurer.
Directors:* Edmond S. Gillette, Jr.
Employer Identification Number: 946062537

220
Hilton (Conrad N.) Foundation ▼
10100 Santa Monica Blvd., Suite 775
Los Angeles 90067   (213) 556-4694

Trust established in 1944; incorporated in 1950 in California.
Donor(s): Conrad N. Hilton.†
Financial data: (yr. ended 2/28/84): Assets, $91,284,615 (M); gifts received, $569,908; expenditures, $9,226,703, including $5,398,676 for 179 grants (high: $1,135,000; low: $50; average: $5,000-$100,000).

Purpose and activities: Broad purposes; giving in four program areas: 1) Support for the human services work of the Catholic Sisters, especially ministries which assist disadvantaged children; 2) Reduction of violence and abuse against children and families; 3) Efforts to improve pre-collegiate public education; and 4) Prevention of substance abuse among young people (currently fully committed to field trials of a prevention education program).
Types of support awarded: Seed money, special projects, matching funds, general purposes.
Limitations: Giving limited to the U.S. No support for religious organizations for the benefit of their own membership, medical research, local branches of national charities, the arts, the elderly. No grants to individuals, or for general fundraising events, exhibits, travel, or surveys; no loans.
Publications: Annual report, program policy statement, application guidelines.
Application information:
  Initial approach: Letter
  Copies of proposal: 1
  Deadline(s): None
  Board meeting date(s): Quarterly
  Write: Donald H. Hubbs, President
Officers: Donald H. Hubbs,* President; W. Kent Holman, Vice-President - Administration and Treasurer; Terry W. McAdam, Vice-President and Program Director; Spearl Ellison,* Vernon Herndon,* Vice-Presidents.
Directors:* Olive W. Wakeman, Chairman; Robert Buckley, M.D., Robert A. Groves, Eric M. Hilton, William Barron Hilton, Thomas R. Wilcox.
Number of staff: 9.
Employer Identification Number: 956038817

221
Hoag Foundation ▼ ⌘
333 South Hope St., 27th Fl.
Los Angeles 90071   (213) 683-6500

Incorporated in 1940 in California.
Donor(s): George Grant Hoag,† Grace E. Hoag, George Grant Hoag II.
Financial data: (yr. ended 12/31/83): Assets, $20,763,107 (M); expenditures, $1,144,463, including $986,811 for 18 grants (high: $400,000; low: $1,725; average: $5,000-$50,000).
Purpose and activities: Broad purposes, with emphasis on the Hoag Memorial Hospital-Presbyterian, Orange County youth organizations and hospitals, medical research, education, and cultural programs, including a music center.
Types of support awarded: Research.
Limitations: Giving primarily in Orange County, CA. No support for government agencies, tax-supported projects, or sectarian or religious organizations for the benefit of their own members. No grants to individuals, or for scholarships, medical assistance, deficit financing, or continuing support; generally no support for student aid or for operating support or capital campaigns.
Application information:
  Initial approach: Letter
  Deadline(s): February 15 and September 15

Board meeting date(s): March and October
Write: W. Dickerson Milliken, Secretary
Officers and Directors: John Macnab, President; W. Dickerson Milliken, Secretary; Albert J. Auer, John Curci, George Grant Hoag II, Patty Hoag, Gwyn Parry.
Employer Identification Number: 956006885

222
Hoffman (The H. Leslie) and Elaine S. Hoffman Foundation
626 Wilshire Blvd.
Los Angeles 90017   (213) 620-0621

Trust established in 1952 in California.
Donor(s): H. Leslie Hoffman.†
Financial data: (yr. ended 12/31/83): Assets, $3,398,526 (M); expenditures, $199,088, including $151,832 for 80 grants (high: $50,000; low: $100).
Purpose and activities: Broad purposes; primarily local giving for higher education, a secondary school, and cancer research; grants also for hospitals and youth agencies.
Limitations: Giving primarily in the Los Angeles, CA, area.
Application information:
  Initial approach: Letter
  Copies of proposal: 1
  Board meeting date(s): As required
  Write: Eugene P. Carver
Trustees: Herbert S. Hazeltine, Elaine S. Hoffman, Jane H. Popovich.
Employer Identification Number: 956048600

223
Hofmann (K. H.) Foundation ⌘
1035 Detroit Ave.
P.O. Box 907
Concord 94522

Established in 1963 in California.
Donor(s): Alta Mortgage Company, Bamia Builders, Hofmann Company, Hofmann Homes Realty, Inc., Ken Inc., Pioneer Village.
Financial data: (yr. ended 7/31/83): Assets, $2,992,844 (M); gifts received, $280,467; expenditures, $493,906, including $150,931 for 41 grants (high: $66,211; low: $70).
Purpose and activities: Giving primarily for health and social services, recreation, and higher education.
Officers: Kenneth H. Hofmann, President; Martha J. Hofmann, Vice-President; Gay Fuller, Secretary-Treasurer.
Employer Identification Number: 946108897

224
Hollywood Canteen Foundation, The ⌘
P.O. Box 2193
Los Angeles 90051

Trust established in 1946 in California.
Financial data: (yr. ended 2/28/83): Assets, $1,470,096 (M); expenditures, $193,975, including $185,715 for 26 grants (high: $37,715; low: $2,500).

Purpose and activities: To promote the well-being of military personnel and veterans and their families through grants to hospitals, colleges, social agencies, and other similar institutions.
Limitations: No grants to individuals.
Application information:
Write: Bertram L. Linz, Executive Secretary
Trustees: Lew R. Wasserman, Chairman; Ralph H. Claire, William K. Howard, Sherman Jones, Arthur Ryan, Doris Stein, John te Groen, Union Bank.
Employer Identification Number: 956023639

225
Holt (William Knox) Foundation
505 Sansome St., Suite 1001
San Francisco 94111   (415) 981-3455

Established in 1967.
Donor(s): William Knox Holt.†
Financial data: (yr. ended 12/31/82): Assets, $7,084,314 (M); expenditures, $612,692, including $526,406 for 10 grants (high: $200,000; low: $5,000).
Purpose and activities: Giving primarily in northern California and southern Texas for higher and secondary education; some support also for museums.
Types of support awarded: Building funds, matching funds, research, special projects, scholarship funds, fellowships.
Limitations: Giving primarily in northern CA and southern TX. No grants for general support, operating budgets, continuing support, annual campaigns, emergency funds, deficit financing, equipment, land acquisition, or endowment funds; no loans.
Application information:
Initial approach: Letter
Copies of proposal: 1
Deadline(s): Submit proposal in January or February; deadline February 15
Board meeting date(s): Quarterly
Final notification: 3 months
Write: Stephen W. Veitch, Secretary
Officers and Directors: Kenneth Van Strum, President and Treasurer; Holt Atherton, Vice-President; Stephen W. Veitch, Secretary; Stevenson Atherton, George M. Malti.
Employer Identification Number: 746084245

226
Hoover (The Margaret W. and Herbert), Jr. Foundation
523 West Sixth St., Suite 450
Los Angeles 90014   (213) 624-4014

Incorporated in 1968 in California.
Donor(s): Herbert Hoover, Jr.,† Margaret W. Hoover.†
Financial data: (yr. ended 12/31/83): Assets, $8,641,941 (M); gifts received, $402,680; expenditures, $499,453, including $404,658 for 16 grants (high: $50,000; low: $1,000; average: $1,000-$30,000).
Purpose and activities: Primarily local giving, with emphasis on medical and scientific research, education, and youth agencies.

Types of support awarded: Continuing support, seed money, emergency funds, equipment, matching funds, research.
Limitations: Giving primarily in CA. No support for performing arts. No grants to individuals, or for endowment funds, building funds, renovation projects, operating budgets, annual campaigns, deficit financing, land acquisition, scholarships or fellowships; no loans.
Publications: Application guidelines.
Application information:
Initial approach: Letter
Copies of proposal: 1
Deadline(s): Submit proposal when requested by the foundation; no set deadline
Board meeting date(s): As required
Final notification: 2 to 3 months
Write: Herbert Hoover III, President
Officers and Trustees: Herbert Hoover III, President; Margaret Hoover Brigham, Vice-President and Secretary; Joan Hoover Vowles, Vice-President and Treasurer; Sally K. Bond, Robert J. Plourde, Vice-Presidents.
Number of staff: 1 part-time professional.
Employer Identification Number: 952560832

227
Howe (Lucile Horton) and Mitchell B. Howe Foundation ¤
180 South Lake Ave.
Pasadena 91101

Incorporated in 1964 in California.
Donor(s): Mitchell B. Howe.
Financial data: (yr. ended 12/31/83): Assets, $1,935,010 (M); expenditures, $142,344, including $137,755 for 96 grants (high: $70,405; low: $18).
Purpose and activities: Broad purposes; giving primarily for youth agencies and social welfare, hospitals, church support, and education, with emphasis on local organizations.
Officers: Mitchell B. Howe, President and Treasurer; Lucile Horton Howe, Vice-President and Secretary.
Employer Identification Number: 956081945

228
Humboldt Area Foundation, The
P.O. Box 632
Eureka 95501   (707) 442-2993

Community foundation established in 1972 in California by declaration of trust.
Donor(s): Vera P. Vietor,† Lynn A. Vietor,† and others.
Financial data: (yr. ended 12/31/83): Assets, $4,600,000 (L); gifts received, $290,000; expenditures, $410,000, including $350,000 for 85 grants (high: $25,000; low: $50) and $2,700 for 6 grants to individuals.
Purpose and activities: Broad purposes; local giving, including grants for prevention of cruelty to children or animals, cultural programs, health, recreation, public safety, education, and human service programs.
Types of support awarded: Special projects, equipment.

Limitations: Giving limited to the north coast area of CA, with preference to Humboldt County. No grants to individuals (except from donor-designated funds); generally no grants for endowment funds, unspecified emergency purposes, deficit financing, or operating budgets.
Publications: Annual report, application guidelines.
Application information: Application form required.
Initial approach: Letter or telephone
Copies of proposal: 8
Deadline(s): February 1, May 1, August 1, and November 1
Board meeting date(s): Monthly; applications reviewed quarterly in January, April, July, and October
Write: Ellen A. Dusick, Executive Director
Officer: Ellen A. Dusick, Executive Director.
Governors: Eve McClaran, Chairman; Monica W. Hadley, Vice-Chairman; Art Dalianes, Secretary; Marjorie Fitzpatrick, Sam B. Merryman, Jr., Edward L. Nilsen.
Trustees: Bank of America, Crocker National Bank, First Interstate Bank, Security Pacific Bank, Wells Fargo Bank.
Employer Identification Number: 237310660

229
Incentive Aid Foundation ¤
c/o McDaniel & McDaniel
2230 East Imperial Hwy., Suite 111
El Segundo 90245

Incorporated in 1953 in California.
Donor(s): George C. Page.
Financial data: (yr. ended 5/31/83): Assets, $2,589,867 (M); expenditures, $164,762, including $153,855 for 16 grants (high: $85,500).
Purpose and activities: To promote the well-being of society by giving the type of aid that will be an incentive to persons to improve themselves by education, work, and creative effort and not depend upon charity, governmental aid, or stultifying gifts. Primarily local giving, with emphasis on a hospital, higher education, cultural programs, and museum building funds.
Limitations: Giving primarily in CA.
Officers and Members: George C. Page, President; Maynard Kambak, Vice-President; Marshall L. McDaniel, Secretary; Ivan McDaniel, Treasurer.
Employer Identification Number: 956091872

230
Irvine (The James) Foundation ▼
One Market Plaza
Steuart Street Tower, Suite 2305
San Francisco 94105   (415) 777-2244
Southern California grant application office:
450 Newport Center Dr., Suite 545, Newport Beach, CA 92660; Tel: (714) 644-1362

Incorporated in 1937 in California.
Donor(s): James Irvine.†
Financial data: (yr. ended 12/31/84): Assets, $306,187,000 (M); expenditures, $17,344,000, including $15,023,000 for 294 grants (high: $1,500,000; low: $1,500).

Purpose and activities: Grants primarily for local higher education, health, youth services, and community and cultural projects.
Types of support awarded: Seed money, building funds, equipment, land acquisition, matching funds, special projects.
Limitations: Giving limited to CA. No support for primary or secondary schools, agencies receiving substantial government support, films, or sectarian religious activities. No grants to individuals, or for operating budgets, continuing support, annual campaign, deficit financing, endowment funds, scholarships, publications, or conferences; no loans.
Publications: Annual report, program policy statement, application guidelines.
Application information: Application form required.
  Initial approach: Letter
  Deadline(s): Proposals from institutions of higher education are reviewed separately in mid-summer; no other deadlines
  Board meeting date(s): March, June, September, and December
  Final notification: 3 months
  Write: Luz A. Vega, Program Director (Northern California office); or Doris C. Jones, Assistant Vice-President (Southern California office)
Officers: Kenneth M. Cuthbertson, President; Jean D. Parmelee, Vice-President and Secretary.
Directors: Morris M. Doyle, Chairman; John V. Newman, Vice-Chairman; Samuel H. Armacost, Edward W. Carter, Myron DuBain, Virginia B. Duncan, Camilla C. Frost, Walter B. Gerken, Roger W. Heyns, Kathryn L. Wheeler.
Number of staff: 7 full-time professional; 1 part-time professional; 6 full-time support; 1 part-time support.
Employer Identification Number: 941236937

231
Irwin (The William G.) Charity
  Foundation ▼ ⌑
1662 Russ Bldg.
235 Montgomery St.
San Francisco 94104   (415) 362-6954

Trust established in 1919 in California.
Donor(s): Fannie M. Irwin,† Helene Irwin Fagan.†
Financial data: (yr. ended 12/31/83): Assets, $32,051,737 (M); expenditures, $2,160,004, including $1,937,587 for 35 grants (high: $300,000; low: $7,000).
Purpose and activities: "... to pay out the net income thereof to ... charitable uses, including medical researches and other scientific uses, designed to promote or improve the physical condition of mankind, ... in the Hawaiian Islands or the State of California." Support for hospitals, cultural programs, education, and social agencies.
Types of support awarded: Building funds, equipment, general purposes, land acquisition, research.
Limitations: Giving limited to HI and Southern CA.
Application information:
  Initial approach: Letter or proposal
  Deadline(s): Approximately 3 weeks prior to board meeting

Board meeting date(s): Approximately every 2 months
  Write: Fred R. Grant, Secretary
Officers: Jane Fagan Olds,* President; Herman Phleger,* Vice-President; Fred R. Grant, Secretary.
Trustees:* Merl McHenry, William Lee Olds, Jr., Atherton Phleger.
Employer Identification Number: 946069873

232
Ishiyama Foundation, The ⌑
465 California St.
San Francisco 94104

Established in 1968 in California.
Donor(s): George S. Ishiyama.
Financial data: (yr. ended 12/31/82): Assets, $3,195,302 (M); expenditures, $468,670, including $459,500 for 13 grants (high: $200,000; low: $500; average: $500-$200,000).
Purpose and activities: Grants to higher and secondary educational institutions in Japan and California.
Types of support awarded: General purposes.
Limitations: Giving primarily in CA and Japan. No grants to individuals.
Application information:
  Initial approach: Letter
  Deadline(s): None
  Final notification: 2 months
  Write: George Ishiyama, President
Officers and Directors: George S. Ishiyama, President; Ralph Bardoff, Vice-President; Setsuko Ishiyama, Secretary; Margaret Raffin.
Employer Identification Number: 941659373

233
Island Foundation
76500 Short Creek Rd.
Covelo 95428

Established in 1976 in Colorado.
Donor(s): Catherine M. Carrithers.
Financial data: (yr. ended 12/31/83): Assets, $1,596,219 (M); gifts received, $100,000; expenditures, $99,247, including $18,000 for 8 grants (high: $5,000; low: $1,000).
Purpose and activities: Giving primarily to conservation and environmental organizations in the Rocky Mountain region.
Limitations: Giving primarily in the Rocky Mountain region, with emphasis on western CO.
Officers and Directors: Ashley K. Carrithers, President; Walter C. Sedgwick, Vice-President; Bruce J. Alexander, Secretary-Treasurer.
Employer Identification Number: 840715001

234
Jackson (Ann) Family Foundation ⌑
P.O. Box 5580
Santa Barbara 93108

Established in 1978.
Donor(s): Ann G. Jackson, Ann Jackson Family Charitable Trust.

Financial data: (yr. ended 5/31/83): Assets, $3,149,499 (M); gifts received, $550,000; expenditures, $185,228, including $174,500 for 29 grants (high: $35,000; low: $500).
Purpose and activities: Primarily local giving, with emphasis on secondary education, health, aid to the handicapped, and prevention of cruelty to children and animals.
Types of support awarded: General purposes.
Limitations: Giving primarily in CA.
Application information:
  Initial approach: Letter
  Write: Palmer G. Jackson, Chief Financial Officer
Officers and Directors: Flora J. Ramsey, President; Peter Jackson, Vice-President; Palmer G. Jackson, Chief Financial Officer.
Employer Identification Number: 953367511

235
Jameson (J. W. and Ida M.)
  Foundation ⌑
481 West Highland Ave.
Sierra Madre 91024   (213) 355-6973

Incorporated in 1955 in California.
Donor(s): J.W. Jameson Corporation.
Financial data: (yr. ended 6/30/83): Assets, $660,065 (M); gifts received, $680,000; expenditures, $692,252, including $680,000 for 90 grants (high: $50,000; low: $1,000).
Purpose and activities: Broad purposes; primarily local giving, with emphasis on higher education, including theological seminaries, hospitals, medical research, cultural programs, and youth agencies; grants also for Protestant church support.
Types of support awarded: Research, general purposes, scholarship funds.
Limitations: Giving primarily in CA.
Application information:
  Write: Arthur W. Kirk, President
Officers and Directors: Arthur W. Kirk, President; Van Alen Pfister, 1st Vice-President; Meta Moore, 2nd Vice-President; Pauline Vetrovec, Secretary; William M. Croxton, Treasurer; Bill B. Betz, Fred L. Leydorf.
Employer Identification Number: 956031465

236
Jefferson (John Percival and Mary C.)
  Endowment Fund
P.O. Box 1418
Santa Barbara 93102

Trust established in 1952 in California.
Donor(s): Mary C. Jefferson.†
Financial data: (yr. ended 3/31/83): Assets, $1,771,512 (M); expenditures, $157,261, including $61,000 for 29 grants (high: $6,300; low: $250).
Purpose and activities: Grants restricted to local use; mainly for family assistance and medical and nursing care.
Limitations: Giving limited to Santa Barbara County, CA.
Application information:
  Write: Patricia M. Brouard, Trustee
Trustees: Steven M. Anders, Patricia M. Brouard, Arthur R. Gaudi.
Employer Identification Number: 956005231

237
Jerome Foundation ⊭
4120 Bandini Blvd.
Los Angeles 90023

Incorporated in 1956 in California.
Donor(s): Members of the Jerome family,
Baker Commodities, Inc., and others.
Financial data: (yr. ended 12/31/83): Assets,
$2,909,487 (M); gifts received, $5,000;
expenditures, $183,023, including $164,319
for 26 grants (low: $100).
Purpose and activities: Primarily local giving,
with emphasis on medical research,
handicapped children's organizations, the blind,
hospitals, youth and health agencies, and the
Jerome Foundation in the Philippines.
Limitations: Giving primarily in CA.
Officers: James M. Andreoli, President; Edward
S. Murakami, Vice-President; Mitchell Ebright,
Secretary and Treasurer.
Employer Identification Number: 956039063

238
Jewett (George Frederick)
Foundation ▼
One Maritime Plaza
The Alcoa Bldg., Suite 1340
San Francisco 94111   (415) 421-1351

Trust established in 1957 in Massachusetts.
Donor(s): George Frederick Jewett.†
Financial data: (yr. ended 12/31/84): Assets,
$16,300,000 (M); expenditures, $1,084,400,
including $944,036 for 144 grants (high:
$50,000; low: $500; average: $1,000-$15,000).
Purpose and activities: To carry on the
charitable interests of the donor, primarily in
the Pacific Northwest, to stimulate, encourage,
and support activities of established, voluntary,
nonprofit organizations which are of
importance to human welfare. Interests include
the performing arts and museums, conservation
of natural resources, higher education,
population planning, health care and medical
research and services, social welfare, religion,
and public affairs.
Types of support awarded: General purposes,
building funds, equipment, land acquisition,
research, matching funds, special projects,
operating budgets.
Limitations: Giving primarily in the Pacific
Northwest, with emphasis on northern ID and
eastern WA, particularly Spokane. No grants to
individuals, or for scholarships, fellowships; no
loans. No emergency grants, except for
disaster relief.
Publications: Annual report, program policy
statement, application guidelines.
Application information:
  Initial approach: Letter
  Copies of proposal: 1
  Deadline(s): November 1
  Board meeting date(s): March, June,
    September, and December (for annual
    distributions)
  Final notification: Annually, at the end of the
    year
  Write: Sara C. Fernandez, Program Director

Officers and Trustees: George Frederick
Jewett, Jr., Chairman; Mary Jewett Gaiser,
Secretary; Margaret Jewett Greer, William
Hershey Greer, Jr., Lucille McIntyre Jewett.
Number of staff: 1 full-time professional; 1
part-time support.
Employer Identification Number: 046013832

239
Johnson (Walter S.) Foundation ▼
525 Middlefield Rd., Suite 200
Menlo Park 94025   (415) 326-0485

Established in 1968 in California.
Donor(s): Walter S. Johnson.†
Financial data: (yr. ended 12/31/83): Assets,
$29,621,357 (M); gifts received, $4,269,939;
expenditures, $1,046,437, including $904,057
for 43 grants (high: $109,962; low: $1,000).
Purpose and activities: Local giving for public
schools and social agencies concerned with the
quality of public education and the social
family experiences of children between
kindergarten and twelfth grade.
Types of support awarded: Operating
budgets, seed money, emergency funds, special
projects, research.
Limitations: Giving primarily in Alameda,
Contra Costa, San Francisco, San Mateo, and
Santa Clara counties in CA; Washoe County,
NV, and Maui County, HI. No support for
religious organizations for sectarian purposes,
or for private schools. No grants to individuals,
or for continuing support, annual campaigns,
deficit financing, memorial funds, capital or
endowment funds, matching gifts, scholarships
and fellowships, publications, or conferences;
no loans.
Publications: Annual report, application
guidelines, program policy statement,
application guidelines.
Application information:
  Initial approach: Telephone or letter
  Copies of proposal: 1
  Deadline(s): Submit proposal 12 weeks
    before board meeting; deadlines April 1,
    August 1, and December 3
  Board meeting date(s): March, July, and
    November
  Final notification: 1 to 4 months
  Write: Donna Terman, Executive Director
Officers: Gloria Eddie,* President; Charles P.
Eddie,* Vice-President; Joseph A. DeMaria,*
Secretary; Elio L. Martin, Treasurer.
Trustees:* Walter S. Johnson, Jr., Walter S.
Johnson III, Leslie L. Luttgens.
Number of staff: 1 full-time professional; 1 full-
time support.
Employer Identification Number: 237003595

240
Jones Foundation, The ▼
One Wilshire Bldg., Suite 1210
624 South Grand Ave.
Los Angeles 90017   (213) 689-9292

Established in 1969 in California.
Donor(s): Fletcher Jones.†

Financial data: (yr. ended 12/31/84): Assets,
$53,500,800 (M); expenditures, $2,940,363,
including $2,328,071 for 38 grants (high:
$400,000; low: $5,000; average: $70,000).
Purpose and activities: Primarily local giving
for private higher educational institutions.
Types of support awarded: Seed money,
building funds, equipment, professorships,
special projects, research, endowment funds,
scholarship funds.
Limitations: Giving primarily in CA. No grants
to individuals or for operating funds, deficit
financing, conferences, travel exhibits, or
projects supported by government agencies.
Publications: Annual report, application
guidelines.
Application information:
  Initial approach: Letter
  Deadline(s): One month prior to board
    meetings
  Board meeting date(s): March, May,
    September, and November
  Final notification: 3 to 6 months
  Write: Harvey L. Price, Executive Director
Officers: John P. Pollock,* President; Houston
Flournoy,* Jess C. Wilson, Jr., Vice-Presidents;
Jack Pettker, Secretary; Harvey L. Price,
Treasurer and Executive Director.
Trustees:* Dean Butler, Dickinson C. Ross,
Robert F. Erburu, Chauncey J. Medberry III,
Rudy J. Munzer, Donald E. Nickelson.
Number of staff: 1 part-time professional; 1
part-time support.
Employer Identification Number: 237030155

241
Joslyn (The Marcellus L.) Foundation
12857 Camino Emparrado
San Diego 92128   (714) 485-7938

Trust established in 1960 in California.
Donor(s): Marcellus L. Joslyn.†
Financial data: (yr. ended 9/30/83): Assets,
$6,374,469 (M); expenditures, $465,034,
including $411,300 for 33 grants (high:
$150,000; low: $900).
Purpose and activities: General purposes;
primarily local giving, with emphasis on
hospitals, higher education, and senior citizens
centers.
Limitations: Giving primarily in CA.
Application information: Funds presently
committed.
  Board meeting date(s): Semiannually in
    either February or March, and September
    or October
  Write: Remy L. Hudson, Chairman, Board of
    Trustees
Trustees: Remy L. Hudson, Chairman; Mary C.
Currivan, Merritt L. Joslyn, John MacIntosh,
Jean Mill.
Employer Identification Number: 952276744

242
Kaiser (The Henry J.) Family
Foundation ▼
525 Middlefield Rd., Suite 200
Menlo Park 94025   (415) 329-1000

Trust established in 1948 in California.

Donor(s): Bess F. Kaiser,† Henry J. Kaiser,† Henry J. Kaiser, Jr.,† and others.
Financial data: (yr. ended 12/31/84): Assets, $250,311,121 (M); expenditures, $13,199,500, including $9,875,242 for 128 grants (high: $2,310,000; low: $1,000) and $44,936 for employee matching gifts.
Purpose and activities: Major share of resources devoted to programs in health and medicine.
Types of support awarded: Seed money, matching funds, scholarship funds, employee matching gifts, special projects, research, fellowships, publications, conferences and seminars, professorships.
Limitations: Giving limited to the San Francisco Bay Area, CA, for the Community Grants Program only; other grants nationwide. No grants to individuals, or for construction, equipment, or capital funds.
Publications: Annual report, application guidelines, program policy statement.
Application information:
Initial approach: Letter or telephone
Copies of proposal: 2
Deadline(s): None
Board meeting date(s): March, June, and October
Final notification: 3 to 6 months
Write: Barbara H. Kehrer, Vice-President
Officers: Alvin R. Tarlov, M.D.,* President; Barbara H. Kehrer, Vice-President; Jean D. Parmelee, Secretary.
Trustees:* Edgar F. Kaiser, Jr., Chairman; Joseph A. Califano, Jr., Edward E. Carlson, Hale Champion, Douglas A. Fraser, Barbara Jordan, Henry M. Kaiser, Kim J. Kaiser, Edwin H. Morgens, Joan E. Morgenthau, M.D., Gerard Piel.
Number of staff: 7 full-time professional; 1 part-time professional; 4 full-time support; 4 part-time support.
Employer Identification Number: 946064808

243
Keck (W. M.) Foundation ▼
555 South Flower St., Suite 3230
Los Angeles 90071   (213) 680-3833

Incorporated in 1954 in Delaware; sole beneficiary of W.M. Keck Trust.
Donor(s): William M. Keck.†
Financial data: (yr. ended 12/31/84): Assets, $500,000,000 (M); expenditures, $21,256,209, including $20,000,000 for 95 grants (high: $1,200,000; low: $15,000; average: $50,000-$500,000).
Purpose and activities: To strengthen studies and programs in educational institutions of higher learning in the areas of sciences, engineering, liberal arts, and medical research (including educational and other institutions). Some consideration, largely in southern California, given to educational institutions at pre-college level, health care and hospitals, arts and cultural institutions, and civic and community affairs institutions which the foundation has traditionally supported.
Types of support awarded: Endowment funds, building funds, seed money, equipment, scholarship funds, special projects, research, fellowships, operating budgets.

Limitations: Giving primarily in western states; restricted to southern CA in all categories except higher education and medical research. No support for umbrella organizations. No grants to individuals, or for fundraising events, or conferences or seminars.
Publications: Annual report, application guidelines, program policy statement.
Application information:
Initial approach: Letter of inquiry
Copies of proposal: 1
Deadline(s): Applications accepted only from April 1 to September 15; deadline September 15 at 4:30 p.m.; requests not considered from September 16 through March 31
Board meeting date(s): December
Final notification: By December 31
Write: Sandra A. Glass, for education grants; Ann D. Gralnek, for arts and culture, health care, and medical research grants; Joan F. DuBois for civic and community affairs grants
Officers: Howard B. Keck,* Chairman, President, and Chief Executive Officer; Paul A. Lower, Vice-President and Secretary; Robert A. Day, Jr.,* Howard B. Keck, Jr.,* W.M. Keck II,* Vice-Presidents; Walter B. Gerken,* Treasurer.
Directors:* Marsh A. Cooper, Naurice G. Cummings, Howard M. Day, Tammis M. Day, Theodore J. Day, Willametta K. Day, Bob Rawls Dorsey, Thomas P. Ford, Max R. Lents, Erin A. Lower, James Paul Lower, Simon Ramo, Arthur M. Smith, Jr., Kerry C. Vaughan, Julian O. Von Kalinowski, Thomas R. Wilcox.
Number of staff: 4 full-time professional; 7 full-time support.
Employer Identification Number: 956092354

244
Kerr (A. H.) Foundation
(formerly Alexander H. Kerr Benevolent Association)
15910 Ventura Blvd., Suite 1027
Encino 91436   (818) 990-2831

Incorporated in 1945 in California.
Donor(s): Ruth Kerr,† A.H. Kerr Corporation, Kerr Glass Corporation, Southern California Protective Society.
Financial data: (yr. ended 12/31/83): Assets, $11,822,731 (L); gifts received, $2,631; expenditures, $487,451, including $161,451 for 50 grants (high: $48,607; low: $350; average: $500-$3,000).
Purpose and activities: Broad purposes; general giving, with emphasis on higher education in California and for church support and religious associations, including foreign missions. Support also for hospitals, health agencies, and social services.
Types of support awarded: Operating budgets, continuing support, annual campaigns, emergency funds, building funds, equipment, land acquisition, publications, conferences and seminars, special projects.
Limitations: No grants to individuals, or for seed money, deficit financing, or demonstration projects; no loans.
Publications: Program policy statement.
Application information:
Initial approach: Full proposal

Copies of proposal: 1
Deadline(s): None
Board meeting date(s): April and October
Final notification: Several months to 2 years
Write: William A. Kerr, Vice-President
Officers and Directors: Alexander H. Kerr, President; William A. Kerr, Vice-President and Treasurer; Ruth K. O'Dell, Secretary.
Number of staff: 1 part-time professional; 1 part-time support.
Employer Identification Number: 956085982

245
Kirchgessner (The Karl) Foundation
10850 Wilshire Blvd., Suite 1200
Los Angeles 90024   (213) 470-2747

Established in 1977 in California.
Donor(s): Karl Kramer,† Nina Kramer.
Financial data: (yr. ended 6/30/83): Assets, $4,337,210 (M); gifts received, $262,051; expenditures, $184,767, including $134,775 for 3 grants (high: $100,000; low: $63,275).
Purpose and activities: "For the advancement of medical research and for the provision of medical and clinical services to disadvantaged persons, particularly the elderly, the young and handicapped." Applicants should be involved with research and/or clinical programs connected with eyesight.
Types of support awarded: Research.
Limitations: Giving limited to the Southern CA area; geographical restriction may be broadened in the future. No grants to individuals, or for fund-raising campaigns.
Application information:
Initial approach: Brief proposal
Deadline(s): None
Board meeting date(s): Grants made once a year, generally on or about June 30
Officers and Directors: Martin H. Webster, President; Amelia Louise Mills, Vice-President; Lewis Whitney, Secretary; Rev. Patrick Cahalan, Karl Kramer, Jr.
Employer Identification Number: 953439716

246
Knudsen (The Tom and Valley) Foundation
P.O. Box 60299, Terminal Annex
Los Angeles 90060   (602) 830-0220

Incorporated in 1951 in California.
Donor(s): Th. R. Knudsen,† Valley M. Knudsen.†
Financial data: (yr. ended 12/31/84): Assets, $4,376,373 (M); gifts received, $148,715; expenditures, $448,544, including $365,714 for 46 grants (high: $15,000; low: $200; average: $5,000).
Purpose and activities: Broad purposes; local giving, with emphasis on private higher educational institutions; grants also for cultural institutions.
Types of support awarded: General purposes, annual campaigns.
Limitations: Giving limited to southern CA. No grants to individuals, or for matching gifts, capital or endowment funds, scholarships and fellowships, research, or special projects; no loans.

Publications: Program policy statement, application guidelines.
Application information:
Initial approach: Full proposal
Copies of proposal: 1
Deadline(s): March 1 and September 1
Board meeting date(s): April and October
Final notification: 2 months
Write: Mrs. Helen B. McGrath, Executive Vice-President
Officers and Directors: J.R. Vaughan, President; Helen B. McGrath, Executive Vice-President, Secretary, and Treasurer; Charles S. Casassa, S.J., Christian Castenskiold, William W. Escherich, Gene Knudsen Hoffman, Doris Holtz, Ernest J. Loebbecke, E. Wilson Lyon, Peter O'Malley, Robert E. Osborne, William G. Schmal, Harold Skou.
Number of staff: None.
Employer Identification Number: 956031188

247
Komes Foundation ⊠
2006 Washington St.
San Francisco 94109

Established in 1965 in California.
Donor(s): Jerome W. Komes, Flora Komes.
Financial data: (yr. ended 12/31/83): Assets, $1,704,506 (M); expenditures, $174,338, including $160,000 for 41 grants (high: $40,000; low: $250).
Purpose and activities: Broad purposes; primarily local giving, with emphasis on hospitals and health agencies, higher education, cultural programs, and Christian welfare organizations.
Limitations: Giving primarily in CA.
Officers: Jerome W. Komes, President; Flora Komes, Vice-President; Michael L. Mellor, Secretary.
Employer Identification Number: 941611406

248
Koret Foundation ▼
201 Filbert St., 5th Fl.
San Francisco 94133   (415) 989-4650

Foundation established in 1966 in California.
Donor(s): Joseph Koret,† Stephanie Koret.†
Financial data: (yr. ended 12/31/83): Assets, $61,285,280 (M); gifts received, $72,771; expenditures, $5,888,228, including $3,341,209 for 206 grants (high: $350,000; low: $100; average: $5,000-$50,000).
Purpose and activities: For the benefit of residents of the San Francisco Bay Area; preference given to social services providing direct aid to youth and the elderly, and to Jewish organizations and institutions of higher education.
Types of support awarded: Operating budgets, continuing support, annual campaigns, seed money, matching funds, scholarship funds, professorships, exchange programs, fellowships, publications, conferences and seminars, special projects, technical assistance, general purposes.

Limitations: Giving limited to the Bay Area counties of San Francisco, Alameda, Contra Costa, Marin, Santa Clara, and San Mateo, CA. No support for arts and humanities, primary or secondary education, medical or scientific research, or for veterans, fraternal, military, religious, or sectarian organizations whose principal activity is for the benefit of their own membership. No grants to individuals, general fundraising campaigns, endowment funds, equipment funds, deficit financing, or emergency funds; no loans.
Publications: Program policy statement, application guidelines, annual report.
Application information: Application form required.
Initial approach: Letter of inquiry
Deadline(s): None
Board meeting date(s): Quarterly
Final notification: 4 months
Write: Jo Anne Vente, Vice-President
Officers: Thaddeus N. Taube,* President and Chief Executive Officer; Kenneth A. Moline, Executive Vice-President and Chief Operating Officer; Jo Anne Vente, Vice-President and Secretary.
Directors:* Susan Koret, Chairman; Eugene L. Friend, Richard L. Greene.
Number of staff: 4 full-time professional; 2 part-time professional; 2 full-time support.
Employer Identification Number: 941624987

249
Koulaieff (The Trustees of Ivan V.) Educational Fund ⊠
c/o Nathan B. Siegel
3406 Geary Blvd.
San Francisco 94118

Incorporated in 1930 in California.
Donor(s): Ivan V. Koulaieff.
Financial data: (yr. ended 12/31/83): Assets, $1,860,912 (M); expenditures, $248,423, including $44,140 for 35 grants (high: $2,450; low: $180) and $57,730 for 62 grants to individuals.
Purpose and activities: Aid to Russian immigrants throughout the world through grants, scholarships, and loans; support also for Russian Orthodox education and churches in the United States.
Types of support awarded: Scholarship funds, loans, grants to individuals.
Officers and Directors: A.S. Mandrusov, President; W.W. Granitow, Secretary; C. Parshootto, Treasurer; R.A. Folkert, Mrs. O.P. Hughes, N.A. Kaliakin, B.J. Koulaieff, A.D. Psiol.
Employer Identification Number: 946088762

250
Kroc Foundation, The ▼
5290 Overpass Rd., Suite 225
Santa Barbara 93111   (805) 967-2302

Incorporated in 1965 in Illinois.
Donor(s): Ray A. Kroc.†
Financial data: (yr. ended 12/31/82): Assets, $56,103,625 (M); gifts received, $24,600; expenditures, $7,808,279, including $5,582,369 for 258 grants (high: $89,896; low: $25; average: $10,000-$40,000).

Purpose and activities: Sponsorship of small group conferences or workshops in any area of medical research or basic science relating to human disease. Grants limited to specific research projects in arthritis, diabetes, and multiple sclerosis.
Types of support awarded: Research.
Limitations: No grants to individuals (except for specific projects by individual medical researchers), or for capital or endowment funds, operating budgets, scholarships and fellowships, or matching gifts; no loans.
Publications: Annual report, newsletter, application guidelines.
Application information: Foundation plans to terminate in 1985; applications for grants not accepted.
Board meeting date(s): Spring and winter
Officers and Directors: Robert L. Kroc, President; Joan B. Kroc, Fred Turner, Vice-Presidents; Ballard F. Smith, Jr., Secretary; Lorraine E. Groh, Treasurer.
Number of staff: 2 full-time professional; 3 full-time support.
Employer Identification Number: 366125258

251
Lakeside Foundation
50 Fremont St., Suite 3825
San Francisco 94105   (415) 768-6022

Incorporated in 1953 in California.
Donor(s): S.D. Bechtel, Mrs. S.D. Bechtel, S.D. Bechtel, Jr., Mrs. Paul L. Davies, Jr., Bechtel Corporation.
Financial data: (yr. ended 12/31/84): Assets, $4,013,399 (M); expenditures, $182,817, including $163,050 for 67 grants (high: $20,000; low: $100).
Purpose and activities: Broad purposes; local giving, principally limited to qualified charitable organizations in the Bay Area, with emphasis on health care, higher education, including international studies, and cultural programs; support also for religious, scientific, and literary purposes, a community fund, and youth agencies.
Types of support awarded: General purposes, operating budgets, continuing support, building funds.
Limitations: Giving primarily in the San Francisco Bay Area, CA. No grants to individuals, or for endowment funds, scholarships, fellowships, or matching gifts; no loans.
Application information:
Initial approach: Full proposal
Copies of proposal: 1
Deadline(s): None
Board meeting date(s): Annually, usually in the spring
Final notification: 6 to 8 weeks
Write: Barbara B. Davies, President
Officers: Barbara B. Davies,* President; D.A. Ruhl, Vice-President and Treasurer; Laura P. Bechtel,* Vice-President; I. Patricia Rublack, Secretary.
Directors:* S.D. Bechtel, Paul L. Davies, Jr., Paul Lewis Davies III, A. Barlow Ferguson, Laura Davies Mateo.
Number of staff: None.
Employer Identification Number: 946066229

252
Layne Foundation
19 Rue Cannes
Newport Beach 92660   (714) 644-6438
Additional telephone number: (714) 644-4059

Incorporated in 1927 in California.
Financial data: (yr. ended 12/31/84): Assets,
$3,657,133 (L); expenditures, $13,900,
including $2,000 for 3 grants (high: $800; low:
$600) and $758,000 for 5 loans.
Purpose and activities: Assistance primarily
through current interest loans given to Christian
churches and religious organizations in
southern California, principally for capital
purposes and to those churches ineligible for
loans from other sources.
Types of support awarded: Loans.
Limitations: Giving primarily in southern CA.
No grants to individuals, or for operating
budgets, building or endowment funds (except
for loans), scholarships or fellowships, or
matching gifts.
Application information: Application form
required.
   Initial approach: Letter
   Copies of proposal: 1
   Deadline(s): None
   Board meeting date(s): November
   Write: Robert H. Mason, President
Officers and Directors: Robert H. Mason,
President; Harold L. Semans, Vice-President;
Welsey M. Mason, Secretary-Treasurer; Richard
H. Nida.
Number of staff: None.
Employer Identification Number: 951765157

253
Lear Siegler Foundation ▼
2850 Ocean Park Blvd.
P.O. Box 2158
Santa Monica 90406   (213) 452-8852

Incorporated in 1953 in Ohio.
Donor(s): Lear Siegler, Inc.
Financial data: (yr. ended 6/30/84): Assets,
$575,297 (M); gifts received, $534,345;
expenditures, $824,813, including $762,505
for 354 grants (high: $40,000; low: $100;
average: $250-$10,000) and $60,463 for 105
employee matching gifts.
Purpose and activities: General giving in areas
of company operations, with emphasis on
community funds and higher education;
support also for cultural and public affairs
organizations, hospitals, and social service and
youth agencies.
Types of support awarded: Annual
campaigns, building funds, continuing support,
emergency funds, employee matching gifts,
equipment, operating budgets, scholarship
funds, seed money, employee related
scholarships.
Limitations: Giving primarily in areas of
company operations, with emphasis on CA and
MI. No support for religious or political
organizations. No grants to individuals, or for
endowment funds, deficit financing, land
acquisition, matching grants, special projects,
research, publications, or conferences; no loans.
Application information:
   Initial approach: Letter

Copies of proposal: 1
Deadline(s): Submit proposal preferably
   between January and March; no set
   deadline
Board meeting date(s): As required
Final notification: 6 to 8 weeks
Write: John V. German, Manager
Directors: Robert T. Campion, Chairman;
Norman A. Barkeley, K. Robert Hahn, James N.
Thayer.
Number of staff: 1 part-time professional; 1
part-time support.
Employer Identification Number: 346555816

254
Leavey (Thomas and Dorothy) Foundation ▼ ⌑
4680 Wilshire Blvd.
Los Angeles 90010   (213) 936-5875

Trust established in 1952 in California.
Donor(s): Thomas E. Leavey,† Dorothy Leavey.
Financial data: (yr. ended 12/31/83): Assets,
$56,933,489 (M); expenditures, $5,515,648,
including $5,216,858 for 59 grants (high:
$2,006,000; low: $1,000; average: $10-
$100,000) and $187,435 for 87 grants to
individuals.
Purpose and activities: Broad purposes;
primarily local giving for hospitals, medical
research, higher and secondary education, and
Catholic church groups; provides scholarships
to children of employees of Farmers Group, Inc.
Types of support awarded: Employee related
scholarships.
Limitations: Giving primarily in southern CA.
Application information:
   Initial approach: Letter
   Copies of proposal: 1
   Board meeting date(s): As required
Officers and Trustees: Dorothy Leavey, Vice-
President; Kathleen Leavey McCarthy,
Secretary; E.W. Boland, M.D., Joseph James
Leavey, J. Thomas McCarthy.
Number of staff: None.
Employer Identification Number: 956060162

255
Lebus (Bertha) Trust
c/o Trust Services of America, Inc.
700 Wilshire Blvd.
Los Angeles 90017

Financial data: (yr. ended 12/31/83): Assets,
$1,630,000 (M); expenditures, $96,200,
including $87,000 for 16 grants (high: $15,000;
low: $500).
Purpose and activities: Grants primarily for
education.
Limitations: No grants to individuals.
Application information:
   Write: M.D. Blood
Trustee: Trust Services of America.
Employer Identification Number: 956022085

256
Ledler Foundation, The ⌑
1800 West Magnolia Blvd.
Burbank 91503

Established in 1966 in California.
Donor(s): Lawrence E. Deutsch,† Lloyd E.
Rigler, Adolph's, Ltd., Adolph's Food Products
Manufacturing Company.
Financial data: (yr. ended 12/31/83): Assets,
$5,945,728 (M); expenditures, $1,060,813,
including $1,010,461 for 13 grants (high:
$876,301; low: $250).
Purpose and activities: Grants mainly for the
arts, particularly music, and a university.
Officers: Lloyd E. Rigler, President and
Director; Simon Miller, Vice-President; Donald
Rigler, Secretary-Treasurer.
Employer Identification Number: 956155653

257
Leonardt Foundation ▼ ⌑
1801 Ave. of the Stars, Suite 811
Los Angeles 90067   (213) 556-3932

Incorporated in 1953 in California.
Donor(s): Amy L. Powell, Clara L. McGinnis.
Financial data: (yr. ended 12/31/83): Assets,
$2,224,654 (M); expenditures, $191,318,
including $159,175 for 77 grants (high:
$22,000; low: $50).
Purpose and activities: Broad purposes; grants
primarily for Roman Catholic church support;
support also for welfare funds, higher and
secondary education, hospitals, and health
agencies.
Limitations: No grants to individuals.
Application information:
   Initial approach: Letter
   Copies of proposal: 1
   Write: Felix S. McGinnis, Jr., President
Officers and Directors: Clara L. McGinnis,
Chairman; Felix S. McGinnis, Jr., President; Carl
L. McGinnis, Vice-President, Secretary, and
Treasurer; Barbara J. McGinnis, J. Frank
McGinnis.
Employer Identification Number: 956045256

258
Levi Strauss Foundation ▼
1155 Battery St.
P.O. Box 7215
San Francisco 94106   (415) 544-6579

Incorporated in 1941 in California.
Donor(s): Levi Strauss & Co.
Financial data: (yr. ended 12/31/83): Assets,
$21,769,943 (M); gifts received, $7,800,000;
expenditures, $9,442,476, including
$4,002,191 for 358 grants (high: $100,000;
low: $100), $171,750 for 204 grants to
individuals and $321,044 for 718 employee
matching gifts.

Purpose and activities: To improve human services, with an emphasis on the communities in which Levi Strauss & Co. has production and distribution facilities, through direct grants and encouragement of employee volunteer activities; also supports education, mainly at the initiative of the foundation. Giving primarily to programs to support and aid the aged, families, the rights of women and Hispanics; higher education, including company employee scholarships and matching gifts; youth, community funds, civic affairs, health, and international development programs.
Types of support awarded: Matching funds, scholarship funds, continuing support, seed money, emergency funds, building funds, equipment, fellowships, exchange programs, internships, employee related scholarships.
Limitations: Giving primarily in areas of company operations. No grants to individuals (except for scholarship programs), or for endowment funds, building funds for national and regional organizations, operating budgets, annual campaigns, deficit financing, land acquisition, renovations, research, production of films, travel, demonstration projects, publications, or conferences; no loans.
Publications: Annual report, application guidelines, program policy statement.
Application information: Application forms required for employee dependent scholarships.
　Initial approach: Letter or full proposal
　Copies of proposal: 1
　Deadline(s): None
　Board meeting date(s): March, June, September, and December
　Final notification: 3 to 6 months
　Write: Katherine B. Durgin, Secretary
Officers: Peter E. Haas,* President; Walter A. Haas, Jr.,* Thomas E. Harris, Vice-Presidents; Katherine B. Durgin, Secretary; David D. Smith, Treasurer.
Directors:* Phyllis K. Friedman, Rhoda H. Goldman, Madeleine Haas Russell.
Number of staff: 6 part-time professional; 13 part-time support.
Employer Identification Number: 946064702

259
Levy (Achille) Foundation
c/o Bank of A. Levy
P.O. Box 272
Oxnard 93032　　　　　(805) 487-6541
Mailing address: P.O. Box 5190, Ventura, CA 93006

Established in 1969 in California.
Donor(s): Bank of A. Levy.
Financial data: (yr. ended 11/30/83): Assets, $68,578 (M); expenditures, $111,784, including $90,100 for 68 grants (high: $25,000; low: $200; average: $1,000-$1,500); $15,000 for 15 grants to individuals and $5,560 for 8 employee matching gifts.
Purpose and activities: Local giving, with emphasis on higher and secondary education, including scholarship funds, youth agencies, cultural programs, including historic preservation, social and health agencies, and a community fund.

Types of support awarded: Operating budgets, annual campaigns, emergency funds, building funds, equipment, employee matching gifts, scholarship funds.
Limitations: Giving limited to Ventura County, CA. No grants for continuing support, seed money, deficit financing, land acquisition, endowment funds, special projects, research, publications, or conferences; no loans.
Application information: Application form required.
　Initial approach: Letter
　Copies of proposal: 1
　Deadline(s): Submit proposal preferably in July or August; deadline August 15
　Board meeting date(s): November
　Final notification: November 30
　Write: Robert L. Mobley, Vice-Chairman
Trustees: A.A. Milligan, Chairman; Robert L. Mobley, Vice-Chairman; Walter H. Hoffman, James F. Koenig, Ben E. Nordman.
Number of staff: None.
Employer Identification Number: 956264755

260
Levy (Hyman Jebb) Foundation ⌑
2222 South Figueroa St.
Los Angeles 90007

Established in 1974.
Donor(s): Hyman J. Levy, Raymond Mallel.
Financial data: (yr. ended 11/30/83): Assets, $2,654,169 (M); expenditures, $437,728, including $430,950 for 28 grants (high: $191,000; low: $500).
Purpose and activities: Grants primarily for Jewish education and temple support in the United States and Israel.
Officer and Director: Hyman J. Levy, President and Treasurer.
Employer Identification Number: 237422872

261
Lewis (Mabelle McLeod) Memorial Fund
P.O. Box 3730
Stanford 94305

Trust established in 1968 in California.
Donor(s): Donald McLeod Lewis.†
Financial data: (yr. ended 3/31/83): Assets, $1,658,047 (M); expenditures, $112,320, including $86,200 for 13 grants to individuals (high: $9,400; low: $4,000).
Purpose and activities: Direct grants to scholars in the humanities affiliated with northern California universities and colleges to bring about the completion of a scholarly dissertation; presently limited to advanced doctoral candidates.
Types of support awarded: Research, fellowships.
Limitations: Giving limited to northern CA. No grants for publication of dissertations.
Publications: Application guidelines, program policy statement.
Application information: Application form required.
　Initial approach: Letter
　Copies of proposal: 2

Deadline(s): Submit application preferably in November or December; deadline January 15
Board meeting date(s): February or March
Final notification: Mid-March
Write: Ms. Phyllis Stephens, Executive Secretary
Officer: Phyllis Stephens, Executive Secretary.
Nominating Committee: William A. Clebsch, Chairman.
Number of staff: 1.
Employer Identification Number: 237079585

262
Litton Industries, Foundation of the ▼
360 North Crescent Dr.
Beverly Hills 90210　　　　(213) 859-5422

Incorporated in 1954 in California.
Donor(s): Litton Industries, Inc., and its subsidiaries.
Financial data: (yr. ended 4/30/83): Assets, $6,146,134 (M); gifts received, $211,760; expenditures, $750,228, including $734,500 for 63 grants (high: $175,000; low: $1,000; average: $5,000).
Purpose and activities: Broad purposes; grants largely for higher education and community funds.
Types of support awarded: Operating budgets, continuing support, annual campaigns, seed money, emergency funds, endowment funds.
Limitations: No grants to individuals, or for deficit financing, capital funds, equipment, land acquisition, renovation projects, matching gifts, scholarships and fellowships, special projects, research, publications, or conferences; no loans.
Application information:
　Initial approach: Letter
　Copies of proposal: 1
　Deadline(s): None
　Board meeting date(s): As required
　Write: Clarence L. Price, President
Officers and Directors:* Clarence L. Price,* President; Janice F. Homer,* Norma E. Nelson,* Vice-Presidents; Mabel B. Herring, Secretary; Cynthia M. Stec, Treasurer.
Number of staff: None.
Employer Identification Number: 956095343

263
Livingston Memorial Foundation
625 North A St.
Oxnard 93030　　　　　(805) 983-0561
Mailing address: P.O. Box 1232, Oxnard, CA 93032

Incorporated about 1974 in California.
Donor(s): Ruth Daily Livingston.†
Financial data: (yr. ended 4/30/84): Assets, $4,876,303 (M); expenditures, $507,752, including $453,000 for 18 grants (high: $250,000; low: $500).
Purpose and activities: Supportive health and health-related activities in Ventura County for the benefit of Ventura County residents.
Limitations: Giving limited to Ventura County, CA. No grants to individuals.
Publications: Application guidelines, program policy statement.

Application information: Application form required.
Initial approach: Letter
Copies of proposal: 8
Deadline(s): Submit proposal preferably in December or January; deadline February 1
Board meeting date(s): As required
Write: Laura K. McAvoy
Officers: Charles M. Hair, M.D., President; W.C. Huff, M.D., Vice-President; Walter W. Hoffman, Secretary-Treasurer.
Directors: James K. Mason, M.D., Ben E. Nordman.
Number of staff: None.
Employer Identification Number: 237364623

264
Lloyd (The Ralph B.) Foundation ▼ ☐
9441 Olympic Blvd.
Beverly Hills 90212   (213) 879-3080

Incorporated in 1939 in California.
Donor(s): Ralph B. Lloyd.†
Financial data: (yr. ended 12/31/83): Assets, $6,807,017 (M); expenditures, $875,657, including $851,549 for 151 grants (high: $100,000; low: $50).
Purpose and activities: Broad purposes; primarily local giving for higher and secondary education, cultural organizations, community funds, Protestant church support, and youth agencies.
Types of support awarded: Building funds, operating budgets, equipment, special projects.
Limitations: Giving primarily in CA, with some support in OR. No grants to individuals.
Application information:
Initial approach: Letter
Officers and Trustees: Eleanor Lloyd Dees, President; Ida Hull Lloyd Crotty, Vice-President; Theresa Von Hagen Bucher, Secretary; Elizabeth Davis Rogers, Treasurer.
Employer Identification Number: 956048100

265
L.L.W.W. Foundation ☐
1600 Huntington Dr.
South Pasadena 91030

Established in 1980 in California.
Donor(s): Laura Lee Whittier Woods.
Financial data: (yr. ended 12/31/83): Assets, $6,850,994 (M); gifts received, $15,615; expenditures, $384,196, including $348,398 for 25 grants (high: $143,000; low: $50).
Purpose and activities: Primarily local giving with emphasis on the arts, including museums; support also for a private college and a medical research institute.
Limitations: Giving primarily in CA.
Officers: Laura Lee Whittier Woods, President; Leland K. Whittier, Vice-President; James E. Greene, Secretary and Treasurer.
Employer Identification Number: 953464689

266
Lockheed Leadership Fund
P.O. Box 551
Burbank 91520   (818) 847-6548

Incorporated in 1953 in California.
Donor(s): Lockheed Corporation.
Financial data: (yr. ended 12/31/84): Assets, $50,000 (M); gifts received, $575,000; expenditures, $580,500, including $401,750 for 109 grants (high: $25,000; low: $1,000; average: $2,000-$5,000) and $178,750 for 18 grants to individuals.
Purpose and activities: Support for higher education through grants, 12 four-year scholarships awarded annually to children of Lockheed employees through the National Merit Scholarship Corporation, two four-year Achievement Scholarships, and two four-year G.I. Forum scholarships for Hispanics annually. Grants principally to support education for engineers, scientists, and managers for aerospace industry.
Types of support awarded: Employee related scholarships, scholarship funds.
Limitations: No grants to individuals (except for scholarship program), or for special projects or matching gifts; no loans.
Application information:
Initial approach: Letter, telephone, or full proposal
Copies of proposal: 1
Deadline(s): Submit proposal preferably in January or February; deadline April 1
Board meeting date(s): May and as required
Write: Howard C. Lockwood, Vice-President
Officers: Norman L. Benjamin,* President; Howard C. Lockwood, Vice-President; James Ryan, Secretary; Robert McKirahan,* Treasurer.
Directors:* S.E. Chaudet, H.I. Fluornoy, R.A. Fuhrman, R.B. Ormsby, L. Shaw, J.G. Twomey, R.H. Wertheim.
Number of staff: 1 part-time professional; 1 part-time support.
Employer Identification Number: 956066086

267
Lurie (Louis R.) Foundation ▼
555 California St., Suite 5100
San Francisco 94104   (415) 392-2470

Incorporated in 1948 in California.
Donor(s): Louis R. Lurie,† Robert A. Lurie, George S. Lurie.†
Financial data: (yr. ended 12/31/83): Assets, $10,399,007 (M); gifts received, $353,534; expenditures, $913,054, including $862,493 for grants (high: $150,000; low: $1,500; average: $5,000-$25,000).
Purpose and activities: Giving primarily in the San Francisco Bay area and Chicago, Illinois, with emphasis on higher and secondary education, Jewish welfare agencies, community and health services, and cultural programs.
Types of support awarded: Annual campaigns, consulting services, continuing support, emergency funds, fellowships, general purposes, matching funds, research, scholarship funds, special projects.

Limitations: Giving limited to the San Francisco Bay, CA, area and the Chicago, IL, metropolitan area. No grants to individuals or for building funds; no loans.
Application information:
Initial approach: Telephone call, followed by letter
Copies of proposal: 1
Deadline(s): 6 weeks prior to board meetings; applicants should contact foundation for exact deadlines
Board meeting date(s): Twice a year, and as needed
Final notification: After board meeting
Write: Eileen Mize, Screening Committee
Officers: Robert A. Lurie,* President; H. Michael Kurzman,* Vice-President; Charles F. Jonas, Secretary.
Directors:* Charles L. Gould, A.R. Zipf.
Number of staff: None.
Employer Identification Number: 946065488

268
Lux (Miranda) Foundation
57 Post St., Suite 604
San Francisco 94104   (415) 981-2966

Incorporated in 1908 in California.
Donor(s): Miranda W. Lux.†
Financial data: (yr. ended 6/30/83): Assets, $2,557,183 (M); expenditures, $192,944, including $166,689 for 18 grants (high: $25,000; low: $250).
Purpose and activities: Local support to promising proposals for preschool through high school (ages: preschool to 18) programs in the fields of prevocational and vocational education and training .
Types of support awarded: Operating budgets, continuing support, seed money, equipment, matching funds, scholarship funds, special projects.
Limitations: Giving limited to San Francisco, CA. No grants to individuals, or for annual campaigns, emergency funds, deficit financing, building or endowment funds, land acquisition, renovations, research, publications, or conferences; no loans.
Publications: Annual report, application guidelines, informational brochure, program policy statement.
Application information:
Initial approach: Letter or telephone
Copies of proposal: 6
Deadline(s): Submit proposal 3 weeks prior to board meeting; no set deadline
Board meeting date(s): January, March, June, September, and November
Final notification: 1 week after board meeting
Write: Lawrence I. Kramer, Jr., Executive Director
Officers: Benson B. Roe, M.D., President; David Wisnom, Jr., Vice-President; Philip F. Spalding, Secretary-Treasurer; Lawrence I. Kramer, Jr., Executive Director.
Trustees: Edmond S. Gillette, Jr., Diana Potter Wolfensperger.
Number of staff: 1 part-time professional.
Employer Identification Number: 941170404

269
Lytel (Bertha Russ) Foundation ▼
P.O. Box 893
Ferndale 95536   (707) 786-4682

Established in 1974 in California.
Donor(s): Bertha Russ Lytel,† L.D. O'Rourke.†
Financial data: (yr. ended 9/30/84): Assets,
$10,141,940 (M); expenditures, $545,334,
including $437,489 for 31 grants (high:
$100,000; low: $1,500).
Purpose and activities: Local giving, with
emphasis on social agencies for the aged and
handicapped, and for local civic and cultural
programs and agricultural and nursing
scholarships.
Types of support awarded: Operating
budgets, continuing support, seed money,
building funds, equipment, scholarship funds,
continuing support.
Limitations: Giving limited to Humboldt
County, CA. No grants to individuals, or for
annual campaigns, emergency or endowment
funds, deficit financing, land acquisition,
renovations, matching gifts, research,
demonstration projects, or publications; no
loans.
Publications: Application guidelines, 990-PF.
Application information: Application form
required.
    Initial approach: Letter
    Copies of proposal: 8
    Deadline(s): 1st Thursday of each month
    Board meeting date(s): Monthly
    Final notification: 30 to 60 days
    Write: George Hindley, Manager
Officers and Directors: Harris R. Connick,*
President; Charles M. Lawrence,* Vice-
President; James K. Morrison,* Secretary;
George Hindley, Manager.
Directors:* Carl Carlson, Clarence Crane, Jr.,
Rex L. McBride, Doris Nairne.
Number of staff: 1 part-time professional.
Employer Identification Number: 942271250

270
MacKenzie Foundation, The
c/o Lloyds Bank of California
595 East Colorado Blvd.
Pasadena 91101

Established about 1978 in California.
Donor(s): Sophia MacKenzie.†
Financial data: (yr. ended 12/31/82): Assets,
$4,748,934 (M); expenditures, $323,626,
including $276,000 for 10 grants (high:
$36,000; low: $6,500).
Purpose and activities: The principal purpose
of the foundation is to make grants for the
benefit of students enrolled in medical schools
located in the state of California.
Limitations: Giving limited to CA.
Trustees: H. Vernon Blankenbaker, Leland J.
Hunnicutt, Philip D. Irwin, Lloyds Bank
California.
Employer Identification Number: 956588350

271
Mahony (Patrick) Charitable Trust ¤
c/o Security Pacific National Bank
P.O. Box 3189, Terminal Annex
Los Angeles 90051

Established in 1981 in California.
Donor(s): Patrick Mahoney.†
Financial data: (yr. ended 6/30/83): Assets,
$1,967,592 (M); gifts received, $243,860;
expenditures, $340,312, including $316,391
for 1 grant.
Purpose and activities: First year of operation
in 1981-82; giving solely to a social science
institute in 1983.
Trustees: Robert Pearson, Security Pacific
National Bank.
Employer Identification Number: 953507273

272
Marini Family Trust ¤
c/o Trust Dept., 9250 VIF
P.O. Box 37000
San Francisco 94137

Trust established about 1970 in California.
Financial data: (yr. ended 4/30/83): Assets,
$2,443,139 (M); expenditures, $196,259,
including $178,500 for 13 grants (high:
$40,000; low: $500).
Purpose and activities: Primarily local giving
for Catholic church support, education, and
social services.
Limitations: Giving primarily in the San
Francisco Bay, CA, area.
Trustee: Bank of America.
Employer Identification Number: 946073636

273
Marshburn Foundation, The ¤
1201 S. Beach Blvd., Suite 105
La Habra 90631

Trust established in 1961 in California.
Financial data: (yr. ended 10/31/83): Assets,
$663,716 (M); gifts received, $2,000;
expenditures, $244,051, including $238,250
for 18 grants (high: $100,000; low: $200).
Purpose and activities: Primarily local giving
for Protestant church support and higher
education.
Limitations: Giving primarily in CA.
Trustees: F.K. Marshburn, L.C. Marshburn.
Employer Identification Number: 956049100

274
Martin (Della) Foundation ¤
c/o Sheppard, Mullin, Richter & Hampton
333 South Hope St., 48th Fl.
Los Angeles 90017   (213) 620-1780

Trust established in 1973 in California.
Donor(s): Della Martin.†
Financial data: (yr. ended 12/31/83): Assets,
$2,838,743 (M); gifts received, $83,000;
expenditures, $100,788, including $67,215 for
3 grants (high: $33,715; low: $15,000).
Purpose and activities: To advance the study
and discovery of cures for all forms of mental
illness primarily through grants for research to
institutions in southern California.
Types of support awarded: Research,
endowment funds.
Limitations: Giving primarily in southern CA.
No grants to individuals or for general support,
capital funds, scholarships, fellowships, or
matching gifts; no loans.
Application information:
    Initial approach: Letter
    Copies of proposal: 7
    Deadline(s): None
    Board meeting date(s): June and December
    Write: Laurence K. Gould, Jr.
Trustees: Frank V. Cahouet, Warren C.
Cordner, Edward J. Flynn, Edward Mills,
Thomas R. Sheppard, Frank Simpson, III.
Number of staff: None.
Employer Identification Number: 237444954

275
Mattel Foundation ▼
5150 Rosecrans Ave.
Hawthorne 90250   (213) 978-5150

Foundation established in 1978 in California.
Donor(s): Mattel, Inc.
Financial data: (yr. ended 1/28/84): Assets,
$611,039 (M); expenditures, $157,404,
including $134,405 for 31 grants (high:
$21,000; low: $375; average: $500-$2,500)
and $21,000 for 93 employee matching gifts.
Purpose and activities: Grants largely for care
and special education of children and the
handicapped in areas of company operations,
primarily in California; support also for national
programs and for employee matching gifts.
Types of support awarded: Operating
budgets, seed money, employee matching gifts,
special projects.
Limitations: Giving limited to areas of
company operations, primarily CA. No support
for religious, fraternal, athletic, social, veterans,
or labor organizations; programs receiving
substantial financial support from federal, state,
or local government agencies; or elementary or
secondary schools. No grants to individuals, or
for capital or endowment funds, equipment,
land acquisition, renovation projects, research,
fundraising activities, or courtesy advertising;
no loans.
Publications: Application guidelines.
Application information:
    Initial approach: Full proposal
    Copies of proposal: 1
    Deadline(s): April 1 and October 1
    Board meeting date(s): June and December
    Final notification: 3 months
    Write: Deanna M. Xavier, Vice-President
Officers: Spencer C. Boise,* President; Robert
E. Anderson,* Deanna M. Xavier, Vice-
Presidents; Timothy P. Reames, Secretary; Ben
J. Little, Treasurer.
Directors:* Roger G. Kennedy, Chairman;
Richard J. Riordan.
Number of staff: 1 part-time professional; 1
part-time support.
Employer Identification Number: 953263647

276
May (Wilbur D.) Foundation ♯
10738 Pico Blvd.
Los Angeles 90064   (213) 475-3501

Incorporated in 1951 in California.
Donor(s): Wilbur D. May.
Financial data: (yr. ended 5/31/83): Assets, $14,956,119 (M); gifts received, $13,026,708; expenditures, $159,106, including $145,050 for 23 grants (high: $25,000; low: $50).
Purpose and activities: General purposes; grants largely for hospitals and medical research, a university, a community fund, and youth agencies in Nevada and California.
Limitations: Giving primarily in CA and NV.
Officers: David May, II, Chairman and President; Aaron Clark, Arthur J. Crowley, Vice-Presidents.
Employer Identification Number: 956038298

277
Mayer (The Louis B.) Foundation ▼
9441 Wilshire Blvd., Suite 616
Beverly Hills 90212   (213) 274-5126

Trust established in 1947 in California.
Donor(s): Louis B. Mayer.†
Financial data: (yr. ended 12/31/82): Assets, $8,057,742 (M); expenditures, $867,448, including $671,508 for 93 grants (high: $50,000; low: $50; average: $500-$25,000).
Purpose and activities: Broad purposes; primarily local giving for medical education and research; higher education, including college film studies programs; and community services and film organizations, particularly historical.
Types of support awarded: Operating budgets, building funds, equipment, research, internships, scholarship funds, fellowships, matching funds, continuing support.
Limitations: Giving primarily in CA; support also for some East Coast colleges and universities. No support for independent film projects. No grants to individuals or for endowment funds; no loans.
Publications: 990-PF.
Application information:
  Initial approach: Letter, full proposal, or telephone
  Copies of proposal: 1
  Deadline(s): January 31 and September 30
  Board meeting date(s): February and October
  Final notification: 2 to 3 weeks after board meeting
  Write: Daniel Mayer Selznick, President
Officers and Trustees: Daniel Mayer Selznick, President; Irene Mayer Selznick, Vice-President; Peter Davis, Secretary; Yvonne Ramus Lenart, Treasurer; Vanessa Reis, Executive Assistant.
Number of staff: 2 full-time professional.
Employer Identification Number: 952232340

278
Mayr (George Henry) Trust ♯
c/o Wells Fargo Bank
P.O. Box 44002
San Francisco 94144

Trust established in 1949 in California.
Donor(s): George Henry Mayr.†

Financial data: (yr. ended 7/31/83): Assets, $5,602,236 (M); expenditures, $412,340, including $349,125 for 34 grants (high: $25,000; low: $2,625).
Purpose and activities: Grants to California educational institutions for scholarships to students resident in California for study principally in the fields of chemistry, chemical and electrical engineering, mechanics, and dentistry.
Types of support awarded: Scholarship funds.
Limitations: Giving primarily in CA. No support for medical education other than dentistry. No grants to individuals.
Advisors: Milo W. Bekins, Brian D. Crahan, Richard Daum.
Trustee: Wells Fargo Bank.
Employer Identification Number: 956062009

279
MCA Foundation Ltd. ♯
100 Universal City Plaza
Universal City 91608

Incorporated in 1956 in California.
Donor(s): MCA Inc.
Financial data: (yr. ended 12/31/82): Assets, $4,774,381 (M); gifts received, $134,967; expenditures, $724,850, including $714,215 for 197 grants (high: $102,000; low: $50).
Purpose and activities: Broad purposes with grants largely for cultural programs, including film and television, higher education, child welfare and youth agencies, and health and medical research organizations.
Officers: Sidney J. Sheinberg,* President; Thomas Wertheimer,* Vice-President; Michael Samuel, Secretary; Ruth S. Cogan,* Treasurer.
Directors:* Lew R. Wasserman.
Employer Identification Number: 136096061

280
McAlister (The Harold) Charitable Foundation ▼
4801 Wilshire Blvd., Suite 232
Los Angeles 90010   (213) 937-0927

Incorporated in 1959 in California.
Donor(s): Harold McAlister.†
Financial data: (yr. ended 5/31/83): Assets, $14,788,177 (M); expenditures, $959,730, including $923,912 for 59 grants (high: $200,000; low: $12; average: $500-$25,000).
Purpose and activities: Local giving, with emphasis on hospitals and social agencies.
Limitations: Giving primarily in Los Angeles, CA. No grants to individuals.
Application information: Applications for grants not invited.
  Board meeting date(s): May and December
Officers: Hobart S. McAlister,* President; Fern Smith McAlister,* Vice-President; Clara D. Nelli, Secretary and Treasurer.
Trustees:* David B. Heyler, Jr., Soni McAlister.
Number of staff: None.
Employer Identification Number: 956050036

281
McBean (The Atholl) Foundation ♯
c/o Main Hurdman
4 Embarcadero Center, Suite 400
San Francisco 94111

Incorporated in 1955 in California.
Donor(s): Atholl McBean.†
Financial data: (yr. ended 12/31/83): Assets, $2,740,717 (M); gifts received, $236,124; expenditures, $133,123, including $106,000 for 3 grants (high: $100,000; low: $1,000).
Purpose and activities: Broad purposes; primarily local giving, with emphasis on hospitals, higher and secondary education, and cultural organizations.
Limitations: Giving primarily in CA. No grants to individuals, or for endowment funds, research, scholarships, or fellowships; no loans.
Application information:
  Initial approach: Letter
  Copies of proposal: 1
  Board meeting date(s): December and as required
  Write: Peter McBean, President
Officers and Directors: Peter McBean, President; George T. Cronin, Vice-President; Ralph L. Preston, Secretary-Treasurer; R. Gwen Follis, Edith McBean, Mrs. Peter McBean.
Employer Identification Number: 946062239

282
McCallum Desert Foundation ♯
101 North Palm Canyon Dr.
P.O. Box 1507
Palm Springs 92262
Application address: c/o Bank of America NT & SA, Trust Dept., P.O. Box 2744, Palm Springs, CA 92263; Tel.: (619) 325-0011

Established in 1966.
Financial data: (yr. ended 2/28/83): Assets, $2,381,711 (M); expenditures, $485,641, including $430,746 for 11 grants (high: $250,000; low: $300).
Purpose and activities: Support primarily for a local hospital; grants also for youth agencies and conservation.
Limitations: Giving limited to the Palm Springs, CA, area. No grants to individuals.
Publications: Application guidelines.
Application information: Application form required.
  Deadline(s): Prior to board meetings
Director-Trustees: Robert G. Bernard, Fred G. Ingram.
Trustees: Leon W. Parma, Bank of America.
Employer Identification Number: 953175567

283
McKesson Foundation, Inc. ▼
One Post St.
San Francisco 94104   (415) 983-8673

Incorporated in 1943 in Florida.
Donor(s): Foremost-McKesson, Inc.

Financial data: (yr. ended 3/31/85): Assets, $4,250,000 (M); expenditures, $1,400,000, including $1,320,000 for 200 grants (high: $50,000; low: $1,500; average: $5,000-$10,000) and $75,000 for 250 employee matching gifts.
Purpose and activities: Charitable purposes; primarily local giving to programs for junior high school students, and emergency services such as food and shelter; limited support for other educational, civic, cultural, and human service programs.
Types of support awarded: Continuing support, emergency funds, employee matching gifts, fellowships, matching funds, operating budgets, seed money, employee related scholarships.
Limitations: Giving primarily in San Francisco, CA. No support for religious organizations or political groups. No grants to individuals, or for endowment funds, advertising, or capital fund drives; no loans.
Publications: Annual report, application guidelines.
Application information:
Initial approach: Letter
Copies of proposal: 1
Deadline(s): Submit initial letter preferably between April and October; submit full proposal upon request
Board meeting date(s): Bimonthly beginning in April
Write: Marcia M. Argyris, President
Officers: Marcia M. Argyris, President; James S. Cohune,* Vice-President; Dena J. Goldberg, Secretary; Garrett A. Scholz, Treasurer.
Trustees:* James I. Johnston, Marvin L. Krasnansky, David L. Ringler.
Number of staff: 1 full-time professional; 1 part-time professional; 1 full-time support; 1 part-time support.
Employer Identification Number: 596144455

284
Mead (Giles W. and Elise G.) Foundation
433 North. Camden Dr., Suite 1000
Beverly Hills 90210   (213) 859-9645

Incorporated in 1961 in California.
Donor(s): Elise G. Mead.†
Financial data: (yr. ended 10/31/83): Assets, $7,066,211 (M); expenditures, $692,211, including $608,296 for 68 grants (high: $35,000; low: $100; average: $1,000-$10,000).
Purpose and activities: Primarily local giving, with emphasis on the arts, including museums and the performing arts; higher and secondary education; and the natural and medical sciences.
Types of support awarded: Seed money, land acquisition, endowment funds, research, scholarship funds, matching funds.
Limitations: Giving primarily in CA. No grants to individuals, or for general operating expenses; no loans.
Application information:
Initial approach: Letter
Copies of proposal: 10
Deadline(s): None
Board meeting date(s): January, and usually in May or June, and September

Final notification: 2 months
Write: Myrna L. Patrick, Executive Secretary
Officers and Directors: Florence M. Benjamin, President; Daniel E. McArthur, George C. Silzer, Jr., Vice-Presidents; Giles W. Mead, Jr., Secretary; Calder M. Mackay, Treasurer; Stafford R. Grady, Katherine Cone Keck, Jane W. Mead.
Number of staff: 1.
Employer Identification Number: 956040921

285
Menlo Foundation ⌐
c/o Sam Menlo
501 S. Fairfax Ave.
Los Angeles 90036

Established in 1978.
Donor(s): Sam Menlo, Vera Menlo.
Financial data: (yr. ended 11/30/83): Assets, $960,815 (M); gifts received, $625,000; expenditures, $587,391, including $585,000 for 33 grants (high: $40,000; low: $10,000).
Purpose and activities: Giving to Jewish welfare funds and educational institutions, and for temple support.
Trustees: Judith Menlo, Sam Menlo, Vera Menlo.
Employer Identification Number: 953388159

286
Merry Mary Charitable Foundation, Inc. ⌐
13809 South Figueroa St.
Los Angeles 90061   (213) 770-1571

Incorporated in 1954 in California.
Donor(s): Merry Mary Fabrics, Inc., Teddi of California, Inc., South Sea Imports, Inc.
Financial data: (yr. ended 3/31/83): Assets, $546,787 (M); gifts received, $145,000; expenditures, $435,641, including $427,528 for 40 grants (high: $236,100; low: $100).
Purpose and activities: Grants mainly for Jewish welfare funds and temple support, higher education in Israel, and hospitals.
Application information:
Initial approach: Letter
Write: Albert Mass, Vice-President
Officers: Stephen Meadow, President; Albert Mass, Vice-President; Samuel Krane, Secretary.
Employer Identification Number: 953263582

287
Meyer (Milton and Sophie) Fund ⌐
c/o Crocker National Bank, Trust Dept.
P.O. Box 38002
San Francisco 94138

Established in 1979.
Donor(s): Milton Meyer.†
Financial data: (yr. ended 12/31/83): Assets, $1,553,927 (M); expenditures, $155,288, including $105,500 for 23 grants (high: $15,000; low: $1,000).
Purpose and activities: Grants primarily for Jewish welfare and educational funds and temple support.
Trustees: Jefferson E. Peyser, Crocker National Bank.
Employer Identification Number: 946480997

288
Mitchell (Edward D. and Anna) Family Foundation ⌐
3700 Wilshire Blvd.
Los Angeles 90010

Established in 1953.
Financial data: (yr. ended 12/31/82): Assets, $1,604,037 (M); gifts received, $9,696; expenditures, $91,635, including $88,455 for 37 grants (high: $35,000; low: $50).
Purpose and activities: Giving primarily for Jewish welfare funds and a community fund.
Officers and Directors: Edward D. Mitchell, President; Kayla Mitchell, Vice-President; Joseph N. Mitchell, Secretary-Treasurer.
Employer Identification Number: 956027618

289
Monterey County, Community Foundation for
(formerly Monterey Peninsula Foundation)
420 Pacific St.
Monterey 93940   (408) 375-9712

Community foundation incorporated in 1945 in California.
Financial data: (yr. ended 12/31/84): Assets, $2,600,000 (M); gifts received, $1,520,000; expenditures, $520,000, including $71,493 for 55 grants (high: $5,000; low: $150; average: $2,000-$5,000), $2,000 for 2 grants to individuals and $22,500 for 3 loans.
Purpose and activities: Primarily local giving for social services, education, including annual awards to teachers and scholarships to high school students, the environment, the arts, health, and other charitable purposes.
Types of support awarded: Operating budgets, continuing support, seed money, emergency funds, building funds, equipment, land acquisition, matching funds, grants to individuals, student aid, loans, special projects, research, conferences and seminars, consulting services, technical assistance, program-related investments.
Limitations: Giving primarily in Monterey County, CA. No grants for annual campaigns, deficit financing, general endowments, employee matching gifts, or publications.
Publications: Annual report, 990-PF, application guidelines, informational brochure, newsletter.
Application information:
Initial approach: Telephone or letter
Copies of proposal: 1
Deadline(s): March 30, June 30, September 30, and December 31
Board meeting date(s): 3rd Tuesday of every month
Final notification: 1 day after each quarterly meeting
Write: Todd Lueders, Executive Director
Director: Todd Lueders, Executive Director.
Board of Governors: Joseph A. Lee, President; Will Shaw, Vice-President.
Number of staff: 2 full-time professional; 2 part-time support.
Employer Identification Number: 941615897

290
Mosher (Samuel B.) Foundation
3278 Loma Riviera Dr.
San Diego 92110   (714) 226-6122

Incorporated in 1951 in California.
Donor(s): Samuel B. Mosher,† Goodwin J. Pelissero, Deborah S. Pelissero.
Financial data: (yr. ended 8/31/83): Assets, $3,133,082 (M); expenditures, $453,503, including $436,000 for 14 grants (high: $325,000; low: $1,000).
Purpose and activities: Broad purposes; giving primarily in Arizona and California, with emphasis on support for capital or building funds; grants mainly for child welfare and church support, higher education, schools, health care, and youth agencies.
Types of support awarded: Building funds.
Limitations: Giving primarily in AZ and CA. No grants to individuals, operating support, endowment funds, scholarships and fellowships, general purposes, or matching gifts; no loans.
Application information:
  Initial approach: Full proposal
  Copies of proposal: 1
  Deadline(s): Submit proposal preferably in May; application deadline June 30
  Board meeting date(s): Quarterly
  Write: Margaret C. Mosher, President
Officers and Trustees:* Margaret C. Mosher,* President; Robert R. Fredrickson, Secretary and Treasurer.
Employer Identification Number: 956037266

291
Muller (Frank), Sr. Foundation ¤
c/o Norby, Sutherland & Muller, No. 318
7080 Hollywood Blvd.
Hollywood 90028

Established in 1965 in California.
Donor(s): Frank Muller.
Financial data: (yr. ended 7/31/83): Assets, $4,353,046 (M); expenditures, $259,451, including $194,715 for 113 grants (high: $25,000; low: $25).
Purpose and activities: Primarily local giving, with emphasis on higher and secondary education, social agencies, Roman Catholic church support, hospitals, and cultural programs.
Limitations: Giving primarily in CA.
Trustees: James Muller, John Muller, T. Muller, Walter Muller, N.M. Thompson, R.A. Vilmure.
Employer Identification Number: 956121774

292
Munger (Alfred C.) Foundation ¤
c/o Richard D. Esbenshade
612 South Flower St., Fifth Fl.
Los Angeles 90017

Established in 1965 in California.
Donor(s): Charles T. Munger, Nancy B. Munger.
Financial data: (yr. ended 11/30/83): Assets, $4,333,521 (M); gifts received, $16,280; expenditures, $198,789, including $197,383 for 39 grants (high: $60,500; low: $100).
Purpose and activities: Grants primarily for higher and secondary education, a family planning and population control institute, and health agencies; giving also for Protestant religious organizations.
Officers and Trustees: Charles T. Munger, President; Richard D. Esbenshade, Vice-President and Secretary; Nancy B. Munger, Treasurer.
Employer Identification Number: 952462103

293
Murdy Foundation ¤
1450 N. Tustin Ave., Suite 200
Santa Ana 92701

Established in 1958.
Donor(s): John A. Murdy, Jr., Norma Murdy Trust B.
Financial data: (yr. ended 12/31/83): Assets, $2,182,547 (M); expenditures, $159,902, including $152,550 for 16 grants (high: $99,000; low: $100).
Purpose and activities: Primarily local giving, with emphasis on higher education and Protestant church support; support also for cultural programs, social agencies, and conservation.
Limitations: Giving primarily in CA.
Officers: George A. Trotter, Jr., President; John A. Murdy III, Vice-President; Maxine Trotter, Secretary; John A. Murdy, Jr., Treasurer.
Employer Identification Number: 956082270

294
Murphey (Lluella Morey) Foundation ¤
c/o Harold S. Voegelin
333 South Grand Ave., 37th Fl.
Los Angeles 90071

Established in 1967.
Donor(s): Lluella Morey Murphey.†
Financial data: (yr. ended 11/30/83): Assets, $2,328,245 (M); expenditures, $157,161, including $107,965 for 31 grants (high: $12,000; low: $500).
Purpose and activities: Primarily local giving, with emphasis on higher and secondary education, youth programs, health, and cultural programs.
Types of support awarded: General purposes, building funds, equipment.
Limitations: Giving primarily in CA.
Trustees: Alfred B. Hastings, Jr., James A. Schlinger, Harold S. Voegelin.
Employer Identification Number: 956152669

295
Murphy (Dan) Foundation ▼
3701 Wilshire Blvd., Rm. 320
Los Angeles 90010   (213) 384-3036
Mailing address: P.O. Box 76026, Los Angeles, CA 90076

Incorporated in 1957 in California.
Donor(s): Mrs. Bernadine Murphy Donohue.†

Financial data: (yr. ended 12/31/82): Assets, $96,196,510 (M); gifts received, $13,800; expenditures, $3,203,134, including $3,003,500 for 48 grants (high: $2,225,000; low: $1,000).
Purpose and activities: Primarily local giving, with emphasis on support of activities and charities of Roman Catholic Church Archdiocese of Los Angeles, including religious orders, colleges and schools, social service agencies, and medical institutions.
Types of support awarded: Continuing support, special projects.
Limitations: Giving primarily in Los Angeles, CA.
Publications: Program policy statement, application guidelines.
Application information: Due to ongoing commitments, the foundation is rarely able to consider unsolicited proposals.
  Initial approach: Letter
  Deadline(s): March 1, June 1, September 1, and December 1
  Board meeting date(s): As needed
  Write: Daniel J. Donohue, President
Officers and Trustees: Daniel J. Donohue, President; Joseph D. Peeler, Vice-President; Richard A. Grant, Jr., Secretary-Treasurer; Rosemary E. Donohue, Msgr. Benjamin G. Hawkes, Oscar T. Lawler.
Employer Identification Number: 956046963

296
Newhall (The Henry Mayo) Foundation
c/o Main Hurdman
Four Embarcadero Center, Suite 400
San Francisco 94111

Incorporated in 1963 in California.
Donor(s): The Newhall Land and Farming Company.
Financial data: (yr. ended 12/31/82): Assets, $3,795,426 (M); expenditures, $251,506, including $217,800 for 30 grants (high: $100,000; low: $150).
Purpose and activities: Broad purposes; primarily local giving, "within the geographic areas that are associated with the career of Henry Mayo Newhall"; support for the Henry Mayo Newhall Hospital and secondary and agricultural education.
Limitations: Giving primarily in CA. No grants to individuals.
Officers: Jane Newhall,* President; Peter McBean,* Henry Kleiser Newhall,* Vice-Presidents; Ralph L. Preston, Secretary.
Directors:* Edith McBean, George Newhall, Scott Newhall, Walter Scott Newhall, Jr., Edwin Newhall Woods.
Employer Identification Number: 946073084

297
Newman (Calvin M. and Racquel H.) Charitable Trust ¤
27500 La Vida Real
Los Altos Hills 94022

Established in 1973.

Financial data: (yr. ended 12/31/83): Assets, $1,619,239 (M); expenditures, $130,480, including $97,972 for 46 grants (high: $40,000; low: $13).
Purpose and activities: Grants primarily for Jewish welfare funds and religious education.
Trustee: Racquel H. Newman.
Employer Identification Number: 476081135

298
Norman (Andrew) Foundation
10960 Wilshire Blvd., Suite 820
Los Angeles 90024   (213) 879-1430

Incorporated in 1958 in California.
Donor(s): Andrew Norman.†
Financial data: (yr. ended 6/30/83): Assets, $8,500,000 (M); expenditures, $530,000, including $450,000 for 15 grants (high: $100,000; low: $500).
Purpose and activities: Broad purposes; primarily local giving, with emphasis on minority group development, environment, education, humanities, arts and community funds; strong interest in seed money.
Types of support awarded: Seed money, special projects, research, publications, loans, matching funds.
Limitations: Giving primarily in CA, with emphasis on the Los Angeles area. No grants to individuals, or for endowment funds, scholarships or fellowships.
Application information: Unsolicited grant requests not accepted.
  Board meeting date(s): May and as required
  Write: Dan Olincy, Secretary-Treasurer
Officers and Trustees: Virginia G. Olincy, President; Bernice G. Kranson, Vice-President; Dan Olincy, Secretary-Treasurer and Legal Counsel.
Number of staff: None.
Employer Identification Number: 953433781

299
Norris (The Kenneth T. and Eileen L.) Foundation ▼
1900 East Ocean Blvd., Suite 1806
Long Beach 90802   (213) 435-8441

Trust established in 1963 in California.
Donor(s): Kenneth T. Norris,† Eileen L. Norris.
Financial data: (yr. ended 11/30/83): Assets, $59,011,879 (M); expenditures, $2,727,777, including $2,406,980 for 193 grants (high: $507,700; low: $100; average: $500-$20,000).
Purpose and activities: Broad purposes; giving limited to Los Angeles County, with emphasis on hospitals, health agencies, higher education, medical research, cultural institutions, and social services.
Types of support awarded: Building funds, equipment, research, scholarship funds, continuing support.
Limitations: Giving limited to Los Angeles County, CA. No grants to individuals; no loans.
Application information:
  Initial approach: Letter
  Copies of proposal: 1
  Deadline(s): None
  Board meeting date(s): As required

  Write: Harry L. Stevens, Jr., Executive Director
Officer and Trustees: Harry L. Stevens, Jr., Executive Director; William G. Corey, Eileen L. Norris, Harlyne J. Norris, Kenneth T. Norris, Jr.
Number of staff: 1 part-time professional; 3 part-time support.
Employer Identification Number: 956080374

300
Nosutch Foundation of California ⌐
c/o T.F.P.M. & K.
1849 Sawtelle Blvd., Suite 500
Los Angeles 90025

Established in 1965.
Financial data: (yr. ended 5/31/83): Assets, $10,235 (M); gifts received, $180,000; expenditures, $176,657, including $176,272 for 102 grants (high: $25,000; low: $60).
Purpose and activities: Giving primarily for the performing arts, especially dance and theater, higher education, and social services.
Trustees: Irving Axelrad, Edward Traubner.
Employer Identification Number: 510175314

301
Oakland Scottish Rite Scaife and Oakland Scottish Rite Scholarship Foundations
1547 Lakeside Dr.
Oakland 94612   (415) 451-1906

Incorporated in 1927 in California.
Donor(s): Irene Jones,† Walter B. Scaife,† S. Sidney Morton.
Financial data: (yr. ended 5/31/83): Assets, $2,400,000 (M); gifts received, $529,900; expenditures, $164,200, including $144,000 for 144 grants to individuals (average: $1,200).
Purpose and activities: Scholarships for graduates of local public high schools only.
Types of support awarded: Student aid.
Limitations: Giving limited to northern CA.
Publications: Informational brochure, program policy statement, application guidelines.
Application information: Application form required.
  Initial approach: Letter
  Copies of proposal: 1
  Deadline(s): Submit proposal preferably in March; deadline March 31
  Board meeting date(s): January, March, May, and August
  Final notification: One month
  Write: Donald H. Madsen, Secretary
Officers and Trustees: Elmer Ross, President; Dale I. Stoops, Vice-President; Donald H. Madsen, Secretary; Alden W. Badal, George Bliss, Paul A. Brom, Elmer E. Ross, Norman Shapiro, Zook Sutton, David S. Tucker, Sr., George Vukasin, Wallace E. York.
Number of staff: 1 part-time professional; 1 part-time support.
Employer Identification Number: 941540333

302
Occidental Petroleum Charitable Foundation, Inc. ⌐
10889 Wilshire Blvd.
Los Angeles 90024   (213) 879-1700

Incorporated in 1959 in New York.
Donor(s): Occidental Petroleum Corporation.
Financial data: (yr. ended 12/31/83): Assets, $145,708 (M); expenditures, $293,920, including $154,285 for 17 grants (high: $60,000) and $137,520 for 347 employee matching gifts.
Purpose and activities: General purposes; grants primarily for higher education, including an employee matching-gifts program.
Types of support awarded: Employee matching gifts.
Limitations: No grants to individuals.
Publications: Application guidelines.
Application information:
  Initial approach: Full proposal
  Copies of proposal: 1
  Board meeting date(s): March, June, September, and December
  Write: Mrs. Evelyn S. Wong, Assistant Secretary
Officers: Arthur Groman, President; Morrie A. Moss, Vice-President; Paul C. Hebner, Secretary-Treasurer.
Directors: A. Robert Abboud, Armand Hammer, Zoltan Merszei.
Employer Identification Number: 166052784

303
Odell (Robert Stewart) and Helen Pfeiffer Odell Fund
49 Geary St., Rm. 244
San Francisco 94102   (415) 391-0292

Established in 1967 in California.
Donor(s): Robert Stewart Odell,† Helen Pfeiffer Odell.
Financial data: (yr. ended 12/31/83): Assets, $13,242,240 (M); expenditures, $614,834, including $480,190 for 67 grants (high: $12,000; low: $250).
Purpose and activities: Primarily local giving, with emphasis on higher education, youth agencies, the handicapped, and child welfare.
Limitations: Giving primarily in the San Francisco Bay Area, CA. No grants to individuals.
Application information:
  Initial approach: Proposal
  Copies of proposal: 1
  Deadline(s): April 15 through November 15
  Board meeting date(s): Monthly
Trustees: John P. Collins, Paul B. Fay, Jr., Wells Fargo Bank.
Employer Identification Number: 946132116

304
Orleton Trust Fund ▼ ⌐
1777 Borel Place, Suite 306
San Mateo 94402   (415) 345-2818
Additional office: c/o Mrs. Anne Johnston Greene, 1101 Runnymede Rd., Dayton, OH 45419

Trust established in 1944 in Ohio.

Donor(s): Miss Mary E. Johnston.†
Financial data: (yr. ended 12/31/82): Assets, $6,470,974 (M); expenditures, $504,059, including $467,170 for 131 grants (high: $50,000; low: $25; average: $1,000-$10,000).
Purpose and activities: Broad purposes; support for higher and secondary education, cultural programs, and Protestant churches, religious associations, and welfare funds; grants also for community funds, population control, youth and social agencies, and ecology.
Types of support awarded: Scholarship funds, building funds, matching funds, annual campaigns, seed money, continuing support.
Limitations: Giving primarily in Dayton, OH, and San Mateo County, CA; educational grants more widely distributed. No grants to individuals.
Application information:
Initial approach: Letter
Copies of proposal: 1
Deadline(s): None
Board meeting date(s): As required
Final notification: 1 month
Write: Mrs. Jean Sawyer Weaver, Trustee
Trustees: Anne Johnston Greene, Jean Sawyer Weaver.
Employer Identification Number: 316024543

305
Ostrow (Seniel and Dorothy)
Foundation ⌑
c/o S. Sanford Ezralow & Co.
9171 Wilshire Blvd., Suite 441
Beverly Hills 90210

Trust established in 1961 in California.
Donor(s): Seniel Ostrow.
Financial data: (yr. ended 7/31/82): Assets, $695,533 (M); gifts received, $549,155; expenditures, $126,515, including $124,823 for 92 grants (high: $16,000; low: $50).
Purpose and activities: Giving primarily for social welfare, higher education, cultural programs, and civic and public affairs.
Trustees: Laurie Ostrow, Seniel Ostrow, Simon Shankin.
Employer Identification Number: 956029169

306
Oxnard Foundation
505 Sansome St., Suite 1001
San Francisco 94111   (415) 981-3455

Established in 1973.
Donor(s): Thomas Thornton Oxnard.†
Financial data: (yr. ended 12/31/82): Assets, $3,411,042 (M); expenditures, $231,520, including $180,000 for 6 grants (high: $40,000; low: $25,000).
Purpose and activities: Giving primarily in four states for medical research, with emphasis on cancer and surgical research.
Types of support awarded: Matching funds, professorships, research.
Limitations: Giving primarily in NY, TX, NM, and northern CA. No grants to individuals, or for general support, capital funds, endowments, scholarships, fellowships, special projects, publications, or conferences; no loans.
Application information:

Initial approach: Letter
Deadline(s): February 15
Board meeting date(s): Quarterly
Final notification: 3 months
Write: Stephen W. Veitch, President
Officer and Directors: Stephen W. Veitch, President; Caroline Meade, Fred C. Smith, Charles H. Thieriot.
Employer Identification Number: 237323007

307
Pacific Western Foundation ⌑
8344 E. Florence, Suite E
Downey 90240

Successor to Western Gear Foundation, incorporated in 1953 in California; name changed in 1982.
Donor(s): Western Gear Corporation.
Financial data: (yr. ended 11/30/83): Assets, $3,185,997 (M); expenditures, $272,358, including $236,360 for 51 grants (high: $106,000; low: $25).
Purpose and activities: Broad purposes; primarily local giving for higher and secondary education, Roman Catholic church support, hospitals, and medical research.
Limitations: Giving primarily in CA.
Officers: Charles F. Bannan, President; Joseph T. Nally, Vice-President; M. Patricia Cruden, Secretary; Elmer L. Stone, Treasurer.
Employer Identification Number: 956097360

308
Packard (The David and Lucile)
Foundation ▼
330 Second St.
P.O. Box 1330
Los Altos 94022   (415) 948-7658

Incorporated in 1964 in California.
Donor(s): David Packard, Lucile Packard.
Financial data: (yr. ended 12/31/83): Assets, $96,287,588 (M); gifts received, $46,582,375; expenditures, $3,834,989, including $3,717,167 for 281 grants (high: $75,000; low: $100; average: $10,000) and $10,800 for 1 loan.
Purpose and activities: Broad purposes; primarily local giving, with emphasis on music, education, youth agencies, minorities, handicapped, and child welfare; national and international giving in areas of conservation, ancient studies, film preservation, and population issues.
Types of support awarded: General purposes, building funds, equipment, land acquisition, research, scholarship funds, internships, matching funds, program-related investments, consulting services, technical assistance, loans, operating budgets.
Limitations: Giving primarily in the San Francisco and Monterey Bay, CA areas; some giving also in the Pueblo area of CO. No grants to individuals; generally no grants for endowment funds.
Publications: Annual report, application guidelines.
Application information:
Initial approach: Proposal
Copies of proposal: 1

Deadline(s): January 7, April 7, July 7, and October 7
Board meeting date(s): March, June, September, and December
Final notification: 2 months
Write: Colburn S. Wilbur, Executive Director
Officers: David Packard,* President; Lucile Packard,* Vice-President and Treasurer; David Woodley Packard,* Vice-President; Nathan C. Finch,* Secretary; Colburn S. Wilbur, Executive Director.
Trustees:* Ernest C. Arbuckle, Nancy Packard Burnett, Robert Glaser, M.D., Susan Packard Orr, Julie E. Packard.
Number of staff: 3 full-time professional; 2 part-time professional; 5 full-time support; 2 part-time support.
Employer Identification Number: 946097114

309
Page (George B.) Foundation
(formerly Mission Linen Foundation)
P.O. Drawer MM
Santa Barbara 93102   (805) 963-1841

Established in 1961 in California.
Donor(s): Mission Linen Companies, Montecito Mfg. Co.
Financial data: (yr. ended 12/31/82): Assets, $1,205,067 (M); expenditures, $51,646, including $37,250 for 23 grants (high: $20,000; low: $100; average: $500).
Purpose and activities: Giving mainly for youth and child welfare agencies and two colleges.
Types of support awarded: Operating budgets, continuing support, annual campaigns, seed money, emergency funds, deficit financing, general purposes, special projects.
Limitations: No grants to individuals, or for endowment funds or matching gifts.
Application information:
Initial approach: Letter
Deadline(s): Submit proposal preferably from January through June; deadline June 30
Board meeting date(s): Annually
Final notification: 6 months
Write: John R. Erickson, Trustee
Trustees: George Castagnola, John R. Erickson, Henry W. Logan, George B. Page, Joe Paxton.
Number of staff: None.
Employer Identification Number: 956121985

310
Parker Foundation, The ▼
1200 Prospect St., Suite 575
La Jolla 92037   (619) 456-3038

Trust established in 1971 in California; incorporated in 1975.
Donor(s): Gerald T. Parker,† Inez Grant Parker.†
Financial data: (yr. ended 9/30/84): Assets, $9,644,683 (M); expenditures, $489,031, including $421,834 for 43 grants (high: $55,000; low: $100; average: $2,000-$20,000).

Purpose and activities: Local giving, with equal emphasis on cultural programs, health and welfare, including medical support and research, adult services, and youth agencies; grants also for education and community activities. Giving largely in the form of partial seed money and matching or challenge grants; generally no support that would make an organization dependent on the foundation.

Types of support awarded: Seed money, matching funds, operating budgets, annual campaigns, emergency funds, building funds, equipment, land acquisition, research, program-related investments, continuing support, special projects, publications.

Limitations: Giving limited to San Diego County, CA. No support for sectarian religious purposes. No grants to individuals, or for endowment funds, scholarships, or fellowships; no loans.

Publications: Annual report, program policy statement, application guidelines.

Application information:
Initial approach: Letter
Copies of proposal: 6
Deadline(s): None
Board meeting date(s): Monthly
Final notification: 2 months
Write: Julie K. Denton, Assistant Secretary

Officers and Directors: Kenneth R. Rearwin, President; V. DeWitt Shuck, Vice-President; William E. Beamer, Secretary and Treasurer; John F. Borchers, Roy M. Drew, Judy McDonald.

Number of staff: None.

Employer Identification Number: 510141231

311

Parsons (The Ralph M.) Foundation ▼

1545 Wilshire Blvd., Suite 300
Los Angeles 90017   (213) 483-8030

Incorporated in 1961 in California.

Donor(s): Ralph M. Parsons.†

Financial data: (yr. ended 12/31/83): Assets, $98,817,396 (M); gifts received, $550,055; expenditures, $4,400,292, including $2,903,497 for 70 grants (high: $200,000; low: $900; average: $2,000-$50,000).

Purpose and activities: Broad purposes; local giving (with the exception of support for some higher educational institutions), for higher education, with emphasis on engineering, technology, management, business, law, science and medicine; and for social impact areas, including assistance to children, battered women, and seniors; grants also for cultural and civic projects.

Types of support awarded: Seed money, equipment, matching funds, professorships, internships, scholarship funds, fellowships.

Limitations: Giving limited to the greater Los Angeles, CA, area, with the exception of grants for higher education. No support for sectarian religious purposes. No grants to individuals, or for operating budgets, continuing support, annual campaigns, emergency, building, or endowment funds; land acquisition, research, demonstration projects, publications, exhibits, surveys, or conferences; no loans.

Publications: Annual report, program policy statement, application guidelines.

Application information:
Initial approach: Telephone or letter
Copies of proposal: 1
Deadline(s): None
Board meeting date(s): Bimonthly beginning in February
Final notification: 2 months
Write: Christine Sisley, Program Director

Officers and Directors: Joseph G. Hurley, President; Leroy B. Houghton, Vice-President and Chief Financial Officer; Everett B. Laybourne, Vice-President; Barbara Stokes Dewey, Secretary and Executive Director; Ira J. Blanco, Albert A. Dorskind, Alex Haley, Edgar R. Jackson, Donald R. Wright.

Number of staff: 2 full-time professional; 1 part-time professional; 3 full-time support.

Employer Identification Number: 956085895

312

Parvin (The Albert) Foundation ⌺

10960 Wilshire Blvd., Suite 816
Los Angeles 90024   (213) 478-0342

Incorporated in 1960 in California.

Donor(s): Albert B. Parvin.

Financial data: (yr. ended 12/31/83): Assets, $4,632,119 (M); expenditures, $302,099, including $274,400 for 38 grants (high: $121,000; low: $25).

Purpose and activities: ''... to promote peace, understanding and goodwill among the nations of the world through education, enlightenment and recognition of achievements toward this objective.'' Supports fellowship programs for young men from new and underdeveloped nations for study at Princeton University and University of California at Los Angeles. Grants also to social agencies, for child welfare services, and medical research.

Types of support awarded: General purposes, fellowships.

Application information:
Deadline(s): None
Write: Albert B. Parvin, Vice-President

Officers and Directors: Arthur J. Goldberg, President; Albert B. Parvin, Vice-President; Phyllis Parvin, Secretary; Alan Shulman.

Employer Identification Number: 952158989

313

Pasadena Area Residential Aid A Corp.

P.O. Box 984
Pasadena 91102

Foundation established in 1948 in California.

Financial data: (yr. ended 7/31/84): Assets, $695,813 (M); gifts received, $1,098,016; expenditures, $952,200, including $952,200 for 500 grants (high: $50,000; low: $10).

Purpose and activities: All contributions initiated by donors; grants largely for higher education, Christian welfare funds and church support; support also for youth agencies and community funds.

Application information: Applications for grants not invited.
Board meeting date(s): Annually

Officers and Directors: Joseph D. Messler, President; Cholmondeley Nelson, Vice-President; Robert Fullerton, III, Secretary; James N. Gamble, Treasurer; Robert R. Huffman, George D. Jagels, Mary W. Johnson, Lee G. Paul.

Number of staff: 1 part-time professional.

Employer Identification Number: 952048774

314

Pasadena Foundation

16 North Marengo Ave., Suite 219
Pasadena 91101   (818) 796-2097

Community foundation established in 1953 in California by resolution and declaration of trust.

Donor(s): Louis A. Webb,† Marion L. Webb,† Helen B. Lockett,† Dorothy I. Stewart.†

Financial data: (yr. ended 12/31/83): Assets, $2,259,726 (M); gifts received, $171,017; expenditures, $293,959, including $265,915 for 134 grants (high: $10,000; low: $603; average: $3,000-$5,000).

Purpose and activities: Grants for capital improvements to established local agencies, with emphasis on child welfare, youth agencies, and senior citizen welfare.

Types of support awarded: Building funds, equipment, matching funds.

Limitations: Giving limited to the Pasadena, CA, area. No grants to individuals, or for operating budgets, continuing support, annual campaigns, emergency funds, seed money, deficit financing, land acquisition, endowment funds, research, special projects, publications, conferences, or scholarships and fellowships; no loans.

Publications: Financial statement, application guidelines.

Application information: Application form required.
Initial approach: Letter
Copies of proposal: 1
Deadline(s): Submit proposal preferably from January to June; deadline July
Board meeting date(s): April and December
Final notification: After December meeting
Write: Mrs. John Stephen, Executive Director

Advisory Board: Orrin K. Earl, Jr., Chairman; Charles Cherniss, Vice-Chairman; Mrs. John Stephen, Executive Director, Secretary, and Treasurer; Berneice A. Anglea, James N. Gamble, Robert V. Hubbard, Sr., Albert C. Lowe, Wallace L. Martin, David K. Robinson, Kyhl S. Smeby.

Trustees: Bank of America, Citizens Commercial Trust and Savings Bank, Lloyds Bank California, Security Pacific National Bank, Interstate Bank.

Number of staff: 1 part-time professional.

Employer Identification Number: 956047660

315

Pattiz Family Foundation ⌺

291 South La Cienega Blvd., Rm. 306
Beverly Hills 90211

Foundation established in 1953 in California.

Donor(s): Oscar S. Pattiz.

Financial data: (yr. ended 1/31/83): Assets, $1,327,289 (M); expenditures, $40,854, including $22,641 for 34 grants (high: $10,330; low: $35).
Purpose and activities: Broad purposes; primarily local giving, with emphasis on education and Jewish welfare funds.
Limitations: Giving primarily in CA.
Officers: Henry A. Pattiz, President; Cathy Lee Pattiz, Vice-President; Leona Pattiz, Secretary and Treasurer.
Employer Identification Number: 956029776

316
Pauley (The Edwin W.) Foundation ⌴
10000 Santa Monica Blvd., Suite 200
Los Angeles 90067

Trust established in 1962 in California.
Donor(s): Edwin W. Pauley.
Financial data: (yr. ended 11/30/83): Assets, $2,033,604 (M); expenditures, $71,811, including $68,155 for 9 grants (high: $23,500; low: $300).
Purpose and activities: Primarily local giving, with grants principally for construction programs for cultural and civic organizations, and educational institutions.
Types of support awarded: Building funds.
Limitations: Giving primarily in CA.
Application information:
 Write: William R. Pagen, Trustee
Trustee: William R. Pagen.
Employer Identification Number: 956039872

317
Peery (Richard T.) Foundation ⌴
2560 Mission College Blvd., Suite 101
Sunnyvale 95050

Established in 1977.
Donor(s): Richard T. Peery.
Financial data: (yr. ended 9/30/83): Assets, $2,935,983 (M); gifts received, $854,600; expenditures, $213,414, including $208,368 for 35 grants (high: $121,418; low: $50).
Purpose and activities: Grants largely for Mormon religious organizations; some support for youth and education.
Directors: John Arrillaga, Mildred D. Peery, Richard T. Peery.
Employer Identification Number: 942460894

318
Peninsula Community Foundation ▼
1204 Burlingame Ave.
P.O. Box 627
Burlingame 94011-0627   (415) 342-2477

Community foundation established as a trust in 1964 in California; incorporated about 1982.
Financial data: (yr. ended 12/31/84): Assets, $7,551,154 (M); gifts received, $1,173,937; expenditures, $1,084,441, including $867,456 for 258 grants (high: $67,166; low: $25; average: $5,000-$20,000) and $29,000 for 1 foundation-administered program.

Purpose and activities: To support local cultural, educational, social service, and health programs; interests include youth, environment, elderly, disabled, civic concerns, and recreation; provides counseling services for local fund seekers.
Types of support awarded: Operating budgets, continuing support, seed money, emergency funds, equipment, matching funds, consulting services, technical assistance, internships, scholarship funds, loans, special projects, research, publications, conferences and seminars.
Limitations: Giving limited to San Mateo County and northern Santa Clara County, CA. No grants for endowment funds.
Publications: Annual report, application guidelines, informational brochure, grants list.
Application information:
 Initial approach: Letter
 Copies of proposal: 1
 Deadline(s): None
 Board meeting date(s): Distribution committee meets in January, March, May, July, September, and November
 Final notification: 3 months
 Write: Bill Somerville, Executive Director
Officer: Bill Somerville, Executive Director.
Distribution Committee: Albert J. Horn, Chairman; Marjorie Bolton, T. Jack Foster, Robert J. Koshland, Aubrey Lee.
Trustee Banks: Bank of America, Borel Bank and Trust Company, The Bank of California, California Canadian Bank, Crocker National Bank, First Interstate Bank of California, The Hibernia Bank, Lloyds Bank California, Pacific Union Bank & Trust Company, University National Bank and Trust Company, Wells Fargo Bank.
Number of staff: 1 full-time professional; 1 part-time professional; 2 full-time support.
Employer Identification Number: 942746687

319
Peppers (The Ann) Foundation ⌴
35 South Raymond Ave., Rm. 400
Pasadena 91105   (818) 449-1821

Established in 1959 in California.
Donor(s): Ann Peppers.†
Financial data: (yr. ended 12/31/83): Assets, $3,289,163 (M); expenditures, $266,928, including $232,505 for 54 grants (high: $28,000; low: $500).
Purpose and activities: Primarily local giving with emphasis on small private colleges and community organizations with limited resources for fund raising; support also for activities that benefit young people and enhance their moral, educational and social well-being; and activities for senior citizens.
Limitations: Giving primarily in the Los Angeles, CA, metropolitan area. No grants to individuals or for endowment funds.
Application information:
 Initial approach: Brief letter
 Copies of proposal: 1
 Deadline(s): None
 Board meeting date(s): Quarterly
 Write: A.L. Burford, Jr., Secretary

Officers and Directors: W. Paul Colwell, President; Giles S. Hall, Vice-President; A.L. Burford, Jr., Secretary; Howard O. Wilson, Treasurer.
Employer Identification Number: 952114455

320
Peters (Leon S.) Foundation
4712 N. Van Ness Blvd.
Fresno 93704

Established in 1959 in California.
Donor(s): Leon S. Peters.
Financial data: (yr. ended 11/30/84): Assets, $105,333 (M); gifts received, $100; expenditures, $277,371, including $249,680 for 55 grants (high: $50,150; low: $10).
Purpose and activities: Broad purposes; primarily local giving, with emphasis on community funds, cultural programs, higher education, youth agencies, and hospitals.
Limitations: Giving primarily in CA.
Officers: Alice Peters, President and Secretary-Treasurer; Pete P. Peters, Vice-President.
Employer Identification Number: 946064669

321
Pfaffinger Foundation ▼
Times Mirror Square
Los Angeles 90053   (213) 972-5743

Incorporated in 1936 in California.
Donor(s): Frank X. Pfaffinger.†
Financial data: (yr. ended 12/31/83): Assets, $35,498,279 (M); expenditures, $1,743,792, including $329,579 for 15 grants (high: $100,000; low: $3,700) and $1,047,818 for 295 grants to individuals.
Purpose and activities: Primarily to assist employees and former employees of The Times Mirror Company; limited support for educational and charitable institutions in Los Angeles and Orange counties when funds are available.
Types of support awarded: Grants to individuals.
Limitations: Giving limited to Los Angeles and Orange counties, CA, for educational and charitable institutions. No grants to individuals other than company employees; no scholarships.
Application information: Application form required.
 Initial approach: Letter
 Copies of proposal: 1
 Deadline(s): Submit proposal preferably between July and September; deadline October 1
 Board meeting date(s): December
 Final notification: Within 1 week of receipt
 Write: Robert N. Bills, President
Officers: Robert N. Bills,* President; Lloyd E. Gallagher, Vice-President; Robert C. Lobdell,* Secretary; Joyce M. Fields, Treasurer.
Trustees:* James C. Boswell, Otis Chandler, Robert F. Erburu, Alfred W. Merkel, Charles R. Redmond, William F. Thomas.
Number of staff: 4 full-time professional; 1 full-time support.
Employer Identification Number: 951661675

322
Pfeiffer (Gustavus and Louise) Research Foundation ▼
2444 Wilshire Blvd., Suite 414
Santa Monica 90403   (213) 829-4773

Incorporated in 1942 in New York.
Donor(s): Gustavus A. Pfeiffer.†
Financial data: (yr. ended 12/31/84): Assets, $10,073,795 (M); expenditures, $783,217, including $624,181 for 27 grants (high: $100,000; low: $5,000; average: $10,000-$25,000).
Purpose and activities: The improvement of public health through the advancement of medicine and pharmacy; the foundation's primary area of interest is in medical and pharmacological research, with support also for medical education.
Types of support awarded: Research, matching funds.
Limitations: No support for national fundraising organizations or publicly financed projects. No grants to individuals, or for building or endowment funds, scholarships, fellowships, travel, conferences, or general purposes; no loans.
Publications: Biennial report, program policy statement, application guidelines.
Application information:
Initial approach: Letter
Copies of proposal: 9
Deadline(s): 1 month before board meeting
Board meeting date(s): Annually, usually in the spring, and as required
Final notification: 1 week after annual board meeting
Write: George R. Pfeiffer, Secretary
Officers and Directors: Paul H. Pfeiffer, M.D., President; H. Robert Herold, II, Matthew G. Herold, Jr., Milton C. Rose, Vice-Presidents; George R. Pfeiffer, Secretary-Treasurer; Lise P. Chapman, Patricia Herold Nagle, Robert H. Pfeiffer.
Number of staff: 1 part-time professional; 1 part-time support.
Employer Identification Number: 136086299

323
Philibosian (Stephen) Foundation
46-930 West Eldorado Dr.
Indian Wells 92260   (619) 568-3920

Trust established in 1969 in Pennsylvania.
Donor(s): Armenian Missionary Association of America.
Financial data: (yr. ended 12/31/82): Assets, $5,091,955 (M); expenditures, $404,259, including $373,070 for 70 grants (high: $207,800; low: $25; average: $100-$5,000).
Purpose and activities: Grants largely for missionary, educational, and social programs of the Armenian-American church, including aid for Armenian schools in the Middle East; support also for child welfare.
Types of support awarded: Continuing support, annual campaigns, endowment funds, scholarship funds.

Limitations: No grants to individuals, or for operating budgets, seed money, emergency funds, deficit financing, building funds, matching gifts, research, special projects, publications, or conferences; no loans.
Application information:
Initial approach: Letter
Copies of proposal: 1
Deadline(s): None
Board meeting date(s): Semiannually in spring and fall
Write: Joyce Stein, Trustee
Trustees: Richard Aijian, Nazar Daghlian, Mrs. Richard Danelian, Albert Momjian, Joyce Stein.
Number of staff: None.
Employer Identification Number: 237029751

324
Phillips Foundation, The ¤
c/o Security Pacific National Bank
P.O. Box 1098
Palm Desert 92260

Incorporated in 1951 in California.
Donor(s): Philip M. Virtue.†
Financial data: (yr. ended 12/31/83): Assets, $1,606,011 (M); expenditures, $100,771, including $81,212 for 24 grants (high: $25,300; low: $25).
Purpose and activities: Broad purposes; grants primarily for research in economics, churches, and higher and secondary education.
Application information:
Write: J. Neil Hastings, Secretary
Officers and Trustees: Tecla M. Virtue, President; Walter H.W. Weiler, Vice-President; J. Neil Hastings, Secretary and Treasurer; Ruth Hastings.
Employer Identification Number: 956042761

325
Pickford (Mary) Foundation ¤
606 Wilshire Blvd., Suite 506
Santa Monica 90401   (213) 395-9951

Established in 1968.
Donor(s): Mary Pickford Rogers.†
Financial data: (yr. ended 5/31/83): Assets, $8,516,333 (M); expenditures, $1,123,187, including $997,134 for 59 grants (high: $100,000; low: $50).
Purpose and activities: Primarily local giving, with grants largely for scholarship funds at colleges and universities, and for "well-established medical or community service organizations."
Types of support awarded: Scholarship funds, general purposes, endowment funds, building funds, equipment.
Limitations: Giving primarily in CA; no grants outside the United States. No grants to individuals.
Application information:
Initial approach: Letter or telephone
Deadline(s): None
Write: Edward C. Stotsenberg, President
Officers and Directors: Edward G. Stotsenberg, President and Chief Executive; Sull Lawrence, Secretary; Charles B. Rogers, Treasurer.
Employer Identification Number: 956093487

326
Potlatch Foundation for Higher Education
c/o George C. Cheek
P.O. Box 3591
San Francisco 94119   (415) 981-5980

Incorporated in 1952 in Delaware.
Donor(s): Potlatch Corporation.
Financial data: (yr. ended 12/31/83): Assets, $83,179 (M); gifts received, $175,000; expenditures, $191,624, including $52,700 for 14 grants (high: $6,000; low: $1,000) and $127,050 for 180 grants to individuals.
Purpose and activities: Educational purposes; grants chiefly for scholarships and fellowships in areas of company operations.
Types of support awarded: Student aid, fellowships.
Limitations: Giving limited to areas of company operations, primarily in AR, ID, and MN. No grants for general support, building or endowment funds, research, or matching gifts; no loans.
Publications: Annual report, program policy statement, application guidelines.
Application information: Application forms will be mailed to students seeking scholarships. Application form required.
Initial approach: Letter
Deadline(s): February 1 for new applications for scholarships; July 1 for scholarship renewals
Board meeting date(s): April
Write: George C. Cheek, President
Officers and Trustees: George C. Cheek, President; George F. Jewett, Jr., Vice-President; Sandra T. Powell, Secretary and Treasurer; Albert L. Alford, Jr., John B. Frazer, Jr., Robert W. Gamble, James B. McMonigle, Kip McQuary, Robert D. Werner.
Employer Identification Number: 826005250

327
Powell (The Charles Lee) Foundation ¤
1320 Columbia St.
San Diego 92101-3416

Established in 1954 in California.
Donor(s): Charles Lee Powell.†
Financial data: (yr. ended 12/31/82): Assets, $9,746,105 (M); expenditures, $2,140,309, including $2,055,000 for 10 grants (high: $475,000; low: $75,000).
Purpose and activities: Grants largely committed to professorships in engineering and for scholarships in engineering, computer science, and applied mathematics at three local universities.
Types of support awarded: Professorships, scholarship funds, equipment.
Limitations: Giving primarily in CA.
Application information: Application information for scholarships available from universities.
Directors: Lawrence Cox, James L. Focht, Herbert Kunzel, William McElroy, Charles Rees.
Employer Identification Number: 237064397

328
Pratt (Arthur P.) and Jeanette Gladys Pratt Memorial Fund
c/o California First Bank
7807 Girard Ave.
La Jolla 92037   (619) 230-4770
Mailing address: P.O. Box 1907, La Jolla, CA 92038

Established in 1973 in California.
Donor(s): Jeanette Gladys Pratt.†
Financial data: (yr. ended 4/30/84): Assets, $2,182,091 (M); expenditures, $174,981, including $159,500 for 38 grants (high: $10,000; low: $500).
Purpose and activities: Local giving, with emphasis on youth agencies and restoration of buildings in a park.
Types of support awarded: Operating budgets, continuing support, annual campaigns, emergency funds, general purposes, building funds, equipment, land acquisition, research, publications, matching funds, employee matching gifts.
Limitations: Giving limited to San Diego County, CA. No grants to individuals, or for endowment funds, or scholarships and fellowships; no loans.
Application information:
  Initial approach: Full proposal
  Copies of proposal: 1
  Deadline(s): None
  Board meeting date(s): March
  Final notification: Immediately after board meeting
  Write: R.A. Cameron, Vice-President
Trustee: California First Bank, Corporate Trustee (R.A. Cameron, Vice-President).
Number of staff: None.
Employer Identification Number: 956464737

329
R & R Foundation, The ⌧
c/o Riordan, Capps & Carbonne
523 West Sixth St., Suite 1234
Los Angeles 90014

Trust established in 1967 in California.
Donor(s): Charles H. Reeves, Richard J. Riordan, Ralph Richley, and others.
Financial data: (yr. ended 2/28/83): Assets, $170,320 (M); gifts received, $647,035; expenditures, $1,005,267, including $1,000,981 for 167 grants (high: $149,999; low: $10).
Purpose and activities: Broad purposes; grants largely for higher education, social and health agencies, including population control, church support and religious associations, cultural programs, a children's institute, and a community fund.
Limitations: No grants to individuals.
Application information: Applications not invited.
Trustees: William E. Gunther, Jr., Charles H. Reeves, Richard J. Riordan.
Employer Identification Number: 956192664

330
R. P. Foundation, Inc. ⌧
3563 7th Ave.
San Diego 92103

Incorporated in 1966 in California.
Donor(s): Robert O. Peterson.
Financial data: (yr. ended 11/30/83): Assets, $1,980,735 (M); expenditures, $128,325, including $125,244 for 6 grants (high: $75,000; low: $75).
Purpose and activities: Primarily local giving in California and New York, with emphasis on cultural programs, including a historic preservation organization; support also for an oceanographic research institute and education.
Limitations: Giving primarily in CA and NY.
Officers and Trustees: Robert O. Peterson, President; Maureen F. O'Connor, Vice-President; John J. McCloskey, Secretary.
Employer Identification Number: 952536736

331
Radin Foundation ⌧
c/o Main Hurdman
4 Embarcadero Center, Suite 400
San Francisco 94111

Established in 1971.
Donor(s): Leta H. Radin.†
Financial data: (yr. ended 12/31/83): Assets, $2,672,735 (M); expenditures, $8,145.
Purpose and activities: No grants awarded in 1982 or 1983; in 1981, support mainly for a local youth organization.
Limitations: Giving primarily in CA.
Officers and Directors: H. Marcus Radin, President; Bruce Rosenblatt, Vice-President; Jefferson Radin Bender, Secretary-Treasurer.
Employer Identification Number: 237155525

332
Richards (The Mabel Wilson) Scholarship Fund ⌧
3333 Glendale Blvd., Suite One
Los Angeles 90039   (213) 661-1396

Trust established in 1951 in California.
Donor(s): Mabel Wilson Richards.†
Financial data: (yr. ended 3/31/83): Assets, $4,847,549 (M); expenditures, $316,300, including $267,771 for 48 grants (high: $20,000; low: $400).
Purpose and activities: Supports scholarship funds for worthy and needy girls of the Los Angeles area recommended by financial aid offices of selected California educational institutions. Awards made directly to schools.
Types of support awarded: Scholarship funds, special projects, student aid.
Limitations: Giving primarily in CA. No grants for building or endowment funds or operating budgets.
Publications: Program policy statement, application guidelines.
Application information: Application form submitted by financial aid office of selected California colleges and universities required for scholarships. Application form required.
  Initial approach: Letter
  Copies of proposal: 1

  Deadline(s): Submit proposal preferably in September; deadline October 15 or February 15
  Board meeting date(s): January, April, July, and October
  Write: Mrs. Ruth G. Walker, Trustee
Trustees: Stanley J. Gallon, Ruth G. Walker, Paul W. Wildman.
Employer Identification Number: 956021322

333
Riverside Community Foundation
P.O. Box 1643
Riverside 92502   (714) 684-4194

Community foundation established as a trust in 1941 in California.
Financial data: (yr. ended 12/31/82): Assets, $3,877,853 (L); gifts received, $42,078; expenditures, $393,871, including $361,828 for 43 grants (high: $63,000; low: $1,000; average: $8,400).
Purpose and activities: Grants for local educational and welfare purposes.
Types of support awarded: Seed money, emergency funds, building funds, equipment, matching funds, scholarship funds, special projects, conferences and seminars.
Limitations: Giving limited to the greater Riverside, CA, area. No grants to individuals, or for endowment funds, operating budgets, continuing support, annual campaigns, deficit financing, land acquisition, fellowships, publications, or research; no loans.
Publications: Program policy statement, application guidelines.
Application information:
  Initial approach: Telephone, letter, or full proposal
  Copies of proposal: 8
  Deadline(s): Submit proposal preferably in February-March, May-August, or October-December; deadlines March 31, August 31, or December 31
  Board meeting date(s): January, April, and September
  Final notification: 1 month after board meetings
  Write: Donald O. Nelson, Executive Director
Officers: Harold D. Wymer, President; Larry L. White, Vice-President; Ray Berry, Secretary-Treasurer; Donald O. Nelson, Executive Director.
Distribution Committee: June Goldware, Jean M. King, Bart R. Singletary, Donald F. Zimmer.
Trustee Bank: Security Pacific National Bank.
Number of staff: 1 part-time professional; 1 part-time support.
Employer Identification Number: 952031692

334
Rosenberg Foundation ▼
210 Post St.
San Francisco 94108   (415) 421-6105

Incorporated in 1935 in California.
Donor(s): Max L. Rosenberg,† Charlotte S. Mack.†

Financial data: (yr. ended 12/31/84): Assets, $20,853,000 (M); expenditures, $1,458,000, including $1,108,000 for 50 grants (high: $65,000; low: $1,000; average: $2,000-$45,000).
Purpose and activities: New and innovative programs benefiting children and youth including 1) early childhood development projects which appear to have unusual promise of encouraging the normal, healthy development of young children both as individuals and as members of a diverse society; 2) adolescent and older youth projects in which young people help to plan and carry out activities of benefit to the community; 3) rural development projects to improve the quality of life in rural California; and 4) projects which identify and address policy issues in the immigration field with particular emphasis on migration from Mexico and its consequences for children and their families in both countries. In 1985 the directors will be reviewing present policies and procedures; new statement of policies and procedures will be available in late 1985.
Types of support awarded: Special projects, research, program-related investments.
Limitations: Giving limited to CA. No grants to individuals, or for endowment or capital funds, operating expenses of established agencies, scholarships and fellowships, continuing support, annual campaigns, seed money, emergency funds, deficit financing, publications, films, matching grants, equipment and materials, land acquisitions, renovation projects, or conferences and seminars.
Publications: Multi-year report, program policy statement, application guidelines.
Application information: The foundation will not consider new proposals until late 1985.
 Initial approach: Letter
 Copies of proposal: 1
 Deadline(s): None
 Board meeting date(s): Monthly except July and August
 Final notification: 1 week to 3 months
 Write: Kirke Wilson, Executive Director
Officers: Norvel L. Smith,* President; Peter F. Sloss,* Vice-President; Kirke Wilson, Executive Director and Secretary; James C. Gaither,* Treasurer.
Directors:* Lewis H. Butler, Phyllis Cook, Herma Hill Kay, William R. Kimball, Leslie L. Luttgens, Cruz Reynoso.
Number of staff: 2 full-time professional.
Employer Identification Number: 941186182

335
Roth Family Foundation
1933 South Broadway, Rm. 251
Los Angeles 90007

Established in 1966 in California.
Donor(s): Louis Roth and Company.
Financial data: (yr. ended 10/31/83): Assets, $3,553,846 (M); expenditures, $289,933, including $270,286 for 118 grants (high: $76,200; low: $10).
Purpose and activities: Primarily local giving, with emphasis on cultural and educational programs. Grants limited to established charities known to the directors.

Limitations: Giving primarily in CA.
Application information: Grants limited to established charities known to the directors.
Officers and Directors: Michael Roth, President; Patricia Roth, Vice-President; Susan Garcetti, Secretary-Treasurer; Gilbert Garcetti, Richard Miller, Susan Roth.
Employer Identification Number: 237008897

336
San Diego Community Foundation
625 Broadway, Suite 1015
San Diego 92101   (619) 239-8815

Established in 1975 in California.
Financial data: (yr. ended 6/30/84): Assets, $7,230,133 (M); gifts received, $2,366,824; expenditures, $693,994, including $537,430 for 85 grants (high: $50,000; low: $165).
Purpose and activities: Local giving to social agencies, cultural activities, education, civic affairs, and recreational activities for youth, the aged, minorities and the handicapped.
Types of support awarded: Seed money, equipment, matching funds, technical assistance, research, conferences and seminars.
Limitations: Giving limited to San Diego County, CA. No support for religious or political purposes. No grants to individuals, or for operating budgets, continuing support, annual campaigns, endowment funds, or land acquisition; no loans.
Publications: Annual report, application guidelines, program policy statement.
Application information: Application form required.
 Initial approach: Telephone or letter
 Copies of proposal: 1
 Deadline(s): January 1, February 1, June 1, and October 1
 Board meeting date(s): Bimonthly beginning in February
 Final notification: 2 months
 Write: Helen Monroe, Executive Director or Pamela Hall, Program Officer
Officers: Joseph W. Hibben, President; Mrs. Jack L. Oatman, Vice-President, Distributions; Walter A. Turner, Jr., Vice-President, Finance; Virgil V. Pedersen, Vice-President, Development; Kevin V. Munnelly, Secretary; James T. Slingsby,* Treasurer.
Board of Governors:* Robert Breitbard, Mrs. John C. Carson, Philip del Campo, Dean R. Dunphy, Michael Ibs Gonzalez, Ronald E. Hahn, William Jeffery, Hope Logan, Dr. Ralph R. Ocampo, Kay Porter, Dwight E. Stanford, James S. Triolo, Donald O. Van Ness, Harold B. Williams.
Number of staff: 1 full-time professional; 2 full-time support.
Employer Identification Number: 952942582

337
San Francisco Foundation, The ▼
500 Washington St., 8th Fl.
San Francisco 94111   (415) 392-0600

Community foundation established in 1948 in California by resolution and declaration of trust.

Financial data: (yr. ended 6/30/84): Assets, $461,040,287 (M); gifts received, $4,728,648; expenditures, $41,152,047, including $37,753,057 for 683 grants (high: $1,000,000; low: $100; average: $5,000-$75,000) and $4,307,903 for 5 loans.
Purpose and activities: Grants principally in five categories: the arts and humanities, community health, education, environment, and urban affairs, for local Bay Area organizations, unless otherwise specified by donors. Technical assistance grants also made, primarily to current recipients.
Types of support awarded: Operating budgets, seed money, building funds, equipment, land acquisition, program-related investments, special projects, loans, technical assistance.
Limitations: Giving limited to the Bay Area, CA counties of Alameda, Contra Costa, Marin, San Francisco, and San Mateo. No support for religious purposes. No grants to individuals, or for continuing support, annual campaigns, films or videotapes, general fundraising campaigns, emergency or endowment funds, deficit financing, matching gifts, scholarships and fellowships (except in Marin County), research, publications, or conferences.
Publications: Annual report, newsletter, application guidelines, program policy statement.
Application information: Application form required.
 Initial approach: Letter
 Copies of proposal: 1
 Deadline(s): None
 Board meeting date(s): Monthly except August; applications are reviewed 6 times each year
 Final notification: 3 to 4 months
 Write: Martin A. Paley, Director
Officer: Martin A. Paley, Director and Secretary.
Distribution Committee: Charles J. Patterson, Chairman; Susan S. Metcalf, Vice-Chairman and Treasurer; Peter H. Behr, Peter E. Haas, Robert C. Harris, Joan F. Lane, Richard B. Madden.
Number of staff: 20 full-time professional; 24 full-time support; 2 part-time support.
Employer Identification Number: 941101547

338
Sandy (George H.) Foundation
P.O. Box 18275
San Francisco 94118   (415) 668-6606

Trust established in 1960 in California.
Donor(s): George H. Sandy.†
Financial data: (yr. ended 12/31/84): Assets, $11,454,101 (M); expenditures, $420,671, including $415,000 for 113 grants (high: $20,000; low: $1,000; average: $3,000).
Purpose and activities: Charitable and educational purposes; primarily local giving, with emphasis on aid to the handicapped and underprivileged.
Types of support awarded: Operating budgets, continuing support.

Limitations: Giving limited to northern CA. No support for other private non-operating foundations. No grants to individuals, or for annual campaigns, seed money, emergency funds, deficit financing, capital, endowment, or building funds, matching gifts, scholarships, fellowships, special projects, research, publications, and conferences; no loans.

Application information:
Initial approach: Letter
Copies of proposal: 1
Board meeting date(s): Quarterly
Final notification: 6 months
Write: Chester R. MacPhee, Jr., Trustee
Trustees: Thomas E. Feeney, Chester R. MacPhee, Jr., The Bank of California.
Number of staff: None.
Employer Identification Number: 946054473

339
Sanguinetti (Annunziata) Foundation
c/o Bank of America
P.O. Box 37121
San Francisco 94137   (415) 622-2211

Trust established in 1958 in California.
Donor(s): Annunziata Sanguinetti.†
Financial data: (yr. ended 9/30/84): Assets, $3,000,000 (M); expenditures, $286,000, including $280,000 for 42 grants (high: $10,000; low: $2,500).
Purpose and activities: Local giving for the benefit of sick, needy children; grants for mental health, rehabilitation, welfare, hospitals, youth and social agencies.
Limitations: Giving limited to San Francisco, CA. No grants to individuals, or for building or endowment funds.
Application information:
Initial approach: Letter, telephone, or full proposal
Copies of proposal: 1
Deadline(s): Submit proposal between July and October; deadline October 30
Board meeting date(s): November or December
Write: Elizabeth Tidmarsh, Trust Officer
Trustee: Bank of America (Elizabeth Tidmarsh, Trust Officer).
Employer Identification Number: 946073762

340
Santa Barbara Foundation ▼
15 East Carrillo St.
Santa Barbara 93101   (805) 963-1873

Community foundation incorporated in 1928 in California.
Financial data: (yr. ended 12/31/82): Assets, $12,754,996 (M); expenditures, $1,556,238, including $963,610 for 110 grants (high: $51,155; low: $314) and $394,217 for 163 loans.
Purpose and activities: Local giving for social services, youth, health services, cultural activities, and student aid loans.
Types of support awarded: Continuing support, emergency funds, building funds, equipment, land acquisition, matching funds, student aid.

Limitations: Giving limited to Santa Barbara County, CA. No support for tax-supported organizations. No grants to individuals, or for operating budgets, annual campaigns, seed money, deficit financing, endowment funds, scholarships, fellowships, special projects, research, publications, or conferences.
Publications: Annual report, application guidelines.
Application information: Application form required.
Initial approach: Letter
Copies of proposal: 1
Deadline(s): None
Board meeting date(s): Monthly except July
Final notification: 2 months
Write: Edward R. Spaulding, Executive Director
Officers and Trustees: John S. Rathbone, D.D.S., President; Robert M. Jones, John V. Pollitt, Vice-Presidents; James L. Free, Jr., Secretary; Lawrence L. Wathey, Treasurer; Fritz Amacher, Mrs. Walter G. Cordero, Mrs. James R. Dow, Warren E. Fenzi, Mrs. Robert G. Ferguson, Edwin F. Froelich, D.D.S., Mrs. John F. Merritt, Mrs. Herman Nelson, P. Paul Riparetti, M.D., Clifford W. Sponsel, Mrs. Howard Vessy, Phillip S. Wilcox.
Fund Managers: Capital Research & Management Company, Crocker National Bank, Security Pacific Investment Managers.
Number of staff: 1 full-time professional; 1 full-time support; 2 part-time support.
Employer Identification Number: 951866094

341
Santa Clara County, Community Foundation of
1691 The Alameda
San Jose 95126   (408) 947-0344

Community foundation established in 1954 in California.
Financial data: (yr. ended 12/31/83): Assets, $1,971,216 (M); gifts received, $1,213,248; expenditures, $693,704, including $478,438 for 144 grants (high: $43,684; low: $50).
Purpose and activities: Giving primarily in Santa Clara County, for the arts, health, higher education (including awards in literature), urban affairs, social services, and the environment.
Types of support awarded: Seed money, emergency funds, matching funds, employee matching gifts, consulting services, technical assistance, student aid, fellowships.
Limitations: Giving primarily in Santa Clara County, CA. No support for religious organizations for sectarian purposes. No grants to individuals, or for operating budgets, continuing support, annual campaigns, deficit financing, building funds, scholarship funds, research, equipment and materials, land acquisition, or endowment funds.
Publications: Annual report, application guidelines.
Application information: Application form required.
Initial approach: Telephone
Deadline(s): 8 weeks prior to board meetings
Board meeting date(s): Second Friday of January, May, and September

Final notification: Within 2 weeks of meetings
Write: Marti Erickson, Executive Director
Directors: C. Lester Hogan, Chairman; Marti Erickson, Executive Director; Ernest C. Arbuckle, Mrs. Paul Davies, Leonard Ely, S. Fred Kaufman, David W. Mitchell, M. Kenneth Oshman, Ernest Renzel, P. Anthony Ridder, Thomas T. Vais, Ray L. Wilbur.
Number of staff: 1 full-time professional; 1 part-time support.
Employer Identification Number: 237112335

342
Santa Cruz County Community Foundation, Greater
7600 Old Dominion Court
Aptos 95003   (408) 662-3676

Community foundation incorporated in 1982 in California.
Financial data: (yr. ended 12/31/83): Assets, $95,084 (M); gifts received, $462,090; expenditures, $402,356, including $346,929 for 55 grants.
Purpose and activities: Giving limited to Santa Cruz County, for social services, health, education, cultural programs, the environment, conservation, and community development programs.
Types of support awarded: General purposes, seed money, operating budgets, emergency funds, equipment, endowment funds, special projects, publications, conferences and seminars, technical assistance.
Limitations: Giving limited to Santa Cruz County, CA. No grants to individuals, or for continuing support, annual campaigns, deficit financing, building funds, land acquisition, student loans, scholarships, fellowships, program-related investments, or research.
Publications: 990-PF, program policy statement, application guidelines.
Application information: Application form required.
Write: Grace Jepsen, Executive Director
Officers: Ian McPhail, President; Grace Jepsen, Executive Director.
Number of staff: 1 full-time professional; 5 part-time support.
Employer Identification Number: 942808039

343
Sassoon (The Vidal) Foundation ⌗
c/o Parks, Adams, & Palmer
8075 W. Third St.
Los Angeles 90048

Established in 1979.
Donor(s): Vidal Sassoon.
Financial data: (yr. ended 12/31/82): Assets, $89,322 (M); gifts received, $258,500; expenditures, $169,369, including $169,320 for 53 grants (high: $30,000; low: $100).
Purpose and activities: Support primarily for Jewish welfare funds and higher education, cultural programs, and youth and social agencies.

Officers: Vidal Sassoon, President; George Shaw, Vice-President and Secretary; Martin Mason, Vice-President and Treasurer; Linda Turner, Vice-President.
Employer Identification Number: 953401086

344
Saturno Foundation
c/o Bank of America
Trust Dept. 9250, P.O. Box 37121
San Francisco 94137   (415) 622-6428

Trust established in 1957 in California.
Donor(s): Joseph Saturno,† Victor Saturno.
Financial data: (yr. ended 10/31/83): Assets, $3,524,647 (M); expenditures, $223,369, including $210,510 for 24 grants (high: $16,841; low: $2,105).
Purpose and activities: Grants to organizations in Italy that assist orphaned children born of Italian mothers and American soldier fathers.
Limitations: Giving primarily in Italy. No grants to individuals, or for general support, building or endowment funds, research, scholarships, fellowships, or matching gifts; no loans.
Publications: 990-PF.
Application information:
  Initial approach: Letter
  Copies of proposal: 1
Trustee: Bank of America (H. Hudspeth, Vice-President).
Employer Identification Number: 946073765

345
Schermer (Frances) Charitable Trust
c/o Security Pacific National Bank
P.O. Box 3189, Terminal Annex
Los Angeles 90051

Trust established in 1980 in California.
Donor(s): Charles I. Schermer,† Frances Schermer.
Financial data: (yr. ended 6/30/83): Assets, $2,081,121 (M); expenditures, $238,690, including $183,784 for 110 grants (high: $5,000; low: $500).
Purpose and activities: Primarily local giving, with emphasis on Jewish welfare funds and Jewish studies, higher education, social agencies, aid to the handicapped, health agencies, and child welfare.
Limitations: Giving primarily in CA and OH.
Trustees: Saul Friedman, James L. Pazol, Security Pacific National Bank.
Employer Identification Number: 956685749

346
Schmidt (Marjorie Mosher) Foundation ♯
15795 Rockfield, Suite G
Irvine 92714

Incorporated in 1956 in California.
Donor(s): Marjorie Mosher Schmidt.
Financial data: (yr. ended 12/31/83): Assets, $1,927,579 (M); expenditures, $180,956, including $159,500 for 47 grants (high: $20,000; low: $500).

Purpose and activities: Broad purposes; primarily local giving, with emphasis on social agencies, health agencies, higher and secondary education, child welfare, aid to the handicapped, and Christian religious organizations.
Limitations: Giving primarily in CA. No grants to individuals.
Application information:
  Initial approach: Letter
  Copies of proposal: 1
  Deadline(s): April 30
  Board meeting date(s): May or June
  Write: Mark F. Scudder, Secretary
Officers and Directors: Valerie Schmidt Scudder, President; John Haas Scudder, Vice-President; Mark F. Scudder, Secretary; Richard Charles Cringle, Treasurer; John T. Kearns, Director.
Employer Identification Number: 956047798

347
Schreiber Family Foundation
433 North Camden Dr., Suite 888
Beverly Hills 90210   (213) 275-5421

Incorporated in 1959 in California.
Donor(s): Bernard A. Greenberg, Lenore S. Greenberg, Taft B. Schreiber,† Rita B. Schreiber, Toby I. Schreiber.
Financial data: (yr. ended 2/28/83): Assets, $60,945 (M); gifts received, $115,663; expenditures, $137,438, including $137,250 for 25 grants (high: $28,000; low: $500).
Purpose and activities: Broad purposes; primarily local giving to projects of interest to the donors, with emphasis on programs for the handicapped, child welfare, Jewish welfare funds, and a hospital.
Types of support awarded: Continuing support, annual campaigns, emergency funds, building funds, endowment funds, research, conferences and seminars.
Limitations: Giving primarily in CA. No grants to individuals, or for operating budgets, seed money, deficit financing, equipment, land acquisition, renovations, matching gifts, scholarships and fellowships, demonstration projects, or publications; no loans.
Application information:
  Initial approach: Letter
  Deadline(s): None
  Board meeting date(s): December and as required
  Final notification: 30 days
  Write: Bernard A. Greenberg, Secretary
Officers and Directors: Rita B. Schreiber, President; Toby I. Schreiber, Vice-President; Bernard A. Greenberg, Secretary; Lenore S. Greenberg, Treasurer.
Number of staff: None.
Employer Identification Number: 956090093

348
Scott (Virginia Steele) Foundation ♯
2 Oak Knoll Terrace
Pasadena 91106

Established in 1974.
Donor(s): Virginia Steele Scott,† Grace C. Steele.†

Financial data: (yr. ended 6/30/83): Assets, $7,543,096 (M); expenditures, $1,249,067, including $1,000,500 for 2 grants (high: $1,000,000; low: $500).
Purpose and activities: Primarily local giving of works of art to a local art museum, and other fine arts organizations.
Limitations: Giving primarily in Pasadena, CA.
Officers: Charles Newton, President; E. Maurice Block, Henry Tanner, Vice-Presidents; Vivian Nichols, Treasurer.
Directors: Blake R. Nevins, Robert R. Wark.
Employer Identification Number: 237365076

349
Scripps (The Ellen Browning) Foundation
California First Bank, P.O. Box B
Rancho Santa Fe 92067   (619) 230-4144

Trust established in 1935 in California.
Donor(s): Ellen Browning Scripps,† Robert Paine Scripps,† Mrs. Margaret C. Hawkins.
Financial data: (yr. ended 6/30/83): Assets, $2,177,963 (M); expenditures, $213,238, including $201,000 for 19 grants (high: $50,000; low: $500).
Purpose and activities: General purposes; primarily local giving, with emphasis on institutions engaged in medical and oceanographic research, higher education, conservation and recreation, and youth and child welfare agencies.
Limitations: Giving primarily in CA.
Application information:
  Initial approach: Full proposal
  Deadline(s): May 1
  Board meeting date(s): June
  Write: E. Douglas Dawson, Vice-President, California First Bank
Trustees: Ellen Scripps Davis, Edward S. Meanley, John P. Scripps, Paul K. Scripps.
Employer Identification Number: 951644633

350
Seaver Institute, The ▼
900 Wilshire Blvd., Suite 1018
Los Angeles 90017   (213) 688-7550

Incorporated in 1955 in California.
Donor(s): Frank R. Seaver.†
Financial data: (yr. ended 6/30/83): Assets, $24,810,344 (M); gifts received, $609,737; expenditures, $1,835,294, including $1,700,285 for 31 grants (high: $300,000; low: $285; average: $1,000-$22,000).
Purpose and activities: Broad purposes; primarily local giving, with emphasis on education, health, the arts, and the community.
Types of support awarded: Seed money, matching funds, special projects, research.
Limitations: Giving primarily in CA. No grants to individuals, or for operating budgets, continuing support, annual campaigns, emergency or endowment funds, scholarships, fellowships, deficit financing, capital or building funds, equipment, land acquisition, publications, or conferences; no loans.
Application information:
  Initial approach: Telephone
  Deadline(s): None

Board meeting date(s): December and June
Final notification: 3 to 6 months
Write: Richard W. Call, President
Officers and Directors: Blanche Ebert Seaver, Chair; Richard C. Seaver, Vice-Chairman; Richard W. Call, President; John F. Hall, Vice-President and Treasurer; Christopher Seaver, Secretary; Richard A. Archer, Myron E. Harpole, Raymond Jallow, Victoria Seaver.
Number of staff: 2 full-time professional; 1 part-time professional.
Employer Identification Number: 956054764

351
Security Pacific Foundation ▼
333 South Hope St.
Los Angeles 90071   (213) 613-6688
Grant application address: P.O. Box 2097, Terminal Annex, Los Angeles, CA 90051

Incorporated in 1977 in California.
Donor(s): Security Pacific Corporation.
Financial data: (yr. ended 12/31/84): Assets, $12,351,994 (M); expenditures, $3,842,070, including $3,581,009 for 741 grants (high: $850,000; low: $50; average: $1,000-$2,500) and $224,269 for 473 employee matching gifts.
Purpose and activities: Established to support charitable efforts in communities throughout California, including grants for community funds, higher education, youth agencies, social welfare, arts and cultural programs, and civic affairs.
Types of support awarded: Annual campaigns, building funds, continuing support, employee matching gifts, operating budgets, employee related scholarships.
Limitations: Giving limited to CA. No support for national agencies, legal defense funds, professional organizations, or churches or religious groups. No grants to individuals (except for company-employee scholarships), or for seed money, emergency funds, deficit financing, land acquisition, equipment, endowments, matching gifts, operational grants for hospitals or health associations, scholarships or fellowships, special projects, research, media projects, or advertising in charitable publications; no loans.
Publications: Annual report, informational brochure, program policy statement, application guidelines.
Application information:
Initial approach: Letter or full proposal
Copies of proposal: 1
Deadline(s): July 15 for capital grant requests; none for operating grants
Board meeting date(s): November
Final notification: 4 to 6 weeks
Write: Mrs. Carol E. Taufer, President
Officers: Carol E. Taufer,* President; Richard J. Flamson III,* John F. Kooken,* George F. Moody,* Richard A. Warner,* Vice-Presidents; Howard B. Stevens, Secretary; Kenneth Sherman, Treasurer.
Directors:* Carl E. Hartnack, Chairman; John J. Duffy, Roy Hartmann, Robert H. Smith.
Number of staff: 2 full-time professional; 2 full-time support.
Employer Identification Number: 953195084

352
See (Charles) Foundation ¤
2222 Ave. of the Stars, Suite 2505
Los Angeles 90067

Incorporated in 1960 in California.
Donor(s): Charles B. See.
Financial data: (yr. ended 12/31/83): Assets, $1,397,711 (M); expenditures, $107,009, including $79,625 for 46 grants (high: $10,000; low: $50).
Purpose and activities: Broad purposes; primarily local giving, with emphasis on mental health, education, hospitals, church support, conservation, and cultural programs.
Limitations: Giving primarily in CA.
Officers and Directors: Charles B. See, President; C.H. Baumhefner, Vice-President; Betty Ann Pettite, Secretary and Treasurer; Harry A. See, Alta B. Underwood.
Employer Identification Number: 956038358

353
Sefton (J. W.) Foundation ¤
P.O. Box 1871
San Diego 92112

Incorporated in 1945 in California.
Donor(s): J.W. Sefton, Jr.†
Financial data: (yr. ended 12/31/83): Assets, $2,554,101 (M); expenditures, $171,648, including $136,437 for 11 grants (high: $50,000; low: $78).
Purpose and activities: Primarily local giving, with emphasis on community development, including grants for the police, museums, and a historical society.
Limitations: Giving primarily in San Diego, CA.
Application information:
Write: Thomas W. Sefton, President
Officers and Trustees: Thomas W. Sefton, President; Donna K. Sefton, Vice-President; Gordon T. Frost, Secretary; Gordon E. McNary, Treasurer; San Diego Trust & Savings Bank.
Employer Identification Number: 951513384

354
Setzer Foundation, The ¤
2555 3rd St., Suite 200
Sacramento 95818

Trust established in 1965 in California.
Donor(s): Members of the Setzer family.
Financial data: (yr. ended 3/31/83): Assets, $1,317,651 (M); expenditures, $128,267, including $115,208 for 101 grants (high: $50,000; low: $25).
Purpose and activities: Primarily local giving, with emphasis on higher education, cultural programs, youth and social agencies, and hospitals.
Limitations: Giving primarily in CA.
Trustees: E.W. Rhoades, G. Cal Setzer, Hardie C. Setzer.
Employer Identification Number: 946115578

355
Seuss (Dr.) Foundation ¤
7301 Encelia Dr.
La Jolla 92037

Incorporated in 1958 in California.
Donor(s): Theodor S. Geisel.
Financial data: (yr. ended 12/31/83): Assets, $1,679,653 (M); expenditures, $154,149, including $141,438 for 70 grants (high: $45,000; low: $50).
Purpose and activities: General purposes; primarily local giving; support for mental health, hospitals, higher education, youth agencies, cultural programs, and the arts.
Limitations: Giving primarily in CA.
Application information: Funds presently committed.
Officers: Theodor S. Geisel, President; R.L. Bernstein, Audrey Geisel, Vice-Presidents; Frank Kockritz, Secretary-Treasurer; Jeanne Jones, Director.
Employer Identification Number: 956029752

356
Shalan Foundation, Inc., The
680 Beach St., Suite 462
San Francisco 94109   (415) 673-8660

Incorporated in 1969 in New York.
Donor(s): A. Stephen Davis.
Financial data: (yr. ended 9/30/84): Assets, $1,139,091 (M); gifts received, $436,723; expenditures, $440,807, including $342,150 for 26 grants (high: $20,000; low: $3,000; average: $10,000-$20,000).
Purpose and activities: Giving primarily in western states except for projects of national importance; interest in groups promoting economic change to increase social justice and to limit practices harmful to the environment.
Types of support awarded: General purposes, operating budgets, continuing support, matching funds, program-related investments.
Limitations: Giving primarily in western states or to projects of national importance. No support for social service programs, or the media. No grants to individuals, or for capital or endowment funds, scholarships, or fellowships.
Publications: Annual report, 990-PF, grants list, program policy statement, application guidelines.
Application information:
Initial approach: Brief description or full proposal
Deadline(s): March 1, July 1, and November 1
Board meeting date(s): March, July, and November
Final notification: 1 to 3 months
Write: Loni Hancock, Executive Director
Officers: Alan Davis,* President; Rochelle Korman,* Vice-President; Loni Hancock,* Secretary-Treasurer and Executive Director.
Directors:* Shane Adler.
Number of staff: 1 full-time professional; 2 part-time support.
Employer Identification Number: 237063923

357
Shea Foundation, The ¤
655 Brea Canyon Rd.
Walnut 91789

Incorporated in 1960 in California.
Donor(s): Members of the Shea family.
Financial data: (yr. ended 11/30/83): Assets,
$1,959,543 (M); expenditures, $105,857,
including $89,000 for 52 grants (high: $10,000;
low: $280).
Purpose and activities: Broad purposes;
primarily local giving, with emphasis on Roman
Catholic church support and religious
associations; support also for secondary
education, and the handicapped.
Limitations: Giving primarily in CA.
Officers: John F. Shea,* President; Patricia Ann
Shea Meek, Vice-President; M.L. Mellor,*
Secretary and Treasurer.
Trustees:* Robert Bridges.
Employer Identification Number: 956027824

358
Shea (J. F.) Company Foundation ¤
655 Brea Canyon Rd.
Walnut 91789

Established in 1967.
Donor(s): J.F. Shea Company.
Financial data: (yr. ended 12/31/83): Assets,
$7,547 (M); gifts received, $5,778;
expenditures, $125,131, including $123,306
for 81 grants (high: $15,000; low: $15).
Purpose and activities: Primarily local giving,
with emphasis on higher and secondary
education, Roman Catholic religious
organizations, health, and recreation.
Limitations: Giving primarily in CA.
Officers: John F. Shea, President and
Treasurer; Edmund H. Shea, Jr., Peter O. Shea,
Vice-Presidents; G.E. Brolin, Secretary.
Employer Identification Number: 952554052

359
Shoong (Milton) Foundation
(formerly The Shoong Foundation)
829 Sacramento St.
San Francisco 94108   (415) 781-6111

Incorporated in 1941 in California.
Donor(s): Joe Shoong,† Rose Shoong,† Milton
W. Shoong, Betty Shoong Bird, Doris Shoong
Lee, National Dollar Stores, Ltd., Richard Tam,
Corinne Shoong.
Financial data: (yr. ended 12/31/83): Assets,
$3,606,160 (M); expenditures, $614,407,
including $423,845 for 140 grants (high:
$100,000; low: $50; average: $5,000) and
$60,000 for 3 employee matching gifts.
Purpose and activities: Originally established
as The Joe Shoong School to provide for the
maintenance of a school or college in China
and scholarships or loans to assist worthy
students. Now primarily local giving, largely to
educational, religious, and welfare institutions,
including the operation of a community center,
principally aiding the local Chinese population.

Types of support awarded: Operating
budgets, seed money, building funds,
equipment, matching funds, scholarship funds,
research.
Limitations: Giving primarily in CA. No grants
to individuals; no loans.
Application information:
  Initial approach: Letter
  Copies of proposal: 1
  Deadline(s): None
  Board meeting date(s): Monthly
  Final notification: 30 days
Officers and Directors: Milton W. Shoong,
President; Jim Ellis, Jerry Fitzpatrick, Paul
Godkin, Ted Lee, Peter Mantegani, Charles
Pius, Vice-Presidents; Dave E. Quan, Vice-
President, Secretary and Treasurer.
Number of staff: None.
Employer Identification Number: 941200291

360
**Signal Companies Charitable
Foundation, The**
11255 North Torrey Pines Rd.
La Jolla 92037   (619) 457-3555

Established in 1978 in California; absorbed
Wheelabrator Foundation in 1984.
Donor(s): The Signal Companies, Inc.
Financial data: (yr. ended 11/30/83): Assets,
$4,510,273 (M); expenditures, $295,261,
including $229,170 for 47 grants (high:
$60,000; low: $250).
Purpose and activities: Support for education,
culture and the arts, health and welfare
agencies, youth and community service
organizations, and civic activities.
Limitations: Giving primarily in areas of
company operations. No grants to individuals.
Application information:
  Initial approach: Letter
  Write: Ted McLin, Secretary, Contributions
    Committee
Trustees: John R. Spencer, Chairman; David H.
Skinner, Secretary; John Bold, Earl Logue,
Evelyn Truitt.
Employer Identification Number: 237002892

361
Simon (The Donald E.) Foundation ¤
1801 Century Park East, Suite 2110
Los Angeles 90067   (213) 277-4772

Trust established in 1961 in California.
Donor(s): Donald Ellis Simon.
Financial data: (yr. ended 12/31/83): Assets,
$753,636 (M); expenditures, $145,914,
including $129,650 for 37 grants (high:
$41,500; low: $100).
Purpose and activities: Support primarily for
Jewish welfare funds, health organizations, and
an Asian society.
Application information: Grants initiated by
the trustees.
  Write: Donald E. Simon
Trustees: John Freidenrich, Bernard A.
Greenberg, Donald Ellis Simon, Lucille Ellis
Simon.
Employer Identification Number: 956035903

362
**Simon, Inc., Foundation Funds of
Norton**
411 West Colorado Blvd.
Pasadena 91105   (818) 449-6840

Incorporated in 1957 in New York.
Donor(s): Norton Simon, Norton Simon, Inc.,
its subsidiaries and predecessors, and members
of the family.
Financial data: (yr. ended 12/31/82): Assets,
$1,297,315 (M); expenditures, $223,037,
including $216,591 for 11 grants (high:
$143,191; low: $200).
Purpose and activities: General purposes;
giving generally for arts, culture, education, and
health.
Types of support awarded: Annual campaigns.
Limitations: Giving primarily in the Los
Angeles, CA, area. No grants to individuals, or
for building or endowment funds, research,
scholarships, fellowships, or matching gifts; no
loans.
Application information: Grants largely
initiated by the foundation.
  Initial approach: Letter
  Copies of proposal: 1
  Deadline(s): None
  Board meeting date(s): As required
  Final notification: 1 month
  Write: Maryanne W. Rex, Vice-President
Officers and Trustees: Norton Simon,
President; Julia R. Mayer, Vice-President and
Secretary; Maryanne W. Rex, Vice-President
and Treasurer; Walter W. Timoshuk, Vice-
President; Jennifer J. Simon.
Number of staff: 1 part-time support.
Employer Identification Number: 136161697

363
Simon (Jennifer Jones) Foundation
(also known as Norton Simon, Inc. Foundation
for Education)
411 West Colorado Blvd.
Pasadena 91105   (818) 499-6840

Foundation established in 1954 in Louisiana.
Donor(s): Norton Simon, Norton Simon, Inc.,
and its subsidiaries and predecessors.
Financial data: (yr. ended 11/30/82): Assets,
$1,753,576 (M); gifts received, $279,990;
expenditures, $127,612, including $67,279 for
grants to individuals and $20,000 for 1
foundation-administered program.
Purpose and activities: Giving primarily to
operate a program of mental health workshops.
Types of support awarded: Annual campaigns.
Limitations: No grants to individuals, or for
building or endowment funds, research,
scholarships, fellowships, or matching gifts; no
loans.
Application information: Grants generally
restricted to programs initiated by the
foundation.
  Initial approach: Letter
  Deadline(s): None
  Board meeting date(s): As required
  Final notification: 1 month
  Write: Maryanne W. Rex, Vice-President

Officers and Trustees: Jennifer J. Simon, Chairman; Norton Simon, President; Julia R. Mayer, Vice-President and Secretary; Maryanne W. Rex, Vice-President and Treasurer.
Number of staff: 3 part-time professional.
Employer Identification Number: 956038539

364
Simon (The Lucille Ellis) Foundation ¤
Hufstedler, Miller, Carlson & Beardsley
700 South Flower St., 16th Fl.
Los Angeles 90017

Incorporated in 1960 in California.
Donor(s): Donald Simon, Lucille Simon, and other members of the Simon family.
Financial data: (yr. ended 12/31/83): Assets, $1,479,155 (M); gifts received, $300,000; expenditures, $204,907, including $188,525 for 44 grants (high: $125,000; low: $25).
Purpose and activities: Broad purposes; primarily local giving, with emphasis on Jewish welfare funds, social agencies, and health agencies.
Limitations: Giving primarily in CA. No grants to individuals.
Application information:
    Write: Lucille Ellis Simon, President
Officers and Trustees: Lucille Ellis Simon, President; Mrs. Sidney Foorman, Vice-President; Jerome Craig, Secretary-Treasurer; Brian E. Lewis, Donald Ellis Simon, Herman Weiner, M.D.
Employer Identification Number: 956035906

365
Simon (Norton) Art Foundation
(formerly Norton Simon, Inc. Museum of Art)
411 West Colorado Blvd.
Pasadena 91105   (818) 449-6840

Incorporated in 1954 in California.
Donor(s): Norton Simon, Norton Simon, Inc., its subsidiaries and predecessors and members of the family.
Financial data: (yr. ended 11/30/82): Assets, $159,275,933 (M); gifts received, $6,767,500; expenditures, $860,639, including $36,029 for 2 grants (high: $36,000; low: $29) and $317,834 for foundation-administered programs.
Purpose and activities: A private operating foundation; local grants generally for arts, education, and health.
Types of support awarded: Annual campaigns.
Limitations: Giving primarily in the Los Angeles, CA, area. No grants to individuals, or for building or endowment funds, research, scholarships, fellowships, or matching gifts; no loans.
Application information: Grants generally initiated by the foundation.
    Initial approach: Letter, followed by proposal
    Copies of proposal: 1
    Deadline(s): None
    Board meeting date(s): As required
    Final notification: 1 month
    Write: Maryanne W. Rex, Vice-President

Officers and Trustees: Norton Simon, President; Julia R. Mayer, Vice-President and Secretary; Maryanne W. Rex, Vice-President and Treasurer; Walter W. Timoshuk, Vice-President; Sara Campbell, Jack R. Clumeck, David J. Mahoney, Eric Simon, Jennifer J. Simon, Herman Weiner, M.D., Billy Wilder, Harold M. Williams.
Number of staff: 3 part-time professional.
Employer Identification Number: 956038921

366
Simon (The Norton) Foundation
411 West Colorado Blvd.
Pasadena 91105   (818) 449-6840

Incorporated in 1952 in California.
Donor(s): Norton Simon, and family members.
Financial data: (yr. ended 12/31/82): Assets, $275,184,024 (M); gifts received, $2,425,000; expenditures, $62,740, including $42,828 for 1 foundation-administered program.
Purpose and activities: A private operating foundation of which the only activity is the purchase of works of art and their loan to major public museums for exhibition.
Types of support awarded: Annual campaigns.
Limitations: No grants to individuals, or for building or endowment funds, research, scholarships, fellowships, or matching gifts; no loans.
Application information:
    Initial approach: Letter
    Copies of proposal: 1
    Deadline(s): None
    Board meeting date(s): As required
    Final notification: 1 month
    Write: Maryanne W. Rex, Vice-President
Officers and Trustees: Norton Simon, President; Julia R. Mayer, Vice-President and Secretary; Maryanne W. Rex, Vice-President and Treasurer; Sara Campbell, David J. Mahoney, Donald Simon, Jennifer Jones Simon, Milton Wexler, Billy Wilder.
Number of staff: 3 part-time professional.
Employer Identification Number: 956035908

367
Simon (The Robert Ellis) Foundation ¤
152 South Lasky Dr.
Beverly Hills 90212

Trust established in 1961 in California.
Donor(s): Robert Ellis Simon,† Norton Simon.
Financial data: (yr. ended 12/31/83): Assets, $2,699,576 (M); expenditures, $282,308, including $249,298 for 10 grants (high: $46,793; low: $3,600).
Purpose and activities: Broad purposes; primarily local giving, with emphasis on social and health agencies, mental health centers, and youth agencies.
Limitations: Giving primarily in CA.
Trustees: Sylvia Simon, Joan G. Willens, Harold M. Williams.
Employer Identification Number: 956035905

368
Sinaiko (Isaac D. and Ruth G.) Foundation ¤
P.O. Box L
Norwalk 90650

Established in 1968 in California.
Donor(s): Isaac D. Sinaiko, Ruth G. Sinaiko.
Financial data: (yr. ended 12/31/83): Assets, $191,541 (M); gifts received, $115,000; expenditures, $103,110, including $101,050 for 17 grants (high: $50,000; low: $150).
Purpose and activities: Giving primarily for Jewish welfare funds and religious organizations; support also for higher education.
Officers: Ruth G. Sinaiko, President; Edward J. Field, Vice-President; Irwin S. Field, Secretary and Treasurer.
Employer Identification Number: 237010727

369
Skaggs (L. J.) and Mary C. Skaggs Foundation ▼
1330 Broadway, 17th Fl.
Oakland 94612   (415) 451-3300

Incorporated in 1967 in California.
Donor(s): L.J. Skaggs,† Mrs. Mary C. Skaggs.
Financial data: (yr. ended 12/31/83): Assets, $13,533,338 (M); expenditures, $1,736,273, including $1,225,960 for 150 grants (high: $125,000; low: $100; average: $5,000-$25,000).
Purpose and activities: General purposes; in 1984-85 giving locally and nationally for the performing arts, projects of historic interest, folklore and folk life, and special projects; giving only to agencies in northern California for social and community concerns with some emphasis on child advocacy and women's projects. Some foreign grants in areas of interest, particularly historic preservation and health and hunger programs at the village level.
Types of support awarded: Seed money, special projects, matching funds, technical assistance, general purposes, continuing support.
Limitations: Giving primarily in northern CA for social and community careers grants. No support for museums and visual arts, higher education, residence home programs, halfway houses, or sectarian religious purposes. No grants to individuals, or for capital or endowment funds, annual fund drives, budget deficits, scholarships, or fellowships; no loans.
Publications: Annual report, program policy statement, application guidelines, grants list.
Application information:
    Initial approach: Letter
    Copies of proposal: 1
    Deadline(s): June 1 for letter of intent, September 1 for proposal
    Board meeting date(s): November
    Final notification: 2 to 3 weeks after board meeting
    Write: Philip M. Jelley, Foundation Manager or David J. Knight, Administrative Assistant
Officers and Directors: Mary C. Skaggs, President; Peter H. Forsham, M.D., Catherine L. O'Brien, Vice-Presidents; Philip M. Jelley, Secretary and Foundation Manager; Stephen J. McKee, Treasurer.
Number of staff: 4 full-time professional.
Employer Identification Number: 946174113

370

Smith (George D.) Fund, Inc. ⌶
555 California St., Suite 5050
San Francisco 94104

Incorporated in 1956 in Delaware.
Donor(s): George D. Smith, Sr.†
Financial data: (yr. ended 12/31/83): Assets,
$9,386,807 (M); expenditures, $405,160,
including $380,100 for 9 grants (high:
$170,000; low: $100).
Purpose and activities: Broad purposes; grants
primarily for higher education, a hospital, and
public television support, largely in California
and Utah.
Limitations: Giving primarily in CA and UT.
Officers and Trustees:* George D. Smith, Jr.,*
President, Secretary, and Treasurer; C.M.
Smith,* Vice-President; H.D. Burgess, Vice-
President and Treasurer.
Employer Identification Number: 136138728

371

Smith (The May and Stanley) Trust ⌶
c/o John P. Collins, Sr.
49 Geary St., Suite 244
San Francisco 94102   (415) 391-0292

Donor(s): May Smith.
Financial data: (yr. ended 12/31/83): Assets,
$1,947,183 (M); expenditures, $64,349,
including $59,200 for 13 grants (high: $5,000;
low: $1,000).
Purpose and activities: Giving primarily in the
San Francisco area, and in England, Scotland,
Canada, and Australia, for church support and
religious welfare funds, including aid to the
handicapped, the aged, and children; support
also for other social agencies.
Types of support awarded: Operating
budgets, building funds, general purposes.
Limitations: Giving primarily in the San
Francisco, CA, area and in Canada, England,
Scotland, and Australia.
Application information:
   Initial approach: Letter
   Deadline(s): None
Trustees: John P. Collins, Sr., John P. Collins,
Jr., J. Ronald Gibbs.
Employer Identification Number: 946435244

372

Smith (The Stanley) Horticultural Trust
49 Geary St., Rm. 244
San Francisco 94102   (415) 391-0292
Application address: Sir George Taylor,
Belhaven House, East Lothian, EH 421 NS,
Scotland

Trust established in 1970 in California.
Donor(s): Mrs. Stanley Smith.
Financial data: (yr. ended 12/31/83): Assets,
$4,230,972 (M); expenditures, $147,233,
including $128,250 for 18 grants (high:
$15,750; low: $2,000).
Purpose and activities: Grants to organizations
for horticultural programs, including education
and research.
Types of support awarded: Building funds,
operating budgets, special projects, research.

Limitations: No grants to individuals or for
endowment funds.
Application information: Application form
required.
   Initial approach: Full proposal
   Copies of proposal: 1
   Deadline(s): None
   Board meeting date(s): As required
   Write: Sir George Taylor, Director
Trustees: John P. Collins, Barbara de Brye,
James R. Gibbs, May Smith, Sir George Taylor.
Employer Identification Number: 946209165

373

**Snelling (The Gustavus J. & Helen
Crowe) Foundation** ⌶
c/o Crocker National Bank
111 Sutter St., 12th Fl.
San Francisco 94104

Established in 1982 in California.
Financial data: (yr. ended 5/31/83): Assets,
$1,330,201 (M); gifts received, $1,283,991;
expenditures, $41,836, including $20,000 for
10 grants (high: $4,000; low: $1,000).
Purpose and activities: Initial year of
operation 1982-83; giving locally and in
Seattle, Washington, for educational and
charitable purposes.
Limitations: Giving primarily in the San
Francisco, CA, area and Seattle, WA.
Trustee: Crocker National Bank.
Employer Identification Number: 946543319

374

Soiland (Albert) Cancer Foundation
c/o Meserve, Mumper & Hughes
5190 Campus Dr., Box 7820
Newport Beach 92660

Incorporated in 1946 in California.
Donor(s): Albert Soiland, M.D.†
Financial data: (yr. ended 6/30/82): Assets,
$1,142,210 (M); expenditures, $215,643,
including $128,153 for 5 grants (high: $60,000;
low: $1,500).
Purpose and activities: Care and treatment of
needy cancer patients; fellowships in
radiological therapy; grants to approved
institutions for cancer research.
Application information:
   Write: J. Robert Meserve, Secretary-Treasurer
Officers and Directors: J. Robert Meserve,
Secretary-Treasurer.
Employer Identification Number: 956027828

375

**Sorensen (The Harvey L.) and Maud C.
Sorensen Foundation**
c/o Bancroft, Avery & McAlister
601 Montgomery St., Suite 900
San Francisco 94111

Incorporated in 1960 in California.
Donor(s): Harvey L. Sorensen,† Maud C.
Sorensen.†
Financial data: (yr. ended 9/30/83): Assets,
$4,557,608 (M); expenditures, $389,228,
including $343,125 for 13 grants (high:
$68,750; low: $5,000).

Purpose and activities: Grants restricted
largely to three hospitals and other local
organizations designated by the donor.
Limitations: Giving primarily in San Francisco,
CA. No grants to individuals; no loans.
Application information: Applications are not
invited and will not be acknowledged.
   Board meeting date(s): 2 or 3 times a year
   Write: James R. Bancroft, President
Officers and Trustees: James R. Bancroft,
President; Edmond S. Gillette, Jr., Vice-
President; John H. Bosche, Secretary; Paul M.
Bancroft.
Employer Identification Number: 941542559

376

**Sprague (Caryll M. and Norman F.)
Foundation**
3600 Wilshire Blvd., Suite 2110
Los Angeles 90010   (213) 387-7311

Trust established in 1957 in California.
Donor(s): Caryll M. Sprague, Norman F.
Sprague, Jr., M.D.
Financial data: (yr. ended 12/31/82): Assets,
$3,085,033 (M); expenditures, $460,692,
including $433,250 for 30 grants (high:
$281,000; low: $250).
Purpose and activities: Broad purposes;
primarily local giving, with emphasis on higher
education including medical education,
secondary education, and museums.
Limitations: Giving primarily in CA. No grants
to individuals.
Application information:
   Initial approach: Letter or telephone
   Board meeting date(s): Annually and as
   required
   Write: Norman F. Sprague, Jr., M.D., Trustee
Trustees: Cynthia S. Holliday, Caryll S. Mingst,
Charles T. Munger, Norman F. Sprague, Jr.,
M.D., Norman F. Sprague III, M.D.
Employer Identification Number: 956021187

377

Stamps (James L.) Foundation, Inc.
P.O. Box 250
Downey 90241   (213) 861-3112

Incorporated in 1963 in California.
Donor(s): James L. Stamps.†
Financial data: (yr. ended 12/31/83): Assets,
$10,033,092 (M); expenditures, $734,013,
including $615,895 for 96 grants (high:
$25,000; low: $400; average: $1,000-$10,000).
Purpose and activities: Broad purposes;
predominantly local giving, as well as in
Arizona, with emphasis on Protestant
evangelical churches, seminaries, associations,
and programs; support also for welfare
agencies, youth agencies, medical research,
and hospitals. Capital fund grants restricted to
Christian organizations; new equipment grants
restricted to Christian organizations and
hospitals; camping grants restricted to Christian
camps.
Types of support awarded: Operating
budgets, continuing support, annual campaigns,
seed money, emergency funds, matching funds,
special projects.

Limitations: Giving limited to CA and AZ. No grants to individuals, or for endowment funds, deficit financing, scholarships, fellowships, publications, or conferences.
Application information: Application form required.
Initial approach: Letter
Deadline(s): 27th of the month preceding board meetings
Board meeting date(s): Bimonthly beginning in January, on the second Tuesday of the month
Final notification: 5 to 10 days
Write: Milan Green, Secretary
Officers and Trustees: Willis R. Leach, President; I.W. Johnson, Vice-President; Milan Green, Secretary and Treasurer; E.C. Boutault, Thomas P. Lynch.
Number of staff: 1 full-time support; 1 part-time support.
Employer Identification Number: 956086125

378
Stans Foundation, The
350 West Colorado Blvd.
Pasadena 91105 (818) 795-5947

Incorporated in 1945 in Illinois.
Donor(s): Maurice H. Stans, Kathleen C. Stans.†
Financial data: (yr. ended 12/31/84): Assets, $3,000,000 (M); expenditures, $243,073, including $222,066 for 80 grants (high: $50,000; low: $25).
Purpose and activities: General giving, with emphasis on a restoration project, a historical society, and a museum; grants also for public service organizations, research, higher education and church support.
Types of support awarded: General purposes, continuing support, annual campaigns, building funds, equipment.
Limitations: No grants to individuals, or for operating budgets, endowment funds, scholarships, fellowships, or matching gifts; no loans.
Application information:
Initial approach: Letter and 1-page proposal
Copies of proposal: 1
Deadline(s): None
Board meeting date(s): August or September
Final notification: 60 days
Write: Maurice H. Stans, President
Officers and Directors: Maurice H. Stans, President and Treasurer; Steven H. Stans, Vice-President; Marie C. Gath, Secretary; Maureen Stans Helmick, Walter Helmick, Terrell Stans Manley, William Manley, Diane Stans, Susan Stans, Theodore M. Stans.
Number of staff: None.
Employer Identification Number: 366008663

379
Stauffer (John and Beverly) Foundation ¤
3255 Wilshire Blvd., Suite 615
Los Angeles 90010 (213) 381-3933

Incorporated in 1954 in California.
Donor(s): John Stauffer.†

Financial data: (yr. ended 12/31/83): Assets, $2,968,348 (M); expenditures, $170,087, including $136,450 for 32 grants (high: $25,450; low: $500).
Purpose and activities: Broad purposes; primarily local giving, with emphasis on higher education, hospitals, medical research, and child welfare.
Types of support awarded: Continuing support, annual campaigns, building funds, equipment, scholarship funds.
Limitations: Giving primarily in the Los Angeles, CA, area. No grants to individuals, or for endowment funds or operating budgets.
Application information:
Initial approach: Letter
Copies of proposal: 1
Board meeting date(s): 3 times a year
Write: Jack R. Sheridan, President
Officers and Directors: Jack R. Sheridan, President; Felix W. Robertson, Vice-President; Mary Ann Frankenhoff, Secretary; Thomas C. Towse, Treasurer; Harriette Hughes, Jack R. Sheridan II.
Employer Identification Number: 952241406

380
Stauffer (John) Charitable Trust ▼
Equitable Plaza, Suite 2500
3435 Wilshire Blvd.
Los Angeles 90010 (213) 385-4345

Trust established in 1974 in California.
Donor(s): John Stauffer.†
Financial data: (yr. ended 5/31/84): Assets, $17,375,970 (M); expenditures, $974,205, including $753,920 for 17 grants (high: $100,000; low: $20,000; average: $20,000-$75,000).
Purpose and activities: Primarily local giving, restricted to hospitals and higher education.
Types of support awarded: Building funds, endowment funds, equipment, fellowships, general purposes, matching funds, professorships, scholarship funds.
Limitations: Giving primarily in CA. No grants to individuals, or for research, special projects, conferences, or publications; no loans.
Publications: Application guidelines, program policy statement.
Application information:
Initial approach: Letter
Copies of proposal: 3
Deadline(s): None
Board meeting date(s): Bimonthly beginning in February
Final notification: 6 to 9 months
Write: Stanley C. Lagerlof, Trustee
Trustees: Carl M. Franklin, A. Richard Kimbrough, Stanley C. Lagerlof.
Number of staff: 1 part-time support.
Employer Identification Number: 237434707

381
Steel (Marshall), Sr. Foundation ¤
P.O. Box 915
Pebble Beach 93953

Trust established in 1957 in California.
Donor(s): Members of the Steel family and family-related businesses.

Financial data: (yr. ended 12/31/83): Assets, $3,295,181 (M); expenditures, $169,339, including $160,400 for 58 grants (high: $10,000; low: $100).
Purpose and activities: General purposes; primarily local giving, with emphasis on higher education and science studies, cultural programs and museums, hospitals, social agencies, and conservation.
Limitations: Giving primarily in CA; no grants outside the U.S. No support for religious purposes. No grants to individuals.
Application information:
Write: Marshall Steel, Jr.
Trustees: Alison Steel, Eric Steel, Gordon Steel, Jane Steel, Lauri Steel, Marshall Steel, Jr.
Employer Identification Number: 946080053

382
Steele (Harry G.) Foundation ▼
441 Old Newport Blvd., Rm. 301
Newport Beach 92663 (714) 631-0418

Incorporated in 1953 in California.
Donor(s): Grace C. Steele.†
Financial data: (yr. ended 10/31/84): Assets, $49,679,082 (M); expenditures, $4,781,255, including $4,595,531 for 58 grants (high: $400,000; low: $500; average: $5,000-$250,000).
Purpose and activities: Primarily local giving, with emphasis on higher and secondary education, including scholarship funds, the fine arts, population control, hospitals and clinics, and youth agencies.
Types of support awarded: Building funds, endowment funds, scholarship funds, matching funds, continuing support, general purposes, special projects, equipment.
Limitations: Giving primarily in CA. No support for tax-supported organizations or private foundations. No grants to individuals; no loans.
Publications: Annual report, program policy statement, application guidelines.
Application information:
Initial approach: Letter, followed by proposal
Copies of proposal: 1
Deadline(s): None
Board meeting date(s): Quarterly
Final notification: 6 months
Write: Richard Steele, Vice-President
Officers and Trustees: Audrey Steele Burnand, President; Richard Steele, Vice-President and Treasurer; Alphonse A. Burnand, III, Secretary; Elizabeth R. Steele, Barbara Steele Williams, Nick B. Williams.
Number of staff: 1 part-time support.
Employer Identification Number: 956035879

383
Stern (Sidney) Memorial Trust ▼
P.O. Box 893
Pacific Palisades 90272

Trust established in 1974 in California.
Donor(s): S. Sidney Stern.†

Financial data: (yr. ended 8/31/83): Assets, $12,485,305 (M); expenditures, $1,065,721, including $941,900 for 108 grants (high: $128,000; low: $150; average: $150-$100,000).

Purpose and activities: Primarily local giving, with emphasis on child welfare, aid to the handicapped, education, cultural programs, and the humanities.

Types of support awarded: Operating budgets, annual campaigns, seed money, emergency funds, deficit financing, building funds, equipment, land acquisition, endowment funds, matching funds, scholarship funds, special projects, research.

Limitations: Giving primarily in CA; all funds must be used within the U.S. No grants to individuals, or for continuing support, publications, or conferences; no loans.

Publications: Program policy statement, application guidelines.

Application information:
Initial approach: Letter or proposal
Copies of proposal: 1
Deadline(s): None
Board meeting date(s): Monthly, except August
Final notification: 3 months
Write: Mrs. Betty Hoffenberg, Chairperson

Officers and Advisors: Betty Hoffenberg, Chairperson; Ira E. Bilson, Secretary; Peter H. Hoffenberg, Marvin Hoffenberg, Edith Lessler, Howard O. Wilson.

Number of staff: None.

Employer Identification Number: 956495222

384
Stewart (Laura May) Trust
3600 Lime St., Bldg. 6, Suite 611
Riverside 92501   (714) 849-7906
Mailing address: Edith Hensell, c/o Laura May Distribution Committee, P.O. Box 574, Banning, CA 92220

Trust established in 1975 in California.
Donor(s): Laura May Stewart.†
Financial data: (yr. ended 5/31/84): Assets, $1,052,673 (M); expenditures, $75,059, including $59,625 for 22 grants (high: $11,914; low: $200).

Purpose and activities: Grants to Banning-Beaumont area only. Emphasis on civic affairs and cultural programs.

Limitations: Giving limited to the Banning-Beaumont, CA, area.

Application information:
Initial approach: Full proposal
Deadline(s): None
Trustee: Bank of America.

Employer Identification Number: 956527634

385
Stuart (Elbridge and Evelyn) Foundation
P.O. Box 3189, Terminal Annex
Los Angeles 90051

Trust established in 1961 in California.
Financial data: (yr. ended 12/31/82): Assets, $5,000,882 (M); expenditures, $413,105, including $370,000 for 30 grants (high: $50,000; low: $500).

Purpose and activities: Primarily local giving, with emphasis on higher and secondary education, hospitals, youth agencies, medical research, and church support.

Limitations: Giving primarily in CA.

Trustees: Clarke A. Nelson, H.E. Olson, Security Pacific National Bank.

Employer Identification Number: 956014019

386
Stuart (Elbridge and Mary) Foundation ▼ ☐
5045 Wilshire Blvd.
Los Angeles 90036   (213) 932-6259

Trust established in 1941 in California.
Donor(s): Elbridge A. Stuart.†
Financial data: (yr. ended 12/31/83): Assets, $32,845,089 (M); expenditures, $1,764,820, including $1,500,300 for 134 grants (high: $100,000; low: $1,100; average: $1,100-$11,000).

Purpose and activities: Broad purposes; primarily local giving, with emphasis on higher education; support also for hospitals, health agencies, youth agencies, and social agencies.

Limitations: Giving primarily in southern CA, with emphasis on Los Angeles. No grants for building funds or past indebtedness.

Application information:
Write: Jonell Hart, Executive Secretary
Advisors: H.E. Olson, Chairman; Dwight L. Stuart, Secretary; E. Hadley Stuart.
Trustee: Crocker National Bank (Gary Nickerson, Trust Officer).

Employer Identification Number: 956019888

387
Stuart (Elbridge) Foundation ▼ ☐
5045 Wilshire Blvd.
Los Angeles 90036

Trust established in 1937 in California.
Donor(s): Elbridge A. Stuart.†
Financial data: (yr. ended 12/31/83): Assets, $40,725,587 (M); expenditures, $2,274,179, including $1,852,700 for 122 grants (high: $270,000; low: $500; average: $1,000-$27,000).

Purpose and activities: Broad purposes; primarily local giving, with emphasis on higher education, hospitals, and health agencies; support also for youth agencies, child welfare, aid to the handicapped, and medical research.

Limitations: Giving primarily in CA, with the exception of educational institutions.

Application information:
Board meeting date(s): Decisions on grants made once annually, toward the end of the year
Write: Jonell Hart, Executive Secretary
Advisors: Dwight L. Stuart, Chairman; H.E. Olson, Secretary; D.L. Stuart, Jr.
Trustee: Crocker National Bank (Gary Nickerson, Trust Officer).

Employer Identification Number: 956019876

388
Stuart (Mary Horner) Foundation ▼ ☐
5045 Wilshire Blvd.
Los Angeles 90036   (213) 932-6259

Trust established in 1941 in Washington.
Donor(s): Elbridge H. Stuart.†
Financial data: (yr. ended 12/31/83): Assets, $19,997,158 (M); expenditures, $1,121,923, including $998,900 for 140 grants (high: $60,600; low: $1,000; average: $1,000-$15,000).

Purpose and activities: Giving primarily locally and in Washington, with emphasis on cultural programs, higher education, hospitals, and health agencies; grants also for youth agencies, and child welfare.

Limitations: Giving primarily in CA and the state of WA. No support for organizations whose teachings are subversive of the fundamental principles of Christianity.

Application information:
Deadline(s): None
Board meeting date(s): Annually, toward end of year
Write: Jonelle Hart
Foundation Advisors: Dwight L. Stuart, E. Hadley Stuart, Jr., E. Hadley Stuart III.
Trustee: Seattle First National Bank.

Employer Identification Number: 916037460

389
Stulsaft (The Morris) Foundation ▼
100 Bush St., Rm. 500
San Francisco 94104   (415) 986-7117

Incorporated in 1953 in California; sole beneficiary of feeder trust created in 1965; assets reflect value of assets of testamentary trust.
Donor(s): The Morris Stulsaft Testamentary Trust.
Financial data: (yr. ended 12/31/84): Assets, $15,346,259 (M); expenditures, $1,510,493, including $1,376,664 for 137 grants (high: $50,000; low: $2,000; average: $5,000-$20,000).

Purpose and activities: Broad purposes; giving restricted to the San Francisco Bay Area, with emphasis on recreational, health, educational, and cultural and social programs for children.

Types of support awarded: Operating budgets, seed money, deficit financing, building funds, equipment, land acquisition, matching funds, scholarship funds, research, special projects, publications, conferences and seminars.

Limitations: Giving limited to the San Francisco Bay area, CA: Alameda, Contra Costa, Marin, San Francisco, Santa Clara, and San Mateo counties. No grants to individuals, or for emergency funding.

Publications: Program policy statement, application guidelines.

Application information: Application form required.
Initial approach: Letter requesting application form
Copies of proposal: 1
Deadline(s): 9 months prior to meetings
Board meeting date(s): January, March, May, July, September, and November

Final notification: Approximately 7 months
Write: Joan Nelson Dills, Administrator
Officers and Directors: J. Boatner
Chamberlain, President; Mrs. William Corvin,
Vice-President; David H. Brodie, Secretary-
Treasurer; Derek F.C. Adams, Mrs. Robert
Corvin, A.C. Gaither, Raymond A. Marks,
Isadore Pivnick.
Number of staff: 2 full-time professional.
Employer Identification Number: 946064379

390
Sundean Foundation ¤
927 Hanover St.
Santa Cruz 95060

Donor(s): Harold A. Sundean, Edith P.
Sundean.
Financial data: (yr. ended 1/31/82): Assets,
$14,130,271 (M); expenditures, $1,917,326,
including $1,233,286 for 23 grants (high:
$752,100; low: $45).
Purpose and activities: Support primarily for
Seventh Day Adventist churches and
missionary activities, with some emphasis on
Central America.
Officers: Harold A. Sundean, President; Harold
C. Sundean, Raymond Nelson, Vice-Presidents;
Carol Nelson, Secretary-Treasurer.
Director: Edith P. Sundean.
Employer Identification Number: 946050302

391
Swig Foundation, The ¤
Fairmont Hotel
San Francisco 94106

Trust established in 1957 in California.
Donor(s): Benjamin H. Swig,† members of the
Swig family.
Financial data: (yr. ended 12/31/83): Assets,
$11,562,725 (M); expenditures, $411,850,
including $319,683 for 62 grants (high:
$65,000; low: $100; average: $1,000-$65,000).
Purpose and activities: Broad purposes;
general giving, with emphasis on higher
education in Israel and the United States; some
support for Jewish welfare funds and cultural
programs.
Trustees: Richard S. Dinner, Melvin M. Swig,
Richard L. Swig.
Employer Identification Number: 946065205

392
Swig (Mae and Benjamin) Charity
Foundation ¤
Fairmont Hotel
California and Powell Sts.
San Francisco 94106

Established in 1955.
Financial data: (yr. ended 12/31/82): Assets,
$3,981,521 (M); expenditures, $331,963,
including $292,770 for 37 grants (high:
$150,000; low: $100).
Purpose and activities: Grants primarily for
Jewish welfare funds and education.
Directors: Richard S. Dinner, Melvin M. Swig,
Richard L. Swig.
Employer Identification Number: 237416746

393
System Development Foundation ▼
181 Lytton Ave., Suite 210
Palo Alto 94301   (415) 328-5120

Incorporated in 1956 in California.
Donor(s): System Development Corporation.
Financial data: (yr. ended 6/30/84): Assets,
$47,000,000 (M); expenditures, $20,500,000,
including $19,402,421 for 66 grants (high:
$5,142,212; low: $1,500).
Purpose and activities: To support basic
research in the principles of information
sciences, biological and machine information
processing, and man-machine interfaces.
Foundation will operate for a finite term; final
grants to be awarded about 1987-88.
Types of support awarded: Publications,
conferences and seminars, research.
Limitations: No grants to individuals, or for
general support, capital or endowment funds,
scholarships and fellowships, or matching gifts;
no loans.
Publications: Annual report, informational
brochure, program policy statement.
Application information: Applications not
accepted.
   Board meeting date(s): February, May,
   August, and December
   Write: Carl M. York, Director of Program
   Administration
Officers and Trustees: Arnold O. Beckman,
Chairman; Ralph W. Tyler, President; Augustus
B. Kinzel, Vice-President; Donald L. Putt,
Secretary; Edwin E. Huddleson, Jr., Lloyd N.
Morrisett.
Number of staff: 2 full-time professional; 2
part-time professional; 2 full-time support.
Employer Identification Number: 951955563

394
Taper (Mark) Foundation ▼
9465 Wilshire Blvd., Suite 900
Beverly Hills 90213

Incorporated in 1952 in California.
Donor(s): S. Mark Taper.
Financial data: (yr. ended 6/30/83): Assets,
$4,966,480 (M); expenditures, $306,594,
including $297,423 for 39 grants (high:
$140,908; low: $25).
Purpose and activities: Broad purposes;
primarily local giving, with emphasis on the
performing arts, higher education, and youth
agencies.
Types of support awarded: General purposes.
Limitations: Giving primarily in CA.
Officers and Directors: S. Mark Taper,
President; Janice A. Lazarof, Barry H. Taper,
Vice-Presidents; Carolyn Mary Kleefeld.
Employer Identification Number: 956027846

395
Teledyne Charitable Trust
Foundation ▼ ¤
1901 Ave. of the Stars, Suite 1800
Los Angeles 90067   (213) 277-3311

Trust established in 1966 in Pennsylvania.
Donor(s): Teledyne Inc., and its subsidiaries
and divisions.

Financial data: (yr. ended 12/31/83): Assets,
$36,328 (L); gifts received, $1,240,335;
expenditures, $1,240,375, including $728,420
for 292 grants (high: $50,000; low: $100;
average: $100-$10,000) and $511,915 for
employee matching gifts.
Purpose and activities: Broad purposes; grants
primarily to higher and secondary education,
community funds, hospitals, and youth agencies.
Types of support awarded: Employee
matching gifts.
Application information: Applications not
invited.
Trustees: Berkley J. Baker, Jack H. Hamilton,
George A. Roberts, G.A. Zitterbart.
Employer Identification Number: 256074705

396
Thagard Foundation ¤
215 E. Commonwealth Ave., Suite A
P.O. Box 171
Fullerton 92632

Established in 1968 in California.
Financial data: (yr. ended 4/30/83): Assets,
$2,506,313 (M); expenditures, $323,990,
including $287,000 for 19 grants (high:
$50,000; low: $1,000).
Purpose and activities: Primarily local giving
for education.
Limitations: Giving primarily in CA.
Officers and Trustees: George F. Thagard, Jr.,
President; Lucille T. Ellis, Roy Reynolds,
Raymond G. Thagard, Vice-Presidents; Richard
L. O'Connor, Secretary-Treasurer; Belle L. Ellis.
Employer Identification Number: 956225425

397
Thomas (Roy E.) Medical Foundation ¤
c/o Security Pacific National Bank
P.O. Box 3189, Terminal Annex
Los Angeles 90051

Established in 1979.
Donor(s): Roy E. Thomas,† Georgia Seaver
Thomas.†
Financial data: (yr. ended 12/31/83): Assets,
$1,314,717 (M); gifts received, $46,308;
expenditures, $74,383, including $60,000 for 1
grant.
Purpose and activities: Primarily local giving
to a hospital for medical equipment.
Limitations: Giving primarily in CA.
Trustees: Seaver T. Page, Richard C. Seaver,
Security Pacific National Bank.
Employer Identification Number: 953190677

398
Thornton Foundation, The
523 West Sixth St., Suite 636
Los Angeles 90014   (213) 629-3867

Incorporated in 1958 in California.
Donor(s): Charles B. Thornton,† Flora L.
Thornton.
Financial data: (yr. ended 12/31/83): Assets,
$1,707,765 (M); gifts received, $37,000;
expenditures, $98,614, including $88,400 for
24 grants (high: $35,000; low: $100).

Purpose and activities: Broad purposes; primarily local giving, with emphasis on higher and secondary education and cultural programs.
Types of support awarded: Operating budgets, continuing support, annual campaigns, building funds, endowment funds, research.
Limitations: Giving primarily in CA. No grants to individuals, or for seed money, emergency funds, deficit financing, equipment, land acquisition, demonstration projects, publications, conferences, scholarships, or fellowships; no loans.
Application information:
 Initial approach: Letter
 Board meeting date(s): As required
 Final notification: 1 month
 Write: Charles B. Thornton, Jr., President
Officers and Trustees:* Charles B. Thornton, Jr.,* President; William Laney Thornton,* Vice-President; Kay J. Evans, Secretary; Danny M. Makos, Chief Financial Officer.
Number of staff: 2 part-time professional; 2 part-time support.
Employer Identification Number: 956037178

399
Ticor Foundation ▼
6300 Wilshire Blvd.
Los Angeles 90048   (213) 852-6311

Incorporated in 1952 in California.
Donor(s): Ticor, and its subsidiaries.
Financial data: (yr. ended 12/31/83): Assets, $2,756,029 (M); gifts received, $2,000; expenditures, $527,035, including $452,725 for 265 grants (high: $25,000; low: $50) and $27,465 for 103 employee matching gifts.
Purpose and activities: Broad purposes; giving primarily in California and the Pacific Northwest, with emphasis on community funds, private higher education, cultural programs and youth agencies.
Types of support awarded: General purposes, continuing support, annual campaigns, building funds, employee matching gifts.
Limitations: Giving primarily in CA and the Pacific Northwest. No support for secondary education. No grants to individuals, or for endowment funds, research, operating grants to organizations receiving money from community funds, or scholarships and fellowships; no loans.
Application information:
 Initial approach: Full proposal
 Copies of proposal: 1
 Deadline(s): Submit proposal preferably in June or December; no set deadline
 Board meeting date(s): February and November
 Final notification: 3 months
 Write: John B. Warner, Executive Vice-President
Officers: Rocco C. Siciliano,* President; John B. Warner, Executive Vice-President and Secretary-Treasurer; William J. Fitzpatrick,* Winston V. Morrow,* Raymond A. Rodeno,* Vice-Presidents.
Trustees:* Ernest J. Loebbecke.
Number of staff: 2.
Employer Identification Number: 956030995

400
Times Mirror Foundation, The ▼
Times Mirror Square
Los Angeles 90053   (213) 972-3936

Incorporated in 1962 in California.
Donor(s): The Times Mirror Company.
Financial data: (yr. ended 12/31/82): Assets, $4,582,942 (M); expenditures, $2,782,080, including $2,770,673 for 94 grants (high: $250,000; low: $2,500).
Purpose and activities: Local giving, largely for higher education and culture.
Limitations: Giving primarily in CA. No support for religious organizations. No grants to individuals, or for publications, conferences, one-time events, or matching gifts; no loans.
Publications: Annual report.
Application information:
 Initial approach: Letter
 Deadline(s): Submit proposal preferably from January to March or from August to October; deadlines April 1 and November 1
 Board meeting date(s): May and December
 Write: Stephen C. Meier, Secretary
Officers: Franklin D. Murphy, M.D.,* President; Otis Chandler,* Robert F. Erburu,* Vice-Presidents; Stephen C. Meier, Secretary; Charles R. Redmond,* Treasurer.
Directors:* Dow W. Carpenter, Jr., John E. Flick, Jack E. Meadows, Phillip L. Williams.
Employer Identification Number: 956079651

401
Timken-Sturgis Foundation
2100 Union Bank Bldg.
525 B St.
San Diego 92101   (619) 699-2782

Incorporated in 1949 in California.
Donor(s): The Timken family, Valerie T. Whitney.†
Financial data: (yr. ended 11/30/83): Assets, $1,535,441 (M); expenditures, $123,235, including $109,500 for 55 grants (high: $15,000; low: $100).
Purpose and activities: Giving primarily in Southern California and Nevada for education, medical research, and health services; support also for cultural programs.
Types of support awarded: Research, professorships.
Limitations: Giving primarily in southern CA and NV. No grants to individuals, or for general support, capital or endowment funds, or matching gifts; no loans.
Application information:
 Initial approach: Letter
 Copies of proposal: 1
 Deadline(s): None
 Board meeting date(s): As required
 Final notification: 1 month
 Write: Frank Kockritz, Secretary-Treasurer
Officers and Directors: George R. Sturgis, President; William T. Sturgis, Vice-President; Frank Kockritz, Secretary-Treasurer.
Number of staff: None.
Employer Identification Number: 956048871

402
Trust Funds Incorporated
100 Broadway, 3rd Fl.
San Francisco 94111   (415) 434-3323

Incorporated in 1934 in California.
Donor(s): Bartley P. Oliver.
Financial data: (yr. ended 12/31/83): Assets, $3,038,264 (M); expenditures, $172,040, including $155,629 for 47 grants (high: $10,000; low: $100; average: $5,000) and $899 for grants to individuals.
Purpose and activities: Broad purposes, primarily local giving, including fostering of Christian religion, education, and social work, primarily through support of institutions and projects related to the Roman Catholic church.
Types of support awarded: General purposes, seed money, emergency funds, research, publications, conferences and seminars, scholarship funds, internships.
Limitations: Giving limited to the San Francisco Bay Area, CA, or to projects of national or global scope. No support for organizations that draw substantial public support. No grants for capital or endowment funds, matching gifts, or annual campaigns; no loans. Generally, no grants to individuals.
Publications: 990-PF, application guidelines, program policy statement.
Application information:
 Initial approach: Telephone, letter, or full proposal
 Copies of proposal: 2
 Deadline(s): None
 Board meeting date(s): Usually in May and December
 Final notification: 2 months
 Write: Albert J. Steiss, President
Officers and Directors: Albert J. Steiss, President; Rev. James J. Ward, Vice-President and Secretary; James T. Healy, Vice-President and Chief Financial Officer.
Number of staff: 1 part-time professional; 1 part-time support.
Employer Identification Number: 946062952

403
Tuohy (Alice Tweed) Foundation ▼
1006 Santa Barbara St.
Santa Barbara 93101   (805) 963-0675
Mailing address: P.O. Box 2578, Santa Barbara, CA 93120

Incorporated in 1956 in California.
Donor(s): Alice Tweed Tuohy.†
Financial data: (yr. ended 6/30/84): Assets, $6,967,114 (M); expenditures, $499,369, including $336,777 for 41 grants (high: $56,850; low: $500; average: $1,000-$10,000).
Purpose and activities: Charitable purposes; primarily local giving, with emphasis on higher education, art as related to higher education, hospital care, patient rehabilitation, and youth programs; substantial support also for the art program at the Duluth campus of the University of Minnesota.
Types of support awarded: Seed money, matching funds, building funds, equipment, land acquisition, scholarship funds, matching funds.

Limitations: Giving limited to the Santa Barbara, CA, area. No support for private foundations. No grants to individuals, or for operating budgets, national campaigns, research, unrestricted purposes, and rarely for endowment funds; no loans.
Publications: Annual report, application guidelines, program policy statement.
Application information:
   Initial approach: Letter
   Copies of proposal: 5
   Deadline(s): Submit proposal between July 1 and September 15; proposals received after deadline may be deferred for a year
   Board meeting date(s): April or May, and November
   Final notification: 2 to 3 months
   Write: Harris W. Seed, President
Officers and Directors: Harris W. Seed, President; Eleanor Van Cott, Vice-President, Secretary, and Treasurer; Lorenzo Dall'Armi, Jr., Raymond W. Darland, Paul W. Hartloff, Jr.
Number of staff: 2 part-time professional.
Employer Identification Number: 956036471

404
Turn On To America
P.O. Box 643
Lafayette 94549

Established in 1981.
Donor(s): Victor Baranco, Jim Sugg, West Oakland Food Coalition, Dreyer's Ice Cream.
Financial data: (yr. ended 10/31/83): Assets, $85 (M); gifts received, $162,796; expenditures, $162,946, including $25,661 for 5 grants (high: $12,538; low: $300) and $130,222 for grants to individuals.
Purpose and activities: Primarily local giving, with emphasis on social services, including foster home care and gifts of food, clothing, and household goods to individuals and charitable organizations.
Types of support awarded: Grants to individuals.
Limitations: Giving primarily in CA.
Officers: Ray Vetterlein, Chairman; Art Friedman, President; Ricci Napoletano, Secretary-Treasurer; Bill Weaver, Executive Director.
Employer Identification Number: 237110313

405
Tyler (Alice C.) Foundation ⌗
c/o Hoag Accountancy Corp.
661 Stone Canyon Rd.
Los Angeles 90077

Established in 1979.
Donor(s): Alice C. Tyler.
Financial data: (yr. ended 11/30/83): Assets, $329,413 (M); gifts received, $162,617; expenditures, $319,402, including $312,200 for 18 grants (high: $205,000; low: $1,000).
Purpose and activities: Primarily local giving, with emphasis on higher education, including an ecology-energy fund at a university, hospitals and medical research, and child welfare.
Limitations: Giving primarily in Los Angeles, CA.

Officers: Alice C. Tyler, President; Mark Townsend, Secretary.
Directors: Frank Clark, Jr., Karl M. Samuelian.
Employer Identification Number: 953432643

406
Union Bank Foundation
P.O. Box 3100
Los Angeles 90051   (213) 236-5823

Trust established in 1953 in California.
Donor(s): Union Bank.
Financial data: (yr. ended 12/31/82): Assets, $158,050 (M); gifts received, $250,000; expenditures, $238,495, including $233,495 for 100 grants (high: $50,000; low: $25) and $5,000 for 37 employee matching gifts.
Purpose and activities: Broad purposes; primarily local giving in areas of company operations, with emphasis on community funds, higher education, hospitals, and cultural programs.
Types of support awarded: General purposes, operating budgets, continuing support, annual campaigns, emergency funds, building funds, equipment, employee matching gifts.
Limitations: Giving primarily in CA, particularly in areas of company operations. No grants to individuals, or for endowment funds, scholarships, fellowships, or research; no loans.
Application information:
   Initial approach: Proposal
   Copies of proposal: 1
   Deadline(s): Submit proposal preferably in January; no set deadline
   Board meeting date(s): Monthly
   Final notification: 3 months
   Write: Christopher I.M. Houser, President
Trustee: Union Bank (Christopher I. M. Houser, President).
Number of staff: 3.
Employer Identification Number: 956023551

407
Union Oil Company of California Foundation ▼
461 South Boylston St.
Los Angeles 90017   (213) 977-6171
Mailing address for applications: P.O. Box 7600, Los Angeles, CA 90051

Incorporated in 1962 in California.
Donor(s): Union Oil Company of California.
Financial data: (yr. ended 12/31/83): Assets, $3,671,415 (M); expenditures, $4,508,031, including $3,960,633 for 484 grants (high: $166,650; low: $300) and $485,211 for 1,256 employee matching gifts.
Purpose and activities: General giving, with emphasis on higher education, community funds, and various scholarship programs; matches employee contributions to colleges and universities up to $5,000 per year per person. Preference given to organizations that serve an area with high concentration of company employees or that are vital to the energy industry. Corporate divisions are located in Colorado, Louisiana, New Mexico, Texas, and Wyoming.

Types of support awarded: Annual campaigns, continuing support, employee matching gifts, fellowships, professorships, research, scholarship funds, seed money, employee related scholarships, building funds, special projects.
Limitations: Giving primarily in areas of company operations in CO, LA, NM, TX, and WY. No support for veterans, fraternal, sectarian, social, religious, athletic, choral, or similar groups; trade or business associations; state agencies and departments; or elementary or secondary education. No grants to individuals (except for company-employee scholarships), or for general purposes, capital funds for education, endowment funds, courtesy advertising, conferences, supplemental operating support to organizations eligible for United Fund support, or for trips or tours; no loans.
Publications: Annual report, application guidelines, program policy statement.
Application information:
   Initial approach: Letter
   Copies of proposal: 1
   Deadline(s): September 15
   Board meeting date(s): As required
   Final notification: 6 to 8 weeks
   Write: R.P. Van Zandt, Vice-President
Officers: Fred L. Hartley,* President; R.P. Van Zandt,* Vice-President; R.O. Hedley,* Secretary; E.H. Powell, Treasurer.
Trustees:* William H. Doheny.
Number of staff: 3.
Employer Identification Number: 956071812

408
Upjohn California Fund, The
P.O. Box 169
Carmel Valley 93924   (408) 659-4662

Incorporated in 1955 in California.
Financial data: (yr. ended 10/31/83): Assets, $1,446,900 (M); expenditures, $143,261, including $112,400 for 60 grants (high: $4,000; low: $500).
Purpose and activities: Broad purposes; primarily local giving, with emphasis on community funds, educational, scientific, and broadly based cultural organizations.
Limitations: Giving primarily in CA. No grants to individuals.
Application information:
   Initial approach: Letter, followed by proposal
   Copies of proposal: 1
   Deadline(s): None
   Board meeting date(s): March, June, September, and December
   Write: Eugene C. Wheary, President
Officers and Directors: Eugene C. Wheary, President and Treasurer; John W. Broad, Vice-President and Secretary.
Employer Identification Number: 946065219

409
Van Camp Foundation ⌗
8316 Marina Pacifica Dr. North
Long Beach 90803

Trust established in 1975 in California.

Donor(s): Gilbert C. Van Camp, Sr. Family Trust.
Financial data: (yr. ended 12/31/83): Assets, $4,195,751 (M); expenditures, $253,037, including $237,000 for 9 grants (high: $115,000; low: $2,000).
Purpose and activities: Primarily local giving for youth agencies, a museum and a university.
Limitations: Giving primarily in CA.
Officers: Gilbert C. Van Camp, Jr., President; Alice Van Camp, Vice-President, Fred Fox, Jr., Secretary-Treasurer.
Employer Identification Number: 956039680

410
van Loben Sels (Ernst D.) - Eleanor Slate van Loben Sels Charitable Foundation
225 Bush St., Rm. 708
San Francisco 94104   (415) 983-1093

Incorporated in 1964 in California.
Donor(s): Ernst D. van Loben Sels.†
Financial data: (yr. ended 12/31/83): Assets, $5,128,263 (M); expenditures, $361,272, including $285,200 for 58 grants (high: $18,000; low: $500; average: $2,000-$3,000).
Purpose and activities: Local giving, with priority given to nonrecurring grants in support of projects which will test potentially useful innovations in the areas of education, health, welfare, humanities, and the environment.
Types of support awarded: Seed money, emergency funds, matching funds, special projects, research, publications, conferences and seminars.
Limitations: Giving limited to northern CA. No support for national organizations unless for a specific local project, or to projects requiring medical, scientific, or other technical knowledge for evaluation. No grants to individuals, or for operating budgets, continuing support, deficit financing, capital or endowment funds, or scholarships and fellowships; no loans.
Publications: Annual report, program policy statement, application guidelines.
Application information:
  Initial approach: Full proposal, letter, or telephone
  Copies of proposal: 3
  Deadline(s): None
  Board meeting date(s): About every 6 weeks
  Final notification: 3 to 4 weeks
  Write: Claude H. Hogan, President
Officers and Directors: Claude H. Hogan, President; Edward A. Nathan, Vice-President; Toni Rembe, Secretary-Treasurer.
Number of staff: None.
Employer Identification Number: 946109309

411
Van Nuys (J. B. and Emily) Charities ⌘
611 West Sixth St., Suite 3320
Los Angeles 90017   (213) 624-6253

Incorporated in 1957 in California.
Donor(s): Emily Van Nuys, J. Benton Van Nuys.

Financial data: (yr. ended 12/31/83): Assets, $379,894 (M); gifts received, $472,489; expenditures, $455,563, including $396,293 for 91 grants (high: $10,000; low: $1,000).
Purpose and activities: Primarily local giving, with emphasis on hospitals and health agencies, child welfare, and youth agencies; support also for the handicapped and social agencies.
Types of support awarded: General purposes.
Limitations: Giving primarily in southern CA.
Application information:
  Initial approach: Proposal
  Deadline(s): None
  Board meeting date(s): Quarterly to award grants
  Write: Robert Gibson Johnson, President
Officers and Trustees: Robert Gibson Johnson, President; Lawrence Chaffin, Vice-President; Donald W. Moulton, Secretary-Treasurer; John M. Heidt, Robert S. Warner.
Employer Identification Number: 956096134

412
Von der Ahe Foundation
4605 Lankershim Blvd., Suite 707
North Hollywood 91602   (213) 877-2454

Incorporated in 1951 in California.
Donor(s): Members of the Von der Ahe family, Von's Grocery Company.
Financial data: (yr. ended 12/31/83): Assets, $4,202,108 (M); expenditures, $335,530, including $305,500 for 54 grants (high: $30,000; low: $100).
Purpose and activities: "To promote scientific and charitable causes"; primarily local giving, with emphasis on Roman Catholic religious institutions and health and welfare services; support also for higher education and a community fund.
Limitations: Giving primarily in CA. No grants to individuals.
Application information:
  Initial approach: Letter
  Board meeting date(s): April and November
Officers and Directors: Wilfred L. Von der Ahe, President; Clyde Von der Ahe, Vice-President; Vincent Von der Ahe, Secretary and Treasurer; Charles K. Von der Ahe, Frederic T. Von der Ahe, Thomas R. Von der Ahe.
Employer Identification Number: 956051857

413
Wade (The Elizabeth Firth) Endowment Fund
P.O. Box BB
200 East Carrillo St.
Santa Barbara 93102

Trust established in 1961 in California; incorporated in 1979.
Donor(s): Elizabeth Firth Wade.†
Financial data: (yr. ended 1/31/83): Assets, $2,052,693 (M); expenditures, $153,968, including $98,200 for 49 grants (high: $17,000; low: $500).
Purpose and activities: Support for youth agencies, the handicapped, education, and cultural programs.
Application information:

Write: Patricia M. Brouard, Secretary-Treasurer
Officers and Directors: Arthur R. Gaudi, President; Steven M. Anders, Vice-President; Patricia M. Brouard, Secretary-Treasurer.
Employer Identification Number: 953610694

414
Walker (T. B.) Foundation ⌘
1280 Columbus Ave.
San Francisco 94133   (415) 775-1245

Incorporated in 1925 in Minnesota; reincorporated partially in 1976 in California.
Donor(s): T.B. Walker,† Gilbert M. Walker.†
Financial data: (yr. ended 9/30/83): Assets, $4,403,491 (M); expenditures, $253,212, including $225,000 for 59 grants (high: $25,333; low: $500).
Purpose and activities: Local giving; interests primarily in the arts and other cultural and educational programs, with some support for population control, and youth and social agencies.
Types of support awarded: Continuing support, annual campaigns, research, special projects.
Limitations: Giving limited to CA. No grants to individuals, and generally not for building funds.
Application information:
  Initial approach: Proposal
  Copies of proposal: 1
  Deadline(s): Submit proposal in August or September
  Board meeting date(s): December
  Write: Brooks Walker, President
Officers and Trustees: Brooks Walker, President; Sylvia S. Walker, 1st Vice-President; Harriet W. Henderson, 2nd Vice-President; Walker Smith, Jr., 3rd Vice-President; Jean S. Goodrich, Secretary; Jean W. Yeates, Treasurer; Calvin Goodrich, Colleen Marsh, Dana C. Smith, John C. Walker.
Employer Identification Number: 521078287

415
Wasserman Foundation ⌘
c/o I.L. Kory Accountancy Corporation
10920 Wilshire Blvd., Suite 1200
Los Angeles 90024

Incorporated in 1956 in California.
Donor(s): Lew R. Wasserman.
Financial data: (yr. ended 12/31/83): Assets, $15,968,639 (M); gifts received, $1,440,780; expenditures, $454,651, including $445,266 for 63 grants (high: $50,000; low: $100).
Purpose and activities: Broad purposes; primarily local giving, with emphasis on hospitals and medical research, Jewish welfare funds, higher education, public policy groups and the performing arts.
Limitations: Giving primarily in CA.
Officers and Directors: Lew R. Wasserman, President and Treasurer; Donald T. Rosenfeld, Allan E. Susman, Edith Wasserman, Vice-Presidents.
Employer Identification Number: 956038762

416
**Watson (Louisa P.) Residuary Trust-
Fund D**
3435 Wilshire Blvd., Suite 1500
Los Angeles 90010

Established in 1973.
Donor(s): Louisa P. Watson.†
Financial data: (yr. ended 6/30/83): Assets,
$4,123,870 (M); expenditures, $422,533,
including $408,829 for 7 grants (high: $60,000;
low: $48,829).
Purpose and activities: Primarily local giving
to colleges, universities, and a youth
organization for scholarship funds.
Types of support awarded: Scholarship funds.
Limitations: Giving primarily in CA. No grants
for general support, building or endowment
funds, or matching gifts; no loans.
Trustees: Albert E. Adams, Howard W.
Hunter, William T. Huston, Gordon L. Lund,
William S. Martin, Jr.
Employer Identification Number: 956420311

417
**Wattis (The Paul L. and Phyllis)
Foundation ▼ ¤**
220 Bush St., Rm. 1016
San Francisco 94104   (415) 989-5426

Incorporated in 1958 in California.
Donor(s): Paul L. Wattis,† Phyllis C. Wattis.
Financial data: (yr. ended 12/31/83): Assets,
$16,465,428 (M); expenditures, $587,849,
including $543,000 for 25 grants (high:
$100,000; low: $3,000; average: $10,000-
$50,000).
Purpose and activities: Primarily local giving,
with emphasis on cultural activities and
secondary education; support also for health
agencies, including services for the
handicapped.
Limitations: Giving primarily in CA, with
emphasis on San Francisco.
Application information:
  Initial approach: Letter
Officers and Directors: Phyllis C. Wattis,
President; W.R. Kimball, Jr., Vice-President;
Paul L. Wattis, Jr., Secretary-Treasurer; H.R.
Horrow, Edmund W. Littlefield, Carol Wattis
Wilmans.
Number of staff: 1 part-time professional.
Employer Identification Number: 946104337

418
**Webb (Torrey H. and Dorothy K.)
Educational and Charitable Trust**
5966 Abernathy Dr.
Los Angeles 90045

Trust established in 1976 in California.
Donor(s): Torrey H. Webb.†
Financial data: (yr. ended 12/31/84): Assets,
$3,071,009 (L); expenditures, $573,332,
including $522,000 for 24 grants (high:
$110,000; low: $1,000; average: $22,000).
Purpose and activities: Primarily local giving,
with emphasis on higher education, health
agencies, and population control.
Limitations: Giving primarily in CA.

Application information:
  Write: Carl M. Franklin, Trustee
Trustee: Carl M. Franklin, Chairman.
Employer Identification Number: 510188579

419
Weiler Foundation, The
(formerly Ralph J. Weiler Foundation)
151 University Ave., Suite 201
Palo Alto 94301

Established in 1961 in California.
Donor(s): Ralph J. Weiler.†
Financial data: (yr. ended 4/30/84): Assets,
$5,252,283 (M); expenditures, $248,423,
including $202,855 for 27 grants.
Purpose and activities: Primarily local giving,
with emphasis on private education, hospitals,
and medical research.
Limitations: Giving primarily in CA.
Publications: Application guidelines.
Application information: Application form
required.
  Initial approach: Proposal
  Copies of proposal: 3
  Deadline(s): March
  Board meeting date(s): Monthly
  Write: Bartlett Burnap, President
Officers: Bartlett Burnap, President; William
Bullis, Vice-President; Elizabeth J. Kelly,
Secretary-Treasurer.
Employer Identification Number: 237418821

420
Weinberg (Adolph and Etta) Foundation
P.O. Box 723
Norwalk 90650

Incorporated in 1952 in California.
Donor(s): Adolph Weinberg, Coast Grain
Company.
Financial data: (yr. ended 9/30/83): Assets,
$1,544,114 (M); expenditures, $113,742,
including $104,095 for 45 grants (high:
$40,000; low: $25).
Purpose and activities: Grants primarily for
Jewish religious organizations and temple
support.
Limitations: No grants to individuals.
Application information:
  Initial approach: Full proposal
  Copies of proposal: 2
  Deadline(s): Submit proposal preferably from
  July through September
Officers and Directors: Adolph Weinberg,
President; Bob Weinberg, Vice-President; Ray
Danielson, Seiso Kawasaki, Ray Moline, George
Ogawa.
Number of staff: 1 part-time support.
Employer Identification Number: 956075855

421
Weingart Foundation ▼
1200 Wilshire Blvd., Suite 305
Los Angeles 90017-1984   (213) 482-4343
Mailing address: P.O. Box 17982, Los Angeles,
CA, 90017-0982

Incorporated in 1951 in California.
Donor(s): Ben Weingart,† Stella Weingart.†

Financial data: (yr. ended 6/30/84): Assets,
$230,297,517 (M); gifts received, $4,724,457;
expenditures, $18,760,713, including
$13,247,828 for 134 grants (high: $2,000,000;
low: $500; average: $10,000-$1,000,000).
Purpose and activities: Broad purposes; giving
only to local non-profit organizations, with
emphasis on community services, medicine,
higher education, and public policy.
Types of support awarded: Seed money,
building funds, equipment, matching funds,
special projects, research.
Limitations: Giving limited to southern CA.
No grants to individuals, or for endowment
funds, normal operating expenses, continuing
support, annual campaigns, emergency funds,
deficit financing, land acquisition, scholarships,
fellowships, seminars, conferences, workshops,
travel, or surveys; no loans.
Publications: Annual report, application
guidelines.
Application information: Application form
required.
  Initial approach: Letter
  Copies of proposal: 10
  Deadline(s): The fifth of each month
  Board meeting date(s): Bimonthly, except
  July and August
  Final notification: 3 to 4 months
  Write: Charles W. Jacobson, Grant
  Administrator
Officers: Morris A. Densmore, President;
Bernardine Helwig, Vice-President and
Treasurer; Laurence A. Wolfe, Vice-President;
Ann Van Dormolen, Assistant Vice-President;
Judy Osborn, Secretary.
Directors:* Harry J. Volk, Chairman; John T.
Gurash, William J. McGill, Sol Price, Marcus H.
Rabwin, M.D.
Number of staff: 6 full-time professional; 2
part-time professional; 6 full-time support.
Employer Identification Number: 956054814

422
Welk (Lawrence) Foundation
1299 Ocean Ave., Suite 800
Santa Monica 90401   (213) 451-5727

Incorporated in 1960 in California.
Donor(s): Teleklen Productions, Inc.
Financial data: (yr. ended 10/30/84): Assets,
$888,125 (M); gifts received, $9,990;
expenditures, $123,251, including $119,650
for 38 grants (high: $15,000; low: $100;
average: $1,000-$10,000).
Purpose and activities: Broad purposes; local
giving for social service agencies, health care
institutions and research.
Types of support awarded: Annual
campaigns, seed money, building funds,
equipment, matching funds, special projects,
research.
Limitations: Giving limited to southern CA.
No grants to individuals, or for endowment
funds, operating budgets, continuing support,
emergency funds, deficit financing,
publications, conferences, scholarships and
fellowships, or employee-matching gifts; no
loans.
Publications: Application guidelines, program
policy statement.

Application information: Application form required.

Initial approach: Letter
Copies of proposal: 2
Deadline(s): Submit proposal preferably from January through August; deadline September 1
Board meeting date(s): October
Final notification: 1 to 10 months
Write: Shirley Fredricks, Executive Director

Officers: Lawrence Welk,* Chairman of the Board; Shirley Fredricks,* President and Executive Director; Theodore Lennon, Secretary-Treasurer.
Directors:* Ronald Gother.
Number of staff: 1 full-time professional.
Employer Identification Number: 956064646

423
Wells Fargo Foundation ▼
420 Montgomery St., MAC 0101-111
San Francisco 94163   (415) 396-7427

Established in 1978 in San Francisco.
Donor(s): Wells Fargo Bank.
Financial data: (yr. ended 12/31/84): Assets, $2,108,508 (M); gifts received, $2,049,000; expenditures, $3,351,926, including $2,864,495 for 260 grants (high: $75,000; low: $100; average: $11,000) and $264,278 for employee matching gifts.
Purpose and activities: Giving primarily in California, with emphasis on art and cultural programs, education, civic affairs organizations, and social service agencies.
Types of support awarded: Special projects, employee matching gifts.
Limitations: Giving primarily in CA. No support for government agencies, United Way-supported agencies, hospitals, national health organizations or organizations with multiple chapters, religious activities, political purposes, or secondary schools (except employee matching gifts). No grants to individuals, or for video tapes, films, publications, research, conferences, or general operating budgets.
Publications: Annual report.
Application information: Application form required.

Initial approach: Telephone or letter
Copies of proposal: 1
Deadline(s): None
Board meeting date(s): Quarterly
Write: Elisa Boone, Vice-President

Officers and Directors:* Ronald E. Eadie,* President; James C. Flood,* Executive Vice-President; Alan C. Gordon,* Lona Jupiter,* Senior Vice-Presidents; Elisa Boone, Thomas E. Peterson,* Frank S. Shepard,* John S. Spiecker,* Vice-Presidents.
Number of staff: 6.
Employer Identification Number: 942549743

424
Whitelight Foundation, The
1875 Century Park East, Ste. 2200
Los Angeles 90067

Established in 1980.
Donor(s): Betty Freeman.

Financial data: (yr. ended 12/31/83): Assets, $59,055 (M); gifts received, $123,470; expenditures, $171,464, including $162,250 for 54 grants (high: $15,000; low: $250).
Purpose and activities: Giving primarily for "assistance to established classical musicians in publishing new compositions, copying scores, and performing new compositions"; support also for cultural programs and social service agencies; grants generally to a limit of $5,000.
Types of support awarded: Grants to individuals.
Application information: Individuals submit brief resume and outline of project, including budget.

Initial approach: Proposal
Write: Betty Freeman, Trustee

Trustee: Betty Freeman.
Employer Identification Number: 953513930

425
Whittell (Elia) Trust for Disabled Veterans of Foreign Wars ⌀
P.O. Box 3747
San Francisco 94119

Established around 1978 in California.
Donor(s): Elia Whittell.†
Financial data: (yr. ended 11/30/83): Assets, $1,872,444 (M); expenditures, $200,317, including $150,000 for 6 grants (high: $40,000; low: $10,000).
Purpose and activities: "To provide maintenance and medical support for disabled French veterans not provided by other sources".
Trustees: Kenneth J. Ashcraft, Edward R. Finch, Jr.
Employer Identification Number: 946449253

426
Whittier Foundation ⌀
1600 Huntington Dr.
South Pasadena 91030

Incorporated in 1955 in California.
Donor(s): Leland K. Whittier, and members of the Whittier family.
Financial data: (yr. ended 4/30/83): Assets, $18,114,320 (M); gifts received, $600,000; expenditures, $807,064, including $720,918 for 8 grants (high: $300,000; low: $500).
Purpose and activities: Broad purposes; primarily local giving, with emphasis on hospitals, aid to the handicapped, and wildlife preservation.
Limitations: Giving primarily in CA.
Officers and Directors: Leland K. Whittier, President; James E. Greene, Vice-President; Linda Sommer, Secretary; Arlo G. Sorensen, Treasurer.
Employer Identification Number: 956027493

427
Wilbur (Brayton) Foundation
320 California St., Suite 200
San Francisco 94104

Incorporated in 1947 in California.

Donor(s): Wilbur-Ellis Company, Connell Bros. Co., Ltd.
Financial data: (yr. ended 12/31/83): Assets, $2,180,878 (M); gifts received, $50,000; expenditures, $143,789, including $132,160 for 43 grants (high: $20,000; low: $450; average: $500-$2,000).
Purpose and activities: Broad purposes; primarily local giving, with emphasis on the arts and on higher and secondary education; grants also for hospitals and church support.
Limitations: Giving primarily in San Francisco, CA.
Application information:

Initial approach: Letter
Write: Brayton Wilbur, Jr., President

Officers and Directors: Brayton Wilbur, Jr., President; Carter P. Thacher, Vice-President; Herbert B. Tully, Secretary-Treasurer.
Employer Identification Number: 946088667

428
Wilbur (Marguerite Eyer) Foundation
P.O. Box B-B
Santa Barbara 93102   (805) 682-6501

Established in 1975 in California.
Donor(s): Marguerite Eyer Wilbur.†
Financial data: (yr. ended 6/30/83): Assets, $2,339,274 (M); gifts received, $412,897; expenditures, $168,349, including $87,050 for 33 grants (high: $10,000; low: $500; average: $1,000-$6,000) and $55,000 for 14 grants to individuals.
Purpose and activities: Grants primarily for higher education, including support for organizations and individuals to publish educational and literary works.
Types of support awarded: Operating budgets, annual campaigns, seed money, emergency funds, matching funds, scholarship funds, exchange programs, special projects, research, publications, conferences and seminars, fellowships.
Limitations: No grants for continuing support, deficit financing, building or endowment funds, or land acquisition; no loans.
Publications: Program policy statement, application guidelines.
Application information:

Initial approach: Full proposal
Copies of proposal: 5
Deadline(s): None
Board meeting date(s): January, April, July and October
Final notification: 30 to 45 days after board meets
Write: Gary R. Ricks, Chief Executive Officer

Officers: Russell Kirk, President; William Longstreth, Vice-President; F. Joseph Frawley, Secretary; Harry J. Haldeman, Jr., Treasurer; Gary R. Ricks, Chief Executive Officer.
Number of staff: 1 full-time professional; 1 full-time support.
Employer Identification Number: 510168214

429
Witter (Dean) Foundation
57 Post St.
San Francisco 94104   (415) 981-2966

Incorporated in 1952 in California.
Donor(s): Dean Witter,† Mrs. Dean Witter, Dean Witter & Company.
Financial data: (yr. ended 11/30/84): Assets, $3,442,298 (M); expenditures, $203,172, including $131,264 for 10 grants (high: $45,000; low: $200).
Purpose and activities: Primary purpose is to support postgraduate research in economics and finance, with a secondary purpose to support local conservation.
Types of support awarded: Research, publications, special projects, building funds, equipment.
Limitations: Giving limited to northern CA. No grants to individuals or for endowment funds.
Publications: Annual report, program policy statement, application guidelines.
Application information:
  Initial approach: Letter, telephone, or full proposal
  Copies of proposal: 6
  Deadline(s): Submit proposal 1 month before board meeting
  Board meeting date(s): January, April, July and October
  Write: Lawrence I. Kramer, Jr., Administrative Director
Officers: Edmond S. Gillette, Jr.,* President; James R. Bancroft,* Vice-President; William D. Witter,* Secretary-Treasurer; Lawrence I. Kramer, Jr., Administrative Director.
Trustees:* Frank H. Roberts, Dean Witter, III.
Number of staff: 1 part-time professional.
Employer Identification Number: 946065150

430
Wollenberg Foundation, The ▼ ⌑
100 Pine St., Suite 1700
San Francisco 94111   (415) 434-4641

Trust established in 1952 in California.
Donor(s): H.L. Wollenberg.†
Financial data: (yr. ended 12/31/83): Assets, $13,015,559 (M); expenditures, $702,500, including $686,250 for 22 grants (high: $330,000; low: $1,000; average: $2,000-$50,000).
Purpose and activities: Primarily to assist non-tax-supported colleges in the United States.
Types of support awarded: Endowment funds, special projects, operating budgets, general purposes.
Limitations: No support for sectarian purposes or religion-affiliated institutions. No grants to individuals; no loans.
Application information: Applications for grants not invited.
  Write: Marc H. Monheimer, Trustee
Trustees: Marc H. Monheimer, J. Roger Wollenberg, Richard P. Wollenberg.
Number of staff: None.
Employer Identification Number: 946072264

431
Wood-Claeyssens Foundation ⌑
c/o Barton E. Clemens, Jr.
200 East Carillo, Suite 400
Santa Barbara 93101

Established in 1980.
Donor(s): Ailene B. Claeyssens.
Financial data: (yr. ended 3/31/83): Assets, $1,718,177 (L); expenditures, $286,904, including $279,379 for 42 grants (high: $90,000; low: $100).
Purpose and activities: Broad purposes; primarily local giving, including support for hospitals and health, welfare, and youth agencies.
Limitations: Giving primarily in CA.
Officers and Directors: Ailene B. Claeyssens,* President; Pierre P. Claeyssens,* 1st Vice-President; Cynthia S. Wood,* 2nd Vice-President; James H. Hurley, Jr., Secretary and Manager; Charles C. Gray, Treasurer.
Employer Identification Number: 953514017

432
Yorkin Foundation, The
250 North Delfern Dr.
Los Angeles 90077

Established in 1979 in California.
Donor(s): Bud Yorkin, Peg Yorkin.
Financial data: (yr. ended 11/30/84): Assets, $180,910 (M); gifts received, $456,692; expenditures, $381,678, including $381,320 for 186 grants (high: $50,000; low: $100; average: $2,050).
Purpose and activities: Primarily local giving, with emphasis on local arts and cultural programs, health, Jewish welfare, and a genetics foundation.
Types of support awarded: Operating budgets, annual campaigns, seed money, emergency funds, special projects, research, publications, conferences and seminars.
Limitations: Giving primarily in Los Angeles, CA. No grants to individuals, or for capital or endowment funds, continuing support, deficit financing, scholarships and fellowships, or matching gifts; no loans.
Application information:
  Initial approach: Letter
  Copies of proposal: 1
  Deadline(s): None
  Board meeting date(s): March
  Final notification: 2 months
  Write: Peg Yorkin, Vice-President
Officers and Directors: Bud Yorkin, President; Peg Yorkin, Vice-President and Secretary; Arthur Greenberg.
Number of staff: None.
Employer Identification Number: 953454331

433
Zellerbach Family Fund, The ▼
260 California St., Suite 1010
San Francisco 94111   (415) 421-2629

Incorporated in 1956 in California.
Donor(s): Jennie B. Zellerbach.†
Financial data: (yr. ended 12/31/84): Assets, $25,474,180 (M); gifts received, $210,000; expenditures, $1,804,612, including $1,339,145 for 155 grants (high: $75,000; low: $500).
Purpose and activities: Primarily local giving for direct-service projects in the arts, health, mental health, and welfare.
Types of support awarded: Continuing support, technical assistance.
Limitations: Giving primarily in the San Francisco Bay area, CA. No grants to individuals, or for capital or endowment funds, research, scholarships, or fellowships; no loans.
Publications: Annual report, application guidelines.
Application information: Applications rarely granted; foundation develops most of its own grant proposals.
  Initial approach: Telephone or full proposal
  Copies of proposal: 1
  Deadline(s): Submit full proposal in 1 copy (art proposal in 8 copies), preferably 2 weeks prior to board meeting
  Board meeting date(s): Quarterly
  Final notification: 1 week for non-art applications; 1 week after board meeting for art applications
  Write: Edward A. Nathan, Executive Director
Officers: William J. Zellerbach,* President; Louis J. Saroni, II,* Vice-President-Treasurer; Robert E. Sinton,* Vice-President; P.S. Ehrlich, Jr., Secretary; Edward A. Nathan,* Executive Director.
Directors:* Rev. Stewart E. Adams, Philip S. Boone, Lucy Ann Geiselman, Verneice Thompson.
Number of staff: 1 full-time professional; 1 part-time professional; 2 full-time support.
Employer Identification Number: 946069482

COLORADO

434
Animal Assistance Foundation
2926 W. Jewell Ave.
Denver 80219   (303) 935-6263

Established in 1976 in Colorado.
Donor(s): Louise C. Harrison.†
Financial data: (yr. ended 7/31/84): Assets, $18,251,547 (M); expenditures, $1,411,572, including $757,380 for 22 grants (high: $120,000; low: $555) and $598,108 for 3 foundation-administered programs.
Purpose and activities: Primarily local giving for animal welfare, especially to prevent cruelty to cats and other small household pets.
Types of support awarded: Research.
Limitations: Giving primarily in CO.
Publications: Annual report.
Application information:
  Initial approach: Letter

Deadline(s): None
Write: Robert A. Williams, Executive Director
Officer and Directors: Robert A. Williams, Executive Director; Charles W. Ennis, Grace Mary B. Greenleaf.
Number of staff: 3 full-time professional; 3 part-time professional; 17 full-time support; 6 part-time support.
Employer Identification Number: 840715412

435
Anschutz Family Foundation, The ▼
2400 Anaconda Tower
555 17th St.
Denver 80202   (303) 293-2338

Established in 1979 in Colorado.
Donor(s): Fred B. Anschutz, Anschutz Land and Livestock Company, Inc., Medicine Bow Ranch Company.
Financial data: (yr. ended 11/30/82): Assets, $5,432,566 (M); expenditures, $866,890, including $825,230 for 67 grants (high: $75,000; low: $2,000; average: $5,000-$50,000).
Purpose and activities: General purposes; primarily local giving, with emphasis on the direct provision of human services, especially for children, the elderly, and the poor, including health services; support also for cultural programs, public policy, and urban development organizations.
Types of support awarded: Special projects, operating budgets, continuing support, annual campaigns, seed money, emergency funds, consulting services, technical assistance, research, publications, conferences and seminars.
Limitations: Giving primarily in CO, especially Denver. No support for programs of educational or research organizations. No grants to individuals, or for building or endowment funds, deficit financing, scholarships, or fellowships.
Publications: 990-PF, application guidelines.
Application information: Grants awarded in November.
Initial approach: Letter
Deadline(s): Submit proposal preferably in May through September; deadline October 1
Board meeting date(s): Spring and October
Final notification: 1 week to 6 months
Write: Robert F. Leduc, Executive Director
Officers: Sue A. Rodgers,* President; Nancy P. Anschutz,* Philip F. Anschutz,* Vice-Presidents; Hugh C. Braly,* Secretary and Treasurer; Robert F. Leduc, Executive Director.
Directors:* Fred B. Anschutz, Melinda A. Rodgers, Melissa A. Rodgers.
Number of staff: 1 full-time professional; 1 full-time support.
Employer Identification Number: 742132676

436
Boettcher Foundation ▼
828 Seventeenth St., Suite 800
Denver 80202   (303) 571-5510

Incorporated in 1937 in Colorado.

Donor(s): C.K. Boettcher,† Mrs. C.K. Boettcher,† Charles Boettcher,† Fannie Boettcher,† Ruth Boettcher Humphreys.†
Financial data: (yr. ended 12/31/84): Assets, $77,801,591 (M); expenditures, $4,020,855, including $3,620,973 for 85 grants (high: $285,000; low: $500).
Purpose and activities: To promote the general well-being of mankind, within Colorado only; grants to higher educational institutions with emphasis on scholarships and fellowships, hospitals, community funds, cultural activities, and welfare programs.
Types of support awarded: Scholarship funds, fellowships, operating budgets, seed money, building funds, equipment, land acquisition, matching funds, general purposes.
Limitations: Giving limited to CO, with emphasis on Denver. No grants to individuals or for endowment funds.
Publications: Annual report, application guidelines.
Application information:
Initial approach: Letter
Copies of proposal: 1
Deadline(s): None
Board meeting date(s): Monthly
Final notification: After board meeting
Write: John C. Mitchell II, President
Officers: John C. Mitchell II,* President and Executive Director; William A. Douglas, Vice-President; Hover T. Lentz,* Secretary; J. William Sorensen,* Treasurer.
Trustees:* Mrs. Charles Boettcher II, Chairman; Walter K. Koch, Vice-Chairman; Hatfield Chilson, Richard A. Kirk, George M. Wilfley.
Number of staff: 2 full-time professional; 3 full-time support.
Employer Identification Number: 840404274

437
Buell (Temple Hoyne) Foundation
730 Fourteenth St.
Denver 80202   (303) 629-6067

Incorporated in 1962 in Colorado.
Donor(s): Temple Hoyne Buell.
Financial data: (yr. ended 6/30/83): Assets, $3,327,000 (M); gifts received, $311,000; expenditures, $128,500, including $105,000 for 15 grants (high: $50,000; low: $1,000).
Purpose and activities: Primarily local giving for higher education, including architecture, and for charitable entities.
Types of support awarded: Operating budgets, continuing support, annual campaigns, seed money, building funds, equipment, land acquisition, endowment funds, professorships, scholarship funds.
Limitations: Giving primarily in CO, with emphasis on Denver. No grants to individuals; no loans.
Publications: Informational brochure, program policy statement, application guidelines.
Application information: Application form required.
Initial approach: Letter
Deadline(s): None
Board meeting date(s): Quarterly
Final notification: 3 to 4 months

Officers and Trustees: Temple Hoyne Buell, President; Sidney Montague, Vice-President and Treasurer; William Walters, Secretary; Ronald Kahler, Jack Kent.
Number of staff: None.
Employer Identification Number: 846037604

438
Carroll Foundation, The ⌑
R.R. 1, Box 159
Franktown 80116

Established in 1978.
Donor(s): International Metals & Machines, Inc., Champion Pneumatic Machinery Co., Inc., Ludlow Industries, Inc., and other companies.
Financial data: (yr. ended 4/30/83): Assets, $2,238,459 (M); gifts received, $10,300; expenditures, $247,187, including $241,801 for 27 grants (high: $201,000; low: $25).
Purpose and activities: Giving largely in Massachusetts and Illinois for higher education and hospitals.
Limitations: Giving primarily in MA and IL.
Trustees: Wallace E. Carroll, Jr., Lelia C. Johnson.
Employer Identification Number: 749930634

439
Carter (Fay S.) Foundation ⌑
1875 Deer Valley Rd.
Boulder 80303

Established in 1964 in Colorado.
Financial data: (yr. ended 11/30/82): Assets, $1,509,455 (M); expenditures, $116,975, including $105,736 for 32 grants (high: $25,000; low: $25; average: $100-$25,000).
Purpose and activities: Broad purposes; primarily local giving, with support for higher education and cultural programs.
Limitations: Giving primarily in CO.
Officers: Fay S. Carter,* President; Sydney N. Freidman, Secretary-Treasurer.
Directors:* Judy Drake, Susan Hedling.
Employer Identification Number: 846041358

440
Colorado Springs Community Trust Fund
Holly Sugar Bldg., Suite 1400
Colorado Springs 80903
Grant application address: Miss Florence Edgerly, Assistant Director, 1622 North Corona, Colorado Springs, CO 80907

Community foundation established in 1928 in Colorado by declaration of trust.
Financial data: (yr. ended 12/31/83): Assets, $2,320,700 (M); gifts received, $403,932; expenditures, $230,329, including $222,171 for 19 grants (high: $50,000; low: $800).
Purpose and activities: Local giving, with emphasis on community funds, youth agencies, and child welfare.
Types of support awarded: Continuing support, annual campaigns, seed money, emergency funds, building funds, equipment.

Limitations: Giving primarily in CO. No grants to individuals, or for operating budgets, deficit financing, land acquisition, endowment funds, matching gifts, scholarships and fellowships, research, demonstration projects, publications, or conferences; no loans.
Application information:
Initial approach: Letter
Board meeting date(s): 3 or 4 times a year
Final notification: 3 to 4 months
Write: Jack W. Foutch, Director
Trustees: Gar L. Anneler, Cres Fleming, Hal V. Littrell, Kent Olin.
Number of staff: None.
Employer Identification Number: 510217708

441
Coors (Adolph) Foundation ▼
350-C Clayton St.
Denver 80206   (303) 388-1636

Incorporated in 1975 in Colorado.
Donor(s): Adolph Coors, Jr.,† Gertrude Coors.†
Financial data: (yr. ended 11/30/84): Assets, $72,528,066 (M); expenditures, $4,425,146, including $3,265,690 for grants.
Purpose and activities: To support religious, charitable, and educational organizations primarily within Colorado, with emphasis on education, arts and humanities, public policy, civic affairs, social services, youth, and health. Giving to national funds is limited and pre-committed.
Types of support awarded: Building funds, general purposes, seed money, program-related investments.
Limitations: Giving primarily in CO. No grants to individuals, or for endowment funds, equipment, research, or scholarships; no loans; only limited giving for building funds.
Publications: Annual report, program policy statement, application guidelines.
Application information:
Initial approach: Letter
Copies of proposal: 1
Deadline(s): 6 weeks prior to meetings
Board meeting date(s): February, May, August, and November
Final notification: 3 months
Write: Linda S. Tafoya, Executive Manager
Officers and Directors: William K. Coors, President; Joseph Coors, Vice-President and Treasurer; Linda S. Tafoya, Secretary and Executive Manager; Jeffrey H. Coors, Peter H. Coors, Robert G. Windsor.
Number of staff: 2 full-time professional; 2 full-time support.
Employer Identification Number: 510172279

442
Denver Foundation, The
1880 Gaylord St.
Denver 80206   (303) 322-5680

Community foundation established in 1925 in Colorado by resolution and declaration of trust.
Financial data: (yr. ended 12/31/83): Assets, $7,831,526 (M); gifts received, $847,214; expenditures, $1,110,857, including $748,763 for 105 grants (high: $60,000; low: $533).

Purpose and activities: To "assist, encourage and promote the well-being of mankind, and primarily of the inhabitants of Metropolitan Denver." Grants made only in the Denver, Colorado area, primarily for education, health and hospitals, social services, and cultural programs.
Limitations: Giving limited to 30-mile radius of Denver, CO. No support for sectarian programs, or projects supported largely by public funds. No grants to individuals, or for debt liquidation, building or endowment funds, or research; no loans.
Publications: Annual report, application guidelines, program policy statement.
Application information: Application form required.
Initial approach: Letter
Copies of proposal: 2
Deadline(s): December 31, March 31, June 30, and August 31
Board meeting date(s): March, June, September, and November
Write: Miss Patricia J. Harrington, Executive Director
Officer: Patricia J. Harrington, Executive Director.
Distribution Committee: Richard P. Brown, Chairman; J. Michael Farley, Vice-Chairman; Sheila S. Bisenius, Donald E. Cordova, Walter C. Emery, Sidney Friedman, Virginia Rockwell, Darlene Silver, Robert S. Sloskey.
Trustee Banks: Central Bank of Denver, Colorado National Bank of Denver, Colorado State Bank, Denver National Bank, First Interstate Bank of Denver, First Trust Corporation, Firstbank of Westland, Guaranty Bank & Trust, IntraWest Bank of Denver, Jefferson Bank and Trust, United Bank of Denver.
Number of staff: 2 full-time professional; 1 full-time support.
Employer Identification Number: 846048381

443
Duncan (John G.) Trust
First Interstate Bank of Denver
P.O. Box 5825 TA
Denver 80217   (303) 293-5324

Trust established in 1955 in Colorado.
Donor(s): John G. Duncan.†
Financial data: (yr. ended 12/31/83): Assets, $1,838,650 (L); expenditures, $17,508.
Purpose and activities: Broad purposes; local giving with emphasis on hospitals, higher and secondary education, youth agencies, cultural programs, and a community fund.
Types of support awarded: Annual campaigns, building funds, equipment, research, operating budgets, continuing support, seed money, emergency funds, special projects.
Limitations: Giving limited to CO. No grants to individuals, or for endowment funds, scholarships, or fellowships; no loans.
Publications: Application guidelines.
Application information:
Initial approach: Letter
Copies of proposal: 1
Deadline(s): Submit proposal in October or November; deadline November 15

Board meeting date(s): December
Final notification: December 31
Write: Yvonne Baca, Vice-President
Trustee: First Interstate Bank of Denver.
Number of staff: None.
Employer Identification Number: 846016555

444
8 South 54 East, Inc.
511 16th St., Suite 700
Denver 80202   (303) 825-6246

Incorporated in 1968 in Colorado.
Donor(s): Samuel Gary.
Financial data: (yr. ended 12/31/82): Assets, $1,991,316 (M); expenditures, $238,048, including $183,816 for 3 grants (high: $110,000; low: $33,816).
Purpose and activities: Primarily local giving.
Types of support awarded: Operating budgets, seed money, emergency funds, program-related investments, loans, general purposes, special projects, technical assistance.
Limitations: Giving primarily in CO. No grants to individuals, or for endowment funds, research, scholarships or fellowships, or matching gifts.
Publications: Application guidelines.
Application information:
Initial approach: Letter
Copies of proposal: 1
Deadline(s): None
Board meeting date(s): As required
Final notification: 4 months
Write: Fern C. Portnoy, Vice-President
Officers: Samuel Gary,* President; Fern C. Portnoy,* Vice-President; Robert J. Hilbert, Secretary-Treasurer.
Directors:* James E. Bye, Nancy Gary, Ronald W. Williams.
Number of staff: None.
Employer Identification Number: 846065732

445
El Pomar Foundation ▼
Ten Lake Circle
P.O. Box 158
Colorado Springs 80901   (303) 633-7733

Incorporated in 1937 in Colorado.
Donor(s): Spencer Penrose,† Mrs. Spencer Penrose.†
Financial data: (yr. ended 12/31/83): Assets, $105,158,074 (M); expenditures, $4,889,548, including $4,631,100 for 80 grants (high: $900,000; low: $1,750; average: $25,000-$50,000).
Purpose and activities: Grants only to local nonprofit organizations for public, educational, health, arts and humanities, and welfare purposes; municipalities may request funds for specific projects.
Types of support awarded: Operating budgets, continuing support, emergency funds, building funds, equipment, land acquisition, scholarship funds, annual campaigns.

Limitations: Giving limited to CO. No grants to individuals, travel, film or other media projects, conferences, deficit financing, endowment funds, research, matching gifts, annual campaigns, seed money, or publications; no loans.
Publications: Annual report, program policy statement, application guidelines.
Application information:
  Initial approach: Letter
  Copies of proposal: 1
  Deadline(s): None
  Board meeting date(s): 5 to 7 times a year
  Final notification: 90 days
  Write: William J. Hybl, President
Officers: William J. Hybl,* President; Ben S. Wendelken,* Vice-President; Jerry Roblewsky,* Secretary; R. Thayer Tutt, Jr.,* Treasurer.
Trustees:* Russell T. Tutt, Chairman; Karl E. Eitel, William Thayer Tutt, Joel A.H. Webb.
Number of staff: 3 part-time professional; 1 part-time support.
Employer Identification Number: 846002373

446
Fairfield (Freeman E.) - Meeker Charitable Trust ¤
Intrawest Bank of Denver
Terminal Annex Box 5825
Denver 80217   (303) 893-2211

Trust established in 1969 in Colorado.
Donor(s): Freeman E. Fairfield.†
Financial data: (yr. ended 11/30/82): Assets, $1,702,828 (M); expenditures, $151,850, including $123,206 for 6 grants (high: $81,306; low: $170; average: $250-$50,000) and $15,380 for 32 grants to individuals.
Purpose and activities: Giving primarily to a community fund; support also for higher educational scholarships to Meeker High School graduates.
Types of support awarded: Student aid.
Limitations: Giving limited to Meeker, CO. No grants for building or endowment funds, research, or matching gifts; no loans.
Application information:
  Initial approach: Letter
  Copies of proposal: 1
  Board meeting date(s): As required
  Write: Randall C. Rieck, Senior Trust Officer
Trustees: James Cook, Steve Harp, Rev. Joseph B. Johns, Steven B. Strang, C.J. Wilson, Intrawest Bank of Denver.
Employer Identification Number: 846068906

447
First Interstate Bank Foundation
(formerly Intrawest Foundation)
c/o Intrawest Bank of Denver, Trust Dept.
Terminal Annex Box 5825
Denver 80217   (303) 293-2211

Established in 1982 in Colorado.
Donor(s): First Interstate Bank of Denver.
Financial data: (yr. ended 9/30/84): Assets, $147,947 (M); gifts received, $293,469; expenditures, $251,487, including $248,545 for 44 grants (high: $115,000; low: $250; average: $2,500-$10,000).

Purpose and activities: Primarily local giving, with emphasis on social services and youth.
Limitations: Giving primarily in CO.
Trustee: First Interstate Bank of Denver.
Employer Identification Number: 846169845

448
Fishback (Harmes C.) Foundation Trust ¤
1675 Broadway, Suite 2600
Denver 80202   (303) 623-2700

Trust established in 1972 in Colorado.
Donor(s): Harmes C. Fishback.†
Financial data: (yr. ended 12/31/83): Assets, $1,345,083 (M); expenditures, $74,580, including $57,150 for 43 grants (high: $5,000; low: $75).
Purpose and activities: Primarily local giving, with emphasis on higher education, hospitals, medical research, cultural programs, and youth agencies.
Limitations: Giving primarily in Denver, CO. No grants to individuals.
Application information:
  Initial approach: Letter
  Write: Benjamin F. Stapleton, Trustee
Trustee: Benjamin F. Stapleton.
Employer Identification Number: 510177270

449
Frost Foundation, Ltd., The ▼
Cherry Creek Plaza II, Suite 940
650 South Cherry St.
Denver 80222   (303) 388-1687

Incorporated in 1959 in Louisiana.
Donor(s): Virginia C. Frost.†
Financial data: (yr. ended 12/31/83): Assets, $13,490,294 (M); expenditures, $946,332, including $727,849 for 45 grants (high: $185,000; low: $1,500).
Purpose and activities: Broad purposes; giving primarily in the Southwest, with emphasis on education, including medical education and business administration; grants also for youth agencies, church support, and cultural programs.
Types of support awarded: Seed money, equipment, endowment funds, matching funds, professorships, internships, scholarship funds, fellowships, special projects, research, publications, conferences and seminars, consulting services, technical assistance.
Limitations: Giving primarily in LA and CO; support also in AR, NM, TX, AZ, and OK. No grants to individuals, or for operating expenses or building funds; no loans.
Publications: Annual report, program policy statement, application guidelines.
Application information:
  Initial approach: Telephone or letter
  Copies of proposal: 4
  Deadline(s): December 1 and July 1
  Board meeting date(s): February and September
  Final notification: 7 to 10 days
  Write: Theodore R. Kauss, Executive Director

Officers: Edwin F. Whited,* President; Theodore R. Kauss, Vice-President and Executive Director; Claude G. Rives, III,* Vice-President; J. Greg Bradley, Secretary-Treasurer.
Directors:* Dallas P. Dickinson, J. Luther Jordan, Jr., John A. LeVan, John W. Loftus, J. Hugh Watson.
Number of staff: 1 full-time professional; 1 part-time professional; 1 part-time support.
Employer Identification Number: 720520342

450
Gates Foundation ▼
155 South Madison, Suite 332
Denver 80209   (303) 388-0871

Incorporated in 1946 in Colorado.
Donor(s): Charles Gates,† Hazel Gates,† John Gates.†
Financial data: (yr. ended 12/31/84): Assets, $63,500,000 (M); expenditures, $3,236,317, including $2,499,535 for 83 grants (high: $250,000; low: $500; average: $20,000-$100,000).
Purpose and activities: Primarily local giving to promote the health, welfare, and broad education of mankind whether by means of research, grants, publications, its own agencies and activities, or through cooperation with agencies and institutions already in existence; grants primarily for education, youth services, including leadership development; public policy, historic preservation, humanities and cultural affairs, health care, including cost reduction; and human services.
Limitations: Giving limited to CO, especially the Denver area, except for foundation-initiated grants. No support for United Way agencies, except through its annual grant to the United Way, or private foundations. No grants to individuals (including scholarships), or for operating budgets, deficit financing, endowment funds, purchase of tickets for fundraising dinners, parties, balls, or other social fundraising events, general purposes, research, scholarships, fellowships, or matching gifts; no loans.
Publications: Annual report, informational brochure, application guidelines, program policy statement.
Application information:
  Initial approach: Telephone
  Copies of proposal: 1
  Deadline(s): February 1, April 15, August 1, and October 15
  Board meeting date(s): April 1, June 15, October 1, December 15
  Final notification: 2 weeks
  Write: F. Charles Froelicher, Executive Director
Officers: Charles C. Gates,* President; Robert G. Bonham,* Vice-President; F. Charles Froelicher, Secretary and Executive Director; Jack E. McCandless, Treasurer.
Trustees:* Brown W. Cannon, Jr., William W. Grant, III, Homer E. Reed, Robert K. Timothy.
Number of staff: 2 full-time professional; 1 full-time support; 1 part-time support.
Employer Identification Number: 840474837

451
Heginbotham (Will E.) Trust ⌗
c/o Harry A. Peach
Holyoke 80734

Trust established in 1968 in Colorado.
Donor(s): Will E. Heginbotham.†
Financial data: (yr. ended 12/31/83): Assets, $4,167,149 (M); expenditures, $411,142, including $394,999 for 17 grants (high: $109,699; low: $267).
Purpose and activities: Primarily local giving, with emphasis on public schools, recreation, hospitals, and community development.
Types of support awarded: Building funds, equipment.
Limitations: Giving primarily in Holyoke, CO.
Trustees: Josephine McWilliams, Harry A. Peach, Glen E. Stenson.
Employer Identification Number: 846053496

452
Hill Foundation ▼
c/o Kutak, Rock & Campbell, 2400 Arco Tower
707 17th St.
Denver 80202   (303) 297-2400

Trust established in 1955 in Colorado.
Donor(s): Virginia W. Hill.†
Financial data: (yr. ended 4/30/84): Assets, $6,504,000 (M); gifts received, $4,887; expenditures, $1,341,645, including $832,900 for 57 grants (high: $45,000; low: $1,000; average: $1,000-$45,000).
Purpose and activities: Giving primarily in Colorado and Wyoming for health care, higher education, services for the elderly, and cultural programs; support also for social service agencies.
Types of support awarded: Scholarship funds, equipment.
Limitations: Giving primarily in CO and WY. No grants to individuals, or for capital improvements other than equipment acquisition for health care and related purposes.
Publications: Program policy statement, application guidelines.
Application information:
  Initial approach: Full proposal
  Deadline(s): August 1 for October grants or February 1 for April grants
  Board meeting date(s): 3rd Tuesday monthly and as required
  Final notification: 120 days
  Write: John R. Moran, Jr., Trustee
Trustees: A.W. Cullen, John R. Moran, Jr., First Interstate Bank of Denver.
Employer Identification Number: 846081879

453
Hogan (Jack) Charitable Foundation
1780 South Bellaire, Suite 614
Denver 80222   (303) 758-2460

Established in 1978 in Colorado.
Donor(s): O.T. Hogan Family Foundation.
Financial data: (yr. ended 11/30/82): Assets, $1,619,433 (M); expenditures, $195,854, including $161,000 for 45 grants (high: $10,000; low: $1,000).

Purpose and activities: Primarily local giving for youth and child welfare agencies, especially for the education, medical care, and counseling of handicapped, disturbed, and abused children.
Limitations: Giving primarily in the Denver, CO metropolitan area.
Application information: Application form required.
  Deadline(s): July 31
  Write: Richard J. Callahan, Vice-President
Officers and Directors: Jack D. Hogan, President and Treasurer; Richard J. Callahan, Vice-President and Secretary; Mary Kaye Hogan, Patricia Hogan Gill, Vice-Presidents.
Employer Identification Number: 840776608

454
Hughes (Mabel Y.) Charitable Trust
c/o The First Interstate Bank of Denver
P.O. Box 5825 TA
Denver 80217   (303) 293-5324

Trust established in 1969 in Colorado.
Donor(s): Mabel Y. Hughes.†
Financial data: (yr. ended 8/31/83): Assets, $6,074,019 (M); expenditures, $390,183, including $357,500 for 18 grants (high: $150,000; low: $5,000).
Purpose and activities: Broad purposes; local giving, with emphasis on hospitals, education, museums, and community funds.
Types of support awarded: Operating budgets, continuing support, annual campaigns, seed money, emergency funds, building funds, equipment, endowment funds, research, special projects.
Limitations: Giving limited to CO, with emphasis on the Denver area. No grants to individuals, or for deficit financing, scholarships, or fellowships; no loans.
Publications: Application guidelines, 990-PF.
Application information:
  Initial approach: Letter
  Copies of proposal: 1
  Deadline(s): Submit proposal preferably in October or November; deadline November 15
  Board meeting date(s): December
  Write: Yvonne J. Baca, Vice-President
Officer: Yvonne J. Baca, Vice-President.
Trustees: Eugene H. Adams, The First Interstate Bank of Denver.
Number of staff: None.
Employer Identification Number: 846070398

455
Hunter (A. V.) Trust, Incorporated ▼
633 Seventeenth St., Suite 1600
Denver 80202   (303) 534-2048

Trust established in 1927; incorporated in 1937 in Colorado.
Donor(s): A.V. Hunter.†
Financial data: (yr. ended 12/31/83): Assets, $15,417,883 (M); expenditures, $518,182, including $461,800 for 53 grants (high: $40,000; low: $300; average: $3,000-$15,000) and $6,160 for grants to individuals.

Purpose and activities: Distributions only for use in Colorado to give aid, comfort, support, or assistance to children or aged persons or indigent adults, crippled, maimed or needy, through charitable organizations rendering such aid to persons in the categories named.
Types of support awarded: General purposes, operating budgets, annual campaigns.
Limitations: Giving limited to CO, with emphasis on Denver. No support for tax-supported institutions.
Publications: 990-PF.
Application information: Application form required.
  Initial approach: Letter
  Copies of proposal: 1
  Deadline(s): Submit proposal preferably in October; deadline November 15
  Board meeting date(s): June and December and as required
  Final notification: Within 15 days after meeting
  Write: Sharon Holt, Secretary
Officers: Eugene H. Adams,* Chairman and Treasurer; G.B. Aydelott,* Vice-President; Sharon Holt, Secretary.
Trustees:* W.R. Alexander, William K. Coors, G.C. Gibson.
Number of staff: 1.
Employer Identification Number: 840461332

456
Jenkins (Alice N.) Foundation ⌗
605 South Alton Way, No. 6C
Denver 80231

Financial data: (yr. ended 9/30/83): Assets, $1,427,700 (M); expenditures, $105,136, including $70,000 for 14 grants (high: $14,000; low: $2,000).
Purpose and activities: To care for and provide shelter for stranded and abandoned domestic and wild animals and fowl, and to protect wildlife.
Limitations: Giving primarily in CO.
Trustees: E.W. Gustafson, C.M. Reese.
Employer Identification Number: 840811678

457
JFM Foundation, The ⌗
P.O. Box 5083
Denver 80217

Established in 1980 in Colorado.
Donor(s): Frederick R. Mayer.
Financial data: (yr. ended 6/30/82): Assets, $210,044 (M); gifts received, $3,000; expenditures, $2,214,390, including $2,210,475 for 33 grants (high: $1,500,000; low: $50).
Purpose and activities: Grants primarily for cultural programs, including museums and performing arts, and secondary and higher education.
Officers: Frederick R. Mayer, President; Jan Perry Mayer, Vice-President, Secretary, and Treasurer.
Directors: Anthony R. Mayer, Frederick M. Mayer.
Employer Identification Number: 840833163

458
Johnson (Helen K. and Arthur E.) Foundation ▼
1700 Broadway, Rm. 2302
Denver 80290   (303) 861-4127

Incorporated in 1948 in Colorado.
Donor(s): Arthur E. Johnson,† Mrs. Helen K. Johnson.
Financial data: (yr. ended 12/31/83): Assets, $44,187,282 (M); expenditures, $2,380,532, including $1,831,209 for 92 grants (high: $300,000; low: $100; average: $5,000-$100,000).
Purpose and activities: "To solve human problems and enrich the quality of human life." Local giving only, with emphasis on operational and capital support for community and social services, education, youth, health, and civic and cultural affairs.
Types of support awarded: Operating budgets, building funds, general purposes, equipment, scholarship funds, continuing support, annual campaigns, seed money, land acquisition, research, technical assistance, matching funds, special projects.
Limitations: Giving limited to CO. No grants to individuals, or for endowment funds, individual scholarships, conferences, or purchase of blocks of tickets; no loans.
Publications: Annual report, application guidelines.
Application information:
   Initial approach: Letter or full proposal
   Copies of proposal: 1
   Deadline(s): 60 days prior to board meetings
   Board meeting date(s): March, June, September, and December
   Final notification: 2 weeks after board meeting
   Write: Robert L. Mitton, Executive Director
Officers: Mrs. James R. Hartley,* President; David R. Murphy,* Vice-President and Treasurer; Robert L. Mitton, Vice-President and Executive Director; Gerald R. Hillyard, Jr.,* Secretary.
Trustees: Lynn H. Campion, Thomas B. Campion, Ralph W. Collins, William H. Kistler, Roger D. Knight, Jr., J. Churchill Owen.
Number of staff: 1 full-time professional; 2 full-time support.
Employer Identification Number: 846020702

459
Joslin-Needham Family Foundation ¤
c/o Farmers State Bank
200 Clayton St.
Brush 80723

Donor(s): Gladys Joslin.†
Financial data: (yr. ended 12/31/82): Assets, $1,931,358 (M); expenditures, $128,612, including $102,973 for 12 grants (high: $45,950; low: $500).
Purpose and activities: Primarily local giving for community development; grants also for a library.
Limitations: Giving primarily in CO.
Officer: Judy Gunnon, Executive Secretary.
Trustee: Farmers State Bank.
Employer Identification Number: 846038670

460
Joslyn (The Carl W. and Carrie Mae) Charitable Trust
c/o The First National Bank of Colorado Springs
P.O. Box 1699
Colorado Springs 80942   (303) 471-5334

Trust established in 1971.
Donor(s): Carl W. Joslyn,† Carrie Mae Joslyn.†
Financial data: (yr. ended 12/31/83): Assets, $1,265,343 (M); expenditures, $69,496, including $60,000 for 17 grants (high: $14,250; low: $400).
Purpose and activities: Local giving; emphasis on aid to the elderly and the handicapped, particularly the blind, including education and rehabilitation programs, and on youth agencies.
Types of support awarded: Operating budgets, annual campaigns, building funds, equipment, special projects.
Limitations: Giving limited to El Paso County, CO, primarily Colorado Springs. No grants to individuals, or for endowment funds, research, scholarships or fellowships, or matching gifts; no loans.
Publications: Application guidelines, 990-PF.
Application information:
   Initial approach: Letter
   Copies of proposal: 1
   Deadline(s): Submit proposal preferably in April or October; deadlines April 30 and October 31
   Board meeting date(s): May and November
   Final notification: July 1 and December 1
   Write: W.F. Gernand, Vice-President
Trustee: The First National Bank of Colorado Springs (W.F. Gernand, Vice-President and Trust Officer).
Number of staff: None.
Employer Identification Number: 237135817

461
Kejr Foundation, Inc. ¤
P.O. Box 264
Woodrow 80757

Incorporated in 1959 in Colorado.
Donor(s): Joseph Kejr,† Mrs. Mary Kejr, Kejr Trust, Kejr Family Foundation of Brookville, Kansas, and others.
Financial data: (yr. ended 12/31/83): Assets, $2,372,050 (M); gifts received, $39,298; expenditures, $205,126, including $176,100 for 34 grants (high: $15,000; low: $50).
Purpose and activities: Support of interdenominational, evangelical religious programs, including radio broadcasting; special services to education, church extension, consultation services, and missionary projects.
Officers and Trustees: Harry J. Kejr, President; Frank G. Kejr, Secretary-Treasurer.
Employer Identification Number: 846023358

462
Levy (The Raphael) Memorial Foundation, Inc. ¤
401 South Buckley Rd.
Aurora 80017

Incorporated in 1944 in Colorado.
Donor(s): Edward Levy, Hannah Levy, Jack H. Levy, Fashion Bar, Inc.
Financial data: (yr. ended 12/31/83): Assets, $996,188 (M); gifts received, $407,451; expenditures, $205,633, including $193,084 for 163 grants (high: $100,000; low: $50).
Purpose and activities: Broad purposes; primarily local giving, with emphasis on hospitals and Jewish welfare funds; support also for higher education and community funds.
Limitations: Giving primarily in CO.
Application information:
   Write: Edward Levy
Officers and Directors: Jack Levy, Chairman; Hannah Levy, President; Robert Levy, Vice-President; Barbara Goldberg, Secretary; John Levy, Treasurer.
Employer Identification Number: 846022586

463
Lowe Foundation
Colorado Judicial Center
Two East 14th Ave.
Denver 80203   (303) 861-1111

Incorporated in 1960 in Colorado.
Donor(s): John G. Lowe,† Edith Eaton Lowe.
Financial data: (yr. ended 11/30/84): Assets, $1,521,108 (M); expenditures, $95,245, including $89,300 for 16 grants (high: $10,000; low: $2,200).
Purpose and activities: Grants to local organizations involved in the treatment and teaching of the mentally retarded and victims of cerebral palsy and research in these areas.
Limitations: Giving primarily in CO. No grants to individuals or for endowment funds.
Publications: 990-PF, application guidelines.
Application information:
   Initial approach: Letter
   Copies of proposal: 5
   Deadline(s): Submit proposal preferably in January; deadline February 28
   Board meeting date(s): March and November
   Write: Luis D. Rovira, President
Trustees: Donald E. Burton, Robert P. Harvey, Richard I. Kaye, Luis D. Rovira.
Employer Identification Number: 846021560

464
McCoy Foundation, The ¤
5040 Lyda Ln.
Colorado Springs 80904

Established in 1979.
Donor(s): Arthur H. McCoy.
Financial data: (yr. ended 11/30/83): Assets, $1,712,983 (M); expenditures, $249,570, including $235,038 for 16 grants (high: $30,003; low: $1,000).
Purpose and activities: Grants for cultural progams, including music, and for hospitals and a university.
Officers: Arthur H. McCoy, President and Treasurer; Barbara M. Gartner, Craig W. McCoy, Vice-Presidents; Virginia G. McCoy, Secretary.
Employer Identification Number: 840802889

465
McHugh Family Foundation, The ⌘
650 S. Cherry St., Suite 1225
Denver 80222 (303) 321-2111

Established in 1980.
Donor(s): Jerome P. McHugh, Kindermac Partnership.
Financial data: (yr. ended 11/30/83): Assets, $38,438 (M); gifts received, $115,000; expenditures, $138,712, including $138,249 for 29 grants (high: $51,500; low: $100).
Purpose and activities: Primarily local giving for education, including higher education; and for social services and cultural programs.
Limitations: Giving primarily in Denver, CO. No grants to individuals.
Application information:
 Initial approach: Proposal
 Deadline(s): None
 Write: Jerome P. McHugh, President
Officers and Directors: Jerome P. McHugh, President and Treasurer; Anabel C. McHugh, Vice-President; Paul D. Hollerman, Secretary; Erin McHugh Gogolak, Jerome P. McHugh, Jr.
Employer Identification Number: 742131272

466
Monfort Charitable Foundation
1325 42nd Ave.
Greeley 80634

Established in 1970.
Financial data: (yr. ended 12/31/83): Assets, $2,272,505 (M); expenditures, $143,907, including $129,997 for 23 grants (high: $43,000; low: $70).
Purpose and activities: Largely local giving to community funds and cultural programs.
Limitations: Giving limited to CO.
Application information:
 Deadline(s): None
 Write: Kyle Monfort Walsh, Secretary
Officers: Kenneth W. Monfort, President; Kaye C. Montera, Vice-President; Kyle Monfort Walsh, Secretary and Treasurer.
Number of staff: None.
Employer Identification Number: 237068253

467
Mullen (The John K. and Catherine S.) Benevolent Corporation
1345 First National Bank Bldg.
Denver 80293 (303) 893-3151

Incorporated in 1924 in Colorado.
Donor(s): John K. Mullen,† Catherine S. Mullen,† The J.K. Mullen Company.
Financial data: (yr. ended 7/31/82): Assets, $1,922,647 (M); expenditures, $204,596, including $199,220 for 4 grants (high: $134,220; low: $500).
Purpose and activities: To support public charities and educational institutions; primarily local giving, with emphasis on Roman Catholic church-affiliated organizations.
Limitations: Giving primarily in Denver, CO. No grants to individuals.
Application information:
 Initial approach: Letter
 Copies of proposal: 1

Board meeting date(s): Annually and as required
 Write: Leon A. Lascor, Secretary
Officers and Directors: J. Kernan Weckbaugh, President; Frank L. Tettemer, 1st Vice-President; J. Kenneth Malo, 2nd Vice-President and Treasurer; Leon A. Lascor, Secretary; John F. Malo, John M. O'Connor, Edith M. Roberts, John K. Weckbaugh, Walter S. Weckbaugh.
Employer Identification Number: 846002475

468
Needmor Fund, The ▼
2129 13th St.
Boulder 80302

Trust established in 1956 in Ohio.
Donor(s): Members of the Stranahan family.
Financial data: (yr. ended 12/31/83): Assets, $4,564,701 (M); gifts received, $1,675,959; expenditures, $2,137,920, including $1,932,810 for 216 grants (high: $200,000; low: $25).
Purpose and activities: Grants made without geographic restriction in these areas: (1) Education: projects which focus on increasing parent, student, and citizen involvement in the governance of public education at the elementary and secondary levels. (2) Individual rights: programs which foster institutional responsiveness to the needs of individuals and help individuals understand and secure their basic rights, protections, and opportunities; and those which help individuals have a voice in the determination of policies. (3) Environment: on a national level, seeks to support non-advocacy efforts to define the boundaries of current knowledge on the environment, to determine the areas where new knowledge is needed, or to ask critical questions concerning the environment in national and international dialogues; also interested in supporting organizations that are attempting to solve environmental problems that directly affect the lives of their members. (4) Population: support for organizations that are examining the impact of population and/or developing new means of controlling and reducing population growth.
Types of support awarded: Seed money, research, technical assistance, general purposes.
Limitations: No grants to individuals, or for capital or endowment funds, scholarships and fellowships, matching gifts, deficit-reduction, or operating support for traditional community services; no loans.
Publications: Annual report, program policy statement, application guidelines.
Application information:
 Initial approach: Letter
 Deadline(s): Usually June 1 and December 1; inquire
 Board meeting date(s): February and August
 Final notification: 2 weeks after board meeting
 Write: Deborah Tuck, Director
Officer: Deborah Tuck, Director.

Advisory Committee: Ann Stranahan, Duane Stranahan, Duane Stranahan, Jr., Eileen B. Stranahan, Frances Stranahan, George S. Stranahan, Josh Stranahan, Mary C. Stranahan, Michael Stranahan, Molly Stranahan, Patricia Q. Stranahan, Patrick J. Stranahan, Stephen Stranahan, Virginia Stranahan.
Trustee: The Toledo Trust Company.
Number of staff: 2 full-time professional; 1 part-time professional.
Employer Identification Number: 346504812

469
Norgren (Carl A.) Foundation
2124 South Birch St.
Denver 80222 (303) 758-8393

Incorporated in 1951 in Colorado.
Donor(s): Carl A. Norgren,† Juliet E. Norgren, C.A. Norgren Company.
Financial data: (yr. ended 12/31/84): Assets, $2,860,000 (M); expenditures, $267,000, including $254,170 for 90 grants (high: $31,000; low: $200).
Purpose and activities: Limited almost exclusively to the local area and to activities in which the board has a direct interest; general giving, with support for education, hospitals, community funds, and youth agencies.
Types of support awarded: General purposes, annual campaigns, emergency funds, building funds, equipment, land acquisition, matching funds.
Limitations: Giving limited to the metropolitan Denver, CO, area. No grants to individuals, or for endowment funds, research, scholarships or fellowships, or matching gifts; no loans.
Publications: Annual report, application guidelines.
Application information:
 Initial approach: Letter
 Copies of proposal: 1
 Board meeting date(s): May and December
 Write: Leigh H. Norgren, President
Officers and Directors: Leigh H. Norgren, President; Juliet E. Norgren, Vice-President; Gene N. Koelbel, Secretary; C. Neil Norgren, Donald K. Norgren, Vanda N. Werner.
Number of staff: None.
Employer Identification Number: 846034195

470
O'Fallon (Martin J. and Mary Anne) Trust ⌘
2800 South University Blvd., Rm. 61
Denver 80210

Trust established in 1951 in Colorado.
Donor(s): Martin J. O'Fallon.†
Financial data: (yr. ended 12/31/83): Assets, $1,894,529 (M); expenditures, $160,657, including $132,947 for 27 grants (high: $13,000; low: $200).
Purpose and activities: Grants to continuing Colorado organizations and agencies to assist cultural programs, health, social, and educational services.
Types of support awarded: Operating budgets, building funds.

Limitations: Giving limited to CO; priority always given to Denver. No grants to individuals, or for endowment funds, research, scholarships, or fellowships; no loans.
Publications: Annual report, application guidelines.
Application information: Grant applications from agencies outside Colorado not accepted. Application form required.
Initial approach: Letter
Copies of proposal: 2
Deadline(s): Submit proposal preferably between May and August
Board meeting date(s): January, April, July, and November, and monthly for other trust business
Write: Alfred O'Meara, Jr., Trustee
Trustees: Margaret H. Carey, Alfred O'Meara, Jr., Brian O'Meara, Patrick E. Purcell.
Employer Identification Number: 840415830

471
Petteys (The Jack) Memorial Foundation ⌀

P.O. Box 324
Brush 80723   (303) 573-5860

Established about 1943 in Colorado.
Financial data: (yr. ended 12/31/82): Assets, $1,849,785 (M); expenditures, $114,771, including $107,010 for 66 grants (high: $8,750; low: $50).
Purpose and activities: Scholarships and grants made primarily to local colleges and educational institutions; support also for hospitals, civic projects, and local churches.
Types of support awarded: Scholarship funds.
Limitations: Giving limited to northeastern CO.
Application information:
Initial approach: Letter
Copies of proposal: 1
Deadline(s): Submit proposal in October and November; deadline December 1
Board meeting date(s): Monthly
Write: Mrs. Robert Gunnon
Committee Members and Trustees: Robert U. Hansen, Robert A. Petteys, Helen C. Watrous, Farmers State Bank (John H. Higgins, Trust Officer).
Employer Identification Number: 846036239

472
Pilot Trust ⌀

c/o Intra-West Bank of Boulder
P.O. Box 227
Boulder 80306   (303) 442-0351

Trust established in 1960 in Colorado.
Donor(s): Roger Calvert.†
Financial data: (yr. ended 12/31/83): Assets, $2,813,359 (M); expenditures, $270,325, including $238,537 for 1 grant.
Purpose and activities: Primarily local giving to organizations that provide opportunities for environmental education for persons generally lacking access to nature and outdoor experiences, including support for the foundation's own outdoor educational facility.
Limitations: Giving primarily in CO. No grants for any purposes except those stated; no loans.
Publications: 990-PF.

Application information:
Initial approach: Letter
Copies of proposal: 1
Board meeting date(s): Semiannually
Write: W. David Zimmerman, Executive Director
Trustees: Dan Calvert, Lawrence Wood, Intra-West Bank of Boulder.
Employer Identification Number: 846030136

473
Piton Foundation, The ▼

511 16th St., Suite 700
Denver 80202   (303) 825-6246

Incorporated in 1976 in Colorado.
Donor(s): Samuel Gary.
Financial data: (yr. ended 11/30/83): Assets, $3,705,070 (L); gifts received, $9,649,102; expenditures, $7,000,324, including $5,660,983 for grants (high: $350,000), $79,992 for 54 grants to individuals and $554,370 for 9 loans.
Purpose and activities: To encourage personal effort toward self-realization, to promote the development of strong cooperative relationships between the public and private sectors with emphasis on local involvement, and to improve conditions and opportunities for persons inadequately served by the institutions of society. Almost exclusively local giving, especially for children, youth, families, community development, especially housing and economic development; support to individual volunteer agencies to encourage improved management and service effectiveness; some giving also for civic, conservation, cultural, educational and health programs.
Types of support awarded: Operating budgets, seed money, emergency funds, consulting services, technical assistance, program-related investments, student aid.
Limitations: Giving primarily in CO, with emphasis on the Denver metropolitan area. No grants for basic research, long-range support, debt reduction, building or endowment funds, media projects, or matching gifts.
Publications: Annual report, program policy statement, application guidelines.
Application information:
Initial approach: Letter
Copies of proposal: 1
Deadline(s): None
Board meeting date(s): As required
Final notification: Approximately 4 months
Write: Fern C. Portnoy, Executive Director
Officers: Samuel Gary,* Chairman and President; Fern C. Portnoy,* Vice-President and Executive Director; Robert J. Hilbert, Secretary-Treasurer.
Directors:* James E. Bye, Nancy Gary, Ronald W. Williams.
Number of staff: 11 full-time professional; 10 full-time support.
Employer Identification Number: 840719486

474
Rabb (Harry W.) Foundation ⌀

6242 S. Elmira Circle
Englewood 80111

Established in 1960.
Financial data: (yr. ended 6/30/83): Assets, $1,717,026 (M); expenditures, $161,854, including $130,812 for 27 grants (high: $66,000).
Purpose and activities: Primarily local giving for hospitals, Jewish welfare funds, and the aged.
Limitations: Giving primarily in Denver, CO.
Officers and Trustees: Jacob B. Kaufman, President; Myles Dolan, Vice-President; Richard A. Zarlengo, Secretary-Treasurer.
Employer Identification Number: 237236149

475
Ray Foundation

600 17th St., Suite 1725N
Denver 80202   (303) 573-8855

Established in 1962 in Montana.
Donor(s): James C. Ray, Joan L. Ray.
Financial data: (yr. ended 6/30/84): Assets, $3,563,951 (L); gifts received, $500,000; expenditures, $177,941, including $70,014 for 13 grants (low: $2,100; average: $2,500-$10,000) and $75,000 for 1 foundation-administered program.
Purpose and activities: Giving primarily for higher education, scientific research, hospitals, and drug abuse prevention for children and adolescents.
Types of support awarded: Operating budgets, continuing support, seed money, emergency funds, building funds, equipment, land acquisition, matching funds, special projects, research, publications, consulting services, technical assistance.
Limitations: No grants to individuals, or for endowment funds or deficit financing; no loans.
Publications: Annual report, application guidelines.
Application information:
Initial approach: Letter or telephone
Copies of proposal: 5
Deadline(s): Submit application in September or April; deadlines September 30 and April 30
Board meeting date(s): November and June
Final notification: Immediately following board meeting
Write: Dr. Phillip J. Swihart, Executive Director
Officers: James C. Ray,* President; Phillip J. Swihart, Executive Director.
Directors:* John Cronkite, Joan L. Ray.
Number of staff: 1 part-time professional; 1 part-time support.
Employer Identification Number: 810288819

476
Sachs Foundation

418 First National Bank Bldg.
Colorado Springs 80903   (303) 633-2353

Incorporated in 1931 in Colorado.
Donor(s): Henry Sachs.†

Financial data: (yr. ended 12/31/84): Assets, $603,113 (M); gifts received, $513,841; expenditures, $497,332, including $415,237 for 274 grants to individuals (high: $3,000; low: $425; average: $1,200-$3,000).
Purpose and activities: Giving only to provide graduate and undergraduate scholarships for black residents of Colorado.
Types of support awarded: Student aid.
Limitations: Giving limited to CO.
Publications: Financial statement, 990-PF, application guidelines.
Application information: Application form required.
   Initial approach: Letter or telephone
   Copies of proposal: 2
   Deadline(s): Submit application preferably in January, February, or March; deadline March 15
   Board meeting date(s): January, June, and September
   Final notification: 3 months after deadline date
   Write: Morris A. Esmiol, President
Officers and Directors:* Morris A. Esmiol,* President; Ben S. Wendelken,* 1st Vice-President; Morris A. Esmiol, Jr.,* 2nd Vice-President; Joy Helm, Secretary-Treasurer.
Number of staff: 3 full-time support.
Employer Identification Number: 840500835

477
Schlessman Foundation, Inc. ▼
1500 Grant St., Suite 400
Denver 80203   (303) 861-8081

Incorporated in 1957 in Colorado.
Donor(s): Greeley Gas Co.
Financial data: (yr. ended 3/31/84): Assets, $11,000,100 (M); gifts received, $40,000; expenditures, $469,300, including $434,811 for 49 grants (high: $150,000; low: $450; average: $1,000-$10,000).
Purpose and activities: Support for higher education, including theological education, cultural programs, and youth agencies.
Types of support awarded: General purposes.
Limitations: No grants to individuals.
Application information: Funds presently committed; no new grants until 1987.
   Initial approach: Letter
   Copies of proposal: 1
   Deadline(s): None
   Board meeting date(s): March, June, September, and December
   Write: Lee E. Schlessman, President
Officers: Lee E. Schlessman, President; Susan M. Duncan, Vice-President; Florence M. Schlessman, Secretary-Treasurer.
Number of staff: None.
Employer Identification Number: 846030309

478
Schramm Foundation, The ⌘
8528 W. 10th Ave.
Lakewood 80215

Established in 1956.

Financial data: (yr. ended 6/30/83): Assets, $2,634,920 (M); expenditures, $141,087, including $119,975 for 49 grants (high: $30,000; low: $500).
Purpose and activities: Primarily local giving for hospitals, education, social services and cultural programs.
Types of support awarded: Equipment, general purposes, scholarship funds, operating budgets.
Limitations: Giving primarily in Denver, CO, and the surrounding area.
Officers: Lesley E. Kring, President; Arnold Tietze, Vice-President; Gary S. Kring, Secretary; Joe Heit, Treasurer.
Employer Identification Number: 846032196

479
Silver Foundation ⌘
1500 First National Bank Bldg.
Denver 80293

Incorporated in 1959 in Colorado.
Donor(s): Harold F. Silver, Silver Corporation.
Financial data: (yr. ended 12/31/83): Assets, $360,868 (M); gifts received, $69,414; expenditures, $1,047,870, including $1,033,200 for 12 grants (high: $1,000,000; low: $500).
Purpose and activities: Broad purposes; primarily local giving, with emphasis on a university and youth agencies.
Limitations: Giving limited to Denver, CO, and UT. No grants to individuals.
Officers and Trustees: Barnard Silver, President; Ruth S. Silver, Vice-President and Secretary; Harold F. Silver, Vice-President and Treasurer; George C. Keely, Vice-President; Mary E. Brickner.
Employer Identification Number: 846036560

480
Sterne-Elder Memorial Trust ⌘
1740 Broadway
Denver 80217

Trust established in 1977 in Colorado.
Donor(s): Charles S. Sterne.
Financial data: (yr. ended 3/31/82): Assets, $2,210,656 (M); expenditures, $204,282, including $188,700 for 48 grants (high: $80,000; low: $50).
Purpose and activities: Largely local giving, with emphasis on the performing arts; support also for a community fund and community development.
Limitations: Giving primarily in CO.
Manager: Dorothy Elder Sterne.
Trustee: United Bank of Denver.
Employer Identification Number: 846143172

481
Swan (The Bal F. and Hilda N.) Foundation ⌘
c/o The First National Bank of Denver
P.O. Box 5825, Terminal Annex
Denver 80217

Established in 1976.
Donor(s): Bal F. Swan.†

Financial data: (yr. ended 12/31/83): Assets, $1,837,349 (M); expenditures, $367,424, including $346,600 for 25 grants (high: $35,000; low: $3,200).
Purpose and activities: Primarily local giving, with emphasis on aid to the handicapped, medical research, child welfare, cultural programs, social agencies, and higher education.
Limitations: Giving primarily in CO.
Trustees: Anthony F. Zarlengo, The First National Bank of Denver.
Employer Identification Number: 742108775

482
Taylor (The Ruth and Vernon) Foundation ▼
1670 Denver Club Bldg.
Denver 80202   (303) 893-5284

Trust established in 1950 in Texas.
Donor(s): Members of the Taylor family.
Financial data: (yr. ended 6/30/84): Assets, $18,495,125 (M); gifts received, $1,209,441; expenditures, $3,209,040, including $3,142,025 for 245 grants (high: $135,000; low: $150; average: $1,000-$50,000).
Purpose and activities: Broad purposes; general giving, with emphasis on higher and secondary education, cultural programs, social services, ecology, youth agencies, and hospitals and medical research.
Types of support awarded: Research, endowment funds, building funds, general purposes.
Limitations: Giving primarily in TX, CO, WY, MT, IL, and the Mid-Atlantic states. No grants to individuals.
Application information:
   Initial approach: Proposal
   Copies of proposal: 1
   Deadline(s): April 30 and July 31
   Board meeting date(s): May and August
   Final notification: 30 days
   Write: Charles A. Schmitt, Trustee, or Miss Friday A. Green, Trustee
Trustees: Ruth Taylor Campbell, Miss Friday A. Green, Charles A. Schmitt, Sara Taylor Swift, Vernon Taylor, Jr.
Number of staff: None.
Employer Identification Number: 846021788

483
Thatcher Foundation, The ⌘
P.O. Box 1401
Pueblo 81002
Scholarship application address: Charlene Burkhard, The Thatcher Foundation, c/o Minnequa Bank of Pueblo, Pueblo, CO 81004

Established in 1924 in Colorado.
Financial data: (yr. ended 12/31/83): Assets, $1,695,783 (M); gifts received, $1,000; expenditures, $154,175, including $110,551 for 27 grants (high: $30,000; low: $100) and $33,360 for 46 grants to individuals.
Purpose and activities: Broad purposes; local giving with emphasis on higher education, including undergraduate scholarships to institutions within the state of Colorado and a chair in music, a community fund, cultural programs, youth agencies, and health.

Types of support awarded: Student aid.
Limitations: Giving limited to Pueblo County, CO.
Application information:
 Deadline(s): Prior to beginning of school year in which assistance is requested
Officers and Trustees: Mahlon T. White, President; Helen T. White, Vice-President; Lester Ward, Jr., Secretary; Adrian Comer, Elizabeth Ensign.
Employer Identification Number: 840581724

484
Weckbaugh (Eleanore Mullen) Foundation ⌑
1779 South Monaco Pkwy.
Denver 80224   (303) 756-0202

Established in 1975.
Donor(s): Eleanore Mullen Weckbaugh.†
Financial data: (yr. ended 3/31/83): Assets, $2,799,439 (M); expenditures, $239,739, including $234,000 for 25 grants (high: $30,000; low: $1,500).
Purpose and activities: Primarily local giving, with emphasis on Roman Catholic church support and welfare funds; grants also for higher and secondary education, the performing arts, health agencies, and a social agency.
Types of support awarded: General purposes.
Limitations: Giving primarily in CO. No grants to individuals.
Application information:
 Initial approach: Letter
 Write: Patricia J. Lascor, Vice-President
Officers: Leon A. Lascor,* President; Patricia J. Lascor,* Vice-President; Dorothy M. Van Pelt, Secretary.
Trustees:* Edward J. Limes.
Employer Identification Number: 237437761

485
Williams Family Foundation, The ⌑
P.O. Box 597
Fort Morgan 80701

Trust established about 1958 in Colorado.
Donor(s): A.F. Williams, M.D.,† Mrs. A.F. Williams.†
Financial data: (yr. ended 12/31/83): Assets, $4,311,472 (M); expenditures, $289,760, including $270,900 for 23 grants (high: $75,000; low: $250).
Purpose and activities: Primarily local giving, with emphasis on support for higher and secondary education, hospitals, and civic affairs.
Limitations: Giving primarily in CO.
Trustees: George A. Epperson, Catherine M. Woodward, Paul E. Woodward.
Employer Identification Number: 846023379

486
Wolf (Marvin and Estelle) Foundation ⌑
3801 E. Florida Ave., Suite 502
Denver 80210

Established in 1980.
Donor(s): Marvin Wolf, Estelle Wolf.

Financial data: (yr. ended 11/30/82): Assets, $1,478,674 (M); expenditures, $150,162, including $142,150 for 7 grants (high: $50,000; low: $1,000).
Purpose and activities: Primarily local giving for higher education and an art museum.
Types of support awarded: Scholarship funds, research, operating budgets, building funds.
Limitations: Giving primarily in Denver, CO.
Officers: Estelle Wolf, President; Lawrence Wolf, Wendy Wolf, Vice-Presidents; Marvin Wolf, Secretary-Treasurer.
Employer Identification Number: 742130149

487
Woodward Governor Company Charitable Trust
c/o United Bank of Fort Collins
P.O. Box 565
Fort Collins 80522   (303) 482-1100
Application address: 5001 North Second St., Rockford, IL 61101; Tel.: (815) 877-7441

Trust established in 1947 in Illinois.
Donor(s): Woodward Governor Company.
Financial data: (yr. ended 12/31/83): Assets, $5,319,439 (M); gifts received, $150,000; expenditures, $284,420, including $266,008 for 80 grants (high: $44,600; low: $64).
Purpose and activities: Grants in areas of company operations for community funds, youth agencies, hospitals and colleges.
Types of support awarded: Continuing support, annual campaigns, seed money, emergency funds, building funds, equipment, land acquisition.
Limitations: Giving primarily in areas of company operations. No grants to individuals, or for endowment funds, research, scholarships and fellowships, special projects, publications, conferences, or matching gifts; no loans.
Application information:
 Initial approach: Letter
 Copies of proposal: 1
 Deadline(s): Submit full proposal preferably in March or July; no set deadline
 Board meeting date(s): As required
 Final notification: 8 weeks
 Write: Chairman, Contributions Committee, Woodward Governor Company
Trustees: Edward Abegg, Forrest Donaldson, Gene Goodall, Maurice O. Nelson, Robert E. Reuterfors.
Number of staff: None.
Employer Identification Number: 846025403

CONNECTICUT

488
Abex Foundation, Inc.
Six Landmark Square
P.O. Box 10268
Stamford 06904-2268   (203) 328-3200

Incorporated in 1951 in New York.
Donor(s): Abex Corporation.
Financial data: (yr. ended 12/31/84): Assets, $18,365 (L); gifts received, $175,000; expenditures, $244,953, including $188,771 for grants (high: $14,000; low: $100), $12,160 for 6 grants to individuals and $44,000 for employee matching gifts.
Purpose and activities: General purposes; grants largely for higher and secondary education, including matching gifts and scholarships; hospitals, health agencies, community funds, and youth agencies in cities where company plants are located.
Types of support awarded: Operating budgets, annual campaigns, emergency funds, building funds, scholarship funds, employee matching gifts, employee related scholarships.
Limitations: Giving limited to cities in which company plants are located. No support for religious, political, veterans', or fraternal organizations. No grants to individuals (except for scholarships to children of company employees), or for endowment funds; no loans.
Application information:
 Initial approach: Letter
 Copies of proposal: 1
 Deadline(s): Submit proposal preferably in August or September; deadline October 31
 Board meeting date(s): February
 Final notification: 60 days
 Write: David C. Christensen, President
Officers: David C. Christensen,* President; S.S. Conway, Jr.,* Vice-President; C.W. Grinnell, Secretary; D. O'Neill, Treasurer.
Directors:* R. Stewart.
Employer Identification Number: 136126219

489
Aetna Life & Casualty Foundation, Inc. ▼
151 Farmington Ave.
Hartford 06156   (203) 273-2465

Incorporated in 1972 in Connecticut.
Donor(s): Aetna Life and Casualty Company.
Financial data: (yr. ended 12/31/83): Assets, $17,983,000 (M); expenditures, $9,356,885, including $8,260,957 for 421 grants (high: $632,000; average: $5,000-$20,000) and $866,068 for 698 employee matching gifts.

Purpose and activities: To help preserve a viable society by supporting programs and organizations that can have a real impact on solving social problems and by providing support that will stimulate other donors. Priority areas for giving are problems of urban public education, improving minority youth employment opportunities, urban neighborhood revitalization, public management, reform of the civil justice system, and responsive philanthropy; support also for education and the arts.
Types of support awarded: Operating budgets, continuing support, seed money, emergency funds, matching funds, employee matching gifts, technical assistance.
Limitations: Giving limited to organizations in the U.S., with emphasis on the greater Hartford, CT, area. No support for religious organizations for religious purposes, or for consolidated fundraising outside of Hartford other than United Way campaigns. No grants to individuals, or for endowment funds, medical research, capital or building funds or renovation projects outside the Hartford area, unrestricted operating funds for colleges, universities, social service agencies, secondary schools, museums, hospitals or other such institutions outside the Hartford area; no grants for computer hardware; no loans.
Publications: Annual report, application guidelines, program policy statement.
Application information:
  Initial approach: Letter
  Copies of proposal: 1
  Deadline(s): None
  Board meeting date(s): February, May, August, and November
  Final notification: 2 months
  Write: Robert H. Roggeveen, Program Officer
Officers: William O. Bailey,* President; Alison G. Coolbrith, Vice-President and Executive Director; Stephen B. Middlebrook, Vice-President; Frederick W. Kingsley, Treasurer.
Directors:* William H. Donaldson, Chairman; Arthur R. Ashe, Jr., Donald G. Conrad, Marian W. Edelman, Barbara Hackman Franklin, Edward K. Hamilton, James T. Lynn, Robert A. Sherman.
Number of staff: 5 full-time professional; 3 full-time support.
Employer Identification Number: 237241940

490
Albers (Josef) Foundation, Inc.
808 Birchwood Dr.
Orange 06477   (203) 795-5525

Incorporated in 1971 in New York.
Donor(s): Josef Albers.†
Financial data: (yr. ended 12/31/82): Assets, $6,147,192 (M); gifts received, $16,150; expenditures, $162,278, including $53,319 for 3 grants (high: $47,879; low: $2,000).
Purpose and activities: Support primarily for art museums which teach and display principles of arts espoused by the late Josef Albers and for activities relating to the donor's own work, including exhibitions, lectures, and publications.
Types of support awarded: Publications, seed money, special projects, research.

Limitations: No grants to individuals, or for operating budgets, continuing support, annual campaigns, emergency funds, deficit financing, building funds, equipment, endowment funds, matching gifts, scholarships or fellowships, or conferences; no loans.
Application information:
  Initial approach: Letter
  Board meeting date(s): Bimonthly
  Final notification: 1 month
  Write: Nicholas F. Weber, Executive Director
Officer and Directors: Nicholas F. Weber, Executive Director; Anni Albers, Lee V. Eastman, Kinglui Wu.
Number of staff: 1 full-time professional; 1 part-time professional; 1 full-time support; 2 part-time support.
Employer Identification Number: 237104223

491
Amax Foundation, Inc. ▼
Amax Center
Greenwich 06836   (203) 629-6901

Incorporated in 1955 in New York.
Donor(s): AMAX Inc.
Financial data: (yr. ended 12/31/83): Assets, $5,044,717 (M); expenditures, $1,496,206, including $1,250,187 for 668 grants (high: $81,000; low: $150; average: $500-$5,000) and $212,100 for 570 employee matching gifts.
Purpose and activities: Grants in areas of company operations for higher education, largely in the fields related to mining, metallurgy, geology, geophysics, and geochemistry; employee matching gift program and Amax Earth Sciences Scholarships for children of employees only; and for health and welfare, especially United Way campaigns; cultural programs, and civic and public affairs.
Types of support awarded: Building funds, continuing support, employee matching gifts, fellowships, general purposes, professorships, research, scholarship funds, employee related scholarships, matching funds.
Limitations: Giving primarily in areas of company operations. No support for fraternal, religious, or sectarian organizations, primary or secondary education, creative arts groups, sports or athletic events, nursing homes, organizations supported by the United Way (unless permission has been granted by the United Way), or governmental or quasi-governmental agencies. No grants to individuals (except company-employee scholarships), or for memorial funds, goodwill advertisements in yearbooks or souvenir programs, charity dinners or special performance events; no support for endowment funds; no loans.
Publications: Application guidelines, program policy statement, informational brochure.
Application information:
  Initial approach: Letter
  Copies of proposal: 1
  Deadline(s): Submit proposal by March 15 for civic and charitable projects; from July 1 to September 1 for educational projects
  Board meeting date(s): May and October and as required
  Final notification: 60 days
  Write: Sonja B. Weill, President

Officers and Directors:* Sonja B. Weill,* President; David George Ball,* Malcolm B. Bayliss,* Lowry Blackburn,* Chester O. Ensign, Jr.,* Rolf Genssler,* John W. Goth,* Pierre Gousseland,* John H. Paul,* Elwin E. Smith,* Vice-Presidents; Helen McCall, Secretary; Dennis Arrouet, Treasurer.
Number of staff: 1 full-time professional; 1 part-time professional; 1 full-time support.
Employer Identification Number: 136111368

492
American Can Company Foundation ▼
American Lane
P.O. Box 3610
Greenwich 06830-3610   (203) 552-2148
Additional telephone: (203) 552-2989

Incorporated in 1960 in New York.
Donor(s): American Can Company.
Financial data: (yr. ended 12/31/83): Assets, $2,425,483 (M); gifts received, $2,591,068; expenditures, $2,041,217, including $1,559,799 for 307 grants (high: $112,115; low: $50; average: $1,000-$30,000), $200,820 for 213 grants to individuals and $181,588 for 305 employee matching gifts.
Purpose and activities: Giving generally in areas of company operations; new policy directions include: 1) The National Themes Program concentrating on economic transition, hunger and nutrition, and public education; 2) The General Grants Program at national, regional, and local levels for health care, human services, education, culture and the arts, civic concerns and international giving; and 3) The Local Contributions Program in areas of company operations, concentrating on the needs of the particular community. In 1984 The Volunteer Awards Program will award fifteen $500 awards to employees and retirees for the volunteer organization of their choice; support for higher education includes employee scholarship and matching gift programs.
Types of support awarded: Operating budgets, seed money, emergency funds, matching funds, employee matching gifts, scholarship funds, employee related scholarships, fellowships, special projects, research, publications, conferences and seminars.
Limitations: No support for strictly recreational, sectarian, or denominational organizations, or political or labor organizations. No grants generally for veterans' or fraternal organizations for their own benefit. No grants to individuals (except for company-employee scholarships), or for building or endowment funds, continuing support, annual campaigns, deficit financing, or land acquisition; no loans. Generally, no grants for capital drives.
Publications: Annual report, program policy statement, application guidelines.
Application information:
  Initial approach: Letter or full proposal
  Copies of proposal: 1
  Deadline(s): None
  Board meeting date(s): Every 8 to 10 weeks
  Final notification: 2 months

Write: Peter Goldberg, Managing Director (Focus: National Themes Program); Ray Reisler, Associate Director (Focus: General Grants and Other Programs)

Officers and Directors: William S. Woodside, President; Frank J. Connor, Sal J. Guidice, Jerry N. Mathis, Vice-Presidents; C. Richard Pedersen, Secretary; Kenneth A. Yarnell, Jr., Treasurer; Joseph Fafian, Jr., Peter Goldberg, Alfred G. Goldstein, David R. Parker.

Number of staff: 4 full-time professional; 2 full-time support.

Employer Identification Number: 136161154

493

American Seamen's Friend Society, The

c/o Connecticut National Bank
888 Main St.
Bridgeport 06601

Founded in 1828.

Financial data: (yr. ended 3/31/84): Assets, $1,488,529 (M); expenditures, $68,772, including $47,996 for 5 grants (high: $28,470; low: $100).

Purpose and activities: To aid maritime museums and organizations concerned with merchant seamen, primarily in Connecticut and New York.

Limitations: Giving primarily in CT and NY.

Officers: William A. Schroeder, President; Charles J. Irwin, Secretary; David W.P. Jewitt, Treasurer.

Employer Identification Number: 135596841

494

Auerbach (The Beatrice Fox)
  Foundation ▼ ⌘

25 Brookside Blvd.
West Hartford 06107

Incorporated in 1941 by special Act of the Connecticut Legislature.

Donor(s): Beatrice F. Auerbach,† Fannie F. Samuels, Standard Investment Company.

Financial data: (yr. ended 12/31/83): Assets, $17,581,696 (M); gifts received, $6,800; expenditures, $818,339, including $756,532 for 51 grants (high: $250,000; low: $100; average: $1,000-$50,000).

Purpose and activities: Broad purposes; primarily local giving for a community fund, youth agencies, health and hospitals, Jewish welfare funds, cultural programs, and higher education.

Types of support awarded: Endowment funds.

Limitations: Giving primarily in the Hartford, CT, area.

Officers and Trustees: Bernard Schiro, Chairman; Richard Koopman, President; Georgette A. Koopman, Vice-President and Secretary; Dorothy A. Schiro, Treasurer; Morton Eisner.

Employer Identification Number: 066033334

495

Barden Foundation, Inc., The ⌘

200 Park Ave.
Danbury 06813

Incorporated in 1959 in Delaware.

Donor(s): The Barden Corporation.

Financial data: (yr. ended 10/31/82): Assets, $257,932 (M); gifts received, $105,050; expenditures, $104,173, including $103,675 for 32 grants (high: $50,000; low: $250).

Purpose and activities: Primarily local giving, with emphasis on higher education, including a scholarship award program administered through colleges and universities; hospitals, and a community fund.

Types of support awarded: Scholarship funds.

Limitations: Giving primarily in CT.

Application information: Application information available for scholarship program. Application form required.

Officers: Stanley Noss, President; Eduard Baruch, Secretary; P.E. Yamont, Treasurer.

Employer Identification Number: 066054855

496

Barnes Foundation, Incorporated, The

P.O. Box 1560
Bristol 06010   (203) 583-7070

Incorporated in 1945 in Connecticut.

Donor(s): Carlyle F. Barnes, Aurelia B. Bristow, Louise B. Adams, Myrtle I. Barnes,† Fuller F. Barnes.†

Financial data: (yr. ended 12/31/84): Assets, $3,798,800 (M); expenditures, $153,945, including $136,007 for 22 grants (high: $20,000; low: $400).

Purpose and activities: General purposes; support largely for private secondary school education within Connecticut; support also for a local hospital.

Types of support awarded: Building funds, equipment.

Limitations: Giving primarily in CT. No grants to individuals, or for endowment funds or operating budgets.

Publications: Annual report, program policy statement, application guidelines.

Application information:

  Initial approach: Letter
  Copies of proposal: 1
  Deadline(s): Submit proposal preferably in early fall
  Board meeting date(s): Usually in January, June, October, and December
  Write: Carlyle F. Barnes, President

Officers and Trustees: Carlyle F. Barnes, President; Aurelia B. Bristow, Vice-President; Sally O'Connor, Secretary; Louise B. Adams, Treasurer.

Employer Identification Number: 066037160

497

Barnes Group Foundation, Inc. ⌘

123 Main St.
Bristol 06010
Scholarship application address: Citizen's Scholarship Foundation of America, One South St., Concord, NH 03301

Incorporated in Connecticut.

Financial data: (yr. ended 12/31/82): Assets, $1,457,587 (M); expenditures, $334,148, including $321,186 for 234 grants (high: $39,850; low: $10).

Purpose and activities: General giving, with emphasis on higher education, community funds, and the environment; scholarships only for children of active and retired company employees.

Types of support awarded: Employee related scholarships.

Application information: Application form required.

  Deadline(s): February 15

Officers: Wallace Barnes, Chairman; Carlyle F. Barnes, President; Jeremiah E. McQuillan, Vice-President; William R. Coombes, Secretary; Eric O. Carlson, Treasurer.

Trustee: United Bank and Trust Company.

Employer Identification Number: 237339727

498

Belgian American Educational
  Foundation, Inc.

195 Church St.
New Haven 06510   (203) 777-5765

Incorporated in 1920 in Delaware.

Donor(s): The Commission for Relief in Belgium.

Financial data: (yr. ended 8/31/84): Assets, $7,039,299 (M); gifts received, $340,617; expenditures, $620,114, including $157,032 for 1 grant (high: $41,500; low: $1,000) and $400,599 for 30 grants to individuals.

Purpose and activities: To promote closer relations between Belgium and the United States through graduate exchange fellowships in diverse fields and to assist higher education, scientific research, and the exchange of intellectual ideas.

Types of support awarded: Exchange programs, fellowships.

Limitations: No grants for general support, endowment funds, or matching gifts; no fellowships (except for Belgian and American graduate students); no loans.

Publications: Financial statement, application guidelines.

Application information: Application form required.

  Initial approach: Letter, full proposal, or telephone
  Copies of proposal: 1
  Deadline(s): Submit proposal preferably in December; deadline December 31
  Board meeting date(s): January, April, June, and October
  Final notification: Before March 31
  Write: Dr. Emile L. Boulpaep, President

Officers and Directors: Gaston Deurinck, Chairman; Emile L. Boulpaep, President; William Moody, Secretary; Sherman Gray, Treasurer; Jacques de Groote, John H.F. Haskell, Jr., Andre Jacques, Daniel Janssen, Herman Liebaers, Andre W.G. Newburg, Shelby H. Page, Marshall Robinson, Edward H. Tuck, Hugo van Itallie, Luc Wauters.

Number of staff: 1 full-time support; 1 part-time support.

Employer Identification Number: 131606002

499
Bennett (Carl and Dorothy) Foundation, Inc. ¤
Green Briar Ln.
Stamford 06903

Established in 1963.
Donor(s): Caldor Inc., Carl Bennett, and others.
Financial data: (yr. ended 6/30/83): Assets, $2,149,022 (M); gifts received, $860,000; expenditures, $392,095, including $370,710 for 14 grants (high: $150,100; low: $35).
Purpose and activities: Primarily local giving, with emphasis on Jewish welfare funds and a hospital.
Limitations: Giving primarily in CT.
Officers and Managers: Carl Bennett, President; Marc Bennett, Vice-President; Dorothy Bennett, Treasurer; Bruce Bennett, Robin Bennett Kanarek, Harold Karun, Malcolm E. Martin, Gerald Roth, Norman Sinrich.
Employer Identification Number: 066051371

500
Bissell (J. Walton) Foundation ¤
One Constitution Plaza, 12th Fl.
Hartford 06103
Application address: 29 Ten Acre Ln., West Hartford, CT; Tel.: (203) 521-6528

Trust established in 1952 in Connecticut.
Donor(s): J. Walton Bissell.†
Financial data: (yr. ended 12/31/82): Assets, $6,970,658 (M); expenditures, $377,425, including $313,412 for 71 grants (high: $29,512; low: $500).
Purpose and activities: General giving, with emphasis on higher and secondary education, including scholarship funds, hospitals, youth agencies, care of the aged, Protestant church support, and historic preservation.
Types of support awarded: Scholarship funds.
Application information:
Initial approach: Letter
Deadline(s): None
Write: W.C. Fenniman
Officer and Trustees: D.M. Rockwell, Secretary; L. Steiner.
Executive Committee: W.G. DeLana, W.C. Fenniman.
Employer Identification Number: 066035614

501
Bodenwein Public Benevolent Foundation ¤
c/o Connecticut National Bank
250 Captain's Walk
New London 06320   (203) 447-6134

Financial data: (yr. ended 12/31/82): Assets, $245,201 (M); gifts received, $131,181; expenditures, $141,684, including $133,816 for 41 grants (high: $14,000; low: $650).
Purpose and activities: Local giving to social service and health agencies, cultural programs, youth agencies, and civic groups.
Limitations: Giving limited to Lyme, Old Lyme, East Lyme, Waterford, New London, Montville, Groton, Ledyard, Stonington, and North Stonington, CT.

Application information: Application form required.
Deadline(s): May 15 and November 15
Write: George H. Swift III
Trustee: Connecticut National Bank.
Employer Identification Number: 066030548

502
Bridgeport Area Foundation, Inc., The
446 University Ave.
Bridgeport 06604   (203) 334-7511

Community foundation incorporated in 1967 in Connecticut.
Financial data: (yr. ended 12/31/83): Assets, $3,319,426 (M); gifts received, $478,586; expenditures, $500,190, including $437,125 for 285 grants (high: $64,000; low: $100; average: $3,000-$5,000).
Purpose and activities: Broad purposes; grants to organizations and for projects that primarily benefit the communities of Bridgeport, Easton, Fairfield, Milford, Monroe, Shelton, Stratford, Trumbull, and Westport.
Types of support awarded: Continuing support, annual campaigns, seed money, emergency funds, building funds, equipment, consulting services, technical assistance, conferences and seminars, special projects.
Limitations: Giving primarily in Bridgeport, Easton, Fairfield, Milford, Monroe, Shelton, Stratford, Trumbull, and Westport, CT. No support for religious purposes. No grants to individuals, or for operating budgets, deficit financing, scholarships, or fellowships; no loans.
Publications: Annual report, program policy statement, application guidelines.
Application information:
Initial approach: Letter
Copies of proposal: 4
Deadline(s): September
Board meeting date(s): April and October; distribution committee meets in March, June, September, and December
Final notification: 2 weeks after committee meetings
Write: Ronald D. Williams, Chairman, Distribution Committee
Officers and Directors: Edward E. Harrison, President; Robert W. Huebner, Vice-President; Ronald D. Williams, Vice-President, Distribution; Peter Wilkinson, Secretary; Henry L. Katz, Treasurer; John P. Bassett, Ronald A. Beilin, Edward F. Bodine, Walter Breslav, Jr., Evelyn M. Conley, Frank G. Elliott, Jr., M.D., Richard F. Freeman, Samuel W. Hawley, Ruth Carlson Horn, Dorothy R. Larson, Donna J. Lockhart, Newman Marsilius, L. Scott Melville, Eddie Rodriguez, Jr.,* Cecil S. Semple, William S. Simpson, Richard I. Steiber, Robert S. Tellalian, Philip Trager, Austin K. Wolf.
Distribution Committee: Ronald D. Williams, Chairman; Marjorie P. Doty, Joan du Pont, William L. Hawkins, Geraldine W. Johnson, Robert C. Lindquist, James E. Marbury, Eddie Rodriguez, Jr., James F. Tomchik, Helen Wasserman.
Trustees: Citytrust, The Connecticut National Bank, Lafayette Bank & Trust Co., Connecticut Bank and Trust Co.
Number of staff: 3 part-time support.
Employer Identification Number: 066103832

503
Carter (Marjorie Sells) Boy Scout Scholarship Fund ¤
c/o Cummings & Lockwood
Ten Stamford Forum
Stamford 06904

Established in 1974.
Donor(s): Marjorie Sells Carter.†
Financial data: (yr. ended 8/31/82): Assets, $794,068 (M); expenditures, $151,854, including $130,875 for 245 grants to individuals.
Purpose and activities: Giving for scholarships.
Types of support awarded: Student aid.
Trustees: Carleton E. Hammond, Union Trust Company.
Employer Identification Number: 066174937

504
Casey (The Annie E.) Foundation ¤
51 Weaver St.
Greenwich Office Park 5
Greenwich 06830

Incorporated in 1948 in California.
Donor(s): Annie E. Casey,† and members of the Casey family.
Financial data: (yr. ended 12/31/82): Assets, $68,891,512 (M); gifts received, $1,257,610; expenditures, $4,839,612, including $100,000 for 1 grant and $2,425,012 for 2 foundation-administered programs.
Purpose and activities: A private operating foundation; giving restricted to the field of child welfare, specifically for the care of foster children; funding largely for the operation of a child care program in Connecticut; grants also for Roman Catholic church support in Seattle, Washington.
Limitations: Giving primarily in CT and WA.
Application information:
Deadline(s): None
Final notification: 2 months
Write: Frank A. Suchomel, Jr., Secretary
Officers and Trustees: George C. Lamb, Jr., Chairman; Paul Oberkotter, Vice-President; Frank A. Suchomel, Jr., Secretary; Walter E. Danielewski, Treasurer; James P. McLaughlin.
Employer Identification Number: 136138589

505
Champion International Foundation, The ▼
One Champion Plaza
Stamford 06921   (203) 358-7656

Incorporated in 1952 in Ohio.
Donor(s): Champion International Corporation.
Financial data: (yr. ended 12/31/82): Assets, $5,410,116 (M); expenditures, $841,769, including $828,977 for 117 grants (high: $103,900; low: $500; average: $1,000-$15,000).
Purpose and activities: General purposes; primary interests currently in higher education, with emphasis on institutions with programs in forestry and pulp and paper technology, and support of the free enterprise business environment; limited support also for cultural, civic, and social agencies.

Types of support awarded: Building funds, continuing support, employee matching gifts, general purposes.
Limitations: Giving primarily in communities where there is a significant number of company employees. No grants to individuals, or for endowment funds or research-related programs; no loans.
Publications: Application guidelines.
Application information:
Initial approach: Full proposal
Copies of proposal: 1
Deadline(s): Submit proposal preferably between January and September
Final notification: 3 months
Write: Thomas H. Latimer, Vice-President
Officers: Donald C. Powell,* President; Thomas H. Latimer, Vice-President; Lester Grotz, Secretary; Frank Long, Treasurer.
Trustees:* Gerald J. Beiser, Karl R. Bendetsen, R. Harcourt Dodds, Philip R. O'Connell.
Number of staff: None.
Employer Identification Number: 316022258

506
Childs (The Jane Coffin) Memorial Fund for Medical Research ▼
333 Cedar St.
New Haven 06510 (203) 785-4612

Trust established in 1937 in Connecticut.
Donor(s): Alice S. Coffin,† Starling W. Childs.†
Financial data: (yr. ended 6/30/84): Assets, $16,500,670 (M); expenditures, $1,245,806, including $1,063,635 for 78 grants (high: $19,750; low: $1,333).
Purpose and activities: "Primarily for medical research into the causes, origins and treatment of cancer." Grants to institutions only for support of individual programs of cancer research and for fellowships.
Types of support awarded: Fellowships, research.
Limitations: No grants to individuals, or for building or endowment funds, matching gifts, or general purposes; no loans.
Publications: Annual report, program policy statement, application guidelines.
Application information: Application form required.
Initial approach: Letter or telephone
Copies of proposal: 17
Deadline(s): January 1
Board meeting date(s): October or November and April or May
Write: Elizabeth M. Ford, Administrative Director
Officers: John W. Barclay,* Secretary; William G. Gridley, Jr.,* Treasurer; Frederic M. Richards, Director.
Managers:* H. Allen Mali, Chairman; Hope S. Childs, Vice-Chairman; Alice C. Anderson, John W. Childs, Starling W. Childs II, Patrick Crossman, Anne Carmichael Childs, J. Vinton Lawrence.
Number of staff: 1 full-time professional; 1 part-time professional; 1 full-time support.
Employer Identification Number: 066034840

507
Connecticut Mutual Life Foundation
140 Garden St.
Hartford 06154 (203) 727-6500

Established in 1976.
Donor(s): Connecticut Mutual Life Insurance Company.
Financial data: (yr. ended 12/31/83): Assets, $8,043,787 (M); expenditures, $791,551, including $769,691 for 102 grants (average: $3,000-$6,000).
Purpose and activities: Primarily local giving, largely for education, housing, and employment purposes; grants also for a community fund, cultural programs, higher and secondary education, health, and community development.
Types of support awarded: Operating budgets, continuing support, annual campaigns, seed money, building funds, matching funds, employee matching gifts, consulting services, technical assistance, program-related investments, scholarship funds, special projects, research, conferences and seminars.
Limitations: Giving primarily in the Hartford, CT, area. No grants to individuals, or for endowment funds, deficit financing, emergency funds, publications, land acquisition, scholarships, or fellowships; no loans.
Publications: 990-PF, program policy statement.
Application information:
Initial approach: Letter, full proposal, or telephone
Copies of proposal: 1
Deadline(s): None
Board meeting date(s): March and November
Final notification: 3 months
Write: Astrida R. Olds, Secretary
Officers: John W. Hennessey, Jr.,* President; Robert R. Googins, Vice-President; Astrida R. Olds, Secretary; William J. Sullivan, Treasurer.
Directors:* Edward B. Bates, Myron P. Curzan, Donald W. Davis, Dean J. Patenaude.
Number of staff: 3 full-time professional; 1 full-time support.
Employer Identification Number: 510192500

508
Conway (Carle C.) Scholarship Foundation ⌑
One Harbor Plaza
P.O. Box 10129
Stamford 06904

Established in 1950.
Donor(s): The Continental Group, Inc.
Financial data: (yr. ended 6/30/82): Assets, $2,309,587 (M); gifts received, $143,181; expenditures, $277,241, including $208,223 for 113 grants to individuals.
Purpose and activities: Grants for scholarships.
Types of support awarded: Student aid.
Officers: S.B. Smart, Jr., President; J.S. Luci, Vice-President; J. Clonan, Secretary; W.R. Good, Treasurer; T.S. Thompson, Member.
Employer Identification Number: 136088936

509
Day (Nancy Sayles) Foundation
c/o Union Trust Company
P.O. Box 1297
Stamford 06904

Trust established in 1964 in Connecticut.
Donor(s): Mrs. Nancy Sayles Day,† Mrs. Lee Day Gillespie.
Financial data: (yr. ended 9/30/83): Assets, $4,757,979 (M); expenditures, $352,783, including $330,758 for 35 grants (high: $117,500; low: $1,000).
Purpose and activities: Primarily local giving; support for music, the arts, higher and secondary education, and youth agencies.
Limitations: Giving primarily in MA. No grants to individuals, or for building or endowment funds, research, or matching gifts; no loans.
Publications: 990-PF.
Application information:
Initial approach: Letter
Copies of proposal: 1
Write: John R. Disbrow, Senior Trust Officer
Trustees: Leonard W. Cronkhite, Jr., M.D., Mrs. Lee Day Gillespie, Union Trust Company.
Employer Identification Number: 066071254

510
Dell (The Hazel) Foundation ⌑
c/o Carroll, Lane & Reed
P.O. Box 771
Norwalk 06852 (203) 853-6565

Incorporated in 1956 in Delaware.
Donor(s): Harry C. McClarity.†
Financial data: (yr. ended 12/31/82): Assets, $1,794,953 (M); expenditures, $177,248, including $150,000 for 74 grants (high: $18,900; low: $100).
Purpose and activities: Broad purposes; grants largely for hospitals, education, aid to the handicapped, and Roman Catholic church support.
Application information:
Deadline(s): None
Write: June M. Powers, President
Officers: June M. Powers,* President; Joy S. Dunlop,* Secretary; Thomas F. Ryan, Treasurer.
Directors:* Gail A. Fallon, Diane Schroeder, William J. Sullivan.
Employer Identification Number: 136161744

511
Dennett (Marie G.) Foundation ⌑
c/o Badger, Fisher, Cohen & Barnett
49 W. Putnam Ave., P.O. Box 1189
Greenwich 06836

Incorporated in 1956 in Illinois.
Donor(s): Marie G. Dennett,† Priscilla D. Ramsey.
Financial data: (yr. ended 8/31/83): Assets, $3,260,293 (M); expenditures, $157,461, including $144,500 for 30 grants (high: $25,000; low: $500).
Purpose and activities: Broad purposes; general giving, with emphasis on hospitals, education, conservation, cultural programs and health agencies.
Application information:

Initial approach: Brief proposal
Deadline(s): September 30
Write: Donat C. Marchand, Secretary
Officers and Directors: Priscilla D. Ramsey, President; Ernest P. Waud III, Vice-President; Donat C. Marchand, Secretary.
Employer Identification Number: 366060748

512
Dexter Corporation Foundation, Inc. ⊐
One Elm St.
Windsor Locks 06096

Established in 1976.
Donor(s): The Dexter Corporation.
Financial data: (yr. ended 12/31/82): Assets, $81,960 (M); gifts received, $300,000; expenditures, $349,563, including $273,825 for 455 grants (high: $12,672; low: $10) and $75,152 for employee matching gifts.
Purpose and activities: Grants largely for higher education, including employee matching gifts, and for community funds, public policy organizations, health and youth agencies, and cultural programs.
Types of support awarded: Employee matching gifts.
Officers: Worth Loomis,* President; Robert E. McGill, III, Secretary.
Directors:* David L. Coffin, Chairman; Jose M. Calhoun, Walter J. Connolly, Jr., Donald W. Davis, William P. Frankenhoff, Ralph H. Martin, Donald R. Roon.
Employer Identification Number: 061013754

513
Dibner Fund, Inc., The ⊐
c/o Burndy Library
Electra Square
Norwalk 06852   (203) 852-6203

Incorporated in 1957 in Connecticut.
Donor(s): Barbara Dibner, Bern Dibner, David Dibner.
Financial data: (yr. ended 12/31/82): Assets, $18,575,531 (M); gifts received, $142,469; expenditures, $623,283, including $596,726 for 33 grants (high: $147,000; low: $500).
Purpose and activities: Broad purposes; support largely for libraries, higher education, and Jewish welfare funds.
Limitations: No grants to individuals, or for building or endowment funds, scholarships, fellowships, or matching gifts; no loans.
Application information:
Initial approach: Letter
Board meeting date(s): May
Officers and Trustees: Bern Dibner, President; Barbara Dibner, Vice-President; David Dibner, Secretary; George M. Szabad, Treasurer.
Employer Identification Number: 066038482

514
Duberg (Dorys McConnell) Charitable Trust ⊐
c/o Citytrust
961 Main St.
Bridgeport 06602

Trust established in 1969 in Connecticut.

Financial data: (yr. ended 1/31/82): Assets, $1,052,256 (M); expenditures, $105,809, including $75,000 for 9 grants (high: $38,000; low: $1,000).
Purpose and activities: Giving for medical education and hospitals; support also for social agencies and religion.
Trustees: H.P.J. Duberg, David Hall Faile, Jr., John B. Faile.
Employer Identification Number: 237016974

515
Eder (The Sidney and Arthur) Foundation, Inc.
P.O. Box 949
New Haven 06504   (203) 934-8381

Incorporated in 1954 in Connecticut.
Donor(s): Sidney Eder, Arthur Eder, Eder Bros., Inc.
Financial data: (yr. ended 12/31/82): Assets, $1,971,179 (M); gifts received, $125,000; expenditures, $115,422, including $83,100 for 42 grants (high: $45,400; low: $25) and $22,159 for 15 grants to individuals.
Purpose and activities: Broad purposes; grants primarily to local Jewish welfare funds; scholarships for children of company employees.
Types of support awarded: Operating budgets, continuing support, annual campaigns, seed money, emergency funds, building funds, employee related scholarships.
Limitations: Giving primarily in CT. No grants for matching gifts or loans.
Application information:
Initial approach: Letter
Board meeting date(s): Semiannually
Officers and Trustees: Sidney Eder, Chairman; Arthur Eder, Secretary; Andrew J. Eder, Richard M. Weiss.
Number of staff: None.
Employer Identification Number: 066035306

516
Educational Foundation of America, The ▼
35 Church Ln.
Westport 06880
Grant application office: c/o Richard W. Hansen, 16250 Ventura Blvd., Suite 445, Encino, CA 91436; Tel.: (818) 990-2724

Trust established in 1959 in New York.
Donor(s): Richard P. Ettinger,† Elsie Ettinger, Richard P. Ettinger, Jr., Elaine P. Hapgood, Paul R. Andrews, Virgil P. Ettinger, Barbara Ettinger, John G. Powers.
Financial data: (yr. ended 12/31/83): Assets, $34,708,363 (M); expenditures, $1,603,051, including $1,284,528 for 42 grants (high: $170,000; low: $1,200; average: $10,000-$50,000).
Purpose and activities: Charitable and educational purposes; grants largely for higher education, including education for American Indians, medical education, and medical research; grants also for population control, children's education, and research in gerontology.

Types of support awarded: General purposes, operating budgets, continuing support, seed money, professorships, internships, scholarship funds, matching funds, special projects, research, publications, conferences and seminars.
Limitations: No grants to individuals, or for capital or endowment funds; no loans.
Publications: Annual report.
Application information:
Initial approach: Letter
Copies of proposal: 1
Deadline(s): None
Board meeting date(s): February, May, August, and November
Final notification: 2 to 3 months
Write: Richard W. Hansen, Executive Director
Officer: Richard W. Hansen, Executive Director.
Trustees: Richard P. Ettinger, Jr., Chairman; Edward E. Harrison, Vice-Chairman; Barbara P. Anderson, Elsie Ettinger, Cyrus Hapgood, Elaine P. Hapgood, Ben Marr Lanman, Frederic Rocco Landesman, Heidi P. Landesman, Erica Pifer.
Number of staff: 1 full-time professional; 5 part-time support.
Employer Identification Number: 136147947

517
EIS Foundation, Inc.
511 Maple Ave.
Old Saybrook 06475   (203) 388-1164

Incorporated in 1951 in Connecticut.
Donor(s): Joseph W. Gilfix, EIS Automotive Inc., Forest City Realty, C.C. Weiss, and members of the Weiss and Schwartz families.
Financial data: (yr. ended 12/31/84): Assets, $2,100,000 (M); gifts received, $65,000; expenditures, $180,400, including $179,600 for 105 grants (low: $25).
Purpose and activities: Grants largely for welfare funds, hospitals, higher education, care of the aged and physically handicapped, and temple support, largely in Connecticut, New York, and Florida.
Limitations: Giving primarily in CT, NY, and FL.
Application information:
Initial approach: Letter
Copies of proposal: 1
Deadline(s): Submit proposal in September
Board meeting date(s): Quarterly
Officers and Directors: Maurice L. Schwarz, President; Bernard M. Schwarz, Vice-President, Secretary and Treasurer; Theresa R. Schwarz.
Employer Identification Number: 066021896

518
Emery Air Freight Educational Foundation, Inc.
Old Danbury Rd.
Wilton 06897   (203) 762-8601

Incorporated in 1965 in Connecticut.
Donor(s): John C. Emery, Sr.,† Mrs. John C. Emery, Sr.,† Emery Air Freight Corporation.
Financial data: (yr. ended 12/31/82): Assets, $1,294,839 (M); expenditures, $113,755, including $3,000 for 1 grant and $103,000 for 39 grants to individuals.

Purpose and activities: Giving limited to general scholarship funds for eligible children of employees of Emery Air Freight Corporation.
Types of support awarded: Employee related scholarships.
Limitations: Giving primarily in CT. No grants to individuals (except eligible children of Emery employees), or for general support, building or endowment funds, research, or matching gifts; no loans.
Publications: Application guidelines.
Application information: Application form required.
  Deadline(s): Submit scholarship application by January testing date for Scholastic Aptitude Tests
  Board meeting date(s): April and October
  Write: John C. Emery, Jr., President
Officers: John C. Emery, Jr.,* President; Denis M. McCarthy,* Vice-President; Daniel J. McCauley, Secretary; Patricia M. Bertrand, Treasurer.
Trustees:* Joseph D. Ardleigh.
Employer Identification Number: 066071565

519
Eno Foundation for Transportation, Inc.
270 Saugatuck Ave.
P.O. Box 2055
Westport 06880   (203) 227-4852

Incorporated in 1921 in Connecticut.
Donor(s): William Phelps Eno.†
Financial data: (yr. ended 12/31/84): Assets, $5,769,102 (M); expenditures, $479,040, including $21,000 for grants (high: $4,000) and $458,040 for foundation-administered programs.
Purpose and activities: A private operating foundation that seeks to help improve transportation in all its aspects through the conduct and encouragement of appropriate research and educational activities and through the publication and distribution of information pertaining to transportation planning, design, operation, and regulation, particularly with support for the publication of "Transportation Quarterly".
Limitations: No grants to individuals.
Publications: 990-PF.
Application information: Applications for grants not invited.
  Board meeting date(s): February, May, August, and October
  Write: Robert S. Holmes, President
Officers and Directors: Wilbur S. Smith, Chairman; Robert S. Holmes, President; Harold F. Hammond, Vice-President; Charlotte K. Munger, Secretary and Treasurer; H. Burr Kelsey, Roland A. Ouellette, Mark D. Robeson.
Number of staff: 5.
Employer Identification Number: 060662124

520
Ensign-Bickford Foundation, Inc., The
660 Hopmeadow St.
P.O. Box 7
Simsbury 06070   (203) 658-4411

Incorporated in 1952 in Connecticut.
Donor(s): Ensign-Bickford Industries, Inc.

Financial data: (yr. ended 12/31/84): Assets, $133,873 (M); gifts received, $125,000; expenditures, $174,076, including $51,746 for grants (high: $10,000; low: $200), $14,750 for grants to individuals, $62,247 for employee matching gifts and $44,640 for foundation-administered programs.
Purpose and activities: Broad purposes; grants for welfare, educational, and cultural projects in areas of company operations; support also for company-employee scholarships and a summer job program for children of company employees and for employee matching gifts.
Types of support awarded: Continuing support, annual campaigns, seed money, building funds, equipment, land acquisition, special projects, scholarship funds, internships, research, publications, conferences and seminars, employee related scholarships, employee matching gifts.
Limitations: Giving primarily in areas of company operations, particularly in the Simsbury and Avon, CT area. No grants to individuals (except for company-employee scholarships), or for general endowment funds, operating budgets, emergency funds, or deficit financing; no loans.
Application information:
  Initial approach: Letter
  Deadline(s): None
  Board meeting date(s): Approximately every two months
  Final notification: 3 months
  Write: Robert E. Darling, Jr., President
Officers: Robert E. Darling, Jr., President; Thornton B. Morris, Vice-President; Linda M. Walsh, Secretary; Hazel H. King, Treasurer.
Directors: John E. Ellsworth, Arnold O. Freas, Blanche C. Skoglund, Frank S. Wilson.
Number of staff: 1 part-time professional.
Employer Identification Number: 066041097

521
Ensworth Charitable Foundation, The
c/o Connecticut National Bank
777 Main St. - MSN 218
Hartford 06115   (203) 728-2274

Trust established in 1949 in Connecticut.
Donor(s): Antoinette L. Ensworth.†
Financial data: (yr. ended 5/31/83): Assets, $5,992,310 (M); expenditures, $370,471, including $331,145 for 79 grants (high: $10,000; low: $35; average: $3,000-$5,000).
Purpose and activities: Local giving to support public or charitable organizations, with emphasis on health and welfare programs, youth activities, enjoyment of the natural environment, religion, arts, and education.
Types of support awarded: Continuing support, seed money, emergency funds, matching funds, conferences and seminars.
Limitations: Giving limited to Hartford, CT and vicinity. No grants to individuals, or for operating budgets, annual campaigns, deficit financing, building or endowment funds, equipment and materials, land acquisition, renovation projects, scholarships and fellowships, research, or publications; no loans.
Publications: 990-PF, program policy statement, application guidelines.

Application information: Application form required.
  Initial approach: Letter or full proposal
  Copies of proposal: 4
  Deadline(s): 18th of month preceding board meetings
  Board meeting date(s): February, May, August, and November
  Final notification: 1 month
  Write: Maxine R. Dean, Community Action Officer
Advisory Committee: William Brown, Jr., Yasha Escalera, Johanna Murphy.
Trustee: Connecticut National Bank.
Number of staff: 1 full-time professional.
Employer Identification Number: 066026018

522
Fairchild (The Sherman) Foundation, Inc. ▼ ⌑
71 Arch St.
Greenwich 06830

Incorporated in 1955 in New York.
Donor(s): May Fairchild,† Sherman Fairchild.†
Financial data: (yr. ended 12/31/82): Assets, $148,282,112 (M); gifts received, $5,036; expenditures, $12,741,084, including $12,075,530 for 24 grants (high: $1,014,352; low: $25,000).
Purpose and activities: General giving, with emphasis on higher education and fine arts and cultural institutions; some support also for medical research and social welfare.
Application information:
  Write: Walter Burke, President
Officers: Walter Burke,* President and Treasurer; Patricia A. Lydon, Vice-President; Richard C. Pugh,* Secretary.
Directors:* Walter F. Burke, III, William Elfers, Lee P. Gagliardi, Fowler Hamilton, Bonnie Himmelman, Samuel H. Woolley.
Employer Identification Number: 131951698

523
Fisher Foundation, Inc. ⌑
36 Brookside Blvd.
West Hartford 06107   (203) 232-2755

Established in 1959.
Donor(s): Stanley D. Fisher Trust, FIP Corporation.
Financial data: (yr. ended 12/31/82): Assets, $3,437 (M); gifts received, $152,000; expenditures, $159,089, including $158,911 for 26 grants (high: $100,000; low: $100).
Purpose and activities: Giving primarily to a Jewish welfare federation, cultural programs, health services, and education.
Limitations: Giving primarily in CT.
Officers: Hinda Fisher, President; George Kaplan, Herbert Krasow, Vice-Presidents.
Employer Identification Number: 066039415

524
Folsom (Maud Glover) Foundation, Inc.
P.O. Box 151
Harwinton 06791   (203) 485-0405

Incorporated in 1957 in New York.
Donor(s): Charles Stuart Folsom.†
Financial data: (yr. ended 7/31/84): Assets, $2,380,368 (M); expenditures, $159,523, including $116,250 for 52 grants to individuals.
Purpose and activities: To provide for the education of selected male students of American ancestry and of Anglo-Saxon or German descent to the age of thirty-five, subject to certain conditions; initial grants of $2,500 annually limited to males between the ages of fourteen to twenty years.
Types of support awarded: Student aid.
Application information: Application form required.
  Initial approach: Letter
  Board meeting date(s): As required
  Write: Leon A. Francisco, President
Officers and Trustees: Leon A. Francisco, President; C. Merrill Austin, Secretary; Barry W. Smith, Treasurer.
Employer Identification Number: 111965890

525
Fox (Jacob L. & Lewis) Foundation Trust ¤
c/o Connecticut National Bank
777 Main St.
Hartford 06115
Scholarship application address: c/o G. William Saxton, Hartford Public Schools, 249 High St., Hartford, CT 06103; Tel.: (230) 722-8725

Trust established about 1951 in Connecticut.
Donor(s): Lewis Fox.†
Financial data: (yr. ended 12/31/82): Assets, $2,139,035 (M); expenditures, $185,271, including $162,164 for 164 grants to individuals.
Purpose and activities: Scholarship awards limited to students graduating from and chosen by Hartford public schools; no other grants awarded.
Types of support awarded: Student aid.
Limitations: Giving limited to Hartford, CT.
Application information: Scholarship application forms and eligibility requirements provided only through Hartford public schools; applications directly to Trust not accepted. Application form required.
  Deadline(s): Usually in late January or early February
Officers and Trustees: G. William Saxton, Chairman; Robert E. Stevens, Treasurer; Amado G. Cruz, Rev. Charles W. Daly, Elizabeth B. Noel, Arthur J. Querido, David W. Parmelee, Lillian Thomas.
Employer Identification Number: 066067700

526
Fry (Lily Palmer) Memorial Trust ¤
c/o State National Bank of Connecticut
240 Greenwich Ave.
Greenwich 06830

Trust established in 1953 in Connecticut.
Donor(s): William Henry Fry.†
Financial data: (yr. ended 12/31/81): Assets, $2,626,014 (M); expenditures, $245,030, including $202,730 for 46 grants (high: $13,000; low: $1,000).
Purpose and activities: To provide summer vacations for the underprivileged and handicapped through grants to youth agencies and relief and social agencies, mainly in Greenwich and New York, and for Protestant church support.
Limitations: Giving primarily in CT.
Trustees: Caroline M. Fry, Evelyn Fry Peterson, State National Bank of Connecticut.
Employer Identification Number: 066033612

527
General Electric Foundation ▼
3135 Easton Turnpike
Fairfield 06431   (203) 373-3216

Trust established in 1952 in New York.
Donor(s): General Electric Company.
Financial data: (yr. ended 12/31/83): Assets, $53,578,000 (M); gifts received, $21,710,000; expenditures, $14,326,412, including $12,606,426 for 746 grants (high: $365,000; low: $1,000; average: $5,000-$50,000) and $1,619,986 for 13,286 employee matching gifts.
Purpose and activities: General purposes; institutional grants primarily in support of education, with emphasis on strengthening of specific areas of work in undergraduate education; graduate-level research and teaching; support for disciplinary fields, including the physical sciences, engineering, computer science, mathematics, industrial management, and business administration; support for minority group education programs, with emphasis on engineering and business; matches educational contributions of employees. Support also for community funds in communities where the company has significant presences, selected arts and cultural centers, public issues research and analysis, equal opportunity, international understanding, and other special grants. Grants are directed toward specific programs authorized by the trustees and most are approved in advance of each calendar year.
Types of support awarded: Annual campaigns, continuing support, employee matching gifts, fellowships, general purposes, publications, research, scholarship funds, seed money, special projects.
Limitations: Giving primarily in the U.S. and its possessions; grants to community funds limited to areas where the company has a significant presence. No grants to individuals or for capital or endowment funds; no loans.
Publications: Annual report.
Application information: Ability to respond to unsolicited requests is extremely limited.
  Initial approach: Full proposal

  Copies of proposal: 1
  Deadline(s): None
  Board meeting date(s): As required
  Final notification: Varies
  Write: Paul M. Ostergard, Secretary
Officers: Paul M. Ostergard, Secretary; W. Richard Fulljames, Treasurer.
Trustees: Walter A. Schlotterbeck, Chairman; Dennis D. Dammerman, Frank P. Doyle, Fred W. Garry, Joyce Hergenhan.
Number of staff: None.
Employer Identification Number: 146015766

528
Gimbel (Bernard F. and Alva B.) Foundation, Inc.
1133 King St.
Greenwich 06830

Incorporated in 1943 in New York.
Donor(s): Bernard F. Gimbel,† Alva B. Gimbel.†
Financial data: (yr. ended 12/31/82): Assets, $1,581,673 (M); expenditures, $86,220, including $74,225 for 24 grants (high: $30,000; low: $100).
Purpose and activities: Giving primarily locally and in New York; charitable and educational purposes; general giving, with emphasis on performing arts, museums, Jewish welfare funds, hospitals, and scientific research.
Limitations: Giving primarily in NY and CT. No grants for scholarships, fellowships, or matching gifts; no loans.
Application information:
  Initial approach: Letter
  Copies of proposal: 1
  Deadline(s): Submit proposal preferably in September; deadline October 31
  Board meeting date(s): November
Officers: Peter R. Gimbel, Robert B. Gimbel, Caral G. Lebworth, Judith G. Mendelsund, Hope G. Solinger, Vice-Presidents; Marion H. Stevenson, Secretary-Treasurer.
Employer Identification Number: 136090843

529
Great Northern Nekoosa Foundation, Inc. ¤
75 Prospect St.
Stamford 06901
Mailing address: P.O. Box 9309, Stamford, CT 06904

Incorporated in 1974 in Connecticut.
Donor(s): Great Northern Nekoosa Corporation.
Financial data: (yr. ended 12/31/82): Assets, $629,853 (M); expenditures, $336,056, including $333,855 for 65 grants (high: $57,545; low: $50).
Purpose and activities: Giving primarily for hospitals, higher education, and youth agencies; support also for the arts.
Application information:
  Deadline(s): None
  Write: Joetta Manzo, Secretary
Officers and Directors:* Robert Hellendale,* President; William R. Laidig,* Gerard E. Veneman,* Peter F. Yacavone,* Vice-Presidents; Joetta Manzo, Secretary; Emery E. Allain,* Treasurer.
Employer Identification Number: 237424336

530
Grubb (Hunter) Foundation, Inc.
P.O. Box 578
Old Lyme 06371

Incorporated in 1968 in Florida.
Donor(s): Anna G. Horn,† Martha G. Moore.†
Financial data: (yr. ended 6/30/84): Assets, $823,263 (M); gifts received, $10,100; expenditures, $128,128, including $120,200 for 32 grants (high: $20,000; low: $400; average: $3,600).
Purpose and activities: Giving primarily for scholarships for medical education.
Types of support awarded: Scholarship funds.
Limitations: No grants to individuals.
Application information: Applications not invited.
Officers and Trustees: Hunter G. Hannum, Chairman; Hildegarde Hannum, Secretary-Treasurer; Sidney Baker, M.D., Hughes Griffis.
Number of staff: None.
Employer Identification Number: 596202749

531
GTE Foundation ▼
(formerly General Telephone & Electronics Foundation)
One Stamford Forum
Stamford 06904   (203) 965-2000

Trust established in 1952 in New York as The Sylvania Foundation; renamed in 1960 as General Telephone & Electronics Foundation; renamed again in 1982.
Donor(s): General Telephone & Electronics Corporation, and subsidiaries.
Financial data: (yr. ended 12/31/82): Assets, $8,696,875 (M); gifts received, $4,356,763; expenditures, $4,380,475, including $4,313,990 for 679 grants (high: $242,000; low: $1,000; average: $1,000-$20,000).
Purpose and activities: General purposes, with emphasis on united funds, hospitals, higher education, and social betterment; giving restricted to institutions located in areas of corporation operations or national organizations deemed to be of broad benefit to GTE companies, employees, shareholders, or customers.
Types of support awarded: Building funds, scholarship funds, fellowships, employee matching gifts, continuing support.
Limitations: Giving limited to areas of company operations and national organizations deemed to be of broad benefit to GTE companies, employees, shareholders, or customers. No grants to individuals, or for research; no loans.
Application information:
  Initial approach: Letter or full proposal
  Deadline(s): September 15
  Board meeting date(s): February, April, June, September, November, and as required
  Final notification: After December 15
  Write: Ann C. Robin, Secretary
Officer: Ann C. Robin, Secretary.

Trustees: Theodore F. Brophy, Chairman; Bruce Carswell, James L. Johnson, Charles R. Lee, Allan L. Rayfield, Alfred C. Viebranz, Manufacturers Hanover Trust Company.
Number of staff: 3 full-time professional; 2 full-time support.
Employer Identification Number: 136046680

532
Hartford Courant Foundation, Incorporated, The ▼
285 Broad St.
Hartford 06115   (203) 241-6472

Foundation established in 1950 in Connecticut.
Donor(s): The Hartford Courant Company.
Financial data: (yr. ended 12/31/83): Assets, $7,012,491 (M); gifts received, $61,000; expenditures, $710,464, including $667,285 for 117 grants (high: $100,000; low: $500; average: $2,000-$10,000).
Purpose and activities: Broad purposes; primarily local giving, with emphasis on arts and cultural programs, education, community funds, health and social agencies, and civic affairs.
Types of support awarded: Annual campaigns, land acquisition, scholarship funds, research, building funds.
Limitations: Giving primarily in the Hartford, CT area. No support for religious organizations (for sectarian purposes), veterans, fraternal, professional, or business associations, member agencies of federated appeals, or political groups. No grants to individuals, or for continuing support, endowment, emergency, or building funds; no loans.
Publications: Annual report, informational brochure, application guidelines.
Application information: Application form required.
  Initial approach: Full proposal
  Copies of proposal: 1
  Deadline(s): January 2, mid-April, July 1, and October 1
  Board meeting date(s): February, June, August, and November
  Final notification: 3 months
  Write: Martha S. Newman, Executive Director
Officers: Worth Loomis,* President; Michael Sudarsky,* Vice-President; Martha S. Newman, Secretary and Executive Director; Richard H. King, Treasurer.
Trustees:* Edward R. Bates, Walter J. Connolly, Jr., Alberto Ibarguen, David Laventhol, Keith L. McGlade, K. Mark Murphy, Millard H. Pryor, Jr., Charles R. Redmond, Glenda C. Reed, Phillip L. Williams.
Number of staff: 1 part-time support.
Employer Identification Number: 060759107

533
Hartford Foundation for Public Giving ▼
45 South Main St.
West Hartford 06107   (203) 233-4443

Community foundation established in 1925 in Connecticut by resolution and declaration of trust.

Financial data: (yr. ended 9/30/84): Assets, $78,130,232 (M); gifts received, $3,959,306; expenditures, $5,106,723, including $4,513,261 for 167 grants (high: $271,062; low: $383; average: $40,000-$50,000).
Purpose and activities: Local giving for demonstration programs and capital purposes, with emphasis on community advancement, educational institutions, youth groups, hospitals, social services, including the aging, and cultural and civic endeavors.
Types of support awarded: Seed money, emergency funds, building funds, equipment, land acquisition, matching funds, scholarship funds, loans, special projects.
Limitations: Giving limited to the greater Hartford, CT, area. No support for sectarian purposes or tax-supported agencies. No grants to individuals, or for operating budgets, continuing support, annual campaigns, deficit financing, endowment funds, research, publications or conferences.
Publications: Annual report, application guidelines, program policy statement.
Application information: Application form required.
  Initial approach: Telephone
  Copies of proposal: 3
  Deadline(s): None
  Board meeting date(s): Monthly except August
  Final notification: 60 to 90 days
  Write: R. Malcolm Salter, Director
Officers: R. Malcolm Salter, Director; Alan E. Green, Assistant Director; William H. Connelly, Director of Development.
Distribution Committee: John S. Murtha, Chairman; Hartzel Z. Lebed, Vice-Chairman; Frederick G. Adams, Treasurer; George Levine, John C. Reagan, Herbert P. Schoen, Judith S. Wawro.
Trustees: The Connecticut Bank and Trust Company, Connecticut National Bank, The Simsbury Bank and Trust Company, United Bank & Trust Company.
Number of staff: 4 full-time professional; 3 part-time professional; 2 full-time support; 1 part-time support.
Employer Identification Number: 060699252

534
Hartford Insurance Group Foundation, Inc., The ▼
Hartford Plaza
Hartford 06115   (203) 547-3924

Incorporated in 1966 in Connecticut.
Donor(s): Hartford Fire Insurance Company, and affiliates.
Financial data: (yr. ended 12/31/82): Assets, $403,763 (M); expenditures, $1,538,090, including $1,410,238 for grants (high: $293,500; low: $10) and $120,135 for employee matching gifts.
Purpose and activities: Broad purposes; primarily local giving, with emphasis on community funds, higher education, health and human services, urban and civic affairs, and the arts.
Types of support awarded: Employee matching gifts.

Limitations: Giving primarily in the Hartford, CT, area. No support for political or religious purposes, United Way member agencies, or public educational organizations (except for matching gifts program). No grants to individuals, or for endowment funds, conferences, courtesy advertising, or capital fund drives outside the greater Hartford area.
Publications: Annual report, program policy statement, application guidelines.
Application information: Application form required.
Initial approach: Letter
Copies of proposal: 1
Deadline(s): None
Board meeting date(s): Quarterly
Write: Roger Dove, Vice-President
Officers: Donald R. Frahm, President; Raymond H. Deck,* Roger Dove,* William M. Giffin,* Vice-Presidents; Michael O'Halloran, Secretary; J. Richard Garrett,* Treasurer.
Directors:* Robert B. Goode, Jr., Michael S. Wilder.
Number of staff: 1 full-time professional; 1 part-time support.
Employer Identification Number: 066079761

535
Hartman (Jesse and Dorothy) Foundation
1453 Bedford St.
Stamford 06905   (203) 323-2101

Established in 1954 in New York.
Donor(s): Jesse Hartman.†
Financial data: (yr. ended 12/31/82): Assets, $2,196,338 (M); gifts received, $2,082,531; expenditures, $111,014, including $108,868 for 13 grants (high: $25,000; low: $1,000).
Purpose and activities: Grants for philanthropic and cultural programs.
Officers: Margot H. Tenney,* President; Charles Looker,* Vice-President; Milton Mann, Secretary-Treasurer.
Trustees:* Delbert Tenney.
Employer Identification Number: 066044501

536
Heritage Foundation, Inc., The ⌐
601 White Plains Rd.
Trumbull 06611

Incorporated in 1967 in Connecticut.
Donor(s): June C.A. Anderson, G.W. Aldeen Charitable Trust, Christian Heritage School, Inc.
Financial data: (yr. ended 12/31/82): Assets, $2,224,961 (M); gifts received, $62,800; expenditures, $12,066, including $1,883 for 1 grant.
Purpose and activities: Broad purposes; primarily local giving for a Protestant church; some support for Christian primary and secondary educational institutions.
Limitations: Giving primarily in CT.
Application information:
Write: Paul H. Anderson, President
Officers and Directors: Paul H. Anderson, President; June C.A. Anderson, Secretary; Bradley S. Anderson, Treasurer; Barton P. Anderson, Timothy J. Anderson.
Employer Identification Number: 066090012

537
Herzog (The Carl J.) Foundation, Inc. ⌐
P.O. Box 15460, Park Square Station
Stamford 06901

Incorporated in 1952 in Connecticut.
Financial data: (yr. ended 12/31/82): Assets, $5,682,628 (M); expenditures, $320,496, including $283,500 for 72 grants (high: $100,000; low: $1,500).
Purpose and activities: To promote medical research, particularly in the field of dermatology.
Officers and Directors: Peter Bentley, President; Nancy W. Alcock, Secretary; John N. Cole, Treasurer.
Employer Identification Number: 510200524

538
Heublein Foundation, Inc. ▼
P.O. Box 388
Farmington 06032   (203) 677-4061

Incorporated in 1960 in Delaware.
Donor(s): Heublein, Inc., KFC Corporation.
Financial data: (yr. ended 12/31/82): Assets, $176,937 (L); gifts received, $1,500,000; expenditures, $1,391,129, including $1,074,553 for 333 grants (high: $100,000; low: $45), $134,325 for 49 grants to individuals and $182,154 for 248 employee matching gifts.
Purpose and activities: Broad purposes; primarily local giving, with emphasis on community funds, higher education, including scholarships for children of company employees, hospitals, and youth agencies.
Types of support awarded: Employee matching gifts, employee related scholarships.
Limitations: Giving primarily in Farmington, CT. No grants for endowment funds.
Application information:
Initial approach: Letter
Deadline(s): Submit proposal preferably in July or August
Board meeting date(s): As required
Write: Nancy B. Zongol, Treasurer
Officers and Directors:* John F. Cox, President; Richard P. Mayer,* John A. Powers,* Vice-Presidents; George J. Caspar,* Secretary; Nancy B. Zongol, Treasurer.
Employer Identification Number: 066051280

539
Howard and Bush Foundation, Inc., The ▼
P.O. Box 31050
Hartford 06103
Application address for organizations in Troy, New York area: Ms. Jean Bolgatz, R.D. 1, Box 145, West Sand Lake, NY 12196

Incorporated in 1961 in Connecticut.
Donor(s): Edith Mason Howard,† Julia Howard Bush.†
Financial data: (yr. ended 12/31/83): Assets, $5,525,153 (M); gifts received, $450,764; expenditures, $874,001, including $824,698 for 64 grants (high: $37,800; average: $5,000-$25,000).

Purpose and activities: Charitable purposes; general giving in the Hartford, Connecticut, and Troy, New York areas, with emphasis on welfare, aid to the handicapped, education, health agencies, hospitals, cultural programs, and youth agencies.
Types of support awarded: Special projects, building funds, equipment, matching funds.
Limitations: Giving primarily in Hartford, CT, and Troy, NY, areas. No support for government agencies, or to colleges, schools, or churches not connected with the founders. No grants to individuals, or for endowment funds, operating budgets, reserve or revolving funds, or deficit financing.
Publications: Annual report, application guidelines.
Application information: Application form required.
Initial approach: Letter
Copies of proposal: 1
Deadline(s): Submit proposal in February, May, August, and November
Board meeting date(s): March, June, September, and December
Write: Charles C. Tomlinson, III, President
Officers: Charles C. Tomlinson, III,* President; George W. McIsaac,* Vice-President; Frederick C. Maynard, Jr.,* Secretary; Connecticut Bank and Trust Company, Treasurer.
Trustees:* Jeremiah H. Bartholomew, Jr., Sara H. Catlin, Thomas S. Melvin.
Number of staff: 1 full-time professional; 1 part-time support.
Employer Identification Number: 066059063

540
Hubbell (The Harvey) Foundation
584 Derby-Milford Rd.
Orange 06477   (203) 789-1100

Trust established in 1959 in Connecticut.
Donor(s): Harvey Hubbell, Incorporated.
Financial data: (yr. ended 12/31/84): Assets, $1,332,363 (M); expenditures, $245,255, including $226,357 for 124 grants (high: $25,400; low: $100) and $16,742 for 109 employee matching gifts.
Purpose and activities: Primarily local giving in areas of company operations, with emphasis on community funds, youth agencies, social services, hospitals, higher educational institutions, and health organizations.
Types of support awarded: Employee matching gifts.
Limitations: Giving primarily in areas of company operations. No grants to individuals.
Application information:
Write: R.A. McRoberts, Trustee
Trustees: F.R. Dusto, R.A. McRoberts, G.J. Ratcliffe.
Employer Identification Number: 066078177

541
Huisking Foundation, Inc., The ⌐
Greenwich Office Park 1
Greenwich 06836   (203) 622-1500

Incorporated in 1946 in New York.
Donor(s): Members of the Huisking family and family-related corporations.

Financial data: (yr. ended 12/31/82): Assets, $2,439,995 (M); gifts received, $47,904; expenditures, $262,226, including $255,930 for 82 grants (high: $50,000; low: $80).
Purpose and activities: Broad purposes; general giving, with emphasis on education, Roman Catholic church support and welfare funds, hospitals, and religious associations.
Limitations: No grants to individuals.
Application information:
Initial approach: Letter
Copies of proposal: 1
Deadline(s): Submit proposal in February and August
Board meeting date(s): March and October
Write: William W. Huisking, Vice-President
Officers: John E. Haigney,* President; William W. Huisking,* Vice-President; Frank R. Huisking, Secretary; Richard Steinschneider, Jr.,* Treasurer.
Directors:* Remick V. Behrens, Evelyn F. Daly, Robert P. Daly, Claire F. Hanavan, Taylor W. Hanavan, Edward P. Huisking, Richard V. Huisking, Jean M. Steinschneider.
Employer Identification Number: 136117501

542
ITT Rayonier Foundation, The
1177 Summer St.
Stamford 06904   (203) 348-7000

Incorporated in 1952 in New York.
Donor(s): ITT Rayonier, Incorporated.
Financial data: (yr. ended 12/31/84): Assets, $2,272,000 (M); expenditures, $287,000, including $230,000 for 80 grants (high: $25,000; low: $500; average: $1,000-$2,500) and $54,000 for 38 grants to individuals.
Purpose and activities: Created as a medium to meet civic responsibilities in the areas of company operations and to educational institutions related to ITT Rayonier recruitment or to forest industry specializations. Grants to individuals for scholarships, including scholarships to children of employees; to educational associations for scholarships and fellowships; to hospitals for buildings and equipment; and to health agencies and community funds.
Types of support awarded: Scholarship funds, employee related scholarships, fellowships, building funds, equipment, operating budgets, continuing support, annual campaigns, seed money, emergency funds, deficit financing, land acquisition, endowment funds, special projects, matching funds, general purposes.
Limitations: Giving primarily in areas of company operations (FL; GA; Fairfield County, CT; SC; and WA). No loans.
Application information:
Initial approach: Letter or full proposal
Copies of proposal: 1
Deadline(s): November 30
Board meeting date(s): February
Final notification: 1 month
Write: Jerome D. Gregoire, Vice-President

Officers: R.M. Gross,* Chairman and President; Jerome D. Gregoire,* C.W. Peacock,* Vice-Presidents; J.B. Canning, Secretary; S.A. Everitt,* Treasurer; G.J. Pollack, Comptroller.
Directors:* W.L. Nutter, D.C. Snyder.
Number of staff: None.
Employer Identification Number: 136064462

543
J.J.C. Foundation, Inc.
One Carney Rd.
West Hartford 06110   (203) 246-6531

Incorporated in 1953 in Connecticut.
Donor(s): Mrs. Florence Carney McGuire,† Mrs. Helen M. Carney.†
Financial data: (yr. ended 11/30/83): Assets, $1,700,000 (M); expenditures, $145,584, including $132,800 for 92 grants (high: $5,000; low: $100).
Purpose and activities: Broad purposes; local giving, with emphasis on higher education, health agencies, and community funds.
Limitations: Giving limited to CT, with emphasis on the Hartford area. No grants to individuals, or for endowment funds, scholarships or fellowships, or matching gifts; no loans.
Application information:
Initial approach: Letter
Copies of proposal: 1
Board meeting date(s): As required
Officers: Francis X. McGuire, President and Treasurer; Grace Carney, Secretary.
Number of staff: None.
Employer Identification Number: 066036358

544
Jones (The Cyrus W. & Amy F.) & Bessie D. Phelps Foundation, Inc.
c/o Tellalian & Tellalian
211 State St.
Bridgeport 06604

Incorporated in Connecticut.
Donor(s): Amy F. Jones.†
Financial data: (yr. ended 9/30/83): Assets, $1,214,937 (M); expenditures, $72,888, including $52,500 for 9 grants (high: $10,000; low: $1,000).
Purpose and activities: Giving largely for local higher education and cultural programs.
Limitations: Giving primarily in CT.
Application information:
Initial approach: Letter
Deadline(s): None
Write: Aram H. Tellalian, Jr., President
Officers and Trustees: Aram H. Tellalian, Jr., Chairman, President, and Treasurer; Alexander R. Nestor, Vice-President; Robert S. Tellalian, Secretary.
Employer Identification Number: 060943204

545
Joseloff (Morris) Foundation, Inc. ¤
125 La Salle Rd., Rm. 200
West Hartford 06107

Incorporated in 1936 in Connecticut.
Donor(s): Lillian L. Joseloff, Morris Joseloff Foundation Trust, Joan Carol Corp., Sycamore Corp.
Financial data: (yr. ended 12/31/82): Assets, $4,407,693 (M); expenditures, $302,758, including $289,430 for 54 grants (high: $68,000; low: $10).
Purpose and activities: Broad purposes; grants largely for Jewish welfare funds, higher and secondary education, and cultural programs, primarily in Connecticut.
Limitations: Giving primarily in CT.
Application information:
Write: Joan J. Kohn, Vice-President
Officers and Directors: Bernhard L. Kohn, Sr., President; Joan J. Kohn, Vice-President, Secretary, and Treasurer; Bernhard L. Kohn, Jr., Katherine K. Masius, Vice-Presidents.
Employer Identification Number: 136062846

546
Jost (Charles & Mabel P.) Foundation, Incorporated ¤
c/o Nestor, Sarka & Schurman
1140 Fairfield Ave.
Bridgeport 06605

Incorporated about 1969.
Financial data: (yr. ended 4/30/83): Assets, $1,949,509 (M); expenditures, $116,963, including $95,000 for 10 grants (high: $19,000; low: $500).
Purpose and activities: Primarily local giving, with emphasis on aid to the handicapped, hospitals, and higher education.
Types of support awarded: Operating budgets.
Limitations: Giving primarily in CT. No grants for scholarships, fellowships, or prizes; no loans.
Application information:
Initial approach: Letter
Deadline(s): None
Write: Alexander R. Nestor, Chairman
Officers and Trustees: Alexander Nestor, Chairman and President; Robert S. Tellalian, Vice-President; Aram H. Tellalian, Jr., Secretary.
Employer Identification Number: 237070398

547
Kayser-Roth Foundation ¤
c/o Gulf & Western Industries, Inc.
High Ridge Park
Stamford 06904

Established in 1956.
Donor(s): Kayser-Roth Corporation, and subsidiaries.
Financial data: (yr. ended 3/31/83): Assets, $1,286 (M); gifts received, $100,290; expenditures, $100,463, including $100,445 for 79 grants (high: $9,000; low: $100).
Purpose and activities: Grants largely for community funds, hospitals, and health agencies; support also for Jewish welfare funds, and youth agencies.

Officers: James I. Spiegel, President; A.N. Briganti, Treasurer; John Bulzacchelli, Principal Manager.
Employer Identification Number: 136104581

548
Kazanjian (The Calvin K.) Economics Foundation, Inc.
P.O. Box 1110
Waterbury 06720   (203) 387-3273
Mailing address: 16 Cleft Rock Ln.,
Woodbridge, CT 06525

Incorporated in 1947 in Connecticut.
Donor(s): Calvin K. Kazanjian.†
Financial data: (yr. ended 12/31/83): Assets, $1,978,691 (M); expenditures, $177,039, including $113,350 for 8 grants (high: $63,000; low: $1,000).
Purpose and activities: To increase man's understanding of economics and to disseminate such knowledge, utilizing various media.
Types of support awarded: Seed money, special projects, research, publications, conferences and seminars.
Limitations: Giving primarily in the U.S. No grants to individuals, or for capital or endowment funds, operating budgets, continuing support, annual campaigns, emergency funds, deficit financing, matching gifts, scholarships, fellowships, or general purposes; no loans.
Publications: 990-PF, program policy statement, application guidelines.
Application information:
Initial approach: General summary letter; if complex, by full proposal
Copies of proposal: 10
Deadline(s): Submit proposal preferably April 1 or October 1; deadline April 15 and October 15
Board meeting date(s): May or June and December
Final notification: 2 weeks after board meetings
Write: Lloyd W. Elston, Treasurer
Officers and Trustees: Mrs. Lloyd W. Elston, President; William A. Forbes, Vice-President; Guerin B. Carmody, Secretary; Lloyd W. Elston, Treasurer; David W. Collins, Richard L. Elston, Thurston H. Graden, Lynn E. Greaves, Worth Loomis.
Number of staff: 1 full-time professional; 1 part-time professional.
Employer Identification Number: 060665174

549
Koopman Fund, Inc., The ⌑
17 Brookside Blvd.
West Hartford 06107   (203) 232-6406

Incorporated in 1963 in Connecticut.
Donor(s): Richard Koopman.
Financial data: (yr. ended 12/31/82): Assets, $4,324,364 (M); expenditures, $313,092, including $292,803 for 112 grants (high: $100,000; low: $10).
Purpose and activities: Broad purposes; primarily local giving, with emphasis on higher and secondary education, Jewish welfare funds, and an art museum.

Limitations: Giving primarily in CT. No grants to individuals.
Application information:
Initial approach: Telephone
Copies of proposal: 1
Board meeting date(s): As required
Write: Richard Koopman, President
Officers and Trustees: Richard Koopman, President; Georgette A. Koopman, Secretary and Treasurer; Dorothy A. Schiro.
Employer Identification Number: 066050431

550
Larrabee Fund Association ⌑
c/o Connecticut National Bank
777 Main St.
Hartford 06115

Established in 1941.
Donor(s): Larrabee Fund, Willie O. Burr.
Financial data: (yr. ended 10/31/82): Assets, $1 (M); gifts received, $146,671; expenditures, $246,584, including $223,290 for grants to individuals.
Purpose and activities: Giving to indigent women.
Types of support awarded: Grants to individuals.
Trustee: Connecticut National Bank.
Employer Identification Number: 066038638

551
List (Albert A.) Foundation, Inc. ▼
207 Byram Shore Rd.
Greenwich 06830   (212) 582-7235

Incorporated in 1953 in Connecticut.
Donor(s): Albert A. List, Vera G. List.
Financial data: (yr. ended 6/30/83): Assets, $12,854,695 (M); gifts received, $50,000; expenditures, $1,171,981, including $1,116,676 for 18 grants (high: $300,000; low: $1,500).
Purpose and activities: Broad purposes; grants largely for Jewish welfare funds, hospitals, and higher education; giving also for the aged, and cultural programs primarily in New York and Connecticut.
Limitations: Giving primarily in NY and CT. No grants to individuals.
Application information:
Initial approach: Letter
Write: Albert A. List, Chairman
Officers: Vera G. List,* President; Stuart Aarons, Secretary; Edward Borsilli, Treasurer.
Directors:* Albert A. List, Chairman; Theodore R. Colborn, Jo Ann List Levinson, Vera G. List, Viki List, Olga List Mack, Carol List Schwartz.
Employer Identification Number: 510188408

552
Long (George A. and Grace L.) Foundation
c/o Connecticut National Bank
777 Main St.
Hartford 06115

Trust established in 1960 in Connecticut.
Donor(s): George A. Long, Grace L. Long.†

Financial data: (yr. ended 12/31/82): Assets, $3,017,346 (M); expenditures, $215,367, including $165,533 for 85 grants (high: $5,000; low: $500).
Purpose and activities: Broad purposes; primarily local giving, with emphasis on cultural programs, education, hospitals, social services, and community funds.
Types of support awarded: Scholarship funds, special projects, building funds.
Limitations: Giving primarily in CT. No grants to individuals, or for operating budgets or endowment funds; no loans.
Application information:
Initial approach: Letter
Copies of proposal: 3
Deadline(s): Submit proposals preferably in January through March or June through August; deadlines March 15 and September or October
Board meeting date(s): April and September or October
Write: J. Harold Williams, Trustee
Trustees: Isabelle C. Shea, J. Harold Williams, Connecticut National Bank.
Employer Identification Number: 066030953

553
MacCurdy-Salisbury Educational Foundation, Inc., The ⌑
Old Lyme 06371   (203) 434-7983

Incorporated in 1893 in Connecticut.
Donor(s): Evelyn MacCurdy Salisbury.
Financial data: (yr. ended 5/31/83): Assets, $2,002,205 (M); expenditures, $117,775, including $10,396 for grants and $92,050 for 98 grants to individuals.
Purpose and activities: Giving to local residents for scholarships; some support for cultural programs.
Types of support awarded: Student aid.
Limitations: Giving limited to Lyme and Old Lyme, CT.
Application information: Application form required.
Deadline(s): April 30; for first semester; November 15 for second semester
Write: Mr. Willis H. Umberger, Secretary-Treasurer
Officer: Willis H. Umberger, Secretary-Treasurer.
Employer Identification Number: 066044250

554
Maguire Foundation, Inc., The ⌑
One Atlantic St., Rm. 414
Stamford 06904

Incorporated in 1948 in Connecticut.
Financial data: (yr. ended 12/31/82): Assets, $5,125,111 (M); expenditures, $434,970, including $400,050 for 37 grants (high: $153,600; low: $100).
Purpose and activities: Broad purposes; primarily local giving, with emphasis on higher and secondary education; grants also for international affairs, hospitals and social services.
Limitations: Giving primarily in CT.

Officers: Sonia S. Maguire, President and Treasurer; Walter L. Maguire, Sr., Vice-President and Secretary; Helen A. Muller, Vice-President.
Employer Identification Number: 066039354

555
Main Street Foundation, Inc. ¤
P.O. Box 58
Southport 06490

Established in 1965.
Financial data: (yr. ended 12/31/83): Assets, $1,777,768 (M); gifts received, $121,837; expenditures, $36,216, including $27,380 for 29 grants (high: $9,000; low: $20).
Purpose and activities: Local giving, mainly for Protestant churches, and for higher and secondary education.
Types of support awarded: Operating budgets, general purposes, scholarship funds.
Limitations: Giving primarily in CT.
Officers: Charles P. Stetson, President and Treasurer; Barbara Stetson, Vice-President and Treasurer.
Director: Charles P. Stetson, Jr.
Employer Identification Number: 066076249

556
Mazer (The Jacob & Ruth) Foundation
c/o David Mazer
Mooreland Rd.
Greenwich 06830

Established in 1961.
Donor(s): Abraham Mazer Foundation.
Financial data: (yr. ended 12/31/84): Assets, $1,715,000 (M); expenditures, $120,000, including $115,000 for 50 grants.
Purpose and activities: Giving primarily for Jewish welfare funds.
Officers: Ruth Mazer, President; David Mazer, Vice-President; Richard Mazer, Secretary and Treasurer.
Employer Identification Number: 136115875

557
Meserve (Albert & Helen) Memorial Fund
c/o Union Trust Co.
P.O. Box 404
New Haven 06502   (203) 773-5832

Established in 1983 in Connecticut.
Donor(s): Albert W. Meserve,† Helen C. Meserve.†
Financial data: (yr. ended 8/31/84): Assets, $2,010,826 (M); expenditures, $221,745, including $193,760 for 30 grants.
Purpose and activities: Charitable purposes.
Limitations: No grants to individuals.
Publications: Application guidelines.
Application information:
   Deadline(s): October 15 and March 1
   Write: Alexander K. Daggett
Trustees: David Clark Murphy, Union Trust Company.
Number of staff: None.
Employer Identification Number: 066254956

558
Moore (Marjorie) Charitable Foundation
c/o Connecticut National Bank
235 Main St., P.O. Box 2140
New Britain 06050   (203) 224-6470

Trust established in 1958 in Connecticut.
Donor(s): Marjorie Moore.†
Financial data: (yr. ended 7/31/84): Assets, $1,154,890 (M); expenditures, $93,038, including $85,224 for 3 grants (high: $55,000; low: $5,224; average: $28,400).
Purpose and activities: To promote local projects of a charitable and civic nature.
Types of support awarded: Operating budgets, continuing support, seed money, building funds, equipment, land acquisition, endowment funds, matching funds, consulting services, special projects.
Limitations: Giving limited to Kensington, CT. No grants to individuals, or for scholarships or fellowships; no loans.
Publications: 990-PF.
Application information:
   Initial approach: Telephone or letter
   Copies of proposal: 1
   Deadline(s): Submit proposal preferably in August; deadline December 1, March 1, June 1, and September 1
   Board meeting date(s): January, April, July, and October
   Final notification: 3 to 6 months
   Write: Miss Rita H. Beaulieu, Trust Officer
Advisory Committee: Pastor, Kensington Congregational Church, and two first deacons; Pastor, Kensington Methodist Church.
Trustee: The New Britain Bank and Trust Company, (Rita H. Beaulieu, Trust Officer).
Number of staff: None.
Employer Identification Number: 066050196

559
New Haven Foundation, The ▼
One State St.
New Haven 06510   (203) 777-2386

Community foundation established in 1928 in Connecticut by resolution and declaration of trust.
Financial data: (yr. ended 12/31/84): Assets, $54,070,122 (M); gifts received, $692,888; expenditures, $3,452,575, including $3,091,223 for 253 grants (high: $120,000; low: $180; average: $40,000) and $295,000 for 7 loans.
Purpose and activities: Public charitable and educational purposes, directed to local communities, with emphasis on support for youth and welfare agencies, hospitals and health agencies, educational institutions, community funds, and the humanities, including music and art.
Types of support awarded: Operating budgets, continuing support, seed money, emergency funds, building funds, equipment, matching funds, consulting services, technical assistance, program-related investments, loans.
Limitations: Giving limited to the greater New Haven, CT, area, and the lower Naugatuck Valley. No grants to individuals, or for annual campaigns, deficit financing, endowment funds, research, or scholarships and fellowships.

Publications: Annual report, application guidelines, newsletter.
Application information: Application form required.
   Initial approach: Telephone
   Copies of proposal: 13
   Deadline(s): January, April, August, and October
   Board meeting date(s): March, June, October, and December
   Final notification: Within 1 week of decision
   Write: Helmer Ekstrom, Associate Director
Distribution Committee: Theodore F. Hogan, Chairman; James Barber, Clare Casher, Terry R. Chatfield, Nancy Ciarleglio, Richard M. Grave, Lawrence M. Liebman, William Muehl, Cheever Tyler.
Trustees: Colonial Bank, The Connecticut Bank and Trust Company, Connecticut National Bank, Union Trust Company.
Number of staff: 3 full-time professional; 1 part-time professional; 2 full-time support.
Employer Identification Number: 066032106

560
Oaklawn Foundation, The
174 Davis Hill Rd.
Weston 06883

Incorporated in 1948 in New York.
Donor(s): Mabel B. Kies, W.S. Kies,† Margaret K. Gibb, and others.
Financial data: (yr. ended 12/31/83): Assets, $7,877,338 (M); gifts received, $28,999; expenditures, $494,088, including $416,510 for grants (average: $2,500-$45,000).
Purpose and activities: Broad purposes; assistance primarily to higher and secondary education, including scholarship funds administered through institutions, undergraduate student exchange organizations, and to youth agencies.
Types of support awarded: Annual campaigns, endowment funds, matching funds, scholarship funds, exchange programs.
Limitations: No grants to individuals, or for operating budgets, deficit financing, emergency funds, capital funds, research, special projects, publications, or conferences; no loans.
Application information:
   Initial approach: Full proposal
   Deadline(s): April 1
   Board meeting date(s): May and October
   Final notification: 2 to 3 months
Officers and Directors: Walter B. Levering, President; John L. Montgomery, Jr., Vice-President; Standish Madina, Secretary; Audrey K. Arnold, M. Emmet, William S. Kies III, A.S. Paight, L. Romanucci.
Number of staff: None.
Employer Identification Number: 136127896

561
Olin Corporation Charitable Trust ▼
120 Long Ridge Rd.
Stamford 06904   (203) 356-3301

Trust established in 1945 in Missouri.
Donor(s): Olin Corporation.

Financial data: (yr. ended 12/31/83): Assets, $11,338,497 (M); expenditures, $1,366,948, including $1,056,233 for 350 grants (high: $70,000; low: $10; average: $500-$10,000), $13,600 for grants to individuals and $236,014 for 1,102 employee matching gifts.
Purpose and activities: Broad purposes; general giving, with emphasis on science and engineering in higher education, community funds, hospitals, youth agencies, and health agencies in areas of corporate operations. Matches employee gifts to education and awards scholarships to children of employees through National Merit Corporation.
Types of support awarded: General purposes, operating budgets, continuing support, annual campaigns, seed money, emergency funds, building funds, equipment, land acquisition, special projects, research, publications, conferences and seminars, internships, scholarship funds, employee related scholarships, fellowships, matching funds, employee matching gifts.
Limitations: Giving primarily in areas of company operations. No grants to individuals (except for scholarships to children of company employees), or for endowment funds; no loans.
Application information:
  Initial approach: Letter or proposal
  Copies of proposal: 1
  Deadline(s): Submit proposal preferably between January and August; no set deadline
  Board meeting date(s): December
  Final notification: 2 to 3 months
  Write: Carmella V. Piacentini, Administrator
Trustees: John M. Henske, James F. Towey, Centerre Trust Company of St. Louis.
Number of staff: 1 full-time professional; 1 full-time support.
Employer Identification Number: 436022750

562
Palmer (The Frank Loomis) Fund
c/o Connecticut National Bank
250 Captain's Walk
New London 06320   (203) 447-6134

Trust established in 1936 in Connecticut.
Donor(s): Virginia Palmer.†
Financial data: (yr. ended 7/31/83): Assets, $7,210,605 (M); expenditures, $420,500, including $420,000 for 48 grants (high: $100,000; low: $155; average: $5,000).
Purpose and activities: Broad purposes; grants exclusively to local institutions, preferably to encourage new projects and to provide seed money, with emphasis on child welfare and family services, youth agencies, and higher and secondary education; support also for civic groups, cultural programs, churches, and hospitals.
Types of support awarded: Seed money, special projects.
Limitations: Giving limited to New London, CT. No grants to individuals, or for endowment funds.
Publications: 990-PF, program policy statement, application guidelines.
Application information: Application form required.
  Initial approach: Telephone

Copies of proposal: 1
Deadline(s): May 15 and November 15
Board meeting date(s): January and July
Final notification: 8 to 14 weeks
Write: George H. Swift, III, Vice-President
Trustee: Connecticut National Bank (George H. Swift, III, Vice-President).
Number of staff: None.
Employer Identification Number: 066026043

563
Panwy Foundation
Greenwich Office Park
P.O. Box 1800
Greenwich 06836   (203) 661-0400

Trust established in 1943 in New York; incorporated in 1951 in New Jersey.
Donor(s): Olga Resseguier, Henry W. Wyman, Maria Wyman, Ralph M. Wyman, Ruth L. Russell, Pantasote Inc., and others.
Financial data: (yr. ended 12/31/84): Assets, $363,435 (M); gifts received, $206,527; expenditures, $258,451, including $252,272 for 315 grants (high: $41,000; low: $25).
Purpose and activities: Charitable purposes; general giving, with emphasis on cultural activities, church support, higher and secondary education, and hospitals.
Types of support awarded: Operating budgets, continuing support, annual campaigns, seed money, emergency funds, endowment funds, building funds, research, equipment, conferences and seminars, scholarship funds, student aid.
Limitations: No grants for matching gifts.
Application information:
  Initial approach: Letter
  Copies of proposal: 1
  Deadline(s): None
  Board meeting date(s): As required
  Final notification: 1 month
  Write: Ralph M. Wyman, Vice-President
Officers and Trustees: Henry W. Wyman, President; Ralph M. Wyman, Vice-President and Treasurer; Barbara K. Eisenberg, Secretary; Virginia A.W. Meyer, Harry A. Russell.
Number of staff: None.
Employer Identification Number: 136130759

564
Patterson (Robert Leet) & Clara Guthrie Patterson Trust
c/o Connecticut National Bank
P.O. Box 1454
Stamford 06904-1454   (203) 358-6159

Established in 1981 in Connecticut.
Donor(s): Robert Patterson Trust No. 2, Robert Leet Patterson,† Clara Guthrie Patterson.†
Financial data: (yr. ended 1/31/84): Assets, $5,769,918 (M); gifts received, $12,804; expenditures, $482,475, including $424,295 for 6 grants (high: $110,000; low: $30,000; average: $50,000).
Purpose and activities: Primarily local giving to hospitals and organizations which are devoted to the advancement of medical science and are engaged in research relating to human diseases.

Types of support awarded: Research, seed money, equipment, matching funds, scholarship funds, professorships, internships, special projects.
Limitations: Giving primarily in CT. No grants to individuals, or for operating budgets, continuing support, annual campaigns, emergency funds, deficit financing, endowment funds, employee-matching gifts, consulting services, technical assistance, demonstration projects, publications, or conferences and seminars; no loans.
Publications: Application guidelines.
Application information: Application form required.
  Initial approach: Letter or proposal
  Copies of proposal: 6
  Deadline(s): April 1st for June meeting and October 1st for December meeting
  Board meeting date(s): June and December
  Final notification: 3 months
  Write: Catherine O. Gagnon, Vice-President
Trustees: John H. McBride, Connecticut National Bank.
Number of staff: None.
Employer Identification Number: 066236358

565
Perkin Fund, The
340 Country Club Rd.
New Canaan 06840   (203) 966-1920

Trust established in 1967 in New York.
Donor(s): Richard S. Perkin.†
Financial data: (yr. ended 12/31/82): Assets, $6,211,649 (M); expenditures, $321,332, including $279,000 for 14 grants (high: $100,000; low: $5,000).
Purpose and activities: Support for advanced education and research, especially in astronomy, biomedicine, and optics.
Limitations: No grants to individuals or for operating budgets; no loans.
Application information:
  Initial approach: Letter
  Copies of proposal: 1
  Board meeting date(s): May and November
  Write: Mrs. Richard S. Perkin, Chairman
Trustees: Mrs. Richard S. Perkin, Chairman; James G. Baker, William F. Close, Winifred P. Gray, John T. Perkin, Richard T. Perkin, Robert S. Perkin, Howard Phipps, Jr., Roderic M. Scott.
Employer Identification Number: 136222498

566
Preston (Evelyn) Trust
One Constitution Plaza
Hartford 06115   (203) 244-4330

Trust established in 1978 in Connecticut.
Donor(s): Mary Yale Bettis,† Evelyn Preston.†
Financial data: (yr. ended 12/31/84): Assets, $1,873,059 (M); expenditures, $134,550, including $128,550 for 35 grants (high: $15,000; low: $460; average: $2,000-$6,000).
Purpose and activities: To provide free band and orchestral concerts in the city of Hartford from June through September.
Limitations: Giving limited to Hartford, CT.
Publications: Application guidelines.

Application information: Application form
required.
  Final notification: 2 months
  Write: Norman E. Armour, Senior Vice-
    President
Trustee: The Connecticut Bank and Trust
Company.
Number of staff: None.
Employer Identification Number: 060747389

567
**Price (Lucien B. and Katherine E.)
Foundation, Incorporated** ⊐
896 Main St.
P.O. Box 790
Manchester 06040

Incorporated in 1922 in Connecticut.
Financial data: (yr. ended 12/31/82): Assets,
$1,596,293 (M); expenditures, $97,839,
including $77,050 for 30 grants (high: $15,000;
low: $300).
Purpose and activities: General giving, with
emphasis on Roman Catholic church support,
religious associations, and church-related
schools, colleges, and hospitals.
Application information:
  Initial approach: Letter
  Write: Rt. Rev. Msgr. Edward J. Reardon,
    President
Officers and Directors: Rt. Rev. Msgr. Edward
J. Reardon, President; Rt. Rev. Msgr. John A.
Brown, Vice-President; Edward P. Flanagan,
Secretary; Morgan P. Ames, Treasurer; Most
Rev. Joseph L. Federal.
Employer Identification Number: 066068868

568
Robinson (Charles Nelson) Fund ⊐
c/o Connecticut Bank and Trust Company
One Constitution Plaza, P.O. Box 3334
Hartford 06103   (203) 244-4295

Trust established in 1928 in Connecticut.
Donor(s): Charles Nelson Robinson.†
Financial data: (yr. ended 6/30/83): Assets,
$1,547,573 (M); expenditures, $114,577,
including $105,242 for 31 grants (high:
$10,000; low: $80).
Purpose and activities: To aid "organized
charities having a principal office in the City of
Hartford"; support for social agencies,
including aid for the aged and youth,
secondary education, and cultural programs.
Limitations: Giving primarily in Hartford, CT.
No grants to individuals or for endowment
funds.
Publications: Application guidelines.
Application information: Application form
required.
  Initial approach: Letter, telephone, or full
    proposal
  Copies of proposal: 5
  Deadline(s): Submit proposal preferably in
    March or September; deadline April 15
    and October 15
  Board meeting date(s): May and November
  Write: Thomas S. Melvin, Vice-President
Trustee: The Connecticut Bank and Trust
Company.
Employer Identification Number: 066029468

569
**Rosenthal (The Richard and Hinda)
Foundation**
High Ridge Park
Stamford 06905   (203) 322-9900

Trust established in 1946 in New York.
Donor(s): Richard L. Rosenthal, and family,
associates, and associated interests.
Financial data: (yr. ended 12/31/83): Assets,
$3,570,564 (M); gifts received, $43,107;
expenditures, $152,013, including $107,046
for 96 grants (high: $20,000; low: $100).
Purpose and activities: Broad purposes, but
particularly to encourage achievement and
excellence in the arts, social sciences, medical
and scientific research, and clinical medicine.
Conceived and annually sponsors the Rosenthal
Awards for Fiction and for Painting through the
American Academy and National Institute of
Arts and Letters; also conceived and sponsors 5
national awards in clinical medicine through
the American College of Physicians, American
Heart Association, American Association for
Cancer Research, and others. Has sponsored
similar "discovery" awards in film through the
National Society of Film Critics and the Society
of Cinematologists.
Types of support awarded: Research,
scholarship funds.
Limitations: No grants to individuals, or for
building or endowment funds, or operating
budgets.
Application information:
  Initial approach: Letter
  Copies of proposal: 1
  Deadline(s): October 31
  Board meeting date(s): Quarterly and as
    required
  Write: Hinda Gould Rosenthal, Vice-President
Officers and Trustees: Richard L. Rosenthal,
President and Treasurer; Hinda Gould
Rosenthal, Vice-President and Secretary;
Richard L. Rosenthal, Jr., Jamie G.R. Wolf, Vice-
Presidents.
Number of staff: 2 part-time professional; 4
part-time support.
Employer Identification Number: 136104817

570
Sachem Fund ⊐
171 Orange St.
New Haven 06510   (203) 773-1291

Trust established in 1969 in Connecticut.
Donor(s): Timothy Mellon.
Financial data: (yr. ended 12/31/82): Assets,
$961,195 (M); expenditures, $263,853,
including $251,125 for 9 grants (high: $50,000;
low: $9,250).
Purpose and activities: Supports primarily
innovative social service programs and land
management projects favoring the Northeast.
Limitations: Giving primarily in the Northeast.
No grants to individuals, or for pure research,
capital projects, endowment funds,
conferences, film projects, publications, or
general operating support.
Publications: Multi-year report.
Application information:
  Initial approach: Letter
  Board meeting date(s): As required

Officers and Trustees: Timothy Mellon,
President; David M. Connors, Secretary;
Nathan W. Pearson, Treasurer; Susan Mellon,
Administrative Trustee.
Employer Identification Number: 066112539

571
Savin Foundation, The ⊐
301 Hartford Ave.
P.O. Box 11190
Newington 06111

Incorporated in 1952 in Connecticut.
Donor(s): A.I. Savin, M.S. Savin, The Balf Co.,
Savin Bros. Inc.
Financial data: (yr. ended 9/30/82): Assets,
$28,133 (M); gifts received, $230,000;
expenditures, $210,957, including $210,947
for 23 grants (high: $191,203; low: $24).
Purpose and activities: Primarily local giving
for Jewish welfare funds.
Limitations: Giving primarily in CT.
Officer and Trustees: Blanche Goldenberg,
Secretary; A.I. Savin, Marvin Savin.
Employer Identification Number: 066038483

572
Schiro Fund, Inc. ⊐
25 Brookside Blvd.
West Hartford 06107

Incorporated in 1963 in Connecticut.
Donor(s): Bernard W. Schiro, Beatrice Fox
Auerbach.†
Financial data: (yr. ended 12/31/82): Assets,
$3,526,701 (M); expenditures, $217,647,
including $192,131 for 79 grants (high:
$136,200).
Purpose and activities: Broad purposes;
primarily local giving, with emphasis on Jewish
welfare funds, higher education.
Limitations: Giving primarily in CT.
Officers and Trustees: Bernard Schiro,
President; Dorothy A. Schiro, Secretary and
Treasurer; Georgette A. Koopman.
Employer Identification Number: 066056977

573
Scott (Walter) Foundation
3 Grand Place
Newtown 06470   (203) 426-4225
Additional mailing address: Chateau Touraine,
P.O. Box 147, Scarsdale, NY 10583

Incorporated in 1903 in New York.
Financial data: (yr. ended 9/30/84): Assets,
$3,611,084 (M); expenditures, $193,430,
including $138,230 for 29 grants (high:
$41,200; low: $150; average: $2,000-$5,000).
Purpose and activities: Grants primarily in the
New York City metropolitan area and lower
Connecticut for aid to institutions concerned
with handicapped children and adults.
Types of support awarded: Operating
budgets, continuing support, annual campaigns,
seed money, emergency funds, building funds,
equipment, endowment funds, research.

Limitations: Giving primarily in the New York, NY, metropolitan area and lower CT. No grants to individuals or for matching gifts; no loans.
Publications: Application guidelines, program policy statement.
Application information:
  Initial approach: Brief letter
  Copies of proposal: 1
  Deadline(s): None
  Board meeting date(s): Semiannually in the spring and early September
  Final notification: 2 to 4 months
  Write: Thorpe A. Nickerson, President
Officers and Directors: Thorpe A. Nickerson, President and Treasurer; Hazel P. Nickerson, Vice-President; Helen L. Hultz, Elizabeth H. Nickerson, Secretary and Executive Manager; Norman A. Hill.
Number of staff: 2 part-time support.
Employer Identification Number: 135681161

574
Scovill Foundation, Inc.
500 Chase Pkwy.
Waterbury 06720   (203) 757-6061

Incorporated in 1961 in Connecticut.
Donor(s): Scovill Manufacturing Company.
Financial data: (yr. ended 12/31/82): Assets, $982,871 (M); expenditures, $376,385, including $373,118 for 126 grants (high: $40,000; low: $500).
Purpose and activities: Broad purposes; general giving, with emphasis on community funds, hospitals, youth agencies, cultural organizations, and educational institutions.
Types of support awarded: Operating budgets, continuing support, seed money, building funds, employee matching gifts.
Limitations: Giving primarily in communities where donor company operates. No grants to individuals.
Application information:
  Initial approach: Proposal
  Copies of proposal: 1
  Deadline(s): Submit proposals in September through November; deadline December 1
  Board meeting date(s): March
  Final notification: 3 months
  Write: Paul Beetz, Secretary
Officers and Trustees: Leonard F. Leganza, President; W.F. Andrews, Vice-President; P.F. Beetz, Jr., Secretary and Treasurer; Bayless Manning, John A. Morgan.
Employer Identification Number: 066022942

575
Singer Company Foundation, The
Eight Stamford Forum
P.O. Box 10151
Stamford 06904   (203) 356-4200

Incorporated in 1960 in Delaware.
Donor(s): The Singer Company.
Financial data: (yr. ended 12/31/84): Assets, $131,371 (M); expenditures, $552,340, including $462,009 for 53 grants (high: $72,750; low: $300) and $90,331 for 896 employee matching gifts.

Purpose and activities: Broad purposes; general giving, with emphasis on higher education and community funds; scholarship support for children of company employees administered by National Merit Scholarship Corporation; support also for hospitals, and civic improvement projects in areas of major Company operations.
Types of support awarded: Employee related scholarships, employee matching gifts.
Limitations: Giving primarily in areas of major company operations. No grants to individuals (except for company-employee scholarships), or for endowment funds.
Publications: Annual report, application guidelines.
Application information:
  Initial approach: Telephone, letter, or proposal
  Copies of proposal: 1
  Board meeting date(s): Annually
  Write: Regina M. Longo, President
Officers: Regina M. Longo, President; Thomas L. Elliott, Jr., Vice-President; Ralph K. Kessler, Secretary; Francis Nicasho, Treasurer; Robert J. Lynch.
Number of staff: 1 full-time professional.
Employer Identification Number: 136065363

576
Society for the Increase of the Ministry, The
120 Sigourney St.
Hartford 06105

Established in 1859.
Donor(s): Sarah Norton Pardee Trust.
Financial data: (yr. ended 8/31/83): Assets, $1,326,485 (M); expenditures, $86,010, including $76,050 for 189 grants to individuals.
Purpose and activities: Grants only to individuals preparing for ordination in the Episcopal church, in an accredited theological seminary.
Types of support awarded: Student aid.
Application information:
  Write: Rev. Canon J.S. Zimmerman, Executive Director
Officers: Rev. H.B. Whitley, President; Howard W. Bornholm, Treasurer.
Employer Identification Number: 066053077

577
Stanley (The Alix W.) Charitable Foundation, Inc.
235 Main St.
New Britain 06051   (203) 224-6473
Mailing address: P.O. Box 1318, New Britain, CT 06050

Incorporated in 1943 in Connecticut.
Donor(s): Alix W. Stanley.†
Financial data: (yr. ended 12/31/84): Assets, $6,755,674 (M); expenditures, $390,276, including $355,173 for 43 grants (high: $50,000; low: $200).
Purpose and activities: Charitable and educational purposes; primarily local giving, with emphasis on cultural programs, community funds, family and youth agencies, and hospitals.

Types of support awarded: Continuing support, annual campaigns, building funds.
Limitations: Giving primarily in New Britain and central CT. No grants to individuals; no loans.
Application information:
  Initial approach: Proposal
  Board meeting date(s): March, June, September, and December
  Write: James P. Carley, Jr., Secretary
Officers: William E. Attwood, President; James P. Carley, Jr., Secretary; Connecticut National Bank, Treasurer.
Trustees: Herbert E. Carlson, Sr., Donald W. Davis, Catherine Rogers, James A. Simpson, Talcott Stanley, Marjorie Wright.
Employer Identification Number: 060724195

578
Stanley Works Foundation, The
c/o Connecticut Bank and Trust Company
P.O. Box 3334
Hartford 06103   (203) 225-5111

Trust established in 1967 in Connecticut.
Donor(s): The Stanley Works.
Financial data: (yr. ended 12/31/82): Assets, $399,000 (M); gifts received, $455,000; expenditures, $539,762, including $369,000 for grants (high: $85,000; low: $200) and $145,762 for 623 employee matching gifts.
Purpose and activities: Broad purposes; giving primarily in areas of company operations for community funds, youth agencies, and higher education; some support also for cultural programs.
Types of support awarded: Operating budgets, continuing support, annual campaigns, seed money, emergency funds, special projects, research, matching funds, employee matching gifts, building funds, internships.
Limitations: Giving primarily in areas of company operations. No grants to individuals, or for deficit financing, equipment, land acquisition, renovation projects, publications, or conferences; no loans.
Publications: Application guidelines.
Application information: Application form required.
  Initial approach: Letter
  Deadline(s): None
  Board meeting date(s): February, May, August, and November
  Write: Ronald F. Gilrain, Vice-President, Public Affairs
Trustee: Connecticut Bank and Trust Company.
Number of staff: None.
Employer Identification Number: 066088099

579
Stone Foundation, Inc., The
P.O. Box 1100
Southport 06430   (203) 655-7918

Incorporated in 1964 in Ohio; reincorporated in 1972 in Connecticut.
Donor(s): Marion H. Stone,† Charles Lynn Stone.†

Financial data: (yr. ended 12/31/83): Assets, $5,106,100 (M); expenditures, $340,771, including $225,375 for 8 grants (high: $100,000; low: $700; average: $25,000-$100,000).
Purpose and activities: Primary interest in seed money for unique projects and programs in medicine, education, and related areas.
Types of support awarded: Seed money, general purposes, building funds, endowment funds.
Limitations: No grants to individuals, or for matching gifts, scholarships, fellowships, or special projects; no loans.
Publications: Program policy statement, application guidelines.
Application information: Funds presently committed; grant requests only from qualified medical schools, colleges, and universities.
    Initial approach: Proposal
    Copies of proposal: 1
    Deadline(s): Submit proposal preferably in September; deadline October 15
    Board meeting date(s): December
    Final notification: By January 31
    Write: Robert B. Milligan, Jr.
Officers and Trustees: Charles Lynn Stone, Jr., President; Edward E. Stone, Vice-President; Robert B. Milligan, Secretary and Treasurer; Paul W. Adams, Mary Stone Parsons, William Parsons, Jr., Judith N. Stone, Sara S. Stone.
Number of staff: 1 part-time professional.
Employer Identification Number: 237148468

580
Stratfield Fund
Ten Middle St., Suite 735
Bridgeport 06604

Trust established in 1955 in Connecticut.
Donor(s): Members of the Hoffman family.
Financial data: (yr. ended 3/31/83): Assets, $1,001,017 (M); gifts received, $264,601; expenditures, $796,686, including $791,797 for 104 grants (high: $230,600; low: $20).
Purpose and activities: Grants primarily for Jewish welfare funds, temple support, and schools and universities; support also for other higher and secondary education.
Trustees: Burton Hoffman, E.R. Hoffman, Laurence K. Hoffman, Sidney Hoffman, Stephen J. Hoffman.
Employer Identification Number: 066046672

581
Sullivan (Ray H. & Pauline)
    Foundation ¤
c/o Connecticut National Bank
777 Main St.
Hartford 06115
Application address: 250 Captain's Walk, New London, CT 06320

Established in 1972 in Connecticut.
Donor(s): Ray H. Sullivan.†
Financial data: (yr. ended 7/31/83): Assets, $5,020,215 (M); expenditures, $198,504, including $169,000 for 18 grants (high: $100,000; low: $500).

Purpose and activities: Giving limited largely to Roman Catholic charities and educational institutions within the diocese of Norwich, Connecticut; some support also for scholarships.
Types of support awarded: Scholarship funds.
Limitations: Giving primarily in the diocese of Norwich, CT.
Application information:
    Deadline(s): May 1
    Write: John C. Curtin
Trustees: David C. Cavicke, James McGuire, Msgr. Paul J. St. Onge, Connecticut National Bank.
Employer Identification Number: 066141242

582
Topsfield Foundation, Inc.
Route 169, P.O. Box 203
Pomfret 06258   (203) 928-2616

Established in 1982 in Connecticut.
Donor(s): Paul J. Aicher.
Financial data: (yr. ended 10/31/84): Assets, $692,871 (M); gifts received, $855,000; expenditures, $236,341, including $183,549 for grants (high: $25,000; low: $500; average: $1,000-$5,000).
Purpose and activities: Giving to grassroots organizations whose purposes include "reversing the arms race, the abolishment of nuclear weapons, and national security issues."
Types of support awarded: Operating budgets, seed money, matching funds.
Limitations: No grants to individuals.
Publications: Informational brochure, application guidelines, annual report, program policy statement.
Application information: Grants are awarded in February, June, and December. Application form required.
    Initial approach: Brief proposal
    Copies of proposal: 2
    Deadline(s): None
    Board meeting date(s): Monthly
    Final notification: 6 to 10 weeks
    Write: Susan Graseck, Executive Director
Members: Paul J. Aicher, Chairman; Joyce Aicher, Peter Aicher, Susan Aicher, Duncan Johnson, Dennis Landis, Kathryn Wright.
Officer: Susan Graseck, Executive Director.
Number of staff: 1 full-time professional; 1 full-time support.
Employer Identification Number: 061074292

583
UMC Industries Foundation, Inc. ¤
c/o UMC Industries, Inc.
P.O. Box 1090
Stamford 06904   (203) 329-6000

Incorporated in 1937 in Delaware; in 1951 in Missouri.
Donor(s): UMC Industries, Inc.
Financial data: (yr. ended 12/31/82): Assets, $1,671,145 (M); expenditures, $157,720, including $152,825 for 202 grants (high: $15,850; low: $25).

Purpose and activities: Charitable and educational purposes; general giving, with emphasis on community funds, higher education, performing arts, youth agencies, and hospitals.
Types of support awarded: General purposes, continuing support, annual campaigns, scholarship funds.
Limitations: No grants to individuals, or for endowment funds, capital funds, or research; no loans.
Application information:
    Board meeting date(s): January, February, April, July, September, October, and November
    Write: Gerard E. Dorsey, Treasurer
Officers: H. Ridgely Bullock,* President; Michael B. McLearn, Vice-President and Secretary; Gerard E. Dorsey, Treasurer.
Directors:* Clarence C. Barksdale, Benton H. Brothers, John L. Burns, Randolph H. Guthrie, John Hawkinson, Jess Nicks, Dudley S. Taft, William M. Weaver.
Employer Identification Number: 436051752

584
UPS Foundation, The ▼
51 Weaver St.
Greenwich Office Park 5
Greenwich 06830   (203) 622-6120

Incorporated in 1951 in Delaware.
Donor(s): United Parcel Service.
Financial data: (yr. ended 12/31/84): Assets, $13,643,674 (M); gifts received, $104,318; expenditures, $3,438,213, including $2,755,000 for 84 grants (high: $250,000; low: $1,000; average: $2,000-$50,000), $413,485 for grants to individuals and $195,184 for employee matching gifts.
Purpose and activities: Support primarily for innovative projects, higher education, health and medicine, human welfare, research, transportation and logistics. Matches gifts of donor's employees to educational and cultural institutions; provides scholarships for qualified children of donor's employees.
Types of support awarded: Operating budgets, continuing support, seed money, equipment, matching funds, employee matching gifts, professorships, internships, scholarship funds, employee related scholarships, exchange programs, fellowships, special projects, research, conferences and seminars.
Limitations: No grants to individuals (except for scholarships to children of company employees), or for building or endowment funds, annual campaigns, emergency funds, deficit financing, land acquisition, renovation projects, or publications; no loans.
Application information:
    Initial approach: Letter or telephone
    Copies of proposal: 1
    Deadline(s): Submit proposal preferably January through August; deadlines March 31 and September 1
    Board meeting date(s): June and late November
    Final notification: 6 weeks
    Write: Robert E. Smith, Administrator

Officers: Paul Oberkotter,* Chairman and Treasurer; George C. Lamb, Jr.,* Vice-Chairman; Preston W. Davis, Secretary; Robert E. Smith, Administrator.
Trustees:* Charles W.L. Foreman, James P. McLaughlin, John W. Rogers.
Number of staff: None.
Employer Identification Number: 136099176

585
Vanderbilt (R. T.) Trust
30 Winfield St.
Norwalk 06855   (203) 853-1400

Trust established in 1951 in Connecticut.
Financial data: (yr. ended 12/31/83): Assets, $4,379,936 (M); expenditures, $206,395, including $181,805 for 97 grants (high: $30,000; low: $50).
Purpose and activities: Broad purposes; general giving in Connecticut and New York, with emphasis on education and conservation; support also for hospitals, cultural programs, and historic preservation.
Types of support awarded: Building funds, endowment funds, operating budgets, special projects.
Limitations: Giving primarily in CT and NY. No grants to individuals.
Application information:
   Initial approach: Proposal
   Copies of proposal: 1
   Deadline(s): Submit proposal preferably in November
   Board meeting date(s): April, June, September, and December
   Write: Hugh B. Vanderbilt, Chairman
Trustees: Hugh B. Vanderbilt, Chairman; Robert T. Vanderbilt, Jr.
Employer Identification Number: 066040981

586
Wahlstrom-Johnson Foundation, Inc., The
(formerly The Wahlstrom Foundation, Inc.)
c/o Wahlson Associates
2425 Post Rd.
Southport 06490   (203) 254-0623

Incorporated in 1956 in Connecticut.
Donor(s): Magnus Wahlstrom.†
Financial data: (yr. ended 7/31/84): Assets, $3,704,741 (M); gifts received, $65,000; expenditures, $377,377, including $337,325 for 97 grants (high: $57,300; low: $50).
Purpose and activities: Broad purposes; general local giving, with emphasis on aid to the handicapped, higher education, hospitals, and youth agencies.
Types of support awarded: Continuing support, seed money, building funds, equipment, research, special projects, matching funds.
Limitations: Giving primarily in the greater Bridgeport, CT, area. No grants to individuals, or for endowment funds, scholarships and fellowships, or operating budgets; no loans.
Publications: Annual report, application guidelines.
Application information:
   Initial approach: Letter

Copies of proposal: 1
Deadline(s): February 15, May 15, August 15, and November 15
Board meeting date(s): March, June, September, and December
Final notification: 3 to 6 months
Write: Eleonora W. McCabe, President
Officers and Directors: Eleonora W. McCabe,* President; Lois J. Hughes,* Secretary and Treasurer.
Employer Identification Number: 066053378

587
Warnaco Fund, Inc. ◻
c/o Corporate Tax Manager
350 Lafayette St.
Bridgeport 06602

Incorporated in 1955 in Connecticut.
Donor(s): Warnaco, Inc.
Financial data: (yr. ended 12/31/82): Assets, $274 (M); gifts received, $147,780; expenditures, $147,780, including $132,150 for 24 grants (high: $25,000; low: $20) and $15,630 for 58 employee matching gifts.
Purpose and activities: Broad purposes, with emphasis on community funds, hospitals, and higher education, including an employees' matching gift fund.
Types of support awarded: Employee matching gifts.
Officers and Directors: Verne L. King, President; John W. Field, Vice-President; Lloyd P. Stauder, Secretary; James C. Walker, William S. Warner.
Employer Identification Number: 066033959

588
Waterbury Foundation
80 Prospect St.
P.O. Box 252
Waterbury 06720   (203) 754-8879

Community foundation incorporated in 1923 by special Act of the Connecticut Legislature.
Donor(s): Katherine Pomeroy,† Edith Chase.†
Financial data: (yr. ended 12/31/83): Assets, $2,651,135 (M); gifts received, $15,399; expenditures, $258,673, including $224,346 for 35 grants (high: $30,000; low: $25; average: $1,000-$30,000).
Purpose and activities: Grants to local organizations, largely for social services, health care, education, youth agencies, community funds, and the arts, with emphasis on providing seed money and venture capital for new projects.
Types of support awarded: Seed money, emergency funds, building funds, equipment, land acquisition, matching funds, research, special projects, publications, conferences and seminars.
Limitations: Giving limited to the greater Waterbury, CT, area. No support for sectarian or religious purposes. No grants to individuals, or for operating expenses, deficit financing, continuing support, annual campaigns, endowment funds, scholarships, or fellowships; no loans.
Publications: Annual report, application guidelines, program policy statement.

Application information: Application form required.
   Initial approach: Telephone or letter
   Copies of proposal: 10
   Deadline(s): 4 weeks prior to board meeting
   Board meeting date(s): February, May, June, July, August, and December; Grants Committee meets 2 weeks prior to board meetings
   Final notification: 2 Months
   Write: Mrs. Ingrid Manning
Officers: Nelson P. Hart,* President; Charles T. Kellogg,* Vice-President; Mrs. Malcolm S. Todt,* Secretary; Christopher A. Brooks,* Treasurer.
Trustees:* Mary Brosnan, Robert N. Davie, M.D., Julia Keggi, Raymond LaMoy, Robert J. Narkis, James C. Smith, Morris Stein, N. Patricia Yarborough.
Trustee Banks: Citytrust, Colonial Bank & Trust Company.
Number of staff: 1 part-time professional; 1 part-time support.
Employer Identification Number: 066038074

589
Wheeler (Wilmot) Foundation, Inc. ◻
P.O. Box 429
Southport 06490

Incorporated in 1941 in Delaware.
Donor(s): Wilmot F. Wheeler,† Mrs. Hulda C. Wheeler.
Financial data: (yr. ended 6/30/83): Assets, $1,835,437 (M); expenditures, $92,405, including $43,130 for 43 grants (high: $10,000; low: $30).
Purpose and activities: Broad purposes; primarily local giving, with emphasis on higher and secondary education, and Protestant church support.
Limitations: Giving primarily in CT.
Officers: Wilmot F. Wheeler, Jr., President; Wilmot F. Wheeler III, Vice-President and Treasurer; Halsted W. Wheeler, Secretary.
Employer Identification Number: 066039119

590
Whitehead Charitable Foundation, The ◻
15 Valley Dr.
Greenwich 06830   (203) 629-4633

Established in 1976.
Donor(s): Edwin C. Whitehead.
Financial data: (yr. ended 11/30/82): Assets, $142,785 (M); gifts received, $250,000; expenditures, $3,616,466, including $3,607,500 for 1 grant.
Purpose and activities: Grants primarily for biomedical research.
Types of support awarded: Research.
Application information:
   Initial approach: Letter
   Write: Arthur Brill, Secretary-Treasurer
Officers and Directors: John Whitehead, President; Peter Whitehead, Vice-President; Arthur W. Brill, Secretary-Treasurer; Susan Whitehead.
Employer Identification Number: 060956618

591
Whitney (Julia A.) Foundation ¤
c/o Thomas P. Whitney, Director
Roxbury Rd., Box 277
Washington 06793

Established in 1965 in New York.
Financial data: (yr. ended 12/31/82): Assets, $1,314,029 (M); expenditures, $52,738, including $41,456 for 8 grants (high: $16,000; low: $1,000).
Purpose and activities: General purposes; grants primarily to foster appreciation and preservation of Russian language, literature, and art, including support for a library of Russian literature; support also for higher education.
Directors: Harrison E. Salisbury, Thomas P. Whitney.
Employer Identification Number: 136192314

592
Widow's Society ¤
c/o Connecticut National Bank
777 Main St.
Hartford 06115

Established in 1907 in Connecticut.
Donor(s): City of Hartford, Sarah W. Pardee Fund.
Financial data: (yr. ended 8/31/83): Assets, $1,370,469 (M); gifts received, $23,492; expenditures, $111,195, including $97,996 for grants to individuals.
Purpose and activities: Aid to needy individuals in the Hartford area.
Types of support awarded: Grants to individuals.
Limitations: Giving primarily in Hartford, CT.
Officers: Mary Hoffer, President; Mrs. Wendell G. Hall, Vice-President; Mrs. John Martin, Secretary.
Employer Identification Number: 066026060

593
Woman's Seamen's Friend Society of Connecticut
74 Forbes Ave.
New Haven 06512   (203) 467-3887

Established in 1859 in Connecticut.
Donor(s): Betsy Forbes Bradley.†
Financial data: (yr. ended 12/31/83): Assets, $1,643,479 (M); expenditures, $106,628, including $62,845 for 103 grants (high: $4,000; low: $400; average: $400).
Purpose and activities: Grants to colleges and universities to provide scholarship aid for students residing in Connecticut or enrolled in Connecticut colleges who are majoring in marine science; support also for public charities which assist needy merchant seamen and their families resident in Connecticut.
Types of support awarded: Seed money, scholarship funds, matching funds, special projects, research.
Limitations: Giving limited to CT. No grants to individuals, or for endowment funds; no loans.
Publications: 990-PF.
Application information:
   Initial approach: Letter
   Copies of proposal: 2

Deadline(s): March or April
Board meeting date(s): February, April, June, October, and December
Final notification: 2 or 3 months
Write: Capt. J.M. Seymour, USN(Ret), Executive Director
Officers and Trustees: Richard Hegel, President; Mrs. Josiah Venter, Secretary; J.M. Seymour, Executive Director; Henry C. Burdick III.
Number of staff: 1 full-time professional; 1 part-time professional.
Employer Identification Number: 060655133

594
Xerox Foundation, The ▼
P.O. Box 1600
Stamford 06904   (203) 329-8700

Incorporated in 1978 in Delaware as successor to Xerox Fund.
Donor(s): Xerox Corporation.
Financial data: (yr. ended 12/31/84): Assets, $9,100,000 (M); expenditures, $10,000,000, including $8,500,000 for grants (high: $1,145,500; low: $250; average: $5,000-$50,000) and $900,000 for 4,800 employee matching gifts.
Purpose and activities: Broad commitment in support of higher education to prepare qualified men and women for careers in business, government, and education; advance knowledge in science and technology; and enhance learning opportunities for minorities and the disadvantaged; also operates employee matching gift program. Support additionally for social, civic, and cultural organizations including United Ways, providing broad-based programs and services in cities where Xerox employees live and work; organizations that foster debate on major national public policy issues; and worldwide, for national leadership efforts around major social problems, education, conservation, and cultural affairs.
Types of support awarded: General purposes, operating budgets, annual campaigns, seed money, emergency funds, deficit financing, research, conferences and seminars, scholarship funds, fellowships, professorships, internships, employee related scholarships, exchange programs, employee matching gifts, program-related investments, consulting services.
Limitations: Giving primarily in areas of company operations. No support for community colleges, organizations supported by United Way, religious organizations, or governmental agencies. No grants to individuals, or for capital or endowment funds, or continuing support; no loans; no donations of machines or related services.
Publications: 990-PF, informational brochure, program policy statement, application guidelines, grants list.
Application information:
   Initial approach: Brief proposal
   Copies of proposal: 1
   Deadline(s): None
   Board meeting date(s): Usually in December and as required
   Final notification: 3 months
   Write: Robert H. Gudger, Vice-President

Officers: Elliott Horton, President; Robert H. Gudger, Vice-President.
Trustees: P. Allaire, David T. Kearns, C. Peter McColough.
Number of staff: 4 full-time professional; 3 full-time support.
Employer Identification Number: 060996443

595
Ziegler (The E. Matilda) Foundation for the Blind, Inc. ¤
41 Harbor Plaza Dr.
P.O. Box 10128
Stamford 06904   (203) 356-9000

Incorporated in 1928 in New York.
Donor(s): Mrs. William Ziegler.†
Financial data: (yr. ended 12/31/82): Assets, $5,605,511 (M); expenditures, $347,269, including $305,000 for 22 grants (high: $135,000; low: $2,500).
Purpose and activities: Giving for charitable and educational work to ameliorate the condition of the blind; support largely for the monthly publication and free distribution of the Matilda Ziegler Magazine for the Blind.
Types of support awarded: General purposes, continuing support, annual campaigns.
Limitations: No grants to individuals, or for endowment funds, research, scholarships, fellowships, or matching gifts; no loans.
Application information:
   Initial approach: Letter
   Copies of proposal: 1
   Deadline(s): Submit proposal prior to December
   Board meeting date(s): December
   Write: William Ziegler III, President
Officers and Directors: William Ziegler III, President; Helen Z. Steinkraus, Secretary; Beatrice H. Page, Treasurer; Lawrence G. Bodkin, Jr., James J. Marett, Frank K. Sanders, Jr.
Employer Identification Number: 136086195

DELAWARE

596
Beneficial Foundation, Inc. ▼
1100 Carr Rd.
P.O. Box 911
Wilmington 19899   (302) 798-0800

Incorporated in 1951 in Delaware.
Donor(s): Beneficial Corporation, and its subsidiaries.
Financial data: (yr. ended 12/31/84): Assets, $4,345,800 (M); gifts received, $350,000; expenditures, $671,205, including $384,550 for 52 grants (high: $100,000; low: $50; average: $1,000-$10,000) and $244,809 for grants to individuals.

Purpose and activities: Broad purposes; grants primarily to educational institutions, hospitals, and for medical research; also a scholarship program for children of employees of Beneficial Corporation or of the Beneficial Finance System. Support also for cultural programs.
Types of support awarded: Employee related scholarships, research, continuing support, annual campaigns, seed money, building funds, equipment, special projects.
Limitations: No grants for endowment funds; no loans.
Application information:
  Initial approach: Full proposal
  Copies of proposal: 1
  Deadline(s): None
  Board meeting date(s): Usually in May and December
  Write: John O. Williams, Vice-President
Officers: Robert A. Tucker,* President; John O. Williams,* Vice-President and Secretary; Kenneth J. Kircher, Treasurer.
Directors:* Freda R. Caspersen.
Number of staff: 2 part-time support.
Employer Identification Number: 516011637

597
Birch (Stephen and Mary) Foundation, Inc. ▼ ☐
306 South State St.
Dover 19901   (302) 734-7528

Incorporated in 1938 in Delaware.
Donor(s): Stephen Birch.†
Financial data: (yr. ended 12/31/82): Assets, $19,500,000 (M); expenditures, $419,542, including $415,000 for 44 grants (high: $20,000; low: $4,500).
Purpose and activities: General giving, with emphasis on health agencies, hospitals, youth agencies, and the blind; support also for cultural programs.
Application information:
  Initial approach: Letter
  Copies of proposal: 1
  Board meeting date(s): Quarterly
  Write: Kay B. Stubbs, Vice-President
Officer and Trustees: Patrick J. Patek, President; Mary B. Patrick, Kay B. Stubbs, Vice-Presidents; Rose B. Patek, Secretary-Treasurer.
Employer Identification Number: 221713022

598
Bishop (Edward E. and Lillian H.) Foundation ☐
c/o Wilmington Trust Company
100 West Tenth St.
Wilmington 19890

Trust established in 1953 in Delaware.
Donor(s): Lillian H. Bishop.
Financial data: (yr. ended 12/31/83): Assets, $1,443,581 (M); expenditures, $97,995, including $90,600 for 33 grants (high: $35,000; low: $100).
Purpose and activities: Grants primarily to organizations in Manatee County, Florida, with emphasis on a museum and planetarium; some support for cultural programs, welfare funds, and care of animals.

Limitations: Giving primarily in Manatee County, FL.
Trustees: Mary E. Parker, Richard W. Pratt, William D. Sugg, Willett Wentzel, P. Woodrow Young, Wilmington Trust Company.
Employer Identification Number: 516017762

599
Carpenter Foundation, Inc., The ☐
Powder Mill Square, Suite 204
3844 Kennett Pike
Greenville 19807

Incorporated in 1942 in Delaware.
Donor(s): William K. Carpenter, and members of the Carpenter family.
Financial data: (yr. ended 12/31/82): Assets, $1,571,296 (M); expenditures, $51,312, including $45,000 for 9 grants (high: $15,000; low: $1,000).
Purpose and activities: Primarily local giving, with emphasis on health services, including hospitals, a secondary school, and a conservation association.
Limitations: Giving primarily in DE.
Officers: Thomas R. Smith,* President and Treasurer; R.R.M. Carpenter, Jr.,* J. Avery Draper,* Vice-Presidents; Betty N. Ginn, Secretary.
Trustees:* William K. Carpenter, Renee C. Draper.
Employer Identification Number: 516015354

600
Chichester du Pont Foundation, Inc. ▼ ☐
1080 DuPont Bldg.
Wilmington 19801   (302) 658-5244

Incorporated in 1946 in Delaware.
Donor(s): Lydia Chichester du Pont,† Mary Chichester du Pont Clark,† A. Felix du Pont, Jr., Alice du Pont Mills.
Financial data: (yr. ended 12/31/82): Assets, $10,135,161 (M); expenditures, $620,460, including $582,000 for 28 grants (high: $190,000; low: $2,000).
Purpose and activities: Giving primarily in the Maryland, Delaware, and Pennsylvania area, with emphasis on welfare, including support for a camp for handicapped children, education, health, cultural programs, and religion; some support for conservation.
Limitations: Giving primarily in the DE, MD, and PA area.
Application information:
  Deadline(s): November 1
  Write: Gregory F. Fields, Secretary
Officers: Alice du Pont Mills,* President; Marka T. du Pont,* Richard C. du Pont, Jr.,* Vice-Presidents; Gregory F. Fields, Secretary; A. Felix du Pont, Jr.,* Treasurer.
Trustees:* Allaire C. du Pont, Caroline J. du Pont, Katharine du Pont Gahagan, James Paul Mills, Phyllis Mills Wyeth.
Employer Identification Number: 516011641

601
Cohen (The Harry) Foundation, Inc. ☐
c/o Charles I. Belfint, Trustee
200 West 9th St. Plaza, Rm. 600
Wilmington 19801

Incorporated in 1959 in Delaware.
Donor(s): Harry Cohen.†
Financial data: (yr. ended 12/31/82): Assets, $1,184,650 (M); expenditures, $159,458, including $122,698 for 13 grants (high: $18,874; low: $500).
Purpose and activities: Primarily local giving, with emphasis on Jewish welfare funds, temple support, and hospitals.
Limitations: Giving primarily in DE.
Officers and Trustees: Sadie C. Toumarkine, President; Charles I. Belfint, Secretary-Treasurer.
Employer Identification Number: 516015783

602
Cohen (Melvin S.) Foundation, Inc. ☐
P.O. Box 2105
Wilmington 19899

Incorporated in 1963 in Wisconsin.
Donor(s): Melvin S. Cohen, Eileen F. Cohen.
Financial data: (yr. ended 12/31/83): Assets, $2,338,100 (M); expenditures, $92,783, including $78,280 for 23 grants (high: $66,000; low: $25).
Purpose and activities: Primarily local giving, with emphasis on Jewish welfare funds.
Types of support awarded: Operating budgets, scholarship funds.
Limitations: Giving primarily in WI.
Officers: Melvin S. Cohen, President; Maryjo Cohen, Vice-President; Eileen F. Cohen, Secretary and Treasurer.
Employer Identification Number: 396075009

603
Common Wealth Trust, The ☐
c/o Bank of Delaware
300 Delaware Ave.
Wilmington 19899

Established in 1978.
Donor(s): Ralph W. Hayes.†
Financial data: (yr. ended 12/31/82): Assets, $4,601,209 (M); expenditures, $336,399, including $185,038 for 5 grants (high: $88,957; low: $1,000) and $72,004 for 5 grants to individuals.
Purpose and activities: Support for a few local organizations, especially a historical society, for educational purposes; also gives distinguished service awards to prominent individuals in literature, the dramatic arts, and communications.
Types of support awarded: Grants to individuals.
Limitations: Giving primarily in DE.
Trustee: Bank of Delaware.
Employer Identification Number: 510232187

604
Copeland Andelot Foundation, Inc. ⌿
2100 DuPont Bldg.
Wilmington 19898

Incorporated in 1953 in Delaware.
Donor(s): Lammot du Pont Copeland.
Financial data: (yr. ended 12/31/82): Assets, $359,243 (M); gifts received, $203,335; expenditures, $208,514, including $196,000 for 19 grants (high: $40,000; low: $1,000).
Purpose and activities: Broad purposes; local giving, with emphasis on hospitals, cultural institutions, community funds, education, and conservation.
Limitations: Giving limited to Wilmington, DE and its 50-mile radius.
Application information:
  Initial approach: Full proposal
  Copies of proposal: 8
  Write: Blaine T. Phillips, President
Officers: Blaine T. Phillips, President; Gerret van S. Copeland, Vice-President; Hugh R. Sharp, Jr., Secretary-Treasurer.
Employer Identification Number: 516001265

605
Crestlea Foundation, Inc.
1004 Wilmington Trust Center
Wilmington 19801

Incorporated in 1955 in Delaware.
Donor(s): Henry B. du Pont.†
Financial data: (yr. ended 12/31/83): Assets, $6,953,931 (M); gifts received, $13,749; expenditures, $328,461, including $303,202 for 34 grants (high: $62,225; low: $1,000).
Purpose and activities: Broad purposes; primarily local giving, with emphasis on higher and secondary education, housing and urban affairs, health agencies, community funds, welfare agencies, and conservation.
Limitations: Giving primarily in DE and CT. No grants to individuals.
Application information:
  Initial approach: Letter
  Copies of proposal: 1
  Board meeting date(s): As required
  Write: Stewart E. Poole, President
Officers: Stewart E. Poole,* President; Elizabeth W. Kane, Secretary; Edward B. du Pont,* Treasurer.
Directors:* Otto C. Fad.
Employer Identification Number: 516015638

606
Crystal Trust ▼
1088 DuPont Bldg.
Wilmington 19898   (302) 774-8421

Trust established in 1947 in Delaware.
Donor(s): Irenee du Pont.†
Financial data: (yr. ended 12/31/84): Assets, $28,000,000 (M); expenditures, $940,000, including $843,260 for 46 grants (high: $100,000; low: $2,000; average: $10,000-$20,000).
Purpose and activities: General purposes; primarily local giving for higher and secondary education and social services.

Types of support awarded: Seed money, building funds, equipment, land acquisition, program-related investments.
Limitations: Giving primarily in DE. No grants to individuals, or for endowment funds, research, scholarships, fellowships, or matching gifts; no loans.
Publications: Application guidelines, program policy statement.
Application information:
  Initial approach: Letter
  Copies of proposal: 1
  Deadline(s): October 1
  Board meeting date(s): November
  Final notification: December 31
  Write: Burt C. Pratt, Director
Officer: Burt C. Pratt, Director.
Trustees: Irenee du Pont, Jr., Mrs. Lucile E. d.P. Flint, David Greenewalt.
Number of staff: 1 part-time professional; 1 part-time support.
Employer Identification Number: 516015063

607
Ederic Foundation, Inc. ⌿
A-102 Greenville Center
3801 Kennett Pike
Wilmington 19807

Incorporated in 1958 in Delaware.
Donor(s): John E. Riegel, Natalie R. Weymouth, Richard E. Riegel, Jr., Mrs. G. Burton Pearson, Jr.
Financial data: (yr. ended 12/31/83): Assets, $52 (M); gifts received, $9,258; expenditures, $270,530, including $270,508 for 87 grants (high: $43,258; low: $100).
Purpose and activities: Broad purposes; primarily local giving, with emphasis on private elementary and secondary schools, hospitals and health care, community funds, cultural institutions, and higher education; grants also for youth agencies and conservation.
Limitations: Giving primarily in DE.
Officers: Mrs. G. Burton Pearson, Jr.,* President; Harry S. Short, Treasurer.
Trustees:* Robert C. McCoy, John E. Riegel, Richard E. Riegel, Jr., Philip B. Weymouth, Jr.
Employer Identification Number: 516017927

608
Gerard (Sumner) Foundation ⌿
100 West Tenth St.
Wilmington 19801

Established in 1963 in Delaware.
Donor(s): Sumner Gerard.†
Financial data: (yr. ended 4/30/83): Assets, $1,434,471 (M); expenditures, $110,977, including $92,200 for 72 grants (high: $18,000; low: $50).
Purpose and activities: General giving, with emphasis on higher and secondary education, hospitals, and church support.
Officers: James W. Gerard, President; C.H. Coster Gerard, Sumner Gerard, Vice-Presidents; John P. Campbell, Secretary and Treasurer.
Employer Identification Number: 136155552

609
Glencoe Foundation, Inc.
Bldg. C, Suite 300
3801 Kennett Pike
Greenville 19807   (302) 654-9933

Established in 1975 in Delaware.
Financial data: (yr. ended 12/31/83): Assets, $1,051,699 (M); gifts received, $363,170; expenditures, $480,962, including $477,960 for 22 grants (high: $318,886; low: $322).
Purpose and activities: Grants "exclusively to Scottish and American charitable organizations, such as museums, hospitals, educational institutions, and other publicly-oriented organizations that promote and preserve Scottish-American traditions and culture."
Types of support awarded: Special projects, general purposes, operating budgets, continuing support, seed money, emergency funds, building funds, equipment, land acquisition, publications.
Limitations: No grants to individuals, or for scholarships, fellowships, or matching gifts; no loans.
Publications: Application guidelines.
Application information: Application form required.
  Initial approach: Full proposal
  Copies of proposal: 1
  Board meeting date(s): Annually and as required
  Final notification: 2 to 3 months
  Write: Ellice McDonald, Jr., President
Officers: Ellice McDonald, Jr.,* President; Rosa H. McDonald,* Vice-President; Curtis J. Frantz, Secretary and Treasurer.
Directors:* Pierre Dupont Hayward, John F. McDonald, Jr., Nestor J. MacDonald, John P. Sinclair.
Employer Identification Number: 510164761

610
Good Samaritan, Inc. ⌿
One Rodney Square
P.O. Box 551
Wilmington 19899   (302) 654-7558

Incorporated in 1938 in Delaware.
Donor(s): Elias Ahuja.†
Financial data: (yr. ended 12/31/83): Assets, $516,561 (M); expenditures, $216,973, including $212,200 for 6 grants (high: $95,200; low: $1,000).
Purpose and activities: Broad purposes; charitable giving, with emphasis on higher education.
Types of support awarded: Building funds, operating budgets, special projects.
Limitations: No grants to individuals.
Application information: Applications for grants not invited.
  Board meeting date(s): As required
  Write: E.N. Carpenter, II, Secretary
Officers and Directors: Rev. Henry Knox Sherrill, President; Elizabeth Lee du Pont, Vice-President; E.N. Carpenter, II, Secretary and Treasurer.
Employer Identification Number: 516000401

611
Israel (A. Cremieux) Foundation, Inc. ☐
229 South State St.
Dover 19901
Mailing address: 110 Wall St., New York, NY
10005

Incorporated in 1967 in Delaware as successor
to the foundation of the same name
incorporated in 1946 in New York.
Donor(s): A.C. Israel.
Financial data: (yr. ended 12/31/83): Assets,
$4,231,604 (M); gifts received, $100,000;
expenditures, $184,801, including $164,050
for 24 grants (high: $50,000; low: $100).
Purpose and activities: Broad purposes; grants
largely for hospitals, and higher and secondary
education.
Limitations: No grants to individuals.
Officers and Directors: A.C. Israel, President;
Barry Gray, Secretary; Thomas C. Israel,
Treasurer.
Employer Identification Number: 516021414

612
Kent (The Ada Howe) Foundation
100 West Tenth St.
Wilmington 19801
Mailing address: c/o John E. Connelly, Jr., 299
Park Ave., 17th Fl., New York, NY 10017

Incorporated in 1962 in Delaware.
Donor(s): Marjorie K. Kilpatrick.†
Financial data: (yr. ended 9/30/82): Assets,
$4,943,858 (M); expenditures, $492,649,
including $429,250 for 20 grants (high:
$78,000; low: $1,500).
Purpose and activities: Broad purposes;
general giving, with emphasis on higher
education and religious organizations carrying
on studies and practical work in comparative
religion; grants also for social agencies.
Officers and Directors: John E. Connelly, Jr.,
President; Henry P. Renard, Vice-President;
John P. Campbell, Secretary and Treasurer.
Employer Identification Number: 136066978

613
Kent-Lucas Foundation, Inc.
101 Springer Bldg.
3411 Silverside Rd.
Wilmington 19810   (302) 478-4383
Mailing address: P.O. Box 7048, Wilmington,
DE 19803

Incorporated in 1968 in Delaware.
Donor(s): Atwater Kent Foundation, Inc.
Financial data: (yr. ended 12/31/83): Assets,
$1,852,421 (M); expenditures, $98,331,
including $84,300 for 80 grants (high: $20,900;
low: $25).
Purpose and activities: Broad purposes; grants
largely for cultural programs, including historic
preservation, hospitals, education, and church
support.
Types of support awarded: General purposes,
operating budgets, continuing support, building
funds.

Limitations: Giving primarily in the
Philadelphia, PA, metropolitan area, ME, and
FL. No grants to individuals or for endowment
funds.
Publications: Application guidelines.
Application information:
  Initial approach: Letter
  Copies of proposal: 1
  Deadline(s): None
  Board meeting date(s): As required
  Final notification: 1 to 3 months
  Write: Mrs. Elizabeth K. Van Alen, President
Officers: Elizabeth K. Van Alen,* President and
Treasurer; William L. Van Alen,* Vice-
President; James R. Weaver, Secretary.
Trustees:* A. Atwater Kent, Jr.
Number of staff: 4.
Employer Identification Number: 237010084

614
Kingsley Foundation, The ☐
c/o Wilmington Trust Company
Rodney Square North
Wilmington 19890

Established in 1961 in Connecticut.
Donor(s): F.G. Kingsley, Ora K. Smith.
Financial data: (yr. ended 12/31/83): Assets,
$2,198,624 (M); gifts received, $195,029;
expenditures, $87,021, including $83,500 for
28 grants (high: $30,000; low: $500).
Purpose and activities: Broad purposes;
support primarily for health, medical education,
social services, and an opera company.
Trustees: Ora Rimes Kingsley, Minot K.
Milliken, R.J. Netter.
Employer Identification Number: 066037966

615
Kutz (Milton and Hattie) Foundation ☐
101 Garden of Eden Rd.
Wilmington 19803

Established in Delaware.
Donor(s): Milton Kutz, Hattie Kutz.
Financial data: (yr. ended 6/30/83): Assets,
$1,686,393 (M); expenditures, $115,768,
including $58,150 for grants (high: $24,700;
low: $500) and $35,000 for grants to
individuals.
Purpose and activities: Giving largely for
Jewish religious organizations and temple
support; grants also for child welfare, social
services, and higher education, including
scholarships to residents of Delaware who will
be college freshmen.
Types of support awarded: Student aid.
Application information: Scholarship
application form required. Application form
required.
  Deadline(s): March 15
Officers and Directors: Alfred J. Greene,
President; Rolf F. Eriksen, Vice-President; Hilda
C. Codor, Secretary; Morris Lapidos, Executive
Secretary; Frank Chaiken, Bennett N. Epstein,
Harold E. May, Irving Morris, Collins Seitz,
Bernard Siegel, Pat Spiegal, Leo Zeftel.
Employer Identification Number: 510187055

616
Laffey-McHugh Foundation ▼
1220 Market Bldg.
P.O. Box 2207
Wilmington 19899   (302) 658-9141

Incorporated in 1959 in Delaware.
Donor(s): Alice L. McHugh,† Marie Louise
McHugh, Frank A. McHugh, Jr.†
Financial data: (yr. ended 12/31/83): Assets,
$23,954,045 (M); expenditures, $1,795,706,
including $1,658,940 for 72 grants (high:
$200,000; low: $1,000).
Purpose and activities: Grants for Roman
Catholic church support and church-related
institutions, including schools, welfare agencies,
religious associations, child welfare agencies,
and a school for the handicapped; support also
for a community fund, higher education, and
hospitals.
Types of support awarded: Annual
campaigns, seed money, emergency funds,
building funds, equipment, land acquisition,
matching funds, general purposes.
Limitations: Giving primarily in DE, with
emphasis on Wilmington. No grants to
individuals, or for operating budgets,
endowment funds, research, demonstration
projects, publications, conferences,
professorships, internships, program-related
investments, consulting services, technical
assistance, scholarships, or fellowships; no
loans.
Publications: 990-PF.
Application information:
  Initial approach: Proposal
  Copies of proposal: 1
  Deadline(s): Submit proposal preferably in
  March or October; deadlines April 1 and
  November 1
  Board meeting date(s): May and November
  Write: Arthur G. Connolly, Sr., President
Officers: Arthur G. Connolly, Sr.,* President;
Marie Louise McHugh,* Collins J. Seitz,* Vice-
Presidents; Thomas S. Lodge, Secretary; Arthur
G. Connolly, Jr.,* Treasurer.
Directors:* Edward J. Goett.
Number of staff: None.
Employer Identification Number: 516015095

617
Lalor Foundation, The
Bldg. B-108
3801 Kennett Pike
Wilmington 19807   (302) 571-1262

Incorporated in 1935 in Delaware.
Donor(s): Members of the Lalor family, Willard
A. Lalor.†
Financial data: (yr. ended 9/30/84): Assets,
$4,207,515 (M); gifts received, $30,000;
expenditures, $162,680, including $131,950
for 12 grants (high: $17,500; low: $7,989;
average: $15,000).
Purpose and activities: Support for
educational and/or scientific research
institutions, for postdoctoral fellowship awards
in the field of mammalian reproductive
physiology research.
Types of support awarded: Fellowships,
research.

Limitations: No support for people over 35 years of age. No grants to individuals, or for operating budgets, capital or endowment funds, continuing support, annual campaigns, seed money, emergency funds, deficit financing, research, or matching gifts; no loans.
Publications: Application guidelines, program policy statement.
Application information: Application form required.
Initial approach: Letter or telephone
Copies of proposal: 1
Deadline(s): Submit proposal in December or January; deadline January 15
Board meeting date(s): November or December
Final notification: March 1 to 15
Write: C. Lalor Burdick, Director
Officers and Trustees: Charles Lee Reese, Jr., President; Rodman Ward, Jr., Vice-President; Lalor Burdick, Treasurer; C. Lalor Burdick, Director; Julian W. Hill, Mrs. James T. Patterson.
Number of staff: 1 part-time support.
Employer Identification Number: 516000153

618
Longwood Foundation, Inc. ▼
1004 Wilmington Trust Center
Wilmington 19801   (302) 654-2477

Incorporated in 1937 in Delaware.
Donor(s): Pierre S. du Pont.†
Financial data: (yr. ended 9/30/83): Assets, $167,901,502 (M); expenditures, $8,295,042, including $7,382,296 for 62 grants (high: $2,667,000; low: $500).
Purpose and activities: Primary obligation is the support, operation, and development of Longwood Gardens, which is open to the public; limited grants generally to educational institutions, and to local hospitals for construction purposes, and social and youth agencies.
Types of support awarded: Annual campaigns, operating budgets, building funds, equipment, land acquisition, endowment funds, research.
Limitations: Giving primarily in DE, with emphasis on Wilmington; some giving also in PA. No grants to individuals or for special projects.
Application information:
Initial approach: Letter
Copies of proposal: 1
Deadline(s): Submit proposal preferably in December, April, or September
Board meeting date(s): January, May, and October
Final notification: At time of next board meeting
Write: Endsley P. Fairman, Executive Secretary
Officers and Trustees: H. Rodney Sharp III, President; Edward B. du Pont, Pierre S. du Pont, Vice-Presidents; Irenee du Pont May, Secretary; Henry H. Silliman, Jr., Treasurer; Gerret van S. Copeland, David L. Craven.
Number of staff: 2 full-time professional; 3 full-time support; 1 part-time support.
Employer Identification Number: 510066734

619
Lovett Foundation, Inc., The ¤
82 Governor Printz Blvd.
Claymont 19703   (302) 798-6604

Incorporated in 1952 in Delaware.
Donor(s): Walter L. Morgan.
Financial data: (yr. ended 11/30/83): Assets, $1,500,412 (M); gifts received, $25,461; expenditures, $143,799, including $129,780 for 141 grants (high: $7,500; low: $50).
Purpose and activities: Broad purposes; giving primarily in Delaware and Pennsylvania, with emphasis on church support, hospitals, cultural programs, and civic affairs; grants also for education and social agencies.
Limitations: Giving primarily in DE and PA.
Application information:
Board meeting date(s): Quarterly
Write: Marie J. Wermuth, Treasurer
Officers: Walter L. Morgan,* President; Michael J. Robinson,* Vice-President; Leanor H. Silver, Secretary; Marie J. Wermuth, Treasurer.
Trustees: * Andrew B. Young.
Employer Identification Number: 236253918

620
Lynch (John B.) Scholarship Foundation
P.O. Box 4248
Wilmington 19807-0248   (302) 654-3444

Trust established in 1963 in Delaware.
Donor(s): John B. Lynch,† Katherine C. Lynch.†
Financial data: (yr. ended 12/31/82): Assets, $2,359,253 (M); expenditures, $183,634, including $6,000 for 1 grant (average: $300-$1,200) and $151,983 for 294 grants to individuals.
Purpose and activities: Scholarships for worthy young persons from the local area .
Types of support awarded: Student aid.
Limitations: Giving limited to DE. No grants for scholarships beyond baccalaureate level.
Publications: Application guidelines.
Application information: Application form required.
Initial approach: Letter
Copies of proposal: 1
Deadline(s): Submit application preferably between January 1 and March 15; deadline March 15
Board meeting date(s): May
Final notification: 3 to 5 months after meeting
Write: Charles A. Robinson, Trustee
Trustees: William Duffy, Jr., Charles A. Robinson, Josephine R. Robinson.
Number of staff: 2 part-time support.
Employer Identification Number: 516017041

621
Marmot Foundation, The ▼
1004 Wilmington Trust Center
Wilmington 19898   (302) 654-2477

Established in 1968 in Delaware.
Donor(s): Margaret F. du Pont Trust.

Financial data: (yr. ended 12/31/82): Assets, $9,828,119 (M); expenditures, $603,265, including $548,000 for 52 grants (high: $42,500; low: $2,500; average: $5,000-$25,000).
Purpose and activities: Giving primarily in Delaware and Florida for hospitals, health, higher and secondary education, community funds, cultural programs, youth agencies, and social services.
Types of support awarded: Emergency funds, building funds, equipment, research, special projects, matching funds, continuing support.
Limitations: Giving primarily in DE and FL. No grants to individuals, or for endowment funds, operating budgets, scholarships, or fellowships; no loans.
Application information:
Initial approach: Letter
Copies of proposal: 1
Deadline(s): Submit proposal preferably in April and October; no set deadline
Board meeting date(s): May and November
Final notification: 2 weeks after board meeting
Write: Endsley P. Fairman, Secretary (for Delaware organizations); William H. du Pont, President (for Florida organizations)
Officers and Trustees: Willis H. du Pont, Chairman; Endsley P. Fairman, Secretary; Miren deA. du Pont, William W. Geddes, George S. Harrington.
Number of staff: None.
Employer Identification Number: 516022487

622
Marshall (Silver) Foundation, Inc. ¤
410 South St.
Dover 19901

Established in 1979.
Donor(s): Russell S. Knapp.
Financial data: (yr. ended 12/31/83): Assets, $369,153 (M); expenditures, $4,299,673, including $4,299,630 for 7 grants (high: $4,297,800; low: $75).
Purpose and activities: Primarily local giving; support largely for Columbia University and small gifts to other educational organizations.
Limitations: Giving primarily in NY.
Officers: Russell S. Knapp, President; Daisy Bedusa, Secretary.
Employer Identification Number: 132979552

623
Milliken (Gerrish H.) Foundation ¤
c/o Wilmington Trust Company
Wilmington 19890

Established in 1962.
Donor(s): Members of the Milliken family.
Financial data: (yr. ended 12/31/83): Assets, $1,328,699 (M); gifts received, $279,454; expenditures, $191,065, including $187,713 for 91 grants (high: $22,000; low: $50).
Purpose and activities: Giving primarily for higher and secondary education and wildlife; grants also for Protestant church support and child welfare.
Types of support awarded: General purposes.

Officer: R.J. Netter, Treasurer.
Trustees: Minot K. Milliken, Phoebe Milliken, Roger Milliken.
Employer Identification Number: 066037106

624
National Vulcanized Fibre Company Community Services Trust Fund ¤
Maryland Ave. and Beech St.
Wilmington 19899

Trust established in 1956 in Delaware.
Donor(s): National Vulcanized Fibre Company.
Financial data: (yr. ended 12/31/83): Assets, $1,340,005 (M); expenditures, $108,468, including $104,625 for 38 grants (high: $35,000; low: $90).
Purpose and activities: Broad purposes; primarily local giving for higher education, cultural programs, and child welfare.
Limitations: Giving primarily in DE.
Trustees: J. Coppersmith, S. Posner, V. Posner.
Employer Identification Number: 516021550

625
Penzance Foundation
100 W. 10th St.
Wilmington 19801
Application address: John M. Emery, c/o Breed, Abbott & Morgan, 153 E. 53rd St., New York, NY 10022; Tel.: (212) 888-0800

Established in 1981 in Delaware.
Donor(s): Edna McConnell Clark.†
Financial data: (yr. ended 4/30/83): Assets, $35,470,537 (M); expenditures, $2,545,614, including $2,485,000 for 6 grants (high: $1,000,000; low: $25,000).
Purpose and activities: First year of giving in 1983; giving primarily in Massachusetts and New York, to a performing arts center, a university, a youth agency, and a hospital.
Types of support awarded: General purposes.
Limitations: Giving primarily in MA and NY.
Application information: Applications not encouraged.
Officers: Hays Clark, President; John M. Emery, Vice-President and Secretary; James McConnell Clark, Vice-President and Treasurer.
Trustees: Hays Clark, James M. Clark, John M. Emery.
Employer Identification Number: 133081557

626
Presto Foundation ¤
P.O. Box 2105
Wilmington 19899

Incorporated in 1952 in Wisconsin.
Donor(s): National Presto Industries, Inc.
Financial data: (yr. ended 5/31/83): Assets, $11,235,940 (M); expenditures, $768,504, including $637,843 for 103 grants (high: $85,000; low: $15) and $72,592 for 25 grants to individuals.

Purpose and activities: Charitable purposes; general giving, with emphasis on higher education, including scholarships for employees' children, educational television, local community funds, health, and social agencies.
Types of support awarded: Employee related scholarships.
Officers and Trustees: Melvin S. Cohen, Chairman and President; R.J. Alexy, Orth I. Dains, Walter Gold, Vice-Presidents; Maryjo Cohen, Secretary and Treasurer; Eileen Phillips Cohen, Kenneth Hansen, Richard Myhers, Lyle Rostad.
Employer Identification Number: 396045769

627
Raskob (The Bill) Foundation, Inc.
P.O. Box 4019
Wilmington 19807   (302) 655-4440

Incorporated in 1928 in Delaware.
Donor(s): John J. Raskob,† Mrs. Helena S. Corcoran.†
Financial data: (yr. ended 12/31/84): Assets, $1,323,200 (M); expenditures, $77,200, including $52,500 for 41 loans (average: $500-$3,000).
Purpose and activities: Giving only for no-interest loans to American students to finance education.
Types of support awarded: Student aid.
Limitations: No grants for any purpose except student loans.
Publications: Application guidelines, program policy statement.
Application information: Request application by April 1; all applicants must first apply for government loans or grants. Currently, no applications accepted from law students, incoming students on any level, foreign students, or American students studying abroad. Application form required.
  Initial approach: Letter or telephone
  Deadline(s): May 1
  Board meeting date(s): Annually
  Final notification: Before September
  Write: Patricia M. Garey, Secretary
Officers: Edward H. Robinson,* President; Gerard S. Garey,* Vice-President; Patricia M. Garey, Secretary; Kathleen D. Smith,* Treasurer.
Directors:* William S. Bremer, Sister Pat Geuting, William F. Raskob III, Anthony L. Robinson, Barbara P. Robinson, Anne M. Stanton, J. Michael Stanton, Jr.
Number of staff: 4 full-time professional.
Employer Identification Number: 510110185

628
Raskob Foundation for Catholic Activities, Inc. ▼
P.O. Box 4019
Wilmington 19807   (302) 655-4440

Incorporated in 1945 in Delaware.
Donor(s): John J. Raskob.†
Financial data: (yr. ended 12/31/84): Assets, $51,920,888 (M); expenditures, $2,424,852, including $1,865,500 for 441 grants (high: $25,000; low: $200; average: $4,230).

Purpose and activities: Support limited to institutions and organizations identified with the Roman Catholic Church. In order to qualify for consideration for large building projects, construction must be underway, a signed construction contract must exist, and 50 percent of the total funds needed must already be committed.
Types of support awarded: Operating budgets, seed money, emergency funds, building funds, equipment, land acquisition, matching funds.
Limitations: No grants to individuals, or for continuing support, annual campaigns, deficit financing (except missions), endowment funds, tuition, scholarships and fellowships, individual research, or building projects prior to the start of construction.
Publications: Annual report, program policy statement, application guidelines.
Application information: Application form required.
  Initial approach: Letter, telephone, or full proposal of 5 pages or less
  Deadline(s): Submit proposals preferably in January, February, July, or August; no set deadlines
  Board meeting date(s): Spring and fall
  Final notification: 6 months
  Write: Gerard S. Garey, Executive Vice-President
Officers and Trustees: Anthony W. Raskob, Chairman; Patsy R. Bremer, President; Gerard S. Garey, Executive Vice-President; Benjamin G. Raskob, First Vice-President; Michael G. Duffy, Second Vice-President; I. Christopher Robinson, Secretary; William F. Raskob, III, Treasurer; Nina B. Bennett, Ann R. Borden, Linda L. Brown, Rosalie M. Parkman, Richard G. Raskob, Kathleen D. Smith, Susan Y. Stanton.
Number of staff: 2 full-time professional; 2 full-time support.
Employer Identification Number: 510070060

629
Red Clay Reservation, Inc.
1004 Wilmington Trust Center
Wilmington 19801

Incorporated in 1962 in Delaware.
Donor(s): Lammot du Pont Copeland, Henry B. du Pont.†
Financial data: (yr. ended 12/31/83): Assets, $4,846,776 (M); gifts received, $142,038; expenditures, $183,003, including $100 for 1 grant and $146,206 for foundation-administered programs.
Purpose and activities: A private operating foundation established to promote the conservation and study of wildlife and game on the North American continent and to maintain wildlife sanctuaries.
Limitations: Giving limited to northern Delaware. No grants to individuals.
Officers and Trustees: Mrs. Lammot du Pont Copeland, President; Mrs. Henry B. du Pont, Vice-President; Edward A. Beacom, Secretary; Edward B. du Pont, Treasurer; Lammot du Pont Copeland, Jr., Blaine T. Phillips.
Number of staff: 1 part-time professional; 1 full-time support; 1 part-time support.
Employer Identification Number: 516017982

630
**Schwartz (The Bernard Lee)
Foundation, Inc.**
P.O. Box 7138
2625 Concord Pike
Wilmington 19803
Address for general information: 7777 Girard
Ave., Suite 201, La Jolla, CA 92037

Incorporated in 1951 in New York.
Donor(s): Bernard L. Schwartz.†
Financial data: (yr. ended 9/30/84): Assets,
$8,931,907 (M); gifts received, $475;
expenditures, $562,189, including $543,697
for 18 grants (high: $395,000; low: $50;
average: $1,000-$50,000).
Purpose and activities: General giving;
support largely to higher education, cultural
programs, and medical tax-exempt institutions,
including hospitals and research facilities.
Types of support awarded: Operating
budgets, continuing support, building funds,
equipment, endowment funds, matching funds,
internships, fellowships, research.
Limitations: No grants to individuals, or for
annual campaigns, seed money, emergency
funds, deficit financing, renovation projects,
land acquisition, demonstration projects,
publications, or conferences; no loans.
Application information:
Initial approach: Letter
Deadline(s): Submit proposal between
January and July 31; deadline July 31
Board meeting date(s): December and as
required
Final notification: 1 month for positive
response
Write: Mrs. Rosalyn R. Schwartz, President
Officers and Directors: Rosalyn R. Schwartz,
President; Donald N. Ravitch, Vice-President;
Tilda R. McGregor, Secretary; Michael L.
Schwartz, Treasurer; Eric A. Schwartz.
Number of staff: 2 part-time support.
Employer Identification Number: 136096198

631
Vale (Ruby R.) Foundation ☒
Bank of Delaware
Milford 19963

Established in 1960 in Delaware.
Donor(s): Ruby R. Vale.†
Financial data: (yr. ended 12/31/83): Assets,
$2,051,650 (M); expenditures, $216,021,
including $198,500 for 20 grants (high:
$35,000; low: $2,000).
Purpose and activities: Grants largely for
higher education.
Application information:
Deadline(s): September 1
Write: Richard E. Menkiewicz, Senior Trust
Administrator
Officers: William G. Vale, President; Robert
Vale, Secretary; Betty McCullough,* Treasurer.
Trustees:* Bank of Delaware (Richard E.
Menkiewicz, Senior Trust Administrator).
Employer Identification Number: 516018883

632
Welfare Foundation, Inc. ▼
1004 Wilmington Trust Center
Wilmington 19801   (302) 654-2477

Incorporated in 1930 in Delaware.
Donor(s): Pierre S. du Pont.†
Financial data: (yr. ended 12/31/83): Assets,
$20,553,793 (M); expenditures, $689,308,
including $545,000 for 30 grants (high:
$193,000; low: $2,000; average: $5,000-
$25,000).
Purpose and activities: General purposes;
emphasis on education, hospitals, a community
fund, and social service agencies.
Types of support awarded: Building funds,
equipment, matching funds, annual campaigns.
Limitations: Giving limited to DE, with
emphasis on the greater Wilmington area. No
grants to individuals, or for endowment funds.
Application information:
Initial approach: Letter
Copies of proposal: 1
Deadline(s): Submit proposal preferably in
April or October; deadlines April 15 and
November 1
Board meeting date(s): May and December
Final notification: 30 to 45 days
Write: Endsley P. Fairman, Executive
Secretary
Officers and Trustees: Robert H. Bolling, Jr.,
President; J. Simpson Dean, Jr., Vice-President;
Mrs. W. Laird Stabler, Jr., Secretary; Edward B.
du Pont, Treasurer.
Number of staff: 2 part-time professional; 2
part-time support.
Employer Identification Number: 516015916

633
Woodstock Foundation, Inc. ☒
3801 Kennett Pike, C-303
Wilmington 19807

Established in 1961.
Financial data: (yr. ended 12/31/83):
Assets, $11,924 (M); gifts received, $111,986;
expenditures, $110,727, including $110,700
for grants.
Purpose and activities: Giving primarily in
Maryland and Delaware for a secondary school
and a church; giving also for a hospital.
Limitations: Giving primarily in DE and MD.
Officers: Allaire C. DuPont, President; Helena
DuPont Wright, Vice-President; Albert J.
Morris, Secretary; Richard C. DuPont, Jr.,
Treasurer.
Employer Identification Number: 510099687

DISTRICT OF COLUMBIA

634
Alvord Foundation, The ☒
918 Sixteenth St., N.W.
Washington 20006

Trust established in 1937 in the District of
Columbia.
Donor(s): Ellsworth C. Alvord.†
Financial data: (yr. ended 12/31/83): Assets,
$3,304,090 (M); expenditures, $380,691,
including $151,125 for 32 grants (high:
$25,000; low: $500).
Purpose and activities: Broad purposes; grants
primarily for higher and secondary education,
performing arts, and hospitals.
Publications: 990-PF.
Application information:
Write: Robert W. Alvord, Vice-President
Officers and Trustees: Ellsworth C. Alvord, Jr.,
President; Robert W. Alvord, Vice-President;
John H. Doyle, Secretary and Treasurer.
Employer Identification Number: 526037194

635
Appleby Foundation, The ☒
c/o Trust Division, National Savings and Trust
Bank
Fifteenth St. and New York Ave., N.W.
Washington 20005

Trust established in 1958 in the District of
Columbia.
Donor(s): Scott B. Appleby.†
Financial data: (yr. ended 12/31/83): Assets,
$4,502,237 (M); expenditures, $331,933,
including $264,410 for 48 grants (high:
$20,000; low: $1,500).
Purpose and activities: Grants primarily for
higher education; giving also for youth
agencies, music, Protestant church support,
cultural programs, and hospitals, largely in
Washington, D.C., Florida, and Georgia.
Limitations: Giving primarily in Washington,
DC, FL and GA.
Trustees: F. Jordan Colby, Sarah P. Williams,
National Savings and Trust Company.
Employer Identification Number: 526026971

636
Appleby (Scott B. and Annie P.) Trust
c/o National Bank of Washington
4340 Connecticut Ave., N.W.
Washington 20008   (202) 537-2176

Trust established in 1948 in the District of
Columbia.
Financial data: (yr. ended 12/31/84): Assets,
$2,179,900 (M); expenditures, $140,930,
including $131,560 for 63 grants (high:
$40,000; low: $120).

Purpose and activities: Broad purposes; emphasis on higher education for the handicapped, primarily in Georgia; some grants for cultural programs and child welfare in Washington, D.C. and Florida.
Limitations: Giving primarily in GA, DC, and FL. No grants to individuals.
Application information:
 Initial approach: Proposal
 Copies of proposal: 1
 Deadline(s): Submit proposal preferably in May; deadline June 1
 Board meeting date(s): July or August
 Write: Beverly Moffett, Trust Officer
Trustees: F. Jordan Colby, Sarah P. Williams, National Bank of Washington.
Employer Identification Number: 526033671

637
April Trust, The
1607 New Hampshire Ave., N.W.
Washington 20009   (202) 462-1155

Charitable lead trust established in 1981 in Washington, DC; trust will terminate June 30, 1991.
Donor(s): Marion Tully Dimick.†
Financial data: (yr. ended 12/31/84): Assets, $0; expenditures, $528,300, including $478,300 for 57 grants (high: $30,000; low: $2,000; average: $1,000-$20,000).
Purpose and activities: Fixed annuity of $500,000 a year either from income or principal of estate must be paid out annually in grants through 1991; primarily local giving, largely as seed money "used to strengthen the quality of leadership, financial viability, and programs of organizations seeking to meet the needs of the community in the arts, education, health care, and other human service areas," with special attention to new and innovative approaches.
Types of support awarded: Seed money.
Limitations: Giving primarily in the greater Washington, DC area. No grants to individuals, or for endowment funds or capital funds.
Publications: Application guidelines, program policy statement.
Application information:
 Initial approach: Brief proposal, letter, or telephone
 Deadline(s): Fall, winter, and spring; call for dates
 Board meeting date(s): February, May, and November
 Write: Judith Y. Downey, Director
Officer: Judith Y. Downey, Director.
Trustees: Rev. John R. Anschutz, Roderic V.O. Boggs, J. Chapman Chester, Clara H. Hendin, Louise H. Neuhoff, Douglas R. Smith, Richard W. Snowdon.
Number of staff: 1 part-time professional; 1 part-time support.

638
Arca Foundation, The ▼
1425 21st St., N.W.
Washington 20036   (202) 822-9193

Incorporated in 1952 in New York.
Donor(s): Nancy S. Reynolds.†
Financial data: (yr. ended 12/31/83): Assets, $10,578,152 (M); expenditures, $801,877, including $643,850 for 47 grants (high: $100,000; low: $500; average: $13,700).
Purpose and activities: "To promote the well-being of mankind through grants to organizations primarily concerned with U.S. foreign policy applications in Central America, toxicity and hazardous wastes, issues of a safe and a healthy environment, community development, and anti-poverty programs. Programs should emphasize network building and decentralization".
Types of support awarded: Operating budgets, continuing support, seed money, technical assistance, publications, conferences and seminars, special projects.
Limitations: No grants to individuals, or for annual campaigns, emergency funds, capital or endowment funds, deficit financing, matching gifts, or scholarships or fellowships; no loans.
Publications: Annual report, application guidelines, program policy statement.
Application information:
 Initial approach: Letter
 Copies of proposal: 3
 Deadline(s): Submit summary of proposal preferably in January, February, July, or August; deadlines March 15 and September 15
 Board meeting date(s): May and November
 Final notification: Up to 6 months
 Write: Margery Tabankin, Executive Director
Officers: Smith Bagley,* President; Russell H. Long,* Vice-President; Mary E. King,* Secretary; Brian Topping,* Treasurer; Margery Tabankin, Executive Director.
Directors:* Dick Clark, Ellsworth Culver, Jane Bagley Lehman, Leslie Lipson.
Number of staff: 1 part-time professional; 2 part-time support.
Employer Identification Number: 132751798

639
Bender Foundation, Inc. ▼ ⌗
1120 Connecticut Ave., N.W., Suite 1200
Washington 20036   (202) 828-9000

Incorporated in 1958 in the District of Columbia.
Donor(s): Jack I. Bender.†
Financial data: (yr. ended 2/28/83): Assets, $7,034,771 (M); gifts received, $215,172; expenditures, $771,337, including $725,000 for 90 grants (high: $101,000; low: $90).
Purpose and activities: Support for higher education, health agencies, Jewish welfare funds and organizations, and social welfare.
Limitations: No grants to individuals.
Application information:
 Initial approach: Letter
 Copies of proposal: 1
 Board meeting date(s): Quarterly

Officers: Sondra D. Bender, President; Howard M. Bender, Executive Vice-President; Stanley S. Bender, Vice-President, Secretary and Treasurer.
Director: Dorothy G. Bender.
Employer Identification Number: 526054193

640
Benton Foundation, The
1776 K St., N.W., Suite 900
Washington 20006   (202) 429-7350

Incorporated in 1948 in New York.
Donor(s): William Benton,† Helen Benton.†
Financial data: (yr. ended 12/31/84): Assets, $10,000,000 (M); expenditures, $582,000, including $299,000 for 51 grants (high: $25,000; low: $100; average: $5,000-$10,000), $11,500 for 4 foundation-administered programs
Purpose and activities: Limited number of grants for communications research and education, and media projects.
Types of support awarded: Matching funds, research, special projects, publications, conferences and seminars, consulting services, technical assistance.
Limitations: No grants to individuals, or for general support, capital funds, scholarships, or fellowships; no loans.
Publications: Multi-year report, program policy statement, application guidelines, informational brochure, grants list.
Application information:
 Initial approach: Letter
 Copies of proposal: 1
 Deadline(s): Submit proposal preferably in December or April
 Board meeting date(s): March, July, and November
 Final notification: About 3 weeks after board meetings
 Write: Carolyn Sachs, Executive Director
Officers and Directors: Charles Benton, President and Chairman; Adrianne Benton, Secretary; Leonard Schrager, Treasurer and General Counsel; John Brademas, Dick Clark, Roy Fisher, Richard Neustadt, Gene Pokorny.
Number of staff: 2 full-time professional; 1 full-time support.
Employer Identification Number: 136075750

641
Bloedorn (Walter A.) Foundation
c/o Reasoner, Davis & Fox
888 Seventeenth St., N.W., Suite 800
Washington 20006   (202) 463-8282

Incorporated in 1966 in the District of Columbia.
Donor(s): Walter A. Bloedorn.†
Financial data: (yr. ended 12/31/83): Assets, $3,935,979 (M); gifts received, $34,926; expenditures, $476,071, including $447,100 for 22 grants (high: $400,000; low: $100).
Purpose and activities: Primarily local giving, with emphasis on higher education, youth agencies, and hospitals; support also for the handicapped, welfare, and a nature conservancy.
Types of support awarded: Continuing support, annual campaigns, endowment funds.

Limitations: Giving primarily in the DC area. No grants to individuals.
Publications: 990-PF.
Application information:
Initial approach: Full proposal
Copies of proposal: 1
Deadline(s): Submit proposal preferably in January and February
Board meeting date(s): April
Final notification: 30 days after board meets
Write: John E. Boice, Jr. Secretary
Officers and Directors: Ethel D. Bloedorn, Chairperson and Vice-President; F. Elwood Davis, President and Treasurer; John E. Boice, Jr., Secretary; Virginia Blair, John H. Bloedorn, Jr.
Number of staff: None.
Employer Identification Number: 520846147

642
Brownley (Walter) Trust
c/o American Security and Trust Company
15th St. and Pennsylvania Ave., N.W.
Washington 20013

Trust established in 1931.
Financial data: (yr. ended 12/31/82): Assets, $1,889,996 (M); expenditures, $163,818, including $144,000 for 12 grants of $12,000 each.
Purpose and activities: Giving restricted solely to Washington, D.C. hospitals.
Limitations: Giving limited to DC hospitals.
Trustee: American Security and Trust Company.
Employer Identification Number: 526028605

643
Cafritz (The Morris and Gwendolyn) Foundation ▼
1825 K St., N.W.
Washington 20006   (202) 862-6800

Incorporated in 1948 in the District of Columbia.
Donor(s): Morris Cafritz.†
Financial data: (yr. ended 4/30/84): Assets, $111,170,647 (M); gifts received, $80,000; expenditures, $5,063,172, including $4,006,476 for 102 grants (high: $650,000; low: $1,000; average: $10,000-$25,000).
Purpose and activities: Broad purposes; giving only for programs of direct assistance to the District of Columbia, with emphasis on community service, cultural programs, education, and health.
Types of support awarded: Operating budgets, continuing support, annual campaigns, seed money, matching funds, scholarship funds, publications, exchange programs.
Limitations: Giving limited to Washington, DC. No grants to individuals, or for emergency funds, deficit financing, capital endowment, or building funds, research, demonstration projects, or conferences; no loans.
Publications: Annual report, application guidelines.
Application information:
Initial approach: Proposal
Copies of proposal: 1
Deadline(s): July 1, November 1, and March 1

Board meeting date(s): May, October, and January
Write: Martin Atlas, Vice-President
Officers: Gwendolyn D. Cafritz,* President; Martin Atlas,* Vice-President and Treasurer; Roger A. Clark, Secretary.
Directors:* William P. Rogers.
Number of staff: 1 part-time professional; 1 part-time support.
Employer Identification Number: 526036989

644
Carnegie Endowment for International Peace
11 Dupont Circle, N.W.
Washington 20036   (202) 797-6400
Additional office: 30 Rockefeller Plaza, New York, NY 10112; Tel.: (212) 572-8200

Founded in 1910 in the District of Columbia; incorporated in 1929 in New York.
Donor(s): Andrew Carnegie.†
Financial data: (yr. ended 6/30/83): Assets, $62,230,658 (M); gifts received, $10,000; expenditures, $4,656,309, including $4,006,941 for foundation-administered programs.
Purpose and activities: A private operating (not a grantmaking) foundation that conducts its own programs of research, discussion, publication, and education in international affairs and American foreign policy. Program activities change periodically and cover a broad range of contemporary policy issues - military, political and economic. Publishes the quarterly "Foreign Policy".
Application information:
Write: Thomas L. Hughes, President
Officers: Thomas L. Hughes,* President; Larry L. Fabian, Secretary; Michael V. O'Hare, Director of Finance and Administration.
Trustees:* John W. Douglas, Chairman; Charles J. Zwick, Vice-Chairman; Charles W. Bailey II, Marjorie Craig Benton, Thomas W. Braden, Kingman Brewster, Anthony J.A. Bryan, Richard A. Debs, Hedley Donovan, Osborn Elliot, C. Clyde Ferguson, Jr., Marion R. Fremont-Smith, James C. Gaither, Robert F. Goheen, Rafael Hernandez-Colon, George N. Lindsay, George C. Lodge, William Macomber, Barbara W. Newell, Wesley W. Posvar, Norman F. Ramsey, Jean Kennedy Smith, Donald B. Straus.
Employer Identification Number: 130552040

645
Cohen-Solomon Family Foundation, Inc. ✄
P.O. Box 1804
Washington 20013

Incorporated in 1959 in the District of Columbia.
Financial data: (yr. ended 12/31/83): Assets, $2,740,346 (M); expenditures, $103,505, including $102,000 for 2 grants (high: $100,000; low: $2,000).
Purpose and activities: Grants primarily for Jewish welfare funds and higher education.
Limitations: Giving primarily in DC.

Officers and Directors: N.M. Cohen, President; Israel Cohen, Vice-President; Emanuel Cohen, Treasurer.
Employer Identification Number: 526054166

646
Council on Library Resources, Inc. ▼
1785 Massachusetts Ave., N.W.
Washington 20036   (202) 483-7474

Incorporated in 1956 in the District of Columbia.
Donor(s): The Ford Foundation, National Endowment for the Humanities, various private foundations.
Financial data: (yr. ended 6/30/84): Assets, $8,116,888 (M); gifts received, $1,433,648; expenditures, $2,482,323, including $1,491,393 for 73 grants (high: $165,000; low: $167) and $902,186 for foundation-administered programs.
Purpose and activities: A private operating foundation; grants only for programs that show promise of helping to provide solutions to problems that affect libraries in general, and academic and research libraries in particular. The Council operates programs of its own to serve the same general purpose.
Types of support awarded: Special projects.
Limitations: No grants for building construction or improvement, indirect costs, purchase of collections or equipment, normal staffing or operational costs, or programs useful only to the institutions in which they take place.
Publications: Annual report, application guidelines, program policy statement, newsletter.
Application information:
Initial approach: Letter
Copies of proposal: 2
Deadline(s): None for general grant applications; deadlines for competitive programs are stated with their announcement
Board meeting date(s): April and November
Write: Warren J. Haas, President
Officers: Warren J. Haas,* President; Deanna Marcum, Vice-President; Mary Agnes Thompson, Secretary and Treasurer.
Directors:* Maximilian W. Kempner, Chairman; Charles D. Churchwell, Vice-Chairman; Page Ackerman, William O. Baker, Patricia Battin, Laura Bornholdt, Harvey Brooks, Fred C. Cole, James S. Coles, Samuel DuBois Cook, Martin M. Cummings, Ruth M. Davis, Caryl P. Haskins, John A. Humphry, Elizabeth T. Kennan, Herman Liebaers, Howard R. Swearer, Robert Vosper, Frederick H. Wagman, Herman B. Wells, Thomas H. Wright.
Number of staff: 11.
Employer Identification Number: 530232831

647
Delmar (The Charles) Foundation
c/o John H. Doyle
918 Sixteenth St., N.W., Suite 203
Washington 20006   (202) 293-2494
Additional telephone number: (202) 393-2266

Trust established in 1957 in the District of Columbia.

Donor(s): Charles Delmar.†
Financial data: (yr. ended 12/31/84): Assets, $1,921,000 (M); expenditures, $96,800, including $77,450 for 95 grants (high: $5,000; low: $100).
Purpose and activities: General giving in Washington, D.C., Puerto Rico, and Latin America. Special interests include inter-American studies, higher education, Roman Catholic and Episcopal churches, hospitals, underprivileged and crippled youth, and general welfare organizations.
Types of support awarded: Continuing support, scholarship funds.
Limitations: Giving primarily in Washington, DC, Puerto Rico, and Latin America. No grants to individuals, building or endowment funds, or matching gifts; no loans.
Application information:
   Initial approach: Letter
   Copies of proposal: 1
   Deadline(s): None
   Board meeting date(s): As required
   Write: Elizabeth Adams del Mar, President
Officers and Trustees: Elizabeth Adams del Mar, President; Mareen D. Hughes, Vice-President; John H. Doyle, Secretary and Treasurer.
Number of staff: None.
Employer Identification Number: 526035345

648
Dimick Foundation, The ⌺
c/o NS & T Bank, Trust Group
15th and New York Ave., N.W.
Washington 20005   (202) 879-6296

Established in 1957 in the District of Columbia.
Financial data: (yr. ended 12/31/83): Assets, $1,769,722 (M); gifts received, $1,350,115; expenditures, $171,821, including $157,400 for 13 grants (high: $100,000; low: $100).
Purpose and activities: Primarily local giving, with emphasis on cultural programs, especially music, and on higher education and social services.
Limitations: Giving primarily in DC.
Application information:
   Deadline(s): None
   Write: Cheryl Williams
Trustees: Joseph Riley, Anita S. Williams.
Employer Identification Number: 526038149

649
Discount Foundation, The ⌺
1819 H St. N.W., Suite 620
Washington 20006

Established in 1977.
Donor(s): Jeffrey W. Zinsmeyer, Garfield Trust.
Financial data: (yr. ended 9/30/83): Assets, $68,834 (M); gifts received, $144,266; expenditures, $318,991, including $289,427 for 28 grants (high: $37,500; low: $1,000).
Purpose and activities: General purposes; "to support public education and organizational activities to lessen community tensions, alleviate poverty and/or combat neighborhood deterioration." Grants mainly for community development, education, civic affairs, and civil rights.

Limitations: Giving primarily in the northeastern U.S.
Application information:
   Initial approach: Proposal
   Deadline(s): December 31 and July 31
   Write: Thomas R. Asher, Secretary-Treasurer
Officers and Directors: Jeffrey W. Zinsmeyer, President; Thomas R. Asher, Secretary-Treasurer; Margery A. Tabankin.
Employer Identification Number: 521095120

650
Dweck (Samuel R.) Foundation ⌺
1730 M St., N.W.
Washington 20036

Donor(s): Samuel R. Dweck, and members of the Dweck family.
Financial data: (yr. ended 12/31/83): Assets, $1,851,985 (M); gifts received, $261,419; expenditures, $86,980, including $70,566 for 72 grants (high: $20,000; low: $25).
Purpose and activities: Grants primarily for Jewish welfare funds.
Officers and Directors: Samuel R. Dweck, President; Rena Dweck, Vice-President; Ralph Dweck.
Employer Identification Number: 526060826

651
Federal National Mortgage Association
   Foundation ⌺
3900 Wisconsin Ave., N.W.
Washington 20016

Established in 1979 in the District of Columbia.
Donor(s): Federal National Mortgage Association.
Financial data: (yr. ended 12/31/83): Assets, $255,926 (M); expenditures, $143,893, including $141,730 for 45 grants (high: $40,000; low: $55).
Purpose and activities: General giving; support primarily for community funds, public affairs, the performng arts, and a graduate center for urban studies.
Limitations: Giving primarily in the Washington, DC, area.
Officers and Directors: David O. Maxwell, Chairman; Robert J. Mylod, President; Douglas M. Bibby, Vice-President; Caryl S. Bernstein, Secretary; Stuart A. McFarland, Treasurer; Samuel S. Simmons, Mallory Walker.
Employer Identification Number: 521172718

652
Felburn Foundation ⌺
c/o Robert Philipson & Company
2000 L St., N.W., Suite 609
Washington 20036

Established in 1978 in Virginia.
Donor(s): J. Phil Felburn, The Aetna Freight Lines, Inc.
Financial data: (yr. ended 12/31/83): Assets, $2,057,696 (M); gifts received, $42,000; expenditures, $34,697, including $2,000 for 2 grants of $1,000 each.
Purpose and activities: Support primarily to organizations in North Carolina.

Limitations: Giving primarily in NC.
Officers and Directors: J. Phil Felburn, President and Treasurer; Charles Freeman, Vice-President; Don H. Norman, Secretary.
Employer Identification Number: 510234331

653
Folger Fund, The
2800 Woodley Rd., N.W.
Washington 20008   (202) 667-2991

Incorporated in 1955 in the District of Columbia.
Donor(s): Eugenia B. Dulin,† Kathrine Dulin Folger.
Financial data: (yr. ended 8/31/83): Assets, $7,413,527 (M); gifts received, $170,509; expenditures, $539,973, including $522,904 for 94 grants (high: $114,000; low: $15).
Purpose and activities: General giving, primarily for an art museum in Tennessee; support also for community funds, hospitals, and the fine arts, mainly in Knoxville, Tennessee, Washington, D.C., and Florida.
Limitations: Giving primarily in Washington, DC; Knoxville, TN; and FL. No grants to individuals.
Publications: Annual report.
Application information: Future funds currently committed.
   Initial approach: Full proposal
   Deadline(s): None
   Board meeting date(s): September
   Final notification: Usually within 3 months
   Write: Kathrine Dulin Folger, President
Officers: Kathrine Dulin Folger, President and Treasurer; Lee Merritt Folger, Vice-President and Secretary.
Trustees: John Dulin Folger, Neil Clifford Folger.
Employer Identification Number: 520794388

654
Foundation for Middle East Peace
1522 K St., N.W., Suite 202
Washington 20005   (202) 347-2558

Incorporated in 1979 in the District of Columbia.
Donor(s): Merle Thorpe, Jr.
Financial data: (yr. ended 9/30/83): Assets, $1,792,000 (M); expenditures, $105,619, including $65,863 for 56 grants (high: $7,000; low: $500; average: $1,000-$5,000).
Purpose and activities: To assist in an understanding of the Israeli-Palestinian conflict, including the identification of United States interests, and to contribute to a just and peaceful resolution of the conflict with security for both peoples. Support directed to elements within the Arab and Jewish communities working for a peaceful resolution of the conflict.
Types of support awarded: Research.
Limitations: No grants to individuals.
Publications: Informational brochure.
Application information: Application form required.
   Initial approach: Letter
   Deadline(s): None
   Board meeting date(s): As required
   Final notification: 30 days

Write: Merle Thorpe, Jr., President
Advisory Committee: Landrum R. Bolling, Stanley Hoffman, Charles W. Yost.
Officers and Trustees: Merle Thorpe, Jr., President; Calvin H. Cobb, Jr., Richard S.T. Marsh, C. Frank Reifsnyder, Mark Sullivan, Jr.
Number of staff: 1 full-time professional; 1 full-time support.
Employer Identification Number: 526055574

655
Fowler (John Edward) Memorial Foundation ▼

1025 Vermont Ave., N.W., Suite 1103
Washington 20005   (202) 347-8978

Incorporated in 1964 in Delaware.
Donor(s): Pearl Gunn Fowler.†
Financial data: (yr. ended 12/31/82): Assets, $4,562,322 (M); expenditures, $643,021, including $593,500 for 40 grants (high: $60,000; low: $1,000).
Purpose and activities: Broad purposes; giving primarily to national organizations or local organizations in the District of Columbia and Maryland, including support for secondary and higher education, health, hospitals, aid to the handicapped, and youth agencies.
Limitations: Giving primarily in Washington, DC, MD, and to national organizations. No grants to individuals, or for academic research programs, building funds, scholarships, or fellowships; no loans.
Application information:
   Initial approach: Full proposal or letter
   Copies of proposal: 2
   Deadline(s): Submit proposal preferably before August
   Board meeting date(s): January, May, August, and October
   Write: Richard H. Lee, President
Officers and Trustees:* Richard H. Lee, President and Treasurer; Carl E. Dunnington, Vice-President; Michael P. Bentzen, Secretary; Jeffrey P. Capron.
Employer Identification Number: 516019469

656
Freed Foundation, Inc., The ▼

(formerly The Allie S. and Frances W. Freed Foundation, Inc.)
1050 Connecticut Ave., N.W., Suite 460
Washington 20036   (202) 296-6406

Incorporated in 1954 in the District of Columbia.
Donor(s): Frances W. Freed.†
Financial data: (yr. ended 5/31/84): Assets, $12,180,192 (M); expenditures, $1,485,509, including $1,089,395 for 56 grants (high: $100,000; low: $100).
Purpose and activities: Broad purposes; support for higher education, hospitals and medical research, social services, the performing arts, and other worthy causes.
Types of support awarded: Annual campaigns, building funds, endowment funds, research, publications, scholarship funds, continuing support.
Limitations: No grants to individuals.
Publications: 990-PF.

Application information: Application form required.
   Initial approach: Letter or telephone
   Copies of proposal: 1
   Deadline(s): April 30
   Board meeting date(s): February, May, August, and November
   Final notification: 1 month
   Write: Gerald A. Freed, President
Officers and Trustees: Gerald A. Freed, President and Treasurer; Harry A. Shubin, Secretary; S. Edward Firestone, Elizabeth Ann Freed, Joan Kahn, Raymond Lowstuter, Sherwood Monahan.
Number of staff: 2 full-time professional; 1 full-time support.
Employer Identification Number: 526047591

657
GEICO Philanthropic Foundation ☐

GEICO Plaza
Washington 20076

Established in 1980 in Washington, D.C.
Donor(s): Criterion Insurance Company, Government Employees Insurance Company, Government Employees Life Insurance Company.
Financial data: (yr. ended 12/31/82): Assets, $624,190 (M); gifts received, $271,264; expenditures, $208,705, including $207,455 for 178 grants (high: $75,000; low: $25).
Purpose and activities: Grants for higher education, a community fund, health agencies, hospitals, cultural programs, child welfare, and youth and social service agencies.
Officers: Donald K. Smith,* President; Harry I. Bond,* Vice-President; John M. O'Connor, Secretary; Albert M. McKenny, Treasurer.
Directors:* Louis A. Simpson, Chairman; Terry L. Baxter, John J. Krieger, Richard C. Lucas, Richard A. Ollen, William B. Snyder, W. Alvon Sparks, Jr.
Employer Identification Number: 521202740

658
Gelman (Melvin and Estelle) Foundation ☐

1620 Eye St., N.W., No. 801
Washington 20006

Established in 1963 in the District of Columbia.
Donor(s): Melvin Gelman,† Towers, Inc.
Financial data: (yr. ended 11/30/83): Assets, $1,551,827 (M); expenditures, $326,030, including $320,366 for 128 grants (high: $150,000; low: $10).
Purpose and activities: Broad purposes; primarily local giving, with emphasis on Jewish welfare funds and a university.
Limitations: Giving primarily in DC.
Officers: Estelle S. Gelman, President and Treasurer; Elise G. Lefkowitz, Elaine G. Miller, Vice-Presidents; Vivian Compton, Secretary.
Employer Identification Number: 526042344

659
German Marshall Fund of the United States ▼

11 Dupont Circle, N.W., Suite 900
Washington 20036   (202) 745-3950
European representives: Jackson Janes, Ahrstrasse 58, 5300 Bonn 2, Federal Republic of Germany. Tel.: 0228-37-66-71; Judith Symonds, c/o TEN, 10 rue Mayet, 75006 Paris, France; Tel.: 01-273-2727

Incorporated in 1972 in the District of Columbia.
Donor(s): Federal Republic of Germany.
Financial data: (yr. ended 5/31/84): Assets, $40,562,851 (M); gifts received, $3,969,829; expenditures, $5,184,912, including $3,786,943 for 223 grants (high: $910,000; low: $450; average: $10,000-$30,000) and $368,830 for 12 grants to individuals.
Purpose and activities: To contribute to the better understanding and resolution of significant, contemporary, or emerging common problems of industrial societies, internally and in their relations with each other and with developing societies, by facilitating and supporting sustained working relationships, studies, cooperation, and contacts by and between persons with shared interests and responsibilities in the United States, Europe and elsewhere. Fund's program areas include common problems, international relations, and European/American comparative studies of industrial societies. Programs must have U.S. and European component, preferably Western Europe. Sponsors postdoctoral research fellowship program on the problems of industrial societies.
Types of support awarded: Continuing support, seed money, employee matching gifts, fellowships, internships, special projects, publications, conferences and seminars, exchange programs, grants to individuals.
Limitations: Giving limited to the U.S. and Western Europe. No support for the arts and humanities, medicine and health, arms control and disarmament, or diplomatic or historical studies. No grants for capital or endowment funds, or for operating budgets, annual campaigns, emergency funds, deficit financing, research, matching gifts, projects sponsored by others, graduate or undergraduate studies, or regular training programs; no loans.
Publications: Program policy statement, application guidelines, multi-year report, newsletter, informational brochure.
Application information: Application form required.
   Initial approach: Letter, telephone, or full proposal
   Copies of proposal: 1
   Deadline(s): November 30 for fellowships; other deadlines vary
   Board meeting date(s): February, May, and October
   Final notification: March for research fellowships; 2 to 3 months for all others
   Write: Frank E. Loy, President

Officers: Frank E. Loy,* President; Elizabeth Midgley,* Vice-Chair and Secretary; Lionel Pincus,* Treasurer; Peter R. Weitz, Director of Programs; Marianne L. Ginsburg, Administrative Officer.
Trustees:* Eugene B. Skolnikoff, Chairman; Harvey Brooks, Robert Ellsworth, Guido Goldman, Andrew Goodpaster, Walter Heller, John E. Kilgore, Jr., Marc E. Leland, Paul McCracken, Joyce D. Miller, Steven Muller, Lois Rice, Richard C. Steadman, Fritz Stern, Walter Stoessel, Russell E. Train, Arnold Weber.
Number of staff: 8 full-time professional; 2 part-time professional; 9 full-time support; 2 part-time support.
Employer Identification Number: 520954751

660
Graham (The Philip L.) Fund ▼
c/o The Washington Post Company
1150 Fifteenth St., N.W.
Washington 20071   (202) 334-6640

Trust established in 1963 in the District of Columbia.
Donor(s): Mrs. Katharine Graham, Frederick S. Beebe,† The Washington Post Company, Newsweek, Inc., Post-Newsweek Stations.
Financial data: (yr. ended 12/31/83): Assets, $27,150,000 (M); expenditures, $1,112,813, including $1,084,598 for 79 grants (high: $63,248; low: $1,500; average: $2,000-$25,000).
Purpose and activities: General purposes, including raising standards of excellence in journalism. Grants also for higher education, social welfare, arts and cultural programs, and youth agencies.
Types of support awarded: Seed money, emergency funds, building funds, equipment, endowment funds, matching funds, general purposes.
Limitations: Giving primarily in metropolitan Washington, DC; New York, NY; Detroit, MI; Miami and Jacksonville, FL; Hartford, CT; and Everett, WA, with the exception of journalism-related grants. No support for national organizations. No grants to individuals, or for annual campaigns or operating expenses; no loans.
Publications: 990-PF, application guidelines, program policy statement.
Application information:
  Initial approach: Letter, telephone or proposal
  Copies of proposal: 1
  Deadline(s): None
  Board meeting date(s): In spring, summer and fall
  Final notification: 6 months
  Write: Mary M. Bellor, Secretary
Officers: Mary M. Bellor, Secretary; Martin Cohen,* Treasurer.
Trustees:* Donald E. Graham, Katharine Graham, Vincent E. Reed, John W. Sweeterman.
Number of staff: 1 part-time professional; 1 part-time support.
Employer Identification Number: 526051781

661
Gudelsky (The Isadore and Bertha) Family Foundation, Inc.
c/o Philip N. Margolius
1503 21st St., N.W.
Washington 20036   (202) 328-0500

Incorporated in 1955 in Maryland.
Donor(s): Members of the Gudelsky family, Contee Sand & Gravel Company, Inc., and others.
Financial data: (yr. ended 4/30/84): Assets, $6,141,079 (M); gifts received, $434,572; expenditures, $528,426, including $469,415 for 16 grants.
Purpose and activities: Broad purposes; primarily local giving, with emphasis on Jewish welfare funds and temple support; grants also for higher education, hospitals, and youth agencies.
Limitations: Giving primarily in DC.
Officers: Arlene G. Zimmerman,* President; Shelley G. Mulitz,* Vice-President; Philip N. Margolius, Secretary-Treasurer.
Directors:* Paul S. Berger.
Employer Identification Number: 526036621

662
Higginson (Corina) Trust
c/o Consortium of Universities
1717 Massachusetts Ave., N.W.
Washington 20036   (202) 265-1313

Trust established in 1962 in the District of Columbia.
Donor(s): Corina Higginson.†
Financial data: (yr. ended 12/31/83): Assets, $1,877,249 (M); expenditures, $157,736, including $135,400 for 22 grants (high: $10,000; low: $500; average: $500-$10,000).
Purpose and activities: Broad purposes; primarily local giving, with emphasis on education and self-help.
Types of support awarded: Operating budgets, continuing support, annual campaigns, seed money, emergency funds, deficit financing, building funds, equipment, land acquisition, matching funds, special projects, research, publications, conferences and seminars.
Limitations: Giving primarily in the Washington, DC, area. No support for medical or health-related programs or organizations. No grants to individuals or for endowment funds; no loans.
Publications: Application guidelines.
Application information:
  Initial approach: Full proposal, letter, or telephone
  Copies of proposal: 5
  Deadline(s): March 1 and September 1
  Board meeting date(s): April and October
  Final notification: 2 months
  Write: Rev. John P. Whalen, Trustee
Trustees: Charles C. Abeles, John Perkins, Jean Sisco, Rev. John P. Whalen, Consortium of Universities.
Number of staff: None.
Employer Identification Number: 526055743

663
Himmelfarb (Paul and Annetta) Foundation, Inc.
733 15th St., N.W., Suite 920
Washington 20005

Incorporated in 1947 in Delaware.
Donor(s): Members of the Himmelfarb family and others.
Financial data: (yr. ended 12/31/83): Assets, $3,710,786 (M); expenditures, $264,358, including $149,530 for 25 grants (high: $30,000; low: $500).
Purpose and activities: Primarily local giving, mainly for Jewish welfare funds, education, and medical research.
Limitations: Giving primarily in the DC area.
Officers and Directors: Ben Greenspoon, President; Ada Naiman, Vice-President; Frances Wolf, Secretary; Bernard Cooper, Treasurer and Manager; Lillian Kronstadt.
Employer Identification Number: 520784206

664
Hyman (The George and Sadie) Foundation ⌀
c/o Benjamin T. Rome
700 New Hampshire Ave., N.W., Apt. 1005
Washington 20037

Incorporated in 1955 in the District of Columbia.
Donor(s): George Hyman,† Mrs. Sadie Hyman.†
Financial data: (yr. ended 12/31/83): Assets, $2,822,535 (M); expenditures, $72,818.
Purpose and activities: Broad purposes; support primarily for higher educational institutions in the Washington, D.C. area. No grants outside of already established program of contributions.
Limitations: Giving primarily in the Washington, DC, area.
Application information: No grants outside of already established program of contributions.
Officers and Trustees: Benjamin T. Rome, President and Treasurer; A. James Clark, Vice-President and Secretary; Milton Gusack.
Employer Identification Number: 526036910

665
Johnston (The James M.) Trust for Charitable and Educational Purposes ▼ ⌀
c/o Riggs National Bank, Trust Dept.
800 17th St., N.W.
Washington 20006
Application address: Harvey B. Gram, Jr., 1101 Vermont Ave., N.W., Washington, DC 20016; Tel.: (202) 289-4996

Trust established in 1968 in the District of Columbia.
Donor(s): James M. Johnston.†
Financial data: (yr. ended 12/31/83): Assets, $34,332,392 (M); expenditures, $498,223, including $143,084 for grants.

Purpose and activities: Grants largely for higher and secondary education, including scholarships and training of nurses, principally to institutions in North Carolina and the District of Columbia area.

Types of support awarded: Scholarship funds, continuing support.

Limitations: Giving primarily in NC and DC. No grants to individuals, or for building or endowment funds, or operating budgets.

Application information:
Initial approach: Letter
Copies of proposal: 1
Board meeting date(s): Monthly

Trustees: Barnum L. Colton, Jr., Harvey B. Gram, Jr., Betty Frost Hayes.

Employer Identification Number: 237019796

666
Kennedy (The Joseph P.), Jr. Foundation ▼
1350 New York Ave., N.W., Suite 500
Washington 20005   (202) 393-1250

Incorporated in 1946 in the District of Columbia.

Donor(s): Joseph P. Kennedy,† Mrs. Joseph P. Kennedy.

Financial data: (yr. ended 12/31/83): Assets, $17,670,909 (M); gifts received, $24,248; expenditures, $2,279,978, including $1,592,319 for 32 grants (high: $586,250; average: $1,000-$30,000) and $115,107 for 10 grants to individuals.

Purpose and activities: Primarily concerned with the rights of the powerless, their treatment by social institutions, the strengthening of the family, the amelioration of conditions concerning mentally retarded individuals, and the ethical implications of genetic and biological discoveries. In the field of mental retardation, sponsors research projects, programs dealing with community living, and Special Olympics, a national and international program of sports training and athletic competition for mentally retarded individuals.

Types of support awarded: Seed money, research, fellowships.

Limitations: No grants to individuals (except for research fellowships), or for building or endowment funds or operating budgets.

Publications: Program policy statement, application guidelines.

Application information: Funds are substantially committed to grants initiated by the foundation; applications considered for research projects.
Initial approach: Letter
Copies of proposal: 1
Deadline(s): None
Board meeting date(s): Usually in February
Final notification: 2 weeks to 1 month
Write: Mrs. Eunice Kennedy Shriver, Executive Vice-President

Officers: Senator Edward M. Kennedy,* President; Eunice Kennedy Shriver,* Executive Vice-President; Joseph E. Hakim, Secretary and Treasurer; Robert M. Montague, Jr., Executive Director.

Trustees:* Patricia Kennedy Lawford, Jean Kennedy Smith.

Number of staff: 2 full-time professional; 3 part-time professional; 4 full-time support.

Employer Identification Number: 136083407

667
Kiplinger Foundation, Inc., The ▼
1729 H St., N.W.
Washington 20006   (202) 887-6400

Incorporated in 1948 in Maryland.

Donor(s): Willard M. Kiplinger.†

Financial data: (yr. ended 12/31/83): Assets, $8,366,862 (M); gifts received, $200,000; expenditures, $530,986, including $459,195 for 116 grants (high: $127,500; low: $5; average: $1,000-$2,000).

Purpose and activities: Broad purposes; primarily local support for higher education, including journalism programs; grants also for cultural groups, community funds, youth agencies, and urban affairs.

Types of support awarded: Operating budgets, continuing support, annual campaigns, building funds, endowment funds, employee matching gifts.

Limitations: Giving primarily in the greater Washington, DC area. No grants to individuals, or for research, seed money, emergency funds, deficit financing, equipment and materials, land acquisition, renovation projects, matching or challenge grants, special projects, publications, conferences, or scholarships and fellowships; no loans.

Publications: 990-PF.

Application information:
Initial approach: Letter
Copies of proposal: 1
Deadline(s): None
Board meeting date(s): March, May, August, and November
Final notification: 3 to 6 months
Write: Arnold B. Barach, Secretary

Officers and Trustees: Austin H. Kiplinger, President; Arnold B. Barach, Secretary; LaVerne C. Kiplinger, James O. Mayo.

Number of staff: 1 part-time support.

Employer Identification Number: 520792570

668
Lehrman (Jacob and Charlotte) Foundation, Inc.
2839 Chesterfield Place, N.W.
Washington 20008   (202) 363-1700

Incorporated in 1953 in the District of Columbia.

Donor(s): Jacob J. Lehrman, Harrisburg Grocery Company.

Financial data: (yr. ended 10/31/84): Assets, $3,692,819 (M); expenditures, $310,365, including $290,000 for 65 grants (high: $115,500; low: $20).

Purpose and activities: Broad purposes; primarily local giving to establish scholarships and fellowships at institutions of learning, and to foster research in medicine and science; grants also for Jewish welfare funds, care of the aged and sick, the establishment of trade schools, the fostering of religious observance, recreation, and aid to refugees.

Types of support awarded: Scholarship funds, fellowships, research.

Limitations: Giving primarily in metropolitan Washington, DC. No grants to individuals or for matching gifts; no loans.

Application information:
Initial approach: Full proposal
Copies of proposal: 2
Deadline(s): Submit proposal preferably in May or September; deadline October 15
Board meeting date(s): May and September or October
Write: Charlotte F. Lehrman, President

Officers: Charlotte F. Lehrman, President; Heidi Berry, Fredrica Lehrman, Samuel Lehrman, Vice-Presidents; Leslie Handler, Secretary; Robert Barry Wertlieb, Treasurer.

Employer Identification Number: 526035666

669
Loughran (Mary and Daniel) Foundation, Inc.
c/o American Security and Trust
15th St. & Pennsylvania Ave., N.W.
Washington 20013   (202) 624-4283

Incorporated in 1967 in the District of Columbia.

Donor(s): John Loughran.†

Financial data: (yr. ended 9/30/81): Assets, $7,932,521 (M); expenditures, $672,608, including $584,000 for 46 grants (high: $40,000; low: $2,500).

Purpose and activities: Grants largely to religious institutions, youth and social agencies, and higher educational institutions within the District of Columbia, Virginia, and Maryland.

Limitations: Giving primarily in DC, VA, and MD. No grants to individuals, or for capital or endowment funds; no loans.

Application information:
Initial approach: Proposal
Copies of proposal: 1
Deadline(s): Submit proposal between January and May; deadline June 1
Board meeting date(s): April, July, August, and December
Write: Roberta Stearns, Assistant Administrator

Officers and Directors: Walter R. Fatzinger, Jr., President; Richard J.M. Poulson, Vice-President and Secretary; F. William Burke, Treasurer and Administrator; Carl L. Gell, A. Linwood Holton, Jr., Joseph L. Whyte.

Trustee: American Security Bank N.A.

Employer Identification Number: 520853980

670
Loyola Foundation, Inc., The ▼
308 C St., N.E.
Washington 20002   (202) 546-9400

Incorporated in 1957 in the District of Columbia.
Donor(s): Members of the Albert Gregory McCarthy, Jr. family.
Financial data: (yr. ended 10/31/84): Assets, $15,202,906 (M); expenditures, $645,456, including $543,108 for 118 grants (high: $40,000; low: $250; average: $5,000).
Purpose and activities: Broad purposes; grants primarily for basic overseas Roman Catholic missionary work and other Catholic activities of special interest to the trustees. Primary interest in nonrecurring requests for capital improvements in the missionary area, which are self-sustaining after completion; special consideration given to requests where there are matching contributions from the missionary area itself.
Types of support awarded: Building funds, equipment, land acquisition, matching funds.
Limitations: Giving primarily in developing nations. No grants to individuals, or for general or annual budgets, endowment funds, research-related programs, continuing support, emergency funds, deficit financing, special projects, publications, conferences, or scholarships and fellowships; no loans.
Publications: 990-PF, application guidelines, program policy statement.
Application information: Application form required.
  Initial approach: Letter, full proposal or telephone
  Copies of proposal: 1
  Deadline(s): Submit proposal preferably in March or September; deadline April 15 and October 15
  Board meeting date(s): June and December
  Write: Albert G. McCarthy III, Secretary
Officers and Trustees: Denise M. Hattler, President and Treasurer; Paul R. Dean, Vice-President; Albert G. McCarthy, III, Secretary; Daniel J. Altobello, Andrea M. Hattler, Russell L. Hauser, Bishop Theodore E. McCarrick, A. Gregory McCarthy, IV, Raymond W. Merritt, Hilary Hattler de Muniz, Rev. Victor R. Yanitelli, S.J.
Number of staff: 1 part-time professional.
Employer Identification Number: 520781255

671
McGregor (Thomas and Frances) Foundation ⌗
c/o Robert Philipson & Company
2000 L St., N.W., Suite 609
Washington 20036

Incorporated in 1961 in the District of Columbia.
Donor(s): Thomas W. McGregor, McGregor Printing Corporation.
Financial data: (yr. ended 2/29/84): Assets, $2,214,334 (M); gifts received, $6,500; expenditures, $112,731, including $107,980 for 59 grants (high: $15,000; low: $50).

Purpose and activities: Primarily local giving, with emphasis on higher and secondary education, hospitals and health agencies, cultural programs, and support for religious organizations.
Limitations: Giving primarily in DC.
Application information:
  Write: Victor Krakower, Manager
Manager: Victor Krakower, Manager.
Employer Identification Number: 526041498

672
Meyer (Eugene and Agnes E.) Foundation ▼
1200 15th St., N.W., Suite 500
Washington 20005   (202) 659-2435

Incorporated in 1944 in New York.
Donor(s): Eugene Meyer,† Agnes E. Meyer.†
Financial data: (yr. ended 12/31/83): Assets, $32,883,330 (M); gifts received, $1,360; expenditures, $1,577,330, including $700,944 for 85 grants (high: $33,750; low: $100; average: $10,000-$25,000).
Purpose and activities: To assist in the development of local community services and facilities; grants principally for welfare, education, health, mental health, the arts, and law and justice, preferably to provide new or improved services rather than to support existing programs.
Types of support awarded: Seed money, emergency funds, matching funds, special projects.
Limitations: Giving primarily in metropolitan Washington, DC area. No support for sectarian purposes, or for programs that are national or international in scope. No grants to individuals, or for operating budgets, continuing support, annual campaigns, deficit financing, building or endowment funds, equipment, land acquisition, renovations, scholarships or fellowships, research, publications, or conferences; no loans.
Publications: Annual report, program policy statement, application guidelines.
Application information: Applications considered only at February, June, and October meetings.
  Initial approach: Letter, telephone, or full proposal
  Copies of proposal: 1
  Deadline(s): December 1, April 1, and August 1
  Board meeting date(s): February, April, June, October, and December
  Final notification: 1 month after meeting
  Write: James O. Gibson, President; grant applications to: Ms. Kathy L. Dwyer, Program Officer
Officers: James O. Gibson, President; Newman T. Halvorson, Jr.,* Secretary-Treasurer.
Directors:* Mallory Walker, Chairman; Delano E. Lewis, Vice-Chairman; Lucy M. Cohen, Charles C. Glover III, Mary Graham, John W. Hechinger, Jr., Theodore C. Lutz, Aubrey E. Robinson, Jr., Pearl Rosser, M.D.
Number of staff: 2 full-time professional; 1 full-time support.
Employer Identification Number: 530241716

673
Miller & Chevalier Charitable Foundation, The
655 15th St., N.W., Suite 900
Washington 20005   (202) 626-5800

Incorporated in 1929 in the District of Columbia.
Donor(s): Robert N. Miller.†
Financial data: (yr. ended 12/31/84): Assets, $1,490,972 (M); expenditures, $129,320, including $109,500 for 48 grants (high: $12,000; low: $1,000).
Purpose and activities: Grants to established charitable organizations working principally in the District of Columbia whose activities are personally known to the directors. Grants also for scholarship funds of schools, particularly law schools.
Types of support awarded: Scholarship funds.
Limitations: Giving primarily in DC. No grants to individuals, or for endowment funds, research, or matching gifts; no loans.
Application information:
  Initial approach: Proposal
  Copies of proposal: 1
  Deadline(s): October
  Board meeting date(s): December
  Final notification: By December, if action is favorable
  Write: John M. Bixler, President
Officers: John M. Bixler,* President; Ronald D. Aucutt, Secretary-Treasurer.
Directors:* Charles T. Akre, Benjamin Lee Bird, James F. Gordy, Barron K. Grier, John S. Nolan, David W. Richmond, Numa L. Smith, Jr.
Number of staff: None.
Employer Identification Number: 526035549

674
National Home Library Foundation
1333 New Hampshire Ave., N.W., Suite 600
Washington 20036   (202) 293-3860

Incorporated in 1932 in the District of Columbia.
Donor(s): Sherman F. Mittell.†
Financial data: (yr. ended 12/31/83): Assets, $1,201,593 (M); expenditures, $127,301, including $98,891 for 13 grants (high: $25,000; low: $1,000).
Purpose and activities: To assist in the distribution of books, pamphlets, and documents to libraries and to community groups with limited access to sources of specific areas of information; to encourage new techniques in the operation of libraries of printed and audio-visual materials and to aid in the wider dissemination of information by use of these techniques; and to encourage projects involving radio and television and other technological improvements in the transmission of information relating primarily to literary and cultural topics.
Limitations: No grants to individuals, or for building or endowment funds, operating budgets, scholarships, fellowships, or matching gifts; no loans.
Publications: Biennial report, program policy statement, application guidelines.
Application information:
  Initial approach: Full proposal

Copies of proposal: 1
Deadline(s): Submit application 3 weeks prior to board meetings
Board meeting date(s): March, June, September, and December
Final notification: 3 months
Write: Leonard H. Marks, President
Officers and Directors: Leonard H. Marks, President; Charles G. Dobbins, Vice-President and Executive Director; Alice B. Popkin, Vice-President; Michael R. Gardner, Secretary-Treasurer; Meredith A. Brokaw, Bernard M.W. Knox, Ann Bradford Mathias, Lynda J. Robb.
Employer Identification Number: 526051013

675
Patterson (Alicia) Foundation
655 Fifteenth St., NW, Suite 320
Washington 20005   (813) 962-6060

Incorporated in 1960 in New York.
Donor(s): Alicia Patterson.†
Financial data: (yr. ended 12/31/83): Assets, $2,411,567 (M); expenditures, $194,383, including $112,000 for grants (high: $20,000) and $25,000 for 7 grants to individuals.
Purpose and activities: General purposes; one-year fellowships for a small number of journalists to examine and write about areas or problems of special interest; candidates must be U.S. citizens who have been working professionally as journalists for five years or longer.
Types of support awarded: Fellowships.
Limitations: No grants for fellowships for academic study.
Publications: Annual report, program policy statement, application guidelines.
Application information: Application form required.
Initial approach: Brief letter, telephone, or full proposal
Copies of proposal: 1
Deadline(s): Submit proposal between June and September; deadline October 1
Board meeting date(s): Annually in the fall
Write: Helen McMaster Coulson, Executive Director
Officers and Directors: Josephine P. Albright, Chairman; Joseph P. Albright, President; Adam M. Albright, Blandina Albright, Maria Casale, Dorothy J. Holdsworth, Vice-Presidents; Helen McMaster Coulson, Secretary and Executive Director; Alice Arlen, Treasurer; Leo Gottlieb.
Number of staff: 2 part-time professional.
Employer Identification Number: 136092124

676
Police Foundation ⌑
1909 K St., N.W., Suite 400
Washington 20006   (202) 833-1460

Incorporated in 1970 in the District of Columbia.
Donor(s): The Ford Foundation, Law Enforcement Assistance Administration.
Financial data: (yr. ended 6/30/83): Assets, $825,488 (M); gifts received, $1,745,175; expenditures, $2,647,910, including $322,000 for 2 grants and $1,179,922 for 1 foundation-administered program.

Purpose and activities: A private operating foundation established to improve the delivery of police services through grants to police departments and projects administered by the Foundation.
Application information:
Initial approach: Cover letter and brief proposal
Deadline(s): None
Board meeting date(s): Semiannually
Write: Patrick V. Murphy, President
Officers: Patrick V. Murphy,* President; William Josephson, Secretary; Clarence M. Kelley,* Treasurer.
Directors:* Francis W. Sargent, Chairman; James Q. Wilson, Vice-Chairman; Henry G. Cisneros, Fred L. Hartley, Robert Kasanof, H. Stuart Knight, Winston V. Morrow, Thomas J. Pownall, Margaret Bush Wilson.
Employer Identification Number: 520906599

677
Post (The Marjorie Merriweather) Foundation
c/o Glassie, Pewett, Dubley, Beebe and Shanks
1317 F St., NW
Washington 20004

Established in 1956.
Donor(s): Marjorie Merriweather Post.†
Financial data: (yr. ended 12/31/82): Assets, $1,781,929 (L); expenditures, $172,389, including $153,000 for 52 grants (high: $15,000; low: $500).
Purpose and activities: Grants primarily for higher and secondary education, cultural programs, international affairs, religious organizations, social agencies, and health agencies.
Officers and Trustees: John A. Logan, Chairman; Henry A. Dudley, Vice-Chairman; Michael J. Ruane, Secretary; Leonard Silverstein, Treasurer; Spottswood P. Dudley, George B. Hertzog, John A. Logan, Jr., Godfrey T. McHugh.
Employer Identification Number: 526054705

678
Post (Marjorie Merriweather) Foundation of D.C.
c/o Rodion Cantacuzene
4155 Linnean Ave., N.W.
Washington 20008   (202) 686-0410

Established in 1967 in the District of Columbia.
Donor(s): Marjorie Merriweather Post.†
Financial data: (yr. ended 12/31/83): Assets, $64,529,685 (M); expenditures, $2,425,724.
Purpose and activities: Support for Hillwood Museum at present time; therefore a period of moratorium on other grants.
Limitations: Giving limited to DC. No grants to individuals.
Publications: Annual report.
Application information: Funds currently committed.
Board meeting date(s): December and as required

Officers and Directors: Adelaide C. Riggs, President; Nedenia H. Robertson, Vice-President; Rodion Cantacuzene, Secretary; Raymond P. Hunter, Treasurer; Ross Barzelay, Eleanor C. Barzin, David P. Close, John A. Logan, E. Brevoort MacNeille, Albert G. Perkins, Stanley Rumbough, Douglas R. Smith, Philip L. Smith.
Employer Identification Number: 526080752

679
Public Welfare Foundation, Inc. ▼
2600 Virginia Ave., N.W., Rm. 505
Washington 20037   (202) 965-1800

Incorporated in 1947 in Texas; reincorporated in 1951 in Delaware.
Donor(s): Charles Edward Marsh,† and others.
Financial data: (yr. ended 10/31/83): Assets, $105,000,000 (M); expenditures, $4,972,233, including $4,402,400 for 225 grants (high: $125,000; low: $1,500; average: $13,000-$20,000).
Purpose and activities: Grants primarily to grass roots organizations in United States and abroad, with emphasis on community services, health, education, economic development, and youth employment; programs must serve low-income population, with preference to short-term needs.
Types of support awarded: Matching funds, operating budgets, seed money, special projects.
Limitations: No support for religious purposes, or the arts. No grants to individuals, or for building funds, capital improvements, endowments, scholarships, graduate work, foreign study, conferences, seminars, publications, films, research, workshops, technical assistance, consulting services, annual campaigns, emergency funds, or deficit financing; no loans.
Publications: Annual report, application guidelines, program policy statement.
Application information:
Initial approach: Full proposal
Copies of proposal: 1
Deadline(s): None
Board meeting date(s): March, June, September, and December
Final notification: 3 months
Write: Charles Glenn Ihrig, Executive Director
Officers and Trustees: Donald T. Warner, Chairman and Vice-President; Charles Davis Haines, President; Charles Glenn Ihrig, Secretary-Treasurer and Executive Director; Edgar F. Berman, M.D., Antoinette M. Haskell, Veronica T. Keating, Claudia Haines Marsh, Everett D. Reese, Thomas J. Scanlon, Herbert Scoville, Jr., Murat W. Williams.
Number of staff: 5 full-time professional; 3 full-time support.
Employer Identification Number: 540597601

680
Ross (Walter G.) Foundation
First American Bank of Washington
740 15th St.
Washington 20005   (202) 637-7880

Trust established about 1964 in the District of Columbia.

Financial data: (yr. ended 12/31/83): Assets, $5,969,267 (M); expenditures, $369,121, including $321,000 for 20 grants (high: $50,000; low: $5,000).
Purpose and activities: Giving generally limited to the Washington, D.C. area and Florida for education, medical research, and care of the sick.
Types of support awarded: Research, general purposes, endowment funds, matching funds.
Limitations: Giving limited to the Washington, DC area and FL. No grants to individuals, or for scholarships or fellowships; no loans.
Publications: Application guidelines.
Application information:
  Initial approach: Letter
  Copies of proposal: 1
  Deadline(s): Submit proposal preferably in August; deadline September 15
  Board meeting date(s): October
  Final notification: 1 month after annual meeting
  Write: Jean L. Warnke, Secretary
Trustees: Glenn Bludworth, Chairman; Eugene L. Bernard, Gladys Bludworth, Lloyd H. Elliott, J. Hillman Zahn, First American Bank of Washington.
Employer Identification Number: 526057560

681
Sapelo Island Research Foundation, Inc. ▼
1425 21st St., N.W.
Washington 20036   (202) 822-9193

Incorporated in 1949 in Georgia.
Donor(s): Richard J. Reynolds.†
Financial data: (yr. ended 6/30/84): Assets, $8,339,401 (M); expenditures, $582,211, including $482,869 for 28 grants (high: $175,000; low: $5,000; average: $17,000) and $16,891 for 40 grants to individuals.
Purpose and activities: A private operating foundation; currently supports a marine research laboratory on Sapelo Island through grants to the University of Georgia; some support also for higher education, and social, economic and environmental issues.
Types of support awarded: Operating budgets, continuing support, annual campaigns, seed money, consulting services, technical assistance, scholarship funds, special projects, research, conferences and seminars, student aid.
Limitations: Giving limited to GA. No grants for capital, emergency, or endowment funds, deficit financing, or publications; no loans.
Publications: Annual report, application guidelines.
Application information:
  Initial approach: Letter
  Deadline(s): March 15 and September 15
  Board meeting date(s): June and December
  Final notification: Up to 6 months
  Write: Margery Tabankin, Executive Director
Officers and Trustees: Annemarie S. Reynolds, President; Richard H. Pough, Vice-Presidents; Smith W. Bagley, Secretary-Treasurer; Jane B. Lehman, Katharine B. Mountcastle.
Number of staff: 1 part-time professional; 2 part-time support.
Employer Identification Number: 580827472

682
Stewart (Alexander and Margaret) Trust ▼
c/o First American Bank of Washington
740 Fifteenth St., N.W.
Washington 20005   (202) 637-7865

Trust established in 1947 in the District of Columbia.
Donor(s): Mary E. Stewart.†
Financial data: (yr. ended 12/31/83): Assets, $13,869,128 (M); expenditures, $990,047, including $902,374 for 16 grants (high: $170,000; low: $10,000).
Purpose and activities: Local giving for the purpose of the prevention of cancer, or the care of those afflicted with cancer.
Types of support awarded: Seed money, equipment, matching funds, continuing support.
Limitations: Giving primarily in the Washington, DC, area. No grants to individuals, or for endowment funds, annual campaigns, deficit financing, building funds, land acquisition, renovation projects, publications, conferences, research, or scholarships and fellowships; no loans.
Publications: Program policy statement, application guidelines.
Application information:
  Initial approach: Letter
  Copies of proposal: 1
  Deadline(s): None
  Board meeting date(s): April, June, September, November, and December
  Write: Gordon Wilson, Secretary
Trustees: Justin Dewitt Bowersock, George E. Hamilton, Jr., First American Bank of Washington.
Number of staff: None.
Employer Identification Number: 526020260

683
Strong (Hattie M.) Foundation
Cafritz Bldg., Suite 409
1625 I St., N.W.
Washington 20006   (202) 331-1619

Incorporated in 1928 in the District of Columbia.
Donor(s): Hattie M. Strong.†
Financial data: (yr. ended 8/31/83): Assets, $12,940,870 (M); gifts received, $1,930; expenditures, $505,763, including $93,095 for 16 grants (high: $10,000; low: $1,500; average: $500-$10,000) and $409,225 for loans.
Purpose and activities: Non-interest-bearing loans to students who are within one year of their degree in college or graduate school and to students from the metropolitan Washington, D.C. area who are enrolled in vocational schools in the Washington area. Maximum loan to vocational school applicants is $2,000; maximum loan to college students is $5,000. Grants program focused primarily on educational programs for the disadvantaged of Washington, D.C.
Types of support awarded: Student aid.

Limitations: Giving primarily in the Washington, DC, area. No grants to individuals (except for loans), or for building or endowment funds, research, scholarships, or fellowships.
Publications: Annual report.
Application information:
  Initial approach: Letter or telephone
  Copies of proposal: 1
  Deadline(s): February 1, April 1, August 1, and November 1
  Board meeting date(s): March, May, September, and December
  Final notification: Within one week
  Write: Thelma L. Eichman, Secretary
Officers: Henry Strong,* Chairman and President; Trowbridge Strong,* Vice-President; Thelma L. Eichman, Secretary; Barbara B. Cantrell, Treasurer.
Directors:* Olive W. Covington, Charles H. Fleischer, Richard S.T. Marsh, John A. Nevius, Barbara K. Strong, C. Peter Strong, Trowbridge Strong, Bennetta B. Washington.
Number of staff: 2 full-time professional; 3 full-time support; 1 part-time support.
Employer Identification Number: 520237223

684
Villers Foundation, Inc., The
1334 G St.
Washington 20005   (202) 628-3030

Incorporated in 1981 in Massachusetts.
Donor(s): Philippe Villers, Katherine Villers.
Financial data: (yr. ended 12/31/84): Assets, $6,600,000 (M); expenditures, $2,890,000, including $1,758,755 for 109 grants (high: $100,000; low: $429; average: $16,000).
Purpose and activities: Giving for the purpose of "nurturing a movement of empowerment among elders;" grants to establish and address the priorities of the aged, particularly those of low income.
Limitations: No grants to individuals.
Publications: Informational brochure, annual report, program policy statement.
Application information:
  Initial approach: Proposal
  Deadline(s): None
  Board meeting date(s): March, June, September, and December
  Write: Ronald F. Pollack, Executive Director
Officers: Philippe Villers,* President; Ronald F. Pollack, Executive Director.
Directors:* Joseph Eaglin, Jr., Carroll Estes, Arthur Flemming, Barney Frank, Douglas A. Fraser, Laura Monroe, Evelyn Murphy, Fernando Torres-Gil, Katherine Villers.
Number of staff: 11 full-time professional; 4 full-time support; 2 part-time support.
Employer Identification Number: 042730934

685
Washington, Inc., The Community Foundation of Greater
3221 M St., N.W., 2nd Fl.
Washington 20007   (202) 338-8993

Community foundation incorporated in 1973 in the District of Columbia.

Financial data: (yr. ended 12/31/83): Assets, $2,458,289 (M); gifts received, $1,181,742; expenditures, $1,834,591, including $792,896 for 101 grants (high: $104,128; low: $250) and $441,248 for 3 foundation-administered programs.
Purpose and activities: To identify the major problems that may be solved to improve the quality of life for the inhabitants of the Greater Washington area; to develop and support projects that effectively contribute to the solution of those problems; and to secure private financial and other resources needed to plan and carry out these projects.
Types of support awarded: Seed money, emergency funds, technical assistance, program-related investments, loans, special projects, research, publications, conferences and seminars.
Limitations: Giving limited to the metropolitan Washington, DC, area. No support for religious purposes. No grants to individuals, or for annual campaigns, endowment funds, continuing support, equipment, land acquisition, renovation projects, scholarships, fellowships, operating budgets, or matching gifts.
Publications: Annual report, program policy statement, application guidelines, informational brochure, newsletter.
Application information:
  Initial approach: Letter
  Copies of proposal: 1
  Deadline(s): None
  Board meeting date(s): March, June, and November
  Final notification: Up to 3 months
  Write: Elizabeth B. Frazier, Grants Coordinator
Officers and Directors: Stephen D. Harlan, Chairman; Kent Cushenberry, Richard Snowdon, Vice-Chairmen; Lawrence S. Stinchcomb, President; Henry Strong, Secretary; John W. Hechinger, Jr., Treasurer; Ronald H. Brown, Sheldon S. Cohen, Allan D. Cors, Arthur S. Flemming, Lee M. Folger, M. Carl Holman, Henry W. Lavine, Gloria Lemos, Mrs. Dale Miller, Robert Nelson, Eleanor Holmes Norton, Robert Petersen, John V. Pollock, Vincent Reed, Joseph H. Riley, Martin Rubenstein, Foster Shannon, Davidson Sommers, Henry Strong, Robert Washington.
Distribution Committee: Winifred Riggs Portenoy, Chairman; Frank W. Bradley, Calvin Franklin, Henry W. Lavine, Edward McCabe, Kevin P. O'Brien, Leonard Pfeiffer IV, Foster Shannon.
Number of staff: 6 full-time professional; 1 part-time professional; 3 full-time support.
Employer Identification Number: 237343119

686
Weir Foundation Trust ☐
c/o American Security and Trust Company
730 15th St. N.W.
Washington 20013

Trust established in 1953 in the District of Columbia.
Donor(s): Davis Weir.

Financial data: (yr. ended 12/31/83): Assets, $1,528,033 (M); expenditures, $61,339, including $59,250 for 57 grants (high: $5,200; low: $100).
Purpose and activities: General giving, primarily for higher education, arts and cultural programs, Protestant church support, and social services.
Trustee: Charles D. Weir.
Employer Identification Number: 526029328

687
Westport Fund, The
1815 Randolph St., N.W.
Washington 20011

Established in 1943.
Donor(s): Milton McGreevy.†
Financial data: (yr. ended 12/31/83): Assets, $1,952,099 (M); gifts received, $12,667; expenditures, $226,914, including $217,374 for 94 grants (high: $40,000; low: $100).
Purpose and activities: Giving primarily to cultural organizations, social services, and education, especially higher education.
Officers: Gail McGreevy Harmon, President; Thomas J. McGreevy, Vice-President and Secretary; Ann McGreevy Heller, Treasurer.
Directors: Jean McGreevy Green, Barbara James McGreevy.
Number of staff: None.
Employer Identification Number: 446007971

688
Wouk (Abe) Foundation, Inc. ☐
3255 N St., N.W.
Washington 20007

Established in 1954.
Donor(s): Betty Sarah Wouk, Herman Wouk.
Financial data: (yr. ended 12/31/83): Assets, $606,825 (M); gifts received, $200,000; expenditures, $162,051, including $160,390 for 137 grants (high: $25,000; low: $25).
Purpose and activities: Grants primarily for higher education, the arts, conservation, and Jewish welfare funds and temple support.
Officers and Trustees: Herman Wouk, President; Joseph Wouk, Nathanial Wouk, Vice-Presidents; Suzanne Stein, Secretary; Betty Sarah Wouk, Treasurer; Charles Rembar.
Employer Identification Number: 136155699

FLORIDA

689
American Foundation, Incorporated, The
P.O. Drawer 3810
Lake Wales 33853   (813) 676-1408

Incorporated in 1925 in Delaware.
Donor(s): Edward W. Bok.†
Financial data: (yr. ended 6/30/84): Assets, $11,980,428 (M); gifts received, $53,368; expenditures, $974,914.
Purpose and activities: A private operating foundation that maintains the Bok Tower Gardens and Singing Tower at Lake Wales, Florida.
Limitations: Giving limited to Lake Wales, FL. No grants to individuals, or for other organizations.
Publications: Annual report.
Application information:
  Board meeting date(s): April and November
  Write: Jonathan A. Shaw, President
Officers: Jonathan A. Shaw, President; Burke Kibler, III, Secretary-Treasurer.
Directors: Guy W. Botts, Chairman; Louise B. Adams, Anthony S. Bok, Mary Ann Bryan, Farris Bryant, H.L. Culbreath, Jean M. Davis, M. Lewis Hall, Jr., Frank M. Hubbard, Peter Lejins, Enid Curtis Bok Schoettle, Emily M. Wallace, Carroll Wetzel, Phoebe Wetzel.
Number of staff: 8 full-time professional; 1 part-time professional; 21 full-time support; 7 part-time support.
Employer Identification Number: 231352009

690
Applebaum Foundation, Inc., The ☐
4925 Collins Ave.
Miami Beach 33140

Incorporated in 1949 in New York.
Donor(s): Joseph Applebaum.
Financial data: (yr. ended 2/29/84): Assets, $3,782,309 (M); gifts received, $185,000; expenditures, $158,269, including $151,355 for 40 grants (high: $41,000).
Purpose and activities: General giving, with emphasis on higher education, hospitals and medical research, Jewish welfare agencies and religious schools, and temple support.
Officer: Joseph Applebaum, President.
Employer Identification Number: 591002714

691
Arison Foundation, Inc. ☐
100 North Biscayne Blvd., Suite 2302
Miami 33132

Incorporated in 1981 in Florida.
Donor(s): Carnival Cruise Lines, Inc., Festivale Maritime, Inc., Intercon Overseas, Inc.

Financial data: (yr. ended 6/30/84): Assets, $14,334 (M); gifts received, $1,752,775; expenditures, $1,766,954, including $1,766,345 for 32 grants (high: $1,423,000; low: $25).
Purpose and activities: Primarily local giving, with emphasis on arts and cultural programs; support also for Jewish welfare funds.
Limitations: Giving primarily in FL.
Officers and Directors: Marilyn Arison, President; William S. Ruben, Vice-President; William D. Parkhurst, Secretary.
Employer Identification Number: 592128429

692
Aurora Foundation, The ▼
P.O. Box 1848
Bradenton 33506   (813) 748-4100

Established in 1969.
Donor(s): Anthony T. Rossi.
Financial data: (yr. ended 6/30/84): Assets, $55,625,504 (M); expenditures, $4,849,332, including $3,484,922 for 87 grants (high: $464,897; low: $100; average: $5,000-$100,000), $246,511 for 84 grants to individuals and $645,164 for 1 foundation-administered program.
Purpose and activities: Support largely for missionary work; grants also for church support, religious associations, education, scholarships for religious study, and other charitable purposes; about $645,000 per year is allotted to an operating program of the Bradenton Missionary Village, a rent-free housing complex.
Types of support awarded: Student aid.
Limitations: No grants for professorships or building funds of schools and colleges.
Application information:
  Initial approach: Letter and full proposal
  Copies of proposal: 1
  Deadline(s): None
  Board meeting date(s): February, May, August, and November
  Final notification: Within 30 days
  Write: Anthony T. Rossi, Chairman
Officers: Anthony T. Rossi,* Chairman and Manager; Francis Aldridge, Secretary.
Trustees:* Frank Erdman, James W. Gray, John E. Kyle, A. Lamar Matthews, Jr., Ed H. Price, Jr.
Number of staff: 9.
Employer Identification Number: 237044641

693
Baker (The George T.) Foundation, Inc.
P.O. Box 6585
Surfside 33154

Incorporated in 1956 in Florida.
Donor(s): George T. Baker.†
Financial data: (yr. ended 5/31/82): Assets, $998,945 (M); expenditures, $143,765, including $121,825 for 86 grants (high: $18,100; low: $100).
Purpose and activities: Broad purposes; general giving, with emphasis on higher education, hospitals, health agencies and medical research; grants also for humane societies, youth agencies, and church support.

Limitations: Giving primarily in Dade County, FL, and Blowing Rock, NC.
Officers and Trustees: Irma Baker Lyons, Chairman; Barbara Baker Hutchens, President; James F. Lyons, M.D., Rev. Oscar Wilsen, Vice-Presidents; Elizabeth J. Wright, Secretary-Treasurer; Patricia A. Corbett, Laura Wilsen.
Employer Identification Number: 596151202

694
Bastien (John E. and Nellie J.) Foundation ¤
(formerly Bastien Foundation)
6991 West Broward Blvd.
Fort Lauderdale 33317

Trust established in 1965 in Florida.
Donor(s): Nellie J. Bastien.†
Financial data: (yr. ended 12/31/83): Assets, $8,240,665 (M); expenditures, $445,450, including $253,905 for 56 grants (high: $25,000; low: $500).
Purpose and activities: Broad purposes; general giving, with emphasis on higher education, including scholarship funds, hospitals, church support, youth agencies, and general welfare.
Types of support awarded: Scholarship funds.
Trustees: Donald L. Kearns, Gene F. Schneider, J. Wallace Wrightson.
Employer Identification Number: 596160694

695
Beattie (Cordelia Lee) Foundation Trust
P.O. Box 267
Sarasota 33578   (813) 953-8272

Trust established in 1975 in Florida.
Donor(s): Cordelia Lee Beattie.†
Financial data: (yr. ended 10/31/84): Assets, $1,536,316 (M); expenditures, $90,453, including $86,652 for 13 grants (high: $15,000; low: $1,527).
Purpose and activities: Local giving for the arts, with emphasis on music.
Types of support awarded: Building funds, equipment, land acquisition, matching funds, scholarship funds, publications, employee matching gifts.
Limitations: Giving limited to Sarasota County, FL. No grants to individuals, or for general support, endowment funds, special projects, research, or conferences; no loans.
Publications: Application guidelines.
Application information:
  Initial approach: Letter
  Copies of proposal: 3
  Deadline(s): Submit proposal from August through January
  Board meeting date(s): Quarterly
  Final notification: 4 to 6 months
  Write: Robert E. Perkins, Administrative Agent
Trustee: Southeast Bank (Jerome A. Jannopoalo, Vice-President).
Number of staff: 1 part-time professional.
Employer Identification Number: 596540711

696
Bible Alliance
P.O. Box 1894
Bradenton 33506

Established in 1972 in Florida.
Donor(s): Anthony T. Rossi, The Aurora Foundation.
Financial data: (yr. ended 6/30/84): Assets, $3,831,842 (M); gifts received, $6,517; expenditures, $437,702, including $319,238 for 106 grants (high: $200,674; low: $23; average: $60-$600).
Purpose and activities: Production and distribution of recorded portions of the Bible and religious messages on cassette tape in various languages for use in missionary outreach.
Limitations: No grants to individuals; no cash grants.
Application information:
  Board meeting date(s): January and as required
  Write: Anthony T. Rossi, President
Officers: Anthony T. Rossi,* President; Francis C. Aldridge, Secretary.
Directors:* Richard W. Cumberland.
Number of staff: 10.
Employer Identification Number: 237178299

697
Blank (Samuel) and Family Foundation ¤
11077 N.W. 36th Ave.
P.O. Box 680310
Miami 33168

Trust established in 1943 in Florida.
Donor(s): Jerome Blank, and members of the Blank family.
Financial data: (yr. ended 12/31/83): Assets, $4,311,772 (M); expenditures, $156,116, including $115,900 for 31 grants (high: $105,000; low: $100).
Purpose and activities: Broad purposes; primarily local giving, with emphasis on Jewish welfare funds, hospitals, higher education, and temple support.
Limitations: Giving primarily in FL.
Trustees: Leonard C. Abess, Jerome Blank, Mark Blank, Marvin S. Florman.
Employer Identification Number: 596128978

698
Briggs Family Foundation, The
2325 Gordon Dr.
Naples 33940   (813) 261-7625

Incorporated in 1957 in Florida.
Donor(s): Stephen F. Briggs,† Beatrice B. Briggs.†
Financial data: (yr. ended 11/30/82): Assets, $2,422,625 (M); expenditures, $180,063, including $160,050 for 19 grants (high: $50,000; low: $100).
Purpose and activities: Broad purposes; primarily local giving, with emphasis on a university, health, education, and conservation.

Types of support awarded: Continuing support, annual campaigns, seed money, building funds, equipment, land acquisition, special projects, research, scholarship funds.
Limitations: Giving primarily in Collier County, FL. No grants to individuals, or for endowment funds, or matching gifts; no loans.
Application information:
  Initial approach: Letter
  Copies of proposal: 1
  Deadline(s): Submit proposal in October; deadline November 1
  Board meeting date(s): As required
  Final notification: 1 month
  Write: John N. Briggs, President
Officers: John N. Briggs, President; James L. Briggs, Secretary-Treasurer.
Number of staff: None.
Employer Identification Number: 596130222

699
Broad (The Shepard) Foundation, Inc. ☒
1108 Kane Concourse
Barnett Bank Bldg.
Bay Harbor Islands 33154

Incorporated in 1956 in Florida.
Donor(s): Shepard Broad, Ruth K. Broad, Morris N. Broad, and many others.
Financial data: (yr. ended 12/31/83): Assets, $2,150,047 (M); gifts received, $181,640; expenditures, $147,810, including $142,775 for 26 grants (high: $81,750; low: $200).
Purpose and activities: Broad purposes; primarily local giving, with emphasis on higher education, Jewish welfare funds and educational organizations, and health services.
Limitations: Giving primarily in FL.
Officers: Shepard Broad, President; Morris N. Broad, Vice-President; Ruth K. Broad, Secretary; Lewis Horwitz, Treasurer.
Employer Identification Number: 590998866

700
Brunner (Fred J.) Foundation
350 Fairway Dr., Suite 110
Deerfield Beach 33441
Grant application address: P.O. Box 610, Deerfield Beach, FL 33441

Incorporated in 1955 in Illinois.
Donor(s): Fred J. Brunner.
Financial data: (yr. ended 12/31/83): Assets, $3,588,438 (M); expenditures, $165,699, including $124,000 for 68 grants (high: $21,500; low: $50).
Purpose and activities: Broad purposes; general giving, with emphasis on education, and social, health, and youth agencies.
Types of support awarded: Continuing support, annual campaigns, seed money, building funds, equipment, research, matching funds.
Limitations: No grants to individuals, or for endowment funds, scholarships, fellowships, or matching gifts; no loans.
Publications: 990-PF.
Application information:
  Initial approach: Full proposal or letter
  Copies of proposal: 1
  Deadline(s): December 15

  Board meeting date(s): December and as required
  Write: A.J. Schwegel, Vice-President
Officers and Directors:* Fred J. Brunner,* President and Treasurer; Ruth Brunner,* Vice-President and Secretary; A.J. Schwegel, Vice-President and General Manager; J.A. Klemeyer, Vice-President.
Employer Identification Number: 366066471

701
Bush (Edyth) Charitable Foundation, Inc. ▼
199 East Welbourne Ave.
P.O. Box 1967
Winter Park 32790-1967   (305) 647-4322

Originally incorporated in 1966 in Minnesota; reincorporated in 1973 in Florida.
Donor(s): Edyth Bush.†
Financial data: (yr. ended 8/31/84): Assets, $40,287,978 (M); expenditures, $2,899,188, including $2,254,585 for 68 grants (high: $200,000; low: $1,000; average: $15,000-$50,000) and $106,921 for 4 foundation-administered programs.
Purpose and activities: Primarily local giving within 100 miles of Winter Park, or for requests that are of special interest to one or more directors, especially family members living in the states of Arizona and California. Support for charitable, educational and health service organizations, with emphasis on human services and health; higher education; the elderly; youth services; the handicapped; and recognized national quality arts or cultural programs within the 100-mile radius. Provides limited number of program-related investment loans for construction, land purchase, emergency or similar purposes to organizations otherwise qualified to receive grants.
Types of support awarded: Seed money, emergency funds, building funds, equipment, land acquisition, loans, conferences and seminars, matching funds, consulting services, technical assistance, program-related investments.
Limitations: Giving primarily in within a 100-mile radius of Winter Park, FL; also AZ and CA if supported by family member directors. No support for alcohol or drug abuse organizations, churches, tax-supported institutions, or advocacy organizations. No grants to individuals, or for endowments, scholarships, fellowships, travel, operating expenses, annual campaigns, or deficit financing.
Publications: 990-PF, program policy statement, application guidelines.
Application information:
  Initial approach: Telephone or full proposal
  Copies of proposal: 2
  Deadline(s): September 1 or January 1; May 30 if funds are available
  Board meeting date(s): Usually in October, March, July, and as required
  Final notification: 3 months after board meeting
  Write: H. Clifford Lee, Executive Vice-President

Officers: Charlotte B. Heuser,* Chairman; David R. Roberts,* President and Chief Executive Officer; H. Clifford Lee,* Executive Vice-President; Frances M. Woodard,* Harold A. Ward III,* Vice-Presidents; Alice J. Rettig, Corporate Secretary; Herbert W. Holm,* Treasurer.
Directors:* William B. Heuser, Hugh F. McKean, Milton P. Woodard.
Number of staff: 2 full-time professional; 1 part-time professional; 4 full-time support.
Employer Identification Number: 237318041

702
Chastain (Robert Lee) and Thomas M. Chastain Charitable Foundation ☒
P.O. Box 190
Palm Beach 33480   (305) 848-6868

Trust established in 1966 in Florida.
Donor(s): Robert Lee Chastain.†
Financial data: (yr. ended 12/31/83): Assets, $2,052,713 (M); expenditures, $112,856, including $97,000 for 13 grants (high: $15,000; low: $3,000).
Purpose and activities: Grants policy confined to community- and publicly managed agencies principally within the Palm Beach and Martin County area, with emphasis given to public higher education, programs in the humanities and sciences, and environmental resource management projects offering benefits to the general population. A few trustee-initiated contributions may exceed these limits.
Limitations: Giving primarily in the Palm Beach and Martin County, FL, area. No support for church-related groups or national charities. No grants to individuals, or for building or endowment funds or appeals in mass circulation.
Application information:
  Initial approach: Full proposal with cover letter
  Copies of proposal: 2
  Board meeting date(s): Quarterly
  Write: Thomas M. Chastain, Trustee
Trustees: Thomas M. Chastain, Harry Johnston, II, Atlantic National Bank of West Palm Beach.
Employer Identification Number: 596171294

703
Childress (The Francis and Miranda) Foundation, Inc. ☒
621 Edward Ball Bldg.
Jacksonville 32202

Established in 1963 in Florida.
Donor(s): Francis B. Childress.†
Financial data: (yr. ended 12/31/83): Assets, $2,201,494 (M); gifts received, $16,713; expenditures, $192,229, including $156,700 for 23 grants (high: $50,000; low: $500).
Purpose and activities: Broad purposes; largely local giving, with emphasis on higher and secondary education, Protestant church support, youth agencies, cultural programs, and hospitals.
Limitations: Giving primarily in FL.

Officers and Trustees:* Miranda Y.
Childress,* President; James A. Cranford,* Vice-
President; Augusta L. Owens, Secretary; Francis
Childress Lee,* Treasurer.
Employer Identification Number: 591051733

704
Conn Memorial Foundation, Inc. ▼
220 East Madison St.
P.O. Box 229
Tampa 33602   (813) 223-3838

Incorporated in 1954 in Florida.
Donor(s): Fred K. Conn,† Edith F. Conn.†
Financial data: (yr. ended 7/31/83): Assets,
$13,854,255 (M); expenditures, $1,234,733,
including $1,007,035 for 83 grants (high:
$100,000; low: $700; average: $1,000-
$25,000).
Purpose and activities: General purposes;
local giving only, with emphasis on education,
health services and rehabilitation, and charities
benefiting youth.
Types of support awarded: Building funds,
continuing support, deficit financing,
equipment, matching funds, operating budgets,
scholarship funds, seed money.
Limitations: Giving limited to the greater
Tampa Bay, FL, area. No grants to individuals
or for endowment funds; no loans.
Publications: 990-PF.
Application information:
 Initial approach: Letter, telephone, or full
  proposal
 Copies of proposal: 4
 Deadline(s): Submit proposal preferably in
  November or May; deadlines November
  30 and May 31
 Board meeting date(s): January and July
 Final notification: One month after board
  meeting
 Write: David B. Frye, President
Officers: David B. Frye,* President and
Treasurer; George W. Ericksen,* Vice-
President; Mary S. Boisselle, Secretary.
Directors:* Charles C. Murphy.
Number of staff: 2 full-time professional; 1
part-time professional.
Employer Identification Number: 590978713

705
**Crane (The Raymond E. and Ellen F.)
Foundation** ¤
P.O. Box 25427
Tamarac 33320

Trust established in 1949 in Pennsylvania.
Donor(s): Raymond E. Crane,† Ellen F. Crane.†
Financial data: (yr. ended 12/31/82): Assets,
$2,124,593 (M); expenditures, $177,329,
including $154,250 for 55 grants (high:
$10,000; low: $250).
Purpose and activities: Broad purposes; giving
primarily in the southeastern states, with
emphasis on higher education and community
funds; grants also for cultural programs,
secondary education, health, and Protestant
church support.
Limitations: Giving primarily in the
southeastern states.

Officer and Trustees: George A. Owen,
Manager; Alpo F. Crane, Robert F. Crane,
Robert F. Crane, Jr.
Employer Identification Number: 596139265

706
Dade Foundation
848 Brickell Ave., Suite 1111
Miami 33131   (305) 371-2711

Community foundation established in 1967 in
Florida.
Financial data: (yr. ended 12/31/83): Assets,
$4,266,409 (M); gifts received, $1,161,405;
expenditures, $846,876, including $728,393
for 112 grants (high: $57,000; low: $100;
average: $6,500).
Purpose and activities: Broad charitable and
educational purposes; grants limited to local
organizations and agencies with preference
given to capital and special projects; support
primarily for youth agencies, social services,
education, hospitals and health agencies, and
the arts.
Types of support awarded: Seed money,
emergency funds, building funds, equipment,
land acquisition, research.
Limitations: Giving limited to Dade County,
FL. No grants to individuals, or for operating
budgets, continuing support, endowment funds,
matching gifts, scholarships and fellowships,
publications, or conferences; no loans.
Publications: Annual report, application
guidelines, program policy statement.
Application information:
 Initial approach: Letter
 Copies of proposal: 1
 Deadline(s): Submit proposal preferably in
  November; deadline December 1
 Board meeting date(s): February, May,
  September, and November
 Final notification: 2 months
 Write: Ruth Shack, Executive Director
Officers: Mrs. Thomas C. Wasmuth,*
Secretary; Thomas M. Chamberlain,* Treasurer;
Ruth Shack, Executive Director.
Governors:* Theodore J. Pappas, Chairman;
Samuel L. Barr, Jr., Vice-Chairman; William H.
Allen, Jr., Carlos J. Arboleya, James K. Batten,
Peter L. Bermont, David Blumberg, Thomas R.
Bomar, Francis J. Christie, Barry G. Hastings,
Lila G. Heatter, Louis J. Hector, Cyrus M.
Jolivette, Charles H. Kimbrell, Norman H.
Lipoff, Byron L. Sparber, Octavio Verdeja,
Robert A. White, George S. Wise.
Trustee Banks: AmeriFirst Florida Trust
Company, Barnett Banks Trust Co., Bessemer
Trust Company of Florida, City National Bank
of Miami, Commercial Bank & Trust Company
of Miami, Flagship National Bank of Miami,
Florida National Bank of Miami, Jefferson
National Bank of Miami Beach, Key Biscayne
Bank and Trust Company, Northern Trust Bank
of Florida, Pan American Bank, Southeast Bank,
Sun Bank of Miami.
Number of staff: 1 full-time professional; 1 full-
time support.
Employer Identification Number: 596183655

707
**Davis (The Arthur Vining)
Foundations** ▼
Haskell Bldg., Suite 520
Oak and Fisk Sts.
Jacksonville 32204   (904) 359-0670

Three trusts established: in 1952 and 1965 in
Pennsylvania; in 1965 in Florida.
Donor(s): Arthur Vining Davis.†
Financial data: (yr. ended 12/31/84): Assets,
$69,902,000 (M); expenditures, $3,239,000,
including $2,601,000 for 36 grants (high:
$247,000; low: $2,000; average: $25,000-
$100,000).
Purpose and activities: Broad purposes;
support largely for private higher education,
hospices, medicine, public television, and
theological education.
Types of support awarded: Building funds,
continuing support, endowment funds,
equipment, fellowships, internships, land
acquisition, matching funds, professorships,
research, scholarship funds.
Limitations: No support for community chests,
institutions primarily supported by government
funds, and projects incurring obligations
extending over many years. No grants to
individuals; no loans.
Publications: Annual report, program policy
statement, application guidelines.
Application information:
 Initial approach: Letter
 Copies of proposal: 1
 Deadline(s): None
 Board meeting date(s): Spring, fall, and winter
 Final notification: 8 to 12 months for
  approvals; within 6 months for rejections
 Write: Max Morris, Executive Director
Officer: Max Morris, Executive Director.
Trustees: Nathanael V. Davis, Chairman; Carl
H. Bruns, Holbrook R. Davis, Joel P. Davis,
Atwood Dunwody, W.E. Dunwody, Jr., The
Rev. Davis Given, Mrs. William B. Given, Jr.,
Mrs. John L. Kee, Jr., W.R. Wright, Southeast
First National Bank of Miami, Mellon Bank.
Number of staff: 2 full-time professional; 4
part-time professional; 2 full-time support.
Employer Identification Number: 256018909

708
**Davis (M. Austin) Family-WD Charities,
Inc.** ¤
5050 Edgewood Ct.
Jacksonville 32205

Incorporated in 1950 in Florida.
Donor(s): Milton Austin Davis.
Financial data: (yr. ended 12/31/83): Assets,
$1,171,627 (M); expenditures, $24,563,
including $20,500 for 4 grants (high: $10,000;
low: $2,500).
Purpose and activities: Giving primarily to
higher education and a community center.
Officers: Milton Austin Davis, President; T.W.
Bishop, Vice-President and Treasurer.
Employer Identification Number: 596128871

709

Davis (The Tine W.) Family - W.D. Charities, Inc. ☼

(formerly Davis (The Tine Wayne) Foundation, Inc.)
5050 Edgewood Court
Jacksonville 32205

Incorporated in 1950 in Florida.
Donor(s): Tine W. Davis, and others.
Financial data: (yr. ended 12/31/83): Assets, $13,856,352 (M); expenditures, $1,106,769, including $559,408 for 113 grants (high: $100,000; low: $25).
Purpose and activities: Broad purposes; grants largely for higher education, church support, youth agencies, medical research, and health and social agencies.
Application information:
   Write: Thomas W. Bishop, Vice-President
Officers and Directors:* Tine W. Davis, Jr.,* President; Thomas W. Bishop, Vice-President and Treasurer.
Employer Identification Number: 590995388

710

Deicke (Edwin F.) Foundation ☼
309 Farmington Dr.
Plantation 33317

Trust established in 1956 in Illinois.
Donor(s): Edwin F. Deicke, Suburban Casualty Company, Pioneer Insurance Company.
Financial data: (yr. ended 12/31/83): Assets, $2,465,384 (M); expenditures, $235,356, including $217,700 for 17 grants (high: $80,050; low: $400).
Purpose and activities: Educational and charitable purposes; general giving, largely in Illinois and Florida, with emphasis on community development, higher education, and youth agencies; grants also for the handicapped and cultural programs.
Limitations: Giving primarily in IL and FL.
Application information:
   Write: Edwin F. Deicke, Chairman
Officer and Trustees: Edwin F. Deicke, Chairman and General Manager; James D. Anderson, Robert E. Covert, Lois L. Deicke, Lois D. Martin.
Employer Identification Number: 366053612

711

Delacorte (George) Fund ☼
11556 Turtle Beach Rd.
North Palm Beach 33408

Established about 1977 in New York.
Donor(s): George T. Delacorte, Jr., and others.
Financial data: (yr. ended 12/31/83): Assets, $3,119,646 (M); gifts received, $502,338; expenditures, $171,492, including $102,250 for 29 grants (high: $54,000; low: $25) and $49,901 for foundation-administered programs.
Purpose and activities: Broad purposes; grants for cultural programs, youth, religious organizations, education, and health; program support annually to maintain and build public monuments in New York City.

Officers: George T. Delacorte, Jr., President; Valerie Delacorte, Vice-President and Treasurer; Albert P. Delacorte, Secretary.
Employer Identification Number: 510202382

712

Dettman (Leroy E.) Foundation, Inc.
108 Southeast Eighth Ave.
Fort Lauderdale 33301   (305) 525-6102

Established in 1978 in Florida.
Donor(s): Leroy E. Dettman.†
Financial data: (yr. ended 10/31/83): Assets, $2,970,825 (M); gifts received, $1,500,000; expenditures, $256,620, including $83,600 for 41 grants (high: $15,500; low: $25; average: $2,000) and $120,060 for 71 grants to individuals.
Purpose and activities: Giving primarily for scholarships to temporary employees of Personnel Pool of America and their children.
Types of support awarded: Continuing support, annual campaigns, equipment, endowment funds, employee related scholarships.
Limitations: No grants for operating budgets, building or emergency funds, seed money, deficit financing, land acquisition, or matching gifts; no loans.
Publications: Application guidelines.
Application information: Application form required.
   Initial approach: Letter
   Deadline(s): March 31
   Board meeting date(s): Quarterly
   Write: Joseph Dyke, Administrator
Officers: Douglas R. Dettman,* President; Barbara Jane Fleming, Vice-President; Gregory L. Dettman,* Secretary; Carolyn Rubin, Treasurer.
Trustees:* Sophie B. Dettman.
Number of staff: 1 full-time support.
Employer Identification Number: 591784551

713

du Pont (Alfred I.) Foundation ☼
803 Edward Ball Bldg.
P.O. Box 1380
Jacksonville 32201   (904) 356-8311

Incorporated in 1936 in Florida.
Donor(s): Jessie Ball du Pont.†
Financial data: (yr. ended 12/31/83): Assets, $10,214,714 (M); gifts received, $600,000; expenditures, $522,691, including $167,140 for 69 grants (high: $25,000; low: $84) and $329,280 for 214 grants to individuals.
Purpose and activities: Charitable giving, including care, treatment, and development for indigent children and elderly adults requiring health, economic, or educational assistance residing in the southeastern United States. Support also for higher education, and medical research.
Types of support awarded: Grants to individuals.
Limitations: Giving primarily in the Southeast.
Application information: Application form required.
   Initial approach: Full proposal
   Copies of proposal: 1

Write: Mrs. Irene Walsh, Secretary
Officers and Directors: Braden Ball, President; J.C. Belin, Vice-President; Irene Walsh, Secretary and Treasurer; Gilbert W. Smith, Hazel O. Willliams.
Employer Identification Number: 591297267

714

Duda Foundation, The ☼
P.O. Box 257
Oviedo 32765

Incorporated in 1953 in Florida.
Donor(s): Members of the Duda family, A. Duda and Sons, Inc.
Financial data: (yr. ended 12/31/83): Assets, $871,597 (M); gifts received, $126,000; expenditures, $428,242, including $426,000 for 10 grants (high: $116,000; low: $1,000).
Purpose and activities: Grants primarily for Protestant church support and church-related institutions.
Officers and Directors: Andrew Duda, Jr., President; Ferdinand Duda, Secretary-Treasurer; Andrew L. Duda, Ferdinand S. Duda, John Duda, John L. Duda.
Employer Identification Number: 596139732

715

Dunspaugh-Dalton Foundation, Inc., The ▼ ☼
35 S.W. Eighth St.
Miami 33130   (305) 373-3355

Incorporated in 1963 in Florida.
Donor(s): Ann V. Dalton.†
Financial data: (yr. ended 12/31/82): Assets, $14,384,785 (M); expenditures, $691,456, including $489,650 for 59 grants (high: $50,000; low: $100).
Purpose and activities: Broad purposes; giving primarily locally and in Monterey, California; grants largely for education, particularly higher education; social service and youth agencies; hospitals; and cultural programs.
Limitations: Giving primarily in Dade County, FL, and Monterey, CA.
Officers and Directors:* William A. Lane, Jr.,* President; Sarah L. Bonner,* Vice-President; Thomas H. Wakefield, Secretary and Treasurer.
Employer Identification Number: 591055300

716

duPont (Jessie Ball) Religious, Charitable and Educational Fund ▼
872 Edward Ball Bldg.
Jacksonville 32202   (904) 353-0890

Trust established in 1976 in Florida.
Donor(s): Jessie Ball duPont.†
Financial data: (yr. ended 10/31/84): Assets, $94,656,500 (M); expenditures, $7,153,477, including $6,408,033 for 92 grants (high: $635,000; low: $1,000; average: $5,000-$100,000).

Purpose and activities: Broad purposes; grants limited to twelve institutions specifically named in the will of the donor and to those institutions to which she contributed personally during the five-year period ending December 31, 1964. Interests include higher and secondary education, cultural programs, social services, hospitals, health agencies, church support and church-related organizations, and youth agencies, with first consideration to organizations in Florida, Delaware, and Virginia.
Types of support awarded: Annual campaigns, seed money, emergency funds, deficit financing, building funds, equipment, land acquisition, special projects, research, publications, professorships, scholarship funds, exchange programs, matching funds, general purposes, continuing support.
Limitations: No support for tax-supported institutions, organizations other than those designated in the donor's will, or those not awarded gifts by the donor from 1960-1964. No grants to individuals; no loans.
Publications: Annual report, informational brochure.
Application information: Applicant must submit proof that a contribution was received from the donor between 1960 and 1964.
Initial approach: Brief proposal
Copies of proposal: 2
Deadline(s): Submit proposal preferably in January or February; deadline March 31
Board meeting date(s): Bimonthly beginning in November
Final notification: 3 to 4 months average
Write: Miss Hazel O. Williams, Executive Secretary
Officer and Trustees: Hazel O. Williams, Executive Secretary; Alexander duBose Juhan, William B. Mills, Florida National Bank (Theodore G. Thoburn, Executive Vice-President and E. Kent Lytle, Vice-President, Trust Department).
Number of staff: 3 full-time support.
Employer Identification Number: 596368632

717
Eagles Memorial Foundation, Inc. ⌑
4710 14th St. West
Bradenton 33511

Established in 1946.
Financial data: (yr. ended 5/31/83): Assets, $6,476,809 (M); gifts received, $288,385; expenditures, $583,973, including $452,488 for 748 grants (high: $150,000; low: $100) and $43,237 for 270 grants to individuals.
Purpose and activities: Grants to organizations through the Golden Eagle Fund, with emphasis on Eagle Village, Inc.; the aged, nutrition, and public libraries. Grants to individuals for student aid and medical and dental care.
Types of support awarded: Grants to individuals, student aid.
Officers and Directors: Maynard Floyd, Chairman; James Bailey, Vice-Chairman; Thomas J. McGriff, Executive Secretary; Joe Cook, Martin Reinhard, Harley Sprague.
Employer Identification Number: 396126176

718
Echlin Foundation ⌑
875 East Camino Real, Apt. 10-H
Boca Raton 33432

Trust established in 1960 in Connecticut.
Donor(s): John E. Echlin.
Financial data: (yr. ended 11/30/83): Assets, $2,263,067 (M); expenditures, $103,467, including $100,000 for 15 grants (high: $41,000; low: $500).
Purpose and activities: Grants largely for higher and secondary education and hospitals.
Officer and Trustees: John E. Echlin, Director; Beryl G. Echlin, John E. Echlin, Jr.
Employer Identification Number: 066037282

719
Eckerd (Jack) Corporation Foundation
P.O. Box 4689
Clearwater 33518 (813) 397-7461

Established in 1973 in Florida.
Donor(s): Jack Eckerd Corporation.
Financial data: (yr. ended 7/28/84): Assets, $391,694 (M); gifts received, $500,000; expenditures, $577,684, including $547,949 for grants (high: $57,000; low: $500) and $29,735 for employee matching gifts.
Purpose and activities: Broad purposes; support for several national health organizations, community funds, hospitals, and for pharmacy scholarships at 24 southern universities.
Types of support awarded: Operating budgets, continuing support, annual campaigns, seed money, emergency funds, building funds, employee matching gifts, scholarship funds.
Limitations: Giving limited to areas of company operations. No grants to individuals, or for endowment funds, deficit financing, equipment, land acquisition, renovation projects, special projects, research, publications, or conferences; no loans.
Publications: Annual report.
Application information:
Initial approach: Letter
Board meeting date(s): Quarterly
Final notification: 4 to 6 months
Write: Michael Zagorac, Jr., Chairman
Trustees: Michael Zagorac, Jr., Chairman; William Bradley, Harry W. Lambert, Burton C. Perfit, James M. Santo.
Number of staff: None.
Employer Identification Number: 237322099

720
Falk (The David) Foundation, Inc.
c/o First National Bank of Florida
P.O. Box 1810
Tampa 33601 (813) 224-1877

Incorporated in 1945 in Florida.
Donor(s): David A. Falk.†
Financial data: (yr. ended 12/31/83): Assets, $1,721,314 (M); expenditures, $118,550, including $68,804 for 15 grants (high: $33,754; low: $100) and $8,400 for 1 foundation-administered program.
Purpose and activities: Local giving, with emphasis on child welfare, youth agencies, social agencies, higher education, hospitals, drug abuse programs, the handicapped, and the aged.
Types of support awarded: Operating budgets, seed money, emergency funds, building funds, equipment, land acquisition, matching funds, publications.
Limitations: Giving limited to the Tampa Bay, FL, area. No support for community funds, electoral or political projects. No grants to individuals, or for continuing support, annual campaigns, deficit financing, general endowments, research, conferences, scholarships, or fellowships; no loans.
Publications: Program policy statement, application guidelines.
Application information: Application form required.
Initial approach: Full proposal
Copies of proposal: 1
Deadline(s): Submit proposal in January, April, July, or October; no set deadline
Board meeting date(s): March, April, June, September, November, and December
Final notification: 90 days after board meeting
Write: John J. Howley, Secretary
Officers and Trustees: Mary Irene McKay Falk, Chairman; Herbert G. McKay, President; John J. Long, Vice-President; John J. Howley, Secretary and Treasurer; David C.G. Kerr, B.G. Smith.
Number of staff: None.
Employer Identification Number: 591055570

721
Fellows (J. Hugh and Earle W.) Memorial Fund
P.O. Box 12950
Pensacola 32576 (904) 432-2451
Loan application office: c/o The President, Pensacola Junior College, 1000 College Blvd., Pensacola, FL 32504; Tel.: (904) 976-5410

Trust established in 1961 in Florida.
Donor(s): Earle W. Fellows-Williamson.†
Financial data: (yr. ended 4/30/83): Assets, $1,600,917 (M); expenditures, $15,909, including $76,000 for 13 loans.
Purpose and activities: To provide low-interest-rate loans to students of medicine, theology, nursing, and medical technology who reside in four northwest Florida counties and who agree to pursue their professions in this area for five years after graduation.
Types of support awarded: Student aid, loans.
Limitations: Giving primarily in Escambia, Santa Rosa, Okaloma and Walton counties, FL.
Application information:
Initial approach: Letter
Copies of proposal: 1
Deadline(s): Submit proposal preferably in March or April; deadline May 31
Board meeting date(s): April and December
Write: C. Roger Vinson, Secretary
Officers and Trustees: Rev. LeVan Davis, Chairman; Lindley M. Camp, Vice-Chairman; C. Roger Vinson, Secretary; W.C. Payne, Jr., M.D., Harold N. Smith.
Employer Identification Number: 596132238

722
Ford (Jefferson Lee) III Memorial Foundation, Inc. ⌧
Sun Bank of Bal Harbour
Bal Harbour 33154

Incorporated in 1950 in Florida.
Donor(s): Jefferson L. Ford, Jr.†
Financial data: (yr. ended 2/29/84): Assets, $2,033,693 (M); expenditures, $192,122, including $171,250 for 48 grants (high: $10,000; low: $500).
Purpose and activities: Support for health agencies, education, medical research, handicapped children, hospitals, and religious institutions.
Application information:
 Write: Herbert L. Kurras, Director
Officers and Directors: Alfonsine Palermo, President; Doris King, Vice-President; David P. Catsman, Herbert L. Kurras, Anthony Palermo.
Employer Identification Number: 526037179

723
Gore Family Memorial Foundation Trust
501 East Las Olas Blvd.
Fort Lauderdale 33302

Trust established in 1973 in Florida.
Donor(s): R.H. Gore Trust.
Financial data: (yr. ended 1/31/84): Assets, $8,234,230 (M); gifts received, $714,368; expenditures, $696,585, including $426,567 for 561 grants (high: $25,000; low: $23) and $139,485 for 106 grants to individuals.
Purpose and activities: Aid to needy and handicapped; aid to needy restricted to Broward County, Florida; scholarships restricted to Broward County residents, except for severely handicapped applicants.
Types of support awarded: Student aid, grants to individuals.
Limitations: Giving primarily in FL, and in Broward County, FL, for aid to the needy. No grants for general programs, capital expenditures, or scholarships for graduate studies (except for the handicapped); no loans.
Publications: 990-PF, informational brochure.
Application information:
 Initial approach: Full proposal
Trustees: George H. Gore, Robert H. Gore, Jr., Theodore T. Gore, Lowell C. Mott, Sun Bank.
Number of staff: 2 full-time support.
Employer Identification Number: 596497544

724
Greenburg (The Harry) Foundation, Inc.
P.O. Box 54-6119
Miami Beach 33154   (305) 864-8639

Incorporated in 1947 in Delaware.
Donor(s): Harry Greenburg.
Financial data: (yr. ended 12/31/84): Assets, $1,858,796 (M); expenditures, $123,761, including $109,370 for 39 grants (high: $50,000; low: $25).
Purpose and activities: Charitable and educational purposes; grants almost entirely for medical research; some support also for hospitals, Jewish welfare funds, and temple support.

Types of support awarded: Operating budgets, continuing support, building funds, research.
Limitations: No grants to individuals, or for endowment funds, special projects, publications, or conferences, generally no scholarships or fellowships; no loans.
Application information:
 Initial approach: Letter
 Copies of proposal: 1
 Deadline(s): None
 Board meeting date(s): January, April, July, and October
 Final notification: 1 to 2 months
 Write: Samuel D. May, President
Officers and Directors: Samuel D. May, President and Treasurer; Peter May, Linda Sklar, Vice-Presidents; Isabel May, Secretary.
Number of staff: 2.
Employer Identification Number: 136162935

725
Greene (Robert Z.) Foundation ⌧
4411 Pinetree Dr.
Miami Beach 33140

Established in 1947.
Donor(s): Robert Z. Greene.
Financial data: (yr. ended 12/31/83): Assets, $778,914 (M); gifts received, $250,630; expenditures, $253,024, including $247,015 for 54 grants (high: $50,000; low: $15).
Purpose and activities: Giving primarily in Florida and New York, with emphasis on higher education, Jewish welfare funds, hospitals, and health agencies.
Limitations: Giving primarily in FL and NY.
Application information:
 Deadline(s): None
Trustees: Monroe Chapin, Nancy J. Greene, Robert Z. Greene.
Employer Identification Number: 136121751

726
Harris Foundation
Melbourne 32919   (305) 727-9378

Incorporated in 1952 in Ohio.
Donor(s): Harris Corporation.
Financial data: (yr. ended 6/30/83): Assets, $302,231 (M); gifts received, $100,000; expenditures, $393,033, including $194,210 for 25 grants (high: $75,000; low: $500) and $194,141 for 1,538 employee matching gifts.
Purpose and activities: General purposes; grants for higher education, including an employee matching gifts program, community funds, cultural programs, youth agencies, and hospitals.
Types of support awarded: General purposes, operating budgets, continuing support, annual campaigns, building funds, research, professorships, scholarship funds, fellowships, employee matching gifts.
Limitations: Giving limited to areas of company operations. No grants to individuals, or for endowment funds; no loans.
Application information:
 Initial approach: Full proposal
 Copies of proposal: 1
 Deadline(s): None

Board meeting date(s): November
Write: O.W. Hudson, Secretary
Officers and Trustees: J.A. Boyd, President; J.T. Hartley, Vice-President; O.W. Hudson, Secretary; M.G. Dowling, Treasurer; R.B. Tullis.
Number of staff: None.
Employer Identification Number: 346520425

727
Hayward (The John T. and Winifred) Foundation Charitable Trust ⌧
c/o First National Bank of Clearwater
P.O. Box 179
Clearwater 33517   (813) 448-3051

Trust established in 1973 in Florida.
Donor(s): John T. Hayward,† Winifred M. Hayward.†
Financial data: (yr. ended 12/31/83): Assets, $4,799,560 (M); expenditures, $375,767, including $332,691 for 2 grants (high: $172,691; low: $160,000).
Purpose and activities: Support for medical research organizations and schools involved in the field of genetics, with emphasis on birth defects and inheritable diseases.
Types of support awarded: Research.
Limitations: No grants to individuals, or for building or endowment funds, or operating budgets.
Publications: Application guidelines.
Application information: Application form required.
 Initial approach: Letter
 Board meeting date(s): January, April, July, and October
 Write: L. Bernard Stephenson, Vice-President
Trustees: William R. LaRosa, M.D., Howard P. Rives, The First National Bank of Clearwater (L. Bernard Stephenson, Vice-President and Trust Officer).
Employer Identification Number: 237363201

728
Hollingsworth (J. E. & Mildred) Foundation, Inc. ⌧
425 Worth Ave.
Palm Beach 33480

Established in 1966.
Financial data: (yr. ended 12/31/83): Assets, $1,301,841 (M); expenditures, $104,790, including $92,280 for 58 grants (high: $15,830; low: $20).
Purpose and activities: Giving primarily for higher education, hospitals and health agencies; support also for a population control organization.
Directors: Mrs. James M. Ballentine, William B. Cudahy, Mildred Hollingsworth, Wyckoff Myers, John Van Ryan.
Employer Identification Number: 596170607

729
Howell (Eric and Jessie) Foundation, Inc. ⌧
P.O. Box 5206
Lighthouse Point 33064   (305) 782-9250
Application address: Manly Thaler, 2720 NE 29 St., Lighthouse Point, FL 33064; Tel.: (305) 782-9250

Incorporated in 1979 in New York.
Donor(s): Eric Howell.†
Financial data: (yr. ended 12/31/83): Assets, $1,216,306 (M); expenditures, $72,973, including $55,880 for 16 grants (high: $21,600; low: $100).
Purpose and activities: Grants primarily to community organizations in Tompkins County, New York, with emphasis on social agencies, including programs for the aged, and a community college.
Limitations: Giving primarily in Thompkins County, NY.
Application information:
  Initial approach: Letter or full proposal
  Deadline(s): None
Officers: Manley Thaler, President; Rachael Thaler, Vice-President; Decisive Thaler, Secretary and Treasurer.
Employer Identification Number: 161116060

730
Jacksonville Community Foundation (Donor-Directed Fund), Greater
924 Barnett Bank Bldg.
Jacksonville 32202   (904) 355-4715

A private foundation established in 1980 under the umbrella of the Greater Jacksonville Community Foundation.
Donor(s): Various individuals.
Financial data: (yr. ended 12/31/83): Assets, $1,426,266 (M); gifts received, $870,920; expenditures, $658,298 for grants.
Purpose and activities: Broad purposes; primarily local giving for religious, educational, and cultural activities.
Limitations: Giving primarily in northeast FL. No grants to individuals.
Application information: Generally, applications not accepted.
  Write: Byon Morris, Executive Vice-President
Officers: Byon Morris, Executive Vice-President; C. Collier McGehee, Jr., Secretary-Treasurer.
Number of staff: 1 full-time professional; 1 part-time professional; 1 full-time support; 1 part-time support.
Employer Identification Number: 591938109

731
Jacksonville Community Foundation, Greater
924 Barnett Bank Bldg.
Jacksonville 32202   (904) 355-4715

Community foundation established in 1964.
Financial data: (yr. ended 12/31/83): Assets, $1,240,105 (M); gifts received, $425,536; expenditures, $526,573, including $390,223 for 115 grants (high: $36,291; low: $25).
Purpose and activities: Primarily local giving for the benefit of the citizens of Jacksonville, Florida.
Limitations: Giving primarily in Jacksonville, FL. No grants to individuals.
Application information:
  Initial approach: Letter
  Write: Byon Morris, Executive Vice-President

Board of Governors: Robert T. Shircliff, Chairman; William K. Hatcher, Vice-Chairman; Douglas W. Maxwell, Secretary; Reese R. Bohn, Treasurer; James L. Ade, H. Jack Bivins, Jr., Louie C. Casey, Jr., George B. Dismore, John W. Donahoo, Jr., Frances B. Kinne, E. Kent Lytle, Thomas R. McGehee, Paul G. Wright, Jr.
Officers: Byon Morris, Executive Vice-President; C. Collier McGehee, Jr., Secretary-Treasurer.
Number of staff: 1 full-time professional; 1 part-time professional.
Employer Identification Number: 596150746

732
Jenkins (George W.) Foundation, Inc. ▼ ⊭
P.O. Box 407
Lakeland 33802   (813) 688-1188

Incorporated in 1967 in Florida.
Donor(s): George W. Jenkins.
Financial data: (yr. ended 12/31/83): Assets, $5,560,377 (M); expenditures, $849,750, including $843,663 for 277 grants (high: $50,000; low: $100; average: $1,000-$5,000).
Purpose and activities: Broad purposes; primarily local giving, with emphasis on youth agencies, health, cultural programs, community funds, higher education, and social service agencies.
Types of support awarded: Building funds, operating budgets, special projects.
Limitations: Giving limited to FL. No grants to individuals.
Application information:
  Initial approach: Proposal
  Copies of proposal: 1
  Deadline(s): None
  Board meeting date(s): Monthly
  Final notification: 2 weeks after first Monday of the month
  Write: George W. Jenkins, President
Officers and Directors: George W. Jenkins, President; Charles H. Jenkins, Sr., Joe Blanton, Vice-Presidents; John A. Turner, Secretary-Treasurer; Jere W. Annis, Barbara O. Hart, Carol Jenkins, Howard Jenkins, Hubert Stockard.
Number of staff: None.
Employer Identification Number: 596194119

733
Johnson (The D. Mead) Foundation, Inc. ⊭
P.O. Box 346
Palm Beach 33480

Incorporated in 1958 in Delaware.
Donor(s): D. Mead Johnson.
Financial data: (yr. ended 12/31/83): Assets, $1,343,328 (M); expenditures, $100,589, including $49,686 for 18 grants (high: $40,000; low: $12).
Purpose and activities: Broad purposes; general giving, primarily local, with emphasis on higher education.
Limitations: Giving primarily in FL.
Officer: D. Mead Johnson, President.
Employer Identification Number: 356021886

734
Koch Foundation, Inc. ▼
625-B N.W. 60th St.
Gainesville 32607   (904) 373-7491

Incorporated in 1979 in Florida.
Donor(s): Carl E. Koch, Paula Koch.
Financial data: (yr. ended 3/31/84): Assets, $43,007,762 (M); expenditures, $2,708,599, including $2,551,510 for 48 grants (high: $800,000; low: $110; average: $5,000-$50,000).
Purpose and activities: Grants only for Roman Catholic religious organizations that propagate the faith.
Types of support awarded: Operating budgets, continuing support, annual campaigns, seed money, building funds, equipment, land acquisition, matching funds, special projects, research, publications, conferences and seminars.
Limitations: No support for health related activities or social service projects, except in needy areas such as exist in the foreign missions; or for building projects of schools and colleges. No grants to individuals, or for endowment funds, deficit financing, emergency funds, or scholarships or fellowships; no loans.
Publications: Annual report, program policy statement, application guidelines.
Application information: Proposals considered at February meeting. Application form required.
  Initial approach: Letter
  Deadline(s): None
  Board meeting date(s): September and last Wednesday of February
  Final notification: 6 months
  Write: Carolyn L. Bomberger, President
Officers and Directors: Carolyn L. Bomberger, President; Cletus Humm, Vice-President, Secretary and Treasurer; John J. Koch, Vice-President; Arthur B. Bomberger, Dorothy C. Bomberger, William A. Bomberger, D. Wallace Fields, Paula Koch, Shari Koch, Inge Vraney, Gerald A. Youngs.
Number of staff: 1 part-time support.
Employer Identification Number: 591885997

735
Kohl (Sidney) Foundation, Inc. ⊭
304 Royal Poinciana Plaza
Palm Beach 33480

Incorporated in 1972 in Wisconsin.
Donor(s): Sidney Kohl.
Financial data: (yr. ended 6/30/83): Assets, $3,157,151 (M); expenditures, $228,980, including $216,243 for 33 grants (high: $155,937; low: $100).
Purpose and activities: Grants primarily for Jewish welfare funds; some support for other charitable and educational organizations.
Publications: 990-PF.
Officers: Sidney Kohl,* President; Mary Kohl,* Vice-President; Arnold Mullen, Secretary and Treasurer.
Directors:* Dorothy Kohl.
Employer Identification Number: 237206459

736

Landegger Charitable Foundation, Inc., The ¤
P.O. Box W
New Smyrna Beach 32069

Established in 1975.
Financial data: (yr. ended 10/31/83): Assets, $6,747,635 (M); expenditures, $262,961, including $231,750 for 14 grants (high: $100,000; low: $250).
Purpose and activities: Grants primarily for higher education and hospitals.
Publications: 990-PF.
Officers and Directors:* Lena Landegger,* President; George Landegger,* Vice-President; John F. Bolt, Secretary; Carl Landegger,* Treasurer.
Employer Identification Number: 510180544

737

Larsh Foundation Charitable Trust
1440 N.E. 79th St. Causeway, Ste. 100E
North Bay Village
Miami 33141

Established in 1980.
Financial data: (yr. ended 2/29/84): Assets, $4,373,989 (M); expenditures, $444,771, including $293,300 for 2 grants (high: $155,300; low: $138,000).
Purpose and activities: Primarily local giving, for Protestant religious groups and marine research.
Limitations: Giving primarily in FL.
Manager: Dana P. Brigham.
Employer Identification Number: 591946342

738

Law (Robert O.) Foundation ¤
2120 N.E. 21st St.
Fort Lauderdale 33305

Incorporated in 1958 in Florida.
Donor(s): Robert O. Law.†
Financial data: (yr. ended 12/31/83): Assets, $2,342,906 (M); expenditures, $202,032, including $103,056 for 29 grants (high: $11,000; low: $100).
Purpose and activities: Broad purposes; giving locally, primarily for youth agencies, health agencies, and hospitals; some support for education.
Limitations: Giving limited to Broward County, FL.
Application information:
    Write: William A. Thacher, Vice-President
Officers: Robert O. Law III,* President; William A. Thacher, Vice-President; William F. Leonard,* Secretary-Treasurer.
Trustees:* Henry E. Kinney, Mary Jane Law, Mary K. Law.
Employer Identification Number: 590914810

739

Leidesdorf Foundation, Inc.
203 South Lake Trail
Palm Beach 33480

Incorporated in 1949 in New York.
Donor(s): Samuel D. Leidesdorf.†
Financial data: (yr. ended 12/31/82): Assets, $988,839 (M); expenditures, $198,073, including $173,325 for 62 grants (high: $50,000; low: $100).
Purpose and activities: Broad purposes; grants primarily in Palm Beach, Florida and New York City for hospitals, health and cancer research, higher education, schools, cultural programs, and social services, particularly Jewish-affiliated agencies and temple support.
Limitations: Giving primarily in Palm Beach, FL, and in New York City, NY.
Application information:
    Write: Arthur D. Leidesdorf, Chairman
Officers: Arthur D. Leidesdorf, Chairman; Tova D. Leidesdorf, Vice-President, Secretary, and Treasurer; Arnold J. Hoffman, Vice-President.
Employer Identification Number: 136075584

740

Leu (Harry P.) Foundation
P.O. Box 2513
Orlando 32802   (305) 843-1251

Established in 1953 in Florida.
Donor(s): Harry P. Leu.†
Financial data: (yr. ended 10/31/83): Assets, $1,727,182 (M); expenditures, $187,490, including $180,000 for 50 grants (high: $50,000; low: $500).
Purpose and activities: Primarily local giving, with emphasis on youth agencies and education.
Limitations: Giving primarily in FL. No grants to individuals, or for scholarships and fellowships, or matching gifts; no loans.
Application information:
    Initial approach: Letter
    Deadline(s): September 15
    Board meeting date(s): October
    Write: Joseph P. Stine, Trustee
Trustees: Mary Jane Leu, Jo Stine, Joseph P. Stine.
Employer Identification Number: 596144721

741

Lewis (Frank J.) Foundation ▼ ¤
P.O. Box 9726
Riviera Beach 33404

Incorporated in 1927 in Illinois.
Donor(s): Frank J. Lewis.†
Financial data: (yr. ended 12/31/83): Assets, $13,341,124 (M); expenditures, $1,100,504, including $1,004,000 for 94 grants (high: $100,000; low: $100; average: $1,000-$15,000).
Purpose and activities: Charitable and educational purposes; to foster, preserve, and extend the Roman Catholic faith; grants largely for Roman Catholic educational institutions, churches, religious orders and church-sponsored programs, and hospitals.

Limitations: No grants to individuals or for endowment funds.
Application information:
    Initial approach: Proposal
    Copies of proposal: 1
    Board meeting date(s): February, May, August, and November
Officers and Trustees: Edward D. Lewis, President; Philip D. Lewis, Vice-President; Victor Hedberg, Treasurer.
Employer Identification Number: 362441931

742

Link Foundation, The
Route 1
Box 195
Fort Pierce 33450

Trust established in 1953 in New York.
Donor(s): Edwin A. Link,† Mrs. Edwin A. Link, Link Division, Singer Co.
Financial data: (yr. ended 6/30/84): Assets, $2,773,498 (M); gifts received, $2,462; expenditures, $215,235, including $181,935 for 20 grants (high: $30,000; low: $500).
Purpose and activities: Sponsors research and development of all facets of aviation, space technology, and oceanography, and supports development of energy resources and conservation. Grants committed through 1986.
Limitations: No grants to individuals.
Publications: Program policy statement, application guidelines.
Application information: Application form required.
    Initial approach: Letter
    Copies of proposal: 1
    Deadline(s): November 1
    Board meeting date(s): June and January
    Write: Marilyn C. Link, Secretary-Treasurer
Officers and Trustees: Lloyd L. Kelly, Chairman; Marilyn C. Link, Secretary-Treasurer; Richard W. Couper, Stuart McCarty, William F. Schmied.
Technical Assistance Board: Ralph E. Flexman, Chairman; Francis E. Drake, Jr., William M. Link, Frederick Seitz, Robert L. Sproull.
Number of staff: 1 part-time support.
Employer Identification Number: 536011109

743

Lowe (The Joe and Emily) Foundation, Inc. ▼
249 Royal Palm Way
Palm Beach 33480   (305) 655-7001

Incorporated in 1949 in New York.
Donor(s): Joe Lowe,† Emily Lowe.†
Financial data: (yr. ended 12/31/83): Assets, $13,265,854 (M); expenditures, $1,220,841, including $1,058,850 for 320 grants (high: $175,000; low: $100; average: $250-$10,000).
Purpose and activities: Broad purposes; giving primarily in the New York metropolitan area and in Florida, with emphasis on Jewish welfare funds, the arts, a museum, higher education including medical education, hospitals, medical research, aid to the handicapped, underprivileged children's organizations, and women's projects.

Types of support awarded: General purposes.
Limitations: Giving primarily in the New York, NY, metropolitan area including NJ, and in FL. No grants to individuals.
Application information:
Initial approach: Letter or brief proposal
Copies of proposal: 1
Deadline(s): None
Board meeting date(s): February and May or June
Final notification: 1 to 3 months
Officers and Trustees: Helen G. Hauben, President; David Fogelson, Vice-President and Secretary; Bernard Stern, Vice-President and Treasurer.
Number of staff: 1 full-time professional.
Employer Identification Number: 136121361

744
Lynn (E. M.) Foundation ⌷
2501 Military Trail
Boca Raton 33431

Established in 1977.
Donor(s): E.M. Lynn, Mrs. E.M. Lynn.
Financial data: (yr. ended 10/31/83): Assets, $6,379,685 (M); gifts received, $5,500,000; expenditures, $262,570, including $253,013 for 60 grants (high: $100,000; low: $25).
Purpose and activities: Primarily local giving for higher education, Protestant church support, and community development.
Types of support awarded: General purposes.
Limitations: Giving primarily in FL.
Trustees: E.M. Lynn.
Employer Identification Number: 591788859

745
Markey (Lucille P.) Charitable Trust
Southeast Financial Center, Suite 4300
Miami 33131-2379   (305) 371-3841

Established in 1983 in Florida; set up to distribute entire estate of donor by 1997.
Donor(s): Lucille P. Markey.†
Financial data: (yr. ended 6/30/84): Assets, $17,372,053 (M); gifts received, $23,027,648; expenditures, $6,314,575, including $5,600,000 for 3 grants (high: $5,000,000; low: $250,000).
Purpose and activities: Initial year of operation 83/84; established solely for the purpose of supporting and encouraging basic medical research.
Types of support awarded: Fellowships, research.
Limitations: No grants to individuals.
Publications: Application guidelines, informational brochure.
Application information:
Initial approach: 2 to 3 page outline of proposal
Board meeting date(s): Quarterly
Trustees: Louis J. Hector, Chairman; William P. Sutter, President; Margaret Glass, Laurette Heraty.
Staff: John H. Dickason, Administrator; Robert J. Glaser, M.D., Director for Medical Science.
Employer Identification Number: 592276359

746
McIntosh Foundation, The ▼
215 Fifth St.
West Palm Beach 33401   (305) 832-8845

Incorporated in 1949 in New York.
Donor(s): Josephine H. McIntosh.†
Financial data: (yr. ended 12/31/82): Assets, $11,080,417 (M); expenditures, $672,062, including $476,500 for 15 grants (high: $224,000; low: $1,000; average: $1,000-$50,000).
Purpose and activities: Broad purposes; grants limited mainly to the support of lawsuits, primarily environmental, brought by public interest law groups. Some giving to education.
Types of support awarded: General purposes.
Limitations: No grants to individuals, or for building or endowment funds.
Publications: Program policy statement, application guidelines.
Application information:
Initial approach: Letter or full proposal
Copies of proposal: 1
Deadline(s): None
Board meeting date(s): Bimonthly
Final notification: 60 to 90 days
Write: Michael A. McIntosh, President
Officers and Directors: Michael A. McIntosh, President; Peter H. McIntosh, Vice-President and Treasurer; Joan H. McIntosh, Winsome D. McIntosh, Vice-Presidents; Frederick A. Terry, Jr., Secretary.
Number of staff: 1 full-time professional; 1 full-time support; 1 part-time support.
Employer Identification Number: 136096459

747
McMannis (William J.) and A. Haskell McMannis Educational Fund
4055 Central Ave.
St. Petersburg 33713   (813) 321-2452

Established in 1974.
Donor(s): Haskell McMannis.†
Financial data: (yr. ended 8/31/84): Assets, $1,792,337 (M); expenditures, $140,322, including $107,208 for grants.
Purpose and activities: Giving for higher education scholarship funds only; grants paid directly to institutions for the benefit of students (U.S. citizens only) who "are enrolled and in good standing".
Types of support awarded: Scholarship funds.
Application information: Application form required.
Copies of proposal: 4
Deadline(s): 120 days prior to commencement of the school term for which aid is requested
Write: Fred B. Sieber, Executive Director
Officer: Fred B. Sieber, Executive Director.
Employer Identification Number: 256164183

748
Meyer (The Baron de Hirsch) Foundation ⌷
407 Lincoln Rd.
Miami Beach 33139   (305) 538-2531

Incorporated in 1940 in Florida.

Donor(s): Baron de Hirsch Meyer.†
Financial data: (yr. ended 12/31/82): Assets, $3,306,772 (M); expenditures, $1,277,402, including $1,230,141 for 25 grants (high: $845,384; low: $30).
Purpose and activities: Primarily local giving, support for religious welfare, with emphasis on Jewish welfare funds, hospitals, medical agencies, child welfare, and the performing arts.
Types of support awarded: Building funds.
Limitations: Giving primarily in FL. No grants to individuals.
Application information:
Initial approach: Proposal or letter
Copies of proposal: 1
Board meeting date(s): February
Officers and Directors: Polly de Hirsch Meyer, President and Treasurer; Marie Williams, Vice-President; Leo Rose, Jr., Secretary.
Employer Identification Number: 596129646

749
Morgan (Louie R. and Gertrude) Foundation ⌷
P.O. Box 550
Arcadia 33821

Established in 1960.
Donor(s): Louie R. Morgan,† Mildred Morgan,† Gertrude Morgan, Eleanor Morgan.
Financial data: (yr. ended 12/31/82): Assets, $2,602,203 (M); expenditures, $136,512, including $110,100 for 5 grants (high: $65,000; low: $100).
Purpose and activities: Grants primarily for local Protestant churches and a hospital.
Limitations: Giving primarily in FL.
Officers: Robert Summerall, Jr.,* Vice-President and Treasurer; Jane Weller, Secretary.
Directors:* Lewis W. Smith.
Employer Identification Number: 596142359

750
Morris (The Allen) Foundation ⌷
One Biscayne Tower, Suite 2600
Miami 33131   (305) 358-1000

Established in 1962 in Florida.
Donor(s): Realty Leasing Corporation of Georgia, and others.
Financial data: (yr. ended 2/29/84): Assets, $1,128,966 (M); gifts received, $120,138; expenditures, $146,585, including $107,858 for 77 grants (high: $10,000; low: $10).
Purpose and activities: Giving primarily for Prostestant religious groups; support also for education, and social services in the Miami area.
Application information:
Initial approach: Proposal
Deadline(s): None
Officers: W. Allen Morris,* President; G. Emerson Travis, Secretary; Ida A. Morris,* Treasurer; Victor C. Glavach, Executive Director.
Directors:* L. Allen Morris, Chairman; Ida M. Bell, James F. Bell, Jr., Diane Y. Morris, Gary L. Rupp, Kathryn Morris Rupp.
Employer Identification Number: 596152420

751
Mote Scientific Foundation, Inc. ¤
580 Spinnaker Ln.
Long Boat Key 33548

Incorporated in 1950 in New York.
Donor(s): William R. Mote, T.R. Bartels, Theodore R. Bartels, and others.
Financial data: (yr. ended 11/30/83): Assets, $1,421,273 (M); gifts received, $58,456; expenditures, $120,454, including $118,100 for 9 grants (high: $103,000; low: $100).
Purpose and activities: Giving mainly for oceanography; support primarily for the Mote Marine Laboratory.
Limitations: Giving primarily in FL.
Manager: William R. Mote.
Employer Identification Number: 136117615

752
Nuveen Benevolent Trust ¤
c/o Walter R. Sundling, Principal Mgr.
7204 13th Ave. West
Bradenton 33529   (813) 794-0432

Trust established in 1936 in Illinois.
Donor(s): John Nuveen V,† and others.
Financial data: (yr. ended 12/31/83): Assets, $1,037,803 (M); expenditures, $62,538, including $46,550 for 68 grants (high: $5,000; low: $200).
Purpose and activities: General giving, with emphasis on higher education.
Trustees: Grace B. Nuveen, Anne Nuveen Reynolds, Walter R. Sundling.
Employer Identification Number: 366069509

753
Phillips (A. P.) Foundation, Inc. ¤
P.O. Box 3628
Orlando 32802

Established in 1965.
Financial data: (yr. ended 6/30/83): Assets, $1,825,530 (M); expenditures, $151,444, including $128,800 for 19 grants (high: $38,500; low: $300).
Purpose and activities: Primarily local giving, with emphasis on youth agencies and child welfare, higher education, and hospitals.
Limitations: Giving primarily in FL.
Application information:
  Initial approach: Proposal
  Deadline(s): None
  Write: M.W. Wells, Jr., President
Officers: M.W. Wells, Jr., President; R.F. Tibbs, Vice-President; J.W. Jordan, Secretary; D.K. Wells, Director.
Employer Identification Number: 596165157

754
Phillips (The Dr. P.) Foundation
60 West Robinson St.
P.O. Box 3753
Orlando 32801   (305) 422-6105

Incorporated in 1953 in Florida.
Donor(s): Mrs. Della Phillips,† Howard Phillips, Dr. Phillips, Inc., and others.

Financial data: (yr. ended 5/31/83): Assets, $11,482,314 (M); gifts received, $294,475; expenditures, $304,151, including $192,712 for 50 grants (high: $41,110; low: $25).
Purpose and activities: Broad purposes; local giving, with emphasis on higher education, hospitals, cultural programs and community development.
Types of support awarded: Building funds, operating budgets, special projects, student aid.
Limitations: Giving limited to Orange County, FL. No grants to individuals (except for loans to residents of Orange County for study of medicine, engineering, or accounting) or for endowment funds.
Publications: Application guidelines.
Application information: Applications for grants not invited; application guidelines available for certain student loans only.
  Initial approach: Letter
  Board meeting date(s): June
Officers: H.E. Johnson, President; J.A. Hinson, Executive Vice-President; Ben Houston, Vice-President; D.L. Baumgardner, Secretary and Treasurer.
Employer Identification Number: 596135403

755
Phipps Florida Foundation
P.O. Box 1351
Tallahassee 32302   (904) 222-2717

Trust established in 1959 in Florida.
Financial data: (yr. ended 11/30/82): Assets, $1,080,000 (M); expenditures, $109,114, including $99,400 for 20 grants (high: $39,000; low: $100; average: $50-$50,000).
Purpose and activities: Primarily local giving, with emphasis on conservation and health.
Types of support awarded: Operating budgets, continuing support, annual campaigns, seed money, emergency funds, building funds, equipment, land acquisition, matching funds, research, publications.
Limitations: Giving primarily in FL. No grants to individuals, or for deficit financing, or scholarships and fellowships; no loans except on an emergency basis.
Application information:
  Initial approach: Letter
  Board meeting date(s): Monthly except in June, July, and August
  Final notification: 2 to 4 months
  Write: Benjamin K. Phipps, Secretary
Officer and Trustees: Benjamin K. Phipps, Secretary; Colin S. Phipps, John E. Phipps.
Number of staff: None.
Employer Identification Number: 596159046

756
Pinellas County Community Foundation
1253 Park St.
Clearwater 33516   (813) 443-3281

Community foundation established in 1969 in Florida by trust agreement.
Financial data: (yr. ended 12/31/84): Assets, $2,508,659 (M); gifts received, $16,545; expenditures, $224,664, including $222,393 for 33 grants (high: $2,500; low: $1,000).

Purpose and activities: Support for charitable activities in Pinellas County.
Limitations: Giving limited to Pinellas County, FL. No grants to individuals, or for endowment funds, research, scholarships and fellowships, or matching gifts; no loans.
Publications: Application guidelines, 990-PF, annual report.
Application information: Application form required.
  Initial approach: Full proposal
  Copies of proposal: 1
  Deadline(s): November 1
  Board meeting date(s): January
  Final notification: 3 months
  Write: Thomas R. Bruckman, Executive Director
Governors: Larry K. Meyer, Chairman; C. Curtis Hess, Vice-Chairman; Connie Marquardt, Secretary; J. Fred Campbell, Jr., Sandra M. Cassidy, Raymond H. Center, M.D., Glenn Kranzow, Stephen R. Miller, Edward R. Turville.
Trustee Banks: Barnett Banks Trust Co., First National Bank of Clearwater, First National Bank of Florida, Florida National Bank, Landmark Union Trust Bank of St. Petersburg, NCNB National Bank of Florida, Pioneer Federal, Rutland Bank, Southeast Banks Trust Co., Sun Bank-Suncoast.
Number of staff: 1 part-time professional.
Employer Identification Number: 237113194

757
Poynter Fund, The
490 First Ave. South
P.O. Box 1121
St. Petersburg 33731

Incorporated in 1953 in the District of Columbia.
Donor(s): Henrietta M. Poynter,† Nelson Poynter.†
Financial data: (yr. ended 11/30/83): Assets, $1,243,472 (M); gifts received, $1,000; expenditures, $104,282, including $68,500 for 8 grants (high: $25,000; low: $1,000) and $31,500 for 36 grants to individuals.
Purpose and activities: Scholarships and fellowships to train, assist, and inspire journalists of all media to improve the reporting and the objective interpretation of news of domestic governments; to link the academic study of political science with the practice of journalism and government. Grants also for educational and cultural projects, primarily in Florida.
Types of support awarded: Fellowships, student aid.
Application information:
  Write: Clifton D. Camp, Jr., Secretary
Officers: Eugene C. Patterson,* President; John B. Lake,* Vice-President; Clifton D. Camp, Jr.,* Secretary; John O'Hearn, Treasurer.
Trustees:* William C. Ballard, Marion K. Poynter, Robert M. Stiff.
Employer Identification Number: 596142547

758
Price (The John E. & Aliese) Foundation, Inc.
1279 Lavin Ln.
P.O. Box 4607
North Fort Myers 33903   (813) 656-0196

Incorporated in 1961 in Florida.
Donor(s): John E. Price, John E. Price, Jr., Mildred Price.
Financial data: (yr. ended 8/31/84): Assets, $3,767,369 (M); gifts received, $2,700; expenditures, $426,241, including $271,681 for 67 grants (high: $112,500; low: $25; average: $1,000-$5,000).
Purpose and activities: Grants primarily for local church support and religious associations, including missionary work; some support for youth agencies, health agencies, and aid to the handicapped.
Types of support awarded: Continuing support, annual campaigns, building funds, matching funds, scholarship funds, research.
Limitations: Giving primarily in FL.
Application information:
   Initial approach: Telephone
   Deadline(s): Submit proposal preferably in July; no set deadline
   Board meeting date(s): January and September
   Write: John E. Price, Sr., Chairman
Officers and Trustees: John E. Price, Sr., Chairman and Treasurer; T. Wainwright Miller, Jr., President; John E. Price, Jr., George F. Sanders, Vice-Presidents; Dennis G. Small, Secretary; Mavis S. Miller, Mildred Price.
Number of staff: 1 part-time support.
Employer Identification Number: 591056841

759
Rainforth Foundation ⌿
3001 Ponce de Leon Blvd.
Coral Gables 33134

Incorporated in 1949 in Florida.
Donor(s): Selden I. Rainforth, Edith Rainforth, Continental Equities, Inc.
Financial data: (yr. ended 12/31/83): Assets, $1,191,739 (M); gifts received, $52,500; expenditures, $84,833, including $33,100 for 7 grants (high: $20,000; low: $100).
Purpose and activities: Primarily local giving for Protestant religious organizations, particularly youth agencies.
Limitations: Giving primarily in FL.
Officers: Tom Maxey, President; Wirt Maxey, Secretary.
Employer Identification Number: 596140259

760
Rinker Companies Foundation, Inc. ⌿
1501 Belvedere Rd.
West Palm Beach 33406   (305) 833-5555

Incorporated in 1957 in Florida.
Donor(s): Rinker Materials Corporation.
Financial data: (yr. ended 3/27/83): Assets, $3,084,532 (M); gifts received, $706,096; expenditures, $370,410, including $260,288 for 14 grants (high: $200,000; low: $25) and $82,273 for 47 grants to individuals.
Purpose and activities: Grants primarily for higher education, including scholarships to individuals who are Florida residents with "business or construction industry related majors;" support also for Protestant churches.
Types of support awarded: Student aid.
Limitations: Giving primarily in FL.
Application information:
   Deadline(s): May and November
Officers: M.E. Rinker, Sr., President and Treasurer; R.A. Krause, Vice-President; M.E. Rinker, Jr., Secretary.
Trustees: W.R. Campbell, J.J. Rinker, K.H. Watson.
Employer Identification Number: 596139266

761
Ritter (R. A.) Foundation ⌿
c/o R.A. Ritter
P.O. Box 1468
Boca Raton 33429

Incorporated in 1957 in Delaware.
Donor(s): Rolland A. Ritter.
Financial data: (yr. ended 12/31/83): Assets, $664,035 (M); expenditures, $114,269, including $103,022 for 62 grants (high: $25,400; low: $15).
Purpose and activities: Broad purposes; general giving, primarily local and in Pennsylvania, with emphasis on higher education, hospitals, youth agencies, and animal care.
Limitations: Giving primarily in FL and PA.
Officers: R.A. Ritter, President; Madeline B. Morrison, Secretary.
Employer Identification Number: 236263338

762
River Branch Foundation ⌿
1514 Nira St.
Jacksonville 32207

Trust established in 1963 in New Jersey.
Donor(s): J. Seward Johnson 1951 and 1961 Charitable Trusts, The Atlantic Foundation.
Financial data: (yr. ended 12/31/83): Assets, $3,627,890 (M); expenditures, $177,999, including $142,000 for 14 grants (high: $25,000; low: $500).
Purpose and activities: Broad purposes; primarily local giving, with emphasis on youth agencies, education, the arts, and cultural programs.
Limitations: Giving primarily in FL. No grants to individuals.
Application information:
   Write: Walter L. Woolfe, Trustee
Directors: Jennifer Johnson Gregg, James Scott Hill.
Trustees: A.M. Foote, Jr., Nathan J. Travassos, Walter L. Woolfe.
Employer Identification Number: 226054887

763
Rosenberg (William J. & Tina) Foundation
2511 Ponce de Leon Blvd., Suite 320
Coral Gables 33134   (305) 444-6121

Application address: c/o Financial Planning and Trust Division, Southeast Bank, 100 South Biscayne Blvd., Miami, FL 33101; Tel.: (305) 577-3744

Established in 1970 in Florida.
Donor(s): Tina Rosenberg.†
Financial data: (yr. ended 4/30/83): Assets, $2,220,154 (M); gifts received, $9,008; expenditures, $140,953, including $118,500 for 9 grants (high: $50,000; low: $1,500).
Purpose and activities: Primarily local giving, with emphasis on social programs, youth agencies, and education.
Limitations: Giving primarily in Miami, FL. No grants to individuals.
Publications: Application guidelines.
Application information:
   Initial approach: Full proposal
   Copies of proposal: 2
   Board meeting date(s): Monthly
   Write: Arne Themmen
Trustees: Jack G. Admire, Southeast Bank (Arne R. Themmen, Vice-President).
Employer Identification Number: 237088390

764
Sample (Adrian M.) Trust No. 2
Sun Bank of St. Lucie County
P.O. Box 8
Fort Pierce 33454   (305) 461-6300
Grant application office: 5311 Burningtree Dr., Orlando, FL 32811; Tel.: (305) 423-0314

Trust established in 1972 in Florida.
Financial data: (yr. ended 12/31/84): Assets, $1,122,613 (M); expenditures, $115,726, including $95,184 for 43 grants to individuals.
Purpose and activities: Grants for scholarship aid to Protestant students who are residents of St. Lucie or Okeechobee counties, Florida.
Types of support awarded: Student aid.
Limitations: Giving limited to residents of St. Lucie or Okeechobee counties, FL.
Publications: Program policy statement, application guidelines.
Application information: Application forms available only through churches in St. Lucie or Okeechobee counties. Application form required.
   Initial approach: Letter
   Copies of proposal: 2
   Deadline(s): April 15
   Board meeting date(s): May, and as required
   Write: Charles W. Sample
Trustees: Charles W. Sample, Sun Bank of St. Lucie County.
Employer Identification Number: 596490788

765
Saunders Foundation
c/o First National Bank of Florida, Trust Dept.
P.O. Box 1810
Tampa 33601   (813) 224-1535

Established in 1970 in Florida.
Donor(s): William N. Saunders,† Ruby Lee Saunders.†

Financial data: (yr. ended 12/31/84): Assets, $6,782,327 (M); expenditures, $464,452, including $364,600 for 24 grants (high: $200,000; low: $500; average: $5,000-$50,000).
Purpose and activities: Primarily local giving, with emphasis on higher education and youth agencies.
Types of support awarded: Scholarship funds, matching funds.
Limitations: Giving primarily in west FL; no grants outside of U.S. No support for travel projects or to organizations which promote sports or athletic competition. No grants for fellowships, or operating funds.
Publications: Application guidelines.
Application information: Application form required.
  Copies of proposal: 2
  Board meeting date(s): 1st Wednesday of each month
  Write: James M. Kelly, Vice-President
Officers and Directors: Herbert G. McKay, President; James M. Kelly, Vice-President and Treasurer; Michael G. Emmanuel, Secretary; Solon F. O'Neal, Jr.
Number of staff: None.
Employer Identification Number: 596152326

766
Selby (William G.) and Marie Selby Foundation ▼
Southeast Bank
P.O. Box 267
Sarasota 33578   (813) 953-8272

Trust established in 1955 in Florida.
Donor(s): William G. Selby,† Marie M. Selby.†
Financial data: (yr. ended 5/31/84): Assets, $24,646,109 (M); expenditures, $1,873,603, including $1,586,962 for 58 grants (high: $100,000; low: $2,000; average: $10,000-$50,000).
Purpose and activities: Broad purposes; emphasis on scholarships and capital grants for giving directly to Florida colleges and universities; local giving also for the aged, hospitals, social agencies, youth agencies, and cultural programs.
Types of support awarded: Building funds, equipment, land acquisition, matching funds, scholarship funds.
Limitations: Giving limited to FL, with emphasis on the Sarasota area. No grants to individuals, or for general support, continuing support, annual campaigns, deficit financing, seed money, emergency funds, operating budgets, endowment funds, special projects, research, publications, or conferences; no loans.
Publications: Informational brochure, program policy statement, application guidelines.
Application information: Application form required.
  Initial approach: Letter
  Copies of proposal: 3
  Deadline(s): Submit proposal preferably in July and December; deadlines August 1 and February 1
  Board meeting date(s): June, September, December, and March
  Final notification: 2 to 6 months
  Write: Robert E. Perkins, Executive Director

Trustee: Southeast Banks Trust Co.
Administrative Committee: James W. Brown, Chairman; Robert E. Perkins, Executive Director; Carl H. Bruns, Anthony DeDeyn, Jerome A. Jannopoulo, Wendel Kent, Charles E. Stottlemyer.
Number of staff: 1 full-time professional; 1 part-time support.
Employer Identification Number: 596121242

767
Shapiro (Carl and Ruth) Foundation ⌗
100 Sunrise Ave., Apartment 501
Palm Beach 33480

Established originally in Massachusetts as Carl Shapiro Foundation.
Financial data: (yr. ended 12/31/83): Assets, $1,525,049 (M); expenditures, $370,989, including $361,715 for 46 grants (high: $125,250; low: $25).
Purpose and activities: Grants primarily for Jewish welfare funds, higher education and hospitals.
Officers: Carl Shapiro, President; Ruth Shapiro, Secretary.
Employer Identification Number: 046135027

768
Sharonsteel Foundation ⌗
6917 Collins Ave.
Miami Beach 33141

Trust established in 1953 in Pennsylvania.
Donor(s): Sharon Steel Corporation.
Financial data: (yr. ended 12/31/82): Assets, $4,419,526 (M); expenditures, $703,893, including $689,840 for 125 grants (high: $101,000; low: $100).
Purpose and activities: Broad purposes; general giving, with emphasis on higher education, Jewish welfare, music, community funds, hospitals, medical research, civic affairs and youth activities.
Trustees: Victor Posner, Chairman; Jack Coppersmith, H.G. Evans, G. McCracken, S. Posner.
Employer Identification Number: 256063133

769
Soref (Samuel M.) Charitable Trust ⌗
4280 North Ocean Blvd., Plaza South, Apt. 17-J
Fort Lauderdale 33308

Trust established in 1969 in Florida.
Donor(s): Samuel M. Soref.
Financial data: (yr. ended 12/31/83): Assets, $5,712,782 (M); gifts received, $108,600; expenditures, $321,769, including $311,705 for 22 grants (high: $70,625; low: $100).
Purpose and activities: Primarily local giving, with emphasis on Jewish welfare funds, temple support, and social agencies; some support also for organizations in Israel.
Limitations: Giving primarily in FL.
Officers: Samuel M. Soref, President and Treasurer; Helene K. Soref, Vice-President; Marvin E. Klitsner, Secretary.
Employer Identification Number: 396107640

770
Southeast Banking Corporation Foundation
One Southeast Financial Center, 22nd Fl.
Miami 33131   (305) 375-7295

Established in 1980.
Donor(s): Southeast Banking Corporation, and its affiliates.
Financial data: (yr. ended 12/31/84): Assets, $520,000 (M); gifts received, $950,000; expenditures, $914,000, including $904,000 for 177 grants (high: $265,000; low: $150; average: $2,500).
Purpose and activities: Broad purposes; primarily statewide giving, with emphasis on community funds, cultural programs, and education.
Types of support awarded: Operating budgets, annual campaigns, seed money, publications, conferences and seminars, scholarship funds, consulting services, technical assistance.
Limitations: Giving primarily in FL. No grants to individuals.
Publications: Annual report, program policy statement, application guidelines.
Application information:
  Initial approach: Telephone, letter, or full proposal
  Copies of proposal: 3
  Deadline(s): None
  Board meeting date(s): Quarterly and as required
  Final notification: 6 to 8 weeks
  Write: Robin Reiter, Executive Director
Officer: Robin Reiter, Executive Director.
Trustees: Rick Atwill, David Aucamp, Bill Klich, Rip DuPont, Joe Thompson, Robert White.
Number of staff: 1 full-time professional; 1 full-time support.
Employer Identification Number: 591172753

771
Southwest Florida Community Foundation, Inc., The
Drawer LL
Fort Myers 33902   (813) 936-1645
Additional telephone number: (813) 232-3315

Community foundation established in 1976 in Florida.
Donor(s): Lorraine Blowstine,† Isabel Kirkpatrick,† Leonard Santini.†
Financial data: (yr. ended 9/30/84): Assets, $2,590,203 (M); gifts received, $6,802; expenditures, $170,191, including $121,968 for 9 grants (high: $25,000; low: $3,857; average: $10,000-$20,000).
Purpose and activities: Primarily local giving for charitable purposes to the citizens of southwest Florida.
Types of support awarded: Seed money, building funds, equipment, matching funds, student aid.
Limitations: Giving primarily in southwest FL. No grants for operating budgets, continuing support, annual campaigns, emergency funds, deficit financing, land acquisition, endowment funds, research, publications, conferences and seminars, or special programs; no loans.

Publications: Multi-year report.
Application information: Application form required.
  Initial approach: Telephone, letter, or proposal
  Copies of proposal: 22
  Deadline(s): February 1 and May 1
  Board meeting date(s): March, June, September, and December
  Final notification: Several days after board meeting
  Write: Christine M. Roberts, Executive Director
Officers and Trustees:* J. Tom Smoot, Jr.,* Chairman and President; Jerry Hussey, Vice-President; Susan Bennett, Secretary-Treasurer; and 18 additional trustees.
Number of staff: 1 part-time professional.
Employer Identification Number: 596580974

772
Staley (Thomas F.) Foundation
75 N.E. Sixth Ave., Suite 208
Delray Beach 33444   (305) 276-2456

Trust established in 1943 in Michigan.
Donor(s): Thomas F. Staley,† Shirley H. Staley.
Financial data: (yr. ended 12/31/84): Assets, $3,480,590 (M); gifts received, $130,000; expenditures, $200,053, including $140,475 for 200 grants (high: $1,100).
Purpose and activities: Support only for Christian scholar lectureship programs on college campuses.
Publications: Program policy statement.
Application information:
  Initial approach: Letter
  Copies of proposal: 1
  Deadline(s): Submit proposal preferably in July or August
  Board meeting date(s): June
  Write: Ms. Teddi Cavanaugh, Secretary
Officer: Teddi Cavanaugh, Secretary.
Trustees: John D. Baker, Jr., Joseph Bishop, Janet S. Howard, Robert G. Howard, Rev. Peter C. Moore, Catherine H. Staley, Shirley H. Staley, Thomas F. Staley, Jr.
Number of staff: 1 full-time professional.
Employer Identification Number: 136071888

773
Stark (Donald A. and Jane C.) Charitable Trust ⌗
c/o B. Wade White, Trustee
5036 Willow Leaf Way
Sarasota 33583

Trust established in 1957 in Ohio.
Financial data: (yr. ended 12/31/83): Assets, $1,175,742 (M); expenditures, $103,717, including $62,000 for 6 grants (high: $20,000; low: $200) and $32,000 for 7 grants to individuals.
Purpose and activities: Grants primarily for student scholarships; support also for botanical gardens and youth organizations.
Types of support awarded: Student aid.
Trustees: Charles E. Manning, Jane C. Stark, B. Wade White.
Employer Identification Number: 346522476

774
Stevens (Ida M.) Foundation, Inc. ⌗
P.O. Box 41222
Jacksonville 32203

Established in 1967.
Donor(s): Virgil A. Stevens.†
Financial data: (yr. ended 12/31/83): Assets, $6,780,546 (M); expenditures, $653,855, including $224,941 for 2 grants (high: $122,666; low: $102,275).
Purpose and activities: A private operating foundation; local giving to a nursing association and a university of nursing.
Limitations: Giving limited to Jacksonville, FL.
Trustees: C.L. Garnett Ashby, David Lemmel, Milne, Hodge & Milne.
Employer Identification Number: 591746148

775
Stickelber Charitable Foundation ⌗
P.O. Box 516
Destin 32541

Incorporated in 1969 in Missouri.
Financial data: (yr. ended 12/31/83): Assets, $1,987,336 (M); expenditures, $142,041, including $107,037 for 28 grants (high: $20,000; low: $300).
Purpose and activities: Grants primarily for social services, hospitals, higher education, church support, and religious associations.
Types of support awarded: General purposes, building funds, equipment, matching funds, employee matching gifts.
Limitations: Giving primarily in Destin, FL, and Mobile and Baldwin counties, AL. No grants to individuals, or for endowment funds, research, scholarships, or fellowships; no loans.
Application information:
  Initial approach: Letter, proposal, or telephone
  Copies of proposal: 1
  Deadline(s): None
  Board meeting date(s): April, July, November, and December
  Write: Merlin C. Stickelber, President
Officers: Merlin C. Stickelber, President; Nelson M. Blohm, Vice-President; John B. Johnson, Secretary-Treasurer.
Trustees: F.H. Dietz, Merlin C. Stickelber, Jr.
Number of staff: 5.
Employer Identification Number: 237062356

776
Storer (The George B.) Foundation, Inc. ⌗
12000 Biscayne Blvd.
P.O. Box 61-8000
Miami 33161-8000   (305) 866-0211

Incorporated in 1955 in Florida.
Financial data: (yr. ended 12/31/83): Assets, $24,434,468 (M); gifts received, $391,584; expenditures, $974,181, including $840,250 for 57 grants (high: $200,000; low: $1,000).
Purpose and activities: Broad purposes; grants for higher education, conservation, the handicapped, hospitals, and a community fund.
Types of support awarded: Research, general purposes, building funds, matching funds.

Limitations: No grants for scholarships or fellowships; no loans.
Application information:
  Initial approach: Letter
  Copies of proposal: 1
  Deadline(s): November 30
  Board meeting date(s): December
  Write: Peter Storer, President
Officers and Directors: Peter Storer, President; William Michaels, Vice-President; James P. Storer, Secretary.
Employer Identification Number: 596136392

777
Stuart (The Edward C.) Foundation Incorporated
P.O. Box 250
Bartow 33830   (813) 533-4196

Incorporated in 1957 in Florida.
Donor(s): The W.H. Stuart family.
Financial data: (yr. ended 5/31/83): Assets, $4,181,762 (M); expenditures, $392,071, including $361,166 for 9 grants (high: $148,780; low: $3,500).
Purpose and activities: Broad purposes; giving primarily to a Protestant religious organization and scholarship funds.
Types of support awarded: General purposes, continuing support, seed money, scholarship funds, matching funds.
Limitations: No grants to individuals, or for building or endowment funds, or special projects.
Publications: Annual report, application guidelines.
Application information: Application form required.
  Initial approach: Letter
  Copies of proposal: 1
  Deadline(s): September 1 and March 1
  Board meeting date(s): Monthly, with decisions on grants in late May and November
  Write: Mrs. Margrette M. Stuart, President
Officers and Directors: Margrette M. Stuart, President; William H. Stuart, Jr., Vice-President; C.A. Boswell, Secretary-Treasurer; Fleetwood T. Lane, Nelle Kennedy Stuart Lane, Nancy S. Stuart, William H. Stuart.
Employer Identification Number: 596142151

778
Sudakoff (The Harry) Foundation, Inc. ⌗
192 North Washington Dr.
Sarasota 33577

Incorporated in 1956 in New York.
Donor(s): The Harry and Ruth Sudakoff Trust, Ruth Sudakoff.†
Financial data: (yr. ended 12/31/82): Assets, $1,088,754 (M); gifts received, $34,062; expenditures, $154,087, including $150,634 for 23 grants (high: $25,000; low: $7).

Purpose and activities: Giving primarily for Jewish welfare funds and other Jewish organizatons and for local cultural and social agencies, particularly a united fund and youth organizations.

Officer: Harry Sudakoff, President and Treasurer.

Employer Identification Number: 116023593

779

Swensrud (S. A.) Charitable Trust ☒

1255 Gulf Shore Blvd., North
Naples 33940   (813) 261-7025

Established in 1955.

Financial data: (yr. ended 12/31/83): Assets, $2,182,521 (M); gifts received, $176,495; expenditures, $146,442, including $146,005 for 53 grants (high: $100,205; low: $24).

Purpose and activities: Giving primarily for population control and public policy organizations.

Limitations: No grants to individuals.

Application information:
Deadline(s): None
Write: Sidney A. Swensrud, Trustee

Trustees: Sidney A. Swensrud, Stephen B. Swensrud.

Employer Identification Number: 256050238

780

Swisher (Carl S.) Foundation, Inc.

P.O. Box 14790
Jacksonville 32238-1790   (904) 389-8320

Incorporated in 1949 in Florida.

Donor(s): Carl S. Swisher.†

Financial data: (yr. ended 12/31/84): Assets, $5,832,574 (M); expenditures, $446,492, including $426,825 for 104 grants (high: $50,000; low: $500).

Purpose and activities: Broad purposes; giving almost entirely in the Jacksonville area, with emphasis on higher education; grants also for youth agencies, hospitals, and social services. Scholarship program for individuals discontinued.

Types of support awarded: General purposes.

Limitations: Giving primarily in the Jacksonville, FL, area. No grants to individuals; no loans.

Application information:
Initial approach: Proposal
Copies of proposal: 1
Board meeting date(s): Usually quarterly
Write: E.A. Middlebrooks, Jr., Secretary

Officers and Trustees: L.D. Hupp, President; George S. Coulter, Harold W. Smith, Vice-Presidents; E.A. Middlebrooks, Jr., Secretary and Treasurer; Kenneth G. Anderson.

Number of staff: 1 part-time professional.

Employer Identification Number: 590998262

781

Sylvester (Harcourt M.) Charitable Fund, Inc. ☒

c/o Trust Company of Florida
P.O. Box 2951
Orlando 32802

Established in 1980 in Florida.

Donor(s): Harcourt M. Sylvester,† Virginia W. Sylvester.

Financial data: (yr. ended 7/31/83): Assets, $3,845,107 (M); gifts received, $520,713; expenditures, $85,975, including $50,000 for 1 grant.

Purpose and activities: Giving primarily to a local college; support also for local social services.

Limitations: Giving primarily in Boca Raton, FL.

Application information:
Initial approach: Proposal
Deadline(s): None
Write: Mena Rogers

Officers and Directors: Harcourt M. Sylvester, Jr., President; Virginia W. Sylvester, Vice-President; Donald E. Brown, Richard Kelly.

Employer Identification Number: 592018824

782

Tampa Cable Television Trust ☒

P.O. Box 320265
Tampa 33679   (813) 875-9461

Established in 1982.

Donor(s): Tampa Cable Television.

Financial data: (yr. ended 12/31/83): Assets, $507,245 (M); gifts received, $250,000; expenditures, $285,171, including $258,591 for 17 grants (high: $50,000; low: $4,000).

Purpose and activities: Local giving for higher education, youth and welfare agencies, and cultural programs.

Limitations: Giving limited to the Tampa, FL, community.

Application information:
Deadline(s): None
Write: Homer Tillery, Chairman

Trustees: Homer Tillery, Chairman; T. Terrell Sessums, Secretary; Laura Blain, Nick Capitano, Robert L. Cromwell, Joseph Garcia, Malinda E. Gray, Robert D. Heide, Rev. Laurence Higgins, Richard S. Hodes, J. Leonard Levy, A. Leon Lowry, Robert Morrison, J. Benton Stewart, Gilbert E. Turner, Donald L. Whittemore, Jr., Sandra H. Wilson.

Employer Identification Number: 592273947

783

Taylor (Jack) Foundation, Inc.

941 Northeast 79th St.
Miami 33138

Established in 1968.

Donor(s): Taylor Development Corp., Jack Taylor, and other members of the Taylor family.

Financial data: (yr. ended 12/31/84): Assets, $6,962,570 (M); gifts received, $406,000; expenditures, $245,967, including $224,129 for 15 grants (high: $85,829; low: $150).

Purpose and activities: Grants primarily for hospitals and health agencies, higher education, and Jewish welfare funds and temple support.

Officers: Jack Taylor,* President; Elly Taylor,* Vice-President and Treasurer.

Directors:* Norman A. Arkin, Victor D. Denbrow, Saul S. Silverman, Mitchell Taylor, Harold Zinn.

Employer Identification Number: 596205187

784

Thomas (Dorothy) Foundation, Inc. ☒

P.O. Box 3436
Tampa 33601

Incorporated in 1960 in Florida.

Donor(s): Wayne Thomas, Robert Thomas, Port Sutton, Inc.

Financial data: (yr. ended 12/31/83): Assets, $2,185,509 (M); expenditures, $50,457, including $42,890 for 8 grants (high: $10,000; low: $1,950).

Purpose and activities: Charitable purposes; primarily local giving for youth, education and health, including church-sponsored organizations.

Limitations: Giving primarily in FL.

Officers and Trustees: Wayne Thomas, Chairman; Michael Thomas, Vice-Chairman; Henry Toland, Secretary and Treasurer.

Employer Identification Number: 596059765

785

Thoresen Foundation, The

9491 Merrimoor Blvd.
Seminole 33543

Trust established in 1952 in Illinois.

Donor(s): William E. Thoresen, Catherine E. Thoresen.

Financial data: (yr. ended 2/28/83): Assets, $2,221,558 (M); gifts received, $9,000; expenditures, $137,577, including $133,750 for 40 grants (high: $35,000; low: $500).

Purpose and activities: Broad purposes; giving primarily to organizations in Florida and Illinois, with emphasis on higher education; grants also for hospitals, social agencies, museums, and cultural programs.

Limitations: Giving primarily in FL and IL. No grants to individuals, or for scholarships.

Application information:
Initial approach: Letter
Board meeting date(s): As required
Write: George V. Berger, Trustee

Trustees: George V. Berger, Katherine Culver, Catherine E. Thoresen, William E. Thoresen.

Employer Identification Number: 366102493

786

Toor (Harold & Harriet) Foundation ☒

100 Sunrise Ave.
Palm Beach 33480

Established in 1947.

Donor(s): Harold O. Toor, Harriet R. Toor.†

Financial data: (yr. ended 12/31/83): Assets, $334,417 (M); gifts received, $81,365; expenditures, $130,993, including $130,325 for 157 grants (high: $51,000; low: $100).

Purpose and activities: Giving to Jewish welfare funds, medical research, and higher eduction.

Officers and Directors: Harold O. Toor, President; Joanne T. Cummings, Vice-President.

Employer Identification Number: 136111662

787
United States Sugar Corporation Charitable Trust
P.O. Drawer 1207
Clewiston 33440

Trust established in 1952 in Florida.
Donor(s): United States Sugar Corporation.
Financial data: (yr. ended 10/31/83): Assets, $2,796,856 (M); gifts received, $243,260; expenditures, $495,657, including $471,843 for 35 grants (high: $128,075; low: $150).
Purpose and activities: Primarily local giving with emphasis on higher education and hospitals.
Limitations: Giving primarily in FL. No grants to individuals, or for scholarships and fellowships; no loans.
Application information:
Initial approach: Full proposal
Board meeting date(s): March, June, September, and December
Trustees: Fleming A. Barbour, M.D., Atwood Dunwody, C.S. Harding Mott.
Employer Identification Number: 596142825

788
Walter (Jim) Corporation Foundation ¤
1500 North Dale Mabry Hwy.
P.O. Box 22601
Tampa 33622

Established in 1966 in Florida.
Donor(s): Jim Walter Corporation, and subsidiaries.
Financial data: (yr. ended 8/31/83): Assets, $2,688,260 (M); expenditures, $133,199, including $126,958 for 109 grants (high: $20,000; low: $10).
Purpose and activities: Broad purposes; grants primarily for community funds; support also for education, youth and social agencies, and hospitals.
Trustees: W.K. Baker, J.B. Cordell, J.W. Kynes.
Employer Identification Number: 596205802

789
Ware Foundation, The ▼
147 Alhambra Circle, Suite 215
Coral Gables 33134

Trust established in 1950 in Pennsylvania.
Donor(s): John H. Ware, Jr.†
Financial data: (yr. ended 12/31/83): Assets, $7,861,703 (M); expenditures, $680,725, including $625,800 for 47 grants (high: $310,000; low: $500).
Purpose and activities: General purposes; support primarily for higher education; grants also for hospitals, historic preservation groups, social service and youth agencies, and religious organizations, with some emphasis on the Mid-Atlantic states, particularly Pennsylvania.
Application information:
Initial approach: Letter or proposal
Deadline(s): None
Final notification: Positive responses only
Trustees: Rhoda C. Ware, Chairman; Rhoda W. Cobb, Nancy W. Pascal, Willard Ware.
Employer Identification Number: 237286585

790
Wells (Lillian S.) Foundation, Inc. ¤
620 East Las Olas Blvd.
Fort Lauderdale 33301

Donor(s): Barbara S. Wells, Preston A. Wells, Jr.
Financial data: (yr. ended 12/31/83): Assets, $3,208,420 (M); expenditures, $118,016, including $114,500 for 5 grants (high: $60,000; low: $5,000).
Purpose and activities: General giving, with emphasis on hospitals.
Officers: Barbara S. Wells, President; Preston A. Wells, Jr., Vice-President; Mary B. Moulding, Secretary; Joseph E. Malecek, Treasurer.
Employer Identification Number: 237433827

791
Whitehall Foundation, Inc. ▼
220 Royal Palm Way, Suite 220
Palm Beach 33480   (305) 655-4474

Incorporated in 1937 in New Jersey.
Donor(s): George M. Moffett,† and others.
Financial data: (yr. ended 9/30/83): Assets, $22,411,164 (M); expenditures, $2,030,131, including $1,749,374 for 61 grants (high: $80,000; low: $3,450; average: $25,000-$38,000).
Purpose and activities: New policy guidelines announced in January 1985. Support for scholarly research in the life sciences, with emphasis on plant physiology, development, genetics and ecology, on ecology and population biology, on invertebrate neurophysiology, on animal behavior and ethology, and on taxonomy and phylogeny; innovative and imaginative projects preferred.
Types of support awarded: Seed money, equipment, technical assistance, special projects, research, publications, grants to individuals.
Limitations: No support for investigators who already have, or expect to receive, substantial support from other quarters. No grants for operating budgets, continuing support, annual campaigns, emergency, building or endowment funds, deficit financing, land acquisition, renovation projects, matching gifts, scholarships, fellowships, or conferences; no loans.
Publications: 990-PF, program policy statement, application guidelines.
Application information: Application form required.
Initial approach: Preliminary letter
Copies of proposal: 1
Deadline(s): March 1, September 1, and December 1
Board meeting date(s): November, but votes by mail in March, June, and December
Final notification: 5 to 9 months
Write: Laurel T. Baker, Secretary
Officers and Trustees: George M. Moffett, II, President and Treasurer; J. Wright Rumbough, Jr., Vice-President; Laurel T. Baker, Secretary; Warren S. Adams II, Kenneth S. Beall, Jr., Helen M. Brooks, Van Vetchen Burger, James A. Moffett.
Number of staff: 2 part-time professional.
Employer Identification Number: 135637595

792
Wilder Foundation, The
P.O. Box 99
Key Biscayne 33149

Incorporated in 1945 in Louisiana.
Donor(s): Candace Mossler,† Jacques Mossler.
Financial data: (yr. ended 12/31/83): Assets, $962,796 (M); expenditures, $178,023, including $126,956 for 18 grants (high: $55,000; low: $80).
Purpose and activities: Primarily local giving, with emphasis on a university and secondary education.
Types of support awarded: General purposes, building funds, endowment funds, research, scholarship funds, matching funds.
Limitations: Giving primarily in FL. No grants to individuals; no loans.
Application information:
Initial approach: Proposal
Copies of proposal: 1
Deadline(s): Submit proposal before September
Board meeting date(s): Monthly
Write: Rita Wilder, President, or Gary Wilder, Vice-President
Officers: Rita Wilder, President; Gary Wilder, Vice-President.
Number of staff: 1 full-time support.
Employer Identification Number: 746049547

793
Williams (Edna Sproull) Foundation ¤
1500 Independent
Jacksonville 32202

Donor(s): Edna Sproull Williams.†
Financial data: (yr. ended 12/31/83): Assets, $6,140,616 (M); gifts received, $5,043,339; expenditures, $294,879, including $281,000 for 17 grants (high: $35,000; low: $1,000).
Purpose and activities: Primarily local giving, with emphasis on youth agencies, Protestant religious organizations, higher education, hospitals, and social services.
Limitations: Giving primarily in FL.
Application information:
Deadline(s): None
Trustees: J.W. Burke, J.W. Burke, Jr., William J. Hamrick, Charles J. Williams III, Patrick M. Williams.
Employer Identification Number: 510198606

794
Winn-Dixie Stores Foundation ▼
P.O. Box B
Jacksonville 32203   (904) 783-5531

Incorporated in 1943 in Florida.
Donor(s): Winn-Dixie Stores, Inc.
Financial data: (yr. ended 12/31/82): Assets, $2,695,997 (M); gifts received, $2,600,000; expenditures, $1,154,282, including $956,910 for 601 grants (high: $40,000; low: $25; average: $50-$5,000) and $194,612 for 360 employee matching gifts.

Purpose and activities: Functions solely as a conduit through which Winn-Dixie Stores, Inc., in its thirteen state trade area, makes contributions to local and national welfare agencies, including community funds, youth agencies, educational institutions, scholarship programs, and hospitals.
Types of support awarded: Annual campaigns, building funds, equipment, matching funds, employee matching gifts, research, special projects, conferences and seminars, continuing support, scholarship funds.
Limitations: Giving primarily in the Southeast, in areas of company operations. No grants to individuals.
Application information:
  Initial approach: Letter
  Deadline(s): None
  Board meeting date(s): As required
  Final notification: 30 days
  Write: Jack P. Jones, President
Officers: Jack P. Jones, President; A. Dano Davis, James E. Davis, Robert D. Davis, F.L. James, Vice-Presidents; D.H. Bragin, Secretary; W.F. Fant, Treasurer.
Number of staff: None.
Employer Identification Number: 590995428

795
Winter Park Community Trust Fund ⌑
c/o Barnett Banks Trust Company
P.O. Box 1000
Winter Park 32790   (305) 646-3290
Scholarship application address: Mrs. Kelly Pflug, 1430 Alabama Dr., Winter Park, FL 32789

Trust established in 1951 in Florida.
Donor(s): Edith F. Davenport,† Cyrus F. Ferald Trust, Henry T. Greene Trust.
Financial data: (yr. ended 11/30/83): Assets, $1,561,105 (M); gifts received, $181,049; expenditures, $152,231, including $116,366 for 28 grants (high: $31,360; low: $50) and $22,160 for 16 grants to individuals.
Purpose and activities: Primarily local giving, with emphasis on health, education, and social services; support also for scholarships and economic assistance to community residents.
Types of support awarded: Continuing support, grants to individuals, student aid, general purposes.
Limitations: Giving limited to the central FL area. No grants for building or endowment funds, or matching gifts; no loans.
Application information:
  Initial approach: Letter
  Copies of proposal: 1
  Deadline(s): None
  Board meeting date(s): Last Thursday of January and July
  Final notification: 1 week
Trustee: Barnett Bank Trust Company.
Number of staff: None.
Employer Identification Number: 596126473

796
Wiseheart Foundation, Inc.
2840 S.W. Third Ave.
Miami 33129   (305) 358-0040

Incorporated in 1953 in Florida.
Donor(s): Malcolm B. Wiseheart,† Dorothy A. Wiseheart.
Financial data: (yr. ended 12/31/83): Assets, $2,051,779 (M); expenditures, $101,109, including $96,775 for grants.
Purpose and activities: Primarily local giving, with emphasis on secondary and higher education, Protestant church support and cultural programs, including a local community television foundation.
Limitations: Giving primarily in FL. No grants to individuals, or for building or endowment funds, or operating budgets.
Application information:
  Initial approach: Full proposal
  Copies of proposal: 2
  Board meeting date(s): Quarterly
  Write: Malcolm B. Wiseheart, Jr., Secretary
Officers and Directors: Dorothy A. Wiseheart, President; Malcolm B. Wiseheart, Jr., Secretary; Elizabeth W. Joyce, Marilyn W. Little, Carolyn W. Milne.
Employer Identification Number: 590992871

797
Wolfson Family Foundation, Inc., The
P.O. Box 4
Jacksonville 32201

Incorporated in 1951 in Florida.
Donor(s): Louis E. Wolfson, Sam W. Wolfson,† Saul Wolfson, Florence M. Wolfson,† Cecil Wolfson.
Financial data: (yr. ended 9/30/82): Assets, $2,347,117 (L); expenditures, $300,480, including $253,940 for 58 grants (high: $100,000; low: $10).
Purpose and activities: Broad purposes; grants, primarily local, for higher education and hospitals, including buildings and equipment, Jewish welfare funds, community funds, and child welfare.
Limitations: Giving primarily in FL.
Officers: Louis E. Wolfson,* Chairman; Saul Wolfson,* Vice-Chairman; M.C. Tomberlin,* Secretary; Robert O. Johnson, Treasurer.
Trustees:* Sylvia W. Degen, Edith W. Edwards, Morris D. Edwards, Rabbi Sidney M. Lefkowitz, Cecil Wolfson, Dennis M. Wolfson, Donald M. Wolfson, Gary L. Wolfson, Nathan Wolfson, Richard J. Wolfson, Stephen P. Wolfson.
Employer Identification Number: 590995431

798
Wolfson (Louis E.) Foundation ⌑
P.O. Box 4
Jacksonville 32201

Trust established in 1951 in Massachusetts.
Donor(s): Louis E. Wolfson, M.D.
Financial data: (yr. ended 12/31/81): Assets, $4,857,226 (M); gifts received, $158,050; expenditures, $168,150, including $160,000 for 4 grants (high: $150,000; low: $1,500).

Purpose and activities: Charitable purposes; support for hospitals, medical education, and Jewish welfare funds.
Trustees: Sidney Gellis, M.D., Lawrence Newman, Louis E. Wolfson, M.D.
Employer Identification Number: 046053295

799
Wray (The Floyd L.) Memorial Foundation, Inc. ⌑
P.O. Box 23274
Fort Lauderdale 33307   (305) 776-4718

Incorporated in 1969 in Florida.
Donor(s): Jane L. Wray.†
Financial data: (yr. ended 9/30/83): Assets, $8,070,553 (M); expenditures, $564,871, including $257,000 for 7 grants (high: $75,000; low: $2,000) and $193,666 for 1 foundation-administered program.
Purpose and activities: Giving for Christian Science church support and higher and secondary education; also maintains the Floyd L. Wray Memorial Gardens, a public nature preserve and zoo.
Application information:
  Board meeting date(s): November, May, and as required
  Write: D. Arnold Phillips, President
Officers and Directors: D. Arnold Phillips, President; Dale Miller, Jr., Vice-President; Ben A. Bollinger, Secretary and Treasurer; Roy L. Aitken, Mary Bayuk, Edwin P. McDonald, Albert A. Will, Jr.
Employer Identification Number: 237112655

800
Yablick Charities, Inc.
c/o Jefferson National Bank
301 Arthur Godfrey Rd.
Miami Beach 33140

Incorporated in 1960 in New Jersey.
Donor(s): Herman Yablick.†
Financial data: (yr. ended 12/31/82): Assets, $1,763,404 (M); expenditures, $166,123, including $115,477 for 91 grants (high: $29,870; low: $10).
Purpose and activities: Grants largely for higher education, hospitals, and cultural programs.
Limitations: Giving primarily in FL and Israel.
Officers: Jerrold F. Goodman, President; Jane Goodman, Ruth Cohen, Vice-Presidents.
Employer Identification Number: 591411171

GEORGIA

801
Anncox Foundation, Inc. ⌗
c/o Cox Enterprises, Inc.
P.O. Box 4689
Atlanta 30302

Incorporated in 1960 in Georgia.
Donor(s): Anne Cox Chambers.
Financial data: (yr. ended 12/31/83): Assets,
$211,385 (M); expenditures, $181,675,
including $177,914 for 39 grants (high:
$50,000; low: $100).
Purpose and activities: Broad purposes;
primarily local giving, with emphasis on
educational associations, museums, animal care
programs, and cultural programs.
Limitations: Giving primarily in GA.
Officers and Directors: Anne Cox Chambers,
President and Treasurer; James Cox Chambers,
Vice-President and Secretary.
Employer Identification Number: 586033966

802
Atlanta Community Foundation, Inc.,
Metropolitan ▼
134 Peachtree St., Suite 710
Atlanta 30303   (404) 688-5525

Community foundation incorporated in 1977 as
successor to Metropolitan Foundation of
Atlanta established in 1951 in Georgia by bank
resolution and declaration of trust.
Financial data: (yr. ended 6/30/84): Assets,
$37,687,985 (M); gifts received, $6,921,100;
expenditures, $6,151,218, including
$3,546,458 for 250 grants (high: $500,000;
low: $50; average: $1,000-$10,000).
Purpose and activities: Organized for the
permanent administration of funds placed in
trust by various donors for charitable purposes.
Grants, unless designated by the donor, are
confined to metropolitan area of Atlanta, with
emphasis on social services, arts and culture,
education, health, and civic purposes.
Types of support awarded: Seed money,
emergency funds, building funds, equipment,
land acquisition, technical assistance, program-
related investments, special projects,
publications.
Limitations: Giving limited to the metropolitan
area of Atlanta, GA and surrounding regions.
No support for religious organizations. No
grants to individuals, or for endowment funds,
continuing support, annual campaigns, deficit
financing, research, films, conferences,
scholarships, or fellowships; generally no grants
for operating budgets or for loans.
Publications: Annual report, program policy
statement, application guidelines.
Application information: Application form
required.
  Initial approach: Letter or telephone
  Copies of proposal: 1
  Deadline(s): December 1, March 1, June 1,
    and September 1

Board meeting date(s): January, April, July,
    and October
Final notification: 6 weeks
  Write: Alicia Philipp, Executive Director
Officer: Alicia Philipp, Executive Director.
Directors: Dan E. Sweat, Jr., President;
Nicholas E. Davies, M.D., Vice-President;
Barbara Asher, Arthur C. Baxter, Howard Ector,
Alston Glenn, Victor A. Gregory, Harrison
Jones II, Russell Osmond, D. Lurton Massee,
Jr., Lee Sessions, Felker W. Ward, Jr., Judson C.
Ward.
Trustees: The Bank of the South, The Citizens
and Southern National Bank, The First National
Bank of Atlanta, The National Bank of Georgia,
Trust Company Bank.
Number of staff: 3 full-time professional; 2 full-
time support.
Employer Identification Number: 581344646

803
Atlanta Foundation
c/o First National Bank of Atlanta
P.O. Box 4148
Atlanta 30302   (404) 588-6677

Community foundation established in 1921 in
Georgia by bank resolution and declaration of
trust.
Financial data: (yr. ended 12/31/83): Assets,
$4,373,794 (M); gifts received, $73,778;
expenditures, $448,776, including $419,111
for 61 grants (high: $25,000; low: $200).
Purpose and activities: Assistance to
charitable and educational institutions only in
Fulton and De Kalb counties for promoting
education and scientific research, and
improving local living conditions. Grants
chiefly for community funds, hospitals,
education, including higher education, cultural
programs, and youth agencies.
Types of support awarded: Research, general
purposes, seed money, emergency funds,
building funds, equipment, land acquisition,
endowment funds, matching funds.
Limitations: Giving limited to Fulton and De
Kalb counties, GA. No grants to individuals, or
for scholarships or fellowships; no loans.
Application information:
  Initial approach: Letter
  Copies of proposal: 1
  Deadline(s): December 15
  Board meeting date(s): January
  Final notification: 1 week
  Write: Arthur C. Baxter, Secretary
Officer: Arthur C. Baxter,* Secretary.
Distribution Committee:* McChesney H.
Jeffries, Chairman; Shirley C. Franklin, Joel
Goldberg, Howard C. Harris, D. Raymond
Riddle.
Trustee: The First National Bank of Atlanta.
Number of staff: None.
Employer Identification Number: 586026879

804
Baker (Clark and Ruby) Foundation ⌗
c/o Bank South, Financial Services Division
P.O. Box 4956
Atlanta 30302   (404) 529-4625
Additional telephone number: (404) 529-4627

Established in 1974.
Donor(s): Clark A. Baker.†
Financial data: (yr. ended 12/31/83): Assets,
$1,066,877 (M); expenditures, $65,607,
including $39,000 for 16 grants (high: $6,000;
low: $300) and $18,000 for 10 grants to
individuals.
Purpose and activities: Primarily local giving,
with emphasis on higher education, including
scholarships; support also for Protestant welfare
funds and pensions for Methodist ministers.
Types of support awarded: Scholarship funds,
endowment funds, conferences and seminars,
general purposes, grants to individuals, student
aid.
Limitations: Giving limited to GA.
Application information:
  Initial approach: Full proposal
  Deadline(s): None
  Write: Odette Capell, Secretary or Tom
    Murphy
Officers: Virlyn B. Moore, Jr., Chairman;
Odette Capell, Secretary.
Trustee: Bank South, N.A.
Employer Identification Number: 581429097

805
Bank South Charitable Trust ⌗
(formerly Fulton Charitable Trust)
Bank South Financial Services Division
55 Marietta St., N.W., P.O. Box 4956
Atlanta 30302

Trust established in 1960 in Georgia.
Donor(s): Bank of the South.
Financial data: (yr. ended 12/31/83): Assets,
$1,461,243 (M); gifts received, $8,615;
expenditures, $104,621, including $94,309 for
1 grant.
Purpose and activities: Local giving primarily
for a community fund.
Limitations: Giving primarily in GA.
Application information: Funds fully
committed.
Trustee: Bank South.
Employer Identification Number: 586031447

806
Bibb Foundation, Inc., The
P.O. Box 4207
Macon 31208   (912) 743-3731

Incorporated in 1930 in Georgia.
Donor(s): The Bibb Company.
Financial data: (yr. ended 8/31/83): Assets,
$1,513,276 (M); expenditures, $235,666,
including $181,792 for 178 grants to
individuals and $35,178 for 36 loans.
Purpose and activities: Giving primarily for
scholarship and student loan program for
employees or children of employees of The
Bibb Company.
Types of support awarded: Employee related
scholarships, student aid.
Limitations: Giving primarily in GA. No grants
to individuals (except for company employees
and children of employees), or for building or
endowment funds, or special projects.
Publications: Program policy statement,
application guidelines.

Application information: Application form for scholarships required. Application form required.

> *Initial approach:* Proposal
> *Copies of proposal:* 2
> *Deadline(s):* April 30
> *Board meeting date(s):* August
> *Write:* Allan V. Davis, Treasurer

Officers and Trustees: W.S. Manning, President; G.R. Dusenberry, E.H. Edmonds, M.O. Thompson, Vice-Presidents; L.W. Belk, Secretary; Allan V. Davis, Treasurer.

Employer Identification Number: 580566140

807
Bradley-Turner Foundation ▼ ⌷
(formerly W. C. and Sarah H. Bradley Foundation)
P.O. Box 140
Columbus 31902   (404) 571-6040

Incorporated in 1943 in Georgia as W.C. and Sarah H. Bradley Foundation; in 1982 absorbed the D.A. and Elizabeth Turner Foundation, Inc., also of Georgia.
Donor(s): W.C. Bradley,† D.A. Turner, Elizabeth B. Turner.†
Financial data: (yr. ended 12/31/82): Assets, $19,474,333 (M); gifts received, $4,287,039; expenditures, $916,802, including $826,126 for 34 grants (high: $100,000; low: $103).
Purpose and activities: Broad purposes; local giving, principally for a community fund, higher education, religious associations, youth and social agencies and a recreation center.
Limitations: Giving primarily in GA. No grants to individuals.
Application information:
> *Initial approach:* Letter
> *Board meeting date(s):* Quarterly
> *Write:* W. Bradley Turner, Jr., Chairman

Officers and Trustees: W. Bradley Turner, Jr., Chairman; Lovick P. Corn, Vice-Chairman; John T. Turner, Secretary; W.B. Turner, Treasurer; Betsy B. Burkholder, C.C. Butler, M.D., Stephen T. Butler, Elizabeth T. Corn, Polly C. Miller, Elizabeth C. Ogie, Sue T. Turner.

Employer Identification Number: 586032142

808
Burke (Thomas C.) Foundation ⌷
P.O. Box 4007
Macon 31213

Established in 1965 in Georgia.
Donor(s): Thomas C. Burke.†
Financial data: (yr. ended 9/30/83): Assets, $2,774,942 (M); gifts received, $7,977; expenditures, $214,378, including $36,650 for 2 grants of $18,325 each and $125,110 for grants to individuals.
Purpose and activities: Grants primarily to needy individuals of Bibb County, Georgia, who are suffering from disease, particularly cancer; some support also for a local Roman Catholic church and academy.
Types of support awarded: Grants to individuals.
Limitations: Giving limited to GA, with emphasis on Bibb County.

Advisory Board Members: Mrs. John D. Comer, Henry E. Marshall, J. Benham Stewart.
Trustee: Citizens and Southern National Bank.
Employer Identification Number: 586047627

809
C B & T Charitable Trust ⌷
P.O. Box 120
Columbus 31902

Established in 1969.
Donor(s): Columbus Bank and Trust Co.
Financial data: (yr. ended 12/31/83): Assets, $17,527 (M); gifts received, $149,250; expenditures, $135,043, including $134,858 for 57 grants (high: $48,300; low: $25).
Purpose and activities: Primarily local giving, with emphasis on youth agencies and education, including higher education, a community fund, and a library.
Limitations: Giving primarily in GA.
Manager: June P. Partain.
Trustees: James H. Blanchard, William B. Turner, James D. Yancey.
Employer Identification Number: 237024198

810
Callaway Foundation, Inc. ▼
209 Broome St.
P.O. Box 790
LaGrange 30241   (404) 884-7348

Incorporated in 1943 in Georgia.
Donor(s): Textile Benefit Association, Callaway Mills, Callaway Institute, Inc.
Financial data: (yr. ended 9/30/84): Assets, $106,604,628 (M); expenditures, $4,670,464, including $4,172,210 for 76 grants (high: $1,050,000; low: $100; average: $1,000-$100,000).
Purpose and activities: Broad purposes; primarily local giving, with grants for education, including buildings and equipment, elementary and secondary schools, libraries, hospitals, community funds, care for the aged, and church support.
Types of support awarded: Continuing support, annual campaigns, general purposes, building funds, equipment, land acquisition, matching funds.
Limitations: Giving primarily in GA, with emphasis on the city of LaGrange and Troup County. No grants to individuals, or for endowment funds, operating expenses, deficit financing, research, or scholarships and fellowships; no loans.
Publications: Annual report, program policy statement, application guidelines.
Application information:
> *Initial approach:* Letter
> *Copies of proposal:* 1
> *Deadline(s):* End of month preceding board meetings
> *Board meeting date(s):* January, April, July, and October
> *Final notification:* 2 months
> *Write:* J.T. Gresham, General Manager

Officers: J.T. Gresham, President, General Manager, and Treasurer; Charles D. Hudson,* Vice-President; C.L. Pitts, Secretary.

Trustees:* Mark Clayton Callaway, J. Philip Cleaveland, Ida Callaway Hudson, James R. Lewis.
Number of staff: 2 part-time professional; 3 part-time support.
Employer Identification Number: 580566147

811
Callaway (Fuller E.) Foundation ▼
209 Broome St.
P.O. Box 790
LaGrange 30241   (404) 884-7348

Incorporated in 1917 in Georgia.
Donor(s): Fuller E. Callaway, Sr.,† and family.
Financial data: (yr. ended 12/31/84): Assets, $22,079,897 (M); expenditures, $1,122,650, including $849,757 for 40 grants (high: $519,730; low: $100) and $136,871 for 59 grants to individuals.
Purpose and activities: Broad purposes; grants to religious and educational institutions in LaGrange and Troup County; scholarships for worthy Troup County students; modest gifts toward operating expenses of local community welfare agencies.
Types of support awarded: Operating budgets, annual campaigns, building funds, equipment, matching funds, general purposes, student aid.
Limitations: Giving primarily in the city of LaGrange and Troup County, GA. No grants for endowment funds or research; no loans.
Publications: Application guidelines.
Application information: Application form required for scholarship program. Application form required.
> *Initial approach:* Letter
> *Copies of proposal:* 1
> *Deadline(s):* End of the month preceding board meeting for grants; February 15 for scholarships
> *Board meeting date(s):* January, April, July and October
> *Final notification:* 60 to 90 days
> *Write:* J.T. Gresham, General Manager

Officers: J.T. Gresham, President, General Manager, and Treasurer; Charles D. Hudson,* Vice-President; C.L. Pitts, Secretary.
Trustees:* Mark Clayton Callaway, J. Philip Cleaveland, Ida Callaway Hudson, James R. Lewis.
Number of staff: 2 part-time professional; 3 part-time support.
Employer Identification Number: 580566148

812
Callaway (Fuller E.) Professorial Chairs, The Trust for
P.O. Box 12448
Atlanta 30355   (404) 262-7191

Trust established in 1968 in Georgia.
Donor(s): Callaway Foundation, Inc.
Financial data: (yr. ended 6/30/81): Assets, $9,700,000 (M); expenditures, $687,200, including $687,200 for 42 grants (high: $25,000; low: $7,250).
Purpose and activities: Establishment of professorial chairs at higher educational institutions in Georgia.

Types of support awarded: Professorships.
Limitations: Giving primarily in GA. No grants to individuals.
Publications: Application guidelines.
Application information: Application form required.
  Initial approach: Letter
  Copies of proposal: 1
  Deadline(s): Submit proposal preferably in July; deadline August 30
  Board meeting date(s): February
  Write: Nancy B. Howard, Secretary
Officer: Nancy B. Howard, Secretary.
Committee Members: Bennett A. Brown, Chairman; Vernon Crawford, James T. Laney, Charles Meredith.
Trustee: The Citizens and Southern National Bank.
Employer Identification Number: 586075259

813
Campbell (J. Bulow) Foundation ▼
1401 Trust Company Tower
25 Park Place, N.E.
Atlanta 30303   (404) 658-9066

Trust established in 1940 in Georgia.
Donor(s): J. Bulow Campbell,† Laura Berry Campbell.†
Financial data: (yr. ended 12/31/83): Assets, $66,001,359 (M); expenditures, $2,400,994, including $2,017,000 for 16 grants (high: $500,000; low: $17,000; average: $25,000-$250,000).
Purpose and activities: Broad purposes; attention focused on Georgia and the (Southern) Presbyterian Church, U.S.; priority given to institutions located in Georgia; aid to Atlanta Presbytery and Synod of Southeast, PCUS, rather than to any local Presbyterian church; grants limited to Georgia, Alabama, Florida, North Carolina, South Carolina, and Tennessee. Concern for improving quality of spiritual and intellectual life, with priority to private agencies undertaking work of regional importance, preferably projects of permanent nature or for capital funds. Gives anonymously and requests no publicity.
Types of support awarded: Building funds, endowment funds, equipment, land acquisition, matching funds.
Limitations: Giving primarily in GA; very limited giving in AL, FL, NC, SC, and TN. No grants to individuals, or for research, scholarships, fellowships, special projects, operating budgets, or recurring items; no loans.
Publications: Application guidelines, program policy statement.
Application information: Submit 1 copy of one-page proposal, 3 copies of tax information.
  Initial approach: Letter or telephone
  Deadline(s): January 15, April 15, July 15, and October 15
  Board meeting date(s): January, April, July, and October
  Final notification: Within 1 week after board meets
  Write: John W. Stephenson, Executive Director
Officer: John W. Stephenson, Executive Director.

Trustees: William A. Parker, Jr., Chairman; Richard W. Courts II, Vice-Chairman; John B. Ellis, Langdon S. Flowers, Mark P. Pentecost, Jr., M.D., Rev. J. Davidson Philips, George E. Smith, Trust Company Bank of Georgia.
Number of staff: 2.
Employer Identification Number: 580566149

814
Chatham Foundation, The ¤
c/o Savannah Sugar Refining Corporation
P.O. Box 339
Savannah 31402

Trust established in 1953 in Georgia.
Donor(s): Savannah Foods & Industries, Inc.
Financial data: (yr. ended 11/30/83): Assets, $2,549,713 (M); expenditures, $99,073, including $87,550 for 11 grants (high: $25,300; low: $500).
Purpose and activities: Broad purposes; support primarily for community funds, higher education, and cultural programs.
Limitations: Giving primarily in Savannah, GA.
Trustees: Walter C. Scott, John E. Simpson, W.W. Sprague, Jr., W.R. Steinhauer, The C & S National Bank, Corporate Trustee.
Employer Identification Number: 586033047

815
Chatham Valley Foundation, Inc., The
1100 Citizens and Southern Nat'l. Bank Bldg.
Atlanta 30335   (404) 572-6605

Incorporated in 1962 in Georgia.
Donor(s): A.J. Weinberg, Elliott Goldstein, W.B. Schwartz, Arthur Jay Schwartz, Robert C. Schwartz.
Financial data: (yr. ended 7/31/84): Assets, $4,842,378 (M); gifts received, $29,614; expenditures, $356,533, including $298,257 for 156 grants (high: $90,000; low: $10).
Purpose and activities: Broad purposes; giving for a local Jewish welfare federation and other Jewish organizations, and broad support for local charitable, educational, cultural and civic activities.
Limitations: Giving primarily in the metropolitan Atlanta, GA area.
Application information:
  Board meeting date(s): Semiannually
  Write: Elliott Goldstein, Secretary
Officers and Trustees: W.B. Schwartz, Jr., Chairman; Sonia Schwartz, Harriet Goldstein, Vice-Chair; Elliott Goldstein, Secretary and Treasurer; Lillian Friedlander, W.B. Schwartz, III.
Employer Identification Number: 586039344

816
Citizens and Southern Fund, The ¤
Citizens and Southern National Bank
P.O. Box 4899, 14 Main St.
Atlanta 30302-4899   (404) 581-3911

Trust established in 1956 in Georgia.
Donor(s): The Citizens and Southern National Bank.

Financial data: (yr. ended 12/31/83): Assets, $80,460 (M); gifts received, $1,200,634; expenditures, $1,139,797, including $1,101,585 for 277 grants (high: $335,000; low: $10) and $37,728 for employee matching gifts.
Purpose and activities: Charitable purposes; grants to community funds, health agencies, youth groups, cultural programs, and educational institutions, including employee matching grants, in cities in which donor banks are located.
Types of support awarded: Employee matching gifts.
Limitations: Giving primarily in areas of company operations. No grants to individuals or for endowment funds.
Application information:
  Initial approach: Letter
  Copies of proposal: 1
  Deadline(s): September
  Board meeting date(s): Semiannually
Officers and Distribution Committee: Lee M. Sessions, Jr., Managing Trustee; Mary P. Catan, Secretary and Treasurer; Willard A. Alexander, Bennett A. Brown, Henry T. Collingsworth, John W. McIntyre, John S. Poelker.
Employer Identification Number: 596025583

817
Cobb (Ty) Educational Fund ¤
P.O. Box 4655
Atlanta 30302   (404) 588-8449
Grant application address: P.O. Box 725, Forest Park, GA 30051

Trust established in 1953 in Georgia.
Donor(s): Tyrus R. Cobb.†
Financial data: (yr. ended 6/20/83): Assets, $3,047,486 (M); expenditures, $210,414, including $176,994 for 318 grants to individuals.
Purpose and activities: Scholarship aid for needy and deserving youth of Georgia who have completed one year in an accredited institution of higher learning, payable to the institution; graduate school scholarships available to law, medical, or dental students.
Types of support awarded: Student aid.
Limitations: Giving limited to GA residents. No grants for building or endowment funds, operating budgets, special projects, or matching gifts; no loans.
Publications: Application guidelines.
Application information: Application form required.
  Initial approach: Letter
  Copies of proposal: 1
  Deadline(s): May 31
  Board meeting date(s): July and January
  Write: Rosie Atkins, Secretary
Officer: Rosie Atkins, Secretary.
Scholarship Board: H. Prentice Miller, Chairman; Harry S. Downs, Merritt E. Hoag, S. Walter Martin.
Trustee: Trust Company Bank.
Employer Identification Number: 586026003

818
Coca-Cola Foundation, The
310 North Ave.
Atlanta 30301   (404) 676-3740

Established in 1984 in Georgia.
Donor(s): Coca-Cola Company.
Financial data: (yr. ended 12/31/84): Assets, $2,285,000 (M).
Purpose and activities: Initial year of operations 1984; emphasis on education, arts and cultural programs, health and wellness, and civic and community affairs, in locations where the greatest number of employees live.
Types of support awarded: Annual campaigns, matching funds, employee matching gifts, professorships, internships, scholarship funds, fellowships.
Limitations: Giving primarily in Atlanta, GA; Houston, TX; New York, NY; and Los Angeles, CA. No grants to individuals, or for operating budgets, building or endowment funds, equipment, or land acquisition; no loans.
Publications: Annual report, application guidelines.
Application information:
 Initial approach: Letter
 Board meeting date(s): February, May, July, and November
 Final notification: 90 to 120 days
 Write: Margaret J. Cox, Executive Director
Officer: Margaret J. Cox, Vice-President and Executive Director.
Employer Identification Number: 581574705

819
Community Enterprises, Inc. ⌀
115 East Main St.
Thomaston 30286

Incorporated in 1944 in Georgia.
Donor(s): Julian T. Hightower, Thomaston Cotton Mills.
Financial data: (yr. ended 6/30/83): Assets, $3,312,593 (M); expenditures, $239,081, including $225,801 for 26 grants (high: $35,000; low: $150).
Purpose and activities: Broad purposes; primarily local giving, with emphasis on higher and secondary education and a hospital; some support for community development.
Limitations: Giving primarily in Thomaston, GA.
Officers and Trustees: William H. Hightower, Jr., President; George H. Hightower, Vice-President; Neil H. Hightower, Secretary and Treasurer.
Employer Identification Number: 586043415

820
Courts Foundation, Inc.
1001 Hurt Bldg.
Atlanta 30303

Incorporated in 1950 in Georgia.
Donor(s): Richard W. Courts, Mrs. Virginia Campbell Courts, Malon C. Courts.†
Financial data: (yr. ended 12/31/83): Assets, $2,521,257 (M); expenditures, $123,429, including $103,500 for 30 grants (high: $19,000; low: $500).

Purpose and activities: When sufficiently large, corpus to be used to provide a home or clinic for elderly people; grants from income for a home for the retired; smaller amounts to local charities, principally universities, youth agencies, and churches.
Limitations: Giving primarily in GA. No grants to individuals.
Application information:
 Write: Francis J. Heazel, Jr., Secretary
Officers and Trustees: Richard W. Courts, President; Richard W. Courts II, Vice-President; Francis J. Heazel, Jr., Secretary and Treasurer; John B. Ellis, William A. Parker, Jr.
Employer Identification Number: 586036859

821
Cousins Foundation, Inc., The ⌀
c/o Thomas G. Cousins
800 N. Omni International
Atlanta 30335

Incorporated in 1963 in Georgia.
Donor(s): Thomas G. Cousins.
Financial data: (yr. ended 3/31/83): Assets, $99,812 (M); gifts received, $117,500; expenditures, $124,220, including $109,108 for 19 grants (high: $100,006; low: $50).
Purpose and activities: Primarily local giving, with emphasis on community activities and Protestant church support.
Limitations: Giving primarily in Atlanta, GA.
Officer: Robert P. Hunter, Jr., Secretary and Treasurer.
Trustees: Thomas G. Cousins, Chairman; Ann D. Cousins, Vice-Chairman; Harry C. Howard.
Employer Identification Number: 586043765

822
Cox (The James M.) Foundation of Georgia, Inc. ⌀
c/o Cox Enterprises, Inc.
72 Marietta St., N.W.
Atlanta 30303

Incorporated in 1957 in Georgia.
Donor(s): Atlanta Newspapers, Inc., Cox Enterprises, Inc.
Financial data: (yr. ended 12/31/82): Assets, $3,702,342 (M); gifts received, $400,000; expenditures, $321,927, including $307,500 for 12 grants (high: $50,000; low: $2,500).
Purpose and activities: Giving primarily locally and in Colorado, with emphasis on higher education, hospitals, and the arts.
Limitations: Giving primarily in GA and CO.
Officers and Trustees:* Anne Cox Chambers,* Chairman; Barbara Cox Anthony,* President; Joseph F. Englert, Secretary-Treasurer; Carl R. Gross, James Cox Kennedy, Daniel J. Mahoney, Jr., William I. Ray, Jr.
Employer Identification Number: 586032469

823
Davis Foundation, Inc., The ⌀
One National Dr.
Atlanta 30336

Established in 1960.

Donor(s): Raleigh Linen Service, Inc., National Distributing Company, Inc., and subsidiaries.
Financial data: (yr. ended 7/31/83): Assets, $173,295 (M); gifts received, $340,000; expenditures, $527,208, including $526,201 for 26 grants (high: $183,300; low: $80).
Purpose and activities: Grants primarily for Jewish welfare funds in the Atlanta area and for higher education.
Officers: Alfred A. Davis, President; Jay M. Davis, Vice-President.
Employer Identification Number: 586035088

824
Day (Cecil B.) Foundation, Inc. ▼
(formerly Day Companies Foundation, Inc.)
6025 The Corners Pkwy., Suite 201
Norcross 30092   (404) 446-1500

Incorporated in 1970 in Georgia.
Donor(s): Cecil B. Day.†
Financial data: (yr. ended 12/31/83): Assets, $15,107,084 (M); gifts received, $1,294,060; expenditures, $1,437,957, including $1,225,598 for 177 grants (high: $250,000; low: $75; average: $500-$10,000).
Purpose and activities: Grants to Christian churches for evangelism, missions, and disciplineships, in the South and New England.
Types of support awarded: Continuing support, annual campaigns, seed money, emergency funds, building funds, equipment, land acquisition, matching funds.
Limitations: Giving primarily in the New England states; special consideration for Georgia, primarily the metropolitan Atlanta area. No grants to individuals, or for deficit financing, endowment funds, scholarships, or fellowships.
Publications: Program policy statement.
Application information:
 Deadline(s): None
 Board meeting date(s): Annually
 Write: Edward L. White, Jr., President
Officers: Edward L. White, Jr.,* President; Ira Q. Craft, R.D. Spear,* Vice-Presidents; JoAnn F. Dollar, Secretary; Charles A. Sanders, Treasurer.
Trustees: Deen Day Smith, Vice-Chairman; C. Burke Day, Jr., Clinton M. Day, Lon L. Day, Jr.
Number of staff: 1 full-time professional.
Employer Identification Number: 581030351

825
Delta Air Lines Foundation
Atlanta Airport
Atlanta 30320   (404) 765-2170

Established in 1968 in Delaware.
Donor(s): Delta Air Lines, Inc.
Financial data: (yr. ended 12/31/83): Assets, $4,582,370 (M); expenditures, $362,192, including $346,000 for 22 grants (high: $200,000; low: $1,000).
Purpose and activities: Giving limited to higher education and educational associations.
Limitations: No grants to individuals.
Application information:
 Initial approach: Full proposal
 Copies of proposal: 1
 Deadline(s): May 1

Board meeting date(s): June and November
Write: Thomas D. Stone, Assistant Secretary
Officers and Trustees: David C. Garrett, Jr., President; James W. Callison, Secretary; R. Oppenlander, Treasurer; Susan Q. Downer, M.O. Galloway, Thomas D. Stone.
Employer Identification Number: 586073119

826
Dobbs (Helen and Howard) Foundation ¤
600 West Peachtree St., N.W.
Atlanta 30308

Financial data: (yr. ended 10/31/83): Assets, $1,098,624 (M); expenditures, $113,842, including $110,000 for 17 grants (high: $50,000; low: $500).
Purpose and activities: Primarily local giving, with emphasis on higher education and Protestant church support.
Limitations: Giving primarily in Atlanta, GA.
Officers and Trustees: R. Howard Dobbs, Jr., Chairman; Jason B. Gilliland, Secretary and Treasurer; Josephine A. Dobbs, E. Cody Laird, Jr.
Employer Identification Number: 586033186

827
Dodson (The James Glenwell and Clara May) Foundation
c/o Trust Dept.
P.O. Box 4655
Atlanta 30302

Trust established in 1967 in Georgia.
Donor(s): Mrs. Clara May Dodson.†
Financial data: (yr. ended 12/31/84): Assets, $1,522,960 (M); expenditures, $147,869, including $138,000 for 21 grants (high: $32,500; low: $500).
Purpose and activities: Broad purposes; primarily local giving to benefit underprivileged children; grants largely for homes and hospitals; support also for education.
Limitations: Giving primarily in GA and SC. No grants to individuals.
Application information:
Initial approach: Typewritten letter
Deadline(s): October 15
Board meeting date(s): November
Write: Cathy I. Solomon, Assistant Vice-President
Managers: Robert F. Bryan, Clara May Godshall, Ellis Godshall, R.L. McConnell, Elenora Richardson, Henry B. Richardson, Jr., Edwin L. Sterne.
Trustee: Trust Company Bank, (Cathy I. Solomon, Assistant Vice-President).
Employer Identification Number: 586074354

828
Dorminy (John Henry) Foundation, Inc. ¤
P.O. Box 870
Fitzgerald 31750

Established in 1962 in Georgia.
Donor(s): John Henry Dorminy, Jr., and members of the Dorminy family.

Financial data: (yr. ended 12/31/83): Assets, $1,519,923 (M); gifts received, $111,000; expenditures, $114,981, including $107,475 for 27 grants (high: $11,500).
Purpose and activities: Support primarily for hospitals and higher education.
Directors: Mrs. John Henry Dorminy, Jr., Chairman and President; W.J. Dorminy, John H. Dorminy, III, Martha Anne D. Verbit, Vice-Chairmen.
Employer Identification Number: 586033324

829
EMSA Fund, Inc.
3929 Tuxedo Rd., N.W.
Atlanta 30342   (404) 233-3455

Incorporated in 1962 in Georgia.
Donor(s): Phoebe Weil Lundeen, and members of the Franklin family.
Financial data: (yr. ended 12/31/83): Assets, $1,269,611 (M); gifts received, $20,087; expenditures, $122,000, including $110,216 for 166 grants (high: $33,333; low: $10).
Purpose and activities: Primarily local giving for human services, cultural, and educational programs, particularly for those who have been neglected or hard to reach in the provision of such programs; some support for environmental programs.
Types of support awarded: General purposes, operating budgets, continuing support, annual campaigns, seed money, emergency funds, building funds, endowment funds, special projects, research.
Limitations: Giving primarily in GA, particularly the Atlanta area. No grants to individuals, or for scholarships, fellowships, or matching gifts; no loans.
Publications: Application guidelines.
Application information:
Initial approach: Full proposal
Copies of proposal: 1
Deadline(s): None
Board meeting date(s): Annually
Final notification: 2 to 4 weeks
Write: Phoebe Weil Lundeen, President
Officers and Trustees: Phoebe Weil Lundeen, President; Andrew D. Franklin, Vice-President; Alice Franklin, Secretary-Treasurer.
Number of staff: 1 part-time professional.
Employer Identification Number: 586043282

830
English (The Florence C. and Harry L.) Memorial Fund
P.O. Box 4418
Atlanta 30302   (404) 588-8246

Established in 1964 in Georgia.
Donor(s): Mrs. Florence Cruft English.†
Financial data: (yr. ended 12/31/83): Assets, $5,411,000 (M); expenditures, $354,000, including $318,000 for 78 grants (high: $10,000; low: $833).
Purpose and activities: Broad purposes; local giving, with grants only for education, health, general welfare, and culture, with emphasis on assisting the aged and chronically ill, the blind, and those persons generally designated as the "underprivileged".

Limitations: Giving limited to the metropolitan Atlanta, GA area. No support for veterans' or political organizations, or organizations which have not been operating without a deficit for at least a year. No grants to individuals.
Publications: Program policy statement, application guidelines.
Application information:
Initial approach: Telephone
Deadline(s): Submit proposal at least 1 month prior to month of committee meetings
Board meeting date(s): January, April, July, and October
Write: Victor A. Gregory, Secretary
Distribution Committee: Robert Strickland, Chairman; Victor A. Gregory, Secretary; E.P. Gould, Jesse S. Hall.
Trustee: Trust Company Bank.
Employer Identification Number: 586045781

831
Equifax Foundation
c/o Equifax Inc.
1600 Peachtree St., N.W.
Atlanta 30309   (404) 885-8000
Mailing address: P.O. Box 4081, Atlanta, GA 30302

Trust established in 1978 in Georgia.
Donor(s): Equifax Inc.
Financial data: (yr. ended 12/31/84): Assets, $7,334 (L); gifts received, $295,000; expenditures, $298,602, including $298,602 for 61 grants (high: $113,300; low: $150).
Purpose and activities: Primarily local giving for higher education, a community fund, and an arts alliance.
Types of support awarded: Operating budgets, continuing support, annual campaigns, seed money, emergency funds, building funds, equipment, land acquisition, endowment funds, scholarship funds, professorships, loans, special projects, research, conferences and seminars.
Limitations: Giving primarily in GA. No grants to individuals, or for deficit financing, fellowships, publications, or matching gifts.
Application information:
Initial approach: Full proposal
Copies of proposal: 1
Deadline(s): None
Board meeting date(s): Approximately every other month
Final notification: 30 days
Write: H.D. Arnold, Staff Vice-President-Corporate Public Affairs
Trustees: H.D. Arnold, W.L. Burge, Robert Strickland.
Number of staff: 2 part-time professional.
Employer Identification Number: 581296807

832
Evans (Lettie Pate) Foundation, Inc. ▼
1400 Peachtree Center Tower
230 Peachtree St., N.W.
Atlanta 30303   (404) 522-6755

Incorporated in 1945 in Georgia.
Donor(s): Mrs. Lettie Pate Evans.†

Financial data: (yr. ended 12/31/83): Assets, $24,933,954 (M); expenditures, $1,177,403, including $1,074,500 for 17 grants (high: $300,000; low: $2,000; average: $63,206).
Purpose and activities: Grants primarily to local institutions, with emphasis on health and higher education, youth programs and child welfare, cultural activities, and civic affairs. Preference is given to one-time capital projects of established private charitable organizations.
Types of support awarded: Building funds, equipment, land acquisition, seed money.
Limitations: Giving primarily in the Atlanta, GA area. No grants to individuals, or for operating expenses, research, scholarships, fellowships, or matching gifts; no loans.
Application information:
Initial approach: Letter of inquiry followed by full proposal
Copies of proposal: 1
Deadline(s): Submit proposal in January or September
Board meeting date(s): April and November
Write: Boisfeuillet Jones, President
Officers: Boisfeuillet Jones, President; Charles H. McTier, Secretary and Treasurer.
Trustees: J.W. Jones, Chairman; Hughes Spalding, Jr., Vice-Chairman; Fillmore B. Eisenberg, James M. Sibley.
Number of staff: 2 part-time professional; 4 part-time support.
Employer Identification Number: 586004644

833
First Atlanta Foundation, Inc. ⌐
c/o The First National Bank of Atlanta, Trust Dept.
P.O. Box 4148
Atlanta 30302

Incorporated in 1976.
Donor(s): First Atlanta Corporation.
Financial data: (yr. ended 12/31/83): Assets, $1,628,181 (M); gifts received, $576,234; expenditures, $537,353, including $535,103 for 225 grants (high: $230,000; low: $25).
Purpose and activities: Giving primarily in the Atlanta area, with emphasis on higher education, community funds, arts and cultural programs, and youth agencies.
Limitations: Giving primarily in the Atlanta, GA area.
Officers: Thomas R. Williams, Chairman and President; William K. Hohlstein, Executive Director and Secretary-Treasurer.
Employer Identification Number: 581274979

834
Foundation for Agronomic Research, Inc.
2801 Buford Hwy., N.E., Suite 401
Atlanta 30329   (404) 634-4274

Donor(s): Potash Corporation of Saskatchewan, Texasgulf Inc., Kalium Chemicals, and others.
Financial data: (yr. ended 12/31/82): Assets, $329,043 (M); gifts received, $512,333; expenditures, $473,528, including $438,795 for 60 grants (high: $15,000; low: $1,000).

Purpose and activities: Grants primarily to universities and research organizations for studies of soil management and improved crop yields.
Types of support awarded: Research, conferences and seminars.
Publications: Program policy statement.
Application information:
Write: Dr. Charles P. Ellington, Vice-President
Officers: Robert E. Wagner,* President; Charles P. Ellington,* Vice-President; Richard T. Roberts, Secretary.
Directors: D.J. Bourne, David Dombowsky, Joe Downey, G.P. Giusti, William F. Hueg, Jr., R.R. Johnson, S.T. Keel, W.L. Nelson, E.T. York, Jr.
Employer Identification Number: 581406074

835
Franklin (John and Mary) Foundation, Inc. ▼
P.O. Box 1134
Atlanta 30301

Incorporated in 1955 in Georgia.
Donor(s): John Franklin, Mary O. Franklin.†
Financial data: (yr. ended 12/31/83): Assets, $14,334,585 (M); expenditures, $1,243,400, including $1,144,100 for 128 grants (high: $65,000; low: $50).
Purpose and activities: Broad purposes; primarily local giving, largely for higher and secondary education, youth agencies, hospitals, and cultural programs.
Types of support awarded: General purposes, scholarship funds, building funds.
Limitations: Giving primarily in GA, with emphasis on the metropolitan Atlanta area; special types of grants awarded to institutions in adjoining states.
Publications: Annual report.
Application information:
Initial approach: Letter
Board meeting date(s): January and July, and as needed
Write: Chairman, Secretary, or any member of the Board of Trustees
Officers: Virlyn B. Moore, Jr.,* Secretary; Robert B. Rountree, Treasurer.
Trustees: W. Kelly Mosley, Chairman; George T. Duncan, Frank M. Malone, Marilu H. McCarty, L. Edmund Rast, Alexander W. Smith, Jr., William M. Suttles, Walter O. Walker.
Employer Identification Number: 586036131

836
Fuqua (J. B.) Foundation, Inc.
c/o Fuqua National Corp.
4900 Georgia-Pacific Center
Atlanta 30303   (404) 659-5318

Incorporated in 1970 in Georgia.
Donor(s): J.B. Fuqua.
Financial data: (yr. ended 9/30/84): Assets, $1,840,719 (M); expenditures, $145,744, including $103,094 for 50 grants (high: $25,000; low: $40).
Purpose and activities: Grants primarily for higher and secondary education.
Limitations: No grants to individuals.
Application information:

Write: J.B. Fuqua, President
Officers: J.B. Fuqua, President; Bennett A. Hall, Vice-President; Dorothy C. Fuqua, Secretary; J. Rex Fuqua, Treasurer.
Number of staff: 1 part-time professional.
Employer Identification Number: 237122039

837
Georgia-Pacific Foundation, Inc. ▼ ⌐
133 Peachtree St., N.E.
Atlanta 30303   (404) 521-5228

Incorporated in 1958 in Oregon.
Donor(s): Georgia-Pacific Corporation, and subsidiaries.
Financial data: (yr. ended 12/31/82): Assets, $958,310 (M); expenditures, $1,185,212, including $648,895 for 354 grants (high: $40,500; low: $20) and $535,714 for grants to individuals.
Purpose and activities: Broad purposes; giving in areas of company operations for higher education, including a scholarship program, and to community funds, health, and youth agencies.
Types of support awarded: Student aid.
Limitations: Giving limited to areas of company operations, with some emphasis on the Atlanta, GA area.
Application information:
Write: Marion L. Talmadge, President
Officers and Trustees: Stanley S. Dennison, Chairman; Marion L. Talmadge, President; T. Marshall Hahn, Jr., Stephen K. Jackson.
Number of staff: 1.
Employer Identification Number: 936023726

838
Gholston (J. K.) Trust ⌐
P.O. Box 992
Athens 30613   (404) 549-8700

Trust established in 1967 in Georgia.
Donor(s): J. Knox Gholston.†
Financial data: (yr. ended 2/29/84): Assets, $2,800,537 (M); expenditures, $243,581, including $219,184 for 77 grants (high: $199,153; low: $100).
Purpose and activities: Support for education, including scholarship funds, and Baptist church support solely within the Comer, Georgia area.
Limitations: Giving limited to the Comer, GA, area.
Application information: Application form required.
Deadline(s): None
Write: Janey Cooley, Trust Officer
Trustee: The Citizens and Southern National Bank (Janey Cooley, Trust Officer).
Employer Identification Number: 586056879

839
Gilbert (Price), Jr. Charitable Trust
c/o First National Bank of Atlanta
P.O. Box 4148
Atlanta 30302   (404) 588-6677

Trust established in 1973 in Georgia.
Donor(s): Price Gilbert, Jr.†

Financial data: (yr. ended 5/31/84): Assets, $3,520,395 (M); expenditures, $271,506, including $242,500 for 26 grants (high: $30,000; low: $1,000).
Purpose and activities: Primarily local giving, with emphasis on secondary and higher education, hospitals, a community fund, and youth agencies.
Limitations: Giving limited to metropolitan Atlanta, GA.
Application information:
Initial approach: Letter
Copies of proposal: 1
Deadline(s): 30 days before each meeting
Board meeting date(s): First week of January, April, July, and October
Write: Frank Rozelle
Trustees: R.W. Courts II, First National Bank of Atlanta.
Employer Identification Number: 586106959

840
Glancy (Lenora and Alfred) Foundation, Inc.
1200 Citizens and Southern National Bank Bldg.
Atlanta 30335   (404) 586-1500

Incorporated in 1954 in Georgia.
Donor(s): Alfred R. Glancy, Sr.†
Financial data: (yr. ended 12/31/84): Assets, $2,939,992 (M); expenditures, $214,246, including $180,000 for 42 grants (high: $20,000; low: $500; average: $500-$20,000).
Purpose and activities: Support for higher and secondary education; grants also for hospitals, medical research, cultural programs, and community funds, largely in Atlanta and Michigan.
Types of support awarded: Operating budgets, continuing support, annual campaigns, seed money, emergency funds, deficit financing, building funds, equipment, land acquisition, endowment funds, general purposes.
Limitations: Giving primarily in Atlanta, GA, and MI. No grants to individuals, or for research, publications, conferences, special projects, matching gifts, scholarships, or fellowships; no loans.
Publications: Application guidelines.
Application information:
Initial approach: Letter or proposal
Copies of proposal: 1
Deadline(s): Submit proposal in October; deadline November 1
Board meeting date(s): November
Write: Benjamin T. White, Assistant Secretary
Officers and Directors: Gerry Hull, Chairman; A.R. Glancy III, Vice-Chairman; Christopher Brandon, Treasurer.
Number of staff: None.
Employer Identification Number: 586041425

841
Glenn (The Wilbur Fisk) Memorial Foundation, Inc. ¤
c/o Trust Company Bank
P.O. Box 4655
Atlanta 30302   (404) 588-7442

Incorporated in 1947 in Georgia.

Financial data: (yr. ended 12/31/83): Assets, $2,858,422 (M); expenditures, $11,117, including $1,000 for 1 grant.
Purpose and activities: Primarily local giving, with support for hospitals and a Methodist church.
Limitations: Giving primarily in the Atlanta, GA area.
Application information:
Initial approach: Letter
Deadline(s): None
Write: Dr. Wadley Glenn
Managers: A.D. Boylston, Charles H. Chandler, Jr., Jack Glenn, Wadley R. Glenn, Wilbur F. Glenn, Trust Company Bank.
Employer Identification Number: 586026020

842
Haley (W. B.) Foundation ¤
c/o First State Bank and Trust Company
333 Broad Ave., P.O. Box 8
Albany 31703

Established in 1973 in Georgia.
Donor(s): W.B. Haley, Jr.†
Financial data: (yr. ended 2/29/84): Assets, $1,638,966 (M); expenditures, $207,648, including $186,940 for 8 grants (high: $174,455; low: $500).
Purpose and activities: Primarily local giving, with emphasis on an art museum.
Limitations: Giving primarily in Albany, GA.
Officers: Eloise Haley, President; Stuart Watson, Secretary.
Trustee: First State Bank and Trust Company.
Employer Identification Number: 586113405

843
Harland (John H. and Wilhelmina D.) Charitable Foundation, Inc.
P.O. Box 105250
Atlanta 30348   (404) 981-9460

Incorporated in 1972 in Georgia.
Donor(s): John H. Harland.†
Financial data: (yr. ended 12/31/84): Assets, $12,856,641 (M); gifts received, $10,000; expenditures, $519,782, including $507,500 for 28 grants (high: $160,500; low: $500).
Purpose and activities: Broad purposes; giving limited to public charities within Georgia, preferably in metropolitan Atlanta, with emphasis on youth agencies, child welfare, higher education, and community funds. Preference given to projects with little chance of gaining popular support, and which increase long-term effectiveness of the grantee.
Types of support awarded: Operating budgets, annual campaigns, building funds, equipment, endowment funds, professorships, scholarship funds, publications.
Limitations: Giving limited to GA, with emphasis on metropolitan Atlanta. No grants to individuals, or for matching gifts; no loans.
Publications: Application guidelines, program policy statement.
Application information:
Initial approach: Letter or telephone
Copies of proposal: 1
Deadline(s): Submit proposal in December through February; deadline March 1

Board meeting date(s): March
Final notification: 3 to 4 weeks after board meeting
Write: John A. Conant, Secretary
Officers and Trustees: Miriam Harland Conant, President; J. William Robinson, Vice-President and Treasurer; John A. Conant, Secretary.
Number of staff: None.
Employer Identification Number: 237225012

844
Harland (John H.) Company Foundation ¤
2939 Miller Rd.
Atlanta 30035

Incorporated in 1957 in Georgia.
Donor(s): John H. Harland Company.
Financial data: (yr. ended 12/31/83): Assets, $1,568,760 (M); gifts received, $302,510; expenditures, $188,241, including $180,446 for 72 grants (high: $30,000; low: $50).
Purpose and activities: Giving for social services, youth agencies, community funds, and higher education.
Types of support awarded: General purposes.
Manager: J. William Robinson.
Employer Identification Number: 586035073

845
Herndon (Alonzo F.) and Norris B. Herndon Foundation, Inc. ¤
Herndon Plaza, 100 Auburn Ave., N.E.
Atlanta 30303

Incorporated in 1950 in Georgia.
Donor(s): Norris B. Herndon.
Financial data: (yr. ended 12/31/83): Assets, $5,359,422 (M); expenditures, $125,206, including $116,688 for 10 grants (high: $81,488; low: $500).
Purpose and activities: Broad purposes; primarily local giving, with emphasis on a museum, higher education, and social services.
Limitations: Giving primarily in GA. No grants to individuals.
Officers and Trustees: Jesse Hill, Jr., President; Henry N. Brown, Secretary; Norris L. Connally, Treasurer; Helen J. Collins, James D. Palmer, Edward L. Simon.
Employer Identification Number: 586036028

846
Hill (Walter Clay) and Family Foundation
P.O. Box 4655
Atlanta 30302   (404) 588-7442

Trust established in 1967 in Georgia.
Donor(s): Rebecca Travers Hill.†
Financial data: (yr. ended 8/31/83): Assets, $2,466,664 (M); expenditures, $148,144, including $135,100 for 18 grants (high: $50,000; low: $1,500; average: $1,500-$50,000).

Purpose and activities: Broad purposes; grants primarily locally and in the southeastern states for the arts, museums, and Protestant church support; support also for higher education and a historical association.
Types of support awarded: General purposes, operating budgets, continuing support, annual campaigns, seed money, emergency funds, deficit financing, building funds, equipment, land acquisition, endowment funds, special projects.
Limitations: Giving primarily in the Southeast, particularly in the Atlanta, GA, area. No grants to individuals, or for research, publications, conferences, scholarships and fellowships, or matching gifts; no loans.
Publications: Application guidelines.
Application information:
Initial approach: Full proposal
Copies of proposal: 1
Deadline(s): Submit proposal preferably from January through June; no set deadline
Board meeting date(s): July or October
Final notification: Immediately after annual meeting if decision is positive
Write: C. Peter Melton, Trust Officer
Trustees: Laura Hill Boland, Walter Clay Hill, Trust Company Bank.
Number of staff: None.
Employer Identification Number: 586065956

847
Hodge Foundation, Inc., The ⌘
P.O. Box 23559
Savannah 31403

Incorporated in 1962 in Georgia.
Donor(s): Mrs. Sarah Mills Hodge.†
Financial data: (yr. ended 7/31/84): Assets, $1,394,045 (M); expenditures, $115,808, including $93,005 for 15 grants (high: $19,475; low: $500).
Purpose and activities: Support limited to local charitable organizations of special interest to the donor and solely to improve the economic condition of the lower income group; grants largely for youth and family services, particularly those assisting black families, and for scholarship funds at local colleges.
Types of support awarded: Scholarship funds.
Limitations: Giving limited to Chatham County, GA.
Application information: Address scholarship applications to presidents of local Armstrong and Savannah State Colleges; no scholarships awarded by foundation directly.
Initial approach: Letter
Copies of proposal: 2
Board meeting date(s): January, April, July, and October
Write: Abram Minis, Jr., President
Officers and Trustees: Abram Minis, Jr., President; Malcolm Bell, John E. Cay III, James E. Hungerpiller, James B. Spencer.
Employer Identification Number: 580909476

848
Illges (A. and M. L.) Memorial Foundation, Inc. ⌘
1345 Second Ave.
P.O. Box 103
Columbus 31902

Incorporated in 1947 in Georgia.
Financial data: (yr. ended 9/30/83): Assets, $2,360,631 (M); expenditures, $175,204, including $158,073 for grants.
Purpose and activities: Broad purposes; primarily local giving, with emphasis on higher education, including scholarship funds, hospitals, church support, and cultural programs.
Limitations: Giving primarily in GA.
Officers and Directors: Howell Hollis, President and Treasurer; J. Barnett Woodruff, Vice-President; John P. Illges, III, Secretary; B.M. Chenoweth, Jr., Martha H. Heinz, Mrs. J.S. Hurt, A. Illges, Jr.
Employer Identification Number: 586033958

849
Illges (John P. and Dorothy S.) Foundation, Inc. ⌘
c/o 1017 First Ave.
P.O. Box 103
Columbus 31902   (404) 323-5342

Incorporated in 1947 in Georgia.
Donor(s): John P. Illges.†
Financial data: (yr. ended 9/30/82): Assets, $2,056,799 (M); expenditures, $170,199, including $155,250 for 7 grants (high: $100,000; low: $1,250).
Purpose and activities: Broad purposes; primarily local giving, with emphasis on a private secondary school and youth agencies.
Limitations: Giving primarily in Columbus, GA. No grants to individuals.
Application information:
Initial approach: Letter
Deadline(s): Submit proposal between June and September; deadline September 1
Board meeting date(s): June and September
Write: John P. Illges, III, President
Officers: John P. Illges, III,* President; Margaret M. Badcock,* Vice-President; Pauline Bryan, Secretary; Custis G. Illges,* Treasurer.
Directors:* Emmy Lou P. Illges, Susan I. Lanier, John W. Mayher, Jr.
Employer Identification Number: 580691476

850
Jinks (Ruth T.) Foundation ⌘
Colquitt 31737

Established in 1955.
Financial data: (yr. ended 11/30/83): Assets, $1,307,445 (M); gifts received, $104,500; expenditures, $129,966, including $126,750 for 54 grants (high: $35,000; low: $100).
Purpose and activities: Primarily local giving for Christian religious organizations and churches, higher education and social services.
Limitations: Giving primarily in GA.
Officers: G.C. Jinks, Sr., Chairman and President; G.C. Jinks, Ruth T. Jinks, Vice-Presidents.
Employer Identification Number: 586043856

851
Lane (Mills Bee) Memorial Foundation, Inc. ⌘
c/o Citizens and Southern National Bank
P.O. Box 9626
Savannah 31402   (912) 233-1108
Additional mailing address: P.O. Box 2364, Savannah, GA 31402

Incorporated in 1947 in Georgia.
Donor(s): Members of the Lane family.
Financial data: (yr. ended 12/31/83): Assets, $5,383,134 (M); expenditures, $191,459, including $175,048 for 34 grants (high: $26,131; low: $50).
Purpose and activities: Primarily local giving; emphasis on higher and secondary education and cultural programs.
Types of support awarded: Seed money, building funds, equipment, land acquisition, professorships, internships, scholarship funds, exchange programs, fellowships, matching funds, employee matching gifts, endowment funds.
Limitations: Giving primarily in the Savannah, GA, area. No grants to individuals or for operating budgets; no loans.
Publications: Application guidelines.
Application information: Application form required.
Initial approach: Letter
Copies of proposal: 1
Deadline(s): Submit proposal in 3-month period prior to each board meeting; deadlines May 15 and November 15
Board meeting date(s): June and December
Final notification: 2 weeks after board meetings
Write: Mills Lane Morrison, Chairman
Officers and Trustees: Mills Lane Morrison, Chairman; Thomas M. Lane, Secretary; Howard Jackson Morrison, Jr., Treasurer.
Number of staff: None.
Employer Identification Number: 586033043

852
Lanier Brothers Foundation ⌘
c/o Trust Company Bank
P.O. Box 4655
Atlanta 30302

Trust established in 1955 in Georgia.
Donor(s): Members of the Lanier family.
Financial data: (yr. ended 12/31/83): Assets, $8,078,971 (M); expenditures, $303,145, including $265,450 for 77 grants (high: $25,000; low: $150).
Purpose and activities: Primarily local giving, with emphasis on higher education, community funds, youth agencies, and hospitals; some support for social welfare.
Limitations: Giving primarily in GA. No grants to individuals.
Application information:
Initial approach: Letter
Deadline(s): December
Trustees: Helen S. Lanier, John Reese Lanier, Sartain Lanier, Trust Company Bank.
Employer Identification Number: 586026033

853
Lee (The Ray M. and Mary Elizabeth) Foundation, Inc.
C & S National Bank
P.O. Box 4899
Atlanta 30302   (404) 897-3153

Incorporated in 1966 in Georgia.
Donor(s): Ray M. Lee,† Mary Elizabeth Lee.†
Financial data: (yr. ended 9/30/84): Assets, $6,023,641 (M); expenditures, $440,000, including $250,000 for 47 grants (high: $38,500; low: $1,000).
Purpose and activities: Broad purposes; primarily local giving, with emphasis on educational institutions, health agencies, hospitals, Protestant church support, and the arts.
Limitations: Giving primarily in GA and the Southeast. No grants to individuals.
Application information:
  Initial approach: Full proposal
  Copies of proposal: 1
  Board meeting date(s): As required
  Write: William B. Stark, President
Officers and Trustees: William B. Stark, President and Treasurer; Donald D. Smith, Secretary; Ronald W. Gann.
Employer Identification Number: 586049441

854
Livingston Foundation, Inc.
55 Park Place, Suite 400
Atlanta 30303   (404) 577-5100

Incorporated in 1964 in Georgia.
Donor(s): Roy N. Livingston,† Mrs. Leslie Livingston Kellar,† Bess B. Livingston.†
Financial data: (yr. ended 9/30/83): Assets, $5,752,981 (L); gifts received, $1,942,582; expenditures, $482,552, including $429,000 for 22 grants (high: $100,000; low: $500).
Purpose and activities: Primarily local giving, with emphasis on cultural organizations.
Types of support awarded: Operating budgets, continuing support, annual campaigns.
Limitations: Giving primarily in the Atlanta, GA area. No grants to individuals, or for endowment funds, scholarships and fellowships, or matching gifts; no loans.
Application information:
  Initial approach: Letter
  Copies of proposal: 1
  Deadline(s): None
  Board meeting date(s): Quarterly
  Final notification: 4 months
  Write: Sol I. Golden, Secretary
Officers and Trustees: Ben W. Brannon, President; Sol I. Golden, Secretary.
Number of staff: 1.
Employer Identification Number: 586044858

855
Loridans (Charles) Foundation, Inc.
1200 Citizens and Southern National Bank Bldg.
35 Broad St., N.W.
Atlanta 30335   (404) 586-1500

Incorporated in 1952 in Georgia.
Donor(s): Charles Loridans,† A.T. Arnold.
Financial data: (yr. ended 12/31/84): Assets, $4,253,128 (M); expenditures, $122,024, including $73,436 for 6 grants (high: $37,000; low: $2,016).
Purpose and activities: Broad purposes; primarily emphasizes assistance to local educational institutions lacking access to general sources of support.
Types of support awarded: Seed money, emergency funds, building funds, equipment, land acquisition, endowment funds, matching funds, scholarship funds, professorships.
Limitations: Giving primarily in GA, with emphasis on the metropolitan Atlanta area. No grants to individuals, or for operating budgets, continuing support, annual campaigns, deficit financing, special projects, research, publications, or conferences; no loans.
Publications: Annual report, program policy statement, application guidelines.
Application information:
  Initial approach: Full proposal
  Copies of proposal: 1
  Board meeting date(s): June and December
  Write: Robert G. Edge, Chairman
Trustees: Robert G. Edge, Chairman; Benjamin T. White, Secretary; Alex P. Gaines, B. Harvey Hill, Jr., Daniel B. Hodgson, Sidney O. Smith, Jr.
Number of staff: None.
Employer Identification Number: 580871627

856
Lubo Fund, Inc.
3910 Randall Mill Rd., N.W.
Atlanta 30327
Application address: c/o H. Simmons, 215 East 62nd St., New York, NY 10021

Incorporated in 1958 in Georgia.
Donor(s): Members of the Bunnen family.
Financial data: (yr. ended 12/31/82): Assets, $1,350,350 (M); gifts received, $20,946; expenditures, $118,364, including $109,045 for 127 grants (high: $15,000; low: $20; average: $20-$15,000).
Purpose and activities: Primarily local giving, with emphasis on cultural programs, including the performing and visual arts; support also for education.
Types of support awarded: General purposes, operating budgets, building funds, equipment, special projects, publications, matching funds, annual campaigns, continuing support, seed money, emergency funds, deficit financing, consulting services.
Limitations: Giving primarily in GA, with emphasis on Atlanta. No grants to individuals, or for land acquisition, renovation projects, endowment funds, scholarships and fellowships, research, or conferences; no loans.
Application information:
  Initial approach: Letter or full proposal
  Copies of proposal: 1
  Deadline(s): None
  Board meeting date(s): July
  Final notification: 1 to 3 months
  Write: Lucinda W. Bunnen, President

Officers: Lucinda W. Bunnen, President; Robert L. Bunnen, Jr., Vice-President; Robert L. Bunnen, Secretary; Phoebe W. Lundeen, Treasurer.
Number of staff: None.
Employer Identification Number: 586043631

857
Marshall (Harriet McDaniel) Trust in Memory of Sanders McDaniel ¤
c/o Trust Company Bank
P.O. Box 4418
Atlanta 30302   (404) 588-8246

Trust established in 1962 in Georgia.
Donor(s): Harriet McDaniel Marshall.
Financial data: (yr. ended 11/30/83): Assets, $2,623,903 (M); expenditures, $136,943, including $119,304 for 35 grants (high: $10,000; low: $500).
Purpose and activities: Primarily local giving, with emphasis on local welfare and higher education; support also for handicapped, and community funds.
Limitations: Giving primarily in GA. No grants to individuals, or for scholarships or fellowships; no loans.
Publications: Application guidelines.
Application information: Application form required.
  Initial approach: Letter
  Copies of proposal: 1
  Deadline(s): Submit proposal at least one month prior to committee meetings
  Board meeting date(s): January, April, July, and October
  Write: Victor A. Gregory, Secretary
Distribution Committee: Robert Strickland, Chairman; Victor A. Gregory, Secretary; E.P. Gould, Jesse S. Hall.
Trustee: Trust Company Bank.
Employer Identification Number: 586089937

858
Mathis (The Alice K.) Memorial Foundation ¤
P.O. Box 88185
Atlanta 30338

Established in 1981 in Georgia.
Donor(s): T. Harvey Mathis.
Financial data: (yr. ended 6/30/83): Assets, $2,376 (M); expenditures, $438,005, including $438,000 for 8 grants (high: $391,000; low: $2,000).
Purpose and activities: Primarily local giving for community development and education.
Types of support awarded: General purposes.
Limitations: Giving primarily in GA.
Trustees: Herschel M. Bloom, Harvey M. Cheatham, Susan W. Mathis, T. Harvey Mathis.
Employer Identification Number: 581444261

859
Moore (James Starr) Memorial Foundation, Inc. ⊐
526 East Paces Ferry Rd., N.E.
Atlanta 30305

Incorporated in 1953 in Georgia.
Donor(s): AMEV Holdings.
Financial data: (yr. ended 12/31/83): Assets, $5,192,520 (M); gifts received, $36,300; expenditures, $301,063, including $215,365 for 110 grants (high: $50,750; low: $25) and $30,917 for 13 grants to individuals.
Purpose and activities: Broad purposes; primarily local giving, with emphasis on cultural programs, higher education, Protestant church support, hospitals, and health agencies. Company scholarship program terminated in 1983.
Limitations: Giving primarily in GA.
Application information:
  Write: James M. Henson, Treasurer
Officers: F.L. Maddox, Secretary; James M. Henson, Treasurer.
Trustees: Sara Giles Moore, Chairman; Monroe F. Swilley, Jr., Vice-Chairman; Starr Moore, Morton S. Hodgson, Jr.
Employer Identification Number: 586033190

860
Murphy (Katherine and John) Foundation
P.O. Box 4655
Atlanta 30302

Trust established in 1954 in Georgia.
Donor(s): Mrs. Katherine M. Riley.
Financial data: (yr. ended 12/31/82): Assets, $1,404,559 (M); expenditures, $114,405, including $103,600 for 14 grants (high: $34,000; low: $500).
Purpose and activities: Primarily local giving, with emphasis on hospitals, cultural programs, health agencies, higher education, youth agencies, and child welfare.
Limitations: Giving primarily in Atlanta, GA. No grants to individuals, or for research, scholarships, fellowships, or matching gifts; no loans.
Application information:
  Initial approach: Letter
  Copies of proposal: 1
  Deadline(s): March 1
  Board meeting date(s): As required
  Write: Dameron Black, Group Vice-President
Managers: A.D. Boylston, Jr., Katherine M. Riley, Ray B. Wilhoit.
Trustee: Trust Company Bank (Dameron Black, Group Vice-President).
Employer Identification Number: 586026045

861
Ottley (Marian W.) Trust - Atlanta ▼
c/o First National Bank of Atlanta
P.O. Box 4148
Atlanta 30302   (404) 588-5485

Trust established in 1975 in Georgia.
Donor(s): Marian W. Ottley.†

Financial data: (yr. ended 5/31/84): Assets, $13,861,281 (M); expenditures, $1,043,522, including $916,500 for 38 grants (high: $100,000; low: $1,500; average: $5,000-$50,000).
Purpose and activities: Primarily local giving, with emphasis on church support, higher and secondary education and hospitals; support also for a community fund and cultural programs.
Types of support awarded: Building funds, emergency funds, endowment funds, equipment, operating budgets, special projects.
Limitations: Giving primarily in Atlanta, GA.
Application information:
  Initial approach: Letter
  Copies of proposal: 1
  Deadline(s): 30 days prior to board meetings
  Board meeting date(s): June and December
  Write: Arthur C. Baxter, Executive Vice-President
Distribution Committee: Edward D. Smith, Chairman; William D. Ellis, Jr., Robert L. Foreman, Jr., Joseph H. Hilsman, James M. Sibley.
Trustee: First National Bank of Atlanta (F.L. Rozelle, Trust Officer).
Number of staff: None.
Employer Identification Number: 586222004

862
Ottley (Marian W.) Trust - Watertown
c/o First National Bank of Atlanta, MC 701
P.O. Box 4148
Atlanta 30302   (404) 588-5485

Trust established in 1975 in Georgia.
Donor(s): Marian W. Ottley.†
Financial data: (yr. ended 5/31/84): Assets, $4,752,826 (M); expenditures, $344,552, including $292,250 for 14 grants (high: $100,000; low: $750).
Purpose and activities: Giving primarily for higher and secondary education, youth agencies, church support, and social services.
Limitations: Giving limited to New England and NY. No grants to individuals.
Application information:
  Write: Arthur C. Baxter, Executive V.P.
Selection Committee: Hemingway Merriman, Edith Pelletier, Edward Thompson.
Trustee: First National Bank of Atlanta (F.L. Rozelle, Trust Officer).
Employer Identification Number: 586222005

863
Patterson-Barclay Memorial Foundation, Inc.
1020 Spring St., N.W.
Atlanta 30309   (404) 876-1022

Incorporated in 1953 in Georgia.
Donor(s): Frederick W. Patterson.
Financial data: (yr. ended 12/31/83): Assets, $3,913,199 (M); expenditures, $311,730, including $296,400 for grants (high: $12,000; average: $1,000-$5,000).

Purpose and activities: Local giving, with emphasis on higher education, hospitals, and church support; grants also for health, social, and youth agencies and for secondary education.
Limitations: Giving limited to the Atlanta, GA metropolitan area. No grants to individuals.
Application information:
  Write: Mrs. Lee Barclay Patterson Allen, Trustee
Trustees: Mrs. Lee Barclay Patterson Allen, J. David Bansley, Ida Brittain Patterson.
Employer Identification Number: 580904580

864
Pattillo Foundation, The ⊐
2053 Mountain Industrial Blvd.
Tucker 30084

Established in 1967.
Financial data: (yr. ended 12/31/83): Assets, $1,310,685 (M); gifts received, $176,500; expenditures, $215,816, including $196,570 for 28 grants (high: $86,000; low: $25).
Purpose and activities: Primarily local giving for higher education and Protestant church support.
Limitations: Giving primarily in GA.
Trustees: D.B. Pattillo, H.G. Pattillo.
Employer Identification Number: 586068757

865
Pickett & Hatcher Educational Fund, Inc.
1800 Buena Vista Rd.
P.O. Box 8169
Columbus 31908   (404) 327-6586

Incorporated in 1938 in Georgia.
Donor(s): Claud A. Hatcher.†
Financial data: (yr. ended 9/30/84): Assets, $12,494,192 (M); expenditures, $1,390,099, including $1,021,860 for 671 loans (average: $1,845).
Purpose and activities: Giving in the southeastern states to encourage worthy students to secure a broad liberal education by providing student loans.
Types of support awarded: Student aid.
Limitations: Giving limited to AL, FL, GA, KY, MS, NC, SC, TN and VA. No support for students planning to enter fields of medicine, law, or the ministry.
Publications: Program policy statement, application guidelines.
Application information: Application form required.
  Initial approach: Letter, telephone, or full proposal
  Deadline(s): July 1 for school year starting in September; for other periods during the year, 2 months prior to beginning of session in which money will be used
  Board meeting date(s): May and November
  Final notification: 2 months
  Write: Robert E. Bennett, Executive Vice-President
Officers: Wilbur H. Glenn,* President; Robert E. Bennett, Executive Vice-President; William T. Smith, Vice-President; Alice V. Haywood, Secretary; C. Alex Sears,* Treasurer.

Trustees:* Guy E. Snavely, Jr., Chairman;
William B. Hardegree, William K. Hatcher,
James W. Key, William T. Miller.
Number of staff: 4 full-time professional; 7 full-time support; 2 part-time support.
Employer Identification Number: 580566216

866
Pitts (William I. H. and Lula E.) Foundation ▼
P.O. Box 4655
Atlanta 30302   (404) 588-8544

Trust established in 1941 in Georgia.
Donor(s): William I.H. Pitts,† Miss Margaret A. Pitts.
Financial data: (yr. ended 12/31/84): Assets,
$7,956,000 (M); expenditures, $560,000,
including $518,000 for 36 grants (high:
$47,000; low: $100; average: $1,000-$47,000).
Purpose and activities: Broad purposes; giving
to local charities, almost exclusively Methodist
church-related institutions; emphasis on higher
education and care of the aged.
Types of support awarded: Building funds,
general purposes, continuing support.
Limitations: Giving limited to GA. No grants
to individuals, or for endowment funds,
research, scholarships and fellowships, or
matching gifts; no loans.
Application information:
   Initial approach: Letter
   Copies of proposal: 1
   Deadline(s): Submit proposal preferably in
      March or October
   Board meeting date(s): April and November
   Write: Marvin R. Benson, Secretary
Officer and Managers: Marvin R. Benson,
Secretary; John H. Boman, Jr., Bishop William
R. Cannon, William D. Greer, Jr., Carroll P.
Jones, Thomas O. Marshall, Walter Y. Murphy,
Margaret A. Pitts, Robert M. Strickland.
Trustee: Trust Company Bank.
Number of staff: None.
Employer Identification Number: 586026047

867
Porter (James Hyde) Testamentary Trust
c/o Trust Company Bank of Middle Georgia
606 Cherry St., P.O. Box 4248
Macon 31208   (912) 741-2265

Trust established in 1949 in Georgia.
Donor(s): James Hyde Porter.†
Financial data: (yr. ended 12/31/83): Assets,
$1,961,137 (M); expenditures, $293,230,
including $281,158 for 29 grants (high:
$50,000; low: $988).
Purpose and activities: To aid local charitable,
educational, and public institutions, with
emphasis on social services, civic affairs,
cultural programs, higher education, and health
agencies.
Limitations: Giving limited to Bibb and
Newton counties, GA. No grants to
individuals, or for endowment funds, research
programs, scholarships, or fellowships; no loans.
Publications: 990-PF, application guidelines.
Application information: Application form
required.
   Initial approach: Telephone

Copies of proposal: 7
Deadline(s): Submit proposal preferably in
   March; deadline April 1
Board meeting date(s): June
Write: William R. Jones, Trust Officer
Managers: W.L. Dobbs, Rabbi Donald M.
Goldstein, Emory Greene, George Israel, E.C.
McMillan, Joe E. Popper, M.M. Pulliam,
Donald G. Stephenson, Roy Varner, Rev. Jack
Wilson.
Trustee: Trust Company Bank of Middle
Georgia (William R. Jones, Trust Officer).
Employer Identification Number: 586034882

868
Ragan and King Charitable Foundation
c/o The First National Bank of Atlanta, Trust
Dept.
P.O. Box 4148
Atlanta 30302   (404) 588-6677

Established in 1972 in Georgia.
Donor(s): Carolyn King Ragan.†
Financial data: (yr. ended 9/30/84): Assets,
$1,595,496 (M); expenditures, $108,776,
including $72,000 for 3 grants (high: $30,000;
low: $12,000).
Purpose and activities: Giving for Baptist
organizations only, to churches, religious
organizations, and theological seminaries, and
for higher education.
Limitations: Giving primarily in GA.
Application information:
   Initial approach: Letter
   Copies of proposal: 1
   Deadline(s): August 1
   Board meeting date(s): Fall
   Write: Frank Rozelle
Trustees: Allen Post, First National Bank of
Atlanta.
Employer Identification Number: 586138950

869
Rainbow Fund ¤
P.O. Box 937
Fort Valley 31030

Trust established in 1954 in Georgia.
Donor(s): Albert L. Luce, Jr., Blue Bird
companies.
Financial data: (yr. ended 3/31/84): Assets,
$4,003 (M); gifts received, $424,250;
expenditures, $423,098, including $422,218
for 117 grants (high: $83,776; low: $100).
Purpose and activities: General giving, with
emphasis on higher education and Protestant
church support including religious
organizations, missionary programs, and
theological education.
Officers: George E. Luce, Chairman; Joseph P.
Luce, Vice-President; Albert L. Luce, Jr.,
Treasurer.
Employer Identification Number: 586043659

870
Rich Foundation, Inc., The ▼
P.O. Box 4539
Atlanta 30302   (404) 586-2488

Incorporated in 1942 in Georgia.
Donor(s): Rich's Inc., and members of the Rich
family.
Financial data: (yr. ended 1/31/84): Assets,
$11,430,815 (M); gifts received, $266,400;
expenditures, $750,037, including $684,333
for 43 grants (high: $373,800; low: $1,000;
average: $1,000-$10,000).
Purpose and activities: Broad purposes;
general giving; grants restricted to the Atlanta
area, with major interests in health, education,
and welfare; emphasis on community funds,
colleges, universities, and private schools, arts
organizations, medical institutions, and youth
organizations.
Types of support awarded: Annual
campaigns, building funds, consulting services,
continuing support, equipment, operating
budgets, technical assistance, employee related
scholarships.
Limitations: Giving limited to Atlanta, GA,
area. No grants to individuals, or for matching
gifts; no loans.
Publications: Application guidelines.
Application information: Application form
required.
   Initial approach: Letter
   Copies of proposal: 1
   Deadline(s): Submit proposal 1 month prior
      to a meeting
   Board meeting date(s): February, May,
      September, and November
   Final notification: 2 weeks
   Write: Anne Poland Berg, Grant Consultant
Officers and Trustees: Harold Brockey,
President; Joel Goldberg, Vice-President;
Michael P. Rich, Secretary-Treasurer; Joseph F.
Asher, Thomas J. Asher, David S. Baker, Joseph
K. Heyman.
Number of staff: None.
Employer Identification Number: 586038037

871
Schwob (Simon) Foundation, Inc.
P.O. Box 1014
Columbus 31902   (404) 327-4582

Incorporated in 1949 in Georgia.
Donor(s): Schwob Manufacturing Company,
Schwob Realty Company, Schwob Company of
Florida.
Financial data: (yr. ended 12/31/82): Assets,
$2,815,359 (M); gifts received, $59,667;
expenditures, $187,681, including $135,000
for 19 grants (high: $50,000; low: $200).
Purpose and activities: Broad purposes;
primarily local giving, with emphasis on higher
education, Jewish welfare funds, music, and
community funds.
Limitations: Giving primarily in OH.
Application information:
   Initial approach: Letter
   Copies of proposal: 1
   Board meeting date(s): Semiannually
   Write: Henry Schwob, President

Officers and Trustees: Henry Schwob, President; Joyce Schwob, Vice-President; Miriam S. Butler, Secretary-Treasurer; Barbara Golden.
Employer Identification Number: 586038932

872
Sewell (Warren P. and Ava F.) Foundation ⌑
Bremen 30110

Trust established in 1948 in Georgia.
Donor(s): Warren P. Sewell.
Financial data: (yr. ended 6/30/83): Assets, $3,734,185 (M); gifts received, $365,000; expenditures, $423,449, including $414,495 for 31 grants (high: $85,000; low: $500).
Purpose and activities: Charitable and educational purposes; grants primarily to Protestant churches, secondary and elementary education, health agencies, and a library in Georgia.
Limitations: Giving primarily in GA.
Trustees: Raymond C. Otwell, Lamar R. Plunkett, Jack Worley.
Employer Identification Number: 586041342

873
Southern Education Foundation, Inc.
340 W. Peachtree St., N.W., Suite 250
Atlanta 30308   (404) 523-0001

Incorporated in 1937 in New York with the merger of Peabody Fund (1867), Slater Fund (1882), Rural School Fund (1907), and Randolph Fund (1938).
Donor(s): George Peabody,† John F. Slater,† Miss Anna T. Jeanes,† Jeanes Teachers of the Southern States.
Financial data: (yr. ended 3/31/84): Assets, $7,907,010 (M); gifts received, $635,045; expenditures, $1,271,047, including $314,446 for 17 grants (high: $50,000) and $674,103 for foundation-administered programs.
Purpose and activities: To advance education, particularly to support equal educational opportunity for Blacks in southern states. Foundation is in a 60-month terminating period as a private foundation, and has gained an IRS advance ruling allowing it to operate as a public charity thereafter.
Types of support awarded: Continuing support, general purposes, seed money, matching funds.
Limitations: Giving limited to the South. No grants to individuals, or for capital or endowment funds, scholarships, or fellowships; no loans.
Publications: Annual report, program policy statement, application guidelines.
Application information:
  Initial approach: Letter
  Copies of proposal: 2
  Deadline(s): Submit proposal preferably in February or September; deadline 6 weeks prior to board meetings
  Board meeting date(s): April and November
  Write: Elridge W. McMillan, President
Officers: Elridge W. McMillan, President; Richard B. Fields,* Secretary; Willie W. Herenton,* Treasurer.

Trustees:* Lisle Carter, Chairman; Elaine B. Alexander, Vice-Chairman; Eula Adams, Adrian Y. Bailey, Jack Bass, Deborah Hodges Bell, Edgar G. Epps, Erwin B. Friedman, Eamon M. Kelly.
Number of staff: 9.
Employer Identification Number: 135562388

874
Steiner (Albert) Charitable Fund
3451 Paces Ferry Rd., N.W.
Atlanta 30327   (404) 237-8736

Trust established in 1919 in Georgia.
Donor(s): Albert Steiner.†
Financial data: (yr. ended 12/31/83): Assets, $1,700,626 (M); expenditures, $159,081, including $136,500 for 12 grants (high: $25,000; low: $500).
Purpose and activities: Grants to institutions to provide hospitalization and medical treatment for the poor of Atlanta.
Types of support awarded: Continuing support, research, general purposes.
Limitations: Giving primarily in GA. No grants to individuals, or for building funds, endowments, scholarships, fellowships, or matching gifts; no loans.
Application information:
  Initial approach: Letter
  Copies of proposal: 1
  Deadline(s): Submit proposal preferably in October
  Board meeting date(s): April, July, October, and December
  Write: L.G. Sherman, Jr., Trustee
Trustees: Bernard S. Lipman, M.D., Lala H. Oberdorfer, L.G. Sherman, Jr.
Employer Identification Number: 586030063

875
Tomlinson (Kate and Elwyn) Foundation, Inc. ⌑
3000 Habersham Rd., N.W.
Atlanta 30303

Incorporated in 1949 in Georgia.
Financial data: (yr. ended 12/31/83): Assets, $1,826,400 (M); expenditures, $214,931, including $91,900 for 50 grants (high: $15,000; low: $100).
Purpose and activities: Broad purposes; primarily local giving, with emphasis on higher and secondary education, arts and culture, hospitals, health agencies, and a community fund.
Limitations: Giving primarily in GA.
Officers: Kathryn Bridges, Chairman; Mark P. Tomlinson, Vice-Chairman.
Employer Identification Number: 580634727

876
Trebor Foundation, Inc. ▼
1400 Peachtree Center Tower
230 Peachtree St., N.W.
Atlanta 30303   (404) 522-6755

Incorporated in 1937 in Delaware.
Donor(s): Robert W. Woodruff, The Acmaro Securities Corporation, and others.

Financial data: (yr. ended 12/31/83): Assets, $32,903,038 (M); expenditures, $1,392,478, including $1,295,385 for 30 grants (high: $300,000; low: $1,000; average: $10,000-$100,000).
Purpose and activities: Grants primarily to local institutions in the fields of health, education, youth programs, the arts, and civic affairs. Preference is given to one-time capital projects of established private charitable organizations.
Types of support awarded: Building funds.
Limitations: Giving primarily in Atlanta, GA. No grants to individuals, or for endowment funds, operating budgets, research, special projects, publications, conferences and seminars, or operating budgets; no loans.
Application information:
  Initial approach: Letter
  Copies of proposal: 1
  Deadline(s): Submit proposal in January or September
  Board meeting date(s): April and November
  Write: Boisfeuillet Jones, President
Officers: Boisfeuillet Jones, President; Charles H. McTier, Secretary; Thomas A. Jackson, Treasurer.
Trustees: Joseph W. Jones, Chairman; James M. Sibley, Vice-Chairman; Ivan Allen, Jr., A.D. Boylston, Jr., James B. Williams.
Number of staff: 2 part-time professional; 4 part-time support.
Employer Identification Number: 586033196

877
Trust Company of Georgia Foundation ⌑
P.O. Box 4418
Atlanta 30302   (404) 588-8246

Trust established in 1959 in Georgia.
Donor(s): Trust Company Bank.
Financial data: (yr. ended 12/31/83): Assets, $3,868,612 (M); gifts received, $1,723,716; expenditures, $608,803, including $575,332 for 335 grants (high: $60,936; low: $10).
Purpose and activities: Primarily local giving, with emphasis on local community welfare and higher education; support also for youth agencies, schools, hospitals, health agencies, and cultural groups.
Types of support awarded: Building funds, equipment, special projects, research.
Limitations: Giving primarily in metropolitan Atlanta, GA. No support for churches. No grants to individuals, or for scholarships or fellowships, maintenance, or debt service; no loans.
Publications: Application guidelines.
Application information: Application form required.
  Initial approach: Letter or telephone
  Copies of proposal: 1
  Deadline(s): 1st of month preceding board meeting
  Board meeting date(s): January, April, July, and October
  Write: Victor A. Gregory, Secretary

Distribution Committee: Robert Strickland, Chairman; Victor A. Gregory, Vice-President and Secretary; E.P. Gould, C.A. McNair, Wade T. Mitchell.
Trustee: Trust Company Bank.
Employer Identification Number: 586026063

878
Tull (The J. M.) Foundation ▼
148 International Blvd., Northeast, Suite 430
Atlanta 30303 (404) 659-7079

Trust established in 1952 in Georgia.
Donor(s): J.M. Tull,† J.M. Tull Metal and Supply Company, Inc.
Financial data: (yr. ended 12/31/84): Assets, $17,468,333 (M); gifts received, $75,000; expenditures, $1,251,282, including $1,097,532 for 126 grants (high: $166,666; low: $50; average: $100-$25,000) and $4,775 for 15 employee matching gifts.
Purpose and activities: General giving locally and regionally, with support for higher and secondary education; grants also for youth and child welfare agencies, community funds, and the arts.
Types of support awarded: Building funds, seed money, endowment funds.
Limitations: Giving primarily in the Southeast, with emphasis on GA. No grants to individuals.
Application information:
 Initial approach: Letter
 Copies of proposal: 1
 Deadline(s): 1st day of month of meeting
 Board meeting date(s): Quarterly
 Write: Pollard Turman, Chairman
Officers and Trustees: Pollard Turman, Chairman; George E. Smith, Secretary-Treasurer; Walter J. Thomas.
Number of staff: 1 part-time support.
Employer Identification Number: 586043871

879
Ward (Harry E.) Foundation ⌧
41 Muscogee Ave., N.W.
Atlanta 30305

Established in 1959.
Donor(s): Elizabeth T. Ward,† Harry E. Ward, Jr.
Financial data: (yr. ended 12/31/82): Assets, $1,217,712 (M); expenditures, $100,266, including $95,000 for 3 grants (high: $75,000; low: $10,000).
Purpose and activities: Grants primarily for higher education.
Managers: George H. Sinnoti, Harry E. Ward, Jr.
Employer Identification Number: 596169469

880
Wardlaw (Gertrude and William C.) Fund, Inc. ⌧
P.O. Box 4655
Trust Company Bank Bldg.
Atlanta 30302

Trust established in 1936 in Georgia; incorporated in 1951.
Donor(s): Gertrude Wardlaw, William C. Wardlaw, Jr.†
Financial data: (yr. ended 12/31/83): Assets, $2,356,176 (M); expenditures, $113,726, including $100,704 for 34 grants (high: $12,000; low: $400).
Purpose and activities: Broad purposes; primarily local giving, with emphasis on higher education, youth agencies, cultural programs, a community fund and a hospital.
Limitations: Giving primarily in Atlanta, GA.
Application information:
 Initial approach: Letter
 Deadline(s): None
Officers: Ednabelle Raine Wardlaw, Vice-Chairman; A. Pinckney Straughn, Secretary; Ray B. Wilhoit.
Trustee: Trust Company Bank.
Employer Identification Number: 586026065

881
Wehadkee Foundation, Inc. ⌧
P.O. Box 150
West Point 31833

Incorporated in 1952 in Alabama.
Donor(s): D.A. Turner.
Financial data: (yr. ended 8/31/83): Assets, $1,166,125 (M); expenditures, $108,018, including $102,350 for 34 grants (high: $25,000; low: $25).
Purpose and activities: Primarily local giving for education, youth agencies, and social services.
Limitations: Giving primarily in GA.
Officers: Bruce N. Lanier, Sr., President; Bruce N. Lanier, Jr., Vice-President; John W. Henderson, Secretary-Treasurer.
Trustees: G.P. Barnwell, Jack Swann.
Employer Identification Number: 636049784

882
West Foundation ⌧
1491 Piedmont Ave., N.E.
Atlanta 30309

Financial data: (yr. ended 12/31/83): Assets, $2,839,249 (M); expenditures, $119,205, including $113,550 for 10 grants (high: $64,625; low: $150).
Purpose and activities: Support for health, cultural programs, and Protestant churches.
Officers and Directors: Charles B. West, President; Charles B. West, Jr., Elizabeth D. West, G. Vincent West, Marian T. West, Marjorie E. West, Mark C. West, Robert Wynne, Vice-Presidents; Marjorie West Wynne, Secretary.
Employer Identification Number: 586073270

883
West Point - Pepperell Foundation, Inc.
P.O. Box 342
West Tenth St.
West Point 31833

Incorporated in 1953 in Georgia as West Point Foundation, Inc.; merged with Sanford Dunson Foundation, Inc. in 1965.
Donor(s): West Point - Pepperell, Inc.

Financial data: (yr. ended 12/31/83): Assets, $961,537 (M); gifts received, $707,892; expenditures, $641,068, including $598,793 for 305 grants (high: $106,400; low: $10).
Purpose and activities: Broad purposes; general giving in areas where West Point Pepperell facilities are located; support for higher and secondary education, hospitals, and health agencies; grants also for youth agencies and community funds.
Limitations: Giving primarily in areas with facilities of West Point Pepperell, Inc. (ME, TX, NC, CA, AL, and SC).
Application information:
 Initial approach: Letter
 Write: H. Hart Cobb, Jr., Vice-President
Officers: Joseph L. Lanier, Jr.,* Chairman and President; H. Hart Cobb, Jr., Vice-President; C. Powers Dorsett, Secretary; C.H. Sauers, Treasurer.
Trustees:* Clarence J. Kjorlien, Harry M. Philpott, Yetta G. Samford, Jr., Kendrick R. Wilson, Jr., C.E. Woodruff.
Employer Identification Number: 580801512

884
Whitehead (Joseph B.) Foundation ▼
1400 Peachtree Center Tower
230 Peachtree St., N.W.
Atlanta 30303 (404) 522-6755

Incorporated in 1937 in Georgia.
Donor(s): Joseph B. Whitehead, Jr.†
Financial data: (yr. ended 12/31/83): Assets, $81,184,569 (M); expenditures, $3,342,209, including $3,026,000 for 40 grants (high: $900,000; low: $1,000; average: $10,000-$50,000).
Purpose and activities: Local giving only, with emphasis on child care and youth programs, education, health, cultural programs, the arts, and civic affairs. Preference is given to one-time capital projects of established private charitable organizations.
Types of support awarded: Seed money, building funds, equipment, land acquisition, general purposes, special projects.
Limitations: Giving limited to metropolitan Atlanta, GA. No grants to individuals, or for endowment funds, research, scholarships, fellowships, or matching gifts; no loans; generally no support for operating expenses.
Application information:
 Initial approach: Letter
 Copies of proposal: 1
 Deadline(s): Submit proposal preferably by the end of February or September; no set deadline
 Board meeting date(s): April and November
 Final notification: Up to one year
 Write: Boisfeuillet Jones, President
Officers: Boisfeuillet Jones, President; Charles H. McTier, Secretary and Treasurer.
Trustees: J.W. Jones, Chairman; James M. Sibley, Vice-Chairman.
Number of staff: 2 part-time professional; 4 part-time support.
Employer Identification Number: 586001954

885
Whitehead (Lettie Pate) Foundation, Inc. ▼
1400 Peachtree Center Tower
230 Peachtree St., N.W.
Atlanta 30303   (404) 522-6755

Incorporated in 1946 in Georgia.
Donor(s): Conkey Pate Whitehead.†
Financial data: (yr. ended 12/31/83): Assets, $61,740,978 (M); expenditures, $2,551,258, including $2,250,000 for 174 grants (high: $50,000; low: $3,000; average: $12,931).
Purpose and activities: Educational and charitable purposes; grants to institutions for scholarships for the education of poor Christian girls and institutional grants for assistance to poor aged Christian women who reside in nine named southeastern states.
Types of support awarded: Scholarship funds.
Limitations: Giving limited to 9 southeastern states. No grants to individuals, or for building or endowment funds, or matching gifts; no loans.
Application information:
  Initial approach: Letter
  Copies of proposal: 1
  Deadline(s): Submit proposal in September
  Board meeting date(s): April and November
  Write: Boisfeuillet Jones, President
Officers: Boisfeuillet Jones, President; Charles H. McTier, Secretary and Treasurer.
Trustees: Hughes Spalding, Jr., Chairman; Herbert A. Claiborne, Jr., M.D., Vice-Chairman; Lyons Gray.
Number of staff: 2 part-time professional; 4 part-time support.
Employer Identification Number: 586012629

886
Wilson (The Frances Wood) Foundation, Inc.
P.O. Box 33188
Decatur 30033   (404) 634-3363

Incorporated in 1954 in Georgia.
Donor(s): Fred B. Wilson,† Mrs. Frances W. Wilson, St. Louis - San Francisco Railroad.
Financial data: (yr. ended 5/31/83): Assets, $15,588,734 (M); expenditures, $2,182,932, including $442,262 for 35 grants (high: $229,212; low: $250).
Purpose and activities: Giving primarily in the southeastern United States, except for programs carried on by The First Church of Christ Scientist, in Boston. Grants largely for child welfare, and religious, civic, health, and higher educational activities, including giving to scholarship funds of colleges.
Types of support awarded: General purposes, operating budgets, continuing support, annual campaigns, seed money, emergency funds, building funds, equipment, land acquisition, scholarship funds.
Limitations: Giving primarily in the southeastern U.S. No grants to individuals, or for endowment funds; no loans.
Publications: Application guidelines, program policy statement.
Application information:
  Initial approach: Full proposal
  Copies of proposal: 1
  Deadline(s): None
  Board meeting date(s): April and October
  Write: Emory K. Crenshaw, President
Officers and Trustees: Emory K. Crenshaw, President; W.T. Wingfield, Executive Vice-President; Michael A. West, Vice-President.
Employer Identification Number: 586035441

887
Woolley (The Vasser) Foundation, Inc. ▼
1200 Citizens and Southern National Bank Bldg.
Atlanta 30335   (404) 586-1500

Incorporated in 1961 in Georgia.
Donor(s): Vasser Woolley.†
Financial data: (yr. ended 12/31/84): Assets, $3,384,113 (M); expenditures, $126,716, including $87,000 for 10 grants (high: $20,000; low: $2,000).
Purpose and activities: Broad purposes; local giving, with emphasis on higher education; support also for the arts, youth agencies, community funds, crime prevention, and aid to the handicapped.
Types of support awarded: Seed money, emergency funds, building funds, equipment, land acquisition, general purposes, professorships, scholarship funds, matching funds.
Limitations: Giving primarily in the metropolitan Atlanta, GA, area. No grants to individuals, or for operating budgets, continuing support, annual campaigns, deficit financing, special projects, research publications, or conferences; no loans.
Publications: Informational brochure, 990-PF, program policy statement, application guidelines.
Application information:
  Initial approach: Letter
  Copies of proposal: 1
  Board meeting date(s): January, April, July, and October
  Final notification: 3 months
  Write: L. Neil Williams, Jr., Chairman
Officers and Trustees: L. Neil Williams, Jr., Chairman; Benjamin T. White, Secretary; John R. Crenshaw, Alex P. Gaines, G. Conley Ingram, John R. Seydel, Paul V. Seydel.
Number of staff: None.
Employer Identification Number: 586034197

HAWAII

888
Amfac Foundation
700 Bishop St.
Honolulu 96813   (808) 945-8465
Mailing address: P.O. Box 3230, Honolulu, HI 96801

Established in 1974 in Hawaii.
Donor(s): Amfac, Inc.
Financial data: (yr. ended 12/31/82): Assets, $269,588 (M); gifts received, $23,904; expenditures, $1,023,944, including $1,000,205 for 187 grants (high: $400,000; low: $50; average: $500-$1,000) and $20,771 for 95 employee matching gifts.
Purpose and activities: Support in areas of company operations, largely for community funds, education, and youth agencies; more than 75 percent of funding is awarded in Hawaii.
Types of support awarded: Operating budgets, continuing support, annual campaigns, seed money, deficit financing, building funds, equipment, endowment funds, employee matching gifts, employee related scholarships.
Limitations: Giving primarily in HI and the continental U.S. in areas of company operations. No grants to individuals; no loans.
Publications: Application guidelines.
Application information: Application form required.
  Initial approach: Full proposal or letter of inquiry
  Copies of proposal: 1
  Deadline(s): 6 months before months in which board meets
  Board meeting date(s): January, April, July, September, and November
  Final notification: 3 months
  Write: Harry Matte, President
Officers: Harry Matte,* President; Charleen K. Ikeda, Vice-President and Secretary; T.R. d'Arcambal,* Daniel A. Curry,* Helen P. Goldsmith,* Karen H. Iwamoto,* D.W. Leibensberger, Barbara Wilson, Vice-Presidents; Thomas Braje, Treasurer.
Directors:* Ronald C. Barr, Richard L. Griffith, Harry Matte, Donald C. Onasch.
Number of staff: 1 full-time professional.
Employer Identification Number: 237418207

889
Anthony (The Barbara Cox) Foundation ⌥
P.O. Box 4316
Honolulu 96813

Incorporated in 1960 in Hawaii.
Donor(s): Barbara Cox Anthony, James M. Cox.†
Financial data: (yr. ended 12/31/82): Assets, $40,566 (M); gifts received, $126,085; expenditures, $108,146, including $108,127 for 60 grants (high: $7,000; low: $25; average: $100-$5,000).
Purpose and activities: Broad purposes; primarily local giving, with emphasis on higher and secondary education, hospitals, and conservation.
Limitations: Giving primarily in HI.
Officers and Directors: Barbara Cox Anthony, President; Garner Anthony, Vice-President, Secretary, and Treasurer; James Cox Kennedy, Blair Parry-Okeden.
Employer Identification Number: 996005049

890
Atherton Family Foundation ▼
c/o Hawaiian Trust Company, Limited
111 South King St.
Honolulu 96813   (808) 525-6512
Mailing address: c/o Hawaiian Trust Company, Limited, P.O. Box 3170, Honolulu, HI 96802

Incorporated in 1976 in Hawaii as successor to Juliette M. Atherton Trust established in 1915; F. C. Atherton Trust merged into the Foundation in 1976.
Donor(s): Juliette M. Atherton,† Frank C. Atherton.†
Financial data: (yr. ended 12/31/83): Assets, $17,760,827 (M); expenditures, $1,749,794, including $1,507,200 for 127 grants (high: $200,000; low: $500) and $49,350 for 58 grants to individuals.
Purpose and activities: Broad purposes; giving limited to institutions and organizations within Hawaii concerned with education, social welfare, culture and the arts, religion, health, and environment. Scholarships for the education of Protestant ministers' children and for theological education.
Types of support awarded: Operating budgets, building funds, student aid.
Limitations: Giving limited to HI. No grants for continuing support.
Publications: Annual report, program policy statement, application guidelines.
Application information:
   Initial approach: Telephone or full proposal
   Copies of proposal: 7
   Deadline(s): 1st day of month preceding board meeting
   Board meeting date(s): 3rd Wednesday of February, April, June, August, October, and December
   Final notification: 1 to 2 months
   Write: Jane R. Giddings, Secretary
Officers and Directors:* Alexander S. Atherton,* President; Judith Dawson, Robert R. Midkiff,* James F. Morgan, Jr.,* Joan H. Rohlfing,* Vice-Presidents; Jane R. Giddings, Secretary; Hawaiian Trust Company, Limited, Treasurer.
Number of staff: 2 part-time professional; 1 part-time support.
Employer Identification Number: 510175971

891
Bohnett (Vi) Memorial Foundation
315 Uluniu St., Rm. 208A
P.O. Box 1361
Kailua 96734

Established in 1969 in California.
Donor(s): F. Newell Bohnett.
Financial data: (yr. ended 12/31/82): Assets, $1,803,859 (M); expenditures, $90,411, including $15,565 for 21 grants (high: $5,000; low: $100; average: $100-$5,000) and $68,250 for 35 grants to individuals.
Purpose and activities: Grants largely for Protestant church support, youth agencies, and education, including scholarships.
Types of support awarded: Student aid, grants to individuals.
Application information:
   Initial approach: Letter requesting information

Managers: F. Newell Bohnett, Owen G. Johnston, James A. Nelson.
Trustees: James N. Bohnett, Joe Bohnett III, Thomas D. Bohnett, William C. Bohnett III.
Employer Identification Number: 956225968

892
Brewer (C.) Charitable Foundation ¤
827 Fort St.
Honolulu 96813

Established in 1980.
Financial data: (yr. ended 12/31/83): Assets, $1,054,125 (M); expenditures, $259,521, including $256,445 for 60 grants (high: $74,725; low: $50).
Purpose and activities: Primarily local giving, with emphasis on community funds, social services, including youth agencies, education, and the arts.
Types of support awarded: General purposes, equipment, emergency funds, building funds, scholarship funds.
Limitations: Giving primarily in HI.
Officers: Harold S.Y. Hee, President; J. Alan Kugle, Vice-President; James G. Higgins, Secretary; Donald E. James, Treasurer.
Employer Identification Number: 990203743

893
Castle (Harold K. L.) Foundation ▼
c/o Kaneohe Ranch
Kaneohe, Oahu 96744   (808) 247-2184

Incorporated in 1962 in Hawaii.
Donor(s): Harold K.L. Castle,† Mrs. Harold K.L. Castle.†
Financial data: (yr. ended 12/31/83): Assets, $35,039,190 (M); expenditures, $986,469, including $711,760 for 10 grants (high: $400,000; low: $5,000; average: $25,000-$100,000).
Purpose and activities: Broad purposes; local giving, with emphasis on education; support also for youth agencies, hospitals, cultural programs, and marine research.
Types of support awarded: Annual campaigns, seed money, emergency funds, building funds, equipment, research, general purposes, continuing support.
Limitations: Giving primarily in HI. No grants to individuals.
Application information:
   Initial approach: Letter
   Copies of proposal: 1
   Deadline(s): Submit proposal preferably in December or January; deadline January 31
   Board meeting date(s): February
   Write: James C. Castle, President
Officers: James C. Castle,* President; David D. Thoma, Vice-President and Treasurer; James C. Castle, Jr., Vice-President; Carol Conrad, Secretary.
Directors:* Virginia C. Baldwin-Dubois, Peter E. Russell.
Employer Identification Number: 996005445

894
Castle (Samuel N. and Mary) Foundation ▼
c/o Hawaiian Trust Company, Ltd.
111 South King St., P.O. Box 3170
Honolulu 96802   (808) 525-8536

Incorporated in 1925 in Hawaii.
Donor(s): Mary Castle.†
Financial data: (yr. ended 12/31/83): Assets, $13,212,975 (M); expenditures, $890,338, including $812,600 for 73 grants (high: $100,000; low: $500; average: $1,000-$5,000).
Purpose and activities: Broad purposes; local giving only, with emphasis on higher and secondary education, Christian outreach, cultural preservation, youth agencies, welfare, and health; special fund for early childhood education programs. Most grants for direct services activities or capital projects.
Types of support awarded: Special projects, building funds, operating budgets, equipment.
Limitations: Giving limited to HI. No grants to individuals, or for endowment funds or scholarships; no loans.
Publications: Annual report, program policy statement, application guidelines.
Application information: Application form required for capital projects over $500,000. Application form required.
   Initial approach: Telephone or full proposal
   Copies of proposal: 6
   Deadline(s): 1st day of month preceding meetings
   Board meeting date(s): 2nd Thursday in March, June, September, and December
   Write: Ms. Jane R. Giddings, Secretary
Officers: W. Donald Castle,* President; James C. Castle,* Vice-President; Jane R. Giddings, Secretary; Hawaiian Trust Company, Limited, Treasurer.
Trustees:* William E. Aull, Zadoc Brown, Robert R. Midkiff.
Number of staff: 2 part-time professional; 2 part-time support.
Employer Identification Number: 996003321

895
Cooke Foundation, Limited ▼
c/o Hawaiian Trust Company, Limited
P.O. Box 3170
Honolulu 96802   (808) 525-8536

Trust established in 1920 in Hawaii; incorporated in 1971.
Donor(s): Anna C. Cooke.†
Financial data: (yr. ended 6/30/84): Assets, $9,615,775 (M); expenditures, $728,351, including $649,500 for 93 grants (high: $50,000; low: $500; average: $1,000-$25,000).
Purpose and activities: Local giving only, with emphasis on culture and the arts, social services, education, programs for youth and the elderly, health, and the environment.
Types of support awarded: Special projects, annual campaigns, building funds, equipment, research, publications, conferences and seminars, matching funds.

Limitations: Giving primarily in HI. No support for churches or religious organizations, unless the trustees' "missionary forebears" were involved with them. No grants to individuals, or for endowment funds, or scholarships or fellowships; no loans.
Publications: Annual report, program policy statement, application guidelines.
Application information:
Initial approach: Telephone or full proposal
Copies of proposal: 7
Deadline(s): For grants of less than $25,000, first week of month preceding board meeting; for grants of over $25,000 or a multi-year commitment, March 1
Board meeting date(s): Fourth Wednesday in January, April, July, and November
Final notification: 2 to 3 months
Write: Jane R. Smith, Assistant Secretary
Officers: Richard A. Cooke, Jr.,* President; Charles C. Spalding,* 1st Vice-President; Samuel A. Cooke,* 2nd Vice-President; Dora C. Derby,* Secretary; Hawaiian Trust Company, Limited, Treasurer.
Trustees:* Betty P. Dunford, Catherine C. Summers.
Employer Identification Number: 237120804

896
Davies Foundation, The ☒
841 Bishop St., P.O. Box 3020
Davies Pacific Center, Suite 2300
Honolulu 96813

Established in 1964.
Financial data: (yr. ended 6/30/83): Assets, $666,895 (M); expenditures, $105,270, including $103,625 for 49 grants (high: $22,000; low: $25).
Purpose and activities: Primarily local giving, with emphasis on higher and secondary education, and a community fund; some support also for cultural programs, youth agencies, and health.
Limitations: Giving primarily in HI.
Officers: D.A. Heenan, President; Francis S. Morgan, Vice-President; Stanley W. Hong, Secretary; Linda K. Kuroda, Treasurer.
Employer Identification Number: 996009108

897
First Hawaiian Foundation ☒
165 S. King St.
Honolulu 96813   (808) 525-8144

Financial data: (yr. ended 12/31/83): Assets, $509,764 (M); gifts received, $460,004; expenditures, $263,721, including $263,162 for 30 grants (high: $89,760; low: $100).
Purpose and activities: Primarily local giving for social services, education, and a community fund.
Types of support awarded: General purposes, operating budgets.
Limitations: Giving primarily in HI.
Application information:
Initial approach: Letter
Deadline(s): None
Write: Herbert E. Wolff, Secretary

Officers: John D. Bellinger, President; Philip H. Ching, Walter A. Dods, Jr., John A. Hoag, Edward Y. Matsumoto, Hugh Pingree, Kennedy Randall, Jr., Vice-Presidents; Herbert E. Wolff, Secretary; Howard H. Karr, Treasurer.
Employer Identification Number: 237437822

898
**Frear (Mary D. and Walter F.)
Eleemosynary Trust**
c/o Bishop Trust Company, Limited
140 South King St.
Honolulu 96813   (808) 523-2111
Mailing address: P.O. Box 2390, Honolulu, HI 96804; Tel.: (808) 523-2233

Trust established in 1936 in Hawaii.
Donor(s): Mary D. Frear,† Walter F. Frear.†
Financial data: (yr. ended 12/31/83): Assets, $6,059,496 (M); expenditures, $374,071, including $272,750 for 106 grants (high: $10,000; low: $350).
Purpose and activities: Broad purposes; primarily local giving for mental health, alcoholism and drug abuse programs, youth development, civic affairs, education, and music.
Types of support awarded: Operating budgets, seed money, building funds, equipment, matching funds, scholarship funds, special projects, conferences and seminars.
Limitations: Giving primarily in HI. No grants to individuals, or for endowment funds, reserve funds, travel, deficit financing, or publications; no loans.
Publications: Annual report, application guidelines.
Application information:
Initial approach: Proposal
Copies of proposal: 4
Deadline(s): January 15, April 15, July 15, and October 15
Board meeting date(s): Distribution committee meets in March, June, September, and December
Final notification: 2 to 3 months
Write: Mrs. Lois C. Loomis, Vice-President
Distribution Committee: Sharon McPhee, Chairman; Edwin L. Carter, Howard Hamamoto.
Trustee: Bishop Trust Company, Limited.
Number of staff: 1 part-time professional; 1 part-time support.
Employer Identification Number: 996002270

899
Hawaiian Foundation, The
111 South King St.
P.O. Box 3170
Honolulu 96802   (808) 525-8548

Community foundation established in 1916 in Hawaii by trust resolution.
Financial data: (yr. ended 12/31/83): Assets, $4,325,152 (M); gifts received, $156,475; expenditures, $521,664, including $357,395 for 61 grants and $28,686 for 75 grants to individuals.

Purpose and activities: To assist charitable, religious, and educational institutions in Hawaii by the distribution of funds, many of which have been restricted for specific purposes and in some instances for specific institutions. General fund priorities are problems of youth, families in crisis, rural area special projects, environmental concerns, and cultural and historic preservation.
Types of support awarded: Operating budgets, continuing support, seed money, deficit financing, equipment, matching funds, technical assistance, scholarship funds, student aid, research, special projects, publications.
Limitations: Giving primarily in HI. No grants for building, endowment funds, or matching gifts; no loans.
Publications: Program policy statement, application guidelines, informational brochure, annual report.
Application information: Application forms required for grants to individuals. Application form required.
Initial approach: Telephone or proposal
Copies of proposal: 9
Deadline(s): First day of month preceding board meeting
Board meeting date(s): January, April, July, and October
Write: Mark J. O'Donnell, Trust Officer
Officer: Jane R. Giddings, Secretary.
Distribution Committee: Samuel A. Cooke, Chairperson; William E. Aull, Robert E. Black, Aaron Chaney, Charlene Graulty, Alice F. Gruld, James F. Morgan, Jr., Theodore F.K. Wong, Clifford H.N. Yee.
Trustee: Hawaiian Trust Company, Limited.
Number of staff: 1 full-time professional; 1 part-time professional; 1 part-time support.
Employer Identification Number: 996003328

900
Ho (Chinn) Foundation ☒
239 Merchant St.
P.O. Box 2668
Honolulu 96803

Established in 1960 in Hawaii.
Donor(s): Chinn Ho.
Financial data: (yr. ended 12/31/83): Assets, $1,366,669 (M); expenditures, $345,140, including $327,788 for 117 grants (high: $50,000; low: $25).
Purpose and activities: Primarily local giving for higher and secondary education and Roman Catholic church support.
Limitations: Giving primarily in HI.
Officers and Trustees: Chinn Ho, President; Stuart Ho, 1st Vice-President; Matsuo Takabuki, 2nd Vice-President; Donald M. Wong, Treasurer; Dean T.W. Ho, Harriet Matsuo.
Employer Identification Number: 996003811

901
Holy Land Charitable Trust ☒
c/o Torkidson, Katz, Jossem, Loden
700 Bishop St., Suite 1512
Honolulu 96813

Established in 1980.

Financial data: (yr. ended 12/31/82): Assets, $1,559,334 (M); expenditures, $336,650, including $284,842 for 7 grants (high: $252,700; low: $4,000).
Purpose and activities: Giving primarily to organizations in Israel.
Trustees: Richard F. Benner, Elliot H. Loden.
Employer Identification Number: 990187302

902
King's Daughters' Foundation
1412 Whitney St.
Honolulu 96822   (808) 944-2807

Established originally as the King's Daughter's Circle in Hawaii in 1906; incorporated as a private foundation in 1978.
Financial data: (yr. ended 12/31/84): Assets, $6,061,354 (M); gifts received, $16,083; expenditures, $433,710, including $259,968 for 257 grants to individuals (low: $20; average: $250).
Purpose and activities: Medical, housing, and general welfare support for needy, aged individuals of Hawaii, who are at least 55 years of age and have been residents of Hawaii for a minimum of 5 years.
Types of support awarded: Grants to individuals.
Limitations: Giving limited to HI.
Publications: Annual report, program policy statement, application guidelines.
Application information: Application form required.
  Initial approach: Telephone
  Deadline(s): 5th of every month
  Board meeting date(s): Monthly
  Final notification: 3rd Friday of the month
  Write: Diana H. Lord, Administrative Assistant
Officers: Ethel McAfee,* President; Virginia May Lewis,* First Vice-President; Diana H. Lord,* Second Vice-President; Mrs. H.M. Taylor, Secretary; First Hawaiian Bank (Kenneth Brown, Treasurer).
Directors:* Iris Hallaran, Chairperson; Margaret Blom, Mrs. W.H. Livingston.
Number of staff: 1 full-time professional.
Employer Identification Number: 990073507

903
McInerny Foundation ▼
Bishop Trust Co., Ltd.
140 South King St.
Honolulu 96813   (808) 523-2111
Mailing address: P.O. Box 2390, Honolulu, HI 96804

Trust established in 1937 in Hawaii.
Donor(s): William H. McInerny,† James D. McInerny,† Ella McInerny.†
Financial data: (yr. ended 9/30/84): Assets, $18,325,509 (M); expenditures, $1,686,113, including $1,221,505 for 151 grants (high: $25,000; low: $1,000).
Purpose and activities: General purposes; giving largely for education, youth services, welfare, health, culture, and arts. Grants only to local secular institutions.

Types of support awarded: Operating budgets, continuing support, seed money, building funds, equipment, matching funds, scholarship funds, special projects.
Limitations: Giving limited to HI. No support for religious institutions. No grants to individuals, or for endowment funds, deficit financing, or research; no loans.
Publications: Annual report, application guidelines.
Application information:
  Initial approach: Full proposal
  Copies of proposal: 7
  Deadline(s): None
  Board meeting date(s): Distribution committee generally meets monthly
  Final notification: 2 months
  Write: Mrs. Lois Loomis, Vice-President and Secretary
Distribution Committee: Edwin L. Carter, Chairman; Henry B. Clark, Jr., Vice-Chairman; Thomas K. Hitch.
Trustee: Bishop Trust Company, Limited.
Number of staff: 1 part-time professional; 1 part-time support.
Employer Identification Number: 996002356

904
Straub (Gertrude S.) Trust Estate
c/o Hawaiian Trust Company, Limited
P.O. Box 3170
Honolulu 96802   (808) 525-8511

Established in 1966.
Donor(s): Gertrude S. Straub.†
Financial data: (yr. ended 9/30/83): Assets, $2,829,337 (M); expenditures, $159,503, including $138,925 for 156 grants to individuals.
Purpose and activities: Scholarship grants to Hawaii high school graduates to attend mainland colleges and major in a subject relating to world peace.
Types of support awarded: Student aid.
Limitations: Giving limited to HI. No grants to individuals (except for scholarships), or for building or endowment funds, or operating budgets.
Publications: Program policy statement, application guidelines.
Application information: Application form required for scholarships. Application form required.
  Initial approach: Telephone or letter of inquiry
  Copies of proposal: 1
  Deadline(s): Submit application preferably between January 1 and March 1; deadline March 1
  Board meeting date(s): April
  Write: Jane R. Giddings, Vice-President
Trustee: Hawaiian Trust Company, Limited.
Number of staff: 1 part-time professional; 1 part-time support.
Employer Identification Number: 996003243

905
Teruya (Albert T. & Wallace T.) Foundation ⌑
1276 Young St.
Honolulu 96814   (808) 521-6946

Financial data: (yr. ended 12/31/82): Assets, $955,424 (M); expenditures, $143,457, including $137,880 for 9 grants (high: $35,000; low: $1,000).
Purpose and activities: Primarily local giving, with capital support largely for secondary and higher education, and hospitals.
Types of support awarded: Building funds.
Limitations: Giving primarily in HI.
Application information:
  Initial approach: Proposal
  Deadline(s): None
  Board meeting date(s): Annually
  Write: Raymond T. Teruya, President
Officers and Trustees: Albert T. Teruya, President; Wallace T. Teruya, Vice-President; Raymond T. Teruya, Secretary; Robert N. Akamine, Treasurer; Roy T. Uyehara.
Employer Identification Number: 996014692

906
Watumull Foundation ⌑
P.O. Box 15638
Honolulu 96815

Financial data: (yr. ended 6/30/83): Assets, $479,677 (M); expenditures, $188,128, including $176,296 for 8 grants (high: $170,840; low: $50).
Purpose and activities: Giving primarily in Hawaii for education.
Limitations: Giving primarily in HI.
Officers and Trustees: Milton Cades, Chairman; Lila Watumull Sahney, President; David Watumull, Vice-President; Radha Watumull Homay, Secretary; Val L. Tennent, Treasurer; J. Russell Cades, Mrs. Lawrence B. Hall, John Jubinsky.
Employer Identification Number: 990080681

907
Watumull (J.) Estate, Inc. ⌑
P.O. Box 3283
Honolulu 96801
Application address: J. Watumull Estate, Inc., 1341 Kapiolani Blvd., Honolulu, HI 96814

Donor(s): Jhamandas Watumull, Gulab Watumull, Indru Watumull, Watumull Brothers, Ltd.
Financial data: (yr. ended 12/31/83): Assets, $1,786,025 (M); gifts received, $170,740; expenditures, $183,543, including $178,000 for 13 grants (high: $50,000; low: $3,000).
Purpose and activities: Primarily local giving, with emphasis on education, including higher education, and on an arts academy and museum.
Types of support awarded: Scholarship funds, endowment funds, special projects, building funds.
Limitations: Giving primarily in HI.
Application information:
  Initial approach: Proposal
  Deadline(s): None

Final notification: 2 months
Write: Jhamandas Watumull, President
Officers and Directors: Jhamandas Watumull, President; Gulab Watumull, Vice-President; Clinton R. Ashford, Secretary; Sundri R. Watumull, Treasurer.
Employer Identification Number: 510205431

908
Wilcox (G. N.) Trust ▼
c/o Bishop Trust Company, Limited
140 South King St.
Honolulu 96813   (808) 523-2111
Mailing address: P.O. Box 2390, Honolulu, HI 96804

Trust established in 1916 in Hawaii.
Donor(s): George N. Wilcox.†
Financial data: (yr. ended 12/31/83): Assets, $9,235,993 (M); expenditures, $619,552, including $553,391 for 122 grants (high: $25,000; low: $300; average: $1,000-$10,000).
Purpose and activities: Broad purposes; emphasis on education and child welfare in Hawaii, particularly on the island of Kauai. Grants also for care of the sick, health agencies, the aged, community funds, delinquency and crime pervention, family service, and Protestant church support.
Types of support awarded: Seed money, building funds, equipment, matching funds, scholarship funds, general purposes, continuing support.
Limitations: Giving limited to HI, particularly the island of Kauai. No support for government agencies or organizations substantially supported by government funds. No grants to individuals, or for endowment or reserve funds, research, publications, deficit financing, or travel; no direct student aid including scholarships to individuals; no loans.
Publications: Annual report, application guidelines.
Application information:
Initial approach: Telephone or full proposal
Copies of proposal: 5
Deadline(s): January 15, April 15, July 15, and October 15
Board meeting date(s): March, June, September, and December
Final notification: 2 months
Write: Mrs. Lois C. Loomis, Vice-President and Corporate Secretary
Committee on Beneficiaries: Rev. Ford G. Coffman, Chairman; Gale Fisher Carswell, Edwin L. Carter.
Trustee: Bishop Trust Company, Limited (Lois C. Loomis, Vice-President and Corporate Secretary).
Number of staff: 1 part-time professional; 1 part-time support.
Employer Identification Number: 996002445

909
Wilcox (S. W.) Trust
c/o Bishop Trust Company, Limited
140 South King St.
Honolulu 96813   (808) 523-2111
Mailing address: P.O. Box 2390, Honolulu, HI 96804

Trust established in 1921 in Hawaii.
Donor(s): Samuel Whitney Wilcox.†
Financial data: (yr. ended 12/31/83): Assets, $2,282,101 (M); expenditures, $124,442, including $115,000 for 7 grants (high: $20,000; low: $5,000).
Purpose and activities: Funds presently committed to the support of local organizations.
Types of support awarded: Continuing support, seed money, building funds.
Limitations: Giving limited to Kauai and Big Island, HI. No grants to individuals, or for research programs, scholarships and fellowships, or matching gifts; no loans.
Application information: No unsolicited proposals considered.
Board meeting date(s): December and as required
Write: Mrs. Lois C. Loomis, Vice-President
Officer: Lois C. Loomis, Vice-President and Secretary.
Trustees: Pamela W. Beck, Gale Fisher Carswell, David W. Pratt.
Number of staff: None.
Employer Identification Number: 996002547

910
Zimmerman (Hans and Clara Davis) Foundation ⌶
c/o Hawaiian Trust Company, Ltd.
P.O. Box 3170
Honolulu 96802

Established in 1963.
Financial data: (yr. ended 12/31/83): Assets, $4,458,414 (M); expenditures, $282,027, including $20,000 for 2 grants and $177,975 for 299 grants to individuals.
Purpose and activities: Giving primarily for scholarships to Hawaiian residents, with preference given to students majoring in medicine, nursing, or related health fields; some support also for medical research.
Types of support awarded: Student aid.
Limitations: Giving primarily in HI.
Publications: Program policy statement, application guidelines.
Application information: Request application forms by February 1. Application form required.
Initial approach: Full proposal
Copies of proposal: 1
Deadline(s): March 1
Trustees: Kenneth E. Young,* Hawaiian Trust Company, Ltd.
Scholarship Committee:* Mary V. Coyne, S.J. Rose, Jetta M. Zimmerman.
Employer Identification Number: 996006669

IDAHO

911
Cunningham (Laura Moore) Foundation, Inc. ⌶
P.O. Box 1157
Boise 83701
Grant application address: 1921 Tallwood, Boise, ID 83706

Incorporated in 1964 in Idaho.
Donor(s): Laura Moore Cunningham.†
Financial data: (yr. ended 8/31/82): Assets, $3,082,147 (M); expenditures, $207,828, including $203,799 for 20 grants (high: $42,099; low: $1,000).
Purpose and activities: Broad purposes; local giving, with emphasis on higher education, particularly for business scholarship funds; support also for hospitals and child welfare.
Limitations: Giving limited to ID.
Application information: Application form required.
Deadline(s): February 28
Board meeting date(s): Spring
Write: Joan Davidson Carley, Secretary-Treasurer
Officers and Directors: Harry Little Bettis, President; Marjorie Moore Davidson, Vice-President; Joan Davidson Carley, Secretary-Treasurer.
Employer Identification Number: 826008294

912
Daugherty Foundation ⌶
P.O. Box 7928
Boise 83707

Established in 1965.
Financial data: (yr. ended 12/31/83): Assets, $2,735,972 (M); expenditures, $111,330, including $100,600 for 6 grants (high: $23,650; low: $1,000).
Purpose and activities: Giving for hospitals and a historical village.
Trustee: Idaho First National Bank.
Employer Identification Number: 826010665

913
Dufresne (The Walter and Leona) Foundation, Inc. ⌶
1150 West State St.
P.O. Box 2833
Boise 83701

Incorporated in 1964 in Idaho.
Donor(s): Walter Dufresne.†
Financial data: (yr. ended 12/31/83): Assets, $1,165,258 (M); expenditures, $110,179, including $98,000 for 7 grants (high: $42,000; low: $3,000).
Purpose and activities: Support primarily for higher education in Idaho.
Limitations: Giving primarily in ID.

Officers: Jess Hawley, President; John T. Hawley, Vice-President; Fred K. O'Brien, Treasurer.
Employer Identification Number: 820266697

914
Morrison (Harry W.) Foundation, Inc. ▼ ¤
(formerly Harry W. Morrison Family Foundation, Inc.)
c/o Richard L. Thomas
P.O. Box 7808
Boise 83729   (208) 345-5000

Incorporated in 1952 in Idaho.
Donor(s): Harry W. Morrison.†
Financial data: (yr. ended 12/31/82): Assets, $8,717,208 (M); expenditures, $1,213,015, including $1,134,965 for 26 grants (high: $997,852; low: $100).
Purpose and activities: Primarily local giving, with emphasis on cultural programs, higher education, medical research, and health.
Limitations: Giving primarily in Boise, ID. No grants to individuals.
Application information:
  Initial approach: Letter of inquiry
  Deadline(s): Early April
  Board meeting date(s): May
  Write: Velma V. Morrison, President, and Richard L. Thomas, Secretary
Officers: Velma V. Morrison, President; Judith V. Roberts, Vice-President; Richard L. Thomas, Secretary-Treasurer.
Directors: Edna M. Allen, Edith Miller Klein, Fred Norman.
Employer Identification Number: 826008111

915
Morrison-Knudsen Employees Foundation, Inc. ¤
One Morrison-Knudsen Plaza
Boise 83729

Established in 1947.
Financial data: (yr. ended 12/31/83): Assets, $1,969,622 (M); gifts received, $3,367; expenditures, $123,010, including $45,000 for 3 grants (high: $15,000) and $76,135 for 28 grants to individuals.
Purpose and activities: Grants primarily to needy company employees and for medical research.
Types of support awarded: Grants to individuals.
Officers: R.K. Woodhead,* President; M.J. Shirley,* Vice-President; J.C. Conway, Secretary-Treasurer.
Director:* John Deagon.
Employer Identification Number: 826005410

916
Whittenberger (Claude R. and Ethel B.) Foundation ¤
P.O. Box 1073
Caldwell 83605   (208) 459-0091

Established in 1970 in Idaho.
Donor(s): Mrs. Ethel B. Whittenberger.†

Financial data: (yr. ended 12/30/82): Assets, $2,261,223 (M); expenditures, $261,084, including $233,916 for 34 grants (high: $46,500; low: $1,000).
Purpose and activities: Giving limited to local institutions, with emphasis on higher and secondary education. Support also for hospitals, cultural programs, and local public libraries.
Types of support awarded: Continuing support, emergency funds, building funds, equipment, fellowships, publications, conferences and seminars.
Limitations: Giving limited to ID. No grants to individuals, or for endowment funds.
Publications: Program policy statement, application guidelines.
Application information: Application form required.
  Initial approach: Letter
  Copies of proposal: 5
  Deadline(s): September 1
  Board meeting date(s): April, July, September, and November
  Write: William J. Rankin, Chairman
Officers and Managers: William J. Rankin, Chairman; Margaret Gigray, Vice-Chairman; Robert A. Johnson, Treasurer; D. Whitman Jones, Joe Miller.
Employer Identification Number: 237092604

ILLINOIS

917
Abbott (The Clara) Foundation ¤
Fourteenth St. and Sheridan Rd.
North Chicago 60064   (312) 937-3840
Grant application address: c/o Abbott Laboratories, D-579, AP6B, North Chicago, IL 60064

Established in 1940 in Illinois.
Financial data: (yr. ended 12/31/83): Assets, $35,990,903 (M); gifts received, $8,275; expenditures, $1,620,921, including $310,732 for 203 grants (high: $30,000; low: $100) and $922,808 for 1,108 grants to individuals.
Purpose and activities: Grants to individuals for scholarships, educational loans to college students, aid to the aged and indigent, and relief grants and loans to employees of Abbott Laboratories who are in financial distress.
Types of support awarded: Student aid, grants to individuals.
Limitations: No loans, except for those currently holding a loan.
Application information: Application form required.
  Deadline(s): Scholarship application deadline, March 15; educational loan application deadline, May 15 (only for those currently holding a loan; no new loans); for other financial aid, no deadline

Write: Herbert S. Wilkinson, President
Officers: Herbert S. Wilkinson,* President; Charles S. Brown,* Michael J. Balma,* Frederick J. Kirchmeyer,* Vice-Presidents; Lael F. Johnson, Secretary; Samuel E. Bradt, Treasurer.
Directors:* Milton J. Henrichs, Richard M. Ross, Bernard H. Semler, Glenn S. Utt, Jr.
Employer Identification Number: 366069632

918
Abbott Laboratories Fund ▼
Abbott Park, AP6C
North Chicago 60064   (312) 937-7075

Incorporated in 1951 in Illinois.
Donor(s): Abbott Laboratories, and others.
Financial data: (yr. ended 12/31/84): Assets, $8,871,000 (M); gifts received, $1,330,000; expenditures, $1,152,156, including $886,201 for 172 grants (high: $207,000; low: $250; average: $500-$10,000) and $231,500 for 1,761 employee matching gifts.
Purpose and activities: Broad purposes; grants primarily to institutions for higher education, including medicine, pharmacy, and nursing, and for medical research and selected health and welfare causes; also matches contributions of Abbott Laboratories employees and retirees to higher educational institutions and hospitals.
Types of support awarded: Operating budgets, continuing support, annual campaigns, seed money, emergency funds, building funds, equipment, matching funds, professorships, scholarship funds, research, conferences and seminars, employee matching gifts, special projects.
Limitations: Giving primarily in areas of company operations. No support for social organizations, political parties or candidates, religious institutions or fundraising events. No grants to individuals, or for deficit financing, land acquisition, demonstration projects, internships, company-employee scholarships, exchange programs, fellowships, or publications; no loans.
Publications: Application guidelines, program policy statement.
Application information:
  Initial approach: Letter
  Copies of proposal: 1
  Deadline(s): None
  Board meeting date(s): April and December
  Final notification: 6 to 8 weeks
  Write: Dr. Charles S. Brown, President
Officers: Charles S. Brown,* President; Herbert S. Wilkinson, Sr.,* Vice-President; Laurence R. Lee,* Vice-President; Paul Roge, Secretary.
Directors:* Charles S. Aschauer, Jr., Duane L. Burnham, James A. Hanley, Milton J. Henrichs, Robert Janicki, Jack W. Schuler.
Number of staff: 2 part-time professional; 2 part-time support.
Employer Identification Number: 366069793

919
Aigner (G. J.) Foundation, Inc. ☐
5617 Dempster St.
Morton Grove 60053   (312) 966-5782

Foundation incorporated in 1957 in Illinois.
Donor(s): George J. Aigner,† Henrietta
Aigner,† G.J. Aigner Company.
Financial data: (yr. ended 4/30/84): Assets,
$1,527,000 (M); expenditures, $60,784,
including $17,150 for 29 grants (high: $5,000;
low: $100) and $13,560 for 15 grants to
individuals.
Purpose and activities: Broad purposes;
primarily local giving, including seed grants for
innovative programs to equip the disabled and
mentally retarded to be self-supporting; for
therapy programs for families with histories of
child abuse and teenagers with conduct
disorders; emergency food assistance; and
scholarships in business, liberal arts, theology,
and for children of company employees.
Types of support awarded: Employee related
scholarships, seed money, special projects.
Limitations: Giving primarily in IL.
Application information: Application forms
available upon request. Application form
required.
 Deadline(s): April 15 for scholarships
 Write: Craig P. Colmar, Secretary-Treasurer
Officers and Directors: Rev. Fred Aigner,
President; Craig P. Colmar, Secretary-Treasurer;
Joyce Aigner Laurence.
Employer Identification Number: 366055199

920
Allen-Heath Memorial Foundation
8500 Sears Tower
233 South Wacker Dr.
Chicago 60606   (312) 876-2130

Incorporated in 1947 in California.
Donor(s): Harriet A. Heath,† John E.S. Heath.†
Financial data: (yr. ended 12/31/84): Assets,
$1,584,204 (M); expenditures, $122,455,
including $99,500 for 18 grants (high: $34,000;
low: $1,000).
Purpose and activities: Grants to a limited
number of educational institutions, hospitals,
museums, air safety organizations, and other
charitable institutions.
Limitations: No support for religious or foreign
organizations. No grants to individuals; no
loans.
Publications: Application guidelines.
Application information:
 Initial approach: Letter
 Copies of proposal: 1
 Deadline(s): Submit proposal in November
 Board meeting date(s): July and December
 Write: Stephen L. Seftenberg, Secretary
Officers and Directors: Charles K. Heath,
President; Ruth R. Hooper, Vice-President;
Stephen L. Seftenberg, Secretary and Treasurer.
Employer Identification Number: 363056910

921
Allied Tube & Conduit Foundation ☐
16100 S. Lathrop Ave.
Harvey 60426

Established in 1982 in Illinois.
Donor(s): Allied Tube & Conduit Corporation.
Financial data: (yr. ended 12/31/83): Assets,
$300,238 (M); gifts received, $270,000;
expenditures, $142,573, including $142,430
for 30 grants (high: $75,000; low: $250).
Purpose and activities: Broad purposes, with
emphasis on Jewish giving.
Officers and Directors: Morris Soble,
President; Allen Grossman, Secretary; Morton
Koch, Treasurer; R. Jerry Conklin, Max
Schrayer, Bernard Semler.
Employer Identification Number: 363205711

922
Allstate Foundation, The ▼
Allstate Plaza, F-3
Northbrook 60062   (312) 291-5502

Incorporated in 1952 in Illinois.
Donor(s): Allstate Insurance Company.
Financial data: (yr. ended 12/31/83): Assets,
$8,345,267 (M); gifts received, $4,976,775;
expenditures, $3,081,621, including
$2,876,351 for 961 grants (high: $161,000;
low: $10; average: $1,000) and $193,612 for
1,131 employee matching gifts.
Purpose and activities: To assist deserving
organizations serving the fields of education,
including colleges and universities; cultural
pursuits, urban and civic affairs; safety; health,
including nursing education; and welfare,
including youth agencies and community
funds. Particular interest in organizations
dedicated to principles of self-help and self-
motivation.
Types of support awarded: Operating
budgets, continuing support, seed money,
employee matching gifts, scholarship funds.
Limitations: No support for primary or
secondary schools, or fraternal or religious
organizations. No grants to individuals, or for
annual campaigns, emergency funds, deficit
financing, building, capital, or endowment
funds; research, special projects, publications,
or conferences; no loans.
Publications: Application guidelines,
informational brochure, program policy
statement.
Application information:
 Initial approach: Full proposal
 Copies of proposal: 1
 Deadline(s): None
 Board meeting date(s): March, June,
  September, and December
 Final notification: 30 to 90 days
 Write: John T. Murphy, Executive Director
Officers and Trustees:* Donald F. Craib, Jr.,*
President; Donald L. Schaffer, Vice-President
and Secretary; Wayne E. Hedien,* Vice-
President and Treasurer; Richard J. Haayen,*
John K. O'Loughlin,* Lawrence H. Williford,
Vice-Presidents; John T. Murphy, Executive
Director.
Number of staff: 2 full-time professional; 1 full-
time support.
Employer Identification Number: 366116535

923
Alsdorf Foundation ☐
4300 West Peterson Ave.
Chicago 60646   (312) 685-2001

Incorporated in 1944 in Illinois.
Donor(s): James W. Alsdorf.
Financial data: (yr. ended 12/31/83): Assets,
$1,212,646 (M); expenditures, $930,331,
including $50,192 for 52 grants (high: $11,105;
low: $20).
Purpose and activities: General purposes;
grants largely for the fine arts and higher
education.
Limitations: No grants to individuals.
Application information:
 Initial approach: Full proposal
 Copies of proposal: 1
 Board meeting date(s): December and as
  required
 Write: James W. Alsdorf, President
Officers and Directors: James W. Alsdorf,
President and Treasurer; Marilynn Alsdorf, Vice-
President; Belle Richard, Secretary.
Employer Identification Number: 366065388

924
Alton Women's Home Association ☐
P.O. Box 552
Alton 62002

Financial data: (yr. ended 12/31/83): Assets,
$1,361,499 (M); gifts received, $1,618;
expenditures, $110,696, including $100,162
for 13 grants (high: $20,000; low: $1,430).
Purpose and activities: A private operating
foundation, established to serve needy women
and children of Madison County; grants to
services for the aged, welfare agencies, and a
hospital.
Limitations: Giving limited to Madison County,
IL. No grants to individuals.
Officers and Directors: June Weinrich,
President; Marty Pfeiffenberger, Vice-President;
Dorothy Davidson, Recording Secretary;
Georgia Whaley, Corresponding Secretary;
Judith Mottaz, Treasurer; and 12 additional
directors.
Employer Identification Number: 370799839

925
American National Bank and Trust
Company of Chicago Foundation ☐
33 North LaSalle St.
Chicago 60602   (312) 661-5000

Trust established in 1955 in Illinois.
Donor(s): American National Bank and Trust
Company of Chicago.
Financial data: (yr. ended 12/31/83): Assets,
$1,728,217 (M); gifts received, $499,958;
expenditures, $467,243, including $459,109
for 173 grants (high: $167,004; low: $15) and
$5,336 for 73 employee matching gifts.
Purpose and activities: Local giving within the
six-county Chicago metropolitan area, with
emphasis on hospitals, the arts, and higher
education; support also for community
organizations, youth agencies, and urban affairs.

Types of support awarded: Employee matching gifts, operating budgets, general purposes, continuing support, annual campaigns, building funds, special projects.
Limitations: Giving limited to the six-county Chicago, IL, metropolitan area. No grants to individuals, or for endowment funds, or fellowships and scholarships; no loans.
Publications: Application guidelines, program policy statement.
Application information:
  Initial approach: Full proposal
  Copies of proposal: 1
  Board meeting date(s): Quarterly; contributions committee meets every 6 to 8 weeks to review applications
  Final notification: 2 to 3 months
  Write: Linda Septow, Public Relations Coordinator
Trustees: Keene H. Addington, Ronald J. Grayheck, Elmer W. Johnson, John F. Reuss, Michael S. Tobin.
Number of staff: None.
Employer Identification Number: 366052269

926
Ameritech Foundation
30 South Wacker Dr., 34th Fl.
Chicago 60606   (312) 750-5223

Established in 1984 in Illinois.
Donor(s): American Information Technologies.
Financial data: (yr. ended 12/31/84): Assets, $15,000,000 (M).
Purpose and activities: Support primarily in the Midwest for economic development, public policy, telecommunications, higher education, and performing arts. Initial year of operation; no grants made in 1984.
Types of support awarded: Employee matching gifts, special projects, research.
Limitations: Giving primarily in IL, WI, IN, MI, and OH. No support for religious organizations for sectarian purposes, political groups, athletics, or health organizations concentrating in one specific area. No grants to individuals, or for general support, capital funds, endowment funds, scholarships, fellowships, consulting, technical assistance, demonstration projects, fund-raising events, publications, or conferences; no loans.
Publications: Application guidelines.
Application information:
  Initial approach: Letter or proposal
  Copies of proposal: 1
  Deadline(s): None
  Board meeting date(s): March, June, September, and December
  Final notification: 3 to 6 months
  Write: Michael E. Kuhlin, Executive Director
Officers: Leighton C. Gilman,* President; Carl G. Koch,* Vice-President and Treasurer; Michael E. Kuhlin, Secretary.
Directors:* Weston R. Christopherson, Thomas J. Reiman, E. Andrew Steffen, Frank R. Zimmerman.
Number of staff: 1 full-time professional; 1 part-time support.
Employer Identification Number: 363350561

927
Amerock Charities Trust ¤
c/o American National Bank & Trust Company
P.O. Box 1537
Rockford 61104
Application address: 4000 Auburn St., Rockford, IL 61104; Tel.: (815) 963-9631

Established in 1952 in Illinois.
Donor(s): Amerock Corporation.
Financial data: (yr. ended 11/30/83): Assets, $90,746 (M); gifts received, $150,000; expenditures, $103,665, including $103,500 for 11 grants (high: $55,000; low: $500).
Purpose and activities: Primarily local giving, with emphasis on hospitals, youth agencies, and a community fund.
Limitations: Giving primarily in Rockford, IL.
Application information:
  Write: Lawrence E. Gloyd, Trustee
Trustees: Carl J. Dargene, John S. Eaton, Ronald H. Entrikin, Karl H. Erikson, Lawrence E. Gloyd, J. Mauritz Johnson, Richard A. Livingston, Richard J. Miller, James S. Waddell, American National Bank & Trust Company.
Employer Identification Number: 366032561

928
Amoco Foundation, Inc. ▼
200 East Randolph Dr.
Chicago 60601   (312) 856-6306

Incorporated in 1952 in Indiana.
Donor(s): Amoco Corp.
Financial data: (yr. ended 12/31/84): Assets, $75,804,476 (M); gifts received, $26,108,915; expenditures, $20,694,291, including $17,849,953 for 1,559 grants (high: $860,000; low: $100; average: $1,000-$25,000), $125,921 for 63 grants to individuals and $1,403,977 for 4,306 employee matching gifts.
Purpose and activities: Approximately 85 percent of grants awarded for higher and pre-college education, primarily in science and engineering, and for community organizations, urban programs, and energy conservation, with emphasis on new initiatives; support also for independent public interest research, a limited program in culture and art, a volunteer program, and an employee educational gift matching program. Limited contributions to foreign charitable and educational institutions.
Types of support awarded: Operating budgets, continuing support, annual campaigns, seed money, emergency funds, building funds, equipment, matching funds, scholarship funds, fellowships, special projects, general purposes.
Limitations: Giving primarily in areas of company representation, for grants to assist communities. No support for primary or secondary education; religious, fraternal, social, and athletic organizations; or generally for organizations already receiving operating support through the United Way. No grants to individuals, or for endowment funds, research, publications, or conferences; no loans.
Publications: Annual report, program policy statement, application guidelines.
Application information:
  Initial approach: Letter or full proposal
  Copies of proposal: 1

Deadline(s): September 1 (for private colleges)
Board meeting date(s): January, March, May, September, and November; contributions committee meets monthly
Final notification: 4 to 6 weeks
Write: Donald G. Schroeter, Executive Director
Officers: H. Laurance Fuller,* President; R.K. Boknecht,* Walter R. Peirson,* Vice-Presidents; Donald G. Schroeter, Secretary and Executive Director; J.S. Ruey, Treasurer.
Directors:* Richard M. Morrow, Chairman; Leland C. Adams, John H. Bryan, Jr., James W. Cozad, Richard J. Ferris, James C. Fletcher, R.H. Leet, Arthur E. Rasmussen.
Number of staff: 4 full-time professional; 3 full-time support.
Employer Identification Number: 366046879

929
Amsted Industries Foundation ▼
3700 Prudential Plaza
Chicago 60601   (312) 645-1700

Trust established in 1953 in Illinois.
Donor(s): Amsted Industries Incorporated.
Financial data: (yr. ended 9/30/84): Assets, $4,528,341 (M); expenditures, $479,124, including $449,340 for 230 grants (high: $52,500; low: $10; average: $1,000-$2,000).
Purpose and activities: Broad purposes; giving primarily in areas of company operations, with emphasis on Chicago; grants largely for community funds and higher education; support also for hospitals, youth agencies, and cultural activities.
Types of support awarded: Operating budgets, continuing support, annual campaigns, emergency funds, building funds, equipment, research, matching funds.
Limitations: Giving primarily in areas of company operations, with emphasis on Chicago, IL. No support for political or religious organizations, or veterans' groups unless funds are for community-wide benefit. No grants to individuals, or for endowment funds, scholarships and fellowships, or courtesy advertising; no loans.
Application information:
  Initial approach: Letter, full proposal, or telephone
  Copies of proposal: 1
  Deadline(s): None
  Board meeting date(s): As required
  Final notification: 45 days
  Write: Eugene W. Anderson, Jr., Director, Public Affairs and Advertising
Trustees: Arthur W. Goetschel, Manager; O.J. Sopranos, G.K. Walter, R.H. Wellington.
Number of staff: 1 part-time professional; 1 part-time support.
Employer Identification Number: 366050609

930
Andersen (Arthur) Foundation ¤
P.O. Box 6
Barrington 60010   (312) 381-8134

Incorporated in 1953 in Illinois.
Donor(s): Arthur A. Andersen.†

Financial data: (yr. ended 10/31/83): Assets, $2,572,690 (M); gifts received, $2,450; expenditures, $269,652, including $219,000 for 15 grants (high: $75,000; low: $1,000).
Purpose and activities: Broad purposes; grants largely for higher and secondary education, hospitals and medical research; support also for a music program.
Officers: Arthur E. Andersen, III, President; Joan N. Andersen, Vice-President and Treasurer; John E. Hicks, Secretary.
Employer Identification Number: 510175922

931
Andrew (Aileen S.) Foundation ▼
10500 West 153rd St.
Orland Park 60462   (312) 349-3300

Incorporated in 1946 in Illinois.
Donor(s): Members of the Andrew family and family-related businesses.
Financial data: (yr. ended 11/30/83): Assets, $28,959,013 (M); expenditures, $2,212,975, including $1,954,136 for 141 grants (high: $727,051; low: $100; average: $100-$25,000) and $183,570 for 82 grants to individuals.
Purpose and activities: Grants limited to individuals and organizations in Orland Park, with giving for higher education, including scholarships for children of Andrew Corporation employees and graduates of a local high school; support also for civic affairs and health.
Types of support awarded: Employee related scholarships, student aid.
Limitations: Giving primarily in Orland Park, IL.
Publications: 990-PF, application guidelines.
Application information: Applications for scholarships accepted only from children of Andrew Corporation employees and graduates of a local high school.
 Write: Richard L. Dybala, Treasurer
Officers and Directors: Robert E. Hord, President; Edward J. Andrew, Vice-President; Juanita A. Hord, Secretary; Richard L. Dybala, Treasurer; Edith G. Andrew, C. Russell Cox.
Number of staff: None.
Employer Identification Number: 366049910

932
Archer-Daniels-Midland Foundation ▼
4666 Faries Pkwy.
P.O. Box 1470
Decatur 62525   (217) 424-5200

Incorporated in 1953 in Minnesota.
Donor(s): Archer-Daniels-Midland Company.
Financial data: (yr. ended 6/30/82): Assets, $5,674,904 (M); gifts received, $2,000,000; expenditures, $1,123,104, including $1,073,923 for 148 grants (high: $100,000; low: $75) and $15,330 for 4 grants to individuals.
Purpose and activities: Broad purposes; grants largely for community funds and higher education; support also for minority group development, cultural activities, hospitals, and youth agencies.
Application information:
 Deadline(s): None
 Board meeting date(s): As needed

Final notification: Upon acceptance; no notification of negative decision
 Write: Doug Snyder
Officers: L.W. Andreas, President; R.L. Erickson, Secretary; D.P. Poboisk, Treasurer; Richard E. Burket, Manager.
Employer Identification Number: 416023126

933
Aronberg (Lester) Foundation ⌑
250 North Washtenaw
Chicago 60612

Financial data: (yr. ended 9/30/83): Assets, $776,565 (M); expenditures, $604,979, including $600,000 for 3 grants of $200,000 each.
Purpose and activities: Grants to universities in Israel, primarily for medical and scientific research.
Types of support awarded: Research.
Limitations: Giving primarily in Israel.
Trustees: E. Cooper, E.A. Epstein, A. Grossman.
Employer Identification Number: 237009157

934
Atwood Foundation ⌑
c/o United Bank of Illinois
P.O. Box 464
Rockford 61105

Incorporated in 1949 in Illinois.
Donor(s): Atwood Vacuum Machine Company, members of the Atwood family.
Financial data: (yr. ended 12/31/83): Assets, $1,393,991 (M); expenditures, $113,600, including $103,600 for 49 grants (high: $40,000; low: $100).
Purpose and activities: Primarily local giving, with emphasis on education, hospitals, a community fund, arts and cultural programs, and youth and health agencies.
Limitations: Giving primarily in Rockford, IL.
Trustees: Bruce T. Atwood, Diane P. Atwood, Seth G. Atwood, Seth L. Atwood, United Bank of Illinois.
Employer Identification Number: 366108602

935
Aurora Foundation, The
32 Water St. Mall
P.O. Box 1247
Aurora 60507   (312) 897-4284

Community foundation incorporated in 1948 in Illinois.
Financial data: (yr. ended 9/30/84): Assets, $3,471,220 (M); gifts received, $185,030; expenditures, $636,840, including $441,930 for grants.
Purpose and activities: To serve the community in and near the Aurora area; grants for scholarships and student loans, colleges and hospitals, youth activities, and community services.
Types of support awarded: Scholarship funds, student aid, matching funds, building funds, equipment, endowment funds, land acquisition.

Limitations: Giving limited to the Aurora, IL area. No grants for operating budgets, research, annual campaigns, or continuing support.
Publications: Annual report, application guidelines.
Application information:
 Initial approach: Telephone
 Copies of proposal: 1
 Deadline(s): None
 Board meeting date(s): May and November; executive committee meets as required
 Write: R. Peter Grometer, Secretary
Officers: John F. McKee II,* President; Frank K. Voris,* Vice-President; R. Peter Grompeter, Secretary; Ruth H. Skaggs, Scholarship Secretary; Louis N. Vago,* Treasurer.
Directors:* George H. Alexander, Anne S. Alschuler, Stephan J. Andras, Ralph A. Andreason, William C. Deisher, Henry C. Fletcher, F. James Garbe, Howard E. Gillette, Karl P. Grube, Vernon H. Haase, Barbara H. Henning, Barbara W. Kaufmann, Theodore R. Landgraf, Albert D. McCoy, John H. McEachern, Jr., Mary Clark Ormond, Neil Ormond, Ralph C. Putnam, Jr., Daniel J. Ruddy, Donald A. Schindlbeck.
Number of staff: 1.
Employer Identification Number: 366086742

936
Barber-Colman Foundation
555 Colman Center Dr.
P.O. Box 7040
Rockford 61125   (815) 397-7400

Trust established in 1951 in Illinois.
Donor(s): Barber Colman Company.
Financial data: (yr. ended 12/31/84): Assets, $546,151 (M); gifts received, $208,150; expenditures, $448,553, including $415,178 for 37 grants (high: $90,000; low: $760) and $28,161 for 183 employee matching gifts.
Purpose and activities: Grants normally made to local, tax-exempt organizations in communities where Barber-Colman Company has plants with 100 or more employees. Except for local United Way campaigns, private educational institutions, and local cultural organizations, grants made only for capital purposes to organizations providing community welfare, health, education, cultural, or economic education services.
Types of support awarded: Operating budgets, continuing support, annual campaigns, seed money, building funds, equipment, land acquisition, employee matching gifts.
Limitations: Giving limited to communities where the company has plants with 100 or more employees. No grants to individuals, or for deficit financing, endowment funds, research, or scholarships or fellowships; no loans.
Publications: Program policy statement, application guidelines.
Application information: Application form required.
 Initial approach: Letter or telephone
 Copies of proposal: 1
 Deadline(s): April 15 and October 15
 Board meeting date(s): Usually in June and December

Final notification: Approximately 9 weeks after deadlines
Write: Nathan D. McClure, Jr., Executive Director
Officer: Nathan D. McClure, Jr., Executive Director.
Trustees: Edwin W. Colman, Janet B. Colman, Richard T. Leighton, Roger M. Sampson, John C. Tower, First National Bank and Trust Company of Rockford, Corporate Trustee.
Number of staff: 1 part-time support.
Employer Identification Number: 366032557

937
Bauer (M. R.) Foundation ⌑
209 South LaSalle St., Rm. 777
Chicago 60604

Established in 1955 in Illinois.
Donor(s): M.R. Bauer, Evelyn M. Bauer.†
Financial data: (yr. ended 12/31/83): Assets, $29,146,709 (M); gifts received, $12,214,838; expenditures, $1,203,552, including $1,000,000 for 79 grants (high: $110,000; low: $500).
Purpose and activities: Grants primarily for higher education, including medical and legal education, hospitals, cultural programs, and youth agencies.
Officers and Directors: A. Charles Lawrence, President; James H. Ackerman, Vice-President and Secretary; Loraine E. Ackerman, Vice-President; Kent Lawrence, Treasurer; Lee James Ackerman, James J. Lawrence.
Employer Identification Number: 366052129

938
Baum (The Alvin H.) Family Fund
134 South LaSalle St.
Chicago 60603

Trust established in 1945; incorporated in 1952 in Illinois.
Donor(s): Members of the Baum family.
Financial data: (yr. ended 12/31/82): Assets, $1,657,502 (M); expenditures, $95,498, including $91,472 for 82 grants (high: $24,000; low: $25).
Purpose and activities: Broad purposes; support largely for higher education, Jewish and Catholic welfare funds, and local temple support.
Limitations: No grants to individuals.
Application information: Funds presently committed.
Initial approach: Letter
Copies of proposal: 1
Board meeting date(s): Annually
Officers: Ann Baum,* President and Treasurer; Edward Neisser, Secretary.
Directors:* Alice S. Baum, Alvin H. Baum, Jr., Nathan Grossman.
Employer Identification Number: 366063093

939
Beatrice Foundation, The ▼
(formerly Esmark, Inc. Foundation)
Two North LaSalle St.
Chicago 60602   (312) 782-3820

Incorporated in 1953 in Illinois as the Esmark, Inc. Foundation.
Donor(s): Esmark, Inc., Beatrice Companies, Inc.
Financial data: (yr. ended 12/31/83): Assets, $7,779,575 (M); expenditures, $1,123,053, including $944,001 for 238 grants (high: $104,000; low: $500; average: $1,000-$5,000), $51,483 for 21 grants to individuals and $73,416 for 400 employee matching gifts.
Purpose and activities: The foundation is undergoing reorganization; grant-making is temporarily suspended. Previous commitments made by the foundation will be honored and new guidelines will be available to grantseekers around June 1, 1985.
Publications: Application guidelines, program policy statement.
Application information:
Deadline(s): February 15, May 15, August 15, and November 15
Board meeting date(s): March, June, September, and December
Final notification: 3 months
Write: Liz Sode, Assistant Vice-President, Public Affairs or Stevelyn Buenger, Manager, Contributions
Officers: Lizabeth Sode,* Vice-President and Treasurer; Patricia Kehoe, Secretary.
Directors:* William P. Carmichael, Harold J. Handley, Anthony Liuso, Donald Rosuck.
Number of staff: 2 part-time professional; 2 part-time support.
Employer Identification Number: 366050467

940
Becker (A. G.) Paribas Foundation
Two First National Plaza
Chicago 60603   (312) 630-5000

Incorporated in 1967 in Illinois.
Donor(s): A.G. Becker Paribas, Inc.
Financial data: (yr. ended 12/31/82): Assets, $1,024,196 (M); gifts received, $16,293; expenditures, $213,778, including $141,050 for 122 grants (high: $2,000; low: $500) and $44,618 for 188 employee matching gifts.
Purpose and activities: Grants for higher education, including matching gifts, community funds, cultural programs, and youth agencies.
Types of support awarded: Employee matching gifts, operating budgets, continuing support, annual campaigns.
Limitations: No grants for seed money, emergency funds, deficit financing, capital funds, or endowment funds.
Application information:
Initial approach: Full proposal
Copies of proposal: 1
Deadline(s): None
Officers: Herve M. Pinet, Chairman; John G. Heimann, Deputy-Chairman; Daniel J. Good, President; Stanley S. Wirt, Executive Director.
Number of staff: None.
Employer Identification Number: 366158978

941
Beidler (Francis) Charitable Trust ⌑
222 West Adams St., Rm. 821
Chicago 60606   (312) 726-0914

Trust established in 1935 in Illinois.
Donor(s): Francis Beidler.†
Financial data: (yr. ended 12/31/83): Assets, $4,345,078 (M); expenditures, $308,868, including $262,330 for 107 grants (high: $8,700; low: $100).
Purpose and activities: To aid public and operating charitable organizations; primarily local giving, with emphasis on care of the aged, crippled, hospitals, youth agencies, child welfare, and education. No beneficiary may receive more than one thirtieth of the net income yearly.
Limitations: Giving primarily in IL. No grants to individuals, or for building funds, research, or matching gifts; no loans.
Application information:
Initial approach: Letter
Copies of proposal: 1
Deadline(s): Submit proposal preferably in September or October; deadline October 31
Board meeting date(s): November or December
Write: Rosemarie Smith, Trustee
Trustees: Francis Beidler II, Thomas B. Dorris, Rosemarie Smith.
Employer Identification Number: 362166969

942
Belden (Joseph C.) Foundation
c/o Belden Wire Products & Belden Electronic Wire and Cable
2000 South Batavia Ave.
Geneva 60134   (312) 232-8900

Established in 1967.
Donor(s): Belden Corporation, J.C. Belden, Jr.
Financial data: (yr. ended 12/31/84): Assets, $1,243,432 (M); expenditures, $109,136, including $79,835 for 61 grants to individuals (high: $3,200; low: $2,700; average: $1,650).
Purpose and activities: Grants only for the education of children of Company employees.
Types of support awarded: Employee related scholarships.
Limitations: Giving primarily in Geneva, IL.
Application information: Applications not invited from any sources except children of company employees.
Board meeting date(s): Quarterly
Write: James D. Eaton
Trustees: Leslie W. Bennett, Arlo E. Carney, Albert C. Fifer, Elsie F. Haan, Robert W. Hawkinson, Helene D. Nelson, Fred O. Weirich.
Number of staff: 1 full-time professional.
Employer Identification Number: 366209342

943
Bell & Howell Foundation
7100 McCormick Rd.
Chicago 60645   (312) 262-1600

Incorporated in 1951 in Illinois.
Donor(s): Bell & Howell Company.

Financial data: (yr. ended 12/31/82): Assets, $31,984 (M); gifts received, $225,000; expenditures, $236,484, including $225,635 for 70 grants (high: $100,000; low: $100) and $10,819 for employee matching gifts.
Purpose and activities: Broad purposes; general giving, with emphasis on community funds and higher education; support for hospitals, cultural programs, youth agencies, and social services.
Limitations: No grants to individuals, or for buildings or endowment funds, research programs, scholarships, fellowships, or special projects; no loans.
Application information: Application form required.
   Initial approach: Full proposal
   Copies of proposal: 2
   Deadline(s): Submit proposal preferably in November; deadline November 30
   Board meeting date(s): April
   Write: Horace J. Schwartz, Treasurer
Officers: James D. Ritchie,* President; Joy Ralph, Secretary; Horace J. Schwartz, Treasurer.
Directors:* Donald N. Frey, J.K. Hudson, Robert B. Huff.
Employer Identification Number: 366095749

944
Berlin (M. H.) Foundation ⌗
c/o Miriam W. Burleson
1603 Orrington Ave.
Evanston 60201

Incorporated in 1954 in Illinois.
Donor(s): M.H. Berlin.
Financial data: (yr. ended 12/31/83): Assets, $1,336,310 (M); expenditures, $144,237, including $126,300 for 31 grants (high: $50,000; low: $100).
Purpose and activities: Primarily local giving, with emphasis on higher education, Jewish welfare funds, hospitals and medical research, and cultural organizations.
Limitations: Giving primarily in IL.
Officers: M.H. Berlin,* President; Arnold M. Berlin,* Secretary; M.A. Erickson, Treasurer.
Directors:* William H. Avery.
Employer Identification Number: 366057143

945
Bersted Foundation, The
c/o Continental Illinois National Bank and Trust Company of Chicago
30 North LaSalle St.
Chicago 60697   (312) 828-8026

Established in 1972 in Illinois.
Donor(s): Alfred Bersted.†
Financial data: (yr. ended 12/31/83): Assets, $6,681,967 (M); expenditures, $276,968, including $225,218 for 14 grants (high: $51,000; low: $450).
Purpose and activities: Broad purposes; giving limited to Kane, DuPage, DeKalb, and McHenry counties in Illinois, with emphasis on community welfare and service agencies, aid to the handicapped, conservation, and youth.
Types of support awarded: Building funds, technical assistance, general purposes, operating budgets.

Limitations: Giving limited to Kane, DuPage, DeKalb, and McHenry counties, IL. No support for religious houses of worship or degree-conferring institutions of higher learning. No grants to individuals.
Publications: Multi-year report.
Application information:
   Initial approach: Letter
   Copies of proposal: 2
   Board meeting date(s): Generally in February, May, August, and November
   Write: A.W. Murray
Trustee: Continental Illinois National Bank and Trust Company of Chicago (R.A. Wiegand, Vice-President).
Employer Identification Number: 366493609

946
Blum (Harry and Maribel G.) Foundation ⌗
c/o H.H. Bregar
500 North Michigan Ave.
Chicago 60611

Established in 1967 in Illinois.
Donor(s): Harry Blum.†
Financial data: (yr. ended 12/31/83): Assets, $8,444,970 (M); expenditures, $329,945, including $272,050 for 29 grants (high: $50,000; low: $300).
Purpose and activities: Grants primarily for hospitals and health agencies, a theological seminary, higher education, and temple support, social services, an art institute, and Jewish welfare funds, largely in Illinois and Miami, Florida.
Limitations: Giving primarily in IL and FL.
Officers and Directors: H. Jonathan Kovler, President; Leo J. Carlin, Peter Kovler, Vice-Presidents; H.H. Bregar, Secretary.
Employer Identification Number: 366152744

947
Blum (The Nathan and Emily S.) Fund ⌗
c/o Harris Bank
111 West Monroe St.
Chicago 60603
Grant application address: c/o Ellen A. Bechthold, Harris Trust and Savings Bank, P.O. Box 755, Chicago, IL 60690

Established in 1980.
Donor(s): Nathan Blum.†
Financial data: (yr. ended 12/31/83): Assets, $4,221,518 (M); expenditures, $329,523, including $301,611 for 10 grants (high: $83,000; low: $3,611).
Purpose and activities: Broad purposes; primarily local giving for hospitals, health and social agencies, including Jewish welfare funds.
Limitations: Giving primarily in Chicago, IL.
Application information:
   Initial approach: Proposal
   Deadline(s): None
Trustee: Harris Trust and Savings Bank.
Employer Identification Number: 366706638

948
Blum-Kovler Foundation ▼ ⌗
500 North Michigan Ave.
Chicago 60611   (312) 828-9777

Incorporated in 1953 in Illinois.
Donor(s): Harry Blum,† Everett Kovler.
Financial data: (yr. ended 12/31/83): Assets, $20,733,372 (M); expenditures, $783,973, including $568,550 for 154 grants (high: $176,500; low: $154; average: $100-$12,000).
Purpose and activities: Broad purposes; primarily local charitable giving, with emphasis on social services, Jewish welfare funds, hospitals, health services, and medical research; support also for higher education, cultural programs, and public interest and civic affairs groups.
Limitations: Giving primarily in IL.
Officers and Directors: Maribel G. Blum, Chairman; Everett Kovler, President; H.H. Bregar, Secretary; H. Jonathan Kovler, Treasurer; Peter Kovler.
Employer Identification Number: 362476143

949
Boothroyd (Charles H. and Bertha L.) Foundation ⌗
135 South LaSalle St., Rm. 1455
Chicago 60603   (312) 346-3833

Incorporated in 1958 in Illinois.
Donor(s): Mary T. Palzkill.†
Financial data: (yr. ended 6/30/83): Assets, $2,150,315 (M); expenditures, $185,083, including $152,000 for 23 grants (high: $23,000; low: $1,000).
Purpose and activities: General purposes; also to provide grants for medical school scholarship funds for research on Parkinson's disease; grants largely for a medical school and other higher educational institutions and hospitals, mainly in Illinois.
Limitations: Giving primarily in IL.
Application information:
   Write: Thomas H. Alcock, President
Officers and Trustees: Thomas H. Alcock, President; William V. Barboorka, Bruce E. Brown, Vice-Presidents; Lorraine Marcus, Secretary.
Employer Identification Number: 366047045

950
Borg-Warner Foundation, Inc. ▼
200 South Michigan Ave.
Chicago 60604   (312) 322-8659

Incorporated in 1953 in Illinois.
Donor(s): Borg-Warner Corporation, its divisions and subsidiaries.
Financial data: (yr. ended 12/31/84): Assets, $658,651 (M); expenditures, $2,113,835, including $1,758,771 for 255 grants (high: $194,000; low: $750; average: $1,000-$10,000) and $355,064 for employee matching gifts.

Purpose and activities: General purposes; primarily local giving for community funds; for private, higher educational institutions, primarily for the education of women and minorities, and of teachers and counselors in early childhood education; and for culture, neighborhood revitalization, social welfare, health agencies, civic affairs, and international programs.
Types of support awarded: General purposes, building funds, equipment, land acquisition, endowment funds, matching funds, professorships, internships, exchange programs, research, special projects, publications, continuing support, employee matching gifts, seed money.
Limitations: Giving primarily in Chicago, IL area. No support for sectarian institutions, foreign-based organizations, governmental agencies, or medical or academic research. No grants to individuals, or for scholarships or fellowships.
Publications: Informational brochure, program policy statement, application guidelines, annual report.
Application information:
Initial approach: Full proposal
Copies of proposal: 1
Deadline(s): None
Board meeting date(s): Quarterly; Contributions Committee meets to consider applications every other month
Final notification: 3 months
Write: Ellen J. Benjamin, Director, Corporate Contributions
Officers: R.O. Bass,* Chairman and President; J.L. Wentz,* Vice-President and Secretary; W.M. Valiant, Treasurer.
Directors:* J.J. Gavin, Jr., L.A. Harvey, R.E. LaRoche, R.A. Morris, R.J. Parsons.
Number of staff: 1 full-time professional; 1 part-time professional; 1 full-time support; 1 part-time support.
Employer Identification Number: 366051857

951
Bowyer (The Ambrose and Gladys) Foundation ▼ ☒
135 South LaSalle St., Suite 1500
Chicago 60603   (312) 346-1030

Incorporated in 1953 in Illinois.
Donor(s): Ambrose Bowyer,† Gladys Bowyer.†
Financial data: (yr. ended 12/31/82): Assets, $2,515,744 (M); expenditures, $433,337, including $417,950 for 47 grants (high: $56,000; low: $600).
Purpose and activities: Broad purposes; general giving, with emphasis on higher education, hospitals, and welfare funds.
Application information:
Write: D.T. Hutchison, President
Officers: D.T. Hutchison, President; R.F. Prendergast, Secretary.
Director: Edward V. Quinn.
Employer Identification Number: 366091247

952
Boynton Gillespie Memorial Fund ☒
Heritage Federal Bldg.
Sparta 62286

Established about 1965.
Donor(s): Bertha Gillespie Boynton,† Charles Otis Boynton.†
Financial data: (yr. ended 12/31/83): Assets, $1,623,013 (M); expenditures, $134,319, including $60,480 for 1 grant and $50,325 for 59 grants to individuals.
Purpose and activities: Grants for a local church and scholarships.
Types of support awarded: Student aid.
Limitations: Giving limited to IL.
Trustees: John Clendenin, John Henderson, Richard Reid.
Employer Identification Number: 376028930

953
Brach (Edwin J.) Foundation ☒
222 Wisconsin Ave., Suite 211
Lake Forest 60045

Incorporated in 1962 in Illinois.
Donor(s): Hazel S. Brodie.
Financial data: (yr. ended 10/31/83): Assets, $2,248,208 (M); expenditures, $72,852, including $69,000 for 33 grants (high: $16,000; low: $1,000).
Purpose and activities: Broad purposes; general giving, with emphasis on local health agencies, child welfare, and hospitals.
Limitations: Giving primarily in IL.
Officers: Hazel S. Brodie, President and Secretary; Bertram Z. Brodie, Vice-President and Treasurer; W.R. Shurtleff, Vice-President.
Employer Identification Number: 366073506

954
Brach (Helen) Foundation ☒
222 Wisconsin Ave., Suite 211
Lake Forest 60045

Established in 1974.
Donor(s): Helen Brach.
Financial data: (yr. ended 3/31/84): Assets, $640,776 (M); gifts received, $220,000; expenditures, $385,274, including $374,700 for 10 grants (high: $150,000; low: $300).
Purpose and activities: Giving limited to animal welfare organizations.
Officers: Helen Brach, President; Charles Vorhees, Vice-President; E.H. Moore, Treasurer.
Employer Identification Number: 237376427

955
Brunswick Foundation, Inc., The ▼
One Brunswick Plaza
Skokie 60077   (312) 470-4645

Incorporated in 1957 in Illinois.
Donor(s): Brunswick Corporation.
Financial data: (yr. ended 12/31/83): Assets, $1,700,000 (M); gifts received, $1,106,000; expenditures, $684,697, including $429,018 for 180 grants (high: $50,000; low: $100), $126,640 for 83 grants to individuals and $103,671 for 249 employee matching gifts.

Purpose and activities: Broad purposes; general giving in areas of company operations, with emphasis on higher education, including scholarship programs for children of Corporation employees, civic and community funds, hospitals, minorities and youth, and business and economics.
Types of support awarded: Employee related scholarships, fellowships, employee matching gifts.
Limitations: Giving primarily in areas of company operations. No support for religious organizations, preschools, primary and secondary schools, fraternal orders, veterans and labor groups, political organizations established to influence legislation, or for trips, tours, tickets or advertising for benefit purposes. No grants to individuals (except for company-sponsored scholarship or fellowship programs), or for endowment or capital funds, or company equipment or products; no loans.
Publications: Program policy statement, application guidelines.
Application information:
Initial approach: Letter
Copies of proposal: 1
Deadline(s): None
Board meeting date(s): About every 6 weeks
Write: Raymond E. Hartstein, Administrator or Wendy L. Fuhs, Coordinator
Officers and Directors: W.L. Niemann, President; E. Vanneman, Jr., Secretary; M.E. McGrath, Treasurer.
Staff: Raymond E. Hartstein, Administrator.
Number of staff: 2 full-time professional.
Employer Identification Number: 366033576

956
Buchanan Family Foundation, The ▼ ☒
222 E. Wisconsin Ave.
Lake Forest 60045

Established in 1967 in Illinois.
Donor(s): D.W. Buchanan, Sr.,† D.W. Buchanan, Jr.
Financial data: (yr. ended 12/31/83): Assets, $21,066,040 (M); expenditures, $881,281, including $855,000 for 45 grants (high: $75,000; low: $5,000; average: $5,000-$50,000).
Purpose and activities: Primarily local giving, with emphasis on hospitals, the arts and cultural programs, community funds, environmental programs, social services, and higher education.
Limitations: Giving primarily in IL.
Officers and Directors: Huntington Eldridge, President; G.M. Walsh, Vice-President and Secretary; D.W. Buchanan, Jr., Treasurer; Kenneth H. Buchanan, Huntington Eldridge, Jr.
Employer Identification Number: 366160998

957
Buehler (A. C.) Foundation
c/o Continental Illinois National Bank and Trust Company of Chicago
30 North LaSalle St.
Chicago 60693   (312) 828-1785

Incorporated in 1972 in Illinois.

Donor(s): Albert C. Buehler.
Financial data: (yr. ended 12/31/83): Assets, $9,210,828 (M); expenditures, $650,422, including $604,000 for 3 grants (high: $225,000; low: $179,000).
Purpose and activities: Primarily local giving for a hospital, health services, and health service education.
Limitations: Giving primarily in metropolitan Chicago, IL.
Application information:
Initial approach: Letter
Write: M.C. Ryan
Officer: Mrs. Fern D. Buehler, President.
Directors: A.C. Buehler, Jr., Carl Buehler, III, Rose B. Grosse, Dale Park, Jr., Barbara B. Ross, James M. Termondt.
Employer Identification Number: 237166014

958
Burgess (The William, Agnes & Elizabeth) Memorial Scholarship Fund ¤
c/o First National Bank
1515 Charleston
Mattoon 61938   (217) 234-7454

Trust established in 1943 in Illinois.
Financial data: (yr. ended 3/31/83): Assets, $1,109,551 (M); expenditures, $91,698, including $41,400 for grants to individuals.
Purpose and activities: Scholarships for graduates of Mattoon, Illinois Community High School.
Types of support awarded: Student aid.
Limitations: Giving limited to Mattoon, IL.
Application information: Application form required.
Deadline(s): March 15
Write: Clark Brogan, Senior Trust Officer
Trustee: First National Bank (Clark Brogan, Vice-President and Senior Trust Officer).
Employer Identification Number: 376024599

959
Burns Family Foundation ¤
c/o Cottle and Cottle, Ltd.
120 S. La Salle St.
Chicago 60603

Incorporated in 1953 in Illinois.
Donor(s): Arthur Keating,† Edward Keating.
Financial data: (yr. ended 12/31/82): Assets, $1,703,068 (M); expenditures, $87,819, including $61,830 for 14 grants (high: $20,000; low: $100).
Purpose and activities: Broad purposes; primarily local giving with emphasis on secondary education, youth agencies, conservation, and a police academy.
Limitations: Giving primarily in CA.
Officers and Directors: Lucy Keating Burns, President; Donald S. Burns, Vice-President; Julie Ann Burns, Secretary; Dennis E. Carpenter, Treasurer.
Employer Identification Number: 366051686

960
Caestecker (The Charles and Marie) Foundation ¤
c/o Frank Karaba
111 West Monroe St., Suite 2200E
Chicago 60603
Scholarship application address: Guidance Counsellor, c/o Green Lake Public High School, Green Lake, WI 54941

Donor(s): Charles E. Caestecker.†
Financial data: (yr. ended 4/30/84): Assets, $4,173,521 (M); gifts received, $32,059; expenditures, $45,343, including $18,080 for 8 grants (high: $5,000; low: $44).
Purpose and activities: Giving for charitable purposes, primarily in Green Lake, Wisconsin, including scholarships to graduates of Green Lake Public High School.
Types of support awarded: Student aid.
Limitations: Giving primarily in Green Lake, WI.
Application information: Application form for scholarships. Application form required.
Deadline(s): February 1 of graduation year
Trustees: Thomas F. Caestecker, Frank Karaba.
Employer Identification Number: 363154453

961
Callner (Milton H.) Foundation ¤
c/o American National Bank and Trust Company of Chicago
33 North LaSalle St.
Chicago 60602

Trust established in 1954 in Illinois.
Donor(s): Members of the Callner family.
Financial data: (yr. ended 1/31/83): Assets, $1,136,419 (M); expenditures, $141,420, including $124,487 for 32 grants (high: $50,000; low: $50).
Purpose and activities: Primarily local giving for higher education, Jewish welfare funds, and health and medical research.
Limitations: Giving primarily in Chicago, IL area.
Trustee: American National Bank and Trust Company of Chicago.
Employer Identification Number: 366034633

962
Camp (Apollos) and Bennet Humiston Trust ¤
300 West Washington St.
Pontiac 61764

Trust established in 1925 in Illinois.
Financial data: (yr. ended 4/30/83): Assets, $5,232,889 (M); expenditures, $363,157, including $217,987 for 8 grants (high: $130,000; low: $1,500).
Purpose and activities: Local giving for a municipal park and other community recreational programs, a youth agency, the aged, and conservation.
Types of support awarded: Operating budgets, equipment, building funds.
Limitations: Giving primarily in Pontiac, IL.
Trustees: Neil C. Bach, Chairman; Delbert R. Gardner, Vice-Chairman; William H. Edwards, William C. Harris, Robert D. Thompson.
Employer Identification Number: 370701044

963
Carlin Fund
8000 Sears Tower
Chicago 60606   (312) 876-8062

Incorporated in 1954 in Illinois.
Donor(s): Leo J. Carlin, Celia Carlin.
Financial data: (yr. ended 12/31/82): Assets, $1,226,659 (M); expenditures, $85,949, including $78,685 for 105 grants (high: $5,000; low: $25).
Purpose and activities: Broad purposes; general giving for higher education, medical research, Jewish welfare funds, temple support, the arts, and civic affairs.
Limitations: No grants to individuals.
Application information: Applications not invited.
Board meeting date(s): September
Write: Leo J. Carlin, President
Officers and Directors: Leo J. Carlin, President and Treasurer; Celia Carlin, Jerome E. Carlin, Vice-Presidents; Florence Epstein, Secretary.
Employer Identification Number: 366057155

964
Carson Pirie Scott Foundation ¤
One South State St.
Chicago 60603   (312) 744-2025

Incorporated in 1959 in Illinois.
Donor(s): Carson Pirie Scott & Company, Carson International Inc.
Financial data: (yr. ended 12/31/83): Assets, $320,641 (M); gifts received, $225,000; expenditures, $285,772, including $284,695 for 141 grants (high: $150,000; low: $50).
Purpose and activities: Giving primarily in Chicago and those communities where Company has operations, with emphasis on community funds; support also for education and the arts. Contributions in proportion to size of Company operations.
Types of support awarded: Continuing support, building funds, scholarship funds, equipment.
Limitations: Giving primarily in Chicago, IL, and communities with company operations. No grants to individuals, or for endowment funds, research, or matching gifts; no loans.
Publications: Program policy statement, application guidelines.
Application information:
Initial approach: Letter
Copies of proposal: 1
Deadline(s): Submit proposal preferably between January and September; deadline 2 months before board meetings
Board meeting date(s): February, May, and September
Final notification: 2 to 3 weeks after meetings
Write: Miss Kathleen Byrnes, Director
Officers: Peter S. Willmott,* President; Daniel M. Fort, Vice-President and Secretary; Charles T. Reice,* Vice-President and Treasurer.
Directors:* Dennis S. Bookshester, Robert P. Bryant, Carroll E. Ebert, Kurt Gasser, Donald J. Gralen, Robert D. Jones, Dean B. McKinney, Robert S. Ruwitch.
Employer Identification Number: 366112629

965
Caterpillar Foundation ☼
100 NE Adams St.
Peoria 61629-1480

Established in 1952 in Illinois.
Financial data: (yr. ended 12/31/83): Assets, $1,006,340 (M); gifts received, $2,200,000; expenditures, $2,953,315, including $2,539,436 for grants and $410,022 for employee matching gifts.
Purpose and activities: Broad purposes; giving primarily to community funds, higher education, and a youth agency; employee matching gift support for cultural and educational institutions.
Types of support awarded: Employee matching gifts.
Officers and Directors:* R.E. Gilmore,* President ; E.J. Schlegel,* Executive Vice-President; B. DeHaan,* H.W. Holling, C.E. Rager, Vice-Presidents; R.R. Thornton, Secretary; A.C. Greer, Treasurer; E.W. Siebert, Manager.
Employer Identification Number: 376022314

966
CBI Foundation
800 Jorie Blvd.
Oak Brook 60521   (312) 654-7000

Incorporated in 1953 in Illinois.
Donor(s): Chicago Bridge & Iron Company.
Financial data: (yr. ended 12/31/83): Assets, $293,386 (L); gifts received, $200,000; expenditures, $249,307, including $236,330 for 180 grants (high: $5,000; low: $50; average: $1,000) and $12,284 for 139 employee matching gifts.
Purpose and activities: General purposes; grants primarily for community funds, scientific and medical research, and hospitals.
Types of support awarded: Continuing support, annual campaigns, emergency funds, employee matching gifts, scholarship funds.
Limitations: No grants to individuals, or for building or endowment funds; no loans.
Application information:
  Initial approach: Letter or full proposal
  Copies of proposal: 1
  Deadline(s): None
  Board meeting date(s): As required
  Final notification: 45 days after board meets
  Write: Barbara Pentecost, Secretary
Officers: R.L. Hull,* President; C.O. Zeimer,* Vice-President; Barbara Pentecost, Secretary; R.L. Brunot,* Treasurer.
Directors:* F.D. Martell, H.R. Fewin.
Number of staff: 2 part-time support.
Employer Identification Number: 366050115

967
Chapin (Frances) Foundation ☼
105 Old Mill Rd.
Barrington 60010

Incorporated in 1966 in New Jersey.
Donor(s): Frances C. Crook.†

Financial data: (yr. ended 3/31/83): Assets, $2,082,744 (M); expenditures, $97,112, including $89,000 for 10 grants (high: $25,000; low: $1,000).
Purpose and activities: Primarily local giving, with emphasis on hospitals, social services, youth, secondary education, and cultural programs.
Limitations: Giving primarily in Barrington, IL.
Officers and Directors: Thomas O. Maxfield, III, President; Robert Gary Maxfield, Vice-President; Naomi Maxfield, Secretary.
Employer Identification Number: 226087456

968
Chicago Community Trust, The ▼
208 South LaSalle St.
Chicago 60604   (312) 372-3356

Community foundation established in 1915 in Illinois by bank resolution and declaration of trust.
Financial data: (yr. ended 9/30/84): Assets, $176,071,827 (M); gifts received, $10,843,375; expenditures, $19,301,203, including $17,310,895 for grants.
Purpose and activities: Established "for such charitable purposes as will . . . best make for the mental, moral, intellectual and physical improvement, assistance and relief of the inhabitants of the County of Cook, State of Illinois." Grants for both general operating support and specific programs and projects in the areas of health and social services, youth agencies, education, particularly higher education, and cultural and civic affairs.
Types of support awarded: Operating budgets, continuing support, seed money, emergency funds, building funds, equipment, land acquisition, matching funds, loans, research, special projects.
Limitations: Giving primarily in Cook County, IL. No support for religious purposes or support of government agencies. No grants to individuals, or for annual campaigns, deficit financing, endowment funds, publications, conferences, scholarships, or fellowships; no support for the purchase of computer hardware; no general operating support for agencies or institutions whose program activities substantially duplicate those already undertaken by others.
Publications: Annual report, informational brochure, program policy statement, application guidelines.
Application information:
  Initial approach: Full proposal
  Copies of proposal: 2
  Deadline(s): None
  Board meeting date(s): March, June or July, September, and December
  Final notification: 90 days after board meeting
  Write: Ms. Barbara L. Massey, Assistant Director
Officer: Bruce L. Newman, Executive Director.
Executive Committee: Mrs. Robert Foote, Chairman; Brooks McCormick, Vice-Chairman; James F. Bere, Franklin A. Cole, J. Ira Harris, Charles E. Lomax, Mrs. Gordon H. Smith, Rev. Kenneth B. Smith, Blaine J. Yarrington.

Trustees: American National Bank and Trust Company of Chicago, Chicago Title and Trust Company, Continental Illinois National Bank and Trust Company of Chicago, The First National Bank of Chicago, Harris Trust and Savings Bank, Heritage-Pullman Bank, LaSalle National Bank, National Boulevard Bank of Chicago, The Northern Trust Company.
Number of staff: 12 full-time professional; 2 part-time professional; 7 full-time support; 1 part-time support.
Employer Identification Number: 362167000

969
Chicago Resource Center ▼
209 W. Jackson Blvd.
Chicago 60606   (312) 461-9333

Established in 1981 in Illinois.
Donor(s): Thomas A. Dennis, Richard J. Dennis.
Financial data: (yr. ended 12/31/83): Assets, $3,226,266 (M); gifts received, $3,315,000; expenditures, $1,137,860, including $1,027,367 for 199 grants (high: $50,000; low: $350; average: $5,500-$7,500).
Purpose and activities: Support for projects dealing with violence against women and families, gay and lesbian issues, and criminal justice.
Types of support awarded: Operating budgets, seed money, emergency funds, equipment, matching funds, continuing support.
Limitations: No grants to individuals, or for annual campaigns, deficit financing, building funds, land acquisition, endowment funds, or scholarships and fellowships; no loans.
Publications: Application guidelines, program policy statement.
Application information:
  Initial approach: Proposal
  Copies of proposal: 1
  Deadline(s): December 21, March 31, June 30, and September 30
  Board meeting date(s): February, May, August, and November
  Final notification: 2 and 1/2 months
  Write: Mary Ann Snyder, Secretary
Officers: Richard J. Dennis, President; Thomas A. Dennis, Vice-President; Mary Ann Snyder, Secretary-Treasurer and Director.
Number of staff: 2 full-time professional; 1 full-time support.
Employer Identification Number: 363121813

970
Chicago Sun-Times Charity Trust
401 North Wabash Ave., Rm. 700
Chicago 60611

Trust established in Illinois.
Donor(s): Racing Industry Charitable Foundation, Inc.
Financial data: (yr. ended 9/30/82): Assets, $717,726 (M); gifts received, $134,445; expenditures, $364,885, including $245,867 for 92 grants (high: $15,200; low: $200).
Purpose and activities: Primarily local giving, with emphasis on higher education, social services, hospitals, and health services; support also for youth agencies and civic affairs.

Limitations: Giving primarily in the Chicago, IL area.
Application information:
Write: Iris J. Krieg, Executive Director
Officers: Margaret C. Baxter, Marshall Field,* Lee Mitchell, Richard Williams,* Vice-Presidents; Thomas M. Tallarico, Secretary and Treasurer.
Trustees:* Richard A. Giesen, Chairman; James Hoge.
Employer Identification Number: 366059459

971
Chicago Title and Trust Company Foundation
111 West Washington St.
Chicago 60602   (312) 630-2911

Trust established in 1951 in Illinois.
Donor(s): Chicago Title and Trust Company.
Financial data: (yr. ended 12/31/83): Assets, $350,000 (M); gifts received, $155,000; expenditures, $155,857, including $135,000 for 33 grants (high: $55,000; low: $500) and $20,000 for 169 employee matching gifts.
Purpose and activities: Broad purposes; giving primarily in the Chicago area with emphasis on community funds, social services, higher education and hospitals.
Types of support awarded: Continuing support, employee matching gifts, special projects.
Limitations: Giving primarily in Chicago, IL. No support for United Way member agencies. No grants to individuals, or for operating budgets, annual campaigns, seed money, emergency funds, deficit financing, building funds, equipment, land acquisition, research, scholarships and fellowships, publications, or conferences; no loans.
Publications: Program policy statement, application guidelines.
Application information: Application form required.
Initial approach: Letter
Copies of proposal: 1
Deadline(s): Submit proposal preferably in February, May, August, or November; deadlines 3rd week of March, June, September, or December
Board meeting date(s): April, July, October, and January
Final notification: 60 days
Write: Carolyn I. Smith
Trustees: Wesley Bass, Alvin Behnke, E. Stanley Enlund, M. Leanne Lachman, Alvin Long, Richard Toft.
Number of staff: 2 part-time professional; 1 full-time support.
Employer Identification Number: 366036809

972
Chicago Tribune Foundation
435 North Michigan Ave.
Chicago 60611   (312) 222-4300
Additional telephone: (312) 222-3825

Incorporated in 1958 in Illinois.
Donor(s): Chicago Tribune Company.

Financial data: (yr. ended 12/31/83): Assets, $588,481 (M); gifts received, $325,170; expenditures, $339,694, including $339,417 for 25 grants (high: $216,500; low: $250).
Purpose and activities: Primarily local giving for a community fund, journalism, higher education, civic affairs, welfare, social services, including aid for the mentally retarded, and cultural programs, including museums; giving includes employee matching gifts program toward higher education and cultural organizations.
Types of support awarded: Employee matching gifts.
Limitations: Giving primarily in the metropolitan Chicago, IL, area. No grants to individuals, or for building or endowment funds, operating budgets, scholarships or fellowships; no loans.
Publications: Application guidelines, program policy statement, informational brochure.
Application information:
Initial approach: Letter
Copies of proposal: 1
Deadline(s): February 1 and September 1
Board meeting date(s): March, June, October, and December
Write: Charles T. Brumback, President
Officers: Charles T. Brumback,* President; Thomas G. Clancy,* Vice-President; Stanley J. Gradowski, Secretary; Larry L. Bloom, Treasurer; J. Nicholas Goodban,* Executive Director.
Directors:* James D. Squires.
Employer Identification Number: 366050792

973
Christiana Foundation, Inc. ☒
69 West Washington St., Rm. 2700
Chicago 60602

Incorporated in 1957 in Illinois.
Donor(s): Lapham Hickey Steel Company.
Financial data: (yr. ended 4/30/83): Assets, $1,155,694 (M); expenditures, $109,320, including $105,375 for grants.
Purpose and activities: Primarily local giving, with emphasis on higher and secondary education, Roman Catholic institutions, health organizations, and youth agencies.
Limitations: Giving primarily in IL.
Officer and Directors: Jerome Frazel, Jr., President; Jerome V. Frazel, Joanne K. Frazel.
Employer Identification Number: 366065745

974
Clark Foundation
2300 Sixth St.
P.O. Box 7000
Rockford 61125   (815) 962-8861

Trust established in 1954 in Illinois.
Donor(s): J.L. Clark Manufacturing Co.
Financial data: (yr. ended 12/31/83): Assets, $5,465,729 (M); expenditures, $719,656, including $679,158 for 146 grants (high: $335,908; low: $100) and $7,475 for 29 employee matching gifts.
Purpose and activities: Broad purposes; emphasis on hospitals, youth agencies, higher education, and community funds.

Types of support awarded: Employee matching gifts, continuing support, annual campaigns, emergency funds, building funds, equipment.
Limitations: Giving primarily in areas of company operations. No grants to individuals, or for endowment funds, research, or scholarships and fellowships; no loans.
Application information:
Initial approach: Full proposal
Copies of proposal: 1
Deadline(s): 1st of each month board meets
Board meeting date(s): January, April, July and October
Write: V.E. Zumhagen, Chairman
Officers and Trustees: V.E. Zumhagen, Chairman; B.J. Peterson, Secretary; M.C. Arne, T.P. Harnois, R.W. Malmgren, W.O. Nelson.
Employer Identification Number: 366032573

975
Coleman Foundation, Inc., The ▼
1137 West Jackson Blvd.
Chicago 60607   (312) 243-2700

Trust established in 1953 in Illinois.
Donor(s): J.D. Stetson Coleman,† Dorothy W. Coleman.†
Financial data: (yr. ended 12/31/84): Assets, $46,360,448 (M); expenditures, $5,189,750, including $4,807,631 for 104 grants (high: $500,000; low: $500; average: $41,200-$51,600).
Purpose and activities: Broad purposes; primarily local giving for social services and civic affairs, education, health services, cultural programs, and scientific research.
Types of support awarded: Operating budgets, annual campaigns, general purposes, seed money, special projects, research, publications, conferences and seminars, building funds, equipment, land acquisition, matching funds, professorships, internships, scholarship funds, fellowships.
Limitations: Giving primarily in the Chicago, IL, metropolitan area. No grants to individuals, or for endowment funds, continuing support, emergency funds, deficit financing, or scholarships and fellowships directly to individuals; no loans.
Publications: Annual report, program policy statement, application guidelines.
Application information:
Initial approach: Concise letter
Deadline(s): September 30
Board meeting date(s): Usually in March, June and October
Final notification: 3 months
Write: Jean D. Thorne, Executive Director
Officers and Directors: John E. Hughes, President and Treasurer; Richard M. Peritz, Executive Vice-President; R. Michael Furlong, Vice-President; Thomas H. Thorne, Secretary; Jean D. Thorne, Executive Director.
Number of staff: 3 full-time professional; 2 part-time professional; 3 full-time support; 3 part-time support.
Employer Identification Number: 363025967

976
Container Corporation of America Foundation ▼
One First National Plaza
Chicago 60603   (312) 580-5500

Incorporated in 1951 in Illinois.
Donor(s): Container Corporation of America.
Financial data: (yr. ended 12/31/84): Assets,
$0 (L); gifts received, $700,000; expenditures,
$767,736, including $698,891 for 250 grants
and $61,765 for 422 employee matching gifts.
Purpose and activities: Local giving; support
for arts and culture, education, health, welfare,
and civic organizations.
Limitations: Giving limited to areas of
operating facilities, primarily in plant
communities. No grants to individuals.
Application information: Unsolicited
proposals (except from Chicago-area
organizations) are not encouraged. A copy of
guidelines should be requested prior to
submission of request.
> *Write:* Catherine Bertini, Vice-President or
> Beth Rohrbach, Administrator

Officer and Trustees: Catherine Bertini, Vice-
President and Manager; and 6 other trustees.
Staff: Beth Rohrbach, Administrator, Corporate
Giving.
Number of staff: None.
Employer Identification Number: 366044227

977
Continental Bank Foundation ▼
231 South LaSalle St.
Chicago 60697   (312) 923-5114

Incorporated in 1962 in Illinois.
Donor(s): Continental Illinois Corporation.
Financial data: (yr. ended 12/31/83): Assets,
$5,763 (M); gifts received, $2,910,000;
expenditures, $2,937,188, including
$2,703,670 for 327 grants (high: $645,000;
low: $100) and $233,518 for 345 employee
matching gifts.
Purpose and activities: All new funding
activity suspended indefinitely in late April,
1984, due to bank's earnings problems;
currently paying out grants previously
authorized. Status of foundation to be
reevaluated in 1986 after review of bank's
performance. Traditionally, charitable
purposes; primarily local giving; grants to tax
exempt organizations, especially for operating
expenses for programs that fall within scope of
following priorities: civic and economic affairs,
culture, education, with emphasis on higher
education, environmental improvement, health,
hospitals, social welfare, and urban affairs.
Limitations: Giving primarily in the Chicago,
IL, metropolitan area. No support for programs
designed to influence legislation, or for tax-
supported educational institutions; pre-school,
elementary, or secondary educational
institutions; sectarian or religious organizations
supporting any one religious group; or grant
making foundations. No grants to individuals,
or for endowment funds, scholarships,
fellowships, or operating expenses of
organizations receiving United Way support; no
loans.

Publications: Annual report, application
guidelines.
Application information: Funds fully
committed; grant applications currently not
accepted; grantmaking programs suspended
indefinitely.
> *Board meeting date(s):* Board meetings
> suspended until foundation is able to
> resume grantmaking operations
> *Write:* Joan F. Neal, 2nd Vice-President,
> Corporate Affairs

Officers: John H. Perkins,* President; John V.
Egan, Jr.,* Vice-President and Chairman of
Contributions Committee; N. Bruce Callow,
Vice-President; David A. Woodworth, 2nd Vice-
President; Kevin J. Hallagan, Secretary; David
G. Taylor, Treasurer.
Directors:* Eugene R. Croisant.
Contributions Committee: Fidel Lopez, Vice-
Chairman; Kenneth K. Chalmers, Thomas
Dowen, Katherine M. Lorenz, Robert O.
McKnew, James J. Nemer, Jr., Roger H.
Sherman.
Number of staff: 4 full-time professional; 1
part-time professional; 2 full-time support.
Employer Identification Number: 366056976

978
Cook (David C.) Foundation ⌑
850 North Grove Ave.
Elgin 60120   (312) 741-2400

Incorporated in 1944 in Illinois.
Donor(s): Frances Kerr Cook Trust.
Financial data: (yr. ended 12/31/83): Assets,
$8,498,103 (M); gifts received, $168,763;
expenditures, $588,172, including $1,500 for 2
grants (high: $1,000; low: $500) and $459,985
for foundation-administered programs.
Purpose and activities: A private operating
foundation working with other agencies to
advance the Christian Gospel through literature,
literacy, mass communications and leadership
training in North America and abroad; projects
and research generally initiated by the
Foundation.
Limitations: No grants to individuals, or for
endowment funds or operating budgets.
Publications: Annual report.
Application information:
> *Initial approach:* Letter
> *Copies of proposal:* 1
> *Board meeting date(s):* April and December
> *Write:* Albert C. Montgomery, Secretary

Officers and Trustees: D. Charles Cook III,
President; Lee Vance, 1st Vice-President;
Joseph T. Bayly, 2nd Vice-President; Bruce L.
Cook, 3rd Vice-President; Albert C.
Montgomery, Secretary; Robert B. Reekie,
Treasurer; Marshall Barnes, Robert S. Laubach,
Frances E. Vance, C. Charles Van Ness.
Employer Identification Number: 366008100

979
Crane Fund, The ⌑
222 West Adams St., Rm. 849
Chicago 60606

Established in 1914.

Financial data: (yr. ended 12/31/83): Assets,
$30,249,804 (M); expenditures, $1,895,311,
including $1,652,230 for 1,209 grants to
individuals.
Purpose and activities: Grants to needy
individuals in the United States, Canada, and
Great Britain.
Types of support awarded: Grants to
individuals.
Limitations: Giving primarily in the United
States, Canada, and Great Britain.
Manager: K.H. Cardoza.
Trustees: C. Dackis, P.R. Hundt, J.F. O'Brien,
R.J. Slater, R.K. Whitley.
Employer Identification Number: 366124341

980
Crane Fund for Widows and Children ⌑
222 West Adams St., Rm. 849
Chicago 60606

Established in 1914 in Illinois.
Financial data: (yr. ended 12/31/83): Assets,
$5,894,114 (M); expenditures, $421,036,
including $363,123 for 232 grants (high:
$15,000; low: $50) and $16,441 for 5 grants
to individuals.
Purpose and activities: General giving,
primarily in the United States to community
funds, hospitals, and for higher education;
limited support also to organizations in Canada;
assistance to needy and indigent persons,
mainly in Illinois.
Limitations: Giving primarily in the U.S. and
Canada; grants to the needy limited to IL.
Manager: K.H. Cardoza.
Trustees: W.C. Dackis, P.R. Hundt, R.J.
Neville, J.F. O'Brien, R.J. Slater.
Employer Identification Number: 366116543

981
Crowell (Henry P.) and Susan C. Crowell Trust ▼
Lock Box 442
Chicago 60690   (312) 372-5202

Trust established in 1927 in Illinois.
Donor(s): Henry P. Crowell.
Financial data: (yr. ended 12/31/83): Assets,
$25,059,088 (M); gifts received, $13,196,142;
expenditures, $1,899,423, including
$1,786,770 for 151 grants (high: $110,000;
low: $3,000; average: $5,000-$25,000).
Purpose and activities: Created to aid
evangelical Christianity by support to
organizations having for their purposes its
teaching, advancement, and active extension at
home and abroad.
Types of support awarded: Emergency funds,
matching funds, operating budgets, building
funds, equipment, scholarship funds.
Limitations: No grants to individuals or for
endowment funds or research; no loans.
Application information:
> *Initial approach:* Full proposal or letter
> *Copies of proposal:* 1
> *Deadline(s):* April 1 and October 1
> *Board meeting date(s):* May and November
> *Final notification:* 1 to 2 months
> *Write:* Lowell L. Kline, Executive Secretary

Officers: Edwin L. Brown, Jr.,* President; LeRoy E. Johnson,* Vice-President; Edwin L. Frizen, Jr.,* Secretary and Treasurer; Lowell L. Kline, Executive Secretary.
Trustees:* John T. Bass, John R. Robinson.
Corporate Trustee: Continental Illinois Bank and Trust Company of Chicago.
Number of staff: 2.
Employer Identification Number: 366038028

982
Crown (Arie and Ida) Memorial ▼
300 West Washington St.
Chicago 60606 (312) 236-6300

Incorporated in 1947 in Illinois.
Donor(s): Members of the Crown family.
Financial data: (yr. ended 12/31/83): Assets, $43,881,764 (M); gifts received, $125,000; expenditures, $1,660,268, including $1,603,525 for 229 grants (high: $450,000; low: $10; average: $100-$50,000).
Purpose and activities: Broad purposes; primarily local giving, with emphasis on Jewish welfare funds, higher and secondary education, music, cultural relations with Israel, temple support, hospitals, community funds, youth agencies, and assistance to the aged and the handicapped.
Types of support awarded: Continuing support, annual campaigns, building funds, equipment, land acquisition, endowment funds, matching funds, professorships, research, special projects.
Limitations: Giving primarily in IL. No grants to individuals; the foundation does not provide consulting services or technical assistance; no loans.
Application information: Funds presently committed; applications for grants currently not invited.
 Board meeting date(s): As required
 Write: Louis J. Levy, Assistant Secretary
Officers: Irving Crown,* President; Lester Crown,* Vice-President; Benjamin Z. Gould, Secretary.
Directors:* Henry Crown, Joanne Crown, John Crown.
Number of staff: None.
Employer Identification Number: 366076088

983
Crown (Edward A.) Charitable Fund
300 West Washington St.
Chicago 60606 (312) 236-6300

Established in 1977 in Illinois.
Donor(s): Edward A. Crown.†
Financial data: (yr. ended 7/31/84): Assets, $5,563,137 (M); expenditures, $270,854, including $262,000 for 6 grants (high: $100,000; low: $1,000).
Purpose and activities: Broad purposes; grants for higher education and Jewish welfare funds.
Types of support awarded: Continuing support, building funds, equipment, land acquisition, endowment funds, matching funds, scholarship funds, fellowships, special projects, research, publications, conferences and seminars.
Limitations: No grants to individuals; no loans.

Application information:
 Initial approach: Letter
 Deadline(s): None
 Board meeting date(s): As required
 Final notification: 2 months
 Write: Lester Crown, Trustee
Trustees: Arie Steven Crown, Barry S. Crown, Bradley David Crown, Bruce Crown, Daniel Morris Crown, David Arden Crown, Debra Lee Crown, Donna Lynn Crown, Elizabeth Ida Crown, Henry Crown, Irving Crown, James Schine Crown, Janet S. Crown, John J. Crown, Laurie Jayne Crown, Lester Crown, Nancy Jean Crown, Patricia Ann Crown, Rebecca Eileen Crown, Sara Beth Crown, Susan Crown, William H. Crown, Barbara N. Goodman, Leonard C. Goodman, Richard Crown Goodman, Suzanne C. Goodman, Irene Crown Merwin, Florence Crown Rothman, Hermine C. Rothman, Michael Crown Rothman, Patricia Rothman.
Number of staff: None.
Employer Identification Number: 362996704

984
Cuneo Foundation, The
Two North Riverside Plaza, Suite 1160
Chicago 60606 (312) 648-5100

Incorporated in 1945 in Illinois.
Donor(s): John F. Cuneo, Milwaukee Golf Development Corporation.
Financial data: (yr. ended 12/31/83): Assets, $10,028,789 (M); expenditures, $286,403, including $252,682 for grants.
Purpose and activities: Broad purposes: primarily local giving, with emphasis on hospitals and Roman Catholic church support, religious associations, and welfare funds; support also for youth agencies and higher education.
Types of support awarded: General purposes, building funds, equipment, matching funds.
Limitations: Giving primarily in the Chicago, IL, metropolitan area. No grants to individuals or for scholarships or fellowships; no loans.
Application information:
 Initial approach: Full proposal
 Copies of proposal: 1
 Deadline(s): May 1 and October 1
 Board meeting date(s): May and October
 Final notification: 2 months
 Write: John F. Cuneo, Jr., President
Officers: John F. Cuneo, Jr.,* President; Charles L. McEvoy,* Vice-President; R.G. De Yong, Secretary and Treasurer.
Directors:* Robert R. Browning, Herta Cuneo, Jr., Rev. Msgr. Harry C. Koenig, Consuela Cuneo McAlister, Rosemary McEvoy.
Number of staff: None.
Employer Identification Number: 362261606

985
D and R Fund ⌐
8000 Sears Tower
Chicago 60606

Incorporated in 1951 in Illinois.
Donor(s): Samuel R. Rosenthal, Marie-Louise Rosenthal, Carolyn S. Dreyfus,† Alice L. Dreyfus.†

Financial data: (yr. ended 12/31/83): Assets, $5,864,351 (M); gifts received, $114,923; expenditures, $223,649, including $197,851 for 54 grants (high: $50,050; low: $100).
Purpose and activities: Broad purposes; grants largely for higher education, hospitals, Jewish welfare funds, and cultural institutions.
Limitations: No grants to individuals, or for building or endowment funds or operating budgets.
Application information: Applications for grants are not invited.
 Write: Samuel R. Rosenthal, President
Officers and Directors: Samuel R. Rosenthal, President; Marie-Louise Rosenthal, Vice-President, Secretary, and Treasurer; Harry H. Hagey, Vice-President; James Glasser, Louise R. Glasser, Donald Lubin, Babette Rosenthal.
Employer Identification Number: 366057159

986
Davee Foundation, The ⌐
1550 Lake Shore Dr., Apartment 23-G
Chicago 60610 (312) 664-4128

Established in 1964 in Illinois.
Donor(s): Ken M. Davee.
Financial data: (yr. ended 12/31/83): Assets, $3,281,536 (M); gifts received, $546,250; expenditures, $104,701, including $103,773 for 22 grants (high: $20,000; low: $25).
Purpose and activities: Primarily local giving, with emphasis on the arts, hospitals, and higher education; support also for civil rights organizations.
Types of support awarded: General purposes.
Limitations: Giving primarily in IL.
Application information:
 Initial approach: Letter
 Deadline(s): None
 Write: Ken M. Davee, President
Officers: Ken M. Davee, President; Adeline B. Davee, Secretary.
Director: J.W. Dugdale.
Employer Identification Number: 366124598

987
Deere (John) Foundation ▼
John Deere Rd.
Moline 61265 (309) 752-4137

Incorporated in 1948 in Illinois.
Donor(s): Deere & Company.
Financial data: (yr. ended 10/31/84): Assets, $4,076,449 (M); gifts received, $6,000,000; expenditures, $3,060,916, including $2,235,208 for 190 grants (high: $420,000; low: $25), $675,800 for 3,264 employee matching gifts and $149,908 for 1 foundation-administered program.
Purpose and activities: Broad purposes; giving in areas of company operations, with grants largely for community funds, higher education, youth agencies, and cultural programs.
Types of support awarded: Annual campaigns, seed money, building funds, equipment, land acquisition, scholarship funds, fellowships, exchange programs, internships, operating budgets, general purposes, employee matching gifts, continuing support.

Limitations: Giving limited to areas where company employees live and work. No grants to individuals or for endowment funds; no loans.
Publications: Annual report, application guidelines.
Application information:
Initial approach: Letter or telephone
Copies of proposal: 1
Deadline(s): None
Board meeting date(s): As required, usually quarterly
Final notification: 30 days after board review
Write: John F. Coy, President
Officers: John F. Coy,* President; Sonja Sterling, Secretary; Eugene L. Schotanus,* Treasurer.
Directors:* Robert W. Boeke, Chairman; Neil O. Christenson, Joseph W. England, David P. Hopley, Michael S. Plunkett, Chester K. Lasell, C.C. Peterson, Milton G. Tiede.
Number of staff: 2.
Employer Identification Number: 366051024

988
Deering Foundation ¤
410 North Michigan Ave., Rm. 590
Chicago 60611

Incorporated in 1956 in Illinois.
Donor(s): Mrs. Barbara D. Danielson, Richard E. Danielson, Jr., Marion D. Campbell, Miami Corporation.
Financial data: (yr. ended 11/30/83): Assets, $4,547,439 (M); expenditures, $503,618, including $412,500 for 20 grants (high: $25,000; low: $1,000).
Purpose and activities: Broad purposes; general giving, chiefly in Massachusetts and Illinois, with emphasis on other foundations, hospitals, education, conservation, and museums.
Types of support awarded: General purposes.
Limitations: Giving primarily in IL and MA.
Officers and Directors: Marion D. Campbell, President; James Deering Danielson, Richard E. Danielson, Jr., Vice-Presidents; Charles E. Schroeder, Secretary and Treasurer.
Employer Identification Number: 366051876

989
DeKalb AgResearch Foundation, The
3100 Sycamore Rd.
DeKalb 60115   (815) 758-3461

Incorporated in 1964 in Illinois.
Donor(s): DeKalb AgResearch, Inc.
Financial data: (yr. ended 8/31/84): Assets, $845,681 (M); gifts received, $53,114; expenditures, $236,119, including $189,823 for 162 grants (high: $15,000; low: $25; average: $50-$50,000) and $44,557 for 137 employee matching gifts.
Purpose and activities: General purposes; grants largely for colleges, civic affairs, social welfare and youth agencies, and community funds in areas of company operations. Educational support limited normally to privately endowed institutions not supported by public tax funds.

Types of support awarded: Continuing support, annual campaigns, seed money, emergency funds, deficit financing, building funds, equipment, land acquisition, endowment funds, matching funds, special projects, employee matching gifts, publications, conferences and seminars.
Limitations: Giving primarily in areas of company operations. No support for religious or labor organizations, policemen's or firemen's ball activities, or publicly-funded educational institutions. No grants to individuals, or for operating budgets, individual travel, study, or similar purposes; no loans.
Publications: Annual report, application guidelines.
Application information:
Initial approach: Letter
Copies of proposal: 1
Deadline(s): None
Board meeting date(s): Bimonthly
Final notification: 2 months
Write: Wayne A. White, Director
Officers and Directors: Bruce Bickner, President; Frank Bauer, Wayne A. White, Vice-Presidents; Ronald Scherer, Secretary; Richard Ryan, Treasurer.
Number of staff: None.
Employer Identification Number: 366117737

990
Demos (N.) Foundation, Inc.
c/o The Northern Trust Company
50 South LaSalle St.
Chicago 60675

Incorporated in 1964 in New York.
Donor(s): Nicholas Demos.†
Financial data: (yr. ended 6/30/82): Assets, $1,482,763 (M); gifts received, $62,500; expenditures, $157,424, including $141,550 for 7 grants (high: $33,000; low: $13,900).
Purpose and activities: Broad purposes; grants limited to organizations in Greece for education and child welfare.
Limitations: Giving limited to Greece.
Publications: Application guidelines.
Application information:
Initial approach: Letter
Write: Mrs. Barbara E. Lundberg, Secretary
Officers: Elizabeth Tieken,* President; Barbara E. Lundberg, Secretary; Robert F. Reusche,* Treasurer.
Directors:* William H. McNeill, Chairman; Mrs. Paul Gebhard, John Heyworth, Bishop Iakovos.
Employer Identification Number: 366165689

991
DeSoto Foundation ¤
1700 South Mt. Prospect Rd.
Des Plaines 60018

Incorporated in 1963 in Illinois.
Donor(s): DeSoto, Inc.
Financial data: (yr. ended 12/31/83): Assets, $655,741 (M); gifts received, $225,000; expenditures, $223,674, including $222,350 for 90 grants (high: $27,200; low: $150).

Purpose and activities: Primarily local giving, with emphasis on community funds, higher education, youth agencies, health agencies and cultural programs.
Limitations: Giving primarily in IL.
Officers: R.R. Missar,* President; J. Barreiro,* Vice-President; C.F. Clemins, Secretary and Treasurer.
Directors:* W.L. Lamey, Jr.
Employer Identification Number: 366097563

992
Dillon Foundation ▼
121 Wallace St.
P.O. Box 108
Sterling 61081   (815) 625-2500

Incorporated in 1953 in Illinois.
Donor(s): Members of the Dillon family, Northwestern Steel and Wire Company.
Financial data: (yr. ended 10/31/83): Assets, $20,618,454 (M); gifts received, $15,485,913; expenditures, $1,218,514, including $1,200,531 for 48 grants (high: $555,931; low: $150; average: $200-$6,000).
Purpose and activities: Broad purposes; primarily local giving, with emphasis on civic and public affairs, education, social services, and youth.
Types of support awarded: Continuing support, annual campaigns, seed money, emergency funds, building funds, scholarship funds, general purposes.
Limitations: Giving primarily in IL. No grants to individuals, or for endowment funds, or matching gifts; no loans.
Application information:
Initial approach: Letter
Copies of proposal: 1
Deadline(s): None
Board meeting date(s): December; committee meets quarterly
Write: W. Martin Dillon, President
Officers and Directors: W. Martin Dillon, President; Peter W. Dillon, Vice-President; John P. Conway, Secretary; John W. Bowman, Treasurer; L.E. Prew.
Number of staff: None.
Employer Identification Number: 366059349

993
Donnelley (Elliott and Ann) Foundation ¤
c/o Isham, Lincoln & Beale
Three First National Plaza, Rm. 5200
Chicago 60602   (312) 558-7414

Incorporated in 1954 in Illinois.
Donor(s): Elliott Donnelley.†
Financial data: (yr. ended 12/31/83): Assets, $1,764,117 (M); expenditures, $80,290, including $75,490 for 67 grants (high: $20,000; low: $10).
Purpose and activities: Primarily local giving, with emphasis on hospitals and education; support also for cultural programs and youth agencies.
Limitations: Giving primarily in IL. No grants to individuals.
Application information: Applications for grants not invited.

Board meeting date(s): As required
Officers and Directors: Ann S. Hardy, President and Treasurer; Robert Wood Tullis, Vice-President and Secretary; Thomas E. Donnelley, II.
Employer Identification Number: 366066894

994
Donnelley (Gaylord and Dorothy) Foundation
(formerly Gaylord Donnelley Foundation)
350 East 22nd St.
Chicago 60616   (312) 326-7255

Incorporated in 1952 in Illinois.
Donor(s): Gaylord Donnelley, Dorothy Ranney Donnelley.
Financial data: (yr. ended 12/31/83): Assets, $3,796,039 (M); gifts received, $95,030; expenditures, $200,598, including $191,439 for 108 grants (high: $6,000; low: $250; average: $1,000-$3,000).
Purpose and activities: General purposes; giving primarily in the Midwest, with emphasis on Chicago, and in South Carolina; grants to educational, cultural, health, conservation, research, religious, animal health and welfare, and general welfare institutions of personal interest to the donors and directors.
Types of support awarded: Operating budgets, continuing support, building funds, research, publications, endowment funds.
Limitations: Giving primarily in the Chicago, IL area, the Midwest, and SC. No grants to individuals, or for seed money, emergency funds, deficit financing, equipment and materials, or matching gifts; no loans.
Publications: Annual report, application guidelines.
Application information:
Initial approach: Letter
Copies of proposal: 1
Deadline(s): None
Board meeting date(s): Spring, summer, and fall
Final notification: 3 weeks
Write: Mrs. Jane Rishel, President
Officers and Directors: Gaylord Donnelley, Chairman; Jane Rishel, President and Treasurer; Dorothy Ranney Donnelley, Vice-President; Middleton Miller, Secretary; Lowell T. Coggeshall, M.D., James E. Gleason, C. Bouton McDougal.
Number of staff: 1 full-time professional.
Employer Identification Number: 366108460

995
Dreier-Penrith Family Foundation ¤
c/o Craig M. Penrith
2401 North Halsted
Chicago 60614

Established in Illinois.
Donor(s): O.T. Hogan.†
Financial data: (yr. ended 10/31/83): Assets, $1,498,513 (M); expenditures, $149,091, including $125,407 for 22 grants (high: $50,000; low: $70).

Purpose and activities: Giving primarily in the Chicago area and Palm Desert, California, with emphasis on education, hospitals, health agencies, and church support.
Limitations: Giving primarily in IL and CA.
Officers: Geraldine I. Dreier, President; Craig Penrith, Secretary; Gary Penrith, Treasurer.
Employer Identification Number: 363012144

996
Eisenberg (The George M.) Foundation ¤
4100 West Fullerton Ave.
Chicago 60639

Trust established in 1945 in Illinois.
Donor(s): George M. Eisenberg, American Decal and Manufacturing Company.
Financial data: (yr. ended 12/31/83): Assets, $3,093,274 (M); gifts received, $255,179; expenditures, $200,038, including $195,063 for 51 grants (high: $50,088; low: $100).
Purpose and activities: Primarily local giving, with emphasis on the aged, hospitals, medical research, and social agencies, particularly those serving the aged, the handicapped, and youth.
Limitations: Giving primarily in IL.
Trustees: George M. Eisenberg, Charles H. Weinman.
Employer Identification Number: 366091694

997
Evinrude (The Ole) Foundation
100 Sea Horse Dr.
Waukegan 60085   (312) 689-5235

Incorporated in 1945 in Wisconsin.
Donor(s): Outboard Marine Corporation.
Financial data: (yr. ended 6/30/84): Assets, $519,936 (M); gifts received, $150,000; expenditures, $187,949, including $153,760 for 40 grants (high: $33,000; low: $200; average: $5,000-$10,000) and $31,000 for 31 grants to individuals.
Purpose and activities: Support of private higher education in states in which the company operates, scholarship aid to children of company employees, and capital grants to hospital and cultural building projects in company locations.
Types of support awarded: Continuing support, annual campaigns, seed money, building funds, equipment, fellowships, special projects, research, scholarship funds, employee related scholarships.
Limitations: Giving limited to areas of company operations. No grants to individuals (except for company-employee scholarships), or for endowment funds, or matching gifts; no loans.
Publications: Program policy statement, application guidelines.
Application information:
Initial approach: Letter
Copies of proposal: 1
Deadline(s): Submit proposal preferably in October; deadline October 31
Board meeting date(s): December
Final notification: 30 days after annual meeting
Write: Edward J. Schroedter, Vice-President

Officers and Directors: Ralph S. Evinrude, President; James C. Chapman, Vice-President; K.A. Pope, Secretary; N. Jacobs, Treasurer; Patrick W. Cotter, Edward J. Schroedter.
Number of staff: None.
Employer Identification Number: 396037139

998
Falk (Dr. Ralph and Marian) Medical Research Foundation ¤
c/o Continental Illinois National Bank and Trust Company of Chicago
30 North LaSalle St.
Chicago 60693   (312) 828-3666

Established in 1974 in Illinois.
Donor(s): Marian C. Falk.
Financial data: (yr. ended 12/31/83): Assets, $2,346,904 (M); expenditures, $260,783, including $243,250 for 10 grants (high: $80,000; low: $50).
Purpose and activities: Support primarily for medical research.
Application information:
Write: M.J. Termondt, Vice-President
Officers and Directors: Marian Falk, President and Treasurer; Carol C. Fullinwider, M.J. Termondt, Vice-Presidents; Nicole Kohl, Secretary; William Graham.
Employer Identification Number: 237380541

999
Farm Foundation
1211 West 22nd St.
Oak Brook 60521   (312) 986-9393

Trust established in 1933 in Illinois.
Donor(s): Alexander Legge,† Frank O. Lowden,† and others.
Financial data: (yr. ended 4/30/84): Assets, $8,032,135 (M); gifts received, $67,409; expenditures, $650,853, including $28,200 for 43 grants to individuals and $267,000 for foundation-administered programs.
Purpose and activities: To improve the conditions of rural life by: (1) stimulating, coordinating, and supplementing the efforts of existing agencies; (2) initiating and conducting research and experimental work for the study of any important economic, social, educational, or scientific problem affecting the rural population of the country; and (3) disseminating the educational and useful information resulting from such study and experimentation. Activities conducted mainly through regional research and extension committees, which include representatives from the state universities in the region and the U.S. Department of Agriculture. Scholarships to extension supervisors for supervisory courses offered at summer schools; fellowships for more extensive study to agricultural extension workers with priority given to administrators and supervisors.
Types of support awarded: Scholarship funds, research, conferences and seminars, publications, fellowships.
Limitations: No grants to individuals (except for scholarships and fellowships), or for building or endowment funds, operating budgets, or special projects.

Publications: Annual report, program policy statement, informational brochure.
Application information:
 Initial approach: Letter
 Board meeting date(s): May or June
 Write: R.J. Hildreth, Managing Director
Officers: R.J. Hildreth, Managing Director; Walter J. Armbruster, Associate Managing Director and Secretary of the Board of Trustees.
Trustees: Joseph P. Sullivan, Chairman; Ben H. Warren, Vice-Chairman, and Chairman of the Executive Committee; and twenty-nine additional trustees.
Number of staff: 4.
Employer Identification Number: 362270048

1000
Fel-Pro/Mecklenburger Foundation
c/o Felt Products Manufacturing Company
7450 North McCormick Blvd.
Skokie 60076   (312) 674-7700

Incorporated in 1959 in Illinois.
Donor(s): Fel-Pro Incorporated, Felt Products Manufacturing Company, Fel-Pro International, Fel-Pro Realty.
Financial data: (yr. ended 12/31/84): Assets, $5,094,798 (M); gifts received, $4,032,600; expenditures, $656,798, including $526,725 for 229 grants (high: $151,080; low: $25; average: $500-$1,500), $100,000 for 200 grants to individuals and $13,979 for 54 employee matching gifts.
Purpose and activities: Grants to local operating organizations, with emphasis on basic human needs, human services, vocational training, corporate social responsibility, minority and inner-city concerns, and the environment; scholarships only awarded through a special automotive technicians' scholarship program.
Types of support awarded: Operating budgets, continuing support, seed money, matching funds, employee matching gifts, special projects, student aid.
Limitations: Giving limited to the Chicago, IL, metropolitan area. No grants to individuals (except for special scholarship program), or for emergency, capital, building or endowment funds, deficit financing, equipment, land acquisition, scholarships, fellowships, research, publications, or conferences; no loans.
Publications: Application guidelines, program policy statement.
Application information: Scholarship applications available through the Citizens' Scholarship Foundation of America, Inc., which selects recipients, or schools' financial aid offices.
 Initial approach: Full proposal
 Copies of proposal: 1
 Deadline(s): None
 Board meeting date(s): Bimonthly beginning in February
 Final notification: 2 months
 Write: Celene Peurye, Foundation Administrator

Officers and Directors: Paul Lehman, President; Harold Heft, Dennis Kessler, Robert Morris, Vice-Presidents; Frances Lehman, Treasurer; Sylvia Radov, Secretary; Celene Peurye, Foundation Administrator.
Number of staff: 1 part-time professional.
Employer Identification Number: 366065607

1001
Field Foundation of Illinois, Inc., The ▼
135 South LaSalle St.
Chicago 60603   (312) 263-3211

Incorporated in 1960 in Illinois.
Donor(s): Marshall Field IV,† The Field Foundation, Inc.
Financial data: (yr. ended 4/30/84): Assets, $22,926,924 (M); expenditures, $1,667,603, including $1,475,357 for 69 grants (high: $60,000; low: $1,000; average: $10,000-$20,000).
Purpose and activities: General purposes; primarily local giving in the fields of health, welfare, education, cultural activities, and civic affairs; grants focused on youth agencies, race relations, and the aged.
Types of support awarded: Building funds, emergency funds, equipment, special projects, land acquisition.
Limitations: Giving primarily in the Chicago, IL area. No support for member agencies of community funds, national health agencies, neighborhood health clinics, small cultural groups, private schools, or for religious purposes. No grants to individuals, or for endowment funds, continuing operating support, medical research, conferences, operating support of day care centers, scholarships, or fellowships; no loans.
Publications: Annual report, program policy statement, application guidelines.
Application information:
 Initial approach: Full proposal
 Board meeting date(s): Quarterly
 Write: Lorraine Madsen, President
Officers: Leland Webber,* Chairman; Lorraine Madsen, President and Treasurer; Gary H. Kline, Secretary.
Directors:* Lowell T. Coggeshall, M.D., Marshall Field, Hanna H. Gray, Paul R. Judy, George A. Ranney, Jr., Arthur E. Rasmussen.
Number of staff: 1 full-time professional; 1 part-time professional; 1 full-time support; 1 part-time support.
Employer Identification Number: 366059408

1002
First National Bank of Chicago Foundation ▼
One First National Plaza
Chicago 60670   (312) 732-6948

Incorporated in 1961 in Illinois.
Donor(s): The First National Bank of Chicago.
Financial data: (yr. ended 12/31/83): Assets, $1,173,834 (M); gifts received, $590,003; expenditures, $676,839, including $508,686 for 70 grants (high: $45,000; low: $250; average: $1,000-$10,000) and $166,608 for 785 employee matching gifts.

Purpose and activities: Broad purposes; general giving, with grants mainly to local organizations in health and welfare, education, youth, culture and the arts, civic and community development ; support also for a local community fund.
Types of support awarded: Operating budgets, continuing support, annual campaigns, building funds, equipment, endowment funds, matching funds, scholarship funds, fellowships, employee matching gifts.
Limitations: Giving primarily in the metropolitan Chicago, IL area. No support for fraternal or religious organizations, preschool, elementary, or secondary education, or tax-supported institutions. No grants to individuals, or for seed money, emergency funds, deficit financing, land acquisition, special projects, research, publications, conferences, or multi-year pledges; no loans.
Publications: Program policy statement, application guidelines.
Application information:
 Initial approach: Letter
 Copies of proposal: 1
 Deadline(s): None
 Board meeting date(s): March, June, September, and December
 Final notification: 3 to 6 months
 Write: Norman A. Ross, President
Officers and Directors:* Norman A. Ross,* President; Clark Burrus,* William S. Lear,* William J. McDonough,* Leo F. Mullin,* David J. Paulus,* Diane M. Smith,* James K. Suhr,* Barry F. Sullivan,* Richard L. Thomas,* David J. Vitale,* Vice-Presidents; Ilona M. Berry, Secretary; Charles H. Montgomery, Treasurer.
Number of staff: 1 full-time professional; 2 full-time support.
Employer Identification Number: 366033828

1003
Fisher Charitable Trust ⌑
First National Bank and Trust Company of Rockford
401 East State St.
Rockford 61104   (815) 962-3771

Trust established in 1951 in Illinois.
Donor(s): Arthur M. Fisher,† and family-related businesses.
Financial data: (yr. ended 12/31/83): Assets, $99 (M); expenditures, $141,209, including $140,807 for 50 grants (high: $25,000; low: $100).
Purpose and activities: Broad purposes; local giving, with emphasis on hospitals, church support and religious associations, and social and youth agencies.
Limitations: Giving limited to the Rockford, IL, area. No grants to individuals, or for endowment funds, research, scholarships, fellowships, or matching gifts; no loans.
Trustees: W.L. Farb, Arthur M. Fisher, Jr., Vera Maureen Fisher, First National Bank and Trust Company of Rockford, Corporate Trustee.
Employer Identification Number: 366032558

1004
Fitzgerald (Father James M.)
Scholarship Trust
c/o Commercial National Bank of Peoria
301 S.W. Adams St.
Peoria 61631

Trust established in 1964 in Illinois.
Donor(s): Father James M. Fitzgerald.†
Financial data: (yr. ended 12/31/83): Assets,
$1,041,000 (M); expenditures, $88,500,
including $83,000 for 45 grants to individuals
(average: $4,000).
Purpose and activities: Grants restricted to
priesthood students who are residents of Illinois
and attend a Catholic university or college.
Types of support awarded: Student aid.
Limitations: Giving limited to residents of IL.
No grants for general purposes, capital or
endowment funds, matching gifts, research,
special projects, publications or conferences;
no loans.
Application information:
 Initial approach: Letter
 Deadline(s): None
 Board meeting date(s): As required
 Final notification: 30 days
Trustees: Rev. Francis Cahill, Commercial
National Bank of Peoria.
Number of staff: None.
Employer Identification Number: 376050189

1005
FMC Foundation ▼
200 East Randolph Dr.
Chicago 60601 (312) 861-6102

Incorporated in 1953 in California.
Donor(s): FMC Corporation.
Financial data: (yr. ended 11/30/83): Assets,
$826,776 (M); gifts received, $37,100;
expenditures, $1,536,565, including
$1,439,895 for 239 grants (high: $60,000; low:
$10) and $60,037 for employee matching gifts.
Purpose and activities: Charitable, scientific
and cultural purposes; general giving, with
emphasis on higher education and community
funds; grants also for economic education and
research, urban affairs, hospitals, cultural
programs, civic groups, and youth agencies in
plant communities.
Types of support awarded: Building funds,
conferences and seminars, continuing support,
employee matching gifts, equipment, program-
related investments, publications, research,
scholarship funds, seed money, special
projects, general purposes, employee related
scholarships.
Limitations: Giving primarily in areas in which
corporate facilities are located. No support for
institutions below the college or university level
or state or regional associations of independent
colleges. No grants to individuals or for
endowment funds; no loans.
Publications: Program policy statement,
application guidelines.
Application information: Application form
required.
 Initial approach: Letter
 Copies of proposal: 1
 Deadline(s): None

Board meeting date(s): December, March,
 June, and September
Final notification: 6 weeks
Write: Edward Kolodziej, Executive Director
Officers: J.L. Kooker, President; Bart R. Van
Eck,* Vice-President; D.N. Schuchardt,
Secretary and Treasurer.
Directors: W.G. Bush, W.J. Kirby, R.H. Malott,
R.C. Tower.
Number of staff: 2 full-time professional; 1 full-
time support.
Employer Identification Number: 946063032

1006
Foote, Cone & Belding Foundation ⌷
401 North Michigan Ave.
Chicago 60611

Incorporated in 1947 in Illinois.
Donor(s): Foote, Cone & Belding
Communications, Inc., and subsidiaries.
Financial data: (yr. ended 12/31/83): Assets,
$51,370 (M); gifts received, $133,000;
expenditures, $126,907, including $126,825
for grants.
Purpose and activities: General purposes;
general giving, with emphasis on higher
education, community funds, cultural programs,
and youth agencies.
Application information:
 Write: Charles H. Gunderson, Secretary-
 Treasurer
Officers and Directors: Willard R. Wirth, Jr.,
President; John E. O'Toole, David Ofner, Vice-
Presidents; Charles H. Gunderson, Secretary-
Treasurer; Thomas E. Arend.
Employer Identification Number: 366116701

1007
Forest Fund, The
Route 1, Box 32, St. Mary's Rd.
Libertyville 60048 (312) 362-2994

Incorporated in 1956 in Illinois.
Donor(s): Marion M. Lloyd.
Financial data: (yr. ended 12/31/82): Assets,
$2,492,169 (M); expenditures, $104,587,
including $101,465 for 108 grants (high:
$12,500; low: $100).
Purpose and activities: Broad purposes; grants
primarily for education, health services, and
cultural programs.
Limitations: No grants to individuals, or for
endowment funds, or scholarships or
fellowships; no loans.
Application information:
 Initial approach: Full proposal
 Copies of proposal: 1
 Deadline(s): Submit proposal preferably in
 May or November
 Board meeting date(s): June and December
 Write: Mrs. Glen A. Lloyd
Officers and Directors: Marion M. Lloyd,
President and Treasurer; Louise A. Baker,
Secretary; Marianne S. Harper.
Employer Identification Number: 366047859

1008
Foundation for Health Enhancement ⌷
c/o Continental Illinois National Bank & Trust
Co. of Chicago
30 North LaSalle St.
Chicago 60693 (312) 828-1785

Established in 1979.
Financial data: (yr. ended 12/31/83): Assets,
$1,202,966 (M); expenditures, $81,372,
including $70,000 for 5 grants (high: $25,000;
low: $5,000).
Purpose and activities: To improve medical
care in the United States, with emphasis on
smaller qualifying applicants located near
Chicago and in the Midwest.
Limitations: Giving primarily in the Chicago,
IL, area.
Application information:
 Initial approach: Letter
 Copies of proposal: 3
 Deadline(s): None
 Write: M.C. Ryan
Officers: Dennis H. Chookaszian,* President;
Jae L. Wittlich,* Vice-President; Paul I.
Wolfman,* 2nd Vice-President and Secretary;
Bernard L. Hengesbaugh,* Treasurer; Mervin
Shalowitz, M.D., Executive Director.
Directors:* John E. Herron, Robert M.
Kohlenbrener, M.D., Donald M. Lowry,
William A. Tech.
Employer Identification Number: 363043628

1009
Frank (Zollie and Elaine) Fund ⌷
6116 North Western Ave.
Chicago 60659

Incorporated in 1953 in Illinois.
Donor(s): Zollie S. Frank, Elaine S. Frank, Z.
Frank, Inc., Four Wheels, Inc., Wheels, Inc.
Financial data: (yr. ended 12/31/83): Assets,
$1,441,263 (M); gifts received, $85,000;
expenditures, $200,902, including $195,814
for 160 grants (high: $67,205; low: $10).
Purpose and activities: Primarily local giving
with emphasis on Jewish welfare funds and
temple support; grants also for higher
education, hospitals, and organized charities.
Limitations: Giving primarily in IL.
Officer and Trustee: Zollie S. Frank, President;
Elaine S. Frank, Vice-President; James S. Frank,
Secretary.
Employer Identification Number: 366118400

1010
Freund (The Erwin O. and Rosalind H.)
Foundation
c/o The Northern Trust Company
50 South LaSalle St.
Chicago 60675

Incorporated in 1944 in Illinois.
Donor(s): Erwin O. Freund,† Rosalind Freund
Kennedy.
Financial data: (yr. ended 12/31/82): Assets,
$582,039 (M); expenditures, $1,152,097,
including $120,250 for 101 grants (high:
$20,000; low: $100).

Purpose and activities: Broad purposes; general giving, primarily in geographic areas in which directors reside; support mainly for hospitals, family services, higher education, and cultural programs.
Limitations: Giving primarily in areas in which directors live. No grants to individuals.
Application information:
Initial approach: Letter
Copies of proposal: 1
Board meeting date(s): October or November
Officers and Directors: Eliot Snider, President; Janet W. Freund, Secretary and Treasurer; Katherine Deane Wright, Ruth F. Snider.
Employer Identification Number: 366064864

1011
Fry (Lloyd A.) Foundation
135 S. La Salle St., Suite 1910
Chicago 60603   (312) 580-0310

Established in 1959 in Illinois.
Donor(s): Lloyd A. Fry.†
Financial data: (yr. ended 2/29/84): Assets, $33,286,395 (M); gifts received, $12,594,731; expenditures, $615,944, including $395,500 for 43 grants (high: $50,000; low: $1,000).
Purpose and activities: General purposes; primarily local giving for education, including secondary and higher education, and for medical research and health education, civic organizations, social services, and cultural programs.
Types of support awarded: Special projects, seed money, equipment, matching funds, research, publications, conferences and seminars.
Limitations: Giving primarily in the Chicago, IL, area. No support for governmental bodies or tax-supported educational institutions for services that fall within their responsibilities, or for fund-raising benefits. No grants to individuals, or for operating budgets, continuing support, annual campaigns, emergency funds, deficit financing, building funds, land acquisition, renovation projects, endowment funds, employee matching gifts, scholarships or fellowships; no loans.
Publications: Application guidelines, annual report.
Application information:
Initial approach: Letter, telephone, or proposal
Copies of proposal: 1
Deadline(s): None
Board meeting date(s): May, August, November, and February
Final notification: 3 months
Write: Ben Rothblatt, Executive Director
Officers and Directors:* Edmund A. Stephen,* Chairman; Roger E. Anderson,* Vice-Chairman; Lloyd A. Fry, Jr.,* President; M. James Termondt, Vice-President and Treasurer; Howard M. McCue III, Secretary; Ben Rothblatt, Executive Director.
Number of staff: 1 full-time professional; 1 full-time support.
Employer Identification Number: 366108775

1012
Furnas Foundation, Inc.
1000 McKee St.
Batavia 60510

Incorporated in 1960 in Illinois.
Donor(s): W.C. Furnas,† Leto M. Furnas.†
Financial data: (yr. ended 9/30/82): Assets, $526,428 (M); gifts received, $212,000; expenditures, $306,902, including $252,001 for 43 grants (high: $150,000; low: $69) and $45,153 for 54 grants to individuals.
Purpose and activities: Broad purposes; primarily local giving, with emphasis on higher education, including a scholarship program limited to undergraduate study and geographically restricted to portions of Illinois and Iowa; support also for health and youth agencies, hospitals, and community funds.
Types of support awarded: Annual campaigns, building funds, equipment, matching funds, student aid.
Limitations: Giving primarily in Batavia, IL and Clarke County, IA. No support for post-graduate students. No grants to individuals (except for scholarships); no loans.
Publications: Informational brochure, program policy statement, application guidelines.
Application information: Application form required.
Initial approach: Full proposal or letter
Copies of proposal: 1
Deadline(s): March 1 for scholarships
Board meeting date(s): January, April, July, and October
Final notification: 2 to 3 months
Officer and Directors: Dale F. Willcox, President; James A. Clark, Elizabeth Hall, Joanne B. Hansen, Richard W. Hansen, William F. Lisman, Gilbert R. Nary.
Number of staff: None.
Employer Identification Number: 366049894

1013
Galter Foundation, The ⌀
215 E. Chicago Ave.
Chicago 60611

Incorporated in 1943 in Illinois.
Donor(s): Dollie Galter, Jack Galter, Spartus Corporation.
Financial data: (yr. ended 12/31/83): Assets, $384,391 (M); gifts received, $200,000; expenditures, $199,977, including $198,616 for 67 grants (high: $50,000; low: $5).
Purpose and activities: Giving for Jewish welfare funds and temple support, hospitals, and the handicapped.
Managers: Dollie Galter, Jack Galter.
Employer Identification Number: 366082419

1014
Galvin (Paul V.) Trust ⌀
c/o Harris Trust and Savings Bank
111 West Monroe St.
Chicago 60603
Grant application address: Ellen A. Bechthold, 7E, Harris Trust and Savings Bank, P.O. Box 755, Chicago, IL 60690

Donor(s): Paul V. Galvin.†

Financial data: (yr. ended 12/31/83): Assets, $2,681,319 (M); expenditures, $922,515, including $908,100 for 25 grants (high: $250,000; low: $2,000).
Purpose and activities: Broad purposes; emphasis on Catholic religious organizations, church support, higher education, and hospitals.
Trustee: Harris Trust and Savings Bank.
Employer Identification Number: 366030329

1015
Galvin (Robert W.) Foundation ⌀
1303 East Algonquin Rd.
Schaumburg 60196   (312) 576-5300

Incorporated in 1953 in Illinois.
Donor(s): Robert W. Galvin.
Financial data: (yr. ended 12/31/83): Assets, $7,338,718 (M); gifts received, $250,000; expenditures, $578,044, including $575,070 for 196 grants (high: $51,010; low: $10).
Purpose and activities: Broad purposes; largely local giving for higher and secondary education, aid to the handicapped, hospitals, and church support; grants also for child welfare agencies.
Limitations: Giving primarily in IL. No grants to individuals.
Application information:
Initial approach: Letter
Board meeting date(s): Annually
Write: Robert W. Galvin, President
Officers and Directors:* Robert W. Galvin,* President; Christopher B. Galvin,* Vice-President; Robert V. Nystrom, Secretary; Mary Barnes Galvin,* Treasurer.
Employer Identification Number: 366065560

1016
Geraldi-Norton Memorial
Corporation ⌀
One First National Plaza, Suite 3148
Chicago 60603

Incorporated in 1952 in Illinois.
Donor(s): Grace Geraldi Norton.†
Financial data: (yr. ended 12/31/83): Assets, $2,167,111 (M); gifts received, $32,840; expenditures, $174,162, including $149,230 for 75 grants (high: $50,000; low: $200).
Purpose and activities: General purposes; primarily local giving for higher education, hospitals, cultural programs, and youth agencies.
Limitations: Giving primarily in the Chicago, IL, area. No grants to individuals.
Application information:
Initial approach: Letter
Deadline(s): None
Write: Roger P. Eklund, President
Officers and Directors: Roger P. Eklund, President and Treasurer; Dariel P. Eklund, Dariel Ann Eklund, Vice-Presidents; Sally S. Eklund, Secretary.
Employer Identification Number: 366069997

1017
Gerber (The Max and Lottie) Foundation, Inc.
4656 W. Touhy Ave.
Chicago 60646

Incorporated in 1942 in Illinois.
Donor(s): Globe Valve Corporation, Kokomo Sanitary Pottery Corporation.
Financial data: (yr. ended 9/30/83): Assets, $231,970 (M); gifts received, $200,000; expenditures, $141,650, including $140,975 for 43 grants (high: $101,000; low: $100).
Purpose and activities: Primarily local giving to Jewish welfare funds and educational organizations.
Limitations: Giving primarily in IL.
Officers: Harriet G. Lewis, President; Robert C. Luker, Secretary; Oscar L. Gerber, Treasurer.
Employer Identification Number: 366091012

1018
Goldenberg (Max) Foundation ⌷
c/o Harris Trust and Savings Bank
111 West Monroe St.
Chicago 60603 (312) 461-2613
Grant application address: P.O. Box 755, Chicago, IL 60626

Trust established in 1946 in Illinois.
Donor(s): Max Goldenberg.†
Financial data: (yr. ended 12/31/83): Assets, $2,242,418 (M); expenditures, $179,997, including $150,000 for 40 grants (high: $10,000; low: $1,000).
Purpose and activities: Broad purposes; primarily local giving, with emphasis on medical research, higher education, and social services, particularly Jewish charities.
Limitations: Giving primarily in IL.
Publications: Annual report.
Application information:
 Initial approach: Full proposal
 Copies of proposal: 3
 Deadline(s): August 31
 Board meeting date(s): October
 Write: Ellen Bechthold, Harris Trust and Savings Bank
Trustees: Harold J. Baer, Marian Goodman, Harris Trust and Savings Bank.
Employer Identification Number: 362471625

1019
Goldman (Morris and Rose) Foundation ⌷
875 N. Michigan Ave.
Chicago 60611

Established in 1965.
Donor(s): Morris Goldman, Rose Goldman.
Financial data: (yr. ended 12/31/83): Assets, $992,921 (M); gifts received, $57,000; expenditures, $215,303, including $212,390 for 148 grants (high: $90,230; low: $7).
Purpose and activities: Giving primarily to Jewish welfare funds, cultural organizations, and social services.
Officers: Morris Goldman, President; Rose Goldman, Vice-President; Shirley Warshaver, Secretary.
Director: Barbara Pine.
Employer Identification Number: 362615047

1020
Gould Inc. Foundation ▼
Ten Gould Center, 9th Fl.
Rolling Meadows 60008 (312) 640-4058

Incorporated in 1951 in Ohio.
Donor(s): Gould Inc.
Financial data: (yr. ended 12/31/84): Assets, $4,272,056 (L); expenditures, $1,316,530, including $1,152,494 for 243 grants (high: $150,000; low: $100), $77,368 for 65 grants to individuals and $86,668 for 428 employee matching gifts.
Purpose and activities: To strengthen the socio-economic environment in areas of corporate operations and of selected educational and scientific institutions; grants largely for community funds, higher education, scholarships for children of employees, hospitals, cultural activities, and youth agencies; support also for national organizations recognized as beneficial to the broader national community.
Types of support awarded: Employee related scholarships, annual campaigns, building funds, equipment, endowment funds, research, employee matching gifts.
Limitations: Giving primarily in areas of corporate operations. No support for political organizations, groups that discriminate against minorities, disease-related organizations, other than special projects undertaken within Gould Inc.; or religious and fraternal groups which do not benefit entire commmunities. No grants to individuals (except company-employee scholarships); no loans.
Publications: Annual report, program policy statement, application guidelines.
Application information: Write to principal manager of local Gould facility.
 Initial approach: Letter or full proposal
 Copies of proposal: 1
 Deadline(s): None
 Board meeting date(s): January and as required
 Write: Gloria E. Eggleston, Vice-President
Officers: William T. Ylvisaker,* President; C.M. Brennan, III,* Gloria E. Eggleston, R.D. Kemplin, G.P. Millington, Jr.,* R.L. Williams, III,* Vice-Presidents; N.R. Jack, Secretary; M.I. Miller, Treasurer.
Trustees:* J.E. Rowe, D. Simpson.
Number of staff: 1 full-time professional; 1 full-time support.
Employer Identification Number: 346525555

1021
Graham Foundation for Advanced Studies in the Fine Arts ▼
Four West Burton Place
Chicago 60610 (312) 787-4071

Incorporated in 1935 in Illinois.
Donor(s): Ernest R. Graham.†
Financial data: (yr. ended 12/31/83): Assets, $11,916,063 (M); expenditures, $1,446,633, including $714,816 for 87 grants (high: $164,000; low: $400; average: $2,000-$10,000).
Purpose and activities: Grants in sums of up to $10,000 for advanced study in contemporary architecture, design, and the study of urban planning, principally to Americans working within the United States who have demonstrated mature, creative talent in the visual arts and have specific work objectives. Fellows are selected by the trustees on the recommendation of the Director and special advisors. Some support for exhibitions, publications, and architectural and urban studies.
Types of support awarded: Research, publications, conferences and seminars, fellowships, grants to individuals, special projects.
Limitations: No grants for building or endowment funds, or for scholarships, or matching gifts; no loans.
Publications: Informational brochure, program policy statement, application guidelines.
Application information:
 Initial approach: Letter or full proposal
 Copies of proposal: 1
 Deadline(s): June 1 and December 1
 Board meeting date(s): June and December
 Final notification: 1 to 4 months
 Write: Carter H. Manny, Jr., Director
Officers: Robert L. Murphy,* President; Michael J. Lane,* Secretary; Roman C. Block,* Treasurer; Carter H. Manny, Jr., Director.
Trustees:* Phillip W. Collins, E.A. Englehardt, Richard S. Jalovec, Robert G. Lamphere, Rita C. Rice.
Number of staff: 1 full-time professional; 1 part-time professional; 1 full-time support; 1 part-time support.
Employer Identification Number: 362356089

1022
Grainger Foundation Inc., The ▼
5500 West Howard St.
Skokie 60077 (312) 982-9000

Incorporated in 1967 in Illinois as successor to the Grainger Charitable Trust established in 1949.
Donor(s): W.W. Grainger,† Hally W. Grainger,† David W. Grainger.
Financial data: (yr. ended 12/31/84): Assets, $38,060,481 (M); gifts received, $631,250; expenditures, $1,481,261, including $1,403,500 for 17 grants (high: $500,000; low: $1,000).
Purpose and activities: Broad purposes; primarily local giving, with emphasis on endowments and capital funds for educational institutions, hospitals, and museums. Grants also for cultural, religious, educational, and medical institutions.
Types of support awarded: Continuing support, building funds, equipment, endowment funds, professorships, research, general purposes.
Limitations: Giving primarily in the Chicago, IL area. No grants to individuals, or for general operating budgets, seed money, emergency funds, deficit financing, special projects, publications, conferences, scholarships, or fellowships; no loans.

Application information: Applications accepted only from organizations in the Chicago area and whose purposes match the Foundation's interest.
Initial approach: Telephone or letter
Copies of proposal: 1
Deadline(s): None
Board meeting date(s): Periodically
Final notification: Primarily on favorable decisions only
Write: Lee J. Flory, Vice-President
Officers and Directors: David W. Grainger, President and Treasurer; Lee J. Flory, Vice-President and Secretary; Juli P. Grainger, Vice-President; John S. Chapman.
Number of staff: None.
Employer Identification Number: 366192971

1023
Griswold (Harry E.) Trust
c/o Millikin National Bank of Decatur
P.O. Box 1278
Decatur 62525   (217) 429-4253

Established in 1978.
Financial data: (yr. ended 3/31/82): Assets, $1,095,690 (M); expenditures, $106,910, including $60,491 for 4 grants (high: $15,123; low: $15,122) and $6,000 for 4 grants to individuals.
Purpose and activities: Two-year scholarships awarded annually to two graduates of local high schools; balance of net income distributed to 4 specified beneficiaries.
Types of support awarded: Operating budgets, continuing support, endowment funds, student aid.
Limitations: No grants for annual campaigns, seed money, emergency or capital funds, deficit financing, matching gifts, special projects, research, publications, or conferences; no loans.
Publications: 990-PF.
Trustees: Millikin National Bank of Decatur.
Number of staff: None.
Employer Identification Number: 376182916

1024
Haffner Foundation
2223 S. Martin Luther King Dr.
Chicago 60616   (312) 326-8043

Incorporated in 1952 in Illinois.
Donor(s): Charles C. Haffner, Jr.,† Mrs. Charles C. Haffner, Jr.,† Charles C. Haffner III.
Financial data: (yr. ended 12/31/83): Assets, $1,354,759 (M); expenditures, $119,624, including $115,000 for 30 grants (high: $15,000; low: $500).
Purpose and activities: To contribute to religious, charitable, and educational organizations of whose activities officers have personal knowledge. Support largely for higher and secondary education, hospitals, social agencies, cultural activities, and health agencies, primarily in Illinois.
Types of support awarded: Operating budgets, continuing support, annual campaigns, seed money, emergency funds, building funds, equipment, endowment funds.

Limitations: Giving primarily in IL. No grants to individuals, or for scholarships, fellowships, or matching gifts; no loans.
Application information: Grant applications not invited.
Board meeting date(s): May
Write: Charles C. Haffner III, President
Officers and Directors: Charles C. Haffner III, President and Treasurer; Clarissa H. Chandler, Vice-President and Secretary; Phoebe H. Andrew, Frances H. Colburn.
Employer Identification Number: 366064770

1025
Hales Charitable Fund, Inc.
120 West Madison St.
Chicago 60602   (312) 641-7016
Application address: 550 Frontage Rd., Suite 3086, Northfield, IL 60093

Incorporated in 1939 in Illinois.
Donor(s): G. Willard Hales,† Burton W. Hales,† William M. Hales.
Financial data: (yr. ended 12/31/82): Assets, $3,562,469 (M); expenditures, $224,486, including $210,187 for 57 grants (high: $150,000; low: $100).
Purpose and activities: Broad purposes; primarily local giving, with emphasis on higher education, Protestant church organizations, and health agencies; support also for cultural programs and social agencies.
Types of support awarded: Operating budgets, continuing support, annual campaigns, emergency funds, building funds, endowment funds, scholarship funds, professorships, research.
Limitations: Giving primarily in IL. No grants to individuals, or for seed money, deficit financing, equipment, land acquisition, renovations, matching gifts, demonstration projects, publications, or conferences; no loans.
Application information:
Initial approach: Letter
Copies of proposal: 1
Board meeting date(s): Annually and as required
Write: Burton W. Hales, Jr., Secretary
Officers and Directors: William M. Hales, President; Burton W. Hales, Jr., Secretary-Treasurer; Marion J. Hales, Mary C. Hales.
Number of staff: None.
Employer Identification Number: 366060632

1026
Hammer (Armand) Foundation ▼
135 South LaSalle St., Suite 1000
Chicago 60603

Established in 1968 in California.
Donor(s): Armand Hammer.
Financial data: (yr. ended 12/31/83): Assets, $23,208,614 (M); gifts received, $1,232,331; expenditures, $5,678,289, including $5,378,118 for 65 grants (high: $3,261,232; low: $150; average: $10,000-$50,000).
Purpose and activities: Giving primarily for higher education, art museums and galleries, and medical research; support also for the state of Israel.
Limitations: No grants to individuals.

Application information:
Initial approach: Letter
Copies of proposal: 2
Deadline(s): None
Board meeting date(s): Annually and as required
Write: David J. Creagan, Jr.
Trustees: Arthur Groman, Armand Hammer, Victor Hammer.
Number of staff: None.
Employer Identification Number: 237010813

1027
Harper (Philip S.) Foundation ¤
c/o Harper-Wyman Company
930 North York Rd.
Hinsdale 60521

Incorporated in 1953 in Illinois.
Donor(s): Philip S. Harper, Harper-Wyman Company.
Financial data: (yr. ended 11/30/83): Assets, $3,174,085 (M); expenditures, $182,826, including $156,350 for 90 grants (high: $6,350; low: $100).
Purpose and activities: Broad purposes; support for higher education, child welfare, health agencies and medical research, cultural programs, including public broadcasting, social welfare, including youth agencies, and Protestant churches.
Officers: Philip S. Harper, Jr., President; Lamar Harper Williams, Vice-President; Charles C. Lamar, Secretary and Treasurer.
Employer Identification Number: 366049875

1028
Harris Bank Foundation
111 West Monroe St.
Chicago 60690   (312) 461-6660

Incorporated in 1953 in Illinois.
Donor(s): Harris Trust and Savings Bank.
Financial data: (yr. ended 12/31/83): Assets, $261,166 (L); gifts received, $365,020; expenditures, $255,600, including $196,075 for 43 grants (high: $15,000; low: $800; average: $1,000-$10,000) and $57,678 for 381 employee matching gifts.
Purpose and activities: Broad purposes; local giving, with emphasis on community funds and higher education, including an employee matching gift program; support also for cultural activities, minority group programs, and hospital capital funds.
Types of support awarded: Operating budgets, continuing support, annual campaigns, seed money, building funds, equipment, matching funds, technical assistance, scholarship funds, special projects, employee related scholarships, professorships, internships, exchange programs, fellowships, employee matching gifts.
Limitations: Giving limited to the Chicago, IL, metropolitan area. No support for sectarian or religious organizations. No grants to individuals, or for emergency or endowment funds, deficit financing, land acquisition, capital grants for higher education, research, publications or conferences; no loans.

Publications: Annual report, program policy statement.
Application information:
Initial approach: Letter
Copies of proposal: 1
Deadline(s): First week of months board meets
Board meeting date(s): January, March, May, June, August, October, and December
Final notification: 2 weeks after board meetings
Write: H. Kris Ronnow, Vice-President
Officers : John L. Stephens,* President; Philip A. Delaney,* Vice-President; H. Kris Ronnow, Vice-President and Secretary-Treasurer.
Directors:* Joan M. Baratta, Cecil R. Coleman, Donald S. Hunt, Nancy M. Sorensen, Edward J. Williams.
Number of staff: 3 part-time support.
Employer Identification Number: 366033888

1029
Harris Family Foundation
333 Skokie Blvd.
Northbrook 60062   (312) 498-1260

Incorporated in 1957 in Illinois.
Donor(s): Neison Harris, and family.
Financial data: (yr. ended 2/28/83): Assets, $4,448,161 (M); expenditures, $290,204, including $275,883 for 134 grants (high: $50,000; low: $25).
Purpose and activities: Broad purposes; primarily local giving, with emphasis on medical research, Jewish welfare funds, cultural programs, higher and secondary education, community funds and social agencies.
Types of support awarded: General purposes, building funds.
Limitations: Giving primarily in the Chicago, IL, area. No grants to individuals.
Application information:
Initial approach: Letter or proposal
Copies of proposal: 1
Deadline(s): Submit proposal preferably in May; no set deadline
Board meeting date(s): May and November
Final notification: 30 days
Write: Neison Harris, President
Officers and Directors: Neison Harris, President and Treasurer; Bette D. Harris, Vice-President and Secretary; Sidney Barrows, Katherine Harris, King Harris, Toni H. Paul.
Number of staff: None.
Employer Identification Number: 366054378

1030
Harris Foundation, The ▼
120 South LaSalle St., Suite 1148
Chicago 60603   (312) 621-0566

Incorporated in 1945 in Minnesota.
Donor(s): Members of the Harris family and others.
Financial data: (yr. ended 12/31/84): Assets, $10,479,847 (M); gifts received, $495,002; expenditures, $547,045, including $431,801 for 272 grants (high: $47,950; low: $60).

Purpose and activities: Charitable and scientific purposes; interests include demonstration and research programs in prevention of family dysfunction, prevention of teenage pregnancy, infant mental health and early childhood development; Jewish and interfaith welfare programs; and educational television.
Types of support awarded: Annual campaigns, seed money, equipment, special projects, research, publications, conferences and seminars.
Limitations: No grants to individuals, or for continuing support, emergency or endowment funds, deficit financing, land acquisition, renovations, or scholarships or fellowships; no loans.
Application information:
Initial approach: Letter
Copies of proposal: 1
Deadline(s): None
Board meeting date(s): Semiannually
Write: Ruth K. Belzer, Executive Director
Officers and Trustees: Irving B. Harris, Chairman; William W. Harris, Vice-Chairman; Benno F. Wolff, Secretary; Sidney Barrows, Roxanne Harris Frank, Joan W. Harris, Neison Harris, Daniel Meyer, Virginia Harris Polsky.
Staff: Ruth K. Belzer, Executive Director.
Number of staff: 1 full-time professional; 1 full-time support.
Employer Identification Number: 366055115

1031
Harris (J. Ira and Nicki) Foundation ¤
8700 Sears Tower
Chicago 60606

Established in 1965.
Financial data: (yr. ended 3/31/83): Assets, $1,770,676 (M); gifts received, $15,685; expenditures, $84,755, including $70,455 for 36 grants (high: $24,000; low: $50).
Purpose and activities: Grants mainly for Jewish welfare funds and education; support also for a foundation for children with learning disabilities.
Officers: J. Ira Harris, President; Nicki Harris, Vice-President; Newton Minow, Secretary-Treasurer.
Employer Identification Number: 366122443

1032
Hart Schaffner & Marx Charitable Foundation ¤
101 North Wacker Dr.
Chicago 60606   (312) 372-6300

Incorporated in 1966 in Illinois.
Donor(s): Hart Schaffner & Marx.
Financial data: (yr. ended 11/30/83): Assets, $464,252 (M); expenditures, $359,374, including $335,755 for 238 grants (high: $60,000; low: $50) and $19,528 for 69 employee matching gifts.
Purpose and activities: Grants primarily for community funds, higher education, and cultural, civic and health programs.
Application information:
Initial approach: Letter
Deadline(s): None

Write: Wayne H. Ahlberg, President
Officers: Wayne H. Ahlberg, President; J.S. Gore,* R.P. Hamilton,* Kay C. Nalbach, Vice-Presidents; C.L. Stewart, Secretary; J.R. Meinert,* Treasurer.
Directors:* Mark J. Lies.
Employer Identification Number: 366152745

1033
Hay (John I.) Foundation ¤
c/o The Northern Trust Company
50 South LaSalle St.
Chicago 60675

Incorporated in 1955 in Illinois.
Donor(s): John I. Hay Trust.
Financial data: (yr. ended 12/31/83): Assets, $2,157,079 (M); expenditures, $100,107, including $80,500 for 2 grants (high: $76,500; low: $4,000).
Purpose and activities: Broad purposes; grants for education and a youth agency.
Officers: Frank P. Markland, President; Arthur H. Vail, Vice-President; Robert Sturtevant, Secretary and Director; John C. Goodall, Jr., Treasurer.
Employer Identification Number: 366103629

1034
Heed Ophthalmic Foundation
303 East Chicago Ave.
Chicago 60611   (312) 649-8152

Trust established in 1946 in Illinois.
Donor(s): Thomas D. Heed,† Mrs. Thomas D. Heed.†
Financial data: (yr. ended 10/31/84): Assets, $2,488,351 (M); gifts received, $10,000; expenditures, $261,000, including $230,400 for 24 grants to individuals (average: $10,000).
Purpose and activities: Fellowships to United States citizens who are graduates of medical schools accredited by the American Medical Association, who have completed a residency in ophthalmology, and who show exceptional promise primarily in the field of eye surgery and secondarily in the field of eye research.
Types of support awarded: Fellowships, grants to individuals.
Publications: Application guidelines.
Application information: Application form required.
Initial approach: Letter or telephone
Copies of proposal: 1
Board meeting date(s): May and November
Write: David Shoch, M.D., Secretary
Officers and Directors: Frank K. Newell, M.D., Chairman; David Shoch, M.D., Secretary.
Trustee: The First National Bank of Chicago.
Number of staff: 1 full-time support.
Employer Identification Number: 366012426

1035
Heller (Florence G.) Foundation ¤
c/o Charles Aaron
3400 Xerox Centre, 55 West Monroe St.
Chicago 60603

Incorporated in 1955 in Illinois.
Donor(s): Florence G. Heller.†

Financial data: (yr. ended 12/31/83): Assets, $1,645,059 (M); expenditures, $573,018, including $506,390 for 24 grants (high: $400,000; low: $200).
Purpose and activities: Broad purposes; with emphasis on higher and secondary education, and Jewish welfare funds.
Officers: Peter E. Heller, President; Charles Aaron, Vice-President and Secretary; Samuel W. Hunt, Jr., Vice-President and Treasurer.
Employer Identification Number: 366061921

1036

Heller (Walter E.) Foundation ▼ ⊭
1540 North Lake Shore Dr.
Chicago 60610 (312) 828-1785
Grant application address: M.C. Ryan, c/o Continental Illinois National Bank and Trust Company of Chicago, 30 North LaSalle St., Chicago, IL 60693

Incorporated in 1955 in Illinois.
Donor(s): Walter E. Heller,† Whico, Inc.
Financial data: (yr. ended 12/31/82): Assets, $3,268,847 (M); expenditures, $1,132,879, including $1,109,974 for 66 grants (high: $676,189; low: $40).
Purpose and activities: Broad purposes; primarily local giving, with emphasis on cultural programs, particularly museums and the performing arts; support also for higher education and health organizations.
Limitations: Giving primarily in IL.
Application information:
Initial approach: Letter
Write: M.C. Ryan
Officer and Directors: Alyce H. DeCosta, President; Edwin J. DeCosta, M.D., Addis E. Hull, Albert E. Jenner, Jr., M. James Termondt.
Employer Identification Number: 366058986

1037

Hermann (The Grover) Foundation ⊭
c/o Schiff, Hardin & Waite, 7200 Sears Tower
233 South Wacker Dr.
Chicago 60606 (312) 876-1000

Incorporated in 1955 in Illinois.
Donor(s): Grover M. Hermann.
Financial data: (yr. ended 12/31/83): Assets, $2,476,738 (M); gifts received, $800,000; expenditures, $1,063,411, including $1,044,600 for 41 grants (high: $250,000; low: $500).
Purpose and activities: Broad purposes; general giving, with emphasis on higher education and social services.
Application information:
Deadline(s): None
Write: Paul K. Rhoads
Officers and Directors: Sarah T. Hermann, President; George B. Pletsch, Vice-President and Treasurer; Harriet R. Thurmond, Secretary.
Employer Identification Number: 366064489

1038

Hightower Charitable Foundation ⊭
1156 Michigan Ave.
Wilmette 60091

Established in 1980.
Financial data: (yr. ended 12/31/83): Assets, $7,410 (M); gifts received, $1,287; expenditures, $110,889, including $109,600 for 36 grants (high: $23,450; low: $100).
Purpose and activities: Giving for Christian religious and welfare organizations.
Officers: Amelia J. Radford, President; Stephen R. Radford, Vice-President; Wesley W. Saul, Secretary-Treasurer.
Employer Identification Number: 363104606

1039

Hoffer Foundation ⊭
255 Wing Blvd.
Elgin 60120

Established in 1966.
Donor(s): Hoffer Plastics Corporation.
Financial data: (yr. ended 11/30/83): Assets, $206,146 (M); gifts received, $216,000; expenditures, $128,066, including $127,780 for 22 grants (high: $33,552; low: $250).
Purpose and activities: Primarily local giving, with emphasis on youth agencies, a community fund, and a college.
Limitations: Giving primarily in IL.
Officers and Trustees: Robert A. Hoffer, President; Helen C. Hoffer, Robert A. Hoffer, Jr.
Employer Identification Number: 366160991

1040

Hokin (The Dave) Foundation ⊭
875 North Michigan Ave., Rm. 3707
Chicago 60611

Incorporated in 1951 in Illinois.
Financial data: (yr. ended 10/31/83): Assets, $814,848 (M); gifts received, $150,000; expenditures, $202,343, including $199,602 for 134 grants (high: $33,000; low: $17).
Purpose and activities: Broad purposes; grants for medical research, hospitals, higher education, cultural organizations, and Jewish welfare funds.
Officers: Myron Hokin, President; Carl K. Heyman, Treasurer.
Employer Identification Number: 366079161

1041

Hoover (The H. Earl) Foundation
1801 Green Bay Rd.
P.O. Box 330
Glencoe 60022 (312) 835-3350

Trust established in 1947 in Illinois.
Donor(s): H. Earl Hoover.
Financial data: (yr. ended 12/31/82): Assets, $1,171,044 (M); gifts received, $10,000; expenditures, $92,260, including $89,600 for grants.

Purpose and activities: Broad purposes; primrily local giving, with emphasis on youth agencies, hospitals, social and welfare agencies, cultural organizations, and Protestant church support.
Limitations: Giving primarily in IL.
Application information:
Initial approach: Letter
Write: H. Earl Hoover, Trustee
Trustees: Edwin C. Austin, Robert L. Foote, H. Earl Hoover, Miriam U. Hoover.
Employer Identification Number: 366063814

1042

Hopper (Bertrand) Memorial Foundation ⊭
319 West Main Cross
Taylorville 62568 (217) 824-3323

Incorporated in 1956 in Illinois.
Donor(s): Bertrand C. Hopper, Hopper Paper Company.
Financial data: (yr. ended 12/31/83): Assets, $1,275,699 (M); expenditures, $78,815, including $72,550 for 34 grants (high: $26,000; low: $100).
Purpose and activities: Broad purposes; primarily local giving, with emphasis on education, including public schools, and youth agencies.
Limitations: Giving primarily in IL.
Application information: Must be organizations listed in Cumulative List of Exempt Organizations.
Initial approach: Letter or telephone
Deadline(s): None
Write: Bertrand C. Hopper, Trustee
Officer and Directors: Bertrand C. Hopper, President; Frederick C. Hopper, William B. Hopper.
Employer Identification Number: 376026794

1043

House (Susan Cook) Educational Trust
Springfield Marine Bank
One East Old Capital Plaza
Springfield 62701 (217) 525-9745

Trust established in 1969 in Illinois.
Financial data: (yr. ended 11/30/83): Assets, $1,704,508 (M); expenditures, $131,612, including $103,500 for 12 grants (high: $20,000; low: $1,000).
Purpose and activities: Primarily local giving, with emphasis on higher and secondary education; support also for the arts and a social agency.
Limitations: Giving primarily in IL.
Publications: Annual report.
Trustees: Phillip W. Vance, Springfield Marine Bank.
Number of staff: None.
Employer Identification Number: 376087675

1044
I and G Charitable Foundation ⋈
120 South LaSalle, Suite 1330
Chicago 60603

Incorporated in 1945 in Illinois.
Donor(s): Members of the Brown family.
Financial data: (yr. ended 12/31/83): Assets, $652,997 (M); gifts received, $25,000; expenditures, $112,334, including $108,550 for 30 grants (high: $55,000; low: $300).
Purpose and activities: Broad purposes; primarily local giving, with emphasis on Jewish welfare funds and higher and secondary education.
Limitations: Giving primarily in IL.
Application information: Applications not invited from hospitals or schools.
  Initial approach: Two-page typewritten letter
  Deadline(s): None
  Write: Roger O. Brown, President
Officers and Directors: Roger O. Brown, President and Treasurer; Howard J. Brown, Vice-President and Secretary; Barbara E. Brown, Elizabeth K. Brown.
Employer Identification Number: 366069174

1045
Illinois Tool Works Foundation
8501 West Higgins Rd.
Chicago 60631   (312) 693-3040

Incorporated in 1954 in Illinois.
Donor(s): Illinois Tool Works Inc.
Financial data: (yr. ended 2/28/85): Assets, $3,000,000 (M); gifts received, $992,000; expenditures, $772,727, including $414,400 for 148 grants (high: $80,500; low: $250; average: $2,800) and $358,327 for 1,026 employee matching gifts.
Purpose and activities: Broad purposes; general giving, with emphasis on higher education, hospitals, community funds, youth agencies, and urban affairs.
Types of support awarded: Operating budgets, continuing support, annual campaigns, seed money, building funds, employee related scholarships, employee matching gifts.
Limitations: Giving primarily in areas of company operations. No grants to individuals, or for endowment funds or research; no loans.
Application information:
  Initial approach: Full proposal
  Copies of proposal: 1
  Board meeting date(s): March, June, September, and December
  Final notification: Same month as board meeting
  Write: Stephen B. Smith, Director
Officers and Directors: Harold Byron Smith, Chairman; Silas S. Cathcart, President; Harold Byron Smith, Jr., Vice-President; Arthur M. Wright, Secretary; David B. Smith, Treasurer; Michael H. Hudson, John D. Nichols, Sidney A. Paige, Stephen B. Smith.
Employer Identification Number: 366087160

1046
IMC Foundation
2315 Sanders Rd.
Northbrook 60062   (312) 564-8600

Incorporated in 1967 in Illinois.
Donor(s): International Minerals & Chemical Corporation.
Financial data: (yr. ended 6/30/84): Assets, $1,327,467 (M); gifts received, $200,000; expenditures, $246,256, including $243,750 for 73 grants (high: $41,800; low: $60).
Purpose and activities: Broad purposes; giving primarily in areas of company operations, with emphasis on arts, cultural activities, world hunger, environment, disaster relief, youth and health agencies, and higher education.
Types of support awarded: General purposes, operating budgets, continuing support, annual campaigns, seed money, emergency funds, special projects.
Limitations: Giving primarily in IL, in areas of company operations. No grants to individuals, or for building or endowment funds, scholarships and fellowships, or matching gifts; no loans.
Publications: Annual report, program policy statement, application guidelines.
Application information:
  Initial approach: Telephone, letter, or full proposal
  Deadline(s): None
  Board meeting date(s): As required
  Final notification: 3 to 4 weeks
  Write: Donald E. Tynan, Executive Vice-President
Officers: George D. Kennedy,* President; Donald E. Tynan,* Executive Vice-President; John F. Sonderegger, Vice-President; Nicholaus Bruns, Jr.,* Secretary; Darrell L. Feaker,* Treasurer.
Directors:* Judson H. Drewry, Paul Faberson, R. Jack Pearce, Oscar T. Stutsman.
Number of staff: None.
Employer Identification Number: 366162015

1047
Ingersoll Foundation, Inc., The
(formerly Ingersoll Foundation, The)
934 North Main St.
Rockford 61103   (815) 964-3242

Trust established in 1948 in Illinois; incorporated in 1983.
Donor(s): The Ingersoll Milling Machine Company.
Financial data: (yr. ended 8/31/83): Assets, $978,267 (M); expenditures, $420,736, including $266,000 for 36 grants (high: $50,000; low: $1,000; average: $1,000-$10,000) and $109,075 for 1 foundation-administered program.
Purpose and activities: Support for local organizations whose activities include direct involvement in character education and/or citizenship education; grants also to organizations outside the Rockford area that have a national impact, and for the Ingersoll Prizes, which include the T.S. Award for Creative Writing and the Richard M. Weaver award for Scholarly Letters.

Types of support awarded: Operating budgets, continuing support, annual campaigns, seed money, special projects, publications, conferences and seminars.
Limitations: Giving primarily in the Rockford, IL, area. No grants to individuals, or for emergency, capital or endowment funds, deficit financing, matching gifts, scholarships and fellowships, or research; no loans.
Publications: Application guidelines, program policy statement.
Application information:
  Initial approach: Letter
  Copies of proposal: 1
  Deadline(s): Submit proposal in September or February; no set deadline
  Board meeting date(s): Spring and fall
  Final notification: 3 weeks after the next board meeting
  Write: John A. Howard, President
Officer and Directors: John A. Howard,* President; Clayton R. Gaylord, Edson I. Gaylord, Robert M. Gaylord, Jr.
Number of staff: None.
Employer Identification Number: 366067555

1048
Inland Steel-Ryerson Foundation, Inc. ▼
30 West Monroe St.
Chicago 60603   (312) 346-0300

Incorporated in 1945 in Illinois as Inland Steel Foundation, Inc.
Donor(s): Inland Steel Company, its subsidiaries and divisions.
Financial data: (yr. ended 12/31/84): Assets, $60,416 (M); gifts received, $1,575,000; expenditures, $1,587,847, including $1,343,220 for 250 grants (high: $341,000; low: $500; average: $500-$25,000) and $217,900 for 250 grants to individuals.
Purpose and activities: Broad purposes; grants to organizations in areas of company operations, particularly Chicago, Illinois, northwest Indiana, and southeast Wisconsin, concerned with education, community welfare, including urban affairs, and civic and cultural activities; and to building funds of certain community welfare organizations; major interest in higher education with support to carefully chosen colleges and universities, with emphasis on business and engineering.
Types of support awarded: Operating budgets, building funds, equipment, scholarship funds, fellowships, employee related scholarships, technical assistance, continuing support.

Limitations: Giving primarily in areas of company operations, particularly Chicago, IL, northwest IN, and the greater Milwaukee, WI, area. Generally no grants for tax-supported or pre-school, primary, or secondary educational institutions; sectarian or religious organizations (except churches under the category of social welfare); or political activities. No grants for endowment funds, matching or challenge grants, publications, conferences, seminars, benefit affairs, or capital projects outside area of primary interest. No grants directly to individuals. Scholarships awarded under the All Inland Scholarship Plan and the National Merit and National Achievement Scholarship programs are restricted to children of company employees. Lawndale Community Scholarships for area high school seniors; nursing scholarships are available only to residents of Lake County, Indiana.

Publications: Annual report, application guidelines, program policy statement.

Application information:
Initial approach: Letter or telephone
Copies of proposal: 1
Deadline(s): Submit proposal preferably in first 9 months of the year; no set deadline
Board meeting date(s): April, August, and December
Final notification: 3 to 4 months
Write: Robert T. Carter, Executive Director

Officers: Warren H. Bacon,* President; John B. Foster,* Vice-President; Jay E. Dittus, Treasurer; Robert T. Carter,* Executive Director and Secretary.

Directors:* O. Robert Nottelmann, Chairman; Philip D. Block III, Frederick G. Jaicks, Frank W. Luerssen, George A. Ranney, George A. Ranney, Jr., Norman A. Robins.

Number of staff: 1 full-time professional; 1 full-time support; 1 part-time support.

Employer Identification Number: 366046944

1049
Interlake Foundation
2015 Spring Rd.
Oak Brook 60521

Incorporated in 1951 in Illinois.
Donor(s): Interlake Inc.
Financial data: (yr. ended 12/31/82): Assets, $2,897,765 (M); gifts received, $310,000; expenditures, $595,174, including $526,940 for 229 grants (high: $82,500; low: $10) and $25,078 for employee matching gifts.
Purpose and activities: General giving, with emphasis on community funds and higher education; support also for youth agencies and cultural programs.
Types of support awarded: Employee matching gifts.
Officers: Reynold C. MacDonald,* President; Robert Jacobs,* Vice-President; I.R. MacLeod, Secretary; R.T. Anderson, Treasurer.
Directors:* Edward J. Williams.
Employer Identification Number: 362590617

1050
Jewel Foundation ▼
5725 East River Rd.
Chicago 60631   (312) 693-6000

Incorporated in 1952 in Illinois.
Donor(s): Jewel Companies, Inc.
Financial data: (yr. ended 12/31/82): Assets, $454,933 (M); gifts received, $1,025,000; expenditures, $1,086,177, including $947,141 for 336 grants (high: $287,500; low: $75; average: $500-$10,000) and $120,477 for employee matching gifts.
Purpose and activities: Grants primarily in areas of company operations for community funds, and for capital fund drives of colleges and universities, hospitals, and youth agencies; support also for an employee matching gifts program and for local social service agencies and cultural and civic organizations.
Types of support awarded: Building funds, equipment, general purposes, continuing support, employee related scholarships, employee matching gifts.
Limitations: Giving primarily in areas of company operations, especially the Chicago, IL, metropolitan area. No support for churches or for public elementary and secondary schools. No grants to individuals, or for endowment funds, or research; no loans.
Publications: Application guidelines.
Application information:
Initial approach: Letter
Copies of proposal: 1
Deadline(s): None
Board meeting date(s): Spring (April or May) and fall (September or October)
Final notification: 1 month
Write: Robert D. Jones, President
Officers: Robert D. Jones,* President; C.E. McClellan, D.S. Scoon,* Vice-Presidents; R.E. Riley, Secretary; J.N. Balch, Treasurer.
Directors:* A.C. Bell, A.T. Dalton, J.T. Fuglestad, T.J. Hanson, J.R. Haugabrook, R.D. Peterson.
Number of staff: None.
Employer Identification Number: 366054067

1051
Johnson (A. D.) Foundation ⌺
30 North LaSalle St., Suite 3520
Chicago 60602

Incorporated in 1965 in Illinois.
Donor(s): A.D. Johnson.†
Financial data: (yr. ended 12/31/83): Assets, $2,057,105 (M); expenditures, $226,347, including $215,000 for 12 grants (high: $75,000; low: $2,000).
Purpose and activities: Broad purposes; primarily local giving, with emphasis on medical research, hospitals, education, and agencies for children and youth; some support for organizations in Florida.
Types of support awarded: General purposes, research.
Limitations: Giving primarily in IL and FL.
Officers and Directors: Fred R. Johnson, President and Treasurer; J. Leonard Johnson, Vice-President; Wayne J. Johnson, Secretary.
Employer Identification Number: 366124270

1052
Joyce Foundation, The ▼
135 South LaSalle St.
Chicago 60603   (312) 782-2464

Incorporated in 1948 in Illinois.
Donor(s): Beatrice Joyce Kean.†
Financial data: (yr. ended 12/31/83): Assets, $200,037,646 (M); expenditures, $8,391,734, including $6,310,857 for 279 grants (high: $100,000; low: $1,000; average: $5,000-$50,000), $3,290 for 17 employee matching gifts and $20,000 for 2 loans.
Purpose and activities: Giving primarily in the Midwest for culture-strengthening organizations of excellence or potential excellence; education - quality four-year institutions and special opportunities for disadvantaged at all levels; health - prevention of adolescent pregnancy; conservation - main focus on preservation of soil and water resources of Midwest and Great Plains region; government - examination of all levels of government on efficiency and effectiveness; and economic development - promotion of long-term employment opportunities for low-income individuals and communities.
Types of support awarded: Operating budgets, continuing support, seed money, emergency funds, matching funds, employee matching gifts, consulting services, technical assistance, program-related investments, scholarship funds, loans, special projects, publications, conferences and seminars.
Limitations: Giving primarily in the Midwestern states including IL, IN, IA, MI, MN, MS, OH, WI; limited number of conservation grants made in ND, SD, KS, and NE. No grants to individuals, or for endowment or building funds, annual campaigns, deficit financing, research, or land acquisition.
Publications: Annual report, program policy statement, application guidelines.
Application information: Program policy and grant proposal guidelines revised in January 1985; completion of questionnaire is required prior to proposal submission in field of higher education; requests should be sent to foundation in November for higher education questionnaire. Application form required.
Initial approach: Letter
Copies of proposal: 1
Deadline(s): January 15 (for April meeting - Education, Economic Development); May 15 (for August meeting - Health and Conservation); September 15 (for December meeting - Culture and Government)
Board meeting date(s): April or May; August or September; and twice in December
Final notification: 3 weeks following meeting
Write: Charles U. Daly, President
Officers: Charles U. Daly,* President; Cushman B. Bissell, Jr.,* Vice-President, Finance and Secretary-Treasurer; R. Craig Kennedy, Vice-President, Program and Planning; Linda K. Schelinski, Vice-President, Administration.

Directors:* John T. Anderson, Cushman B. Bissell, Sr., Co-Chairmen; Raymond Wearing, Vice-Chairman; Lewis Butler, Richard K. Donahue, Marion T. Hall, Jessica T. Matthews.
Number of staff: 9 full-time professional; 4 full-time support.
Employer Identification Number: 366079185

1053
Joyce (The John M. and Mary A.) Foundation
P.O. Box 2007
Joliet 60434   (815) 741-7777
Additional address: c/o Timothy J. Joyce, Joyce Rd., New Rochelle, NY 10802

Incorporated in 1956 in Illinois.
Donor(s): John M. Joyce, Mary McCann Joyce,† Seven-Up Bottling Company.
Financial data: (yr. ended 7/31/83): Assets, $3,458,477 (L); expenditures, $355,711, including $336,360 for 77 grants (high: $41,500; low: $260).
Purpose and activities: Broad purposes; general giving, largely in Illinois and New York, with emphasis on church support, schools, and hospitals.
Types of support awarded: Matching funds, continuing support, emergency funds, building funds.
Limitations: Giving primarily in IL and NY. No grants to individuals, or for endowment funds, or scholarships and fellowships.
Application information:
  Board meeting date(s): March, June, September, and December
  Write: William J. Davito, Secretary
Officers and Trustees:* John M. Joyce,* President and Treasurer; Sidney P. Mudd,* John M. Joyce, III,* Timothy J. Joyce,* Vice-Presidents; William J. Davito, Secretary.
Employer Identification Number: 366054112

1054
JSR Foundation ⌐
1360 N. Sandburg Terrace, Suite 2201
Chicago 60610

Established in 1979.
Donor(s): Harold L. Miller, Beatrice R. Miller.
Financial data: (yr. ended 11/30/83): Assets, $11,781 (M); gifts received, $6,500; expenditures, $110,403, including $107,739 for 16 grants (high: $100,000; low: $25).
Purpose and activities: Giving primarily to social services and Jewish welfare funds.
Officers and Directors: Harold L. Miller, President; Judith B. Schectman, Vice-President; Robert F. Miller, Secretary; Beatrice R. Miller, Treasurer.
Employer Identification Number: 363053757

1055
Kaplan (Mayer and Morris) Foundation
191 Waukegan Rd.
Northfield 60062   (312) 441-6630

Incorporated in 1957 in Illinois.
Donor(s): Alice B. Kaplan, Sealy Mattress Company of Illinois.

Financial data: (yr. ended 10/31/83): Assets, $1,177,037 (M); gifts received, $210,000; expenditures, $187,083, including $182,260 for 180 grants (high: $60,000; low: $25; average: $500-$1,000) and $600 for 4 employee matching gifts.
Purpose and activities: Support primarily for Jewish welfare funds, community funds, higher education, and cultural programs.
Types of support awarded: Operating budgets, continuing support, annual campaigns, endowment funds, employee matching gifts, scholarship funds, professorships, internships, employee related scholarships, exchange programs, fellowships.
Limitations: Giving primarily in the Chicago, IL, area. No grants to individuals, or for seed money, emergency funds, deficit financing, building funds, equipment and materials, land acquisition, general endowments, matching grants, research, demonstration projects, publications, or conferences and seminars.
Application information:
  Initial approach: Letter
  Board meeting date(s): Annually
  Final notification: 1 month
  Write: Sharon Osterberg
Officers: Morris A. Kaplan, President; Anthony B. Grublesky, Secretary; Burton B. Kaplan, Treasurer.
Number of staff: None.
Employer Identification Number: 366099675

1056
Keating Family Foundation, Inc. ⌐
640 Winnetka Mews
Winnetka 60093

Incorporated in 1967 in Illinois.
Donor(s): Edward Keating.
Financial data: (yr. ended 12/31/83): Assets, $2,505,214 (M); expenditures, $125,780, including $86,940 for 40 grants (high: $15,000; low: $50).
Purpose and activities: Charitable purposes; primarily local giving, with emphasis on hospitals, health and mental health agencies, child welfare, church support, and Jewish welfare funds.
Limitations: Giving primarily in IL.
Application information:
  Write: Gerald H. Galler, Secretary
Officers and Directors: Edward Keating, President; Lynne E. Temme-Keating, Arthur E. Keating, Lee B. Keating, Vice-Presidents; Gerald H. Galler, Secretary.
Employer Identification Number: 366198002

1057
Keebler Company Foundation
One Hollow Tree Ln.
Elmhurst 60126   (312) 833-2900

Established in 1968 in Illinois.
Donor(s): Keebler Company.
Financial data: (yr. ended 12/31/82): Assets, $13,815 (M); gifts received, $216,900; expenditures, $208,622, including $193,391 for 105 grants (high: $41,516; low: $10) and $15,066 for 64 employee matching gifts.

Purpose and activities: General giving, in areas where the company has major facilities, with emphasis on community funds; support also for minority programs and employee matching gifts for higher education.
Types of support awarded: Employee matching gifts.
Limitations: Giving primarily in areas where the company has major operations. No grants to individuals, or for endowment funds, research programs, or scholarships and fellowships; no loans.
Application information:
  Write: A.G. Bland, Vice-President
Officers: T.M. Garvin,* President; A.G. Bland, Vice-President and Treasurer; W.S. Maker,* Secretary.
Directors:* C.A. Gerber.
Employer Identification Number: 362658310

1058
Kellstadt Foundation
c/o UnibancTrust Company
Sears Tower
Chicago 60606

Established in 1977 in Illinois.
Donor(s): Charles Kellstadt Trust.
Financial data: (yr. ended 9/30/83): Assets, $4,613,329 (M); expenditures, $426,050, including $400,000 for 6 grants (high: $100,000; low: $25,000; average: $100,000).
Purpose and activities: Grants for private institutions of higher education, with emphasis on graduate education in business, primarily in the Midwest.
Limitations: Giving primarily in the Midwest. No grants to individuals.
Application information:
  Initial approach: Letter
  Deadline(s): None
  Board meeting date(s): March and September
  Write: Emory Williams, Trustee
Trustees: Leo Arnstein, Emory Williams, UnibancTrust Company.
Number of staff: None.
Employer Identification Number: 362897620

1059
Kemper Educational and Charitable Fund
20 North Wacker Dr., Rm. 3800
Chicago 60606   (312) 580-1024

Incorporated in 1961 in Illinois.
Donor(s): James S. Kemper.†
Financial data: (yr. ended 9/30/83): Assets, $4,660,420 (M); gifts received, $653,256; expenditures, $288,316, including $160,000 for 17 grants (high: $50,000; low: $1,000).
Purpose and activities: Charitable and educational purposes; giving primarily for educational programs; support also for hospitals.
Limitations: No grants to individuals, or for building or endowment funds; no loans.
Application information: Applications not encouraged.
  Initial approach: Full proposal
  Copies of proposal: 3
  Board meeting date(s): Annually and as required

Write: Maurice F. Thunack, Secretary
Officers and Trustees: Gertrude Z. Kemper, Chairperson; Dale Park, Jr., President; Mildred K. Terrill, Vice-President; Maurice F. Thunack, Secretary-Treasurer; Margaret M. Archambault, Leslie N. Christensen, Mark Kemper, Raymond T. Smith, Frank D. Stout, William G. Stratton, John Van Cleave.
Employer Identification Number: 366054499

1060
Kemper (The James S.) Foundation ▼
c/o Kemper Insurance
Route 22
Long Grove 60049   (312) 540-2846

Incorporated in 1942 in Illinois.
Donor(s): James S. Kemper,† and others, Lumbermens Mutual Casualty Company, American Motorists Insurance Company, American Manufacturers Mutual Insurance Company.
Financial data: (yr. ended 7/31/84): Assets, $10,343,903 (M); gifts received, $20; expenditures, $786,056, including $523,472 for 74 grants (high: $50,000; low: $250; average: $250-$15,000).
Purpose and activities: The Kemper Scholars Program has two purposes: to provide undergraduate and graduate financial aid for students in the fields of business and nursing, and to provide educationally relevant summer work experience in a large corporation for students oriented toward a career in business.
Types of support awarded: Scholarship funds, fellowships.
Limitations: No grants to individuals, or for any purposes other than scholarships and fellowships at participating institutions.
Publications: Annual report, application guidelines.
Application information: Applicants are screened by committees at participating universities. Application form required.
  Initial approach: Letter or telephone
  Board meeting date(s): November and May
  Write: John H. Barcroft, Executive Director
Officers: Joseph E. Luecke,* President; Robert F. Ballus, Vice-President; Donald R. Clark, Secretary and Treasurer; John H. Barcroft, Executive Director.
Trustees:* James S. Kemper, Jr., Chairman; Thomas R. Anderson, J. Reed Coleman, Raymond E. Farley, David C. Jones, George D. Kennedy, Rudolph F. Landolt, Joseph B. Lanterman, Shirley N. Pettis, Kenneth A. Randall, Richard N. Rosett, Charles B. Stauffacher, John C. Stetson.
Number of staff: 1 full-time professional; 2 full-time support.
Employer Identification Number: 366007812

1061
Kendall (The George R.) Foundation ▼
State National Bank
P.O. Box 1670
Evanston 60204   (312) 491-6000

Trust established in 1969 in Illinois.
Donor(s): George R. Kendall.†

Financial data: (yr. ended 11/30/83): Assets, $14,692,237 (M); expenditures, $657,259, including $624,632 for 14 grants (high: $187,500; low: $3,000; average: $10,000-$100,000).
Purpose and activities: Primarily local giving, with emphasis on higher education; support also for social agencies and child welfare.
Types of support awarded: General purposes.
Limitations: Giving primarily in IL. No grants to individuals, or for endowment funds, scholarships, fellowships, or matching gifts; no loans.
Application information:
  Initial approach: Proposal
  Copies of proposal: 1
  Deadline(s): Submit proposals preferably in January, February, or March; deadline September 1
  Board meeting date(s): April and October
  Final notification: After October 31 if acted upon
  Write: C. David Howell, Vice-President and Trust Officer
Trustees: Helen K. Johnson, G. Preston Kendall, George P. Kendall, Jr., Thomas C. Kendall, State National Bank (C. David Howell, Vice-President and Trust Officer).
Number of staff: None.
Employer Identification Number: 366403376

1062
Kern Foundation Trust ⌑
c/o Northern Trust Company
50 S. LaSalle St.
Chicago 60675

Financial data: (yr. ended 12/31/83): Assets, $10,720,577 (M); expenditures, $633,186, including $576,781 for 4 grants (high: $431,920; low: $32,000).
Purpose and activities: Giving primarily to societies for the study of religions, with emphasis on Eastern religions and theosophy.
Trustees: John C. Kern, Northern Trust Company.
Employer Identification Number: 366107250

1063
Kirkland & Ellis Foundation ⌑
200 E. Randolph Dr.
Chicago 60601

Established in 1981.
Donor(s): Fred H. Bartlitt, Jr., Frank Cicero, Jr., Thomas A. Gottschalk, Glen E. Hess, William R. Jentes, Elmer W. Johnson, Donald G. Kempf, Jr., Howard G. Krane, Jack S. Levin, Karl F. Nygren, Daniel W. Vittum, Jr.
Financial data: (yr. ended 12/31/83): Assets, $18,423 (M); gifts received, $266,000; expenditures, $286,999, including $286,828 for grants.
Purpose and activities: Charitable purposes.
Officers: Elmer W. Johnson, President; Melvin S. Adess, William R. Jentes, J. Landis Martin, James H. Schink, Vice-Presidents; Stephen C. Neal, Secretary and Treasurer.
Employer Identification Number: 363160355

1064
Koehler (John G.) Fund
103 North Main St.
Pontiac 61764
Grant application address: Stephen Herr, Citizens Bank Bldg., Chatsworth, IL; Tel.: (815) 635-3134

Established in 1975.
Financial data: (yr. ended 12/31/83): Assets, $1,048,496 (M); expenditures, $85,597, including $53,350 for 50 grants to individuals.
Purpose and activities: Giving for scholarships only to Chatsworth High School graduates.
Types of support awarded: Student aid.
Limitations: Giving limited to Chatsworth, IL.
Application information: Application form required.
  Initial approach: Full proposal
  Deadline(s): June 1
  Write: Stephen Herr, Trustee
Trustees: Stephen F. Herr, Clair Koehler, Robert Koehler.
Employer Identification Number: 376141953

1065
Lasky (Harry and Sadie) Foundation ⌑
30 N. Michigan Ave., Suite 1813
Chicago 60602

Incorporated in 1958 in Illinois.
Donor(s): Sadie Lasky.
Financial data: (yr. ended 12/31/83): Assets, $1,177,004 (M); expenditures, $99,630, including $96,000 for 4 grants (high: $74,000; low: $3,500).
Purpose and activities: Giving for Jewish welfare funds.
Officers: Harry Lasky, President and Treasurer; Sadie Lasky, Vice-President and Secretary.
Directors: Alex A. Lathorn, Isadore Solomon.
Employer Identification Number: 366105123

1066
Layman Trust for Evangelism ⌑
2047 Vermont St.
Quincy 62301

Trust established in 1938 in Illinois.
Donor(s): Edgar V. Moorman,† Jessie Moorman,† Moorman Manufacturing Company.
Financial data: (yr. ended 12/31/83): Assets, $1,437,783 (M); expenditures, $106,743, including $102,000 for 5 grants (high: $30,000; low: $12,000).
Purpose and activities: "To conduct evangelism, by spreading, preaching and promulgating, along interdenominational lines, the exclusive yet complete gospel of Jesus Christ as taught in the New Testament, especially recognizing the divinity of Jesus Christ and the prime necessity of individual conversion for salvation." Giving limited to Protestant evangelical associations for missionary work.
Application information: Application must include certification of IRS eligibility and that applicant is not a private foundation.
  Initial approach: Letter or full proposal
  Deadline(s): None
  Final notification: Usually in November

Write: Robert H. Langerhans, Secretary-Treasurer
Officers and Trustees: Robert F. Gillhouse, President; Robert H. Langerhans, Secretary-Treasurer; John R. Read, James A. Wooldridge.
Employer Identification Number: 376037837

1067
Lederer (The Francis L.) Foundation ¤
c/o Leo H. Arnstein
7500 Sears Tower
Chicago 60606

Established in 1966 in Illinois.
Financial data: (yr. ended 12/31/83): Assets, $1,639,703 (M); expenditures, $119,856, including $105,460 for 24 grants (high: $14,000; low: $460).
Purpose and activities: Primarily local giving, with emphasis on higher and secondary education, medical education and research, Jewish welfare funds, and the arts.
Limitations: Giving primarily in IL.
Officers and Directors: Anne P. Lederer, President; Francis L. Lederer II, Vice-President and Treasurer; Leo H. Arnstein, Secretary.
Employer Identification Number: 362594937

1068
Lehmann (Otto W.) Foundation ¤
105 North Green Bay Rd.
Lake Bluff 60044

Incorporated in 1967 in Illinois.
Donor(s): Otto W. Lehmann.†
Financial data: (yr. ended 7/31/82): Assets, $1,283,321 (M); gifts received, $1,339; expenditures, $127,911, including $109,650 for 81 grants (high: $5,000; low: $100).
Purpose and activities: Broad purposes; local giving, with emphasis on youth agencies and child welfare, including aid for the handicapped, higher education, health agencies, social agencies, and rehabilitation.
Limitations: Giving limited to the Chicago, IL area.
Application information:
Write: Robert O. Lehmann, Managing Trustee
Trustees: Robert O. Lehmann, Managing Trustee; James E. Elworth, Marguerite S. Lehmann.
Employer Identification Number: 366160836

1069
Leslie Fund, Inc.
3600 West Lake Ave.
Glenview 60025 (312) 724-6100

Incorporated in 1956 in Illinois.
Donor(s): Members of the Leslie family.
Financial data: (yr. ended 3/31/84): Assets, $2,888,943 (M); expenditures, $93,553, including $85,600 for 58 grants (high: $20,000; low: $50).
Purpose and activities: Broad purposes; primarily local giving, with emphasis on cultural programs, aid to the handicapped, education, youth agencies, conservation and social welfare agencies, and hospitals.

Limitations: Giving primarily in IL. No grants to individuals.
Application information:
Initial approach: Letter
Copies of proposal: 1
Deadline(s): None
Board meeting date(s): January, April, July, and October
Write: John H. Leslie, President
Officers: John H. Leslie,* President; Virginia A. Leslie, Vice-President; Barbara Laskin, Secretary-Treasurer.
Directors:* James W. Leslie, Robert W. Wright.
Number of staff: 1 part-time support.
Employer Identification Number: 366055800

1070
Levie (Marcus and Theresa) Educational Fund
c/o Jewish Federation of Metropolitan Chicago
One South Franklin St.
Chicago 60606 (312) 346-6700

Trust established in 1959 in Illinois.
Donor(s): Maude M. Levie,† Jerome M. Levie,† Charles M. Levie.†
Financial data: (yr. ended 7/31/84): Assets, $1,746,656 (M); expenditures, $143,800, including $143,800 for 58 grants to individuals.
Purpose and activities: Scholarships awarded to Jewish students who are residents of Cook County and who have financial need to complete their professional or vocational training in the helping professions.
Types of support awarded: Student aid.
Limitations: Giving limited to Cook County, IL. No grants for general support, or for building or endowment funds, research, or matching gifts; no loans.
Publications: Application guidelines, program policy statement.
Application information: Application form required.
Initial approach: Letter or telephone
Copies of proposal: 2
Deadline(s): Submit scholarship application between November and February; deadline March 1
Board meeting date(s): As required, usually in July and August
Final notification: July or August
Write: Ruth Elbaum, Secretary
Officer: Ruth Elbaum, Secretary.
Distribution Committee (1984-1985): Mrs. Herman Finch, Chair; Robert L. Adler, Mrs. Stanley D. Braun, Rabbi Herbert Bronstein, Michael Cahr, Sanford Cantor, Midge Feinberg, Susan Feit, Mrs. Zollie S. Frank, Mrs. Melvin Hecktman, Mrs. Bernard Kaye, Mrs. Buryl Lazar, Mrs. Maurice L. Lewis, Sylvia Margolies, Mrs. Arnold Newberger, Mark Ratner, Harold Saffir, Mrs. Jerold S. Solovy.
Trustee: Chicago Title and Trust Company.
Number of staff: 14 part-time professional; 1 full-time support; 1 part-time support.
Employer Identification Number: 366010074

1071
Levy (Chas. and Ruth) Foundation ¤
1200 North Branch St.
Chicago 60622

Incorporated in 1959 in Illinois.
Donor(s): Charles Levy, Charles Levy Circulating Company, and several other Levy companies.
Financial data: (yr. ended 6/30/84): Assets, $1,650,770 (M); gifts received, $212,818; expenditures, $179,207, including $161,078 for 80 grants (high: $85,000; low: $25).
Purpose and activities: General giving, largely local, with emphasis on Jewish welfare funds, higher education, and performing arts.
Limitations: Giving primarily in IL.
Officers and Directors: Charles Levy, President and Treasurer; Ruth Levy, Vice-President.
Employer Identification Number: 366032324

1072
Lingle (Bowman C.) Trust ¤
c/o Harris Trust and Savings Bank
111 West Monroe St.
Chicago 60690 (312) 461-2613

Trust established in 1959 in Illinois.
Donor(s): Bowman C. Lingle.†
Financial data: (yr. ended 12/31/82): Assets, $4,211,470 (M); expenditures, $205,968, including $199,168 for 18 grants (high: $50,000; low: $1,000).
Purpose and activities: For the benefit of agencies which are or, through pioneering ventures, will be involved in improving public welfare or public administration within the Chicago area.
Limitations: Giving limited to the Chicago, IL area. No grants to individuals, or for endowment funds, matching gifts, scholarships, or fellowships; no loans.
Publications: Application guidelines.
Application information:
Initial approach: Letter
Copies of proposal: 1
Board meeting date(s): March, June, September, and December
Write: Miss Ellen A. Bechthold, Trust Administrator
Trustee: Harris Trust and Savings Bank (Ellen A. Bechthold, Trust Administrator).

1073
Listeman (Marguerite) Foundation ¤
c/o Northern Trust Company
50 South LaSalle St.
Chicago 60675

Trust established in 1958 in Wisconsin.
Donor(s): Kurt Listeman.†
Financial data: (yr. ended 12/31/83): Assets, $1,128,332 (M); expenditures, $78,333, including $65,613 for 18 grants (high: $12,000; low: $725).
Purpose and activities: Grants primarily for community development, including support for buildings and equipment for parks and recreation areas and cultural facilities in the Clark County-Neillsville, Wisconsin area.

Types of support awarded: Building funds, equipment.
Limitations: Giving limited to the Clark County-Neillsville, WI area.
Officer and Advisors: Mike Krultz, Jr., Secretary; Bruce Beilfuss, Bradley Larson, James Musil, Heron Van Gordon, Fred Wall.
Trustee: Northern Trust Company.
Employer Identification Number: 366028439

1074
Lizzadro (Joseph) Family Foundation
105 Center Mall
Oak Brook 60521

Incorporated in 1957 in Illinois.
Donor(s): Members of the Lizzadro family and others.
Financial data: (yr. ended 12/31/83): Assets, $3,797,032 (M); expenditures, $96,046, including $80,650 for 16 grants (low: $200; average: $1,000).
Purpose and activities: Broad purposes; local giving, with emphasis on a museum of lapidary art, hospitals, and health agencies.
Limitations: Giving limited to Oak Brook, IL. No grants to individuals or for endowment funds.
Application information:
  Initial approach: Letter
  Copies of proposal: 1
  Deadline(s): Submit proposal in November; deadline November 30
  Board meeting date(s): March and December
  Write: John S. Lizzadro, Treasurer
Officers and Directors: Mary Lizzadro, President; Joseph Lizzadro, Jr., Vice-President; Angela Anderson, Secretary; John S. Lizzadro, Treasurer; Bonita Hay, Frank C. Lizzadro, Diane Nicholas.
Employer Identification Number: 366047939

1075
Lumpkin Foundation, The ☒
7200 Sears Tower
233 S. Wacker Dr.
Chicago 60606   (217) 235-3361

Incorporated in 1953 in Illinois.
Donor(s): Besse Adamson Lumpkin, Richard Adamson Lumpkin, Illinois Consolidated Telephone Company.
Financial data: (yr. ended 12/31/82): Assets, $2,278,197 (M); gifts received, $90,000; expenditures, $149,527, including $140,600 for 44 grants (high: $25,000; low: $100).
Purpose and activities: Broad purposes; grants primarily for higher and secondary education, hospitals, and health agencies; support also for public libraries.
Limitations: No grants to individuals.
Application information:
  Board meeting date(s): June, December, and as required
  Write: Richard Adamson Lumpkin, President
Officers and Directors: Richard Adamson Lumpkin, President; Mary G. Lumpkin, Vice-President and Secretary; Richard Anthony Lumpkin, Treasurer.
Employer Identification Number: 376028909

1076
MacArthur (J. Roderick) Foundation
9333 N. Milwaukee Ave.
Niles 60648   (312) 966-0143

Established in 1976 in Illinois.
Donor(s): J. Roderick MacArthur,† Bradford Exchange AG.
Financial data: (yr. ended 1/31/85): Assets, $22,626,530 (M); gifts received, $15,356,792; expenditures, $2,679,222, including $1,004,531 for 75 grants (high: $20,000; low: $25; average: $2,000-$20,000).
Purpose and activities: The foundation seeks to "aid those who are inequitably or unjustly treated by established institutions" by "protecting and encouraging freedom of expression, human rights, civil liberties, and social justice; and by eliminating political, economic, social, religious, and cultural oppression".
Types of support awarded: Operating budgets, seed money, emergency funds, equipment, research, publications.
Limitations: No support for ongoing social services, government programs, or religious, church-based activities. No grants to individuals, or for capital projects, endowments, development campaigns, statues or memorials, annual campaigns, conferences, continuing support, deficit financing, land acquisition, endowments, matching gifts, consulting services, technical assistance, scholarships, fellowships, or seminars; no loans.
Publications: Financial statement, program policy statement, application guidelines, grants list.
Application information: Application form required.
  Initial approach: Letter, proposal, or telephone
  Copies of proposal: 1
  Deadline(s): None
  Board meeting date(s): Approximately every 1 or 2 months
  Final notification: 1 to 2 months
  Write: Lance Lindblom, President
Officers and Directors:* Solange MacArthur,* Chairman; Gregoire MacArthur,* Vice-Chairman; Lance Lindblom, President; John R.C.G. MacArthur,* Secretary-Treasurer.
Number of staff: 4.
Employer Identification Number: 510214450

1077
MacArthur (John D. and Catherine T.) Foundation ▼
140 South Dearborn St.
Chicago 60603   (312) 726-8000

Incorporated in 1970 in Illinois.
Donor(s): John D. MacArthur.†
Financial data: (yr. ended 12/31/83): Assets, $1,920,260,560 (M); gifts received, $3,000; expenditures, $49,946,231, including $34,266,505 for 413 grants (high: $3,000,000; low: $1,000) and $3,931,013 for 94 grants to individuals.

Purpose and activities: Broad purposes; four major initiatives currently authorized: MacArthur Fellows Program, for highly talented individuals in any field of endeavor (self-initiated or outside nominations not considered); the Health Program, primarily for research in mental health and the psychological and behavioral aspects of health and rehabilitation; the General Grants Program, primarily for education, governance, public affairs, civil and criminal justice, and mass communication; and the Special Grants Program, for support of cultural and community activities in the Chicago metropolitan area.
Types of support awarded: Matching funds, general purposes, operating budgets, special projects, research, fellowships.
Limitations: No support for churches or religious programs. No grants for capital or endowment funds, conferences, publications, films, debt retirement, development campaigns, fund-raising appeals, scholarships, fellowships (except those sponsored by the foundation); no loans.
Publications: Annual report, program policy statement, application guidelines.
Application information: Direct applications for Prize Fellows Program not accepted.
  Initial approach: Letter
  Copies of proposal: 1
  Board meeting date(s): Monthly, except August
  Write: James M. Furman, Executive Vice-President
Officers: Paul D. Doolen,* Chairman; William T. Kirby,* Vice-Chairman and Secretary; John E. Corbally,* President; James M. Furman, Executive Vice-President; Joseph A. Diana, Vice-President for Administration and Treasurer; William Bevan, Vice-President and Director of Health Program; David M. Murdoch, Vice-President, Finance.
Directors:* Weston R. Christopherson, Robert P. Ewing, Gaylord Freeman, Murray Gell-Mann, Paul Harvey, Shirley Mount Hufstedler, Edward H. Levi, J. Roderick MacArthur, Jonas Salk, M.D., Jerome B. Weisner.
Number of staff: 19 full-time professional; 2 part-time professional; 19 full-time support; 3 part-time support.
Employer Identification Number: 237093598

1078
Maltz (B. N.) Foundation ☒
180 North LaSalle St.
Chicago 60601

Incorporated in 1948 in Illinois.
Donor(s): Ben N. Maltz, Medal Distilled Products Company, Inc.
Financial data: (yr. ended 12/31/83): Assets, $1,394,229 (M); gifts received, $45,230; expenditures, $141,518, including $134,590 for 114 grants (high: $30,050; low: $25).
Purpose and activities: Broad purposes; grants largely for Jewish welfare funds, hospitals, and health agencies; support also for higher education.
Officers: B.N. Maltz, President; M.M. Maltz, Treasurer.
Employer Identification Number: 956034307

1079
Manilow (Nathan) Foundation
754 N. Milwaukee Ave.
Chicago 60622   (312) 829-3655

Incorporated in 1955 in Illinois.
Donor(s): Nathan Manilow,† Lewis Manilow.
Financial data: (yr. ended 5/31/84): Assets,
$2,887,733 (M); expenditures, $424,109,
including $378,372 for 29 grants (high:
$341,697; low: $100).
Purpose and activities: Broad purposes;
primarily local giving, with emphasis on Jewish
welfare funds, a museum, and education;
grants also for temple support and child welfare.
Limitations: Giving primarily in IL.
Officers and Trustees: Lewis Manilow,
President and Treasurer; Norman Altman, Vice-
President and Secretary.
Employer Identification Number: 366079220

1080
Mansfield (Albert & Anne) Foundation ☐
c/o Much, Shelist, Freed, et al.
135 S. LaSalle St., Suite 2323
Chicago 60603

Established in 1976.
Financial data: (yr. ended 12/31/83): Assets,
$1,216,886 (M); expenditures, $67,402,
including $51,500 for 7 grants (high: $12,000;
low: $2,500).
Purpose and activities: Broad purposes;
primarily local giving, with emphasis on higher
education.
Limitations: Giving primarily in Chicago, IL.
Application information:
  Initial approach: Proposal
  Write: Lawrence Kasakoff, Trustee
Trustees: Marlene Hopmayer, Lawrence
Kasakoff, Anne Mansfield, Benetta Mansfield,
Seymour Mansfield, Harris Trust & Savings
Bank.
Employer Identification Number: 366151176

1081
Maremont Corporation Foundation ☐
200 East Randolph Dr.
Chicago 60601   (312) 861-4031

Established in 1957 in Illinois.
Donor(s): Maremont Corporation.
Financial data: (yr. ended 12/31/83): Assets,
$242,590 (M); gifts received, $150,000;
expenditures, $173,518, including $148,967
for 167 grants (high: $10,000; low: $15) and
$20,650 for 21 grants to individuals.
Purpose and activities: Charitable purposes;
grants mainly for community funds, higher
education, including scholarships for children
of company employees, cultural programs, and
health.
Types of support awarded: Employee related
scholarships.
Limitations: Giving primarily in IL.
Application information: Application
information available for scholarship program.
Application form required.
  Deadline(s): January 1
  Write: Shari Cedron

Officers and Directors:* Byron O. Pond,*
President; Milton Shapiro,* Vice-President and
Treasurer; Raymond P. Mack,* Vice-President;
Jon S. Kubiak, Secretary.
Employer Identification Number: 366162616

1082
Marquette Charitable Organization ☐
2141 South Jefferson St.
Chicago 60616

Incorporated in 1923 in Illinois.
Financial data: (yr. ended 12/31/83): Assets,
$6,162,754 (M); expenditures, $491,659,
including $438,360 for 96 grants (high:
$74,500; low: $50).
Purpose and activities: Charitable and
educational purposes; general giving, with
emphasis on secondary and higher education
and cultural programs, including historic
preservation; support also for Christian religious
organizations, health agencies, youth and child
welfare, and public policy organizations.
Officers: Henry Regnery,* President; William
H. Regnery II,* Vice-President; Betty Basile,
Secretary-Treasurer.
Directors:* David R. Meyers.
Employer Identification Number: 366055852

1083
Martin (Bert William) Foundation ☐
c/o The Northern Trust Company
50 South LaSalle St.
Chicago 60675

Incorporated in 1946 in Illinois.
Donor(s): Bert W. Martin, Ada La May Martin.
Financial data: (yr. ended 12/31/83): Assets,
$2,537,234 (M); gifts received, $17,612;
expenditures, $143,165, including $104,048
for 27 grants (low: $100).
Purpose and activities: Broad purposes; grants
largely for hospitals and health services in
Mount Vernon, Ohio and in California.
Limitations: Giving primarily in CA and Mount
Vernon, OH.
Officers and Directors: Ada La May Martin,
President; Joseph J. Regan, Vice-President;
James W. Fisher, Secretary and Treasurer;
Winston C. Moore, Winifred M. Warden.
Employer Identification Number: 366060591

1084
Mason Charitable Foundation ☐
One First National Plaza, Suite 5000
Chicago 60603

Established in 1980 in Illinois.
Donor(s): Marian Tyler.
Financial data: (yr. ended 1/31/84): Assets,
$1,260,409 (M); gifts received, $5,000;
expenditures, $42,976, including $37,500 for 5
grants (high: $10,000; low: $2,500).
Purpose and activities: Grants primarily for
public television and social services.
Trustees: Katheryn Cowles Douglass, Kingman
Scott Douglass, Louise J. Douglass, Robert Dun
Douglass, Timothy P. Douglass.
Employer Identification Number: 363101263

1085
Material Service Foundation
300 West Washington St.
Chicago 60606

Established about 1952 in Illinois; incorporated
in 1960 in Illinois.
Donor(s): Material Service Corporation, and
various subsidiaries of General Dynamics
Corporation.
Financial data: (yr. ended 12/31/84): Assets,
$144,708 (M); gifts received, $301,500;
expenditures, $296,314, including $295,774
for 171 grants (high: $69,000; low: $25).
Purpose and activities: Broad purposes;
primarily local giving, with emphasis on
community funds; grants also for community
development, youth agencies, education, health
agencies, and cultural activities.
Limitations: Giving primarily in IL, with
emphasis on Chicago. No grants to individuals.
Application information:
  Initial approach: Letter
  Board meeting date(s): As required
  Write: Lester Crown, Manager
Manager: Lester Crown.
Employer Identification Number: 366062106

1086
Mayer (Oscar G. and Elsa S.) Charitable Trust ▼
c/o Hugo J. Melvoin
115 South LaSalle St., Rm. 2500
Chicago 60603   (312) 332-3682

Trust established in 1965 in Illinois.
Donor(s): Oscar G. Mayer, Sr.,† Elsa S.
Mayer.†
Financial data: (yr. ended 12/31/83): Assets,
$7,641,672 (M); expenditures, $644,133,
including $555,000 for 39 grants (high:
$50,000; low: $5,000; average: $5,000-
$25,000).
Purpose and activities: Grants limited to
charitable institutions in which the donors did
or their descendants do actively participate,
including higher education, hospitals, music,
and museums in Wisconsin and Illinois .
Types of support awarded: General purposes.
Limitations: Giving primarily in the Chicago, IL
metropolitan area and in WI. No grants to
individuals.
Application information:
  Initial approach: Letter
  Copies of proposal: 1
  Deadline(s): None
  Board meeting date(s): As required
  Final notification: 2 weeks
  Write: Oscar G. Mayer, Managing Trustee
Trustees: Oscar G. Mayer, Managing Trustee;
Allan C. Mayer, Harold F. Mayer, Harold M.
Mayer.
Number of staff: 1 part-time professional; 1
part-time support.
Employer Identification Number: 366134354

1087
Mazza Foundation ¤
801 North Clark St.
Chicago 60610

Incorporated in 1957 in Illinois.
Donor(s): Leonard M. Lavezzorio,† Louise T. Mazza Trust.
Financial data: (yr. ended 11/30/83): Assets, $2,367,609 (M); gifts received, $813,746; expenditures, $148,953, including $144,100 for 10 grants (high: $100,000; low: $100).
Purpose and activities: Broad purposes; primarily local giving, with emphasis on support for churches, religious organizations, and social agencies.
Limitations: Giving primarily in Chicago, IL.
Officers: Neil Vernasco, President; Joseph O. Rubinelli, Vice-President; Stanley Pukelis, Secretary and Treasurer; Tina Lavezzorio, Director.
Employer Identification Number: 366054751

1088
McCormick (Chauncey and Marion Deering) Foundation ▼ ¤
410 North Michigan Ave., Rm. 590
Chicago 60611   (312) 644-6720

Incorporated in 1957 in Illinois.
Donor(s): Brooks McCormick, Brooks McCormick Trust, Charles Deering McCormick Trust, Roger McCormick Trust.
Financial data: (yr. ended 7/31/84): Assets, $10,086,965 (M); gifts received, $12,500; expenditures, $1,792,205, including $624,000 for 31 grants (high: $150,000; low: $1,000; average: $1,000-$60,000).
Purpose and activities: Broad purposes; primarily local giving, with emphasis on higher and secondary education, hospitals, and cultural institutions, including an art museum; support also for conservation and child welfare.
Limitations: Giving primarily in Chicago, IL.
Officers and Directors: Charles Deering McCormick, President; Brooks McCormick, Vice-President; Charles E. Schroeder, Secretary and Treasurer; James McCormick.
Employer Identification Number: 366054815

1089
McCormick (Robert R.) Charitable Trust ▼
435 North Michigan Ave., Suite 1231
Chicago 60611   (312) 222-3512

Trust established in 1955 in Illinois.
Donor(s): Robert R. McCormick.†
Financial data: (yr. ended 12/31/83): Assets, $38,100,581 (M); expenditures, $5,487,636, including $5,137,485 for 115 grants (high: $395,000; low: $5,000; average: $10,000-$30,000).

Purpose and activities: Broad purposes; largest contributions for higher education and aid to specific educational projects; grants to hospitals, including the endowment of free beds; to projects aimed at serving young people, as well as cultural and community activities, and for medical research. Grants for operating purposes and other grants of less than $10,000 are distributed through Robert R. McCormick Foundation from funds received from the Charitable Trust.
Types of support awarded: Building funds, equipment, endowment funds, research, scholarship funds, fellowships, matching funds, conferences and seminars, continuing support, emergency funds.
Limitations: Giving primarily in the Chicago, IL, metropolitan area. No support for primary or secondary education. No grants to individuals, or for operating budgets, or seed money; no loans; no gifts to the same institution for more than 3 successive years.
Publications: Annual report, application guidelines.
Application information:
    Deadline(s): Submit proposal preferably in January, April, July, and October; deadline February 1, May 1, August 1, and November 1
    Board meeting date(s): March, June, September, and December
    Final notification: 3 months
    Write: William N. Clark, Executive Director
Officer: William N. Clark, Executive Director.
Trustees: Robert M. Hunt, Chairman; Charles T. Brumback, Stanton R. Cook, Clayton Kirkpatrick, John W. Madigan.
Number of staff: 1 part-time professional; 1 full-time support; 1 part-time support.
Employer Identification Number: 366046974

1090
McCormick (Robert R.) Foundation
435 North Michigan Ave., Suite 1231
Chicago 60611   (312) 222-3512

Incorporated in 1953 in Illinois.
Donor(s): Robert R. McCormick,† Robert R. McCormick Charitable Trust.
Financial data: (yr. ended 12/31/84): Assets, $348 (L); gifts received, $441,480; expenditures, $444,797, including $438,405 for 94 grants (high: $10,000; low: $500; average: $2,000-$5,000).
Purpose and activities: Broad purposes; local giving, with emphasis on youth, social, and health agencies, music, and cultural programs.
Types of support awarded: Operating budgets, continuing support, annual campaigns, emergency funds, general purposes.
Limitations: Giving limited to the Chicago, IL, metropolitan area. No support for primary or secondary education. No grants to individuals, or for building or endowment funds, research, scholarships, fellowships, or matching gifts; no loans.
Publications: Annual report, application guidelines.
Application information:
    Initial approach: Letter
    Copies of proposal: 1

    Deadline(s): February 1, May 1, August 1, or November 1
    Board meeting date(s): March, June, September, and December
    Write: William N. Clark, Executive Director
Officers and Directors: Robert M. Hunt, President; Clayton Kirkpatrick, John W. Madigan, Vice-Presidents; Charles T. Brumback, Treasurer; Stanton R. Cook.
Number of staff: 1 part-time professional; 1 full-time support; 1 part-time support.
Employer Identification Number: 366046973

1091
McDonnell (Everett N.) Foundation
150 North Wacker Dr., Rm. 2700
Chicago 60606

Incorporated in 1946 in Illinois.
Donor(s): Everett N. McDonnell.†
Financial data: (yr. ended 10/31/84): Assets, $2,046,865 (M); expenditures, $128,951, including $112,474 for 57 grants (high: $70,000; low: $100).
Purpose and activities: Broad purposes; giving for hospitals, health agencies, church support, and higher education.
Limitations: Giving primarily in IL and GA.
Application information: Proposals for grants not invited.
Officers and Directors: Florence L. McDonnell, President and Treasurer; John D. Marshall, Vice-President; Roswell H. Chrisman, Secretary.
Employer Identification Number: 366109359

1092
McFarland Charitable Foundation ¤
c/o Havana National Bank
112 South Orange St.
Havana 62644
Scholarship application address: c/o Kathy Tarvin, Director of Nursing Service, Mason District Hospital, 520 East Franklin St., Havana, IL 62644; Tel.: (309) 543-4431

Established in 1960 in Illinois.
Financial data: (yr. ended 12/31/83): Assets, $1,423,491 (M); gifts received, $5,000; expenditures, $143,958, including $124,737 for 30 grants to individuals.
Purpose and activities: Primarily local giving; scholarships to student nurses for tuition and expenses; support also for schools of nursing, and The McFarland Medical Trust.
Types of support awarded: Student aid.
Limitations: Giving primarily in central IL.
Publications: Application guidelines.
Application information: Application is mailed to applicant by Director of Nursing Services. Application form required.
    Deadline(s): May 1
    Board meeting date(s): June
Trustee: Havana National Bank (F.S. Cook, Jr., Trust Officer).
Employer Identification Number: 376022376

1093

McGaw (Foster G.) Foundation ⌉
c/o The Northern Trust Company
50 S. LaSalle St.
Chicago 60675   (312) 461-7560

Trust established in 1970 in Illinois.
Donor(s): Foster G. McGaw.
Financial data: (yr. ended 12/31/82): Assets, $2,662,862 (M); expenditures, $222,118, including $205,500 for 92 grants (high: $24,000; low: $100).
Purpose and activities: Primarily local giving, with emphasis on higher education, Protestant church support and religious associations, social service agencies, and economic and public policy studies.
Limitations: Giving primarily in IL.
Trustee: The Northern Trust Company.
Employer Identification Number: 366031834

1094

McGraw Foundation ▼
3436 North Kennicott Ave.
Arlington Heights 60004   (312) 870-8014
Mailing address: P.O. Box 307 B, Wheeling, IL 60090

Incorporated in 1948 in Illinois.
Donor(s): Alfred Bersted,† Carol Jean Root, Maxine Elrod,† Donald S. Elrod, Max McGraw,† Richard F. McGraw,† McGraw-Edison Co., and others.
Financial data: (yr. ended 12/31/83): Assets, $11,482,334 (M); gifts received, $92,569; expenditures, $695,092, including $559,889 for 73 grants (high: $39,000; low: $500; average: $3,000-$25,000).
Purpose and activities: Broad purposes; general giving, primarily for higher education, youth agencies, hospitals, and medical research, child welfare, cultural programs, and the handicapped.
Types of support awarded: Operating budgets, annual campaigns, building funds, equipment, fellowships, scholarship funds, research, matching funds, seed money, continuing support, employee related scholarships.
Limitations: Giving limited to organizations in the U.S. No grants to individuals (except fellowships relating to specific program areas), or for endowment funds; no loans.
Publications: Program policy statement, application guidelines.
Application information:
   Initial approach: Letter
   Copies of proposal: 1
   Deadline(s): Submit proposal between December 1 and February 1
   Board meeting date(s): June; contribution committee meets annually in March
   Final notification: 30 days to 1 year
   Write: James F. Quilter, Vice-President

Officers and Directors: Scott M. Elrod, President; James F. Quilter, Vice-President, Secretary, Treasurer, and Executive Director; William W. Mauritz, Vice-President; Dennis Fitzgerald, Raymond H. Giesecke, Jerry D. Jones, Catherine Nelson, Bernard B. Rinella, Leah K. Robson.
Number of staff: 1 part-time professional; 1 part-time support.
Employer Identification Number: 362490000

1095

McGraw-Edison Foundation ⌉
1701 Golf Rd.
Rolling Meadows 60008

Established in 1981.
Financial data: (yr. ended 12/31/83): Assets, $194,481 (M); gifts received, $31,500; expenditures, $661,951, including $659,848 for 401 grants (high: $179,037; low: $25).
Purpose and activities: Support for higher education, hospitals, youth and social agencies, cultural programs, and community funds.
Officers: Edward J. Williams, President; George L. Faulstich, William R. Rawson, Vice-Presidents; Nancy Yde, Secretary.
Employer Identification Number: 363116163

1096

Mellinger (Edward Arthur) Educational Foundation, Inc.
1025 East Broadway
P.O. Box 278
Monmouth 61462   (309) 734-2419

Incorporated in 1959 in Delaware.
Donor(s): Mrs. Inez M. Hensleigh.†
Financial data: (yr. ended 12/31/84): Assets, $9,415,526 (M); expenditures, $863,313, including $264,813 for 947 grants to individuals and $353,575 for 323 loans.
Purpose and activities: Scholarships for undergraduate college students and loans primarily to graduate students. Giving only to students residing in or attending college in the Midwest.
Types of support awarded: Student aid.
Limitations: Giving limited to students residing in or attending college in the Midwest.
Publications: Application guidelines, program policy statement.
Application information: Application form required.
   Initial approach: Letter
   Deadline(s): Submit proposal preferably from February through May; deadline June 1
   Board meeting date(s): Scholarship committee meets in July
   Final notification: 1 month after meeting
Officers and Trustees: Lloyd C. Stevenson, President; David D. Fleming, Arthur W. Murray, II, Merle R. Yontz, Vice-Presidents; Tom Johnson, Secretary; William G. Hart, Lawrence C. Stevenson, Jackie D. Upton.
Number of staff: 6.
Employer Identification Number: 362428421

1097

Meyer-Ceco Foundation, The ⌉
1400 Kensington Rd.
Oak Brook 60521

Trust established in 1946 in Nebraska.
Donor(s): C. Louis Meyer, Ceco Steel Products Corporation.
Financial data: (yr. ended 12/31/83): Assets, $2,523,863 (M); gifts received, $200,000; expenditures, $215,480, including $209,650 for 125 grants (high: $29,000; low: $100).
Purpose and activities: Charitable purposes; general giving, with emphasis on higher education, community funds, hospitals, youth agencies, and civic affairs.
Limitations: Giving primarily in IL.
Trustees: Mrs. Joseph L. Davidson, Heidi Hall Jones, Ned A. Ochiltree, Jr.
Employer Identification Number: 366053404

1098

Millard (Adah K.) Charitable Trust ⌉
c/o The Northern Trust Company
50 South LaSalle St.
Chicago 60675   (312) 444-3856

Trust established in 1976 in Illinois.
Donor(s): Adah K. Millard.†
Financial data: (yr. ended 12/31/83): Assets, $3,067,870 (M); expenditures, $235,113, including $214,241 for 16 grants (high: $24,741; low: $1,000).
Purpose and activities: Giving restricted to Omaha and Douglas county, Nebraska, with emphasis on youth agencies, social welfare groups, and cultural programs.
Types of support awarded: General purposes, continuing support, seed money, building funds, equipment.
Limitations: Giving limited to Omaha and Douglas counties, NE. No grants to individuals, or for endowment funds, scholarships, fellowships, or matching gifts; generally no grants for operating budgets; no loans.
Publications: Application guidelines.
Application information:
   Initial approach: Letter or full proposal
   Copies of proposal: 6
   Deadline(s): February 28, and September 30
   Board meeting date(s): April and November
   Final notification: 6 months
   Write: John C. Goodall, Jr., Vice-President
Trustee: The Northern Trust Company.
Number of staff: None.
Employer Identification Number: 366629069

1099

Millikin (James) Trust ▼
P.O. Box 1278
Decatur 62525   (217) 424-6327

Trust established in 1910 in Illinois.
Donor(s): James Millikin.†
Financial data: (yr. ended 12/31/83): Assets, $9,434,493 (M); expenditures, $683,025, including $577,213 for 8 grants (high: $380,000; low: $2,000; average: $2,000-$100,000).

Purpose and activities: Primarily local giving, with emphasis on a university and a hospital; grants also for a community fund and youth organizations.
Types of support awarded: Operating budgets.
Limitations: Giving primarily in Decatur, IL.
Application information:
   Initial approach: Proposal
   Deadline(s): None
   Board meeting date(s): 3rd Wednesday of each month
   Write: R. Wayne Gill, Secretary
Officer: R. Wayne Gill, Secretary.
Trustees: Wayne S. Martin, Chairman; Hugh L. Baker, G. William Harner, Jack Hunter, James W. Moore, Bernard Wright.
Number of staff: None.
Employer Identification Number: 370661226

1100
Monticello College Foundation, The
The Evergreens
Godfrey 62035   (618) 466-7911

Incorporated in 1843 in Illinois as Monticello College; reorganized as a foundation in 1971.
Financial data: (yr. ended 6/30/83): Assets, $5,675,453 (M); expenditures, $362,388, including $314,694 for 23 grants (high: $160,000; low: $1,000).
Purpose and activities: Support for programs that assist advancing education for women.
Types of support awarded: Scholarship funds, special projects, fellowships, internships.
Limitations: No support for social service agencies, foreign schools, or foreign-based American schools. No grants to individuals, or for capital funds, operating expenses, endowed chairs, conferences and seminars, or exchange students.
Publications: Annual report, program policy statement, application guidelines.
Application information:
   Initial approach: Full proposal
   Copies of proposal: 14
   Deadline(s): Submit proposal preferably in July or February; deadline 8 weeks before board meeting
   Board meeting date(s): Third week of September and April
   Final notification: 2 weeks after board meeting
   Write: Winifred G. Delano, Executive Director
Officers: Mrs. Vaughan Morrill,* Secretary; Karl K. Hoagland, Jr.,* Treasurer; Winifred G. Delano, Executive Director.
Trustees:* Harry N. Schweppe, Jr., Chairman; Mrs. William J. Barnard, Vice-Chairman; Robert R. Anschuetz, M.D., Mrs. Robert R. Anschuetz, Mrs. Leland F. Kreid, Jr., Mrs. Robert H. Levis II, Nancy C. McCaig, M. Ryrie Milnor, Mrs. John C. Pritzlaff, Jr.
Number of staff: 1 part-time professional.
Employer Identification Number: 370681538

1101
Moorman Company Fund ▼
1000 North 30th St.
Quincy 62301-3496   (217) 222-7100

Incorporated in 1952 in Illinois.
Donor(s): Moorman Manufacturing Company.
Financial data: (yr. ended 12/31/83): Assets, $1,499,805 (M); gifts received, $250,000; expenditures, $503,285, including $498,300 for 107 grants (high: $79,286; low: $100; average: $100-$16,000).
Purpose and activities: Limited mainly to local and community activities in areas where the company has facilities; general giving, with emphasis on higher education, educational associations, community funds, youth agencies, health associations, hospitals, and welfare organizations; support for local colleges and land-grant universities in company's market area for scholarships in agriculture.
Types of support awarded: Scholarship funds, operating budgets, general purposes, building funds, equipment.
Limitations: Giving limited to areas of company operations, with emphasis on Adams County, IL. No grants to individuals.
Application information:
   Initial approach: Letter
   Deadline(s): None
   Board meeting date(s): Third Wednesday of each month
   Write: C.F. Bearden, Secretary
Officers: C. Dean Thomas,* President; C.F. Bearden, Secretary; R.K. McClelland,* Treasurer.
Directors:* S. Kent Adams, H.C. Eaton, Robert B. Hulsen, H.D. Hutchinson, R.S. Kilbride, Richard A. Liebig, T.L. Shade.
Number of staff: None.
Employer Identification Number: 376026253

1102
Moorman Foundation, The ▼ ⌑
Illinois State Bank Bldg., Rm. 605
Quincy 62301   (217) 222-8636

Incorporated in 1942 in Illinois.
Donor(s): C.A. Moorman,† Mrs. C.A. Moorman,† Moorman Manufacturing Company.
Financial data: (yr. ended 3/31/83): Assets, $41,827,026 (M); expenditures, $2,948,050, including $2,923,000 for 18 grants (high: $800,000; low: $6,300).
Purpose and activities: Foundation has applied for change in status; giving currently limited to specified list of 29 organizations, with emphasis on higher education, medical institutions, youth agencies, social services, and a hospital.
Types of support awarded: Special projects, building funds, operating budgets, equipment.
Limitations: Giving primarily in IL. No grants to individuals, or for endowments, ongoing programs, or capital expansion; no loans.
Application information: Applications not invited.
   Write: Robert H. Langerhans, Executive Director

Officers and Directors: Richard A. Liebig, President; Elmer H. Wilson, Vice-President; Jean B. Suhren, Secretary; Douglas A. Dulaney, Treasurer; Robert H. Langerhans, Executive Director; Harry C. Eaton, Robert B. Hulsen, Carl G. Schmiedeskamp, Ross Warden, Earl Zenge.
Employer Identification Number: 376026254

1103
Morton (The Sterling) Charitable Trust ⌑
c/o The Northern Trust Company
50 South LaSalle St.
Chicago 60675

Trust established in 1958 in Illinois.
Donor(s): Sterling Morton,† The Morton Fund.
Financial data: (yr. ended 12/31/83): Assets, $13,899,448 (M); expenditures, $690,475, including $644,500 for 35 grants (high: $170,000; low: $200).
Purpose and activities: Broad purposes; giving primarily in Chicago and Santa Barbara, California, with emphasis on higher education, cultural institutions, including museums, and hospitals.
Limitations: Giving primarily in Chicago, IL, and Santa Barbara, CA.
Trustees: Suzette M. Davidson, Charles C. Haffner III, Northern Trust Company.
Employer Identification Number: 366065833

1104
Motorola Foundation ▼
1303 East Algonquin Rd.
Schaumburg 60196   (312) 576-6200

Incorporated in 1953 in Illinois.
Donor(s): Motorola Inc.
Financial data: (yr. ended 12/31/83): Assets, $3,926,119 (M); gifts received, $1,500,000; expenditures, $1,525,690, including $1,349,000 for 356 grants (high: $130,000; low: $100) and $167,073 for 374 employee matching gifts.
Purpose and activities: Broad purposes; general giving primarily in major plant communities, with emphasis on community funds, higher education, including an employee matching gifts program, and hospitals; support also for cultural programs.
Types of support awarded: Operating budgets, seed money, building funds, scholarship funds, employee matching gifts, fellowships, general purposes, continuing support.
Limitations: Giving primarily in communities where the company has major facilities, with emphasis on IL and AZ. No support for strictly sectarian or denominational religious organizations, national health organizations or their local chapters; secondary schools, trade schools, or state institutions. No grants to individuals, or for endowment funds, research, benefit events, courtesy advertising, operating expenses of organizations receiving United Way funding, or capital fund drives of colleges or universities; no loans.

Publications: Informational brochure, application guidelines, program policy statement, grants list.
Application information:
Initial approach: Letter, telephone, or full proposal
Copies of proposal: 1
Deadline(s): October (for capital requests)
Board meeting date(s): December and as required
Final notification: 2 to 3 months
Write: Marilyn J. Doyle, Assistant Director
Officers and Directors:* Robert W. Galvin,* President; John T. Hickey,* Vice-President and Executive Director; Victor R. Kopidlansky, Secretary; Donald R. Jones, Treasurer.
Number of staff: 1 full-time professional.
Employer Identification Number: 366109323

1105
Nalco Foundation, The ▼
2901 Butterfield Rd.
Oak Brook 60521   (312) 887-7500

Incorporated in 1953 in Illinois.
Donor(s): Nalco Chemical Company.
Financial data: (yr. ended 12/31/83): Assets, $2,194,672 (M); expenditures, $1,653,805, including $1,640,910 for 266 grants (high: $59,500; low: $250; average: $500-$5,000).
Purpose and activities: General purposes; grants largely for private institutions of higher education, community funds, youth agencies, hospitals, health agencies, and cultural activities, including museums, generally in geographic areas where the company is involved.
Types of support awarded: Operating budgets, continuing support, annual campaigns, seed money, emergency funds, building funds, equipment, land acquisition.
Limitations: Giving primarily in areas of company operations. No support for state-supported colleges or universities, political activities, secondary or elementary schools, churches, or religious education. No grants to individuals, or for endowments, research, scholarships, fellowships, or matching gifts; no loans.
Publications: Annual report, application guidelines, program policy statement.
Application information:
Initial approach: Full proposal
Copies of proposal: 1
Deadline(s): Submit proposal preferably in January, April, July, or September; deadline October 1
Board meeting date(s): Quarterly
Final notification: 3 to 6 months
Write: Ms. Rita J. Secor, President
Officers: Rita J. Secor,* President; Clifford J. Carpenter, Vice-President and Treasurer; Pauline A. Russ, Secretary.
Directors:* Lloyd J. Palmer.
Number of staff: 1 full-time professional; 1 full-time support.
Employer Identification Number: 366065864

1106
National Institute for the Food Service Industry
20 North Wacker Dr.
Chicago 60606   (312) 782-1703

Established in 1971 in Illinois.
Financial data: (yr. ended 12/31/83): Assets, $861,660 (M); gifts received, $644,850; expenditures, $716,099, including $172,500 for 150 grants to individuals.
Purpose and activities: A private operating foundation which "develops courses, programs, and textbooks on topics related to the food service industry." Grants to individuals for scholarships and fellowships for the food service field, as well as work-study grants to teachers and administrators.
Types of support awarded: Student aid, fellowships.
Publications: Application guidelines, program policy statement.
Application information: Application form required.
Deadline(s): April 1 for fellowships and scholarships; December 31 for work-study grants
Officers: Richard Hauer, Executive Director; Harold Kelly, Director of Operations; Paul F. Martin, Director of Instructional Planning; Charles Sandler, Director of Educational Information.
Employer Identification Number: 366103388

1107
New Prospect Foundation
7450 North McCormick Blvd.
Skokie 60076
Additional address: 86 Prospect, Highland Park, IL 60035

Established in 1969 in Illinois.
Donor(s): Elliot Lehman, Frances Lehman, Fel-Pro Incorporated.
Financial data: (yr. ended 12/31/84): Assets, $4,158,073 (M); gifts received, $631,700; expenditures, $329,712, including $311,695 for 103 grants (high: $42,500; low: $25; average: $2,500-$4,000).
Purpose and activities: Support for activities directed toward the improvement of housing, employment, health, welfare, and the economic viability of urban and inner city neighborhoods, specifically in the Chicago metropolitan area. Funding priority given to organizations with modest budgets that may not qualify for traditional sources of financial assistance; also supports efforts undertaken in the public interest.
Types of support awarded: General purposes, operating budgets, continuing support, seed money, emergency funds, special projects, matching funds.
Limitations: Giving limited to the Chicago, IL, metropolitan area. Generally no funding for the arts or higher education. No grants to individuals, or for capital or endowment funds, basic research, scholarships, or fellowships; no loans.
Publications: Application guidelines, program policy statement.
Application information:

Initial approach: Letter, full proposal, or telephone
Copies of proposal: 1
Deadline(s): 1 month before board meetings
Board meeting date(s): March, June, October, and December
Final notification: 3 months
Write: Frances Lehman, President
Officer and Directors: Frances Lehman, President; Elliot Lehman, Kenneth Lehman, Lucy Lehman, Paul Lehman, Ronna Stamm Lehman, Kay Schlozman, Stanley Schlozman.
Number of staff: 1 part-time professional.
Employer Identification Number: 237032384

1108
Northern Trust Company Charitable Trust, The ▼
50 South LaSalle St.
Chicago 60675   (312) 444-3538

Trust established in 1966 in Illinois.
Donor(s): The Northern Trust Company.
Financial data: (yr. ended 12/31/84): Assets, $839,322 (M); expenditures, $983,899, including $827,236 for 200 grants (high: $67,500; low: $100; average: $2,000-$5,000) and $152,803 for 915 employee matching gifts.
Purpose and activities: Broad purposes; local giving with emphasis on community organizations, higher education, hospitals and health, civic and cultural programs, and welfare agencies.
Types of support awarded: Operating budgets, continuing support, annual campaigns, seed money, emergency funds, building funds, equipment, land acquisition, employee matching gifts, consulting services, technical assistance, special projects.
Limitations: Giving limited to the metropolitan Chicago, IL, area and locations of company subsidiaries. No support for national organizations, elementary or secondary schools, or health organizations concentrating efforts in one area of human disease. No grants to individuals, or for scholarships or fellowships; no loans. Grants rarely for endowment funds.
Publications: Application guidelines, 990-PF, annual report.
Application information:
Initial approach: Brief proposal
Copies of proposal: 1
Deadline(s): Hospitals: end of calendar year for March consideration; Universities: end of March for June consideration
Board meeting date(s): Bimonthly
Final notification: 2 months
Write: Marjorie W. Lundy, Second Vice-President
Contributions Committee: William N. Setterstrom, Chairman; Kathleen M. Almaney, Donald H. Choate, Buell C. Cole, Beverly M. Glenn, Susan R. Hunt, William E. McClintic, Perry R. Pero, Sue A. Rageas.
Trustee: The Northern Trust Company (Marjorie W. Lundy, Second Vice-President).
Number of staff: 1 part-time professional; 1 full-time support; 1 part-time support.
Employer Identification Number: 366147253

1109
Northwest Industries Foundation, Inc. ▼
6300 Sears Tower
Chicago 60606 (312) 876-7000

Incorporated in 1958 in New York.
Donor(s): Northwest Industries, Inc., and subsidiaries.
Financial data: (yr. ended 12/31/83): Assets, $702,508 (M); gifts received, $1,089,250; expenditures, $805,849, including $724,334 for 279 grants (high: $50,000; low: $100; average: $1,000-$15,000) and $78,406 for 423 employee matching gifts.
Purpose and activities: Broad purposes; general giving in areas of company operations, particularly locally, and to national organizations; emphasis on higher education, community funds, cultural programs, civic affairs, social services, hospitals, and youth agencies.
Types of support awarded: Operating budgets, continuing support, annual campaigns, building funds, employee matching gifts, scholarship funds, fellowships, research, special projects.
Limitations: Giving limited to areas of company operations, with some emphasis on the Chicago, IL, metropolitan area, and to national organizations. No grants to individuals; no loans.
Publications: Program policy statement, application guidelines.
Application information:
Initial approach: Full proposal
Copies of proposal: 1
Deadline(s): None
Board meeting date(s): As required
Final notification: 3 months
Write: Jerome B. Scherer, Assistant Treasurer
Officers and Directors:* Ben W. Heineman,* President; Brendan M. O'Neill,* Vice-President; R.J. Hill, Secretary; Bernard Firestone,* Treasurer.
Number of staff: None.
Employer Identification Number: 136100754

1110
Offield Family Foundation, The ⌑
(formerly Dorothy Wrigley Offield Charity Fund, Inc.)
410 North Michigan Ave., Rm. 942
Chicago 60611

Incorporated in 1940 in Illinois.
Donor(s): Dorothy Wrigley Offield.
Financial data: (yr. ended 6/30/83): Assets, $10,197,198 (M); gifts received, $60,000; expenditures, $651,896, including $591,586 for 35 grants (high: $107,337; low: $500).
Purpose and activities: Broad purposes; primarily local giving, with emphasis on hospitals, a population control agency, education, and cultural programs.
Limitations: Giving primarily in Chicago, IL area and MI. No grants to individuals.
Officers and Directors: Wrigley Offield, President; Edna Jean Offield, Vice-President; Marie Larson, Secretary; James E. Elworth, Treasurer; James S. Offield, Paxson H. Offield.
Employer Identification Number: 366066240

1111
Oppenheimer Family Foundation, The ⌑
One IBM Plaza, Suite 4500
Chicago 60606

Incorporated in 1953 in Illinois.
Donor(s): Seymour Oppenheimer.
Financial data: (yr. ended 12/31/83): Assets, $1,771,187 (M); expenditures, $149,532, including $134,400 for 48 grants (high: $10,000; low: $500).
Purpose and activities: Primarily local giving, with emphasis on medical research, hospitals, and education.
Limitations: Giving primarily in IL.
Officers and Directors: Edward Oppenheimer, President; James Oppenheimer, Vice-President; Harry D. Oppenheimer, Vice-President-Treasurer.
Employer Identification Number: 366054015

1112
Page (The Ruth) Foundation ⌑
c/o Jenner & Block
One IBM Plaza
Chicago 60611

Incorporated in 1970 in Illinois.
Donor(s): Ruth Page.
Financial data: (yr. ended 6/30/83): Assets, $3,787,728 (M); gifts received, $145,850; expenditures, $457,862, including $2,240 for 6 grants (high: $1,000; low: $50) and $438,692 for foundation-administered programs.
Purpose and activities: A private operating foundation to develop ballet as an art, including the training and education of ballet dancers and choreographers and the production of ballet performances.
Officers and Directors: Ruth Page, President and Treasurer; Jerold S. Solovy, Vice-President and Secretary; Ronald I. Reicin.
Employer Identification Number: 237069159

1113
Payne (Frank E.) and Seba B. Payne Foundation ▼
Continental Illinois National Bank and Trust Company of Chicago
30 North LaSalle St.
Chicago 60697 (312) 828-8026

Trust established in 1962 in Illinois.
Donor(s): Seba B. Payne.†
Financial data: (yr. ended 6/30/83): Assets, $39,800,629 (M); expenditures, $1,647,399, including $1,510,260 for 36 grants (high: $305,000; low: $1,000; average: $5,000-$15,000).
Purpose and activities: Broad purposes; local giving and in Pennsylvania, primarily for education, hospitals, and cultural programs.
Types of support awarded: Equipment, operating budgets, building funds, general purposes.
Limitations: Giving primarily in the metropolitan Chicago, IL, area and PA. No grants to individuals, or for endowment funds, or fellowships; no loans.
Publications: Application guidelines.
Application information:
Initial approach: Proposal
Copies of proposal: 1
Deadline(s): None
Board meeting date(s): Generally in spring and fall, and as required
Final notification: 4 months
Write: A.W. Murray
Trustees: Susan Hurd Cumings, George A. Hurd, Sr., Priscilla Payne Hurd, Charles M. Nisen, Continental Illinois National Bank and Trust Company of Chicago.
Number of staff: None.
Employer Identification Number: 237435471

1114
Pearson (The Patsy) Memorial Fund ⌑
c/o Alton W. Potter
20110 Governors Dr.
Olympia Fields 60461

Incorporated in 1927 in Illinois.
Donor(s): Harry C. Pearson,† Ferne L. Pearson.†
Financial data: (yr. ended 12/31/83): Assets, $1,056,833 (M); expenditures, $46,398, including $36,000 for 1 grant.
Purpose and activities: Broad purposes; support for religious organizations, including missionary programs and Bible studies.
Officers and Directors: John W. Harper, President; Alton W. Potter, Secretary; W. Gordon Haresign, Treasurer.
Employer Identification Number: 366131031

1115
Perkins (Kitty M.) Foundation
c/o Kent Lawrence
209 South LaSalle St., Rm. 777
Chicago 60604 (312) 372-1947

Incorporated in 1966 in Illinois.
Donor(s): Edwin E. Perkins,† Kitty M. Perkins.†
Financial data: (yr. ended 12/31/82): Assets, $4,519,386 (M); expenditures, $77,504, including $50,000 for 3 grants (high: $32,000; low: $3,000).
Purpose and activities: Broad purposes; grants largely for two hospitals in Minnesota and Nebraska, and for higher education and medical research.
Limitations: No grants to individuals or for matching gifts; no loans.
Application information: Grant applications not encouraged.
Board meeting date(s): Semiannually
Officers and Directors: Ome C. Shoemaker, President; Kent Lawrence, William Shoemaker, Vice-Presidents; A. Charles Lawrence, Secretary and Treasurer; Robert J. Lawrence, George Franklin Shoemaker.
Employer Identification Number: 366154399

1116
Perlman (Louis & Anita) Family Foundation ⌑
P.O. Box 96
Arlington Heights 60006

Established in 1969.

Financial data: (yr. ended 12/31/83): Assets, $842,330 (M); gifts received, $25,000; expenditures, $143,410, including $139,850 for 18 grants (high: $30,000; low: $100).
Purpose and activities: Giving primarily locally and in Ft. Lauderdale, Florida, for Jewish welfare funds and higher education.
Limitations: Giving primarily in IL and Ft. Lauderdale, FL.
Officers: Anita M. Perlman, President and Treasurer; Theodore F. Perlman, Vice-President and Secretary.
Employer Identification Number: 362670190

1117
Peterborough Foundation
c/o Edwin H. Watkins, Manager
333 West Wacker Dr.
Chicago 60606 (312) 321-2607

Established in 1979 in Illinois.
Financial data: (yr. ended 12/31/83): Assets, $578,121 (M); gifts received, $368,000; expenditures, $397,476, including $375,557 for 28 grants (high: $150,000; low: $500).
Purpose and activities: Broad purposes; grants primarily for education, cultural programs, and health; support also for a wildlife organization.
Types of support awarded: Endowment funds, annual campaigns, general purposes, research, special projects, operating budgets, continuing support, seed money, building funds.
Limitations: No grants to individuals, or for emergency funds, deficit financing, equipment, land acquisition, renovation projects, publications, conferences, scholarships, fellowships, or matching gifts; no loans.
Application information:
Initial approach: Letter or full proposal
Copies of proposal: 1
Deadline(s): None
Board meeting date(s): As required
Final notification: 6 months
Write: Royall Victor or John Pirovano, Trustees
Trustees: John Pirovano, Royall Victor.
Manager: Edwin H. Watkins.
Number of staff: None.
Employer Identification Number: 363013372

1118
Petersen (Esper A.) Foundation ⌑
c/o Bertha Matthews
4241 Kirk St.
Skokie 60076 (312) 677-0049

Incorporated in 1944 in Illinois.
Donor(s): Esper A. Petersen.†
Financial data: (yr. ended 12/31/83): Assets, $4,450,205 (M); expenditures, $340,468, including $160,009 for 25 grants (high: $35,000; low: $70) and $25,349 for grants to individuals.
Purpose and activities: General giving, primarily in Illinois and California, with emphasis on higher education, including local scholarships, a community fund, heart research, and aid to the handicapped.
Types of support awarded: General purposes, research, building funds, student aid.
Limitations: Giving primarily in IL and CA.
Publications: Program policy statement, application guidelines.
Application information: Application form required.
Initial approach: Letter
Deadline(s): January 1
Write: Bertha Matthews
Directors: Ann S. Christie, Daniel H. Foster, Stephen A. Malato, Bertha Matthews, Anna M. Petersen, Esper A. Petersen, Jr.
Employer Identification Number: 366125570

1119
Pick (The Albert), Jr. Fund
30 North Michigan Ave., Suite 819
Chicago 60602 (312) 236-1192

Incorporated in 1947 in Illinois.
Donor(s): Albert Pick, Jr.†
Financial data: (yr. ended 12/31/83): Assets, $7,458,880 (M); gifts received, $1,500; expenditures, $603,422, including $481,340 for 145 grants (high: $30,000; low: $1,000; average: $2,000-$5,000).
Purpose and activities: Primarily local giving for cultural programs, education, health and social services, community organizations, and civic affairs.
Types of support awarded: Operating budgets, emergency funds, special projects, student aid, seed money.
Limitations: Giving primarily in Chicago, IL. No support for religious purposes. No grants to individuals, or for building or endowment funds, advertising, deficit financing, long-term projects, or advertising.
Publications: Program policy statement, application guidelines.
Application information:
Initial approach: Brief proposal
Copies of proposal: 1
Deadline(s): February 1, April 1, July 1, October 1
Board meeting date(s): March or April, June, September, December, and as required
Write: Nadine Van Sant, Executive Director
Officers and Directors: Corinne F. Pick, President; Alan J. Altheimer, Albert Pick III, Vice-Presidents; Nadine Van Sant, Executive Director and Secretary; Ralph Lewy, Treasurer; Arthur W. Brown, Jr., Edward Neisser.
Employer Identification Number: 366071402

1120
Pittway Corporation Charitable Foundation ⌑
333 Skokie Blvd.
P.O. Box 602
Northbrook 60062

Established in 1966 in Illinois.
Financial data: (yr. ended 2/29/84): Assets, $4,646,441 (M); gifts received, $1,000,000; expenditures, $1,176,532, including $901,949 for 135 grants (high: $250,000; low: $100) and $265,229 for employee matching gifts.
Purpose and activities: Broad purposes; support for higher education, health associations, community funds, and social agencies, including child welfare organizations; support also for an early childhood education institute, and cultural programs.
Limitations: Giving primarily in IL. No grants to individuals.
Application information:
Deadline(s): None
Write: Paul R. Gauvreau, Treasurer
Officers: Neison Harris,* President; Peter E. Downing, Secretary; Paul R. Gauvreau, Treasurer.
Directors:* Irving B. Harris, Chairman; Sidney Barrows, Edwin A. Bergman, Maurice Fulton, William W. Harris.
Employer Identification Number: 366149938

1121
Polk Brothers Foundation, Inc. ▼ ⌑
8311 West North Ave.
Melrose Park 60160 (312) 287-1011

Incorporated in 1957 in Illinois.
Donor(s): Members of the Polk family, Rand Realty and Development Co., Polk Brothers, Inc., and others.
Financial data: (yr. ended 12/31/83): Assets, $13,203,874 (M); expenditures, $536,760, including $477,543 for 1,045 grants (high: $100,000; low: $35; average: $50-$5,000).
Purpose and activities: Broad purposes; primarily local giving, with emphasis on social service and health agencies, including the handicapped and hospitals, Jewish welfare funds and religious organizations, and higher education.
Limitations: Giving primarily in the Chicago, IL, area.
Application information:
Initial approach: Letter
Officers: Sol Polk, President; Morris G. Polk, Secretary and Treasurer.
Employer Identification Number: 366108293

1122
Prince (Abbie Norman) Trust ⌑
First National Plaza, Rm. 4950
Chicago 60603

Established in 1949 in Illinois.
Financial data: (yr. ended 12/31/83): Assets, $8,676,354 (M); expenditures, $777,161, including $717,650 for 66 grants (high: $75,000; low: $250).
Purpose and activities: General purposes; support for higher and secondary education, cultural programs, hospitals, youth organizations, and social services, with some emphasis on the Chicago area.
Trustees: Charles S. Potter, William Wood Prince.
Employer Identification Number: 362411865

1123
Prince Foundation ¤
One First National Plaza, Rm. 4950
Chicago 60603

Incorporated in 1955 in Illinois.
Donor(s): Central Manufacturing Distributors, Produce Terminal Corporation, Union Stock Fund & Transit Company.
Financial data: (yr. ended 12/31/82): Assets, $1,018,516 (M); expenditures, $206,232, including $197,365 for 10 grants (high: $82,500; low: $1,000).
Purpose and activities: Support primarily for higher education and a community fund.
Officers: William Wood Prince,* President; Thomas S. Tyler,* Secretary; Charles E. Hanley, Treasurer.
Trustees:* David J. Hardy.
Employer Identification Number: 366116507

1124
Pritzker Foundation ▼
Two First National Plaza, 30th Fl.
Chicago 60603   (312) 621-4200

Incorporated in 1944 in Illinois.
Donor(s): Members of the Pritzker family.
Financial data: (yr. ended 12/31/82): Assets, $5,068,803 (M); gifts received, $31,379; expenditures, $3,105,922, including $3,000,842 for 258 grants (high: $923,200; low: $10).
Purpose and activities: Grants largely for higher education, including medical education and religious welfare funds; giving also for hospitals, temple support, and cultural programs.
Limitations: No grants to individuals.
Application information: Funds fully committed, applications not accepted.
    Board meeting date(s): December and as required
    Write: Simon Zunamon
Officers: A.N. Pritzker, President; Robert A. Pritzker, Vice-President; Nicholas Pritzker, Secretary; Thomas Pritzker, Treasurer.
Number of staff: None.
Employer Identification Number: 366058062

1125
Pullman (George M.) Educational Foundation
5020 South Lake Shore Dr.
Chicago 60615   (312) 363-6191

Incorporated in 1949 in Illinois.
Donor(s): George Mortimer Pullman,† Harriet Sanger Pullman.†
Financial data: (yr. ended 7/31/83): Assets, $11,507,463 (M); expenditures, $700,433, including $2,250 for 1 grant and $477,603 for 629 grants to individuals.

Purpose and activities: From 1915 to 1950 the income of this fund was used to operate the Pullman Free School of Manual Training. The Foundation, as successor of the School, has focused its resources on college scholarships. Any resident of Cook County, Illinois or child or grandchild of graduates of the Pullman Free School of Manual Training is eligible for consideration.
Types of support awarded: Student aid.
Limitations: Giving limited to IL.
Publications: Biennial report, informational brochure.
Application information: Application form required.
    Board meeting date(s): Semiannually
    Write: John H. Munger, Executive Director
Officers: Phillip Lowden Miller,* President; Warner A. Wick,* Secretary; Robert C. McCormack, Treasurer; John H. Munger, Executive Director.
Directors:* Edward McCormick Blair, Florence Lowden Miller, Warren Pullman Miller, Harry M. Oliver, Jr., Rev. Sam A. Portaro, Jr., George A. Ranney, Jr., John S. Runnells.
Employer Identification Number: 362216171

1126
Quaker Oats Foundation, The ▼
345 Merchandise Mart Plaza
Chicago 60654   (312) 222-7033

Incorporated in 1947 in Illinois.
Donor(s): The Quaker Oats Company.
Financial data: (yr. ended 6/30/83): Assets, $2,013 (M); gifts received, $2,000,000; expenditures, $2,131,519, including $1,423,097 for 263 grants (high: $129,875; low: $500; average: $1,000-$10,000) and $706,838 for 2,158 employee matching gifts.
Purpose and activities: Broad purposes; general giving in areas of company operations, with emphasis on higher education, including scholarship and employee matching gifts programs, and guaranteeing of loans through United Student Aid Funds (USAF); civic affairs, community funds, youth agencies, hospitals, arts and culture, child development, economics and public policy.
Types of support awarded: General purposes, building funds, equipment, land acquisition, internships, scholarship funds, employee related scholarships, fellowships, employee matching gifts, operating budgets, special projects, matching funds, annual campaigns, publications, conferences and seminars, continuing support.
Limitations: Giving primarily in areas of company operations, particularly IL. No support for religious organizations. No grants to individuals or for advertising; no loans, except for USAF program.
Publications: Annual report, informational brochure, application guidelines, program policy statement.
Application information:
    Initial approach: Proposal
    Copies of proposal: 1
    Deadline(s): None
    Board meeting date(s): September, December, March, and June
    Final notification: 6 to 8 weeks

Write: W. Thomas Phillips, Secretary
Officers: Frank J. Morgan,* President; Luther C. McKinney,* Vice-President; W. Thomas Phillips, Secretary; Richard D. Jaquith, Treasurer.
Directors:* William D. Smithburg, Chairman; William J. Kennedy III, Vernon R. Loucks, Jr., Kenneth Mason, Gertrude G. Michelson, Walter J. Salmon.
Number of staff: 1 full-time professional; 1 full-time support; 2 part-time support.
Employer Identification Number: 366084548

1127
Quarrie (William F., Mabel E., and Margaret K.) Charitable Trust No. 2 ¤
c/o The Northern Trust Company
50 South LaSalle St.
Chicago 60675

Financial data: (yr. ended 12/31/83): Assets, $2,114,691 (M); expenditures, $155,017, including $136,627 for 3 grants (high: $69,947; low: $2,733).
Purpose and activities: Grants mainly to a hospital and a local community foundation.
Limitations: Giving primarily in Chicago, IL, and New York City, NY.
Trustee: The Northern Trust Company.
Employer Identification Number: 366646474

1128
R. F. Foundation
One First National Plaza, Rm. 4700
Chicago 60603   (815) 758-3461
Mailing address: c/o DeKalb AgResearch, Inc., Sycamore Rd., DeKalb, IL 60115

Incorporated in 1953 in Illinois.
Donor(s): Thomas H. Roberts, Thomas H. Roberts, Jr., Eleanor T. Roberts, Mary R. Roberts.
Financial data: (yr. ended 12/31/84): Assets, $3,566,690 (M); expenditures, $164,128, including $150,000 for 11 grants (high: $52,000; low: $500; average: $8,000-$50,000).
Purpose and activities: Broad purposes; primarily local giving, with emphasis on a community health center.
Types of support awarded: Operating budgets, continuing support, annual campaigns, building funds, equipment.
Limitations: Giving primarily in the DeKalb County, IL, area. No grants to individuals, or for seed money, emergency funds, deficit financing, land acquisition, renovations, endowment funds, matching gifts, scholarships, fellowships, special projects, research, publications, or conferences; no loans.
Application information:
    Initial approach: Proposal
    Copies of proposal: 1
    Deadline(s): Submit proposal preferably from August through October
    Board meeting date(s): September and October
    Final notification: By December 31
    Write: H. Blair White, President

Officers and Directors: H. Blair White, President; Mary Eleanor Roberts, Vice-President; Charles C. Roberts, Secretary; Thomas H. Roberts, Jr., Treasurer.
Number of staff: None.
Employer Identification Number: 366069098

1129
Reade Industrial Fund ⌧
c/o Harris Trust and Savings Bank
111 W. Monroe St.
Chicago 60690   (312) 641-6145

Trust established in 1946 in Illinois.
Donor(s): Edith M. Reade.†
Financial data: (yr. ended 12/31/82): Assets, $1,703,400 (M); expenditures, $136,139, including $115,934 for 64 grants to individuals (high: $5,000; low: $80).
Purpose and activities: Grants of up to $5,000 are given only to "individuals of good moral character, who are or have been employed in Industry in the State of Illinois, and who shall by reason of an emergency beyond their control, such as accidental injury, illness of themselves or family members, inability to obtain any employment, or sudden and involuntary cessation of employment, be unable to care for themselves and their spouse and children and be in need of aid."
Types of support awarded: Grants to individuals.
Limitations: Giving limited to IL, particularly to Chicago and its surrounding area.
Application information: Application form required.
  Write: Ellen A. Bechthold, Assistant Vice-President
Trustee: Harris Trust and Savings Bank (Ellen A. Bechthold, Assistant Vice-President).
Employer Identification Number: 366048673

1130
Regenstein Foundation, The ▼
3450 North Kimball Ave.
Chicago 60618   (312) 463-4355

Incorporated in 1950 in Illinois.
Donor(s): Joseph Regenstein,† Helen Regenstein.†
Financial data: (yr. ended 12/31/84): Assets, $61,197,616 (M); gifts received, $110,970; expenditures, $2,617,936, including $2,315,165 for 33 grants (high: $1,500,000; low: $500; average: $500-$1,500,000).
Purpose and activities: Giving primarily for music, art, higher education, and medical research.
Types of support awarded: Building funds, equipment, research, endowment funds, special projects.
Limitations: Giving primarily in the Chicago, IL, metropolitan area. No grants to individuals, or for scholarships, fellowships, annual campaigns, seed money, emergency funds, deficit financing, land acquisition, publications, conferences, matching gifts, or operating support; no loans.
Publications: Program policy statement, application guidelines.

Application information: Most grants made on the initiative of the trustees.
  Initial approach: Letter
  Copies of proposal: 1
  Deadline(s): None
  Board meeting date(s): May and as required
  Final notification: 30 days
  Write: Joseph Regenstein, Jr., President
Officers and Directors: Joseph Regenstein, Jr., President; Betty R. Hartman, Vice-President; John Eggum, Secretary-Treasurer.
Number of staff: 2 full-time professional; 1 full-time support.
Employer Identification Number: 366056362

1131
Relations Foundation ⌧
927 Fischer Ln.
Winnetka 60093

Established in 1969.
Donor(s): Felt Products Manufacturing Co., and others.
Financial data: (yr. ended 12/31/83): Assets, $2,139,068 (M); gifts received, $503,000; expenditures, $231,522, including $193,610 for 72 grants (high: $55,000; low: $100).
Purpose and activities: Giving primarily to Jewish welfare funds; support also for medical research and social service agencies.
Officers: Lewis C. Weinberg, President; Sylvia M. Radon, Vice-President; Barbara Kessler, Secretary; David A. Weinberg, Treasurer.
Employer Identification Number: 237032294

1132
Retirement Research Foundation, The ▼
325 Touhy Ave.
Park Ridge 60068   (312) 823-4133

Incorporated in 1950 in Michigan.
Donor(s): John D. MacArthur.†
Financial data: (yr. ended 12/31/83): Assets, $67,534,152 (M); expenditures, $3,606,605, including $2,383,166 for 63 grants (high: $200,000; low: $3,451; average: $10,000-$75,000).
Purpose and activities: Support principally to improve the quality of life of older persons in the U.S. Priority interests are innovative model projects and research designed to: (1) increase the availability and effectiveness of community programs to maintain older persons in independent living environments; (2) improve the quality of nursing home care; (3) provide volunteer and employment opportunities for the elderly; and (4) seek causes and solutions to significant problems of the aged.
Types of support awarded: Seed money, matching funds, fellowships, research, special projects.
Limitations: Giving limited to the U.S. No grants to individuals, or for construction, general operating expenses of established organizations, endowment or developmental campaigns, emergency funds, deficit financing, land acquisition, publications, conferences, scholarships, media productions, dissertation research, annual campaigns, or renovation projects; no loans.

Publications: Multi-year report, program policy statement, application guidelines.
Application information:
  Initial approach: Letter or full proposal
  Copies of proposal: 3
  Deadline(s): Submit proposal preferably in January, April, or July; deadlines February 1, May 1, and August 1
  Board meeting date(s): January, April, July, and October
  Final notification: 3 months
  Write: Marilyn Hennessy, Executive Director
Officers and Trustees: Edward J. Kelly, President; Thomas P. Rogers, Vice-President, Secretary and Treasurer; Paul D. Doolen, Robert P. Ewing, William T. Kirby, Joe L. Parkin, John F. Santos, Sister Stella Louise, C.S.F.N.; George E. Weaver.
Number of staff: 2 full-time professional; 1 part-time professional; 2 full-time support.
Employer Identification Number: 362429540

1133
Rhoades (Otto L. and Hazel T.) Fund ⌧
c/o Leo J. Carlin
8000 Sears Tower
Chicago 60606

Established in 1978.
Donor(s): Otto L. Rhoades.
Financial data: (yr. ended 12/31/83): Assets, $1,130,820 (M); expenditures, $165,798, including $157,750 for 12 grants (high: $68,750; low: $1,000).
Purpose and activities: Primarily local giving, with an emphasis on religious support, including a Christian communications organization, higher education, and health.
Limitations: Giving primarily in IL.
Officers and Directors: Hazel T. Rhoades, President; Harry M. Coffman, Vice-President; Leo J. Carlin, Secretary-Treasurer.
Employer Identification Number: 362994856

1134
Rice Foundation ⌧
222 Waukegan Rd.
Glenview 60025   (312) 998-6666

Incorporated in 1947 in Illinois.
Donor(s): Daniel F. Rice,† and others.
Financial data: (yr. ended 12/31/83): Assets, $14,292,749 (M); gifts received, $11,308,352; expenditures, $199,843, including $65,100 for 41 grants (high: $7,000; low: $500).
Purpose and activities: Broad purposes; primarily local giving, with emphasis on higher education, including medical education, hospitals, and youth agencies.
Limitations: Giving primarily in IL. No grants to individuals.
Application information:
  Initial approach: Proposal
  Deadline(s): None
  Write: Mr. Arthur A. Nolan, Jr., President
Officers and Directors: Arthur A. Nolan, Jr., President; Beatrice Rice Sheridan, Vice-President; James P. Doherty, Jr., Secretary and Treasurer; Donald M. Graham, James H. Ingersoll, Dorance L. Kirtland, Barbara M.J. Wood.
Employer Identification Number: 366043160

1135
Roper Foundation ⋈
1905 West Court St.
Kankakee 60901   (815) 937-6000

Incorporated in 1965 in Illinois.
Donor(s): Roper Corporation.
Financial data: (yr. ended 7/31/83): Assets, $174,096 (M); expenditures, $236,074, including $186,744 for 75 grants (high: $20,000; low: $200) and $48,900 for grants to individuals.
Purpose and activities: Broad purposes; general giving, with emphasis on youth agencies, community funds, hospitals, and higher education, including National Merit scholarships to children of company employees.
Types of support awarded: Employee related scholarships.
Limitations: Giving primarily in IL, KY, MD, SC, TN, and GA. No grants to individuals (except for company-employee scholarships) or for endowment funds; no loans.
Application information:
  Initial approach: Letter
  Copies of proposal: 1
  Board meeting date(s): December and May or July
  Write: R.L. Wood, Secretary
Officers and Directors: J.M. Stumbras, President; G.W. Waites, Vice-President; R.L. Wood, Secretary; D.C. Stark, Treasurer; R.E. Cook, H.W. Harris, C.M. Hoover, W.J. McGrath, R.E. Nickels.
Employer Identification Number: 366136001

1136
Rosenthal (Benjamin J.) Foundation ⋈
36 South State St., Rm. 1400
Chicago 60603

Incorporated in 1922 in Illinois.
Donor(s): Benjamin J. Rosenthal.†
Financial data: (yr. ended 12/31/83): Assets, $3,101,817 (M); expenditures, $131,862, including $104,025 for 102 grants (high: $35,000; low: $50).
Purpose and activities: General giving, primarily local, with emphasis on youth and social service agencies.
Limitations: Giving primarily in Chicago, IL.
Officers and Directors: Gladys R. Tartiere, President; Elaine R. Moseley, Vice-President; Maurice A. Riskind, Secretary; Jacob M. Shapiro, Treasurer.
Employer Identification Number: 362523643

1137
Sang (Elsie O. and Philip D.) Foundation
180 East Pearson St., Apt. 5805
Chicago 60611

Established in 1954.
Financial data: (yr. ended 10/31/83): Assets, $3,200,000 (M); expenditures, $292,000, including $273,000 for 36 grants (high: $100,000; low: $50).
Purpose and activities: Broad purposes; grants primarily for Jewish welfare funds; support also for hospitals and higher education.
Limitations: No grants to individuals.

Application information: Applications for grants not invited.
  Board meeting date(s): As required
Officers: Elsie O. Sang, President; Bernard Sang, Secretary.
Number of staff: None.
Employer Identification Number: 366214200

1138
Santa Fe Southern Pacific Foundation ▼
(formerly Santa Fe Industries Foundation, Inc.; Southern Pacific Foundation)
224 South Michigan Ave.
Chicago 60604   (312) 347-2676

Incorporated in 1953 in Illinois.
Donor(s): Santa Fe Industries, Inc., and subsidiary companies.
Financial data: (yr. ended 12/31/83): Assets, $1,513,496 (M); gifts received, $1,000,000; expenditures, $1,636,491, including $1,383,492 for 367 grants (high: $175,000; low: $100; average: $100-$5,000), $8,890 for grants to individuals and $235,468 for 907 employee matching gifts.
Purpose and activities: Giving to non-profit organizations serving areas of company operations, with emphasis on higher education, community funds, health and human services and cultural programs.
Types of support awarded: Scholarship funds, employee matching gifts, employee related scholarships.
Limitations: Giving limited to areas of company operations. No support for religious organizations for sectarian purposes; public educational institutions, pre-school, primary, and secondary educational institutions; organizations already receiving United Way support; fraternal or war veteran organizations; hospitals; national health or cultural organizations; or community and other grantmaking foundations. No grants to individuals (except for company-employee scholarships), or for travel expenses, testimonial dinners, or endowment funds.
Publications: Informational brochure, program policy statement.
Application information: Proposals are accepted and reviewed continuously, except for major requests (over $20,000) which are reviewed annually in the fall.
  Initial approach: Proposal
  Deadline(s): September 1
  Board meeting date(s): February and in the fall
  Write: George D. Scheckel, Vice-President
Officers: F.N. Grossman,* President; Glenn W. Dodd, Vice-President and Treasurer; George D. Scheckel,* Vice-President and Executive Director; J.D. Jackson, Secretary.
Directors:* L. Cena, W.R. Denton, W.T. Eskew, O.G. Linde, T.M. Orth, J.E. Stevens, R.T. Zitting.
Number of staff: 2 full-time professional; 1 full-time support.
Employer Identification Number: 366051896

1139
Sara Lee Foundation ▼
(formerly The Consolidated Foods Foundation)
3 First National Plaza
Chicago 60602-4260   (312) 558-8448

Incorporated in 1981 in Illinois.
Donor(s): Sara Lee Corporation.
Financial data: (yr. ended 6/30/84): Assets, $5,294,781 (M); gifts received, $5,500,000; expenditures, $1,702,661, including $1,280,729 for 80 grants (high: $193,462; low: $1,000; average: $1,000-$5,000), $48,958 for 10 grants to individuals and $372,974 for 1,200 employee matching gifts.
Purpose and activities: Primarily local giving for organizations assisting economically disadvantaged, underprivileged, or handicapped persons, and for arts and cultural organizations; support also for youth and civic affairs organizations and for higher education.
Types of support awarded: Employee related scholarships, employee matching gifts, special projects, operating budgets, annual campaigns, seed money, emergency funds, deficit financing, building funds, equipment, land acquisition, matching funds, continuing support.
Limitations: Giving primarily in Chicago, IL. No support for fraternities or veterans groups, political organizations, elementary or secondary schools, religious organizations, or disease-related health organizations. No grants to individuals (except for company-employee scholarships administered by National Merit), or for fundraising events, goodwill advertising, or endowments.
Publications: Company report, application guidelines.
Application information: Application form required.
  Initial approach: Letter or telephone
  Copies of proposal: 1
  Deadline(s): 1st of March, June, September, or December
  Board meeting date(s): Quarterly
  Final notification: After board meetings
  Write: Elizabeth E. Skalla, Executive Director or Gretchen R. Reimel, Coordinator of Community Relations
Officers: Robert L. Lauer,* President; Barbara A. Quinn, Vice-President; Gordon H. Newman, Vice-President and Secretary; Mark J. McCarville, Treasurer; Elizabeth E. Skalla, Executive Director; Gretchen R. Reimel, Coordinator.
Directors:* John H. Bryan, Jr., Robert E. Elberson, Michael E. Murphy.
Number of staff: 3 part-time professional; 2 part-time support.
Employer Identification Number: 363150460

1140
Scheinfeld (Sylvia and Aaron) Foundation
1040 North Lake Shore Dr., No. 37-A
Chicago 60611

Incorporated in 1955 in Illinois.
Donor(s): Mrs. Sylvia R. Scheinfeld, Aaron Scheinfeld.†

Financial data: (yr. ended 12/31/83): Assets, $847,506 (M); gifts received, $114,434; expenditures, $556,823, including $416,660 for 97 grants (high: $385,187; low: $50), $17,600 for grants to individuals and $35,000 for 1 foundation-administered program.

Purpose and activities: Broad purposes; giving in midwestern urban areas, particularly metropolitan Milwaukee and Chicago; support for an urban policy research institute and to organizations that aim to empower people to control and improve the quality of their lives, largely through experimental programs and community-based organizations seeking to meet social needs in housing, hunger, job training, employment, neighborhood reinvestment, women's equality, ethnic and racial equality, and legal services for minorities, the poor, and the public interest.

Limitations: Giving limited to midwestern urban areas, with emphasis on metropolitan Milwaukee, WI, and Chicago, IL. No support for religious activities, medical institutions, government agencies, or fine arts programs. No grants to individuals, or for building or endowment funds, investments, or program advertising; no loans.

Publications: Multi-year report, program policy statement.

Application information: Scholarship grants to individuals discontinued; applications not accepted.

   Board meeting date(s): 3 times a year
   Write: Mrs. Sylvia R. Scheinfeld, President
Officers: Sylvia R. Scheinfeld,* President; James D. Scheinfeld,* Vice-President; Ruth S. Pollak,* Secretary; Stephen J. Pollak,* Treasurer.
Directors:* Daniel R. Scheinfeld, Kathleen M. Scheinfeld, Sandra J.P. Scheinfeld.
Employer Identification Number: 366056338

1141
Schmitt (Arthur J.) Foundation ▼
Two North LaSalle St., Suite 2010
Chicago 60602   (312) 236-5089

Incorporated in 1941 in Illinois.
Donor(s): Arthur J. Schmitt.†
Financial data: (yr. ended 6/30/83): Assets, $14,777,672 (M); expenditures, $1,502,046, including $1,398,300 for 60 grants (high: $200,000; low: $100; average: $1,000-$30,000).

Purpose and activities: General purposes; primarily local giving, with emphasis on scholarships and fellowships established at certain selected universities to aid students to pursue graduate degrees, with preference given to those engaged or seriously expecting to engage in teaching; grants also to social services.

Types of support awarded: Endowment funds, scholarship funds, fellowships, general purposes, continuing support.

Limitations: Giving limited to the Chicago, IL metropolitan area, except for a few selected colleges and universities. No grants to individuals, or for capital or building funds, research, or matching gifts; no loans.

Publications: Application guidelines.

Application information:
   Initial approach: Full proposal

   Copies of proposal: 3
   Deadline(s): Submit proposal preferably in July, October, January, and April
   Board meeting date(s): February, April, June, September, and December
   Final notification: 1 month
   Write: John A. Donahue, Executive Secretary
Officers: John J. Gearen, President; John A. Donahue, Executive Secretary.
Directors: Richard C. Becker, William A. Maloney, Daniel E. Mayworm, Edmund A. Stephan, Peter J. Wrenn.
Number of staff: 1 part-time professional.
Employer Identification Number: 362217999

1142
Scholl (Dr.) Foundation ▼
11 South LaSalle St., Suite 2100
Chicago 60603   (312) 782-5210

Incorporated in 1947 in Illinois.
Donor(s): William M. Scholl, M.D.†
Financial data: (yr. ended 12/31/84): Assets, $88,567,861 (M); expenditures, $6,220,274, including $5,052,625 for 193 grants (high: $1,000,000; low: $500; average: $13,500) and $225,000 for 50 grants to individuals.

Purpose and activities: Charitable purposes; support for private education at all levels, including elementary, secondary, and post-secondary schools, colleges and universities, and medical and nursing institutions; medical and scientific research; general charitable programs, including grants to hospitals, and programs for children, the developmentally disabled, and senior citizens; civic, cultural, social welfare, economic, and religious activities.

Types of support awarded: Employee related scholarships, equipment, research, conferences and seminars, special projects.

Limitations: Giving primarily in IL. No support for public education. No grants to individuals (except for scholarships to children of company employees), or for endowment or building funds, general support, continuing support, operating budgets, deficit financing, or unrestricted purposes.

Publications: Program policy statement, application guidelines.

Application information: Application form required.
   Initial approach: Full proposal
   Copies of proposal: 1
   Deadline(s): May 15
   Board meeting date(s): January, April, July, and October
   Final notification: In November
   Write: Jack E. Scholl, Executive Director
Officers and Trustees: William H. Scholl,* President; Jack E. Scholl,* Vice-President, Secretary, and Executive Director; L.J. Knirko, Treasurer; Ernst Bittner, William T. Branham, M.R. Brecknock, Paul Eiseman, Neil Flanagin, William B. Jordan, Charles F. Scholl.
Number of staff: 2 full-time professional; 2 part-time professional; 3 full-time support.
Employer Identification Number: 366068724

1143
Seabury Foundation, The ▼ ¤
c/o The Northern Trust Company
50 South LaSalle St.
Chicago 60675

Trust established in 1947 in Illinois.
Donor(s): Charles Ward Seabury,† Louise Lovett Seabury.†
Financial data: (yr. ended 12/31/82): Assets, $9,710,021 (M); expenditures, $539,956, including $517,870 for 132 grants (high: $50,000; low: $500).

Purpose and activities: Primarily local giving, with emphasis on hospitals, cultural programs, including music, higher and secondary education, aid to the handicapped, youth agencies and child welfare.

Limitations: Giving primarily in IL.

Officers and Trustees: Clara Seabury Boone, Executive Secretary; John Ward Seabury, Executive Director; Daniel J. Boone, Charles B. Fisk, Elizabeth Seabury Mitchell, Louis Fisk Morris, Charlene B. Seabury.
Employer Identification Number: 366027398

1144
Searle (G. D.) & Co. Charitable Trust
c/o G.D. Searle & Co.
P.O. Box 1045
Skokie 60076

Established in 1983 in Illinois.
Donor(s): G.D. Searle & Co.
Financial data: (yr. ended 12/31/83): Assets, $3,000,000 (M); gifts received, $3,000,000.
Purpose and activities: Initial year of operation, 1983; no grants made.
Application information:
   Write: Mrs. Susan Sittnick, Manager
Officers and Directors: John E. Robson, Chairman; William I. Greener, Secretary; James M. Denny, Marcel Durot, Tod Hullin, Hollis Schoepke, Donald L. Seeley, Robert Shapiro, Bernard Windon.
Trustee: Northern Trust Company.
Employer Identification Number: 366785886

1145
Sears-Roebuck Foundation, The ▼
Sears Tower, Dept. 903--BSC 37-20
Chicago 60684   (312) 875-8464

Incorporated in 1923 in Illinois as Sears Agricultural Foundation; re-chartered in 1941.
Donor(s): Sears, Roebuck and Co.
Financial data: (yr. ended 1/31/85): Assets, $4,555,466 (M); expenditures, $2,965,849, including $2,948,920 for grants.
Purpose and activities: To aid and support the formal system of education at the higher and lower levels generally by funding projects initiated by the Foundation.
Types of support awarded: General purposes, continuing support, annual campaigns, seed money, emergency funds, deficit financing, special projects.

Limitations: Giving limited to the U.S. No support for religious groups for religious purposes. No grants to individuals, or to colleges for building or endowment funds, operating budgets, scholarships, fellowships, or matching gifts; no loans.
Publications: Annual report.
Application information: Grant applications not accepted.
Board meeting date(s): January
Write: William L. Whitsitt, Vice-President and Executive Director
Officers: Gene Harmon,* President; William L. Whitsitt, Vice-President and Executive Director; Richard K. Hartung, Vice-President and Program Director; William Kenney, Vice-President and Controller; John H. Blalock,* Donald A. Deutsch,* Guy F. Eberhart,* Philo K. Holland, Jr.,* C.W. Rule,* Vice-Presidents; Sarah Q. Hargrave, Vice-President and Treasurer; Julie A. Hansen, Secretary.
Directors:* Edward R. Telling, Chairman; William I. Bass, Edward A. Brennan, Howard B. Dean, Richard M. Jones, Jr., Vincent M. Jones, Philip M. Knox, Jr., Henry D. Sunderland, Lawrence H. Williford.
Number of staff: 2.
Employer Identification Number: 366032266

1146
Seeley Foundation, The
115 South LaSalle St., Rm. 2500
Chicago 60604

Incorporated in 1945 in Michigan.
Donor(s): Halsted H. Seeley,† Laurel H. Seeley.
Financial data: (yr. ended 12/31/83): Assets, $2,054,104 (M); expenditures, $262,544, including $247,300 for 6 grants (high: $180,000; low: $1,000).
Purpose and activities: General purposes; continuing support of fellowship and research funds set up in memory of John Harper Seeley, largely in the field of mental health.
Officers and Directors: Miles G. Seeley, President; Jane P. Seeley, Vice-President; Hugo J. Melvoin, Secretary and Treasurer; Judith S. Fales, Miles P. Seeley.
Employer Identification Number: 366049991

1147
Shapiro (Charles and M. R.) Foundation, Inc. ⌑
330 West Diversey Pkwy., No. 1801
Chicago 60657

Incorporated in 1956 in Illinois.
Donor(s): Charles Shapiro,† Mary Shapiro.†
Financial data: (yr. ended 7/31/83): Assets, $11,276,173 (M); expenditures, $730,693, including $677,367 for 83 grants (high: $125,000; low: $25).
Purpose and activities: Giving primarily for Jewish welfare funds and temple support.
Officers: Morris R. Shapiro, President and Treasurer; Joseph Muskal, Vice-President and Director; Alfred I. Schwerdlin, Secretary.
Employer Identification Number: 366109757

1148
Shapiro (Isaac and Fannie) Memorial Foundation, Inc. ⌑
7575 South Kostner Ave.
Chicago 60652

Incorporated in 1947 in Maryland.
Donor(s): Henry Shapiro, Sweetheart Paper Products Co., Inc., and others.
Financial data: (yr. ended 8/31/83): Assets, $526,681 (M); gifts received, $135,000; expenditures, $317,193, including $315,166 for 7 grants (high: $274,500; low: $1,500).
Purpose and activities: Charitable purposes; grants largely for Jewish welfare funds.
Officers: Arthur H. Shapiro, President; Earl Shapiro, Vice-President; Henry Shapiro, Secretary-Treasurer.
Employer Identification Number: 366062358

1149
Shaw (Arch W.) Foundation
135 South LaSalle St.
Chicago 60603

Trust established in 1949 in Illinois.
Financial data: (yr. ended 12/31/83): Assets, $2,412,444 (M); expenditures, $125,851, including $122,500 for 55 grants (high: $35,000; low: $100).
Purpose and activities: Charitable and educational purposes; grants largely for higher education, local hospitals, and cultural programs.
Limitations: Giving primarily in IL. No grants to individuals.
Trustees: John I. Shaw, Roger D. Shaw.
Employer Identification Number: 366055262

1150
Sherman (Nate H.) Foundation ⌑
919 North Michigan Ave.
Chicago 60611

Established in 1967 in Illinois.
Donor(s): Nate H. Sherman, Midas-International Corporation, Midas-International Corporation Foundation.
Financial data: (yr. ended 12/31/83): Assets, $2,068,093 (M); expenditures, $129,993, including $122,900 for 24 grants (high: $60,000; low: $25).
Purpose and activities: Primarily local giving, with emphasis on Jewish welfare funds.
Types of support awarded: General purposes.
Limitations: Giving primarily in IL.
Officers and Directors: Sarita Warshawsky, President and Treasurer; Bette Lou Seidner, Vice-President; David Silbert, Secretary.
Employer Identification Number: 366194153

1151
Shirk (The Russell and Betty) Foundation ⌑
103 North Robinson St.
Bloomington 61701 (309) 827-8580

Established in 1968.
Financial data: (yr. ended 12/31/83): Assets, $1,723,836 (M); gifts received, $500,000; expenditures, $54,965, including $51,183 for 38 grants (high: $10,000; low: $25).
Purpose and activities: Primarily local giving, including support for building funds, with emphasis on higher education, youth agencies, and health.
Types of support awarded: Operating budgets, scholarship funds, building funds.
Limitations: Giving primarily in IL.
Application information:
Write: James A. Shirk, Trustee
Trustees: Merrick C. Hayes, James A. Shirk, Russell O. Shirk.
Employer Identification Number: 237022709

1152
Signode Foundation, Inc.
3600 West Lake Ave.
Glenview 60025 (312) 724-6100

Incorporated in 1951 in Illinois.
Donor(s): Signode Corporation, Reichel & Drews, Inc.
Financial data: (yr. ended 12/31/83): Assets, $283,231 (M); gifts received, $105,040; expenditures, $309,632, including $269,275 for 110 grants (high: $92,000; low: $90) and $39,231 for employee matching gifts.
Purpose and activities: Broad purposes; general giving primarily in areas of company operations, for community services, higher education, including scholarships for children of company employees, hospitals, youth agencies, community funds, and cultural programs.
Types of support awarded: Employee related scholarships, employee matching gifts, continuing support, building funds.
Limitations: No grants to individuals (except scholarships for children of company employees) or for endowment funds.
Publications: Application guidelines.
Application information: Application form required.
Initial approach: Letter, telephone, or full proposal
Copies of proposal: 1
Board meeting date(s): As required
Write: Linda J. Noyle, Director of Community Affairs
Officers and Trustees: J. Thomas Schanck, President and Treasurer; Linda J. Noyle, Vice-President; Thurman Jordan, Secretary; John H. Leslie, John G. Powers.
Employer Identification Number: 366051140

1153
Siragusa Foundation, The
840 North Michigan Ave., Suite 615
Chicago 60611 (312) 280-0833

Trust established in 1950 in Illinois; incorporated in 1980.
Donor(s): Ross D. Siragusa.
Financial data: (yr. ended 12/31/84): Assets, $7,479,056 (M); expenditures, $378,269, including $268,300 for 44 grants (high: $50,000; low: $250) and $109,969 for foundation-administered programs.

Purpose and activities: Broad purposes; general giving, with emphasis on higher education and medical research; support also for cultural activities, child development programs, education of the handicapped, and care of the elderly. Preference given to ongoing programs of established organizations in the Midwest, particularly in the metropolitan Chicago area.

Types of support awarded: Operating budgets, building funds, equipment, matching funds, research, special projects.

Limitations: Giving primarily in in the Midwest, with preference to the Chicago, IL, metropolitan area. No grants to individuals, or for endowment funds, scholarships, or fellowships; no loans.

Publications: Program policy statement, application guidelines.

Application information: Submit proposal only when invited.

  Initial approach: Letter
  Copies of proposal: 1
  Board meeting date(s): February, May, August, and November
  Final notification: 2 to 3 months
  Write: Melvin T. Tracht, Secretary-Treasurer

Officers and Directors: Ross D. Siragusa, President; Melvin T. Tracht, Secretary-Treasurer; Roy M. Adams, George E. Driscoll, Alfred A. Medica, Melvyn H. Schneider, John R. Siragusa, Martha P. Siragusa, Richard D. Siragusa, Ross D. Siragusa III, James B. Wilson.

Number of staff: 1 full-time professional; 1 full-time support.

Employer Identification Number: 363100492

1154
Skidmore, Owings & Merrill Foundation ⌑
33 W. Monroe St.
Chicago 60603

Established in 1978.
Donor(s): Skidmore, Owings & Merrill.
Financial data: (yr. ended 8/31/83): Assets, $1,211,257 (M); gifts received, $402,583; expenditures, $50,439, including $22,700 for 3 grants (high: $10,000; low: $5,000) and $21,000 for 7 grants to individuals.
Purpose and activities: Grants "for the purpose of education, research, or publications in or directly related to the fields of Architecture or Architectural Engineering".
Types of support awarded: Fellowships, general purposes.
Application information:
  Initial approach: Proposal
  Deadline(s): None
  Write: Robert A. Hutchins, Secretary
Officers and Directors: Bruce J. Graham, Chairman; Michael A. McCarthy, Marc E. Goldstein, Vice-Chairmen; Robert A. Hutchins, Secretary-Treasurer; David M. Childs, James R. DeStefano, Raul de Armas, Lawrence S. Doane.
Employer Identification Number: 362969068

1155
Smail Family Foundation ⌑
1000 N. Lakeshore Plaza, Apt. 27A
Chicago 60611

Established in 1965.
Financial data: (yr. ended 6/30/83): Assets, $629 (M); gifts received, $168,000; expenditures, $167,875, including $166,100 for 24 grants (high: $75,000; low: $60).
Purpose and activities: "To further the prevention and relief of human suffering"; primarily local giving, with emphasis on hospitals, social services, and education.
Limitations: Giving primarily in IL.
Trustee: Anne W. Smail.
Employer Identification Number: 366136148

1156
Smith Charitable Trust ⌑
c/o David S. Paddock
850 North Church St.
Rockford 61103

Trust established in 1956 in Illinois.
Donor(s): Smith Oil Corporation, Carl A. Smith,† Byron C. Marlowe.
Financial data: (yr. ended 12/31/83): Assets, $2,127,628 (M); gifts received, $16,488; expenditures, $125,802, including $118,675 for 76 grants (high: $20,000; low: $25).
Purpose and activities: Primarily local giving, with emphasis on hospitals, higher education, and youth and child welfare; grants also for cultural activities and civic affairs.
Limitations: Giving primarily in IL.
Trustees: David S. Paddock, C. Gordon Smith.
Employer Identification Number: 366078557

1157
Snite (Fred B.) Foundation ⌑
4800 North Western Ave.
Chicago 60625

Incorporated in 1945 in Illinois.
Donor(s): Fred B. Snite,† Local Loan Co.
Financial data: (yr. ended 6/30/83): Assets, $5,566,183 (M); expenditures, $156,371, including $115,415 for 18 grants (high: $39,815; low: $100).
Purpose and activities: Broad purposes; grants largely for Roman Catholic church support and church-related educational institutions.
Officers: Terrance J. Dillon,* President; Mary L. Dillon,* Katherine B. Williams,* Vice-Presidents; Lawrence X. Pusateri, Secretary; Allen E. Eliot, Treasurer.
Directors: * Nicholas Rassas.
Employer Identification Number: 366084839

1158
Solo Cup Foundation ⌑
7431 East End Ave.
Chicago 60649

Established in 1959 in Illinois.
Donor(s): Solo Cup Company.

Financial data: (yr. ended 3/31/83): Assets, $290,324 (M); gifts received, $297,003; expenditures, $204,576, including $203,050 for grants.
Purpose and activities: Grants primarily for higher and secondary education and Christian religious organizations.
Officers: L.J. Hulseman, President; J.F. Hulseman, Vice-President; R.L. Hulseman, Secretary-Treasurer.
Employer Identification Number: 366062327

1159
Sonntag (Christine and Alfred) Foundation for Cancer Research ⌑
853 Dundee Ave.
Elgin 60120

Trust established in 1962 in Connecticut.
Donor(s): Alfred Sonntag,† Christine Sonntag.†
Financial data: (yr. ended 9/30/83): Assets, $294,870 (M); gifts received, $4,125; expenditures, $208,509, including $207,270 for 2 grants (high: $107,270; low: $100,000).
Purpose and activities: Charitable and scientific purposes; grants to institutions for basic cancer cell research.
Trustees: Barry J. Carroll, Wallace E. Carroll.
Employer Identification Number: 066050572

1160
Spencer Foundation, The ▼
875 North Michigan Ave.
Chicago 60611   (312) 337-7000

Incorporated in 1962 in Illinois.
Donor(s): Lyle M. Spencer.†
Financial data: (yr. ended 3/31/84): Assets, $126,341,823 (M); expenditures, $5,093,873, including $3,645,193 for 90 grants (high: $360,050; low: $1,250; average: $60,000).
Purpose and activities: Supports the investigation of learning and the improvement of education through behavioral science research.
Types of support awarded: Research.
Limitations: No grants to individuals (except those working under the auspices of an institution), or for capital funds, general purposes, operating and continuing support, sabbatical supplements, work in instructional or curriculum development, or any kind of training or service program; scholarships, travel fellowships, endowment funds, postdoctoral research, or matching gifts; no loans.
Publications: Annual report, application guidelines, program policy statement.
Application information: Submit full proposal upon request.
  Initial approach: Letter
  Copies of proposal: 2
  Deadline(s): May 1, August 1, November 1, and February 1
  Board meeting date(s): April, July, October, and January
  Final notification: After 1 quarterly period
  Write: Mrs. Marion M. Faldet, Vice-President
Officers: H. Thomas James,* President; Marion M. Faldet, Vice-President and Secretary; Farwell Smith,* Treasurer.

Directors:* Frank L. Bixby, Chairman;
Catherine M. Spencer, Vice-Chair; Lawrence A.
Cremin, Jacob W. Getzels, Patricia Albjerg
Graham, George A. Ranney, Jr., Lyle M.
Spencer, Jr., Ralph W. Tyler, Franklin H.
Williams.
Number of staff: 4 full-time professional; 1
part-time professional; 4 full-time support.
Employer Identification Number: 366078558

1161
Sprague (The Otho S. A.) Memorial Institute ▼
c/o The Northern Trust Company
50 South LaSalle St.
Chicago 60675   (312) 630-6000

Incorporated in 1910 in Illinois.
Donor(s): The Sprague family.
Financial data: (yr. ended 12/31/83): Assets,
$9,693,847 (M); expenditures, $454,025,
including $391,000 for 5 grants (high:
$125,000; low: $6,000).
Purpose and activities: To investigate the
cause of disease and the prevention and relief
of human suffering caused by disease in the
city of Chicago. In accordance with the wishes
of the founder, support primarily to the major
private, medical teaching and research
universities in Chicago.
Types of support awarded: Research, special
projects.
Limitations: Giving limited to Chicago, IL. No
grants to individuals, or for building or
endowment funds, general purposes,
scholarships, fellowships, or matching gifts; no
loans.
Publications: Annual report, application
guidelines.
Application information: Application form
required.
  Initial approach: Letter
  Copies of proposal: 4
  Deadline(s): Submit proposal preferably from
    December through February; deadline
    February 28
  Board meeting date(s): Semiannually in the
    spring and fall
  Write: Mrs. Shirley T. Antes
Officers and Trustees: John P. Bent, President;
Vernon Armour, Vice-President; Stewart S.
Dixon, Secretary; Van R. Gathany, Treasurer;
Harry N. Beaty, M.D., Charles F. Clark, Jr.,
Charles C. Haffner III, Leo M. Henikoff, M.D.,
Leon O. Jacobson, M.D.
Number of staff: None.
Employer Identification Number: 366068723

1162
Square D Foundation ▼ ¤
1415 South Roselle Rd.
Palatine 60067   (312) 397-2600

Incorporated in 1956 in Michigan.
Donor(s): Square D Company.
Financial data: (yr. ended 12/31/83): Assets,
$1,125,534 (M); gifts received, $950,000;
expenditures, $1,005,390, including $962,943
for 263 grants (high: $100,000; low: $250),
$13,943 for grants to individuals and $27,373
for employee matching gifts.

Purpose and activities: Broad purposes;
general giving, with emphasis on community
funds, higher education, and youth; support
also for hospitals, and health agencies.
Types of support awarded: Building funds,
employee related scholarships, equipment,
employee matching gifts.
Limitations: Giving primarily in areas of
company operations, with emphasis on the
Midwest and South.
Application information:
  Write: Donald E. Wilson, Secretary-Treasurer
Officers: D.L. Knauss,* President; Robert E.
King, Vice-President; Donald E. Wilson,*
Secretary-Treasurer.
Directors:* Donald C. Clark, David B. Meeker,
William C. Messinger, Gustave H. Moede, Jr.
Employer Identification Number: 366054195

1163
Staley (A. E.), Jr. Foundation ¤
c/o Citizens National Bank of Decatur
236 North Water St.
Decatur 62525

Trust established in 1955 in Illinois.
Donor(s): Augustus Eugene Staley, Jr.
Financial data: (yr. ended 12/31/83): Assets,
$2,951,140 (M); expenditures, $116,809,
including $110,796 for 37 grants (high:
$32,700; low: $70).
Purpose and activities: Primarily local giving,
with emphasis on higher education, hospitals, a
community fund and health agencies.
Limitations: Giving primarily in IL.
Trustee: Citizens National Bank of Decatur.
Employer Identification Number: 376023961

1164
Staley (Emma L.) Foundation ¤
c/o The Northern Trust Company
50 South LaSalle St.
Chicago 60675

Trust established in 1957 in Illinois.
Donor(s): Emma L. Staley.
Financial data: (yr. ended 12/31/81): Assets,
$2,551,495 (M); expenditures, $134,643,
including $125,000 for 3 grants (high:
$100,000; low: $12,500).
Purpose and activities: Primarily local giving,
with emphasis on higher education and
hospitals.
Limitations: Giving primarily in IL.
Trustee: The Northern Trust Company.
Employer Identification Number: 376023963

1165
Stanadyne Foundation ¤
c/o Oak Park Trust & Savings Bank
Village Mall Plaza
Oak Park 60301

Trust established in 1958 in Illinois.
Donor(s): Stanadyne, Inc.
Financial data: (yr. ended 12/31/83): Assets,
$319,647 (M); gifts received, $250,000;
expenditures, $306,341, including $303,236
for 79 grants (high: $26,000; low: $1,000).

Purpose and activities: Broad purpose funds;
general giving in areas of company operations,
with emphasis on community funds, higher
education, including scholarships, hospitals and
health associations, cultural programs and
youth agencies.
Trustee: Oak Park Trust and Savings Bank.
Employer Identification Number: 237421900

1166
State Farm Companies Foundation ▼
One State Farm Plaza
Bloomington 61701   (309) 766-2039

Incorporated in 1963 in Illinois.
Donor(s): State Farm Insurance Companies.
Financial data: (yr. ended 12/31/83): Assets,
$3,104,306 (M); expenditures, $675,782,
including $660,427 for 117 grants (high:
$131,201; low: $37; average: $500-$10,000).
Purpose and activities: Support for higher
education, including scholarships for children
of employees, a business fellowship program,
exceptional student fellowships, and promotion
of educational activities related to the insurance
business; grants are generally to national
organizations; support also for community
funds, hospitals, and a center for automobile
safety.
Types of support awarded: Fellowships,
scholarship funds, employee related
scholarships.
Limitations: No grants to individuals (except
for company employee scholarship programs).
Publications: Informational brochure, grants
list, application guidelines.
Application information: Funds largely
committed; no direct appeals accepted;
scholarship and fellowship recipients must be
nominated by their schools. Application form
required.
  Deadline(s): For scholarships, December 31;
    for fellowships, February 28; for doctoral
    program, March 31
  Board meeting date(s): March, June,
    September, and December
  Write: William I. Grogg, Assistant Vice-
    President, Programs
Officers: Edward B. Rust,* Chairman,
President, and Treasurer; Edward B. Rust, Jr.,*
Vice-President and Secretary; Dallas Reynolds,
Vice-President-Programs.
Directors:* Paul G. Anderson, Jr., Robert S.
Eckley, Thomas C. Morrill.
Number of staff: None.
Employer Identification Number: 366110423

1167
Stern (Irvin) Foundation
53 W. Jackson Blvd., Suite 930
Chicago 60604   (312) 346-0236

Trust established in 1957 in Illinois.
Donor(s): Irvin Stern.†
Financial data: (yr. ended 9/30/84): Assets,
$5,350,026 (M); expenditures, $400,446,
including $355,830 for 66 grants (high:
$84,000; low: $100; average: $3,000-$20,000).

Purpose and activities: General purposes; emphasis on meeting the needs of the Jewish community in the United States and Israel; support for efforts to combat heart disease, mental illness, and cancer; for vocational training and help for the aged; and for improving urban living conditions via neighborhood organizations.

Types of support awarded: Operating budgets, continuing support, seed money, emergency funds, matching funds, conferences and seminars.

Limitations: Giving primarily in Chicago, IL; New York, NY; and San Diego, CA. No support for religious and political purposes. No grants to individuals, or for endowment funds, deficit financing, or advertising or program books.

Publications: 990-PF, application guidelines, program policy statement.

Application information: Application form required.

  Initial approach: Letter
  Deadline(s): Submit proposal preferably in March or August; deadlines April 1 and September 1
  Board meeting date(s): April and October
  Write: Mrs. Rae W. Epstein, Secretary

Officer: Rae W. Epstein,* Secretary.

Trustees: E. Allan Epstein, Jeffrey Epstein, Stuart Epstein, Dorothy G. Winter, Arthur Winter, Richard Winter, Stanley Winter.

Number of staff: 1 part-time support.

Employer Identification Number: 366047947

1168

Stewart-Warner Foundation ☒
1826 Diversey Pkwy.
Chicago 60614   (312) 883-6000

Incorporated in 1950 in Illinois.

Donor(s): Stewart-Warner Corporation, The Bassick Company.

Financial data: (yr. ended 12/31/83): Assets, $43,899 (M); gifts received, $65,000; expenditures, $219,009, including $218,265 for 73 grants (high: $45,000; low: $100).

Purpose and activities: General purposes; grants primarily for community funds; support also for higher education, hospitals, cultural programs, and youth agencies.

Limitations: Giving primarily in IL; some support in other areas of company operations. No grants to individuals.

Application information:

  Initial approach: Full proposal
  Copies of proposal: 1
  Deadline(s): None
  Board meeting date(s): As required
  Write: J.C. Morrison, President

Officers: J.C. Morrison, President; H.L. Parker, Vice-President and Treasurer; R.M. Demouth, Secretary.

Trustees: J.S. Kemper, Jr., T.L. Martin, Jr., W.F. Murray, J.C. Stetson, D.J. Terra.

Employer Identification Number: 366109737

1169

Stone Foundation, Inc. ☒
360 North Michigan Ave.
Chicago 60601

Incorporated in 1944 in Illinois.

Donor(s): Stone Container Corporation.

Financial data: (yr. ended 12/31/83): Assets, $764,754 (M); expenditures, $211,804, including $192,359 for 36 grants (high: $120,000; low: $25) and $16,000 for 8 grants to individuals.

Purpose and activities: Broad purposes; general giving, with emphasis on Jewish welfare funds; higher education, including scholarships; hospitals; and cultural activities.

Directors: Jerome H. Stone, Marvin H. Stone, Norman H. Stone, Roger W. Stone.

Employer Identification Number: 366063761

1170

Stone (W. Clement and Jessie V.) Foundation
111 East Wacker Dr., Suite 510
Chicago 60601   (312) 565-1100

Incorporated in 1958 in Illinois.

Donor(s): W. Clement Stone, Jessie V. Stone.

Financial data: (yr. ended 12/31/84): Assets, $269,459 (M); gifts received, $762,000; expenditures, $763,201, including $118,325 for 28 grants (high: $15,000; low: $80; average: $5,000).

Purpose and activities: Broad purposes; "making this world a better place in which to live" through programs which seek to put "Positive Mental Attitude" philosophy into action in the areas of education, mental health, religion, and youth work.

Types of support awarded: Consulting services, technical assistance.

Limitations: No grants to individuals, or for building or endowment funds, or scholarships and fellowships.

Publications: Annual report, informational brochure.

Application information: Funds presently committed, but consulting services are available. Application form required.

  Initial approach: Letter
  Copies of proposal: 1
  Deadline(s): None
  Board meeting date(s): April
  Final notification: 90 days
  Write: Maree G. Bullock, Executive Director

Officers and Directors: W. Clement Stone, Chairman; Donna J. Stone, President; Clement Stone, Vice-President and Secretary; Mrs. Jessie V. Stone, Vice-President and Treasurer; Barbara Stone, Norman C. Stone, LeRoy A. Pesch, M.D., Vice-Presidents; Maree G. Bullock, Executive Director; Myron L. Boardman, Jack Early, Mary Conway Kohler, James L. McGaugh, Karl A. Menninger, M.D., Ralph Newman, Gerald Pugh, Billy B. Sharp, Ralph Tyler, Harold Blake Walker.

Number of staff: 5 full-time professional; 3 full-time support; 3 part-time support.

Employer Identification Number: 362498125

1171

Stump (Jacob), Jr. and Clara Stump Memorial Scholarship Fund
c/o Central National Bank of Mattoon
Broadway and Charleston at 14th St.
Mattoon 61938   (217) 234-6434

Trust established in 1967 in Illinois.

Donor(s): Jacob Stump, Jr.†

Financial data: (yr. ended 7/31/83): Assets, $1,133,679 (M); expenditures, $180,924, including $143,265 for grants to individuals.

Purpose and activities: To provide scholarships to high school graduates from four local counties to attend any state-supported college or university in Illinois.

Types of support awarded: Student aid.

Limitations: Giving limited to high school graduates from Coles, Cumberland, Douglas, and Moultrie counties, IL, attending state-supported colleges and universities in IL.

Application information: Application form required.

  Deadline(s): April 1
  Write: Malcolm O'Neill, Trust Officer

Trustee: Central National Bank of Mattoon (Malcolm F. O'Neill, Trust Officer).

Employer Identification Number: 376064295

1172

Sullivan (Bolton) Fund ☒
One Northfield Plaza, Rm. 310
Northfield 60093   (312) 446-1500

Incorporated in 1948 in Illinois.

Donor(s): Bolton Sullivan, Constance Sullivan, Jennie M. Sullivan, Skil Corporation.

Financial data: (yr. ended 12/31/83): Assets, $2,015,347 (M); expenditures, $168,391, including $142,000 for 34 grants (high: $50,000; low: $500).

Purpose and activities: Broad purposes; grants largely for higher education, Roman Catholic church support, church-related institutions, and hospitals.

Limitations: No grants to individuals.

Application information:

  Initial approach: Letter
  Deadline(s): None
  Board meeting date(s): Usually in April
  Write: Bolton Sullivan, President

Officers and Directors: Bolton Sullivan, President; John W. Sullivan, Vice-President; Charles R. Beauregard, Secretary-Treasurer; Gieriet S. Carroll, Martin C. Carroll, Thomas A. Dean, Joan K. Hanly, Constance Sullivan, Susan R. Sullivan.

Employer Identification Number: 366064523

1173

Sulzer Family Foundation ☒
1940 West Irving Park Rd.
Chicago 60613

Incorporated in 1956 in Illinois.

Donor(s): Miss Grace E. Sulzer.

Financial data: (yr. ended 12/31/83): Assets, $1,553,097 (M); expenditures, $231,553, including $87,000 for 63 grants (high: $5,000; low: $100).

Purpose and activities: General purposes; primarily local giving, with emphasis on church support and religious organizations, secondary education, hospitals, and youth agencies.
Limitations: Giving primarily in IL.
Officer: John J. Hoellen, President.
Employer Identification Number: 362466016

1174
Sundstrand Corporation Foundation ▼ ¤
4751 Harrison Ave.
P.O. Box 7003
Rockford 61125　　　　　(815) 226-6000

Incorporated in 1952 in Illinois.
Donor(s): Sundstrand Corporation.
Financial data: (yr. ended 10/31/83): Assets, $2,399,639 (M); gifts received, $960,000; expenditures, $740,358, including $721,975 for 110 grants (high: $112,750; low: $400; average: $500-$10,000).
Purpose and activities: General purposes; grants for community funds, education, particularly higher education, hospitals, and youth agencies in areas of Company operations; support also for the handicapped, social service and health agencies, and a company-employee scholarship program; some support for cultural programs.
Types of support awarded: Building funds, equipment, scholarship funds, employee related scholarships.
Limitations: Giving primarily in areas of company operations. No support for projects of a religious or political nature. No grants to individuals or for operating funds.
Application information:
　Initial approach: Letter
　Copies of proposal: 1
　Deadline(s): None
　Board meeting date(s): March, June, September, and December
　Final notification: 2 months
　Write: John A. Thayer, Secretary
Officers: Don R. O'Hare, President; Philip W. Polgreen, Vice-President; John A. Thayer, Secretary; Ted L. Ross, Treasurer.
Employer Identification Number: 366072477

1175
Susman and Asher Foundation ¤
c/o Norman Asher
134 North LaSalle St., Suite 1900
Chicago 60602

Incorporated in 1949 in Illinois.
Donor(s): Louis Susman, and members of the Asher family.
Financial data: (yr. ended 12/31/83): Assets, $1,234,261 (M); gifts received, $120,757; expenditures, $222,492, including $216,084 for 21 grants (high: $148,754; low: $100).
Purpose and activities: General giving, with emphasis on higher, including religious education, and Jewish welfare funds.
Officer and Trustees: Norman Asher, President; Donald Asher, Gilbert Asher, Helen Asher, Robert Asher, Louis Susman.
Employer Identification Number: 366049760

1176
Svenson (Ernest J.) Foundation
P.O. Box 219
Rockford 61105　　　　　(815) 987-8900

Established in 1975 in Illinois.
Financial data: (yr. ended 2/29/84): Assets, $2,621,364 (M); expenditures, $237,928, including $215,000 for 7 grants (high: $105,000; low: $1,000).
Purpose and activities: Primarily local giving, with emphasis on higher education and medical research.
Limitations: Giving primarily in the Rockford, IL, area.
Application information: Funds entirely committed through 1990.
　Write: Thomas Johnson
Directors: Thomas Johnson, David W. Knapp, Shirley Ritchie, Irene Svenson.
Number of staff: None.
Employer Identification Number: 362550629

1177
TYF Foundation, Inc. ¤
c/o The Northern Trust Company
Chicago 60675

Established in 1968.
Donor(s): Bruce E. McArthur.
Financial data: (yr. ended 8/31/83): Assets, $1,194,244 (M); expenditures, $131,494, including $117,500 for 38 grants (high: $30,000; low: $500).
Purpose and activities: Support for education, including higher education, Protestant religious organizations, conservation, and social services.
Officers and Directors: Bruce E. McArthur, President; Charlotte A. McArthur, Vice-President; David M. McArthur, Secretary.
Employer Identification Number: 237041854

1178
Tyndale House Foundation ¤
336 Gundersen Dr., Box 80
Wheaton 60187　　　　　(312) 293-0179

Established in 1964 in Illinois.
Donor(s): Kenneth N. Taylor.
Financial data: (yr. ended 12/31/83): Assets, $43,444 (M); gifts received, $60,000; expenditures, $185,138, including $172,800 for 26 grants (high: $135,000; low: $300).
Purpose and activities: Grants primarily for Christian literature projects and Bible translation.
Types of support awarded: General purposes, special projects, publications.
Limitations: No support for libraries. No grants to individuals, or for building or endowment funds, scholarships, fellowships, personnel support, or matching or challenge grants.
Publications: Program policy statement, application guidelines.
Application information: Applications severely restricted. New grants awarded on a limited basis. Application form required.
　Initial approach: Letter or telephone
　Copies of proposal: 1
　Deadline(s): February 15 and September 15
　Board meeting date(s): March and October

　Write: Mrs. Mary Kleine Yehling, Executive Director
Officers and Managers: Mark D. Taylor, President; Harold Shaw, Vice-President; Margaret W. Taylor, Secretary-Treasurer; Edwin L. Frizen, Jr., Wendell C. Hawley, Paul A. Leetz, Bernard Palmer, Kenneth N. Taylor,* Sam Wolgemuth.
Trustees:* Elmhurst National Bank.
Employer Identification Number: 362555516

1179
United Air Lines Foundation ▼
P.O. Box 66100
Chicago 60666　　　　　(312) 952-5714

Incorporated in 1951 in Illinois.
Donor(s): United Air Lines, Inc.
Financial data: (yr. ended 12/31/83): Assets, $1,219,681 (M); gifts received, $1,000,000; expenditures, $521,304, including $517,621 for 123 grants (high: $50,539; low: $1,000; average: $1,000-$50,000).
Purpose and activities: Due to budget cutbacks, in 1982 the foundation suspended all annual grants, with the exception of United Way agencies in cities served by the company, pledges committed in prior years and payable in 1983, and scholarship programs for children of employees.
Types of support awarded: Annual campaigns, building funds, exchange programs, fellowships, operating budgets, research, scholarship funds, employee related scholarships, employee matching gifts.
Limitations: Giving limited to areas of company operations. No support for organizations established to influence legislation, labor unions, or fraternal or veterans organizations, or for propaganda. No grants to individuals, or for endowments, advertising campaigns, purchase of tickets or tables for fundraising dinners or similar events; club memberships, conferences, or travel; no loans.
Publications: Annual report, program policy statement, application guidelines.
Application information:
　Initial approach: Brief proposal
　Copies of proposal: 1
　Deadline(s): 60 days prior to board meetings
　Board meeting date(s): March, June, September, and December
　Final notification: 1 month
　Write: Eileen M. Younglove, Vice-President and Secretary
Officers: Monte Lazarus,* President; Eileen M. Younglove,* Vice-President and Secretary; G.J. Helbig, Treasurer.
Directors:* John M. Batten, Richard J. Ferris, James J. Hartigan, Hugo J. Moriano.
Number of staff: 3.
Employer Identification Number: 366109873

1180
UOP Foundation ¤
Ten UOP Plaza
Des Plaines 60016　　　　　(312) 391-2288

Incorporated in 1965 in Illinois.
Donor(s): UOP Inc.

Financial data: (yr. ended 12/31/83): Assets, $1,568,085 (M); gifts received, $400,000; expenditures, $544,057, including $449,581 for 257 grants (high: $53,000; low: $25), $37,500 for grants to individuals and $29,580 for employee matching gifts.
Purpose and activities: Charitable purposes; general giving, in the Chicago metropolitan area and locations where the company has operating facilities, with emphasis on higher education, including technological education; support also for community funds, cultural programs, hospitals, youth and health agencies, and aid to the handicapped.
Types of support awarded: Employee related scholarships, operating budgets, continuing support, annual campaigns, building funds, equipment, research, conferences and seminars, employee matching gifts, scholarship funds, fellowships.
Limitations: Giving primarily in the Chicago, IL, metropolitan area and locations where the company has operating facilities. No grants to individuals (except scholarships for the children of company employees) or for endowment funds; no loans.
Application information:
Initial approach: Letter or full proposal
Copies of proposal: 1
Deadline(s): Submit proposal in February, March, May, or June
Board meeting date(s): April, July, October, and January
Final notification: 2 months
Write: Donald E. Lewan, Executive Director
Officers: Donald E. Lewan,* President and Executive Director; Susan M. Larsen, Secretary; Ray Butner, Treasurer.
Trustees:* G.E. Illingworth, John D. Ring, Karl J. Youtsey.
Number of staff: 2.
Employer Identification Number: 366134569

1181
Upton (Frederick S.) Foundation ⌑
c/o The First National Bank of Chicago
One First National Plaza, Suite 0111
Chicago 60670

Trust established in 1954 in Illinois.
Donor(s): Frederick S. Upton.
Financial data: (yr. ended 12/31/83): Assets, $7,769,495 (M); expenditures, $346,081, including $325,900 for 34 grants (high: $159,000; low: $100).
Purpose and activities: Broad purposes; emphasis on higher education; grants also for cultural programs, youth agencies, and church support.
Limitations: Giving primarily in MI.
Trustees: Priscilla U. Byrns, David F. Upton, Frederick S. Upton, Stephen E. Upton, The First National Bank of Chicago.
Employer Identification Number: 366013317

1182
USG Foundation, Inc. ▼
(formerly United States Gypsum Foundation, Inc.)
101 South Wacker Dr.
Chicago 60606   (312) 321-3706

Incorporated in 1978 in Illinois.
Donor(s): United States Gypsum Company.
Financial data: (yr. ended 12/31/83): Assets, $1,318,185 (M); expenditures, $565,436, including $473,610 for 116 grants (high: $95,366; average: $1,000-$5,000) and $89,378 for employee matching gifts.
Purpose and activities: Primarily local giving for higher education and community funds; support also for cultural organizations, hospitals, youth agencies, and public interest organizations.
Types of support awarded: Continuing support, annual campaigns, building funds, equipment, research, matching funds, employee matching gifts, technical assistance, general purposes.
Limitations: Giving primarily in Chicago, IL, and areas of company operations. No support for sectarian organizations that are exclusively religious, or for political parties, offices, or candidates; fraternal or veterans' organizations; primary or secondary schools, or generally organizations receiving funds from united campaigns. No grants to individuals; no loans.
Publications: Informational brochure, program policy statement, application guidelines.
Application information:
Initial approach: Full proposal
Copies of proposal: 1
Deadline(s): None
Board meeting date(s): Quarterly
Final notification: 3 months
Write: Eugene Miller, President
Officers: Eugene Miller,* President; Stanton T. Hadley,* R.C. Joynes,* Vice-President; Thaddeus S. Snell, Secretary; W.R. Hogan, Treasurer.
Directors:* Chuck Campbell, H.E. Pendexter.
Number of staff: 2 part-time professional; 2 part-time support.
Employer Identification Number: 362984045

1183
Walgreen Benefit Fund ▼
200 Wilmot Rd.
Deerfield 60015   (312) 946-2931

Incorporated in 1939 in Illinois.
Donor(s): Walgreen Co.
Financial data: (yr. ended 4/30/83): Assets, $7,533,294 (M); expenditures, $648,288, including $414,265 for 511 grants (high: $10,000; low: $10; average: $100-$2,500) and $208,763 for grants to individuals.
Purpose and activities: Charitable purposes; general giving, primarily in areas of company operations, with emphasis on a welfare fund for present and former Walgreen employees and their families; balance of income distributed for higher education, with preference to pharmacy colleges, and to community funds, hospitals and medical research, minorities, and social, cultural, and youth agencies, basically in Walgreen market areas.

Types of support awarded: Annual campaigns, continuing support, emergency funds, general purposes, grants to individuals.
Limitations: Giving primarily in areas of Walgreen markets; no support outside of the U.S. No support for religious organizations. No grants for capital or endowment funds, research-related programs or matching gifts; no loans.
Application information:
Initial approach: Letter or proposal
Copies of proposal: 1
Deadline(s): None
Board meeting date(s): Monthly and as required
Final notification: 30 to 60 days
Write: Edward H. King, Vice-President
Officers: Emily Koulogeorge,* President; Edward H. King,* William Thien, Vice-Presidents; Clarence Hall, Secretary-Treasurer.
Directors:* R.E. Engler.
Number of staff: 1 part-time professional; 1 part-time support.
Employer Identification Number: 366051130

1184
Ward (The A. Montgomery) Foundation
c/o Continental Illinois National Bank and Trust Company of Chicago
30 North LaSalle St.
Chicago 60697   (312) 828-8026

Trust established in 1959 in Illinois.
Donor(s): Mrs. Marjorie Montgomery Ward Baker.†
Financial data: (yr. ended 6/30/83): Assets, $6,153,998 (M); expenditures, $450,081, including $392,343 for 18 grants (high: $150,000; low: $5,000).
Purpose and activities: Broad purposes; primarily local giving, with emphasis on hospitals; support also for higher education, youth agencies, cultural activities, and social agencies.
Limitations: Giving primarily in IL. No grants to individuals.
Publications: Application guidelines.
Application information:
Initial approach: Letter
Copies of proposal: 2
Board meeting date(s): May and November
Write: A.W. Murray, Secretary
Trustees: Richard A. Beck, John A. Hutchings, Continental Illinois National Bank and Trust Company of Chicago.
Employer Identification Number: 362417437

1185
Ward (Montgomery) Foundation
Montgomery Ward Plaza, 20-N
Chicago 60671   (312) 467-7663

Established in 1968 in Illinois.
Donor(s): Montgomery Ward & Co., Inc.
Financial data: (yr. ended 12/31/84): Assets, $263,184 (M); gifts received, $759,000; expenditures, $619,000, including $259,200 for 53 grants (high: $200,000; low: $500) and $159,800 for 606 employee matching gifts.

Purpose and activities: Broad purposes; giving currently limited to support of Chicago organizations, including United Way, arts and cultural programs, and civic and welfare programs in the immediate corporate headquarters' neighborhood; support also for employee matching gifts to higher education, cultural institutions, and public television and radio.
Types of support awarded: Employee matching gifts, annual campaigns, seed money, emergency funds, continuing support, general purposes.
Limitations: Giving limited to Chicago, IL. No grants to individuals, or for building or endowment funds.
Publications: 990-PF, program policy statement.
Application information:
Initial approach: Letter or telephone
Copies of proposal: 1
Deadline(s): Submit proposal preferably between January and May; deadline September
Board meeting date(s): March, June, September, and December
Final notification: Up to 7 months
Write: Nan Kilkeary, Executive Secretary
Officers and Directors:* M.M. Stern, President; J.A. Sarnowski, Vice-President and Treasurer; A. Raives, D. Snell, Vice-Presidents; Nan Kilkeary, Executive Secretary.
Employer Identification Number: 362670108

1186
Warner Electric Foundation ⌘
c/o William W. Keefer Trust
449 Gardner St.
Beloit 61080

Trust established in 1964 in Illinois.
Donor(s): Warner Electric Brake & Clutch Company.
Financial data: (yr. ended 12/31/83): Assets, $172,650 (M); gifts received, $130,000; expenditures, $103,497, including $102,833 for 27 grants (high: $27,500; low: $50).
Purpose and activities: Primarily local giving for higher education, cultural programs, youth agencies, and social services.
Limitations: Giving primarily in Beloit, IL.
Trustees: T.E. Berger, W.W. Keefer.
Employer Identification Number: 366142884

1187
Werner (Clara and Spencer) Foundation, Inc. ⌘
616 South Jefferson St.
Paris 61944

Incorporated in 1953 in Illinois.
Donor(s): Clara B. Werner, Spencer Werner, Illinois Cereal Mills, Inc.
Financial data: (yr. ended 6/30/83): Assets, $4,882,601 (M); expenditures, $419,754, including $410,000 for 9 grants (high: $300,000; low: $5,000).
Purpose and activities: Broad purposes; grants limited to Lutheran programs, including theological education.
Limitations: No grants to individuals.

Officers and Directors: Clara B. Werner, Chairman; W. Frank Wiggins, President; Joseph W. Hasler, Secretary; Herman M. Kurrelmeier, Treasurer; Robert L. Gibson.
Employer Identification Number: 376046119

1188
White (W. P. and H. B.) Foundation
540 Frontage Rd., Suite 332
Northfield 60693   (312) 446-1441

Incorporated in 1953 in Illinois.
Donor(s): William P. White,† Hazel B. White.†
Financial data: (yr. ended 12/31/83): Assets, $9,761,486 (M); expenditures, $543,096, including $459,690 for 163 grants (high: $25,000; low: $500; average: $1,000-$25,000).
Purpose and activities: General purposes; primarily local giving for higher education, hospitals, Roman Catholic church support and church-related institutions, inner city programs, and community funds.
Types of support awarded: Operating budgets, continuing support, annual campaigns, seed money, emergency funds, building funds, equipment, professorships, scholarship funds, special projects, research.
Limitations: Giving primarily in metropolitan Chicago, IL. No grants to individuals, or for land acquisition, endowment funds, publications, conferences, deficit financing, or matching gifts; no loans.
Application information:
Initial approach: Letter or full proposal
Copies of proposal: 1
Deadline(s): None
Board meeting date(s): March, June, September, and December
Final notification: Several weeks
Write: John H. McCortney, Vice-President
Officers and Directors: Roger B. White, President; John H. McCortney, Vice-President and Treasurer; Steven R. White, Secretary; Paul M. Plunkett, Robert P. White.
Number of staff: 1 part-time professional; 1 part-time support.
Employer Identification Number: 362601558

1189
Wieboldt Foundation
79 West Monroe St., Suite 810
Chicago 60603   (312) 726-1553

Incorporated in 1921 in Illinois.
Donor(s): William A. Wieboldt,† Mrs. Anna Krueger Wieboldt.†
Financial data: (yr. ended 12/31/83): Assets, $90 (M); expenditures, $587,402, including $396,550 for 46 grants (high: $35,000; low: $750).
Purpose and activities: Interest focused on community organizations, resources for community groups, and change-oriented agencies.
Types of support awarded: General purposes, continuing support, research.
Limitations: Giving limited to Chicago, IL. No grants to individuals, or for endowment funds, scholarships or fellowships.
Publications: Annual report, program policy statement, application guidelines.

Application information:
Initial approach: Letter or telephone
Copies of proposal: 1
Deadline(s): 1st of each month
Board meeting date(s): Monthly
Final notification: 1 to 2 months
Write: George Todd, Executive Director
Officers: John W. Straub,* President; Stanley J. Hallett,* Nydia W. Hohf,* Vice-Presidents; George E. Todd, Secretary and Executive Director; Nancy A. Wieboldt,* Treasurer.
Directors:* Rosalyn J. Averette, Kathryn Sieck Bloom, Anita S. Darrow, Jill C. Darrow, Carol W. Higgins, David C. Hilliard, Lawrence E. Kennon, Mary W. Sample, Rita Simo, Dolores J. Smith, Joan E. Straub.
Members: Donald A. Bloom, Cecil C. Butler, Anita S. Darrow, Robert P. Taylor, Raymond C. Wieboldt, Jr.
Number of staff: 2.
Employer Identification Number: 362167955

1190
Wilkie Brothers Foundation ⌘
254 North Laurel Ave.
Des Plaines 60016

Incorporated in 1951 in Illinois.
Donor(s): Leighton A. Wilkie, Robert J. Wilkie, James W. Wilkie, and their business interests.
Financial data: (yr. ended 12/31/82): Assets, $831,320 (M); expenditures, $746,317, including $722,911 for 30 grants (high: $264,210; low: $50) and $7,919 for 1 foundation-administered program.
Purpose and activities: Grants primarily for tool history and higher education; support also for hospitals and museums.
Application information:
Write: Philip J. Weber, Treasurer
Officers and Directors:* Leighton A. Wilkie,* President; Robert J. Wilkie,* James W. Wilkie,* Vice-Presidents; Charles T. Peterson, Secretary; Philip J. Weber, Treasurer.
Employer Identification Number: 362226189

1191
Willett (Howard L.) Foundation, Inc. ⌘
69 West Washington St., Rm. 2000
Chicago 60602

Incorporated in 1973 in Illinois.
Donor(s): Howard L. Willett,† Howard L. Willett, Jr.†
Financial data: (yr. ended 12/31/83): Assets, $3,042,612 (M); expenditures, $257,016, including $242,900 for 65 grants (high: $25,000; low: $500).
Purpose and activities: Broad purposes; primarily local giving with emphasis on higher education, health agencies, support for the aged, secondary education and cultural organizations.
Limitations: Giving primarily in IL.
Officer: John R. Covington, Manager.
Employer Identification Number: 237311429

1192
Wolf (Harry H.), Sr. & Jr. Foundation
1000 Skokie Blvd., Suite 325
Wilmette 60091

Incorporated in 1956 in Illinois.
Donor(s): Jockey International, Inc., Harry H. Wolf, Jr.
Financial data: (yr. ended 10/31/84): Assets, $1,025,023 (M); expenditures, $192,583, including $186,000 for 2 grants (high: $185,000; low: $1,000).
Purpose and activities: General giving, with emphasis on hospitals; grants also for higher education, church support and youth agencies.
Officers: Harry H. Wolf, Jr., President; Mary W. Bogue, Donna W. Steigerwaldt, Vice-Presidents.
Employer Identification Number: 366050373

1193
Woods Charitable Fund, Inc. ▼
Three First National Plaza, Suite 3050
Chicago 60602   (312) 782-2698
For applications from Nebraska: Margaret Small, P.O. Box 81309, Lincoln, NE 68501; Tel.: (402) 474-0707

Incorporated in 1941 in Nebraska.
Donor(s): Frank H. Woods,† Nelle C. Woods,† Sahara Coal Company, Inc.
Financial data: (yr. ended 12/31/84): Assets, $30,171,295 (M); gifts received, $90,150; expenditures, $2,070,266, including $1,673,695 for 97 grants (high: $200,000; low: $1,250; average: $17,255).
Purpose and activities: Broad charitable and educational purposes; giving primarily to enhance life in Chicago and Lincoln, particularly for the most disadvantaged residents, and largely through citizens' community-based organizations and public interest groups. Interests in both cities include public policy, culture, and education; giving in Chicago with emphasis on public schools, government accountability, and public policy as it affects families; giving in Lincoln for the arts and humanities, the family, historic preservation, and community improvement and leadership. Social service projects should have a clear public policy strategy or be expressly planned for wide duplication.
Types of support awarded: Operating budgets, seed money, matching funds, special projects, research, consulting services.
Limitations: Giving primarily in IL and NE, with emphasis on the Chicago and Lincoln metropolitan areas. No support for medical or scientific research, religious activities, health care institutions, recreation programs, government agencies or projects, or national health, welfare, educational or cultural organizations or their state or local affiliates. No grants to individuals, or for endowments, scholarships, fellowships, fund raising benefits, capital campaigns or large capital projects, residential care, program advertising, or research.
Publications: Annual report, application guidelines, 990-PF.

Application information: Capital campaigns and projects considered only at December meeting.
Initial approach: Telephone or letter
Copies of proposal: 1
Deadline(s): 8 weeks (Chicago) or 5 weeks (Lincoln) before board meetings
Board meeting date(s): March 13, June 18, September 11, and December 3
Final notification: 1 week after board meeting
Write: Jean Rudd, Executive Director, or Martin P. Adams (Chicago area); Margaret Small (Nebraska)
Officers: Thomas C. Woods, Jr.,* President; George Kelm,* Thomas C. Woods, III,* Vice-Presidents; Charles N. Wheatley, Secretary-Treasurer; Jean Rudd, Executive Director.
Trustees:* Lucia Woods Lindley.
Number of staff: 2 full-time professional; 1 part-time professional; 1 full-time support.
Employer Identification Number: 476032847

1194
Wurlitzer (The Farny R.) Foundation
P.O. Box 387
Sycamore 60178   (815) 756-2771

Established about 1948; incorporated in 1962 in New York.
Donor(s): Farny R. Wurlitzer,† Grace K. Wurlitzer.†
Financial data: (yr. ended 12/31/82): Assets, $2,784,585 (M); expenditures, $184,738, including $173,017 for 49 grants (high: $10,000; low: $100; average: $2,000-$10,000).
Purpose and activities: Broad purposes; general local giving, with emphasis on music education, music organizations, civic and community projects, and higher education.
Types of support awarded: Operating budgets, continuing support, annual campaigns, emergency funds, deficit financing, building funds, equipment, land acquisition, endowment funds, special projects, research.
Limitations: Giving primarily in IL and the Midwest. No grants to individuals, or for scholarships and fellowships, seed money, publications, or conferences; no loans.
Application information:
Initial approach: Full proposal
Copies of proposal: 1
Deadline(s): Submit proposal preferably between January and March or between July and September
Board meeting date(s): May and November
Final notification: 90 days
Write: William A. Rolfing, President
Officers and Directors: William A. Rolfing, President; W.S. Turner, Vice-President; C.P. O'Kane, Secretary-Treasurer; H.L. Evans, W.G. Olson, J.D. Ovitz.
Number of staff: None.
Employer Identification Number: 363079264

INDIANA

1195
Anderson (John W.) Foundation ▼
402 Wall St.
Valparaiso 46383   (219) 462-4611

Trust established in 1967 in Indiana.
Donor(s): John W. Anderson.†
Financial data: (yr. ended 12/31/83): Assets, $62,006,881 (M); expenditures, $3,602,314, including $3,016,079 for 117 grants (high: $475,076; low: $450; average: $2,000-$25,000) and $135,786 for grants to individuals.
Purpose and activities: General giving primarily in Lake and Porter counties in northwest Indiana, with emphasis on youth agencies; support also for higher education, community funds, aid to the handicapped, and hospitals.
Types of support awarded: Operating budgets, continuing support, emergency funds, building funds, matching funds, research, special projects, employee related scholarships.
Limitations: Giving primarily in Lake and Porter counties in northwest IN. No grants to individuals (except for company-employee scholarships), or for endowment funds, annual campaigns, seed money, deficit financing, scholarships, or renovation projects; no loans.
Publications: 990-PF.
Application information:
Initial approach: Letter
Copies of proposal: 5
Deadline(s): None
Board meeting date(s): February, April, June, August, October, and December
Final notification: 1 month
Write: Harold G. Rudd, Secretary
Officers and Trustees: Richard S. Melvin, Chairman; Wilfred G. Wilkins, Vice-Chairman; Harold G. Rudd, Secretary; Paul G. Wallace, Bruce W. Wargo.
Number of staff: 2 part-time professional; 4 full-time support.
Employer Identification Number: 356070695

1196
Arvin Foundation, Inc., The ⊠
1531 East 13th St.
Columbus 47201   (812) 372-7271

Incorporated in 1951 in Indiana.
Donor(s): Arvin Industries, Inc.
Financial data: (yr. ended 12/31/83): Assets, $761,902 (M); gifts received, $255,000; expenditures, $326,607, including $324,842 for 123 grants (high: $125,000; low: $25).
Purpose and activities: Giving primarily for higher education, community funds, youth organizations, and cultural programs.
Types of support awarded: General purposes, building funds, operating budgets, continuing support, equipment, special projects.

Limitations: No grants to individuals, or for endowment funds, scholarships, fellowships, or matching gifts; no loans.
Publications: Annual report.
Application information:
Initial approach: Full proposal
Copies of proposal: 1
Deadline(s): None
Board meeting date(s): May and October
Final notification: 8 weeks
Write: W. Fred Meyer, Vice-President, Public Affairs
Officers and Directors: James K. Baker, Chairman and President; W. Fred Meyer, Vice-President, Public Affairs; Martha J. Schrader, Secretary; Stanley R. Wheeler, Treasurer; Clyde R. Davis, L.K. Evans, Richard L. Hendricks, V. William Hunt, J. William Kendall, John P. Sohn, Charles H. Watson.
Number of staff: 6.
Employer Identification Number: 356020798

1197
Ayres Foundation, Inc.
1-15 West Washington St.
Indianapolis 46204

Incorporated in 1944 in Indiana.
Donor(s): L.S. Ayres and Company, Theodore B. Griffith, Mrs. Theodore B. Griffith, Ayr-Way Stores, Inc.
Financial data: (yr. ended 1/28/83): Assets, $961,395 (M); gifts received, $93,250; expenditures, $167,855, including $160,950 for 52 grants (high: $64,000; low: $100) and $1,441 for 3 grants to individuals.
Purpose and activities: Primarily local giving, with emphasis on community funds, cultural activities, and higher education; also provides relief to needy company employees, ex-employees, and their dependents.
Limitations: Giving primarily in IN, with emphasis on Indianapolis.
Application information: Applications not invited.
Deadline(s): None
Officers and Directors: John E.D. Peacock, President; John L. Hoerner, Vice-President; Herbert A. Abbott, Jr., Secretary-Treasurer; Lyman S. Ayres, Joseph F. Bornhorst, Daniel F. Evans, Alvin C. Fernandes, Jr., James A. Gloin, William J. Stout, Gunnar Vanays.
Employer Identification Number: 356018437

1198
Baber (Weisell) Foundation, Inc. ⌖
535 South Broadway
Peru 46970   (317) 473-7526

Incorporated in 1958 in Indiana.
Donor(s): Avanella Baber,† Weisell Baber.†
Financial data: (yr. ended 12/31/83): Assets, $2,026,460 (M); expenditures, $110,086, including $56,300 for 33 loans.
Purpose and activities: Grants primarily for student loans to graduates of one of the Miami County, Indiana, high schools.
Types of support awarded: Student aid.
Limitations: Giving limited to Miami County, IN.

Application information: Applicants must apply in person.
Write: Roger D. Baber, President
Officers and Directors: Roger D. Baber, President; Eric R. Baber, Ruth R. Bowland, Vice-Presidents; Naomi R. Baber, Secretary.
Employer Identification Number: 356024561

1199
Ball Brothers Foundation ▼
520 Merchants Bank Bldg.
Muncie 47305   (317) 747-0948

Incorporated in 1926 in Indiana.
Donor(s): Edmund B. Ball,† Frank C. Ball,† George A. Ball,† Lucius L. Ball, M.D.,† William A. Ball.†
Financial data: (yr. ended 12/31/84): Assets, $57,049,000 (M); gifts received, $12,653,000; expenditures, $2,084,269, including $1,502,683 for 53 grants (high: $100,000; low: $500).
Purpose and activities: Broad purposes; emphasis on higher education, hospitals, social services, and cultural programs.
Types of support awarded: Matching funds, professorships, research, publications, conferences and seminars, special projects.
Limitations: Giving limited to IN. No grants to individuals.
Publications: 990-PF.
Application information:
Initial approach: Letter or full proposal
Copies of proposal: 1
Deadline(s): Submit proposal preferably before June; no set deadline
Board meeting date(s): Quarterly and as necessary
Write: Douglas A. Bakken, Executive Director
Officers: Edmund F. Ball,* President; Alexander M. Bracken,* John W. Fisher,* Vice-Presidents; Reed D. Voran,* Secretary; Douglas J. Foy,* Treasurer; Douglas A. Bakken, Executive Director.
Directors:* Frank E. Ball, Lucina B. Moxley, Edmund F. Petty, John J. Pruis.
Number of staff: 1 full-time professional; 2 part-time professional.
Employer Identification Number: 350882856

1200
Ball (George and Frances) Foundation ▼
520 Merchants National Bank Bldg.
Muncie 47305   (317) 289-2792

Incorporated in 1937 in Indiana.
Donor(s): George A. Ball.†
Financial data: (yr. ended 12/31/83): Assets, $11,702,940 (M); gifts received, $6,608,478; expenditures, $2,477,409, including $2,446,985 for 22 grants (high: $1,986,380; low: $50; average: $1,000-$15,000).
Purpose and activities: Primarily local giving, with emphasis on higher education.
Limitations: Giving primarily in Muncie, IN.
Application information: Application form required.
Initial approach: Proposal
Deadline(s): None
Write: Alexander M. Bracken, President

Officers: Alexander M. Bracken,* President; John J. Pruis,* Vice-President; Reed D. Voran,* Secretary; Douglas J. Foy, Treasurer.
Directors:* Rosemary B. Bracken, Doris Frederichs.
Employer Identification Number: 356033917

1201
Beardsley Foundation, The
(formerly Andrew Hubble Beardsley and Walter Raper Beardsley Foundation)
c/o First National Bank
301 South Main St.
Elkhart 46514

Trust established in 1955 in Indiana.
Donor(s): Walter R. Beardsley.†
Financial data: (yr. ended 12/31/84): Assets, $3,639,599 (M); gifts received, $5,000; expenditures, $107,500, including $77,500 for 17 grants (high: $20,000; low: $1,000).
Purpose and activities: A private operating foundation giving primarily locally for a museum, cultural programs and social services.
Limitations: Giving primarily in IN.
Application information:
Write: Richard C. Spaulding, Treasurer
Officers and Directors: Robert B. Beardsley, President; John F. Dille, Jr., Vice-President; John R. Harman, Secretary; Richard C. Spaulding, Treasurer; Rev. George Minnix.
Number of staff: 8 part-time support.
Employer Identification Number: 351170807

1202
Bowsher-Booher Foundation, The ⌖
112 West Jefferson Blvd.
South Bend 46601   (219) 237-3314

Established in 1980.
Financial data: (yr. ended 5/31/83): Assets, $1,200,074 (M); expenditures, $97,921, including $90,832 for 11 grants (high: $20,000; low: $5,000).
Purpose and activities: Local giving primarily for social services.
Limitations: Giving primarily in Grants limited to the South Bend area and St. Joseph County, IN.
Application information:
Initial approach: Letter
Copies of proposal: 1
Deadline(s): April 1 for consideration in May; October 1 for consideration in November
Write: Robert R. Cleppe
Trustee: National Bank & Trust Company.
Employer Identification Number: 310979401

1203
Bronstein (The Sol and Arlene) Foundation ⌖
c/o National City Bank of Evansville
Evansville 47705

Established in 1979 in Indiana.
Donor(s): Sol Bronstein,† Laketon Asphalt Refining Co.

Financial data: (yr. ended 12/31/83): Assets, $3,895,494 (M); expenditures, $354,387, including $320,000 for 26 grants (high: $117,000; low: $1,000).
Purpose and activities: Primarily local giving for Jewish organizations, with emphasis on temple support, Jewish education, and Jewish welfare funds; also giving for higher education.
Limitations: Giving primarily in IN.
Trustees: Hubert De Jong, National City Bank of Evansville.
Advisors: Leonard Pearson, Sidney Shane, Howard Treckman, Congregation B'Nai Israel, Hebrew Union Jewish Institute of Religion.
Employer Identification Number: 356313412

1204
Central Newspapers Foundation
307 N. Pennsylvania St.
Indianapolis 46204

Incorporated in 1935 in Indiana.
Donor(s): Eugene C. Pulliam, Central Newspapers, Inc., Indianapolis Newspapers, Inc., Phoenix Newspapers, Inc.
Financial data: (yr. ended 4/30/84): Assets, $208,683 (M); gifts received, $114,000; expenditures, $287,355, including $116,518 for 29 grants (high: $14,184; low: $100) and $84,500 for 56 grants to individuals.
Purpose and activities: Broad purposes; limited activities, including aid to the blind of central Indiana; support for higher education with emphasis on the states of Indiana and Arizona; and a scholarship program for children of employees of member newspapers.
Types of support awarded: Employee related scholarships.
Limitations: Giving primarily in IN and AZ.
Application information: Applications not invited.
Board meeting date(s): Annually
Officers and Directors: William A. Dyer, Jr., President; Eugene S. Pulliam, Vice-President; Frank E. Russell, Secretary-Treasurer; Raymond E. Houk, Shirley A. Shideler.
Employer Identification Number: 356013720

1205
Central Soya Foundation ⌑
900 Fort Wayne National Bank Bldg.
Fort Wayne 46802

Trust established in 1954 in Indiana.
Donor(s): Central Soya Company, Inc.
Financial data: (yr. ended 8/31/83): Assets, $577,390 (M); gifts received, $500,000; expenditures, $364,718, including $360,470 for 118 grants (high: $26,000; low: $60).
Purpose and activities: Giving primarily in areas of company operations, with emphasis on higher education, health and social agencies, community funds, and youth agencies.
Limitations: Giving primarily in areas of company operations.
Trustee: Fort Wayne National Bank.
Employer Identification Number: 356020624

1206
Clowes Fund, Inc., The ▼
250 East 38th St.
Indianapolis 46205 (317) 923-3264

Incorporated in 1952 in Indiana.
Donor(s): Edith W. Clowes,† George H.A. Clowes,† Allen W. Clowes.
Financial data: (yr. ended 12/31/83): Assets, $15,893,885 (M); expenditures, $552,005, including $485,000 for 27 grants (high: $150,000; low: $1,000; average: $2,500-$50,000).
Purpose and activities: Broad purposes; giving locally for maintenance of the Clowes Collection of Old Master Paintings in Clowes Pavilion, Indianapolis Museum of Art, and in Boston, Massachusetts; grants largely for the arts, music, higher education, and marine biology; support also for social services.
Types of support awarded: Operating budgets, continuing support, building funds, endowment funds, scholarship funds, special projects, research.
Limitations: Giving primarily in Indianapolis, IN, and Boston, MA. No grants to individuals, or for publications, or conferences; no loans.
Publications: Application guidelines.
Application information:
Initial approach: Letter or full proposal
Copies of proposal: 2
Deadline(s): Submit proposal between September and January; deadline January 31
Board meeting date(s): Between February 1 and June 1, once a year
Final notification: 1 month after board meeting
Write: Allen W. Clowes, President
Officers and Directors: Allen W. Clowes, President and Treasurer; Margaret J. Clowes, Vice-President; Thomas M. Lofton, Secretary; Margaret C. Bowles, Alexander W. Clowes, George H.A. Clowes, Jr., Bryon P. Hollett, John J. vanBenten.
Number of staff: 2 full-time professional; 1 part-time support.
Employer Identification Number: 351079679

1207
Cole (Olive B.) Foundation, Inc. ▼
3242 Mallard Cove Ln.
Fort Wayne 46804 (219) 436-2182

Incorporated in 1954 in Indiana.
Donor(s): Richard R. Cole,† Olive B. Cole.
Financial data: (yr. ended 3/31/84): Assets, $12,778,283 (M); expenditures, $672,557, including $337,462 for 28 grants (high: $70,000; low: $1,000; average: $12,052) and $118,018 for grants to individuals.
Purpose and activities: Broad purposes; for the benefit of residents of the Kendallville, Noble County, Indiana area. Grants largely for education, including scholarships, hospitals, civic affairs, youth agencies, and cultural programs.
Types of support awarded: Seed money, building funds, equipment, land acquisition, student aid, matching funds, program-related investments, general purposes, continuing support.

Limitations: Giving limited to the Kendallville, Noble County, IN, area. No grants for endowment funds, or research; no loans.
Publications: Application guidelines, program policy statement.
Application information: Application form required.
Initial approach: Letter
Copies of proposal: 7
Deadline(s): None
Board meeting date(s): February, May, August, and November
Final notification: 4 months
Write: John E. Hogan, Jr., Executive Vice-President
Officers and Directors: John N. Pichon, Jr., President; John E. Hogan, Jr., Executive Vice-President and Treasurer; Maclyn T. Parker, Secretary; Thomas Alberts, Duane L. Axel, Robert Borger, Matt Dalton, Paul Schirmeyer.
Scholarship Administrator: Gwendlyn I. Tipton.
Number of staff: 1 full-time professional; 1 full-time support.
Employer Identification Number: 356040491

1208
Credithrift Financial - Richard E. Meier Foundation, Inc.
P.O. Box 59
Evansville 47701 (812) 424-8031

Incorporated in 1958 in Indiana.
Donor(s): Credithrift Financial Corporation, and subsidiaries.
Financial data: (yr. ended 12/31/84): Assets, $846,461 (M); expenditures, $249,552, including $248,711 for 93 grants (high: $20,000; low: $25; average: $500-$1,000).
Purpose and activities: Broad purposes; support for community funds and privately endowed colleges and universities within the operating areas of the corporation. Most grants awarded on pre-established formula to the United Way and state associations of private colleges.
Types of support awarded: Operating budgets, continuing support, annual campaigns, building funds, employee related scholarships.
Limitations: Giving primarily in areas of company operations. No grants to individuals (except for 3 scholarships to dependents of employees), or for seed money, emergency or endowment funds, deficit financing, equipment, land acquisition, matching gifts, special projects, research, publications, or conferences; no loans.
Application information:
Initial approach: Letter
Copies of proposal: 1
Deadline(s): None
Board meeting date(s): April
Final notification: 2 to 3 weeks
Write: Owen M. Hamilton, Vice-President
Officers: Wendell L. Dixon,* President; Owen M. Hamilton,* Vice-President; Lysle I. Abbott, Secretary; Arthur D. Holley,* Treasurer.
Directors:* Louis Durfee, Gaylord E. Francis, Harold S. Hook, Fred S. Kohlruss, Robert Plummer, Michael J. Poulos, H. Norris Robinson.
Number of staff: None.
Employer Identification Number: 356042566

1209
CTS Foundation
905 North West Blvd.
Elkhart 46514 (219) 293-7511

Trust established in 1953 in Indiana.
Donor(s): CTS Corporation.
Financial data: (yr. ended 6/30/83): Assets, $1,865,000 (M); expenditures, $71,000, including $60,000 for 16 grants (high: $20,000; low: $250) and $206,000 for 170 loans.
Purpose and activities: Principal activity is to make interest-free student loans to employees and children of employees of CTS and its subsidiaries for undergraduate college education. Support also for educational and charitable organizations in communities in which the company is located, primarily in Indiana; some support for community funds, civic, and health agencies.
Types of support awarded: Annual campaigns, student aid.
Limitations: Giving primarily in areas of company operations, primarily in IN.
Application information:
Initial approach: Full proposal
Deadline(s): None
Board meeting date(s): Semiannually and as needed
Write: James S. Taylor, Chairman
Officers and Trustees: James S. Taylor, Chairman; Joseph DiGirolamo, Vice-Chairman; David K. Sentman, Treasurer; Clinton W. Hartman, Robert D. Hostetler, Charles C. Smith.
Number of staff: None.
Employer Identification Number: 356014484

1210
Cummins Engine Foundation ▼
Box Number 3005
Columbus 47202-3005 (812) 377-3560

Incorporated in 1954 in Indiana.
Donor(s): Cummins Engine Company, Inc.
Financial data: (yr. ended 12/31/83): Assets, $2,769,442 (M); expenditures, $2,171,925, including $1,711,063 for 120 grants (high: $272,296; low: $500; average: $2,500-$15,000), $118,657 for 103 grants to individuals and $184,941 for employee matching gifts.
Purpose and activities: Giving focused primarily on local community needs, youth, civil rights, and education, including an employee matching gifts program and a company employee scholarship program; grants also for national needs which combine equal opportunity and excellence.
Types of support awarded: Annual campaigns, conferences and seminars, continuing support, emergency funds, endowment funds, matching funds, operating budgets, program-related investments, publications, seed money, technical assistance, employee related scholarships, special projects, grants to individuals, student aid.
Limitations: Giving primarily in areas of company operations, particularly the Columbus, IN, area. No support for denominational religious purposes. No grants to individuals (except scholarships for children of company employees).

Publications: Annual report, program policy statement, application guidelines.
Application information:
Initial approach: Full proposal or letter
Copies of proposal: 1
Deadline(s): None
Board meeting date(s): February, July, September, and December
Final notification: 1 to 3 months
Write: David L. Dodson, Executive Director
Officers and Directors: Henry B. Schacht, Chairman; Richard B. Stoner, Vice-Chairman; James A. Henderson, President; Ted L. Marston, Secretary; John T. Hackett, Treasurer; David L. Dodson, Executive Director; Michael F. Brewer, Hanna Gray, James A. Joseph, J. Irwin Miller, Michael H. Walsh, B. Joseph White.
Number of staff: 2 full-time professional; 2 part-time professional; 1 full-time support; 1 part-time support.
Employer Identification Number: 356042373

1211
Decio (Arthur J.) Foundation ¤
c/o Skyline Corporation
2520 By-Pass Rd.
Elkhart 46514

Established in 1970 in Indiana.
Donor(s): Arthur J. Decio.
Financial data: (yr. ended 9/30/83): Assets, $1,697,890 (M); expenditures, $103,957, including $102,002 for 31 grants (high: $16,402).
Purpose and activities: Primarily local giving, with emphasis on education and cultural programs.
Limitations: Giving primarily in IN.
Application information:
Write: Ronald F. Kloska, Trustee
Trustees: Arthur J. Decio, Patricia C. Decio, Ronald F. Kloska, Andrew McKenna, Richard M. Treckelo.
Employer Identification Number: 237083597

1212
English-Bonter-Mitchell Foundation ▼ ¤
900 Fort Wayne National Bank Bldg.
Fort Wayne 46802

Established in 1972 in Indiana.
Donor(s): Mary Tower English, Louise Bonter, and others.
Financial data: (yr. ended 12/31/83): Assets, $26,108,755 (M); expenditures, $1,464,221, including $1,367,500 for 45 grants (high: $155,000; low: $500; average: $2,000-$50,000).
Purpose and activities: Primarily local giving with emphasis on cultural programs and programs for youth; support also for higher education, hospitals, churches and religious organizations, social services, health, and community development.
Limitations: Giving primarily in Fort Wayne, IN.
Officer: Mary E. Mitchell, Advisor.
Trustee: Fort Wayne National Bank.
Employer Identification Number: 356247168

1213
Foellinger Foundation, Inc. ▼ ¤
5800 Fairfield Ave., Suite 230
Fort Wayne 46807 (219) 456-4441

Incorporated in 1958 in Indiana.
Donor(s): Esther A. Foellinger,† Helene R. Foellinger, News Publishing Company.
Financial data: (yr. ended 8/31/83): Assets, $15,682,808 (M); gifts received, $318,000; expenditures, $1,138,468, including $1,072,690 for 37 grants (high: $400,000; low: $150; average: $1,000-$15,000).
Purpose and activities: Primarily local giving, with emphasis on cultural organizations, higher education, parks and recreation, social services, and a community fund.
Types of support awarded: Operating budgets, building funds, special projects.
Limitations: Giving primarily in the Fort Wayne, IN area. No grants to individuals.
Application information:
Initial approach: Letter or proposal
Copies of proposal: 1
Board meeting date(s): As required
Final notification: Varies, depending on request
Write: Helene R. Foellinger, President
Officers and Directors: Helene R. Foellinger, President; Ernest E. Williams, Vice-President; Walter P. Helmke, Secretary; Harry V. Owen, Treasurer; Carl Rolfson.
Number of staff: 2.
Employer Identification Number: 356027059

1214
Fort Wayne Foundation, Inc., The
116 E. Wayne St.
Fort Wayne 46802 (219) 429-2167

Community foundation incorporated in 1956 in Indiana.
Financial data: (yr. ended 12/31/83): Assets, $2,154,264 (M); gifts received, $168,514; expenditures, $170,048, including $152,406 for 21 grants.
Purpose and activities: Primarily local giving; discretionary grant-making preference given to "projects expected to generate substantial benefits for the greater Fort Wayne area," including capital projects, demonstration projects, and projects promoting effective management, efficient use of community resources or volunteer participation.
Types of support awarded: Seed money, emergency funds, building funds, equipment, land acquisition, matching funds, consulting services, conferences and seminars, special projects.
Limitations: Giving primarily in Allen County, IN. No support for religious purposes, hospitals or medical research, or private schools. No grants to individuals, or for operating budgets, continuing support, annual campaigns, deficit financing, endowment funds, technical assistance, scholarships, fellowships, research, or publications; no loans.
Publications: Biennial report, application guidelines.
Application information:
Initial approach: Proposal, letter, or telephone

Copies of proposal: 1
Deadline(s): None
Board meeting date(s): February, May,
    August, and November
Final notification: 3 months
Write: Mrs. Joyce Schlatter, Director-Grants
Staff: Barbara Burt, Executive Director; Paul
Clarke, Director-Special Projects; Joyce
Schlatter, Director-Grants.
Number of staff: 3 part-time professional.
Employer Identification Number: 351119450

1215
Froderman Foundation, Inc., The ⌑
18 S. Ninth St.
Terre Haute 47808

Donor(s): Harvey Froderman.†
Financial data: (yr. ended 6/30/84): Assets,
$5,037,359 (M); expenditures, $315,915,
including $266,102 for 27 grants (high:
$50,000; low: $100).
Purpose and activities: Primarily local giving
for church support, medical education, and
youth organizations.
Types of support awarded: Building funds,
equipment, scholarship funds, operating
budgets, publications.
Limitations: Giving primarily in IN.
Application information: Application form
required.
    Initial approach: Letter
    Deadline(s): None
    Write: Carl M. Froderman, Director
Directors: Carl M. Froderman, Esten P. Fuson.
Employer Identification Number: 356025283

1216
Gershon Ben-Ephraim Fund ⌑
One Indiana Square
Indianapolis 46266
Application address: 445 N. Pennsylvania St.,
Rm. 908, Indianapolis, IN 46204; Tel.: (317)
632-7359

Established in 1981 in Indiana.
Donor(s): Clarence W. Efroymson.
Financial data: (yr. ended 4/30/83): Assets,
$10,140,159 (M); gifts received, $1,162,985;
expenditures, $264,199, including $260,000
for 3 grants (high: $150,000; low: $50,000).
Purpose and activities: Charitable purposes
with emphasis on giving to Israel.
Application information:
    Initial approach: Proposal
Distribution Committee: Clarence W.
Efroymson, Robert A. Efroymson.
Trustee: Indiana National Bank.
Employer Identification Number: 356370113

1217
Griffith (The W. C.) Foundation
c/o Merchants National Bank & Trust Company
P.O. Box 5031
Indianapolis 46255   (317) 267-7281

Trust established in 1959 in Indiana.
Donor(s): William C. Griffith,† Ruth Perry
Griffith.

Financial data: (yr. ended 11/30/84): Assets,
$3,729,116 (M); expenditures, $217,381,
including $200,400 for 60 grants (high:
$25,000; low: $250; average: $1,000).
Purpose and activities: Primarily local giving,
with emphasis on hospitals, church support,
art, community funds, and higher and
secondary education.
Limitations: Giving primarily in Indianapolis,
IN. No grants to individuals, or for
scholarships and fellowships.
Publications: 990-PF.
Application information:
    Initial approach: Letter
    Copies of proposal: 1
    Deadline(s): None
    Write: Mike Miner, Vice-President and Trust
        Officer
Trustee: Merchants National Bank & Trust
Company (Mike Miner, Vice-President).
Advisors: C. Perry Griffith, Jr., W.C. Griffith,
Jr., Walter Stuhr Griffith, William C. Griffith, III.
Number of staff: None.
Employer Identification Number: 356007742

1218
Habig (Arnold F.) Foundation, Inc. ⌑
c/o Arnold F. Habig
1301 St. Charles St.
Jasper 47546

Established in 1967.
Financial data: (yr. ended 12/31/83): Assets,
$2,122,774 (M); gifts received, $9,201;
expenditures, $47,219, including $19,957 for
63 grants (high: $3,955; low: $3).
Purpose and activities: Grants mainly for
education and Roman Catholic religious
organizations.
Limitations: Giving primarily in IN.
Officers: Arnold F. Habig, President; John B.
Habig, Secretary; Thomas L. Habig, Treasurer.
Director: Douglas Habig.
Employer Identification Number: 356074146

1219
Habig Foundation Inc., The
1600 Royal St.
Jasper 47546

Incorporated in 1951 in Indiana.
Donor(s): Kimball International, Inc.
Financial data: (yr. ended 6/30/84): Assets,
$639,637 (M); gifts received, $134,750;
expenditures, $277,292, including $214,309
for 120 grants (high: $60,000; low: $25) and
$61,000 for 35 grants to individuals.
Purpose and activities: Primarily local giving,
with emphasis on higher education, including
scholarships for children of company
employees only, civic affairs, church support
and cultural programs.
Types of support awarded: Employee related
scholarships.
Limitations: Giving primarily in IN.

Officers and Directors: Thomas L. Habig,
Chairman; Douglas A. Habig, President; H.E.
Thyen, Secretary; James C. Thyen, Treasurer;
Anthony P. Habig, Arnold F. Habig, John B.
Habig, Maurice R. Kuper, Leonard B. Marshall,
Jr., Patricia H. Snyder, Ronald J. Thyen, Jack R.
Wentworth.
Employer Identification Number: 356022535

1220
**Hayes (Stanley W.) Research
    Foundation, Inc.**
801 Elks Rd.
P.O. Box 1404
Richmond 47374   (317) 962-4894

Incorporated in 1959 in Indiana.
Donor(s): Stanley W. Hayes.†
Financial data: (yr. ended 6/30/84): Assets,
$4,120,000 (M); expenditures, $299,800,
including $5,800 for 21 grants (high: $500;
low: $75) and $294,000 for 1 foundation-
administered program.
Purpose and activities: Educational purposes;
a private operating foundation which maintains
the Hayes Regional Arboretum as a laboratory
for ecological research by educational
institutions, a source of regional flora for civic
improvement, and a teaching center for
biological sciences; some limited support for
local cultural organizations, youth agencies,
and other organizations interested in education
about and preservation of Indiana plants.
Limitations: Giving limited to IN, particularly
the Richmond area. No grants to individuals.
Publications: Program policy statement,
application guidelines.
Application information: No grants over $500
considered. Application form required.
    Initial approach: Letter
    Deadline(s): Between June 1 and September 1
    Board meeting date(s): September
    Write: Stephen H. Hayes, President
Officers and Directors: Stephen H. Hayes,
President and Treasurer; Edmund B. Hayes,
Vice-President; Robert E. McClure, Secretary;
James B. Cope, Donald R. Hendricks, Patricia
A. Mayer, William H. Reller.
Employer Identification Number: 351061111

1221
Hayner Foundation
c/o Lincoln National Bank and Trust Company
116 East Berry St.
Fort Wayne 46802   (219) 423-6419

Established in 1966 in Indiana.
Donor(s): John F. Hayner.†
Financial data: (yr. ended 12/31/82): Assets,
$1,137,339 (M); expenditures, $85,872,
including $79,120 for 15 grants (high: $51,500;
low: $150; average: $1,000).
Purpose and activities: Local grants for health,
including health education services, and
cultural activities.
Types of support awarded: Operating
budgets, continuing support, seed money,
equipment, matching funds.

Limitations: Giving limited to Allen County, IN. No grants to individuals, or for annual campaigns, emergency, building, or endowment funds, deficit financing, land acquisition, scholarships or fellowships, research, special projects, publications, or conferences; no loans.
Publications: 990-PF.
Application information:
Initial approach: Letter
Deadline(s): None
Board meeting date(s): Monthly
Final notification: 6 weeks
Write: Alice Kopfer, Trust Officer
Trustee: Lincoln National Bank and Trust Company.
Number of staff: None.
Employer Identification Number: 356064431

1222
Heritage Fund of Bartholomew County, Inc.
P.O. Box 1371
Columbus 47202   (812) 376-7772

Community foundation established in 1977 in Indiana.
Financial data: (yr. ended 12/31/83): Assets, $3,074,169 (M); gifts received, $1,150; expenditures, $83,199, including $9,938 for 4 grants.
Purpose and activities: Primarily local giving for education, social services, health, cultural programs, and civic affairs.
Types of support awarded: Operating budgets, continuing support, seed money, emergency funds, deficit financing, building funds, equipment, land acquisition, matching funds, consulting services, technical assistance, scholarship funds, program-related investments, special projects, research, publications, conferences and seminars.
Limitations: Giving primarily in Bartholomew County, IN. No grants to individuals, or for annual campaigns or endowment funds.
Publications: Program policy statement, application guidelines, annual report.
Application information:
Write: Edward F. Sullivan, Executive Director
Director: Edward F. Sullivan, Executive Director.
Number of staff: 1 full-time professional; 2 part-time support.
Employer Identification Number: 351343903

1223
Hillenbrand (John A.) Foundation, Inc.
Hwy. 46
Batesville 47006

Incorporated in 1950 in Indiana.
Donor(s): Hillenbrand Industries, Inc.
Financial data: (yr. ended 11/30/84): Assets, $3,400,000 (M); gifts received, $100,000; expenditures, $218,000, including $201,000 for 34 grants (high: $49,000; low: $500).
Purpose and activities: Broad purposes; local giving with emphasis on civic programs, church support, and education; some support for youth agencies.

Limitations: Giving limited to Batesville, IN, and Ripley County.
Application information:
Initial approach: Letter (typewritten)
Deadline(s): None
Write: William A. Hillenbrand, President
Officers and Directors: William A. Hillenbrand, President; W. August Hillenbrand, Vice-President, Secretary, and Treasurer; Daniel A. Hillenbrand, George C. Hillenbrand, John A. Hillenbrand II, Vice-Presidents; George M. Hillenbrand, Ray J. Hillenbrand.
Employer Identification Number: 356042242

1224
Honeywell Foundation, Inc., The
275 West Market St.
P.O. Box 432
Wabash 46992   (219) 563-1102

Incorporated in 1941 in Indiana.
Donor(s): Mark C. Honeywell,† Eugenia H. Honeywell,† Della D. Hubbard,† and others.
Financial data: (yr. ended 9/30/84): Assets, $15,121,469 (M); expenditures, $709,722, including $114,605 for 17 grants (high: $65,809; low: $130; average: $6,700) and $533,195 for 1 foundation-administered program.
Purpose and activities: A private operating foundation; operates a community center, which includes a variety of educational and cultural programs, and makes local grants only, with emphasis on education, recreation, the arts, and social service.
Types of support awarded: Operating budgets, continuing support, seed money, emergency funds, building funds, equipment, land acquisition, endowment funds, matching funds, special projects, research, publications, conferences and seminars, consulting services, technical assistance.
Limitations: Giving limited to Wabash County, IN. No grants to individuals, or for scholarships or fellowships.
Publications: Annual report, application guidelines.
Application information: Application form required.
Initial approach: Telephone, letter, or full proposal
Copies of proposal: 1
Deadline(s): 1st day of each month
Board meeting date(s): Monthly
Final notification: 30 to 45 days
Write: Donald F. Knapp, Executive Director
Officers: Charles R. Tiede,* President; J. Douglas Craig,* Vice-President; Donald F. Knapp, Secretary and Executive Director; Henry A. Leander,* Treasurer.
Directors:* Kim Clark, Larry Curless, Joseph H. Nixon, Linda Robertson, Mrs. L.W. Yoder.
Number of staff: 2 full-time professional; 10 full-time support; 6 part-time support.
Employer Identification Number: 350390706

1225
Indiana Chemical Trust ⌶
c/o The Merchants National Bank of Terre Haute
701 Wabash Ave.
Terre Haute 47808

Trust established in 1953 in Indiana.
Donor(s): Indiana Gas & Chemical Corporation, Terre Haute Gas Corporation, Tribune-Star Publishing Company.
Financial data: (yr. ended 12/31/83): Assets, $3,124,621 (M); gifts received, $11,300; expenditures, $297,426, including $287,500 for 14 grants (high: $236,000; low: $1,000).
Purpose and activities: Local giving; grants primarily to civic, charitable, and educational institutions in Vigo County, Indiana, with emphasis on an institute of technology.
Limitations: Giving primarily in Vigo County, IN.
Committee Members: Joseph R. Cloutier, Rex R. Detar, Mary F. Holman.
Trustee: The Merchants National Bank of Terre Haute.
Employer Identification Number: 356024816

1226
Indianapolis Foundation, The ▼
615 North Alabama St., Rm. 119
Indianapolis 46204   (317) 634-7497

Community foundation established in 1916 in Indiana by resolution of trust.
Donor(s): James Proctor,† James E. Roberts,† Delavan Smith,† Charles N. Thompson,† Georgeanna Zumpfe.†
Financial data: (yr. ended 12/31/84): Assets, $26,860,375 (M); gifts received, $1,474,881; expenditures, $2,296,860, including $2,106,736 for 71 grants (high: $300,000; low: $300).
Purpose and activities: Promoting the welfare of Indianapolis residents by providing assistance in the areas of health, welfare, education, character building, and culture through grants for services to youth and children; health, hospitals, and the handicapped; family and neighborhood services; nursing and nursing education; civic and cultural programs; research and community planning; and general education.
Types of support awarded: Matching funds, consulting services, program-related investments, seed money, general purposes, building funds, equipment, land acquisition, special projects, conferences and seminars, annual campaigns.
Limitations: Giving limited to Indianapolis and Marion County, IN. No support for religious or sectarian purposes, elementary or secondary private schools, or sectarian pre-school or day-care centers. No grants to individuals, or for endowment funds; no loans.
Publications: Annual report, program policy statement, application guidelines.
Application information:
Initial approach: Telephone or letter
Copies of proposal: 7
Deadline(s): Submit proposal by last day of January, March, May, July, September, or November

Board meeting date(s): February, April, June, August, October, and December
Final notification: 6 weeks to 2 months
Write: Kenneth I. Chapman, Executive Director
Officers and Trustees: Richard I. Blankenbaker, Chairman; Rexford C. Early, Vice-Chairman; Matthew E. Welsh, Secretary; Robert A. Efroymson, Louis S. Hensley, Jr., Charles A. Pechette.
Trustee Banks: American Fletcher National Bank and Trust Company, First Bank & Trust Company, Indiana National Bank, Merchants National Bank & Trust Company, Peoples Bank & Trust Company.
Number of staff: 1 full-time professional; 1 part-time professional; 2 part-time support.
Employer Identification Number: 350868115

1227
Inland Container Corporation Foundation, Inc.
151 North Delaware St.
P.O. Box 925
Indianapolis 46206   (317) 262-0308

Incorporated in 1951 in Indiana.
Donor(s): Inland Container Corporation, Temple-Inland, Inc.
Financial data: (yr. ended 12/31/84): Assets, $5,303,125 (M); gifts received, $700,000; expenditures, $416,443, including $334,985 for 287 grants (high: $34,000; low: $100) and $81,458 for 41 grants to individuals.
Purpose and activities: Giving primarily in areas of plant locations, with emphasis on community funds and education; grants also for cultural programs and youth agencies.
Limitations: Giving primarily in areas of plant locations. No grants to individuals (except for company-employee scholarships), or for building or endowment funds.
Application information:
Initial approach: Letter
Copies of proposal: 1
Deadline(s): Submit proposal in October; deadline November 1
Board meeting date(s): May and November
Write: F.F. Hirschman, President
Officers and Directors: F.F. Hirschman, President; C.G. Ames, Jr., J.M. Areddy, B.J. Lancashire, Vice-Presidents; P.A. Foley, Secretary and Treasurer.
Employer Identification Number: 356014640

1228
Irwin-Sweeney-Miller Foundation ▼
420 Third St.
P.O. Box 808
Columbus 47202   (812) 372-0251

Incorporated in 1952 in Indiana.
Donor(s): Members of the Irwin, Sweeney, and Miller families.
Financial data: (yr. ended 12/31/83): Assets, $3,402,249 (M); gifts received, $106,611; expenditures, $747,079, including $652,155 for 44 grants (high: $249,900; low: $100; average: $2,000-$5,000).

Purpose and activities: Broad purposes; new funding presently limited to grants in the local area; emphasis on creative programs in social justice, religion, the arts, and improving family stability.
Types of support awarded: Conferences and seminars, continuing support, operating budgets, seed money, technical assistance, special projects.
Limitations: Giving limited to the Columbus, IN area for all new funding. No grants to individuals, or for deficit financing, research, scholarships, or fellowships; no loans.
Publications: Biennial report.
Application information:
Initial approach: Letter or full proposal
Copies of proposal: 1
Deadline(s): March 1 and September 1
Board meeting date(s): April and October
Final notification: 1 month
Write: Sarla Kalsi, Secretary-Treasurer
Officers: Richard B. Stoner,* President; Sarla Kalsi, Secretary and Treasurer.
Directors:* Clementine M. Tangeman, Chair; Lynne Maguire, Robert Alan Melting, Catherine G. Miller, Elizabeth G. Miller, Hugh Thomas Miller, J. Irwin Miller, Margaret I. Miller, William I. Miller, Xenia S. Miller, George W. Newlin, Jonathan D. Schiller, John T. Tangeman.
Number of staff: 1 part-time support.
Employer Identification Number: 356014513

1229
Jenn Foundation ⌘
8900 Keystone Crossing, Suite 401
Indianapolis 46240

Established in 1963.
Financial data: (yr. ended 12/31/83): Assets, $1,054,851 (L); expenditures, $123,824, including $116,350 for 32 grants (high: $25,000; low: $150).
Purpose and activities: Giving primarily for higher education, hospitals, youth agencies, and a community fund.
Officers and Directors: Louis J. Jenn, Chairman and President; Gerald R. Jenn, Vice-President; Leslie E. Howell, Secretary; Clarence Long, Treasurer; George Doyle.
Employer Identification Number: 356037030

1230
Jordan (Arthur) Foundation ⌘
1230 North Delaware St.
Indianapolis 46202   (317) 635-1378

Trust established in 1928 in Indiana.
Donor(s): Arthur Jordan.†
Financial data: (yr. ended 12/31/83): Assets, $6,798,066 (M); expenditures, $640,094, including $557,781 for 31 grants (high: $80,000; low: $250).
Purpose and activities: Broad purposes; local giving only, primarily for private colleges and universities and fine arts.
Types of support awarded: Operating budgets, general purposes, continuing support, annual campaigns, building funds, endowment funds, matching funds.

Limitations: Giving limited to Marion County, IN. No support for medical research. No grants to individuals, or for endowment funds, research, scholarships, or fellowships; no loans.
Publications: Application guidelines.
Application information:
Initial approach: Letter
Copies of proposal: 3
Deadline(s): Submit proposal preferably in April or October; deadlines May 1 and November 1
Board meeting date(s): May and November
Final notification: 30 days
Write: Margaret F. Sallee, Administrative Assistant
Officers: Frank E. Russell,* Secretary; Eugene M. Busche,* Treasurer; Margaret F. Sallee, Administrative Assistant.
Trustees:* Ben J. Weaver, Chairman; Boris E. Meditch, Vice-Chairman; Richard B. DeMars, Richard A. Steele.
Number of staff: 1.
Employer Identification Number: 350428850

1231
Kilbourne (E. H.) Residuary Charitable Trust
c/o Lincoln National Bank Trust Dept.
116 East Berry St.
Fort Wayne 46802   (219) 423-6419

Trust established in Indiana.
Donor(s): Edgar Kilbourne.†
Financial data: (yr. ended 1/31/83): Assets, $4,764,664 (M); expenditures, $372,815, including $199,924 for 27 grants (high: $33,667; low: $1,000) and $131,078 for grants to individuals.
Purpose and activities: Local giving for higher education, including scholarships for graduating high school seniors, youth agencies, and Protestant church support.
Types of support awarded: Student aid.
Limitations: Giving limited to Allen County, IN. No grants for general support, capital or endowment funds, matching gifts, special projects, research, publications, or conferences; no loans.
Publications: 990-PF, application guidelines.
Application information: Application form required.
Initial approach: Letter
Deadline(s): April 15 for scholarships
Final notification: 6 weeks
Write: Alice Kopfer, Trust Officer
Trustee: Lincoln National Bank & Trust Company.
Number of staff: None.
Employer Identification Number: 356332820

1232
Koch (George) Sons Foundation, Inc.
P.O. Box 358
Evansville 47744

Incorporated in 1945 in Indiana.
Donor(s): Gibbs Die Casting Aluminum, Corp., George Koch Sons, Inc., Santa Claus Land.

Financial data: (yr. ended 12/31/83): Assets, $3,541,438 (M); gifts received, $250,000; expenditures, $127,674, including $119,885 for 70 grants (high: $10,000; low: $100).
Purpose and activities: Local giving, with emphasis on relief for needy families designated by charitable institutions; grants also to cultural and educational institutions, museums, churches, and youth camps, with particular emphasis on underprivileged children.
Limitations: Giving limited to IN, with emphasis on the Evansville-Vanderburgh County area.
Application information:
Write: Robert L. Koch, II, Secretary
Officers and Directors: Robert L. Koch, President and Treasurer; W.A. Koch, Vice-President; Robert L. Koch, II, Secretary; J.J. Hunsinger, L.J. Koch, Jr., J.H. Muelbauer.
Employer Identification Number: 356023372

1233
Krannert Charitable Trust ▼
P.O. Box 1021
Indianapolis 46206   (317) 634-9857

Trust established in 1960 in Indiana.
Donor(s): Herman C. Krannert,† Ellnora D. Krannert.†
Financial data: (yr. ended 12/31/84): Assets, $30,535,816 (M); expenditures, $12,309,897, including $11,792,000 for 22 grants (high: $2,000,000; low: $15,000; average: $100,000-$500,000).
Purpose and activities: Support mainly for capital programs in the areas of higher education, medical research, health care, performing and visual arts, and civic improvements, primarily in Indiana and particularly in Indianapolis. Foundation will be terminating and distributing its assets within the next few years. Organizations to which final distributions will be made have already been decided.
Types of support awarded: General purposes, operating budgets, continuing support, annual campaigns, building funds, endowment funds, research, equipment.
Limitations: Giving primarily in IN, with emphasis on Indianapolis. No grants to individuals, or for scholarships and fellowships, or matching gifts; no loans.
Application information: Funds fully committed; no new proposals accepted.
Board meeting date(s): April, August, and November
Write: Don B. Earnhart, Administrative Trustee
Officers and Trustees: George B. Elliott, Chairman; Don B. Earnhart, Administrative Trustee, Secretary and Treasurer; Robert S. Ashby, Charles Fisch, M.D., The Indiana National Bank.
Number of staff: 2.
Employer Identification Number: 356014651

1234
Kuehn Foundation ¤
P.O. Box 207
Evansville 47702

Established in 1968 in Indiana.
Financial data: (yr. ended 12/31/83): Assets, $2,104,725 (M); expenditures, $55,510, including $52,250 for 25 grants (high: $20,500; low: $250).
Purpose and activities: Giving largely for higher and secondary education.
Limitations: Giving primarily in IN.
Trustees: Mary Catherine Powell, Chairman; George E. Powell, Jr., Vice-Chairman; Nicholas K. Powell, Secretary.
Employer Identification Number: 237021199

1235
Leighton-Oare Foundation, Inc.
307 National Bank Bldg.
112 West Jefferson Blvd.
South Bend 46601

Incorporated in 1955 in Indiana.
Donor(s): Mary Morris Leighton.
Financial data: (yr. ended 12/31/83): Assets, $5,327,000 (M); expenditures, $295,000, including $157,000 for 33 grants (high: $5,000; low: $100).
Purpose and activities: Primarily local giving, with emphasis on higher education and health; grants also for the arts and community funds.
Types of support awarded: Continuing support.
Limitations: Giving primarily in IN. No grants to individuals, or for capital, endowment or emergency funds, operating budgets, annual campaigns, seed money, deficit financing, matching gifts, scholarships or fellowships; no loans.
Publications: 990-PF.
Application information:
Initial approach: Letter
Deadline(s): None
Board meeting date(s): February, May, August, and November
Final notification: 90 to 120 days
Officers and Directors: Mary Morris Leighton, President; James F. Thornburg, Vice-President; Judd Leighton, Secretary-Treasurer.
Number of staff: None.
Employer Identification Number: 356034243

1236
Liberty Fund, Inc.
7440 North Shadeland Ave., Suite 100
Indianapolis 46250   (317) 842-0880

Incorporated in 1960 in Indiana.
Donor(s): Pierre F. Goodrich,† Enid Goodrich, John B. Goodrich.†
Financial data: (yr. ended 4/30/84): Assets, $66,671,363 (M); expenditures, $2,743,690, including $115,000 for 9 grants (high: $20,000; low: $5,000) and $1,965,200 for 1 foundation-administered program.
Purpose and activities: To promote education concerned with human liberty mainly through an operating program.

Types of support awarded: Operating budgets, continuing support, special projects.
Limitations: No grants to individuals, or for annual campaigns, seed money, emergency funds, deficit financing, capital or endowment funds, matching gifts, scholarships and fellowships, research, demonstration projects, publications, or conferences; no loans.
Application information:
Initial approach: Letter or full proposal
Copies of proposal: 1
Deadline(s): None
Board meeting date(s): Monthly
Final notification: 1 to 2 weeks if denied; after April meeting if considered further
Write: A. Neil McLeod, President
Officers: A. Neil McLeod,* Chairman, President, and Treasurer; Enid Goodrich,* Vice-Chairman; Helen W. Garlotte, Secretary.
Directors:* W.W. Hill, Jr., Ralph W. Husted, Roseda D. Martin, Irwin H. Reiss, R.A. Ware, Don E. Welch.
Number of staff: 8 full-time professional.
Employer Identification Number: 351320021

1237
Lilly (Eli) and Company Foundation ▼
Lilly Corporate Center
Indianapolis 46285   (317) 261-2489

Incorporated in 1968 in Indiana.
Donor(s): Eli Lilly and Company.
Financial data: (yr. ended 12/31/83): Assets, $4,600,309 (M); gifts received, $1,200,000; expenditures, $1,633,458, including $1,623,598 for 55 grants (high: $680,000; low: $1,000).
Purpose and activities: Giving primarily in areas of company operations for health, civic and cultural activities, and medical and pharmaceutical education.
Types of support awarded: General purposes, operating budgets, building funds, equipment, land acquisition, matching funds, professorships, internships, fellowships.
Limitations: Giving primarily in Indianapolis, IN; also in Roanoke, VA and other areas of company operations. No grants to individuals, or for endowment funds, special projects, research, publications, or conferences; no loans.
Application information:
Initial approach: Full proposal
Copies of proposal: 1
Deadline(s): None
Board meeting date(s): Quarterly
Final notification: 3 weeks to 3 months
Write: Ms. Marilee Fraser, Secretary
Officers: Edgar G. Davis, President; James M. Cornelius, Vice-President and Treasurer; Daniel P. Carmichael, Vice-President; Marilee Fraser, Secretary.
Directors: V.D. Bryson, R.E. Crandall, Earl B. Herr, Jr., Melvin Perelman, Cornelius W. Pettinga, Eugene L. Step, Richard D. Wood, J. Richard Zapapas.
Number of staff: None.
Employer Identification Number: 356202479

1238
Lilly Endowment, Inc. ▼
2801 North Meridian St.
P.O. Box 88068
Indianapolis 46208   (317) 924-5471

Incorporated in 1937 in Indiana.
Donor(s): J.K. Lilly, Sr.,† Eli Lilly,† J.K. Lilly.†
Financial data: (yr. ended 12/31/84): Assets,
$889,437,000 (M); expenditures, $29,620,266,
including $24,271,000 for 172 grants (high:
$1,500,000; low: $7,500; average: $10,000-
$500,000).
Purpose and activities: "The promotion and
support of religious, educational or charitable
purposes." Giving emphasizes projects that
depend on private support, with a limited
number of grants to government institutions
and tax-supported programs. Special interest in
innovative programs that seek to produce
positive changes in human society, promote
human development, strengthen independent
institutions, encourage responsive government
at local, state, and national levels, and improve
quality of life in Indianapolis and Indiana.
Grants for arts and culture are limited to
Indianapolis and Indiana. Grants to
international programs are restricted to a small
number of developmental and informational
programs.
Types of support awarded: Annual
campaigns, seed money, research, fellowships,
matching funds, general purposes.
Limitations: Giving limited to IN, especially
Indianapolis, for art and culture; international
giving in other areas. No support for health
care, housing, transportation, environment,
population control, films, biological or physical
science research, or other mass media. No
grants to individuals or for endowment funds or
scholarships; no loans.
Publications: Annual report, program policy
statement, application guidelines.
Application information:
   Initial approach: Letter of 2 pages or less
   Copies of proposal: 1
   Deadline(s): None
   Board meeting date(s): February, April, June,
      September, and November; executive
      committee meets in January, March, May,
      July, October, and December
   Write: James T. Morris, President
Officers: James T. Morris, President; Robert W.
Lynn, Executive Vice-President; William C.
Bonifield, Vice-President, Education; Michael
A. Carroll, Vice-President, Community
Development; Charles A. Johnson, Vice-
President, Development; William M. Goodwin,
Secretary-Treasurer.
Directors: Thomas H. Lake, Chairman; Otis R.
Bowen, M.D., Byron P. Hollett, Eli Lilly II,
Eugene F. Ratliff, Margaret Chase Smith,
Herman B. Wells, Richard D. Wood.
Number of staff: 17 full-time professional; 1
part-time professional; 18 full-time support.
Employer Identification Number: 350868122

1239
**Lincoln National Life Foundation, Inc.,
The**
P.O. Box 1110
1300 South Clinton St.
Fort Wayne 46801   (219) 427-3271

Established in 1928; incorporated in 1962 in
Indiana.
Donor(s): The Lincoln National Life Insurance
Company, Lincoln National Corporation.
Financial data: (yr. ended 12/31/84): Assets,
$1,719,393 (M); gifts received, $327,623;
expenditures, $133,204, including $31,802 for
16 grants (high: $7,000; low: $150; average:
$2,000) and $37,000 for 3 loans.
Purpose and activities: General purposes;
maintains The Lincoln Library and Museum;
grants primarily to higher educational
institutions, including scholarships for minority
students selected by local minority
representatives. Support mainly limited to the
Fort Wayne area, except for Lincoln Scholar
actuarial science grants.
Types of support awarded: Scholarship funds.
Limitations: Giving limited to the Fort Wayne,
IN area, except for annual actuarial science
grants. No grants to individuals, or for building
or endowment funds, research, matching gifts.
Publications: Application guidelines.
Application information:
   Initial approach: Letter
   Copies of proposal: 1
   Deadline(s): None
   Board meeting date(s): May and December
   Final notification: 45 to 60 days after meeting
   Write: Marilyn A. Vachon, Vice-President
Officers: Ian M. Rolland,* President; Marilyn
A. Vachon,* Vice-President and Secretary; Max
A. Roesler, Treasurer.
Directors:* P. Kenneth Dunsire, Harlan K.
Holly, Mark E. Neely, Jr., M. Joyce Schlatter, C.
David Silletto, Howard E. Steele, Thomas M.
West.
Number of staff: None.
Employer Identification Number: 356042099

1240
Martin Foundation Inc., The ▼
500 Simpson St.
Elkhart 46515   (219) 295-3343

Incorporated in 1953 in Indiana.
Donor(s): Ross Martin, Esther Martin, Lee
Martin, Geraldine F. Martin, Nibco Inc.
Financial data: (yr. ended 6/30/83): Assets,
$15,876,651 (M); expenditures, $937,586,
including $788,700 for 56 grants (high:
$254,500; low: $200; average: $500-$50,000).
Purpose and activities: Broad purposes;
primarily local giving, with emphasis on
education, particularly higher education, and
social services.
Limitations: Giving primarily in IN, with
emphasis on Elkhart. No grants to individuals.
Application information:
   Deadline(s): None
   Board meeting date(s): As required
   Final notification: 3 to 6 weeks
   Write: Geraldine F. Martin

Officers and Directors: Geraldine F. Martin,
President; Elizabeth Martin, Secretary; Jennifer
Martin, Treasurer; Casper Martin, Lee Martin.
Number of staff: None.
Employer Identification Number: 351070929

1241
McMillen Foundation, Inc. ▼ ⌑
1500 Fort Wayne Bank Bldg.
Fort Wayne 46802

Incorporated in 1947 in Indiana.
Donor(s): Dale W. McMillen,† members of the
McMillen family.
Financial data: (yr. ended 12/31/82): Assets,
$7,691,429 (M); expenditures, $820,777,
including $714,021 for 18 grants (high:
$172,630; low: $500).
Purpose and activities: Broad purposes;
primarily local giving, with emphasis on
recreation and education; some support for
youth agencies and churches.
Limitations: Giving primarily in IN.
Officers and Directors: Dale W. McMillen,
Jr., President; John F. McMillen, Vice-President;
Mary Jane Crowe, Secretary and Treasurer;
Barry W. McMillen, Harold W. McMillen.
Employer Identification Number: 356021003

1242
**Mead Johnson & Company Foundation,
Inc.**
2404 West Pennsylvania St.
Evansville 47721   (812) 426-6428

Incorporated in 1955 in Indiana.
Donor(s): Mead Johnson & Company.
Financial data: (yr. ended 12/31/84): Assets,
$614,527 (M); expenditures, $765,757,
including $674,033 for 93 grants (high:
$300,000; low: $300), $24,000 for 8 grants to
individuals and $66,600 for employee
matching gifts.
Purpose and activities: Broad purposes;
primarily local giving, largely for higher
education, including scholarships (for children
of employees or administered by university
only) and employee matching gifts, and for
community funds, cultural activities, health
agencies, and youth agencies.
Types of support awarded: Employee related
scholarships, employee matching gifts,
scholarship funds.
Limitations: Giving primarily in IN. No grants
to individuals (except children of employees).
Application information:
   Initial approach: Letter or full proposal
   Copies of proposal: 1
   Deadline(s): Submit proposal preferably in
      the summer
   Board meeting date(s): April and as required
   Final notification: 2 months
   Write: Rolland M. Eckels, President
Officers: Rolland M. Eckels, President; Edward
F. Hassee, Vice-President and Treasurer; Joel
M. Lasker, Secretary.
Number of staff: 1 part-time professional; 1
part-time support.
Employer Identification Number: 356017067

1243
Miles Laboratories Foundation ⌑
1127 Myrtle St.
P.O. Box 40
Elkhart 46515   (219) 264-8225

Trust established in 1953 in Indiana.
Donor(s): Miles Laboratories, Inc.
Financial data: (yr. ended 12/31/83): Assets, $22,265 (M); gifts received, $267,000; expenditures, $246,887, including $219,772 for 25 grants (high: $40,000; low: $100) and $2,400 for 8 grants to individuals.
Purpose and activities: Broad purposes; primarily local giving, with emphasis on higher education including scholarship grants, community funds in areas of company operations, and hospitals.
Limitations: Giving primarily in IN, with some support for organizations in other areas of company operations.
Application information:
  Initial approach: Letter
  Deadline(s): None
  Board meeting date(s): Quarterly
  Write: Lehman F. Beardsley, Chairman
Officers and Trustees: Lehman F. Beardsley, Chairman; Franklin E. Breckenridge, Secretary; George E. Davy, John R. Gildea, Joseph H. Rosloff.
Employer Identification Number: 356026510

1244
Minear (Ruth M.) Educational Trust ⌑
c/o First National Bank in Wabash
202 S. Wabash St.
Wabash 46992   (219) 563-1116

Established in 1977.
Financial data: (yr. ended 2/29/84): Assets, $1,312,135 (M); expenditures, $125,732, including $114,200 for grants to individuals.
Purpose and activities: Giving to graduates of Wabash High School attending accredited post-secondary schools in Indiana.
Types of support awarded: Student aid.
Limitations: Giving limited to graduates of Wabash High School, Wasbash, IN.
Application information: Submit Indiana financial aid forms.
  Deadline(s): Middle of February
  Write: Allen P. Spring, Sr., Vice-President
Trustees: First National Bank in Wabash.
Employer Identification Number: 356335021

1245
Moore Foundation ▼
9100 Meridian Square
50 East 91st St.
Indianapolis 46240   (317) 848-2013

Incorporated in 1960 in Indiana.
Donor(s): Frank M. Moore.†
Financial data: (yr. ended 3/31/83): Assets, $11,211,958 (M); expenditures, $569,394, including $328,593 for 72 grants (high: $40,000; low: $250; average: $1,000-$30,000) and $9,000 for 6 grants to individuals.

Purpose and activities: Broad purposes; primarily local giving, with emphasis on support of free enterprise system, the development of curriculum at the elementary and secondary school levels, and the support of religious organizations oriented toward youth; small scholarship program previously implemented has been phased out completely.
Types of support awarded: Operating budgets, continuing support, matching funds, special projects, conferences and seminars.
Limitations: Giving primarily in IN. No grants to individuals, or for capital or endowment funds, annual campaigns, seed money, emergency funds, deficit financing, publications, scholarships, or fellowships; no loans.
Application information:
  Initial approach: Letter, full proposal, or telephone
  Copies of proposal: 1
  Deadline(s): None
  Board meeting date(s): May and November; executive committee meets monthly
  Final notification: 1 to 2 months
  Write: Mrs. Joan R. Barrett, Program Coordinator
Officers: Martin J. Moore,* President; Albert M. Campbell,* Executive Vice-President; Brenda B. Moore,* Vice-President, Executive Secretary, and Treasurer; Joan R. Barrett, Program Coordinator.
Directors:* Stephen Keith, Edward C. McKeown, Mark B. Moore, John M. Rohm.
Number of staff: 1 full-time professional.
Employer Identification Number: 356013824

1246
Noyes (Nicholas H.), Jr. Memorial Foundation, Inc. ⌑
307 East McCarty St.
Indianapolis 46285   (317) 261-3172

Incorporated in 1951 in Indiana.
Donor(s): Nicholas H. Noyes,† Marguerite Lilly Noyes.†
Financial data: (yr. ended 12/31/83): Assets, $5,986,313 (M); expenditures, $298,733, including $273,650 for 45 grants (high: $30,000; low: $500).
Purpose and activities: Broad purposes; general giving, primarily local, with emphasis on higher and secondary education, museums and cultural programs, a community fund, church support, hospitals, and youth agencies.
Types of support awarded: Operating budgets, endowment funds, scholarship funds, matching funds.
Limitations: Giving primarily in IN. No grants to individuals or for building funds; no loans.
Application information:
  Initial approach: Full proposal
  Copies of proposal: 1
  Board meeting date(s): Semiannually
  Write: A. Malcolm McVie, President
Officers and Directors: A. Malcolm McVie, President and Treasurer; Frederic D. Anderson, Vice-President; Evan L. Noyes, Jr., Secretary; Janet Noyes Adams, Frederic M. Ayres, Janet A. Carrington, David L. Chambers, Jr.
Employer Identification Number: 351003699

1247
Oliver Memorial Trust Foundation
112-114 West Jefferson Blvd.
South Bend 46601   (219) 237-3321

Trust established in 1959 in Indiana.
Donor(s): C. Frederick Cunningham,† Mrs. Gertrude Oliver Cunningham, Walter C. Steenburg,† Jane Warriner, J. Oliver Cunningham.
Financial data: (yr. ended 12/31/83): Assets, $3,899,000 (M); gifts received, $200,000; expenditures, $306,750, including $290,250 for 32 grants (high: $50,000; low: $300; average: $5,000-$10,000).
Purpose and activities: Broad purposes; primarily local giving, with emphasis on hospitals, higher education, particularly college endowments, community funds, and youth agencies.
Types of support awarded: Continuing support, annual campaigns, building funds, endowment funds, matching funds, research.
Limitations: Giving primarily in IN. No grants to individuals, or for equipment and materials, land acquisition, publications, conferences, special projects or scholarships and fellowships; no loans.
Application information:
  Initial approach: Telephone
  Deadline(s): Submit proposal in January; deadline March 1
  Board meeting date(s): Quarterly or as required
  Final notification: 9 months to 1 year
  Write: William E. Rozycki, Vice-President, The National Bank and Trust Company of South Bend
Distribution Committee: Gertrude Oliver Cunningham, Chairman; J. Oliver Cunningham, Anne Cunningham Downey.
Trustee: The National Bank and Trust Company of South Bend (William E. Rozycki, Vice-President).
Number of staff: None.
Employer Identification Number: 356013076

1248
Plumsock Fund, The
510 Guaranty Bldg.
Indianapolis 46204   (317) 632-3405

Incorporated in 1959 in Indiana.
Donor(s): Evelyn L. Lutz,† Herbert B. Lutz, Sarah L. Lutz.
Financial data: (yr. ended 12/31/83): Assets, $1,205,530 (M); gifts received, $200,000; expenditures, $468,995, including $465,400 for grants (high: $100,000; low: $50).
Purpose and activities: Broad purposes; general giving for cultural programs, higher and secondary education, anthropology, youth agencies, and welfare and health agencies, with some emphasis on Central America.
Limitations: No grants to individuals, or for scholarships or fellowships; no loans.
Application information:
  Initial approach: Telephone, letter or full proposal
  Copies of proposal: 3
  Board meeting date(s): Annually and as required

Write: John G. Rauch, Jr., Secretary
Officers and Directors: Daniel A. Wolf, President; Kenneth Chapman, Vice-President; John G. Rauch, Jr., Secretary-Treasurer; Edwin Fancher, Christopher H. Lutz.
Employer Identification Number: 356014719

1249
Pott (Robert and Elaine) Foundation ¤
Citizens National Bank
P.O. Box 719
Evansville 47705

Established in Indiana.
Financial data: (yr. ended 3/31/84): Assets, $2,052,527 (M); expenditures, $142,107, including $130,000 for 5 grants (high: $75.000; low: $10,000).
Purpose and activities: Grants to higher education institutions for scholarships.
Types of support awarded: Scholarship funds.
Trustee: Citizens National Bank.
Employer Identification Number: 356290997

1250
Reilly Foundation
1510 Market Square Center
151 North Delaware St.
Indianapolis 46204

Trust established in 1962 in Indiana.
Donor(s): Reilly Tar & Chemical Corporation.
Financial data: (yr. ended 12/31/83): Assets, $557,681 (M); gifts received, $250,000; expenditures, $185,298, including $150,944 for 39 grants (high: $16,500; low: $250) and $33,540 for 67 grants to individuals.
Purpose and activities: Giving primarily for higher education, community funds, hospitals, and social agencies; educational grants and scholarships limited to children of company employees.
Types of support awarded: Employee related scholarships.
Trustees: Ineva R. Baldwin, Elizabeth B. Reilly, Peter C. Reilly, Lorraine D. Schroeder.
Employer Identification Number: 352061750

1251
Rock Island Refining Foundation ¤
5000 West 86th St.
P.O. Box 68007
Indianapolis 46268

Established in 1973.
Financial data: (yr. ended 11/30/83): Assets, $1,602,551 (M); expenditures, $143,362, including $138,726 for 78 grants (high: $27,600; low: $50).
Purpose and activities: Primarily local giving, with emphasis on community funds, hospitals, higher education, and youth agencies.
Limitations: Giving primarily in IN.
Trustees: F.W. Grube, William E. Huff, Louis E. Kincannon.
Employer Identification Number: 356264479

1252
Schurz Communications Foundation, Inc. ¤
225 West Colfax Ave.
South Bend 46601

Incorporated in 1940 in Indiana.
Donor(s): Schurz Communications, Inc., South Bend Tribune.
Financial data: (yr. ended 12/31/83): Assets, $916,184 (M); gifts received, $61,807; expenditures, $110,742, including $109,133 for 27 grants (high: $30,000; low: $100).
Purpose and activities: Primarily local giving, with emphasis on higher education, including scholarships and community funds.
Limitations: Giving primarily in IN.
Officers: W.G. Wheeler, President; J.G. Young, Vice-President; R.M. Zitter, Secretary-Treasurer.
Employer Identification Number: 356024357

1253
Smock (Frank L. and Laura L.) Foundation
c/o Lincoln National Bank and Trust Company
116 East Berry St.
Fort Wayne 46802   (219) 423-6419

Trust established in 1953 in Indiana.
Donor(s): Mrs. Laura L. Smock.†
Financial data: (yr. ended 12/31/82): Assets, $4,780,837 (M); expenditures, $253,368, including $50,230 for 10 grants and $179,955 for 28 grants to individuals.
Purpose and activities: Broad purposes; to "promote the health, welfare and happiness of ailing or needy or crippled or blind or elderly and aged men and women of the Presbyterian faith throughout the State of Indiana"; support also for Presbyterian churches and a college.
Types of support awarded: Grants to individuals.
Limitations: Giving limited to IN. No grants for general or operating support, capital, building, or endowment funds, or matching gifts; no loans.
Publications: Application guidelines.
Application information: Application form required.
  Initial approach: Letter
  Deadline(s): None
  Board meeting date(s): Monthly
  Final notification: 6 weeks
  Write: Alice Kopfer, Trust Officer
Advisory Committee: Lisle D. Hodell, Rev. George Mather, John Walley.
Trustee: Lincoln National Bank and Trust Company.
Number of staff: None.
Employer Identification Number: 356011335

1254
Somers (Byron H.) Foundation ¤
5814 Reed Rd.
Fort Wayne 46815

Established in 1977.
Financial data: (yr. ended 11/30/83): Assets, $3,378,241 (M); gifts received, $350,000; expenditures, $245,693, including $232,300 for 11 grants (high: $100,000; low: $1,000).

Purpose and activities: Primarily local giving, with emphasis on youth agencies, education, and cultural programs.
Limitations: Giving limited to IN.
Trustees: Norman E. Baker, Druscilla S. Doehrman, Robert W. Gibson.
Employer Identification Number: 351410969

1255
Stokely (The William B.), Jr. Foundation
8900 Keystone Crossing, Suite 1010
Indianapolis 46240   (317) 843-3800

Incorporated in 1951 in Indiana.
Donor(s): W.B. Stokely, Jr.†
Financial data: (yr. ended 12/31/84): Assets, $7,361,000 (M); expenditures, $442,044, including $288,926 for 92 grants (high: $250,000; low: $100).
Purpose and activities: Broad purposes; general local giving, with emphasis on higher education; some support also for hospitals, health agencies, and cultural programs.
Limitations: Giving primarily in IN and the Southeast. No grants to individuals.
Application information:
  Initial approach: Letter or full proposal
  Copies of proposal: 1
  Deadline(s): Submit proposal preferably in the fall
  Board meeting date(s): February, May, August, and November
  Write: William B. Stokely III, President
Officers: William B. Stokely III,* President; Kay H. Stokely,* Executive Vice-President; Alfred J. Stokely,* Vice-President; Donna J. Graham, Secretary; K. Marvin Eberts, Jr.,* Treasurer.
Directors:* Mrs. Horace Burnett, W. Foster McKenney.
Number of staff: 1 full-time professional.
Employer Identification Number: 356016402

1256
Thirty Five Twenty, Inc.
7440 North Shadeland
Indianapolis 46250   (317) 842-0880

Incorporated in 1965 in Indiana.
Donor(s): Enid Goodrich.
Financial data: (yr. ended 4/30/84): Assets, $1,083,953 (M); expenditures, $47,979, including $35,000 for 5 grants (high: $20,000; low: $1,000).
Purpose and activities: "To further educational activities which concern themselves with human liberty and individual freedom within a free society"; grants largely for higher education and cultural programs.
Types of support awarded: Operating budgets, continuing support, special projects.
Limitations: No grants to individuals, or for annual campaigns, seed money, emergency funds, deficit financing, capital or endowment funds, scholarships and fellowships, matching gifts, research, demonstration projects, publications, or conferences; no loans.
Application information:
  Initial approach: Letter
  Copies of proposal: 1
  Deadline(s): Submit proposal preferably in March; deadline April 1

Board meeting date(s): April and September
Final notification: 1 to 2 weeks if denied; after April meeting if favorable
Write: A. Neil McLeod, Chairman
Officers and Directors: A. Neil McLeod, Chairman, President and Treasurer; Enid Goodrich, Vice-Chairman; Helen W. Garlotte, Secretary; Ruth E. Connolly, Ralph W. Husted, Chris L. Talley.
Number of staff: 2 part-time professional.
Employer Identification Number: 356056960

1257
Thrush (H. A.) Foundation, Inc. ¤
P.O. Box 185
Peru 46970

Incorporated in 1936 in Delaware.
Donor(s): Homer A. Thrush.†
Financial data: (yr. ended 7/31/83): Assets, $2,080,150 (M); expenditures, $162,419, including $142,506 for 38 grants (high: $84,300; low: $50).
Purpose and activities: Broad purposes; primarily local giving, with emphasis on higher education, youth agencies, Protestant church support, health agencies and cultural programs.
Limitations: Giving primarily in IN.
Officers and Directors: Paul F. Thompson, President and Treasurer; Pauline Thrush Thompson, Vice-President; Robert L. Thompson, Secretary; Dean A. Thompson, Jerry T. Thompson.
Employer Identification Number: 356018476

1258
Tyson Fund ¤
One Indiana Square, No. 733
Indianapolis 46266
Application address: 409 Willis Dr., Versailles, IN 47042

Trust established in 1930 in Indiana.
Donor(s): James H. Tyson.
Financial data: (yr. ended 12/31/83): Assets, $3,989,504 (M); expenditures, $111,252, including $99,629 for 11 grants (high: $24,634; low: $200).
Purpose and activities: Grants limited to organizations in Versailles, Indiana, and vicinity, with emphasis on education, community services and a library.
Limitations: Giving limited to Versailles, IN.
Application information:
Initial approach: Letter
Deadline(s): September 1
Write: Richard E. Helton
Trustees: Richard E. Helton, Indiana National Bank.
Employer Identification Number: 356009973

IOWA

1259
Aliber Foundation ¤
1200 Carriers Bldg.
Des Moines 50309

Established in 1963 in Iowa.
Donor(s): Elizabeth Gordon,† M.M. Aliber Trust.
Financial data: (yr. ended 3/31/84): Assets, $2,285,910 (M); expenditures, $1,340,035, including $1,320,000 for 16 grants (high: $1,000,000; low: $1,000).
Purpose and activities: Primarily local giving, with emphasis on higher education, Jewish welfare funds, and temple support.
Limitations: Giving primarily in IA.
Officers and Directors: Richard L. Sharpnack, President; M.D. Christensen, Vice-President; Charles E. Harris, Secretary; Phillip Burns, Treasurer; Nate Bernstein, Thomas Hall, Harlan D. Hockenberg, Ercell K. Penniwell, Karl R. Penniwell.
Employer Identification Number: 426073199

1260
Blank (The Myron and Jacqueline) Charity Fund ¤
414 Insurance Exchange Bldg.
505 Fifth Ave.
Des Moines 50309

Incorporated in 1948 in Iowa.
Donor(s): A.H. Blank, Myron N. Blank, and others.
Financial data: (yr. ended 12/31/83): Assets, $4,629,288 (M); expenditures, $208,242, including $189,272 for 79 grants (high: $75,000; low: $30).
Purpose and activities: Primarily local giving, with emphasis on Jewish welfare funds, higher education, and cultural programs.
Limitations: Giving primarily in IA.
Application information: Applications are not invited.
Officers and Directors: Myron N. Blank, President and Treasurer; Jacqueline N. Blank, Vice-President and Secretary; Steven N. Blank.
Employer Identification Number: 237423791

1261
Bohen Foundation, The
1716 Locust St.
Des Moines 50336   (515) 284-2556

Incorporated in 1958 in Iowa.
Donor(s): Mildred M. Bohen Charitable Trust, Edna E. Meredith Charitable Trust.
Financial data: (yr. ended 6/30/83): Assets, $4,387,036 (M); gifts received, $110,000; expenditures, $310,034, including $283,900 for 18 grants (high: $154,000; low: $500).

Purpose and activities: Charitable and educational purposes; general giving, with emphasis on higher and secondary education, conservation, and the performing arts.
Limitations: No grants to individuals.
Application information:
Initial approach: Letter
Copies of proposal: 1
Board meeting date(s): As required
Write: Marilyn Dillivan, Assistant Secretary
Officers and Directors:* Mildred M. Bohen,* President; Frederick B. Henry,* Vice-President and Treasurer; Irene Anderson, Secretary.
Employer Identification Number: 426054774

1262
Cowles (Gardner and Florence Call) Foundation, Inc. ▼
P.O. Box 957
Des Moines 50304   (515) 284-8116

Incorporated in 1934 in Iowa.
Donor(s): Gardner Cowles, Sr.,† Florence C. Cowles.
Financial data: (yr. ended 12/31/84): Assets, $12,073,622 (M); gifts received, $3,700; expenditures, $1,397,701, including $1,280,700 for 16 grants (high: $400,000; low: $200; average: $200-$400,000).
Purpose and activities: General purposes; giving confined to Iowa institutions; grants largely for higher education, including buildings and equipment, an art center, and a civic center.
Types of support awarded: Operating budgets, continuing support, seed money, building funds, endowment funds, matching funds.
Limitations: Giving primarily in IA, with emphasis on Des Moines. No grants to individuals, or for scholarships or fellowships; no loans.
Publications: 990-PF.
Application information:
Initial approach: Full proposal or letter
Copies of proposal: 1
Deadline(s): None
Board meeting date(s): Annually and as required
Write: David Kruidenier, President
Officers and Trustees: David Kruidenier, President; Kenneth MacDonald, Vice-President; Luther L. Hill, Jr., Secretary; Elizabeth S. Kruidenier, Treasurer; Morley Cowles Ballantine, Charles C. Edwards, Jr.
Number of staff: None.
Employer Identification Number: 426054609

1263
Des Moines Community Foundation, Greater
800 High St.
Des Moines 50307   (515) 286-4958

Community foundation incorporated in 1969 in Iowa.
Financial data: (yr. ended 12/31/83): Assets, $341,549 (M); gifts received, $223,829; expenditures, $234,375, including $229,261 for 15 grants.

Purpose and activities: Primarily local giving to provide seed money for human services.
Types of support awarded: Operating budgets, annual campaigns, seed money, emergency funds, matching funds, scholarship funds, internships, special projects, conferences and seminars.
Limitations: Giving primarily in the greater Des Moines, IA, area. No grants to individuals, or for continuing support.
Publications: Annual report.
Application information:
Write: Monroe L. Colston, Secretary
Officer: Monroe L. Colston, Secretary.
Employer Identification Number: 237043870

1264
E & M Charities ⌧
c/o C. Maxwell Stanley
Stanley Bldg.
Muscatine 52761

Incorporated in 1979 in Iowa.
Donor(s): C. Maxwell Stanley, Elizabeth M. Stanley.
Financial data: (yr. ended 12/31/83): Assets, $1,994,669 (M); expenditures, $115,346, including $109,700 for 13 grants (high: $38,500; low: $400).
Purpose and activities: Support for a university, Methodist churches, and a community fund.
Officers and Directors: C. Maxwell Stanley, President and Treasurer; David M. Stanley, Vice-President; Elizabeth M. Stanley, Secretary; Richard H. Stanley, Jane S. Buckles.
Employer Identification Number: 421129959

1265
Fahrney Education Foundation ⌧
c/o Union Bank, Trust Dept.
123 East Third St.
Ottumwa 52501   (515) 683-1641

Established in 1979 in Iowa.
Donor(s): Helen Fahrney.†
Financial data: (yr. ended 2/29/84): Assets, $1,562,892 (M); expenditures, $129,028, including $101,874 for 78 grants to individuals.
Purpose and activities: Local giving to residents of Wapello County for scholarships.
Types of support awarded: Student aid.
Limitations: Giving limited to residents of Wapello County, IA.
Publications: Application guidelines.
Application information: Application form required.
Deadline(s): February 15
Trustee: Union Bank & Trust Co.
Employer Identification Number: 426295370

1266
Fisher (Gramma) Foundation ▼
112 West Church St.
Marshalltown 50158
Mailing address: c/o The Jaspar Corporation, The Bullitt House, Easton, MD 21601; Tel.: (301) 822-8450

Incorporated in 1957 in Iowa.

Donor(s): J. William Fisher.
Financial data: (yr. ended 12/31/83): Assets, $5,804,500 (M); gifts received, $531,922; expenditures, $1,087,569, including $983,890 for 13 grants (high: $379,900; low: $800; average: $1,000-$75,000).
Purpose and activities: Broad purposes; grants mainly for support and sponsorship of opera.
Application information:
Write: William T. Hunter, Secretary-Treasurer
Officers and Trustees: J. William Fisher, Chairman; Christine F. Hunter, Vice-Chairman; William T. Hunter, Secretary-Treasurer.
Employer Identification Number: 426068755

1267
Gazette Foundation ⌧
500 Third Ave., S.E.
Cedar Rapids 52401

Established in 1960 in Iowa.
Donor(s): The Gazette Company.
Financial data: (yr. ended 12/31/83): Assets, $306,188 (M); gifts received, $98,025; expenditures, $129,520, including $128,450 for 47 grants (high: $13,500; low: $50).
Purpose and activities: Primarily local giving, with emphasis on higher education and a community fund; support also for youth agencies and cultural programs.
Limitations: Giving primarily in IA.
Officers: J.F. Hladky, III, President; William Crawford, Vice-President; John L. Donnelly, Treasurer; J.F. Hladky, Jr., Director.
Employer Identification Number: 426075177

1268
Glazer (Madelyn L.) Foundation ⌧
312 Hubbell Bldg.
Des Moines 50309

Established in 1957.
Financial data: (yr. ended 12/31/83): Assets, $2,699,884 (M); expenditures, $371,601, including $330,755 for 42 grants (high: $105,200; low: $10).
Purpose and activities: Primarily local giving for higher education, cultural programs, welfare, and Jewish welfare funds.
Limitations: Giving primarily in Des Moines, IA.
Officers: Madelyn L. Glazer, President; Edward Glazer, Vice-President; Richard Toran, Secretary; William Toran, Treasurer.
Employer Identification Number: 426052426

1269
Hall Foundation, Inc., The ▼
803 Merchants National Bank Bldg.
Cedar Rapids 52401   (319) 362-9079

Incorporated in 1953 in Iowa.
Donor(s): Members of the Hall family.
Financial data: (yr. ended 12/31/83): Assets, $31,897,077 (M); gifts received, $718,208; expenditures, $1,793,353, including $1,652,993 for 37 grants (high: $680,000; low: $500; average: $5,000-$50,000).

Purpose and activities: Broad purposes; local giving, with emphasis on cultural programs, higher education, social agencies, youth agencies, a community fund, and health services.
Types of support awarded: Operating budgets, continuing support, annual campaigns, seed money, emergency funds, building funds, equipment, land acquisition, special projects, research.
Limitations: Giving limited to Cedar Rapids, IA and the immediate trade area. No grants to individuals, or for deficit financing, endowment funds, scholarships, or fellowships; no loans.
Publications: Informational brochure, program policy statement, application guidelines.
Application information:
Initial approach: Letter
Copies of proposal: 1
Deadline(s): None
Board meeting date(s): The third Tuesday in June, and as required
Final notification: 3 months
Write: John G. Lidvall, Executive Director
Officers and Directors: Beahl T. Perrine, Chairman; William P. Whipple, President and Treasurer; Joseph R. Loufek, Vice-President; George C. Foerstner, Irene H. Perrine, Vice-Presidents; Darrel A. Morf, Secretary; John G. Lidvall, Executive Director; E.J. Buresh, James E. Coquillette, Carleen Grandon, Alex Meyer.
Number of staff: 2 full-time professional.
Employer Identification Number: 426057097

1270
Hawley Foundation ⌧
700 Sixth Ave.
Des Moines 50309   (515) 245-7413
Grant application office: 1520 Financial Center, Des Moines, IA 50307

Incorporated in 1927 in Iowa.
Donor(s): Henry B. Hawley,† Mrs. Henry B. Hawley.†
Financial data: (yr. ended 12/31/83): Assets, $1,656,483 (M); expenditures, $109,442, including $83,950 for 16 grants (high: $20,000; low: $500).
Purpose and activities: Broad purposes; to serve mankind, strengthen family life, and give assistance to organizations without regard to race, religion, or other affiliations as a community trust for Des Moines and the state of Iowa; support primarily for youth agencies, a children's home, and child and social agencies.
Limitations: Giving primarily in the greater Des Moines, IA, area. No support for individual churches or religious orders. No grants to individuals, or for endowment funds or operating budgets, and rarely for building funds; no loans.
Application information:
Initial approach: Letter or telephone
Copies of proposal: 1
Deadline(s): Submit proposal in September or October if requested by the foundation
Board meeting date(s): Quarterly and as required
Write: Amos C. Pearsall, Jr., Executive Director

Officers and Trustees: William Z. Proctor, President; Bernard D. Kurtz, Vice-President; Amos C. Pearsall, Jr., Secretary and Executive Director; Robb B. Kelley, Treasurer; Ray E. Cassell, Daniel F. Crowley, Robert J. Fleming, William Friedman, Jr., James W. Hubbell, Jr.
Employer Identification Number: 426056159

1271
Jay (George S. & Grace A.) Memorial Trust ◻
612 Sheridan Ave.
Shenandoah 51601   (712) 246-3399
Address for loan applications: 612 1/2 West Sheridan Ave., Shenandoah, IA 51601

Trust established in 1963 in Iowa.
Financial data: (yr. ended 3/31/84): Assets, $1,428,992 (M); expenditures, $129,875, including $81,200 for 87 loans.
Purpose and activities: Student loans to graduates of Shenandoah, Essex, and Farragut, Iowa high schools, only for higher education at an accredited college, univerisity or trade school; some support also for colleges and universities.
Types of support awarded: Student aid.
Limitations: Giving limited to IA.
Application information: Loan application information available; telephone inquiries accepted on Tuesdays only, during regular business hours. Application form required.
    Deadline(s): May 31
    Final notification: 1 month
    Write: Pauline Morton
Trustees: Francis Braley, William A. Longman, Robert Read.
Employer Identification Number: 426061515

1272
Kinney-Lindstrom Foundation, Inc. ▼ ◻
P.O. Box 520
Mason City 50401   (515) 896-3888

Incorporated in 1957 in Iowa.
Donor(s): Ida Lindstrom Kinney.†
Financial data: (yr. ended 12/31/83): Assets, $5,885,396 (M); expenditures, $1,911,492, including $1,716,469 for 81 grants (high: $330,000; low: $200; average: $2,500-$50,000).
Purpose and activities: Broad purposes; grants primarily for building funds for libraries in Iowa towns; support also for health, youth agencies, and education.
Types of support awarded: Building funds.
Limitations: Giving primarily in IA. No grants to individuals, or for endowment funds, operating budgets, or research; no loans.
Application information:
    Initial approach: Letter
    Copies of proposal: 1
    Deadline(s): None
    Board meeting date(s): 10 times a year
    Final notification: 2 weeks after interview
    Write: Lowell K. Hall, Secretary
Officer: Lowell K. Hall, Secretary and Treasurer.
Trustees: Thor Jenson, Ira Stinson.
Number of staff: 1 full-time professional.
Employer Identification Number: 426037351

1273
Kuyper (Peter H.) and E. Lucille Gaass Foundation ◻
c/o Rolscreen Company
Pella 50219   (515) 628-1000

Established in 1970 in Iowa.
Donor(s): Peter H. Kuyper, E. Lucille Gaass Kuyper.
Financial data: (yr. ended 4/30/84): Assets, $6,350,138 (M); expenditures, $252,643, including $242,571 for 23 grants (high: $150,000; low: $270).
Purpose and activities: Primarily local support for a college and for Christian welfare funds.
Limitations: Giving primarily in IA.
Application information:
    Deadline(s): None
    Write: Joan Kuyper Farber
Officer and Directors: Mary Joan Farver, President; LeRoy Baughman, Thomas W. Carpenter, David C. Lennartz.
Employer Identification Number: 237068402

1274
Lee Foundation ◻
130 East Second St.
Davenport 52801

Incorporated in 1962 in Iowa.
Financial data: (yr. ended 9/30/83): Assets, $1,321,431 (M); expenditures, $153,319, including $150,350 for 39 grants (high: $60,000; low: $333).
Purpose and activities: Broad purposes; grants largely for higher education, hospitals, youth agencies, cultural programs, and journalism.
Types of support awarded: Endowment funds, building funds.
Officers and Directors: Lloyd G. Schermer, President; James E. Burgess, Vice-President; Richard P. Galligan, Secretary; John S. Stemlar, Treasurer; Richard Belkin.
Employer Identification Number: 426057173

1275
Levitt (Richard S.) Foundation ◻
312 Hubbell Bldg.
Des Moines 50309

Established in 1957.
Donor(s): Members of the Levitt Family.
Financial data: (yr. ended 12/31/83): Assets, $1,944,839 (M); gifts received, $17,500; expenditures, $152,539, including $134,258 for 38 grants (high: $30,025; low: $10).
Purpose and activities: Primarily local giving for higher education, cultural programs, and welfare.
Limitations: Giving primarily in Des Moines, IA.
Officers: Richard Levitt, President and Treasurer; Mark Levitt, Randall Levitt, Vice-Presidents; Jeanne Levitt, Secretary.
Employer Identification Number: 426052427

1276
Maytag Company Foundation, Inc., The
c/o The Maytag Company
403 West Fourth St. North
Newton 50208   (515) 792-7000

Incorporated in 1952 in Iowa.
Donor(s): The Maytag Company.
Financial data: (yr. ended 12/31/84): Assets, $933,860 (M); gifts received, $300,000; expenditures, $411,511, including $247,716 for 80 grants (high: $46,700; low: $200), $125,331 for 175 grants to individuals and $29,129 for 80 employee matching gifts.
Purpose and activities: Broad purposes; contributes to worthwhile undertakings to help fulfill the Company's role as a responsible corporate citizen. Principal interest in scholarships and career education awards for students in Newton High School and children of Company employees, with cost-of-education supplements to colleges attended by scholarship winners; matches Company employees' gifts to approved colleges up to $1,000 annually per employee; makes other grants to college funds and educational organizations. Supports community betterment, including community funds and cultural activities in Newton/Central Iowa area, and other localities in which Company has plants or offices.
Types of support awarded: Student aid, employee matching gifts, employee related scholarships, scholarship funds.
Limitations: Giving limited to areas of company operations for community projects.
Publications: Program policy statement, financial statement, informational brochure.
Application information:
    Initial approach: Letter or telephone inquiry
    Copies of proposal: 1
    Board meeting date(s): March and as required
    Final notification: Varies
    Write: Miss Betty J. Dickinson, Executive Director
Officers: Daniel J. Krumm,* President; Francis C. Miller,* Vice-President; Donald C. Byers, Secretary and Treasurer; Betty J. Dickinson, Executive Director.
Trustees:* J.C. Enyart, Karl F. Langrock, Jack D. Levin, Donald R. Runger, Sterling O. Swanger.
Employer Identification Number: 426055722

1277
Maytag (The Fred) Family Foundation ▼
P.O. Box 39
Newton 50208   (515) 792-7000

Trust established in 1945 in Iowa.
Donor(s): Fred Maytag II,† Members of the Maytag family.
Financial data: (yr. ended 12/31/83): Assets, $16,426,364 (M); expenditures, $681,835, including $610,153 for 66 grants (high: $200,000; low: $50; average: $50-$200,000).
Purpose and activities: Primarily local giving for higher education, arts and culture, public affairs, and social services.

Types of support awarded: Operating budgets, continuing support, annual campaigns, seed money, building funds, equipment, land acquisition, matching funds, research, special projects.
Limitations: Giving primarily in Des Moines and Newton, IA. No grants to individuals, or for emergency funds, deficit financing, endowment funds, scholarships and fellowships, demonstration projects, publications, or conferences; no loans.
Application information:
    Initial approach: Letter
    Copies of proposal: 1
    Deadline(s): Submit proposal preferably in April or May; deadline May 31
    Board meeting date(s): June or July
    Final notification: 30 days after meeting
    Write: Francis C. Miller, Secretary
Trustees: Ellen Pray Maytag Madsen, Frederick L. Maytag III, Kenneth P. Maytag.
Officer: Francis C. Miller, Manager and Secretary.
Number of staff: 2 part-time support.
Employer Identification Number: 426055654

1278
Meredith (Edwin T.) Foundation ¤
1716 Locust St.
Des Moines 50309   (515) 284-2545

Incorporated in 1946 in Iowa.
Donor(s): Meredith Publishing Company.
Financial data: (yr. ended 12/31/83): Assets, $4,293,326 (M); gifts received, $204,562; expenditures, $373,024, including $335,623 for 52 grants (high: $50,000; low: $200).
Purpose and activities: Charitable and educational purposes; grants largely for youth agencies, higher education, cultural programs and a historic preservation area; some support for hospitals and health agencies, and conservation.
Limitations: No grants to individuals.
Application information: Grants are initiated by the foundation.
    Board meeting date(s): June
    Write: E.T. Meredith III, President
Officers: E.T. Meredith III, President and Director; Katherine C. Meredith, Vice-President; Gerald Thornton, Secretary; Marilyn Dillivan, Treasurer.
Employer Identification Number: 426059818

1279
National By-Products Foundation, Inc.
P.O. Box 615
1020 Locust St.
Des Moines 50303   (515) 288-2166

Incorporated in 1966 in Iowa.
Donor(s): National By-Products, Inc.
Financial data: (yr. ended 9/30/83): Assets, $367,888 (M); expenditures, $150,889, including $149,600 for 54 grants (high: $35,000; low: $20).
Purpose and activities: Giving primarily in areas of company operations, with emphasis on higher education and community funds; support also for community development, hospitals, and youth agencies.

Types of support awarded: Operating budgets, continuing support, annual campaigns, building funds.
Limitations: Giving limited to areas of company operations. No grants to individuals, or for matching gifts, scholarships and fellowships, special projects, research, publications, or conferences; no loans.
Application information:
    Initial approach: Letter
    Deadline(s): None
    Final notification: 30 days
    Write: C. Dean Carlson, President
Officers and Directors: C. Dean Carlson, President; Milt Riese, Secretary; Paul Bohlig, Treasurer; R.J. Fleming.
Number of staff: None.
Employer Identification Number: 420924487

1280
Pella Rolscreen Foundation ▼
c/o Rolscreen Company
Pella 50219   (515) 628-1000

Trust established in 1952 in Iowa.
Donor(s): Rolscreen Company.
Financial data: (yr. ended 12/31/83): Assets, $3,501,641 (M); gifts received, $949,000; expenditures, $491,097, including $469,355 for 94 grants (high: $100,000; low: $70; average: $500-$10,000) and $12,406 for grants to individuals.
Purpose and activities: Broad purposes; primarily local giving, with emphasis on higher education and hospitals; some support for cultural programs and social agencies.
Types of support awarded: Annual campaigns, building funds, scholarship funds, employee related scholarships.
Limitations: Giving primarily in areas of company operations, with emphasis on Pella and Des Moines, IA. No grants to individuals (except for company-employee scholarships), or for endowment funds, research, or matching gifts; no loans.
Publications: Informational brochure, application guidelines.
Application information:
    Initial approach: Proposal
    Deadline(s): None
    Board meeting date(s): Quarterly
    Final notification: 1 month
    Write: Clifford M. White, Assistant Secretary-Treasurer
Officers and Directors: Mary Joan Farver, President; J. Wayne Bevis, Secretary and Treasurer.
Number of staff: 1 part-time support.
Employer Identification Number: 237043881

1281
Ruan (John) Foundation Trust ¤
3200 Ruan Center
Des Moines 50304

Trust established in 1955 in Iowa.
Donor(s): John Ruan.
Financial data: (yr. ended 6/30/83): Assets, $3,910,034 (M); gifts received, $12,984; expenditures, $215,499, including $214,228 for 90 grants (high: $60,000; low: $25).

Purpose and activities: Primarily local giving, with emphasis on higher education, cultural programs, youth agencies, child welfare, and health agencies.
Limitations: Giving primarily in Des Moines, IA.
Application information:
    Write: John Ruan, Trustee
Trustee: Elizabeth J. Ruan, John Ruan.
Employer Identification Number: 426059463

1282
Salsbury (Dr. J. E.) Foundation
2000 Rockford Rd.
Charles City 50616   (515) 257-2422

Trust established in 1950 in Iowa.
Donor(s): Members of the Dr. J.E. Salsbury family and others.
Financial data: (yr. ended 12/31/83): Assets, $4,668,627 (M); gifts received, $50,000; expenditures, $260,605, including $231,265 for 16 grants (high: $125,000; low: $250) and $16,225 for 20 grants to individuals.
Purpose and activities: Principally for the advancement of education and the promotion of scientific research in animal health; scholarships are limited to children of employees of Salsbury Laboratories, Inc., and its subsidiaries.
Types of support awarded: Employee related scholarships, continuing support, building funds, research, matching funds.
Limitations: No grants for scholarships (except for children of company employees) or for endowment funds; no loans.
Application information:
    Initial approach: Letter
    Copies of proposal: 1
    Deadline(s): February 1 for scholarships
    Board meeting date(s): As required
    Write: John G. Salsbury, Trustee
Trustees: Doris J. Salsbury, John G. Salsbury, Frances I. Zbornik, Jim J. Zbornik.
Employer Identification Number: 426061190

1283
Sherman (Mabel E.) Educational Fund ¤
212 West Willow St.
Cherokee 51012   (712) 225-5131

Established in 1977 in Iowa.
Financial data: (yr. ended 6/30/83): Assets, $1,661,983 (M); expenditures, $98,274, including $66,863 for 4 grants (high: $22,288; low: $11,143).
Purpose and activities: Grants to four local colleges for student loans, preferably to residents of Ida or Cherokee counties, Iowa.
Types of support awarded: Student aid.
Limitations: Giving limited to Ida and Cherokee counties, IA.
Trustee: Cherokee State Bank.
Employer Identification Number: 426278859

1284
Stanley Foundation, The
420 East Third St.
Muscatine 52761   (319) 264-1500

Incorporated in 1956 in Iowa.
Financial data: (yr. ended 12/31/84): Assets, $15,718,400 (M); gifts received, $5,261; expenditures, $3,125,700, including $2,708,300 for foundation-administered programs.
Purpose and activities: A private operating foundation, the Stanley Foundation encourages study, research, and education in international relations with emphasis on world organizations. Sponsors conferences for policymakers and opinion shapers; publishes conference reports and essays by various authors, both distributed free, and a monthly news magazine of excerpts from the foreign press - available by subscription; produces a radio program on world issues; conducts an international education model in the Muscatine schools and community.
Limitations: No grants for any purposes; no scholarships.
Application information: Applications not accepted since foundation does not make grants.
   Write: Richard H. Stanley, President, or Kenton L. Allen, Secretary and Treasurer
Officers: Richard H. Stanley,* President; Elizabeth M. Stanley,* Vice-President; Kenton L. Allen, Secretary and Treasurer.
Directors:* Jane Stanley Buckles, David M. Stanley, Mary Jo Stanley.
Number of staff: 10 full-time professional; 1 part-time professional; 3 full-time support; 2 part-time support.
Employer Identification Number: 426071036

1285
Van Buren Foundation, Inc., The
c/o Farmers State Bank
Keosauqua 52565   (319) 293-3794

Incorporated in 1959 in Iowa.
Donor(s): Ralph S. Roberts.†
Financial data: (yr. ended 12/31/83): Assets, $2,107,602 (M); gifts received, $5,000; expenditures, $163,335, including $135,781 for 40 grants (high: $24,200; low: $260) and $10,292 for grants to individuals.
Purpose and activities: Local giving only for religious and educational purposes; grants for local community development, education, including scholarships, aid for the aged, and recreation programs.
Types of support awarded: Special projects, building funds, general purposes, student aid.
Limitations: Giving limited to Van Buren County, IA.
Application information:
   Initial approach: Full proposal
   Copies of proposal: 1
   Board meeting date(s): As required
   Write: For general grants: John A. Manning, Chairman; for educational grants: Arthur P. Ovrum, Treasurer

Officers: John A. Manning, Chairman; Norwood Teal, Vice-Chairman; Davis E. Pollock, President; John R. Nickelson, 1st Vice-President; Rex Strait, 2nd Vice-President; Richard H. Lytle, Secretary; Arthur P. Ovrom, Treasurer.
Employer Identification Number: 426062589

1286
Vermeer Charitable Foundation, Inc.
c/o Vermeer Manufacturing Company
P.O. Box 200
Pella 50219   (515) 628-3141

Established in 1977 in Iowa.
Donor(s): Vermeer Manufacturing, Vermeer Sales and Service of Iowa, Vermeer Farms Inc.
Financial data: (yr. ended 12/31/84): Assets, $2,714,660 (M); gifts received, $524,927; expenditures, $77,648, including $74,600 for 8 grants (high: $20,000; low: $100).
Purpose and activities: Local giving primarily for Christian religious organizations and higher education.
Types of support awarded: General purposes, seed money, building funds.
Limitations: Giving limited to the Pella, IA, area. No grants to individuals, or for endowment funds, scholarships and fellowships, or matching gifts; no loans.
Application information: Applications not encouraged.
   Board meeting date(s): December and as required
   Write: Mary Andringa, Director
Directors: Dale Andringa, Mary Andringa, Gary Vermeer, Matilda Vermeer.
Number of staff: None.
Employer Identification Number: 421087640

1287
Vermeer Foundation Co.
(formerly The Vermeer Foundation)
c/o Vermeer Manufacturing Company
P.O. Box 200
Pella 50219   (515) 628-3141

Trust established in 1958 in Iowa.
Donor(s): Vermeer Manufacturing Company.
Financial data: (yr. ended 12/31/84): Assets, $2,510,002 (M); gifts received, $506,317; expenditures, $140,187, including $136,500 for 40 grants (high: $27,500; low: $50).
Purpose and activities: Emphasis on local church-related institutions and community projects.
Types of support awarded: General purposes, annual campaigns, seed money, building funds, endowment funds.
Limitations: Giving primarily in Pella, IA. No grants to individuals, or for research, scholarships and fellowships, or matching gifts; no loans.
Application information: Applications not invited from any group which does not know a director personally. Application form required.
   Initial approach: Letter
   Board meeting date(s): December and as required
   Final notification: 1 month
   Write: Stanley J. Vermeer, President

Officer and Directors: Stanley J. Vermeer, President and Secretary; Robert L. Vermeer, Treasurer; Carl E. Boat.
Number of staff: None.
Employer Identification Number: 426059566

1288
Wahlert Foundation
Sixteenth and Sycamore Sts.
Dubuque 52001   (319) 588-5400
Grant application office: c/o FDL Foods, Inc., P.O. Box 898, Dubuque, IA 52001

Incorporated in 1948 in Iowa.
Donor(s): Dubuque Packing Co., FDL Foods, Inc., H.W. Wahlert,† and officers of the Foundation.
Financial data: (yr. ended 11/30/84): Assets, $1,896,000 (M); gifts received, $5,783; expenditures, $163,400, including $144,000 for 13 grants (high: $62,000; low: $540).
Purpose and activities: Broad purposes; local giving, with emphasis on education; grants also for hospitals, social agencies, and cultural activities.
Types of support awarded: Continuing support, annual campaigns, seed money, emergency funds, building funds, equipment, land acquisition.
Limitations: Giving limited to the Dubuque, IA, metropolitan area. No grants to individuals, or for endowment funds, operating budgets, deficit financing, special projects, research, publications, conferences, scholarships and fellowships, or matching gifts; no loans.
Application information:
   Initial approach: Full proposal
   Copies of proposal: 1
   Deadline(s): November 30
   Board meeting date(s): December
   Final notification: January 30
   Write: R.H. Wahlert, Treasurer
Officers and Trustees: R.C. Wahlert, President; Al E. Hughes, Secretary; R.H. Wahlert, Treasurer; Jean Stoltz, Donald Strausse, David Wahlert, Donna Wahlert, Jim Wahlert.
Number of staff: None.
Employer Identification Number: 426051124

1289
Witte (John H.), Jr. Foundation ¤
c/o First National Bank
201 Jefferson St., P.O. Box 1088
Burlington 52601   (319) 752-2761

Donor(s): John H. Witte, Jr.†
Financial data: (yr. ended 8/31/83): Assets, $3,349,446 (M); expenditures, $150,908, including $138,190 for 31 grants (high: $20,000; low: $163).
Purpose and activities: Local giving, with emphasis on social service and youth agencies, education, and a community fund.
Limitations: Giving primarily in Burlington, IA.
Application information:
   Write: Robert C. Matsch
Trustee: First National Bank.
Employer Identification Number: 426297940

1290
Younkers Foundation, Inc.
c/o Younker Brothers
Seventh and Walnut Sts., Box 1495
Des Moines 50397   (515) 244-1112

Incorporated in 1968 in Iowa.
Donor(s): Younkers, Inc.
Financial data: (yr. ended 12/31/84): Assets, $0 (L); gifts received, $378,206; expenditures, $378,206, including $378,206 for grants.
Purpose and activities: Primarily local giving with emphasis on community funds; grants also for higher education and Jewish welfare funds; some support for cultural activities.
Limitations: Giving primarily in IA. No grants to individuals.
Application information: Applications for grants not invited.
Officers: Fred Hubbell, President; Robert Lubetkin, Don Thomas, Vice-Presidents; John Cavins, Secretary and Treasurer.
Employer Identification Number: 420937873

KANSAS

1291
Abell (Jennie G. and Pearl) Education Trust
723 1/2 Main St.
P.O. Box 487
Ashland 67831   (316) 685-2228

Trust established in 1975 in Kansas.
Donor(s): P.G. Abell.†
Financial data: (yr. ended 5/31/83): Assets, $1,924,359 (M); expenditures, $167,875, including $138,365 for 91 grants to individuals.
Purpose and activities: Grants only for scholarships for graduates of Clark County, Kansas high schools.
Types of support awarded: Student aid.
Limitations: Giving limited to Clark County, KS.
Publications: Program policy statement.
Application information: Application form required.
 Initial approach: Full proposal
 Copies of proposal: 1
 Deadline(s): Submit application in April through May or November through December; deadlines June 15 and December 15
 Board meeting date(s): Monthly
 Write: Sarah D. Shattuck, Manager
Trustees: Juanita Abell Pyle, Sarah D. Shattuck, W.A. Shattuck, W.H. Stevenson.
Employer Identification Number: 237454791

1292
Baker (J. H.) Trust ♯
c/o Farmers and Merchants State Bank
La Crosse 67548   (913) 222-2513

Established in 1976.
Donor(s): J.H. Baker.†
Financial data: (yr. ended 12/31/83): Assets, $1,196,075 (M); expenditures, $25,773, including $14,555 for 20 loans.
Purpose and activities: Grants primarily for student loans.
Types of support awarded: Student aid.
Trustee: Farmers and Merchants State Bank.
Employer Identification Number: 510210925

1293
Baughman Foundation ▼ ♯
112 W. 3rd
P.O. Box 1356
Liberal 67901   (316) 624-1371

Incorporated in 1958 in Kansas.
Donor(s): Robert W. Baughman,† The John W. Baughman Farms Company.
Financial data: (yr. ended 12/31/83): Assets, $9,957,771 (M); expenditures, $514,900, including $385,613 for 38 grants (high: $80,000; low: $100).
Purpose and activities: Primarily local giving, with emphasis on higher education, including a community junior college, youth agencies, and civic projects.
Types of support awarded: Building funds, endowment funds, operating budgets, special projects, scholarship funds.
Limitations: Giving primarily in KS, with emphasis on Liberal. No grants to individuals.
Application information:
 Initial approach: Letter or telephone
 Copies of proposal: 3
 Deadline(s): Prior to second Wednesday of each month
 Board meeting date(s): Monthly
 Final notification: 30 days
 Write: Eugene W. Slaymaker, President
Officers and Trustees: Eugene W. Slaymaker, President; Oliver S. Brown, Vice-President; James R. Yoxall, Secretary-Treasurer.
Number of staff: None.
Employer Identification Number: 486108797

1294
Beech Aircraft Foundation
9709 East Central Ave.
Wichita 67201   (316) 681-8177

Incorporated in 1966 in Kansas.
Donor(s): Beech Aircraft Corporation.
Financial data: (yr. ended 9/30/84): Assets, $5,190,000 (M); expenditures, $438,000, including $412,800 for 150 grants (high: $50,000; low: $25) and $20,000 for employee matching gifts.
Purpose and activities: Grants made only to communities where company has factories, with emphasis on higher education, community funds, youth agencies, and hospitals; some support for cultural activities, conservation, and the handicapped.

Limitations: Giving primarily in communities with company facilities. No grants to individuals, or for endowment funds, research, or matching gifts; no loans.
Application information: Applications for grants not invited.
 Board meeting date(s): January, April, July, and October
 Write: Larry E. Lawrence, Secretary-Treasurer
Officers and Directors: O.A. Beech, Chairman; Frank E. Hedrick, President; Austin Rising, Vice-President; Larry E. Lawrence, Secretary-Treasurer; J.A. Elliott, James S. Walsh, Lucille Winters.
Employer Identification Number: 486125881

1295
Breidenthal (Willard J. and Mary G.) Foundation
Commercial National Bank, Trust Div.
P.O. Box 1400
Kansas City 66117

Trust established in 1962 in Kansas.
Donor(s): Willard J. Breidenthal,† Mary G. Breidenthal,† and members of the Breidenthal family.
Financial data: (yr. ended 12/31/84): Assets, $2,182,000 (M); expenditures, $156,000, including $149,000 for 40 grants (high: $10,000; low: $250; average: $3,725).
Purpose and activities: Primarily local giving, with emphasis on higher education and hospitals; support also for agriculture, child welfare, youth agencies, and cultural programs.
Limitations: Giving primarily in the Kansas City, KS area.
Application information:
 Initial approach: Letter
 Deadline(s): Submit proposal preferably in September or October; deadline October 31
 Board meeting date(s): November
 Write: William C. Tempel
Trustees: George Gray Breidenthal, Mary P. Breidenthal, Ruth B. Snyder, Commercial National Bank.
Number of staff: None.
Employer Identification Number: 486103376

1296
Brown (Samuel M. and Laura H.) Charitable Trust ♯
c/o First National Bank
P.O. Box One
Wichita 67201

Trust established in 1974 in Kansas.
Donor(s): S.M. Brown.†
Financial data: (yr. ended 11/30/83): Assets, $1,172,549 (M); expenditures, $80,851, including $71,477 for 14 grants (high: $6,000; low: $2,700).
Purpose and activities: Primarily local giving, with emphasis on cultural programs, especially music, higher education, and church support.
Limitations: Giving primarily in Wichita, KS.
Trustees: Robert G. Braden, Roetzel Jochems, First National Bank (W.A. Byerley, Senior Vice-President and Trust Officer).
Employer Identification Number: 486193416

1297
Cessna Foundation, Inc.
5800 East Pawnee Rd.
P.O. Box 1521
Wichita 67201   (316) 685-9111

Incorporated in 1952 in Kansas.
Donor(s): The Cessna Aircraft Company.
Financial data: (yr. ended 12/31/83): Assets,
$6,255,855 (M); expenditures, $459,049,
including $433,675 for 66 grants (high:
$115,000; low: $150; average: $500-$1,000)
and $7,314 for 26 employee matching gifts.
Purpose and activities: Broad purposes; grants
largely for United Ways, higher education, and
youth agencies, primarily in areas of Company
operations; support also for cultural programs,
including museums.
Types of support awarded: Employee
matching gifts, building funds, equipment.
Limitations: Giving primarily in areas of
company operations. No grants to individuals.
Application information:
   Initial approach: Letter
   Copies of proposal: 1
   Deadline(s): Submit proposals preferably in
      December or January
   Board meeting date(s): February and
      September
   Write: D.R. Edwards, Secretary
Officers and Trustees: Russell W. Meyer, Jr.,
President; John E. Moore, Vice-President; D.R.
Edwards, Secretary and Treasurer; Dean
Humphrey, R.W. Van Sant.
Employer Identification Number: 486108801

1298
Coleman Charitable Trust, Inc. ¤
250 North St. Francis St.
Wichita 67201

Incorporated in 1944 in Kansas.
Donor(s): The Coleman Company, Inc.
Financial data: (yr. ended 12/31/83): Assets,
$303,983 (M); gifts received, $135,500;
expenditures, $366,713, including $174,960
for 97 grants (high: $42,000; low: $25) and
$5,025 for 17 employee matching gifts.
Purpose and activities: Primarily local giving,
with emphasis on a community fund, higher
education, youth and social agencies.
Types of support awarded: Matching funds,
operating budgets, scholarship funds, building
funds, annual campaigns, special projects.
Limitations: Giving primarily in Wichita, KS.
Officers and Directors: Sheldon Coleman,
Chairman; Clarence Coleman, Frank Shaw,
Vice-Presidents; G. Lawrence Keller, Secretary;
Lawrence M. Jones, Treasurer; Don Berchtold,
R.A. Curry, Wesley H. Sowers, Duane Wallace.
Employer Identification Number: 486104738

1299
Darby (Edith and Harry) Foundation ¤
First St. and Walker Ave.
Kansas City 66110

Incorporated in 1961 in Kansas.
Donor(s): Harry Darby Foundation, and others.

Financial data: (yr. ended 9/30/83): Assets,
$1,609,009 (M); gifts received, $22,407;
expenditures, $112,863, including $103,334
for 97 grants (high: $30,000; low: $50).
Purpose and activities: Broad purposes; giving
largely in Kansas and Missouri with emphasis
on higher education, hospitals, church support,
community development, and cultural
programs.
Limitations: Giving primarily in KS and MO.
Officers and Directors: Harry Darby,
President; Sam W. Sinderson, Vice-President
and Secretary; L.A. Randall, Treasurer.
Employer Identification Number: 486103395

1300
Davis (James A. and Juliet L.)
Foundation, Inc. ¤
P.O. Box 2027
Hutchinson 67501-2027   (316) 663-5021

Incorporated in 1954 in Kansas.
Financial data: (yr. ended 12/31/83): Assets,
$1,697,159 (M); expenditures, $133,463,
including $61,780 for 25 grants (high: $15,000;
low: $100) and $31,500 for 23 grants to
individuals.
Purpose and activities: Primarily local giving,
with emphasis on higher education, including
scholarships, cultural programs, and child
welfare.
Types of support awarded: Student aid.
Limitations: Giving limited to the Hutchinson,
KS, area.
Application information: Scholarships limited
to students attending Hutchinson High School.
   Deadline(s): March 15
   Write: William Y. Chalfant, Secretary-
      Treasurer
Officers and Trustees: Peter M. Macdonald,
President; Merl F. Sellers, Vice-President;
William Y. Chalfant, Secretary-Treasurer; Kent
Longenecker.
Employer Identification Number: 486105748

1301
DeVore Foundation, Inc. ¤
P.O. Box 118
Wichita 67201

Incorporated in 1953 in Kansas.
Donor(s): Floyd DeVore, Western Drilling Tool
Company, and others.
Financial data: (yr. ended 11/30/83): Assets,
$1,309,607 (M); gifts received, $37,312;
expenditures, $84,748, including $68,853 for
51 grants (high: $31,600; low: $25).
Purpose and activities: Primarily local giving,
with emphasis on youth agencies, Protestant
church support, higher education, and social
services.
Limitations: Giving primarily in Wichita, KS.
Officers: Richard A. DeVore, President and
Secretary; William D. DeVore, Vice-President
and Treasurer.
Director: Donald R. Miller.
Employer Identification Number: 486109754

1302
Doskocil Family Foundation, Inc.,
The ¤
2909 McNew Rd.
Hutchinson 67501

Incorporated in 1983 in Kansas.
Donor(s): Lawrence D. Doskocil, William L.
Rogers, Wendel Strong, Orvin Miller.
Financial data: (yr. ended 12/31/83): Assets,
$1,300,000 (M); gifts received, $1,300,000.
Purpose and activities: First year of operation
in 1983; no grants awarded.
Officers: Larry D. Doskocil, President;
Jacquelin Doskocil, Secretary-Treasurer.
Employer Identification Number: 480970383

1303
Fink Foundation ¤
800 First National Bank Tower
Topeka 66603   (913) 233-0541

Incorporated in 1962 in Kansas.
Donor(s): H. Bernerd Fink, Ruth G. Fink.
Financial data: (yr. ended 12/31/83): Assets,
$1,368,145 (M); expenditures, $68,148,
including $68,065 for 4 grants (high: $68,000;
low: $15).
Purpose and activities: Broad purposes;
primarily local giving, with emphasis on a local
private foundation.
Types of support awarded: Operating
budgets, building funds, scholarship funds.
Limitations: Giving primarily in KS. No grants
to individuals.
Application information:
   Initial approach: Letter
   Copies of proposal: 1
   Deadline(s): Submit proposal in April,
      August, or September
   Board meeting date(s): May and December
   Write: Ruth G. Fink, President
Officers: Ruth G. Fink,* President; H. Bernerd
Fink,* Vice-President; Jack H. Hamilton,
Secretary; Larry D. Riggins, Treasurer.
Trustees:* Marcia F. Anderson, Bruce G.
Cochener.
Employer Identification Number: 486113919

1304
First National Bank in Wichita
Charitable Trust ¤
Box one
Wichita 67201

Established in 1952 in Kansas.
Donor(s): First National Bank in Wichita.
Financial data: (yr. ended 12/31/83): Assets,
$215,465 (M); gifts received, $120,000;
expenditures, $183,304, including $183,300
for 33 grants (high: $25,000; low: $500).
Purpose and activities: Local giving for higher
education, youth agencies, a community fund,
and social services.
Types of support awarded: General purposes,
building funds.
Limitations: Giving limited to KS, with
emphasis on Wichita.
Trustee: First National Bank in Wichita.
Employer Identification Number: 486102412

1305
Fourth National Bank in Wichita Charitable Trust
P.O. Box 1122
Wichita 67201 (316) 261-4361

Trust established in 1952 in Kansas.
Donor(s): The Fourth National Bank and Trust Company.
Financial data: (yr. ended 11/30/84): Assets, $2,012,529 (M); gifts received, $200,000; expenditures, $322,600, including $307,000 for 53 grants (high: $79,000; low: $200).
Purpose and activities: Primarily local giving, with emphasis on community funds, youth agencies, higher education, hospitals, aid to the handicapped, music, and civic projects.
Types of support awarded: Building funds, equipment, endowment funds, scholarship funds.
Limitations: Giving primarily in KS, with emphasis on Wichita. No support for political or religious organizations, fraternal groups, or organizations which receive a major portion of their support from government funds. No grants to individuals, or for general support, operating budgets, dinners, travel, annual campaigns, seed money, emergency funds, deficit financing, publications, conferences, or matching gifts; no loans.
Publications: Application guidelines.
Application information:
 Initial approach: Full proposal
 Copies of proposal: 1
 Deadline(s): None
 Board meeting date(s): December, March, June, and September
 Final notification: Up to 3 months
 Write: Michael R. Ritchey, Executive Vice-President
Trustees: A. Dwight Button, Wilson Cadman, Jordan Haines, Frank Lowman, Richard Price, The Fourth National Bank and Trust Company, (Michael R. Ritchey, Executive Vice-President and Senior Trust Officer).
Number of staff: None.
Employer Identification Number: 486103519

1306
Francis (Parker B.) III Foundation
9401 Indian Creek Pkwy.
P.O. Box 25905
Overland Park 66225-5905 (913) 661-0444

Established in 1962 in Missouri.
Donor(s): Parker B. Francis III.†
Financial data: (yr. ended 12/31/83): Assets, $20,081,434 (M); expenditures, $896,786, including $813,579 for 61 grants (high: $116,000; low: $195).
Purpose and activities: Giving primarily for medical research through the Parker B. Francis Fellowship Program on a national basis.
Types of support awarded: Fellowships.
Application information:
 Initial approach: Letter
 Write: Carlene Adams, Assistant Secretary-Treasurer
Trustees: W. Coleman Branton, Burton A. Dole, Jr., Thomas A. Reed, Daniel C. Weary.
Employer Identification Number: 436050408

1307
Garvey Foundation ▼
R. H. Garvey Bldg., Suite 1000
300 West Douglas St.
Wichita 67202 (316) 261-5384

Incorporated in 1949 in Kansas.
Donor(s): Members of the Garvey family and family-related businesses.
Financial data: (yr. ended 12/31/84): Assets, $7,040,209 (M); gifts received, $473,500; expenditures, $123,541, including $45,981 for 109 grants (high: $4,000; low: $10).
Purpose and activities: Broad purposes; local giving, with emphasis on higher education, community funds, and nutrition research.
Types of support awarded: Operating budgets, annual campaigns, seed money, building funds, equipment, research, conferences and seminars, scholarship funds, matching funds, continuing support, general purposes.
Limitations: Giving primarily in KS, with emphasis on Wichita. No grants to individuals or for endowment funds; no loans.
Application information:
 Initial approach: Letter
 Copies of proposal: 1
 Deadline(s): None
 Board meeting date(s): Monthly
 Final notification: 6 weeks
 Write: D. Clifford Allison, Executive Vice-President
Officers and Trustees:* Olive W. Garvey,* President; D. Clifford Allison, Executive Vice-President; Ruth G. Fink,* James S. Garvey,* Olivia G. Lincoln,* Vice-Presidents; Willard W. Garvey,* Secretary-Treasurer.
Number of staff: None.
Employer Identification Number: 486105223

1308
Garvey Kansas Foundation
R. H. Garvey Bldg., Suite 1000
300 West Douglas
Wichita 67202 (316) 261-5411

Incorporated in 1964 in Kansas.
Donor(s): Willard W. Garvey.
Financial data: (yr. ended 11/30/82): Assets, $2,210,793 (M); gifts received, $114,106; expenditures, $176,723, including $169,090 for 74 grants (high: $76,000; low: $10).
Purpose and activities: Primarily local giving for secondary and higher education and Protestant church support; support also for community funds and legal foundations.
Limitations: Giving primarily in KS. No grants to individuals or for endowment funds; no loans.
Application information:
 Initial approach: Letter
 Copies of proposal: 1
 Board meeting date(s): January, April, July, and October
 Write: Jean K. Garvey, President
Officers: Jean K. Garvey,* President; Willard W. Garvey,* Vice-President; James A. Childers, Secretary-Treasurer.
Trustees:* Emily Garvey Bonavia, John K. Garvey.
Employer Identification Number: 486115213

1309
Hansen (Dane G.) Foundation ▼ ⋈
P.O. Box 187
Logan 67646 (913) 689-4816

Incorporated in 1965 in Kansas.
Donor(s): Dane G. Hansen.†
Financial data: (yr. ended 9/30/82): Assets, $16,170,210 (M); expenditures, $1,965,133, including $1,372,679 for 116 grants (high: $120,000; low: $150).
Purpose and activities: Charitable and educational purposes; for the benefit of the town of Logan, Phillips County, and northwest Kansas generally. Grants largely for higher education including scholarship funds, youth agencies, the handicapped, civic affairs, hospitals, and Protestant church support.
Types of support awarded: Building funds, equipment, operating budgets, publications, general purposes, continuing support, scholarship funds.
Limitations: Giving primarily in northwest KS. No grants to individuals.
Application information:
 Write: Ralph E. Reitz, President
Officers and Trustees: Ralph E. Reitz, President; McDill Boyd, Vice-President; Ross Beach, Secretary; Oscar F. Belin, Treasurer; James W. Baird, Dane G. Bales, W.R. Lappin.
Employer Identification Number: 486121156

1310
Helvering (R. L. and Elsa) Trust ⋈
c/o Robert F. Galloway
P.O. Box 468, 1100 Broadway
Marysville 66508 (913) 562-2375

Trust established about 1980.
Donor(s): R. L. Helvering,† Elsa Helvering.†
Financial data: (yr. ended 3/31/83): Assets, $1,458,293 (M); expenditures, $23,932, including $21,866 for 5 grants (high: $8,846; low: $750) and $750 for 1 grant to an individual.
Purpose and activities: Local giving, largely for civic and community development projects; one four-year scholarship for a Kansas college or university awarded each year to a graduating senior from a high school in Marshall County, Kansas.
Limitations: Giving primarily in KS.
Application information: Scholarship application form required. Application form required.
 Deadline(s): May 1
 Write: Robert F. Galloway, Trustee
Trustee: Robert F. Galloway.
Employer Identification Number: 480924200

1311
Hesston Foundation, Inc.
P.O. Box 4000
Hesston 67062 (316) 327-6760

Incorporated in 1965 in Kansas.
Donor(s): Hesston Corporation, and others.

Financial data: (yr. ended 12/31/84): Assets, $1,206,449 (L); expenditures, $110,915, including $101,175 for 14 grants (high: $35,000; low: $500; average: $1,000) and $5,567 for 86 employee matching gifts.

Purpose and activities: Grants are primarily made to causes within the "community of responsibility," including programs of direct impact on company employees, with emphasis on higher education; church-supported activities; hospitals, nursing homes and health services; youth agencies; public music and fine arts agencies; and community and general welfare assistance agencies.

Types of support awarded:
Operating budgets, continuing support, annual campaigns, seed money, building funds, equipment, matching funds, special projects, research, employee matching gifts.

Limitations: Giving primarily in in areas where company employees live and work. No grants to individuals, or for emergency funds, deficit financing, land acquisition, or scholarships and fellowships; no loans.

Application information:
Initial approach: Full proposal
Copies of proposal: 1
Deadline(s): February 28, May 31, August 31, and November 30
Board meeting date(s): March, June, September, and December
Final notification: 2 to 3 weeks after board meetings
Write: Raymond C. Schlichting, President

Officers: Raymond C. Schlichting,* Chairman and President; Harold P. Dyck,* Lyle E. Yost,* Vice-Presidents; Roberta M. Oliver, Secretary-Treasurer.

Directors:* Howard L. Brenneman, William L. Friesen, John Siemens, Jr., Kenneth G. Speir.

Number of staff: 1 part-time support.

Employer Identification Number: 480698307

1312
Jellison (Arthur D. and Maude S.) Charitable Trust ¤
c/o First National Bank of Topeka
P.O. Box 88
Topeka 66601

Trust established in 1965 in Kansas.
Financial data: (yr. ended 3/31/83): Assets, $821,175 (M); expenditures, $136,184, including $116,587 for 34 grants (high: $44,500; low: $350).

Purpose and activities: Grants mainly for higher education and a youth agency.

Trustees: Dean A. Cassity, Robert K. Weary, First National Bank of Topeka.

Employer Identification Number: 486120194

1313
Jones (Walter S. and Evan C.) Foundation ¤
515 Citizens National Bank Bldg.
Emporia 66801   (316) 342-1714

Established in 1974 in Kansas.
Donor(s): Walter S. and Evan C. Jones Trust.

Financial data: (yr. ended 3/31/84): Assets, $1,350 (M); gifts received, $1,295,850; expenditures, $1,298,498, including $1,256,342 for grants to individuals.

Purpose and activities: Grants only to children of Osage, Coffey, and Lyon counties, Kansas, who have resided there continuously for one year, for educational and medical expenses.

Types of support awarded: Grants to individuals, student aid.

Limitations: Giving limited to residents of Osage, Coffey, and Lyon counties, KS.

Publications: Program policy statement.

Application information:
Initial approach: Letter
Deadline(s): Submit proposal preferably in May; deadline July 1
Board meeting date(s): Monthly
Final notification: 2 months
Write: Dorothy E. Melander, General Manager

Officers: Kenneth B. Thomas, President; James Teichgraeber, Vice-President; David W. Evans, Jr., Secretary; Ken Calhoun, Treasurer; Dorothy E. Melander, General Manager.

Trustees: Stephen Jones, Mary McKinney, Max Stewart, Jr.

Number of staff: 2.

Employer Identification Number: 237384087

1314
Jordaan Foundation Trust
c/o First State Bank & Trust Company
111 East 84th St., P.O. Box 360
Larned 67550   (316) 285-3157

Trust established in 1970 in Kansas.
Donor(s): J.D. Jordaan.†
Financial data: (yr. ended 12/31/84): Assets, $1,865,432 (M); expenditures, $295,158, including $243,775 for 6 grants (high: $200,000; low: $1,000) and $30,000 for 20 grants to individuals.

Purpose and activities: Charitable giving; local support for educational and civic development, with emphasis on community programs, an historical society, and scholarships to graduates of a local high school.

Types of support awarded: General purposes, operating budgets, building funds, equipment, land acquisition, matching funds, consulting services, scholarship funds, special projects, research, publications, conferences and seminars, student aid.

Limitations: Giving limited to organizations and individuals in Pawnee County, KS. No grants for endowment funds; no loans.

Publications: Application guidelines.

Application information:
Initial approach: Telephone or letter
Copies of proposal: 5
Deadline(s): 1st Tuesday of every month
Board meeting date(s): Monthly
Final notification: 2 days
Write: Glee S. Smith, Chairman

Advisory Board: Glee S. Smith, Chairman; Edward B. Boyd, Ned M. Brown, Walter M. Crawford, Reed Peters.

Trustee Bank: First State Bank and Trust Co. of Larned.

Number of staff: None.

Employer Identification Number: 486155003

1315
Kansas Gas and Electric Charitable Foundation ¤
201 North Market St.
P.O. Box 208
Wichita 67201

Incorporated in 1952 in Kansas.
Donor(s): Kansas Gas and Electric Company.
Financial data: (yr. ended 12/31/82): Assets, $209,344 (M); gifts received, $50,000; expenditures, $128,479, including $127,110 for 48 grants (high: $51,500; low: $100).

Purpose and activities: Broad purposes; primarily local giving largely for community funds, higher education, youth agencies, social services, and cultural programs.

Limitations: Giving primarily in southeastern KS.

Officers and Trustees:* Wilson K. Cadman,* President; Dennis L. Evans,* Marjorie I. Setter,* Vice-Presidents; W.B. Walker, Secretary; R.E. Tate, Treasurer.

Employer Identification Number: 486116437

1316
Koch (Charles G.) Charitable Foundation ¤
4111 E. 37th St. North
Wichita 67220   (316) 832-5227
Application address: P.O. Box 2256, Wichita, KS 67201

Established in 1981 in Kansas.
Donor(s): Charles G. Koch, Fred C. Koch Foundation, Fred C. Koch Trusts for Charity.
Financial data: (yr. ended 12/31/83): Assets, $4,019,952 (M); gifts received, $1,293,452; expenditures, $158,290, including $155,319 for 4 grants (high: $100,000; low: $1,000).

Purpose and activities: Grants mainly for higher education.

Limitations: No grants to individuals.

Application information:
Initial approach: Proposal
Deadline(s): None
Write: George Pearson, Administrator

Officers and Directors:* Charles Koch,* President; Elizabeth Koch,* Vice-President; George Pearson,* Secretary; Florence Stockwell, Treasurer.

Employer Identification Number: 480918408

1317
Koch (The Fred C.) Foundation, Inc.
P.O. Box 2256
Wichita 67201

Incorporated in 1955 in Kansas.
Donor(s): Fred C. Koch,† Mary R. Koch, Koch Industries, Inc.
Financial data: (yr. ended 12/31/83): Assets, $6,547,997 (M); gifts received, $36,000; expenditures, $362,694, including $333,606 for 29 grants (high: $95,051; low: $100) and $20,000 for 20 grants to individuals.

Purpose and activities: Grants for research in social sciences and for cultural programs. Scholarship program for dependents of employees of Koch Industries.

Types of support awarded: Employee related scholarships.
Limitations: No grants to individuals, except for dependents of Koch Industries employees.
Application information:
  Initial approach: Letter
  Copies of proposal: 1
  Deadline(s): Submit proposal preferably in February
  Board meeting date(s): March
  Write: George H. Pearson, President
Officers: George H. Pearson, President; Mary R. Koch,* Vice-President; Frederick Hansen, Secretary; Florence Stockwell, Treasurer.
Directors:* S. Hazard Gillespie, Robert L. Howard, David H. Koch, William I. Koch.
Employer Identification Number: 486113560

1318
Krause (Henry) Charitable Foundation
305 South Monroe St.
Hutchinson 67501

Incorporated in 1959 in Kansas.
Donor(s): Krause Plow Corporation, Inc.
Financial data: (yr. ended 9/30/83): Assets, $757,674 (M); gifts received, $123,450; expenditures, $154,209, including $152,775 for 30 grants (high: $25,000; low: $100).
Purpose and activities: Broad purposes; primarily local giving, with emphasis on higher education, cultural programs, and a community fund.
Limitations: Giving primarily in KS.
Officers and Directors: Norman L. Krause, President; Gilbert R. Rains, Vice-President; Lowell Haldeman, Secretary; Donald D. Wiggins, Treasurer; Lila L. Gatlin, Margaret A. Sames.
Employer Identification Number: 486105132

1319
Marley Fund, The
5800 Foxridge Dr.
Mission 66202   (913) 362-1818

Incorporated in 1961 in Missouri.
Donor(s): Marley Company.
Financial data: (yr. ended 4/30/83): Assets, $904,710 (M); gifts received, $6,000; expenditures, $251,651, including $209,315 for 601 grants (high: $19,250; low: $15), $32,025 for 51 grants to individuals and $7,732 for 50 employee matching gifts.
Purpose and activities: Broad purposes; emphasis on higher education, including scholarships, community funds, health agencies and hospitals, and social agencies.
Types of support awarded: Operating budgets, continuing support, annual campaigns, building funds, equipment, employee matching gifts, employee related scholarships.
Limitations: Giving limited to areas of company operations. No grants to individuals (except for company-employee scholarships), or for seed money, emergency funds, deficit financing, land acquisition, endowment funds, scholarships and fellowships, special projects, research, publications, and conferences; no loans.

Publications: Application guidelines, program policy statement.
Application information:
  Initial approach: Letter
  Copies of proposal: 1
  Deadline(s): None
  Board meeting date(s): Monthly
  Final notification: 1 month
  Write: G.W. Cantrell, President
Officers: G.W. Cantrell, President; J.P. Way, Vice-President; B.L. Paine, Secretary; G.L. Wilson, Treasurer.
Number of staff: None.
Employer Identification Number: 446012343

1320
Mingenback (The Julia J.) Foundation, Inc. ⌺
P.O. Drawer 927
McPherson 67460

Incorporated in 1959 in Kansas.
Donor(s): E.C. Mingenback.†
Financial data: (yr. ended 12/31/83): Assets, $3,158,154 (M); expenditures, $167,557, including $123,825 for 12 grants (high: $25,000; low: $500).
Purpose and activities: Primarily local giving, with emphasis on higher education.
Limitations: Giving primarily in KS.
Officers: Willda Coughenour, President; Ruth Lancaster, Treasurer.
Employer Identification Number: 486109567

1321
Muchnic Foundation ⌺
107 North 6th St., Suite 32
P.O. Box 329
Atchison 66002

Trust established in 1946 in Kansas.
Donor(s): Valley Company, Inc., Helen Q. Muchnic,† H.E. Muchnic.
Financial data: (yr. ended 11/30/83): Assets, $3,134,358 (M); expenditures, $146,640, including $138,420 for 51 grants (high: $28,000; low: $20).
Purpose and activities: Primarily local giving for higher education, health, cultural programs, including museums, and civic affairs.
Limitations: Giving primarily in KS. No grants to individuals.
Application information:
  Board meeting date(s): As required
  Write: Francis M. Bush, Secretary-Treasurer
Officer and Trustees: Francis M. Bush, Secretary-Treasurer; E.M. Mize, William H. Muchnic.
Employer Identification Number: 486102818

1322
Nelson (The Ludvig and Selma) Religious, Educational and Charitable Trust ⌺
118 North Main St.
Lindsborg 67456

Trust established in 1948 in Kansas.
Donor(s): Ludvig Nelson,† Selma Nelson.

Financial data: (yr. ended 12/31/83): Assets, $1,278,218 (M); expenditures, $265,804, including $169,300 for 29 grants (high: $48,000; low: $250).
Purpose and activities: Grants only to non-tax-supported institutions within Kansas; emphasis on higher education, hospitals, Protestant churches, and an historical society.
Limitations: Giving primarily in KS.
Trustees: John Anderson, Jr., Swen Burk, Robert W. Wise.
Employer Identification Number: 486107965

1323
Powell Family Foundation, The ▼
10990 Roe Ave.
P.O. Box 7270
Shawnee Mission 66207   (913) 345-3000

Established in 1969 in Missouri.
Donor(s): George E. Powell, Sr.†
Financial data: (yr. ended 12/31/83): Assets, $44,354,020 (M); expenditures, $1,324,043, including $1,191,538 for 119 grants (high: $147,400; low: $200).
Purpose and activities: Local grants for educational, religious, community and youth-oriented activities.
Types of support awarded: Operating budgets, annual campaigns, seed money, emergency funds, equipment, program-related investments, conferences and seminars, scholarship funds, matching funds, general purposes.
Limitations: Giving limited to Kansas City, KS and the surrounding community. No grants to individuals, or for endowment funds; no loans except for program-related investments.
Publications: Annual report, application guidelines.
Application information:
  Initial approach: Letter
  Copies of proposal: 2
  Deadline(s): 30 days preceding board meeting
  Board meeting date(s): Usually in January, April, July, and October
  Final notification: 60 days
  Write: Marjorie P. Allen, President
Officers and Trustees: George E. Powell, Jr., Chairman; Marjorie P. Allen, President; Marilyn P. McLeod, Vice-President and Secretary; George E. Powell III, Treasurer; Nicholas K. Powell.
Number of staff: 1 part-time professional; 1 full-time support; 1 part-time support.
Employer Identification Number: 237023968

1324
Puritan-Bennett Foundation ▼
(formerly The Parker B. Francis Foundation)
9401 Indian Creek Pkwy.
Overland Park 66225-5905
Address application to: c/o S. Marsh Tenney, M.D., Executive Vice-President, Puritan-Bennett Foundation, Remsen Bldg., Rm. 621, Dartmouth Medical School, Hanover, NH 03756; Tel.: (603) 646-7730

Trust established in 1951 in Missouri.
Donor(s): Parker B. Francis,† Mary B. Francis.†

Financial data: (yr. ended 12/31/83): Assets, $16,987,713 (M); expenditures, $1,471,749, including $1,179,979 for 56 grants (high: $42,497; low: $7,600; average: $20,000-$25,000).

Purpose and activities: To promote improved understanding and treatment of diseases of the lungs through support of research fellowships in pulmonary medicine and anesthesiology. Grants to institutions with approved programs.

Types of support awarded: Fellowships.

Limitations: Giving limited to the US and Canada. No grants to individuals, or for operating budgets, building and endowment funds, or matching gifts; no loans.

Publications: Annual report, informational brochure, program policy statement.

Application information: Application form required.

  Initial approach: Letter
  Copies of proposal: 10
  Deadline(s): Submit proposal preferably in August; deadline September 15
  Board meeting date(s): Council of Scientific Advisors meets in December
  Final notification: December
  Write: S. Marsh Tenney, M.D., Executive Vice-President

Scientific Advisors: S. Marsh Tenney, M.D., Chairman; and 7 others.

Officers: John B. Francis,* President; S. Marsh Tenney, M.D., Executive Vice-President; Daniel C. Weary,* Vice-President, Secretary and Treasurer.

Trustees:* William Coleman Branton, C.M. Carson, Burton A. Dole, Jr., Thomas A. Reed.

Number of staff: 1.

Employer Identification Number: 436049228

1325
Rice (Ethel and Raymond F.) Foundation ⌗
700 Massachusetts St.
Lawrence 66044

Financial data: (yr. ended 12/31/83): Assets, $4,296,656 (M); gifts received, $58,052; expenditures, $199,355, including $164,300 for 54 grants (high: $15,000; low: $500).

Purpose and activities: Primarily local giving, with emphasis on higher education, health, youth agencies, and social agencies.

Limitations: Giving limited to the Lawrence, KS area.

Application information:

  Initial approach: Full proposal
  Deadline(s): November 15
  Write: Robert B. Oyler, President or George M. Clem, Treasurer

Officers: Robert B. Oyler, President; R.W. McClure, Vice-President; James W. Paddock, Secretary; George M. Clem, Treasurer.

Employer Identification Number: 237156608

1326
Rouback Family Foundation ⌗
P.O. Box 713
Russell 67665   (913) 483-3123

Trust established in 1969 in Kansas.
Donor(s): Hannah Rouback.†

Financial data: (yr. ended 12/31/83): Assets, $1,143,530 (M); expenditures, $169,467, including $147,713 for 28 grants (high: $50,000; low: $60).

Purpose and activities: Primarily local giving, with emphasis on a hospital, a college, and a speech institute; grants also for youth agencies and Protestant church-related schools.

Limitations: Giving primarily in KS.

Application information: Funds presently committed.

Trustee: Russell State Bank.

Employer Identification Number: 486143203

1327
Schowalter Foundation, Inc., The
716 Main St.
Newton 67114   (316) 283-3720

Incorporated in 1953 in Kansas.
Donor(s): J.A. Schowalter.†

Financial data: (yr. ended 12/31/82): Assets, $1,501,451 (L); expenditures, $347,595, including $192,160 for 49 grants (high: $15,000; low: $200).

Purpose and activities: To assist retired ministers and missionaries, theological seminaries and church-related schools (including scholarships); grants also for peace and international cooperation and for technical assistance abroad. Activities related to the Mennonite Church, with giving generally limited to the Midwest.

Types of support awarded: Technical assistance, scholarship funds.

Limitations: Giving limited to the Midwest. No grants to individuals, or for endowment funds, fellowships, operating budgets, travel, or matching gifts; no loans.

Publications: Program policy statement, application guidelines.

Application information:

  Initial approach: Full proposal
  Copies of proposal: 1
  Deadline(s): Submit proposal preferably in February or August; deadlines March 1 and September 1
  Board meeting date(s): April and October
  Write: William L. Friesen, President

Officers and Trustees: Daniel Kauffman, Chairman; William L. Friesen, President; Raymond Becker, Alvin Funk, W.W. Graber, Adin Holdeman, Warren W. Oswald.

Employer Identification Number: 480623544

1328
Smoot Charitable Foundation ⌗
1700 East Iron
Salina 67401

Established in 1976.
Financial data: (yr. ended 6/30/83): Assets, $4,359,525 (M); expenditures, $321,559, including $305,423 for 36 grants (high: $72,500; low: $300).

Purpose and activities: Primarily local giving, with emphasis on youth agencies and higher education.

Limitations: Giving primarily in KS.

Officers: Joe C. Cloud, President; Dr. Robert W. Weber, Vice-President; Thomas J. Kennedy, Secretary-Treasurer.

Employer Identification Number: 480851141

1329
Sosland Foundation, The
P.O. Box 29155
Shawnee Mission 66201   (913) 236-7300

Incorporated in 1955 in Missouri.
Donor(s): Members of the Sosland family.

Financial data: (yr. ended 11/30/83): Assets, $2,461,313 (M); gifts received, $14,616; expenditures, $334,840, including $319,178 for 84 grants (high: $100,000; low: $25; average: $1,000-$4,000).

Purpose and activities: Primarily local giving to Jewish welfare funds; some grants for higher and secondary education, the arts, temple support, civic causes, and social welfare.

Types of support awarded: General purposes, operating budgets, continuing support, annual campaigns, seed money, emergency funds, deficit financing, building funds, equipment, land acquisition, endowment funds, matching funds, consulting services, technical assistance, scholarship funds, special projects, research.

Limitations: Giving primarily in MO. No grants to individuals, or for publications, or conferences; no loans.

Application information:

  Initial approach: Letter
  Deadline(s): None
  Board meeting date(s): March, June, September, and December
  Final notification: 3 months

Officers and Directors:* H.J. Sosland, President; Neil Sosland,* Vice-President; Morton I. Sosland,* Secretary-Treasurer.

Number of staff: 1 part-time professional.

Employer Identification Number: 446007129

1330
Wiedemann (K. T.) Foundation, Inc. ▼
300 Page Court
Wichita 67202   (316) 265-9311

Incorporated in 1959 in Kansas.
Donor(s): K.T. Wiedemann Trust.

Financial data: (yr. ended 2/28/84): Assets, $18,817 (M); gifts received, $531,900; expenditures, $514,740, including $483,850 for 146 grants (high: $50,000; low: $10; average: $100-$10,000).

Purpose and activities: Broad purposes; primarily local giving, with emphasis on higher education, youth agencies, social service organizations, hospitals, cultural programs, and Protestant church support; giving also for health-related associations.

Types of support awarded: Annual campaigns, seed money, emergency funds, equipment, endowment funds, research, scholarship funds, matching funds, general purposes, continuing support, building funds.

Limitations: Giving primarily in south-central KS, with emphasis on Wichita. No grants to individuals.

Application information:

  Initial approach: Letter

Copies of proposal: 1
Deadline(s): None
Board meeting date(s): Weekly
Final notification: 10 days
Write: Kenneth Pringle, Secretary
Officers and Trustees: Gladys H.G. Wiedemann, President and Treasurer; Kenneth Pringle, Secretary; Douglas S. Pringle.
Number of staff: None.
Employer Identification Number: 486117541

KENTUCKY

1331
Appalachian Fund, Inc.
P.O. Box 2277, College Station
Berea 40404

Incorporated in 1950 in Kentucky.
Donor(s): Herbert A. Faber,† Mrs. Herbert A. Faber.†
Financial data: (yr. ended 12/31/83): Assets, $6,114,764 (M); gifts received, $3,373; expenditures, $419,413, including $367,440 for 33 grants (high: $35,000; low: $2,000) and $11,000 for 11 grants to individuals.
Purpose and activities: "To promote and establish whatsoever may improve the general education, health, and physical well-being mainly of the inhabitants of the Appalachian Mountain area and surrounding territory." Emphasis on higher education, including assistance to medical and dental school students who will return to the area to practice, and on hospitals.
Types of support awarded: Operating budgets, continuing support, equipment, scholarship funds, student aid.
Limitations: Giving primarily in the Appalachian Mountains in KY. No grants for endowment funds; no loans.
Application information:
Initial approach: Letter
Copies of proposal: 1
Deadline(s): November 1
Board meeting date(s): May and December
Write: Mrs. Norbert F. Stammer, Director
Officers and Trustees: Stuart L. Faber, President and Treasurer; Mrs. Stuart L. Faber, Vice-President; Mrs. Norbert F. Stammer, Director and Secretary; Mary P. Fox, Charles R. Harris, Norbert F. Stammer.
Number of staff: 1 part-time support.
Employer Identification Number: 616018384

1332
Ashland Foundation, Inc., Greater
1212 Bath Ave.
P.O. Box 2096
Ashland 41105   (606) 324-3888

Community foundation incorporated in 1972 in Kentucky.
Financial data: (yr. ended 12/31/83): Assets, $2,428,519 (M); gifts received, $158,046; expenditures, $291,741.
Purpose and activities: Giving for charitable, educational, and scientific purposes in the greater Ashland area.
Types of support awarded: Operating budgets, continuing support, seed money, emergency funds, consulting services, technical assistance.
Limitations: Giving limited to the tri-state area of Ashland, KY, Ironton, OH, and Huntington, WV. No grants to individuals, or for annual campaigns, deficit financing, building or endowment funds, scholarships, or fellowships.
Publications: Annual report.
Application information: Application form required.
Initial approach: Letter
Copies of proposal: 1
Board meeting date(s): June
Write: Linda L. Ball, Executive Director
Officers and Trustees:* Joel Watson,* President; Elsie Dysard,* Vice-President; Linda L. Ball, Secretary and Executive Director; William Stinnett,* Treasurer.
Number of staff: 1 full-time professional; 1 full-time support; 1 part-time support.
Employer Identification Number: 610729266

1333
Ashland Oil Foundation, Inc., The ▼
1409 Winchester Ave.
Ashland 41101   (606) 329-4525

Incorporated in 1968 in Delaware.
Donor(s): Ashland Oil, Inc.
Financial data: (yr. ended 12/31/83): Assets, $5,399,583 (M); gifts received, $4,628,000; expenditures, $1,395,676, including $655,108 for 106 grants (high: $93,700; low: $500) and $683,789 for 564 employee matching gifts.
Purpose and activities: Broad purposes; giving primarily through an employee matching gifts program to higher education and community funds; direct support only to educational organizations, mainly colleges and universities; some support also for cultural programs.
Types of support awarded: Employee matching gifts, professorships, scholarship funds, employee related scholarships, fellowships.
Limitations: No grants to individuals, or for building or endowment funds; no loans.
Application information:
Initial approach: Telephone or letter
Deadline(s): Submit proposal preferably in October or November; deadline November 31
Board meeting date(s): February
Write: Judy B. Dailey, President
Officers: Robert D. Bell,* Chairman; Judy B. Dailey,* President; Franklin P. Justice, Jr.,* Charles M. Russell, Jr.,* Vice-Presidents; Donald C. Wheeler, Secretary; Larry K. Wessel, Treasurer.
Trustees:* James V. Marcum.
Employer Identification Number: 616057900

1334
Bank of Louisville Charities, Inc. ☐
P.O. Box 1101
Louisville 40201

Established in 1973.
Donor(s): Bank of Louisville.
Financial data: (yr. ended 12/31/83): Assets, $3,066,947 (M); expenditures, $207,617, including $200,730 for 68 grants (high: $32,000; low: $30).
Purpose and activities: Primarily local giving, with emphasis on cultural programs, especially in the arts, education, health, civic affairs, and a community fund.
Limitations: Giving primarily in KY.
Officer: Marian Wimsett, Secretary.
Directors: Joe D. Holladay, Bertram W. Klein, Samuel H. Klein.
Employer Identification Number: 237423454

1335
Bingham Enterprises Foundation of Kentucky, Inc. ▼
525 West Broadway
Louisville 40202   (502) 582-4507

Incorporated in 1951 in Kentucky.
Donor(s): George Barry Bingham, Mary C. Bingham.
Financial data: (yr. ended 12/31/83): Assets, $295,049 (M); gifts received, $1,020,338; expenditures, $959,025, including $957,653 for 45 grants (high: $250,000; low: $100).
Purpose and activities: Broad purposes; giving locally and in southern Indiana, with emphasis on community funds, higher education, social services, civic affairs, and cultural activities.
Types of support awarded: General purposes, operating budgets, continuing support, annual campaigns, seed money, emergency funds, deficit financing, building funds, equipment, matching funds, employee matching gifts, research, conferences and seminars, special projects.
Limitations: Giving limited to KY and southern IN. No grants to individuals, or for scholarships or fellowships; no loans.
Publications: 990-PF.
Application information: Application form required.
Initial approach: Letter
Deadline(s): 1 month prior to board meetings
Board meeting date(s): March, June, September, and December
Final notification: 3 months
Write: John L. Richards, Secretary
Officers and Trustees:* George Barry Bingham,* President; George Barry Bingham, Jr.,* Mary C. Bingham,* George N. Gill,* Cyrus MacKinnon, Eleanor Bingham Miller, Vice-Presidents; John L. Richards, Secretary and Treasurer.
Number of staff: None.
Employer Identification Number: 616029022

1336
Brown (James Graham) Foundation, Inc. ▼ ⊐⊏
132 E. Gray St.
Louisville 40202   (502) 583-4085

Trust established in 1943 in Kentucky; incorporated in 1954.
Donor(s): J. Graham Brown,† Agnes B. Duggan.†
Financial data: (yr. ended 12/31/83): Assets, $141,922,971 (M); expenditures, $7,069,369, including $6,098,546 for 57 grants (high: $1,625,600).
Purpose and activities: Broad purposes; primarily local giving, with emphasis on higher and secondary education, health agencies, a community fund, civic affairs, and youth agencies.
Limitations: Giving primarily in KY.
Application information: Application form required.
    Initial approach: Letter
    Board meeting date(s): Monthly
    Write: Dan C. Ewing, Grants Chairman
Officers: Ray E. Loper,* President; H. Curtis Craig,* Vice-President; Charles F. Wood,* Secretary; Harold E. Hawkins, Treasurer.
Trustees:* Dan C. Ewing, Stanley F. Hugenberg, Jr., Arthur Keeney, M.D., Graham B. Loper, Joe M. Rodes, Robert L. Royer.
Employer Identification Number: 610724060

1337
Brown (W. L. Lyons) Foundation ⊐⊏
850 Dixie Hwy.
Louisville 40210

Incorporated in 1962 in Kentucky.
Donor(s): W.L. Lyons Brown.†
Financial data: (yr. ended 12/31/83): Assets, $3,386,304 (M); expenditures, $180,276, including $174,184 for 30 grants (high: $36,667; low: $250).
Purpose and activities: Broad purposes; primarily local giving, with emphasis on education, conservation, cultural activities, and the arts.
Limitations: Giving primarily in KY.
Application information:
    Write: Benjamin H. Morris, Secretary
Officers and Trustees: Ina B. Johnson, President; Benjamin H. Morris, Secretary; Owsley Brown, II, Treasurer; Martin S. Brown, W.L. Lyons Brown, Jr., Mrs. W.L. Lyons Brown, Earl L. Dorsey, David L. McDonald.
Employer Identification Number: 610598511

1338
Citizens Fidelity Foundation, Inc. ⊐⊏
Citizens Fidelity Bank and Trust Co.
Louisville 40296   (502) 581-3342

Incorporated in 1980 in Kentucky.
Donor(s): Citizens Fidelity Bank and Trust Company.
Financial data: (yr. ended 12/31/83): Assets, $351,576 (M); gifts received, $165,000; expenditures, $332,399, including $331,877 for 29 grants (high: $126,000; low: $500).

Purpose and activities: Primarily local giving, with emphasis on cultural programs, a community fund, education, including higher education, and social services.
Limitations: Giving primarily in Louisville, KY.
Publications: Application guidelines.
Application information: Application form required.
    Deadline(s): None
    Write: C. Alan Irvin, Treasurer
Officers and Directors: Rose L. Rubel, President; E. Frederick Zopp, Secretary; C. Alan Irvin, Treasurer; James H. Davis, Warner L. Jones, Jr., Harry LaViers, Jr., Lawrence L. Smith, Jefferson D. Stewart, Jr., James Thompson.
Employer Identification Number: 310999030

1339
Cooke (V. V.) Foundation Corporation
3901 Atkinson Dr., Suite 200
Louisville 40218   (502) 459-3968

Incorporated in 1947 in Kentucky.
Donor(s): V.V. Cooke,† Cooke Chevrolet Company, Cooke Pontiac Company, and others.
Financial data: (yr. ended 8/31/84): Assets, $4,762,893 (M); expenditures, $364,418, including $309,960 for 73 grants (high: $60,000; low: $50).
Purpose and activities: Broad purposes; primarily local giving, with emphasis on Baptist church support and higher education.
Types of support awarded: Continuing support, annual campaigns, emergency funds, building funds, equipment, endowment funds, professorships.
Limitations: Giving primarily in KY. No grants to individuals, or for general endowment funds, research, scholarships, or fellowships; no loans.
Application information: Personal interviews not granted.
    Initial approach: Full proposal
    Copies of proposal: 1
    Board meeting date(s): Monthly
    Write: Charles H. Wells, Executive Secretary
Officers: V.V. Cooke, Jr.,* President; Joe D. Cross,* Vice-President; Robert L. Hook,* Secretary; Elva Cooke,* Treasurer; Charles H. Wells, Executive Secretary.
Directors:* Lori Cooke, Jane C. Cross, June C. Hook.
Number of staff: 1 full-time professional.
Employer Identification Number: 616033714

1340
Gheens Foundation, Inc., The ⊐⊏
746 Starks Bldg.
Louisville 40202   (502) 584-4650

Incorporated in 1957 in Kentucky.
Donor(s): C. Edwin Gheens.†
Financial data: (yr. ended 10/31/83): Assets, $4,392,590 (M); gifts received, $10,795; expenditures, $2,652,279, including $2,389,155 for 39 grants (high: $1,850,650; low: $400).
Purpose and activities: Broad purposes; primarily local giving, with emphasis on higher education, hospitals, cultural programs, mental health, and health agencies.
Limitations: Giving primarily in KY.

Publications: Application guidelines.
Application information: Application form required.
    Initial approach: Letter with 1 to 2 page outline
    Deadline(s): None
    Write: John M. Smith, Treasurer
Officers and Trustees: Joseph E. Stopher, President; Laramie L. Leatherman, Vice-President; Oscar S. Bryant, Jr., Secretary; John M. Smith, Treasurer; Bernard H. Barnett, Donald W. Doyle, William M. Rue.
Employer Identification Number: 616031406

1341
Honey Locust Foundation ⊐⊏
P.O. Box 35110
Louisville 40232

Incorporated in 1952 in Illinois.
Donor(s): Vermont American Corporation, and the trustees.
Financial data: (yr. ended 12/31/82): Assets, $1,915,985 (M); expenditures, $60,635, including $55,000 for 5 grants (high: $20,000; low: $5,000).
Purpose and activities: Broad purposes; primarily local giving, with emphasis on higher, secondary, and elementary education.
Limitations: Giving primarily in KY.
Directors: Lee B. Thomas, Sr., Chairman; Wallace H. Dunbar, Mrs. Wallace H. Dunbar, A. Scott Hamilton, Mrs. A. Scott Hamilton, Lee B. Thomas, Jr., Mrs. Lee B. Thomas, Jr.
Employer Identification Number: 616025781

1342
Hope (Blanche and Thomas) Fund ⊐⊏
P.O. Box 1270
Ashland 41101

Financial data: (yr. ended 12/31/83): Assets, $1,570,625 (M); expenditures, $142,988, including $115,850 for 216 grants to individuals.
Purpose and activities: Funds distributed exclusively as scholarships to individuals.
Types of support awarded: Student aid.
Application information: Application form required.
    Deadline(s): March 1
Trustees: Kenneth Ater, Harold Conley, Charles Sinnette, Stephen Towler, John W. Woods, III.
Employer Identification Number: 616067105

1343
Houchens Foundation, Inc. ⊐⊏
900 Church St.
Bowling Green 42101   (502) 843-3252

Incorporated in 1954 in Kentucky.
Donor(s): Houchens Markets, Inc., B.G. Wholesale, Inc.
Financial data: (yr. ended 5/31/83): Assets, $2,980,136 (M); gifts received, $550,000; expenditures, $154,945, including $153,037 for 646 grants (high: $21,350; low: $10) and $976,552 for 59 loans.

Purpose and activities: Broad purposes; primarily local giving, including loans, with emphasis on Protestant church support, including loans, community funds, youth agencies, and education.
Types of support awarded: Loans.
Limitations: Giving limited to southwest KY.
Application information:
  Initial approach: Letter with comprehensive details
  Deadline(s): None
  Write: Roger M. Page, Secretary-Treasurer
Officers and Directors: E.G. Houchens, Chairman; Roger M. Page, Secretary-Treasurer; Covella M. Biggers.
Employer Identification Number: 610623087

1344
Humana Foundation, Inc., The ¤
1800 First National Tower
P.O. Box 1438
Louisville 40201

Incorporated in 1981 in Kentucky.
Donor(s): Humana Inc.
Financial data: (yr. ended 8/31/82): Assets, $5,382,689 (M); gifts received, $5,000,000; expenditures, $37.
Purpose and activities: First year of operation in 1982; no purposes announced.
Officers and Directors:* David A. Jones,* Chairman; Wendell Cherry,* President; Thomas J. Flynn, Senior Vice-President; William C. Ballard, Jr., Carl F. Pollard,* Executive Vice-Presidents; William H. Lomicka, Vice-President; Alice F. Newton, Secretary; Henry J. Werronen, Foundation Manager.
Employer Identification Number: 611004763

1345
LaViers (Harry and Maxie) Foundation, Inc.
P.O. Box 332
Irvine 40336

Established in 1977.
Donor(s): Harry LaViers.†
Financial data: (yr. ended 8/31/84): Assets, $1,981,552 (M); expenditures, $161,222, including $157,350 for 44 grants (high: $20,000; low: $500).
Purpose and activities: Primarily local giving, with emphasis on Protestant church support, higher education, and medical research.
Limitations: Giving primarily in rural eastern KY. No support for national programs. No grants to individuals or for scholarships.
Officers and Directors: Harry LaViers, Jr., President; Elizabeth LaViers Owen, Vice-President; Barbara P. LaViers, Secretary-Treasurer.
Employer Identification Number: 310902455

1346
Louisville Community Foundation, Inc., The
(formerly The Louisville Foundation, Inc.)
Three Riverfront Plaza
Louisville 40202   (502) 585-4649

Established in 1916 in Kentucky; reorganized in 1984.
Financial data: (yr. ended 6/30/84): Assets, $1,131,113 (M); gifts received, $44,934; expenditures, $169,879, including $107,224 for 26 grants (high: $37,500; low: $450; average: $4,000-$6,000).
Purpose and activities: Local giving for social services, arts and humanities, education, and environment; support also for scholarships and student loans and a teacher awards program.
Types of support awarded: Student aid, consulting services, technical assistance, seed money, special projects, emergency funds.
Limitations: Giving limited to the greater Louisville, KY, area. No grants for operating budgets, continuing support, annual campaigns, deficit financing, capital funds, matching gifts, research, publications, or conferences and seminars.
Publications: Annual report, program policy statement, application guidelines.
Application information: Application form required.
  Initial approach: Letter
  Copies of proposal: 10
  Deadline(s): Submit proposal preferably in April or October; deadlines May 1 and November 1
  Board meeting date(s): September, December, March, and June
  Final notification: Within 2 weeks after June and December meetings
  Write: Darrell L. Murphy, Executive Director
Administrator: Darrell L. Murphy, Executive Director.
Directors: Wilson W. Wyatt, Sr., Chairman; Baylor Landrum, President; Mary Norton Shands, Secretary; John E. Brown, Treasurer; and 31 additional directors.
Number of staff: 1 full-time professional; 1 part-time support.
Employer Identification Number: 616019497

1347
Margaret Hall Foundation, Inc. ¤
291 South Ashland Ave.
Lexington 40502   (606) 269-2236

Incorporated in 1980 in Kentucky.
Donor(s): Margaret Hall School.
Financial data: (yr. ended 6/30/83): Assets, $1,247,000 (M); expenditures, $106,402, including $50,000 for 10 grants (high: $7,000; low: $3,500).
Purpose and activities: To award grants to private secondary schools for innovative programming and scholarships.
Types of support awarded: Scholarship funds, special projects.
Limitations: No grants to individuals, or for building or endowment funds.
Publications: Application guidelines.
Application information:
  Initial approach: Letter
  Write: Helen R. Burg, Executive Director
Officer: Helen R. Burg, Executive Director.
Directors: John R. Mink, Chairman and President; Sister Andrea, The Rev. Sister Columba Gilliss, Sister Jean, Sister Josephine, A.P. Lawing, Jr., Susanna P. Turner.
Employer Identification Number: 611006412

1348
Mills (Ralph E.) Foundation ¤
c/o Drawer M
Frankfort 40601

Incorporated in 1947 in Kentucky.
Donor(s): Ralph E. Mills.
Financial data: (yr. ended 12/31/83): Assets, $1,823,585 (M); gifts received, $50,000; expenditures, $92,025, including $86,800 for 52 grants (high: $20,000; low: $25).
Purpose and activities: Primarily local giving with emphasis on higher education, hospitals, churches, and social services.
Limitations: Giving primarily in KY.
Officers and Trustees: Ralph E. Mills, President; Bernard H. Barnett, Secretary; Charles Barnett, John E. Brown, Thomas R. McDonald, Mary Wilson.
Employer Identification Number: 610529834

1349
Norton (The George W.) Foundation, Inc.
1212 Citizens Plaza, 500 West Jefferson St.
Louisville 40202   (502) 589-1248

Incorporated in 1958 in Kentucky.
Donor(s): Mrs. George W. Norton.
Financial data: (yr. ended 12/31/83): Assets, $3,950,967 (M); gifts received, $200,000; expenditures, $168,670, including $162,200 for 35 grants (high: $36,000; low: $500).
Purpose and activities: Broad purposes; primarily local giving, with emphasis on a community fund, education, health, cultural programs, youth agencies, and social services.
Limitations: Giving primarily in KY. No grants to individuals.
Application information:
  Initial approach: Full proposal
  Deadline(s): None
  Board meeting date(s): Quarterly
  Final notification: 90 days
  Write: Miss Willodyne Miller, Executive Director
Officers and Directors: Jane Morton Norton, President; Rucker Todd, Vice-President; Willodyne Miller, Secretary, Treasurer, and Executive Director.
Employer Identification Number: 616024040

1350
Ogden College Fund, The
P.O. Box 930
Bowling Green 42101   (502) 781-2121
Application address: c/o Cooper R. Smith, Jr., Route 4, P.O. Box 380A, Bowling Green, KY 42101

Financial data: (yr. ended 10/31/84): Assets, $2,038,715 (M); expenditures, $133,849, including $10,000 for 1 grant (high: $10,000; low: $204) and $91,279 for 394 grants to individuals.
Purpose and activities: Scholarship grants for students residing in Kentucky and attending Ogden College of Western Kentucky University; limited support also for Kentucky colleges and universities, primarily for equipment.

Types of support awarded: Student aid, equipment.
Limitations: Giving limited to KY.
Application information:
   Write: Alvis Temple, Executive Secretary
Officers and Trustees: Cooper R. Smith, Jr., Regent; Alvis Temple, Executive Secretary; Jerry E. Cohron, Jo Tilden Orendorf, Marvin W. Russell, Herbert J. Smith.
Employer Identification Number: 237078715

1351
Robinson (E. O.) Mountain Fund
425 Holiday Rd.
Lexington 40502   (606) 233-0817

Incorporated in 1922 in Kentucky.
Donor(s): Edward O. Robinson.†
Financial data: (yr. ended 6/30/84): Assets, $5,282,946 (M); expenditures, $474,781, including $370,684 for 47 grants (high: $25,000; low: $400; average: $5,000-$10,000).
Purpose and activities: To help the people, particularly the youth, of the mountain region of eastern Kentucky improve their living conditions; grants largely to hospitals and health agencies for medical care and to higher educational institutions for scholarships.
Types of support awarded: Scholarship funds.
Limitations: Giving primarily in eastern KY. No grants to individuals.
Application information:
   Initial approach: Full proposal
   Copies of proposal: 9
   Deadline(s): Submit proposal 3 months in advance
   Board meeting date(s): Every 4 months
   Write: Juanita Stollings, Secretary-Treasurer
Officers: Lyman V. Ginger,* President; N. Mitchell Meade,* Vice-President; Juanita Stollings, Secretary-Treasurer.
Directors:* Mary P. Fox, C.A. Gerst, Francis S. Hutchins, Burl Phillips, Robert A. Sparks, Jr., Vinson A. Watts.
Employer Identification Number: 610449642

1352
Schneider (Al J.) Foundation Corporation ⌑
3720 Seventh St. Rd.
Louisville 40216

Incorporated in 1957 in Kentucky.
Donor(s): Al J. Schneider.
Financial data: (yr. ended 2/28/83): Assets, $301,821 (M); gifts received, $221,625; expenditures, $146,888, including $146,610 for 95 grants (high: $30,000; low: $15).
Purpose and activities: Primarily local giving, with emphasis on church support, health, cultural programs, youth agencies, and education, particularly higher education.
Limitations: Giving primarily in KY.
Trustee: Al J. Schneider.
Employer Identification Number: 610621591

1353
Vogt (The Henry) Foundation, Inc.
1000 West Ormsby Ave.
Louisville 40210   (502) 634-1511
Mailing address: P.O. Box 1918, Louisville, KY 40201

Incorporated in 1958 in Kentucky.
Donor(s): Henry Vogt Machine Company.
Financial data: (yr. ended 6/30/83): Assets, $1,341,219 (M); gifts received, $175,000; expenditures, $119,333, including $116,993 for 42 grants (high: $22,000; low: $25).
Purpose and activities: Broad purposes; primarily local giving, with emphasis on community development, education, and a community fund.
Types of support awarded: General purposes, continuing support, annual campaigns, building funds, equipment, land acquisition, research.
Limitations: Giving limited to KY, with emphasis on the Louisville area. No grants to individuals, or for endowment funds, scholarships, fellowships, or matching gifts; no loans.
Application information:
   Initial approach: Letter or telephone
   Copies of proposal: 1
Officers: Henry V. Heuser, Jr.,* President; Marshall V. Heuser,* Leland D. Schlegel, Jr.,* Vice-Presidents; Margaret S. Culver, Secretary-Treasurer.
Directors:* Henry V. Heuser, Donald G. White.
Number of staff: None.
Employer Identification Number: 237416717

LOUISIANA

1354
Baton Rouge Area Foundation
P.O. Box 14553
Baton Rouge 70898   (504) 766-5992

Community foundation incorporated in 1964 in Louisiana.
Financial data: (yr. ended 12/31/84): Assets, $3,087,574 (M); gifts received, $167,239; expenditures, $271,616, including $238,113 for 74 grants (high: $32,500; low: $100; average: $5,000).
Purpose and activities: Broad purposes; preference given to those projects in the Baton Rouge area which promise to affect a broad segment of the population or which tend to help a segment of the citizenry who are not being adequately served by the community's resources.
Types of support awarded: Seed money, emergency funds, research, equipment, matching funds.

Limitations: Giving limited to the Baton Rouge, LA, area, including East Baton Rouge, West Baton Rouge, Livingston, Ascension, Iberville, Pointe Coupee, East Feliciana, and West Feliciana parishes. No grants to individuals, or for endowment funds, continuing support, annual campaigns, deficit financing, land acquisition, conferences, scholarships, fellowships, or operating budgets; no loans.
Publications: Annual report, application guidelines, newsletter.
Application information:
   Initial approach: Telephone, letter, or full proposal
   Copies of proposal: 7
   Deadline(s): None
   Board meeting date(s): Usually in March, June, September, and December
   Final notification: 2 to 4 months
   Write: Myron Falk, Executive Director
Officers: Jake L. Netterville,* Chairman; J. Luther Jordon, Jr.,* Vice-Chairman; Dan H. Hoffman,* Secretary; Roland M. Toups,* Treasurer; Myron Falk, Executive Director.
Directors:* Dr. Charles Belleau, Robert P. Breazeale, Allan R. Brent, Mrs. E.D. Brockett, John S. Kean, William H. LeBlanc, Jonathan C. Lee, Rosalind B. McKenzie, John B. Noland, Henry D. Salassi, Jr., T.P. Singletar, Kenneth E. Uffman, Robert E. Wales, Huey J. Wilson, Milton Womack.
Trustee Banks: American Bank and Trust Company, Baton Rouge Bank & Trust Company, Capital Bank and Trust Company, City National Bank, Fidelity National Bank, Louisiana National Bank.
Number of staff: 1 part-time professional.
Employer Identification Number: 726030391

1355
Brown (Joe W. & Dorothy Dorsett) Foundation ⌑
1801 Pere Marquette Bldg.
New Orleans 70112

Established in 1959 in Louisiana.
Donor(s): Mrs. Joe W. Brown, Dorothy Dorsett Brown.
Financial data: (yr. ended 12/31/83): Assets, $3,086,061 (L); gifts received, $600,000; expenditures, $213,583, including $97,614 for 36 grants (high: $15,000; low: $300) and $28,682 for 9 grants to individuals.
Purpose and activities: Primarily local giving for scholarships, a community fund, and welfare.
Types of support awarded: Grants to individuals, building funds, operating budgets, equipment, research, student aid.
Limitations: Giving primarily in LA.
Application information:
   Initial approach: Full proposal
   Deadline(s): None
Officers: Mrs. Joe W. Brown, President; B.P. Spencer, Vice-President; E.K. Hunter, Secretary and Treasurer.
Trustee: W.P. Thompson.
Employer Identification Number: 726027232

1356
Burton (The William T. and Ethel Lewis) Foundation
101 North Huntington St.
Sulphur 70663　　　　　(318) 527-5221

Incorporated in 1963 in Louisiana.
Donor(s): William T. Burton, Wm. T. Burton Industries, Inc.
Financial data: (yr. ended 5/31/83): Assets, $2,836,774 (M); expenditures, $345,350, including $249,040 for 13 grants (high: $225,000; low: $100) and $91,214 for 75 grants to individuals.
Purpose and activities: Broad purposes; primarily local giving, with emphasis on scholarships for Sulphur High School graduates to encourage them to continue their education; grants also for church support.
Types of support awarded: Student aid.
Limitations: Giving primarily in Sulphur, LA. No grants for endowment funds, or for matching gifts; no loans.
Application information:
　Initial approach: Letter
　Copies of proposal: 3
　Board meeting date(s): April and August
Officers: Jack E. Lawton,* President; Charles W. Carwile,* Vice-President; Charles M. Drost,* Secretary.
Directors:* William B. Lawton, Chairman; Thomas S. Leary, Billy Moses, Sam L. Puckett, Allen J. Rhorer.
Employer Identification Number: 726027957

1357
Cahn Family Foundation ⌑
P.O. Box 52005
New Orleans 70152

Incorporated in 1957 in Louisiana.
Donor(s): Dixie Mill Supply Co., Inc.
Financial data: (yr. ended 12/31/83): Assets, $1,625,153 (M); expenditures, $76,681, including $74,250 for 21 grants (high: $28,000; low: $250).
Purpose and activities: Primarily local giving, with emphasis on Jewish welfare funds.
Limitations: Giving primarily in LA.
Directors: Emile L. Cahn, Jules L. Cahn.
Employer Identification Number: 726020106

1358
Favrot (Clifford F.) Family Fund
203 Carondelet St.
New Orleans 70130　　　　(504) 581-9025

Incorporated in 1959 in Louisiana.
Donor(s): Members of the Favrot family.
Financial data: (yr. ended 12/31/83): Assets, $1,936,060 (M); gifts received, $76,240; expenditures, $130,240, including $127,869 for 76 grants (high: $27,950; low: $14).
Purpose and activities: Broad purposes; primarily local giving, with emphasis on higher and secondary education, a community fund, and Protestant church support.
Limitations: Giving primarily in LA. No grants to individuals, or for scholarships, fellowships, research, special projects, publications, or conferences; no loans.

Application information: Applications not requested.
　Board meeting date(s): Spring and December
　Write: D. Blair Favrot, Director
Officers and Directors: Clifford F. Favrot, President; Clifford F. Favrot, Jr., Secretary; C. Allen Favrot, D. Blair Favrot, Thomas B. Favrot.
Number of staff: None.
Employer Identification Number: 726018687

1359
First National Family Foundation, Inc. ⌑
400 Texas St.
Shreveport 71101

Incorporated in 1955 in Louisiana.
Donor(s): First National Bank of Shreveport.
Financial data: (yr. ended 6/30/83): Assets, $621,666 (M); gifts received, $75,000; expenditures, $135,887, including $126,899 for 56 grants (high: $25,284; low: $50).
Purpose and activities: Primarily local giving for community development, cultural programs, and a community fund; support also for higher and secondary education, public policy organizations, and health agencies.
Limitations: Giving primarily in LA.
Officers: J. Hugh Watson, President; Jerry Boughton, Vice-President; Chouttie Haxter, Secretary; J.M. Catanese, Treasurer.
Employer Identification Number: 726022876

1360
Frazier Foundation, Inc.
P.O. Box 1175
Minden 71055　　　　　(318) 377-0182

Established in 1974 in Louisiana.
Donor(s): J. Walter Frazier.
Financial data: (yr. ended 11/30/82): Assets, $5,397,462 (M); expenditures, $1,282,980, including $1,264,880 for 58 grants (high: $109,304; low: $1,000).
Purpose and activities: Support primarily for Church of Christ churches, religious organizations, and educational institutions.
Limitations: No grants to individuals, or for endowment funds; no loans.
Publications: Application guidelines, 990-PF.
Application information:
　Initial approach: Letter or proposal
　Copies of proposal: 1
　Deadline(s): Submit proposal preferably in April or October; deadlines May 1 and November 1
　Board meeting date(s): June and December
　Write: James Walter Frazier, Jr., President
Officers: James Walter Frazier, Jr., President; Rudith A. Drennan, Vice-President; Betty Mikal Frazier, Secretary; Altie Don Drennan, Treasurer.
Employer Identification Number: 720760891

1361
Freeman (The Ella West) Foundation
P.O. Box 50400
New Orleans 70150

Trust established about 1940 in Louisiana.

Donor(s): Richard W. Freeman,† Alfred B. Freeman.†
Financial data: (yr. ended 12/31/84): Assets, $10,975,587 (M); expenditures, $547,755, including $255,450 for 7 grants (high: $250,000; low: $400) and $128,053 for 1 foundation-administered program.
Purpose and activities: General purposes; primarily local giving, with emphasis on higher education and civic affairs; also supports a museum.
Limitations: Giving primarily in the greater New Orleans, LA, area. No grants to individuals.
Application information:
　Initial approach: Proposal
　Deadline(s): None
　Board meeting date(s): Approximately every 4 months beginning in spring
　Write: Richard W. Freeman, Jr., Secretary
Trustees: Mrs. Montine McD. Freeman, Louis M. Freeman, Richard W. Freeman, Jr., Tina F. Woollam.
Employer Identification Number: 726018322

1362
German Protestant Orphan Asylum Association ⌑
476 Metairie Rd., Rm. 213
Metairie 70005

Established in 1943.
Financial data: (yr. ended 11/30/82): Assets, $3,646,398 (M); expenditures, $327,700, including $284,686 for 18 grants (high: $34,358; low: $1,500).
Purpose and activities: Primarily local giving, with emphasis on youth, social services, and family services; giving also for medical purposes.
Types of support awarded: Building funds, operating budgets, general purposes, equipment.
Limitations: Giving primarily in LA.
Officers: George J. Mayer, President; P.W. Bohne, Vice-President; J. Gary Haller, Secretary; Robert L. Hattier, Treasurer; Ferdinand Grayson, Executive Director.
Directors: Albert J. Flettrich, Walter C. Flowers III, T. Frank Haller, Walter W. May, Charles B. Mayer, Charles Wirth III.
Employer Identification Number: 720423621

1363
Goldring Family Foundation ⌑
809 Jefferson Ave.
Jefferson 70121

Incorporated in 1955 in Louisiana.
Donor(s): Magnolia Liquor Co., Inc., Sazerac Co., Inc., Great Southern Liquor Co., Inc., N. Goldring Corp.
Financial data: (yr. ended 11/30/81): Assets, $1,326,626 (M); gifts received, $166,000; expenditures, $115,583, including $110,960 for 31 grants (high: $30,000; low: $250).
Purpose and activities: Primarily local giving, with emphasis on Jewish welfare funds and education; some support also for health agencies and community funds.
Limitations: Giving primarily in LA.
Officer: Stephen Goldring, President.
Employer Identification Number: 726022666

1364
Gray (The Matilda Geddings) Foundation ⌐
714 Esplanade
New Orleans 70116 (504) 581-5396

Established in 1969 in Louisiana.
Donor(s): Matilda Geddings Gray,† Matilda Gray Stream.
Financial data: (yr. ended 10/31/82): Assets, $2,496,442 (M); expenditures, $287,098, including $11,081 for 3 grants (high: $10,000; low: $81) and $162,916 for 5 foundation-administered programs.
Purpose and activities: A private operating foundation that works with local universities to promote art exhibits and the study of art and art history at educational institutions throughout Louisiana, especially in the fields of graphic, literary, and plastic arts; support also for research in local agricultural methods.
Limitations: Giving primarily in LA.
Application information:
Deadline(s): None
Write: Steven Carter
Officers and Trustees: Matilda Gray Stream, President; Harold H. Stream II, Vice-President; Harold H. Stream III, Secretary; Alice K. Arguello, Treasurer; Edward M. Carmouche, Sandra Stream Miller.
Employer Identification Number: 237072892

1365
Helis Foundation, The ⌐
912 Whitney Bldg.
New Orleans 70130

Incorporated in 1955 in Louisiana.
Donor(s): Members of the William G. Helis family.
Financial data: (yr. ended 12/31/83): Assets, $7,579,569 (M); gifts received, $100,000; expenditures, $259,264, including $233,400 for 29 grants (high: $60,000; low: $250).
Purpose and activities: Broad purposes; primarily local giving for music and the arts, community funds, religious associations, civic agencies, and youth agencies.
Limitations: Giving primarily in LA.
Application information:
Write: A.E. Armbruster, Vice-President and Treasurer
Officers and Trustees: William G. Helis, Jr.,* President; A.E. Armbruster, Vice-President and Treasurer; Virginia Helis Droulia, Bettie Conley Hanemann, Esther Helis Henry, David A. Kerstein,* Nathan Wallfisch.
Members:* Cassandra Marie Helis.
Employer Identification Number: 726020536

1366
Heymann (Mr. and Mrs. Jimmy) Special Account ⌐
1201 Canal St.
New Orleans 70112

Incorporated in 1958 in Louisiana.
Donor(s): Jimmy Heymann, Mrs. May H. Wolf.

Financial data: (yr. ended 12/31/83): Assets, $2,847,049 (M); gifts received, $35,000; expenditures, $175,299, including $169,774 for 55 grants (high: $52,500; low: $7).
Purpose and activities: General purposes; primarily local giving, with emphasis on education, a community fund, health services, youth activities, and cultural programs.
Limitations: Giving primarily in LA.
Officers: Mrs. Jimmy Heymann, President and Secretary; Jimmy Heymann, Vice-President; Jerry Heymann, Treasurer.
Employer Identification Number: 726019367

1367
Heymann-Wolf Foundation ⌐
1201 Canal St.
New Orleans 70112

Incorporated in 1947 in Louisiana.
Donor(s): Leon Heymann,† Mrs. Leon Heymann,† Leon M. Wolf,† Mrs. May H. Wolf, Jimmy Heymann, Mrs. Jimmy Heymann, Krauss Company, Ltd.
Financial data: (yr. ended 12/31/83): Assets, $2,534,937 (M); expenditures, $137,115, including $132,550 for 10 grants (high: $35,000; low: $500).
Purpose and activities: Broad purposes; primarily local giving, with emphasis on a university, a community fund, hospitals, and cultural programs.
Limitations: Giving primarily in LA.
Officers: Jerry Heymann, President; Jimmy Heymann, Vice-President; Mrs. Jimmy Heymann, Secretary-Treasurer.
Employer Identification Number: 726019363

1368
Holmes (D. H.) Foundation ⌐
819 Canal St.
New Orleans 70112

Established in 1965.
Donor(s): D.H. Holmes Company, Limited.
Financial data: (yr. ended 7/31/83): Assets, $2,413 (M); gifts received, $119,500; expenditures, $119,757, including $119,734 for 49 grants (high: $27,500; low: $100).
Purpose and activities: General giving, primarily in Louisiana, with emphasis on community funds, music, and education.
Types of support awarded: Building funds.
Limitations: Giving primarily in LA.
Officers and Directors: Hugh McC. Evans, Chairman; T. Robert Fiddler, President; James E. Ammon, Senior Vice-President and Chief Executive Officer; Robert L. Karem, Executive Vice-President; E. Stewart Maunsell, Vice-President; George W. Dodge, Secretary; Frank J. Beuscher, Albert J. Flettrich, Donald J. Nalty, Frank E. Schmidt, John L. Toler, George G. Westfeldt, Norris S.L. Williams.
Employer Identification Number: 726028216

1369
Hurley (Ed E. and Gladys) Foundation ⌐
c/o The First National Bank of Shreveport
P.O. Box 1116
Shreveport 71102

Trust established in 1954 in Louisiana.
Donor(s): Ed E. Hurley.†
Financial data: (yr. ended 12/31/83): Assets, $2,163,941 (M); expenditures, $94,974, including $32,425 for 1 grant.
Purpose and activities: Grants for residents of any state attending Scarritt College in Tennessee and loans to students residing in Arkansas, Louisiana, and Texas, to attend any other college.
Types of support awarded: Student aid.
Trustee: The First National Bank of Shreveport.
Employer Identification Number: 726018854

1370
Jones (Eugenie and Joseph) Family Foundation
835 Union St., Suite 333
New Orleans 70112 (504) 581-2424

Incorporated in 1955 in Louisiana.
Donor(s): Joseph M. Jones,† Eugenie P. Jones.†
Financial data: (yr. ended 6/30/84): Assets, $4,800,859 (M); expenditures, $306,792, including $247,800 for 35 grants (high: $75,000; low: $100).
Purpose and activities: Broad purposes; primarily local giving, with emphasis on higher education; grants also for church support and a community fund.
Types of support awarded: Annual campaigns, building funds, equipment, endowment funds, matching funds, scholarship funds, professorships, fellowships.
Limitations: Giving primarily in LA. No grants to individuals, or for land acquisition, operating budgets, continuing support, special projects, research, publications, conferences, start-up or emergency funds, or deficit financing; no loans.
Application information:
Initial approach: Full proposal
Copies of proposal: 1
Deadline(s): Submit proposal preferably in June; deadline June 30
Board meeting date(s): July and December
Final notification: 6 months
Write: Joseph M. Jones, Jr., Vice-President
Officers and Trustees: Eugenie Jones Huger, President; Joseph Merrick Jones, Jr., Susan Jones Lane, Vice-Presidents; H. Merritt Lane, Jr., Secretary-Treasurer; George Denegre, Killian L. Huger, A.J. Waechter, Jr.
Number of staff: None.
Employer Identification Number: 720507534

1371
Keller Family Foundation ⌐
909 International Bldg.
611 Gravier St.
New Orleans 70130

Trust established in 1949 in Louisiana.
Donor(s): Charles Keller, Jr., Rosa F. Keller.

Financial data: (yr. ended 12/31/83): Assets, $1,458,049 (M); expenditures, $62,989, including $59,050 for 26 grants (high: $11,000; low: $100).
Purpose and activities: Primarily local giving for public policy organizations and higher education; support also for cultural programs, community development, a community fund, and a secondary school.
Limitations: Giving primarily in LA.
Trustees: Charles Keller, Jr., Chairman; Julie F. Breitmeyer, Rosa F. Keller, Caroline K. Loughlin, Mary K. Zervigon.
Employer Identification Number: 726027426

1372
Libby-Dufour Fund ⌑
321 Hibernia Bank Bldg., Suite 202
New Orleans 70112

Incorporated in 1952 in Louisiana.
Donor(s): Edith Libby Dufour.†
Financial data: (yr. ended 5/31/83): Assets, $4,462,322 (M); expenditures, $368,898, including $347,050 for 22 grants (high: $160,000; low: $5,000).
Purpose and activities: Educational and charitable purposes; local giving, with emphasis on Christian charities, including support for churches, church-related education, and Christian welfare funds.
Limitations: Giving limited to the New Orleans, LA, area. No grants to individuals, or for endowment funds, or operating budgets.
Application information:
  Initial approach: Full proposal
  Copies of proposal: 1
  Board meeting date(s): Quarterly
  Write: James A. Stouse, President
Officers and Trustees: James A. Stouse, President; Eben Hardie, Secretary; E.T. Colton II, Jackson P. Ducournau, E. James Kock, Jr., Robert P. Lockett, Jr., Ernest C. Villere.
Employer Identification Number: 726027406

1373
Louisiana Land and Exploration Company Foundation, The
P.O. Box 60350
New Orleans 70160

Established in 1979 in Louisiana.
Donor(s): The Louisiana Land and Exploration Company.
Financial data: (yr. ended 12/31/82): Assets, $3,943,095 (M); expenditures, $632,109, including $623,070 for 174 grants (high: $229,000; low: $100).
Purpose and activities: Support primarily for higher education, including matching gifts and a scholarship program administered by selected Louisiana colleges and universities; support also for community funds, and social service or civic agencies.
Types of support awarded: Matching funds, scholarship funds.
Officers and Directors: John G. Phillips, President; E.L. Williamson, Vice-President; Eugene M. Parrish, Secretary and Treasurer.
Employer Identification Number: 720866443

1374
Magale Foundation, The ⌑
P.O. Box 21116
Shreveport 71154   (318) 226-2382

Incorporated in 1957 in Louisiana.
Donor(s): John F. Magale.
Financial data: (yr. ended 11/30/83): Assets, $1,411,915 (M); expenditures, $136,949, including $101,500 for 21 grants (high: $15,000; low: $1,000) and $7,875 for 13 loans.
Purpose and activities: Charitable and educational purposes; grants for higher education, social services, and the performing arts, principally in Louisiana and Arkansas; loans are also made to students who reside in Arkansas, Louisiana, and Texas.
Limitations: Giving limited to residents of LA, TX and AR.
Application information: Application form required.
  Initial approach: Letter
  Deadline(s): April 1
  Write: Mrs. Mary J. Fain, Treasurer
Officer: Mary J. Fain, Treasurer.
Employer Identification Number: 726025096

1375
Morgan City Fund, The ⌑
P.O. Box 949
Morgan City 70380

Incorporated in 1955 in Louisiana.
Donor(s): Byrnes M. Young.†
Financial data: (yr. ended 12/31/82): Assets, $3,943,957 (M); expenditures, $260,068, including $207,085 for 14 grants (high: $47,000; low: $1,000) and $500 for 2 grants to individuals.
Purpose and activities: Charitable purposes; local giving only, with emphasis on parks, landscaping, and recreational facilities; support also for a public library, secondary schools, primarily for scholarship programs, and a hospital.
Limitations: Giving limited to Morgan City, LA.
Officers and Directors: C.R. Brownell, Jr., M.D., President; Eugene B. Garber, Vice-President; Anna Pearl Squires, Secretary.
Employer Identification Number: 726029365

1376
New Orleans Regional Foundation, The Greater
c/o Richard A. Fusco, Executive Director
2515 Canal St.
New Orleans 70119   (504) 822-4906

Established in 1924 in Louisiana, as the Community Chest; became a community foundation in 1983.
Financial data: (yr. ended 12/31/83): Assets, $3,601,685 (M); gifts received, $247,449; expenditures, $86,350, including $26,299 for 10 grants.
Purpose and activities: Local giving for health, social services, cultural programs, and education.
Types of support awarded: Emergency funds, technical assistance, seed money, special projects.

Limitations: Giving limited to the greater New Orleans, LA, area. No support for religious organizations. No grants to individuals, or for operating budgets, annual fund campaigns, continuing support, endowment funds, or deficit financing.
Publications: Annual report, application guidelines, program policy statement.
Application information: Application form required.
  Initial approach: Proposal
Officers: Donald W. Doyle, Chairman; Robert C. McIntyre, Vice-Chairman; Brooke H. Duncan, Secretary; Harley B. Howcott, Jr., Treasurer; Richard A. Fusco, Executive Director.
Number of staff: 1 part-time professional.
Employer Identification Number: 720408921

1377
Physicians New Orleans Foundation
3715 Prytania St., Suite 403
New Orleans 70115   (504) 897-6125

Incorporated in 1981 in Louisiana.
Financial data: (yr. ended 12/31/83): Assets, $13,953,179 (M); expenditures, $951,420, including $583,542 for 49 grants (high: $50,000; low: $500).
Purpose and activities: Primarily local giving, with emphasis on Jewish welfare funds, religion, community development, and social services.
Types of support awarded: Building funds, equipment, research, scholarship funds, special projects, matching funds.
Limitations: Giving primarily in LA.
Application information: Application form required.
  Initial approach: Brief proposal
  Deadline(s): None
  Board meeting date(s): Monthly
  Write: Lori Glover
Officers: Arnold Lupin, President; Louis Levy II, Vice-President; Sam Lupin, Secretary; Richard Brown, Director.
Number of staff: 1 full-time support.
Employer Identification Number: 720940770

1378
Poindexter Foundation, Inc. ⌑
P.O. Box 1692
Shreveport 71164

Established in 1960.
Donor(s): R.D. Poindexter, Superior Iron Works & Supply Company, Inc.
Financial data: (yr. ended 11/30/83): Assets, $1,304,539 (M); expenditures, $158,708, including $155,115 for 49 grants (high: $105,000; low: $25).
Purpose and activities: Primarily local giving to youth and health agencies, and education.
Types of support awarded: General purposes.
Limitations: Giving primarily in LA.
Officers: R.D. Poindexter, President; John Shuey, Vice-President; Johnny B. Addison, Secretary; T.C. Poindexter, Treasurer.
Employer Identification Number: 726019174

1379
Reily Foundation
P.O. Box 60296
New Orleans 70160

Established in 1962.
Donor(s): Wm. B. Reily & Company, Inc.
Financial data: (yr. ended 12/31/82): Assets,
$1,640,286 (M); gifts received, $300,000;
expenditures, $525,412, including $522,350
for 31 grants (high: $400,000; low: $150).
Purpose and activities: Primarily local giving
for higher education, including a medical
school, and for organizations "to encourage
civic responsibility".
Limitations: Giving primarily in LA.
Application information:
   Write: H.E. Reily, President
Officers and Directors: H.E. Reily, President;
R.D. Reily, Vice-President; William B. Reily, III,
Secretary and Treasurer.
Employer Identification Number: 726029179

1380
RosaMary Foundation, The ▼
P.O. Box 50400
New Orleans 70150

Trust established in 1939 in Louisiana.
Donor(s): Members of the A.B. Freeman family.
Financial data: (yr. ended 12/31/84): Assets,
$17,378,314 (M); expenditures, $767,826,
including $727,334 for 15 grants (high:
$300,000; low: $250; average: $1,500-
$25,000).
Purpose and activities: General purposes;
primarily local giving, with emphasis on a
community fund, higher and secondary
education, including church-related schools,
civic affairs, and cultural programs.
Limitations: Giving primarily in the greater
New Orleans, LA, area. No grants to
individuals.
Application information:
   Initial approach: Proposal in letter form
   Copies of proposal: 1
   Deadline(s): None
   Board meeting date(s): Approximately 3
      times a year beginning in spring
   Write: Louis M. Freeman, Chairman
Trustees: Louis M. Freeman, Chairman;
Adelaide W. Benjamin, Richard W. Freeman,
Jr., Charles Keller, Jr., Rosa F. Keller, Mary
Elizabeth Wisdom.
Number of staff: 1 part-time support.
Employer Identification Number: 726024696

1381
Schlieder (Edward G.) Educational
   Foundation ▼
One Shell Square, Suite 4424
New Orleans 70139   (504) 581-6179

Incorporated in 1945 in Louisiana.
Donor(s): Edward G. Schlieder.†
Financial data: (yr. ended 12/31/83): Assets,
$8,871,602 (M); expenditures, $685,378,
including $570,378 for 21 grants (high:
$100,000; low: $12,100; average: $10,000-
$30,000).

Purpose and activities: To aid schools,
colleges, and universities in Louisiana only;
grants largely to universities for medical
research.
Types of support awarded: Research.
Limitations: Giving limited to LA. No grants to
individuals, or for general purposes, building or
endowment funds, scholarships, fellowships, or
operating budgets; no loans.
Publications: Annual report.
Application information:
   Initial approach: Letter
   Copies of proposal: 3
   Deadline(s): Submit proposal preferably in
      February; no set deadline
   Board meeting date(s): As required
   Final notification: 30 to 45 days
   Write: T. Sterling Dunn, Executive Consultant
Officers: Donald J. Nalty,* President; Louis G.
Lemle,* Vice-President; George G. Westfeldt,
Jr.,* Secretary-Treasurer; T. Sterling Dunn,
Executive Consultant.
Directors:* Morgan L. Shaw, William H.
Sullivan, Jr.
Number of staff: 1 part-time professional; 1
part-time support.
Employer Identification Number: 720408974

1382
Scott Foundation, Inc. ⌘
P.O. Box 4948
Monroe 71201

Incorporated in Louisiana.
Financial data: (yr. ended 7/31/83): Assets,
$1,338,103 (M); gifts received, $64,000;
expenditures, $11,640, including $11,233 for
45 grants (high: $3,000; low: $10).
Purpose and activities: Primarily local giving,
with emphasis on a community fund and youth
agencies.
Limitations: Giving primarily in LA.
Officers: T.H. Scott, President; G.J. Berohin,
Secretary-Treasurer.
Trustees: Betty Scott Cummings, S. Berton
Heard, Mayme P. Scott, Rupert R. Scott, T.H.
Scott, Jr.
Employer Identification Number: 726027563

1383
Shreveport-Bossier, The Community
   Foundation of
2950 Hearne Ave.
Shreveport 71103   (318) 635-2135

Community foundation incorporated in 1961 in
Louisiana.
Financial data: (yr. ended 12/31/84): Assets,
$2,601,482 (M); gifts received, $2,269,291;
expenditures, $339,430, including $300,916
for 13 grants (high: $30,500; low: $300).
Purpose and activities: Broad purposes; grants
to organizations in the Caddo and Bossier
parishes, with emphasis on health services,
welfare, youth agencies, higher education, and
cultural programs.
Types of support awarded: Special projects,
equipment, building funds.
Limitations: Giving limited to the Caddo and
Bossier parishes. No grants to individuals.
Publications: Application guidelines.

Application information:
   Initial approach: Letter
   Copies of proposal: 8
   Deadline(s): December 1
   Board meeting date(s): Bimonthly, beginning
      in February
   Final notification: Immediately after board
      meetings
   Write: Mrs. Ida Hayden, Executive Director
Officers and Directors: Virginia K. Shehee,
Chair; Donald P. Weiss, Vice-Chair; Louis C.
Pendleton, Secretary; John D. Caruthers, Jr.,
Treasurer; Ida Hayden, Executive Director;
James C. Gardner, Margaret W. Kinsey.
Trustee Banks: Bossier Bank & Trust Company,
Commercial National Bank in Shreveport, First
National Bank of Bossier, The First National
Bank of Shreveport, Louisiana Bank & Trust
Company, Pioneer Bank & Trust Company.
Number of staff: 1 part-time professional.
Employer Identification Number: 726022365

1384
Virlane Foundation
1055 St. Charles Ave.
New Orleans 70130

Incorporated in 1958 in Louisiana.
Financial data: (yr. ended 9/30/83): Assets,
$3,915,272 (M); gifts received, $785,588;
expenditures, $335,853, including $82,008 for
21 grants (high: $30,000; low: $100) and
$245,343 for 1 foundation-administered
program.
Purpose and activities: A private operating
foundation; primarily local giving, with
emphasis on maintaining a sculpture plaza to
encourage and foster the creation of art and
sculpture; grants also for welfare funds, cultural
programs, and community funds.
Limitations: Giving primarily in LA.
Officers and Directors: Jac Stich, President;
Charles T. Althaus, Secretary-Treasurer; Walda
Besthoff, and others.
Number of staff: None.
Employer Identification Number: 726019440

1385
Wheless Foundation, The ⌘
c/o Commercial National Bank in Shreveport
P.O. Box 21119
Shreveport 71152

Trust established in 1945 in Louisiana.
Donor(s): N. Hobson Wheless.†
Financial data: (yr. ended 10/31/82): Assets,
$1,740,800 (M); expenditures, $182,278,
including $133,016 for 51 grants (high:
$58,250; low: $50).
Purpose and activities: Broad purposes;
primarily local giving, with emphasis on higher
education, church support, a community fund,
and youth agencies.
Limitations: Giving primarily in LA.
Board of Control: Nicholas Hobson Wheless,
Jr., Chairman; Robert L. Berryman, Robert E.
King.
Trustee: Commercial National Bank in
Shreveport.
Employer Identification Number: 726017724

1386
Williams (Kemper and Leila) Foundation
P.O. Box 50580
New Orleans 70112   (504) 895-3939

Incorporated in 1974 in Louisiana.
Donor(s): L. Kemper Williams,† Mrs. Leila M.
Williams,† and others.
Financial data: (yr. ended 3/31/83): Assets,
$34,028,853 (M); gifts received, $187,084;
expenditures, $4,560,489, including $111,132
for 2 grants (high: $110,132; low: $1,000) and
$2,380,757 for 3 foundation-administered
programs.
Purpose and activities: Foundation was
established to fund a museum, research library,
and historic home, all located in the French
Quarter of New Orleans.
Limitations: Giving limited to New Orleans, LA.
Application information: Applications not
accepted.
Officers and Directors: Benjamin W. Yancey,
President; Ernest C. Villere, Vice-President;
Fred M. Smith, Secretary and Treasurer; Mary
Lou M. Christovich, G. Henry Person, Jr., John
A. Rodgers.
Employer Identification Number: 237336090

1387
**Woldenberg (Dorothy & Malcolm)
Foundation** ⌧
2100 St. Charles Ave., PHC
New Orleans 70140

Incorporated in 1959 in Louisiana as
Woldenberg Charitable and Educational
Foundation.
Donor(s): Malcolm Woldenberg, Magnolia
Liquor Co., Inc., Sazerac Company, Inc., Great
Southern Liquor Co., Duval Spirits, Inc.
Financial data: (yr. ended 12/31/83): Assets,
$389,088 (M); expenditures, $207,441,
including $204,756 for 21 grants (high:
$52,081; low: $1,000).
Purpose and activities: Grants largely for
Jewish welfare funds, temple support, and
higher and secondary educational institutions.
Officer: Malcolm Woldenberg.
Employer Identification Number: 726022665

1388
Woolf (William C.) Foundation ⌧
P.O. Box 21119
Shreveport 71152

Incorporated in 1959 in Louisiana.
Donor(s): William C. Woolf,† Geraldine H.
Woolf.†
Financial data: (yr. ended 2/28/83): Assets,
$1,979,437 (M); expenditures, $282,069,
including $245,213 for 44 grants (high:
$100,000; low: $250).
Purpose and activities: Broad purposes;
primarily local giving, including church support,
higher education, social service agencies, and
youth agencies.
Limitations: Giving primarily in Shreveport, LA.
Application information:
Write: Nicholas H. Wheless, Jr., Chairman

Officer: Bobby L. Miller, Secretary.
Trustees: Nicholas H. Wheless, Jr., Chairman;
Claude G. Rives III, C. Lane Sartor.
Employer Identification Number: 726020630

1389
Zemurray Foundation ▼
335 Whitney Bank Bldg.
New Orleans 70130   (504) 525-0091

Incorporated in 1951 in Louisiana.
Donor(s): Mrs. Sarah W. Zemurray.
Financial data: (yr. ended 12/31/82): Assets,
$28,131,452 (M); expenditures, $1,287,774,
including $1,074,134 for 49 grants (high:
$400,000; low: $100).
Purpose and activities: Broad purposes; grants
primarily for education, particularly higher
education, cultural programs, and hospitals.
Application information:
Initial approach: Full proposal
Copies of proposal: 1
Deadline(s): October
Board meeting date(s): Usually in November
Write: Walter J. Belsom, Jr., Treasurer
Officers and Directors: Roger T. Stone,
President; Doris Z. Stone, Vice-President and
Secretary; Walter J. Belsom, Jr., Treasurer;
Thomas B. Lemann.
Employer Identification Number: 720539603

1390
Zigler (Fred B. and Ruth B.) Foundation
P.O. Box 986
Jennings 70546   (318) 824-2413

Incorporated in 1956 in Louisiana.
Donor(s): Fred B. Zigler,† Ruth B. Zigler.†
Financial data: (yr. ended 12/31/84): Assets,
$3,535,366 (L); expenditures, $275,000,
including $160,015 for 49 grants (high:
$25,000; low: $35; average: $4,600) and
$64,987 for 44 grants to individuals.
Purpose and activities: Broad purposes;
primarily local giving, with emphasis on higher
and secondary education, including
scholarships for local students, and youth
agencies; support also for a museum.
Types of support awarded: Operating
budgets, building funds, general purposes,
equipment, student aid, grants to individuals.
Limitations: Giving primarily in Jefferson Davis
Parish, LA. No grants to individuals (except
scholarships for graduates of Jefferson Davis
Parish high schools).
Application information:
Initial approach: Full proposal or letter
Copies of proposal: 1
Deadline(s): 3 weeks prior to board
meetings; scholarship deadline March 10
Board meeting date(s): Bimonthly beginning
in January
Write: Margaret Cormier, Secretary-Treasurer
Officers: Paul E. Brummett,* President;
Margaret Cormier, Secretary-Treasurer.
Trustees:* Dale Elmore.
Employer Identification Number: 726019403

MAINE

1391
Alfond (The Harold) Trust ⌧
P.O. Box 353
Dexter 04930

Trust established in 1950 in Maine.
Donor(s): Harold Alfond, Dexter Shoe
Company.
Financial data: (yr. ended 12/31/82): Assets,
$3,825,297 (M); gifts received, $1,200,000;
expenditures, $250,429, including $240,646
for 64 grants (high: $100,000; low: $10).
Purpose and activities: Grants largely for
secondary and higher education, youth
agencies, and hospitals, primarily in Maine and
Massachusetts.
Limitations: Giving primarily in ME and MA.
Trustees: Dorothy Alfond, Harold Alfond,
Theodore Alfond.
Employer Identification Number: 016010672

1392
Davenport (George P.) Trust Fund
55 Front St.
Bath 04530   (207) 443-3431

Trust established in 1927 in Maine.
Donor(s): George P. Davenport.†
Financial data: (yr. ended 12/31/84): Assets,
$3,795,128 (M); expenditures, $326,499,
including $220,638 for 28 grants (high:
$50,000; low: $300) and $73,800 for 57 grants
to individuals.
Purpose and activities: Broad purposes; grants
limited exclusively to institutions in Bath, with
emphasis on higher education (for Bath area
students), hospitals, and community
development.
Types of support awarded: Operating
budgets, seed money, emergency funds,
building funds, matching funds, student aid.
Limitations: Giving limited to Bath, ME. No
grants to individuals (other than for scholarships
to Bath area high school graduates), or for
continuing support, annual campaigns, deficit
financing, equipment, land acquisition,
endowment funds, program support, research,
demonstration projects, publications, or
conferences; no loans.
Application information:
Initial approach: Telephone
Copies of proposal: 1
Deadline(s): 5th of each month
Final notification: 2 months
Trustees: John W. Coombs, Leland R. Patton,
Harold D. Perry.
Number of staff: 1 part-time support.
Employer Identification Number: 016009246

1393
Gannett (Guy) Foundation ⌯
390 Congress St.
Portland 04101

Established in 1968 in Maine.
Donor(s): Guy Gannett Publishing Co., and subsidiaries.
Financial data: (yr. ended 12/31/82): Assets, $1,201,600 (M); gifts received, $127,500; expenditures, $181,240, including $163,388 for 37 grants (high: $71,625; low: $100).
Purpose and activities: Primarily local giving for community funds, cultural programs, especially a museum and a library, education, and health and social agencies.
Limitations: Giving primarily in ME.
Officers and Directors: Jean Gannett Hawley, President; James E. Baker, Treasurer; John R. Dimatteo, John H. Gannett.
Employer Identification Number: 016003797

1394
Market Trust ⌯
c/o Maine National Bank
P.O. Box 3555
Portland 04104

Trust established in 1959 in Maine.
Donor(s): Brockton Public Market, Inc., George C. Shaw Company, and subsidiaries.
Financial data: (yr. ended 12/31/81): Assets, $1,138,400 (M); gifts received, $721,500; expenditures, $177,688, including $177,205 for 46 grants (high: $25,000; low: $250).
Purpose and activities: General purposes; giving for community funds, hospitals, youth agencies, and arts and cultural programs.
Limitations: Giving primarily in New England.
Trustee: Maine National Bank.
Employer Identification Number: 016008389

1395
Monks (G. G.) Foundation
178 Middle St.
Portland 04101

Trust established in 1962 in Massachusetts.
Donor(s): Millicent S. Monks, Robert A.G. Monks, and members of the Monks family.
Financial data: (yr. ended 12/31/84): Assets, $19,631 (M); gifts received, $169,461; expenditures, $383,752, including $380,969 for 49 grants (high: $82,873; low: $50; average: $7,775).
Purpose and activities: Primarily local giving to private charitable foundations, higher and secondary education, and cultural programs.
Types of support awarded: General purposes.
Limitations: Giving primarily in ME.
Application information:
  Write: David Lakari, Trustee
Trustees: Austin D. Higgins, David Lakari, Robert A.G. Monks.
Number of staff: None.
Employer Identification Number: 046018033

1396
Mulford (The Clarence E.) Trust
Eight Portland St.
Fryeburg 04037   (207) 935-2061

Trust established in 1950 in Maine.
Donor(s): Clarence E. Mulford.†
Financial data: (yr. ended 12/31/82): Assets, $2,378,576 (M); expenditures, $205,198, including $170,905 for 36 grants (high: $127,055; low: $100).
Purpose and activities: Primarily local giving, with emphasis on schools; grants also for church support, community services and welfare programs, libraries, and youth agencies.
Limitations: Giving primarily in Fryeburg, ME, and neighboring towns. No grants to individuals, or for building or endowment funds, scholarships, fellowships, or matching gifts; no loans.
Application information:
  Initial approach: Letter
  Copies of proposal: 3
  Deadline(s): Submit proposal preferably in June or December; deadlines June 30 and December 31
  Board meeting date(s): January and July
Trustees: David R. Hastings II, Peter G. Hastings.
Employer Identification Number: 010247548

1397
Unionmutual Charitable Foundation
2211 Congress St.
Portland 04122   (207) 780-6225

Established in 1969 in Maine.
Donor(s): Unionmutual Stock Life Insurance Co. of America.
Financial data: (yr. ended 12/31/84): Assets, $983,359 (M); gifts received, $1,059,508; expenditures, $712,255, including $686,557 for 85 grants (high: $127,751; low: $50; average: $5,000) and $20,338 for 174 employee matching gifts.
Purpose and activities: Primarily local giving, with emphasis on health agencies, arts and cultural programs, secondary education, including employee matching gifts, and community development.
Types of support awarded: Employee matching gifts.
Limitations: Giving primarily in ME. No support for religious organizations, fundraising or athletic events, goodwill advertising, or community funds. No grants to individuals, or for endowments.
Application information: Application form required.
  Copies of proposal: 9
  Deadline(s): None
  Board meeting date(s): Trustees meet quarterly for grants over $25,000; Contributions Committee meets 1st Tuesday of each month for grants under $25,000
  Final notification: Within 2 weeks
  Write: Barbara J. Reidman, Secretary
Officers: Colin C. Hampton,* President; David Emery Hughes,* Vice-President; Barbara J. Reidman,* Secretary; Timothy Ludden, Treasurer.

Trustees:* Kenneth Dolley, John N. Hastings, Phyllis Kenniston, Jean Mattimore, William O. Wagner, Robin A. Weeks.
Contributions Committee: Douglas Allen, Wilma Bott, Brian Davis, Waldo Hayes, Sarah MacColl, Mary Spugnardi.
Number of staff: 2 full-time professional; 1 full-time support.
Employer Identification Number: 237026979

1398
Warren Memorial Foundation ⌯
R.R. 1, Box 645
North Windham 04062   (207) 892-8832

Incorporated in 1929 in Maine.
Donor(s): Susan C. Warren.†
Financial data: (yr. ended 12/31/82): Assets, $1,503,538 (M); expenditures, $88,106, including $25,708 for 15 grants (high: $10,000; low: $400) and $5,983 for 1 foundation-administered program.
Purpose and activities: A private operating foundation; giving restricted to programs offering some benefit to local residents, in education and the arts. Giving primarily for cultural and children's programs and secondary education; operates a local public library.
Limitations: Giving limited to Westbrook, ME. No grants to individuals, or for endowment funds.
Application information:
  Initial approach: Letter
  Copies of proposal: 1
  Board meeting date(s): Usually monthly
  Write: Lawrence B. Abbiati, Treasurer
Officers and Directors: Rudolph T. Greep, President; Joseph G. Hakanson, Clerk; Lawrence B. Abbiati, Treasurer; Henry J. Roehner, Clarence Van Orman.
Employer Identification Number: 010220759

MARYLAND

1399
Abell (The A. S.) Company Foundation, Inc. ▼
1116 Fidelity Bldg.
210 N. Charles St.
Baltimore 21201-4013   (301) 332-6096

Incorporated in 1953 in Maryland.
Donor(s): A.S. Abell Company, Harry C. Black.†
Financial data: (yr. ended 12/31/84): Assets, $12,746,567 (M); expenditures, $610,257, including $483,800 for 38 grants (high: $72,000; low: $500; average: $5,000), $33,912 for 24 grants to individuals and $63,526 for 38 employee matching gifts.

Purpose and activities: Grants largely to local capital campaigns of educational, cultural, and medical institutions; support also for community funds, scholarships for children of company employees, and an employee matching gifts program for higher and secondary education.

Types of support awarded: Endowment funds, employee matching gifts, employee related scholarships.

Limitations: Giving limited to MD. No grants to individuals (except for company-employee scholarships), or for operating budgets, sponsorships, memberships, sustaining funds, or deficit financing.

Application information:
  Initial approach: Letter
  Copies of proposal: 1
  Deadline(s): February 1, May 1, August 1, and November 1
  Board meeting date(s): Quarterly
  Write: Anne La Farge Culman, Executive Director

Officers: Donald H. Patterson,* President; C. Ruth Kratz, Secretary and Treasurer; Anne La Farge Culman, Executive Director.

Trustees:* Gary Black, Sr., Chairman; Williams S. Abell, Jr., Gary Black, Jr., George L. Bunting, Jr., Robert Garrett.

Number of staff: 1 part-time professional; 1 part-time support.

Employer Identification Number: 526036106

1400
Baker (Clayton) Trust
c/o John B. Powell, Jr.
Sun Life Bldg., 3rd Fl.
Baltimore 21201

Established in 1960.

Donor(s): Susan Vaughan Clayton,† Julia C. Baker.

Financial data: (yr. ended 12/31/83): Assets, $238,331 (M); gifts received, $237,321; expenditures, $140,365, including $137,500 for 13 grants (high: $40,000; low: $1,000).

Purpose and activities: General giving, with support for local environment, population control, and improved housing; support also for arms control.

Managers: Julia C. Baker, John B. Powell, Jr.

Employer Identification Number: 526054237

1401
Baker (The William G.), Jr. Memorial Fund
c/o Mercantile-Safe Deposit and Trust Company
P.O. Box 2257, Two Hopkins Plaza
Baltimore 21201   (301) 237-5551

Established in 1964 in Maryland.

Financial data: (yr. ended 8/31/84): Assets, $8,997,000 (M); expenditures, $490,600, including $445,300 for 50 grants (high: $30,000; low: $653; average: $8,900).

Purpose and activities: Broad purposes; primarily local giving, with emphasis on education and community funds.

Types of support awarded: Operating budgets, seed money, emergency funds, building funds, equipment, land acquisition, endowment funds.

Limitations: Giving limited to the Baltimore, MD metropolitan area. No grants to individuals, or for annual campaigns, deficit financing, scholarships, or fellowships; no loans.

Publications: Application guidelines.

Application information:
  Initial approach: Full proposal
  Copies of proposal: 6
  Deadline(s): Submit proposal 2 months before board meetings
  Board meeting date(s): February, May, August, and November
  Final notification: 3 months
  Write: H. Louis French, Executive Director

Officer: H. Louis French, Executive Director.

Governors: Mary Ellen Imboden, John T. King, III, Walter Sondheim, Jr., Semmes G. Walsh,* Bruce P. Wilson.

Trustees:* Mercantile-Safe Deposit and Trust Company, Corporate Trustee.

Number of staff: None.

Employer Identification Number: 526057178

1402
Baldwin (Summerfield), Jr. Foundation
c/o Mercantile-Safe Deposit and Trust Company
P.O. Box 2257, Two Hopkins Plaza
Baltimore 21201

Trust established in 1946 in Maryland.

Financial data: (yr. ended 12/31/83): Assets, $1,894,082 (M); expenditures, $127,462, including $115,557 for 14 grants (high: $35,000; low: $150).

Purpose and activities: Charitable purposes; primarily local giving, with emphasis on Protestant Episcopal church support, church-sponsored secondary schools, and a hospital.

Limitations: Giving primarily in MD.

Trustee: Mercantile-Safe Deposit and Trust Company.

Employer Identification Number: 526023112

1403
Baltimore Area, Inc., The Community Foundation of the Greater
Six East Hamilton St.
Baltimore 21202   (301) 332-4171

Community foundation incorporated in 1972 in Maryland.

Financial data: (yr. ended 12/31/82): Assets, $4,890,340 (M); gifts received, $1,830,233; expenditures, $661,011, including $606,144 for 126 grants (high: $73,000; low: $100).

Purpose and activities: To meet the civic, cultural, health, and other needs of the Greater Baltimore community. Grants primarily for pilot projects and to increase organizational effectiveness and self-sufficiency.

Limitations: Giving primarily in MD. No loans.

Publications: Annual report, application guidelines.

Application information:
  Initial approach: Letter

Board meeting date(s): March, June, September, and December
  Write: Eugene C. Struckhoff, Executive Director

Officers: W. Wallace Lanahan, Jr.,* Vice-President and Treasurer; Timothy D. Armbruster, Secretary.

Trustees:* Donald L. DeVries, Chairman; Herbert M. Katzenberg, Vice-Chairman; J. Owen Cole, Alonzo G. Decker, Jr., Sheldon Goldseker, Mary Ellen Imboden, Robert H. Levi, Joseph Meyerhoff, Jack Moseley, James W. Rouse, Jacques T. Schlenger, Maryland National Bank (John M. Nelson III); Mercantile-Safe Deposit & Trust Company (Bruce P. Wilson).

Employer Identification Number: 237180620

1404
Blaustein (The Jacob and Hilda) Foundation, Inc. ▼ ¤
Blaustein Bldg.
P.O. Box 238
Baltimore 21203

Incorporated in 1957 in Maryland.

Donor(s): Jacob Blaustein.†

Financial data: (yr. ended 12/31/83): Assets, $41,035,133 (M); gifts received, $829,600; expenditures, $2,381,219, including $2,245,800 for 26 grants (high: $605,000; low: $500).

Purpose and activities: Grants for Jewish welfare funds and higher education, primarily in New York and Maryland.

Limitations: Giving primarily in MD and NY.

Application information:
  Initial approach: Letter
  Deadline(s): None
  Board meeting date(s): Every 4 to 6 weeks
  Write: Morton K. Blaustein, President

Officers: Morton K. Blaustein,* President; David Hirschhorn,* Henry A. Rosenberg, Jr., Louis B. Thalheimer, Vice-Presidents; J. Warren Weiss, Secretary and Treasurer.

Trustees:* Barbara B. Hirschhorn, Ruth B. Rosenberg, Elizabeth B. Roswell.

Number of staff: None.

Employer Identification Number: 526038382

1405
Blaustein (The Louis and Henrietta) Foundation, Inc. ¤
Blaustein Bldg.
P.O. Box 238
Baltimore 21203

Incorporated in 1938 in Maryland.

Donor(s): Louis Blaustein,† Henrietta Blaustein,† American Trading and Production Corporation, and members of the Blaustein family.

Financial data: (yr. ended 12/31/83): Assets, $6,531,154 (M); gifts received, $118,000; expenditures, $555,112, including $536,676 for 53 grants (high: $167,000; low: $700).

Purpose and activities: Broad purposes; local charitable giving, mainly to recipients already known to the trustees; emphasis on higher and secondary education, Jewish welfare funds, museums, music and the arts, and a community fund.
Limitations: Giving primarily in the greater Baltimore, MD, metropolitan area.
Application information:
Initial approach: Letter
Deadline(s): None
Write: Morton K. Blaustein
Officers and Trustees: * Ruth B. Rosenberg,* Chairman; Morton K. Blaustein,* President; Henry A. Rosenberg, Jr.,* David Hirschhorn,* Louis B. Thalheimer,* Vice-Presidents; J. Warren Weiss, Secretary and Treasurer.
Employer Identification Number: 526038381

1406
Chertkof (David W. and Annie) Mitzvah Fund, Inc. ¤
19 West Franklin St.
Baltimore 21201

Incorporated in 1952 in Maryland.
Donor(s): David W. Chertkof.
Financial data: (yr. ended 12/31/83): Assets, $1,120,789 (M); expenditures, $471,291, including $459,129 for grants.
Purpose and activities: Grants for Jewish-sponsored educational programs, temple support, and Jewish welfare funds, largely in Maryland, New York, and Florida.
Limitations: Giving primarily in MD, NY, and FL.
Officers: Ethel Posnick, President; Helen C. Gimbel, Ethel C. Posnick, Vice-Presidents; Howard L. Chertkof, Secretary; Stephanie Prince, Treasurer.
Employer Identification Number: 526035353

1407
Clark-Winchcole Foundation ▼ ¤
7315 Wisconsin Ave., Suite 345N
Bethesda 20814   (301) 654-3607

Established in 1964 in the District of Columbia.
Donor(s): Dorothy C. Winchcole, Elizabeth G. Clark.†
Financial data: (yr. ended 12/31/82): Assets, $13,360,150 (M); expenditures, $1,312,369, including $1,215,000 for 40 grants (high: $333,000; low: $5,000).
Purpose and activities: Giving primarily in the Washington, D.C. area, with emphasis on higher education, hospitals, health agencies, cultural programs, social services, aid to the handicapped, and Protestant church support.
Limitations: Giving primarily in the Washington, DC area.
Officers and Trustees: * Charles Emory Phillips,* President; Vincent E. Burke, Jr.,* Joseph H. Riley, Thomas C. Thompson, Jr.,* Vice-Presidents; E. Marie Lund, Secretary; Dorothy C. Winchcole,* Treasurer.
Employer Identification Number: 526058340

1408
Commercial Credit Companies Foundation, Inc. ¤
300 St. Paul Place
Baltimore 21202   (301) 332-3444

Incorporated in 1951 in Delaware.
Donor(s): Commercial Credit Company, and subsidiaries.
Financial data: (yr. ended 12/31/83): Assets, $410,615 (M); expenditures, $254,949, including $237,183 for 82 grants (high: $118,000; low: $50) and $15,110 for employee matching gifts.
Purpose and activities: Broad purposes; primarily local giving for the arts and cultural programs, higher education, and economic development with emphasis on jobs and training for disadvantaged youth and a community fund.
Types of support awarded: Employee matching gifts.
Limitations: Giving primarily in metropolitan Baltimore, MD, area.
Application information:
Initial approach: Proposal
Copies of proposal: 2
Deadline(s): Submit proposal between May and June; deadline July 1
Board meeting date(s): As required
Write: John P. Moe, President
Officers: John P. Moe,* President; Brenda K. Shelley, Manager.
Trustees: * F. Barton Harvey, Jr., Donald S. Jones, William D. Rowe, L.S. Willard.
Employer Identification Number: 526043604

1409
Crown Central Petroleum Foundation, Inc. ¤
One North Charles St.
Baltimore 21201

Donor(s): Crown Central Petroleum Corporation.
Financial data: (yr. ended 12/31/83): Assets, $13,555 (M); gifts received, $50,000; expenditures, $181,371, including $175,396 for 62 grants (high: $35,000; low: $50) and $5,311 for 21 employee matching gifts.
Purpose and activities: Primarily local giving in Maryland and Texas with emphasis on higher education, community funds and community development.
Limitations: Giving primarily in MD and TX.
Officers: W.R. Snyder, President; Ted M. Jackson, Vice-President and Treasurer; N.K. Cooper, Secretary.
Employer Identification Number: 521203348

1410
Dean (Joel) Foundation, Inc. ¤
c/o Jurrien Dean
7422 Hampden Ln.
Bethesda 20014

Established in 1957 in New York.
Donor(s): Joel Dean, Joel Dean Associates Corp.

Financial data: (yr. ended 12/31/83): Assets, $1,492,508 (M); expenditures, $69,885, including $52,750 for 36 grants (high: $15,500; low: $150).
Purpose and activities: Grants primarily for higher education and cultural programs.
Officers and Directors: Jurrien Dean, President; Gretchen Dean, Vice-President; Gillian Dean, Joel Dean, Jr.
Employer Identification Number: 136097306

1411
Duncan (Harry F.) Foundation, Inc.
1007 Ripley St.
Silver Spring 20910

Incorporated in 1955 in Delaware.
Donor(s): Harry F. Duncan.
Financial data: (yr. ended 12/31/83): Assets, $679,277 (M); expenditures, $162,630, including $160,525 for 51 grants (high: $42,000; low: $25).
Purpose and activities: Broad purposes; grants for youth agencies, church support, and other religious programs; some support also for education and civic affairs, primarily in the District of Columbia and Missouri.
Limitations: Giving primarily in MD, MO, and DC. No grants to individuals, or for endowment funds, operating budgets, or special projects.
Application information: Funds fully committed at present.
Write: Harry F. Duncan, President
Officers and Trustees: Harry F. Duncan, President and Treasurer; Robert F. McFadden, Vice-President; George P. Mathieson, Secretary; Anneliese H. Duncan.
Number of staff: 2 part-time support.
Employer Identification Number: 526054187

1412
Egenton Home ¤
200 Padonia Rd. East
Timonium 21093

Financial data: (yr. ended 6/30/83): Assets, $1,425,063 (M); expenditures, $105,970, including $19,690 for 7 grants (high: $5,000; low: $1,690).
Purpose and activities: Foundation primarily operates a home; some local giving for secondary education and other charitable purposes.
Limitations: Giving primarily in MD.
Officers and Trustees: Norvell E. Miller III, President; Thomas H. Hedrick, Secretary; Richard M. Drought, Treasurer; Cecil B. Bishop, Jr., Mrs. Henry F. Cassidy, Haswell Franklin, Curtis Janzen, William H. McCormick, Herbert R. Preston, Jr., David Rice, Kent Rutley, David Wallace, Mrs. David Wallace.
Employer Identification Number: 520600233

1413

Equitable Bank Foundation, Inc., The

(formerly Equitable Trust Company Foundation, Inc.)

100 South Charles St.
Baltimore 21201   (301) 547-4395

Incorporated in 1964 in Maryland.
Donor(s): The Equitable Bank.
Financial data: (yr. ended 12/31/83): Assets, $570,249 (M); gifts received, $500,000; expenditures, $288,973, including $286,003 for 44 grants (high: $104,000; low: $100).
Purpose and activities: Broad purposes; primarily local giving, with emphasis on community funds, higher education, youth agencies, hospitals, and arts and culture.
Limitations: Giving primarily in MD.
Application information:
  Write: Barbara B. Lucas, Secretary
Officers: H. Grant Hathaway, President; John C. Ruxton, Vice-President; Barbara B. Lucas, Secretary; Laura J. Bortle, Treasurer.
Employer Identification Number: 526060268

1414

Fairchild Industries Foundation, Inc.

20301 Century Blvd.
Germantown 20874

Incorporated in 1953 in Maryland.
Donor(s): Fairchild Industries, Inc.
Financial data: (yr. ended 12/31/83): Assets, $901,051 (M); gifts received, $300,000; expenditures, $411,250, including $328,100 for 146 grants (high: $30,000; low: $250) and $36,135 for 250 employee matching gifts.
Purpose and activities: Giving primarily in areas where company has facilities; emphasis on higher education, including employee matching gifts, community funds, and civic affairs; support also for scholarships to children of employees and aid to needy employees or retired employees.
Types of support awarded: Operating budgets, continuing support, annual campaigns, seed money, emergency funds, building funds, equipment, land acquisition, endowment funds, matching funds, scholarship funds, professorships, internships, employee related scholarships, exchange programs, fellowships, employee matching gifts.
Limitations: Giving primarily in areas of company operations. No grants to individuals (except to aid needy employees or retirees), or for deficit financing; no loans.
Application information:
  Initial approach: Letter
  Copies of proposal: 1
  Deadline(s): Submit proposal in September or October
  Board meeting date(s): January or as required
  Write: Charles Collis, President
Officers: Charles Collis,* President; Frank J. Schmidt, Vice-President; Hazel S. Chilcote, Secretary; William H. Buckland, Treasurer.
Trustees:* Charles A. Kuper, Deming Lewis, T.H. Moorer.
Number of staff: 1 part-time professional.
Employer Identification Number: 526043638

1415

First Maryland Foundation, Inc.

25 South Charles St.
Baltimore 21203   (301) 244-4907

Incorporated in 1967 in Maryland.
Donor(s): The First National Bank of Maryland.
Financial data: (yr. ended 12/31/83): Assets, $938,480 (M); gifts received, $295,000; expenditures, $367,160, including $364,222 for 120 grants (high: $90,000; low: $10; average: $3,000).
Purpose and activities: Charitable purposes; primarily local giving, with emphasis on community funds; support also for higher education, music, youth agencies, and hospitals.
Limitations: Giving primarily in the Baltimore, MD area. No grants to individuals, or for endowment funds, scholarships and fellowships or matching gifts; no loans.
Application information:
  Initial approach: Letter
  Copies of proposal: 1
  Deadline(s): March 31
  Board meeting date(s): March, June, September, and December
  Write: Robert W. Schaefer, Secretary-Treasurer
Officers and Trustees: J. Owen Cole, President; Charles W. Cole, Jr., Vice-President; Robert W. Schaefer, Secretary-Treasurer.
Employer Identification Number: 526077253

1416

France (The Jacob and Annita) Foundation, Inc. ▼

Charles Fountain Professional Bldg., Suite 7
6301 North Charles St.
Baltimore 21212   (301) 377-5251

Incorporated in 1959 in Maryland.
Donor(s): Jacob France,† Annita A. France.†
Financial data: (yr. ended 5/31/84): Assets, $33,521,993 (M); gifts received, $174,894; expenditures, $716,089, including $438,508 for 57 grants (high: $100,000; low: $75; average: $500-$10,000).
Purpose and activities: Broad purposes; primarily local giving, within 5 program areas: higher education, secondary education, social services and health, historic preservation, and arts and culture.
Types of support awarded: General purposes.
Limitations: Giving limited to MD, with emphasis on Baltimore. No grants to individuals.
Application information:
  Initial approach: Letter
  Copies of proposal: 1
  Board meeting date(s): As required
  Write: Vernon T. Pittinger, Vice-President
Officers and Directors: Robert G. Merrick, Sr., President; Vernon T. Pittinger, Vice-President, Secretary and Treasurer; Donna Silbersack, Mary Balladarsh, The Equitable Trust Co.
Number of staff: 2 full-time professional; 2 full-time support; 2 part-time support.
Employer Identification Number: 520794585

1417

Freeman (Carl M.) Foundation, Inc. ⌕

11325 Seven Locks Rd.
Potomac 20854

Established in 1962.
Donor(s): Carl M. Freeman.
Financial data: (yr. ended 12/31/83): Assets, $1,591,132 (M); expenditures, $96,418, including $78,035 for 37 grants (high: $10,000; low: $35).
Purpose and activities: Primarily local giving, with emphasis on cultural programs and Jewish welfare agencies.
Types of support awarded: Operating budgets.
Limitations: Giving primarily in MD and DC.
Officers and Trustees: Carl M. Freeman, President; Albert E. Arent, Vice-President; Virginia Freeman, Secretary.
Employer Identification Number: 526047536

1418

Giant Food Foundation, Inc. ▼

6300 Sheriff Rd.
Landover 20785   (301) 341-4100
Mailing address: P.O. Box 1804, Washington, DC 20013

Incorporated in 1950 in the District of Columbia.
Donor(s): Giant Food Inc.
Financial data: (yr. ended 1/31/84): Assets, $358,878 (M); gifts received, $700,000; expenditures, $593,730, including $593,011 for 155 grants (high: $300,500; low: $100; average: $100-$1,000).
Purpose and activities: Primarily local giving in Washington and Baltimore metropolitan areas; funds largely committed for continuing support, in fields of community service, community funds, health and mental health, education, the arts and humanities.
Types of support awarded: General purposes, continuing support.
Limitations: Giving primarily in the Baltimore, MD, and Washington, DC, metropolitan areas; normally no grants to programs of national or international scope. No grants to individuals, or for scholarships and fellowships, or matching gifts; no loans.
Application information:
  Initial approach: Proposal
  Copies of proposal: 1
  Deadline(s): None
  Board meeting date(s): Monthly
Officers: Israel Cohen, Charlotte Lehrman, Vice-Presidents; Emanuel Cohen, Treasurer.
Number of staff: None.
Employer Identification Number: 526045041

1419

Goldseker (Morris) Foundation of Maryland, Inc. ▼

300 North Charles St.
Baltimore 21201   (301) 837-5100

Incorporated in 1973 in Maryland.
Donor(s): Morris Goldseker.†

Financial data: (yr. ended 4/30/84): Assets, $26,005,727 (M); expenditures, $3,141,759, including $922,601 for 32 grants (high: $54,000; low: $5,000).
Purpose and activities: Primarily local giving; grants to nonprofit institutions operating or initiating programs in community affairs, education, housing, medicine and public health, and human services, primarily benefiting economically disadvantaged persons.
Types of support awarded: Seed money, emergency funds, matching funds, consulting services, technical assistance, loans, special projects.
Limitations: Giving limited to the Baltimore, MD, area. No support for advocacy or political action groups, religious purposes, or for cultural affairs. No grants to individuals, or for building or endowment funds, equipment, land acquisition, renovations, deficit financing, annual campaigns, research, scholarships, fellowships, publications, or conferences.
Publications: Annual report, program policy statement, application guidelines.
Application information: Submit preliminary letter as early as possible before deadlines.
  Initial approach: Brief letter
  Copies of proposal: 1
  Deadline(s): April 1, August 1, and December 1
  Board meeting date(s): Distribution committee meets 3 times a year in March, June, and October
  Final notification: After board meeting
  Write: Timothy D. Armbruster, Executive Director
Officers: Sheldon Goldseker,* President; Samuel Goldseker, Vice-President and Secretary; Simon Goldseker,* Vice-President and Treasurer; Timothy D. Armbruster, Vice-President and Executive Director.
Trustees:* John C. Ruxton, The Equitable Trust Company.
Selection Committee: Earl Richardson, President, Morgan State University; Shoshana Cardin, President, Associated Jewish Charities and Welfare Fund; Steven Muller, President, The Johns Hopkins University.
Number of staff: 3 full-time professional.
Employer Identification Number: 520983502

1420
Gudelsky (The Homer and Martha) Family Foundation, Inc. ⌻
11900 Tech Rd.
Silver Spring 20904

Incorporated in 1968 in Maryland.
Donor(s): Members of the Gudelsky family, Percontee, Inc., Axcorp, Inc.
Financial data: (yr. ended 12/31/83): Assets, $6,514,932 (M); gifts received, $7,500; expenditures, $172,899, including $170,635 for 33 grants (high: $50,000; low: $35).
Purpose and activities: Broad purposes; grants largely for higher education, and local temple support, and Jewish welfare funds.
Officers: Homer Gudelsky,* President; Martha Gudelsky,* Vice-President; John Gudelsky, Secretary-Treasurer.
Directors:* Winston T. Brundige, Medda Yarowsky, Jack C. Merriman.
Employer Identification Number: 520885969

1421
Hechinger (Sidney L.) Foundation
3500 Pennsy Dr.
Landover 20785   (301) 341-0404

Incorporated in 1955 in the District of Columbia.
Donor(s): Hechinger Company, members of the Hechinger family.
Financial data: (yr. ended 6/30/83): Assets, $1,551,838 (M); gifts received, $902,102; expenditures, $853,655, including $849,113 for 387 grants (high: $150,666; low: $20).
Purpose and activities: General giving, with emphasis on Jewish welfare funds and United Way; support for music and other cultural programs, aid to the handicapped, and youth and social agencies in areas of company operations in Maryland, Virginia, Pennsylvania, and the District of Columbia.
Limitations: Giving limited to areas of company operations.
Application information:
  Final notification: 8 to 10 weeks
  Write: John W. Hechinger
Managers and Trustees: Lois H. England, Richard England, John W. Hechinger, June R. Hechinger.
Employer Identification Number: 526054428

1422
Hecht-Levi Foundation, Inc., The ⌻
1300 Mercantile Bank & Trust Bldg.
Two Hopkins Plaza
Baltimore 21201   (301) 237-5581

Incorporated in 1958 in Maryland.
Donor(s): Alexander Hecht,† Selma H. Hecht,† Robert H. Levi, Ryda H. Levi.
Financial data: (yr. ended 12/31/83): Assets, $4,704,709 (M); expenditures, $292,596, including $258,525 for 53 grants (high: $85,000; low: $150).
Purpose and activities: Charitable purposes; primarily local giving, with emphasis on Jewish welfare funds, cultural programs, including music, and higher education.
Limitations: Giving primarily in the Baltimore, MD, metropolitan area. No grants to individuals.
Application information:
  Initial approach: Full proposal
  Copies of proposal: 1
  Deadline(s): Submit proposal preferably in March or September
  Board meeting date(s): June and December
  Write: Robert H. Levi, President
Officers and Directors: Robert H. Levi, President; Ryda H. Levi, Frank A. Kaufman, Vice-Presidents; Wilbert H. Sirota, Secretary; Richard H. Levi, Treasurer; Sandra L. Gerstung, Alexander H. Levi.
Employer Identification Number: 526035023

1423
Hoffberger Foundation, Inc. ▼
900 Garrett Bldg.
237 East Redwood St.
Baltimore 21202   (301) 752-1284

Incorporated in 1941 in Maryland.

Donor(s): The Hoffberger family.
Financial data: (yr. ended 12/31/83): Assets, $8,062,208 (M); expenditures, $489,198, including $486,213 for 22 grants (high: $376,063; low: $300; average: $500-$10,000).
Purpose and activities: General purposes; emphasis on local Jewish health and welfare agencies, and social service and higher educational organizations and institutions.
Types of support awarded: Annual campaigns, seed money, building funds, equipment, endowment funds, scholarship funds, fellowships, matching funds, general purposes, continuing support.
Limitations: Giving primarily in Baltimore, MD. No grants to individuals or for operating budgets; no loans.
Application information:
  Initial approach: Full proposal
  Copies of proposal: 1
  Deadline(s): 30 days prior to board meetings
  Board meeting date(s): June and December
  Final notification: 6 months
  Write: LeRoy E. Hoffberger, President
Officers and Directors: LeRoy E. Hoffberger, President; Charles H. Hoffberger, Vice-President and Secretary; Jerold C. Hoffberger, Treasurer; Morton J. Hollander.
Employer Identification Number: 520794249

1424
Kelly (Ensign C. Markland), Jr. Memorial Foundation, Inc.
1224 Fidelity Bldg.
Baltimore 21201   (301) 837-8822

Incorporated in 1946 in Maryland.
Donor(s): C. Markland Kelly,† Kelly Buick Sales Corporation.
Financial data: (yr. ended 12/31/83): Assets, $3,381,080 (M); expenditures, $251,007, including $155,432 for 39 grants (high: $31,888; low: $100).
Purpose and activities: Broad purposes; local giving to support elementary and secondary education, and youth activities; support also for music and social agencies.
Types of support awarded: Annual campaigns, building funds, equipment, endowment funds, special projects, scholarship funds, matching funds.
Limitations: Giving limited to the greater Baltimore, MD, metropolitan area. No grants to individuals, or for operating budgets, research, fellowships, or travel; no loans.
Publications: Informational brochure, program policy statement, application guidelines.
Application information:
  Initial approach: Full proposal
  Copies of proposal: 3
  Deadline(s): None
  Board meeting date(s): Monthly
  Final notification: 6 months
  Write: Herbert E. Witz, President
Officers and Directors: Herbert E. Witz, President; Bowen P. Weisheit, Vice-President and Secretary; Warren A. Burdette, Treasurer; Bowen P. Weisheit, Jr.
Number of staff: 2.
Employer Identification Number: 526033330

1425
Kentland Foundation, Inc. ☐
P.O. Box 4689
Rockville 20850

Incorporated about 1966 in Maryland.
Donor(s): Otis Beall Kent.†
Financial data: (yr. ended 12/31/83): Assets, $4,963,119 (M); expenditures, $612,452, including $147,150 for 26 grants (high: $36,250; low: $250).
Purpose and activities: Primarily local giving for the National Geographic Society and church support.
Limitations: Giving primarily in MD.
Officers: Helene D. Kent, President; William H. Loren, Vice-President; Helene Walker, Secretary-Treasurer.
Director: Steven O'Neil.
Employer Identification Number: 526070323

1426
Knapp Educational Fund, Inc. ☐
P.O. Box O
St. Michaels 21663   (301) 745-5660

Established about 1979 in Maryland.
Donor(s): The Knapp Foundation, Inc.
Financial data: (yr. ended 12/31/83): Assets, $1,896,498 (M); expenditures, $94,817, including $60,100 for 57 grants to individuals.
Purpose and activities: Scholarships for children of employees of Macmillan, Inc. only.
Types of support awarded: Employee related scholarships.
Application information:
   Write: Mrs. Antoinette Vodjvoda, President
Officers and Trustees: Antoinette P. Vojvoda, President; Robert K. Vojvoda, Vice-President and Treasurer; Sylvia V. Penny, Secretary; Ruth Capranica, Frank M. Dahne.
Employer Identification Number: 132970128

1427
Knapp Foundation, Inc., The
c/o Robert B. Vojvoda
Box O
St. Michaels 21663   (301) 745-5660

Incorporated in 1929 in North Carolina.
Donor(s): Joseph Palmer Knapp.†
Financial data: (yr. ended 12/31/83): Assets, $7,045,761 (M); gifts received, $707,000; expenditures, $310,794, including $268,800 for 28 grants (high: $100,000; low: $100).
Purpose and activities: Grants primarily for conservation, libraries, historic preservation, health projects, and preservation of birds and animals.
Limitations: Giving limited to the United States. No grants to individuals, or for endowment funds, scholarships, or fellowships; no loans.
Publications: 990-PF, application guidelines.
Application information:
   Initial approach: Letter
   Copies of proposal: 1
   Board meeting date(s): January and August
   Write: Robert B. Vojvoda, Vice-President

Officers and Trustees: Antoinette P. Vojvoda, President; Robert B. Vojvoda, Vice-President and Treasurer; Ruth M. Capranica, Secretary; Margaret P. Newcombe, Sylvia V. Penny.
Number of staff: 1 part-time professional.
Employer Identification Number: 136001167

1428
Knott (The Marion I. and Henry J.) Foundation, Inc. ▼
Two West University Pkwy.
Baltimore 21218   (301) 235-7068

Incorporated in 1977 in Maryland.
Donor(s): Henry J. Knott, Marion I. Knott.
Financial data: (yr. ended 12/31/84): Assets, $16,000,000 (M); expenditures, $679,872, including $596,860 for 42 grants (high: $100,000; low: $35; average: $2,000-$50,000).
Purpose and activities: Local giving for higher and secondary education, religious welfare organizations, especially Roman Catholic organizations, and community development.
Types of support awarded: Operating budgets, continuing support, seed money, emergency funds, deficit financing, endowment funds, research, publications, special projects, matching funds, general purposes, building funds, equipment.
Limitations: Giving limited to Baltimore, MD and five surrounding counties. No support for organizations that provide abortion services, or for public schools. No grants to individuals, or for annual campaigns, continuing support over three years, demonstration projects, conferences, or scholarships and fellowships; no loans.
Publications: Application guidelines, program policy statement.
Application information:
   Initial approach: Letter
   Copies of proposal: 2
   Deadline(s): Submit proposal preferably in June or January; deadlines March 1 and September 1
   Board meeting date(s): May and December
   Final notification: 2 to 5 months
   Write: Margaret K. Riehl, Secretary
Officers and Directors: Henry J. Knott, Chairman; Marion I. Knott, Vice-Chairman; Rose Marie K. Porter, President; Margaret K. Riehl, Secretary; James F. Knott, Treasurer; Marion K. Beckman, Francis X. Knott, Henry J. Knott, Jr., Martin G. Knott, Patricia K. Smyth, Alice K. Voelkel, Catherine K. Wies.
Number of staff: 1 part-time support.
Employer Identification Number: 521097109

1429
Krieger Fund, Inc., The ☐
c/o Wolpoff & Company
1111 North Charles St.
Baltimore 21201

Incorporated in 1944 in Maryland.
Donor(s): Abraham Krieger.
Financial data: (yr. ended 12/31/83): Assets, $1,255,063 (M); expenditures, $84,611, including $81,150 for 15 grants (high: $50,000; low: $250).

Purpose and activities: Broad purposes; primarily local giving, with emphasis on Jewish welfare funds; support also for secondary education and cultural programs.
Limitations: Giving primarily in MD.
Officer: Jane K. Schapiro, President; Joann C. Fruchtman, Vice-President and Secretary; Howard K. Cohen, Vice-President and Treasurer.
Employer Identification Number: 526035537

1430
Leidy (John J.) Foundation, Inc. ☐
c/o Pierson & Pierson
Ten Light St., 30th Fl.
Baltimore 21202   (301) 727-7733

Incorporated in 1957 in Maryland.
Donor(s): John J. Leidy.†
Financial data: (yr. ended 12/31/83): Assets, $3,572,990 (M); expenditures, $171,894, including $134,770 for 137 grants (high: $14,252; low: $5).
Purpose and activities: Primarily local giving, with emphasis on child welfare, hospitals, higher education, including scholarship funds, and social agencies.
Limitations: Giving primarily in MD. No grants to individuals.
Application information:
   Initial approach: Proposal
   Deadline(s): None
   Write: Edward Pierson, President
Officers and Trustees: Edward Pierson, President; W. Michel Pierson, Vice-President; Allan H. Fisher, Secretary; Henry E. Pear, Treasurer.
Employer Identification Number: 526034785

1431
Loats Foundation, Inc.
P.O. Box 240
Frederick 21701   (301) 662-2191
Application address: c/o Evangelical Lutheran Church, E. Church St., Frederick, MD 21701; Tel.: (301) 663-6361

Established in 1881 in Maryland.
Donor(s): John Loats.†
Financial data: (yr. ended 5/31/83): Assets, $1,871,187 (M); expenditures, $134,183, including $37,645 for 11 grants (high: $12,645; low: $500) and $83,792 for 92 grants to individuals.
Purpose and activities: To provide for the care and education of needy children and orphans resident in Frederick County only; giving primarily for scholarships.
Types of support awarded: Student aid.
Limitations: Giving limited to Frederick County, MD.
Publications: Program policy statement, application guidelines.
Application information: Application form required.
   Deadline(s): Contact Evangelical Lutheran Church office for deadlines
   Board meeting date(s): Annually and as required
   Write: Glenn E. Biehl, Treasurer

Officers: W. Philip Fogarty,* President; Warner
L. Brittain, Vice-President; Melvin H. Derr,*
Secretary; Glenn E. Biehl, Treasurer.
Trustees:* Garland P. Ferga, C. Richard Miller,
Jr., Charles E. Tressler.
Employer Identification Number: 520610535

1432
M. E. Foundation, The ⌑
Rutherford Plaza
7133 Rutherford Rd.
Baltimore 21207

Established in 1966 in New York.
Donor(s): Mrs. Margaret Brown Trimble, Miss
Frances Carroll Brown.
Financial data: (yr. ended 12/31/83): Assets,
$10,068,096 (M); expenditures, $566,229,
including $552,098 for 27 grants (high:
$60,000; low: $5,000).
Purpose and activities: Broad purposes; grants
to organizations in the United States and
abroad for Protestant evangelistic missionary
work and Bible studies.
Officers and Directors: Margaret Brown
Trimble, President and Secretary; Frances
Carroll Brown, Vice-President and Treasurer;
Stuart Garver, Louis King, Burton Smoliar.
Employer Identification Number: 136205356

1433
Marriott (The J. Willard) Foundation
(formerly The J. Willard Marriott Family
Foundation)
10400 Fernwood Rd.
Bethesda 20058

Established in 1966 in the District of Columbia.
Donor(s): J. Willard Marriott, Alice S. Marriott.
Financial data: (yr. ended 12/31/84): Assets,
$4,650,000 (M); expenditures, $457,257,
including $415,000 for 59 grants (high:
$325,000; low: $100; average: $100-$2,000).
Purpose and activities: Grants primarily to
local, previously supported charities, and a few
general scholarship funds.
Types of support awarded: Continuing
support, scholarship funds.
Limitations: Giving primarily in DC. No grants
to individuals, including scholarships.
Application information: Applications for
grants not invited.
Initial approach: Letter
Copies of proposal: 1
Trustees: Sterling D. Colton, Alice S. Marriott,
J. Willard Marriott, J. Willard Marriott, Jr.,
Richard E. Marriott.
Number of staff: 1 part-time support.
Employer Identification Number: 526068678

1434
Marshall (George Preston) Foundation
(also known as Redskin Foundation, Inc.)
5454 Wisconsin Ave., Suite 1455
Chevy Chase 20815   (301) 654-7774

Incorporated in 1972 in the District of
Columbia.
Donor(s): George Preston Marshall.†

Financial data: (yr. ended 12/31/83): Assets,
$0 (M); gifts received, $414,333; expenditures,
$427,855, including $399,476 for 63 grants
(high: $32,700; low: $300).
Purpose and activities: "For the health,
welfare, education and improvement of
conditions of children in the District of
Columbia and in the states of Maryland and
Virginia".
Limitations: Giving limited to DC, MD, and
VA. No grants to individuals.
Publications: Annual report, application
guidelines, program policy statement.
Application information:
Initial approach: Full proposal
Copies of proposal: 1
Deadline(s): 1st of month preceding board
meetings
Board meeting date(s): Bimonthly, beginning
in January
Write: Elizabeth B. Frazier, Executive Director
Officers: James C. McKay,* President; William
D. Foote,* Vice-President; J. Paull Marshall,*
Secretary; G. Dewey Arnold, Jr.,* Treasurer;
Elizabeth B. Frazier, Executive Director.
Directors:* John W. Sweeterman.
Employer Identification Number: 237173302

1435
**Martin Marietta Corporation
Foundation** ⌑
6801 Rockledge Dr.
Bethesda 20034

Trust established in 1955 in Maryland.
Donor(s): Martin Marietta Corporation.
Financial data: (yr. ended 12/31/83): Assets,
$53,455 (M); gifts received, $480,000;
expenditures, $450,022, including $445,866
for 155 grants to individuals.
Purpose and activities: Primary interest in
higher education, particularly through support
of scholarships for children of Corporation
employees.
Types of support awarded: Employee related
scholarships.
Application information: Application form
required.
Deadline(s): February 15
Trustees: Wayne Shaner, James D. Simpson,
Peter F. Warren.
Employer Identification Number: 136161566

1436
**Maryland National Foundation, Inc.,
The** ⌑
Ten Light St.
Baltimore 21202

Incorporated in 1965 in Maryland.
Donor(s): Maryland National Bank.
Financial data: (yr. ended 12/31/82): Assets,
$1,615,488 (M); gifts received, $100,000;
expenditures, $414,707, including $412,146
for 84 grants (high: $131,000; low: $200).
Purpose and activities: Broad purposes;
primarily local giving, with emphasis on
community funds; support also for higher
education, music, and hospitals.
Limitations: Giving primarily in MD.

Officers: Robert D.H. Harvey, President;
Henry A. Baker, Jr., Secretary; John M. Nelson,
III, Treasurer.
Employer Identification Number: 526062721

1437
**Mendelson (Alfred G. and Ida) Family
Foundation, Inc.** ⌑
8300 Pennsylvania Ave.
P.O. Box 398
Forestville 20747-0398

Incorporated in 1970 in the District of
Columbia.
Donor(s): Murry's Steaks, Inc., and subsidiaries.
Financial data: (yr. ended 3/31/83): Assets,
$224,531 (M); gifts received, $295,492;
expenditures, $151,663, including $151,555
for 61 grants (high: $55,250; low: $25).
Purpose and activities: Giving primarily in
Maryland and the District of Columbia, with
emphasis on temple support, Jewish welfare
agencies, and social services.
Limitations: Giving primarily in MD and DC.
Officers: Ida Mendelson, President; David
Luftig, Vice-President; Murry Mendelson,
Secretary.
Employer Identification Number: 237068870

1438
**Merrick (Robert G. and Anne M.)
Foundation, Inc.** ⌑
c/o Wolpoff & Company
1111 North Charles St.
Baltimore 21201

Established in 1962.
Donor(s): Robert G. Merrick, Sr., Anne M.
Merrick,† Homewood Holding Company.
Financial data: (yr. ended 10/31/83): Assets,
$1,678,643 (M); gifts received, $15,968;
expenditures, $469,939, including $456,113
for 38 grants (high: $110,000; low: $10).
Purpose and activities: Primarily local giving,
with emphasis on cultural programs and higher
education.
Limitations: Giving primarily in Baltimore, MD.
Officers: Robert G. Merrick, Sr., President;
Robert G. Merrick, Jr., Vice-President; Mary
Plaggemeyer, Secretary-Treasurer.
Employer Identification Number: 526072964

1439
Meyerhoff (The Joseph) Fund, Inc. ▼
25 South Charles St.
Baltimore 21201   (301) 727-3200

Incorporated in 1953 in Maryland.
Donor(s): Joseph Meyerhoff, Mrs. Joseph
Meyerhoff.
Financial data: (yr. ended 12/31/83): Assets,
$14,299,543 (M); gifts received, $846,140;
expenditures, $1,588,727, including
$1,493,567 for 106 grants (high: $632,400;
low: $250).

Purpose and activities: Primarily local giving and in New York City and Israel to support and encourage cultural and higher educational programs and institutions and to facilitate immigration and absorption of new immigrants into Israel.
Types of support awarded: Annual campaigns, seed money, emergency funds, deficit financing, building funds, land acquisition, endowment funds, research, publications, professorships, scholarship funds, matching funds, continuing support.
Limitations: Giving primarily in Baltimore, MD, and New York City, NY; some grants to organizations in Israel. No grants to individuals.
Application information: Application form required.
Initial approach: Letter
Copies of proposal: 1
Deadline(s): Submit proposal preferably from August to September
Board meeting date(s): May and October and as required
Final notification: 2 weeks to 1 month
Write: Louis L. Kaplan, Executive Vice-President
Officers and Directors:* Harvey M. Meyerhoff,* Vice-President and Treasurer; Louis L. Kaplan, Executive Vice-President; Marvin S. Williams, Secretary.
Number of staff: 1 part-time professional; 1 part-time support.
Employer Identification Number: 526035997

1440
Middendorf Foundation, Inc.
803 Cathedral St.
Baltimore 21201

Incorporated in 1953 in Maryland.
Donor(s): J. William Middendorf, Jr.,† Mrs. Alice C. Middendorf.†
Financial data: (yr. ended 3/31/84): Assets, $8,841,750 (M); expenditures, $404,304, including $309,750 for 49 grants (high: $75,000; low: $750).
Purpose and activities: Charitable and religious purposes; primarily local giving, with emphasis on cultural programs, including historic preservation and museums, higher and secondary education, Protestant church support, and conservation; support also for hospitals and the handicapped.
Types of support awarded: Matching funds, annual campaigns, endowment funds, professorships.
Limitations: Giving primarily in MD. No grants to individuals.
Application information:
Write: E. Phillips Hathaway, President
Officers and Trustees: E. Phillips Hathaway, President; Roger B. Hopkins, Jr., Vice-President; Robert B. Russell, II, Secretary; Craig Lewis, Treasurer; Peter B. Middendorf.
Employer Identification Number: 526048944

1441
Mulford (Vincent) Foundation ⌧
c/o Mercantile Safe Deposit & Trust Company
Two Hopkins Plaza
Baltimore 21201

Trust established in 1951 in New Jersey.
Donor(s): Vincent S. Mulford,† Edith Mulford.†
Financial data: (yr. ended 12/31/83): Assets, $1,545,603 (M); expenditures, $134,799, including $125,000 for 60 grants (high: $20,000; low: $250).
Purpose and activities: Broad purposes; giving primarily in New Jersey, Connecticut and New York, with emphasis on the arts, higher and secondary education, Protestant church support, and social agencies.
Limitations: Giving primarily in NY, NJ, and CT.
Trustees: Walter E. Moor, Donald L. Mulford, Vincent S. Mulford, Jr., Thomas L. Pulling, Christian R. Sonne.
Employer Identification Number: 226043594

1442
Mullan (The Thomas F. and Clementine L.) Foundation, Inc. ⌧
15 Charles Plaza, Suite 400
Baltimore 21201

Incorporated in 1958 in Maryland.
Donor(s): Thomas F. Mullan, Sr.,† and his corporations.
Financial data: (yr. ended 11/30/83): Assets, $2,707,424 (M); expenditures, $168,587, including $157,040 for 107 grants (high: $15,000; low: $50).
Purpose and activities: To assist charitable institutions; primarily local giving, with emphasis on hospitals and health agencies, higher and secondary education, and Roman Catholic church support.
Limitations: Giving primarily in Baltimore, MD.
Officers: Thomas F. Mullan, Jr., President; Charles A. Mullan, Vice-President; C. Louise Mullan, Secretary; Joseph Mullan, Treasurer.
Employer Identification Number: 526050776

1443
NFL Alumni Foundation Fund ⌧
c/o Sigmund M. Hyman
100 South Charles St., Suite 870
Baltimore 21201   (301) 332-0560

Established in 1969.
Donor(s): NFL Charities, NFL Alumni Association.
Financial data: (yr. ended 5/31/83): Assets, $69,402 (M); gifts received, $25,000; expenditures, $119,010, including $112,388 for 25 grants to individuals.
Purpose and activities: Grants to physically or mentally disabled former National Football League alumni; support also for death benefits and medical expenses.
Application information:
Initial approach: Letter, including proof of income
Deadline(s): None
Trustees: Pete Rozelle, Chairman; William Bidwell, James Castiglia, William Dudley, George Halas, John Panelli, Arthur Rooney.
Employer Identification Number: 237087489

1444
Noxell Foundation, Inc., The
P.O. Box 1799
Baltimore 21203   (301) 628-7300

Incorporated in 1951 in Maryland.
Donor(s): Noxell Corporation.
Financial data: (yr. ended 12/31/84): Assets, $2,000,000 (M); gifts received, $1,000,000; expenditures, $1,208,195, including $1,200,000 for 91 grants (high: $498,000; low: $250) and $6,195 for 46 employee matching gifts.
Purpose and activities: Primarily local giving, with emphasis on higher education, cultural programs, and hospitals; some support for youth agencies and community funds.
Types of support awarded: Annual campaigns, seed money, emergency funds, building funds, equipment, land acquisition, employee matching gifts, internships.
Limitations: Giving primarily in MD. No grants to individuals, or for operating budgets, continuing support, or deficit financing; no loans.
Publications: Application guidelines.
Application information:
Initial approach: Full proposal
Copies of proposal: 1
Deadline(s): None
Board meeting date(s): Quarterly
Final notification: 3 months
Write: Robert W. Lindsay, Treasurer
Officers: G. Lloyd Bunting, President; C. Gordon Haines, Leslie G. Schek, Vice-Presidents; George L. Bunting, Jr., Secretary; Robert W. Lindsay, Treasurer.
Number of staff: None.
Employer Identification Number: 526041435

1445
Pearlstone (The Peggy Meyerhoff) Foundation, Inc.
100 East Pratt St.
Baltimore 21202   (301) 727-1030

Established in 1975 in Maryland.
Donor(s): Peggy Meyerhoff Pearlstone,† Monumental Corporation.
Financial data: (yr. ended 2/28/83): Assets, $2,981,459 (M); expenditures, $208,675, including $195,760 for 18 grants (high: $52,760; low: $500).
Purpose and activities: Primarily local giving; support mainly for Jewish welfare funds, youth, and the arts, with emphasis on the performing arts.
Types of support awarded: Operating budgets, continuing support, annual campaigns, seed money, emergency funds, deficit financing, building funds, endowment funds, matching funds, publications, special projects.
Limitations: Giving primarily in Baltimore, MD. No grants to individuals, or for scholarships and fellowships; no loans.
Publications: 990-PF.
Application information:
Initial approach: Letter
Copies of proposal: 3
Deadline(s): Submit proposal preferably from September to January
Board meeting date(s): August

Final notification: 60 days
Write: Richard L. Pearlstone, President
Officers: Richard L. Pearlstone, President;
Eleen P. Leary, Secretary-Treasurer.
Number of staff: None.
Employer Identification Number: 521035731

1446
PHH Group Foundation Incorporated
P.O. Box 2174
Baltimore 21203
Principal office: 11333 McCormick Rd., Hunt
Valley, MD 21031

Established in 1962 in Maryland.
Donor(s): PHH Group, Inc.
Financial data: (yr. ended 4/30/83): Assets,
$195,000 (M); gifts received, $325,000;
expenditures, $354,300, including $247,000
for 122 grants (high: $25,000; low: $100;
average: $500) and $17,300 for 104 employee
matching gifts.
Purpose and activities: Grants mainly for arts
and cultural programs, community funds,
higher education, and health.
Types of support awarded: Operating
budgets, continuing support, annual campaigns,
seed money, emergency funds, building funds,
equipment, land acquisition, employee
matching gifts, scholarship funds.
Limitations: No support for governmental,
political, or religious organizations. No grants
to individuals, or for deficit financing,
endowment funds, matching or challenge
grants, research, special projects, publications,
or conferences; no loans.
Publications: Program policy statement,
application guidelines.
Application information: Application form
required.
Initial approach: Letter
Copies of proposal: 1
Deadline(s): None
Board meeting date(s): June, September,
December, and March
Final notification: 3 months
Write: Dudley G. Davis, President
Officers: Dudley G. Davis, President; Peter
Sollenne,* First Vice-President; Barbara Novak,
Secretary; Charles G. Wise, III, Treasurer.
Directors:* Eugene Arbaugh, Don Freiert, Jr.,
Jack Gottsman, Richard E. Sells.
Number of staff: 12 full-time professional; 1
full-time support.
Employer Identification Number: 526040911

1447
Plitt (Clarence Manger & Audrey
Cordero) Trust ⊠
c/o First National Bank of Maryland
25 South Charles St., P.O. Box 1596
Baltimore 21201

Financial data: (yr. ended 10/31/83): Assets,
$4,288,533 (M); expenditures, $606,409,
including $565,000 for 15 grants (high:
$75,000; low: $20,000).
Purpose and activities: Grants to educational
institutions for student loans.
Trustees: Mary Kirgan, First National Bank of
Maryland.
Employer Identification Number: 526195778

1448
Polinger (Howard and Geraldine)
Foundation, Inc.
5530 Wisconsin Ave.
Chevy Chase 20815   (301) 657-3600

Incorporated in 1968 in Maryland.
Donor(s): Howard and Geraldine Polinger.
Financial data: (yr. ended 6/30/83): Assets,
$1,084,491 (M); gifts received, $200,000;
expenditures, $53,670, including $51,393 for
17 grants (high: $9,000; low: $1,000).
Purpose and activities: Giving primarily in the
District of Columbia for Jewish welfare funds
and cultural programs.
Limitations: Giving primarily in DC. No grants
to individuals.
Application information:
Write: Howard Polinger
Number of staff: None.
Employer Identification Number: 526078041

1449
Price (T. Rowe) Associates
Foundation ⊠
100 E. Pratt St.
Baltimore 21202

Established in 1982.
Donor(s): T. Rowe Price Associates, Inc.
Financial data: (yr. ended 12/31/82): Assets,
$169,583 (M); gifts received, $349,700;
expenditures, $193,501, including $193,401
for 167 grants (high: $27,500; low: $100).
Purpose and activities: Primarily local giving
for higher and secondary education, cultural
programs, and social services.
Types of support awarded: General purposes.
Limitations: Giving primarily in MD.
Officers: David T. Fehsenfeld, President; M.
Jenkins Cromwell, Vice-President; Mary Louise
Williams, Secretary-Treasurer.
Employer Identification Number: 521231953

1450
Rosenberg (The Henry and Ruth
Blaustein) Foundation, Inc. ⊠
Blaustein Bldg.
P.O. Box 238
Baltimore 21203

Incorporated in 1959 in Maryland.
Donor(s): Ruth Blaustein Rosenberg, Henry A.
Rosenberg, Jr.
Financial data: (yr. ended 12/31/83): Assets,
$5,223,241 (M); gifts received, $385,700;
expenditures, $411,243, including $394,125
for 60 grants (high: $204,000; low: $250).
Purpose and activities: Primarily local giving,
with emphasis on higher education, music and
other performing arts, and Jewish welfare funds.
Limitations: Giving primarily in the greater
Baltimore, MD, area.
Application information:
Initial approach: Letter
Deadline(s): None
Write: Henry A. Rosenberg, Jr.
Officers: Henry A. Rosenberg, Jr.,* President;
J. Warren Weiss, Secretary and Treasurer.
Trustees:* Ruth Blaustein Rosenberg,
Chairman; Judith R. Hoffberger, Ruth R. Marder.
Employer Identification Number: 526038384

1451
Ryan Family Charitable Foundation,
Inc., The
Teachers Bldg., Suite 214
Columbia 21044   (301) 730-6868

Incorporated in 1977 in Maryland.
Donor(s): James P. Ryan.
Financial data: (yr. ended 11/30/84): Assets,
$386,438 (M); gifts received, $1,912,500;
expenditures, $1,617,496, including
$1,551,102 for 83 grants (high: $457,000; low:
$300; average: $5,500).
Purpose and activities: Primarily local giving,
with emphasis on needs of the poor, the
developmentally disabled, and affiliates of
religious organizations.
Types of support awarded: General purposes,
seed money, special projects, scholarship funds.
Limitations: Giving primarily in Baltimore,
MD. No support for the arts. No grants to
individuals, or for building or endowment
funds, publications, or matching gifts; no loans.
Publications: Program policy statement,
application guidelines.
Application information:
Initial approach: Letter
Copies of proposal: 8
Deadline(s): None
Board meeting date(s): February, April, June,
August, October, and December
Final notification: Within 1 month after
board meeting
Write: Kay W. Martin, Executive Secretary
Officers: Linda M. Ryan, President; James P.
Ryan, Vice-President.
Directors: George Kalivrentos, Barbara M.
Ryan, Daniel M. Ryan, James P. Ryan, Jr.,
Kathleen C. Ryan, Peter D. Ryan.
Number of staff: 1 part-time professional.
Employer Identification Number: 521102104

1452
Shapiro Brothers Charitable
Foundation, Inc. ⊠
10100 Reisterstown Rd.
Owings Mills 21117

Incorporated in 1953 in Maryland.
Donor(s): Joseph Shapiro, Maryland Cup
Corporation, and others.
Financial data: (yr. ended 8/31/83): Assets,
$2,498,330 (M); gifts received, $315,600;
expenditures, $389,068, including $374,416
for 50 grants (high: $175,000; low: $25).
Purpose and activities: Primarily local giving,
with emphasis on Jewish welfare funds; grants
also for a community fund, and higher
education.
Limitations: Giving primarily in the greater
Baltimore, MD area.
Officers and Trustees: Albert Shapiro,
President; Merrill L. Bank, Vice-President; Irving
F. Cohn, Secretary; Eugene Foreman, Treasurer.
Employer Identification Number: 526037720

1453
Shapiro (Ida & Joseph) Foundation, Inc. ⌕
c/o Irving F. Cohn
9 W. Mulberry St.
Baltimore 21201

Established in 1967.
Financial data: (yr. ended 3/31/84): Assets, $442,226 (M); gifts received, $612,962; expenditures, $1,819,954, including $1,818,594 for 24 grants (high: $888,880; low: $250).
Purpose and activities: Primarily local giving for Jewish welfare funds and cultural programs.
Officers: Dr. Albert Shapiro,* President; Merrill Bank,* Vice-President; Irving F. Cohn,* Secretary; Eugene Foreman, Treasurer.
Trustees:* Helen Bank.
Employer Identification Number: 526076584

1454
Sheridan (The Thomas B. and Elizabeth M.) Foundation, Inc.
Executive Plaza II, Suite 604
11350 McCormick Rd.
Hunt Valley 21031   (301) 667-0475

Incorporated in 1962 in Maryland.
Donor(s): Thomas B. Sheridan,† Elizabeth M. Sheridan.†
Financial data: (yr. ended 12/31/84): Assets, $3,935,998 (M); expenditures, $183,764, including $113,075 for 20 grants (high: $50,000; low: $275).
Purpose and activities: Primarily local giving, with emphasis on private secondary schools and cultural organizations.
Types of support awarded: Continuing support, annual campaigns, building funds, equipment, land acquisition, endowment funds, scholarship funds.
Limitations: Giving primarily in the greater Baltimore, MD, area. No grants to individuals or for matching gifts; no loans.
Publications: Application guidelines, program policy statement.
Application information: Application form required.
  Initial approach: Letter
  Copies of proposal: 1
  Deadline(s): None
  Board meeting date(s): Monthly
  Write: Mrs. Elizabeth S. Sinclair, Executive Director
Officers and Trustees: James L. Sinclair, President; Elizabeth S. Sinclair, Vice-President and Executive Director; John B. Sinclair, Secretary; J. Robert Kenealy, Treasurer; L. Patrick Deering.
Number of staff: 1 full-time professional; 1 part-time professional; 1 part-time support.
Employer Identification Number: 526075270

1455
Stewart (J. C.) Memorial Trust
8901 Annapolis Rd.
Lanham 20706   (301) 459-4200

Trust established in 1973 in Maryland.
Donor(s): Anna L. Stewart.†

Financial data: (yr. ended 11/30/83): Assets, $4,728,544 (M); expenditures, $326,511, including $75,500 for 1 grant, $6,000 for 2 grants to individuals and $153,600 for 81 loans.
Purpose and activities: Local giving primarily for a legal services agency; support also for student loans to Maryland residents.
Types of support awarded: Student aid.
Limitations: Giving primarily in MD.
Application information:
  Write: Robert S. Hoyert, Trustee
Trustees: Robert S. Hoyert, Bill L. Yoho.
Employer Identification Number: 237357104

1456
Straus (The Aaron) and Lillie Straus Foundation, Inc. ▼
101 West Mt. Royal Ave.
Baltimore 21201   (301) 752-6209

Incorporated in 1926 in Maryland.
Donor(s): Aaron Straus,† Lillie Straus.†
Financial data: (yr. ended 12/31/83): Assets, $30,500,572 (M); expenditures, $3,158,800, including $1,726,638 for 55 grants (high: $732,807; low: $100; average: $1,500-$100,000).
Purpose and activities: Broad purposes; primarily local giving, with emphasis on Jewish welfare funds, medicine and public health, education, community development, and social services.
Types of support awarded: Seed money, research.
Limitations: Giving primarily in Baltimore, MD, metropolitan area. No grants to individuals, or for capital or endowment funds; no loans.
Application information:
  Initial approach: Full proposal
  Copies of proposal: 2
  Deadline(s): February 1, May 1, August 1, and November 1
  Board meeting date(s): March, June, September, and December
  Final notification: 7 days
  Write: Jan Rivitz, Executive Director
Officers: S. Meyer Barnett,* President; Lewis Hamburger,* Vice-President; Alfred I. Coplan,* Secretary; Bessie Urwick,* Treasurer; Jan Rivitz, Executive Director.
Trustees:* Henry L. Abraham, Richard M. Barnett.
Number of staff: 1 part-time professional; 2 part-time support.
Employer Identification Number: 520563083

1457
Tauber Foundation, Inc. ⌕
5401 Westbard Ave.
Bethesda 20816

Established in 1958.
Financial data: (yr. ended 12/31/83): Assets, $3,420,608 (M); gifts received, $64,150; expenditures, $114,759, including $112,738 for 9 grants (high: $52,888; low: $100).
Purpose and activities: Support for Jewish welfare funds.
Types of support awarded: General purposes, building funds.

Officers: Laszlo N. Tauber, President; Alfred I. Tauber, Vice-President and Secretary; Ingrid D. Tauber, Treasurer.
Employer Identification Number: 526054648

1458
Thalheimer (The Alvin and Fanny Blaustein) Foundation, Inc. ▼ ⌕
Blaustein Bldg.
P.O. Box 238
Baltimore 21203   (301) 685-4230

Incorporated in 1958 in Maryland.
Donor(s): American Trading and Production Corporation.
Financial data: (yr. ended 2/28/83): Assets, $5,269,135 (M); gifts received, $268,700; expenditures, $521,386, including $511,000 for 7 grants (high: $280,525; low: $7,000).
Purpose and activities: Charitable purposes; primarily local giving, with emphasis on Jewish welfare funds, art education, and the arts.
Types of support awarded: General purposes.
Limitations: Giving primarily in Baltimore, MD. No grants to individuals.
Application information:
  Initial approach: Letter
  Deadline(s): None
  Board meeting date(s): 6 times a year
  Write: Louis B. Thalheimer, President
Officers: Louis B. Thalheimer,* President; Morton K. Blaustein, Henry A. Rosenberg, Jr., Vice-Presidents; J. Warren Weiss, Secretary and Treasurer.
Trustees:* Marjorie Thalheimer Coleman, Ruth B. Rosenberg, Elizabeth T. Wachs.
Number of staff: None.
Employer Identification Number: 526038383

1459
Town Creek Foundation, Inc.
P.O. Box 159
Oxford 21654

Established in 1981 in Maryland.
Donor(s): Edmund A. Stanley, Jr.
Financial data: (yr. ended 12/31/84): Assets, $12,126,835 (M); gifts received, $645,000; expenditures, $750,574, including $639,000 for 26 grants (high: $150,000; low: $3,000; average: $3,000-$150,000).
Purpose and activities: Support for local and national environmental protection, and public policy organizations.
Types of support awarded: Operating budgets, continuing support, seed money, research, publications, conferences and seminars, special projects.
Limitations: Giving primarily in MD and the Washington, DC, area. No grants to individuals, or for annual campaigns, emergency funds, deficit financing, building funds, equipment and materials, land acquisition, renovation projects, endowments, matching grants, consulting services, technical assistance, or program-related investments; no loans.
Publications: Informational brochure, application guidelines, program policy statement.
Application information:

Initial approach: Letter of inquiry
Deadline(s): Submit proposal preferably between March and October; deadline November 1
Board meeting date(s): March and October
Final notification: 2 months
Write: Edmund A. Stanley, Jr., President
Officers and Trustees: Edmund A. Stanley, Jr., President; Jennifer Stanley, Vice-President; Philip E.L. Dietz, Jr., Secretary-Treasurer; Lisa A. Stanley.
Number of staff: None.
Employer Identification Number: 521227030

1460
U.S.F. & G. Foundation, The
100 Light St.
Baltimore 21202   (301) 547-3000

Foundation established in 1980 in Maryland.
Donor(s): United States Fidelity and Guaranty Company.
Financial data: (yr. ended 12/31/83): Assets, $597,418 (M); gifts received, $581,000; expenditures, $953,015, including $948,832 for 37 grants (high: $281,000; low: $200; average: $5,000-$10,000).
Purpose and activities: Primarily local giving; support largely for a community fund, arts and cultural programs, and higher education.
Types of support awarded: Operating budgets, continuing support, annual campaigns, building funds, equipment, scholarship funds, special projects, endowment funds.
Limitations: Giving primarily in MD. No grants to individuals (except for scholarships), or for seed money, emergency funds, deficit financing, land acquisition, matching gifts, research, publications, or conferences; no loans.
Publications: Program policy statement.
Application information: Application form required.
Initial approach: Proposal
Copies of proposal: 1
Deadline(s): None
Board meeting date(s): As required
Final notification: 3 to 4 weeks
Write: Jack Moseley, President
Officers and Trustees:* Jack Moseley,* President; Paul J. Scheel,* Vice-President; William F. Spliedt, Secretary-Treasurer.
Number of staff: None.
Employer Identification Number: 521197155

1461
Warfield (Anna Emory) Memorial Fund, Inc.
103 West Monument St.
Baltimore 21201   (301) 547-0612

Incorporated in 1928 in Maryland.
Donor(s): S. Davies Warfield.†
Financial data: (yr. ended 12/31/84): Assets, $2,092,627 (M); expenditures, $135,328, including $121,750 for 46 grants to individuals (high: $3,250; low: $250).
Purpose and activities: Organized exclusively to assist aged and dependent women, primarily locally.
Types of support awarded: Grants to individuals.

Limitations: Giving primarily in the Baltimore, MD, metropolitan area. No grants for capital or endowment funds, general support, matching gifts, scholarships and fellowships, or research; no loans.
Publications: Application guidelines.
Application information: Application form required.
Initial approach: Telephone
Copies of proposal: 1
Deadline(s): None
Board meeting date(s): April and October
Final notification: 2 months
Write: Mrs. Thelma K. O'Neal, Secretary
Officers: Charles B. Reeves, Jr.,* President; Braxton D. Mitchell,* Vice-President; Thelma K. O'Neal, Secretary; Michael E. Yaggy,* Treasurer.
Trustees:* Mrs. W. Page Dame, Jr., Mrs. William E. Grose, Louis W. Hargrave, Mrs. Thomas H. Maddux, Mrs. William F. Schmick, Jr., Mrs. John R. Sherwood, William C. Trimble.
Number of staff: 1 part-time support.
Employer Identification Number: 520785672

1462
Wasserman (George) Foundation, Inc.
5454 Wisconsin Ave., Suite 1300
Chevy Chase 20815

Established in 1948.
Donor(s): George Wasserman.†
Financial data: (yr. ended 12/31/83): Assets, $2,295,439 (M); expenditures, $228,645, including $222,200 for 34 grants (high: $75,000; low: $50).
Purpose and activities: Grants primarily for Jewish welfare funds, theological studies, and temple support.
Officers: Louis C. Grossberg, President and Treasurer; C. Richard Byeda, Julius I. Fox, Vice-Presidents; Solomon Grossberg, Secretary.
Employer Identification Number: 526035888

1463
Weinberg (The Harry and Jeanette) Foundation, Incorporated
5518 Baltimore National Pike
Baltimore 21228

Incorporated in 1959 in Maryland.
Donor(s): Harry Weinberg.
Financial data: (yr. ended 2/29/84): Assets, $7,134,098 (M); gifts received, $1,908,270; expenditures, $459,713, including $446,004 for 20 grants (high: $303,000; low: $50).
Purpose and activities: Broad purposes; giving largely in Hawaii; Baltimore, Maryland; and Scranton, Pennsylvania, with emphasis on Jewish welfare funds; grants also for temple support, and higher education.
Limitations: Giving primarily in HI; Baltimore, MD; and Scranton, PA.
Officers and Directors: Harry Weinberg, President and Treasurer; Nathan Weinberg, Vice-President and Secretary; Jeanette Weinberg, William Weinberg, Joel Winegarden.
Employer Identification Number: 526037034

1464
Wilson (Thomas) Sanitarium for Children of Baltimore City
Stegman & Associates
36 S. Charles St.
Baltimore 21201

Trust established in 1879 in Maryland.
Donor(s): Thomas Wilson.†
Financial data: (yr. ended 1/31/83): Assets, $1,826,705 (M); expenditures, $127,639, including $110,194 for 9 grants (high: $22,500; low: $1,000).
Purpose and activities: Local giving, with emphasis on hospitals, medical and educational research, and social services, largely relating to children.
Limitations: Giving primarily in MD.
Application information:
Write: Charles L. Stout, President
Officers: Charles L. Stout, President; Jean Stifler, Vice-President; William C. Trimble, Jr., Secretary; Allan P. Hoblitzell, Treasurer.
Trustees: Edward C. Dunn, Guy T.O. Holiday, B. Carter Randall, Blanchard Randall, William C. Whitridge, Ralph N. Willis, David E. Wood.
Employer Identification Number: 526044885

1465
Wye Institute, Inc.
Cheston-on-Wye
Queenstown 21658   (301) 827-7401

Incorporated in 1963 in Maryland.
Donor(s): Arthur A. Houghton, Jr.
Financial data: (yr. ended 12/31/83): Assets, $4,570,677 (M); gifts received, $200,000; expenditures, $157,521, including $19,797 for 6 grants (high: $8,883; low: $125) and $48,231 for foundation-administered programs.
Purpose and activities: A private operating foundation to assist in the advancement of local education, culture, and the economy of the eastern shore of Maryland.
Limitations: Giving limited to the eastern shore of MD. No grants to individuals.
Application information:
Board meeting date(s): Semiannually
Write: James G. Nelson, President
Officers: James G. Nelson, President and Manager; Rowland Stebbins, III, Vice-President and Treasurer; Richard Garrett, Secretary.
Trustees:* Arthur A. Houghton, Jr., Chairman; Sylvia H. Garrett, Nina R. Houghton, John R. Kimberly, John F. White.
Number of staff: 6.
Employer Identification Number: 520799244

MASSACHUSETTS

1466
Acushnet Foundation, The
P.O. Box 916
New Bedford 02742   (617) 997-2811

Trust established in 1953 in Massachusetts.
Donor(s): Acushnet Company.
Financial data: (yr. ended 6/30/84): Assets, $3,577,693 (M); expenditures, $194,403, including $172,530 for 44 grants (high: $38,750; low: $250; average: $1,000-$5,000).
Purpose and activities: Primarily local giving for community funds, hospitals, higher education, and youth agencies.
Types of support awarded: Continuing support, annual campaigns, seed money, emergency funds, building funds, professorships, scholarship funds.
Limitations: Giving limited to the Greater New Bedford, MA area. No grants to individuals, or for endowment funds, operating budgets, deficit financing, or matching gifts.
Application information:
  Initial approach: Letter
  Copies of proposal: 1
  Board meeting date(s): As required
  Final notification: 4 to 6 weeks
  Write: Richard B. Young, Trustee
Trustees: William Bommer, Graeme L. Flanders, John T. Ludes, Thomas C. Weaver, Richard B. Young.
Number of staff: 1 part-time support.
Employer Identification Number: 046032197

1467
Adams (Frank W. and Carl S.) Memorial Fund
c/o The First National Bank of Boston
P.O. Box 1890
Boston 02105   (617) 434-5669

Trust established in 1955 in Massachusetts.
Donor(s): Charles E. Adams,† Caroline J. Adams.†
Financial data: (yr. ended 5/31/84): Assets, $5,202,610 (M); expenditures, $395,984, including $350,298 for grants.
Purpose and activities: One half of the net income is distributed for general purposes, entirely within the city of Boston, in the fields of health, welfare, the humanities, and education; the balance of income is designated to assist needy and deserving students selected by Massachusetts Institute of Technology and the Harvard Medical School.
Types of support awarded: General purposes, scholarship funds, building funds, operating budgets.
Limitations: Giving limited to the city of Boston, MA.
Application information:
  Initial approach: Full proposal
  Copies of proposal: 1
  Deadline(s): Last day of month prior to board meetings

Board meeting date(s): January, April, July, and October
Write: Miss Sharon M. Driscoll, Trust Officer
Trustee: The First National Bank of Boston (Miss Sharon M. Driscoll, Trust Officer).
Employer Identification Number: 046011995

1468
Alden (George I.) Trust ▼
370 Main St., Suite 1250
Worcester 01608   (617) 757-9243

Trust established in 1912 in Massachusetts.
Donor(s): George I. Alden.†
Financial data: (yr. ended 12/31/83): Assets, $51,857,270 (M); expenditures, $2,417,868, including $2,144,871 for 150 grants (high: $100,000; low: $500).
Purpose and activities: For the promotion of education in schools, colleges or other educational institutions, with a preference for industrial, vocational or professional education, for the promotion of the work carried on by the Young Men's Christian Association, or its successors, either in this country or abroad, for the benefit of the Worcester Trade Schools and the Worcester Polytechnic Institute; some support also for cultural programs.
Types of support awarded: Annual campaigns, seed money, emergency funds, building funds, equipment, land acquisition, research, publications, conferences and seminars, scholarship funds, internships, professorships, matching funds, general purposes.
Limitations: No grants to individuals or for endowment funds; no loans.
Publications: Program policy statement, application guidelines.
Application information:
  Copies of proposal: 1
  Board meeting date(s): Bimonthly beginning in January
  Write: Paris Fletcher, Chairman
Trustees: Paris Fletcher, Chairman; Robert G. Hess, Vice-Chairman; George W. Hazzard, Secretary; Francis H. Dewey III, Treasurer.
Number of staff: None.
Employer Identification Number: 046023784

1469
Association for the Relief of Aged Women of New Bedford ⌁
P.O. Box B939
New Bedford 02741

Established in 1866.
Financial data: (yr. ended 3/31/83): Assets, $3,529,964 (M); gifts received, $35,625; expenditures, $166,526, including $142,651 for 21 grants to individuals.
Purpose and activities: A private operating foundation; grants to needy aged women in New Bedford, Massachusetts.
Types of support awarded: Grants to individuals.
Limitations: Giving limited to New Bedford, MA.
Officers: Mrs. Edgar Earle, President; Mrs. Philip C. Douglas, Secretary; Mrs. Frank Simpson, Treasurer.
Employer Identification Number: 046056367

1470
Babson (The Paul and Edith) Foundation ⌁
28 State St.
Boston 02109   (617) 523-5700

Trust established in 1957 in Massachusetts.
Donor(s): Paul T. Babson.†
Financial data: (yr. ended 12/31/82): Assets, $2,867,284 (M); expenditures, $125,791, including $112,500 for 53 grants (high: $10,000; low: $200).
Purpose and activities: Broad purposes; primarily local giving, with emphasis on education, health, and youth agencies.
Limitations: Giving primarily in MA. No grants to individuals, or for endowment funds.
Application information:
  Initial approach: Letter
  Copies of proposal: 1
  Deadline(s): Submit proposal in September; deadline September 30
  Board meeting date(s): October or November
  Write: Richard M. Nichols, Trustee
Trustees: Edith Y. Babson, James R. Nichols, Richard M. Nichols.
Employer Identification Number: 046037891

1471
Babson-Webber-Mustard Fund ⌁
c/o Hutchins & Wheeler
1 Boston Place
Boston 02108

Established in 1962 in Massachusetts.
Financial data: (yr. ended 12/31/82): Assets, $1,542,575 (M); expenditures, $89,842, including $71,100 for 125 grants to individuals (high: $800; low: $250).
Purpose and activities: Primarily local giving to aid needy individuals.
Types of support awarded: Grants to individuals.
Limitations: Giving primarily in Boston, MA.
Trustees: Robert S. Hoffman, Jessie M. Putman, John O. Rhome.
Employer Identification Number: 042307820

1472
Bacon (Charles F.) Trust ⌁
c/o Bank of New England
28 State St.
Boston 02107   (617) 973-1798

Trust established in 1928 in Massachusetts.
Donor(s): Charles F. Bacon.†
Financial data: (yr. ended 12/31/82): Assets, $1,493,230 (M); expenditures, $89,010, including $59,100 for 13 grants (high: $10,000; low: $1,000) and $17,000 for 9 grants to individuals.
Purpose and activities: One third of grants to assist needy retired employees of Conrad & Chandler Company; one third to local charitable organizations for elderly women; and one third to other local charitable organizations.
Types of support awarded: Grants to individuals, general purposes, seed money, matching funds, building funds, equipment, land acquisition.
Limitations: Giving primarily in MA.

Publications: Application guidelines.
Application information:
Initial approach: Letter
Copies of proposal: 1
Deadline(s): Submit proposal preferably in
November; deadline December 1
Board meeting date(s): February
Final notification: 2 months
Write: John M. Dolan, Senior Trust Officer
Trustee: Bank of New England (John M. Dolan,
Senior Trust Officer).
Number of staff: None.
Employer Identification Number: 046024467

1473
Bank of Boston Corporation Charitable Foundation ▼

(formerly First National Boston Corporation
Foundation)
100 Federal St.
Boston 02110   (617) 434-2171

Trust established in 1961 in Massachusetts for
First National Bank of Boston Charitable
Foundation; absorbed into First National Boston
Corporation Foundation in 1983; present name
adopted in 1983.
Donor(s): Bank of Boston Corporation.
Financial data: (yr. ended 12/31/84): Assets,
$6,000,000 (M); gifts received, $5,000,000;
expenditures, $1,450,510, including
$1,269,044 for 185 grants (high: $50,000; low:
$500; average: $500-$20,000) and $181,466
for 1,404 employee matching gifts.
Purpose and activities: Broad purposes; giving
limited to local organizations with impact on
the inner city, education, health, welfare, and
the arts and culture. In 1984, contributions
directly from corporate funds totaled an
additional $684,486, including $181,466 in
employee matching gifts.
Types of support awarded: Annual
campaigns, emergency funds, building funds,
land acquisition, general purposes, matching
funds, operating budgets, special projects,
continuing support.
Limitations: Giving limited to metropolitan
Boston, MA area, with emphasis on Suffolk
County and inner-city organizations. No
support for religious or partisan causes or
nationally organized health programs. No
grants to individuals, or for endowment funds,
research, fund-raising events, or scholarships
and fellowships; no loans.
Publications: Application guidelines.
Application information:
Initial approach: Full proposal or letter of
inquiry
Copies of proposal: 1
Deadline(s): None
Board meeting date(s): March, June,
September, and December
Final notification: 2 months
Write: Judith Kidd, Coordinator, Corporate
Contributions
Trustees: William L. Brown, T. McLean Griffin,
Richard D. Hill.
Number of staff: 2 full-time professional.
Employer Identification Number: 046013168

1474
Bayrd (Adelaide Breed) Foundation

c/o John A. Plummer
Eight Wilson Rd.
Stoneham 02180   (617) 438-6619

Incorporated in 1927 in Massachusetts.
Donor(s): Frank A. Bayrd,† Blanche S. Bayrd.†
Financial data: (yr. ended 12/31/84): Assets,
$1,112,012 (M); gifts received, $190,000;
expenditures, $269,442, including $216,900
for 61 grants (high: $30,000; low: $150).
Purpose and activities: To aid those causes in
which the donor's mother was interested;
primarily supports local cultural activities .
Types of support awarded: Operating
budgets, annual campaigns, emergency funds,
building funds, equipment, endowment funds,
research, special projects.
Limitations: Giving primarily in the greater
Boston, MA, area, with emphasis on Malden.
No support for national or out-of-state
organizations. No grants to individuals, or for
matching or challenge grants, demonstration
projects, conferences, or publications; no loans.
Publications: Annual report.
Application information:
Initial approach: Full proposal
Deadline(s): Submit proposal preferably in
January or December; deadline February 15
Board meeting date(s): First Tuesday in
February; special meetings usually held in
March and in the fall to consider grant
requests
Final notification: Generally in April or May
Write: John A. Plummer, President
Officers and Trustees: John A. Plummer,
President; Russell E. Watts, Treasurer and Clerk;
Florence C. Burns, Katharine W. Hughes, C.
Henry Kezer, Susan C. Mansur, William H.
Marshall, Gaynor K. Rutherford, H. Allen
Stevens.
Number of staff: 1 full-time support; 1 part-
time support.
Employer Identification Number: 046051258

1475
Beveridge (The Frank Stanley) Foundation, Inc. ▼

333 Western Ave.
Westfield 01085   (413) 562-3631

Trust established in 1947 in Massachusetts;
incorporated in 1956.
Donor(s): Frank Stanley Beveridge,† Stanhome
Inc.
Financial data: (yr. ended 12/31/83): Assets,
$14,496,388 (M); gifts received, $21,000;
expenditures, $1,093,200, including
$1,021,544 for 85 grants (high: $350,000; low:
$25).
Purpose and activities: A portion of the
income designated for maintenance of a local
park; the balance for general local giving, with
emphasis on higher education, youth agencies,
and community development.
Types of support awarded: Operating
budgets, seed money, emergency funds,
equipment, building funds, land acquisition,
publications, conferences and seminars,
matching funds.

Limitations: Giving primarily in Hampden and
Hampshire counties, MA. No grants to
individuals, or for endowment funds,
scholarships, or fellowships; no loans.
Application information:
Initial approach: Letter
Copies of proposal: 1
Deadline(s): March and September
Board meeting date(s): April and October
Write: Theresa V. Gusek, Administrator
Officers: Homer G. Perkins,* President; Evelyn
Beveridge Russell,* Secretary; Latimer B. Eddy,
Treasurer.
Directors:* Philip Caswell, Pamela Everets,
Joseph J. Geehern, Joseph B. Palmer, H.L.
Tower.
Employer Identification Number: 046032164

1476
Bird Companies Charitable Foundation, Inc. ⌑

Washington St.
East Walpole 02032   (617) 668-2500

Incorporated in 1967 in Massachusetts.
Donor(s): Bird & Son, Inc., Bird Machine
Company, Inc.
Financial data: (yr. ended 12/31/81): Assets,
$1,162,068 (M); expenditures, $550,998,
including $475,289 for 277 grants (high:
$36,250; low: $10).
Purpose and activities: Broad purposes; grant
emphasis on community development,
education, cultural programs, and natural
resources. Additional consideration to projects
related to corporate locations as determined by
local committees. Emphasis on seed monies.
Types of support awarded: Seed money.
Limitations: Giving primarily in MA. No grants
to individuals.
Publications: Program policy statement,
application guidelines.
Application information:
Initial approach: Letter, telephone, or
proposal
Copies of proposal: 1
Board meeting date(s): February, May,
August, and October
Final notification: 1 to 6 months
Officers: Robert Jenkins,* President; Marilyn A.
Buffington, Secretary; Ronald G. Babcock,
Treasurer.
Directors:* Perkins Bass, Robert P. Bass, Jr.,
Charles S. Bird, David Bird, Richard P.
Chapman, Weston Howland, Jr., Calvin A.
King, Mary Bird Phillips, Charles W. Schmidt.
Employer Identification Number: 237067725

1477
Birmingham Foundation ⌑

c/o Paul Mark Ryan, Trustee
28 State St., Suite 3780
Boston 02109

Donor(s): John P. Birmingham.†
Financial data: (yr. ended 12/31/82): Assets,
$4,476,672 (M); expenditures, $301,335,
including $278,100 for 35 grants (high:
$50,000; low: $200).

Purpose and activities: Primarily local giving for Roman Catholic welfare funds and secondary education; some support also for other social agencies.
Limitations: Giving primarily in MA.
Trustees: Leona C. Birmingham, Paul J. Birmingham, Paul Mark Ryan.
Employer Identification Number: 046050748

1478
Blake (Curtis) Foundation
33 Mill Rd.
Longmeadow 01106   (413) 567-1574

Established in 1972 in Massachusetts.
Donor(s): Curtis Blake.
Financial data: (yr. ended 12/31/82): Assets, $1,404,776 (M); expenditures, $164,645, including $149,450 for 17 grants (high: $75,000; low: $100).
Purpose and activities: Primarily local giving, with emphasis on higher education, museuems, and programs for the learning disabled.
Limitations: Giving primarily in MA. No grants to individuals.
Application information:
  Initial approach: Letter
  Write: Curtis L. Blake, Trustee
Trustees: Curtis L. Blake, Alfred W. Fuller.
Employer Identification Number: 237204498

1479
Blake (S. P.) Foundation ☐
734 Bliss Rd.
Longmeadow 01106   (413) 543-2400

Established in 1972 in Massachusetts.
Donor(s): S. Prestley Blake.
Financial data: (yr. ended 12/31/82): Assets, $2,604,140 (M); expenditures, $292,515, including $284,347 for 30 grants (high: $100,000; low: $10).
Purpose and activities: Educational purposes; giving primarily in Massachusetts, with emphasis on higher education and historic preservation, including a museum.
Limitations: Giving primarily in MA. No grants to individuals.
Application information:
  Initial approach: Letter
  Copies of proposal: 1
  Board meeting date(s): Monthly
  Final notification: 2 months
  Write: S. Prestley Blake, Trustee
Trustees: Benson Blake, S. Prestley Blake.
Employer Identification Number: 237185871

1480
Blanchard Foundation, The
c/o Boston Safe Deposit and Trust Company
One Boston Place
Boston 02106   (617) 722-7340

Trust established in 1943 in Massachusetts.
Donor(s): Arthur F. Blanchard.†
Financial data: (yr. ended 12/31/84): Assets, $6,589,020 (M); expenditures, $353,125, including $343,125 for 12 grants (high: $100,000; low: $5,000).

Purpose and activities: Broad purposes; grants restricted to charitable purposes within Massachusetts, with focus primarily on the needs of metropolitan Boston, and principally in the areas of community development, human services, and education.
Types of support awarded: General purposes, seed money, emergency funds, building funds, equipment, land acquisition, research, special projects, matching funds.
Limitations: Giving limited to MA, with emphasis on the Boston metropolitan area. No support for health or hospital projects, or programs for children or youth. No grants to individuals, or for endowment funds, scholarships, or fellowships; no loans.
Publications: Program policy statement, application guidelines.
Application information:
  Initial approach: Proposal
  Copies of proposal: 1
  Deadline(s): February 1, May 1, August 1, and November 1
  Board meeting date(s): March, June, September, and December
  Final notification: 3 months
  Write: Jane C. Williams, Vice-President
Trustee: Boston Safe Deposit and Trust Company (Jane C. Williams, Vice-President).
Number of staff: None.
Employer Identification Number: 046093374

1481
Boston Fatherless & Widows Society
c/o Goodwin, Procter & Hoar
28 State St.
Boston 02109

Established in 1837 in Massachusetts.
Financial data: (yr. ended 11/30/83): Assets, $2,547,710 (M); gifts received, $13,900; expenditures, $124,251, including $101,875 for 14 grants (high: $4,000; low: $25).
Purpose and activities: Local giving primarily for aid to indigent widows and orphans.
Types of support awarded: Grants to individuals.
Limitations: Giving limited to the Boston, MA area.
Officers: Mrs. John S. Clapp,* President; Mrs. H. Stephen Kott,* Vice-President; Mrs. Vernon S. Dick,* Secretary; Richard Wengren, Treasurer.
Trustees:* Mrs. Robert B. Bachman, Mrs. David T. Dinwoody, Mrs. Urban H. Eversole, Mrs. John M. Gepson, Mrs. Clinton H. Shattuck, Mrs. Robert H. Traylor.
Employer Identification Number: 046006506

1482
Boston Foundation ▼
(formerly Permanent Charity Fund of Boston)
One Boston Place, Rm. 3005
Boston 02108   (617) 723-7415

Community foundation established in 1915 in Massachusetts by agreement and declaration of trust; incorporated in 1917.

Financial data: (yr. ended 6/30/84): Assets, $115,292,184 (M); gifts received, $8,652,144; expenditures, $10,401,867, including $8,649,620 for 637 grants (high: $250,000; low: $50; average: $5,000-$50,000).
Purpose and activities: To support local health, welfare, educational, cultural, and recreational programs and institutions; grants for start-up expenses of new or experimental programs of both established and new institutions, as well as for capital needs and for coordination and planning projects.
Types of support awarded: Building funds, emergency funds, equipment, land acquisition, matching funds, research, seed money, special projects.
Limitations: Giving limited to metropolitan Boston, MA. No support for religious purposes. No grants to individuals, or for general operating funds, medical, scientific, or academic research; publications, films, scholarships, conferences, or multi-million dollar capital campaigns with a national focus; no loans.
Publications: Annual report, program policy statement, application guidelines, newsletter.
Application information:
  Initial approach: Letter or full proposal
  Copies of proposal: 1
  Deadline(s): 10 weeks prior to board meetings
  Board meeting date(s): February, April, June, September, and December
  Write: Anna Faith Jones, Director
Officers: Dwight L. Allison, Jr.,* President; William W. Wolbach,* Vice-President; Anna Faith Jones, Secretary-Treasurer and Director.
Committee Members:* Carol R. Goldberg, G. Rosalyn Johnson, Msgr. Francis J. Lally, Gael Mahony, Lawrence T. Perera, David R. Pokross, Sr., Muriel S. Snowden, John Larkin Thompson, Paul N. Ylvisaker.
Trustee Banks: Bank of New England, Bank of Boston, Boston Safe Deposit and Trust Company, Shawmut Bank, State Street Bank.
Number of staff: 4 full-time professional; 1 part-time professional; 4 full-time support.
Employer Identification Number: 042104021

1483
Boston Globe Foundation, The ▼
The Boston Globe Bldg.
Boston 02107   (617) 929-2895

Incorporated in 1981 in Massachusetts.
Donor(s): Affiliated Publications, Inc.
Financial data: (yr. ended 11/30/82): Assets, $978,499 (M); gifts received, $784,550; expenditures, $773,483, including $755,254 for 263 grants (high: $140,000; low: $25) and $5,370 for employee matching gifts.
Purpose and activities: Primarily local giving, with emphasis on community services, including a community fund, cultural programs, the arts, and education; support also for summer camps and communications organizations.
Types of support awarded: Employee matching gifts, operating budgets, special projects, building funds.

Limitations: Giving primarily in the Boston, MA, metropolitan area. No grants to individuals.
Publications: Annual report, application guidelines.
Application information: Very detailed proposal requirements are provided in the Guidelines brochure.
   Deadline(s): None
   Board meeting date(s): In 1984, January, March, April, May, June, September, October, and November
   Final notification: After November meeting
   Write: George M. Collins, Jr., Exec. Director
Officers and Directors: William O. Taylor, President; John Giuggio, Treasurer; George M. Collins, Jr., Executive Director; Dexter D. Eure, Catherine E.C. Henn, John I. Taylor, William Davis Taylor.
Number of staff: 2.
Employer Identification Number: 042731195

1484
Boynton (John W.) Fund
c/o State St. Bank and Trust Company
P.O. Box 351
Boston 02101   (617) 654-3343

Trust established in 1950 in Massachusetts.
Donor(s): Dora C. Boynton.†
Financial data: (yr. ended 12/31/84): Assets, $1,420,183 (M); expenditures, $81,320, including $63,690 for 34 grants (high: $3,000; low: $950).
Purpose and activities: Grants principally to organizations in eastern Massachusetts serving low income elderly and the handicapped; special consideration also to the town of Athol, Massachusetts and a limited number of other grants.
Types of support awarded: Operating budgets, seed money, building funds, general purposes, equipment.
Limitations: Giving primarily in eastern MA, with emphasis on Athol, MA. No grants to individuals, or for endowment funds, research, scholarships, fellowships, or matching gifts; no loans.
Publications: Application guidelines.
Application information:
   Initial approach: Proposal
   Copies of proposal: 1
   Deadline(s): March 15, June 15, September 15, or December 15
   Board meeting date(s): April, July, October, and January
   Final notification: 3 months
   Write: Deborah A. Robbins, Vice-President, State Street Bank and Trust Company
Trustee: State Street Bank and Trust Company.
Number of staff: 1 part-time professional; 1 part-time support.
Employer Identification Number: 046036706

1485
Braitmayer Foundation, The
c/o North American Management Corp.
28 State St., Suite 3854
Boston 02109

Trust established in 1964 in Massachusetts.

Donor(s): Marian S. Braitmayer.
Financial data: (yr. ended 12/31/82): Assets, $1,715,856 (M); expenditures, $141,583, including $121,000 for 22 grants (high: $12,000; low: $500).
Purpose and activities: Support primarily in New England for the advancement of higher education, particularly in developing techniques of instruction in the humanities and liberal arts.
Limitations: No grants for building or endowment funds, scholarships, fellowships, or matching gifts; no loans.
Application information:
   Initial approach: Letter
   Copies of proposal: 1
   Board meeting date(s): Annually and as required
   Write: John W. Braitmayer or Anne B. Webb, Trustees
Trustees: John W. Braitmayer, Karen L. Braitmayer, Anne B. Webb, R. Davis Webb, Jr.
Employer Identification Number: 046112131

1486
Brandegee Charitable Foundation
50 Federal St., Rm. 520
Boston 02110   (617) 423-7157

Trust established in 1949 in Massachusetts.
Donor(s): Mary B. Brandegee.†
Financial data: (yr. ended 12/31/82): Assets, $1,200,000 (M); expenditures, $77,306, including $7,000 for 2 grants (high: $5,000; low: $2,000; average: $2,500) and $29,257 for 1 foundation-administered program.
Purpose and activities: Broad purposes; almost all expenditures currently to maintain Mary B. Brandegee Mansion for leasing space to charitable organizations; support also for a school and a nature preservation fund.
Types of support awarded: Operating budgets, annual campaigns, research, special projects.
Limitations: Giving limited to the Boston, MA, area. No grants to individuals, or for continuing support, seed money, emergency funds, deficit financing, matching gifts, capital or endowment funds, scholarships or fellowships, demonstration projects, publications or conferences; no loans.
Application information:
   Initial approach: Letter
   Deadline(s): None
   Board meeting date(s): As required
   Final notification: 1 month
Trustees: Martina L. Albright, Charles S. Boit, Ernest E. Monrad.
Number of staff: 1 full-time support; 1 part-time support.
Employer Identification Number: 042103930

1487
Bright (Horace O.) Charitable Fund
c/o Boston Safe Deposit and Trust Company
One Boston Place
Boston 02106   (617) 722-7336

Trust established in 1952 in Massachusetts.
Donor(s): Horace O. Bright.

Financial data: (yr. ended 12/31/82): Assets, $1,365,517 (M); expenditures, $89,293, including $87,000 for 18 grants (high: $10,000; low: $1,000).
Purpose and activities: Grants largely committed to charities of personal interest to the trustees, with some emphasis on education and the environment.
Limitations: No grants to individuals, or for scholarships, fellowships, or matching gifts; no loans.
Application information:
   Initial approach: Full proposal
   Copies of proposal: 1
   Deadline(s): February, May, August, and November
   Board meeting date(s): March, June, September, and December
   Write: A. Lyman Parson, Trust Officer
Trustees: Horace O. Bright, Edward W. Weld.
Employer Identification Number: 046013966

1488
Cabot Corporation Foundation, Inc. ▼
125 High St.
Boston 02110   (617) 423-6000

Incorporated in 1953 in Massachusetts.
Donor(s): Cabot Corporation.
Financial data: (yr. ended 9/30/83): Assets, $1,843,635 (M); gifts received, $1,000,000; expenditures, $1,436,812, including $1,434,370 for 183 grants (high: $60,000; low: $15; average: $500-$50,000).
Purpose and activities: Broad purposes; emphasis on science and technology, higher education, including matching employee gifts, community development, community funds, and public policy.
Types of support awarded: Annual campaigns, seed money, building funds, equipment, land acquisition, scholarship funds, fellowships, special projects, matching funds, general purposes, employee matching gifts.
Limitations: Giving primarily in communities near Cabot corporate installations in TX; Douglas County, IL; Howard and Elkhart counties, IN; Henderson County, KY; St. Mary Parish and Evangeline Parish, LA; Reading and Boyertown, PA; Kanawha County, West Virginia; and Boston, MA. No grants to individuals.
Publications: Annual report, application guidelines.
Application information:
   Initial approach: Letter or full proposal
   Copies of proposal: 1
   Deadline(s): 1 month prior to meetings
   Board meeting date(s): March, June, September, and December
   Final notification: 3 months
   Write: Ruth C. Scheer, Executive Director
Officers: Thomas D. Cabot,* President; Norton O. Sloan,* Vice-President and Treasurer; Leslye A. Arsht,* Louis W. Cabot,* Robert A. Charpie,* Vice-Presidents; Althea M. Burpos, Secretary; Ruth C. Scheer,* Executive Director.
Directors:* Maryellen Cabot, Michael J. Widmer.
Number of staff: 1 full-time professional; 1 full-time support.
Employer Identification Number: 046035227

1489
Cabot Family Charitable Trust ▼
125 High St.
Boston 02110 (617) 423-6000

Trust established in 1942 in Massachusetts.
Donor(s): Godfrey L. Cabot.†
Financial data: (yr. ended 12/31/83): Assets,
$8,743,605 (M); expenditures, $849,897,
including $405,250 for 45 grants (high:
$50,000; low: $250; average: $2,000-$10,000).
Purpose and activities: Program interests
include urban programs, youth and family
services, higher and other education, cultural
programs, conservation, hospitals, and
population-related projects.
Types of support awarded: Annual
campaigns, seed money, building funds,
equipment, land acquisition, endowment funds,
general purposes, continuing support.
Limitations: Giving limited to the Boston, MA,
area. No support for computer-related
projects. No grants to individuals, or for
medical or scientific research, scholarships,
fellowships, or matching gifts; no loans.
Publications: Annual report.
Application information:
  Initial approach: Full proposal
  Copies of proposal: 1
  Deadline(s): None
  Board meeting date(s): June, September, and
    December
  Final notification: 3 to 5 months
  Write: Ruth C. Scheer, Manager
Trustees: Louis W. Cabot, Thomas D. Cabot,
Arthur H. Phillips.
Number of staff: 1.
Employer Identification Number: 046036446

1490
Cabot-Saltonstall Charitable Trust ⌑
225 Franklin St., Rm. 2920
Boston 02110

Trust established in 1936 in Massachusetts.
Donor(s): Paul C. Cabot, Virginia C. Cabot,
Charles C. Cabot.
Financial data: (yr. ended 12/31/82): Assets,
$3,229,599 (M); expenditures, $258,486,
including $255,915 for 69 grants (high:
$50,000; low: $25).
Purpose and activities: Primarily local giving,
with emphasis on higher and secondary
education, hospitals, and a community fund.
Limitations: Giving primarily in the Boston,
MA area.
Trustees: Paul C. Cabot, Paul C. Cabot, Jr.,
Virginia C. Cabot.
Employer Identification Number: 046042037

1491
Cambridge Foundation, The
99 Bishop Richard Allen Dr.
Cambridge 02139 (617) 876-5214

Community foundation established in 1916 in
Massachusetts by declaration of trust.

Financial data: (yr. ended 12/31/83): Assets,
$2,118,568 (M); gifts received, $34,535;
expenditures, $190,532, including $165,899
for 41 grants (high: $13,000; low: $800;
average: $1,000-$3,500).
Purpose and activities: To promote the
mental, moral, and physical welfare of the
inhabitants of Cambridge (or elsewhere, if
specified by the donor), through grants to
community agencies, generally for health and
welfare.
Types of support awarded: Operating
budgets, general purposes, special projects,
seed money, building funds, equipment.
Limitations: Giving primarily in Cambridge,
MA, except as specified by donors. No
support for municipal, state, or federal
agencies. No grants to individuals, or for
scholarships, endowment funds, research
studies, conferences, films, or matching gifts;
no loans.
Publications: Annual report, application
guidelines, program policy statement.
Application information:
  Initial approach: Telephone
  Copies of proposal: 6
  Deadline(s): Submit proposal preferably in
    February through April and September
    through October; deadline April 15 and
    October 15
  Board meeting date(s): Distribution
    committee meets in June and December
  Write: Phyllis Simpkins, Secretary
Distribution Committee: Marion Eiseman,
Chair; Phyllis Simpkins, Secretary; Melville
Chapin, Lawrence F. Feloney, Mrs. Herbert
Pratt, Mrs. Leonard Wheeler.
Trustees: Bay Bank Harvard Trust Company,
Cambridge Trust Company.
Employer Identification Number: 046012492

1492
**Campbell (Bushrod H.) and Adah F.
Hall Charity Fund**
c/o Palmer & Dodge
One Beacon St.
Boston 02108 (617) 227-4400

Trust established in 1956 in Massachusetts.
Donor(s): Bushrod H. Campbell,† Adah F.
Hall.†
Financial data: (yr. ended 5/31/84): Assets,
$5,236,065 (M); gifts received, $451;
expenditures, $385,685, including $279,978
for 57 grants (high: $35,175; low: $500;
average: $7,000).
Purpose and activities: Broad purposes; grants
limited to organizations in the greater Boston
area devoted to aid to the elderly, for
population control, special projects in major
Boston hospitals, and medical research grants
administered through The Medical Foundation.
Grants made primarily for services and
programs.
Types of support awarded: Operating
budgets, continuing support, seed money,
building funds, equipment, scholarship funds,
fellowships, research, conferences and
seminars, special projects.

Limitations: Giving limited to greater Boston,
MA, area. No grants to individuals, or for
annual campaigns, emergency funds, deficit
financing, land acquisition, demonstration
projects, publications, general endowments, or
matching gifts; no loans.
Publications: 990-PF, application guidelines.
Application information:
  Initial approach: Telephone or letter
  Copies of proposal: 1
  Deadline(s): 1st week of February, May,
    September, or November
  Board meeting date(s): February, May,
    September, and November
  Write: Casimir de Rham, Jr., Trustee
Trustees: Donald J. Barker, Casimir de Rham,
Jr., Curtis Prout.
Number of staff: None.
Employer Identification Number: 046013598

1493
**Canaday (Ward M. & Mariam C.)
Educational and Charitable Trust**
c/o Bank of Boston
P.O. Box 1890
Boston 02105 (617) 434-3348

Trust established in 1945 in Ohio.
Donor(s): Ward M. Canaday,† Mariam C.
Canaday.†
Financial data: (yr. ended 12/31/82): Assets,
$6,162,535 (M); gifts received, $30,842;
expenditures, $194,420, including $174,339
for 3 grants (high: $112,095; low: $5,359).
Purpose and activities: Educational and
charitable purposes; grants for higher
education. Funds fully committed.
Application information: Grant applications
not accepted.
  Board meeting date(s): Quarterly
  Write: R.H. Frey, Vice-President
Trustees: Doreen Spitzer, Lyman Spitzer, Jr.,
N.C. Spitzer, Bank of Boston (R.H. Frey, Vice-
President).
Number of staff: None.
Employer Identification Number: 346523619

1494
CarEth Foundation
3 Church St.
Cambridge 02138 (617) 354-8343

Incorporated in 1967 in Connecticut.
Donor(s): G. Sterling Grumman.†
Financial data: (yr. ended 12/31/83): Assets,
$1,241,417 (M); gifts received, $49,992;
expenditures, $123,627, including $106,100
for 44 grants (high: $7,000; low: $250;
average: $2,000-$4,000).
Purpose and activities: Grants "only for
programs promoting world peace" including
religious, educational and public policy
organizations.
Types of support awarded: General purposes,
operating budgets, special projects, research.
Limitations: No grants to individuals.
Publications: Application guidelines, program
policy statement.
Application information: Application form
required.
  Initial approach: Letter

Copies of proposal: 1
Deadline(s): 8 weeks before board meetings
Board meeting date(s): January and late spring; specific dates decided semiannually
Write: Elizabeth S. Grumman, Secretary
Officers and Directors: Helen Burr Grumman, President; Carol B. Grumman, Vice-President; Elizabeth S. Grumman, Secretary; Paul Martin Grumman, Treasurer; Paul Deats, Jr., Gregory Finger, Sandra Martin Grumman.
Number of staff: None.
Employer Identification Number: 042433914

1495
Charlesbank Homes ¤
c/o Thomas W. Lynch
470 Pleasant St.
Milton 02186
Application address: John B. Kenerson, President, 23 Ravine Rd., Wellesley Hills, MA 02181

Established in 1911.
Donor(s): Edwin Ginn.†
Financial data: (yr. ended 4/30/82): Assets, $3,453,187 (M); gifts received, $199,500; expenditures, $387,553, including $197,500 for 12 grants (high: $60,000; low: $2,500).
Purpose and activities: Primarily local giving with emphasis on low- and moderate-income housing; support also for youth and social agencies.
Limitations: Giving primarily in the greater Boston, MA, area.
Application information:
Initial approach: Letter
Write: John B. Kenerson, President
Officers and Trustees: John B. Kenerson, President; Dudley H. Bradlee II, Vice-President; Peter S. Damon, Secretary; Thomas W. Lynch, Treasurer; William C. Allison IV, F. William Andres, Edward D. Rowley, Mark C. Wheeler.
Employer Identification Number: 042103755

1496
Charlton (Earle P.), Jr. Charitable Trust
c/o The First National Bank of Boston
P.O. Box 1890
Boston 02105

Trust established in 1973 in Massachusetts.
Donor(s): Earle P. Charlton, Jr.†
Financial data: (yr. ended 12/31/83): Assets, $3,384,326 (M); expenditures, $240,543, including $200,000 for 2 grants of $100,000 each.
Purpose and activities: Local giving primarily to hospitals.
Limitations: Giving primarily in Boston, MA.
Application information: Funds currently committed.
Trustee: The First National Bank of Boston (Arthur H. Veasey, Trust Officer).
Employer Identification Number: 046334412

1497
Chase (The Alfred E.) Charity Foundation ¤
c/o New England Merchants National Bank
28 State St.
Boston 02107   (617) 973-1798

Trust established in 1956 in Massachusetts.
Donor(s): Alfred E. Chase.
Financial data: (yr. ended 10/31/83): Assets, $2,822,811 (M); expenditures, $218,346, including $199,250 for 20 grants (high: $36,000; low: $2,000).
Purpose and activities: Giving primarily to local organizations, with particular interest in social service organizations and programs for children and youth; grants also to hospitals.
Limitations: Giving limited to MA, primarily the Greater Boston and North Shore areas. No grants to individuals, or for research, scholarships, or fellowships; no loans.
Publications: Application guidelines.
Application information:
Initial approach: Telephone
Copies of proposal: 1
Deadline(s): Submit proposal preferably in January; deadline February 1
Board meeting date(s): April
Write: John M. Dolan, Senior Trust Officer
Trustee: Bank of New England (John M. Dolan, Senior Trust Officer).
Employer Identification Number: 046026314

1498
Chase (Alice P.) Trust
Boston Safe Deposit & Trust Co.
One Boston Place
Boston 02106   (617) 722-7340

Trust established in 1956 in Massachusetts.
Donor(s): Alice P. Chase,† Alfred E. Chase.†
Financial data: (yr. ended 8/31/84): Assets, $2,640,641 (M); expenditures, $172,545, including $169,445 for 17 grants (high: $32,000; low: $2,000).
Purpose and activities: Primarily local giving for social welfare agencies providing health, educational, recreational, and other support services to mentally, economically, or physically disadvantaged youth and the aged.
Limitations: Giving primarily in Lynn, MA, and the North Shore area. No grants to individuals, or for matching gifts; no loans.
Publications: Application guidelines.
Application information:
Initial approach: Letter or proposal
Copies of proposal: 1
Deadline(s): Submit proposal preferably 2 months prior to board meetings
Board meeting date(s): March, June, September, and December
Write: Jane C. Williams
Trustee: Boston Safe Deposit & Trust Co.
Employer Identification Number: 046093897

1499
Childs (Roberta M.) Charitable Foundation ¤
73 Tremont St., Rm. 835
Boston 02108

Trust established in 1978 in Massachusetts.
Donor(s): Roberta M. Childs.†
Financial data: (yr. ended 3/31/83): Assets, $2,112,991 (M); expenditures, $104,634, including $88,750 for 53 grants (high: $10,500; low: $250).
Purpose and activities: Primarily local giving, with emphasis on aid to the indigent, child welfare, education, and the prevention of cruelty to animals.
Limitations: Giving primarily in MA. No grants to individuals.
Application information:
Initial approach: Letter
Copies of proposal: 1
Board meeting date(s): Monthly
Trustee: John R.D. McClintock.
Employer Identification Number: 042660275

1500
Codman (The Ogden) Trust
31 Milk St., Suite 62
Boston 02109   (617) 723-4535

Established in 1968 in Massachusetts.
Donor(s): Dorothy S.F.M. Codman.†
Financial data: (yr. ended 12/31/84): Assets, $1,263,795 (M); expenditures, $116,733, including $109,557 for 6 grants (high: $59,163; low: $9,000; average: $250).
Purpose and activities: Giving restricted to tax-exempt organizations in the town of Lincoln, Massachusetts, for educational, recreational, and other community projects.
Types of support awarded: Operating budgets, emergency funds, building funds, equipment, land acquisition, matching funds.
Limitations: Giving limited to Lincoln, MA. No grants to individuals, or for continuing support, annual campaigns, seed money, deficit financing, endowment funds, scholarships, or fellowships; no loans.
Application information:
Initial approach: Telephone
Board meeting date(s): 1st week of March, June, September, and December
Final notification: 2 to 3 weeks
Write: Daniel W. Fawcett, Trustee
Trustees: Daniel W. Fawcett, William B. Tyler, Walter G. Van Dorn.
Number of staff: 1 part-time support.
Employer Identification Number: 046225360

1501
Colgan (The James W.) Fund
(formerly The James W. Colgan Trust)
c/o Bank of New England - West
1391 Main St., P.O. Box 9003
Springfield 01101   (413) 787-8700

Trust established in 1944 in Massachusetts.
Donor(s): James W. Colgan.†

Financial data: (yr. ended 12/31/83): Assets, $1,766,245 (M); gifts received, $150; expenditures, $241,368, including $214,807 for 318 loans.
Purpose and activities: Student loan program to aid needy, deserving young men and women who are residents of Massachusetts, at an undergraduate level of study.
Types of support awarded: Student aid.
Limitations: Giving limited to MA. No grants for general purposes, capital funds, endowment funds, matching gifts, scholarships, or fellowships.
Application information: Application form required.
  Initial approach: Letter or telephone
  Copies of proposal: 1
  Deadline(s): Submit proposal preferably between April and June; deadline June 30
  Board meeting date(s): During summer as required
  Write: Suzanne Renault-Morgan, Trust Officer
Distribution Committee: Suzanne Renault-Morgan, Trust Officer; Raymond F. Chudy, William Coulter, Mitchell Garabedian, John B. Shea.
Trustee: Bank of New England - West.
Number of staff: None.
Employer Identification Number: 046032781

1502
Cook (John Brown) Foundation Inc.

P.O. Box 246
Monument Beach 02553   (617) 759-3188

Incorporated in 1952 in Connecticut.
Donor(s): John Brown Cook,† Marian Miner Cook, Wallace L. Cook,† Whitney Blake Company, Reliable Electric Company.
Financial data: (yr. ended 10/31/84): Assets, $1,395,461 (M); expenditures, $358,726, including $304,500 for 15 grants (high: $150,000; low: $1,000).
Purpose and activities: Grants to institutions only, including colleges and universities, educational associations, and public policy research organizations relating to preservation of the American economic system and national defense.
Types of support awarded: General purposes, continuing support, seed money, publications, conferences and seminars.
Limitations: No grants to individuals, or for building or endowment funds, scholarships, fellowships, or matching gifts; no loans.
Application information:
  Initial approach: Telephone
  Copies of proposal: 1
  Board meeting date(s): June, December, and as required
  Write: Harold C. Ripley, President
Officers and Trustees:* Harold C. Ripley,* President and Treasurer; Leo C. McKenna,* Vice-President; William R. Murphy, Secretary; Gregory M. Cook, Marcia Cook Hart, Boston Safe Deposit and Trust Company.
Employer Identification Number: 066022958

1503
Cove Charitable Trust, The

c/o Sherburne, Powers & Needham
One Beacon St.
Boston 02108   (617) 523-2700

Established in 1964 in Massachusetts.
Donor(s): Aileen Kelly Pratt,† Edwin H.B. Pratt.†
Financial data: (yr. ended 12/31/84): Assets, $1,422,522 (M); expenditures, $78,873, including $71,540 for 22 grants (high: $10,000; low: $500; average: $1,000-$2,000).
Purpose and activities: Primarily local giving, with emphasis on schools, social services, particularly for disadvantaged youth, and urban programs.
Types of support awarded: General purposes, special projects, operating budgets, continuing support, annual campaigns, seed money, building funds, matching funds.
Limitations: Giving primarily in MA. No grants to individuals, or for scholarships, fellowships, emergency funds, deficit financing, equipment and materials, land acquisition, renovation projects, endowments, program-related investments, research, demonstration projects, publications, or conferences and seminars; no loans.
Application information:
  Initial approach: Letter
  Deadline(s): October 1
  Board meeting date(s): Occasionally
  Final notification: 6 months
  Write: F. Stanton Deland, Trustee
Trustees: F. Stanton Deland, Jr., Charlotte P. Sudduth.
Number of staff: None.
Employer Identification Number: 046118955

1504
Cowan (The Lillian L. and Harry A.) Foundation Corporation

P.O. Box 733
Norwood 02062

Incorporated in 1962 in Massachusetts.
Donor(s): Harry A. Cowan.†
Financial data: (yr. ended 4/30/84): Assets, $2,088,649 (M); expenditures, $159,558, including $131,225 for 28 grants (high: $5,000; low: $1,000).
Purpose and activities: To aid the blind and aid physically and emotionally handicapped children in Massachusetts.
Limitations: Giving primarily in the greater Boston, MA, area. No grants to individuals.
Application information:
  Initial approach: Full proposal
  Copies of proposal: 1
  Deadline(s): None
  Board meeting date(s): Semiannually, usually in April and October
Officers and Trustees: Albert Slavin, President and Treasurer; Ellen Glazer, Marjorie Herson, Beatrice Slavin, Vice-Presidents; Donald Glazer.
Employer Identification Number: 046130077

1505
Cox Foundation, Inc. ¤

c/o Gaston, Snow & Ely Bartlett
One Federal St.
Boston 02110

Established in 1970.
Donor(s): William C. Cox, Jr.
Financial data: (yr. ended 12/31/82): Assets, $1,535,283 (M); gifts received, $227,938; expenditures, $41,116, including $37,782 for 16 grants (high: $10,000; low: $500).
Purpose and activities: Primarily local giving, with emphasis on private schools and hospitals.
Limitations: Giving primarily in MA.
Officers: William C. Cox, Jr., President; William A. Lowell, Secretary; Martha W. Cox, Treasurer.
Employer Identification Number: 237068786

1506
Cox (Jessie B.) Charitable Trust ▼

100 Franklin St., 7th Fl.
Boston 02110   (617) 357-1516
Additional telephone number: (617) 357-1500

Split-interest trust established in 1982 in Boston, Massachusetts.
Donor(s): Jessie B. Cox.†
Financial data: (yr. ended 10/31/83): Assets, $48,352,411 (M); expenditures, $4,271,757, including $4,173,350 for 45 grants (high: $500,000; low: $6,000; average: $30,000-$100,000).
Purpose and activities: Giving primarily in the Northeast, with emphasis on education, health, and the protection of the environment.
Types of support awarded: Seed money, internships, special projects, research.
Limitations: Giving primarily in the Northeast, with emphasis on eastern MA. No support for sectarian religious activities, or efforts usually supported by the general public. No grants to individuals, or for capital or building funds, equipment and materials, land acquisition, renovation projects, deficit financing, operating budgets, continuing support, annual campaigns, general endowments, or matching or challenge grants; no loans.
Publications: Annual report, application guidelines, program policy statement.
Application information:
  Initial approach: Brief concept paper
  Copies of proposal: 3
  Deadline(s): January 31, April 30, July 15, and October 31
  Board meeting date(s): March, June, September, and December
  Final notification: Within 3 months of deadline
  Write: Administrators
Administrators: Newell Flather, Mary Phillips, Ala H. Reid.
Trustees: William C. Cox, Jr., Roy A. Hammer, Jane Cox MacElree, George T. Shaw.
Number of staff: 3 part-time professional; 1 full-time support.
Employer Identification Number: 046478024

1507
Crabtree, Trustees under the Will of Lotta M.
73 Tremont St.
Boston 02108

Trust established in 1928; incorporated in 1929 in Massachusetts.
Donor(s): Lotta M. Crabtree.†
Financial data: (yr. ended 12/31/81): Assets, $3,363,952 (M); expenditures, $383,169, including $213,483 for grants.
Purpose and activities: Grants distributed from seven funds for charitable purposes, including hospitals in Boston only, musical education at New England Conservatory of Music only, dumb animals, and Christmas gifts; assistance to graduates of the University of Massachusetts, Stockbridge School of Agriculture, College of Food and Natural Resources, or related programs, in order to establish themselves in agriculture; and to needy actors and discharged convicts.
Limitations: Giving limited to MA.
Trustees: Thomas F. Donohue, Edward C. Hamaty, Michael J. Harney.
Employer Identification Number: 042105770

1508
Dana (Herman) Charitable Trust ⌑
Three Center Plaza
Boston 02108

Trust established in 1969 in Massachusetts.
Donor(s): Herman Dana.†
Financial data: (yr. ended 12/31/82): Assets, $3,019,798 (M); expenditures, $554,270, including $60,000 for 3 grants (high: $25,000; low: $15,000).
Purpose and activities: Primarily local giving, with emphasis on Jewish welfare funds, a medical school, and hospitals.
Limitations: Giving primarily in MA.
Trustees: Lester Harold Dana, David L. Stone.
Employer Identification Number: 046209497

1509
Daniels (Fred Harris) Foundation, Inc.
c/o The Mechanics Bank of Worcester, Trust Dept.
P.O. Box 987
Worcester 01613 (617) 798-6443

Incorporated in 1949 in Massachusetts.
Donor(s): F.H. Daniels,† Riley Stoker Company.
Financial data: (yr. ended 10/31/83): Assets, $4,989,678 (M); expenditures, $332,994, including $309,200 for 70 grants (high: $35,000; low: $500; average: $1,000-$125,000).
Purpose and activities: Broad purposes, including the advancement of promotion of sciences, medicine, and literature; primarily local giving for education, hospitals, community funds and services, museums, and Protestant church support.

Types of support awarded: Operating budgets, continuing support, annual campaigns, emergency funds, building funds, equipment, land acquisition, endowment funds, matching funds, professorships, internships, scholarship funds, fellowships, special projects.
Limitations: Giving primarily in the Worcester, MA area. No grants to individuals, or for seed money or deficit financing; no loans.
Application information:
  Initial approach: Letter
  Copies of proposal: 1
  Deadline(s): March 1, June 1, September 1, and December 1
  Board meeting date(s): March, June, September, and December
  Final notification: 1 to 2 1/2 months
  Write: Edward S. Lewis, Trust Officer
Officers and Directors: Bruce G. Daniels, Chairman and President; F. Turner Blake, Jr., Secretary; Clarence W. Daniels, Jr., Treasurer; Johnathan D. Blake, Eleanor D. Bronson, Sarah D. Morse, William S. Nicholson, William O. Pettit, Jr., Meridith D. Wesby.
Number of staff: None.
Employer Identification Number: 046014333

1510
Davenport Memorial Foundation
70 Salem St.
Malden 02148 (617) 324-0150

Trust established in 1946 in Massachusetts.
Donor(s): Alice M. Davenport.†
Financial data: (yr. ended 5/31/84): Assets, $6,034,085 (M); gifts received, $1,600; expenditures, $392,392, including $45,009 for 24 grants (high: $2,000; low: $100; average: $600) and $344,912 for 1 foundation-administered program.
Purpose and activities: To operate and maintain a perpetual home for the reception, care, support, and maintenance of married couples, citizens of the United States and of Protestant religious affiliation; also to contribute 85 per cent of surplus funds to charities named in will, with 15 per cent to go to other Malden charities at the discretion of the Trustees.
Limitations: Giving primarily in Malden, MA. No grants to individuals.
Application information:
  Initial approach: Telephone or letter
  Copies of proposal: 1
  Deadline(s): Submit proposal preferably in April; deadline May 1
  Board meeting date(s): Monthly, except in July and August
  Write: Heber Wells, President
Officers and Trustees: Heber Wells, President; Elliot Gerrish, Vice-President; Carroll R. Libby, Treasurer; Muriel Weldon, Clerk; Mrs. J. Allen Barrig, Dana Bill, Donald E. Brunelli, Frederick L. Fish, Mrs. Robert Gabriel, Katharine W. Hughes, Geraldine Jackson, Charles Kezar, Donald E. MacCuish, Arthur R. Marshall, John A. Plummer, Robert L. Shannon, Hallie Strong.
Number of staff: 21.
Employer Identification Number: 042104142

1511
Davis (Irene E. and George A.) Foundation
American Saw and Manufacturing Company
301 Chestnut St.
East Longmeadow 01028 (413) 525-3961

Established in 1970 in Massachusetts.
Donor(s): American Saw and Manufacturing Company, Irene E. Davis.
Financial data: (yr. ended 12/31/82): Assets, $2,922,862 (M); gifts received, $100,000; expenditures, $272,999, including $251,925 for 56 grants (high: $25,000; low: $40).
Purpose and activities: Primarily locl giving, with emphasis on higher education and Roman Catholic institutions, including churches; grants also for social services, hospitals, and a community fund.
Types of support awarded: Operating budgets, continuing support, annual campaigns, seed money, emergency funds, building funds, land acquisition.
Limitations: Giving primarily in MA. No grants to individuals, or for deficit financing, equipment, endowment funds, matching gifts, scholarships and fellowships, research, special projects, publications, or conferences; no loans.
Application information:
  Initial approach: Letter
  Copies of proposal: 1
  Deadline(s): None
  Board meeting date(s): As required
  Final notification: 1 month
  Write: James E. Davis, Trustee
Trustees: James E. Davis, John H. Davis, Arthur L. Duquette, Robert R. Lepak, David R. Sayles.
Number of staff: None.
Employer Identification Number: 237102734

1512
DeLoura Family Trust, The ⌑
c/o Shawmut Bank of Boston
P.O. Box 4276
Boston 02211

Established in 1981.
Financial data: (yr. ended 1/31/83): Assets, $1,223,813 (M); gifts received, $3,437; expenditures, $100,250, including $84,553 for 1 grant.
Purpose and activities: Supports a scholarship fund for residents of Martha's Vineyard only.
Types of support awarded: Scholarship funds.
Limitations: Giving limited to Martha's Vineyard, MA.
Trustee: Shawmut Bank of Boston.
Employer Identification Number: 046460749

1513
Demoulas Foundation ⌑
875 East St.
Tewksbury 01876

Trust established in 1964 in Massachusetts.
Donor(s): Members of the Demoulas family.
Financial data: (yr. ended 12/31/82): Assets, $8,604,019 (M); gifts received, $780,000; expenditures, $508,309, including $469,819 for 294 grants.

Purpose and activities: Charitable purposes; grants largely for Greek Orthodox church support, higher and secondary education, and youth agencies.
Application information:
Initial approach: Letter
Write: Telemachus A. Demoulas, Trustee
Trustee: Telemachus A. Demoulas.
Employer Identification Number: 046122337

1514
Devonshire Associates ◻
50 Federal St.
Boston 02110

Incorporated in 1949 in Massachusetts.
Donor(s): Melita S. Howland, Weston Howland III, Thomas Power.
Financial data: (yr. ended 12/31/82): Assets, $1,105,004 (M); gifts received, $115,500; expenditures, $127,199, including $111,500 for 18 grants (high: $35,000; low: $500).
Purpose and activities: General purposes; primarily local giving with emphasis on a college and an aquarium; support also for cultural programs, higher education and youth agencies.
Limitations: Giving primarily in MA.
Officers and Trustees: Weston Howland, Jr., President; William H. MacCrellish, Jr., Secretary; Donald M. DeHart, Treasurer; Lewis H. Parks.
Employer Identification Number: 046004808

1515
Dexter (Eugene A.) Charitable Fund
c/o BayBank Valley Trust Company
1500 Main St.
Springfield 01115   (413) 781-7575
Grant application address: Robert J. Van Wart, Secretary, Community Funds Advisory Committee, 1365 Main St., Springfield, MA 01103

Trust established in 1946 in Massachusetts.
Donor(s): Henrietta F. Dexter.†
Financial data: (yr. ended 12/31/83): Assets, $5,579,024 (M); expenditures, $543,012, including $493,900 for 32 grants (high: $120,000; low: $564).
Purpose and activities: Grants for public charitable purposes in the city of Springfield only, including health, welfare, the humanities, and education; emphasis on the physically and mentally handicapped, minorities, youth and child welfare agencies, and health services.
Types of support awarded: Building funds, equipment, land acquisition, conferences and seminars, publications, matching funds, special projects.
Limitations: Giving limited to the city of Springfield, MA. No grants to individuals, or for endowment funds, operating budgets, scholarships, fellowships, or general purposes; no loans.
Publications: Application guidelines.
Application information:
Initial approach: Telephone, letter, or proposal
Copies of proposal: 12

Deadline(s): Submit proposals preferably in December, April, or August; deadline first Monday in January and May and first Tuesday in September
Board meeting date(s): March, July, and November
Final notification: 4 months
Write: Robert J. Van Wart, Secretary
Trustee: BayBank Valley Trust Company, (Peter Weston, Vice-President).
Number of staff: 1 part-time professional; 1 part-time support.
Employer Identification Number: 046018698

1516
Doehla (Harry) Foundation, Inc. ◻
c/o Singer and Lusardi
370 Main St.
Worcester 01608   (617) 756-4657

Incorporated in 1950 in Delaware.
Donor(s): Harry Doehla.†
Financial data: (yr. ended 3/31/82): Assets, $1,405,145 (M); expenditures, $278,990, including $261,500 for 22 grants (high: $52,000; low: $500).
Purpose and activities: Support for higher education, aid to the handicapped, including the blind, and mental health.
Officers: Henry Lusardi, President; Philip Straus, Vice-President; Paul Singer, Secretary; Philip H. Steckler, Jr., Treasurer.
Employer Identification Number: 026014132

1517
Donaldson (Oliver S. and Jennie R.) Charitable Trust
c/o Durfee Attleboro Bank
Ten North Main St.
Fall River 02722   (617) 679-8311

Trust established in 1969 in New York.
Donor(s): Oliver S. Donaldson.†
Financial data: (yr. ended 12/31/82): Assets, $7,914,215 (M); gifts received, $838,749; expenditures, $817,208, including $718,605 for 63 grants (high: $100,000; low: $500).
Purpose and activities: Interests include cancer research and treatment, child welfare and youth agencies, hospitals and health agencies, elementary, secondary, and higher education, and the town of Pawling, New York; eleven named institutions are given first consideration.
Limitations: No grants to individuals.
Publications: Application guidelines.
Application information: Application form required.
Initial approach: Proposal
Copies of proposal: 3
Board meeting date(s): Quarterly
Write: Stephen C. Williams, Senior Vice-President, Durfee Attleboro Bank
Officers and Trustees: William E. Murray, Chairman; Wilson W. Curtis, Vice-Chairman; Marjorie Atwood, Elizabeth A. Lawrence, Durfee Attleboro Bank.
Employer Identification Number: 046229044

1518
Eastern Associated Foundation, The ▼
One Beacon St.
Boston 02108   (617) 742-9200

Established in 1964 in Massachusetts.
Donor(s): Eastern Gas and Fuel Associates, Boston Gas Company, Eastern Associated Coal Corp., Midland Affiliated Co., Western Associated Coal Corp., Western Associated Development Corp.
Financial data: (yr. ended 12/31/83): Assets, $0 (M); gifts received, $496,667; expenditures, $508,381, including $406,950 for 146 grants (high: $169,000; low: $500; average: $500-$10,000) and $89,431 for 200 employee matching gifts.
Purpose and activities: Broad purposes; giving generally confined to areas of company operations in Greater Boston, Appalachia, and the Mississippi River Valley; emphasis on community funds, higher education, hospitals, youth agencies, and cultural programs.
Types of support awarded: Annual campaigns, building funds, emergency funds, employee matching gifts, equipment, general purposes, seed money.
Limitations: Giving limited to areas of company operations in greater Boston, MA, Appalachia, and the Mississippi River Valley. No grants to individuals, or for endowment funds, scholarships, fellowships, or research; no loans.
Publications: Program policy statement, application guidelines.
Application information:
Initial approach: Cover letter with brief proposal
Copies of proposal: 1
Deadline(s): Submit proposal preferably in October; budget prepared in November and December for the following year
Board meeting date(s): January and as required
Final notification: 2 to 3 months
Write: Jesse R. Mohorovic, Secretary
Officer: Jesse R. Mohorovic, Secretary.
Trustees: J.J. Bacon, R.H. Freeman, J.D. Geary, R.C. O'Brien, W.J. Pruyn, R.W. Weinig.
Number of staff: 2 part-time professional.
Employer Identification Number: 046109087

1519
Eaton (Georgina Goddard) Memorial Fund
c/o Welch and Forbes
73 Tremont St.
Boston 02108   (617) 523-1635

Trust established in 1917 in Massachusetts.
Financial data: (yr. ended 6/30/83): Assets, $4,425,328 (M); expenditures, $396,237, including $329,550 for 6 grants (high: $299,350; low: $1,245).
Purpose and activities: Primarily local giving, with emphasis on support for a rehabilitation agency.
Limitations: Giving primarily in MA. No grants to individuals, or for endowment funds, or matching gifts; no loans.
Application information:
Initial approach: Letter

Copies of proposal: 1
Board meeting date(s): As required
Write: Kenneth S. Safe, Jr., Trustee
Trustees: Augustus P. Loring, Kenneth S. Safe, Jr., Welch and Forbes.
Employer Identification Number: 046112820

1520
Edwards Scholarship Fund ☼
One Federal St.
Boston 02110   (617) 426-4434

Trust established in 1939 in Massachusetts.
Donor(s): Miss Grace M. Edwards.†
Financial data: (yr. ended 7/31/83): Assets, $3,107,201 (M); gifts received, $1,140; expenditures, $246,374, including $199,150 for 236 grants to individuals.
Purpose and activities: To assist young men and women, under the age of 25, whose families live within the city of Boston. Scholarship loans to students, with preference for undergraduates enrolled in a program leading to a bachelor's or advanced degree at an accredited college or university. Maximum aid $1,000, but most in range of $200-$800 a year for not more than six years. No grants to individuals attending junior colleges, community colleges, or hospital schools of nursing. Students to repay grant when financially able.
Types of support awarded: Student aid.
Limitations: Giving limited to families of students living in Boston.
Application information:
    Deadline(s): March 31
    Write: Mrs. Warren Rabb, Executive Secretary
Officer: Mrs. Warren Rabb, Executive Secretary.
Trustees: Richard Ely, Edward Kirk, Stephen Little.
Employer Identification Number: 046002496

1521
EG&G Foundation ☼
c/o EG&G, Inc.
45 William St.
Wellesley 02181

Established in 1979 in Massachusetts.
Donor(s): EG&G, Inc.
Financial data: (yr. ended 6/30/83): Assets, $3,404,360 (M); expenditures, $629,719, including $561,593 for 136 grants (high: $100,000; low: $18) and $68,126 for 213 employee matching gifts.
Purpose and activities: Charitable purposes; grants primarily for higher education and community funds, including an employee matching gifts program.
Types of support awarded: Employee matching gifts.
Officer: Kathleen M. Russo, Trust Administrator.
Trustees: M. Theresa Kelly, Richard F. Murphy, Bernard J. O'Keefe, Eugene J. White.
Employer Identification Number: 042683042

1522
Ellison Foundation, The ☼
129 South St.
Boston 02111

Trust established in 1952 in Massachusetts.
Donor(s): Eben H. Ellison.†
Financial data: (yr. ended 12/31/82): Assets, $1,118,746 (M); gifts received, $18,000; expenditures, $133,197, including $127,014 for 38 grants (high: $35,457; low: $40).
Purpose and activities: Primarily local giving, with emphasis on higher education, hospitals and medical research, a community fund, church support, and cultural programs.
Limitations: Giving primarily in MA.
Application information:
    Write: Wendell R. Freeman, Trustee
Trustees: William P. Ellison, Wendell R. Freeman, Ellery W. Rogers, Harriet E. Rogers.
Employer Identification Number: 046050704

1523
Ellsworth (Ruth H. and Warren A.) Foundation
370 Main St.
Worcester 01608   (617) 798-8621

Trust established in 1964 in Massachusetts.
Donor(s): Ruth H. Ellsworth.†
Financial data: (yr. ended 12/31/83): Assets, $5,841,850 (M); expenditures, $248,029, including $231,385 for 38 grants (high: $75,000; low: $250; average: $1,000-$3,000).
Purpose and activities: Broad purposes; primarily local giving, with emphasis on higher education, scientific research, youth agencies, and hospitals.
Types of support awarded: Operating budgets, general purposes, continuing support, annual campaigns, seed money, emergency funds, deficit financing, building funds, equipment, land acquisition.
Limitations: Giving primarily in the Worcester, MA area. No grants to individuals, or for endowment funds, scholarships and fellowships, special projects, research, publications, conferences, or matching gifts; no loans.
Application information:
    Initial approach: Full proposal
    Copies of proposal: 1
    Deadline(s): Submit proposal preferably in June; deadline November 30
    Board meeting date(s): July and December
    Final notification: By December 28
    Write: Sumner B. Tilton, Jr., Trustee
Trustees: David H. Ellsworth, Sumner B. Tilton, Jr., Robert H. Wetzel.
Number of staff: 1 part-time professional.
Employer Identification Number: 046113491

1524
Endowment for Biblical Research, Boston
(formerly Zion Research Foundation)
P.O. Box 993
Boston 02123   (617) 267-1593

Established in 1920 in Massachusetts.
Donor(s): Mary Beecher Longyear.†

Financial data: (yr. ended 6/30/83): Assets, $1,438,984 (M); expenditures, $87,188, including $69,480 for 5 grants (high: $20,000; low: $1,500) and $2,654 for 1 foundation-administered program.
Purpose and activities: To facilitate and advance research in the Bible and the history of the Christian church, including archaeological digs, publications, lecture tours, and aid to theological libraries; mantains the Zion Research Library.
Types of support awarded: Publications, research.
Publications: Informational brochure, application guidelines.
Application information: Funds largely committed, but proposals invited.
    Board meeting date(s): April and October
    Final notification: May and November
    Write: Marjory I. Anderson, Secretary
Trustees: Elaine H. Harkness, Richard M. Harley, Stephen R. Howard, J. Alden Manley, Virginia Stopfel.
Number of staff: 1 full-time professional.
Employer Identification Number: 042104439

1525
Evans (Wilmot Roby) Corporation
Palmer & Dodge
One Beacon St., Rm. 2200
Boston 02108   (617) 227-4400

Incorporated in 1953 in Massachusetts.
Donor(s): Florence Evans Bushee.†
Financial data: (yr. ended 12/31/83): Assets, $1,804,070 (M); expenditures, $121,686, including $3,000 for 4 grants (high: $1,500; low: $350; average: $866) and $75,050 for 110 grants to individuals.
Purpose and activities: Charitable purposes; grants to charitable institutions in the Newburyport area of interest to the donor during her lifetime; scholarship grants to college students from the Newburyport area.
Types of support awarded: Student aid.
Limitations: Giving limited to the Newburyport, MA, area. No grants for building or endowment funds, or operating budgets; no loans.
Publications: Informational brochure.
Application information: Application form required.
    Initial approach: Letter or telephone
    Copies of proposal: 1
    Deadline(s): May 1
    Board meeting date(s): March, April, May, June, and as required
    Write: Ann Reidy, Legal Assistant
Officers and Trustees:* Marion Brown,* President; Judith Robertson,* Vice-President; Casimir de Rham,* Treasurer.
Number of staff: None.
Employer Identification Number: 046035327

1526
Farnsworth (Charles H.) Trust ☼
c/o State Street Bank & Trust Co.
225 Franklin St., P.O. Box 351
Boston 02101

Trust established in 1930; became a charitable trust in 1978.
Donor(s): Charles H. Farnsworth.†
Financial data: (yr. ended 9/30/82): Assets, $7,956,842 (M); gifts received, $6,761,172; expenditures, $231,580, including $199,680 for 12 grants (high: $56,400; low: $2,200).
Purpose and activities: First year of operations in 1982; primarily local giving for urban development, the aged, hospitals, and a medical school.
Limitations: Giving primarily in MA.
Trustee: State Street Bank & Trust.
Employer Identification Number: 046096075

1527
Feldberg Family Foundation, The
770 Cochituate Rd.
P.O. Box 910
Framingham 01701   (617) 620-2318

Trust established in 1951 in Massachusetts.
Donor(s): Max Feldberg, Morris Feldberg.†
Financial data: (yr. ended 11/30/83): Assets, $2,379,764 (M); expenditures, $165,949, including $165,289 for 8 grants (high: $50,000; low: $1,000).
Purpose and activities: Broad purposes; primarily local giving, with emphasis on Jewish welfare funds, hospitals, and higher education.
Limitations: Giving primarily in MA. No grants to individuals.
Application information:
  Initial approach: Letter
  Copies of proposal: 1
  Board meeting date(s): As required
  Write: Sumner Feldberg, Trustee
Trustees: Stanley H. Feldberg, Sumner Feldberg.
Employer Identification Number: 046065393

1528
Fidelity Foundation
82 Devonshire St.
Boston 02109

Trust established in 1965 in Massachusetts.
Donor(s): Fidelity Management & Research Co.
Financial data: (yr. ended 12/31/82): Assets, $4,724,893 (M); gifts received, $890,231; expenditures, $844,535, including $825,675 for 62 grants (high: $468,750; low: $100).
Purpose and activities: Primarily local giving, largely for building funds, operating support, special projects, and endowments, to organizations working in the fields of community development, education, health, and cultural affairs.
Types of support awarded: Building funds, operating budgets, special projects, endowment funds.
Limitations: Giving primarily in MA, especially the Boston area. No grants to individuals.
Application information:
  Initial approach: Full proposal
  Copies of proposal: 1
  Board meeting date(s): Late fall
  Write: Ross E. Sherbrooke, Trustee
Trustees: Edward C. Johnson, III, Caleb Loring, Jr., Ross E. Sherbrooke.
Employer Identification Number: 046131201

1529
Filene (Lincoln and Therese) Foundation, Inc. ▼
c/o Nutter, McClennen & Fish
600 Atlantic Ave., 18th Fl.
Boston 02110   (617) 973-9700

Incorporated in 1937 in Massachusetts.
Donor(s): Lincoln Filene.†
Financial data: (yr. ended 1/31/83): Assets, $7,143,272 (M); gifts received, $50,424; expenditures, $475,220, including $438,350 for 12 grants (high: $125,000; low: $100; average: $5,000-$100,000).
Purpose and activities: General purposes, including particularly the scientific investigation of the causes of economic distress; grants largely for higher education, music, the performing arts, and public policy issues. Funds largely committed to long-term support of existing projects.
Types of support awarded: Continuing support, emergency funds, equipment, matching funds, operating budgets, special projects.
Limitations: No grants to individuals, or for endowment funds, or scholarships and fellowships; no loans.
Application information: Funds largely committed.
  Initial approach: Letter
  Copies of proposal: 1
  Deadline(s): April 15 and October 15
  Board meeting date(s): May and November
  Final notification: After next semiannual meeting
  Write: John K.P. Stone III, Secretary
Officers and Directors: John J. Robertson, President; Lincoln F. Ladd, Vice-President; John K.P. Stone, III, Secretary-Treasurer; George E. Ladd, Jr., George E. Ladd, III, George M. Ladd, Robert M. Ladd, David A. Robertson, Jr., Catherine F. Shouse, Benjamin A. Trustman.
Number of staff: None.
Employer Identification Number: 237423946

1530
Foster (Joseph C. and Esther) Foundation, Inc. ⌗
Two Center Plaza, Suite 200
Boston 02108

Established in 1961 in Massachusetts.
Donor(s): Esther Foster.
Financial data: (yr. ended 12/31/82): Assets, $1,777,823 (M); gifts received, $15,000; expenditures, $149,211, including $137,145 for 18 grants (high: $110,000; low: $100).
Purpose and activities: Grants for higher education, mainly in Israel; giving also for Jewish welfare funds and cultural programs.
Officers and Directors: Leo Scheinbart, President; Esther J. Foster, Treasurer; Jacob Chatkis, Samuel Rappaporte, Jr., Marcia Scheinbart.
Employer Identification Number: 046114436

1531
Friendship Fund, Inc.
c/o Boston Safe Deposit & Trust Co.
One Boston Place, OBP-2
Boston 02106   (617) 722-7538

Incorporated in 1918 in New York.
Donor(s): Charles R. Crane.†
Financial data: (yr. ended 6/30/84): Assets, $1,700,000 (M); expenditures, $101,000, including $86,000 for 75 grants (high: $5,000; low: $200; average: $1,000-$2,000).
Purpose and activities: "For the advancement of the humanities and the sciences and for the welfare of humanity;" emphasis on local giving for environmental protection, social services, and international affairs. Funds largely committed in advance.
Types of support awarded: Seed money, building funds, equipment, land acquisition, publications, special projects.
Limitations: No grants to individuals or for scholarships.
Publications: Program policy statement, application guidelines.
Application information:
  Initial approach: One-page proposal summary and budget
  Copies of proposal: 1
  Deadline(s): Submit proposal only in May; deadline May 31
  Board meeting date(s): August
  Final notification: September (positive responses only)
Officers and Trustees: Mrs. Bruce C. Fisher, President; Sylvia Crane, Vice-President; Elizabeth McLane-Bradley, Secretary and Treasurer.
Number of staff: None.
Employer Identification Number: 136089220

1532
Fuller Foundation, Inc., The
112 Fulton St.
Boston 02109   (617) 523-0737

Incorporated in 1936 in Massachusetts.
Donor(s): Alvan T. Fuller, Sr.†
Financial data: (yr. ended 12/31/82): Assets, $5,554,990 (M); expenditures, $408,552, including $372,508 for 135 grants (high: $25,000; low: $100; average: $1,000-$2,500).
Purpose and activities: To aid religious and educational organizations; giving primarily in Boston and southeastern New Hampshire to medical, educational, and religious institutions.
Types of support awarded: Operating budgets, continuing support, annual campaigns, emergency funds, deficit financing, building funds, equipment, land acquisition, endowment funds, matching funds, professorships, internships, scholarship funds, employee related scholarships, special projects, research.
Limitations: Giving primarily in Boston, MA and southeastern NH. No grants to individuals, or for seed money, publications, or conferences; no loans.
Publications: Application guidelines.
Application information:
  Initial approach: Full proposal
  Copies of proposal: 1
  Deadline(s): None

Board meeting date(s): May, September, and December
Final notification: 1 to 6 months
Write: Gaynor K. Rutherford, Executive Director
Officers and Trustees: Peter Fuller, President; Gaynor K. Rutherford, Executive Director; Samuel S. Talbot, Treasurer; Miranda Fuller Bocko, John T. Bottomley, Lydia Fuller Bottomley, Pamela Bottomley, Ann Fuller Donovan, Peter D. Fuller, Jr., James D. Henderson, Mary Fuller Henderson, Lydia B. Langeley, Hope Halsey Swasey, Melinda F. Van den Heuvel.
Number of staff: 1 part-time professional; 1 part-time support.
Employer Identification Number: 042241130

1533
Fuller (George F. and Sybil H.) Foundation ▼ ☒
105 Madison St.
Worcester 01610   (617) 869-2106

Trust established in 1955 in Massachusetts.
Donor(s): George F. Fuller.†
Financial data: (yr. ended 12/31/83): Assets, $115,630,000 (M); expenditures, $3,531,727, including $3,335,687 for 110 grants (low: $500; average: $2,000-$50,000).
Purpose and activities: Primarily local giving, with emphasis on higher education, cultural institutions, historic preservation, hospitals, community funds, and youth organizations; support also for social agencies and schools.
Types of support awarded: Annual campaigns, seed money, emergency funds, general purposes, building funds, endowment funds, research, continuing support.
Limitations: Giving primarily in MA, with emphasis on Worcester. No grants to individuals, or for scholarships and fellowships, or matching gifts; no loans.
Application information:
  Initial approach: Letter or telephone
  Copies of proposal: 1
  Deadline(s): None
  Board meeting date(s): May, September, and December
  Final notification: Varies
  Write: Russell E. Fuller, Treasurer
Officers and Trustees: Sacket R. Duryee, Chairman; Paris Fletcher, Vice-Chairman; Robert P. Hallock, Jr., Secretary; Russell E. Fuller, Treasurer; Ernest M. Fuller.
Number of staff: 1.
Employer Identification Number: 046125606

1534
GenRad Foundation
300 Baker Ave.
Concord 01742   (617) 369-4400

Trust established in 1934 in Massachusetts.
Donor(s): GenRad, Inc.
Financial data: (yr. ended 12/31/83): Assets, $16,689,794 (M); expenditures, $720,335, including $622,650 for 320 grants (high: $81,000; low: $20) and $69,477 for employee matching gifts.

Purpose and activities: Broad purposes; primarily local giving, with emphasis on social services, hospitals, cultural programs, higher and secondary education, and public broadcasting.
Types of support awarded: Employee matching gifts.
Limitations: Giving primarily in MA. No grants to individuals.
Publications: Application guidelines.
Application information: Full proposal limited to 5 pages.
  Initial approach: Request for application guidelines
  Copies of proposal: 1
  Board meeting date(s): Monthly
  Write: Linda B. Smoker, Administrator
Officers and Trustees: Constantine J. Lahanas, Vice-President; John L. Steele, Jr., Secretary.
Number of staff: 1 full-time professional; 1 part-time support.
Employer Identification Number: 046043570

1535
Gillette Charitable and Educational Foundation, The ☒
c/o The Gillette Company
Prudential Tower Bldg.
Boston 02199   (617) 421-7722

Trust established in 1952 in Massachusetts.
Donor(s): The Gillette Company.
Financial data: (yr. ended 12/31/82): Assets, $662,275 (M); gifts received, $4,000; expenditures, $118,731, including $113,000 for 11 grants (high: $30,000; low: $1,500).
Purpose and activities: To assist charitable organizations in areas of company operations, with emphasis on higher education and a hospital.
Limitations: Giving primarily in areas of Company operations. No grants to individuals, or for medical or scientific research.
Application information:
  Initial approach: Proposal
  Copies of proposal: 1
  Deadline(s): Submit proposal preferably between October and December; deadline December 15
  Board meeting date(s): January and June
  Write: Charles O. Lynch, Manager of Civic Affairs
Trustees: Robert W. Hinman, William J. McMorrow, Robert F. Sama, Manufacturers Hanover Trust Company.
Employer Identification Number: 136047626

1536
Goldberg (Israel and Matilda) Family Foundation ☒
211 Congress St.
Boston 02110

Trust established in 1952 in Massachusetts.
Donor(s): Israel Goldberg, Albert S. Goldberg, Herbert A. Goldberg, and others.
Financial data: (yr. ended 12/31/82): Assets, $2,400,574 (M); gifts received, $129,000; expenditures, $210,542, including $205,591 for 123 grants (high: $50,000; low: $10).

Purpose and activities: General giving, with emphasis on local Jewish welfare funds and temple support.
Limitations: Giving primarily in the Boston, MA area.
Trustees: Joseph H. Baron, Albert S. Goldberg, Herbert A. Goldberg, Matilda Goldberg, Saul T. Hahn.
Employer Identification Number: 046047066

1537
Gorin (The Nehemias) Foundation
c/o William Gorin
1400 Soldiers Field Rd.
Brighton 02135

Established in 1964 in Massachusetts.
Donor(s): Nehemias Gorin.†
Financial data: (yr. ended 11/30/83): Assets, $2,500,000 (M); expenditures, $259,000, including $236,350 for grants (high: $56,000; low: $200).
Purpose and activities: Primarily local giving, with emphasis on hospitals, Jewish welfare funds, higher education, the handicapped, cultural programs, community funds, and health agencies.
Limitations: Giving primarily in MA.
Trustees: Bertha G. Fritz, William Gorin, Myer Israel, Ruth G. Katz, Ida G. Leckart.
Employer Identification Number: 046119939

1538
Grass Foundation, The
77 Reservoir Rd.
Quincy 02170   (617) 773-0002

Incorporated in 1955 in Massachusetts.
Donor(s): Grass Instrument Company, Albert M. Grass, Ellen R. Grass, Cannon Manufacturing Company, and others.
Financial data: (yr. ended 12/31/82): Assets, $3,485,658 (M); gifts received, $274,000; expenditures, $450,114, including $372,914 for 25 grants (high: $124,666; low: $1,000).
Purpose and activities: To encourage research in neurophysiology and allied fields of science and medicine; grants primarily for fellowships for summer study at a marine biological laboratory, lectureships, and for higher education.
Types of support awarded: Fellowships, research, lectureships.
Application information:
  Write: Mary G. Grass, Secretary
Officers and Directors: Ellen R. Grass, President; Albert M. Grass, Vice-President; Mary G. Grass, Secretary; Richmond B. Woodward, Treasurer; George H. Acheson, M.D., Albert J. Aquayo, M.D., Sidney Goldring, M.D., Henry J. Grass, M.D., Bernice Grafstein, Donald B. Lindsley, Fiorindo A. Simeone, M.D., Charles F. Stevens, M.D., Torsten N. Wiesel, M.D.
Employer Identification Number: 046049529

1539
Green Island, Inc. ♯
c/o Grabill & Ley, Inc.
Ten Post Office Square
Boston 02109

Incorporated in 1979 in Massachussetts.
Donor(s): W. Van Alan Clark, Jr.
Financial data: (yr. ended 2/28/82): Assets,
$1,147,731 (M); expenditures, $134,933,
including $106,636 for 5 grants (high: $42,516;
low: $7,800).
Purpose and activities: Support largely for
higher education, conservation, and cultural
programs.
Officers and Directors: W. Van Alan Clark,
Jr., President; Elliott V. Grabill, Treasurer; Mary
H. Clark.
Employer Identification Number: 042670568

1540
Grossman Family Trust ♯
P.O. Box 207
Nantucket 02554

Trust established in 1938 in Massachusetts.
Donor(s): Members of the Grossman family
and family-controlled businesses.
Financial data: (yr. ended 12/31/82): Assets,
$2,103,071 (M); expenditures, $171,598,
including $119,000 for 4 grants (high:
$108,900; low: $100).
Purpose and activities: Broad purposes; giving
primarily for Jewish welfare funds.
Trustees: Bernard D. Grossman, Everett P.
Grossman, Joseph B. Grossman, Joseph B.
Grossman II, Maurice Grossman, Morton S.
Grossman, Nissie Grossman.
Employer Identification Number: 046041134

1541
Hamilburg (Joseph M.) Foundation ♯
c/o Plymouth Rubber Co.
Revere St.
Canton 02021

Established in 1963.
Donor(s): Daniel M. Hamilburg.
Financial data: (yr. ended 12/31/82): Assets,
$1,363,741 (M); expenditures, $77,292,
including $74,928 for 75 grants (high: $10,200;
low: $10).
Purpose and activities: Primarily local giving
for health agencies, hospitals, and the
performing arts; support also for higher
education.
Limitations: Giving primarily in MA.
Trustee: Daniel M. Hamilburg.
Employer Identification Number: 046128210

1542
Harrington (Francis A. & Jacquelyn H.) Foundation
370 Main St.
Worcester 01608

Trust established in 1965 in Massachusetts.
Donor(s): Francis A. Harrington, Charles A.
Harrington Foundation.

Financial data: (yr. ended 12/31/84): Assets,
$3,000,000 (M); expenditures, $173,000,
including $163,000 for 30 grants (high:
$20,000; low: $500).
Purpose and activities: Broad purposes;
primarily local giving for higher and secondary
education, a science center, scientific and
medical research, and hospitals.
Limitations: Giving primarily in Worcester, MA.
Application information:
  Copies of proposal: 1
  Deadline(s): December 1
  Board meeting date(s): December 15
  Final notification: December 31
  Write: Sumner B. Tilton, Jr., Trustee
Trustees: Francis A. Harrington, Francis A.
Harrington, Jr., Jacquelyn H. Harrington, James
H. Harrington, Sumner B. Tilton, Jr.
Employer Identification Number: 046125088

1543
Harrington (George) Trust ♯
c/o Boston Safe Deposit and Trust Company
One Boston Place
Boston 02106   (617) 722-7318

Trust established in 1936 in Massachusetts.
Donor(s): George Harrington.†
Financial data: (yr. ended 12/31/82): Assets,
$1,454,362 (M); expenditures, $98,268,
including $83,919 for 3 grants (high: $70,000;
low: $3,919).
Purpose and activities: "To stimulate major
new efforts in the understanding, prevention,
and treatment of the mental disorders of
adolescents and young adults through the
George Harrington Professorship in Clinical and
Epidemiologic Psychiatry at Harvard Medical
School".
Types of support awarded: Professorships.
Limitations: Giving limited to Cambridge, MA.
No grants to individuals.
Publications: 990-PF.
Application information:
  Initial approach: Letter
  Deadline(s): Februaru, May, August, and
    November
  Board meeting date(s): March, June,
    September, and December
  Write: Ms. Jane Williams
Trustees: John G. Cornish, William W.
Wolbach.
Employer Identification Number: 046037725

1544
Harvard Apparatus Foundation, Inc. ♯
c/o Palmer & Dodge
One Beacon St.
Boston 02108

Established in 1938.
Financial data: (yr. ended 3/31/83): Assets,
$1,161,630 (M); expenditures, $100,791,
including $83,000 for 1 grant.
Purpose and activities: Grants to promote the
teaching of physiology.
Officers: A. Clifford Barger, President; Ranier
Beeuwkes III, Treasurer.
Trustees: J. Fray, Benjamin Kamier, Nancy
Millborne, John Mitchell, Richard Walker.
Employer Identification Number: 042104293

1545
Harvard Musical Association ♯
c/o Hobart W. Spring, Jr.
73 Tremont St., Rm. 921
Boston 02108   (617) 523-2897
Application address: c/o Chairman of Awards
Committee, Harvard Musical Association, 57A
Chestnut St., Boston, MA 02108

Established in 1837.
Financial data: (yr. ended 6/30/83): Assets,
$2,225,562 (M); gifts received, $2,931;
expenditures, $127,770, including $20,050 for
19 grants (high: $1,500; low: $50).
Purpose and activities: Primarily local giving
for music, including scholarship funds at music
schools.
Types of support awarded: Scholarship funds.
Limitations: Giving primarily in the greater
Boston, MA, area.
Application information:
  Deadline(s): April 1
Officers: Abram J. Collier, President; George
Butterworth, Secretary; Sherwood E. Bain,
Treasurer.
Employer Identification Number: 042104284

1546
Harvard-Yenching Institute
2 Divinity Ave.
Cambridge 02138   (617) 495-3369

Incorporated in 1928 in Massachusetts.
Donor(s): Trustees of Estate of Charles Martin
Hall.
Financial data: (yr. ended 6/30/84): Assets,
$29,545,448 (M); expenditures, $1,462,762,
including $1,304,310 for 70 grants (high:
$452,600; low: $1,400).
Purpose and activities: To aid the
development of higher education in eastern
and southern Asia, concentrating on the
humanities and social sciences; grants to
support teaching, research, and study by Asians
in these fields; and to sponsor fellowships for
research at Harvard University, or scholarships
for graduate study, by younger faculty
members of selected Asian institutions; also
helps to support East Asian studies at Harvard
through publication of the Harvard Journal of
Asiatic Studies, and through the Harvard-
Yenching Library, which became an integral
part of Harvard University as of July 1, 1976.
Grants given only for research or study by
faculty members of invited universities in East
and Southeast Asia.
Types of support awarded: Scholarship funds,
research, fellowships.
Limitations: Giving primarily in Asia and
Cambridge, MA. No grants to individuals.
Publications: Application guidelines, program
policy statement.
Application information: Application form
required for scholarships; applicants nominated
by participating universities. Application form
required.
  Initial approach: Letter
  Copies of proposal: 1
  Deadline(s): Submit proposal in September or
    October for following autumn; deadlines
    October 1 for Visiting Scholars; January 10
    for Doctoral Scholarships

Board meeting date(s): Usually in December and April
Write: Albert M. Craig, Director
Officers: Albert M. Craig, Director; Roderick MacDougall, Treasurer.
Trustees: Henry Rosovsky, Chairman; F. Gregg Bemis, T. Jefferson Coolidge, Jr., Bong Hak Hyun, Daniel H.H. Ingalls, Paul T. Lauby, John C. Pelzel, Nathan M. Pusey, A. Michael Spence.
Number of staff: 1 full-time professional; 1 part-time professional; 2 full-time support; 1 part-time support.
Employer Identification Number: 042062394

1547
Henderson Foundation
P.O. Box 420
Sudbury 01776 (617) 443-4646

Trust established in 1947 in Massachusetts.
Donor(s): Ernest Henderson,† George B. Henderson,† J. Brooks Fenno,† Ernest Henderson III.
Financial data: (yr. ended 12/31/84): Assets, $5,946,767 (M); expenditures, $288,453, including $246,600 for 64 grants (high: $9,500; low: $500).
Purpose and activities: Charitable purposes; general giving, with emphasis on education, intercultural relations, health and hospitals, religion, and youth agencies.
Types of support awarded: Continuing support, general purposes.
Limitations: No grants to individuals or for scholarships or fellowships.
Application information:
Initial approach: Letter
Copies of proposal: 1
Deadline(s): Submit proposal in October
Board meeting date(s): As required
Write: Ernest Henderson III, Trustee
Trustees: Barclay G.S. Henderson, Ernest Henderson III, Joseph Carlton Petrone, Jr.
Employer Identification Number: 046051095

1548
Henderson (The George B.) Foundation
c/o Herrick & Smith
100 Federal St.
Boston 02110 (617) 357-9000

Established in 1964 in Massachusetts.
Donor(s): George B. Henderson.†
Financial data: (yr. ended 12/31/82): Assets, $2,675,464 (M); expenditures, $147,667, including $137,000 for 4 grants (high: $80,000; low: $5,000).
Purpose and activities: Grants for enhancement of the physical appearance of the city of Boston.
Limitations: Giving limited to Boston, MA. No grants to individuals, or for endowment funds, maintenance, operating budgets, research, scholarships, fellowships, or general purposes; no loans.
Application information: Application form required.
Initial approach: Letter or proposal
Copies of proposal: 1
Board meeting date(s): As required

Write: John T. Galvin, Secretary, Board of Designators
Trustees: Henry R. Guild, Jr., Ernest Henderson III, Gerard C. Henderson.
Employer Identification Number: 046089310

1549
Heydt (Nan and Matilda) Fund
c/o BayBank Valley Trust Company
1500 Main St.
Springfield 01115 (413) 781-7575
Grant application address: Robert J. Van Wart, Secretary, Community Funds Advisory Committee, 1365 Main St., Springfield, MA 01103

Trust established in 1966 in Massachusetts.
Donor(s): Matilda L. Heydt.†
Financial data: (yr. ended 12/31/83): Assets, $2,361,491 (M); expenditures, $247,813, including $224,562 for 12 grants (high: $60,000; low: $1,450).
Purpose and activities: Grants for public charitable purposes in Hampden County, including health, welfare, the humanities, and education; emphasis on child welfare and youth agencies, community funds, and aid to the handicapped.
Limitations: Giving limited to Hampden County, MA. No grants to individuals, or for endowment funds, scholarships, fellowships, or operating budgets; no loans.
Publications: Application guidelines.
Application information:
Initial approach: Telephone, letter, or proposal
Copies of proposal: 12
Deadline(s): Submit proposal preferably in December, April, or August; deadline first Monday in January and May, and first Tuesday in September
Board meeting date(s): March, July, and November
Final notification: 4 months
Write: Robert J. Van Wart, Secretary, Community Funds Advisory Committee
Trustee: Baybank Valley Trust Company (Peter Weston, Vice-President).
Number of staff: 1 part-time professional; 1 part-time support.
Employer Identification Number: 046136421

1550
Hiatt (Jacob and Frances) Foundation, Inc. ☒
P.O. Box 1657, Station C
Worcester 01607

Incorporated in 1951 in Massachusetts.
Donor(s): Jacob Hiatt, Estey Charitable Income Trust, Rand-Whitney Packaging Corporation, Frances L. Hiatt.
Financial data: (yr. ended 8/31/82): Assets, $790,190 (M); gifts received, $471,188; expenditures, $555,521, including $530,525 for 27 grants (high: $200,000; low: $50).
Purpose and activities: Broad purposes; primarily local giving, with emphasis on higher education, cultural programs, and Jewish welfare funds.
Limitations: Giving primarily in Worcester, MA.

Officers: Jacob Hiatt,* President and Treasurer; Frances L. Hiatt,* Vice-President; Violet E. Robinson, Secretary.
Directors:* Myra H. Kraft, Robert K. Kraft.
Employer Identification Number: 046050716

1551
Higgins (Aldus C.) Foundation ☒
c/o Fiduciary Trust Company
175 Federal St.
Boston 02110

Trust established in 1946 in Massachusetts.
Donor(s): Higgins Trust No. 13, Mary S. Higgins Trust No. 2, and others.
Financial data: (yr. ended 9/30/83): Assets, $2,171,499 (M); expenditures, $137,562, including $126,000 for 8 grants (high: $50,000; low: $1,000).
Purpose and activities: Primarily local giving, with emphasis on higher and secondary education and cultural programs.
Limitations: Giving primarily in Worcester, MA.
Trustee: Richard Chapin, Milton P. Higgins, Ruth H. Tucker.
Employer Identification Number: 046049262

1552
Home for Aged Men in the City of Brockton ☒
c/o John Creedon
Shawmut Bank Bldg., 90 Main St.
Brockton 02401

Trust established in Massachusetts.
Donor(s): Horace Howard.†
Financial data: (yr. ended 3/31/83): Assets, $1,706,189 (M); gifts received, $9,746; expenditures, $134,836, including $60,000 for 5 grants (high: $20,000; low: $10,000).
Purpose and activities: Grants for local homes for the aged and hospitals to encourage development of the facilities' public assistance programs.
Limitations: Giving primarily in MA.
Officers: John Creedon, President; Anthony Froio, Treasurer.
Employer Identification Number: 042103796

1553
Hood (Charles H.) Foundation
29 Commonwealth Ave., Suite 801
Boston 02116 (617) 262-2206

Fund established in 1931; incorporated in 1942 in New Hampshire.
Donor(s): Charles H. Hood.†
Financial data: (yr. ended 12/31/84): Assets, $13,249,618 (M); expenditures, $311,265, including $291,819 for 14 grants (high: $30,000; low: $16,330).
Purpose and activities: Supports projects concerned with child health in New England through its Child Health Advisory Committee; emphasis on the initiation or furtherance of medical research and related projects contributing to a reduction of the health problems and health needs of large numbers of children.
Types of support awarded: Research.

Limitations: Giving limited to New England. No support for nutrition, public health, mental health, education, or social or general welfare. No grants to individuals, or for building or endowment funds, operating budgets, general support, publications, scholarships, fellowships, fund-raising campaigns, or matching gifts; no loans.
Publications: Annual report, program policy statement, application guidelines.
Application information: Application form required.
  Initial approach: Letter or telephone
  Copies of proposal: 9
  Deadline(s): Submit proposal after February 1 for April 15 deadline, and after August 1 for October 15 deadline
  Board meeting date(s): Usually in June and December
  Final notification: 60 to 70 days
  Write: Merle W. Mudd, Executive Director
Officers: Charles H. Hood, 2nd,* President and Treasurer; Merle W. Mudd, Secretary and Executive Director; John R. McLane, Jr., Clerk.
Members:* Roswell M. Boutwell, 3rd, John O. Parker, Henry M. Sanders.
Number of staff: 1 part-time professional.
Employer Identification Number: 046036790

1554
Hood (Charles H.) Fund ¤
500 Rutherford Ln.
Boston 02129

Foundation established in 1981.
Financial data: (yr. ended 12/31/81): Assets, $1,276,766 (M); expenditures, $56,027, including $24,150 for 7 grants (high: $4,000; low: $150) and $18,000 for 6 grants to individuals.
Purpose and activities: Giving primarily in New England for higher education, including scholarships.
Types of support awarded: Student aid.
Limitations: Giving primarily in New England.
Officers: Charles H. Hood,* Chairman and Member; June S. Fountain, Secretary; Marius deVos,* Treasurer.
Directors:* Barbara Normine.
Members: Robert Cushman, Warren Donovan, Eastman F. Heywood, Paul Varney.
Employer Identification Number: 046036788

1555
Hopedale Foundation, The
43 Hope St.
Hopedale 01747   (617) 473-0820

Trust established in 1946 in Massachusetts.
Donor(s): Draper Corporation, Thomas H. West,† John D. Gannett.†
Financial data: (yr. ended 10/31/84): Assets, $7,986,611 (M); expenditures, $194,128, including $132,894 for 21 grants (high: $50,000; low: $1,000) and $52,600 for 44 loans.

Purpose and activities: Emphasis on area community funds and hospitals; support also for health agencies, youth services, and higher education; student loans limited to local high school graduates. New grants only to organizations having direct impact on the local community.
Types of support awarded: Loans, student aid.
Limitations: Giving primarily in MA. No grants for endowment funds.
Application information:
  Initial approach: Letter
  Copies of proposal: 1
  Board meeting date(s): April, August, and December
  Write: Thad R. Jackson, Treasurer
Officers and Trustees: William K. Child, Chairman; Robert D. Donley, Secretary; Thad R. Jackson, Treasurer; W. Gregory Burrill, Peter S. Ellis, William B. Gannett, Thomas H. West, Jr.
Employer Identification Number: 046044779

1556
Hornblower (Henry) Fund, Inc. ¤
c/o H & W Agency, Inc.
24 Federal St.
Boston 02110

Incorporated in 1945 in Massachusetts.
Donor(s): Hornblower & Weeks - Hemphill, Noyes, members of the Hornblower family.
Financial data: (yr. ended 12/31/82): Assets, $1,259,241 (M); expenditures, $97,698, including $86,150 for 47 grants (high: $5,000; low: $150) and $1,380 for 1 grant to an individual.
Purpose and activities: Broad purposes; primarily local giving, with emphasis on higher and secondary education, hospitals, and cultural programs; support also for needy individuals presently or formerly employed by Hornblower & Weeks.
Limitations: Giving primarily in Boston, MA.
Directors: Richard Blomfield, Dudley Bradlee II, Martin J. Carew, Karl Grace, Henry Hornblower II, Ralph Hornblower, Jr., George Larson, Nathan Withington.
Employer Identification Number: 237425285

1557
Horne (Mabel A.) Trust
c/o The First National Bank of Boston
P.O. Box 1890
Boston 02105   (617) 434-5669

Trust established in 1964 in Massachusetts.
Donor(s): Mabel A. Horne.†
Financial data: (yr. ended 9/30/83): Assets, $2,273,805 (M); expenditures, $112,500, including $92,500 for 20 grants (high: $10,000; low: $1,000).
Purpose and activities: Broad purposes; grants limited to organizations operating in Massachusetts, with emphasis on giving within Boston.
Limitations: Giving limited to MA, with emphasis on Boston. No grants to individuals.
Publications: Application guidelines.
Application information: Application form required.

  Initial approach: Letter
  Copies of proposal: 1
  Deadline(s): Submit proposal preferably in December, May, June or September; deadline is last day of month prior to meetings
  Board meeting date(s): January, April, July, and October
  Write: Miss Sharon M. Driscoll, Trust Officer
Trustee: The First National Bank of Boston (Sharon M. Driscoll, Trust Officer).
Employer Identification Number: 046089241

1558
Housen Foundation, Inc.
c/o Erving Paper Mills
47 East Main St.
Erving 01344   (617) 544-2711

Incorporated in 1968 in Massachusetts.
Donor(s): Erving Paper Mills.
Financial data: (yr. ended 12/31/83): Assets, $283,115 (M); gifts received, $150,625; expenditures, $125,841, including $125,382 for 30 grants (high: $75,000; low: $20).
Purpose and activities: Local giving, with emphasis on Jewish welfare funds, community funds, and higher education including scholarships to children of Erving Paper Mill employees.
Types of support awarded: Employee related scholarships.
Limitations: Giving limited to MA. No grants to individuals (except scholarships for employees' children only).
Application information: Grant applications not accepted.
  Board meeting date(s): January
  Write: Ms. Dawn Williams
Officers and Directors: Charles B. Housen, President; Leo J. Roiko, Vice-President; Ellen C. Rutan, Treasurer; Morton Slavin, Clerk.
Number of staff: None.
Employer Identification Number: 046183673

1559
Howard Benevolent Society ¤
14 Beacon St., Rm. 507
Boston 02108

Established in 1812.
Donor(s): Elisha V. Ashton.†
Financial data: (yr. ended 9/30/82): Assets, $1,070,681 (M); gifts received, $24,000; expenditures, $102,310, including $74,977 for 200 grants to individuals.
Purpose and activities: Local giving to aid sick and destitute individuals.
Types of support awarded: Grants to individuals.
Limitations: Giving limited to the Boston, MA, metropolitan area.
Officers: Horace Besecker, Jr., President; Carol Tibbetts, Secretary; Howard Bacon, Treasurer.
Employer Identification Number: 042129132

1560
Humane Society of the Commonwealth of Massachusetts ☒
177 Milk St.
Boston 02109

Established in 1785.
Financial data: (yr. ended 3/31/83): Assets, $1,431,325 (M); expenditures, $87,341, including $36,121 for grants.
Purpose and activities: Primarily local giving for medical education and research.
Limitations: Giving primarily in MA.
Officers and Trustees: John E. Lawrence, President; Charles Devens, Secretary; Henry E. Russell, Treasurer; Charles F. Adams, Francis H. Burr, Ferdinand Colloredo-Mansfeld, Richard M. Cutler, John H. Finley, George P. Gardner, Jr., Frederick S. Moseley, III, Lawrence T. Perera, Curtis Prout.
Employer Identification Number: 042104291

1561
Hyams (Godfrey M.) Trust ▼
One Boston Place, 33rd Fl.
Boston 02108 (617) 725-1520

Trust established in 1921 in Massachusetts.
Donor(s): Godfrey M. Hyams.†
Financial data: (yr. ended 12/31/83): Assets, $36,856,565 (M); gifts received, $206,425; expenditures, $2,793,499, including $2,481,387 for 170 grants (high: $87,000; low: $2,500; average: $5,000-$20,000).
Purpose and activities: Giving locally only, with emphasis on youth agencies and neighborhood centers; support also for other social service and community development purposes; limited grants to cultural organizations and mental health programs.
Types of support awarded: Operating budgets, continuing support, annual campaigns, seed money, building funds, equipment, land acquisition, matching funds.
Limitations: Giving limited to the Boston, MA, metropolitan area. No support for municipal, state, or federal agencies; to institutions of higher learning for standard educational programs; or to national or regional health organizations. No grants to individuals, or for endowment funds, deficit financing, fellowships, publications, or conferences; no loans.
Publications: Annual report, application guidelines.
Application information: Application form required.
  Initial approach: Full proposal
  Copies of proposal: 6
  Deadline(s): Submit proposal preferably in fall or winter; no set deadline
  Board meeting date(s): 5 to 6 times a year regularly from October through June
  Final notification: 2 to 6 months
  Write: Joan M. Diver, Executive Director
Officer: Joan M. Diver, Executive Director.

Trustees: William N. Swift, Chairman; John H. Clymer, Theresa J. Morse, John O. Rhome, Lewis H. Spence, Roslyn M. Watson, Boston Safe Deposit and Trust Company (Michael W. Christian, Executive Vice-President).
Number of staff: 2 full-time professional; 1 full-time support; 1 part-time support.
Employer Identification Number: 042214849

1562
Hyams (Sarah A.) Fund, Inc.
One Boston Place, 33rd Fl.
Boston 02108 (617) 725-1520

Incorporated in 1929 in Massachusetts.
Donor(s): Godfrey M. Hyams Trust.
Financial data: (yr. ended 12/31/83): Assets, $2,461,837 (M); gifts received, $33,693; expenditures, $186,059, including $150,800 for 30 grants (high: $10,000; low: $500; average: $1,000-$5,000).
Purpose and activities: Grants only to Massachusetts charitable corporations serving the needs of residents of metropolitan Boston, with emphasis on operating expenses and capital funds for summer youth programs.
Types of support awarded: Operating budgets, building funds.
Limitations: Giving limited to MA organizations serving residents of metropolitan Boston. No support for municipal, state or federal agencies, institutions of higher learning for standard educational programs, or national or regional health organizations. No grants to individuals, or for endowment funds, research, scholarships and fellowships, or matching gifts; no loans.
Publications: Annual report, application guidelines.
Application information: Application form required.
  Initial approach: Proposal
  Copies of proposal: 6
  Deadline(s): Submit proposal in February or March; no set deadline
  Board meeting date(s): 5 to 6 times a year between October and June
  Final notification: 2 to 6 months
  Write: Joan M. Diver, Executive Director
Officers: William N. Swift,* President and Treasurer; Theresa J. Morse,* Secretary; Joan M. Diver, Executive Director.
Trustees:* Michael W. Christian, John H. Clymer, John O. Rhome, Lewis H. Spence, Roslyn M. Watson.
Number of staff: 2 full-time professional; 1 full-time support; 1 part-time support.
Employer Identification Number: 046013680

1563
Jackson (Marion Gardner) Charitable Trust
c/o The First National Bank of Boston
P.O. Box 1890
Boston 02105

Financial data: (yr. ended 12/31/83): Assets, $4,310,292 (M); expenditures, $226,900, including $211,900 for 22 grants (high: $25,000; low: $2,000).

Purpose and activities: Giving largely in capital funds for youth, social, and health agencies, higher education, and arts and cultural programs.
Types of support awarded: Building funds.
Limitations: Giving primarily in Adams County, IL.
Application information:
  Write: Sharon M. Driscoll, Trust Officer
Trustee: The First National Bank of Boston (Sharon M. Driscoll, Trust Officer).
Employer Identification Number: 046010559

1564
Jaffe Foundation, The
350 North Main St.
P.O. Box 227
Fall River 02720 (617) 679-2151

Trust established in 1962 in Massachusetts.
Donor(s): Meyer Jaffe,† Edwin A. Jaffe.
Financial data: (yr. ended 6/30/84): Assets, $1,959,929 (M); gifts received, $186,738; expenditures, $181,980, including $171,094 for 46 grants (high: $45,000; low: $250; average: $1,000).
Purpose and activities: Broad purposes; primarily local giving.
Limitations: Giving primarily in MA. No grants to individuals.
Application information:
  Initial approach: Letter
  Copies of proposal: 1
  Board meeting date(s): January and July
  Write: Edwin A. Jaffe, Trustee
Trustees: Edwin A. Jaffe, Chairman; Lola Jaffe, Vice-Chairman; David S. Greer, Donna Jaffe, Robert Jaffe.
Employer Identification Number: 046049261

1565
Johnson (Edward C.) Fund ☒
c/o Edward C. Johnson, 2nd
82 Devonshire St.
Boston 02109

Trust established in 1964 in Massachusetts.
Donor(s): Edward C. Johnson, 2nd, Edward C. Johnson, 3rd.
Financial data: (yr. ended 12/31/82): Assets, $4,034,998 (M); gifts received, $1,010,073; expenditures, $742,530, including $726,561 for 60 grants (high: $125,000; low: $50).
Purpose and activities: Primarily local giving, with emphasis on cultural programs including fine arts and historic preservation, animal welfare agencies, religious organizations, higher education, and health services.
Limitations: Giving primarily in MA.
Trustees: Edward C. Johnson, 2nd, Edward C. Johnson, 3rd, Caleb Loring, Jr.
Employer Identification Number: 046108344

1566
Johnson (The Howard) Foundation
One Howard Johnson Plaza
Dorchester 02125 (617) 847-2000
Mailing address: c/o Howard B. Johnson, 720 Fifth Ave., 13th Fl., New York, NY 10019

Trust established in 1961 in Massachusetts.
Donor(s): Howard D. Johnson.†
Financial data: (yr. ended 12/31/84): Assets, $2,427,864 (M); expenditures, $204,280, including $188,500 for 83 grants (high: $25,000; low: $500; average: $2,200).
Purpose and activities: Broad purposes; grants primarily for higher and secondary education and hospitals; support also for museums, churches, and religious welfare agencies.
Limitations: No grants to individuals.
Application information:
Initial approach: Letter
Copies of proposal: 1
Deadline(s): Submit proposal early in calendar year
Board meeting date(s): Quarterly
Write: Howard B. Johnson
Officer: Eugene J. Durgin, Secretary.
Trustees: Dorothy J. Henry, Howard B. Johnson, John T. Noonan.
Number of staff: 1 part-time support.
Employer Identification Number: 046060965

1567
Kelley (Edward Bangs) and Elza Kelley Foundation, Inc.
243 South St.
P.O. Drawer M
Hyannis 02601 (617) 775-3117

Incorporated in 1954 in Massachusetts.
Donor(s): Edward Bangs Kelley,† Elza deHorvath Kelley.†
Financial data: (yr. ended 12/31/83): Assets, $2,500,000 (M); expenditures, $170,000, including $115,000 for 25 grants (high: $20,000; low: $1,000; average: $1,000-$10,000) and $35,000 for 35 grants to individuals.
Purpose and activities: To promote health and welfare of inhabitants of Barnstable County, Massachusetts; grants for higher education, including scholarships and particularly for medical and paramedical education; hospitals, youth agencies, and libraries.
Types of support awarded: Operating budgets, continuing support, seed money, emergency funds, building funds, equipment, matching funds, scholarship funds, internships, professorships, special projects, research, student aid.
Limitations: Giving limited to Barnstable County, MA. No grants to individuals (except for scholarships), or for annual campaigns, deficit financing, land acquisition, endowment funds, exchange programs, fellowships, publications, or conferences; no loans.
Publications: Informational brochure, application guidelines, annual report.
Application information: Application form required.
Initial approach: Letter, followed by full proposal
Copies of proposal: 8
Deadline(s): April 30 for scholarships; no deadline for grants
Board meeting date(s): January, April, July, and October
Final notification: 3 weeks
Write: Henry L. Murphy, Jr., Administrative Manager

Officers and Directors: Frank L. Nickerson, President; Walter G. Robinson, Vice-President; Milton L. Penn, Treasurer; Mary Susich, Clerk; Henry L. Murphy, Jr., Administrative Manager; Palmer Davenport, Frank W. Garran, Jr., M.D., Townsend Hornor, Esther Howes, Frederick V. Lawrence, Katherine A. Leland, M.D., Kenneth S. MacAffer, Jr., Henry L. Murphy, Jr., E. Carlton Nickerson.
Number of staff: None.
Employer Identification Number: 046039660

1568
Kendall Company Foundation ¤
One Federal St.
Boston 02101

Trust established in 1959 in Massachusetts.
Donor(s): The Kendall Company.
Financial data: (yr. ended 12/31/82): Assets, $10,169 (M); gifts received, $162,000; expenditures, $169,285, including $132,072 for 46 grants (high: $58,761; low: $150) and $36,059 for employee matching gifts.
Purpose and activities: Giving primarily for community funds, hospitals, and a matching gifts program for higher education; some support also for social agencies.
Types of support awarded: Employee matching gifts.
Trustees: Andrew R. Cay, R.W. MacLeod, J.D. Sherratt.
Employer Identification Number: 046048626

1569
Kendall (The Henry P.) Foundation ▼
One Boston Place
Boston 02108 (617) 723-8727

Trust established in 1957 in Massachusetts.
Donor(s): Henry P. Kendall family.
Financial data: (yr. ended 12/31/82): Assets, $37,264,065 (M); gifts received, $253,146; expenditures, $2,122,107, including $1,861,111 for 84 grants (high: $480,585; low: $600; average: $1,000-$50,000).
Purpose and activities: General purposes; with special emphasis on matters concerning the natural environment, energy, natural resources, the nuclear arms race, and other public interest issues; support also for higher education and a whaling museum.
Types of support awarded: Operating budgets, seed money, emergency funds, research, special projects, publications, conferences and seminars, loans, continuing support.
Limitations: No grants to individuals, or for capital or endowment funds, scholarships and fellowships, or matching gifts.
Publications: Program policy statement, application guidelines.
Application information:
Initial approach: Letter
Copies of proposal: 1
Deadline(s): None
Board meeting date(s): As required
Final notification: 2 months
Write: Robert L. Allen, Vice-President
Officer: Robert L. Allen, Vice-President.

Trustees: Henry W. Kendall, John P. Kendall, Anne G. Plimpton.
Number of staff: 1 full-time professional.
Employer Identification Number: 046029103

1570
Kenwood Foundation ¤
c/o Woodstock Service Corp.
100 Federal St.
Boston 02110

Established in 1960.
Donor(s): Edith LaCroix Dabney, and others.
Financial data: (yr. ended 12/31/82): Assets, $214,759 (M); gifts received, $185,900; expenditures, $217,041, including $210,000 for 53 grants (high: $40,000; low: $100).
Purpose and activities: Primarily local giving for higher and secondary education, hospitals, and cultural programs, including music.
Limitations: Giving primarily in MA.
Trustees: Edith L. Dabney, Charles P. Knowles, James T. Knowles, Jean L. Knowles, John H. Knowles, Jr., Richard D. Phippen, Edith K. Williams, Thomas M. Williams.
Employer Identification Number: 046012784

1571
King (Charles A.) Trust ¤
c/o Bank of New England
28 State St.
Boston 02107 (617) 973-1793

Trust established in 1938 in Massachusetts.
Donor(s): Charles A. King.†
Financial data: (yr. ended 12/31/82): Assets, $6,161,506 (M); expenditures, $376,018, including $339,500 for 30 grants (high: $17,000; low: $7,400).
Purpose and activities: To encourage and support medical and surgical research projects carried on by charitable or educational corporations within Massachusetts. Grants are awarded for postdoctoral research fellowships.
Types of support awarded: Research, fellowships.
Limitations: Giving primarily in MA. No grants to individuals.
Publications: Application guidelines.
Application information: Application form required.
Initial approach: Telephone
Copies of proposal: 17
Deadline(s): Submit proposals preferably in March or September; deadlines April 15 and October 15
Board meeting date(s): June and December
Final notification: 2 months
Write: John M. Dolan, Senior Trust Officer
Trustees: Edward N. Dane, Richard H. Lovell, Bank of New England.
Number of staff: None.
Employer Identification Number: 046012742

1572
Knistrom (Fanny and Svante) Foundation
3 Holbrook Rd.
Wayland 01778

Established in 1972 in New Jersey.
Donor(s): Svante Knistrom,† Fanny Knistrom.
Financial data: (yr. ended 5/31/82): Assets, $3,638,664 (M); expenditures, $237,024, including $193,000 for 40 grants (high: $38,000; low: $1,000).
Purpose and activities: Primarily local giving, with emphasis on health agencies; grants also for the American Indian, youth agencies, and higher education.
Limitations: Giving primarily in NJ.
Application information:
  Write: Charles J. Beusing, President
Officers and Trustees: Charles J. Beusing, President; Ann Buesing, Secretary; Gregory P. Buesing, Guy K. Buesing, Donald Kreuzberger, Virginia Kreuzberger, Richard W. Stickel.
Employer Identification Number: 222011417

1573
Lend A Hand Society ⋈
34 1/2 Beacon St.
Boston 02108

Established in 1870.
Financial data: (yr. ended 12/31/82): Assets, $1,053,515 (M); gifts received, $1,762; expenditures, $92,092, including $3,800 for 5 grants (high: $1,500; low: $300) and $57,198 for 397 grants to individuals.
Purpose and activities: Charitable purposes; primarily local giving to aid needy individuals.
Types of support awarded: Grants to individuals.
Limitations: Giving primarily in Boston, MA.
Officers and Directors: Richard S. Chute, President; Mrs. Vincent H. Hazard, 1st Vice-President; Mrs. Rhys Williams, 2nd Vice-President; Edward C. Huebner, Treasurer; Mrs. Paul Carnes, Thomas H. Dahill, Mary Ann Daily, Mrs. Dana McLean Greely, Roland D. Grimm, Mrs. James H. Jackson, Henry J. Mascarello, Donald W. Moreland, Thomas B. Williams.
Employer Identification Number: 042104384

1574
Levinson (Max and Anna) Foundation
1318 Beacon St., Rm. 6
Brookline 02146   (617) 731-1602

Incorporated in 1956 in Delaware.
Donor(s): Max Levinson,† Carl A. Levinson.
Financial data: (yr. ended 9/30/83): Assets, $4,462,000 (M); gifts received, $2,000; expenditures, $708,783, including $479,225 for 61 grants (high: $25,000; low: $500; average: $500-$20,000).

Purpose and activities: Broad purposes; toward the development of a more humane and rewarding democratic society, in which people have greater ability and opportunity to determine directions for the future. Seeks to encourage projects that are concerned with promoting social change and social justice, either by developing and testing alternatives or by responsibly modifying existing systems, institutions, conditions and attitudes that block promising innovation. Grants mainly for projects of national and international impact in the areas of world peace, arms control, energy, environment, civil liberties, human rights, and the Jewish community.
Types of support awarded: Seed money, program-related investments, special projects.
Limitations: No grants to individuals, or for capital and endowment funds, travel, projects of primarily local community significance, expansion of existing services, matching gifts, or scholarships and fellowships; no loans.
Publications: Informational brochure, application guidelines, program policy statement.
Application information:
  Initial approach: Full proposal
  Copies of proposal: 1
  Deadline(s): March 1 and September 1
  Board meeting date(s): May and November
  Final notification: 2 weeks after board meeting
  Write: Sidney Shapiro, Executive Director
Officers and Directors: Helen L. Doroshow,* President; James E. Doroshow,* Vice-President; Charles A. Hunt,* Secretary; Carl A. Levinson,* Treasurer; Donald Bean, Carol A. Doroshow, William Doroshow, Anna B. Levinson, Lynda B. Levinson.
Number of staff: 1 full-time professional; 1 full-time support.
Employer Identification Number: 236282844

1575
Levy (June Rockwell) Foundation Incorporated
100 Federal St., Rm. 2900
Boston 02110

Incorporated in 1947 in Connecticut.
Donor(s): Austin T. Levy.†
Financial data: (yr. ended 12/31/82): Assets, $8,725,744 (M); expenditures, $417,823, including $342,470 for 60 grants (high: $45,000; low: $1,000).
Purpose and activities: General purposes; grants largely for hospitals, medical research, and higher and secondary education; support also for youth agencies, cultural programs, and the handicapped, primarily in Rhode Island.
Limitations: Giving primarily in RI. No support for religious purposes.
Application information:
  Initial approach: Letter
  Write: James W. Noonan, Secretary
Officers: Edward H. Osgood,* Chairman and President; Robert S. Swain,* Vice-President; James W. Noonan,* Secretary; Edwin W. Dennis, Treasurer.
Trustees:* George T. Helm, Winifred H. Thompson.
Employer Identification Number: 046074284

1576
Lindsay (Agnes M.) Trust ▼
38 Newbury St.
Boston 02116   (617) 266-2741

Trust established in 1938 in New Hampshire.
Donor(s): Agnes M. Lindsay.†
Financial data: (yr. ended 12/31/82): Assets, $11,503,129 (M); expenditures, $928,555, including $838,500 for 156 grants (high: $20,000; low: $500).
Purpose and activities: Charitable and educational purposes in northern New England, including child welfare and education of poor and deserving students from rural areas; support largely for higher education, health agencies, agencies for the handicapped, and welfare institutions.
Types of support awarded: Scholarship funds, building funds, equipment, special projects, operating budgets, deficit financing, matching funds, general purposes.
Limitations: Giving limited to ME, MA, NH, and VT. No grants to individuals.
Application information:
  Initial approach: Full proposal
  Deadline(s): None
  Board meeting date(s): Infrequently
  Write: Wilbur W. Bullen, Trustee
Trustees: Wilbur W. Bullen, Robert L. Chiesa, Franklin D. Jerome.
Number of staff: 3.
Employer Identification Number: 026004971

1577
Lipsky (Fred & Sarah) Charitable Foundation ⋈
46 Pleasant St.
Malden 02148

Trust established in 1960 in Massachusetts.
Donor(s): Fred Lipsky.†
Financial data: (yr. ended 1/31/82): Assets, $1,320,237 (M); gifts received, $146,363; expenditures, $72,981, including $40,950 for 72 grants (high: $2,000; low: $100).
Purpose and activities: Primarily local giving, with emphasis on Jewish welfare funds and temple support; support also for secondary education, hospitals, and youth agencies.
Limitations: Giving primarily in MA.
Trustee: First National Bank of Malden.
Employer Identification Number: 046072512

1578
Little (The Arthur D.) Foundation
25 Acorn Park
Cambridge 02140   (617) 864-5770

Trust established in 1953 in Massachusetts.
Donor(s): Arthur D. Little, Inc.
Financial data: (yr. ended 12/31/82): Assets, $452,797 (M); gifts received, $316,800; expenditures, $422,026, including $418,798 for 132 grants (high: $75,000; low: $300).

Purpose and activities: Broad purposes; grants primarily for education, including higher education, vocational and special projects; scientific and other research; health care; and community charities, with preference to innovative programs in areas of company operations that benefit company employees.
Types of support awarded: Continuing support, annual campaigns, seed money, emergency funds, deficit financing, research, special projects, publications, conferences and seminars, consulting services, technical assistance.
Limitations: Giving primarily in areas of company operations. No support for religious, fraternal, or veterans' organizations, the arts, or the alleviation of natural disasters. No grants to individuals, building or endowment funds, or matching gifts; no loans.
Publications: Program policy statement, application guidelines.
Application information:
  Initial approach: Letter
  Copies of proposal: 2
  Deadline(s): Submit proposal preferably in April or September
  Board meeting date(s): May and October
  Write: Standish Bradford, Jr., Secretary
Officer and Trustees: Standish Bradford, Jr., Secretary; Theodore P. Heuchling, Judith C. Harris, D. Reid Weedon, Jr.
Employer Identification Number: 046079132

1579
Lowell Institute, Trustees of the
73 Tremont St.
Boston 02108   (617) 523-1635

Established in 1917.
Financial data: (yr. ended 7/31/83): Assets, $10,579,116 (M); expenditures, $597,846, including $506,740 for 5 grants (high: $225,000; low: $15,000).
Purpose and activities: Local giving; grants largely for higher education and cultural programs.
Types of support awarded: Conferences and seminars, lectureships.
Limitations: Giving primarily in MA. No grants to individuals, or for operating budgets, building or endowment funds, scholarships or fellowships, or matching gifts; no loans.
Application information:
  Initial approach: Telephone or full proposal
  Copies of proposal: 1
  Write: Mary L. O'Toole
Manager and Trustee: John Lowell.
Number of staff: 1.
Employer Identification Number: 042105771

1580
Massachusetts Charitable Mechanic Association ¤
20 Providence St.
Boston 02116   (617) 426-7907

Established in 1806.
Financial data: (yr. ended 12/31/82): Assets, $2,716,453 (M); gifts received, $172,211; expenditures, $163,181, including $57,861 for 14 grants.

Purpose and activities: Primarily local giving for the handicapped, vocational education, and social services.
Limitations: Giving primarily in MA.
Application information:
  Write: Raymond J. Purdy, Secretary-Treasurer
Officer: Raymond J. Purdy, Secretary-Treasurer.
Employer Identification Number: 042023566

1581
McEvoy (Mildred H.) Foundation ▼
370 Main St.
Worcester 01608   (617) 798-8621

Trust established in 1963 in Massachusetts.
Donor(s): Mildred H. McEvoy.†
Financial data: (yr. ended 12/31/83): Assets, $10,985,964 (M); expenditures, $382,378, including $362,200 for 45 grants (high: $75,000; low: $100; average: $250-$2,000).
Purpose and activities: Broad purposes; primarily local giving in Worcester, Massachusetts and Boothbay Harbor, Maine; grants largely for higher education, museums and historic preservation, scientific and medical research, and hospitals.
Limitations: Giving primarily in Worcester, MA, and Boothbay Harbor, ME. No grants to individuals, or for endowment funds or operating budgets.
Application information:
  Initial approach: Letter
  Copies of proposal: 1
  Deadline(s): Submit proposal in April; no set deadline
  Write: Sumner B. Tilton, Jr., Trustee
Trustees: George A. McEvoy, George H. McEvoy, Sumner B. Tilton, Jr.
Number of staff: None.
Employer Identification Number: 046069958

1582
Melville (The David B.) Foundation ¤
30 Colpitts Rd.
Weston 02193

Foundation established in 1962 in Massachusetts.
Donor(s): David B. Melville.
Financial data: (yr. ended 6/30/81): Assets, $956,203 (M); gifts received, $264,010; expenditures, $249,235, including $247,587 for 4 grants (high: $232,187; low: $1,000).
Purpose and activities: Giving largely for a secondary school and Christian missionary work.
Trustees: Robert W. Hanlon, Aubrey E. Jones, E. Christopher Palmer.
Employer Identification Number: 042680388

1583
Merkert (E. F.) Foundation ¤
c/o Eugene F. Merkert
500 Turnpike St.
Canton 02021

Established in 1960.
Donor(s): Merkert Enterprises, Inc., Eugene F. Merkert.

Financial data: (yr. ended 12/31/82): Assets, $94,364 (M); gifts received, $125,000; expenditures, $121,347, including $121,105 for 38 grants (high: $50,000; low: $75).
Purpose and activities: Broad purposes; giving primarily in Massachusetts for higher education, social services, and medical organizations, including research and hospitals.
Types of support awarded: Endowment funds, research.
Limitations: Giving primarily in MA.
Trustee: Eugene F. Merkert.
Employer Identification Number: 046111832

1584
Morgan-Worcester, Inc.
15 Belmont St.
Worcester 01605   (617) 755-6111

Incorporated in 1953 in Massachusetts.
Donor(s): Morgan Construction Company.
Financial data: (yr. ended 9/30/83): Assets, $1,301,666 (M); gifts received, $150,000; expenditures, $292,368, including $251,438 for 58 grants (high: $73,000; low: $100) and $40,930 for 254 employee matching gifts.
Purpose and activities: Local giving with emphasis on civic affairs, cultural programs, education, health, and community funds.
Types of support awarded: Employee matching gifts, operating budgets, continuing support, annual campaigns, seed money, emergency funds, building funds, equipment, land acquisition.
Limitations: Giving primarily in the greater Worcester, MA, area. No grants to individuals, or for endowment funds, special projects, research, publications, conferences, scholarships, or fellowships; no loans.
Application information:
  Initial approach: Letter
  Copies of proposal: 1
  Deadline(s): None
  Board meeting date(s): December, March, June, and September
  Final notification: Within 3 months
  Write: Peter S. Morgan, President
Officers and Directors: Peter S. Morgan, President and Treasurer; Daniel M. Morgan, Paul B. Morgan, Jr., Paul S. Morgan, Philip R. Morgan, Gavin D. Robertson.
Number of staff: None.
Employer Identification Number: 046111693

1585
Naurison (James Z.) Scholarship Fund
c/o Bank of New England - West
P.O. Box 9006
Springfield 01102-9006   (413) 787-8745

Trust established in 1973 in Massachusetts.
Donor(s): James Z. Naurison.†
Financial data: (yr. ended 7/31/83): Assets, $4,062,791 (M); expenditures, $403,415, including $349,600 for 573 grants to individuals (average: $500-$700).
Purpose and activities: Scholarship awards to local students only.
Types of support awarded: Student aid.

Limitations: Giving limited to residents of Hampden, Hampshire, Franklin, and Berkshire counties, MA; and Enfield and Suffield, CT.
Publications: Application guidelines.
Application information: Application form required.

Initial approach: Letter
Deadline(s): Submit application between December and April; deadline May 1
Board meeting date(s): February and June
Final notification: July 1
Write: Phyllis J. Farrell, Administrator
Trustees: Bank of New England - West.
Number of staff: 1 full-time professional.
Employer Identification Number: 046329627

1586
New England Peabody Home for Crippled Children
c/o Norman C. Nicholson, Jr.
One Boston Place
Boston 02106   (617) 722-7086

Established in 1894 in Massachusetts.
Financial data: (yr. ended 9/30/82): Assets, $4,765,666 (M); gifts received, $12,000; expenditures, $296,753, including $256,894 for 9 grants (high: $72,600; low: $4,100).
Purpose and activities: Grants primarily for medical research relating to handicapped children in the Boston area.
Limitations: Giving primarily in the Boston, MA, area.
Officers and Trustees: F. Stanton Deland, President; Norman C. Nicholson, Jr., Vice-President and Treasurer; William V. Tripp III, Vice-President and Clerk; Dorothy A. Brown, Mrs. Paul F. Burdon, Mrs. John L. Damon, Charles F. Eaton, Jr., Mrs. Francis B. Haydock, John H. Hewitt, Paul W. Hugenberger, M.D., Sally D. Hurlbut, Anna P. Revere, Mrs. Stephen D. Paine.
Employer Identification Number: 042104767

1587
Noonan (Deborah Munroe) Memorial Fund
c/o Bank of New England
28 State St.
Boston 02106   (617) 973-1798

Trust established in 1947 in Massachusetts.
Donor(s): Frank M. Noonan.†
Financial data: (yr. ended 9/30/83): Assets, $3,269,303 (M); expenditures, $267,960, including $245,000 for 8 grants (high: $100,000; low: $5,000).
Purpose and activities: Grants principally to local hospitals.
Limitations: Giving limited to the greater Boston, MA, area. No grants to individuals, or for scholarships or fellowships; no loans.
Publications: Application guidelines.
Application information:

Initial approach: Full proposal
Copies of proposal: 1
Board meeting date(s): Distribution committee meets as required

Write: Sharon M. Driscoll, Assistant Trust Officer
Trustee: Bank of New England (John M. Dolan, Senior Trust Officer).
Employer Identification Number: 046025957

1588
Norton Company Foundation ▼
One New Bond St.
Worcester 01606   (617) 853-1000

Trust established in 1953 in Massachusetts; incorporated in 1975.
Donor(s): Norton Company.
Financial data: (yr. ended 12/31/82): Assets, $79,393 (M); gifts received, $101,000; expenditures, $1,485,783, including $1,210,674 for 555 grants (high: $165,000; low: $30) and $259,074 for 1,076 employee matching gifts.
Purpose and activities: Primarily local giving, with emphasis on community funds, higher education, hospitals, youth agencies, and cultural programs in areas of company operations.
Limitations: Giving primarily in MA. No grants to individuals, or for endowment funds, scholarships, or fellowships; no loans.
Publications: 990-PF, application guidelines.
Application information:

Initial approach: Full proposal
Copies of proposal: 1
Deadline(s): March 1, June 1, September 1 and December 1
Board meeting date(s): March, June, September, and December
Write: Deborah A. Kaufman, Secretary
Officers and Director: Donald R. Melville, President; Deborah A. Kaufman, Secretary; Richard J. Flynn, Treasurer.
Employer Identification Number: 237423043

1589
Old Colony Charitable Foundation
c/o First National Bank of Boston
P.O. Box 1890
Boston 02105   (617) 434-5669

Community foundation established in 1955 in Massachusetts by declaration of trust.
Financial data: (yr. ended 12/31/83): Assets, $1,251,936 (M); gifts received, $384,168; expenditures, $304,199, including $290,608 for grants (average: $1,000-$7,500).
Purpose and activities: Grants to local organizations; consideration given to core programming and capital support in the areas of human services, urban programs, youth and elderly, special education, family services, and health care programs.
Types of support awarded: Operating budgets, continuing support, seed money, building funds, equipment.

Limitations: Giving limited to the greater Boston, MA area. No support for national organizations or film production. No grants to individuals, or for conferences, travel, endowment funds, matching gifts, scholarships, research not under aegis of recognized charitable organization, publications, or projects requiring multi-year commitment; no loans.
Publications: Annual report, application guidelines.
Application information: Application form required.

Initial approach: Full proposal
Copies of proposal: 1
Deadline(s): February 28 and August 31
Board meeting date(s): May and November
Final notification: 1 week
Write: Miss Sharon Driscoll, Trust Officer
Committee: Lawrence K. Fish, Chairman; Joseph Auerbach, Mrs. Norman L. Cahners, Caroline Chang, Joseph S. Mitchell, Jr.
Trustee: The First National Bank of Boston.
Number of staff: 1 full-time support.
Employer Identification Number: 046010342

1590
Pappas (Bessie) Charitable Foundation, Inc.
(formerly Pappas Family Foundation)
P.O. Box 318
Belmont 02540

Trust established in 1960 in Massachusetts.
Donor(s): Thomas Anthony Pappas Charitable Foundation.
Financial data: (yr. ended 12/31/81): Assets, $578,026 (M); gifts received, $657,000; expenditures, $698,349, including $685,000 for 9 grants (high: $405,000; low: $1,000).
Purpose and activities: General purposes; primarily local giving with emphasis on higher and secondary education.
Limitations: Giving primarily in MA. No grants to individuals.
Officers and Directors: Charles A. Pappas, President and Treasurer; Helen K. Pappas, Vice-President; Betsy Z. Pappas, Clerk and Director of Development; James S. Hekemian.
Number of staff: 2 full-time professional.
Employer Identification Number: 222540702

1591
Pappas (Thomas Anthony) Charitable Foundation, Inc. ▼
P.O. Box 463
Belmont 02178

Incorporated in 1975 in Massachusetts.
Donor(s): Thomas A. Pappas.
Financial data: (yr. ended 12/31/82): Assets, $12,494,472 (M); expenditures, $1,526,432, including $1,238,200 for 80 grants (high: $225,000; low: $450; average: $500-$25,000).
Purpose and activities: Largely local giving, with emphasis on higher education, hospitals, cultural programs, Greek Orthodox church support, religious associations, and youth and social service agencies.

Types of support awarded: Annual campaigns, building funds, endowment funds, research, professorships, scholarship funds, fellowships, continuing support.
Limitations: Giving primarily in MA. No grants to individuals.
Publications: Program policy statement, application guidelines.
Application information:
  Initial approach: Letter or full proposal
  Deadline(s): Submit proposal preferably in March or September; deadline September 30
  Board meeting date(s): March, June, September, and December
  Final notification: December 31
Officers and Directors: Charles A. Pappas, President and Treasurer; Helen K. Pappas, Vice-President; Betsy Z. Pappas, Clerk and Director of Development; James S. Hekemian.
Number of staff: 3 full-time professional; 1 part-time professional.
Employer Identification Number: 510153284

1592
Parker (The Theodore Edson) Foundation
100 Franklin St.
Boston 02110   (617) 357-1500

Incorporated in 1944 in Massachusetts.
Donor(s): Theodore Edson Parker.†
Financial data: (yr. ended 12/31/84): Assets, $6,300,000 (M); expenditures, $435,000, including $376,188 for 35 grants (high: $35,000; low: $2,500; average: $10,748).
Purpose and activities: Broad purposes; local giving largely for social services, arts, housing, and community development.
Types of support awarded: Seed money, building funds, equipment, special projects.
Limitations: Giving limited to the greater Boston and Lowell, MA, area. No grants to individuals, or for operating budgets, continuing support, annual campaigns, emergency funds, deficit financing, matching gifts, scholarships, or fellowships; no loans.
Publications: 990-PF, program policy statement, application guidelines.
Application information:
  Initial approach: Telephone, full proposal, or letter
  Copies of proposal: 1
  Deadline(s): Submit proposal preferably in spring, summer, or fall
  Board meeting date(s): Spring, summer, and late fall
  Final notification: 4 to 5 months
  Write: Ala H. Reid, Administrator
Officers and Trustees: Newell Flather, President; Andrew C. Bailey, Secretary and Treasurer; Allen C. Barry, Thomas E. Leggat, Leon F. Sargent.
Number of staff: 1 part-time professional; 1 part-time support.
Employer Identification Number: 046036092

1593
Peabody (Amelia) Foundation
60 State St.
Boston 02109   (617) 723-5393

Trust established in 1942 in Massachusetts.
Donor(s): Amelia Peabody.
Financial data: (yr. ended 12/31/82): Assets, $3,095,513 (M); expenditures, $202,214, including $175,500 for 14 grants (high: $85,000; low: $1,000).
Purpose and activities: To assist local charitable and educational organizations, with emphasis on secondary education, hospitals, youth agencies, cultural programs, and conservation.
Limitations: Giving limited to MA. No grants to individuals, or for endowment funds, scholarships or fellowships; no loans.
Application information:
  Initial approach: Letter
  Copies of proposal: 1
  Board meeting date(s): As required
  Write: Lloyd B. Waring, Trustee
Trustees: James St. Clair, Bayard D. Waring.
Employer Identification Number: 046036558

1594
Perini (Joseph) Memorial Foundation
73 Mt. Wayte Ave.
Framingham 01701   (617) 875-6171

Incorporated in 1953 in Massachusetts.
Donor(s): Joseph R. Perini.†
Financial data: (yr. ended 12/31/83): Assets, $9,171,187 (M); gifts received, $65,000; expenditures, $251,202, including $224,860 for 68 grants (high: $25,000; low: $100) and $16,000 for 1 foundation-administered program.
Purpose and activities: Broad purposes; primarily local giving, with emphasis on education, the family, church support and religious associations, and youth agencies.
Limitations: Giving primarily in MA. No grants to individuals, or for endowment funds, research, scholarships, fellowships, matching gifts, or operating budgets; no loans.
Application information:
  Initial approach: Letter
  Deadline(s): October 1
  Board meeting date(s): December
  Write: Joseph R. Perini, Jr., Secretary
Officers: Harold M. Hill, President; Thomas B. Perini, Vice-President; Joseph R. Perini, Jr., Secretary-Treasurer.
Employer Identification Number: 046139986

1595
Perini Memorial Foundation, Inc.
73 Mt. Wayte Ave.
Framingham 01701   (617) 875-6171

Incorporated in 1953 in Massachusetts.
Financial data: (yr. ended 12/31/83): Assets, $4,346,418 (M); gifts received, $65,000; expenditures, $192,936, including $141,651 for 75 grants (high: $7,600; low: $100) and $16,000 for 1 foundation-administered program.

Purpose and activities: Charitable purposes; primarily local giving, with emphasis on higher education, Roman Catholic church support and religious associations, and hospitals.
Limitations: Giving primarily in MA. No grants to individuals, or for research, scholarships, fellowships, or matching gifts; no loans.
Application information:
  Initial approach: Letter
  Copies of proposal: 1
  Deadline(s): October 1
  Board meeting date(s): December
  Write: Bart W. Perini, Treasurer
Officers: David B. Perini, President; Charles B. Perini, Vice-President; Charles B. Molineaux, Jr., Secretary; Bart W. Perini, Treasurer.
Employer Identification Number: 046118587

1596
Perpetual Benevolent Fund, The
c/o BayBank Middlesex
300 Washington St.
Newton 02158   (617) 894-6500

Charitable trust established in 1932 in Massachusetts; activated in 1957.
Donor(s): Nathan P. Cutler,† William H. Cutler,† and others.
Financial data: (yr. ended 8/31/84): Assets, $1,459,286 (M); expenditures, $113,664, including $81,929 for 306 grants (high: $6,000; low: $50; average: $300-$500) and $10,000 for 22 grants to individuals.
Purpose and activities: To assist local needy individuals. Individuals are referred by health, welfare, hospitals, or other organizations.
Types of support awarded: Grants to individuals.
Limitations: Giving limited to Newton, Waltham, and adjacent communities in MA. No grants for scholarships.
Publications: Application guidelines.
Application information: Application form required.
  Initial approach: Telephone or full proposal
  Copies of proposal: 1
  Deadline(s): None
  Board meeting date(s): October
  Final notification: 1 week
  Write: Marjorie M. Kelley, Secretary
Officer: Marjorie M. Kelley, Secretary.
Trustee: BayBank Middlesex (Norman E. MacNeil, Chairman).
Number of staff: 1.
Employer Identification Number: 237011723

1597
Persky (Joseph) Foundation ¤
c/o Singer & Lusardi
370 Main St.
Worcester 01608

Incorporated in 1944 in Massachusetts.
Donor(s): David Persky, Hardwick Knitted Fabrics, Inc.
Financial data: (yr. ended 12/31/82): Assets, $1,318,911 (M); gifts received, $55,000; expenditures, $104,214, including $98,850 for 43 grants (high: $10,000; low: $50).

Purpose and activities: Grants largely for hospitals; support also for higher education, Jewish welfare funds, health agencies, and biological research.
Officers: David Persky, President and Treasurer; Suzanne Persky, Secretary.
Trustees: Marguerite Persky, Warren Persky.
Employer Identification Number: 046057747

1598
Phillips (Edwin) Trust ☐
c/o Bank of New England
28 State St.
Boston 02107

Financial data: (yr. ended 12/31/82): Assets, $4,100,101 (M); expenditures, $129,789, including $104,650 for 2 grants (high: $54,650; low: $50,000).
Purpose and activities: Giving for the treatment of handicapped children.
Trustees: Marvin Bernstein, Archbishop Humberto Madeiros, John Silber, Bank of New England.
Employer Identification Number: 046025549

1599
Pierce (Harold Whitworth) Charitable Trust ☐
c/o Nichols and Pratt
28 State St., 19th Fl.
Boston 02109

Trust established in 1960 in Massachusetts.
Donor(s): Harold Whitworth Pierce.†
Financial data: (yr. ended 11/30/82): Assets, $6,574,815 (M); expenditures, $428,626, including $379,563 for 44 grants (high: $102,563; low: $2,000).
Purpose and activities: Primarily local giving, with emphasis on hospitals, higher and secondary education, youth agencies, cultural activities, and conservation.
Limitations: Giving primarily in MA.
Trustees: Robert U. Ingalls, Richard M. Nichols.
Employer Identification Number: 046019896

1600
Pilgrim Foundation, The
8 Perkins Ave.
Brockton 02401 (617) 586-6100

Established in 1926 in Massachusetts; incorporated in 1927.
Donor(s): Edgar B. Davis.†
Financial data: (yr. ended 12/31/82): Assets, $1,929,603 (M); gifts received, $1,568; expenditures, $194,647, including $14,303 for 10 grants (high: $4,500; low: $298) and $137,177 for 185 grants to individuals.
Purpose and activities: Primarily to aid children by assisting needy families through grants to individuals, providing camping and memberships in character-building facilities, and scholarships for higher education; restricted to local beneficiaries; limited grants also to organizations.
Types of support awarded: Student aid, grants to individuals.
Limitations: Giving limited to Brockton, MA.

Application information: Application form required.
 Deadline(s): April 1 for graduating high school students; May 1 for returning college students
 Write: Sherry Yuskaitis, Executive Director
Officers and Trustees: Gerald Kelleher, President; Dorothy H. Trower, Secretary; Charles N. Fuller, Treasurer; David E. Crosby, Lincoln K. Davis, Alice Lamond, Oscar Pratt.
Employer Identification Number: 042104834

1601
Pneumo Foundation ☐
4800 Prudential Tower
Boston 02799

Established in 1953.
Financial data: (yr. ended 11/30/83): Assets, $15,739 (M); gifts received, $165,000; expenditures, $195,283, including $194,430 for 217 grants (high: $30,400; low: $25).
Purpose and activities: Grants primarily for community funds; support also for higher education, cultural programs, hospitals, and health and youth agencies.
Officers: Gerard A. Fulham,* President; James A. Wood,* Vice-President; C.L. Hoffman, Secretary; D.J. Mahoney, Treasurer.
Trustees:* C.L. Pecchenino.
Employer Identification Number: 346549528

1602
Polaroid Foundation, Inc. ▼
28 Osborn St., 4th Fl.
Cambridge 02139 (617) 577-4035

Incorporated in 1971 in Massachusetts.
Donor(s): Polaroid Corporation.
Financial data: (yr. ended 12/31/83): Assets, $0 (M); gifts received, $1,771,931; expenditures, $1,771,931, including $906,536 for grants (high: $280,000; low: $50; average: $100-$10,000) and $265,395 for employee matching gifts.
Purpose and activities: Primarily local giving, with emphasis on community funds and welfare agencies, including programs for the urban poor, and higher education, including matching gifts; grants also for cultural programs and youth agencies.
Types of support awarded: Matching funds, employee matching gifts, employee related scholarships, seed money, emergency funds, internships, scholarship funds, exchange programs, fellowships, general purposes.
Limitations: Giving primarily in MA, particularly greater Boston and Cambridge. No grants to individuals or for endowment funds.
Publications: Annual report, application guidelines, program policy statement.
Application information: Application form required.
 Initial approach: proposal
 Copies of proposal: 2
 Deadline(s): None
 Board meeting date(s): Monthly
 Final notification: 2 to 3 months after board meeting
 Write: Marcia Schiff, Executive Director

Officers: Christopher Ingraham, President; Charles E. Zerwekh, Jr., Vice-President; Marcia Schiff, Secretary and Executive Director; Harvey H. Thayer,* Treasurer.
Trustees:* I.M. Booth, Sheldon A. Buckler, Richard F. deLima, Milton S. Dietz, Owen Gaffney, John Harlor, William J. McCune, Jr., William J. O'Neill, Jr., Howard G. Rogers.
Number of staff: 2 full-time professional; 2 full-time support.
Employer Identification Number: 237152261

1603
Prouty (Olive Higgins) Foundation, Inc. ☐
c/o Bank of New England
28 State St.
Boston 02107

Incorporated in 1952 in Massachusetts.
Donor(s): Olive Higgins Prouty.†
Financial data: (yr. ended 12/31/82): Assets, $1,207,914 (M); expenditures, $87,032, including $77,000 for 28 grants (high: $15,000; low: $1,000).
Purpose and activities: General purposes; primarily local giving, with emphasis on hospitals, higher and secondary education, music, and museums.
Limitations: Giving primarily in MA.
Officers and Trustees: Richard Prouty, President; Jane Prouty Smith, Vice-President; Richard C. Doll, Treasurer; Harold T. Davis, Clerk.
Employer Identification Number: 046046475

1604
Ram Island, Inc. ☐
c/o Grabill & Ley, Inc.
Ten Post Office Square
Boston 02109

Incorporated in 1979 in Massachusetts.
Donor(s): W. Van Alan Clark, Jr.
Financial data: (yr. ended 2/28/83): Assets, $1,224,811 (M); expenditures, $318,532, including $259,000 for 9 grants (high: $50,000; low: $4,000).
Purpose and activities: General giving; support primarily for education, including higher education, and a youth agency.
Types of support awarded: General purposes.
Limitations: Giving primarily in MA.
Officers and Directors: W. Van Alan Clark, Jr., President; Robert Howle, Treasurer; Mary H. Clark, Elliott V. Grabill.
Employer Identification Number: 042670567

1605
Ratshesky (A. C.) Foundation
40 Court St.
Boston 02108 (617) 742-7443

Incorporated in 1916 in Massachusetts.
Donor(s): A.C. Ratshesky,† and family.
Financial data: (yr. ended 12/31/84): Assets, $1,556,075 (M); expenditures, $170,000, including $145,625 for 74 grants (high: $5,000; low: $1,000; average: $2,000).

Purpose and activities: Giving to organizations whose work is done principally in or for people of greater Boston, with emphasis on education, cultural programs, and social agencies; some support for hospitals and youth agencies.

Types of support awarded: Operating budgets, emergency funds, building funds, equipment, matching funds, technical assistance, scholarship funds.

Limitations: Giving primarily in the greater Boston, MA area. No support for scientific research. No grants to individuals, or for continuing support, annual campaigns, general endowments, seed money, deficit financing, land acquisition, special projects, research, publications, or conferences; no loans.

Publications: Application guidelines.

Application information:

Initial approach: Full proposal
Copies of proposal: 1
Deadline(s): None
Board meeting date(s): April, June, September, and December
Final notification: 4 months
Write: John Morse, Sr., President, or Bette Finkelstein, Executive Director

Officers and Trustees: John Morse, Sr., President; John Morse, Jr., Vice-President; J. Robert Morse, Secretary and Treasurer; Hetty L.R. Kaffenburgh, Alan R. Morse, Jr., Eric Robert Morse, Theresa J. Morse.

Number of staff: 1 part-time professional.

Employer Identification Number: 046017426

1606
Ribakoff (Eugene J. and Corinne A.) Charitable Foundation ⌑
c/o the Day Bldg.
306 Main St., Suite 1000
Worcester 01608

Trust established in 1960 in Massachusetts.

Donor(s): Auto Rental Corporation, Trucklease Corporation, Eugene J. Ribakoff.

Financial data: (yr. ended 5/31/83): Assets, $211,414 (M); gifts received, $165,000; expenditures, $129,560, including $128,712 for 50 grants (high: $73,500; low: $10).

Purpose and activities: Broad purposes; primarily local giving, with emphasis on Jewish welfare funds and temple support; some support also for hospitals.

Limitations: Giving primarily in Worcester, MA.

Trustees: Corinne A. Ribakoff, Eugene J. Ribakoff, Harold Seder.

Employer Identification Number: 046055498

1607
Rice (The Albert W.) Charitable Foundation ⌑
c/o Shawmut Worcester County Bank, Trust Dept.
446 Main St.
Worcester 01608

Established in 1959.

Donor(s): Albert W. Rice.†

Financial data: (yr. ended 12/31/82): Assets, $2,531,986 (M); expenditures, $166,615, including $147,220 for 5 grants (high: $38,720; low: $15,000).

Purpose and activities: Primarily local giving for historic preservation, higher education, and a community foundation.

Limitations: Giving primarily in MA.

Trustee: Shawmut Worcester County Trust.

Employer Identification Number: 046028085

1608
Riley Foundation, The ▼
100 Franklin St.
Boston 02110   (617) 357-1514

Foundation established in 1971 in Massachusetts as the Mabel Louise Riley Trust.

Donor(s): Mabel Louise Riley.†

Financial data: (yr. ended 5/31/84): Assets, $17,063,251 (M); expenditures, $1,502,663, including $1,323,670 for 42 grants (high: $150,000; low: $5,000; average: $10,000-$100,000).

Purpose and activities: Grants to charities incorporated in Massachusetts; interest in new approaches to old problems, with an emphasis on improved social services and race relations; special interest in programs for children and youth; selective support for schools, community and neighborhood development, and for cultural, employment, and housing programs.

Types of support awarded: Seed money, building funds, equipment, land acquisition, endowment funds, special projects, scholarship funds, loans, consulting services.

Limitations: Giving limited to MA, with emphasis on the greater Boston area. No grants to individuals, or for operating budgets, continuing support, annual campaigns, emergency funds, deficit financing, research, publications, conferences, professorships, internships, exchange programs, fellowships, or matching gifts.

Publications: Application guidelines.

Application information:

Initial approach: Full proposal
Copies of proposal: 1
Deadline(s): Submit proposal preferably in February or August; deadlines March 1 and September 1
Board meeting date(s): April and October
Final notification: 1 month after board meetings
Write: Newell Flather, Administrator

Officers: Newell Flather, Administrator.

Trustees: Andrew C. Bailey, Douglas Danner, Robert W. Holmes, Jr., Boston Safe Deposit and Trust Company (Guy R. Sturgeon, Trust Officer).

Number of staff: 1 part-time professional; 1 part-time support.

Employer Identification Number: 046278857

1609
Rodgers (Elizabeth Killam) Trust ⌑
c/o John B. Newhall and Nathan Newbury III
530 Atlantic Ave.
Boston 02110

Established in 1977.

Financial data: (yr. ended 4/30/83): Assets, $3,045,580 (M); expenditures, $295,461, including $271,800 for 3 grants (high: $210,000; low: $10,000).

Purpose and activities: Primarily local giving for conservation and a university.

Types of support awarded: General purposes.

Limitations: Giving primarily in MA.

Trustees: John B. Newhall, Nathan Newbury III.

Agency: Nutter McClennen and Fish.

Employer Identification Number: 046385523

1610
Rogers Family Foundation, The ⌑
100 Turnpike St.
North Andover 01845   (617) 685-1000
Mailing address: P.O. Box 100, Lawrence, MA 01842

Trust established in 1957 in Massachusetts.

Donor(s): Irving E. Rogers, Eagle-Tribune Publishing Company.

Financial data: (yr. ended 12/31/82): Assets, $2,448,299 (M); gifts received, $258,133; expenditures, $173,767, including $167,122 for 25 grants (high: $40,500; low: $500).

Purpose and activities: Broad purposes; primarily local giving, with emphasis on hospitals, higher and secondary education, and community funds.

Limitations: Giving primarily in MA. No grants to individuals, or for endowment funds, research, scholarships, fellowships, or matching gifts; no loans.

Application information: Funds largely committed.

Initial approach: Letter
Write: Irving E. Rogers, Trustee

Trustees: Alexander H. Rogers, II, Irving E. Rogers, Irving E. Rogers, Jr., Richard M. Wyman.

Employer Identification Number: 046063152

1611
Rowland Foundation, Inc. ▼
P.O. Box 13
Cambridge 02138   (617) 497-4632

Incorporated in 1960 in Delaware.

Donor(s): Edwin H. Land, Helen M. Land.

Financial data: (yr. ended 11/30/83): Assets, $26,573,619 (M); expenditures, $1,574,990, including $1,383,168 for 45 grants (high: $653,000; low: $2,000; average: $2,000-$35,000).

Purpose and activities: Broad purposes; support mainly for a scientific research institute; grants also for education, health, social welfare, ecology, and cultural programs.

Types of support awarded: Conferences and seminars, continuing support, deficit financing, emergency funds, general purposes, professorships, research.

Limitations: Giving primarily in the Boston-Cambridge, MA area. No grants to individuals, or for capital or endowment funds, or matching gifts; no loans.

Application information:

Initial approach: Letter
Copies of proposal: 1
Deadline(s): None

Board meeting date(s): As required
Write: Philip DuBois, Vice-President
Officers: Edwin H. Land,* President; Helen M. Land,* Vice-President and Treasurer; Philip DuBois,* Vice-President; Julius Silver, Secretary.
Trustees:* Jennifer Land DuBois, Valerie Land Smallwood.
Number of staff: None.
Employer Identification Number: 046046756

1612
Rubenstein (Lawrence J. and Anne) Charitable Foundation
50 Longwood Ave., Suite 816
Brookline 02146

Trust established in 1963 in Massachusetts.
Donor(s): Lawrence J. Rubenstein,† Anne Rubinstein.
Financial data: (yr. ended 5/31/83): Assets, $6,510,114 (M); expenditures, $334,307, including $315,000 for 10 grants (high: $75,000; low: $10,000).
Purpose and activities: Primarily local giving, with emphasis on hospitals, higher education, and medical research and education.
Limitations: Giving primarily in MA.
Application information:
Write: Richard I. Kaner, Trustee
Trustees: Richard I. Kaner, Frank Kopelman, Anne C. Rubenstein.
Employer Identification Number: 046087371

1613
Rubin (Cele H. and William B.) Family Fund, Inc. ⌖
32 Monadnock Rd.
Wellesley Hills 02181

Incorporated in 1943 in New York.
Donor(s): Members of the Joseph Rubin family, The Sweets Company of America, Inc., Joseph Rubin and Sons, Inc., and others.
Financial data: (yr. ended 12/31/82): Assets, $3,613,503 (M); gifts received, $125,000; expenditures, $186,477, including $145,625 for 36 grants (high: $70,000; low: $100).
Purpose and activities: Broad purposes; grants for higher education including medical education, secondary schools and social agencies, including Jewish welfare funds, primarily in New York and Massachusetts.
Limitations: Giving primarily in MA and NY.
Application information:
Deadline(s): None
Write: Ellen R. Gordon, President
Officers: Ellen R. Gordon,* President; Melvin J. Gordon,* Vice-President; M. Drangel, Secretary; Barbara Reynolds,* Treasurer.
Directors:* Jacob Gordon, J.T. Hand.
Employer Identification Number: 116026235

1614
Russell (Josephine G.) Trust
c/o Clifford E. Elias
316 Essex St.
Lawrence 01840   (617) 686-3918

Trust established in 1934.

Financial data: (yr. ended 12/31/82): Assets, $2,817,992 (M); expenditures, $197,459, including $169,865 for 16 grants (high: $60,000; low: $25).
Purpose and activities: Giving only in the greater Lawrence area, with emphasis on hospitals and a community fund.
Types of support awarded: General purposes, annual campaigns, emergency funds, building funds, equipment, publications, scholarship funds.
Limitations: Giving limited to the greater Lawrence, MA, area. No grants to individuals or for matching gifts; no loans.
Application information:
Initial approach: Letter or full proposal
Copies of proposal: 3
Deadline(s): Submit proposal preferably in January or February; deadline March
Board meeting date(s): Quarterly
Write: Clifford E. Elias, Trustee
Trustees: Archer L. Bolton, Jr., Roger N. Bower, Clifford E. Elias.
Employer Identification Number: 042136910

1615
Sagamore Foundation ⌖
c/o Woodstock Service Corporation
100 Federal St.
Boston 02110

Trust established in 1947 in Massachusetts.
Donor(s): Nelson J. Darling, Jr., Members of the LaCroix family.
Financial data: (yr. ended 12/31/82): Assets, $819,548 (M); expenditures, $160,028, including $151,810 for 22 grants (high: $25,000; low: $560).
Purpose and activities: Broad purposes; primarily local giving, with emphasis on higher education, hospitals, arts and cultural programs, particularly museums, and a community fund.
Limitations: Giving primarily in MA.
Trustees: Bigelow Crocker, Jr., Jeanne LaCroix Crocker, Edith LaCroix Dabney, Nelson J. Darling, Jr., Ruth LaCroix Darling, Richard D. Phippen, Susanne LaCroix Phippen.
Employer Identification Number: 046027799

1616
Sailors' Snug Harbor of Boston ⌖
111 Devonshire St., 3rd Fl.
Boston 02109   (617) 426-7320

Established in 1852 in Massachusetts.
Financial data: (yr. ended 4/30/83): Assets, $3,385,633 (M); expenditures, $193,348, including $154,778 for 16 grants (high: $20,000; low: $1,000) and $3,078 for 1 grant to an individual.
Purpose and activities: Primarily local giving for the health and welfare of the aged, sailors, and others; grants to individuals for the relief and support of aged sailors; some support also for cultural programs.
Limitations: Giving primarily in the Boston, MA, area.
Application information:
Initial approach: Full proposal
Deadline(s): November 15, February 15, and April 15

Write: Lincoln B. Hansel, President
Officers and Trustees: Lincoln B. Hansel, President; Charles E. Rogerson, II, Secretary and Treasurer; John R. Chapin, Charles K. Cobb, Jr., Warren A. Dodge, G. Lincoln Dow, Jr., Joseph E. Eaton, C. Russell Eddy, Charles R. Eddy, Jr., Francis B. Lothrop, Francis B. Lothrop, Jr., Everett Morss, Jr., John A. Perkins, R. Forbes Perkins, William L. Saltonstall, Henry Wheeler, Ralph B. Williams, Thomas B. Williams, Jr., Samuel H. Wolcott, Jr.
Employer Identification Number: 042104430

1617
Sawyer Charitable Foundation ⌖
209 Columbus Ave., Fifth Fl.
Boston 02116

Trust established in 1957 in Massachusetts.
Donor(s): Frank Sawyer, William Sawyer, The Brattle Company Corp., St. Botolph Holding Company, First Franklin Parking Corp., and others.
Financial data: (yr. ended 12/31/83): Assets, $2,535,075 (M); gifts received, $110,400; expenditures, $208,730, including $141,615 for 64 grants (high: $25,000; low: $25).
Purpose and activities: General giving, including Jewish and Roman Catholic welfare funds, community funds, health agencies, hospitals, and aid to the handicapped.
Officer and Managers: Carol S. Packs, Executive Director; Frank Sawyer, Mildred F. Sawyer.
Employer Identification Number: 046088774

1618
Schrafft (William E.) and Bertha E. Schrafft Charitable Trust ▼
One Financial Center
Boston 02111   (617) 350-6100

Trust established in 1946 in Massachusetts.
Donor(s): William E. Schrafft,† Bertha E. Schrafft.†
Financial data: (yr. ended 12/31/84): Assets, $9,551,280 (M); expenditures, $500,800, including $441,000 for 87 grants (high: $60,000; low: $1,000).
Purpose and activities: To assist charitable corporations within Massachusetts; grants largely for hospitals, higher and secondary education, community funds, cultural programs and youth agencies.
Types of support awarded: General purposes, operating budgets, continuing support, annual campaigns, endowment funds, scholarship funds.
Limitations: Giving limited to MA, with emphasis on the Boston metropolitan area. No grants to individuals, or for matching gifts, seed money, emergency funds, or deficit financing; no loans.
Publications: Annual report, application guidelines.
Application information:
Initial approach: Full proposal
Copies of proposal: 3
Deadline(s): Submit proposal preferably from January through July; no set deadline
Board meeting date(s): About 6 times a year

Final notification: 2 months
Write: Hazen H. Ayer, Trustee
Trustees: Hazen H. Ayer, Robert H. Jewell, John M. Wood, Jr.
Number of staff: None.
Employer Identification Number: 046065605

1619
Sears (Clara Endicott) Trust
c/o Bank of New England
28 State St.
Boston 02109   (617) 973-1793

Trust established in 1962.
Donor(s): Clara Endicott Sears.†
Financial data: (yr. ended 12/31/83): Assets, $4,146,883 (M); expenditures, $261,000, including $238,000 for 5 grants (high: $198,000; low: $3,000).
Purpose and activities: Giving restricted to Harvard, Massachusetts mainly to support "Fruitlands and the Wayside Museums, Inc."; some minor support for other charities in Harvard.
Limitations: Giving limited to the town of Harvard, MA. No grants to individuals.
Trustees: F. Murray Forbes, Jr., Francis C. Welch, Bank of New England (John M. Dolan, Senior Trust Officer).
Employer Identification Number: 046025576

1620
Shapiro (Abraham) Charity Fund
65 Sprague St.
Boston 02163   (617) 361-1200

Trust established in 1945 in Massachusetts.
Donor(s): Abraham Shapiro, and various companies.
Financial data: (yr. ended 12/31/82): Assets, $4,658,262 (M); gifts received, $50,950; expenditures, $237,939, including $187,420 for 17 grants (high: $80,000; low: $200).
Purpose and activities: Primarily local giving, with emphasis on Jewish welfare funds, higher education, and hospitals.
Limitations: Giving primarily in MA. No grants to individuals, or for scholarships and fellowships, or matching gifts; no loans.
Application information:
Board meeting date(s): Quarterly
Write: George Shapiro, Trustee
Trustees: Arthur S. Goldberg, George Shapiro, Phillip Shir.
Employer Identification Number: 046043588

1621
Shaw Fund for Mariners' Children
50 Congress St., Rm. 800
Boston 02109

Incorporated in 1853 in Massachusetts.
Donor(s): Robert Gould Shaw.†
Financial data: (yr. ended 12/31/81): Assets, $1,524,662 (M); expenditures, $107,797, including $94,352 for grants to individuals.
Purpose and activities: To aid mariners, mariners' wives or widows, and their children who are in distress and are residents of Massachusetts.

Types of support awarded: Grants to individuals.
Limitations: Giving limited to MA. No grants for building or endowment funds, operating budgets, special projects, research, scholarships, fellowships, or matching gifts; no loans.
Application information:
Initial approach: Letter
Copies of proposal: 1
Write: Francis G. Shaw, President
Officers and Members: Francis G. Shaw, President; Thomas Whiteside, Vice-President; Andrew A. Hunter, Clerk; James B. Ames, Walter Amory, Mrs. George B. Blake, Mrs. William G. Constable, Edward D. Cook, Jr., Ingersoll Cunningham, Mrs. Raymond J. Montminy, Norman C. Nicholson, Jr., Clement C. Sawtell, Marguerite G. Shaw, S. Parkman Shaw III, Howell R. Wood, Jr.
Employer Identification Number: 042104861

1622
Shaw (Gardiner Howland) Foundation
19 Temple Place, 5th Fl.
Boston 02111   (617) 451-9206

Trust established in 1959 in Massachusetts.
Donor(s): Gardiner Howland Shaw.†
Financial data: (yr. ended 4/30/84): Assets, $5,872,475 (M); expenditures, $311,248, including $235,800 for 33 grants (high: $17,500; low: $670; average: $5,000-$10,000).
Purpose and activities: Local giving for the study, prevention, correction, and alleviation of crime and delinquency, and the rehabilitation of adult and juvenile offenders. Awards grants in 3 categories: 1) 50 percent of available funds to programs that expand use of alternative sentencing and dispute resolution in the criminal courts, explore the use of substitutes for confinement, or strengthen the role of the community in the courts; 2) 30 percent of funds awarded to previous recipients with effective community programs for adult or juvenile offenders; priority to programs serving minority or female offenders and those helping committed adults or juveniles return to the community; and 3) 20 percent of funds awarded to programs that test new ideas or approaches to criminal justice issues and attract new agencies or resources into the criminal justice field. Foundation participates in Emergency Loan Fund.
Types of support awarded: Operating budgets, continuing support, seed money, emergency funds, matching funds, consulting services, technical assistance, loans, research.
Limitations: Giving limited to MA. No support for drug or mental health programs, or the arts. No grants to individuals, or for capital and building funds, equipment, land acquisition, renovations, endowment funds, or scholarships and fellowships.
Publications: Annual report, program policy statement, application guidelines.
Application information:
Initial approach: Concept paper or full proposal
Copies of proposal: 1
Deadline(s): 1st day of January, May and September

Board meeting date(s): February, June and October
Final notification: 60 days
Write: Neil Houston, Director
Officer: Neil Houston, Director.
Trustees: James D. Colt, F. Murray Forbes, Jr., John Lowell, Kenneth S. Safe, Jr., Francis C. Welch.
Number of staff: 1 part-time professional; 1 part-time support.
Employer Identification Number: 046111826

1623
Shawmut Charitable Foundation, The
(formerly Warren Charitable Trust)
c/o Shawmut Bank of Boston, 10th Fl.
One Federal St.
Boston 02211   (617) 292-3748

Trust established in 1961 in Massachusetts.
Donor(s): Shawmut Bank of Boston.
Financial data: (yr. ended 12/31/84): Assets, $63,430 (M); gifts received, $435,775; expenditures, $513,226, including $413,000 for 80 grants (high: $198,700; low: $250; average: $2,500) and $10,000 for 127 employee matching gifts.
Purpose and activities: Local giving, with emphasis on United Way, community services, health, education, and cultural organizations.
Types of support awarded: Operating budgets, building funds, special projects, matching funds.
Limitations: Giving limited to Suffolk County, MA. No support for national medical foundations. No grants to individuals.
Publications: Program policy statement.
Application information:
Initial approach: Telephone and/or letter
Copies of proposal: 1
Deadline(s): None
Board meeting date(s): Quarterly
Write: Ms. Win Barnard, Administrator, Contributions
Agent: Shawmut Bank of Boston.
Trustees: Warren S. Berg, John P. La Ware, Carter H. Harrison.
Number of staff: 1 full-time professional; 1 part-time support.
Employer Identification Number: 046023794

1624
Shawmut Worcester County Bank Charitable Foundation, Inc. ¤
c/o Eugene J. Schwartz, Secretary
446 Main St.
Worcester 01608

Incorporated in 1982 in Massachusetts.
Donor(s): Shawmut Worcester County Bank.
Financial data: (yr. ended 12/31/82): Assets, $10,089 (M); gifts received, $149,788; expenditures, $140,020, including $140,000 for 56 grants (high: $22,500; low: $300).
Purpose and activities: First year of operation in 1982; primarily local giving for community funds and for higher education; support also for cultural programs and youth agencies.
Limitations: Giving primarily in MA.

Officers and Directors:* Neal F. Finnegan,*
President; John D. Hunt,* Vice-President;
Eugene J. Schwartz, Secretary; Harry I.
Spencer, Jr.,* Treasurer.
Employer Identification Number: 042746775

1625
Sheraton Foundation, Inc. ⌑
60 State St.
Boston 02109   (617) 367-5531

Incorporated in 1950 in Massachusetts.
Donor(s): The Sheraton Corporation.
Financial data: (yr. ended 12/31/82): Assets,
$1,885,163 (M); gifts received, $249,515;
expenditures, $207,120, including $177,298
for 57 grants (high: $49,515; low: $100).
Purpose and activities: Broad purposes; grants
primarily for community funds; some support
to educational institutions, including scholarship
funds; health agencies; youth agencies; and
hospitals.
Types of support awarded: General purposes,
continuing support, annual campaigns,
research, scholarship funds.
Limitations: No grants to individuals, or for
endowment or capital funds, research, or
matching gifts; no loans.
Application information: Applicants for
scholarship funds must be enrolled in hotel
administration and/or restaurant management.
  Initial approach: Proposal
  Copies of proposal: 1
  Board meeting date(s): April, July,
    September, and December
  Final notification: 6 months
  Write: Donald P. Summers, Treasurer
Officers and Directors: Howard P. James,
President; James D. McGraw, Donald E.
Stephenson, Vice-Presidents; Donald P.
Summers, Treasurer; N. Ronald Silberstein,
Clerk; Joseph F. Cotter, Roger C. Senter, John
R. Young.
Employer Identification Number: 046039510

1626
**Sherman (George and Beatrice) Family
  Charitable Trust** ⌑
c/o Goulston & Storrs
One Federal St.
Boston 02110

Trust established in 1969.
Donor(s): George Sherman.†
Financial data: (yr. ended 6/30/83): Assets,
$2,881,513 (M); expenditures, $317,459,
including $239,468 for 93 grants (high:
$35,000; low: $25).
Purpose and activities: Primarily local giving,
with emphasis on Jewish welfare funds, temple
support, higher education, and hospitals.
Limitations: Giving primarily in MA.
Trustees: David H. Greenberg, Jacob Lewiton,
Beatrice B. Sherman, Norton L. Sherman,
Marvin Sparrow.
Employer Identification Number: 046223350

1627
Shipley Foundation, Inc., The
75 Federal St.
Newton 02110

Established in 1969.
Donor(s): Charles R. Shipley, Lucia H. Shipley.
Financial data: (yr. ended 12/31/82): Assets,
$1,100,862 (M); expenditures, $28,228,
including $22,900 for 41 grants (high: $2,500;
low: $100).
Purpose and activities: Broad purposes;
primarily local giving, with emphasis on support
for the Shipley Institute of Medicine; some
support also for secondary education and
health.
Limitations: Giving primarily in MA.
Officers and Directors: Charles Shipley,
President; Richard C. Shipley, Vice-
President; Lucia Shipley, Treasurer; William H.
MacCrellish, Jr., Clerk.
Employer Identification Number: 237015570

1628
**Smith (Richard and Susan)
  Foundation** ⌑
27 Boylston St.
Chestnut Hill 02167

Trust established in 1970 in Massachusetts.
Donor(s): Marion Smith, Richard A. Smith.
Financial data: (yr. ended 4/30/83): Assets,
$55,146 (M); gifts received, $180,455;
expenditures, $195,602, including $190,675
for 24 grants (high: $50,000).
Purpose and activities: Grants largely for
Jewish studies and welfare funds; some support
also for education, hospitals, and a symphony
orchestra.
Types of support awarded: General purposes.
Trustees: Amy S. Berylson, Debra S. Smith,
Robert A. Smith, Susan M. Smith.
Employer Identification Number: 237090011

1629
State Street Boston Charitable Fund ⌑
c/o State Street Bank and Trust Company
P.O. Box 351
Boston 02101

Trust established in 1963 in Massachusetts.
Donor(s): State Street Bank and Trust Company.
Financial data: (yr. ended 12/31/82): Assets,
$449,569 (M); gifts received, $408,423;
expenditures, $282,677, including $281,750
for 55 grants (high: $126,750; low: $500).
Purpose and activities: Grants to organizations
helping to improve the quality of life for
residents of the greater Boston area, with
emphasis on community funds, cultural
programs, higher education, community
development, and health.
Limitations: Giving primarily in MA.
Trustee: State Street Bank and Trust Company.
Employer Identification Number: 046401847

1630
Stearns (Artemas W.) Trust
c/o Clifford E. Elias
316 Essex St.
Lawrence 01840   (617) 686-3918

Trust established in 1896 in Massachusetts.
Donor(s): Artemas W. Stearns.†
Financial data: (yr. ended 12/31/82): Assets,
$1,717,139 (M); expenditures, $144,039,
including $124,645 for 26 grants (high:
$27,500; low: $500).
Purpose and activities: Local giving only, with
emphasis on hospitals; support also for
community projects and secondary schools.
Limitations: Giving limited to the greater
Lawrence, MA area. No grants to individuals,
or for endowment funds or matching gifts; no
loans.
Application information: Submit proposal
preferably in January or February.
  Initial approach: Letter or full proposal
  Copies of proposal: 3
  Deadline(s): March
  Board meeting date(s): Quarterly
  Write: Clifford E. Elias, Trustee
Trustees: Joseph F. Bacigalupo, Clifford E.
Elias, Vincent P. Morton, Jr.
Employer Identification Number: 042137061

1631
Stearns Charitable Trust ⌑
c/o Ropes and Gray
225 Franklin St.
Boston 02110

Trust established in 1947 in Massachusetts.
Donor(s): Russell B. Stearns.†
Financial data: (yr. ended 12/31/82): Assets,
$1,617,764 (M); expenditures, $118,654,
including $110,000 for 21 grants (high:
$30,000; low: $500).
Purpose and activities: Primarily local giving,
with emphasis on cultural programs, including a
science museum; some support for hospitals,
education, and a community fund.
Limitations: Giving primarily in MA. No grants
to individuals.
Application information:
  Initial approach: Letter
  Board meeting date(s): As required
Trustees: Russell S. Beade, Andree B. Stearns.
Employer Identification Number: 046036697

1632
Steiger (Albert) Memorial Fund, Inc. ⌑
1477 Main St.
Springfield 01101   (413) 781-4211

Incorporated in 1953 in Massachusetts.
Donor(s): Ralph A. Steiger, Chauncey A.
Steiger, Albert Steiger, Inc.
Financial data: (yr. ended 12/31/83): Assets,
$1,377,810 (M); expenditures, $105,194,
including $90,375 for 22 grants (high: $29,000;
low: $750).

Purpose and activities: Educational and charitable purposes, particularly for the benefit of persons residing in the vicinity of Hampden County; grants recommended by the Community Funds Advisory Committee of the Community Council, primarily for community funds, social agencies, cultural programs and higher education.
Types of support awarded: Special projects, building funds.
Limitations: Giving primarily in Hampden County, MA. No grants to individuals, or for endowment funds, or operating budgets.
Application information: Submit proposal betwen May and November.
  Initial approach: Letter
  Copies of proposal: 1
  Board meeting date(s): As required
  Write: Albert A. Steiger, Jr., President
Officers and Trustees: Albert A. Steiger, Jr., President; Ralph A. Steiger II, Vice-President; Hugh J. Corcoran, Clerk; Allen Steiger, Treasurer; William H. Low, Chauncey A. Steiger, Philip C. Steiger, Jr., Robert R. Steiger.
Employer Identification Number: 046051750

1633
Stevens (The Abbot and Dorothy H.) Foundation
P.O. Box 111
North Andover 01845   (617) 688-7211

Trust established in 1953 in Massachusetts.
Donor(s): Abbot Stevens.†
Financial data: (yr. ended 12/31/84): Assets, $6,349,600 (M); expenditures, $465,078, including $404,137 for 51 grants (high: $50,000; low: $500; average: $2,000-$5,000).
Purpose and activities: Primarily local giving, with emphasis on education, health, welfare, youth organizations, arts and humanities, conservation, and historic preservation.
Limitations: Giving limited to MA, with emphasis on the greater Lawrence area. No grants to individuals, or for scholarships and fellowships; no loans.
Publications: Program policy statement, application guidelines.
Application information:
  Initial approach: Full proposal
  Copies of proposal: 1
  Board meeting date(s): Monthly except July and August
  Write: Elizabeth A. Beland
Trustees: Phebe S. Miner, Christopher W. Rogers, Samuel S. Rogers.
Employer Identification Number: 046107991

1634
Stevens (The Nathaniel and Elizabeth P.) Foundation
P.O. Box 111
North Andover 01845   (617) 688-7211

Trust established in 1943 in Massachusetts.
Donor(s): Nathaniel Stevens.†
Financial data: (yr. ended 12/31/84): Assets, $5,527,448 (M); expenditures, $394,227, including $343,620 for 47 grants (high: $50,000; low: $750; average: $2,000-$5,000).

Purpose and activities: Primarily local giving, with emphasis on education, historic preservation, the arts, social services, health, and conservation.
Types of support awarded: General purposes, seed money, emergency funds, building funds, equipment, land acquisition, endowment funds, research, special projects, matching funds, program-related investments.
Limitations: Giving limited to MA, with emphasis on the greater Lawrence area. No grants to individuals, or for scholarships and fellowships; no loans.
Publications: Program policy statement, application guidelines.
Application information:
  Initial approach: Full proposal
  Copies of proposal: 1
  Deadline(s): None
  Board meeting date(s): Monthly except in July and August
  Final notification: 2 months
  Write: Elizabeth A. Beland
Trustees: Phebe S. Miner, Christopher W. Rogers, Samuel S. Rogers.
Number of staff: 1.
Employer Identification Number: 042236996

1635
Stoddard Charitable Trust, The ▼
370 Main St., Suite 1250
Worcester 01608   (617) 757-9243

Trust established in 1939 in Massachusetts.
Donor(s): Harry G. Stoddard.†
Financial data: (yr. ended 12/31/83): Assets, $60,418,118 (M); expenditures, $1,484,752, including $1,440,000 for 61 grants (high: $200,000; low: $400).
Purpose and activities: Primarily local giving, with emphasis on education, cultural programs, historical associations, youth agencies, and a community fund.
Types of support awarded: Annual campaigns, seed money, emergency funds, building funds, equipment, land acquisition, research, scholarship funds, fellowships, professorships, internships, matching funds, general purposes.
Limitations: Giving primarily in Worcester, MA. No grants to individuals.
Application information:
  Initial approach: Full proposal
  Copies of proposal: 1
  Deadline(s): Submit proposal between January and November
  Board meeting date(s): As required
  Write: Paris Fletcher, Secretary
Officers and Trustees: Robert W. Stoddard, Chairman; Paris Fletcher, Secretary and Treasurer; Marion S. Fletcher, Warner S. Fletcher, Judith S. King, Valerie S. Loring, Helen E. Stoddard.
Employer Identification Number: 046023791

1636
Stone (Albert H. & Reuben S.) Fund ¤
c/o Nichols & Stone
232 Sherman St.
Gardner 01440

Established in 1948.
Financial data: (yr. ended 12/31/82): Assets, $1,772,669 (M); expenditures, $153,138, including $127,460 for 188 grants to individuals.
Purpose and activities: Giving for scholarships to local residents.
Types of support awarded: Student aid.
Limitations: Giving limited to residents of Gardner, MA.
Application information: Application form required.
  Initial approach: Proposal
  Deadline(s): Early in second semester
  Write: Carlton Nichols or Carlton Nichols, Jr., Trustees
Trustees: Richard C. Higgins, Carlton E. Nichols, Carlton E. Nichols, Jr.
Employer Identification Number: 046050419

1637
Stone Charitable Foundation, Inc., The
P.O. Box 728
Wareham 02571

Incorporated in 1948 in Massachusetts.
Donor(s): Dewey D. Stone,† Stephen A. Stone.
Financial data: (yr. ended 11/30/84): Assets, $4,319,517 (M); gifts received, $35,296; expenditures, $509,939, including $471,273 for 66 grants (high: $155,000; low: $25).
Purpose and activities: Broad purposes; giving largely for Jewish welfare funds; grants also for hospitals, higher education, and cultural programs.
Types of support awarded: General purposes, research, endowment funds, scholarship funds, building funds, land acquisition, equipment.
Limitations: Giving primarily in MA. No grants to individuals.
Application information:
  Board meeting date(s): As required
Officers and Trustees: Stephen A. Stone, President; Alfred P. Rudnick, Treasurer; Theodore Teplow.
Number of staff: None.
Employer Identification Number: 046052313

1638
Stoneman (Anne and David) Charitable Foundation, Inc. ¤
One Federal St.
Boston 02110   (617) 482-0497

Incorporated in 1957 in Massachusetts.
Donor(s): Anne Stoneman.
Financial data: (yr. ended 7/31/83): Assets, $1,423,772 (M); expenditures, $364,087, including $361,165 for 58 grants (high: $250,000; low: $25).
Purpose and activities: Giving primarily to Jewish welfare funds and hospitals; some support also for education.
Application information:

Write: S. Sidney Stoneman
Officers: Miriam H. Stoneman, President; Jean R. Fitzpatrick, Treasurer.
Employer Identification Number: 046047379

1639
Stop & Shop Charitable Foundation, The
P.O. Box 369
Boston 02101

Trust established in 1951 in Massachusetts.
Donor(s): Stop & Shop Companies, Inc., and subsidiaries.
Financial data: (yr. ended 12/31/83): Assets, $4,941,427 (M); gifts received, $654,633; expenditures, $404,340, including $400,759 for 102 grants (high: $108,686).
Purpose and activities: General giving, primarily to charitable organizations in Massachusetts, Rhode Island, and Connecticut, with emphasis on community funds, higher education, religious welfare funds, and hospitals.
Limitations: Giving primarily in MA, RI, and CT.
Trustees: Albert F. Frager, Avram J. Goldberg, Carol R. Goldberg, Irving W. Rabb, Sidney R. Rabb.
Employer Identification Number: 046039593

1640
Stride Rite Charitable Foundation, Inc., The
Five Cambridge Center
Cambridge 02142

Incorporated in 1953 in Massachusetts as J.A. and Bessie Slosberg Charitable Foundation, Inc.
Donor(s): Stride Rite Corporation.
Financial data: (yr. ended 9/30/84): Assets, $755,000 (M); gifts received, $400,000; expenditures, $273,000, including $272,000 for 60 grants (high: $75,000; low: $200).
Purpose and activities: Broad purposes; primarily local giving, with emphasis on child welfare; support also for cultural programs and community funds.
Limitations: Giving limited to MA, with emphasis on the Boston area.
Officers and Directors: Miles J. Slosberg, President; Arnold Hiatt, Treasurer.
Employer Identification Number: 046059887

1641
Sudbury Foundation ☐
c/o Mechanics Bank Trust Dept.
P.O. Box 987
Worcester 01613

Trust established in 1952 in Massachusetts.
Donor(s): Esther M. Atkinson,† Herbert J. Atkinson.†
Financial data: (yr. ended 12/31/82): Assets, $3,743,588 (M); expenditures, $246,924, including $3,022 for 5 grants and $188,680 for 86 loans.
Purpose and activities: Grants primarily to individuals for student loans; some support for local social services and secondary education.
Types of support awarded: Student aid.
Limitations: Giving primarily in Sudbury, MA.

Application information:
Initial approach: Letter
Deadline(s): None
Write: Alan Newton
Trustees: Alton Clark, John E. Taft, Mechanics Bank.
Employer Identification Number: 046037026

1642
Tamarack Foundation ☐
c/o Woodstock Service Corporation
100 Federal St.
Boston 02110

Trust established in 1958 in Massachusetts.
Donor(s): Nelson J. Darling, Jr., Ruth A. Darling, Morris F. Darling, Thomas W. Darling, William H. Darling, Esther D. Mulroy, Sarah D. Pruett, Jeannette C. Darling.
Financial data: (yr. ended 12/31/82): Assets, $785,862 (M); gifts received, $479,938; expenditures, $268,730, including $256,700 for 82 grants (high: $50,000; low: $200).
Purpose and activities: Primarily local giving, with emphasis on cultural programs, including music, and on hospitals and education.
Limitations: Giving primarily in MA.
Trustees: Andrew Cox, Nelson J. Darling, Jr., Ruth L. Darling, Richard D. Phippen.
Employer Identification Number: 046027800

1643
Thompson (Thomas) Trust
31 Milk St., Suite 620
Boston 02109   (617) 723-4535

Trust established in 1869 in Massachusetts.
Donor(s): Thomas Thompson.†
Financial data: (yr. ended 5/31/84): Assets, $5,464,147 (M); expenditures, $336,666, including $286,095 for 11 grants (high: $70,000; low: $834; average: $3,000-$15,000).
Purpose and activities: To assist poor seamstresses, needlewomen, and shop girls in temporary need. Pursuant to the authorized adoption of the doctrine of cy pres, funds may be distributed "to those charitable organizations... deemed to be directed toward the promotion of health, education, or the general social or civic betterment".
Types of support awarded: Annual campaigns, emergency funds, building funds, equipment, land acquisition, matching funds, special projects.
Limitations: Giving primarily in Winham County, VT, particularly in the town of Brattleboro, and in Dutchess County, NY, particularly in the town of Rhinebeck. No grants to individuals, or for operating budgets, continuing support, seed money, deficit financing, endowment funds, scholarships, or fellowships; no loans.
Application information: Application form required.
Initial approach: Telephone
Copies of proposal: 1
Deadline(s): None
Board meeting date(s): Monthly except August, and as required
Final notification: 6 weeks

Write: Daniel W. Fawcett or William B. Tyler, Trustees
Trustees: Daniel W. Fawcett, William B. Tyler.
Number of staff: 1 part-time professional.
Employer Identification Number: 030179429

1644
Travelli (Charles Irwin) Fund ▼
c/o Sumner R. Andrews
77 Franklin St.
Boston 02110

Incorporated in 1914 in Massachusetts.
Donor(s): Charles I. Travelli,† Emma R. Travelli.†
Financial data: (yr. ended 11/30/83): Assets, $499,299 (M); gifts received, $437,309; expenditures, $498,829, including $474,395 for 31 grants (high: $48,000; low: $800).
Purpose and activities: "...furnishing aid and comfort to the deserving poor; contribute to the support of other Massachusetts charitable corporations or associations, and generally for the doing and carrying on of educational, charitable, benevolent and religious work." Grants largely to New England higher educational institutions for scholarship funds administered by the recipient institutions.
Types of support awarded: Scholarship funds.
Limitations: Giving primarily in the New England area for higher education; grants to other organizations mainly in MA, particularly Boston.
Application information:
Initial approach: Letter
Deadline(s): None
Board meeting date(s): As required
Officers: Sumner R. Andrews, President; Marshall G. Bolster, Treasurer; Oliver R. Andrews, Jr., Executive Director.
Number of staff: 1 part-time professional.
Employer Identification Number: 042260155

1645
Urann Foundation
P.O. Box 1788
Brockton 02403   (617) 588-7744

Established in 1963 in Massachusetts.
Financial data: (yr. ended 12/31/83): Assets, $1,533,251 (M); expenditures, $121,544, including $45,000 for 2 grants of $22,500 each and $29,800 for 14 grants to individuals.
Purpose and activities: Giving for scholarships and payment of medical bills to members of Massachusetts families engaged in cranberry production; remainder of giving to a specified university and hospital.
Types of support awarded: Student aid, grants to individuals.
Limitations: Giving limited to MA.
Application information: Telephone during weekday mornings; scholarship applications also available at guidance offices of high schools; scholarship status decided anew each year; other beneficiaries already specified. Application form required.
Initial approach: Telephone or letter
Deadline(s): April 15 for scholarship; none for medical bill grants
Board meeting date(s): Varies

Write: Howard Whelan, Administrator
Trustees: Balfour Bassett, Reginald T. Cole, Ellen Stillman.
Employer Identification Number: 046115599

1646
Vingo Trust II ☐
238 Main St., Rm. 303
Cambridge 02142   (617) 354-1454

Trust established in 1954 in Massachusetts as successor to Vingo Trust.
Donor(s): Amory Coolidge,† William A. Coolidge.
Financial data: (yr. ended 12/31/82): Assets, $8,000,000 (M); expenditures, $745,000, including $680,000 for 100 grants (high: $100,000; low: $500).
Purpose and activities: Support for community-run neighborhood projects in Boston, Cambridge, Somerville, and Chelsea.
Types of support awarded: Operating budgets, special projects, building funds, equipment.
Limitations: Giving limited to Boston, Somerville, and Chelsea, MA. No grants to individuals, or for endowment funds, scholarships, or fellowships; no loans.
Publications: Informational brochure, application guidelines.
Application information: Program currently under re-evaluation by trustees.
    Write: Mary Sargent, Secretary
Officer: Mary Sargent, Secretary.
Trustees: Francis H. Burr, Gloria Coolidge, T. Jefferson Coolidge, William A. Coolidge, George H. Kidder, John Lastavica.
Employer Identification Number: 046027982

1647
Wallace (The George R.) Foundation
c/o Boston Safe Deposit and Trust Co.
One Boston Place
Boston 02106   (617) 523-5700
Mailing address: 28 State St., Rm. 2400, Boston, MA 02109

Trust established in 1963 in Massachusetts.
Donor(s): George R. Wallace.†
Financial data: (yr. ended 12/31/83): Assets, $3,431,912 (M); expenditures, $245,886, including $211,100 for 30 grants (high: $50,000; low: $100).
Purpose and activities: Giving primarily in Massachusetts, with emphasis on education.
Types of support awarded: General purposes, annual campaigns, seed money, building funds, equipment, land acquisition, endowment funds, matching funds.
Limitations: Giving primarily in MA. No grants to individuals, or for or scholarships and fellowships; no loans.
Application information:
    Initial approach: Letter
    Copies of proposal: 3
    Deadline(s): None
    Board meeting date(s): Semiannually
    Final notification: 6 months
    Write: George R. Wallace 3rd, Chairman
Trustees: John Grado, Jr., Henry B. Shepard, Jr., George R. Wallace 3rd.

Custodian: Boston Safe Deposit and Trust Company.
Number of staff: None.
Employer Identification Number: 046130518

1648
Walsh (Blanche M.) Charity Trust
174 Central St., Suite 329
Lowell 01852   (617) 454-5654

Trust established in 1973 in Massachusetts.
Financial data: (yr. ended 12/31/83): Assets, $2,042,051 (M); expenditures, $172,312, including $156,130 for 43 grants (high: $10,000; low: $500; average: $1,000-$5,000).
Purpose and activities: Giving limited to Roman Catholic organizations, including educational institutions and welfare organizations.
Types of support awarded: Operating budgets, seed money, building funds, equipment, scholarship funds, publications, conferences and seminars.
Limitations: No grants to individuals, or for endowment funds, continuing support, annual campaigns, deficit financing, or matching gifts; no loans.
Publications: Application guidelines.
Application information: Application form required.
    Initial approach: Letter
    Copies of proposal: 1
    Deadline(s): December 1
    Board meeting date(s): December and as required
    Write: Robert F. Murphy, Jr., Trustee
Trustees: Ruth F. Cowdrey, John E. Leggat, Robert F. Murphy, Jr.
Number of staff: 3 part-time professional.
Employer Identification Number: 046311841

1649
Warren Benevolent Fund, Inc.
342 Eliot St.
P.O. Box 46
Ashland 01721   (617) 881-2077

Incorporated in 1953 in Massachusetts.
Donor(s): Henry E. Warren.†
Financial data: (yr. ended 12/31/82): Assets, $515,535 (M); expenditures, $266,596, including $212,988 for 5 grants (high: $56,000; low: $2,000) and $16,500 for loans.
Purpose and activities: Charitable purposes; primarily local giving, with emphasis on youth agencies; support also for scholarship loans to Ashland High School students only.
Types of support awarded: Student aid.
Limitations: Giving primarily in Ashland, MA. No grants for building or endowment funds.
Application information:
    Initial approach: Letter
    Copies of proposal: 7
    Board meeting date(s): Quarterly
    Write: Mrs. Ann Thurston, Treasurer
Officers and Directors: Robert Rutherford, President; James Poitras, Vice-President; Ann Thurston, Clerk and Treasurer; John P. Chase, David Livingston, Finlay H. Perry.
Employer Identification Number: 042309470

1650
Waters Foundation, The ☐
1153 Grove St.
Framingham 01701

Trust established in 1958 in Massachusetts.
Financial data: (yr. ended 12/31/82): Assets, $1,795,357 (M); gifts received, $364,000; expenditures, $133,566, including $110,919 for 13 grants (high: $51,000; low: $200).
Purpose and activities: Grants largely for a psychological research organization and education.
Trustees: Barbara F. Waters, Faith P. Waters, James L. Waters, Richard C. Waters.
Employer Identification Number: 046115211

1651
Weber (The Frederick E.) Charities Corporation
50 Congress St., Rm. 742
Boston 02109   (617) 523-1455

Incorporated in 1902 in Massachusetts.
Donor(s): Frederick E. Weber.†
Financial data: (yr. ended 3/31/84): Assets, $3,251,071 (M); expenditures, $178,877, including $138,676 for 114 grants (high: $15,000; low: $25; average: $300-$1,000).
Purpose and activities: Giving primarily in the greater Boston area, with emphasis on social service agencies, for emergency financial assistance to indigent families or individuals.
Limitations: Giving primarily in MA. No grants to individuals or for research, capital projects, or equipment.
Publications: Annual report, program policy statement.
Application information:
    Initial approach: Letter
    Copies of proposal: 1
    Deadline(s): None
    Board meeting date(s): Monthly except in August
    Final notification: 30 days
Officers and Directors: Donald W. Moreland, President; Robert H. Baldwin, Doris L. Burke, Lawrence Coolidge, John G. Cushman, Franklin T. Hammond, Jr., William F. Kehoe, Patrick V. Riley, Peter E. Reinhold, William C. Swan, Daniel P. Wise.
Number of staff: 1 part-time support.
Employer Identification Number: 042133244

1652
Webster (Edwin S.) Foundation ▼
Accounting Service Corporation
75 Federal St.
Boston 02110   (617) 426-3750

Trust established in 1948 in Massachusetts.
Donor(s): Edwin S. Webster.†
Financial data: (yr. ended 12/31/83): Assets, $10,145,778 (M); expenditures, $515,448, including $476,000 for 38 grants (high: $60,000; low: $1,000; average: $5,000-$40,000).

Purpose and activities: Charitable purposes; giving primarily in the New England area, with emphasis on hospitals, medical research, higher and secondary education, youth agencies, cultural activities, community funds, and programs relating to alcoholism, the handicapped, and minorities.
Types of support awarded: Operating budgets, continuing support, annual campaigns, building funds, equipment, land acquisition, endowment funds, matching funds, scholarship funds, professorships, internships, fellowships, special projects, research.
Limitations: Giving primarily in New England. No grants to individuals, or for seed money, emergency funds, deficit financing, publications, or conferences; no loans.
Publications: 990-PF, program policy statement.
Application information: Application form required.
Initial approach: Full proposal
Copies of proposal: 1
Deadline(s): Submit proposal preferably in March or September; no set deadline
Board meeting date(s): May or June and November or December to consider proposals; March and September for general business
Final notification: 10 days after meetings on grant proposals
Write: Richard Harte, Jr., Secretary
Officer and Trustees: Richard Harte, Jr., Secretary; Henry U. Harris, Jr., Edwin W. Hiam, James H. Orr.
Number of staff: 1 part-time professional; 1 part-time support.
Employer Identification Number: 046000647

1653
Weld Foundation ¤
201 Devonshire St.
Boston 02110

Trust established in 1952 in Massachusetts.
Donor(s): Mary Weld Pingree.†
Financial data: (yr. ended 12/31/82): Assets, $2,005,723 (M); expenditures, $213,925, including $190,000 for 8 grants (high: $50,000; low: $10,000).
Purpose and activities: Broad purposes; local giving, with emphasis on schools, museums, and a hospital.
Limitations: Giving limited to MA.
Application information:
Write: Samuel H. Wolcott, Jr., Trustee
Trustees: Augustus P. Loring, Samuel H. Wolcott, Jr.
Employer Identification Number: 046039173

1654
Wellman (Arthur O. & Gullan M.) Foundation ¤
c/o Shawmut Bank of Boston
P.O. Box 4276
Boston 02211

Established in 1974.
Donor(s): Arthur Wellman Foundation.

Financial data: (yr. ended 12/31/82): Assets, $3,863 (M); gifts received, $747,400; expenditures, $745,537, including $731,846 for 47 grants (high: $46,400; low: $10).
Purpose and activities: Primarily local giving for hospitals and a medical school in Florida.
Limitations: Giving primarily in MA.
Trustee: Shawmut Bank of Boston.
Employer Identification Number: 046358222

1655
Wellman Foundation, The ¤
c/o Shawmut Bank of Boston
One Federal St.
Boston 02211

Established in 1951.
Donor(s): Wellman, Inc.
Financial data: (yr. ended 12/30/82): Assets, $3,840 (M); gifts received, $150,000; expenditures, $154,600, including $151,450 for 95 grants (high: $15,000; low: $50).
Purpose and activities: Giving primarily locally and in South Carolina, with emphasis on higher education and Protestant church support; some support also for hospitals, health agencies, secondary education, and an institute for research into alternate sources of energy.
Limitations: Giving primarily in MA and SC.
Trustee: Shawmut Bank of Boston.
Employer Identification Number: 046020616

1656
Wells (Fred W.) Trust Fund ¤
Bank of New England-Franklin, Trust Dept.
One Federal St.
Greenfield 01301   (413) 772-0281

Donor(s): Fred W. Wells.†
Financial data: (yr. ended 6/30/83): Assets, $1,951,182 (M); expenditures, $131,985, including $50,598 for 9 grants (high: $13,000; low: $60) and $64,914 for 125 grants to individuals.
Purpose and activities: Local giving, with grants for medical and other health care programs, and agricultural accomplishment prizes. Scholarships available to residents of Greenfield, Deerfield, Shelburne, Ashfield, Montague, Buckland, Charlemont, Heath, Leyden, Gill, Northfield, Conway, Bernardston, Hawley, Rowe, and Monroe.
Types of support awarded: Student aid.
Limitations: Giving limited to Franklin County, MA.
Publications: Application guidelines.
Application information: Application form required for education grants.
Initial approach: Letter
Deadline(s): May 1 for education grants
Write: Gordon W. Leavis, Trust Officer
Officers and Trustees: Beda A. Langevin, Chairman; Christopher Maniatty, Treasurer; Ann B. Abbott, Douglas Angelman, Judith K. Boerman, Kathryn Brown, Albert W. Charsky, Jean B. Cummings, John F. Dahowski, Ralph Haskins, Donald J. LaPierre, Gordon W. Leavis, Peter C. Mackin, Newland F. Smith, Jr., Wendell E. Streeter.
Employer Identification Number: 046412350

1657
Wheelwright Scientific School
c/o Chase & Lunt
47 State St.
Newburyport 01950   (617) 462-4434

Established in 1882.
Financial data: (yr. ended 6/30/82): Assets, $1,298,665 (M); gifts received, $84,567; expenditures, $84,567, including $62,629 for 28 grants to individuals.
Purpose and activities: Giving only for scholarships to financially aid young, Protestant men of Newburyport in obtaining a scientific education.
Types of support awarded: Student aid.
Limitations: Giving limited to Newburyport, MA.
Application information: Application form required.
Initial approach: Full proposal
Copies of proposal: 1
Deadline(s): Submit proposal preferably in March; deadline April 1
Board meeting date(s): April and November
Write: Josiah H. Welch, Secretary
Officers and Trustees: Elliot P. Knight, President; Josiah H. Welch, Secretary; Douglas Sloane IV, Treasurer; John H. Pramberg, Jr., Richard E. Sullivan, James G. Zafris, Jr.
Employer Identification Number: 046004390

1658
Williams (Arthur Ashley) Foundation
345 Union Ave.
P.O. Box 665
Framingham 01701   (617) 429-1149

Incorporated in 1951 in Massachusetts.
Donor(s): Arthur A. Williams.†
Financial data: (yr. ended 12/31/84): Assets, $2,992,220 (M); expenditures, $300,292, including $164,460 for 25 grants (high: $20,000; low: $200; average: $5,000-$10,000) and $54,250 for 44 grants to individuals.
Purpose and activities: Grants primarily for higher education, especially for financial aid to students in need and for churches, social welfare and youth agencies.
Types of support awarded: Student aid.
Publications: Application guidelines.
Application information: Application form required.
Initial approach: Letter
Copies of proposal: 1
Deadline(s): Submit proposal preferably in December; deadline 1 week prior to board meetings
Board meeting date(s): January, April, July, and October
Write: Frederick Cole, Chairman
Officers and Trustees: Frederick Cole, Chairman; Elbert F. Tuttle, Secretary; Clement T. Lambert, Treasurer; Arthur A. Williams, Jr., David S. Williams, William Williams, Hayden R. Wood.
Employer Identification Number: 046044714

1659
Worcester Community Foundation, Inc., Greater
332 Main St., Suite 722
Worcester 01608   (617) 755-0980

Community foundation incorporated in 1975 in Massachusetts.

Financial data: (yr. ended 12/31/83): Assets, $2,695,917 (M); gifts received, $282,537; expenditures, $276,551, including $224,760 for 80 grants (high: $15,000; low: $200; average: $1,000-$10,000) and $6,500 for 7 grants to individuals.

Purpose and activities: Broad purposes; "to help meet the health, educational, social welfare, cultural and civic needs of the people of Greater Worcester, including, but not limited to, assisting charitable and educational institutions; for the needy, sick, aged or helpless; for the care of children; for the betterment of living and working conditions; for recreation for all classes, and for such other public and/or charitable uses and purposes as will best make for mental, moral and physical improvement, or contribute to the public welfare."

Types of support awarded: Seed money, emergency funds, equipment, matching funds, internships, scholarship funds.

Limitations: Giving limited to the greater Worcester, MA, area. No grants for endowment funds, general operating expenses, continuing support, annual campaigns, deficit financing, building funds, land acquisition, or research; no loans.

Publications: Annual report, program policy statement, application guidelines.

Application information: Application form required.

  Initial approach: Telephone or letter
  Copies of proposal: 2
  Deadline(s): Submit 8 copies of Foundation summary sheet, plus 2 copies of proposal in July; deadline July 31
  Board meeting date(s): February, April, August, November, and as required
  Final notification: 3 1/2 months
  Write: Ms. Kay M. Seivard, Executive Director

Officers and Directors: Robert H. Wetzel, President; Jean F. Hazzard, Vice-President; Robert K. Massey, Treasurer; John Adam, Jr., Helen A. Bowditch, Joseph J. Butare, Jr., Harold N. Cotton, Robert Cushman, Bayard T. DeMallie, Thomas S. Green, Ernest S. Hayeck, Louis C. Iandoli, Howard Jacobson, Austin W. Keane, Barry L. Krock, Shirley M. Maguire, Melvin M. Rosenblatt, Edward D. Simsarian, Evangeline Tierney, Sumner B. Tilton, Jr.

Distribution Committee: Michael P. Angelini, Martha A. Cowan, Charles Dodson, Barbara Greenberg, Abraham Haddad, David Stephens, Meridith Wesby.

Trustee Banks: Guaranty Bank and Trust Company, Mechanics Bank, Shawmut Worcester County Bank.

Number of staff: 1 full-time professional; 1 part-time professional; 2 part-time support.

Employer Identification Number: 042572276

1660
Wyman-Gordon Foundation
105 Madison St.
Worcester 01613   (617) 756-5111

Established in 1966 in Delaware.

Donor(s): Wyman-Gordon Co.

Financial data: (yr. ended 12/31/84): Assets, $4,236,659 (M); gifts received, $900,000; expenditures, $915,733, including $829,375 for 83 grants (high: $150,000; low: $100), $68,500 for 20 grants to individuals and $17,695 for 120 employee matching gifts.

Purpose and activities: General purposes; giving locally and in plant communities, with emphasis on community funds, cultural programs, higher education, hospitals, and youth agencies.

Types of support awarded: General purposes, operating budgets, continuing support, annual campaigns, seed money, emergency funds, deficit financing, building funds, equipment, land acquisition, employee matching gifts, scholarship funds, employee related scholarships, fellowships.

Limitations: Giving primarily in MA, with emphasis on the Worcester area, and plant communities (Harvey and Danville, IL; Jackson, MI; Cedartown, GA; McAllen, TX; South Gate, CA). No grants to individuals, or for endowment funds, special projects, research, publications, or conferences; no loans.

Application information:

  Initial approach: Letter or full proposal
  Copies of proposal: 1
  Board meeting date(s): February, April, June, August, October, and December
  Write: John J.L. Matson, Assistant Secretary-Treasurer

Officers and Directors: Richard Bullock, President; Joseph R. Carter, Vice-President; Donald L. Marshall, Secretary-Treasurer; Edward W. Bettke, Sacket R. Duryee.

Number of staff: 1 part-time professional; 1 part-time support.

Employer Identification Number: 046142600

1661
Zayre Foundation, Inc.
c/o Zayre Corp.
Community Affairs Dept.
Framingham 01701   (617) 651-6200

Incorporated in 1966 in Massachusetts.

Donor(s): Zayre Corporation.

Financial data: (yr. ended 1/31/83): Assets, $25,806 (M); gifts received, $110,000; expenditures, $104,959, including $104,912 for 89 grants (high: $10,500; low: $100; average: $1,000).

Purpose and activities: Giving primarily to community funds, hospitals, Jewish welfare funds, and cultural programs.

Limitations: Giving limited to areas of company operations.

Application information:

  Write: Stanley Berkovitz, Vice-President

Officers and Directors: Stanley H. Feldberg, President; Maurice Segall, Vice-President; Sumner Feldberg, Treasurer.

Employer Identification Number: 042399760

MICHIGAN

1662
Aeroquip Foundation
300 South East Ave.
Jackson 49203-1972   (517) 787-8121

Incorporated in 1962 in Michigan.

Donor(s): Aeroquip Corporation.

Financial data: (yr. ended 12/31/83): Assets, $2,162,941 (M); expenditures, $189,027, including $171,900 for 59 grants (high: $31,300; low: $150).

Purpose and activities: Grants largely for united funds, regional independent college funds, local cultural organizations, hospitals, and youth agencies in communities where Aeroquip Corporation plants are located.

Types of support awarded: Continuing support, annual campaigns, building funds, equipment, land acquisition.

Limitations: Giving limited to areas of company operations. No support for sectarian or religious purposes. No grants to individuals, or for endowment funds, research, scholarships, fellowships, or matching gifts; no loans.

Publications: Annual report, program policy statement, application guidelines.

Application information:

  Initial approach: Letter
  Copies of proposal: 1
  Deadline(s): Submit proposal preferably between May and December
  Board meeting date(s): As required
  Final notification: 1 month
  Write: David E. Rainey, Secretary-Treasurer

Officers and Trustees: H.A. Bancroft, President; Lloyd C. Preston, Vice-President; David E. Rainey, Secretary-Treasurer; G.W. Moody, J.L. Price.

Number of staff: 1.

Employer Identification Number: 386061520

1663
Americana Foundation
c/o Manufacturers National Bank of Detroit
1166 North Woodward Ave.
Birmingham 48011

Trust established in 1960 in New York.

Donor(s): Adolph H. Meyer, Ida M. Meyer Charitable Remainder Annuity Trust.

Financial data: (yr. ended 12/31/83): Assets, $3,376,916 (M); gifts received, $257,078; expenditures, $144,449, including $115,000 for 14 grants.

Purpose and activities: Primarily local giving, with emphasis on education related to agricultural and environmental programs.

Types of support awarded: General purposes, equipment, annual campaigns, research.

Limitations: Giving primarily in MI.

Application information:

  Write: Sinclair J. Harcus, Secretary

Officers and Directors: Gary Rentrop, President; Sinclair J. Harcus, Secretary; Thomas F. Ranger, Treasurer; Jack Barnes, Gordon E. Guyer, Thomas McMullen.
Employer Identification Number: 382269431

1664
Ann Arbor Area Foundation
2301 Platt Rd.
Ann Arbor 48104   (313) 971-2355

Community foundation incorporated in 1963 in Michigan.
Financial data: (yr. ended 12/31/84): Assets, $1,993,994 (M); gifts received, $43,669; expenditures, $124,247, including $71,022 for 21 grants.
Purpose and activities: Support for innovative programs and projects in charitable, religious, scientific, civic, moral, literary, cultural, social, economic, and educational areas. Limited to the Ann Arbor area and Ann Arbor residents only.
Types of support awarded: Seed money, emergency funds, building funds, equipment, matching funds, scholarship funds, program-related investments, research, special projects, publications, conferences and seminars.
Limitations: Giving limited to the Ann Arbor, MI, area. No grants to individuals, or for operating budgets, continuing support, annual campaigns, deficit financing, land acquisition, endowment funds, consulting services, technical assistance, fellowships, or program-related investments; no loans.
Publications: Annual report, program policy statement, application guidelines.
Application information: Application form required.
  Initial approach: Telephone
  Deadline(s): Middle of month prior to meetings
  Board meeting date(s): January, March, May, September, and November
  Final notification: 30 to 60 days
  Write: Robert B. Kerschbaum, Executive Director
Officer: Robert B. Kerschbaum, Executive Director.
Distribution Committee: Robert E. Bonfield, Chairman; Anne Amendt, Herbert O. Ellis, John Eman, James Frenza, James Irwin, Fran Jelinek, Terry Martin, Mark Ouimet.
Trustees: Russell W. Reister, President; Susan Westerman, Vice-President; Stephen Dobson, Secretary; John Burtt, Treasurer; George H. Cress, Richard A. Hadler, William Kulenkamp, Charles E. Leahy, Norma Sarns.
Number of staff: 1 part-time support.
Employer Identification Number: 386087967

1665
Avery (Charles Shirley) Foundation
c/o Manufacturers National Bank of Detroit
100 Renaissance Center
Detroit 48243   (313) 222-5509

Established in 1972 in Michigan.
Donor(s): Charles Shirley Avery.†

Financial data: (yr. ended 6/30/84): Assets, $2,099,274 (M); expenditures, $187,853, including $165,000 for 11 grants of $15,000 each.
Purpose and activities: Support for local social and health agencies, including medical research and aid to the handicapped.
Limitations: Giving limited to MI.
Trustees: Raymond T. Huetteman, Jr., Manufacturers National Bank of Detroit.
Employer Identification Number: 386218309

1666
Baldwin Foundation ⌗
Old Kent Bank Bldg.
320 Old Kent
Grand Rapids 49502

Trust established in 1964 in Michigan.
Donor(s): Members of the Baldwin family.
Financial data: (yr. ended 11/30/83): Assets, $1,837,047 (M); expenditures, $91,357, including $79,171 for 32 grants (high: $10,000; low: $215).
Purpose and activities: Primarily local giving, with emphasis on arts and cultural programs, higher education, and social agencies.
Limitations: Giving primarily in MI.
Trustees: Julie B. Baldwin, Melvin D. Baldwin II, Ralph B. Baldwin, Carol Curlin, John R. Davies, Margaret Johnson, Frances Mulnix, Old Kent Bank & Trust Company.
Employer Identification Number: 386085641

1667
Bargman (Theodore and Mina) Foundation
29201 Telegraph Rd., Suite 500
Southfield 48034

Incorporated in 1954 in Michigan.
Donor(s): Mina Bargman.†
Financial data: (yr. ended 12/31/83): Assets, $3,187,875 (M); expenditures, $148,893, including $138,260 for 56 grants (high: $19,300; low: $100).
Purpose and activities: Broad purposes; primarily religious giving, with emphasis on Jewish welfare funds, higher education in Israel, and temple support.
Types of support awarded: Continuing support, annual campaigns, general purposes, building funds.
Limitations: No grants for endowment funds, scholarships and fellowships, or matching gifts; no loans.
Officers and Directors: Joseph H. Jackier, President; Lawrence S. Jackier, Vice-President; Maxwell E. Katzen, Secretary; Bruce R. Mayhew, Treasurer.
Employer Identification Number: 386087158

1668
Barstow Foundation, The
c/o Chemical Bank and Trust Company
333 East Main St.
Midland 48640   (517) 631-9200

Trust established in 1967 in Michigan.
Donor(s): Florence K. Barstow.†

Financial data: (yr. ended 12/31/84): Assets, $1,405,396 (M); expenditures, $84,945, including $80,167 for 9 grants (high: $25,000; low: $3,333; average: $5,000-$10,000).
Purpose and activities: Primarily to support Midland Community Center with secondary interest in local organizations and in other charitable organizations engaged in alleviating poverty and hunger on a national or world basis.
Types of support awarded: Operating budgets, annual campaigns, seed money, emergency funds, equipment, endowment funds, matching funds, special projects.
Limitations: Giving primarily in Midland County, MI. No grants to individuals, or for research, continuing support, deficit financing, building funds, scholarships, or fellowships; no loans.
Publications: 990-PF.
Application information:
  Initial approach: Full proposal
  Copies of proposal: 2
  Deadline(s): Submit proposal preferably from August through October; deadline October 31
  Board meeting date(s): November
  Final notification: After annual meeting
  Write: Eugene B. Skeebo, Senior Vice-President, Chemical Bank and Trust Company
Trustees: Ormond E. Barstow, Frederick E. Barstow, Mrs. Ruth B. Dixon, Chemical Bank and Trust Company.
Number of staff: None.
Employer Identification Number: 386151026

1669
Battle Creek Foundation, Greater
512 Michigan National Bank Bldg.
Battle Creek 49017   (616) 962-2181

Community foundation established in 1973 in Michigan.
Financial data: (yr. ended 4/30/84): Assets, $1,683,628 (M); gifts received, $212,484; expenditures, $170,018, including $112,616 for 20 grants (high: $50,000; low: $100; average: $5,630).
Purpose and activities: For the general welfare of the residents of the greater Battle Creek area and to that end to support charitable, scientific, literary, and educational programs of all kinds that will foster improvement of the physical environment and the living, working, and social conditions.
Types of support awarded: Seed money, emergency funds, building funds, equipment, land acquisition, scholarship funds, special projects, program-related investments, publications, conferences and seminars, endowment funds.
Limitations: Giving limited to the greater Battle Creek, MI, area. No grants to individuals, or for operating budgets, deficit financing, endowments, matching gifts, consulting services, technical assistance, or research; no loans.
Publications: Annual report.
Application information: Application form required.
  Initial approach: Letter

Copies of proposal: 10
Deadline(s): March 1 and October 1
Board meeting date(s): Monthly
Write: Harry R. Davidson, Executive Director
Officer: Harry R. Davidson, Executive Director.
Number of staff: 1 part-time professional.
Employer Identification Number: 382045459

1670
Bauervic (Charles M.) Foundation, Inc. ⌐
2885 Coolidge, Suite 107
Troy 48084

Incorporated in 1967 in Michigan.
Donor(s): Charles M. Bauervic.†
Financial data: (yr. ended 12/31/83): Assets, $6,294,749 (M); expenditures, $456,247, including $352,400 for 32 grants (high: $60,000; low: $500).
Purpose and activities: Local giving for hospitals, higher and secondary education, churches, child welfare and youth development organizations, and cultural organizations.
Limitations: Giving primarily in MI.
Application information:
Deadline(s): October 1
Officers: Rose D. Bauervic-Wright, President; Patricia A. Leonard, Vice-President; Beverly M. Paisley, Secretary; Peggy L. Carroll, Treasurer.
Employer Identification Number: 386146352

1671
Bentley (Alvin M.) Foundation
312 W. Main St.
P.O. Box 458
Owosso 48867   (517) 723-5114

Incorporated in 1961 in Michigan.
Donor(s): Alvin M. Bentley,† Arvella D. Bentley.†
Financial data: (yr. ended 7/31/84): Assets, $1,625,034 (M); gifts received, $5,000; expenditures, $106,138, including $65,100 for 8 grants (high: $42,600; low: $450) and $24,808 for grants to individuals.
Purpose and activities: Broad purposes; largely local giving, with emphasis on higher education, including scholarships for students attending one of 17 Michigan colleges and universities, and community funds.
Types of support awarded: Student aid, grants to individuals.
Limitations: Giving primarily in MI. No grants to individuals (except for scholarships), or for building or endowment funds, or matching gifts.
Application information: Application form for scholarships is required; scholarships restricted to 17 colleges or universities in Michigan. Application form required.
Initial approach: Letter
Copies of proposal: 1
Deadline(s): March 1 for scholarships
Board meeting date(s): Quarterly when possible
Write: Dorothy Cross, Secretary-Treasurer
Officers: Mark C. Stevens,* President; Veda Anderson,* Vice-President; Dorothy Cross, Secretary-Treasurer.

Trustees:* Alvin M. Bentley IV, Ann Bentley, Clark H. Bentley, Michael D. Bentley, Paul Brown, Mrs. Helen Bentley Crowell, Jerry L. Des Jardins, William J. Edwards, John R. Francis, Paul G. Goebel, Jr.
Employer Identification Number: 386076280

1672
Besser Foundation
314 East Chisholm St.
Alpena 49707   (517) 354-4722

Incorporated in 1944 in Michigan.
Donor(s): J.H. Besser,† Besser Company.
Financial data: (yr. ended 12/31/83): Assets, $6,679,349 (M); expenditures, $561,871, including $293,542 for 46 grants (high: $120,431; low: $250).
Purpose and activities: General purposes; giving limited primarily to the Alpena area; grants to local schools and colleges, health and social agencies, and churches; also full support of Besser Museum, a local historical and art museum.
Types of support awarded: Scholarship funds, matching funds, seed money.
Limitations: Giving primarily in the Alpena, MI area. No grants to individuals, or for endowment funds or research; no loans.
Publications: Program policy statement.
Application information:
Initial approach: Telephone, letter, or full proposal
Copies of proposal: 1
Deadline(s): None
Board meeting date(s): Bimonthly, beginning in February
Write: Carl F. Reitz, Secretary-Treasurer
Officers and Trustees: Frederick T. Johnston, President; Rev. Robert M. Barksdale, Vice-President; Carl F. Reitz, Secretary-Treasurer; J.R. Wilson.
Employer Identification Number: 386071938

1673
Besser (Jesse) Fund, Inc.
150-C N. State St.
Alpena 49707   (517) 354-4722

Incorporated in 1960 in Michigan.
Donor(s): Besser Company.
Financial data: (yr. ended 12/31/84): Assets, $3,166,000 (M); expenditures, $183,038, including $157,863 for 24 grants (high: $12,500; low: $1,000).
Purpose and activities: Charitable giving primarily in Alpena, with emphasis on health, community funds, and social agencies.
Types of support awarded: Operating budgets, continuing support, annual campaigns, seed money, emergency funds, equipment, matching funds.
Limitations: Giving primarily in the Alpena, MI, area. No grants to individuals or for endowment funds; no loans.
Publications: Annual report, program policy statement, application guidelines.
Application information: Application form required.
Initial approach: Letter, telephone, or full proposal

Copies of proposal: 1
Board meeting date(s): Bimonthly, beginning in February
Write: Carl F. Reitz, Secretary-Treasurer
Officers and Trustees: Edward Adams, Jr., President; Harold A. Ruemenapp, Vice-President; Carl F. Reitz, Secretary-Treasurer.
Number of staff: None.
Employer Identification Number: 386061035

1674
Bishop (A. G.) Charitable Trust
Genesee Merchants Bank & Trust Co.
One East First St.
Flint 48502   (313) 766-8307

Trust established in 1944 in Michigan.
Donor(s): Arthur Giles Bishop.†
Financial data: (yr. ended 12/31/84): Assets, $2,943,323 (M); expenditures, $158,000, including $146,000 for 45 grants (high: $20,000; low: $500).
Purpose and activities: Local giving, with emphasis on a hospital, a community fund, youth agencies, higher education, and social and health agencies.
Types of support awarded: Operating budgets, continuing support, annual campaigns, seed money, emergency funds, deficit financing, building funds, equipment, land acquisition, research.
Limitations: Giving limited to the Flint-Genesee County, MI community. No grants to individuals, or for endowment funds, scholarships, fellowships, or matching gifts; no loans.
Application information:
Initial approach: Letter
Copies of proposal: 1
Deadline(s): Submit proposal preferably June through August
Board meeting date(s): Annually in the fall
Final notification: 2 weeks
Write: C. Ann Barton, Personal Trust Administrator
Trustees: Mrs. Robert H. Bellairs, A. William Bishop, Genesee Merchants Bank & Trust Co. (C. Ann Barton, Personal Trust Administrator).
Number of staff: 1 part-time professional.
Employer Identification Number: 386040693

1675
Boutell (Arnold and Gertrude) Memorial Fund ⌐
c/o Second National Bank of Saginaw
101 North Washington Ave.
Saginaw 48607   (517) 755-3411

Trust established in 1961 in Michigan.
Donor(s): Arnold Boutell,† Gertrude Boutell.†
Financial data: (yr. ended 3/31/83): Assets, $5,329,844 (M); expenditures, $934,576, including $895,723 for 51 grants (high: $100,000; low: $111).
Purpose and activities: Charitable and educational purposes; local grants only, largely for a community fund, education, cultural programs, community development, and hospitals.

Limitations: Giving limited to Saginaw County, MI. No grants to individuals, or for endowment funds.
Application information: Application form required.
  Initial approach: Letter
  Copies of proposal: 1
  Board meeting date(s): Monthly
Trustee: Second National Bank of Saginaw.
Employer Identification Number: 386040492

1676
Bray (Viola E.) Charitable Trust
c/o Genesee Merchants Bank & Trust Co.
One East First St.
Flint 48502   (313) 766-8370

Trust established in 1961 in Michigan.
Donor(s): Viola E. Bray.
Financial data: (yr. ended 9/30/84): Assets, $2,029,061 (M); expenditures, $88,024, including $73,110 for 12 grants (high: $20,000; low: $450).
Purpose and activities: Local giving, with emphasis on the fine arts.
Types of support awarded: Continuing support, annual campaigns, seed money, emergency funds, building funds, equipment, matching funds.
Limitations: Giving limited to the Flint, MI, area. No grants to individuals, or for research, scholarships, or fellowships; no loans.
Publications: 990-PF, program policy statement, application guidelines.
Application information:
  Initial approach: One-page proposal
  Copies of proposal: 3
  Deadline(s): None
  Board meeting date(s): As required
  Final notification: 2 months
  Write: Webb F. Martin, Sr., Vice-President
Trustee: Genesee Merchants Bank & Trust Co. (Webb F. Martin, Sr., Vice-President).
Employer Identification Number: 386039741

1677
Bundy Foundation, The ⌗
333 West Fort St., 20th Fl.
Detroit 48226   (313) 964-4244

Incorporated in 1952 in Michigan.
Donor(s): Bundy Corporation.
Financial data: (yr. ended 12/31/83): Assets, $4,324,798 (M); gifts received, $310,000; expenditures, $464,940, including $402,920 for 94 grants (high: $90,000; low: $100) and $1,325 for 16 employee matching gifts.
Purpose and activities: Grants only to tax-exempt organizations, with emphasis on community funds, education, hospitals, and cultural programs, usually in areas where employees of the Bundy Corporation and Divisions reside.
Types of support awarded: Matching funds, operating budgets.
Limitations: Giving primarily in areas of company operations. No support for organizations currently receiving funds from other organizations which the foundation supports. No grants to individuals.
Application information:

Initial approach: Letter
Copies of proposal: 1
Deadline(s): None
Board meeting date(s): As required
Write: Robert E. Barton, Secretary
Officers and Trustees: Wendell W. Anderson, Jr., President; John W. Anderson II, Vice-President; Robert E. Barton, Secretary and Treasurer.
Employer Identification Number: 386053694

1678
Chamberlin (Gerald W.) Foundation, Inc. ⌗
18301 East Eight Mile Rd., Suite 212
East Detroit 48021

Incorporated in 1955 in Michigan.
Donor(s): Gerald W. Chamberlin,† Myrtle F. Chamberlin,† Donald F. Chamberlin, Joanne M. Chamberlin, Chamberlin Products.
Financial data: (yr. ended 12/31/83): Assets, $1,931,524 (M); expenditures, $187,638, including $147,250 for 54 grants (high: $25,000; low: $100).
Purpose and activities: Primarily local giving for Protestant church support, youth agencies, higher and secondary education, and cultural programs.
Limitations: Giving primarily in MI.
Officers: Donald F. Chamberlin, President; John W. Butler, Vice-President; Joy C. Robbins, Secretary-Treasurer.
Employer Identification Number: 386055730

1679
Chrysler Corporation Fund ▼
P.O. Box 1919
Detroit 48288   (313) 956-5194
Office address: 12000 Chrysler Dr., Highland Park, MI 48203

Incorporated in 1953 in Michigan.
Donor(s): Chrysler Corporation.
Financial data: (yr. ended 12/31/83): Assets, $1,166,219 (M); expenditures, $1,679,403, including $1,519,900 for 155 grants (high: $312,500; low: $100) and $159,503 for 971 employee matching gifts.
Purpose and activities: Broad purposes; general giving in areas where the company has a substantial number of employees, with emphasis on community funds, higher education, civic affairs, and cultural programs.
Types of support awarded: Operating budgets, continuing support, annual campaigns, emergency funds, special projects, employee matching gifts, building funds, employee related scholarships.
Limitations: Giving primarily in areas where the company has a substantial number of employees. No grants to individuals (except for scholarships to children of company employees), or for endowment funds, fellowships, deficit financing, equipment and materials, or research; capital funds supported mainly through United Ways; no loans.
Publications: Program policy statement, application guidelines.
Application information:
  Initial approach: Letter

Copies of proposal: 1
Deadline(s): None
Board meeting date(s): As required, usually quarterly; educational grants approved at fall meeting
Final notification: 1 to 2 months
Write: Ms. Lynn A. Feldhouse, Administrator
Officers: J.L. Tolley,* President; R.S. Miller, Jr.,* Vice-President and Treasurer; M.M. Glusac, Secretary and Executive Director.
Trustees:* B.E. Bidwell, R. Goodyear, S. Sharf, G.E. White, J.D. Withrow, Jr.
Number of staff: 1 full-time professional; 2 part-time support.
Employer Identification Number: 386087371

1680
Cook (Peter C. and Emajean) Charitable Trust ⌗
c/o Peter C. Cook
2660 28th St., SE
Grand Rapids 49508

Trust established in 1959 in Michigan.
Donor(s): Peter C. Cook, Emajean Cook.
Financial data: (yr. ended 12/31/83): Assets, $1,258,495 (M); gifts received, $242,000; expenditures, $237,860, including $232,682 for 45 grants (high: $50,000; low: $24).
Purpose and activities: Primarily local giving, with emphasis on higher education, including a theological seminary, and Protestant religious organizations; support also for youth agencies and cultural programs.
Limitations: Giving primarily in MI.
Trustee: Peter C. Cook.
Employer Identification Number: 386065735

1681
Dalton (Dorothy U.) Foundation, Inc.
c/o American National Bank and Trust Company
151 East Michigan Ave.
Kalamazoo 49007   (616) 383-6958

Incorporated in 1978 in Michigan as successor to Dorothy U. Dalton Foundation Trust.
Donor(s): Dorothy U. Dalton.†
Financial data: (yr. ended 12/31/82): Assets, $9,844,012 (M); expenditures, $754,406, including $706,693 for 57 grants (high: $191,272; low: $100; average: $100-$88,000).
Purpose and activities: Broad purposes; primarily local giving, with emphasis on higher education, mental health, youth agencies, cultural programs and a community fund.
Types of support awarded: Operating budgets, continuing support, seed money, emergency funds, deficit financing, building funds, equipment, land acquisition, matching funds, research, special projects.
Limitations: Giving primarily in Kalamazoo County, MI. No grants to individuals, or for annual campaigns, scholarships, fellowships, publications, or conferences; no loans.
Publications: 990-PF.
Application information:
  Initial approach: Full proposal
  Copies of proposal: 5
  Deadline(s): April and October
  Board meeting date(s): May and November

Final notification: 30 days after board meetings

Write: Ronald N. Kilgore, Secretary and Treasurer

Officers and Trustees: Suzanne D. Parish, President; Howard Kalleward, Vice-President; Ronald N. Kilgore, Secretary and Treasurer; Thompson Bennett, Arthur F. Homer.
Number of staff: None.
Employer Identification Number: 382240062

1682
DeRoy (The Helen L.) Foundation ¤
3274 Penobscot Bldg.
Detroit 48226   (313) 961-3814

Incorporated in 1946 in Michigan.
Donor(s): Helen L. DeRoy.
Financial data: (yr. ended 12/31/83): Assets, $3,256,867 (M); gifts received, $52,900; expenditures, $93,820, including $61,770 for 102 grants (high: $12,500; low: $50).
Purpose and activities: Broad purposes; primarily local giving, with emphasis on Jewish welfare funds and higher education; grants also for child welfare.
Types of support awarded: Operating budgets, general purposes, annual campaigns, research, emergency funds, scholarship funds, building funds.
Limitations: Giving primarily in MI.
Application information:
Deadline(s): None
Write: Arthur Rodecker, President, or Leonard H. Weiner, Vice-President
Officers and Trustees: Arthur Rodecker, President; Leonard H. Weiner, Vice-President; Bernice Michel, Secretary.
Employer Identification Number: 386082108

1683
DeRoy Testamentary Foundation ¤
3274 City National Bank Bldg.
Detroit 48226

Established in 1979 in Michigan.
Donor(s): Helen DeRoy.†
Financial data: (yr. ended 12/31/83): Assets, $8,749,285 (M); expenditures, $344,975, including $301,200 for 45 grants (high: $100,000; low: $500).
Purpose and activities: Primarily local giving, with emphasis on higher education; support also for Jewish welfare funds, hospitals, and social and youth agencies.
Limitations: Giving primarily in MI.
Officers and Trustees: Leonard H. Weiner, Chairman; Gilbert Michel, President; Arthur Rodecker, Vice-President; Bernice Michel, Secretary.
Employer Identification Number: 382208833

1684
Detroit Community Trust, The
c/o Comerica Bank - Detroit
211 West Fort St.
Detroit 48231   (313) 222-3300

Community foundation established in 1915 in Michigan.

Financial data: (yr. ended 12/31/83): Assets, $1,200,000 (M); expenditures, $72,000, including $61,000 for 27 grants (high: $4,000; low: $1,000).
Purpose and activities: Primarily local giving to youth agencies, hospitals, cultural programs and social welfare.
Limitations: Giving primarily in Detroit, MI. No support for organizations included in the United Fund. No grants to individuals, or for building or endowment funds, or research.
Application information:
Initial approach: Letter with brief supporting material
Copies of proposal: 1
Deadline(s): Submit proposal preferably in March or April; deadline May 10
Board meeting date(s): May
Trustee: The Detroit Bank and Trust Company.
Disbursing Board: Andrew W. Barr, Rt. Rev. Edward J. Hickey, Charles S. Himelhoch, James M. McMillan, Cleveland Thurber.
Employer Identification Number: 386042433

1685
DeVlieg (The Charles B. and Charles R.) Foundation
c/o deVlieg Machine Company
Fair St.
Royal Oak 48068   (313) 280-1100

Incorporated in 1961 in Michigan.
Donor(s): Charles B. DeVlieg,† Charles R. DeVlieg, DeVlieg Machine Company.
Financial data: (yr. ended 12/31/83): Assets, $2,387,430 (M); expenditures, $231,197, including $206,100 for 35 grants (high: $25,000; low: $300) and $14,000 for grants to individuals.
Purpose and activities: Primarily local giving; support largely for higher education, including grants to a university for fellowships and a scholarship program for local high school graduates; grants for community funds, hospitals, and youth agencies.
Types of support awarded: Fellowships, general purposes, scholarship funds, employee related scholarships.
Limitations: Giving primarily in southeastern MI. No grants to individuals (except for company-employee scholarships), or for endowment funds, research programs, or matching gifts; no loans.
Application information: Application form required.
Initial approach: Full proposal
Copies of proposal: 2
Board meeting date(s): Semiannually
Write: S.T. Segesta, Secretary-Treasurer
Officers: Charles R. DeVlieg,* President; Herbert A. Beyer,* Vice-President; S.T. Segesta, Secretary-Treasurer.
Trustees:* Janet M. Irvine.
Employer Identification Number: 386075696

1686
DeVos (The Richard and Helen) Foundation ▼
7154 Windy Hill Rd., S.E.
Grand Rapids 49506

Incorporated in 1969 in Michigan.
Donor(s): Richard M. DeVos, Helen J. DeVos.
Financial data: (yr. ended 12/31/82): Assets, $12,900,052 (M); gifts received, $1,255,063; expenditures, $1,101,011, including $1,096,322 for 76 grants (high: $150,000; low: $30).
Purpose and activities: Charitable purposes; giving largely for religious programs and associations, church support, music, higher education, and social welfare.
Application information:
Write: Richard M. DeVos, President
Officers: Richard M. DeVos, President; Helen J. DeVos, Vice-President; William J. Halliday, Jr., Secretary; C. Dale Discher, Treasurer.
Employer Identification Number: 237066873

1687
DeWaters Charitable Trust ▼
c/o Michigan National Bank
519 South Saginaw St.
Flint 48502   (313) 762-5563

Trust established in 1963 in Michigan.
Donor(s): Enos A. DeWaters.†
Financial data: (yr. ended 12/31/84): Assets, $1,242,517 (M); expenditures, $417,846, including $398,688 for 8 grants (high: $126,125; low: $5,000; average: $5,000-$75,000).
Purpose and activities: Broad purposes; local giving for education, including a scholarship fund, mental health and community health programs; grants also for youth agencies, cultural institutions, community funds, and other programs .
Types of support awarded: Seed money, building funds, equipment, matching funds, scholarship funds.
Limitations: Giving limited to Genesee County, MI. No grants to individuals, or for endowment funds, or research; no loans.
Publications: Multi-year report.
Application information:
Initial approach: Letter, telephone, or full proposal
Copies of proposal: 1
Deadline(s): December 1
Board meeting date(s): January
Final notification: 2 weeks after board meeting
Write: John D. Logan, Executive Director
Officer: John D. Logan, Executive Director.
Distribution Committee: Thomas C. Robberson, Chairman; Phillip Dutcher, H. Samuel Greenawalt, Elmer Knopf, Olivia Maynard, Michael D. Melet.
Trustee: Michigan National Bank.
Number of staff: 1 part-time professional; 1 part-time support.
Employer Identification Number: 386069997

1688
Dow Chemical Company Foundation, The ▼
2030 Dow Bldg.
Midland 48640   (517) 636-1162

Established in 1979 in Michigan.
Donor(s): The Dow Chemical Company.
Financial data: (yr. ended 12/31/83): Assets, $1,695,115 (M); expenditures, $2,591,235, including $2,571,301 for 183 grants (high: $178,578; low: $500; average: $1,000-$70,000).
Purpose and activities: Grants primarily for higher education, especially chemical research.
Limitations: No grants to individuals.
Publications: Annual report.
Application information:
   Write: Dr. Earl F. Engles, Jr., Program Manager
Officers: P.F. Oreffice,* President; D.P. Sheetz, Vice-President; A.H. Jenkins, Secretary; E.C. Yehle, Treasurer; Earl F. Engles, Jr., Program Manager.
Trustees:* R.W. Lundeen, Chairman; H.D. Doan, H.H. Dow, H.W. Henry, R.M. Keill, D.L. Rooke.
Employer Identification Number: 382314603

1689
Dow (Herbert H. and Barbara C.) Foundation ¤
2301 W. Sugnet Rd.
Midland 48642

Incorporated in 1957 in Michigan.
Donor(s): Herbert H. Dow.
Financial data: (yr. ended 12/31/83): Assets, $3,555,715 (M); expenditures, $178,482, including $145,345 for 24 grants (high: $50,000; low: $90).
Purpose and activities: Charitable purposes; primarily local giving, with emphasis on higher education, cultural programs, and community funds.
Types of support awarded: Equipment, continuing support, general purposes.
Limitations: Giving primarily in MI.
Application information:
   Initial approach: Letter
   Board meeting date(s): Annually
   Write: Herbert H. Dow II, President
Officers and Trustees: Herbert H. Dow II, President; Barbara C. Dow, Secretary and Treasurer; Willard H. Dow III.
Employer Identification Number: 386058513

1690
Dow (The Herbert H. and Grace A.) Foundation ▼
P.O. Box 2184
Midland 48641-2184   (517) 636-2482

Trust established in 1936 in Michigan.
Donor(s): Mrs. Grace A. Dow.†
Financial data: (yr. ended 12/31/83): Assets, $118,156,203 (M); expenditures, $8,757,936, including $7,699,154 for 34 grants (high: $1,686,281; low: $16; average: $5,000-$150,000).

Purpose and activities: For the benefit of the residents of Midland and the people of the state of Michigan; emphasis on "support of the arts, and especially of the symbiotic relationship between the arts and sciences." Grants largely for education, particularly higher education, community and social services, civic improvement, conservation, scientific research, church support, and cultural programs; maintains a public horticultural garden.
Types of support awarded: General purposes, building funds, equipment, operating budgets, annual campaigns, endowment funds, research, special projects.
Limitations: Giving limited to MI, primarily Midland County. No grants to individuals, or for scholarships, travel, or conferences; no loans.
Publications: Annual report, application guidelines, program policy statement.
Application information:
   Initial approach: Full proposal
   Copies of proposal: 1
   Deadline(s): None
   Board meeting date(s): Bimonthly
   Final notification: 20 months
   Write: Herbert H. Dow, President
Officers and Trustees: Herbert H. Dow, President and Treasurer; Dorothy D. Arbury, Vice-President; Herbert D. Doan, Secretary; Michael L. Dow, I. Frank Harlow, Margaret Ann Riecker.
Number of staff: None.
Employer Identification Number: 381437485

1691
Earhart Foundation ▼
Plymouth Bldg., Suite 204
2929 Plymouth Rd.
Ann Arbor 48105   (313) 761-8592

Incorporated in 1929 in Michigan.
Donor(s): Harry Boyd Earhart.†
Financial data: (yr. ended 12/31/83): Assets, $29,397,440 (M); expenditures, $2,034,483, including $791,090 for 88 grants (high: $53,602; low: $475) and $885,826 for 130 grants to individuals.
Purpose and activities: Broad purposes; grants through a special nominating process for graduate study fellowships, and by application for research fellowships and individual projects in economics, history, international affairs, and political science; grants also to educational and research organizations.
Types of support awarded: Professorships, fellowships, research, publications, conferences and seminars, grants to individuals.
Limitations: No grants for capital or endowment funds, operating budgets, continuing support, annual campaigns, seed money, emergency funds, deficit financing, or matching gifts; no loans.
Publications: Annual report, program policy statement, application guidelines, financial statement.
Application information: Direct applications from candidates or sponsors for H.B. Earhart Fellowships are not accepted.
   Initial approach: Letter
   Copies of proposal: 1
   Deadline(s): None

   Board meeting date(s): Monthly except in August
   Final notification: 90 to 120 days
   Write: Richard A. Ware, President
Officers: Richard A. Ware,* President; David B. Kennedy,* Vice-President; Anthony T. Sullivan, Secretary; Earl H. Miner, Treasurer.
Trustees:* William D. Laurie, Chairman; Dennis L. Bark, Henry T. Bodman, Peter B. Clark, Stephen M. DuBrul, Earl I. Heenan.
Number of staff: 2 full-time professional; 2 full-time support.
Employer Identification Number: 386008273

1692
Earl-Beth Foundation ¤
63 Kercheval Ave., Suite 201-A/B
Grosse Pointe Farms 48236   (313) 882-1577

Incorporated in 1944 in Michigan.
Donor(s): Earl Holley, Mrs. Earl Holley, Holley Carburetor Company.
Financial data: (yr. ended 12/31/83): Assets, $5,079,002 (M); expenditures, $207,029, including $134,729 for 108 grants (high: $15,000; low: $50).
Purpose and activities: Broad purposes; primarily local giving, with emphasis on higher and secondary education, hospitals, child welfare, cultural programs including music, and health.
Limitations: Giving primarily in MI. No grants to individuals or for endowment funds.
Application information:
   Initial approach: Letter or telephone
   Copies of proposal: 1
   Board meeting date(s): January, April, July, and October
   Write: Danforth Holley, President
Officers: Danforth Holley, President and Treasurer; Lisa Holley,* Vice-President; Theodore Oldham, Secretary.
Trustees:* Danforth Earl Holley, Deborah Holley.
Employer Identification Number: 386055542

1693
Eddy (C. K.) Family Memorial Fund ¤
c/o Second National Bank of Saginaw
101 North Washington Ave.
Saginaw 48607

Trust established in 1925 in Michigan.
Donor(s): Arthur D. Eddy.†
Financial data: (yr. ended 6/30/83): Assets, $6,738,003 (M); expenditures, $443,310, including $402,903 for 12 grants (high: $212,000; low: $1,000).
Purpose and activities: Charitable and educational purposes; local giving, with emphasis on hospitals, a community fund, musical and cultural activities, and aid to Saginaw public schools.
Limitations: Giving limited to Saginaw County, MI.
Publications: Application guidelines.
Application information:

Deadline(s): For student loans, May 1; for grants under $5,000, the Monday before the weekly Thursday meeting; for grants over $5,000, 2 weeks prior to the bimonthly meeting on the last Wednesday of the month
Write: Barbara Strasz (Grants); Lois Knapp (Student Loans)
Trustee: Second National Bank of Saginaw.
Employer Identification Number: 386040506

1694
Ex-cell-o Corporation Foundation
2855 Coolidge Rd.
Troy 48084   (313) 637-1022

Foundation established in 1968 in Michigan as The McCord Corporation Foundation.
Donor(s): Ex-cell-o Corporation.
Financial data: (yr. ended 8/31/84): Assets, $2,986,987 (M); gifts received, $1,000,000; expenditures, $534,671, including $530,264 for 182 grants (high: $75,000; low: $50; average: $1,000-$3,500).
Purpose and activities: Grants in areas of company operations, primarily for community funds, higher education, and hospitals; support also for cultural programs.
Types of support awarded: Fellowships, professorships, research.
Limitations: Giving limited to areas of company operations. No grants to individuals, or for goodwill advertising, or operating budgets of United Fund supported organizations; no loans.
Application information:
 Initial approach: Letter
 Copies of proposal: 1
 Deadline(s): None
 Board meeting date(s): Semi-monthly
 Final notification: 2 months
 Write: T.J. Stuart, Vice-President
Officers and Trustees: E.P. Casey, President; T.J. Stuart, Vice-President and Treasurer; A.D. MacDonald, Secretary.
Number of staff: None.
Employer Identification Number: 381874763

1695
Faigle (Ida M.) Charitable Foundation ¤
100 Renaissance Center, Suite 1780
Detroit 48243

Established in 1978.
Donor(s): Ida M. Faigle.†
Financial data: (yr. ended 12/31/83): Assets, $1,103,201 (M); expenditures, $155,223, including $100,000 for 25 grants (high: $15,000; low: $500).
Purpose and activities: Primarily local giving, with emphasis on higher education, including adult education; support also for youth and social agenices, cultural programs, and health agencies.
Limitations: Giving primarily in MI.
Officers and Trustees: Michael M. Wild, Chairman; Richard Fox, Secretary; Walter E. Krell, Treasurer.
Employer Identification Number: 237366145

1696
Federal-Mogul Corporation Charitable Trust
c/o National Bank of Detroit
611 Woodward Ave.
Detroit 48232   (313) 354-9928

Established in 1952 in Michigan.
Donor(s): Federal-Mogul Corporation.
Financial data: (yr. ended 10/31/83): Assets, $199,643 (M); gifts received, $240,500; expenditures, $269,100, including $240,358 for 132 grants (high: $38,000; low: $25) and $25,227 for 64 employee matching gifts.
Purpose and activities: Support largely for educational and cultural projects, including employee matching gifts programs.
Types of support awarded: Employee matching gifts, building funds, continuing support, annual campaigns, research, matching funds.
Limitations: No grants to individuals, or for endowments, scholarships or fellowships; no loans.
Application information:
 Initial approach: Letter
 Copies of proposal: 1
 Board meeting date(s): May
 Write: David T. Snyder, Secretary, Corporation Contributions Committee
Board of Control: E.W. Anderson, L. Gay, R.W. Hague, David T. Snyder.
Trustee: National Bank of Detroit.
Employer Identification Number: 386046512

1697
Fink (George R. and Elise M.) Foundation
20550 Vernier Rd., Suite 101
Harper Woods 48225   (313) 886-5302

Incorporated in 1955 in Michigan.
Donor(s): George R. Fink.†
Financial data: (yr. ended 11/30/83): Assets, $1,460,000 (M); expenditures, $175,000, including $133,000 for 32 grants (high: $52,000; low: $100).
Purpose and activities: Broad purposes; primarily local giving, with emphasis on secondary education, Protestant church support, and church-related institutions.
Limitations: Giving primarily in MI. No grants to individuals or for scholarships or fellowships; no loans.
Publications: Annual report.
Application information:
 Initial approach: Full proposal
 Copies of proposal: 1
 Board meeting date(s): March, June, September, and December
 Write: Frank J. Cernak, Secretary
Officers: Elise M. Fink,* President and Treasurer; Peter M. Fink,* Vice-President; Frank J. Cernak, Secretary.
Trustees:* W. Merritt Jones, Jr.
Employer Identification Number: 386059952

1698
Flint Public Trust, The
902-3 Citizen's Banking Center-South
Flint 48502   (313) 232-7241

Community foundation incorporated in 1950 in Michigan.
Financial data: (yr. ended 12/31/84): Assets, $1,996,234 (M); gifts received, $556,584; expenditures, $91,006, including $68,627 for 26 grants (high: $7,500; low: $100; average: $500-$5,000).
Purpose and activities: Giving for charitable purposes to benefit the citizens of Genesee County.
Types of support awarded: Seed money, matching funds, special projects.
Limitations: Giving limited to Genesee County, MI. No grants to individuals, or for operating budgets, continuing support, annual campaigns, emergency funds, consulting services, building funds, equipment and materials, land acquisition, endowments, deficit financing, technical assistance, program-related investments, research, publications, or conferences and seminars; no loans.
Publications: Annual report, program policy statement, application guidelines.
Application information: Application form required.
 Initial approach: Letter
 Copies of proposal: 10
 Deadline(s): Last Monday in December, March, June, and September
 Board meeting date(s): 2nd Thursday in January, April, July, and October
 Final notification: 1 month after board meeting
 Write: Raymond Finley, Secretary-Treasurer
Officers: C. Rees Dean,* President; John Butler,* Vice-President; Raymond Finley, Secretary-Treasurer.
Trustees:* William Crick, Dana A. Czmer, David Doherty, Helen Harris, John D. Logan, Helen Philpott, Margaret Stewart.
Number of staff: 1 part-time professional.
Employer Identification Number: 386052394

1699
Ford (Benson and Edith) Fund ¤
100 Renaissance Center, 34th Fl.
Detroit 48243

Incorporated in 1943 in Michigan as the Hotchkiss Fund.
Donor(s): Benson Ford.†
Financial data: (yr. ended 12/31/83): Assets, $4,286,791 (M); gifts received, $145,079; expenditures, $308,971, including $301,200 for grants.
Purpose and activities: Broad purposes; general giving, with primary emphasis on education, hospitals, community funds, and the arts, including museums; grants also for church support, child welfare, and youth agencies.
Application information: Funds currently committed.
Officers and Trustees:* Lynn F. Alandt,* President; Pierre V. Heftler,* Secretary; Richard M. Cundiff, Treasurer.
Employer Identification Number: 386066333

1700
Ford (Eleanor and Edsel) Fund ▼
100 Renaissance Center, 34th Fl.
Detroit 48243

Incorporated in 1944 in Michigan.
Donor(s): Eleanor Clay Ford.†
Financial data: (yr. ended 12/31/83): Assets,
$7,763,751 (M); expenditures, $456,715,
including $440,000 for 8 grants (high: $80,000;
low: $10,000).
Purpose and activities: Broad purposes;
primarily local giving, with emphasis on higher
and secondary education, the arts, including
museums, music, and hospitals.
Types of support awarded: Building funds,
scholarship funds, general purposes.
Limitations: Giving primarily in MI, with
emphasis on Detroit. No grants to individuals.
Application information:
  Deadline(s): Prior to annual meeting
  Board meeting date(s): October or November
  Final notification: Within 1 month
Officers: William Clay Ford,* President; Pierre
V. Heftler,* Secretary; Richard M. Cundiff,
Treasurer.
Trustees:* Henry Ford II, Josephine F. Ford.
Number of staff: None.
Employer Identification Number: 386066331

1701
Ford (The Henry) II Fund ▼ ⌑
100 Renaissance Center, 34th Fl.
Detroit 48243

Incorporated in 1953 in Michigan.
Donor(s): Henry Ford II.
Financial data: (yr. ended 12/31/83): Assets,
$6,148,877 (M); gifts received, $207,965;
expenditures, $527,487, including $498,788
for 33 grants (high: $190,000; low: $25;
average: $500-$25,000).
Purpose and activities: Broad purposes;
general giving with primary emphasis on higher
education, Jewish welfare funds, the arts, a
community fund, minority development,
religion, welfare, and youth agencies.
Limitations: No grants to individuals.
Application information: Funds presently
committed.
Officers and Trustees: Henry Ford II,
President; Pierre V. Heftler, Secretary; Richard
M. Cundiff, Treasurer.
Employer Identification Number: 386066332

1702
Ford Motor Company Fund ▼
The American Rd.
Dearborn 48121   (313) 845-8711

Incorporated in 1949 in Michigan.
Donor(s): Ford Motor Company.
Financial data: (yr. ended 12/31/84): Assets,
$47,579,311 (M); gifts received, $20,028,018;
expenditures, $10,093,830, including
$8,470,745 for 926 grants (high: $1,015,000;
low: $40) and $1,460,436 for 10,084
employee matching gifts.

Purpose and activities: General purposes;
support largely for education, including
matching gifts for colleges and universities and
basic research grants; community funds and
urban affairs; hospitals; and civic and cultural
programs.
Types of support awarded: Matching funds,
research, annual campaigns, building funds,
equipment, general purposes, publications,
conferences and seminars, employee matching
gifts, continuing support.
Limitations: Giving primarily in areas of
company operations, with special emphasis on
Detroit and the rest of MI. No grants to
individuals, or for building or endowment
funds, scholarships or fellowships.
Publications: Annual report, application
guidelines.
Application information:
  Initial approach: Letter
  Copies of proposal: 1
  Deadline(s): None
  Board meeting date(s): January, April, June,
    and October
  Final notification: 6 months
  Write: Leo J. Brennan, Jr., Executive Director
Officers: Donald E. Petersen,* President; Will
Scott,* Robert A. Taub, Vice-Presidents; Sidney
Kelly, Secretary; John Sagan, Treasurer.
Trustees:* Will M. Caldwell, William Clay
Ford, A.D. Gilmour, David N. McCammon,
Henry R. Nolte, Jr., Peter J. Pestillo, Harold
Poling.
Number of staff: 5.
Employer Identification Number: 381459376

1703
Ford (Walter and Josephine) Fund
100 Renaissance Center, 34th Fl.
Detroit 48243

Incorporated in 1951 in Michigan.
Donor(s): Josephine F. Ford.
Financial data: (yr. ended 12/31/83): Assets,
$2,662,768 (M); gifts received, $22,570;
expenditures, $375,527, including $361,083
for 69 grants (high: $55,000; low: $50).
Purpose and activities: Broad purposes;
primarily local giving, with emphasis on
education, community funds, the arts, including
museums, and hospitals; grants also for
Protestant church support, medical research,
and youth and social agencies.
Limitations: Giving primarily in MI. No grants
to individuals.
Application information: Funds currently
committed.
Officers: Walter B. Ford II,* President;
Josephine F. Ford,* Vice-President; Pierre V.
Heftler,* Secretary; Richard M. Cundiff,
Treasurer.
Trustees:* John C. Gibbs.
Employer Identification Number: 386066334

1704
Ford (William and Martha) Fund ⌑
100 Renaissance Center, 34th Fl.
Detroit 48243

Incorporated in 1953 in Michigan.
Donor(s): William Clay Ford.

Financial data: (yr. ended 12/31/83): Assets,
$2,385,650 (M); gifts received, $58,033;
expenditures, $404,280, including $395,891
for 54 grants (high: $100,000; low: $100).
Purpose and activities: Broad purposes;
general giving, with emphasis on education;
grants also for the arts, hospitals and medical
research, community funds, child welfare,
church support, and youth agencies.
Limitations: No grants to individuals.
Application information: Funds presently
committed.
Officers: William Clay Ford,* President; Pierre
V. Heftler,* Secretary; Richard M. Cundiff,
Treasurer.
Trustees:* Martha F. Ford.
Employer Identification Number: 386066335

1705
Fremont Area Foundation, The
108 South Stewart
Fremont 49412   (616) 924-5350

Community foundation incorporated in 1951 in
Michigan.
Financial data: (yr. ended 12/31/84): Assets,
$17,072,806 (M); gifts received, $144,780;
expenditures, $899,516, including $667,138
for 49 grants (high: $251,300; low: $199),
$24,369 for 43 grants to individuals and
$23,955 for 1 foundation-administered program.
Purpose and activities: To benefit the people
of Newaygo County; grants for youth groups,
hospitals, education, a library, and a new civic
center.
Types of support awarded: Operating
budgets, seed money, emergency funds,
student aid, matching funds.
Limitations: Giving primarily in Newaygo
County, MI. No grants to individuals (except
for scholarships), or for building or endowment
funds, or research; no loans.
Publications: Annual report, application
guidelines.
Application information:
  Initial approach: Letter or telephone to
    arrange interview
  Copies of proposal: 8
  Deadline(s): Submit proposal preferably by
    October 15
  Board meeting date(s): Usually in February,
    April, July, and November
  Final notification: 3 months
  Write: Bertram W. Vermeulen, Executive
    Director
Officers: Kenneth B. Peirce,* President;
Maynard DeKryger,* Vice-President; Virginia
Gerber,* Treasurer; Bertram W. Vermeulen,
Secretary and Executive Director.
Trustees:* Sally DeShetler, Richard
Hogancamp, Douglas M. Jeannero, L. Max Lee,
Gerald E. Martin, Dean H. Morehouse, William
A. Rottman, Ross G. Scott, Robert A. Stewart,
Peggie Stone, David H. Warm, John Williams.
Number of staff: 2 full-time professional; 1
part-time support.
Employer Identification Number: 381443367

1706
Fruehauf Corporation Charitable Fund, Inc.
10900 Harper Ave.
Detroit 48213

Incorporated in 1963 in Michigan.
Donor(s): Fruehauf Corporation.
Financial data: (yr. ended 12/31/83): Assets, $1,271 (M); expenditures, $357,790, including $340,782 for 104 grants (high: $18,334; low: $45) and $17,008 for 67 employee matching gifts.
Purpose and activities: Broad purposes; general giving, with emphasis on community funds; support also for higher education, youth agencies, and the arts.
Officers and Trustees: Robert D. Rowan,* President; Frank P. Coyer, Jr., Vice-President and Treasurer; T. Neal Combs, Secretary.
Charitable Fund Committee:* John P. Grace, Russell G. Howell, Thomas J. Reghanti, John D. Schapiro.
Employer Identification Number: 381785381

1707
Fruehauf Foundation, The ☐
3900 Guardian Bldg.
Detroit 48226   (313) 964-5333

Incorporated in 1968 in Michigan.
Donor(s): Angela Fruehauf, and others.
Financial data: (yr. ended 12/31/83): Assets, $1,575,885 (M); expenditures, $121,226, including $111,680 for 93 grants (high: $18,750; low: $50).
Purpose and activities: Broad purposes; grants primarily for educational institutions, cultural programs, hospitals, health agencies, welfare including youth agencies, economic research, and churches and religious programs.
Limitations: Giving primarily in MI.
Application information:
   Initial approach: Letter
   Deadline(s): Monthly
   Board meeting date(s): As required
   Write: Elizabeth J. Woods, Assistant Secretary
Officers and Trustees: Harvey C. Fruehauf, Jr., President; Ann F. Bowman, Vice-President and Treasurer; Barbara F. Bristol, Vice-President; Frederick R. Keydel, Secretary.
Employer Identification Number: 237015744

1708
Garb Foundation, The ☐
c/o E. James Gamble
35th Fl., 400 Renaissance Center
Detroit 48243

Established in 1983 in Michigan.
Financial data: (yr. ended 1/31/84): Assets, $145,440 (M); gifts received, $252,000; expenditures, $125,000, including $125,000 for 12 grants (high: $50,000; low: $500).
Purpose and activities: Giving primarily for Jewish welfare funds.
Types of support awarded: General purposes.
Officers and Trustees: Melvin Garb, President; Harrison Levin, Secretary; Genesse G. Levin, Treasurer.
Employer Identification Number: 382450840

1709
General Motors Cancer Research Foundation, Inc.
13-138 General Motors Bldg.
Detroit 48202   (313) 556-4260

Established about 1978 in Michigan.
Donor(s): General Motors Corporation.
Financial data: (yr. ended 12/31/82): Assets, $1,547,782 (M); gifts received, $2,001,550; expenditures, $885,630, including $305,725 for 3 grants to individuals (average: $100,000).
Purpose and activities: Awards to individuals for "contributions to the prevention, detection, or treatment of cancer in order to stimulate further research in this field." Candidates for prizes must be nominated by invited proposers.
Publications: Application guidelines.
Application information:
   Deadline(s): October, for prize nominations
   Board meeting date(s): April or May
Officers: J.G. Fortner, President; J.B. Cook, Secretary; J.R. Edman, Treasurer.
Trustees: R.B. Smith, Chairman; H.H. Kehrl, Vice-Chairman; W.O. Baker, J.E. Rhoads, L.S. Rockefeller, B.C. Schmidt, C.H. Townes.
Number of staff: 1.
Employer Identification Number: 382219731

1710
General Motors Foundation ▼
3044 West Grand Blvd., Rm. 13-145
Detroit 48202   (313) 556-4260

Incorporated in 1976 in Michigan.
Donor(s): General Motors Corporation.
Financial data: (yr. ended 12/31/84): Assets, $123,278,321 (M); gifts received, $30,000; expenditures, $33,999,853, including $31,441,533 for grants (average: $25,000-$50,000).
Purpose and activities: General purposes; grants largely for higher education, community funds, social services, hospitals, health, cancer research, cultural programs, and urban and civic affairs.
Types of support awarded: Operating budgets, continuing support, annual campaigns, seed money, emergency funds, building funds, equipment, land acquisition, research, publications, conferences and seminars, special projects.
Limitations: Giving primarily in plant cities where company has significant operations. No support for special interest groups. No grants to individuals, or for deficit financing, endowment funds, matching gifts, scholarships, or fellowships; no loans.
Publications: Application guidelines.
Application information:
   Initial approach: Letter
   Copies of proposal: 1
   Deadline(s): None
   Board meeting date(s): Contributions committee meets annually
   Final notification: 2 months
   Write: Mr. R.J. Winkley, Manager
Officers: J.R. Edman, President; J.B. Cook, Secretary; C.F. Jones, Treasurer.

Trustees: F.A. Smith, Chairman; D.J. Atwood, A.A. Cunningham, H.H. Kehrl, F.J. McDonald, R.B. Smith.
Number of staff: 2 full-time professional; 1 full-time support.
Employer Identification Number: 382132136

1711
Gerber Baby Foods Fund
445 State St.
Fremont 49412   (616) 928-2227

Incorporated in 1952 in Michigan.
Donor(s): Gerber Products Company.
Financial data: (yr. ended 5/31/84): Assets, $8,409,018 (M); gifts received, $69,971; expenditures, $424,590, including $293,022 for 200 grants (high: $5,000; low: $50; average: $100-$5,000), $96,775 for 277 grants to individuals and $20,928 for employee matching gifts.
Purpose and activities: General purposes; grants largely for education, including scholarships for company employees or children of employees, community funds and hospitals in areas of company operations, some support for medical education, nursing, public health, family service, and research in chemistry, agriculture, and the biological sciences.
Types of support awarded: Operating budgets, continuing support, annual campaigns, building funds, matching funds, scholarship funds, employee related scholarships, conferences and seminars.
Limitations: Giving limited to cities where company has major operations. No grants for seed money, emergency funds, deficit financing, equipment, land acquisition, renovations, endowment funds, research, demonstration projects, or publications; no loans.
Publications: Program policy statement.
Application information:
   Initial approach: Telephone or letter
   Copies of proposal: 1
   Deadline(s): Submit proposal preferably in December or January
   Board meeting date(s): February, May, July, and September
   Write: John B. Whitlock, President
Officers and Trustees: John B. Whitlock, President; George Purvis, Vice-President; Joseph Pinnick, Secretary; Richard Dunning, Treasurer; Jerry Britt, Leo D. Goulet, Floyd Head, Jack Leaver, Yvonne Lee, William L. McKinley, Kenneth Peirce, Carl Smith, Frank Sondeen.
Number of staff: None.
Employer Identification Number: 386068090

1712
Gerstacker (The Rollin M.) Foundation ▼
P.O. Box 1945
Midland 48640

Incorporated in 1957 in Michigan.
Donor(s): Eda U. Gerstacker,† Carl A. Gerstacker.

Financial data: (yr. ended 12/25/83): Assets, $26,942,634 (M); expenditures, $1,612,553, including $1,578,393 for 54 grants (high: $1,000,000; low: $1,000; average: $5,000-$25,000).

Purpose and activities: To assist community projects, primarily in Michigan and Ohio, with emphasis on the aged and youth; grants also for higher education (including seminaries), health care, a medical research institute,and a hospital.

Types of support awarded: Annual campaigns, seed money, emergency funds, building funds, equipment, endowment funds, research, matching funds, general purposes, continuing support, land acquisition.

Limitations: Giving primarily in MI and OH. No grants to individuals, or for scholarships and fellowships; no loans.

Publications: Annual report.

Application information:
Initial approach: Letter
Copies of proposal: 1
Deadline(s): June 1 and December 1
Board meeting date(s): June and December
Final notification: Varies
Write: E.N. Brandt, Secretary

Officers and Trustees: Gail E. Brink, President; Carl A. Gerstacker, Vice-President and Treasurer; Theodore M. Greenhoe, I. Frank Harlow, Vice-Presidents; E.N. Brandt, Secretary; Gilbert A. Currie, Lisa J. Gerstacker, Julius Grosberg, Paul F. Oreffice, William D. Schuette.

Number of staff: None.

Employer Identification Number: 386060276

1713
Gilmore Foundation
c/o American National Bank and Trust Company of Michigan
151 East Michigan Ave.
Kalamazoo 49007   (616) 383-6956

Trust established in 1956 in Michigan.

Donor(s): Irving S. Gilmore.

Financial data: (yr. ended 12/31/83): Assets, $4,686 (M); gifts received, $226,600; expenditures, $230,286, including $30,952 for 2 grants (high: $17,352; low: $13,600) and $177,527 for 88 grants to individuals.

Purpose and activities: Limited primarily to benevolence grants to low-income individuals residing in local area who are unable to care for themselves due to physical limitations or advanced age.

Types of support awarded: Grants to individuals.

Limitations: Giving primarily in the Kalamazoo, MI, area.

Application information: Application form required.
Initial approach: Telephone
Deadline(s): None
Write: Floyd L. Parks, Senior Vice-President

Trustee: American National Bank and Trust Company (Floyd L. Parks, Senior Vice-President).

Disbursing Committee: Harold H. Holland, Floyd L. Parks, John C. Schaberg.

Employer Identification Number: 386052803

1714
Gordon Christian Foundation ¤
P.O. Box 1787
Grand Rapids 49501

Established in 1967.

Donor(s): Gordon Food Service, Inc.

Financial data: (yr. ended 12/31/82): Assets, $330,474 (M); gifts received, $71,500; expenditures, $103,434, including $102,295 for 36 grants (high: $35,000; low: $500).

Purpose and activities: Giving for Christian missionary work, programs, and education.

Officers and Directors: Ruth H. Gordon, President; Phillip W. Gordon, Vice-President; Paul B. Gordon, Secretary; William D. Lanning, Treasurer.

Employer Identification Number: 386123463

1715
Grand Rapids Foundation ▼
300-E Waters Bldg.
161 Ottawa NW
Grand Rapids 49503   (616) 454-1751

Community foundation established in 1922 in Michigan by resolution and declaration of trust.

Financial data: (yr. ended 6/30/84): Assets, $23,081,708 (M); gifts received, $556,252; expenditures, $1,295,724, including $1,122,617 for 55 grants (high: $134,300; low: $83; average: $500-$100,000), $51,904 for grants to individuals and $80,500 for 37 loans.

Purpose and activities: To provide support for projects or causes designed to benefit the people and the quality of life in the Grand Rapids community and its environs, including grants for social welfare, youth agencies, cultural programs, health, recreation, and education.

Types of support awarded: Seed money, emergency funds, building funds, equipment, land acquisition, matching funds, scholarship funds, student aid, loans.

Limitations: Giving limited to Kent County, MI. No grants to individuals (except for scholarships and student loans), or for operating budgets, continuing support, annual campaigns, deficit financing, or endowment funds.

Publications: Annual report, informational brochure, program policy statement, application guidelines.

Application information: Application form required.
Initial approach: Letter or telephone
Copies of proposal: 10
Deadline(s): Submit student loan applications between January 1 and April 1; deadline for all other applications 4 weeks preceding board meeting
Board meeting date(s): Bimonthly beginning in August
Final notification: 1 month; June 15 for student loans
Write: Patricia H. Edison, Executive Director

Officer: Patricia H. Edison, Executive Director.

Trustees: Ernest A. Mika, Chairman; Jane H. Idema, Vice-Chairman; Sue Blandford, James W. Carpenter, Norman De Graaf, R. Park Johnston, David B. La Claire, Robert L. Sadler, Herbert Vander Mey.

Trustee Banks: Michigan National Bank, National Bank of Detroit, Old Kent Bank and Trust Company, Union Bank and Trust Company.

Number of staff: 1 part-time professional; 1 part-time support.

Employer Identification Number: 386032912

1716
Harder Foundation
18301 East Eight Mile Rd., Suite 213
East Detroit 48021   (313) 772-4433
Address for applicants in western states: c/o Del N. Langbauer, Vice-President, Harder Foundation Western Office, P.O. Box 7407, Tacoma, WA 98407-7407

Incorporated in 1955 in Michigan.

Donor(s): Delmar S. Harder.†

Financial data: (yr. ended 12/31/84): Assets, $8,015,632 (M); gifts received, $21,000; expenditures, $234,984, including $142,500 for 23 grants (high: $20,000; low: $100; average: $6,195).

Purpose and activities: Support for environmental projects only.

Types of support awarded: Operating budgets, continuing support, annual campaigns, seed money, emergency funds, land acquisition, endowment funds, matching funds.

Limitations: No grants to individuals, or for deficit financing, building funds, equipment, renovation projects, scholarships or fellowships, research, publications, or conferences; no loans.

Publications: Annual report, application guidelines.

Application information: Grants considered February through July at western office. Application form required.
Initial approach: Letter, full proposal, or telephone
Copies of proposal: 1
Deadline(s): July 31 for western office; no deadline for Michigan office
Board meeting date(s): July
Final notification: 4 months
Write: Nathan B. Driggers, President; Del N. Langbauer, Vice-President, for applicants in western states

Officers and Trustees: Nathan B. Driggers, President; Lucille E. Langbauer, Vice-President and Treasurer; Elizabeth Harder, Del N. Langbauer, Vice-Presidents; Jay A. Herbst, Secretary.

Number of staff: 2 part-time professional; 1 part-time support.

Employer Identification Number: 386048242

1717
Herman (John and Rose) Foundation ¤
3001 West Big Beaver Rd., Suite 404
Troy 48084

Established in 1967 in Michigan.

Financial data: (yr. ended 12/31/83): Assets, $1,699,995 (M); expenditures, $123,966, including $114,254 for 54 grants (high: $16,000; low: $100).

Purpose and activities: Grants largely for Jewish welfare funds and temple support; some support also for education.

Officers: Rose Herman, President; Hortense Alper, Donald Herman, Vice-Presidents; Harold S. Tobias, Secretary; James E. Fuller, Treasurer.
Employer Identification Number: 237041624

1718
Herrick Foundation ▼
2500 Comerica Bldg.
Detroit 48226   (313) 963-6420

Incorporated in 1949 in Michigan.
Donor(s): Ray W. Herrick,† Hazel M. Herrick.†
Financial data: (yr. ended 9/30/83): Assets, $134,305,920 (M); expenditures, $5,096,308, including $4,885,925 for 136 grants (high: $500,000; low: $500; average: $5,000-$125,000).
Purpose and activities: Broad purposes; primarily local giving, with emphasis on higher and secondary education, including scholarship and capital funds, Protestant church support, cultural programs, youth agencies, hospitals, and health and welfare agencies.
Types of support awarded: Building funds, equipment, land acquisition, research, scholarship funds, special projects, general purposes.
Limitations: Giving primarily in MI. No grants to individuals.
Application information:
  Initial approach: Letter
  Deadline(s): None
  Board meeting date(s): Every 2 to 3 months
  Write: Kenneth G. Herrick, President, or Emmett E. Eagan, Secretary
Officers and Trustees:* Kenneth G. Herrick,* Chairman, President, and Treasurer; Emmett E. Eagan,* Vice-President and Secretary; Todd W. Herrick, Vice-President; Catherine R. Cobb,* Richard B. Gushee*.
Number of staff: None.
Employer Identification Number: 386041517

1719
Himmel (The Clarence and Jack) Foundation ⌗
3000 Town Center, Suite 2550
Southfield 48075

Established in 1975 in Michigan.
Donor(s): Clarence Himmel.†
Financial data: (yr. ended 10/31/83): Assets, $1,188,362 (M); expenditures, $112,871, including $87,100 for 70 grants (high: $5,000; low: $250).
Purpose and activities: General local giving, with emphasis on family and child welfare services and youth agencies; grants also for hospitals, Jewish welfare funds, health agencies, cultural programs, and the handicapped.
Limitations: Giving primarily in MI.
Officers and Directors: Robert A. Karbel, President and Secretary; Sidney J. Karbel, Vice-President; Ronald A. Rothstein, Treasurer.
Employer Identification Number: 510140773

1720
Holden (James and Lynelle) Fund ▼
1428 Buhl Bldg.
Detroit 48226   (313) 962-4757

Incorporated in 1941 in Michigan.
Donor(s): James S. Holden,† Lynelle A. Holden.†
Financial data: (yr. ended 12/31/84): Assets, $7,295,161 (M); expenditures, $718,668, including $612,346 for 43 grants (high: $65,000; low: $500).
Purpose and activities: General purposes; primarily local giving; support for medical research, including medical schools and hospitals; aid to youth agencies, minority and underprivileged children, education, and care of the aged; support also for cultural programs.
Types of support awarded: Annual campaigns, general purposes, building funds, equipment, research, scholarship funds, fellowships, matching funds, continuing support, operating budgets.
Limitations: Giving primarily in MI, with emphasis on Detroit. No grants to individuals, or for endowment funds; no loans.
Application information:
  Initial approach: Letter
  Copies of proposal: 1
  Deadline(s): None
  Board meeting date(s): January, April, July, and October
  Final notification: Several weeks
  Write: Joseph Freedman, President
Officers and Trustees: Joseph Freedman, President and Secretary; Louis F. Dahling, Vice-President; Herbert J. Wilson, Treasurer.
Number of staff: 1 full-time professional; 1 part-time professional.
Employer Identification Number: 386052154

1721
Honigman Foundation, Inc.
c/o Jason L. Honigman
2290 First National Bldg.
Detroit 48226   (313) 256-7500

Incorporated in 1955 in Michigan.
Donor(s): Jason L. Honigman, Edith Honigman.
Financial data: (yr. ended 10/31/83): Assets, $2,988,988 (M); expenditures, $323,687, including $315,327 for 52 grants (high: $270,000; low: $10).
Purpose and activities: Primarily local giving, with emphasis on Jewish welfare funds; grants also for higher and secondary education, including institutions in Israel, and a local cancer research foundation.
Limitations: Giving primarily in MI.
Officers: Jason L. Honigman, President; Edith Honigman, Vice-President; Daniel M. Honigman, Secretary; Julie R. Levy, Treasurer.
Employer Identification Number: 386059254

1722
Hudson-Webber Foundation ▼
(formerly three foundations including Richard H. and Eloise Jenks Webber Charitable Fund and Eloise and Richard Webber Foundation)
333 West Fort St.
Detroit 48226   (313) 963-8991

Incorporated in 1943 in Michigan; in 1983 absorbed The Richard H. and Eloise Jenks Webber Charitable Fund, Inc., and the Eloise and Richard Webber Foundation.
Donor(s): Eloise Webber, Richard Webber, The J.L. Hudson Company, The Richard H. and Eloise Jenks Webber Charitable Fund, The Eloise and Richard Webber Foundation, and members of the Webber family.
Financial data: (yr. ended 12/31/84): Assets, $53,327,446 (M); gifts received, $8,719; expenditures, $2,987,275, including $2,176,592 for 62 grants (high: $213,000; low: $2,400; average: $10,000-$30,000), $188,871 for 236 grants to individuals and $43,946 for 11 employee matching gifts.
Purpose and activities: Concentrates efforts and resources in support of projects within six program missions, which impact upon the vitality and quality of life of the community: 1) growth and development of the Detroit Medical Center, 2) physical revitalization of downtown Detroit, 3) reduction of crime in Detroit, 4) economic development of southeastern Michigan, with emphasis on the creation of additional employment opportunities, 5) enhancement of major art and cultural resources in Detroit, and 6) charitable assistance of J. L. Hudson Company employees needing help to overcome personal crises and misfortunes.
Types of support awarded: Operating budgets, continuing support, annual campaigns, seed money, building funds, matching funds, research, special projects, program-related investments, employee matching gifts, grants to individuals.
Limitations: Giving primarily in the Wayne, Oakland, and Macomb tri-county area of southeastern MI, particularly Detroit. No support for educational institutions, unless they fall within current program priorities. No grants to individuals (except for J.L. Hudson Company employees), or for emergency funds, deficit financing, endowment funds, scholarships or fellowships, publications, conferences, fundraising social events, or exhibits; no loans.
Publications: Biennial report, program policy statement, application guidelines.
Application information:
  Initial approach: Full proposal
  Copies of proposal: 1
  Deadline(s): April 15, August 15, and December 15
  Board meeting date(s): March, July, and December
  Final notification: 1 week after board decision
  Write: Gilbert Hudson, President
Officers and Trustees: Joseph L. Hudson, Jr., Chairman; Gilbert Hudson, President and Chief Executive Officer; Frank A. Colombo, Vice-President; Charles Wright, III, Secretary; Frank M. Hennessey, Treasurer; Lawrence P. Doss, Hudson Holland, Jr., Richard L. Measelle, Philip J. Meathe, Theodore H. Mecke, Jr., John W. Paynter, Mrs. Alan E. Schwartz.
Number of staff: 2 full-time professional; 1 full-time support; 1 part-time support.
Employer Identification Number: 386052131

1723
Hunter (Edward and Irma) Foundation
423 Sycamore St.
P.O. Box 906
Niles 49120   (616) 684-3248

Established in 1968 in Michigan.
Donor(s): Edward Hunter,† Irma Hunter.†
Financial data: (yr. ended 12/31/83): Assets,
$2,762,936 (M); gifts received, $43,475;
expenditures, $395,799, including $362,500
for 9 grants (high: $268,000; low: $1,000).
Purpose and activities: Local giving primarily
for economic development and area
employment, including support for social
services and welfare organizations.
Types of support awarded: Annual
campaigns, emergency funds, building funds,
equipment, land acquisition, matching funds.
Limitations: Giving limited to the Niles and
Buchanan, MI, area. No grants to individuals,
or for operating budgets, continuing support,
seed money, deficit financing, endowment
funds, scholarships, fellowships, program
support, research, demonstration projects,
publications, or conferences; no loans.
Publications: Informational brochure, 990-PF,
application guidelines, program policy
statement.
Application information:
  Initial approach: Letter
  Copies of proposal: 6
  Deadline(s): Second week of February, May,
    August, and November
  Board meeting date(s): 4th Monday of
    February, May, August, and November
  Final notification: 1 week
  Write: Donald F. Walter, President
Officers and Trustees: Donald F. Walter,
President; Philip A. Hadsell, Jr., Vice-President;
William S. White, Secretary; Gerald H. Frieling,
Jr., Treasurer; J. Edward French, Paul W. Jedele.
Employer Identification Number: 237065471

1724
Hurst Foundation, The
775 West Michigan
Jackson 49201   (517) 788-8600

Trust established in 1955 in Michigan.
Donor(s): Peter F. Hurst,† Elizabeth S. Hurst.
Financial data: (yr. ended 12/31/84): Assets,
$4,402,835 (M); expenditures, $241,311,
including $215,487 for 24 grants (high:
$50,000; low: $500).
Purpose and activities: Charitable and
religious purposes; local giving, with emphasis
on higher and secondary education, a museum,
social services, community development, and
youth agencies.
Types of support awarded: Operating
budgets, seed money, building funds,
equipment, special projects.
Limitations: Giving limited to Jackson County,
MI. No grants to individuals, or for
endowment funds, scholarships, fellowships, or
matching gifts; no loans.
Application information:
  Initial approach: Letter
  Copies of proposal: 2
  Deadline(s): Submit proposal preferably in
    October; deadline November 10

Board meeting date(s): December and as
  required
Final notification: 60 days
Write: Mrs. Jody Bacon
Trustees: Anthony P. Hurst, Elizabeth S. Hurst,
Ronald F. Hurst.
Number of staff: 1 part-time professional.
Employer Identification Number: 386089457

1725
**Imerman (Stanley) Memorial
  Foundation** ☼
29201 Telegraph Rd., Suite 500
Southfield 48034

Established in 1971 in Michigan.
Donor(s): Stanley Imerman.†
Financial data: (yr. ended 12/31/83): Assets,
$1,884,156 (M); expenditures, $89,759,
including $78,500 for 35 grants (high: $15,000;
low: $100).
Purpose and activities: Grants largely for
Jewish welfare funds, higher education, and
health agencies.
Types of support awarded: Continuing
support, annual campaigns, building funds,
general purposes.
Limitations: Giving primarily in MI. No grants
to individuals, or for endowment funds,
scholarships or fellowships, or matching gifts;
no loans.
Officers and Trustees: Joseph H. Jackier,
President and Treasurer; Lawrence S. Jackier,
Vice-President and Secretary; Dale G. Rands,
Vice-President; Mark E. Schlussel.
Employer Identification Number: 237152760

1726
Jackson Foundation, The
505 Wildwood Ave.
Jackson 49201   (517) 787-1321

Community foundation incorporated in 1948 in
Michigan.
Donor(s): Residents of Jackson County,
Michigan.
Financial data: (yr. ended 12/31/84): Assets,
$1,771,764 (M); gifts received, $46,053;
expenditures, $179,530, including $146,402
for 11 grants (high: $75,000; low: $500;
average: $500-$3,000).
Purpose and activities: General purposes;
support for community improvement and other
programs for the benefit of the residents of
Jackson County.
Types of support awarded: Seed money,
building funds, equipment, land acquisition,
matching funds, consulting services, technical
assistance, loans, special projects, research.
Limitations: Giving limited to Jackson County,
MI. No support for religious purposes. No
grants to individuals, or for endowment funds,
scholarships and fellowships, publications, or
conferences.
Publications: Annual report.
Application information: Application form
required.
  Initial approach: Letter or telephone
  Copies of proposal: 1

Deadline(s): Submit proposal preferably in
  January, April, July, or October; deadlines
  February 1, May 1, August 1, and
  November 1
Board meeting date(s): March, June,
  September, and December
Final notification: 6 weeks
Write: Mrs. Jody Bacon, Executive Director
Officers: John D. Selby,* President; Carl F.
Spaeth, Jr.,* Vice-President; Douglas L.
Burdick,* Secretary-Treasurer; Mrs. Jody Bacon,
Executive Director.
Trustees:* Charles H. Aymond, Charles E.
Drury, Gloria B. Federer, Richard Firestone,
Donna Hardy, Ueal E. Patrick, Mark Rosenfeld,
John D. Selby, William Sigmund, Max Videto,
Susan Wrzesinski.
Number of staff: 1 part-time professional; 1
part-time support.
Employer Identification Number: 386070739

1727
**Jeffers (Michael) Memorial
  Foundation** ☼
c/o Second National Bank of Saginaw
101 North Washington Ave.
Saginaw 48607   (517) 776-7353

Established in 1967 in Michigan.
Donor(s): John Jeffers.†
Financial data: (yr. ended 12/31/83): Assets,
$2,385,831 (M); expenditures, $135,074,
including $103,750 for loans.
Purpose and activities: Funds limited solely
for educational loans to students from Saginaw
County.
Types of support awarded: Student aid.
Limitations: Giving primarily in Saginaw City,
MI.
Application information:
  Deadline(s): June 1 for renewals, June 15 for
    new applications
  Write: Louis Knapp
Officers: Alvin G. Benson, President; E.B.
Morley, Jr., Vice-President; Thomas G. Deibel,
Secretary-Treasurer; Second National Bank of
Saginaw.
Employer Identification Number: 237059762

1728
Kalamazoo Foundation ▼
332 Comerica Bank Bldg.
151 South Rose St.
Kalamazoo 49007   (616) 381-4416

Community foundation established in 1925;
incorporated in 1930 in Michigan.
Financial data: (yr. ended 12/31/84): Assets,
$44,001,846 (M); gifts received, $2,236,093;
expenditures, $4,559,219, including
$3,944,638 for 204 grants (high: $500,000;
low: $25; average: $5,000-$100,000).
Purpose and activities: To assist primarily
local educational and charitable institutions;
grants largely for capital purposes, for higher
education, child welfare, youth agencies, music
and the arts, a civic auditorium, and hospitals;
support also for housing, care of the aged, aid
to the handicapped, recreation, public health,
and community development.

Types of support awarded: Seed money, building funds, general purposes, emergency funds, research, publications, matching funds.
Limitations: Giving primarily in Kalamazoo County, MI. No support for religious organizations. No grants to individuals, or for endowment funds, scholarships, or fellowships.
Publications: Annual report, program policy statement, application guidelines, informational brochure.
Application information: Application form required.
  Initial approach: Telephone or letter
  Copies of proposal: 8
  Deadline(s): April 1, August 1, or December 1
  Board meeting date(s): January, May, and September
  Final notification: 2 months
  Write: Howard D. Kalleward, Executive Director
Officers: William J. Lawrence, Jr.,* President; Martha G. Parfet,* Vice-President; Howard D. Kalleward, Executive Director.
Trustees and Distribution Committee:* Joseph J. Dunnigan, Judson A. Knapper, Elizabeth S. Upjohn.
Trustee Banks: The American National Bank and Trust Company of Michigan, Comerica Bank - Kalamazoo, First of America Bank - Michigan.
Number of staff: 2 full-time professional; 2 full-time support.
Employer Identification Number: 386048002

1729
Kantzler Foundation, The
900 Center Ave.
Bay City 48706   (517) 892-0591

Incorporated in 1974 in Michigan.
Donor(s): Leopold J. Kantzler.†
Financial data: (yr. ended 12/31/83): Assets, $2,684,723 (M); expenditures, $153,392, including $125,948 for 6 grants (high: $39,619; low: $5,600).
Purpose and activities: To support local projects and capital improvements of charitable, artistic, educational, and cultural organizations.
Types of support awarded: Seed money, building funds, equipment, land acquisition, matching funds.
Limitations: Giving limited to the greater Bay City, MI area. No grants to individuals, or for endowment funds, operating budgets, continuing support, annual campaigns, special projects, publications, conferences, emergency funds, deficit financing, research, or scholarships and fellowships; no loans.
Publications: Program policy statement, application guidelines.
Application information:
  Initial approach: Full proposal
  Copies of proposal: 1
  Deadline(s): None
  Board meeting date(s): Approximately 10 times a year
  Final notification: 2 months
  Write: Robert D. Sarow, Secretary

Officers: Jack Steinmetz,* President; Clifford C. Van Dyke,* Vice-President; Robert D. Sarow, Secretary; Arthur E. Hagen, Jr.,* Treasurer.
Trustees:* Robbie L. Baker, Arthur E. Hagen.
Number of staff: None.
Employer Identification Number: 237422733

1730
Kaufman (Louis G.) Endowment Fund
c/o First National Bank and Trust Co.
Drawer 10-Trust Dept.
Marquette 49855   (906) 228-7900

Trust established in 1927 in Michigan.
Donor(s): L.G. Kaufman Trust.
Financial data: (yr. ended 12/31/82): Assets, $1,634,233 (M); expenditures, $158,050, including $121,421 for 15 grants (high: $55,000; low: $300; average: $1,000-$50,000).
Purpose and activities: Primarily local giving, with emphasis on secondary education, community development, youth agencies, and recreation.
Types of support awarded: Operating budgets, annual campaigns, seed money, emergency funds, scholarship funds, special projects.
Limitations: Giving primarily in Marquette, MI. No grants to individuals, or for continuing support, deficit financing, land acquisition, endowment funds, matching gifts, research, publications, or conferences; no loans.
Application information:
  Initial approach: Letter
  Copies of proposal: 5
  Deadline(s): May 1
  Board meeting date(s): As required
  Write: Harold D. Herlich, Jr., Senior Vice-President, First National Bank and Trust Company
Trustee: First National Bank and Trust Company (Harold N. Herlich, Jr., Senior Vice-President and Trust Officer).
Employer Identification Number: 386048505

1731
Kellogg Company 25-Year Employees Fund, Inc. ▼
235 Porter St.
Battle Creek 49016   (616) 966-2000

Established in 1944 in Michigan.
Donor(s): W.K. Kellogg.†
Financial data: (yr. ended 12/31/83): Assets, $11,633,962 (M); expenditures, $525,573, including $1,000 for 1 grant (high: $32,389; low: $719; average: $4,741) and $445,567 for 96 grants to individuals.
Purpose and activities: Grants for living and medical expenses of current and former company employees and their dependents only.
Types of support awarded: Grants to individuals.
Limitations: Giving primarily in MI. No support for organizations; grants only to Kellogg 25-year employees and their dependents.
Publications: Program policy statement, application guidelines, 990-PF.
Application information: Application form required.
  Initial approach: Letter

Copies of proposal: 1
Deadline(s): Submit proposal preferably in April; deadline June 1
Board meeting date(s): January, April, July, and October
Write: D.E. Kinnisten, President
Officers: D.E. Kinnisten,* President; P.A. Humiston,* Vice-President; J.G. Jacobs,* Secretary; M. Wu, Treasurer.
Trustees:* B.A. Haefner, W.T. Redmond, J.M. Stewart, J.M. Zorbo.
Number of staff: 1 full-time support.
Employer Identification Number: 386039770

1732
Kellogg (W. K.) Foundation ▼
400 North Ave.
Battle Creek 49017-3398   (616) 968-1611

Incorporated in 1930 in Michigan.
Donor(s): W.K. Kellogg.†
Financial data: (yr. ended 8/31/84): Assets, $1,291,843,298 (M); expenditures, $64,604,912, including $59,505,689 for 689 grants (high: $3,430,500; low: $10; average: $75,000-$250,000), $26,572 for employee matching gifts and $1,303,618 for 20 foundation-administered programs.
Purpose and activities: "To receive and administer funds for educational and charitable purposes." Aid limited to programs concerned with application of existing knowledge rather than research. Grants only to institutions and agencies of the United States, Latin America, and the Caribbean, as well as to international fellowship programs in other countries. Supports pilot projects which, if successful, can be continued by initiating organization and emulated by other communities or organizations with similar problems. Current funding priorities include projects designed to improve human well-being through: adult continuing education; betterment of health (health promotion/disease prevention/public health); community-wide, coordinated, cost-effective health services; a wholesome food supply; and broadening leadership capacity of individuals. In Michigan only, projects are supported for economic development and opportunities for youths.
Types of support awarded: Seed money, fellowships.
Limitations: Giving primarily in the United States and Latin America. No support for religious purposes. No grants to individuals, or for building or endowment funds, research, development campaigns, films, publications, conferences, or radio and television programs unless they are an integral part of a project already being funded; operating budgets, continuing support, annual campaigns, emergency funds, deficit financing, land acquisition, or renovation projects; no loans.
Publications: Annual report, application guidelines, program policy statement, newsletter.
Application information:
  Initial approach: Letter
  Copies of proposal: 1
  Deadline(s): None
  Board meeting date(s): Monthly
  Final notification: 3 months to 2 years

Write: Robert D. Sparks, President
Officers: Russell G. Mawby,* Chairman and Chief Executive Officer; Robert D. Sparks,* President and Chief Programming Officer; Laura A. Davis, Vice-President--Administration and Corporate Secretary; Lloyd E. Holt, Vice-President--Finance and Treasurer; James M. Richmond, Vice-President.
Trustees:* Alphonse H. Aymond, Chris T. Christ, William N. Hubbard, Jr., Dorothy A. Johnson, Howard R. Sims, Durwood B. Varner, Jonathan T. Walton.
Number of staff: 27 full-time professional; 1 part-time professional; 33 full-time support; 4 part-time support.
Employer Identification Number: 381359264

1733
Kennedy (Elizabeth E.) Fund
500 City Center Bldg.
Ann Arbor 48104   (313) 761-3780

Incorporated in 1954 in Michigan.
Donor(s): Elizabeth E. Kennedy.
Financial data: (yr. ended 12/31/83): Assets, $1,175,765 (M); expenditures, $82,501, including $72,000 for 16 grants (high: $10,000; low: $1,500).
Purpose and activities: Broad purposes; primarily local giving, with emphasis on higher education, the arts, conservation, health and family planning.
Types of support awarded: Seed money.
Limitations: Giving primarily in MI, with emphasis on less populated areas of the state.
Application information:
Initial approach: Letter
Deadline(s): None
Write: John S. Dobson, Secretary
Officers and Trustees: Elizabeth E. Kennedy, President; John S. Dobson, Secretary; Ann K. Irish, Joan K. Slocum, William W. Slocum.
Employer Identification Number: 386063463

1734
Kresge Foundation, The ▼
P.O. Box 3151
3215 West Big Beaver Rd.
Troy 48007-3151   (313) 643-9630

Incorporated in 1924 in Michigan.
Donor(s): Sebastian S. Kresge.†
Financial data: (yr. ended 12/31/84): Assets, $813,648,263 (M); gifts received, $11,773,896; expenditures, $45,475,819, including $43,145,000 for 150 grants (high: $3,000,000; low: $25,000).

Purpose and activities: Broad purposes; challenge grants only for building construction or renovation projects, major, movable capital equipment having a unit cost of not less than $75,000, and purchase of real estate; grants generally to well-established, financially sound, and fully accredited institutions involved in higher (four-year) and graduate education, hospitals and health-related services, social services, science and conservation, the arts and humanities, and public policy. Initial funds considered essential and support not given for total project costs; grants on a challenge basis for a portion of the funds remaining to be raised.
Types of support awarded: Building funds, equipment, land acquisition, matching funds.
Limitations: No grants to individuals, operating or special project budgets, conferences or seminars, church building programs, endowment funds, student aid, scholarships, fellowships, research, debt retirement, substantially completed projects, or general purposes; no loans.
Publications: Annual report, informational brochure, program policy statement, application guidelines.
Application information: Application form required.
Initial approach: Letter or telephone
Copies of proposal: 1
Deadline(s): Applications must be postmarked between January 1 and February 15
Board meeting date(s): Monthly
Final notification: July
Write: Alfred H. Taylor, Jr., President
Officers: Alfred H. Taylor, Jr.,* President and Secretary of the Board of Trustees; John E. Marshall III, Executive Vice-President; Thomas W. Herbert, Vice-President and Treasurer.
Trustees:* William H. Baldwin, Chairman; Stanley S. Kresge, Honorary Chairman; Bruce A. Kresge, M.D., Vice-President; George E. Cartmill, Edward H. Lerchen, Wilbur K. Pierpont.
Number of staff: 7 full-time professional; 7 full-time support.
Employer Identification Number: 381359217

1735
Lansing Foundation, The Greater
c/o First of America Bank-Central
P.O. Box 21007
Lansing 48909   (517) 374-5438

Established as community foundation in 1947 in Michigan; status changed in 1980 to independent foundation.
Financial data: (yr. ended 12/31/83): Assets, $1,600,983 (M); gifts received, $3,000; expenditures, $142,300, including $115,667 for 43 grants (high: $9,688; low: $559).
Purpose and activities: To promote the well-being of the inhabitants of Ingam, Clinton, and Eaton counties by distributing income from bequests to local charitable, public, or educational institutions. Grants mainly for capital expenditures.
Types of support awarded: Building funds, land acquisition, equipment.

Limitations: Giving limited to Ingam, Clinton, and Eaton counties, MI. No grants to individuals, or for operating budgets, or endowment funds.
Publications: Application guidelines, program policy statement.
Application information: Application form required.
Initial approach: Telephone
Copies of proposal: 6
Deadline(s): Submit application form preferably in April; deadline May 15
Board meeting date(s): Usually in June or July
Write: Ms. Dorothy L. Vartanian, Secretary
Officer: Gregory Deliyanne, Chairman; Joanne Hacker, Vice-Chairman; Dorothy L. Vartanian, Secretary.
Distribution Committee: Donald Hines, J. Michael Hofmann, Chester Kennedy.
Trustee Bank: First of America Bank-Central.
Employer Identification Number: 386057513

1736
La-Z-Boy Chair Foundation
1284 North Telegraph Rd.
P.O. Box 713
Monroe 48161   (313) 242-1444

Incorporated in 1953 in Michigan.
Donor(s): E.M. Knabusch, E.J. Shoemaker, Herman F. Gertz, La-Z-Boy Chair Company.
Financial data: (yr. ended 12/31/83): Assets, $5,179,900 (M); gifts received, $70,000; expenditures, $242,610, including $234,654 for 129 grants (high: $45,000; low: $30).
Purpose and activities: Broad purposes; primarily local giving in areas of Company operations, with emphasis on church support, community funds, hospitals, higher education, and youth agencies.
Types of support awarded: Operating budgets, building funds, professorships.
Limitations: Giving primarily in MI in areas of company operations. No grants to individuals, or for travel, continuing support, annual campaigns, seed money, emergency or endowment funds, deficit financing, equipment, land acquisition, matching gifts, research, special projects, publications, or conferences; no loans.
Publications: Annual report, program policy statement, application guidelines.
Application information:
Initial approach: Letter
Copies of proposal: 1
Deadline(s): February 15, May 15, August 15, and November 15
Board meeting date(s): March, June, September, and December
Final notification: 60 days
Write: Herman F. Gertz, Foundation Administrator

Officers and Trustees: E.M. Knabusch, Chairman; C.T. Knabusch, President; F.H. Jackson, Vice-President-Finance; Patrick H. Norton, Vice-President-Sales and Marketing; E.J. Shoemaker, Vice-President-Engineering; L.G. Stevens, Vice-President-Manufacturing; Gene M. Hardy, Secretary-Treasurer; Herman F. Gertz, Foundation Administrator; Warren W. Gruber, D.K. Hehl, R.E. Lipford, John F. Weaver.
Number of staff: 1 full-time professional.
Employer Identification Number: 386087673

1737
Levy Foundation, The ¤
8800 Dix Ave.
Detroit 48209

Financial data: (yr. ended 5/31/82): Assets, $463,223 (M); expenditures, $194,723, including $191,605 for grants.
Purpose and activities: Giving for charitable purposes.
Officers: Janet Ardnoff, Secretary; Edward C. Levy, Jr., Treasurer.
Employer Identification Number: 591865316

1738
Loutit Foundation, The
c/o Michigan National Bank
P.O. Box 1707
Grand Rapids 49501   (616) 451-7688

Incorporated in 1957 in Michigan.
Donor(s): William R. Loutit.†
Financial data: (yr. ended 12/31/84): Assets, $2,939,864 (M); expenditures, $228,860, including $194,500 for 29 grants (high: $25,000; low: $400).
Purpose and activities: Broad purposes; primarily concerned with programs and projects related to the welfare of the citizens in the Grand Haven area of western Michigan; emphasis on hospitals, public schools and higher education, including buildings and equipment, a library, youth agencies, aid to the handicapped, cultural programs, and community funds.
Types of support awarded: General purposes, operating budgets, continuing support, annual campaigns, seed money, emergency funds, deficit financing, building funds, equipment, land acquisition, endowment funds, matching funds, scholarship funds, fellowships, special projects.
Limitations: Giving limited to MI, with emphasis on the western area of the state. No grants to individuals or for research; no loans.
Publications: Biennial report, program policy statement.
Application information:
  Initial approach: Letter or full proposal
  Copies of proposal: 6
  Deadline(s): 1 week prior to board meeting
  Board meeting date(s): February, May, August, and November
  Final notification: 1 week after meeting
  Write: R. Park Johnston, Secretary

Officers and Trustees: Paul A. Johnson, President; Harvey L. Scholten, Vice-President; R. Park Johnston, Secretary and Treasurer; Jon W. Eshleman, Eugene O. Harbeck, Jr.
Number of staff: None.
Employer Identification Number: 386053445

1739
Lyon Foundation, Inc. ¤
1295 Villa
Birmingham 48008

Incorporated in 1951 in Michigan.
Donor(s): G. Albert Lyon, Sr.
Financial data: (yr. ended 12/31/83): Assets, $1,029,066 (M); expenditures, $56,493, including $46,680 for 43 grants (high: $7,300; low: $150).
Purpose and activities: Primarily local giving for cultural activities, higher and secondary education, hospitals, and youth agencies.
Types of support awarded: Research, operating budgets.
Limitations: Giving primarily in MI.
Officers: Alberta L. Judd, Vice-President; I. Terrill Judd, Secretary; A. Randolph Judd, Treasurer.
Agent: National Bank of Detroit.
Employer Identification Number: 386121075

1740
Mallery (J. Harvey) Trust ¤
(also known as Mallery Charitable Trust)
c/o Michigan National Bank
P.O. Box 1707
Grand Rapids 49501   (313) 762-5563

Trust established in 1970 in Michigan.
Donor(s): Harvey J. Mallery.
Financial data: (yr. ended 6/30/83): Assets, $893,443 (M); expenditures, $125,090, including $112,450 for 7 grants (high: $48,300; low: $2,000).
Purpose and activities: Local giving, primarily for education, cultural programs, and recreation, including a youth agency.
Limitations: Giving limited to Genessee County, MI. No grants to individuals, or for endowment funds, scholarships, or fellowships; no loans.
Application information:
  Initial approach: Proposal, letter or telephone
  Copies of proposal: 2
  Board meeting date(s): Quarterly
  Write: Susan K. Koory, Administrator
Officer: Susan K. Koory, Administrator.
Trustees: Thomas C. Robberson, Chairman; Mary Davis, H. Samuel Greenawalt, Michigan National Bank.
Employer Identification Number: 386039907

1741
Manoogian (Alex and Marie)
  Foundation ▼ ¤
21001 Van Born Rd.
Taylor 48180   (313) 274-7400

Incorporated in 1942 in Michigan.
Donor(s): Alex Manoogian, Marie Manoogian.

Financial data: (yr. ended 12/31/82): Assets, $25,948,904 (M); expenditures, $1,146,921, including $1,093,078 for 85 grants (high: $201,800; low: $25; average: $100-$50,000).
Purpose and activities: Support primarily for Armenian welfare funds and religious institutions, higher and secondary education; support also for cultural programs.
Types of support awarded: Building funds, equipment, operating budgets, seed money, emergency funds, matching funds, endowment funds, scholarship funds, fellowships, research.
Limitations: No grants for annual campaigns, or for deficit financing, land acquisition, publications, or conferences and seminars.
Application information:
  Initial approach: Letter
  Deadline(s): None
  Board meeting date(s): Twice a year
  Final notification: 1 month
  Write: Alex Manoogian, President
Officers and Directors: Alex Manoogian, President and Treasurer; Richard A. Manoogian, Vice-President; H.S. Derderian, Secretary.
Number of staff: None.
Employer Identification Number: 386089952

1742
Mardigian Foundation ¤
1525 Tottenham
Birmingham 48009

Incorporated in 1955 in Michigan.
Donor(s): Edward S. Mardigian, Helen Mardigian.
Financial data: (yr. ended 12/31/82): Assets, $1,698,634 (M); gifts received, $127,000; expenditures, $64,747, including $59,833 for 25 grants (high: $28,300; low: $48).
Purpose and activities: Broad purposes; grants largely for Armenian church and cultural support, religious associations, and welfare funds.
Officers and Directors: Edward S. Mardigian Sr., President; Helen Mardigian, Marilyn Varbedian.
Employer Identification Number: 386048886

1743
Masco Screw Products Company
  Charitable Trust ¤
c/o Detroit Bank and Trust Company
211 West Fort St.
Detroit 48231

Trust established in 1952 in Michigan.
Donor(s): Masco Screw Products Company.
Financial data: (yr. ended 12/31/83): Assets, $167,902 (M); gifts received, $600,000; expenditures, $595,072, including $593,000 for 30 grants (high: $195,000; low: $2,000).
Purpose and activities: Broad purposes; largely local giving, with emphasis on the arts, higher education, museums, communications, and church support.
Limitations: Giving primarily in MI.
Board of Control: Owen Koning, Richard G. Mosteller, John C. Nicholls, Jr.
Trustee: Comerica Bank-Detroit.
Employer Identification Number: 386043605

1744
McGregor Fund ▼
333 West Fort Bldg., Suite 1380
Detroit 48226   (313) 963-3495

Incorporated in 1925 in Michigan.
Donor(s): Tracy W. McGregor,† Mrs. Tracy
W. McGregor.†
Financial data: (yr. ended 6/30/84): Assets,
$42,570,064 (M); expenditures, $2,683,095,
including $2,163,770 for 71 grants (high:
$200,000; low: $2,000; average: $10,000-
$50,000).
Purpose and activities: A general purpose
foundation supporting education, welfare,
including health and youth agencies,
humanities, and sciences with emphasis on
higher education. Support limited principally to
Michigan, largely to institutions located in the
metropolitan Detroit area; grants also to private
colleges and universities located within the
states of Indiana, Michigan, and Ohio.
Types of support awarded: Operating
budgets, annual campaigns, seed money,
emergency funds, building funds, equipment,
special projects.
Limitations: Giving limited to IN, OH, and MI,
with emphasis on the Detroit metropolitan
area. No grants to individuals, or for
continuing support, deficit financing, land
acquisition, endowment funds, matching gifts,
scholarships and fellowships, research, travel,
workshops, publications, or conferences; no
loans.
Publications: Annual report, application
guidelines.
Application information:
 Initial approach: Full proposal
 Copies of proposal: 1
 Deadline(s): January 1, March 1, August 1,
  and October 1
 Board meeting date(s): February, April, June,
  September, and November
 Final notification: 45 days
 Write: Jack L. Otto, Executive Director
Officers: Elliot H. Phillips,* President; Lem W.
Bowen,* Vice-President; W. Warren Sheldon,*
Secretary; Raymond T. Perring,* Treasurer; Jack
L. Otto, Executive Director.
Trustees:* Carlton M. Higbie, Jr., Peter W.
Stroh, Robert M. Surdam, Donald N. Sweeny,
Jr., M.D., Peter P. Thurber.
Number of staff: 1 full-time professional; 2 full-
time support.
Employer Identification Number: 380808800

1745
McIntyre (B. D. and Jane E.) Foundation
c/o National Bank of Detroit
Detroit 48232   (313) 225-3124

Trust established in 1961 in Michigan.
Donor(s): Members of the McIntyre family.
Financial data: (yr. ended 11/30/83): Assets,
$1,967,137 (M); expenditures, $148,860,
including $130,450 for 6 grants (high: $77,000;
low: $450).
Purpose and activities: Charitable purposes;
primarily local giving, with emphasis on
education, Episcopal church support, and a
community fund.

Limitations: Giving primarily in Monroe, MI.
No grants to individuals.
Application information:
 Initial approach: Letter
 Copies of proposal: 1
 Deadline(s): Submit proposal preferably in
  August or November
 Board meeting date(s): As required
Trustee: National Bank of Detroit.
Managers: Dic L. Dorney, Rocque E. Lipford,
Jane E. McIntyre, Therese M. Thorn.
Employer Identification Number: 386046718

1746
McIntyre (C. S. and Marion F.) Foundation
c/o National Bank of Detroit
Detroit 48232   (313) 225-3124

Trust established in 1961 in Michigan.
Donor(s): Members of the McIntyre family.
Financial data: (yr. ended 11/30/83): Assets,
$1,157,371 (M); expenditures, $9,046.
Purpose and activities: Charitable purposes;
primarily local giving, with emphasis on higher
education.
Limitations: Giving primarily in MI, with
emphasis on the Monroe, MI, area. No grants
to individuals.
Application information:
 Initial approach: Full proposal
 Copies of proposal: 4
 Deadline(s): Submit proposal between August
  and November
 Board meeting date(s): As required
 Write: Therese M. Thorn, Managing Trustee
Managers: Dil L. Dorney, Rocque E. Lipford,
David L. McIntyre, Edwin R. Stroh, III.
Trustee: National Bank of Detroit (Therese M.
Thorn, Trust Officer).
Employer Identification Number: 386046733

1747
Michigan Standard Alloys - Arthur S. Mendel Foundation ☒
777 Riverview Dr.
Benton Harbor 49022

Established in 1964 in Michigan.
Financial data: (yr. ended 4/30/81): Assets,
$1,305,539 (M); gifts received, $38,713;
expenditures, $72,239, including $72,200 for
26 grants (high: $50,200; low: $25).
Purpose and activities: Primarily local giving,
with emphasis on Jewish welfare funds,
religious associations, and temple support;
grants also for music.
Limitations: Giving primarily in MI.
Officers: Herbert D. Mendel, President; Edwin
J. Mendel, Vice-President.
Employer Identification Number: 386099787

1748
Midland Foundation
117 McDonald St.
P.O. Box 289
Midland 48640   (517) 839-9661

Community foundation established in 1973 in
Michigan.

Financial data: (yr. ended 12/31/84): Assets,
$6,602,276 (L); gifts received, $1,214,757;
expenditures, $999,448, including $886,599
for 34 grants (high: $800,000; low: $60;
average: $26,000), $21,210 for 35 grants to
individuals and $25,946 for 54 loans.
Purpose and activities: "To support the
charitable, cultural, educational, and scientific
needs of the Midland area."
Types of support awarded: Seed money,
emergency funds, equipment, matching funds,
scholarship funds, student aid, grants to
individuals.
Limitations: Giving limited to Midland County,
MI. No grants to individuals (except for
student loans and scholarships), or for
operating budgets, continuing support, annual
campaigns, deficit financing, building funds,
land acquisition, or endowment funds.
Publications: Annual report, application
guidelines.
Application information:
 Initial approach: Telephone
 Copies of proposal: 1
 Deadline(s): Submit proposal in November;
  deadlines January 1, April 1, and
  November 1
 Board meeting date(s): January, April,
  November, and as required
 Final notification: 2 months
 Write: Firmin A. Paulus, Executive Director
Officers: Mary M. Neely,* President; E. Ned
Brandt, Roy M. Goethe, M.D.,* Vice-
Presidents; James A. Kendall,* Secretary; Julius
Grosberg,* Treasurer; Firmin A. Paulus,
Executive Director.
Trustees:* Arnold Butterworth, O. James Clark,
L.C. Dorman, Frank Gerace, Bernard C.
Lorimer, William V. Mapes, John E. Riecker,
Norman Rumple, Tina Van Dam.
Number of staff: 1 part-time professional; 1
part-time support.
Employer Identification Number: 382023395

1749
Miller (Albert L. and Louise B.) Foundation, Inc.
155 West Van Buren St.
Battle Creek 49016   (616) 964-7161

Incorporated in 1963 in Michigan.
Donor(s): Mrs. Louise B. Miller,† Robert B.
Miller.
Financial data: (yr. ended 2/28/84): Assets,
$5,791,706 (M); gifts received, $98,333;
expenditures, $688,171, including $100,625
for 32 grants (high: $18,000; low: $400;
average: $3,000).
Purpose and activities: Broad purposes;
primarily local giving, with emphasis on higher
education, public schools, and local municipal
improvements.
Types of support awarded: Annual
campaigns, seed money, emergency funds,
building funds, equipment, land acquisition,
endowment funds, matching funds, program-
related investments, scholarship funds,
exchange programs, loans, publications.
Limitations: Giving primarily in the Battle
Creek, MI, area. No grants to individuals or for
operating budgets.
Publications: Annual report.

Application information: Application form required.
Initial approach: Letter
Copies of proposal: 10
Deadline(s): None
Board meeting date(s): Monthly
Final notification: 2 months
Write: Robert B. Miller, Chairman
Officers and Trustees: Robert B. Miller, Chairman; W. James McQuiston, President; Rebecca A. Engelhardt, Secretary; Arnold Van Zanten, Treasurer; Arthur W. Angood, Barbara L. Comai, Gary E. Costley, Dale G. Griffin, Olive T. Miller, Robert B. Miller, Jr.
Number of staff: 1 part-time support.
Employer Identification Number: 386064925

1750

Mills (Frances Goll) Fund
101 N. Washington Ave.
Saginaw 48607

Established in 1982 in Michigan.
Donor(s): Frances Goll Mills.†
Financial data: (yr. ended 9/30/83): Assets, $2,440,528 (M).
Purpose and activities: First year of operation in 1982-83; no grants awarded.
Types of support awarded: Operating budgets, continuing support, seed money, emergency funds, building funds, equipment, land acquisition, matching funds, consulting services.
Limitations: Giving primarily in Saginaw County, MI. No grants to individuals, or for annual campaigns, deficit financing, endowments, special programs, scholarships, fellowships, professorships, or internships; no loans.
Publications: Annual report, application guidelines.
Application information:
Initial approach: Letter or proposal
Copies of proposal: 1
Deadline(s): 10 days prior to board meeting
Board meeting date(s): Bimonthly, beginning in February
Final notification: 1 week after meeting
Write: Denice McGlaughlin
Trustee: Second National Bank of Saginaw.
Number of staff: None.
Employer Identification Number: 382434002

1751

Morley Brothers Foundation
330 Brockway Place
Saginaw 48602   (517) 792-1427

Incorporated in 1948 in Michigan.
Donor(s): Ralph Chase Morley, Sr.,† Mrs. Ralph Chase Morley, Sr.†
Financial data: (yr. ended 12/31/82): Assets, $1,978,659 (M); expenditures, $133,306, including $120,114 for 35 grants (high: $30,000; low: $100; average: $100-$12,000).
Purpose and activities: Educational and charitable purposes; giving generally local, with emphasis on higher and secondary education, community funds, the arts, youth agencies, and hospitals.

Types of support awarded: Operating budgets, continuing support, annual campaigns, seed money, emergency funds, building funds, equipment, scholarship funds, exchange programs, special projects, research, matching funds, employee matching gifts.
Limitations: Giving primarily in the greater Saginaw, MI, area. No grants to individuals, or for endowment funds, deficit financing, land acquisition, renovation projects, publications, or conferences; no loans.
Application information:
Initial approach: Letter
Copies of proposal: 1
Deadline(s): Submit proposal preferably in December or January
Board meeting date(s): April, July, October, and December
Final notification: 3 months
Write: Edward B. Morley, Jr., President
Officers: Edward B. Morley, Jr.,* President; Lucy M. Thomson,* Vice-President; Lois K. Guttowsky, Secretary; George B. Morley,* Treasurer.
Trustees:* Burrows Morley, Burrows Morley, Jr., Peter B. Morley, Robert S. Morley.
Number of staff: 1 part-time professional.
Employer Identification Number: 386055569

1752

Mott (Charles Stewart) Foundation ▼
1200 Mott Foundation Bldg.
Flint 48502-1851   (313) 238-5651

Incorporated in 1926 in Michigan.
Donor(s): Charles Stewart Mott,† and family.
Financial data: (yr. ended 12/31/84): Assets, $569,037,725 (M); expenditures, $32,747,358, including $26,513,612 for 356 grants (high: $4,000,000; low: $1,000; average: $10,000-$200,000) and $140,015 for 257 employee matching gifts.
Purpose and activities: Supports community improvement through grants for expressing individuality; expanding personal horizons; citizenship; volunteer action; counteracting root causes of alienation; community identity and stability; community renewal; environmental management; fostering institutional openness; better delivery of services; and training in and improving practices of leadership. Pioneer in community education concept.
Types of support awarded: Annual campaigns, conferences and seminars, continuing support, deficit financing, emergency funds, employee matching gifts, loans, matching funds, operating budgets, program-related investments, publications, seed money, special projects.
Limitations: No grants to individuals, or generally for building or endowment funds, research, scholarships, or fellowships.
Publications: Annual report, program policy statement, application guidelines.
Application information:
Initial approach: Letter
Copies of proposal: 1
Deadline(s): None
Board meeting date(s): March, June, September, and December
Final notification: 60 to 90 days

Write: Frank Gilsdorf, Vice-President for Program Administration
Officers: William S. White,* President and Chief Executive Officer; Ray B. Loeschner, Vice-President and Chief Administrative Officer; Willard J. Hertz, Vice-President for Program Planning and Dissemination; Robert E. Swaney, Jr., Vice-President for Investments; Frank Gilsdorf, Vice-President for Program Administration; Richard K. Rappleye, Secretary and Treasurer.
Trustees:* C.S. Harding Mott, Chairman; Marjorie Powell Allen, Joseph A. Anderson, Charles B. Cumings, C.S. Harding Mott, II, Maryanne Mott, Willa B. Player, John W. Porter, Harold P. Rodes, George L. Whyel.
Number of staff: 25 full-time professional; 3 part-time professional; 23 full-time support.
Employer Identification Number: 381211227

1753

Mott (Ruth) Fund ▼
1726 Genesee Towers
Flint 48502   (313) 232-3180

Incorporated in 1979 in Michigan.
Donor(s): Ruth R. Mott.
Financial data: (yr. ended 12/31/83): Assets, $386,484 (M); gifts received, $1,287,805; expenditures, $1,173,479, including $999,339 for 128 grants (high: $50,000; low: $25; average: $10,000-$15,000).
Purpose and activities: Support for programs that focus on topics of emerging significance, exemplify originality, and offer the potential for application on a broader scale within four broad areas: 1) arts and special interests, including arts as a means to a greater educational, humanistic, or social goal with emphasis on youth, and for beautification of Flint, Michigan; 2) environment programs addressing toxic substance issues, including emphasis on public participation in policy-making, preventive action, and alternatives to the proliferation of toxic substances; 3) health promotion, with emphasis on nutrition or stress control, especially preventive approaches and programs that can have a beneficial effect on attitudes and lifestyles affecting health, and programs with the potential to benefit youth; and 4) prevention of nuclear war including educational programs, joint projects, and projects to increase the public's understanding of the scientific complexities.
Types of support awarded: Operating budgets, continuing support, seed money, matching funds, special projects, research, publications, conferences and seminars.
Limitations: No support for film or television projects about the documented or probable effects of nuclear war. No grants to individuals, or for capital or endowment funds, annual campaigns, emergency funds, deficit financing, scholarships, or fellowships; no loans.
Publications: Multi-year report, program policy statement, application guidelines.
Application information: Application form required.
Initial approach: Letter or telephone
Deadline(s): None
Board meeting date(s): February, June, and October

Final notification: 3 to 4 months
Write: James R. Kettler, Executive Director
Officers: Maryanne Mott,* President; Stewart Dansby,* Secretary; Stewart R. Mott,* Treasurer; James R. Kettler, Executive Director.
Trustees:* Sarah R. Molla, Chair; Sandra Butler, Norman Cousins, Howard Hiatt, Helen Milliken, C.S. Harding Mott, Ruth R. Mott, George Woodwell.
Number of staff: 3 full-time professional; 1 part-time support.
Employer Identification Number: 382284264

1754
Muskegon County Community Foundation, Inc.
Frauenthal Center, Suite 304
407 W. Western Ave.
Muskegon 49440   (616) 722-4538

Community foundation incorporated in 1961 in Michigan.
Donor(s): Harold Frauenthal,† Charles Goodnow.†
Financial data: (yr. ended 3/31/84): Assets, $7,206,219 (M); gifts received, $687,013; expenditures, $593,530, including $373,094 for 46 grants (high: $58,600; low: $200; average: $1,000-$5,000) and $163,259 for 192 grants to individuals.
Purpose and activities: To assist worthwhile projects for the betterment of Muskegon County, with some emphasis on health care, the arts, education and training, and human services. Priority support for pilot projects, seed money, and challenge gifts.
Types of support awarded: Seed money, special projects, matching funds, building funds, equipment, land acquisition, scholarship funds, loans, research, publications, conferences and seminars, endowment funds, student aid, annual campaigns.
Limitations: Giving limited to Muskegon County, MI. No grants to individuals (except for scholarships), or for operating budgets, continuing support, emergency funds, or deficit financing.
Publications: Annual report, application guidelines.
Application information: Application form required.
Initial approach: Letter or telephone
Copies of proposal: 12
Deadline(s): January, April, July, or October
Board meeting date(s): February, May, August, and November
Final notification: 2 to 3 weeks
Write: Patricia B. Johnson, Executive Director
Officers: George W. Bartlett, President; Robert Tuttle, Vice-President; Patricia B. Johnson, Secretary-Treasurer and Executive Director.
Distribution Committee: Daniel Thill, Chairman; Ellen Hanley, Associate Chairman; George Arwady, Eugene Fisher, Robert Hilleary, Robert Jewell, Richard Johnson, William Marietti, Antoinette Reynolds, Donald Seyferth.
Trustee Banks: Comerica Bank & Trust, First of America Bank, FMB Lumbermans' Bank.
Number of staff: 1 full-time professional; 1 full-time support; 2 part-time support.
Employer Identification Number: 386114135

1755
National Bank of Detroit Charitable Trust ▼
c/o National Bank of Detroit
611 Woodward Ave.
Detroit 48232   (313) 225-2682

Trust established in 1963 in Michigan.
Donor(s): National Bank of Detroit.
Financial data: (yr. ended 12/31/83): Assets, $704,599 (M); expenditures, $404,749, including $337,075 for 40 grants (high: $62,000; low: $500; average: $1,000-$15,000) and $54,471 for 93 employee matching gifts.
Purpose and activities: Primarily local giving, with emphasis on community funds; support also for cultural programs, higher education, and civic organizations.
Types of support awarded: Employee matching gifts.
Limitations: Giving primarily in MI, with emphasis on the Detroit area.
Application information:
Initial approach: Letter
Deadline(s): None
Board meeting date(s): Every 2 weeks, except July and August
Write: Dennis Kembel, Public Relations
Board of Control: Henry T. Bodman, Joseph L. Hudson, Jr., Ralph T. McElvenny, Ellis B. Merry, Robert M. Surdam, Donald F. Valley.
Trustee: National Bank of Detroit (Therese M. Thorn, Managing Trustee).
Employer Identification Number: 386059088

1756
Pagel (William M. and Mary E.) Trust
c/o National Bank of Detroit
611 Woodward Ave.
Detroit 48232   (313) 225-3124

Financial data: (yr. ended 12/31/82): Assets, $4,066,461 (M); expenditures, $287,602, including $267,378 for 8 grants (high: $53,475; low: $26,737).
Purpose and activities: Primarily local giving, with emphasis on hospitals, child welfare, aid to the handicapped, and Protestant church support; support also for a social agency.
Limitations: Giving primarily in MI, with emphasis on Detroit.
Trustee: National Bank of Detroit (Therese M. Thorn, Manager).
Employer Identification Number: 386046204

1757
Pardee (Elsa U.) Foundation ▼
P.O. Box 1866
Midland 48640   (517) 832-3691

Incorporated in 1944 in Michigan.
Donor(s): Elsa U. Pardee.†
Financial data: (yr. ended 12/25/83): Assets, $22,181,974 (M); expenditures, $1,055,608, including $1,027,214 for 26 grants (high: $110,000; low: $1,000).
Purpose and activities: To promote the cure and control of cancer; grants to hospitals, universities, and institutes for cancer research and control.
Types of support awarded: Research.

Limitations: No grants to individuals, or for capital or endowment funds, equipment (except when used in a specific project), scholarships and fellowships, general purposes, matching gifts, or fundraising campaigns; no loans.
Publications: Annual report, program policy statement, application guidelines.
Application information: Application form required.
Initial approach: Letter
Copies of proposal: 7
Board meeting date(s): 3 times a year
Final notification: 4 to 6 months
Write: William W. Allen, Vice-President
Officers and Trustees: Gail E. Brink, President; William W. Allen, Vice-President and Secretary; Carl A. Gerstacker, Vice-President and Treasurer; W. James Allen, Maynard B. Chenoweth, M.D., Lisa J. Gerstacker, I. Frank Harlow, James A. Kendall, Richard J. Kociba, Michael S. Leahy, M.D., Patrick J. Oriel, Norman C. Rumple, William H. Staub, M.D., Charles H. Willison, M.D.
Number of staff: 1 part-time support.
Employer Identification Number: 386065799

1758
Plym Foundation ⌐
Star Bldg.
Niles 49120   (616) 683-8300

Incorporated in 1952 in Michigan.
Donor(s): Mrs. Francis J. Plym.
Financial data: (yr. ended 9/30/83): Assets, $3,378,953 (M); expenditures, $162,316, including $149,600 for 5 grants (high: $100,000; low: $5,000) and $4,600 for 1 grant to an individual.
Purpose and activities: Broad purposes; primarily local giving, with emphasis on education, including a community education center, the arts, and scholarships.
Limitations: Giving primarily in MI.
Application information:
Initial approach: Letter including goals, resources, and amount required
Copies of proposal: 1
Write: Murray C. Campbell, Secretary
Officers and Trustees: Lawrence J. Plym, President; Murray C. Campbell, Secretary.
Employer Identification Number: 386069680

1759
Prentis (The Meyer and Anna) Family Foundation, Inc.
c/o Lester J. Morris
6785 Telegraph Rd., Suite 320
Birmingham 48010   (313) 540-4340

Incorporated in 1955 in Michigan.
Donor(s): Members of the Prentis family.
Financial data: (yr. ended 12/31/82): Assets, $6,578,890 (M); expenditures, $526,240, including $513,280 for 39 grants (high: $221,300; low: $100).
Purpose and activities: Broad purposes; primarily local giving, with emphasis on Jewish welfare funds, higher education, medical research, temple support, and a museum.

Limitations: Giving primarily in MI. No grants to individuals, or for endowment funds, scholarships and fellowships, or matching gifts; no loans.
Application information:
Initial approach: Letter
Copies of proposal: 1
Board meeting date(s): July and December
Write: Lester J. Morris, Secretary
Officers and Trustees: Beverly J. Prentis, President; Barbara P. Frenkel, Vice-President; Lester J. Morris, Secretary and Treasurer; Denise L. Farber, Dale P. Frenkel, Marvin A. Frenkel, Jewell P. Morris, Robert P. Morris.
Employer Identification Number: 386090332

1760
Prince Foundation ☐
1057 S. Shore Dr.
Holland 49423

Established in 1977.
Financial data: (yr. ended 6/30/83): Assets, $519,752 (M); gifts received, $125,000; expenditures, $186,297, including $185,250 for 39 grants (high: $28,250; low: $100).
Purpose and activities: Primarily local giving to Christian organizations and churches, and higher education.
Limitations: Giving primarily in MI.
Trustee: Edgar D. Prince.
Employer Identification Number: 382190330

1761
Ransom Fidelity Company ☐
702 Michigan National Tower
Lansing 48933

Incorporated in 1915 in Michigan.
Donor(s): Ransom E. Olds.†
Financial data: (yr. ended 12/31/83): Assets, $6,939,534 (M); expenditures, $415,940, including $338,169 for 79 grants (high: $50,500; low: $350).
Purpose and activities: Charitable purposes; primarily local giving, with emphasis on higher and secondary education, hospitals, youth agencies, cultural programs, Protestant church support, a conservation organization, and the handicapped.
Limitations: Giving primarily in MI.
Officers and Directors: J. Woodward Roe, President and Treasurer; R.E. Olds Anderson, Vice-President and Secretary.
Employer Identification Number: 381485403

1762
Ratner (Milton M.) Foundation ☐
400 Renaissance Center, 35th Fl.
Detroit 48243   (313) 568-6655

Incorporated in 1968 in Michigan.
Donor(s): Milton M. Ratner Trust.
Financial data: (yr. ended 8/31/83): Assets, $3,639,788 (M); expenditures, $184,926, including $151,950 for 42 grants (high: $10,000; low: $200).

Purpose and activities: Giving primarily in Michigan and Georgia, with emphasis on higher education, including scholarship and loan funds, hospitals, and medical research.
Limitations: Giving primarily in MI and GA. No grants to individuals.
Application information:
Initial approach: Full proposal
Copies of proposal: 1
Deadline(s): Submit proposal in August or September; deadline October 1
Board meeting date(s): October
Write: Thomas L. Munson, Vice-President
Officers and Trustees: Mary Jo Corley, President; Thomas L. Munson, Vice-President and Secretary; J. Beverly Langford, Treasurer.
Employer Identification Number: 386160330

1763
Royal (May Mitchell) Foundation ☐
c/o Comerica Bank
201 McDonald St.
Midland 48640
Application address: Richard O. Hartley, Chairman, Grant Committee, 414 Townsend St., Midland, MI 48640; Tel.: (517) 631-1025

Established in 1981 in Michigan.
Donor(s): May Mitchell Royal Trust.
Financial data: (yr. ended 9/30/82): Assets, $1,010,194 (M); gifts received, $55,000; expenditures, $126,022, including $110,000 for 10 grants (high: $30,000; low: $1,000).
Purpose and activities: Giving primarily in Michigan and Hawaii for hospitals and for eye research and treatment.
Limitations: Giving primarily in MI and HI.
Application information: Application form required.
Initial approach: Letter
Write: John M. Walsh, Senior Vice-President
Trust Officer: John M. Walsh.
Grant Committee: Richard O. Hartley, Chairman; Tyrone W. Gillespie, Ruth C. Lishman.
Employer Identification Number: 382387140

1764
Sage Foundation ▼ ☐
2500 Comerica Bldg.
Detroit 48226   (313) 963-6420

Incorporated in 1954 in Michigan.
Donor(s): Charles F. Sage,† Effa L. Sage.†
Financial data: (yr. ended 12/31/83): Assets, $33,557,939 (M); expenditures, $1,350,213, including $1,270,050 for 164 grants (high: $50,000; low: $350; average: $1,000-$10,000).
Purpose and activities: Broad purposes; primarily local giving, with emphasis on higher and secondary education and hospitals; grants also for aid to the handicapped, Roman Catholic religious and charitable organizations, child welfare, church support, and youth agencies.
Limitations: Giving primarily in MI.
Application information:
Initial approach: Letter
Deadline(s): None
Write: Robert F. Sage, President, or Emmett E. Eagan, Sr., Secretary

Officers: Robert F. Sage,* Chairman, President, and Treasurer; Emmett E. Eagan,* Vice-President and Secretary; Melissa Sage Booth, John W. Gelder, Vice-Presidents.
Trustees:* Emmett E. Eagan, Jr., Donato F. Sarapo.
Number of staff: None.
Employer Identification Number: 386041518

1765
Scott (Lillian H. and Karl W.) Foundation ☐
46410 Van Dyke Ave.
Utica 48087

Established in 1963 in Michigan.
Financial data: (yr. ended 10/31/83): Assets, $1,367,806 (M); expenditures, $102,323, including $64,191 for 95 grants (high: $7,350; low: $100).
Purpose and activities: Grants primarily to local institutions concerned with the care and education of children and youth.
Limitations: Giving primarily in MI.
Officers and Directors: B.A. Chaplow, President and Treasurer; Ted Vincent, Secretary; Thomas J. Chaplow.
Employer Identification Number: 386065953

1766
Sebastian Foundation, The ☐
2000 Robinson Rd., S.E.
Grand Rapids 49506   (616) 451-6403
Application address: 82 Ionia, N.W., Suite 360, Grand Rapids, MI 49503

Established in 1980.
Donor(s): Audrey M. Sebastian, James R. Sebastian.
Financial data: (yr. ended 8/31/83): Assets, $1,385,977 (M); gifts received, $158,738; expenditures, $117,353, including $106,000 for 6 grants (high: $35,000; low: $1,000).
Purpose and activities: Primarily local giving.
Limitations: Giving primarily in the Grand Rapids and Kent County areas, MI. No grants to individuals.
Application information:
Initial approach: Full proposal
Deadline(s): None
Write: James R. Sebastian, Trustee
Trustees: Audrey M. Sebastian, James R. Sebastian, John O. Sebastian.
Employer Identification Number: 382340219

1767
Seidman (The Thomas Erler) Foundation ☐
700 Union Bank Bldg.
Grand Rapids 49503

Trust established in 1950 in Michigan.
Donor(s): Frank E. Seidman,† Esther L. Seidman.†
Financial data: (yr. ended 12/31/83): Assets, $1,790,644 (M); expenditures, $104,278, including $93,475 for 36 grants (high: $30,000; low: $100).

Purpose and activities: Charitable purposes; largely local giving, with emphasis on cultural programs and higher education; support also for social agencies.
Types of support awarded: General purposes, building funds, endowment funds, annual campaigns, equipment.
Limitations: Giving primarily in MI. No grants to individuals.
Trustees: Augusta Eppinga, L. William Seidman, Philip K. Seidman.
Employer Identification Number: 136098204

1768
Seymour and Troester Foundation ¤
21500 Harper
St. Clair Shores 48080

Incorporated in 1945 in Michigan.
Donor(s): Charles E. Troester.†
Financial data: (yr. ended 12/31/83): Assets, $3,058,336 (M); expenditures, $216,941, including $119,055 for 22 grants (high: $50,000; low: $500).
Purpose and activities: Broad purposes; grants largely for higher and secondary educational institutions and Roman Catholic charitable and religious organizations.
Officers and Trustees: Mrs. B.A. Seymour, Sr., Chairman; B.A. Seymour, Jr., President and Treasurer; Isabel Fitzer, Vice-President and Secretary; Kathleen Froelich, Marcella Lilly.
Employer Identification Number: 386062647

1769
Shapero (The Nate S. and Ruth B.) Foundation ¤
1927 Twelfth St.
Detroit 48216

Established in 1949 in Michigan.
Donor(s): Nate S. Shapero, Ray A. Shapero.
Financial data: (yr. ended 4/30/83): Assets, $1,423,607 (M); expenditures, $162,772, including $154,477 for 29 grants (high: $58,000; low: $67).
Purpose and activities: Primarily local giving, with emphasis on Jewish welfare funds, higher education, and the arts, including music.
Types of support awarded: General purposes.
Limitations: Giving primarily in MI.
Officers and Trustees: Ruth B. Shapero, Vice-Chairman; J.E. Shapero, Secretary; Ray A. Shapero, Treasurer; Alan E. Schwartz, Marianne S. Schwartz.
Employer Identification Number: 386041567

1770
Shelden (Elizabeth, Allan and Warren) Fund
333 West Fort Bldg., Suite 1870
Detroit 48226   (313) 963-2356

Incorporated in 1937 in Michigan.
Donor(s): Elizabeth Warren Shelden,† Allan Shelden III,† W. Warren Shelden.
Financial data: (yr. ended 12/31/83): Assets, $1,852,768 (M); expenditures, $144,167, including $140,000 for 14 grants (high: $42,500; low: $1,000).

Purpose and activities: Broad purposes; primarily local giving, with emphasis on hospitals, community funds, higher and secondary education, youth agencies, and cultural organizations.
Types of support awarded: Continuing support, annual campaigns, building funds, equipment, endowment funds, research, general purposes.
Limitations: Giving primarily in MI. No grants to individuals, or for scholarships or fellowships, or matching gifts; no loans.
Application information:
  Initial approach: Full proposal
  Copies of proposal: 1
  Deadline(s): Submit proposal in October or November; no set deadline
  Board meeting date(s): December or January
  Write: W. Warren Shelden, President
Officers: W. Warren Shelden,* President; Frances W. Shelden,* Vice-President; Robert W. Emke, Jr., Secretary; William W. Shelden, Jr.,* Treasurer.
Trustees:* William G. Butler, Robert M. Surdam.
Number of staff: 1 part-time professional; 1 part-time support.
Employer Identification Number: 386052198

1771
Shiffman Foundation, The
1040 West Fort St.
Detroit 48226

Incorporated in 1948 in Michigan.
Donor(s): Abraham Shiffman.
Financial data: (yr. ended 9/30/83): Assets, $1,901,274 (M); expenditures, $199,381, including $180,482 for 78 grants (high: $33,300; low: $100).
Purpose and activities: Charitable and educational purposes; primarily local giving, with emphasis on Jewish welfare funds; some support for higher education in the United States and Israel, hospitals, community funds, and temple support.
Limitations: Giving primarily in Detroit, MI. No grants to individuals.
Application information:
  Write: N. James Levey, President
Officers and Trustees: N. James Levey, President; Richard Levey, Robert I. Kohn, Jr., Vice-Presidents; Janet S. Kohn, Milton J. Miller, Secretaries; Jason L. Honigman, Treasurer; Max M. Fisher.
Employer Identification Number: 381396850

1772
Simpson Foundation, The
c/o City Bank & Trust Company
One Jackson Square
Jackson 49201

Established in 1980 in Michigan.
Donor(s): Robert J. Simpson.†
Financial data: (yr. ended 9/30/84): Assets, $1,937,419 (M); expenditures, $130,505, including $100,445 for grants (average: $10,000).

Purpose and activities: Local giving for education, health, scientific, and religious purposes.
Types of support awarded: Seed money, emergency funds, building funds, equipment, matching funds, consulting services, technical assistance, special projects.
Limitations: Giving limited to Hillsdale County or to programs benefiting Hillsdale County, MI. No grants to individuals, or for endowment funds, operating budgets, continuing support, annual campaigns, deficit financing, land acquisition, scholarships and fellowships, research, publication, or conferences.
Application information: Application form required.
  Initial approach: Full proposal, letter, or telephone
  Deadline(s): Submit proposal preferably in August or September
  Board meeting date(s): October
  Final notification: 30 to 60 days
  Write: Robert E. Carlson, V.P. & Trust Officer
Trustee: City Bank & Trust Company.
Number of staff: None.
Employer Identification Number: 386054058

1773
Skillman Foundation, The ▼
333 West Fort St., Suite 1350
Detroit 48226   (313) 961-8853

Incorporated in 1960 in Michigan.
Donor(s): Rose P. Skillman.†
Financial data: (yr. ended 12/31/83): Assets, $1,174,756 (M); gifts received, $3,750,000; expenditures, $2,598,806, including $2,568,600 for 121 grants (high: $165,000; low: $100; average: $1,000-$150,000).
Purpose and activities: Primarily local giving, with emphasis on educational institutions of college and higher level; social service agencies involved primarily with child welfare and youth assistance; and health care facilities and institutions.
Types of support awarded: Operating budgets, continuing support, annual campaigns, emergency funds, building funds, equipment, professorships, scholarship funds.
Limitations: Giving primarily in southeastern MI, with emphasis on metropolitan Detroit, including Oakland County. No support for elementary or secondary schools, or for long-term projects not being aided by other sources. No grants to individuals, or for endowment funds, or matching funds; no loans.
Publications: Annual report, application guidelines.
Application information:
  Initial approach: Letter
  Copies of proposal: 6
  Deadline(s): Submit proposal preferably in February, March, August, or September; deadlines March 15 and September 15
  Board meeting date(s): April and October
  Final notification: Within 1 month of receipt of proposal or 1 week after board meeting
  Write: Leonard W. Smith, President

Officers: Milton Pilhashy,* Chairman; Leonard W. Smith,* President and Secretary; Samuel C. Kovan,* Vice-President; Jean E. Gregory, Administrative Officer.
Trustees:* Mandell L. Berman, William M. Brodhead, William E. Hogland.
Number of staff: 2 full-time professional; 2 full-time support.
Employer Identification Number: 381675780

1774
Slaughter (William E.), Jr. Foundation, Inc. ⌗
32949 Bingham Ln.
Birmingham 48010

Incorporated in 1959 in Michigan.
Donor(s): William E. Slaughter, Jr.
Financial data: (yr. ended 12/31/83): Assets, $1,626,295 (M); expenditures, $259,792, including $226,847 for 58 grants (high: $104,950; low: $10).
Purpose and activities: Grants primarily for youth agencies, higher education, Protestant church support, cultural programs, disease research, and social agencies.
Officers: William E. Slaughter, Jr.,* President and Treasurer; Betty P. Slaughter,* Vice-President; Miles Jaffe, Secretary.
Directors:* Herbert E. Everett.
Employer Identification Number: 386065616

1775
Steelcase Foundation ▼
c/o Steelcase, Inc.
P.O. Box 1967
Grand Rapids 49501   (616) 247-2229

Trust established in 1951 in Michigan.
Donor(s): Steelcase, Inc.
Financial data: (yr. ended 11/30/84): Assets, $14,746,790 (M); gifts received, $3,000,000; expenditures, $1,591,897, including $1,545,976 for 75 grants (high: $200,000; low: $450; average: $1,000-$50,000).
Purpose and activities: Giving limited to local projects or programs operating in areas of company operations, with emphasis on a community fund, higher education, cultural programs, and youth and social agencies.
Limitations: Giving limited to MI and areas of company operations, including Orange County, CA; Ashville, NC; Athens, AL; and Toronto, Canada. No grants to individuals or for endowment funds.
Publications: Annual report, application guidelines.
Application information: Application form required.
  Initial approach: Letter
  Deadline(s): None
  Board meeting date(s): Quarterly and as required
  Write: Clifford O. Boyce, Vice-President, Community Relations
Trustees: David D. Hunting, Sr., David D. Hunting, Jr., Frank H. Merlotti, Robert C. Pew, Peter M. Wege, Old Kent Bank and Trust Company.
Number of staff: 1 full-time support; 1 part-time support.
Employer Identification Number: 386050470

1776
Stephenson (The Edward C. and Hazel L.) Foundation
505 Hampton Rd.
Grosse Pointe Woods 48236   (313) 886-2659

Incorporated in 1969 in Michigan.
Donor(s): Edward C. Stephenson,† Hazel Stephenson.†
Financial data: (yr. ended 12/31/83): Assets, $2,485,543 (M); expenditures, $164,637, including $147,000 for 13 grants (high: $50,000; low: $2,000).
Purpose and activities: Grants to colleges and universities in four states for scholarships to individual students selected by the financial aid officer of the respective institutions.
Types of support awarded: Operating budgets, scholarship funds.
Limitations: Giving limited to MI, IN, OH, and KY; new grants generally only in MI. No grants to individuals or for capital funds or matching gifts.
Application information:
  Initial approach: Letter
  Copies of proposal: 1
  Deadline(s): Submit proposal in October or November; deadline November 15
  Board meeting date(s): December
  Final notification: About 30 days
  Write: Ludger A. Beauvais, Vice-President
Officers and Trustees: Henry K. Wallstrom, President and Treasurer; Charles R. Kinnaird, Vice-President and Secretary; Ludger A. Beauvais, Vice-President.
Number of staff: None.
Employer Identification Number: 386172669

1777
Stewart (Sarah A.) Foundation
P.O. Box 36358
Grosse Pointe Woods 48236

Established in 1980 in California.
Financial data: (yr. ended 9/30/82): Assets, $2,605,320 (M); expenditures, $67,721, including $56,000 for 4 grants (high: $40,000; low: $2,000).
Purpose and activities: Giving for charitable purposes, including a cancer research center.
Limitations: Giving primarily in CA.
Officers: Elizabeth Gibbs, President; Daniel M. Gibbs, M.D., Vice-President; Mary P. Daniel, Secretary; Nancy Richard, Treasurer.
Employer Identification Number: 953705192

1778
Stollman Foundation, The ⌗
2900 West Maple Rd.
Troy 48084

Incorporated in 1953 in Michigan.
Donor(s): Phillip Stollman, Max Stollman.
Financial data: (yr. ended 4/30/84): Assets, $196,903 (M); gifts received, $150,000; expenditures, $128,084, including $127,142 for 46 grants (high: $40,000; low: $100).

Purpose and activities: Grants largely for education, including religious education and higher education in Israel, temple support, and Jewish welfare funds, primarily in Michigan and New York.
Limitations: Giving primarily in MI and NY.
Officers and Directors: Max Stollman, President; Bernard Stollman, Gerald Stollman, Vice-Presidents; Phillip Stollman, Secretary and Treasurer.
Employer Identification Number: 386086417

1779
Stroh Brewery Foundation ⌗
1881 First National Bldg.
Detroit 48226

Established in 1965 in Michigan.
Donor(s): Stroh Brewery Company.
Financial data: (yr. ended 3/31/84): Assets, $455,352 (M); expenditures, $189,026, including $187,250 for 56 grants (high: $25,000; low: $500).
Purpose and activities: Primarily local giving, with support for cultural institutions, education, including higher education, social services, and a local community fund.
Limitations: Giving primarily in MI.
Officers and Trustees: Eric W. Stroh, President; David V. Van Howe, Secretary; Gari M. Stroh, Jr., Treasurer; John W. Stroh, Jr., Peter W. Stroh.
Employer Identification Number: 386108732

1780
Strosacker (The Charles J.) Foundation ▼
P.O. Box 2164
Midland 48641-2164

Incorporated in 1957 in Michigan.
Donor(s): Charles J. Strosacker.†
Financial data: (yr. ended 12/31/84): Assets, $10,912,000 (M); expenditures, $683,000, including $662,000 for 39 grants (high: $200,000; low: $400).
Purpose and activities: Primarily local giving, to assist and benefit political subdivisions of the state of Michigan and religious, charitable, artistic, or educational organizations.
Types of support awarded: General purposes, fellowships, endowment funds, building funds, operating budgets, special projects.
Limitations: Giving primarily in MI, with emphasis on the city of Midland. No grants to individuals, or for matching gifts; no loans.
Publications: Annual report, program policy statement, application guidelines.
Application information:
  Initial approach: Full proposal or letter
  Copies of proposal: 1
  Deadline(s): Submit proposal preferably in October or November
  Board meeting date(s): February, May, August, and November
  Write: Eugene C. Yehle, Chairman
Officers: Martha G. Arnold,* President; Ralph A. Cole, Vice-President and Treasurer; Patricia E. McKelvey, Secretary.

Trustees:* Eugene C. Yehle, Chairman; James B. Arnold, John S. Ludington, Donna T. Morris, Charles J. Thrune.
Number of staff: 1 part-time professional.
Employer Identification Number: 386062787

1781
Student Aid Foundation of Michigan ¤
8146 Macomb Rd.
Grosse Ile 48138

Incorporated in 1939 in Michigan.
Donor(s): Katherine Tuck Fund, The Hundred Club of Detroit, McGregor Fund, and others.
Financial data: (yr. ended 6/30/83): Assets, $67,356 (M); gifts received, $158,000; expenditures, $176,286, including $165,212 for 63 grants to individuals.
Purpose and activities: Giving limited to scholarships to graduating high school seniors from Wayne, Oakland, Macomb, Monroe, and Washtenaw counties, Michigan.
Types of support awarded: Student aid.
Limitations: Giving limited to Wayne, Oakland, Macomb, Monroe, and Washtenaw counties, MI.
Application information: Application form required.
  Deadline(s): February, for the school year beginning in September
  Write: William W. Wattenberg, M.D., President
Officers and Trustees: William W. Wattenberg, M.D., President; William L. Simpson, M.D., Vice-President; Robert H. Gregg, M.D., Secretary; James W. Furlong, Treasurer; Richard F. Huegli.
Employer Identification Number: 381497206

1782
Tiscornia Foundation, Inc., The
643 Graves St.
St. Joseph 49085   (616) 982-2335

Incorporated in 1942 in Michigan.
Donor(s): Auto Specialties Manufacturing Company, Lambert Brake Corporation, James W. Tiscornia,† Waldo V. Tiscornia.†
Financial data: (yr. ended 11/30/82): Assets, $2,060,541 (M); gifts received, $45,284; expenditures, $139,621, including $103,155 for 51 grants (high: $33,880; low: $25) and $12,219 for 9 grants to individuals.
Purpose and activities: Primarily local giving, with emphasis on health, youth, community funds, and higher education.
Types of support awarded: Continuing support, annual campaigns, seed money, emergency funds, building funds, equipment, employee related scholarships.
Limitations: Giving primarily in MI. No grants to individuals (except for scholarships to children of company employees), or for endowment funds, research, or matching gifts; no loans.
Application information:
  Initial approach: Letter or full proposal
  Copies of proposal: 1
  Deadline(s): Submit proposal preferably in October; deadline October 31
  Board meeting date(s): January

Write: Laurianne T. Davis, Secretary
Officers and Trustees: Lester Tiscornia, President; Howard H. Paxson, Vice-President; Laurianne T. Davis, Secretary; Henry H. Tippett, Treasurer; Robert C. Miller, Victor C. Palenske.
Employer Identification Number: 381777343

1783
Towsley (The Harry A. and Margaret D.) Foundation ▼
670 City Center Bldg.
220 East Huron St.
Ann Arbor 48104   (313) 662-6777

Incorporated in 1959 in Michigan.
Donor(s): Margaret D. Towsley.
Financial data: (yr. ended 12/31/84): Assets, $13,260,098 (M); expenditures, $776,201, including $732,500 for 28 grants (high: $100,000; low: $1,000; average: $5,000-$25,000).
Purpose and activities: Broad purposes; local giving, with emphasis on medical and preschool education, social services, and continuing education and research in the health sciences.
Types of support awarded: Continuing support, annual campaigns, building funds, endowment funds, matching funds, special projects.
Limitations: Giving limited to MI, with emphasis on Ann Arbor and Washtenaw County. No grants to individuals, or for travel, scholarships, fellowships, or conferences; no loans.
Publications: Annual report, application guidelines.
Application information:
  Initial approach: Letter and proposal
  Copies of proposal: 2
  Deadline(s): Submit proposal between January and March; deadline March 31
  Board meeting date(s): April, July, September, and December
  Final notification: 60 to 90 days
  Write: Margaret Ann Riecker, President
Officers: Margaret Ann Riecker,* President; Margaret D. Towsley,* Vice-President; John E. Riecker, Secretary; C. Wendell Dunbar,* Treasurer.
Trustees:* Harry A. Towsley, M.D., Chairman; Judith T. Alexander, Robert L. Bring, Lynn T. Hamblin, Janis T. Poteat, Susan T. Wyland.
Number of staff: None.
Employer Identification Number: 386091798

1784
Tracy (Emmet and Frances) Fund ¤
400 Renaissance Center, 35th Fl.
Detroit 48243

Incorporated in 1951 in Michigan.
Donor(s): Alma Piston Company, G.P.D., Inc., Snow Manufacturing Company.
Financial data: (yr. ended 11/30/83): Assets, $964,396 (M); gifts received, $500,000; expenditures, $665,426, including $662,081 for 241 grants (high: $100,000; low: $75).

Purpose and activities: Broad purposes; emphasis on Roman Catholic religious organizations and missionary groups; some support for hospitals and education.
Limitations: Giving primarily in MI.
Officers: Emmet E. Tracy, President; Frances A. Tracy, Vice-President; Paul R. Trigg, Jr., Secretary; Emmet E. Tracy, Jr., Treasurer.
Employer Identification Number: 386057796

1785
Tuck (Katherine) Fund
2500 Comerica Bldg.
Detroit 48226   (313) 963-6420

Incorporated in 1935 in Michigan.
Donor(s): Katherine Tuck.
Financial data: (yr. ended 12/31/82): Assets, $6,199,567 (M); expenditures, $1,072,262, including $1,000,800 for 37 grants (high: $500,000; low: $100).
Purpose and activities: Broad purposes; primarily local giving, with emphasis on handicapped children, the blind, music and musical education, and scholarship funds; support also for nursing, youth and social agencies, and health services.
Types of support awarded: General purposes, building funds, operating budgets, scholarship funds.
Limitations: Giving primarily in MI. No grants to individuals.
Application information:
  Initial approach: Letter
  Copies of proposal: 1
  Board meeting date(s): Quarterly
  Write: Cleveland Thurber, President
Officers and Trustees: Cleveland Thurber, President; Peter P. Thurber, Vice-President and Secretary; George E. Parker, III, Vice-President; Richard B. Gushee, Treasurer.
Employer Identification Number: 386040079

1786
Upjohn (The Harold and Grace) Foundation
c/o The American National Bank and Trust Company of Michigan
P.O. Box 2769
Kalamazoo 49003   (616) 383-6956

Incorporated in 1958 in Michigan.
Donor(s): Grace G. Upjohn.†
Financial data: (yr. ended 10/31/82): Assets, $3,532,569 (M); expenditures, $258,213, including $233,500 for 19 grants (high: $35,000; low: $2,000).
Purpose and activities: Charitable purposes; primarily local giving, with emphasis on youth agencies, family service agencies, health services, higher education, and population control; grants primarily for specific projects, especially to provide seed money for new projects whose continuing expenses will be met by other sources.
Types of support awarded: Seed money, special projects.
Limitations: Giving primarily in MI. No grants to individuals, or for operating budgets, or annual campaigns.

Publications: Annual report, program policy statement, application guidelines.
Application information:
Initial approach: Full proposal
Copies of proposal: 1
Board meeting date(s): Semiannually as required
Write: Floyd L. Parks, Secretary-Treasurer
Officers: Christopher U. Light,* President; Edwin E. Meader,* Vice-President; Floyd L. Parks, Secretary-Treasurer.
Trustees:* Gene R. Conrad, James C. Cristy, William A. Kirkpatrick.
Employer Identification Number: 386052963

1787
Upjohn (W. E.) Unemployment Trustee Corporation
300 South Westnedge Ave.
Kalamazoo 49007   (616) 343-5541

Incorporated in 1932 in Michigan.
Donor(s): W.E. Upjohn.†
Financial data: (yr. ended 12/31/84): Assets, $23,202,800 (M); expenditures, $1,752,703, including $111,162 for 7 grants (high: $33,500; low: $2,500) and $731,680 for 4 foundation-administered programs.
Purpose and activities: A private operating foundation; supports research into the causes, effects, prevention, and alleviation of unemployment; funds used to support W.E. Upjohn Institute for Employment Research.
Types of support awarded: Research.
Limitations: No grants for building or for endowment funds, operating budgets, or matching gifts; no loans.
Publications: Program policy statement, application guidelines.
Application information:
Initial approach: Letter
Copies of proposal: 2
Deadline(s): None
Board meeting date(s): May and December
Final notification: 90 days
Write: Robert G. Spiegelman, Director
Officers and Trustees: P.S. Parish, Chairman; J.H. Duncan, Secretary-Treasurer; John T. Bernhard, David Breneman, C.C. Gibbons, Genevieve U. Gilmore, Mrs. Ray T. Parfet, Jr., Paul H. Todd, E. Gifford Upjohn, M.D.
Number of staff: 25 full-time professional; 25 full-time support; 3 part-time support.
Employer Identification Number: 381360419

1788
VanAndel (Jay and Betty) Foundation ¤
7186 Windy Hill Rd. Southeast
Grand Rapids 49506

Established in 1963.
Donor(s): Jay VanAndel, Betty VanAndel.
Financial data: (yr. ended 12/31/83): Assets, $5,160,794 (M); gifts received, $300,000; expenditures, $447,462, including $439,400 for 83 grants (high: $30,000; low: $50).
Purpose and activities: Largely local giving, with emphasis on Christian religious activities, including higher and secondary education.
Limitations: Giving primarily in MI.

Officers and Trustees: Jay VanAndel, President; Betty VanAndel, Vice-President; William J. Halliday, Jr., Secretary; C. Dale Discher, Treasurer.
Employer Identification Number: 237066716

1789
Vicksburg Foundation
c/o First of America-Michigan
Kalamazoo 49007   (616) 383-9291

Incorporated in 1943 in Michigan.
Financial data: (yr. ended 12/31/84): Assets, $1,700,000 (M); expenditures, $90,000, including $74,000 for grants (high: $34,000; low: $500).
Purpose and activities: To coordinate and unify the charitable and benevolent activities of the incorporators; primarily local giving, with emphasis on community programs.
Types of support awarded: Operating budgets, special projects.
Limitations: Giving primarily in MI. No grants for endowment funds.
Application information:
Initial approach: Letter or full proposal
Copies of proposal: 1
Deadline(s): Submit proposal in February, May, August, or November
Board meeting date(s): March, June, September, and December
Write: Frederick S. Kirkpatrick, Secretary-Treasurer
Officers: Maxwell D. Bardeen,* President; Frederick S. Kirkpatrick, Secretary-Treasurer.
Directors:* Dennis Boyle, Meredith Clark, Gordon Daniels, William Oswalt.
Employer Identification Number: 386065237

1790
Vollbrecht (Frederick A.) Foundation ¤
770 S. Adams Rd., Suite 210
Birmingham 48011   (313) 646-7440

Incorporated in 1959 in Michigan.
Donor(s): Frederick A. Vollbrecht.†
Financial data: (yr. ended 12/31/82): Assets, $1,338,326 (M); expenditures, $110,996, including $97,000 for 24 grants (high: $30,000; low: $2,000).
Purpose and activities: Broad purposes; primarily local giving, with emphasis on higher education; support also for health agencies, youth agencies, social services, and aid to the handicapped.
Limitations: Giving primarily in MI. No grants to individuals.
Application information:
Initial approach: Proposal
Copies of proposal: 1
Deadline(s): None
Board meeting date(s): June
Write: Carl W. McConkey, Vice-President
Officers and Trustees: Mervyn B. Walsh, President and Treasurer; Carl W. McConkey, Vice-President; George R. Waltensperger, Secretary.
Employer Identification Number: 386056173

1791
Walker (L. C. and Margaret) Foundation ▼
(formerly The Shaw-Walker Foundation)
c/o Comerica Bank-Hackley
161 Muskegon Mall
Muskegon 49443

Incorporated in 1951 in Michigan.
Donor(s): Louis Carlisle Walker,† Shaw Walker Company.
Financial data: (yr. ended 12/31/82): Assets, $12,228,363 (M); expenditures, $1,597,218, including $1,421,513 for 21 grants (high: $700,000; low: $1,000).
Purpose and activities: Broad purposes, with emphasis on secondary and higher education.
Officers: Shaw Walker,* President and Treasurer; Betty Walker, Vice-President; Monica Bauman, Secretary.
Trustees:* Walker McKinney, Margaret Walker Spofford, Amy Walker.
Employer Identification Number: 386060045

1792
Wenger (Henry E. and Consuelo S.) Foundation, Inc. ¤
8916 Gale Rd.
Pontiac 48054

Incorporated in 1959 in Michigan.
Donor(s): Consuelo S. Wenger.
Financial data: (yr. ended 12/31/83): Assets, $4,094,682 (M); expenditures, $336,586, including $259,414 for 75 grants (high: $25,000; low: $150).
Purpose and activities: Support for secondary and higher education, hospitals, and cultural programs.
Officers and Directors:* Henry Penn Wenger,* President; Miles Jaffe, Diane Wenger Wilson,* Vice-Presidents; William E. Slaughter, Jr.,* Treasurer.
Employer Identification Number: 386077419

1793
Whirlpool Foundation ▼
2000 U.S. 33, North
Benton Harbor 49022   (616) 926-3461

Incorporated in 1951 in Michigan.
Donor(s): Whirlpool Corporation.
Financial data: (yr. ended 12/31/84): Assets, $9,575,556 (M); gifts received, $2,400,000; expenditures, $2,208,206, including $1,831,082 for 283 grants (high: $105,500; low: $100; average: $250-$30,000), $233,500 for 110 grants to individuals and $109,398 for employee matching gifts.
Purpose and activities: Broad purposes; grants generally limited to institutions located in plant communities, including community funds, youth and social welfare agencies, cultural programs, and higher education, including scholarships for children of corporation employees and employee matching gifts.
Types of support awarded: Matching funds, operating budgets, annual campaigns, emergency funds, building funds, equipment, research, employee related scholarships, continuing support, employee matching gifts.

Limitations: Giving limited to communities where major company units are located. No grants to individuals (except company-employee scholarships), or for endowment funds; no loans.

Application information:

Initial approach: Letter or telephone

Copies of proposal: 1

Board meeting date(s): As required

Final notification: 30 to 60 days

Write: Patricia O'Day, Secretary

Officers: George E. Wardeberg,* President; Stephen E. Upton,* Vice-President; Patricia O'Day, Secretary; William B. Naylor, Treasurer.

Trustees:* William K. Emery, David R. Whitwam.

Number of staff: 1 full-time professional.

Employer Identification Number: 386077342

1794

White Foundation, The ☒

4800 Avondale
Bloomfield Hills 48013

Established in 1945.

Financial data: (yr. ended 12/31/83): Assets, $584,039 (M); gifts received, $42,220; expenditures, $182,830, including $104,970 for 15 grants (high: $26,725; low: $50).

Purpose and activities: Primarily local giving to Christian churches and a college.

Types of support awarded: General purposes.

Limitations: Giving primarily in MI.

Officer: Hugh A. White, President.

Employer Identification Number: 386054883

1795

Whiteley (The John and Elizabeth) Foundation ☒

c/o First of America Bank-Central
101 S. Washington Square
Lansing 48933   (517) 374-5436

Incorporated in 1955 in Michigan.

Donor(s): Mrs. Nellie M. Zimmerman.†

Financial data: (yr. ended 12/31/83): Assets, $1,544,188 (M); expenditures, $106,692, including $37,155 for 6 grants (high: $8,980; low: $750) and $15,000 for 12 grants to individuals.

Purpose and activities: To aid needy and deserving students of Ingham County to acquire a business education; grants largely for scholarships and Protestant church support.

Types of support awarded: Student aid.

Limitations: Giving limited to Ingham County, MI.

Application information: Application form required for scholarships.

Deadline(s): None

Write: Joseph A. Caruso

Trustees: Hubert B. Bates, Richard F. Burmeister, Romayne E. Hicks, Harry D. Hubbard, Richard P. Lyman, Jonathan R. White.

Employer Identification Number: 381558108

1796

Whiting Foundation, The ☒

901 Citizens Bank Bldg.
Flint 48502   (313) 238-2701

Incorporated in 1940 in Michigan.

Donor(s): Members of the Johnson family.

Financial data: (yr. ended 6/30/83): Assets, $5,772,493 (M); gifts received, $139,450; expenditures, $349,159, including $326,103 for 38 grants (high: $100,000; low: $100).

Purpose and activities: Broad purposes; largely local giving to further secular and religious education and research of all kinds; to aid and improve the physical, financial, mental, and moral condition of the poor, the sick, the young, the aged, and the disabled among all classes. Support nationally for cancer research.

Limitations: Giving primarily in MI.

Application information:

Initial approach: Concise proposal

Copies of proposal: 1

Deadline(s): April 30

Write: Donald E. Johnson, Secretary

Officers and Trustees: Alice D. Johnson, President; Max M. Greenfield, Vice-President; Donald E. Johnson, Secretary and Treasurer; Mary Alice J. Heaton, Donald E. Johnson, Jr., Linda W.J. Utley.

Employer Identification Number: 386056693

1797

Whiting (Macauley and Helen Dow) Foundation ☒

121-1/2 McDonald St.
Midland 48640
Mailing address: P.O. Box 1980, Sun Valley, ID 83353

Incorporated in 1957 in Michigan.

Financial data: (yr. ended 12/31/81): Assets, $1,842,442 (M); expenditures, $154,812, including $147,366 for 18 grants (high: $45,000; low: $500).

Purpose and activities: Charitable purposes, with emphasis on higher education and hospitals; grants only to institutions with which trustees are familiar.

Limitations: Giving primarily in MI. No grants to individuals.

Application information:

Initial approach: Letter

Copies of proposal: 1

Board meeting date(s): At least twice a year

Write: Helen Dow Whiting, Treasurer

Officers and Trustees: Macauley Whiting, President; Mary Macauley Whiting, Secretary; Helen Dow Whiting, Treasurer.

Employer Identification Number: 386058078

1798

Wickes (Harvey Randall) Foundation ▼

Plaza North, Suite 472
4800 Fashion Square Blvd.
Saginaw 48604   (517) 799-1850

Incorporated in 1945 in Michigan.

Donor(s): Harvey Randall Wickes,† members of the Wickes family, and others.

Financial data: (yr. ended 12/31/83): Assets, $13,252,916 (M); expenditures, $637,658, including $551,167 for 35 grants (high: $170,000; low: $50).

Purpose and activities: Primarily local giving for education, including higher education; a community fund and civic affairs, hospitals and a rehabilitation center, cultural activities, social services and youth agencies .

Types of support awarded: Building funds, continuing support, equipment, operating budgets, scholarship funds.

Limitations: Giving limited to the Saginaw, MI, area. No grants to individuals.

Application information:

Initial approach: Letter

Copies of proposal: 1

Deadline(s): Submit proposal preferably one month prior to meeting

Board meeting date(s): January, April, June, and October

Write: Melvin J. Zahnow, President

Officers and Trustees: Melvin J. Zahnow, President and Treasurer; G.A. Barber, Vice-President; J.V. Finkbeiner, Secretary; F.N. Andersen, R.G. App, H.E. Braun, Jr., M.P. Heavenrich, Jr., F.M. Johnson, William Kessel, D.F. Wallace, L.J. Yeo.

Number of staff: 1 full-time professional; 1 part-time support.

Employer Identification Number: 386061470

1799

Wilson (Lula C.) Trust

c/o National Bank of Detroit
1116 West Long Lake Rd.
Bloomfield Hills 48013   (313) 645-6600

Trust established in 1963 in Michigan.

Donor(s): Lula C. Wilson.†

Financial data: (yr. ended 12/31/84): Assets, $1,303,417 (M); expenditures, $106,000, including $87,674 for 20 grants (high: $10,000; low: $1,550; average: $2,000-$5,000).

Purpose and activities: Local giving with emphasis on higher and secondary education, cultural programs, youth agencies, and community service agencies.

Types of support awarded: Operating budgets, continuing support, annual campaigns, seed money, emergency funds, building funds, equipment.

Limitations: Giving limited to Pontiac and Oakland County, MI. No grants to individuals, or for endowment funds, research, deficit financing, land acquisition, special projects, publications, conferences, scholarships and fellowships, or matching gifts; no loans.

Publications: 990-PF.

Application information:

Initial approach: Letter

Copies of proposal: 1

Deadline(s): None

Board meeting date(s): As required

Final notification: 1 month

Write: Frederick H. Gravelle, Vice-President

Trustee: National Bank of Detroit (Frederick H. Gravelle, Vice-President).

Number of staff: None.

Employer Identification Number: 386058895

1800
Wilson (Matilda R.) Fund ☒
100 Renaissance Center, Suite 3377
Detroit 48243   (313) 259-3232

Incorporated in 1944 in Michigan.
Donor(s): Matilda R. Wilson,† Alfred G.
Wilson.†
Financial data: (yr. ended 12/31/83): Assets,
$19,645,455 (M); expenditures, $806,277,
including $682,900 for 25 grants (high:
$110,000; low: $1,000).
Purpose and activities: Broad purposes;
primarily local giving, with emphasis on
medical research, higher education, the arts,
and social and youth agencies.
Types of support awarded: Operating
budgets, general purposes, building funds,
equipment, endowment funds, research, special
projects, scholarship funds, matching funds.
Limitations: Giving primarily in MI. No grants
to individuals; no loans.
Application information:
 Initial approach: Full proposal
 Copies of proposal: 1
 Board meeting date(s): January, April, July,
  and October
 Write: Frederick C. Nash, President
Officers and Trustees: Frederick C. Nash,
President; Pierre V. Heftler, Vice-President;
Henry T. Bodman, Treasurer.
Employer Identification Number: 386087665

1801
**Winkelman Brothers Apparel
 Foundation** ☒
25 Parsons St.
Detroit 48201

Trust established in 1954 in Michigan.
Donor(s): Winkelman Stores, Inc.
Financial data: (yr. ended 12/31/83): Assets,
$239,119 (M); gifts received, $100,000;
expenditures, $188,332, including $187,637
for 66 grants (high: $84,000; low: $100).
Purpose and activities: Primarily local giving,
with emphasis on a Jewish welfare fund, higher
education, community funds, and community
development.
Limitations: Giving primarily in MI.
Trustees: Alan E. Schwartz, E.S. Simon,
Anthony J. Vinci, Stanley J. Winkelman.
Employer Identification Number: 386041568

1802
**Winship Memorial Scholarship
 Foundation** ☒
c/o Comerica Bank-Battle Creek, Trust Division
25 W. Michigan Mall
Battle Creek 49017   (616) 966-6340

Established in 1961 in Michigan.
Financial data: (yr. ended 12/31/83): Assets,
$1,675,189 (M); gifts received, $1,000;
expenditures, $126,406, including $109,060
for 92 grants to individuals.
Purpose and activities: Local giving for
scholarships.
Types of support awarded: Student aid.
Limitations: Giving limited to Battle Creek, MI.

Application information: Application form
required.
 Deadline(s): November 15
Trustee: Comerica Bank-Battle Creek.
Employer Identification Number: 386092543

1803
Wolverine Charitable Foundation ☒
c/o Union Bank & Trust Co.
200 Ottawa N.W.
Grand Rapids 49503

Trust established in 1959 in Michigan.
Donor(s): Wolverine Shoe and Tanning
Corporation.
Financial data: (yr. ended 12/31/83): Assets,
$383,275 (M); gifts received, $225,000;
expenditures, $284,289, including $279,641
for 148 grants (high: $106,300; low: $10).
Purpose and activities: Giving primarily for
higher education; support also for community
funds, cultural programs, youth agencies, and
social services.
Officer: Lester Hyde, Manager.
Trustee: Union Bank & Trust Co.
Employer Identification Number: 386056939

1804
Youth Foundation of America, The
7 Pennsylvania Plaza
Petoskey 49770   (616) 347-3907

Incorporated in 1947 in Michigan.
Financial data: (yr. ended 12/31/82): Assets,
$172,180 (M); gifts received, $166,478;
expenditures, $153,062, including $132,000
for 19 grants (high: $17,000; low: $1,500).
Purpose and activities: Support of local
summer camps for underprivileged and
handicapped children.
Limitations: Giving limited to MI. No grants to
individuals.
Application information:
 Initial approach: Letter
 Copies of proposal: 1
 Board meeting date(s): Annually
 Write: Paul W. Brown, Vice-President
Officers and Trustees: Clarine R. Bales,
President; Paul W. Brown, Vice-President and
Secretary-Treasurer; Kimberly Hines.
Number of staff: None.
Employer Identification Number: 386090960

MINNESOTA

1805
**Alliss (Charles and Ellora) Educational
 Foundation** ▼
c/o First Trust Company of St. Paul
W-555 First National Bank Bldg.
St. Paul 55101   (612) 291-5114

Trust established in 1958 in Minnesota.
Donor(s): Charles C. Alliss,† Ellora Martha
Alliss.†
Financial data: (yr. ended 12/31/84): Assets,
$38,700,000 (M); expenditures, $2,940,370,
including $2,791,900 for 22 grants (high:
$404,400; low: $30,000; average: $30,000-
$200,000).
Purpose and activities: To further the
education of young people by granting
scholarships, fellowships, gifts, and awards;
grants made in lump sums solely to Minnesota
institutions in support of undergraduate aid
programs administered by the grantee
institutions.
Types of support awarded: Scholarship funds,
continuing support.
Limitations: Giving limited to MN. No grants
to individuals, or for general purposes, capital
funds, endowment funds, research, operating
budgets, special projects, matching gifts; no
loans.
Application information:
 Initial approach: Letter with background
 Copies of proposal: 1
 Deadline(s): Submit proposal preferably in
  August and September; no set deadline
 Board meeting date(s): March, June,
  September, and December
 Final notification: 3 months
 Write: Jeffrey T. Peterson, Secretary
Trustees: Elmer L. Anderson, Sidney Barrows,
Richard L. Gunderson, Frank Hammond, Harry
L. Holtz, First Trust Company of St. Paul.
Number of staff: None.
Employer Identification Number: 416011054

1806
**Alworth (Marshall H. and Nellie)
 Memorial Fund**
604 Alworth Bldg.
Duluth 55802   (218) 722-9366

Incorporated in 1949 in Minnesota.
Donor(s): Marshall W. Alworth.†
Financial data: (yr. ended 12/31/83): Assets,
$2,574,746 (M); gifts received, $1,740,450;
expenditures, $603,078, including $504,420
for 538 grants to individuals.
Purpose and activities: To assist high school
graduates from Duluth and northern Minnesota
who intend to specialize in the sciences,
including chemistry, physics, mathematics,
geology, biological sciences, engineering, and
medicine.
Types of support awarded: Student aid.

Limitations: Giving limited to students in Duluth and northern MN. No grants for building or endowment funds, or matching gifts; no loans.
Publications: Program policy statement, application guidelines.
Application information: Application form required.
  Initial approach: Letter
  Copies of proposal: 1
  Deadline(s): Submit proposal preferably in December through February; deadline March 1
  Board meeting date(s): June
  Final notification: In July
  Write: Raymond W. Darland, President
Officers: Raymond W. Darland, President and Executive Director; Mrs. John H. Lewman, Jr.,* Vice-President; John M. Donovan,* Secretary; Donald B. Crassweller,* Treasurer.
Directors:* James H. Claypool, Evan R. Danson, William E. Jacott, M.D., Joseph A. Pittel.
Number of staff: 2 full-time professional.
Employer Identification Number: 410797340

1807
American Hoist and Derrick Foundation
63 South Robert St.
St. Paul 55107   (612) 293-4959

Incorporated in 1958 in Minnesota.
Donor(s): American Hoist & Derrick Company, Machinery Investment Corporation.
Financial data: (yr. ended 12/31/82): Assets, $162,411 (M); gifts received, $400,000; expenditures, $321,434, including $321,413 for 46 grants (high: $130,000).
Purpose and activities: General purposes; giving largely to community funds and higher education including support for company-employee scholarships; additional support for civic and social agencies.
Types of support awarded: Operating budgets, annual campaigns, building funds, scholarship funds, employee related scholarships.
Limitations: No grants for matching gifts; no loans.
Application information:
  Initial approach: Full proposal
  Copies of proposal: 2
  Deadline(s): None
  Board meeting date(s): As required
  Final notification: 30 days
  Write: William B. Faulkner, President
Officers: Robert P. Fox, Chairman; William B. Faulkner, President; Charles G. Truzinski, Secretary-Treasurer.
Number of staff: None.
Employer Identification Number: 416080179

1808
Andersen (Elmer L. & Eleanor J.) Foundation
First Trust Company
1st National Bank Bldg.
St. Paul 55101   (612) 291-5114

Established in Minnesota.

Donor(s): Elmer L. Andersen, Eleanor J. Andersen.
Financial data: (yr. ended 11/30/84): Assets, $1,863,017 (M); expenditures, $104,254, including $99,040 for 36 grants (high: $33,540; low: $200).
Purpose and activities: Primarily local giving for higher education and community services.
Types of support awarded: Operating budgets, publications.
Limitations: Giving primarily in MN. No grants to individuals.
Publications: 990-PF.
Application information:
  Initial approach: Proposal
  Deadline(s): Submit proposal in February, May, August and November; deadline 1 week before board meetings
  Board meeting date(s): December 15, March 15, June 15, and September 15
  Final notification: 3 months
  Write: Jeffrey Peterson
Officers: Elmer L. Andersen, President; Eleanor J. Andersen, Vice-President; Samuel H. Morgan, Secretary.
Directors: Julian Andersen, Barbara B. Miller.
Number of staff: 1 part-time professional.
Employer Identification Number: 416032984

1809
Andersen Foundation ▼
c/o Andersen Corporation
Bayport 55003   (612) 439-5150

Incorporated in 1959 in Minnesota.
Donor(s): Fred C. Andersen.†
Financial data: (yr. ended 12/31/82): Assets, $35,945,614 (M); gifts received, $646,713; expenditures, $2,419,567, including $2,353,172 for 61 grants (high: $65,000; low: $200).
Purpose and activities: General giving, with emphasis on higher education; grants also for the handicapped, medical research, youth agencies, and hospitals.
Application information:
  Board meeting date(s): As required
  Write: Earl C. Swanson, Vice-President
Officers and Directors: Katherine B. Andersen, President; Earl C. Swanson, Vice-President and Secretary; Roy H. Sakrison, Treasurer; Keith R. Clements.
Employer Identification Number: 416020920

1810
Andersen (Hugh J.) Foundation
c/o Baywood Corporation
287 Central Ave.
Bayport 55003   (612) 439-1557

Established in 1962.
Donor(s): Hugh J. Andersen,† Jane K. Andersen.
Financial data: (yr. ended 2/29/84): Assets, $8,559,967 (M); gifts received, $100,000; expenditures, $383,362, including $366,399 for 40 grants (high: $108,000; low: $50).
Purpose and activities: Primarily local giving, with emphasis on social agencies, youth agencies, cultural programs, education, and medical research.

Types of support awarded: Research, operating budgets, seed money, building funds, special projects.
Limitations: Giving primarily in MN. No grants to individuals, or for endowment funds, scholarships, fellowships, or matching gifts; no loans.
Publications: Application guidelines.
Application information:
  Initial approach: Letter or proposal
  Copies of proposal: 1
  Deadline(s): Submit proposal preferably in March, June, September, or December
  Board meeting date(s): May, August, November, and February
  Write: Carol F. Andersen, President
Officers: Carol F. Andersen, President; Sarah J. Andersen, Vice-President; Christine E. Andersen, Treasurer.
Number of staff: 2.
Employer Identification Number: 416020914

1811
Andreas Foundation, The ☐
c/o Archer-Daniels-Midlands Co.
Third and Harper Sts., Box 728
Mankato 56001   (507) 625-7947

Incorporated in 1945 in Iowa.
Donor(s): Dwayne O. Andreas, Lowell W. Andreas, Glenn A. Andreas, and others.
Financial data: (yr. ended 11/30/83): Assets, $1,762,803 (M); gifts received, $408,000; expenditures, $1,166,704, including $1,147,320 for 121 grants (high: $204,600; low: $25).
Purpose and activities: Broad purposes; general giving, with emphasis on higher and secondary education, civil rights and economic opportunities for minority groups, and cultural programs; some support for hospitals, public policy research, churches, and youth agencies.
Limitations: No grants to individuals.
Application information:
  Initial approach: Full proposal
  Copies of proposal: 1
  Deadline(s): Submit proposal in first quarter of year
  Board meeting date(s): Meets as required
  Write: Dwayne O. Andreas, President
Officers and Trustees: Dwayne O. Andreas, President; Lowell W. Andreas, Executive Vice-President and Treasurer; Michael D. Andreas, Vice-President and Secretary; Dorothy Inez Andreas, Terry Lynn Bevis, Sandra Andreas McMurtrie.
Employer Identification Number: 416017057

1812
Apache Foundation
730 Second Ave. South
Minneapolis 55402-2498   (612) 347-8700

Established in 1960 in Minnesota.
Donor(s): Dean G. Newman, Apache Corporation, and subsidiaries.
Financial data: (yr. ended 12/31/84): Assets, $16,512 (M); gifts received, $165,899; expenditures, $165,985, including $165,985 for 125 grants (high: $27,850; low: $25).

Purpose and activities: Primarily local giving, with emphasis on programs and agencies that have the potential to create new approaches to meet changing social needs; support for community funds, higher education, public policy associations, youth agencies, and cultural programs.
Types of support awarded: Matching funds, general purposes, operating budgets, annual campaigns.
Limitations: Giving primarily in MN, with emphasis on areas of Apache Corporation operations.
Application information:
  Initial approach: Full proposal
  Deadline(s): None
  Write: Dean G. Newman, President
Officers: Dean G. Newman,* President; Beatrice L. Huston, Vice-President and Secretary; John Buske, Treasurer.
Directors:* John A. Kocur, Chairman; S. James Nelson.
Employer Identification Number: 416031039

1813
Athwin Foundation
901 Midwest Plaza East
Minneapolis 55402   (612) 340-3618

Trust established in 1956 in Minnesota.
Donor(s): Atherton Bean, Winifred W. Bean.
Financial data: (yr. ended 12/31/84): Assets, $4,131,844 (M); expenditures, $437,678, including $424,197 for 48 grants (high: $72,500; low: $50; average: $1,000-$5,000).
Purpose and activities: Broad purposes; primarily local giving; support for educational, cultural, religious, and community welfare programs.
Types of support awarded: Operating budgets, special projects.
Limitations: Giving primarily in Minneapolis-St. Paul, MN; Phoenix, AZ; and Claremont, CA. No grants to individuals, or for scholarships and fellowships; no loans.
Publications: Annual report.
Application information:
  Initial approach: Proposal
  Copies of proposal: 5
  Deadline(s): None
  Board meeting date(s): Quarterly
  Final notification: 60 days
  Write: Atherton Bean, Trustee
Trustees: Atherton Bean, Bruce W. Bean, Eleanor Nolan, Mary F. Bean, Winifred W. Bean.
Number of staff: 1 part-time support.
Employer Identification Number: 416021773

1814
Baker Foundation
4900 IDS Center
Minneapolis 55402   (612) 332-7691

Trust established in 1947; incorporated in 1954 in Minnesota.
Donor(s): Morris T. Baker.†
Financial data: (yr. ended 12/31/83): Assets, $1,659,387 (M); expenditures, $157,159, including $148,733 for 32 grants (high: $25,000; low: $100).

Purpose and activities: Broad purposes; primarily local giving, with emphasis on medical research, higher education, community funds, conservation, youth agencies, and music.
Limitations: Giving primarily in MN. No grants to individuals.
Application information:
  Initial approach: Letter
  Copies of proposal: 1
  Board meeting date(s): As required
  Write: William M. Baker, President
Officers: William M. Baker,* President; Roger L. Baker,* David C. Sherman,* Vice-Presidents; Margaret M. Rieck, Secretary; James W. Peter,* Treasurer.
Directors:* Morris T. Baker, Mrs. William M. Baker, Mary Baker-Philbin, Tobias R. Philbin, Charles C. Pineo III, Linda Baker Pineo, Sandra B. Sherman.
Employer Identification Number: 416022591

1815
Bayport Foundation, Inc. ▼ ⌑
c/o Andersen Corporation
Bayport 55003   (612) 439-1557

Incorporated in 1941 in Minnesota.
Donor(s): Andersen Corporation, and the Andersen families.
Financial data: (yr. ended 11/30/83): Assets, $9,476,744 (M); expenditures, $956,053, including $914,601 for 107 grants (high: $500,000; low: $100; average: $500-$15,000).
Purpose and activities: Broad purposes; primarily local giving, with emphasis on medical education and research, educational programs, community projects, hospitals, youth agencies, and religious organizations.
Limitations: Giving primarily in MN. No grants to individuals.
Application information:
  Write: W.A Wellman, President
Officers and Trustees: W.A. Wellman, President; A.D. Hulings, Mary A. Hulings, Harold C. Meissner, Vice-Presidents; Loren R. Croone, Secretary and Treasurer; Katherine B. Andersen, Earl C. Swanson.
Employer Identification Number: 416020912

1816
Beim Foundation, The
6750 France Ave. South
Minneapolis 55435   (612) 920-1556

Incorporated in 1957 in Minnesota.
Donor(s): N.C. Beim,† R.N. Beim.
Financial data: (yr. ended 12/31/83): Assets, $2,298,000 (M); gifts received, $33,300; expenditures, $95,200, including $95,000 for 38 grants (high: $6,000; low: $250; average: $1,000-$5,000).
Purpose and activities: Broad purposes; local giving primarily for capital expenditures rather than operating expenses. Giving to youth agencies, the handicapped, and higher education.
Types of support awarded: Seed money, building funds, equipment.

Limitations: Giving limited to Minneapolis, MN and vicinity. No grants to individuals, or for operating budgets, continuing support, annual campaigns, emergency funds, deficit financing; no loans.
Application information:
  Initial approach: Full proposal
  Copies of proposal: 1
  Deadline(s): September 30
  Board meeting date(s): October and December
  Final notification: By December 15th
  Write: William H. Beim, President
Officers and Directors: William H. Beim, President; Raymond N. Beim, Vice-President; William H. Beim, Jr., Secretary-Treasurer; Judith McKim.
Number of staff: None.
Employer Identification Number: 416022529

1817
Bell (James F.) Foundation ⌑
10000 Hwy. 55 West, Suite 450
Minneapolis 55441

Trust established in 1955 in Minnesota.
Donor(s): James Ford Bell.†
Financial data: (yr. ended 12/31/83): Assets, $5,348,816 (M); expenditures, $367,575, including $300,628 for 40 grants (high: $60,000; low: $250).
Purpose and activities: Primarily local giving, with emphasis on a local university library and cultural programs; support also for wildlife preservation and conservation, and youth agencies.
Limitations: Giving primarily in MN.
Officer: L.L. Arnevik, Executive Secretary.
Trustees: Charles H. Bell, Ford W. Bell, Samuel H. Bell.
Employer Identification Number: 416023099

1818
Bemis Company Foundation ▼
800 Northstar Center
Minneapolis 55402   (612) 340-6018

Trust established in 1959 in Missouri.
Donor(s): Bemis Company, Inc.
Financial data: (yr. ended 12/31/82): Assets, $385,962 (M); gifts received, $502,000; expenditures, $486,925, including $409,720 for 106 grants (high: $52,582; low: $100) and $75,174 for 188 employee matching gifts.
Purpose and activities: Grants largely for higher and secondary education, community funds, hospitals, and cultural and civic affairs programs.
Types of support awarded: Annual campaigns, building funds, employee related scholarships, employee matching gifts, continuing support.
Limitations: No grants to individuals, or for endowment funds or research; no loans.
Publications: Application guidelines.
Application information:
  Initial approach: Full proposal
  Copies of proposal: 1
  Deadline(s): None
  Board meeting date(s): March, June, September, and December

Write: Edward J. Dougherty, Executive Director

Officer and Trustees: Edward J. Dougherty, Executive Director; Benjamin R. Field, Alvin L. Park.

Number of staff: 2.

Employer Identification Number: 416038616

1819
Bend Foundation
510 Baker Bldg.
Minneapolis 55403   (612) 332-2454
Application address: 416 Northeast
Greenwood, Bend, OR 97701

Trust established in 1947 in Illinois.

Donor(s): Brooks-Scanlon, Inc.

Financial data: (yr. ended 12/31/83): Assets, $1,578,234 (M); expenditures, $166,868, including $126,111 for 11 grants (high: $30,000; average: $1,000-$5,000) and $23,120 for 4 grants to individuals.

Purpose and activities: Local giving for higher education, cultural programs, and a community fund.

Types of support awarded: Continuing support, annual campaigns, seed money, building funds, equipment, land acquisition, matching funds, student aid.

Limitations: Giving limited to central OR, with preference for the city of Bend and Deschutes County. No grants for operating budgets, deficit financing, endowment funds, special projects, research, publications, or conferences; no loans.

Application information:
Initial approach: Letter or full proposal
Copies of proposal: 1
Deadline(s): Submit proposal preferably in December
Board meeting date(s): February or March
Final notification: A few months
Write: James L. Crowell

Trustees: Conley Brooks, Conley Brooks, Jr., Michael P. Hollern, William L. Smith.

Number of staff: None.

Employer Identification Number: 416019901

1820
Bigelow (F. R.) Foundation ▼
1120 Norwest Center
St. Paul 55101   (612) 224-5463

Trust established in 1934; incorporated in 1946 in Minnesota.

Donor(s): F.R. Bigelow,† Eileen Bigelow.

Financial data: (yr. ended 12/31/83): Assets, $29,120,109 (M); gifts received, $72,500; expenditures, $1,192,694, including $1,094,171 for 77 grants (high: $100,000; low: $1,000).

Purpose and activities: Broad purposes; local giving, with emphasis on cultural programs, higher and secondary education, social services, community funds, and health.

Types of support awarded: Seed money, emergency funds, equipment, land acquisition, building funds, scholarship funds, matching funds, special projects, continuing support.

Limitations: Giving limited to the greater St. Paul, MN metropolitan area. No grants to individuals, or for endowment funds; giving rarely for operating budgets; no loans.

Publications: Annual report, application guidelines.

Application information: Application form required.
Initial approach: Telephone, letter, or full proposal
Copies of proposal: 1
Deadline(s): Submit proposal preferably from January through April or July through October; deadlines April 1 and October 1
Board meeting date(s): June and December
Final notification: 3 to 4 months
Write: Paul A. Verret, Secretary

Officers: Paul A. Verret, Secretary; John L. Jerry, Treasurer.

Trustees: Ronald M. Hubbs, Chairman; Carl B. Drake, Jr., Vice-Chairman; Richard L. Gunderson, Malcolm W. McDonald, Kathleen Culman Ridder, Roger B. Shepard, Jr.

Number of staff: None.

Employer Identification Number: 416011519

1821
Blandin (Charles K.) Foundation ▼
100 Pokegama Ave. N.
Grand Rapids 55744   (218) 326-0523

Incorporated in 1941 in Minnesota.

Donor(s): Charles K. Blandin.†

Financial data: (yr. ended 12/31/84): Assets, $17,651,437 (M); gifts received, $6,000,000; expenditures, $5,984,056, including $4,192,734 for 152 grants (high: $450,000; low: $500), $215,071 for 378 grants to individuals and $110,000 for 2 loans.

Purpose and activities: Broad purposes; local giving for scholarships and higher education, community projects, health and welfare services, arts and humanities, recreation, economic development, and research in forestry.

Types of support awarded: Seed money, emergency funds, matching funds, scholarship funds, loans, program-related investments, special projects, consulting services, technical assistance.

Limitations: Giving limited to MN, with emphasis on the northeastern area. No support for medical research, or travel. No grants to individuals other than for scholarships, or for operating budgets, continuing support, annual campaigns, deficit financing, capital funds, endowments, publications, conferences, or seminars.

Publications: Annual report, application guidelines, program policy statement.

Application information:
Initial approach: Letter
Copies of proposal: 1
Deadline(s): Submit proposal preferably 2 months prior to board meetings; deadlines March 1, June 1, September 1, and December 1
Board meeting date(s): First week of February, May, August, and November
Final notification: 2 weeks after board meeting
Write: Paul M. Olson, Executive Director

Officers: James R. Oppenheimer,* President; Henry Doerr,* Harold F. Zigmund,* Vice-Presidents; Russell E. Virden, Vice-President and Treasurer; Margaret Matalamaki, Secretary; Paul M. Olson, Executive Director.

Trustees:* Warren H. Anderson, Robert L. Bullard, Robert L. Comstock, Jr., Peter A. Heegaard, Mary Jo Jess, George A. Rossman, Eugene F. Rothstein, Bruce Stender.

Number of staff: 3 full-time professional; 2 full-time support; 1 part-time support.

Employer Identification Number: 416038619

1822
Bremer (Otto) Foundation ▼
55 East Fifth St., Suite 700
St. Paul 55101   (612) 227-8036

Trust established in 1944 in Minnesota.

Donor(s): Otto Bremer.†

Financial data: (yr. ended 12/31/84): Assets, $59,000,000 (M); expenditures, $2,765,228, including $2,394,772 for 412 grants (high: $80,000; low: $40; average: $5,000-$6,000).

Purpose and activities: Broad purposes; grants limited to communities with Bremer Bank affiliates; emphasis on post-secondary education, human services, health, religion, and community affairs.

Types of support awarded: Operating budgets, continuing support, annual campaigns, seed money, emergency funds, deficit financing, building funds, equipment, land acquisition, special projects, matching funds, employee matching gifts, scholarship funds, conferences and seminars, employee related scholarships.

Limitations: Giving limited to MN, ND, and WI where there are Bremer Bank affiliates. No support for national health organizations. No grants to individuals, or for endowment funds, or medical research.

Publications: Annual report, application guidelines.

Application information:
Initial approach: Letter or telephone
Copies of proposal: 1
Deadline(s): Submit proposal at least 3 months before funding decision is desired
Board meeting date(s): Monthly
Final notification: 3 months
Write: John Kostishack, Executive Director

Officer: John Kostishack, Executive Director.

Trustees: William H. Lipschultz, Robert J. Reardon, Gordon Shepard.

Number of staff: 3 full-time professional.

Employer Identification Number: 416019050

1823
Bush Foundation, The ▼
East 900 First National Bank Bldg.
St. Paul 55101   (612) 227-0891

Incorporated in 1953 in Minnesota.

Donor(s): Archibald Bush,† Mrs. Archibald Bush.†

Financial data: (yr. ended 11/30/84): Assets, $261,919,051 (M); expenditures, $15,374,028, including $11,251,711 for 157 grants (high: $1,000,000; low: $5,000; average: $20,000-$500,000) and $1,113,956 for 106 grants to individuals.

Purpose and activities: General purposes; support largely for higher education, performing arts and humanities, delivery of health care, social service and welfare agencies in Minnesota and the Dakotas. Also operates the Bush Leadership Fellows Program in Minnesota, the Dakotas, and western Wisconsin, the Bush Fellowships for Artists in Minnesota, and the Bush Clinical Fellows program in rural Minnesota and the Dakotas.

Types of support awarded: Fellowships, matching funds, endowment funds, special projects, seed money.

Limitations: Giving primarily in MN, ND, and SD; no grants outside the U.S. No support for other private foundations, or for research in biomedical and health sciences. No grants to individuals (except for fellowships), or for deficit financing; generally no grants for continuing operating support; no loans.

Publications: Annual report, application guidelines, program policy statement.

Application information:
Initial approach: Letter or telephone
Copies of proposal: 2
Deadline(s): 3 1/2 months before board meetings
Board meeting date(s): February, April, June, and October
Final notification: 10 days after board meetings
Write: Humphrey Doermann, President

Officers: Thomas J. Clifford,* Chairman; James P. Shannon,* First Vice-Chairman; Ellen Z. Green, M.D.,* Second Vice-Chairman; Humphrey Doermann, President; John F. Nash,* Secretary; Frank B. Wilderson, Jr.,* Treasurer.

Directors:* Phyllis B. France, Thomas E. Holloran, Hess Kline, Herbert E. Longenecker, Diana E. Murphy, Harry P. Sweitzer.

Number of staff: 6 full-time professional; 5 full-time support.

Employer Identification Number: 416017815

1824
Butler (Patrick and Aimee) Family Foundation
West 1380 First National Bank Bldg.
St. Paul 55101   (612) 222-2565

Incorporated in 1951 in Minnesota.
Donor(s): Patrick Butler, and family.
Financial data: (yr. ended 12/31/84): Assets, $5,066,334 (M); expenditures, $347,852, including $315,860 for 118 grants (high: $25,760; low: $350).
Purpose and activities: Broad purposes; primarily local giving, with emphasis on Catholic institutions, higher education, chemical dependency, visual arts, cultural institutions, health, women, social services, and human services.

Types of support awarded: Continuing support, annual campaigns, building funds, matching funds, special projects, endowment funds.

Limitations: Giving primarily in the Saint Paul and Minneapolis, MN, area; limited support for national organizations and institutions in MA. No support for criminal justice, secondary and elementary education, medical research, performing arts, employment, vocational programs, or economic education. No grants to individuals; no loans.

Publications: Program policy statement, application guidelines.

Application information:
Initial approach: Letter
Copies of proposal: 1
Deadline(s): Submit proposal preferably in January, June, and October; deadlines February 1, July 1, and November 1
Board meeting date(s): February, July, November, and as required
Final notification: 3 to 6 months
Write: Sandra K. Butler, Program Officer

Officers: Patrick Butler,* President; Peter M. Butler,* Vice-President and Treasurer; T.N. Doyle, Secretary.

Trustees:* Patrick Butler, Jr., Sandra K. Butler, Kate B. Peterson.

Number of staff: 1 part-time support.

Employer Identification Number: 416009902

1825
Cargill Foundation, The ▼
P.O. Box 9300
Minneapolis 55440   (612) 475-6122

Incorporated in 1952 in Minnesota.
Donor(s): Cargill Charitable Trust, Cargill Incorporated.
Financial data: (yr. ended 12/31/83): Assets, $20,097,040 (M); gifts received, $750,000; expenditures, $1,529,128, including $1,396,285 for 109 grants (high: $210,000; low: $110; average: $1,000-$5,000).
Purpose and activities: Primarily local giving in the seven county Minneapolis-St. Paul metropolitan area, with emphasis on education, social programs, health, cultural programs, and civic affairs.
Types of support awarded: Operating budgets, continuing support, general purposes, special projects, building funds.
Limitations: Giving primarily in the seven county Minneapolis-St. Paul, MN, metropolitan area. No support for religious organizations for religious purposes. No grants to individuals, or for equipment and materials, land acquisition, endowment funds, matching gifts, research, demonstration projects, publications, conferences, scholarships, or fellowships; no loans.
Application information: Application form required.
Initial approach: Telephone
Copies of proposal: 1
Deadline(s): February 15 for educational grants; April 15 for social programs; July 15 for health grants; October 15 for cultural programs
Board meeting date(s): April, June, September, and December

Final notification: 2 weeks to 2 months after board meetings
Write: Calvin J. Anderson, Executive Director
Officers and Directors:* Gordon L. Alexander,* President; J.R. Cargill,* Peter Dorsey,* Cargill MacMillan, Jr.,* Clinton Morrison,* Vice-Presidents; Calvin J. Anderson, Secretary-Treasurer and Executive Director.
Number of staff: 1 part-time professional; 1 full-time support.
Employer Identification Number: 416020221

1826
Carlson (The Curtis L.) Foundation ⌿
12755 State Hwy. 55
Minneapolis 55441

Incorporated in 1959 in Minnesota.
Donor(s): Curtis L. Carlson.
Financial data: (yr. ended 12/31/82): Assets, $147,688 (M); gifts received, $28,430; expenditures, $384,056, including $368,051 for 71 grants (high: $60,000; low: $25).
Purpose and activities: Primarily local giving for music and the arts, social agencies and recreational facilities, higher education and schools, and Scandinavian intercultural organizations.
Limitations: Giving primarily in MN.
Officers: Curtis L. Carlson, President; Arleen E. Carlson, Vice-President; Alan E. Cleland, Secretary.
Employer Identification Number: 416028973

1827
Carolyn Foundation ▼
2106 First Bank Place West
Minneapolis 55402   (612) 339-7101

Trust established in 1964 in Minnesota.
Donor(s): Carolyn McKnight Christian.†
Financial data: (yr. ended 12/31/83): Assets, $11,667,597 (M); expenditures, $849,645, including $748,563 for 36 grants (high: $170,000; low: $1,000; average: $35,000).
Purpose and activities: Charitable purposes; grants limited largely to metropolitan areas of New Haven, Connecticut, and Minneapolis-St. Paul, Minnesota; priorities include education, culture, health and welfare, including child welfare, the environment and the disadvantaged.
Types of support awarded: Operating budgets, seed money, building funds, equipment, land acquisition, matching funds, scholarship funds, special projects.
Limitations: Giving primarily in the metropolitan areas of New Haven, CT and Minneapolis-St. Paul, MN. No support for political or veterans' groups, fraternal societies, or religious organizations for religious purposes. No grants to individuals, or for endowment funds, annual fund drives, deficit funding or continuing support; no loans.
Publications: Program policy statement, application guidelines, annual report.
Application information:
Initial approach: Letter
Copies of proposal: 1

Deadline(s): Submit proposal between January and March for minor grants (under $10,000) and between January and August for major grants ($10,000 and larger); board awards major grants at its December meeting; deadlines April 1 for minor grants; September 15 for major grants

Board meeting date(s): May or June and December

Write: C. John Kirsch, Executive Director

Officers and Trustees: Lucy C. Mitchell, Chairperson; Guido Calabresi, Vice-Chairman; C. John Kirsch, Secretary-Treasurer and Executive Director; Beatrice C. Booth, Edwin L. Crosby, Franklin M. Crosby III, G. Christian Crosby, Sumner McK. Crosby, Jr., Thomas M. Crosby, Jr., Carolyn C. Graham.

Number of staff: None.

Employer Identification Number: 416044416

1828
Cenex Foundation ☖

5600 Cenex Dr.
Inver Grove Heights 55075 (612) 451-5105

Trust established in 1947 in Minnesota.

Donor(s): Central Exchange Agency.

Financial data: (yr. ended 11/30/83): Assets, $3,110,394 (M); expenditures, $372,322, including $230,830 for 133 grants (high: $25,000; low: $50) and $124,537 for 43 grants to individuals.

Purpose and activities: General purposes; grants largely for research and education, including scholarship funds; assistance to needy former employees of affiliated organizations; grants also to youth agencies and community funds.

Types of support awarded: Scholarship funds, grants to individuals.

Limitations: Giving limited to MN, ND, SD, WI, WA, ID, WY, MT, and OR. No grants for endowment funds.

Application information: Application form required.

Initial approach: Letter
Copies of proposal: 1
Board meeting date(s): Quarterly
Write: Sharon A. Blaiser, Manager

Officers: Joseph Larson,* President; John Broste,* Vice-President; Dale Johnson,* Secretary; Darrell Moseson, Treasurer; Sharon A. Blaiser, Manager.

Trustees:* Lloyd Kaercher, Roy Kopperud, Edward J. Melby, Doane Mortenson, Lester Peter, Herbert Pomplun, Dixie Lee Riddle, Kermit Veum, Elroy Webster, Arnold Weisenbeck.

Employer Identification Number: 416025858

1829
Chadwick Foundation ☖

4122 IDS Center
Minneapolis 55402

Established in 1967 in Minnesota.

Donor(s): Members of the Dayton family.

Financial data: (yr. ended 12/31/83): Assets, $4,054,210 (M); gifts received, $2,495; expenditures, $235,277, including $173,775 for 60 grants (high: $15,000; low: $250).

Purpose and activities: Broad purposes; primarily local giving, with emphasis on secondary and higher education, community services, cultural programs, conservation, hospitals and medical research, arts and Protestant church support.

Types of support awarded: Research, general purposes.

Limitations: Giving primarily in MN.

Officers and Directors: Donald C. Dayton, President and Treasurer; Edward N. Dayton, John W. Dayton, Robert J. Dayton, Vice-Presidents; Lucy J. Dayton, Secretary.

Employer Identification Number: 416080619

1830
Charity, Inc.

7350 Commerce Ln.
Minneapolis 55432 (612) 571-7350

Incorporated in 1962 in Minnesota.

Donor(s): Mrs. Rose Totino, Pillsbury Corporation.

Financial data: (yr. ended 2/28/83): Assets, $773,726 (M); gifts received, $1,165,000; expenditures, $1,399,900, including $1,386,009 for 39 grants (high: $504,893; low: $1,000).

Purpose and activities: Primarily local giving for higher and secondary education and Christian organizations.

Limitations: Giving primarily in MN.

Application information:

Initial approach: Full proposal or letter
Copies of proposal: 1
Board meeting date(s): Monthly

Officers and Directors:* Rose Totino, President and Treasurer; Joanne Elwell,* John M. Metcalfe,* Vice-Presidents; Leonard M. Addington, Secretary.

Employer Identification Number: 410636273

1831
Circle Foundation, The ☖

c/o First Trust Company of St. Paul
W-555 First National Bank Bldg.
St. Paul 55101 (612) 291-5128

Established in 1975.

Donor(s): Ursula Jaeger, Robert Jaeger.

Financial data: (yr. ended 12/31/82): Assets, $980,133 (M); gifts received, $35,000; expenditures, $118,222, including $111,143 for 15 grants (high: $15,000; low: $4,200).

Purpose and activities: Giving exclusively in western Pennsylvania; grants largely for social agencies, with emphasis on aid to the mentally handicapped.

Limitations: Giving limited to western PA.

Application information:

Initial approach: Letter

Officers and Directors: Robert Jaeger, President; Ursula Jaeger, Vice-President; John L. Jerry, Secretary-Treasurer.

Employer Identification Number: 510147632

1832
Cowles (John and Elizabeth Bates) Foundation ☖

329 Portland Ave.
Minneapolis 55415

Incorporated in 1954 in Minnesota.

Donor(s): John Cowles,† and members of the Cowles family.

Financial data: (yr. ended 2/29/84): Assets, $1,215,966 (M); gifts received, $611,976; expenditures, $33,116, including $27,250 for 7 grants (high: $15,000; low: $250).

Purpose and activities: Grants primarily to local organizations, with emphasis on education, a community fund, and a historical society.

Limitations: Giving primarily in Minneapolis, MN, and New York, NY. No grants to individuals.

Application information:

Write: Norton L. Armour, Vice-President

Officers and Directors: John Cowles, Jr., President; Norton L. Armour, Vice-President and Secretary; Philip S. Sherburne, Vice-President and Treasurer; Russell Cowles II, Sage Fuller Cowles, Otto A. Silha, Vice-Presidents; Morley Cowles Ballantine, Sarah Cowles Doering.

Employer Identification Number: 416031374

1833
Davis (Edwin W. and Catherine M.) Foundation ▼

2100 First National Bank Bldg.
St. Paul 55101 (612) 228-0935

Incorporated in 1956 in Minnesota.

Donor(s): Samuel S. Davis,† Edwin W. Davis,† Frederick W. Davis.

Financial data: (yr. ended 12/31/83): Assets, $5,497,209 (M); gifts received, $338,195; expenditures, $629,877, including $608,490 for 81 grants (high: $75,000; low: $250; average: $5,000-$20,000).

Purpose and activities: The foundation is concerned with "the amelioration of social problems and increasing the opportunities available to disadvantaged people," with particular interest in the fields of education, social welfare, mental health, the arts, and environmental problems. Educational grants primarily for colleges and universities; support also for religious youth groups.

Types of support awarded: Annual campaigns, continuing support, operating budgets, scholarship funds.

Limitations: No grants to individuals, or for emergency funds, capital outlay, building and equipment, or endowments; no loans.

Publications: Annual report, program policy statement, application guidelines.

Application information:

Initial approach: Letter
Copies of proposal: 1
Deadline(s): None
Board meeting date(s): May or June and as required
Final notification: 4 to 6 weeks
Write: Frederick W. Davis, President

Officers and Directors: Frederick W. Davis, President; Bette D. Moorman, Vice-President; Mary E. Davis, Secretary; Albert J. Moorman, Treasurer; Joseph S. Micallef.
Number of staff: None.
Employer Identification Number: 416012064

1834
Dayton Hudson Foundation ▼
777 Nicollet Mall
Minneapolis 55402   (612) 370-6553

Incorporated in 1917 in Minnesota.
Donor(s): Dayton Hudson Corporation, and operating companies.
Financial data: (yr. ended 1/31/85): Assets, $9,112,008 (M); gifts received, $12,381,000; expenditures, $11,042,179, including $11,018,720 for 789 grants (high: $1,000,000; low: $250; average: $1,000-$5,000).
Purpose and activities: Support for the arts and social-action programs to assist socially disadvantaged adults in overcoming barriers to self-sufficiency, or that prepare socially disadvantaged young people for adult self-sufficiency in areas of Corporation operations.
Types of support awarded: Operating budgets, continuing support, annual campaigns, building funds, equipment, matching funds, consulting services, technical assistance, special projects, publications.
Limitations: Giving primarily in areas of company operations; grants rarely for national organizations or programs. No support for religious organizations for religious purposes; grants rarely made to health organizations, educational institutions, advocacy, or tax-supported activities. No grants to individuals, or for seed money, emergency funds, land acquisition, scholarships, fellowships, research, conferences, or loans; grants rarely for endowment funds.
Publications: Company report, informational brochure, program policy statement, application guidelines.
Application information: Organizations located outside Minnesota should apply to local headquarters office of Dayton Hudson Corporation.
Initial approach: Letter with proposal
Copies of proposal: 1
Deadline(s): None
Board meeting date(s): March, June, September, and December
Final notification: Within 60 days, although decisions are generally not made between January 31 and April 15
Write: Vivian K. Stuck, Administrative Officer
Officers and Managers: Peter C. Hutchinson,* Chairman; Cynthia Mayeda, Managing Director; Willard C. Shull, III,* Vice-President and Treasurer; William E. Harder, Secretary.
Trustees:* Bruce G. Allbright, William A. Andres, Gerald R. Gallagher, James T. Hale, Peter C. Hutchinson, J.F. Kilmartin, K.A. Macke, P. Gerald Mills, Boake A. Sells.
Number of staff: 4 full-time professional; 2 full-time support.
Employer Identification Number: 416017088

1835
DeLuxe Check Printers Foundation ▼
P.O. Box 64399
St. Paul 55164   (612) 483-7842
Street address: 1080 West County Rd. "F", St. Paul, MN 55112

Incorporated in 1952 in Minnesota.
Donor(s): DeLuxe Check Printers, Inc.
Financial data: (yr. ended 12/31/84): Assets, $2,050,933 (M); gifts received, $2,000,000; expenditures, $2,007,254, including $1,903,503 for 451 grants (high: $25,000; low: $1,000; average: $1,000-$10,000) and $89,877 for 589 employee matching gifts.
Purpose and activities: Broad purposes; giving in areas of company operations for private higher education, particularly independent college funds, and for medical services, youth organizations, social welfare agencies, civic groups, and cultural organizations; grants largely for capital purposes, including buildings, renovations, or equipment and for operations, programs, special projects, and an employee matching gifts program.
Types of support awarded: Building funds, equipment, operating budgets, special projects, employee matching gifts, scholarship funds.
Limitations: Giving primarily in areas of company operations. No support for primary or secondary schools, religious or political organizations. No grants to individuals, or for annual campaigns or research; no loans.
Publications: Annual report, program policy statement, application guidelines.
Application information: Application form required.
Initial approach: Letter or telephone
Copies of proposal: 1
Deadline(s): None
Board meeting date(s): February; regional meetings at least twice a year
Final notification: 3 months
Write: Michael J. Welch, Executive Director
Officers and Trustees: Eugene R. Olsen, President; Harold V. Haverty, Vice-President; F.H. Cloutier, Secretary-Treasurer; Michael J. Welch, Executive Director; J.R. Cross, Michael J. Einan, William J. Oliver, Charles M. Osborne.
Number of staff: 1 full-time professional; 1 part-time professional; 1 part-time support.
Employer Identification Number: 416034786

1836
Donaldson Foundation, The
P.O. Box 1299
Minneapolis 55440   (612) 887-3007

Established in 1966 in Minnesota.
Donor(s): Donaldson Company, Inc.
Financial data: (yr. ended 7/31/83): Assets, $511,542 (M); gifts received, $200,000; expenditures, $293,988, including $286,720 for 65 grants (high: $50,000; low: $300) and $5,480 for 16 employee matching gifts.
Purpose and activities: Giving primarily in areas of company operations; support for community funds, youth agencies, arts and cultural organizations, schools, and higher education; grants also for educational associations, environmental protection, community development, and health services.

Limitations: Giving primarily in areas of company operations. No support for religious organizations. No grants to individuals.
Publications: Application guidelines.
Application information:
Initial approach: Letter
Copies of proposal: 1
Board meeting date(s): August, November, February, and May
Write: Raymond Vodovnik, Secretary
Officers: Raymond Vodovnik,* Secretary; Ernest W. Andberg, Treasurer.
Trustees:* Erland Anderson, F.A. Donaldson, Arlene Louton, Betsy Lund, Kenneth Riesberg, Robert Schweitzer, William West.
Employer Identification Number: 416052950

1837
Driscoll Foundation
2100 First National Bank Bldg.
St. Paul 55101   (612) 228-0935

Incorporated in 1962 in Minnesota.
Donor(s): Members of the Driscoll family.
Financial data: (yr. ended 2/28/83): Assets, $1,731,023 (M); gifts received, $460,018; expenditures, $236,331, including $224,850 for 15 grants (high: $50,000; low: $1,200).
Purpose and activities: Broad purposes; giving primarily locally and in the area of San Francisco, California, with emphasis on higher and secondary education, hospitals, the arts, Protestant church support, conservation, and community funds.
Limitations: Giving primarily in the metropolitan areas of St. Paul-Minneapolis, MN and San Francisco, CA. No grants to individuals, or for conferences, travel, publications, or films.
Publications: Annual report, application guidelines.
Application information:
Initial approach: Letter
Copies of proposal: 1
Board meeting date(s): Annually and as required
Final notification: 3 to 4 weeks
Write: W. John Driscoll, President
Officers: W. John Driscoll,* President; Rudolph W. Driscoll,* Vice-President; Joseph S. Micallef, Secretary; Gordon E. Hed, Treasurer.
Directors:* Elizabeth S. Driscoll, Margot H. Driscoll.
Number of staff: None.
Employer Identification Number: 416012065

1838
Dye (The Glen M.) - Pako Foundation ⌷
c/o First National Bank of Minneapolis
120 South Sixth St.
Minneapolis 55480   (612) 540-6207

Trust established in 1958 in Minnesota.
Donor(s): Glen M. Dye, Marjorie D. Getsch, Pako Corporation.
Financial data: (yr. ended 12/31/83): Assets, $6,360,139 (M); expenditures, $643,305, including $600,000 for 115 grants (high: $95,000; low: $500).

Purpose and activities: Charitable purposes; general giving, primarily in Wisconsin and Minnesota, with emphasis on higher education, a secondary school, youth agencies, and Protestant church support.
Limitations: Giving primarily in MN. No grants to individuals, or for endowment funds.
Application information: Applications not invited.
   Write: Kenneth M. Knopf, Trustee
Trustees: Glen M. Dye, Harry M. Dye, Marjorie D. Getsch, William C. Getsch, Amy D. Knopf, Kenneth M. Knopf, The First National Bank of Minneapolis.
Directors: Charles B. Woehrle.
Employer Identification Number: 416016362

1839
Eddy Foundation ⌘
c/o Trust Dept., Norwest Bank Duluth
P.O. Box 488
Duluth 55802   (218) 723-2773

Established in 1982 in Minnesota.
Donor(s): Edwin H. Eddy, Jr.†
Financial data: (yr. ended 6/30/84): Assets, $1,664,667 (M); expenditures, $136,253, including $83,737 for 9 grants (high: $38,440; low: $654) and $29,268 for 21 grants to individuals.
Purpose and activities: Local giving for research into and treatment of individuals with speech or hearing disorders; also scholarships for residents of Duluth studying in the field of communication disorders and for non-residents attending the University of Minnesota at Duluth.
Types of support awarded: Student aid.
Limitations: Giving limited to the Duluth, MN, area.
Application information:
   Initial approach: Proposal
   Copies of proposal: 8
   Write: Murray George
Trustees: Rodney J. Edwards, Eben S. Spencer, Norwest Bank Duluth.
Employer Identification Number: 416242226

1840
Edwards Memorial Trust ▼
c/o First Trust Company of St. Paul
W-555 First National Bank Bldg.
St. Paul 55101   (612) 291-5114

Trust established in 1961 in Minnesota.
Donor(s): Ray Edwards.†
Financial data: (yr. ended 12/31/84): Assets, $8,291,244 (M); expenditures, $592,356, including $558,500 for 48 grants (high: $75,000; low: $1,000).
Purpose and activities: Primarily local giving, with emphasis on public hospitals, including the maintaining of free beds; some support for social services and health agencies, including the handicapped, and cultural programs.
Types of support awarded: General purposes.
Limitations: Giving primarily in the Minneapolis-St. Paul, MN, area.
Application information:
   Initial approach: Letter
   Deadline(s): None

Write: Jeffrey T. Peterson, Vice-President
Trustee: First Trust Company of St. Paul (Jeffrey T. Peterson, Vice-President).
Employer Identification Number: 416011292

1841
Fingerhut Family Foundation, The
5354 Parkdale Dr., No. 310
Minneapolis 55416   (612) 545-3000

Incorporated in 1960 in Minnesota.
Donor(s): Manny Fingerhut, Rose Fingerhut.
Financial data: (yr. ended 8/31/83): Assets, $140,608 (M); expenditures, $863,704, including $857,175 for 69 grants (high: $447,500; low: $100).
Purpose and activities: Broad purposes; primarily local giving, with emphasis on Jewish welfare funds, social agencies, and medical research.
Limitations: Giving primarily in MN, especially the Twin Cities. No grants for building funds.
Application information:
   Initial approach: Letter and brief proposal
   Copies of proposal: 1
   Write: Ronald Fingerhut, Vice-President
Officers and Directors: Manny Fingerhut, President; Ronald Fingerhut, Rose Fingerhut, Vice-Presidents; Stanley Nemer, Secretary-Treasurer; Beverly Deikel.
Number of staff: 1 part-time professional; 1 part-time support.
Employer Identification Number: 416030930

1842
First Bank System Foundation ▼
1300 First Bank Place East
P.O. Box 522
Minneapolis 55480   (612) 370-5080

Established about 1979.
Donor(s): First Bank of Minneapolis, First Bank of Saint Paul, and other First Banks and Trust Companies in the North Central States.
Financial data: (yr. ended 12/31/84): Assets, $234,375 (M); gifts received, $2,246,313; expenditures, $2,224,286, including $2,203,530 for 200 grants (high: $125,000; low: $600; average: $1,000-$10,000) and $20,756 for employee matching gifts.
Purpose and activities: Giving primarily in Minnesota, Montana, North Dakota, and South Dakota for higher education, cultural programs, community funds, social service, youth and human service agencies.
Types of support awarded: Operating budgets, continuing support, annual campaigns, emergency funds, building funds, equipment, employee matching gifts, employee related scholarships, special projects.
Limitations: Giving primarily in MN, MT, ND, and SD. No support for religious organizations. No grants to individuals, or for seed money, deficit financing, land acquisition, endowment funds, publications, conferences, trips, tours, or research; no loans.
Publications: Annual report, application guidelines.
Application information: Application form required.
   Initial approach: Letter or telephone

Deadline(s): 2 months before committee meetings
Board meeting date(s): March, June, September, and November
Final notification: 1 month after committee meetings
Write: Lloyd L. Brandt, President, general information; Sally Sumner, Administrative Assistant, grant applications
Officers: Lloyd L. Brandt,* President; Eugene R. Mason, Treasurer.
Directors:* George H. Dixon, Chairman; DeWalt H. Ankeny, Jr., Dennis E. Evans, Darrell G. Knutson, James E. Ulland.
Number of staff: 1 part-time professional; 2 part-time support.
Employer Identification Number: 411359579

1843
First National Bank of Minneapolis Foundation ▼
First Bank Place
Minneapolis 55480   (612) 370-4099

Trust established in 1969 in Minnesota.
Donor(s): First National Bank of Minneapolis.
Financial data: (yr. ended 12/31/84): Assets, $0 (L); gifts received, $1,889,718; expenditures, $1,889,718, including $1,831,580 for 314 grants (high: $385,000; low: $300; average: $1,500) and $29,069 for 344 employee matching gifts.
Purpose and activities: Local giving for a community fund and in the general areas of culture, education, health, housing, environment, and human and social relations.
Types of support awarded: Employee matching gifts, annual campaigns.
Limitations: Giving primarily in the Minneapolis, MN area. No support for religious organizations for religious purposes, political organizations, or national or local disease-related organizations. No grants to individuals, or for endowment funds, research, travel, or fundraising campaigns.
Publications: Annual report, application guidelines.
Application information:
   Initial approach: Letter or full proposal
   Copies of proposal: 1
   Deadline(s): 15 days before board meetings
   Board meeting date(s): March, June, September, and December
   Final notification: 2 weeks after board meeting
   Write: James L. Hetland, Jr., Senior Vice-President
Trustee: First National Bank of Minneapolis (James L. Hetland, Jr., Senior Vice-President).
Number of staff: 1 part-time professional; 1 part-time support.
Employer Identification Number: 416093462

1844
Fiterman (The Jack and Bessie) Foundation ⌘
5600 North County Rd. 18
Minneapolis 55428

Established in 1966 in Minnesota.

Donor(s): Fidelity File Box, Inc., Liberty Carton Company, Safco Products Company, Shamrock Industries, Inc.
Financial data: (yr. ended 5/31/83): Assets, $197,412 (M); gifts received, $180,000; expenditures, $151,604, including $151,140 for 20 grants (high: $74,460; low: $35).
Purpose and activities: Broad purposes; giving primarily for Jewish welfare funds.
Officers and Directors: Michael Fiterman, President; Sylvia Sorkin, Vice-President; Ben Fiterman, Secretary.
Employer Identification Number: 416058465

1845
Gamble (The B. C.) and P. W. Skogmo Foundation ▼
(formerly B. C. Gamble Foundation; P. W. Skogmo Foundation)
c/o Minneapolis Foundation
821 Marquette Ave., 500 Foshay Tower
Minneapolis 55402   (612) 339-7343

B.C. Gamble Foundation incorporated in Minnesota in 1948; P.W. Skogmo Foundation also incorporated in 1948 in Minnesota and merged with P.W. Skogmo Charitable Trust in 1962; B.C. Gamble Foundation merged with P.W. Skogmo Foundation in 1982 and became supporting organization of The Minneapolis Foundation.
Donor(s): P.W. Skogmo,† B.C. Gamble.
Financial data: (yr. ended 3/31/84): Assets, $14,622,361 (M); expenditures, $1,622,546, including $1,524,164 for 79 grants (high: $250,000; low: $1,000).
Purpose and activities: Charitable purposes; primarily local giving, with emphasis on disadvantaged youth and their families, the handicapped, programs in the field of aging, health care, including research and education, and higher and secondary educational institutions in the Twin Cities metropolitan area.
Types of support awarded: Operating budgets, special projects.
Limitations: Giving limited to the Minneapolis-St. Paul, MN, metropolitan area. No support for political organizations, veterans' organizations, fraternal societies, national fundraising campaigns, religious organizations for religious purposes, or for membership in civic or trade organizations. No grants to individuals, or for endowment funds, courtesy advertising, conferences, or tickets for benefits.
Publications: Annual report, program policy statement, application guidelines.
Application information:
 Initial approach: Proposal of 5 pages or less
 Copies of proposal: 10
 Deadline(s): April 1 and October 1
 Board meeting date(s): May and November
 Final notification: As soon as possible following board meeting
 Write: Marion G. Etzwiler, Secretary and Treasurer
Officers: Henry T. Rutledge,* President; Philip B. Harris,* Vice-President; Marion G. Etzwiler, Secretary and Treasurer.
Trustees:* Donald G. Dreblow, Robert H. Engels, Bertin C. Gamble, Timothy G. Johnson, Raymond O. Mithun.
Employer Identification Number: 411410675

1846
Gelco Foundation, The
One Gelco Dr.
Eden Prairie 55344   (612) 828-2614

Incorporated in 1973 in Minnesota.
Donor(s): Gelco Corporation.
Financial data: (yr. ended 6/30/83): Assets, $1,249,550 (M); expenditures, $285,491, including $281,328 for 117 grants (high: $50,000; low: $100).
Purpose and activities: Primarily local giving, with emphasis on the arts, communications, higher education, social agencies and a community fund.
Limitations: Giving primarily in MN, with emphasis on the Minneapolis-St. Paul area. No support for political or fraternal organizations, or for religious organizations for sectarian purposes. No grants to individuals, or for scholarships and fellowships, fundraising events, or matching gifts; no loans.
Publications: Application guidelines.
Application information:
 Initial approach: Letter
 Copies of proposal: 1
 Deadline(s): May 1
 Board meeting date(s): Usually in January and July
 Write: James P. Johnson, Executive Director
Officers: N. Bud Grossman,* President and Chairman; James P. Johnson, Executive Director.
Directors:* Stanley Chason, Andrew Grossman, Richard McFerran, Kevin Mitchell, Morton Zalk.
Employer Identification Number: 237302799

1847
General Mills Foundation ▼
9200 Wayzata Blvd.
Minneapolis 55426   (612) 540-3337
Address for proposals or requests for information: Executive Director, P.O. Box 1113, Minneapolis, MN 55440

Incorporated in 1954 in Minnesota.
Donor(s): General Mills, Inc.
Financial data: (yr. ended 5/31/84): Assets, $12,642,443 (L); gifts received, $5,800,000; expenditures, $6,217,062, including $5,237,552 for 577 grants (high: $494,000; low: $500; average: $2,500-$5,000) and $600,198 for 1,745 employee matching gifts.
Purpose and activities: Broad purposes; grants for higher and secondary education, social services, community funds, health and hospitals, and civic and cultural activities.
Types of support awarded: Operating budgets, seed money, emergency funds, matching funds, employee matching gifts, scholarship funds, employee related scholarships, special projects.

Limitations: Giving primarily in areas of major company operations, with emphasis on the Minneapolis, MN area. No support for religious or lobbying organizations, recreation, or national or local campaigns to eliminate or control specific diseases. No grants to individuals, or for endowment or building funds for education, continuing support for operating purposes, research, publications, conferences, seminars, workshops, symposia, travel, fundraising campaigns, or deficit financing; no loans.
Publications: Annual report, application guidelines, program policy statement.
Application information: Preliminary telephone calls or personal visits discouraged.
 Initial approach: Proposal with brief cover letter
 Deadline(s): None
 Board meeting date(s): 4 to 6 times a year and as required
 Final notification: 4 weeks
 Write: James P. Shannon, Executive Director
Officers: H. Brewster Atwater, Jr.,* President; James P. Shannon, Vice-President and Executive Director; Paul L. Parker,* Vice-President; Clifford L. Whitehill, Secretary; Eugene P. Preiss, Treasurer.
Trustees:* F. Caleb Blodgett, Mark H. Willes.
Number of staff: 3 full-time professional; 3 full-time support; 1 part-time support.
Employer Identification Number: 416018495

1848
General Service Foundation ▼
c/o Macalester College
14 Carnegie Hall
St. Paul 55105   (612) 696-6504
Principal office: 3080 First National Bank Bldg., St. Paul, MN 55101; Tel.: (612) 222-3789

Incorporated in 1946 in Illinois.
Donor(s): Clifton R. Musser,† Margaret K. Musser.†
Financial data: (yr. ended 12/31/83): Assets, $20,658,658 (M); expenditures, $1,118,805, including $989,500 for 58 grants (high: $68,000; low: $500; average: $10,000-$30,000).
Purpose and activities: Major areas of interest include population, resources, education, and non-military aspects of international peace, with new guidelines in each area. In 1983-84, approximately two-thirds of grants were in area of resources, with emphasis on water quality and management in the United States and food and agriculture in developing countries. Preferred contributions support experimental, demonstration, or research projects on a national and international level, particularly in Latin America, Mexico, the Caribbean, and other developing areas; grants for education primarily to inner-city schools and rural public schools having a substantial percentage of minorities, to colleges and universities, and to developing countries.
Types of support awarded: Special projects, research.

Limitations: No grants to individuals, or for general purposes, capital funds, relief, deficit financing, emergency funds, continuing support, seed money, operating budgets, endowments, scholarships and fellowships, matching gifts, or the annual campaigns of established organizations; no loans.
Publications: Annual report, application guidelines.
Application information:
　Initial approach: Letter or telephone
　Copies of proposal: 1
　Deadline(s): Submit proposal preferably in March and September; deadline at least one month prior to board meetings
　Board meeting date(s): April and November
　Final notification: 6 months
　Write: David A. Lanegran, Ph.D., Program Associate
Officers: John M. Musser,* President and Treasurer; Marion M. Lloyd,* Vice-President; Ruth Hezzelwood, Secretary.
Directors:* Harland Cleveland, Mary Estrin, Robert L. Estrin, Christian G. Halby, John M. Lloyd, Janet H. Malone, Elizabeth W. Musser, Marcie J. Musser, Robert W. Musser, Phillips Talbot, Gilbert F. White.
Number of staff: 1 full-time professional; 1 part-time professional; 1 full-time support; 1 part-time support.
Employer Identification Number: 366018535

1849
Graco Foundation, The
P.O. Box 1441
Minneapolis 55440　　　　(612) 623-6617

Incorporated in 1958 in Minnesota.
Donor(s): Graco Inc.
Financial data: (yr. ended 12/31/84): Assets, $865,300 (M); gifts received, $158,000; expenditures, $572,625, including $564,430 for 125 grants (high: $200,000; low: $100; average: $500-$5,000) and $8,195 for 65 employee matching gifts.
Purpose and activities: Support for social and educational programs with emphasis on community funds, youth agencies, higher and secondary education, and economic education in Minneapolis and areas of corporate operation.
Types of support awarded: Operating budgets, continuing support, annual campaigns, building funds, equipment, matching funds, employee related scholarships, research, special projects, employee matching gifts.
Limitations: Giving primarily in MN, with emphasis on Minneapolis and in areas of company operations. No support for political or religious purposes. No grants to individuals (except for company-employee scholarships), or for seed money, emergency funds, deficit financing, land acquisition, endowment funds, publications, or conferences; no loans.
Application information:
　Initial approach: Letter, full proposal, or telephone
　Copies of proposal: 1
　Deadline(s): None
　Board meeting date(s): March, June, September, and December
　Final notification: 2 months

Write: Charles F. Murphy, Executive Director
Officers and Directors: David A. Koch, President; Charles F. Murphy, Secretary, Treasurer, and Executive Director; Maynard B. Hasselquist.
Number of staff: 1 part-time support.
Employer Identification Number: 416023537

1850
Grain Terminal Foundation ⌑
1667 Snelling Ave., North
P.O. Box 43594
St. Paul 55164

Incorporated in 1947 in Minnesota.
Donor(s): The Terminal Agency, Inc.
Financial data: (yr. ended 5/31/83): Assets, $2,909,259 (M); expenditures, $269,288, including $218,025 for 85 grants (high: $27,500; low: $200) and $1,800 for 2 grants to individuals.
Purpose and activities: Broad purposes; grants largely for higher education, particularly in agriculture, with preference given to scholarship funds for studies in agricultural vocations in land-grant colleges in Minnesota, Iowa, North and South Dakota, Montana, Idaho, and Washington; support also for youth organizations and community funds.
Types of support awarded: Scholarship funds.
Limitations: Giving primarily in MN, IA, ID, MT, ND, SD, and WA.
Application information:
　Initial approach: Letter
　Copies of proposal: 1
　Write: Mr. R.L. Zabel, Treasurer
Officers: Audrey J. Dieter, Secretary; R.L. Zabel,* Treasurer.
Trustees:* Allen D. Hanson, Chairman; Donald F. Giffey, Vice-Chairman; Milo Dunn, Fred G. Ehlers, Edward Ellison, Olaf Haugo, Myron Just, Gerald Kuster, Lester G. Larson, George L. Mann, Gordon H. Matheson, Raymond Neuhauser, Gerald G. Redlin, Philip Testerman.
Employer Identification Number: 416039613

1851
Greystone Foundation, The
510 Baker Bldg.
Minneapolis 55402　　　　(612) 332-2454

Established in 1948 in Minnesota.
Donor(s): Members of the Paul A. Brooks family.
Financial data: (yr. ended 12/31/83): Assets, $1,537,554 (M); gifts received, $373,283; expenditures, $300,221, including $294,165 for 97 grants (high: $47,000; low: $40; average: $1,000-$10,000).
Purpose and activities: Broad purposes; primarily local giving for health and medical research, community funds and a community foundation, private secondary education, animal care and preservation, and arts and cultural programs.
Types of support awarded: Operating budgets, continuing support, annual campaigns, seed money, emergency funds, deficit financing, building funds, equipment, land acquisition, special projects, research, publications, conferences and seminars.

Limitations: Giving primarily in MN. No grants to individuals, or for endowment funds, matching gifts, or scholarships and fellowships; no loans.
Application information:
　Initial approach: Letter
　Deadline(s): None
　Board meeting date(s): As required
　Write: John M. Hollern, Trustee
Trustees: John M. Hollern, Michael P. Hollern.
Number of staff: None.
Employer Identification Number: 416027765

1852
Griggs (Mary Livingston) and Mary Griggs Burke Foundation ▼
1400 Northwestern National Bank Bldg.
55 East Fifth St.
St. Paul 55101　　　　(612) 227-7683

Established in 1966 in Minnesota.
Donor(s): Mary L. Griggs.†
Financial data: (yr. ended 6/30/84): Assets, $9,141,647 (M); expenditures, $704,614, including $611,498 for 68 grants (high: $50,000; low: $500; average: $500-$50,000).
Purpose and activities: General giving, primarily in New York and locally, with emphasis on higher and secondary education, an Asian cultural society, museums, conservation, and the arts.
Types of support awarded: Fellowships.
Limitations: Giving primarily in MN and NY. No grants to individuals, or for special projects or research.
Application information:
　Initial approach: Letter
　Copies of proposal: 1
　Board meeting date(s): Quarterly
　Final notification: 10 days to 3 months
　Write: Marvin J. Pertzik, Secretary
Officers and Directors: Mary Griggs Burke, President; Richard A. Moore, Vice-President; Marvin J. Pertzik, Secretary; Orley R. Taylor, Treasurer; Eleanor Griggs, C.F. Bayliss Griggs.
Number of staff: None.
Employer Identification Number: 416052355

1853
Grotto Foundation, Inc.
West 2090 First National Bank Bldg.
St. Paul 55101　　　　(612) 224-9431

Incorporated in 1964 in Minnesota.
Donor(s): Louis W. Hill, Jr.
Financial data: (yr. ended 4/30/84): Assets, $2,545,888 (M); gifts received, $25,987; expenditures, $146,642, including $97,865 for 28 grants (high: $16,000; low: $115; average: $3,000-$5,000).
Purpose and activities: Broad purposes; local giving, with emphasis on education, especially higher education; cultural programs, welfare, and health; grants also for special projects relating to American Indians, recent American immigrants, and racially mixed families.
Types of support awarded: Seed money, emergency funds, scholarship funds, internships, special projects, research.

Limitations: Giving limited to MN, adjoining Midwestern states, and, on a lesser basis, to AK. No support for writing projects, political activity, government projects, or art programs. No grants to individuals, or for capital or endowment funds, travel, continuing support, operating budgets (except to aid in initiating occasional programs), annual campaigns, deficit financing, student research, matching gifts, publications, or conferences; no loans.
Publications: Annual report, program policy statement, application guidelines.
Application information: Application form required.
  Initial approach: Letter or full proposal
  Copies of proposal: 2
  Deadline(s): 60 days prior to months in which board meets
  Board meeting date(s): March, June, September, and December, and as required
  Final notification: 2 months
  Write: A.A. Heckman, Executive Director
Officers: Louis W. Hill, Jr.,* President; Irving Clark,* Vice-President; A.A. Heckman,* Secretary and Executive Director; Jeffery Peterson, Treasurer.
Directors:* John Diehl, Malcolm McDonald, William B. Randall.
Number of staff: 1 full-time professional; 1 part-time support.
Employer Identification Number: 416052604

1854
Groves Foundation ▼ ¤
(formerly Groves Fund)
10,000 Highway 55 West
P.O. Box 1267
Minneapolis 55440   (612) 546-6943

Incorporated in 1952 in Minnesota.
Donor(s): S.J. Groves & Sons Company, Frank M. Groves.†
Financial data: (yr. ended 9/30/83): Assets, $10,026,422 (M); expenditures, $767,454, including $677,390 for 22 grants (high: $317,286; low: $100; average: $100-$30,000) and $31,117 for 20 grants to individuals.
Purpose and activities: General purposes; primarily local giving for the arts, education, including scholarships for immediate dependents of Company and subsidiary Company employees, and social services.
Types of support awarded: Employee related scholarships, annual campaigns.
Limitations: Giving primarily in the Minneapolis, MN, area. No grants to individuals (except for company-employee scholarships), or for capital or endowment funds, or matching gifts; no loans.
Application information:
  Initial approach: Letter
  Copies of proposal: 1
  Deadline(s): None
  Board meeting date(s): November and as required
  Write: Elfriede M. Lobeck, Executive Director
Officers and Trustees: F.N. Groves, President; C.T. Groves, Vice-President; H.A. Beltz, Secretary and Treasurer; Elfriede M. Lobeck, Executive Director; J.L. Mann.
Number of staff: 1.
Employer Identification Number: 416038512

1855
Hamm Foundation
1120 Norwest Center
St. Paul 55101   (612) 222-3565

Incorporated in 1952 in Minnesota.
Donor(s): Various companies formerly owned by the Hamm family.
Financial data: (yr. ended 6/30/83): Assets, $7,124,691 (M); gifts received, $64,100; expenditures, $569,738, including $45,000 for 1 grant and $318,839 for 1 foundation-administered program.
Purpose and activities: A private operating foundation; primarily operates a local charitable out-patient psychiatric clinic; does not award grants.
Limitations: Giving primarily in St. Paul, MN.
Application information: Applications not invited.
  Board meeting date(s): Quarterly
  Write: Paul A. Verret, Secretary
Officers: Sally A. Anson,* President; William H. Hamm, III,* 1st Vice-President; Cynthia K. O'Neill,* 2nd Vice-President; Paul A. Verret, Secretary-Treasurer.
Directors:* DeWalt H. Ankeny, Jr., Marie H. Ankeny, Barbara L. Cochran, Edward H. Hamm, James E. Kelley, Margaret H. Kelley, Sarah F. Lang, Theodora Lang, Mrs. Kendall A. Mix, Phoebe A. Mix, Kelley M. O'Neill.
Number of staff: 3 full-time professional; 6 part-time professional; 3 full-time support; 1 part-time support.
Employer Identification Number: 416008892

1856
Hartz Foundation
Northern State Bank Bldg.
P.O. Box 642
Thief River Falls 56701

Incorporated in 1956 in Minnesota.
Financial data: (yr. ended 7/31/83): Assets, $3,597,762 (M); expenditures, $182,322, including $180,073 for 67 grants (high: $20,000; low: $34).
Purpose and activities: Primarily local giving, with emphasis on Protestant church support, higher and secondary education, hospitals, community development, and public broadcasting.
Limitations: Giving primarily in MN. No grants to individuals, or for building or endowment funds; no loans.
Application information: Application form required.
  Initial approach: Full proposal
  Copies of proposal: 1
  Deadline(s): Submit proposal preferably in the fall or winter
  Board meeting date(s): September
Officers: L.B. Hartz, President; Onealee Hartz, Secretary and Treasurer; G. Beito, Vice-President.
Employer Identification Number: 416041638

1857
Hartzell Foundation ¤
2515 Wabash Ave.
St. Paul 55114

Established in 1969.
Donor(s): Hartzell Corporation, and its subsidiaries.
Financial data: (yr. ended 9/30/83): Assets, $299,796 (M); gifts received, $150,000; expenditures, $160,271, including $159,284 for 70 grants (high: $20,070; low: $15).
Purpose and activities: Primarily local giving, with emphasis on social agencies, cultural programs, secondary education, hospitals, Protestant church support, and an organization that aids the handicapped.
Limitations: Giving primarily in MN.
Officers: James R. Hartzell, President and Treasurer; Robert Hartzell, Vice-President.
Employer Identification Number: 237059886

1858
Hawthorne Foundation Incorporated ¤
Peninsula Rd. Dellwood
White Bear Lake 55110

Established in 1953.
Donor(s): Herbert R. Galloway.
Financial data: (yr. ended 12/31/83): Assets, $197,044 (M); gifts received, $99,537; expenditures, $123,156, including $121,968 for 37 grants (high: $30,000; low: $100).
Purpose and activities: Primarily local support for education, youth organizations, cultural programs and community funds.
Types of support awarded: General purposes.
Limitations: Giving primarily in the St. Paul, MN, area.
Officers: Herbert R. Galloway, President and Treasurer; Janice T. Galloway, Vice-President; Victoria G. Holmen, Secretary .
Member: Richard B. Galloway.
Employer Identification Number: 416038264

1859
Heilicher (Menahem) Charitable Foundation ¤
850 Decatur Ave., North
Minneapolis 55427

Incorporated in 1963 in Minnesota.
Donor(s): Amos Heilicher, Daniel Heilicher, Advance Carter Co.
Financial data: (yr. ended 9/30/83): Assets, $106 (M); expenditures, $164,543, including $156,445 for 39 grants (high: $107,850; low: $10).
Purpose and activities: Broad purposes; primarily local giving, with emphasis on Jewish welfare funds and religious education.
Limitations: Giving primarily in MN.
Officers: Amos Heilicher, President; Daniel Heilicher, Vice-President and Treasurer; Marvin Borman, Elisa Kane, Secretaries.
Employer Identification Number: 416043457

1860
Hersey Foundation ♯
408 St. Peter St., Rm. 440
St. Paul 55102

Established about 1968 in Minnesota.
Donor(s): William Hamm, Jr.†
Financial data: (yr. ended 12/31/83): Assets, $3,964,975 (M); expenditures, $127,087, including $115,260 for 27 grants (high: $30,600; low: $70).
Purpose and activities: Largely local giving, with emphasis on historic preservation, youth agencies, and urban affairs.
Limitations: Giving primarily in MN.
Officers: Edward H. Hamm, President and Treasurer; Austin Chapman, Vice-President; Joseph A. Maun, Secretary.
Employer Identification Number: 237001771

1861
Honeywell Foundation ▼
(formerly Honeywell Fund)
P.O. Box 524
Minneapolis 55440   (612) 870-6821
Grant application address: for local agencies, send proposals to nearest company manufacturing facility

Incorporated in 1958 in Minnesota.
Donor(s): Honeywell Inc.
Financial data: (yr. ended 12/31/84): Assets, $13,201,841 (M); gifts received, $3,125,000; expenditures, $5,488,640, including $4,554,653 for 680 grants (high: $500,000; low: $125) and $724,519 for 1,600 employee matching gifts.
Purpose and activities: Broad purposes; grants in areas of company operations for higher education, community funds, cultural programs, and youth agencies. Additional charitable support through direct corporate contributions.
Types of support awarded: Operating budgets, continuing support, annual campaigns, seed money, building funds, equipment, employee matching gifts, scholarship funds, fellowships, special projects.
Limitations: Giving limited to cities where company has major facilities, with emphasis on Minneapolis, MN. No grants to individuals, or for general endowment funds, deficit financing, land acquisition, matching or challenge grants, research, demonstration projects, or conferences; no loans.
Publications: Annual report, application guidelines.
Application information:
  Initial approach: Full proposal
  Copies of proposal: 1
  Deadline(s): 15th of month preceding board meetings
  Board meeting date(s): March, June, September, and December
  Final notification: 2 to 3 weeks
  Write: Patricia Hoven, Director
Officers: Ronald K. Speed,* President; Richard E. Weber,* Vice-President; Sigurd Ueland, Jr., Secretary; Louis E. Navin, Treasurer.

Contribution Committee:* Patricia Hoven, Director; Fosten A. Boyle, Richard J. Boyle, Charles E. Brown, W. Donald Conley, Gerald P. Dinneen, James J. Grierson, Charles W. Johnson, Dean B. Randall, Curtis B. Thompson, Richard P. Versoi.
Number of staff: 1 full-time professional; 1 full-time support.
Employer Identification Number: 416023933

1862
Hormel (George A.) Testamentary Trust
501 Sixteenth Ave., N.E.
Austin 55912   (507) 437-5663

Trust established in 1946 in Minnesota.
Donor(s): George A. Hormel.†
Financial data: (yr. ended 12/31/83): Assets, $1,167,826 (M); expenditures, $124,121, including $119,080 for 6 grants (high: $50,000; low: $2,500).
Purpose and activities: Broad purposes; local giving, with emphasis on building maintenance of youth agencies, especially YMCA.
Types of support awarded: Operating budgets, continuing support, annual campaigns, seed money, emergency funds, building funds, equipment, matching funds.
Limitations: Giving limited to Austin, MN. No grants to individuals, or for endowment funds, research, scholarships, fellowships, deficit financing, land acquisition, publications, or conferences; no loans.
Publications: 990-PF.
Application information:
  Initial approach: Letter
  Copies of proposal: 1
  Board meeting date(s): Monthly
  Final notification: 1 month
  Write: E.C. Alsaker, Treasurer
Officers and Members: I.J. Holton, Chairman; R.F. Lichty,* Vice-Chairman; K.F. Hoversten,* Secretary; E.C. Alsaker,* Treasurer; D.R. Brezicka, R.T. Holman, J.G. Huntting, Jr., R.L. Knowlton, J.R. Mueller, R.B. Ondov, N.A. Perry, P. Richardson, W.J. Sheehy, R. Strommer, M.B. Thompson*.
Trustee:* The Hormel Foundation.
Number of staff: None.
Employer Identification Number: 416026834

1863
Hotchkiss (W. R.) Foundation ♯
1080 W. County Rd. F
St. Paul 55112
Scholarship application address: Michael J. Welch, W.R. Hotchkiss Scholarship Plan, P.O. Box 4399, St. Paul, MN 55164-0399; Tel.: (612) 483-7111

Established in 1959.
Donor(s): Agnes M. Gates.†
Financial data: (yr. ended 6/30/83): Assets, $5,334,197 (M); expenditures, $515,014, including $326,289 for 36 grants (high: $40,000; low: $166) and $176,453 for 81 grants to individuals.

Purpose and activities: Primarily local giving for higher and secondary education, youth organizations, and social services; scholarships for children of employees and ex-employees of Deluxe Check Printers, Inc.
Types of support awarded: Employee related scholarships.
Limitations: Giving primarily in MN.
Application information: Application form required.
  Deadline(s): January 31 for scholarships
Officers and Trustees: M.J. Welch, President; J.R. Cross, Vice-President; S.L. Peterson, Secretary; F.H. Cloutier, Treasurer; W.N. Hanson, R.L. Keen, D.J. Pearson, T.J. Quigley.
Employer Identification Number: 416038562

1864
Hubbard Foundation, The ♯
3415 University Ave., S.E.
Minneapolis 55114

Incorporated in 1958 in Minnesota.
Donor(s): Stanley E. Hubbard, KSTP, Inc., Hubbard Broadcasting, Inc.
Financial data: (yr. ended 11/30/83): Assets, $4,772,429 (M); expenditures, $312,157, including $305,361 for 162 grants (high: $11,000; low: $25).
Purpose and activities: Broad purposes; primarily local giving, with emphasis on youth agencies, recreation, community funds, hospitals, and higher and secondary education.
Limitations: Giving primarily in MN.
Officers: Stanley E. Hubbard,* President; Stanley S. Hubbard,* Vice-President and Treasurer; Karen H. Hubbard,* Vice-President; Gerald D. Deeney, Secretary.
Trustees:* Phillip A. Dufrene.
Employer Identification Number: 416022291

1865
Hulings (Mary Andersen) Foundation ♯
c/o Baywood Corporation
287 Central Ave.
Bayport 55003   (612) 439-1557

Established in 1962.
Donor(s): Mary Andersen Hulings, Fred Andersen,† Katherine B. Andersen.
Financial data: (yr. ended 2/29/84): Assets, $4,169,468 (M); gifts received, $100,000; expenditures, $201,256, including $191,665 for 62 grants (high: $35,000; low: $100).
Purpose and activities: Primarily local giving, with emphasis on youth and social agencies, cultural programs, and education.
Types of support awarded: General purposes, operating budgets, seed money, building funds, program-related investments, research.
Limitations: Giving primarily in MN, with emphasis on Bayport. No grants to individuals, or for endowment funds, scholarships, fellowships, or matching gifts; no loans.
Publications: Application guidelines.
Application information: Application form required.
  Initial approach: Letter or proposal
  Copies of proposal: 2

Deadline(s): Submit proposal preferably in March, June, September, or December; no set deadline
Board meeting date(s): May, August, November, and February
Final notification: 3 months
Write: Mary A. Hulings, President
Officers: Mary Andersen Hulings, President; Albert D. Hulings, Vice-President; Kathleen R. Conley, Secretary; William J. Begin, Treasurer.
Number of staff: 2.
Employer Identification Number: 416020911

1866
International Multifoods Charitable Foundation
Multifoods Tower, Box 2942
Minneapolis 55402   (612) 340-3302

Incorporated in 1970 in Delaware.
Donor(s): International Multifoods.
Financial data: (yr. ended 2/29/84): Assets, $632,909 (M); gifts received, $162,000; expenditures, $224,198, including $148,021 for 36 grants (high: $20,000; low: $1,000; average: $1,200-$3,200) and $74,491 for 94 employee matching gifts.
Purpose and activities: Support for local higher education, cultural programs, community funds, youth agencies, health, and public education.
Types of support awarded: Operating budgets, continuing support, annual campaigns, emergency funds, building funds, employee matching gifts.
Limitations: Giving primarily in MN, with emphasis on the Saint Paul-Minneapolis metropolitan area. No support for religious purposes or political campaigns. No grants to individuals, or for deficit financing, equipment, land acquisition, endowment funds, scholarships and fellowships, research, demonstration projects, publications, or conferences; no loans.
Publications: Annual report, program policy statement, application guidelines.
Application information:
Initial approach: Letter
Copies of proposal: 1
Deadline(s): None
Board meeting date(s): Quarterly or as required
Final notification: 10 days after meeting
Write: Frances A. Kolb
Officers: William G. Phillips,* President; Richard H. King,* Vice-President and Treasurer; Thomas P. Brennan, Secretary.
Directors:* Atherton Bean.
Number of staff: None.
Employer Identification Number: 237064628

1867
Inter-Regional Financial Group, Inc., Foundation
100 Dain Tower
Minneapolis 55402   (612) 371-7750
Mailing address: P.O. Box 1160, Minneapolis, MN 55440

Incorporated in 1961 in Minnesota.

Donor(s): Dain, Kalman and Quail, Incorporated, Inter-Regional Financial Group, Inc.
Financial data: (yr. ended 12/31/84): Assets, $204,400 (M); gifts received, $303,755; expenditures, $260,222, including $248,099 for grants (high: $38,000; low: $15) and $11,893 for employee matching gifts.
Purpose and activities: Giving primarily in areas of company operations for social services, community funds, cultural and civic affairs, health, and education, with an emphasis on economic education and community and business development.
Types of support awarded: Employee matching gifts, general purposes, continuing support, annual campaigns, seed money, building funds.
Limitations: Giving primarily in areas of company operations. No grants to individuals, or for endowment funds, research, scholarships, or fellowships; no loans.
Publications: Program policy statement, application guidelines.
Application information:
Initial approach: Full proposal
Copies of proposal: 1
Deadline(s): November 15 and August 15
Board meeting date(s): February and October
Write: Donna Knight, Executive Director
Officers: Thomas E. Holloran,* President; Lutz Pape, Secretary-Treasurer; Donna Knight, Executive Director.
Directors:* Douglas R. Coleman, Joseph J. Gallick, R. Goodfellow, Noel P. Rahn.
Number of staff: 2 part-time professional; 2 part-time support.
Employer Identification Number: 416030639

1868
Jerome Foundation ▼
West-2090 First National Bank Bldg.
St. Paul 55101   (612) 224-9431

Incorporated in 1964 in Minnesota.
Donor(s): J. Jerome Hill.†
Financial data: (yr. ended 4/30/83): Assets, $24,104,386 (M); gifts received, $35,012; expenditures, $1,503,996, including $1,071,722 for 89 grants (high: $84,300; low: $750; average: $5,000-$20,000) and $116,679 for 1 foundation-administered program.
Purpose and activities: Program focus on arts and humanities in the New York City area and in Minnesota.
Types of support awarded: Special projects, general purposes, fellowships.
Limitations: Giving limited to New York, NY, and to MN. Generally no support for crafts or for educational programs in the arts and humanities. No grants to individuals (except for New York City film and video artists), or for travel, undergraduate or graduate student research projects, capital or endowment funds, equipment, scholarships, or matching gifts.
Publications: Annual report, program policy statement, application guidelines.
Application information:
Initial approach: Letter or full proposal
Copies of proposal: 1
Deadline(s): None
Board meeting date(s): Bimonthly

Final notification: 3 to 4 months
Write: Cynthia Gehrig, President
Officers: A.A. Heckman,* Chairman and Treasurer; Irving Clark,* Vice-Chairman; Cynthia Gehrig, President and Secretary.
Directors:* Patricia Bratnober, Gaylord W. Glarner, Thelma Hunter, Archibald Leyasmeyer.
Number of staff: 2 full-time professional; 2 full-time support.
Employer Identification Number: 416035163

1869
J.N.M. 1966 Gift Trust ⊭
c/o Norwest Bank Duluth, Trust Dept.
Duluth 55802

Trust established in 1966 in Minnesota as successor to J.N.M. Gift Trust established in 1949.
Donor(s): Newell Marshall.
Financial data: (yr. ended 12/31/83): Assets, $1,158,674 (M); expenditures, $248,138, including $242,225 for 19 grants (high: $47,500; low: $100).
Purpose and activities: Primarily local giving, with emphasis on higher education and cultural programs; support also for international cooperation.
Limitations: Giving primarily in MN.
Trustees: Caroline Marshall, Newell Marshall.
Employer Identification Number: 416050249

1870
Jostens Foundation, Inc., The
5501 Norman Center Dr.
Minneapolis 55437   (612) 830-8429
Application address: P.O. Box 20367, Bloomington, MN 55420; Scholarship application address: Citizens Scholarship Foundation of America, Inc., Box 112A, Londonberry Turnpike RFD No. 7, Manchester, NH 03104; Tel.: (603) 627-3870

Established in 1976 in Minnesota.
Donor(s): Jostens Inc.
Financial data: (yr. ended 6/30/83): Assets, $509,607 (M); gifts received, $607,428; expenditures, $545,102, including $272,451 for 139 grants (high: $27,000; low: $200), $110,000 for 220 grants to individuals and $59,650 for 185 employee matching gifts.
Purpose and activities: Support mainly for local youth and social agencies, arts and cultural programs, a community fund, and secondary and higher education, including a scholarship program and employee matching gifts.
Types of support awarded: Employee matching gifts, student aid.
Limitations: Giving primarily in MN, particularly the Twin Cities area; matching gift programs have a national scope. No grants for endowment funds; no loans.
Publications: Annual report, application guidelines, program policy statement.
Application information:
Initial approach: Telephone
Copies of proposal: 1
Deadline(s): Last day of the month preceding board meeting

Board meeting date(s): Bimonthly begining in January
Write: Ellis F. Bullock, Jr., Director
Officers and Directors: H. William Lurton, Chairman; Robert Leslie, Vice-Chairman; Don C. Lein, President; Orville E. Fisher, Jr., Secretary; James J. Sellner, Jr., Treasurer; Ellis F. Bullock, Jr., Executive Director.
Employer Identification Number: 411280587

1871
Kasal (Father) Charitable Trust
c/o Minnesota Trust Company
107 West Oakland Ave., P.O. Box 463
Austin 55912   (507) 437-3231

Trust established in 1963 in Minnesota.
Financial data: (yr. ended 9/30/83): Assets, $1,639,094 (M); expenditures, $129,798, including $97,380 for 35 grants (high: $14,000; low: $500; average: $2,782).
Purpose and activities: Support for Catholic charities in the United States and for education of young men and women for religious life.
Types of support awarded: Matching funds, scholarship funds.
Limitations: No grants to individuals, or for building or endowment funds, or research; no loans.
Publications: Annual report, program policy statement, application guidelines.
Application information: Application form required.
Initial approach: Letter
Copies of proposal: 2
Deadline(s): Submit proposal preferably in January, April, or July; deadline 10th of month in which board meets
Board meeting date(s): January, April, July, October, and November
Final notification: 6 months
Write: Warren F. Plunkett, President
Officers and Trustees: Warren F. Plunkett, President; Mary Matuska, Secretary; Rt. Rev. Msgr. B.P. Mangan, Treasurer; Minnesota Trust Company.
Number of staff: None.
Employer Identification Number: 416031334

1872
Kennedy (Augustus H.) Memorial Fund Trust ¤
c/o First Trust Company of St. Paul
W-555 First National Bank Bldg.
St. Paul 55101

Trust established about 1977 in Minnesota.
Donor(s): Augustus H. Kennedy.†
Financial data: (yr. ended 8/31/83): Assets, $1,959,083 (M); gifts received, $125,072; expenditures, $124,520, including $113,632 for 5 grants (high: $34,090; low: $5,682).
Purpose and activities: Local giving to religious organizations, a medical research organization, and a foundation.
Limitations: Giving limited to Minneapolis, St. Paul, and Rochester, MN, and Miami, FL.
Application information: Distributions are committed exclusively to four specific organizations and a foundation.
Trustee: First Trust Company of St. Paul.
Employer Identification Number: 411328800

1873
Lang (Helen) Charitable Trust ¤
c/o First Trust Company of Saint Paul
W-555 First National Bank Bldg.
St. Paul 55101

Established in 1980.
Donor(s): Helen Lang.†
Financial data: (yr. ended 8/31/83): Assets, $1,401,411 (M); expenditures, $30,791, including $20,000 for 1 grant.
Purpose and activities: Primarily local support for education.
Limitations: Giving primarily in MN.
Application information:
Initial approach: Written form only
Deadline(s): None
Write: Paul J. Kelly, Secretary
Trustees: Andrew Scott, First Trust Company of St. Paul.
Employer Identification Number: 416231202

1874
Larson (Joseph N.) Foundation ¤
c/o Tax Division
Norwest Bank, Minneapolis
Minneapolis 55479

Financial data: (yr. ended 3/31/83): Assets, $14,924 (M); gifts received, $1,848; expenditures, $105,706, including $100,000 for 5 grants (high: $25,000; low: $5,000).
Purpose and activities: Primarily local giving for Protestant church support and organizations.
Limitations: Giving primarily in MN.
Application information: Applications not invited.
Trustees: Gordon Larson, Harold Larson, Ingvold B. Sorenson, Rueben Waltov, Norwest Bank Minneapolis.
Employer Identification Number: 416198979

1875
Lieberman-Okinow Foundation, The
9549 Penn Ave. South
Minneapolis 55431

Incorporated in 1961 in Minnesota.
Donor(s): Carousel Snack Bars of Minnesota, Inc., Lieberman Enterprises, Incorporated.
Financial data: (yr. ended 9/30/83): Assets, $1,712 (M); gifts received, $283,172; expenditures, $289,766, including $289,753 for 106 grants (high: $125,000; low: $25).
Purpose and activities: Primarily local giving, with emphasis on Jewish welfare funds; some support for community funds.
Limitations: Giving primarily in MN.
Officers and Directors: Adele Lieberman, President; David Lieberman, Vice-President; Stephen Lieberman, Secretary; Harold Okinow, Treasurer; Sara Lieberman, Sheila Lieberman, Sandra Okinow.
Employer Identification Number: 416036200

1876
Lilly (Richard Coyle) Foundation
c/o First Trust Company of Saint Paul
W-555 First National Bank Bldg.
St. Paul 55101   (612) 291-5061

Incorporated in 1941 in Minnesota.
Donor(s): Richard C. Lilly.†
Financial data: (yr. ended 12/31/83): Assets, $2,899,500 (M); expenditures, $106,338, including $95,800 for 51 grants (high: $6,000; low: $200).
Purpose and activities: Broad purposes; primarily local giving, with emphasis on education.
Types of support awarded: General purposes, continuing support, annual campaigns, seed money, building funds, equipment, land acquisition, endowment funds, research, special projects, publications, matching funds.
Limitations: Giving primarily in St. Paul, MN. No grants to individuals, or for fellowships or scholarships; no loans.
Application information:
Initial approach: Full proposal or letter
Copies of proposal: 2
Deadline(s): None
Board meeting date(s): December
Final notification: 6 weeks
Write: James P. Donner, Vice-President
Officers and Directors: David M. Lilly, President; Elizabeth M. Lilly, Vice-President; Bruce A. Lilly, David M. Lilly, Jr., Susanne Lilly Hutcheson.
Employer Identification Number: 416038717

1877
Lutheran Brotherhood Foundation
625 4th Ave. South
Minneapolis 55415   (612) 340-5821

Established in 1982 in Minnesota.
Donor(s): Lutheran Brotherhood, Lutheran Brotherhood Research Corp.
Financial data: (yr. ended 12/31/84): Assets, $6,998,021 (M); gifts received, $2,030,757; expenditures, $332,259, including $151,236 for 7 grants (high: $25,000; low: $6,455; average: $10,000-$15,000).
Purpose and activities: Grants for Lutheran churches and religious organizations only, including higher education and innovative pilot projects in leadership development and volunteerism.
Types of support awarded: Seed money, conferences and seminars.
Limitations: No grants to individuals, or for operating budgets, continuing support, annual campaigns, emergency funds, deficit financing, building funds, equipment and materials, land acquisition, renovation projects, endowments, matching or challenge grants, scholarships or fellowships, program support, research, or publications; no loans.
Publications: Program policy statement, application guidelines.
Application information: Application form required.
Initial approach: Letter of not more than 3 typewritten pages
Deadline(s): March 1 and October 1
Board meeting date(s): Quarterly

Final notification: 2 months after deadlines
Write: Linda Paulson
Officers: Helen M. Thal,* President; Kent Eklund, Executive Director and Vice-President; Woodrow P. Langhaug,* Rolf F. Bjelland, Vice-Presidents; Norman M. Lorentzen,* Secretary; Edward A. Lindell,* Treasurer.
Trustees:* Clair E. Strommen, Lloyd Svendsbye.
Number of staff: 1.
Employer Identification Number: 411449680

1878
Marbrook Foundation
510 Baker Bldg.
Minneapolis 55402   (612) 332-2454

Trust established in 1948 in Minnesota.
Donor(s): Edward Brooks,† Markell C. Brooks,† Markell C. Brooks Charitable Trust.
Financial data: (yr. ended 12/31/84): Assets, $3,913,465 (M); gifts received, $10,000; expenditures, $278,330, including $240,000 for 55 grants (high: $30,000; low: $250; average: $500-$2,500).
Purpose and activities: General purposes; support primarily to established local organizations with ongoing programs, with emphasis on education, visual and performing arts, social welfare, health and medicine, and conservation and recreation.
Types of support awarded: Operating budgets, continuing support, annual campaigns, seed money, emergency funds, building funds, endowment funds, matching funds, professorships, internships, research, conferences and seminars, special projects.
Limitations: Giving primarily in Minneapolis-St. Paul, MN, area. No support for religious purposes. No grants to individuals, or for deficit financing, equipment, land acquisition, scholarships or fellowships, demonstration projects, or publications; no loans.
Publications: Annual report, application guidelines.
Application information:
Initial approach: Letter
Copies of proposal: 1
Deadline(s): Submit proposal preferably in March or September; deadlines May 15 and October 15
Board meeting date(s): May and November
Final notification: 3 weeks after meeting
Write: Conley Brooks, Jr., Executive Director
Trustees: Conley Brooks, Jr., Executive Director; John E. Andrus III, Conley Brooks, William R. Humphrey, Jr.
Number of staff: None.
Employer Identification Number: 416019899

1879
Mardag Foundation ▼
1120 Norwest Center
St. Paul 55101   (612) 224-4849

Trust established in 1969 in Minnesota.
Donor(s): Agnes E. Ober.†
Financial data: (yr. ended 12/31/83): Assets, $15,333,924 (M); expenditures, $665,595, including $563,823 for 65 grants (high: $50,000; low: $1,000; average: $3,000-$25,000).

Purpose and activities: General purposes; local giving for social agencies, conservation, programs to benefit senior citizens, arts and cultural programs, and education.
Types of support awarded: Special projects, building funds, research, seed money, deficit financing, matching funds, equipment, emergency funds, general purposes.
Limitations: Giving limited to MN. No support for sectarian religious programs. No grants to individuals, or for continuing support, annual campaigns, endowment funds, scholarships, or fellowships.
Publications: Annual report, 990-PF, program policy statement, application guidelines.
Application information:
Initial approach: Telephone, letter, or full proposal
Copies of proposal: 1
Deadline(s): None
Board meeting date(s): Quarterly and as required
Final notification: 90 days
Write: Paul A. Verret, Secretary
Officers: Thomas G. Mairs,* Principal Officer; Stephen S. Ober,* Financial Officer; Paul A. Verret, Secretary.
Trustees:* James E. Davidson, Virginia G. Davidson, James C. Otis.
Number of staff: None.
Employer Identification Number: 237022429

1880
McKnight Foundation, The ▼
410 Peavey Bldg.
Minneapolis 55402   (612) 333-4220

Incorporated in 1953 in Minnesota.
Donor(s): William L. McKnight,† Maude L. McKnight,† Virginia M. Binger, James H. Binger.
Financial data: (yr. ended 12/31/84): Assets, $509,422,638 (M); gifts received, $60,566,178; expenditures, $29,863,192, including $11,945,119 for 200 grants (high: $700,000; low: $250; average: $5,000-$500,000), $3,519,338 for 53 grants to individuals and $12,209,244 for 2 loans.
Purpose and activities: Emphasis on grantmaking in the areas of human and social services in the seven-county Twin Cities metropolitan area and in Minnesota; has multi-year comprehensive programs in the arts, mental health, and developmental disabilities; supports nation-wide scientific research programs in areas of (1) neuroscience, particularly for research in memory and diseases affecting memory, and (2) basic plant biology (applications for these programs are solicited periodically through announcements in scientific journals and directly to institutions carrying out research programs). Also supports programs for the chronically mentally ill in 4 different communities.
Types of support awarded: Research, operating budgets, building funds, seed money, emergency funds, equipment, matching funds, program-related investments, continuing support.

Limitations: Giving limited to organizations in MN, primarily in the seven-county metropolitan area of Minneapolis and St. Paul. No support for religious organizations for religious purposes, or biomedical research (except for awards in neuroscience). No grants to individuals (except for the McKnight Awards in Neuroscience and Plant Biology), or for endowment funds, scholarships and fellowships, or national fundraising campaigns; no loans.
Publications: Annual report, informational brochure, program policy statement, application guidelines.
Application information: Application form required.
Initial approach: Letter
Copies of proposal: 7
Deadline(s): March 1, June 1, September 1, and December 1
Board meeting date(s): February, May, August, and November
Final notification: Two and a half months
Write: Russell V. Ewald, Executive Vice-President
Officers and Directors: Virginia M. Binger, President; Russell V. Ewald, Executive Vice-President and Secretary; James H. Binger, Vice-President and Treasurer; James M. Binger, Judith Binger, Cynthia Boynton.
Number of staff: 2 full-time professional; 2 part-time professional; 4 full-time support.
Employer Identification Number: 410754835

1881
McKnight (The Sumner T.) Foundation ⌺
c/o Northwestern National Bank of Minneapolis, Trust Dept.
Eighth and Marquette Ave.
Minneapolis 55479

Incorporated in 1956 in Minnesota.
Donor(s): Sumner T. McKnight,† H. Turney McKnight.
Financial data: (yr. ended 12/31/83): Assets, $3,447,935 (M); gifts received, $24,096; expenditures, $273,700, including $239,600 for 35 grants (high: $30,000; low: $1,000).
Purpose and activities: Broad purposes; primarily local giving, with emphasis on music, fine arts, conservation and recreation, historical societies, higher and secondary education, inner-city programs, and community funds.
Limitations: Giving primarily in MN. No support for religion. No grants to individuals or for endowment funds.
Application information:
Initial approach: Full proposal
Board meeting date(s): January and midyear
Write: Malcolm G. Pfunder, Secretary
Officers and Directors: H. Turney McKnight, President; Peter Heegaard, Sumner T. McKnight, Eugene Trumble, Vice-Presidents; Malcolm G. Pfunder, Secretary and Treasurer; Duane E. Joseph, Christina M. Kippen, John T. Westrom, Wheelock Whitney.
Employer Identification Number: 416022360

1882
McNeely Foundation, The
444 Lafayette Rd.
St. Paul 55101   (612) 228-4444

Established in 1981 in Minnesota.
Donor(s): Lee and Rose Warner Foundation.
Financial data: (yr. ended 12/31/82): Assets,
$2,600,000 (M); expenditures, $150,000,
including $120,000 for 20 grants (high:
$40,000; low: $500; average: $3,000-$5,000)
and $30,000 for 130 employee matching gifts.
Purpose and activities: Primarily local giving
for Christian church support and religious
institutions; support also for community funds
and higher education.
Types of support awarded: Operating
budgets, continuing support, annual campaigns,
seed money, emergency funds, building funds,
endowment funds, employee matching gifts,
program-related investments.
Limitations: Giving primarily in the St. Paul-
Minneapolis, MN, area. No grants to
individuals, or for deficit financing, equipment,
land acquisition, renovation projects,
scholarships and fellowships, research,
demonstration projects, publications, or
conferences; no loans.
Application information:
  Initial approach: Letter
  Copies of proposal: 1
  Deadline(s): Submit proposal preferably in
    September or December
  Board meeting date(s): March, June,
    September, and December
  Write: Malcolm W. McDonald
Trustees: Frank A. Koscielack, Gregory
McNeely, Harry G. McNeely.
Number of staff: None.
Employer Identification Number: 411392221

1883
Meadowood Foundation
4122 IDS Center
Minneapolis 55402

Established in 1968.
Financial data: (yr. ended 12/31/83): Assets,
$2,945,206 (M); gifts received, $2,495;
expenditures, $137,870, including $135,180
for 16 grants (high: $70,000; low: $100).
Purpose and activities: Primarily local giving
for education, cultural programs, and a youth
organization.
Types of support awarded: General purposes,
building funds.
Limitations: Giving primarily in MN.
Officers and Directors: Douglas J. Dayton,
President; Shirley D. Dayton, Vice-President;
Ronald N. Gross, Secretary; Bruce C. Dayton,
David D. Dayton, Steven J. Melander-Dayton.
Employer Identification Number: 410943749

1884
Medtronic Foundation, The ▼
3055 Old Highway Eight
P.O. Box 1453
Minneapolis 55440   (612) 574-3024

Established in 1979 in Minnesota.
Donor(s): Medtronic, Inc.

Financial data: (yr. ended 4/30/84): Assets,
$2,421,894 (M); gifts received, $1,018,000;
expenditures, $769,600, including $664,868
for 92 grants (high: $45,000; low: $1,000;
average: $1,000-$10,000) and $30,621 for 242
employee matching gifts.
Purpose and activities: Giving primarily in
areas of company facilities, with emphasis on
physical health promotion, the elderly,
education, arts and culture, social agencies and
community funds.
Types of support awarded: Operating
budgets, continuing support, annual campaigns,
seed money, matching funds, scholarship
funds, fellowships, special projects, employee
matching gifts.
Limitations: Giving primarily in areas of
company operations. No support for United
Way member agencies, primarily social
organizations, religious activities, primary health
care, health research. No grants to individuals,
or for deficit financing, capital funds, research,
travel, fund-raising events, advertising, or
publications; generally no grants for
endowment funds, conferences, or operating
support for smaller arts groups.
Publications: Annual report, application
guidelines.
Application information:
  Initial approach: Telephone
  Copies of proposal: 1
  Deadline(s): Submit proposal between
    September and March; no set deadline
  Board meeting date(s): June, August,
    October, December, and April
  Final notification: 60 days
  Write: Jan Schwarz, Manager
Officers and Directors: John A. Meslow,
Chairman; Raymond J. Dittrich, Vice-Chairman;
David L. Duclos, Secretary; B. Kristine Johnson,
Treasurer; Bobby I. Griffin, Gerard C.
Planchon, Franklin R. Rick, Jeffrey O. Stewart.
Number of staff: 1 part-time professional; 1
part-time support.
Employer Identification Number: 411306950

1885
Melamed Foundation, The ⌷
820 Midwest Plaza Bldg.
Minneapolis 55402

Incorporated in 1947 in Minnesota.
Donor(s): Members of the Melamed family.
Financial data: (yr. ended 12/31/83): Assets,
$764,322 (M); gifts received, $25,706;
expenditures, $117,316, including $109,372
for 56 grants (high: $35,050; low: $13).
Purpose and activities: Broad purposes;
emphasis on Jewish welfare funds; grants also
for higher education, temple support, and
hospitals.
Officers and Trustees: Arthur C. Melamed,
President and Treasurer; Ruth H. Melamed,
Vice-President and Secretary; Arthur D.
Melamed, Robert L. Melamed, Vice-Presidents.
Employer Identification Number: 416019581

1886
Miller (The Gladys and Rudolph) Foundation
5112 IDS Center
Minneapolis 55402

Established in 1980.
Donor(s): R.W. Miller, Miller Felpar Corp.
Financial data: (yr. ended 11/30/83): Assets,
$1,954,540 (M); gifts received, $4,760;
expenditures, $255,676, including $252,454
for 7 grants (high: $130,000; low: $500).
Purpose and activities: Grants primarily for
medical organizations, Jewish giving, and the
performing arts.
Officers and Directors: R.W. Miller, President
and Treasurer; Sidney Lovber, Vice-President
and Secretary; Sidney Barrows.
Employer Identification Number: 411388774

1887
Minneapolis Foundation, The ▼
500 Foshay Tower
821 Marquette Ave.
Minneapolis 55402   (612) 339-7343

Community foundation incorporated in 1915 in
Minnesota.
Financial data: (yr. ended 3/31/83): Assets,
$29,561,647 (M); gifts received, $1,583,292;
expenditures, $3,109,034; including
$2,596,126 for 534 grants (high: $50,000; low:
$50; average: $5,000-$15,000).
Purpose and activities: To aid groups to
provide services for the benefit of local
residents; grants largely for human services,
community affairs, education, arts and health.
Types of support awarded: Seed money,
emergency funds, equipment, technical
assistance, loans, special projects.
Limitations: Giving primarily in the
Minneapolis-St. Paul, MN, seven-county
metropolitan area. No support for national
campaigns, religious organizations for religious
purposes, veterans or fraternal organizations, or
to organizations within umbrella organizations.
No grants to individuals, or for operating
budgets, continuing support, annual campaigns,
deficit financing, building or endowment funds,
land acquisition, matching gifts, scholarships
and fellowships, research, publications,
conferences, courtesy advertising, benefit
tickets, telephone solicitations, or memberships.
Publications: Annual report, application
guidelines, program policy statement.
Application information: Undesignated funds
considered in June and December; requests to
the McKnight-Neighborhood Self-Help
Initiatives Program reviewed in March and
September. Application form required.
  Initial approach: Letter or telephone
  Copies of proposal: 14
  Deadline(s): 6 weeks before distribution
    committee meeting
  Board meeting date(s): Semiannually;
    distribution committee meets quarterly
  Final notification: 4 months
  Write: Marion Etzwiler, Executive Director

Officers and Trustees:* Marvin Borman,* President; Edward C. Lund,* Frances Naftalin,* Vice-Presidents; Conley Brooks,* Secretary; Clinton Morrison,* Treasurer; Marion Etzwiler, Executive Director; and 29 additional trustees.
Distribution Committee: Mary Lee Dayton, Chair.
Trustee Banks: First National Bank of Minneapolis, Northwestern National Bank of Minneapolis.
Number of staff: 5 full-time professional; 2 part-time professional; 3 full-time support.
Employer Identification Number: 416029402

1888
Minneapolis Star and Tribune Foundation
329 Portland Ave.
Minneapolis 55415   (612) 375-7034

Incorporated in 1945 in Minnesota.
Donor(s): Minneapolis Star and Tribune Company.
Financial data: (yr. ended 2/25/84): Assets, $854,650 (M); expenditures, $128,570, including $118,508 for 8 grants (high: $31,000; low: $2,508).
Purpose and activities: Support of educational, scientific, and charitable organizations in the Minneapolis area, including higher education, civic agencies, and journalism; support also for a community fund and a youth organization.
Limitations: Giving limited to the Minneapolis, MN, area. No grants to individuals, or for operating budgets or special projects.
Publications: 990-PF, program policy statement, application guidelines.
Application information:
  Initial approach: Letter, or telephone
  Copies of proposal: 1
  Board meeting date(s): February, April, June, August, October, and December
Officers and Directors: David Kruidenier, Chairman; Roger Parkinson, President; James A. Alcott, David C. Cox, Vice-Presidents; Norton L. Armour, Secretary; John Cole, Treasurer; Hazel Reinhardt, Otto A. Silha.
Employer Identification Number: 416031373

1889
Minnesota Foundation
1120 Norwest Center
St. Paul 55101   (612) 224-5463

Incorporated in 1949 in Minnesota.
Financial data: (yr. ended 6/30/83): Assets, $3,351,642 (M); gifts received, $35,851; expenditures, $169,871, including $124,047 for 11 grants (high: $70,000; low: $241) and $29,935 for 1 foundation-administered program.
Purpose and activities: As of January 1, 1984, the foundation is a supporting organization of the Saint Paul Foundation.
Limitations: Giving primarily in MN.
Application information:
  Board meeting date(s): Quarterly or as required
  Write: Paul A. Verret, President

Officers: Paul A. Verret, President; Mariam C. Noland, Vice-President; Robert S. Davis,* Treasurer.
Trustees:* Frank Hammond, Chairman; Emily Anne Staples, Vice-Chairman; Robert L. Bullard, Nancy N. Weyerhaeuser, Leonard H. Wilkening.
Employer Identification Number: 410832480

1890
Minnesota Mining and Manufacturing Foundation, Inc. ▼
3M Center
St. Paul 55144   (612) 736-3781

Incorporated in 1953 in Minnesota.
Donor(s): Minnesota Mining & Manufacturing Company.
Financial data: (yr. ended 12/31/83): Assets, $6,552,577 (M); gifts received, $5,000,000; expenditures, $4,791,091, including $4,326,208 for 656 grants (high: $564,723; low: $25; average: $500-$1,000) and $453,022 for 1,536 employee matching gifts.
Purpose and activities: Giving in areas of company operations, with emphasis on community funds, higher education, the arts, youth agencies, and hospitals.
Types of support awarded: Operating budgets, continuing support, annual campaigns, emergency funds, matching funds, employee matching gifts, scholarship funds, professorships, internships, fellowships, special projects, research.
Limitations: Giving primarily in areas where the company has facilities. No support for projects of specific religious denominations or sects, or conduit agencies. No grants to individuals, or for capital or endowment funds, loans or investments, propaganda and lobbying efforts, fundraising events and associated advertising, travel, publications unrelated to foundation-funded projects, seed money, deficit financing, or conferences; no loans.
Publications: Company report, program policy statement, application guidelines.
Application information: Application form required.
  Initial approach: Letter
  Deadline(s): 6 weeks prior to month in which board meets
  Board meeting date(s): March, June, September, and December
  Final notification: 3 months
  Write: E.W. Steele, Manager, Contributions Programs
Officers: D.E. Garretson,* President; D.W. Larson,* Vice-President and Secretary; R.D. Ebbott, Treasurer.
Directors:* R.M. Adams, R.W. Brust, Charlton Dietz, A.F. Jacobson, L.W. Lehr, D.R. Osmon, J.E. Robertson, S.W. Thiele, J.A. Thwaits.
Number of staff: 9.
Employer Identification Number: 416038262

1891
Neilson (George W.) Foundation
805 Builders Exchange
Minneapolis 55402   (612) 327-6717

Trust established in 1962 in Minnesota.
Donor(s): George W. Neilson,† Mrs. Katharine Neilson Cram.
Financial data: (yr. ended 12/31/84): Assets, $1,430,552 (M); expenditures, $87,982, including $32,700 for 11 grants (high: $5,000; low: $450; average: $2,454).
Purpose and activities: Local giving, with emphasis on matching funds for community needs, including recreation, educational facilities and support for conservation.
Types of support awarded: General purposes, building funds, research, matching funds.
Limitations: Giving primarily in MN. No grants to individuals, or for endowment funds, scholarships, or fellowships; no loans.
Application information:
  Initial approach: Letter
  Copies of proposal: 1
  Deadline(s): July 1
  Board meeting date(s): July or August
  Write: Henry Doerr, Treasurer
Officers: Katharine Neilson Cram, President; Edward M. Arundel, Secretary; Henry Doerr, Treasurer.
Number of staff: None.
Employer Identification Number: 416022186

1892
North Star Research Foundation
805 Builders Exchange
Minneapolis 55402   (612) 339-8101

Established in 1982 in Minnesota.
Financial data: (yr. ended 12/31/84): Assets, $1,462,000 (L); expenditures, $72,000, including $50,000 for 2 foundation-administered programs and $22,000 for 2 loans.
Purpose and activities: Giving limited to Minnesota and surrounding states; grants will be for the support of scientific research leading to new technology or new businesses to produce or retain jobs to strengthen the region; also loans to businesses or individuals in the form of program-related investments.
Types of support awarded: Seed money, equipment, program-related investments, loans, research.
Limitations: Giving limited to MN and surrounding states. No grants to individuals, or for operating budgets, continuing support, annual campaigns, emergency funds, deficit financing, building or endowment funds, land acquisition, renovation, matching gifts, scholarships, fellowships, special projects, publications, or conferences.
Application information: Application form required.
  Initial approach: Telephone or letter
  Deadline(s): None
  Board meeting date(s): January, April, July, and October
  Final notification: 120 days
  Write: Henry Doerr, Consultant

Officers and Directors: John N. Dempsey, President; Henry T. Rutledge, Vice-President; John E. Haaland, Secretary; Philip B. Harris, Treasurer; and 17 additional directors.
Number of staff: None.
Employer Identification Number: 411408469

1893
Northern Star Foundation ⊠
440 Hamm Bldg.
St. Paul 55102

Incorporated in 1960 in Minnesota.
Donor(s): Members of the Hamm family.
Financial data: (yr. ended 10/31/83): Assets, $2,499,659 (M); expenditures, $124,099, including $112,102 for 63 grants (high: $15,000; low: $25).
Purpose and activities: Primarily local giving, with emphasis on secondary and higher education, including scholarship funds, cultural programs, youth agencies, and a community fund.
Limitations: Giving primarily in MN and CA.
Application information:
  Write: William H. Hamm, President
Officers and Directors: William H. Hamm,* President; Edward H. Hamm,* Vice-President and Treasurer; Candace S. Hamm, Vice-President; Joseph A. Maun, Secretary.
Employer Identification Number: 416030832

1894
Northwest Area Foundation ▼
West 975 First National Bank Bldg.
St. Paul 55101   (612) 224-9635

Incorporated in 1934 in Minnesota as Lexington Foundation; name changed to Louis W. and Maud Hill Family Foundation in 1950; present name adopted 1975.
Donor(s): Louis W. Hill, Sr.,† and other members of the Hill family.
Financial data: (yr. ended 2/29/84): Assets, $134,830,898 (M); expenditures, $7,462,822, including $6,967,105 for 196 grants (high: $250,000; low: $150; average: $20,000-$60,000).
Purpose and activities: To aid in development of new bodies of knowledge; to develop and improve liaison between research and practice; to encourage utilization and correlation of existing bodies of knowledge; to pioneer and assist pioneering organizations in the fields of the arts and humanities, environmental and physical sciences, medical sciences and health, human services, social sciences, youth and higher education. Grants generally for experimental and demonstration projects which promise significant impact but for which there is not now general support; giving limited to an eight-state region that includes Idaho, Iowa, Minnesota, Montana, North Dakota, Oregon, South Dakota, and Washington; funding for the arts program limited primarily to metropolitan St. Paul and Minneapolis, Minnesota.
Types of support awarded: Special projects, research, consulting services, technical assistance, program-related investments.

Limitations: Giving primarily in ID, IA, MN, MT, ND, OR, SD, and WA; funding for the Arts Program limited to metropolitan St. Paul and Minneapolis, MN. No support for religious programs. No grants to individuals, or for scholarships, fellowships, endowment or capital funds, films, travel, lobbying, propaganda, overhead, physical plants, equipment, publications, operating budgets, continuing support, annual campaigns, emergency funds, deficit financing, building funds, land acquisition, renovation projects, or conferences.
Publications: Annual report, program policy statement, application guidelines.
Application information:
  Initial approach: Telephone, letter, or proposal
  Copies of proposal: 2
  Deadline(s): Varies according to field
  Board meeting date(s): Bimonthly beginning in February
  Final notification: 60 to 90 days
  Write: Terry Tinson, President
Officers: W. John Driscoll,* Chairman and Treasurer; Irving Clark,* Vice-Chairman; Terry Tinson Saario, President and Secretary; Martha G. Butt, Judith K. Healey, Vice-Presidents.
Trustees: Irving Clark, W. John Driscoll, Sheila ffolliot, Louis W. Hill, Jr., Maud Hill Schroll.
Directors: Shirley M. Clark, Joseph T. Ling, Norman Lorentzsen, Carlos Luis, Francis B. Tiffany, M.D., Jean M. West, Stanley E. Williams.
Number of staff: 3 full-time professional; 6 full-time support.
Employer Identification Number: 410719221

1895
Norwest Foundation
1200 Peavey Bldg.
Minneapolis 55479   (612) 372-0990

Established in 1979 in Minnesota.
Donor(s): Norwest Corporation, and affiliated banks.
Financial data: (yr. ended 12/31/84): Assets, $783,822 (M); gifts received, $999,907; expenditures, $863,758, including $863,758 for 85 grants (high: $80,000; low: $500; average: $5,000-$15,000).
Purpose and activities: Giving primarily for higher education; support also for cultural programs, public communications, and social agencies.
Limitations: Giving limited to organizations in the Midwest or national organizations that benefit that region. No grants to individuals, or for endowment funds, or matching gifts; no loans.
Application information:
  Initial approach: Letter
  Copies of proposal: 1
  Board meeting date(s): January, April, July, and October
  Write: David W. Cost, President
Officers and Directors: David W. Cost, President; Stanley S. Stroup, Secretary; David Jarvis, Treasurer.
Number of staff: 1 full-time professional; 2 full-time support.
Employer Identification Number: 411367441

1896
O'Brien (Alice M.) Foundation
324 Forest
Mahtomedi 55115   (612) 426-2143

Incorporated in 1951 in Minnesota.
Donor(s): Miss Alice M. O'Brien.†
Financial data: (yr. ended 12/31/83): Assets, $2,004,855 (M); expenditures, $156,812, including $139,650 for 24 grants (high: $25,000; low: $125).
Purpose and activities: Local giving, with emphasis on secondary and higer education, including medical education and research; some support for social services and cultural programs.
Types of support awarded: Operating budgets, annual campaigns, seed money, building funds, equipment, research.
Limitations: Giving limited to MN. No grants to individuals, or for endowment funds, scholarships, fellowships, or matching gifts; no loans.
Application information:
  Initial approach: Full proposal
  Copies of proposal: 1
  Deadline(s): Submit proposal in May or November; deadlines June 1 and December 1
  Board meeting date(s): June and December
  Final notification: 6 months
  Write: Julia O'Brien Wilcox, President
Officers and Directors: Julia O'Brien Wilcox, President; Richard S. Wilcox, Jr., Vice-President; Thomond R. O'Brien, Treasurer; Eleanor M. O'Brien, Terance G. O'Brien, William J. O'Brien.
Number of staff: None.
Employer Identification Number: 416018991

1897
Onan Family Foundation
310 Shelard Plaza West
435 Ford Rd.
Minneapolis 55426   (612) 544-4702

Incorporated in 1942 in Minnesota.
Donor(s): Members of the Onan family.
Financial data: (yr. ended 12/31/83): Assets, $2,908,433 (M); expenditures, $159,485, including $119,800 for 28 grants (high: $33,000; low: $100).
Purpose and activities: To improve the physical, cultural, and educational condition of mankind; primarily local giving, with emphasis on social welfare agencies, cultural and civic organizations, educational institutions, and church support.
Limitations: Giving primarily in the Twin Cities, MN, metropolitan area. No grants to individuals, or for capital or endowment funds, research, scholarships, fellowships, trips, or matching gifts; no loans.
Publications: Annual report, program policy statement, application guidelines.
Application information:
  Initial approach: Letter
  Copies of proposal: 1
  Deadline(s): Submit proposal in April or September
  Board meeting date(s): Semiannually
  Write: David W. Onan, II, President

Officers and Trustees: David W. Onan, II, President and Treasurer; Bruce R. Smith, Secretary; David W. Onan, III, Elizabeth H. Onan, Lois C. Onan, Geraldine O. Smith.
Number of staff: 1 part-time professional.
Employer Identification Number: 416033631

1898
O'Neil (The Casey Albert T.) Foundation
(formerly The Albert T. O'Neil Foundation)
c/o First Trust Company of St. Paul
W-555 First National Bank Bldg.
St. Paul 55101   (612) 291-5114

Trust established in 1965 in Minnesota.
Donor(s): Albert T. O'Neil.
Financial data: (yr. ended 6/30/84): Assets, $1,462,234 (M); expenditures, $223,647, including $221,600 for 34 grants (high: $30,000; low: $500).
Purpose and activities: Primarily local giving, with emphasis on Roman Catholic religious assocations and missions, health agencies, and aid to handicapped children.
Types of support awarded: Operating budgets, continuing support, annual campaigns, seed money, emergency funds, scholarship funds.
Limitations: Giving primarily in St. Paul, MN. No grants to individuals, or for deficit financing, capital or endowment funds, matching gifts, research, special projects, publications, or conferences; no loans.
Application information:
    Initial approach: Full proposal
    Deadline(s): None
    Board meeting date(s): As required
    Final notification: 3 months
    Write: Jeffrey T. Peterson
Trustees: Thomas J. Dwight, John F. Kelly, Casey A. T. O'Neil, First Trust Company of Saint Paul.
Number of staff: None.
Employer Identification Number: 416044079

1899
Ordean Foundation ▼
501 Ordean Bldg.
Duluth 55802   (218) 726-4785

Incorporated in 1933 in Minnesota.
Donor(s): Albert Ordean,† Louise Ordean.†
Financial data: (yr. ended 12/31/84): Assets, $11,988,000 (M); expenditures, $1,133,000, including $817,744 for 54 grants (high: $136,000; low: $300; average: $1,000-$25,000) and $75,000 for 1 loan.
Purpose and activities: To administer and furnish relief and charity for the local worthy poor; to make grants to local organizations performing services or providing facilities in certain areas of health and youth activities.
Types of support awarded: Building funds, scholarship funds, loans, operating budgets, matching funds, program-related investments.
Limitations: Giving limited to Duluth and contiguous cities and towns in St. Louis County, MN. No grants to individuals, or for endowment funds, or research.
Publications: Annual report, application guidelines.

Application information: Application form required.
    Initial approach: Telephone, letter, or full proposal
    Copies of proposal: 10
    Deadline(s): 15th of each month
    Board meeting date(s): Monthly
    Final notification: Within 30 days of board meeting
    Write: Ernest S. Petersen, Executive Director
Officers and Directors: Arthur C. Josephs, President; Arend J. Sandbulte, Vice-President; Ernest S. Petersen, Secretary, Treasurer, and Executive Director; Cynthia Albright, Roger M. Bowman, Howard P. Clarke, Dennis W. Dunne, Robert M. Fischer, Donald G. Wirtanen.
Number of staff: 1 full-time professional; 2 full-time support.
Employer Identification Number: 410711611

1900
O'Shaughnessy (I. A.) Foundation, Inc. ▼ ⌀
c/o Paul Kelly
W-555 First National Bank Bldg.
St. Paul 55101   (612) 222-2323

Incorporated in 1941 in Minnesota.
Donor(s): I.A. O'Shaughnessy,† John F. O'Shaughnessy, Globe Oil and Refining Companies, Lario Oil and Gas Company.
Financial data: (yr. ended 12/31/82): Assets, $19,169,535 (M); gifts received, $298,651; expenditures, $1,035,877, including $962,000 for 46 grants (high: $125,000; low: $1,000).
Purpose and activities: Broad purposes; giving for higher and secondary education, the arts, social welfare, and Roman Catholic religious organizations.
Types of support awarded: Annual campaigns, building funds, equipment, endowment funds, research, general purposes, continuing support.
Limitations: Giving limited to the U.S., with emphasis on MN, IL, KS, and TX. No support for religious missions or individual parishes. No grants to individuals, or for scholarships, fellowships, matching gifts; no loans.
Publications: Application guidelines.
Application information: Grants usually initiated by the directors.
    Initial approach: Letter
    Copies of proposal: 1
    Deadline(s): Submit proposal preferably in January or February; no set deadline
    Board meeting date(s): June and November
    Final notification: 6 months
    Write: Paul J. Kelly, Secretary-Treasurer
Officers and Directors:* John F. O'Shaughnessy,* President; Donald E. O'Shaughnessy,* Eileen O'Shaughnessy,* Marion O'Shaughnessy Burke,* Vice-Presidents; Paul J. Kelly, Secretary-Treasurer.
Employer Identification Number: 416011524

1901
Paper (Lewis and Annie F.) Foundation
P.O. Box 65186
St. Paul 55165-0186   (612) 631-1111

Incorporated in 1947 in Minnesota.
Donor(s): Members of the Paper family, Paper, Calmenson and Company.
Financial data: (yr. ended 12/31/83): Assets, $2,323,000 (M); expenditures, $281,406, including $274,800 for 42 grants (high: $116,300; low: $50).
Purpose and activities: Broad purposes; primarily local giving, with emphasis on community funds, Jewish welfare funds, and higher and secondary education; grants also for hospitals and health agencies, youth agencies, and temple and church support.
Types of support awarded: Operating budgets, continuing support, annual campaigns, seed money, emergency funds, deficit financing, building funds, equipment, land acquisition, endowment funds.
Limitations: Giving primarily in St. Paul, MN. No support for organizations that are part of the United Way of the St. Paul Area, Inc., or whose programs come within the scope of the United Way. No grants to individuals, or for scholarships, fellowships, research, special projects, publications, conferences, or matching gifts; no loans.
Publications: Annual report, application guidelines.
Application information:
    Initial approach: Full proposal or letter
    Copies of proposal: 1
    Deadline(s): Submit proposal preferably in January or February; deadline March 1
    Board meeting date(s): April
    Final notification: 6 months
    Write: Lewis Paper, President
Officers and Trustees: Lewis Paper, President; Lewis R. Harris, Vice-President; Roxanne P. Forman, Secretary and Treasurer; Willis M. Forman.
Employer Identification Number: 416019288

1902
Paulucci Family Foundation, The ⌀
525 Lake Ave., South
Duluth 55806   (218) 727-8871

Incorporated in 1966 in Minnesota.
Donor(s): Jeno F. Paulucci.
Financial data: (yr. ended 12/31/83): Assets, $1,506,877 (M); gifts received, $153,853; expenditures, $182,164, including $160,000 for 14 grants (high: $55,000; low: $1,000).
Purpose and activities: Broad purposes; general giving, with emphasis on higher education, medical research, and support of Italian-American cultural and charitable activities.
Limitations: No grants to individuals.
Application information:
    Initial approach: Letter
    Copies of proposal: 1
    Board meeting date(s): Annually

Officers and Directors: Jeno F. Paulucci, President; Lois M. Paulucci, Michael J. Paulucci, Vice-Presidents; Robert Heller, Secretary; Robert L. Cotton, Treasurer; Gina J. Paulucci, Cynthia Paulucci Soderstrom.
Employer Identification Number: 416054004

1903
Phillips Foundation, The ▼
100 Washington Sq., Suite 1650
Minneapolis 55401   (612) 331-6230

Incorporated in 1944 in Minnesota.
Donor(s): Jay Phillips, and members of his family.
Financial data: (yr. ended 12/31/83): Assets, $42,282,857 (M); expenditures, $2,038,215, including $1,765,329 for 212 grants (high: $122,500; low: $15).
Purpose and activities: Broad purposes; giving largely in Minnesota and the Middle West for higher education, including medical and theological education, hospitals and medical research, Jewish welfare funds, cultural programs, and social services, including community funds.
Types of support awarded: Building funds, equipment, research, scholarship funds, fellowships, professorships, matching funds, student aid.
Limitations: Giving primarily in MN and the Middle West. No grants to individuals, or for endowment funds.
Application information:
  Initial approach: Letter
  Copies of proposal: 1
  Deadline(s): None
  Board meeting date(s): As required
  Final notification: 30 days
  Write: Thomas P. Cook, Executive Director
Officers and Trustees: Jay Phillips, President; Rose Phillips, Vice-President; Samuel H. Maslon, Secretary; Morton B. Phillips, Treasurer; Thomas P. Cook, Executive Director; Paula Bernstein, William Bernstein, Helen P. Levin, Jack I. Levin, Pauline Phillips.
Number of staff: 4.
Employer Identification Number: 416019578

1904
Phipps (William H.) Foundation
c/o First Trust Company of Saint Paul
W-555 First National Bank Bldg.
St. Paul 55101
Application address: P.O. Box 106, Hudson, WI 54016; Tel.: (715) 386-5848

Incorporated in 1946 in Wisconsin.
Donor(s): Helen Clark Phipps,† Stephen C. Phipps.†
Financial data: (yr. ended 4/30/84): Assets, $7,334,211 (M); expenditures, $430,721, including $423,811 for 13 grants (high: $183,209; low: $550).
Purpose and activities: Support for a hospital, an arts center, a church group, and civic organizations.
Limitations: Giving limited to the Hudson, WI, area. No grants to individuals.
Application information:
  Initial approach: Letter

Copies of proposal: 1
  Deadline(s): None
  Final notification: Three months
  Write: Hugh F. Gwin, Secretary
Officers and Directors: Hugh G. Bryce, President; Frederick E. Nagel, Vice-President; Hugh F. Gwin, Secretary-Treasurer; Jack Erdmann.
Employer Identification Number: 396043312

1905
Pillsbury Company Foundation, The ▼
Mail Station 3775
200 South Sixth St.
Minneapolis 55402-1464   (612) 330-7230

Incorporated in 1957 in Minnesota.
Donor(s): The Pillsbury Company.
Financial data: (yr. ended 5/31/84): Assets, $6,173,910 (M); gifts received, $2,811,219; expenditures, $3,057,608, including $2,800,423 for 350 grants (high: $175,000; low: $100; average: $500-$25,000), $69,550 for 52 grants to individuals and $187,635 for employee matching gifts.
Purpose and activities: Grants only in areas where the company has plants and subsidiaries inside the U.S., with emphasis on four major areas of giving: community service, with emphasis on federated appeals, including matching employee gifts, and youth programs; food and nutrition, including nutrition research; higher education, including matching employee gifts and support for minority programs, scholarships, and faculty; arts and culture, including operating support to established, leading performing arts organizations in Minneapolis/St. Paul, Dallas, and Miami, and support for public radio and television organizations and educational museums in company locations. Corporate charitable contributions including foundation giving in fiscal 1983 totaled more than $3.4 million.
Types of support awarded: Continuing support, annual campaigns, conferences and seminars, scholarship funds, employee related scholarships, matching funds, employee matching gifts.
Limitations: Giving limited to areas where the company has plants and subsidiaries in the U.S. No support for religious denominations or sects. No grants to individuals (except for scholarships to children of company employees), or for operating, capital or endowment funds (of individual colleges and universities), fundraising, conduit organizations, travel, research, film, radio and television programs, propaganda or lobbying efforts, publications, or other media presentations (unless related to projects supported by the foundation); no loans.
Publications: Company report, application guidelines, program policy statement, annual report.
Application information:
  Initial approach: Letter
  Copies of proposal: 1
  Deadline(s): None
  Board meeting date(s): Quarterly
  Final notification: 3 months

Officers: William H. Spoor,* President; Edward C. Stringer,* Vice-President; Lynn M. Seifert, Treasurer.
Directors:* Diana L. Doshan, N. Jean Fountain, Joel Levine, Philip J. Lindau, Gerald L. Olson, Lynn M. Seifert.
Number of staff: 3 full-time professional; 3 full-time support.
Employer Identification Number: 416021373

1906
Quinlan (The Elizabeth C.) Foundation, Inc.
417 Minnesota Federal Bldg.
Minneapolis 55402   (612) 333-8084

Incorporated in 1945 in Minnesota.
Donor(s): Elizabeth C. Quinlan.†
Financial data: (yr. ended 12/31/83): Assets, $2,000,981 (M); expenditures, $264,147, including $202,885 for 64 grants (high: $20,000; low: $250).
Purpose and activities: Grants largely for Roman Catholic institutions, higher and secondary education, cultural programs, and community funds for use exclusively within Minnesota.
Types of support awarded: Operating budgets, continuing support, annual campaigns, seed money, emergency funds, deficit financing, building funds, equipment, land acquisition, endowment funds, research, scholarship funds, matching funds, general purposes, special projects.
Limitations: Giving limited to MN. No grants to individuals; no loans.
Publications: Annual report, application guidelines.
Application information:
  Initial approach: Full proposal or letter
  Copies of proposal: 1
  Deadline(s): Submit proposal preferably in May or June; deadline September
  Board meeting date(s): October
  Final notification: December 1
  Write: Richard A. Klein, President
Officers and Trustees: Richard A. Klein, President and Treasurer; Eugene P. McCahill, Vice-President; Mary Elizabeth Lahiff, Secretary; Lucia L. Crane, Eileen L. Grundman, Anne L. Klein, Alice M. Lahiff.
Number of staff: 2 part-time support.
Employer Identification Number: 410706125

1907
Rauenhorst (Gerald) Family Foundation
100 South Fifth St., Suite 2200
Minneapolis 55402

Incorporated in 1965 in Minnesota.
Donor(s): Gerald A. Rauenhorst, Henrietta Rauenhorst, Rauenhorst Corporation.
Financial data: (yr. ended 12/31/82): Assets, $6,720,695 (M); expenditures, $293,985, including $287,764 for 28 grants (high: $64,378; low: $1,000).
Purpose and activities: Primarily local giving, with emphasis on higher education, Roman Catholic church support and church-related institutions, and chemical dependency programs.

Limitations: Giving primarily in MN. No grants to individuals.
Application information:
Initial approach: Letter
Copies of proposal: 1
Board meeting date(s): June and December
Write: Michael P. Manning, Vice-President
Officers and Directors:* Gerald A. Rauenhorst,* President; Michael P. Manning, Vice-President and Managing Director; Henrietta Rauenhorst,* Executive Vice-President; Judith Mahoney,* Secretary; Mark Rauenhorst,* Treasurer.
Employer Identification Number: 410080773

1908
Red Wing Shoe Company Foundation
419 Bush St.
Red Wing 55066   (612) 388-8211

Incorporated in 1955 in Minnesota.
Donor(s): Red Wing Shoe Company, Inc.
Financial data: (yr. ended 12/31/83): Assets, $472,401 (M); gifts received, $220,000; expenditures, $186,071, including $186,071 for 51 grants (high: $42,500; low: $45).
Purpose and activities: Broad purposes; primarily local giving, with emphasis on youth agencies; support also for environmental education, and higher and secondary education.
Limitations: Giving primarily in MN.
Application information:
Initial approach: Letter
Write: Joseph P. Goggin, Vice-President
Officers: W.D. Sweasy, President; Joseph P. Goggin, Vice-President; Terrance G. Shelstad, Secretary-Treasurer.
Employer Identification Number: 416020177

1909
Rivers (Margaret) Fund ⌗
c/o William D. Klapp
First National Bank Bldg.
Stillwater 55082

Incorporated in 1948 in Minnesota.
Donor(s): Robert E. Slaughter.†
Financial data: (yr. ended 12/31/83): Assets, $9,092,205 (M); expenditures, $398,036, including $346,950 for 167 grants (high: $25,000; low: $200).
Purpose and activities: A private operating foundation; broad purposes; primarily local giving, with emphasis on hospitals, church support, youth agencies, aid to the handicapped, and care of the aged; grants also for cultural programs and conservation.
Limitations: Giving primarily in MN.
Officers and Trustees:* William D. Klapp,* President; Helen Moelter, Secretary; Robert G. Briggs, Treasurer.
Employer Identification Number: 416017102

1910
Rochester Area Foundation
First Bank Bldg., Suite 436
201 S.W. First Ave.
Rochester 55902   (507) 282-0203

Community foundation established in 1944 in Minnesota by resolution of trust.
Donor(s): Laura Anderson,† H.J. Harwick,† Priscilla Keely.†
Financial data: (yr. ended 12/31/83): Assets, $1,029,900 (M); gifts received, $15,118; expenditures, $85,576, including $63,436 for 20 grants.
Purpose and activities: To help launch new projects which represent innovative approaches to community needs, support special purposes of established organizations, promote volunteer and citizen involvement in community, respond to current human needs in community, and support projects without other sources of support; giving in areas of health, education, social services, and civic and cultural affairs.
Types of support awarded: Seed money, emergency funds, building funds, equipment, matching funds, technical assistance, conferences and seminars.
Limitations: Giving limited to Olmsted County, MN. No support for religious organizations for sectarian purposes. No grants to individuals, or for endowment funds, annual campaigns, operating budgets, continuing support, land acquisition, conferences and seminars, deficit financing, employee matching gifts, consulting services, scholarships, fellowships, or research; no loans.
Publications: Annual report, program policy statement, application guidelines.
Application information: Application form required.
Initial approach: Letter
Copies of proposal: 11
Deadline(s): Submit proposals in January, April, July, and October; deadline first working day of the month
Board meeting date(s): February, May, August, and November
Final notification: 1 week
Write: Isabel C. Huizenga, Executive Director
Trustees: H.T. Stewart, Chairman; Curt Taylor, Margaret S. Thompson, Vice-Chairmen; Barbara B. Withers, Secretary; Theodore G. Martens, M.D., Treasurer; Betty A. Beck, William C. Boyne, Vera M. Elgin, Ann Ferguson, Jean H. Freeman, Clifford M. Johnson, Jennings O. Johnson, Sue Norris, Herbert M. Stellner, Jr., James L. Talen, Charles R. Von Wald.
Number of staff: 2 part-time support.
Employer Identification Number: 416017740

1911
Rodman Foundation, The ⌗
2100 First National Bank Bldg.
St. Paul 55101   (612) 228-0935

Established in 1969 in Minnesota.
Donor(s): Members of the Titcomb family.
Financial data: (yr. ended 12/31/83): Assets, $747,755 (M); gifts received, $210,556; expenditures, $141,119, including $126,100 for 37 grants (high: $17,000; low: $250).
Purpose and activities: Primarily local giving, with emphasis on higher and secondary education, historic preservation, and a science museum; grants also for cultural programs, hospitals, community funds, and youth agencies.

Types of support awarded: Operating budgets, building funds, scholarship funds.
Limitations: Giving primarily in MN. No grants to individuals.
Publications: Annual report.
Application information:
Initial approach: Letter
Copies of proposal: 1
Deadline(s): None
Board meeting date(s): As required
Final notification: 2 to 3 weeks
Write: E. Rodman Titcomb, Jr., President
Officers: E. Rodman Titcomb, Jr.,* President; Julie C. Titcomb,* Vice-President; Joseph S. Micallef, Secretary; Gordon E. Hed, Treasurer.
Directors:* Edward R. Titcomb.
Number of staff: None.
Employer Identification Number: 237025570

1912
Saint Paul Foundation, The ▼
1120 Norwest Center
St. Paul 55101   (612) 224-5463

Community foundation established in 1940 in Minnesota by adoption of a plan; incorporated in 1964.
Financial data: (yr. ended 12/31/84): Assets, $73,859,367 (M); gifts received, $17,556,052; expenditures, $15,601,929, including $13,033,824 for 381 grants (high: $9,967,964; low: $60; average: $500-$50,000), $372,893 for 125 grants to individuals, $714,374 for 60 foundation-administered programs and $324,168 for 7 loans.
Purpose and activities: Support for educational, charitable, cultural, or benevolent purposes of a public nature as will promote the well-being of mankind and, preferably, the inhabitants of St. Paul and its vicinity. Grants largely to cultural, educational, health, and welfare agencies.
Types of support awarded: Seed money, emergency funds, building funds, equipment, research, matching funds, special projects, scholarship funds, fellowships, program-related investments, employee related scholarships.
Limitations: Giving limited to the St. Paul, MN, metropolitan area. No support for sectarian religious programs, except from designated funds. No grants for operating budgets, continuing support, annual campaigns, or deficit financing; no student loans. No support for endowment funds except through designated funds.
Publications: Annual report, application guidelines.
Application information:
Initial approach: Telephone, letter, or full proposal
Copies of proposal: 1
Deadline(s): 3 months before next board meeting
Board meeting date(s): Generally in March, June, September, November, and December
Write: Paul A. Verret, President
Officers: Paul A. Verret, President; Ronald M. Hubbs,* Treasurer.

Distribution Committee:* Richard A. Moore, Chairman; Sam Singer, Vice-Chairman; Virginia D. Brooks, David M. Craig, M.D., Willis M. Formon, John D. Healy, Jr., Reatha Clark King, Richard A. Klingen, Richard H. Kyle, Jr., James W. Reagan, Barbara B. Roy, J. Thomas Simonet, Frederick T. Weyerhaeuser.
Corporate Trustees: American National Bank and Trust Company, First Trust Company of Saint Paul, Norwest Bank Saint Paul.
Number of staff: 16 full-time professional; 1 part-time professional; 9 full-time support; 1 part-time support.
Employer Identification Number: 416031510

1913
Southways Foundation, The ¤

c/o Sargent Management Company
1300 TCF Tower
Minneapolis 55402   (612) 338-3871

Incorporated in 1950 in Minnesota.
Donor(s): John S. Pillsbury,† and family.
Financial data: (yr. ended 12/31/83): Assets, $5,938,650 (M); gifts received, $2,543; expenditures, $240,660, including $217,763 for 38 grants (high: $62,000; low: $100).
Purpose and activities: Broad purposes; primarily local giving, with emphasis on secondary and higher education, cultural activities, and community funds.
Limitations: Giving primarily in MN.
Application information:
Deadline(s): None
Write: Donald K. Morrison
Officers: John S. Pillsbury, Jr.,* President; John S. Pillsbury III,* Donald K. Morrison, Vice-Presidents; George S. Pillsbury,* Secretary-Treasurer.
Trustees:* Mrs. Thomas M. Crosby, Lucy C. Mitchell, Mrs. John S. Pillsbury.
Employer Identification Number: 416018502

1914
Sweatt (The Harold W.) Foundation ¤

1500 Bracketts Point Rd.
Wayzata 55391

Trust established in 1968 in Minnesota as successor in part to The Sweatt Foundation established in 1951.
Donor(s): Harold W. Sweatt.†
Financial data: (yr. ended 2/29/84): Assets, $1,438,484 (M); expenditures, $75,931, including $64,708 for 65 grants (high: $10,000; low: $20).
Purpose and activities: Broad purposes; emphasis on higher and secondary education, Protestant churches and religious organizations, and the arts.
Trustees: A. Lachlan Reed, Martha S. Reed, William S. Reed.
Employer Identification Number: 416075860

1915
Tennant Company Foundation

701 North Lilac Dr.
P.O. Box 1452
Minneapolis 55440   (612) 540-1207

Established in 1972 in Minnesota.
Donor(s): Tennant Company.
Financial data: (yr. ended 12/31/84): Assets, $144,592 (M); gifts received, $400,611; expenditures, $274,855, including $248,565 for 135 grants (high: $10,000; low: $100; average: $1,970), $8,380 for 11 grants to individuals and $9,135 for 88 employee matching gifts.
Purpose and activities: Primarily local giving for community funds, social service and youth agencies, higher education, and cultural programs including the arts and public broadcasting; limited support for conservation and health.
Types of support awarded: General purposes, building funds, equipment, employee related scholarships, employee matching gifts.
Limitations: Giving primarily in the greater Minneapolis-St. Paul, MN, metropolitan area. No support for agencies funded through umbrella organizations, or for religious organizations for religious purposes. No grants to individuals, or for travel, benefit tickets, or courtesy advertising.
Publications: Annual report, application guidelines, program policy statement.
Application information:
Initial approach: Full proposal or telephone
Copies of proposal: 1
Deadline(s): 3 weeks prior to board meetings
Board meeting date(s): Usually in April, July, October, and December
Final notification: 3 months
Write: Donna Anderson, Administrator, or Robert D. Langford, President
Officers and Directors: Robert D. Langford, President; Joseph A. Shaw, Secretary and Treasurer; Roger L. Hale, Kenneth Hall, George T. Pennock.
Number of staff: 1 part-time professional; 1 part-time support.
Employer Identification Number: 237297045

1916
Thorpe (James R.) Foundation

8085 Wayzata Blvd.
Minneapolis 55426   (612) 545-1111

Incorporated in 1974 in Minnesota.
Donor(s): James R. Thorpe.†
Financial data: (yr. ended 11/30/83): Assets, $4,944,426 (M); expenditures, $260,121, including $220,500 for 44 grants (high: $12,500; low: $500; average: $2,000-$5,000).
Purpose and activities: Broad purposes; primarily local giving, with emphasis on youth and social agencies, arts and cultural programs, and education; support also for health and religious organizations.
Types of support awarded: Operating budgets, annual campaigns, seed money, building funds, equipment, endowment funds, consulting services, scholarship funds.

Limitations: Giving primarily in MN, with emphasis on Minneapolis and St. Paul. No grants to individuals, or for continuing support, emergency funds, deficit financing, land acquisition, matching gifts, special projects, research, publications, or conferences; no loans.
Publications: Annual report, program policy statement, application guidelines.
Application information:
Initial approach: Letter outlining proposal
Copies of proposal: 1
Deadline(s): March 1 and September 1
Board meeting date(s): May and November
Final notification: 1 week
Write: Mrs. Edith D. Thorpe, President
Officers and Directors: Edith D. Thorpe, President; Leonard M. Addington, Samuel A. Cote, Vice-Presidents; Mary C. Boos, Secretary; Samuel S. Thorpe III, Treasurer.
Number of staff: 1 part-time professional.
Employer Identification Number: 416175293

1917
Tozer Foundation, Inc. ¤

c/o Lawson, Ranum & Raleigh
104 North Main St.
Stillwater 55082
Application address for grants other than scholarships: W-555 First National Bank Bldg., St. Paul, MN 55101; Tel.: (612) 291-5134

Incorporated in 1946 in Minnesota.
Donor(s): David Tozer.†
Financial data: (yr. ended 10/31/83): Assets, $10,695,452 (M); expenditures, $752,936, including $201,634 for 28 grants (high: $50,000; low: $100) and $497,595 for 635 grants to individuals.
Purpose and activities: Broad purposes; chiefly interested in educational projects, including scholarships to graduating high school students in three counties in Minnesota as well as undergraduate and graduate scholarships in various colleges in the state; support also for cultural programs, community funds, and aid to the handicapped; activities largely confined to Minnesota.
Types of support awarded: Student aid.
Limitations: Giving primarily in MN.
Application information: Candidates must apply for scholarships through selected high schools.
Initial approach: Letter
Copies of proposal: 1
Board meeting date(s): Monthly
Write: Grant T. Waldref, President
Officers and Directors: Grant T. Waldref, President; Robert S. Davis, Vice-President; Harry L. Holtz, James W. Oppenheimer, J. Thomas Simonet, Earl C. Swanson, John F. Thoreen.
Employer Identification Number: 416011518

1918
Valspar Foundation, The

1101 Third St. South
Minneapolis 55415
Scholarship application address: Linda Dempsey, Valspar Scholarship Committee, Personnel Dept., P.O. Box 1461, Minneapolis, MN 55440

Established in 1979.
Donor(s): Valspar Corporation.
Financial data: (yr. ended 9/30/84): Assets, $209,180 (M); expenditures, $179,712, including $169,187 for 132 grants (high: $12,500; low: $50) and $10,000 for 10 grants to individuals.
Purpose and activities: Primarily local giving for community funds, community development, higher education, including scholarships for children of Valspar employees, and cultural programs.
Types of support awarded: Employee related scholarships.
Limitations: Giving primarily in Minneapolis, MN.
Application information: Application form required.
    Deadline(s): June 1
Officers: C.A. Wurtele, President; H.F. Denker, Vice-President and Secretary; S. Guerrera, Vice-President and Treasurer.
Employer Identification Number: 411363847

1919
Van Evera (Dewitt) Foundation
Route 2
St. Joseph 56374   (612) 363-8388

Established in 1959.
Donor(s): Dewitt Van Evera.†
Financial data: (yr. ended 12/31/83): Assets, $1,321,777 (M); expenditures, $95,505, including $90,900 for 8 grants (high: $29,300; low: $500).
Purpose and activities: Giving primarily in Minnesota and Wisconsin for higher and secondary education, and for projects to aid youth, the arts, and the disadvantaged. Almost all funding distributed on a continuing basis to ongong projects.
Types of support awarded: Continuing support, general purposes, building funds, endowment funds, scholarship funds.
Limitations: Giving primarily in MN and WI. No grants to individuals, or for matching gifts; no loans.
Application information:
    Initial approach: Letter
    Copies of proposal: 1
    Deadline(s): Submit proposal preferably in September through December
    Board meeting date(s): February and September
    Write: Laura Jane V.E. La Fond, Advisor
Advisors: Laura Jane V.E. La Fond, Robert W. Van Evera, William P. Van Evera.
Trustee: First Interstate Bank of Utah.
Number of staff: None.
Employer Identification Number: 876117907

1920
Walker (Archie D. and Bertha H.) Foundation
1121 Hennepin Ave.
Minneapolis 55403   (612) 332-3556

Incorporated in 1953 in Minnesota.
Donor(s): Archie D. Walker,† Bertha H. Walker.†

Financial data: (yr. ended 12/31/83): Assets, $3,891,080 (M); expenditures, $245,874, including $218,800 for 56 grants (high: $35,100; low: $500).
Purpose and activities: Primarily local giving to support programs dealing with chemical dependency (chiefly alcoholism); grants also for organizations that combat racism in the white community.
Types of support awarded: Special projects, general purposes, building funds, research.
Limitations: Giving primarily in the seven-county Minneapolis-St. Paul, MN, metropolitan area. No support for private foundations. No grants to individuals, or for building or endowment funds.
Publications: Annual report, program policy statement, application guidelines.
Application information:
    Initial approach: Proposal
    Copies of proposal: 1
    Deadline(s): Submit proposal preferably by December 31
    Board meeting date(s): 2 or 3 times a year in February or March, September, and as required
    Write: David H. Griffith, President
Officers and Trustees: David H. Griffith, President; Louise Walker McCannel, Berta Walker, Vice-Presidents; Walter W. Walker, Secretary; Harriet W. Heron, Treasurer; Louise W. Davy, Katherine W. Griffith, Teri M. Lamb, Laurie H. McCannel, Amy C. Walker, Archie D. Walker, Jr., Archie D. Walker III, Elaine B. Walker, Lita L. Walker, Suzanne Walker.
Number of staff: None.
Employer Identification Number: 416022758

1921
Warner (Lee and Rose) Foundation ☒
444 Lafayette Rd.
St. Paul 55101   (612) 222-7792

Incorporated in 1959 in Minnesota.
Donor(s): Mrs. Rose Warner.†
Financial data: (yr. ended 12/31/82): Assets, $5,107,644 (M); expenditures, $255,256, including $245,850 for 20 grants (high: $70,000; low: $200).
Purpose and activities: Broad purposes; primarily local giving to a nature center, a science museum, and several universities.
Limitations: Giving primarily in MN. No grants to individuals, or for endowment funds, research programs, or scholarships or fellowships; no loans.
Application information:
    Initial approach: Letter
    Copies of proposal: 1
    Deadline(s): None
    Board meeting date(s): September and December
Officers and Trustees: Frank A. Koscielack, Adelaide F. McNeely, Donald G. McNeely.
Number of staff: None.
Employer Identification Number: 416011523

1922
Wasie Foundation, The ▼
909 Foshay Tower
Minneapolis 55402   (612) 332-3883

Incorporated in 1966 in Minnesota.
Donor(s): Donald A. Wasie,† Stanley L. Wasie,† Marie F. Wasie.
Financial data: (yr. ended 12/31/83): Assets, $10,682,360 (M); expenditures, $1,415,811, including $1,127,182 for 73 grants (high: $800,000; low: $25).
Purpose and activities: Primarily local giving for higher education, including scholarship funds at selected institutions for qualified students of Polish ancestry, Roman Catholic religious associations, and hospitals and health organizations.
Types of support awarded: Operating budgets, continuing support, seed money, emergency funds, building funds, equipment, land acquisition, endowment funds, special projects, research, publications, conferences and seminars, professorships, scholarship funds, fellowships.
Limitations: Giving limited to MN, with emphasis on Minneapolis and St. Paul. No grants to individuals; no loans.
Publications: Application guidelines.
Application information: Application form required.
    Initial approach: Telephone
    Copies of proposal: 8
    Deadline(s): Varies
    Board meeting date(s): As required
    Final notification: 2 weeks after board meetings
    Write: David A. Odahowski, Executive Director
Officers and Directors: Marie F. Wasie, President and Treasurer; J.J. Choromanski, Vice-President and Secretary; David A. Odahowski, Executive Director; Andrew J. Leemhuis, Medical Director; Thelma G. Haynes, Ina N. Reed, Audrey D. Smith.
Number of staff: 1 full-time professional; 1 part-time support.
Employer Identification Number: 410911636

1923
Weyand (Louis F. and Florence H.) 1977 Charitable Trust
(formerly Louis F. and Florence H. Weyand Charitable Trust)
c/o First Trust Company of St. Paul
W-555 First National Bank Bldg.
St. Paul 55101

Established in 1977.
Donor(s): Louis F. Weyand,† Florence H. Weyand.
Financial data: (yr. ended 9/30/84): Assets, $1,024,888 (M); expenditures, $71,050, including $69,800 for 48 grants (high: $5,000; low: $75).
Purpose and activities: Giving primarily for the arts; support also for education.
Limitations: Giving limited to MI, FL, and CA.
Application information:
    Initial approach: Letter

Write: Jeffrey T. Peterson
Trustees: Lois Bachman, Carolyn Yorston, First Trust Company of St. Paul.
Employer Identification Number: 942473421

1924
Weyerhaeuser (The Charles A.) Memorial Foundation
2100 First National Bank Bldg.
St. Paul 55101   (612) 228-0935

Incorporated in 1959 in Minnesota.
Donor(s): Carl A. Weyerhaeuser trusts, Sarah-Maud W. Sivertsen trusts.
Financial data: (yr. ended 2/28/83): Assets, $620,272 (M); gifts received, $800,913; expenditures, $537,254, including $283,000 for 8 grants (high: $50,000; low: $3,000).
Purpose and activities: Broad purposes; primarily local giving, with emphasis on art, music, higher education, and community funds.
Limitations: Giving primarily in MN. No grants to individuals.
Publications: 990-PF.
Application information:
  Initial approach: Letter
  Copies of proposal: 1
  Board meeting date(s): As required
  Final notification: 5 to 6 weeks
  Write: Walter S. Rosenberry, III, President
Officers and Directors: Walter S. Rosenberry, III, President; Robert J. Sivertsen, Vice-President; Joseph S. Micallef, Secretary and Treasurer; Elise R. Donohue, Richard E. Kyle, Lucy R. McCarthy.
Employer Identification Number: 416012063

1925
Weyerhaeuser Foundation, Inc.
2100 First National Bank Bldg.
St. Paul 55101   (612) 228-0935

Incorporated in 1950 in Minnesota.
Donor(s): Members of the Weyerhaeuser family.
Financial data: (yr. ended 12/31/82): Assets, $4,782,428 (M); gifts received, $118,024; expenditures, $300,574, including $240,106 for 19 grants (high: $30,000; low: $400).
Purpose and activities: Grants restricted to support of national and international programs and services, with the exception of Foundation-initiated grants to two theological seminaries for programs in religion and psychiatry; emphasis on education for members of minority races, conservation, population control, self-help programs, and the promotion of world cooperation and understanding.
Types of support awarded: Seed money, special projects.
Limitations: No grants to individuals, or for building or endowment funds, operating budgets, scholarships and fellowships, or matching gifts; no loans.
Publications: Annual report, application guidelines, program policy statement.
Application information:
  Initial approach: Letter
  Copies of proposal: 1
  Deadline(s): Submit proposal between January and June; deadline July 1

Board meeting date(s): Program committee meets annually in late summer to review proposals; board meets usually in November
Write: Julie C. Titcomb, President
Officers and Trustees: Julie C. Titcomb, President; George F. Jewett, Jr., Vice-President; Nancy N. Weyerhaeuser, Secretary; Walter S. Rosenberry, III, Treasurer; Lynn W. Day, Mary J. Greer, Sara T. Greer, Elizabeth S. Driscoll, Elizabeth W. Meadowcroft, Joseph S. Micallef, Bette D. Moorman, Charles A. Weyerhaeuser, Ginnie Weyerhaeuser, William T. Weyerhaeuser.
Employer Identification Number: 416012062

1926
Weyerhaeuser (The Frederick and Margaret L.) Foundation
2100 First National Bank Bldg.
St. Paul 55101   (612) 228-0935

Incorporated in 1963 in Minnesota.
Donor(s): Margaret Weyerhaeuser Harmon.
Financial data: (yr. ended 6/30/83): Assets, $453,857 (M); gifts received, $556,808; expenditures, $392,301, including $390,180 for 25 grants (high: $150,000; low: $500).
Purpose and activities: Broad purposes; primarily local giving for a college chair of chaplaincy, a theological seminary, and religious welfare.
Limitations: Giving primarily in MN. No grants to individuals.
Publications: 990-PF.
Application information:
  Initial approach: Letter
  Copies of proposal: 1
  Board meeting date(s): June and December
  Final notification: 4 to 5 weeks
  Write: Frederick T. Weyerhaeuser, President
Officers and Directors:* Frederick T. Weyerhaeuser,* President; Charles L. Weyerhaeuser, Vice-President; Joseph S. Micallef,* Secretary; Gordon E. Hed,* Treasurer.
Number of staff: None.
Employer Identification Number: 416029036

1927
Whiteside (Robert B. and Sophia) Scholarship Fund ⌳
c/o First Bank Duluth
306 West Superior St.
Duluth 55801

Established in 1976.
Financial data: (yr. ended 12/31/83): Assets, $4,876,462 (M); expenditures, $906,886, including $810,547 for 294 grants to individuals.
Purpose and activities: Grants for scholarships to individuals from the top five percent of graduating classes of Duluth.
Types of support awarded: Student aid.
Limitations: Giving limited to Duluth, MN.
Application information: Applications are submitted to local high school counselors. Application form required.
Trustees: First Bank Duluth, Fryberger, Buchanan, Smith & Frederick.
Employer Identification Number: 411288761

1928
Wilder (Amherst H.) Foundation
919 Lafond Ave.
St. Paul 55104   (612) 642-4000

Incorporated in 1910 in Minnesota.
Donor(s): Amherst H. Wilder,† Mrs. Amherst H. Wilder,† Cornelia Day Wilder Appleby.†
Financial data: (yr. ended 6/30/84): Assets, $173,516,712 (M); gifts received, $1,144,246; expenditures, $21,410,781, including $83,779 for grants and $21,327,002 for 38 foundation-administered programs.
Purpose and activities: A private operating foundation aiding the poor, sick, aged, or otherwise needy people of the greater metropolitan St. Paul area by financing and operating various community services.
Limitations: Giving limited to the greater metropolitan St. Paul, MN, area.
Publications: Annual report.
Application information:
  Board meeting date(s): Monthly
  Write: Leonard H. Wilkening, President
Officers and Directors: Frank Hammond, Chairman; G. Richard Slade, 1st Vice-Chair; Mary Bigelow McMillan, 2nd Vice-Chair; Leonard H. Wilkening, President; H. James Seesel, Jr., Secretary-Treasurer; Anthony L. Andersen, Elisabeth W. Doermann, Elizabeth M. Kiernat, Malcolm W. McDonald.
Employer Identification Number: 410693889

1929
Wood-Rill Foundation ⌳
4122 IDS Center
Minneapolis 55402

Established in 1967 in Minnesota.
Donor(s): Bruce B. Dayton, Lucy B. Dayton.
Financial data: (yr. ended 12/31/83): Assets, $249,670 (M); gifts received, $117,820; expenditures, $279,630, including $279,230 for 30 grants (high: $100,000; low: $100).
Purpose and activities: Broad purposes; primarily local giving with emphasis on the arts, particularly on fine arts and the performing arts; support also for education and civic affairs.
Types of support awarded: General purposes.
Limitations: Giving primarily in MN.
Officers and Directors:* Bruce B. Dayton,* President; Anne S. Dayton,* Brandt W. Dayton,* Lucy B. Dayton,* Mark B. Dayton,* Virginia Y. Dayton,* Vice-Presidents; Ronald N. Gross, Secretary-Treasurer.
Employer Identification Number: 416080487

MISSISSIPPI

1930
Bacot Foundation, Inc.
3007 Magnolia St.
P.O. Box 1959
Pascagoula 39567   (601) 762-2490

Incorporated in 1978 in Mississippi.
Donor(s): Edward H. Bacot.†
Financial data: (yr. ended 10/31/83): Assets,
$1,305,997 (M); expenditures, $28,029,
including $14,400 for 2 grants (high: $10,000;
low: $4,400).
Purpose and activities: Primarily local giving
for higher education.
Limitations: Giving primarily in Jackson
County, MS.
Application information:
 Initial approach: Full proposal
 Deadline(s): None
 Write: John G. Corlew, Secretary
Officers and Directors: Bertha P. Bacot,
President; Douglass L. Fontaine, Vice-President;
John G. Corlew, Secretary; David M. Peeples,
Treasurer; Alf F. Dantzler, Jr., Jerry St. Pe, Ted
VonSprecker.
Employer Identification Number: 640620054

1931
Chisholm Foundation, The ⌑
P.O. Box 2766
Laurel 39400

Established in 1960 in Mississippi.
Donor(s): A.F. Chisholm.†
Financial data: (yr. ended 12/31/82): Assets,
$3,950,671 (M); gifts received, $21,000;
expenditures, $236,334, including $201,000
for 31 grants (high: $50,000; low: $1,000).
Purpose and activities: Primarily local giving
largely for education and Protestant
organizations; support also for health, cultural
programs, youth, and community funds.
Limitations: Giving primarily in MS.
Officers: Jean C. Lindsey, President; Cynthia C.
Saint-Amand, Secretary; Margaret A. Chisholm,
Treasurer.
Director: Nathan F. Sain.
Employer Identification Number: 646014272

1932
Community Foundation, Inc., The ⌑
P.O. Box 924
Jackson 39205   (601) 372-2227

Incorporated in 1963 in Mississippi.
Donor(s): W.K. Paine.
Financial data: (yr. ended 12/31/83): Assets,
$3,530,350 (M); gifts received, $190,400;
expenditures, $161,136, including $153,500
for 22 grants (high: $20,000; low: $500).
Purpose and activities: Primarily local giving,
with emphasis on Protestant religious
associations, higher education, and social
agencies.

Limitations: Giving primarily in MS.
Application information:
 Initial approach: Proposal
 Final notification: Usually within 2 months
 Write: W.K. Paine, President
Officers: W.K. Paine, President and Treasurer;
Carolyn P. Davis, Vice-President; Werdna
McClurkin, Secretary.
Employer Identification Number: 237033813

1933
Day (Carl and Virginia Johnson) Trust
108 West Madison St.
Yazoo City 39194   (601) 746-4901

Trust established in 1948 in Mississippi.
Donor(s): Carl Day, M.D.†
Financial data: (yr. ended 12/31/83): Assets,
$2,212,557 (M); expenditures, $26,830,
including $208,182 for 142 loans (high:
$2,500; low: $200).
Purpose and activities: Student loans to
residents of Mississippi who attend Mississippi
schools.
Types of support awarded: Student aid.
Limitations: Giving limited to MS.
Application information:
 Initial approach: Letter
 Deadline(s): December 15 and August 15
 Write: J.C. Lamkin, Manager
Manager: J.C. Lamkin.
Trustees: W.R. Bridgforth, R.B. Harris, Hugh
M. Love, Sr., R.J. Parks, Jr., F.M. Patty, Jr.
Employer Identification Number: 640386095

1934
Deposit Guaranty Foundation ⌑
One Deposit Guaranty Plaza
P.O. Box 1200
Jackson 39201   (601) 354-8114

Incorporated in 1962 in Mississippi.
Donor(s): Deposit Guaranty National Bank.
Financial data: (yr. ended 1/31/84): Assets,
$20,866 (M); gifts received, $247,781;
expenditures, $195,154, including $194,465
for 83 grants (high: $48,146; low: $9).
Purpose and activities: Local giving, with
emphasis on higher education and a
community fund; support also for youth and
social agencies, hospitals, and the arts.
Limitations: Giving limited to MS. No grants
to individuals.
Application information:
 Initial approach: Letter
 Copies of proposal: 1
 Board meeting date(s): Annually
 Write: John P. Maloney, Vice-President
Officers and Directors: E.B. Robinson, Jr.,
President; James S. Lenoir, Vice-President;
Robert G. Barnett, Secretary; David Harcharik,
Treasurer; Lowell F. Stevens.
Employer Identification Number: 646026793

1935
Feild Co-Operative Association, Inc.
P.O. Box 5054
Jackson 39216   (601) 362-3180

Incorporated in 1919 in Tennessee.
Donor(s): Sons of the late Dr. and Mrs.
Monfort Jones.
Financial data: (yr. ended 12/31/83): Assets,
$4,939,185 (M); expenditures, $671,452,
including $23,400 for 13 grants (high: $10,000;
low: $900) and $233,230 for loans.
Purpose and activities: General purposes;
interest-bearing student loans to Mississippi
residents who are juniors or seniors in college,
graduate and professional students, or students
in special fields; some grants to local hospitals
and social agencies.
Types of support awarded: Student aid.
Limitations: Giving limited to MS residents.
No grants for building or endowment funds,
operating budgets, or special projects.
Publications: Informational brochure,
application guidelines.
Application information: Application form
required for student loans.
 Initial approach: Letter
 Copies of proposal: 1
 Deadline(s): Submit proposal in September or
  October; deadline 6 to 8 weeks before
  semester begins
 Board meeting date(s): Semiannually
 Write: Mrs. Glenn Pate
Officers and Directors: Hobson C. McGehee,
President; Bernard B. Jones II, 1st Vice-
President; Hobson C. McGehee, Jr., 2nd Vice-
President; B. Bryan Jones III, 3rd Vice-
President; Mrs. Glenn Pate, Secretary-
Treasurer; William M. Link, Kenneth Wills.
Number of staff: 3.
Employer Identification Number: 640155700

1936
First Mississippi Corporation Foundation, Inc.
700 North St.
P.O. Box 1249
Jackson 39205   (601) 948-7550

Incorporated in 1975 in Mississippi.
Donor(s): First Mississippi Corporation.
Financial data: (yr. ended 6/30/84): Assets,
$890,485 (L); expenditures, $255,420,
including $219,599 for 37 grants (high:
$50,000; low: $500), $6,525 for 14 grants to
individuals and $27,238 for 48 employee
matching gifts.
Purpose and activities: Grants primarily
locally and in areas of company operations,
with emphasis on higher education, including
scholarships limited to valedictorians of local
high schools, and employee matching gifts,
community funds, excellence awards to
workers (chosen by peer committee) in
experimental agriculture programs, and youth
agencies.
Types of support awarded: Operating
budgets, continuing support, annual campaigns,
emergency funds, building funds, equipment,
land acquisition, endowment funds, matching
funds, employee matching gifts, scholarship
funds, special projects, research.

Limitations: Giving primarily in MS, in areas of company operations. No support for health or church-related programs. No grants for seed money, deficit financing, publications, or conferences; no loans.
Application information:
  Initial approach: Letter
  Copies of proposal: 1
  Deadline(s): Submit education proposals preferably between February and July and all others between August and January; deadline 1 month prior to board meetings
  Board meeting date(s): February and August
  Final notification: 2 weeks after meetings
  Write: J. Kelley Williams, President
Officers: J. Kelley Williams,* President; James W. Crook,* C.M. McAuley, R.M. Summerford, Vice-Presidents; J.B. Lange, Secretary-Treasurer.
Trustees:* Jack W. Castino, Owen Cooper, Robert P. Guyton, Dwain G. Luce, Charles Moreton, William H. Mounger, Paul W. Murrill, LeRoy P. Percy, Maurice T. Reed, Jr., Frank G. Smith, Jr., Leland R. Speed.
Number of staff: None.
Employer Identification Number: 510152783

1937
Hardin (Phil) Foundation
P.O. Box 3429
Meridian 39301   (601) 483-4282

Incorporated in 1964 in Mississippi.
Donor(s): Philip Bernard Hardin,† Hardin's Bakeries Corp.
Financial data: (yr. ended 12/31/83): Assets, $12,912,048 (M); expenditures, $469,277, including $342,664 for 28 grants (high: $150,000; low: $500; average: $12,000) and $88,850 for loans.
Purpose and activities: To improve education for residents of the state of Mississippi. Grants primarily to schools, institutions of higher education, museums, and other educational institutions and programs.
Types of support awarded: Operating budgets, continuing support, seed money, building funds, equipment, endowment funds, matching funds, program-related investments, professorships, scholarship funds, fellowships, student aid, special projects, research, publications, conferences and seminars.
Limitations: Giving primarily in MS, but also to out-of-state organizations or programs of benefit to the people of MS. No grants to individuals (except for limited student loans), or for deficit financing or land acquisition.
Publications: Application guidelines, program policy statement.
Application information:
  Initial approach: Telephone, letter, or proposal
  Copies of proposal: 2
  Deadline(s): None
  Board meeting date(s): As required, usually at least every 2 months
  Final notification: 3 months
  Write: C. Thompson Wacaster, Vice-President

Officers and Directors:* S.A. Rosenbaum,* President; Mark M. Porter,* Vice-President; C. Thompson Wacaster, Vice-President for Educational Programs; R.B. Deen, Jr.,* Secretary; Archie R. McDonnell,* Treasurer.
Number of staff: 1 full-time professional; 1 part-time support.
Employer Identification Number: 646025706

1938
Irby (Elizabeth M.) Foundation ¤
P.O. Box 1819
Jackson 39205

Incorporated in 1952 in Mississippi.
Donor(s): Mrs. J.L. Milam, Irby Construction Company, Stuart C. Irby Company.
Financial data: (yr. ended 12/31/83): Assets, $2,203,917 (M); gifts received, $341,949; expenditures, $349,173, including $341,789 for 60 grants (high: $81,862; low: $200).
Purpose and activities: Grants primarily for higher education, including a theological seminary, and Protestant church support and religious organizations.
Officers: Stuart C. Irby, Jr.,* President; Stuart M. Irby,* Vice-President; William D. Nutt, Secretary and Treasurer.
Trustees:* Margaret L. Irby, Elizabeth J. Milam.
Employer Identification Number: 646020278

1939
Walker (W. E.) Foundation ¤
3800 I-55 North
Jackson 39206   (601) 981-7171

Established in 1972 in Mississippi.
Donor(s): W.E. Walker, Jr., W.E. Walker Stores, Inc.
Financial data: (yr. ended 12/31/83): Assets, $1,283,406 (M); gifts received, $1,222,002; expenditures, $366,909, including $314,415 for 57 grants (high: $70,000; low: $25) and $21,000 for 7 grants to individuals.
Purpose and activities: Primarily local giving for independent schools, Protestant churches, higher education, and youth agencies; grants also for cultural programs, health, and welfare agencies.
Types of support awarded: General purposes, student aid.
Limitations: Giving primarily in MS.
Application information:
  Write: Dave N. Stoner
Trustees: Edmund L. Brunini, Justina W. McLean, Gloria M. Walker, W.E. Walker, Jr.
Employer Identification Number: 237279902

MISSOURI

1940
Anheuser-Busch Charitable Trust ▼
One Busch Place
St. Louis 63118   (314) 577-2454

Trust established in 1951 in Missouri.
Donor(s): August A. Busch, Jr., Alice Busch, Anheuser-Busch, Inc., August A. Busch & Co. of Massachusetts, Inc.
Financial data: (yr. ended 9/30/83): Assets, $11,019,597 (M); expenditures, $1,640,187, including $1,599,800 for 18 grants (high: $500,000; low: $1,000; average: $10,000-$50,000).
Purpose and activities: General giving, especially for a community fund, higher education, hospitals, cultural programs, and youth agencies, primarily in cities where Anheuser-Busch has manufacturing facilities .
Types of support awarded: Annual campaigns, seed money, emergency funds, deficit financing, building funds, equipment, land acquisition, endowment funds, employee matching gifts, professorships, internships, scholarship funds, research, conferences and seminars, employee related scholarships.
Limitations: Giving primarily in areas of company operations, with emphasis on the St. Louis, MO area. No grants to individuals (except for company-employee scholarships), or for operating budgets, continuing support, demonstration projects, or publications; no loans.
Application information:
  Initial approach: Full proposal
  Copies of proposal: 1
  Deadline(s): None
  Board meeting date(s): As required
  Final notification: 6 to 8 weeks
  Write: Jobeth Brown, Assistant Secretary
Board of Control: August A. Busch, Jr., August A. Busch III, Jerry E. Ritter.
Trustee: Centerre Trust Co. of St. Louis.
Number of staff: None.
Employer Identification Number: 436023453

1941
Block (The H & R) Foundation
4410 Main St.
Kansas City 64111   (816) 932-8424

Incorporated in 1974 in Missouri.
Donor(s): H & R Block, Inc.
Financial data: (yr. ended 12/31/83): Assets, $3,739,311 (M); gifts received, $733,000; expenditures, $330,397, including $233,955 for 131 grants (high: $26,000; low: $50; average: $500-$25,000), $60,000 for 30 grants to individuals and $5,100 for 22 employee matching gifts.
Purpose and activities: Local giving, with emphasis on civic, cultural, and welfare programs; scholarships for children of company employees only.

Types of support awarded: General purposes, building funds, equipment, land acquisition, matching funds, employee matching gifts, program-related investments, employee related scholarships, operating budgets, continuing support, annual campaigns, seed money, emergency funds, deficit financing.
Limitations: Giving limited to the 50-mile area around Kansas City, KS. No support for religious purposes, single disease agencies, or historic preservation projects. No grants to individuals (except for scholarships to children of company employees), or for endowment funds, travel, telethons, research, demonstration projects, publications, or conferences; no loans.
Publications: Informational brochure, program policy statement, application guidelines.
Application information:
Initial approach: Full proposal
Copies of proposal: 1
Deadline(s): 45 days prior to meetings
Board meeting date(s): March, June, September, and December
Final notification: 2 weeks after board meeting
Write: I.J. Mnookin, Secretary
Officers and Directors: Henry W. Bloch, President and Treasurer; I.J. Mnookin, Secretary; Edward A. Smith, Morton I. Sosland.
Number of staff: 1 full-time professional; 1 full-time support.
Employer Identification Number: 237378232

1942
Boatmen's National Bank of St. Louis Irrevocable Charitable Trust ▱
P.O. Box 7365
St. Louis 63166   (314) 425-7707

Established in 1966 in Missouri.
Donor(s): Boatmen's National Bank of St. Louis.
Financial data: (yr. ended 12/31/83): Assets, $789,325 (M); gifts received, $224,000; expenditures, $332,174, including $328,788 for 60 grants (high: $73,300; low: $25).
Purpose and activities: Broad purposes; primarily local giving, with emphasis on higher education, the arts, social agencies, hospitals, and a community fund.
Limitations: Giving primarily in MO.
Application information:
Deadline(s): None
Write: John L. Phillips, Jr.
Trustee: Boatmen's National Bank of St. Louis.
Employer Identification Number: 436065511

1943
Boone County Community Trust
c/o Boone County National Bank
P.O. Box 678
Columbia 65205   (314) 874-8100
Additional telephone: (314) 449-4576

Established in 1976 in Missouri.
Donor(s): R.B. Price, Jr.,† Noma S. Brown.†
Financial data: (yr. ended 5/31/84): Assets, $1,113,228 (M); gifts received, $1,740; expenditures, $52,149, including $42,194 for 7 grants (high: $12,944; low: $1,000; average: $6,000-$7,000).

Purpose and activities: Local giving for education, social services, and broad charitable purposes.
Types of support awarded: Equipment, general purposes, seed money, emergency funds, building funds, land acquisition, professorships, internships, scholarship funds, exchange programs, fellowships, special projects, research, publications, conferences and seminars.
Limitations: Giving limited to Boone County, MO. No grants to individuals, or for operating budgets, continuing support, annual campaigns, deficit financing, endowment funds, or matching gifts; no loans.
Publications: Application guidelines, program policy statement.
Application information:
Initial approach: Telephone or letter
Copies of proposal: 1
Deadline(s): None
Board meeting date(s): As needed
Final notification: 6 weeks
Write: Jerry Epple, Trust Administrator
Trustee: Boone County National Bank (Jerry Epple, Trust Administrator).
Number of staff: None.
Employer Identification Number: 436182354

1944
Brown (George Warren) Foundation
8400 Maryland Ave.
St. Louis 63105   (314) 854-4120

Trust established in 1921 in Missouri.
Donor(s): George Warren Brown.†
Financial data: (yr. ended 12/31/84): Assets, $2,655,442 (M); expenditures, $274,722, including $267,640 for 43 grants (high: $60,000; low: $50).
Purpose and activities: Grants largely to provide pensions for Brown Group, Inc. employees; also primarily local giving to colleges and universities, hospitals, and youth agencies.
Types of support awarded: General purposes, operating budgets, continuing support, annual campaigns, seed money, emergency funds, deficit financing, building funds, equipment, land acquisition, scholarship funds.
Limitations: Giving primarily in areas of company operations. No grants for endowment funds, matching gifts, program support, research, special projects, publications or conferences; no loans.
Application information:
Initial approach: Full proposal
Copies of proposal: 1
Deadline(s): None
Board meeting date(s): January, March, June, September, October, and December
Final notification: 1 to 2 months
Write: Hiram S. Liggett, Jr., Treasurer
Trustees: B.A. Bridgewater, Jr., Chairman; W.L. Hadley Griffin, William E. Maritz, Edward L. O'Neill, Harry E. Rich, Warren McK. Shapleigh, Richard W. Schomaker, Armand C. Stalnaker, Daniel R. Toll.
Number of staff: None.
Employer Identification Number: 436027798

1945
Brown Group, Inc. Charitable Trust ▼
8400 Maryland Ave.
St. Louis 63105   (314) 854-4120

Trust established in 1951 in Missouri.
Donor(s): Brown Group, Inc.
Financial data: (yr. ended 9/30/84): Assets, $6,381,941 (M); gifts received, $1,300,000; expenditures, $1,264,415, including $1,160,915 for 224 grants (high: $200,000; low: $100; average: $100-$200,000) and $103,500 for 165 employee matching gifts.
Purpose and activities: Broad purposes; general giving in areas of company operations, with emphasis on community funds, hospitals, higher education, the arts, and youth agencies.
Types of support awarded: General purposes, operating budgets, continuing support, annual campaigns, seed money, emergency funds, deficit financing, building funds, equipment, land acquisition, employee matching gifts, scholarship funds.
Limitations: Giving limited to areas of company's major operations, with emphasis in St. Louis, MO. No grants to individuals, or for endowment funds, special projects, research, publications, or conferences; no loans.
Publications: 990-PF.
Application information:
Initial approach: Full proposal
Copies of proposal: 1
Deadline(s): None
Board meeting date(s): As needed
Final notification: 1 to 3 months
Write: Hiram S. Liggett, Jr., Secretary
Control Committee: Hiram S. Liggett, Jr.,* Secretary; B.A. Bridgewater, Jr.,* W.L. Hadley Griffin,* Richard W. Shomaker*.
Trustees:* Centerre Trust Company.
Number of staff: None.
Employer Identification Number: 237443082

1946
Butler Manufacturing Company Foundation ▼
BMA Tower - P.O. Box 917
Penn Valley Park
Kansas City 64141   (816) 968-3000

Incorporated in 1952 in Missouri.
Donor(s): Butler Manufacturing Company.
Financial data: (yr. ended 12/31/83): Assets, $2,431,279 (M); expenditures, $552,505, including $281,472 for 102 grants, $74,166 for 38 grants to individuals, $21,596 for 81 employee matching gifts and $4,550 for 5 loans.
Purpose and activities: General purposes; specifically for the furtherance of education, learning, research, assistance for minorities and the handicapped, preserving urban neighborhoods, the development and improvement of agriculture and industry by establishing endowments, fellowships, and scholarships at educational institutions or through grants to individuals; assistance to persons in need, including employees, former employees, and their dependents. Grants largely for higher education, hospitals, and community funds located in communities where employees of the company reside.

Types of support awarded: Annual campaigns, seed money, emergency funds, building funds, equipment, research, publications, scholarship funds, fellowships, internships, matching funds, program-related investments, general purposes, special projects, employee related scholarships.
Limitations: No grants to individuals (except for scholarships to children of company employees), or for endowment funds; no loans.
Publications: Annual report, informational brochure, program policy statement, application guidelines.
Application information:
Initial approach: Telephone or letter
Copies of proposal: 1
Deadline(s): Submit proposal preferably in month prior to board meeting
Board meeting date(s): March, June, September, and December
Final notification: 6 months
Write: Monroe Taliaferro, Vice-President
Officers: George C. Dillon,* President; Robert H. West,* Monroe Taliaferro,* Vice-Presidents; Richard O. Ballentine,* Secretary; Leslie V. Rist, Treasurer.
Trustees:* John A. Morgan, Donald H. Pratt.
Number of staff: None.
Employer Identification Number: 440663648

1947
Calkins (Ina) Board
c/o The First National Bank of Kansas City
Kansas City 64183 (816) 221-2800

Established in 1930 in Missouri.
Donor(s): Ina Calkins Trust.
Financial data: (yr. ended 12/31/84): Assets, $251,327 (M); gifts received, $221,341; expenditures, $254,888, including $218,674 for 4 grants (high: $120,000; low: $3,000) and $31,500 for 72 grants to individuals.
Purpose and activities: Local giving, with emphasis on a social agency; grants also for youth agencies, and child welfare.
Limitations: Giving limited to Kansas City, MO.
Publications: 990-PF, program policy statement, application guidelines.
Application information:
Initial approach: Telephone
Copies of proposal: 1
Deadline(s): Submit proposal one month before board meets
Board meeting date(s): January, April, July, and October
Write: David P. Ross, Secretary
Officers: Clark G. McCorkle, President; David P. Ross, Secretary and Treasurer.
Employer Identification Number: 237377909

1948
Centerre Bank N.A. Charitable Trust ▼
One Centerre Plaza, MS 28-03
St. Louis 63101 (314) 554-6873
Grant application office: P.O. Box 267, St. Louis, MO 63166

Trust established in 1951 in Missouri.
Donor(s): Centerre Bank, N.A.
Financial data: (yr. ended 12/31/84): Assets, $3,280,111 (M); expenditures, $657,567, including $653,132 for 65 grants (high: $252,000; low: $100) and $4,435 for 42 employee matching gifts.
Purpose and activities: Broad purposes; primarily local giving, with emphasis on a community fund, higher education, hospitals, cultural programs, and youth agencies.
Types of support awarded: General purposes, operating budgets, continuing support, annual campaigns, building funds, employee matching gifts.
Limitations: Giving primarily in the St. Louis, MO metropolitan area. No grants to individuals, or for endowment funds, research, scholarships, or fellowships; no loans.
Application information:
Initial approach: Full proposal
Copies of proposal: 1
Deadline(s): None
Board meeting date(s): March, June, September, and December
Final notification: 3 months
Write: Alfred H. Kerth III, Vice-President
Contributions Committee: Clarence C. Barksdale, Alfred H. Kerth III, John Peters McCarthy, Wayne Muskopf, Paul Ross.
Trustee: Centerre Trust Company in St. Louis.
Number of staff: 1.
Employer Identification Number: 436023492

1949
Chance Foundation, The
123 North Rollins St.
Centralia 65240 (314) 682-5511

Trust established in 1947 in Missouri.
Donor(s): A.B. Chance Company, F. Gano Chance,† Nathan A. Toalson.
Financial data: (yr. ended 12/31/83): Assets, $1,742,578 (M); expenditures, $144,980, including $74,919 for 33 grants (high: $35,000; low: $100).
Purpose and activities: Broad purposes; general giving, with emphasis on higher education, church support, religious associations, and youth agencies.
Trustees: Arthur H. Allen, Joseph M. Arndt, James T. Ausmus, John H. Chance, Phillip G. Chance, L.C. Hansen, M.J. Johnson, Nathan A. Toalson.
Employer Identification Number: 436028959

1950
Chromalloy American Foundation ⌘
120 South Central Ave.
St. Louis 63105 (314) 726-9200

Established in 1968 in Missouri.
Financial data: (yr. ended 12/31/83): Assets, $4,382 (M); gifts received, $16,010; expenditures, $113,461, including $113,050 for 5 grants (high: $100,000; low: $250).
Purpose and activities: Primarily local giving, with emphasis on hospitals, health agencies, and recreation.
Limitations: Giving primarily in St. Louis, MO. No grants to individuals, or for building or endowment funds, research, scholarships, fellowships, or matching gifts; no loans.
Application information:
Initial approach: Proposal
Copies of proposal: 1
Board meeting date(s): May
Officers and Directors: W.E. Stevens, President; D.M. Carolan, Vice-President; J.F. Krupsky, Secretary; T.G. Barnett, Treasurer.
Employer Identification Number: 430908776

1951
Commerce Foundation, The ⌘
P.O. Box 13686
Kansas City 64199 (816) 234-2300

Incorporated in 1952 in Missouri.
Donor(s): Commerce Bank of Kansas City.
Financial data: (yr. ended 12/31/83): Assets, $122,226 (M); gifts received, $165,000; expenditures, $280,361, including $279,100 for 65 grants (high: $70,000; low: $200).
Purpose and activities: Primarily local giving, with emphasis on community funds, the performing arts, higher education, music, youth agencies, and hospitals.
Types of support awarded: Continuing support, annual campaigns, seed money, building funds, endowment funds, special projects, professorships.
Limitations: Giving primarily in MO. No grants to individuals, or for operating budgets or matching gifts; no loans.
Application information:
Initial approach: Letter
Copies of proposal: 1
Board meeting date(s): As required
Write: Warren W. Weaver, Vice-President
Officers and Directors: James M. Kemper, Jr., President; Charles E. Templer, Vice-President and Treasurer; Warren W. Weaver, Vice-President; T. Alan Peschka, Secretary.
Number of staff: None.
Employer Identification Number: 446012453

1952
Cowden (Louetta M.) Foundation
c/o The First National Bank of Kansas City
14 West Tenth St.
Kansas City 64105 (816) 221-2800
Mailing address: P.O. Box 38, Kansas City, MO 64183

Trust established in 1964 in Missouri.
Donor(s): Louetta M. Cowden.†
Financial data: (yr. ended 12/31/84): Assets, $3,566,738 (M); expenditures, $202,566, including $180,000 for 6 grants (high: $50,000; low: $10,000).
Purpose and activities: Broad purposes; grants restricted to local institutions with emphasis on capital fund grants.
Types of support awarded: Building funds, equipment, land acquisition, seed money, emergency funds.
Limitations: Giving limited to MO. No grants to individuals, or for endowment funds, scholarships or fellowships, or matching gifts; no loans.
Publications: 990-PF, application guidelines.
Application information:
Initial approach: Telephone
Copies of proposal: 1

Deadline(s): Submit proposal in February, August, or November
Board meeting date(s): March, June, September, and December
Final notification: 2 months
Write: David P. Ross, Senior Vice-President
Trustees: Menefee D. Blackwell, Arthur H. Bowen, Jr., The First National Bank of Kansas City (David P. Ross, Senior Vice-President).
Number of staff: 1.
Employer Identification Number: 436052617

1953
Craig (The E. L.) Foundation, Inc. ¤
P.O. Box 1404
Joplin 64801

Incorporated in 1960 in Missouri.
Donor(s): Tamko Asphalt Products, Inc., Royal Brand Roofing, Inc.
Financial data: (yr. ended 7/31/83): Assets, $1,029,034 (M); expenditures, $68,836, including $63,679 for 23 grants (high: $35,000; low: $25).
Purpose and activities: Primarily local giving; interests include higher education, economics, freedom-liberty programs, youth agencies, and hospitals.
Limitations: Giving primarily in Joplin, MO. No grants to individuals.
Application information:
Write: J.P. Humphreys, Vice-President
Officers and Directors: Mary Ethel Craig, President; J.P. Humphreys, Vice-President; Ethel Mae Craig Humphreys, Secretary-Treasurer.
Employer Identification Number: 446015127

1954
Cross Foundation, Inc., The ¤
1734 East 63rd St., Suite 414
Kansas City 64110   (816) 333-1730

Incorporated in 1955 in Missouri.
Donor(s): Mrs. Annette Cross Murphy.
Financial data: (yr. ended 12/31/83): Assets, $1,316,910 (M); expenditures, $164,307, including $133,300 for 14 grants (high: $50,000; low: $200).
Purpose and activities: General purposes; grants largely for medical research, higher education, and health-related programs and programs for youth.
Types of support awarded: Operating budgets, research, building funds, endowment funds.
Application information:
Initial approach: Full proposal
Deadline(s): Applications are reviewed between April 15 and December 15
Write: Mrs. Martha O. Lever, Executive Director
Officers: Annette Cross Murphy, President; Lyman Field,* Vice-President and Secretary; Martha O. Lever, Executive Director.
Directors:* Robert R. Cross, Walter M. Cross III, George E. Murphy, M.D., Gertrude F. Oliver, David Oliver.
Employer Identification Number: 440613382

1955
Danforth Foundation, The ▼
231 South Bemiston Ave.
St. Louis 63105   (314) 862-6200

Incorporated in 1927 in Missouri.
Donor(s): William H. Danforth,† Mrs. William H. Danforth.†
Financial data: (yr. ended 5/31/84): Assets, $149,581,061 (M); expenditures, $11,317,131, including $9,548,176 for 112 grants (high: $6,732,697; low: $212; average: $50,000), $367,382 for 90 grants to individuals, $105,056 for 27 employee matching gifts and $907,294 for 5 foundation-administered programs.
Purpose and activities: Dedicated to enhancing the humane dimensions of life through activities which emphasize the theme of improving the quality of teaching and learning. Serves higher education nationally through sponsorship of staff-administered programs; precollegiate education nationally through grant-making and program activities; and urban affairs in metropolitan St. Louis .
Types of support awarded: Employee matching gifts, consulting services, technical assistance, fellowships, general purposes.
Limitations: Giving limited to St. Louis, MO area for urban affairs grants; otherwise, nationally, for secondary education. No grants for building or endowment funds, special projects, or operating budgets; no loans.
Publications: Annual report, informational brochure, program policy statement, application guidelines.
Application information: Graduate fellowship program to be terminated in 1986; no new nominations accepted.
Initial approach: Letter
Copies of proposal: 1
Deadline(s): None
Board meeting date(s): January, May, and October, and as required
Final notification: 4 weeks
Write: Gene L. Schwilck, President
Officers: Gene L. Schwilck,* President; Bruce Anderson, John B. Ervin, Vice-Presidents; Melvin C. Bahle, Treasurer.
Trustees:* William H. Danforth, Chairman; James R. Compton, Vice-Chairman and Secretary; Virginia S. Brown, George H. Capps, Donald Danforth, Jr., Charles Guggenheim, George E. Pake, P. Roy Vagelos.
Number of staff: 4 full-time professional; 4 full-time support.
Employer Identification Number: 430653297

1956
Deer Creek Foundation
818 Olive St.
St. Louis 63101   (314) 241-3228

Established in 1964 in Missouri.
Financial data: (yr. ended 12/31/83): Assets, $1,270,167 (M); gifts received, $40,000; expenditures, $178,946, including $101,900 for 22 grants (high: $12,000; low: $1,000).

Purpose and activities: Support primarily for programs to preserve and advance majority rule in this society, with protections provided for minorities by the Constitution and the Bill of Rights; grants primarily to "action programs" with promise of making a significant national or regional impact; some preference to projects in Missouri.
Limitations: No grants to individuals, or for building or endowment funds, equipment, or operating budgets.
Publications: Application guidelines, program policy statement.
Application information:
Initial approach: Full proposal
Copies of proposal: 1
Deadline(s): None
Board meeting date(s): March, June, September, and December
Write: Mary Stake Hawker, Administrator
Trustees: Lattie F. Coor, Aaron Fischer, M. Peter Fischer, Teresa M. Fischer, Philip B. Kurland.
Number of staff: 1 full-time professional; 1 part-time support.
Employer Identification Number: 436052774

1957
Edison Brothers Stores Foundation
P.O. Box 14020
St. Louis 63178

Incorporated in 1956 in Missouri.
Donor(s): Members of the Edison family, Edison Brothers Stores, Inc., and its subsidiaries.
Financial data: (yr. ended 5/31/83): Assets, $566,119 (M); expenditures, $263,613, including $258,175 for 128 grants (high: $100,000; low: $100).
Purpose and activities: Broad purposes; general giving, primarily in St. Louis, with emphasis on community and Jewish welfare funds, higher education, and cultural organizations.
Limitations: Giving primarily in St. Louis, MO.
Officers and Directors: Bernard Edison, President; Eric P. Newman, Vice-President and Secretary; Louis Melchior, Vice-President and Treasurer; Julian Edison, Andrew Newman, Vice-Presidents.
Employer Identification Number: 436047207

1958
Edison (Harry) Foundation ▼ ¤
400 Washington Ave.
St. Louis 63102   (314) 444-6525

Incorporated in 1949 in Illinois.
Donor(s): Harry Edison.†
Financial data: (yr. ended 12/31/82): Assets, $12,738,358 (M); expenditures, $642,349, including $620,522 for 55 grants (high: $300,000; low: $15).
Purpose and activities: Broad purposes; primarily local giving, with emphasis on higher education, Jewish welfare funds, a community fund, and hospitals.
Types of support awarded: Professorships, building funds, annual campaigns.
Limitations: Giving primarily in St. Louis, MO. No grants to individuals.

Application information:
   Write: Eric P. Newman, Secretary
Officers and Directors: Irving Edison, President and Treasurer; Eric P. Newman, Secretary; Henry Kohn.
Employer Identification Number: 436027017

1959
Emerson Charitable Trust ▼ ⌀
c/o Emeron Electric Co.
8000 W. Florissant, P.O. Box 4100
Saint Louis 63136

Established in 1944 in Missouri as Emerson Electric Manufacturing Company Charitable Trust; present name adopted in 1981.
Donor(s): Emerson Electric Company.
Financial data: (yr. ended 9/30/83): Assets, $5,682,224 (M); expenditures, $3,291,824, including $3,143,050 for 766 grants (high: $261,000; low: $25; average: $25-$50,000) and $97,000 for 194 grants to individuals.
Purpose and activities: Grants for community funds, higher education, cultural programs, hospitals and health agencies, public policy organizations, and youth agencies.
Types of support awarded: Employee matching gifts, employee related scholarships.
Application information:
   Initial approach: Letter
   Deadline(s): None
   Write: Ned Taddeucci, Director of Public Affairs
Trustee: Centerre Trust Co.
Principal Officer: L.L. Browning, Jr., Chairman, Board of Control.
Employer Identification Number: 526200123

1960
Enright Foundation, Inc. ⌀
7508 Main
Kansas City 64114

Established in 1965.
Donor(s): Joseph J. Enright.
Financial data: (yr. ended 3/31/83): Assets, $2,040,346 (M); expenditures, $168,217, including $137,328 for 42 grants (high: $35,000; low: $18).
Purpose and activities: Primarily local giving, with emphasis on Roman Catholic religious organizations, hospitals, child welfare, and social agencies.
Limitations: Giving primarily in MO.
Officers: Anna M. Cassidy, President; John J. Conron, Vice-President; Thomas E. King, Secretary; L.J. Cassidy, Treasurer.
Employer Identification Number: 436067639

1961
Feld (Milton W.) Charitable Trust ⌀
1000 United Missouri Bank Bldg.
Kansas City 64106

Established in 1977.
Financial data: (yr. ended 8/31/83): Assets, $3,087,889 (M); gifts received, $74,121; expenditures, $1,223,809, including $1,157,393 for 27 grants (high: $260,000; low: $1,000).

Purpose and activities: Primarily local giving to Jewish welfare and religious organizations, social service agencies, hospitals, higher education, and cultural programs.
Limitations: Giving primarily in MO.
Trustees: Selma S. Feld, Abraham Margolin, Irving S. Selber.
Employer Identification Number: 431155236

1962
Fischer-Bauer-Knirps Foundation ⌀
c/o St. Louis County National Bank
8000 Forsyth Blvd.
Clayton 63105
Application address: 6800 Manchester Rd., St. Louis, MO 63143

Incorporated in 1959 in Illinois.
Financial data: (yr. ended 12/31/83): Assets, $1,251,391 (M); expenditures, $86,949, including $74,800 for 204 grants (high: $2,000; low: $200).
Purpose and activities: Primarily local giving, with emphasis on hospitals, higher education, church support, and health agencies.
Limitations: Giving primarily in MO.
Application information:
   Write: Carl Bauer, President
Officers and Directors: Carl Bauer, President and Treasurer; Richard E. Fister, Secretary; Dorothy Anderson, Roger P. Eklund, Katherine Gebhard.
Employer Identification Number: 436036524

1963
Flarsheim (Louis and Elizabeth) Charitable Foundation
c/o First National Bank of Kansas City
14 West Tenth St.
Kansas City 64183

Donor(s): Louis Flarsheim.
Financial data: (yr. ended 11/30/84): Assets, $1,762,063 (M); expenditures, $101,141, including $99,475 for 8 grants (high: $25,000; low: $2,000).
Purpose and activities: Broad purposes including support for the performing and visual arts; primarily local giving.
Limitations: Giving primarily in the Kansas City, MO, area.
Trustee: The First National Bank of Kansas City.
Employer Identification Number: 436223957

1964
Garvey (Edward Chase) Memorial Foundation
c/o Commerce Bank of St. Louis County
8000 Forsyth Blvd., P.O. Box 11356
Clayton 63105   (314) 726-2255

Trust established in 1970 in Missouri.
Donor(s): Edward C. Garvey.†
Financial data: (yr. ended 9/30/83): Assets, $1,448,590 (M); expenditures, $157,245, including $143,500 for 33 grants (high: $24,000; low: $500).

Purpose and activities: Broad purposes; primarily local giving for higher and secondary education, music, the performing arts, and youth agencies.
Limitations: Giving primarily in MO. No grants to individuals.
Application information:
   Initial approach: Full proposal
   Copies of proposal: 1
   Board meeting date(s): Annually, in the summer
   Write: Michael C. Erb, Vice-President, Commerce Bank of St. Louis County
Trustees: Bliss Shands, Commerce Bank of St. Louis County (Michael C. Erb, Vice-President).
Employer Identification Number: 436132744

1965
Gaylord (The Catherine Manley) Foundation
314 North Broadway, Rm. 1230
St. Louis 63102   (314) 421-0181

Trust established about 1959 in Missouri.
Donor(s): Catherine M. Gaylord.†
Financial data: (yr. ended 6/30/84): Assets, $2,968,667 (M); expenditures, $359,675, including $282,162 for 54 grants (high: $35,000; low: $100).
Purpose and activities: Broad purposes; primarily local giving, with emphasis on private higher education, Protestant and Roman Catholic church support, youth and child welfare agencies, civic affairs, social services, and music and art.
Types of support awarded: Operating budgets, continuing support, annual campaigns, seed money, emergency funds, deficit financing, building funds, equipment, endowment funds, matching funds, scholarship funds, special projects, publications, conferences and seminars.
Limitations: Giving primarily in the St. Louis, MO, metropolitan community. No grants to individuals; no loans.
Publications: Annual report, program policy statement, application guidelines.
Application information:
   Initial approach: Letter
   Copies of proposal: 1
   Deadline(s): None
   Board meeting date(s): Monthly
   Final notification: 30 days
   Write: Donald E. Fahey, Trustee
Trustees: Donald E. Fahey, Leigh Gerdine, Herbert F. Kalbfleisch.
Number of staff: 1 full-time professional; 1 part-time support.
Employer Identification Number: 436029174

1966
Gaylord (Clifford Willard) Foundation ▼ ⌀
c/o Boatmen's National Bank
P.O. Box 7365, Main Post Office
St. Louis 63166

Trust established in 1948 in Missouri.
Donor(s): Clifford W. Gaylord.†

Financial data: (yr. ended 12/31/83): Assets, $5,061,844 (M); expenditures, $480,076, including $433,000 for 72 grants (high: $25,000; low: $1,000).
Purpose and activities: Broad purposes; primarily local giving, with emphasis on higher education, hospitals, social agencies, youth agencies, child welfare, health agencies, and cultural programs.
Limitations: Giving primarily in St. Louis, MO. No grants to individuals.
Application information:
 Deadline(s): None
 Write: George H. Halpin, Jr.
Trustees: H. Sam Priest, President; Frances M. Barnes III, Gaylord Fauntleroy.
Agent for Trustees: Boatmen's National Bank of St. Louis.
Employer Identification Number: 436027517

1967
Green (Allen P. & Josephine B.) Foundation
P.O. Box 523
Mexico 65265 (314) 581-5568

Trust established in 1941 in Missouri.
Donor(s): Allen P. Green,† Mrs. Allen P. Green.†
Financial data: (yr. ended 12/31/84): Assets, $4,924,644 (M); expenditures, $239,418, including $199,500 for 17 grants (high: $20,000; low: $1,000) and $25,000 for 2 foundation-administered programs.
Purpose and activities: Broad purposes; primarily local giving for health care and educational programs for children, and cultural and preservation projects.
Types of support awarded: Continuing support, seed money, emergency funds, building funds, equipment, endowment funds, scholarship funds, special projects, research, publications, conferences and seminars.
Limitations: Giving primarily in MO. No grants to individuals, or for operating budgets; no loans.
Publications: Annual report, program policy statement, application guidelines.
Application information:
 Initial approach: Letter
 Copies of proposal: 1
 Deadline(s): April 1 or October 1
 Board meeting date(s): May and November
 Final notification: 1 month
 Write: Walter G. Staley, Secretary-Treasurer
Officers and Directors: George C. Willson, III, President; Homer E. Sayad, Vice-President; Walter G. Staley, Secretary-Treasurer; Christopher S. Bond, Elizabeth G. Bond, Robert R. Collins, James F. McHenry, Martha G. Staley, Walter G. Staley, Jr., Robert A. Wood.
Number of staff: 1 part-time support.
Employer Identification Number: 436030135

1968
Hall Family Foundations ▼
(formerly Hallmark Educational Foundations)
Charitable & Crown Investment - 323
P.O. Box 580
Kansas City 64141 (816) 274-5615

Hallmark Educational Foundation incorporated in 1943 in Missouri; Hallmark Education Foundation of Kansas incorporated in 1954 in Kansas; combined funds known as Hallmark Educational Foundations.
Donor(s): Hallmark Cards, Inc., Joyce C. Hall,† E.A. Hall,† R.B. Hall.†
Financial data: (yr. ended 12/31/83): Assets, $117,877,180 (M); gifts received, $35,747,932; expenditures, $4,667,266, including $3,768,407 for 52 grants (high: $1,966,921; low: $1,000; average: $35,000), $155,550 for 110 grants to individuals and $130,600 for 89 loans.
Purpose and activities: Broad purposes; giving restricted to local area, within four main areas of interest: 1) youth, especially education and programs that promote social welfare, health and character building of young people; 2) economic development; 3)the performing and visual arts; and 4) the elderly.
Types of support awarded: Operating budgets, seed money, emergency funds, building funds, equipment, special projects, matching funds, general purposes, student aid, employee related scholarships.
Limitations: Giving limited to the Kansas City, MO area. No support for international or religious organizations. No grants to individuals (except for emergency aid to company employees, and scholarships and student loans for their children), or for endowment funds, travel, operating deficits, conferences, scholarly research, or fundraising campaigns such as telethons.
Publications: Annual report, informational brochure, program policy statement, application guidelines.
Application information:
 Initial approach: Letter
 Copies of proposal: 1
 Deadline(s): 4 weeks before board meetings
 Board meeting date(s): March, June, September, and December
 Final notification: 4 to 6 weeks
 Write: Sarah V. Hutchison, Margaret H. Pence, or Wendy Hockaday, Program Officers
Officers: William A. Hall, President; John A. McDonald, Vice-President and Treasurer; Eleanor Angelbeck, Secretary.
Directors: Donald J. Hall, Chairman; Irvine O. Hockaday, David H. Hughes, John P. Mascotte, Morton I. Sosland, W. Clarke Wescoe, M.D.
Number of staff: 3 full-time professional; 1 part-time professional.
Employer Identification Number: 446006291

1969
H.B.S. Fund ⊭
10 South Broadway, Suite 500
St. Louis 63102 (314) 241-2100

Incorporated in 1969 in Missouri.
Donor(s): Harriet B. Spoehrer.
Financial data: (yr. ended 11/30/83): Assets, $435,890 (M); gifts received, $200,000; expenditures, $928,785, including $923,985 for 41 grants (high: $302,985; low: $500).

Purpose and activities: Broad purposes; primarily local giving, with emphasis on higher education, hospitals, youth agencies, cultural programs, and social agencies.
Limitations: Giving primarily in MO. No grants to individuals.
Application information:
 Initial approach: Letter
 Copies of proposal: 1
 Deadline(s): Submit proposal in September
 Board meeting date(s): May and October
 Write: Ned O. Lemkemeier, Secretary
Officers and Directors: Harriet B. Spoehrer, President; Jane S. Tschudy, Vice-President; Ned O. Lemkemeier, Secretary; Charles H. Spoehrer.
Employer Identification Number: 237098540

1970
Ilgenfritz (May H.) Testamentary Trust ⊭
P.O. Box 311
Sedalia 65301 (816) 826-3310

Trust established in 1941 in Missouri.
Financial data: (yr. ended 12/31/83): Assets, $1,440,581 (M); expenditures, $89,641, including $15,000 for 1 grant and $62,179 for 100 grants to individuals.
Purpose and activities: Primarily local giving, with emphasis on scholarships and on a hospital for handicapped children.
Types of support awarded: Student aid.
Limitations: Giving primarily in MO.
Application information:
 Deadline(s): None
 Write: John Pelham, Trustee
Trustees: John Pelham, Third National Bank.
Employer Identification Number: 440663403

1971
Ingram (Joe) Trust
Centerre Bank of Kansas City
900 Walnut, P.O. Box 666
Kansas City 64141
Grant application address: Joe W. Ingram Trust Office, 111 West Third St., Salisbury, MO 65281; Tel.: (816) 388-5555

Trust established in 1960 in Missouri.
Donor(s): Joe Ingram.†
Financial data: (yr. ended 12/31/83): Assets, $5,172,530 (M); expenditures, $411,374, including $900 for 9 grants to individuals and $342,107 for 127 loans.
Purpose and activities: Giving restricted to Chariton County, primarily for student loans; some support for local civic projects.
Types of support awarded: Grants to individuals, student aid.
Limitations: Giving limited to Chariton County, MO.
Application information:
 Initial approach: Letter
 Write: C.E. Griswold
Trustees: Centerre Bank of Kansas City.
Trust Fund Committee:* Elmer Arnsperger, Leroy Baker, Elmer E. Bills, Jr., D.T. Blake, Thomas H. Ehrhardt, W.D. Hollis, F.B. Manion, W.D. Richards III, Robert H. Sweeney, George S. Thompson.
Employer Identification Number: 446006475

1972
Interco, Inc. Charitable Trust ▼ ⌑
P.O. Drawer 387
St. Louis 63166   (314) 425-2667

Trust established in 1944 in Missouri.
Donor(s): Interco, Inc., and subsidiaries.
Financial data: (yr. ended 12/31/83): Assets,
$14,857,292 (M); gifts received, $545,202;
expenditures, $637,572, including $565,853
for 45 grants (high: $115,000; low: $400;
average: $1,000-$10,000).
Purpose and activities: Primarily local giving,
with emphasis on a community fund and
higher education; support also for hospitals,
cultural programs, and social agencies.
Limitations: Giving primarily in St. Louis, MO.
Application information:
    Write: Herschel Lynch, Administrator
Trustees: Robert T. Hensley, Jr., Norfleet H.
Rand, Mercantile Trust Company.
Employer Identification Number: 436020530

1973
Jordan (Mary Ranken) and Ettie A.
  Jordan Charitable Foundation ▼
c/o Mercantile Trust Company
P.O. Box 387
St. Louis 63166   (314) 425-2672

Trust established in 1957 in Missouri.
Donor(s): Mrs. Mary Ranken Jordan.†
Financial data: (yr. ended 12/31/83): Assets,
$11,752,410 (M); expenditures, $483,492,
including $419,733 for 57 grants (high:
$45,000; low: $1,000; average: $1,000-
$10,000).
Purpose and activities: Giving limited to
charitable and eleemosynary institutions within
Missouri, with emphasis on higher education
and hospitals; grants also for social services,
secondary education, health services, and
cultural programs.
Types of support awarded: Building funds,
operating budgets, special projects, continuing
support.
Limitations: Giving limited to MO, with
emphasis on St. Louis. No grants to individuals
or for endowment funds.
Publications: Application guidelines.
Application information:
    Initial approach: Letter
    Copies of proposal: 3
    Deadline(s): Submit proposal preferably in
      November; deadline November 30
    Board meeting date(s): January
    Final notification: After January 15
    Write: H. Jill Fivecoat, Trust Officer
Trustee: Mercantile Trust Company.
Advisory Committee: Fred Arnold, Robert
Neill.
Employer Identification Number: 436020554

1974
Kemper (The David Woods) Memorial
  Foundation
720 Main St.
P.O. Box 13686
Kansas City 64199   (816) 234-2345

Incorporated in 1946 in Missouri.

Donor(s): James M. Kemper, James M.
Kemper, Jr.
Financial data: (yr. ended 12/31/84): Assets,
$1,896,857 (M); expenditures, $146,807,
including $139,303 for 135 grants (high:
$12,000; low: $15).
Purpose and activities: Broad purposes;
primarily local giving, with emphasis on cultural
programs, higher and secondary education,
population control, Protestant church support,
youth agencies, and community funds.
Limitations: Giving primarily in MO.
Application information:
    Write: James M. Kemper, Jr., President
Officers and Directors: James M. Kemper, Jr.,
President; Laura Kemper Fields, Vice-President
and Treasurer; Mildred Lane Kemper, Secretary.
Employer Identification Number: 446012535

1975
Kemper (Enid and Crosby)
  Foundation ▼ ⌑
c/o United Missouri Bank of Kansas City
Tenth St. and Grand Ave., P.O. Box 226
Kansas City 64141   (816) 556-7722

Established in 1972 in Missouri.
Donor(s): Enid J. Kemper, R. Crosby Kemper,
Sr.†
Financial data: (yr. ended 12/31/83): Assets,
$27,261,255 (M); expenditures, $2,034,194,
including $1,806,458 for 55 grants (high:
$695,900; low: $100; average: $500-$50,000).
Purpose and activities: Broad purposes;
primarily local giving for cultural programs,
including museums and performing arts, higher
and secondary education, and an agricultural
organization; some support also for health.
Types of support awarded: General purposes.
Limitations: Giving primarily in KS and MO.
No support for medical institutions. No grants
for capital funds.
Application information:
    Initial approach: Telephone
    Copies of proposal: 1
    Board meeting date(s): Quarterly and as
      needed
    Final notification: 3 days after board
      meetings
    Write: Melanie Alm
Trustees: Mary S. Kemper, R. Crosby Kemper,
Jr., Richard C. King, United Missouri Bank of
Kansas City.
Employer Identification Number: 237279896

1976
Kemper (R. C.) Charitable Trust &
  Foundation ⌑
c/o United Missouri Bank of Kansas City
Tenth & Grand Ave.
Kansas City 64141

Trust established in 1953 in Missouri.
Donor(s): R. Crosby Kemper, Sr.†
Financial data: (yr. ended 12/31/83): Assets,
$8,230,446 (M); expenditures, $268,378,
including $200,000 for 1 grant.
Purpose and activities: Broad purposes;
primarily local giving, with emphasis on cultural
activities, higher education, including
scholarship funds, and youth agencies.

Limitations: Giving primarily in MO.
Trustees: Pamela K. Graborsky, Mary S.
Kemper, R. Crosby Kemper, Jr., Trust
Committee of United Missouri Bank of Kansas
City.
Employer Identification Number: 446010318

1977
Laclede Gas Charitable Trust
720 Olive St., Rm. 812
St. Louis 63101   (314) 342-0643

Trust established in 1966 in Missouri.
Donor(s): Laclede Gas Company.
Financial data: (yr. ended 9/30/83): Assets,
$5,028,440 (M); expenditures, $466,640,
including $450,505 for 122 grants (high:
$117,500; low: $100) and $4,895 for 43
employee matching gifts.
Purpose and activities: Support of public
charitable organizations; giving primarily in area
of company operations, with emphasis on
community funds, higher and secondary
education, the arts, hospitals, and youth
agencies.
Types of support awarded: Matching funds,
operating budgets, scholarship funds, building
funds, equipment, emergency funds,
conferences and seminars, special projects.
Limitations: Giving primarily in areas of
company operations. No support for religious
or sectarian organizations, political
organizations, or veterans groups. No grants to
individuals.
Publications: Informational brochure.
Application information: Application form
required.
    Initial approach: Full proposal
    Copies of proposal: 1
    Deadline(s): March 15
    Board meeting date(s): March, June,
      September, and December
    Write: Wildeth McShane, or David L.
      Gardner, Trustee
Trustees: David L. Gardner, Lee M. Liberman,
D.A. Novatny.
Number of staff: None.
Employer Identification Number: 436068197

1978
LaRue (George A. and Dolly F.) Trust
c/o Commerce Bank of Kansas City
P.O. Box 248
Kansas City 64141   (816) 234-2568
Application address: Janice C. Kreamer, Kansas
City Association of Trusts and Foundations, 406
Board of Trade, Kansas City, MO 64105

Trust established in 1973 in Missouri.
Donor(s): George A. LaRue,† Dolly F. LaRue.†
Financial data: (yr. ended 12/31/83): Assets,
$1,913,448 (M); expenditures, $114,100,
including $102,125 for 7 grants (high: $35,000;
low: $5,000).
Purpose and activities: Broad purposes;
primarily local giving, including grants for
cultural organizations, conservation, and a
community service organization.

Limitations: Giving primarily in MO, with emphasis on Kansas City.
Trustee: Commerce Bank of Kansas City.
Number of staff: None.
Employer Identification Number: 436122865

1979
Leader Foundation, The ¤
1025 S. Brentwood Blvd.
St. Louis 63117

Established in 1944.
Financial data: (yr. ended 1/31/84): Assets, $1,829,133 (M); expenditures, $142,567, including $56,465 for 12 grants and $71,764 for 32 grants to individuals.
Purpose and activities: Local giving, primarily to individuals for pensions.
Types of support awarded: Grants to individuals.
Limitations: Giving primarily in St. Louis, MO.
Officers: Donald Ray, President; J.A. Baer II, John Quinn, Edwin Shifrin, Vice-Presidents; Richard Eaton, Secretary-Treasurer.
Employer Identification Number: 436036864

1980
Long (R. A.) Foundation
127 West Tenth St., Suite 500
Kansas City 64105   (816) 842-2315

Incorporated in 1958 in Missouri.
Donor(s): Loula Long Combs,† Sally Long Ellis.†
Financial data: (yr. ended 11/30/84): Assets, $2,021,234 (M); expenditures, $126,010, including $112,824 for 35 grants (high: $12,951; low: $200).
Purpose and activities: Primarily local giving, largely for services for youth, including child welfare, recreation, rehabilitation, and education.
Limitations: Giving primarily in KS and MO. No grants to individuals, or for endowment funds, research programs, or scholarships and fellowships; no loans.
Publications: Application guidelines.
Application information:
  Initial approach: Letter
  Copies of proposal: 1
  Deadline(s): April 30 and October 30
  Board meeting date(s): May and November
  Write: James H. Bernard, Treasurer
Officers: R.A.L. Ellis,* President; Jack B. O'Hara,* Hayne Ellis III, Vice-Presidents; James R. Mueller, Secretary; James H. Bernard,* Treasurer.
Directors:* Ann J. Thompson.
Employer Identification Number: 446014081

1981
Loose (Carrie J.) Trust
(formerly Carrie J. Loose Fund)
406 Board of Trade Bldg.
Tenth and Wyandotte Sts.
Kansas City 64105   (816) 842-0944

Trust established in 1927 in Missouri.
Donor(s): Harry Wilson Loose,† Carrie J. Loose.†

Financial data: (yr. ended 12/31/84): Assets, $5,667,582 (M); expenditures, $350,169, including $309,647 for 19 grants (high: $35,000; low: $3,809).
Purpose and activities: Broad purposes; grants to established local educational, health, and welfare institutions; support for research into the community's social and cultural needs and for experimental and demonstration projects. A member trust of the Kansas City Association of Trusts and Foundations.
Types of support awarded: Research, special projects.
Limitations: Giving limited to Kansas City, MO. No grants to individuals, or for building funds, matching gifts, endowment funds, general support, scholarships, or fellowships; no loans.
Publications: Annual report, program policy statement, application guidelines.
Application information:
  Initial approach: Letter or full proposal
  Copies of proposal: 1
  Deadline(s): 6 weeks prior to board meetings
  Board meeting date(s): April, July, October, and December
  Write: Janice C. Kreamer, Administrative Officer
Officer: Janice C. Kreamer, Administrative Officer.
Trustees: Taylor S. Abernathy, Boatmen's First National Bank of Kansas City.
Number of staff: 1 full-time professional; 1 part-time support.
Employer Identification Number: 446009246

1982
Loose (Harry Wilson) Trust
406 Board of Trade Bldg.
Tenth and Wyandotte Sts.
Kansas City 64105   (816) 842-0944

Trust established in 1927 in Missouri.
Donor(s): Harry Wilson Loose.†
Financial data: (yr. ended 12/31/84): Assets, $2,331,768 (M); expenditures, $207,058, including $180,675 for 10 grants (high: $67,500; low: $5,000).
Purpose and activities: Primarily local giving, with emphasis on civic and community development in Kansas City, including grants for the arts and cultural programs. A member trust of the Kansas City Association of Trusts and Foundations.
Types of support awarded: Research, special projects, conferences and seminars, professorships, internships, exchange programs.
Limitations: Giving primarily in Kansas City, MO. No grants to individuals, or for endowment funds, general support, building funds, matching gifts, scholarships, or fellowships; no loans.
Publications: Annual report, application guidelines, program policy statement.
Application information:
  Initial approach: Letter or full proposal
  Copies of proposal: 1
  Deadline(s): 6 weeks before board meetings
  Board meeting date(s): April, July, October, and December
  Write: Janice C. Kreamer, President, Kansas City Association of Trusts and Foundations

Trustees: Robert T.H. Davidson, Donald H. Chisholm, Boatmen's First National Bank of Kansas City.
Number of staff: 1 full-time professional; 1 part-time support.
Employer Identification Number: 446009245

1983
Loose (Jacob L. and Ella C.) Foundation
406 Board of Trade Bldg.
Tenth and Wyandotte Sts.
Kansas City 64105   (816) 842-0944

Trust established in 1924 in Missouri.
Donor(s): Jacob L. Loose,† Ella C. Loose.†
Financial data: (yr. ended 12/31/83): Assets, $4,507,239 (M); expenditures, $340,576, including $227,474 for 8 grants (high: $102,900; low: $1,500).
Purpose and activities: "To relieve personal distress and sickness among the poor and needy of Kansas City, Missouri, especially among children"; support for social research into community needs; assists organizations operating in the fields of care of sick, medical education and mental health, family service, and relief to persons in need.
Types of support awarded: Research, special projects, publications, conferences and seminars, technical assistance, consulting services.
Limitations: Giving limited to Kansas City, MO. No grants to individuals, or for endowment funds, general support, building funds, matching gifts, scholarships, or fellowships; no loans.
Publications: Annual report, application guidelines, program policy statement.
Application information:
  Initial approach: Letter or full proposal
  Copies of proposal: 1
  Deadline(s): 6 weeks prior to board meetings
  Board meeting date(s): April, July, October, and December
  Final notification: 3 months
  Write: Janice C. Kreamer, Administrative Officer
Officers and Directors: Floyd R. Gibson, President; Herman R. Sutherland, Gordon E. Wells, Vice-Presidents; Menefee D. Blackwell, Secretary; James P. Sunderland, Treasurer; Janice C. Kreamer, Administrative Officer; John S. Ayres, Donald H. Chisholm, Jerry T. Duggan, Robert A. Olson, Byron T. Shutz, R. Hugh Uhlmann, Robert W. Wagstaff, Louis L. Ward.
Number of staff: 1 full-time professional; 1 part-time support.
Employer Identification Number: 436050347

1984
Lopata (Stanley and Lucy) Foundation ¤
7751 Carondelet
St. Louis 63105

Established in 1968.
Donor(s): Stanley Lopata, Lucy Lopata.
Financial data: (yr. ended 12/31/82): Assets, $1,632,792 (M); gifts received, $300,000; expenditures, $137,422, including $131,460 for 122 grants (high: $30,000; low: $10).

Purpose and activities: Giving primarily for Jewish welfare funds and temple support.
Manager: Stanley Lopata.
Trustees: Lucy Lopata, Monte L. Lopata.
Employer Identification Number: 436099972

1985
Love (John Allan) Charitable Foundation
c/o Edgar G. Boedecker
120 South Central Ave.
Clayton 63105   (314) 863-6900

Established in 1966 in Missouri.
Donor(s): John Allan Love Trusts.
Financial data: (yr. ended 12/31/82): Assets, $1,350,359 (M); expenditures, $98,691, including $83,000 for 27 grants (high: $10,000; low: $200).
Purpose and activities: Primarily local giving, including aid for the handicapped and medical research, higher education, and cultural programs; grants also for a community fund and a child welfare society.
Limitations: Giving primarily in MO.
Officers: Rumsey Ewing, President; William Boyd, Vice-President; James G. Forsyth, Treasurer.
Directors: William W. Boyd, C. Venable Minor, W. Anderson Payne.
Employer Identification Number: 436066121

1986
Lowenstein Brothers Foundation
1008 Commerce Bank Bldg.
Kansas City 64106

Trust established in 1956 in Missouri.
Financial data: (yr. ended 10/31/83): Assets, $1,919,454 (M); expenditures, $196,259, including $188,205 for 43 grants (high: $62,800; low: $50).
Purpose and activities: Primarily local giving, with emphasis on Jewish welfare funds; support also for secondary education.
Limitations: Giving primarily in MO.
Trustees: Marjorie Sue Kaplan, Sharon Lowenstein, William B. Lowenstein.
Employer Identification Number: 436055404

1987
Mallinckrodt (Edward), Jr. Foundation ⊭
9312 Tesson Ferry Rd.
St. Louis 63123
Application address: 611 Olive, Suite 1400, St. Louis, MO 63101

Incorporated in 1953 in Missouri.
Donor(s): Edward Mallinckrodt, Jr.†
Financial data: (yr. ended 9/30/83): Assets, $11,374,094 (M); expenditures, $563,105, including $417,424 for 6 grants (high: $125,000; low: $50,000) and $45,000 for 1 grant to an individual.
Purpose and activities: Broad purposes; grants largely for bio-medical education and research, including grants to individual researchers under the Scholar Program.
Types of support awarded: Research.
Application information:

Deadline(s): None
Write: Charles C. Allen, Jr., Secretary
Officers and Directors: Oliver M. Langenberg, President and Treasurer; Tom Cori, Vice-President; Charles C. Allen, Jr., Secretary; Eugene H. Bricker, Juan Traveras.
Employer Identification Number: 436030295

1988
Mallinckrodt Fund, Inc., The
675 McDonnell Blvd.
P.O. Box 5840
St. Louis 63134

Incorporated in 1968 in Missouri.
Donor(s): Mallinckrodt, Inc.
Financial data: (yr. ended 12/31/83): Assets, $1,017 (M); gifts received, $450,850; expenditures, $452,502, including $452,501 for 143 grants (high: $112,000; low: $25).
Purpose and activities: Grants for community funds, higher education, hospitals, youth agencies, and cultural programs.
Application information:
Deadline(s): None
Officers: Donald G. Sillies,* Chairman and President; C. Ray Holman,* Vice-President; Patricia F. Hicks, Secretary; Bruce A. Beeler, Treasurer.
Directors:* Raymond F. Bentele, Grace J. Fishel, Walter W. Thulin, John L. Ufheil.
Employer Identification Number: 430909558

1989
Mathews Foundation, The ⊭
c/o Centerre Trust Co., 510 Locust St.
P.O. Box 14737
St. Louis 63178

Trust established in 1959 in Illinois.
Donor(s): Harry B. Mathews, Jr. Trust.
Financial data: (yr. ended 11/30/83): Assets, $1,294,287 (M); expenditures, $143,724, including $132,050 for grants.
Purpose and activities: Broad purposes; giving largely in Missouri and Arizona, primarily for Protestant church support including church-related higher and secondary education; support also for cultural programs including historic preservation, hospitals, the handicapped and social agencies.
Limitations: Giving primarily in MO and AZ.
Trustees: Margaret B. Jenks, John P. MacCarthy, Harry B. Mathews III.
Employer Identification Number: 376040862

1990
May (The Morton J.) Foundation ⊭
c/o Famous Barr Company
Sixth and Olive Sts., Suite 2062
St. Louis 63101

Trust established in 1959 in Missouri.
Donor(s): Morton J. May.†
Financial data: (yr. ended 3/31/83): Assets, $5,960,535 (M); expenditures, $495,652, including $453,386 for 46 grants (high: $145,000; low: $50).

Purpose and activities: Broad purposes; primarily local giving, with emphasis on Jewish welfare funds, music and art, higher education, a community fund, hospitals, and social agencies.
Limitations: Giving primarily in St. Louis, MO.
Application information:
Write: Frank J. Reilly, Trustee
Trustees: Betty McNichols, Frank J. Reilly, Sarah Jane May Waldheim.
Employer Identification Number: 436027519

1991
May Stores Foundation, Inc., The ▼ ⊭
Sixth and Olive Sts.
St. Louis 63101   (314) 247-0300

Incorporated in 1945 in New York.
Donor(s): May Department Stores Company.
Financial data: (yr. ended 12/31/83): Assets, $26,733,786 (M); gifts received, $15,600,000; expenditures, $1,979,061, including $1,932,263 for 96 grants (high: $309,925; low: $500; average: $1,000-$50,000).
Purpose and activities: Grants to charitable and educational institutions throughout the country, with emphasis on community funds in areas of company operations; support also for cultural programs and hospitals.
Limitations: Giving primarily in areas of company operations.
Application information:
Initial approach: Letter
Deadline(s): None
Write: Richard A. Smith, Vice-President
Officers: Jerome T. Loeb,* President; William R.H. Martin,* Vice-President and Secretary; Richard A. Smith,* Vice-President and Treasurer; Alfred F. Dougherty, Jr.,* David C. Farrell,* Henry A. Lay, Vice-Presidents.
Director:* Robert F. Cerulli.
Number of staff: None.
Employer Identification Number: 436028949

1992
McDavid (G. N. and Edna) Dental Education Trust ⊭
c/o Mercantile Trust Company
P.O. Box 387, Main Post Office
St. Louis 63166   (314) 425-2672

Established in 1975.
Financial data: (yr. ended 12/31/83): Assets, $1,113,348 (M); expenditures, $67,604, including $53,470 for 26 loans.
Purpose and activities: Loans to students in an accredited dental school in Missouri, with preference given to residents of Madison County, Missouri.
Types of support awarded: Student aid.
Limitations: Giving limited to MO, with preference to residents of Madison County.
Application information:
Write: Ms. Jill Fivecoat
Trustee: Mercantile Trust Company.
Employer Identification Number: 436192984

1993
McDonnell Douglas Foundation ▼ ☐

P.O. Box 516
St. Louis 63166　　　　　　　(314) 232-5595

Incorporated in 1977 as successor to McDonnell Aerospace Foundation, a trust established in 1963 in Missouri.

Donor(s): McDonnell Douglas Corporation.
Financial data: (yr. ended 6/30/83): Assets, $42,084,205 (M); expenditures, $4,116,420, including $3,786,896 for 177 grants (high: $530,000; low: $90; average: $100-$50,000) and $218,052 for employee matching gifts.
Purpose and activities: General giving, with emphasis on higher education and community funds; support also for hospitals, aerospace and aviation organizations, and civic and cultural affairs.
Types of support awarded: General purposes, scholarship funds, special projects, employee matching gifts.
Application information:
　Deadline(s): None
　Write: Michael Witunski, Secretary
Officers: James S. McDonnell III,* Vice-President; Michael Witunski, Secretary; Stanley J. Sheinbein, Treasurer.
Directors:* Sanford N. McDonnell, Chairman; John F. McDonnell, R.L. Harmon.
Employer Identification Number: 431128093

1994
McDonnell (James S.) Foundation ▼ ☐
(formerly McDonnell Foundation, Inc.)
P.O. Box 516
St. Louis 63166　　　　　　　(314) 232-0232

Incorporated in 1950 in Missouri.
Donor(s): James S. McDonnell, James S. McDonnell III, John F. McDonnell.
Financial data: (yr. ended 12/31/82): Assets, $76,585,895 (M); gifts received, $5,688,036; expenditures, $8,732,353, including $8,443,972 for 21 grants (high: $5,790,000; low: $500).
Purpose and activities: Broad purposes; giving for education, primarily higher education, and research in parapsychology.
Application information:
　Write: Michael Witunski, President
Officers: Michael Witunski, President; James S. McDonnell III,* Vice-President; Stanley J. Sheinbein,* Secretary-Treasurer.
Directors:* John F. McDonnell.
Employer Identification Number: 436030988

1995
McGee Foundation, The
4900 Oak St.
Kansas City 64112　　　　　　　(816) 753-4900

Incorporated in 1951 in Missouri.
Donor(s): Joseph J. McGee,† Mrs. Joseph J. McGee,† Frank McGee,† Mrs. Frank McGee, Louis B. McGee,† Old American Insurance Co., Thomas McGee and Sons.
Financial data: (yr. ended 12/31/83): Assets, $3,032,223 (M); gifts received, $237,627; expenditures, $154,488, including $148,600 for 30 grants (high: $35,000; low: $200).

Purpose and activities: Broad purposes; local giving only, with emphasis on health care, education, and Roman Catholic church support.
Types of support awarded: General purposes, operating budgets, continuing support, annual campaigns, seed money, emergency funds, deficit financing, building funds, equipment, land acquisition.
Limitations: Giving limited to the greater Kansas City, MO, area. No support for the visual or performing arts; historic preservation; community development or rehabilitation; public information programs; united appeals; or telethons or national organizations with wide support. No grants to individuals, or for scholarships, fellowships, endowment funds, matching gifts, special projects, research, publications or conferences; no loans.
Publications: Program policy statement, application guidelines, annual report.
Application information:
　Initial approach: Letter
　Copies of proposal: 1
　Deadline(s): None
　Board meeting date(s): February, May, August, and November
　Final notification: 1 1/2 months
　Write: Joseph J. McGee, Jr., Chairman
Officers and Directors: Joseph J. McGee, Jr., Chairman; Thomas F. McGee, Jr., Vice-Chairman; Edward J. Reardon, Secretary; Thomas R. McGee, Treasurer.
Members: T. Eugene Crawford, Mrs. Bernard J. Duffy, Jr., Henry J. Massman, III.
Number of staff: None.
Employer Identification Number: 446006285

1996
Mercantile Trust Company Charitable Trust ☐
c/o Mercantile Trust Company
P.O. Box 387
St. Louis 63166

Trust established in 1952 in Missouri.
Donor(s): Mercantile Trust Company.
Financial data: (yr. ended 2/29/84): Assets, $2,949,736 (M); expenditures, $423,692, including $398,200 for 31 grants (high: $48,950; low: $2,000).
Purpose and activities: Primarily local giving, with emphasis on higher education, hospitals, and cultural programs; support also for youth agencies, and community development.
Limitations: Giving primarily in MO.
Trustee: Neal J. Farrell, Donald E. Lasater, Mercantile Trust Company.
Employer Identification Number: 436020630

1997
MFA Foundation ☐
201 S. Seventh St.
Columbia 65201　　　　　　　(314) 876-5395

Established in 1958.
Donor(s): Shelter Insurance Companies, MFA Incorporated, MFA Oil Company.
Financial data: (yr. ended 6/30/83): Assets, $2,631,032 (M); gifts received, $101,863; expenditures, $236,738, including $224,859 for 213 grants to individuals.

Purpose and activities: Primarily local giving in areas of company operations for scholarships; some support also for higher education and youth organizations.
Types of support awarded: Student aid.
Limitations: Giving primarily in MO, and in areas of company operations.
Publications: Application guidelines.
Application information: Application form required.
　Deadline(s): April 15
　Write: Ormal C. Creach, President
Officers: Ormal C. Creach,* President; Eric G. Thompson,* Vice-President; Mary F. Gonnerman, Secretary-Treasurer.
Directors:* Hilton Bracey, Dale Creach, James Cunningham, B.L. Frew, James L. Halsey, Alfred Hoffman, David Jobe, Fred Koenig, Loren Morey, R.A. Young.
Employer Identification Number: 436026877

1998
Millstone Foundation
8510 Eager Rd.
St. Louis 63144　　　　　　　(314) 961-8500

Incorporated in 1955 in Missouri.
Donor(s): I.E. Millstone, Mrs. Goldie G. Millstone.
Financial data: (yr. ended 5/31/83): Assets, $1,695,024 (M); gifts received, $95,000; expenditures, $172,552, including $154,019 for 69 grants (high: $95,000; low: $50).
Purpose and activities: General purposes; local giving, with emphasis on higher education.
Types of support awarded: General purposes, operating budgets, continuing support, annual campaigns, emergency funds, deficit financing, research, special projects.
Limitations: Giving primarily in St. Louis, MO. No grants to individuals, or for scholarships and fellowships, demonstration projects, publications, conferences, or matching gifts; no loans.
Application information:
　Initial approach: Letter
　Copies of proposal: 1
　Deadline(s): None
　Board meeting date(s): Monthly
　Final notification: 1 month
　Write: I.E. Millstone, President
Officers and Directors: I.E. Millstone, Chairman and President; David S. Millstone, Vice-President; Goldie G. Millstone, Secretary; Harry Hammerman, Treasurer.
Number of staff: None.
Employer Identification Number: 436027373

1999
Monsanto Fund ▼
800 North Lindbergh Blvd.
St. Louis 63167　　　　　　　(314) 694-2742

Incorporated in 1964 in Missouri as successor to Monsanto Charitable Trust.
Donor(s): Monsanto Company.
Financial data: (yr. ended 12/31/83): Assets, $1,002,397 (M); gifts received, $6,948,851; expenditures, $7,075,190, including $6,761,251 for 2,114 grants (high: $640,640; low: $25; average: $100-$20,000).

Purpose and activities: General giving,
principally for higher education, community
funds, hospitals, cultural programs, social
services, and youth agencies, chiefly in cities in
which the company operates.
Types of support awarded: General purposes,
building funds, equipment, operating budgets,
annual campaigns, seed money, fellowships,
special projects, employee matching gifts,
continuing support.
Limitations: Giving primarily in areas of
company operations, with emphasis on St.
Louis, MO. No grants to individuals or for
endowment funds.
Publications: Application guidelines.
Application information:
  Initial approach: Proposal
  Copies of proposal: 1
  Deadline(s): None
  Board meeting date(s): 4 to 6 times a year
  Final notification: 2 to 4 months
  Write: Sharen R. Bull, Secretary
Officers: William F. Symes, President; Richard
W. Duesenberg,* Vice-President; Sharen R.
Bull, Secretary; L.B. Skatoff, Treasurer.
Directors:* Joseph T. Nolan, Chairman; Robert
E. Berra, Japnell D. Braun, Louis Fernandez, E.J.
Hawk, L.W. McKenna, R.G. Potter, Francis A.
Si, M.P. Wilkins.
Number of staff: 4 full-time professional; 2 full-
time support.
Employer Identification Number: 436044736

2000
Nichols (Miller) Foundation ⌿
310 Ward Pkwy.
Kansas City 64112

Established in 1960.
Donor(s): Miller Nichols.
Financial data: (yr. ended 12/31/83): Assets,
$1,901,154 (M); gifts received, $34,653;
expenditures, $36,250, including $34,822 for
48 grants (high: $10,000; low: $10).
Purpose and activities: Primarily local giving
for charitable purposes, with emphasis on civic
and cultural organizations.
Limitations: Giving primarily in Kansas City,
MO.
Trustees: Kay Nichols Callison, Walter C.
Janes, Jeannette Nichols, Miller Nichols.
Employer Identification Number: 446015540

2001
Olin (John M.) Charitable Trust
7701 Forsyth Blvd.
Clayton 63105   (314) 863-2266

Trust established in 1945 in Missouri.
Donor(s): John M. Olin.†
Financial data: (yr. ended 12/31/83): Assets,
$1,252,445 (M); expenditures, $125,335,
including $119,000 for 8 grants (high: $30,000;
low: $1,000).
Purpose and activities: Broad purposes; grants
primarily for medical research, hospitals,
museums, cultural programs, and youth
agencies.
Limitations: No grants to individuals, or for
building funds, endowment funds or special
projects.

Application information:
  Write: Mrs. Constance B. Josse, Trustee
Trustees: Constance B. Josse, St. Louis Union
Trust Company.
Employer Identification Number: 436022769

2002
Olin (Spencer T. and Ann W.) Foundation ▼
1239 Pierre Laclede Bldg.
7701 Forsyth Blvd.
St. Louis 63105   (314) 727-6202

Incorporated in 1957 in Delaware.
Donor(s): Spencer T. Olin, Ann W. Olin.†
Financial data: (yr. ended 12/31/84): Assets,
$29,925,418 (M); gifts received, $304,491;
expenditures, $1,637,170, including
$1,452,675 for 31 grants (high: $600,000; low:
$750; average: $1,000-$50,000).
Purpose and activities: Giving primarily
locally for higher education, medical education
and research, health services, and community,
cultural, and social service agencies.
Types of support awarded: Annual
campaigns, research, general purposes.
Limitations: Giving primarily in the
metropolitan St. Louis, MO area. No support
for national health or welfare organizations,
religious groups, or generally for secondary
education, or projects which are substantially
financed by public tax funds. No grants to
individuals, or for building or endowment
funds, deficit financing, operating budgets,
conferences, travel, exhibits, scholarships and
fellowships, or matching gifts; no loans.
Publications: Annual report.
Application information:
  Initial approach: Letter
  Copies of proposal: 1
  Deadline(s): None
  Board meeting date(s): Usually in April
  Final notification: 2 weeks
  Write: Rolla J. Mottaz, President
Officers and Trustees: Rolla J. Mottaz,
President; J. Lester Willemetz, Treasurer; Eunice
Olin Higgins, Mary Olin Pritzlaff, Barbara Olin
Taylor.
Number of staff: 2 part-time professional; 1
part-time support.
Employer Identification Number: 376044148

2003
Oppenstein Brothers Foundation
Commerce Bank Bldg., Rm. 617
922 Walnut St.
Kansas City 64106   (816) 421-2647

Trust established in 1975 in Missouri.
Donor(s): Michael Oppenstein.†
Financial data: (yr. ended 3/31/84): Assets,
$10,736,884 (M); expenditures, $676,948,
including $573,440 for 54 grants (high:
$75,000; low: $1,000; average: $4,000-
$10,000).

Purpose and activities: Broad purposes;
primarily local giving, with emphasis on
welfare, education and health care programs,
emphasizing the prevention of illness and
abuse, and programs which enhance the ability
of individuals to remain or become self-
sufficient.
Types of support awarded: Operating
budgets, general purposes, seed money,
emergency funds, equipment, special projects,
matching funds.
Limitations: Giving primarily in the
Kansas City, MO metropolitan area. No
support for medical research. No grants to
individuals, or for endowment funds,
scholarships, or fellowships; no loans.
Publications: Multi-year report, application
guidelines, program policy statement.
Application information:
  Initial approach: Telephone or letter
  Copies of proposal: 2
  Deadline(s): Submit proposal 2 weeks
    preceding board meetings; no set deadline
  Board meeting date(s): Usually in February,
    April, June, August, October and December
  Final notification: 2 to 4 months
  Write: Karen M. Herman, Program Officer
Officer: Karen M. Herman, Program Officer.
Disbursement Committee: John Morgan,
Chairman; Roger Hurwitz, Mildred Kemper,
Estelle Sosland, Suzanne Statland.
Trustee: Commerce Bank of Kansas City.
Number of staff: 1 part-time professional; 1
part-time support.
Employer Identification Number: 436203035

2004
Orscheln Industries Foundation, Inc. ⌿
339 North Williams
Moberly 65270
Scholarship application address: William E.
Clark, Orscheln Industries Foundation
Scholarship Committee, P.O. Box 266,
Moberly, MO 65270; Tel.: (816) 263-6693

Established in 1971.
Donor(s): Orscheln Industries, and its
subsidiaries.
Financial data: (yr. ended 9/30/83): Assets,
$1,783,723 (M); gifts received, $391,853;
expenditures, $214,882, including $203,374
for 147 grants (high: $121,633; low: $15) and
$8,716 for 18 grants to individuals.
Purpose and activities: Primarily local giving,
with emphasis on Roman Catholic church
support and religious organizations, community
funds, and higher education, including
scholarships.
Types of support awarded: Student aid.
Limitations: Giving primarily in MO;
scholarships restricted to graduates of Cairo,
Higbee, Moberly, and Westran high schools, in
Randolph County.
Publications: Informational brochure,
application guidelines, program policy
statement.
Application information: Application form
and informational brochure available for
scholarship applicants. Application form
required.
  Deadline(s): April 1 for scholarships

Officers: G.A. Orscheln, President; Phillip A. Orscheln, W.L. Orscheln, Vice-President; D.W. Orscheln, Secretary.
Employer Identification Number: 237115623

2005
Parrott (William G.) Foundation ⊠
515 Commerce Bldg.
Kansas City 64106

Incorporated in 1962 in Missouri.
Donor(s): William G. Parrott.†
Financial data: (yr. ended 7/31/83): Assets, $208,598 (M); gifts received, $173,244; expenditures, $249,284, including $248,100 for 28 grants (high: $35,000; low: $100).
Purpose and activities: Broad purposes; grants largely for higher secondary education, performing arts programs, religious organizations, and youth agencies.
Limitations: Giving primarily in MO.
Officers and Directors: Patricia P. Willits, President; William G. Parrott, Jr., Vice-President; Guy A. Magruder, Secretary; Robert W. Willits, Treasurer.
Employer Identification Number: 435048680

2006
Pendergast-Weyer Foundation, The
P.O. Box 23245
Kansas City 64141

Established about 1976 in Missouri.
Donor(s): Mary Louise Weyer Pendergast,† Thomas J. Pendergast, Jr.
Financial data: (yr. ended 6/30/84): Assets, $3,007,737 (M); expenditures, $162,226, including $120,496 for 26 grants (high: $22,299; low: $200).
Purpose and activities: Support primarily for local Roman Catholic church-related day care centers, pre-schools, elementary schools, high schools, and religious organizations. A minimum of 80 percent of all grants must go to Catholic institutions with a maximum of 20 percent available for institutions of other religious denominations.
Types of support awarded: Operating budgets, continuing support, emergency funds, equipment.
Limitations: Giving limited to towns or cities in MO with populations under 100,000. No support for clergymen, chanceries, or church foundations. No grants to individuals, or for annual campaigns, seed money, building funds, land acquisition, renovation projects, endowment funds, matching gifts, scholarships, fellowships, research, special projects, publications, conferences, or salaries; no loans.
Application information: Application form required.
Initial approach: Letter
Copies of proposal: 1
Deadline(s): Submit proposal in March or September; deadline, March 31 and September 30
Board meeting date(s): June
Write: Grant Selection Committee

Officers and Directors: Taylor L. Bowen, Chairman; Thomas J. Pendergast, Jr., President and Treasurer; Deborah Rouchka, Secretary; Sister Miriam Victor Jansen, Charles A. Pfeiffer, Stephen Rouchka, Monsignor Emmet R. Summers, Jeanne Verssue.
Number of staff: None.
Employer Identification Number: 431070676

2007
Pillsbury Foundation, The ▼ ⊠
Six Oakleigh Ln.
St. Louis 63124

Incorporated in 1944 in Missouri.
Donor(s): Edwin S. Pillsbury,† Harriette Brown Pillsbury.†
Financial data: (yr. ended 12/31/83): Assets, $11,257,749 (M); expenditures, $551,625, including $487,744 for 73 grants (high: $160,046; low: $50; average: $100-$10,000).
Purpose and activities: Broad purposes; primarily local giving, with emphasis on higher education, Baptist church support and religious associations, and social services.
Limitations: Giving primarily in the St. Louis, MO, area.
Officers: Joyce S. Pillsbury, President; Fred H. Pillsbury, Vice-President; William E. Pillsbury, Secretary-Treasurer.
Number of staff: None.
Employer Identification Number: 436030335

2008
Pitzman Fund ⊠
P.O. Box 1369
St. Louis 63101

Established in 1944.
Financial data: (yr. ended 9/30/83): Assets, $1,212,532 (M); gifts received, $9,814; expenditures, $81,363, including $76,000 for 56 grants (high: $7,000; low: $500).
Purpose and activities: Broad purposes; primarily local giving for education, cultural programs, Protestant church support, social services, and youth agencies.
Limitations: Giving primarily in St. Louis, MO.
Trustees: Pauline Fads, Robert H. McRoberts, Centerre Trust Company.
Employer Identification Number: 436023901

2009
Pott (Phenie R. & Herman T.) Foundation
c/o Mercantile Trust Company
P.O. Box 387
St. Louis 63166   (314) 231-5525

Trust established in 1963 in Missouri.
Financial data: (yr. ended 12/31/84): Assets, $5,134,000 (M); expenditures, $356,000, including $311,000 for 44 grants (high: $50,000; low: $500; average: $1,000-$5,000).
Purpose and activities: Primarily local giving, with emphasis on a community fund, youth agencies, health agencies, hospitals, and social agencies.

Limitations: Giving primarily in MO, particularly the St. Louis area. No grants to individuals.
Application information:
Initial approach: Letter
Copies of proposal: 1
Deadline(s): None
Board meeting date(s): Quarterly
Write: John P. Fechter, Executive Director
Trustee: Mercantile Trust Company.
Advisory committee: James Collins, Roy Collins, Richard Conerly, John Fechter, Mary Greco, William Guerri, Jane Murphy, Phenie Pott.
Number of staff: 1 part-time professional.
Employer Identification Number: 436041541

2010
Ralston Purina Trust Fund ▼
Checkerboard Square
St. Louis 63164   (314) 982-3219

Trust established in 1951 in Missouri.
Donor(s): Ralston Purina Company.
Financial data: (yr. ended 8/31/83): Assets, $1,529,662 (M); gifts received, $1,000,000; expenditures, $1,634,291, including $1,614,342 for grants.
Purpose and activities: Broad purposes; grants principally to community funds in areas in which the company has offices; support also for education, hospitals, cultural programs, and youth agencies. Foundation support represents about one half of the company's charitable giving which includes funds for an employee matching gift program and company-employee scholarships.
Types of support awarded: General purposes, employee matching gifts, employee related scholarships.
Limitations: Giving primarily in areas of company facilities, especially St. Louis, MO. No grants to individuals.
Application information:
Initial approach: Proposal
Copies of proposal: 1
Deadline(s): None
Board meeting date(s): Monthly
Final notification: 30 days
Write: George H. Kyd, Member, Board of Control
Board of Control: M.C. Bahle, J.P. Baird, George H. Kyd, A.J. Reimers.
Trustee: Centerre Trust Company of St. Louis.
Number of staff: 1 part-time professional; 1 full-time support.
Employer Identification Number: 436023455

2011
Reynolds (The J. B.) Foundation ▼ ⊠
3520 Broadway
P.O. Box 139
Kansas City 64111   (816) 753-7000

Incorporated in 1961 in Missouri.
Donor(s): Walter Edwin Bixby, Sr., Pearl G. Reynolds.†
Financial data: (yr. ended 12/31/82): Assets, $5,821,734 (M); expenditures, $478,998, including $467,250 for 73 grants (high: $35,000; low: $248).

Purpose and activities: Broad purposes; grants largely for local higher education, medical research, social service and youth agencies, and community projects; support also for cultural programs.
Types of support awarded: Annual campaigns, seed money, emergency funds, building funds, equipment, land acquisition, research, publications, conferences and seminars, continuing support.
Limitations: Giving primarily in a 150-mile radius of Kansas City, MO. No grants to individuals.
Application information:
  Initial approach: Telephone
  Copies of proposal: 1
  Board meeting date(s): May and December
  Write: Walter E. Bixby, Vice-President
Officers: Joseph Reynolds Bixby,* President; Walter E. Bixby,* Vice-President and Treasurer; Richard L. Finn, Secretary.
Trustees:* Kathryn Bixby, Ann Bixby Oxler.
Employer Identification Number: 446014359

2012
Roblee (Joseph H. and Florence A.) Foundation
c/o Centerre Trust Company
510 Locust St.
St. Louis 63101

Trust established in 1970 in Missouri.
Donor(s): Louise Roblee McCarthy,† Florence Roblee Trust.
Financial data: (yr. ended 12/31/82): Assets, $6,023,288 (M); expenditures, $394,947, including $348,257 for 103 grants (high: $34,000; low: $500; average: $1,000-$15,000).
Purpose and activities: Primarily local giving, with emphasis on ecumenical projects, educational projects generally outside the academic area (such as intercultural global understanding, citizen education, and leadership development), health (primarily mental health), and pressing social problems.
Types of support awarded: Seed money, building funds, equipment, endowment funds, scholarship funds, exchange programs.
Limitations: Giving primarily in MO. No grants to individuals, or for research programs, or matching gifts; no loans.
Application information:
  Initial approach: Full proposal
  Copies of proposal: 2
  Deadline(s): Submit proposal preferably in April or August; deadlines May 1 and September 1
  Board meeting date(s): June and October
  Write: Marjorie M. Robins, Trustee, or Roy Blair, Trust Officer
Trustees: Carol M. Duhme, Marjorie M. Robins, Centerre Trust Company (Roy Blair, Trust Officer).
Number of staff: None.
Employer Identification Number: 436109579

2013
Sachs Fund ⌺
16300 Justus Post Rd.
Chesterfield 63017

Trust established in 1957 in Missouri.
Donor(s): Samuel C. Sachs, Sachs Electric Corporation, and others.
Financial data: (yr. ended 4/30/83): Assets, $2,283,802 (M); gifts received, $50,000; expenditures, $195,590, including $189,090 for 55 grants (high: $65,000; low: $25).
Purpose and activities: Broad purposes; primarily local giving, with emphasis on Jewish welfare funds, community funds, higher education, cultural programs, and hospitals.
Limitations: Giving primarily in MO.
Trustees: Louis S. Sachs, Lewis H. Sachs, Jerome W. Sandweiss.
Employer Identification Number: 436032385

2014
Shoenberg Foundation, Inc.
500 North Broadway
St. Louis 63102   (314) 421-2247

Incorporated in 1955 in Missouri.
Donor(s): Sydney M. Shoenberg.†
Financial data: (yr. ended 12/31/83): Assets, $4,457,338 (M); expenditures, $481,966, including $470,550 for 32 grants (high: $120,000; low: $100).
Purpose and activities: Broad purposes; primarily local giving, with emphasis on hospitals, community funds, Jewish welfare funds, and art.
Limitations: Giving primarily in MO. No grants to individuals.
Application information:
  Initial approach: Letter
  Write: William W. Ross, Secretary
Officers and Directors: Sydney M. Shoenberg, Jr., Chairman; Robert H. Shoenberg, President; E. L. Langenberg, Vice-President; William W. Ross, Secretary and Treasurer.
Employer Identification Number: 436028764

2015
Smith (Ralph L.) Foundation
c/o The First National Bank of Kansas City
14 West Tenth St.
Kansas City 64105   (816) 221-2800
Mailing address: P.O. Box 38, Kansas City, MO 64183

Trust established in 1952 in Missouri.
Donor(s): Harriet T. Smith,† Ralph L. Smith.†
Financial data: (yr. ended 12/31/84): Assets, $3,610,066 (M); expenditures, $298,905, including $276,500 for 57 grants (high: $20,000; low: $500).
Purpose and activities: Broad purposes; grants largely for education, hospitals and medical research, youth agencies, and conservation.
Limitations: No grants to individuals.
Application information: Applications for grants will not be acknowledged.
  Initial approach: Telephone
  Copies of proposal: 1
  Board meeting date(s): Quarterly
  Write: David P. Ross, Senior Vice-President

Managers: Margaret S. Denison, Anne S. Douthat, Ralph L. Smith, Jr.
Trustee: The First National Bank of Kansas City (David P. Ross, Senior Vice-President).
Employer Identification Number: 446008508

2016
Souers (Sidney W. and Sylvia N.) Charitable Trust ⌺
c/o Centerre Trust Company of St. Louis
510 Locust St., P.O. Box 14737
St. Louis 63178

Trust established in 1955 in Missouri.
Donor(s): Sylvia N. Souers.
Financial data: (yr. ended 12/31/83): Assets, $6,978,922 (M); expenditures, $367,668, including $340,000 for 23 grants (high: $10,000; low: $1,000).
Purpose and activities: Broad purposes; giving primarily in Missouri and Washington, D.C., with emphasis on higher education and hospitals.
Limitations: Giving primarily in MO and Washington, DC.
Grantor: Sylvia N. Souers.
Trustee: Centerre Trust Co. of St. Louis.
Employer Identification Number: 436079817

2017
Speas (John W. and Effie E.) Memorial ⌺
c/o First National Bank of Kansas City
14 W. 10th St.
Kansas City 64141
Application address: David P. Ross, First National Bank of Kansas City, P.O. Box 38, Kansas City, MO 64183; Tel.: (816) 221-2800

Trust established in 1947 in Missouri.
Donor(s): Effie E. Speas,† Victor E. Speas,† Speas and Company.
Financial data: (yr. ended 12/31/83): Assets, $14,638,436 (M); expenditures, $1,229,065, including $1,119,609 for 24 grants (high: $200,000; low: $800).
Purpose and activities: Primarily local giving for hospitals and health services, higher education in the health professions, and medical research.
Types of support awarded: Building funds, special projects, equipment, research, conferences and seminars, general purposes, operating budgets, scholarship funds.
Limitations: Giving primarily in the Kansas City, MO, metropolitan area.
Application information:
  Deadline(s): None
  Final notification: 2 months
Trustee: First National Bank of Kansas City.
Employer Identification Number: 446008249

2018
Speas (Victor E.) Foundation ▼
c/o The First National Bank of Kansas City
14 West Tenth St.
Kansas City 64183   (816) 221-2800

Trust established in 1947 in Missouri.

Donor(s): Effie E. Speas,† Victor E. Speas,† Speas Company.
Financial data: (yr. ended 12/31/84): Assets, $14,875,233 (M); expenditures, $1,198,800, including $1,087,216 for 31 grants (high: $200,000; low: $1,000; average: $5,000-$50,000).
Purpose and activities: Broad purposes; primarily local giving largely for hospitals, rehabilitation, medically related higher education, preventive health care, and medical research; grants also for agencies serving the elderly and handicapped, and the family church.
Types of support awarded: Operating budgets, seed money, emergency funds, building funds, equipment, land acquisition, research, continuing support, student aid, special projects.
Limitations: Giving limited to Jackson, Clay, Platt, and Cass counties in MO. No grants for endowment funds; no loans or scholarships except to medical students at the University of Missouri at Kansas City.
Publications: 990-PF, program policy statement, application guidelines.
Application information:
  Initial approach: Telephone
  Copies of proposal: 1
  Deadline(s): None
  Board meeting date(s): Weekly
  Final notification: 2 months
  Write: David P. Ross, Senior Vice-President
Trustee: The First National Bank of Kansas City (David P. Ross, Senior Vice-President).
Number of staff: 1 full-time professional.
Employer Identification Number: 446008340

2019
Springmeier Foundation
1116 Cass Ave.
St. Louis 63106   (314) 241-0860

Incorporated in 1967 in Missouri.
Donor(s): Clara G. Springmeier.†
Financial data: (yr. ended 12/31/82): Assets, $636,746 (M); expenditures, $173,842, including $160,795 for 51 grants (high: $25,000; low: $100).
Purpose and activities: Primarily local giving, with emphasis on child welfare, youth agencies, hospitals and health services, education, and religious organizations.
Limitations: Giving primarily in MO. No grants to individuals.
Application information:
  Write: William B. Trost, President
Officers: William B. Trost, President; R.F. Kroeger, Vice-President; Virginia M. Andrews, Secretary and Treasurer.
Employer Identification Number: 436073755

2020
St. Louis Community Foundation
818 Olive St.
St. Louis 63101   (314) 241-2703

Community foundation established in 1915 in Missouri.

Financial data: (yr. ended 12/31/84): Assets, $3,713,595 (M); gifts received, $281,423; expenditures, $399,097, including $327,189 for 77 grants (high: $27,500; low: $415).
Purpose and activities: Purposes include, but are not limited to, the promotion of education, social and scientific research, the care of the sick, aged, infirm and handicapped, the care of children, the improvement of living, working, recreation and environmental conditions or facilities, cultural programs, and such other charitable, educational, and social purposes that will assist the betterment of the mental, moral, and social and physical conditions of the inhabitants of the St. Louis metropolitan area.
Types of support awarded: Research, seed money, scholarship funds, operating budgets, emergency funds.
Limitations: Giving primarily in the St. Louis, MO, metropolitan area. No support for sectarian religious programs. No grants to individuals, or for deficit financing, or endowment funds; grants for operating expenses only during an organization's start-up.
Publications: Annual report, program policy statement, application guidelines.
Application information:
  Initial approach: Proposal
  Copies of proposal: 1
  Deadline(s): January 15, April 15, July 15, and October 15
  Board meeting date(s): Quarterly
  Final notification: Usually within 1 week of board meetings
  Write: Ms. Mary Brucker, Executive Director
Officers: Edwin S. Jones,* Treasurer; Mary Brucker, Executive Director.
Board of Directors:* George S. Rosborough, Jr., Chairman; Josephine Throdahl, Vice-Chairman; Laurance L. Browning, Jr., Thomas N. DePew, Walter F. Gray, Henry O. Johnston, John F. Lashly, Hubert C. Moog, Ben H. Wells.
Trustees: Boatmen's National Bank of St. Louis, Boatmen's Trust Company, Centerre Trust Company of St. Louis, Commerce Bank of St. Louis County, Commerce Bank of Tower Grove, First Missouri Bank and Trust Company of Creve Coeur, Guaranty Trust Company of Missouri, Mercantile Trust Company.
Number of staff: 2 full-time professional.
Employer Identification Number: 436023126

2021
St. Louis Post - Dispatch Foundation ⌑
900 North Tucker Blvd.
St. Louis 63101   (314) 622-7337

Incorporated in 1963 in Missouri.
Donor(s): The Pulitzer Publishing Company.
Financial data: (yr. ended 12/31/83): Assets, $323,874 (M); gifts received, $383,110; expenditures, $403,109, including $402,120 for 37 grants (high: $100,000).
Purpose and activities: Broad purposes; primarily local giving, with emphasis on music, cultural programs, a community fund, and higher education, including a scholarship fund for black students attending the University of Missouri Journalism School.
Limitations: Giving primarily in MO.

Application information: Application form required.
  Deadline(s): March 1
  Write: Jim Millstone
Officers and Directors: Joseph Pulitzer, Jr., Chairman; Michael E. Pulitzer, President; Glenn A. Christopher, Vice-President; Ronald H. Ridgway, Secretary-Treasurer; David Lipman.
Employer Identification Number: 436052854

2022
Steadley (Kent D. & Mary L.) Memorial Trust ⌑
c/o CharterBank of Carthage
231 S. Main
Carthage 64836   (417) 358-9011

Established in 1970.
Financial data: (yr. ended 12/31/83): Assets, $2,501,285 (M); gifts received, $141,300; expenditures, $338,796, including $333,000 for 1 grant.
Purpose and activities: Local giving for community development.
Limitations: Giving limited to Carthage, MO.
Application information:
  Deadline(s): None
  Final notification: Usually within 2 months
  Write: Linda M. Hodge
Trustee: CharterBank of Carthage.
Employer Identification Number: 436120866

2023
Stupp Bros. Bridge & Iron Co. Foundation ⌑
P.O. Box 6600
St. Louis 63125

Trust established about 1952 in Missouri.
Donor(s): Stupp Bros. Bridge & Iron Co.
Financial data: (yr. ended 10/31/83): Assets, $4,324,920 (M); expenditures, $255,886, including $252,005 for 168 grants (high: $30,000; low: $50).
Purpose and activities: Primarily local giving to hospitals, community funds, higher education and educational associations; with support for cultural, health and welfare programs.
Limitations: Giving primarily in MO.
Trustees: Erwin P. Stupp, Jr., John P. Stupp, Robert P. Stupp.
Employer Identification Number: 237412437

2024
Stupp (Norman J.) Foundation ⌑
c/o Commerce Bank of Tower Grove
3134 S. Grand
St. Louis 63118

Established about 1952 in Missouri.
Donor(s): Norman J. Stupp.
Financial data: (yr. ended 6/30/84): Assets, $782,626 (M); expenditures, $145,319, including $119,500 for 27 grants (high: $50,000; low: $500).
Purpose and activities: Primarily local giving to hospitals, youth agencies, and social services.
Limitations: Giving primarily in MO.
Trustee: Commerce Bank of Tower Grove.
Employer Identification Number: 436027433

2025
Sunderland (Lester T.) Foundation
9225 Ward Pkwy., Suite 106
Kansas City 64114   (913) 381-8900

Incorporated in 1945 in Missouri.
Donor(s): Lester T. Sunderland.†
Financial data: (yr. ended 12/31/84): Assets, $8,533,004 (L); gifts received, $850,200; expenditures, $362,689, including $337,925 for 100 grants (high: $30,000; low: $25).
Purpose and activities: Broad purposes; giving primarily in Missouri, Nebraska, and Kansas, with emphasis on building funds for higher education; support also for youth agencies, hospitals, and community funds.
Types of support awarded: Operating budgets, continuing support, annual campaigns, seed money, emergency funds, deficit financing, building funds, equipment, land acquisition, endowment funds.
Limitations: Giving primarily in MO, KS, and NE. No grants to individuals; no loans.
Application information:
 Initial approach: Letter
 Copies of proposal: 1
 Board meeting date(s): As required
 Write: James P. Sunderland, Vice-President
Officers and Trustees: Paul Sunderland, President; James P. Sunderland, Vice-President and Secretary; Robert Sunderland, Vice-President and Treasurer; Charles Sunderland, Whitney P. Sunderland.
Number of staff: None.
Employer Identification Number: 446011082

2026
Sunmark Foundation ☐
10795 Watson Rd.
St. Louis 63127

Established in 1964.
Donor(s): Sunmark, Inc.
Financial data: (yr. ended 1/31/84): Assets, $488,901 (M); gifts received, $200,000; expenditures, $174,872, including $173,907 for 49 grants (high: $25,000; low: $200).
Purpose and activities: Primarily local giving for civic affairs, higher education, social services, and conservative public policy and anti-labor organizations.
Limitations: Giving primarily in MO.
Trustees: Frank H. McCracken, John J. Reed, Menlo F. Smith.
Employer Identification Number: 436061564

2027
Sunnen Foundation ▼
7910 Manchester Ave.
St. Louis 63143   (314) 781-2100

Incorporated in 1953 in Missouri.
Donor(s): Joseph Sunnen.†
Financial data: (yr. ended 12/31/83): Assets, $17,296,511 (M); expenditures, $1,943,663, including $1,835,789 for 50 grants (high: $400,000; low: $100; average: $5,000-$50,000).

Purpose and activities: Grants for specific goal-oriented activities, the purpose of which is to protect individual freedom of association; freedom of choice in religious beliefs, particularly contraception and pregnancy termination; freedom from censorship (especially textbooks); freedom from union coercion and compulsory membership; separation of church and state; separation of church and schools; and economic education. Projects also for learning programs for the handicapped and disadvantaged; youth and child welfare agencies; and medical research and health programs. Project should have an overall impact on the field of concern involved.
Types of support awarded: Seed money, emergency funds, equipment, matching funds, special projects, publications.
Limitations: No support for religious bodies, educational institutions, environmental organizations, hospitals, medical charities, or the arts (except for specific projects related to the foundation's area of concern); generally no support for charities with broad-based public appeal. No grants to individuals, or for building or endowment funds, scholarships, fellowships, annual campaigns, land acquisition, research, or conferences; no loans.
Publications: Program policy statement, application guidelines.
Application information:
 Initial approach: Letter
 Deadline(s): Submit proposal preferably in December and January; no set deadline
 Board meeting date(s): June and December; grants committee meets continuously
 Final notification: 2 to 3 weeks
 Write: Samuel G. Landfather, Chairman, Grants Committee
Officers: Robert M. Sunnen,* President; James P. Berthold,* Vice-President; C. Diane Kates, Secretary; Samuel G. Landfather,* Treasurer and Executive Director.
Directors:* Esther S. Kreider, Helen S. Sly.
Number of staff: None.
Employer Identification Number: 436029156

2028
Swift (John S.) Company, Inc. Charitable Trust ☐
c/o Mercantile Trust Company
P.O. Box 387
St. Louis 63166   (314) 425-2667

Trust established in 1952 in Missouri.
Donor(s): John S. Swift Company, Inc.
Financial data: (yr. ended 12/31/83): Assets, $1,250,102 (M); expenditures, $64,948, including $57,435 for 64 grants (high: $5,000; low: $25).
Purpose and activities: General giving; grants largely for higher and secondary education, cultural programs, including museums, and hospitals.
Application information:
 Write: Herschel Lynch
Trustees: Charles E. Schoelhamer, Hampden Swift, Mercantile Trust Company.
Employer Identification Number: 436020812

2029
Swinney (Edward F.) Trust
406 Board of Trade Bldg.
Tenth and Wyandotte Sts.
Kansas City 64105   (816) 842-0944

Trust established in 1946 in Missouri.
Donor(s): Edward F. Swinney.†
Financial data: (yr. ended 12/31/83): Assets, $7,349,951 (M); expenditures, $324,264, including $253,265 for 12 grants (high: $180,000; low: $2,000; average: $25,000-$50,000).
Purpose and activities: To further and develop local charitable and educational purposes; grants for mental health, higher education, hospitals, rehabilitation, and other health and welfare programs; supports research into the community's social and cultural needs. Giving for demonstration and experimental projects, extension and improvement of human services, with preference in the voluntary sector; planning and cooperation among voluntary agencies and between public and private agencies, and for education and training in community service. A member trust of the Kansas City Association of Trusts and Foundations.
Types of support awarded: Operating budgets, seed money, emergency funds, consulting services, technical assistance, special projects, research, publications, conferences and seminars.
Limitations: Giving limited to MO. No grants to individuals, or for building or endowment funds, annual campaigns, scholarships, fellowships, or matching gifts; generally no grants for base support or deficit financing; no loans.
Publications: Annual report, application guidelines, program policy statement.
Application information:
 Initial approach: Letter or full proposal
 Copies of proposal: 1
 Deadline(s): 2 months prior to board meeting
 Board meeting date(s): First Tuesday in April, July, October, and December
 Final notification: 10 days after board meetings
 Write: Janice C. Kreamer, Administrative Officer
Officer: Janice C. Kreamer, Administrative Officer.
Trustees: Boatmen's First National Bank of Kansas City.
Number of staff: 1 full-time professional; 1 part-time support.
Employer Identification Number: 446009264

2030
Sycamore Tree Trust ☐
P.O. Box 11264
Clayton 63105

Trust established about 1953 in Missouri.
Donor(s): Katherine M. Walsh, Dorothy M. Moore, Adelaide M. Schlafly, Thomas F. Schlafly, Daniel L. Schlafly, Jr.
Financial data: (yr. ended 12/31/83): Assets, $223,977 (M); gifts received, $246,065; expenditures, $528,979, including $528,533 for 93 grants (high: $107,503; low: $50).

Purpose and activities: Broad purposes; primarily local giving with emphasis on Roman Catholic church support and religious associations; support also for the arts and cultural programs, higher education, and a community fund; some support also for international affairs organizations.
Limitations: Giving primarily in MO.
Trustees: R.J. Connors, M.L. Hyde, C.L. Mayer.
Employer Identification Number: 436026719

2031
Tension Envelope Foundation ⌑
819 East 19th St., 5th Fl.
Kansas City 64108

Incorporated in 1954 in Missouri.
Donor(s): Tension Envelope Corporations.
Financial data: (yr. ended 11/30/83): Assets, $2,119,619 (M); gifts received, $112,000; expenditures, $259,719, including $239,943 for 161 grants (high: $24,250; low: $100).
Purpose and activities: Broad purposes; general giving in areas of company operations, with emphasis on Jewish welfare funds; support also for community funds, higher education, and hospitals.
Officers and Directors: Richard L. Berkley, President; Walter Hiersteiner, Vice-President; Eliot S. Berkley, Secretary; E.B. Berkley, Treasurer.
Employer Identification Number: 446012554

2032
Tilles (Rosalie) Nonsectarian Charity Fund
705 Olive St., Suite 906
St. Louis 63101

Trust established in 1926 in Missouri.
Donor(s): Cap Andrew Tilles.
Financial data: (yr. ended 6/30/83): Assets, $1,771,755 (M); expenditures, $271,207, including $1,000 for 2 grants (high: $600; low: $400) and $234,799 for 197 grants to individuals.
Purpose and activities: To aid deserving girls and boys residing in the city or county of St. Louis who are in need of physical or educational help, including scholarships to local high schools, and to any of the 5 participating higher education institutions: St. Louis University; University of Missouri's Columbia, Rolla, and St. Louis campuses; and Washington University.
Types of support awarded: Student aid.
Limitations: Giving primarily in St. Louis City and St. Louis County, MO.
Publications: Application guidelines.
Application information: Application guidelines issued for University Scholarship Program.
  Board meeting date(s): Scholarships approved by the trustees at June meeting
  Write: Sue Lott, Secretary
Officers and Trustees: H. Sam Priest, Chairman; Mercantile Trust Company, Treasurer; Archbishop John L. May, Rabbi Alvan D. Rubin.
Employer Identification Number: 436020833

2033
Townsend (R. E.) Educational Fund
P.O. Box 147
St. Joseph 64502   (816) 279-2721

Trust established in 1931 in Missouri.
Donor(s): R.E. Townsend.†
Financial data: (yr. ended 6/30/81): Assets, $2,360,282 (M); expenditures, $98,655, including $89,559 for 19 grants (high: $54,357; low: $220).
Purpose and activities: To assist needy youth between the ages of six and twenty-two, who reside in Buchanan and Andrew counties, Missouri, and Doniphan County, Kansas, and who attend grade, high, or vocational schools, "to make a better life with their hands" through vocational training; assistance also to young women interested in teaching grade school or high school.
Limitations: Giving limited to Buchanan and Andrew counties, MO, and Doniphan County, KS. No grants to individuals.
Application information: Solicitations for grants are not invited.
  Board meeting date(s): As required
Trustees: Mary Lynn Brown, David H. Morton, The First National Bank (Trust Department).
Employer Identification Number: 446012857

2034
Union Electric Company Charitable Trust ▼
1901 Gratiot St.
P.O. Box 149
St. Louis 63166   (314) 621-3222

Trust established in 1944 in Missouri.
Donor(s): Union Electric Company.
Financial data: (yr. ended 12/31/84): Assets, $770,719 (M); expenditures, $585,424, including $547,050 for 24 grants (high: $230,000; low: $1,650; average: $5,000-$25,000), $3,860 for 2 grants to individuals and $32,682 for 120 employee matching gifts.
Purpose and activities: General giving in areas served by the Company (Missouri, Illinois, and Iowa), largely for community funds and higher education; grants also for hospitals.
Types of support awarded: Annual campaigns, building funds, emergency funds, employee matching gifts, equipment, general purposes, land acquisition, operating budgets, employee related scholarships, scholarship funds, fellowships.
Limitations: Giving limited to areas served by the company: MO, IL, and IA. No grants to individuals (except for company employee scholarships), or for endowment funds, or research-related programs; no loans.
Publications: Application guidelines.
Application information:
  Initial approach: Letter
  Copies of proposal: 1
  Deadline(s): None
  Board meeting date(s): 2 or 3 times a year
  Final notification: 60 to 90 days
  Write: Ms. Patricia Barrett, Manager--Community Affairs

Trustees: William E. Cornelius, Centerre Trust Company of St. Louis.
Number of staff: 1 full-time professional; 2 part-time professional; 1 part-time support.
Employer Identification Number: 436022693

2035
Vatterott Foundation ⌑
10449 St. Charles Rock Rd.
St. Ann 63074

Trust established in 1948 in Missouri.
Donor(s): Charles F. Vatterott, Jr., Joseph A. Vatterott.
Financial data: (yr. ended 5/31/83): Assets, $874,167 (M); gifts received, $19,125; expenditures, $131,154, including $101,778 for 37 grants (high: $16,500; low: $300).
Purpose and activities: Broad purposes; general giving with emphasis on Roman Catholic church support and church-related institutions, and on higher education.
Trustees: William H. Erker, Edward M. Harris, Jr., J. Harvey Vatterott, John C. Vatterott, Joseph H. Vatterott.
Employer Identification Number: 436031155

2036
Voelkerding (Walter and Jean) Charitable Trust ⌑
P.O. Box 81
Dutzow 63342

Trust established in 1968 in Missouri.
Donor(s): Walter J. Voelkerding.†
Financial data: (yr. ended 2/29/84): Assets, $3,314,242 (M); expenditures, $167,142, including $134,520 for 2 grants (high: $130,000; low: $4,520).
Purpose and activities: Support for churches and religious welfare organizations.
Trustees: William Marquart, Steven J. Maune, David J. Voelkerding, Victor F. Voelkerding, William J. Zollman III.
Employer Identification Number: 237015780

2037
Webb Foundation
1034 South Brentwood, Suite 1660
St. Louis 63117   (314) 721-1976

Established in 1969 in Missouri.
Donor(s): Francis M. Webb,† Pearl M. Webb.†
Financial data: (yr. ended 12/31/84): Assets, $5,070,056 (M); expenditures, $342,228, including $337,500 for 45 grants (high: $20,000; low: $1,000; average: $3,000-$15,000).
Purpose and activities: Giving in the Midwest, with emphasis on child welfare, social agencies, higher and secondary education, and health and hospitals.
Types of support awarded: Operating budgets, continuing support, annual campaigns, seed money, building funds, equipment, scholarship funds, fellowships, research.

Limitations: Giving limited to the Midwest. No grants to individuals, or for emergency funds, deficit financing, land acquisition, endowment funds, matching gifts, special projects, publications, or conferences; no loans.
Publications: Program policy statement.
Application information:
  Initial approach: Letter, full proposal, or telephone
  Copies of proposal: 2
  Deadline(s): Submit proposals preferably in April or September; deadline end of May and October
  Board meeting date(s): June and November
  Final notification: After board meetings
  Write: Richard E. Fister, Secretary
Officer and Advisory Committee: Richard E. Fister, Secretary; Virginia M. Fister, Bernice Hock, Donald D. McDonald, Evelyn M. McDonald.
Trustee: Company Bank of Tower Grove.
Number of staff: None.
Employer Identification Number: 237028768

2038
Westlake (James L. & Nellie M.) Scholarship Fund ☒
c/o Mercantile Trust Company
P.O. Box 387
St. Louis 63166

Established in 1980.
Financial data: (yr. ended 9/30/82): Assets, $8,829,296 (M); gifts received, $69,059; expenditures, $303,413, including $145,150 for 265 grants to individuals.
Purpose and activities: Giving for higher education scholarships.
Types of support awarded: Student aid.
Limitations: Giving limited to high school graduates who are residents of MO.
Selection Committee: Daniel Schlafly, Chairman; Virginia Brown, Vice-Chairman; Oliver Wagner, Secretary.
Employer Identification Number: 436248269

2039
Whitaker (Mr. and Mrs. Lyndon C.) Charitable Foundation ▼ ☒
c/o Urban C. Bergbauer, Jr.
7711 Bonhomme Ave., Suite 201
St. Louis 63105

Trust established in 1975 in Missouri.
Donor(s): Mae M. Whitaker.†
Financial data: (yr. ended 4/30/83): Assets, $10,667,041 (M); expenditures, $760,828, including $624,819 for 35 grants (high: $113,794; low: $140; average: $2,000-$25,000).
Purpose and activities: Primarily local giving, with emphasis on handicapped children, medical research, cultural programs including music, and hospitals; grants also for youth agencies, and education.
Limitations: Giving primarily in St. Louis, MO.
Trustee: Urban C. Bergbauer, Jr.
Advisory Board: Cyril J. Costello, James D. Cullen, George T. Guernsey, James C. Thompson, Jr., Anita D. Vincel.
Employer Identification Number: 510173109

2040
Wolff (The John M.) Foundation ☒
c/o County Bank of Tower Grove
3134 South Grand Blvd.
St. Louis 63118

Trust established in 1956 in Missouri.
Donor(s): John M. Wolff, Jr.
Financial data: (yr. ended 12/31/83): Assets, $1,531,036 (M); expenditures, $133,663, including $122,000 for 39 grants (high: $25,000; low: $250).
Purpose and activities: primarily local giving, with emphasis on hospitals, higher education, and social services.
Limitations: Giving primarily in MO.
Trustees: Edith D. Wolff, John M. Wolff III, County Bank of Tower Grove.
Employer Identification Number: 436026247

2041
Woods (James H.) Foundation ☒
c/o Centerre Trust Company of St. Louis
510 Locust St.
St. Louis 63178

Trust established in 1958 in Missouri.
Donor(s): James H. Woods.†
Financial data: (yr. ended 11/30/83): Assets, $5,164,901 (M); expenditures, $321,134, including $278,500 for 31 grants (high: $75,000; low: $1,000).
Purpose and activities: Broad purposes; giving primarily in the Midwest, with emphasis on secondary and higher education, conservation, youth agencies, and church support.
Limitations: Giving primarily in the midwestern states.
Trustees: Elizabeth W. Bradbury, David L. Woods, James H. Woods, Jr., John R. Woods, Centerre Trust Company of St. Louis.
Employer Identification Number: 436024866

2042
Yellow Freight System Foundation ☒
1500 Commerce Bank Bldg., 922 Walnut St.
Kansas City 64106

Donor(s): Yellow Freight System, Inc.
Financial data: (yr. ended 12/31/83): Assets, $461,435 (M); gifts received, $171,947; expenditures, $281,863, including $279,415 for 61 grants (high: $74,135; low: $100).
Purpose and activities: Primarily local giving, with emphasis on cultural programs, social services, and education.
Limitations: Giving primarily in MO.
Officers and Directors:* George E. Powell, Jr.,* President; Donald L. McMorris,* Vice-President; Raymond A. Stewart, Jr.,* Secretary; P.A. Spangler, Treasurer.
Employer Identification Number: 237004674

MONTANA

2043
Bair (Charles M.) Memorial Trust ☒
c/o First Trust Company of Montana
P.O. Box 30678
Billings 59115   (406) 657-8124

Established in 1978.
Donor(s): Marguerite B. Lamb.†
Financial data: (yr. ended 1/31/84): Assets, $13,185,681 (M); expenditures, $584,251, including $459,000 for 5 grants (high: $150,000; low: $10,000) and $98,719 for 36 grants to individuals.
Purpose and activities: Primarily local giving for hospitals and Protestant churches; scholarships limited to high school students from Meagher and Wheatland counties, Montana.
Types of support awarded: Student aid.
Limitations: Giving primarily in MT.
Trustees: Alberta M. Bair, First Trust Company of Montana.
Employer Identification Number: 810370774

2044
Fortin Foundation of Montana ☒
P.O. Box 2416
Billings 59103

Incorporated in 1961 in Montana.
Donor(s): Philip N. Fortin, Dorothy Fortin.†
Financial data: (yr. ended 12/31/83): Assets, $5,138,612 (M); gifts received, $300,000; expenditures, $226,173, including $211,010 for 68 grants (high: $57,400; low: $20).
Purpose and activities: Broad purposes; grants largely for hospitals, higher education, and youth agencies, primarily in Montana and Florida.
Limitations: Giving primarily in MT and FL. No grants to individuals or for scholarships.
Application information:
  Write: Mary Alice Fortin, President
Officers: Mary Alice Fortin,* President and Treasurer; Leslie Stockard Smith,* Vice-President; Susan Stockard Channing, Secretary.
Directors:* Emil A. Fried.
Employer Identification Number: 816009207

2045
Haynes Foundation ☒
P.O. Box 746
Bozeman 59715

Incorporated in 1958 in Montana.
Donor(s): J.E. Haynes.†
Financial data: (yr. ended 3/31/84): Assets, $1,464,359 (M); gifts received, $25,000; expenditures, $69,976, including $60,000 for 6 grants of $10,000 each.
Purpose and activities: Primarily local giving to universities for scholarships.
Types of support awarded: Scholarship funds.
Limitations: Giving primarily in MT.

Application information: Application should be made through universities.
Officers and Trustees: J.I. Forbes, President and Treasurer; I.M. Haynes, Vice-President; John R. Kline, Secretary.
Employer Identification Number: 816013577

2046
Heisey Foundation, The ¤
c/o The First National Bank
P.O. Box 5000
Great Falls 59401   (406) 761-7200

Established about 1940 in Montana.
Donor(s): Charles E. Heisey.†
Financial data: (yr. ended 12/31/83): Assets, $1,377,536 (M); expenditures, $73,108, including $65,150 for 348 grants.
Purpose and activities: Giving limited to students attending specific schools located in the Foundation's trade area, with emphasis on awards for academic improvement for high school and college students.
Types of support awarded: Scholarship funds.
Limitations: Giving limited to the Great Falls, MT, trade area.
Publications: Application guidelines, program policy statement.
Application information:
Deadline(s): October 5 for high schools to provide necessary information for awards to foundation
Board meeting date(s): Annually
Write: John Reichel, Trustee
Trustees: Myra Norman, John Reichel, John D. Stephenson.
Employer Identification Number: 816009624

2047
Sample Foundation, Inc. ¤
3203 Third Ave. North, Suite 300
Billings 59103

Incorporated in 1956 in Florida.
Donor(s): Helen S. Sample.
Financial data: (yr. ended 10/31/83): Assets, $2,313,252 (M); expenditures, $181,911, including $136,800 for 41 grants (high: $31,000; low: $100).
Purpose and activities: Broad purposes; grants for higher education, museums, social services, youth agencies, hospitals, and community funds.
Officers: Joseph S. Sample, President; Sally Sample Aall, Vice-President and Treasurer.
Employer Identification Number: 596138602

2048
Sweet (Lloyd D.) Foundation
c/o Chinook Public High School
528 Ohio St.
Chinook 59523

Financial data: (yr. ended 12/31/84): Assets, $1,402,028 (M); expenditures, $169,820, including $166,380 for 168 grants to individuals.
Purpose and activities: Scholarships for graduates of Chinook High School in Montana.
Types of support awarded: Student aid.
Limitations: Giving limited to Chinook, MT.

Application information: Application form required.
Deadline(s): March 1 for academic scholarships; May 18 for summer scholarships; August 1 for continuing education scholarships
Officers: Gail Swant, President; Frank Pehrson, Jr., Vice-President; Betty Sprinkle, Secretary and Treasurer.
Directors: Norman Mosser, Betty Munson, Nellie Jo Nicholson, Bill Solem, Ellen Solem, William M. Solem.
Employer Identification Number: 237131688

NEBRASKA

2049
Abel Foundation, The ¤
P.O. Box 80268
Lincoln 68501

Trust established in 1951.
Donor(s): Abel Construction Company.
Financial data: (yr. ended 12/31/83): Assets, $498,702 (M); gifts received, $56,336; expenditures, $107,780, including $105,059 for 82 grants (high: $25,000; low: $25).
Purpose and activities: Primarily local giving, with emphasis on higher education, community development programs, community funds, and Protestant religious organizations.
Types of support awarded: Building funds.
Limitations: Giving limited to NE, particularly Lincoln.
Officers: George Abel, President; Gene Tallman, Vice-President; C.W. Hansen, Secretary-Treasurer.
Directors: Alice Abel, Elizabeth Abel, Ann Bradbeer, Hazel Tallman.
Employer Identification Number: 476041771

2050
Blumkin Foundation, Incorporated ¤
c/o Ben F. Shrier
400 First National Bank Bldg.
Omaha 68102

Incorporated in 1956 in Omaha, Nebraska.
Donor(s): Louis Blumkin, Rose Blumkin, Nebraska Furniture Mart, Inc.
Financial data: (yr. ended 11/30/83): Assets, $609,824 (M); gifts received, $435,000; expenditures, $183,990, including $182,418 for 137 grants (high: $10,550; low: $25).
Purpose and activities: Giving primarily for Jewish welfare funds, higher education, and cultural programs.
Limitations: Giving primarily in NE.
Officers: Rose Blumkin, Chairman; Louis Blumkin, President; Norman B. Batt, Vice-President; Ben F. Shrier, Secretary-Treasurer.
Employer Identification Number: 476030726

2051
Buckley (Thomas D.) Trust
P.O. Box 647
Chappell 69129

Established about 1980 in Nebraska.
Donor(s): Thomas D. Buckley.†
Financial data: (yr. ended 5/31/84): Assets, $4,805,261 (M); expenditures, $275,583, including $234,237 for 19 grants (high: $181,976; low: $500).
Purpose and activities: Primarily local giving, with emphasis on community development programs, Christian churches, and health services.
Limitations: Giving primarily in NE, particularly Chappell, and CO.
Trustees: Bill M. Hughes, James P. Jacobs, Walter W. Peterson.
Employer Identification Number: 476121041

2052
Buffett Foundation, The ¤
1440 Kiewit Plaza
Omaha 68131

Incorporated in 1964 in Nebraska.
Donor(s): Warren E. Buffett, Berkshire Hathaway Inc.
Financial data: (yr. ended 6/30/83): Assets, $1,824,182 (M); gifts received, $364,141; expenditures, $522,146, including $507,897 for 67 grants (high: $50,000; low: $8).
Purpose and activities: Broad purposes; grants primarily for higher education.
Officers and Directors: Susan T. Buffett, President; Warren E. Buffett, Vice-President and Treasurer; Gladys Kaiser, Secretary; Shirley S. Anderson, Executive Director.
Employer Identification Number: 476032365

2053
ConAgra Charitable Foundation, Inc. ¤
One Central Park Plaza
Omaha 68102

Donor(s): ConAgra, Inc.
Financial data: (yr. ended 5/27/84): Assets, $131,190 (M); gifts received, $450,000; expenditures, $423,706, including $422,793 for 75 grants (high: $50,000; low: $50).
Purpose and activities: Primarily local giving, with emphasis on higher education, youth agencies, community funds, and cultural programs.
Limitations: Giving primarily in Omaha, NE.
Officers: C.M. Harper,* President; M.G. Colladay,* Vice-President and Secretary; J.P. O'Donnell, Treasurer.
Directors:* R.B. Daugherty.
Employer Identification Number: 362899320

2054
Cooper Foundation
504 Cooper Plaza
Twelfth and P Sts.
Lincoln 68508   (402) 476-7571

Incorporated in 1934 in Nebraska.
Donor(s): Joseph H. Cooper.†

Financial data: (yr. ended 12/31/84): Assets, $7,425,553 (M); expenditures, $561,714, including $269,854 for 55 grants (high: $50,000; low: $200).

Purpose and activities: Charitable purposes; grants largely for programs benefiting children and young people, primarily in education and the arts.

Types of support awarded: Annual campaigns, seed money, emergency funds, research, scholarship funds, matching funds.

Limitations: Giving primarily in NE, with emphasis on Lincoln and Lancaster County. No grants to individuals, or for endowment funds; no loans.

Publications: Biennial report, application guidelines, program policy statement.

Application information: Application form required.

  Initial approach: Proposal
  Copies of proposal: 1
  Deadline(s): None
  Board meeting date(s): Monthly
  Final notification: 1 month
  Write: Elwood N. Thompson, President

Officers and Trustees: Elwood N. Thompson, President; Peg Huff, Secretary; Richard Knudsen, Counsel; Jack Campbell, Robert Dobson, Kathryn Druliner, E.J. Faulkner, Harold Hoppe, W.W. Nuernberger, John Olsson, E. Arthur Thompson, Norton E. Warner, Burnham Yates.

Number of staff: 3 full-time professional.

Employer Identification Number: 470401230

2055
Criss (Dr. C. C. and Mabel L.) Memorial Foundation ▼ ⌺
800 Commercial Federal Tower
72nd and Mercy Rd.
Omaha 68124   (402) 392-1500

Trust established in 1978 in Nebraska.

Donor(s): C.C. Criss, M.D.,† Mabel L. Criss.†

Financial data: (yr. ended 2/29/84): Assets, $22,436,495 (M); expenditures, $1,816,663, including $1,592,333 for 15 grants (high: $801,000; low: $2,000; average: $10,000-$100,000).

Purpose and activities: Educational and scientific purposes; primarily to meet the needs of Creighton University's medical center; support also for education, including higher education, cultural agencies, youth and social agencies, and a hospital.

Limitations: Giving primarily in NE.

Application information:

  Write: Joseph J. Vinardi, Trustee

Trustees: M. Thomas Crummer, Richard L. Daly, Gale E. Davis, Joseph J. Vinardi, The Omaha National Bank.

Employer Identification Number: 470601105

2056
Frohm (Carl) Memorial Foundation ⌺
c/o Omaha National Bank, Estate and Trust Division
17th and Farnam St.
Omaha 68102

Established about 1980 in Nebraska.

Donor(s): Carl Frohm Insurance Trust.

Financial data: (yr. ended 12/31/83): Assets, $1,209,457 (M); expenditures, $86,218, including $72,500 for 4 grants (high: $57,500; low: $5,000).

Purpose and activities: Funds primarily for a Jewish retirement home and temple support.

Limitations: Giving limited to Omaha, NE.

Application information:

  Write: Donald W. Engdahl

Trustee: Omaha National Bank.

Employer Identification Number: 470607603

2057
Hitchcock (Gilbert M. and Martha H.) Foundation ▼
Kennedy Holland Bldg.
10306 Regency Parkway Dr.
Omaha 68114   (402) 397-0203

Incorporated in 1943 in Nebraska.

Donor(s): Mrs. Martha H. Hitchcock.†

Financial data: (yr. ended 12/31/84): Assets, $6,541,874 (M); expenditures, $495,000, including $445,500 for 38 grants (high: $117,046; low: $1,000; average: $1,000-$15,000).

Purpose and activities: Broad purposes; local giving for private secondary and higher education; support also for cultural programs and youth and social agencies.

Types of support awarded: Annual campaigns, building funds, endowment funds, matching funds, general purposes, scholarship funds.

Limitations: Giving limited to NE and western IA, with emphasis on Omaha. No grants to individuals or for research-related programs.

Publications: Application guidelines.

Application information:

  Initial approach: Full proposal or letter
  Copies of proposal: 8
  Deadline(s): December 1
  Board meeting date(s): January and as required
  Final notification: After January board meeting
  Write: Thomas R. Burke, Secretary

Officers: Denman Kountze,* President; Neely Kountze,* Vice-President; Thomas R. Burke, Secretary; Tyler B. Gaines,* Treasurer.

Trustees:* Mary Jennings, Charles Kountze.

Number of staff: None.

Employer Identification Number: 476025723

2058
InterNorth Foundation, The ▼
2223 Dodge St.
Omaha 68102   (402) 633-5812

Established in 1979 in Nebraska.

Donor(s): InterNorth, Inc.

Financial data: (yr. ended 12/31/84): Assets, $8,670,000 (M); gifts received, $2,000,000; expenditures, $2,504,000, including $2,310,000 for 373 grants (high: $150,000; low: $20; average: $2,900) and $193,984 for 482 employee matching gifts.

Purpose and activities: General purposes; support primarily for higher education, community funds and civic organizations, social and youth agencies, culture and the arts, including the InterNorth Art Foundation.

Types of support awarded: General purposes, operating budgets, continuing support, annual campaigns, seed money, emergency funds, deficit financing, building funds, matching funds, conferences and seminars, employee matching gifts, special projects.

Limitations: Giving limited to areas of company operations, with preference given to the Midwest. No support for religious organizations that are not educational. No grants to individuals or for scholarships and fellowships; generally no grants for endowment funds; no loans.

Publications: Application guidelines.

Application information:

  Initial approach: Full proposal, letter, or telephone
  Copies of proposal: 1
  Deadline(s): 3 weeks before board meeting
  Board meeting date(s): March, June, September, and December
  Final notification: Within 10 days following board meetings
  Write: James J. Finnegan, Executive Director

Officers and Directors: W.A. Strauss, Chairman; S.F. Segnar, President; J.J. McClymond, Vice-President; James J. Finnegan, Executive Director.

Number of staff: 2 full-time professional; 1 full-time support.

Employer Identification Number: 470615943

2059
Kiewit (Peter) Foundation ▼
Woodmen Tower, Suite 900
Farnam at Seventeenth
Omaha 68102   (402) 344-7890

Established in 1975 in Nebraska.

Donor(s): Peter Kiewit.

Financial data: (yr. ended 6/30/84): Assets, $65,302,823 (M); expenditures, $7,211,398, including $6,353,912 for grants.

Purpose and activities: Broad purposes; primarily local giving, with emphasis on civic affairs and community development, higher education, health and social agencies, youth, cultural programs, and a Presbyterian missionary organization. Contributions almost always made as challenge grants.

Types of support awarded: Matching funds, student aid.

Limitations: Giving limited to NE and western IA; Sheridan, WY; and Rancho Mirage, CA; college scholarships available to high school students in the Omaha, NE--Council Bluffs, IA, area only. No support for elementary or secondary education, churches, religious groups, or tax-supported public facilities. No grants to individuals (except for scholarships), or for endowment funds, construction, renovation, operating budgets or annual campaigns.

Publications: Annual report, program policy statement, application guidelines.

Application information: For scholarships, request application form from high school principal who makes scholarship selection for his or her school. Application form required.

Deadline(s): June 30, September 30, December 31, and March 3

Board meeting date(s): September, December, March, and June

Final notification: Within 30 days of board meeting

Write: Ray L. Daniel, Jr., Executive Director

Officers and Trustees: Marjorie H. Kiewit, Chairman; Richard L. Coyne, Vice-Chairman; Ray L. Daniel, Jr., Executive Director; Robert B. Dougherty, Peter Kiewit, Jr., Omaha National Bank.

Number of staff: 3.

Employer Identification Number: 476098282

2060
Kiewit (The Peter) Sons Company Foundation ▼ ¤
1000 Kiewit Plaza
Omaha 68131

Established in 1963 in Nebraska.

Donor(s): Peter Kiewit Sons Company, Wytana Inc., Big Horn Coal Co.

Financial data: (yr. ended 12/31/83): Assets, $8,870,221 (M); gifts received, $2,634,625; expenditures, $1,421,236, including $1,407,499 for 131 grants (high: $250,250; low: $25).

Purpose and activities: Charitable purposes; grants largely for youth agencies, higher education, community funds, hospitals, cultural programs, including a zoo, and civic affairs.

Trustee: The Omaha National Bank.

Employer Identification Number: 476029996

2061
Lane (Winthrop and Frances) Foundation
c/o Omaha National Bank
17th & Farnham St.
Omaha 68102   (402) 348-6350

Established in 1976.

Financial data: (yr. ended 12/31/83): Assets, $1,524,375 (M); gifts received, $2,264; expenditures, $135,948, including $23,800 for 6 grants (high: $6,000; low: $500) and $99,393 for 63 grants to individuals.

Purpose and activities: Giving limited to students enrolled at Creighton School of Law, the University of Nebraska College of Law, and for educational programs at these institutions.

Types of support awarded: Student aid, research, conferences and seminars.

Limitations: Giving limited to Omaha and Lincoln, NE.

Application information: Application form required.

Deadline(s): None

Trustee: Omaha National Bank.

Employer Identification Number: 470581778

2062
Lincoln Family Foundation ¤
P.O. Box 80269
Lincoln 68501

Established in 1963 in Kansas.

Financial data: (yr. ended 12/31/83): Assets, $1,449,097 (M); expenditures, $75,565, including $75,025 for 2 grants (high: $75,000; low: $25).

Purpose and activities: Broad purposes; grants primarily in Nebraska and Kansas for higher education, Protestant church support, a charitable foundation, and a youth agency.

Limitations: Giving primarily in NE and KS.

Officers and Trustees:* George A. Lincoln,* President; Olivia G. Lincoln,* Vice-President; Ardean A. Arnot, Secretary; Bill C. Macy, Treasurer.

Employer Identification Number: 476034708

2063
Lincoln Foundation Inc. ▼
215 Centennial Mall South
Lincoln 68508   (402) 474-2345

Community foundation incorporated in 1955 in Nebraska.

Financial data: (yr. ended 12/31/84): Assets, $11,099,458 (M); gifts received, $1,781,037; expenditures, $1,651,728, including $1,137,835 for grants (high: $241,500; low: $100).

Purpose and activities: To promote the mental, moral, intellectual, and physical improvement, assistance and relief of the inhabitants of Lincoln and Lancaster County in particular, and elsewhere in the U.S. where funds are available; giving mainly in the areas of civic and community affairs, cultural programs, health and welfare, and higher education.

Types of support awarded: Scholarship funds, seed money, emergency funds, research, matching funds, continuing support, special projects.

Limitations: Giving primarily in Lincoln and Lancaster County, NE. No grants to individuals, or for building or endowment funds, or operating budgets.

Publications: Annual report, program policy statement, application guidelines, newsletter.

Application information:

Initial approach: Telephone

Copies of proposal: 12

Board meeting date(s): Quarterly and as required

Write: John H. Frey, President

Officers and Directors: James C. Constance, Chairman; Robert S. Milligan, 1st Vice-Chairman; David T. Calhoun, 2nd Vice-Chairman; John H. Frey, President; Mary Arth, Secretary; James F. Nissen, Treasurer; Alice Abel, Roger L. Anderson, Charles Barton, Glenn Clements, Robert Haag, Robert L. Hans, Ron Harris, Martin Massengale, Gates Minnick, Lu Pansing, Harriet Potter, Robert Saffer, Kent Seacrest, William C. Smith, Robert E. Swett, L.T. Womack, Thomas C. Woods III, Alan Young.

Number of staff: 3 full-time professional; 1 part-time professional; 2 full-time support; 1 part-time support.

Employer Identification Number: 470458128

2064
Livingston (The Milton S. and Corinne N.) Foundation, Inc.
300 Overland Wolf Center
6910 Pacific St.
Omaha 68106   (402) 558-1112

Incorporated in 1948 in Nebraska.

Donor(s): Milton S. Livingston.†

Financial data: (yr. ended 12/31/83): Assets, $2,692,489 (M); expenditures, $383,960, including $354,650 for 47 grants (high: $145,000; low: $100).

Purpose and activities: Grants largely for local Jewish welfare funds; interests also include higher education and temple support.

Types of support awarded: Continuing support, building funds, general purposes.

Limitations: Giving primarily in NE. No grants to individuals.

Application information:

Initial approach: Letter

Copies of proposal: 1

Board meeting date(s): May and October

Write: Yale Richards, Secretary

Officers: Jule M. Newman,* President; Morton A. Richards,* Vice-President; Yale Richards, Secretary; Stanley J. Slosburg,* Treasurer.

Trustees:* Robert I. Kully, Murray H. Newman.

Employer Identification Number: 476027670

2065
Omaha National Bank Charitable Trust ¤
c/o The Omaha National Bank
1620 Farnam St.
Omaha 68102

Trust established in 1962 in Nebraska.

Donor(s): The Omaha National Bank.

Financial data: (yr. ended 12/31/83): Assets, $1,839,244 (M); expenditures, $204,717, including $201,375 for 88 grants (high: $25,000; low: $100).

Purpose and activities: Primarily local giving, with emphasis on a community fund, higher education, cultural programs, and youth agencies.

Limitations: Giving primarily in Ohama, NE.

Trustee: The Omaha National Bank.

Employer Identification Number: 476020716

2066
Omaha World-Herald Foundation, The ▼
c/o Omaha World-Herald Company
14th and Dodge Sts.
Omaha 68102   (402) 444-1000

Trust established in 1968 in Nebraska.

Donor(s): Omaha World-Herald Company.

Financial data: (yr. ended 12/31/83): Assets, $2,908,139 (M); gifts received, $900,000; expenditures, $494,020, including $480,424 for 117 grants (high: $76,055; low: $25; average: $500-$10,000).
Purpose and activities: Broad purposes; local giving to institutions involved with education, civic, health, welfare, and cultural programs.
Types of support awarded: Seed money, building funds, land acquisition, internships, scholarship funds, matching funds.
Limitations: Giving limited to the Omaha, NE area. No grants to individuals, or for endowment funds, or research; no loans.
Publications: 990-PF.
Application information:
Initial approach: Letter
Copies of proposal: 1
Board meeting date(s): As required
Final notification: 2 months
Write: John Gottschalk, Vice-President
Distribution Committee: Harold W. Andersen, John Gottschalk, G. Woodson Howe.
Trustee: Norwest Capital Management and Trust Co. Nebraska.
Employer Identification Number: 476058691

2067
Phelps County Community Foundation, Inc.
c/o Tim Anderson
P.O. Box 466
Holdrege 68949   (308) 995-6191

Community foundation incorporated in 1976 in Nebraska.
Financial data: (yr. ended 2/29/84): Assets, $1,395,499 (M); gifts received, $240,249; expenditures, $204,914, including $199,272 for 6 grants.
Purpose and activities: Local giving for charitable and educational purposes for the benefit of the residents of Phelps County.
Types of support awarded: Seed money, emergency funds, building funds, equipment, matching funds, scholarship funds, student aid.
Limitations: Giving limited to NE, particularly Phelps County. No grants for operating budgets, continuing support, annual campaigns, deficit financing, land acquisition, endowments, program support, research, demonstration projects, publications, or conferences and seminars; no loans.
Publications: Program policy statement, application guidelines.
Application information: Application form required.
Initial approach: Letter
Officer: Mary L. Stephenson, Treasurer.
Number of staff: None.
Employer Identification Number: 470577414

2068
Quivey-Bay State Foundation ⌷
1515 East 20th St.
Scottsbluff 69361   (308) 632-2168

Established in 1948 in Nebraska.
Donor(s): M.B. Quivey, Mrs. M.B. Quivey.

Financial data: (yr. ended 1/31/84): Assets, $1,561,738 (M); expenditures, $130,800, including $121,132 for 55 grants (high: $10,000; low: $100).
Purpose and activities: Primarily local giving, with emphasis on higher education, church support, and youth and child welfare agencies; support also for historic preservation.
Limitations: Giving primarily in NE. No grants to individuals or for endowment funds.
Application information:
Initial approach: Letter
Copies of proposal: 1
Deadline(s): Submit proposal in September; deadline October 15
Board meeting date(s): October and November
Officers and Trustees: Earl R. Cherry, President; Ted Cannon, Secretary-Treasurer.
Employer Identification Number: 476024159

2069
Reynolds (Edgar) Foundation, Inc. ⌷
204 North Walnut St.
Grand Island 68801   (308) 384-0957

Established in 1977.
Donor(s): Edgar Reynolds.†
Financial data: (yr. ended 12/31/83): Assets, $2,766,647 (M); gifts received, $85,000; expenditures, $159,851, including $158,750 for 9 grants (high: $50,000; low: $2,250).
Purpose and activities: Grants primarily to local hospitals, youth agencies, and welfare programs.
Limitations: Giving primarily in NE.
Application information:
Write: Fred M. Glade, Jr., Chairman
Officers and Directors: Fred M. Glade, Jr., Chairman; William Marshall, Jr., Vice-Chairman; Frances Reynolds, Secretary-Treasurer; Jon F. Luebs.
Employer Identification Number: 470589941

2070
Rogers Foundation
925 Stuart Bldg.
Lincoln 68508   (402) 477-3725

Established in 1954 in Nebraska.
Donor(s): Richard H. Rogers.†
Financial data: (yr. ended 12/31/84): Assets, $3,662,642 (M); expenditures, $156,377, including $141,000 for 33 grants (high: $26,000; low: $250).
Purpose and activities: Primarily local giving, with emphasis on support for cultural programs, civic affairs, youth and health agencies, and education.
Limitations: Giving primarily in Lincoln and Lancaster County, NE. No support for religious activities, national organizations, or organizations supported by government agencies. No grants to individuals, or for fundraising benefits, program advertising, endowments, or continuing support; no loans.
Publications: Application guidelines.
Application information:
Initial approach: Proposal
Write: Eloise R. Agee or Richard W. Agee

Officers and Directors: Richard W. Agee, President; Eloise R. Agee, Vice-President; Richard R. Agee, Marie M. Rogers.
Employer Identification Number: 476026897

2071
Steinhart Foundation, Inc., The
1000 Terrace Dr.
Nebraska City 68410

Incorporated in 1954 in Nebraska.
Donor(s): Morton Steinhart,† Ella S. Steinhart.
Financial data: (yr. ended 12/31/83): Assets, $4,273,192 (M); expenditures, $200,718, including $154,500 for 42 grants (high: $40,000; low: $100).
Purpose and activities: General purposes; primarily local giving, with emphasis on civic projects.
Limitations: Giving primarily in southeastern NE.
Application information: Funds presently committed.
Board meeting date(s): Annually
Write: Garry Ailes, Trustee
Officers and Trustees: Byrl Thostesen, President and Treasurer; Gladys Wenzel, Vice-President; Garry Ailes, Secretary; Mary Ellen Bosworth, Deroy Harshman, John H. Nelson, Mrs. Karl H. Nelson, Henry B. Pierpont, Henry Schwake.
Employer Identification Number: 476025185

2072
Storz (Robert Herman) Foundation ⌷
Eighth Fl., Kiewit Plaza
Omaha 68131

Established in 1957.
Donor(s): Robert Herman Storz.
Financial data: (yr. ended 12/31/83): Assets, $3,055,167 (M); gifts received, $600,000; expenditures, $237,152, including $166,850 for 16 grants (high: $75,000; low: $100).
Purpose and activities: Primarily local giving, with support for hospitals, a cathedral, and cultural programs.
Limitations: Giving primarily in NE.
Trustees: Susan Storz Butler, Mildred T. Storz, Robert Herman Storz.
Employer Identification Number: 476025980

2073
Swanson (Carl and Caroline) Foundation, Inc.
8701 West Dodge Rd., Suite 304
Omaha 68114   (402) 391-8400

Trust established in 1945; incorporated in 1953 in Nebraska.
Donor(s): Members of the Carl A. Swanson family.
Financial data: (yr. ended 12/31/84): Assets, $1,381,244 (M); expenditures, $398,576, including $364,545 for 3 grants (high: $356,245; low: $100).
Purpose and activities: Funds presently committed to the Swanson Center for Nutrition.
Limitations: Giving limited to Omaha, NE.

Application information:
Board meeting date(s): Quarterly
Write: Frederick S. Bucholz, Secretary
Officers and Directors: Gretchen Swanson Velde, President; Frederick S. Bucholz, Vice-President and Secretary; Edson L. Bridges, Vice-President and Treasurer.
Employer Identification Number: 476024644

2074
Valmont Foundation, The ⌑
c/o Valmont Industries, Inc.
Valley 68064

Established in 1976.
Donor(s): Valmont Industries, Inc.
Financial data: (yr. ended 2/29/84): Assets, $12,014 (M); gifts received, $170,000; expenditures, $178,885, including $178,885 for 63 grants (high: $26,000; low: $100).
Purpose and activities: Primarily local giving to higher education, youth agencies, community funds, and cultural programs.
Limitations: Giving primarily in NE.
Officers: Robert B. Daugherty, President; Paul F. Leineimann, Secretary; Terry J. McClain, Treasurer.
Director: R.A. Wahl, Jr.
Employer Identification Number: 362895245

2075
Weller Foundation, Inc. ⌑
East Highway 20
P.O. Box 636
Atkinson 68713   (402) 925-2803

Incorporated in 1979 in Nebraska.
Donor(s): E.C. Weller, Frances W. Weller.
Financial data: (yr. ended 10/31/83): Assets, $4,143,012 (M); expenditures, $198,639, including $162,150 for 304 grants to individuals.
Purpose and activities: Scholarships for students attending one of the Technical Community Colleges in Nebraska, or other vocational education such as nursing.
Types of support awarded: Student aid.
Limitations: Giving limited to NE, with primary consideration for residents of Holt, Boyd, Brown, Rock, Keya Paha, and Garfield counties. No grants for scholarships for education toward a Bachelor's degree.
Publications: Application guidelines.
Application information: Application form required.
Deadline(s): June 1 and November 1
Officers and Directors: Robert Clifford, President; Ernest J. Gottschall, Vice-President; Dean Fleming, Secretary-Treasurer; Clayton Goeke, Frances Weller.
Employer Identification Number: 470611350

NEVADA

2076
Bing Fund Corporation ▼
302 East Carson Ave., Suite 617
Las Vegas 89101   (702) 386-6183

Incorporated in 1977 in Nevada as partial successor to Bing Fund, Inc., incorporated in New York.
Donor(s): Leo S. Bing,† Mrs. Anna Bing Arnold, Peter S. Bing.
Financial data: (yr. ended 5/31/84): Assets, $20,326,195 (M); expenditures, $1,168,209, including $1,112,330 for 472 grants (high: $100,000; low: $100; average: $100-$1,000).
Purpose and activities: Giving primarily for higher education, museums, the arts, secondary education, hospitals, and population control.
Limitations: Giving primarily in southern CA.
Officers: Anna H. Bing, President; Peter S. Bing, Vice-President and Treasurer; Robert D. Burch, Secretary.
Employer Identification Number: 942476169

2077
Bing Fund Inc. ⌑
One East First St., Suite 1203
Reno 89501

Incorporated in 1977 in Nevada as partial successor to Bing Fund, Inc., incorporated in New York.
Donor(s): Leo S. Bing,† Mrs. Anna Bing Arnold, Peter S. Bing.
Financial data: (yr. ended 5/31/83): Assets, $1,464,475 (M); expenditures, $57,396, including $55,000 for 2 grants (high: $50,000; low: $5,000).
Purpose and activities: Primarily local giving with emphasis on medical education and youth agencies.
Limitations: Giving primarily in NV.
Officers and Trustees: Peter S. Bing, President and Treasurer; Margaret Churn, Vice-President and Secretary; Robert D. Burch, Anna Mandelstam.
Employer Identification Number: 942496050

2078
ELW Foundation, The
One E. First St., Suite 800
Reno 89501   (702) 322-2242

Established in 1982 in Nevada.
Donor(s): Ann K. Wiegand,† Edwin L. Wiegand.†
Financial data: (yr. ended 10/31/84): Assets, $21,716,141 (M); gifts received, $100,000; expenditures, $1,416,526, including $1,204,200 for 46 grants (high: $100,000; low: $2,400).

Purpose and activities: Giving primarily in Nevada for Roman Catholic organizations, including health care and education; support also for medical research, equipment, cultural projects, and public affairs.
Types of support awarded: Equipment, building funds.
Limitations: Giving primarily in NV.
Application information:
Initial approach: Letter
Deadline(s): None
Write: Raymond C. Avansino, Jr., President
Officers: Raymond C. Avansino, Jr.,* Chairman, President, and Secretary; Norbert F. Stanny,* Vice-President; N. Callaghan Stanny, Treasurer.
Trustees:* Harvey C. Fruehauf, Jr.
Employer Identification Number: 942839372

2079
Golden Nugget Scholarship Fund, Inc.
P.O. Box 610
129 E. Fremont St.
Las Vegas 89125   (702) 385-7111

Established in 1981 in Nevada.
Donor(s): Golden Nugget, Inc.
Financial data: (yr. ended 5/31/84): Assets, $3,041,943 (M); expenditures, $209,381, including $179,800 for 122 grants to individuals.
Purpose and activities: Scholarships to graduates of high schools in Nevada and New Jersey for college studies at accredited public or private institutions located in the United States.
Types of support awarded: Student aid.
Limitations: Giving limited to students in NV and NJ.
Application information: Application form required.
Deadline(s): March 10
Write: Elaine Wynn, Vice-Chairperson
Officers and Trustees: Mike O'Callaghan, Chairman and President; Elaine Wynn, Vice-Chairperson and Treasurer; Alfred J. Luciani, Secretary; Pat Wayson, Stephen A. Wynn.
Employer Identification Number: 942768861

2080
Hawkins (Robert Z.) Foundation ⌑
One East Liberty St., Suite 509
Reno 89505   (702) 786-4646

Established in 1980.
Financial data: (yr. ended 12/31/83): Assets, $8,122,184 (M); expenditures, $333,568, including $226,020 for 24 grants (high: $43,660; low: $350).
Purpose and activities: Local giving, with emphasis on education, including a university, youth agencies and child welfare, and church support.
Limitations: Giving limited to NV.
Application information:
Deadline(s): None
Write: Paul O. Wiig, Chairman
Officer: Prince A. Hawkins, Secretary.

Trustees: Paul O. Wiig, Chairman; Kathryn A. Hawkins, Robert M. Hawkins, Bill A. Ligon, Security Bank of Nevada (T.A. Nigro, Representative).
Employer Identification Number: 880162645

2081
Sells (Carol Buck) Foundation
P.O. Drawer CE
Incline Village 89450 (702) 831-6366

Foundation incorporated in 1979 in Nevada.
Donor(s): Carol B. Sells, John E. Sells.
Financial data: (yr. ended 11/30/84): Assets, $4,232,177 (M); gifts received, $250,000; expenditures, $416,276, including $344,500 for 10 grants (high: $50,000; low: $5,000).
Purpose and activities: Support for the visual and performing arts, especially music, and for education in the arts, largely in the western United States.
Types of support awarded: Operating budgets, continuing support, annual campaigns, seed money, building funds, matching funds, endowment funds.
Limitations: Giving primarily in the western U.S. No grants to individuals, or for emergency funds, deficit financing, equipment, land acquisition, renovations, scholarships and fellowships, special projects, research, publications, or conferences; no loans.
Application information:
Initial approach: Letter or telephone
Copies of proposal: 1
Deadline(s): April 1 or October 1
Board meeting date(s): End of April and end of October
Final notification: 3 months
Write: Marya A. Beam, Administrative Assistant or Carol B. Sells, President
Officers and Trustees: Carol B. Sells, President; John E. Sells, Vice-President and Secretary; Christian P. Erdman, Vice-President and Treasurer; John M. Barry.
Number of staff: 1 full-time professional; 1 part-time professional.
Employer Identification Number: 880163505

NEW HAMPSHIRE

2082
Barker Foundation Inc., The ⌑
P.O. Box 328
Nashua 03061 (603) 889-1763

Incorporated in 1954 in Maine.
Donor(s): Walter Barker,† Irene L. Barker.
Financial data: (yr. ended 12/31/82): Assets, $1,980,113 (M); expenditures, $162,102, including $140,350 for 61 grants (high: $25,000; low: $150) and $10,297 for grants to individuals.
Purpose and activities: Broad purposes; primarily local giving, with emphasis on hospitals and health associations, higher education, including scholarships, church support, and youth agencies.
Types of support awarded: Scholarship funds.
Limitations: Giving limited to NH.
Application information:
Write: Allan M. Barker, Trustee
Officers and Trustees: Allan M. Barker, President; Elizabeth M. Bucknam, Susan B. Moran, Vice-Presidents; Gilbert Bucknam, Treasurer; Dorothy A. Barker, Edward P. Moran, Jr.
Employer Identification Number: 026005885

2083
Bean (Norwin S. and Elizabeth N.) Foundation ⌑
c/o New Hampshire Charitable Fund
1 South St., P.O. Box 1335
Concord 03301 (603) 225-6641

Trust established in 1957 in New Hampshire; later became an affiliated trust of the New Hampshire Charitable Fund.
Donor(s): Norwin S. Bean,† Elizabeth N. Bean.†
Financial data: (yr. ended 12/31/82): Assets, $5,298,067 (M); expenditures, $306,440, including $274,691 for 31 grants (high: $75,000; low: $350; average: $500-$5,000) and $12,000 for 1 loan.
Purpose and activities: Religious, educational and charitable purposes in Amherst and Manchester, New Hampshire; grants for health, education, welfare, and cultural activities and other qualified nonprofit purposes.
Types of support awarded: General purposes, seed money, emergency funds, building funds, equipment, land acquisition, special projects, conferences and seminars, matching funds, loans, program-related investments, consulting services.
Limitations: Giving limited to Amherst and Manchester, NH. No grants to individuals, or for scholarships and fellowships, operating budgets, deficit financing, or endowment funds.
Publications: Program policy statement, application guidelines.
Application information:
Initial approach: Letter or telephone
Copies of proposal: 6
Deadline(s): February 15, May 15, August 15, and November 15
Board meeting date(s): March, June, September, and December
Write: Deborah Cowan, Associate Director
Officers and Trustees: John R. McLane, Jr., Chairman; Frederick W. Griffin, Secretary; James A. Shanahan, Jr., Treasurer; Hilda W. Fleisher, Ann Snow.
Employer Identification Number: 026013381

2084
Cogswell Benevolent Trust
875 Elm St.
Manchester 03101 (603) 622-4013

Trust established in 1929 in New Hampshire.
Donor(s): Leander A. Cogswell.†
Financial data: (yr. ended 12/31/83): Assets, $6,034,787 (M); expenditures, $288,695, including $257,214 for 78 grants (high: $25,000; low: $100).
Purpose and activities: Broad purposes; grants principally for higher education, including student loans and scholarship aid, youth agencies, community funds, hospitals, and church support. At least ninety percent of the annual income must be used for charitable purposes in New Hampshire.
Types of support awarded: Student aid, special projects.
Limitations: Giving primarily in NH. No grants to individuals, or for endowment funds or operating budgets.
Application information: Application form required for scholarship assistance.
Initial approach: Letter
Copies of proposal: 1
Deadline(s): None
Board meeting date(s): Usually weekly and as required
Final notification: 30 days
Write: Winthrop Wadleigh, Trustee
Officer: Mary Stimans, Secretary.
Trustees: David P. Goodwin, Owen Johnson, Winthrop Wadleigh.
Number of staff: 1.
Employer Identification Number: 020235690

2085
Freygang (Walter Henry) Foundation ⌑
P.O. Box 768
Wolfeboro 03894

Incorporated in 1949 in New Jersey.
Donor(s): Walter Henry Freygang,† Marie A. Freygang, and others.
Financial data: (yr. ended 8/31/83): Assets, $2,802,742 (M); gifts received, $1,307,113; expenditures, $97,699, including $83,029 for 43 grants (high: $10,700; low: $250).
Purpose and activities: Grants primarily for higher education and hospitals; some support also for welfare.
Officers: Gustav G. Freygang, Jr., President and Treasurer; Dorothea F. Drennan, Vice-President; Dorothy B. Freygang, Secretary.
Trustees: Joseph A. Drennan, Dale G. Freygang, Katherine A. Freygang, W. Nicholas Freygang.
Employer Identification Number: 226027952

2086
Hubbard Farms Charitable Foundation ⌑
P.O. Box 505
Walpole 03608

Donor(s): Hubbard Farms, Inc.
Financial data: (yr. ended 12/31/82): Assets, $814,152 (M); gifts received, $95,000; expenditures, $146,128, including $138,703 for grants.
Purpose and activities: Support for education, including scholarships, youth agencies, and social services.
Types of support awarded: Scholarship funds.

Trustees: Leslie S. Hubbard, Chairman; Dr. James H. Smith, Vice-Chairman and Treasurer; Lowell R. Blass, Orland Fluharty, Jane F. Kelly, John J. Linney, Carl R. Weston.
Employer Identification Number: 026015114

2087
Hunt (Samuel P.) Foundation
c/o Merchants National Bank
P.O. Box 267
Manchester 03105   (603) 668-5000
Application address: 1000 Elm St., Manchester, NH 03101

Trust established in 1951 in New Hampshire.
Donor(s): Samuel P. Hunt.†
Financial data: (yr. ended 9/30/83): Assets, $3,778,480 (M); expenditures, $155,681, including $139,270 for 19 grants (high: $25,000; low: $600).
Purpose and activities: Broad purposes; local giving only, with emphasis on higher education, community funds, youth agencies, and cultural programs.
Types of support awarded: Continuing support, annual campaigns, seed money, emergency funds, building funds, equipment, land acquisition, publications, conferences and seminars, matching funds.
Limitations: Giving limited to NH. No grants to individuals, or for operating budgets, endowment funds, scholarships, or fellowships; no loans.
Publications: Program policy statement, application guidelines.
Application information:
  Initial approach: Letter or proposal
  Copies of proposal: 1
  Deadline(s): March 1 and September 1
  Board meeting date(s): March and September
  Final notification: 2 weeks after meeting
  Write: Therese A. Benoit, Assistant Vice-President
Trustees: Ralph A. McIninch, Merchants National Bank (Therese A. Benoit, Assistant Vice-President).
Number of staff: None.
Employer Identification Number: 026004471

2088
Institute of Current World Affairs, Inc.
(also known as The Crane-Rogers Foundation)
Four West Wheelock St.
Hanover 03755   (603) 643-5548

Incorporated in 1925 in New York.
Donor(s): Charles R. Crane family.
Financial data: (yr. ended 2/29/84): Assets, $952,079 (M); gifts received, $354,063; expenditures, $322,149, including $41,383 for 4 grants (high: $36,356; low: $1,000) and $110,681 for 8 grants to individuals.
Purpose and activities: A private operating foundation; includes support for a limited number of long-term fellowships to persons of exceptional ability to enable them to work on foreign or problem areas of significance to the United States; activities center around the research and study programs of its fellows, including special programs in journalism and forestry.

Types of support awarded: Fellowships.
Limitations: Giving limited to U.S. organizations. No support for formal education.
Publications: Informational brochure, application guidelines, program policy statement, annual report.
Application information:
  Initial approach: Letter
  Board meeting date(s): May and November
  Final notification: 6 months to 4 years
  Write: Peter Bird Martin, Executive Director
Officers and Trustees: Warren W. Unna, Chairman; David Binder, Vice-Chairman; Thomas Crane, Secretary; Edmond H. Sutton, Treasurer; Peter Bird Martin, Executive Director; Richard J. Balzer, Barbara Bright, Richard Dudman, David Hapgood, Edwin S. Munger, Richard H. Nolte, John O'Neil, Roger Reynolds, Stefan Robock, Anatole Shub.
Number of staff: 1 part-time professional; 1 part-time support.
Employer Identification Number: 131621044

2089
Jameson (Oleonda) Trust
One Eagle Square
P.O. Box 709
Concord 03301

Established in 1977 in New Hampshire.
Financial data: (yr. ended 12/31/84): Assets, $1,683,944 (M); expenditures, $140,108, including $109,702 for 45 grants (high: $15,000; low: $100).
Purpose and activities: Giving primarily for higher education, community funds, social agencies, hospitals, and cultural programs.
Limitations: Giving primarily in NH.
Trustees: Malcolm McLane, Dudley W. Orr, Robert H. Reno.
Employer Identification Number: 026048930

2090
Kingsbury Fund ¤
c/o Kingsbury Machine Tool Corp.
80 Laurel St.
Keene 03431   (603) 352-5212

Trust established in 1952 in New Hampshire.
Donor(s): Kingsbury Machine Tool Corporation, Kingsbury Manufacturing Company, Fitchburg Foundry, Inc.
Financial data: (yr. ended 12/31/82): Assets, $1,459,363 (M); gifts received, $300,000; expenditures, $95,444, including $86,360 for 72 grants (high: $20,000; low: $10).
Purpose and activities: Local giving for higher education, including scholarships for children of employees, youth agencies, and social services.
Types of support awarded: Matching funds, employee related scholarships.
Limitations: Giving limited to Keene, Chesire County, and the Monadnock region of NH.
Application information: Application form for scholarships only.
  Deadline(s): April 20 for scholarships
  Write: Roger W. Hetherman, Executive Trustee

Trustees: Roger W. Hetherman, Executive Trustee; John S. Cookson, Priscilla K. Frechette, Charles J. Hanrahan, James L. Koontz.
Employer Identification Number: 026004465

2091
Lord (Henry C.) Scholarship Fund Trust ¤
c/o Amoskeag National Bank and Trust Company
P.O. Box 150
Manchester 03105   (603) 624-3608

Trust established in 1978 in New Hampshire.
Donor(s): Henry C. Lord.†
Financial data: (yr. ended 6/30/83): Assets, $4,775,936 (M); expenditures, $321,090, including $271,772 for 420 grants to individuals.
Purpose and activities: Scholarships for needy residents of Peterborough, New Hampshire.
Types of support awarded: Student aid.
Limitations: Giving limited to residents of Peterborough, NH, and contiguous towns. No grants for general support, capital or endowment funds, or matching gifts; no loans.
Application information: Application form required.
  Initial approach: Letter
  Deadline(s): Submit proposal from March through May; deadline April 30 (for following academic year)
  Write: Leslie H. Goodnow, Jr.
Trustee: Amoskeag National Bank and Trust Company (Leslie H. Goodnow, Jr., Assistant Trust Officer).
Employer Identification Number: 026051741

2092
New Hampshire Charitable Fund, The ▼
One South St.
P.O. Box 1335
Concord 03301   (603) 225-6641

Community foundation incorporated in 1962 in New Hampshire.
Financial data: (yr. ended 12/31/83): Assets, $16,022,204 (M); gifts received, $2,470,947; expenditures, $1,917,250, including $1,239,056 for 354 grants (high: $207,966; low: $78), $187,428 for 205 grants to individuals and $349,636 for 175 loans.
Purpose and activities: Primarily local giving; broad charitable and educational purposes including the arts, humanities, the environment, health, and social and community services; grants primarily to inaugurate new programs and strengthen existing charitable organizations, with emphasis on program rather than capital needs; support also for college scholarships.
Types of support awarded: Seed money, loans, student aid, scholarship funds, general purposes, special projects, grants to individuals.
Limitations: Giving limited to NH. No grants to individuals (except for student aid); generally no grants for building funds, endowments, operating support, or deficit financing.
Publications: Annual report, program policy statement, application guidelines, newsletter.

Application information:
  Initial approach: Telephone
  Deadline(s): February 1, May 1, August 1, and November 1
  Board meeting date(s): March, June, September, and December
  Final notification: 4 to 6 weeks
  Write: Deborah Cowan, Associate Director
Officers and Directors: Walter J. Dunfey, Chairperson; Sylvio Dupuis, Vice-Chairperson; William B. Hart, Jr., President; Elizabeth McLane-Bradley, Secretary; Robert H. Reno, Treasurer; Irene Gallen, Hollis E. Harrington, Jr., C. Robertson Trowbridge, Kimon S. Zachos.
Number of staff: 4 full-time professional; 4 full-time support.
Employer Identification Number: 026005625

2093
Phillips (Ellis L.) Foundation
13 Dartmouth College Hwy.
Lyme 03768   (603) 795-2790

Incorporated in 1930 in New York.
Donor(s): Ellis L. Phillips.†
Financial data: (yr. ended 6/30/84): Assets, $4,198,892 (M); expenditures, $330,849, including $268,658 for 45 grants (high: $30,158; low: $1,000; average: $1,000-$10,000).
Purpose and activities: Grants for education on public issues, particularly economic education, and for religion, education, social services, the arts, historic preservation, conservation, and medical research, generally in the northeastern states.
Types of support awarded: Operating budgets, continuing support, annual campaigns, seed money, emergency funds, endowment funds, internships, fellowships, research, conferences and seminars.
Limitations: Giving primarily in in the Northeast. No grants to individuals, or for scholarships and fellowships, or matching gifts; no loans.
Publications: Annual report, application guidelines.
Application information:
  Initial approach: Letter of 1 to 3 pages
  Copies of proposal: 1
  Board meeting date(s): October, February, and May
  Write: Ellis L. Phillips, Jr., President
Officers and Directors: Ellis L. Phillips, Jr., President; Marion G. Phillips, Vice-President; Ellis L. Phillips III, Secretary; George C. Thompson, Treasurer; David L. Grumman, Laurence W. Lougee, Janet S. Stevenson, Edward E. Watts III, Elise Phillips Watts.
Number of staff: 1 part-time professional.
Employer Identification Number: 135677691

2094
Putnam Foundation ¤
150 Congress St.
P.O. Box 323
Keene 03431   (603) 352-1130

Trust established in 1952 in New Hampshire.

Financial data: (yr. ended 10/31/83): Assets, $3,409,963 (M); expenditures, $200,654, including $176,343 for 38 grants (high: $25,000; low: $50).
Purpose and activities: Primarily local giving, with emphasis on civic affairs, cultural programs, historic preservation, ecological maintenance, youth agencies, education, and conservation.
Limitations: Giving primarily in NH.
Application information:
  Initial approach: Letter
  Deadline(s): None
  Write: Robert C. Mensel, Secretary
Officer: Robert C. Mensel, Secretary.
Trustees: David F. Putnam, James A. Putnam, Rosamond P. Putnam.
Employer Identification Number: 026011388

2095
Smyth (Marion C.) Trust
875 Elm St., Rm. 615
Manchester 03101   (603) 623-3420

Established in 1946 in New Hampshire.
Donor(s): Marion C. Smyth.†
Financial data: (yr. ended 12/31/84): Assets, $2,665,555 (M); expenditures, $190,068, including $153,820 for 95 grants (high: $15,000; low: $50).
Purpose and activities: To establish and maintain the Frederick Smyth Institute of music; giving also for musical education, including scholarships in the city of Manchester (a) for the cultural benefit of the citizens of Manchester and the state of New Hampshire and (b) to aid and encourage deserving youth of Manchester and adjacent towns to increase their knowledge of the field of music.
Types of support awarded: Continuing support, equipment, scholarship funds.
Limitations: Giving limited to NH, primarily Manchester.
Application information: Application form required for student scholarships.
  Initial approach: Letter
  Copies of proposal: 1
  Board meeting date(s): As required
  Write: Lyford B. MacEwen, Chairman
Trustees: Lyford B. MacEwen, Chairman; J. Fred French, Roger E. Sundeen.
Number of staff: 1 part-time support.
Employer Identification Number: 026005793

2096
Standex Foundation of New York, Inc. ¤
c/o Standex International Corporation
Six Manor Pkwy.
Salem 03079

Incorporated in 1959 in New York as Wire-O Foundation, Inc.
Donor(s): Standex International Corporation.
Financial data: (yr. ended 12/31/82): Assets, $117,385 (M); expenditures, $105,635, including $104,758 for 78 grants (high: $9,500).

Purpose and activities: General giving, with emphasis on community funds, higher education, hospitals, health agencies, church support and church-related organizations, and youth agencies.
Application information:
  Deadline(s): None
  Write: Jack Wall, Vice-President for Industrial Relations
Officers and Directors: Thomas L. King, President and Treasurer; Warren S. Cooper, Vice-President; Robert E. Masotta, Secretary.
Employer Identification Number: 510243945

2097
Wagner (Edward) and George Hosser Scholarship Fund Trust ¤
c/o Amoskeag National Bank & Trust Company
P.O. Box 150
Manchester 03105   (603) 624-3608

Trust established in 1964 in New Hampshire.
Donor(s): Ottilie Wagner Hosser.†
Financial data: (yr. ended 6/30/83): Assets, $2,366,197 (M); expenditures, $154,296, including $125,301 for 295 grants to individuals.
Purpose and activities: Scholarship grants for college or professional education to worthy boys and young men residing in Manchester and vicinity.
Types of support awarded: Student aid.
Limitations: Giving limited to Manchester, NH.
Application information: Application form required.
  Deadline(s): April 30
  Write: Leslie H. Goodnow, Jr., Assistant Trust Officer
Trustee: Amoskeag National Bank & Trust Company.
Employer Identification Number: 026005491

NEW JERSEY

2098
Allied Corporation Foundation ▼
Columbia Rd. and Park Ave.
P.O. Box 2245R
Morristown 07960   (201) 455-2671

Incorporated in 1963 in New York; in 1982 absorbed Bunker Ramo Foundation; in 1984 absorbed Bendix Foundation.
Donor(s): Allied Corporation.
Financial data: (yr. ended 12/31/83): Assets, $411,426 (M); expenditures, $3,700,000, including $3,036,474 for 859 grants (high: $86,000; low: $1,000; average: $1,500-$5,000) and $396,919 for 2,881 employee matching gifts.

Purpose and activities: General purposes; giving primarily in areas of company operations for higher education, including fellowship and scholarship programs, and community funds; grants also for health, aging, human services, youth agencies, urban affairs, and cultural programs.

Types of support awarded: Operating budgets, continuing support, annual campaigns, seed money, emergency funds, deficit financing, building funds, equipment, land acquisition, employee matching gifts, consulting services, technical assistance, fellowships, professorships, internships, employee related scholarships, special projects, research, scholarship funds.

Limitations: Giving primarily in areas of company operations. No support for church-related programs. No grants to individuals, or for endowment funds; no loans.

Publications: Annual report.

Application information:
Initial approach: Letter
Copies of proposal: 1
Deadline(s): Submit proposal preferably in September and October; no set deadline
Board meeting date(s): February
Final notification: 3 months
Write: Margaret C. Petri, Manager-Administration

Officers: David G. Powell,* President; Alan S. Painter,* Vice-President and Executive Director; Brian D. Forrow, Edwin M. Halkyard,* Vice-Presidents; Heather M. Mullett,* Secretary; William T. Loftus,* Treasurer.

Directors:* Edward L. Hennessy, Jr., Chairman; Alan Belzer, A.H. Brockie, L. James Colby, Jr., A. Clark Johnson, Jr., W.C. Purple, J.M. Reynolds, G.L. Seelig.

Number of staff: 1 full-time professional; 1 full-time support.

Employer Identification Number: 136132567

2099
Armour Family Foundation, The
c/o Schotz Simon Miller & Co.
100 Hamilton Plaza, Suite 1400
Paterson 07505

Established in 1981.

Donor(s): George and Frances Armour Foundation, Inc.

Financial data: (yr. ended 3/31/83): Assets, $1,434,585 (M); gifts received, $138,032; expenditures, $126,368, including $96,835 for 21 grants (high: $51,000; low: $200).

Purpose and activities: General giving, with emphasis on Jewish sociological areas, medical research and hospitals, and secondary education; some support also for social agencies.

Officers: Robert N. Armour, President; David Armour, Lynne Armour, Frederick Sudekum, Margaret Armour Sudekum, Vice-Presidents; Joan Armour, Secretary.

Employer Identification Number: 510257055

2100
Atlantic Foundation, The ▼
16 Farber Rd.
Princeton 08540   (609) 799-8530

Incorporated in 1964 in New Jersey.

Donor(s): J. Seward Johnson.†

Financial data: (yr. ended 12/31/82): Assets, $80,081,613 (M); gifts received, $601,031; expenditures, $2,382,022, including $1,535,000 for 4 grants (high: $950,000; low: $85,000).

Purpose and activities: Supports marine science research and education. Available funds presently committed through 1986 for marine research off the Florida coast.

Types of support awarded: Research.

Limitations: Giving primarily in FL.

Application information: Funds committed through 1986.
Write: Trudy Puglia, Assistant Secretary

Officers and Directors: J. Seward Johnson, Jr., Chairman, President, and Treasurer; Carl Schafer, Vice-President; Marilyn C. Link, Secretary; Joyce S. Combs, Louis R. Hewitt, Gertrude Puglia.

Number of staff: 25 full-time professional.

Employer Identification Number: 226054882

2101
Belasco (The Edna & Jack) Foundation
P.O. Box 100
135 High St.
Mount Holly 08060   (609) 234-8462

Established in 1977 in New Jersey.

Donor(s): Edna R. Belasco.†

Financial data: (yr. ended 3/31/85): Assets, $1,158,004 (M); expenditures, $312,814, including $301,630 for 88 grants (high: $15,000; low: $500; average: $2,500-$10,000).

Purpose and activities: Grants for social service and youth organizations, hospitals and health agencies, education, and Protestant church support.

Types of support awarded: Building funds, special projects, scholarship funds, continuing support, seed money, emergency funds, equipment, land acquisition, matching funds, professorships, internships, scholarship funds, research, conferences and seminars.

Limitations: Giving primarily in the Delaware Valley (NJ and PA). No grants to individuals, or for operating budgets, annual campaigns, deficit financing, endowment funds, consulting services, technical assistance, exchange programs, fellowships, demonstration projects, or publications; no loans.

Application information:
Initial approach: Letter, telephone, or proposal
Copies of proposal: 1
Deadline(s): Submit proposal preferably in January or February; deadline February 28
Board meeting date(s): March and September
Final notification: Within fiscal year
Write: Peggy Maitland Henry, Executive Director

Officer: Peggy Maitland Henry, Executive Director.

Trustees: William H. Wells, Provident National Bank.

Number of staff: 1 part-time professional.

Employer Identification Number: 236656485

2102
Bergen (Frank and Lydia) Foundation
c/o First Fidelity Bank
55 Madison Ave.
Morristown 07960   (201) 829-7111

Incorporated in 1983 in New Jersey.

Donor(s): Charlotte V. Bergen.†

Financial data: (yr. ended 12/31/84): Assets, $2,363,411 (M); gifts received, $121,972; expenditures, $211,955, including $193,255 for 13 grants (high: $56,505; low: $1,000).

Purpose and activities: For the benefit of the musical arts; support for traditional music entertainment without profit to the foundation; aid for worthy students of music to gain musical education through scholarships to institutions; and assistance to organizations, such as symphony orchestras, in their public performances.

Types of support awarded: Seed money, matching funds, scholarship funds.

Limitations: Giving primarily in the NJ area, except for projects of nationwide impact. No grants for annual campaigns, deficit financing, land acquistion, renovation projects, endowment funds, or employee matching gifts; no loans.

Publications: Annual report, application guidelines, informational brochure.

Application information:
Initial approach: Letter or telephone
Copies of proposal: 1
Deadline(s): 15th of February, May, August, and November
Board meeting date(s): April, July, October, and January
Write: Jane Donnelly, Administrator

Officers and Trustee Committee: Robert H. Dunker, Chairman; A. Daniel D'Ambrosio, Vice-Chairman; Jeffrey T. Osmun, Secretary; Peter T. Lillard, Treasurer.

Trustee: First Fidelity Bank.

Staff: Jane Donnelly, Administrator.

Number of staff: 1 full-time professional.

Employer Identification Number: 226359304

2103
Berger (Sol and Margaret) Foundation ¤
140 Hepburn Rd.
Clifton 07012

Trust established in 1962 in New York.

Donor(s): Sol Berger.

Financial data: (yr. ended 4/30/83): Assets, $1,461,800 (M); expenditures, $114,632, including $100,854 for 82 grants (high: $34,000; low: $25).

Purpose and activities: Broad purposes; primarily local giving, with emphasis on medical education, youth agencies, Jewish welfare, and health agencies.

Limitations: Giving primarily in NJ and NY.

Trustees: Sandye Berger Aidner, Margaret Berger, Sol Berger, Renee Berger Kurtz, Richard Kurtz.
Employer Identification Number: 136118516

2104
Borden (The Mary Owen) Memorial Foundation
c/o Mrs. Mary L. Miles
11 Wisteria Dr.
Fords 08863   (201) 225-2178

Incorporated in 1934 in New Jersey.
Donor(s): Bertram H. Borden,† Victory Memorial Park Foundation.
Financial data: (yr. ended 12/31/83): Assets, $5,251,519 (M); expenditures, $262,079, including $218,407 for 50 grants (high: $25,000; low: $50; average: $5,000) and $24,000 for 4 grants to individuals.
Purpose and activities: Grants for programs focusing on special needs of youth which include: family planning counselling to teenagers; assistance to unwed, teenage mothers; day care centers for young, disadvantaged parents; assistance to families where instability prevails; assistance to institutions or programs aiding delinquent youth; and innovative or alternative forms of criminal justice for youthful offenders. Support also for health care, education, welfare, and music.
Types of support awarded: Seed money, matching funds, special projects.
Limitations: Giving limited to NJ, particularly Monmouth and Mercer Counties. No grants to individuals, or for scholarships (except to graduates of Rumson-Fair Haven New Jersey Regional High School) or fellowships; no loans.
Publications: Application guidelines.
Application information:
  Initial approach: Letter
  Copies of proposal: 1
  Deadline(s): March and August
  Board meeting date(s): May and October
  Final notification: 3 months
  Write: Mrs. Mary L. Miles, Secretary
Officers: Mrs. Q.A.S. McKean,* President; William H. Borden,* Vice-President; Mary L. Miles, Secretary; Mrs. Marvin Broder,* Treasurer; John C. Borden, Jr.,* Executive Director.
Trustees: * Stuart A. Young, Jr.
Employer Identification Number: 136137137

2105
Brady Foundation
P.O. Box 351
Gladstone 07934   (201) 234-1900

Incorporated in 1953 in New Jersey.
Donor(s): Helen M. Cutting,† Nicholas Brady.
Financial data: (yr. ended 12/31/84): Assets, $2,900,000 (M); expenditures, $270,000, including $231,000 for 30 grants (high: $40,000; low: $750).
Purpose and activities: Primarily local giving, with emphasis on hospitals, youth agencies, museums, and religious organizations.
Limitations: Giving primarily in NJ.
Application information:

Initial approach: Letter
Deadline(s): None
Board meeting date(s): Quarterly
Write: Joseph A. Gaunt, Secretary
Officers: James C. Brady, Jr.,* President and Treasurer; Joseph A. Gaunt, Secretary.
Trustees: * Anderson Fowler.
Number of staff: 2 part-time professional; 2 part-time support.
Employer Identification Number: 136167209

2106
Bunbury Company, Inc., The ▼
169 Nassau St.
Princeton 08542   (609) 683-1414

Incorporated in 1952 in New York.
Donor(s): Dean Mathey.†
Financial data: (yr. ended 12/31/83): Assets, $8,794,682 (M); expenditures, $740,342, including $567,426 for 23 grants (high: $437,500; low: $50).
Purpose and activities: Broad purposes; grants primarily for higher and secondary education, mainly in New Jersey, and for youth agencies.
Limitations: Giving primarily in NJ. No grants to individuals, or for building or endowment funds, scholarships, fellowships, or matching gifts; no loans.
Publications: Annual report.
Application information:
  Initial approach: Full proposal
  Copies of proposal: 1
  Deadline(s): 1 month before board meetings
  Board meeting date(s): February, May, July, and October
  Final notification: 1 to 2 weeks after board meeting
  Write: Samuel W. Lambert, III, President; Howard W. Stepp, Chairman; or Barbara L. Kesely, Assistant Secretary
Officers and Directors: Howard W. Stepp, Chairman; Samuel W. Lambert, III, President; Edward J. Toohey, Vice-President; Frank H. Dickison, Secretary; James R. Cogan, Treasurer; Charles B. Atwater, Stephan A. Morse, William B. Wright.
Number of staff: 10 part-time professional.
Employer Identification Number: 136066172

2107
Campbell Soup Fund ▼
Campbell Place
Camden 08101   (609) 342-6431

Incorporated in 1953 in New Jersey.
Donor(s): Campbell Soup Company.
Financial data: (yr. ended 6/30/83): Assets, $4,795,442 (M); gifts received, $3,000,000; expenditures, $1,433,761, including $1,406,047 for 100 grants (high: $100,000; low: $5,000; average: $5,000).
Purpose and activities: Capital grants to private institutions of higher education, and to hospitals and other health care facilities; support also for cultural programs, social service and youth agencies, community funds, and public interest groups, with emphasis on giving in areas where the company has major plants, particularly the Camden-Philadelphia area.

Types of support awarded: Building funds, employee matching gifts, matching funds, equipment.
Limitations: Giving primarily in areas of company operations, with emphasis on the Camden, NJ, and Philadelphia, PA, areas. No grants to individuals, or for operating budgets, continuing support, annual campaigns, seed money, emergency funds, deficit financing, land acquisition, endowment funds, or scholarships or fellowships; no loans.
Application information:
  Initial approach: Letter
  Copies of proposal: 1
  Deadline(s): None
  Board meeting date(s): As required
  Final notification: 4 to 8 weeks
  Write: Frank G. Moore, Vice-President
Officers and Trustees: Raymond S. Page, Jr., President; D.H. Springer, Vice-President and Treasurer; John T. Dorrance, Jr., Frank G. Moore, J.F. O'Brien, Vice-Presidents; R.L. Baker, Secretary.
Number of staff: 2 part-time professional; 2 part-time support.
Employer Identification Number: 216019196

2108
Cape Branch Foundation
c/o Dancer, Balaam & Frank
P.O. Box 419
Dayton 08810   (201) 821-7400

Established in 1964 in New Jersey.
Financial data: (yr. ended 12/31/83): Assets, $3,036,753 (M); expenditures, $244,053, including $226,205 for 11 grants (high: $50,000; low: $2,000; average: $20,500).
Purpose and activities: Primarily local giving for secondary education, conservation, museums, and a university.
Types of support awarded: Research, building funds, land acquisition, general purposes.
Limitations: Giving primarily in NJ. No grants to individuals.
Publications: 990-PF.
Application information:
  Initial approach: Brief letter
  Deadline(s): None
  Board meeting date(s): Annually
  Write: Dorothy Frank
Directors: Gretchen W. Johnson,* James L. Johnson.
Trustees: * John R. Wittenborn.
Number of staff: None.
Employer Identification Number: 226054886

2109
Carnegie Foundation for the Advancement of Teaching, The
Five Ivy Ln.
Princeton 08540   (609) 452-1780

Established in 1905 under New York State charter; incorporated in 1906 under an Act of Congress.
Donor(s): Andrew Carnegie.†

Financial data: (yr. ended 6/30/84): Assets, $36,073,656 (M); gifts received, $1,031,087; expenditures, $2,870,061, including $1,547,339 for foundation-administered programs.
Purpose and activities: A private operating foundation established to provide retirement allowances for teachers of universities, colleges, and technical schools in the United States and Canada; and in general, to do all things necessary to encourage, uphold, and dignify the profession of teaching and the cause of higher education in the United States and Canada. At present part of its income is still committed to the pension program, although the list of eligibles closed in 1931. A limited number of grants are given for research and policy studies on higher education.
Types of support awarded: Consulting services, technical assistance, research.
Limitations: No grants to individuals, or for general support, capital or endowment funds, matching gifts, scholarships, fellowships, special projects, publications, or conferences; no loans.
Publications: Annual report.
Application information: Grants usually initiated by the foundation.
Initial approach: Letter
Deadline(s): None
Board meeting date(s): April and November
Final notification: 90 days
Write: Verne A. Stadtman, Vice-President
Officers: Ernest L. Boyer,* President; Verne A. Stadtman, Vice-President - General Services; Jean Van Gorden, Secretary and Treasurer.
Trustees:* Adele Simmons, Chairperson; Frank H.T. Rhodes, Vice-Chairperson; Ernest L. Boyer, Eugene Cola-Robles, Lawrence A. Cremin, Alonzo Crim, William R. Dill, Robert Edwards, Nell P. Eurich, Daniel J. Evans, Norman Francis, Patricia A. Graham, David W. Hornbeck, Stanley Ikenberry, Leslie Koltai, Walter Leonard, Marigold Linton, Mary Patterson McPherson, Frank Newman, Robert M. O'Neil, Alan Pifer, Donald C. Platten, Lauren Resnick, Barbara Uehling, John C. Whitehead.
Number of staff: 7 full-time professional; 1 part-time professional; 9 full-time support.
Employer Identification Number: 131623924

2110
Carroll Foundation ⌑
70 Enterprise Ave.
Secaucus 07094

Established in 1980.
Donor(s): Milton Petrie.
Financial data: (yr. ended 12/31/81): Assets, $61,296 (M); gifts received, $350,000; expenditures, $343,795, including $342,750 for 61 grants to individuals.
Purpose and activities: Grants primarily to assist needy individuals; some giving also for education and Roman Catholic church support.
Types of support awarded: Grants to individuals.
Directors: Carroll Petrie, Milton Petrie.
Employer Identification Number: 222299776

2111
Caspersen (O. W.) Foundation for Aid to Health and Education, Inc.
76 Route 206
P.O. Box 800
Andover 07821 (201) 786-5354

Incorporated in 1964 in Delaware.
Donor(s): O.W. Caspersen.†
Financial data: (yr. ended 12/31/84): Assets, $1,595,076 (M); expenditures, $221,578, including $221,500 for 12 grants (high: $50,000; low: $1,000).
Purpose and activities: General purposes; giving mainly on the East Coast for higher and secondary education and hospitals. Present policy to make grants only to those educational and health-oriented institutions with which the Foundation has had extensive previous experience.
Types of support awarded: Operating budgets, continuing support, annual campaigns, emergency funds, building funds, equipment, land acquisition, research.
Limitations: Giving primarily in the eastern coastal states. No grants to individuals, or for seed money, scholarships, fellowships, or matching gifts; no loans.
Application information:
Initial approach: Letter
Copies of proposal: 1
Board meeting date(s): January and July
Write: Finn M.W. Caspersen, Vice-President
Officers and Directors: Freda R. Caspersen, President; Finn M.W. Caspersen, Vice-President and Treasurer; Barbara M. Caspersen.
Number of staff: None.
Employer Identification Number: 510101350

2112
C.I.T. Foundation, Inc., The
650 C.I.T. Dr.
Livingston 07039

Incorporated in 1955 in New York.
Donor(s): C.I.T. Financial Corporation, and its subsidiaries.
Financial data: (yr. ended 12/31/84): Assets, $220,039 (M); expenditures, $135,822, including $106,902 for 24 grants (high: $45,000; low: $50) and $28,920 for 95 employee matching gifts.
Purpose and activities: Charitable and educational purposes; support largely for community funds and education; giving limited to areas of C.I.T. operations.
Limitations: Giving limited to areas of company operations. No grants to individuals.
Officers and Directors:* Todd G. Cole,* President; John J. Carroll, H.A. Ittleson,* C.L. Wingfield, Vice-Presidents; J.O. Gregory, Secretary.
Employer Identification Number: 136083856

2113
CPC Educational Foundation ⌑
International Plaza
P.O. Box 8000
Englewood 07632 (201) 894-2249

Established in 1961.
Financial data: (yr. ended 11/30/82): Assets, $1,709,747 (M); expenditures, $143,121, including $132,600 for 96 grants to individuals.
Purpose and activities: Giving for college scholarships.
Types of support awarded: Student aid.
Publications: Application guidelines, program policy statement.
Application information: Application form required.
Write: Linda Salcito
Officers: William F. Cody,* President; Luis Schuchinski, Vice-President; John B. Meagher, Secretary; James J. Nicholson,* Treasurer.
Directors:* Richard P. Bergeman, Clifford B. Storms.
Employer Identification Number: 136103949

2114
Crum and Forster Foundation ▼
305 Madison Ave.
P.O. Box 2387
Morristown 07960 (201) 285-7247

Incorporated in 1953 in California as the Industrial Indemnity Foundation.
Donor(s): Crum and Forster, and affiliated companies.
Financial data: (yr. ended 12/31/83): Assets, $600,000 (M); expenditures, $1,105,795, including $1,105,750 for 808 grants (high: $36,000; low: $50; average: $500).
Purpose and activities: General giving, with emphasis on community funds, youth agencies, health agencies, higher and secondary education, hospitals, safety, culture and the arts, and civic affairs.
Limitations: No support for political organizations or candidates, or religious organizations or activities. No grants to individuals or for matching gifts; no loans.
Application information:
Initial approach: Letter or full proposal
Deadline(s): Submit proposal preferably from September through November; deadline November 30
Board meeting date(s): March and as required
Write: John A. Douglas, Vice-President
Officers: John K. Lundberg,* President; John A. Douglas, Vice-President; Antoinette C. Bentley,* Secretary; George J. Rachmiel, Treasurer.
Trustees:* Sidney F. Wentz, Chairman; Walter T. Biel, B.P. Russell.
Employer Identification Number: 946065476

2115
Diller (The William & Helen) Charitable Foundation ⌑
9614 Third Ave.
Stone Harbor 08247

Established in 1972.
Donor(s): William J. Diller.†
Financial data: (yr. ended 9/30/83): Assets, $1,177,804 (M); expenditures, $76,496, including $9,224 for 15 grants (high: $2,500).
Purpose and activities: Local giving for charitable purposes.
Limitations: Giving primarily in NJ.
Employer Identification Number: 237200648

2116
Dodge (Geraldine R.) Foundation, Incorporated ▼
95 Madison Ave.
P.O. Box 1239R
Morristown 07960 (201) 540-8442

Incorporated in 1974 in New Jersey.
Donor(s): Geraldine R. Dodge.†
Financial data: (yr. ended 12/31/84): Assets, $97,285,629 (M); expenditures, $4,353,304, including $4,015,288 for 199 grants (high: $285,500; average: $5,000-$100,000).
Purpose and activities: Grant-making emphasis in New Jersey, on secondary education, performing and visual arts and other cultural activities, projects in population, environment, energy, and other critical areas, and programs in the public interest, including development of volunteerism, communications, and study of public issues. Interest in independent secondary schools in New England and Middle Atlantic states and in projects on the national level that are likely to lead to significant advances in secondary education. Commitment to animal welfare concentrates on national strategies for coping with problems posed by burgeoning populations of pets and stray dogs and cats. Interest in the development of a gentler ethic and reduced societal and domestic violence.
Types of support awarded: Seed money, conferences and seminars, matching funds, general purposes, special projects, publications, continuing support.
Limitations: Giving primarily in NJ, with some giving in the other Middle Atlantic states, New England, and to national organizations. No support for religion, higher education, health, international programs, or conduit organizations. No grants to individuals, or for capital projects, endowment funds, deficit financing, scholarships, or fellowships.
Publications: Annual report.
Application information:
Initial approach: Letter or full proposal
Copies of proposal: 1
Deadline(s): Submit proposal preferably in March, June, September, or December; deadlines January 1 for animal welfare and local projects; April 1 for secondary education; July 1 for the arts; and October 1 for critical issues/public interest
Board meeting date(s): March, June, September, and December
Final notification: By the end of the month in which board meetings are held
Write: Scott McVay, Executive Director
Officers: William Rockefeller,* Chairman and President; Scott McVay, Executive Director.
Trustees:* Robert H.B. Baldwin, Barbara Knowles Debs, Henry U. Harder, Robert LeBuhn, David Hunter McAlpin, Walter J. Neppl, Paul J. O'Donnell, Edwin J. Sayres.
Number of staff: 4 full-time professional; 3 full-time support; 1 part-time support.
Employer Identification Number: 237406010

2117
Dow Jones Newspaper Fund, Inc., The
P.O. Box 300
Princeton 08540 (609) 452-2820

Incorporated in 1958 in Delaware.
Donor(s): Dow Jones & Company, Inc., and other news companies.
Financial data: (yr. ended 12/31/84): Assets, $383,641 (M); gifts received, $368,703; expenditures, $351,720, including $123,261 for 30 grants (high: $20,986; low: $2,000), $69,978 for 193 grants to individuals and $16,305 for 3 foundation-administered programs.
Purpose and activities: Major effort devoted to practical newspaper experience for college students and journalism training for inner-city high school students, high school teachers of journalism, and high school publications advisors. Scholarships for 40 college juniors and 10 minority seniors completing summer work on a newspaper. Names National High School Journalism Teacher of the Year. Sponsors a journalism career information program.
Types of support awarded: Fellowships, special projects, student aid.
Limitations: No grants for building or endowment funds, research, special projects, publications, or conferences and seminars; no loans.
Publications: Annual report, application guidelines.
Application information: Grant application guidelines available for minority high school programs. Application form required.
Initial approach: Letter
Copies of proposal: 1
Deadline(s): Submit proposal preferably in September; deadline October 1
Board meeting date(s): May and November
Final notification: December 1
Write: Thomas E. Engleman, Executive Director
Officers and Directors: Edward R. Cony, President; Everett Groseclose, Vice-President and Secretary; Warren H. Phillips, Vice-President; Thomas E. Engleman, Executive Director; Donnel E. Carter, Betty Duval, Jay Harris, Linda Martelli, Paul S. Swensson, Frederick Taylor.
Number of staff: 3 full-time professional; 2 full-time support.
Employer Identification Number: 136021439

2118
Duke (The Doris) Foundation, Inc. ⌑
Duke Farms
P.O. Box 2030
Somerville 08876

Incorporated in 1934 in Delaware.
Donor(s): Doris Duke.
Financial data: (yr. ended 12/31/82): Assets, $913,872 (M); expenditures, $253,455, including $232,855 for 24 grants (high: $100,000; low: $250).
Purpose and activities: General purposes; grants to charitable institutions on an annual basis, with priority given to agencies in New York, New Jersey, and California; support for social service programs, improved services for the aging, child welfare and aid to agencies giving relief and medical care; support also for cultural organizations.
Limitations: Giving primarily in NJ, NY, and CA. No support for religious organizations for sectarian purposes. No grants to individuals, or for building or capital funds, publications, or general operating expenses.
Officer and Directors: Doris Duke, President; Lloyd A. Pantages.
Employer Identification Number: 131655241

2119
Edison (Charles) Fund
101 South Harrison St.
East Orange 07018 (201) 675-9000

Incorporated in 1948 in Delaware.
Donor(s): Charles Edison,† and others.
Financial data: (yr. ended 12/31/84): Assets, $15,651,099 (M); gifts received, $148,143; expenditures, $779,244, including $278,885 for 43 grants (high: $40,000; low: $50) and $172,869 for 8 foundation-administered programs.
Purpose and activities: Grants largely for historic preservation, with emphasis on the homes of Thomas Alva Edison; and for education, medical research, and hospitals. Support also for foundation-sponsored exhibits at over 80 museums throughout the U.S., for science education teaching kits in over 20,000 classrooms, and for cassette re-recording of antique phonograph records for schools and museums.
Types of support awarded: Operating budgets, continuing support, seed money, special projects, research.
Limitations: No grants to individuals, or for building or endowment funds, scholarships and fellowships, or matching gifts; no loans.
Publications: Informational brochure, application guidelines.
Application information:
Initial approach: Letter or full proposal
Copies of proposal: 1
Deadline(s): 30 days prior to board meetings
Board meeting date(s): March, June, September, and December
Write: Paul J. Christiansen, President
Officers and Trustees: Paul J. Christiansen, President; Roger M. Dolan, Vice-President; David O. Schantz, Secretary-Treasurer; Nancy M. Arnn, James E. Howe, Howard G. Kafer, Alice F. Stevenson, John D. Venable, Melvin J. Weig.
Number of staff: 2 full-time professional; 1 part-time professional; 2 full-time support.
Employer Identification Number: 221514861

2120
Elizabeth Foundation, The ¤
c/o Lum, Biunno & Tompkins
550 Broad St.
Newark 07102   (201) 622-2300

Incorporated in 1974 in New Jersey.
Donor(s): The Fund for New Jersey.
Financial data: (yr. ended 3/31/84): Assets, $2,543,918 (M); expenditures, $214,186, including $187,000 for 32 grants (high: $20,000; low: $1,000).
Purpose and activities: General giving, particularly in South Carolina and other southern states, with emphasis on aid to the aged, youth, and minorities; grants also for hospitals, education, and social agencies.
Limitations: Giving primarily in SC and other southern states.
Application information:
  Initial approach: Letter
  Write: William B. Lum, Executive Director
Officers: Elizabeth W. Ellis, President; Raymond G. Ellis, Vice-President, Secretary, and Treasurer; William B. Lum, Vice-President and Executive Director.
Employer Identification Number: 237379321

2121
Engelhard (The Charles) Foundation ▼ ¤
P.O. Box 427
Far Hills 07931   (201) 766-7224

Incorporated in 1940 in New Jersey.
Donor(s): Charles Engelhard,† Engelhard Hanovia, Inc., and others.
Financial data: (yr. ended 12/31/83): Assets, $61,688,308 (M); expenditures, $4,533,540, including $4,038,040 for 106 grants (high: $550,000; low: $1,000; average: $5,000-$50,000).
Purpose and activities: General giving, with emphasis on higher and secondary education, and cultural, medical, religious, wildlife, and conservation organizations.
Limitations: No grants to individuals.
Application information:
  Initial approach: Proposal
  Copies of proposal: 1
  Deadline(s): None
  Board meeting date(s): Quarterly
  Final notification: Varies
  Write: Elaine Catterall, Secretary
Officers: Jane B. Engelhard,* President; Elaine Catterall, Secretary; Edward G. Beimfohr,* Treasurer.
Trustees:* Charlene B. Engelhard, Sophie Engelhard, Michael J. Mansfield, Susan O'Connor, Sally E. Pingree, Anne E. Reed.
Employer Identification Number: 226063032

2122
Fidelity Union Foundation ¤
c/o Fidelity Union Bank, Trustee
765 Broad St.
Newark 07101

Established in 1955 in New Jersey.
Donor(s): Fidelity Union Bank.

Financial data: (yr. ended 12/31/82): Assets, $151,596 (M); expenditures, $209,984, including $209,951 for 32 grants (high: $100,000; low: $10).
Purpose and activities: Primarily local giving, with emphasis on a community fund and community development; support also for education and youth agencies.
Limitations: Giving primarily in NJ.
Application information:
  Initial approach: Letter
  Deadline(s): None
Trustee: Fidelity Union Bank.
Employer Identification Number: 226019976

2123
Frelinghuysen Foundation, The ¤
P.O. Box 726
Far Hills 07931

Incorporated in 1950 in New Jersey.
Donor(s): The Frelinghuysen family.
Financial data: (yr. ended 12/31/82): Assets, $974,314 (M); expenditures, $196,657, including $150,500 for 37 grants (high: $20,000; low: $500).
Purpose and activities: Charitable giving, primarily in New York and New Jersey, with emphasis on higher and secondary education, cultural programs, and hospitals.
Limitations: Giving primarily in NJ and NY.
Application information:
  Deadline(s): None
  Write: Frederick Frelinghuysen, Vice-President
Officers and Directors: George L.K. Frelinghuysen, President; Frank E. Carr, Frederick Frelinghuysen, H.O.H. Frelinghuysen, Peter Frelinghuysen, Vice-Presidents; John F. Szczepanski, Secretary; Barratt Frelinghuysen, Mrs. H.O.H. Frelinghuysen, Mrs. Peter H.B. Frelinghuysen, Rodney P. Frelinghuysen, Beatrice van Roijen.
Employer Identification Number: 221723755

2124
Frisch Foundation, Inc., The ¤
1600 Parker Ave.
Fort Lee 07024
Mailing address: c/o A. Kadish, 501 East 79th St., New York, NY 10021

Foundation incorporated in 1961 in New York.
Donor(s): Alfred M. Frisch, Ethel Frisch.
Financial data: (yr. ended 6/30/81): Assets, $2,040,479 (M); expenditures, $456,786, including $437,823 for 96 grants (high: $125,000; low: $10).
Purpose and activities: Grants largely for Jewish welfare funds and temple support in the United States and Israel, higher education, women's organizations, and hospitals.
Officer and Trustee: Alfred M. Frisch, President.
Employer Identification Number: 136113829

2125
Fund for New Jersey, The ▼
57 Washington St.
East Orange 07017   (201) 676-5905

Incorporated in 1969 in New Jersey as successor to The Florence Murray Wallace Fund established in 1958.
Donor(s): Charles F. Wallace,† and members of his family.
Financial data: (yr. ended 12/31/83): Assets, $15,464,718 (M); expenditures, $1,096,037, including $906,634 for 37 grants (high: $34,000; low: $3,500).
Purpose and activities: Charitable purposes; giving primarily to local organizations, with emphasis on projects which provide the basis for public action on state or local problems by way of research, litigation, citizen action, or government supervision.
Types of support awarded: Seed money, research, special projects, publications, conferences and seminars, matching funds, general purposes.
Limitations: Giving primarily in NJ or to regional programs that benefit NJ residents. No support for recreation, day care centers, drug treatment programs, health care delivery, or curricular changes in educational institutions. No grants to individuals, or for capital projects, equipment, endowment funds, scholarships and fellowships, or debt reduction; no loans.
Publications: Annual report, informational brochure, program policy statement, application guidelines.
Application information:
  Initial approach: Letter
  Copies of proposal: 1
  Deadline(s): None
  Board meeting date(s): March, June, September, and December
  Final notification: 2 weeks after board meeting
  Write: Robert P. Corman, Executive Director
Officers: Jos. C. Cornwall,* Chairman and Treasurer; Richard J. Sullivan,* President; John J. Gibbons,* Vice-President; Robert P. Corman, Executive Director and Secretary.
Trustees:* William O. Baker, Barbara W. Cornwall, Dickinson R. Debevoise, David F. Freeman, Robert F. Goheen, Gustav Heningburg, Mary S. Strong, Jane W. Thorne.
Number of staff: 2 full-time professional; 1 part-time professional; 1 full-time support.
Employer Identification Number: 221895028

2126
Geist Foundation, The
c/o J. H. Cohn & Company
810 Broad St.
Newark 07102   (201) 624-6300

Incorporated about 1959 in New Jersey.
Donor(s): Irving Geist.†
Financial data: (yr. ended 9/30/82): Assets, $1,431,050 (M); expenditures, $196,071, including $190,988 for 33 grants (high: $90,828; low: $60).
Purpose and activities: Primarily local grants, largely for Jewish welfare funds; support also for higher education and medical research.

Limitations: Giving primarily in NJ and NY.
No grants to individuals.
Publications: 990-PF.
Application information:
 Initial approach: Letter
 Copies of proposal: 1
 Board meeting date(s): As required
 Write: Louis Rones, President
Officers and Trustees: Louis Rones, President;
Steven Rones, Vice-President; Benjamin Alpert,
Secretary and Treasurer.
Employer Identification Number: 226059859

2127
Grassmann (E. J.) Trust
P.O. Box 4470
Watchung 07060   (201) 753-2440

Trust established in 1979 in New Jersey.
Donor(s): Edward J. Grassmann.†
Financial data: (yr. ended 12/31/83): Assets,
$24,145,081 (M); gifts received, $12,297;
expenditures, $1,868,193, including
$1,626,600 for 62 grants (high: $135,000; low:
$2,500).
Purpose and activities: Giving primarily
locally and in Georgia, with grants for hospitals,
higher and secondary education, ecology and
social agencies, especially child welfare, and
religious and historical associations. Preference
given to organizations with low administration
costs, and which show efforts to achieve a
broad funding base.
Types of support awarded: Endowment
funds, scholarship funds, building funds,
equipment, land acquisition.
Limitations: Giving primarily in NJ, particularly
Union County, and in GA. No grants to
individuals, or for operating expenses.
Publications: Application guidelines.
Application information:
 Initial approach: Letter
 Deadline(s): April 20 and October 15
 Board meeting date(s): May and November
 Write: William V. Engel, Executive Director
Officer: William V. Engel, Executive Director.
Trustees: Charles Danzig, Edward G. Engel,
Joseph G. Engel, John B. Harris, Haydn H.
Murray.
Employer Identification Number: 226326539

2128
Grupe (William F.) Foundation, Inc.
22 Old Short Hills Rd.
Livingston 07039   (201) 740-1919

Established in 1967.
Donor(s): William F. Grupe.†
Financial data: (yr. ended 12/31/82): Assets,
$1,057,505 (M); expenditures, $158,768,
including $143,450 for 162 grants to
individuals.
Purpose and activities: Medical and nursing
scholarships for New Jersey residents planning
to practice within the state.
Types of support awarded: Student aid.
Limitations: Giving limited to NJ.
Publications: Application guidelines.
Application information: Two letters of
recommendation required. Application form
required.

 Deadline(s): March 1
 Write: Abdol H. Islami, M.D., President
Officers: Abdol H. Islami, M.D., President;
George P. Moser, Vice-President; Edward C.
Klein, Jr., M.D., Vice-President and Treasurer;
Lynn Van Borkulo, Secretary.
Employer Identification Number: 226094704

2129
Hackett Foundation, Inc., The ▼
2124 Oak Tree Rd.
Edison 08820   (201) 548-3686

Incorporated in 1975 in New York.
Donor(s): William J. Hackett.
Financial data: (yr. ended 12/31/82): Assets,
$7,752,418 (M); expenditures, $591,842,
including $457,917 for 26 grants (high:
$31,500; low: $3,025; average: $20,000).
Purpose and activities: Grants primarily to
Catholic foreign missions; also giving to
Catholic health and social service agencies
located in New Jersey, New York, and
Pennsylvania.
Types of support awarded: General purposes,
building funds, equipment, operating budgets,
continuing support, annual campaigns, seed
money, emergency funds, deficit financing,
special projects.
Limitations: Giving limited to NJ, NY, PA, and
Catholic missions overseas. No grants to
individuals, or for land acquisition, endowment
funds, matching gifts, scholarships, fellowships,
research, demonstration projects, publications,
or conferences; no loans.
Publications: Application guidelines.
Application information: Application form
required.
 Initial approach: Letter
 Deadline(s): April 30 and October 30
 Board meeting date(s): 30th of each month
 Final notification: 60 days
 Write: Alice T. Hackett, Chair, Grant
  Committee
Officers: R. Kevin Hackett, President; Dennis
Hackett, Vice-President and Treasurer; Alice T.
Hackett, Secretary.
Trustees: Rev. Denis Hackett, Sister Patricia
Mary Hackett.
Number of staff: 2 full-time professional.
Employer Identification Number: 132840750

2130
Harris Brothers Foundation ⌗
Stonewyck Sutton Rd., RD2
Lebanon 08833

Established in 1956 in Delaware.
Donor(s): Members of the Harris family.
Financial data: (yr. ended 12/31/82): Assets,
$1,952,156 (M); gifts received, $3,500;
expenditures, $120,537, including $105,600
for 44 grants (high: $100,600; low: $40).
Purpose and activities: Giving primarily for
local Protestant church support.
Limitations: Giving primarily in NJ.
Officers: Walter I. Harris, President; George
W. Harris, Vice-President; Barbara Harris,
Secretary and Treasurer.
Trustee: Lois J. Stilwell.
Employer Identification Number: 136167230

2131
Hoffmann-La Roche Foundation, The
P.O. Box 278
Nutley 07110   (201) 235-3797

Trust established in 1945 in New Jersey.
Donor(s): Hoffmann-La Roche, Inc.
Financial data: (yr. ended 12/31/84): Assets,
$49 (M); gifts received, $223,417;
expenditures, $223,417, including $223,417
for 15 grants (high: $75,000; low: $1,000).
Purpose and activities: Giving for medical and
scientific research at post-doctoral level at
leading universities and teaching hospitals.
Types of support awarded: Research,
fellowships.
Limitations: No grants to individuals, or for
general support, operating budgets, capital or
endowment funds, matching gifts, special
projects, publications, or conferences; no loans.
Publications: Application guidelines.
Application information:
 Initial approach: Letter
 Copies of proposal: 1
 Board meeting date(s): As required
 Final notification: 4 to 6 weeks
 Write: Rosemary Bruner, Administrative
  Director
Officer: H.F. Boardman, Secretary.
Trustees: E.B. Anderson, R.G. Kuntzman, I.
Lerner, M.F. Stadler, J. Weber.
Number of staff: None.
Employer Identification Number: 226063790

2132
Hoyt Foundation, The ⌗
Half Acre Rd.
Cranbury 08512

Incorporated in 1957 in Delaware.
Financial data: (yr. ended 6/30/83): Assets,
$3,105,672 (M); expenditures, $129,310,
including $122,000 for 20 grants (high:
$22,000; low: $1,000).
Purpose and activities: Educational and
charitable purposes; grants primarily for higher
and secondary education, with emphasis on
medical education and research; support also
for health agencies and hospitals, the
handicapped, and music, largely in New Jersey
and New York.
Limitations: Giving primarily in NJ and NY.
No grants to individuals.
Officers and Trustees: Henry H. Hoyt,
President; Frank M. Berger, M.D., Vice-
President; Charles O. Hoyt, Secretary; Henry
H. Hoyt, Jr., Treasurer; Suzanne H. Weil.
Employer Identification Number: 136110857

2133
Huber Foundation, The ▼
P.O. Box 277
Rumson 07760   (201) 842-3733

Incorporated in 1949 in New Jersey.
Donor(s): Marion Huber, Hans W. Huber,†
Catherine G. Huber, Robert E. Mertens,
Gertrude H. Mertens, and others.

Financial data: (yr. ended 12/31/83): Assets, $15,011,031 (M); expenditures, $804,536, including $696,000 for 40 grants (high: $125,000; low: $2,000; average: $1,000-$20,000).
Purpose and activities: Grants primarily to organizations working in the areas of family planning, reproductive freedom and population control.
Types of support awarded: Annual campaigns, matching funds, operating budgets, seed money, special projects.
Limitations: Giving limited to the U.S. No grants to individuals, or for scholarships or fellowships, research, or building or endowment funds; no loans.
Publications: Annual report.
Application information:
  Initial approach: Letter
  Copies of proposal: 1
  Deadline(s): None
  Board meeting date(s): 4 times a year, dates not fixed
  Final notification: 3 months
  Write: Lorraine Barnhart, Program Director
Officers: Hans A. Huber,* President; David G. Huber,* Vice-President; Michael W. Huber, Secretary; Julia Ann Nagy, Treasurer.
Trustees:* Marion Huber, Gertrude H. Mertens.
Number of staff: 1 part-time professional.
Employer Identification Number: 210737062

2134
Hyde and Watson Foundation, The ▼
(formerly The Lillia Babbitt Hyde Foundation; The John Jay and Eliza Jane Watson Foundation)
437 Southern Blvd.
Chatham Township 07928   (201) 966-6024

The Lillia Babbitt Hyde Foundation incorporated in 1924 in New York; The John Jay and Eliza Jane Watson Foundation incorporated in 1949; consolidation of two foundations into Hyde and Watson Foundation in 1983.
Donor(s): Lillia Babbitt Hyde,† Eliza Jane Watson.†
Financial data: (yr. ended 12/31/83): Assets, $33,429,783 (M); expenditures, $2,177,691, including $1,787,520 for 123 grants (high: $50,000; low: $500) and $57,220 for 1 foundation-administered program.
Purpose and activities: Broad purposes; support primarily for facilities, equipment and other developmental capital needs and projects of educational and religious institutions, and of social and health agencies, primarily in the New York-New Jersey metropolitan area. Includes projects designed to increase the efficiency, quality, or capacity of important programs and services or to provide primarily capital seed money to establish new programs and services to meet important public needs.
Types of support awarded: Seed money, emergency funds, building funds, equipment, land acquisition, matching funds, research.
Limitations: Giving primarily in the NY-NJ metropolitan area. No grants to individuals, or generally for operating budgets, continuing support, annual campaigns, endowment funds, deficit financing, or scholarships.

Publications: Annual report, application guidelines, program policy statement.
Application information: Application format required if proposal is considered by grants committee. Application form required.
  Initial approach: Letter
  Copies of proposal: 1
  Deadline(s): Submit preliminary letter of appeal by February 15 for spring meeting and by September 15 for fall meeting
  Board meeting date(s): April/May and November/December
  Write: Robert W. Parsons, Jr., President
Officers and Trustees: John G. MacKechnie, Chairman; Robert W. Parsons, Jr., President and Principal Officer; Roger B. Parsons, Vice-President and Secretary; Hunter W. Corbin, Vice-President; John W. Holman, Jr., Treasurer; Joseph G. Engel, David G. Ferguson, G. Morrison Hubbard, Jr., Richard W. KixMiller.
Number of staff: 7 full-time professional.
Employer Identification Number: 222425725

2135
International Foundation, The ▼
c/o John D. Carrico & Associates
10 Park Place, P.O. Box 88
Butler 07405   (201) 838-4664
Grant application office: c/o Chandler McC. Brooks, M.D., Box 31, Downstate Medical Center, 450 Clarkson Ave., Brooklyn, NY 11203; Tel.: (718) 270-3106

Incorporated in 1948 in Delaware.
Financial data: (yr. ended 12/31/84): Assets, $10,500,000 (M); expenditures, $518,000, including $413,750 for 22 grants (high: $60,000; low: $1,000).
Purpose and activities: To conduct and/or support medical, educational, humanitarian, scientific, technical, cultural, and other enterprises in the United States which focus on international matters.
Types of support awarded: Seed money, building funds, equipment, publications, conferences and seminars, continuing support.
Limitations: No grants to individuals, or for endowment funds, operating budgets, scholarships and fellowships, or matching gifts; no loans.
Publications: Program policy statement.
Application information:
  Initial approach: Letter
  Copies of proposal: 2
  Deadline(s): Submit proposal preferably from November to March
  Board meeting date(s): January, April, July, and October
  Final notification: 6 months
  Write: Chandler McC. Brooks, M.D., Chairman, Grants Committee
Officers: Wallace S. Jones,* President; Frank Madden,* Vice-President; John D. Carrico, Secretary-Treasurer.
Trustees:* Chandler McC. Brooks, M.D., Duncan W. Clark, M.D., J. Carter Hammel, Edward Holmes.
Number of staff: 1 part-time support.
Employer Identification Number: 131962255

2136
Ix Foundation, The ⌘
560 Sylvan Ave.
Englewood Cliffs 07632

Incorporated in 1948 in New Jersey.
Donor(s): Franklin Ix and Sons.
Financial data: (yr. ended 12/31/82): Assets, $1,308,379 (M); expenditures, $163,776, including $143,002 for 91 grants (high: $20,000; low: $16).
Purpose and activities: Primarily local grants for higher and secondary education, Roman Catholic church support, hospitals, and community development.
Limitations: Giving primarily in NJ and areas of company operations.
Application information: Apply to local personnel manager. Application form required.
  Deadline(s): None
Managers: Alexander E. Ix, Jr., Douglas E. Ix, Mary Catherine Gaynor, Barbara E. Leis.
Employer Identification Number: 221713050

2137
Jeffery (Clara L. D.) Charitable Residuary Trust ⌘
c/o Summit & Elizabeth Trust Company
367 Springfield Ave.
Summit 07901

Trust established in 1969.
Donor(s): Clara L.D. Jeffery.†
Financial data: (yr. ended 12/31/82): Assets, $4,271,776 (M); expenditures, $406,498, including $301,500 for 17 grants (high: $90,000; low: $1,000).
Purpose and activities: Grants largely to organizations for prevention of cruelty to animals and for higher education.
Application information: Applications not invited.
Trustees: Coleman Burke, Leslie A. Wagner, Summit & Elizabeth Trust Company.
Employer Identification Number: 226138410

2138
Jockey Hollow Foundation, Inc., The
P.O. Box 134
Bernardsville 07924

Incorporated in 1960 in New Jersey.
Donor(s): Carl Shirley, Mrs. Carl Shirley.
Financial data: (yr. ended 3/31/83): Assets, $6,676,537 (M); gifts received, $204,025; expenditures, $493,976, including $408,527 for 49 grants (high: $78,000; low: $500).
Purpose and activities: Broad purposes; primarily local giving, with emphasis on scholarship funds, secondary education, conservation, hospitals, and cultural programs.
Types of support awarded: Scholarship funds.
Limitations: Giving primarily in NJ and NY.
Officers and Trustees: Betsy S. Michel, President and Secretary; Charles B. Laing, Vice-President and Treasurer; Joanne S. Forkner, Carl Shirley, Vice-Presidents; Virginia L. Hartmann, Clifford L. Michel, Betsy B. Shirley.
Employer Identification Number: 221724138

2139
Johnson & Johnson Family of Companies Contribution Fund ▼

One Johnson & Johnson Plaza
New Brunswick 08933   (201) 524-6747

Incorporated in 1953 in New Jersey.
Donor(s): Johnson and Johnson, and subsidiary companies.
Financial data: (yr. ended 12/31/83): Assets, $760,000 (M); gifts received, $6,070,000; expenditures, $5,366,000, including $4,000,000 for 300 grants (high: $625,000; low: $200; average: $1,000-$25,000) and $1,366,000 for 1,800 employee matching gifts.
Purpose and activities: General purposes; grants for projects or organizations which advance science and technology in the health care and medical fields. Support also for higher education, arts and cultural programs, civic affairs and public interest organizations, social welfare, including community funds, and an employee matching gifts program.
Types of support awarded: Operating budgets, continuing support, annual campaigns, emergency funds, matching funds, fellowships, research, technical assistance, special projects, employee matching gifts.
Limitations: Giving primarily in areas where company has facilities, to both national and local organizations. No grants to individuals, or for deficit financing, capital or endowment funds, demonstration projects, or publications; no loans.
Publications: Application guidelines, program policy statement.
Application information:
  Initial approach: Telephone or letter
  Copies of proposal: 1
  Deadline(s): None
  Board meeting date(s): March, June, September, and December
  Final notification: 2 months
  Write: Herbert T. Nelson, Vice-President
Officers and Trustees: John J. Heldrich, President; Herbert T. Nelson, William J. Ryan, Vice-Presidents; Andrew J. Markey, Treasurer; G.M. Gorran.
Number of staff: 2 full-time professional; 2 full-time support.
Employer Identification Number: 226062811

2140
Johnson (The Robert Wood) Foundation ▼

P.O. Box 2316
Princeton 08540   (609) 452-8701

Incorporated in 1936 in New Jersey.
Donor(s): Robert Wood Johnson.†
Financial data: (yr. ended 12/31/84): Assets, $1,173,836,335 (M); gifts received, $1,100; expenditures, $65,825,380, including $57,737,244 for 208 grants (high: $1,194,608; low: $5,319) and $5,038 for employee matching gifts.

Purpose and activities: Improvement of health services in the United States, with emphasis on projects to improve access to personal health care for the most underserved population groups; to make health care arrangements more effective and affordable; and to help people maintain or regain maximum attainable function in their everyday lives. Within these areas, support provided for the development and testing of previously untried approaches; demonstrations to assess objectively the operational effectiveness of approaches shown to be effective in more limited settings; and the broader diffusion of programs objectively shown to improve health status or make health care more affordable.
Types of support awarded: Seed money, research, special projects, fellowships, continuing support.
Limitations: Giving limited to the U.S. No support for international activities, programs or institutions concerned solely with a specific disease; basic biomedical research, or broad public health problems, except as they might relate to the foundation's areas of interest. No grants to individuals, or for ongoing general operating expenses, endowment funds, construction, or equipment (except for local purchases).
Publications: Annual report, informational brochure, program policy statement, application guidelines.
Application information:
  Initial approach: Letter
  Copies of proposal: 1
  Deadline(s): None
  Board meeting date(s): February, May, July, October, and December
  Final notification: 6 to 12 months
  Write: Edward H. Robbins, Proposal Manager
Officers: David E. Rogers, M.D.,* President; Leighton E. Cluff, M.D., Executive Vice-President; Robert J. Blendon, Senior Vice-President; J. Warren Wood III, Vice-President and Secretary; William R. Walsh, Jr., Vice-President and Treasurer; Frank Karel, III, Vice-President for Communications; Terrance Keenan, Vice-President for Special Programs; Linda H. Aiken, Vice-President; Ruby P. Hearn, Vice-President.
Trustees:* Gustav O. Lienhard, Chairman; Robert J. Dixson, Edward R. Eberle, Leonard F. Hill, Philip B. Hofmann, Wayne J. Holman, Jr., William McChesney Martin, Jr., George H. Murphy, Robert H. Myers, Richard B. Ogilvie, Norman Rosenberg, M.D., Richard B. Sellars, Foster B. Whitlock.
Number of staff: 33 full-time professional; 1 part-time professional; 52 full-time support; 6 part-time support.
Employer Identification Number: 226029397

2141
Kennedy (The John R.) Foundation, Inc. ⌷

75 Chestnut Ridge Rd.
Montvale 07645

Incorporated in 1951 in Delaware.
Donor(s): John R. Kennedy, Sr., Luke A. Mulligan.†

Financial data: (yr. ended 12/31/82): Assets, $4,134,029 (M); gifts received, $75,000; expenditures, $213,794, including $206,975 for 41 grants (high: $20,000).
Purpose and activities: Broad purposes; grants largely for higher education, Roman Catholic church-related programs, and social services.
Officer: John R. Kennedy, Sr., President.
Employer Identification Number: 221714822

2142
Kerney (The James) Foundation ⌷

143 East State St.
P.O. Box 1413
Trenton 08607-1413

Incorporated in 1934 in New Jersey.
Donor(s): Members of the Kerney family.
Financial data: (yr. ended 12/31/82): Assets, $1,472,462 (M); expenditures, $66,652, including $54,250 for 15 grants (high: $5,000; low: $100).
Purpose and activities: Broad purposes; local giving, with emphasis on hospitals, youth agencies, higher education and Roman Catholic church support.
Types of support awarded: Scholarship funds, building funds.
Limitations: Giving limited to Trenton, NJ, and its surrounding area. No grants to individuals, or for operating budgets.
Application information:
  Write: Albert B. Kahn, Secretary
Officers and Trustees: Raymond L. Steen, President and Treasurer; James C. Kerney, James P. Stewart, Vice-Presidents; Albert B. Kahn, Secretary; Joseph R. Comly, III, Sheila McNeil Priory.
Employer Identification Number: 226055884

2143
Kirby (F. M.) Foundation, Inc. ▼

17 De Hart St.
Morristown 07960   (201) 538-4800
IRS filing address: Delaware

Incorporated in 1931 in Delaware.
Donor(s): F.M. Kirby,† Allan P. Kirby, Sr.,† Fred M. Kirby II.
Financial data: (yr. ended 12/31/83): Assets, $97,648,842 (M); expenditures, $4,267,582, including $4,106,988 for 401 grants.
Purpose and activities: Broad purposes; giving largely in New York, New Jersey, Pennsylvania, and Virginia for higher and secondary education, health and hospitals, community funds, historic preservation, church support and church-related organizations, social services, conservation, public policy organizations and population control. Education grants limited to organizations associated with present or former foundation directors.
Types of support awarded: Building funds, endowment funds, operating budgets, special projects, general purposes.
Limitations: Giving primarily in NY, NJ, PA, and VA. No grants to individuals; no loans.
Publications: Application guidelines, informational brochure.
Application information:

Initial approach: Brief proposal; no telephone solicitations accepted
Copies of proposal: 1
Deadline(s): October 31
Board meeting date(s): Irregularly
Final notification: By December 31; positive responses only
Write: Fred M. Kirby II, President
Officers: Fred M. Kirby II,* President; Allan P. Kirby, Jr.,* Vice-President; Paul B. Mott, Jr., Secretary and Executive Director; Robert N. Lindblom, Treasurer.
Directors:* Grace K. Culbertson, Ann K. Kirby.
Number of staff: 1 part-time professional; 1 part-time support.
Employer Identification Number: 516017929

2144
Komar (Charles & Esther) Foundation ¤
259 N. Stevens Ave.
South Amboy 08879

Incorporated in 1952 in New Jersey.
Donor(s): Charles Komar and Sons.
Financial data: (yr. ended 7/31/83): Assets, $40,019 (M); gifts received, $78,000; expenditures, $105,769, including $105,460 for 95 grants (high: $65,000; low: $25).
Purpose and activities: Giving primarily for Jewish welfare funds, hospitals, and higher education.
Employer Identification Number: 226063002

2145
Large Foundation, The ¤
117 Main St.
Flemington 08822

Incorporated in 1957 in New Jersey.
Donor(s): George K. Large,† and members of the Large family.
Financial data: (yr. ended 12/31/82): Assets, $2,855,578 (M); expenditures, $257,356, including $239,988 for 30 grants (high: $50,000; low: $250).
Purpose and activities: Charitable purposes; primarily local giving, with emphasis on health agencies; grants also for social agencies, youth agencies, and historic preservation.
Limitations: Giving primarily in NJ, particularly Hunterdon County.
Officers and Trustees: Edwin K. Large, Jr., President; Lloyd B. Wescott, Vice-President; Scott Scammell II, Secretary; George R. Hanks, Treasurer; Robert F. Danziger, Alfred R. Dorf, Miss Frances Engeman, Edward Grant, H. Seely Thomas, Jr.
Employer Identification Number: 226049246

2146
Lautenberg Foundation, The ¤
P.O. Box 9
Roseland 07068

Established in 1967 in New Jersey.
Donor(s): Frank R. Lautenberg, Henry Taub, Joseph Taub, Frank R. Lautenberg Charitable Trusts.
Financial data: (yr. ended 12/31/83): Assets, $1,778,913 (M); expenditures, $104,378, including $100,115 for 46 grants (high: $30,000; low: $25).
Purpose and activities: Grants largely for Jewish welfare funds, education, and cultural programs, primarily in the New Jersey and New York area; support also for educational and cultural institutions in Israel.
Limitations: Giving primarily in the NJ and NY area, and Israel.
Officers and Directors:* Frank R. Lautenberg,* President; Lois Lautenberg,* Vice-President; Fred S. Lafer, Secretary.
Employer Identification Number: 226102734

2147
Levin (The Philip & Janice) Foundation ¤
893 Route 22
North Plainfield 07060

Incorporated in 1963 in New Jersey.
Donor(s): Philip J. Levin.†
Financial data: (yr. ended 8/31/83): Assets, $2,707,796 (M); gifts received, $451,200; expenditures, $304,665, including $291,133 for 10 grants (high: $77,800; low: $1,000).
Purpose and activities: General giving, primarily in New Jersey and New York City, with emphasis on higher education, Jewish welfare funds, and the arts.
Limitations: Giving primarily in NJ and New York, NY.
Trustees: Adam K. Levin, Janice H. Levin, Susan J. Levin, Catherine Levin Ward.
Employer Identification Number: 226075837

2148
L'Hommedieu (Frances B. and Paige D.) Trust ▼ ¤
One Palmer Square, Rm. 231
Princeton 08540
Application address: c/o Danser, Balaam, and Frank, P.O. Box 419, Dayton, NJ 08810; Tel.: (201) 821-7400

Trust established in 1966 in New Jersey.
Donor(s): Paige D. L'Hommedieu.†
Financial data: (yr. ended 12/31/83): Assets, $45,344 (M); gifts received, $32,175; expenditures, $518,714, including $500,815 for 13 grants (high: $100,000; low: $4,000; average: $4,000-$45,000).
Purpose and activities: Broad purposes; primarily local giving, with emphasis on higher education; grants also for youth and health agencies, and historic preservation.
Limitations: Giving primarily in NJ.
Application information:
Initial approach: Brief letter
Deadline(s): None
Board meeting date(s): November
Final notification: Varies
Trustees: Paige B. L'Hommedieu, Chair; John J. Heldrich, Leonard F. Hill, Frances B. L'Hommedieu, Gustav O. Lienhard, William R. Walsh.
Employer Identification Number: 226088414

2149
Lindberg Foundation, The
c/o General Drafting Co., Inc.
Convent Station 07961 (201) 538-7600

Incorporated in 1961 in New Jersey.
Donor(s): Otto G. Lindberg.†
Financial data: (yr. ended 12/31/83): Assets, $1,359,607 (M); expenditures, $64,948, including $60,500 for 68 grants (high: $5,000; low: $500).
Purpose and activities: Primarily local giving, with emphasis on higher education, hospitals, community funds, youth agencies, and health agencies.
Types of support awarded: Building funds, equipment.
Limitations: Giving primarily in Morris County and northern NJ. No grants to individuals, or for endowment funds, scholarships and fellowships, or matching gifts; no loans.
Publications: 990-PF, application guidelines.
Application information:
Initial approach: Letter
Copies of proposal: 1
Deadline(s): Submit application preferably in September; deadline November 1
Board meeting date(s): March and December
Final notification: January
Write: R.E. Hueston, Treasurer
Officers and Trustees: Richard E. Scully, President; Clyde Copeland, Jr., Vice-President; Margaret M. Murray, Secretary; R.E. Hueston, Treasurer; M.B. Bennett, Charles J. Gaffney, Edward H. Hein.
Number of staff: None.
Employer Identification Number: 226058169

2150
Lipton (Thomas J.) Foundation, Inc. ¤
c/o Thomas J. Lipton, Inc.
800 Sylvan Ave.
Englewood Cliffs 07632

Incorporated in 1952 in Delaware.
Donor(s): Thomas J. Lipton, Inc.
Financial data: (yr. ended 12/31/82): Assets, $331,052 (M); gifts received, $200,000; expenditures, $483,074, including $464,675 for 196 grants (high: $65,000; low: $15) and $17,217 for 40 employee matching gifts.
Purpose and activities: Broad purposes; general giving, with emphasis on research in nutrition, community funds, higher education, including scholarship aid, hospitals, and youth agencies.
Types of support awarded: Research, scholarship funds, employee matching gifts.
Officers: H.M. Tibbetts, President; J.W. Riehm, Vice-President and Secretary; J. McPeak, Vice-President and Treasurer; E. Feliciotti, C.B. Fuller, W.K. Godfrey, D.W. St. Clair, Vice-Presidents.
Employer Identification Number: 226063094

2151
Mamiye Foundation, Inc. ⋈
26 Englehard Ave.
Avenel 07001

Incorporated in 1982 in New Jersey.
Donor(s): Mamiye Brothers, Inc.
Financial data: (yr. ended 12/31/82): Assets,
$1,393 (M); gifts received, $110,400;
expenditures, $109,007, including $108,267
for 133 grants (high: $5,000; low: $20).
Purpose and activities: First year of operation
1982; grants mainly for Jewish education and
social service agencies.
Officers: Jack C. Mamiye, President; Charles
Mamiye, Michael Mamiye, Vice-Presidents;
David Mamiye, Secretary.
Employer Identification Number: 222405277

2152
Martin (The Sylvia) Foundation, Inc.
40 Eisenhower Dr.
Paramus 07652   (201) 845-6161

Incorporated in 1962 in New York.
Donor(s): The Martin Foundation, Inc., Sylvia
Martin.†
Financial data: (yr. ended 12/31/81): Assets,
$4,417,425 (M); expenditures, $453,127,
including $301,197 for 141 grants (high:
$60,000; low: $250).
Purpose and activities: Foundation currently
undergoing complete reorganization in 1985;
corpus expected to split; information to be
available in 1986.
Limitations: No grants to individuals, or for
endowment funds, scholarships, or fellowships;
no loans.
Application information: Applications
currently not accepted.
   Board meeting date(s): June and December
   Write: R. Allan Martin, Executive Vice-
   President
Officers and Trustees:* R. Allan Martin,*
Executive Vice-President and Secretary; Alana
Martin Frumkes, Vice-President.
Number of staff: 3 full-time support; 2 part-
time support.
Employer Identification Number: 136130140

2153
McCutchen Foundation, The ⋈
209 West Second St.
Plainfield 07060

Trust established in 1956 in New Jersey.
Donor(s): Brunson S. McCutchen, Charles W.
McCutchen, Margaret W. McCutchen.
Financial data: (yr. ended 12/31/82): Assets,
$1,140,522 (M); expenditures, $89,521,
including $87,500 for 28 grants (high: $60,000;
low: $100).
Purpose and activities: Primarily local giving
for religious welfare funds, with emphasis on a
home maintained by The Religious Society of
Friends.
Limitations: Giving primarily in NJ.
Trustees: Brunson S. McCutchen, Charles W.
McCutchen, Marilyn R. Jaeger.
Employer Identification Number: 226050116

2154
McGraw (The Curtis W.) Foundation
c/o Smith, Lambert, Hicks and Miller
P.O. Box 627
Princeton 08542   (609) 921-6336

Established in 1964 in New Jersey.
Donor(s): Elizabeth McGraw Webster.
Financial data: (yr. ended 12/31/84): Assets,
$8,578,516 (M); expenditures, $414,174,
including $401,111 for 58 grants (high:
$30,000; low: $1,000).
Purpose and activities: Grants primarily for
hospitals, educational institutions, and churches
in the Princeton, New Jersey and Vail,
Colorado areas. Grants usually to charities
which are of interest to the officers.
Limitations: Giving limited to the Princeton,
NJ, and Vail, CO, areas. No grants to
individuals, or for endowment funds, research,
scholarships or fellowships, or matching gifts;
no loans.
Publications: 990-PF.
Application information:
   Initial approach: Letter or full proposal
   Copies of proposal: 1
   Deadline(s): October 15
   Board meeting date(s): November or
   December and as required
   Write: Samuel W. Lambert III, Secretary
Officers and Trustees: Elizabeth McGraw
Webster, President; George R. Webster, Vice-
President and Treasurer; David Leventritt,
Harold W. McGraw, Jr., John L. McGraw,
Curtis M. Webster, Vice-Presidents; Samuel W.
Lambert III, Secretary; Charles L. Jaffin.
Number of staff: None.
Employer Identification Number: 221761678

2155
Merck Company Foundation, The ▼
P.O. Box 2000
Rahway 07065-0900   (201) 574-4375

Incorporated in 1957 in New Jersey.
Donor(s): Merck & Co., Inc.
Financial data: (yr. ended 12/31/83): Assets,
$883,000 (M); gifts received, $3,675,000;
expenditures, $3,054,000, including
$2,367,000 for 283 grants (high: $55,000; low:
$200; average: $1,000-$10,000), $437,000 for
3,340 employee matching gifts and $241,000
for 1 foundation-administered program.
Purpose and activities: Support of education,
primarily medical and including the Merck
Sharp & Dohme International Fellowships in
Clinical Pharmacology; community funds,
hospitals, health agencies, civic organizations,
and colleges in localities where the Company
has major operations; state and regional
associations of independent colleges; a program
for matching gifts of Company employees to
colleges, secondary schools, and hospitals.
Types of support awarded: Seed money,
building funds, equipment, employee matching
gifts, fellowships.

Limitations: Giving primarily in areas of
company operations. No grants to individuals
(except for fellowships in clinical
pharmacology), or for operating budgets,
continuing support, annual campaigns,
emergency or endowment funds, deficit
financing, land acquisition, special projects,
research, publications, travel, or conferences;
no loans.
Publications: Annual report.
Application information: Grants usually made
at the initiative of the foundation.
   Initial approach: Full proposal
   Copies of proposal: 1
   Deadline(s): None
   Board meeting date(s): Semiannually and as
   required
   Final notification: 2 months
   Write: Vernon B. Baker, Executive Vice-
   President
Officers: William B. Van Buren, President;
Vernon B. Baker, Executive Vice-President and
Secretary; Richard F. Phillips, Treasurer.
Trustees: John J. Horan, Chairman; Frank T.
Cary, John T. Connor, Lloyd C. Elam, M.D.,
Jacques Genest, M.D., Marian S. Heiskell, John
L. Huck, Reginald H. Jones, John K. McKinley,
Albert W. Merck, Ruben F. Mettler, Glenn S.
Pound, Paul G. Rogers.
Number of staff: 2 full-time professional; 4 full-
time support.
Employer Identification Number: 226028476

2156
**Messing (The Morris M. and Helen F.)
Foundation** ⋈
c/o Vanguard Research Associates
239 St. Nicholas Ave.
South Plainfield 07080

Incorporated in 1957 in New Jersey.
Donor(s): Morris M. Messing.
Financial data: (yr. ended 12/31/82): Assets,
$1,289,438 (M); expenditures, $151,182,
including $147,891 for 56 grants (high:
$30,000; low: $500).
Purpose and activities: Broad purposes; grants
largely for Jewish welfare funds, temple
support, medical research, and higher
education.
Trustees: Herbert Burstein, John J. Elliott,
Morris M. Messing, Robert H. Messing.
Employer Identification Number: 226045391

2157
**Meyer (Aaron and Rachel) Memorial
Foundation, Inc.** ⋈
Ten Rooney Circle
West Orange 07052   (201) 736-9380

Incorporated in 1964 in New Jersey.
Donor(s): Bertram Meyer.†
Financial data: (yr. ended 3/31/83): Assets,
$3,334,984 (M); expenditures, $331,887,
including $268,750 for 29 grants (high:
$47,500; low: $2,000).
Purpose and activities: Broad purposes;
primarily local giving, with grants largely for
hospitals and youth agencies.
Limitations: Giving primarily in Passaic
County, NJ. No grants to individuals.

Application information:
Board meeting date(s): 7 or 8 times a year
Write: Robert S. Mortenson, Secretary
Officers and Trustees: Philip B. Lowy, President; A.L. Levine, Julius Samuels, Vice-Presidents; Robert S. Mortenson, Secretary.
Employer Identification Number: 226063514

2158
Mueller (C. F.) Company Scholarship Foundation ¤
180 Baldwin Ave.
Jersey City 07306   (201) 653-3800

Incorporated in 1967 in New Jersey.
Donor(s): C.F. Mueller Company.
Financial data: (yr. ended 6/30/83): Assets, $236,248 (M); gifts received, $125,000; expenditures, $205,747, including $203,103 for 137 grants to individuals.
Purpose and activities: Scholarships, grants-in-aid, awards, and student loans to Company employees and their children to continue their education on a preparatory, college, university, graduate, or professional level.
Types of support awarded: Employee related scholarships.
Publications: 990-PF.
Application information:
Deadline(s): Submit application between January 1 and April 30; students must reapply every year
Board meeting date(s): January and July
Write: Edwin J. Geils, Treasurer
Officers and Trustees:* Lester R. Thurston, Jr.,* President; Junior C. Buck,* David S. Kane,* Samuel M. Kinney, Jr.,* William R. Vanderbilt,* Vice-Presidents; John D. Keith, Secretary; Edwin J. Geils,* Treasurer; Rev. Edward Glynn, G. Clinton Merrick.
Employer Identification Number: 226100054

2159
Nabisco Foundation ¤
195 River Rd.
East Hanover 07936

Incorporated in 1953 in New Jersey.
Donor(s): Nabisco, Inc.
Financial data: (yr. ended 12/31/82): Assets, $8,642,792 (M); gifts received, $1,300,000; expenditures, $578,698, including $417,724 for 106 grants (high: $50,000; low: $200) and $132,456 for employee matching gifts.
Purpose and activities: Broad purposes; giving largely for higher education and community funds; support also for hospitals and cultural programs.
Types of support awarded: Building funds, scholarship funds, fellowships, employee matching gifts.
Application information: Applications for grants not invited.
Write: Ms. Marian Sheslow, Director of Contributions
Administrative Committee: R.M. Schaeberle, W.H. Weber, Jr.
Trustee: Bankers Trust Company.
Employer Identification Number: 136042595

2160
National Starch & Chemical Foundation, Inc. ¤
10 Finderne Ave.
Bridgewater 08807

Incorporated in 1968 in New York.
Donor(s): National Starch & Chemical Corporation.
Financial data: (yr. ended 12/31/82): Assets, $7,618 (M); gifts received, $224,412; expenditures, $225,679, including $218,074 for 132 grants (high: $20,000; low: $25) and $7,560 for employee matching gifts.
Purpose and activities: General giving primarily in areas of company operations, with emphasis on higher education, including scholarships to children of company employees, hospitals, community funds, and youth agencies.
Types of support awarded: Employee related scholarships, employee matching gifts.
Limitations: Giving primarily in areas of company operations.
Officers: H.R. Sampson, President; J.C. Clay, Vice-President; H.J. Baumgarten, Secretary; R.B. Albert,* Treasurer.
Directors:* D.D. Pascal, S.A. Segal.
Employer Identification Number: 237010264

2161
New Jersey, Community Foundation of
439 Main St.
Orange 07050   (201) 676-3552

Community foundation incorporated in 1979 in New Jersey.
Financial data: (yr. ended 6/30/84): Assets, $1,872,649 (M); gifts received, $1,648,218; expenditures, $166,316, including $110,741 for 32 grants (high: $51,063; low: $50).
Purpose and activities: Support "for innovative programs which can exert a multiplier effect or which through research may contribute to the solution or easing of important community problems." Areas of interest include cultural programs, education, environment and conservation, health, religion, and social services.
Types of support awarded: Seed money, matching funds, technical assistance, special projects, research, publications, conferences and seminars.
Limitations: Giving limited to NJ. No grants to individuals, or for capital or endowment funds, operating budgets, continuing support, annual campaigns, emergency funds, deficit financing, scholarships, or fellowships; no loans.
Publications: Annual report, program policy statement, application guidelines.
Application information:
Write: Sheila C. Williamson, Executive Director
Officers: Bernard S. Berkowitz,* President; Alfred C. Clapp,* Vice-President; Tilly-Jo B. Emerson,* Secretary; S. Jervis Brinton, Jr.,* Treasurer; Sheila C. Williamson, Executive Director.

Trustees:* George L. Bielitz, Jr., Robert P. Corman, Adrian M. Foley, Jr., Harold H. Helm, Hilda Hidalgo, Audrey C. McBratney, Donald F. McCormick, Frederick G. Meissner, Jr., Robert B. O'Brien, Jr., Elizabeth W.V. Penick, Dillard H. Robinson, Richard W. Roper, Christine T. Whitman, Charles D. Worthington.
Employer Identification Number: 222281783

2162
Newcombe (The Charlotte W.) Foundation
231 Nassau St.
Princeton 08540   (609) 924-7022
Fellowship application address: Newcombe Fellowships, Woodrow Wilson National Fellowships Foundation, P.O. Box 642, Princeton, NJ 08540

Trust established in 1979 in Pennsylvania.
Donor(s): Charlotte W. Newcombe.†
Financial data: (yr. ended 12/31/84): Assets, $22,693,152 (L); expenditures, $1,875,424, including $1,532,125 for 68 grants (high: $459,125; low: $5,000; average: $5,000-$30,000).
Purpose and activities: Grants available to colleges and universities for scholarship or fellowship aid only in 4 programs: 1) doctoral dissertation fellowships awarded annually for degree candidates in the humanities and social sciences whose work focuses on ethics and religion (national selection process administered by Woodrow Wilson National Fellowship Foundation); 2) scholarships for physically disabled students, restricted to colleges and universities in Pennsylvania, New Jersey, New York City, Maryland, Delaware, and Washington, D.C.; 3) scholarships for mature second-career women in the same states with no grants in this program to 2-year colleges or to theological seminaries; 4) scholarships for economically disadvantaged or minority students attending colleges related to the Presbyterian Church in the U.S. Scholarships for undergraduate and graduate students only; no aid available for post-doctoral fellowships. Selection of student recipients and scholarship administration are responsibility of academic institution.
Types of support awarded: Scholarship funds, fellowships.
Limitations: No support for colleges except for scholarship and fellowship programs. No grants to individuals, or for staffing, program development, or building funds; scholarships to institutions only; no loans.
Publications: Annual report, program policy statement, application guidelines.
Application information: Application materials available from mid-June through mid-October; fellowship applicants should request applications by December 15.
Initial approach: Letter or telephone
Copies of proposal: 5
Deadline(s): November 1; January 1 for fellowships
Board meeting date(s): February, April, June, September, and December
Final notification: 5 months
Write: Janet A. Fearon, Executive Director

Officer and Trustees: Janet A. Fearon, Executive Director and Trustee; Robert M. Adams, Aaron E. Gast, Millard E. Gladfelter, Thomas P. Glassmoyer.
Number of staff: 2 full-time professional; 1 part-time support.
Employer Identification Number: 232120614

2163
Ohl (George A.), Jr. Trust ☒
c/o First National State Bank of New Jersey
24 Commerce St.
Newark 07102   (201) 565-3751

Trust established in 1947 in New Jersey.
Financial data: (yr. ended 12/31/82): Assets, $2,690,134 (M); expenditures, $175,725, including $145,823 for 34 grants (high: $47,350; low: $50).
Purpose and activities: Local giving, with emphasis on higher and secondary education, health agencies, and a medical and dental school; support also for the handicapped and cultural programs.
Types of support awarded: General purposes, continuing support, annual campaigns, seed money, equipment, research, publications, conferences and seminars, scholarship funds, matching funds.
Limitations: Giving limited to NJ. No grants to individuals; no loans.
Publications: 990-PF, application guidelines.
Application information:
  Initial approach: Proposal or letter
  Copies of proposal: 1
  Deadline(s): Submit proposal preferably in June or November; deadline June 1 and November 1
  Board meeting date(s): July and December
  Final notification: 1 month after board meets
  Write: Joseph J. Cardinal, Senior Trust Officer
Trustees: Mathilda Young, First National State Bank of New Jersey (Joseph J. Cardinal, Senior Trust Officer).
Employer Identification Number: 226024900

2164
Orange Orphan Society, The
c/o A.H. Hardwick, Jr.
57 Egbert St.
Bay Head 08742

Established in 1855 in New Jersey.
Financial data: (yr. ended 12/31/82): Assets, $2,877,792 (M); expenditures, $151,602, including $124,687 for 18 grants (high: $24,200; low: $1,200).
Purpose and activities: Grants to local child welfare and youth agencies.
Limitations: Giving limited to the Orange, NJ area.
Officers and Trustees: A.H. Hardwick, Jr., President; Clarence E. Williams, Vice-President; Mrs. George H. Wilder, Recording Secretary; Mrs. W. Clayton Farris, Jr., Corresponding Secretary; and 20 additional trustees.
Employer Identification Number: 221711513

2165
Penick (Albert) Fund ☒
271 East Bradford Ave.
Cedar Grove 07009

Trust established in 1951 in New York.
Donor(s): A.D. Penick,† Mrs. Albert D. Penick.
Financial data: (yr. ended 12/31/82): Assets, $1,596,551 (M); expenditures, $99,047, including $91,950 for grants.
Purpose and activities: Broad purposes; grants largely for higher and secondary education, hospitals, and cultural organizations.
Trustees: Nancy P. Corcoran, K. Philip Dresdner, S. Barksdale Penick, Jr., V. Susan Penick, Horizon Trust Co.
Employer Identification Number: 136161137

2166
Perkins (F. Mason) Trust ☒
P.O. Box 547
Hackensack 07602

Established in 1971.
Donor(s): F. Mason Perkins.†
Financial data: (yr. ended 12/31/82): Assets, $1,337,204 (M); expenditures, $124,530, including $112,886 for 13 grants (high: $17,126; low: $1,500).
Purpose and activities: Giving exclusively in Italy for aid to the poor and handicapped, particularly children, and for the protection of animals; 50 per cent of giving to six organizations specified by court order.
Limitations: Giving limited to Italy.
Trustee: United Jersey Bank.
Employer Identification Number: 226040411

2167
Prudential Foundation, The ▼
4 Prudential Plaza
Newark 07101   (201) 877-7354

Incorporated in 1977 in New Jersey.
Donor(s): Prudential Insurance Company of America, Prudential Property and Casualty Company.
Financial data: (yr. ended 8/31/84): Assets, $38,864,000 (M); gifts received, $62,000; expenditures, $6,837,299, including $5,657,381 for 600 grants (high: $198,000; low: $1,000; average: $5,000-$10,000) and $1,179,918 for 4,000 employee matching gifts.
Purpose and activities: Program interests include business and economic research and education, conservation and ecology, culture, education, health, public affairs, and urban and community affairs; support also for federated-type drives in areas of Company operations.
Types of support awarded: Operating budgets, continuing support, annual campaigns, seed money, emergency funds, deficit financing, building funds, equipment, matching funds, employee matching gifts, consulting services, technical assistance, employee related scholarships, research, special projects.

Limitations: Giving primarily in areas of company operations, especially Newark, NJ. No support for labor, religious, political, fraternal, or athletic groups, or single-disease health organizations seeking funds independently of federated drives. No grants to individuals or for endowment funds; no loans.
Publications: Annual report, application guidelines.
Application information: Additional information will be requested as needed.
  Initial approach: Letter with brief description of program
  Copies of proposal: 1
  Deadline(s): None
  Board meeting date(s): March, June, September, and December
  Final notification: 4 to 6 weeks
  Write: Donald N. Treloar, Secretary
Officers: Alex J. Plinio, President; William M. Bethke, George V. Franks, Vice-Presidents; Donald N. Treloar, Secretary; Joyce R. Leibowitz, Treasurer.
Trustees: William H. Tremayne, Chairman; Robert A. Beck, Adrian M. Foley, Jr., Margery S. Foster, Donald E. Procknow, Robert C. Winters, David L. Yunich, Edward D. Zinbarg.
Number of staff: 4 full-time professional; 1 part-time professional; 4 full-time support; 1 part-time support.
Employer Identification Number: 222175290

2168
Psychists, Inc. ☒
1100 West Blancke St.
Linden 07036

Incorporated in 1943 in New York.
Donor(s): Richard L. Parish,† American Flange & Manufacturing Co., Inc.
Financial data: (yr. ended 8/31/83): Assets, $1,913,480 (M); expenditures, $201,084, including $194,000 for 46 grants (high: $50,000; low: $500).
Purpose and activities: General purposes; grants largely for higher and secondary education, hospitals and health agencies.
Officers and Directors: Diana McKissock, Chairman; Richard L. Parish, Jr., President and Treasurer; David L. McKissock, Vice-President and Secretary; Richard L. Parish III.
Employer Identification Number: 131869530

2169
Quaker Hill Foundation, The
c/o King, King & Goldsack
120 West 7th St.
Plainfield 07060

Trust established in 1948 in New Jersey.
Donor(s): Edith S. Stevens, John P. Stevens, Jr.†
Financial data: (yr. ended 12/31/83): Assets, $1,677,315 (M); expenditures, $118,109, including $94,100 for 21 grants (high: $15,000; low: $50) and $2,905 for employee matching gifts.

Purpose and activities: Charitable and educational purposes; grants restricted to organizations in which trustees have an active interest, especially for higher and secondary education.
Application information: Applications not invited.
Trustees: Edith S. Sheldon, Edith Stevens, John P. Stevens, III.
Employer Identification Number: 136088786

2170
Reeves Brothers Foundation, Inc., The ☐
115 Summit Ave.
Summit 07901

Incorporated in 1944 in Delaware.
Donor(s): J.E. Reeves, J.M. Reeves Brothers, Reeves Brothers Mills, Reeves Brothers, Inc.
Financial data: (yr. ended 6/30/82): Assets, $11,540,394 (M); gifts received, $17,284; expenditures, $458,819, including $280,009 for 192 grants (high: $50,000; low: $25) and $77,050 for 85 loans.
Purpose and activities: General giving, with emphasis on higher education, including scholarship loan grants, community funds, youth agencies, and Jewish welfare funds.
Types of support awarded: Student aid.
Officers and Trustees: John E. Reeves, President; Jerry H. Wyatt, Joseph D. Moore, Vice-Presidents; William E. Smith, Secretary; John E. Reeves, Jr., Treasurer.
Employer Identification Number: 131891781

2171
Rippel (Fannie E.) Foundation ▼
333 Main St.
Madison 07940   (201) 377-5333

Incorporated in 1953 in New Jersey.
Donor(s): Julius S. Rippel.†
Financial data: (yr. ended 4/30/84): Assets, $40,559,081 (M); expenditures, $4,506,761, including $4,001,677 for 46 grants (high: $150,000; low: $12,181; average: $10,000-$150,000).
Purpose and activities: To aid hospitals, organizations for the relief and care of aged women, and organizations for treatment of and/or research concerning heart disease and cancer.
Types of support awarded: Equipment, research, building funds.
Limitations: Giving primarily in the eastern seaboard states, particularly NJ, and New York, NY. No grants to individuals, or for general support, operating budgets, continuing support, annual campaigns, seed money, emergency funds, deficit financing, scholarships, fellowships, endowment funds or matching gifts; support rarely for building or renovation funds; no loans.
Publications: Annual report, program policy statement, application guidelines.
Application information:
  Initial approach: Letter, telephone, or full proposal
  Copies of proposal: 1
  Deadline(s): None

Board meeting date(s): 10 to 11 times a year
Write: Herbert C. Englert, President
Officers: Herbert C. Englert,* President; Eric R. Rippel,* Vice-President and Secretary; Janet E. Luther, Treasurer.
Trustees:* Julius A. Rippel, Chairman; Jay E. Bailey, S. Jervis Brinton, Jr., G. Frederick Hockenjos, John Kean, Clifford W. Starrett.
Number of staff: 3 full-time professional; 2 part-time professional; 1 full-time support.
Employer Identification Number: 221559427

2172
Rosenhaus (The Sarah and Matthew) Peace Foundation, Inc. ▼ ☐
Picatinny Rd.
Morristown 07960   (201) 267-6583

Incorporated in 1959 in New York.
Donor(s): Sarah Rosenhaus,† Matthew B. Rosenhaus.†
Financial data: (yr. ended 7/31/82): Assets, $8,611,108 (M); gifts received, $3,000; expenditures, $742,390, including $669,481 for 93 grants (high: $50,000; low: $50; average: $1,000-$25,000).
Purpose and activities: To promote world peace and understanding; general giving, primarily in New Jersey and New York, with emphasis on higher education, including theological education, international peace organizations, health agencies, Jewish welfare funds, the performing arts, temple support, and social agencies.
Limitations: Giving primarily in NJ and NY.
Application information:
  Write: Irving Rosenhaus, Managing Director
Officers and Directors: Gila Rosenhaus Chester, Chair; Lawrence Rosenhaus, President; Harriet Rosenhaus Bobrow, Secretary; Robert Bobrow, Treasurer; Irving Rosenhaus, Managing Director; Annetta Rosenhaus Chester, Jerome Cossman, Albert Rosenhaus, Roger Schultz.
Number of staff: 1.
Employer Identification Number: 136136983

2173
Roth (Stanley & Elsie) Foundation, Inc.
975 Scioto Dr.
Franklin Lakes 07417

Incorporated in 1974 in New Jersey.
Donor(s): Stanley Roth, Sr.†
Financial data: (yr. ended 12/31/82): Assets, $1,337,517 (M); expenditures, $158,929, including $154,500 for 12 grants (high: $48,000; low: $2,500).
Purpose and activities: Giving largely for Jewish welfare funds, hospitals, and a community fund.
Limitations: No grants to individuals.
Publications: 990-PF.
Application information:
  Initial approach: Letter
  Deadline(s): None
  Board meeting date(s): May 5 and November 11
  Final notification: 60 days
  Write: Stanley Roth, Jr., President

Officers and Directors: Stanley Roth, Jr., President; Elsie Roth, Vice-President; Joseph S. Iseman, Secretary and Treasurer; Richard Borisoff, Robert Roth.
Number of staff: None.
Employer Identification Number: 237400784

2174
Sandoz Foundation of America ☐
Rte. Ten
E. Hanover 07936

Incorporated in 1965 in Delaware.
Donor(s): Sandoz, Inc.
Financial data: (yr. ended 12/31/82): Assets, $3,743,603 (M); expenditures, $468,758, including $306,466 for 29 grants (high: $25,000; low: $1,000).
Purpose and activities: Grants primarily to educational and charitable institutions engaged in medical research.
Limitations: No grants to individuals, or for building or endowment funds, or operating budgets.
Publications: Application guidelines.
Application information:
  Initial approach: Letter
  Copies of proposal: 1
  Deadline(s): None
  Board meeting date(s): As required
  Write: Craig D. Burrell, M.D., Vice-President
Officers: Albert J. Frey,* President; Kenneth L. Brewton, Jr., Craig D. Burrell, M.D., Vice-Presidents; Herbert J. Brennan, Secretary.
Trustees:* William C. Warren, Chairman; Botond Berde, Marc Moret, Ulrich H. Oppikofer, Daniel C. Wagniere.
Employer Identification Number: 136193034

2175
Sawtelle (Virginia Harkness) Foundation ☐
c/o Summit and Elizabeth Trust Company
367 Springfield Ave.
Summit 07901
Application address: 33 North Fullerton Ave., Montclair, NJ 07042

Established in 1966 in New Jersey.
Donor(s): Virginia Harkness Sawtelle.
Financial data: (yr. ended 4/30/83): Assets, $18,625 (M); gifts received, $55,099; expenditures, $279,476, including $234,267 for 22 grants (high: $50,000; low: $500) and $32,749 for 25 grants to individuals.
Purpose and activities: Giving primarily for scholarship awards, cultural programs, and youth agencies, largely in New Jersey.
Types of support awarded: Student aid, special projects.
Limitations: Giving primarily in NJ.
Application information: Application form available for scholarships.
  Initial approach: Full proposal
  Deadline(s): April 1
  Write: Elizabeth R. Perkins, Executive Director

Officers: Virginia Harkness Sawtelle,* President; Kate B. Wood,* Rev. John Owens,* Vice-Presidents; Elizabeth R. Perkins, Secretary and Executive Director; John Walker,* Treasurer.
Trustees:* Gilman S. Burke, James B. Burke.
Employer Identification Number: 226103008

2176
Schamach (The Milton) Foundation, Inc.
810 Belmont Ave.
North Haledon 07508

Incorporated in 1969 in New Jersey.
Donor(s): Milton Schamach.†
Financial data: (yr. ended 8/31/84): Assets, $1,671,527 (M); expenditures, $151,685, including $122,895 for 26 grants (high: $18,500; low: $100).
Purpose and activities: Primarily local giving for medical research and hospitals; support also for health agencies and Jewish welfare funds.
Limitations: Giving primarily in NJ. No grants to individuals.
Application information:
Initial approach: Letter
Deadline(s): May 31
Board meeting date(s): 3 or 4 times a year as required
Final notification: 3 to 4 months
Write: Jack Goodman, Secretary
Officers and Trustees: Gene Schamach, President; Jack Goodman, Secretary and Treasurer; Andrew E.R. Frommelt, Jr., Jay Rubenstein, Howard Schamach, Robert Schamach, Sanford Schamach.
Number of staff: 2.
Employer Identification Number: 237051147

2177
Schenck (Lillian P.) Fund ⌑
c/o Midlantic National Bank
Metro Park Plaza, P.O. Box 608
Edison 08818

Trust established in 1960 in New Jersey.
Donor(s): Lillian Pitkin Schenck.†
Financial data: (yr. ended 8/31/83): Assets, $5,895,464 (M); expenditures, $397,445, including $369,500 for 35 grants (high: $30,000; low: $1,000).
Purpose and activities: Broad purposes; grants restricted to institutions in the immediate local area, including support for youth and social agencies, and cultural programs.
Types of support awarded: General purposes, operating budgets, special projects, building funds.
Limitations: Giving primarily in NJ. No grants to individuals, or for endowment funds.
Application information:
Initial approach: Full proposal
Copies of proposal: 3
Deadline(s): Submit proposal between April and July; deadline August 1
Board meeting date(s): September
Trustees: Mary P. Oenslager, Elizabeth N. Thatcher, Midlantic National Bank.
Employer Identification Number: 226040581

2178
Schering-Plough Foundation, Inc. ▼
One Giralda Farms
P.O. Box 1000
Madison 07940-1000 (201) 822-7407

Incorporated in 1955 in Delaware.
Donor(s): Schering Corporation, The Plough Foundation.
Financial data: (yr. ended 12/31/84): Assets, $13,185,346 (L); expenditures, $1,265,370, including $951,250 for 68 grants (high: $50,000; low: $1,000; average: $10,000-$15,000) and $255,916 for 842 employee matching gifts.
Purpose and activities: Primary objective is support of institutional activities devoted to improving the quality and delivery of health care, through medical and allied education. Selective support to higher education, hospitals and health care institutions, and cultural organizations, primarily in those geographic locations in which the corporate sponsor has major facilities. Matching gift plan includes accredited higher and secondary educational institutions, and hospitals. Grants made both directly and through national granting groups.
Types of support awarded: Employee matching gifts, annual campaigns, seed money, building funds, equipment, research, internships, fellowships, general purposes, professorships, continuing support, operating budgets, scholarship funds.
Limitations: Giving limited to the U.S., primarily in areas of company operations. No grants to individuals or for endowment funds, deficit financing, publications, or conferences; no loans.
Publications: Annual report, application guidelines, program policy statement.
Application information:
Initial approach: Letter
Copies of proposal: 1
Deadline(s): Submit proposal preferably in January-February or June-August; deadline March 1 and September 1
Board meeting date(s): Semiannually in spring and fall
Final notification: 6 months
Write: Richard J. Kinney, Secretary
Officers: Allan S. Kushen,* President; Richard J. Kinney, Secretary; J. Martin Comey, Treasurer.
Trustees:* Hugh A. D'Andrade, Harold R. Hiser, Jr., R. Lee Jenkins, Richard J. Kogan, Robert P. Luciano, William H. Scholl.
Number of staff: 1 full-time professional; 1 part-time professional; 2 part-time support.
Employer Identification Number: 221711047

2179
Schultz Foundation, The
697 Route 46
Clifton 07015 (201) 365-6558

Incorporated in 1966 in Delaware.
Donor(s): Mrs. Mabel L. Schultz.†
Financial data: (yr. ended 6/30/84): Assets, $5,933,579 (M); expenditures, $290,297, including $239,144 for 37 grants (high: $51,944; low: $100).
Purpose and activities: Charitable purposes; emphasis on community improvement in the local area.
Types of support awarded: General purposes, operating budgets, continuing support, seed money, emergency funds, building funds, matching funds, scholarship funds, internships, fellowships, research, special projects, publications.
Limitations: Giving primarily in the north central area of NJ. No grants to individuals, or for endowment funds, deficit financing, equipment, or land acquisition; no loans.
Publications: Application guidelines.
Application information: Submit proposal not exceeding 3 pages. Application form required.
Initial approach: Telephone or letter
Copies of proposal: 1
Deadline(s): None
Board meeting date(s): April and September
Final notification: 1 to 6 months
Write: Mary S. Strong, Executive Director
Officers: George L. Schultz,* President and Treasurer; Elizabeth Schultz Rigg,* Vice-President; Margaret F. Schultz,* Secretary; Mary S. Strong, Executive Director.
Trustees:* Katharine Schultz Ambrose, John K. Bangs, John Barker, Margaret Schultz Bilotti, Marilyn Schultz Blackwell, Elizabeth Schultz Vanderlinde.
Number of staff: 1 part-time professional; 1 part-time support.
Employer Identification Number: 226103387

2180
Schultz (The William Lightfoot) Foundation
697 Route 46
Clifton 07015 (201) 365-6558

Incorporated in 1952 in New Jersey.
Donor(s): Members of the family of the late William L. Schultz.
Financial data: (yr. ended 6/30/84): Assets, $4,750,410 (M); expenditures, $259,516, including $213,936 for 18 grants (high: $70,000; low: $100).
Purpose and activities: Charitable purposes; emphasis on medical research in the local area.
Types of support awarded: Research, scholarship funds, operating budgets, continuing support, general purposes, seed money, emergency funds, building funds, matching funds, internships, employee related scholarships, fellowships, special projects, publications, conferences and seminars.
Limitations: Giving primarily in north central NJ. No grants to individuals or for endowment funds; no loans.
Publications: Application guidelines.
Application information: Submit proposal not exceeding 3 pages. Application form required.
Initial approach: Telephone or letter
Copies of proposal: 1
Deadline(s): None
Board meeting date(s): September and April
Final notification: 1 to 6 months
Write: Mary S. Strong, Executive Director
Officers: George L. Schultz,* President and Treasurer; Elizabeth Schultz Rigg,* Vice-President; Margaret F. Schultz,* Secretary; Mary S. Strong, Executive Director.

Trustees:* Katharine Schultz Ambrose, John K. Bangs, John Barker, Margaret Schultz Bilotti, Marilyn Schultz Blackwell, Elizabeth Schultz Vanderlinde.
Number of staff: 1 part-time professional; 1 part-time support.
Employer Identification Number: 226025636

2181
Schumann (The Florence and John) Foundation ▼
33 Park St.
Montclair 07042   (201) 783-6660

Incorporated in 1961 in New Jersey.
Donor(s): Mrs. Florence F. Schumann, John J. Schumann, Jr.†
Financial data: (yr. ended 12/31/83): Assets, $52,758,721 (M); expenditures, $3,153,504, including $2,829,939 for 120 grants (high: $300,000; low: $1,000; average: $10,000-$25,000).
Purpose and activities: Grants for health, higher and secondary education, and community development programs.
Types of support awarded: Operating budgets, continuing support, seed money, emergency funds, building funds, matching funds.
Limitations: No grants to individuals, or for annual campaigns, deficit financing, equipment, land acquisition, or endowment funds; no loans.
Publications: Annual report, application guidelines.
Application information:
  Initial approach: Letter
  Copies of proposal: 1
  Deadline(s): January 15, April 15, August 15, and October 15
  Board meeting date(s): March, June, October, and December
  Final notification: 2 to 3 months
  Write: William B. Mullins, President
Officers and Trustees: Robert F. Schumann, Chairman; William B. Mullins, President; Howard D. Brundage, Financial Vice-President; Caroline S. Mark, W. Ford Schumann, Vice-Presidents; David S. Bate, Secretary and Treasurer; Aubin Z. Ames, Robert D.B. Carlisle, Charles B. Sanders, John C. Whitehead.
Staff: Patricia McCarthy, Administrative Officer.
Number of staff: 2 full-time professional; 2 part-time support.
Employer Identification Number: 226044214

2182
Schwartz (The Arnold A.) Foundation ☐
Kunzman, Coley, Yospin & Bernstein
15 Mountain Blvd.
Warren 07060   (201) 757-7927

Incorporated in 1953 in New Jersey.
Donor(s): Arnold A. Schwartz.†
Financial data: (yr. ended 11/30/83): Assets, $2,256,462 (M); expenditures, $212,783, including $144,925 for 47 grants (high: $21,000; low: $500).

Purpose and activities: Primarily local giving, with emphasis on elementary and secondary schools, community services, youth agencies, hospitals, and child welfare.
Limitations: Giving primarily in northern NJ. No support for religious purposes. No grants to individuals or for endowment funds; no loans.
Application information:
  Initial approach: Letter
  Copies of proposal: 2
  Deadline(s): Submit proposal in July or August; deadline September 30
  Board meeting date(s): February, June, September, and November
  Write: Edwin D. Kunzman, President
Officers and Trustees: Edwin D. Kunzman, President; Louis Harding, Vice-President; Steven Kunzman, Secretary and Treasurer; Victor Dileo, David Lackland, Robert Shapiro, Kenneth Turnbull.
Employer Identification Number: 226034152

2183
Schwartz (David) Foundation, Inc. ▼
50 Terminal Rd.
Secaucus 07094   (201) 867-9350

Incorporated in 1945 in New York.
Donor(s): Jonathan Logan, Inc., David Schwartz, and others.
Financial data: (yr. ended 5/31/83): Assets, $9,822,096 (M); gifts received, $200,000; expenditures, $856,525, including $769,960 for 45 grants (high: $150,000; low: $100).
Purpose and activities: Broad purposes; general giving, primarily in New York City with emphasis on cultural programs and hospitals; grants also for Jewish welfare funds and health agencies.
Types of support awarded: General purposes.
Limitations: Giving primarily in NY, with emphasis on New York City. No grants to individuals.
Application information: Funds currently committed.
  Board meeting date(s): At least once a year, usually in May or June
  Write: Walter L. Krieger, Assistant Secretary
Officers and Directors: David Schwartz, President; Richard J. Schwartz, Vice-President; Lois R. Zenkel, Secretary; Stephen D. Gardner, Irene Schwartz, Bruce Zenkel.
Number of staff: None.
Employer Identification Number: 226075974

2184
Simon (Richard and Betty) Foundation ☐
415 N. Douglas Ave.
Margate 08404

Established in 1978.
Donor(s): Richard Simon, Jacob Simon, Renee Simon, Valerie Simon, Herman Zell.
Financial data: (yr. ended 12/31/82): Assets, $8,824 (M); gifts received, $156,300; expenditures, $131,507, including $131,500 for 10 grants (high: $40,000; low: $500).
Purpose and activities: Giving for Jewish welfare funds and educational organizations.
Trustees: Herman Zell, Jacob Zell, Marsha Zell.
Employer Identification Number: 222209101

2185
South Branch Foundation, The ▼
c/o Gillen & Johnson
P.O. Box 477
Somerville 08876   (201) 722-6400

Trust established in 1960 in New Jersey.
Donor(s): J. Seward Johnson, The J. Seward Johnson Charitable Trust.
Financial data: (yr. ended 12/31/82): Assets, $6,863,003 (M); expenditures, $628,118, including $621,168 for 37 grants (high: $175,000; low: $500; average: $1,000-$50,000).
Purpose and activities: Broad purposes; general giving, with emphasis on civil rights, education, international relations, conservation, protection of animals, cultural programs, and health.
Types of support awarded: Continuing support, fellowships, research, scholarship funds, special projects.
Limitations: No grants to individuals or for building funds.
Application information:
  Initial approach: Proposal
  Copies of proposal: 1
  Deadline(s): Submit proposal preferably in November or December; deadline December 31
  Board meeting date(s): January
  Final notification: 45 days
  Write: Peter S. Johnson
Officer and Trustees: Esther U. Johnson, Director; James L. Johnson, John D. Mack, Deyan M. Popvic.
Employer Identification Number: 226029434

2186
Stern (Max) Foundation, Inc. ▼ ☐
600 South Fourth St.
Harrison 07029

Incorporated in 1945 in Delaware.
Donor(s): Max Stern,† Stanley Stern.
Financial data: (yr. ended 9/30/82): Assets, $5,071,144 (M); gifts received, $38,521; expenditures, $649,861, including $635,228 for 52 grants (high: $600,000; low: $25).
Purpose and activities: Broad purposes; grants largely for higher and secondary education, including religious education, Jewish welfare funds, and organizations in Israel, particularly a hospital.
Officers and Directors: Leonard N. Stern, President, Vice-President, and Treasurer; Armand Lindenbaum, Secretary; Ghity Stern.
Employer Identification Number: 136161280

2187
Subaru of America Foundation
7040 Central Hwy.
Pennsauken 08109   (609) 488-5099

Established in 1984 in New Jersey.
Donor(s): Subaru of America, Inc.

Financial data: (yr. ended 10/31/84): Assets, $694,501 (M); gifts received, $862,000; expenditures, $197,346, including $192,460 for 69 grants (high: $17,500; low: $250; average: $1,000-$2,500) and $4,177 for 33 employee matching gifts.
Purpose and activities: Giving in areas of company operations for cultural programs, health and hospitals, social services, education, and civic organizations.
Types of support awarded: Operating budgets, continuing support, annual campaigns, seed money, emergency funds, building funds, equipment, employee matching gifts, special projects.
Limitations: Giving limited to areas of company operations, primarily southern NJ. No support for religious, fraternal, or veterans' groups. No grants to individuals, or for land acquisition, endowment funds, scholarships, fellowships, research, publications, or conferences and seminars; no loans.
Publications: Annual report, program policy statement, application guidelines.
Application information:
  Initial approach: Letter, telephone, or proposal
  Copies of proposal: 1
  Deadline(s): None
  Board meeting date(s): March, June, September, and December
  Final notification: 2 months
  Write: Denise L. Middleman, Administrator
Officers and Trustees: Harvey H. Lamm, President; Thomas R. Gibson, Vice-President; Marvin S. Reisenbach, Secretary; Robert L. Reich, Treasurer.
Contributions Committee: Eugene L. Egan, Chairman; John J. Coyle, Patricia D. Hohwald, Drew K. Kapur, Joanne A. Welde, Deborah P. Weinstein, Gilbert N. Zitin.
Administrator: Denise L. Middleman.
Number of staff: 1 full-time professional; 1 part-time professional.
Employer Identification Number: 222531774

2188
Sullivan (The Algernon Sydney) Foundation ¤
55 Maple Ave.
Morristown 07960   (201) 539-8412

Incorporated in 1930 in New York.
Donor(s): Mrs. Algernon Sydney Sullivan,† George Hammond Sullivan,† Zilph P. Devereaux,† and others.
Financial data: (yr. ended 12/31/82): Assets, $5,636,059 (M); gifts received, $52,142; expenditures, $325,679, including $259,850 for 48 grants (high: $18,500; low: $250).
Purpose and activities: Grants largely for higher education, almost entirely in the Southeast.
Types of support awarded: Scholarship funds.
Limitations: Giving primarily in the Southeast. No grants to individuals, or for capital construction.
Application information:
  Initial approach: Proposal
  Copies of proposal: 1
  Board meeting date(s): May and November
  Write: William E. Bardusch, Jr., President

Officers and Trustees: William E. Bardusch, Jr., President; John S. Chapman, Jr., Vice-President; Charles W. Cook, Secretary; Frederick L. Redpath, Treasurer; Walter G. Dunnington, Jr., Hiram B. Ely, Jr., G. Rives Shaffer, Gray Williams, Jr., Emmett Wright, Jr.
Employer Identification Number: 136084596

2189
Taub (The Henry and Marilyn) Foundation ¤
c/o Wiss & Company
354 Eisenhower Pkwy.
Livingston 07039

Established in 1967 in Delaware.
Donor(s): Henry Taub.
Financial data: (yr. ended 12/31/83): Assets, $1,048,243 (M); gifts received, $1,034,637; expenditures, $592,239, including $574,867 for 94 grants (high: $117,451; low: $15).
Purpose and activities: Grants largely for Jewish welfare funds; some support for higher education, temples, social agencies, and hospitals.
Limitations: Giving primarily in NY.
Officers and Directors:* Henry Taub,* President; Fred S. Lafer, Secretary; Marilyn Taub,* Treasurer.
Employer Identification Number: 226100525

2190
Taub (Joseph and Arlene) Foundation ¤
c/o Wiss & Company
33 Evergreen Place
East Orange 07018

Established in 1968 in Delaware.
Donor(s): Joseph Taub.
Financial data: (yr. ended 12/31/82): Assets, $950,306 (M); gifts received, $397,815; expenditures, $1,001,810, including $989,786 for 39 grants (high: $276,250; low: $10).
Purpose and activities: Grants for Jewish welfare funds, including temple support and education, and the handicapped.
Officers and Directors: Joseph Taub, President; Fred S. Lafer, Secretary; Arlene Taub, Treasurer; Abraham H. Nechemie.
Employer Identification Number: 226104545

2191
Terner Foundation, Inc. ¤
P.O. Box 1060
Piscataway 08854

Established in 1953.
Donor(s): Emmanuel M. Terner.
Financial data: (yr. ended 7/31/83): Assets, $722,377 (M); gifts received, $100,000; expenditures, $142,079, including $127,930 for 55 grants (high: $40,000; low: $80).
Purpose and activities: Giving primarily for Jewish welfare funds and temple support, higher and secondary education, and hospitals.
Officer: Emmanuel M. Terner, President.
Employer Identification Number: 221605265

2192
Thomas & Betts Charitable Trust, The ¤
c/o Robert V. Berry
920 Route 202
Raritan 08869   (201) 685-1600

Trust established in 1948 in New Jersey.
Donor(s): Thomas & Betts Corporation.
Financial data: (yr. ended 12/31/82): Assets, $496,573 (M); expenditures, $304,862, including $298,080 for 142 grants (high: $27,000; low: $25).
Purpose and activities: Broad purposes; serves community near company facility; grants for higher education and local community funds, health services, hospitals, and youth agencies.
Limitations: Giving limited to the area of company operations in Raritan, NJ. No grants to individuals, or for endowment funds, research, scholarships, or fellowships; no loans.
Publications: Annual report, application guidelines, informational brochure.
Application information:
  Initial approach: Letter
  Copies of proposal: 1
  Deadline(s): October 1
  Board meeting date(s): October and December and as required
  Write: Robert V. Berry, Vice-President, Finance
Trustees: J. David Parkinson, Chairman of Board; Robert V. Berry, Vice-President, Finance; Edward D. Thomas, Vice-President, Corporate Development.
Employer Identification Number: 226032533

2193
Turrell Fund ▼
33 Evergreen Place
East Orange 07018   (201) 678-8580

Incorporated in 1935 in New Jersey.
Donor(s): Herbert Turrell,† Margaret Turrell.†
Financial data: (yr. ended 12/31/84): Assets, $54,869,610 (M); expenditures, $3,898,974, including $3,243,547 for 227 grants (high: $78,900; low: $750; average: $14,000) and $253,517 for 1 foundation-administered program.
Purpose and activities: Grants to organizations dedicated to service to or care of children and youth under 18 years of age, with emphasis on the needy, the socially maladjusted, and the disadvantaged.
Types of support awarded: Operating budgets, seed money, emergency funds, building funds, equipment, land acquisition, matching funds, scholarship funds.
Limitations: Giving limited to NJ, particularly the northern urban areas centered in Essex County, and to VT. No support for advocacy work, most hospital work, or health delivery services; generally no support for cultural activities. No grants to individuals, or for endowment funds, publications, conferences, or research; no loans.
Publications: Annual report, program policy statement, application guidelines.
Application information:
  Initial approach: Letter
  Copies of proposal: 1

Deadline(s): Submit proposal preferably in January or February or between June and September; deadline February 15 and September 15 for first time applicants; March 1 and October 1 for others
Board meeting date(s): May and November or December
Final notification: 3 months after deadlines
Write: Carl Fjellman, Executive Director
Officers and Trustees: S. Whitney Landon, Chairman; Frank J. Hoenemeyer, President; Harry W. Lindeman, Vice-President; Carl Fjellman, Secretary, Treasurer, and Executive Director; Paul J. Christiansen, Ann G. Dinse, Richard R. Hough, Ernest D. North, J. Henry Smith, E. Belvin Williams.
Number of staff: 2 full-time professional; 1 part-time professional; 3 full-time support.
Employer Identification Number: 221551936

2194
Union Camp Charitable Trust ▼
c/o Union Camp Corporation
1600 Valley Rd.
Wayne 07470   (201) 628-2232

Trust established in 1951 in New York.
Donor(s): Union Camp Corporation.
Financial data: (yr. ended 12/31/83): Assets, $1,317,388 (M); gifts received, $650,000; expenditures, $1,007,745, including $998,566 for 1,112 grants (high: $106,500; low: $10; average: $100-$25,000) and $4,253 for 46 employee matching gifts.
Purpose and activities: General purposes; grants in areas of company operations and to national organizations, largely for community funds, higher education, including company-employee scholarships and matching gifts; health services, social agencies, civic affairs, youth agencies, and hospitals.
Types of support awarded: Employee matching gifts, employee related scholarships, operating budgets, continuing support, annual campaigns, building funds, equipment, special projects, research.
Limitations: Giving primarily in areas of company operations and to national organizations. No grants to individuals; no loans.
Application information:
Initial approach: Proposal
Copies of proposal: 1
Deadline(s): Submit proposal preferably from January through August
Board meeting date(s): November
Write: Harold Hoss, Treasurer
Trustees: Alexander Calder, Jr., Hugh D. Camp, Thomas D. Dunn, Morgan Guaranty Trust Company of New York, Corporate Trustee.
Employer Identification Number: 136034666

2195
Union Foundation ▼
P.O. Box 4470
Watchung 07060   (201) 753-2440

Incorporated in 1951 in New Jersey.
Donor(s): E.J. Grassmann,† and others.

Financial data: (yr. ended 11/30/83): Assets, $7,425,711 (M); expenditures, $552,928, including $507,800 for 62 grants (high: $30,000; low: $1,500).
Purpose and activities: Broad purposes; primarily local giving, with emphasis on hospitals, social and youth agencies, privately-supported higher and secondary education, conservation, the humanities, and denominational giving.
Types of support awarded: Endowment funds, building funds, equipment.
Limitations: Giving primarily in NJ, particularly Union County. No grants to individuals or for operating budgets.
Publications: Application guidelines.
Application information:
Copies of proposal: 1
Deadline(s): October 15
Board meeting date(s): November
Write: William V. Engel, Secretary
Officers and Trustees: Joseph G. Engel, President; Edward G. Engel, Vice-President; William V. Engel, Secretary; Thomas H. Campbell, Treasurer; Haydn H. Murray, Suzanne B. Richard, William O. Wuester, M.D.
Employer Identification Number: 226046454

2196
Upton (Lucy and Eleanor S.) Charitable Foundation ☒
744 Broad St., Suite 700
Newark 07102

Established in 1965.
Donor(s): Eleanor S. Upton.†
Financial data: (yr. ended 12/31/82): Assets, $3,069,542 (M); expenditures, $164,532, including $133,500 for 11 grants (high: $58,000; low: $1,000).
Purpose and activities: Primarily local giving to hospitals and cultural programs.
Types of support awarded: General purposes, research.
Limitations: Giving primarily in NJ.
Application information:
Write: Thomas L. Morrissey, Trustee
Trustees: William B. Cater, Thomas L. Morrissey, Samuel C. Williams, Jr.
Employer Identification Number: 226074947

2197
Victoria Foundation, Inc. ▼
40 South Fullerton Ave.
Montclair 07042   (201) 783-4450

Incorporated in 1924 in New Jersey.
Donor(s): Hendon Chubb.†
Financial data: (yr. ended 12/31/84): Assets, $50,233,934 (M); expenditures, $2,979,658, including $2,676,850 for 141 grants (high: $65,000; low: $5,000; average: $10,000-$25,000).
Purpose and activities: Grants primarily for local welfare and education programs, including urban problems, neighborhood development, youth agencies, and behavioral rehabilitation; support also for certain statewide environmental projects.

Types of support awarded: Operating budgets, continuing support, seed money, emergency funds, deficit financing, building funds, matching funds, scholarship funds, special projects, research, consulting services, technical assistance.
Limitations: Giving primarily in the greater Newark, NJ, area. No support for organizations dealing with specific diseases or afflictions. No grants to individuals, or for endowment funds, annual campaigns, publications, conferences, or land acquisition; no loans.
Publications: Annual report, application guidelines.
Application information: Application form required.
Initial approach: Proposal
Copies of proposal: 1
Deadline(s): Submit proposal in January through March or June through September; deadlines March 15 and September 15
Board meeting date(s): May and December
Final notification: Within 1 week after board meeting if accepted; within 30 days after board meeting if not accepted
Write: Howard E. Quirk, Executive Officer
Officers: Percy Chubb III,* President; Margaret H. Parker,* Vice-President; Howard E. Quirk, Secretary and Executive Officer; Kevin Shanley,* Treasurer.
Trustees:* Matthew G. Carter, Corinne A. Chubb, Sally Chubb, Mary Coggeshall, Robert M. Curvin, Haliburton Fales II, Jean Felker, Robert D. Lilley, Gordon A. Millspaugh, Jr., Bernard M. Shanley, William Turnbull.
Number of staff: 2 full-time professional; 1 full-time support.
Employer Identification Number: 221554541

2198
Visceglia-Summit Associates Foundation
(formerly Vincent and Anna Visceglia Foundation)
Raritan Plaza II
Raritan Center
Edison 08818   (201) 225-2900

Incorporated in 1953 in New Jersey.
Donor(s): Vincent Visceglia, Diego R. Visceglia, John B. Visceglia.
Financial data: (yr. ended 3/31/84): Assets, $1,813,102 (M); expenditures, $187,993, including $183,516 for 173 grants (high: $18,626; low: $25).
Purpose and activities: Broad purposes; primarily local giving, with emphasis on hospitals, higher education, church support, and religious associations; some support also for community funds, music, opera, ballet, and other performing arts, and youth agencies.
Limitations: Giving primarily in Essex and Middlesex Counties, NJ. No grants to individuals.
Application information: No new applications accepted.
Officers: Diego R. Visceglia, President; Vincent Visceglia, Vice-President; John B. Visceglia, Secretary.
Employer Identification Number: 226041608

2199
Vollmer Foundation, Inc. ▼
95 River St., Suite 411
Hoboken 07030   (201) 420-8961

Incorporated in 1965 in New York.
Donor(s): Alberto F. Vollmer.†
Financial data: (yr. ended 12/31/83): Assets, $6,822,074 (M); expenditures, $851,599, including $716,856 for 29 grants (high: $132,530; low: $1,650) and $19,305 for 2 grants to individuals.
Purpose and activities: General purposes; support for charitable, scientific and educational activities dedicated primarily to Latin America and particularly to Venezuela. Support also for international youth organizations, for the Catholic church in Venezuela, and for Venezuelan individuals engaged in research.
Types of support awarded: Annual campaigns, seed money, equipment, research, program-related investments, general purposes, continuing support.
Limitations: Giving primarily in Latin America, particularly Venezuela. No grants for building funds or for matching gifts; no loans.
Publications: Program policy statement, application guidelines.
Application information:
    Initial approach: Letter
    Copies of proposal: 2
    Deadline(s): Submit proposal preferably between December and March
    Board meeting date(s): As required
    Final notification: 2 to 3 months
    Write: Albert L. Ennist, Assistant Secretary
Officers and Directors: Gustavo J. Vollmer, President; Alberto J. Vollmer, Vice-President and Treasurer.
Number of staff: 1 full-time professional; 2 part-time support.
Employer Identification Number: 132620718

2200
Warner-Lambert Foundation, The ▼
201 Tabor Rd.
Morris Plains 07950   (201) 540-2243

Incorporated in 1969 in Delaware.
Donor(s): Warner-Lambert Company.
Financial data: (yr. ended 12/31/82): Assets, $23,638 (M); gifts received, $2,000,000; expenditures, $1,930,259, including $1,929,497 for 220 grants (high: $125,000; low: $480; average: $1,000-$25,000).
Purpose and activities: Grants primarily in areas of company operations, largely for community funds, higher education, medical research and education, and pharmacology; some support for hospitals, civil rights, and social welfare and youth agencies.
Types of support awarded: Annual campaigns, building funds, continuing support, emergency funds, equipment, matching funds, operating budgets, professorships, seed money, research.
Limitations: Giving primarily in communities where company plants are located. No grants to individuals, or for endowment funds, demonstration projects, research (other than for medical research) or conferences; no loans.

Application information:
    Initial approach: Letter
    Copies of proposal: 1
    Deadline(s): Submit proposal preferably between July and September; deadline September
    Board meeting date(s): Quarterly
    Write: Ewart V. Thomas, Secretary-Treasurer
Officers: Robert J. Dircks,* President; David Alton, 1st Vice-President; Richard Pecheur,* 2nd Vice-President; Melvin R. Goodes,* 3rd Vice-President; Ewart V. Thomas, Secretary-Treasurer.
Directors:* Ronald E. Zier, Chairman; Paul Gerhart.
Number of staff: 1 full-time professional; 1 part-time support.
Employer Identification Number: 237038078

2201
Westfield Foundation, The
210 Orchard St.
Westfield 07091

Incorporated in 1975 in New Jersey.
Financial data: (yr. ended 12/31/84): Assets, $1,111,015 (M); gifts received, $20,947; expenditures, $111,238, including $77,015 for 16 grants (high: $20,000; low: $150; average: $100-$10,000) and $35,000 for 1 loan.
Purpose and activities: Charitable giving to programs that benefit the local community.
Types of support awarded: Annual campaigns, equipment, matching funds, scholarship funds.
Limitations: Giving limited to Westfield, NJ. No support for churches or religious programs. No grants to individuals, or for operating expenses or endowments.
Publications: Annual report, informational brochure.
Application information:
    Initial approach: Letter
    Copies of proposal: 2
    Deadline(s): January 1, April 1, July 1, and October 1
    Board meeting date(s): February, May, August, and November
    Final notification: 1 week after board meeting
    Write: E. Alfred Herberich, Executive Director
Officers and Trustees:* H. Emerson Thomas,* President; Charles H. Frankenbach, Jr., Robert H. Mulreany, Vice-Presidents; E. Alfred Herberich,* Secretary and Executive Director; Donn A. Snyder,* Treasurer.
Number of staff: None.
Employer Identification Number: 222155896

2202
Wetterberg (The Harold) Foundation ⌺
c/o Hannoch, Weisman, Stern et al.
744 Broad St.
Newark 07102   (609) 452-9555
Application address: P.O. Box 30, Princeton, NJ

Incorporated in 1961 in New Jersey.
Donor(s): Harold Wetterberg.†

Financial data: (yr. ended 11/30/83): Assets, $1,375,775 (M); expenditures, $199,428, including $173,075 for 9 grants (high: $52,084; low: $4,500).
Purpose and activities: Broad purposes; grants primarily to higher educational institutions and a science organization, with emphasis on research programs in the veterinary sciences.
Types of support awarded: Research.
Application information: Application form required.
    Deadline(s): None
    Write: Henry K. Parsons, Trustee
Officers and Trustees: Albert G. Besser, President; George C. Poppensick, Vice-President; Norbert R. Murphy, Secretary; Henry K. Parsons, Treasurer.
Employer Identification Number: 226042915

2203
Wilf Family Foundation ⌺
1640 Vauxhall Rd.
Union 07083

Established in 1964.
Donor(s): Harry Wilf, Joseph Wilf.
Financial data: (yr. ended 10/31/82): Assets, $170,918 (M); gifts received, $253,750; expenditures, $120,838, including $120,453 for 36 grants (high: $34,931; low: $100).
Purpose and activities: Grants for Jewish welfare funds, including educational programs.
Officers: Harry Wilf, President; Joseph Wilf, Secretary.
Trustees: Elizabeth Wilf, Judith Wilf.
Employer Identification Number: 226075840

2204
Willits Foundation, The ⌺
731 Central Ave.
Murray Hill 07974   (201) 277-8259

Incorporated in 1963 in New Jersey.
Donor(s): Members of the Willits family.
Financial data: (yr. ended 11/30/83): Assets, $2,044,815 (M); gifts received, $1,250; expenditures, $190,960, including $173,658 for 107 grants (high: $15,000; low: $50).
Purpose and activities: Broad purposes; emphasis on grants to higher educational institutions for scholarships, and on Protestant church support and religious activities, schools, social agencies, and hospitals.
Types of support awarded: Scholarship funds.
Limitations: Giving primarily in NJ. No grants to individuals.
Application information:
    Initial approach: Proposal
    Copies of proposal: 1
    Deadline(s): Submit proposal preferably between August and October
    Board meeting date(s): November and as required
    Write: Harris L. Willits, President
Officers and Trustees: Harris L. Willits, President; Barbara W. Evans, Vice-President; Emily D. Lawrence, Secretary-Treasurer; John H. Evans, Rev. William H. Felmeth, Itto A. Willits, John F. Willits.
Employer Identification Number: 226063106

2205
Youths' Friends Association, Inc.
c/o J. K. Smit & Sons, Inc.
571 Central Ave.
Murray Hill 07974   (201) 464-3700

Incorporated in 1950 in New York.
Donor(s): Johan J. Smit, Mrs. Johan J. Smit.†
Financial data: (yr. ended 12/31/83): Assets, $3,158,000 (M); expenditures, $180,000, including $155,000 for 120 grants (high: $4,000; low: $200).
Purpose and activities: Broad purposes; grants largely for character-building, with emphasis on higher and secondary education, health agencies, hospitals, youth agencies, child welfare, and music, largely in New York and New Jersey; some support also for churches and religious associations.
Limitations: Giving primarily in NY and NJ. No grants to individuals.
Application information:
Initial approach: Letter
Copies of proposal: 1
Deadline(s): None
Board meeting date(s): Semiannually
Write: Herman J. Meinert, President
Officers and Directors: Herman J. Meinert, President; Sheila Smit, Vice-President; Walter Graver, Secretary; Andrew J. Morris, Treasurer; Marion Meinert, Johan J. Smit, Stephen C. Smit.
Employer Identification Number: 136097828

NEW MEXICO

2206
Bellamah (Dale J.) Foundation ▼
P.O. Box 36600, Station D
Albuquerque 87176   (505) 265-3741

Established around 1972 in New Mexico.
Donor(s): Dale J. Bellamah.†
Financial data: (yr. ended 12/31/83): Assets, $8,691,579 (M); expenditures, $606,023, including $406,000 for 9 grants (high: $100,000; low: $5,000).
Purpose and activities: Giving for higher education, health, an organization providing care of the mentally retarded, and youth agencies.
Types of support awarded: Scholarship funds, equipment.
Limitations: No grants to individuals.
Application information:
Initial approach: Letter
Deadline(s): None
Board meeting date(s): As necessary
Write: A.F. Potenziani, Chairman and President

Officers and Directors: A.F. Potenziani, Chairman and President; Frank A. Potenziani, Vice-President; William Potenziani, Secretary-Treasurer; Martha M. Potenziani, Kathleen P. Stetson.
Number of staff: None.
Employer Identification Number: 237177691

2207
Bynner (The Witter) Foundation for Poetry, Inc.
660 East Garcia
P.O. Box 2188
Santa Fe 87504   (505) 988-3251

Incorporated in 1972 in New Mexico.
Donor(s): Witter Bynner.†
Financial data: (yr. ended 5/31/83): Assets, $1,793,120 (M); expenditures, $151,370, including $110,397 for 14 grants (high: $25,000; low: $2,493; average: $1,000-$25,000).
Purpose and activities: To make grants, particularly as seed money, in support of poetry and poetry translation to non-profit organizations and institutions.
Types of support awarded: Seed money, matching funds, special projects, research, conferences and seminars.
Limitations: No support for poetry readings or publication projects. No grants to individuals, or for building or endowment funds, continuing support, or operating expenses; no loans.
Publications: Annual report, application guidelines, program policy statement.
Application information: Application form required.
Initial approach: Letter or telephone
Copies of proposal: 3
Deadline(s): Submit proposals preferably in January; deadline February 1
Board meeting date(s): April or May
Final notification: 2 weeks after annual meeting
Write: Steven Schwartz, Administrator
Officers and Trustees: Douglas W. Schwartz, President; Art Gallaher, Jr., Vice-President; Thomas B. Catron, III, Secretary and Treasurer; Vera Zorina Lieberson.
Number of staff: 3 part-time support.
Employer Identification Number: 237169999

2208
Carlsbad Foundation, Inc.
405 W. Greene St.
Carlsbad 88220   (505) 887-1131

Incorporated in 1977 in New Mexico.
Financial data: (yr. ended 6/30/83): Assets, $2,464,031 (M); gifts received, $75,850; expenditures, $249,513, including $62,853 for grants, $92,781 for grants to individuals and $400,000 for 1 loan.

Purpose and activities: A private operating foundation; supports recruitment and education activities of the medical profession and health care services in the South Eddy County and Carlsbad, New Mexico, area through an educational loan program for medical and paramedical students relocating to that area; support also for civic groups and charitable organizations.
Types of support awarded: Loans, operating budgets, seed money, emergency funds, building funds, equipment, endowment funds, matching funds, employee matching gifts, consulting services, technical assistance, scholarship funds, program-related investments, special projects, publications, conferences and seminars.
Limitations: Giving limited to South Eddy County, NM. No grants for annual campaigns, deficit financing, land aquisitions or continuing support.
Publications: Annual report, program policy statement, application guidelines.
Application information:
Write: John Mills, Executive Director
Officer: John Mills, Executive Director.
Number of staff: 1 full-time professional; 1 part-time professional; 1 part-time support.
Employer Identification Number: 850206472

2209
Maddox (J. F.) Foundation
P.O. Box 5410
Hobbs 88241   (505) 393-6338

Established in 1968 in New Mexico.
Donor(s): J.F. Maddox,† Mabel S. Maddox.
Financial data: (yr. ended 6/30/84): Assets, $16,711,274 (M); gifts received, $6,993,963; expenditures, $1,331,911, including $1,086,500 for 33 grants (high: $800,000; low: $500) and $27,658 for 24 loans.
Purpose and activities: Giving primarily in west Texas and New Mexico for higher education, including student loans; support also for cultural programs and youth organizations.
Limitations: Giving primarily in NM and west TX.
Application information: Application form required for student loans.
Deadline(s): None
Write: Robert Socolofsky, Executive Director
Officers and Directors: Donovan Maddox, President; Don Maddox, Vice-President; James M. Maddox, Secretary-Treasurer; Harry M. Lynch, Mabel S. Maddox.
Number of staff: 1 full-time professional; 3 part-time support.
Employer Identification Number: 756023767

2210
Phillips (Waite and Genevieve) Charitable Trust ☐
P.O. Box 5726
Santa Fe 87502

Established in 1980 in New Mexico.
Donor(s): Genevieve E. Phillips.†

Financial data: (yr. ended 5/31/83): Assets, $6,433,472 (M); expenditures, $373,926, including $311,500 for 25 grants (high: $100,000; low: $500).
Purpose and activities: General giving, with emphasis on an art center; giving also for social services, education, higher education, medical research facilities, and hospitals.
Trustees: Elliott Phillips, Virginia Phillips.
Employer Identification Number: 856086754

2211
Picker (James) Foundation ▼
P.O. Box 9101
Albuquerque 87119

Incorporated in 1947 in New York.
Donor(s): James Picker,† Harvey Picker.
Financial data: (yr. ended 12/31/82): Assets, $10,711,317 (M); expenditures, $636,771, including $542,381 for 9 grants (high: $300,000; low: $10,586).
Purpose and activities: Support devoted to the Picker Program in the "Human Qualities of Medicine".
Types of support awarded: Research.
Limitations: No grants for professorships.
Publications: Program policy statement.
Application information: Only invited proposals are considered.
    Board meeting date(s): Annually in early spring
    Write: Robert D. Moseley, Jr., M.D., President
Officers and Directors: Robert D. Moseley, Jr., M.D., President; Jean Picker, Secretary; Harvey Picker, Treasurer; Julius R. Krevans, M.D., Margaret Mahoney, Russell H. Morgan, M.D.
Employer Identification Number: 136046374

2212
Sizemore (Luther A.) Foundation ☒
6010 Lomas Blvd., NE
Albuquerque 87110

Established in 1977.
Financial data: (yr. ended 12/31/83): Assets, $1,186,404 (M); expenditures, $106,382, including $81,673 for 32 grants (high: $14,500; low: $200).
Purpose and activities: Primarily local giving for higher education, Christian religious organizations, and cultural programs, with emphasis on a natural history museum.
Limitations: Giving primarily in Albuquerque, NM.
Officers: Marcial Rey, President; Wilfred Padilla, Vice-President; Clinton Abel, Secretary and Treasurer.
Employer Identification Number: 510206540

2213
Wurlitzer (The Helene) Foundation of New Mexico
P.O. Box 545
Taos 87571   (505) 758-2413

Incorporated in 1956 in New Mexico.
Donor(s): Mrs. Howard E. Wurlitzer.†

Financial data: (yr. ended 3/31/82): Assets, $1,153,314 (M); gifts received, $3,475; expenditures, $68,524, including $215 for 5 grants (high: $100; low: $15) and $46,521 for 20 grants to individuals.
Purpose and activities: A private operating foundation established to encourage and stimulate creative work in the humanities, arts, and allied fields through the provision of rent-free and utilities-free housing in Taos, New Mexico.
Types of support awarded: Grants to individuals.
Limitations: Giving limited to Taos, NM.
Application information: Application form required.
    Initial approach: Letter
    Deadline(s): None
    Board meeting date(s): As required
    Final notification: Several weeks
    Write: Henry A. Sauerwein, Jr., President
Officers and Trustees: Henry A. Sauerwein, Jr., President and Executive Director; Burton Phillips, Vice-President and Treasurer; Jean Harrison, Secretary; Sumner S. Koch, Dolores Montoya, Kenneth Peterson, Toni Tarleton.
Number of staff: None.
Employer Identification Number: 850128634

NEW YORK

2214
Abrams (Benjamin and Elizabeth) Foundation, Inc. ☒
645 Madison Ave.
New York 10022

Incorporated in 1943 in New York.
Donor(s): Benjamin Abrams,† Elizabeth Abrams Kramer.
Financial data: (yr. ended 12/31/83): Assets, $1,353,292 (M); expenditures, $128,324, including $94,870 for 60 grants (high: $20,784; low: $50).
Purpose and activities: General purposes; primarily local giving, and in Palm Beach County, Florida, with emphasis on higher education, including medical education, hospitals, Jewish welfare funds, and cultural programs.
Limitations: Giving primarily in NY, and in Palm Beach County, FL.
Officers and Directors: Elizabeth Abrams Kramer, President; Geraldine Kory, Secretary and Treasurer; Marjorie Hyman.
Employer Identification Number: 136092960

2215
Abrons (Louis and Anne) Foundation, Inc. ▼
c/o First Manhattan Co.
437 Madison Ave.
New York 10022   (212) 832-4376

Incorporated in 1950 in New York.
Donor(s): Anne S. Abrons,† Louis Abrons.†
Financial data: (yr. ended 4/30/84): Assets, $21,584,000 (M); expenditures, $1,647,217, including $1,423,250 for 125 grants (high: $360,000; low: $500; average: $5,000-$10,000).
Purpose and activities: General support; primarily local giving for social welfare agencies, major institutions, civic improvement and environmental projects.
Types of support awarded: Operating budgets, continuing support, annual campaigns, seed money, matching funds, general purposes, special projects, scholarship funds, fellowships.
Limitations: Giving primarily in New York, NY, metropolitan area. No grants to individuals.
Application information:
    Initial approach: Letter or full proposal
    Copies of proposal: 1
    Deadline(s): None
    Board meeting date(s): January, April, and September
    Final notification: 1 month
    Write: Richard Abrons, President
Officers and Directors*: Richard Abrons,* President and Treasurer; Herbert Abrons, Vice-President; Rita Aranow,* Vice-President; Edward Aranow, Secretary.
Number of staff: None.
Employer Identification Number: 136061329

2216
Abrons (Richard & Mimi) Foundation, Inc. ☒
c/o Oppenheim, Appel, Dixon & Co.
One New York Plaza
New York 10004

Established in New York.
Financial data: (yr. ended 12/31/82): Assets, $301,921 (M); expenditures, $109,245, including $107,040 for 43 grants (high: $94,000; low: $25).
Purpose and activities: Primarily local giving, with emphasis on an environmental council.
Types of support awarded: Research, conferences and seminars.
Limitations: Giving primarily in NY.
Employer Identification Number: 136184029

2217
ACF Foundation, Inc.
750 Third Ave.
New York 10017   (212) 986-8600

Incorporated in 1954 in New York.
Donor(s): ACF Industries, Inc.
Financial data: (yr. ended 4/30/83): Assets, $869,547 (M); expenditures, $384,473, including $349,650 for 191 grants (high: $38,000; low: $250; average: $250-$2,500), $17,450 for 7 grants to individuals and $15,355 for 98 employee matching gifts.

Purpose and activities: General giving, with emphasis on private higher education, community funds, health and youth agencies, urban affairs, and the arts, primarily in areas of company operations in Pennsylvania, Missouri, West Virginia, and Texas.
Types of support awarded: Annual campaigns, building funds, employee matching gifts, employee related scholarships.
Limitations: Giving primarily in areas of company operations in St. Louis, MO; Houston, TX; Milton and Reading, PA; and Huntington, WV. No support for primary and secondary education, public colleges and universities (except for matching gifts), sports or athletic events, organizations supported by United Way, municipal, state, and federal agencies, nursing homes, religious functions of sectarian or religious organizations. No grants to individuals (except for company-employee scholarships), or for operating budgets, continuing support, seed money, emergency funds, deficit financing, equipment, land acquisition, endowment funds, special projects, research, publications, or conferences; no loans.
Publications: Application guidelines, program policy statement.
Application information:
  Initial approach: Full proposal
  Copies of proposal: 1
  Deadline(s): Submit proposal preferably in February and March; no set deadline
  Board meeting date(s): Usually in June
  Final notification: After June meeting
  Write: Bruce A. Gustafsen, Secretary
Officers: Ivan A. Burns,* Chairman; J. Donald Brinkerhoff,* President; Eric F. Jensen,* Vice-President; Bruce A. Gustafsen, Secretary-Treasurer.
Directors:* Irma L. Beckley, Curtiss E. Frank, Martha T. Muse.
Number of staff: None.
Employer Identification Number: 136085065

2218
Achelis Foundation, The ▼
c/o Morris & McVeigh
767 Third Ave.
New York 10017   (212) 418-0588

Incorporated in 1940 in New York.
Donor(s): Elizabeth Achelis.†
Financial data: (yr. ended 12/31/83): Assets, $12,549,485 (M); gifts received, $13,438; expenditures, $868,743, including $771,000 for 41 grants (high: $30,000; low: $6,000).
Purpose and activities: Broad purposes; primarily local giving, including support for education, health and hospitals, youth and social agencies, the arts, and cultural programs.
Types of support awarded: Building funds, general purposes, operating budgets, matching funds, equipment, land acquisition.
Limitations: Giving primarily in the NY area. No grants to individuals, or for research, experimental projects, films, travel, publications, or conferences; no loans.
Publications: Biennial report, application guidelines.
Application information:
  Initial approach: Letter or full proposal
  Copies of proposal: 1

  Deadline(s): None
  Board meeting date(s): As required
  Write: Mary E. Caslin, Sec. and Exec. Dir.
Officers and Trustees: Guy G. Rutherfurd, President; Peter Frelinghuysen, Vice-President and Treasurer; Mary E. Caslin, Secretary and Executive Director; George A. Braga, Walter J.P. Curley, Jr., Mary S. Phipps.
Employer Identification Number: 136022018

2219
Adams (Emma J.) Memorial Fund, Inc.
c/o Finch & Schaefler
36 W. 44th St.
New York 10036   (212) 840-3636

Incorporated in 1932 in New York.
Donor(s): Emma J. Adams.†
Financial data: (yr. ended 12/31/82): Assets, $2,061,507 (M); expenditures, $124,984, including $107,878 for 25 grants (high: $25,000; low: $100; average: $1,500) and $9,913 for 9 loans.
Purpose and activities: Giving primarily in New York to aid the elderly and indigent through church-sponsored meals program and ecumenical medical care; also very limited grants to needy individuals on a non-recurring basis, and where agency-sponsored.
Types of support awarded: Emergency funds.
Limitations: Giving primarily in the New York, NY, metropolitan area. No grants for operating budgets, administrative expenses, building funds, special programs, or endowments.
Application information: Application form required.
  Initial approach: Letter
  Copies of proposal: 1
  Deadline(s): September 1
  Board meeting date(s): May and October
  Final notification: Usually within 60 days
  Write: Edward R. Finch, Jr.
Directors: Edward R. Finch, Jr., Pauline Swayze Finch, Mary D.F. Haskell, Trumbull Higgins, Donald W. Scholle, Harold L. Suttle.
Number of staff: 1 part-time professional; 2 part-time support.
Employer Identification Number: 136116503

2220
Ades Foundation, Inc. ⌑
17 East 37th St.
New York 10016

Incorporated in 1945 in New York.
Donor(s): Joseph Ades, Isaac Ades, Irving Baron, Barney Bernstein, Joseph Karp.
Financial data: (yr. ended 12/31/82): Assets, $98,704 (M); gifts received, $78,000; expenditures, $288,445, including $283,484 for 50 grants (high: $109,500; low: $50).
Purpose and activities: Broad purposes; grants largely for Jewish welfare funds, temple support, and education.
Officers: Joseph Ades, President; Robert Ades, Secretary; Albert Ades, Treasurer.
Employer Identification Number: 136077369

2221
Adler Foundation, Inc.
Purchase Ln.
Rye 10580   (914) 967-3335

Incorporated in 1951 in New York.
Donor(s): Morton M. Adler, Helen R. Adler, Harry Rosenthal.†
Financial data: (yr. ended 9/30/83): Assets, $3,165,023 (M); gifts received, $144,078; expenditures, $139,110, including $126,453 for 27 grants (high: $39,000; low: $10).
Purpose and activities: Broad purposes; grants chiefly for medical education and for medical research in diabetes and ophthalmology.
Types of support awarded: Research.
Limitations: No grants to individuals.
Application information:
  Initial approach: Letter
  Copies of proposal: 2
  Board meeting date(s): Annually
  Write: Morton M. Adler, President
Officers and Trustees: Morton M. Adler, President; John Adler, Vice-President; Edward H. Potter, Financial Vice-President; Joel I. Berson, Secretary; Helen R. Adler, Treasurer; Katherine A. Astrove, Robert F. Bradley, George F. Cahill, Jr., Charles E. Eble, Frederic de Hoffmann, William G. Kuhns, Alexander Marble, Robert H. McCooey, Helen A. Potter, Edwin H. Smith.
Employer Identification Number: 136087869

2222
Adler (Louis and Bessie) Foundation, Inc. ⌑
100 Park Ave.
New York 10017

Incorporated in 1946 in New York.
Donor(s): Louis Adler,† Louis Adler Realty Company, Inc.
Financial data: (yr. ended 12/31/81): Assets, $1,250,174 (M); expenditures, $739,355, including $154,925 for 31 grants (high: $25,000; low: $175).
Purpose and activities: Charitable purposes; primarily local giving, with emphasis on Jewish welfare funds, higher and secondary education, hospitals, youth agencies, and museums.
Limitations: Giving primarily in NY.
Application information:
  Write: Seymour M. Klein, Chairman
Officers and Directors: Seymour M. Klein, Chairman and President; Ruth Klein, Vice-President and Secretary; Robert Liberman, Treasurer.
Employer Identification Number: 131880122

2223
Aeroflex Foundation, The ⌑
500 Fifth Ave., 47th Fl.
New York 10110   (212) 947-8000

Established in 1964 in New York.
Donor(s): The Aeroflex Corporation.
Financial data: (yr. ended 9/30/83): Assets, $3,369,449 (M); expenditures, $324,661, including $193,500 for 14 grants (high: $45,000; low: $2,000).

Purpose and activities: Broad purposes; general giving with emphasis on cultural programs and higher education.
Limitations: No grants to individuals.
Application information:
 Initial approach: Letter
 Copies of proposal: 1
 Deadline(s): September
 Board meeting date(s): Quarterly
Trustees: Kay Knight Clarke, Neil Hussey, William A. Perlmuth.
Employer Identification Number: 136168635

2224
Agway Foundation
333 Butternut Dr.
P.O. Box 4933
Syracuse 13221   (315) 477-6506

Established in 1967 in New York.
Donor(s): Agway, Inc.
Financial data: (yr. ended 6/30/84): Assets, $2,067,742 (M); expenditures, $269,126, including $269,110 for 107 grants (high: $40,000; low: $50).
Purpose and activities: Broad purposes; general giving, with emphasis on northeastern agriculture, community funds, and rural youth organizations.
Types of support awarded: Continuing support, annual campaigns, seed money, emergency funds, building funds, equipment.
Limitations: Giving primarily in the northeastern states. No support for educational, religious, or political organizations. No grants to individuals or for operating budgets.
Publications: Application guidelines.
Application information:
 Initial approach: Letter
 Copies of proposal: 1
 Deadline(s): None
 Board meeting date(s): Every 6 to 8 weeks
 Write: Arthur J. Fogerty, Chairman
Officers and Trustees: Arthur J. Fogerty, Chairman; Robert J. Ryan, Secretary-Treasurer; Arnon C. Greif.
Number of staff: 1 part-time professional; 1 part-time support.
Employer Identification Number: 166089932

2225
AKC Fund, Inc.
145 E. 74th St., Suite 1C
New York 10021   (212) 737-1011

Incorporated in 1955 in New York.
Donor(s): Members of the Childs and Lawrence families.
Financial data: (yr. ended 3/31/84): Assets, $1,763,903 (M); expenditures, $97,987, including $84,650 for 45 grants (high: $5,750; low: $500; average: $1,500-$2,500).
Purpose and activities: Broad purposes; grants largely for elementary, secondary, and higher education; support also for conservation, hospitals, and the arts.
Limitations: Giving primarily in New England, with emphasis on CT. No grants to individuals.
Application information:

Initial approach: Letter, telephone, or full proposal
Copies of proposal: 1
Deadline(s): April 30
Board meeting date(s): May and occasionally between November and January
Write: Ann Brownell Sloane, Administrator
Officers and Directors: Barbara Childs Lawrence, President; Edward C. Childs, Richard S. Childs, Richard S. Childs, Jr., Vice-Presidents; James Vinton Lawrence, Secretary; John W. Childs, Treasurer; Timothy W. Childs.
Employer Identification Number: 136091321

2226
Albany's Hospital for Incurables
P.O. Box 3628, Executive Park
Albany 12203   (518) 459-7711

Established in 1974 in New York.
Financial data: (yr. ended 12/31/84): Assets, $2,552,000 (M); expenditures, $188,736, including $166,150 for 16 grants (high: $25,000; low: $5,000) and $19,106 for 1 loan.
Purpose and activities: Grants to facilitate the development of better health care for Albany, Schenectady, Rensselaer, and Saratoga Counties; support for hospitals, nursing homes, medical colleges, community health centers, and regional health planning groups.
Types of support awarded: General purposes, building funds, equipment, land acquisition, matching funds, loans.
Limitations: Giving limited to Albany, Schenectady, Rensselaer, and Saratoga Counties, NY. No grants to individuals, or for deficit financing, endowment funds, scholarships or fellowships.
Publications: Annual report, program policy statement, application guidelines.
Application information: Application form required.
 Initial approach: Telephone, letter, or full proposal
 Deadline(s): 30 days before board meetings
 Board meeting date(s): January, April, June, and September
 Final notification: 5 days after board meets
 Write: Arnold Cogswell, President
Officers and Trustees: Arnold Cogswell, President and Treasurer; Thomas L. Hawkins, Jr., M.D., Secretary; William Barnet, II, Albert Hessberg, II, Mrs. Lewis Muhlfelder, Mrs. Donald M. Slingerland, Richard F. Sonneborn, Mrs. Dorann Zimicki.
Number of staff: None.
Employer Identification Number: 14136443

2227
Alexander (Joseph) Foundation
400 Madison Ave., Suite 906
New York 10017   (212) 355-3688

Established in 1960 in New York.
Donor(s): Joseph Alexander.†
Financial data: (yr. ended 10/31/83): Assets, $11,129,330 (M); gifts received, $2,244; expenditures, $1,264,054, including $1,094,500 for 96 grants (high: $85,000; low: $500).

Purpose and activities: Primarily local giving for education, medical research, hospitals, and Jewish welfare and religious organizations.
Types of support awarded: General purposes, operating budgets, building funds, equipment, research.
Limitations: Giving primarily in New York, NY. No grants to individuals.
Application information:
 Deadline(s): Submit proposal preferably in February through August
 Board meeting date(s): January, April, July, and October
 Write: Alfred Mackler, President
Officers and Directors: Alfred Mackler, President; Helen Mackler, Vice-President; Arthur Alfert, Secretary; Robert Weintraub, Treasurer; Harvey Mackler.
Employer Identification Number: 510175951

2228
Allen (Frances) Foundation ⌷
711 Fifth Ave.
New York 10022   (212) 832-8000

Trust established in 1959 in New York.
Donor(s): Members of the Allen family, Allen & Company, Incorporated.
Financial data: (yr. ended 12/31/82): Assets, $2,906,429 (L); expenditures, $312,342, including $304,200 for 59 grants (high: $100,000; low: $500).
Purpose and activities: Broad purposes; primarily local giving, with emphasis on medical research and youth agencies; interests also include higher education, Jewish welfare funds, and hospitals.
Limitations: Giving primarily in NY. No grants to individuals.
Application information:
 Initial approach: Proposal
 Copies of proposal: 1
 Board meeting date(s): Monthly
Trustees: C. Robert Allen III, Charles Allen, Jr., Herbert Allen, Herbert Anthony Allen.
Employer Identification Number: 136104670

2229
Allen (Rita) Foundation, Inc.
550 Park Ave.
New York 10021

Incorporated in 1953 in New York.
Donor(s): Rita Allen Cassel.†
Financial data: (yr. ended 12/31/82): Assets, $6,570,238 (M); expenditures, $260,399, including $256,061 for 39 grants (high: $60,000; low: $100).
Purpose and activities: Charitable purposes; primarily medical grants, with emphasis on research in the fields of cancer, multiple sclerosis, cerebral palsy, and euphorics and analgesics related to the terminally ill; some support for recognized welfare and religious organizations.
Limitations: No grants to individuals (except university research scientists), or for building funds, or operating budgets.
Application information:
 Copies of proposal: 1
 Deadline(s): January 15

Board meeting date(s): Annually and as required
Write: Milton E. Cassel, President
Officers and Directors: Milton E. Cassel, President and Treasurer; Moore Gates, Jr., Secretary; George S. Johnston.
Employer Identification Number: 136116429

2230
Allied Stores Foundation, Inc.
1114 Ave. of the Americas
New York 10036 (212) 764-2333

Incorporated in 1945 in New York.
Donor(s): Allied Stores Corporation.
Financial data: (yr. ended 12/31/83): Assets, $3,384,378 (M); gifts received, $1,000; expenditures, $218,841, including $207,290 for 85 grants (high: $30,000; low: $500).
Purpose and activities: Broad purposes, including relief of needy company employees; health grants usually confined to national health agencies and academic grants primarily confined to regional educational associations in areas where stores are located.
Types of support awarded: Scholarship funds, continuing support, annual campaigns, research, grants to individuals.
Limitations: No support for individual colleges. No grants for building or endowment funds, operating budgets, or special projects; no scholarships to individuals.
Application information:
Initial approach: Letter
Deadline(s): Submit proposal preferably in November
Board meeting date(s): January
Write: Patrick Edwards, Vice-President
Officers and Directors: Thomas M. Macioce,* President; Patrick Edwards,* Vice-President and Secretary; Howard E. Hassler,* George C. Kern, Jr.,* Vice-Presidents; JoAnn Abma, Treasurer; Lillian Berkman*.
Employer Identification Number: 136102820

2231
Allyn Foundation, Inc. ⌑
P.O. Box 22
Skaneateles 13152
Grant application address: c/o Mrs. Marie Infanger, RD No. 1, Cayuga, NY 13034; Tel.: (315) 252-7618

Incorporated in 1956 in New York.
Financial data: (yr. ended 12/31/82): Assets, $2,019,860 (M); expenditures, $147,719, including $135,550 for 45 grants (high: $15,000; low: $200).
Purpose and activities: Primarily local giving, with emphasis on higher education, including medical education; grants also for Protestant church support, youth agencies, arts and culture, and hospitals.
Limitations: Giving primarily in NY.
Application information:
Initial approach: Letter
Deadline(s): None
Officers and Directors: William G. Allyn, President; Lou F. Allyn, William F. Allyn, Donald Kreiger, Vice-Presidents; Marie Infanger, Secretary-Treasurer and Executive Director; Dawn Allyn, Janet Allyn, Sonya Allyn, Robert C. Heaviside, Rev. Stephen A. Kish, Ruth Penchoen, Elsa A. Soderberg, Peter Soderberg, Robert C. Soderberg.
Employer Identification Number: 156017723

2232
Altman Foundation ▼ ⌑
361 Fifth Ave.
New York 10016 (212) 679-7800

Incorporated in 1913 in New York.
Donor(s): Benjamin Altman,† Colonel Michael Friedsam.†
Financial data: (yr. ended 12/31/83): Assets, $10,338,080 (M); expenditures, $877,340, including $791,600 for 62 grants (high: $110,000; low: $1,000; average: $1,000-$50,000).
Purpose and activities: To aid charitable and educational institutions in New York State, with emphasis on religious associations and welfare funds; support also for hospitals, higher and secondary education, youth agencies, and child welfare.
Limitations: Giving limited to NY, with emphasis on the New York City metropolitan area.
Application information:
Write: John S. Burke, Jr., President
Officers: John S. Burke, Jr.,* President; Marion C. Baer, Secretary; Thomas C. Burke,* Treasurer.
Trustees:* Thomas F. Moore, Jr., Jane B. O'Connell, Maurice A. Selinger, Jr., Martin F. Shea.
Employer Identification Number: 131623879

2233
Altschul Foundation, The ▼
342 Madison Ave., Suite 1002
New York 10017 (212) 697-3525

Incorporated in 1941 in New York.
Donor(s): Louis Altschul,† Mrs. Jeanette Cohen Altschul.†
Financial data: (yr. ended 6/30/83): Assets, $3,620,095 (M); expenditures, $808,525, including $487,175 for 57 grants (high: $170,000; low: $125; average: $1,000-$10,000).
Purpose and activities: General purposes; primarily local giving, with emphasis on Jewish welfare funds; support also for higher education, community funds, health agencies, youth agencies, social services, and hospitals.
Limitations: Giving primarily in New York City, NY.
Application information:
Deadline(s): June 1 and September 1
Board meeting date(s): June and September
Write: Leonard Rodney
Officers and Trustees: Gerald A. Rothstein, President; Louis Rothstein, Secretary; Phyllis Rothstein, Treasurer; Israel Goldstein, Vivian Reichman.
Number of staff: None.
Employer Identification Number: 136400009

2234
American Conservation Association, Inc.
30 Rockefeller Plaza, Rm. 5510
New York 10112 (212) 247-3700

Incorporated in 1958 in New York.
Donor(s): Laurance S. Rockefeller, Laurance Rockefeller, Rockefeller Brothers Fund.
Financial data: (yr. ended 12/31/83): Assets, $724,455 (M); gifts received, $358,000; expenditures, $369,800, including $257,500 for 13 grants (high: $60,000; low: $15,000) and $2,815 for 2 foundation-administered programs.
Purpose and activities: A private operating foundation organized to advance knowledge and understanding of conservation and to preserve the beauties of the landscape and the natural and living resources in areas of the United States and elsewhere; to educate the public in the proper use of such areas.
Limitations: Giving limited to the U.S. No grants to individuals, or for building funds, endowments, or scholarships and fellowships; no loans.
Application information:
Initial approach: Letter or full proposal
Copies of proposal: 1
Deadline(s): Submit proposal preferably early in the year
Board meeting date(s): September or October; executive committee meets frequently
Write: George R. Lamb, Executive Vice-President
Officers: Laurance S. Rockefeller,* Chairman; Laurance Rockefeller,* President; George R. Lamb,* Executive Vice-President; Gene W. Setzer,* Vice-President; Franklin E. Parker, Secretary; Ruth C. Haupert, Treasurer.
Trustees:* Nash Castro, William G. Conway, Dana S. Creel, Mrs. Lyndon B. Johnson, Fred I. Kent III, W. Barnabas McHenry, Patrick F. Noonan, Story Clark Resor, Russell E. Train, William H. Whyte, Jr., Conrad L. Wirth.
Number of staff: 3 part-time professional; 1 part-time support.
Employer Identification Number: 131874023

2235
American Express Foundation ▼
American Express Plaza
New York 10004 (212) 323-3477

Incorporated in 1954 in New York.
Donor(s): American Express Company, and its subsidiaries.
Financial data: (yr. ended 12/31/84): Assets, $555,903 (M); gifts received, $5,759,260; expenditures, $5,994,700, including $5,112,782 for grants (high: $250,000; low: $100; average: $5,000-$25,000), $131,597 for grants to individuals and $396,728 for employee matching gifts.

Purpose and activities: Broad purposes; committed to efforts for creating public-private partnerships, primarily in support of education, employment and training programs in the financial services, travel and tourism industries; support for education includes employee matching gift program and children of employee scholarship program administered by the National Merit Scholarship Corporation; grants to local organizations for health and welfare, urban affairs, and community development; support also for innovative programs to promote understanding of the world's cultural diversity and its shared heritage.
Types of support awarded: Special projects, continuing support, employee related scholarships, employee matching gifts.
Limitations: No support for religious, veterans', or fraternal organizations. No grants to individuals (except for company-employee scholarships), or for building or endowment funds, operating funds (of United Way member agencies), or fundraising events; no loans.
Publications: Company report, program policy statement, application guidelines.
Application information: Application form required.
> *Initial approach:* Proposal
> *Copies of proposal:* 1
> *Deadline(s):* None
> *Board meeting date(s):* March and September
> *Final notification:* 8 weeks
> *Write:* Mary Beth Salerno, Director
Officers: Stephen S. Halsey, President; Dee Topal, Vice-President; Mary Beth Salerno, Secretary; F. Gregory Fitz-Gerald, Treasurer.
Trustees: L.V. Gerstner, James D. Robinson, III, Robert F. Smith, Sanford I. Weill.
Number of staff: 8 full-time professional; 1 part-time professional; 4 full-time support; 1 part-time support.
Employer Identification Number: 136123529

2236
American Friends of Israel ⌑
10 Rockefeller Plaza, Suite 612
New York 10020

Established in 1948.
Financial data: (yr. ended 12/31/82): Assets, $2,344,020 (M); expenditures, $135,155, including $133,250 for 7 grants (high: $100,000; low: $750).
Purpose and activities: Primarily local giving, with emphasis on higher education in Israel.
Limitations: Giving primarily in NY.
Officers: Cary Shwartz, President; Alexander J. Katz, Secretary; Julian B. Venezky, Treasurer.
Employer Identification Number: 136113746

2237
American-Standard Foundation ▼
40 West 40th St.
New York 10018   (212) 703-5188

Trust established in 1952 in Pennsylvania as Westinghouse Air Brake Foundation; name changed in 1977.
Donor(s): American-Standard Inc.

Financial data: (yr. ended 12/31/83): Assets, $8,678,861 (M); gifts received, $335,574; expenditures, $1,154,368, including $967,488 for 225 grants (high: $100,000; low: $500; average: $1,000-$10,000) and $108,166 for 229 employee matching gifts.
Purpose and activities: Charitable purposes; grants largely in areas of company operations for community funds, higher education, including employee matching gifts, and civic affairs; support also for cultural programs, health organizations, and youth agencies.
Types of support awarded: Employee matching gifts, annual campaigns, general purposes, endowment funds, continuing support.
Limitations: Giving primarily in areas of significant company operations. No grants to individuals, or for capital funds, research, or scholarships and fellowships; no loans.
Publications: Program policy statement.
Application information:
> *Initial approach:* Letter
> *Copies of proposal:* 1
> *Deadline(s):* None
> *Board meeting date(s):* Quarterly
> *Final notification:* 3 to 6 months
> *Write:* Jeanne M. Golly, President
Officer and Trustees: Jeanne M. Golly, President; Richard H. Francis, John F. Geer.
Number of staff: None.
Employer Identification Number: 256018911

2238
AMETEK Foundation, Inc.
410 Park Ave.
New York 10022   (212) 935-8640

Incorporated in 1960 in New York.
Donor(s): AMETEK, Inc.
Financial data: (yr. ended 12/31/83): Assets, $3,087,199 (M); gifts received, $500,000; expenditures, $504,605, including $500,228 for 90 grants (high: $70,000; low: $250).
Purpose and activities: Charitable and educational purposes; general giving, with emphasis on community funds, hospitals, higher education, welfare, and medical research.
Types of support awarded: Annual campaigns, building funds, research, employee related scholarships.
Limitations: No grants to individuals, or for endowment funds, or matching gifts; no loans.
Application information:
> *Initial approach:* Letter
> *Copies of proposal:* 1
> *Deadline(s):* Submit proposal preferably in February or September; deadlines February 28 and September 30
> *Board meeting date(s):* April and November
> *Final notification:* 2 weeks after board meets
> *Write:* Robert J. Coffman, Assistant Secretary-Treasurer
Officers: John H. Lux,* President; Robert L. Noland, Vice-President; B.E. Brandes,* Secretary and Treasurer.
Directors:* H.N. Friedlaender, Samuel Hoffman, Anthony A. Sirna, III.
Number of staff: None.
Employer Identification Number: 136095939

2239
Anderson (Douglas G.) - Leigh R. Evans Foundation ⌑
1420 College Ave.
Elmira 14902   (607) 734-2281

Incorporated in 1960 in New York.
Donor(s): Hardinge Brothers, Inc.
Financial data: (yr. ended 10/31/83): Assets, $1,187,509 (M); gifts received, $175,000; expenditures, $386,282, including $380,850 for 25 grants (high: $60,000; low: $2,000).
Purpose and activities: Broad purposes; primarily local giving, with emphasis on higher education, hospitals, community funds, and the performing arts.
Types of support awarded: General purposes, building funds, equipment.
Limitations: Giving primarily in Elmira, NY. No grants to individuals.
Application information:
> *Initial approach:* Proposal
> *Copies of proposal:* 1
> *Board meeting date(s):* Semiannually and as required
> *Write:* Robert G. Prochnow, President
Officers: Robert G. Prochnow,* President; John D. Anderson,* Vice-President; Bela C. Tifft,* Secretary; Malcolm L. Gibson, Treasurer.
Trustees:* Robert E. Agan, Charles R. Bauman, E. Martin Gibson, Douglas A. Greenlee, Joseph C. Littleton, Boyd McDowell, J. Ralph Murray, Whitney S. Powers, Maurice P. Whitney.
Employer Identification Number: 166024690

2240
Anderson Foundation, Inc., The ⌑
c/o Chemung Canal Trust Co., Trust Dept.
P.O. Box 1522
Elmira 14902

Incorporated in 1960 in New York.
Donor(s): Jane G. Anderson, Douglas G. Anderson.†
Financial data: (yr. ended 4/30/83): Assets, $2,489,953 (M); expenditures, $197,211, including $184,700 for 25 grants (high: $50,000; low: $1,000).
Purpose and activities: Primarily local giving, with emphasis on cultural and social service organizations.
Types of support awarded: Scholarship funds, operating budgets, deficit financing, equipment.
Limitations: Giving primarily in Elmira, NY.
Officers and Trustees: John D. Anderson, President; Charles A. Winding, Vice-President; Bela C. Tifft, Secretary; Bertha A. Greenlee, Treasurer; Robert T. Jones, Ethel A. Whittaker.
Employer Identification Number: 166024689

2241
Appleman Foundation, Inc., The ⌑
c/o Bessemer Trust Co.
630 Fifth Ave., 39th Fl.
New York 10111

Incorporated in 1952 in Delaware.
Donor(s): Nathan Appleman, and members of the Appleman family.

Financial data: (yr. ended 12/31/82): Assets, $697,958 (M); gifts received, $528,875; expenditures, $373,162, including $311,626 for 67 grants (high: $75,000; low: $10).
Purpose and activities: Primarily local giving in New York and Palm Beach, Florida, for Jewish welfare funds, higher education, including a Jewish theological seminary, hospitals, social services, and temple support.
Limitations: Giving primarily in NY and Palm Beach, FL.
Application information:
 Write: Joe Copko
Officer: Nathan Appleman, President.
Employer Identification Number: 136154978

2242
Archbold (Adrian & Jessie) Charitable Trust ▼ ☒
Chemical Bank, Administrative Services Dept.
30 Rockefeller Plaza
New York 10012   (212) 621-2143

Trust established in 1976 in New York.
Donor(s): Mrs. Adrian Archbold.†
Financial data: (yr. ended 11/30/83): Assets, $10,488,788 (M); expenditures, $812,395, including $684,074 for 164 grants (high: $235,000; low: $100).
Purpose and activities: Grants primarily for hospitals and health-related organizations, higher education, youth and social agencies, and a recreation center.
Types of support awarded: General purposes, continuing support, program-related investments, research, publications, conferences and seminars.
Limitations: No grants to individuals, or for endowment funds, scholarships or fellowships, or building funds; no loans.
Application information:
 Initial approach: Proposal
 Copies of proposal: 1
 Board meeting date(s): As required
 Final notification: 3 to 6 months
 Write: Barbara Strohmeier
Trustees: Arthur J. Mahon, Chemical Bank.
Employer Identification Number: 510179829

2243
Arkell Hall Foundation Incorporated ▼
55 Montgomery St.
Canajoharie 13317   (518) 673-5417

Incorporated in 1948 in New York.
Donor(s): Mrs. F.E. Barbour,† and others.
Financial data: (yr. ended 11/30/84): Assets, $18,550,382 (M); gifts received, $1,605; expenditures, $1,097,767, including $663,000 for 48 grants (high: $85,000; low: $400).
Purpose and activities: Broad purposes; to erect and maintain a residence and home for needy elderly women who are residents of Montgomery County; also general local giving, with emphasis on higher education, including scholarship funds, hospitals, and health and social services including youth agencies.
Types of support awarded: Scholarship funds, building funds.

Limitations: Giving primarily in NY (outside the City of New York). No grants to individuals, or for matching gifts, special projects, publications, conferences, or research; no loans.
Application information:
 Initial approach: Full proposal
 Copies of proposal: 1
 Deadline(s): October 15
 Board meeting date(s): January, March, June, and October
 Write: Franklin L. Fero, President
Officers and Trustees: Franklin L. Fero, President; Edward W. Shineman, Jr., Vice-President; William B. MacKenzie, Vice-President; Edward Spraker, Secretary; Robert H. Wille, Treasurer; James R. Dern, Ferdinand C. Kaiser, Richard G. Kimmerer, William T. Martin.
Number of staff: None.
Employer Identification Number: 141343077

2244
Aron (J.) Charitable Foundation, Inc. ▼
126 East 56th St.
New York 10022   (212) 832-3405

Incorporated in 1934 in New York.
Donor(s): Members of the Aron family.
Financial data: (yr. ended 12/31/83): Assets, $21,063,073 (M); expenditures, $1,300,017, including $1,179,153 for 234 grants (high: $130,000; low: $100).
Purpose and activities: Broad purposes; grants primarily in New York and New Orleans for hospitals and medical schools, religious welfare funds, health agencies, education, including scholarship funds, and cultural programs.
Limitations: Giving primarily in NY and New Orleans, LA. No grants to individuals.
Application information:
 Initial approach: Full proposal
 Copies of proposal: 1
 Board meeting date(s): January, April, July, September or October, and December
 Write: Peter A. Aron, Executive Director
Officers: Jack R. Aron,* President; Peter A. Aron,* Vice-President and Executive Director; Robert Aron,* Vice-President; Hans P. Jepson, Secretary and Treasurer.
Directors:* Jacqueline A. Morrison, Ronald J. Stein.
Number of staff: 1 part-time support.
Employer Identification Number: 136068230

2245
ARW Foundation, The
c/o Pinkerton's, Inc.
100 Church St.
New York 10007   (212) 285-4890

Incorporated in 1966 in Delaware.
Donor(s): Robert A. Pinkerton.†
Financial data: (yr. ended 12/31/82): Assets, $5,957,788 (M); expenditures, $418,310, including $363,883 for grants to individuals.
Purpose and activities: Broad purposes; assistance to employees and former employees of Pinkerton's, Inc. and scholarships for children of employees.
Types of support awarded: Grants to individuals, employee related scholarships.

Publications: 990-PF.
Application information:
 Initial approach: Letter
 Copies of proposal: 1
 Deadline(s): Submit proposal preferably in March or October
 Board meeting date(s): June and December
 Write: Joan Colello, Executive Director
Officers and Trustees: Louise C. Pinkerton Marshall, Chairman; Edward J. Bednarz, President; Joan Colello, Secretary and Executive Director; Eugene C. Fey, Treasurer; George J. Gillespie, III.
Employer Identification Number: 136206601

2246
ASARCO Foundation ▼
120 Broadway
New York 10271   (212) 699-1284

Incorporated in 1956 in New York.
Donor(s): ASARCO Incorporated.
Financial data: (yr. ended 12/31/82): Assets, $636,891 (M); expenditures, $499,705, including $387,645 for 103 grants (high: $40,500; low: $45) and $95,569 for employee matching gifts.
Purpose and activities: General purposes; a limited program, including support for community funds, scholarship programs of colleges and universities with emphasis on mineral technology and engineering, hospitals, cultural activities, and an employee matching gifts program for education.
Types of support awarded: Employee matching gifts, scholarship funds, fellowships, general purposes, continuing support.
Limitations: Giving limited to areas of company operations. No grants to individuals, or for endowment funds, research, or operating budgets; no loans.
Publications: Program policy statement, application guidelines.
Application information:
 Initial approach: Letter
 Board meeting date(s): As required
 Final notification: 2 to 3 months
 Write: Rose J. Schwing, Vice-President
Officers: Francis R. McAllister,* President; Rose J. Schwing, Douglas H. Soutar,* Vice-Presidents; Alexander J. Gillespie, Jr.,* Secretary; Stephen P. McCandless,* Treasurer.
Directors and Members:* George W. Anderson, Ralph L. Hennebach, Robert J. Muth, Richard deJ. Osborne, T.C. Osborne.
Number of staff: 1 part-time support.
Employer Identification Number: 136089860

2247
Associated Metals and Minerals Foundation, Inc. ☒
30 Rockefeller Plaza, 26th Fl.
New York 10020

Incorporated in 1951 in New York.
Donor(s): Associated Metals and Minerals Corp.
Financial data: (yr. ended 12/31/82): Assets, $1,026,626 (M); expenditures, $184,426, including $177,500 for 2 grants (high: $175,000; low: $2,500).

Purpose and activities: Broad purposes; grants largely for local Jewish welfare funds.
Limitations: Giving primarily in NY.
Officers: F.A. Lissauer, President; S.E. Eliel, Vice-President; T.A. Aron, Secretary.
Employer Identification Number: 136161478

2248
Astor (The Vincent) Foundation ▼
405 Park Ave.
New York 10022   (212) 758-4110

Incorporated in 1948 in New York; reincorporated in 1974 in Delaware.
Donor(s): Vincent Astor.†
Financial data: (yr. ended 12/31/84): Assets, $33,989,449 (M); expenditures, $7,242,479, including $6,702,833 for 106 grants (high: $1,250,000; low: $2,500; average: $25,000-$200,000).
Purpose and activities: Broad purposes; primarily confined to institutions and projects in New York City or projects significantly affecting New York City residents; support for certain cultural institutions (except programs involving the performing arts), parks and landmark preservation, neighborhood revitalization projects, community-based programs, especially those involving or affecting children and older people, and to a limited extent, for educational programs.
Types of support awarded: Operating budgets, continuing support, seed money, building funds, equipment, land acquisition, endowment funds, matching funds, scholarship funds, professorships.
Limitations: Giving primarily in New York City, NY. No support for performing arts, medicine, mental health, or private schools. No grants to individuals, or for annual campaigns, emergency funds, deficit financing, research, film production, publications, or conferences; no loans.
Publications: Annual report, program policy statement, application guidelines.
Application information:
  Initial approach: Letter or telephone
  Copies of proposal: 1
  Deadline(s): None
  Board meeting date(s): April, October, and December
  Final notification: 6 months
  Write: Linda L. Gillies, Director
Officers: Mrs. Vincent Astor,* President; Anthony D. Marshall,* Vice-President; Peter P. McN. Gates, Secretary; Fergus Reid III,* Treasurer; Linda L. Gillies,* Director; Mary Earle, Program Officer.
Trustees:* Thomas R. Coolidge, Henry N. Ess III, Howard Phipps, Jr., John Pierrepont, Felix Rohatyn.
Advisory Trustees: Peter S. Paine, David W. Peck, Richard S. Perkins.
Number of staff: 1 full-time professional; 2 full-time support; 2 part-time support.
Employer Identification Number: 237167124

2249
AT&T Foundation
550 Madison Ave.
New York 10022   (212) 605-6734

Established in 1984 in New York.
Donor(s): American Telephone & Telegraph Co., Western Electric Fund.
Financial data: (yr. ended 12/31/84): Assets, $86,336,346 (M); expenditures, $16,249,518, including $15,170,300 for 903 grants (high: $400,000; low: $1,000) and $962,099 for 6,000 employee matching gifts.
Purpose and activities: General purposes; principal source of philanthropy for AT&T and its subsidiaries; scope is national, emphasizing support of private higher education, and institutions and projects in the areas of health care, social action, and the arts. Aid to local communities provided primarily through the United Way.
Types of support awarded: Building funds, equipment, matching funds, employee matching gifts, special projects, research.
Limitations: No support for religious organizations for sectarian purposes; local chapters of national organizations; elementary or secondary schools, social sciences or health sciences programs, medical or nursing schools, or junior and community colleges; industrial affiliate programs or technical trade associations; medical research projects, disease-related health associations, or for operating expenses or capital campaigns of local health or human service agencies other than hospitals; or sports, teams, or athletic competitions. No grants to individuals, or for operating budgets, annual campaigns, seed money, emergency funds, deficit financing, land acquisition, endowment funds, scholarships, fellowships, publications, or conferences; does not purchase advertisements or donate equipment.
Publications: Biennial report, application guidelines, program policy statement.
Application information: Detailed program limitations provided in guidelines; first biennial report (1984-85) due out in early 1986.
  Initial approach: Letter or proposal
  Copies of proposal: 1
  Deadline(s): None
  Board meeting date(s): February, April, June, August, October, and December
  Final notification: 90 days
  Write: Ms. Dorothy E. Francis, Secretary
Officers: Reynold Levy,* President; Richard W. Arnold, Senior Vice-President; Dorothy E. Francis, Secretary; Robert E. Angelica, Treasurer.
Directors:* Edward M. Block, Chairman; W. Frank Blount, J.W. Cannon, R.D. Dalziel, N.J. Dreicer, M.J. Eisen, J.F. Healy, A.J. Izzo, M. Laurie, C.K.N. Patel, L.W. Plekenpol, T.L. Porter, K.O. Raschke, N. Rhinehart, Jr.
Number of staff: 9 full-time professional; 8 part-time professional; 2 full-time support; 2 part-time support.
Employer Identification Number: 133166495

2250
Atran Foundation, Inc.
23-25 E. 21st St., 3rd Fl.
New York 10010   (212) 505-9677

Incorporated in 1945 in New York.
Donor(s): Frank Z. Atran.†
Financial data: (yr. ended 11/30/83): Assets, $4,975,114 (M); expenditures, $593,739, including $465,630 for grants.
Purpose and activities: General purposes, including research relating to labor and labor relations, art, science, literature, economics, and sociology; support of publications furthering these purposes; endowment for chairs of learning in these fields.
Types of support awarded: Continuing support, annual campaigns, seed money, emergency funds, endowment funds, research, publications, conferences and seminars, scholarship funds, professorships, internships, exchange programs, matching funds.
Limitations: No grants to individuals.
Application information:
  Initial approach: Full proposal
  Copies of proposal: 4
  Deadline(s): October 31
  Board meeting date(s): Between November and January and as required
  Write: Julius A. Bell, Secretary
Officers: Max Atran, President; Julius A. Bell, Secretary and Treasurer.
Employer Identification Number: 135566548

2251
Avon Products Foundation, Inc. ▼
Nine West 57th St.
New York 10019   (212) 546-6733

Incorporated in 1955 in New York.
Donor(s): Avon Products, Inc.
Financial data: (yr. ended 12/31/83): Assets, $131,000 (M); gifts received, $1,700,000; expenditures, $1,867,665, including $1,670,037 for 630 grants (high: $100,000; low: $250; average: $2,500-$5,000), $123,635 for 68 grants to individuals and $73,993 for 384 employee matching gifts.
Purpose and activities: Broad purposes; support for institutions and agencies whose main focus is on individuals, particularly women, minorities and the disadvantaged; support also for hospitals, education, cultural organizations, urban programs, and civic projects. Scholarship program limited to named school districts in areas of company operations and to children of company employees.
Types of support awarded: General purposes, operating budgets, fellowships, employee related scholarships, matching funds, technical assistance, special projects.

Limitations: Giving limited to areas immediately surrounding company operations in New York City, Rye, and Suffern, NY; Newark, DE; Atlanta, GA; Springdale, OH; Pasadena, CA; Morton Grove, IL; and Newport News, VA. No support for individual member agencies of United Way and United Fund, or national health and welfare organizations. No grants to individuals (except for scholarships for children of company employees), or for capital or endowment funds; no loans.
Publications: Application guidelines.
Application information:
Initial approach: Letter
Copies of proposal: 1
Deadline(s): January 15 (health); May 15 (education and humanities); July 15 (community and social services); and October 15 (women and minority economic development)
Write: Glenn S. Clarke, President
Officers and Directors: Glenn S. Clarke, President; Hicks B. Waldron, Vice-President; John F. Cox, Secretary; Margo R. Long, Treasurer; William R. Chaney, Philip J. Davis, James E. Preston.
Number of staff: 3 full-time professional; 2 full-time support.
Employer Identification Number: 136128447

2252
Axe-Houghton Foundation
875 Third Ave., 23rd Fl.
New York 10022   (212) 909-6000

Incorporated in 1965 in New York.
Donor(s): Emerson W. Axe.†
Financial data: (yr. ended 2/29/84): Assets, $1,255,723 (M); expenditures, $107,857, including $69,000 for 18 grants (high: $9,000; low: $1,000; average: $2,000-$5,000).
Purpose and activities: To encourage the improvement of spoken English in all its manifestations, including remedial speech, public speaking, and speaking as an art form.
Types of support awarded: Seed money, research, special projects, conferences and seminars.
Limitations: No grants to individuals, or for operating budgets, continuing support, annual campaigns, emergency funds, deficit financing, capital funds, endowment funds, matching gifts, scholarships and fellowships, or publications; no loans.
Publications: Program policy statement, application guidelines.
Application information:
Initial approach: Letter
Copies of proposal: 1
Deadline(s): Submit full proposal preferably in October or November; deadline November 1
Board meeting date(s): May and December
Final notification: 1 month
Write: William A. Hance, President
Officers: William A. Hance,* President; Robert B. von Mehren,* Richard A. Norman,* Vice-Presidents; Harold A. Gunn, Secretary; Thomas J. McDonald, Treasurer.

Directors:* Alfred Berman, Howard A. Cutler, Remington P. Patterson, Suzanne Schwartz.
Number of staff: 1 part-time professional; 3 part-time support.
Employer Identification Number: 136200200

2253
Bache Corporation Foundation ⌑
(formerly Bache Halsey Stuart Shields Foundation)
100 Gold St.
New York 10292

Incorporated in 1965 in New York.
Donor(s): Bache Halsey Stuart Shields Inc.
Financial data: (yr. ended 1/31/83): Assets, $72,297 (M); gifts received, $156,800; expenditures, $159,314, including $159,180 for 86 grants (high: $20,000; low: $200).
Purpose and activities: General giving, with emphasis on social services, higher education, hospitals, cultural programs, and Jewish and Roman Catholic welfare funds.
Officers: John J. Curran,* Secretary; Bruno G. Bissetta, Treasurer.
Directors:* George McGough, Leland Paton.
Employer Identification Number: 136193023

2254
Bache (H. L.) Foundation ⌑
c/o R.A. Eisner & Co.
380 Madison Ave.
New York 10017

Incorporated in 1945 in New York.
Donor(s): Alice K. Bache, Harold L. Bache,† Bache & Co.
Financial data: (yr. ended 12/31/82): Assets, $534,773 (M); expenditures, $124,805, including $115,100 for 19 grants (high: $25,000; low: $500).
Purpose and activities: Primarily local giving, with emphasis on intercultural relations, hospitals, medical education, cultural programs, including a museum and a zoological society, and some social service agencies.
Limitations: Giving primarily in NY.
Officers and Directors: John E. Leslie, Vice-President; Maurice C. Greenbaum, Secretary-Treasurer.
Employer Identification Number: 136082714

2255
Bachmann Foundation, Inc., The ⌑
c/o Danziger, Bangser & Klipstein
230 Park Ave.
New York 10017   (212) 867-6500

Incorporated in 1949 in New York.
Donor(s): Louis Bachmann, Thomas W. Strauss.
Financial data: (yr. ended 12/31/82): Assets, $1,933,780 (M); gifts received, $178,500; expenditures, $223,284, including $215,540 for 122 grants (high: $41,000; low: $25).
Purpose and activities: Primarily local giving, with emphasis on Jewish welfare funds, higher and secondary education, hospitals, and children's welfare and development programs.
Limitations: Giving primarily in NY. No grants to individuals.

Application information:
Write: Louis Bachmann, President
Officers and Directors: Louis Bachmann, President; Barbara Bachmann Strauss, Vice-President; Richard M. Danziger, Secretary; Thomas W. Strauss, Treasurer.
Employer Identification Number: 136043497

2256
Badgeley (Rose M.) Residuary Charitable Trust ▼ ⌑
c/o Marine Midland Bank
250 Park Ave.
New York 10177   (212) 949-6707

Trust established about 1977 in New York.
Donor(s): Rose Badgeley.†
Financial data: (yr. ended 1/31/83): Assets, $9,288,063 (M); gifts received, $60,335; expenditures, $953,419, including $873,938 for 44 grants (high: $69,888; low: $2,000; average: $5,000-$32,000).
Purpose and activities: Local giving, with emphasis on hospitals and health associations, particularly those concerned with medical research; higher education, cultural programs, and social agencies, including youth agencies.
Limitations: Giving limited to the New York, NY, metropolitan area.
Application information:
Initial approach: Full proposal
Deadline(s): 30 day before board meets
Board meeting date(s): Quarterly
Write: Leonard J. Risi, Vice-President
Trustees: John Duffy, Marine Midland Bank (Leonard J. Risi, Vice-President).
Number of staff: 1 full-time professional; 1 part-time professional; 1 full-time support; 1 part-time support.
Employer Identification Number: 136744781

2257
Baier (Marie) Foundation, Inc.
150 Fifth Ave., Rm. 420
New York 10011   (212) 989-7733

Donor(s): John F. Baier.†
Financial data: (yr. ended 1/31/83): Assets, $5,909,186 (M); gifts received, $250,000; expenditures, $443,315, including $402,000 for 20 grants (high: $30,000; low: $10,000).
Purpose and activities: Grants primarily for higher and secondary education, cultural programs, and youth agencies; support also for German-American organizations, and a home for the aged.
Limitations: No grants to individuals.
Application information:
Initial approach: Letter
Write: Berteline Baier Dale, President
Officers and Directors: Berteline Baier Dale, President; John F. Baier, Jr., Vice-President; Erich H. Markel, Treasurer; Carl H. Ficke, Guenter F. Metsch, William M. Parkhurst, Sidney Sirkin.
Employer Identification Number: 136267032

2258
Baird (The Cameron) Foundation ▼
8877 Jennings Rd.
Eden 14057   (716) 992-9128

Trust established in 1960 in New York.
Donor(s): Members of the family of Cameron Baird.
Financial data: (yr. ended 12/31/82): Assets, $7,664,568 (M); expenditures, $623,771, including $574,265 for 47 grants (high: $120,000; low: $250).
Purpose and activities: Broad purposes; primarily local giving, with emphasis on music and cultural programs, higher and secondary education, social services, population control, conservation, and a civil rights organization.
Limitations: Giving primarily in the New York, NY, area. No grants to individuals.
Application information:
Initial approach: Letter
Copies of proposal: 1
Deadline(s): Submit proposal in the fall
Board meeting date(s): Annually
Write: Jane D. Baird, Trustee
Trustees: Brian T. Baird, Bridget B. Baird, Bruce C. Baird, Jane D. Baird, Bronwyn Baird Clauson, Brenda Baird Senturia.
Employer Identification Number: 166029481

2259
Baird (David, Josephine, & Winfield) Foundation, Inc. ⌐
c/o Lawrence E. Brinn, President
781 Fifth Ave.
New York 10022

Incorporated in 1944 in New York.
Donor(s): David G. Baird.
Financial data: (yr. ended 12/31/81): Assets, $1,757,569 (M); expenditures, $132,014, including $49,890 for 21 grants (high: $10,000; low: $100).
Purpose and activities: Grants largely for youth agencies, including a boys town in Israel; some support for higher education, hospitals, health agencies and a social agency.
Officers: Lawrence E. Brinn, President and Treasurer; David G. Baird, Jr., Vice-President; Mildred Cunningham, Secretary.
Employer Identification Number: 132757293

2260
Baird Foundation, The ▼ ⌐
1880 Elmwood Ave.
Buffalo 14207   (716) 876-8100

Trust established in 1947 in New York.
Donor(s): Flora M. Baird,† Frank B. Baird, Jr., Cameron Baird,† William C. Baird.
Financial data: (yr. ended 12/31/82): Assets, $5,718,627 (M); expenditures, $268,239, including $228,157 for 61 grants (high: $58,500; low: $100).
Purpose and activities: Primarily local giving, with emphasis on higher education, church support, cultural programs, and hospitals.
Types of support awarded: Endowment funds, research, scholarship funds, fellowships, matching funds, general purposes.

Limitations: Giving primarily in Erie County, NY. No grants to individuals; no loans.
Application information:
Initial approach: Letter
Copies of proposal: 1
Deadline(s): None
Board meeting date(s): About 6 times a year
Final notification: 1 month
Write: William C. Baird, Manager
Officer and Trustees: William C. Baird, Manager; Carl E. Gruber, Robert J.A. Irwin, Jr.
Number of staff: None.
Employer Identification Number: 166023080

2261
Baird (Winfield) Foundation ⌐
c/o Lawrence E. Brinn, President
781 Fifth Ave.
New York 10022

Trust established in 1936 in New York.
Donor(s): Winfield Baird.†
Financial data: (yr. ended 12/31/82): Assets, $5,094,520 (M); expenditures, $261,429, including $134,355 for 43 grants (high: $35,000; low: $100).
Purpose and activities: General charitable giving, chiefly in New York City, with emphasis on the performing arts, hospitals, youth agencies, religious associations, and higher education.
Limitations: Giving primarily in NY.
Officers: Lawrence E. Brinn, President and Treasurer; David G. Baird, Jr., Vice-President; Mildred Cunningham, Secretary.
Employer Identification Number: 136608843

2262
Baker (The George F.) Trust ▼
245 Park Ave., Suite 2770
New York 10167   (212) 661-1470

Trust established in 1937 in New York.
Donor(s): George F. Baker.†
Financial data: (yr. ended 12/31/83): Assets, $15,941,881 (L); expenditures, $1,024,590, including $756,360 for 39 grants (high: $100,000; low: $1,000) and $24,060 for grants to individuals.
Purpose and activities: Broad purposes; general charitable giving, with emphasis on higher and secondary education, hospitals, youth agencies, and conservation; some emphasis on institutions in the New York City area traditionally supported by the donor and his family.
Types of support awarded: Matching funds, general purposes.
Limitations: Giving primarily in the New York, NY, area. No grants to individuals, or for building or endowment funds, scholarships or fellowships, research, or special projects; no loans.
Publications: Annual report.
Application information:
Initial approach: Letter with brief outline of proposal
Board meeting date(s): June and November
Write: Miss Rocio Suarez, Executive Director

Officer: Miss Rocio Suarez, Executive Director.
Trustees: Anthony K. Baker, George F. Baker III, Citibank.
Employer Identification Number: 136056818

2263
Banbury Fund, Inc. ⌐
c/o Curtis, Mallet-Prevost, Colt & Mosle
101 Park Ave., 35th Fl.
New York 10178

Incorporated in 1946 in New York.
Donor(s): Marie H. Robertson.†
Financial data: (yr. ended 12/31/82): Assets, $12,183,494 (M); gifts received, $2,412,970; expenditures, $199,825, including $101,467 for 7 grants (high: $61,467; low: $5,000).
Purpose and activities: General purposes; primarily local giving, with emphasis on secondary and higher education, hospitals, welfare agencies, and scientific research.
Limitations: Giving primarily in NY. No grants to individuals.
Application information:
Initial approach: Proposal
Copies of proposal: 3
Board meeting date(s): July and January
Write: William S. Robertson, President
Officers and Directors: William S. Robertson, President; Robert Ernst, Townsend J. Knight, Vice-Presidents; Katherine R. Ernst, Secretary; Anne R. Meier, Treasurer; Walter C. Meier, John L. Robertson.
Employer Identification Number: 136062463

2264
Barker (J. M. R.) Foundation
630 Fifth Ave.
New York 10111   (212) 541-6970

Established in 1968 in New York.
Donor(s): James M. Barker,† Margaret R. Barker,† Robert R. Barker.
Financial data: (yr. ended 12/31/83): Assets, $9,484,202 (M); expenditures, $492,928, including $390,350 for 38 grants (high: $100,000; low: $500).
Purpose and activities: Support primarily for local educational and cultural programs, generally to organizations that have previously been evaluated by one or more directors.
Types of support awarded: Operating budgets, continuing support, annual campaigns, seed money, general purposes, building funds, endowment funds, special projects, research.
Limitations: Giving primarily in the greater New York City, NY, area. No grants to individuals, or for scholarships and fellowships, or matching gifts; no loans.
Application information:
Initial approach: Full proposal
Copies of proposal: 1
Deadline(s): Submit proposal in May or October
Board meeting date(s): June and December
Final notification: 3 months
Write: Robert R. Barker, President
Officers: Robert R. Barker,* President; Elizabeth S. Barker,* James R. Barker,* Dwight E. Lee,* Vice-Presidents; Cynthia C. Dousman, Secretary; Robert P. Connor,* Treasurer.

Directors:* Margaret W. Barker, W.B. Barker, John W. Holman, Jr., Richard D. Kahn, Ann B. Kolvig.
Number of staff: None.
Employer Identification Number: 136268289

2265
Barker Welfare Foundation, The ▼
c/o Charles C. Hickox
26 Broadway
New York 10004   (516) 625-0465
Application address for Chicago agencies: c/o Philip D. Block, III, Inland Steel Container Company, 30 West Monroe St., Chicago, IL 60603; for New York and national agencies: c/o Mrs. Walter L. Ross, II, P.O. Box 2, Glen Head, NY 11545

Incorporated in 1934 in Illinois.
Donor(s): Mrs. Charles V. Hickox.†
Financial data: (yr. ended 9/30/83): Assets, $24,435,881 (M); expenditures, $1,486,566, including $1,076,690 for 156 grants (high: $100,000; low: $1,000; average: $5,000).
Purpose and activities: Broad purposes; grants to established organizations and charitable institutions, primarily in Chicago and New York, with emphasis on arts and culture, including museums, youth agencies, health, welfare, aid to the handicapped, and recreation.
Types of support awarded: Operating budgets, continuing support, annual campaigns, building funds, equipment, land acquisition, matching funds, publications, special projects.
Limitations: Giving primarily in Chicago, IL and New York, NY. No grants to individuals, or for endowment funds, seed money, emergency funds, deficit financing, scholarships, fellowships, research, or conferences.
Publications: Program policy statement, application guidelines.
Application information:
  Initial approach: Letter or telephone
  Copies of proposal: 1
  Deadline(s): Submit proposal preferably between September and December; deadline February 1
  Board meeting date(s): May
  Final notification: After annual meeting for positive response; from September to May for negative response
  Write: Mrs. Walter L. Ross, II, President (New York and national agencies); Philip D. Block (Chicago agencies)
Officers: Mrs. Walter L. Ross, II,* President; Mrs. Charles Becker,* Vice-President and Secretary; Mrs. John A. Garrettson,* Vice-President; Charles C. Hickox, Treasurer.
Directors: Philip D. Block, III, James R. Donnelley, Kenneth Fryar, David Granger, Mrs. Edward A. Hansen, Mrs. Charles C. Hickox, John B. Hickox, Victor D. Palmer.
Number of staff: 1 part-time support.
Employer Identification Number: 366018526

2266
Barrington Foundation, Inc., The ¤
c/o Rubin, Baum, Levin, et al.
645 Fifth Ave.
New York 10022

Established in 1978.
Donor(s): Samuel A. Strassler,† Gary M. Strassler, R.C.M. Corporation, Weston Associates.
Financial data: (yr. ended 12/31/82): Assets, $492,100 (M); gifts received, $382,000; expenditures, $485,220, including $484,205 for 203 grants (high: $90,000; low: $25).
Purpose and activities: Giving primarily for Jewish welfare funds, higher education, and cultural programs.
Officers: Robert B. Strassler, Secretary; David H. Strassler, Treasurer.
Employer Identification Number: 132930849

2267
Barth (The Theodore H.) Foundation, Inc. ▼ ¤
530 Fifth Ave.
New York 10036

Incorporated in 1953 in Delaware.
Donor(s): Theodore H. Barth.†
Financial data: (yr. ended 12/31/83): Assets, $9,316,061 (M); expenditures, $581,357, including $495,950 for 55 grants (high: $67,000; low: $200; average: $1,000-$20,000) and $15,331 for 19 grants to individuals.
Purpose and activities: Broad purposes; grants for higher education, including scholarships, hospitals, religion, health agencies, and social services; support also for the arts and cultural organizations, civic affairs and conservation.
Types of support awarded: Student aid.
Application information:
  Deadline(s): None
  Write: Irving P. Berelson, Vice-President
Officers and Directors: Irving P. Berelson, W. Latimer Gray, Vice-Presidents; Charlton T. Barth.
Employer Identification Number: 136103401

2268
Bat Hanadiv Foundation, No. 3 ▼ ¤
c/o Carter, Ledyard & Milburn
2 Wall St.
New York 10005
Application address outside Israel: Mr. M. Rowe, Trustee, 5 Rue Pedro Mevlan, Geneva, Switzerland; in Israel: Mr. A. Fried, 16 Ibn Gvirol St., Jerusalem 92430

Established in 1981.
Financial data: (yr. ended 12/31/83): Assets, $111,205,993 (M); expenditures, $4,425,794, including $3,458,222 for 32 grants (high: $622,895; low: $750; average: $5,000-$500,000).
Purpose and activities: General giving, primarily in Israel, with emphasis on hospitals, cultural programs, higher education, and social services.
Types of support awarded: Operating budgets, equipment, special projects.

Limitations: Giving primarily in Israel. No grants to individuals.
Application information:
  Initial approach: Letter
  Deadline(s): None
Trustees: M. Rowe, Doder Trust Limited.
Employer Identification Number: 133091620

2269
Bausch & Lomb Foundation, Inc. ¤
One Lincoln First Square
Rochester 14601

Incorporated in 1927 in New York.
Donor(s): Bausch & Lomb Incorporated, and others.
Financial data: (yr. ended 12/31/82): Assets, $479,247 (M); gifts received, $112,836; expenditures, $342,638, including $339,500 for 35 grants (high: $97,500; low: $400).
Purpose and activities: Grants limited to local giving, with emphasis on higher education, community funds, and cultural programs.
Limitations: Giving primarily in NY.
Application information:
  Initial approach: Letter
  Write: Daniel E. Gill, President
Officers and Directors: Daniel E. Gill, President; Thomas C. McDermott, Stanley W. Merrell, Harland L. Mischler, Vice-Presidents; Jay T. Holmes, Secretary; W. Henry Aughey, III, Treasurer.
Employer Identification Number: 166039442

2270
Bay (Charles Ulrick and Josephine) Foundation, Inc. ▼
14 Wall St., Suite 1600
New York 10005   (212) 815-7500

Incorporated in 1950 in New York.
Donor(s): Charles Ulrick Bay,† Josephine Bay.†
Financial data: (yr. ended 12/31/84): Assets, $8,560,077 (M); expenditures, $769,421, including $553,815 for 67 grants (high: $100,000; low: $500; average: $2,000-$15,000).
Purpose and activities: Broad purposes; grants primarily for the arts, especially art museums; education, with emphasis on pre-college children's projects, and medical sciences, particularly veterinary medicine.
Types of support awarded: Operating budgets, seed money, research, scholarship funds, matching funds, general purposes.
Limitations: No support for the performing arts, or for other than publicly supported charities. No grants to individuals, or for capital or endowment funds; no loans.
Publications: 990-PF.
Application information:
  Initial approach: Full proposal
  Copies of proposal: 1
  Deadline(s): Submit proposal preferably in January or August
  Board meeting date(s): March and October
  Final notification: 5 months
  Write: Robert W. Ashton, Executive Director

Officers and Directors: Synnova B. Hayes, President; Raymonde I. Paul, Vice-President; Frederick Bay, Secretary; Robert W. Ashton, Executive Director; Ira Butler.
Number of staff: 2 part-time professional.
Employer Identification Number: 135646283

2271
Bayne (The Howard) Fund
c/o Simpson Thacher & Bartlett
One Battery Park Plaza
New York 10004

Incorporated in 1960 in New York.
Donor(s): Louise Van Beuren Bayne Trust.
Financial data: (yr. ended 12/31/82): Assets, $3,936,299 (M); expenditures, $281,527, including $223,000 for 73 grants (high: $11,000; low: $500).
Purpose and activities: General giving, with emphasis on music, cultural programs, education, conservation, and hospitals.
Application information: Applications not invited.
Officers: Gurdon B. Wattles,* President; Daphne B. Shih,* Vice-President; Donald P. Wefer, Secretary and Treasurer.
Directors:* Diana de Vegh, Pierre J. de Vegh, Daisy Paradis, Elizabeth B. Shields, Richard Shields, Elizabeth C.S. Wattles.
Employer Identification Number: 136100680

2272
Bedford Fund, Inc., The
c/o M.E. Brody
Two Overhill Rd.
Scarsdale 10583   (914) 725-3591

Incorporated in 1919 in Connecticut.
Donor(s): Edward T. Bedford.†
Financial data: (yr. ended 6/30/83): Assets, $5,368,244 (M); expenditures, $475,479, including $438,000 for 19 grants (high: $100,000; low: $1,000).
Purpose and activities: Giving limited to the Westport, CT, area, largely for hospitals, a youth agency, community funds and the handicapped; support also for secondary education, and conservation.
Limitations: Giving limited to the local area surrounding Westport, CT.
Officers: Ruth T. Bedford,* President; Edward B. Lloyd,* Vice-President; Marjorie E. Brody, Secretary; John Fearnley,* Treasurer.
Trustees:* Mariana L. Clark, William B. Lloyd, Helen B. McCashin.
Employer Identification Number: 066032006

2273
Bedminster Fund, Inc., The
1270 Ave. of the Americas, Rm. 2300
New York 10020   (212) 315-8300

Incorporated in 1948 in New York.
Financial data: (yr. ended 6/30/84): Assets, $1,888,774 (M); expenditures, $364,160, including $352,000 for 16 grants (high: $100,000; low: $500).
Purpose and activities: Broad purposes; general giving, with emphasis on education, hospitals, the arts, and welfare agencies. Grants only to present beneficiary organizations and to special proposals developed by the directors; additional requests seldom considered.
Limitations: No grants to individuals; no loans.
Application information: Applications not invited.
  Board meeting date(s): November and as required
  Write: Robert F. Quick, Treasurer
Officers: Mrs. Dorothy Dillon Eweson,* President; Philip D. Allen,* David H. Peipers,* Vice-Presidents; Joan Waldron, Secretary; Robert F. Quick, Treasurer.
Directors:* Christine Allen, Douglas E. Allen, Judith Leonard, Anne Zetterberg.
Number of staff: None.
Employer Identification Number: 136083684

2274
Beefeater Foundation ⌂
134 East 40th St.
New York 10016   (212) 490-9300

Established in 1972.
Financial data: (yr. ended 12/31/82): Assets, $493,464 (M); gifts received, $139,600; expenditures, $173,986, including $149,605 for 603 grants (high: $14,125; low: $15).
Purpose and activities: Giving for health and social agencies, and for awards in recognition of outstanding works of literature relating to British or American culture; support also for education, religion, hospitals, and youth agencies.
Application information:
  Write: R.C. Kopf, President
Officers and Directors: R.C. Kopf, President and Treasurer; John Bush, Vice-President; Charles S. Mueller, Secretary.
Employer Identification Number: 237309965

2275
Beinecke (Edwin J.) Trust ▼
14-16 Elm Place
Rye 10058   (914) 967-6960

Trust established in 1970 in Connecticut.
Donor(s): Edwin J. Beinecke.†
Financial data: (yr. ended 2/29/84): Assets, $23,212,029 (M); expenditures, $2,135,549, including $1,713,500 for 43 grants (high: $300,000; low: $1,000).
Purpose and activities: General giving, locally and in Connecticut, with emphasis on higher and secondary education, a center for vocational rehabilitation and special education of the handicapped, and hospitals; support also for youth agencies, community programs, and historic preservation.
Types of support awarded: Operating budgets, building funds, equipment, endowment funds, research, scholarship funds, matching funds, continuing support.
Limitations: Giving primarily in the NY-CT area. No grants to individuals; no loans.
Publications: Financial statement.
Application information:

Initial approach: Letter
Copies of proposal: 1
Deadline(s): None
Board meeting date(s): Spring and fall
Final notification: 30 days
  Write: John R. Robinson, Chairman
Trustees: John R. Robinson, Chairman; Theodore H. Ashford, William O. Beers, Sylvia B. Robinson.
Number of staff: 1 full-time professional; 1 part-time professional; 1 part-time support.
Employer Identification Number: 066129683

2276
Beir Foundation, The ⌂
630 Fifth Ave.
New York 10020

Incorporated in 1944 in New York.
Donor(s): Members of the Beir family.
Financial data: (yr. ended 12/31/82): Assets, $2,197,705 (M); expenditures, $145,937, including $132,103 for 37 grants (high: $57,925; low: $25).
Purpose and activities: General local giving, with emphasis on elementary, secondary, and higher education, Jewish welfare funds, hospitals, and social agencies.
Limitations: Giving primarily in the NY area.
Officers and Directors: Robert L. Beir, President; Joan S. Beir, Vice-President and Secretary; James H. Mathias, Treasurer.
Employer Identification Number: 136084093

2277
Belfer Foundation, Inc., The ⌂
One Dag Hammarskjold Plaza
New York 10017

Incorporated in 1951 in New York.
Donor(s): Members of the Belfer family, Belfer Corporation.
Financial data: (yr. ended 12/31/82): Assets, $3,052,450 (M); expenditures, $99,905, including $98,237 for 62 grants (high: $25,000; low: $10).
Purpose and activities: Charitable purposes; primarily local giving, with emphasis on health agencies, higher education and Jewish welfare funds.
Limitations: Giving primarily in NY.
Officers: Arthur B. Belfer, President; Lawrence Ruben, Vice-President; Robert A. Belfer, Secretary; Jack Saltz, Treasurer.
Employer Identification Number: 136086711

2278
Bendheim (Charles and Els) Foundation ⌂
Ten Columbus Circle
New York 10019

Incorporated in 1947 in New York.
Donor(s): Nannette Bendheim,† and others.
Financial data: (yr. ended 1/31/83): Assets, $663,236 (M); gifts received, $139,850; expenditures, $222,171, including $219,815 for 269 grants (high: $40,000; low: $10).

Purpose and activities: Broad purposes; grants primarily to Jewish-sponsored religious and educational institutions and Jewish welfare funds.
Officer: Charles H. Bendheim, President.
Employer Identification Number: 136103769

2279
Bennett (The James Gordon) Memorial Corporation ⌑
200 Park Ave., Rm. 4320
New York 10166 (212) 755-8310
Scholarship application address: Eleanor H. Keil, New York University, 23 W. 4th St., P.O. Box 901, Cooper Station, New York, NY 10003; Tel.: (212) 598-2844

Incorporated in 1919 in New York.
Donor(s): James Gordon Bennett.†
Financial data: (yr. ended 12/31/82): Assets, $2,502,317 (M); expenditures, $197,359, including $165,206 for 109 grants to individuals.
Purpose and activities: Direct aid to journalists unable to provide for themselves because of old age, infirmity, or lack of means; limited to employees for ten years or more of a daily newspaper published in New York City, with preference for employees of newspapers in Manhattan; if funds are sufficient, employees of daily newspapers in any borough are eligible, together with their immediate families; any surplus funds to be applied to scholarship aid to children of these persons.
Types of support awarded: Grants to individuals, student aid.
Limitations: Giving limited to employees (and their immediate families) of New York City dailies. No grants for building or endowment funds, operating budgets, or special projects.
Publications: Program policy statement, application guidelines.
Application information: Application form required.
   Initial approach: Letter
   Deadline(s): March 1 for scholarships
   Board meeting date(s): May and December
   Write: Patrick T. Finnegan, President
Officers and Directors: William A. Casselman, Chairman; Patrick T. Finnegan, President; William R. White, Treasurer; Samuel C. Blackman, Edward A. Forte, Jack R. Howard, Joseph W. McGovern, John Mortimer, A.H. Raskin.
Employer Identification Number: 136150414

2280
Berlin (Irving) Charitable Fund, Incorporated ⌑
1290 Ave. of the Americas
New York 10019

Incorporated in 1947 in New York.
Donor(s): Irving Berlin.
Financial data: (yr. ended 12/31/82): Assets, $1,277,819 (M); gifts received, $54,000; expenditures, $131,836, including $127,050 for 13 grants (high: $100,000; low: $250).
Purpose and activities: Giving primarily to a music school, an opera association, and to Jewish welfare funds.

Limitations: Giving primarily in NY.
Officers and Directors: Irving Berlin, President and Treasurer; Ellin Berlin, Vice-President; T. Newman Lawler, Secretary.
Employer Identification Number: 136092592

2281
Berlinger (Rhonie & George) Foundation, Incorporated ⌑
1120 Park Ave.
New York 10128

Incorporated in 1958 in New York.
Donor(s): George F. Berlinger, Rhonie H. Berlinger.
Financial data: (yr. ended 5/31/83): Assets, $323,030 (M); gifts received, $108,388; expenditures, $108,056, including $102,740 for 86 grants (high: $25,000; low: $25).
Purpose and activities: Primarily local giving, with emphasis on health agencies, children, cultural programs, education, and Jewish welfare funds.
Officers: George F. Berlinger, President; Rhonie H. Berlinger, Secretary-Treasurer.
Employer Identification Number: 136084411

2282
Bernhill Fund, The
c/o Joint Foundation Support
122 East 42nd St., Suite 922
New York 10168 (212) 661-4080

Incorporated in 1977 in New York as partial successor to The Bernhard Foundation, Inc.
Donor(s): The Bernhard Foundation, Inc.
Financial data: (yr. ended 10/31/84): Assets, $874,738 (M); expenditures, $298,212, including $285,900 for 54 grants (high: $135,000; low: $250; average: $2,000-$5,000).
Purpose and activities: Grants to community organizations and service delivery projects in New York City; support also for institutions of particular interest to the trustees. Annual report published within annual report of Joint Foundation Support, Inc.
Types of support awarded: Operating budgets, continuing support, seed money, special projects.
Limitations: Giving primarily in New York, NY. No grants to individuals, or for annual campaigns, emergency funds, deficit financing, building or endowment funds, matching gifts, scholarships, fellowships, research, demonstration projects, publications, or conferences; no loans.
Publications: Annual report.
Application information:
   Initial approach: Letter or proposal
   Copies of proposal: 1
   Deadline(s): 2 to 3 times a year in spring, fall, and winter
   Final notification: 3 to 6 months
   Write: Patricia Hewitt, Executive Director
Officers and Directors:* William L. Bernhard,* President; Catherine G. Cahill,* Vice-President and Secretary; William C. Breed III,* Treasurer; Patricia Hewitt, Executive Director.
Number of staff: 6.
Employer Identification Number: 132898599

2283
Bezalel Foundation, Inc.
The Clock Tower Bldg.
Two Madison Ave.
Larchmont 10538 (914) 833-0425

Incorporated in 1940 in Maryland; in 1981 merged with Ferdinand W. Breth Foundation.
Donor(s): Henry Sonneborn III, Rudolf G. Sonneborn, Gustave Schindler.
Financial data: (yr. ended 6/30/83): Assets, $1,158,323 (M); gifts received, $101,500; expenditures, $94,894, including $83,979 for 113 grants (high: $5,025; low: $15).
Purpose and activities: Broad purposes; general giving, with emphasis on Jewish welfare funds and higher education, including institutions in Israel; support also for hospitals, music, and museums.
Limitations: No grants to individuals.
Application information: Applications for grants not invited.
   Write: Henry Sonneborn III, President
Officers and Directors: Henry Sonneborn, III, President; Gustave Schindler, Rudolf G. Sonneborn, Vice-Presidents; Clara L. Sonneborn, Secretary; Amalie S. Katz, Hans Schindler.
Employer Identification Number: 136096042

2284
Biddle (Margaret T.) Foundation ⌑
c/o Cusack & Stiles
61 Broadway, Rm. 2912
New York 10006

Incorporated in 1952 in New York.
Donor(s): Margaret T. Biddle.†
Financial data: (yr. ended 12/31/82): Assets, $1,868,090 (M); expenditures, $148,136, including $131,500 for 13 grants (high: $30,000; low: $2,000).
Purpose and activities: Broad purposes; emphasis on research in plant diseases, aid to refugees from Communist countries, cancer research and treatment, the handicapped, and health agencies.
Limitations: No grants to individuals.
Officers: William T. Smith,* President; Lawrence X. Cusack,* Vice-President and Secretary; Richard A. Smith,* Vice-President; James F. O'Brien, Treasurer.
Directors:* Catherine H. Jacobus.
Employer Identification Number: 131936016

2285
Bieber (The Siegfried & Josephine) Foundation, Inc. ⌑
70 Pine St.
New York 10005

Incorporated in 1960 in New York.
Donor(s): Siegfried Bieber,† Josephine Bieber.†
Financial data: (yr. ended 12/31/82): Assets, $1,523,772 (M); expenditures, $274,519, including $249,000 for 68 grants (high: $20,000; low: $500).
Purpose and activities: Primarily local giving, with emphasis on religious welfare funds, social services, hospitals and medical research, the performing arts, education, and museums.

Limitations: Giving primarily in NY.
Application information:
   Write: Rene Loeb, President
Officers and Directors: Rene Loeb, President;
Leonard Wacksman, Secretary; Stephen M.
Kellen, Treasurer; Stephen Connolly.
Employer Identification Number: 136162556

2286
Bingham's (Mr.) Trust for Charity
c/o U.S. Trust Company of New York
45 Wall St.
New York 10005
Mailing address: c/o Robert T. Barr, Trustee,
21 Ann St., Old Greenwich, CT 06870; Tel.:
(203) 637-2178

Trust established in 1934 in New York.
Donor(s): William Bingham, 2nd.†
Financial data: (yr. ended 12/31/83): Assets,
$18,641,205 (M); gifts received, $9,200;
expenditures, $1,062,918, including $770,778
for 10 grants (high: $325,000; low: $10,000).
Purpose and activities: Grants awarded to
invited institutions only for projects in the
following fields: (1) archetypal depth
psychology; (2) archeology of early man in
North America, pre-13,000 B.P.; and (3)
writing proficiency in elementary and
secondary school.
Types of support awarded: Operating
budgets, seed money, matching funds,
special projects, research.
Limitations: No grants to individuals, or for
scholarships or fellowships.
Application information: Applications
currently not invited.
   Board meeting date(s): Monthly
   Write: Robert T. Barr, Trustee
Trustees: Robert T. Barr, Robert T.H.
Davidson, U.S. Trust Company of New York.
Number of staff: 2 part-time professional.
Employer Identification Number: 136069740

2287
Blackmer (Henry M.) Foundation, Inc. ⌀
14 Wall St., Rm. 2500
New York 10005

Incorporated in 1952 in Delaware.
Donor(s): Henry M. Blackmer.†
Financial data: (yr. ended 12/31/83): Assets,
$1,950,879 (M); expenditures, $107,539,
including $85,750 for 22 grants (high: $15,000;
low: $500).
Purpose and activities: Grants generally
limited to a small list of institutional donees
who have received grants from the Foundation
in the past.
Officers and Trustees: Morton Moskin,
President; W. Perry Neff, Vice-President; David
W. Swanson, Secretary-Treasurer; Henry M.
Blackmer II.
Employer Identification Number: 136097357

2288
Bleibtreu (Jacob) Foundation, Incorporated ⌀
c/o Oppenheim, Appel, Dixon & Co.
One New York Plaza
New York 10004

Incorporated in 1945 in New York.
Donor(s): Helen R. Bleibtreu, Jacob Bleibtreu.†
Financial data: (yr. ended 9/30/82): Assets,
$69,861 (M); gifts received, $216,481;
expenditures, $245,046, including $240,045
for 28 grants (high: $50,000; low: $10).
Purpose and activities: Primarily local giving
to hospitals, with emphasis on St. Luke's-
Roosevelt, and Jewish welfare funds, including
a youth recreation program.
Limitations: Giving primarily in NY.
Officers: Helen R. Bleibtreu, President; John
Bleibtreu, Vice-President; Alexander Abraham,
Secretary-Treasurer.
Employer Identification Number: 136065942

2289
Bliss (Cornelius N.) Memorial Fund ⌀
c/o U.S. Trust Co. of NY, Tax Dept.
45 Wall St.
New York 10005

Incorporated in 1917 in New York.
Donor(s): Cornelius N. Bliss,† Elizabeth M.
Bliss, Lizzie P. Bliss, William B. Markell.
Financial data: (yr. ended 12/31/82): Assets,
$1,053,323 (M); gifts received, $4,287;
expenditures, $87,640, including $76,550 for
16 grants (high: $15,500; low: $1,000).
Purpose and activities: Primarily local giving
to cultural programs, hospitals, and secondary
education.
Limitations: Giving primarily in NY.
Officers: Cornelius N. Bliss, Jr., President;
Elizabeth B. Parkinson, Vice-President; Anthony
A. Bliss, Secretary-Treasurer.
Directors: Cornelius N. Bliss III, John Parkinson.
Employer Identification Number: 136400075

2290
Bloomingdale (Samuel J.) Foundation ⌀
641 Lexington Ave., 29th Fl.
New York 10022

Incorporated in 1951 in New York.
Donor(s): Samuel J. Bloomingdale,† Rita G.
Bloomingdale,† Richard C. Ernst, Susan B.
Ernst,† Edgar M. Cullman, Louise B. Cullman.
Financial data: (yr. ended 12/31/82): Assets,
$1,321,466 (M); gifts received, $7,085;
expenditures, $104,993, including $104,000
for 9 grants (high: $50,000; low: $250).
Purpose and activities: Broad purposes;
primarily local giving, with emphasis on Jewish
welfare funds, education, and a wildlife fund.
Limitations: Giving primarily in NY.
Officers: Edgar M. Cullman,* President; John
C. Emmert, Vice-President and Treasurer;
Richard C. Ernst,* Vice-President; Patricia
Castaybert, Secretary.
Directors:* Louise B. Cullman.
Employer Identification Number: 136099790

2291
Blum (Edith C.) Foundation ▼ ⌀
300 Park Ave.
New York 10022

Trust established in 1976 in New York.
Donor(s): Albert Blum,† Edith C. Blum.†
Financial data: (yr. ended 9/30/82): Assets,
$9,197,082 (M); expenditures, $523,208,
including $447,443 for 100 grants (high:
$99,333; low: $100).
Purpose and activities: Primarily local giving,
with emphasis on cultural programs, including
the performing arts and museums; higher
education, including legal education; and public
interest organizations.
Limitations: Giving primarily in NY.
Application information:
   Write: Wilbur H. Friedman, Trustee
Trustee: Wilbur H. Friedman.
Employer Identification Number: 132871362

2292
Blythmour Corporation ⌀
c/o Breed, Abbott & Morgan
153 East 53rd St.
New York 10022

Established in 1951 in New York.
Donor(s): Lloyd S. Gilmour.
Financial data: (yr. ended 12/31/82): Assets,
$1,005,575 (M); expenditures, $75,668,
including $69,500 for 34 grants (high: $10,000;
low: $200).
Purpose and activities: Grants primarily for
medical research, hospitals, and youth agencies.
Officers and Directors:* Margery B.
Gilmour,* President; Lloyd S. Gilmour, Jr.,*
Blyth G. Patel,* Vice-Presidents; David F.
Kroenlein, Secretary and Treasurer.
Employer Identification Number: 136157750

2293
Bobst (The Elmer and Mamdouha) Foundation, Inc. ▼
c/o The Elmer Holmes Bobst Library, New
York University
70 Washington Square South
New York 10012

Incorporated in 1968 in New York.
Donor(s): Elmer H. Bobst.†
Financial data: (yr. ended 12/31/82): Assets,
$12,393,071 (M); gifts received, $1,157,882;
expenditures, $903,331, including $855,925
for 27 grants (high: $600,000; low: $25).
Purpose and activities: General giving, with
emphasis on the promotion of health and
medical research services, higher education,
cultural programs, and youth agencies,
nationally and internationally.
Application information:
   Write: Mamdouha S. Bobst, President
Officers: Mamdouha S. Bobst,* President and
Treasurer; Arthur J. Mahon, Secretary.
Directors:* Farouk As-Sayid, Raja Kabbani,
Mary Rockefeller, Milton C. Rose.
Employer Identification Number: 132616114

2294
Bodman Foundation, The ▼
c/o Morris & McVeigh
767 Third Ave.
New York 10017   (212) 418-0500

Incorporated in 1945 in New Jersey.
Donor(s): George M. Bodman,† Louise C. Bodman.†
Financial data: (yr. ended 12/31/83): Assets, $33,217,334 (M); expenditures, $2,779,302, including $2,584,700 for 67 grants (high: $110,000; low: $7,500).
Purpose and activities: Broad purposes; primarily local giving, largely for cultural and educational institutions, youth and social agencies, and hospitals.
Types of support awarded: Building funds, equipment.
Limitations: Giving primarily in the New York City, NY area. No support for colleges or universities, performing arts groups, museums, or national health or mental health organizations. No grants to individuals, or for conferences, publications, travel, or film; no loans.
Publications: Biennial report, application guidelines, program policy statement.
Application information:
 Initial approach: Letter
 Copies of proposal: 1
 Deadline(s): None
 Board meeting date(s): Three times a year and as required
 Write: Mary E. Caslin, Secretary and Executive Director
Officers: Guy G. Rutherfurd,* President and Treasurer; Marguerite S. Nichols,* Vice-President; Mary E. Caslin, Secretary and Executive Director.
Trustees:* Harry W. Albright, Jr., Mary B. Braga, Gordon S. Braislin, Peter S. Paine.
Number of staff: 1 full-time professional.
Employer Identification Number: 136022016

2295
Boehm Foundation, The
500 Fifth Ave.
New York 10110-0296   (212) 354-9292
Application mailing address: c/o Nancy Coster, 4 Sparks Place, Cambridge, MA 02138

Trust established in 1963 in New York.
Donor(s): Robert L. Boehm, Frances Boehm.
Financial data: (yr. ended 12/31/83): Assets, $1,165,490 (L); expenditures, $292,164, including $289,750 for 107 grants (high: $63,000; low: $250; average: $3,000).
Purpose and activities: Charitable purposes; primarily local giving, with emphasis on legal research and training, race relations and civil liberties, arms control socio-political studies, community funds, and higher education.
Types of support awarded: Continuing support, seed money, emergency funds, matching funds, internships, scholarship funds, fellowships, publications.
Limitations: Giving primarily in NY. No grants to individuals, or for capital or endowment funds, operating budgets, annual campaigns, or deficit financing.

Publications: Annual report, program policy statement, application guidelines.
Application information:
 Initial approach: Letter
 Copies of proposal: 3
 Deadline(s): None
 Board meeting date(s): Monthly
 Final notification: 1 month
 Write: Nancy Coster, Executive Director, or Robert L. Boehm, Trustee
Trustees: Nancy L. Coster, Executive Director; Judy Austermiller, Robert L. Boehm, Bernard D. Fischman, Joseph Rosenblatt.
Number of staff: 1 full-time professional.
Employer Identification Number: 136145943

2296
Booth Ferris Foundation ▼
30 Broad St.
New York 10004   (212) 269-3850

Trusts established in 1957 and 1958 in New York; merged in 1964.
Donor(s): Chancie Ferris Booth,† Willis H. Booth.†
Financial data: (yr. ended 12/31/84): Assets, $81,681,833 (M); expenditures, $5,514,746, including $4,821,625 for 114 grants.
Purpose and activities: Broad purposes; grants primarily for private education, especially smaller colleges, and independent secondary schools; limited support also for theological education, urban programs, social agencies, and cultural activities in the New York City metropolitan area.
Types of support awarded: Continuing support.
Limitations: Giving limited to the U.S.; no grants to social service agencies or cultural organizations outside the New York, NY, metropolitan area. No support for federated campaigns, community chests, or for work with specific diseases or disabilities. No grants to individuals or for research; generally no grants to educational institutions for scholarships, fellowships, or unrestricted endowments; no loans.
Publications: Annual report, program policy statement.
Application information:
 Initial approach: Telephone, letter, or full proposal
 Copies of proposal: 1
 Board meeting date(s): Bimonthly
 Write: Robert J. Murtagh, Trustee
Trustees: Robert J. Murtagh, Morgan Guaranty Trust Company of New York.
Number of staff: 3 part-time professional.
Employer Identification Number: 136170340

2297
Bostwick (The Albert C.) Foundation ⋈
Hillside Ave. and Bacon Rd.
P.O. Box A
Old Westbury 11568   (516) 224-5566

Trust established in 1958 in New York.
Donor(s): Albert C. Bostwick.†

Financial data: (yr. ended 12/31/82): Assets, $1,442,706 (M); expenditures, $136,447, including $125,000 for 61 grants (high: $25,000; low: $50).
Purpose and activities: Broad purposes; primarily local giving, with emphasis on hospitals, youth agencies, aid to the handicapped, health agencies, and medical research.
Limitations: Giving primarily in NY. No grants to individuals.
Application information:
 Initial approach: Letter
 Board meeting date(s): Anually
 Write: Albert C. Bostwick, Jr., Trustee
Trustees: Albert C. Bostwick, Jr., Eleanor P. Bostwick, Andrew G.C. Sage, III.
Employer Identification Number: 116003740

2298
Botwinick-Wolfensohn Foundation, Incorporated ⋈
176 E. 71 St., Apt. 6C
New York 10021

Established in 1952.
Donor(s): James D. Wolfensohn.
Financial data: (yr. ended 5/31/82): Assets, $706,666 (M); gifts received, $210,000; expenditures, $241,787, including $239,964 for 114 grants (high: $25,000; low: $50).
Purpose and activities: Giving primarily in New York and Florida, with emphasis on Jewish welfare funds, music, higher and secondary education, and cultural programs.
Limitations: Giving primarily in NY and FL.
Officers: Benjamin Botwinick, President; Edward Botwinick, James D. Wolfensohn, Vice-Presidents; Bessie Botwinick, Secretary-Treasurer.
Employer Identification Number: 136111833

2299
Bowne (Robert) Foundation, Inc., The
345 Hudson St.
New York 10014   (212) 924-5500

Incorporated in 1968 in New York.
Donor(s): Edmund A. Stanley, Jr., Emily Stanley, Bowne & Co., Inc., and members of the Stanley family.
Financial data: (yr. ended 12/31/84): Assets, $3,274,080 (M); gifts received, $1,080,625; expenditures, $231,726, including $190,000 for 42 grants (high: $16,000; low: $500).
Purpose and activities: To improve the social and economic conditions of the disadvantaged in New York City, with emphasis on youth.
Types of support awarded: Operating budgets, seed money, special projects.
Limitations: Giving limited to New York City, NY, especially the boroughs outside Manhattan. No grants to individuals.
Publications: Application guidelines, program policy statement, annual report.
Application information:
 Initial approach: Letter
 Deadline(s): Submit proposal January 1 through November 1; deadline November 1
 Board meeting date(s): Varies

Final notification: 3 months
Write: Dianne Kangisser, Vice-President
Officers and Trustees: Edmund A. Stanley, Jr., President; Dianne Kangisser, Jennifer Stanley, Vice-Presidents; C.R. Pite, Treasurer; Thomas O. Stanley, Franz von Ziegesar.
Number of staff: 1 part-time professional.
Employer Identification Number: 132620393

2300
Brand (The Martha and Regina) Foundation, Inc. ¤
521 Fifth Ave., Rm. 1805
New York 10175

Established in 1962 in New York.
Donor(s): Martha Brand.†
Financial data: (yr. ended 12/31/82): Assets, $1,348,876 (M); expenditures, $112,881, including $84,725 for 41 grants (high: $35,450; low: $65).
Purpose and activities: Primarily local giving, with emphasis on Jewish welfare funds, temple support, and a theological seminary; support also for a museum.
Limitations: Giving primarily in NY.
Application information:
Write: Nathan B. Kogan, President
Officer: Nathan B. Kogan, President.
Employer Identification Number: 136159106

2301
Brencanda Foundation
358 Fifth Ave.
New York 10001

Established in 1979.
Donor(s): Members of the Brenninkmeyer family and affiliated entities.
Financial data: (yr. ended 11/30/81): Assets, $173,190 (M); gifts received, $460,000; expenditures, $350,892, including $284,100 for 22 grants (high: $35,000; low: $600).
Purpose and activities: Broad purposes; grants largely for Roman Catholic religious organizations in the United States and Canada.
Application information:
Write: Peter S. Robinson, Executive Vice-President
Officers: Anthony Brenninkmeyer,* President; Peter S. Robinson, Executive Vice-President; Miles P. Fischer, Vice-President and Secretary; Kenneth R. Allex, Vice-President and Treasurer.
Directors:* Roland M. Brenninkmeyer, Derick Brenninkmeyer, Felix G.M. Brenninkmeyer, Johannes A.P. Brenninkmeyer, Michael L.M. Brenninkmeyer, H.J.H. Cloudt.
Employer Identification Number: 133005012

2302
Bristol-Myers Fund, Inc., The ▼
345 Park Ave., 43rd Fl.
New York 10154 (212) 546-4331

Trust established in 1953 in New York; the successor fund incorporated in 1982 in Florida as Bristol-Myers Fund, Inc.
Donor(s): Bristol-Myers Company, divisions and subsidiaries.
Financial data: (yr. ended 12/31/83): Assets, $2,084,335 (M); gifts received, $3,000,000; expenditures, $3,322,559, including $2,947,544 for 299 grants (high: $160,576; low: $1,000), $160,576 for grants to individuals and $160,842 for 753 employee matching gifts.
Purpose and activities: Broad purposes; general giving, with emphasis on medical research, community funds, higher education, including company employee scholarships and matching gifts, and health care; support also for civic affairs, minority and women's organizations, youth agencies, and the arts.
Types of support awarded: Annual campaigns, research, employee related scholarships, fellowships, scholarship funds, general purposes, employee matching gifts.
Limitations: Giving limited to areas of company operations, and to national organizations. No support for political, fraternal, social, or veterans organizations; religious or sectarian organizations not engaged in a significant project benefiting the entire community; or organizations receiving support through federated campaigns. No grants to individuals (except for company employee scholarships), or for endowment funds; no loans.
Publications: Application guidelines.
Application information:
Initial approach: Letter
Copies of proposal: 1
Deadline(s): Submit proposal preferably between February and September; deadline October 1
Board meeting date(s): December and as needed
Final notification: 2 to 3 months
Write: Marilyn L. Gruber, Vice-President
Officer and Directors: Patrick F. Crossman, President; J. Richard Edmondson, Bruce S. Gelb, Richard L. Gelb, Marilyn L. Gruber, William R. Miller, Jonathan B. Morris.
Number of staff: 1 full-time professional; 1 part-time professional; 2 full-time support.
Employer Identification Number: 133127947

2303
Bronfman (Ann L.) Foundation ¤
c/o Main Hurdman
55 E. 52nd St.
New York 10055

Established in 1958.
Donor(s): Ann L. Bronfman.
Financial data: (yr. ended 7/31/83): Assets, $274,533 (M); gifts received, $1,165; expenditures, $181,714, including $177,785 for 10 grants (high: $68,000; low: $1,000).
Purpose and activities: Giving primarily for cultural programs and groups working to better international relations.
Application information:
Write: L. Foster
Officers: Ann L. Bronfman, President; Alan M. Stroock, Vice-President; Ronald J. Stein, Secretary; John L. Loeb, Treasurer.
Employer Identification Number: 136085595

2304
Bronfman (The Samuel) Foundation, Inc. ▼
c/o Claire Cullen, Secretary
375 Park Ave.
New York 10152 (212) 572-7799

Incorporated in 1951 in Delaware.
Donor(s): Joseph E. Seagram and Sons, Inc.
Financial data: (yr. ended 12/31/82): Assets, $16,327,530 (M); expenditures, $3,063,696, including $3,030,950 for 44 grants (high: $640,000).
Purpose and activities: Broad purposes; formed to perpetuate the ideals of American democracy; finances research programs for the study of democratic business enterprise by means of fellowships and professorships in colleges and universities; grants also for Jewish welfare funds and medical education.
Limitations: No grants to individuals, or for building or endowment funds, or operating budgets.
Application information:
Initial approach: Full proposal
Copies of proposal: 1
Deadline(s): None
Board meeting date(s): January, April, July, and October
Final notification: 6 to 8 weeks
Write: William K. Friedman, Director
Officers: Edgar M. Bronfman,* President; Claire Cullen, Secretary; Richard Karl Goeltz,* Treasurer; William K. Friedman,* Director.
Trustees:* Philip E. Beekman, David G. Sacks.
Employer Identification Number: 136084708

2305
Brookdale Foundation, The
126 East 56th St.
New York 10022 (212) 308-7355

Incorporated in 1950 in New York.
Donor(s): Henry L. Schwartz,† and his brothers.
Financial data: (yr. ended 6/30/83): Assets, $2,961,008 (M); expenditures, $896,988, including $654,500 for 8 grants (average: $40,000-$519,000).
Purpose and activities: Broad purposes; primarily local giving for gerentological and geriatric research and innovative service programs.
Types of support awarded: Seed money, emergency funds, deficit financing, building funds, equipment, land acquisition, endowment funds, matching funds, scholarship funds, fellowships, professorships, internships, exchange programs, conferences and seminars, publications, special projects, research, employee related scholarships.
Limitations: Giving primarily in the metropolitan New York, NY area. No grants to individuals, or for operating budgets, continuing support, or annual campaigns; no loans.
Publications: Multi-year report.
Application information: No unsolicited grant applications accepted.
Board meeting date(s): Monthly except in July and August
Write: Stephen L. Schwartz, President

Officers: Stephen L. Schwartz,* President; Estelle Greenberg, Mary Ann Van Clief, Vice-Presidents; Horace P. Clark, Secretary and Treasurer.
Directors:* Stanley Epstein, Arthur Norman Field, Harold Resnik, Rebecca Schwartz, John Winthrop.
Number of staff: 1 full-time professional; 1 part-time professional; 2 part-time support.
Employer Identification Number: 136076863

2306
Brooklyn Benevolent Society ⌺
84 Amity St.
Brooklyn 11201

Incorporated in 1845 in New York.
Donor(s): Cornelius Heaney.†
Financial data: (yr. ended 12/31/81): Assets, $1,435,304 (M); expenditures, $84,942, including $50,005 for 47 grants (high: $2,000; low: $100).
Purpose and activities: For the support, maintenance, and education of poor orphan children and for supplying clothing, shoes, and fuel to poor persons resident in Brooklyn only. Grants primarily to agencies of the Roman Catholic Diocese of Brooklyn.
Limitations: Giving primarily in Brooklyn, NY.
Officers: Cornelius A. Heaney, Secretary; Thomas C. Powers, Treasurer.
Employer Identification Number: 111661344

2307
Brooklyn Home for Aged Men ⌺
32 Court St.
Brooklyn 11201

Established in 1878 in New York.
Financial data: (yr. ended 12/31/83): Assets, $1,107,229 (M); gifts received, $22,941; expenditures, $192,848, including $170,000 for 9 grants (high: $35,000; low: $10,000).
Purpose and activities: Support for homes for the aged.
Officers and Directors: Crawford Young, Chairman; Robert W. Ciulla, President; Elsa Ciulla, Alice Owens, Vice-Presidents; Gertrude Young, Secretary; Helen Gilman Smith, Treasurer; George Olsen.
Employer Identification Number: 111630754

2308
Brooks (Gladys) Foundation
90 Broad St.
New York 10004   (212) 943-3217

Established in 1981 in New York.
Donor(s): Gladys Brooks Thayer.†
Financial data: (yr. ended 12/31/84): Assets, $14,000,000 (M); expenditures, $736,027, including $565,000 for 14 grants (high: $100,000; low: $5,000; average: $50,000-$100,000).
Purpose and activities: Grants largely for libraries, higher education, and hospitals and clinics.
Limitations: Giving limited to the Northeast. No grants to individuals, or for research.

Publications: Annual report, program policy statement.
Application information: Application form required.
  Copies of proposal: 4
  Deadline(s): June 28
  Final notification: November
  Write: Ms. Jessica L. Rutledge, Administrative Assistant
Board of Governors: James J. Daly,* Harman Hawkins,* Robert E. Hill*.
Trustees:* U.S. Trust Company of New York (Richard J. Bushelon, Vice-President).
Employer Identification Number: 132955337

2309
Bruner Foundation, Inc. ▼
132 West 43rd St.
New York 10036   (212) 719-3110

Incorporated in 1963 in New York.
Donor(s): Rudy Bruner,† Martha Bruner.
Financial data: (yr. ended 12/31/82): Assets, $5,270,548 (M); expenditures, $583,998, including $496,100 for 18 grants (high: $98,000; low: $5,000; average: $5,000-$50,000).
Purpose and activities: Primarily local giving. Historically, aid has been given to innovative programs, particularly for health care and public health/preventive medicine, including care for the aged. In the future, the foundation will continue to make limited grants in these areas; however, the emphasis will be on projects involving children and adolescents and racial and religious intergroup relations. Funds primarily for evaluation of projects; the foundation is actively involved in improving the assessment of the impact of social programs.
Types of support awarded: Loans, special projects.
Limitations: Giving primarily in NY. No grants to individuals, or for general support, building or endowment funds, scholarships, or fellowships.
Publications: Multi-year report, program policy statement, application guidelines.
Application information:
  Initial approach: Letter and brief outline of proposal, including budget
  Copies of proposal: 1
  Deadline(s): None
  Board meeting date(s): As required
  Final notification: 1 month
  Write: Janet Carter, Executive Director
Officers: Martin C. Barell,* Chairman and Treasurer; Martha Bruner,* President; R. Simeon Bruner,* Vice-President; Richard J.L. Herson, Executive Vice-President and Secretary.
Trustees:* Joshua E. Bruner, Jerome S. Katzin.
Number of staff: 1 full-time professional.
Employer Identification Number: 136180803

2310
Brunner (The Robert) Foundation
63 Wall St., Suite 1903
New York 10005   (212) 344-0050

Incorporated in 1949 in New York.
Donor(s): Robert Brunner.†

Financial data: (yr. ended 12/31/82): Assets, $3,572,731 (M); expenditures, $196,601, including $160,100 for 6 grants (high: $89,600; low: $2,500).
Purpose and activities: Grants for Roman Catholic institutions in the United States and Belgium, but principally for educational and religious organizations founded by the donor.
Limitations: No grants to individuals, or for building or endowment funds.
Application information:
  Initial approach: Letter
  Board meeting date(s): May and December
  Write: John M. Bruderman, Jr., Treasurer
Officers and Directors: John M. Bruderman,* President; William F. Ray,* Vice-President; Eugene F. Rowan,* Secretary; John M. Bruderman, Jr.,* Treasurer; Patrick Bonnewyn*.
Members:* Madeleine DeKan, Donald J. Guarino.
Employer Identification Number: 136067212

2311
Buffalo Foundation, The ▼
237 Main St.
Buffalo 14203   (716) 852-2857

Community foundation established in 1919 in New York by resolution and declaration of trust.
Financial data: (yr. ended 12/31/84): Assets, $18,655,826 (M); gifts received, $740,821; expenditures, $1,669,742, including $1,289,111 for 123 grants (high: $109,050; low: $78) and $245,263 for 421 grants to individuals.
Purpose and activities: To administer trust funds for charitable, educational, and civic purposes, primarily for the benefit of residents of Erie County. Grants restricted to the Buffalo area unless the donor directs otherwise; scholarships awarded to local residents only; grants for educational institutions, scholarships, family and child welfare, health services and hospitals, the arts, and community development.
Types of support awarded: Operating budgets, seed money, emergency funds, building funds, equipment, land acquisition, special projects, matching funds, consulting services, technical assistance, scholarship funds, research, publications, conferences and seminars, general purposes.
Limitations: Giving primarily in Erie County, NY. No grants to individuals (except scholarships), or for annual campaigns, deficit financing, or endowment funds; no loans.
Publications: Annual report, application guidelines.
Application information: Application forms for scholarship applicants only, and must be requested between March 1 and May 10. Application form required.
  Initial approach: Proposal
  Copies of proposal: 1
  Deadline(s): March 31, June 30, September 30, or December 31 for grants; May 25 for scholarships
  Board meeting date(s): First Wednesday of February, May, August, and November
  Final notification: 1st meeting after submission
  Write: W.L. Van Schoonhoven, Director

Officer: William L. Van Schoonhoven, Director and Secretary.
Governing Committee: Philip M. Marshall, Chairman; Edwin Polokoff, Vice-Chairman; Ronald J. Anthony, Robert T. Bongi, Mrs. Robert S. Grantham, Mrs. Warren W. Lane, Richard B. McCormick.
Trustee Banks: The Bank of New York-Western Region, Key Trust Co., Liberty Norstar, Manufacturers and Traders Trust Company, Marine Midland Bank - Western Region.
Number of staff: 1 full-time professional; 2 full-time support; 1 part-time support.
Employer Identification Number: 160743935

2312
Bulova (The Arde) Memorial Fund, Inc. ⌀
1081 Palmer Ave.
Larchmont 10538

Established in 1962.
Donor(s): Louise B. Guilden.
Financial data: (yr. ended 12/31/82): Assets, $1,255,431 (M); expenditures, $85,001, including $73,500 for 6 grants (high: $30,000; low: $2,000).
Purpose and activities: Primarily local giving for higher education and the handicapped.
Limitations: Giving primarily in NY. No grants to individuals.
Application information:
  Initial approach: Letter or proposal
  Write: Joseph P. Catera, Secretary
Officers and Directors: Louise B. Guilden, President; Paul B. Guilden, Vice-President; Joseph P. Catera, Secretary; Edward Gale, Treasurer; Joan G. Gale, Ben Lipton.
Employer Identification Number: 136117194

2313
Bulova Fund, Inc. ⌀
370 Lexington Ave.
New York 10017
Application address; Edward Gale, c/o Arrow Manufacturing Co., 767 52nd St., West New York, NJ 07093

Incorporated in 1955 in New York.
Donor(s): Members of the Bulova family.
Financial data: (yr. ended 12/31/82): Assets, $6,608,370 (M); expenditures, $509,749, including $480,000 for 1 grant.
Purpose and activities: Giving largely in the New York metropolitan area, primarily for a school of watchmaking; some support also for higher education.
Limitations: Giving primarily in the New York, NY, metropolitan area. No grants to individuals.
Application information:
  Initial approach: Letter or proposal
  Final notification: Applicants notified only when an application is accepted
Officers and Directors: Joy Henshel, President; Paul Guilden, Vice-President; Edward Gale, Secretary; Ira Guilden, Treasurer; Henry Henshel.
Employer Identification Number: 131974650

2314
Burchfield (Charles E.) Foundation, Inc.
43 Court St., Rm. 210
Buffalo 14202   (716) 853-7338

Incorporated in 1966 in New York.
Donor(s): Charles E. Burchfield.†
Financial data: (yr. ended 12/31/82): Assets, $2,615,790 (M); expenditures, $129,040, including $53,233 for 7 grants (high: $25,000; low: $358; average: $5,000-$10,000).
Purpose and activities: Broad giving; support for Lutheran religious and charitable organizations, including a local program for disadvantaged youth and international programs for relief and medical assistance.
Types of support awarded: Operating budgets, continuing support, building funds, matching funds.
Limitations: No grants to individuals, or for endowment funds, scholarships, or fellowships; no loans.
Publications: Annual report.
Application information:
  Initial approach: Letter
  Deadline(s): None
  Board meeting date(s): Spring and fall
  Write: Robert J. Schutrum, Sr., Treasurer
Officers and Directors: C. Arthur Burchfield, President; Catherine Parker, Vice-President; Robert Mustain, Secretary; Robert J. Schutrum, Sr., Treasurer; Sally Ferris.
Number of staff: 1 full-time professional; 2 part-time professional.
Employer Identification Number: 166073522

2315
Burden (Florence V.) Foundation ▼
630 Fifth Ave., Suite 2900
New York 10111   (212) 489-1063

Incorporated in 1967 in New York.
Donor(s): Mrs. Florence V. Burden,† and members of her family.
Financial data: (yr. ended 12/31/83): Assets, $15,422,723 (M); expenditures, $823,650, including $622,457 for 43 grants (high: $50,000; low: $500; average: $20,000).
Purpose and activities: All new grants to be made in two fields of concentration: problems of the elderly and crime and justice; emphasis on practical approaches for solving problems, management improvement, policy research, and demonstration projects.
Types of support awarded: Seed money, special projects, research, publications, conferences and seminars.
Limitations: Giving limited to the United States. No grants to individuals, or for capital or endowment funds, operating expenses, continuing support, annual campaigns, emergency funds, deficit financing, scholarships, fellowships, or matching gifts; no loans.
Publications: Annual report, program policy statement, application guidelines.
Application information: Application form required.
  Initial approach: Letter of intent
  Copies of proposal: 1

Deadline(s): Submit letter of intent by December 1, April 1, or August 1; deadlines January 1, May 1, and September 1
Board meeting date(s): February, June, and October
Final notification: 2 weeks after board meeting
Write: David M. Nee, Executive Director
Officers and Directors: Donald P. Moriarty, Vice-President and Treasurer; Shirley C. Burden, Vice-President; Daniel R. Childs, Secretary; David M. Nee, Executive Director; Robert R. Barker, Marvin Bower, Carter Burden, Margaret L. Burden, Ordway P. Burden, Susan L. Burden, Margaret B. Childs, Robert F. Higgins, John W. Holman, Jr., William L. Musser, Jr., Stephen R. Petschek, John H. Watts, III.
Number of staff: 2 full-time professional.
Employer Identification Number: 136224125

2316
Burnham (Alfred G.) Donor Fund, Inc. ⌀
c/o Stein Danziger & Co.
1180 Ave. of the Americas
New York 10036

Incorporated in 1953 in New York.
Donor(s): Alfred G. Burnham,† Rae O. Burnham.
Financial data: (yr. ended 10/31/83): Assets, $2,437,665 (M); expenditures, $165,688, including $156,000 for 36 grants (high: $18,000; low: $1,000).
Purpose and activities: Charitable and educational purposes; grants largely for higher education, medical research, Jewish welfare funds, and population control. Grants only to established charities.
Limitations: No grants to individuals, or for building or endowment funds, or special projects.
Application information:
  Initial approach: Letter
  Board meeting date(s): September or October
  Write: Wirth H. Koenig, Secretary
Officers and Directors: Rae O. Burnham, President and Treasurer; Patrick J. James, Vice-President; Wirth H. Koenig, Secretary; Alicia Byington.
Employer Identification Number: 136097278

2317
Burns (Jacob) Foundation, Inc. ⌀
(formerly Burns Foundation, Inc.)
c/o Jacob Burns
60 E. 42nd St.
New York 10165

Incorporated in 1957 in New York.
Donor(s): Mary Elizabeth Hood,† Jacob Burns.
Financial data: (yr. ended 12/31/83): Assets, $6,298,862 (M); expenditures, $125,232, including $83,705 for 68 grants (high: $10,000; low: $25).

Purpose and activities: Broad purposes; primarily local giving for education, Jewish organizations, law and civil rights organizations, cultural programs, religious organizations, and hospitals and medical research.
Limitations: Giving primarily in NY.
Officers: Jacob Burns, President and Treasurer; Rosalie A. Goldberg, Vice-President and Secretary.
Employer Identification Number: 136114245

2318
Butler (J. Homer) Foundation
10 West 17th St.
New York 10011   (212) 807-7363

Incorporated in 1961 in New York.
Donor(s): Mabel A. Tod.†
Financial data: (yr. ended 12/31/83): Assets, $2,800,398 (M); expenditures, $102,932, including $92,350 for grants (high: $12,000; low: $100).
Purpose and activities: Broad purposes; grants primarily to Roman Catholic missions and religious orders for the relief, care, and assistance of leprosy victims only.
Application information: Applications not invited.
Officers and Directors: Rev. Joseph J. Walter, S.J., President; J. Homer Butler, Vice-President; Geraldine Fremer, Secretary-Treasurer; Rev. Edwin J. Brooks, S.J., Daniel H. Coleman, M.D., Martha S. Collin, Rev. Timothy A. Curtin, S.J., Peter F. DeGaetano, Fausto Gonzalez, William F. Hibberd, F. Patrick Rogers, Robert T. Ross, Rev. Henry J. Zenorini, S.J.
Employer Identification Number: 136126669

2319
Bydale Foundation, The ▼
500 Fifth Ave., Rm. 2140
New York 10110   (212) 719-9393

Incorporated in 1965 in Delaware.
Donor(s): James P. Warburg.†
Financial data: (yr. ended 12/31/83): Assets, $8,073,558 (M); expenditures, $1,253,733, including $1,126,611 for 126 grants (high: $250,000; low: $250; average: $2,500-$15,000).
Purpose and activities: Broad purposes; general giving, with emphasis on international understanding, public policy research, environmental quality, cultural programs, the law and civil rights, social services, and higher education.
Types of support awarded: Operating budgets, continuing support, seed money, matching funds, research, publications, conferences and seminars, special projects.
Limitations: No grants to individuals, or for annual campaigns, emergency funds, deficit financing, endowment funds, demonstration projects, capital funds, or scholarships and fellowships; no loans.
Application information:
  Initial approach: Letter or full proposal
  Copies of proposal: 1
  Deadline(s): Submit proposal preferably in July or August; deadline November 1

Board meeting date(s): June, November, and December
Final notification: 2 or 3 weeks
Write: Milton D. Solomon, Vice-President
Officers: Joan M. Warburg,* President; Milton D. Solomon,* Vice-President and Secretary; Frank J. Kick, Treasurer.
Trustees:* Sarah W. Bliumis, James P. Warburg, Jr., Jenny Warburg, Philip N. Warburg.
Number of staff: None.
Employer Identification Number: 136195286

2320
Calder (The Louis) Foundation ▼
Ten Rockefeller Plaza, Rm. 601
New York 10020   (212) 757-8710

Trust established in 1951 in New York.
Donor(s): Louis Calder.†
Financial data: (yr. ended 10/31/84): Assets, $67,111,897 (M); expenditures, $4,408,981, including $3,877,000 for 193 grants (high: $200,000; low: $5,000; average: $10,000-$25,000).
Purpose and activities: To support mainly those programs deemed best calculated to promote health, education, and welfare through grants to established organizations, with preference given to organizations or projects in or beneficial to the people of New York City or environs or in which the founder was interested. Grants for cultural programs to well-known and established institutions only.
Types of support awarded: Operating budgets, equipment, special projects, research, scholarship funds, general purposes.
Limitations: Giving primarily in the New York, NY metropolitan area. No support for publicly-operated educational or medical institutions, private foundations or governmental organizations; cultural grants only to well-known and established institutions. No grants to individuals; generally no grants for building or endowment funds, capital development or continuing support.
Publications: Annual report, program policy statement, application guidelines.
Application information:
  Initial approach: Letter
  Copies of proposal: 1
  Deadline(s): Submit proposal from January through March; deadline March 31
  Board meeting date(s): As required
  Write: Reinhold Dreher, Trustee
Trustees: Reinhold Dreher, J. Quincy Hunsicker III, Manufacturers Hanover Trust Company.
Number of staff: 2 full-time professional; 1 full-time support; 1 part-time support.
Employer Identification Number: 136015562

2321
Campe (The Ed Lee and Jean) Foundation, Inc. ¤
c/o Frankenthaler, Kohn & Schneider
26 Broadway, Suite 200
New York 10004   (212) 269-4310

Incorporated in 1944 in New York.
Donor(s): Ed Lee Campe,† Jean Campe.†

Financial data: (yr. ended 12/31/82): Assets, $1,186,270 (M); expenditures, $88,011, including $78,050 for 89 grants (high: $7,500; low: $100).
Purpose and activities: Broad purposes; largely local giving for higher education, including scholarship funds and musical education, community funds, Jewish welfare funds, and youth and social agencies.
Types of support awarded: Scholarship funds, general purposes, continuing support, building funds, endowment funds, special projects.
Limitations: Giving primarily in NY. No grants to individuals, or for matching gifts; no loans.
Application information:
  Initial approach: Letter
  Copies of proposal: 1
  Deadline(s): Submit proposal between January and March
  Board meeting date(s): April
  Write: Henry Kohn, President
Officers and Directors: Henry Kohn, President; Anne F. Kohn, Vice-President; Herbert A. Schneider, Secretary.
Number of staff: None.
Employer Identification Number: 136123929

2322
Capital Cities Foundation, Inc. ▼ ¤
24 East 51st St.
New York 10022   (212) 421-9595

Incorporated in 1974 in Delaware.
Donor(s): Capital Cities Communications, Inc.
Financial data: (yr. ended 11/30/82): Assets, $544,012 (M); gifts received, $1,000,000; expenditures, $1,233,274, including $1,230,559 for 118 grants (high: $200,000; low: $500).
Purpose and activities: Grants for higher education, hospitals, health agencies, and local minority development; some support for cultural programs and youth agencies.
Application information:
  Write: Andrew Jackson
Officers: Thomas S. Murphy, President; Daniel B. Burke, Vice-President and Treasurer; Gerald Dickler, Secretary.
Employer Identification Number: 237443020

2323
Caritas Fund ¤
c/o Yohalem, Gillman, Field & Agler
655 Third Ave.
New York 10017

Incorporated in 1951 in New York.
Donor(s): Walter N. Rothschild,† Carola W. Rothschild.
Financial data: (yr. ended 12/31/82): Assets, $110,211 (M); gifts received, $43,635; expenditures, $129,245, including $126,500 for 10 grants (high: $53,000; low: $2,000).
Purpose and activities: Broad purposes; grants largely for population control, higher education, including that for minorities, a Jewish welfare fund, and local social agencies.
Officers and Directors: Carola W. Rothschild, President; Walter N. Rothschild, Jr., Vice-President and Treasurer; Carol R. Noyes, Vice-President; Alan M. Stroock, Secretary.
Employer Identification Number: 136121435

2324
Carnahan-Jackson Foundation ⌑
Fourth and Pine Bldg.
Jamestown 14701   (716) 483-1015

Trust established in 1972 in New York.
Donor(s): Katharine J. Carnahan.†
Financial data: (yr. ended 7/31/83): Assets,
$6,253,857 (M); expenditures, $370,226,
including $334,500 for 26 grants (high:
$102,500; low: $1,000).
Purpose and activities: Broad purposes; grants
for higher education, hospitals, youth agencies,
community development, and church support,
primarily in the western New York area and
particularly Chautauqua County; some support
for certain prior interests of the donor.
Limitations: Giving primarily in western NY,
particularly Chautauqua County. No grants to
individuals.
Application information:
Initial approach: Letter outlining needs and
use of grant
Copies of proposal: 2
Deadline(s): Submit proposal preferably in
January, April, July, or October
Board meeting date(s): June and December
Write: David H. Carnahan, Chairman
Advisory Committee: David H. Carnahan,*
Chairman; Mrs. M.B. Franks, John D. Hamilton,
Dorothy Johnston, Samuel P. Price.
Trustees:* Lincoln First Bank, First National
Division.
Employer Identification Number: 166151608

2325
Carnegie Corporation of New York ▼
437 Madison Ave.
New York 10022   (212) 371-3200

Incorporated in 1911 in New York.
Donor(s): Andrew Carnegie.†
Financial data: (yr. ended 9/30/84): Assets,
$503,942,991 (M); expenditures, $23,765,880,
including $18,967,451 for 189 grants (high:
$1,528,500; low: $4,800) and $567,788 for 6
foundation-administered programs.

Purpose and activities: The advancement and
diffusion of knowledge and understanding
among the peoples of the United States and
certain countries that have been members of
the British Overseas Commonwealth. In 1984
the foundation announced four new sets of
program goals: 1) The avoidance of nuclear
war and improvement in U.S.-Soviet Union
relations. Support for science-based analyses
of ways in which the risk of nuclear war can be
diminished and efforts to ensure that the results
of such analyses are widely known and
understood. This program emphasizes the
mobilization of the best possible intellectual,
technical, and moral resources to work toward
this objective. 2) The education of all
Americans, especially youth, for a scientifically
and technologically based economy, linking the
movement for educational reform to changes in
society and the economy. This program draws
upon the Corporation's past interests in the
education of children, youth, and adults and
particularly its commitment to equity for
women and members of minority groups. (3)
The prevention of damage to children from
birth through early adolescence. This program
focuses on ways to prevent the development of
serious problems for children and young
teenagers, especially school failure and school-
age pregnancy, and secondarily on childhood
injury and substance abuse. It continues the
foundation's interests in early education and
child care. (4) Strengthening human resources
in developing countries. This program aims to
engage the scientific and scholarly communities
in the United States and developing countries
in this effort and to heighten American
understanding of Third World development.
Giving primarily to academic and research
institutions.
Types of support awarded: Operating
budgets, continuing support, seed money,
emergency funds, program-related investments,
loans, special projects, research, publications,
conferences and seminars.
Limitations: No support for the arts, operating
budgets of educational institutions or day care
centers, or general support for social service
agencies. No grants for annual campaigns,
deficit financing, capital, building, or
endowment funds, scholarships, or fellowships.
Publications: Annual report, informational
brochure, program policy statement.
Application information:
Initial approach: Telephone or letter
Deadline(s): None
Board meeting date(s): October, December,
February, April, and June
Final notification: 6 months
Write: Sara L. Engelhardt, Secretary
Officers: David A. Hamburg,* President;
David Z. Robinson, Executive Vice-President;
Barbara D. Finberg, Vice-President, Program;
Sara L. Engelhardt, Secretary; Richard W.
Greene, Treasurer.
Trustees:* Helene Kaplan, Chairman; Jack G.
Clarke, Vice-Chairman; Thomas A. Arciniega,
Bruce Bliss Dayton, Richard B. Fisher, James
Lowell Gibbs, Jr., John G. Gloster, Ruth Simms
Hamilton, Caryl P. Haskins, Fred M.
Hechinger, Joshua Lederberg, Ann R. Leven,
Ray Marshall, Margaret Carnegie Miller,
Margaret K. Rosenheim, Judy P. Rosenstreich,
Thomas A. Troyer, Sheila E. Widnall.

Number of staff: 32 full-time professional; 5
part-time professional; 14 full-time support; 3
part-time support.
Employer Identification Number: 131628151

2326
Carter Fund, The ⌑
c/o Citibank, Sort 4850
641 Lexington Ave.
New York 10043

Trust established in 1958 in New York.
Donor(s): James W. Carter, Margaret W. Carter.
Financial data: (yr. ended 12/31/82): Assets,
$1,363,029 (M); gifts received, $500,000;
expenditures, $1,110,873, including
$1,076,000 for 14 grants (high: $500,000; low:
$2,500).
Purpose and activities: Broad purposes;
primarily local giving, with emphasis on a
museum of natural history, historic
preservation, including a historical society, and
Protestant church support.
Limitations: Giving primarily in NY.
Trustee: Citibank.
Employer Identification Number: 136057027

2327
Cary (Mary Flagler) Charitable Trust ▼
350 Fifth Ave., Rm. 6622
New York 10118   (212) 563-6860

Trust established in 1968 in New York.
Donor(s): Mary Flagler Cary.†
Financial data: (yr. ended 6/30/84): Assets,
$73,366,533 (M); expenditures, $5,884,049,
including $4,789,025 for 57 grants (high:
$100,000; low: $3,000; average: $44,000).
Purpose and activities: Charitable purposes;
primarily regional giving; restricted to (1)
maintenance of three family collections of
books and manuscripts; (2) music in New York
City (including a limited number of professional
performing organizations, the training of
orchestral musicians, new music, and the
teaching of music in several conservatories and
community music schools); and (3) the
conservation of natural resources (including
support for the operations of The Cary
Arboretum in Millbrook, NY, and for the
preservation of barrier islands along the Atlantic
and Gulf coasts).
Types of support awarded: Operating
budgets, continuing support, land acquisition,
matching funds, special projects, program-
related investments.
Limitations: Giving primarily in the New York,
NY, metropolitan region for music and the
eastern coastal states for conservation. No
support for private foundations, hospitals,
religious organizations, primary or secondary
schools, or colleges and universities. No grants
to individuals, or for scholarships, fellowships,
capital funds, annual campaigns, seed money,
emergency funds, deficit financing, or
endowment funds; no loans to individuals.
Publications: Biennial report, program policy
statement, application guidelines.
Application information:
Initial approach: Letter with brief proposal
Copies of proposal: 1

Deadline(s): None
Board meeting date(s): Usually every 3 weeks
Final notification: 2 months
Write: Edward A. Ames, Trustee
Trustees: Edward A. Ames, William R. Grant, Herbert J. Jacobi, Helen LaFetra Stanton.
Number of staff: 1 part-time professional; 1 full-time support.
Employer Identification Number: 136266964

2328
Cattell (James McKeen) Fund
c/o Robert L. Thorndike
525 West 120th St.
New York 10027   (212) 678-3358

Trust established in 1942 in New York.
Donor(s): James McKeen Cattell.†
Financial data: (yr. ended 12/31/84): Assets, $1,673,217 (M); expenditures, $112,719, including $101,215 for 6 grants to individuals.
Purpose and activities: Grants for postdoctoral training to supplement sabbatical allowances of psychologists in universities.
Types of support awarded: Fellowships.
Limitations: Giving limited to the United States and Canada. No grants for building or endowment funds, operating budgets, or special projects.
Publications: Annual report, application guidelines.
Application information: Application form required.
Initial approach: Letter
Copies of proposal: 1
Deadline(s): Submit proposal preferably in October or November; deadline December 1
Board meeting date(s): January or February
Write: Robert L. Thorndike, Secretary
Officers and Trustees: Robert L. Thorndike, Secretary-Treasurer; Lyle V. Jones, Managing Trustee; Edward Jones, Gregory Kimble, Janet Spence.
Employer Identification Number: 136129600

2329
CBS Foundation Inc. ▼
51 West 52nd St.
New York 10019   (212) 975-5791

Incorporated in 1953 in New York.
Donor(s): CBS Inc.
Financial data: (yr. ended 12/31/82): Assets, $1,721,184 (M); gifts received, $593,997; expenditures, $1,487,784, including $1,479,000 for 17 grants (high: $250,000; low: $2,500; average: $50,000-$150,000).
Purpose and activities: General purposes; grants primarily for higher education, cultural affairs, the performing and fine arts, and civic affairs in areas of company operations.
Limitations: No grants to individuals, or for building or endowment funds, or matching gifts; no loans.
Application information:
Initial approach: Letter
Copies of proposal: 1
Deadline(s): None
Board meeting date(s): Quarterly and as required

Final notification: 4 months
Write: Helen M. Brown, Executive Director
Officers: John W. Kiermaier, President; Charles T. Bates, Secretary; Louis J. Rauchenberger, Treasurer; Helen M. Brown, Executive Director.
Directors: Marietta Tree, Chairman; Walter L. Cronkite, Newton N. Minnow, Benno C. Schmidt, Franklin A. Thomas.
Number of staff: None.
Employer Identification Number: 136099759

2330
Centennial Foundation ⌑
c/o Joel E. Sammet & Co.
19 Rector St.
New York 10006

Incorporated in 1965 in New York.
Donor(s): Henry H. Arnhold, Arnold S. Bleienroeder.
Financial data: (yr. ended 12/31/83): Assets, $570,442 (M); gifts received, $50,072; expenditures, $105,482, including $103,609 for 99 grants (high: $10,000; low: $100).
Purpose and activities: Charitable purposes; primarily local giving, with emphasis on hospitals and health agencies, international relations, community development, the performing arts, and education.
Limitations: Giving primarily in New York, NY.
Officers and Trustees: Stephen M. Kellen, Chairman; Henry H. Arnhold, President; Adele Siegel, Secretary; Gilbert Kerlin, Michael Kellen.
Employer Identification Number: 136189397

2331
Central New York Community Foundation, Inc. ▼
500 South Salina St., Suite 330
Syracuse 13202   (315) 422-9538

Community foundation incorporated in 1927 in New York; reorganized in 1951.
Financial data: (yr. ended 3/31/84): Assets, $6,929,994 (M); gifts received, $2,189,212; expenditures, $1,693,663, including $1,565,081 for 340 grants (high: $209,961; low: $25; average: $5,000).
Purpose and activities: Broad purposes; unrestricted funds limited to use only within Onondaga and Madison counties, with grants primarily to existing agencies for health, welfare, educational, recreational or cultural purposes.
Types of support awarded: Operating budgets, continuing support, seed money, emergency funds, building funds, equipment, special projects, matching funds, employee matching gifts, publications.
Limitations: Giving limited to Onondaga and Madison counties, NY. No grants to individuals, or for scholarships or fellowships, land acquisition, or research; no loans.
Publications: Annual report, application guidelines.
Application information: Application form required.
Initial approach: Letter or telephone
Copies of proposal: 10
Deadline(s): 3 weeks before board meetings

Board meeting date(s): March, June, September, and December
Final notification: 5 weeks
Write: John S. Dietz, Secretary
Officers: Nancy F. Marquardt,* President; Martha H. Northrup,* First Vice-President; Richard C. Pietrafesa, Sr.,* Second Vice-President; John S. Dietz, Secretary and Chief Executive Officer; Vaughn A. Skinner,* Treasurer.
Directors:* Douglas Cagwin, N. Earle Evans, Michael J. Falcone, Edward S. Green, Richard I. Heiligman, H. Follett Hodgkins, Jr., Dorothy R. Irish, Edward Jenner, John F. Marsellus, Ernest L. Sarason, Virginia Small, Jay W. Wason, Chris J. Witting.
Number of staff: 2 full-time professional.
Employer Identification Number: 150626910

2332
Chadwick (Dorothy Jordan) Fund
c/o U.S. Trust Company of New York
45 Wall St.
New York 10005   (212) 425-4500

Trust established in 1957 in New York.
Donor(s): Dorothy J. Chadwick,† Dorothy R. Kidder.
Financial data: (yr. ended 5/31/83): Assets, $4,722,193 (M); gifts received, $214,267; expenditures, $312,998, including $220,000 for 28 grants (high: $50,000; low: $14).
Purpose and activities: Grants largely for the arts and performing arts in New York City and Washington, D.C.
Limitations: Giving primarily in New York City, NY, and Washington, DC.
Application information:
Initial approach: Full proposal
Copies of proposal: 1
Deadline(s): February 1
Board meeting date(s): As required
Trustees: Berkeley D. Johnson, Jr., Dorothy R. Kidder, U.S. Trust Company of New York.
Employer Identification Number: 136069950

2333
Chait (The Sara) Memorial Foundation, Inc.
217 West 36th St.
New York 10018

Incorporated in 1959 in New York.
Donor(s): Abraham Chait,† Murray Backer,† Burton D. Chait, Mrs. Marilyn Chait, and others.
Financial data: (yr. ended 12/31/83): Assets, $1,836,968 (M); expenditures, $195,614, including $188,000 for 19 grants (high: $50,600; low: $150).
Purpose and activities: Broad purposes; grants to higher educational institutions to aid worthy students training primarily for careers in medicine; support also for medical research.
Officers: Seymour Sobel, President; Richard May, Vice-President; Marilyn Chait, Secretary and Treasurer.
Employer Identification Number: 136121596

2334
Chanin Family Foundation, Inc. ⌑
122 East 42nd St.
New York 10168

Incorporated in 1953 in New York.
Donor(s): Irwin S. Chanin, Henry I. Chanin, and family-related companies.
Financial data: (yr. ended 1/31/83): Assets, $461,020 (M); gifts received, $23,000; expenditures, $126,978, including $126,905 for 22 grants (high: $50,000; low: $25).
Purpose and activities: Broad purposes; primarily local giving, with emphasis on Jewish welfare funds; support also for higher education and hospitals.
Limitations: Giving primarily in NY.
Officers: Irwin S. Chanin, President; Marcy Chanin, Paul R. Chanin, Vice-Presidents.
Employer Identification Number: 136183052

2335
Charina Foundation, Inc. ⌑
c/o Goldman, Sachs & Co.
85 Broad St.
New York 10004

Incorporated in 1980 in New York.
Donor(s): Richard L. Menschel, The Menschel Foundation.
Financial data: (yr. ended 8/31/83): Assets, $3,407,208 (M); gifts received, $375,000; expenditures, $134,914, including $132,135 for 139 grants (high: $23,000; low: $100).
Purpose and activities: Broad purposes; emphasis on arts and culture.
Officers and Directors: Richard L. Menschel, President and Treasurer; Ronay Menschel, Secretary; Eugene P. Polk.
Employer Identification Number: 133050294

2336
Charlpeg Foundation, Inc., The ⌑
c/o Meyer Handelman Company
80 Pine St.
New York 10005 (212) 269-2840

Incorporated in 1958 in New York.
Donor(s): Charles M. Grace.
Financial data: (yr. ended 10/31/83): Assets, $33,780 (M); gifts received, $108,853; expenditures, $111,319, including $109,150 for grants.
Purpose and activities: Broad purposes; primarily local giving, with emphasis on Roman Catholic religious associations and church support and higher and secondary education; grants also for youth agencies, conservation, and cultural programs, including Irish-American cultural programs.
Limitations: Giving primarily in NY. No grants to individuals, or for endowment funds or operating budgets.
Application information:
Initial approach: Letter
Copies of proposal: 1
Board meeting date(s): Monthly
Officers and Directors: Charles M. Grace, President; Margaret V. Grace, Vice-President; John R. Young, Secretary; Donald E. Handelman, Treasurer; William R. Handelman.
Employer Identification Number: 136076805

2337
Chase Manhattan International Foundation, The
One Chase Manhattan Plaza
New York 10081 (212) 552-4411

Incorporated in 1969 in New York.
Donor(s): The Chase Manhattan Bank.
Financial data: (yr. ended 12/31/83): Assets, $950,347 (M); gifts received, $687,000; expenditures, $258,183, including $211,000 for 31 grants (high: $20,000; low: $2,000) and $42,204 for 10 grants to individuals.
Purpose and activities: General purposes; grants primarily for child welfare, health care, hunger and disaster relief, education, and other community, economic, and human resource development by organizations that operate largely outside the continental United States; also funds a company-employee scholarship program.
Types of support awarded: Operating budgets, continuing support, annual campaigns, seed money, emergency funds, building funds, employee related scholarships, special projects.
Limitations: Giving limited to organizations that operate largely outside the continental United States. No grants to individuals (except for company employee-childrens' scholarships), or for deficit financing, equipment, land acquisition, endowment funds, or matching gifts; no loans.
Publications: Annual report, application guidelines.
Application information: Application form required.
Initial approach: Letter or full proposal
Copies of proposal: 1
Deadline(s): Submit proposal preferably in January or June; deadline October 1
Board meeting date(s): 5 times a year
Final notification: 6 months
Write: John R. Meekin, Secretary
Officers: Willard C. Butcher,* President; Fraser P. Seitel,* Francis X. Stankard,* Vice-Presidents; John R. Meekin, Secretary and Treasurer.
Trustees:* A. Edward Allinson, Elaine R. Bond, Richard J. Boyle, James H. Carey, Robert R. Douglass, A. Wright Elliott, John C. Haley, Frederick S. Hammer, Joseph J. Harkins, John H. Hooper, Thomas G. Labrecque, Alan F. Lafley, Arthur F. Ryan, Anthony P. Terraciano, J. Richard Zecher.
Number of staff: None.
Employer Identification Number: 237049738

2338
Chatlos Foundation, Inc., The ▼
11 Penn Plaza, Rm. 2121
New York 10001

Incorporated in 1953 in New York.
Donor(s): Bristol Door and Lumber Company, Inc., William F. Chatlos.†
Financial data: (yr. ended 12/31/83): Assets, $57,100,000 (M); gifts received, $50,300; expenditures, $2,333,961, including $1,777,633 for 102 grants (high: $130,000; low: $200; average: $10,000-$25,000).
Purpose and activities: Broad purposes; grants largely for higher education, including religious education and religious associations; giving also for hospitals, health agencies, and child welfare.
Types of support awarded: Operating budgets, continuing support, annual campaigns, emergency funds, equipment, land acquisition, matching funds, scholarship funds, special projects, publications.
Limitations: No grants to individuals, or for seed money, deficit financing, building or endowment funds, research, or conferences; no loans.
Publications: Application guidelines, program policy statement.
Application information:
Initial approach: Letter or full proposal
Copies of proposal: 1
Deadline(s): February 1, May 1, August 1, and November 1
Board meeting date(s): February, May, August, and November
Final notification: 60 days after board meeting
Write: William J. Chatlos, President
Officers and Trustees: Alice E. Chatlos, Chairman, Vice-President, and Treasurer; William J. Chatlos, President; Kathryn A. Randle, Secretary; Joy E. D'Arata, Charles O. Morgan, Carol J. Williams Pesa, Michele C. Roach.
Number of staff: 7 full-time professional.
Employer Identification Number: 136161425

2339
Chautauqua Region Community Foundation, Inc.
812 Hotel Jamestown Bldg.
Jamestown 14701

Incorporated in 1978 in New York.
Financial data: (yr. ended 4/30/84): Assets, $1,603,790 (M); gifts received, $278,317; expenditures, $155,897, including $81,359 for 39 grants (high: $7,500; low: $105) and $18,687 for 43 grants to individuals.
Purpose and activities: Local giving for cultural, educational, civic, and charitable projects.
Types of support awarded: Operating budgets, continuing support, seed money, emergency funds, equipment, publications, conferences and seminars, student aid.
Limitations: Giving limited to the Chautauqua, NY, area. No support for religious or sectarian purposes. No grants to individuals (except for scholarship grants); no loans.
Publications: Annual report.
Application information: Application form required.
Initial approach: Letter or telephone
Copies of proposal: 1
Deadline(s): April 30
Board meeting date(s): May
Final notification: Early June
Write: Francis B. Grow, Manager

Officers and Directors: Kenneth W. Strickler, President; Marian Panzarella, Vice-President; Elizabeth S. Lonna, Secretary; Miles L. Lasser, Treasurer; Craig P. Colburn, Betty Erickson, Marilyn Gruel, Frederick J.W. Heft.
Number of staff: 1 full-time professional; 2 part-time support.
Employer Identification Number: 161116837

2340
Cheatham (Owen) Foundation
540 Madison Ave.
New York 10022   (212) 753-4733

Incorporated in 1957 in New York as successor to Owen R. Cheatham Foundation, a trust established in 1934 in Georgia.
Donor(s): Owen Robertson Cheatham,† Celeste W. Cheatham.†
Financial data: (yr. ended 12/31/83): Assets, $6,766,026 (M); expenditures, $549,691, including $360,750 for 60 grants (high: $100,000; low: $50).
Purpose and activities: Broad purposes; primarily to assist programs that might not otherwise be achieved; grants mainly for education, health, the arts, and welfare.
Officers and Directors:* Celeste C. Weisglass,* President; Stephen S. Weisglass,* Vice-President and Treasurer; Thomas P. Ford,* Vice-President; Ilse C. Meckauer, Secretary.
Employer Identification Number: 136097798

2341
Chernow (Michael) Trust for the Benefit of Charity Dated 03/13/75 ¤
c/o Schapiro, Wisan and Krassner
122 East 42nd St.
New York 10168-0057

Trust established in 1975.
Financial data: (yr. ended 6/30/83): Assets, $2,683,631 (M); gifts received, $1,011,311; expenditures, $218,157, including $181,200 for 9 grants (high: $75,000; low: $500).
Purpose and activities: Giving primarily for Jewish welfare funds, higher education, and health, and medical research.
Trustees: Morris I. Chernofsky, Martin P. Krassner, Lynn A. Streim.
Employer Identification Number: 136758226

2342
Chernow (Michael) Trust for the Benefit of Charity Dated 4/16/68 ¤
c/o Schapiro, Wisan & Krassner
122 East 42nd St.
New York 10168-0057

Trust established in 1968.
Financial data: (yr. ended 6/30/83): Assets, $1,663,912 (M); expenditures, $95,732, including $73,000 for 4 grants (high: $50,000; low: $3,000).
Purpose and activities: Primarily local giving, with emphasis on Jewish welfare funds, medical education and research, and a blood bank.

Limitations: Giving primarily in NY.
Trustees: Albert Krassner, Martin P. Krassner, Morris I. Chernofsky.
Employer Identification Number: 136758228

2343
Children's Foundation of Erie County, Inc. ¤
c/o Lewis F. Hazel
One Marine Midland Center
Buffalo 14240

Incorporated in 1836 in New York.
Financial data: (yr. ended 12/31/82): Assets, $1,021,205 (M); expenditures, $98,496, including $93,522 for 34 grants (high: $7,500; low: $500).
Purpose and activities: Local giving, largely for child welfare, youth agencies, recreation, and a hospital.
Limitations: Giving primarily in NY.
Officers: Thomas B. Healy, Jr., President; Calvin J. Haller, Vice-President; Charles J. Hahn, Secretary; Lewis F. Hazel, Treasurer.
Employer Identification Number: 166000171

2344
China Medical Board of New York, Inc. ▼
622 Third Ave., 34th Fl.
New York 10017   (212) 682-8000

Incorporated in 1928 in New York.
Donor(s): The Rockefeller Foundation.
Financial data: (yr. ended 6/30/84): Assets, $63,327,000 (M); expenditures, $4,085,000, including $3,010,000 for 35 grants (high: $300,000; low: $5,000).
Purpose and activities: "To extend financial aid to the Peking Union Medical College and/or like institutions in the Far East or the United States of America." The Board's activities are: 1) to assist institutions in improving the health levels and services in Asian societies and 2) to assist institutions in improving the quality and increasing the numbers of appropriate health practitioners in these societies. Supports programs in medical research, staff development, cooperative planning and library endowment only at designated national medical schools, nursing schools, and schools of public health in Hong Kong, Indonesia, Korea, Malaysia, the Philippines, Singapore, Taiwan, Thailand, and the People's Republic of China.
Types of support awarded: Conferences and seminars, matching funds, scholarship funds, research, fellowships.
Limitations: Giving limited to East and Southeast Asia, including the People's Republic of China, Hong Kong, Indonesia, Korea, Malaysia, the Philippines, Singapore, Taiwan, and Thailand. No support for governments, professional societies, or research institutes not directly under medical school control. No grants to individuals, or for capital facilities, operational activities for medical care, special projects, or the basic equipping of medical schools, nursing schools, or schools of public health that are the responsibility of various governments or universities; no loans.

Publications: Annual report.
Application information: Submit request through dean's office of Asian institution in which foundation has a program of support.
  Initial approach: Letter
  Deadline(s): None
  Board meeting date(s): June and December
  Write: Patrick A. Ongley, M.D., President
Officers: Patrick A. Ongley, M.D.,* President; Mary Ann Cramer, Secretary; Frances M. Harrison, Treasurer.
Trustees:* W. Clarke Wescoe, M.D., Chairman; J. Robert Buchanan, M.D., Vice-Chairman; Mary Brown Bullock, Loring Catlin, Walter G. Ehlers, John R. Hogness, M.D., Bayless A. Manning, Gloria H. Spivak, Phillips Talbot.
Number of staff: 4 full-time professional; 3 full-time support.
Employer Identification Number: 131659619

2345
Cintas Foundation, Inc.
140 Broadway, Rm. 4500
New York 10005   (212) 820-1100
Grant application address: Robert F. Morris, Cintas Fellowship Program, Institute of International Education, 809 United Nations Plaza, New York, NY 10017

Incorporated in 1957 in New York as Cuban Art Foundation, Inc.
Donor(s): Oscar B. Cintas.†
Financial data: (yr. ended 8/31/83): Assets, $2,001,060 (M); expenditures, $126,272, including $90,000 for 18 grants to individuals (average: $7,000).
Purpose and activities: To foster and encourage art within Cuba and art created by persons of Cuban citizenship or lineage within or outside of Cuba. Present activities restricted to fostering art and granting fellowships to those in the above categories living outside of Cuba who show professional achievement in music, literature, or the arts; students pursuing academic programs are not eligible.
Types of support awarded: Fellowships.
Limitations: No grants for building or endowment funds, operating budgets, or special projects.
Publications: Application guidelines.
Application information: Application form required.
  Initial approach: Letter
  Deadline(s): Submit application from December through February; deadline March 1
  Board meeting date(s): May or June, late October or November, and as required
  Final notification: 4 to 5 months
  Write: Maria Heilbron Richter, Secretary
Officers and Directors: Ethan D. Alyea, President; William B. Warren, Vice-President; Maria Heilbron Richter, Secretary; Paul A. McManus, Treasurer; Riva Castleman, Ulises Giberga, Hortensia Sampedro, Daniel Serra-Badue, Roger D. Stone.
Number of staff: None.
Employer Identification Number: 131980389

2346
Clark (The Edna McConnell) Foundation ▼
250 Park Ave., Rm. 900
New York 10017   (212) 986-7050

Incorporated in 1950 in New York and 1969 in Delaware; the New York corporation merged into the Delaware corporation in 1974.
Donor(s): Edna McConnell Clark,† W. Van Alan Clark.†
Financial data: (yr. ended 9/30/84): Assets, $274,305,565 (M); gifts received, $2,550,000; expenditures, $17,858,613, including $14,065,132 for 140 grants (high: $1,840,000; low: $1,500; average: $103,000).
Purpose and activities: Programs presently narrowly defined and directed towards four specific areas: 1) reducing unnecessary removal of children from troubled families by establishing better family preservation policies and services; supporting courts, agencies, and advocates in implementation of specific foster care and adoption reforms; 2) improving the school-to-work transition of disadvantaged urban youth by: developing model work-education programs among private industry, schools, community organizations and unions, and monitoring government initiatives particularly as they relate to disadvantaged youth; 3) seeking more rational, humane, and effective ways of dealing with those in criminal justice system by developing alternatives to unnecessary incarceration, supporting litigation to correct abuses and to establish standards of care, and exploring ways to reduce the length of prison sentences for offenders who present little threat to society; and 4) helping millions in the developing world through a targeted research program aimed at controlling the tropical diseases, schistosomiasis, trachoma, and onchocerciasis.
Types of support awarded: Consulting services, continuing support, research, seed money, technical assistance.
Limitations: No grants to individuals, or for capital funds, construction and equipment, endowments, scholarships and fellowships, annual appeals, deficit financing, or matching gifts; no loans.
Publications: Annual report, informational brochure, program policy statement, application guidelines.
Application information: Action-oriented projects preferred; research support primarily in Tropical Disease program.
Initial approach: Letter
Copies of proposal: 1
Deadline(s): None
Board meeting date(s): February, April, June, September, and December
Final notification: 3 weeks for declination; 2 months on positive action
Write: John R. Coleman, President
Officers: James M. Clark,* Chairman and Treasurer; John R. Coleman,* President; Peter W. Forsythe, Vice-President; Patricia Carry Stewart, Vice-President and Secretary.

Trustees:* Hays Clark, Eleanor T. Elliott, John M. Emery, Lucy Nesbeda, Walter N. Rothschild, Jr., Sidney J. Weinberg, Jr., O. Meredith Wilson.
Number of staff: 11 full-time professional; 11 full-time support; 1 part-time support.
Employer Identification Number: 237047034

2347
Clark Foundation, The ▼
30 Wall St.
New York 10005   (212) 269-1833

Incorporated in 1931 in New York; merged with Scriven Foundation, Inc. in 1973.
Donor(s): Members of the Clark family.
Financial data: (yr. ended 6/30/84): Assets, $136,973,711 (M); gifts received, $2,928,275; expenditures, $6,800,160, including $3,294,941 for 130 grants (high: $125,000; low: $1,000), $1,462,256 for 657 grants to individuals and $240,316 for 1 foundation-administered program.
Purpose and activities: Support for a hospital and museums in Cooperstown, New York; grants also for charitable, welfare, and educational purposes, including undergraduate scholarships to students residing in Cooperstown area. Support also for health, educational, youth, cultural, and community welfare organizations and institutions and for medical and convalescence care of needy individuals.
Types of support awarded: Operating budgets, continuing support, annual campaigns, seed money, emergency funds, building funds, equipment, special projects, student aid.
Limitations: Giving primarily in upstate NY and New York City. No grants for deficit financing, or matching gifts; no loans.
Publications: Program policy statement, application guidelines.
Application information:
Initial approach: Letter
Copies of proposal: 1
Deadline(s): None
Board meeting date(s): October and May
Final notification: 2 to 6 months
Write: Edward W. Stack, Secretary
Officers: Stephen C. Clark, Jr.,* President; Michael A. Nicolais,* Vice-President; Edward W. Stack, Secretary; John J. Burkly, Treasurer.
Directors:* Alfred C. Clark, Miss Jane F. Clark II, William M. Evarts, Jr., Henry R. Labouisse, Archie F. MacAllaster, Mrs. Edward B. McMenamin, A. Pennington Whitehead.
Number of staff: 4 full-time professional; 2 part-time professional; 18 full-time support; 1 part-time support.
Employer Identification Number: 135616528

2348
Clark (Frank E.) Charitable Trust
c/o Manufacturers Hanover Trust Company
600 Fifth Ave.
New York 10020

Trust established in 1936 in New York.
Donor(s): Frank E. Clark.†

Financial data: (yr. ended 12/31/83): Assets, $2,606,163 (M); expenditures, $187,643, including $174,500 for 36 grants (high: $14,100; low: $400).
Purpose and activities: Charitable and religious purposes; income distributed to the parent body of major religious denominations for aid to needy churches; support also for health, welfare, and other charitable organizations.
Limitations: Giving primarily in NY.
Application information:
Initial approach: Proposal
Copies of proposal: 1
Deadline(s): August 31
Board meeting date(s): November
Write: Helen M. Thome, Vice-President
Trustee: Manufacturers Hanover Trust Company (Helen M. Thome, Vice-President).
Employer Identification Number: 136049032

2349
Clark (Robert Sterling) Foundation, Inc. ▼
112 East 64th St.
New York 10021   (212) 308-0411

Incorporated in 1952 in New York.
Donor(s): Robert Sterling Clark.†
Financial data: (yr. ended 10/31/84): Assets, $34,791,345 (M); expenditures, $2,371,375, including $1,754,129 for 83 grants (high: $120,000; low: $2,000; average: $25,000-$30,000).
Purpose and activities: The foundation supports projects that: 1) encourage permanence and stability for children in, or at risk of, foster care; 2) strengthen the management of cultural institutions in New York City and the greater metropolitan area; 3) ensure the effectiveness and accountability of public agencies in New York City and State; and 4) protect reproductive freedom.
Types of support awarded: Loans, special projects, research, publications.
Limitations: Giving primarily in New York, with emphasis on New York City. No grants to individuals, or for operating budgets, annual campaigns, seed money, emergency funds, deficit financing, capital or endowment funds, matching gifts, scholarships, fellowships, or conferences.
Publications: Annual report, application guidelines, program policy statement.
Application information:
Initial approach: Full proposal
Copies of proposal: 1
Deadline(s): None
Board meeting date(s): January, April, July, and October
Final notification: 1 to 6 months
Write: Margaret C. Ayers, Executive Director
Officers: Winslow M. Lovejoy, Jr.,* President and Treasurer; Miner D. Crary, Jr.,* Secretary; Margaret C. Ayers, Executive Director.
Directors:* Lewis Mack, Charles G. Meyer, Jr., Winthrop R. Munyan, Richardson Pratt, Jr., Philip Svigals, Sandra S. Weiksner.
Number of staff: 3 full-time professional; 1 part-time professional; 1 full-time support.
Employer Identification Number: 131957792

2350
Cobble Pond Foundation ¤
c/o Irving Trust Company
Church Street Station, P.O. Box 12446
New York 10249

Trust established in 1968 in Connecticut.
Donor(s): Harold A. Hatch, Margaret Milliken Hatch.†
Financial data: (yr. ended 5/31/83): Assets, $4,226,873 (M); gifts received, $1,540,003; expenditures, $441,770, including $429,500 for 20 grants (high: $175,000; low: $2,000).
Purpose and activities: Broad purposes; primarily local giving to institutions of interest to the original donors, with emphasis on international understanding and welfare, higher education, and Protestant church support.
Limitations: Giving primarily in NY. No grants for building funds.
Application information:
 Initial approach: Letter
 Copies of proposal: 1
 Deadline(s): Submit proposal in January or June
 Board meeting date(s): April and September
 Write: H.R. Patch, Jr., Vice-President
Trustees: Irving Trust Company.
Employer Identification Number: 136283813

2351
Cohen (Elias A.) Foundation, Inc. ¤
c/o Joseph Schlang
45 John St.
New York 10038 (212) 425-1313

Incorporated in 1951 in New York.
Donor(s): Elias A. Cohen,† David Schlang, Joseph Schlang, Maurice Schlang, Cohen Family Fund.
Financial data: (yr. ended 12/31/82): Assets, $1,210,022 (M); expenditures, $78,437, including $75,700 for grants.
Purpose and activities: Broad purposes; primarily local giving, with emphasis on a camp; grants also for higher education, temple support, and Jewish welfare funds.
Limitations: Giving primarily in NY. No grants to individuals.
Application information:
 Initial approach: Proposal
 Copies of proposal: 1
 Deadline(s): Submit proposal preferably in September or October
 Board meeting date(s): Quarterly
 Write: Joseph Schlang, Treasurer
Officers: Estelle Frindel, President; Sylvan Lawrence, Vice-President; Pearl Miller, Secretary; Joseph Schlang, Treasurer.
Employer Identification Number: 136113003

2352
Cohen (Sherman & Edward Baron) Foundation, Inc. ¤
805 Third Ave., 14th Fl.
New York 10022

Established in 1979.
Donor(s): Edward Baron Cohen, Sherman Cohen.

Financial data: (yr. ended 12/31/82): Assets, $1,437 (M); gifts received, $101,000; expenditures, $101,590, including $101,450 for 4 grants (high: $100,000; low: $300).
Purpose and activities: Support primarily for a Jewish welfare fund in Israel.
Officers: Sherman Cohen, President; Edward Baron Cohen, Secretary-Treasurer.
Employer Identification Number: 132994580

2353
Cohen (Wilfred P.) Foundation, Inc.
1290 Ave. of the Americas, Suite 1614
P.O. Box 53
New York 10104

Incorporated in 1956 in New York.
Donor(s): Wilfred P. Cohen.
Financial data: (yr. ended 3/31/83): Assets, $2,222,023 (M); expenditures, $78,641, including $77,610 for 34 grants (high: $35,000; low: $50).
Purpose and activities: Educational and charitable purposes; primarily local giving, with emphasis on Jewish welfare funds; grants also for temple support, community funds, higher education, and aid to the handicapped.
Limitations: Giving primarily in the New York, NY metropolitan area.
Officers and Directors: Wilfred P. Cohen, President; Jack Greenberg, Secretary; Rose J. Cohen, Treasurer.
Employer Identification Number: 136108635

2354
Cohn (Herman & Terese) Foundation ¤
c/o Lincoln First Bank of Rochester
P.O. Box 1412
Rochester 14603

Trust established in 1954 in New York.
Donor(s): Herman M. Cohn.†
Financial data: (yr. ended 12/31/82): Assets, $3,457,370 (M); expenditures, $240,056, including $221,000 for 11 grants (high: $50,000; low: $1,000).
Purpose and activities: Broad purposes; primarily local giving for higher education, medical research, the family, and community funds.
Limitations: Giving primarily in NY.
Trustee: Lincoln First Bank of Rochester.
Employer Identification Number: 166015300

2355
Cohn (Peter A. and Elizabeth S.) Foundation, Inc. ¤
c/o Dammann, Edelman & Engel
60 E. 42nd St.
New York 10165

Established in 1955.
Donor(s): Peter A. Cohn.
Financial data: (yr. ended 6/30/83): Assets, $1,494,013 (M); gifts received, $100,000; expenditures, $41,885, including $34,215 for 15 grants (high: $12,000; low: $200).
Purpose and activities: Primarily local giving for hospitals, Jewish welfare agencies, and higher education.

Limitations: Giving primarily in New York, NY.
Officers and Directors: Peter A. Cohn, President; Elizabeth S. Cohn, Vice-President and Treasurer; Edna M. Hoffman, Secretary.
Employer Identification Number: 136117647

2356
Coleman Foundation, The
551 Fifth Ave.
New York 10176 (212) 986-9751

Trust established in 1962 in New York.
Donor(s): Janet M. Coleman, Martin S. Coleman.
Financial data: (yr. ended 11/30/83): Assets, $1,264,490 (M); expenditures, $120,124, including $88,466 for 38 grants (high: $32,000; low: $100).
Purpose and activities: Broad purposes; primarily local giving, with emphasis on higher education, Jewish welfare funds, social agencies, and hospitals.
Limitations: Giving primarily in NY. No grants to individuals or for endowment funds.
Application information:
 Initial approach: Letter
 Copies of proposal: 1
 Board meeting date(s): Semiannually
 Write: Martin S. Coleman, Trustee
Trustees: Janet M. Coleman, Martin S. Coleman.
Employer Identification Number: 136126040

2357
Coleman (George E.), Jr. Foundation ¤
c/o Alexander and Green
299 Park Ave.
New York 10017

Established in 1979 in New York.
Donor(s): George E. Coleman, Jr.†
Financial data: (yr. ended 12/31/81): Assets, $2,266,117 (M); expenditures, $224,797, including $191,000 for 41 grants (high: $35,000; low: $500).
Purpose and activities: Broad purposes; grants largely for educational institutions and associations, historic preservation, cultural organizations, and conservation.
Trustees: Daniel Oliver, Louise Oliver.
Employer Identification Number: 133025258

2358
Coles Foundation, The ▼
983 Park Ave.
New York 10028 (212) 288-2397

Trust established in 1966 in New York.
Donor(s): Jerome S. Coles, Geraldine H. Coles, Marilyn Haykin, Helene Stein.
Financial data: (yr. ended 12/31/82): Assets, $1,129,092 (M); expenditures, $725,885, including $643,345 for 65 grants (high: $422,250; low: $25).
Purpose and activities: Broad purposes, grants largely for higher education and religious welfare funds, principally Jewish; support also for the arts and public recreational park facilities.

Types of support awarded: Operating budgets, annual campaigns, seed money, building funds, equipment, land acquisition, endowment funds, professorships, scholarship funds, fellowships, student aid, special projects, research.
Limitations: No grants to individuals or for matching gifts.
Publications: 990-PF.
Application information: Applications for grants in excess of $5,000 are not considered; major gifts awarded at the initiative of the trustees.
  Initial approach: Letter
  Copies of proposal: 1
  Deadline(s): None
  Board meeting date(s): Semiannually
  Write: Jerome S. Coles, M.D., Managing Trustee
Trustees: Geraldine H. Coles, Jerome S. Coles, Howard Haykin, Marilyn Haykin, Alvin Schulman, Helene Stein, Sidney Stein.
Number of staff: 1 part-time support.
Employer Identification Number: 136213654

2359
Collins (Joseph) Foundation
One Citicorp Center
153 East 53rd St.
New York 10022

Incorporated in 1951 in New York.
Donor(s): Joseph Collins, M.D.†
Financial data: (yr. ended 6/30/83): Assets, $5,084,187 (M); expenditures, $264,590, including $242,500 for 165 grants (high: $2,500; low: $600).
Purpose and activities: Grants for tuition and/or subsistence to needy undergraduate medical students on the recommendation of medical school authorities.
Types of support awarded: Fellowships.
Publications: Annual report, program policy statement, application guidelines.
Application information: Application form required.
  Initial approach: Full proposal
  Copies of proposal: 1
  Deadline(s): Submit proposal between January and March
  Board meeting date(s): November and as required
  Write: Mrs. Augusta L. Packer, Secretary
Officers and Trustees: Mark F. Hughes, President; W. Graham Knox, M.D., John A. Lawler, M.D., Mark Saxton, Vice-Presidents; Augusta L. Packer, Secretary and Treasurer.
Number of staff: None.
Employer Identification Number: 136404527

2360
Colt Industries Charitable Foundation, Inc. ▼
430 Park Ave.
New York 10022   (212) 940-0565

Incorporated in 1963 in Delaware.
Donor(s): Colt Industries Operating Corp., Crucible Inc.

Financial data: (yr. ended 6/30/84): Assets, $11,730 (M); gifts received, $540,000; expenditures, $561,712, including $537,386 for 186 grants (high: $55,000; low: $100; average: $2,000-$3,000).
Purpose and activities: General giving, with emphasis on community funds, higher education, hospitals, cultural programs, and youth agencies.
Types of support awarded: Building funds, operating budgets.
Limitations: Giving primarily in areas of company operations. No grants to individuals.
Application information:
  Initial approach: Letter
  Copies of proposal: 1
  Deadline(s): Submit proposal preferably in September or October
  Board meeting date(s): Quarterly
  Final notification: 3 months
  Write: John F. Campbell
Officers and Directors: David I. Margolis, President; William D. Ford, Vice-President and Secretary; Salvatore J. Cozzolino, Vice-President and Treasurer, Andrew C. Hilton, George A. Strichman.
Number of staff: 2.
Employer Identification Number: 256057849

2361
Colt (James J.) Foundation, Inc. ⌖
375 Park Ave.
New York 10152

Incorporated in 1952 in New York.
Donor(s): James J. Colt.†
Financial data: (yr. ended 12/31/83): Assets, $2,360,684 (M); expenditures, $180,551, including $146,510 for 15 grants (high: $73,260; low: $100).
Purpose and activities: Broad purposes; primarily local giving, with emphasis on medical education, hospitals, Jewish welfare funds, health agencies, and church support.
Limitations: Giving primarily in NY.
Officers and Directors: Anita C. Heard, President; Thomas H. Heard, Vice-President; Miss Lottie L. Jeffers, Secretary and Treasurer; Caesar P. Kimmel, Judson W. Pearl.
Employer Identification Number: 136112997

2362
Commonwealth Fund, The ▼
One East 75th St.
New York 10021   (212) 535-0400

Incorporated in 1918 in New York.
Donor(s): Mrs. Stephen V. Harkness,† Edward S. Harkness,† Mrs. Edward S. Harkness.†
Financial data: (yr. ended 6/30/84): Assets, $158,118,231 (M); expenditures, $14,456,341, including $7,149,958 for grants (average: $5,000-$350,000) and $1,000,000 for 25 grants to individuals.

Purpose and activities: Support for research and analysis that will help the nation's academic health centers to meet their public responsibilities during a period of major institutional change, aid health care institutions in New York City to use available funds to best advantage in assuring care for residents, and assist in developing new approaches to several critical national concerns, including: problems facing Americans who are both functionally dependent and poor in old age; problems facing low-income families attempting to finance their medical care; problems facing individuals whose personal habits could lead to major disability and premature death; problems facing working mothers with young children; and problems facing minorities looking toward careers in the health professions. The Commonwealth Fund Book Program on the Frontiers of Science initiated in 1982 to encourage books by working scientists on subjects related to human health for lay literate audiences. Harkness Fellowships awarded by selection committees in each country to young potential leaders from the United Kingdom, Australia, and New Zealand for study and travel in the United States.
Types of support awarded: Research, special projects, fellowships.
Limitations: Giving limited to New York, NY for health care institutions and agencies; Harkness fellowships available only to citizens of the United Kingdom, Australia, and New Zealand. No grants to individuals (except for Harkness fellowships), or for building or endowment funds, general support, capital funds, construction or renovation of facilities, purchase of equipment, or assistance with operating budgets or deficits of established programs or institutions, scholarships or matching gifts; no loans.
Publications: Annual report, program policy statement, application guidelines.
Application information: Harkness Fellowships awarded by selection committees in each country.
  Initial approach: Letter or full proposal
  Copies of proposal: 3
  Deadline(s): None
  Board meeting date(s): April, July and November
  Write: Cynthia H. Woodcock, Program Officer-Grants Management
Officers: Margaret E. Mahoney,* President; Thomas W. Moloney, Senior Vice-President; John Craig, Vice-President and Treasurer; Gail Potter Neale, Secretary.
Directors:* C. Sims Farr, Chairman; Harriet B. Belin, Robert J. Glaser, M.D., R.L. Ireland III, Roswell B. Perkins, Robert L. Sproull, Alfred R. Stern, Blenda J. Wilson.
Number of staff: 9 full-time professional; 1 part-time professional; 15 full-time support; 3 part-time support.
Employer Identification Number: 131635260

2363
Compton Foundation, Inc. ▼
Ten Hanover Square
New York 10005   (212) 510-5039

Incorporated in 1972 in New York as successor to The Compton Trust.
Donor(s): Members of the Compton family.
Financial data: (yr. ended 12/31/83): Assets, $29,813,521 (M); expenditures, $1,549,338, including $1,434,100 for 436 grants (high: $125,000; low: $25; average: $25-$10,000).
Purpose and activities: To coordinate the family giving to community, national, and international programs in areas of its special interests, including peace and world order, higher education, population control, race relations, welfare, and the arts.
Types of support awarded: Endowment funds, fellowships, general purposes, matching funds, scholarship funds, operating budgets, continuing support, annual campaigns, seed money, special projects.
Limitations: No grants to individuals, or for capital building funds; no loans.
Publications: Biennial report.
Application information:
Initial approach: Letter
Deadline(s): None
Board meeting date(s): May and November
Final notification: 6 months, favorable replies only
Write: Randolph P. Compton, Chairman
Officers and Directors: Randolph P. Compton, Chairman and Treasurer; James R. Compton, President; Ann C. Stephens, Vice-President and Secretary; Arthur L. Bowen, Kenneth W. Thompson.
Number of staff: 1 part-time support.
Employer Identification Number: 237262706

2364
Constans-Culver Foundation
c/o Manufacturers Hanover Trust Company
600 Fifth Ave.
New York 10020

Trust established in 1965 in New York.
Donor(s): Erne Constans Culver.†
Financial data: (yr. ended 12/31/83): Assets, $2,858,782 (M); expenditures, $294,936, including $277,250 for 91 grants (high: $28,000; low: $500; average: $1,000-$2,000).
Purpose and activities: Primarily local giving, with emphasis on church support, civic and cultural organizations, and higher education.
Limitations: Giving primarily in NY. No grants to individuals or for endowment funds.
Application information:
Initial approach: Letter
Copies of proposal: 1
Deadline(s): Submit proposal preferably in September
Board meeting date(s): December and as required
Write: Robert Rosenthal, Vice-President
Trustees: J. Victor Herd, Pauline May Herd, Pauline Hoffmann Herd, Victoria Prescott Herd, Manufacturers Hanover Trust Company (Robert Rosenthal, Vice-President).
Number of staff: None.
Employer Identification Number: 136048059

2365
Continental Corporation Foundation, The ▼
180 Maiden Ln.
New York 10038   (212) 440-7729

Incorporated in 1957 in New York.
Donor(s): The Continental Corporation.
Financial data: (yr. ended 12/31/83): Assets, $16,153,775 (M); expenditures, $1,259,992, including $1,060,140 for 97 grants (high: $324,000; low: $150; average: $150-$10,000) and $137,805 for 691 employee matching gifts.
Purpose and activities: General purposes; grants largely for community funds and colleges and universities, including matching gifts and college scholarship programs for children of Continental Corporation employees, and for health and social welfare.
Types of support awarded: General purposes, building funds, employee related scholarships, employee matching gifts, scholarship funds.
Limitations: Giving limited to the U.S. No support for religious, political, or professional groups. No grants to individuals (except for scholarships to children of employees), research, courtesy advertising, or endowment funds; no loans.
Publications: Annual report, informational brochure, program policy statement, application guidelines.
Application information:
Initial approach: Letter
Copies of proposal: 1
Deadline(s): Submit proposal preferably between September and November
Board meeting date(s): March, June, September, and December
Write: Kathleen P. Mellon, Manager, Community Affairs
Officers: John P. Mascotte,* Chairman and Chief Executive Officer; William F. Gleason, Jr., Secretary; Edward J. Harvey, Treasurer.
Trustees:* Drummond C. Bell, Alec Flamm, John B. Ricker, Jr., J. Edwin Smart, Patricia Carry Stewart.
Number of staff: 1 full-time professional; 1 full-time support.
Employer Identification Number: 136090280

2366
Continental Grain Foundation ⌑
277 Park Ave.
New York 10172

Incorporated in 1961 in New York.
Donor(s): Continental Grain Company.
Financial data: (yr. ended 1/31/83): Assets, $3,199 (M); gifts received, $100,000; expenditures, $113,867, including $109,830 for 21 grants (high: $33,065; low: $1,250) and $4,000 for 5 grants to individuals.
Purpose and activities: Broad purposes; giving to universities and individual students for exchange programs between the United States and other countries.
Types of support awarded: Exchange programs.

Officers: Michel Fribourg, President; Marvin B. Berenblum, Dwight C. Coffin, Walter M. Goldschmidt, Donald L. Staheli, Vice-Presidents; John Q. Deaver, Secretary; Hendrik J. Laverge, Treasurer.
Employer Identification Number: 136160912

2367
Cornell (Peter C.) Trust
1600 Main Place Tower
Buffalo 14202   (716) 856-5500

Established in 1949 in New York.
Donor(s): Peter C. Cornell, M.D.†
Financial data: (yr. ended 9/30/84): Assets, $3,424,502 (M); expenditures, $386,936, including $365,150 for 83 grants (high: $25,000; low: $250; average: $3,000-$5,000).
Purpose and activities: General giving, with emphasis on local eleemosynary, social, education, and health needs; some grants to national agencies in those fields.
Types of support awarded: Operating budgets, continuing support, annual campaigns, seed money, emergency funds, building funds, equipment, land acquisition, matching funds.
Limitations: Giving primarily in Buffalo and Erie County, NY. No grants to individuals, or for program support, research, demonstration projects, publications, or conferences; no loans.
Publications: Application guidelines.
Application information:
Initial approach: Full proposal
Copies of proposal: 3
Deadline(s): October 1
Board meeting date(s): May and November
Final notification: 6 months
Write: Joseph H. Morey, Jr., Trustee
Trustees: Alice K. Busch, S. Douglas Cornell, Joseph H. Morey, Jr.
Number of staff: None.
Employer Identification Number: 951660344

2368
Corning Glass Works Foundation ▼
Main Plant, HF021
Corning 14831   (607) 974-8719

Incorporated in 1952 in New York.
Donor(s): Corning Glass Works.
Financial data: (yr. ended 12/31/84): Assets, $2,472,762 (M); gifts received, $1,796,148; expenditures, $1,789,987, including $1,437,750 for 246 grants (high: $130,000; low: $100; average: $100-$5,000) and $352,237 for 3,133 employee matching gifts.
Purpose and activities: To improve quality of life through support of educational, civic, cultural, health and social service institutions; special interest in efforts to improve the social and visual environment; emphasis on programs in communities where the donor has manufacturing plants. Limited support for national and international organizations.
Types of support awarded: Operating budgets, seed money, equipment, endowment funds, employee matching gifts, scholarship funds, fellowships, special projects, publications, conferences and seminars.

Limitations: Giving primarily in areas of company operations. No support for elementary or secondary schools outside of school systems in plant communities. No grants to individuals; no loans.
Publications: Annual report, program policy statement, application guidelines.
Application information:
Initial approach: Letter
Copies of proposal: 1
Deadline(s): None
Board meeting date(s): February, June, September, and December
Final notification: 2 months
Write: Kristin A. Swain, Program Manager
Officers: Richard B. Bessey,* President; James L. Flynn,* Vice-President and Treasurer; A. John Peck, Jr., Secretary.
Trustees:* Thomas S. Buechner, Chairman; Roger G. Ackerman, Van C. Campbell, John B. Coburn, George W. Douglas, Richard Dulude, E. Martin Gibson, Amory Houghton, Jr., James R. Houghton, William H. Hudson, Susan B. King, Thomas C. MacAvoy, Conrad Stemski, William C. Ughetta.
Number of staff: 2 full-time professional; 2 full-time support.
Employer Identification Number: 166051394

2369
Cowles Charitable Trust, The
630 Fifth Ave., Suite 1612
New York 10111   (212) 765-6262

Trust established in 1948 in New York.
Donor(s): Gardner Cowles.
Financial data: (yr. ended 12/31/83): Assets, $7,645,076 (M); expenditures, $928,351, including $823,018 for 47 grants (high: $250,250).
Purpose and activities: General purposes; primarily local giving, largely for art museums, higher and secondary education, hospitals, and community funds.
Types of support awarded: Operating budgets, continuing support, annual campaigns, seed money, emergency funds, building funds, equipment, endowment funds, matching funds.
Limitations: Giving primarily in NY. No grants to individuals; no loans.
Publications: Annual report.
Application information:
Initial approach: Full proposal or letter
Deadline(s): None
Board meeting date(s): January, April, July and October
Write: Martha Roby Stephens, Secretary
Officers: Gardner Cowles,* President; Martha Roby Stephens,* Secretary; Mary Croft, Treasurer.
Trustees:* Charles Cowles, Gardner Cowles III, Jan S. Cowles, Lois Cowles Harrison, Virginia Cowles Kurtis, Kate Cowles Nichols, Marvin C. Whatmore.
Number of staff: 2.
Employer Identification Number: 136090295

2370
Craigmyle Foundation, The ⌧
110 Wall St.
New York 10005

Trust established in 1951 in New York.
Donor(s): Ronald M. Craigmyle.
Financial data: (yr. ended 12/31/82): Assets, $1,154,445 (M); expenditures, $129,713, including $123,000 for 59 grants (high: $20,000; low: $25).
Purpose and activities: Charitable purposes; primarily local giving, with emphasis on higher and secondary education, Protestant church support, youth agencies, and hospitals.
Limitations: Giving primarily in NY.
Application information:
Write: Ronald M. Craigmyle, President
Officer and Trustees: Ronald M. Craigmyle, President; William C. Blind, Louise Craigmyle.
Employer Identification Number: 136109205

2371
Crane (Josephine B.) Foundation ⌧
781 Fifth Ave.
New York 10022

Incorporated in 1955 in New York.
Donor(s): Mrs. Josephine B. Crane.†
Financial data: (yr. ended 12/31/82): Assets, $1,970,781 (M); expenditures, $111,139, including $86,130 for 6 grants (high: $30,000; low: $3,130).
Purpose and activities: Broad purposes; emphasis on social and cultural advancement; grants for research in marine biology, an institute sponsoring Chinese studies, musical education, a museum, a social agency, and a hospital, primarily in New York and Massachusetts.
Limitations: Giving primarily in NY and MA.
Application information:
Write: Lawrence E. Brinn, Vice-President
Officers and Directors: Louise B. Crane, President and Treasurer; Lawrence E. Brinn, Vice-President and Secretary; Bruce Crane, Vice-President.
Employer Identification Number: 136156264

2372
Cranshaw Corporation ⌧
c/o White and Case
14 Wall St.
New York 10005   (212) 732-1040

Incorporated in 1954 in Delaware.
Donor(s): Helen Babbott Sanders.†
Financial data: (yr. ended 12/31/82): Assets, $1,235,433 (M); expenditures, $22,382, including $18,000 for 5 grants (high: $9,000; low: $2,000).
Purpose and activities: Broad purposes; primarily local giving, with emphasis on higher education.
Limitations: Giving primarily in NY. No grants to individuals.
Application information:
Deadline(s): None
Write: Edward F. Rover, Vice-President

Officers and Directors: Frederick B. Payne, President; Edward F. Rover, Vice-President, Secretary, and Treasurer; Robert I. MacDonald, Vice-President.
Employer Identification Number: 136110555

2373
Crary (Bruce L.) Foundation, Inc.
Hand House, River St.
P.O. Box 396
Elizabethtown 12932   (518) 873-6496

Incorporated in 1973 in New York.
Donor(s): Crary Public Trust, Bruce L. Crary.†
Financial data: (yr. ended 6/30/84): Assets, $3,470,763 (M); expenditures, $217,584, including $12,446 for 11 grants (high: $1,500; low: $500; average: $1,130), $108,137 for 297 grants to individuals and $21,225 for 2 foundation-administered programs.
Purpose and activities: Emphasis on scholarship aid for post-secondary education, limited to residents of Clinton, Essex, Franklin, Hamilton, and Warren counties; some support for educational and social agencies, in Essex County only. In fiscal 1978-79 the Foundation initiated a ''Citizen Information Service'' at its headquarters in Elizabethtown patterned after the British ''Citizen Advice Bureaux''.
Types of support awarded: Student aid.
Limitations: Giving limited to Clinton, Essex, Franklin, Hamilton, and Warren Counties, NY, for higher education scholarships, and to Essex County, NY, for educational and social agencies.
Application information: Application form required for scholarships. Application form required.
Initial approach: Letter or telephone
Copies of proposal: 1
Deadline(s): March for scholarships
Board meeting date(s): Monthly
Final notification: 30 to 60 days for grants; scholarships awarded in early July
Write: Richard W. Lawrence, Jr., President
Officers and Governors: Richard W. Lawrence, Jr., President; G. Gordon Davis, Vice-President and Secretary; Arthur V. Savage, Vice-President and Treasurer; Thomas Hale, Euphemia V. Hall, John W. Nason.
Number of staff: 1 full-time professional; 1 part-time professional; 1 full-time support.
Employer Identification Number: 237366844

2374
Culpeper (Charles E.) Foundation, Inc. ▼
866 United Nations Plaza, Rm. 408
New York 10017   (212) 755-9188

Incorporated in 1940 in Connecticut; in 1955 in New York.
Donor(s): Charles E. Culpeper.†
Financial data: (yr. ended 12/31/84): Assets, $86,779,027 (M); gifts received, $2,155; expenditures, $4,610,211, including $3,754,878 for 164 grants (high: $330,000; low: $500; average: $10,000-$150,000).

Purpose and activities: Grants to organizations concerned with health, education, science and technology, arts and letters, cultural programs, and administration of justice.
Types of support awarded: Research, professorships, fellowships, general purposes, equipment.
Limitations: No grants to individuals, or for conferences, conduit organizations, operating budgets, or travel; no loans. Limited support only for endowment or building funds.
Publications: Informational brochure, program policy statement, application guidelines, multi-year report.
Application information:
Initial approach: Full proposal
Copies of proposal: 1
Deadline(s): Submit proposal preferably between February and September; no set deadline
Board meeting date(s): Usually in March, May, September, and December
Final notification: 3 weeks
Write: Mrs. Helen D. Johnson, President
Officers and Directors: Francis J. McNamara, Jr., Chairman; Helen D. Johnson, President; Nicholas J. Nardi, Vice-President and Treasurer; Philip M. Drake, Secretary; Colin G. Campbell, John A. Huston.
Number of staff: 4.
Employer Identification Number: 131956297

2375
Cummings (Frances & Edwin) Memorial Fund ⌖

c/o Irving Trust Company
12446 Church St. Station
New York 10249

Established in 1982 in New York.
Donor(s): Edwin Cummings.†
Financial data: (yr. ended 7/31/83): Assets, $12,641,695 (M); gifts received, $8,876,118; expenditures, $350,350, including $350,000 for 4 grants (high: $150,000; low: $25,000).
Purpose and activities: Giving primarily in New York for medical and disease research, and for a hospital.
Types of support awarded: Research, general purposes.
Limitations: Giving primarily in NY.
Trustee: Irving Trust Company.
Employer Identification Number: 136814491

2376
Cummings (James H.) Foundation, Inc. ▼

1807 Elmwood Ave., Rm. 112
Buffalo 14203   (716) 874-0040

Incorporated in 1962 in New York.
Donor(s): James H. Cummings.†
Financial data: (yr. ended 5/31/84): Assets, $8,752,264 (M); expenditures, $565,660, including $461,427 for 25 grants (high: $61,875; low: $196; average: $2,500-$40,000).

Purpose and activities: Exclusively for charitable purposes in advancing medical science, research, and education in the United States and Canada and for charitable work among underprivileged boys and girls and aged and infirm persons in designated areas.
Types of support awarded: Building funds, seed money, equipment, land acquisition, matching funds, consulting services, research.
Limitations: Giving limited to the vicinity of the cities of Buffalo, NY, Hendersonville, NC, and Toronto, Ontario. No grants to individuals, or for annual campaigns, program support, endowment funds, operating budgets, emergency funds, deficit financing, scholarships, fellowships, publications, conferences, or continuing support; no loans.
Publications: Annual report, program policy statement, application guidelines.
Application information:
Initial approach: Letter of not more than 2 pages or by telephone
Copies of proposal: 7
Deadline(s): February 15, May 15, August 15, and November 15
Board meeting date(s): March, June, September, and December
Final notification: 4 to 8 weeks
Write: Robert J. Lyle, Executive Director
Officers: Robert S. Scheu,* President; William G. Gisel,* Vice-President; Robert J. Lyle, Secretary and Executive Director; Robert J.A. Irwin,* Treasurer.
Directors:* Kenneth M. Alford, M.D., John Naughton, M.D., John N. Walsh, Jr.
Number of staff: 1 full-time professional.
Employer Identification Number: 160864200

2377
Curtice-Burns/Pro-Fac Foundation

P.O. Box 681
Rochester 14603   (716) 325-1020

Trust established in 1966 in New York.
Donor(s): Curtice-Burns, Inc.
Financial data: (yr. ended 6/29/84): Assets, $778,775 (M); gifts received, $240,000; expenditures, $320,561, including $316,861 for 268 grants (high: $13,357; low: $100).
Purpose and activities: Broad purposes; primarily local giving, with emphasis on higher education, including scholarship funds, hospitals, community funds, and youth agencies.
Types of support awarded: General purposes, operating budgets, annual campaigns, building funds, equipment, endowment funds, scholarship funds, fellowships, professorships, internships, special projects, research, conferences and seminars.
Limitations: Giving primarily in areas of company operations. No support for religious organizations. No grants to individuals, or for seed money, emergency funds, deficit financing, land acquisition, matching gifts, or publications; no loans.
Application information:
Initial approach: Full proposal
Copies of proposal: 1
Deadline(s): None
Board meeting date(s): Usually in January, March, May, August, October, and December

Final notification: 2 months
Write: Marilyn T. Helmer, Secretary
Officer: Marilyn T. Helmer, Secretary.
Trustees: Don Wickham, Chairman; Betty E. Hawthorne, Theodore J. Holmgren.
Number of staff: 1 part-time support.
Employer Identification Number: 166071142

2378
Dammann Fund, Inc., The

60 East 42nd St., Suite 3014
New York 10165   (212) 687-0880

Incorporated in 1946 in New York.
Donor(s): Members of the Dammann family.
Financial data: (yr. ended 11/30/84): Assets, $7,457,578 (M); expenditures, $567,027, including $536,556 for 367 grants (high: $50,000; low: $10).
Purpose and activities: Broad purposes; grants to hospitals, health and welfare agencies, and religious and educational institutions.
Types of support awarded: Continuing support, annual campaigns, seed money, building funds, endowment funds, general purposes, special projects.
Limitations: No grants to individuals, or for scholarships, fellowships, or matching gifts; no loans.
Application information:
Initial approach: Letter
Copies of proposal: 1
Deadline(s): None
Board meeting date(s): March, June, September, and December
Write: Richard W. Dammann, President
Officers and Directors: Richard W. Dammann, President and Secretary-Treasurer; Margaret D. Eisner, Vice-President.
Number of staff: 2 part-time support.
Employer Identification Number: 136089896

2379
Dana (The Charles A.) Foundation, Incorporated ▼

150 East 52nd St., 23rd Fl.
New York 10022   (212) 223-4040

Incorporated in 1950 in Connecticut.
Donor(s): Charles A. Dana,† Eleanor N. Dana.†
Financial data: (yr. ended 12/31/84): Assets, $123,006,858 (M); expenditures, $8,350,737, including $6,725,712 for 61 grants (high: $500,000; low: $5,000; average: $10,000-$250,000).
Purpose and activities: Broad purposes; principal interests in private higher education at four-year liberal arts colleges in the eastern United States, and health.
Types of support awarded: Seed money, matching funds, scholarship funds, professorships, internships, fellowships, research.
Limitations: Giving primarily in the eastern United States. No support for professional organizations. No grants to individuals, or for capital or endowment funds, operating budgets, continuing support, annual campaigns, emergency funds, deficit financing, publications, conferences, demonstration projects, or colloquia; no loans.

Publications: Annual report, program policy statement, application guidelines.
Application information:
  Initial approach: Letter
  Deadline(s): None
  Board meeting date(s): April, June, October, and December
  Final notification: 2 to 3 months
  Write: Robert N. Kreidler, President
Officers and Directors: David J. Mahoney, Chairman; Robert N. Kreidler, President; Walter G. Corcoran, Vice-President; Clark M. Whittemore, Jr., Secretary-Treasurer; Edward C. Andrews, Jr., Wallace L. Cook, Charles A. Dana, Jr., James H. French, William S. Hirschberg, Donald B. Marron, Donald C. Platten.
Number of staff: 3 full-time professional; 2 part-time professional; 4 full-time support.
Employer Identification Number: 066036761

2380
Daniel (Gerard & Ruth) Foundation, Inc. ♯
Five Plain Ave.
New Rochelle 10801

Donor(s): Gerard Daniel & Company.
Financial data: (yr. ended 12/31/84): Assets, $2,238,153 (M); gifts received, $200,000; expenditures, $112,494, including $109,535 for 28 grants (high: $46,000; low: $25).
Purpose and activities: Grants primarily for Jewish welfare funds, cultural and educational organizations, and temple support; support also for museums.
Officers and Directors: Gerard Daniel, President; Ruth Daniel, Vice-President; Joseph S. Iseman, Secretary.
Employer Identification Number: 136207879

2381
Darrah (Jessie S.) Charitable Trust
c/o Citibank
One Citicorp Center, Sort 2439, PB & I Division
New York 10043

Donor(s): Jessie S. Darrah.†
Financial data: (yr. ended 12/31/84): Assets, $1,462,000 (M); expenditures, $150,000, including $140,000 for 25 grants (high: $10,000; low: $500).
Purpose and activities: Giving primarily in Chautauqua County, New York, with emphasis on youth agencies, child welfare, and Methodist church support.
Limitations: Giving primarily in Chautauqua County, NY.
Trustees: Howard A. Johnson, Wesley H. Nord, Charles N. Price, Richard F. Reading, Richard L. Swanson, Citibank, (Kent H. Parker, Senior Trust Officer).
Employer Identification Number: 136129875

2382
Davenport-Hatch Foundation, Inc., The ♯
c/o Security Trust Company
One East Ave.
Rochester 14638

Incorporated in 1952 in New York.
Donor(s): Augustus Hatch.†
Financial data: (yr. ended 5/31/82): Assets, $7,715,712 (M); expenditures, $416,333, including $388,245 for 75 grants (high: $40,000; low: $550).
Purpose and activities: Broad purposes; primarily local giving, with emphasis on community development, higher education, the aged, welfare, youth agencies, hospitals, and church support.
Limitations: Giving primarily in the Rochester, NY, area.
Officers and Directors: Austin E. Hildebrandt, President; John W. Ross, Vice-President; Helen H. Heller, Secretary and Treasurer; Earl W. Brinkman, Robert J. Brinkman, J. Wallace Ely, William L. Ely, A. Thomas Hildebrandt, Elizabeth H. Hildebrandt, David H. Taylor, Douglas F. Taylor, Hart Taylor.
Employer Identification Number: 166027105

2383
Davidson-Krueger Foundation Inc., The ♯
(formerly The Philip Davidson Foundation, Inc.)
5002 Second Ave.
Brooklyn 11232

Incorporated in 1955 in New York.
Donor(s): Philip Davidson, Davidson Pipe Company, Inc., and others.
Financial data: (yr. ended 11/30/83): Assets, $1,019,965 (M); gifts received, $50,000; expenditures, $163,427, including $159,120 for grants.
Purpose and activities: Primarily local giving, with emphasis on Jewish welfare funds, hospitals, and education in Israel.
Limitations: Giving primarily in NY.
Officers: H. Peter Davidson, President; Nancy Brookman, Vice-President; Stuart Krueger, Secretary-Treasurer.
Employer Identification Number: 116005674

2384
Davis (The Leonard and Sophie) Foundation, Inc. ▼ ♯
555 Madison Ave.
New York 10022

Incorporated in 1961 in New York.
Donor(s): Leonard Davis, Sophie Davis.
Financial data: (yr. ended 12/31/82): Assets, $8,840,389 (M); gifts received, $950,000; expenditures, $973,624, including $940,800 for 66 grants (high: $400,000; low: $50).
Purpose and activities: Charitable purposes; grants largely for higher education, Jewish welfare funds and the arts.
Application information:
  Write: Mrs. Zmira Goodman, President

Officers: Mrs. Zmira Goodman, President; Sophie Davis, Vice-President and Secretary; Leonard Davis, Vice-President and Treasurer; Eugene Rose, Vice-President.
Employer Identification Number: 136062579

2385
Davis (Shelby Cullom) Foundation ▼ ♯
70 Pine St.
New York 10270   (212) 425-3212

Incorporated in 1962 in New York.
Donor(s): Shelby Cullom Davis, Shelby M. Cullom Davis.
Financial data: (yr. ended 11/30/82): Assets, $17,371,128 (M); expenditures, $1,045,335, including $807,228 for 78 grants (high: $125,000; low: $15).
Purpose and activities: Broad purposes; interest primarily in higher education, economic research, and public policy.
Officers and Trustees: Shelby Cullom Davis, Chairman and Treasurer; Shelby M. Cullom Davis, Secretary.
Director: Kenneth C. Ebbitt.
Employer Identification Number: 136165382

2386
Davis (Simon and Annie) Foundation ▼ ♯
c/o Davis & Gilbert
850 Third Ave.
New York 10022

Incorporated in 1946 in New York.
Donor(s): Abraham M. Davis,† Meyer Davis,† Ruth Davis.
Financial data: (yr. ended 12/31/82): Assets, $2,829,634 (M); expenditures, $850,063, including $830,650 for 17 grants (high: $700,000; low: $1,500).
Purpose and activities: Broad purposes; primarily local giving, with emphasis on Jewish welfare funds and higher education in the United States and Israel.
Limitations: Giving primarily in NY.
Officers and Directors: Paul B. Gibney, Jr., President and Treasurer; Leonard Schwartz, Secretary; Robert K. Knox.
Employer Identification Number: 136069454

2387
de Hirsch (The Baron) Fund
130 East 59th St.
New York 10022   (212) 980-1000
Fellowship application address: Fellowship Committee, Baron de Hirsch Fund, Ministry of Agriculture, Tel Aviv, Israel

Incorporated in 1891 in New York.
Donor(s): Baron Maurice de Hirsch,† Baroness Clara de Hirsch.†
Financial data: (yr. ended 8/31/83): Assets, $5,291,695 (M); expenditures, $451,380, including $311,000 for 14 grants (high: $37,500; low: $10,000; average: $21,000) and $42,925 for 37 grants to individuals.

Purpose and activities: To assist in the economic assimilation of Jewish immigrants in the United States and Israel, their instruction in trades and agriculture, and promotion of agriculture among them; aids other agencies that work to obtain education and jobs for immigrants.

Types of support awarded: Operating budgets, continuing support, seed money, emergency funds, scholarship funds, exchange programs, fellowships, loans, special projects, research, conferences and seminars, student aid, grants to individuals.

Limitations: No grants to individuals (except for study grants), or for annual campaigns, deficit financing, capital or endowment funds, scholarships and fellowships, matching gifts, or publications.

Publications: Application guidelines.

Application information:
Initial approach: Letter
Copies of proposal: 1
Deadline(s): Submit proposal preferably between May and August; deadline September 1
Board meeting date(s): October
Final notification: 2 weeks after board meeting
Write: Robert B. Goldmann, Managing Director

Officers: Ezra P. Mager,* President; Francis Rosenbaum, Jr.,* Vice-President; E. Gabriel Perle,* Secretary; James A. Block,* Treasurer; Robert B. Goldmann, Managing Director.

Trustees:* Martin Blumenthal, Gail Chasin, Alan Davies, Thomas Frank, William W. Heineman, Walter W. Hess, Jr., Myron S. Isaacs, Robert Morgenthau, George W. Naumburg, Jr., Theodore Norman, Christopher C. Schwabacher, Arthur Sporn, Mrs. Laurence Tisch.

Number of staff: 1 part-time professional; 1 part-time support.

Employer Identification Number: 135562971

2388
De Jur (Harry) Foundation, Inc. ⌑
c/o Pavia & Harcourt
600 Madison Ave.
New York 10022

Incorporated in 1958 in New York.
Donor(s): Harry De Jur.†
Financial data: (yr. ended 11/30/82): Assets, $1,920,635 (M); gifts received, $4,000; expenditures, $343,408, including $330,605 for 76 grants (high: $80,700; low: $40).
Purpose and activities: Broad purposes; primarily local giving, with emphasis on higher education, both in Israel and the United States, social agencies, Jewish welfare funds, and youth agencies.
Limitations: Giving primarily in NY.
Officers: Robert Greenberg, President; Marian De Jur, Benjamin Neuwirth, Vice-Presidents; David Botwinik, Secretary.
Employer Identification Number: 136110844

2389
de Kay Foundation, The
c/o Manufacturers Hanover Trust Company
600 Fifth Ave.
New York 10020   (212) 957-1668

Trust established in 1967 in Connecticut.
Donor(s): Mrs. Helen M. de Kay.†
Financial data: (yr. ended 2/28/83): Assets, $11,558,872 (M); expenditures, $695,868, including $408,833 for 3 grants (high: $204,416; low: $102,208) and $192,803 for 83 grants to individuals.
Purpose and activities: To encourage and promote the well-doing and well-being of men and women of culture or refined heritage who are in real need of financial assistance, particularly sick, old, or disabled persons who are not being otherwise properly cared for; after distribution of two-thirds of the income to specified institutions, balance is allocated for above purpose. Generally limited to residents of Connecticut, New York, and New Jersey.
Types of support awarded: Continuing support, grants to individuals.
Limitations: Giving limited to NY, NJ, and CT. No grants for building or endowment funds, scholarships or fellowships, or matching gifts; no loans.
Application information: Application form required.
Initial approach: Letter requesting application form
Copies of proposal: 1
Board meeting date(s): Quarterly
Final notification: 1 or 2 months
Write: Lloyd Saltus, II, Vice-President, Manufacturers Hanover Trust Company
Advisory Committee: Howard S. Tuthill, Chairman; Betsy Devecchi, Robert F. Longley, Rev. Hays Rockwell, Lloyd Saltus, II, Jerome Shaw.
Trustees: Manufacturers Hanover Trust Company, Morgan Guaranty Trust Company of New York.
Employer Identification Number: 136203234

2390
de Rothschild (B.) Foundation for the Advancement of Science in Israel ⌑
One Rockefeller Plaza, Rm. 2814
New York 10020

Incorporated in 1958 in New York.
Donor(s): Mrs. Bethsabee de Rothschild.
Financial data: (yr. ended 5/31/83): Assets, $1,134,286 (M); expenditures, $82,432, including $58,684 for 8 grants (high: $20,000; low: $1,014).
Purpose and activities: Grants for seminars on scientific research in Israel.
Limitations: Giving limited to Israel.
Officers and Directors:* Bethsabee de Rothschild,* President; Joram Piatigorsky,* Vice President; G. Peter Fleck, Secretary.
Employer Identification Number: 136075582

2391
de Rothschild (The Edmond) Foundation ▼
300 Park Ave., Rm. 2100
New York 10022   (212) 909-7724

Incorporated in 1963 in New York.
Donor(s): Edmond de Rothschild.
Financial data: (yr. ended 2/28/83): Assets, $11,088,713 (M); gifts received, $1,300,000; expenditures, $1,048,739, including $968,232 for 44 grants (high: $407,445; low: $500; average: $1,000-$50,000).
Purpose and activities: General purposes; grants largely for Jewish welfare funds, higher education, and organizations concerned with Israeli affairs in the U.S. and abroad; support also for cultural programs, hospitals, and scientific research in the U.S., Israel, and France.
Limitations: Giving primarily in New York City, NY and in France. No grants to individuals.
Application information:
Initial approach: Letter
Copies of proposal: 1
Board meeting date(s): As required
Write: Paul H. Epstein, Secretary
Officers and Directors: Edmond de Rothschild, Chairman; George M. Shapiro, President; George C. Karlweis, Vice-President; Paul H. Epstein, Secretary and Treasurer.
Number of staff: None.
Employer Identification Number: 136119422

2392
DeCamp (The Ira W.) Foundation ▼
c/o Mudge Rose Guthrie Alexander & Ferdon
20 Broad St.
New York 10005   (212) 701-1558

Trust established in 1975 in New York.
Donor(s): Elizabeth DeCamp McInerny.†
Financial data: (yr. ended 10/31/83): Assets, $41,897,806 (M); expenditures, $2,585,585, including $2,098,627 for 39 grants (high: $200,000; low: $2,000; average: $10,000-$100,000).
Purpose and activities: Grants for health care facilities and equipment and for medical research and education.
Types of support awarded: Building funds, equipment, matching funds, professorships, seed money, research, special projects.
Limitations: No grants to individuals, or for general support, land acquisition, publications, conferences, endowment funds, operating budgets, continuing support, annual campaigns, emergency funds, or deficit financing; no loans.
Application information:
Initial approach: Letter
Copies of proposal: 3
Deadline(s): None
Board meeting date(s): Quarterly
Final notification: 3 Months
Write: William J. Kramer
Trustees: Herbert H. Faber, James H. McInerny.
Number of staff: None.
Employer Identification Number: 510138577

2393
Delany (Beatrice P.) Charitable Trust ▼ ☒
c/o The Chase Manhattan Bank
1211 Ave. of the Americas
New York 10036   (212) 730-3088

Trust established about 1977 in New York.
Donor(s): Beatrice P. Delany.†
Financial data: (yr. ended 10/31/82): Assets, $23,239,181 (M); expenditures, $1,422,753, including $1,245,000 for 54 grants (high: $425,000; low: $800).
Purpose and activities: Giving largely for higher education, hospitals, and health organizations.
Trust Committee: Thomas A. Reynolds, Jr., Mrs. Thomas A. Reynolds, Jr., Andrew Thomson, M.D.
Trustee: The Chase Manhattan Bank.
Employer Identification Number: 136748171

2394
Delmas (The Gladys Krieble) Foundation
40 West 57th St.
New York 10019   (212) 603-2302

Established in 1976 in New York.
Donor(s): Gladys Krieble Delmas.
Financial data: (yr. ended 12/31/83): Assets, $1,140,577 (M); gifts received, $125,000; expenditures, $229,193, including $133,852 for 4 grants (high: $10,000; low: $500; average: $3,000-$10,000) and $85,770 for 35 grants to individuals.
Purpose and activities: Grants primarily to individuals for research in Venice, Italy, and for travel; support also for a local library.
Types of support awarded: Research, fellowships.
Limitations: No grants for general support, building or endowment funds, or matching gifts; no loans.
Publications: Program policy statement, application guidelines.
Application information:
  Initial approach: Full proposal
  Copies of proposal: 8
  Deadline(s): Submit proposal preferably in October or November; deadline December 15
  Board meeting date(s): March
  Final notification: By April 1
  Write: Joan Squires, Administrative Assistant
Trustees: Gladys Krieble Delmas, Patricia Labalme, David H. Stam.
Number of staff: 1 part-time support.
Employer Identification Number: 510193884

2395
Deloitte Haskins & Sells Foundation ▼
1114 Ave. of the Americas
New York 10036   (212) 790-0588

Incorporated in 1928 in New York.
Donor(s): Charles Stewart Ludlam,† Charles C. Croggon,† Weldon Powell,† Haskins & Sells.

Financial data: (yr. ended 8/31/83): Assets, $4,128,791 (M); gifts received, $521,601; expenditures, $838,823, including $205,853 for 10 grants (high: $60,000; low: $1,300), $220,411 for 48 grants to individuals and $367,374 for 2,723 employee matching gifts.
Purpose and activities: To further accounting education in the United States, including faculty development grants and research in accounting through support of the Doctoral Fellowship Program and the Graduate Research Assistant Program.
Types of support awarded: Employee matching gifts, scholarship funds, fellowships, research, conferences and seminars.
Limitations: No grants for general support, capital or endowment funds, matching gifts, special programs, or publications; no loans.
Publications: Informational brochure.
Application information: Application form required.
  Initial approach: Letter
  Copies of proposal: 1
  Deadline(s): October 15 for Doctoral Fellowship Program
  Board meeting date(s): Semiannually
  Write: William G. Cole, Assistant Secretary
Officers and Directors: Charles G. Steele, Chairman and President; C. Howard Kast, Vice-President and Treasurer; James L. McGregor, Jerry W. Kolb, Raymond Spinola, Vice-Presidents; Robert W. Pivik, Secretary.
Number of staff: None.
Employer Identification Number: 136400341

2396
Dent (Harry) Family Foundation, Inc.
1607 Statler Bldg.
Buffalo 14202   (716) 856-0975

Incorporated in 1954 in New York.
Donor(s): Harry M. Dent.†
Financial data: (yr. ended 10/31/83): Assets, $2,782,695 (M); expenditures, $196,191, including $145,500 for 6 grants (high: $125,000; low: $500).
Purpose and activities: Broad purposes; grants to local organizations, principally for medical research purposes, with emphasis on a neurological institute; some support for community funds.
Limitations: Giving limited to western NY. No grants to individuals.
Application information: Funds presently committed.
  Board meeting date(s): Semiannually
  Write: Miss Jane E. Gailey, Secretary
Officers and Directors: Harry M. Dent, Jr., President; L. Nelson Hopkins, Vice-President; Jane E. Gailey, Secretary; John C. Trefts, Jr., Treasurer; Max Becker, Jr., Theodore H. Booth, Gloria G. Dent, Lucy Dent, Helen Dent Lenahan, Herman E. Moecker, Gilbert J. Pedersen, Graham Wood Smith.
Employer Identification Number: 160849923

2397
Dewar (James A. and Jessie Smith) Foundation, Inc. ☒
c/o Rutsom R. Henderson
45 Dietz St.
Oneonta 13820

Incorporated in 1947 in New York.
Donor(s): Jessie Smith Dewar.†
Financial data: (yr. ended 12/31/82): Assets, $11,189,322 (M); expenditures, $386,893, including $358,296 for 52 grants (high: $80,000; low: $500).
Purpose and activities: Primarily local giving, with emphasis on civic and charitable organizations, including support for cultural organizations, youth agencies, Protestant churches, education, and child welfare.
Limitations: Giving primarily in Oneonta, NY.
Officer and Trustees: Rutson R. Henderson, President and Treasurer; Richard Applebaugh, Charles H. Bissell, Frank Getman.
Employer Identification Number: 166054329

2398
Dewey (John) Foundation
570 Seventh Ave., Suite 1007
New York 10018   (212) 391-2396

Established in 1964 in Delaware.
Donor(s): Mrs. John Dewey.†
Financial data: (yr. ended 12/31/83): Assets, $1,040,224 (M); expenditures, $212,716, including $190,263 for 7 grants (high: $57,350; low: $500).
Purpose and activities: General purposes; grants for the promotion of academic endeavor relating to the philosophy of John Dewey.
Publications: 990-PF.
Application information: Application form required.
  Initial approach: Letter
  Copies of proposal: 3
  Deadline(s): Submit proposal preferably from June through September; deadline October 1
  Board meeting date(s): October and March
Officers and Directors: Steven Cahn, President; Ernest Nagel, Secretary; Sidney Hook, Treasurer.
Employer Identification Number: 136172348

2399
Dillon (Clarence and Anne) Dunwalke Trust ▼
1270 Ave. of the Americas, Rm. 2300
New York 10020   (212) 315-8343

Trust established in 1969 in New York.
Donor(s): Clarence Dillon.†
Financial data: (yr. ended 6/30/84): Assets, $11,003,057 (M); expenditures, $628,666, including $558,000 for 14 grants (high: $125,000; low: $1,000).
Purpose and activities: Broad purposes; giving primarily locally and in New Jersey, with emphasis on education, hospitals, the arts, and welfare agencies. Grants only to present beneficiary organizations and for special proposals developed by the trustees.

Types of support awarded: Fellowships, endowment funds, equipment, research, annual campaigns, operating budgets, building funds, special projects, general purposes.
Limitations: Giving primarily in NJ and NY. No grants to individuals; no loans.
Application information: New requests seldom considered.
Deadline(s): None
Board meeting date(s): November and as required
Write: Crosby R. Smith, Trustee
Officer: Robert F. Quick, Administrative Secretary.
Trustees: Christine Allen, Philip D. Allen, Mark McC. Collins, Jr., Phyllis Dillon Collins, C. Douglas Dillon, Dorothy Dillon Eweson, David H. Peipers, Crosby R. Smith.
Number of staff: 1 part-time professional.
Employer Identification Number: 237043773

2400
Dillon Fund, The ▼
1270 Ave. of the Americas, Rm. 2300
New York 10020 (212) 315-8343

Incorporated in 1922 in New York.
Donor(s): Clarence Dillon,† C. Douglas Dillon.
Financial data: (yr. ended 12/31/84): Assets, $1,407,048 (M); gifts received, $2,713,863; expenditures, $2,605,229, including $2,571,700 for 88 grants (high: $1,500,000; low: $1,000).
Purpose and activities: Broad purposes; general giving, with emphasis on education and the arts.
Types of support awarded: Continuing support, annual campaigns, building funds, operating budgets, publications, endowment funds, general purposes.
Limitations: No grants to individuals; no loans.
Application information: New applications seldom considered; giving only to present beneficiaries and for special proposals developed by the directors.
Deadline(s): None
Board meeting date(s): May and as required
Write: Crosby R. Smith, President
Officers: Crosby R. Smith,* President; Robert F. Quick, Vice-President and Treasurer; Margaret Florio, Secretary.
Directors:* Mark M. Collins, Jr., Phyllis Dillon Collins, C. Douglas Dillon, Susan S. Dillon.
Number of staff: 1 part-time professional.
Employer Identification Number: 136400226

2401
Dobson Foundation, Inc., The ⌑
Four East 66th St., Suite 1E
New York 10021

Incorporated in 1961 in New York.
Donor(s): Walter M. Jeffords, Jr.
Financial data: (yr. ended 12/31/82): Assets, $2,770,795 (M); expenditures, $324,489, including $311,400 for 44 grants (high: $170,000; low: $50).
Purpose and activities: Broad purposes; general giving, with emphasis on conservation; support also for hospitals, higher education, sports museums and Catholic church support, largely in New York State and Maine.
Limitations: Giving primarily in NY and ME.
Officers and Directors: Walter M. Jeffords, Jr., President; Kathleen McL. Jeffords, Vice-President, Secretary, and Treasurer; George V. McL. Jeffords.
Employer Identification Number: 136168259

2402
Dodge (Cleveland H.) Foundation, Inc. ▼
670 West 247th St.
Riverdale 10471 (212) 543-1220

Incorporated in 1917 in New York.
Donor(s): Cleveland H. Dodge.†
Financial data: (yr. ended 12/31/83): Assets, $15,547,000 (M); gifts received, $392,938; expenditures, $1,074,163, including $831,300 for 96 grants (high: $50,000; low: $500; average: $5,000-$10,000) and $26,000 for 24 employee matching gifts.
Purpose and activities: "To promote the well-being of mankind throughout the world." Grants for a selected list of international purposes, especially confined to the Near East; grants also to a selected few national agencies in the United States and the balance for the most part to organizations located in New York City. Most grants in the United States for higher and secondary education, youth agencies and child welfare, and cultural programs.
Types of support awarded: Building funds, equipment, endowment funds, matching funds.
Limitations: Giving primarily in New York, NY, the Near East, and national organizations. No support for health care or medical research. No grants to individuals, or for general purposes, research, scholarships, or fellowships; no loans.
Publications: Annual report, program policy statement.
Application information:
Initial approach: Letter
Copies of proposal: 1
Deadline(s): Submit proposal preferably prior to the 15th of January, April, July, or October
Board meeting date(s): February, May, August, and November
Write: Miss Louise H. Kerr, Administrative Director
Officers: Cleveland E. Dodge, Jr.,* President; Alfred H. Howell,* Vice-President; John Rulon-Miller,* Secretary; Louise H. Kerr, Administrative Director and Treasurer.
Directors:* David S. Dodge, Margaret Dodge Garrett, Robert Garrett, Gilbert Kerlin, Cleveland D. Rea, William Dodge Rueckert, Mary Rea Weidlein.
Number of staff: 1 full-time professional; 1 full-time support.
Employer Identification Number: 136015087

2403
Doft (Beryl H.) Foundation, Inc. ⌑
124 Fulton St.
Lawrence 11559

Established in 1947.
Donor(s): Members of the Doft family and others.
Financial data: (yr. ended 12/31/82): Assets, $252,155 (M); gifts received, $111,452; expenditures, $153,665, including $152,185 for 55 grants (high: $23,475).
Purpose and activities: Giving primarily locally and in Israel for Jewish religious organizations, temple support, and education.
Limitations: Giving primarily in NY and Israel.
Officers: Emanuel Doft, President; Alan Doft, Avrom Doft, Vice-Presidents; Barry Escott, Secretary; Pauline Doft, Treasurer.
Employer Identification Number: 116035628

2404
Doherty (The Henry L. and Grace) Charitable Foundation, Inc.
61 Broadway, Rm. 724
New York 10006 (212) 269-3870

Incorporated in 1947 in Delaware.
Donor(s): Mrs. Henry L. Doherty,† Mrs. Helen Lee Lassen.†
Financial data: (yr. ended 12/31/83): Assets, $4,276,806 (M); expenditures, $128,420, including $58,725 for 31 grants (high: $5,000; low: $100).
Purpose and activities: Primarily to promote research in the marine sciences and to assist institutions engaged in oceanographic activities. Only limited expansion of activities is anticipated in the foreseeable future.
Types of support awarded: Research.
Limitations: No grants to individuals.
Application information: Available funds presently committed.
Initial approach: Letter
Copies of proposal: 1
Deadline(s): None
Board meeting date(s): As required
Write: James R. Billingsley, Vice-President
Officers: Walter R. Brown,* President; James R. Billingsley,* Vice-President and Treasurer; Dorothy R. McCall,* George G. Vest,* Vice-Presidents; Joan B. Cadmus, Secretary.
Trustees:* Helen Lee Billingsley, Kiyoko O. Brown.
Number of staff: 2 part-time support.
Employer Identification Number: 136401292

2405
Donner (The William H.) Foundation, Inc. ▼
630 Fifth Ave., Rm. 2452
New York 10111 (212) 765-1695

Incorporated in 1961 in the District of Columbia.
Donor(s): William H. Donner.†
Financial data: (yr. ended 10/31/84): Assets, $37,050,432 (M); expenditures, $2,277,573, including $1,700,799 for 47 grants (high: $165,585; low: $8,125; average: $15,000-$75,000).

Purpose and activities: Concerned with 1) Canadian studies in the United States in order to increase awareness and understanding of the differences in language, history, and government which exist between the two countries; 2) programs to strengthen the management of the nation's coastal ocean and inland water resources; 3) education of physicians and the public of the role nutrition plays in maintaining health.
Types of support awarded: Seed money, matching funds, research, conferences and seminars, publications.
Limitations: No grants to individuals, or for operating budgets, continuing support, annual campaigns, emergency, capital, or endowment funds; deficit financing, charitable drives, scholarships, fellowships, or special projects; no loans. The foundation does not provide consulting services or technical assistance.
Publications: Annual report, program policy statement, application guidelines.
Application information:
Initial approach: Letter or telephone
Copies of proposal: 1
Deadline(s): Submit proposal preferably in November, March, or July; deadlines 8 weeks prior to board meetings
Board meeting date(s): February, June, and October
Final notification: Immediately after board meetings
Write: Philip S. Jessup, II, Vice-President
Officers: Donald S. Rickerd, President; Joseph W. Donner,* Robert Donner, Jr.,* Philip S. Jessup II, Vice-Presidents; Curtin Winsor, Jr.,* Secretary; William D. Roosevelt,* Treasurer.
Trustees:* Stephen Stamas, Chairman; Jill K. Conway, Gilbert Grosvenor.
Number of staff: 3 full-time professional; 1 full-time support.
Employer Identification Number: 231611346

2406
Donovan Leisure Newton & Irvine Foundation, Inc. ⊭
30 Rockefeller Plaza
New York 10112

Established in 1977.
Donor(s): Donovan Leisure Newton & Irvine.
Financial data: (yr. ended 5/31/83): Assets, $106,027 (M); gifts received, $150,000; expenditures, $104,906, including $95,950 for 20 grants (high: $25,000; low: $250) and $8,630 for 14 employee matching gifts.
Purpose and activities: Grants largely for programs in law and justice and civil rights; supports an employee matching gifts program, primarily to law schools; support also for a community fund.
Types of support awarded: Employee matching gifts.
Officers and Directors: John E. Tobin, President; John J. McCann, Secretary and Treasurer; John C. Baity, Kenneth N. Hart, Andrew J. Kilcarr, George S. Leisure, Jr., Sanford M. Litvack, Louis C. Lustenberger, Jr., Samuel W. Murphy, Jr., Stuart B. Peerce.
Employer Identification Number: 132900457

2407
Dorot Foundation ⊭
100 Park Ave.
New York 10017

Incorporated in 1958 in New York as Joy and Samuel Ungerleider Foundation.
Donor(s): Joy G. Mayerson, D.S and R.H. Gottesman Foundation.
Financial data: (yr. ended 3/31/83): Assets, $9,470,179 (M); expenditures, $527,159, including $467,100 for 39 grants (high: $157,000; low: $100).
Purpose and activities: Grants primarily for Jewish welfare funds, including organizations in Israel; support also for higher education and educational organizations.
Limitations: Giving primarily in the U.S. and Israel.
Officers: Joy Ungerleider-Mayerson,* President; Philip Mayerson,* Edgar Wachenheim III, Vice-Presidents; Peter C. Siegfried, Secretary; Benjamin Glowatz, Treasurer.
Directors:* Milton Gottesman.
Employer Identification Number: 136116927

2408
Dorr Foundation
P.O. Box 281
Bedford 10506

Trust established in 1940 in Connecticut.
Donor(s): John Dorr.
Financial data: (yr. ended 12/31/83): Assets, $1,469,679 (M); gifts received, $25,200; expenditures, $81,000, including $57,840 for 9 grants (high: $25,000; low: $2,350).
Purpose and activities: Grants primarily for conservation of natural areas and wildlife organizations; support also for special education projects for youth and/or the aged with emphasis on conservation and environment.
Types of support awarded: Seed money, emergency funds, building funds, equipment, land acquisition, special projects, matching funds, research, publications.
Limitations: Giving primarily in the northeast U.S.; selective national and international grants. No grants to individuals, or for operating budgets, continuing support, annual campaigns, deficit financing, general endowment funds, conferences and seminars, or scholarships and fellowships; no loans.
Application information: Foundation does not respond to requests for guidelines or other publications.
Initial approach: Full proposal, including a 1- to-2 page summary
Copies of proposal: 6
Deadline(s): None
Board meeting date(s): December and as required
Final notification: 3 months
Write: Hugh McMillan, Chairman
Officer and Trustees: Hugh McMillan, Chairman and Treasurer; Allen Hardon, Secretary; Roger Hardon, Virginia Maxwell, William Phillips, Shirley M. Punzeit, Perry D. Trafford.
Number of staff: None.
Employer Identification Number: 136017294

2409
Doubleday (Russell and Janet) Fund ⊭
c/o Citibank
641 Lexington Ave.
New York 10043

Established in 1965 in New York.
Donor(s): Janet Doubleday.†
Financial data: (yr. ended 10/31/83): Assets, $3,394,557 (M); expenditures, $214,263, including $195,072 for 9 grants (high: $80,072; low: $2,500).
Purpose and activities: Primarily local giving, with emphasis on a library, higher education, biological research, population control, and youth agencies. Grants generally limited to charities of particular interest to the donor during her lifetime.
Limitations: Giving primarily in NY.
Application information: Applications for grants not invited.
Trustees: Albert L. Lingelbach, Roger D. Smith, Citibank, (W.B. Reid, Assistant Vice-President).
Employer Identification Number: 136207874

2410
Dow Jones Foundation
22 Cortlandt St.
New York 10007   (212) 285-5000

Trust established in 1954 in New York.
Donor(s): Dow Jones & Company, Inc.
Financial data: (yr. ended 12/31/84): Assets, $4,678,111 (M); expenditures, $212,250, including $212,250 for 11 grants (high: $89,250; low: $1,000; average: $1,000-$5,000).
Purpose and activities: General giving, with emphasis on community funds, and higher education, largely in areas of company operations.
Types of support awarded: Continuing support, annual campaigns, employee related scholarships.
Limitations: Giving primarily in areas of company operations. No support for medical or scientific research, or cultural activities. No grants to individuals (except for company-employee scholarships), or for endowment funds or operating budgets.
Publications: Application guidelines.
Application information:
Copies of proposal: 1
Deadline(s): Submit proposal preferably in August or September; deadline November 1
Board meeting date(s): Usually in the last quarter
Write: Leonard E. Doherty, Administrative Officer
Advisory Committee: Bettina Bancroft, Jane B. Cook, Frederick G. Harris, Warren H. Phillips.
Trustee: United States Trust Company of New York.
Number of staff: None.
Employer Identification Number: 136070158

2411
Dreyfus (The Camille and Henry) Foundation, Inc. ▼
445 Park Ave.
New York 10022   (212) 753-1760

Incorporated in 1946 in New York.
Donor(s): Camille Dreyfus.†
Financial data: (yr. ended 12/31/84): Assets, $29,743,566 (M); expenditures, $3,161,346, including $2,794,479 for 56 grants (high: $1,000,000; low: $5,000).
Purpose and activities: "To advance the sciences of chemistry, biochemistry, chemical engineering, and related sciences as a means of improving human relations and circumstances throughout the world"; assists organizations which afford facilities for the production, collection, or dissemination of scientific information; support mainly for post-secondary academic institutions through sponsorship of Newly Appointed Young Faculty in Chemistry Program, Dreyfus Teacher-Scholar Grant Program, and Special Grants Program.
Types of support awarded: Seed money, equipment, scholarship funds, research, special projects.
Limitations: No support for health, medicine, or biology. No grants to individuals, or for building or endowment funds, operating budgets, continuing support, emergency funds, deficit financing, land acquisition, renovation projects, publications, conferences, or matching gifts; no loans.
Publications: Annual report, informational brochure.
Application information: Candidates for Teacher-Scholar grants and Young Faculty grants must be nominated by applying academic institution. Application form required.
    Initial approach: Letter in 3 copies, preferably in January through May
    Copies of proposal: 3
    Deadline(s): April 15 for Teacher-Scholar Grant Program, May 15 for Newly Appointed Young Faculty in Chemistry Program, and June 15 for Special Grants Program
    Board meeting date(s): April, July, September, and October
    Final notification: 6 months
    Write: William L. Evers, Executive Director
Officers: Jean Dreyfus Boissevain,* President; Harold Blancke,* Vice-President; Henry B. Guthrie,* Secretary-Treasurer; William L. Evers, Executive Director.
Directors:* John R.H. Blum, Elizabeth Guthrie, Joshua Lederberg, Robert L. Mitchell, Grayson M-P. Murphy, H. Marshall Schwarz, Reiner G. Stoll, Henry C. Walter.
Number of staff: 2 full-time professional; 6 part-time professional; 1 part-time support.
Employer Identification Number: 135570117

2412
Dreyfus (Jean and Louis) Foundation, Inc. ¤
c/o Decker, Hubbard and Welden
30 Rockefeller Plaza
New York 10112

Incorporated about 1978 in New York.

Donor(s): Louis Dreyfus.†
Financial data: (yr. ended 12/31/82): Assets, $7,287,748 (M); expenditures, $374,583, including $334,000 for 26 grants (high: $100,000; low: $1,000).
Purpose and activities: Grants primarily to established institutions of the arts and medical research.
Application information:
    Initial approach: Proposal
    Board meeting date(s): Spring
    Write: Thomas J. Hubbard, Secretary
Officers: Valli V. Dreyfus Firth, President; Thomas J. Sweeney, Vice-President and Treasurer; Nicholas L.D. Firth, Vice-President; Thomas J. Hubbard, Secretary.
Employer Identification Number: 132947180

2413
Dreyfus (The Max and Victoria) Foundation, Inc. ▼
575 Madison Ave.
New York 10022   (212) 605-0354

Incorporated in 1965 in New York.
Donor(s): Victoria Dreyfus.†
Financial data: (yr. ended 12/31/83): Assets, $28,666,723 (M); expenditures, $1,729,159, including $1,383,900 for 158 grants (high: $120,000; low: $500; average: $5,000-$15,000).
Purpose and activities: Broad purposes, including support for hospitals, medical research, education, health and social services, with emphasis on youth and aid to the aged and handicapped, and cultural programs.
Types of support awarded: Research, special projects.
Limitations: No grants to individuals.
Application information: Submit proposal upon request by the foundation only.
    Initial approach: Letter
    Deadline(s): 10 weeks prior to board meeting dates
    Board meeting date(s): Usually in mid-February, June and October
    Final notification: 2 weeks after board meetings
    Write: Ms. Lucy Gioia, Administrative Assistant
Officers and Directors: David J. Oppenheim, President; Nancy E. Oddo, Norman S. Portenoy, Vice-Presidents; Winifred Riggs Portenoy, Secretary-Treasurer.
Number of staff: 1 full-time support.
Employer Identification Number: 131687573

2414
Dula (The Caleb C. and Julia W.) Educational and Charitable Foundation ▼ ¤
c/o Manufacturers Hanover Trust Company
600 Fifth Ave.
New York 10020

Trust established in 1939 in New York.
Donor(s): Julia W. Dula.†
Financial data: (yr. ended 12/31/82): Assets, $11,204,909 (M); expenditures, $556,684, including $396,000 for 77 grants (high: $100,000; low: $500).

Purpose and activities: Grants to charities which the Dulas supported during their lifetime, with emphasis on higher and secondary education, hospitals, libraries, social agencies, child welfare, church support, cultural programs, and historic preservation, primarily in New York and St. Louis, Missouri.
Limitations: Giving primarily in NY and St. Louis, MO.
Application information:
    Board meeting date(s): Usually spring and fall
    Write: M.J.A. Smith, Administrative Officer
Trustees: Margaret C. Taylor, Julia P. Wightman, Orrin S. Wightman III, Manufacturers Hanover Trust Company (M.J.A. Smith, Vice-President).
Employer Identification Number: 136045790

2415
Dun & Bradstreet Corporation Foundation, The ▼
299 Park Ave.
New York 10171   (212) 593-6746

Incorporated in 1953 in Delaware.
Donor(s): The Dun & Bradstreet Group.
Financial data: (yr. ended 12/31/82): Assets, $4,510,434 (M); gifts received, $800,000; expenditures, $1,795,356, including $1,070,455 for 371 grants (high: $350,000; low: $50; average: $100-$10,000) and $661,103 for 1,231 employee matching gifts.
Purpose and activities: General purposes; to assist charitable and educational institutions, with emphasis on cultural programs, community funds, higher education, health and welfare, and youth agencies.
Types of support awarded: Operating budgets, continuing support, annual campaigns, general purposes, employee related scholarships, employee matching gifts.
Limitations: No grants to individuals (except for company-employee scholarships), or for building or endowment funds, or research; no loans.
Application information:
    Initial approach: Letter or full proposal
    Copies of proposal: 1
    Deadline(s): Submit proposal preferably in August or September; no set deadline
    Board meeting date(s): Semiannually
    Final notification: 4 weeks
    Write: Juliann Gill, Administrator
Officers: Charles W. Moritz,* President; Robert G. Wallace, Secretary; Frank L. Alexander, Treasurer; Juliann Gill, Administrator.
Trustees:* Edwin A. Bescherer, Jr., Harrington Drake.
Number of staff: None.
Employer Identification Number: 136148188

2416
Dutchess County, The Area Fund of
Nine Vassar St.
Poughkeepsie 12601   (914) 452-3077

Community foundation established in 1969 in New York.
Donor(s): McCann Foundation, Lester Freer,† and others.

Financial data: (yr. ended 12/31/83): Assets, $8,123,526 (M); gifts received, $81,801; expenditures, $60,644, including $26,547 for 23 grants (high: $2,624; low: $20).
Purpose and activities: Emergency and special grants, particularly as "seed money," to non-profit organizations operating principally within Dutchess County, which were established for charitable, cultural, and educational purposes. Limited funds available for grantmaking as bulk of assets is in non-income producing properties.
Types of support awarded: Seed money, emergency funds, equipment, scholarship funds, special projects, research, publications, conferences and seminars.
Limitations: Giving primarily in Dutchess County, NY. No grants to individuals, or for endowment funds, capital campaigns, building funds, land acquisition, matching gifts, deficit financing, operating budgets, or where amount of grant will not make a significant impact on a project; no loans.
Publications: Annual report, application guidelines.
Application information:
  Initial approach: Letter or telephone
  Copies of proposal: 1
  Deadline(s): Submit proposal one and a half months before board meetings; no set deadlines
  Board meeting date(s): February, May, September, and November
  Final notification: 3 months
  Write: Caroline H. Morse, Administrator
Officers and Trustees: Steele C. Cameron, President; James S. Hedges II, Vice-President; Mrs. Arthur Gellert, Secretary; Owen T. Clarke, Jr., Treasurer; Stephen P. Becker, Charles A. Butts, Mrs. Edward V.K. Cunningham, Jr., Daniel F. Curtin, Mrs. Tyler Dann, J. James Fahey, Lloyd W. Hapeman, Mrs. C.K. Howe, Joseph P. Jordan, Roy C. Ketcham, Maurice E. Kinkade, Natalie J. Marshall, Mrs. Victor O. Morris, John P. O'Shea, Oliver E. Porter, James J. Ritterskamp, Jr., Richard J. Staats, Eric K. Stoutenburgh, Richard M. Whalen, Mrs. H. Clifton Wilson, Rabbi Erwin Zimet.
Number of staff: 1 full-time professional.
Employer Identification Number: 237026859

2417
Dyson Foundation
230 Park Ave., Rm. 659
New York 10169

Trust established in 1949 in New York; incorporated in 1958 in Delaware.
Donor(s): Charles H. Dyson, Margaret M. Dyson, The Dyson-Kissner-Moran Corporation.
Financial data: (yr. ended 12/31/83): Assets, $1,162,216 (M); gifts received, $1,297,000; expenditures, $1,319,132, including $1,318,475 for 59 grants (high: $80,000; low: $250).
Purpose and activities: Grants primarily for medical research, with emphasis on pediatrics; support also for education and cultural programs. The foundation does not consider unsolicited requests for funds of any kind.
Types of support awarded: Building funds, general purposes, research.

Application information: Unsolicited applications of any kind are not accepted.
  Write: Anne E. Dyson, M.D., President
Officers and Directors: Anne E. Dyson, M.D., President; Charles H. Dyson, John S. Dyson, Margaret M. Dyson, Peter L. Dyson, Robert R. Dyson, Ernest H. Lorch, Joseph V. Mariner, John A. Moran, Vice-Presidents; Elizabeth L. Darney, Secretary; Robert L. Wallace, Treasurer.
Employer Identification Number: 136084888

2418
Eastman Kodak Charitable Trust ▼
c/o Lincoln First Bank of Rochester
P.O. Box 1412
Rochester 14603   (716) 724-3127

Trust established in 1952 in New York.
Donor(s): Eastman Kodak Company.
Financial data: (yr. ended 12/31/83): Assets, $36,865,533 (M); expenditures, $7,089,435, including $7,009,592 for 135 grants (high: $2,500,000; low: $100; average: $25,000-$250,000).
Purpose and activities: Charitable purposes; primarily local giving at the initiative of the foundation for a community chest, higher education, and a local photographic museum.
Types of support awarded: Annual campaigns, research, general purposes, continuing support.
Limitations: Giving primarily in the Rochester, NY area. No grants to individuals, or for building or endowment funds, scholarships, fellowships, or matching gifts; no loans.
Application information:
  Initial approach: Letter, full proposal, or telephone
  Copies of proposal: 1
  Deadline(s): None
  Board meeting date(s): Monthly
  Final notification: 4 weeks
  Write: Stanley C. Wright, Secretary, Financial Aid Committee
Trustee: Lincoln First Bank of Rochester (Patricia Bonawitz, Trust Officer).
Number of staff: None.
Employer Identification Number: 166015274

2419
Ebsary Charitable Foundation, The
80 Rock Wood Place
Rochester 14610   (716) 244-0256

Incorporated in 1949 in New York.
Donor(s): Frederick G. Ebsary,† Mrs. Margaret E. Ebsary,† F.G. Ebsary, Inc.
Financial data: (yr. ended 7/31/84): Assets, $918,429 (M); expenditures, $171,022, including $148,378 for 107 grants (high: $10,000; low: $250; average: $1,000-$2,000).
Purpose and activities: Broad purposes; primarily local giving, with emphasis on higher education, including scholarship funds, hospitals, Protestant and Roman Catholic church support and welfare funds, youth and social agencies, and cultural organizations.
Types of support awarded: Research, scholarship funds.

Limitations: Giving primarily in NY, especially Monroe and surrounding counties. No grants to individuals, or for endowment funds, or matching gifts; no loans.
Application information:
  Initial approach: Proposal
  Copies of proposal: 2
  Deadline(s): May
  Board meeting date(s): Quarterly
  Write: Charles F. Seuffert, President
Officers and Directors: Charles F. Seuffert, President; Evelyn C. Madara, Secretary; Rockwood Jenkins, Edna M. Winslow.
Employer Identification Number: 166013209

2420
Elsmere Foundation, Inc. ⊭
55 Water St.
New York 10041

Incorporated in 1955 in New York.
Donor(s): Kate S. Heming, Henry L. Heming, Henry A. Cohn, Abraham S. Platt, Richard H. Baer, Walter W. Hess, Jr., Herbert H. Weitsman,† Chester W. Viale, Stephen Kovacs.
Financial data: (yr. ended 12/31/82): Assets, $769,035 (M); gifts received, $133,100; expenditures, $181,752, including $178,170 for 101 grants (high: $100,000; low: $25).
Purpose and activities: Broad purposes; primarily local giving, with emphasis on Jewish welfare funds, social agencies, cultural programs, and hospitals. Applications for grants not invited.
Limitations: Giving primarily in NY.
Application information: Applications for grants not invited.
  Write: Walter W. Hess, President
Officers and Directors: Walter W. Hess, Jr., President; Alexander Bing III, Vice-President and Treasurer; Stephen Kovacs, Robert Schoenthal, Chester Viale.
Employer Identification Number: 136061343

2421
Emerson (Fred L.) Foundation, Inc. ▼
63 Genesee St.
P.O. Box 307
Auburn 13021   (315) 253-9621

Incorporated in 1932 in Delaware.
Donor(s): Fred L. Emerson.†
Financial data: (yr. ended 12/31/84): Assets, $32,292,550 (M); expenditures, $1,670,086, including $1,506,133 for 51 grants (high: $175,000; low: $60).
Purpose and activities: Broad purposes; primarily local giving, with emphasis on colleges and universities (primarily for scholarships or building funds), hospitals, community funds, and a library building fund; grants also for youth and health agencies, church support, cultural programs, and social service agencies.
Types of support awarded: Building funds, matching funds, continuing support, annual campaigns, emergency funds, equipment, endowment funds, scholarship funds, special projects, research.

Limitations: Giving primarily in the central NY area. No grants to individuals, or for operating budgets, seed money, or deficit financing; no loans.
Publications: Program policy statement, application guidelines.
Application information:
Initial approach: Letter, telephone, or full proposal
Copies of proposal: 1
Deadline(s): 2 months prior to board meetings
Board meeting date(s): June and December
Final notification: 2 to 3 weeks after board meetings (positive replies only)
Write: Ronald D. West, Executive Director
Officers and Directors: William V. Emerson, President; Peter J. Emerson, Vice-President; David E. Newell, Secretary; Thomas S. Tallman, Treasurer; David L. Emerson, E. Paul Flynn, J. David Hammond, James Richard B. Secrest, Ronald D. West.
Number of staff: 1 full-time professional; 1 full-time support.
Employer Identification Number: 156017650

2422
Erpf (The Armand G.) Fund, Inc.
c/o Sue Erpf Van de Bovenkamp
640 Park Ave.
New York 10021

Incorporated in 1951 in New York.
Donor(s): Armand G. Erpf.†
Financial data: (yr. ended 11/30/82): Assets, $3,874,237 (M); expenditures, $353,051, including $261,459 for 48 grants (high: $44,590; low: $50).
Purpose and activities: Broad purposes; primarily local support for environment and conservation, education, and cultural programs.
Limitations: Giving primarily in NY. No grants to individuals or for endowment funds.
Application information:
Initial approach: Full proposal
Copies of proposal: 1
Board meeting date(s): Quarterly
Write: Sue Erpf Van de Bovenkamp, President
Officers and Trustees: Sue Erpf Van de Bovenkamp, President; Gerrit P. Van de Bovenkamp, Exec. Vice-President; John G. Clancy, Secretary; Carl Kempner, Treasurer; Douglas Campbell, Henry B. Hyde, Roger D. Stone, Alan M. Stroock.
Employer Identification Number: 136085594

2423
Ettinger Foundation, Inc., The ⋈
420 Lexington Ave., Rm. 2320
New York 10170

Incorporated in 1949 in Delaware.
Donor(s): Members of the Ettinger family.
Financial data: (yr. ended 12/31/83): Assets, $3,465,870 (M); expenditures, $187,968, including $152,100 for 46 grants (high: $10,000; low: $300).

Purpose and activities: Broad purposes; general giving, with emphasis on higher and secondary education, including scholarship funds; grants also for community funds, health, and youth agencies.
Limitations: No grants to individuals, or for general support, or building or endowment funds; no loans.
Application information:
Initial approach: Letter
Copies of proposal: 1
Board meeting date(s): February, May, August, and November
Write: Richard P. Ettinger, Jr., President
Officers: Richard P. Ettinger, Jr., President and Treasurer; Elsie A. Ettinger, Vice-President; Ralph F. Anthony, Secretary.
Trustees: Virginia E. Andrews, Elaine Hapgood.
Employer Identification Number: 066038938

2424
Evans (The T. M.) Foundation, Inc.
300 Park Ave.
New York 10022   (212) 644-3715

Incorporated in 1951 in Delaware.
Donor(s): Thomas Mellon Evans.
Financial data: (yr. ended 12/31/84): Assets, $4,007,111 (M); expenditures, $341,490, including $293,325 for 37 grants (high: $75,000; low: $125).
Purpose and activities: Broad purposes; grants primarily for museums and historic preservation, higher education, hospitals, medical research, and music.
Limitations: No grants to individuals or for scholarships or fellowships; no loans.
Application information:
Initial approach: Full proposal
Copies of proposal: 1
Board meeting date(s): December
Write: L.F. Cerrone, Assistant Secretary
Officers and Trustees: Thomas Mellon Evans, President; James H. Fraser, Secretary-Treasurer; Betty B. Evans, Edward P. Evans, Thomas M. Evans, Jr.
Employer Identification Number: 256012086

2425
Everett (Fred M. and Ora H.) Charitable Trust ⋈
c/o The Bank of Auburn
120 Genesee St.
Auburn 13021   (315) 253-2731

Trust established in 1957 in New York.
Donor(s): Fred M. Everett, Ora H. Everett.
Financial data: (yr. ended 12/31/82): Assets, $1,232,518 (M); expenditures, $85,548, including $78,095 for 13 grants (high: $31,597; low: $500).
Purpose and activities: Grants restricted to charitable organizations in Auburn and Cayuga County, New York; support for a community fund, youth agencies, Protestant church support, and hospitals.
Limitations: Giving primarily in NY. No grants to individuals.
Application information:
Initial approach: Letter
Copies of proposal: 1

Deadline(s): Submit proposal preferably in October; deadline November 1
Board meeting date(s): December
Write: Ronald D. West, Trust Officer
Trustee: The Bank of Auburn (Ronald D. West, Vice-President and Trust Officer).
Employer Identification Number: 156018093

2426
Exxon Education Foundation ▼
111 West 49th St.
New York 10020   (212) 398-2273

Incorporated in 1955 in New Jersey.
Donor(s): Exxon Corporation, and affiliated companies.
Financial data: (yr. ended 12/31/83): Assets, $60,014,000 (M); gifts received, $32,484,000; expenditures, $31,684,152, including $21,698,742 for 555 grants (high: $325,000; low: $300; average: $15,000-$20,000) and $5,662,682 for 10,000 employee matching gifts.
Purpose and activities: To aid education in the United States through various programs in the areas of general education, integrative studies, innovations in teaching and learning, and economic research and management of higher education. Grants are to public and private colleges and universities and to professional educational associations. Also matches Exxon employee and annuitant contributions to colleges and universities up to $5,000 each per year on a $3-to-$1 basis.
Types of support awarded: Special projects, publications, conferences and seminars, employee matching gifts, general purposes, professorships, matching funds, operating budgets.
Limitations: No grants to individuals, or for capital or building funds, equipment, land acquisition, renovation projects, endowments, institutional scholarships or fellowships, or standard course or curriculum development activities normally covered by institutional budgets; no loans.
Publications: Annual report, program policy statement, application guidelines.
Application information: Applications for funding under the Research and Training Program, the Organizational and Institutional Support Program, or for pre-college funds in the Curriculum and Teaching Program are by foundation invitation only.
Initial approach: Full proposal or letter of no more than 5 typewritten, letter-sized pages
Copies of proposal: 5
Deadline(s): None
Board meeting date(s): Usually in March, June, September, and December
Final notification: 2 to 3 months
Write: Robert L. Payton, President
Officers: Robert L. Payton, President; Walter Kenworthy, Vice-President and Secretary; A.B. McDougall, J.E. Remmert,* Vice-Presidents; C.W. Williams, Treasurer; L.J. Brown, Controller.

Trustees*: S. Stamas, Chairman; R.H. Beresford, E.R. Cattarulla, R.E. Faggioli, H.J. Lartique, Jr., U.J. LeGrange, P.J. Lucchesi, G.B. McCullough, T.S. McDonagh, E.A. Robinson.
Number of staff: 6 full-time professional; 4 full-time support.
Employer Identification Number: 136082357

2427
Faith Home Foundation ⌑
32 Court St., Rm. 807
Brooklyn 11201   (212) 875-1952

Incorporated in 1878 in New York.
Financial data: (yr. ended 2/28/83): Assets, $1,302,210 (M); expenditures, $124,698, including $92,500 for 30 grants (high: $5,000; low: $2,100).
Purpose and activities: Charitable purposes; primarily local giving, with emphasis on the aged and child welfare agencies.
Limitations: Giving primarily in NY.
Officers and Trustees: Waldemar J. Neumann, President; Charles H. Heinlein, Frank Mullen, Vice-Presidents; Dorothy C. Beckmann, Secretary; Owen E. Brooks, Gordon M. Brown, William F. de Neergaard, Kenneth Heiberg, Elwin S. Larson, Eugene B. Martens, Jr., George C. Schaefer, William P. Tucker.
Employer Identification Number: 111776032

2428
Falk (Michael David) Foundation, Inc. ⌑
569 Broadway
New York 10012

Established in 1968.
Donor(s): Isidore Falk.
Financial data: (yr. ended 12/31/82): Assets, $1,522,543 (M); expenditures, $59,411, including $57,800 for 14 grants (high: $25,000; low: $250).
Purpose and activities: Grants largely for higher education and Jewish welfare funds.
Managers: Isidore Falk, Maurice Falk.
Employer Identification Number: 136265854

2429
Faulkner (Marianne Gaillard) Trust ⌑
c/o Manufacturers Hanover Trust Company
600 Fifth Ave.
New York 10020   (212) 957-1595

Trust established in 1959 in Vermont.
Donor(s): Marianne Gaillard Faulkner.†
Financial data: (yr. ended 12/31/82): Assets, $3,919,833 (M); expenditures, $280,894, including $237,017 for 7 grants (high: $124,255; low: $101).
Purpose and activities: Grants primarily to Vermont institutions, with emphasis on a recreation center and other community development projects, particularly in the town of Woodstock.
Types of support awarded: Matching funds, operating budgets.

Limitations: Giving primarily in VT, mostly in the town of Woodstock. No grants to individuals, or for endowment funds, or operating budgets.
Application information: Prefer matching or one-time grants.
 Initial approach: Proposal
 Copies of proposal: 4
 Board meeting date(s): As required
 Write: J.J. Kindred III, Vice-President
Trustee: Manufacturers Hanover Trust Company, (J.J. Kindred III, Vice-President).
Employer Identification Number: 136047458

2430
Ferkauf (The Eugene and Estelle) Foundation
c/o Fredric A. Kleinberg
522 Fifth Ave., 22nd Fl.
New York 10036   (212) 382-0080

Established in 1967 in New York.
Donor(s): Eugene Ferkauf, Estelle Ferkauf.
Financial data: (yr. ended 12/31/83): Assets, $3,551,352 (M); expenditures, $424,602, including $359,018 for 58 grants (high: $40,500; low: $100).
Purpose and activities: Grants primarily for education, medical facilities, and medical research.
Limitations: No grants to individuals.
Publications: Application guidelines.
Application information:
 Initial approach: Letter
 Copies of proposal: 1
 Deadline(s): Submit proposal preferably in January, July, or December
 Board meeting date(s): As required
 Write: Fredric A. Kleinberg
Trustees: Lenore Bronstein, Robert Bronstein, Richard M. Dicke, Barbara Dor, Estelle Ferkauf, Eugene Ferkauf, Amy Shapira.
Employer Identification Number: 132621094

2431
FFHS & J Fund, Inc. ⌑
One New York Plaza
New York 10004

Incorporated in 1982 in New York.
Donor(s): Members of the firm of Fried, Frank, Harris, Shriver & Jacobson.
Financial data: (yr. ended 12/31/82): Assets, $18,433 (M); gifts received, $533,550; expenditures, $519,550, including $518,980 for 53 grants (high: $200,000; low: $30).
Purpose and activities: First year of operations in 1982; giving primarily in New York and Washington, D.C., for Jewish welfare funds, public interest law and civil rights associations, and law schools; also supports a community fund.
Limitations: Giving primarily in New York, NY and DC.
Officer and Trustees: William Josephson, President; Leslie A. Jacobsen, Herbert Hirsch, David E. Birenbaum.
Employer Identification Number: 133111495

2432
Field Foundation, Inc., The ▼
100 East 85th St.
New York 10028   (212) 535-9915

Incorporated in 1940 in New York.
Donor(s): Marshall Field III.†
Financial data: (yr. ended 9/30/84): Assets, $9,796,000 (M); expenditures, $5,494,527, including $4,497,770 for 168 grants (high: $145,000; low: $500) and $487,000 for 5 foundation-administered programs.
Purpose and activities: Broad charitable purposes; major interests in race relations, including social justice and civil rights; education, child welfare, poverty within the United States, reduction of nuclear armaments and military spending, and programs directed towards world peace.
Types of support awarded: Conferences and seminars, general purposes, publications, research, seed money, special projects, technical assistance.
Limitations: Giving primarily in the U.S., largely for national organizations. No support for medical research. No grants to individuals, or for annual campaigns or ordinary expense budgets of health and welfare agencies, building or endowment funds, scholarships, or fellowships; no loans.
Publications: Biennial report, application guidelines.
Application information:
 Initial approach: Letter
 Copies of proposal: 1
 Deadline(s): None
 Board meeting date(s): About 2 times a year
 Write: Richard W. Boone, Secretary
Officers: John R. Kramer,* President; Justine W. Polier,* M. Carl Holman,* Milton J.E. Senn,* Vice-Presidents; Richard W. Boone, Secretary and Executive Director; Seth Glickenhaus,* Treasurer.
Directors:* Ruth P. Field, Chairman; William B. Cannon, James P. Comer, Vine Deloria, Jr., Adrian DeWind, Willard Gaylin, S.M. Miller, Robert L. Phipps, Aaron Shirley.
Number of staff: 7.
Employer Identification Number: 131624003

2433
Fife (Elias and Bertha) Foundation, Inc.
37-18 Northern Blvd.
Long Island City 11101

Incorporated in 1959 in New York.
Donor(s): Members of the Fife family, Standard Motor Products, Incorporated.
Financial data: (yr. ended 4/30/83): Assets, $3,409,294 (M); gifts received, $120,000; expenditures, $105,667, including $104,515 for 94 grants (high: $76,500; low: $100).
Purpose and activities: Charitable purposes; support for Jewish welfare funds and national and local health and welfare agencies.
Officers and Directors: Bernard Fife, President; Nathaniel L. Sills, Secretary and Treasurer; Arlene Fife, Ruth Sills.
Employer Identification Number: 116035634

2434
Fink Foundation, Inc. ⌗
1212 Ave. of the Americas, Rm. 2204
New York 10036

Incorporated in 1956 in New York.
Donor(s): David Fink, Nathan Fink.
Financial data: (yr. ended 12/31/82): Assets,
$1,949,453 (M); gifts received, $60,950;
expenditures, $151,669, including $108,743
for 69 grants (high: $25,000; low: $10).
Purpose and activities: Grants largely to
Jewish-sponsored organizations, with emphasis
on education and welfare.
Officers: Nathan Fink, President; Vivian R.
Fink, Secretary-Treasurer.
Employer Identification Number: 136135438

2435
First Boston Foundation Trust, The
c/o The First Boston Corporation
Park Ave. Plaza
New York 10055   (212) 909-2000
Mailing address: One Federal St., Boston, MA
02110

Trust established in 1959 in Massachusetts.
Donor(s): The First Boston Corporation.
Financial data: (yr. ended 12/31/83): Assets,
$1,300,000 (M); expenditures, $520,000,
including $400,000 for 102 grants (high:
$85,000; low: $100) and $120,000 for
employee matching gifts.
Purpose and activities: Broad purposes;
emphasis on community funds and higher
education; support also for cultural programs,
community development, and groups seeking
to improve international relations.
Types of support awarded: Employee
matching gifts.
Limitations: No grants to individuals.
Application information:
 Initial approach: Letter
 Deadline(s): None
 Write: Morgan C. Brown, III
Officers and Trustees: William E. Mayer,
Chairman; Morgan C. Brown, III, Secretary;
John R. Carhuff, Roderick J. Kirkpatrick, George
A. Needham, Andrew N. Overby, Alexander C.
Tomlinson.
Employer Identification Number: 046059692

2436
Fischbach Foundation Incorporated ⌗
Timber Trail
Rye 10580

Incorporated in 1944 in New York.
Donor(s): Members of the Fischbach family.
Financial data: (yr. ended 12/31/82): Assets,
$1,366,052 (M); gifts received, $1,500;
expenditures, $106,352, including $103,650
for 44 grants (high: $50,000; low: $50).
Purpose and activities: To aid the health,
welfare, and education of poor and needy
people; primarily local giving for higher
education, including education in Israel, and
hospitals; some support for Jewish welfare
funds.

Limitations: Giving primarily in NY.
Officers: Jerome Fischbach, President; Beatrice
Levinson, Secretary.
Employer Identification Number: 237416874

2437
Fischel (Harry and Jane) Foundation
276 Fifth Ave.
New York 10001   (212) 684-2626

Incorporated in 1932 in New York.
Donor(s): Harry Fischel.†
Financial data: (yr. ended 12/31/83): Assets,
$4,288,546 (M); expenditures, $337,055,
including $181,925 for 30 grants (high:
$160,300; low: $10).
Purpose and activities: Organized to develop
Talmudic research to aid Jewish knowledge and
present the Orthodox Jewish contributions to
civilization. Grants largely to two educational
institutions initiated by the donor.
Limitations: No grants to individuals.
Application information: Applications not
invited.
 Write: Simeon H.F. Goldstein, Executive
 Director
Officers and Directors: Rabbi O. Asher
Reichel, Chairman; Gabriel F. Goldstein, Acting
President and Vice-President; Frederic S.
Goldstein, Secretary and Treasurer; Simeon
H.F. Goldstein, Executive Director; Rabbi Shear
Yashuv Cohen, Seth M. Goldstein, Harry
Grossman, Michael Jaspan, Norman Jaspan,
Ronald Jaspan, Rabbi Aaron I. Reichel.
Number of staff: 1 full-time professional; 2
part-time support.
Employer Identification Number: 135677832

2438
Fish (Vain and Harry) Foundation, Inc. ⌗
66 East 79th St.
New York 10021

Incorporated in 1972 in New York.
Donor(s): Vain B. Fish,† Harry Fish.†
Financial data: (yr. ended 12/31/81): Assets,
$2,269,106 (M); expenditures, $239,492,
including $197,372 for 59 grants (high:
$15,000; low: $500).
Purpose and activities: General purposes;
primarily local giving, with emphasis on higher
education and hospitals; grants also for cultural
activities, youth agencies, the handicapped,
and church support.
Limitations: Giving primarily in NY.
Application information:
 Write: Alexander W. Gentleman, President
Officers: Alexander W. Gentleman, President;
Vivian F. Gentleman, Vice-President and
Secretary; Bernard Leegant, Treasurer.
Employer Identification Number: 132723211

2439
Flemm (John J.) Foundation, Inc. ⌗
c/o Sidney Horn
225 West 34 St.
New York 10001

Established in 1974.

Donor(s): John J. Flemm.†
Financial data: (yr. ended 1/31/83): Assets,
$1,775,616 (M); expenditures, $210,489,
including $183,800 for 65 grants (high:
$15,000; low: $50).
Purpose and activities: Giving primarily for
Jewish welfare and educational funds in the
United States and Israel, and temple support;
support also for higher education.
Officers and Trustees: Judah J. Harris,
President; Robert Post, Vice-President; Judith
Post, Secretary; Daniel Harris, Treasurer; Avery
Harris, Michael Harris, Rose Harris, Leona Post.
Employer Identification Number: 237348789

2440
Forbes Foundation
60 Fifth Ave.
New York 10011   (212) 620-2248

Established in 1979 in New Jersey.
Donor(s): Forbes, Inc.
Financial data: (yr. ended 12/31/83): Assets,
$2,383,825 (M); gifts received, $1,450,000;
expenditures, $1,415,538, including
$1,410,482 for grants (high: $1,013,440).
Purpose and activities: Giving primarily for
higher and secondary education, hospitals,
cultural programs, including museums, and
welfare funds.
Types of support awarded: General purposes,
building funds, endowment funds.
Limitations: No grants to individuals or for
matching gifts; no loans.
Publications: 990-PF.
Application information:
 Initial approach: Letter
 Copies of proposal: 1
 Deadline(s): Submit proposal in January;
 deadline January 31
 Board meeting date(s): As required
 Final notification: 90 days
 Write: Leonard H. Yablon, Secretary
Officers: Malcolm S. Forbes, President;
Malcolm S. Forbes, Jr., Vice-President; Leonard
H. Yablon, Secretary and Treasurer.
Number of staff: None.
Employer Identification Number: 237037319

2441
Forbes (Herman) Charitable Trust ⌗
c/o Chase Bank Tax Dept.
1211 Ave. of the Americas
New York 10036

Incorporated in 1982 in New York.
Donor(s): Herman Forbes.†
Financial data: (yr. ended 3/31/83): Assets,
$3,095,107 (M); gifts received, $2,824,784;
expenditures, $245,312, including $240,000
for 17 grants (high: $25,000; low: $5,000).
Purpose and activities: First year of operation
1982-83; initial grants primarily for social
services, particularly Jewish welfare agencies.
Trustees: Sidney Richman, David L. Silverman,
Chase Manhattan Bank.
Employer Identification Number: 136814404

2442
Forchheimer Foundation, Inc. ▼
c/o Weitzner, Levine & Louis
230 Park Ave.
New York 10169

Established in New York.
Donor(s): Leo Forchheimer.†
Financial data: (yr. ended 12/31/82): Assets,
$3,135,875 (M); gifts received, $9,622,523;
expenditures, $7,200,592, including
$7,194,068 for 45 grants (high: $1,000,000;
low: $10; average: $100-$250,000).
Purpose and activities: Giving primarily in
New York City and Israel for hospitals, health
agencies, higher education, including medical
and technical education, Jewish welfare funds,
museums, and social services.
Limitations: Giving primarily in New York, NY,
and Israel.
Officers: Julia Forchheimer, President; Ludwig
Jesselson, Vice-President and Treasurer;
Rudolph Forchheimer, Secretary.
Employer Identification Number: 136075112

2443
Ford (The Edward E.) Foundation ▼
c/o Manufacturers Hanover Trust Company
600 Fifth Ave.
New York 10020
Mailing address: 20 Nassau St., Princeton, NJ
08542; Tel.: (609) 921-1126

Trust established in 1957 in New York.
Donor(s): Edward E. Ford.†
Financial data: (yr. ended 9/30/84): Assets,
$37,196,281 (M); expenditures, $2,635,049,
including $2,380,233 for 77 grants (high:
$35,000; low: $20,000; average: $15,000-
$35,000).
Purpose and activities: Primary interest in
independent secondary education.
Independent secondary schools must hold
membership in National Association of
Independent Schools to be eligible for
consideration.
Types of support awarded: Annual
campaigns, seed money, building funds,
equipment, land acquisition, endowment funds,
matching funds, professorships, scholarship
funds, special projects, research, publications.
Limitations: Giving limited to the United States
and its protectorates. No support for
elementary or college-level schools, or to
organizations that have been recipients within
the last 3 years. No grants to individuals, or
for emergency funds or deficit financing.
Publications: Annual report, application
guidelines.
Application information: Application form
required.
Initial approach: Letter
Copies of proposal: 10
Deadline(s): Submit proposal preferably in
March, May, or October; deadlines
February 1, April 1, and September 15
Board meeting date(s): April, June, and
November
Final notification: 6 weeks for formal reply;
informal reply sooner
Write: Lawrence L. Hlavacek, Executive
Director

Officer: Lawrence L. Hlavacek, Executive
Director.
Advisory Board: William C. Fowle, Chairman;
H. Ward Reighley, Vice-Chairman; Gillian
Attfield, Frank H. Detweiler, Edward F.
Menard, Julia F. Menard.
Trustee: Manufacturers Hanover Trust
Company.
Number of staff: 1 full-time professional; 1 full-
time support.
Employer Identification Number: 136047243

2444
Ford Foundation, The ▼
320 East 43rd St.
New York 10017   (212) 573-5000

Incorporated in 1936 in Michigan.
Donor(s): Henry Ford,† Edsel Ford.†
Financial data: (yr. ended 9/30/84): Assets,
$3,497,800,000 (M); expenditures,
$185,684,672, including $113,102,009 for
1,510 grants (high: $7,075,000; low: $1,200;
average: $20,000-$200,000), $8,981,052 for
foundation-administered programs and
$6,607,672 for 11 loans.
Purpose and activities: To advance the public
well-being by identifying and contributing to
the solution of problems of national and
international importance. Grants primarily to
institutions for experimental, demonstration,
and developmental efforts that are likely to
produce significant advances within the
Foundation's six major fields of interest: urban
poverty and the disadvantaged--including
community and neighborhood self-help
initiatives, improvement of secondary
education, educational and employment
programs for disadvantaged youth and for
welfare recipients, child care, health and
nutrition services, reduction of street crime and
arson, housing rehabilitation, and research on
urban problems; rural poverty and resources--
largely focused on developing countries and
including community-based efforts, national
policy planning, income-generating projects,
improvement of opportunities for women, the
landless, and migrants, and management of
land and water resources; human rights and
social justice--including civil rights, sex
discrimination, and the rights of refugees and
migrants; education--principally support for
excellence and equity in higher education;
international politics and economic issues--
analysis, research, dialogue, and public
education on such issues as policies affecting
immigrants and refugees, arms control and
international security, and the changing world
economy; and governance and public policy--
including governmental and public policy
issues, experiments in delivering government
services, and development strategies of Third
World countries.
Types of support awarded: Conferences and
seminars, consulting services, exchange
programs, general purposes, matching funds,
professorships, program-related investments,
publications, research, seed money, special
projects, technical assistance.

Limitations: No support for programs receiving
substantial governmental support, or religious
activities. No grants for routine operating
costs, construction or maintenance of buildings,
or undergraduate scholarships; support for
internships to institutions only; graduate
fellowships generally channeled through grants
to universities or organizations.
Publications: Annual report, newsletter,
informational brochure, program policy
statement, application guidelines.
Application information: Foreign applicants
should contact foundation for addresses of its
overseas offices, through which they must
apply.
Initial approach: Letter, full proposal or
telephone
Copies of proposal: 1
Deadline(s): None
Board meeting date(s): December, March,
June, and September
Final notification: Initial indication as to
whether proposal falls within program
interests within 1 month
Write: Barron M. Tenny, Secretary
Officers: Franklin A. Thomas,* President;
Barron M. Tenny, Vice-President, General
Counsel, and Secretary; Susan V. Berresford,
William D. Carmichael, John W. English, Vice-
Presidents; John Koprowski, Treasurer; Louis
Winnick, Barry D. Gaberman, John D. Gerhart,
Deputy Vice-Presidents.
Trustees:* Alexander Heard, Chairman;
Rodrigo Botero, Ralf Dahrendorf, Nina G.
Garsoian, A. Bartlett Giamatti, Donald F.
McHenry, Robert S. McNamara, Paul F. Miller,
Jr., William G. Milliken, Donald S. Perkins,
Barbara Scott Preiskel, Harriet S. Rabb, Irving S.
Shapiro, Edson W. Spencer, Glenn E. Watts,
Thomas H. Wyman.
Number of staff: 511.
Employer Identification Number: 131684331

2445
Foundation for Child Development ▼
345 East 46th St., Rm. 700
New York 10017   (212) 697-3150

Incorporated as a voluntary agency in New
York in 1900 and established as the
Association for the Aid of Crippled Children in
1908; current name adopted in 1972, affirming
a broader focus on children at risk.
Donor(s): Milo M. Belding,† Annie K.
Belding,† and others.
Financial data: (yr. ended 3/31/84): Assets,
$32,785,138 (M); gifts received, $4,768;
expenditures, $2,202,509, including
$1,203,330 for 51 grants (high: $126,611; low:
$353; average: $5,000-$65,000) and $156,710
for 9 foundation-administered programs.
Purpose and activities: Supports research,
policy studies, advocacy projects, and service
experiments that increase knowledge about
children and help to translate this knowledge
into policies that affect their daily lives and
those of their families.
Types of support awarded: Continuing
support, fellowships, special projects, research,
publications, general purposes.

Limitations: Giving limited to NY for service-related projects; no other geographic limitations. No grants to individuals, or for capital or endowment funds, annual campaigns, conferences, or matching gifts; no loans.
Publications: Annual report.
Application information:
  Initial approach: Proposal
  Copies of proposal: 1
  Deadline(s): None
  Board meeting date(s): June, September, December, and March
  Final notification: 1 to 3 weeks for unfavorable replies; 2 to 6 months for favorable replies
  Write: Jane Dustan, Vice-President
Officers: Gerard Piel,* Chairman; E. Mavis Hetherington,* Vice-Chairman; Orville G. Brim, Jr.,* President; Jane Dustan, Vice-President; Richard D. Kahn,* Secretary; John H. Hobbs,* Treasurer.
Directors:* Eleanor T. Elliott, John W. Holman, Jr., Charlayne Hunter-Gault, Julius B. Richmond, Henry W. Riecken, Gilbert Y. Steiner, Candace L. Straight.
Number of staff: 3 full-time professional; 1 part-time professional; 6 full-time support; 1 part-time support.
Employer Identification Number: 131623901

2446
Foundation for Microbiology
c/o National Multiple Sclerosis Society
205 East 42nd St.
New York 10017   (212) 986-3240

Incorporated in 1951 in New Jersey.
Donor(s): Selman A. Waksman,† Deborah B. Waksman.†
Financial data: (yr. ended 12/31/84): Assets, $1,117,048 (M); expenditures, $85,327, including $60,500 for 9 grants (high: $38,000; low: $500).
Purpose and activities: Grants for lectureships, courses, meetings, unusual projects, and publication of monographs in microbiological sciences.
Types of support awarded: Special projects, publications, conferences and seminars, professorships, exchange programs.
Limitations: No grants to individuals, or for fellowships, conventional research projects, travel, general or operating support, or capital or endowment funds; no loans.
Publications: 990-PF.
Application information:
  Initial approach: Letter
  Copies of proposal: 1
  Deadline(s): None
  Board meeting date(s): May or June
  Final notification: 3 to 6 months
  Write: Byron H. Waksman, M.D., President
Officers and Trustees: Byron H. Waksman, M.D., President; Harlyn O. Halvorson, Secretary-Treasurer; Edward A. Adelberg, Herman N. Eisen, J. Oliver Lampen, Arthur P. Pardee, Kenneth V. Thimann, Dudley Watson.
Number of staff: None.
Employer Identification Number: 226057913

2447
Foundation for the Needs of Others, Inc. ¤
c/o Patterson, Belknap, Webb & Tyler
30 Rockefeller Plaza, Suite 3500
New York 10112   (212) 541-4000

Incorporated in 1953 in New York.
Donor(s): Mrs. Helen W. Buckner, Walker G. Buckner, Thomas W. Buckner.
Financial data: (yr. ended 12/31/83): Assets, $3,293,708 (M); expenditures, $322,227, including $299,675 for 37 grants (high: $50,000; low: $100).
Purpose and activities: Broad purposes; primarily local giving, with emphasis on conservation, higher and secondary education, and cultural programs; grants also for social agencies.
Limitations: Giving primarily in New York, NY. No grants to individuals.
Publications: 990-PF.
Application information:
  Initial approach: Letter
  Write: Mimi Kaplansky
Officers and Trustees: Helen W. Buckner, President; Thomas W. Buckner, Vice-President; Walker G. Buckner, Jr., Secretary; Mary B. Shea, Treasurer; Elizabeth B. Buckner.
Employer Identification Number: 136119874

2448
Frank (Ernst & Elfriede) Foundation ¤
1221 Ave. of the Americas
New York 10020

Financial data: (yr. ended 8/31/83): Assets, $2,564,033 (M); expenditures, $79,492, including $77,841 for 40 grants (high: $14,000; low: $21).
Purpose and activities: Primarily local giving for social services and cultural programs.
Limitations: Giving primarily in NY.
Employer Identification Number: 136106471

2449
Frankel (George and Elizabeth F.) Foundation, Inc. ¤
60 East 42nd St.
New York 10165

Incorporated in 1945 in New York.
Donor(s): George Frankel,† Elizabeth F. Frankel,† G. David Frankel, Charles Korn.
Financial data: (yr. ended 3/31/83): Assets, $3,864,860 (M); gifts received, $226,163; expenditures, $261,068, including $236,890 for 97 grants (high: $60,770; low: $100).
Purpose and activities: Broad purposes; primarily local giving, with emphasis on medical education, health and medical research agencies, and Jewish welfare funds.
Limitations: Giving primarily in NY.
Officers and Trustees: G. David Frankel, President; Doris F. Tulcin, Secretary; Elizabeth F. Bock, Charles Korn, Geraldine F. Merksamer.
Employer Identification Number: 136126076

2450
Frasch (Herman) Foundation for Chemical Research
c/o United States Trust Company of New York
45 Wall St.
New York 10005   (212) 425-4500
Mailing address for application forms: c/o Dr. Justin Collat, Head, Dept. of Research Grants and Awards, American Chemical Society, 1155 16th St., N.W., Washington, DC 20036; Tel.: (202) 872-4487

Trust established in 1924 in New York.
Donor(s): Mrs. Elizabeth Blee Frasch.†
Financial data: (yr. ended 12/31/82): Assets, $3,719,896 (M); expenditures, $257,719, including $180,080 for 65 grants (high: $16,173; low: $2,150).
Purpose and activities: Grants for research in agricultural chemistry made for five-year periods to nonprofit incorporated institutions in the United States selected by the Trust Company with the advice of the American Chemical Society.
Types of support awarded: Research.
Limitations: No grants to individuals, or for endowment funds, building funds, operating budgets, scholarships or fellowships, or matching gifts; no loans.
Application information: Next application period April 1, 1986 to August 1, 1986. Application form required.
  Initial approach: Letter or telephone
  Copies of proposal: 7
  Board meeting date(s): Every 5 years in November
Trustee: United States Trust Company of New York.
Employer Identification Number: 136073145

2451
French (D. E.) Foundation, Inc. ¤
120 Genesee St., Rm. 602
Auburn 13021

Incorporated in 1955 in New York.
Donor(s): Clara M. French,† D.E. French.†
Financial data: (yr. ended 12/31/83): Assets, $1,865,964 (M); expenditures, $115,110, including $100,615 for 47 grants (high: $15,000; low: $15).
Purpose and activities: Broad purposes; primarily local giving, with emphasis on Protestant church support, youth agencies, and education.
Limitations: Giving primarily in Auburn, NY.
Officers and Directors: H. Randolph Seymour, President; J. Douglas Pedley, Vice-President and Treasurer; Ronald D. West, Secretary; Frederick J. Atkins, John Y. Critchley, Burke W. W. Drummond.
Employer Identification Number: 166052246

2452
Frese (Arnold D.) Foundation, Inc. ¤
30 Rockefeller Plaza, Suite 1938
New York 10022

Established in 1966.
Donor(s): Arnold D. Frese.†

Financial data: (yr. ended 12/31/82): Assets, $10,848,249 (M); gifts received, $1,684,163; expenditures, $2,940,021, including $571,500 for 16 grants (high: $205,000; low: $1,000).
Purpose and activities: Primarily local giving in New York City and Greenwich, Connecticut; support for hospitals, cultural programs, especially an opera company, and higher education.
Limitations: Giving primarily in New York, NY, and Greenwich, CT.
Officers: James S. Smith, President and Treasurer; Hector G. Dowd, Secretary.
Trustees: Ines Frese, Chairman; Henry D. Mercer, Jr., Emil Mosbacher, Jr.
Employer Identification Number: 136212507

2453
Fribourg Foundation, Inc.
277 Park Ave., 8th Fl.
New York 10172

Incorporated in 1953 in New York.
Donor(s): Michel Fribourg, Lucienne Fribourg, Arrow Steamship Company, Inc., Continental Grain Co.
Financial data: (yr. ended 12/31/82): Assets, $1,941,502 (M); gifts received, $75,000; expenditures, $181,042, including $169,250 for 100 grants (high: $50,000; low: $100).
Purpose and activities: Broad purposes; primarily local giving, with emphasis on higher and secondary education, cultural relations with France and Israel, and Jewish welfare funds; some support for community funds and the performing arts.
Limitations: Giving primarily in NY.
Application information: Applications not accepted.
Officers: Michel Fribourg,* President; Sheldon L. Berens,* Vice-President; John Q. Deaver, Secretary; Hendrik J. Laverge, Treasurer.
Directors:* Mary Ann Fribourg, Bernard Steinweg.
Employer Identification Number: 136159195

2454
Frohlich (Ludwig W.) Charitable Trust ▼ ♯
c/o Chadbourne, Parke, Whiteside & Wolff
30 Rockefeller Plaza
New York 10112

Trust established in 1969 in New York.
Donor(s): Ludwig W. Frohlich.†
Financial data: (yr. ended 12/31/82): Assets, $5,813,698 (M); expenditures, $556,194, including $436,470 for 25 grants (high: $100,000; low: $500).
Purpose and activities: Giving primarily to organizations located in New York City, with emphasis on hospitals, medical research, cultural programs, and social and youth agencies.
Limitations: Giving primarily in New York, NY.
Application information: Applications not invited.
Trustees: Kathleen B. Buddenhagen, Ingrid Lilly Burns, Thomas R. Burns, Richard B. Leather.
Employer Identification Number: 136288404

2455
Frueauff (Charles A.) Foundation, Inc. ▼
70 Pine St.
New York 10005   (212) 422-4799

Incorporated in 1950 in New York.
Donor(s): Charles A. Frueauff.†
Financial data: (yr. ended 12/31/84): Assets, $42,891,197 (M); expenditures, $2,814,483, including $2,632,725 for 185 grants (high: $250,000; low: $1,000; average: $5,000-$25,000).
Purpose and activities: Broad purposes; interest in health, including hospitals, mental health, and other health services; grants for welfare purposes, including services to children, the indigent, and the handicapped; support for higher education, including student aid.
Types of support awarded: Operating budgets, annual campaigns, emergency funds, building funds, equipment, endowment funds, scholarship funds, matching funds, general purposes, continuing support.
Limitations: Giving primarily in the U.S. No grants to individuals or for research; no loans.
Publications: 990-PF, program policy statement, annual report.
Application information:
    Initial approach: Full proposal, telephone, or letter
    Copies of proposal: 1
    Deadline(s): Submit proposal between September and March; deadline March 31
    Board meeting date(s): May
    Final notification: After annual meeting
    Write: Katherine R. Pawson, Secretary-Treasurer
Officers: Harry D. Frueauff,* President; Charles T. Klein,* James P. Farrell,* Vice-Presidents; Katherine R. Pawson, Secretary-Treasurer.
Trustees:* James P. Fallon, Charles T. Klein, Elaine Perry.
Number of staff: 1 full-time support; 3 part-time support.
Employer Identification Number: 135605371

2456
Fuchsberg (Abraham) Family Foundation, Inc. ♯
250 Broadway
New York 10007

Established in 1978.
Donor(s): Abraham Fuchsberg, Fuchsberg & Fuchsberg, Fuchsberg Family Foundation.
Financial data: (yr. ended 10/31/83): Assets, $2,224,541 (M); gifts received, $60,000; expenditures, $294,578, including $278,685 for 18 grants (high: $150,000; low: $125).
Purpose and activities: Giving primarily for Jewish welfare funds.
Officers: Abraham Fuchsberg, President; Seymour Fuchsberg, Secretary; Meyer Fuchsberg, Treasurer.
Employer Identification Number: 132966385

2457
Fuchsberg Family Foundation, Inc. ♯
250 Broadway
New York 10007

Incorporated in 1954 in New York.
Donor(s): Jacob D. Fuchsberg, Abraham Fuchsberg, Shirley Fuchsberg, Fuchsberg & Fuchsberg.
Financial data: (yr. ended 12/31/82): Assets, $3,762,993 (M); gifts received, $125,000; expenditures, $330,273, including $323,112 for 36 grants (high: $150,000; low: $15).
Purpose and activities: Broad purposes; to engage in research and promote the study, analysis, and interpretation of legal systems and concepts in order to improve the judicial procedures and techniques of trials in the courts of New York State and of the United States; support also for Jewish welfare funds and higher education, primarily in the New York area.
Officers and Directors: Meyer Fuchsberg, President; Shirley Fuchsberg, Vice-President.
Employer Identification Number: 136165600

2458
Fuld (Helene) Health Trust ▼
c/o Marine Midland Bank
250 Park Ave.
New York 10177   (212) 949-6707
Grants address: c/o Sage Gray Todd & Sims, Two World Trade Center, 100th Fl., New York, NY 10048; Tel.: (212) 466-9000

Trust established in 1951 in New Jersey; activated in 1969 as successor to Helene Fuld Health Foundation incorporated in 1935.
Donor(s): Leonhard Felix Fuld,† Florentine M. Fuld.†
Financial data: (yr. ended 9/30/84): Assets, $54,076,161 (M); expenditures, $3,886,310, including $3,158,131 for 69 grants (high: $187,500; low: $3,500; average: $10,000-$75,000).
Purpose and activities: Grants to state-accredited nursing schools affiliated with accredited hospitals to promote the health, education, and welfare of enrolled student nurses who are being taught to care for the sick and injured at bedside.
Types of support awarded: Equipment, publications, special projects.
Limitations: No grants to individuals, or for endowment funds, operating expenses, matching gifts, or general purposes; no loans.
Publications: 990-PF, application guidelines, program policy statement.
Application information: Application form required.
    Initial approach: Letter
    Copies of proposal: 1
    Deadline(s): October 31
    Board meeting date(s): March, June, September, and December
    Final notification: 3 to 6 months
    Write: Robert C. Miller
Trustee: Marine Midland Bank (Terence McKeever, Jr., Vice-President).
Number of staff: 1 full-time professional; 4 part-time professional.
Employer Identification Number: 136309307

2459
Fullerton Foundation, The ▼ ⌑
c/o Wilson & Bradbury Sales Corporation
104 W. 40th St.
New York 10018
Application address: W.E. Cavell, Executive
Director, The Fullerton Foundation, P.O. Box
1146, Gaffney, SC 29342; Tel.: (803) 489-6678

Established in 1954.
Donor(s): Alma H. Fullerton.†
Financial data: (yr. ended 11/30/83): Assets,
$18,933,043 (M); gifts received, $251,104;
expenditures, $1,158,839, including
$1,037,000 for 15 grants (high: $320,000; low:
$1,000).
Purpose and activities: Giving in South
Carolina, North Carolina, New York, and
Florida, for hospitals, health care, and medical
research; some support for higher education.
Types of support awarded: Building funds,
equipment.
Limitations: Giving limited to SC, NC, NY, and
FL.
Application information:
Initial approach: Letter
Deadline(s): April 1 and August 1
Write: W.E. Cavell, Executive Director
Officer: Walter E. Cavell, Executive Director.
Trustees: Catherine Hamrick Beattie, Charles F.
Hamrick, John Hamrick, Wylie L. Hamrick,
Volina Cline Valentine.
Employer Identification Number: 136162551

2460
Fund for the City of New York, Inc.
419 Park Ave. South, 16th Fl.
New York 10016   (212) 689-1240

Incorporated in 1968 in New York.
Donor(s): The Ford Foundation, Russell Sage
Foundation.
Financial data: (yr. ended 9/30/84): Assets,
$998,472 (M); gifts received, $2,295,027;
expenditures, $2,172,486, including $306,875
for 35 grants (high: $50,000; low: $500) and
$1,672,127 for 31 foundation-administered
programs.
Purpose and activities: A private operating
foundation supporting public and private projects
designed to improve the effectiveness
of government and the quality of life in New
York City, with particular emphasis on public
service productivity, accountability,
performance monitoring, and computer
assistance; operates a program of assistance to
public managers; also runs a cash flow loan
program against governmental grants and
contracts.
Types of support awarded: Technical
assistance, loans.
Limitations: Giving limited to the New York,
NY area. No grants to individuals (except for
public service awards), or for conferences,
ongoing service programs, academic research,
building or endowment funds, scholarships,
fellowships, matching gifts, special projects, or
studies that do not show promise of leading
directly to policy or program improvement.
Publications: Multi-year report, 990-PF,
program policy statement, application
guidelines.

Application information:
Initial approach: Full proposal
Copies of proposal: 1
Deadline(s): None
Board meeting date(s): Approximately 5
times a year in December, February, April,
June, and September
Write: Anita Nager, Grants Administrator
Officers: R. Palmer Baker, Secretary; Joyce
Phillips Austin,* Treasurer; Gregory R. Farrell,
Executive Director.
Directors:* Kenneth S. Axelson, Chairman;
Evan A. Davis, Vice-Chairman; Amalia V.
Betanzos, Roscoe Brown, Jr., Paul Gibson,
Stephen Lefkowitz, Martin E. Segal, Donna E.
Shalala, Most Rev. Joseph M. Sullivan, Peter
Swords, Gus Tyler.
Number of staff: 18 full-time professional; 2
part-time professional; 7 full-time support.
Employer Identification Number: 132612524

2461
Furst (Sol and Hilda) Foundation ⌑
One Old Country Rd.
Carle Place 11514

Incorporated in 1951 in New York.
Donor(s): Sol Furst.†
Financial data: (yr. ended 4/30/83): Assets,
$1,286,452 (M); gifts received, $50,000;
expenditures, $106,404, including $87,864 for
128 grants (high: $45,940; low: $10).
Purpose and activities: Broad purposes;
primarily local giving, with emphasis on higher
education, Jewish welfare funds, and hospitals.
Limitations: Giving primarily in NY.
Officers and Directors: Hilda Furst, President;
Gerald Furst, Vice-President and Secretary;
Violet Furst, Treasurer.
Employer Identification Number: 136107416

2462
**Gaisman (The Catherine and Henry J.)
Foundation** ⌑
P.O. Box 277
Ridge Rd.
Hartsdale 10530

Incorporated in 1934 in Delaware.
Donor(s): Henry J. Gaisman.†
Financial data: (yr. ended 12/31/82): Assets,
$3,390,307 (M); expenditures, $253,407,
including $246,400 for 14 grants (high:
$100,000; low: $100).
Purpose and activities: Broad purposes;
primarily local giving, with emphasis on
hospitals, including ophthalmologic research,
and for Catholic church support.
Limitations: Giving primarily in NY.
Officers and Directors: Catherine V. Gaisman,
President; Mildred B. Coleman, Secretary;
Robert Arias, Lawrence X. Cusack, Leon
Ginzburg, M.D., Eric W. Waldman.
Employer Identification Number: 136129464

2463
Gannett Foundation, Inc. ▼
Lincoln Tower
Rochester 14604   (716) 262-3315

Incorporated in 1935 in New York.
Donor(s): Frank E. Gannett.†
Financial data: (yr. ended 12/31/84): Assets,
$386,416,619 (M); expenditures, $15,971,464,
including $12,692,850 for 2,119 grants (high:
$413,051; low: $152; average: $4,000-
$6,000), $177,676 for 111 grants to
individuals, $270,388 for 747 employee
matching gifts and $667,461 for 1 foundation-
administered program.
Purpose and activities: Grants to non-profit
educational, charitable, civic, cultural, health,
and social service institutions and organizations
in areas served by daily newspapers, broadcast
stations, outdoor advertising companies, and
other properties of Gannett Company, Inc. in
the United States and Canada. Primary
national interests are support of journalism-
related programs and the advancement of
philanthropy and volunteerism. The foundation
also operates the Gannett Center for Media
Studies, the nation's first institute for the
advanced study of mass media and society,
located at Columbia University in New York.
Types of support awarded: Operating
budgets, continuing support, seed money,
emergency funds, deficit financing, building
funds, equipment, land acquisition, employee
matching gifts, scholarship funds, employee
related scholarships, special projects,
publications, conferences and seminars, general
purposes.
Limitations: Giving primarily in the U.S. and
Canada. No support for national or regional
organizations, or research programs unrelated
to journalism, religious organizations for
religious purposes, elementary or secondary
schools, fraternal groups, athletic teams, bands,
veterans' organizations, volunteer fire
departments, or organizations providing
information on abortion. No grants to
individuals (except for scholarships to children
of employees), annual campaigns (other than
United Ways), matching fund commitments,
research, or endowment funds; no loans.
Publications: Annual report, application
guidelines, informational brochure.
Application information: Grant proposals
from organizations in communities served by
Gannett properties should be directed to the
Chief Executive of the local property; Executive
Committee of board approves grants monthly
or as required. Journalism proposals should be
directed to Gerald M. Sass, Vice-
President/Education.
Initial approach: Letter or full proposal
Copies of proposal: 1
Deadline(s): None
Board meeting date(s): 3 to 4 times a year,
and as required; annual meeting in April or
May
Final notification: 2 to 4 months
Write: Eugene C. Dorsey, President; or local
Gannett Co., Inc. chief executives or
publishers, for requests originating in areas
served by Gannett Co., Inc.

Officers: Eugene C. Dorsey,* President and Chief Executive Officer; Christy C. Bulkeley, Harvey S. Cotter, Vice-Presidents; Calvin Mayne, Vice-President - Grants Administration; Gerald M. Sass, Vice-President - Education; Marilyn A. Stein, Vice-President - Communications; Thomas L. Chapple, Secretary; Jimmy L. Thomas, Treasurer.
Trustees:* John A. Scott, Chairman; Martin F. Birmingham, Bernard B. Brody, M.D., Harry W. Brooks, Jr., John E. Heselden, Madelyn P. Jennings, Sally Gannett McAdam, Douglas H. McCorkindale, Dillard Munford, Allen H. Neuharth, Frank H.T. Rhodes, Josefina A. Salas-Porras, Samuel J. Stabins, M.D., Robert B. Whittington.
Number of staff: 13 full-time professional; 2 part-time professional; 4 full-time support.
Employer Identification Number: 166027020

2464
Gannett (Frank) Newspapercarrier Scholarships, Inc.

Lincoln Tower
Rochester 14604   (716) 262-3315

Incorporated in 1952 in New York.
Donor(s): Gannett Foundation, Inc.
Financial data: (yr. ended 12/31/83): Assets, $3,333 (L); gifts received, $378,369; expenditures, $425,990, including $377,050 for grants to individuals.
Purpose and activities: College scholarships, on a competitive basis, to newspaper carriers of participating Gannett newspapers.
Types of support awarded: Employee related scholarships.
Limitations: No grants for general support, capital or endowment funds, matching gifts, program support, research, special projects, publications, or conferences; no loans.
Publications: 990-PF, program policy statement, application guidelines.
Application information: Application form required.
  Board meeting date(s): April, June, and either October, November, or December
  Write: Debra J. Buckett, Scholarships Administrator
Officers and Directors: D. Robert Frisina, President; Alice H. Young, Vice-President; Gerald M. Sass, Secretary-Treasurer; Betty J. Altier, William H. Dermody, M.D., Eugene C. Dorsey, John A. Scott.
Number of staff: None.
Employer Identification Number: 160766965

2465
Gebbie Foundation, Inc. ▼

Hotel Jamestown Bldg., Rm. 308
Jamestown 14701   (716) 487-1062

Incorporated in 1963 in New York.
Donor(s): Marion B. Gebbie,† Geraldine G. Bellinger.†
Financial data: (yr. ended 9/30/83): Assets, $31,814,701 (M); expenditures, $1,997,389, including $1,790,022 for 65 grants (high: $201,000; low: $140; average: $1,000-$50,000) and $84,200 for 2 loans.

Purpose and activities: Grants for medical and scientific research to alleviate human suffering and ills related to metabolic diseases of the bone; some support for hospitals, libraries, local youth agencies, cultural programs, social agencies, and a community fund. Interested in programs of preventive medicine as they relate to diseases of children, to detection of deafness, and to training and education of the deaf.
Types of support awarded: Annual campaigns, seed money, building funds, equipment, matching funds, general purposes, loans.
Limitations: Giving primarily in Chautauqua County and, secondly, in neighboring areas of western NY; giving in other areas only when the project is consonant with program objectives that cannot be developed locally. No support for higher education, except to institutions that were recipients of lifetime contributions of the donor. No grants to individuals, or for endowment funds.
Publications: Multi-year report, program policy statement, application guidelines.
Application information:
  Initial approach: Letter
  Copies of proposal: 9
  Deadline(s): None
  Board meeting date(s): November, May, and September
  Final notification: 1 to 4 months
  Write: John D. Hamilton, President
Officers and Directors: John D. Hamilton, President; Myron B. Franks, Vice-President; William I. Parker, Secretary; Gerald E. Hunt, Treasurer; Charles T. Hall, Robert E. Halsted, Geraldine Parker, Paul W. Sandberg, Jennie Vimmerstedt.
Number of staff: 1 full-time professional; 2 part-time professional; 1 part-time support.
Employer Identification Number: 166050287

2466
Gelb (Lawrence M.) Foundation, Inc.

300 Park Ave., Rm. 2100
New York 10022

Established in 1957 in New York.
Donor(s): Lawrence M. Gelb.†
Financial data: (yr. ended 12/31/82): Assets, $838,973 (M); gifts received, $417,000; expenditures, $322,110, including $302,000 for 24 grants (high: $150,000; low: $500).
Purpose and activities: Support primarily for private secondary and higher education; some support also for cultural programs.
Officers and Directors: Richard L. Gelb, Chairman and Treasurer; Bruce S. Gelb, President; Wilbur M. Friedman, Secretary; John T. Gelb, Lawrence N. Gelb, Robert M. Kaufman.
Employer Identification Number: 136113586

2467
General Foods Fund, Inc., The ▼

250 North St.
White Plains 10625   (914) 335-7961

Incorporated in 1953 in New York.
Donor(s): General Foods Corporation.

Financial data: (yr. ended 3/31/84): Assets, $5,302,782 (M); gifts received, $5,775,000; expenditures, $2,753,493, including $2,174,511 for 99 grants (high: $250,000; low: $1,000; average: $5,000-$75,000) and $578,982 for 1,680 employee matching gifts.
Purpose and activities: Grants primarily for education in nutrition and food sciences including: (a) training future health professionals, (b) continuing education of practicing health professionals, (c) graduate fellowships in nutrition and food sciences, (d) nutrition training for primary and secondary school educators, (e) public information about food and nutrition. Support also for colleges and universities through restricted grants for well-defined academic programs in areas of specific relevance to General Foods Corporation's businesses, and a matching grant program for educational institutions available to employees of General Foods Corporation. Grants on a highly selective basis to: (a) national programs addressing needs of women, the elderly, youth, minorities, and the disadvantaged with focus on health care (diet and exercise), youth unemployment and upward mobility, (b) nationally prominent cultural organizations, (c) not-for-profit organizations engaged in research, evaluation, resolution of issues important to public policy generally and/or the food industry in particular.
Types of support awarded: Continuing support, annual campaigns, seed money, employee matching gifts, professorships, scholarship funds, employee related scholarships, fellowships, internships, exchange programs, special projects.
Limitations: Giving limited to the U.S. No grants to individuals, or for capital or endowment funds, publications, conferences, or research; no loans.
Publications: Company report, program policy statement, application guidelines.
Application information:
  Initial approach: Letter
  Copies of proposal: 1
  Deadline(s): None
  Board meeting date(s): Bimonthly beginning in January
  Final notification: 3 to 4 months
  Write: Kathryn Krause, Secretary
Officers: David M. Brush,* President; C.R. Blundell,* Vice-President; Kathryn Krause,* Secretary; R.B. Hostetler, Treasurer.
Trustees:* E.J. Guardia, S.B. Morris.
Number of staff: 1 full-time professional; 2 full-time support.
Employer Identification Number: 136089667

2468
Gibbs Brothers Foundation

c/o Morgan Guaranty Trust Company of New York
Nine West 57th St.
New York 10019   (212) 826-7615

Trust established in 1957 in New York.
Donor(s): Gibbs & Cox, Inc.
Financial data: (yr. ended 12/31/84): Assets, $2,233,023 (M); expenditures, $266,801, including $249,000 for 54 grants (high: $25,000; low: $250).

Purpose and activities: Broad purposes; grants largely for continuing support of organizations including maritime museums and seamen's institutes, hospitals, colleges and universities, naval engineering societies, and legal organizations.
Types of support awarded: Operating budgets, research.
Limitations: No grants to individuals, or for annual campaigns, seed money, emergency funds, deficit financing, capital and endowment funds, matching gifts, scholarships or fellowships, program support, demonstration projects, publications, or conferences; no loans.
Application information: No inquiries or applications for assistance will be acknowledged.
  Copies of proposal: 1
  Board meeting date(s): May
  Write: Joseph A. DeLosa, Trust Officer
Advisory Committee: M. Bernard Aidinoff, Richard M. Ehrlich, Walter Malmstrom, Edward J. Willi.
Trustee: Morgan Guaranty Trust Company of New York (Joseph A. DeLosa, Trust Officer).
Number of staff: None.
Employer Identification Number: 136037653

2469
Gifford (The Rosamond) Charitable Corporation ▼

731 James St., Rm. 404
Syracuse 13203   (315) 474-2489

Incorporated in 1954 in New York.
Donor(s): Rosamond Gifford.†
Financial data: (yr. ended 12/31/82): Assets, $9,439,946 (M); expenditures, $797,467, including $683,373 for 32 grants (high: $100,000; low: $1,000).
Purpose and activities: Broad purposes; local giving, with emphasis on urban problems, higher and secondary education, health research, hospital construction and equipment, youth agencies, rehabilitation of alcoholics, the aged, general welfare, a community fund, and cultural programs.
Types of support awarded: Operating budgets, annual campaigns, seed money, emergency funds, building funds, equipment, research.
Limitations: Giving limited to organizations serving the residents of Syracuse and Onondaga County, NY. No grants to individuals, or for endowment funds, continuing support, deficit financing, land aquisition, special projects, matching gifts, or scholarships and fellowships; no loans.
Publications: Program policy statement, application guidelines, multi-year report.
Application information:
  Initial approach: Letter or telephone
  Copies of proposal: 2
  Deadline(s): None
  Board meeting date(s): Monthly
  Final notification: 2 months
  Write: Dean A. Lesinski, Executive Director
Officers: Francis A. Feil,* President; Roger L. MacDonald,* Vice-President and Treasurer; Virginia Z. Lynch,* Vice-President; Virginia B. Coughlin,* Secretary; Dean A. Lesinski, Executive Director.

Directors:* Charles J. Miller, John H. Lynch.
Number of staff: 2 full-time professional; 1 part-time support.
Employer Identification Number: 150572881

2470
Gilman (The Howard) Foundation, Inc. ⌺

111 W. 50th St.
New York 10020   (212) 246-3300

Incorporated in 1982 in New York.
Donor(s): Gilman Foundation, Inc.
Financial data: (yr. ended 4/30/83): Assets, $10,139,150 (M); gifts received, $52,872; expenditures, $656,172, including $379,680 for 95 grants (high: $53,000; low: $50).
Purpose and activities: Primarily local giving for hospitals, higher education, music, cultural programs, social services, and for wildlife preservation.
Limitations: Giving primarily in New York, NY.
Application information:
  Deadline(s): None
  Write: Howard Gilman, President
Officers: Howard Gilman,* President; N. Moody, Secretary.
Directors:* B. Bergreen, Sylvia Gilman, William C. Warren.
Employer Identification Number: 133097486

2471
Gimbel-Saks Trust Fund ⌺

c/o Gimbel Brothers, Inc.
1275 Broadway
New York 10001

Trust established about 1959 in New York.
Donor(s): Gimbel Brothers Foundation.
Financial data: (yr. ended 1/31/82): Assets, $352,515 (M); expenditures, $197,590, including $196,265 for 53 grants (high: $20,000; low: $250).
Purpose and activities: Grants mainly for community funds, civic affairs, and youth agencies.
Trustee: Angelo Rosato.
Employer Identification Number: 136129705

2472
Ginsberg (Moses) Family Foundation, Inc. ⌺

80 Broad St.
New York 10004

Incorporated in 1946 in New York.
Donor(s): Moses Ginsberg.†
Financial data: (yr. ended 12/31/81): Assets, $1,986,036 (M); gifts received, $204,000; expenditures, $244,745, including $241,000 for 11 grants (high: $175,000; low: $500).
Purpose and activities: Primarily local giving, with emphasis on Jewish welfare funds.
Limitations: Giving primarily in NY.
Officers: Calmon J. Ginsberg, President; Morris Ginsberg, Secretary; Samuel S. Jaffe, Treasurer.
Employer Identification Number: 237418806

2473
Gleason Fund, Inc. ⌺

1000 University Ave.
Rochester 14692

Established in 1934 in New York.
Financial data: (yr. ended 12/31/82): Assets, $6,841,325 (M); expenditures, $128,176, including $91,744 for 57 grants to individuals.
Purpose and activities: Primarily local giving to needy individuals for medical insurance premiums.
Types of support awarded: Grants to individuals.
Limitations: Giving primarily in NY.
Officers and Directors: Gerald E. Douglas, President; Roy L. Cole, Vice-President; Ralph E. Harper, Secretary; Richard S. Tallo, Treasurer; Walter E. Andras, James Gleason, Albert W. Moore, Royden J. Smith.
Employer Identification Number: 166023234

2474
Gleason Memorial Fund, Inc. ▼ ⌺

1000 University Ave.
Rochester 14692   (716) 473-1000

Incorporated in 1959 in New York.
Donor(s): Miriam B. Gleason.†
Financial data: (yr. ended 12/31/82): Assets, $27,676,164 (M); expenditures, $1,902,016, including $1,696,657 for 77 grants (high: $210,000; low: $400).
Purpose and activities: Broad purposes; giving primarily in the Rochester metropolitan area, with emphasis on higher education; support also for community funds, urban programs, and cultural activities.
Limitations: Giving primarily in the Rochester, NY, metropolitan area.
Publications: Application guidelines.
Application information:
  Initial approach: Proposal
  Write: Calvin A. Miller, Vice-President for Administration
Officers and Directors: Sterling L. Weaver, Chairman; James S. Gleason, President; Robert L. Galbraith, Vice-President; Calvin A. Miller, Vice-President for Administration; Ralph E. Harper, Secretary; John F. Hasenauer, Treasurer; Walter E. Andrus, Louis A. Langie, Jr.
Employer Identification Number: 166023235

2475
Glenn (Paul F.) Foundation for Medical Research, Inc.

72 Virginia Dr.
Manhasset 11030

Established in 1965.
Financial data: (yr. ended 9/30/84): Assets, $1,948,251 (M); expenditures, $104,875, including $82,118 for 10 grants (high: $14,950; low: $1,000) and $15,000 for grants to individuals.

Purpose and activities: Grants to 1) encourage and accelerate research on the biology of aging; 2) assist those engaged in research on causes of the aging process, with the objective of delaying or preventing the onset of senility and prolonging the human life span; 3) increase the stature of the field of gerontology; 4) broaden public understanding of aging; and 5) educate the public on ways to delay or prevent senility and prolong the human life span. The Foundation is particularly interested in the investigation of proper nutrition as a factor in the aging process.
Types of support awarded: Research, general purposes, grants to individuals.
Limitations: No support for sociological, as opposed to biological, aging projects.
Application information:
  Initial approach: Proposal
  Copies of proposal: 3
  Write: Barbara Boyd, Vice-President
Officers: Paul F. Glenn,* Chairman, President, and Treasurer; Richard Hochschild, Vice-President; Barbara Boyd,* Vice-President, Secretary, and Executive Director.
Directors:* Florence S. Mahoney, Mary E. Ruth.
Number of staff: 3 part-time professional.
Employer Identification Number: 136191732

2476
Glens Falls Foundation, The
237 Glen St.
P.O. Box 311
Glens Falls 12801   (518) 792-1151

Community foundation established in 1939 in New York by declaration of trust.
Financial data: (yr. ended 12/31/82): Assets, $1,296,000 (M); gifts received, $10,500; expenditures, $86,013, including $73,369 for 29 grants (high: $10,000; low: $35) and $7,500 for 27 grants to individuals.
Purpose and activities: Broad purposes, including the promotion of the mental, moral, and its physical improvement of the people of Glens Falls and environs. Grants to graduating seniors from area high schools and for assistance with medical expenses not covered by government programs or insurance.
Types of support awarded: Scholarship funds, seed money, emergency funds, building funds, equipment, research, publications, conferences and seminars, special projects, matching funds, consulting services, technical assistance, grants to individuals, student aid.
Limitations: Giving limited to Warren, Washington, and Saratoga counties, NY. No grants for endowment funds; no loans.
Application information:
  Initial approach: Letter, telephone, or full proposal
  Copies of proposal: 8
  Deadline(s): Submit proposal preferably in December, March, June, or September; deadline 1st day of months in which board meets
  Board meeting date(s): 2nd Wednesday in January, April, July, and October
  Final notification: 2 days after quarterly meetings
  Write: G. Nelson Lowe, Secretary

Officer: G. Nelson Lowe, Secretary.
Distribution Committee: John D. Toomey, Chairman; Marilyn Cohen, Ruth Fratus, John V. Hallett, Burt M. Keene, Daniel F. O'Keefe, M.D., Floyd H. Rourke.
Trustee: The First National Bank of Glens Falls.
Number of staff: None.
Employer Identification Number: 146036390

2477
Glickenhaus Foundation, The
100 Dorchester Rd.
Scarsdale 10583

Incorporated in 1960 in New York.
Donor(s): Glickenhaus & Company.
Financial data: (yr. ended 11/30/81): Assets, $117,679 (M); gifts received, $25,309; expenditures, $120,890, including $117,204 for 175 grants (high: $10,000; low: $25).
Purpose and activities: Grants primarily for higher education, social welfare, international peace organizations, a fusion energy society, and a community development project.
Officers: Nancy G. Pier, President; James Glickenhaus, Vice-President; Herb Ackerman, Treasurer.
Employer Identification Number: 136160941

2478
Gloeckner (The Fred C.) Foundation, Inc. ¤
15 East 26th St.
New York 10010

Foundation incorporated in 1960 in New York.
Donor(s): Frederick C. Gloeckner.
Financial data: (yr. ended 10/31/82): Assets, $898,971 (M); gifts received, $65,150; expenditures, $143,883, including $136,612 for grants.
Purpose and activities: To further research in floriculture and related fields through fellowships; grants to higher educational and agricultural research institutions.
Types of support awarded: Fellowships.
Officers and Directors: Frederick C. Gloeckner, President; Gustav H. Poesch, Vice-President and Treasurer; T. Newman Lawler, Secretary; Richard K. Charlesworth, Paul L. Daum, Douglas K. Dillon, Phillip J. Kurlich, Roy Larson, John G. Seeley.
Employer Identification Number: 136124190

2479
Golden (John) Fund, Inc.
274 Madison Ave.
New York 10016

Incorporated in 1944 in New York.
Donor(s): John Golden.†
Financial data: (yr. ended 12/31/82): Assets, $1,118,500 (M); expenditures, $98,400, including $91,700 for 30 grants (high: $20,000; low: $500).

Purpose and activities: For the advancement of playwriting for the American legitimate theater or of the individuals in any way associated with it, through improvement of the teaching of drama in universities and colleges, and through other organizations and workshops, prize awards to playwrights engaged in, or in training for, dramatic playwriting in colleges, and promotion of theatrical productions for young people through organizations only.
Types of support awarded: Scholarship funds.
Limitations: No grants to individuals, or for building or endowment funds, research programs, or matching gifts.
Application information:
  Initial approach: Full proposal
  Copies of proposal: 1
  Board meeting date(s): May and November
  Write: Mrs. Zilla Lippmann, President
Officers and Directors: Zilla Lippmann, President; Norman J. Stone, Treasurer; Jean Dalrymple, John Houseman, John Lippman, Edwin Wilson.
Employer Identification Number: 136065978

2480
Golden (Sibyl and William T.) Foundation
40 Wall St., Rm. 4201
New York 10005   (212) 425-0333

Incorporated in 1952 in New York.
Donor(s): William T. Golden, Sibyl L. Golden.†
Financial data: (yr. ended 12/31/84): Assets, $12,079,046 (M); gifts received, $1,750,032; expenditures, $563,592, including $563,000 for 145 grants (high: $100,000; low: $100).
Purpose and activities: General purposes; to support a broad range of programs in higher education, science, public affairs, and other cultural areas.
Limitations: No grants to individuals.
Application information:
  Initial approach: Letter
  Copies of proposal: 1
  Deadline(s): None
  Board meeting date(s): January and as required
  Write: William T. Golden, President
Officers and Directors: William T. Golden, President; Sibyl R. Golden, Vice-President; Helene L. Kaplan, Secretary; Ralph E. Hansmann, Treasurer.
Number of staff: None.
Employer Identification Number: 237423802

2481
Goldman (Herman) Foundation ▼
120 Broadway, Suite 2945
New York 10271   (212) 571-1425

Incorporated in 1943 in New York.
Donor(s): Herman Goldman.†
Financial data: (yr. ended 2/28/83): Assets, $37,418,826 (M); expenditures, $2,214,608, including $1,931,343 for 87 grants (high: $150,000; low: $1,000).

Purpose and activities: Broad purposes; primarily local giving, but some aid for programs relating to nation-wide problems; emphasis on aiding economically and socially deprived persons through innovative grants in four main areas: health, to achieve effective delivery of physical and mental health care services; social justice, to develop organizational, social, and legal approaches to aid deprived or handicapped people; education, for new or improved counseling for effective pre-school, vocational and paraprofessional training; and the arts, to increase opportunities for talented youth to receive training and for less affluent individuals to attend quality presentations.
Limitations: Giving primarily in the New York, NY, metropolitan area. No support for religious organizations. No grants to individuals.
Publications: Annual report, application guidelines.
Application information:
Initial approach: Full proposal
Copies of proposal: 1
Deadline(s): None
Board meeting date(s): Monthly
Final notification: 1 to 2 months
Write: Raymond H. Lux, Executive Director
Officers: Raymond S. Baron,* President; Elias Rosenzweig,* Vice-President; Michael L. Goldstein,* Secretary; Raymond H. Lux, Treasurer and Executive Director.
Directors:* Jules M. Baron, Paul Bauman, David A. Brauner, Robert N. Davies, Emanuel Goldstein, Stanley M. Klein, Seymour H. Kligler, Howard A. Scribner, Jr., Norman Sparber.
Number of staff: 3.
Employer Identification Number: 136066039

2482
Goldman (The William P.) and Brothers Foundation, Inc. ⊭
1270 Ave. of the Americas, Rm. 1801
New York 10036

Incorporated in 1951 in New York.
Donor(s): William P. Goldman,† William P. Goldman & Bros., Inc.
Financial data: (yr. ended 12/31/83): Assets, $2,726,684 (M); expenditures, $340,403, including $309,550 for 90 grants (high: $40,000; low: $100).
Purpose and activities: Primarily local giving, with emphasis on Jewish welfare funds; support also for hospitals and medical research.
Limitations: Giving primarily in NY.
Officers: Sidney Kraines, President and Secretary; Byron Goldman, Vice-President; Justin Goldman, Treasurer.
Employer Identification Number: 136163100

2483
Goldsmith (Horace W.) Foundation ▼ ⊭
c/o Paskus, Gordon, & Hyman
45 Rockefeller Plaza
New York 10111   (212) 841-0260

Incorporated in 1955 in New York.
Donor(s): Horace Goldsmith.†

Financial data: (yr. ended 12/31/82): Assets, $110,266,965 (M); gifts received, $33,087,158; expenditures, $2,272,348, including $2,140,000 for 34 grants (high: $250,000; low: $25,000).
Purpose and activities: Giving primarily in New York City, Massachusetts, and Arizona, with support for cultural programs, including the performing arts and museums; Jewish welfare funds, including higher education and temple support; hospitals, education, and a geriatric center.
Limitations: Giving primarily in New York City, NY, MA, and AZ.
Application information: Foundation initiates grants.
Write: Robert R. Slaughter, Chief Executive
Officers and Directors: Grace R. Goldsmith, Chairperson; Robert R. Slaughter, Chief Executive; Richard Menschel, Robert B. Menschel, James C. Slaughter.
Employer Identification Number: 136107758

2484
Golub Foundation, The ⊭
501 Duanesburg Rd.
Schenectady 12306

Established in 1981 in New York.
Donor(s): Golub Corporation.
Financial data: (yr. ended 3/31/83): Assets, $23,780 (M); gifts received, $196,500; expenditures, $217,327, including $217,302 for grants to individuals.
Purpose and activities: Scholarship awards to high school graduates in areas served by the company.
Types of support awarded: Student aid.
Limitations: Giving limited to the Price Chopper Supermarket marketing area.
Publications: Informational brochure.
Application information: Application form required.
Deadline(s): April 1
Final notification: By May 21
Trustees: Lewis Golub, Sue Ann Ritchko, Stephen Wasser.
Employer Identification Number: 222341421

2485
Goodman Family Foundation, The
c/o Roy M. Goodman, President
1035 Fifth Ave.
New York 10028

Trust established in 1970 in New York as one of two successor trusts to the Matz Foundation.
Donor(s): Israel Matz.†
Financial data: (yr. ended 6/30/82): Assets, $1,870,692 (M); expenditures, $179,239, including $170,585 for 184 grants (high: $34,550; low: $10).
Purpose and activities: Broad purposes; primarily local giving, with emphasis on higher education and Jewish welfare funds; grants also for temple and church support, social agencies, and arts organizations.
Limitations: Giving primarily in NY.
Trustee: Roy M. Goodman.
Employer Identification Number: 136355553

2486
Goodman (Joseph C. and Clare F.) Memorial Foundation, Inc. ⊭
230 Park Ave., Rm. 2300
New York 10017

Incorporated in 1969 in New York.
Donor(s): Clare F. Goodman.†
Financial data: (yr. ended 9/30/83): Assets, $1,360,862 (M); expenditures, $112,306, including $106,000 for 13 grants (high: $20,000; low: $500).
Purpose and activities: Grants for the handicapped, hospitals, and education.
Limitations: Giving primarily in NY.
Officers: Sidney A. Wolff, President and Treasurer; Joyce N. Eichenberg, Vice-President and Secretary.
Employer Identification Number: 237039999

2487
Goodstein (David) Family Foundation, Inc. ⊭
Ten West 20th St.
New York 10011

Incorporated in 1944 in New York.
Donor(s): Members of the Goodstein family and family-related businesses.
Financial data: (yr. ended 2/28/83): Assets, $3,383,217 (M); expenditures, $223,792, including $207,553 for 100 grants (high: $57,700; low: $15).
Purpose and activities: Broad purposes; primarily local giving, with emphasis on Jewish welfare funds, hospitals, and higher education, including medical education.
Types of support awarded: General purposes, continuing support, annual campaigns, emergency funds, building funds, equipment, scholarship funds.
Limitations: Giving primarily in NY. No grants to individuals, or for matching gifts; no loans.
Application information:
Board meeting date(s): Quarterly
Officers and Directors: Albert Goodstein, President; William Goodstein, Treasurer; Robert Goodstein, Herman D. Raabin, Marilyn Ruttenberg.
Employer Identification Number: 136094685

2488
Goodyear (Josephine) Foundation
c/o E.W. Dann Stevens, Secretary
1920 Liberty Bank Bldg.
Buffalo 14202   (716) 856-2112

Incorporated in 1913 in New York.
Donor(s): Josephine L. Goodyear.
Financial data: (yr. ended 12/31/83): Assets, $1,999,160 (M); expenditures, $140,781, including $115,639 for 19 grants (high: $20,000; low: $300; average: $200-$50,000).
Purpose and activities: Local giving to promote the health, education, and welfare of indigent women and children; emphasis on hospitals, child welfare, youth agencies, and community funds.

Types of support awarded: Seed money, emergency funds, building funds, equipment, land acquisition, matching funds, employee matching gifts.
Limitations: Giving limited to the Buffalo, NY, area. No grants to individuals, or for operating budgets, continuing support, annual campaigns, deficit financing, endowment funds, or scholarships or fellowships; no loans.
Application information:
Initial approach: Letter
Copies of proposal: 3
Deadline(s): Submit proposal preferably in August; deadline September 15
Board meeting date(s): February and September or October
Final notification: 6 to 9 months
Officers and Directors: Kevin M. Wyckoff, President; Dorothy G. Wyckoff, Robert M. Goodyear, Vice-Presidents; E.W. Dann Stevens, Secretary; Robert S. Scheu, Treasurer; Frank H. Goodyear, Clinton R. Wyckoff, Jr.
Number of staff: None.
Employer Identification Number: 160755234

2489
Gordon Fund ▼
c/o William N. Loverd
10 Hanover Square
New York 10005

Trust established in 1954 in New York.
Donor(s): Members of the Gordon family.
Financial data: (yr. ended 12/31/82): Assets, $1,301,310 (M); gifts received, $581,205; expenditures, $651,315, including $649,367 for 155 grants (high: $100,000; low: $100).
Purpose and activities: Broad purposes; general giving, with emphasis on elementary, secondary, and higher education; support also for youth agencies, religion and hospitals.
Application information: Applications for grants not necessarily acknowledged.
Trustees: Albert F. Gordon, William N. Loverd.
Employer Identification Number: 136085919

2490
Gordon (Isaac) Foundation, Inc. ⌑
c/o D. Margolis
500 Reynolds Arcade
Rochester 14614

Incorporated in 1951 in New York.
Financial data: (yr. ended 9/30/83): Assets, $2,072,302 (M); expenditures, $202,508, including $158,960 for 7 grants (high: $134,000; low: $250).
Purpose and activities: Broad purposes; primarily local giving, with emphasis on a Jewish welfare fund and secondary education.
Limitations: Giving primarily in NY.
Officers: Robert Gordon, President; Robert Clark, Vice-President; Beryl Nusbaum, Secretary; Donald Margolis, Treasurer.
Employer Identification Number: 237425361

2491
Gottesman (D. S. and R. H.) Foundation ⌑
100 Park Ave.
New York 10017

Incorporated in 1941 in New York.
Donor(s): D. Samuel Gottesman.†
Financial data: (yr. ended 10/31/83): Assets, $1,661,607 (M); expenditures, $476,962, including $472,816 for 4 grants (high: $312,500; low: $316).
Purpose and activities: Broad purposes; major support currently for a local public library; support traditionally for Jewish welfare funds and higher education.
Limitations: Giving primarily in New York City, NY.
Officers: Ira D. Wallach,* President; Armand P. Bartos,* Joy G. Ungerleider-Mayerson,* Edgar Wachenheim III, James G. Wallach, Vice-Presidents; Peter C. Siegfried, Secretary; Benjamin Glowatz, Treasurer.
Directors:* Celeste G. Bartos, Philip Mayerson, Miriam G. Wallach.
Employer Identification Number: 136101701

2492
Gottlieb (Adolph and Esther) Foundation, Inc.
380 West Broadway
New York 10012 (212) 226-0581

Established in 1976 in New York.
Donor(s): Adolph Gottlieb,† Esther Gottlieb.
Financial data: (yr. ended 6/30/84): Assets, $2,600,000 (M); expenditures, $204,394, including $100,000 for 10 grants to individuals.
Purpose and activities: Grants to mature painters and sculptors with a 20-year minimum professional background in their field, who are in current need of financial support in order to continue their art. Emergency assistance is also given, on a one-time basis, to artists who have a financial need in excess of and unrelated to their normal economic situation.
Types of support awarded: Grants to individuals.
Limitations: No support for organizations.
Publications: Annual report.
Application information: Application form required.
Initial approach: Letter
Copies of proposal: 1
Deadline(s): Submit proposal between September and December; deadline December 31
Board meeting date(s): Quarterly
Final notification: Early March
Officers and Directors: Esther Gottlieb, President; Dick Netzer, Treasurer; Sanford Hirsch, Secretary and Administrator; Lawrence Alloway, Palmer Wald.
Employer Identification Number: 132853957

2493
Gould (Edwin) Foundation for Children ▼
126 East 31st St.
New York 10016 (212) 481-0170

Incorporated in 1923 in New York.
Donor(s): Edwin Gould.†
Financial data: (yr. ended 12/31/83): Assets, $28,267,374 (M); gifts received, $4,000; expenditures, $1,616,584, including $603,673 for 41 grants (high: $140,000; low: $2,000) and $257,000 for 6 foundation-administered programs.
Purpose and activities: "To promote the welfare of children...and to improve social and living conditions in the United States of America"; support primarily to children's services in the local area, with priority to agencies formerly affiliated with the Foundation; some scholarship support to institutions for young people who have passed through foundation-affiliated institutions only.
Types of support awarded: Operating budgets, continuing support, seed money, special projects, conferences and seminars, scholarship funds.
Limitations: Giving primarily in New York, NY. No grants to individuals, or for building or endowment funds, or matching gifts; no loans.
Publications: Multi-year report, informational brochure, program policy statement.
Application information: Grant applications not encouraged.
Initial approach: Letter or proposal
Copies of proposal: 1
Deadline(s): None
Board meeting date(s): Monthly except July and August
Final notification: Less than 1 month
Write: Schuyler M. Meyer, Jr., President
Officers and Trustees: Daniel W. Joy, Chairman; Schuyler M. Meyer, Jr., President and Treasurer; Martha M. Innes, Vice-President; Herschel E. Sparks, Jr., Secretary; Brandt R. Allen, Robert Coulson, Malcolm J. Edgerton, Jr., Frances K. Field, Megan E. McLaughlin, Newton P.S. Merrill, Elsie V. Newburg, Michael W. Osheowitz, George C. Seward, Richard H. Valentine, Virginia N. Wilking, M.D.
Number of staff: 9.
Employer Identification Number: 135675642

2494
Gould (Florence) Arts Foundation, Inc.
80 Pine St., 17th Fl.
New York 10005

Incorporated in 1957 in New York.
Donor(s): Florence J. Gould.†
Financial data: (yr. ended 12/31/83): Assets, $2,689,718 (M); expenditures, $24,773, including $24,512 for grants.
Purpose and activities: Grants primarily for language and literature studies, including an annual poetry prize; support also for a museum association.
Limitations: No grants to individuals (except for annual poetry prize, candidates for which are nominated by publishers in France).

Officers and Directors: John R. Young, President; Joan Murtaugh Frankel, Vice-President and Treasurer; Suzanne Goodson, Secretary.
Employer Identification Number: 136161616

2495
Goulds Pumps Foundation ¤
240 Fall St.
Seneca Falls 13148   (315) 568-2811

Incorporated in 1964 in New York.
Donor(s): Goulds Pumps, Inc.
Financial data: (yr. ended 12/31/82): Assets, $75,382 (M); gifts received, $100,000; expenditures, $138,624, including $126,628 for 72 grants (high: $15,000; low: $15) and $10,550 for 22 grants to individuals.
Purpose and activities: Primarily local giving; grants largely for higher education, including scholarships for children of Company employees; some support also for health associations and a community fund.
Types of support awarded: Employee related scholarships.
Limitations: Giving limited to the Seneca Falls, NY, area.
Application information:
  Write: Bryan Rogers, Vice-President, Administrative Services-Scholarship Committee
Trustee: Security Trust Company.
Donation Committee: Eugene B. Bradshaw, J.A. Nelson, Robert L. Tarnow.
Scholarship Committee: Edward Boudreau, Joseph Coffee, Samuel M. Kilpatrick, Frank M. Knight, David M. Rice.
Employer Identification Number: 166054041

2496
Grace Foundation Inc. ▼
1114 Ave. of the Americas
New York 10036-7794   (212) 819-6316

Incorporated in 1961 in New York.
Donor(s): W.R. Grace & Co.
Financial data: (yr. ended 12/31/83): Assets, $2,132,579 (M); gifts received, $2,825,000; expenditures, $3,989,147, including $3,761,989 for 561 grants (high: $333,334; low: $1,000; average: $1,000-$10,000) and $209,358 for 1,000 employee matching gifts.
Purpose and activities: General purposes; grants primarily to national organizations for higher education, urban and minority affairs, cultural programs, including performing arts, community funds, and hospitals.
Types of support awarded: Operating budgets, continuing support, annual campaigns, building funds, equipment, matching funds, employee matching gifts, scholarship funds, employee related scholarships, fellowships.

Limitations: Giving primarily in New York City and to national organizations; grants to local organizations outside New York City are made generally on the recommendation of local operating groups or affiliates of W.R. Grace & Co. No grants to individuals, or for endowment funds, seed money, emergency, deficit financing, land acquisition, publications, demonstration projects, conferences, or for specific research projects.
Publications: Program policy statement, application guidelines.
Application information:
  Initial approach: Letter
  Copies of proposal: 1
  Deadline(s): None
  Board meeting date(s): February, April, June, October, and December
  Final notification: 2 to 3 months
  Write: William A. Baker, Vice-President
Officers: Thomas M. Doyle,* Chairman and Treasurer; Richard I. Morris,* President; John J. Meehan,* Vice-President and Secretary; William A. Baker, Vice-President.
Directors:* James W. Frick, Paul F. Hellmuth, Ethel Mann, Charles W. Miller, Paul D. Paganucci, Eben W. Pyne, Harold A. Stevens, John R. Young.
Number of staff: 2 full-time professional; 3 part-time professional; 3 full-time support.
Employer Identification Number: 136153305

2497
Gramercy Park Foundation Incorporated, The
(formerly Gramercy Park Foundation)
c/o Lawrence S. Karnbad
225 Broadway
New York 10007   (212) 964-4140

Incorporated in 1952 in New York.
Donor(s): Benjamin Sonnenberg, Helen Sonnenberg Tucker.
Financial data: (yr. ended 12/31/83): Assets, $1,885,186 (M); expenditures, $188,175, including $137,525 for 59 grants (high: $34,850; low: $50).
Purpose and activities: Grants primarily for arts and cultural programs in the New York City area, with emphasis on libraries and the performing arts; support also for higher education, including music education.
Limitations: Giving primarily in the New York City, NY, area. No grants to individuals.
Officers: Helen Tucker, President and Treasurer; Steven Tucker, Vice-President; Benjamin Sonnenberg, Secretary.
Number of staff: 1 part-time support.
Employer Identification Number: 132507282

2498
Grant (Charles M. & Mary D.) Foundation ¤
c/o Morgan Guaranty Trust Company of New York
23 Wall St.
New York 10015   (212) 483-2248

Trust established in 1967 in New York.
Donor(s): Mary D. Grant.†

Financial data: (yr. ended 12/31/83): Assets, $3,719,373 (M); expenditures, $230,863, including $175,000 for 10 grants (high: $25,000; low: $10,000).
Purpose and activities: Broad purposes; grants limited to institutions in the southern part of the United States, with emphasis on higher education and hospitals.
Types of support awarded: Operating budgets, continuing support, seed money, building funds, equipment, land acquisition, publications, special projects, general purposes.
Limitations: Giving primarily in the southern U.S. No grants to individuals, or for research, endowment funds, or matching gifts; generally no scholarships and fellowships; no loans.
Application information:
  Initial approach: Full proposal, letter, or telephone
  Copies of proposal: 1
  Deadline(s): August 1
  Board meeting date(s): May and August
  Write: Robert F. Longley, Senior Vice-President
Trustee: Morgan Guaranty Trust Company of New York (Robert F. Longley, Senior Vice-President).
Number of staff: 5.
Employer Identification Number: 136264329

2499
Grant (William T.) Foundation ▼
919 Third Ave.
New York 10022   (212) 752-0071

Incorporated in 1936 in Delaware.
Donor(s): William T. Grant.†
Financial data: (yr. ended 12/31/84): Assets, $97,300,000 (M); expenditures, $6,800,000, including $4,900,000 for 93 grants (high: $200,000; low: $750; average: $5,000-$200,000) and $966,000 for 6 grants to individuals.
Purpose and activities: Support nationally and internationally for research, professional training, and social policy and advocacy projects concerned with the healthy psychological and social development of children and youth. Current emphasis on research projects dealing with stress and coping of school-age children. Preference given to the support of new programs in their initial stages of development. Support is channeled through three mechanisms: Investigator-initiated projects, Faculty Scholars Program, and the Action Research Program. Awards limited number of small one-time grants for small-scale research, training, and service projects in the New York City metropolitan area.
Types of support awarded: Continuing support, seed money, research, special projects, fellowships.
Limitations: No grants to individuals (except Faculty Scholars Program), or for annual fundraising campaigns, deficit financing, equipment and materials, land acquisition, renovation projects, capital funds, operating budgets of on-going service agencies or educational institutions or matching gifts; no loans.

Publications: Annual report, informational brochure, program policy statement, application guidelines.
Application information:
Initial approach: Letter
Copies of proposal: 5
Deadline(s): December 1, March 1, and August 1
Board meeting date(s): February, May, September, and December
Write: Robert Johns Haggerty, M.D., President
Officers: Robert Johns Haggerty, M.D.,* President; E. Jeanne Merkling, Senior Vice-President; Lynn Russell, Vice-President for Program and Secretary; Lynda M. Pickett, Vice-President for Administration; William H. Chisholm,* Treasurer.
Trustees: Robert P. Patterson, Jr., Chairman; William Bevan, Ellis T. Gravette, Jr., Beatrix A. Hamburg, M.D., R. McAllister Lloyd, Martha L. Minow, Henry W. Riecken, Rivington R. Winant.
Number of staff: 5 full-time professional; 9 full-time support.
Employer Identification Number: 131624021

2500
Green Fund, Inc., The ▼
501 Fifth Ave., Suite 1615
New York 10017   (212) 697-9531

Incorporated in 1947 in New York.
Donor(s): Evelyn Green Davis, Louis A. Green.†
Financial data: (yr. ended 1/31/84): Assets, $25,125,351 (M); gifts received, $437,600; expenditures, $1,216,888, including $936,862 for 145 grants (high: $165,500; low: $50).
Purpose and activities: Charitable purposes; primarily local giving, with emphasis on Jewish welfare funds, hospitals within the Jewish Federation network, services to the aged and mentally handicapped, higher and secondary education, the performing arts, and youth agencies.
Limitations: Giving primarily in the New York, NY, metropolitan area. No grants to individuals.
Application information: Grants initiated by the fund's members; solicitations not welcome.
Write: Cynthia Green Colin, President
Officers: Cynthia Green Colin, President; S. William Green, Treasurer.
Number of staff: 1 part-time support.
Employer Identification Number: 136160950

2501
Greenberg (The Alan C.) Foundation, Inc. ⌑
55 Water St.
New York 10041

Established in 1964.
Donor(s): Alan C. Greenberg.
Financial data: (yr. ended 12/31/82): Assets, $391,936 (M); gifts received, $1,030,380; expenditures, $875,603, including $869,174 for 53 grants (high: $785,528; low: $50).
Purpose and activities: Primarily local giving in New York and Israel, for Jewish welfare funds and higher education.
Limitations: Giving primarily in NY and Israel.

Officers and Directors: Alan C. Greenberg, President and Treasurer; Maynard Greenberg, Vice-President and Secretary.
Employer Identification Number: 136271740

2502
Greene (The David J.) Foundation, Inc.
c/o Ms. Florence B. Weingart
30 Wall St.
New York 10005   (212) 344-5180

Incorporated in 1966 in New York.
Donor(s): Members of the Greene family.
Financial data: (yr. ended 12/31/83): Assets, $3,486,755 (M); gifts received, $1,877,307; expenditures, $367,125, including $354,368 for 205 grants (high: $74,270; low: $25).
Purpose and activities: Broad purposes; primarily local giving, with emphasis on grants for hospitals, higher and secondary education, aid to children and blind, and Jewish welfare funds.
Limitations: Giving primarily in the New York, NY area. No grants to individuals.
Application information:
Initial approach: Letter
Board meeting date(s): March, June, September, and December
Officers and Directors: Alan I. Greene, President; Robert J. Ravitz, Vice-President; Florence B. Weingart, Secretary; Richard G. Spring, Treasurer; Irving A. Greene.
Employer Identification Number: 136209280

2503
Greene (The Jerome L.) Foundation, Inc. ⌑
c/o Rosenman Colin, et al.
575 Madison Ave.
New York 10022

Established in 1978.
Donor(s): Jerome L. Greene.
Financial data: (yr. ended 11/30/82): Assets, $1,153,539 (M); gifts received, $1,000,000; expenditures, $2,043,935, including $2,021,970 for 30 grants (high: $846,995; low: $300).
Purpose and activities: Grants primarily for higher education and cultural programs; support also for Jewish welfare funds.
Officer and Directors: Jerome L. Greene, President; Howard Bindeglass, Dawn Greene.
Employer Identification Number: 132960852

2504
Greenebaum (The Charles and Estelle) Foundation, Inc. ⌑
555 Fifth Ave.
New York 10017

Incorporated in 1944 in New York.
Donor(s): Leon C. Greenebaum,† Charles L. Greenebaum, and others.
Financial data: (yr. ended 12/31/82): Assets, $1,414,451 (M); expenditures, $170,358, including $136,900 for 44 grants (high: $35,500; low: $100).

Purpose and activities: Charitable purposes; primarily local giving, with emphasis on health agencies, Jewish welfare funds, higher and secondary education, and temple support.
Limitations: Giving primarily in NY.
Application information:
Write: Richard M. Ticktin, Secretary
Officers and Directors: Charles L. Greenebaum, President and Treasurer; Richard M. Ticktin, Vice-President and Secretary.
Employer Identification Number: 136097729

2505
Greenwall Foundation, The ▼
245 Park Ave., 31st Fl.
New York 10017   (212) 661-0833

Incorporated in 1949 in New York.
Donor(s): Anna A. Greenwall,† Frank K. Greenwall.
Financial data: (yr. ended 12/31/84): Assets, $21,307,086 (L); gifts received, $366,061; expenditures, $1,393,641, including $1,084,124 for 35 grants (high: $240,000; average: $10,000-$75,000).
Purpose and activities: Broad purposes; primarily local giving, with current emphasis on medical education and research, especially in bone cancer, diabetes and geriatric care; education, especially scholarships through institutions, and the arts and humanities.
Types of support awarded: Continuing support, seed money, emergency funds, equipment, matching funds, scholarship funds, professorships, fellowships, research, special projects.
Limitations: Giving primarily in New York, NY. No grants to individuals, or for building or endowment funds, operating budgets, annual campaigns, deficit financing, publications, or conferences; no loans.
Publications: Program policy statement, application guidelines, annual report.
Application information:
Initial approach: Letter
Copies of proposal: 1
Deadline(s): Submit proposal preferably in January or August; no set deadline
Board meeting date(s): May and November
Write: John L. Dugan, Jr., Executive Director
Officers and Directors: Oscar M. Ruebhausen, Chairman; Frank K. Greenwall, President; Lawrence H. Greenwald, Donald Pascal, Vice-Presidents; Edith Levett, Corporate Secretary; C. Richard MacGrath, Treasurer; John L. Dugan, Jr., Executive Director; Chester Billings, George Bugliarello, Andrew A. MacGrath, Francis F. MacGrath, Susan A. MacGrath, Richard L. Salzer, Richard L. Salzer, Jr., M.D., William S. Vaun, M.D.
Number of staff: 1 full-time professional.
Employer Identification Number: 136082277

2506
Greve (The William and Mary) Foundation, Inc. ▼
One East 53rd St.
New York 10022   (212) 758-8032

Incorporated in 1964 in New York.
Donor(s): Mary P. Greve.†

Financial data: (yr. ended 12/31/83): Assets, $14,640,018 (M); expenditures, $1,065,466, including $712,388 for 37 grants (high: $100,000; low: $1,000; average: $5,000-$20,000).
Purpose and activities: Grants largely for education and related fields, including East-West relations, the performing arts, and Off-Broadway nonprofit theater.
Types of support awarded: Seed money, endowment funds, research, matching funds, general purposes, building funds.
Limitations: No grants to individuals, or for scholarships or fellowships; no loans.
Publications: Program policy statement, application guidelines.
Application information:
  Initial approach: Letter
  Copies of proposal: 1
  Deadline(s): None
  Board meeting date(s): February, May, August, and November
  Final notification: 2 months
  Write: Irving H. Becker, Executive Vice-President
Officers and Directors: John W. Kiser III, Chairman; Anthony C.M. Kiser, President; Irving H. Becker, Executive Vice-President; John J. Tommaney, Secretary; John A. Buckbee, James W. Sykes, Jr.
Number of staff: 3 full-time professional; 1 part-time professional.
Employer Identification Number: 136020724

2507
Griffis Foundation, Inc., The
29 East 61st St.
New York 10021   (212) 759-8693

Incorporated in 1943 in New York.
Donor(s): Stanton Griffis,† Nixon Griffis.
Financial data: (yr. ended 12/31/83): Assets, $7,342,658 (M); gifts received, $54,513; expenditures, $521,231, including $355,091 for 53 grants (high: $150,779; low: $50; average: $250-$3,000).
Purpose and activities: Broad purposes; general giving, with emphasis on continuing projects in conservation, education, humanities, health, and research in oceanographic fields.
Types of support awarded: Operating budgets, continuing support, seed money, deficit financing, professorships, fellowships, research, publications.
Limitations: No grants to individuals, or for capital or endowment funds, annual campaigns, emergency funds, matching gifts, or conferences; no loans.
Publications: Program policy statement, application guidelines.
Application information:
  Initial approach: Full proposal
  Copies of proposal: 1
  Deadline(s): Submit proposal preferably between January and May; deadline October 1
  Board meeting date(s): 10 months per year
  Final notification: 2 months
  Write: Nixon Griffis, President

Officers and Directors: Nixon Griffis, President; Elizabeth H.G. Amory, Vice-President; Hughes Griffis, Secretary; William G. Conway.
Number of staff: 1 full-time support.
Employer Identification Number: 135678764

2508
Grossinger (Jennie) Foundation, Inc. ⌒
271 Madison Ave., 22nd Fl.
New York 10016

Established in 1970.
Financial data: (yr. ended 6/30/83): Assets, $47,313 (M); gifts received, $2,000; expenditures, $114,577, including $113,414 for 69 grants (high: $10,000; low: $75).
Purpose and activities: Primarily local giving for Jewish organizations, particularly temple support, education, and social services.
Limitations: Giving primarily in NY.
Officers: Joseph Alpert, Secretary; Charles Alpert, Treasurer.
Employer Identification Number: 132726085

2509
Gruber (Lila) Research Foundation ⌒
19 Laurel Dr.
Great Neck 11091

Established in 1962.
Donor(s): Barry Gruber, Daryl Gruber, Murray Gruber.
Financial data: (yr. ended 12/31/82): Assets, $1,456,089 (M); gifts received, $140,000; expenditures, $156,090, including $152,988 for 26 grants (high: $50,000; low: $15).
Purpose and activities: Primarily local giving for Jewish religious and educational institutions and for medical research; support also for social services, particularly a Jewish welfare fund.
Limitations: Giving primarily in NY.
Trustees: Morris L. Green, Murray Gruber.
Employer Identification Number: 116035223

2510
Grumbacher (Stanley and Kathleen) Foundation, Inc. ⌒
460 West 34th St.
New York 10001

Incorporated in 1951 in New York.
Financial data: (yr. ended 4/30/83): Assets, $974,561 (M); expenditures, $167,629, including $163,695 for 56 grants (high: $40,000; low: $30).
Purpose and activities: Grants largely for hospitals and Jewish welfare funds.
Officers and Directors: Kathleen Grumbacher Silberstein, President and Treasurer; Alex Silberstein, Vice-President; Jack J. Roland, Secretary.
Employer Identification Number: 136161277

2511
Gruss (Oscar and Regina) Charitable and Educational Foundation, Inc. ⌒
c/o Oscar Gruss & Son
74 Broad St.
New York 10004

Incorporated in 1952 in New York.
Donor(s): Emanuel Gruss, Oscar Gruss,† Regina Gruss.
Financial data: (yr. ended 3/31/83): Assets, $4,605,765 (M); gifts received, $1,160,540; expenditures, $157,289, including $154,995 for 28 grants (high: $34,000; low: $10).
Purpose and activities: Broad purposes; grants largely for education, Jewish welfare funds and temple support.
Officers: Regina Gruss, President; Elizabeth Goldberg, Vice-President; Emanuel Gruss, Secretary; Riane Gruss, Treasurer.
Employer Identification Number: 136061333

2512
Guggenheim (The Daniel and Florence) Foundation ▼
950 Third Ave., 30th Fl.
New York 10022   (212) 755-3199

Incorporated in 1924 in New York.
Donor(s): Daniel Guggenheim,† Florence Guggenheim.†
Financial data: (yr. ended 3/31/85): Assets, $5,822,795 (M); expenditures, $662,475, including $553,750 for 13 grants (high: $185,000; low: $1,000; average: $20,000-$30,000).
Purpose and activities: To advance public welfare, civic betterment, and the well-being of mankind throughout the world; support primarily in the area of criminal justice, particualarly for training programs; grants also for health and welfare agencies.
Types of support awarded: Continuing support, annual campaigns, seed money, matching funds, research.
Limitations: No grants to individuals, or for scholarships and fellowships.
Publications: Multi-year report.
Application information:
  Initial approach: Letter
  Copies of proposal: 1
  Deadline(s): March 15 and September 10
  Board meeting date(s): May and October
  Final notification: 2 weeks
  Write: Oscar S. Straus II, President
Officers: Oscar S. Straus II,* President; Oscar S. Straus III,* Joan Van de Maele,* Vice-Presidents; Rowley Bialla, Secretary; John T. Barnes, Treasurer.
Directors:* Michael B. Davies, Dana Draper, Daniel Guggenheim, Robert Guggenheim, Jr., Mrs. Max A. Hart, James S. Lanigan, Henry C. Marshall, Pamela H. Metcalf, Alfred Ogden, Henry Patton, Oscar Schafer, Albert C. Van de Maele.
Number of staff: 1 part-time professional; 2 part-time support.
Employer Identification Number: 135562232

2513
Guggenheim (The Harry Frank) Foundation ▼

Woolworth Bldg.
233 Broadway, 17th Fl.
New York 10279   (212) 267-3860

Incorporated in 1929 in New York.
Donor(s): Harry Frank Guggenheim.†
Financial data: (yr. ended 6/30/83): Assets, $26,210,680 (M); expenditures, $1,509,038, including $780,877 for 54 grants (high: $37,500; low: $250; average: $15,000-$25,000).
Purpose and activities: Grants for research projects at the post-doctoral level (though not necessarily requiring a Ph.D.) directed toward providing a better understanding of man and his nature, particularly his tendencies toward violence, aggression, and dominance; giving includes Career Development Awards, to recognize an outstanding young scientist or academic leader, and support for higher education.
Types of support awarded: Research, seed money, general purposes.
Limitations: No grants for capital or endowment funds, or for matching gifts; no loans. No funds for overhead costs of institutions, travel to professional meetings, publications, subsidiaries, self-education, elaborate fixed equipment, or pre-doctoral support (apart from that indirectly involved in research assistantships).
Publications: Multi-year report, application guidelines.
Application information:
  Initial approach: Letter
  Copies of proposal: 5
  Deadline(s): February 1 and August 1
  Board meeting date(s): June and December
  Final notification: Within 3 days of meeting
  Write: Karen Colvard, Program Officer
Officers and Directors: Peter O. Lawson-Johnston, Chairman; Floyd Ratliff, President; William O. Baker, James B. Edwards, George J. Fountaine, Leo Gottlieb, Donald R. Griffin, James M. Hester, Peter Lawson-Johnston II, Theodore D. Lockwood, John A. Peeples, Rudy L. Ruggles, Jr., Roger W. Straus, Jr., Joan G. Van de Maele, William C. Westmoreland.
Number of staff: 4 full-time professional; 5 part-time professional.
Employer Identification Number: 136043471

2514
Guggenheim (John Simon) Memorial Foundation ▼

90 Park Ave.
New York 10016   (212) 687-4470

Incorporated in 1925 in New York.
Donor(s): Simon Guggenheim,† Mrs. Simon Guggenheim.†
Financial data: (yr. ended 12/31/83): Assets, $105,418,870 (M); expenditures, $7,964,251, including $5,959,000 for 317 grants to individuals.

Purpose and activities: "To add to the educational, literary, artistic and scientific power of this country, and also to provide for the cause of better international understanding" through providing "opportunities for both men and women to carry on advanced study in any field of knowledge, or in any of the fine arts, including music...under the freest possible conditions, and to make available for the public benefit the results of such studies." Assistance to individuals through fellowships broader in concept than the usual fellowship, awarded by the trustees upon nomination by a Committee of Selection. Awards are made to citizens and permanent residents of the United States and Canada, of all the other American states, of the Caribbean, of the Philippines and of the French, Dutch, and British possessions in the Western Hemisphere. Fellowships in music are awarded only to composers of music or scholars in the history or theory of music. Guggenheim fellowships may not be held concurrently with other fellowships.
Types of support awarded: Fellowships.
Limitations: No grants for building or endowment funds, or for operating budgets, or special projects.
Publications: Annual report, informational brochure, program policy statement, application guidelines.
Application information: Application form required.
  Initial approach: Letter
  Deadline(s): October 1 for U.S. and Canada; December 1 for Western Hemisphere and the Philippines
  Board meeting date(s): March and May and as required
  Final notification: Approximately 6 months
  Write: Joel Conarroe, President
Officers: Joel Conarroe,* President; G. Thomas Tanselle, Vice-President; Stephen L. Schlesinger, Secretary; Robert P. Bergin, Treasurer.
Trustees:* W. Clarke Wescoe, Chairman; Richard W. Couper, Edward E. David, Jr., Helene L. Kaplan, Robert V. Lindsay, Carl M. Mueller, Charles Andrew Ryskamp, Malcolm B. Smith, Roger W. Straus, Jr., Lewis Thomas.
Number of staff: 10 full-time professional; 6 full-time support.
Employer Identification Number: 135673173

2515
Guinzburg Fund, The ⌿

Three West 29th St.
New York 10001

Incorporated in 1955 in New York.
Donor(s): Harold K. Guinzburg.†
Financial data: (yr. ended 12/31/82): Assets, $1,773,847 (M); expenditures, $139,889, including $100,731 for 107 grants (high: $20,000; low: $10).
Purpose and activities: Broad purposes; primarily local giving, with emphasis on hospitals, higher education, cultural activities, and community development.
Limitations: Giving primarily in NY.
Officer and Director: Thomas H. Guinzburg, President and Treasurer.
Employer Identification Number: 136108425

2516
Gulf + Western Foundation, Inc.

One Gulf + Western Plaza
New York 10023   (212) 333-4394

Incorporated in 1954 in New York.
Donor(s): Gulf + Western Industries, Inc.
Financial data: (yr. ended 7/31/84): Assets, $7,569 (M); gifts received, $1,049,301; expenditures, $1,055,348, including $897,863 for 155 grants (high: $75,000; low: $500) and $151,438 for 452 employee matching gifts.
Purpose and activities: Broad purposes; administers philanthropic giving of operating units on behalf of the corporation in areas of company operations. Grants principally to national organizations, for an employee matching gifts program, and for the foundation's Major Awards Program which supports projects that demonstrate new concepts of public service within specific areas of interest selected yearly.
Types of support awarded: Operating budgets, continuing support, employee matching gifts, internships, employee related scholarships, special projects.
Limitations: Giving primarily in areas of company operations. No grants to individuals, or for annual campaigns, seed money, emergency funds, deficit financing, equipment, land acquisition, renovation, endowment funds, research, demonstration projects, publications, or conferences; no loans.
Publications: Application guidelines.
Application information:
  Initial approach: Letter
  Copies of proposal: 1
  Deadline(s): Submit proposal preferably in June; no set deadline
  Board meeting date(s): January, May, September, and December
  Final notification: 6 weeks to 6 months
  Write: Gloria S. White, Executive Director
Officers and Directors:* Samuel J. Silberman,* President; Lawrence E. Levinson,* Executive Vice-President and Secretary; David H. Lissy, Treasurer.
Number of staff: 2 full-time professional; 1 part-time professional; 2 full-time support.
Employer Identification Number: 136089816

2517
Gulton Foundation, Inc. ⌿

c/o A. P. Bersohn & Co.
One Blue Hill Plaza, No. 1606
Pearl River 10965-8606

Incorporated in 1961 in New York.
Donor(s): Leslie K. Gulton,† Marian G. Malcolm.
Financial data: (yr. ended 10/31/82): Assets, $1,378,754 (M); gifts received, $25,000; expenditures, $193,155, including $183,300 for 8 grants (high: $138,000; low: $1,000).
Purpose and activities: Broad purposes; grants largely for higher education and mental health services in Israel.
Officers: Edith Gulton, President; Marian G. Malcolm, Vice-President and Treasurer; Daniel Malcolm, Secretary.
Employer Identification Number: 136105207

2518
Gurwin (J.) Foundation, Inc.
934 Middle Neck Rd.
Great Neck 11024 (516) 466-3800

Incorporated in 1959 in New York.
Donor(s): Joseph Gurwin, Kings Point Industries Inc.
Financial data: (yr. ended 7/31/83): Assets, $2,462,986 (M); gifts received, $257,500; expenditures, $262,978, including $257,700 for 46 grants (high: $211,650; low: $10).
Purpose and activities: Charitable purposes; primarily local giving, with emphasis on Jewish welfare funds; grants also for temple support and hospitals.
Limitations: Giving primarily in NY. No grants to individuals.
Application information:
Board meeting date(s): As required
Officers and Directors: Joseph Gurwin, President; Eric Gurwin, Vice-President; Rosalind Gurwin, Secretary-Treasurer; Laura Gurwin Flug.
Employer Identification Number: 136059258

2519
Gutfreund Foundation, Inc., The
c/o Joint Foundation Support, Inc.
122 East 42nd St., Suite 922
New York 10168 (212) 661-4080

Incorporated in 1967 in New York.
Donor(s): John H. Gutfreund.
Financial data: (yr. ended 4/30/84): Assets, $1,110,571 (M); gifts received, $137,100; expenditures, $109,212, including $86,500 for 17 grants (high: $10,000; low: $1,500; average: $5,000-$10,000).
Purpose and activities: Broad purposes; small grants (averaging $8,000) to support projects designed to ensure civil rights and civil liberties, encourage self-help, and promote equality of opportunity for the urban and rural poor; giving primarily in the New York City area, including grants to groups organizing for change at the community level, as well as to organizations seeking new ways to deliver services. Grants sometimes made outside the New York City area to organizations that do not have access to larger sources of funding. Occasional larger grants to projects or institutions of personal interest to the trustees.
Types of support awarded: Operating budgets, continuing support, seed money.
Limitations: Giving primarily in New York, NY. No grants to individuals, or for building or endowment funds, scholarships or fellowships, matching gifts, or program support; no loans.
Publications: Annual report, application guidelines.
Application information:
Initial approach: Letter
Copies of proposal: 1
Deadline(s): None
Board meeting date(s): Semiannually in spring and fall
Final notification: 3 to 6 months
Write: Patricia Hewitt, Executive Director, Joint Foundation Support
Officers and Trustees: John H. Gutfreund, President; Lawrence B. Buttenwieser, Secretary-Treasurer.
Number of staff: 1.
Employer Identification Number: 136227515

2520
Gutman (Edna and Monroe C.) Foundation, Inc.
c/o Hertz, Herson & Company
2 Park Ave.
New York 10016

Incorporated in 1947 in New York.
Donor(s): Edna C. Gutman,† Monroe C. Gutman.†
Financial data: (yr. ended 6/30/83): Assets, $2,579,976 (M); expenditures, $256,085, including $238,250 for 11 grants (high: $125,000; low: $1,000).
Purpose and activities: Broad purposes; grants largely for secondary and higher education, and a hospital.
Officers and Directors: Margaret S. Nathan, President; Alvin W. Pearson, Vice-President and Treasurer; Philip Kimmel, Vice-President; George Siegel, Secretary.
Employer Identification Number: 136094013

2521
Guttman (Stella and Charles) Foundation, Inc. ▼ ⌑
c/o Gassman, Rebhun, and Company
350 Fifth Ave.
New York 10118 (212) 239-1280

Incorporated in 1959 in New York.
Donor(s): Charles Guttman,† Stella Guttman.†
Financial data: (yr. ended 12/31/82): Assets, $15,470,236 (M); expenditures, $799,345, including $719,000 for 117 grants (high: $100,000; low: $500).
Purpose and activities: Broad purposes; support largely for higher education, including grants to colleges and universities for a scholarship program; grants for medical research; and general local giving, with emphasis on religious welfare funds, hospitals, social agencies, health agencies, and the handicapped.
Limitations: Giving primarily in the New York, NY, metropolitan area for health and welfare; nationally for education.
Application information:
Board meeting date(s): As required
Write: Robert S. Gassman, Treasurer
Officers and Directors: Abraham Rosenberg, President; Edgar H. Brenner, Vice-President; Sonia Rosenberg, Secretary; Robert S. Gassman, Treasurer; Charles S. Brenner, P. Fred Fox, Peter A. Herbert.
Employer Identification Number: 136103039

2522
Hackett (Charlotte Cuneen) Charitable Trust ⌑
c/o Marine Midland Bank
Trust Operations Center, P.O. Box 4203
Buffalo 14240

Established in 1971.
Financial data: (yr. ended 12/31/83): Assets, $1,115,315 (M); expenditures, $98,678, including $85,970 for 5 grants (high: $34,276; low: $1,921).
Purpose and activities: Giving primarily to youth agencies.
Trustee: Marine Midland Bank.
Employer Identification Number: 237215233

2523
Hagedorn Fund, The
c/o Manufacturers Hanover Trust Company
600 Fifth Ave.
New York 10020 (212) 957-1500

Trust established in 1953 in New York.
Donor(s): William Hagedorn.†
Financial data: (yr. ended 12/31/83): Assets, $3,097,216 (M); expenditures, $288,370, including $255,000 for 64 grants (high: $17,500; low: $1,000; average: $1,000-$5,000).
Purpose and activities: General local giving, with emphasis on higher and secondary education, theological seminaries, and church support; grants also for religious associations, hospitals and health agencies, the aged, youth agencies, and social welfare.
Types of support awarded: Operating budgets.
Limitations: Giving limited to the New York, NY, metropolitan area. No grants to individuals, or for continuing support, annual campaigns, seed money, emergency funds, deficit financing, capital or endowment funds, matching gifts, scholarships, fellowships, research, special projects, publications, or conferences; no loans.
Application information:
Initial approach: Full proposal
Copies of proposal: 1
Deadline(s): Submit proposal preferably in November; deadline November 15
Board meeting date(s): December
Final notification: 1 month
Write: Robert Rosenthal, Assistant Vice-President
Trustees: Gilbert C. Freeauf, Ruth Marie Hagedorn, Manufacturers Hanover Trust Company.
Number of staff: None.
Employer Identification Number: 136048718

2524
Haggin (Margaret Voorhies) Trust in Memory of her late husband, James Ben Ali Haggin ▼ ⌑
c/o The Bank of New York
48 Wall St.
New York 10015

Trust established in 1938 in New York.
Donor(s): Mrs. Margaret Voorhies Haggin.†
Financial data: (yr. ended 12/31/82): Assets, $8,469,671 (M); expenditures, $698,834, including $621,470 for 23 grants (high: $89,795; low: $650).
Purpose and activities: Charitable purposes; local giving largely for higher education and hospitals.
Limitations: Giving limited to KY.

Application information:
Write: Peter Bingenheimer
Trustees: Laura C. Christianson, The Bank of New York.
Employer Identification Number: 136078494

2525
Hahn Family Foundation ☐
1800 M & T Plaza
Buffalo 14203   (716) 885-4931

Established in 1965.
Financial data: (yr. ended 12/31/82): Assets, $1,276,987 (M); expenditures, $62,387, including $44,920 for 6 grants (high: $10,420; low: $3,000).
Purpose and activities: Primarily local giving, with emphasis on ecology, particularly in the areas of renewable energy sources, organic farming, preservation of farmland, integrated pest management, and radioactive, toxic, and other wastes; grants also to local cultural and higher educational institutions.
Limitations: Giving primarily in Buffalo and Erie County, NY. No grants to individuals or for operating expenses.
Application information:
Initial approach: Letter or proposal
Write: Anne D. Hahn, Trustee
Trustees: Anne D. Hahn, Anne S. Hahn, Charles J. Hahn, Charles O. Hahn, Eric S. Hahn.
Employer Identification Number: 166128499

2526
Harding Educational and Charitable Foundation, The ☐
c/o Chase Manhattan Bank
1211 Ave. of the Americas
New York 10036

Trust established in 1945 in New York.
Donor(s): Henry J. Harding, Robert L. Harding.
Financial data: (yr. ended 12/31/83): Assets, $3,178,118 (M); gifts received, $10,000; expenditures, $105,566, including $99,300 for 12 grants (high: $50,000; low: $1,000).
Purpose and activities: Broad purposes; primarily local giving; funds presently committed to organizations of interest to the donors.
Limitations: Giving primarily in NY.
Application information:
Write: Henry J. Harding, Trustee
Trustees: Arthur R. Douglass, Henry J. Harding, Robert L. Harding, Jr., The Chase Manhattan Bank.
Employer Identification Number: 136083440

2527
Harriman (Mary W.) Foundation ▼
63 Wall St., 23rd Fl.
New York 10005   (212) 483-8182

Trust established in 1925 in New York; incorporated in 1973.
Donor(s): Mary W. Harriman.†

Financial data: (yr. ended 12/31/83): Assets, $12,432,960 (M); expenditures, $754,331, including $672,369 for 117 grants (high: $50,000; low: $1,000; average: $1,000-$20,000).
Purpose and activities: General giving, primarily in the New York metropolitan area, with emphasis on higher and secondary education, hospitals and health agencies, cultural organizations, public policy, social agencies and youth agencies.
Limitations: Giving primarily in the New York, NY, metropolitan area. No grants to individuals.
Application information:
Initial approach: Proposal
Copies of proposal: 1
Deadline(s): None
Board meeting date(s): December
Final notification: 1 month
Write: William F. Hibberd, Secretary
Officers: W. Averell Harriman,* President; William Rich III, Vice-President; William F. Hibberd, Secretary; William J. Corcoran, Treasurer.
Directors: Mary A. Fisk, Elbridge T. Gerry, Sr., Pamela C. Harriman, John B. Madden, Edward H. Northrop.
Employer Identification Number: 237356000

2528
Hartford (The John A.) Foundation, Inc. ▼
405 Lexington Ave., 55th Fl.
New York 10174   (212) 661-2828

Established in 1929; incorporated in 1942 in New York.
Donor(s): John A. Hartford,† George L. Hartford.†
Financial data: (yr. ended 12/31/84): Assets, $155,170,232 (M); expenditures, $7,995,029, including $4,160,842 for 52 grants (high: $207,514; low: $5,000; average: $50,000-$150,000), $1,323,000 for 35 grants to individuals, $145,614 for 105 employee matching gifts and $100,000 for 1 loan.
Purpose and activities: Broad purposes; Health Care Financing Program: grants to improve the effectiveness of the health care system by stimulating the payment system and associated organizational reforms; Aging and Health Program: grants to address specific needs of the elderly, including improved diagnostic techniques and coordination of care for long-term, chronic health problems; Hartford Geriatric Faculty Development Awards Program: provides retraining of physicians who are planning academic careers in geriatrics; John A. and George L. Hartford Fellowship Program: grants to train and develop young physicians who wish to pursue careers in medical research.
Types of support awarded: Operating budgets, continuing support, employee matching gifts, program-related investments, fellowships, special projects, research, publications, conferences and seminars, loans.
Limitations: No grants to individuals (except for fellowships), or for annual campaigns, seed money, emergency, capital, or endowment funds, or deficit financing.

Publications: Annual report, newsletter.
Application information: Application form required.
Initial approach: Proposal in 3 to 4 pages (for Health Care and Aging and Health programs)
Copies of proposal: 2
Deadline(s): For Fellows Program, submit required application form by June
Board meeting date(s): April, July, September, and December; annual meeting for Fellows Program in September
Final notification: 6 weeks
Write: John Billings, Executive Director
Officers: Byron Jay,* Secretary and Treasurer; John Billings, Executive Director.
Trustees:* Leonard Dalsemer, Chairman; William Corbus, James D. Farley, Vice-Chairmen; Michael D. Dingman, Perry E. Gresham, Birny Mason, Jr., Charles Moeller, Jr., Robert H. Mulreany, Charles E. Murphy, Jr., Nuala Pell, Norman Volk, Matthew E. Welsh.
Number of staff: 6 full-time professional; 6 full-time support; 1 part-time support.
Employer Identification Number: 131667057

2529
Hasenfeld (A. & Z.) Foundation, Inc. ☐
580 Fifth Ave.
New York 10036

Established in 1969.
Donor(s): Alexander Hasenfeld, Zissy Hasenfeld.
Financial data: (yr. ended 3/31/83): Assets, $38,508 (M); gifts received, $201,000; expenditures, $232,731, including $232,646 for 205 grants (high: $40,721; low: $10).
Purpose and activities: Grants for Jewish welfare funds and temple support.
Officers and Trustees: Alexander Hasenfeld, President; Zissy Hasenfeld, Treasurer.
Employer Identification Number: 237017589

2530
Hastings (Merrill G. and Emita E.) Foundation ☐
c/o Conceptual Planning, Inc.
285 Madison Ave.
New York 10017   (212) 679-6001

Trust established in 1966 in New York.
Donor(s): Emita E. Hastings.†
Financial data: (yr. ended 2/28/83): Assets, $1,891,931 (M); expenditures, $131,629, including $90,260 for 21 grants (high: $39,000; low: $100).
Purpose and activities: Broad purposes; primarily local giving for cultural programs, including museums, and for education and conservation.
Limitations: Giving primarily in the New York, NY, area. No grants to individuals, or for endowment funds.
Publications: 990-PF.
Application information:
Initial approach: Letter
Copies of proposal: 1
Deadline(s): None
Board meeting date(s): As required

Write: Lee R. Robins, Accountant
Trustees: Elizabeth H. Peterfreund, Joshua Peterfreund.
Employer Identification Number: 136203465

2531
Hatch (Margaret Milliken) Charitable Trust ⌷

c/o Irving Trust Company
One Wall St.
New York 10015

Trust established in 1970 in New York.
Donor(s): Margaret Milliken Hatch.†
Financial data: (yr. ended 10/31/82): Assets, $3,622,516 (M); expenditures, $157,458, including $137,000 for 29 grants (high: $10,000; low: $1,000).
Purpose and activities: Giving primarily in New York and Connecticut, with emphasis on higher education, international welfare and understanding, and hospitals; support also for the aged, social agencies, and Protestant churches. Grants almost entirely limited to institutions originally favored by creators of the Trust.
Limitations: Giving primarily in NY and CT. No grants to individuals or for building funds.
Application information:
Initial approach: Letter
Copies of proposal: 1
Deadline(s): Submit proposal in January or June
Board meeting date(s): April and September
Write: H.R. Patch, Jr., Vice-President
Trustees: Mrs. Rakia I. Hatch, Richard L. Hatch, Irving Trust Company.
Employer Identification Number: 136330533

2532
Hausman Belding Foundation, Inc. ⌷

(formerly Belding Hausman Foundation, Inc.)
1430 Broadway
New York 10018

Established in 1953.
Donor(s): Belding Heminway Company, Inc.
Financial data: (yr. ended 12/31/82): Assets, $754 (M); gifts received, $253,833; expenditures, $256,860, including $256,860 for 119 grants (high: $50,000; low: $25).
Purpose and activities: Grants primarily for Jewish welfare funds; support also for hospitals, health agencies, and education.
Manager: C.L. Randazzo.
Employer Identification Number: 136119189

2533
Havens Relief Fund Society, The

105 East 22nd St., Suite 805
New York 10010   (212) 475-1991

Incorporated in 1870 in New York.
Donor(s): Charles G. Havens.†
Financial data: (yr. ended 12/31/83): Assets, $7,513,437 (M); expenditures, $473,881, including $323,644 for 2,436 grants (high: $3,900; low: $10).

Purpose and activities: A private operating foundation established for "the relief of poverty and distress, and especially the affording of temporary relief to unobtrusive suffering endured by industrious or worthy persons." Income distributed by almoners, appointed by the Society, who are responsible for distribution of their respective grants among individual beneficiaries of their own selection in greater New York City.
Limitations: Giving limited to New York, NY. No support for institutions.
Application information: Grant requests from individuals not accepted; individuals are not referred to almoners.
Board meeting date(s): February and November
Officers: Thomas Thacher, President; Arthur V. Savage, Vice-President; William S. Ellis, Secretary; Paul J. Brignola, Treasurer.
Employer Identification Number: 135562382

2534
Hayden (Charles) Foundation ▼

One Bankers Trust Plaza
130 Liberty St.
New York 10006   (212) 938-0790

Incorporated in 1937 in New York.
Donor(s): Charles Hayden.†
Financial data: (yr. ended 9/30/84): Assets, $97,349,352 (M); expenditures, $5,361,578, including $4,299,488 for 112 grants (high: $150,000; low: $3,363; average: $5,000-$100,000).
Purpose and activities: To assist young people; emphasis on helping to provide physical facilities and equipment for organizations primarily concerned with the mental, moral, and physical development of youth in the New York City and Boston metropolitan areas .
Types of support awarded: Building funds, equipment, land acquisition, matching funds.
Limitations: Giving limited to the New York, NY and Boston, MA metropolitan areas. No support for day care centers, labor groups, fraternal groups, religious organizations for other than community youth-related projects, or hospitals, hospices, and projects essentially medical in nature. No grants to individuals, or for endowment funds, operating budgets, general support, continuing support, transportation equipment, scholarships, fellowships, research, special projects, annual campaigns, seed money, emergency funds, deficit financing, program support, demonstration projects, publications, or conferences; no loans.
Publications: Annual report, program policy statement, application guidelines.
Application information:
Initial approach: Full proposal
Copies of proposal: 1
Deadline(s): None
Board meeting date(s): Monthly
Final notification: 4 to 6 weeks
Write: William T. Wachenfeld, President

Officers and Trustees: William T. Wachenfeld, President; David B. Stone, Vice-President; Howard F. Cerny, Secretary; John L. Kidde, Treasurer; Andrew Arditol.
Number of staff: 5 full-time professional; 2 part-time professional; 1 part-time support.
Employer Identification Number: 135562237

2535
Hazen (The Edward W.) Foundation, Inc.

16 East 34th St.
New York 10016   (212) 889-1616

Incorporated in 1925 in Connecticut.
Donor(s): Edward Warriner Hazen,† Helen Russell Hazen,† Lucy Abigail Hazen,† Mary Hazen Arnold.†
Financial data: (yr. ended 12/31/84): Assets, $7,021,575 (M); expenditures, $651,848, including $369,848 for 43 grants (high: $27,500; low: $50; average: $20,000).
Purpose and activities: Support focused on young people and their values, primarily in community agencies and educational programs at the secondary level that include action and/or research in: the quality of education of adolescents in general and of at-risk youngsters, especially from disadvantaged minorities; youth development through community institutions; and community service by young people and by adult volunteers who serve youth. Exploratory fields include improvement of writing, juvenile justice, and youth in the armed forces.
Types of support awarded: Seed money, matching funds, special projects.
Limitations: Giving limited to the U.S. No support for programs or projects in medicine or health sciences, engineering, law, or public and business administration. No grants to individuals, or for operating budgets, continuing support, annual campaigns, deficit financing, capital or endowment funds, scholarships, fellowships, publications, or conferences; no loans.
Publications: Application guidelines, biennial report, informational brochure.
Application information: Request guidelines for detailed program and support limitations. Application form required.
Initial approach: Letter
Copies of proposal: 2
Deadline(s): January 15 and July 15
Board meeting date(s): April and October
Final notification: 3 days
Write: Richard Magat, President
Officers and Trustees: A. Richard Turner, Chairman; Richard Magat, President; Manuel R. Guerrero, Vice-President; Vilma S. Martinez, Secretary; Harry Wugalter, Treasurer; Carol Anastasio, Adrienne Y. Bailey, Edward E. Booher, Mary Bundy, Richard Green, Edward M. Harris, Jr., Paul N. Ylvisaker.
Number of staff: 1 full-time professional; 1 full-time support; 1 part-time support.
Employer Identification Number: 060646671

2536
Hazen (Joseph H.) Foundation ⌷
645 Madison Ave.
New York 10022

Incorporated in 1957 in New York.
Donor(s): Joseph H. Hazen.
Financial data: (yr. ended 12/31/82): Assets,
$1,271,445 (M); gifts received, $75,000;
expenditures, $236,178, including $228,975
for 56 grants (high: $75,000; low: $25).
Purpose and activities: General purposes;
giving primarily for the support of organizations
in Israel and New York City, with emphasis on
Jewish welfare funds, cultural organizations,
and educational institutions; support also
for museums and hospitals.
Limitations: Giving primarily in New York, NY,
and Israel.
Officers and Directors: Joseph H. Hazen,
President; Cynthia H. Polsky, Vice-President;
Robert Anthoine, Secretary; Lita A. Hazen.
Employer Identification Number: 136161536

2537
Hearst Foundation, Inc., The ▼
888 Seventh Ave.
New York 10106   (212) 586-5404
*Mailing address for applications from west of
the Mississippi River:* c/o Charles L. Gould,
690 Market St., Suite 502, San Francisco, CA
94104

Incorporated in 1945 in New York.
Donor(s): William Randolph Hearst.†
Financial data: (yr. ended 12/31/83): Assets,
$73,260,917 (M); expenditures, $3,191,924,
including $2,474,700 for 274 grants (high:
$50,000; low: $2,500; average: $5,000-
$30,000).
Purpose and activities: Broad purposes; giving
for programs to aid poverty-level and minority
groups, educational programs at all levels,
health-delivery systems and medical research,
and cultural programs with records of public
support. Organizations serving larger
geographic areas generally favored over those
of a narrow community nature.
Types of support awarded: Operating
budgets, building funds, equipment,
endowment funds, research, scholarship funds,
fellowships, matching funds.
Limitations: Giving limited to the U.S. and its
territories. No support for political purposes.
No grants to individuals; no loans.
Publications: Program policy statement,
application guidelines.
Application information:
Initial approach: Letter or full proposal
Copies of proposal: 1
Deadline(s): January 15, April 15, July 15,
    and October 15
Board meeting date(s): March, June,
    September, and December
Final notification: 4 to 6 weeks
Write: Robert M. Frehse, Jr., Executive
    Director

Officers: Randolph A. Hearst,* President;
Robert M. Frehse, Jr., Vice-President and
Executive Director; Charles L. Gould, Vice-
President and Senior Executive; Harvey L.
Lipton,* Vice-President and Secretary; Frank A.
Bennack, Jr.,* George Hearst, Jr.,* William R.
Hearst, Jr.,* Frank Massi,* Vice-Presidents;
Ralph J. Cuomo, Treasurer.
Directors:* Richard E. Deems, David W.
Hearst, John R. Hearst, Jr., J. Kingsbury-Smith,
Gilbert C. Maurer, Raymond J. Petersen,
Franklin C. Snyder.
Number of staff: 6 full-time professional; 3 full-
time support; 3 part-time support.
Employer Identification Number: 136161746

2538
Hearst (William Randolph)
Foundation ▼
888 Seventh Ave.
New York 10106   (212) 586-5404
*Mailing address for applications from west of
the Mississippi River:* c/o Charles L. Gould,
690 Market St., Suite 502, San Francisco, CA
94104

Incorporated in 1949 in California.
Donor(s): William Randolph Hearst.†
Financial data: (yr. ended 12/31/84): Assets,
$162,642,764 (M); expenditures, $8,989,072,
including $6,165,500 for 271 grants (high:
$200,000; low: $2,500; average: $5,000-
$50,000) and $691,584 for 2 foundation-
administered programs.
Purpose and activities: Broad purposes;
programs to aid poverty-level and minority
groups, educational programs at all levels,
health delivery systems and medical research,
and cultural programs with records of public
support; support also through an operating
program for journalism scholarships.
Organizations serving larger geographic areas
generally favored over those of a narrow
community nature.
Types of support awarded: Building funds,
equipment, endowment funds, operating
budgets, research, scholarship funds,
fellowships, matching funds, general purposes.
Limitations: Giving limited to the U.S. and its
territories. No grants to individuals; generally
no grants for start-up funds; no loans.
Publications: Program policy statement,
application guidelines.
Application information:
Initial approach: Letter or full proposal
Copies of proposal: 1
Deadline(s): January 15, April 15, July 15,
    and October 15
Board meeting date(s): March, June,
    September, and December
Final notification: 4 to 6 weeks
Write: Robert M. Frehse, Jr., Executive
    Director

Officers and Directors:* David W. Hearst,*
President; Robert M. Frehse, Jr., Vice-President
and Executive Director; Charles L. Gould, Vice-
President and Senior Executive; Harvey L.
Lipton,* Vice-President and Secretary; Frank A.
Bennack, Jr.,* Richard E. Deems,* George R.
Hearst, Jr.,* Randolph A. Hearst,* William R.
Hearst, Jr.,* J. Kingsbury-Smith,* Frank Massi,*
Gilbert C. Maurer,* Raymond J. Petersen,*
Franklin C. Snyder,* Vice-Presidents; Ralph J.
Cuomo, Treasurer.
Number of staff: 6 full-time professional; 3 full-
time support; 3 part-time support.
Employer Identification Number: 136019226

2539
Hebrew Technical Institute ⌷
235 Park Ave. South
New York 10003

Established in 1884.
Financial data: (yr. ended 12/31/82): Assets,
$1,250,147 (M); gifts received, $22,560;
expenditures, $86,463, including $73,103 for 5
grants (high: $35,830; low: $4,400).
Purpose and activities: Giving primarily in
New York to organizations in the field of
vocational education; support also for an
educational institution in Israel.
Limitations: Giving primarily in NY.
Officer: Myron S. Gallef, Treasurer.
Employer Identification Number: 135562240

2540
Heckscher Foundation for Children,
The ▼
17 East 47th St.
New York 10017   (212) 371-7775

Incorporated in 1921 in New York.
Donor(s): August Heckscher.†
Financial data: (yr. ended 12/31/84): Assets,
$21,929,781 (M); expenditures, $1,004,226,
including $914,092 for 122 grants (high:
$150,000; low: $45; average: $500-$25,000).
Purpose and activities: To promote the
welfare of children; grants particularly for child
welfare and family service agencies, education,
recreation, music, hospitals, summer youth
programs and camps, and aid to the
handicapped.
Types of support awarded: Seed money,
emergency funds, building funds, equipment,
land acquisition.
Limitations: Giving limited to the greater New
York, NY, area. No grants to individuals, or for
operating budgets, continuing support, annual
campaigns, deficit financing, scholarships and
fellowships, special projects, research,
publications, or endowment funds; no loans.
Publications: Application guidelines.
Application information: Application form
required.
Initial approach: Letter or full proposal
Copies of proposal: 1
Deadline(s): Submit proposal preferably at
    beginning of year
Board meeting date(s): Monthly except July
    and August
Final notification: 1 month
Write: Virginia Sloane, President

Officers and Trustees: Ruth Smadbeck, Chairman; Virginia Sloane, President; Howard G. Sloane, Vice-President and Treasurer; Louis Smadbeck, Vice-President; William D. Hart, Jr., Secretary; Mrs. J. Clarence Davies, Jr., Richard N. Kerst, John D. MacNeary, John M. O'Mara, Gail Meyers, Howard Grant Sloane, Arthur J. Smadbeck, Mrs. Louis Smadbeck, Paul Smadbeck, Florence Wallach.
Number of staff: 1 full-time professional; 1 part-time professional; 1 part-time support.
Employer Identification Number: 131820170

2541
Heineman Foundation for Research, Educational, Charitable and Scientific Purposes, Inc.
475 Park Ave.
New York 10022   (212) 688-2028

Incorporated in 1947 in Delaware.
Donor(s): Dannie N. Heineman.†
Financial data: (yr. ended 12/31/83): Assets, $4,417,220 (M); expenditures, $320,452, including $268,859 for 19 grants (high: $80,000; low: $5,000).
Purpose and activities: General purposes; support for research programs in mathematical sciences and medicine; grants for higher education, Jewish welfare funds, specialized libraries (including the Heineman Library of Rare Books and Manuscripts given to The Pierpont Morgan Library, New York), music schools and two annual physics awards.
Application information:
 Initial approach: Letter
 Deadline(s): June 30
 Board meeting date(s): September-October
 Write: James H. Heineman, President
Officers and Directors: James H. Heineman, President; Marian Rose, Vice-President; Agnes Gautier, Secretary; Sibylle Evelt, Robert O. Fehr, Treasurer; Hans Tauber, M.D.
Employer Identification Number: 136082899

2542
Heller (Dr. Bernard) Foundation ¤
c/o Herman Mark Harris
239 E. 79th St.
New York 10021

Established in 1977.
Donor(s): Bernard Heller.†
Financial data: (yr. ended 3/31/83): Assets, $6,746,412 (M); gifts received, $6,318,787; expenditures, $380,686, including $339,200 for 4 grants (high: $113,550; low: $63,550).
Purpose and activities: Grants to local Jewish theological and educational institutions.
Limitations: Giving primarily in New York, NY.
Publications: 990-PF.
Trustees-Managers: Herman Mark Harris, Arthur H. Shaffer.
Employer Identification Number: 132887370

2543
Helmsley (The Harry B.) Foundation, Inc. ¤
60 East 42nd St.
New York 10165

Incorporated in 1954 in New York.
Donor(s): Harry B. Helmsley.
Financial data: (yr. ended 5/31/83): Assets, $4,954,114 (M); gifts received, $3,123,874; expenditures, $260,059, including $256,358 for 49 grants (high: $32,000; low: $25).
Purpose and activities: General purposes; grants largely for higher education, hospitals, medical research, and religious organizations.
Officers and Directors: Harry B. Helmsley, President; Leona M. Helmsley, Vice-President and Treasurer.
Employer Identification Number: 136123336

2544
HEM Charitable Trust, The
c/o Pannell Kerr Forster
420 Lexington Ave.
New York 10170

Trust established in 1962 in New York.
Financial data: (yr. ended 12/31/83): Assets, $2,722,901 (M); expenditures, $556,071, including $369,200 for 7 grants (high: $184,000; low: $2,000).
Purpose and activities: Giving with emphasis on higher education and performing arts; grants usually limited to previous recipients.
Publications: 990-PF.
Application information:
 Board meeting date(s): As required
Trustee: George E. Lien.
Employer Identification Number: 116010743

2545
Hendrickson Bros. Foundation, Inc. ¤
63 North Central Ave.
Valley Stream 11582

Incorporated in 1955 in New York.
Donor(s): Hendrickson Bros., Inc., Rason Asphalt, Inc.
Financial data: (yr. ended 12/31/81): Assets, $2,084,139 (M); gifts received, $10,000; expenditures, $90,077, including $89,137 for 55 grants (high: $38,385; low: $25).
Purpose and activities: Primarily local giving with emphasis on youth agencies; grants also for health agencies, higher education, and hospitals.
Limitations: Giving primarily in NY.
Application information:
 Write: Milton A. Hendrickson, President
Officers and Directors: Milton A. Hendrickson, President; John C. Hendrickson, Secretary; Arthur J. Hendrickson, Treasurer.
Employer Identification Number: 116006297

2546
Hess Foundation, Inc. ▼ ¤
1185 Ave. of the Americas
New York 10036   (212) 997-8500

Incorporated in 1954 in Delaware.
Donor(s): Leon Hess.
Financial data: (yr. ended 11/30/82): Assets, $66,422,290 (M); expenditures, $3,854,151, including $3,795,985 for 56 grants (high: $2,420,000; low: $500).
Purpose and activities: General giving, with emphasis on a disaster relief fund and higher education; grants also for hospitals, temple support, youth and child welfare agencies, and the performing arts.
Officers and Directors: Leon Hess, President; John B. Hess, Vice-President; H.W. McCollum, Vice-President and Secretary; Norma Hess, Vice President and Treasurer.
Employer Identification Number: 221713046

2547
Hettinger Foundation
P.O. Box 3106
New York 10185

Trust established in 1961 in New York.
Donor(s): Albert J. Hettinger, Jr.†
Financial data: (yr. ended 12/31/82): Assets, $3,405,142 (M); gifts received, $200,000; expenditures, $79,787, including $71,081 for 4 grants (high: $55,081; low: $750).
Purpose and activities: Broad purposes; grants largely for higher and secondary education at certain schools with which there is a long-standing relationship, including scholarship funds; some support for welfare agencies.
Types of support awarded: General purposes, scholarship funds.
Limitations: No grants to individuals.
Trustees: Albert J. Hettinger III, William R. Hettinger.
Employer Identification Number: 136097726

2548
Hickrill Foundation, Inc.
215 East 62nd St.
New York 10021

Incorporated in 1946 in New York.
Donor(s): The Norman Foundation, Frank A. Weil.
Financial data: (yr. ended 12/31/82): Assets, $1,207,733 (M); gifts received, $1,190; expenditures, $82,271, including $65,594 for 78 grants (high: $15,000; low: $25).
Purpose and activities: Broad purposes; grants primarily for higher education, with emphasis on a school for government studies.
Officers: Frank A. Weil, President; Denie S. Weil, Vice-President; Deborah W. Harrington, Secretary.
Employer Identification Number: 136002949

2549
Hidary (Jacob) Foundation, Inc. ⌘
10 West 33rd St.
New York 10001

Donor(s): M. Hidary Company, Inc., and members of the Hidary family.
Financial data: (yr. ended 12/31/84): Assets, $425,486 (M); gifts received, $286,488; expenditures, $189,221, including $188,407 for 456 grants (high: $5,000; low: $18).
Purpose and activities: Grants primarily for Jewish welfare and educational funds and temple support.
Officers: Moses Hidary, Vice-President; Isaac Hidary, Secretary; Abraham Hidary, Treasurer.
Employer Identification Number: 136125420

2550
High Winds Fund, Inc. ▼
200 Park Ave., 34th Fl.
New York 10166   (212) 907-6900

Incorporated in 1966 in New York.
Donor(s): Lila Acheson Wallace.
Financial data: (yr. ended 12/31/82): Assets, $6,634,350 (M); gifts received, $1,508,994; expenditures, $17,960,697, including $17,909,307 for 14 grants (high: $14,872,500; low: $8,500; average: $8,000-$50,000).
Purpose and activities: Giving primarily in the Northeast, with emphasis on the New York metropolitan area; grants to preserve and maintain places of beauty including buildings of historical interest, art museums, and sanctuaries; direct program support for performing arts and general support for conservation activities.
Types of support awarded: Operating budgets.
Limitations: Giving primarily in the Northeast, with emphasis on the New York, NY metropolitan area. No support for private foundations or corporations. No grants to individuals or for capital projects.
Application information: Funds fully committed.
  Board meeting date(s): Semiannually
  Write: Barnabas McHenry, Secretary
Officers and Directors: Lila Acheson Wallace, President and Treasurer; Barnabas McHenry, Secretary; John A. O'Hara, Laurance S. Rockefeller, Frank Stinchfield.
Number of staff: None.
Employer Identification Number: 136203421

2551
Hillman (The Alex) Family Foundation
630 Fifth Ave.
New York 10111   (212) 265-3115

Incorporated in 1966 in New York.
Donor(s): Alex L. Hillman,† Mrs. Rita K. Hillman.
Financial data: (yr. ended 12/31/84): Assets, $3,250,692 (M); gifts received, $46,550; expenditures, $88,599, including $78,740 for 30 grants (high: $25,675; low: $50).
Purpose and activities: Educational purposes, including encouragement of the arts; primarily local grants for higher education, art museums, and music.

Limitations: Giving primarily in NY. No grants to individuals or for continuing support.
Publications: Annual report.
Application information:
  Initial approach: Letter
  Copies of proposal: 1
  Deadline(s): None
  Board meeting date(s): Semiannually
  Final notification: 2 months
  Write: Mrs. Rita K. Hillman, President
Officers and Directors: Rita K. Hillman, President; William M. Griffin, Vice-President.
Number of staff: None.
Employer Identification Number: 132560546

2552
Hirschl (Irma T.) Trust for Charitable Purposes ▼
c/o Manufacturers Hanover Trust Company
600 Fifth Ave.
New York 10020   (212) 957-1664

Trust established in 1973 in New York.
Donor(s): Irma T. Hirschl.†
Financial data: (yr. ended 10/31/83): Assets, $24,290,593 (M); expenditures, $2,050,943, including $1,816,000 for 88 grants (high: $95,000; low: $1,000; average: $15,000-$50,000).
Purpose and activities: Grants primarily to eight medical schools in New York City for partial funding of selected medical research projects; annual medical scholarships to four designated medical schools in New York City; support also for 14 designated social, welfare, and health agencies in New York City.
Types of support awarded: Research, scholarship funds.
Limitations: Giving primarily in New York City, NY. No support for private foundations. No grants to individuals.
Application information: All applications submitted by designated medical schools.
  Deadline(s): None
  Board meeting date(s): Around December 1
  Final notification: Promptly after board meeting
  Write: Michael J.A. Smith
Trustees: Arthur M. Kriedmann, John M. Lewis, Manufacturers Hanover Trust Company.
Employer Identification Number: 136356381

2553
Hochschild Fund, Inc. ▼
c/o Yohalem, Gillman, Field & Agler
655 Third Ave.
New York 10017

Incorporated in 1948 in New York.
Donor(s): Members of the Hochschild family.
Financial data: (yr. ended 12/31/83): Assets, $4,295,223 (M); gifts received, $158,375; expenditures, $343,550, including $329,099 for 149 grants (high: $125,000; low: $18; average: $100-$4,000).
Purpose and activities: Charitable purposes; primarily local giving, with emphasis on higher and secondary education, international exchange programs, museums, social agencies, hospitals, music, cultural activities, health and youth agencies, and aid for the handicapped.

Types of support awarded: General purposes, building funds, matching funds, exchange programs.
Limitations: Giving primarily in New York, NY, and northeastern NY. No grants to individuals, or for endowment funds, scholarships or fellowships, or research; no loans.
Application information:
  Initial approach: Full proposal
  Copies of proposal: 1
  Deadline(s): Submit proposal preferably in May or October; deadlines June 1 and November 1
  Board meeting date(s): June and November
  Final notification: 1 month after board meeting
  Write: Alan D. Spiegel
Officers and Directors: Adam Hochschild, President; Kathrin S. Hochschild, Kira Sergievsky, Vice-Presidents; Joseph Mische, Secretary and Treasurer; Lynn H. Boillot, Arlie R. Hochschild, George Labalme, Jr.
Number of staff: None.
Employer Identification Number: 136091737

2554
Hochschild (Harold K.) Foundation ▼
(also known as H.K.H. Foundation)
c/o Yohalem, Gillman, Field & Agler
655 Third Ave.
New York 10017

Foundation established in 1980 in New York.
Donor(s): Harold K. Hochschild.†
Financial data: (yr. ended 12/31/83): Assets, $24,275,115 (M); expenditures, $1,585,973, including $1,394,000 for 35 grants (high: $600,000; low: $1,500).
Purpose and activities: Support primarily for Adirondack Historical Association; additional support as determined by the trustees.
Limitations: Giving primarily in NY.
Application information:
  Write: Alan D. Spiegel
Trustees: Jane Carroll, Adam Hochschild, Joseph Mische, Frederick A. Terry, Jr., Robert R. Worth.
Employer Identification Number: 136784950

2555
Hochstein Foundation, Inc. ⌘
6 E. 45th St.
New York 10017

Established in 1960.
Financial data: (yr. ended 12/31/82): Assets, $19,357 (M); gifts received, $133,975; expenditures, $141,170, including $138,405 for 23 grants (high: $25,625; low: $100).
Purpose and activities: Giving for Jewish educational organizations, including theological education, religious congregations, and welfare.
Types of support awarded: Operating budgets, general purposes.
Officer: Bernard Hochstein, President.
Employer Identification Number: 136161765

2556
Hoernle (A. W.) Foundation
630 Central Park Ave.
Yonkers 10704

Established in 1978 in New York.
Donor(s): Adolph W. Hoernle.
Financial data: (yr. ended 5/31/84): Assets,
$4,400,000 (M); gifts received, $40,000;
expenditures, $175,000, including $175,000
for 10 grants (high: $50,000; low: $500).
Purpose and activities: Local giving primarily
for hospitals and health, cultural programs,
education, and social agencies.
Limitations: Giving limited to NY and FL. No
grants to individuals.
Application information:
  Board meeting date(s): Annually
Officers: Adolph W. Hoernle, President; Fred
W. Lessing, Secretary-Treasurer.
Number of staff: None.
Employer Identification Number: 132945331

2557
Holmes Foundation, Inc. ⌺
100 Park Ave.
New York 10017   (212) 889-8480

Incorporated in 1935 in New York.
Donor(s): Carl Holmes,† Mrs. Christian R.
Holmes,† Jay Holmes.†
Financial data: (yr. ended 12/31/81): Assets,
$1,320,329 (M); expenditures, $94,668,
including $69,500 for 48 grants (high: $10,000;
low: $100).
Purpose and activities: Broad purposes;
support for music, education, a museum,
hospitals, and youth agencies, primarily in New
York, California, and Florida.
Limitations: Giving primarily in NY, CA, and
FL.
Application information:
  Initial approach: Letter or proposal
  Copies of proposal: 1
  Board meeting date(s): Annually, or as
    necessary
Officers and Directors: Carl Holmes,
Vice-President; Henry Hyde, Treasurer.
Employer Identification Number: 131946867

2558
Holtzmann (Jacob L. and Lillian)
  Foundation ⌺
c/o Holtzmann, Wise & Shepard
745 Fifth Ave.
New York 10022

Trust established in 1958 in New York.
Donor(s): Jacob L. Holtzmann,† Lillian
Holtzmann,† Howard M. Holtzmann.
Financial data: (yr. ended 12/31/81): Assets,
$1,796,525 (M); gifts received, $55,090;
expenditures, $66,555, including $55,525 for
22 grants (high: $30,000; low: $100).
Purpose and activities: Grants largely for local
Jewish welfare funds and higher education,
including a theological seminary.
Limitations: Giving primarily in NY.
Trustees: Howard M. Holtzmann, Benjamin C.
O'Sullivan, Susan H. Richardson.
Employer Identification Number: 136174349

2559
Homan (B. H.), Jr. Trust ⌺
c/o Morgan Guaranty Trust Company of New
York
Nine West 57th St.
New York 10019

Trust established in 1978 in New York.
Donor(s): Benjamin Homan, Jr.†
Financial data: (yr. ended 5/31/83): Assets,
$6,882,127 (M); expenditures, $409,196,
including $360,000 for 6 grants of $60,000
each.
Purpose and activities: Broad purposes;
primarily local giving for higher education,
including medical education.
Limitations: Giving primarily in NY.
Trustees: Leon Shaefler, Morgan Guaranty
Trust Company of New York.
Employer Identification Number: 136741112

2560
Homeland Foundation, Inc. ⌺
c/o Kelley, Drye & Warren
101 Park Ave.
New York 10178   (212) 808-7800

Incorporated in 1938 in New York.
Donor(s): Chauncey Stillman, and others.
Financial data: (yr. ended 4/30/83): Assets,
$442 (M); gifts received, $172,546;
expenditures, $170,316, including $165,546
for 29 grants (high: $20,000; low: $500).
Purpose and activities: Broad purposes; giving
predominantly for Roman Catholic church
support, and to Catholic welfare organizations
in the United States and abroad, and Catholic
educational institutions.
Types of support awarded: General purposes,
building funds, operating budgets, lectureships,
scholarship funds.
Application information:
  Initial approach: Letter
Trustees: Chauncey Stillman, Chairman;
Theodora Stillman Budnick, Msgr. Eugene V.
Clark, John J. Costello, Louis B. Warren.
Employer Identification Number: 136113816

2561
Hopkins (Josephine Lawrence)
  Foundation ⌺
61 Broadway, Rm. 2912
New York 10006

Incorporated in 1968 in New York.
Donor(s): Josephine H. Graeber.†
Financial data: (yr. ended 12/31/82): Assets,
$2,887,883 (M); expenditures, $266,276,
including $219,500 for 29 grants (high:
$52,500; low: $500).
Purpose and activities: Broad purposes;
primarily local giving, with emphasis on
hospitals and medical research, Roman
Catholic church support, animal welfare, youth
agencies, and cultural programs including the
performing arts.
Limitations: Giving primarily in NY. No grants
to individuals; no loans.

Officers and Directors: Ivan Obolensky,
President and Treasurer; Lawrence X. Cusack,
Vice-President and Secretary; Vera Colage,
Meredith N. Stiles, Jr., Susan H. Whitmore,
Vice-Presidents.
Employer Identification Number: 136277593

2562
Houghton Foundation, Inc., The
Two East Market St.
Corning 14830   (607) 962-6876

Incorporated in 1955 in New York.
Donor(s): Arthur A. Houghton, Jr., Amory
Houghton.†
Financial data: (yr. ended 11/30/82): Assets,
$1,472,246 (M); gifts received, $29,031;
expenditures, $217,755, including $203,600
for 15 grants (high: $125,000; low: $1,000).
Purpose and activities: Broad purposes;
primarily local giving, including support for a
community foundation, education, and
Protestant churches.
Limitations: Giving primarily in NY.
Officers: Amory Houghton, Jr.,* President;
Alanson B. Houghton, II,* James R. Houghton,*
Vice-Presidents; Thomas Waaland, Treasurer.
Trustees:* Arthur A. Houghton, Jr., Chairman;
Laura R. Houghton, Rowland Stebbins, III.
Employer Identification Number: 166028719

2563
House of St. Giles the Cripple, The ⌺
One Hanson Place
Brooklyn 11217

Donor(s): Louis W. Arnold,† Marvin Leavens,†
Jesse Ridley,† and others.
Financial data: (yr. ended 3/31/82): Assets,
$6,194,924 (M); gifts received, $115,380;
expenditures, $577,336, including $486,000
for 7 grants (high: $225,000; low: $12,000).
Purpose and activities: Grants for hospitals
and organizations to help the handicapped.
Types of support awarded: Equipment,
research, general purposes.
Officers: Richard T. Arkwright, President; John
H. Livingston, Vice-President; George W. Clark,
Secretary; Samuel H. Owens, Treasurer.
Employer Identification Number: 111630806

2564
Howard (Cecil) Charitable Trust
111 Broadway, Suite 512
New York 10006   (212) 732-7075

Trust established in 1968 in New York.
Donor(s): Cecil A. Howard.†
Financial data: (yr. ended 6/30/82): Assets,
$1,196,880 (M); gifts received, $40,000;
expenditures, $186,688, including $111,950
for 55 grants (high: $10,000; low: $100).
Purpose and activities: Grants primarily for
historic preservation, largely in New York and
Vermont.
Types of support awarded: General purposes,
seed money, special projects, conferences and
seminars, matching funds, program-related
investments.

Limitations: Giving primarily in NY and VT. No grants to individuals, or for capital or endowment funds, scholarships, or fellowships; no loans.
Publications: 990-PF, application guidelines.
Application information:
   Initial approach: Letter
   Copies of proposal: 1
   Deadline(s): April 1 and November 1
   Board meeting date(s): May and December
   Write: George B. Cameron, Trustee
Trustees: George B. Cameron, Robert A. Sincerbeaux.
Number of staff: 4.
Employer Identification Number: 136266200

2565
Hoyt (Stewart W. & Willma C.) Foundation
1000 Security Mutual Bldg.
80 Exchange St.
Binghamton 13901   (607) 722-6706

Established in 1970 in New York.
Donor(s): Willma C. Hoyt.†
Financial data: (yr. ended 12/31/84): Assets, $8,495,640 (M); gifts received, $7,700,208; expenditures, $488,616, including $461,260 for 41 grants (high: $100,000; low: $1,400; average: $1,500-$30,000).
Purpose and activities: Broad purposes; local giving for the arts and humanities, education, health, and social and human services, with preference for capital campaigns, special projects, seed money, and operating expenses.
Types of support awarded: General purposes, building funds, matching funds, seed money, special projects, operating budgets, continuing support, emergency funds, equipment, technical assistance, consulting services, scholarship funds, conferences and seminars.
Limitations: Giving limited to Broome County, NY. No support for religious purposes. No grants to individuals, or for annual campaigns, deficit financing, land acquisition, general endowments, employee matching gifts, research, or publications; no loans.
Publications: Annual report, informational brochure, program policy statement, application guidelines.
Application information: No grants considered at January meeting.
   Initial approach: Telephone or letter
   Copies of proposal: 1
   Deadline(s): The 1st of months prior to board meetings
   Board meeting date(s): Bimonthly, beginning in January
   Final notification: 1 to 3 days following board meetings
   Write: Judith C. Peckham, Executive Director
Officers and Directors: William S. Chittenden, Chairman; Shirley W. Keller, Vice-Chairman; William Rincker, Secretary-Treasurer; John M. Keeler, Stuart McCarty, Jane M. Park, John F. Russell.
Trustee: Chase Lincoln First Bank.
Number of staff: 1 part-time professional.
Employer Identification Number: 237072539

2566
Hughes (The Charles Evans) Memorial Foundation, Inc.
40 Wall St.
New York 10005

Incorporated in 1962 in New York.
Donor(s): Mrs. Chauncey L. Waddell,† Chauncey L. Waddell.†
Financial data: (yr. ended 7/31/83): Assets, $3,711,224 (M); expenditures, $278,730, including $225,800 for 18 grants (high: $75,000; low: $300).
Purpose and activities: Support for education, legal aid, and organizations combatting prejudice based on race, color, or religious belief.
Application information:
   Write: Mitchel J. Valicenti, President
Officers and Directors:* Mitchel J. Valicenti,* President and Treasurer; William T. Gossett,* Vice-President; Helen Brownlee, Secretary; Mrs. William H. Johnson, Betty J. Stebman, Theodore H. Waddell.
Number of staff: 1 part-time support.
Employer Identification Number: 136159445

2567
Hunter (Graham) Foundation ⌑
c/o Thomas G. Burke & Company
230 Park Ave.
New York 10169

Established in 1946 in New York.
Donor(s): Graham Hunter.†
Financial data: (yr. ended 12/31/82): Assets, $1,059,895 (M); gifts received, $17,130; expenditures, $77,249, including $50,697 for 19 grants (high: $25,097; low: $100).
Purpose and activities: Grants primarily for higher education, including medical education; support also for cultural programs.
Officer and Trustees: Herbert C. Smyth, Thomas G. Burke, Carol J.G. Kelley, Nellie S. Kinneyman.
Employer Identification Number: 136161726

2568
Hutchins (Mary J.) Foundation, Inc. ⌑
110 William St.
New York 10038   (212) 233-5559

Incorporated in 1935 in New York.
Donor(s): Mary J. Hutchins,† Caspar J. Voorhis.†
Financial data: (yr. ended 12/31/82): Assets, $13,396,120 (M); gifts received, $1,527,816; expenditures, $542,761, including $450,000 for 48 grants (high: $50,000; low: $750) and $35,830 for 15 grants to individuals.
Purpose and activities: To assist the poor and needy; grants also largely to hospitals, community funds, and religious welfare funds, primarily in the New York area.
Types of support awarded: Grants to individuals.
Limitations: Giving primarily in the New York, NY, area. No support for educational purposes or national health funds. No grants for seed money, scholarships, or annual campaigns.
Application information:

Initial approach: Proposal
   Write: John F. Hirsch, 3rd, Senior Vice-President
Officers: Waldo Hutchins, Jr.,* President; John F. Hirsch, 3rd,* Senior Vice-President; Richard J. Mirabella,* Vice-President and Treasurer; Robert A. Frommel,* Waldo Hutchins, III,* Vice-Presidents; Julia L. Zeller, Secretary.
Directors:* Henry C. Johnston.
Employer Identification Number: 136083578

2569
Hutton (Edward F.) Foundation
One Battery Park Plaza
New York 10004   (212) 742-5806

Incorporated in 1960 in Delaware.
Donor(s): E.F. Hutton and Company, Inc.
Financial data: (yr. ended 12/31/82): Assets, $316,532 (M); expenditures, $453,390, including $441,608 for 370 grants (high: $262,000; low: $10).
Purpose and activities: General purposes; grants largely for higher education and community funds; some support for youth agencies, health agencies, and hospitals.
Limitations: No grants to individuals, or for building or endowment funds, research programs, scholarships, fellowships, or matching gifts; no loans.
Application information:
   Board meeting date(s): As required
Officers and Trustees: Robert Fomon, Chairman and President; Thomas P. Lynch, Vice-President, Secretary, and Treasurer; Thomas W. Rae, Vice-President; Gerald Daffner.
Employer Identification Number: 136091161

2570
Hycliff Foundation, Inc., The
122 East 42nd St., Suite 922
New York 10168   (212) 661-4080

Incorporated in 1977 in Delaware as partial successor to The Bernhard Foundation, Inc.
Donor(s): The Bernhard Foundation, Inc.
Financial data: (yr. ended 2/28/84): Assets, $900,719 (M); expenditures, $137,684, including $114,500 for 18 grants (high: $7,500; low: $3,500; average: $5,000).
Purpose and activities: General giving, with emphasis on small experimental projects in New York City, including civil rights and civil liberties. Report on foundation included in annual report of Joint Foundation Support which administers the foundation.
Types of support awarded: Operating budgets, continuing support, seed money.
Limitations: Giving primarily in New York, NY. No grants to individuals, or for building or endowment funds, scholarships and fellowships, or matching gifts; no loans.
Publications: Annual report.
Application information:
   Initial approach: Full proposal
   Copies of proposal: 1
   Deadline(s): None
   Board meeting date(s): Spring, fall, and winter
   Final notification: Up to 6 months
   Write: Patricia Hewitt, Executive Director

Officers and Directors: Robert A. Bernhard, President; Michael R. Bernhard, Vice-President and Treasurer; Joan M. Bernhard, Vice-President; Adele Bernhard, Secretary; Steven G. Bernhard, Susan Bernhard Collins.
Number of staff: 3 part-time professional; 3 full-time support.
Employer Identification Number: 132893039

2571
IFF Foundation, Inc., The ⊠
521 West 57th St.
New York 10019

Incorporated in 1963 in New York.
Donor(s): International Flavors & Fragrances, Inc.
Financial data: (yr. ended 12/31/82): Assets, $104,790 (M); gifts received, $150,000; expenditures, $284,116, including $265,272 for 87 grants (high: $35,000; low: $50) and $17,737 for employee matching gifts.
Purpose and activities: Broad purposes; grants primarily for higher education, including medical education and matching gifts; support also for research in chemistry and international affairs, and for mental health and a community fund.
Types of support awarded: Research, employee matching gifts.
Officers: H.G. Walter, Jr., President; S.J. Spitz, Jr., Vice-President; E.P. Grisanti, Secretary; J.P. Winandy, Treasurer.
Employer Identification Number: 136159094

2572
Indian Head Foundation ⊠
1211 Ave. of the Americas
New York 10036

Incorporated in 1972 in New York.
Donor(s): Indian Head Inc.
Financial data: (yr. ended 12/31/81): Assets, $23,732 (M); gifts received, $180,000; expenditures, $171,773, including $171,243 for 106 grants (high: $20,000; low: $100).
Purpose and activities: Broad purposes; giving primarily for community funds, education, youth agencies, hospitals, and cultural activities.
Officers and Directors:* Ralph E. Pounds,* President; Charles H. Chatfield, Jr., Vice-President and Treasurer; Richard J. Cutler, John E. Haegele,* Lawrence A. Johnes,* Robert B. Levine, Vice-Presidents; Weaver H. Gaines, Jr., Secretary.
Employer Identification Number: 132732880

2573
Initial Teaching Alphabet Foundation, Inc.
32 Thornwood Ln.
Roslyn Heights 11577   (516) 621-6772

Incorporated in 1965 in New York.
Donor(s): Eugene Kelly.†
Financial data: (yr. ended 12/31/84): Assets, $7,267,762 (M); expenditures, $471,512, including $181,123 for 18 grants (high: $32,011; low: $506) and $225,385 for foundation-administered programs.

Purpose and activities: Educational and charitable purposes; to promote, maintain, and advance education, in all its fields, and in particular, but without limiting the generality of the foregoing, by the development, standardization, propagation, dissemination, teaching, and use of the Initial Teaching Alphabet, with the aim of improving reading and writing skills. Grants presently limited to support of projects and programs in support of the Initial Teaching Alphabet.
Types of support awarded: Special projects, research, publications, consulting services, technical assistance.
Limitations: No grants to individuals, or for building or endowment funds, general support, scholarships, fellowships, or matching gifts; no loans.
Publications: 990-PF, informational brochure, program policy statement.
Application information:
 Initial approach: Letter or telephone
 Copies of proposal: 3
 Deadline(s): Submit proposal preferably in March or April; deadline April 15
 Board meeting date(s): May
 Final notification: 1 month
 Write: Betty E. Thompson, Executive Director
Officers and Directors: Frank G. Jennings, President; Gerald L. Knieter, Vice-President; Maurice S. Spanbock, Secretary-Treasurer; Betty E. Thompson, Executive Director; Max Bogart, Rebecca W. Stewart.
Number of staff: 1 full-time professional; 1 part-time professional.
Employer Identification Number: 112074243

2574
International Paper Company Foundation ▼
International Paper Company Plaza
77 West 45th St.
New York 10036   (212) 536-6580
Address for grant applications from company communities: c/o local company mill or plant manager

Incorporated in 1952 in New York.
Donor(s): International Paper Company.
Financial data: (yr. ended 12/31/83): Assets, $16,039,913 (M); gifts received, $161,921; expenditures, $2,267,160, including $1,786,281 for 160 grants (high: $400,000; low: $500; average: $3,000-$20,000) and $231,833 for employee matching gifts.
Purpose and activities: Broad purposes; grants primarily for model projects in Company communities and selected programs with potental national impact, with focus on pre-college levels of economic and career education, programs for minorities and women in engineering, health and welfare, and community and cultural affairs. Operates own program EDCORE (Education and Community Resource Program) in selected International Paper communities for public schools.
Types of support awarded: Seed money, special projects, annual campaigns, research, publications, conferences and seminars, scholarship funds, matching funds, employee matching gifts, continuing support.

Limitations: Giving primarily in communities where there are company plants and mills; no grants outside the U.S. No support for athletic organizations or religious groups. No grants to individuals, or for endowment funds, capital expenses (except in company communities), or general operating expenses of health and welfare agencies or higher educational institutions; no loans.
Publications: Program policy statement, annual report, application guidelines.
Application information: Address requests from organizations in company communities to the local company mill or plant manager; no applications accepted for EDCORE (Education and Community Resource Program) or for fellowships.
 Initial approach: Letter, telephone, or full proposal
 Copies of proposal: 1
 Deadline(s): Previous summer for next calender year
 Board meeting date(s): Spring, fall, and as required
 Final notification: 6 to 8 weeks
 Write: Gladys F. Waltemade, Vice-President
Officers: Arthur Wallace, President; Gladys F. Waltemade, Vice-President; Brent Bullock, Secretary; Rosalie J. Wolf, Treasurer.
Directors: Herbert Elish, Edwin A. Gee, John A. Georges.
Trustee: State Street Bank and Trust Company.
Number of staff: 6.
Employer Identification Number: 136155080

2575
Irving One Wall Street Foundation, Inc.
One Wall St.
New York 10005   (212) 487-6268

Incorporated in 1968 in New York.
Donor(s): Irving Trust Company.
Financial data: (yr. ended 12/31/82): Assets, $1,500,934 (M); expenditures, $431,847, including $396,001 for 58 grants (high: $190,000; low: $500) and $31,817 for 254 employee matching gifts.
Purpose and activities: Charitable purposes; primarily local giving, with emphasis on community funds, higher education, urban affairs, cultural programs, hospitals, and health agencies.
Types of support awarded: Matching funds, general purposes, operating budgets, continuing support, annual campaigns, emergency funds, employee matching gifts.
Limitations: Giving primarily in NY. No grants to individuals, or for endowment funds, research programs, scholarships, or fellowships; no loans.
Publications: Annual report.
Application information:
 Initial approach: Letter
 Copies of proposal: 1
 Deadline(s): None
 Board meeting date(s): Monthly
 Write: Peter D. Crawford, Vice-President

Officers and Directors:* Philip D. Barksdale, Jr.,* President; Peter D. Crawford, William R. Hamcke,* Robert W. Stone,* Vice-Presidents; William F. Connell, Secretary; Alvin L. Begleiter, Treasurer.
Number of staff: 1.
Employer Identification Number: 132623378

2576
Ittleson Foundation, Inc. ▼
14 East 60th St., Suite 704
New York 10022   (212) 838-5010

Trust established in 1932 in New York.
Donor(s): Henry Ittleson,† Blanche F. Ittleson,† Henry Ittleson, Jr.,† Lee F. Ittleson, Nancy S. Ittleson.
Financial data: (yr. ended 12/31/83): Assets, $11,933,469 (M); expenditures, $1,220,371, including $941,289 for 102 grants (high: $250,000; low: $50; average: $25,000-$100,000).
Purpose and activities: For the promotion of the well-being of mankind throughout the world, including research, publication, and the establishment, maintenance, and aid of charitable activities and institutions; interests include health, welfare, and education for health and welfare, with special emphasis on mental health and psychiatric research.
Types of support awarded: Operating budgets, seed money, matching funds, professorships, special projects, research, publications, conferences and seminars.
Limitations: Giving limited to the U.S. No support for humanities or for cultural projects, general education, or to social agencies offering direct service to people in local communities. No grants to individuals, or for continuing support, scholarships, fellowships, annual campaigns, travel, emergency, capital, or endowment funds, or deficit financing; no loans.
Publications: Informational brochure, program policy statement, application guidelines.
Application information:
  Initial approach: Letter
  Copies of proposal: 1
  Deadline(s): None
  Board meeting date(s): May and December
  Final notification: 3 weeks to 3 months
  Write: William T. Beaty II, Executive Director
Officers: H. Anthony Ittleson,* Chairman and President; Mrs. Henry Ittleson, Jr.,* Pamela Lee Syrmis,* Vice-Presidents; William T. Beaty II, Secretary and Executive Director; Bernard W. Schwartz, Treasurer.
Directors:* Mrs. H. Anthony Ittleson, Lionel I. Pincus, Victor Syrmis, M.D.
Number of staff: 1 part-time professional; 1 part-time support.
Employer Identification Number: 510172757

2577
Jackson Hole Preserve, Incorporated
30 Rockefeller Plaza, Rm. 5510
New York 10112   (212) 247-3700

Incorporated in 1940 in New York.
Donor(s): John D. Rockefeller, Jr.,† Laurance S. Rockefeller, Rockefeller Brothers Fund, Inc.

Financial data: (yr. ended 12/31/82): Assets, $29,375,520 (L); expenditures, $542,837, including $272,500 for 6 grants (high: $200,000; low: $7,500) and $105,683 for 6 foundation-administered programs.
Purpose and activities: A private operating foundation. General purposes; to restore, protect, and preserve for the benefit of the public the primitive grandeur and natural beauties of the landscape in areas notable for picturesque scenery; through investments in its wholly owned subsidiaries, such as Grand Teton Lodge Company and Caneel Bay Plantation, Inc., to provide facilities for the public use, understanding, appreciation, and enjoyment of such areas; and to promote, encourage, and conduct other activities germane to these purposes.
Types of support awarded: Land acquisition, matching funds, publications.
Limitations: No grants to individuals, or for building or endowment funds, scholarships, or fellowships; no loans.
Application information:
  Initial approach: Letter or full proposal
  Copies of proposal: 1
  Deadline(s): Submit proposal preferably early in the year
  Board meeting date(s): September or October; executive committee meets frequently
  Write: George R. Lamb, Executive Vice-President
Officers: Laurance S. Rockefeller,* President; George R. Lamb,* Executive Vice-President; Gene W. Setzer,* Vice-President; Franklin E. Parker,* Secretary; Ruth C. Haupert, Treasurer.
Trustees:* Nash Castro, Henry L. Diamond, Clayton W. Frye, Jr., Mrs. Lyndon B. Johnson, Howard Phipps, Laurance Rockefeller, Fred Smith, Conrad L. Wirth.
Number of staff: 3 part-time professional; 1 part-time support.
Employer Identification Number: 131813818

2578
JDR 3rd Fund, Inc., The ▼
30 Rockefeller Plaza, Rm. 5600
New York 10112   (212) 247-3700

Incorporated in 1963 in New York.
Donor(s): John D. Rockefeller 3rd.†
Financial data: (yr. ended 8/31/84): Assets, $960,276 (M); gifts received, $5,000,000; expenditures, $6,817,216, including $6,789,782 for 7 grants (high: $3,211,875; low: $2,907).
Purpose and activities: A private operating foundation. The Fund is currently limited to meeting its prior commitments, and no new grant proposals are being considered. Future program under review. Asian Cultural Program now established as an independent organization known as the Asian Cultural Council.
Types of support awarded: Exchange programs.
Application information:
  Board meeting date(s): October
  Write: Nancy C. Quarto, Assistant Secretary

Officers: Mrs. John D. Rockefeller 3rd,* President; Elizabeth J. McCormack,* Vice-President and Secretary; David G. Fernald, Treasurer.
Trustees:* Hope Aldrich, Donal C. O'Brien, Jr., Alida Rockefeller Dayton.
Number of staff: None.
Employer Identification Number: 131988876

2579
Jehovah Jireh, Inc. ⌷
12 Summit Park
Ballston Lake 12019   (518) 371-6611

Financial data: (yr. ended 3/31/83): Assets, $724,964 (M); gifts received, $530,350; expenditures, $704,183, including $589,615 for grants (high: $443,400) and $11,394 for 30 grants to individuals.
Purpose and activities: Grants for Protestant religious support, including a biblical studies school, missionary programs, and grants to theological students.
Types of support awarded: Student aid.
Application information:
  Initial approach: Proposal
  Deadline(s): None
  Write: Larry Deason, Director
Director: Larry Deason.
Employer Identification Number: 222239206

2580
Jephson Educational Trust No. 1
c/o The Chase Manhattan Bank
1211 Ave. of the Americas
New York 10036   (212) 730-3795

Trust established in 1946 in New York.
Donor(s): Lucretia Davis Jephson.†
Financial data: (yr. ended 12/31/82): Assets, $2,020,100 (M); expenditures, $179,336, including $154,000 for 58 grants (high: $5,000; low: $1,000).
Purpose and activities: To support 4-year educational institutions through scholarship aid for youth throughout the United States.
Types of support awarded: Scholarship funds.
Limitations: No grants to individuals or for matching gifts; no loans.
Trustees: Dermod Ives, J. Stanley Parkin, The Chase Manhattan Bank.
Employer Identification Number: 136023169

2581
Jephson Educational Trust No. 2
c/o Chase Manhattan Bank
1211 Ave. of the Americas
New York 10036   (212) 730-3795

Trust established in 1979 in New York.
Donor(s): Lucretia Davis Jephson.†
Financial data: (yr. ended 9/30/82): Assets, $2,020,100 (M); expenditures, $179,336, including $154,000 for 58 grants (high: $6,000; low: $1,000).
Purpose and activities: Grants for higher and secondary education, including scholarship aid for worthy but needy students.

Types of support awarded: Scholarship funds, general purposes, building funds, endowment funds.
Limitations: No grants to individuals or for matching gifts; no loans.
Application information:
  Initial approach: Full proposal
  Copies of proposal: 1
  Deadline(s): Submit proposal preferably in March or April; deadline April 30
  Board meeting date(s): June and October
  Final notification: 6 months
  Write: William R. Baird, Vice-President
Trustees: Dermod Ives, J. Stanley Parkins, The Chase Manhattan Bank.
Number of staff: 1.
Employer Identification Number: 136777236

2582
Jesselson Foundation ▼ ♯
1221 Ave. of the Americas
New York 10020

Incorporated in 1955 in New York.
Donor(s): Ludwig Jesselson.
Financial data: (yr. ended 4/30/82): Assets, $11,061,952 (M); gifts received, $809,750; expenditures, $1,017,193, including $981,926 for 293 grants (high: $431,570; low: $15).
Purpose and activities: Broad purposes; grants largely for temple support, Jewish welfare funds, including a hospital in Israel, and Jewish-sponsored educational and charitable institutions.
Officers: Ludwig Jesselson, President and Treasurer; Erica Jesselson, Vice-President and Secretary; Michael Jesselson, 2nd Vice-President.
Employer Identification Number: 136075098

2583
Jewish Foundation for Education of Women
330 West 58th St., 5J
New York 10019   (212) 265-2565

Incorporated in 1884 in New York.
Financial data: (yr. ended 6/30/84): Assets, $10,966,180 (M); gifts received, $108,733; expenditures, $721,160, including $576,418 for 509 grants to individuals (average: $500-$2,000) and $83,885 for 74 loans.
Purpose and activities: To provide scholarship assistance to women in the form of grants and loans for undergraduate, graduate, and professional studies. Applicants must be legal residents of the greater New York City metropolitan area.
Types of support awarded: Student aid.
Limitations: Giving limited to the greater New York, NY, metropolitan area. No grants for general support, operating budgets, capital or endowment funds, matching gifts, research, special projects, publications, or conferences.
Publications: Application guidelines.
Application information: Application form required.
  Initial approach: Letter
  Copies of proposal: 1

Deadline(s): Submit proposal preferably between October and January; deadline January 31
  Board meeting date(s): October, January, June, and as required
  Final notification: 6 weeks to 4 months
  Write: Florence Wallach, Executive Director
Officers and Directors: Charles J. Tanenbaum, Chairman; Mrs. Warren R. Goldsmith, President; Ellen B. Phillips, 1st Vice-President; Mrs. Frederick H. Block, James Wood, Vice-Presidents; Marion Spanbock, Secretary; Alan R. Kahn, Treasurer; Jack Ackerman, Sylvia Biederman, Martin Blumenthal, Alan Cohn, Lasalle Felheim, Linda Gabriel, Mrs. Carl Goldmark, Jr., Irving Kahn, Suzanne Keusch, Essie Lee, Brenda L. Lehman, Nadine Liebhardt, Marjorie Madonick, Ruth Messinger, Morton Pepper, David Rosenberg, Susan J. Schatz, Ann Freda Thomas.
Number of staff: 1 full-time professional; 1 full-time support; 1 part-time support.
Employer Identification Number: 131860415

2584
J.M. Foundation, The ▼
60 East 42nd St., Rm. 1651
New York 10165   (212) 687-7735

Incorporated in 1924 in New York.
Donor(s): Jeremiah Milbank,† Katharine S. Milbank.†
Financial data: (yr. ended 12/31/84): Assets, $25,756,630 (M); expenditures, $4,253,346, including $3,402,367 for 135 grants (high: $200,000; low: $5,000) and $21,135 for 23 employee matching gifts.
Purpose and activities: Broad purposes; concentrates support in medical research and education, rehabilitation centers, and selected projects which focus on strengthening traditional values essential to the preservation of a free society, such as free enterprise, voluntarism, and the two-party system; grants also for youth opportunity and a matching gifts program for foundation employees and the board of directors.
Types of support awarded: Research, special projects, publications, internships, scholarship funds, matching funds, conferences and seminars, technical assistance, employee matching gifts.
Limitations: Giving primarily in New York, NY, and Washington, DC, areas, although there are no prescribed geographic limitations. No support for the arts. No grants to individuals, or for operating expenses, international activities, annual fundraising campaigns, capital campaigns, or endowment funds; no loans.
Publications: Annual report, informational brochure, program policy statement, application guidelines.
Application information:
  Initial approach: Letter acompanied by full proposal
  Copies of proposal: 1
  Deadline(s): Submit proposal preferably in March, July, or October; deadlines 45 days prior to meetings
  Board meeting date(s): January, May, September, and December
  Write: Jack Brauntuch, Executive Director

Officers: Jeremiah Milbank, Jr.,* President; Mrs. H. Lawrence Bogert,* Vice-President; Daniel G. Tenney, Jr.,* Secretary; Allan Hoover,* Treasurer; Jack Brauntuch, Executive Director.
Directors:* William Lee Hanley, Jr., Frank J. Shakespeare.
Number of staff: 3 full-time professional; 3 full-time support; 1 part-time support.
Employer Identification Number: 136068340

2585
Jockey Club Foundation ♯
380 Madison Ave.
New York 10017

Incorporated in 1943 in New York.
Donor(s): New York Racing Association, Clark Foundation.
Financial data: (yr. ended 12/31/82): Assets, $2,129,952 (M); gifts received, $216,718; expenditures, $108,262, including $97,820 for 54 grants to individuals.
Purpose and activities: To support indigent employees of turf and racing clubs.
Types of support awarded: Grants to individuals.
Trustees: James B. Moseley, Managing Trustee; Stephen Clark, Jr., Charles H. Thieriot.
Employer Identification Number: 136124094

2586
Johnson (Barbara Piasecka) Foundation ♯
c/o Shearman & Sterling
153 E. 53rd St.
New York 10022   (212) 940-3387

Financial data: (yr. ended 12/31/82): Assets, $1,272,813 (M); gifts received, $6,881; expenditures, $106,102, including $57,648 for 6 grants (high: $20,000; low: $2,195) and $34,458 for 2 grants to individuals.
Purpose and activities: To defray expenses of scientific and artistic endeavors, including grants to individuals and colleges.
Types of support awarded: Grants to individuals, equipment.
Application information: Application form required.
  Deadline(s): None
  Write: Nina S. Zagat, Secretary
Officers and Directors: Barbara P. Johnson, President and Trustee; J.S. Johnson, Vice-President, Treasurer, and Trustee; Nina S. Zagat, Secretary; Gregory Gorzynski, Grzegorz Piasecki.
Employer Identification Number: 510201795

2587
Johnson (Christian A.) Endeavor Foundation ▼
1060 Park Ave.
New York 10128   (212) 534-6620

Incorporated in 1952 in New York.
Donor(s): Christian A. Johnson.†

Financial data: (yr. ended 9/30/84): Assets, $45,549,024 (M); expenditures, $1,871,575, including $1,560,379 for 41 grants (high: $300,000; low: $1,000; average: $25,000-$50,000) and $222,236 for 1 foundation-administered program.
Purpose and activities: Concentrates on the improvement of the cultural and intellectual environments of American society; emphasis on education, particularly liberal arts at the baccalaureate level; primary concern in the arts for developing new talent and bringing the arts to young people.
Types of support awarded: Operating budgets, seed money, building funds, equipment, matching funds, professorships, scholarship funds.
Limitations: Giving limited to the eastern U.S. No support for government agencies, or for community or neighborhood projects. No grants to individuals, or for continuing support, annual campaigns, emergency funds, deficit financing, land acquisitions, research, demonstration projects, publications, or conferences; no loans.
Publications: Annual report, application guidelines, program policy statement.
Application information:
  Initial approach: Letter with proposal summary
  Deadline(s): Submit proposal upon foundation's request; deadline March 1
  Board meeting date(s): Fall, winter, spring, and early summer
  Final notification: 9 months
  Write: Mrs. Wilmot H. Kidd, President
Officers and Trustees: Mrs. Christian A. Johnson, Chair; Mrs. Wilmot H. Kidd, President; Marie Jordan, Secretary; Charles H. Harff.
Number of staff: 1 part-time professional; 2 full-time support; 1 part-time support.
Employer Identification Number: 136147952

2588
Johnson (The J. S.) & Barbara Piasecka Johnson Charitable Trust ¤
c/o Citibank, N.A.
153 East 53rd St.
New York 10022

Established in New York in 1981.
Financial data: (yr. ended 12/31/81): Assets, $2,220,128 (M); gifts received, $2,220,128.
Purpose and activities: Charitable purposes.
Application information:
  Write: James Carey, Trust Officer
Officer: James Carey.
Employer Identification Number: 136802742

2589
Johnson (R. B.) Foundation, Inc.
c/o Smith, Barney, Harris, Upham and Company, Inc.
1345 Ave. of the Americas
New York 10105   (212) 399-6204

Incorporated in 1955 in Delaware.
Donor(s): Ralph B. Johnson.†

Financial data: (yr. ended 12/31/82): Assets, $271,448 (M); expenditures, $123,635, including $120,387 for 115 grants (high: $10,000; low: $30).
Purpose and activities: Broad purposes; grants largely for higher and secondary education, hospitals, community services, and church support.
Limitations: No grants to individuals; no loans.
Application information:
  Board meeting date(s): May and September or October, and as required
  Write: Fred Comas, President
Officers and Directors: Fred Comas, President; Mary Alyce Clancy, Secretary; Jerry Cusumano, Treasurer; Marlene Ratti, David Steele.
Employer Identification Number: 136162735

2590
Johnson (Willard T. C.) Foundation, Inc. ¤
c/o Shea & Gould
330 Madison Ave.
New York 10017   (212) 370-8000

Incorporated in 1979 in New York.
Donor(s): Willard T.C. Johnson.†
Financial data: (yr. ended 12/31/82): Assets, $15,318,803 (M); expenditures, $1,557,271, including $1,424,000 for 10 grants (high: $1,000,000; low: $3,000).
Purpose and activities: Broad purposes, with emphasis on hospitals, cultural programs, social services, and a zoological society.
Application information:
  Deadline(s): None
  Write: Seymour M. Klein, President
Officers and Directors: Betty W. Johnson, Chairman; Seymour M. Klein, President; Robert J. Mortimer, Vice-President, Secretary, and Treasurer.
Employer Identification Number: 132993310

2591
Jones (Daisy Marquis) Foundation ▼
945 Crossroads Office Bldg.
Two State St.
Rochester 14614   (716) 263-3331

Established in 1968 in New York.
Donor(s): Daisy Marquis Jones.†
Financial data: (yr. ended 12/31/84): Assets, $16,388,234 (M); gifts received, $20,000; expenditures, $1,449,799, including $1,284,716 for 105 grants (high: $250,000; low: $200; average: $500-$25,000).
Purpose and activities: Grants primarily to improve the quality of health care available to residents of Monroe and Yates counties; support also for services for senior citizens, women and youth, with special emphasis on the disadvantaged; support also toward improving the administration of justice. Special attention to preventive programs.
Types of support awarded: Operating budgets, seed money, emergency funds, building funds, equipment, land acquisition, matching funds, consulting services, technical assistance, special projects, publications, conferences and seminars.

Limitations: Giving limited to Monroe and Yates counties, NY. No support for the arts or for religious purposes. No grants to individuals, or for endowment funds, research, continuing support, scholarships, fellowships, annual campaigns, or deficit financing; no loans.
Publications: Informational brochure, application guidelines, program policy statement, grants list.
Application information: Application form required.
  Initial approach: Letter
  Copies of proposal: 1
  Deadline(s): None
  Board meeting date(s): Monthly
  Final notification: 2 to 3 months
  Write: Pearl W. Rubin, Director
Trustees: Leo M. Lyons, Chairman; Pearl W. Rubin, Director; Helen G. Whitney, Marine Midland Bank.
Number of staff: 1 part-time professional; 1 part-time support.
Employer Identification Number: 237000227

2592
Joselow Foundation
(formerly The Joselow Foundation)
c/o Burns Summit Rovins & Feldesman
445 Park Ave.
New York 10022   (212) 702-2356

Established in 1967 in New York.
Donor(s): Irving Joselow,† Florence Joselow.†
Financial data: (yr. ended 12/31/82): Assets, $1,535,236 (M); gifts received, $265,187; expenditures, $153,661, including $149,500 for 30 grants (high: $12,500; low: $1,000; average: $1,000-$10,000).
Purpose and activities: Giving to selected organizations, including support for Jewish welfare and educational funds; support also for international activities and higher education.
Limitations: No grants to individuals.
Application information:
  Initial approach: Letter or full proposal
  Copies of proposal: 1
  Deadline(s): None
  Write: Mildred Robbins Leet and Jacquin D. Bierman
Trustees: Jacquin D. Bierman, Mildred Robbins Leet.
Number of staff: None.
Employer Identification Number: 237028908

2593
Julia R. and Estelle L. Foundation, Inc. ▼ ¤
P.O. Box 97, Market Station
Buffalo 14203

Incorporated in 1941 in New York.
Donor(s): Peter C. Cornell Trust, John R. Oishei.†
Financial data: (yr. ended 12/31/83): Assets, $11,557,550 (M); gifts received, $430,000; expenditures, $936,395, including $900,300 for 117 grants (high: $70,000; low: $100).

Purpose and activities: Religious and educational purposes; primarily local giving, with emphasis on higher and secondary education, medical research, and hospitals; some support for welfare funds, health agencies, child welfare and youth agencies and cultural programs.
Types of support awarded: General purposes, research, building funds.
Limitations: Giving primarily in Buffalo, NY.
Officers and Directors: R. John Oshei, President; Julian R. Oishei, Vice-President; Rupert Warren, Vice-President and Secretary-Treasurer.
Members: Peter T. Allen, Patricia Q. Colby, Carl E. Larson.
Number of staff: None.
Employer Identification Number: 166027507

2594
Jurodin Fund, Inc. ⌑
60 East 42nd St., Rm. 5010
New York 10017

Incorporated in 1960 in Delaware.
Donor(s): Julius Silver.
Financial data: (yr. ended 12/31/81): Assets, $3,587,350 (M); gifts received, $274,158; expenditures, $319,173, including $265,650 for 36 grants (high: $60,000).
Purpose and activities: Broad purposes; grants largely for hospitals, higher education, and Jewish welfare funds primarily in New York.
Limitations: Giving primarily in NY.
Officers: Julius Silver, President and Treasurer; Roslyn Silver, Enid Winslow, Vice-Presidents; Milton Solomon, Secretary.
Employer Identification Number: 136169166

2595
Jurzykowski (Alfred) Foundation, Inc. ▼
21 East 40th St.
New York 10016 (212) 689-2460
Address for award nominations by scholarly and cultural institutions: Cultural Advisory Committee, 59 East 66th St., New York, NY 10021

Incorporated in 1960 in New York.
Donor(s): Alfred Jurzykowski.†
Financial data: (yr. ended 12/31/84): Assets, $12,228,794 (M); expenditures, $904,601, including $739,651 for 65 grants (high: $100,000; low: $825; average: $5,000-$15,000) and $56,000 for 15 grants to individuals.
Purpose and activities: Broad purposes; grants primarily for projects in the fields of culture, medical research, and education. Annual awards, by nomination only, for achievement in science, the arts, medicine, and literary translations by Poles living in Poland or abroad.
Types of support awarded: Research, operating budgets, annual campaigns, special projects, general purposes, publications, conferences and seminars, exchange programs, matching funds, continuing support.
Limitations: No grants to individuals (for travel, study, scholarships, publications, or other similar purposes), or for endowment funds; no loans.
Publications: Application guidelines.
Application information: Awards to individuals by nomination only.
Initial approach: Telephone or full proposal
Copies of proposal: 1
Deadline(s): 1 month before board meetings
Board meeting date(s): January, May, and September
Final notification: 2 weeks after board meeting
Write: Bluma D. Cohen, Executive Director
Officers and Trustees: Yolande L. Jurzykowski, Executive Vice-President; Bluma D. Cohen, Vice-President and Executive Director; M. Christine Jurzykowski, Secretary and Treasurer; Karin Falencki, William Pyka, M.D., Walter A.L. Thompson, M.D.
Number of staff: None.
Employer Identification Number: 136192256

2596
Kade (Annette) Fund
c/o Citibank
641 Lexington Ave., 4th Fl.
New York 10043

Established in 1978 in New York.
Donor(s): Annette Kade.†
Financial data: (yr. ended 12/31/83): Assets, $1,323,748 (M); expenditures, $93,143, including $81,336 for 1 grant.
Purpose and activities: Support for education of U.S. students studying in France or Germany, or for French or German students studying in the United States.
Application information:
Write: J.B. Ballantine, Assistant Vice-President
Trustees: Dinsmore Adams, Gilbert Frei, Citibank.
Employer Identification Number: 136754615

2597
Kade (Max) Foundation, Inc. ▼
100 Church St., Rm. 1604
New York 10007 (212) 964-7980

Incorporated in 1944 in New York.
Donor(s): Max Kade.†
Financial data: (yr. ended 12/31/82): Assets, $24,412,235 (M); expenditures, $1,894,034, including $1,625,770 for 75 grants (high: $600,000; low: $400).
Purpose and activities: Broad purposes; grants primarily to higher educational institutions, with present emphasis on postdoctoral research exchange programs between the United States and Europe in medicine or in the natural and physical sciences. Foreign scholars and scientists are selected by the sponsoring universities upon nomination by the respective Academy of Sciences. Grants also for visiting faculty exchange programs, the training of language teachers, and the development of language centers at qualified colleges and universities.
Types of support awarded: Exchange programs.
Limitations: No grants to individuals, or for operating budgets, capital funds, development campaigns, or endowment funds; no loans.
Application information:
Board meeting date(s): As required
Write: Erich H. Markel, President
Officers and Directors: Erich H. Markel, President; Edgar Schwaibold, Vice-President; Reimer Koch-Weser, Secretary; Carl F. Bayerschmidt, Treasurer; Hans G. Hachmann, Fritz Kade, Fritz Kade, Jr., M.D.
Employer Identification Number: 135658082

2598
Kaplan (The J. M.) Fund, Inc. ▼
330 Madison Ave.
New York 10017 (212) 661-8485

Incorporated in 1948 in New York as Faigel Leah Foundation, Inc.; The J.M. Kaplan Fund, Inc., a Delaware corporation, merged with it in 1975 and was renamed The J.M. Kaplan Fund, Inc.
Donor(s): Members of the J.M. Kaplan family.
Financial data: (yr. ended 11/30/84): Assets, $57,900,000 (M); expenditures, $4,889,014, including $3,324,800 for 117 grants (high: $250,000; low: $1,000; average: $20,000) and $448,500 for 35 employee matching gifts.
Purpose and activities: Interest primarily in programs in architecture and urban planning, preservation, parks and other urban amenities; local cultural institutions and selected arts projects; and certain civil liberties and human needs programs; support also for trustee matching gifts program.
Types of support awarded: Employee matching gifts, continuing support, seed money, emergency funds, matching funds, special projects, publications, technical assistance.
Limitations: Giving primarily in NY, with emphasis on New York City. No support for education, medicine, or science. No grants to individuals, or for personal ventures such as books, dances, plays or works of art; films or video; building, operating, or endowment funds; annual campaigns; deficit financing; equipment and materials; land acquisition; renovation projects; or scholarships, fellowships, conferences, research, prizes, study, or travel; no loans.
Publications: Annual report, application guidelines.
Application information:
Initial approach: Telephone, full proposal, or letter
Copies of proposal: 1
Deadline(s): Submit proposal only from March to November; deadline November 1
Board meeting date(s): As required
Final notification: 2 months
Write: Joan K. Davidson, President
Officers: Joan K. Davidson,* President; Elizabeth K. Fonseca,* Mary E. Kaplan,* Richard D. Kaplan,* Vice-Presidents; John Matthew Davidson,* Secretary; Lothar Stiefel,* Treasurer; Suzanne Davis, Administrative Director.

Trustees:* Maurice Austin, Betsy Davidson, Bradford Davidson, Peter Davidson, Isabel Fonseca, Quina Fonseca, Alice M. Kaplan, Henry C. Kaplan, Jacob M. Kaplan, Maurice C. Kaplan.
Number of staff: 1 full-time professional; 1 part-time support.
Employer Identification Number: 136090286

2599
Kaplun (Morris J. and Betty) Foundation ⌑
c/o Zvi Levavy & Company
50 East 42nd St.
New York 10017

Incorporated in 1955 in New York.
Donor(s): Morris J. Kaplun.†
Financial data: (yr. ended 8/31/83): Assets, $1,436,690 (M); expenditures, $139,748, including $107,450 for 22 grants (high: $36,000; low: $200).
Purpose and activities: General purposes; grants largely for Jewish-sponsored higher education and welfare funds.
Officers and Trustees: Zvi Levavy,* President; Bernard Grossman,* Larry Marin,* Herbert Rothman,* Aaron Seligson,* Moshe Sheinbaum,* Vice-Presidents; Gloria Isakower, Secretary.
Employer Identification Number: 136096009

2600
Karagheusian (The Howard) Commemorative Corporation
386 Park Ave. South, Suite 1601
New York 10016   (212) 725-0973

Incorporated in 1921 in New York.
Donor(s): Miran Karagheusian,† Mrs. Zabelle Karagheusian,† Miss Leila Karagheusian, Vartan H. Jinishian,† and others.
Financial data: (yr. ended 12/31/84): Assets, $10,630,000 (M); expenditures, $674,000, including $29,750 for 17 grants (high: $15,000; low: $100) and $537,000 for foundation-administered programs.
Purpose and activities: A private operating foundation established to promote child welfare, public health services, and relief programs in Armenian refugee communities of Greece, Lebanon, and Syria and, on a smaller scale, in native Moslem Arab groups in the same communities.
Limitations: No grants to individuals; no loans.
Publications: Annual report.
Application information: Applications for scholarships and research projects discouraged.
  Write: Walter C. Bandazian, Executive Director
Officers: Leila Karagheusian,* President; Pergrouhi Svajian,* Vice-President; Walter J. Corno,* Secretary and Treasurer; Walter C. Bandazian, Executive Director.
Directors: Harry A. Dorian, Richard M. Dorian, Edgar M. Housepian, Edward Janjigian, Vasken L. Parsegian, Alan G. Philibosian, Richard J. Varadian.
Employer Identification Number: 136149578

2601
Karpas Family Foundation, Inc.
c/o M.J. Stillman & Co.
111 John St.
New York 10038   (212) 233-4990

Incorporated in 1947 in Delaware.
Financial data: (yr. ended 12/31/82): Assets, $1,043,981 (M); expenditures, $98,448, including $92,855 for 14 grants (high: $60,000; low: $25).
Purpose and activities: Primarily local giving for hospitals and Jewish welfare organizations.
Limitations: Giving primarily in NY.
Officers: Irving D. Karpas, Jr., President; Suzanne T. Karpas, Vice-President; Bruce T. Karpas, Secretary-Treasurer.
Employer Identification Number: 136116217

2602
Kassin (Otsar) Foundation, Inc. ⌑
10 West 33rd St.
New York 10001

Established in 1974.
Donor(s): Members of the Kassin family.
Financial data: (yr. ended 11/30/81): Assets, $29,973 (M); gifts received, $98,600; expenditures, $185,341, including $182,844 for 67 grants (high: $32,000; low: $200).
Purpose and activities: Grants primarily for Jewish educational institutions.
Directors: Abe Kassin, Jack Kassin, Saul Kassin.
Employer Identification Number: 510168548

2603
Katzenberger Foundation, Inc., The ⌑
c/o Golieb & Golieb
6 East 43rd St.
New York 10017   (212) 687-3340

Incorporated in 1952 in New York.
Donor(s): Walter B. Katzenberger,† Helen Katherine Katzenberger,† The Advertising Checking Bureau, Inc.
Financial data: (yr. ended 11/30/82): Assets, $2,929,761 (M); gifts received, $25,000; expenditures, $189,131, including $170,000 for 30 grants (high: $42,500; low: $250).
Purpose and activities: Grants for church support, welfare, higher and secondary education, the performing arts, and youth agencies.
Limitations: No grants to individuals.
Application information:
  Initial approach: Letter
  Copies of proposal: 2
  Deadline(s): Submit proposal preferably between July and October; deadline October 31
  Board meeting date(s): November and May
  Write: Abner J. Golieb, President
Officers and Directors: Abner J. Golieb, President; Bertram Isaacs, Secretary; Earl Swanson, Treasurer.
Employer Identification Number: 136094434

2604
Kaufman (Henry & Elaine) Foundation, Inc. ⌑
One New York Plaza
New York 10004

Established in 1969.
Donor(s): Henry Kaufman.
Financial data: (yr. ended 12/31/82): Assets, $2,589,991 (M); gifts received, $394,000; expenditures, $189,482, including $171,060 for 48 grants (high: $100,000; low: $50).
Purpose and activities: Grants primarily for higher education and Jewish welfare funds and temple support.
Officers and Directors: Henry Kaufman, President and Treasurer; Elaine Kaufman, Vice-President; George DeSipio, Secretary; Glen Kaufman.
Employer Identification Number: 237045903

2605
Kaufmann (Henry) Foundation ▼
300 Park Ave.
New York 10022   (212) 909-7000

Incorporated in 1928 in New York.
Donor(s): Henry Kaufmann.†
Financial data: (yr. ended 12/31/82): Assets, $6,303,069 (M); expenditures, $567,035, including $510,000 for 26 grants (high: $50,000; low: $1,500; average: $2,500-$25,000).
Purpose and activities: Broad purposes; capital grants principally for camping and community centers in Pittsburgh and New York City.
Types of support awarded: Building funds, equipment, general purposes.
Limitations: Giving primarily in the New York City, NY, metropolitan area and Pittsburgh, PA. No grants to individuals, or for endowment funds, operating budgets, scholarships and fellowships, or matching gifts; no loans.
Publications: 990-PF.
Application information:
  Initial approach: Full proposal
  Copies of proposal: 2
  Deadline(s): Submit proposal preferably 1 or 2 months before board meeting dates; no set deadline
  Board meeting date(s): May and November
  Final notification: after board meetings
  Write: Peter E. Yaeger, Secretary
Officers: Walter Mendelsohn,* President; Maurice B. Hexter,* Vice-President and Treasurer; Peter E. Yaeger, Secretary.
Directors: Leonard N. Block, Mary S. Froelich, William T. Golden, Charles Looker, John M. Wolfe.
Number of staff: None.
Employer Identification Number: 136034179

2606
Kautz (Charles P. and Pauline M.) Foundation ⌑
United National Bank
Callicoon 12723

Established in 1976 in New York.

Donor(s): Charles P. Kautz.†
Financial data: (yr. ended 12/31/82): Assets, $1,423,044 (M); expenditures, $109,900, including $99,750 for 86 grants to individuals (high: $3,000; low: $500).
Purpose and activities: Grants for college scholarships to graduates of Delaware Valley High School.
Types of support awarded: Student aid.
Limitations: Giving limited to the Delaware Valley, NY, area.
Application information:
  Deadline(s): May 15
  Write: Robert C. Curtis, President
Officers and Directors: Robert C. Curtis, President; Edith C. Craig, Secretary; Sylvia F. Mitterwager, Treasurer; William H. Metzger, Frederick W.V. Schadt.
Employer Identification Number: 141579429

2607
Keck (William M.), Jr. Foundation ☒
c/o Shearman & Sterling
153 East 53rd St.
New York 10022

Incorporated in 1958 in Delaware.
Donor(s): William M. Keck, Jr.
Financial data: (yr. ended 12/31/82): Assets, $6,395,484 (M); expenditures, $403,588, including $398,937 for 20 grants (high: $83,625; low: $1,000).
Purpose and activities: Charitable purposes; emphasis on higher and secondary education, hospitals, cultural programs and church support.
Officers and Directors: Thomas P. Ford, President; Arthur Logan, Vice-President and Secretary; William M. Keck II, Vice-President and Treasurer.
Employer Identification Number: 136097874

2608
Kempner Foundation, Inc., The ☒
c/o Main Hurdman c/s
55 E. 52nd St.
New York 10022

Incorporated in 1955 in New York.
Donor(s): Alan H. Kempner, Margaret L. Kempner, Thomas L. Kempner, and others.
Financial data: (yr. ended 11/30/82): Assets, $408,096 (M); gifts received, $24,774; expenditures, $140,044, including $134,513 for 169 grants (high: $20,000; low: $20).
Purpose and activities: Giving largely for higher education, hospitals, and Jewish welfare funds; support also for youth agencies.
Officers: Margaret L. Kempner, President; Alan H. Kempner, Vice-President; Charles H. Guggenheimer, Secretary.
Employer Identification Number: 136085600

2609
Kenan (William R.), Jr. Charitable Trust ▼
120 Broadway, Rm. 3046
New York 10271   (212) 732-3151

Trust established in 1965 in New York.
Donor(s): William R. Kenan, Jr.†

Financial data: (yr. ended 12/31/83): Assets, $143,000,000 (M); expenditures, $8,000,000, including $7,439,000 for 20 grants (high: $1,600,000).
Purpose and activities: To support education, primarily teaching excellence, at private universities and colleges of recognized high quality in the U.S.; also challenge grant support to independent secondary schools which meet trustees' requirements and are located in states selected by trustees.
Types of support awarded: Endowment funds, matching funds, professorships.
Limitations: Giving limited to the U.S. No support for medical, public health, or social welfare agencies; or for designated educational programs, or independent day schools. No grants to individuals, or for building funds, operating budgets, scholarships and fellowships, research, or special programs.
Publications: Annual report, informational brochure, program policy statement.
Application information: Application by invitation only.
  Board meeting date(s): As required
  Write: Hamilton C. Hoyt, Trust Administrator
Trustees: Frank H. Kenan, Thomas S. Kenan III, Morgan Guaranty Trust Company of New York.
Trust Administrator: Hamilton C. Hoyt.
Number of staff: 2 full-time professional; 1 part-time support.

2610
Kerry Foundation, Inc., The
14-16 Elm Place
Rye 10508   (914) 967-2385

Incorporated in 1966 in New York.
Donor(s): Sylvia B. Robinson.
Financial data: (yr. ended 12/31/83): Assets, $3,265,557 (M); gifts received, $409,151; expenditures, $419,913, including $351,201 for 104 grants (high: $26,000; low: $70; average: $100-$5,000).
Purpose and activities: Broad purposes; with emphasis on secondary and higher education, conservation, and Protestant church support.
Limitations: No grants to individuals; no loans.
Application information:
  Write: John R. Robinson, President
Officers and Directors: John R. Robinson, President and Treasurer; Sylvia B. Robinson, Vice-President; Theodore H. Ashford.
Number of staff: 1 part-time support.
Employer Identification Number: 136201175

2611
Kevorkian (Hagop) Fund ▼ ☒
1411 Third Ave.
New York 10028   (212) 988-9304

Trust established in 1950; incorporated in 1951 in New York.
Donor(s): Hagop Kevorkian.†
Financial data: (yr. ended 12/31/82): Assets, $8,217,268 (M); expenditures, $932,204, including $690,139 for 8 grants (high: $325,200; low: $3,000).

Purpose and activities: To promote interest in Near and Middle Eastern art through exhibitions and through fellowships administered by the recipient institutions for research and study in this field.
Types of support awarded: Fellowships, research.
Application information:
  Write: Ralph D. Minasian, Secretary-Treasurer
Officers and Trustees: Stephen Chan, Chairman and Executive Vice-President; Marjorie Kevorkian, President and Curator; Joseph Huber, Vice-President; Ralph D. Minasian, Secretary-Treasurer; Miriam Chan.
Employer Identification Number: 131839686

2612
Kidder Peabody Foundation, The ☒
c/o Kidder, Peabody & Co., Inc.
20 Exchange Place
New York 10005

Incorporated in 1959 in New York.
Donor(s): Kidder, Peabody & Co.
Financial data: (yr. ended 12/31/83): Assets, $2,189,623 (M); gifts received, $1,099,787; expenditures, $1,013,325, including $1,011,035 for 846 grants (high: $167,000; low: $100).
Purpose and activities: Broad purposes; general giving, with emphasis on higher and secondary education; support also for arts and culture and hospitals.
Limitations: No grants to individuals.
Application information:
  Write: William N. Loverd, Treasurer
Officers and Directors: Albert H. Gordon, Chairman; Erwin A. Stuebner, President; William N. Loverd, Treasurer.
Employer Identification Number: 136085918

2613
Killough (Walter H. D.) Trust ☒
c/o Marine Midland Bank
250 Park Ave.
New York 10017   (212) 949-6707

Trust established in 1929 in New York.
Donor(s): Walter H.D. Killough.†
Financial data: (yr. ended 7/31/83): Assets, $1,644,174 (M); expenditures, $118,869, including $94,632 for 21 grants (high: $25,419; low: $847).
Purpose and activities: Specific grants to designated educational and humane organizations; discretionary grants restricted primarily to hospitals and homes for the aged; scholarships limited to graduates of Erasmus High School, Brooklyn, New York.
Application information:
  Deadline(s): May 15
Trustees: Joseph Campbell, Rt. Rev. Jonathan G. Sherman, Marine Midland Bank.
Employer Identification Number: 136063894

2614
Kimmelman Foundation ☒
745 Fifth Ave., Suite 2204
New York 10022

Established in 1958.
Financial data: (yr. ended 12/31/82): Assets, $241,685 (M); gifts received, $19,095; expenditures, $153,362, including $150,135 for 85 grants (high: $25,000; low: $10).
Purpose and activities: Grants primarily for higher education; support also for health and hospitals, cultural programs, and Jewish welfare funds.
Officers and Directors: Milton Kimmelman, President; Helen Kimmelman, Treasurer.
Employer Identification Number: 136107240

2615
Klau (The David and Sadie) Foundation ▼ ☒
c/o Harry Goodkin & Company
P.O. Box 5428, Grand Central Station
New York 10017

Incorporated in 1942 in New York.
Donor(s): David W. Klau.†
Financial data: (yr. ended 12/31/82): Assets, $10,614,133 (M); expenditures, $742,014, including $696,317 for 143 grants (high: $150,000; low: $10).
Purpose and activities: Broad purposes; primarily local giving, with emphasis on hospitals, Jewish welfare funds, a theological seminary, higher education, and temple support.
Limitations: Giving primarily in NY.
Application information:
Write: Mrs. Sadie K. Klau, President
Officers and Directors: Sadie K. Klau, President; Paula K. Oppenheim, Vice-President, Secretary, and Treasurer; Lucille K. Carothers, James D. Klau, Felice K. Shea.
Employer Identification Number: 136161378

2616
Klee (The Conrad and Virginia) Foundation, Inc. ☒
700 Security Mutual Bldg.
80 Exchange St.
Binghamton 13901   (607) 723-5341

Incorporated in 1957 in New York.
Donor(s): Conrad C. Klee,† Virginia Klee.†
Financial data: (yr. ended 12/31/82): Assets, $2,787,968 (M); gifts received, $415,236; expenditures, $135,876, including $121,550 for 22 grants (high: $55,000; low: $400).
Purpose and activities: Broad purposes; primarily local giving, with emphasis on community funds, Protestant church support, and higher education.
Limitations: Giving primarily in NY, especially Broome County and Guilford. No grants to individuals.
Application information:
Initial approach: Letter
Copies of proposal: 1
Deadline(s): None
Board meeting date(s): April and November
Write: Clayton M. Axtell, Jr., President

Officers and Directors: Clayton M. Axtell, Jr., President; Richard R. Millar, Vice-President; David K. Patterson, Secretary; Peter Gordan, John E. Gwyn, Douglas R. Johnson, Robert J. Nash.
Employer Identification Number: 156019821

2617
Klein (David L.), Jr. Memorial Foundation Inc. ☒
700 Park Ave.
New York 10021

Incorporated in 1959 in New York.
Donor(s): David L. Klein,† Miriam Klein, Endo Laboratories, Inc.
Financial data: (yr. ended 2/28/83): Assets, $1,411,791 (M); expenditures, $323,718, including $301,395 for 110 grants (high: $222,500; low: $10).
Purpose and activities: Primarily local giving, with emphasis on hospitals, medical research, Jewish welfare funds, temple support, higher education, and cultural activities.
Limitations: Giving primarily in NY. No grants to individuals.
Officer and Trustees: Miriam Klein, President; Saretta Barnet, Marjorie Traub.
Employer Identification Number: 136085432

2618
Klingenstein (The Esther A. and Joseph) Fund, Inc. ▼
200 Park Ave.
New York 10166   (212) 578-0285

Incorporated in 1945 in New York.
Donor(s): Esther A. Klingenstein,† Joseph Klingenstein.†
Financial data: (yr. ended 9/30/84): Assets, $33,761,440 (M); gifts received, $67,258; expenditures, $4,030,680, including $3,834,897 for 57 grants (high: $330,000; low: $2,500; average: $5,000-$50,000).
Purpose and activities: Charitable purposes; primary interests in neuroscientific research bearing on epilepsy; independent secondary education; and public policy issues relating to the free enterprise economic system. Some support also for other education, health care, and social welfare.
Types of support awarded: Research, special projects, publications, conferences and seminars, fellowships.
Limitations: No grants to individuals (except in Fund's own programs in neuroscience and independent secondary education), or for building or endowment funds, or matching gifts; generally no grants for operating budgets; no loans.
Publications: Informational brochure, program policy statement.
Application information:
Initial approach: Letter or full proposal
Copies of proposal: 1
Deadline(s): None
Board meeting date(s): Generally 5 or 6 times a year
Final notification: 2 months
Write: John Klingenstein, President

Officers and Directors: John Klingenstein, President and Treasurer; Frederick A. Klingenstein, Vice-President and Secretary; Patricia D. Klingenstein, Sharon L. Klingenstein.
Number of staff: 3 part-time professional; 1 full-time support.
Employer Identification Number: 136028788

2619
Klosk (Louis & Rose) Fund ☒
c/o Chemical Bank
30 Rockefeller Plaza, 60th Fl.
New York 10112   (212) 621-2143

Trust established in 1970 in New York.
Donor(s): Louis Klosk.†
Financial data: (yr. ended 12/31/82): Assets, $2,129,558 (M); expenditures, $186,327, including $167,000 for 22 grants (high: $37,000; low: $750).
Purpose and activities: Primarily local giving, with emphasis on Jewish welfare funds, hospitals, care for the aged, arts and higher education.
Limitations: Giving primarily in NY.
Application information:
Write: Barbara Strohmeier
Trustees: Laurence Klosk, Chemical Bank.
Employer Identification Number: 136328994

2620
Knapp Fund, The
c/o James C. Edwards & Co., Inc.
805 Third Ave., 8th Fl.
New York 10022   (212) 319-8488

Incorporated in 1917 in New York.
Donor(s): George O. Knapp.†
Financial data: (yr. ended 8/31/84): Assets, $1,475,591 (M); expenditures, $81,861, including $67,000 for 11 grants (high: $20,000; low: $1,000).
Purpose and activities: Activities largely confined to support for higher and secondary educational institutions.
Types of support awarded: General purposes, continuing support, annual campaigns, building funds, research, scholarship funds, special projects.
Limitations: No grants to individuals, or for matching gifts; no loans.
Publications: 990-PF.
Application information: Funds largely committed.
Initial approach: Letter
Copies of proposal: 1
Board meeting date(s): September
Write: George O. Knapp II, President
Officers: George O. Knapp II,* President; Frank A. Sprole,* Vice-President; Grace C. Gregoire, Secretary-Treasurer.
Directors:* James C. Edwards, George O. Knapp III, Frank Jared Sprole.
Number of staff: None.
Employer Identification Number: 136068384

2621
Knox Gelatine Foundation ¤
P.O. Box 387
Johnstown 12095

Incorporated in 1961 in New York.
Donor(s): Eleanor E. Knox,† Knox Gelatine, Inc.
Financial data: (yr. ended 12/31/82): Assets,
$3,077,590 (M); expenditures, $205,757,
including $188,000 for 109 grants (high:
$20,000; low: $100).
Purpose and activities: Broad purposes, with
emphasis on higher and secondary education,
hospitals, Protestant church support, and social
welfare.
Officers and Directors: John B. Knox,
Chairman; George A. Graham, President and
Treasurer; Nora K. Graham, Secretary; John G.
Armstrong, Roseann K. Armstrong, Charles K.
Brumley, Richard W. Hallock.
Employer Identification Number: 146017797

2622
Knox (The Seymour H.) Foundation, Inc.
3750 Marine Midland Center
Buffalo 14203   (716) 854-6811

Incorporated in 1945 in New York.
Donor(s): Seymour H. Knox, Marjorie K.C.
Klopp,† Dorothy K.G. Rogers.†
Financial data: (yr. ended 12/31/82): Assets,
$7,240,113 (M); expenditures, $285,300,
including $178,668 for 54 grants (high:
$30,000; low: $25).
Purpose and activities: Broad purposes;
primarily local giving with emphasis on the arts,
higher and secondary education, and
community funds.
Limitations: Giving primarily in the Buffalo,
NY, area. No grants to individuals.
Application information:
  Initial approach: Letter
  Copies of proposal: 1
  Board meeting date(s): May and December
  Write: Seymour H. Knox, President
Officers and Directors: Seymour H. Knox,
President; Seymour H. Knox III, Northrup R.
Knox, Hazard K. Campbell, Vice-Presidents;
Samuel Magavern, Secretary; Robert Scheu,
Treasurer.
Employer Identification Number: 160839066

2623
Kopf (Elizabeth Christy) Foundation ¤
134 E. 40th St.
New York 10016

Established in 1982 in New York.
Donor(s): R.C. Kopf.
Financial data: (yr. ended 12/31/82): Assets,
$490,291 (M); gifts received, $561,500;
expenditures, $105,050, including $105,000
for 7 grants (high: $100,000; low: $5,000).
Purpose and activities: First year of operation
in 1982; support for a social service
organization and a church.
Limitations: Giving primarily in NY.
Officers: R.C. Kopf, President; Patricia
Colagiuri, Vice-President; Brenda Helies,
Secretary; Nancy Sue Mueller, Treasurer.
Employer Identification Number: 133127936

2624
Kopf Foundation, Inc. ¤
c/o Siegel
600 Fifth Ave., 19th Fl.
New York 10020

Incorporated in 1967 in New York.
Financial data: (yr. ended 12/31/81): Assets,
$1,188,056 (M); gifts received, $275,000;
expenditures, $338,384, including $330,525
for 11 grants (high: $300,000; low: $25).
Purpose and activities: Grants primarily for a
local hospital, church support, and higher
education.
Officers and Directors: R.C. Kopf, Chairman;
Patricia Ann Colagiuri, Vice-President; Nancy
Sue Mueller, Secretary; Brenda Christy Helies,
Treasurer; Patrick Colagiuri, Anthony Helies,
Charles S. Mueller.
Employer Identification Number: 136228036

2625
Kraft (E. A.) Charitable Trust ¤
c/o Chemical Bank
30 Rockefeller Plaza, 60th Fl.
New York 10112   (212) 621-2143

Established in 1978.
Financial data: (yr. ended 7/29/83): Assets,
$859,315 (M); expenditures, $414,419,
including $404,270 for 32 grants (high:
$35,000; low: $1,000).
Purpose and activities: Primarily local giving
for secondary and higher education, hospitals
and health, social services, cultural programs,
and Episcopal religious organizations.
Limitations: Giving primarily in New York, NY.
Application information:
  Deadline(s): None
  Write: Mrs. Barbara Strohmeier
Trustees: Alfred Ferguson, Logan Fulrath, Jr.,
Chemical Bank.
Employer Identification Number: 136761770

2626
Kramer (C. L. C.) Foundation ¤
c/o Zabelle, Schechter & Marks
1780 Broadway
New York 10019

Established in 1966.
Donor(s): Catherine Kramer.†
Financial data: (yr. ended 9/30/82): Assets,
$3,271,748 (M); gifts received, $2,370,000;
expenditures, $580,250, including $575,000
for 8 grants (high: $150,000; low: $25,000).
Purpose and activities: Primarily local giving
for hospitals and health agencies.
Limitations: Giving primarily in New York, NY.
Officers: Robert Zabelle, President; Charles
Looker, Secretary; David Marks, Treasurer.
Employer Identification Number: 136226513

2627
Kramer Foundation ¤
500 Fifth Ave., Rm. 1802
New York 10110

Established about 1951 in New York.

Financial data: (yr. ended 12/31/83): Assets,
$1,505,329 (M); expenditures, $92,699,
including $84,035 for 78 grants (high: $10,000;
low: $12).
Purpose and activities: Primarily local giving,
with emphasis on Jewish welfare funds and
higher education including medical education.
Limitations: Giving primarily in NY.
Manager: Saul Kramer.
Employer Identification Number: 221713053

2628
Kresevich Foundation, Inc., The ¤
184 West 237th St.
Bronx 10463

Incorporated in 1953 in New York.
Donor(s): Stella D'Oro Biscuit Co., Inc.
Financial data: (yr. ended 11/30/82): Assets,
$809,976 (M); gifts received, $2,700;
expenditures, $148,573, including $146,521
for 105 grants (high: $40,000; low: $10).
Purpose and activities: Charitable purposes;
grants largely for Roman Catholic religious
associations, church support, and secondary
education.
Officer: Felice Zambetti, President; E.V.
Cerutti, Treasurer.
Employer Identification Number: 136082003

2629
Kress (Samuel H.) Foundation ▼
174 East 80th St.
New York 10021   (212) 861-4993

Incorporated in 1929 in New York.
Donor(s): Samuel H. Kress,† Claude W.
Kress,† Rush H. Kress.†
Financial data: (yr. ended 8/31/84): Assets,
$40,642,935 (M); expenditures, $2,757,272,
including $2,085,930 for 175 grants (high:
$218,000; low: $500; average: $5,000-
$12,500) and $280,149 for 60 grants to
individuals.
Purpose and activities: Giving through six
main programs: 1) fellowships for pre-doctoral
research in art history; 2) advanced training
and research in conservation of works of art; 3)
development of scholarly resources in the fields
of art history and conservation; 4) conservation
and restoration of monuments overseas; 5)
archaeological fieldwork emphasizing art
history; 6) occasional related projects.
Types of support awarded: Matching funds,
professorships, internships, fellowships,
research, publications, conferences and
seminars.
Limitations: No support for art history
programs below the pre-doctoral level, or the
purchase of works of art. No grants for living
artists, or for operating budgets, continuing
support, annual campaigns, endowments,
deficit financing, capital funds, or films; no
loans.
Publications: Annual report, application
guidelines, program policy statement.
Application information:
  Initial approach: Proposal
  Copies of proposal: 1

Deadline(s): November 30, for research
fellowships in art history; January 31, for
fellowships in art conservation
Board meeting date(s): Usually in October
and May
Final notification: 3 months
Write: Dr. Marilyn Perry, President
Officers: Marilyn Perry,* President; John C.
Fontaine,* W. Clarke Wescoe, M.D.,* Vice-
Presidents; Robert A. Cassans, Secretary and
Treasurer.
Trustees:* Franklin D. Murphy, M.D.,
Chairman; Lyman Field.
Number of staff: 3 full-time professional; 1
part-time professional; 2 full-time support.
Employer Identification Number: 131624176

2630
**Krim (The Mathilde and Arthur B.)
Foundation, Inc.** ⌐
c/o Orion Pictures
711 Fifth Ave.
New York 10022

Donor(s): Arthur B. Krim.
Financial data: (yr. ended 12/31/82): Assets,
$145,518 (M); gifts received, $119,375;
expenditures, $178,307, including $176,575
for 108 grants (high: $35,000; low: $40).
Purpose and activities: Primarily local giving,
with emphasis on higher education, cultural
programs, health agencies, public policy, social
services, civil rights, Jewish organizations, and
an institute of sociology.
Limitations: Giving primarily in NY.
Director: Arthur B. Krim.
Employer Identification Number: 136219851

2631
**Kriser (Charles and Bertha) Foundation,
Inc.** ⌐
211 E. 43rd St.
New York 10017

Established in New York.
Donor(s): Sidney P. Kriser, Richard Feldstein,
Judy Feldstein, R.C. Mahon & Company, and
others.
Financial data: (yr. ended 5/31/83): Assets,
$1,827,470 (M); gifts received, $507,000;
expenditures, $240,902, including $240,779
for 85 grants (high: $35,000; low: $36).
Purpose and activities: Primarily local giving,
with emphasis on Jewish welfare organizations;
support also for health and hospitals, cultural
programs, and higher education.
Limitations: Giving primarily in NY.
Officers: David Kriser, President; Sidney Kriser,
Secretary; Leonard Kriser, Treasurer.
Employer Identification Number: 136188243

2632
**Kunstadter (The Albert) Family
Foundation**
1035 Fifth Ave.
New York 10028   (212) 249-1733
Additional telephone: (212) 593-0274

Incorporated in 1952 in Illinois.
Donor(s): Members of the Kunstadter family.

Financial data: (yr. ended 12/31/83): Assets,
$2,080,797 (M); expenditures, $199,510,
including $173,200 for 43 grants (high:
$50,000; low: $1,000; average: $2,000-
$6,000).
Purpose and activities: Broad purposes; local,
national, and, where possible, international
giving, including support for education and the
arts.
Types of support awarded: Operating
budgets, endowment funds, special projects,
general purposes.
Limitations: Giving primarily in east coast
states between Boston, MA, and Washington,
DC. No support for religious purposes. No
grants to individuals, or for deficit financing,
building funds, land acquisition, scholarships
and fellowships, or matching gifts; no loans.
Publications: Annual report.
Application information:
Initial approach: Letter
Copies of proposal: 1
Deadline(s): Submit short proposal preferably
before November
Board meeting date(s): June and as required
Final notification: 2 weeks for negative
responses, 1 to 3 months for positive ones
Write: John W. Kunstadter, President or
Geraldine S. Kunstadter, Vice-President
Officers and Directors: Peter Kunstadter,
Chairman; John W. Kunstadter, President and
Treasurer; Geraldine S. Kunstadter, Vice-
President and Secretary; Sally Lennington
Kunstadter, Vice-President; Christopher
Kunstadter, Elizabeth Kunstadter, John W.
Kunstadter, Jr., Lisa Kunstadter.
Number of staff: None.
Employer Identification Number: 366047975

2633
L and L Foundation ⌐
781 Fifth Ave.
New York 10022

Incorporated in 1963 in New York.
Donor(s): Lawrence E. Brinn.
Financial data: (yr. ended 12/31/82): Assets,
$3,737,755 (M); gifts received, $3,500;
expenditures, $247,905, including $184,545
for 48 grants (high: $35,200; low: $100).
Purpose and activities: Broad purposes;
emphasis on hospitals, higher education,
cultural programs, including the performing
arts, and youth and child welfare agencies,
largely in New York.
Limitations: Giving primarily in NY.
Application information:
Write: Lawrence E. Brinn, President
Officers and Directors: Lawrence E. Brinn,
President and Treasurer; Mildred F.
Cunningham, Vice-President.
Employer Identification Number: 136155758

2634
La Sala (The Stefano) Foundation, Inc.
371 North Ave.
New Rochelle 10801   (914) 235-1974

Incorporated in 1956 in New York.
Donor(s): Members of the La Sala family, La
Sala Contracting Company, Inc., and others.

Financial data: (yr. ended 11/30/82): Assets,
$1,447,509 (M); expenditures, $138,183,
including $126,507 for 75 grants (high:
$16,700; low: $50).
Purpose and activities: Religious and
charitable purposes; primarily local giving, with
emphasis on higher and secondary education
and hospitals; grants also for Roman Catholic
church support, social agencies and a school
for the handicapped.
Limitations: Giving primarily in the New York,
NY, area.
Application information:
Write: A. Stephen La Sala
Trustees: A. Stephen La Sala, Andrew J. La
Sala, Anthony La Sala, Frank La Sala.
Number of staff: 1 part-time professional; 1
part-time support.
Employer Identification Number: 136110920

2635
Lakeview Fund, Inc. ▼
200 Park Ave., 34th Fl.
New York 10166   (212) 972-6070

Incorporated in 1966 in New York.
Donor(s): DeWitt Wallace.†
Financial data: (yr. ended 12/31/82): Assets,
$5,475,668 (M); expenditures, $3,840,339,
including $3,779,174 for 67 grants (high:
$1,182,000; low: $425; average: $10,000-
$25,000).
Purpose and activities: Support primarily for
independent schools and activities fostering
qualities of leadership and character in young
people, including scholarships, summer camps,
experiences abroad, explorations, projects
promoting an understanding of the history and
economy of the United States, and special
medical and educational projects; grants also
for hospitals and cultural programs.
Types of support awarded: Operating
budgets, continuing support, matching funds,
consulting services, internships, scholarship
funds, exchange programs, special projects.
Limitations: No grants to individuals, or for
annual campaigns, seed money, emergency or
capital funds, deficit financing, research,
demonstration projects, publications, or
conferences; no loans.
Application information: Funds fully
committed.
Board meeting date(s): Semiannually
Final notification: 6 months
Write: Barnabas McHenry, Secretary
Officers: John A. O'Hara,* President; Barnabas
McHenry,* Secretary and Treasurer.
Directors:* Edward T. Thompson, Lila
Acheson Wallace.
Number of staff: None.
Employer Identification Number: 136203422

2636
Lang (Eugene M.) Foundation
122 East 42nd St.
New York 10168   (212) 687-4741

Established in 1968 in New York.
Donor(s): Eugene M. Lang.

Financial data: (yr. ended 12/31/84): Assets, $14,897,000 (M); gifts received, $1,039,000; expenditures, $930,000, including $820,000 for 61 grants (high: $440,000; low: $100).
Purpose and activities: Primarily local giving, with emphasis on higher education, cultural programs, and hospitals.
Types of support awarded: Operating budgets, continuing support, annual campaigns, seed money, emergency funds, scholarship funds, professorships, internships, fellowships, special projects, conferences and seminars.
Limitations: Giving primarily in NY and neighboring area. No grants to individuals, or for capital or endowment funds, deficit financing, publications, research, or matching gifts; no loans.
Application information:
Initial approach: Letter
Board meeting date(s): April and November
Write: Eugene M. Lang, Trustee
Trustees: David A. Lang, Eugene M. Lang, Stephen Lang, Theresa Lang, Jane Lang McGrew.
Number of staff: 1 part-time professional; 1 full-time support.
Employer Identification Number: 136153412

2637
Langeloth (The Jacob and Valeria) Foundation ▼
One East 42nd St.
New York 10017 (212) 687-3760

Incorporated in 1915 in New York as the Valeria Home; renamed in 1975.
Donor(s): Jacob Langeloth.†
Financial data: (yr. ended 11/30/84): Assets, $21,651,495 (M); expenditures, $1,584,939, including $1,210,000 for 20 grants (high: $100,000; low: $10,000; average: $39,000-$82,000).
Purpose and activities: Grants to nonprofit hospitals and health-care facilities in the New York metropolitan area and Westchester County, primarily to defray costs incurred by in-patients who are "people of education," or are involved in the arts.
Types of support awarded: General purposes, continuing support.
Limitations: Giving primarily in NY, with emphasis on New York City and Westchester County. No grants to individuals.
Application information: Applications invited only from previous recipients.
Initial approach: Letter
Copies of proposal: 1
Deadline(s): September 1
Board meeting date(s): February and September
Write: William R. Cross, Jr., President
Officers and Directors: John L. Loeb, Chairman; William R. Cross, Jr., President and Executive Director; George Labalme, Jr., Vice-President; Julian B. Beaty, Jr., Secretary; Henry A. Loeb, Treasurer; Mrs. Claude Boillot, Adam Hochschild, John L. Loeb, Jr., Peter K. Loeb, Richard G. Poole.
Number of staff: 1 part-time professional; 2 full-time support.
Employer Identification Number: 131773646

2638
Larsen Fund, Inc.
Time & Life Bldg., Rm. 3949
New York 10020 (212) 841-2665

Incorporated in 1941 in New York.
Donor(s): Roy E. Larsen.†
Financial data: (yr. ended 12/31/83): Assets, $3,307,778 (M); expenditures, $336,869, including $307,181 for grants (high: $100,956; low: $500).
Purpose and activities: Broad purposes; grants largely for higher education and conservation; support also for a library and a hospital, primarily in the New York area and Massachusetts.
Limitations: Giving primarily in the New York, NY, area, and MA. No grants to individuals.
Application information:
Initial approach: Letter
Copies of proposal: 1
Deadline(s): Submit proposal preferably between April and July
Board meeting date(s): May and December
Write: Robert R. Larsen, President
Officers: Robert R. Larsen,* President and Secretary; Ann Larsen Simonson,* Christopher Larsen,* Vice-Presidents; Marcelle Coudrai, Treasurer.
Directors:* Jonathan Z. Larsen.
Employer Identification Number: 136104430

2639
Lasdon Foundation, Inc. ⌥
45 Rockefeller Plaza, Suite 2355
New York 10111 (212) 977-8420

Incorporated in 1946 in Delaware.
Donor(s): W.S. Lasdon, Stanley S. Lasdon, J.S. Lasdon,† M.S. Lasdon.†
Financial data: (yr. ended 11/30/82): Assets, $2,995,742 (M); expenditures, $232,863, including $137,005 for 83 grants (high: $25,000; low: $50).
Purpose and activities: To further research in the medical sciences through grants to universities and medical institutions; support also for the performing arts and Jewish welfare funds.
Types of support awarded: Research, matching funds, continuing support, annual campaigns.
Limitations: No grants to individuals, or for building or endowment funds, operating budgets, or program support.
Publications: Application guidelines.
Application information: Application form required.
Initial approach: Letter
Copies of proposal: 2
Deadline(s): Submit proposal preferably in March or September; no set deadline
Board meeting date(s): Quarterly
Final notification: 3 months
Write: Stanley S. Lasdon, Vice-President
Officers and Directors: William S. Lasdon, President; Stanley S. Lasdon, Vice-President and Secretary-Treasurer.
Number of staff: 2 full-time support.
Employer Identification Number: 131739997

2640
Lasker (Albert and Mary) Foundation, Inc. ⌥
865 First Avenue, 14A
New York 10017 (212) 421-9010

Incorporated in 1942 in New York.
Donor(s): Albert D. Lasker,† Mary W. Lasker.
Financial data: (yr. ended 12/31/82): Assets, $4,065,191 (M); gifts received, $172,453; expenditures, $671,612, including $251,294 for 38 grants (high: $50,000; low: $50) and $159,656 for 1 foundation-administered program.
Purpose and activities: Broad purposes; primarily concerned with medical research; annual Lasker awards given to honor and encourage outstanding medical research; support also for a beautification program in New York City, health programs, and the arts.
Application information:
Deadline(s): None
Write: Mary W. Lasker, President
Officers and Directors: Mary W. Lasker, President; Alice Fordyce, William McC. Blair, Catherine G. Blair, Vice-Presidents; James W. Fordyce, Secretary and Treasurer; Christopher Brody, Anne B. Fordyce, Anna R. Hoffman, David Morse.
Employer Identification Number: 131680062

2641
Lastfogel (Abe and Frances) Foundation ⌥
c/o Wallin, Simon, Black and Company
1350 Ave. of the Americas
New York 10019

Established in 1972 in California.
Donor(s): Abe Lastfogel, Frances Lastfogel.†
Financial data: (yr. ended 12/31/82): Assets, $796,124 (M); gifts received, $116,630; expenditures, $257,940, including $257,715 for 166 grants (high: $50,000; low: $250).
Purpose and activities: Grants primarily in the Los Angeles area and in New York for Jewish welfare funds, education, health and social service agencies, including those affiliated with the motion picture industry.
Limitations: Giving primarily in the Los Angeles, CA, area and NY.
Officers and Directors:* Morris Stoller,* Chairman and Treasurer; Sam Weisbord,* President; Roger Davis,* Lee Stevens,* Walter Zifkin,* Vice-Presidents; Lawrence Lewis, Secretary.
Employer Identification Number: 237146829

2642
Lauder Foundation, The ▼ ⌥
767 Fifth Ave.
New York 10022 (212) 572-4217

Incorporated in 1962 in New York.
Donor(s): Mrs. Estee Lauder, Joseph H. Lauder,† Leonard A. Lauder, Ronald S. Lauder.
Financial data: (yr. ended 11/30/82): Assets, $6,600,619 (M); expenditures, $949,059, including $934,745 for 57 grants (high: $178,150; low: $1,000).

Purpose and activities: To provide creative playgrounds for the children of New York City, featuring educational and recreational facilities under supervision; support also for social agencies, museums, cultural programs, medical research, and education, primarily in the New York City metropolitan area.
Limitations: Giving primarily in the New York, NY, metropolitan area.
Application information:
Write: Jeannine Boullier
Officers and Directors: Estee Lauder, President; Ronald S. Lauder, Vice-President; Leonard A. Lauder, Secretary-Treasurer.
Employer Identification Number: 136153743

2643
Lavanburg (Fred L.) Foundation
950 Third Ave., 30th Fl.
New York 10022   (212) 371-5060

Incorporated in 1927 in New York.
Donor(s): Fred L. Lavanburg.†
Financial data: (yr. ended 12/31/84): Assets, $1,564,899 (M); gifts received, $1,480; expenditures, $109,898, including $43,033 for 3 grants (high: $33,033; low: $5,000; average: $5,000-$10,000).
Purpose and activities: Major objectives related to the improvement of low- and middle-income housing and design, the development of neighborhood, city, and regional planning, and the movement to resolve problems associated with family and community living
Types of support awarded: Seed money, matching funds, special projects, publications, conferences and seminars.
Limitations: No grants to individuals, or for endowment funds, scholarships, fellowships, or operating budgets; no loans.
Application information: Foundation initiates most of its own programs.
Initial approach: Brief proposal
Copies of proposal: 1
Deadline(s): Submit proposal preferably in April or August
Board meeting date(s): May and September
Final notification: 2 weeks
Write: Oscar S. Straus II, President
Officers and Trustees: Oscar S. Straus II, President; Rowley Bialla, Secretary; Richard M. Rossbach, Treasurer; Pauline Falk, Leonard A. Hockstader II, James A. Kingsland, Peter O. Lawson-Johnston, Oscar S. Schafer, Jr., Roger Schafer, Oscar Straus, III, Harold S. Williams.
Number of staff: 1 part-time professional; 2 part-time support.
Employer Identification Number: 131850830

2644
Lavanburg-Corner House, Inc., The
130 East 59th St., Rm. 902
New York 10022   (212) 980-1000

Incorporated in 1928 in New York.
Donor(s): Fred L. Lavanburg,† Sara Lavanburg Strauss.
Financial data: (yr. ended 12/31/83): Assets, $2,319,750 (M); expenditures, $220,411, including $212,609 for 51 grants (high: $17,000; low: $2,000; average: $3,000).

Purpose and activities: Local grants to community agencies and schools for demonstration, innovative pilot projects dealing with welfare and health services to seriously disadvantaged children and youth through high school.
Types of support awarded: Seed money, matching funds, scholarship funds, special projects.
Limitations: Giving limited to metropolitan New York, NY. No grants to individuals, or for operating budgets, continuing support, annual campaigns, emergency funds, deficit financing, capital or endowment funds, research, publications, or conferences; no loans.
Publications: Application guidelines.
Application information:
Initial approach: Letter, full proposal, or telephone
Copies of proposal: 1
Deadline(s): Submit proposal preferably in February or September; deadline 6 weeks prior to board meetings
Board meeting date(s): May and December
Final notification: 1 week after board meetings
Write: Robert B. Goldmann, Staff Consultant
Officers and Directors: Robert L. Popper, President; Ira H. Lustgarten, Vice-President; Herbert Millman, Secretary; Mrs. Leonard H. Bernheim, Henry Kohn, Mark D. Litt, Mrs. Henry A. Loeb, Millard L. Midonick, Ann Sand, Sanford Solender.
Number of staff: 1 part-time professional.
Employer Identification Number: 131960060

2645
L.A.W. Fund, Inc. ▼
200 Park Ave., 34th Fl.
New York 10166   (212) 907-6900

Incorporated in 1956 in New York.
Donor(s): Lila Acheson Wallace.
Financial data: (yr. ended 12/31/82): Assets, $8,342,238 (M); gifts received, $1,104,254; expenditures, $6,342,409, including $6,289,254 for 39 grants (high: $1,689,254; low: $1,000; average: $10,000).
Purpose and activities: Giving primarily in the New York metropolitan area for preservation, restoration, and maintenance of places of beauty, museums, and sanctuaries; direct project support for the performing arts and general support for conservation activities. Giving indirectly for same purposes through a New York community foundation.
Types of support awarded: Operating budgets, continuing support, land acquisition, publications, conferences and seminars, endowment funds, special projects.
Limitations: Giving primarily in the New York, NY, metropolitan area. No support for radio, film, or video projects. No grants to individuals, or for annual campaigns, seed money, emergency or building funds, deficit financing, equipment, matching gifts, scholarships or fellowships, or research; no loans.
Publications: Program policy statement, application guidelines.
Application information: Funds fully committed.

Deadline(s): None
Board meeting date(s): Semiannually
Final notification: 4 weeks
Write: Barnabas McHenry, Secretary
Officers and Directors: Lila Acheson Wallace, President and Treasurer; Barnabas McHenry, Secretary; Richard H. Howland, Laurance S. Rockefeller, Edward T. Thompson, John Walker.
Number of staff: None.
Employer Identification Number: 136086859

2646
Lazar Foundation, The
680 Madison Ave.
New York 10021

Incorporated in 1957 in Delaware.
Donor(s): Jack Lazar, and others.
Financial data: (yr. ended 12/31/83): Assets, $5,180,000 (L); gifts received, $18,825; expenditures, $275,000, including $229,000 for 41 grants (high: $100,000; low: $100).
Purpose and activities: Broad purposes; primarily local giving, with emphasis on welfare funds, higher education, including medical education, and hospitals.
Limitations: Giving primarily in NY.
Officers and Trustees: Jack Lazar, President; Celien Hibbel, Vice-President; Helen B. Lazar, Secretary-Treasurer.
Employer Identification Number: 136088182

2647
Lebensfeld Foundation, The ⌑
600 Fifth Ave.
New York 10020

Incorporated in 1959 in New York.
Donor(s): Harry Lebensfeld.
Financial data: (yr. ended 8/31/83): Assets, $1,299,151 (M); expenditures, $139,257, including $136,190 for 42 grants (high: $50,000; low: $50).
Purpose and activities: Broad purposes; grants primarily for higher and secondary education, hospitals, and Jewish welfare funds.
Application information:
Write: Andrew G. Pietrini, Vice-President
Officers: Harry Lebensfeld, President; Andrew G. Pietrini, Vice-President and Secretary; Joseph F. Arrigo, Vice-President and Treasurer; Lynne Pasculano, Vice-President.
Employer Identification Number: 136086169

2648
LeBrun Foundation ⌑
2100 Main Place Tower
Buffalo 14202

Established in 1974.
Donor(s): Jennifer L. Jacobs.
Financial data: (yr. ended 6/30/83): Assets, $1,818,097 (M); gifts received, $77,000; expenditures, $126,282, including $107,091 for 8 grants (high: $36,000; low: $2,995).

Purpose and activities: Grants primarily for international welfare and justice organizations, including those under Roman Catholic and Jewish auspices and an amnesty organization.
Trustees: Thomas R. Beecher, Jr., Jennifer L. Jacobs.
Employer Identification Number: 237408547

2649
Lee (James T.) Foundation, Inc.
219 East 70th St.
P.O. Box 509, Lenox Hill Station
New York 10021

Incorporated in 1958 in New York.
Donor(s): James T. Lee.†
Financial data: (yr. ended 11/30/82): Assets, $3,041,783 (M); expenditures, $185,483, including $164,500 for 18 grants (high: $20,000; low: $2,500).
Purpose and activities: Broad purposes; primarily local giving, with emphasis on higher education, including medical education, hospitals, religious associations, and child welfare.
Types of support awarded: Continuing support, annual campaigns, emergency funds, deficit financing, scholarship funds, special projects, research.
Limitations: Giving primarily in NY. No grants to individuals, or for operating budgets, seed money, capital or endowment funds, publications, or conferences; no loans.
Application information:
 Initial approach: Letter
 Copies of proposal: 1
 Deadline(s): Submit proposal preferably in September; deadline October 1
 Board meeting date(s): February, May, August, and November
 Final notification: 3 months
 Write: James Bloor, President
Officers and Directors: James Bloor, President; Robert Rivel, Vice-President and Treasurer; Randolph C. Larsen, Vice-President; John J. Duffy, Secretary; Verne S. Atwater, John B. Bridgwood, Robert Graber, Benjamin Grund, Raymond T. O'Keefe.
Number of staff: None.
Employer Identification Number: 131878496

2650
Leff Foundation, Inc. ⌖
c/o National Spinning Co., Inc.
183 Madison Ave.
New York 10016

Incorporated in 1942 in New York.
Donor(s): Carl Leff, Phillip Leff, National Spinning Co., Inc.
Financial data: (yr. ended 12/31/82): Assets, $893,652 (M); gifts received, $83,500; expenditures, $124,520, including $123,220 for grants.
Purpose and activities: Support primarily for Jewish welfare funds and educational and religious organizations, including institutions in Israel.
Officers: Carl Leff, President; Eleanor Leff, Lilian Leff, Vice-Presidents; Joseph Leff, Secretary-Treasurer.
Employer Identification Number: 116007845

2651
Lefrak (Samuel J. & Ethel) Foundation, Inc. ⌖
97-77 Queens Blvd.
Rego Park 11374

Established in 1963.
Donor(s): Park Lane Associates.
Financial data: (yr. ended 12/31/82): Assets, $187,716 (M); gifts received, $17,100; expenditures, $227,736, including $227,646 for 102 grants (high: $152,623; low: $10).
Purpose and activities: Primarily local support for Jewish schools and temples, and for cultural programs and social services; support also for a university.
Limitations: Giving primarily in New York, NY.
Officer: Simon J. Lefrak, President.
Employer Identification Number: 116043788

2652
Lehman (Edith and Herbert) Foundation, Inc.
c/o Davis, Wind & Co.
41 E. 42nd St.
New York 10017 (212) 599-1818

Incorporated in 1952 in New York.
Donor(s): Mrs. Edith A. Lehman,† Herbert Lehman.†
Financial data: (yr. ended 9/30/84): Assets, $2,542,579 (M); expenditures, $136,613, including $123,750 for 9 grants (high: $50,000; low: $3,500).
Purpose and activities: Broad purposes; grants largely for welfare and health services.
Officers and Directors: John R. Lehman, President; Arthur G. Altschul, Arthur M. Master, Jr., Vice-Presidents; George DeSipio, Secretary-Treasurer; Wendy Lash, Stephanie Wise.
Employer Identification Number: 136094015

2653
Lehman (Robert) Foundation, Inc. ▼ ⌖
c/o Kelly, Drye & Warren
600 Fifth Ave., 19th Fl.
New York 10028

Incorporated in 1943 in New York.
Donor(s): Robert Lehman.†
Financial data: (yr. ended 9/30/82): Assets, $23,051,353 (M); expenditures, $1,328,253, including $1,187,936 for 15 grants (high: $641,056; low: $1,000).
Purpose and activities: Broad purposes; for the maintenance, conservation, and preservation of the Robert Lehman collection of the Metropolitan Museum of Art; some support also for higher education and cultural programs, with emphasis on visual arts and related teaching activities and publications.
Limitations: Giving primarily in New York, NY.
Application information:
 Deadline(s): None
 Write: Paul C. Guth, Executive Secretary

Officers and Directors: Alvin W. Pearson, President; Charles Zadok, Vice-President; Paul C. Guth, Executive Secretary; Philip H. Isles, Treasurer; Robert A. Bernhard, James M. Hester, Michael Thomas, Edwin L. Weisl, Jr.
Number of staff: None.
Employer Identification Number: 136094018

2654
Leir (Henry J. and Erna D.) Foundation, Inc. ⌖
c/o Oppenheim, Appel, Dixon & Company
101 Park Ave.
New York 10178
Additional address: 3 Place Winston Churchill, Luxembourg City, Luxembourg

Established in 1972.
Financial data: (yr. ended 12/31/82): Assets, $1,907,909 (M); expenditures, $969,024, including $931,175 for 44 grants (high: $170,503; low: $640).
Purpose and activities: Giving limited to the Duchy of Luxembourg for social welfare, with emphasis on homes, handicapped, and youth agencies.
Limitations: Giving limited to Luxembourg.
Directors: Edmond Israel, Henry J. Leir, Jacques Zaesch, Henry Loutsch, Paul-Henri Mayers, Leon Schaus, Antoine Wehenkel.
Employer Identification Number: 237176054

2655
Lemberg Foundation, Inc. ⌖
400 Madison Ave., Rm. 909
New York 10017 (212) 355-2727

Incorporated in 1945 in New York.
Donor(s): Samuel Lemberg, Samuel Fields.
Financial data: (yr. ended 12/31/82): Assets, $2,121,627 (M); expenditures, $217,170, including $197,260 for 50 grants (high: $32,100; low: $10).
Purpose and activities: Broad purposes; primarily local giving, with emphasis on Jewish welfare funds, higher education, temple support, and the performing arts.
Types of support awarded: Building funds, endowment funds, special projects, research, scholarship funds, fellowships.
Limitations: Giving primarily in NY. No grants to individuals, or for matching gifts; no loans.
Application information:
 Initial approach: Letter, proposal, or telephone
 Copies of proposal: 1
 Board meeting date(s): As required
 Write: Suzanne Usdan, President
Officers: Suzanne Usdan, President; Norman Silverson, Secretary; John Usdan, Treasurer.
Number of staff: 1.
Employer Identification Number: 136082064

2656
Leonhardt Foundation, Inc., The ⌖
One Chase Manhattan Plaza, 47th Fl.
New York 10005

Incorporated in 1953 in New York.
Donor(s): Frederick H. Leonhardt.

Financial data: (yr. ended 7/31/83): Assets, $13,207,219 (M); expenditures, $772,875, including $631,250 for 42 grants (high: $225,000; low: $1,000).
Purpose and activities: Support primarily for higher and secondary education and cultural programs, including a museum; grants also for social services and hospitals.
Limitations: Giving primarily in NY and CT for social services and hospitals; wider distribution for other areas of support.
Application information:
    Board meeting date(s): Fourth Monday in September
Officers and Directors: Frederick H. Leonhardt, President; Joanne L. Cassullo, Dorothea L. Demetrion, Frederick Leonhardt, Vice-Presidents; Richard A. Stark, Secretary-Treasurer; Alexander D. Forger.
Employer Identification Number: 136123271

2657
Lever Brothers Company Foundation, Inc.
390 Park Ave.
New York 10022   (212) 688-6000

Incorporated in 1952 in New York.
Donor(s): Lever Brothers Company.
Financial data: (yr. ended 12/31/84): Assets, $420,991 (M); gifts received, $200,000; expenditures, $193,317, including $192,793 for 138 grants (high: $15,000; low: $50; average: $1,000).
Purpose and activities: Broad purposes; grants largely for health and human services, higher education, civil rights, hospitals, community development, civic affairs, and cultural programs in areas of company operations .
Types of support awarded: Operating budgets.
Limitations: Giving primarily in areas of company operations. No support for religious or international organizations. No grants to individuals, or for building funds (except for hospitals), or endowment funds; no loans.
Publications: Application guidelines.
Application information:
    Initial approach: Letter or full proposal
    Copies of proposal: 1
    Deadline(s): December 31
    Board meeting date(s): February
    Final notification: 1 month after meeting
    Write: Humphrey Sullivan, Contributions Committee
Officers: Paul W. Cook,* President; J. Handler, Secretary.
Directors:* D. Lunghino, C. Roberts.
Number of staff: 1 part-time professional; 1 part-time support.
Employer Identification Number: 136122117

2658
Levinson (Morris L.) Foundation, Inc. ⌐
c/o Becker Ross Stone DeStefano and Klein
41 East 42nd St.
New York 10017

Incorporated in 1952 in New York.
Donor(s): Morris L. Levinson, Associated Products, Inc.

Financial data: (yr. ended 6/30/84): Assets, $2,210,038 (M); expenditures, $80,104, including $78,039 for 42 grants (high: $25,000; low: $15).
Purpose and activities: Broad purposes; emphasis on local Jewish welfare funds, temple support, and higher education in Israel.
Limitations: Giving primarily in NY and Israel. No grants to individuals.
Application information:
    Write: Morris L. Levinson, President
Officers and Directors: Morris L. Levinson, President; Barbara S. Levinson, Vice-President; Daniel G. Ross, Secretary.
Employer Identification Number: 136132727

2659
Leviton Foundation, Inc. - New York ⌐
59-25 Little Neck Pkwy.
Little Neck 11362

Incorporated in 1952 in New York.
Donor(s): Leviton Manufacturing Company, American Insulated Wire Corporation.
Financial data: (yr. ended 12/31/81): Assets, $1,351,208 (M); gifts received, $140,000; expenditures, $209,245, including $209,145 for 29 grants (high: $75,000; low: $25).
Purpose and activities: Charitable purposes; giving primarily in Rhode Island and New York, with emphasis on Jewish welfare funds; some support for education and community funds.
Limitations: Giving primarily in NY and RI.
Officers: Harold Leviton, President; Jack Amsterdam, Secretary and Treasurer.
Employer Identification Number: 116006368

2660
Levitt Foundation, The
57 Northern Blvd.
Greenvale 11548

Incorporated in 1949 in New York.
Donor(s): Levitt and Sons, Inc., and others.
Financial data: (yr. ended 4/30/83): Assets, $4,519,394 (M); expenditures, $388,347, including $388,225 for 74 grants (high: $25,400; low: $100).
Purpose and activities: Broad purposes; support primarily for higher education, medical research, relief agencies, and aid to the handicapped.
Officers and Trustees: William J. Levitt, President and Treasurer; Simone H. Levitt, Vice-President.
Employer Identification Number: 136128226

2661
Levy (Isaac Youssef) Family Foundation ⌐
c/o Jerome Kamerman
500 Fifth Ave.
New York 10110

Established in 1969.
Donor(s): James Levy, Lucien Levy, Mary Levy.
Financial data: (yr. ended 4/30/82): Assets, $11,100 (M); gifts received, $108,655; expenditures, $108,769, including $108,655 for 13 grants (high: $100,000; low: $40).

Purpose and activities: Giving primarily in New York City and in Switzerland for Jewish educational and welfare organizations.
Limitations: Giving primarily in New York, NY, and Switzerland.
Trustee: Jerome Kamerman.
Employer Identification Number: 237015550

2662
Levy (The Jerome) Foundation ⌐
Warshaw, Burstein, Cohen, Schleisinge
555 Fifth Ave.
New York 10017

Trust established in 1955 in New York.
Donor(s): Leon Levy, S. Jay Levy.
Financial data: (yr. ended 10/31/84): Assets, $16,381 (M); gifts received, $329,198; expenditures, $476,240, including $464,563 for 67 grants (high: $200,000; low: $13).
Purpose and activities: Broad purposes; grants largely for Jewish welfare funds, the fine arts, and higher education; support also for organizations interested in freedom of expression.
Trustees: Leon Levy, S. Jay Levy.
Employer Identification Number: 136159573

2663
Lewis Foundation, Inc., The ⌐
c/o S.B. Lewis and Company
76 Beaver St.
New York 10005

Incorporated in 1952 in New York.
Donor(s): Salim L. Lewis,† Diana B. Lewis.
Financial data: (yr. ended 8/31/83): Assets, $1,633,241 (M); expenditures, $118,883, including $110,770 for 63 grants (high: $25,000; low: $10).
Purpose and activities: Broad purposes; primarily local giving, with emphasis on higher and secondary education, Jewish welfare funds, and child development.
Limitations: Giving primarily in NY.
Officers: Salim B. Lewis, President; Barbara Lewis, Vice-President; Milton B. Eulau, Secretary and Treasurer.
Employer Identification Number: 136062713

2664
Li Foundation, Inc., The ⌐
63 Herbill Rd.
Glen Cove 11542

Established in 1944.
Financial data: (yr. ended 12/31/83): Assets, $4,245,278 (M); expenditures, $256,934, including $208,999 for 44 grants to individuals.
Purpose and activities: Giving entirely for scholarships to Chinese students.
Types of support awarded: Student aid.
Application information: Application form required.
    Deadline(s): None
    Write: John C. Li, Vice-President
Officers and Director:* John C. Li,* Vice-President; Helen Coe Convisser, Treasurer; Lucy Li, Financial Director.
Employer Identification Number: 136098783

2665
Liebowitz (J. S.) Foundation, Inc. ⌑
1270 Ave. of the Americas
New York 10020

Incorporated in 1945 in New York.
Donor(s): J.S. Leibowitz.
Financial data: (yr. ended 11/30/82): Assets,
$745,337 (M); expenditures, $193,400,
including $180,615 for 33 grants (high:
$60,000; low: $15).
Purpose and activities: Grants primarily for
Jewish welfare funds, higher education, and
health agencies.
Officers: J.S. Liebowitz, President and
Treasurer; Shirley W. Liebowitz, Vice-President;
Bernard Kashdan, Secretary.
Employer Identification Number: 136100091

2666
LILCO Charitable Trust ⌑
250 Old Country Rd.
Mineola 11501   (516) 228-2081

Trust established in 1966 in New York.
Donor(s): Long Island Lighting Company.
Financial data: (yr. ended 12/31/82): Assets,
$2,311 (M); gifts received, $450,000;
expenditures, $450,748, including $449,850
for 57 grants (high: $275,000; low: $500).
Purpose and activities: Charitable and
educational purposes; grants primarily for
community funds, higher education, hospitals,
and health agencies, mainly in areas of
company operations on Long Island.
Limitations: Giving primarily in areas of
company operations on Long Island, NY. No
grants to individuals, or for endowment funds,
research programs, scholarships, fellowships, or
matching gifts; no loans.
Application information:
   Initial approach: Letter
   Copies of proposal: 1
   Board meeting date(s): Usually in March,
      May, July, and November
   Write: Kenneth A. Hutcheson, Secretary
Trustees: Edward M. Barrett, Frank C. Mackay,
George C. Soos.
Employer Identification Number: 116082329

2667
Lincoln Fund, The
292 Madison Ave., 24th Fl.
New York 10017   (212) 889-4109

Incorporated in 1898 in New York.
Financial data: (yr. ended 6/30/84): Assets,
$3,663,816 (M); expenditures, $184,412,
including $149,500 for 13 grants (high:
$22,000; low: $5,000).
Purpose and activities: Local giving for aid to
the elderly, education, nursing, and medical
programs; grants limited to pilot projects,
demonstrations, and expansion of programs.
Types of support awarded: Continuing
support, seed money, matching funds,
scholarship funds, special projects.
Limitations: Giving limited to New York, NY.
No grants to individuals, or for building or
endowment funds, operating budgets, or
general corporate purposes.

Application information:
   Initial approach: Letter
   Copies of proposal: 10
   Deadline(s): May 1
   Board meeting date(s): September,
      December, March, and June
   Final notification: 3 to 4 months
   Write: Mrs. James C. Sargent, President
Officers and Directors: Mrs. James C. Sargent,
President; Mrs. Duer McLanahan, Vice-
President; Mrs. William Brown, Secretary;
Lawrence L. Lanier, Treasurer; Mrs. Paule R.
Alexander, Jean M. Green, E. Eldred Hill, Mrs.
Thomas D. Warren.
Number of staff: 1 part-time support.
Employer Identification Number: 131740466

2668
Lindemann Foundation, Inc., The ⌑
66 East 34th St.
New York 10016

Incorporated in 1943 in New York.
Donor(s): Joseph S. Lindemann.
Financial data: (yr. ended 12/31/82): Assets,
$1,928,278 (M); expenditures, $189,972,
including $160,784 for 76 grants (high:
$100,000; low: $10).
Purpose and activities: Charitable purposes;
general giving, with emphasis on higher
education in Israel and the United States and
Jewish welfare funds.
Officers and Directors: Joseph S. Lindemann,
President; Lilyan S. Lindemann, Vice-President;
George L. Lindemann, Secretary-Treasurer;
Murry C. Becker, Jack Greisman, Carol G.
Lindemann, Harold Rand, Barbara L. Schlei.
Employer Identification Number: 136140249

2669
Linder (Albert A. & Bertram N.)
Foundation, Inc.
305 East 40th St., PH C
New York 10016   (212) 986-7983

Incorporated in 1947 in New York.
Donor(s): Bertram N. Linder.
Financial data: (yr. ended 5/31/84): Assets,
$1,044,451 (M); expenditures, $66,185,
including $64,783 for 57 grants (high: $10,000;
low: $10).
Purpose and activities: Broad purposes; local
giving in New York and Scranton,
Pennsylvania, with emphasis on Jewish welfare
funds, community funds, higher education,
hospitals, and church and temple support.
Limitations: Giving primarily in NY and
Scranton, PA. No grants to individuals, or for
scholarships, fellowships, or matching gifts; no
loans.
Application information:
   Initial approach: Letter
   Copies of proposal: 1
   Deadline(s): Submit application preferably in
      April or early May; deadline May 15
   Board meeting date(s): June and December
   Write: Bertram N. Linder, Vice-President
Officers and Trustees: Mary Ellen Linder,
President and Treasurer; Bertram N. Linder,
Vice-President and Secretary; Robert Allen
Linder, Vice-President.
Employer Identification Number: 136100590

2670
Lindner (Fay J.) Foundation ⌑
1161 Meadowbrook Rd.
North Merrick 11566

Established in 1966.
Donor(s): Fay J. Lindner.
Financial data: (yr. ended 8/31/83): Assets,
$230,700 (M); gifts received, $100,000;
expenditures, $100,606, including $100,150
for 22 grants (high: $20,000; low: $20).
Purpose and activities: Primarily local giving
for hospitals and health agencies; grants also to
a university and a Jewish welfare agency.
Limitations: Giving primarily in Long Island,
NY.
Officer: Fay J. Lindner, President.
Employer Identification Number: 116043320

2671
Lingnan University, Trustees of
1290 Ave. of the Americas, Rm. 3450
New York 10104   (212) 397-4800

Established in 1893 in New York.
Financial data: (yr. ended 6/30/84): Assets,
$5,136,692 (M); gifts received, $5,388;
expenditures, $577,727, including $497,595
for 8 grants (high: $193,715; low: $2,685;
average: $2,500-$75,000).
Purpose and activities: Grants limited to Hong
Kong and China; support of higher education of
Chinese and other Far Eastern students.
Types of support awarded: Operating
budgets, continuing support, seed money,
professorships, internships, exchange programs,
research, publications, conferences and
seminars.
Limitations: Giving limited to support for
projects in Hong Kong and People's Republic
of China. No grants to individuals, or for
annual campaigns, emergency, capital, or
endowment funds; no loans.
Application information:
   Initial approach: Full proposal or letter
   Copies of proposal: 1
   Deadline(s): None
   Board meeting date(s): May and November
   Final notification: 6 months after meetings
   Write: Douglas P. Murray, Executive Director
Officers and Trustees: Russell A. Phillips, Jr.,
President; Ralph E. Lerner, Secretary;
Stuyvesant Wainwright, III, Treasurer; and 21
other trustees.
Number of staff: 1 part-time professional; 1
part-time support.
Employer Identification Number: 136400470

2672
Link (George), Jr. Foundation, Inc. ▼
c/o Emmet, Marvin and Martin
48 Wall St.
New York 10005   (212) 530-1974

Incorporated in 1980 in New York.
Donor(s): George Link, Jr.†
Financial data: (yr. ended 12/31/83): Assets,
$18,053,532 (M); gifts received, $5,563,851;
expenditures, $1,732,297, including
$1,625,850 for 95 grants (high: $260,000; low:
$500; average: $10,000).

Purpose and activities: Giving primarily for hospitals and medical research, higher and secondary education, and welfare.
Types of support awarded: Building funds, scholarship funds, fellowships, endowment funds.
Limitations: No grants to individuals, or for general support, operating budgets, continuing support, annual campaigns, seed money, emergency funds, deficit financing, equipment, land acquisition, renovation projects, or matching gifts; no loans.
Application information:
  Initial approach: Full proposal
  Copies of proposal: 5
  Deadline(s): None
  Board meeting date(s): Monthly except July and August
  Final notification: 6 weeks
  Write: Michael J. Catanzaro, Vice-President
Officers and Directors: Eleanor Irene Higgins Link, Chairman; Robert Emmet Link, Vice-Chairman; Bernard F. Joyce, Vice-President and Secretary; Michael J. Catanzaro, Vice-President and Treasurer; Coleman Clougherty, Vice-President.
Number of staff: None.
Employer Identification Number: 133041396

2673
Lipchitz (Jacques and Yulla) Foundation, Inc. ⌖
c/o H. D. Mott
6 E. 43rd St.
New York 10017

Established in 1962.
Donor(s): Yulla Lipchitz.
Financial data: (yr. ended 2/28/83): Assets, $3,451,782 (M); expenditures, $587,123, including $587,000 for grants.
Purpose and activities: Gifts of works of art by Jacques Lipchitz to various museums.
Officers: Yulla Lipchitz, President; Hanno D. Mott, Vice-President.
Employer Identification Number: 136151503

2674
Lippman Rose Schnurmacher Fund, Inc. ⌖
1114 First Ave.
New York 10021

Incorporated in 1945 in New York.
Donor(s): Rose Schnurmacher.†
Financial data: (yr. ended 12/31/82): Assets, $948,458 (M); expenditures, $982,354, including $952,645 for 17 grants (high: $307,500; low: $100).
Purpose and activities: Broad purposes; primarily local giving, with emphasis on Jewish welfare funds and hospitals; grants also for an optometric center.
Limitations: Giving primarily in NY.
Managers: Adolph Schnurmacher, Irwin Schnurmacher.
Employer Identification Number: 136126002

2675
Littauer (The Lucius N.) Foundation, Inc. ▼
60 East 42nd St., Suite 2910
New York 10165   (212) 697-2677

Incorporated in 1929 in New York.
Donor(s): Lucius N. Littauer.†
Financial data: (yr. ended 12/31/83): Assets, $13,534,666 (M); expenditures, $701,409, including $496,796 for 30 grants (high: $125,000; low: $200; average: $2,500-$10,000).
Purpose and activities: Charitable and educational purposes, with emphasis on the social sciences and the humanities; support for higher education with emphasis on Jewish and Middle Eastern studies, and refugee aid, including resettlement and rehabilitation; other interests include history and biography, language and literature, philosophy, economics, political science, and religion.
Types of support awarded: Research, publications, conferences and seminars, endowment funds, matching funds.
Limitations: No grants to individuals.
Application information:
  Initial approach: Full proposal
  Copies of proposal: 1
  Deadline(s): None
  Board meeting date(s): Semiannually and as required
  Final notification: 3 months
  Write: William Lee Frost, President
Officers and Directors: Harry Starr, Chairman and Treasurer; William Lee Frost, President; Issai Hosiosky, Vice-President and Secretary; Charles Berlin, Lee B. Harris, Henry A. Lowet, Peter J. Solomon.
Number of staff: 2 full-time professional; 1 part-time professional.
Employer Identification Number: 131688027

2676
Loeb (Frances and John L.) Foundation ⌖
375 Park Ave.
New York 10022

Incorporated in 1937 in New York.
Donor(s): John L. Loeb, Frances L. Loeb.
Financial data: (yr. ended 10/31/82): Assets, $2,230,521 (M); gifts received, $9,970; expenditures, $675,687, including $662,336 for 101 grants (high: $203,000; low: $100).
Purpose and activities: Broad purposes; with emphasis on higher education, hospitals, cultural programs, including museums, and the performing arts, Jewish welfare funds, and international activities.
Officers and Trustees: John L. Loeb, President and Treasurer; Frances L. Loeb, Vice-President; John L. Loeb, Jr., Secretary; Deborah L. Brice, Ann L. Bronfman.
Employer Identification Number: 136085598

2677
Loews Foundation ⌖
666 Fifth Ave.
New York 10103   (212) 841-1277

Trust established in 1957 in New York.
Donor(s): Loews Corporation, and subsidiaries.
Financial data: (yr. ended 12/31/82): Assets, $9,273 (M); expenditures, $835,826, including $809,304 for 37 grants (high: $509,181; low: $100) and $9,453 for employee matching gifts.
Purpose and activities: Charitable and educational purposes; grants primarily for Jewish welfare funds, higher education, including matching gifts and company-employee scholarships, and cultural organizations.
Types of support awarded: Employee matching gifts, employee related scholarships.
Trustees: Roy Posner, C.G. Sposato, Jr., Laurence A. Tisch.
Employer Identification Number: 136082817

2678
Lopin (The Sam and Anna) Foundation, Inc. ⌖
936 Fifth Ave.
New York 10021

Established in 1968.
Donor(s): Sam Lopin,† Anna Lopin.
Financial data: (yr. ended 6/30/83): Assets, $1,061,684 (M); expenditures, $133,761, including $128,327 for 71 grants (high: $100,000; low: $25).
Purpose and activities: Primarily local giving, with emphasis on a Jewish welfare fund and Jewish educational institutions; support also for social services.
Limitations: Giving primarily in NY.
Officer and Director: Anna Lopin, Vice-President and Secretary.
Employer Identification Number: 136275108

2679
Lounsbery (Richard) Foundation, Inc. ▼
159A East 61st St.
New York 10021   (212) 319-7033

Incorporated in 1959 in New York.
Donor(s): Richard Lounsbery Foundation, Inc. Trust.
Financial data: (yr. ended 12/31/83): Assets, $11,971,410 (M); gifts received, $1,106,517; expenditures, $1,803,827, including $1,427,486 for 54 grants (high: $100,000; low: $2,500; average: $500-$50,000).
Purpose and activities: Broad purposes; support primarily for higher and secondary education, international studies, science and cultural organizations, and medical research.
Types of support awarded: Seed money, emergency funds, matching funds, scholarship funds, fellowships, research, special projects, publications, conferences and seminars.
Limitations: No grants to individuals, or for capital, building, or endowment funds; no loans.
Application information: Funds mainly committed to projects developed by the directors; applications not encouraged.

Initial approach: Letter
Board meeting date(s): January, April, July, and October
Final notification: 2 months
Write: Alan F. McHenry, President
Officers and Directors: Alan F. McHenry, President and Treasurer; Benjamin J. Borden, Vice-President and Secretary; William J. McGill, Frederick Seitz, Lewis Thomas, M.D.
Number of staff: 1.
Employer Identification Number: 136081860

2680
Lowenstein (Leon) Foundation, Inc. ▼
1430 Broadway
New York 10018   (212) 930-5000

Incorporated in 1941 in New York.
Donor(s): Leon Lowenstein.†
Financial data: (yr. ended 12/31/82): Assets, $24,862,699 (M); gifts received, $485,000; expenditures, $1,017,056, including $845,513 for 123 grants (high: $260,000; low: $98).
Purpose and activities: Broad purposes; local giving, with emphasis on hospitals, higher education and social welfare.
Limitations: Giving limited to NY.
Officers: Robert Bendheim, President; John M. Bendheim, Vice-President; Bernard R. Rapoport, Secretary and Treasurer.
Employer Identification Number: 136015951

2681
Lubin (Joseph I. and Evelyn J.)
Foundation, Inc. ⌑
c/o Elk Realty, Inc.
145 Huguenot St.
New Rochelle 10801

Incorporated in 1948 in New York.
Donor(s): Evelyn J. Lubin, Joseph I. Lubin.†
Financial data: (yr. ended 12/31/84): Assets, $4,497,216 (M); gifts received, $400,000; expenditures, $216,925, including $184,025 for 27 grants (high: $35,000; low: $1,000).
Purpose and activities: Broad purposes; general giving, with emphasis on Jewish welfare funds and higher education; grants also for temple support and health and social agencies.
Officers and Directors: Alfred R. Goldstein, President; Frank Perry, Vice-President; Barbara Goldsmith, Secretary; Ann L. Goldstein, Treasurer; Hirschel E. Levine.
Employer Identification Number: 136075755

2682
Luce (The Henry) Foundation, Inc. ▼
111 West 50th St.
New York 10020   (212) 489-7700

Incorporated in 1936 in New York.
Donor(s): Henry R. Luce.†
Financial data: (yr. ended 12/31/83): Assets, $181,681,509 (M); gifts received, $120,000; expenditures, $6,455,828, including $4,572,096 for 108 grants (high: $750,000; low: $5,000; average: $25,000-$300,000), $179,576 for 15 grants to individuals and $108,370 for 90 employee matching gifts.

Purpose and activities: Grants for specific projects in the broad areas of Asian affairs, higher education and scholarships, theology, the arts, and public affairs. The Luce Scholars Program gives a select group of young American professionals, not Asian specialists, a year's work/study experience in the Far East. The Henry R. Luce Professorship Program provides five- or eight-year support for a limited number of integrative academic programs in the humanities and social sciences at private colleges and universities. The Luce Fund for Chinese Scholars provides support for leading humanists and social scientists from the People's Republic of China at 17 designated China studies centers. The Luce Fund for Scholarship in American Art, working through 43 pre-selected American museums, encourages research and scholarship with direct support of specific projects. International activities confined to East and Southeast Asia .
Types of support awarded: Seed money, employee matching gifts, special projects, research, professorships, internships, exchange programs, fellowships.
Limitations: Giving for international activities limited to East and Southeast Asia. No support for journalism or media projects. No grants to individuals (except for the Luce Scholars Program), or for endowment or domestic building funds, general support, scholarships and fellowships, or annual fund drives; no loans.
Publications: Annual report, application guidelines.
Application information: Nominees for scholars programs accepted from institutions only; individual applications cannot be considered.
Initial approach: Letter
Deadline(s): April 1 for Luce Professorship proposals; June 15 for Luce Fund for Scholarship in American Art proposals (by invitation only); first Monday in December for Luce Scholar Nominations; none for Program Grants
Board meeting date(s): June and December
Final notification: 1 month to 1 year; program grants awarded in late fall
Write: Robert E. Armstrong, Executive Director
Officers and Directors: Henry Luce III, President; Charles L. Stillman, Vice-President and Secretary-Treasurer; Robert E. Armstrong, Vice-President and Executive Director; John C. Evans, Mrs. Maurice T. Moore, Vice-Presidents; David V. Ragone, Charles C. Tillinghast, Jr.
Number of staff: 6 full-time professional; 4 full-time support.
Employer Identification Number: 136001282

2683
Lucerna Fund
85 Channel Dr.
Port Washington 11050   (516) 883-1775

Incorporated in 1965 in New York.
Donor(s): LuEsther T. Mertz.

Financial data: (yr. ended 12/31/84): Assets, $5,350,000 (M); expenditures, $363,000, including $2,000 for 1 grant and $310,000 for 1 foundation-administered program.
Purpose and activities: A private operating foundation established for the production and distribution of recording for the blind, visually impaired, and physically handicapped.
Limitations: No grants to individuals.
Publications: 990-PF.
Application information: Funds presently committed to a single project.
Board meeting date(s): April
Write: LuEsther T. Mertz, President
Officers and Directors: LuEsther T. Mertz, President; Robert W. Gilmore, Vice-President; William J. Rennert, Secretary; Robert I. Williams, Treasurer; Georgia Delano, Peter B. Putnam, Paul D. Richards, Robert W. Russell.
Number of staff: 3 full-time professional; 3 part-time professional.
Employer Identification Number: 116044099

2684
Lurcy (Georges) Charitable and
Educational Trust ⌑
c/o Bienstock, Friedman, Frank Grossman
30 Broad St.
New York 10004

Donor(s): Georges Lurcy.†
Financial data: (yr. ended 6/30/83): Assets, $9,720,168 (M); gifts received, $6,481; expenditures, $579,968, including $471,961 for 17 grants (high: $108,525; low: $1,775).
Purpose and activities: Support primarily for higher education.
Trustees: Daniel L. Bernstein, Edward M. Bernstein, George L. Bernstein, Seth E. Frank, Sidney O. Friedman.
Employer Identification Number: 136372044

2685
Macdonald (James A.) Foundation
One North Broadway
White Plains 10601   (914) 428-9305

Incorporated in 1966 in New York.
Donor(s): Flora MacDonald Bonney.†
Financial data: (yr. ended 12/31/84): Assets, $3,429,817 (M); expenditures, $319,003, including $287,355 for 254 grants (high: $25,000; low: $100; average: $200-$600).
Purpose and activities: Broad purposes; primarily local giving, with emphasis on Protestant church support, secondary education, community funds, hospitals, youth agencies, and historic preservation.
Types of support awarded: Operating budgets, continuing support, annual campaigns, seed money, emergency funds, building funds, equipment, land acquisition, endowment funds, scholarship funds, special projects, research, fellowships.
Limitations: Giving primarily in NY. No grants to individuals or for matching gifts; no loans.
Application information:
Initial approach: Letter
Copies of proposal: 1
Deadline(s): None

Board meeting date(s): Irregularly, but at least quarterly
Write: Walter J. Handelman, Secretary
Officers: Blanche B. Handelman,* President; Walter J. Handelman,* Secretary; Alan L. Model, Treasurer.
Directors:* Alice H. Model.
Number of staff: None.
Employer Identification Number: 136199690

2686
MacDonald (Marquis George) Foundation, Inc.
c/o Miss Virginia Sauer
1211 Ave. of the Americas, 37th Fl.
New York 10036   (212) 730-3994

Incorporated in 1951 in New York.
Donor(s): Marquis George MacDonald.†
Financial data: (yr. ended 12/31/82): Assets, $2,908,502 (M); expenditures, $135,096, including $72,000 for 53 grants (high: $5,500; low: $250).
Purpose and activities: Broad purposes; local giving, with emphasis on higher and secondary education, church support, religious associations, hospitals, welfare funds, and organizations providing benefit to the community and serving the public interest. Grant applications not accepted.
Limitations: Giving limited to NY. No grants to individuals or for matching gifts; no loans.
Application information: Grant applications not accepted.
Board meeting date(s): May, July, and December
Officers and Directors: Gerald MacDonald, President; Catherine MacDonald, Kevin McDonald, Vice-Presidents; Joseph MacDonald, Helen McDonald, Lee McDonald.
Employer Identification Number: 131957181

2687
MacKall (The Paul) & Evanina Evans Bell MacKall Trust ☐
Morgan Guaranty Tr. Co. of New York
9 W. 57th St.
New York 10019

Established in 1982.
Financial data: (yr. ended 8/31/83): Assets, $4,934,647 (M); gifts received, $4,683,708.
Purpose and activities: Giving limited to medical facilities.
Application information:
Initial approach: Letter
Write: Robert F. Longley, Senior Vice-President
Trustee: Morgan Guaranty Trust Company of New York.
Employer Identification Number: 136794686

2688
Macmillan Foundation, The
866 Third Ave.
New York 10022   (212) 935-2017

Incorporated in 1967 in Delaware.
Donor(s): Macmillan Inc.

Financial data: (yr. ended 12/31/82): Assets, $1,800,000 (M); expenditures, $115,000, including $100,000 for 45 grants (high: $10,000; low: $250).
Purpose and activities: General giving, primarily in the metropolitan New York area, with emphasis on cultural organizations, including the performing arts and libraries, and higher education.
Types of support awarded: General purposes, operating budgets, annual campaigns, endowment funds.
Limitations: Giving primarily in NY, particularly in the New York City metropolitan area. No grants to individuals, or for building funds, scholarships, fellowships, or matching gifts; no loans.
Application information:
Initial approach: Proposal
Copies of proposal: 1
Board meeting date(s): As required
Final notification: 2 months
Write: Paul Chenet, Assistant Treasurer
Officers and Directors: Edward P. Evans, Chairman and President; Philip E. Hoversten, Vice-President-Finance; Beverly C. Chell, Secretary; Eric C. Fast, Treasurer; William F. Reilly.
Number of staff: None.
Employer Identification Number: 136260248

2689
Macy (Josiah), Jr. Foundation ▼
44 East 64th St.
New York 10021   (212) 486-2424

Incorporated in 1930 in New York.
Donor(s): Mrs. Kate Macy Ladd.†
Financial data: (yr. ended 6/30/84): Assets, $60,415,411 (M); expenditures, $3,682,521, including $2,289,465 for 31 grants (high: $556,731; low: $3,000), $40,000 for 27 employee matching gifts and $136,423 for 1 foundation-administered program.
Purpose and activities: Major interest in medicine and health. Major grant programs are Minorities in Medicine, Innovations in Medical School Curriculum and Teaching Practices, and New Academic Offerings for Students in Biomedical Sciences; support also for Macy Symposia.
Types of support awarded: Special projects, employee matching gifts.
Limitations: No grants to individuals, or for travel, capital or endowment funds, operating budgets, continuing support, annual fund appeals, seed money, emergency funds, deficit financing, research, publications, matching gifts, conferences not run by the foundation, or scholarships and fellowships; no loans.
Publications: Annual report, informational brochure, program policy statement, application guidelines.
Application information:
Initial approach: Letter
Copies of proposal: 1
Board meeting date(s): January, May, and September
Final notification: Within 1 month
Write: James G. Hirsch, M.D., President

Officers: Clarence F. Michalis,* Chairman and Treasurer; James G. Hirsch, M.D.,* President; Rina Forlini, Corporate Secretary.
Directors:* Lawrence K. Altman, Harold Amos, Louis Auchincloss, Alexander G. Bearn, E. Virgil Conway, Charles B. Finch, Elbridge T. Gerry, Jr., S. Parker Gilbert, Patricia A. Graham, Bernard W. Harleston, Lawrence S. Huntington, David L. Luke III, George B. Mackaness, Mary Patterson McPherson, Walter N. Rothschild, Jr.
Number of staff: 5 full-time professional; 2 full-time support.
Employer Identification Number: 135596895

2690
Mad River Foundation ☐
500 Fifth Ave., Rm. 2410
New York 10110

Incorporated in 1961 in Delaware.
Donor(s): Godfrey S. Rockefeller.
Financial data: (yr. ended 12/31/82): Assets, $1,063,080 (M); gifts received, $121,870; expenditures, $102,327, including $99,650 for 68 grants (high: $10,000; low: $100).
Purpose and activities: Support primarily for higher and secondary education, including a medical school, welfare programs, and social agencies; support also for conservation and wildlife preservation.
Application information:
Write: Waldemar O. Peltzer, Secretary
Officers: Godfrey S. Rockefeller,* President; Waldemar O. Peltzer, Secretary and Treasurer.
Directors:* Audrey R. Blair, Marion R. Stone.
Employer Identification Number: 136097034

2691
Magowan Family Foundation, Inc., The ☐
165 Broadway
New York 10080
Application address: c/o Safeway Stores, Inc., Oakland, CA 94660; Tel.: (415) 891-3400

Incorporated in 1954 in New York.
Donor(s): Charles E. Merrill,† Robert A. Magowan, Doris M. Magowan, Merrill L. Magowan, Robert A. Magowan, Jr.
Financial data: (yr. ended 10/31/83): Assets, $3,047,056 (M); expenditures, $174,470, including $146,950 for 170 grants (high: $15,650; low: $100).
Purpose and activities: Broad purposes; grants largely for higher and secondary education, hospitals, church support, and cultural programs, primarily in New York, California, and Florida.
Limitations: Giving primarily in NY, CA, and FL.
Application information:
Initial approach: Letter
Deadline(s): None
Write: Jeane Hickerson Calhoun, Assistant Treasurer
Officers: Robert A. Magowan, President; Doris M. Magowan, Merrill L. Magowan, Peter A. Magowan, Stephen C. Magowan, Vice-Presidents; Bernat Rosner, Secretary; Calvin A. Gogolin, Treasurer.
Employer Identification Number: 136085999

2692
Maguire (The Russell) Foundation, Inc. ☒
c/o Berman and Hecht
500 Fifth Ave., 47th Fl.
New York 10110

Incorporated in 1941 in New York.
Donor(s): Russell Maguire,† and others.
Financial data: (yr. ended 12/31/82): Assets, $2,092,974 (M); gifts received, $2,000; expenditures, $201,225, including $155,060 for 59 grants (high: $25,000; low: $10).
Purpose and activities: Giving largely in Connecticut and New York, with emphasis on arts and cultural programs; support also for a community fund, education, and social agencies.
Limitations: Giving primarily in NY and CT.
Officers: Alexander L. Caccia, Secretary; Natasha B. Ford III,* Treasurer.
Directors:* Elizabeth S. Gale, Suzanne S. Maguire, F. Richards Ford III.
Employer Identification Number: 136162698

2693
Mailman (A. L.) Family Foundation, Inc.
707 Westchester Ave.
White Plains 10604   (914) 681-4448

Foundation established in 1976 in Florida as The Dr. Marilyn M. Segal Foundation, Inc.
Donor(s): Abraham L. Mailman,† The Mailman Foundation, Inc.
Financial data: (yr. ended 12/31/83): Assets, $9,475,530 (M); gifts received, $327,588; expenditures, $630,968, including $501,816 for 35 grants (high: $100,000; low: $55).
Purpose and activities: Support primarily for programs committed to the preservation and strengthening of the family, with a special interest in children and youth who are disadvantaged by socio-economic status, race, and emotional or physical disabilities; giving also for educational efforts to stimulate moral and intellectual growth and the development of social responsibility; and for research in and refinement of developmental, individualized education.
Types of support awarded: Seed money, matching funds, special projects, research, publications.
Limitations: No grants to individuals, or for operating budgets, capital or endowment funds, continuing support, annual campaigns, emergency funds, deficit financing, or scholarships and fellowships; no loans.
Publications: Annual report, program policy statement, application guidelines.
Application information:
    Initial approach: Letter
    Copies of proposal: 1
    Deadline(s): Submit proposal preferably in September and February; deadline March 1 and October 1
    Board meeting date(s): January and June
    Final notification: 5 months
    Write: Luba H. Lynch, Executive Director
Officers: Richard D. Segal,* President; Vito G. DiCristina,* Patricia S. Lieberman,* Vice-Presidents; Kurt Lichten, Secretary and Treasurer.

Trustees:* Marilyn M. Segal, Chairman; Betty Bardige, Jonathan Gordon, Jay B. Langner, Wendy Masi.
Number of staff: 1 full-time professional; 1 part-time professional; 1 part-time support.
Employer Identification Number: 510203866

2694
Mailman Foundation, Inc., The ▼
460 Park Ave.
New York 10022   (212) 751-7171

Incorporated in 1943 in Delaware.
Donor(s): Joseph L. Mailman, Abraham L. Mailman.†
Financial data: (yr. ended 12/31/83): Assets, $3,421,560 (M); gifts received, $70,000; expenditures, $539,675, including $510,411 for 97 grants (high: $200,000; low: $30).
Purpose and activities: General giving, with emphasis on Jewish welfare funds, hospitals, higher education, temple support, and the arts.
Application information:
    Write: Hilda Schultz
Officers and Trustees: Joseph L. Mailman, President; Phyllis Mailman, Vice-President; Vito G. DiCristina, Secretary and Treasurer; Joseph S. Mailman, Joshua L. Mailman, Joan M. Wolfe.
Employer Identification Number: 136161556

2695
Mandeville Foundation, Inc., The ▼ ☒
230 Park Ave.
New York 10169   (212) 986-3377

Incorporated in 1963 in Connecticut.
Donor(s): Ernest W. Mandeville.
Financial data: (yr. ended 12/31/82): Assets, $5,634,297 (M); gifts received, $155; expenditures, $632,070, including $505,760 for 79 grants (high: $76,642; low: $50).
Purpose and activities: Broad purposes; general giving, primarily in Connecticut and New York, with emphasis on higher and secondary education, cultural programs, and social agencies.
Limitations: Giving primarily in NY and CT.
Application information:
    Deadline(s): None
    Final notification: 90 days
    Write: Hubert T. Mandeville, President
Officers and Directors: Hubert T. Mandeville, President and Treasurer; P. Kempton Mandeville, Vice-President; Maurice C. Greenbaum, Secretary; Meredith M. Hollis, Deborah S. Mandeville.
Number of staff: 2.
Employer Identification Number: 066043343

2696
Manealoff Foundation, Inc. ☒
c/o Maxwell Shmerler & Co.
630 Third Ave.
New York 10017

Incorporated in 1956 in New York.
Donor(s): Dorothy Manealoff,† William Manealoff, Adams Fabricated Steel Corporation, J.B. Kendall Company, and others.

Financial data: (yr. ended 4/30/84): Assets, $1,142,597 (M); expenditures, $140,443, including $107,625 for 8 grants (high: $50,000).
Purpose and activities: Grants primarily for higher education, Jewish welfare and educational funds, and hospitals.
Officers: William Manealoff, President; Molly Manealoff, Vice-President and Secretary.
Employer Identification Number: 136067649

2697
Manning (The James Hilton) and Emma Austin Manning Foundation
c/o Ernst & Co.
100 Wall St., 19th Fl.
New York 10005
Mailing address: P.O. Box 1092, Dunedin, FL 33528; Tel.: (813) 734-5274

Incorporated in 1958 in New York.
Donor(s): Beatrice Austin Manning.†
Financial data: (yr. ended 7/31/84): Assets, $4,000,000 (M); expenditures, $425,000, including $424,500 for 9 grants (high: $175,000; low: $5,000).
Purpose and activities: Charitable purposes; support only for "medical research in human physiology and the diseases thereof".
Types of support awarded: Research.
Limitations: Giving limited to U.S. organizations. No grants to individuals, or for student aid, general support, capital or endowment funds, scholarships, fellowships, or matching gifts; no loans.
Application information: Funds presently committed; applications not invited.
    Board meeting date(s): Semiannually
    Write: Elizabeth R. Cohen, Secretary
Officers: Leon I. Cohen, President; Leonard T. Scully, Vice-President and Treasurer; Ella A. Severin, Vice-President; Elizabeth R. Cohen, Secretary.
Number of staff: 1 part-time professional.
Employer Identification Number: 136123540

2698
Manufacturers Hanover Foundation ▼
c/o Manufacturers Hanover Trust Company
600 Fifth Ave.
New York 10020   (212) 286-7124

Trust established in 1956 in New York.
Donor(s): Manufacturers Hanover Trust Company.
Financial data: (yr. ended 12/31/83): Assets, $12,542,903 (M); expenditures, $1,231,233, including $924,000 for 83 grants (high: $412,500; low: $1,000; average: $1,000-$25,000) and $274,993 for 537 employee matching gifts.
Purpose and activities: Broad purposes; interests include a community fund, higher and secondary education, hospitals, cultural programs, youth agencies, public policy and community development organizations, and health agencies.
Types of support awarded: Employee matching gifts, annual campaigns, building funds, endowment funds, general purposes, continuing support.

Limitations: Giving primarily in areas in which the company operates. No grants to individuals, or for scholarships, fellowships, or special projects; no loans.
Publications: Annual report.
Application information:
Initial approach: Letter
Copies of proposal: 1
Deadline(s): Submit proposal preferably between September and December; deadline March 31
Board meeting date(s): May
Final notification: June 1
Write: John R. Price, Jr., Agent
Advisory Committee: John F. McGillicudy, Chairman.
Trustee: Manufacturers Hanover Trust Company (John R. Price, Jr., Agent).
Employer Identification Number: 136143284

2699
Marcus (James S.) Foundation ⊭
c/o Goldman, Sachs & Co.
85 Broad St.
New York 10004

Established in 1969.
Donor(s): James S. Marcus.
Financial data: (yr. ended 5/31/83): Assets, $1,350,082 (M); expenditures, $213,938, including $210,378 for 95 grants (high: $153,000; low: $12).
Purpose and activities: Primarily local giving, with emphasis on arts and cultural programs, particularly opera; some support for health agencies, social services, and higher education.
Limitations: Giving primarily in NY.
Trustees: James S. Marcus, Ellen F. Marcus, H. Frederick Krimendahl II.
Employer Identification Number: 237044611

2700
Markle (The John and Mary R.)
Foundation ▼
50 Rockefeller Plaza, Suite 940
New York 10020   (212) 489-6655

Incorporated in 1927 in New York.
Donor(s): John Markle.†
Financial data: (yr. ended 6/30/84): Assets, $59,886,308 (M); expenditures, $4,330,531, including $3,473,180 for 50 grants (high: $950,000; low: $2,650; average: $30,000-$100,000).
Purpose and activities: In 1969 program shifted from medical education to the improvement of mass communications including services growing out of new technologies for the processing and transfer of information. Grants for expanding research on the role of mass communications in society; analyzing public issues and questions of public interest; improving the performance of professionals involved in the mass communications industry; exploring the relationship between the media and politics; and enriching the quality of print and electronic journalism.
Types of support awarded: Research, special projects.

Limitations: No grants to individuals (except for pensions to specified beneficiaries); generally no grants for general support, operating budgets, continuing support, annual campaigns, seed money, emergency funds, equipment, land acquisition, renovations, capital or endowment funds, matching gifts, or scholarships and fellowships; no loans. No grants generally for publications, conferences, or film and video production.
Publications: Annual report, informational brochure, program policy statement, application guidelines.
Application information:
Initial approach: Letter or full proposal
Copies of proposal: 1
Deadline(s): 6 weeks prior to board meeting
Board meeting date(s): March, June, and November
Final notification: 2 weeks to 2 months
Write: Lloyd N. Morrisett, President
Officers: Lloyd N. Morrisett,* President; Dolores E. Miller, Secretary; Lee J. Moran, Treasurer.
Directors:* D. Ronald Daniel, Chairman; David O. Beim, Joel L. Fleishman, Barbara Hauptfuhrer, Alice S. Ilchman, Maximilian W. Kempner, Gertrude G. Michelson, William M. Rees, Richard E. Stewart, George B. Weiksner.
Number of staff: 3 full-time professional; 1 part-time professional; 5 full-time support.
Employer Identification Number: 131770307

2701
Martinson (Joseph) Memorial
Foundation
(formerly Joseph Martinson Memorial Fund)
c/o Citibank, Co-Trustee No.147376
One Citicorp Center, 19th Fl.
New York 10043

Trust established in 1950 in New York.
Donor(s): Joseph B. Martinson.†
Financial data: (yr. ended 12/31/84): Assets, $1,200,000 (M); expenditures, $125,000, including $120,000 for 35 grants.
Purpose and activities: Support largely for the performing arts and museums.
Trustees: Paul Martinson, Howard Graff, Frances Sirota, Citibank.
Employer Identification Number: 136161532

2702
Mastronardi (The Charles A.)
Foundation ⊭
c/o Morgan Guaranty Trust Company
Nine West 57th St.
New York 10019

Established in 1964 in New York.
Donor(s): Charles A. Mastronardi.†
Financial data: (yr. ended 12/31/82): Assets, $4,947,668 (M); gifts received, $205,000; expenditures, $408,852, including $368,500 for 48 grants (high: $85,000; low: $500).
Purpose and activities: Giving largely for higher education, child welfare, hospitals, and Roman Catholic church support.

Officers: Carrie Mastronardi, President; Alfred C. Turino, Executive Vice-President; Edward F. Bennett, Daniel R. Mastronardi, Nicholas D. Mastronardi, Vice-Presidents; Olga De Felippo, Secretary; Joseph Mastronardi, Treasurer.
Employer Identification Number: 136167916

2703
Mather (The Richard) Fund
c/o Key Trust Company
201 South Warren St.
Syracuse 13202   (315) 470-5222

Trust established in 1955 in New York.
Donor(s): Flora Mather Hosmer,† R.C. Hosmer, Jr.,† Hosmer Descendants Trust.
Financial data: (yr. ended 12/31/83): Assets, $1,855,966 (M); gifts received, $16,585; expenditures, $98,843, including $83,650 for 11 grants (high: $33,500; low: $150).
Purpose and activities: Primarily local giving, with emphasis on cultural organizations.
Limitations: Giving primarily in central NY, with emphasis on Syracuse. No grants to individuals.
Application information: Funds substantially committed.
Initial approach: Letter
Copies of proposal: 1
Board meeting date(s): As required
Write: John S. Hancock, Trustee
Trustees: William L. Broad, John S. Hancock, S. Sterling McMillan III, Elizabeth H. Schaefer.
Number of staff: None.
Employer Identification Number: 156018423

2704
Mathers (G. Harold & Leila) Charitable
Foundation ⊭
c/o Meyer Handelman Company
80 Pine St.
New York 10005

Established in 1975 in New York.
Financial data: (yr. ended 12/31/83): Assets, $58,850,313 (M); gifts received, $53,156,447; expenditures, $5,140,609, including $230,500 for 21 grants (high: $50,000; low: $500).
Purpose and activities: General giving, with emphasis on higher education, social services, including youth agencies, cultural programs, and an international relief agency.
Officers and Trustee: Donald E. Handelman, President; William R. Handelman, John Hay, Vice-Presidents; Don Fizer, Secretary; Joseph W. Handelman, Treasurer; John R. Young.
Employer Identification Number: 237441901

2705
Mathis-Pfohl Foundation ⊭
5-46 46th Ave.
Long Island City 11101

Incorporated in 1947 in Iowa.
Donor(s): Members of the Pfohl family and associated companies.
Financial data: (yr. ended 11/30/84): Assets, $2,010,671 (M); gifts received, $35,000; expenditures, $94,455, including $91,187 for 113 grants (high: $5,000; low: $25).

Purpose and activities: Broad purposes; grants for higher and secondary education, hospitals, religious institutions and welfare funds.
Application information:
Board meeting date(s): As required
Officers and Trustees: Louis H. Pfohl, President; James Mathis Pfohl, Vice-President; Ann Pfohl Kirby, Secretary-Treasurer; Lynn Pfohl Quigley.
Employer Identification Number: 116013764

2706
Matthews (Hale) Foundation ⊐
100 Park Ave., 33rd Fl.
New York 10017

Established in 1963.
Donor(s): Hale Matthews.†
Financial data: (yr. ended 12/31/82): Assets, $1,218,585 (M); expenditures, $110,593, including $97,000 for 8 grants (high: $25,000; low: $1,000).
Purpose and activities: Primarily local giving, with emphasis on the theatre and the performing arts.
Types of support awarded: Matching funds, fellowships, general purposes.
Limitations: Giving primarily in NY.
Application information:
Initial approach: Proposal
Officers and Directors: William Ashbey, President; Helen Brann, Secretary; Richard G. Hewitt, Treasurer.
Employer Identification Number: 136157267

2707
Matz Foundation (Edelman Division) ⊐
253 Broadway
New York 10007

Trust established in 1970 in New York as one of two successor trusts to the Matz Foundation.
Donor(s): Israel Matz.†
Financial data: (yr. ended 6/30/84): Assets, $1,692,580 (M); expenditures, $209,167, including $183,850 for 42 grants (high: $75,100; low: $300).
Purpose and activities: Broad purposes; primarily local giving, with emphasis on Jewish welfare funds and cultural institutions, higher education, and hospitals.
Limitations: Giving primarily in NY.
Trustees: Ethel M. Edelman, Richard Edelman, Louise E. Sagalyn.
Employer Identification Number: 237082997

2708
Matz (Israel) Foundation
14 East 4th St.
New York 10012

Trust established in 1925 in New York.
Donor(s): Israel Matz.†
Financial data: (yr. ended 12/31/83): Assets, $1,768,469 (M); expenditures, $154,433, including $105,322 for 45 grants (high: $18,000; low: $250).

Purpose and activities: To extend financial grants-in-aid to indigent Hebrew scholars, writers, and public workers and their dependents; also to publish Hebrew classics.
Types of support awarded: Grants to individuals, publications.
Application information:
Write: Dr. Rivka Friedman, Executive-Secretary
Officer: Rivka Friedman, Executive Secretary.
Trustees: Milton Arfa, Chairman; Z. Almog, S.D. Braun, R. Friedman, Abraham S. Halkin, Hayim Leaf, S. Sharan.
Employer Identification Number: 136121533

2709
Mazer (Joseph & Ceil) Foundation, Inc. ⊐
c/o Becker, Ross, Stone, et al.
41 East 42nd St.
New York 10017

Established in 1941.
Donor(s): Joseph M. Mazer.†
Financial data: (yr. ended 12/31/82): Assets, $350,759 (M); gifts received, $1,700,250; expenditures, $1,704,300, including $1,704,050 for 22 grants (high: $662,500; low: $100).
Purpose and activities: Grants primarily for Jewish welfare and educational funds in the United States and Israel.
Officers and Directors: William Mazer, President; Daniel Ross, Vice-President; Jesse Margolin, Secretary and Treasurer.
Employer Identification Number: 136111730

2710
Mazer (William and Helen) Foundation, Inc. ⊐
944 Fifth Ave.
New York 10021

Incorporated in 1979 in New York.
Donor(s): Abraham Mazer Family Fund, Inc.
Financial data: (yr. ended 9/30/84): Assets, $1,170,604 (M); expenditures, $165,877, including $162,466 for 55 grants (high: $50,000; low: $15).
Purpose and activities: Broad purposes; emphasis on gifts to higher education, including medical education, and hospitals; support also for the performing arts, Jewish welfare organizations, and a peace fund.
Officers and Directors: William Mazer, President; Helen Mazer, Vice-President and Secretary; Linda M. Berkowitz, Frank B. Mazer, Robert C. Mazer.
Employer Identification Number: 133029517

2711
McCaddin-McQuirk Foundation, Inc., The ⊐
1002 Madison Ave.
New York 10021   (212) 772-9090

Incorporated in 1902 in New York.
Donor(s): Rt. Rev. John McQuirk,† Ann Eliza McCaddin Walsh.†

Financial data: (yr. ended 12/31/81): Assets, $1,043,905 (M); expenditures, $120,140, including $113,100 for 57 grants.
Purpose and activities: Grants to bishops and seminaries for the education of students in the priesthood of the Roman Catholic Church throughout the world.
Application information:
Initial approach: Letter
Deadline(s): Generally August 31
Write: Robert W. Dumser, Secretary
Officers: John G. Scott, President; Thomas R. Hardart, Vice-President; Robert W. Dumser, Secretary; William A. White, Treasurer.
Trustees: Most Rev. John W. Comber, Leo A. Egan, Frederic J. Fuller, Francis M. Hartman, Henry J. Humphreys, Richard M. Mumma, Thomas A. Turley, Douglas W. Wyatt.
Employer Identification Number: 136134444

2712
McCann (James J.) Charitable Trust ▼
35 Market St.
Poughkeepsie 12601   (914) 452-3085

Trust established in 1969 in New York.
Donor(s): James J. McCann.†
Financial data: (yr. ended 12/31/84): Assets, $20,119,111 (M); expenditures, $1,886,061, including $1,610,580 for grants (high: $10,000; low: $100; average: $1,000-$10,000).
Purpose and activities: Broad purposes; giving limited to the local area, with emphasis on secondary and higher education, including scholarship funds, recreation, civic projects, social services, cultural programs, church support and religious associations, and hospitals.
Types of support awarded: Continuing support, annual campaigns, seed money, building funds, equipment, land acquisition, scholarship funds, fellowships, publications, conferences and seminars.
Limitations: Giving limited to Poughkeepsie and Dutchess County, NY. No grants to individuals, or for operating budgets, emergency or endowment funds, deficit financing, or matching gifts; no loans.
Publications: Annual report.
Application information:
Initial approach: Letter or proposal
Copies of proposal: 1
Deadline(s): Submit proposal preferably in February or August; no deadline
Board meeting date(s): January and July
Final notification: 60 days
Write: John J. Gartland, Jr., Trustee
Officers and Trustees:* John J. Gartland, Jr.,* President; William L. Gardner, Jr.,* Vice-President; Richard V. Corbally, Secretary.
Number of staff: 1 part-time professional; 1 full-time support.
Employer Identification Number: 146050628

2713
McCarthy Charities, Inc., The ⊐
P.O. Box 576
Troy 12181

Incorporated in 1917 in New York.
Donor(s): Robert H. McCarthy, Lucy A. McCarthy.†

Financial data: (yr. ended 12/31/82): Assets, $2,211,942 (M); expenditures, $131,576, including $124,240 for 55 grants (high: $10,500; low: $25).
Purpose and activities: Broad purposes; primarily local giving, with emphasis on Roman Catholic church support and church-related education and welfare agencies; support also for community funds, social agencies, and hospitals.
Limitations: Giving primarily in NY.
Officers and Directors: Peter F. McCarthy, President and Treasurer; James A. McCarthy, Vice-President; Marion P. McCarthy, Secretary.
Employer Identification Number: 146019064

2714
McCarthy (The Michael W.) Foundation ¤
One Liberty Plaza, 27th Fl.
New York 10080

Trust established in 1958 in New York.
Donor(s): Michael W. McCarthy, Margaret E. McCarthy.
Financial data: (yr. ended 12/31/82): Assets, $2,026,125 (M); expenditures, $219,984, including $210,563 for 34 grants (high: $53,000; low: $80).
Purpose and activities: Broad purposes; support largely for higher education and for Roman Catholic church support and religious associations.
Trustee: Michael W. McCarthy.
Employer Identification Number: 136150919

2715
McConnell (Neil A.) Foundation, Inc.
113 East 55th St.
New York 10022

Incorporated in 1960 in New York.
Donor(s): Neil A. McConnell.
Financial data: (yr. ended 3/31/83): Assets, $2,661,253 (M); expenditures, $323,298, including $276,000 for 9 grants (high: $100,000; low: $16,000).
Purpose and activities: Broad purposes; local giving for special educational projects identified or developed by the Foundation.
Types of support awarded: Special projects.
Limitations: Giving limited to the greater New York, NY metropolitan area. No grants to individuals.
Application information:
   Initial approach: Letter
   Copies of proposal: 1
   Deadline(s): None
   Board meeting date(s): Semiannually and as required
   Write: R. Scott Asen, Executive Director
Officers and Trustees:* Neil A. McConnell,* President; Serena Balfour,* B. Scott McConnell,* James G. Niven,* Vice-Presidents; Douglas F. Williamson, Jr., Secretary; Sidney Mathews,* Treasurer; R. Scott Asen, Executive Director.
Employer Identification Number: 136114121

2716
McCrory Foundation, Inc., The
c/o Simona Ackerman
595 Madison Ave., 37th Fl.
New York 10022

Incorporated in 1960 in New York.
Donor(s): McCrory Corporation.
Financial data: (yr. ended 6/30/84): Assets, $2,549,550 (M); gifts received, $900,000; expenditures, $171,140, including $168,850 for 37 grants (high: $30,000; low: $350).
Purpose and activities: General giving, with emphasis on Jewish welfare funds, children, and education.
Application information:
   Initial approach: Letter
Officers: Simona Ackerman, President; Meshulam Riklis, Haim Bernstein, Vice-Presidents; Avigdor Shwartzstein, Secretary and Treasurer.
Employer Identification Number: 136163061

2717
McDonald (Frederick) Trust
c/o State Bank of Albany, Trust Dept.
69 State St.
Albany 12201

Established in 1950.
Financial data: (yr. ended 12/31/83): Assets, $1,504,435 (M); expenditures, $98,931, including $96,500 for 20 grants (high: $26,000; low: $1,000).
Purpose and activities: Local giving, primarily for hospitals and health agencies; support also for youth agencies and a community fund.
Limitations: Giving limited to Albany, NY. No grants to individuals.
Application information: Application form required.
   Initial approach: Letter
   Deadline(s): Submit proposal preferably May through September; deadline October 1
   Board meeting date(s): October and December
Trustee: State Bank of Albany.
Number of staff: None.
Employer Identification Number: 146014233

2718
McDonald (J. M.) Foundation, Inc. ▼
2057 East River Rd.
Cortland 13045   (607) 756-9283
Western grant office: Fountain Plaza Office Bldg., Suite 112E, 7340 East Shoeman Ln., Scottsdale, AZ 85251

Incorporated in 1952 in Nebraska.
Donor(s): James M. McDonald, Sr.†
Financial data: (yr. ended 12/31/83): Assets, $13,304,000 (M); expenditures, $888,319, including $808,000 for 48 grants (high: $75,000; low: $3,000; average: $5,000-$30,000).
Purpose and activities: Religious and educational purposes; grants for the aged, orphans, and children who are sick, infirm, blind, or crippled; youth and child care in an effort to combat juvenile delinquency and to aid underprivileged, mentally or physically handicapped children; other interests include hospitals and educational institutions.
Types of support awarded: Annual campaigns, building funds, equipment, research, general purposes, continuing support.
Limitations: Giving limited to the U.S. No grants to individuals, or for seminars, workshops, endowment funds, scholarships, fellowships, travel, exhibits, or conferences; no loans.
Publications: Application guidelines, program policy statement.
Application information:
   Initial approach: Letter, full proposal, or telephone
   Copies of proposal: 1
   Deadline(s): April 15 and September 15
   Board meeting date(s): May and October
   Write: Reed L. McJunkin, Secretary
Officers and Trustees: Eleanor F. McJunkin, President; Future H. McDonald, Vice-President; Reed L. McJunkin, Secretary; James M. McDonald III, Treasurer; Donald C. Berry, Jr.
Number of staff: 2 part-time support.
Employer Identification Number: 470431059

2719
McGonagle (Dextra Baldwin) Foundation, Inc.
445 Park Ave.
New York 10022   (212) 758-8970

Incorporated in 1967 in New York.
Donor(s): Mrs. Dextra Baldwin McGonagle.
Financial data: (yr. ended 12/31/83): Assets, $4,290,918 (M); expenditures, $282,492, including $245,550 for 111 grants (high: $25,000; low: $100; average: $2,000).
Purpose and activities: Giving in New York and California for hospitals and higher education; grants also for social agencies, religious organizations, and cultural programs.
Types of support awarded: Annual campaigns, seed money, building funds, equipment.
Limitations: Giving primarily in NY and CA. No grants to individuals or for matching gifts.
Application information:
   Initial approach: Letter
   Copies of proposal: 1
   Deadline(s): None
   Board meeting date(s): As required
   Final notification: 3 months
   Write: David B. Spanier, President
Officers and Directors:* Maury L. Spanier,* Chairman; David B. Spanier,* President; Paul Corash, Vice-President; Helen G. Spanier,* Vice-President, Secretary and Treasurer.
Number of staff: 4 part-time support.
Employer Identification Number: 136219236

2720
McGraw (The Donald C.) Foundation, Inc. ⌑
46 Summit Ave.
Bronxville 10708

Incorporated in 1963 in New York.
Donor(s): Donald C. McGraw.†
Financial data: (yr. ended 1/31/83): Assets, $1,055,730 (L); gifts received, $121,689; expenditures, $216,143, including $213,350 for 25 grants (high: $50,000; low: $1,000).
Purpose and activities: Broad purposes; grants largely for hospitals and medical research, education, church support, cultural programs and social agencies mainly in New York and New Jersey.
Limitations: Giving primarily in NY and NJ.
Application information:
  Write: John L. Cady, Vice-President
Officers and Directors: Donald C. McGraw, Jr., President; John L. McGraw, Vice-President and Treasurer; John L. Cady, Vice-President and Secretary.
Employer Identification Number: 136165603

2721
McGraw-Hill Foundation, Inc., The ▼
1221 Ave. of the Americas
New York 10020   (212) 512-6113

Incorporated in 1978 in New York.
Donor(s): McGraw-Hill, Inc.
Financial data: (yr. ended 12/31/83): Assets, $704,000 (M); expenditures, $1,322,699, including $679,216 for 134 grants (high: $91,650; low: $500; average: $1,000-$7,500), $90,951 for grants to individuals and $547,928 for 2,309 employee matching gifts.
Purpose and activities: Broad purposes; program emphasis is on education; significant support also given in the areas of health and welfare, civic activities, and arts and cultural organizations. Grants limited to national organizations and organizations located in the immediate vicinity of Company operations.
Types of support awarded: General purposes, operating budgets, continuing support, annual campaigns, seed money, emergency funds, special projects, research, publications, conferences and seminars, internships, scholarship funds, employee related scholarships, exchange programs, fellowships, matching funds, employee matching gifts.
Limitations: Giving limited to areas of company operations, or to national organizations. No support for religious organizations, or United Way member agencies. No grants to individuals (except for company-employee scholarships), or for capital, building, or endowment funds; conferences, travel, courtesy advertising, films or publications; no loans.
Publications: Annual report, program policy statement, application guidelines.
Application information:
  Initial approach: Proposal
  Copies of proposal: 1
  Board meeting date(s): March, June, September, and December
  Final notification: 2 weeks
  Write: Ann M. Hardwick, Administrator

Officers and Directors:* Theodore S. Weber, Jr.,* President; John B. Cave,* Dan Lacy,* Robert N. Landes,* Donald S. Rubin, Vice-Presidents; John L. Cady,* Secretary; Ralph J. Webb, Treasurer.
Number of staff: 2 full-time professional; 1 full-time support; 1 part-time support.
Employer Identification Number: 132955464

2722
Mellon (The Andrew W.) Foundation ▼
140 East 62nd St.
New York 10021   (212) 838-8400

Trust established in 1940 in Delaware as Avalon Foundation; incorporated in 1954 in New York; merged with Old Dominion Foundation and renamed The Andrew W. Mellon Foundation in 1969.
Donor(s): Ailsa Mellon Bruce,† Paul Mellon.
Financial data: (yr. ended 12/31/84): Assets, $1,016,625,922 (M); expenditures, $65,215,251, including $61,066,230 for 230 grants (high: $5,000,000; low: $7,500; average: $25,000-$1,000,000).
Purpose and activities: Broad purposes; grants on selective basis in higher education, medical, public health, and population education and research, cultural affairs, including historic preservation, the humanities, museums, and performing arts, and in certain environmental and public affairs areas. Graduate fellowship program in the humanities administered by the Woodrow Wilson National Fellowship Foundation, which makes all awards.
Types of support awarded: Endowment funds, research, professorships, internships, fellowships, matching funds.
Limitations: No grants to individuals, including scholarships and fellowships, or to primarily local organizations; no loans.
Publications: Annual report, program policy statement.
Application information:
  Initial approach: Descriptive letter or full proposal
  Copies of proposal: 1
  Deadline(s): None
  Board meeting date(s): March, June, October, and December
  Write: J. Kellum Smith, Jr., Vice-President
Officers: John E. Sawyer,* President; J. Kellum Smith, Jr., Vice-President and Secretary; Kenneth J. Herr, Treasurer.
Trustees:* William O. Baker, Chairman; Hanna Holborn Gray, Paul Mellon, Timothy Mellon, Arjay Miller, Frank H.T. Rhodes, Charles A. Ryskamp, John R. Stevenson.
Number of staff: 7 full-time professional; 10 full-time support.
Employer Identification Number: 131879954

2723
Melohn Foundation, Inc., The ⌑
105 W. 55th St.
New York 10019

Established in 1965.

Financial data: (yr. ended 7/31/83): Assets, $73,698 (M); expenditures, $233,849, including $233,827 for 13 grants (high: $54,500).
Purpose and activities: Primarily local giving, for Jewish schools and temple support.
Limitations: Giving primarily in NY.
Manager: Alfons Melohn.
Employer Identification Number: 136197827

2724
Memton Fund, Inc., The
One East 75th St.
New York 10021   (212) 570-4814

Incorporated in 1936 in New York.
Donor(s): Albert G. Milbank,† Charles M. Cauldwell.†
Financial data: (yr. ended 12/31/84): Assets, $4,231,836 (M); expenditures, $286,474, including $217,400 for 109 grants (high: $15,000; low: $150; average: $1,000-$5,000).
Purpose and activities: Charitable purposes; in practice makes grants in those fields in which the founders were interested, with emphasis on higher education, cultural organizations, community funds, health agencies, youth agencies, and child welfare.
Types of support awarded: General purposes, operating budgets, continuing support, annual campaigns, seed money, emergency funds, deficit financing, endowment funds, scholarship funds.
Limitations: No grants to individuals, or for building funds, equipment, land acquisition, renovation projects, matching gifts, special projects, research, publications, or conferences; no loans.
Application information:
  Initial approach: Telephone
  Copies of proposal: 1
  Deadline(s): February
  Board meeting date(s): March and October
  Write: Lillian Daniels, Secretary-Treasurer
Officers and Directors: David L. Milbank, President; Samuel L. Milbank, Vice-President; Lillian I. Daniels, Secretary and Treasurer; Elenita M. Drumwright, Marjorie M. Farrar, Francis H. Musselman, Samuel S. Polk, Daphne M. White.
Number of staff: 1 full-time professional; 2 part-time professional.
Employer Identification Number: 136096608

2725
Menschel (The Robert B.) Foundation
c/o Goldman, Sachs & Co.
85 Broad St.
New York 10004

Established in 1958 in New York.
Donor(s): Robert B. Menschel.
Financial data: (yr. ended 10/31/84): Assets, $2,219,000 (M); expenditures, $155,322, including $155,204 for 125 grants (high: $10,000; low: $100).
Purpose and activities: General giving, with emphasis on social welfare, the arts, hospitals, and higher education.
Application information: All grants initiated by the foundation.

Officers: Robert B. Menschel, President and Treasurer; Joyce F. Menschel, Vice-President and Secretary.
Employer Identification Number: 136098443

2726
Merck (John) Fund
c/o Hughes, Hubbard & Reed
One Wall St.
New York 10005   (212) 709-7703

Established in 1970 in New York.
Donor(s): Serena S. Merck.†
Financial data: (yr. ended 12/31/83): Assets, $9,034,120 (M); expenditures, $312,001, including $230,000 for 3 grants (high: $100,000; low: $30,000).
Purpose and activities: Grants are made principally to medical teaching hospitals for research in connection with developmental disabilities in children.
Types of support awarded: Research.
Limitations: No grants to individuals.
Application information: Grants usually made at the initiation of the foundation; applications not invited.
Write: Orville H. Schell
Trustees: Francis W. Hatch, Serena M. Hatch, Huyler C. Held, Richard A. Kimball, Jr., Robert M. Pennoyer, Orville H. Schell.
Number of staff: None.
Employer Identification Number: 237082558

2727
Merrill (The Ingram) Foundation ⌑
c/o Bankers Trust Company
P.O. Box 1297, Church Street Station
New York 10015

Trust established in 1956 in New York.
Donor(s): James I. Merrill.
Financial data: (yr. ended 12/31/81): Assets, $263,915 (M); gifts received, $100,000; expenditures, $237,711, including $217,875 for 33 grants to individuals (high: $12,000; low: $3,000).
Purpose and activities: General purposes; concerned primarily with the advancement of the cultural and fine arts; aids individuals, educational institutions, and performing groups.
Selection Committee: Harry Ford, Chairman; John Myers, Secretary; John Hollander, David M. Kalstone.
Trustees: Huyler C. Held, Robert A. Magowan, Jr., Bankers Trust Company.
Employer Identification Number: 136042498

2728
Merrill Lynch & Co. Foundation, Inc.
One Liberty Plaza
165 Broadway
New York 10080   (212) 637-8165

Incorporated in 1950 in Delaware.
Donor(s): Merrill Lynch, Pierce, Fenner & Smith, Inc.

Financial data: (yr. ended 12/31/83): Assets, $7,230,193 (M); gifts received, $2,500,000; expenditures, $821,281, including $783,000 for 76 grants (high: $75,000; low: $5,000; average: $10,000).
Purpose and activities: General giving, with emphasis on higher education, the performing arts, hospitals, and health services.
Types of support awarded: Continuing support, annual campaigns, building funds, research.
Limitations: No grants to individuals, or for operating budgets, seed money, emergency funds, deficit financing, land acquisition, matching gifts, special projects, publications, or conferences; no loans.
Publications: Application guidelines.
Application information:
Initial approach: Full proposal
Copies of proposal: 1
Deadline(s): None
Board meeting date(s): March, June, September, and December
Final notification: 3 months
Write: Thomas B. Jones, Secretary
Officers: James E. Murphy,* President; Roger E. Birk,* Dakin B. Ferris,* William A. Schreyer,* Vice-Presidents; Thomas B. Jones, Secretary; Calvin A. Gogolin, Treasurer.
Trustees:* John J. Boland.
Number of staff: 2 full-time professional; 1 full-time support.
Employer Identification Number: 136139556

2729
Mertz (Martha) Foundation, Inc. ⌑
c/o Allen and Brown
60 East 42nd St., Suite 1743
New York 10165

Incorporated in 1939 in New York.
Donor(s): DeWitt W. Mertz.†
Financial data: (yr. ended 12/31/82): Assets, $2,607,623 (M); expenditures, $118,586, including $85,000 for 8 grants (high: $28,700; low: $1,700).
Purpose and activities: To administer to, provide for, and rehabilitate unmarried girls who have become mothers or prostitutes, or who, from such causes, shall be homeless or in fear of becoming homeless or social outcasts; grants to local agencies only.
Limitations: Giving primarily in NY. No grants to individuals.
Application information:
Deadline(s): None
Write: Jonathan Reilly, President
Officers and Directors: Jonathan Reilly, President; Mrs. Paul Kammerer, Vice-President and Secretary; Mrs. David Kubie, Barbara Lee Cudd, Mrs. Richard Harris, Mrs. Louis Otten, Jonathan B. Reilly, Vice-Presidents; Richard H. Pershan, Wendy Pyle, Mrs. Samuel Rubin.
Employer Identification Number: 136129085

2730
Mertz-Gilmore (Joyce) Foundation ▼
218 East 18th St.
New York 10003

Incorporated in 1959 in New York.
Donor(s): Joyce Mertz Gilmore.†
Financial data: (yr. ended 12/31/84): Assets, $24,563,167 (M); gifts received, $6,839,442; expenditures, $1,554,901, including $1,251,318 for 83 grants (high: $277,500; low: $500; average: $1,000-$15,000).
Purpose and activities: Current concerns include: civil and human rights and democratic values; cultural and civic improvements in the New York metropolitan area; education; emergency aid to refugees; education for humane treatment of animals; nuclear arms control and nuclear disarmament; peace and international affairs; population issues; and protection of the environment.
Types of support awarded: Operating budgets, general purposes.
Limitations: No grants to individuals, or for capital or endowment funds, conferences, scholarships, fellowships, or matching gifts; no loans.
Publications: 990-PF, program policy statement, application guidelines.
Application information:
Initial approach: Brief explanatory letter
Deadline(s): Submit proposal upon request of foundation only; no set deadline
Board meeting date(s): Quarterly
Write: Larry E. Condon, Executive Director
Officers and Directors: LuEsther T. Mertz, President; Elizabeth Burke Gilmore, Secretary and Treasurer; Larry E. Condon, Executive Director; Charles Bloomstein, Harlan Cleveland, Robert W. Gilmore, C. Virgil Martin, Richard J. Mertz, Bayard Rustin, Franklin W. Wallin.
Number of staff: 2 full-time professional; 2 full-time support.
Employer Identification Number: 132872722

2731
Metcalf (Stanley W.) Foundation, Inc. ⌑
120 Genesee St.
Auburn 13021

Established in 1962.
Donor(s): Stanley W. Metcalf.†
Financial data: (yr. ended 12/31/83): Assets, $3,654,131 (M); expenditures, $244,418, including $196,800 for 8 grants (high: $141,800; low: $1,000).
Purpose and activities: Primarily local giving, with emphasis on youth organizations and church support; grants also for hospitals, welfare, and education.
Limitations: Giving primarily in NY.
Officers and Directors: H. Randolph Seymour, President; J. Douglas Pedley, Vice-President and Treasurer; Ronald D. West, Vice-President; Madeline M. Schneider, Secretary; Herbert T. Anderson, Marjorie S. Pedley.
Employer Identification Number: 156017859

2732
Metropolitan Life Foundation ▼
One Madison Ave.
New York 10010   (212) 578-6272

Incorporated in 1976 in New York.
Donor(s): Metropolitan Life Insurance Company.
Financial data: (yr. ended 12/31/84): Assets, $73,326,121 (M); expenditures, $6,206,116, including $5,244,959 for 1,450 grants (high: $232,600; low: $100; average: $1,000-$10,000), $414,390 for 2,109 employee matching gifts and $300,000 for 3 foundation-administered programs.
Purpose and activities: To make donations for higher education, health, including medical sciences and substance abuse programs; civic purposes, and community funds; grants also for cultural programs.
Types of support awarded: Operating budgets, continuing support, seed money, employee matching gifts, research.
Limitations: No support for private foundations, religious, fraternal, athletic, social, or veterans organizations; organizations already receiving support through United Way campaigns; local chapters of national organizations; disease-specified organizations; labor groups; organizations with international programs; organizations primarily engaged in patient care or direct treatment, drug treatment centers and community health clinics; hospital capital fund campaigns; or elementary or secondary schools. No grants to individuals.
Publications: Annual report, informational brochure, program policy statement, application guidelines.
Application information:
  Initial approach: Letter
  Copies of proposal: 1
  Deadline(s): Varies for competitive awards programs; none for grants
  Board meeting date(s): About 6 times a year
  Final notification: 8 to 10 weeks
  Write: Sibyl C. Jacobson, President
Officers: Sibyl C. Jacobson,* President; Paul S. Entmacher, M.D.,* Vice-President; William J. Howard, Secretary; Arthur G. Typermass,* Treasurer.
Directors:* John J. Creedon, Chairman; Richard W. Keough, Donald A. Odell.
Number of staff: 7 full-time professional; 4 full-time support.
Employer Identification Number: 132878224

2733
Metzger-Price Fund ¤
230 Park Ave.
New York 10169   (212) 686-4638

Trust established in 1970 in New York.
Donor(s): Estelle Metzger.†
Financial data: (yr. ended 6/30/82): Assets, $2,961 (M); gifts received, $140,156; expenditures, $137,736, including $125,000 for 63 grants (high: $5,000; low: $500).

Purpose and activities: Giving primarily in New York and New Jersey, with emphasis on higher and secondary education, including medical education, aid to the handicapped, and health services; support also for child welfare and social agencies, and recreation.
Limitations: Giving primarily in New York, NY. No grants to individuals.
Application information:
  Initial approach: Letter
  Copies of proposal: 1
  Deadline(s): Submit proposal preferably 1 month before board meetings
  Board meeting date(s): January, April, July, and October
  Write: Marie Mallot, Secretary-Treasurer
Officers and Directors: Algernon D. Black, President; Rabbi Ronald B. Sobel, Vice-President; Marie Mallot, Secretary-Treasurer.
Employer Identification Number: 237072764

2734
Meyer (The Andre and Bella) Foundation, Inc. ▼ ¤
c/o Patrick Gerschel
122 East 42nd St.
New York 10168   (212) 697-7565

Incorporated in 1950 in New York.
Donor(s): Patrick Gerschel, Laurent Gerschel, Andre Meyer,† Lazard Freres & Co., and others.
Financial data: (yr. ended 12/31/82): Assets, $19,311,395 (M); expenditures, $552,838, including $460,000 for 3 grants (high: $420,000; low: $10,000).
Purpose and activities: General purposes; grants largely for medical research and higher education.
Officers and Directors: Philippe Meyer, President; Laurent Gerschel, Marianne Gerschel, Patrick Gerschel, Vice-Presidents; George J. Ames, Secretary and Treasurer.
Employer Identification Number: 136094945

2735
Michel (Barbara and Clifford) Foundation, Inc.
80 Pine St.
New York 10005   (212) 344-3090

Incorporated in 1951 in New York.
Donor(s): Mrs. Barbara R. Michel, Clifford W. Michel.†
Financial data: (yr. ended 12/31/83): Assets, $691,500 (M); gifts received, $60,000; expenditures, $114,000, including $112,500 for 26 grants (high: $25,000; low: $1,000).
Purpose and activities: Broad purposes; emphasis on private higher and secondary education; grants also for local hospitals, churches, and cultural programs.
Types of support awarded: Operating budgets, continuing support, annual campaigns, building funds, equipment, endowment funds.
Limitations: No grants to individuals, or for seed money, emergency funds, deficit financing, land acquisition, demonstration projects, publications, conferences, research, scholarships or fellowships; no loans.
Publications: 990-PF.
Application information:

  Initial approach: Letter
  Board meeting date(s): June and December
  Final notification: 2 to 3 weeks
Officers and Directors: Clifford L. Michel, President; Alan R. McFarland, Ellen Michel McFarland, Vice-Presidents; Lynn R. Falcone, Secretary; James E. Alexander, Treasurer.
Number of staff: None.
Employer Identification Number: 136082879

2736
Milbank (The Dunlevy) Foundation, Inc.
c/o Sullivan & Cromwell
125 Broad St.
New York 10004   (212) 558-3724

Incorporated in 1941 in New York.
Donor(s): Dunlevy Milbank.†
Financial data: (yr. ended 12/31/84): Assets, $3,764,946 (M); expenditures, $2,104,805, including $2,050,000 for 19 grants (high: $1,000,000; low: $5,000).
Purpose and activities: Broad purposes; local giving, with emphasis on hospitals, a zoological society, and a public library.
Limitations: Giving primarily in New York City, NY. No grants to individuals.
Application information:
  Initial approach: Letter
  Copies of proposal: 1
  Deadline(s): October
  Board meeting date(s): November or December and as required
  Final notification: 1 to 2 months
  Write: Donald R. Osborn, Secretary
Officers and Directors: William Ward Foshay, President; Barbara Foshay Duke, Vice-President; Donald R. Osborn, Secretary and Treasurer.
Number of staff: None.
Employer Identification Number: 136096738

2737
Milbank Memorial Fund ▼
One East 75th St.
New York 10021   (212) 570-4805

Incorporated in 1905 in New York.
Donor(s): Elizabeth Milbank Anderson.†
Financial data: (yr. ended 12/31/84): Assets, $26,709,562 (M); expenditures, $2,000,011, including $69,298 for 7 grants (high: $50,000; low: $400) and $742,857 for 2 foundation-administered programs.
Purpose and activities: A private operating foundation; primary activity is the Milbank Scholar Program, whose purpose is to bring the discipline of epidemiology into closer union with clinical medicine. Support for those already appointed as Scholars will continue, but no new awards within this program will be made. At present, only modest, short-term grants will be considered for funding, and these will be consistent with the Fund's interest in the uses of epidemiology in clinical training. It is anticipated that a new grants policy for the Fund will be announced early in 1986.
Types of support awarded: Research, fellowships.

Limitations: No grants to individuals, or for annual campaigns, building or endowment funds, deficit financing, dissertation research, operating budgets, sabbatical leaves, general purposes, or matching gifts; no new scholarships or fellowships; no loans.
Publications: Annual report, program policy statement, application guidelines, informational brochure.
Application information:
Initial approach: Letter
Copies of proposal: 1
Deadline(s): 4 to 6 weeks prior to meetings
Board meeting date(s): March, May, October, and December
Final notification: 4 weeks after meetings
Write: Sidney S. Lee, M.D., President
Officers: Sidney S. Lee, M.D.,* President and Executive Director; John S. Baugh, Executive Vice-President, Secretary, and Treasurer.
Directors:* Francis H. Musselman, Vice-Chairman; Leroy E. Burney, M.D., Robert H. Ebert, M.D., Ellen V. Futter, John W. Hennessey, Jr., Sidney S. Lee, M.D., Samuel L. Milbank, Thomas I. Parkinson, Jr.
Number of staff: 4 full-time professional; 4 full-time support; 1 part-time support.
Employer Identification Number: 135562282

2738
Millbrook Tribute Garden, Inc. ¤
Franklin Ave.
P.O. Box AC
Millbrook 12545

Incorporated in 1943 in New York.
Financial data: (yr. ended 9/30/82): Assets, $13,368,338 (M); expenditures, $341,699, including $294,000 for 27 grants (high: $55,000; low: $1,000).
Purpose and activities: Primarily local giving, with emphasis on secondary education, church support, child welfare, hospitals, and civic projects.
Limitations: Giving primarily in Millbrook, NY.
Officers: Oakleigh B. Thorne, President; Daryl Parshall, Vice-President; Vincent N. Turletes, Secretary; George T. Whalen, Jr., Treasurer.
Trustees: Mrs. Oakleigh B. Thorne, Robert W. Whalen.
Employer Identification Number: 141340079

2739
Miller (Kathryn & Gilbert) Fund, Inc. ¤
c/o Peat, Marwick, Mitchell & Company
345 Park Ave.
New York 10154

Incorporated in 1952 in New York.
Donor(s): Kathryn B. Miller.†
Financial data: (yr. ended 3/31/83): Assets, $2,065,659 (M); gifts received, $495,850; expenditures, $440,646, including $433,500 for 27 grants (high: $70,000; low: $500).
Purpose and activities: Grants primarily for cultural programs, hospitals and medical research, and higher and secondary education.
Officers and Directors: Charles Looker, President; Philip J. Hirsch, Vice-President and Treasurer; Jerold Zieselman, Secretary.
Employer Identification Number: 136121254

2740
Milliken Foundation ▼ ¤
1045 Ave. of the Americas
New York 10018

Trust established in 1945 in New York.
Donor(s): Milliken & Company, and others.
Financial data: (yr. ended 12/31/82): Assets, $1,336,179 (M); gifts received, $350,717; expenditures, $1,144,970, including $1,133,976 for 158 grants (high: $140,000; low: $50).
Purpose and activities: Broad purposes; general giving, with emphasis on higher and secondary education, community funds, public affairs, and youth agencies.
Advisory Committee: F.G. Kingsley, Minot K. Milliken, Roger Milliken, R.J. Netter.
Trustee: Citibank.
Employer Identification Number: 136055062

2741
Minerals Industry Educational Foundation, The
200 Park Ave., 36th Fl.
New York 10166   (212) 953-6900

Trust established in 1971 in New York.
Donor(s): The Anaconda Company, ASARCO Foundation, Amax Foundation, Newmont Mining Corporation, Phelps Dodge Foundation, and others.
Financial data: (yr. ended 12/31/82): Assets, $76,327 (M); gifts received, $113,100; expenditures, $118,658, including $118,300 for 12 grants (high: $18,650; low: $3,750).
Purpose and activities: Grants for higher education, with emphasis on schools of mining and technology.
Limitations: No grants to individuals.
Application information:
Initial approach: Letter
Copies of proposal: 1
Board meeting date(s): June
Officer: H.T. Read, Treasurer.
Trustees: J.E. Thompson, Chairman; Jack Anderson, E.D. Frost, Jr., W.R. Heinke, Ralph L. Hennebach, F.C. Kroft, Jr., John Towers, Milton H. Ward.
Employer Identification Number: 136346617

2742
Mitrani Family Foundation, Inc. ¤
c/o Benjamin Nadel & Company
437 Fifth Ave.
New York 10016

Incorporated in 1959 in New York.
Donor(s): Members of the Mitrani family, Milco Industries, Inc., and others.
Financial data: (yr. ended 12/31/81): Assets, $1,489,244 (M); gifts received, $128,509; expenditures, $249,817, including $249,111 for 188 grants (high: $20,000; low: $10).
Purpose and activities: Broad purposes; grants largely for Jewish-sponsored higher and secondary education and for vocational and technological training schools in Israel and the United States; support also for Jewish welfare funds, non-secular colleges and universities, and social and health agencies.

Officers and Directors: Marco Mitrani, President; Benjamin Nadel, Secretary; Isadore Minkin, Samuel Seidel.
Employer Identification Number: 246018102

2743
Mobil Foundation, Inc. ▼
150 East 42nd St.
New York 10017   (212) 883-2174

Incorporated in 1965 in New York.
Donor(s): Mobil Oil Corporation.
Financial data: (yr. ended 12/31/84): Assets, $19,736,302 (M); gifts received, $18,022,000; expenditures, $15,045,000, including $11,350,000 for 1,427 grants and $3,134,000 for 8,310 employee matching gifts.
Purpose and activities: Charitable and educational purposes; support for worthy charities and art and cultural programs in areas of company operations, with emphasis on higher education, including grants in fields relating to the petroleum and chemical industries, a scholarship program for children of employees, and a matching-gift program; support for community funds, civic affairs, social welfare, health agencies, and hospitals.
Types of support awarded: Employee related scholarships, employee matching gifts, research, exchange programs, general purposes.
Limitations: Giving primarily in areas of company operations. No grants to individuals, or for building or endowment funds, or operating budgets; no loans.
Publications: Financial statement, application guidelines.
Application information:
Initial approach: Letter or full proposal
Copies of proposal: 1
Deadline(s): None
Board meeting date(s): Monthly
Final notification: 6 to 8 weeks
Write: Richard G. Mund, Executive Director
Officers: Dede Thompson Bartlett,* President; Edward P. Hardin,* Vice-President; Richard G. Mund, Secretary and Executive Director; Anthony L. Cavaliere, Treasurer.
Directors:* Rex D. Adams, Harry H. Hinkle, Seymour L. Meisel, John B. Merrell, Robert C. Musser, A.F. Stancell.
Number of staff: 3 full-time professional; 6 full-time support.
Employer Identification Number: 136177075

2744
Mocquereau (The Dom) Foundation, Inc.
c/o Davis, Polk and Wardwell
499 Park Ave.
New York 10022   (212) 688-7771

Incorporated about 1926 in New York.
Donor(s): Justine B. Ward.†
Financial data: (yr. ended 9/30/83): Assets, $1,577,574 (M); expenditures, $437,489, including $299,867 for 14 grants (high: $112,648; low: $5,000).

Purpose and activities: Support for teaching of Gregorian chant by gifts to charitable organizations in the United States, France, Switzerland, Holland, Italy, and Portugal, and by direct payment of salary of teachers of Gregorian chant.
Limitations: No grants for scholarships; no loans.
Application information:
  Initial approach: Letter
  Deadline(s): None
  Write: James F. Dolan, President
Officers: James F. Dolan,* President; Theodore Marier, Executive Vice-President; Bernard F. Curry,* 2nd Vice-President and Treasurer; Maureen S. Bateman,* Secretary.
Directors: Jean Lallemand, Thomas Mastrosanni, Martin F. Shea.
Employer Identification Number: 237118643

2745
Model (Jane & Leo) Foundation, Inc. ¤
100 Gold St.
New York 10038

Incorporated in 1954 in New York.
Donor(s): Leo Model.†
Financial data: (yr. ended 12/31/81): Assets, $1,268,309 (M); expenditures, $87,761, including $72,121 for 59 grants (high: $13,421; low: $10).
Purpose and activities: Grants primarily for Jewish welfare and educational funds in the United States and Israel; support also for a creative arts rehabilitation center.
Officer: John A. Nevins, Secretary and Treasurer.
Employer Identification Number: 136034032

2746
Monell (The Ambrose) Foundation ▼ ¤
c/o Harmon Duncombe
30 Rockefeller Plaza, Rm. 3217
New York 10112   (212) 586-0700

Incorporated in 1952 in New York.
Donor(s): Mrs. Maude Monell Vetlesen.†
Financial data: (yr. ended 12/31/82): Assets, $62,533,729 (M); expenditures, $3,676,120, including $3,440,700 for 127 grants (high: $250,000; low: $1,000; average: $5,000-$75,000).
Purpose and activities: For the "improvement of the physical, mental, and moral condition of humanity throughout the world"; general giving, largely for hospitals and health services, medical, chemical, and geophysical research, museums, performing arts, and other cultural activities, and higher education; support also for research in political science, mental health, aid to the handicapped, social services, and population control.
Officers and Directors: Harmon Duncombe, President and Treasurer; George Rowe, Jr., Vice-President and Secretary; Henry G. Walter, Jr.
Employer Identification Number: 131982683

2747
Monterey Fund, Inc. ▼ ¤
c/o Bear, Stearns & Co.
5 Hanover Square, 9th Fl.
New York 10004

Incorporated in 1967 in New York.
Donor(s): Bear, Stearns & Co., employees of Bear, Stearns & Co.
Financial data: (yr. ended 4/30/83): Assets, $786,617 (M); gifts received, $1,595,379; expenditures, $1,812,441, including $1,806,845 for 1,358 grants (high: $40,000; low: $20).
Purpose and activities: Broad purposes; support largely for Jewish welfare funds, hospitals, and higher and secondary education; grants also for social service agencies and cultural programs.
Officers and Directors: Carleton Holstrom, President; Alvin Einbender, Secretary; Paul Weissman, Treasurer.
Employer Identification Number: 136255661

2748
Moore (Edward S.) Foundation, Inc.
c/o Alexander and Green
299 Park Ave.
New York 10171   (212) 758-6900

Foundation established in 1957 in New York.
Donor(s): Edward S. Moore, Jr.,† Evelyn N. Moore,† Carolyn N. Moore, and others.
Financial data: (yr. ended 12/31/82): Assets, $14,776,590 (M); gifts received, $1,487,232; expenditures, $871,252, including $705,500 for 64 grants (high: $50,000; low: $500; average: $1,000-$25,000).
Purpose and activities: Support largely in New York and Connecticut for youth agencies, hospitals, education, and cultural programs, including museums.
Types of support awarded: Operating budgets, continuing support, annual campaigns, seed money, emergency funds, building funds, equipment, land acquisition, endowment funds, matching funds, internships, scholarship funds, special projects, research.
Limitations: Giving primarily in NY and CT. No grants to individuals, or for deficit financing, publications, or conferences; no loans.
Application information:
  Initial approach: Letter
  Deadline(s): None
  Board meeting date(s): January, April, July, and October
  Final notification: 3 to 6 months
  Write: Donald Vail, Secretary
Officers and Directors: John W. Cross, III, President; Marion Moore Gilbert, Vice-President; Donald Vail, Secretary; Alexander Jackson, Treasurer.
Number of staff: 2 full-time professional.
Employer Identification Number: 136127365

2749
Morania Foundation, Inc. ¤
c/o Morgan Guaranty Trust Company
9 West 57th St.
New York 10019

Incorporated in 1960 in New York.
Financial data: (yr. ended 10/31/82): Assets, $4,433,500 (M); expenditures, $307,383, including $291,500 for 21 grants (high: $150,000; low: $1,000).
Purpose and activities: Broad purposes; grants largely for Roman Catholic church-related institutions, foreign missions, and welfare funds.
Officers and Directors: William J. McCormack, President and Treasurer; Jacob I. Goodstein, Secretary; Julie M. Greenough.
Employer Identification Number: 136141577

2750
Morgan Guaranty Trust Company of New York Charitable Trust ▼
23 Wall St.
New York 10015   (212) 483-2058

Trust established in 1961 in New York.
Donor(s): Morgan Guaranty Trust Company of New York.
Financial data: (yr. ended 12/31/84): Assets, $12,139,562 (M); gifts received, $4,000,000; expenditures, $4,451,488, including $3,764,784 for 368 grants (high: $80,000; low: $1,000; average: $1,000-$25,000) and $677,328 for 4,000 employee matching gifts.
Purpose and activities: General purposes; emphasis is on helping to find solutions to social problems and needs through support of competent agencies in fields of health, social services, education, cultural resources, urban affairs, and the environment; special attention to job training, housing, economic development, advocacy and citizen involvement programs in New York City. Matches employee gifts to educational and cultural institutions and to hospitals.
Types of support awarded: Employee matching gifts, operating budgets, annual campaigns, seed money, building funds, equipment, land acquisition, special projects, matching funds, technical assistance, general purposes.
Limitations: Giving primarily in the New York City, NY, area, except for selected institutions of higher education. No support for organizations working with specific disabilities or diseases. No grants to individuals, or for endowment funds or scholarships and fellowships; no loans.
Publications: Annual report, application guidelines, program policy statement.
Application information: Application form required.
  Initial approach: Full proposal
  Copies of proposal: 1
  Deadline(s): None
  Board meeting date(s): Monthly
  Final notification: 2 months
  Write: Robert F. Longley, Senior Vice-President, Morgan Guaranty Trust Company of New York

Advisory Committee: Boris S. Berkovitch, Robert V. Lindsay, Lewis T. Preston, Dennis Weatherstone.
Trustee: Morgan Guaranty Trust Company of New York (Robert F. Longley, Senior Vice-President).
Number of staff: 5 full-time professional; 6 full-time support.
Employer Identification Number: 136037931

2751
Morgan Stanley Foundation
1251 Ave. of the Americas, 21st Fl.
New York 10020   (212) 974-2522

Trust established in 1961 in New York.
Donor(s): Morgan Stanley & Co., Inc.
Financial data: (yr. ended 12/31/84): Assets, $2,733,125 (M); expenditures, $700,000, including $575,000 for 70 grants (high: $100,000; low: $1,000; average: $2,500-$5,000) and $125,000 for employee matching gifts.
Purpose and activities: Broad purposes; primarily local giving for programs in minority education; grants also for business schools, cultural programs, and hospitals.
Types of support awarded: Operating budgets, continuing support, annual campaigns, seed money, employee matching gifts.
Limitations: Giving primarily in the New York, NY, metropolitan area. No grants to individuals, or for emergency, endowment or building funds; deficit financing, equipment, land acquisition, scholarships, fellowships, special projects, research, publications, or conferences; no loans.
Application information:
    Initial approach: Letter
    Copies of proposal: 1
    Deadline(s): None
    Board meeting date(s): Quarterly and as required
    Final notification: 3 months
    Write: Patricia Schaefer, Foundation Officer
Trustees: John Barr, Anson Beard, Edward Dunn, Joseph Tompkins, John Wilson.
Officer: Patricia Schaefer, Foundation Officer.
Number of staff: 1 part-time professional.
Employer Identification Number: 136155650

2752
Morgenstern (Morris) Foundation ▼ ☐
100 Merrick Rd., Rm. 506E
Rockville Centre 11570   (516) 536-3030

Trust established in 1949 in New York.
Donor(s): Morris Morgenstern.†
Financial data: (yr. ended 12/31/83): Assets, $10,013,691 (M); gifts received, $11,800; expenditures, $1,531,923, including $1,242,949 for 136 grants (high: $370,000; low: $15; average: $50-$10,000).

Purpose and activities: Broad purposes, including various public programs of its own, such as a national art contest for the physically handicapped and a drive against bigotry. Morris Morgenstern Student Loan funds are established at a number of colleges and universities to aid undergraduates with short-term emergency loans. Support for Jewish welfare funds; religious institutions, particularly synagogues; religious and secular education and youth agencies in New York and vicinity.
Types of support awarded: General purposes, student aid.
Limitations: Giving primarily in the New York, NY, metropolitan area.
Application information:
    Write: Hannah Klein, Executive Director
Officer: Hannah Klein, Executive Director.
Trustee: Frank N. Morgenstern.
Employer Identification Number: 131635719

2753
Morris (Norman M.) Foundation, Inc. ☐
Six Corporate Dr.
White Plains 10604

Incorporated in 1947 in New York.
Donor(s): Norman M. Morris.
Financial data: (yr. ended 12/31/83): Assets, $3,435,278 (L); expenditures, $215,698, including $205,340 for 187 grants (high: $75,000; low: $20).
Purpose and activities: Primarily local giving, with emphasis on Jewish welfare funds, higher education, and hospitals.
Limitations: Giving primarily in NY.
Officers and Directors: Norman M. Morris, President; Marvin Lubin, Vice-President; Edward L. Morris, Secretary; Robert E. Morris, Treasurer; Arline J. Lubin, Adele G. Morris.
Employer Identification Number: 136119134

2754
Morris (The William T.) Foundation, Inc. ▼ ☐
P.O. Box 5786
New York 10163

Trust established in 1937; incorporated in 1941 in Delaware.
Donor(s): William T. Morris.†
Financial data: (yr. ended 6/30/83): Assets, $22,592,161 (M); expenditures, $1,421,717, including $1,058,110 for 123 grants (high: $45,000; low: $1,000), $8,000 for 4 grants to individuals and $57,220 for loans.
Purpose and activities: Broad purposes; giving largely in New York and Connecticut with emphasis on higher education, including loans and scholarships; hospitals; and health agencies, youth agencies, and cultural programs.
Types of support awarded: Student aid.
Limitations: Giving primarily in in areas of American Chain and Cable Company operations, especially in NY and CT.
Application information:
    Write: Arthur C. Laske, President

Officers and Directors: Arthur C. Laske, President; E.A. Antonelli, Executive Vice-President and Treasurer; W.F. Wheeler, Jr., Vice-President; P.W. Krehbiel, Secretary; A.C. Laske, Jr.
Employer Identification Number: 131600908

2755
Morton Foundation, Inc. ☐
c/o Charles Triebwasser
855 Ave. of the Americas
New York 10001

Established in 1961.
Donor(s): J. Morton Davis.
Financial data: (yr. ended 12/31/82): Assets, $4,208,895 (M); expenditures, $79,979, including $76,014 for 25 grants (high: $20,000).
Purpose and activities: Primarily local giving, with emphasis on Jewish education and temple support; support also for higher education.
Limitations: Giving primarily in NY.
Officers and Directors: Rosalind Davidowitz, President and Treasurer; Ruki Renov, Secretary; Esther Stanley.
Employer Identification Number: 136107817

2756
Mosbacher (Emil), Jr. Foundation, Inc.
515 Madison Ave.
New York 10022

Incorporated in 1974 in New York.
Donor(s): Emil Mosbacher, Jr., Emil Mosbacher, III, John D. Mosbacher, R. Bruce Mosbacher.
Financial data: (yr. ended 11/30/84): Assets, $1,226,594 (M); expenditures, $81,683, including $80,200 for 141 grants (high: $5,000; low: $25).
Purpose and activities: Support primarily for higher education and hospitals.
Officers: Emil Mosbacher, Jr., President and Treasurer; Patricia Mosbacher, Vice-President and Secretary.
Employer Identification Number: 237454106

2757
Mosbacher Foundation, Inc. ☐
515 Madison Ave.
New York 10022

Incorporated in 1948 in New York.
Donor(s): Emil Mosbacher, Gertrude Mosbacher, Emil Mosbacher, Jr.
Financial data: (yr. ended 12/31/82): Assets, $214,886 (M); gifts received, $140,000; expenditures, $118,884, including $118,112 for 84 grants (high: $15,000; low: $20).
Purpose and activities: Grants primarily for higher education, cultural programs, including museums, and international studies.
Officers: Robert Mosbacher, President; Barbara Mosbacher, Secretary and Treasurer.
Employer Identification Number: 136155392

2758

Moses (Henry and Lucy) Fund, Inc. ▼

c/o Moses and Singer
1271 Ave. of the Americas
New York 10020   (212) 246-3700

Incorporated in 1942 in New York.
Donor(s): Henry L. Moses,† Mrs. Lucy G. Moses.
Financial data: (yr. ended 12/31/83): Assets, $8,026,164 (M); gifts received, $1,950,000; expenditures, $1,553,588, including $1,528,531 for 127 grants (high: $200,000; low: $200; average: $1,000-$25,000).
Purpose and activities: Broad purposes; primarily local giving, including support for hospitals and medical schools, Jewish welfare funds, higher education, youth, minority, and social agencies, the aged, the handicapped, cultural programs, and a park in New York City.
Types of support awarded: Building funds, endowment funds, research, scholarship funds, fellowships, general purposes, matching funds, professorships.
Limitations: Giving primarily in the New York, NY, metropolitan area. No grants to individuals; no loans.
Application information:
   Initial approach: Letter followed by proposal
   Copies of proposal: 1
   Deadline(s): None
   Board meeting date(s): Usually in February, May, August, and October
   Final notification: 3 months
   Write: Henry Schneider, Treasurer
Officers and Directors: Lucy G. Moses, President; Alfred W. Bressler, Arthur M. Fishberg, M.D., Felix A. Fishman, Vice-Presidents; Lillian E. Rachlin, Secretary; Henry Schneider, Treasurer.
Number of staff: 1 full-time support; 2 part-time support.
Employer Identification Number: 136092967

2759

Mosler (Edwin H.), Jr. Foundation ¤

307 Fifth Ave., 12th Fl.
New York 10016

Trust established in 1962 in New York.
Donor(s): Edwin H. Mosler, Jr.†
Financial data: (yr. ended 11/30/82): Assets, $41,602 (M); gifts received, $412,665; expenditures, $152,974, including $22,447 for 10 grants (high: $12,500; low: $52) and $128,129 for 1 foundation-administered program.
Purpose and activities: Broad purposes; general giving, with emphasis on support for the U.S. Olympic Committee, sports and recreation activities, youth agencies, and Jewish welfare agencies.
Trustees: Edmund W. Badgely, Joan Johnson, Monroe Steinhacker.
Employer Identification Number: 136108682

2760

Mossman (J. Malcolm) Charitable Trust ¤

c/o Chemical Bank
30 Rockefeller Plaza
New York 10112   (212) 621-2143

Established in 1971.
Financial data: (yr. ended 12/31/82): Assets, $851,024 (M); expenditures, $117,315, including $108,225 for 48 grants (high: $15,000; low: $225).
Purpose and activities: Broad purposes; primarily local giving for social service and youth agencies, higher and secondary education, cultural programs, health, and church support, with some emphasis on Roman Catholic organizations.
Limitations: Giving primarily in NY.
Application information:
   Initial approach: Letter
   Deadline(s): None
   Write: Mrs. Barbara Strohmeier
Trustees: Irving Goodstein, Chemical Bank.
Employer Identification Number: 136354042

2761

Mostazafan Foundation of New York, The

24 West 40th St.
New York 10018   (212) 944-8333

Incorporated in 1973 in New York.
Donor(s): Bank Melli of Iran.
Financial data: (yr. ended 3/31/84): Assets, $40,065,481 (M); expenditures, $9,179,269, including $1,348,497 for 150 grants, $535,200 for grants to individuals and $235,978 for foundation-administered programs.
Purpose and activities: To provide scholarships to Iranian students studying in the United States, counsel students, and conduct research in the areas of Islamic religion and economic development; and publishing and distributing educational and religious books, for scientific and educational research and activities.
Types of support awarded: Student aid, fellowships.
Publications: Program policy statement, application guidelines.
Application information: Application form required.
   Board meeting date(s): Annually
Officers and Directors: M. Hossein Mahallati, President; Mohammad Badr-Taleh, Treasurer.
Employer Identification Number: 237345978

2762

Mostyn Foundation Inc. ¤

c/o J. F. Lambert
645 Madison Ave., Suite 1800
New York 10022   (212) 832-3919

Trust established in 1949 in New York; incorporated in 1965.
Donor(s): Harvey D. Gibson,† Mrs. Harvey D. Gibson,† Mrs. Whitney Bourne Atwood.

Financial data: (yr. ended 12/31/82): Assets, $2,386,831 (M); expenditures, $243,600, including $213,625 for 116 grants (high: $65,000; low: $25).
Purpose and activities: Broad purposes; grants largely for Protestant church support and religious associations, social agencies, higher education, health agencies, hospitals, and youth agencies.
Limitations: No grants to individuals.
Application information: Applications for grants not invited.
   Write: Mrs. Whitney Bourne Atwood, President
Officers and Trustees: Mrs. Whitney Bourne Atwood, President; Arthur B. Choate, Charles C. Newbery, Vice-Presidents; William G. Rabe, Secretary-Treasurer.
Employer Identification Number: 136171217

2763

Mott (Stewart R.) Charitable Trust

1133 Fifth Ave.
New York 10028   (212) 289-0006

Trust established in 1968 in New York.
Donor(s): Stewart R. Mott, Ruth R. Mott.
Financial data: (yr. ended 12/31/82): Assets, $3,072,023 (M); gifts received, $1,847,064; expenditures, $166,104, including $156,050 for 82 grants (high: $10,000; low: $250; average: $1,000).
Purpose and activities: Support primarily for arms control and international family planning.
Limitations: No grants to individuals.
Application information:
   Initial approach: Proposal
   Copies of proposal: 4
   Deadline(s): None
   Write: Stewart R. Mott, Trustee
Trustees: Stewart R. Mott, K.J. Wells, John P. Hodgkin.
Number of staff: 4 full-time professional; 3 full-time support.
Employer Identification Number: 237002554

2764

Muehlstein (The Herman) Foundation, Inc.

130 E. 59th St., Rm. 902
New York 10022   (212) 980-1000

Incorporated in 1947 in New York.
Donor(s): Herman Muehlstein.†
Financial data: (yr. ended 11/30/84): Assets, $274,452 (M); expenditures, $212,143, including $193,000 for 18 grants (high: $25,000; low: $5,000).
Purpose and activities: Educational and charitable purposes; grants largely for higher education, including scholarship funds and medical education, Jewish welfare funds, and youth agencies, primarily in New York.
Types of support awarded: Scholarship funds.
Limitations: Giving primarily in NY. No grants to individuals, or for building funds or operating budgets.
Application information:
   Initial approach: Telephone
   Board meeting date(s): May
   Write: Norman P. Auburn, President

Officers and Directors: Caryl B. Muehlstein, Chairman; Norman P. Auburn, President; Sanford Solender, Vice-President; Lawrence B. Buttenwieser, Secretary; Donald Wilson, Treasurer; Wilma Tisch.
Number of staff: 1 part-time professional; 1 part-time support.
Employer Identification Number: 136146516

2765
Musica Aeterna, Inc. ⊭
c/o Choate, Moore, Hahn, McGarry & Nemeth
420 Lexington Ave.
New York 10164

Incorporated in 1960 in Delaware.
Donor(s): Alice Tully.
Financial data: (yr. ended 12/31/81): Assets, $25,628 (M); gifts received, $185,911; expenditures, $178,159, including $165,844 for 1 grant.
Purpose and activities: The advancement of classical music through subsidies for two series of concerts in New York City; grants also for musical commissions.
Limitations: Giving primarily in NY.
Officers and Directors: James McGarry, President; Catherine E. Finnegan, Treasurer; Stephen Rauch, Secretary.
Employer Identification Number: 131933437

2766
Muskiwinni Foundation, The
c/o Joint Foundation Support
122 E. 42nd St., Suite 922
New York 10168   (212) 661-4080

Trust established in 1969 in New York.
Financial data: (yr. ended 12/31/82): Assets, $67,916 (M); expenditures, $289,085, including $250,000 for 1 grant.
Purpose and activities: Support currently to local and national programs in four areas: 1) Equal Employment Opportunity for Women; 2) Support Systems for Women, including child care and child custody; 3) Pro-Choice issues; and 4) Women's Role in National Affairs; particular interest in projects which address the special needs of low income and minority women and ensure women's involvement in the political process.
Publications: Informational brochure, program policy statement, application guidelines, grants list.
Application information:
Initial approach: Letter or proposal
Deadline(s): None
Board meeting date(s): Generally twice in fall and twice in spring
Write: Patricia Hewitt, Executive Director
Employer Identification Number: 136279928

2767
Napier Foundation, The ⊭
c/o Chemical Bank
30 Rockefeller Plaza, 60th Fl.
New York 10112   (212) 621-2143

Donor(s): Napier Company.

Financial data: (yr. ended 7/29/83): Assets, $1,883,083 (M); gifts received, $6,713; expenditures, $133,579, including $123,850 for 61 grants (high: $5,000; low: $300).
Purpose and activities: Primarily local giving, with emphasis on higher and secondary education, youth and social agencies, hospitals, and cultural programs.
Limitations: Giving primarily in Meriden, CT, and New England.
Application information:
Deadline(s): None
Write: Barbara Strohmeier
Trustees: John E. Benison, Eugene E. Bertolli, Michael G. Consolini, Eleanor S. Cooney, Ronald J. Meoni, Robert M. Meyers, Howard C. Schaefer, John A. Shulga, Carter H. White, Chemical Bank.
Employer Identification Number: 136029883

2768
Nathanson-Abrams Family Foundation ⊭
c/o Roberta Abrams
345 East 46th St.
New York 10017

Established in 1980.
Financial data: (yr. ended 2/28/83): Assets, $1,130,345 (M); expenditures, $113,262, including $106,263 for grants.
Purpose and activities: Support for museums, universities, and public charities.
Officer: Roberta Abrams, Treasurer.
Employer Identification Number: 133030314

2769
National City Foundation, The ⊭
c/o Corporate Tax Dept.
399 Park Ave.
New York 10043

Financial data: (yr. ended 12/31/82): Assets, $1,951,094 (M); gifts received, $4,266; expenditures, $178,857, including $33,563 for 42 grants to individuals (high: $1,500; low: $250).
Purpose and activities: Support entirely for scholarship stipends to individuals.
Types of support awarded: Student aid.
Officers: Walter B. Wriston,* Chairman; William I. Spencer,* President; Henry R. Brenner, Wade H. Coleman III, Richard G. Paton, Frederick A. Roesch,* Vice-Presidents; Stephen C. Eyre,* Secretary.
Directors:* Doris Margonine, Managing Director.
Employer Identification Number: 136097628

2770
Nelco Foundation, Inc. ⊭
164 W. 25th St.
New York 10001

Incorporated in 1953 in New York.
Donor(s): Leon Jolson, Nelco Sewing Machine Sales Corp.

Financial data: (yr. ended 5/31/83): Assets, $578,524 (M); gifts received, $152,000; expenditures, $161,485, including $160,401 for 57 grants (high: $118,000; low: $10).
Purpose and activities: Primarily local giving, with emphasis on the Holocaust Survivors Memorial Foundation and Jewish welfare and educational organizations.
Limitations: Giving primarily in NY.
Manager: Leon Jolson.
Employer Identification Number: 136089850

2771
Neu (Hugo and Doris) Foundation, Inc. ⊭
380 Madison Ave.
New York 10017

Incorporated in 1955 in New York.
Donor(s): Hugo Neu, Union Minerals & Alloys Corporation, Hugo Neu & Sons, Inc.
Financial data: (yr. ended 12/31/82): Assets, $1,276,711 (M); expenditures, $118,139, including $114,320 for 53 grants (high: $50,000; low: $25).
Purpose and activities: Primarily local giving, with emphasis on Jewish welfare funds; support also for hospitals and higher and secondary education.
Limitations: Giving primarily in NY.
Officers and Directors: Hugo Neu, President and Treasurer; Doris Neu, Vice-President and Secretary; Herman Caro, John Neu, Richard Neu, Donald Schapiro, David Simon.
Employer Identification Number: 136107504

2772
Neuberger (Roy R. and Marie S.) Foundation, Inc.
522 Fifth Ave.
New York 10036   (212) 790-9676

Incorporated in 1954 in New York.
Donor(s): Roy R. Neuberger, Marie S. Neuberger.
Financial data: (yr. ended 12/31/84): Assets, $3,800,452 (M); expenditures, $291,220, including $276,200 for 220 grants (high: $50,000; low: $25; average: $1,258).
Purpose and activities: Broad purposes; grants primarily for the fine arts, and higher education.
Limitations: No grants to individuals.
Application information:
Initial approach: Letter
Board meeting date(s): April
Write: Roy R. Neuberger, President
Officers and Directors: Roy R. Neuberger, President and Treasurer; Marie S. Neuberger, Vice-President; Charles H. Levitt, Secretary; James A. Neuberger, Mary Piatoff.
Number of staff: None.
Employer Identification Number: 136066102

2773
New World Foundation, The ▼
100 East 85th St.
New York 10028   (212) 249-1023

Incorporated in 1954 in Illinois.
Donor(s): Anita McCormick Blaine.†

Financial data: (yr. ended 9/30/84): Assets, $19,557,578 (M); expenditures, $2,456,359, including $1,579,700 for 145 grants (high: $50,000; low: $500; average: $1,000-$25,000).
Purpose and activities: Program places emphasis on (a) equal rights and opportunity, with emphasis on minorities rights; (b) public education, especially the roles of parents and the community working together; (c) public health, particularly helping the disadvantaged, and raising occupational health and safety standards and reducing environmental hazards to health; (d) community initiative for rural and urban communities; and (e) avoidance of war, especially nuclear war, and seeking peace.
Types of support awarded: Special projects, conferences and seminars, program-related investments, technical assistance.
Limitations: No support for cultural, arts, or media programs, organizations which discriminate against women or members of ethnic minority groups, or that do not have an affirmative action policy and practice. No grants to individuals, or for general operating budgets, deficit financing, continuing support, capital, building, or endowment funds, research that is not action- or policy-oriented with regard to current issues and is not of limited scope or duration, scholarships or fellowships, or matching gifts.
Publications: Biennial report, program policy statement, application guidelines, informational brochure.
Application information:
  Initial approach: Letter
  Copies of proposal: 1
  Deadline(s): None
  Board meeting date(s): 3 times a year
  Final notification: 3 months
  Write: David Ramage, Jr., President
Officers: David Ramage, Jr., President and Executive Vice-Chair; Lucile F. Newman,* Secretary; David V.B. Britt, Treasurer.
Directors:* Peter B. Edelman, Chair; Kenneth W. Haskin, Vice-Chair; Hillary Rodham Clinton, Maria Echaveste, Harold C. Fleming, Alfred Gellhorn, M.D., David B. Harrison, John W. Hatch, Karl Mathiasen, III, Linda A. Randolph.
Number of staff: 3 full-time professional; 3 full-time support.
Employer Identification Number: 131919791

2774
New York Community Trust, The ▼
415 Madison Ave.
New York 10017   (212) 758-0100

Community foundation established in 1923 in New York by resolution and declaration of trust.
Financial data: (yr. ended 12/31/83): Assets, $369,988,918 (M); gifts received, $11,528,899; expenditures, $40,743,387, including $37,239,322 for 3,780 grants (high: $1,000,000; low: $100; average: $20,000-$25,000).

Purpose and activities: A composite of many charitable funds. The grant program of each fund is handled separately, designed to meet objectives suggested by founder where requested. Priority given to applications for special support for projects having particular significance for New York City area. Community Funds, Inc. handles charitable funds of a special nature or smaller size.
Types of support awarded: Seed money, matching funds, employee matching gifts, consulting services, technical assistance, special projects, research, publications, conferences and seminars, loans.
Limitations: Giving limited to New York, NY. No support for religious purposes, projects in areas of the environment (except for environmental internship program), transportation, manpower development, summer youth programs, or addiction services and treatment. No grants to individuals, or for endowments, capital projects, building fund campaigns, deficit financing, emergency funds, general operating support, scholarships, fellowships, or annual giving.
Publications: Annual report, program policy statement, application guidelines, newsletter.
Application information:
  Initial approach: Full proposal
  Copies of proposal: 1
  Deadline(s): None
  Board meeting date(s): February, April, June, July, October, and December
  Final notification: 4 months
  Write: Herbert B. West, Director or Richard Mittenthal, Assistant Director - Program
Officers: Herbert B. West,* Director; James R. Dumpson, Karen Metcalf, Richard Mittenthal, Lorie Slutsky, Sidney S. Whelan, Jr., Assistant Directors; Lawrence R. Wirth, Treasurer; Kieran J. Lawler, Controller.
Distribution Committee:* William Parsons, Chairman; Arthur G. Altschul, Le Roy Carmichael, Duncan W. Clark, M.D., Frank H. Detweiler, William M. Evarts, Jr., Barry Garfinkel, Judah Gribetz, John B. Madden, Barbara S. Preiskel, Mrs. Laurance S. Rockefeller.
Trustees: The Bank of New York, Bankers Trust Company, Barclays Bank of New York, Brown Brothers Harriman Trust Co., Chase Lincoln First Bank, Chase Manhattan Bank, Chemical Bank, CitiBank, Fiduciary Trust Company of New York, Irving Trust Company, Long Island Trust Company, Manufacturers Hanover Trust Company, Marine Midland Bank, Morgan Guaranty Trust Company, National Westminster Bank, Republic National Bank, J. Henry Schroder Bank and Trust Company, United States Trust Company.
Number of staff: 19 full-time professional; 2 part-time professional; 18 full-time support; 2 part-time support.
Employer Identification Number: 133062214

2775
New York Foundation ▼
369 Lexington Ave.
New York 10017   (212) 599-0330

Incorporated in 1909 in New York.

Donor(s): Louis A. Heinsheimer,† Alfred M. Heinsheimer,† Lionel J. Salomon.†
Financial data: (yr. ended 12/31/84): Assets, $32,687,000 (M); expenditures, $2,179,000, including $1,613,000 for 80 grants (high: $50,000; low: $10,000; average: $20,000).
Purpose and activities: General purposes; local giving for projects designed to improve the quality of life for disadvantaged, handicapped, and minority populations, with extra emphasis on youth and the elderly, especially projects with a strong community base. Some support for advocacy and coalition work.
Types of support awarded: Operating budgets, continuing support, seed money, matching funds, technical assistance, publications, conferences and seminars.
Limitations: Giving primarily in the New York, NY, metropolitan area. No support for the arts, medical research, or films. No grants to individuals, or for annual campaigns, renovations, emergency funds, deficit financing, building or endowment funds, equipment, scholarships or fellowships, land acquisition, research, or demonstration projects; no loans.
Publications: Annual report, application guidelines, program policy statement.
Application information:
  Initial approach: Letter
  Copies of proposal: 1
  Deadline(s): November 1, March 1, and July 1
  Board meeting date(s): February, June, and October
  Final notification: 3 to 6 months
  Write: Ms. Madeline Lee, Executive Director
Officers and Trustees: Malcolm B. Smith, Chairman; Barbara D. Finberg, Vice-Chair; Rebecca S. Straus, Secretary; Michael M. Kellen, Treasurer; Myron S. Falk, Jr., Charles V. Hamilton, Stephen D. Heyman, Theodora Jackson, John E. Jacob, Josephine Morales, Archibald R. Murray, Stephanie K. Newman, John B. Oakes.
Number of staff: 2 full-time professional; 3 full-time support.
Employer Identification Number: 135626345

2776
New York Life Foundation ▼ ⌗
51 Madison Ave.
New York 10010   (212) 576-7341

Established in 1979 in New York.
Donor(s): New York Life Insurance Company.
Financial data: (yr. ended 12/31/83): Assets, $17,314,060 (M); expenditures, $1,856,656, including $1,813,790 for 400 grants (high: $340,000; low: $100).
Purpose and activities: Grants to national and local organizations. Broad purposes; emphasis on higher education, including medical and insurance education, community funds, community development and urban affairs, hospitals, cultural programs and social agencies.
Types of support awarded: General purposes, scholarship funds, operating budgets, building funds, special projects.

Limitations: No support for public educational institutions; athletic organizations; religious or sectarian organizations; pre-school, primary, or secondary educational institutions; or United Way-member organizations already receiving foundation support. No grants to individuals, or for seminars, conferences, trips, memorials, endowments, research-related programs, or matching gifts; no loans.
Publications: Application guidelines.
Application information:
Initial approach: Letter
Copies of proposal: 1
Deadline(s): None
Final notification: Varies
Write: Carol J. Reuter, Executive Director
Officers: Jacob B. Underhill,* President; Edmund Harnedy,* Secretary; William E. Keiter,* Treasurer; Carol J. Reuter, Executive Director.
Directors:* Donald K. Ross, Chairman; George A.W. Bundschuh, John De Bardeleben, Harry G. Hohn, Malcolm MacKay, Walter Shur, John H. Stimpson.
Number of staff: 2 full-time professional; 1 full-time support.
Employer Identification Number: 132989476

2777
New York Times Company Foundation, Inc., The ▼
229 West 43rd St.
New York 10036   (212) 556-1091

Incorporated in 1955 in New York.
Donor(s): The New York Times Company.
Financial data: (yr. ended 12/31/83): Assets, $995,646 (M); gifts received, $1,890,000; expenditures, $1,826,891, including $1,465,200 for 295 grants (high: $200,000; low: $500) and $155,671 for 370 employee matching gifts.
Purpose and activities: General local giving, with emphasis on higher and secondary education, including support for minority education and a matching gifts program; support also for urban affairs, cultural programs, journalism, and environmental concerns.
Types of support awarded: Annual campaigns, conferences and seminars, continuing support, emergency funds, employee matching gifts, endowment funds, exchange programs, fellowships, general purposes, internships, operating budgets, publications, research, scholarship funds, seed money, employee related scholarships.
Limitations: Giving primarily in the New York, NY, metropolitan area and in localities served by affiliates of the company. No support for sectarian religious institutions or for health-related purposes; grants for urban affairs seldom made on the neighborhood level. No grants to individuals, or for capital and building funds; no loans.
Publications: Annual report, program policy statement, application guidelines.
Application information:
Initial approach: Letter
Copies of proposal: 1
Deadline(s): Submit proposal in the early part of the year; no set deadline

Board meeting date(s): March and October, and as required
Write: Fred M. Hechinger, President
Officers: Fred M. Hechinger,* President; David L. Gorham, Michael E. Ryan, Senior Vice-Presidents; Solomon B. Watson IV, Secretary; Denise K. Fletcher, Treasurer.
Directors:* Arthur Ochs Sulzberger, Chairman; William R. Cross, Jr., Richard L. Gelb, Sydney Gruson, Marian S. Heiskell, Ruth S. Holmberg, Judith S. Levinson, M.D., Walter E. Mattson, William F. May, William W. Scranton, George L. Shinn, Iphigene Ochs Sulzberger, Cyrus R. Vance.
Number of staff: 3.
Employer Identification Number: 136066955

2778
Newhouse (Samuel I.) Foundation, Inc. ▼ ☐
c/o Paul Schener
360 Madison Ave.
New York 10017

Incorporated in 1945 in New York.
Donor(s): Samuel I. Newhouse,† Mitzi E. Newhouse.
Financial data: (yr. ended 10/31/83): Assets, $46,255,102 (M); gifts received, $5,000; expenditures, $5,048,249, including $4,944,149 for 298 grants (high: $2,000,000; low: $100).
Purpose and activities: Establishment of Newhouse Communications Center at Syracuse University for education and research in mass communications; general giving, largely in areas of Newhouse newspaper operations, for community funds, hospitals, Jewish welfare funds, higher and secondary education, music and the arts, and youth agencies; support also for journalism associations.
Application information: Applications are not encouraged.
Officers and Directors: Mitzi E. Newhouse, President; Donald E. Newhouse, Samuel I. Newhouse, Jr., Vice-Presidents; Norman N. Newhouse, Secretary; Theodore Newhouse, Treasurer; Richard E. Diamond.
Employer Identification Number: 116006296

2779
New-Land Foundation, Inc., The ▼
200 Park Ave., Suite 3014
New York 10166   (212) 867-5500

Incorporated in 1941 in New York.
Donor(s): Joseph Buttinger, Muriel M. Buttinger.†
Financial data: (yr. ended 12/31/82): Assets, $9,698,366 (M); gifts received, $42,246; expenditures, $1,063,733, including $899,169 for 123 grants (high: $50,000; low: $500).
Purpose and activities: Broad purposes; grants for civil rights, mental health, environmental preservation, arms control and disarmament, cultural programs, minority and medical education, and social services.
Types of support awarded: General purposes, annual campaigns, seed money, research.
Limitations: No grants to individuals; no loans.
Publications: Application guidelines.

Application information:
Initial approach: Proposal
Copies of proposal: 2
Board meeting date(s): Spring and fall
Final notification: 2 weeks after board meeting
Write: Robert Wolf, President
Officers and Directors: Robert Wolf, President; Renee G. Schwartz, Secretary-Treasurer; Constance Harvey, Hal Harvey, Joan Harvey, Anna Frank Loeb, Albert Solnit.
Number of staff: None.
Employer Identification Number: 136086562

2780
Newman (Jerome A. and Estelle R.) Assistance Fund, Inc. ☐
345 Park Ave., 7th Fl.
New York 10154

Incorporated in 1954 in New York.
Donor(s): Howard A. Newman, Jerome A. Newman.†
Financial data: (yr. ended 6/30/83): Assets, $7,591,710 (M); expenditures, $656,505, including $499,979 for 46 grants (high: $120,000; low: $50).
Purpose and activities: Broad purposes; primarily local giving, with emphasis on higher education, hospitals, aid to the handicapped, Jewish welfare funds, and the performing arts.
Limitations: Giving primarily in NY. No grants to individuals or loans to individuals.
Officers and Directors: Howard A. Newman, President and Treasurer; Patricia Nanon, Elizabeth L. Newman, William C. Newman, Vice-Presidents; Robert H. Haines, Secretary; William C. Scott.
Employer Identification Number: 136096241

2781
Nias (Henry) Foundation, Inc. ▼
c/o Henry L. Fleischman
639 Seney Ave.
Mamaroneck 10543   (914) 698-5036

Incorporated in 1955 in New York.
Donor(s): Henry Nias.†
Financial data: (yr. ended 11/30/83): Assets, $6,928,489 (M); expenditures, $536,419, including $467,000 for 54 grants (high: $28,000; low: $1,000; average: $5,000-$12,000).
Purpose and activities: Primarily local giving in the New York metropolitan area, with emphasis on hospitals, aid to the handicapped, medical school student loan funds, cultural programs, youth and the aged, and Jewish welfare funds.
Limitations: Giving limited to the New York City, NY, metropolitan area.
Application information: Applications by invitation only.
Deadline(s): August 31
Board meeting date(s): September and October
Final notification: Grants paid in November
Write: Stanley Edelman, M.D., Medical Activities; Albert J. Rosenberg, Educational Activities; Henry L. Fleischman, General Activities

Officers and Directors: Henry L. Fleischman, President and Treasurer; Stanley Edelman, M.D., Vice-President; Albert J. Rosenberg, Secretary; Charles D. Fleischman, William F. Rosenberg.
Number of staff: None.
Employer Identification Number: 136075785

2782
Nichols Foundation, Inc.
630 Fifth Ave., Rm. 352
New York 10111 (212) 581-1160

Incorporated in 1923 in New York.
Donor(s): Members of the Nichols family.
Financial data: (yr. ended 1/31/83): Assets, $5,827,388 (M); expenditures, $490,612, including $443,286 for 53 grants (high: $125,000; low: $750).
Purpose and activities: Broad purposes; mainly local giving, with emphasis on higher and secondary education, research in chemistry, biology, and the medical sciences, conservation, hospitals, child welfare, youth agencies, and social agencies.
Types of support awarded: Research, matching funds, continuing support, annual campaigns, building funds, equipment, endowment funds, scholarship funds, fellowships.
Limitations: Giving primarily in the New York, NY, metropolitan area. No grants to individuals; no loans.
Application information:
Initial approach: Letter
Copies of proposal: 1
Deadline(s): Submit proposal preferably in April or October; deadlines April 30 and October 31
Board meeting date(s): June and December
Final notification: 4 months to 1 year
Write: Charles W. Nichols, Jr., President
Officers and Directors:* Charles W. Nichols, Jr.,* President; Marguerite Sykes Nichols,* Kathleen Nichols Van Pelt,* Vice-Presidents; Mary H. Vinton, Secretary; Charles W. Nichols, III,* Treasurer.
Number of staff: 1.
Employer Identification Number: 136400615

2783
NL Industries Foundation, Inc., The ▼
1230 Ave. of the Americas
New York 10020 (212) 621-9370

Incorporated in 1953 in New York.
Donor(s): NL Industries, Inc.
Financial data: (yr. ended 12/31/84): Assets, $2,500,000 (M); expenditures, $1,426,000, including $1,286,000 for 450 grants (high: $35,000; low: $100; average: $500-$5,000) and $84,000 for 450 employee matching gifts.
Purpose and activities: General purposes; grants for community programs and projects, including United Way, and for higher education, hospitals, health and welfare agencies, culture, and art. Priority consideration given to proposals endorsed by local managers of company operations.
Types of support awarded: Operating budgets, continuing support, annual campaigns, seed money, emergency funds, building funds, employee matching gifts, scholarship funds, employee related scholarships, fellowships, research.
Limitations: Giving primarily in areas of company operations. No grants to individuals, or for deficit financing, equipment, land acquisition, renovations, endowment funds, special projects, publications, or conferences; no loans.
Publications: Application guidelines, program policy statement.
Application information:
Initial approach: Full proposal
Copies of proposal: 1
Deadline(s): None
Board meeting date(s): As required
Final notification: 2 months
Write: Richmond W. Unwin, Jr., President
Officers: Theodore C. Rogers,* Chairman; Richmond W. Unwin, Jr., President; Ilan Kaufthal,* Vice-President and Treasurer; Robert J. Hurley,* Vice-President and Secretary.
Directors:* James A. Heely, Michael L. Moore.
Number of staff: 1 part-time professional; 1 part-time support.
Employer Identification Number: 136085835

2784
Noble (Edward John) Foundation, Inc. ▼
32 East 57th St.
New York 10022 (212) 759-4212
Business office address: P.O. Box 162, Washington Depot, CT 06794

Trust established in 1940 in Connecticut; incorporated in 1982.
Donor(s): Edward John Noble.†
Financial data: (yr. ended 12/31/83): Assets, $65,241,238 (M); expenditures, $5,035,438, including $4,292,406 for 56 grants (high: $2,691,000; low: $250).
Purpose and activities: Grants for programs in the arts encouraging the development of outstanding talent (the current priority is in music), primarily in the metropolitan New York area with the exception of some foundation-generated projects. Selected projects concerned with conservation and ecology primarily related to activities on an island off the coast of Georgia. Supports private college and university environmental studies programs in Northeast and programs to improve educational opportunity for gifted and talented disadvantaged children in New York City. Programs in health education efforts related to family planning and the problems of overpopulation.
Types of support awarded: Seed money, internships, scholarship funds, matching funds, general purposes, endowment funds.
Limitations: Giving primarily in the metropolitan New York, NY, area for arts organizations and educational programs; St. Catherine's Island, GA, for conservation projects; the Eastern states for conservation and population control; the Northeast for private colleges and universities. No support for television, films, or performances. No grants to individuals, or for building or equipment funds, or publications; no loans.
Publications: Annual report, application guidelines.
Application information:
Initial approach: Letter or full proposal
Copies of proposal: 1
Deadline(s): 6 weeks before board meeting dates
Board meeting date(s): June and December
Final notification: 3 weeks
Write: June Noble Larkin, Chairman
Officers: June Noble Larkin,* Chairman and President; Nancy K. Breslin,* Secretary; Frank Y. Larkin,* Treasurer; John F. Joline III, Executive Director.
Directors:* Mimi Coleman, Robert G. Goelet, Howard Phipps, Jr., Frank P. Piskor, E.J. Noble Smith, Jeremy T. Smith, Carroll L. Wainwright, Jr., Alan N. Weeden.
Number of staff: 2 full-time professional; 2 full-time support.
Employer Identification Number: 061055586

2785
Noble (John H. and Ethel G.) Charitable Trust ⌑
c/o Bankers Trust Company
P.O. Box 1297, Church St. Station
New York 10015

Trust established in 1969 in Connecticut.
Donor(s): Ethel G. Noble.†
Financial data: (yr. ended 5/31/83): Assets, $7,738,436 (M); expenditures, $455,395, including $405,000 for 1 grant.
Purpose and activities: Giving to a local home for the aged.
Limitations: Giving primarily in CT.
Application information: Funds presently committed.
Trustees: Thomas R. Wagner, Bankers Trust Company.
Employer Identification Number: 136307313

2786
Noguchi (Isamu) Foundation, Inc. ⌑
32-37 Vernon Blvd.
Long Island City 11106

Incorporated in 1980 in New York.
Donor(s): Isamu Noguchi, and others.
Financial data: (yr. ended 12/31/82): Assets, $4,410,916 (M); gifts received, $35,000; expenditures, $15,504.
Purpose and activities: Grants of art objects to museums.
Officers and Trustees: Isamu Noguchi, President; Charles H. Lieb, Secretary; Bernard Bergstein, Treasurer; Priscilla Morgan, Shoji Sadao.
Employer Identification Number: 133059538

2787
Norman Foundation, Inc. ▼
215 East 62nd St.
New York 10021   (212) 759-7185

Incorporated in 1935 in New York.
Donor(s): Aaron E. Norman,† and directors of the Foundation.
Financial data: (yr. ended 12/31/82): Assets, $12,903,112 (M); gifts received, $5,000; expenditures, $547,375, including $360,250 for 62 grants (high: $25,000; low: $100; average: $7,500-$15,000).
Purpose and activities: Major interests include the protection of civil rights and civil liberties and, in general, broadening and improving the quality of citizen participation in the political, economic, and social processes of American communities. A major portion of grants are currently being made to projects which address the economic plight of the working and non-working poor and which enable them to have more voice in the institutions which allocate jobs and resources in their communities.
Types of support awarded: General purposes, matching funds, seed money, special projects.
Limitations: Giving limited to the U.S. No support for programs having broad public support, or for media or art projects, direct social service agencies, community fund drives, schools, or hospitals. No grants to individuals, or for building or endowment funds, continuing support, conferences, research, or scholarships and fellowships; no loans.
Publications: Application guidelines, program policy statement, multi-year report.
Application information:
  Initial approach: Letter or full proposal
  Copies of proposal: 1
  Deadline(s): None
  Board meeting date(s): Quarterly
  Final notification: 1 to 5 months
  Write: Hildy Simmons, Program Director
Officers: Frank A. Weil,* President; Lucinda W. Bunnen,* Phoebe W. Lundeen,* Vice-Presidents; Nancy N. Lassalle,* Secretary; Hildy Simmons, Treasurer and Program Director.
Directors:* Andrew E. Norman, Chairman; Melissa Bunnen, Robert L. Bunnen, Jr., Alice F. Cohen, Andrew D. Franklin, Deborah Weil Harrington, Diana Lassalle, Honor Lassalle, Philip Lassalle, Abigail Norman, Margaret Norman, Rebecca Norman, Sarah Norman, Belinda Bunnen Reusch, Amanda Weil, Sandison Weil, William Weil.
Number of staff: 1 part-time professional; 1 full-time support.
Employer Identification Number: 131862694

2788
Normandie Foundation, Inc.
215 East 62nd St.
New York 10021   (212) 759-7185

Incorporated in 1966 in New York.
Donor(s): Andrew E. Norman, The Aaron E. Norman Fund, Inc.
Financial data: (yr. ended 12/31/83): Assets, $1,251,374 (M); expenditures, $56,741, including $52,018 for 17 grants (high: $25,000; low: $30).

Purpose and activities: Grants primarily for cultural programs, with emphasis on a school for circus arts, and for civil liberties, and minority and civil rights organizations.
Types of support awarded: General purposes.
Limitations: No grants to individuals, or for building or endowment funds, scholarships and fellowships, or matching gifts; no loans.
Application information:
  Initial approach: Letter
  Copies of proposal: 1
  Deadline(s): None
  Board meeting date(s): June and December
  Final notification: 6 months
  Write: Hildy J. Simmons, Administrator
Officers: Andrew E. Norman, President and Treasurer; Nancy N. LaSalle, Vice-President and Secretary; Helen D. Norman, Vice-President.
Number of staff: None.
Employer Identification Number: 136213564

2789
Norstar Bank of Upstate NY Foundation
(formerly State Bank of Albany Foundation)
c/o Norstar Bank of Upstate NY
69 State St.
Albany 12201   (518) 447-4162

Trust established in 1962 in New York.
Donor(s): Norstar Bank of Upstate NY.
Financial data: (yr. ended 9/30/84): Assets, $275,137 (M); gifts received, $236,068; expenditures, $227,108, including $225,980 for 60 grants (high: $103,480; low: $25).
Purpose and activities: Primarily local giving, with emphasis on community funds, higher education, health associations, and youth agencies.
Types of support awarded: Building funds, equipment, land acquisition, research.
Limitations: Giving primarily in the Albany, NY, area. No grants to individuals, or for endowment funds, scholarships, fellowships, or matching gifts; no loans.
Application information:
  Initial approach: Proposal
  Copies of proposal: 2
  Deadline(s): None
  Board meeting date(s): Distribution committee meets 3 or 4 times a year as required
  Final notification: Shortly after meeting
  Write: Frank H. Odell, President
Trustee: Norstar Bank of Upstate NY (Richard F. Galvin, Vice-President and Trust Officer).
Number of staff: None.
Employer Identification Number: 146014607

2790
Northeastern Pooled Common Fund for Education in the Social Sciences and the Arts
c/o Gaye Fugate, MGF Management, Inc.
One Rockefeller Plaza, Suite 1505
New York 10020

Established in 1973.

Financial data: (yr. ended 12/31/82): Assets, $1,799,073 (M); expenditures, $38,180, including $28,000 for 2 grants (high: $25,000; low: $3,000).
Purpose and activities: Support for special projects in the arts and social sciences, primarily at colleges and universities.
Trustees: Lewis Cabot, Guido Goldman, Kenworth Moffett, Abraham L. Udovitch.
Employer Identification Number: 237345848

2791
Norwood Foundation, Inc.
c/o Bessemer Trust Company
630 Fifth Ave.
New York 10111
Mailing address: P.O. Box 238, East Norwich, NY 11732

Incorporated in 1952 in New York.
Donor(s): T.M. Bancroft, E.W. Bancroft.
Financial data: (yr. ended 12/31/84): Assets, $1,332,299 (M); expenditures, $118,000, including $110,000 for 8 grants (high: $60,000; low: $1,000).
Purpose and activities: Grants primarily for secondary education and hospitals.
Types of support awarded: Operating budgets, continuing support, annual campaigns, seed money, building funds, equipment, endowment funds, scholarship funds.
Limitations: No grants to individuals, or for emergency funds, exchange programs, deficit financing, land acquisition, matching gifts, fellowships, professorships, internships, special projects, research, publications, or conferences; no loans.
Application information:
  Initial approach: Letter
  Deadline(s): None
Officer: Thomas M. Bancroft, Jr., President and Treasurer.
Number of staff: None.
Employer Identification Number: 136111530

2792
Noyes (Jessie Smith) Foundation, Inc. ▼
16 East 34th St.
New York 10016   (212) 684-6577

Incorporated in 1947 in New York.
Donor(s): Charles F. Noyes.†
Financial data: (yr. ended 12/31/84): Assets, $50,576,877 (M); expenditures, $3,588,572, including $2,951,844 for 135 grants (high: $81,540; average: $30,000-$45,000).
Purpose and activities: Educational purposes through student aid. Grants to tax-exempt institutions beyond the high school level for scholarships, fellowships, and internships within programs concerned with specific aspects of health care, population control, environment, and education.
Types of support awarded: Internships, scholarship funds, fellowships.

Limitations: Giving limited to the U.S. No grants to individuals, or for general operating expenses, capital or endowment funds, matching gifts, faculty or administrative salaries, continuing support, annual campaigns, seed money, emergency funds, deficit financing, special projects, conferences, or publishing; no loans.
Publications: Annual report, program policy statement, application guidelines.
Application information: Applications not accepted for discretionary or founder-designated funds.
Initial approach: 1 or 2-page letter of inquiry, including budget
Copies of proposal: 1
Deadline(s): November 1, March 1, and August 1
Board meeting date(s): January, May, and October
Final notification: 2 months
Write: Marilyn L. Gross, Program Administrator
Officers and Directors: Edith N. Muma, Chairperson; Ann F. Wiener, Vice-Chairperson; Dan M. Martin, President; Barbara B. Dow, Duncan M. Findlay, Nicholas Jacangelo, Vice-Presidents; George W. McGrath, Secretary and Treasurer; Rowland H.S. Bedell, M.D., Dorothy E. Muma.
Number of staff: 3 full-time professional; 1 part-time support.
Employer Identification Number: 135600408

2793
N've Shalom Foundation, Inc. ⌷
411 Fifth Ave.
New York 10016

Incorporated about 1938 in New York.
Donor(s): Joseph Attie.
Financial data: (yr. ended 12/31/82): Assets, $1,881,690 (M); expenditures, $129,498, including $120,840 for 67 grants (high: $8,000; low: $20).
Purpose and activities: Primarily local giving, with emphasis on Jewish educational institutions and welfare funds.
Limitations: Giving primarily in NY.
Officers: Joseph Shalom, President; Henry Shalom, Vice-President and Secretary; Stephen Shalom, Treasurer.
Employer Identification Number: 136168301

2794
O.C.F. Foundation, Inc. ⌷
122 East 42nd St.
New York 10017

Incorporated in 1940 in New York.
Donor(s): International Minerals and Metals Corporation.
Financial data: (yr. ended 12/31/82): Assets, $1,438,435 (M); expenditures, $147,736, including $136,310 for 33 grants (high: $45,000; low: $75).
Purpose and activities: Broad purposes; primarily local giving, with emphasis on Jewish welfare funds and cultural activities.
Limitations: Giving primarily in NY.

Officers: H. Fred Baerwald, President; Anne Halpern, Vice-President; Philip J. Maron, Secretary; Gregor Leinsdorf, Treasurer.
Employer Identification Number: 136007727

2795
O'Connor (A. Lindsay and Olive B.) Foundation ▼
P.O. Box D
Hobart 13788   (607) 538-9248

Trust established in 1965 in New York.
Donor(s): Olive B. O'Connor.†
Financial data: (yr. ended 12/31/82): Assets, $26,497,846 (M); gifts received, $245,000; expenditures, $1,488,181, including $1,262,964 for 45 grants (high: $500,000; low: $500; average: $1,000-$20,000).
Purpose and activities: Broad purposes; local giving, with emphasis on "quality of life," including hospitals, libraries, community centers, higher education, nursing and other vocational education, youth agencies, religious organizations, and historic restorations; support for town, village, and environmental improvement.
Types of support awarded: General purposes, continuing support, annual campaigns, seed money, emergency funds, building funds, equipment, land acquisition, endowment funds, special projects, research, publications, conferences and seminars, scholarship funds, matching funds, loans, technical assistance, program-related investments.
Limitations: Giving primarily in Delaware County, NY, and contiguous rural counties in upstate NY. No grants to individuals, or for operating budgets.
Publications: 990-PF, multi-year report, program policy statement, application guidelines.
Application information: Application form required.
Initial approach: Letter
Copies of proposal: 1
Deadline(s): April 1
Board meeting date(s): May or June and September or October; committee meets monthly to consider grants under $5,000
Final notification: 1 week to 10 days after semiannual meeting
Write: Donald F. Bishop, II, Executive Director
Officer: Donald F. Bishop, II, Executive Director.
Advisory Committee: Olive B. Price, Chairman; Robert L. Bishop, II, Vice-Chairman; Robert L. Bishop, Executive Secretary; Donald F. Bishop, Charlotte B. Hill, William J. Murphy, Eugene E. Peckham.
Trustee: First-City Division of Lincoln First Bank.
Number of staff: 2.
Employer Identification Number: 166063485

2796
Oestreicher (Sylvan and Ann) Foundation, Inc.
645 Madison Ave.
New York 10022   (212) 759-8500

Incorporated in 1948 in New York.
Donor(s): Sylvan Oestreicher.†
Financial data: (yr. ended 4/30/83): Assets, $2,145,007 (M); expenditures, $44,698, including $39,094 for 110 grants (high: $5,000; low: $10).
Purpose and activities: Broad purposes; grants primarily for religious welfare funds, hospitals, and higher education; support also for the handicapped, youth agencies, religious associations, and cultural programs.
Officers: Ann Oestreicher,* President; Merwin Lewis,* Vice-President; Robert F. Welch,* Secretary.
Directors:* Gunhilde Carroad.
Employer Identification Number: 136085974

2797
Ogden (Ralph E.) Foundation, Inc. ▼ ⌷
Pleasant Hill Rd.
Mountainville 10953

Incorporated in 1947 in Delaware.
Donor(s): Ralph E. Ogden,† H. Peter Stern, Margaret H. Ogden.†
Financial data: (yr. ended 12/31/83): Assets, $14,563,507 (M); expenditures, $452,159, including $409,801 for 20 grants (high: $273,401; low: $1,000; average: $1,000-$7,500).
Purpose and activities: Broad purposes; support primarily for the arts, especially a local art center.
Limitations: Giving primarily in Mountainville, NY, and New York City.
Officers: H. Peter Stern,* President; W.C. Von Staden,* Vice-President; Spencer L. Koslan, Secretary; Eugene L. Cohan,* Treasurer.
Trustees:* Leslie A. Jacobson, Frederick Lubcher, David Sachs.
Employer Identification Number: 141455902

2798
Olin Foundation, Inc. ▼
805 Third Ave.
New York 10022   (212) 832-0508
Minnesota address: 415 Foshay Tower, Minneapolis, MN 55402, Tel.: (612) 341-2581

Incorporated in 1938 in New York.
Donor(s): Franklin W. Olin.†
Financial data: (yr. ended 12/31/83): Assets, $134,598,916 (M); expenditures, $5,880,039, including $5,229,000 for 5 grants (average: $1,500,000-$5,000,000).
Purpose and activities: Primarily for constructing and equipping new academic buildings and libraries at private 4-year, accredited, degree-granting colleges and universities, with a preference for funding undergraduate buildings. Authorizes grants of up to $5,000,000 payable over several years. Awards limited to institutions with enrollment of more than 500 full-time students.

Types of support awarded: Building funds, equipment.
Limitations: No support for colleges and universities with enrollments of less than 500 full-time students. No grants to individuals, or for operating budgets, building renovations or additions, research, scholarships, fellowships, matching gifts, special projects, general support, or non-academic buildings and facilities; no loans.
Publications: Program policy statement, application guidelines.
Application information: Submit original application to New York office and 1 copy to Minneapolis office; geographic location is given negative weight for proposals in areas of previous foundation support, especially during the last five years.
  Initial approach: Letter of five pages or less
  Copies of proposal: 2
  Deadline(s): Submit applications from January 1 to October 1; deadline October 31
  Board meeting date(s): As required
  Final notification: June 30 of following year
  Write: Lawrence W. Milas, President
Officers: Lawrence W. Milas,* President; Robert D. Moss,* Assistant to the President; William B. Norden, Secretary; William J. Schmidt, Treasurer.
Directors:* Carlton T. Helming, William B. Horn.
Number of staff: 1 full-time professional; 5 part-time professional.
Employer Identification Number: 131820176

2799
Olin (John M.) Foundation, Inc. ▼
100 Park Ave.
New York 10017   (212) 661-2670

Incorporated in 1953 in Delaware.
Donor(s): John M. Olin.†
Financial data: (yr. ended 12/31/83): Assets, $71,557,477 (M); gifts received, $120,000; expenditures, $4,943,697, including $4,166,638 for 97 grants (high: $302,412; average: $5,000-$25,000).
Purpose and activities: Support for public policy research and education with emphasis on the application of fundamental American principles of freedom and justice.
Types of support awarded: Seed money, research, special projects, publications, conferences and seminars, general purposes, professorships, fellowships, continuing support.
Limitations: No grants to individuals, or for capital or endowment funds; no loans.
Publications: Annual report, program policy statement, application guidelines.
Application information:
  Initial approach: Proposal
  Deadline(s): None
  Board meeting date(s): 5 times a year
  Final notification: Within 90 days
  Write: Michael S. Joyce, Executive Director
Officers: William E. Simon,* President; George J. Gillespie, III,* Secretary-Treasurer; Michael S. Joyce,* Executive Director.

Trustees:* Richard M. Furlaud, John J. McCloy, Eugene F. Williams, Jr.
Number of staff: 6 full-time professional; 1 full-time support.
Employer Identification Number: 376031033

2800
Olive Bridge Fund, Inc. ⌐
40 Wall St., Rm. 4201
New York 10005

Incorporated in 1952 in New York.
Donor(s): Harold F. Linder.†
Financial data: (yr. ended 12/31/83): Assets, $4,226,098 (M); gifts received, $15,000; expenditures, $421,719, including $378,800 for 58 grants (high: $250,000; low: $100).
Purpose and activities: Grants primarily for higher education and Jewish welfare funds.
Officers: Daniel F. Steiner, President; William T. Golden, Vice-President and Treasurer; May L. Linder, Secretary.
Directors: Anna Lou Dehavenon, Susan E. Linder, Prudence L. Steiner.
Employer Identification Number: 136161669

2801
O'Neil (Cyril F. and Marie E.) Foundation ⌐
c/o Richards O'Neil & Allegaert
660 Madison Ave.
New York 10021

Incorporated in 1957 in Ohio.
Donor(s): Members of the O'Neil family.
Financial data: (yr. ended 12/31/82): Assets, $1,769,775 (M); expenditures, $85,212, including $71,450 for 20 grants (high: $50,000; low: $100).
Purpose and activities: Broad purposes; grants largely for higher and secondary education, and Catholic church support.
Limitations: Giving primarily in NY and OH.
Officers and Directors: Ralph M. O'Neil, President; Cyril F. O'Neil, Vice-President and Treasurer.
Employer Identification Number: 346523819

2802
Oppenheimer (Leo) and Flora Oppenheimer Haas Trust ⌐
c/o Chase Bank Tax
1211 Ave. of the Americas
New York 10036

Trust established in 1950 in New York.
Donor(s): Mrs. Flora Oppenheimer Haas.†
Financial data: (yr. ended 12/31/82): Assets, $5,182,721 (M); expenditures, $442,835, including $385,844 for 15 grants (high: $110,000; low: $5,000).
Purpose and activities: Grants, out of income only, for the care, aid, and comfort of needy children of the Hebrew faith through grants to established agencies in the New York metropolitan area.
Limitations: Giving primarily in the New York, NY, metropolitan area.
Trustees: Maurice Josephberg, Jacob M. Robbins, Chase Manhattan Bank.
Employer Identification Number: 136013101

2803
Osborn (Edward B.) Charitable Trust ⌐
c/o United States Trust Company of New York
45 Wall St.
New York 10005

Trust established in 1961 in New York.
Donor(s): Edward B. Osborn.
Financial data: (yr. ended 10/31/82): Assets, $2,476,738 (L); expenditures, $103,811, including $100,500 for 21 grants (high: $30,000; low: $1,000).
Purpose and activities: Primarily local giving for hospitals and medical research, with some support for cultural programs, secondary schools, parks, and youth agencies.
Limitations: Giving primarily in NY and FL.
Officer and Trustees: James W. Anderson, Vice-President; Mrs. Edward B. Osborn, United States Trust Company of New York.
Employer Identification Number: 136071296

2804
Osceola Foundation, Inc. ⌐
51 E. 42nd St., Suite 1601
New York 10017

Incorporated in 1963 in New York.
Donor(s): Katherine Sperry Beinecke Trust.
Financial data: (yr. ended 12/31/83): Assets, $2,670,619 (M); expenditures, $399,615, including $370,442 for 34 grants (high: $129,000; low: $20).
Purpose and activities: Giving primarily for higher education and historic preservation, including a rare book library; some support for performing arts organizations.
Officers and Directors: Walter Beinecke, Jr., President and Treasurer; Perry Ashley, Secretary; Barbara Collar, Deborah Kinseila, Ann Oliver.
Employer Identification Number: 136094234

2805
O'Toole (Theresa and Edward) Foundation ▼ ⌐
c/o The Bank of New York
48 Wall St.
New York 10015

Established in 1971.
Donor(s): Theresa O'Toole.†
Financial data: (yr. ended 6/30/83): Assets, $14,143,682 (M); gifts received, $526,712; expenditures, $2,744,849, including $1,437,710 for 273 grants (high: $50,000; low: $1,000).
Purpose and activities: Grants primarily for Roman Catholic welfare, church support, educational funds, hospitals, and higher education.
Types of support awarded: Continuing support, annual campaigns, emergency funds, building funds, special projects, research, matching funds.
Limitations: No grants for endowment funds, scholarships or fellowships; no loans.
Trustees: Chris Degheri, The Bank of New York.
Employer Identification Number: 136350175

2806
Ottinger Foundation, Inc., The
370 Lexington Ave.
New York 10017   (212) 532-0617

Incorporated in 1945 in New York.
Donor(s): Lawrence Ottinger.†
Financial data: (yr. ended 12/31/82): Assets, $2,764,146 (M); expenditures, $273,450, including $243,750 for 52 grants (high: $15,000; low: $100; average: $50-$30,000).
Purpose and activities: Supports selected projects designed to advance democracy, social justice, civil liberty, civil rights, and ecological balance.
Types of support awarded: Continuing support, seed money, emergency funds, special projects, research, conferences and seminars.
Limitations: No grants to individuals, or for operating budgets, capital campaigns, annual campaigns, deficit financing, building or endowment funds, equipment and materials, land acquisition, matching gifts, publications, or scholarships and fellowships; no loans.
Publications: Application guidelines.
Application information:
  Initial approach: Letter
  Copies of proposal: 1
  Deadline(s): None
  Board meeting date(s): January or February and in spring and fall
  Final notification: 2 weeks
  Write: David R. Hunter, Executive Director
Officers: Louise L. Ottinger,* President; Patricia Chernoff,* Betty Ann Ottinger,* Richard L. Ottinger,* Vice-Presidents; David R. Hunter, Executive Director.
Trustees: Karen Heath, Sharon Kalemkiarian, Lawrence Ottinger, Randy Ottinger, Ronald Ottinger, Sharon Ottinger.
Employer Identification Number: 136118423

2807
Overbrook Foundation, The ▼
521 Fifth Ave.
New York 10175   (212) 661-8710

Incorporated in 1948 in New York.
Donor(s): Frank Altschul,† Helen G. Altschul, Arthur G. Altschul, Margaret A. Lang.
Financial data: (yr. ended 12/31/84): Assets, $14,060,276 (M); gifts received, $2,650,000; expenditures, $648,712, including $565,650 for 153 grants (high: $62,500; low: $100).
Purpose and activities: General purposes; grants largely for Jewish welfare funds, higher and secondary education, hospitals, and a community fund; support also for international relations.
Types of support awarded: General purposes.
Limitations: Giving primarily in NY and CT. No grants to individuals.
Application information:
  Initial approach: Letter
  Deadline(s): None
  Write: M. Sheila McGoldrick
Officers and Directors: Arthur G. Altschul, President and Treasurer; Helen G. Altschul, Vice-President; Diana L. Altschul, Secretary; Edith A. Graham, Margaret A. Lang, Bethuel M. Webster.
Number of staff: 6.
Employer Identification Number: 136088860

2808
Paley (William S.) Foundation, Inc. ⌑
51 West 52nd St., Rm. 3490
New York 10019   (212) 765-3333

Incorporated in 1936 in New York.
Donor(s): William S. Paley.
Financial data: (yr. ended 12/31/82): Assets, $8,988,098 (M); expenditures, $768,371, including $373,750 for 21 grants (high: $125,000; low: $250).
Purpose and activities: Broad purposes; primarily local giving, with emphasis on a museum of broadcasting, education, cultural programs, and health services.
Types of support awarded: General purposes, fellowships.
Limitations: Giving primarily in NY. No grants to individuals.
Application information:
  Deadline(s): None
  Write: John S. Minary, Secretary
Officers and Directors: William S. Paley, President; John S. Minary, Secretary; Sidney W. Harl, Treasurer.
Employer Identification Number: 136085929

2809
Palisano (The Vincent H. "Jim") Foundation ⌑
c/o V.M. Di Angelo
135 Huntley Rd.
Buffalo 14215

Established in 1962 in New York.
Financial data: (yr. ended 5/31/83): Assets, $1,664,141 (M); expenditures, $93,434, including $65,133 for 10 grants (high: $28,333; low: $800).
Purpose and activities: Broad purposes; primarily local giving, with emphasis on higher and secondary education, including scholarship aid for selected colleges and high schools in Erie County administered through The Buffalo Foundation; support also for Roman Catholic associations and a hospital.
Types of support awarded: Scholarship funds.
Limitations: Giving primarily in NY.
Trustees: James G. Hurley, Charles J. Palisano, Harriet A. Palisano, Joseph S. Palisano.
Employer Identification Number: 166052186

2810
Palmer (Francis Asbury) Fund ⌑
47 East 88th St.
New York 10028

Incorporated in 1897 in New York.
Donor(s): Francis Asbury Palmer.†
Financial data: (yr. ended 4/30/83): Assets, $1,910,241 (M); expenditures, $111,812, including $105,000 for 11 grants (high: $10,000; low: $5,000).
Purpose and activities: To support home missions and educational institutions, to assist Christian ministers and workers, to help needy persons desiring to become Christian ministers, teachers, or workers to acquire a suitable education, and to establish in colleges and schools Bible teachers and lecturers. Current grants to institutions only.

Limitations: No grants to individuals.
Application information:
  Initial approach: Letter
  Copies of proposal: 1
  Deadline(s): Submit proposal preferably in April or October
  Board meeting date(s): May and November
  Write: William A. Chisolm, Secretary
Officers and Directors: John H. Washburn, President; Frederic D. Carter, Jr., Vice-President; William A. Chisolm, Secretary and Treasurer; E. Gayle McGuigan, Jr., Robert P. Patterson, Jr., William H. Sword.
Employer Identification Number: 136400635

2811
Parapsychology Foundation, Inc.
228 East 71st St.
New York 10021   (212) 628-1550

Incorporated in 1951 in Delaware.
Financial data: (yr. ended 12/31/84): Assets, $2,844,433 (M); expenditures, $313,720, including $16,377 for 10 grants (high: $3,000; low: $500; average: $1,500), $3,000 for 1 grant to an individual and $73,113 for 3 foundation-administered programs.
Purpose and activities: A private operating foundation; to conduct and further research in parapsychology through an operating program of its own and grants to educational institutions throughout the world.
Types of support awarded: Research.
Limitations: No grants for building or endowment funds, or operating budgets.
Publications: Application guidelines.
Application information: Application form required.
  Initial approach: Letter
  Copies of proposal: 2
  Deadline(s): Submit proposal preferably between January and March; no set deadline
  Board meeting date(s): Quarterly
  Final notification: 4 to 6 weeks
  Write: Mrs. Eileen Coly, President
Officers and Trustees: Eileen Coly, President; Lisette Coly, Vice-President; Robert Coly, Secretary-Treasurer; Allan Angoff, William Martin, Irving Rosen.
Number of staff: 6.
Employer Identification Number: 131677742

2812
Park Foundation, The ⌑
200 Park Ave., Rm. 3021
New York 10166

Incorporated in 1949 in the District of Columbia.
Financial data: (yr. ended 12/31/81): Assets, $6,635 (M); gifts received, $127,000; expenditures, $130,977, including $130,829 for 65 grants (high: $15,000;

Purpose and activities: Assistance to "the indigent, sick, and infirm;" general giving largely in New York, Massachusetts, and the District of Columbia, with emphasis on higher and secondary education and child welfare; support also for rehabilitation of the handicapped, Roman Catholic welfare agencies, and cultural programs.
Limitations: Giving primarily in NY, MA, and DC.
Officers: Jean K. Smith,* Vice-President; Joseph E. Hakim, Treasurer.
Trustees:* Stephen E. Smith.
Employer Identification Number: 136163065

2813
Parshelsky (Moses L.) Foundation
26 Court St., Rm. 904
Brooklyn 11242   (718) 875-8883

Trust established in 1949 in New York.
Donor(s): Moses L. Parshelsky.
Financial data: (yr. ended 12/31/84): Assets, $4,285,860 (M); expenditures, $383,937, including $288,400 for 65 grants (high: $28,000; low: $100).
Purpose and activities: Broad purposes; grants primarily to organizations located in or providing benefits for persons resident or employed in the boroughs of Brooklyn and Queens, with emphasis on hospitals, higher and secondary education, and temple support and religious activities; grants also for care of the aged, the handicapped, youth agencies, mental health, and Jewish welfare funds.
Limitations: Giving primarily in Brooklyn and Queens, NY. No grants to individuals, or for building or endowment funds, or operating budgets.
Application information:
  Initial approach: Letter
  Copies of proposal: 1
  Board meeting date(s): Monthly
  Write: Josephine B. Krinsky, Trustee
Trustees: Tony B. Berk, Josephine B. Krinsky, Robert D. Krinsky.
Number of staff: 1 part-time professional.
Employer Identification Number: 111848260

2814
Paul (Josephine Bay and C. Michael) Foundation, Inc.
c/o Gaston Snow Beekman & Bogue
14 Wall St.
New York 10005   (212) 227-8200

Incorporated in 1962 in New York.
Donor(s): Josephine Bay Paul.†
Financial data: (yr. ended 1/31/85): Assets, $2,329,770 (M); expenditures, $219,074, including $139,100 for 20 grants (high: $80,000; low: $1,200; average: $3,000) and $12,146 for 1 foundation-administered program.
Purpose and activities: Broad purposes; grants primarily for chamber music.
Publications: Program policy statement.
Application information:
  Initial approach: Letter
  Copies of proposal: 1
  Board meeting date(s): April and October
  Write: Robert W. Ashton, Executive Director

Officers and Directors: Raymonde I. Paul, President; Synnova B. Hayes, Vice-President; Frederick Bay, Secretary; Robert W. Ashton, Executive Director.
Number of staff: 1 part-time professional; 1 part-time support.
Employer Identification Number: 131991717

2815
PBP Foundation of New York, Inc. ⌑
c/o Wilkie, Farr and Gallagher
153 E. 53 St.
New York 10022

Incorporated in 1978 in New York.
Donor(s): Fiona F. Beck.
Financial data: (yr. ended 12/31/82): Assets, $20,064 (M); gifts received, $220,783; expenditures, $209,098, including $173,280 for 28 grants (high: $12,500; low: $1,000).
Purpose and activities: Broad purposes; emphasis on public policy, equal rights, and political science; support also for media and for higher education.
Types of support awarded: General purposes, annual campaigns, building funds, operating budgets, special projects, fellowships.
Application information:
  Initial approach: Letter
  Deadline(s): None
  Write: Arthur D. Kowaloff, Vice-President
Officers and Directors:* Stuart J. Beck,* President; Fiona F. Beck,* Vice-President; Susan Trabosh, Vice-President and Secretary; Arthur D. Kowaloff,* Vice-President and Treasurer.
Employer Identification Number: 132939192

2816
Pearlman (Henry and Rose) Foundation, Inc. ⌑
c/o Ralph Levitt
510 Fifth Ave.
New York 10036

Incorporated in 1953 in New York.
Donor(s): Henry Pearlman,† Rose Pearlman, Eastern Cold Storage Insulation Company, Inc.
Financial data: (yr. ended 11/30/82): Assets, $10,323,551 (M); gifts received, $336,500; expenditures, $4,210, including $3,800 for 20 grants (high: $1,000; low: $50).
Purpose and activities: A private operating foundation; grants locally for museums, arts organizations, and social agencies.
Limitations: Giving primarily in NY.
Officers and Directors: Rose Pearlman, President; Alex W. Pearlman, Vice-President; Marge Schever, Secretary; Dorothy Edelman, Treasurer.
Employer Identification Number: 136159092

2817
Peat, Marwick, Mitchell Foundation, The ▼
345 Park Ave.
New York 10154   (212) 758-9700

Trust established in 1968 in New York.

Donor(s): Peat, Marwick, Mitchell & Co., and its partners and employees.
Financial data: (yr. ended 6/30/84): Assets, $3,274,926 (L); gifts received, $3,440,936; expenditures, $3,090,989, including $1,114,746 for 525 grants (high: $58,000; low: $50; average: $1,000-$25,000) and $1,958,103 for employee matching gifts.
Purpose and activities: To assist the company in providing outstanding service to the profession by conducting programs to strengthen the profession's educational and research resources; grants restricted to educational purposes related to the company's functional areas of practice - accounting, auditing, taxation, management consulting - private business advisory services, including the Research Opportunities in Auditing Program (ROA).
Types of support awarded: Employee matching gifts, scholarship funds, special projects, lectureships, research, professorships, conferences and seminars.
Limitations: No support for athletic purposes. No grants to individuals.
Publications: Informational brochure, program policy statement, application guidelines.
Application information:
  Initial approach: Full proposal
  Copies of proposal: 1
  Deadline(s): Submit proposal preferably between April and June for most grants, and between September 1 and November 30 for RDA Program
  Board meeting date(s): August and January
  Final notification: 4 months for most proposals; ROA Program grants announced in February
  Write: F. David Fowler, Secretary
Officers and Trustees: K. Dane Brooksher, Chairman; F. David Fowler, Secretary and Treasurer; James E. Gilleran, T.E. Hanson, W.H. Moody.
Number of staff: 1 full-time professional; 1 part-time professional; 1 part-time support.
Employer Identification Number: 136262199

2818
Peierls Foundation, Inc., The ⌑
c/o Bankers Trust Company
P.O. Box 1297, Church Street Station
New York 10015

Incorporated in 1956 in New York.
Donor(s): Edgar S. Peierls.†
Financial data: (yr. ended 10/31/81): Assets, $1,572,907 (M); expenditures, $88,720, including $80,900 for 38 grants (high: $4,400; low: $600).
Purpose and activities: Grants primarily for youth and social agencies, aid to the handicapped, minority rights and opportunities programs, higher education, medical research, and population control.
Officers: E.J. Peierls, President; Ethel Peierls, Vice-President and Treasurer; Brian E. Peierls, Secretary.
Employer Identification Number: 136082503

2819
Penney (James C.) Foundation, Inc.
1301 Ave. of the Americas, 4th Fl.
New York 10019   (212) 957-6920

Incorporated in 1954 in New York.
Donor(s): James C. Penney.†
Financial data: (yr. ended 12/31/83): Assets,
$3,832,528 (M); expenditures, $310,308,
including $236,375 for 50 grants (high: $7,500;
low: $2,500).
Purpose and activities: Grants in the
Northeast and Appalachia primarily for special
projects, with emphasis on community-based
organizations and state or national coalitions
operating in the areas of environment,
especially toxic waste clean-up, housing,
domestic violence, child abuse, economic
development, employment, homelessness,
peace and social justice.
Limitations: Giving limited to the Northeast
and Appalachia. No grants to individuals.
Publications: Annual report.
Application information:
  Initial approach: Letter
  Copies of proposal: 1
  Deadline(s): None
  Board meeting date(s): March, May,
    September, and November
  Final notification: 1 to 6 months
  Write: Judith M. Friedman, Managing Director
Administrator: Judith M. Friedman, Managing
Director.
Officers and Directors: Carol P. Guyer,
President; Andrew W. Bisset, Secretary; Mary
Frances Wagley, Treasurer; Anne W. Gow,
Alissa C. Guyer, Shelly D. Guyer, Caroline A.
Penney, Mary F.K. Wagley.
Number of staff: 1 full-time professional.
Employer Identification Number: 136114301

2820
PepsiCo Foundation, Inc. ▼
Purchase 10577   (914) 253-3153

Incorporated in 1962 in New York.
Donor(s): PepsiCo, Inc., Frito-Lay, Inc.
Financial data: (yr. ended 12/31/83): Assets,
$502,664 (M); gifts received, $2,801,403;
expenditures, $2,895,280, including
$2,646,038 for 392 grants (high: $226,750;
low: $25; average: $25-$30,000), $72,520 for
20 grants to individuals and $175,000 for
1,000 employee matching gifts.
Purpose and activities: General giving, with
emphasis on health and human services,
including fitness education for youth and fitness
research; education, including graduate
business schools, minority education, and
economic education; the arts, community
funds, and other philanthropic activities.
Types of support awarded: Employee
matching gifts.
Limitations: Giving primarily in areas of
company operations. No grants to individuals,
or for building funds.
Publications: Informational brochure, program
policy statement, application guidelines.
Application information:
  Initial approach: Full proposal
  Deadline(s): None
  Board meeting date(s): At least annually

  Write: Jacqueline R. Millan, Vice-President
Officers: Max L. Friedersdorf,* President;
Jacqueline R. Millan, Vice-President,
Contributions; Thomas H. Tamoney, Jr.,
Secretary; Claudia Morf, Treasurer.
Directors:* Donald M. Kendall, Chairman;
Victor A. Bonomo, D. Wayne Calloway, Arthur
G. Gunther, Michael H. Jordan, William C.
Korn, Andrall E. Pearson, Harvey C. Russell,
Peter K. Warren.
Number of staff: 3 full-time professional; 2 full-
time support.
Employer Identification Number: 136163174

2821
Perkins (The George W.) Memorial
Foundation ⌑
660 Madison Ave.
New York 10021

Incorporated in 1961 in New York.
Donor(s): Mrs. George W. Perkins.
Financial data: (yr. ended 12/31/82): Assets,
$4,728,335 (M); expenditures, $328,699,
including $300,000 for 52 grants (high:
$20,000; low: $500).
Purpose and activities: Grants largely for
higher and secondary education, hospitals, and
conservation.
Officers: Linn M. Perkins, President; Anne P.
Cabot,* George W. Perkins, Jr.,* Penelope P.
Wilson,* Vice-Presidents; Antoinette Burns,*
Secretary and Treasurer.
Trustees:* Arthur V. Savage.
Employer Identification Number: 136085859

2822
Pettus-Crowe Foundation, Inc.
c/o Cahill Gordon & Reindel
80 Pine St.
New York 10005

Incorporated in 1968 in New York.
Donor(s): Irene P. Crowe.
Financial data: (yr. ended 12/31/83): Assets,
$1,311,041 (M); expenditures, $75,841,
including $65,498 for 15 grants (high: $20,000;
low: $1,000).
Purpose and activities: Support for family
planning agencies and women's rights
organizations.
Application information:
  Write: John R. Young, Vice-President
Officers and Directors:* Irene P. Crowe,*
President; John R. Young, Vice-President and
Secretary; Irene Crowe,* Mary Crowe,* Phillipa
C. Neilson,* Vice-Presidents.
Employer Identification Number: 237025310

2823
Pfizer Foundation, Inc., The ▼
235 East 42nd St.
New York 10017   (212) 573-3351

Incorporated in 1953 in New York.
Donor(s): Pfizer Inc.

Financial data: (yr. ended 12/31/84): Assets,
$4,996,441 (M); gifts received, $2,000,000;
expenditures, $2,144,458, including
$2,134,672 for 442 grants (high: $62,500; low:
$500; average: $1,000-$20,000).
Purpose and activities: Broad purposes; grants
primarily to national and certain local New
York City organizations classified into five
major categories: education, health, civic and
community welfare, culture, and international
affairs.
Types of support awarded: Operating
budgets, continuing support, annual campaigns,
seed money, emergency funds, building funds,
equipment, matching funds, professorships,
internships, scholarship funds, fellowships,
special projects, research, publications,
conferences and seminars.
Limitations: No support for religious
organizations, veterans organizations, non tax-
exempt foundations, fraternal or labor
organizations. No grants to individuals, or for
deficit financing, employee matching gifts,
goodwill advertising, or land acquisition; no
loans.
Publications: Annual report, program policy
statement, application guidelines.
Application information:
  Initial approach: Full proposal
  Copies of proposal: 1
  Deadline(s): None
  Board meeting date(s): As required
  Final notification: 3 months
  Write: S. Wyndham Anderson, Vice-President
Officers and Directors: Robert A. Wilson,
President; Richard C. Allen, Executive Vice-
President; S. Wyndham Anderson, Vice-
President; Terence J. Gallagher, Secretary; John
J. Morrison, Treasurer.
Number of staff: None.
Employer Identification Number: 136083839

2824
Pforzheimer (The Carl and Lily)
Foundation, Inc.
70 Pine St., Rm. 3030
New York 10270   (212) 422-5484

Incorporated in 1942 in New York.
Donor(s): Members of the Pforzheimer family
and others.
Financial data: (yr. ended 12/31/83): Assets,
$15,627,568 (M); expenditures, $1,193,295,
including $808,533 for 15 grants (high:
$400,000; low: $2,500).
Purpose and activities: General purposes;
collaborates with established libraries and
educational institutions in connection with the
Carl H. Pforzheimer Library, acquired upon the
death of one of its founders, in the general field
of American and English literature; also
supports charitable and educational institutions,
with emphasis on higher education, medical
associations, libraries, hospitals, and
community agencies.
Limitations: No grants to individuals, or for
building or endowment funds, research
programs, or matching gifts; no loans.
Application information:
  Initial approach: Letter or full proposal
  Copies of proposal: 1

Deadline(s): Submit proposal in March, May, September, or November

Board meeting date(s): April, June, October, and December

Write: Carl H. Pforzheimer, Jr., President

Officers: Carl H. Pforzheimer, Jr.,* President; Carl H. Pforzheimer, III,* Vice-President and Treasurer; Martin F. Richman, Secretary.

Directors:* Nancy Aronson, Richard W. Couper, George Frelinghuysen, Jill L. Leinbach, Carol K. Pforzheimer.

Number of staff: 5 full-time professional; 2 full-time support.

Employer Identification Number: 135624374

2825
Phelps Dodge Foundation ▼

300 Park Ave.
New York 10022   (212) 940-6446

Incorporated in 1953 in New York.

Donor(s): Phelps Dodge Corporation, and subsidiaries.

Financial data: (yr. ended 12/31/83): Assets, $10,426,400 (M); expenditures, $1,093,100, including $885,200 for 273 grants (high: $41,200; low: $50; average: $5,000-$10,000) and $180,900 for 522 employee matching gifts.

Purpose and activities: Broad purposes; general giving, with emphasis on higher education, community funds, health and welfare, civic activities, and cultural programs, mainly in areas of operations of Phelps Dodge Corporation and its subsidiaries.

Types of support awarded: Continuing support, annual campaigns, endowment funds, employee matching gifts, professorships, scholarship funds, fellowships.

Limitations: Giving primarily in areas of company operations. No grants to individuals, or for operating budgets, seed money, emergency funds, deficit financing, capital funds, matching or challenge grants, research, special projects, publications, or conferences; no loans.

Application information:
Initial approach: Letter or full proposal
Copies of proposal: 1
Deadline(s): Submit proposal preferably in March, June, or September; deadline November 30
Board meeting date(s): April
Final notification: 3 to 4 months
Write: Edwin D. Frost, Jr., President

Officers: Edwin D. Frost, Jr., President; Richard W. Pendleton, Jr., Vice-President; Anita H. Laudone, Secretary; Renny D. Warren, Treasurer.

Directors: William H. Chisholm, Cleveland E. Dodge, Jr., Warren E. Fenzi, George B. Munroe, Edward L. Palmer, Lawrason Riggs III, John P. Schroeder.

Number of staff: None.

Employer Identification Number: 136077350

2826
Philippe Foundation, Inc.

122 East 42nd St.
New York 10168   (212) 687-3290

Incorporated in 1953 in New York.

Donor(s): Pierre Philippe.

Financial data: (yr. ended 12/31/83): Assets, $1,791,463 (M); gifts received, $16,200; expenditures, $230,134, including $222,615 for 106 grants to individuals (average: $1,000-$6,000).

Purpose and activities: Grants to individuals for advanced study and scientific research.

Types of support awarded: Internships, exchange programs, research, conferences and seminars, grants to individuals, fellowships.

Publications: Application guidelines.

Application information:
Initial approach: Letter
Deadline(s): First day of board meeting months
Board meeting date(s): March, June, September, and December
Final notification: 3 months

Officers and Directors: Beatrice Philippe, President; Merton Holman, Vice-President, Secretary and Treasurer; Anne Marie Philippe, Vice-President; Marie-Josette Larrieu, Irving London, Alain Philippe, Anne Philippe, Helene P. Grenier, Pierre Philippe.

Number of staff: None.

Employer Identification Number: 136087157

2827
Phillips (Charlotte Palmer) Foundation, Inc.

c/o Alexander & Green
299 Park Ave.
New York 10171

Incorporated in 1958 in New York.

Donor(s): Charlotte Palmer Phillips.†

Financial data: (yr. ended 12/31/83): Assets, $1,300,204 (M); expenditures, $76,308, including $56,600 for 41 grants (high: $6,000; low: $50; average: $100-$6,000).

Purpose and activities: Grants primarily for higher and secondary education and church support.

Types of support awarded: Operating budgets, continuing support, building funds, equipment, endowment funds.

Limitations: No loans.

Application information: Applications not invited.
Board meeting date(s): May
Write: Robert L. Strong, President

Officers and Trustees: Robert L. Strong, President and Treasurer; James R. Cogan, Secretary; Rev. George Cook, John R. Miller, Charles E. Rogers.

Number of staff: 1 part-time professional.

Employer Identification Number: 136100994

2828
Phillips-Van Heusen Foundation, Inc.

1290 Ave. of the Americas
New York 10104   (212) 541-5200

Incorporated in New York in 1969.

Donor(s): Phillips-Van Heusen Corporation, and others.

Financial data: (yr. ended 12/31/83): Assets, $712,277 (M); gifts received, $261,505; expenditures, $179,674, including $178,075 for 96 grants (high: $21,000; low: $100).

Purpose and activities: General giving, with emphasis on Jewish organizations, including those in Israel, community funds, health and hospitals, and higher education; support also for child welfare, youth and social agencies, and international affairs.

Types of support awarded: Operating budgets, continuing support, annual campaigns, emergency funds, building funds, special projects, research.

Limitations: No grants to individuals.

Publications: 990-PF.

Application information:
Initial approach: Letter
Board meeting date(s): September
Write: Lawrence S. Phillips, President

Officers and Directors:* Seymour J. Phillips, Chairman; Lawrence S. Phillips,* President; Robert F. Reilly,* Vice-President; Albert R. Bongiovi, Secretary and Treasurer.

Number of staff: None.

Employer Identification Number: 237104639

2829
Pinewood Foundation ⌑

100 Park Ave.
New York 10017

Incorporated in 1956 in New York as Celeste and Armand Bartos Foundation.

Donor(s): Celeste G. Bartos, D.S. and R.H. Gottesman Foundation.

Financial data: (yr. ended 10/31/83): Assets, $7,600,487 (M); expenditures, $392,810, including $360,472 for 35 grants (high: $61,472; low: $1,000).

Purpose and activities: Broad purposes; primarily local giving for higher education and cultural programs, with emphasis on the arts.

Limitations: Giving primarily in New York, NY.

Officers: Celeste G. Bartos,* President; Armand P. Bartos,* Edgar Wachenheim III, Vice-Presidents; Peter C. Siegfried, Secretary; Benjamin Glowatz, Treasurer.

Directors:* Adam Bartos.

Employer Identification Number: 136101581

2830
Pinkerton Foundation, The

725 Park Ave.
New York 10021   (212) 772-6110

Incorporated in 1966 in Delaware.

Donor(s): Robert A. Pinkerton.†

Financial data: (yr. ended 12/31/82): Assets, $6,165,691 (M); expenditures, $318,212, including $299,133 for 21 grants (high: $50,000; low: $300).

Purpose and activities: Broad purposes, including the prevention of crime and juvenile delinquency; primarily local giving, with emphasis on youth training and employment programs and special education.
Limitations: Giving primarily in NY. No grants to individuals.
Publications: 990-PF.
Application information:
  Initial approach: Letter
  Copies of proposal: 1
  Deadline(s): Submit proposal preferably in April or October
  Board meeting date(s): June and December
  Write: Ms. Joan Colello, Secretary
Officers and Trustees: Louise C.P. Marshall, Chairman; Edward J. Bednarz, President; Joan Colello, Secretary and Executive Director; Eugene C. Fey, Treasurer; George J. Gillespie III, Thomas J. Sweeney, Augustus J. Young.
Employer Identification Number: 136206624

2831
Pioneer Fund, Inc., The
299 Park Ave.
New York 10171   (212) 207-1800

Incorporated in 1937 in New York.
Donor(s): Wickliffe P. Draper.†
Financial data: (yr. ended 12/31/82): Assets, $4,747,563 (M); expenditures, $461,531, including $418,974 for 8 grants (high: $91,200; low: $12,000).
Purpose and activities: Education and research in heredity and eugenics.
Limitations: No grants to individuals.
Publications: Program policy statement.
Application information:
  Copies of proposal: 1
  Board meeting date(s): Annually
  Write: Harry F. Weyher, President
Officers and Directors: Harry F. Weyher, President; John B. Trevor, Treasurer; Marion A. Parrott, Randolph L. Speight, William D. Miller.
Employer Identification Number: 510242968

2832
Pisces Foundation, The
210 South St.
New York 10002   (212) 619-6255

Incorporated in 1951 in New York.
Donor(s): Dorothy Schiff, New York Post Corporation.
Financial data: (yr. ended 12/31/83): Assets, $4,657,210 (M); gifts received, $131,000; expenditures, $227,831, including $199,710 for 60 grants (high: $30,000; low: $50).
Purpose and activities: General purposes; primarily local giving with emphasis on education, hospitals, public television, and juvenile crime prevention.
Limitations: Giving primarily in NY. No grants to individuals, or for endowment or capital funds, or matching gifts; no loans.
Application information:
  Initial approach: Letter
  Board meeting date(s): Monthly except August
  Write: Mrs. Adele Hall Sweet, Vice-President

Officers: Dorothy Schiff, President; Adele Hall Sweet, Vice-President; Sarah Ann Kramarsky, Secretary; Mortimer W. Hall, Treasurer.
Employer Identification Number: 136018311

2833
Plant (Henry B.) Memorial Fund, Inc. ☒
c/o United States Trust Company of New York
45 Wall St.
New York 10005

Incorporated in 1947 in New York.
Donor(s): Mrs. Amy P. Statter.
Financial data: (yr. ended 12/31/82): Assets, $1,955,384 (M); expenditures, $153,447, including $134,613 for 49 grants (high: $15,000; low: $200).
Purpose and activities: Broad purposes; primarily local giving, with emphasis on hospitals, population control, cultural programs, the environment, and health agencies.
Limitations: Giving primarily in NY.
Officers: Phyllis S. Oxman, President; Mrs. J. Philip Lee, Vice-President; Amy P. Clarke, Secretary.
Employer Identification Number: 136077327

2834
Pluta Family Foundation, Inc.
3385 Brighton Henriette Town Line Rd.
Rochester 14623

Incorporated in 1966 in New York.
Donor(s): James Pluta, Helen Pluta, Mr. & Mrs. Peter Pluta, General Circuits, Inc., Pluta Manufacturing Corp.
Financial data: (yr. ended 12/31/82): Assets, $2,810,558 (M); gifts received, $25,000; expenditures, $156,259, including $148,418 for 22 grants (high: $75,000; low: $500).
Purpose and activities: Local giving only, for higher education, including scholarship funds, and to hospitals.
Limitations: Giving limited to Monroe County, NY.
Application information:
  Initial approach: Letter
  Board meeting date(s): Semiannually
Directors: Andrew Pluta, John Pluta, Peter Pluta.
Employer Identification Number: 510176213

2835
Pope Foundation, The ▼ ☒
211 West 56th St., Suite 5-E
New York 10019

Incorporated in 1947 in New York.
Donor(s): Generoso Pope.†
Financial data: (yr. ended 12/31/82): Assets, $15,210,254 (M); expenditures, $1,749,312, including $1,492,060 for 64 grants (high: $385,000; low: $60).
Purpose and activities: Broad purposes; giving primarily in the New York metropolitan area including Westchester County, with emphasis on Roman Catholic church support, religious associations and welfare funds, higher and secondary education, and hospitals.

Limitations: Giving primarily in the New York, NY metropolitan area, including Westchester County.
Application information:
  Write: Fortune Pope, Vice-President
Officers and Directors: Catherine Pope, President; Anthony Pope, Vice-President and Secretary; Fortune Pope, Vice-President and Treasurer.
Employer Identification Number: 136096193

2836
Potts Memorial Foundation, The
J. Warren Van Duesen
Joslen Blvd.
Hudson 12534   (518) 828-3366

Incorporated in 1922 in New York.
Financial data: (yr. ended 12/31/82): Assets, $1,810,739 (M); expenditures, $102,795, including $88,377 for 5 grants (high: $43,927; low: $1,000).
Purpose and activities: A private operating foundation established to provide for the care, treatment, and rehabilitation of persons afflicted with tuberculosis; support for tuberculosis eradication, including fellowship programs for physicians.
Types of support awarded: Continuing support, seed money, building funds, equipment, land acquisition, research, special projects, publications, conferences and seminars, professorships, internships, scholarship funds, fellowships.
Limitations: No grants to individuals, or for endowment funds, or matching gifts; no loans.
Application information:
  Initial approach: Full proposal
  Copies of proposal: 8
  Board meeting date(s): May and October
  Write: Charles E. Inman, Secretary
Officers and Trustees: Carl G. Whitbeck, M.D., President; James M. Blake, M.D., Vice-President; Charles E. Inman, Secretary; J. Warren Van Deusen, Treasurer; Stanley Bardwell, M.D., Gerald D. Dorman, M.D., Frank C. Maxon, Jr., M.D.
Employer Identification Number: 141347714

2837
Pratt-Northam Foundation, The ☒
c/o Bond, Schoeneck & King
One Lincoln Center
Syracuse 13202   (315) 422-0121

Incorporated in 1962 in New York.
Donor(s): Hazel Northam.†
Financial data: (yr. ended 12/31/82): Assets, $1,599,217 (M); expenditures, $110,451, including $79,430 for 28 grants (high: $15,058; low: $320) and $12,500 for 9 grants to individuals.
Purpose and activities: Grants provided for educational, cultural or charitable objectives that benefit the Black River Valley Region of northern New York.
Types of support awarded: Student aid, grants to individuals.
Limitations: Giving limited to the Black River Valley region of NY.
Application information:

Deadline(s): None
Write: John A. Beach, Director
Directors: John A. Beach, Andrew J. Behr, Richard C. Cummings, Lee Hirschey, Lyle W. Hornbeck, Donald M. Hunt, Livingston Lansing, Edward Sieber.
Employer Identification Number: 166088207

2838
Pren-Hall Foundation, Inc., The ☒
420 Lexington Ave., Rm. 2320
New York 10170

Incorporated in 1949 in Delaware.
Donor(s): Prentice-Hall, Inc.
Financial data: (yr. ended 12/31/82): Assets, $3,383,212 (M); expenditures, $185,139, including $135,190 for 69 grants (high: $27,750; low: $50) and $28,912 for 144 employee matching gifts.
Purpose and activities: Charitable and educational purposes; general giving, with emphasis on hospitals, community funds, and higher education, including an employee educational matching-gift program.
Types of support awarded: Employee matching gifts.
Limitations: No grants to individuals, or for endowment funds, scholarships, or fellowships; no loans.
Application information:
Initial approach: Letter
Board meeting date(s): November or December
Officers: Frank J. Dunnigan,* President; Ralph F. Anthony,* Vice-President and Secretary; Vera E. Sharpe, Treasurer.
Trustees:* Colin Gunn.
Employer Identification Number: 516015053

2839
Price (The Louis and Harold) Foundation, Inc. ▼
654 Madison Ave., Suite 2005
New York 10023   (212) 753-0240

Incorporated in 1951 in New York.
Donor(s): Louis Price,† Harold Price.
Financial data: (yr. ended 12/31/83): Assets, $14,253,750 (M); expenditures, $1,371,551, including $1,304,750 for 273 grants (high: $900,000; low: $25; average: $100-$2,500).
Purpose and activities: Charitable and educational purposes; general giving, largely in New York and California, with emphasis on a business institute, Jewish welfare funds, hospitals, community funds, and higher education, including scholarship funds; grants also for youth agencies, camps for children, temple support, medical research, the arts, and services for the blind and other handicapped.
Types of support awarded: Endowment funds, operating budgets, scholarship funds, special projects.
Limitations: Giving primarily in metropolitan New York, NY and Los Angeles, CA. No grants to individuals or for building funds.
Application information:
Initial approach: Letter or full proposal
Copies of proposal: 1
Deadline(s): None

Board meeting date(s): February, May, and as required
Final notification: 1 to 3 months
Write: Harold Price, President
Officers and Trustees: Harold Price, President and Treasurer; Pauline Price, Vice-President and Secretary; Edwin M. Appel, Vice-President; Melvin Brodie, M.D., David Gerstein, Rosemary L. Guidone, Milton Slotkin, Linda Vitti.
Number of staff: 1 part-time support.
Employer Identification Number: 136121358

2840
Price Waterhouse Foundation ▼
1251 Ave. of the Americas
New York 10020   (212) 489-8900

Incorporated in 1956 in New York.
Donor(s): Active and retired partners and employees of Price Waterhouse.
Financial data: (yr. ended 12/31/83): Assets, $22,232 (M); gifts received, $864,180; expenditures, $885,405, including $882,646 for 441 grants (high: $37,500; low: $25; average: $1,000-$8,000).
Purpose and activities: The advancement of higher education in the field of accountancy; grants to four-year and postgraduate degree-granting colleges and universities for aid to teachers, scholarships, fellowships, and student loans; support for an employee matching gifts program and for research programs, libraries, and other facilities.
Types of support awarded: Professorships, fellowships, scholarship funds, research, employee matching gifts.
Limitations: Giving limited to the U.S. No grants to individuals, or for general purposes, or capital funds; no loans.
Publications: Program policy statement.
Application information: Applications should be made through local offices of Price Waterhouse.
Initial approach: Letter and summary of proposal
Copies of proposal: 1
Deadline(s): Submit letter of inquiry and summary of proposal preferably prior to July; no set deadline
Board meeting date(s): 3 to 4 times a year
Write: S.C. Biggs, Jr., Secretary
Officers: R.G. Nichols,* President; S.C. Biggs, Jr.,* Vice-President and Secretary; H. Haddock, Jr., Treasurer.
Directors:* R.C. Lauver, R.A. Mulshine, W.D. Pugh, A. Siegel, J.W. Zick.
Number of staff: None.
Employer Identification Number: 136119208

2841
Propp (Morris and Anna) Sons Fund, Inc. ☒
405 Park Ave.
New York 10022

Incorporated in 1944 in New York.
Donor(s): Members of the Propp family.

Financial data: (yr. ended 12/31/82): Assets, $1,820,976 (M); expenditures, $91,266, including $87,099 for 106 grants (high: $23,100; low: $10).
Purpose and activities: Broad purposes; giving primarily for Jewish welfare funds, temple support, and religious education; some support for higher education.
Officers: M.J. Propp, President; Seymour Propp, Vice-President; Ephraim Propp, Treasurer.
Employer Identification Number: 136099110

2842
Prospect Hill Foundation, Inc., The ▼
420 Lexington Ave., Suite 3020
New York 10170   (212) 370-1144

Incorporated in 1960 in New York; absorbed The Frederick W. Beinecke Fund in 1983.
Donor(s): William S. Beinecke.
Financial data: (yr. ended 12/31/84): Assets, $22,451,327 (M); expenditures, $1,680,571, including $1,302,000 for 59 grants (high: $330,000; low: $2,500; average: $2,500-$25,000) and $56,870 for 132 employee matching gifts.
Purpose and activities: Broad purposes; general giving, primarily in the northeastern United States, with emphasis on higher and secondary education, museums, recreation, performing arts and cultural programs, youth agencies, and social agencies. Absorbed the purposes of The Frederick W. Beinecke Fund in 1983, including grants for environment, conservation, wildlife preservation, and historic preservation.
Types of support awarded: Annual campaigns, seed money, emergency funds, deficit financing, building funds, land acquisition, endowment funds, research, continuing support.
Limitations: Giving primarily in the northeastern US. No grants to individuals; no loans.
Application information:
Initial approach: 2 or 3 page letter
Copies of proposal: 1
Deadline(s): None
Board meeting date(s): June, September, and November
Final notification: 4 weeks
Write: Paul B. Mott, Jr., Executive Director
Officers: William S. Beinecke,* President; Elizabeth G. Beinecke,* John B. Beinecke,* Vice-Presidents; Paul B. Mott, Jr., Secretary and Executive Director; Thomas P. McConnell, Treasurer.
Directors:* Frederick W. Beinecke, Frances Beinecke Elston, Sarah Beinecke Richardson.
Number of staff: 1 part-time professional; 1 part-time support.
Employer Identification Number: 136075567

2843

R and D Fund, Inc., The ☒
1700 Broadway, Rm. 1702
New York 10019

Incorporated in 1952 in New York.
Donor(s): Members of the Straus family.
Financial data: (yr. ended 12/31/82): Assets,
$126,607 (M); gifts received, $190,829;
expenditures, $226,558, including $223,521
for 163 grants (high: $80,000; low: $10).
Purpose and activities: Grants only to
charities of personal interest to the donors, with
emphasis on fine arts and cultural programs,
international affairs, higher education, and
hospitals.
Officers: Ralph I. Straus, President; Donald B.
Straus, Vice-President; John L. Peper, Secretary-
Treasurer.
Employer Identification Number: 136118829

2844

Raisler (The Harold K.) Foundation, Inc.
875 Third Ave.
New York 10022   (212) 986-9200

Incorporated in 1957 in New York.
Financial data: (yr. ended 12/31/82): Assets,
$1,295,000 (M); expenditures, $132,600,
including $90,098 for 85 grants (high: $25,000;
low: $10).
Purpose and activities: Charitable purposes;
grants for higher education, hospitals, temple
support, and Jewish welfare funds; support also
for the blind.
Limitations: No grants to individuals.
Application information:
  Initial approach: Letter
  Copies of proposal: 2
  Board meeting date(s): May
  Write: Harold K. Raisler, President
Officer and Directors: Harold K. Raisler,
President; Herbert A. Raisler, Robert K. Raisler.
Employer Identification Number: 136094406

2845

Raisler (The Robert K.) Foundation, Inc.
875 Third Ave.
New York 10022   (212) 319-2660

Incorporated in 1958 in New York.
Financial data: (yr. ended 12/31/82): Assets,
$1,372,601 (M); expenditures, $127,808,
including $121,639 for 78 grants (high:
$49,000; low: $10).
Purpose and activities: Charitable purposes;
general giving, with emphasis on higher
education, Jewish welfare funds, hospitals,
temple support, and health agencies.
Officers and Directors: Robert K. Raisler,
President and Treasurer; Harold K. Raisler, Vice-
President and Secretary.
Employer Identification Number: 136094433

2846

Ramapo Trust ▼
126 East 56 St.
New York 10022   (212) 308-7355

Trust established in 1973 in New York.
Donor(s): Henry L. Schwartz,† Montebello
Trust.
Financial data: (yr. ended 6/30/83): Assets,
$36,747,203 (M); expenditures, $2,817,177,
including $2,621,324 for 55 grants (high:
$250,000; low: $50,000).
Purpose and activities: Broad purposes;
primarily local giving for gerontological and
geriatric research and innovative services.
Types of support awarded: Seed money,
emergency funds, equipment, matching funds,
professorships, internships, scholarship funds,
fellowships, special projects, research,
publications, conferences and seminars.
Limitations: Giving primarily in the
metropolitan New York, NY, and NJ areas. No
grants to individuals, or for operating budgets,
continuing support, annual campaigns, or
deficit financing; no loans.
Application information: Unsolicited
proposals not accepted.
  Board meeting date(s): Monthly
Trustees: Arthur Norman Field, Harold Resnik,
Andrew M. Schreier, William Schreier, Stephen
L. Schwartz, Mary Ann Van Clief.
Number of staff: 1 full-time professional; 1
part-time professional; 2 part-time support.
Employer Identification Number: 136594279

2847

**Raskin (Hirsch and Braine) Foundation,
Inc.** ☒
270 Madison Ave., Rm. 1204
New York 10016

Incorporated in 1957 in New York.
Donor(s): Hirsch Raskin,† Braine Raskin.†
Financial data: (yr. ended 2/28/83): Assets,
$1,376,054 (M); expenditures, $139,849,
including $127,500 for 5 grants (high: $50,000;
low: $12,500).
Purpose and activities: Charitable purposes;
grants largely for Israeli higher educational and
scientific institutions and for Jewish welfare
funds.
Officers and Directors: Rose Raskin,
President; William W. Prager, Vice-President
and Secretary.
Employer Identification Number: 136085867

2848

Rauch Foundation, Inc.
118 Huntington Rd.
Port Washington 11050   (516) 944-5244

Incorporated in 1960 in New York.
Donor(s): Philip Rauch, Louis Rauch.
Financial data: (yr. ended 11/30/84): Assets,
$2,456,773 (M); gifts received, $155,600;
expenditures, $196,051, including $191,050
for 74 grants (high: $50,000; low: $100).

Purpose and activities: Primarily local giving,
with emphasis on higher and secondary
education, hospitals and medical research,
Protestant church support, cultural groups, and
health and welfare agencies.
Limitations: Giving primarily in NY.
Application information:
  Write: Dr. Nancy Douzinas
Officers: Louis Rauch, President; Philip Rauch,
Vice-President.
Employer Identification Number: 112001717

2849

Raymond Foundation
P.O. Box 277
Greene 13778   (607) 656-2494

Trust established in 1964 in New York.
Donor(s): George Raymond.†
Financial data: (yr. ended 12/31/82): Assets,
$1,040,363 (M); gifts received, $20,000;
expenditures, $70,251, including $67,596 for
44 grants (high: $10,000; low: $50).
Purpose and activities: Grants for community
funds, higher education, and youth agencies in
areas where Raymond Corporation facilities are
located.
Limitations: Giving limited to areas of
company operations. No grants to individuals,
or for endowment funds, or operating budgets;
no loans.
Publications: 990-PF, application guidelines,
program policy statement, annual report.
Application information: Grant proposals are
not invited.
  Board meeting date(s): March, June,
    September, and December
  Write: Pete Raymond, Executive Secretary
Officers: Pete Raymond,* Executive Secretary;
Marilyn W. Palmiter, Treasurer.
Trustees:* Stephen S. Raymond, Chairman;
James F. Barton, Vice-Chairman; Robert T.
Cline, Robert Eldred, George G. Raymond, Jr.,
Jean C. Raymond, John Riley, Jeanette L.
Williamson, Lee J. Wolf, Madeleine R. Young.
Employer Identification Number: 166047847

2850

Read (The Charles L.) Foundation ☒
c/o Joseph Eisenberg
122 E. 42nd St.
New York 10168

Trust established in 1954 in New Jersey.
Donor(s): Charles L. Read.
Financial data: (yr. ended 12/31/82): Assets,
$1,384,733 (M); expenditures, $129,280,
including $89,600 for 56 grants (high: $10,000;
low: $250).
Purpose and activities: Grants for hospitals,
education, and religious welfare funds,
primarily in New York and New Jersey.
Limitations: Giving primarily in NJ and NY.
Officers: Fred Herrigel, Jr., President; Joseph
Eisenberg, Vice-President; Fred Herrigel III,
Secretary; Saul Eisenberg, Treasurer.
Employer Identification Number: 226053510

2851
Reader's Digest Foundation ▼
Pleasantville 10570 (914) 241-5360

Incorporated in 1938 in New York.
Donor(s): The Reader's Digest Association, Inc., DeWitt Wallace,† Lila Acheson Wallace.†
Financial data: (yr. ended 12/31/84): Assets, $14,544,333 (M); gifts received, $500,000; expenditures, $1,191,764, including $760,974 for 133 grants (high: $40,000; low: $20; average: $50-$10,000) and $319,619 for 866 employee matching gifts.
Purpose and activities: Broad purposes; particular interest in journalism education; support also for programs that offer pre-college youth a variety of character-building experiences, public affairs, cultural programs, and employee matching gifts.
Types of support awarded: Employee matching gifts, general purposes.
Limitations: Giving primarily in the U.S. No grants to individuals, or for capital funds, operating budgets, annual campaigns, seed money, emergency funds, deficit financing, special projects, publications, or conferences; no loans.
Application information:
Initial approach: Letter of inquiry
Copies of proposal: 1
Deadline(s): None
Board meeting date(s): Quarterly
Final notification: About 2 months
Write: Kent Rhodes, Chairman
Officers: Kent Rhodes,* Chairman; Virginia Lawton, Secretary; William J. Cross,* Treasurer.
Directors:* John T. Beaudouin, Kenneth O. Gilmore, George V. Grune, W. Barnabas McHenry, Edward T. Thompson.
Number of staff: 1 part-time professional; 2 full-time support.
Employer Identification Number: 136120380

2852
Reed (Philip D.) Foundation, Inc.
375 Park Ave., Rm. 2709
New York 10152

Incorporated in 1955 in New York.
Donor(s): Philip D. Reed.
Financial data: (yr. ended 6/30/83): Assets, $2,195,527 (M); expenditures, $70,453, including $67,900 for 66 grants (high: $7,500; low: $100).
Purpose and activities: Broad purposes; grants mainly for hospitals, institutions of higher education, international studies, public policy organizations, and community funds.
Limitations: No grants to individuals.
Officers and Trustees: Philip D. Reed, President and Chairman; Patricia Anderson, Secretary; Philip D. Reed, Jr., Treasurer.
Employer Identification Number: 136098916

2853
Reicher (Anne & Harry J.) Foundation ☒
1776 Broadway
New York 10019

Established in 1961 in Pennsylvania.

Financial data: (yr. ended 12/31/82): Assets, $1,107,442 (M); expenditures, $74,083, including $70,583 for 37 grants (high: $50,000; low: $10).
Purpose and activities: Giving primarily to hospitals, particularly a hospital for joint diseases, and to Jewish welfare funds.
Officers: Harry J. Reicher, President and Treasurer; Hermia Gould, Secretary.
Employer Identification Number: 136115086

2854
Reimann (Kurt P.) Foundation, Inc. ☒
c/o Benjamin Nadel & Company
437 Fifth Ave.
New York 10016

Established in 1971.
Donor(s): Auguste Reimann,† Kurt P. Reimann, Mrs. Kurt P. Reimann.
Financial data: (yr. ended 11/30/82): Assets, $1,246,014 (M); gifts received, $121,500; expenditures, $261,901, including $256,467 for 15 grants (high: $50,000; low: $1,500).
Purpose and activities: Grants mainly for cultural programs, with emphasis on music and the performing arts; support also for a college.
Officers: Reimer Koch-Weser, President; Anna Ellsam, Vice-President; Benjamin Nadel, Treasurer.
Employer Identification Number: 221712688

2855
Reiss (Jacob L.) Foundation ☒
c/o Irving Trust Company
P.O. Box 12446, Church Street Station
New York 10249

Trust established in 1953 in New York.
Donor(s): Jacob L. Reiss.†
Financial data: (yr. ended 12/31/81): Assets, $1,526,816 (M); gifts received, $10,000; expenditures, $99,919, including $94,000 for 15 grants (high: $41,000; low: $1,000).
Purpose and activities: Broad purposes; grants largely for hospitals and Roman Catholic, educational and welfare organizations; some support for the handicapped and aged, primarily in New York, New Jersey, and Wisconsin.
Limitations: Giving primarily in NY, NJ, and WI. No grants to individuals.
Application information: Grants limited to charities of interest to the donor.
Board meeting date(s): As required
Advisory Committee: Raymond H. Reiss, Robert R. Reiss, Marion R. Tietje.
Trustee: Irving Trust Company.
Employer Identification Number: 136044123

2856
Resnick (Louis and Mildred) Foundation ☒
c/o L. Spitalnik
124 South Main St.
Ellenville 12428

Established in 1977.
Donor(s): Louis Resnick.

Financial data: (yr. ended 8/31/83): Assets, $53,711 (M); gifts received, $479,500; expenditures, $475,818, including $471,090 for 50 grants (high: $235,000; low: $250).
Purpose and activities: Grants primarily for Jewish welfare funds; support also for higher education, hospitals, and civic organizations.
Trustees: Louis Resnick, Mildred Resnick.
Employer Identification Number: 132915626

2857
Revlon Foundation, Inc.
Roger Shelley, President
767 Fifth Ave.
New York 10153 (212) 572-5000

Incorporated in 1955 in New York.
Donor(s): Revlon, Inc., and its subsidiaries.
Financial data: (yr. ended 12/31/82): Assets, $74,187 (M); gifts received, $450,000; expenditures, $445,366, including $403,050 for 58 grants (high: $58,850; low: $300) and $42,316 for 231 employee matching gifts.
Purpose and activities: Broad purposes; general giving, with emphasis on women's interest groups, minorities and health care which are national in scope or where company has subsidiaries, and cultural organizations which focus on main areas of interest listed above; support also for higher education and community funds.
Types of support awarded: Employee matching gifts.
Limitations: No grants to individuals; employee matching gifts awarded to educational institutions only.
Application information:
Write: Roger Shelley, President
Officers: Roger Shelley,* President; Enzo J. Vialardi, Vice-President and Treasurer; Sander P. Alexander,* Vice-President; Samuel L. Simmons,* Secretary.
Directors:* Jay I. Bennett.
Employer Identification Number: 136126130

2858
Revson (Charles H.) Foundation, Inc. ▼
444 Madison Ave., 30th Fl.
New York 10022 (212) 935-3340

Incorporated in 1956 in New York.
Donor(s): Charles H. Revson.†
Financial data: (yr. ended 12/31/84): Assets, $74,660,000 (M); gifts received, $230,973; expenditures, $5,952,721, including $4,939,580 for 68 grants (high: $350,000; low: $3,325; average: $72,000).
Purpose and activities: Grants for urban affairs and public policy; with a special emphasis on New York City problems as well as national policy issues; education, including higher education; biomedical research policy; and Jewish philanthropy and education. Particular emphasis within these program areas on the future of New York City, accountability of government, the changing role of women (especially leadership development for public life), minority groups, law and justice, and the role of modern communications in education and other aspects of society.

Types of support awarded: Research, fellowships, internships, special projects.
Limitations: Giving primarily in New York, NY. No support for local health appeals. No grants to individuals, or for building or endowment funds, general support, or matching gifts; no loans.
Publications: Biennial report, application guidelines.
Application information:
Initial approach: Letter or full proposal
Copies of proposal: 1
Deadline(s): None
Board meeting date(s): April, June, October, and December
Final notification: 4 months
Write: Eli N. Evans, President
Officers and Directors: Simon H. Rifkind, Chairman; Eli N. Evans, President; Harry Meresman, Secretary and Treasurer; Victor J. Barnett, Benjamin J. Buttenwieser, Alice Chandler, Adrian W. DeWind, Paul A. Marks, Robert B. McKay, Charles H. Revson, Jr., John C. Revson.
Number of staff: 3 full-time professional; 1 part-time professional; 2 full-time support; 3 part-time support.
Employer Identification Number: 136126105

2859
Reynolds (The Christopher) Foundation, Inc.
121 East 61st St.
New York 10021   (212) 838-2920

Incorporated in 1952 in New York.
Donor(s): Mrs. Libby Holman Reynolds.†
Financial data: (yr. ended 1/31/84): Assets, $13,655,119 (M); expenditures, $914,110, including $745,963 for grants (high: $248,790; low: $1,000; average: $20,000-$100,000).
Purpose and activities: Grants primarily in the field of international relations, particularly peace and disarmament, with a current focus on Southeast Asia, including Vietnam, Laos, and Cambodia.
Types of support awarded: Continuing support, conferences and seminars.
Limitations: Giving primarily in Southeast Asia, primarily Indochina. No grants to individuals, or for capital or endowment funds, operating budgets, annual campaigns, seed money, emergency funds, deficit financing, special projects, research, publications, scholarships and fellowships, or matching gifts; no loans.
Publications: Annual report, application guidelines.
Application information:
Initial approach: Letter
Copies of proposal: 4
Deadline(s): Submit proposal preferably 30 days prior to board meeting
Board meeting date(s): March, June, September, and December
Final notification: 1 week
Write: Jack Clareman, Executive Director

Officers and Directors: Michael Kahn, President; Margaret Neustadt Randol, Senior Vice-President; John R. Boettiger, Vice-President; Jack Clareman, Secretary-Treasurer and Executive Director.
Number of staff: 1 full-time professional; 1 full-time support.
Employer Identification Number: 136129401

2860
Reynolds (Edith Grace) Estate Residuary Trust ⌘
c/o Key Trust Co.
60 State St., P.O. Box 1965
Albany 12207

Financial data: (yr. ended 3/31/83): Assets, $1,189,310 (M); expenditures, $125,230, including $12,350 for 13 grants (high: $3,000; low: $100) and $103,725 for 311 grants to individuals.
Purpose and activities: Local giving, primarily for scholarships for higher education; some support also for local community development.
Types of support awarded: Student aid.
Limitations: Giving limited to School District 1, in Rensselaer County, NY.
Application information:
Initial approach: Application and high school transcript for scholarships
Deadline(s): February 15 for scholarship applications
Write: Richard Weiskotten, Trust Officer
Trustee: Key Trust Co. (Richard Weiskotten, Trust Officer).
Employer Identification Number: 237170056

2861
Rice (Jacob & Sophie) Family Foundation, Inc. ⌘
Milton Gold & Company
1250 Broadway, Rm. 1801
New York 10001

Incorporated in 1968 in New York.
Donor(s): Miss Mathilde T. Rice.†
Financial data: (yr. ended 12/31/82): Assets, $1,354,700 (M); expenditures, $124,035, including $107,500 for 13 grants (high: $25,000; low: $2,000).
Purpose and activities: Support largely for hospitals and Roman Catholic welfare funds; some grants also for higher education.
Trustees: Richard Keneven, Edwin McMahon Singer.
Employer Identification Number: 136264756

2862
Rich Foundation, Inc. ⌘
1145 Niagra St.
P.O. Box 245
Buffalo 14240

Established in 1961.
Financial data: (yr. ended 12/31/82): Assets, $353,638 (M); gifts received, $270,000; expenditures, $143,899, including $137,571 for 125 grants (high: $30,000; low: $12).

Purpose and activities: Primarily local giving, with emphasis on community funds, the arts, hospitals, church support, and education, especially higher education.
Limitations: Giving primarily in NY.
Officer: David A. Rich, Executive Director.
Employer Identification Number: 166026199

2863
Richardson (Anne S.) Fund ▼
c/o Chemical Bank
30 Rockefeller Plaza
New York 10112   (212) 621-2143

Trust established in 1965 in Connecticut.
Donor(s): Anne S. Richardson.†
Financial data: (yr. ended 7/31/83): Assets, $6,137,048 (M); expenditures, $442,531, including $408,200 for 116 grants (high: $25,000; low: $300).
Purpose and activities: Interests include conservation, education, and cultural programs, primarily in Connecticut and New York.
Limitations: Giving primarily in CT and NY. No grants to individuals, or for endowment funds, scholarships or fellowships; no loans.
Publications: 990-PF.
Application information:
Initial approach: Letter or full proposal
Copies of proposal: 2
Deadline(s): Submit proposal preferably in January, March, June, or October; no set deadline
Board meeting date(s): February, April, July, and November
Write: Mrs. Barbara Strohmeier
Trustees: Ernest Brooks, Jr., Chemical Bank (Frederick W. Arnold, Trust Officer).
Employer Identification Number: 136192516

2864
Richmond (The Frederick W.) Foundation, Inc.
245 East 58th St., Suite 8-G
New York 10022   (212) 752-1668

Incorporated in 1962 in New York.
Donor(s): Frederick W. Richmond.
Financial data: (yr. ended 6/30/84): Assets, $2,882,503 (M); expenditures, $279,539, including $199,427 for 40 grants (high: $37,500; low: $150; average: $1,000) and $20,025 for 3 loans.
Purpose and activities: Major interest in pilot projects in the social, arts, and economic research areas, including emphasis on unemployment, the elderly, education, and the performing arts.
Types of support awarded: Special projects, seed money, loans.
Limitations: No grants to individuals, or for matching gifts, scholarships, or fellowships.
Publications: 990-PF, program policy statement.
Application information:
Initial approach: Letter
Copies of proposal: 1
Deadline(s): None
Board meeting date(s): September and March
Final notification: 3 months
Write: Timothy E. Wyman, President

Officers: Timothy E. Wyman,* President;
William J. Butler,* Secretary; Beatriz Mirich,
Treasurer.
Directors:* Barbara Bode, Helen Fioratti,
Steven N. Kaufmann, Frederick W. Richmond.
Number of staff: 1 full-time support; 1 part-
time support.
Employer Identification Number: 136124582

2865
Ridgefield Foundation, The
820 Second Ave.
New York 10017   (212) 692-9570

Incorporated in 1956 in New York.
Donor(s): Henry J. Leir, Erna D. Leir,
Continental Ore Corporation, International Ore
and Fertilizer Corporation.
Financial data: (yr. ended 2/29/84): Assets,
$2,053,628 (M); expenditures, $110,037,
including $60,000 for 33 grants (high: $5,000;
low: $100).
Purpose and activities: Broad purposes;
general giving, with emphasis on education,
including that in Israel, Jewish welfare funds,
social agencies and cultural programs.
Limitations: No grants to individuals, or for
scholarships, fellowships, or matching gifts; no
loans.
Application information:
  Initial approach: Letter
  Copies of proposal: 2
  Deadline(s): Submit proposal preferably in
    September
  Board meeting date(s): October or November
  Write: Mrs. Marguerite M. Riposanu,
    Treasurer
Officers: Henry J. Leir,* President; Louis J.
Lipton,* Vice-President; Samuel Sitkoff,*
Secretary; Marguerite M. Riposanu, Treasurer.
Directors:* Arthur S. Hoffman, Erna D. Leir,
Jean Mayer, Jerome Shelby.
Number of staff: 1 part-time professional.
Employer Identification Number: 136093563

2866
Ridley (Jessie) Foundation, Inc. ¤
250 W. 57th St.
New York 10019

Incorporated in 1973 in New York.
Financial data: (yr. ended 12/31/82): Assets,
$1,141,425 (M); expenditures, $124,308,
including $102,878 for 13 grants (high:
$12,530; low: $2,000).
Purpose and activities: Grants to higher
educational institutions, primarily for
scholarships for physically handicapped
students selected by the institutions.
Types of support awarded: Scholarship funds.
Limitations: No grants to individuals.
Officers and Trustees: Murry Kalik, President;
P. Douglass Martin, Vice-President; Mark Kalik,
Secretary; Edward Ridley Finch, Jr., Treasurer;
Elizabeth Lathrop Finch, Lawrence Kalik,
Richard W. Martin.
Employer Identification Number: 237379436

2867
Ritter Foundation, Inc., The
1776 Broadway
New York 10019   (212) 757-4646

Incorporated in 1947 in New York.
Donor(s): Gladys Ritter Livingston, Irene
Ritter,† Lena Ritter,† Louis Ritter,† Sidney
Ritter.†
Financial data: (yr. ended 11/30/83): Assets,
$2,862,883 (M); gifts received, $29,500;
expenditures, $237,327, including $174,393
for 133 grants (high: $26,635; low: $20).
Purpose and activities: Broad purposes; grants
largely for higher education, including medical
education, and local Jewish welfare funds.
Limitations: No grants to individuals.
Application information: Applications not
currently accepted; funds committed through
1990.
  Board meeting date(s): May and November
  Write: Toby G. Ritter, Secretary
Officers and Trustees: Gladys Ritter
Livingston, President; David Ritter, Vice-
President; Toby G. Ritter, Vice-President and
Secretary; Alan I. Ritter, Treasurer; Frances R.
Weisman.
Employer Identification Number: 136082276

2868
Ritter (The Gerald & May Ellen)
Memorial Fund ▼
c/o Proskauer Rose Goetz & Mendelsohn
300 Park Ave.
New York 10022   (212) 909-7708

Fund established in 1980 in New York.
Donor(s): May Ellen Ritter,† Gerald Ritter.†
Financial data: (yr. ended 4/30/83): Assets,
$3,812,295 (M); gifts received, $807,673;
expenditures, $1,045,972, including
$1,009,550 for 38 grants (high: $400,000; low:
$500; average: $500-$50,000).
Purpose and activities: Primarily local giving
and in Israel, with emphasis on higher
education, cultural organizations, including
music and other performing arts, medical
research, youth agencies and Jewish welfare
funds.
Types of support awarded: General purposes,
building funds, equipment, land acquisition,
endowment funds, matching funds, scholarship
funds, fellowships, research, loans,
publications, conferences and seminars,
continuing support.
Limitations: Giving primarily in New York, NY
and Israel. No grants to individuals.
Application information:
  Initial approach: Letter or full proposal
  Deadline(s): None
  Board meeting date(s): Quarterly
  Final notification: Varies
  Write: Gerald Silbert, President
Officers and Directors:* Gerald Silbert,*
Chairman and President; Lawrence Lachman,*
Ramie Silbert,* Vice-Presidents; Aileen R.
Leventon, Secretary; Herbert T. Weinstein,*
Treasurer.
Number of staff: None.
Employer Identification Number: 133037300

2869
Ritter (May Ellen and Gerald)
Foundation ¤
c/o Emma A. Daniels
9411 Shore Rd.
Brooklyn 11209

Foundation established in 1980 in New York.
Donor(s): Gerald Ritter,† May Ellen Ritter.†
Financial data: (yr. ended 12/31/82): Assets,
$4,971,002 (M); gifts received, $1,000,000;
expenditures, $318,513, including $239,250
for 15 grants (high: $150,000; low: $150).
Purpose and activities: Giving primarily for
health agencies and Roman Catholic welfare
funds.
Limitations: No grants to individuals.
Application information:
  Initial approach: Letter and proposal
  Board meeting date(s): Quarterly
Officers: Emma A. Daniels, President; Vincent
Rohan, First Vice-President; John Parker,
Second Vice-President; Helen Rohan, Secretary.
Number of staff: None.
Employer Identification Number: 136114269

2870
Robert Alan Foundation, Inc., The ¤
520 Madison Ave.
New York 10022   (212) 399-8870

Incorporated in 1956 in New York.
Donor(s): Robert V. Tishman, Alan V. Tishman,
David Tishman.†
Financial data: (yr. ended 11/30/84): Assets,
$1,698,299 (M); expenditures, $65,398,
including $57,460 for 67 grants (high: $10,950;
low: $100).
Purpose and activities: Primarily local giving,
with emphasis on Jewish welfare funds; support
also for education.
Types of support awarded: General purposes,
continuing support, emergency funds, building
funds, endowment funds, professorships.
Limitations: Giving primarily in NY. No grants
to individuals, or for research or matching gifts;
no loans.
Application information:
  Initial approach: Letter
  Board meeting date(s): Semiannually
  Write: Robert V. Tishman, President, or Alan
    V. Tishman, Vice-President
Officers: Robert V. Tishman, President; Alan
V. Tishman, Vice-President.
Employer Identification Number: 136099395

2871
Robison (The Ellis H. and Doris B.)
Foundation
155-167 River St.
Troy 12181   (518) 274-6000

Trust established in 1980 in New York.
Donor(s): Ellis Robison.†
Financial data: (yr. ended 12/31/83): Assets,
$1,433,753 (M); expenditures,
$67,103, including $67,103 for 36 grants (high:
$20,000; low: $500).
Purpose and activities: Grants for local
educational, religious, and medical purposes
initiated solely by the president.

Types of support awarded: Continuing support, building funds, general purposes.
Limitations: Giving limited to Rensselaer County, NY. No grants to individuals, or for endowment funds, scholarships, fellowships, or matching gifts; no loans.
Application information:
Write: Elissa R. Prout, Secretary-Treasurer
Officers and Directors: James A. Robison, President; Richard G. Robison, Vice-President; Elissa R. Prout, Secretary-Treasurer; Doris B. Robison, Barbara R. Sporck.
Employer Identification Number: 222470695

2872
Roche (Edward & Ellen) Relief Foundation

c/o U.S. Trust Company of New York
45 Wall St.
New York 10005   (212) 806-4316

Established in 1930 in New York.
Donor(s): Edward Roche.†
Financial data: (yr. ended 12/31/83): Assets, $2,535,636 (M); expenditures, $214,413, including $109,700 for 50 grants (high: $12,000; low: $1,000).
Purpose and activities: Primarily local giving, with emphasis on aid to destitute women and children, grants largely for child welfare, youth organizations, and social agencies.
Limitations: Giving primarily in NY, CT and NJ. No grants to individuals, or for building or endowment funds, operating budgets, research, scholarships, fellowships, or matching gifts; no loans.
Application information:
Initial approach: Full proposal or telephone
Copies of proposal: 1
Deadline(s): Mid-May and mid-November
Board meeting date(s): May and November
Write: Anne L. Smith, Assistant Vice-President
Trustee: United States Trust Company of New York.
Employer Identification Number: 135622067

2873
Rochester Area Foundation

335 Main St. East, Suite 402
Rochester 14604   (716) 325-4353

Incorporated in 1983 in New York.
Financial data: (yr. ended 2/29/84): Assets, $3,644,036 (M); gifts received, $978,259; expenditures, $312,740, including $221,335 for 214 grants and $8,960 for 85 grants to individuals.
Purpose and activities: Local giving only for broad purposes related to community betterment.
Types of support awarded: Seed money, emergency funds, equipment, fellowships.
Limitations: Giving limited to Monroe, Livingston, Ontario, Orleans, and Genesee counties, NY. No support for religious projects. No grants to individuals (except from restricted funds), or for operating budgets, continuing support, annual campaigns, deficit financing, building funds, land acquisition, endowment funds, matching gifts, research, or conferences and seminars; no loans.

Publications: Annual report, program policy statement, application guidelines.
Application information: Application form required.
Board meeting date(s): January, March, May, July, September, and November
Write: Linda S. Weinstein, President
Officers and Directors: Malinda B. Fischer, Chairman; Linda S. Weinstein, President; Harris H. Rusitsky, John Swett, Vice-Presidents; Norman Leenhouts, Secretary; Steven G. Schwartz, Treasurer; and 25 other directors.
Number of staff: 1 full-time professional; 1 part-time professional; 1 full-time support; 1 part-time support.
Employer Identification Number: 237250641

2874
Rochester Female Charitable Society ¤

c/o Lincoln First Bank
P.O. Box 1412
Rochester 14603
Grant appplication address: Mrs. J. Peter Bush, 179 Hollywood Ave., Rochester, NY 14618; Tel.: (716) 244-4945

Established in 1822.
Financial data: (yr. ended 3/31/83): Assets, $1,126,801 (M); expenditures, $45,867, including $39,984 for 42 grants (high: $3,500; low: $50).
Purpose and activities: Local giving, with emphasis on recreation programs and facilities for youth, child welfare, hospitals, and social agencies.
Limitations: Giving limited to the greater Rochester, NY, area.
Application information:
Initial approach: Letter
Deadline(s): None
Trustee: Lincoln First Bank.
Employer Identification Number: 237166180

2875
Rockefeller Brothers Fund ▼

1290 Ave. of the Americas
New York 10104   (212) 397-4800

Incorporated in 1940 in New York.
Donor(s): John D. Rockefeller, Jr.,† Mrs. Martha Baird Rockefeller,† Mrs. Abby Rockefeller Mauze,† David Rockefeller, John D. Rockefeller 3rd,† Laurance S. Rockefeller, Nelson A. Rockefeller,† Winthrop Rockefeller.†
Financial data: (yr. ended 12/31/83): Assets, $160,055,365 (M); gifts received, $47,430; expenditures, $28,763,752, including $26,208,888 for 143 grants (high: $15,000,000; low: $2,000; average: $10,000-$75,000).

Purpose and activities: "Support of efforts in the United States and abroad that contribute ideas, develop leaders, and encourage institutions in the transition to global interdependence and that counter world trends of resource depletion, militarization, protectionism, and isolation which now threaten to move humankind everywhere further away from cooperation, trade and economic growth, arms restraint, and conservation." There are four major giving catagories: 1) One World, with two major components: resources management and security, including issues related to arms control and those involving international relations, development, trade, and finance; 2) New York City; 3) the well-being of the non-profit sector; and 4) "special concerns".
Types of support awarded: General purposes, seed money, special projects, conferences and seminars, internships, exchange programs, matching funds, employee matching gifts, consulting services, continuing support.
Limitations: No support for churches, hospitals, or community centers. No grants to individuals, or for endowments or building funds; no loans.
Publications: Annual report, program policy statement, application guidelines.
Application information:
Initial approach: Letter, full proposal, or telephone
Copies of proposal: 1
Deadline(s): None
Board meeting date(s): June and November
Final notification: 3 months
Write: Benjamin R. Shute, Jr., Secretary
Officers: William M. Dietel,* President; Russell A. Phillips, Jr., Executive Vice-President; Benjamin R. Shute, Jr., Secretary; David G. Fernald, Treasurer.
Trustees: David Rockefeller, Chairman; Abby M. O'Neill, Vice-Chairman; Laurance S. Rockefeller, Advisory Trustee; Thornton F. Bradshaw, Laura R. Chasin, Mark B. Dayton, Peggy Dulany, James H. Evans, Peter C. Goldmark, Jr., Henry A. Kissinger, George Putnam, David Rockefeller, Jr., Laurance Rockefeller, Rodman C. Rockefeller, S. Frederick Starr, Russell E. Train, Jeremy P. Waletzky.
Number of staff: 7 full-time professional; 1 part-time professional; 18 full-time support; 2 part-time support.
Employer Identification Number: 131760106

2876
Rockefeller Family Fund, Inc. ▼

1290 Ave. of the Americas, Rm. 3450
New York 10104   (212) 397-4844

Incorporated in 1967 in New York.
Donor(s): Members of the Rockefeller family.
Financial data: (yr. ended 12/31/84): Assets, $20,108,085 (M); gifts received, $464,259; expenditures, $2,106,127, including $1,478,358 for 72 grants (high: $65,000; low: $1,250; average: $5,000-$40,000).

Purpose and activities: Broad purposes, with special emphasis on arms control, conservation litigation, the women's movement, and public-interest activities centered on institutional responsiveness.
Types of support awarded: Operating budgets, continuing support, seed money, special projects, conferences and seminars.
Limitations: No grants to individuals, or for capital or endowment funds, matching gifts, scholarships, or fellowships; no loans.
Publications: Annual report, program policy statement, application guidelines.
Application information:
   Initial approach: Letter or full proposal
   Copies of proposal: 1
   Deadline(s): None
   Board meeting date(s): April and December; executive committee usually meets every 8 weeks
   Final notification: 1 to 3 months
   Write: Donald K. Ross, Director
Officers: Richard M. Chasin,* President; Anne Bartley,* Nancy Anderson,* Peggy Dulany,* Diana N. Rockefeller,* Jeremy P. Waletzky,* Vice-Presidents; David G. Fernald, Treasurer; Donald K. Ross, Director.
Trustees:* Hope Aldrich, Clare P. Buden, Alida Dayton, Eileen R. Growald, Gail O'Neill, Laurance Rockefeller, Richard G. Rockefeller, Wendy Rockefeller, Laura Thorn.
Number of staff: 1 full-time professional; 2 part-time professional; 2 full-time support.
Employer Identification Number: 136257658

2877
Rockefeller Foundation, The ▼
1133 Ave. of the Americas
New York 10036   (212) 869-8500

Incorporated in 1913 in New York.
Donor(s): John D. Rockefeller, Sr.†
Financial data: (yr. ended 12/31/84): Assets, $1,101,856,013 (M); expenditures, $50,533,399, including $26,603,379 for 516 grants (high: $987,500; low: $1,025), $4,174,820 for 284 grants to individuals and $7,111,758 for 6 foundation-administered programs.
Purpose and activities: "To promote the well-being of mankind throughout the world." Concentrates its activities on fields of fundamental importance to mankind through the following six program areas: 1) agricultural sciences, 2) population sciences, 3) health sciences, 4) international relations, 5) equal opportunity, and 6) arts and humanities. A "Special Interests and Explorations" category exists to maintain flexibility in grantmaking. Programs are carried out through the awarding of grants and fellowships, and the dissemination of knowledge through publications and close association with the media.
Types of support awarded: Matching funds, fellowships, research, publications, conferences and seminars, special projects.

Limitations: No support for appraising or subsidizing cures or inventions; for the establishment of local hospitals, churches, schools, libraries, or welfare agencies or for their building or operating funds; financing altruistic movements involving private profit; propaganda or attempts to influence legislation; or investing in securities on a philanthropic basis. No grants for personal aid to individuals, or for capital or endowment funds, general support, or scholarships; no loans.
Publications: Annual report, informational brochure, newsletter, program policy statement, application guidelines, grants list.
Application information:
   Initial approach: Letter
   Copies of proposal: 1
   Deadline(s): Specified in individual brochures for fellowship programs
   Board meeting date(s): Usually in April, June, September, and December
   Write: Simon P. Gourdine, Secretary
Officers: Richard W. Lyman,* President; Laurence D. Stifel, Vice-President; Nan S. Robinson, Vice-President for Administration; Simon P. Gourdine, Secretary; Jack R. Meyer, Treasurer.
Trustees:* Clifton R. Wharton, Jr., Chairman; W. Michael Blumenthal, John Brademas, Harold Brown, Kenneth N. Dayton, John R. Evans, Herman E. Gallegos, James P. Grant, W. David Hopper, Tom Johnson, Robert C. Maynard, Eleanor Holmes Norton, Victor H. Palmieri, Alice M. Rivlin, Eleanor B. Sheldon, Billy Taylor, James D. Wolfensohn, Harry Woolf.
Number of staff: 49 full-time professional; 1 part-time professional; 73 full-time support; 2 part-time support.
Employer Identification Number: 131659629

2878
Rohatyn (Felix G.) Foundation, Inc. ⋈
c/o Lazard Freres & Co.
1 Rockefeller Plaza
New York 10020

Established in 1968.
Donor(s): Felix G. Rohatyn.
Financial data: (yr. ended 12/31/83): Assets, $1,654,166 (M); gifts received, $200,000; expenditures, $97,001, including $93,600 for 42 grants (high: $10,000; low: $200).
Purpose and activities: Primarily local giving, with emphasis on education, particularly higher education, the performing arts, community development, international affairs organizations, and public policy groups.
Types of support awarded: General purposes, equipment.
Limitations: Giving primarily in the New York, NY, area.
Officers: Felix G. Rohatyn, President; Elizabeth Rohatyn, Vice-President; Melvin L. Heineman, Secretary-Treasurer.
Employer Identification Number: 737015644

2879
Romerovski (Martin) Foundation, Inc. ⋈
812 Fifth Ave.
New York 10021

Established in 1965.
Donor(s): Martin Romerovski, Romerovski Brothers, Inc.
Financial data: (yr. ended 12/31/82): Assets, $762 (M); gifts received, $159,000; expenditures, $197,192, including $197,159 for 59 grants (high: $70,100; low: $10).
Purpose and activities: Giving primarily for Jewish welfare funds and educational institutions, both in the United States and Israel.
Officers: Martin Romerovski, President; Rose Romerovski, Vice-President and Secretary; Philip Maron, Treasurer.
Employer Identification Number: 136172511

2880
Romill Foundation ▼ ⋈
c/o R. J. Netter
1045 Sixth Ave.
New York 10018

Trust established in 1960 in South Carolina.
Donor(s): Roger Milliken.
Financial data: (yr. ended 12/31/83): Assets, $1,364,130 (M); gifts received, $509,431; expenditures, $912,506, including $903,533 for 40 grants (high: $270,000; low: $150; average: $1,000-$25,000).
Purpose and activities: Broad purposes; grants largely for educational associations and higher education.
Types of support awarded: General purposes, endowment funds.
Limitations: Giving primarily in Spartanburg County, SC.
Application information:
   Initial approach: Letter
   Deadline(s): None
Officer: R.J. Netter, Treasurer.
Trustees: Gerrish H. Milliken, Justine V.R. Milliken, Minot K. Milliken.
Number of staff: None.
Employer Identification Number: 136102069

2881
Roothbert Fund, Inc., The
360 Park Ave. South, 15th Fl.
New York 10010   (212) 679-2030

Incorporated in 1958 in New York.
Donor(s): Albert Roothbert,† Toni Roothbert.†
Financial data: (yr. ended 12/31/83): Assets, $1,883,727 (M); expenditures, $86,155, including $58,000 for grants to individuals.
Purpose and activities: To assist college or university students who are primarily motivated by spiritual values, with preference to those considering teaching as a vocation.
Types of support awarded: Student aid.
Limitations: No grants for capital or endowment funds, operating budgets, general support, special projects, or matching gifts; no loans.
Publications: Annual report, application guidelines.

Application information: Application process includes interview with Scholarship Committee in New York City. Application form required.
   Initial approach: Letter
   Copies of proposal: 1
   Deadline(s): Submit Fund form in January or February; deadline March 1
   Board meeting date(s): April and October; awards grants annually in April
   Final notification: 1 month
   Write: Carl Solberg, President
Officers and Directors: Carl Solberg, President and Secretary; Lowell W. Livezey, Vice-President; Blake T. Newton, III, Treasurer; Catherine Abbott, Robert C. Bates, John E. Baumann, Sylvia A. Boone, James P. Carse, Janette H. Harris, Michael Mooney, Robert M. Perry, Susan S. Purdy, Gilmore Stott, Warren Van Horne, Elizabeth Vermey.
Number of staff: None.
Employer Identification Number: 136162570

2882
Rose (Billy) Foundation, Inc. ▼ ♯
1 Dag Hammarskjold Plaza
New York 10017

Incorporated in 1958 in New York.
Donor(s): Billy Rose.†
Financial data: (yr. ended 12/31/83): Assets, $10,285,893 (M); expenditures, $1,694,995, including $1,611,500 for 81 grants (high: $500,000; low: $1,000; average: $2,000-$50,000).
Purpose and activities: Broad purposes; support for museums, particularly a museum in Israel, the performing and fine arts, higher education, and medical research, with emphasis on organizations in New York City.
Types of support awarded: Research, special projects.
Limitations: Giving primarily in New York, NY.
Officers and Directors: Morris Shilensky, Chairman and Secretary; Charles Wohlstetter, President; James R. Cherry, Vice-President and Treasurer; Arthur Cantor, Vice-President.
Employer Identification Number: 136165466

2883
Rosen (Joseph) Foundation, Inc. ♯
P.O. Box 334, Lenox Hill Station
New York 10021   (212) 249-1550

Incorporated in 1948 in New York.
Financial data: (yr. ended 6/30/83): Assets, $4,374,338 (M); expenditures, $341,681, including $236,395 for 231 grants (high: $15,000; low: $25).
Purpose and activities: Broad purposes; grants largely for Jewish welfare funds, child welfare, higher education and cultural organizations, especially the performing arts.
Officers and Directors: Abraham A. Rosen, President; Jonathan P. Rosen, Vice-President and Secretary; Miriam Rosen, Treasurer.
Employer Identification Number: 136158412

2884
Rosenberg (Sunny and Abe) Foundation, Inc. ♯
c/o R. Gassman
350 Fifth Ave.
New York 10001

Incorporated in 1966 in New York.
Donor(s): Abraham Rosenberg.
Financial data: (yr. ended 12/31/82): Assets, $3,493,304 (M); gifts received, $500,000; expenditures, $416,662, including $400,353 for grants.
Purpose and activities: Grants largely for Jewish welfare funds, higher education, and hospitals.
Officers and Trustees: Abraham Rosenberg, President and Treasurer; Sonia Rosenberg, Vice-President and Secretary.
Employer Identification Number: 136208158

2885
Rosenblatt Family Foundation, Inc. ♯
155 Riverside Dr.
New York 10024

Incorporated in 1956 in New York.
Donor(s): Marcus Retter, Betty Retter, C. Rosenblatt.
Financial data: (yr. ended 11/30/82): Assets, $449,287 (M); expenditures, $102,809, including $101,628 for 250 grants (high: $24,000).
Purpose and activities: Broad purposes; giving to Jewish welfare funds and educational organizations, both in the United States and Israel.
Officers: Marcus Retter, President; Betty Retter, Vice-President; Mary Schreiber, Secretary-Treasurer.
Employer Identification Number: 136145385

2886
Rosenstiel Foundation, The ▼ ♯
99 Park Ave., Suite 2200
New York 10016

Incorporated in 1950 in Ohio.
Donor(s): Lewis S. Rosenstiel.†
Financial data: (yr. ended 12/31/82): Assets, $7,844,843 (M); expenditures, $553,197, including $499,650 for 101 grants (high: $102,500; low: $200).
Purpose and activities: Broad purposes; giving primarily in New York and Florida, with grants largely for Polish cultural programs, the performing arts, health organizations, hospitals, and higher education.
Limitations: Giving primarily in NY and FL.
Application information:
   Write: Seymour Roberts, Treasurer
Officers: Blanka A. Rosenstiel, President; Elizabeth R. Kabler, Vice-President; Maurice Greenbaum, Secretary; Seymour Roberts, Treasurer.
Employer Identification Number: 066034536

2887
Rosenthal (Benj.) Foundation, Inc.
680 Fifth Ave., Suite 1207
New York 10019   (212) 541-4262

Incorporated in 1943 in New York.
Donor(s): Benjamin Rosenthal.†
Financial data: (yr. ended 12/31/83): Assets, $898,201 (M); expenditures, $274,206, including $161,100 for 17 grants (high: $70,000; low: $250).
Purpose and activities: To provide emergency relief in the face of collective suffering arising from extraordinary conditions; to aid philanthropic institutions in meeting extraordinary and emergency conditions, including deficit financing; support provided to national or international organizations rather than to local chapters of charitable institutions. Interests include demonstration projects, particularly in the field of child guidance, mental health, and care of the sick.
Types of support awarded: Emergency funds, deficit financing, special projects.
Limitations: No grants to individuals or for endowment funds.
Publications: Annual report, program policy statement.
Application information:
   Initial approach: Letter
   Copies of proposal: 1
   Board meeting date(s): Quarterly
   Write: Edmund A. Rosenthal, President
Officers: Edmund A. Rosenthal,* President and Treasurer; Jane S. Rosenthal,* Vice-President; Donald C. Platten, Secretary.
Trustees:* Martha R. Wolf.
Employer Identification Number: 131664999

2888
Rosenthal (The Ida and William) Foundation, Inc.
90 Park Ave.
New York 10016   (212) 953-1415

Incorporated in 1953 in New York.
Donor(s): Mrs. Ida Rosenthal, William Rosenthal,† and others.
Financial data: (yr. ended 8/31/83): Assets, $3,856,555 (M); expenditures, $470,248, including $205,675 for grants (high: $50,000; low: $50).
Purpose and activities: Grants primarily to scholarship funds for higher educationand for arts and theatre and dance groups in New York; gifts also to community funds and youth agencies in New York, New Jersey, West Virginia, and Puerto Rico.
Types of support awarded: General purposes, continuing support, annual campaigns, seed money, endowment funds, scholarship funds.
Limitations: Giving primarily in NY. No grants to individuals, or for building funds or matching gifts; no loans.
Application information:
   Initial approach: Letter
   Copies of proposal: 1
   Deadline(s): June 30
   Board meeting date(s): As required
   Write: Mrs. Beatrice Coleman, President

Officers and Directors: Beatrice Coleman, President; Henry C. Heppen, Vice-President and Secretary; David C. Masket, Vice-President and Treasurer; Catherine Coleman Brawer, Vice-President.
Number of staff: 1.
Employer Identification Number: 136141274

2889
Rosenwald (The William) Family Fund, Inc. ♯
122 East 42nd St., Rm. 3400
New York 10168

Incorporated in 1938 in Connecticut.
Donor(s): The William Rosenwald family.
Financial data: (yr. ended 12/31/82): Assets, $9,092,412 (M); expenditures, $499,949, including $467,834 for 31 grants (high: $303,500; low: $100).
Purpose and activities: General purposes; primarily local giving, with emphasis on Jewish welfare funds; some support for higher education, including medical education, cultural activities, and hospitals.
Limitations: Giving primarily in NY.
Officers and Directors: William Rosenwald, President and Treasurer; Mary K. Rosenwald, Nina Rosenwald, Alice R. Sigelman, Elizabeth R. Varet, Vice-Presidents; Frank D. Williams, Secretary; Hulbert S. Aldrich, Samuel Hoffman, Henry Z. Steinway.
Employer Identification Number: 131635289

2890
Ross (Arthur) Foundation, Inc. ♯
c/o Yohalem, Gillman, Field & Agler
655 Third Ave.
New York 10017

Incorporated in 1955 in New York.
Donor(s): Arthur Ross.
Financial data: (yr. ended 12/31/82): Assets, $2,842,079 (M); expenditures, $237,802, including $195,411 for grants.
Purpose and activities: Broad purposes; primarily local giving, with emphasis on higher education, and cultural institutions, especially museums and parks.
Limitations: Giving primarily in NY.
Officers and Directors: Arthur Ross, President and Treasurer; Clifford A. Ross, Vice-President; William T. Goldin, Leo Gottlieb, Ralph M. Sussman, Paul E. Taylor, Jr., Edgar Wachenheim III.
Employer Identification Number: 136121436

2891
Ross (The Dorothea Haus) Foundation
Booth Bldg.
80 West Ave.
Brockport 14420   (716) 637-2230

Established in 1979 in New York.
Donor(s): Dorothea Haus Ross.
Financial data: (yr. ended 5/31/84): Assets, $1,120,248 (M); expenditures, $118,560, including $98,060 for 32 grants (high: $7,641; low: $200; average: $3,064).

Purpose and activities: To advance the moral, mental, and physical well-being of children of all races and creeds in all parts of the world; to aid and assist in providing for the basic needs of food, shelter, and education of such children by whatever means and methods necessary or advisable; to prevent by medical research or otherwise the mental and physical handicaps of children.
Types of support awarded: Seed money, equipment, matching funds, special projects, research, publications.
Limitations: No grants to individuals, or for building or endowment funds, operating budgets, continuing support, annual campaigns, deficit financing, land acquisition, conferences, scholarships, or fellowships; no emergency funds outside Monroe County, NY; no loans.
Publications: Annual report, program policy statement, application guidelines.
Application information: 1 copy only of appendix material.
  Initial approach: Telephone, letter, or full proposal
  Copies of proposal: 4
  Deadline(s): None
  Board meeting date(s): Quarterly
  Final notification: 2 months
  Write: Wayne S. Cook or Patricia Hans, Directors
Officer and Trustees: Dorothea Haus Ross, Philetus M. Chamberlain, Marine Midland Bank.
Directors: Wayne S. Cook, Patricia Hans.
Number of staff: 2 part-time professional.
Employer Identification Number: 161080458

2892
Rothschild (Robert and Maurine) Fund, Inc. ♯
c/o David Tarlow & Co.
60 East 42nd St.
New York 10165

Incorporated in 1948 in New York.
Donor(s): Herbert M. Rothschild,† Nannette F. Rothschild, and others.
Financial data: (yr. ended 12/31/83): Assets, $1,459,871 (M); expenditures, $70,312, including $56,553 for 112 grants (high: $25,000; low: $10).
Purpose and activities: Broad purposes; general giving, with emphasis on the arts, including museums, community development, and higher education.
Application information:
  Deadline(s): None
Directors: Katherine Jackson, Maurine Rothschild, Peter Rothschild, Robert F. Rothschild.
Employer Identification Number: 136059064

2893
Ruben Family Foundation ♯
600 Madison Ave.
New York 10022

Established in 1982 in New York.
Donor(s): Lawrence Ruben, Selma Ruben.

Financial data: (yr. ended 12/31/82): Assets, $105,900 (M); gifts received, $211,000; expenditures, $105,100, including $105,100 for 10 grants (high: $50,000; low: $500).
Purpose and activities: Grants for higher education, especially medical education, and Jewish welfare funds.
Officers: Lawrence Ruben, President; Richard Gordon Ruben, Vice-President; Selma Ruben, Secretary and Treasurer.
Employer Identification Number: 133124700

2894
Rubenstein (Frank) Foundation, Inc. ♯
c/o Albert Rubenstein
781 Fifth Ave.
New York 10022

Incorporated in 1951 in New York.
Donor(s): Mrs. Frank Rubenstein,† Albert Rubenstein, Denia Levin, and others.
Financial data: (yr. ended 12/31/82): Assets, $908,685 (M); expenditures, $138,401, including $133,146 for 72 grants (high: $67,200; low: $10).
Purpose and activities: Charitable purposes; general giving, with emphasis on Jewish welfare funds, hospitals, temple support, and education.
Officers: Albert Rubenstein, President; Denia Levin, Secretary and Treasurer.
Employer Identification Number: 136103808

2895
Rubin (Samuel) Foundation, Inc. ▼
777 United Nations Plaza
New York 10017   (212) 697-8945

Incorporated in 1949 in New York.
Donor(s): Samuel Rubin.†
Financial data: (yr. ended 12/31/83): Assets, $20,412,728 (M); expenditures, $1,965,577, including $1,722,022 for 77 grants (high: $500,000; low: $1,000).
Purpose and activities: Grants to national and international organizations primarily for programs concerned with the pursuit of peace and justice, the search for an equitable reallocation of the world's resources, and the fullest implementation of social, economic, political, civil, and cultural rights for all of the world's people; some emphasis on organizations located in New York City and Washington, DC.
Types of support awarded: Endowment funds, research, conferences and seminars, scholarship funds, fellowships, professorships, exchange programs, matching funds, general purposes.
Limitations: No grants to individuals or for capital funds.
Publications: Program policy statement.
Application information: Funds largely committed.
  Initial approach: Full proposal
  Copies of proposal: 1
  Deadline(s): None
  Board meeting date(s): February, June, September, and December
  Final notification: 2 weeks after board meetings
  Write: Cora Weiss, President

Officers and Directors: J. Sinclair Armstrong, Chairman and Secretary; Cora Weiss, President; Peter Weiss, Vice-President; Reed Rubin, Treasurer; Jane Gregory Rubin.
Number of staff: 3.
Employer Identification Number: 131990017

2896
Rubinstein (Helena) Foundation, Inc. ▼
405 Lexington Ave.
New York 10174   (212) 986-0806

Incorporated in 1953 in New York.
Donor(s): Helena Rubinstein Gourielli.†
Financial data: (yr. ended 5/31/84): Assets, $33,248,504 (M); expenditures, $3,382,478, including $2,723,526 for 198 grants (high: $220,000; average: $5,000-$25,000).
Purpose and activities: Broad-based activities with strong focus on projects that benefit women and children and the developing role of women in society. Funding primarily for education, community services, health care and medical research, and the arts.
Types of support awarded: Operating budgets, seed money, equipment, matching funds, professorships, internships, scholarship funds, fellowships, special projects, research, publications, technical assistance.
Limitations: Giving primarily in New York City, NY. No support for film or television projects. No grants to individuals; no loans. Only occasional support for building or endowment funds.
Publications: Annual report, program policy statement, application guidelines.
Application information:
Initial approach: Letter
Copies of proposal: 1
Deadline(s): None
Board meeting date(s): November and May
Final notification: 1 to 5 months
Write: Mrs. Diane Moss, Executive Director
Officers and Directors: Roy V. Titus, Chairman; Oscar Kolin, President; Diane Moss, Vice-President and Executive Director; Robert S. Friedman, Secretary and Treasurer; Gertrude G. Michelson, Martin E. Segal, Mrs. Roy V. Titus.
Number of staff: 4 full-time professional; 2 full-time support.
Employer Identification Number: 136102666

2897
Rudin Foundation, Inc. ⊄
345 Park Ave.
New York 10154

Incorporated in 1960 in New York.
Donor(s): Many local businesses.
Financial data: (yr. ended 12/31/82): Assets, $612,191 (M); gifts received, $477,400; expenditures, $200,425, including $197,471 for 149 grants (high: $7,500; low: $100).
Purpose and activities: Broad purposes; primarily local giving for higher education, community development, and cultural organizations.
Limitations: Giving primarily in NY.
Officer: Jack Rudin, President.
Employer Identification Number: 136113064

2898
Rudin (The Louis and Rachel) Foundation, Inc.
345 Park Ave.
New York 10154

Incorporated in 1968 in New York.
Financial data: (yr. ended 7/31/83): Assets, $5,173,079 (M); expenditures, $394,783, including $377,500 for 11 grants (high: $68,000; low: $10,000).
Purpose and activities: Grants for local medical and nursing schools.
Limitations: Giving primarily in NY.
Officers and Directors: Jack Rudin, President; Lydia Heimlich, Vice-President; Lewis Rudin, Secretary and Treasurer; Donald Heimlich, Lewis Steinman.
Employer Identification Number: 237039549

2899
Rudin (Samuel and May) Foundation, Inc.
345 Park Ave.
New York 10154

Incorporated in 1976 in New York.
Donor(s): Samuel Rudin.†
Financial data: (yr. ended 6/30/83): Assets, $1,037,432 (M); gifts received, $1,038,265; expenditures, $474,166, including $455,916 for 25 grants (high: $60,000; low: $5,000).
Purpose and activities: Primarily local giving, with emphasis on higher education, social agencies, including religious welfare funds, hospitals, museums, performing arts and other cultural programs.
Types of support awarded: General purposes, scholarship funds, research.
Limitations: Giving primarily in the New York, NY, metropolitan area.
Officers and Directors: May Rudin, Chairman; Jack Rudin, President; Lewis Rudin, Executive Vice-President; Beth DeWoody, Eric Rudin, Vice-Presidents; Madeline Rudin, William Rudin.
Employer Identification Number: 132906946

2900
Russ Togs Foundation, The ⊄
1411 Broadway
New York 10018

Established in 1960 in New York.
Donor(s): Russ Togs, Inc.
Financial data: (yr. ended 12/31/82): Assets, $3,802 (M); gifts received, $150,000; expenditures, $154,401, including $154,338 for 94 grants (high: $41,640; low: $50).
Purpose and activities: General giving, with emphasis on Jewish welfare funds, hospitals, and the aged; support also for higher education and youth.
Trustees: Eli L. Rousso, Irving L. Rousso, Louis E. Rousso, Herman Saporta.
Employer Identification Number: 136086149

2901
Ryan (The Nina M.) Foundation, Inc. ⊄
Two Durham Rd.
Bronxville 10708

Incorporated in 1947 in New York.
Financial data: (yr. ended 12/31/82): Assets, $1,303,429 (M); gifts received, $2,765; expenditures, $115,274, including $110,010 for 87 grants (high: $15,000; low: $25).
Purpose and activities: Grants primarily for cultural programs, with emphasis on music and music education, and for higher education; support also for community funds.
Officers: R.F. Bell, President; M.H. Sander, Vice-President; T.R. Berner, Treasurer.
Employer Identification Number: 136111038

2902
Sage (Russell) Foundation ▼
112 East 64th St.
New York 10021   (212) 750-6000

Incorporated in 1907 in New York.
Donor(s): Mrs. Russell Sage.†
Financial data: (yr. ended 9/30/84): Assets, $67,203,498 (M); expenditures, $4,452,549, including $1,135,705 for 50 grants (high: $158,773; low: $4,000) and $1,187,227 for 3 foundation-administered programs.
Purpose and activities: A private operating foundation created for "the improvement of social and living conditions in the United States." Currently exploring gender in American institutions. Primary attention in recent years to the application of social science research to social policy formation. The Foundation maintains a professional staff of resident and visiting social scientists who engage in their own research and also advise on Foundation policies and projects; provides support for other scholars and collaborates with other granting agencies and academic institutions in studies of social problems; sponsors special seminars on current social problems; participates in the planning and operation of each study or program and usually reserves the right to publish any resulting manuscripts; assures widespread dissemination of the research it sponsors through publication of books and monographs; and conducts a Visiting Scholar Program, under which persons working in the areas of current interest to the Foundation join the staff for one year to consult and continue their own research and writing.
Types of support awarded: Seed money, special projects, fellowships, research, publications, conferences and seminars.
Limitations: No grants to individuals, or for capital or endowment funds, independent ongoing activities of other institutions, scholarships, matching gifts, annual campaigns, emergency funds, deficit financing, operating budgets, or continuing support; no loans.
Publications: Biennial report, informational brochure, program policy statement, application guidelines, newsletter.
Application information:
Initial approach: Letter
Copies of proposal: 1
Deadline(s): None

Board meeting date(s): November, March, and June
Final notification: 3 months
Write: Marshall A. Robinson, President
Officers: Marshall A. Robinson,* President; Peter E. de Janosi, Vice-President; Doris Fennell, Secretary; Loren D. Ross, Treasurer.
Trustees:* John S. Reed, Chair; Carl Kaysen, Vice-Chair; Robert McCormick Adams, Earl F. Cheit, Philip E. Converse, Renee Fox, Herma Hill Kay, Patricia A. King, Gardner Lindzey, Gary E. MacDougal, James G. March, Frederick Mosteller, Madelon Talley, Mortimer B. Zuckerman.
Number of staff: 23 full-time professional; 17 part-time professional; 5 full-time support; 3 part-time support.
Employer Identification Number: 131635303

2903
Saks Fifth Avenue - Gimbel Brothers Foundation, Inc. ⊭
1275 Broadway
New York 10001   (212) 564-3300

Incorporated in 1945 in New York.
Donor(s): Gimbel Brothers, Inc.
Financial data: (yr. ended 12/31/82): Assets, $200,384 (M); expenditures, $391,909, including $389,744 for 76 grants (high: $84,700; low: $50).
Purpose and activities: Broad purposes; general charitable giving, primarily to community funds in areas where the donor operates stores. Support also for cultural organizations and education.
Limitations: Giving primarily in areas in which the donor operates stores, including Milwaukee, WI, New York, NY, and Pittsburgh and Philadelphia, PA. No grants to individuals.
Application information:
Initial approach: Letter
Copies of proposal: 1
Board meeting date(s): As required
Officers and Directors:* Angelo Rosato,* Vice-President, Secretary, and Treasurer; Robert J. Suslow, Vice-President; Hugh V. Cochrane*.
Employer Identification Number: 136129702

2904
Salomon (The William R. and Virginia F.) Family Foundation, Inc. ⊭
c/o Salomon Brothers
One State St. Plaza, 42nd Fl.
New York 10004   (212) 747-7000

Incorporated in 1954 in New York.
Donor(s): William R. Salomon.
Financial data: (yr. ended 12/31/82): Assets, $1,384,219 (M); expenditures, $199,026, including $183,759 for 79 grants (high: $45,150; low: $15).
Purpose and activities: General purposes; primarily local giving, with emphasis on Jewish welfare funds, higher education, and hospitals.
Limitations: Giving primarily in NY.
Application information:
Board meeting date(s): Annually
Write: William R. Salomon, President

Officers and Directors: William R. Salomon, President and Treasurer; Virginia F. Salomon, Vice-President; Susan S. Havens.
Employer Identification Number: 136088823

2905
Samuels (The Fan Fox and Leslie R.) Foundation, Inc. ▼
30 Rockefeller Plaza, Suite 1936
New York 10112   (212) 315-2940

Incorporated in 1959 in Utah; reincorporated in 1983 in New York.
Donor(s): Leslie R. Samuels,† Fan Fox Samuels.†
Financial data: (yr. ended 7/31/84): Assets, $19,454,534 (M); gifts received, $17,548,801; expenditures, $1,111,607, including $936,904 for 15 grants (high: $300,000; low: $200).
Purpose and activities: Charitable purposes; primarily local giving, with grants largely for cultural programs; support also for health and welfare funds.
Types of support awarded: General purposes, operating budgets, continuing support, annual campaigns, seed money, emergency funds, building funds, equipment, research, matching funds.
Limitations: Giving primarily in New York, NY. No grants to individuals, or for scholarships and fellowships; no loans.
Publications: Annual report, 990-PF.
Application information:
Initial approach: Letter
Copies of proposal: 1
Deadline(s): None
Board meeting date(s): October, January, April, July, and as necessary
Final notification: 1 month
Write: Ms. Gerry Levinson, Associate
Officers and Directors: Morton J. Bernstein, President; Carlos D. Moseley, Vice-President; Joseph C. Mitchell, Secretary; Marvin A. Kaufman, Treasurer.
Number of staff: 2 full-time professional.
Employer Identification Number: 133124818

2906
Santa Maria Foundation, Inc. ⊭
c/o John Meehan, Secretary
43 W. 42nd St.
New York 10036

Established in 1978.
Donor(s): J. Peter Grace, Margaret F. Grace.
Financial data: (yr. ended 12/31/83): Assets, $1,529,648 (M); gifts received, $492,752; expenditures, $63,556, including $53,053 for 11 grants (high: $10,000; low: $53).
Purpose and activities: Broad purposes; support largely for higher education and Roman Catholic religious organizations.
Limitations: Giving primarily in NY.
Officers and Directors: J. Peter Grace, President; John J. Meehan, Secretary; Thomas M. Doyle, Treasurer.
Employer Identification Number: 132938749

2907
Sarne Charitable Trust ⊭
c/o Abraham Sarway
20 West 33rd St.
New York 10001

Established in 1977.
Donor(s): Abraham Sarway, Sarne Handbag Company, Inc.
Financial data: (yr. ended 12/31/82): Assets, $162,267 (M); gifts received, $150,000; expenditures, $126,283, including $126,161 for 38 grants (high: $20,000; low: $52).
Purpose and activities: Grants primarily for local Jewish welfare and educational funds and temple support.
Limitations: Giving primarily in NY.
Trustees: Abraham Sarway.
Employer Identification Number: 132886431

2908
Sasco Foundation
c/o Manufacturers Hanover Trust Company
600 Fifth Ave.
New York 10020

Trust established in 1951 in New York.
Donor(s): Mrs. Leila E. Riegel,† Mrs. Katherine R. Emory.
Financial data: (yr. ended 12/31/82): Assets, $2,949,804 (M); expenditures, $180,239, including $155,250 for 89 grants (high: $25,000; low: $500).
Purpose and activities: Broad purposes; grants primarily in New York, Connecticut, and Maine for hospitals, higher and secondary education, youth agencies, cultural programs, and conservation.
Limitations: Giving primarily in NY, CT, and ME.
Trustees: Katherine R. Emory, Frank M. Foley, Manufacturers Hanover Trust Company.
Employer Identification Number: 136046567

2909
Sayour (Elias) Foundation, Inc. ⊭
185 Madison Ave.
New York 10016

Incorporated in 1951 in New York.
Donor(s): Elias Sayour,† George Sayour, and associates.
Financial data: (yr. ended 10/31/83): Assets, $1,211,930 (M); expenditures, $142,602, including $131,150 for 66 grants (high: $32,000; low: $100).
Purpose and activities: Grants primarily for Roman Catholic church support, welfare funds, and religious organizations; support also for hospitals.
Officers: Jeanette Sayour, President; Peter Sayour, Vice-President.
Employer Identification Number: 136109953

2910
Schaefer (B. F. S.) Foundation, Inc. ¤
c/o Franklin Schaefer
30 Glen Head Rd., P.O. Box 144
Glen Head 11545

Established in 1961.
Financial data: (yr. ended 3/31/83): Assets,
$342,626 (M); expenditures, $127,835,
including $123,120 for 15 grants (high:
$100,000; low: $35).
Purpose and activities: Major giving for higher
education; additional support locally for a
hospital and other charitable organizations.
Limitations: Giving primarily in NY.
Managers: Franklin Schaefer, Stephen Schaefer.
Employer Identification Number: 510205694

2911
Schalkenbach (Robert) Foundation, Inc. ▼
Five East 44th St.
New York 10017   (212) 986-8684

Incorporated in 1925 in New York.
Donor(s): Robert Schalkenbach.†
Financial data: (yr. ended 6/30/84): Assets,
$4,779,839 (M); gifts received, $54,347;
expenditures, $291,803, including $156,493
for 14 grants (high: $40,554; low: $108) and
$17,071 for 3 foundation-administered
programs.
Purpose and activities: A private operating
foundation established to teach the social and
economic philosophy of Henry George,
especially his views concerning the single tax
on land values and international free trade,
primarily through publication of books and
other forms of educational work, including
research.
Types of support awarded: Continuing
support, matching funds, research, publications,
conferences and seminars.
Limitations: No grants to individuals, or for
capital funds, operating budgets, annual
campaigns, demonstration projects, start-up or
emergency funds, or deficit financing; no loans.
Publications: Annual report.
Application information:
  Initial approach: Letter or full proposal
  Copies of proposal: 1
  Deadline(s): None
  Board meeting date(s): Bimonthly, beginning
    in February
  Final notification: 2 months
  Write: Oscar B. Johannsen, Secretary
Officers and Directors: Lancaster M. Greene,
President; Gabriel Kerekes, Vice-President;
Oscar Johannsen, Secretary and Executive
Director; Thomas A. Larkin, Treasurer; Charles
Abramovitz, T.H. Bonaparte, Steven B. Cord,
William P. Davidson, Karl Falk, Roy A. Foulke,
Jr., Violetta G. Graham, J. Ted Gwartney, C.
Lowell Harriss, A.L. Hydeman, Jr., John M.
Kelly, Will Lissner, Richard Noyes, Pierrepont I.
Prentice, Walter Rybeck, Frances Soriero.
Number of staff: 2 full-time professional; 1 full-
time support; 1 part-time support.
Employer Identification Number: 131656331

2912
Schepp (Leopold) Foundation
15 East 26th St., Suite 1900
New York 10010   (212) 889-9737

Incorporated in 1925 in New York.
Donor(s): Leopold Schepp,† Miss Florence L.
Schepp.†
Financial data: (yr. ended 2/28/84): Assets,
$6,112,983 (M); expenditures, $454,159,
including $324,450 for grants to individuals.
Purpose and activities: Primarily to assist
young men and women of character and ability
who have insufficient means to complete their
vocational or professional education.
Undergraduate scholarships to individuals
under 30 years of age; graduate scholarships to
individuals under 40 years of age; a small
number of postdoctoral fellowships for
independent study and research awarded
annually to individuals in the arts and literature,
medicine, and oceanography.
Types of support awarded: Fellowships,
student aid.
Publications: Program policy statement,
application guidelines.
Application information: Application form
required.
  Initial approach: Letter
  Copies of proposal: 1
  Deadline(s): Submit application request
    between June and December; deadline
    December 31
  Board meeting date(s): May and October
  Final notification: 1st week in May
  Write: Mrs. Edythe Bobrow, Executive
    Secretary
Officers: Barbara Tweed Estill,* President;
Elizabeth N. Gaillard,* Charles E. Hodges,*
Howard F. Ordman,* Vice-Presidents; Edythe
Bobrow, Executive Secretary; Henry E.
Gaillard,* Treasurer.
Trustees:* Katherine W. Barnes, Carvel H.
Cartmell, Christopher E. Doyle, Clementine Z.
Estes, Anne Linville, C. Edwin Linville, Julius
Maldutis, Julia Markham, Barbara McLendon,
Thomas W. McNealy, Margaret Ogden,
Priscilla C. Perkins, Benjamin Phillips, Samuel
Thorne, Jr., Eugenia B. Willard.
Number of staff: 1 full-time professional; 2 full-
time support.
Employer Identification Number: 135562353

2913
Scherman Foundation, Inc., The ▼
250 West 57th St., Suite 2122
New York 10107   (212) 489-7143

Incorporated in 1941 in New York.
Donor(s): The Scherman family.
Financial data: (yr. ended 12/31/83): Assets,
$38,061,969 (M); expenditures, $2,531,178,
including $2,119,000 for 153 grants (high:
$100,000; low: $3,000; average: $5,000-
$25,000).
Purpose and activities: Grants largely for
conservation, disarmament and peace, family
planning, human rights and liberties, the arts,
and social welfare; priority given to New York
City organizations in the arts and social welfare
fields.

Types of support awarded: Operating
budgets, continuing support, seed money,
emergency funds, matching funds, program-
related investments, special projects, loans,
general purposes.
Limitations: Giving primarily in New York, NY
for arts and social welfare grants. No support
for colleges or universities. No grants to
individuals, or for building or endowment
funds, scholarships or fellowships.
Publications: Annual report, program
policy statement, application guidelines.
Application information:
  Initial approach: Full proposal
  Copies of proposal: 1
  Deadline(s): None
  Board meeting date(s): Quarterly
  Final notification: 3 months
  Write: David F. Freeman, Executive Director
Officers: Axel G. Rosin,* President; Katharine
S. Rosin,* Secretary; David F. Freeman,
Treasurer and Executive Director.
Directors:* Helen Edey, M.D., Joseph S.
Iseman, Archibald R. Murray, Anthony M.
Schulte, Sandra Silverman, Karen R. Sollins,
Marcia Thompson.
Number of staff: 1 full-time professional; 1
part-time professional; 1 full-time support.
Employer Identification Number: 136098464

2914
Scheuer (S. H. and Helen R.) Family Foundation, Inc. ▼ ¤
350 Fifth Ave., Suite 3410
New York 10118

Incorporated in 1943 in New York.
Donor(s): Members of the Scheuer family.
Financial data: (yr. ended 11/30/83): Assets,
$19,634,293 (M); gifts received, $1,489,112;
expenditures, $2,407,536, including
$2,323,562 for 327 grants (high: $175,000;
low: $50; average: $1,000-$10,000).
Purpose and activities: Broad purposes;
general giving, with emphasis on local Jewish
welfare funds and higher education; some
support for social services and cultural
programs, including music and museums.
Limitations: Giving primarily in New York, NY.
Application information: Applications for
grants not invited.
  Write: Norbert Krailik
Officer and Directors: Amy S. Cohen, Harold
Cohen, George H. Heyman, Jr., Leon Meyers,
Richard J. Scheuer.
Employer Identification Number: 136062661

2915
Schieffelin (Sarah I.) Residuary Trust ¤
c/o The Bank of New York
48 Wall St.
New York 10015

Established in 1976.
Donor(s): Sarah I. Schieffelin.†
Financial data: (yr. ended 3/31/83): Assets,
$4,111,818 (M); expenditures, $264,136,
including $230,803 for 26 grants (high:
$23,080; low: $1,000).

Purpose and activities: Primarily local giving for conservation and wildlife preservation; cultural programs, health, and church support. Giving generally limited to continuing support for specified recipients.
Limitations: Giving primarily in NY.
Trustees: Thomas Fenlon, Bank of New York.
Employer Identification Number: 136724459

2916
Schiff Foundation, The
420 Madison Ave., 13th Fl.
New York 10017   (212) 751-3180

Incorporated in 1946 in New York.
Donor(s): John M. Schiff, Edith B. Schiff,† David T. Schiff, Peter G. Schiff, Northwood Finance and Realty Corporation.
Financial data: (yr. ended 12/31/84): Assets, $7,000,000 (M); expenditures, $243,140, including $243,140 for 196 grants (high: $25,000; low: $25).
Purpose and activities: Broad purposes; primarily local giving, with emphasis on special medical programs, certain youth agencies, museums and the performing arts, and education.
Limitations: Giving primarily in NY. No grants to individuals.
Application information: Reluctant to take on new commitments at this time.
 Initial approach: Proposal
 Copies of proposal: 1
 Deadline(s): Submit proposal preferably between May and October
 Write: Deborah Henry Onello, Secretary
Officers and Directors:* John M. Schiff,* President; David T. Schiff,* Peter G. Schiff,* Vice-Presidents; Deborah H. Onello, Secretary; Humberto Lopez, Treasurer.
Employer Identification Number: 136088221

2917
Schimmel Foundation, The ⌑
20 Cooper Square
New York 10003

Incorporated 1n 1960 in New York.
Donor(s): Norbert Schimmel.
Financial data: (yr. ended 12/31/82): Assets, $1,148,986 (M); gifts received, $438,750; expenditures, $134,434, including $126,512 for 21 grants (high: $52,500).
Purpose and activities: Giving primarily to art museums, including donations of works of art.
Directors: Norbert Schimmel, Manager; Alan Bloom, Earl Morse, Lee Pomeranz, Evelyn Schimmel, Stanley Wagman.
Employer Identification Number: 136145185

2918
Schimper (Frederick and Amelia) Foundation
805 Third Ave., 20th Fl.
New York 10022   (212) 702-5700

Incorporated in 1943 in New York.
Donor(s): Amelia S. Ehrmann.†

Financial data: (yr. ended 12/31/83): Assets, $1,286,553 (M); expenditures, $89,403, including $74,000 for 5 grants (high: $25,000; low: $2,000; average: $5,000-$25,000).
Purpose and activities: Giving primarily for seed money for significant research designed to benefit indigent, aged persons.
Types of support awarded: Continuing support, seed money, research, publications.
Limitations: No grants to individuals, or for building or endowment funds, annual campaigns, emergency funds, deficit financing, equipment, land acquisition, matching gifts, special projects, conferences, scholarships, fellowships, or operating budgets; no loans.
Publications: Application guidelines.
Application information:
 Initial approach: Letter of inquiry or full proposal
 Copies of proposal: 3
 Deadline(s): None
 Board meeting date(s): June and December
 Final notification: 1 to 2 months
 Write: William E. Friedman, President
Officers and Directors: William E. Friedman, President and Treasurer; Myles A. Cane, Vice-President and Secretary; Stanley S. Weithorn.
Number of staff: None.
Employer Identification Number: 136108507

2919
Schlumberger Foundation, Inc. ▼
277 Park Ave.
New York 10172   (212) 350-9439

Schlumberger Foundation established as a trust in Texas in 1954; terminated in 1982 and assets transferred to Schlumberger Horizons, Inc., a Delaware foundation; in 1982 name changed from Schlumberger Horizons, Inc. to Schlumberger Foundation, Inc.
Donor(s): Schlumberger, Limited.
Financial data: (yr. ended 3/31/83): Assets, $17,875,810 (M); expenditures, $2,013,696, including $1,753,143 for 111 grants (high: $200,000; low: $500).
Purpose and activities: Broad purposes; grants limited to selected colleges and universities for scholarships, fellowships, and endowed professorships in engineering and other scientific fields; support also for cultural institutions.
Types of support awarded: Scholarship funds, fellowships, professorships, general purposes.
Limitations: No grants to individuals, or for building funds, or operating budgets.
Application information:
 Initial approach: Letter
 Deadline(s): None
 Board meeting date(s): February or March
 Write: Arthur W. Alexander, Executive Secretary
Officers: Arthur W. Alexander,* Executive Secretary.
Managers: G.H. Jewell, A. Lindenauer, R. Shourd.
Trustees:* First City National Bank of Houston.
Number of staff: 1.
Employer Identification Number: 237033142

2920
Schwartz (Arnold and Marie) Fund for Education and Health Research ▼ ⌑
465 Park Ave.
New York 10022

Incorporated in 1971 in Delaware.
Donor(s): Arnold Schwartz Charitable Trust.
Financial data: (yr. ended 3/31/83): Assets, $7,260,616 (M); gifts received, $25,356; expenditures, $1,563,757, including $1,468,620 for 84 grants (high: $650,100; low: $15; average: $25-$25,000).
Purpose and activities: General purposes; grants largely for higher education, hospitals, medical research, music, and religious organizations.
Limitations: Giving primarily in the New York City, NY, area.
Application information: Applications not solicited; all funds are committed.
Officer: Marie D. Schwartz, President.
Employer Identification Number: 237115019

2921
Schwarz (Jakob, Louise and Kurt) Charitable Trust
c/o Morgan Guaranty Trust Company of New York
9 West 57th St.
New York 10019   (212) 483-2248

Trust established in 1974 in New York.
Donor(s): Kurt Schwarz.†
Financial data: (yr. ended 11/30/83): Assets, $210,181 (M); expenditures, $146,470, including $142,000 for 3 grants (high: $112,000; low: $15,000).
Purpose and activities: To provide for the Jewish sick, blind, and needy in the state of Israel.
Types of support awarded: General purposes, operating budgets, continuing support, seed money, building funds, equipment, special projects.
Limitations: No grants to individuals, or for endowment funds, research programs, scholarships, fellowships, or matching gifts; no loans.
Application information:
 Initial approach: Full proposal
 Copies of proposal: 1
 Deadline(s): October 1
 Board meeting date(s): August or December
 Write: Robert F. Longley, Senior Vice-President
Trustees: William H. Miller, Morgan Guaranty Trust Company of New York (Robert F. Longley, Senior Vice-President.
Employer Identification Number: 510199188

2922
Schweckendieck (Edith M.) Trusts
Private Banking Division
Sort 2439
New York 10043   (212) 715-0178

Trust established in 1922 in New York; second trust established in 1936 in New York.
Donor(s): Edith M. Schweckendieck.†

Financial data: (yr. ended 12/31/84): Assets, $1,800,000 (M); expenditures, $160,000, including $160,000 for 20 grants (high: $15,000; low: $5,000).
Purpose and activities: Grants to local charitable institutions, to provide assistance for care and maintenance of the aged and feeble; care, maintenance, and education of crippled children; and prevention and relief of cancer.
Types of support awarded: General purposes, building funds, endowment funds.
Limitations: Giving limited to NY. No grants to individuals.
Application information:
  Initial approach: Letter
  Deadline(s): Submit proposal preferably in July; deadline August 31
  Board meeting date(s): October
  Write: Kent H. Parker, Senior Trust Officer
Trustee: Citibank (Kent H. Parker, Senior Trust Officer).
Employer Identification Number: 136055135

2923
Schweitzer (Louis) Charitable Trust ⌷
c/o Hecht & Company, P.C.
1500 Broadway
New York 10036

Trust established in 1972 in New York.
Donor(s): Louis Schweitzer.†
Financial data: (yr. ended 4/30/83): Assets, $1,232,384 (M); expenditures, $95,309, including $91,150 for 3 grants (high: $80,000; low: $2,000).
Purpose and activities: Grants largely for a theater foundation.
Application information: Applications for grants not invited.
Trustees: Daniel G. Ross, Lucille Schweitzer, M. Peter Schweitzer.
Employer Identification Number: 136517711

2924
SCM Foundation, Inc.
299 Park Ave.
New York 10171   (212) 752-2700

Incorporated in 1955 in New York.
Donor(s): SCM Corporation.
Financial data: (yr. ended 12/31/83): Assets, $104,220 (M); gifts received, $129,500; expenditures, $119,365, including $119,365 for 377 employee matching gifts.
Purpose and activities: Support only for an employee matching gift program for higher education; contributions are matched or doubled depending on the institution's status, up to a maximum of $2,500 a year.
Types of support awarded: Employee matching gifts.
Limitations: No grants to individuals, or for endowment funds, capital funds, general support, operating budgets, scholarships, fellowships, or research; no loans.
Publications: Program policy statement, application guidelines.
Application information: Application form required.
  Initial approach: Letter
  Copies of proposal: 1

Write: Gerard F. Stoddard, Chairman
Officers: Gerard F. Stoddard, Chairman and President; James Balph, 1st Vice-President; Herbert Egli, 2nd Vice-President; Richard Sexton, Vice-President and Secretary; Paul Elicker, George E. Hall, Vice-Presidents; William V. Cawley, Treasurer.
Employer Identification Number: 166039441

2925
Sexauer Foundation, The ⌷
P.O. Box 1000
White Plains 10602

Incorporated in 1961 in Delaware.
Donor(s): John A. Sexauer.†
Financial data: (yr. ended 8/31/82): Assets, $1,581,579 (M); expenditures, $196,464, including $156,910 for 147 grants (high: $15,000; low: $50).
Purpose and activities: General giving, with emphasis on hospitals and higher education; support also for churches.
Officers and Trustees: James M. Sexauer, President; John B. Schmitt, Vice-President; Howard G. Kafer, Mae M. Sexauer.
Employer Identification Number: 136156256

2926
Sharp (The Evelyn) Foundation ⌷
1370 Ave. of the Americas
New York 10019   (212) 371-4888

Incorporated in 1952 in New York.
Donor(s): Mrs. Evelyn Sharp, and others.
Financial data: (yr. ended 6/30/83): Assets, $3,009,440 (M); expenditures, $129,029, including $125,800 for 33 grants (high: $10,000; low: $1,000).
Purpose and activities: Broad purposes; primarily local giving, with emphasis on the performing arts and museums, education, population control, and medical research and hospitals.
Limitations: Giving primarily in NY.
Officers and Trustees: Evelyn Sharp, President; Mrs. Philip Bastedo, Mary Cronson, Emerson Foote, Albert Francqe III, Jeremiah Milbank, Jr., Peter Sharp, Vice-Presidents.
Employer Identification Number: 136119532

2927
Shatford (J. D.) Memorial Trust ⌷
c/o Chemical Bank
30 Rockefeller Plaza
New York 10112   (212) 621-2148

Trust established in 1955 in New York.
Financial data: (yr. ended 12/31/82): Assets, $1,881,635 (M); expenditures, $168,002, including $33,301 for 8 grants (high: $17,542; low: $331) and $113,406 for grants to individuals.
Purpose and activities: Broad purposes, with emphasis on scholarship aid, secondary education, and charities in Hubbards, Nova Scotia.
Types of support awarded: Student aid, grants to individuals.

Limitations: Giving limited to Nova Scotia, Canada.
Application information: Application form available for scholarship grants.
  Deadline(s): None
  Write: Mrs. Barbara Strohmeier
Trustees: Willard R. Brown, Chemical Bank.
Employer Identification Number: 136029993

2928
Sheafer (Emma A.) Charitable Trust ⌷
c/o Morgan Guaranty Trust Company of New York
23 Wall St.
New York 10015   (212) 483-2248

Trust established in 1975 in New York.
Donor(s): Emma A. Sheafer.†
Financial data: (yr. ended 12/31/83): Assets, $2,124,173 (M); expenditures, $136,472, including $120,000 for 7 grants (high: $25,000; low: $3,000).
Purpose and activities: Giving locally to performing arts groups.
Types of support awarded: General purposes, continuing support, seed money, deficit financing, building funds, equipment, land acquisition, endowment funds.
Limitations: Giving limited to NY. No grants to individuals, or for research, scholarships and fellowships, or matching gifts; no loans.
Application information:
  Initial approach: Proposal
  Copies of proposal: 1
  Deadline(s): Mid-April and mid-October
  Board meeting date(s): June and December
  Final notification: 2 months
  Write: Robert F. Longley, Senior Vice-President
Trustees: John C. Russell, Morgan Guaranty Trust Company of New York (Robert F. Longley, Senior Vice-President).
Number of staff: None.
Employer Identification Number: 510186114

2929
Shiah (C. D.) Charitable Foundation ⌷
75 Rockefeller Plaza, Suite 1501
New York 10019   (212) 484-8780

Established in 1981 in New York.
Financial data: (yr. ended 6/30/83): Assets, $1,005,262 (M); gifts received, $1,000,300; expenditures, $249,154, including $249,100 for 11 grants (high: $90,725; low: $2,000).
Purpose and activities: General giving, with emphasis on Chinese-American programs, secondary and higher education, and performing arts.
Application information:
  Initial approach: Proposal
  Write: Oded Aboodi, Trustee
Trustee: Oded Aboodi.
Employer Identification Number: 133076929

2930
Shubert Foundation, Inc., The ▼
234 West 44th St.
New York 10036   (212) 944-3777

Incorporated in 1945 in Delaware.
Donor(s): Lee Shubert,† J.J. Shubert.†
Financial data: (yr. ended 5/31/84): Assets,
$47,100,910 (M); gifts received, $168,065;
expenditures, $2,430,997, including $902,760
for 69 grants (high: $175,000; low: $5,000;
average: $10,000-$20,000) and $125,168 for 1
foundation-administered program.
Purpose and activities: To build and
perpetuate the live performing arts, particularly
the professional theater, in the United States.
Support both of theatrical institutions and of
those other elements of the performing arts and
related institutions necessary to maintain and
support the theater. Grants almost always
made exclusively for general operating funds.
Types of support awarded: Operating budgets.
Limitations: Giving primarily in the U.S. No
grants to individuals, or for building or
endowment funds, research, conduit
organizations, audience development, direct
subsidies to reduce admission prices,
productions for specialized audiences,
scholarships and fellowships, or matching gifts;
no loans.
Publications: Annual report, program policy
statement, application guidelines.
Application information: Application form
required.
  Initial approach: Letter or telephone
  Copies of proposal: 2
  Deadline(s): Submit proposal preferably in
    October or November; deadline
    December 1
  Board meeting date(s): Monthly
  Final notification: May
  Write: Mrs. Lynn L. Seidler, Executive
    Director
Officers and Directors:* Gerald Schoenfeld,*
Chairman; John W. Kluge,* Kerttu H. Shubert,*
Michael I. Sovern,* Vice-Presidents; Irving M.
Wall,* Secretary; Lee J. Seidler,* Treasurer;
Lynn L. Seidler, Executive Director.
Number of staff: 1 full-time professional; 1
part-time support.
Employer Identification Number: 136106961

2931
Silberman (The Lois and Samuel) Fund, Inc.
133 East 79th St.
New York 10021   (212) 737-8500

Incorporated in 1951 in New York.
Donor(s): Samuel J. Silberman.
Financial data: (yr. ended 7/31/84): Assets,
$2,260,000 (M); gifts received, $228,000;
expenditures, $219,500, including $155,500
for 8 grants (high: $62,500; low: $3,800;
average: $10,000).
Purpose and activities: Project grants with
sole interest in social welfare manpower
development.

Limitations: Giving limited to the U.S. No
grants to individuals, or for building or
endowment funds, general purposes, operating
budgets, scholarships, fellowships, or matching
gifts.
Publications: Multi-year report, program policy
statement, application guidelines, annual report.
Application information:
  Initial approach: Preliminary 2-page request
  Copies of proposal: 15
  Deadline(s): Submit proposal preferably in
    June or January; deadlines August and
    March
  Board meeting date(s): Semiannually
  Final notification: 6 months
  Write: Mrs. Lois V. Silberman, Vice-President
Officers and Trustees: Samuel J. Silberman,
President; Lois V. Silberman, Vice-President;
Allen H. Russell, Secretary; J. Robert Baylis,
Treasurer; Herbert L. Abrons, Seymour Milstein.
Number of staff: None.
Employer Identification Number: 136097931

2932
Silbermann (Max) Foundation ¤
c/o Shea & Gould
330 Madison Ave.
New York 10017

Established in 1961.
Donor(s): Joachim Silbermann.
Financial data: (yr. ended 12/31/82): Assets,
$1,001,434 (M); expenditures, $110,513,
including $108,225 for 9 grants (high: $50,000;
low: $25).
Purpose and activities: Support primarily for
higher education and temple support.
Application information:
  Write: Milton S. Gould, Trustee
Trustee: Milton S. Gould.
Employer Identification Number: 136085205

2933
Simon Foundation, Inc. ¤
c/o Charles Simon
One New York Plaza
New York 10004

Incorporated in 1954 in New York.
Donor(s): Charles Simon.
Financial data: (yr. ended 12/31/82): Assets,
$1,193,261 (M); expenditures, $275,755,
including $264,216 for 76 grants (high:
$50,000; low: $26).
Purpose and activities: Broad purposes;
primarily local giving, with emphasis on cultural
programs and museums, higher education,
hospitals, and youth agencies.
Types of support awarded: General purposes,
scholarship funds.
Limitations: Giving primarily in NY.
Officers and Directors: Charles Simon,
President-Treasurer; George DeSipio, Vice-
President and Secretary; Daniel M. Kelly.
Employer Identification Number: 136088838

2934
Simon (Sidney, Milton and Leoma) Foundation ¤
23 Crestview Dr.
Pleasantville 10570

Established in 1964.
Donor(s): Milton Simon.†
Financial data: (yr. ended 5/31/83): Assets,
$10,396,065 (M); gifts received, $287,548;
expenditures, $563,244, including $415,000
for 65 grants (high: $15,000; low: $1,000).
Purpose and activities: Grants primarily for
the handicapped, performing arts, medical
research, Jewish welfare funds, and hospitals.
Types of support awarded: Research.
Application information:
  Write: Joseph C. Warner, Trustee
Trustees: Joseph C. Warner, Meryll Warner,
Alan Wechsler.
Employer Identification Number: 136175218

2935
Sinsheimer (The Alexandrine and Alexander L.) Fund
c/o Manufacturers Hanover Trust Company
600 Fifth Ave.
New York 10020

Trust established in 1959 in New York.
Donor(s): Alexander L. Sinsheimer,† Mrs.
Alexandrine Sinsheimer.†
Financial data: (yr. ended 4/30/83): Assets,
$5,439,097 (M); expenditures, $397,574,
including $380,096 for 18 grants (high:
$56,199; low: $15,000).
Purpose and activities: To support scientific
research relating to prevention and cure of
human disease; grants to medical schools in
New York only.
Limitations: Giving limited to NY.
Application information:
  Write: T.E. Roepe
Trustee: Manufacturers Hanover Trust
Company (T.E. Roepe, Vice-President).
Employer Identification Number: 136047421

2936
Slade Foundation, Inc., The ¤
55 Water St.
New York 10041

Incorporated in 1952 in New York.
Donor(s): John H. Slade.
Financial data: (yr. ended 7/31/83): Assets,
$564,976 (M); gifts received, $333,620;
expenditures, $259,292, including $250,425
for 50 grants (high: $100,000; low: $20).
Purpose and activities: Primarily local giving,
for Jewish welfare funds and organizations, and
for cultural programs and social services;
support also for organizations in Israel.
Limitations: Giving primarily in New York, NY
and Israel.
Officers and Directors:* John Slade,*
President; Milton B. Eulau,* Vice-President;
Ursula Schneider, Secretary-Treasurer.
Employer Identification Number: 136065039

2937
Slifka (Joseph & Sylvia) Foundation ⌐
477 Madison Ave.
New York 10022

Established in 1944.
Financial data: (yr. ended 10/31/82): Assets,
$1,158,400 (M); gifts received, $75,000;
expenditures, $66,869, including $59,785 for
52 grants (high: $23,410; low: $25).
Purpose and activities: A private operating
foundation; grants largely for Jewish welfare
funds, hospitals, and cultural programs.
Officer: Joseph Slifka, President.
Employer Identification Number: 136106433

2938
Sloan (Alfred P.) Foundation ▼
630 Fifth Ave.
New York 10111   (212) 582-0450

Incorporated in 1934 in Delaware.
Donor(s): Alfred P. Sloan, Jr.,† Irene Jackson
Sloan,† New Castle Corporation.
Financial data: (yr. ended 12/31/84): Assets,
$371,148,237 (M); expenditures, $20,451,687,
including $16,986,340 for 182 grants (high:
$500,000; low: $1,250; average: $10,000-
$300,000), $2,771,380 for 130 grants to
individuals and $97,350 for 5 foundation-
administered programs.
Purpose and activities: Broad purposes;
interests in science and technology, education,
economics and management, and related
problems of society; Sloan fellowships for basic
research in the sciences are administered
entirely through institutions.
Types of support awarded: General purposes,
seed money, research, fellowships, matching
funds.
Limitations: No support for the creative or
performing arts, humanities (except through the
New Liberal Arts Program), medical research,
religion, or primary or secondary education.
No grants to individuals directly, or for
endowment or building funds, or equipment
not related directly to foundation-supported
projects; no loans.
Publications: Annual report, informational
brochure, program policy statement,
application guidelines.
Application information: Nomination forms
available for fellowship candidates; direct
applications not accepted.
  Initial approach: Letter
  Copies of proposal: 1
  Deadline(s): September 15 for fellowship
    program
  Board meeting date(s): 5 times a year
  Final notification: Within 3 months
  Write: Albert Rees, President
Officers: Albert Rees,* President; Arthur L.
Singer, Jr., James D. Koerner, Vice-Presidents;
Stewart F. Campbell, Secretary and Treasurer.
Trustees:* Thomas A. Murphy, Chairman;
Lucy Wilson Benson, R. Manning Brown, Jr.,
Lloyd C. Elam, Howard W. Johnson, Cathleen
S. Morawetz, Ellmore C. Patterson, Frank A.
Petito, Frank Press, James D. Robinson, III,
Charles J. Scanlon, Harold T. Shapiro.
Number of staff: 8 full-time professional; 11
full-time support.
Employer Identification Number: 131623877

2939
Smart Family Foundation
335 Madison Ave., 18th Fl.
New York 10017   (212) 682-7073

Trust established in 1951 in Illinois.
Donor(s): David A. Smart,† A.D. Elden,† Vera
Elden,† John Smart, Edgar G. Richards,
Florence Richards.
Financial data: (yr. ended 12/31/84): Assets,
$32,443,836 (M); expenditures, $1,510,787,
including $1,090,242 for 37 grants (high:
$500,000; low: $1,000).
Purpose and activities: Goals of foundation
currently being reevaluated; likely focus will be
education.
Types of support awarded: Research,
publications, conferences and seminars, special
projects.
Limitations: No grants to individuals.
Application information:
  Initial approach: Proposal or letter
  Copies of proposal: 1
  Board meeting date(s): Fall and spring
  Write: Deborah Wadsworth, Executive
    Director
Officer: Deborah Wadsworth, Executive
Director.
Trustees: John Smart, Chairman; A.L. Blinder,
President; Ralph S. Brown, Robert Feitler, Mary
S. Kitrosner, Bernard Krauss, Edgar G. Richards.
Number of staff: 1 full-time professional; 2
part-time professional; 1 full-time support.
Employer Identification Number: 366008282

2940
Smith, Barney Foundation, The ⌐
1345 Ave. of the Americas
New York 10019

Incorporated in 1965 in New York.
Donor(s): Smith Barney, Harris Upham &
Company, Inc.
Financial data: (yr. ended 12/31/81): Assets,
$58,885 (M); gifts received, $150,000;
expenditures, $118,172, including $118,162
for grants.
Purpose and activities: Broad purposes; grants
primarily for community funds, higher
education, including business education, youth
agencies, urban affairs, and the arts.
Officers and Directors:* Robert A. Powers,*
Chairman; John A. Orb,* President; Jean M.
Anderson, Secretary; Jack L. Billhardt, William
E. Fay, Jr., Theodore L. Haff, Jr.
Employer Identification Number: 136187938

2941
**Smithers (The Christopher D.)
Foundation, Inc.**
Box 67, Oyster Bay Rd.
Mill Neck 11765   (516) 676-0067

Incorporated in 1952 in New York.
Donor(s): Christopher D. Smithers,† Mrs.
Mabel B. Smithers,† R. Brinkley Smithers.
Financial data: (yr. ended 12/31/83): Assets,
$4,372,724 (M); gifts received, $989,655;
expenditures, $1,005,600, including $889,560
for 43 grants (high: $110,000; low: $200;
average: $20,000).

Purpose and activities: Supports organizations
performing prevention, educational service,
treatment, and research in the field of
alcoholism; initiates its own projects in this field
primarily by writing and publishing specialized
booklets for industry, educational organizations,
and the general public.
Types of support awarded: Operating
budgets, special projects, research, conferences
and seminars.
Limitations: No grants to individuals, or for
building or endowment funds, or matching
gifts; no loans.
Publications: Annual report.
Application information:
  Initial approach: Full proposal
  Copies of proposal: 2
  Deadline(s): Submit proposal between
    September and December; no set deadline
  Board meeting date(s): May
  Write: R. Brinkley Smithers, President
Officers and Directors: R. Brinkley Smithers,
President; Adele C. Smithers, Vice-President;
Henry S. Ziegler, Secretary; Charles F.
Smithers, Treasurer; Shirley B. Klesener.
Number of staff: 2 full-time support.
Employer Identification Number: 131861928

2942
Snow (The John Ben) Foundation, Inc.
P.O. Box 376
Pulaski 13142   (315) 298-6401
New Jersey office: 202 Mountain Ave.,
Westfield, NJ 07090

Incorporated in 1948 in New York.
Donor(s): John Ben Snow.†
Financial data: (yr. ended 3/31/84): Assets,
$3,175,900 (M); expenditures, $307,000,
including $257,600 for 13 grants (high:
$45,000; low: $1,000; average: $3,500) and
$1,000,000 for 1 loan.
Purpose and activities: Primarily local giving
for higher and secondary educational
institutions, youth agencies, hospitals, and
community betterment projects.
Limitations: Giving limited to central NY, with
emphasis on Oswego County. No grants to
individuals, or for operating budgets,
endowment funds, or contingency financing.
Publications: Program policy statement,
application guidelines.
Application information: Application form
required.
  Initial approach: Letter
  Copies of proposal: 1
  Deadline(s): Submit proposal between
    September and April; deadline April 15
  Board meeting date(s): June
  Write: Vernon F. Snow, President
Officers: Vernon F. Snow, President; Allen R.
Malcolm, Executive Vice-President, Secretary
and Treasurer; Ralph W. Snow, Vice-President.
Number of staff: 2 part-time professional; 2
part-time support.
Employer Identification Number: 136112704

2943
Snow (John Ben) Memorial Trust ▼
P.O. Box 378
Pulaski 13142   (315) 298-6401

Trust established in 1974 in New York.
Donor(s): John Ben Snow.†
Financial data: (yr. ended 12/31/83): Assets,
$14,002,000 (M); expenditures, $1,070,000,
including $805,350 for 35 grants (high:
$100,000; low: $4,000) and $750,000 for 1
loan.
Purpose and activities: Primarily local giving
for education, especially scholarships; cultural
institutions, especially libraries; medical and
health organizations; and environment.
Types of support awarded: Seed money,
equipment, research, publications, scholarship
funds, fellowships, matching funds.
Limitations: Giving primarily in central NY and
New York City. No grants to individuals or for
endowment funds.
Publications: Program policy statement,
application guidelines.
Application information: Application form
required.
  Initial approach: Letter
  Copies of proposal: 1
  Deadline(s): Submit proposal preferably from
     January through April; deadline April 15
  Final notification: 3 months
  Write: Vernon F. Snow, Trustee
Trustees: Rollan D. Melton, Vernon F. Snow,
Irving Trust Company.
Number of staff: 2 part-time support.
Employer Identification Number: 136633814

2944
Snyder (The Valentine Perry) Fund ¤
c/o Morgan Guaranty Trust Company of New
York
23 Wall St.
New York 10015   (212) 483-2248

Trust established in 1942 in New York.
Donor(s): Mrs. Sheda T. Snyder.†
Financial data: (yr. ended 12/31/83): Assets,
$3,742,063 (M); expenditures, $266,220,
including $246,100 for 18 grants (high:
$20,000; low: $300).
Purpose and activities: Broad purposes; giving
in the local area for social services, including
religious welfare organizations, child welfare,
community development, and church support.
Types of support awarded: General purposes,
operating budgets, continuing support, seed
money, emergency funds, building funds,
equipment, land acquisition, endowment funds,
special projects.
Limitations: Giving primarily in the New York,
NY, metropolitan area. No grants to
individuals, or for research-related programs,
scholarships, fellowships, or matching gifts; no
loans.
Application information:
  Initial approach: Proposal, letter, or
     telephone
  Copies of proposal: 1
  Deadline(s): None
  Board meeting date(s): May and November
  Write: Robert F. Longley, Senior Vice-
     President

Trustee: Morgan Guaranty Trust Company of
New York (Robert F. Longley, Senior Vice-
President).
Number of staff: 1.
Employer Identification Number: 136036765

2945
Sony Corporation of America
Foundation, Inc.
Nine West 57th St.
New York 10019   (212) 371-5800

Established in 1972 in New York.
Donor(s): Sony Corporation of America.
Financial data: (yr. ended 12/31/84): Assets,
$72,920 (M); gifts received, $360,000;
expenditures, $371,284, including $360,941
for 200 grants (high: $62,500; low: $25) and
$9,940 for 2 grants to individuals.
Purpose and activities: Grants largely for
hospitals, higher education, including
scholarships for children of company
employees, community funds, the performing
arts, and Japanese and other cultural programs.
Types of support awarded: General purposes,
operating budgets, continuing support, annual
campaigns, seed money, emergency funds,
deficit financing, building funds, equipment,
land acquisition, endowment funds, employee
matching gifts, internships, employee related
scholarships.
Limitations: No grants to individuals (except
for scholarships for children of company
employees), or for special projects, research,
publications, or conferences; no loans.
Application information:
  Initial approach: Letter
  Copies of proposal: 1
  Deadline(s): None
  Board meeting date(s): Quarterly
  Final notification: 1 week
  Write: Kenneth L. Nees, Vice-President
Officers and Directors: Akio Morita,
Chairman; Kenji Tamiya, President; Kenneth L.
Nees, Vice-President and Secretary; Robert D.
Dillon, Jr., Norio Ohga, Harvey L. Schein, Vice-
Presidents.
Number of staff: None.
Employer Identification Number: 237181637

2946
Soros (George) Charitable Trust ¤
10 Columbus Circle
New York 10019

Established in 1968.
Donor(s): George Soros.
Financial data: (yr. ended 12/31/82): Assets,
$107,374 (M); gifts received, $87,000;
expenditures, $107,905, including $107,409
for 21 grants (high: $38,880; low: $100).
Purpose and activities: Primarily local giving
for higher education, cultural programs, and an
African relief agency.
Limitations: Giving primarily in New York, NY.
Officer: George Soros, Administrator.
Employer Identification Number: 237012841

2947
Sperry Corporation Foundation ▼
1290 Ave. of the Americas
New York 10104   (212) 484-4209

Trust established in 1953 in New York as
Remington Rand Foundation, Inc.
Donor(s): Sperry Corporation.
Financial data: (yr. ended 12/31/82): Assets,
$327,517 (M); gifts received, $157,127;
expenditures, $1,867,891, including
$1,759,640 for 362 grants (high: $200,000;
low: $250) and $104,423 for 703 employee
matching gifts.
Purpose and activities: Charitable and
educational purposes; general giving, with
emphasis on community funds, higher
education, cultural organizations, hospitals, and
health agencies.
Limitations: No grants to individuals; no loans.
Application information:
  Initial approach: Full proposal
  Copies of proposal: 1
  Deadline(s): Submit proposal preferably in
     October
  Board meeting date(s): March and September
Manager: Katherine Harrington.
Trustee: The Chase Manhattan Bank.
Employer Identification Number: 136028101

2948
Spingold (Nate B. and Frances)
Foundation, Inc. ▼
c/o James R. Halperin
One Dag Hammarskjold Plaza
New York 10017   (212) 940-8324

Incorporated in 1955 in New York.
Donor(s): Frances Spingold,† Nathan B.
Spingold.†
Financial data: (yr. ended 11/30/82): Assets,
$11,249,788 (M); gifts received, $513,750;
expenditures, $1,478,021, including $961,920
for 70 grants (high: $88,750; low: $450;
average: $500-$25,000).
Purpose and activities: Primarily local giving,
as well as the state of Israel, to improve the
human condition through health and human
services, with emphasis on meeting pediatric,
geriatric and gerentological needs; expand
opportunities for research and higher
education, particularly in the medical sciences;
and foster the development of the visual,
performing and communication arts by
providing opportunities for talented young
artists, and by making arts available to more
people.
Types of support awarded: Conferences and
seminars, fellowships, internships, matching
funds, professorships, research, scholarship
funds, special projects.
Limitations: Giving primarily in the New York,
NY, metropolitan area and in Israel. No
support for international activities. No grants to
individuals, or for building or endowment
funds, annual campaigns, or general operating
purposes; no loans.
Publications: Annual report, application
guidelines.
Application information:
  Initial approach: Full proposal
  Copies of proposal: 1

Deadline(s): None
Board meeting date(s): Monthly
Final notification: 90 days
Write: James R. Halperin, Executive Vice-President
Officers and Directors: Samuel Strasbourger, President; James R. Halperin, Executive Vice-President, Secretary, and Treasurer; Melvyn C. Levitan, Vice-President.
Number of staff: None.
Employer Identification Number: 136107659

2949
Sprague (The Seth) Educational and Charitable Foundation ▼
c/o U.S. Trust Company of New York
45 Wall St.
New York 10005   (212) 806-4500

Trust established in 1939 in New York.
Donor(s): Seth Sprague.†
Financial data: (yr. ended 12/31/82): Assets, $22,571,906 (M); expenditures, $1,830,802, including $1,430,000 for 434 grants (high: $25,000; low: $500; average: $2,500).
Purpose and activities: Broad purposes; general giving locally and in Massachusetts as well, with emphasis on hospitals, health organizations and medical research, social welfare agencies, cultural organizations, including museums and performing arts, youth and child welfare agencies, and higher and secondary education.
Types of support awarded: Operating budgets, continuing support, seed money.
Limitations: Giving primarily in NY and MA. No grants to individuals, or for capital or endowment funds, matching gifts, scholarships or fellowships, special projects, research, publications, or conferences; no loans.
Publications: Application guidelines.
Application information:
Initial approach: Telephone
Copies of proposal: 1
Deadline(s): Mid-May and mid-October
Board meeting date(s): March, June, September, and November
Final notification: Up to 6 months
Write: Maureen Augusciak, Vice-President or Anne L. Smith, Assistant Vice-President
Trustees: Walter G. Dunnington, Jr., Arline Ripley Greenleaf, Jacqueline N. Simpkins, United States Trust Company of New York (Maureen Augusciak, Vice-President).
Number of staff: None.
Employer Identification Number: 136071886

2950
St. Faith's House Foundation
P.O. Box 7189
Ardsley-on-Hudson 10503   (914) 631-0053
Grant application office: c/o Ms. Ann D. Phillips, 16 Crest Dr., Tarrytown, NY 10591

Incorporated in 1901 in New York as St. Faith's House; reorganized in 1973.
Financial data: (yr. ended 6/30/84): Assets, $3,472,473 (M); expenditures, $170,902, including $142,500 for 21 grants (high: $12,000; low: $2,000; average: $6,000-$10,000).

Purpose and activities: To make grants for services to and for children and young people in Westchester County.
Types of support awarded: Continuing support, seed money, emergency funds, equipment, matching funds, special projects.
Limitations: Giving limited to Westchester County, NY. No grants to individuals, or for building or endowment funds, or operating budgets.
Publications: Application guidelines, 990-PF.
Application information: Application form required.
Initial approach: Letter
Copies of proposal: 11
Deadline(s): Submit proposal preferably in August, November, or January; deadlines September 1, December 1, and March 1
Board meeting date(s): October, January, and April
Write: Ms. Ann D. Phillips, Grants Committee Chairman
Officers and Directors: Mrs. William Shore, President; Mrs. J.B. Stewart, Vice-President; Horace J. McAfee, Secretary; Daniel H. Childs, Treasurer; Mrs. Frederick Childs, Mrs. Robert W. Lyman, Mrs. Arthur O. Mojo, Robert C. Myers, Ann D. Phillips, Mrs. Maarten van Hengel.
Number of staff: None.
Employer Identification Number: 131740123

2951
Standard Brands Charitable, Scientific and Educational Foundation, The
625 Madison Ave.
New York 10022   (212) 759-4400

Trust established in 1945 in New York.
Donor(s): Standard Brands, Inc.
Financial data: (yr. ended 2/28/83): Assets, $769,788 (M); expenditures, $208,919, including $203,700 for 13 grants (high: $48,000; low: $2,000).
Purpose and activities: Grants primarily to charities in which the donor is interested, including institutions concerned with nutrition, higher education, a performing arts center, and community funds.
Types of support awarded: Continuing support, annual campaigns, research, fellowships.
Limitations: No grants to individuals.
Application information:
Initial approach: Full proposal
Copies of proposal: 1
Deadline(s): Submit proposal preferably in January; deadline January 31
Board meeting date(s): May
Write: Michael M. Masterpool, Senior Vice-President, Corporate Affairs
Trustees: Walter G. Dunnington, Jr., F. Ross Johnson, George F. Karch, S. Lanier, W. Earle McLaughlin, Ellmore C. Patterson, Manufacturers Hanover Trust Company.
Employer Identification Number: 136046118

2952
Stanley-Timolat Foundation, Inc., The
122 East 42nd St., Suite 3902
New York 10168   (212) 697-8917

Foundation incorporated in 1960 in New York.
Donor(s): Alma Timolat Stanley.†
Financial data: (yr. ended 12/31/83): Assets, $1,443,956 (M); expenditures, $118,022, including $106,500 for 25 grants (high: $17,000; low: $1,000).
Purpose and activities: Broad purposes; primarily local giving, with emphasis on arts and culture, hospitals and health agencies, and a secondary school.
Limitations: Giving limited to Staten Island, NY, and Monmouth and Morris counties, NJ. No grants to individuals.
Application information:
Initial approach: Letter
Copies of proposal: 2
Deadline(s): November 25
Board meeting date(s): December
Final notification: 15 to 20 days
Write: Robert Crooks Stanley, Jr., President
Officers: Robert Crooks Stanley, Jr.,* President; Robert C. Stanley, III,* Colton P. Wagner,* Vice-Presidents; Teresa Thomson, Secretary and Treasurer.
Trustees:* Virginia Anne Kehoe, Alma W. Wood.
Number of staff: 1.
Employer Identification Number: 136163112

2953
Starr (Anne and Jacob) Foundation ⌑
2101 Broadway
New York 10023

Incorporated in 1964 in New York.
Donor(s): Jacob Starr.
Financial data: (yr. ended 11/30/82): Assets, $922,665 (M); expenditures, $264,895, including $245,286 for 19 grants (high: $28,150; low: $150).
Purpose and activities: Grants mainly for Jewish welfare funds and educational organizations.
Officers: Melvin Starr, President; Lita Starr, Vice-President; Morris Carsons, Secretary.
Employer Identification Number: 136193022

2954
Starr Foundation, The ▼
70 Pine St.
New York 10270   (212) 770-6882

Incorporated in 1955 in New York.
Donor(s): Cornelius V. Starr,† related corporations, and others.
Financial data: (yr. ended 12/31/83): Assets, $258,384,711 (M); gifts received, $35,338; expenditures, $14,240,216, including $13,537,906 for 178 grants (high: $2,000,000; low: $150; average: $1,000-$50,000) and $417,991 for 219 grants to individuals.

Purpose and activities: Broad purposes; grants largely for education with emphasis on higher education, including scholarships under specific programs; also limited contributions to hospitals and medical research, cultural programs, international affairs organizations, and social services.
Types of support awarded: Continuing support, annual campaigns, building funds, endowment funds, professorships, student aid, scholarship funds, fellowships, research.
Limitations: No grants to individuals (except through foundation's scholarship program), or for matching gifts; no loans.
Publications: 990-PF.
Application information:
Initial approach: Letter
Copies of proposal: 1
Deadline(s): None
Board meeting date(s): February and September
Write: Ta Chun Hsu, President
Officers: Ta Chun Hsu,* President; Marion I. Breen,* Vice-President; Ida E. Galler, Secretary; Frank R. Tengi, Treasurer.
Directors: Maurice R. Greenberg, Chairman; Houghton Freeman, Edwin A.G. Manton, John J. Roberts, Ernest E. Stempel.
Number of staff: 1 full-time professional; 3 full-time support.
Employer Identification Number: 136151545

2955
Statler Foundation, The ▼
Statler Tower, Suite 508
Buffalo 14202 (716) 852-1104

Trust established in 1934 in New York.
Donor(s): Ellsworth Milton Statler.†
Financial data: (yr. ended 12/31/84): Assets, $16,877,714 (M); expenditures, $716,840, including $368,390 for 18 grants (high: $200,000; low: $250).
Purpose and activities: Education and research for the benefit of the hotel industry in the United States. Income used for endowments, scholarship funds, and awards to colleges and schools teaching hotel techniques and for grants to schools and others for research projects and for programs to train and increase the proficiency of hotel workers. The foundation also provides funds to local social service agencies to support food services to the needy.
Types of support awarded: Endowment funds, scholarship funds, research, building funds, professorships, program-related investments, equipment.
Limitations: Giving primarily in upstate NY.
Application information: Application form required for scholarships in the hospitality field.
Initial approach: Letter
Deadline(s): April 15
Write: Peter J. Crotty, Chairman
Trustees: Peter J. Crotty, Chairman; M. Robert Koren, Arthur F. Musarra.
Number of staff: 1 full-time professional.
Employer Identification Number: 131889077

2956
Stebbins Fund, Inc., The
R.D. Box 1792, Route 106
Syosset 11791 (212) 267-8181

Incorporated in 1947 in New York.
Donor(s): Members of the Stebbins family.
Financial data: (yr. ended 12/31/82): Assets, $1,353,845 (M); expenditures, $89,933, including $76,250 for 39 grants (high: $8,600; low: $100).
Purpose and activities: Broad purposes; support to charitable organizations of personal interest to the officers.
Limitations: No grants to individuals or for endowment funds; no loans.
Application information: Applications for grants are not invited.
Board meeting date(s): June
Write: James F. Stebbins, President
Officers: James F. Stebbins,* President; Jane S. Greenleaf,* Vice-President and Treasurer; Mary Emma Stebbins,* Theodore E. Stebbins,* Vice-Presidents; Meredith M. Brown, Secretary.
Directors: Francis T.P. Plimpton, J. Wright Rumbough, Jr.
Employer Identification Number: 116021709

2957
Steele-Reese Foundation, The ▼
c/o Davidson, Dawson & Clark
330 Madison Ave., 35th Fl.
New York 10017 (212) 557-7700
Additional addresses: John R. Bryden, Director for Appalachia, 760 Malabu Dr., Lexington, KY 40502; Lydia Schofield, Scholarship Director for Idaho, 602 First St. North, Salmon, ID 83467; Robert T.H. Davidson, Correspondent for Northwestern Grants, 65 Parker Hill Rd. Ext., Killingworth, CT 06417

Trust established in 1955 in New York.
Donor(s): Eleanor Steele Reese,† Emmet P. Reese.†
Financial data: (yr. ended 8/31/84): Assets, $14,982,147 (M); gifts received, $727,445; expenditures, $588,581, including $410,000 for 26 grants (high: $80,000; low: $750).
Purpose and activities: Principally to aid organized charities in southern Appalachia and Idaho and adjacent states. Giving for higher education, with some support for conservation, cultural programs, and general education.
Types of support awarded: Operating budgets, equipment, endowment funds, matching funds, professorships, scholarship funds.
Limitations: Giving primarily in southern Appalachia, as well as ID and adjacent states; scholarship program limited to students from Lemhi and Custer counties, ID. No grants to individuals, or for continuing support, annual campaigns, seed money, emergency or building funds, deficit financing, research, or land acquisition; no loans.
Publications: Program policy statement, application guidelines.
Application information:
Initial approach: Letter
Copies of proposal: 3
Deadline(s): Submit proposal between March and May; deadline May 31

Board meeting date(s): Monthly
Final notification: 3 to 6 months
Write: William T. Buice, III, Trustee
Trustees: William T. Buice, III, Robert T.H. Davidson, Morgan Guaranty Trust Company of New York.
Number of staff: 3 part-time support.
Employer Identification Number: 136034763

2958
Stein (Joseph F.) Foundation, Inc.
28 Aspen Rd.
Scarsdale 10583 (914) 725-1770

Incorporated in 1954 in New York.
Donor(s): Joseph F. Stein,† and others.
Financial data: (yr. ended 12/31/84): Assets, $4,225,000 (M); gifts received, $283,000; expenditures, $288,000, including $279,000 for 150 grants (high: $10,000; low: $50; average: $500).
Purpose and activities: Broad purposes; grants largely for local Jewish welfare and social activities; some support for higher and secondary education, including religious education, and medical research.
Types of support awarded: General purposes, building funds, scholarship funds, equipment, research.
Limitations: Giving primarily in NY. No grants to individuals, or for scholarships, fellowships, or matching gifts; no loans.
Application information:
Initial approach: Letter
Copies of proposal: 1
Board meeting date(s): Monthly
Write: Melvin M. Stein, Vice-President
Officers and Directors: Melvin M. Stein, Vice-President; Allen A. Stein, Secretary.
Number of staff: None.
Employer Identification Number: 136097095

2959
Steinbach (Ruth and Milton) Fund, Inc. ⌺
c/o Harry Goodkin & Company
60 East 42nd St.
New York 10165

Incorporated in 1950 in New York.
Donor(s): Milton Steinbach.†
Financial data: (yr. ended 10/31/83): Assets, $3,751,010 (M); expenditures, $197,469, including $185,650 for 14 grants (high: $40,000; low: $500).
Purpose and activities: Charitable purposes; grants largely for Jewish welfare funds, secondary and higher education, hospitals and a social science research institute.
Limitations: Giving primarily in NY.
Officers and Directors: Ruth A. Steinbach, President; John Klingenstein, John S. Hilson, Vice-Presidents; Frederick A. Klingenstein, Treasurer.
Employer Identification Number: 136028785

2960
Stern Fund
370 Lexington Ave.
New York 10017   (212) 532-0617

Incorporated in 1936 in Louisiana.
Donor(s): Members of the Stern family.
Financial data: (yr. ended 12/31/83): Assets,
$1,264,162 (M); expenditures, $666,359,
including $363,500 for 21 grants (high:
$40,000; low: $2,000).
Purpose and activities: Broad purposes; to
foster democracy and social and institutional
responsiveness in the public and private arenas
of America. To this end seeks to identify and
support energetic, strategically rational,
theoretically well-grounded efforts to effect
appropriate institutional development or
change; to develop new ways of life and work;
to redress the imbalances and inequities of
American life; and to defend existing
constitutional and institutional protections of
freedom.
Types of support awarded: Seed money,
matching funds, research, publications, special
projects, general purposes, loans.
Limitations: No grants to individuals, or for
building or endowment funds, or scholarships
and fellowships.
Publications: Application guidelines.
Application information:
  Initial approach: Full proposal or letter
  Copies of proposal: 1
  Deadline(s): None
  Board meeting date(s): Semiannually in the
    fall and spring
  Final notification: Within 3 weeks if proposal
    is not considered
  Write: David R. Hunter, Executive Director
Officers: Thomas A. Troyer,* Secretary; David
R. Hunter, Executive Director.
Directors:* Helen Hess, Susan Hess, William
D. Hess, Sandra MacIver, William MacIver,
David Stern, Eve Stern, Henry Stern, Paula
Stern, Philip M. Stern, Dale Wiehoff.
Number of staff: 4.
Employer Identification Number: 720467504

2961
**Stern (Jerome L. and Jane) Foundation,
Inc.** ⌑
745 Fifth Ave.
New York 10022

Incorporated in 1944 in New York.
Donor(s): Members of the Stern family.
Financial data: (yr. ended 2/28/83): Assets,
$1,640,130 (M); gifts received, $132,775;
expenditures, $116,510, including $114,437
for grants.
Purpose and activities: Primarily local giving,
with emphasis on Jewish religious education,
temple support, and Jewish welfare funds;
some support also for museums.
Limitations: Giving primarily in NY.
Officers: Jerome L. Stern, Chairman and Vice-
President; Jane M. Stern, President; Henriette J.
Stern, Treasurer.
Employer Identification Number: 136127063

2962
**Stevens (J. P.) & Co., Inc.
Foundation** ▼ ⌑
1185 Ave. of the Americas
New York 10036   (212) 930-2526

Incorporated in 1959 in New York.
Donor(s): J.P. Stevens & Co., Inc.
Financial data: (yr. ended 10/31/83): Assets,
$1,633,596 (M); gifts received, $518,000;
expenditures, $902,743, including $741,888
for 433 grants (high: $60,000; low: $25;
average: $25-$5,000) and $137,238 for 169
employee matching gifts.
Purpose and activities: Broad purposes; grants
for higher and secondary education,
community funds, hospitals and health
agencies, church support, social and civic
agencies, including youth programs, and
cultural programs.
Types of support awarded: Employee
matching gifts.
Limitations: Giving primarily in areas of
company operations, especially NC, SC, and
New York City, NY. No grants to individuals
or for building funds.
Application information:
  Initial approach: Letter
  Copies of proposal: 1
  Deadline(s): Submit proposal preferably in
    September; deadline October 1
  Board meeting date(s): Semiannually and as
    required
  Final notification: 1 to 2 months
  Write: James R. Franklin, Administrator
Officers: John W. Wagner,* President and
Treasurer; Whitney Stevens,* Vice-President;
Margaret T. Hulz, Secretary; James R. Franklin,
Administrator.
Directors:* Ward Burns, Henry Ponder.
Number of staff: None.
Employer Identification Number: 136150183

2963
Stony Wold - Herbert Fund, Inc.
136 East 57th St., Rm. 1705
New York 10022   (212) 753-6565

Incorporated in 1974 in New York.
Financial data: (yr. ended 12/31/84): Assets,
$3,120,320 (M); gifts received, $3,454;
expenditures, $227,920, including $113,657
for 14 grants (high: $12,310; low: $1,250;
average: $8,000) and $40,875 for 15 grants to
individuals.
Purpose and activities: Grants for local
hospitals and medical research in the
respiratory field; pulmonary fellowship grants;
and scholarships for college and vocational
school students with respiratory ailments.
Types of support awarded: Continuing
support, deficit financing, fellowships, special
projects, research, conferences and seminars,
student aid.
Limitations: Giving primarily in NY. No grants
for capital or endowment funds, or for
operating budgets, annual campaigns, seed
money, emergency funds, or matching gifts; no
loans.
Publications: Application guidelines.
Application information: Application form
required.

Initial approach: Letter or telephone
Copies of proposal: 6
Deadline(s): October 15 for research and
  fellowship grants
Board meeting date(s): November, March,
  and June
Final notification: 2 to 3 weeks
Write: Mrs. Cheryl S. Friedman, Executive
  Director
Officers: William C. Breed, III, President;
Cheryl S. Friedman, Executive Director.
Number of staff: 1 part-time professional.
Employer Identification Number: 132784124

2964
Stott (Robert L.) Foundation, Inc. ⌑
20 Broad St.
New York 10005

Incorporated in 1957 in New York.
Donor(s): Robert L. Stott.†
Financial data: (yr. ended 12/31/81): Assets,
$1,233,854 (M); expenditures, $90,045,
including $81,500 for 25 grants (high: $10,000;
low: $1,000).
Purpose and activities: Broad purposes; grants
largely for aid to hospitals and secondary
education, primarily in New York and Palm
Beach, Florida.
Limitations: Giving primarily in NY, and in
Palm Beach, FL.
Officers and Directors: Robert L. Stott, Jr.,
President; Leonard Wagner, Vice-President;
Donald B. Stott, Secretary and Treasurer.
Employer Identification Number: 136061943

2965
**Straus (Martha Washington) - Harry H.
Straus Foundation, Inc.** ⌑
Sky Meadow Farm, Lincoln Ave.
Port Chester 10573

Incorporated in 1949 in North Carolina.
Donor(s): Harry H. Straus, Sr.†
Financial data: (yr. ended 12/31/82): Assets,
$1,514,000 (M); expenditures, $127,197,
including $122,450 for 98 grants (high:
$16,000; low: $100).
Purpose and activities: Broad purposes; grants
for medical research, higher education,
including medical education, hospitals, and
health and welfare funds.
Limitations: No grants to individuals.
Application information: Application for
grants not encouraged.
  Board meeting date(s): As required
  Write: Roger J. King, Secretary
Officers and Trustees: Louise Straus King,
President; Betty B. Straus, Vice-President; Roger
J. King, Secretary and Treasurer; Harry H.
Straus III.
Employer Identification Number: 560645526

2966
**Straus (The Philip A. and Lynn)
Foundation, Inc.** ⌑
1037 Constable Dr. South
Mamaroneck 10543

Incorporated about 1957 in New York.

Donor(s): Philip A. Straus.
Financial data: (yr. ended 3/31/83): Assets, $2,883,724 (M); expenditures, $211,807, including $205,920 for 83 grants (high: $52,850; low: $50).
Purpose and activities: Broad purposes; primarily local giving, with emphasis on higher education, Jewish welfare funds, international cooperation, child welfare, civil rights organizations, and cultural programs.
Limitations: Giving primarily in NY.
Application information:
  Write: Philip A. Straus, President
Officers and Trustees: Philip A. Straus, President; Lynn Straus, Vice-President and Treasurer; John W. Herz, Secretary.
Employer Identification Number: 136161223

2967
Stuart Foundation, Inc., The
126 E. 56th St.
New York 10022   (212) 753-0800

Incorporated in 1951 in New York.
Donor(s): Members of the Stuart family.
Financial data: (yr. ended 12/31/83): Assets, $1,411,251 (M); expenditures, $85,331, including $57,245 for grants.
Purpose and activities: Broad purposes; primarily local giving.
Limitations: Giving primarily in NY and New England.
Application information:
  Write: James M. Stuart, Treasurer
Officers and Directors:* Elizabeth L. Stuart,* President; Alan L. Stuart,* Vice-President; Beatrice M. Smith, Secretary; James M. Stuart,* Treasurer and Manager.
Employer Identification Number: 136066191

2968
Sullivan (William Matheus) Musical Foundation, Inc.
c/o Hugh Ross
410 East 57th St.
New York 10022

Incorporated in 1956 in New York.
Donor(s): William Matheus Sullivan,† Arcie Lubetkin.†
Financial data: (yr. ended 12/31/82): Assets, $1,798,135 (M); gifts received, $10,497; expenditures, $115,138, including $72,250 for 8 grants (high: $50,000; low: $500) and $7,900 for 32 grants to individuals.
Purpose and activities: To advance the careers of gifted young singers, who have completed their formal music training, either directly or by finding engagements for them via assistance given to orchestras, operatic societies, or other musical groups; grants based on financial need of applicant.
Types of support awarded: Grants to individuals, continuing support, special projects.
Limitations: No support for general fields of music education and vocal or instrument training. No grants for building or endowment funds, or for operating budgets.
Publications: Application guidelines.

Application information: Requests for New York auditions should be accompanied by resume and copy of contract for at least one engagement with full orchestra after November; West Coast auditions may be reestablished soon. Application form required.
  Initial approach: Letter or proposal, detailing educational and musical experience
  Copies of proposal: 1
  Deadline(s): Submit proposal preferably between September and June; deadline October 10 for New York audition requests
  Board meeting date(s): 5 or 6 times a year as required
  Write: Hugh Ross, Executive Director
Officers and Trustees: Spencer Byard, President; Hugh Ross, Vice-President and Executive Director; Jose T. Moscoso, Secretary; George L. Boveroux, Jr., Treasurer; Richard Gaddes, David Lloyd, Barbara B. Mestre, Maria M. Moore, Lowell Wadmond.
Employer Identification Number: 136069096

2969
Sulzberger Foundation, Inc., The
229 West 43rd St.
New York 10036   (212) 556-1878

Incorporated in 1956 in New York.
Donor(s): Arthur Hays Sulzberger,† Mrs. Iphigene Ochs Sulzberger.
Financial data: (yr. ended 12/31/83): Assets, $5,471,900 (M); gifts received, $500,000; expenditures, $388,715, including $358,585 for grants (high: $36,500; low: $100).
Purpose and activities: Broad purposes; grants largely for education, cultural programs, hospitals, community funds, and welfare funds.
Limitations: Giving primarily in NY and Chattanooga, TN. No grants to individuals, or for endowment funds, or matching gifts; no loans.
Application information:
  Initial approach: Telephone
  Board meeting date(s): January and as required
Officers and Directors: Marian S. Heiskell, President; Arthur Ochs Sulzberger, Vice-President, Secretary, and Treasurer; Judith S. Levinson, Ruth S. Holmberg, Vice-Presidents; Iphigene Ochs Sulzberger.
Employer Identification Number: 136083166

2970
Summerfield (Solon E.) Foundation, Inc. ▼ ⌑
270 Madison Ave.
New York 10016   (212) 685-5524

Incorporated in 1939 in New York.
Donor(s): Solon E. Summerfield.†
Financial data: (yr. ended 12/31/82): Assets, $16,688,189 (M); expenditures, $989,820, including $752,880 for 102 grants (high: $283,337; low: $100).
Purpose and activities: Broad purposes; three-fourths of funds paid to designated recipients; remaining one-fourth distributed largely for higher education; some support, primarily local, for social services.

Application information: Funds largely committed; no applications accepted.
  Write: William W. Prager, President
Officers and Directors: William W. Prager, President; Clarence R. Treeger, Vice-President; Joseph A. Tiano, Secretary and Treasurer.
Employer Identification Number: 131797260

2971
Sun Chemical Foundation ⌑
200 Park Ave.
New York 10166

Established in 1967.
Donor(s): Sun Chemical Corporation.
Financial data: (yr. ended 12/31/83): Assets, $161,169 (M); gifts received, $103,750; expenditures, $111,798, including $111,350 for 38 grants (high: $45,000; low: $50).
Purpose and activities: Primarily local giving to Jewish welfare funds, higher education, and social services.
Limitations: Giving primarily in NY.
Officer: Norman E. Alexander, Principal Manager.
Employer Identification Number: 237000821

2972
Surdna Foundation, Inc. ▼
250 Park Ave., Rm. 528
New York 10177   (212) 697-0630

Incorporated in 1917 in New York.
Donor(s): John E. Andrus.†
Financial data: (yr. ended 6/30/83): Assets, $243,073,565 (M); gifts received, $1,247,665; expenditures, $15,381,271, including $14,724,555 for 100 grants (high: $250,000; low: $3,374; average: $10,000-$100,000).
Purpose and activities: Broad purposes; support primarily for higher education, medical education, health care delivery, medical research, social concerns, and cultural affairs.
Types of support awarded: Seed money, emergency funds, equipment, matching funds, internships, scholarship funds, fellowships, special projects, research.
Limitations: Giving limited to the northeastern US, with emphasis on NY. No grants to individuals, or for operating budgets, continuing support, annual campaigns, deficit financing, building funds, land acquisition, publications, or conferences; no loans.
Publications: Biennial report, program policy statement, application guidelines.
Application information:
  Initial approach: Letter
  Copies of proposal: 1
  Deadline(s): July 1, October 1, January 1, and April 1
  Board meeting date(s): February, May, September, and November
  Final notification: 2 weeks
  Write: Mrs. Lindsley Homrighausen, Administrator for Grants
Officers: Edward F. McGee,* President; Leonard A. Blue,* Vice-President and Secretary; Russell R. Roetger,* Vice-President; Donald R. Spaidal,* Treasurer; Mrs. Lindsley Homrighausen, Administrator for Grants.

Directors:* John E. Andrus III, Chairman; Peter B. Benedict, Lawrence S.C. Griffith, Julia A. Moon, Robert H. Taylor.
Number of staff: 1 full-time professional; 1 full-time support.
Employer Identification Number: 136108163

2973
Sussman (Otto) Trust ☐
c/o Sullivan and Cromwell
125 Broad St.
New York 10004

Trust established in 1947 in New York.
Donor(s): Otto Sussman.†
Financial data: (yr. ended 12/31/83): Assets, $1,538,377 (M); expenditures, $76,672, including $52,114 for 25 grants to individuals.
Purpose and activities: Assistance to persons in need due to death or illness in their immediate families or some other unusual or unfortunate circumstance.
Types of support awarded: Grants to individuals, student aid.
Limitations: Giving limited to residents of NY, NJ, OK, and PA.
Application information: Application form required.
Deadline(s): None
Trustees: Arthur H. Dean, Edward S. Miller, Erwin A. Weil.
Employer Identification Number: 136075849

2974
Swanson Foundation, The ☐
122 East 42nd St.
New York 10017

Incorporated in 1952 in New York.
Donor(s): Glen E. Swanson.
Financial data: (yr. ended 12/31/82): Assets, $2,132,081 (M); expenditures, $130,071, including $126,400 for 18 grants (high: $50,000; low: $100).
Purpose and activities: General giving, largely in southern California, with emphasis on medical research and hospitals.
Limitations: Giving primarily in CA.
Officer: Glen E. Swanson, President.
Employer Identification Number: 136108509

2975
Switzer Foundation
5 Beekman St., Rm. 512
New York 10038   (212) 964-1034

Incorporated in 1909 in New York.
Donor(s): Margaret Switzer,† Sarah Switzer.†
Financial data: (yr. ended 12/31/84): Assets, $2,810,788 (M); expenditures, $197,258, including $152,634 for grants.
Purpose and activities: To provide scholarships for girls and women, particularly nursing students, through grants directly to schools primarily in the New York metropolitan area.
Types of support awarded: Scholarship funds.

Limitations: Giving primarily in the New York, NY, metropolitan area. No grants to individuals, or for building or endowment funds, operating budgets, or special projects.
Publications: Annual report, informational brochure, program policy statement, application guidelines.
Application information: Application form required.
Initial approach: Letter
Copies of proposal: 1
Deadline(s): Submit proposal preferably between January and June; deadline June 30
Board meeting date(s): April and October
Final notification: 3 months
Write: Mrs. Mary D. Butler, Secretary
Officers: Francis L. Dougan, President; John A. Bamonte, Vice-President; Mary D. Butler, Secretary and Treasurer.
Number of staff: 2 full-time professional.
Employer Identification Number: 135596831

2976
Taconic Foundation, Inc. ▼
745 Fifth Ave., Suite 1111
New York 10151   (212) 758-8673

Incorporated in 1958 in Delaware.
Donor(s): Stephen R. Currier,† Mrs. Stephen R. Currier.†
Financial data: (yr. ended 12/31/83): Assets, $14,874,839 (M); expenditures, $1,058,478, including $585,653 for 32 grants (high: $230,800; low: $1,300; average: $2,000-$15,000), $222,908 for 1 foundation-administered program and $140,491 for 3 loans.
Purpose and activities: Grants, primarily in the New York City area, for programs furthering equal opportunity; current emphasis on housing and youth employment.
Types of support awarded: Seed money, program-related investments, general purposes, continuing support.
Limitations: Giving primarily in the New York City, NY, area. No support for higher education, arts and cultural programs, mass media, crime and justice, health, medicine, mental health, ecology and the enviroment, individual economic development projects, or local community programs outside New York City. No grants to individuals, or for building and endowment funds, scholarships, or fellowships; no loans.
Publications: Program policy statement, application guidelines.
Application information:
Initial approach: Letter or proposal
Copies of proposal: 1
Deadline(s): None
Board meeting date(s): 4 to 6 times a year
Final notification: 2 to 3 months
Write: Mrs. Jane Lee J. Eddy, Executive Director
Officers and Directors: John G. Simon, President and Treasurer; Lloyd K. Garrison, Vice-President; Jane Lee J. Eddy, Executive Director and Secretary; Michael S. Currier, Alan J. Dworsky, Harold C. Fleming, Dorothy Hirshon, Vernon E. Jordan, Jr.

Number of staff: 1 full-time professional; 1 part-time professional; 2 full-time support; 1 part-time support.
Employer Identification Number: 131873668

2977
Tananbaum (Martin) Foundation, Inc. ☐
261 Madison Ave., 16th Fl.
New York 10017   (212) 687-3440

Incorporated in 1958 in New York.
Donor(s): Martin Tananbaum.†
Financial data: (yr. ended 12/31/82): Assets, $2,322,870 (M); expenditures, $421,000, including $329,382 for 107 grants (high: $81,850; low: $50).
Purpose and activities: Grants largely for Jewish welfare funds, theological education, and health agencies.
Limitations: No grants to individuals, or for building or endowment funds.
Application information:
Initial approach: Letter
Copies of proposal: 7
Deadline(s): Submit proposal between October and April
Board meeting date(s): Monthly
Write: Arnold Alperstein, President
Officers and Directors: Arnold Alperstein, President; Elbert Brodsky, Vice-President; Florence Levine, Secretary; Minnie Lee Tananbaum, Treasurer; Barbara Tananbaum DeGeorge, Ida Goldstick.
Members: Eileen Alperstein, Amy Colon.
Employer Identification Number: 136162900

2978
Taylor (Fred and Harriett) Foundation ☐
c/o Lincoln First Bank of Rochester
P.O. Box 1412
Rochester 14603

Trust established in New York.
Donor(s): Fred C. Taylor.†
Financial data: (yr. ended 12/31/82): Assets, $5,005,883 (M); expenditures, $329,947, including $307,524 for 18 grants (high: $23,356; low: $1,393).
Purpose and activities: Local giving in the Hammondsport, New York area, with emphasis on education, hospitals, Protestant church support and religious associations, youth agencies, and health associations.
Limitations: Giving limited to the Hammondsport, NY, area.
Trustee: Lincoln First Bank of Rochester.
Employer Identification Number: 166205365

2979
Teagle Foundation, Incorporated, The ▼
30 Rockefeller Plaza, Rm. 2835
New York 10112   (212) 247-1946

Incorporated in 1944 in Connecticut.
Donor(s): Walter C. Teagle,† Rowena Lee Teagle,† Walter C. Teagle, Jr.†

Financial data: (yr. ended 5/31/83): Assets, $48,039,139 (M); gifts received, $1,440; expenditures, $3,233,899, including $1,416,000 for 73 grants (high: $55,000; low: $500; average: $10,000-$35,000) and $1,214,895 for grants to individuals.

Purpose and activities: Scholarships to children of employees of Exxon Corporation and its affiliates (program administered by College Scholarship Service, Princeton, (N.J.); grants to educational institutions for financial aid programs in the areas of general, medical, nursing, and theological scholarships (selection of recipient and amount of stipend determined by the school). Support also for community organizations and youth activities and direct assistance grants to needy employees, annuitants and widows of deceased employees of the corporation.

Types of support awarded: Seed money, equipment, scholarship funds, research, employee related scholarships, grants to individuals.

Limitations: No support for primary or secondary education. No grants for operating budgets, continuing support, annual campaigns, building or endowment funds, deficit financing, emergency funds, land acquisition, renovation projects, publications, conferences, special projects, or matching gifts; no loans.

Publications: Annual report.

Application information:

Initial approach: Letter or full proposal
Copies of proposal: 1
Deadline(s): Prior to board meetings; scholarship deadline November 1 for receipt by College Scholarship Service
Board meeting date(s): October, January, and May
Final notification: 2 weeks after board meeting
Write: Mary R. Williams, Chairman

Officers: George T. Piercy,* President; Trygve H. Tonnessen, Executive Vice-President; Dean W. Malott, Vice-President; Margaret B. Sullivan, Secretary; Maurice J. Boland, Treasurer.

Directors:* Mary R. Williams,* Chairman; George Bugliarello, John S. Chalsty, Jackson O. Hall, Deane W. Malott, Vincent J. Motto, Jansen Noyes, Jr., Stephen Stamas, Walter C. Teagle III, Albert J. Wetzel.

Number of staff: 2 full-time professional; 1 part-time professional; 3 full-time support.

Employer Identification Number: 131773645

2980

Tebil Foundation, Inc., The ⌘

660 Madison Ave.
New York 10024

Established in 1959.

Donor(s): Edna L. Jacobs,† William K. Jacobs, Jr.

Financial data: (yr. ended 12/31/83): Assets, $67,806 (M); expenditures, $113,187, including $112,440 for grants.

Purpose and activities: Primarily local giving for museums, hospitals and health agencies, cultural programs, and social services.

Limitations: Giving primarily in NY.

Officers: William K. Jacobs, Jr., President and Treasurer; George Disipio, Secretary.

Employer Identification Number: 136082546

2981

Texaco Philanthropic Foundation Inc. ▼

2000 Westchester Ave.
White Plains 10650   (914) 253-4000

Incorporated in 1979 in Delaware.

Donor(s): Texaco, Inc.

Financial data: (yr. ended 12/31/83): Assets, $38,020,214 (M); expenditures, $7,881,235, including $7,138,055 for 481 grants (high: $3,054,950; low: $500; average: $1,000-$25,000), $138,265 for grants to individuals and $437,454 for 1,500 employee matching gifts.

Purpose and activities: Grants to enhance the quality of life; broad purposes, support primarily for cultural programs, higher education, social welfare and civic organizations, and hospitals and health agencies.

Types of support awarded: Conferences and seminars, employee matching gifts, fellowships, general purposes, research, employee related scholarships.

Limitations: No support for religious organizations. No grants to individuals (except for company-employee scholarships), or for capital funds or endowments (except for selected private non-profit hospitals), or for propaganda; no loans.

Publications: Annual report, program policy statement, application guidelines, informational brochure.

Application information:

Initial approach: Full proposal
Copies of proposal: 1
Deadline(s): None
Board meeting date(s): March, June, October, and December
Final notification: 2 months
Write: Maria Mike-Mayer, Secretary

Officers: William C. Weitzel, Jr.,* President; Maria Mike-Mayer, Secretary; E.W. Wolaham, Treasurer.

Directors:* Lorene L. Rogers, Chairman; John D. Ambler, William S. Barrack, Jr., Paul B. Hicks, Jr., George Parker, Jr., .

Number of staff: 6.

Employer Identification Number: 133007516

2982

Thompson (J. Walter) Company Fund, Inc.

466 Lexington Ave.
New York 10017   (212) 210-7000

Incorporated in 1953 in New York.

Donor(s): J. Walter Thompson Company.

Financial data: (yr. ended 11/30/84): Assets, $1,033,180 (M); gifts received, $150,000; expenditures, $163,822, including $40,460 for 11 grants (high: $10,000; low: $1,000; average: $3,700) and $62,097 for 147 employee matching gifts.

Purpose and activities: Giving to arts and educational organizations, including an educational matching gifts program. Grants generally restricted to organizations which have received longstanding support from the Fund.

Types of support awarded: Employee matching gifts.

Limitations: Giving limited to the U.S. No grants to individuals.

Application information:

Deadline(s): Submit proposal preferably before February
Board meeting date(s): February-March
Write: Hugh P. Connell, Secretary

Officers and Directors: Don Johnston, President; Hugh P. Connell, Vice-President and Secretary; Nancy Fitzpatrick, John E. Peters.

Employer Identification Number: 136020644

2983

Thorne Foundation, The ⌘

435 East 52nd St.
New York 10022

Incorporated in 1930 in New York.

Donor(s): Landon K. Thorne,† Mrs. Julia L. Thorne.†

Financial data: (yr. ended 12/31/83): Assets, $2,335,073 (M); expenditures, $104,351, including $73,199 for 49 grants (high: $25,000; low: $50).

Purpose and activities: Broad purposes; primarily local giving, with emphasis on higher education, museums, and cultural programs.

Limitations: Giving primarily in NY.

Officers: Miriam Thorne, President; David H. Thorne, Vice-President; John B. Jessup, Secretary and Treasurer.

Employer Identification Number: 136109955

2984

Thorne (The Oakleigh L.) Foundation

1633 Broadway, 30th Fl.
New York 10019

Incorporated in 1959 in New York.

Donor(s): Commerce Clearing House, Inc.

Financial data: (yr. ended 12/31/83): Assets, $342,568 (M); gifts received, $200,000; expenditures, $270,319, including $269,450 for 100 grants (high: $90,000; low: $200).

Purpose and activities: Broad purposes; general giving, with emphasis on community funds, hospitals, health agencies, higher and secondary education, youth agencies, conservation programs, and cultural programs.

Types of support awarded: General purposes, operating budgets, continuing support, annual campaigns, seed money, emergency funds, deficit financing, building funds, equipment, land acquisition, endowment funds, special projects, research, publications, conferences and seminars, consulting services.

Limitations: No grants to individuals, or for scholarships and fellowships, or matching gifts; no loans.

Application information:

Initial approach: Letter
Copies of proposal: 1
Deadline(s): None
Board meeting date(s): Quarterly

Final notification: 6 months
Write: Oakleigh B. Thorne, President
Officers and Directors: Oakleigh B. Thorne,
President and Treasurer; Horace C.
Stephenson, Ellen L. Klingener, Vice-Presidents.
Number of staff: None.
Employer Identification Number: 136108384

2985
Tiffany (Louis Comfort) Foundation
P.O. Box 480
Canal Street Station
New York 10013　　　　　(212) 431-9880

Association established in 1918 in New York.
Donor(s): Louis Comfort Tiffany.†
Financial data: (yr. ended 12/31/82): Assets,
$3,086,019 (M); expenditures, $208,098,
including $29,950 for 6 grants (high: $10,000;
low: $2,200) and $130,000 for 13 grants to
individuals.
Purpose and activities: To encourage talented
and advanced professionals of the fine arts
(painting, sculpture, and the graphic arts) and
the industrial crafts (ceramics, textile design,
glass design, metal crafts) by awarding a limited
number of grants annually. Grants also to
museums for acquisition of specific craft and
art objects.
Types of support awarded: Grants to
individuals.
Limitations: No grants for general support, or
capital or endowment funds.
Application information: Nominations only;
no direct applications accepted.
　Write: Angela Westwater, President
Officers and Trustees: Angela Westwater,
President; Paul J. Smith, Vice-President; Gerard
E. Jones, Secretary; Robert Meltzer, Treasurer;
William Bailey, Mildred Baker, Robert
Blackburn, Thomas Buechner, Amanda Burden,
Roseanne Clark, Herbert Fink, Xavier Gonzalez,
Stephen Greene, Lewis Iselin, Bill Lacy, Roy
Lichtenstein, Hugh McKean, Diane Waldman.
Number of staff: None.
Employer Identification Number: 131689389

2986
Tinker Foundation Incorporated, The ▼
645 Madison Ave.
New York 10022　　　　　(212) 421-6858

Trust established in 1959 in New York;
incorporated in 1975 in New York.
Donor(s): Edward Larocque Tinker.†
Financial data: (yr. ended 12/31/84):
Assets, $36,255,437 (M); expenditures,
$2,349,815, including $1,458,200 for 51
grants (high: $150,000; low: $3,500; average:
$5,000-$50,000) and $82,486 for 8 grants to
individuals.

Purpose and activities: Broad purposes; to
promote better understanding among the
peoples of the United States, Latin America,
Portugal and Spain. Grants in aid of projects in
the social sciences, international relations,
marine sciences, and natural resource
development. Support also offered for
conferences, meetings, seminars, and public
affairs programs and occasionally for programs
furthering the education of the Spanish- and
Portuguese-speaking peoples in the U.S.
Awards postdoctoral fellowships in an annual
competition.
Types of support awarded: Special projects,
research, conferences and seminars,
fellowships, internships, exchange programs,
matching funds.
Limitations: No grants to individuals (except
for postdoctoral fellowships), or for building or
endowment funds, annual campaigns, or
operating budgets.
Publications: Annual report, application
guidelines, program policy statement.
Application information:
　Initial approach: Letter
　Copies of proposal: 1
　Deadline(s): Submit proposal preferably in
　　January, February, September, and
　　October; deadline March 31 and October
　　14; for fellowships, January 15; for field
　　research grants, October 1
　Board meeting date(s): April, June,
　　September, and December
　Final notification: 2 weeks after June and
　　December meetings
　Write: Martha T. Muse, Chairman and
　　President
Officers and Directors: Martha T. Muse,
Chairman and President; Grayson Kirk, Vice-
President; Raymond L. Brittenham, Secretary;
Joshua B. Powers, Treasurer; John N. Irwin II,
Gordon T. Wallis, W. Clarke Wescoe.
Number of staff: 5 full-time professional; 3 full-
time support.
Employer Identification Number: 510175449

2987
Tisch Foundation, Inc. ▼
666 Fifth Ave.
New York 10019　　　　　(212) 841-1547

Incorporated in 1957 in Florida.
Donor(s): Hotel Americana, Tisch Hotels, Inc.,
members of the Tisch family, and closely held
corporations.
Financial data: (yr. ended 12/31/83): Assets,
$9,271,029 (M); expenditures, $1,174,697,
including $1,123,688 for 105 grants (high:
$750,275; low: $36; average: $100-$10,000).
Purpose and activities: Broad purposes;
general giving, with emphasis on higher
education including institutions in Israel, and
research related programs; support also for
museums, Jewish welfare funds, and secondary
education.
Types of support awarded: Continuing
support, building funds, equipment, research.
Limitations: No grants to individuals, or for
endowment funds, scholarships or fellowships,
or matching gifts; no loans.
Application information:
　Initial approach: Full proposal

　Copies of proposal: 1
　Deadline(s): None
　Board meeting date(s): March, June,
　　September, December, and as required
　Final notification: 1 to 2 months
　Write: Laurence A. Tisch, Senior Vice-
　　President
Officers and Directors: Preston R. Tisch,
President; Laurence A. Tisch, Senior Vice-
President; Anthony J. DiNome, Vice-President
and Secretary-Treasurer; Joan H. Tisch, Wilma
S. Tisch.
Number of staff: None.
Employer Identification Number: 591002844

2988
Titan Industrial Foundation, Inc., The ¤
745 Fifth Ave.
New York 10151

Incorporated in 1951 in New York.
Donor(s): Titan Industrial Corporation,
Dominion Steel Export Co., Ltd.
Financial data: (yr. ended 11/30/82): Assets,
$332,294 (M); gifts received, $150,000;
expenditures, $156,624, including $155,074
for 61 grants (high: $39,600; low: $10).
Purpose and activities: Primarily local giving,
with emphasis on Jewish welfare funds; support
also for higher education, including a science
institute in Israel, and health agencies.
Limitations: Giving primarily in NY.
Officers and Directors: Jerome A. Siegel,
President; Edward M. Siegel, Vice-President
and Treasurer; Arthur Siegel, Secretary.
Employer Identification Number: 136066216

2989
Todd (W. Parsons) Foundation, Inc.
405 Park Ave.
New York 10022

Incorporated in 1949 in New Jersey.
Donor(s): W. Parsons Todd.
Financial data: (yr. ended 12/31/82): Assets,
$2,096,251 (M); expenditures, $80,466,
including $73,401 for 9 grants (high: $64,276;
low: $125).
Purpose and activities: Broad purposes;
emphasis on an historical museum; grants also
for church support.
Limitations: Giving limited to the Morris
County, NJ, and Houghton County, MI, areas.
Application information:
　Write: E.A. Deckenbach, Trustee
Officers and Trustees: Mortimer J. Propp,
President and Treasurer; H.T. Todd, Vice-
President; B. Paul Gladston, Secretary; E.A.
Deckenbach, Seymour Propp.
Employer Identification Number: 136116488

2990
Towbin Fund ¤
c/o Belmont Towbin
55 Water St.
New York 10041

Trust established in 1955 in New York.
Donor(s): Belmont Towbin, and others.

Financial data: (yr. ended 6/30/83): Assets, $239,079 (M); gifts received, $174,906; expenditures, $113,133, including $109,318 for 104 grants (high: $30,500; low: $10).
Purpose and activities: Broad purposes; grants largely for hospitals, cultural programs and higher education.
Trustee: Belmont Towbin.
Employer Identification Number: 136158005

2991
Transway International Foundation
81 Main St.
White Plains 10601   (914) 682-7100

Established in 1974 in New York.
Donor(s): Transway International Corporation, and subsidiaries.
Financial data: (yr. ended 12/31/84): Assets, $95,520 (M); gifts received, $162,323; expenditures, $166,168, including $155,553 for 84 grants (high: $15,000; low: $50) and $10,208 for 36 employee matching gifts.
Purpose and activities: Grants primarily for hospitals, health agencies, youth agencies, cultural programs, including museum support, and community funds; support also for a higher education matching gifts program and welfare organizations.
Types of support awarded: Employee matching gifts.
Limitations: No grants to individuals; no loans.
Application information:
 Initial approach: Letter or proposal
 Copies of proposal: 1
 Board meeting date(s): March, June, September, and December
 Write: Karen E. Jones, Secretary
Officers and Directors: J.W. Wolcott, Chairman; D.C. Bevan, Jr., President; Karen E. Jones, Secretary; A. Gregor, Treasurer; L. Berman.
Employer Identification Number: 237411179

2992
Trump (The Fred C.) Foundation ⌑
c/o Durben & Haskel
200 Garden City Plaza
Garden City 11530

Incorporated in 1952 in New York.
Donor(s): Beach Haven Apartments, Inc., Green Park Essex, Inc., Shore Haven Apartments, Inc., Trump Village Construction Corporation, and others.
Financial data: (yr. ended 12/31/81): Assets, $13,141 (M); gifts received, $178,500; expenditures, $170,676, including $170,645 for 104 grants (high: $14,200; low: $40).
Purpose and activities: Broad purposes; primarily local giving, with emphasis on hospitals, higher education, Jewish welfare funds, and youth and health agencies.
Limitations: Giving primarily in NY.
Directors: Irwin Durben, Donald Trump, Fred C. Trump.
Employer Identification Number: 116015006

2993
Tuch (Michael) Foundation, Inc.
c/o Eugene Tuck
122 E. 42nd St., No. 1616
New York 10168   (212) 986-9082

Incorporated in 1946 in New York.
Donor(s): Michael Tuch.†
Financial data: (yr. ended 12/31/83): Assets, $3,708,397 (M); expenditures, $200,000, including $162,052 for 90 grants (high: $11,000; low: $500; average: $1,000).
Purpose and activities: Broad purposes; primarily local giving, with emphasis on higher education, cultural programs, including the performing arts, Jewish welfare funds, and child welfare.
Types of support awarded: Endowment funds, scholarship funds, fellowships.
Limitations: Giving primarily in New York, NY. No support for religion or health. No grants for study, or new general support.
Officers: Eugene Tuck, President and Executive Director; Elizabeth Tuck, 1st Vice-President.
Employer Identification Number: 136002848

2994
Tudor Foundation, Inc. ⌑
551 Fifth Ave.
New York 10176   (212) 682-8490

Incorporated in 1945 in New York.
Donor(s): Aaron Rabinowitz.†
Financial data: (yr. ended 3/31/83): Assets, $2,978,807 (M); expenditures, $289,979, including $277,750 for 52 grants (high: $30,000; low: $500).
Purpose and activities: To promote a better understanding among peoples of all races, creeds, and backgrounds; grants to institutions promoting the above purposes, with emphasis on institutions of higher learning for the establishment of student loan funds; support also for Jewish welfare funds and Jewish theological education.
Types of support awarded: General purposes, building funds, endowment funds, matching funds.
Limitations: No grants to individuals.
Application information:
 Initial approach: Letter
 Copies of proposal: 1
 Deadline(s): Submit proposal in February or March; deadline April 15
 Board meeting date(s): June
 Write: Edwin A. Malloy, Treasurer
Officers and Directors: Simon H. Rifkind, President; Joseph A. Weinberger, Vice-President and Secretary; Clara G. Rabinowitz, Vice-President; Edwin A. Malloy, Treasurer; Nathan A. Perilman, Ann Sheffer Reich, Ralph Sheffer.
Employer Identification Number: 136119193

2995
Twentieth Century Fund, Inc.
41 East 70th St.
New York 10021   (212) 535-4441

Incorporated in 1919 in Massachusetts.
Donor(s): Edward A. Filene.†

Financial data: (yr. ended 6/30/83): Assets, $40,310,000 (M); expenditures, $1,911,872, including $544,878 for 50 foundation-administered programs.
Purpose and activities: A private operating foundation engaged in research and public education on significant contemporary issues, with an emphasis on communications, economic and social questions, and international affairs.
Limitations: Generally no grants to individuals or institutions.
Publications: Annual report, program policy statement, application guidelines.
Application information: Generally, no grants to institutions or individuals, but foundation will review independent project proposals within program guidelines as well as soliciting its own.
 Initial approach: Letter
 Copies of proposal: 1
 Deadline(s): Submit proposal preferably in December, March, or September
 Board meeting date(s): January, May, and November
 Write: M.J. Rossant, Director
Officers: August Heckscher,* Secretary; David B. Truman,* Treasurer; Matina S. Horner,* Clerk; M.J. Rossant, Director.
Trustees:* Peter A.A. Berle, Chairman; Brewster Denny, Vice-Chairman; Morris B. Abram, Jonathan B. Bingham, Jose A. Cabranes, Hodding Carter, III, Brewster C. Denny, Daniel J. Evans, Charles V. Hamilton, James A. Leach, Georges-Henri Martin, P. Michael Pitfield, Richard Ravitch, Arthur M. Schlesinger, Jr., Harvey I. Sloane, M.D., James Tobin, Shirley Williams.
Number of staff: 11 full-time professional; 1 part-time professional; 10 full-time support; 3 part-time support.
Employer Identification Number: 131624235

2996
Ungar (S. J.) Foundation ⌑
299 Broadway
New York 10007

Incorporated in 1958 in New York.
Donor(s): Sidney J. Ungar.
Financial data: (yr. ended 6/30/83): Assets, $2,348,878 (M); expenditures, $18,092, including $11,275 for 20 grants (high: $3,000; low: $25).
Purpose and activities: Primarily local giving; emphasis on Jewish welfare funds, with some support for health agencies and hospitals.
Limitations: Giving primarily in NY.
Application information: Applications are not invited.
Officer: Helen Ungar, President and Secretary.
Employer Identification Number: 136188247

2997
Union Pacific Foundation ▼
345 Park Ave.
New York 10154   (212) 418-7926

Incorporated in 1955 in Utah.
Donor(s): Union Pacific Corporation.

Financial data: (yr. ended 12/31/84): Assets, $543,960 (M); expenditures, $5,920,876, including $5,908,200 for 775 grants (high: $140,000; low: $500).
Purpose and activities: Grants primarily to non-tax-supported institutions in communities where Union Pacific corporate subsidiary operations are located, with emphasis on private higher education, health, social welfare, arts, and cultural institutions.
Types of support awarded: Operating budgets, continuing support, annual campaigns, building funds, equipment, matching funds.
Limitations: Giving primarily in areas of company operations, particularly in the western United States. No support for tax-supported institutions or affiliates, or for specialized national health and welfare organizations, political, religious, social clubs, or labor groups. No grants to individuals, or for deficit financing, land acquisition, endowment funds, demonstration projects, special events, publications, or conferences; no loans.
Publications: Application guidelines, program policy statement.
Application information: Application form required.
Initial approach: Letter
Copies of proposal: 1
Deadline(s): August 15
Board meeting date(s): December
Final notification: 6 to 9 months
Write: Charles N. Olsen, President
Officers: Charles N. Olsen, President and Secretary; J.R. Mendenhall, Vice-President, Taxes; W.F. Surette, Vice-President, Finance; L.W. Matthews, III, Treasurer.
Trustees: W.S. Cook, Chairman; James H. Evans, Vice-Chairman; and twenty-two additional trustees.
Number of staff: 2 full-time professional; 2 full-time support.
Employer Identification Number: 136406825

2998
United Brands Foundation ¤
1271 Ave. of the Americas
New York 10020   (212) 397-4489

Incorporated in 1954 in Illinois.
Donor(s): United Fruit Company, John Morrell and Company, United Brands Company.
Financial data: (yr. ended 12/31/82): Assets, $147,851 (M); expenditures, $146,111, including $121,550 for 14 grants (high: $35,000) and $19,835 for employee matching gifts.
Purpose and activities: Broad purposes; general giving, primarily in the United States and Latin America, with emphasis on a Latin American agricultural school; support also for Latin American churches and for community funds, primarily in areas of Company operations.
Limitations: No grants to individuals or for endowment funds.
Application information:
Initial approach: Letter
Copies of proposal: 1
Board meeting date(s): As required
Write: Julie A. de la Quintana, Administrator

Officers and Directors:* Seymour Milstein,* President; Max M. Fisher,* Paul Milstein,* G. Burke Wright,* Vice-Presidents; Herman M. Beltzer, Treasurer.
Employer Identification Number: 366051081

2999
United Merchants Foundation, Inc.
1407 Broadway, 6th Fl.
New York 10018   (212) 930-3915

Incorporated in 1944 in New York.
Financial data: (yr. ended 6/30/83): Assets, $1,387,387 (M); expenditures, $74,258, including $71,745 for 29 grants (high: $25,800; low: $50).
Purpose and activities: Broad purposes; primarily local giving, with emphasis on Jewish welfare funds, community funds, higher education, and hospitals.
Limitations: Giving primarily in NY. No grants to individuals.
Application information:
Initial approach: Letter
Copies of proposal: 1
Board meeting date(s): December
Write: Lawrence Marx, Jr., President
Officers and Directors:* Lawrence Marx, Jr.,* President; Martin J. Schwab,* Vice-President; Oliver G. Seidman,* Secretary; Stephen Greenwald, Treasurer.
Employer Identification Number: 136077135

3000
United States Trust Company of New York Foundation
45 Wall St.
New York 10005   (212) 806-4420

Trust established in 1955 in New York.
Donor(s): United States Trust Company of New York.
Financial data: (yr. ended 12/31/84): Assets, $197,000 (L); gifts received, $111,000; expenditures, $283,972, including $237,000 for 81 grants (high: $45,000; low: $500; average: $1,000-$5,000) and $44,472 for 244 employee matching gifts.
Purpose and activities: Giving largely in the New York metropolitan area and other primary market areas, with emphasis on cultural, health, educational, and civic and urban affairs organizations that assist in building or maintaining an improved quality of life for citizens in U.S. Preference given to innovative, broad-based, privately supported, and efficient organizations in which company employees are active.
Types of support awarded: Operating budgets, continuing support, annual campaigns, seed money, building funds, equipment, land acquisition, endowment funds, matching funds, employee matching gifts, special projects, research.
Limitations: Giving primarily in the New York metropolitan area and other primary market areas of the company; no grants awarded outside the United States. No support for religious or political organizations. No grants to individuals, or for emergency funds, deficit financing, scholarships, or fellowships; no loans.

Publications: Program policy statement, application guidelines.
Application information:
Initial approach: Letter or full proposal in 1 copy
Copies of proposal: 1
Deadline(s): April 1
Board meeting date(s): February, June, September, and December
Final notification: 2 to 3 months
Write: Carol A. Strickland, Vice-President
Officer: Carol A. Strickland, Vice-President and Corporate Secretary.
Number of staff: 1 part-time professional; 2 part-time support.
Employer Identification Number: 136072081

3001
United States-Japan Foundation ▼
560 Lexington Ave.
New York 10022   (212) 688-6363
Tokyo, Japan office address: Nihon Shobo Kaikan, 9th Fl., 2-9-16 Toranomon, Minato-ku, Tokyo; Tel.: 03-591-4002

Foundation incorporated in 1980 in New York.
Donor(s): The Japan Shipbuilding Industry Foundation.
Financial data: (yr. ended 2/28/83): Assets, $38,854,383 (M); gifts received, $10,778,185; expenditures, $2,663,650, including $1,237,442 for 40 grants (high: $100,000; low: $2,000).
Purpose and activities: To strengthen cooperation and understanding between the people of the United States and Japan through grants in: 1) Exchange of persons and ideas, involving leaders in labor, management, minorities, the media, local and state governments, women and farm groups; 2) Education, with emphasis on pre-college education; and 3) Nongovernmental dialogue in such fields as energy, technology, international finance, and defense.
Types of support awarded: Exchange programs, conferences and seminars, research, special projects, publications, internships, fellowships, matching funds.
Limitations: Generally no support for projects in the arts involving performances, exhibitions, or productions. No grants to individuals, or for building or endowment funds; no loans.
Publications: Annual report, program policy statement, application guidelines.
Application information:
Initial approach: Letter
Deadline(s): None
Board meeting date(s): January
Final notification: 6 months to 1 year
Write: Ronald Aqua, Program Director
Officers: Richard W. Petree,* President; Hironobu Shibuya, Executive Director; William Pickens, III, Secretary.

Trustees:* Angier Biddle Duke, Chairman; Kiichi Saeki, Vice-Chairman; William D. Eberle, Orville L. Freeman, Tadao Ishikawa, Hiroyuki Itami, James A. Linen, Robert S. McNamara, Isao Nakauchi, Shizuo Saito, Robert W. Sarnoff, Yohei Sasakawa, Ryuzo Sejima, Ayako Sono, Phillips Talbot, Joseph D. Tydings, Henry G. Walter, Jr.
Number of staff: 5 full-time professional; 1 part-time professional; 4 full-time support.
Employer Identification Number: 133054425

3002
Unterberg (Bella & Israel) Foundation, Inc. ⌶
c/o Leipziger & Breskin
230 Park Ave.
New York 10169

Incorporated in 1948 in New York.
Donor(s): Members of the Unterberg family.
Financial data: (yr. ended 12/31/84): Assets, $753,740 (M); gifts received, $401,805; expenditures, $147,180, including $137,977 for 95 grants (high: $20,000; low: $10).
Purpose and activities: Giving primarily for Jewish welfare funds, higher education, hospitals, and community development.
Limitations: No grants to individuals.
Officers: Clarence Unterberg, President and Treasurer; Ann Blumenstein, Selma Unterberg, Thomas Unterberg, Vice-Presidents.
Employer Identification Number: 136099080

3003
Uris Brothers Foundation, Inc. ▼
300 Park Ave.
New York 10022   (212) 407-9508

Incorporated in 1956 in New York.
Donor(s): Percy Uris,† Harold D. Uris,† and related business interests.
Financial data: (yr. ended 10/31/84): Assets, $18,513,682 (M); expenditures, $1,596,154, including $1,485,950 for 82 grants (high: $450,000; low: $30; average: $1,000-$25,000).
Purpose and activities: Special focus on New York City institutions, including grants for higher and secondary educational institutions, hospitals, the arts, and social service agencies.
Types of support awarded: Building funds, research, scholarship funds.
Limitations: Giving primarily in New York, NY. No grants to individuals, or for endowment funds, or matching gifts; no loans.
Publications: Application guidelines.
Application information:
    Initial approach: Letter
    Copies of proposal: 1
    Deadline(s): None
    Board meeting date(s): Quarterly
    Write: Mrs. Alice Paul, Program Director
Officers: Susan Halpern,* President; Jane Nye, Linda Sanger, Vice-Presidents; Milton Copland,* Secretary; Benjamin Gessula, Treasurer.
Directors:* Ruth Uris, Chairman; Robert H. Abrams, Robert L. Bachner.
Number of staff: 1 full-time professional.
Employer Identification Number: 136115748

3004
Ushkow Foundation, Inc. ⌶
Eight Blue Sea Ln.
Great Neck 11024

Incorporated in 1956 in New York.
Donor(s): Joseph Ushkow.
Financial data: (yr. ended 10/31/81): Assets, $3,228,137 (M); expenditures, $160,770, including $152,455 for 82 grants (high: $25,000; low: $10).
Purpose and activities: Charitable purposes; primarily local giving, with emphasis on hospitals, higher education, and Jewish welfare funds.
Limitations: Giving primarily in NY. No grants to individuals.
Application information:
    Board meeting date(s): Quarterly
Officer: Joseph Ushkow, President.
Employer Identification Number: 116006274

3005
Utica Foundation, Inc.
233 Genesee St.
Utica 13501   (315) 797-9200

Community foundation incorporated in 1952 in New York.
Financial data: (yr. ended 12/31/83): Assets, $1,363,946 (L); gifts received, $29,385; expenditures, $112,824, including $96,356 for 37 grants (high: $5,000; low: $500).
Purpose and activities: General purposes; support for organizations benefiting the residents of Utica, Oneida, and Herkimer counties, with emphasis on social and health services, scholarship aid for local students, and cultural programs.
Types of support awarded: General purposes, seed money, building funds, equipment, conferences and seminars, professorships, matching funds, student aid.
Limitations: Giving limited to Utica, Oneida, and Herkimer counties, NY. No grants to individuals (except for scholarships), or for endowment funds, or operating budgets; no loans.
Publications: Annual report, application guidelines.
Application information: Application form required.
    Initial approach: Letter
    Copies of proposal: 7
    Board meeting date(s): 3 to 4 times a year, in May and as required
    Final notification: 2 to 3 months
    Write: Addison M. White, President
Officers and Directors: Addison M. White, President; Mrs. Thomas G. Hineline, Arthur H. Turner, Vice-Presidents; William L. Schrauth, Secretary; James S. Kernan, Jr., Treasurer; Rev. P. Arthur Brindisi, Vincent R. Corrou, Jr., Irving Cramer, M.D., Victor T. Ehre, John L. Knower, Harold J. Moore, Burrel Samuels, Msgr. Charles Sewall, Dwight E. Vicks, Jr., William B. Westcott, Jr.
Trustee Banks: Marine Midland Bank, Oneida National Bank & Trust Company of Central New York.
Number of staff: 1 part-time support.
Employer Identification Number: 156016932

3006
van Ameringen Foundation, Inc. ▼
509 Madison Ave.
New York 10022   (212) 758-6221

Incorporated in 1950 in New York.
Donor(s): Arnold Louis van Ameringen.†
Financial data: (yr. ended 12/31/84): Assets, $19,170,417 (M); expenditures, $1,167,070, including $1,011,789 for 37 grants (high: $100,000; low: $1,250; average: $30,000).
Purpose and activities: Grants chiefly to promote mental health and social welfare through preventive measures, treatment, and rehabilitation; some general local giving. Grants made largely in the urban Northeast, from Boston to Washington, D.C.; occasional grants in other parts of the country.
Types of support awarded: Operating budgets, continuing support, seed money, matching funds, special projects, research, publications, conferences and seminars.
Limitations: Giving primarily in the urban northeast from Boston, MA, to Washington, DC. No support for international activities and institutions in other countries, or for mental retardation, the physically handicapped, drug abuse, or alcoholism. No grants to individuals, or for annual campaigns, deficit financing, or emergency, capital, or endowment funds; or scholarships or fellowships; no loans.
Publications: Annual report, program policy statement, application guidelines.
Application information:
    Initial approach: Full proposal
    Copies of proposal: 1
    Deadline(s): 2 months before board meetings
    Board meeting date(s): February, June, and November
    Final notification: Within 60 days
    Write: Patricia van A. Kind, President
Officers and Directors: Patricia van A. Kind, President, Treasurer, and Chief Executive Officer; Lily van A. Auchincloss, Vice-President; Harmon Duncombe, Secretary; Mrs. Arnold L. van Ameringen, Honorary Chairman; Henry P. van Ameringen, Henry G. Walter, Jr.
Number of staff: 1 part-time professional; 1 full-time support.
Employer Identification Number: 136125699

3007
van Ameringen (H.) Foundation ⌶
30 Rockefeller Plaza, Rm. 3217
New York 10112

Established in 1950.
Donor(s): Henry van Ameringen, Mrs. Arnold L. van Ameringen.
Financial data: (yr. ended 12/31/82): Assets, $69,612 (M); expenditures, $130,376, including $128,900 for 13 grants (high: $25,000; low: $500).
Purpose and activities: Primarily local giving, with emphasis on cultural programs, conservation, mental health, education, and social services.
Limitations: Giving primarily in NY.
Trustee: Henry van Ameringen.
Employer Identification Number: 136215329

3008
van Ameringen (Hedwig) Foundation ⌗
680 Madison Ave.
New York 10021

Established in 1972 in New York.
Donor(s): Mrs. Arnold L. van Ameringen.
Financial data: (yr. ended 12/31/82): Assets,
$7,890 (M); gifts received, $75,000;
expenditures, $126,936, including $125,000
for 1 grant.
Purpose and activities: Primarily local giving,
with emphasis on cultural programs, mental
health, and social agencies.
Limitations: Giving primarily in NY.
Trustee: Mrs. Arnold L. van Ameringen.
Employer Identification Number: 237181576

3009
Vanneck-Bailey Foundation, The ⌗
100 Park Ave.
New York 10017   (212) 725-2850

Established in 1971 in New York through the
consolidation of The Vanneck Foundation,
incorporated in 1949 in New York, and The
Frank and Marie Bailey Foundation.
Donor(s): John Vanneck,† Barbara Bailey
Vanneck.
Financial data: (yr. ended 12/31/82): Assets,
$3,820,514 (M); expenditures, $297,582,
including $291,445 for 111 grants (high:
$45,000; low: $25).
Purpose and activities: Emphasis on higher
and secondary education, hospitals, and youth
agencies.
Types of support awarded: Continuing
support, research.
Limitations: No grants to individuals.
Application information:
 Initial approach: Letter
 Copies of proposal: 1
 Board meeting date(s): Monthly
 Write: John B. Vanneck, Vice-President
Officers: Barbara Bailey Vanneck, President;
John B. Vanneck, Vice-President; Jeanne M.
Wiedenman, Secretary; William P. Vanneck,
Treasurer.
Employer Identification Number: 237165285

3010
Vernon (Miles Hodsdon) Fund, Inc. ⌗
49 Beekman Ave.
North Tarrytown 10591   (914) 631-4226

Incorporated in 1953 in New York.
Donor(s): Miles Hodsdon Vernon,† Martha
Hodsdon Kinney,† Louise Hodsdon.†
Financial data: (yr. ended 12/31/83): Assets,
$2,081,654 (M); expenditures, $123,624,
including $97,425 for 28 grants (high: $30,000;
low: $250).
Purpose and activities: Charitable purposes;
grants for medical research, especially on
encephalitis and other brain disorders; support
also for youth agencies, aid for the aged, and
education.
Application information:
 Initial approach: Proposal
 Deadline(s): None
 Write: Robert C. Thomson, Jr., President

Officers and Directors: Robert C. Thomson,
Jr., President and Treasurer; Dennis M.
Fitzgerald, Vice-President and Secretary;
Eleanor C. Thomson, Gertrude Whalen.
Employer Identification Number: 136076836

3011
Vetlesen (G. Unger) Foundation ▼ ⌗
c/o Harmon Duncombe
30 Rockefeller Plaza, Rm. 3217
New York 10112   (212) 586-0700

Incorporated in 1955 in New York.
Donor(s): George Unger Vetlesen.†
Financial data: (yr. ended 12/31/83): Assets,
$16,665,895 (M); expenditures, $830,851,
including $754,018 for 26 grants (high:
$200,000; low: $5,000; average: $10,000-
$50,000).
Purpose and activities: Broad purposes;
established a biennial international science
award for discoveries in the earth sciences;
grants for medical, biological, and geological
research, higher education, including
scholarships, and cultural organizations,
particularly those emphasizing Norwegian-
American relations and maritime interests.
Support also for public policy research,
museums, libraries, and social services.
Types of support awarded: General purposes,
special projects.
Application information:
 Initial approach: Proposal
 Deadline(s): December 1
 Board meeting date(s): December
 Final notification: Positive determination, by
  December 31; negative determination, no
  response
Officers and Directors: Henry G. Walter, Jr.,
President; Harmon Duncombe, Vice-President
and Treasurer; Christian J. Mohn, Vice-
President; George Rowe, Jr., Secretary.
Number of staff: None.
Employer Identification Number: 131982695

3012
Vidda Foundation, The
c/o Carter, Carter, & Rupp
10 E. 40th St.
New York 10016   (212) 696-4050

Established in 1979 in New York.
Donor(s): Ursula Corning.
Financial data: (yr. ended 5/31/83): Assets,
$2,771,260 (M); gifts received, $1,217,013;
expenditures, $550,610, including $468,595
for 12 grants (high: $144,525; low: $1,500).
Purpose and activities: Giving primarily to
educational projects, cultural programs,
including an educational film-making company,
church music funds, conservation, and a
hospital.
Types of support awarded: General purposes,
building funds, special projects, endowment
funds, research.
Limitations: Giving primarily in NY. No grants
to individuals.
Application information:
 Initial approach: Letter or proposal
 Copies of proposal: 3

Deadline(s): Submit proposal preferably in
  October and April; deadlines October 15
  and April 15
 Board meeting date(s): November and May
 Final notification: 2 months
 Write: Gerald E. Rupp, Manager
Trustees: Gerald E. Rupp, Manager; Ann Fraser
Brewer, Ursula Corning, Christophe Velay.
Number of staff: None.
Employer Identification Number: 132981105

3013
Vidor (Doris Warner) Foundation, Inc. ⌗
317 East 64th St.
New York 10021

Established in 1972.
Financial data: (yr. ended 11/30/83): Assets,
$1,759,322 (M); expenditures, $191,983,
including $181,039 for 87 grants (high:
$40,000; low: $20).
Purpose and activities: Primarily local giving,
with emphasis on cultural and civic programs;
support also for secondary education, and
social agencies.
Limitations: Giving primarily in the greater
New York, NY, metropolitan area.
Officers: Warner Leroy, President; Quentin
Vidor, Vice-President; Lewis Brian Vidor,
Secretary; Linda Janklow, Treasurer.
Employer Identification Number: 237252504

3014
Villa Banfi Foundation, The ⌗
1111 Cedar Swamp Rd.
Old Brookville 11545

Established in 1982 in New York.
Donor(s): Banfi Products Corp.
Financial data: (yr. ended 12/31/82): Assets,
$4,000,656 (M); gifts received, $4,000,000.
Purpose and activities: First year of operation
in 1982; no grants disbursed.
Application information:
 Write: John G. Troiano, Executive Director
Officers: Lydia K. Taylor, Secretary; Alexander
C. D'Atri, Treasurer; John G. Troiano,*
Executive Director.
Directors:* Harry F. Mariani, John Mariani.
Employer Identification Number: 112622792

3015
Vinmont Foundation, Inc.
888 East 19th St.
Brooklyn 11230

Incorporated in 1947 in New York.
Donor(s): Lily H. Weinberg,† Robert C.
Weinberg.†
Financial data: (yr. ended 12/31/83): Assets,
$1,078,083 (M); expenditures, $108,330,
including $106,600 for 79 grants (high: $6,000;
low: $100; average: $500-$2,000).
Purpose and activities: Giving primarily for
black and Native American development
nationally; and social agencies, urban planning,
and restoration in metropolitan New York.

Types of support awarded: Operating budgets, continuing support, annual campaigns, seed money, emergency funds.
Limitations: No grants to individuals, or for capital or endowment funds, research, special projects, publications, conferences, scholarships and fellowships, or matching gifts; no loans.
Publications: Program policy statement.
Application information: Rarely funds unsolicited proposals.
  Initial approach: Letter or proposal
  Copies of proposal: 1
  Board meeting date(s): February, April, September, and November
  Final notification: 6 months
  Write: William R. Nye, Treasurer
Officers and Directors: Myron S. Isaacs, President; Marian K. Weinberg, Vice-President; Ethel Wortis, Secretary; William R. Nye, Treasurer; Paul S. Bayard, Bruce L. Bozeman, L. Franklyn Lowenstein, Carolyn Whittle.
Number of staff: None.
Employer Identification Number: 131577203

3016
Vogler (The Laura B.) Foundation, Inc.
P.O. Box 94
Bayside 11361   (718) 423-3000

Incorporated in 1959 in New York.
Donor(s): Laura B. Vogler,† John J. Vogler.†
Financial data: (yr. ended 10/31/84): Assets, $2,338,679 (M); expenditures, $141,793, including $102,102 for 33 grants (high: $7,500; low: $500; average: $1,000-$5,000).
Purpose and activities: Local giving for education, youth assistance, and health care.
Types of support awarded: Seed money, emergency funds, special projects, research, scholarship funds.
Limitations: Giving limited to the New York metropolitan area. No grants to individuals, or for building or endowment funds, annual fundraising campaigns, or matching gifts; no loans.
Publications: Annual report, application guidelines.
Application information: Application form required.
  Initial approach: Letter
  Deadline(s): Thirty days prior to board meeting
  Board meeting date(s): January, April, July, and October
  Final notification: 2 to 3 months
  Write: D. Donald D'Amato, President
Officers and Trustees: D. Donald D'Amato, President and Chief Executive Officer; Lawrence L. D'Amato, Secretary-Treasurer; Donald P. D'Amato, Max L. Kupferberg, I. Jerry Lasurdo, Stanley Pearson, Louis L. Theiss, Jr.
Number of staff: 2 part-time professional.
Employer Identification Number: 116022241

3017
Waldbaum (The I.) Family Foundation, Incorporated ⋈
c/o Stuart and Simel
10 Cutter Mill Rd.
Great Neck 11021

Incorporated in 1961 in New York.
Donor(s): Bernice Waldbaum, Ira Waldbaum, Waldbaum, Inc.
Financial data: (yr. ended 12/31/83): Assets, $1,729,821 (M); gifts received, $35,151; expenditures, $35,936, including $35,730 for 49 grants (high: $10,000; low: $25).
Purpose and activities: Giving chiefly to Jewish welfare funds including temple support, and to cultural programs.
Officers: Ira Waldbaum, President; Bernice Waldbaum, Treasurer.
Employer Identification Number: 136145916

3018
Walker (The George Herbert) Foundation
c/o Convoy Hewitt O'Brien and Boardman
100 Park Ave., 10th Fl.
New York 10017

Trust established in 1954 in New York.
Donor(s): G.H. Walker, Jr.
Financial data: (yr. ended 12/31/82): Assets, $1,058,804 (M); expenditures, $60,947, including $50,700 for 14 grants (high: $19,000; low: $100).
Purpose and activities: Grants primarily for higher and secondary education and Protestant church support.
Application information:
  Write: Winslow M. Lovejoy, Trustee
Trustees: Winslow M. Lovejoy, G.H. Walker, III, Mary Carter Walker.
Employer Identification Number: 136084806

3019
Wallace (DeWitt) Fund, Inc. ▼
200 Park Ave., 34th Fl.
New York 10166   (212) 906-6900

Incorporated in 1965 in New York.
Donor(s): DeWitt Wallace.†
Financial data: (yr. ended 12/31/82): Assets, $7,828,323 (M); gifts received, $9,334,053; expenditures, $3,116,075, including $3,034,873 for 56 grants (high: $1,182,000; low: $2,000; average: $10,000-$25,000).
Purpose and activities: Support primarily for independent schools and activities fostering qualities of leadership and character in young people, including scholarships, summer camps, experiences abroad, explorations, international exchange programs, projects promoting an understanding of the history and economy of the United States, and special medical and educational projects. Grants also for a community fund and cultural programs.
Types of support awarded: Operating budgets, continuing support, matching funds, consulting services, internships, scholarship funds, exchange programs.

Limitations: No grants to individuals, or for annual campaigns, seed money, emergency or capital funds, deficit financing, research, demonstration projects, publications, or conferences; no loans.
Application information: Funds fully committed.
  Board meeting date(s): Semiannually
  Write: Barnabas McHenry, Secretary
Officers and Directors: John A. O'Hara, President; Barnabas McHenry, Secretary and Treasurer; Albert L. Cole, Edward T. Thompson, Lila Acheson Wallace.
Number of staff: None.
Employer Identification Number: 136183757

3020
Wallace Genetic Foundation, Inc. ▼
Farvue Farm
South Salem 10590   (914) 763-3523
Grant application address: Joan D. Murray, Research Secretary, 4801 Massachusetts Ave., Suite 400, Washington, DC 20016

Incorporated in 1959 in New York.
Donor(s): Henry A. Wallace.†
Financial data: (yr. ended 12/31/83): Assets, $25,642,235 (M); gifts received, $540,000; expenditures, $1,268,073, including $1,164,144 for 55 grants (high: $403,500; low: $1,000).
Purpose and activities: Support for agricultural research and preservation of farmland, nutrition, ecology and conservation, higher education, and health research.
Limitations: No grants to individuals, or for scholarships or operating expenses.
Application information:
  Initial approach: Letter
  Board meeting date(s): As required
Officer: Jean W. Douglas, President.
Directors: Henry B. Wallace, Robert B. Wallace.
Employer Identification Number: 136162575

3021
Wallach (Miriam and Ira D.) Foundation ⋈
100 Park Ave.
New York 10017

Incorporated in 1956 in New York.
Financial data: (yr. ended 10/31/83): Assets, $10,802,108 (M); expenditures, $1,576,487, including $1,528,899 for 90 grants (high: $250,000; low: $50).
Purpose and activities: Broad purposes; primarily local giving, with emphasis on Jewish welfare funds, cultural programs, international relations, including peace, and higher education.
Limitations: Giving primarily in NY.
Officers: Ira D. Wallach,* President; Edgar Wachenheim III,* Miriam G. Wallach,* James G. Wallach,* Kenneth L. Wallach,* Vice-Presidents; Peter C. Siegfried, Secretary; Benjamin Glowatz, Treasurer.
Directors:* Sue W. Wachenheim, Kate B. Wallach, Mary K. Wallach, Susan S. Wallach.
Employer Identification Number: 136101702

3022
Warner (Albert and Bessie) Fund
P.O. Box 649
Bridgehampton 11932   (516) 537-3713

Trust established in 1955 in New York.
Donor(s): Albert Warner,† Mrs. Albert Warner,† and the Steel family.
Financial data: (yr. ended 12/31/82): Assets, $1,906,942 (M); expenditures, $215,841, including $179,633 for 188 grants (high: $25,000; low: $100).
Purpose and activities: Broad purposes; grants largely for education, cultural programs, hospitals, civil liberties and health agencies, primarily in New York City and Suffolk County.
Limitations: Giving primarily in New York City and Suffolk County, NY. No grants to individuals, or for building or endowment funds.
Application information: Applications not accepted.
  Board meeting date(s): February, May, August, and November
  Write: Arthur J. Steel, Trustee
Trustees: Arthur J. Steel, Lewis M. Steel, Ruth M. Steel.
Number of staff: 1 part-time support.
Employer Identification Number: 131095213

3023
Warner Communications Foundation, Inc.
c/o Warner Communications, Inc.
75 Rockefeller Plaza
New York 10019   (212) 484-8022

Established in 1959.
Donor(s): Warner Communications, Inc.
Financial data: (yr. ended 9/30/82): Assets, $4,535,196 (M); gifts received, $5,000,000; expenditures, $1,144,653, including $1,144,500 for 14 grants (high: $500,000; low: $2,500).
Purpose and activities: Primarily local giving, with emphasis on hospitals, museums, cultural programs and historic preservation, and education. Due to changes within the company, no new grants currently being awarded; foundation continues to make payments on earlier commitments.
Limitations: Giving primarily in NY.
Application information: Applications currently not accepted.
  Write: Mary E. McCarthy, Director of Corporate Contributions
Officers and Directors:* Deane F. Johnson, Chairman; Eli T. Bruno, Secretary; David R. Haas,* Treasurer.
Administrator: Mary E. McCarthy, Director of Corporate Contributions.
Employer Identification Number: 136085361

3024
Warren (Riley J. and Lillian N.) and Beatrice W. Blanding Foundation ¤
Six Ford Ave.
Oneonta 13820   (607) 432-6720

Trust established in 1972 in New York.
Donor(s): Beatrice W. Blanding.

Financial data: (yr. ended 12/31/82): Assets, $3,549,278 (M); gifts received, $150,000; expenditures, $373,785, including $346,500 for 28 grants (high: $50,000; low: $500).
Purpose and activities: Primarily local giving, with emphasis on higher and secondary education; support also for churches and civic affairs programs.
Limitations: Giving primarily in NY.
Application information:
  Initial approach: Letter
  Deadline(s): November 1
  Write: Joseph P. Molinari, Jr., Fdn. Mgr.
Officer and Trustees: Joseph P. Molinari, Jr., Manager and Secretary; Beatrice W. Blanding.
Employer Identification Number: 237203341

3025
Wasserman (The David) Foundation, Inc.
107 Division St.
Amsterdam 12010   (518) 843-2800

Incorporated in 1953 in New York.
Donor(s): David Wasserman.†
Financial data: (yr. ended 2/28/83): Assets, $1,153,679 (M); expenditures, $102,274, including $87,700 for 5 grants (high: $26,500; low: $750).
Purpose and activities: Grants for scientific, educational, and charitable purposes within Montgomery County, including a scholarship fund.
Limitations: Giving limited to Montgomery County, NY. No grants for operating budgets.
Application information:
  Initial approach: Letter
  Copies of proposal: 1
  Deadline(s): Submit proposal preferably in January
  Board meeting date(s): Monthly
  Write: Norbert J. Sherbunt, President
Officers and Directors: Norbert J. Sherbunt, President and Treasurer; Judith M. Sherbunt, Vice-President and Secretary; Peter W. Hosner.
Employer Identification Number: 237183522

3026
Wasserman (Lucius P.) Foundation, Inc. ¤
c/o Wasserman, Chinitz, Geffner & Green
535 Fifth Ave.
New York 10017

Incorporated in 1951 in New York.
Donor(s): L.P. Wasserman,† and others.
Financial data: (yr. ended 12/31/82): Assets, $2,720,801 (M); expenditures, $133,428, including $117,915 for 71 grants (high: $35,000).
Purpose and activities: Primarily local giving, with emphasis on higher and secondary education, Jewish welfare funds, hospitals, and social agencies.
Limitations: Giving primarily in NY. No grants to individuals, or for building or endowment funds, operating budgets, or special projects.
Application information:
  Initial approach: Letter
  Board meeting date(s): As required
  Write: Bernard A. Green, Secretary

Officers and Trustees:* Peter Wasserman,* President; Judith Soley,* Robert Soley, Judith Wasserman, Vice-Presidents; Bernard A. Green,* Secretary; J.S. Chinitz, Treasurer.
Employer Identification Number: 136098895

3027
Watertown Foundation, Inc.
216 Washington St., Chase Lincoln First Bank Bldg.
Watertown 13601   (315) 782-7110

Community foundation incorporated in 1929 in New York.
Financial data: (yr. ended 2/29/84): Assets, $1,270,263 (L); gifts received, $685,277; expenditures, $683,677, including $431,677 for 89 grants (high: $33,000; low: $125; average: $125-$10,000) and $252,000 for 203 grants to individuals.
Purpose and activities: To promote charitable, educational, cultural, recreational, and health programs in Watertown and Jefferson County through grants to community organizations and agencies and a student scholarship program.
Types of support awarded: Operating budgets, continuing support, annual campaigns, seed money, emergency funds, building funds, equipment, land acquisition, matching funds, student aid, special projects, research, publications.
Limitations: Giving limited to Watertown and Jefferson County, NY. No grants for endowment funds, or for deficit financing, or conferences.
Publications: Annual report, program policy statement, application guidelines.
Application information:
  Initial approach: Letter
  Copies of proposal: 1
  Deadline(s): February 1 for March meeting; August 1 for September meeting
  Board meeting date(s): March, June, September, and December; grants considered at March and September meetings only
  Final notification: 1 to 2 months
  Write: James E. McVean, Executive Director
Officers: James B. Fish, M.D.,* President; Richard O. Flechtner,* Vice-President; Frank A. Empsall,* Secretary-Treasurer; James E. McVean, Executive Director.
Directors:* Frances P. Carter, Floyd J. Chandler, William C. Couch, John Doldo, Jr., Barbara D. Hanrahan, James W. Higgins, Robert G. Horr, Jr., P. Owen Willaman.
Number of staff: 1 full-time professional; 1 full-time support; 1 part-time support.
Employer Identification Number: 156020989

3028
Weatherhead Foundation, The ▼
420 Lexington Ave., Rm. 1660
New York 10170   (212) 687-2130

Incorporated in 1953 in Ohio; foundation is income beneficiary of a perpetual trust; assets reflect assets of both feeder trust and foundation.
Donor(s): Albert J. Weatherhead, Jr.†

Financial data: (yr. ended 12/31/84): Assets, $15,973,640 (M); gifts received, $974,759; expenditures, $1,062,872, including $926,362 for 6 grants (high: $500,000; low: $2,000).
Purpose and activities: Grants for endowments or programs, principally to universities and research organizations.
Types of support awarded: Endowment funds, special projects, research.
Limitations: No support for religious purposes or for general support of church or denominational institutions. No grants to individuals.
Publications: Annual report, application guidelines, informational brochure.
Application information: Funds fully committed through 1988.
Board meeting date(s): Spring and fall, and as required
Write: Richard W. Weatherhead, President
Officers and Trustees: Richard W. Weatherhead,* President; Albert J. Weatherhead, III,* Vice-President and Secretary; Richard Eells,* Vice-President and Treasurer; Don K. Price,* Henry Rosovsky,* Stanley Salmen,* Dwight S. Weatherhead,* John P. Weatherhead,* Vice-Presidents; Muriel A. Golden, Administrative Director.
Number of staff: 1 full-time professional.
Employer Identification Number: 132711998

3029
Weezie Foundation, The ⌑
c/o Morgan Guaranty Trust Company of New York
Nine West 57th St.
New York 10019
Application address: Robert Schwecherl, Secretary, 499 Park Ave., 24th Fl., New York, NY 10022

Trust established in 1961 in New York.
Donor(s): Adelaide T. Corbett.†
Financial data: (yr. ended 12/31/83): Assets, $8,685,045 (M); gifts received, $500; expenditures, $537,862, including $469,640 for 20 grants (high: $75,000; low: $4,800).
Purpose and activities: Broad purposes; support for education, hospitals, the handicapped and youth agencies.
Application information:
Initial approach: Letter
Deadline(s): None
Write: Robert Schwecherl, Secretary
Officer and Trustees: Robert Schwecherl, Secretary and Treasurer; Morgan Guaranty Trust Company of New York.
Committee: D. Nelson Adams, Adelrick Benziger, Jr., James F. Dolan, Mrs. George F. Fiske, Jr., Mrs. William H. Hays III, Charles H. Thieriot, Lucile T. Walker.
Employer Identification Number: 136090903

3030
Wegman (John F.) Foundation, Inc.
335 E. Main St., Suite 402
Rochester 14604   (716) 325-4353

Incorporated in 1953 in New York.
Donor(s): John F. Wegman.†

Financial data: (yr. ended 12/31/83): Assets, $1,181,578 (M); expenditures, $97,382, including $95,150 for 27 grants (high: $10,000; low: $400; average: $2,500).
Purpose and activities: To support "any charitable, philanthropic and educational purpose which will make for the welfare of the Rochester and Monroe County community, and particularly giving assistance in the care of the aged, ... and to character building agencies, ... and in developing through educational work and otherwise, better relationship between capital and labor." Grants made primarily for youth agencies and higher education, including scholarship funds; grants also for child welfare agencies and health.
Types of support awarded: Seed money, emergency funds, building funds, equipment, special projects, scholarship funds.
Limitations: Giving limited to Monroe County, NY, with emphasis on Rochester. No grants to individuals, or for endowment funds, or operating budgets; no loans.
Publications: Program policy statement, application guidelines.
Application information: Application form required.
Initial approach: Letter
Copies of proposal: 3
Deadline(s): Submit proposal preferably in September, December, or March; no set deadline
Board meeting date(s): 4 to 5 times a year as required
Final notification: 3 months
Write: Linda S. Weinstein, Administrator
Officers: Anthony R. Palermo, President; Michael Harren, Vice-President; Rev. Charles Thurman, Secretary; Neil S. Norry, Linda S. Weinstein, Administrative Secretary.
Directors: Mary Ann Benincasa, John S. Gilman, Harold S. Hacker, Francena L. Miller, Rudolph Miller, Fred Neisner, Robert D. Skerritt, Carolyn R. Zaroff.
Number of staff: 1 part-time professional.
Employer Identification Number: 160834311

3031
Weiler (F.) Charity Fund ⌑
c/o Jack D. Weiler
1114 Ave. of the Americas
New York 10036

Trust established in 1946 in New York.
Donor(s): The Weiler family and associates.
Financial data: (yr. ended 12/31/83): Assets, $936,415 (M); gifts received, $180,000; expenditures, $133,307, including $124,700 for 73 grants (high: $45,000; low: $25).
Purpose and activities: Broad purposes; primarily local giving, with emphasis on Jewish welfare funds, religious education, and temple support.
Limitations: Giving primarily in NY.
Trustees: Robert H. Arnow, Alan G. Weiler, Jack D. Weiler.
Employer Identification Number: 136161247

3032
Weinberg (The John L.) Foundation
c/o Goldman, Sachs & Co.
85 Broad St.
New York 10004

Trust established in 1959 in New York.
Donor(s): John L. Weinberg.
Financial data: (yr. ended 4/30/84): Assets, $4,554,343 (M); gifts received, $1,106,250; expenditures, $201,448, including $196,482 for 98 grants (high: $50,000; low: $25).
Purpose and activities: Broad purposes; general giving, with emphasis on hospitals, secondary and higher education, and Jewish welfare funds.
Trustees: Arthur G. Altschul, John L. Weinberg, Sue Ann Weinberg, John C. Whitehead.
Employer Identification Number: 136028813

3033
Weinstein (The Alex J.) Foundation, Inc. ⌑
c/o Laventhol & Horwath
919 Third Ave.
New York 10022

Established in 1953.
Financial data: (yr. ended 11/30/82): Assets, $1,656,711 (M); expenditures, $232,645, including $219,025 for 19 grants (high: $155,000; low: $25).
Purpose and activities: Support largely for hospitals and higher education.
Officers and Directors: Samuel M. Miller, President; Herbert D. Feinberg, Secretary; Barrie W. Selesko, Treasurer.
Employer Identification Number: 136160964

3034
Weinstein (J.) Foundation, Inc.
c/o Sal Capuzzo, Secretary
Rockridge Farm, Route 52
Carmel 10512

Incorporated in 1948 in New York.
Donor(s): Joe Weinstein,† J.W. Mays, Inc., and others.
Financial data: (yr. ended 12/31/83): Assets, $1,407,817 (M); expenditures, $76,792 for 72 grants (high: $33,150; low: $10).
Purpose and activities: Primarily local giving, with support for higher education in the United States and Israel, temple support, hospitals, and Jewish welfare funds.
Limitations: Giving primarily in NY.
Officers: Max L. Shulman, President; Lloyd J. Shulman, Sylvia W. Shulman, Vice-Presidents; Sal Capuzzo, Secretary; Alex Slobodin, Treasurer.
Employer Identification Number: 116003595

3035
Wellington Foundation, Inc. ⌑
120 Broadway
New York 10005

Incorporated in 1955 in New York.
Donor(s): Herbert G. Wellington,† Herbert G. Wellington, Jr., Elizabeth D. Wellington.†

Financial data: (yr. ended 12/31/82): Assets, $1,907,259 (M); expenditures, $284,202, including $279,500 for 23 grants (high: $60,000; low: $1,000).

Purpose and activities: To support recognized medical, educational, and cultural programs.

Application information: Grants limited to institutions known to the Foundation, and no expansion of activities is anticipated in the forseeable future.

Officers and Directors: Herbert G. Wellington, Jr., President and Treasurer; Patricia B. Wellington, Vice-President; Thomas D. Wellington, Secretary.

Employer Identification Number: 136110175

3036
Wendt (The Margaret L.) Foundation ▼

1325 Liberty Bank Bldg.
Buffalo 14202   (716) 855-2146

Trust established in 1956 in New York.

Donor(s): Miss Margaret L. Wendt.†

Financial data: (yr. ended 1/31/84): Assets, $21,708,580 (M); expenditures, $1,374,099, including $1,060,261 for 58 grants (high: $100,000; low: $446).

Purpose and activities: Broad purposes; primarily local giving, with emphasis on education, hospitals and health organizations, the arts, and social services; support also for churches and religious organizations.

Limitations: Giving primarily in Buffalo and western NY. No grants to individuals or for scholarships.

Application information:
Initial approach: Letter
Copies of proposal: 4
Deadline(s): 1 month prior to board meeting
Board meeting date(s): Quarterly; no fixed dates
Final notification: Usually 4 to 6 months
Write: Robert J. Kresse, Secretary

Officers and Trustees: Ralph W. Loew, Chairman; Robert J. Kresse, Secretary; Thomas D. Lunt.

Number of staff: 1 part-time support.

Employer Identification Number: 166030037

3037
Wenner-Gren Foundation for Anthropological Research, Incorporated

1865 Broadway
New York 10023   (212) 957-8750

Incorporated in 1941 in Delaware.

Donor(s): Axel L. Wenner-Gren.†

Financial data: (yr. ended 12/31/83): Assets, $30,739,622 (M); expenditures, $1,730,535, including $471,958 for 126 grants (high: $12,000; low: $400) and $462,328 for foundation-administered programs.

Purpose and activities: A private operating foundation; international support of research in anthropology and in closely related disciplines so far as they pertain to the problems of the science of man; grants-in-aid for programs of research; subsidizes conferences for anthropologists to promote reporting on results of research; publishes a monograph series and journal and provides clearinghouse services for anthropological information.

Types of support awarded: Research, conferences and seminars, seed money, emergency funds, publications, fellowships, grants to individuals.

Limitations: No support for intermediary funding agencies. No grants for building or endowment funds, operating budgets, capital funds, or matching gifts; no loans.

Publications: Annual report, program policy statement, application guidelines.

Application information: Deadline schedule varies; contact Foundation for most recent information. Application form required.
Initial approach: Letter
Copies of proposal: 5
Deadline(s): April 1 for projects to begin January 1 through December 31
Board meeting date(s): April and November
Final notification: Approximately 6 months after deadline
Write: Mrs. Lita Osmundsen, Director of Research

Officers and Directors: Frank W. Wadsworth, Chairman; Richard Scheuch, Vice-Chairman; Lita Osmundsen, President, Director of Research, and Secretary; Hiram F. Moody, Jr., Treasurer; E.V. Ekman, Donald M. Engelman, W.T. Jones, Harold C. Martin, Dana H. Smith, Tracy Westen.

Number of staff: 2 full-time professional; 1 part-time professional; 9 full-time support; 2 part-time support.

Employer Identification Number: 131813827

3038
Werblow (Nina W.) Charitable Trust

c/o Ehrenkranz, Ehrenkranz and Schultz
375 Park Ave.
New York 10152

Trust established in New York.

Donor(s): Nina W. Werblow.†

Financial data: (yr. ended 2/28/83): Assets, $2,241,806 (M); expenditures, $193,965, including $146,500 for 54 grants (high: $19,000; low: $500).

Purpose and activities: Primarily local giving, with emphasis on hospitals, Jewish welfare organizations, higher education, social agencies, and cultural programs.

Limitations: Giving primarily in NY.

Trustees: Lillian Ahrens Carver, Joel S. Ehrenkranz, Roger A. Goldman.

Employer Identification Number: 136742999

3039
Western New York Foundation, The

Main-Seneca Bldg., Suite 1402
Buffalo 14203   (716) 847-6440

Incorporated in 1951 in New York.

Donor(s): Welles V. Moot.†

Financial data: (yr. ended 7/31/84): Assets, $2,714,338 (M); expenditures, $221,816, including $162,132 for 27 grants (high: $25,000; low: $100; average: $6,000).

Purpose and activities: Broad purposes; grants to local nonprofit institutions, with emphasis on capital needs, new projects, or expanding services. Support primarily for the performing arts, youth agencies, the natural sciences, and social agencies.

Types of support awarded: Building funds, equipment, land acquisition, endowment funds, special projects, publications, conferences and seminars, matching funds, loans.

Limitations: Giving limited to the 8th Judicial District of NY (Erie, Niagara, Genesee, Wyoming, Allegany, Cattaraugus, and Chautauqua Counties). No support for hospitals or religious organizations. No grants to individuals, or for scholarships and fellowships.

Publications: Annual report.

Application information: Application form required.
Initial approach: Letter, including copy of IRS exemption letter
Copies of proposal: 1
Deadline(s): None
Board meeting date(s): 3 or 4 times a year
Final notification: 4 to 6 weeks
Write: Welles V. Moot, Jr., President

Officers and Trustees: Welles V. Moot, Jr., President; Richard Moot, Robert S. Scheu, Vice-Presidents; John R. Moot, Secretary; Cecily M. Johnson, Treasurer.

Number of staff: 1.

Employer Identification Number: 160845962

3040
Westvaco Foundation Trust ▼ ¤

299 Park Ave.
New York 10171   (212) 688-5000

Trust established in 1951 in New York.

Donor(s): Westvaco Corporation.

Financial data: (yr. ended 12/31/83): Assets, $96,846 (M); gifts received, $550,000; expenditures, $611,112, including $548,550 for 132 grants (high: $43,500; low: $110) and $61,860 for employee matching gifts.

Purpose and activities: General giving, with emphasis on community funds, higher education, and hospitals.

Types of support awarded: Employee matching gifts.

Application information: Grants initiated primarily by plant managers; grant applications not invited.
Write: Donald C. Smith, Assistant Treasurer, Westvaco Corporation

Trustees: George Cruser, John A. Luke, Irving Trust Company.

Number of staff: 1 part-time professional; 1 part-time support.

Employer Identification Number: 136021319

3041
Whitehead Foundation, The ☐
c/o Goldman, Sachs & Co.
85 Broad St.
New York 10004

Established in 1982 in New York.
Donor(s): John C. Whitehead Foundation.
Financial data: (yr. ended 6/30/83): Assets,
$4,205,255 (M); gifts received, $2,000,000;
expenditures, $226,270, including $211,325
for 46 grants (high: $25,000; low: $150).
Purpose and activities: Giving primarily in
New York and New Jersey for higher
education, church support, the arts, and civic
organizations.
Limitations: Giving primarily in NY and NJ.
Trustees: Arthur G. Altschul, John L. Weinberg,
Jaan W. Whitehead, John C. Whitehead.
Employer Identification Number: 133119344

3042
Whiting (Mrs. Giles) Foundation ▼
30 Rockefeller Plaza
New York 10112   (212) 541-4000

Incorporated in 1963 in New York.
Donor(s): Mrs. Giles Whiting.†
Financial data: (yr. ended 11/30/84): Assets,
$14,491,000 (M); expenditures, $795,660,
including $645,000 for 8 grants (high: $90,000;
low: $25,000).
Purpose and activities: Charitable purposes;
grants only to seven higher educational
institutions conducting programs of Whiting
Fellowships in the Humanities.
Types of support awarded: Fellowships.
Limitations: No grants to individuals, or for
general support, capital funds, matching gifts,
research, special projects, publications, or
conferences; no loans.
Publications: Multi-year report.
Application information: Applications for
grants not invited.
   Board meeting date(s): May and November
   Write: Robert H.M. Ferguson, Secretary
Officer: Robert H.M. Ferguson, Secretary and
Treasurer.
Trustees: Mary St. John Douglas, Harry W.
Havemeyer, Robert Pennoyer.
Number of staff: 2 part-time professional.
Employer Identification Number: 136154484

3043
Whitney (The Helen Hay)
Foundation ▼
450 East 63rd St.
New York 10021   (212) 751-8228

Trust established in 1947; incorporated in 1951
in New York.
Donor(s): Mrs. Charles S. Payson.†
Financial data: (yr. ended 6/30/84): Assets,
$20,377,947 (M); expenditures, $1,314,544,
including $951,701 for 71 grants to individuals
(high: $25,240; low: $3,750).

Purpose and activities: To support beginning
postdoctoral training in basic biomedical
research; grants research fellowships for
postdoctoral candidates (age limit 35;
fellowships awarded to individuals but funds
administered largely by research institution;
American citizenship not required, but
applications not accepted from individuals or
organizations outside North America).
Types of support awarded: Fellowships.
Limitations: Giving limited to North America.
Publications: Annual report, program policy
statement, application guidelines.
Application information: Application form
required.
   Initial approach: Letter or telephone
   Copies of proposal: 7
   Deadline(s): Submit proposal in August;
      deadline August 15
   Board meeting date(s): January and June
   Final notification: 5 months
   Write: Barbara M. Hugonnet, Administrative
      Director
Officers: Mrs. Henry B. Middleton,* President;
Maclyn McCarty, M.D.,* Vice-President and
Chairman, Scientific Advisory Committee;
William A. Cameron,* Secretary; Jeffrey S.
Maurer,* Treasurer; Barbara M. Hugonnet,
Administrative Director.
Trustees:* Alexander G. Bearn, M.D., Charles
L. Christian, M.D., Sandra deRoulet, Thomas A.
Melfe, Lisa A. Steiner, M.D., Frank Streeter.
Number of staff: 1 full-time professional; 6
part-time professional; 1 part-time support.
Employer Identification Number: 131677403

3044
Wien (Lawrence A.) Foundation, Inc. ☐
c/o Wien, Lane & Malkin
60 East 42nd St.
New York 10165

Incorporated in 1953 in New York.
Donor(s): Lawrence A. Wien, Mae L. Wien,
and others.
Financial data: (yr. ended 6/30/83): Assets,
$3,463,666 (M); expenditures, $557,656,
including $548,804 for 213 grants (high:
$81,030; low: $100).
Purpose and activities: Broad purposes; grants
primarily for higher education, Jewish welfare
funds, and cultural programs; support also for
hospitals, largely in New York.
Application information:
   Write: Lawrence A. Wien, President
Officers and Directors: Lawrence A. Wien,
President and Treasurer; Peter L. Malkin,
Secretary; Isabel W. Malkin, Enid W. Morse,
Lester S. Morse, Jr., Mae L. Wien.
Employer Identification Number: 136095927

3045
Wikstrom Foundation
c/o Norstar Bank of Upstate New York, Trust
Dept.
69 State St.
Albany 12201   (518)447-4357

Established in 1960 in New York.
Donor(s): A.S. Wikstrom.†

Financial data: (yr. ended 12/31/84): Assets,
$1,895,004 (M); gifts received, $416,038;
expenditures, $328,907, including $285,145
for 43 grants (high: $50,000; low: $400;
average: $1,000-$20,000).
Purpose and activities: Grants primarily for
cultural programs and higher education;
support also for programs for the elderly, and
for Roman Catholic organizations, including
church support.
Types of support awarded: Operating
budgets, annual campaigns, building funds,
equipment, endowment funds, matching funds.
Limitations: Giving limited to NY. No grants
to individuals, or for continuing support, seed
money, emergency funds, deficit financing,
land acquisition, special projects, research,
publications, scholarships, fellowships, or
conferences; no loans.
Application information:
   Initial approach: Letter
   Final notification: 6 months
Trustee: Norstar Bank of Upstate New York.
Number of staff: None.
Employer Identification Number: 146014286

3046
Wilson (Elaine P. and Richard U.)
Foundation ☐
c/o Lincoln First Bank of Rochester
P.O. Box 1412
Rochester 14603

Established in 1963 in New York.
Donor(s): Katherine M. Wilson.†
Financial data: (yr. ended 12/31/82): Assets,
$4,404,781 (M); expenditures, $146,348,
including $137,000 for 16 grants (high:
$25,000; low: $1,000).
Purpose and activities: Charitable purposes;
primarily local giving, with emphasis on higher
and secondary education, Protestant church
support, cultural programs, and museums.
Limitations: Giving primarily in NY.
Trustee: Lincoln First Bank of Rochester.
Employer Identification Number: 166042023

3047
Wilson (The H. W.) Foundation, Inc. ☐
950 University Ave.
Bronx 10452   (212) 588-8400

Incorporated in 1952 in New York.
Donor(s): H.W. Wilson,† Mrs. H.W. Wilson,†
The H.W. Wilson Company, Inc.
Financial data: (yr. ended 11/30/82): Assets,
$3,694,794 (M); expenditures, $153,428,
including $140,834 for 41 grants (high:
$13,000; low: $500).
Purpose and activities: Broad purposes; grants
largely to accredited library schools for
scholarships; support also for cultural programs,
including historical societies, and a public
policy association.
Types of support awarded: Continuing
support, seed money, research, conferences
and seminars, scholarship funds.
Limitations: No grants for building or
endowment funds or operating budgets.
Application information:
   Initial approach: Letter

Copies of proposal: 1
Board meeting date(s): January, March, May, July, and October
Final notification: 3 months
Write: Leo M. Weins, President, or James Humphrey III, Vice-President
Officers and Directors: Howard Haycraft, Chairman; Leo M. Weins, President and Treasurer; James Humphrey III, Vice-President and Secretary; Florence A. Arnold, John Fall, Rutherford D. Rogers, William A. Ziegler.
Employer Identification Number: 237418062

3048
Wilson (Marie C. and Joseph C.) Foundation ▼
160 Allens Creek Rd.
Rochester 14618   (716) 461-4699

Trust established in 1963 in New York.
Donor(s): Katherine M. Wilson,† Joseph C. Wilson.†
Financial data: (yr. ended 12/31/83): Assets, $6,600,287 (M); expenditures, $466,627, including $400,466 for 36 grants (high: $50,000; low: $100; average: $1,000-$25,000).
Purpose and activities: Broad purposes; primarily local giving, with emphasis on social services, health and medical research, education, housing and youth agencies.
Types of support awarded: Operating budgets, continuing support, annual campaigns, seed money, emergency funds, deficit financing, building funds, endowment funds, matching funds, internships, scholarship funds, fellowships, special projects, research, conferences and seminars.
Limitations: Giving primarily in Rochester, NY. No grants to individuals, or for equipment, land acquisition, or publications; no loans.
Publications: Annual report, application guidelines.
Application information: Application form required.
Initial approach: Letter
Copies of proposal: 10
Deadline(s): 4 weeks before board meeting
Board meeting date(s): February, May, and September
Final notification: 3 months
Write: Ruth H. Fleischmann, Executive Director
Officer: Ruth H. Fleischmann, Executive Director.
Board of Managers: Deidre W. Garton, Chairperson; Joan W. Dalbey, Marie O. Dalbey, Judith W. Martin, Katherine W. Roby, J. Christine Wilson, J. Richard Wilson, Marie C. Wilson.
Trustee: Lincoln First Bank of Rochester.
Number of staff: 1 part-time professional; 1 part-time support.
Employer Identification Number: 166042022

3049
Wilson (Robert and Marillyn) Foundation ▼
250 West 57th St.
New York 10107   (212) 586-7620

Trust established in 1964 in New York.
Donor(s): Robert W. Wilson, Marillyn B. Wilson.
Financial data: (yr. ended 12/31/83): Assets, $199,859 (M); expenditures, $960,336, including $928,670 for 68 grants (high: $135,000; low: $20).
Purpose and activities: Primarily local giving, with emphasis on music, especially opera, social services, historic preservation, population control, the arts, and conservation.
Types of support awarded: Building funds, equipment, land acquisition, matching funds, loans.
Limitations: Giving primarily in New York City, NY. No grants to individuals, or for endowment funds, research, scholarships, or fellowships.
Publications: Annual report.
Application information:
Initial approach: Telephone or proposal
Copies of proposal: 1
Deadline(s): Submit proposal preferably in January or February; no set deadline
Board meeting date(s): As required
Write: Robert W. Wilson, Trustee
Trustees: Richard Gilder, Marillyn B. Wilson, Robert W. Wilson.
Number of staff: None.
Employer Identification Number: 116037280

3050
Winfield Foundation ⌘
680 Fifth Ave., Rm. 1706
New York 10019   (212) 245-7580

Incorporated in 1941 in New York.
Donor(s): Frasier W. McCann, Mrs. Helena M. Charlton.†
Financial data: (yr. ended 9/30/82): Assets, $1,038,429 (M); expenditures, $73,930, including $55,500 for 20 grants (high: $20,000; low: $500).
Purpose and activities: Broad purposes; primarily local giving, with emphasis on historic preservation, music, and hospitals.
Limitations: Giving primarily in NY. No grants to individuals, or for research-related programs, scholarships or fellowships, or matching gifts; no loans.
Application information:
Initial approach: Letter
Copies of proposal: 1
Board meeting date(s): Semiannually
Write: Frasier W. McCann, President
Officers and Directors: Frasier W. McCann, President; Franklin W. McCann, D. Chase Troxell, Vice-Presidents; Evelyn B. Field, Margaret G. Maher, Secretaries; Gordon S. Gavan, Treasurer.
Employer Identification Number: 136158017

3051
Winston (Harry) Research Foundation, Inc. ⌘
718 Fifth Ave.
New York 10019

Incorporated in 1964 in New York.
Donor(s): Harry Winston,† Ronald Winston.
Financial data: (yr. ended 12/31/82): Assets, $73,387,003 (M); gifts received, $71,128,917; expenditures, $180,590, including $111,900 for 9 grants (high: $100,000; low: $100).
Purpose and activities: Broad purposes; primarily local giving with emphasis on programs of scientific research in the field of genetics and related medical research; includes support for hospitals and higher education.
Types of support awarded: Research.
Limitations: Giving primarily in NY.
Officers: Ronald Winston, President; Robert Holtzman, Vice-President; Gerald Schultz, Secretary-Treasurer.
Employer Identification Number: 136168266

3052
Winston (The Norman and Rosita) Foundation, Inc. ⌘
c/o Robinson, Perlman and Kirschner
32 East 57th St.
New York 10022

Incorporated in 1954 in New York.
Donor(s): Norman K. Winston,† The N.K. Winston Foundation, Inc.
Financial data: (yr. ended 12/31/83): Assets, $26,176,616 (M); gifts received, $8,321; expenditures, $1,844,173, including $1,665,000 for 57 grants (high: $550,000; low: $1,000).
Purpose and activities: Broad purposes; largely local giving, with emphasis on Jewish welfare organizations, higher education, including medical and theological education, hospitals, cultural programs, and secondary education.
Types of support awarded: General purposes.
Limitations: Giving primarily in NY. No grants to individuals.
Application information:
Initial approach: Proposal
Copies of proposal: 1
Deadline(s): October 1
Board meeting date(s): 2 to 4 times a year
Final notification: By the end of December
Write: Joel M. Rudell, Secretary
Officers and Trustees:* Simon H. Rifkind, President; Arthur Levitt, Jr.,* Vice-President; Joel Rudell,* Secretary; Julian S. Perlman, Treasurer.
Employer Identification Number: 136161672

3053
Witco Foundation, The ▼
(formerly Witco Chemical Corporation Foundation)
520 Madison Ave.
New York 10022   (212) 605-3843

Incorporated in 1951 in Illinois.
Donor(s): Witco Chemical Corporation.

Financial data: (yr. ended 12/31/82): Assets, $5,357,795 (M); gifts received, $623,000; expenditures, $499,465, including $483,286 for 198 grants (high: $127,300; low: $25).
Purpose and activities: Broad purposes; grants largely for religious, charitable, scientific and educational purposes, including support for hospitals and local organizations; grants also for higher education, community funds, Jewish welfare funds.
Types of support awarded: Annual campaigns, endowment funds, research, conferences and seminars, scholarship funds, fellowships, employee related scholarships, general purposes.
Limitations: No grants to individuals (except for company-employee scholarships), or for matching gifts; no loans.
Application information: Requests from outside New York City must be forwarded through local offices of the corporation.
Initial approach: Full proposal
Copies of proposal: 1
Deadline(s): None
Board meeting date(s): Monthly
Final notification: 6 to 8 weeks
Write: Earl L. Hogard, Secretary, for national and NY organizations; local company offices for local organizations
Officers: William Wishnick,* President; Thomas J. Bickett, Vice-President; Earl L. Hogard,* Secretary; William J. Ashe,* Treasurer.
Directors: Robert L. Bachner, Simeon Brinberg, Charles H. Tally.
Employer Identification Number: 136068668

3054
Wohlgemuth (Esther & Martin) Foundation, Inc. ⌑
P.O. Box 595
Monroe 10950

Incorporated in 1956 in New York.
Donor(s): Morton Wohlgemuth,† Esther Wohlgemuth, Alexander Wohlgemuth, Robert Wohlgemuth.
Financial data: (yr. ended 12/31/82): Assets, $1,375,797 (M); expenditures, $78,652, including $66,400 for 48 grants (high: $15,500; low: $100).
Purpose and activities: Primarily local giving for Jewish welfare funds, higher education, and health agencies.
Limitations: Giving primarily in NY.
Officer and Directors: Alexander Wohlgemuth, Vice-President; Esther Wohlgemuth, Robert Wolgemuth.
Employer Identification Number: 136086849

3055
Wolfowski Foundation, Inc. ▼ ⌑
One State St. Plaza
New York 10004

Incorporated in 1953 in New York.
Financial data: (yr. ended 12/30/82): Assets, $280,480 (M); expenditures, $146,537, including $146,119 for 39 grants (high: $58,000; low: $25).

Purpose and activities: Grants largely for Jewish welfare funds, Jewish religious education in the United States and Israel, and temple support.
Manager: Zev W. Wolfson.
Employer Identification Number: 136168759

3056
Wolfson (Erwin S. and Rose F.) Foundation, Inc. ⌑
c/o Proskauer, Rose, Goetz, & Mendelsohn
300 Park Ave.
New York 10022

Incorporated in 1958 in New York.
Donor(s): Erwin S. Wolfson,† Rose F. Wolfson, 100 Church Street Management Corporation, Wolfson Management Corporation.
Financial data: (yr. ended 12/31/82): Assets, $508,789 (M); expenditures, $227,263, including $211,845 for 94 grants (high: $100,000; low: $50).
Purpose and activities: General purposes; grants largely for higher education, Jewish welfare funds, and medical research.
Limitations: No grants to individuals.
Application information:
Write: Wilbur H. Friedman, Vice-President
Officers and Directors: Rose F. Wolfson, President and Treasurer; Wilbur H. Friedman, Vice-President and Secretary; John Wolfson, Vice-President.
Employer Identification Number: 136117678

3057
Wood Kalb Foundation ⌑
One Rockefeller Plaza, Suite 2100
New York 10020

Trust established in 1953 in New York.
Donor(s): Social Research Foundation, Inc.
Financial data: (yr. ended 12/31/83): Assets, $419,711 (M); expenditures, $209,937, including $194,652 for 20 grants (high: $30,000; low: $100).
Purpose and activities: Grants largely for higher education, medical research, and social services, including youth agencies.
Trustee: Ethan A. Hitchcock.
Employer Identification Number: 136105376

3058
Woodland Foundation, Inc. ⌑
c/o Bankers Trust Company
280 Park Ave.
New York 10017

Incorporated in 1950 in Delaware.
Donor(s): William Durant Campbell.
Financial data: (yr. ended 12/31/83): Assets, $2,330,428 (M); gifts received, $4,000; expenditures, $150,751, including $134,087 for 46 grants (high: $25,000; low: $200).
Purpose and activities: Broad purposes; general giving, with emphasis on higher and secondary education; grants also for youth agencies, Protestant church support, and hospitals.
Application information:
Deadline(s): None

Write: Harvey G. Burney, Treasurer
Officers and Trustees: William Durant Campbell, President; Jeremiah M. Bogert, Margot C. Bogert, Vice-Presidents; Winthrop Rutherford, Jr., Secretary; Harvey G. Burney, Treasurer; Beatrice Campbell, George W. Knight, Richard A. Nelson.
Employer Identification Number: 136018244

3059
Wooley-Clifford Foundation, The
c/o G. A. Wolf
745 Fifth Ave., Rm. 601
New York 10151

Incorporated in 1953 in Delaware.
Donor(s): Stewart B. Clifford, Cornelia W. Clifford.
Financial data: (yr. ended 12/31/82): Assets, $553,938 (M); gifts received, $188,946; expenditures, $166,583, including $162,596 for 51 grants (high: $69,246; low: $100).
Purpose and activities: Broad purposes; support primarily for higher education and private secondary schools; giving locally for social services and cultural programs; support also for a Protestant church.
Limitations: Giving primarily in NY.
Manager: Stewart B. Clifford.
Employer Identification Number: 136100412

3060
Wrightson-Ramsing Foundation, Inc.
375 Park Ave., Suite 3408
New York 10152

Incorporated in 1952 in New York.
Donor(s): Martha Wrightson Ramsing.
Financial data: (yr. ended 12/31/82): Assets, $1,235,792 (M); expenditures, $167,426, including $151,280 for 57 grants (high: $25,500; low: $100).
Purpose and activities: Grants primarily for cultural programs and museums, higher education, and welfare.
Application information:
Initial approach: Letter
Officers: Thor H. Ramsing,* President and Treasurer; Martha Wrightson Ramsing,* Vice-President; Anthony A. Bliss, Secretary.
Directors: Byron L. Ramsing, Martha R. Zoubek.
Employer Identification Number: 131967462

3061
Wunsch Foundation, Inc. ⌑
861 Sixty-third St.
Brooklyn 11220

Incorporated in 1943 in New York.
Donor(s): Joseph W. Wunsch, Eric M. Wunsch, Samuel Wunsch.
Financial data: (yr. ended 12/31/81): Assets, $2,044,232 (M); gifts received, $128,262; expenditures, $167,021, including $163,700 for 18 grants (high: $60,000; low: $100).

Purpose and activities: For advancement of the study of engineering through scholarship funds and scientific research; also general charitable giving, with emphasis on higher education and Jewish welfare funds.
Types of support awarded: Research, scholarship funds.
Application information:
Write: Eric M. Wunsch, Vice-President
Officers and Directors: Joseph W. Wunsch, President; Eric M. Wunsch, Vice-President; Ethel Wunsch, Secretary.
Employer Identification Number: 116006013

3062
Young & Rubicam Foundation, The
c/o R. John Cooper, President
285 Madison Ave.
New York 10017   (212) 210-3000

Incorporated in 1955 in New York.
Donor(s): Young & Rubicam, Inc.
Financial data: (yr. ended 12/31/83): Assets, $39,057 (M); gifts received, $323,936; expenditures, $320,137, including $264,350 for grants and $55,787 for 316 employee matching gifts.
Purpose and activities: Grants primarily for a matching gifts program; foundation directors initiate contributions for selected community funds, cultural programs, including the performing arts, community development, and youth agencies.
Types of support awarded: Employee matching gifts.
Limitations: No grants to individuals, or for capital or endowment funds, scholarships and fellowships, operating budgets, continuing support, annual campaigns, seed money, emergency funds, deficit financing, special projects, research, publications, or conferences; no loans.
Application information: Applications not accepted.
Board meeting date(s): June and November
Write: Alice M. Saunders, Secretary
Officers and Directors: R. John Cooper, President; Joan Hafey, Mark Stroock, Vice-Presidents; Alice M. Saunders, Secretary; William J. Beihl, Treasurer.
Number of staff: 5 part-time support.
Employer Identification Number: 136156199

3063
Youth Foundation, Inc.
36 West 44th St.
New York 10036

Incorporated in 1940 in New York.
Donor(s): Alexander M. Hadden,† Mrs. Alexander M. Hadden,† and others.
Financial data: (yr. ended 12/31/82): Assets, $2,507,634 (M); gifts received, $4,560; expenditures, $222,192, including $14,250 for 54 grants (high: $2,000; low: $100) and $150,000 for 100 grants to individuals.

Purpose and activities: Emphasis on assisting young people to a richer experience in living. Approximately 50 Alexander and Maude Hadden Scholarships of $1,500 each awarded annually to undergraduate students who have demonstrated need as well as ability.
Types of support awarded: Student aid.
Limitations: No support for post-graduate studies.
Publications: Application guidelines, program policy statement.
Application information: All entries must include self-addressed stamped envelope. Application form required.
Initial approach: Letter
Copies of proposal: 1
Deadline(s): April 15
Write: Edward F.L. Bruen, Vice-President
Officers and Directors: Mrs. Guy Norman Robinson, President; Edward F.L. Bruen, Vice-President; Henry S. Middendorf, Jr., Secretary; Jack L. Rubin, Treasurer; Mrs. C. Kenneth Clinton, John L. Clinton, Edwin B. Colwell, John L. Fenton, James W. Gerard, Mrs. James W. Gerard, J. Campbell Henry, Mrs. Donald M. Liddell, Jr., Asa E. Phillips, Jr., Harry Roberts, Horace B.B. Robinson.
Employer Identification Number: 136093036

3064
Yulman (Morton & Helen) Trust ¤
c/o Schenectady Trust Company
P.O. Box 380
Schenectady 12301

Established in 1955.
Donor(s): Morton Yulman, Helen Yulman, Sealy of Minnesota, Inc., Sealy of Eastern New York, Inc.
Financial data: (yr. ended 12/31/82): Assets, $1,102,580 (M); gifts received, $104,000; expenditures, $108,438, including $104,150 for 28 grants (high: $50,000; low: $100).
Purpose and activities: Giving locally and in Florida, primarily to Jewish welfare organizations, social services, and a college.
Limitations: Giving primarily in upstate NY and FL.
Trustee: Schenectady Trust Co.
Employer Identification Number: 146015572

3065
Zacharia (Isaac Herman) Foundation, Inc. ¤
c/o Weinick, Sanders and Company
1515 Broadway
New York 10036

Incorporated in 1953 in New York.
Donor(s): Isaac H. Zacharia, and others.
Financial data: (yr. ended 12/31/82): Assets, $1,503,016 (M); gifts received, $66,220; expenditures, $99,835, including $91,498 for 42 grants (high: $30,000; low: $10).
Purpose and activities: Broad purposes; primarily local giving, with emphasis on education, including religious education; grants also for aid to the handicapped, temple support, Jewish welfare funds, and recreation.

Limitations: Giving primarily in NY.
Officers: Isaac H. Zacharia, President; Sarah Marmorstein, Secretary.
Employer Identification Number: 510108212

3066
Zarkin (Charles) Memorial Foundation, Inc.
c/o Wachtell, Lipton, Rosen & Katz
299 Park Ave.
New York 10171

Incorporated in 1969 in New York.
Donor(s): Fay Zarkin.†
Financial data: (yr. ended 12/31/83): Assets, $2,514,425 (M); expenditures, $177,795, including $140,000 for grants (high: $50,000; low: $5,000).
Purpose and activities: Primarily local giving, with emphasis on Jewish welfare funds, youth agencies, hospitals, higher education, and cultural programs.
Limitations: Giving primarily in New York, NY. No grants to individuals.
Application information:
Board meeting date(s): December
Officers: Martin Lipton, President; Leonard Rosen, Estelle Oleck, Vice-Presidents; Constance Monte, Secretary.
Trustees: Robert B. McKay, Lester Pollack.
Number of staff: None.
Employer Identification Number: 237149277

3067
Zilkha Foundation, Inc., The
30 Rockefeller Plaza
New York 10112-0153   (212) 765-8661

Incorporated in 1948 in New York.
Donor(s): Selim K. Zilkha, Ezra K. Zilkha, Zilkha & Sons, Inc.
Financial data: (yr. ended 8/31/83): Assets, $1,385,287 (M); expenditures, $352,754, including $335,173 for 54 grants (high: $202,563; low: $15).
Purpose and activities: A small family foundation of which a large part of funds are designated for specific charities; grants primarily for higher education, Jewish welfare and educational funds, the performing arts, and intercultural organizations; support also for a hospital.
Limitations: No grants to individuals.
Application information: Grants awarded largely at the initiative of the officers.
Initial approach: Letter
Deadline(s): August 31
Board meeting date(s): December
Write: Ezra K. Zilkha, President
Officers: Ezra K. Zilkha, President and Treasurer; Selim K. Zilkha, Vice-President; Cecile E. Zilkha, Secretary.
Number of staff: None.
Employer Identification Number: 136090739

3068
Zimmermann (Marie and John) Fund, Inc. ⌐
c/o U.S. Trust Company of New York
45 Wall St.
New York 10005

Incorporated in 1942 in New York.
Donor(s): Marie Zimmermann,† Frank A. Zunio, Jr.
Financial data: (yr. ended 12/31/82): Assets, $3,173,107 (M); expenditures, $192,787, including $166,000 for 4 grants (high: $97,000; low: $8,000).
Purpose and activities: Charitable purposes; grants primarily for higher education, particularly medical education.
Officers and Directors: John C. Zimmermann III, President; Thomas Parsons, III, Secretary; Robert E. Hill, Treasurer; J. Robert Buchanan, M.D., Henry W. Grady, Jr., Anne C. Heller, A. Parks McCombs, Thomas H. Meikle, Jr., Robert Perret, Jr.
Employer Identification Number: 136158767

3069
Zimtbaum (Arthur) Foundation, Inc. ⌐
c/o Elihu H. Modlin
1050 Franklin Ave.
Garden City 11530

Incorporated in 1955 in New York.
Donor(s): Arthur Zimtbaum,† Rose B. Levantine.
Financial data: (yr. ended 12/31/82): Assets, $905,887 (M); expenditures, $134,854, including $110,300 for 17 grants (high: $25,000; low: $600).
Purpose and activities: Primarily local giving for hospitals, cultural programs, and higher education.
Limitations: Giving primarily in NY.
Manager: Rose B. Levantine.
Employer Identification Number: 116016391

3070
Zlinkoff (Sergei S.) Fund for Medical Research and Education, Inc. ⌐
c/o Guggenheimer & Untermyer
80 Pine St.
New York 10005

Incorporated in 1956 in New York.
Donor(s): Sergei S. Zlinkoff.†
Financial data: (yr. ended 10/31/83): Assets, $1,680,789 (M); expenditures, $204,756, including $190,300 for 16 grants (high: $25,000; low: $1,500).
Purpose and activities: Grants primarily for higher education, including medical education and research.
Officers: Mack Lipkin, President; Milton Handsky, Vice-President.
Directors: Victor Brudney, Jerome Cohen, Ralph E. Hansmann, John O. Lipkin, Mack Lipkin, Jr.
Employer Identification Number: 136094651

NORTH CAROLINA

3071
ABC Foundation
P.O. Box 120
Charlotte 28255

Trust established in 1944 in North Carolina.
Donor(s): Cone Mills Corporation.
Financial data: (yr. ended 10/31/82): Assets, $3,930,995 (M); gifts received, $200,000; expenditures, $401,804, including $377,350 for 71 grants (high: $32,500; low: $100).
Purpose and activities: Charitable purposes; grants for higher education, community funds, cultural and child welfare programs in areas of Corporation operations.
Limitations: Giving limited to areas of company operations. No grants to individuals.
Application information:
 Initial approach: Letter
 Copies of proposal: 1
 Board meeting date(s): Annually and as required
Trustees: Lacy G. Baynes, W.O. Leonard, Dewey L. Trogdon, North Carolina National Bank.
Employer Identification Number: 566040774

3072
Akers Foundation, Inc. ⌐
P.O. Box 2726
Gastonia 28053

Incorporated in 1955 in North Carolina.
Financial data: (yr. ended 12/31/83): Assets, $1,399,048 (M); expenditures, $162,814, including $146,495 for 54 grants (high: $25,500; low: $85).
Purpose and activities: Primarily local giving for Protestant church support, higher education, and social services; support also for cultural programs.
Limitations: Giving primarily in NC.
Officers and Directors: John M. Akers, President and Treasurer; C. Scott Akers, Vice-President; Charles W. Akers, Secretary.
Employer Identification Number: 566044428

3073
Akzona Foundation, The
Sand Hill Rd.
Enka 28728   (704) 667-6485

Trust established in 1952 in North Carolina.
Donor(s): American Enka Corporation.
Financial data: (yr. ended 12/31/84): Assets, $385,767 (M); expenditures, $214,234, including $172,868 for 21 grants (high: $50,000; low: $2,500) and $41,366 for 137 employee matching gifts.

Purpose and activities: Broad purposes; giving primarily in North Carolina and in areas of company operations, for scholarships, fellowships, and matching contributions of employees to accredited colleges, universities, and preparatory schools; support also for community funds, health, and youth agencies in areas of company operations.
Types of support awarded: Employee matching gifts, scholarship funds, fellowships.
Limitations: Giving primarily in NC and in areas of company operations. No grants to individuals.
Publications: Application guidelines.
Application information: Submit proposal in October.
 Initial approach: Letter
 Copies of proposal: 4
 Board meeting date(s): December
 Write: Mortimer Ryon, Secretary
Officer: Mortimer Ryon, Secretary.
Trustees: G. John Coli, Vinson A. Parsons, Met R. Poston.
Employer Identification Number: 566061194

3074
Anderson (Robert C. and Sadie G.) Foundation
c/o North Carolina National Bank
Charlotte 28255   (704) 374-5721

Trust established in 1952 in North Carolina.
Donor(s): Robert C. Anderson,† Sadie Gaither Anderson.†
Financial data: (yr. ended 12/31/83): Assets, $1,767,663 (M); expenditures, $148,593, including $135,000 for 18 grants (high: $55,000; low: $1,500).
Purpose and activities: Support only for Presbyterian causes or institutions within North Carolina.
Limitations: Giving limited to NC. No grants to individuals, or for operating budgets, building or endowment funds, or matching gifts; no loans.
Publications: Program policy statement.
Application information:
 Initial approach: Letter
 Copies of proposal: 10
 Deadline(s): Submit proposal in February; deadline March 1
 Board meeting date(s): April
 Write: John F. Renger, Jr., Vice-President, North Carolina National Bank
Directors: William M. M. Barnhardt, Katherine M. Belk, Voit Gilmore, Carl Horn, Jr., P. Greer Johnson, Ralph S. Robinson, Jr., J.M. Trotter.
Trustee: North Carolina National Bank (John F. Renger, Jr., Vice-President).
Employer Identification Number: 566065233

3075
Babcock (Mary Reynolds) Foundation, Incorporated ▼
102 Reynolda Village
Winston-Salem 27106-5123   (919) 748-9222

Incorporated in 1953 in North Carolina.
Donor(s): Mrs. Mary Reynolds Babcock,† Charles H. Babcock.†

Financial data: (yr. ended 8/31/84): Assets, $40,601,750 (M); expenditures, $3,921,773, including $3,127,491 for 156 grants (high: $175,000; low: $1,000; average: $10,000-$50,000) and $200,000 for 2 loans.
Purpose and activities: Broad purposes; grants primarily for education, social services, including community development and youth employment, the environment, and citizen participation in the development of public policy.
Types of support awarded: Operating budgets, seed money, emergency funds, special projects, program-related investments.
Limitations: Giving primarily in NC and the southeastern United States, and to national organizations. No support for medical research, public health, international activities, or local or county projects. No grants to individuals, or for capital or endowment funds, scholarships or fellowships, or matching gifts; no student loans.
Publications: Annual report, program policy statement, application guidelines.
Application information: Application form required.
  Initial approach: Letter, full proposal, or telephone
  Copies of proposal: 1
  Deadline(s): Submit proposal between December and February or June and August; deadlines March 1 and September 1
  Board meeting date(s): May and November
  Final notification: First week of the month following a board meeting
  Write: William L. Bondurant, Executive Director
Officers: Katharine B. Mountcastle,* President; Zachary T. Smith,* Vice-President; Barbara B. Millhouse,* Secretary; Kenneth F. Mountcastle, Jr.,* Treasurer; William L. Bondurant, Executive Director.
Directors:* Betsy M. Babcock, Bruce M. Babcock, Charles H. Babcock, Jr., Wallace Carroll, Kenneth F. Mountcastle, III, L. Richardson Preyer, Milton C. Rose, Paul N. Ylvisaker.
Number of staff: 3 full-time professional; 2 full-time support.
Employer Identification Number: 560690140

3076
BarclaysAmerican/Foundation, Inc.
201 South Tryon St.
P.O. Box 31488
Charlotte 28231   (704) 372-0060

Incorporated in 1959 in North Carolina.
Donor(s): BarclaysAmerican Corporation, and subsidiaries.
Financial data: (yr. ended 12/31/84): Assets, $1,246,596 (M); gifts received, $429,010; expenditures, $368,458, including $346,596 for 360 grants (high: $40,000; low: $100) and $21,862 for 124 employee matching gifts.
Purpose and activities: Broad purposes; grants in areas of Company operations, largely for education and community funds; support also for youth agencies, the arts, and medical institutions.

Types of support awarded: Operating budgets, continuing support, annual campaigns, building funds, equipment, matching funds.
Limitations: Giving limited to areas of company operations. No grants to individuals, or for endowment funds, scholarships, fellowships, or research; no loans.
Application information:
  Initial approach: Letter
  Copies of proposal: 2
  Deadline(s): None
  Board meeting date(s): April and December
  Final notification: 6 months
  Write: Robert V. Knight, Jr., Secretary
Officers and Directors: Graeme M. Keith, President and Chairman; Robert V. Knight, Jr., Secretary and Treasurer; Jack A. Reeder, Bland W. Worley.
Employer Identification Number: 566060973

3077
Belk Foundation, The ⌷
P.O. Box 32245
800 Briar Creek Rd.
Charlotte 28232

Trust established in 1928 in North Carolina.
Donor(s): The Belk mercantile corporations.
Financial data: (yr. ended 5/31/82): Assets, $9,057,446 (M); gifts received, $348,513; expenditures, $891,755, including $868,400 for 31 grants (high: $100,000; low: $400).
Purpose and activities: Broad purposes; grants largely for higher education and community funds; support also for youth agencies and cultural programs, mainly in North and South Carolina.
Limitations: Giving primarily in NC and SC.
Trustee: I.N. Howard.
Advisors: Thomas M. Belk, Chairman; Irwin Belk, John M. Belk, John Belk Stevens.
Employer Identification Number: 566046450

3078
Biddle (The Mary Duke) Foundation ▼
1044 W. Forest Hills Blvd.
Durham 27707   (919) 493-5591

Trust established in 1956 in New York.
Donor(s): Mary Duke Biddle.†
Financial data: (yr. ended 12/31/84): Assets, $10,753,746 (M); expenditures, $858,396, including $646,370 for 64 grants (high: $14,500; low: $500; average: $2,500-$10,000).
Purpose and activities: Grants restricted to New York City and North Carolina, with emphasis on higher and secondary education, specified churches, cultural programs, particularly music, projects in the arts, and aid to the community and to the handicapped; half of the income is committed to Duke University.
Types of support awarded: Seed money, research, conferences and seminars, scholarship funds, fellowships, professorships, general purposes, matching funds, emergency funds.
Limitations: Giving limited to New York, NY, and NC. No grants to individuals, or for building or endowment funds, or operating budgets; no loans.

Publications: Annual report, application guidelines, program policy statement.
Application information:
  Initial approach: Letter
  Copies of proposal: 1
  Deadline(s): None
  Board meeting date(s): March, June, September, and December
  Final notification: Approximately 90 days for negative responses
  Write: Dr. James H. Semans, Chairman
Officers and Trustees: James H. Semans, M.D., Chairman; Mary D.B.T. Semans, Vice-Chairman; T.S. Kenan III, Secretary and Treasurer; Archie K. Davis, Mary Duke Trent Jones.
Number of staff: 4 part-time professional; 4 part-time support.
Employer Identification Number: 136068883

3079
Blue Bell Foundation
c/o Blue Bell, Inc.
P.O. Box 21488
Greensboro 27420   (919) 373-3476

Trust established in 1944 in North Carolina.
Donor(s): Blue Bell, Inc.
Financial data: (yr. ended 9/30/83): Assets, $3,528,548 (M); expenditures, $354,248, including $319,315 for 194 grants (high: $25,000; low: $25) and $26,592 for 129 employee matching gifts.
Purpose and activities: Grants for higher and secondary education, including matching gifts, community funds, hospitals and cultural programs in the localities in which the corporation has plants.
Types of support awarded: Employee matching gifts.
Limitations: Giving primarily in areas where corporation has plants.
Application information:
  Initial approach: Letter
  Deadline(s): None
  Write: Edward K. Crothers, Jr., Chairman
Advisory Committee: E.K. Crothers, Jr., Chairman; E.F. Lucas, L.K. Mann, R.M. Odear, P.B. Thompson, B.T. Toben, K.E. Tutterow.
Trustee: Wachovia Bank and Trust Company.
Employer Identification Number: 566041057

3080
Blumenthal Foundation, The
P.O. Box 34689
Charlotte 28234   (704) 377-6555

Trust established in 1953 in North Carolina.
Donor(s): I.D. Blumenthal,† Herman Blumenthal, Radiator Specialty Company.
Financial data: (yr. ended 4/30/83): Assets, $14,579,741 (M); expenditures, $881,875, including $848,789 for 142 grants (high: $437,000; low: $15).
Purpose and activities: Broad purposes; primarily local giving for higher education, Jewish welfare organizations, and programs in the arts and humanities; also supports Wildacres, a conference center in North Carolina, which invites groups in a variety of disciplines to use its facilities.

Limitations: Giving primarily in NC. No grants to individuals, or for scholarships or fellowships; no loans.
Application information:
Initial approach: Letter or full proposal
Copies of proposal: 1
Deadline(s): 15 days before board meetings
Board meeting date(s): March, June, and October
Final notification: 1 to 3 months
Write: Herman Blumenthal, Trustee
Trustees: Herman Blumenthal, Chairman; Alan Blumenthal, Anita Blumenthal, Philip Blumenthal, Samuel Blumenthal.
Employer Identification Number: 560793667

3081
Broyhill Foundation, Inc. ▼
P.O. Box 700
Lenoir 28633   (704) 758-3111

Incorporated in 1945 in North Carolina.
Donor(s): Broyhill Furniture Industries, Inc., James E. Broyhill, and family.
Financial data: (yr. ended 12/31/83): Assets, $18,697,186 (M); gifts received, $67,480; expenditures, $610,444, including $573,059 for 244 grants (high: $100,000; low: $50; average: $500-$5,000) and $54,520 for 51 loans.
Purpose and activities: Broad purposes; originally intended to assist deserving children to obtain a college education through loans; local giving largely for education; support also for health, child development and welfare, civic and community services, and the free enterprise system. The foundation is no longer funding new student loans directly to individuals. A special Investment Loan Program is now available through the College Foundation, Inc.
Types of support awarded: Scholarship funds, special projects.
Limitations: Giving primarily in NC. No grants to individuals.
Application information: Application forms for student loans available from foundation. Applications considered within calendar year submitted. Application form required.
Initial approach: Letter
Board meeting date(s): Quarterly
Final notification: Within calendar year
Write: Paul H. Broyhill, President
Officers and Directors: James E. Broyhill, Chairman; Paul H. Broyhill, President; E.D. Beach, Secretary-Treasurer; Mrs. Lee E. Pritchard, M. Hunt Broyhill.
Employer Identification Number: 566054119

3082
Bryan (James E. and Mary Z.) Foundation, Inc.
First Citizens Bank and Trust Company
P.O. Box 151
Raleigh 27602   (919) 755-7101

Incorporated in 1954 in North Carolina.
Donor(s): James E. Bryan,† Mary Z. Bryan.†

Financial data: (yr. ended 6/30/84): Assets, $2,885,040 (M); expenditures, $327,427, including $307,500 for 17 grants (high: $75,000; low: $1,500).
Purpose and activities: To aid needy students who are residents of North Carolina through grants to trade schools, colleges, or universities in or outside the state; support also to secondary schools.
Types of support awarded: Scholarship funds.
Limitations: Giving limited to NC. No grants to individuals, or for general support, capital or endowment funds, or matching gifts; no loans.
Application information:
Initial approach: Full proposal
Copies of proposal: 3
Deadline(s): Submit proposal preferably in November or December
Board meeting date(s): January or February
Write: Byron E. Bryan, President
Officers and Directors: Byron E. Bryan, President; James M. Zealy, Vice-President; Lewis R. Holding, Secretary-Treasurer.
Number of staff: 2 part-time support.
Employer Identification Number: 560686194

3083
Bryan (The Kathleen Price and Joseph M.) Family Foundation, Inc.
P.O. Box 1349
Greensboro 27402   (919) 275-7275

Incorporated in 1955 in North Carolina.
Donor(s): Joseph M. Bryan, Kathleen Price Bryan,† and family.
Financial data: (yr. ended 12/31/84): Assets, $1,566,000 (M); expenditures, $115,650, including $105,500 for 29 grants (high: $10,000; low: $1,000; average: $1,000-$10,000).
Purpose and activities: Broad purposes; primarily local giving, with grants principally to religious and educational institutions and for community projects and cultural programs of personal interest to the family.
Types of support awarded: Continuing support, seed money, building funds, program-related investments.
Limitations: Giving primarily in NC. No grants to individuals or to private foundations, or for endowment funds, scholarships, fellowships, or matching gifts; no loans.
Application information:
Initial approach: Letter
Copies of proposal: 1
Deadline(s): March 15 and September 15
Board meeting date(s): Usually in March, May, and November
Final notification: 3 months after board meeting
Write: Richard L. Wharton, Executive Secretary
Officers and Trustees: Kathleen Bryan Edwards, President; Joseph M. Bryan, Jr., Nancy Bryan Faircloth, Vice-Presidents; Richard L. Wharton, Executive Secretary and Treasurer.
Number of staff: 1 part-time professional.
Employer Identification Number: 566046952

3084
Burlington Industries Foundation ▼
P.O. Box 21207
3330 West Friendly Ave.
Greensboro 27420   (919) 379-2515

Trust established in 1943 in North Carolina.
Donor(s): Burlington Industries, Inc., and subsidiary companies.
Financial data: (yr. ended 9/30/84): Assets, $9,589,604 (M); expenditures, $1,856,617, including $1,510,592 for 525 grants and $344,065 for 1,686 employee matching gifts.
Purpose and activities: To support educational, charitable, cultural, and similar causes in areas of company operations. Grants to colleges and universities generally in the geographical area of plants, where the company recruits annually for employees. Grants to various community and civic causes based upon recommendation of the company's local management.
Types of support awarded: Matching funds, annual campaigns, building funds, professorships, scholarship funds, fellowships, employee matching gifts.
Limitations: Giving primarily in areas of company operations in NC, SC, and VA. Generally no grants for sectarian or denominational religious organizations. No grants to individuals (except for company employees and their families in distress), or for conferences, seminars, workshops, films, or documentaries; no loans.
Publications: Program policy statement, application guidelines.
Application information:
Initial approach: Telephone, letter, or full proposal
Copies of proposal: 1
Deadline(s): 1 month prior to board meetings
Board meeting date(s): Generally in March, June, September, and December
Final notification: 30 to 90 days
Write: Park R. Davidson, Executive Director
Officer and Trustees: Park R. Davidson, Executive Director; J.C. Cowan, Jr., Charles A. McLendon, Jr.
Number of staff: 1 full-time support.
Employer Identification Number: 566043142

3085
Burroughs Wellcome Fund, The ▼
3030 Cornwallis Rd.
Research Triangle Park 27709   (919) 248-4136

Incorporated in 1955 in New York.
Donor(s): Burroughs Wellcome Co.
Financial data: (yr. ended 4/30/84): Assets, $9,517,874 (M); gifts received, $1,500,000; expenditures, $1,855,818, including $1,739,207 for 80 grants (high: $250,000; low: $500; average: $5,000-$20,000).

Purpose and activities: Primarily to give financial aid for the advancement of research in the medical sciences within the U.S.: (1) support for clinical pharmacology through a competitive annual award, now $250,000 paid over five years, and an annual series of Creasy Visiting Professorships of Clinical Pharmacology; (2) an annual competitive Toxicology Scholar Award of $200,000 paid over five years; (3) an annual competitive Molecular Parasitology Award of $200,000 paid over five years; (4) Wellcome Visiting Professorships in the Basic Medical Sciences administered by the Federation of American Societies for Experimental Biology; (5) Wellcome Visiting Professorships in Microbiology administered by the American Society of Microbiology; (6) Wellcome Visiting Professorships in Cell Biology administered by the American Society of Cell Biology; (7) Wellcome Research Travel Grants to Britain/Ireland; (8) competitive awards for postdoctoral research fellowships administered by national medical organizations; (9) Pharmacoepidemiology Scholar Award of $250,000 payable over 5 years; occasional, modest grants made on a short-term basis to "institutions for specially talented investigators and innovative research projects in the basic medical sciences".

Types of support awarded: Seed money, emergency funds, consulting services, scholarship funds, special projects, research, professorships.

Limitations: Giving limited to the United States. No grants to individuals, or for building or endowment funds, operating budgets, continuing support, annual campaigns, deficit financing, publications, conferences or matching gifts; no loans.

Publications: Annual report, program policy statement, application guidelines.

Application information: Application form required for Wellcome Research travel grants only. Application form required.

Initial approach: Letter
Copies of proposal: 2
Deadline(s): None
Board meeting date(s): Bimonthly, beginning in January
Final notification: 6 weeks
Write: Martha G. Peck, Executive Director

Officers: George H. Hitchings,* President; Martha G. Peck, Secretary and Executive Director; Theodore E. Haigler, Jr.,* Treasurer.

Directors:* Fred A. Coe, Jr., Pedro Cuatrecasas, M.D., A.J. Shepperd, Gordon Smith, M.D., William M. Sullivan, John R. Vane.

Number of staff: 2 full-time professional; 1 part-time professional.

Employer Identification Number: 237225395

3086
Cannon Foundation, Inc., The ▼
P.O. Box 548
Concord 28026-0548   (704) 786-8216

Incorporated in 1943 in North Carolina.
Donor(s): Charles A. Cannon,† Hearne Swink,† Cannon Mills Company.

Financial data: (yr. ended 9/30/84): Assets, $61,458,376 (M); expenditures, $3,173,194, including $2,756,593 for 59 grants (high: $1,000,000; low: $500; average: $1,000-$25,000).

Purpose and activities: Broad purposes; primarily local giving, with emphasis on hospitals, community funds, higher and secondary education, and cultural programs; grants also for Protestant church support, social services, and youth agencies.

Types of support awarded: Annual campaigns, building funds, equipment, matching funds.

Limitations: Giving primarily in NC, especially in the Cabarrus County area. No grants to individuals, or for operating support, continuing support, seed money, emergency funds, deficit financing, land acquisition, endowment funds, demonstration projects, research, publications, conferences, seminars, scholarships, or fellowships; no loans.

Publications: Application guidelines.

Application information: Application form required.

Initial approach: Letter
Copies of proposal: 1
Deadline(s): Submit proposal in January and July; deadline January 15 and July 15
Board meeting date(s): March, June, September, and December
Final notification: 3 to 6 months
Write: Dan L. Gray, Executive Director

Officers and Directors: Mariam C. Hayes, President; W.C. Cannon, Vice-President; T.C. Haywood, Secretary-Treasurer; Dan L. Gray, Executive Director; G.A. Batte, Jr., W.S. Fisher, T.L. Ross.

Number of staff: 1 full-time professional; 1 full-time support.

Employer Identification Number: 566042532

3087
Carolina Steel Foundation ⌑
National Bank of North Carolina
Charlotte 28255

Trust established in 1948 in North Carolina.
Donor(s): Carolina Steel Corporation, Salem Steel Company.
Financial data: (yr. ended 12/31/83): Assets, $1,202,725 (M); expenditures, $116,549, including $105,118 for 80 grants (high: $21,386; low: $25).
Purpose and activities: Broad purposes; primarily local giving, with emphasis on higher education and community funds.
Limitations: Giving primarily in NC.
Trustee: National Bank of North Carolina.
Directors: N.P. Hayes, Jr., N.G. Ridenhour, E.H. Webster.
Employer Identification Number: 566040772

3088
Chapin Foundation of Myrtle Beach, S.C. ⌑
c/o North Carolina National Bank
One North Carolina National Bank Plaza
Charlotte 28255

Trust established in 1943 in South Carolina.

Donor(s): S.B. Chapin.
Financial data: (yr. ended 7/31/83): Assets, $2,731,621 (M); expenditures, $122,122, including $118,131 for 33 grants (high: $20,000; low: $500).
Purpose and activities: Support for local Protestant churches and libraries.
Limitations: Giving limited to the Myrtle Beach, SC area.
Trustee: North Carolina National Bank.
Board of Advisors: Harold C. Clardy, Chairman; Claude M. Epps, Jr., Secretary.
Employer Identification Number: 566039453

3089
Chatham Foundation, Inc.
Elkin 28621   (919) 835-2211

Incorporated in 1943 in North Carolina.
Donor(s): Chatham and Hanes families and corporations.
Financial data: (yr. ended 12/31/83): Assets, $1,134,221 (M); expenditures, $85,274, including $53,567 for 29 grants (high: $10,000; low: $100) and $22,500 for 16 grants to individuals.

Purpose and activities: Broad purposes; primarily local giving, with emphasis on a hospital building program; grants also for higher and secondary education, including scholarships to children of Chatham Manufacturing Company employees, Protestant church support, youth agencies, and alcoholism programs.

Types of support awarded: Operating budgets, continuing support, annual campaigns, building funds, employee related scholarships.
Limitations: Giving primarily in Elkin, NC, and vicinity. No grants to individuals (except for company-employee scholarships), or for endowment funds, research, or matching gifts; no loans.

Application information:
Initial approach: Letter
Copies of proposal: 1
Deadline(s): None
Board meeting date(s): As required
Final notification: 30 days
Write: William M. Butler, Secretary

Officers and Directors: Hugh Gwyn Chatham II, Chairman; Richard T. Chatham, President; William M. Butler, Secretary; Thomas L. Chatham.

Number of staff: None.
Employer Identification Number: 560771852

3090
Connemara Fund
P.O. Box 20124
Greensboro 27420

Established in 1968 in North Carolina.
Donor(s): Mary R. Jackson.†
Financial data: (yr. ended 6/30/84): Assets, $2,612,595 (M); expenditures, $139,961, including $123,600 for 39 grants (high: $25,000; low: $500; average: $1,000-$10,000).

Purpose and activities: Grants primarily for church support and religious welfare associations; support also for child welfare, social services, and cultural programs; some emphasis on local giving.
Types of support awarded: Annual campaigns, emergency funds, endowment funds, scholarship funds, fellowships, research, building funds.
Limitations: Giving primarily in the New England area. No grants to individuals.
Application information:
  Initial approach: Full proposal or letter
  Copies of proposal: 1
  Deadline(s): April 15 and October 15
  Board meeting date(s): May and November
  Final notification: 2 months
  Write: Herrick Jackson, Trustee
Trustees: Herrick Jackson, Robert W. Jackson, Alison Jackson Van Dyk.
Number of staff: None.
Employer Identification Number: 566096063

3091
Daniels (The Josephus) Charitable Foundation ⋈
215 South McDowell St.
Raleigh 27602

Established in 1964 in North Carolina.
Donor(s): The News and Observer Publishing Company.
Financial data: (yr. ended 12/31/83): Assets, $1,083,926 (M); gifts received, $370,589; expenditures, $371,250, including $369,166 for 73 grants (high: $202,900; low: $15).
Purpose and activities: Primarily local giving, with emphasis on higher education and community development.
Limitations: Giving primarily in NC.
Officers: Frank A. Daniels, President; Frank A. Daniels, Jr., Vice-President.
Employer Identification Number: 566065260

3092
Dickson Foundation, Inc., The ⋈
2000 Jefferson First Union Plaza
Charlotte 28282   (704) 372-5404

Incorporated in 1944 in North Carolina.
Donor(s): American and Efird Mills, Inc.
Financial data: (yr. ended 12/31/83): Assets, $7,637,212 (M); expenditures, $388,037, including $368,570 for 220 grants (high: $25,000; low: $50).
Purpose and activities: Broad purposes; primarily local giving, with emphasis on secondary and higher education, including scholarship funds, Protestant church support, community funds, youth agencies, and hospitals.
Limitations: Giving primarily in NC. No grants to individuals, or for building or endowment funds.
Application information:
  Initial approach: Letter
  Board meeting date(s): Annually and as required
  Write: F.H. McKinney, Secretary-Treasurer

Officers and Directors: Alan T. Dickson, President; R. Stuart Dickson, Vice-President; F.H. McKinney, Secretary-Treasurer; Rush S. Dickson, III, Thomas W. Dickson, F.B. Helms.
Employer Identification Number: 566022339

3093
Dickson (Rush S.) Family Foundation, Inc. ⋈
2000 Jefferson First Union Plaza
Charlotte 28282   (704) 373-5404

Incorporated in 1953 in North Carolina.
Donor(s): Rush S. Dickson.†
Financial data: (yr. ended 12/31/83): Assets, $4,260,785 (M); expenditures, $196,412, including $188,945 for 66 grants (high: $25,000; low: $100).
Purpose and activities: Broad purposes; primarily local giving, with emphasis on higher and secondary education, hospitals, community funds, youth agencies, and church support.
Limitations: Giving primarily in NC. No grants to individuals, or for building or endowment funds.
Application information:
  Initial approach: Letter
  Deadline(s): None
  Board meeting date(s): Annually and as required
  Write: F.H. McKinney, Secretary
Officers: R. Stuart Dickson,* President; Alan T. Dickson,* Vice-President; F.H. McKinney, Secretary and Treasurer.
Directors:* Rush S. Dickson, III, Thomas W. Dickson, F.B. Helms.
Employer Identification Number: 566047850

3094
Dover Foundation, Inc., The ⋈
c/o Dover Mill Company
Shelby 28150

Incorporated in 1944 in North Carolina.
Donor(s): Dover Mill Company, Ora Mill Company.
Financial data: (yr. ended 8/31/83): Assets, $6,968,810 (M); gifts received, $359,520; expenditures, $373,315, including $339,352 for 116 grants (high: $111,174; low: $25).
Purpose and activities: Broad purposes; primarily local giving, with emphasis on higher and secondary education, church support, and social agencies.
Limitations: Giving primarily in NC.
Officers: Charles I. Dover, President.
Employer Identification Number: 560769897

3095
Duke Endowment, The ▼
200 South Tryon St., Suite 1100
Charlotte 28202   (704) 376-0291
Additional office: 3329 Chapel Hill Blvd., P.O. Box 8816, Durham, NC 27707

Trust established in 1924 in New Jersey.
Donor(s): James Buchanan Duke.†
Financial data: (yr. ended 12/31/84): Assets, $551,459,647 (M); expenditures, $37,815,633, including $32,999,108 for 734 grants.

Purpose and activities: "To make provision in some measure for the needs of mankind along physical, mental, and spiritual lines." Grants to nonprofit hospitals and child care institutions in North and South Carolina; rural United Methodist churches and retired ministers in North Carolina; and Duke, Furman, and Johnson C. Smith universities, and Davidson College.
Types of support awarded: Operating budgets, seed money, emergency funds, matching funds, professorships, internships, scholarship funds, fellowships, endowment funds, research, special projects, publications, conferences and seminars, consulting services, technical assistance, continuing support.
Limitations: Giving primarily in North and South Carolina. No grants to individuals (except for retired ministers and their dependents) or for deficit financing; no loans.
Publications: Annual report, application guidelines.
Application information:
  Initial approach: Letter
  Deadline(s): None
  Board meeting date(s): Monthly except in January and August
  Final notification: Varies
  Write: John F. Day, Executive Director, or Billy G. McCall, Deputy Executive Director
Officers: John F. Day, Executive Director and Treasurer; Billy G. McCall, Deputy Executive Director and Secretary.
Trustees: Mary D.B.T. Semans, Chairman; William B. McGuire, Louis C. Stephens, Jr., Vice-Chairmen; Hugh M. Chapman, Archie K. Davis, John D. deButts, Doris Duke, James R. Felts, Jr., W. Kenneth Goodson, Frank H. Kenan, Juanita M. Kreps, Charles F. Myers, Jr., Marshall I. Pickens, James C. Self, Charles Byrd Wade, Jr.
Number of staff: 22 full-time professional; 13 full-time support.
Employer Identification Number: 560529965

3096
Elizabeth City Foundation ⋈
P.O. Box 220
Elizabeth City 27909

Community trust.
Financial data: (yr. ended 7/31/83): Assets, $1,464,614 (M); gifts received, $65,153; expenditures, $94,399, including $48,880 for 17 grants (high: $17,000; low: $500) and $26,731 for grants to individuals.
Purpose and activities: Giving locally for education and civic improvement; support also for scholarships for local students.
Types of support awarded: Student aid.
Limitations: Giving limited to the Albemarle area of northeastern NC for grants and Camden County, NC, for scholarships.
Application information: Application form required.
  Deadline(s): April 1 for scholarships; May 15 and December 15 for other grants
  Board meeting date(s): January
  Write: Dewey W. Wells, Executive Director
Officer: Dewey W. Wells, Executive Director.

Trustees: First Union National Bank, First Citizens Bank and Trust, Peoples Bank and Trust, Wachovia Bank and Trust Co.
Employer Identification Number: 237076018

3097
Ferebee (Percy B.) Endowment
c/o Wachovia Bank & Trust Company
P.O. Box 3099
Winston-Salem 27150   (919) 748-5269

Established in 1973 in North Carolina.
Donor(s): Percy Ferebee.†
Financial data: (yr. ended 12/31/84): Assets, $1,550,000 (M); expenditures, $159,833, including $97,833 for 14 grants (high: $40,000; low: $1,338; average: $5,000) and $62,000 for 55 grants to individuals.
Purpose and activities: Primarily local giving, with emphasis on scholarships to individuals, and educational, cultural, and civic development.
Types of support awarded: Annual campaigns, seed money, emergency funds, building funds, equipment, land acquisition, student aid.
Limitations: Giving primarily in western NC communities. No grants to individuals (except for scholarships), or for endowment funds, matching gifts, special projects, publications, conferences, or research; no loans.
Publications: Program policy statement, application guidelines.
Application information: Application form required.
   Initial approach: Full proposal
   Copies of proposal: 1
   Deadline(s): Submit proposal preferably in September; deadline for scholarships, February 15; for grants, October 1
   Board meeting date(s): May and November
   Final notification: 10 days
Awards Committee: John Parris, Chairman; Mrs. Frela Owl Beck, Ty W. Burnette, J. Smith Howell, John Waldroup, Bill Walker.
Trustee: Wachovia Bank and Trust Company.
Number of staff: None.
Employer Identification Number: 566118992

3098
Fieldcrest Foundation ¤
c/o D.R. Tebbs
326 East Stadium Rd.
Eden 27288   (919) 623-2123
Application address: M.B. Franklin, c/o Fieldcrest Mills, Inc., General Office, Eden, NC 27288; Tel.: (919) 627-3046

Incorporated in 1959 in North Carolina.
Donor(s): Fieldcrest Mills, Inc.
Financial data: (yr. ended 12/31/83): Assets, $1,286,032 (M); gifts received, $200,000; expenditures, $379,848, including $302,889 for 69 grants (high: $66,956; low: $50) and $73,500 for 5 grants to individuals.
Purpose and activities: Scholarships for children of company employees; grants primarily to community funds, youth agencies, and higher education, including building funds, in areas of plant operations.

Types of support awarded: Employee related scholarships, building funds.
Limitations: Giving primarily in in areas of company operations.
Application information: Application form required.
   Deadline(s): March 1 for scholarships; July 1 for grants-in-aid
   Board meeting date(s): Quarterly
Officers: F.X. Larkin,* President; L.H. Lance,* Vice-President; M.B. Franklin, Secretary; K.W. Fraser, Jr.,* Treasurer.
Directors:* T.W. Graves, Jr., C.G. Horn, H.H. Newton.
Employer Identification Number: 566046659

3099
Finch (The Doak) Foundation
P.O. Box 120
Charlotte 28255

Trust established in 1961 in North Carolina.
Donor(s): Doak Finch.
Financial data: (yr. ended 10/31/82): Assets, $1,807,875 (M); expenditures, $172,739, including $160,250 for 14 grants (high: $25,000; low: $2,500).
Purpose and activities: Broad purposes; primarily local giving primarily to schools and social service and cultural organizations.
Limitations: Giving primarily in NC.
Trustee: North Carolina National Bank.
Employer Identification Number: 566042823

3100
Finch (Thomas Austin) Foundation
c/o Wachovia Bank and Trust Company
P.O. Box 3099
Winston-Salem 27150   (919) 748-5991

Trust established in 1944 in North Carolina.
Donor(s): Ernestine L. Finch Mobley,† Thomas Austin Finch, Jr.
Financial data: (yr. ended 12/31/83): Assets, $1,842,026 (M); expenditures, $88,220, including $71,500 for 6 grants (high: $60,000; low: $500; average: $10,000).
Purpose and activities: Local charitable and educational purposes; interests include higher and secondary education, Protestant church support and church-related schools, and community funds.
Types of support awarded: Operating budgets, continuing support, annual campaigns, seed money, building funds, equipment, land acquisition.
Limitations: Giving limited to Thomasville, NC. No grants to individuals, or for emergency funds, deficit financing, endowment funds, or fellowships; no loans.
Publications: Application guidelines.
Application information: Application form required for all grants over $5,000.
   Copies of proposal: 1
   Deadline(s): February 15 and October 15
   Board meeting date(s): March and November
   Final notification: 2 weeks
   Write: Warren C. Hodges, Account Mgr., Wachovia Bank and Trust Co.

Foundation Committee: David Finch, Chairman; Kermit Cloninger, John Finch, Meredith Slane Finch, Sumner Finch.
Trustee: Wachovia Bank and Trust Company, (Warren C. Hodges, Account Mgr.).
Number of staff: None.
Employer Identification Number: 566037907

3101
Finley (A. E.) Foundation, Inc. ¤
P.O. Box 27785
Raleigh 27611

Incorporated in 1957 in North Carolina.
Donor(s): A.E. Finley.
Financial data: (yr. ended 11/30/83): Assets, $3,639,252 (M); gifts received, $250,070; expenditures, $143,082, including $135,025 for 35 grants (high: $50,000; low: $75).
Purpose and activities: Broad purposes; primarily local giving, with emphasis on higher education and youth agencies.
Limitations: Giving primarily in NC.
Officers and Directors: A.E. Finley, President; R.C. Brown, Secretary-Treasurer; D.J. Jones.
Employer Identification Number: 566057379

3102
Foundation for the Carolinas ▼
(formerly The Greater Charlotte Foundation, Inc.)
301 South Brevard St.
Charlotte 28202   (704) 376-9541

Community foundation incorporated in 1958 in North Carolina.
Financial data: (yr. ended 12/31/84): Assets, $13,552,003 (M); gifts received, $4,169,387; expenditures, $2,659,496, including $2,385,853 for 1,225 grants (high: $209,800; low: $100; average: $500-$10,000), $12,398 for 15 grants to individuals and $4,000 for 4 loans.
Purpose and activities: Broad purposes; giving only to organizations serving the citizens of North and South Carolina; grants for education, human services, religion, youth programs, senior programs, the arts, and health and medical research.
Types of support awarded: Operating budgets, seed money, emergency funds, building funds, equipment, matching funds, consulting services, student aid, technical assistance, scholarship funds, land acquisition, special projects, research.
Limitations: Giving primarily in NC and SC. No grants to individuals (except for limited scholarships and student loans).
Publications: Annual report, application guidelines, informational brochure, newsletter.
Application information: Application form required.
   Initial approach: Letter
   Copies of proposal: 11
   Deadline(s): None
   Board meeting date(s): Quarterly, with annual meeting in March; distribution committee meets monthly
   Final notification: 1 to 2 months
   Write: Gordon Berg, Executive Director

Officers: William M. Barnhardt,* President; C.C. Cameron,* Monroe T. Gilmour,* Vice-Presidents; Robin L. Hinson,* Secretary; Graeme M. Keith,* Treasurer; Gordon Berg, Executive Director.
Distribution Committee:* Frances V. Bryant, Chair; David Taylor, Vice-Chair; S. Walter Byuarm, Robert D. Culbertson, William F. Drew, Jr., Gwendolyn D. Cunningham, James O. Funderburk, Robert Kirby, Samuel H. Smith, Jr., Ann D. Thomas, William H. Williamson, III.
Number of staff: 3 full-time professional; 2 part-time professional; 2 full-time support; 1 part-time support.
Employer Identification Number: 566047886

3103
Garrison Community Foundation of Gaston County, Inc.
P.O. Box 123
Gastonia 28053   (704) 864-0927

Community foundation incorporated in 1978 in North Carolina.
Financial data: (yr. ended 12/31/83): Assets, $1,257,234 (M); gifts received, $167,281; expenditures, $88,674, including $77,534 for 13 grants and $6,214 for 15 grants to individuals.
Purpose and activities: Local giving for charitable purposes in Gaston County; and in the state of North Carolina for medical grants to children 18 or under.
Types of support awarded: Operating budgets, seed money, emergency funds, building funds, equipment, land acquisition, endowment funds, matching funds, employee matching gifts, scholarship funds, special projects, publications, conferences and seminars, grants to individuals.
Limitations: Giving limited to NC, particularly Gaston County. No grants for exchange programs, fellowships, program-related investments, research, annual campaigns, deficit financing, continuing support, consulting services, technical assistance, professorships, internships, company-employee scholarships, or demonstration projects; no loans.
Publications: Annual report.
Application information:
 Write: Harold T. Sumner, Executive Director
Officer: Harold T. Sumner, Executive Director.
Employer Identification Number: 589830716

3104
Ginter (Karl and Anna) Foundation ¤
c/o North Carolina National Bank
P.O. Box 120
Charlotte 28255

Established in 1968 in North Carolina.
Donor(s): Karl Ginter Trust.
Financial data: (yr. ended 12/31/83): Assets, $1,332,629 (M); expenditures, $94,881, including $85,150 for 13 grants (high: $20,000; low: $400).
Purpose and activities: Primarily local giving, with emphasis on higher education; grants also for cultural programs.
Limitations: Giving primarily in NC.

Directors: Stamford R. Brookshire, Joseph W. Grier, Jr.
Trustee: North Carolina National Bank.
Employer Identification Number: 566094355

3105
Hanes (James G.) Memorial Fund/Foundation ▼
c/o Wachovia Bank and Trust Company
P.O. Box 3099
Winston-Salem 27150   (919) 748-5269

Trusts established in 1957 and 1972 in North Carolina.
Donor(s): Mary Ruffin Hanes,† James Gordon Hanes,† Gordon Hanes.
Financial data: (yr. ended 12/31/84): Assets, $8,217,592 (M); gifts received, $689,726; expenditures, $1,300,053, including $1,300,053 for 39 grants (high: $125,000; low: $1,000; average: $1,000-$50,000).
Purpose and activities: Broad purposes; support largely for local and regional health and education projects, with emphasis on art schools and art museums, higher and secondary education, cultural programs, conservation, and community programs.
Types of support awarded: Annual campaigns, seed money, emergency funds, building funds, equipment, land acquisition, matching funds, special projects, research, program-related investments, publications, endowment funds.
Limitations: Giving primarily in NC. No grants to individuals, or for general operational or maintenance purposes.
Publications: Application guidelines, program policy statement.
Application information: Application form required.
 Initial approach: Proposal
 Copies of proposal: 1
 Deadline(s): First day of month in which board meets; prefers to receive applications in preceding month
 Board meeting date(s): January, April, July and October
 Final notification: 10 days
 Write: E. Ray Cope, Vice-President
Distribution Committee: Eldridge C. Hanes, Chairman; Joseph F. Abely, Jr., James G. Hanes III, Douglas R. Lewis, Drewry Hanes Nostitz, Frank F. Willingham.
Trustee: Wachovia Bank and Trust Company (E. Ray Cope, Vice-President).
Number of staff: None.
Employer Identification Number: 566036987

3106
Hanes (The John W. and Anna H.) Foundation ▼
c/o Wachovia Bank and Trust Company
P.O. Box 3099
Winston-Salem 27150   (919) 748-5269

Trust established in 1947 in North Carolina.
Donor(s): James G. Hanes,† Robert M. Hanes,† Lucy Hanes Chatham,† Daisy Hanes Lassiter, John W. Hanes, Ralph P. Hanes, Hugh G. Chatham.†

Financial data: (yr. ended 12/31/84): Assets, $8,166,267 (M); expenditures, $454,576, including $454,576 for 24 grants (high: $100,000; low: $1,000; average: $1,000-$25,000).
Purpose and activities: General purposes; local giving largely for cultural programs, historic preservation, higher education, youth, child welfare, and social services.
Types of support awarded: Annual campaigns, seed money, emergency funds, building funds, equipment, land acquisition, endowment funds, matching funds, special projects, research, publications.
Limitations: Giving limited to NC, particularly Forsyth County. No grants to individuals, or for scholarships and fellowships, operating budgets, continuing support, deficit financing, or conferences; no loans.
Publications: Program policy statement, application guidelines.
Application information: Application form required.
 Initial approach: Telephone or letter
 Deadline(s): 15th day of month preceeding board meeting
 Board meeting date(s): January, April, July, and October
 Final notification: 10 days
 Write: E. Ray Cope, Vice-President
Trustees: Frank Borden Hanes, Frank Borden Hanes, Jr., Gordon Hanes, R. Philip Hanes, Jr., Wachovia Bank and Trust Company (E. Ray Cope, Vice-President).
Number of staff: None.
Employer Identification Number: 566037589

3107
Hillsdale Fund, Inc.
P.O. Box 20124
Greensboro 27420   (919) 274-5471

Incorporated in 1963 in North Carolina.
Donor(s): The L. Richardson family.
Financial data: (yr. ended 12/31/83): Assets, $6,082,066 (M); expenditures, $381,260, including $311,100 for 39 grants (high: $40,000; low: $1,000).
Purpose and activities: Broad purposes; interests include the general fields of education, preservation, the arts and humanities.
Limitations: Giving primarily in NC and the southeastern states. No grants to individuals or for operating budgets.
Application information:
 Initial approach: Letter
 Copies of proposal: 1
 Deadline(s): Submit proposal in March or September
 Board meeting date(s): Usually in May and November
 Write: Sion A. Boney, Administrative Vice-President
Officers and Trustees: Lunsford Richardson, Jr., President; Sion A. Boney, Administrative Vice-President and Secretary-Treasurer; Betsy R. Boney, Vice-President; J. Peter Gallagher, Laurinda V. Lowenstein, Beatrix W. Richardson, Eudora L. Richardson, Molly R. Smith, Richard G. Smith, III, Margaret R. White.
Employer Identification Number: 566057433

3108
Jenkins-Tapp Foundation, Inc. ⊨
P.O. Box 667
Kinston 28501

Incorporated in 1961 in North Carolina.
Financial data: (yr. ended 12/31/83): Assets,
$1,263,824 (M); expenditures, $154,466,
including $81,000 for 35 grants (high: $20,000;
low: $500).
Purpose and activities: Primarily local giving,
with emphasis on Protestant church support,
higher and secondary education, and local fire
departments.
Limitations: Giving primarily in NC.
Officer: Elizabeth C. Jenkins, President and
Treasurer; Lee B. Jenkins, Vice-President and
Secretary; Coleman J. Hardy, John T. Jenkins,
Jr., Vice-Presidents.
Employer Identification Number: 560845817

3109
Kellenberger (May Gordon Latham)
Historical Foundation ⊨
c/o North Carolina National Bank
One North Carolina Nat'l. Bank Plaza
Charlotte 28255

Established in 1979.
Financial data: (yr. ended 11/30/83): Assets,
$3,690,227 (M); expenditures, $338,022,
including $311,927 for 26 grants (high:
$100,000; low: $1,000).
Purpose and activities: Local giving "to aid
and support projects related to Tryon Palace
and Historical New Bern," with emphasis on
building, restoration, and preservation.
Types of support awarded: Building funds,
special projects.
Limitations: Giving limited to New Bern, NC.
Trustee: North Carolina National Bank.
Directors: Gertrude Carraway, R.D. Douglas,
Jr., Mrs. H. Dail Holderness, Raymond C.
Houghton.
Employer Identification Number: 581360279

3110
Lamb (Kirkland S. and Rena B.)
Foundation, Inc. ⊨
c/o Austin Falls & Hamel
114 W. Bland St.
Charlotte 28203
Application address: Wendell G. Johnston,
President, 645 Catalina, Fullerton, CA 92635

Incorporated in 1961 in North Carolina.
Donor(s): Rena B. Lamb,† Kirkland S. Lamb.†
Financial data: (yr. ended 12/31/83): Assets,
$6,272,638 (M); gifts received, $20,000;
expenditures, $258,914, including $245,827
for 21 grants (high: $89,307; low: $300).
Purpose and activities: Charitable and
religious purposes; grants largely for Protestant
church support, theological studies, and
evangelical activities.
Application information:
Initial approach: Letter
Deadline(s): September
Board meeting date(s): November
Write: Wendell G. Johnston, President

Officers: Wendell G. Johnston, President;
Lillian L. Williams, Vice-President; Martha L.
Johnston, Secretary; Richard A. Williams,
Treasurer.
Employer Identification Number: 566062394

3111
Lance Foundation
P.O. Box 120
Charlotte 28255

Trust established in 1956 in North Carolina.
Donor(s): Lance, Inc., and members of the Van
Every family.
Financial data: (yr. ended 6/30/83): Assets,
$3,056,697 (M); gifts received, $262,102;
expenditures, $203,713, including $182,700
for 45 grants (high: $26,000; low: $200).
Purpose and activities: Broad purposes;
primarily local giving, with emphasis on higher
education, medical research and community
services; some support also in South Carolina
and southeastern states.
Limitations: Giving primarily in NC, SC, and
southeastern states. No grants to individuals,
or for scholarships or fellowships; no loans.
Application information:
Initial approach: Full proposal or letter
Copies of proposal: 1
Deadline(s): None
Board meeting date(s): As required
Final notification: 2 to 3 months
Directors: C.J. Buchanan, T.B. Horack, James
S. Howell, Albert F. Sloan.
Trustee: North Carolina National Bank.
Number of staff: 1.
Employer Identification Number: 566039487

3112
Lineberger Foundation, Inc. ⊨
Landsdale Bldg.
P.O. Box 1126
Belmont 28012

Incorporated in 1944 in North Carolina.
Donor(s): Henry A. Lineberger,† Acme
Spinning Company, Linford Mills, Inc.,
Perfection Spinning Company, and others.
Financial data: (yr. ended 12/31/83): Assets,
$5,004,993 (M); gifts received, $217,800;
expenditures, $212,870, including $194,750
for 19 grants (high: $50,000; low: $500).
Purpose and activities: Broad purposes;
primarily local giving, with emphasis on higher
and secondary education, including theological
education, a hospital, and a museum.
Limitations: Giving primarily in NC.
Officers and Directors: J. Harold Lineberger,
President; John R. Crawford, Vice-President;
Joseph W. Lineberger, Secretary-Treasurer.
Employer Identification Number: 566049464

3113
Love (Martha and Spencer)
Foundation ⊨
National Bank of North Carolina
Charlotte 28255

Trust established in 1947 in North Carolina.

Donor(s): J. Spencer Love,† Mrs. Martha E.
Love Ayers.
Financial data: (yr. ended 12/31/83): Assets,
$1,807,417 (M); expenditures, $276,849,
including $259,000 for 26 grants (high:
$50,000; low: $1,000).
Purpose and activities: Broad purposes;
general giving, with emphasis on higher
education, the arts, Protestant church support,
and social welfare programs, largely in North
Carolina.
Limitations: Giving primarily in NC.
Trustee: National Bank of North Carolina.
Directors: Howard Holderness, Charles E.
Love, Cornelia S. Love, Julian Love, Lela Porter
Love, Martin E. Love, E.R. Zane.
Employer Identification Number: 566040789

3114
Martin Marietta Philanthropic Trust
c/o Wachovia Bank and Trust Company
P.O. Box 3099
Winston-Salem 27150   (919) 748-5269
Application address: John F. Long, Jr., Dir.
Gov't Affairs, Martin Marietta Aggregates, P.O.
Box 30013, Raleigh, NC 27622; Tel.: (919)
781-4550

Trust established in 1952 in North Carolina.
Donor(s): Superior Stone Company.
Financial data: (yr. ended 12/31/84): Assets,
$1,374,644 (M); expenditures, $145,399,
including $134,930 for 167 grants (high:
$25,000; low: $50; average: $800).
Purpose and activities: Broad purposes;
primarily local giving in areas of company
operations, with emphasis on community
funds, higher education, and youth agencies.
Limitations: Giving primarily in the Southeast
and the Midwest, especially in areas of
company operations. No grants to individuals
or for courtesy advertising, tickets for
fundraising, or memberships in local chambers
of commerce or other civic groups.
Publications: Annual report, newsletter.
Application information:
Initial approach: Letter
Copies of proposal: 0
Deadline(s): None
Board meeting date(s): None
Write: John F. Long, Jr., Director,
Governmental Affairs
Advisory Committee: John F. Long, Jr., James
D. Simpson.
Trustee: Wachovia Bank and Trust Company.
Employer Identification Number: 566035971

3115
McAdenville Foundation, Inc., The
McAdenville 28101   (704) 824-3551

Incorporated in 1944 in North Carolina.
Donor(s): Local textile mills.
Financial data: (yr. ended 12/31/82): Assets,
$1,835,447 (M); gifts received, $194,000;
expenditures, $367,617, including $58,567 for
grants (high: $33,000; low: $50) and $162,872
for foundation-administered programs.

Purpose and activities: A private operating foundation with broad purposes; local giving; primarily operates community social and recreational facilities; grants to churches, and church-affiliated colleges.
Limitations: Giving limited to McAdenville, NC. No grants to individuals, or for endowment funds, research, scholarships, fellowships, or matching gifts.
Application information: Applications for grants not encouraged.
   Board meeting date(s): May and December
   Write: W.J. Pharr, President
Officers and Trustees: W.J. Pharr, President and Treasurer; Daniel J. Stowe, Vice-President and Secretary; J.M. Carstarphen, Vice-President.
Employer Identification Number: 560623961

3116
McClure (James G. K.) Educational and Development Fund, Inc.
P.O. Box 1490
Woodfin St.
Asheville 28802   (704) 254-3566

Incorporated in 1944 in North Carolina.
Financial data: (yr. ended 12/31/84): Assets, $1,558,486 (M); gifts received, $7,244; expenditures, $123,228, including $61,069 for 125 grants (high: $2,500; low: $200) and $4,500 for 4 foundation-administered programs.
Purpose and activities: Support primarily for scholarship funds and educational projects, a nurse recruitment program in the mountain counties of North Carolina, and other activities for the welfare of the people of western North Carolina.
Types of support awarded: Scholarship funds.
Limitations: Giving primarily in western NC. No grants to individuals, or for endowment funds; no loans.
Publications: Biennial report, application guidelines.
Application information: Application form required.
   Initial approach: Letter
   Copies of proposal: 1
   Board meeting date(s): January and July
   Write: John Curtis Ager, Executive Director
Officers and Trustees: Julian A. Woodcock, Jr., President; Harold L. Bacon, M.D., Vice-President; James McClure Clarke, Secretary; Martha Guy, Treasurer; John Curtis Ager, Executive Director; Mrs. John C. Ager, Jr., Mrs. Burnham S. Colburn, Richard G. Jennings, Jr.
Number of staff: 1 full-time professional; 1 full-time support.
Employer Identification Number: 560690982

3117
Memorial Fund, Inc., The ⊐
127 Fairly St.
P.O. Box 399
Laurinburg 28352

Incorporated in 1943 in North Carolina.
Donor(s): Local businesses.
Financial data: (yr. ended 8/31/83): Assets, $194,434 (M); gifts received, $81,476; expenditures, $142,641, including $141,960 for 12 grants (high: $70,000; low: $25).

Purpose and activities: Broad purposes; primarily local giving, with emphasis on higher education and Protestant church support. Grants also to community development programs and youth agencies.
Limitations: Giving primarily in NC.
Application information:
   Initial approach: Letter
Officers and Directors: C.E. Beman, President; McNair Evans, R.F. McCoy, Vice-Presidents; J.H. Muse, Secretary-Treasurer; James H. Pou Bailey, Jr., E. Hervey Evans, Jr., Halbert M. Jones, Jr.
Employer Identification Number: 560772091

3118
Morehead (The John Motley) Foundation ▼ ⊐
P.O. Box 348
Chapel Hill 27514   (919) 962-1201

Trust established in 1945 in New York.
Donor(s): John Motley Morehead.†
Financial data: (yr. ended 6/30/83): Assets, $48,906,055 (M); expenditures, $3,366,525, including $875,496 for 12 grants (high: $631,270; low: $187) and $1,425,396 for 300 grants to individuals.
Purpose and activities: "The advancement of education, learning and/or research for public benefit, in the United States, particularly in North Carolina and the South, but not limited thereto." Currently makes awards for undergraduate study only at the University of North Carolina at Chapel Hill to graduates of North Carolina high schools and preparatory schools, of selected preparatory schools outside the state, and of twenty-four selected public schools in England; candidates for undergraduate scholarships must be nominated by their secondary schools; awards fellowships for graduate and professional study only at the University of North Carolina at Chapel Hill.
Types of support awarded: Scholarship funds, internships, special projects, equipment, fellowships.
Limitations: Giving primarily in the South, particularly NC.
Publications: Annual report.
Application information: Nomination form required. Application form required.
   Initial approach: By nomination only; no one may apply directly for Morehead Award
   Deadline(s): November 1
   Board meeting date(s): September, November, February, and April
   Final notification: March 1
   Write: Mebane M. Pritchett, Executive Director
Officers: Charles E. Lovelace, Jr., Treasurer; Mebane M. Pritchett, Executive Director.
Trustees: Hugh G. Chatham, Chairman; Alan Thomas Dickson, Vice-Chairman; Robert Cluett, Frank Borden Hanes, Jean M. Larkin.
Number of staff: 5 full-time professional; 1 part-time professional; 4 full-time support; 1 part-time support.
Employer Identification Number: 560599225

3119
Morgan Trust for Charity, Religion, and Education, The
Laurel Hill 28351   (919) 462-2016

Trust established in 1949 in North Carolina.
Donor(s): Edwin Morgan,† Elise McK. Morgan, Morgan Mills, Inc.
Financial data: (yr. ended 4/30/84): Assets, $3,978,084 (M); gifts received, $26,500; expenditures, $241,895, including $204,150 for 32 grants (high: $25,000; low: $50).
Purpose and activities: Broad purposes; primarily local giving, with emphasis on higher education, a theological seminary, and Protestant church support.
Types of support awarded: Continuing support, annual campaigns, seed money, building funds, matching funds, endowment funds.
Limitations: Giving primarily in NC. No grants to individuals, or for scholarships and fellowships; no loans. No grants generally for operating budgets.
Application information:
   Initial approach: Letter
   Copies of proposal: 1
   Deadline(s): None
   Board meeting date(s): As required
   Write: James L. Morgan, Chairman
Officers and Trustees: James L. Morgan, Chairman; William R. Dulin, Secretary and Treasurer; Elizabeth E. Morgan, M. Morrison Morgan.
Number of staff: None.
Employer Identification Number: 566056812

3120
Morris (E. A.) Charitable Foundation ⊐
c/o Duke Univ. Medical Center
P.O. Box 2901
Durham 27710   (919) 684-5332

Established in 1980.
Donor(s): E.A. Morris, Mrs. E.A. Morris.
Financial data: (yr. ended 12/31/83): Assets, $4,530,814 (M); expenditures, $473,974, including $439,760 for 103 grants (high: $25,000; low: $10).
Purpose and activities: Giving mainly for Christian missionary organizations, education and churches; some support also for national public policy research organizations concerned with free enterprise and government.
Application information:
   Initial approach: Letter
   Deadline(s): None
   Write: John S. Thomas, Vice-President
Officers and Directors: E.A. Morris, President; John S. Thomas, Vice-President and Executive Director; Mrs. E.A. Morris, Vice-President; Mary Lou Morris, Secretary; Joseph E. Morris, Treasurer.
Employer Identification Number: 581413060

3121
Myers-Ti-Caro Foundation, Inc. ☐
Jenkins St.
P.O. Box 699
Gastonia 28053-0699   (704) 867-7271

Incorporated in 1950 in North Carolina.
Donor(s): Textiles, Incorporated, Threads, Incorporated.
Financial data: (yr. ended 10/1/83): Assets, $4,286,364 (M); expenditures, $371,369, including $284,023 for 72 grants (high: $25,000; low: $500), $62,328 for 36 grants to individuals and $16,159 for 9 loans.
Purpose and activities: Broad purposes; grants for higher and secondary education in communities where company mills are located, including scholarships and student loans to children and other eligible dependents of Ti-Caro, Inc. employees.
Types of support awarded: Employee related scholarships.
Limitations: Giving limited to communities where company mills are located.
Application information: Application form required.
Deadline(s): September
Write: Lee O. Waters
Officers and Directors: A.G. Myers, Jr., President; J.H. Martin, Jr., Vice-President; J.R. Helms, Secretary and Treasurer; A.L. Brunnemer, R.P. Caldwell, J.C. Fry, Don Maddox, B. Frank Matthews II.
Employer Identification Number: 560770083

3122
P & B Foundation ☐
3041 Valencia Terrace
Charlotte 28211

Established in 1970.
Donor(s): C. Wilbur Peters.
Financial data: (yr. ended 8/31/83): Assets, $1,251,248 (M); expenditures, $106,951, including $100,000 for 1 grant.
Purpose and activities: Primarily local giving, with emphasis on Baptist church-related educational and religious institutions.
Limitations: Giving primarily in NC.
Application information: Applications not invited.
Officer: Duane G. Hansen, Secretary and Treasurer.
Manager: C. Wilbur Peters.
Employer Identification Number: 237083912

3123
Reynolds (Kate B.) Charitable Trust ▼
P.O. Box 3099
Winston-Salem 27150   (919) 748-5274
Grant application address for health care: Kate B. Reynolds Health Care Trust, 910 First Union National Bank Bldg., Winston-Salem, NC 27101; Tel.: (919) 723-1456

Trust established in 1946 in North Carolina.
Donor(s): Kate B. Reynolds.†
Financial data: (yr. ended 8/31/84): Assets, $82,966,723 (M); expenditures, $3,599,418, including $3,394,497 for 104 grants (high: $175,000; low: $685).

Purpose and activities: Seventy-five percent of net income to be distributed for the health care of those in need within North Carolina; twenty-five percent for the benefit of poor and needy residents of Winston-Salem and Forsyth County.
Types of support awarded: Operating budgets, continuing support, annual campaigns, seed money, emergency funds, scholarship funds, matching funds.
Limitations: Giving primarily in NC, with emphasis on Winston-Salem and Forsyth County. No grants to individuals, or for endowment funds; grants seldom awarded for construction of facilities or purchase of equipment.
Publications: Annual report, program policy statement, application guidelines.
Application information: For grants concerning poor and needy, submit proposal in 8 copies; for grants in health care, submit 1 copy of proposal. Application form required.
Initial approach: Full proposal
Deadline(s): January 31, April 30, July 31, and October 31 for social welfare grants; April 1 and October 1 for health care grants
Board meeting date(s): Advisory committee for social welfare grants meets in February, May, August, and November; advisory committee for health care grants meets in May and November
Final notification: 1 week after committee meeting
Write: Joyce T. Adger, Vice-President (for poor and needy); W. Vance Frye, Executive Secretary, Kate B. Reynolds Health Care Trust (for health care)
Trustees: Wachovia Bank and Trust Company (E. Ray Cope, Vice-President, Charitable Funds Section).
Number of staff: 1 full-time professional; 1 part-time professional.
Employer Identification Number: 566036515

3124
Reynolds (Z. Smith) Foundation, Inc. ▼
101 Reynolda Village
Winston-Salem 27106-5199   (919) 725-7541

Incorporated in 1936 in North Carolina.
Donor(s): Mrs. Nancy S. Reynolds, Mrs. Mary Reynolds Babcock,† Richard J. Reynolds,† William N. Reynolds.†
Financial data: (yr. ended 12/31/83): Assets, $103,581,285 (M); gifts received, $6,209,987; expenditures, $6,365,066, including $6,051,555 for 161 grants (high: $1,700,000; low: $746; average: $34,000).
Purpose and activities: General charitable purposes; local giving primarily for colleges, including scholarships, the arts, health care, youth, social services, public policy, environment, and improvement of the criminal justice system.
Types of support awarded: Operating budgets, continuing support, annual campaigns, seed money, emergency funds, building funds, equipment, land acquisition, endowment funds, matching funds, special projects, publications, conferences and seminars, scholarship funds.

Limitations: Giving limited to NC. No grants to individuals, or for research or program-related investments; no loans. Very limited support for scholarships to institutions only.
Publications: Annual report, application guidelines.
Application information:
Initial approach: Letter, telephone, or full proposal
Copies of proposal: 1
Deadline(s): February 1 and August 1
Board meeting date(s): Second Friday in May and November
Final notification: 4 months
Write: Thomas W. Lambeth, Executive Director
Officers: Smith W. Bagley,* President; Zachary T. Smith,* Vice-President; Thomas W. Lambeth, Secretary and Executive Director; Joseph G. Gordon,* Treasurer.
Trustees:* Nancy S. Reynolds, Honorary Chairman; Daniel G. Clodfelter, Hubert Humphrey, Katharine B. Mountcastle, Mary Mountcastle, Stephen L. Neal, Jane S. Patterson, Sherwood H. Smith, Jr.
Number of staff: 2 full-time professional; 2 full-time support.
Employer Identification Number: 586038145

3125
Richardson (Grace Jones) Trust
P.O. Box 20124
Greensboro 27420

Trust established in 1962 in Connecticut.
Donor(s): Mrs. Grace Jones Richardson.†
Financial data: (yr. ended 12/31/83): Assets, $9,435,482 (M); expenditures, $143,072, including $109,865 for 110 grants (high: $10,865; low: $50).
Purpose and activities: Broad purposes; primarily local giving, with emphasis on community funds.
Limitations: Giving primarily in NC. No grants to individuals.
Application information: Applications not invited.
Board meeting date(s): As required
Write: H. Smith Richardson, Jr., Trustee
Trustees: H. Smith Richardson, Jr., Robert R. Richardson.
Number of staff: None.
Employer Identification Number: 066023003

3126
Richardson (H. Smith) Charitable Trust ▼
c/o Piedmont Financial Company
P.O. Box 20124
Greensboro 27420

Trust established in 1976 in North Carolina.
Donor(s): H. Smith Richardson.†
Financial data: (yr. ended 6/30/84): Assets, $14,015,868 (M); expenditures, $837,555, including $753,095 for 41 grants (high: $60,000; low: $1,000).
Purpose and activities: Support primarily for higher education, educational organizations, and public policy research.
Application information:

Initial approach: Proposal
Write: H. Smith Richardson, Jr., Trustee
Trustees: C.W. Cheek, H. Smith Richardson, Jr., R.R. Richardson, Stuart S. Richardson.
Number of staff: 1 part-time professional.
Employer Identification Number: 237245123

3127
Richardson (The Mary Lynn) Fund
P.O. Box 20124
Greensboro 27420

Trust established in 1940 in North Carolina.
Donor(s): Mary Lynn Richardson.†
Financial data: (yr. ended 12/31/83): Assets, $2,090,246 (M); expenditures, $150,888, including $130,460 for 26 grants (high: $8,000; low: $900) and $7,800 for 6 grants to individuals.
Purpose and activities: To distribute income equally between: (1) domestic charities to include aged indigents mostly in North Carolina and the South; new grants to individuals made directly to institutions to carry out this purpose; and (2) foreign missions for religious, charitable, or educational application.
Types of support awarded: General purposes, scholarship funds.
Limitations: Giving primarily in NC for domestic programs. No grants for building funds, research programs, or matching gifts; no loans.
Application information:
Initial approach: Full proposal
Copies of proposal: 1
Deadline(s): Submit proposal preferably between January and March; deadline April 1 and October 1
Board meeting date(s): In late spring and the fall
Write: Bess R. Boney, Trustee
Manager: James F. Connolly.
Trustees: Lisa V. Beaman, Bess R. Boney, Eric R. Calhoun, William Y. Preyer, Jr., Adele Richardson Ray.
Employer Identification Number: 066025946

3128
Richardson (Smith) Foundation, Inc. ▼
5000 Laurinda Dr.
P.O. Box 3265
Greensboro 27402   (919) 288-7230

Incorporated in 1935 in North Carolina.
Donor(s): H.S. Richardson, Sr.,† Mrs. Grace Jones Richardson.†
Financial data: (yr. ended 12/31/84): Assets, $107,448,490 (M); expenditures, $4,864,947, including $4,021,987 for 83 grants (high: $1,331,330).

Purpose and activities: The grants-in-aid program has two main thrusts: 1) a public affairs program, aimed at supporting and promoting a vigorous economy and free society, mainly through support of public policy research projects and educational programs focusing on business and the economy; 2) to aid in developing the qualities of leadership that will make society fully responsive to the great demands being placed upon it in today's world, through support of the Center for Creative Leadership in Greensboro, North Carolina.
Types of support awarded: Research, publications, conferences and seminars, seed money.
Limitations: No support for programs in the arts, historic restoration, programs concerning employment, recreation, or regional or community health and welfare. No grants to individuals, or for deficit financing, building funds, scholarships, fellowships, operating budgets, or research in the physical sciences; no loans.
Publications: Annual report.
Application information: Most projects funded are initiated by the foundation.
Initial approach: Proposal
Copies of proposal: 1
Deadline(s): None
Board meeting date(s): Usually in March, June, September, and December
Final notification: 30 to 60 days
Write: Dorothy W. Hurley, Coordinator
Officers: Randolph R. Richardson,* President; Charles W. Cheek,* Vice-President, Secretary, and Treasurer.
Trustees:* H. Smith Richardson, Jr., Chairman; Robert H. Mulreany, Stuart S. Richardson.
Number of staff: 3 full-time professional; 1 part-time professional; 3 full-time support; 1 part-time support.
Employer Identification Number: 560611550

3129
Rixson (Oscar C.) Foundation, Inc. ⊭
535 Glendale Dr.
Statesville 28677

Incorporated in 1925 in New York.
Financial data: (yr. ended 12/31/83): Assets, $1,445,307 (M); expenditures, $118,016, including $73,150 for 250 grants (high: $10,000; low: $100).
Purpose and activities: To render financial assistance to certain religious and charitable organizations and needy active and retired religious workers.
Officers and Directors: Walter J. Munro, Sr., President; Walter J. Munro, Jr., Vice-President; Nathan Dunkerton, Secretary; Thomas Elliott, William R. Kusche, Jr., Paul Tully.
Employer Identification Number: 136129767

3130
Rogers (The Florence) Charitable Trust
P.O. Box 36006
Fayetteville 28303   (919) 484-2033

Trust established in 1961 in North Carolina.
Donor(s): Florence L. Rogers.†

Financial data: (yr. ended 3/31/84): Assets, $3,191,362 (M); expenditures, $126,389, including $126,389 for 16 grants (high: $36,300; low: $708).
Purpose and activities: Broad purposes; primarily local giving, with emphasis on art programs, education, recreation, child welfare, and the general quality of life in the area. Preference is given to seed money for new ideas.
Types of support awarded: Seed money, matching funds, research.
Limitations: Giving primarily in Fayetteville, Cumberland County, and southeastern NC. No grants to individuals, or for building or endowment funds, operating budgets, or scholarships and fellowships; no loans.
Publications: Informational brochure, program policy statement, application guidelines.
Application information:
Initial approach: Letter or telephone
Copies of proposal: 1
Board meeting date(s): Monthly
Final notification: 3 months
Write: JoAnn M. Barnette, Administrator
Officer: JoAnn M. Barnette, Administrator.
Trustees: Nolan P. Clark, John C. Tally.
Number of staff: 1.
Employer Identification Number: 566074515

3131
Salisbury Community Foundation, Inc.
P.O. Box 1327
Salisbury 28144   (704) 636-5211

Community foundation incorporated in 1944 in North Carolina.
Financial data: (yr. ended 12/31/81): Assets, $1,852,211 (M); gifts received, $728,531; expenditures, $624,676, including $595,351 for 397 grants (high: $52,000; low: $10).
Purpose and activities: Grants primarily for capital projects in Rowan County; some seed-money grants for special projects.
Types of support awarded: Building funds, special projects, seed money.
Limitations: Giving primarily in NC. No grants to individuals, or for endowment funds or operating budgets.
Application information:
Initial approach: Proposal
Copies of proposal: 1
Deadline(s): 10 days before board meetings
Board meeting date(s): February, May, August, and November
Write: W.A. Sherrill, Secretary-Treasurer
Officers and Trustees: W.C. Stanback, President; W.A. Sherrill, Secretary-Treasurer; Wiley Lash, Reid Leonard, Irvin Oestreicher, Joe Rutledge, Miles J. Smith, Sr., Fred J. Stanback, Jr., C.H. Wentz, J.G. Whitton.
Trustee Bank: Security Bank & Trust Company.
Employer Identification Number: 560772117

3132
Sternberger (Sigmund) Foundation, Inc.
P.O. Box 3111
Greensboro 27402   (919) 378-1791

Incorporated in 1957 in North Carolina.
Donor(s): Sigmund Sternberger.†

Financial data: (yr. ended 3/31/84): Assets, $6,090,943 (M); expenditures, $299,105, including $251,679 for 54 grants (high: $25,000; low: $200; average: $1,000-$10,000) and $13,878 for 14 grants to individuals.
Purpose and activities: Broad purposes; primarily local giving, with emphasis on higher education, including scholarship funds, and individual scholarships for children of members of the Revolution Masonic Lodge; grants also for the arts and human service agencies.
Types of support awarded: Seed money, emergency funds, special projects, deficit financing, building funds, equipment, matching funds, scholarship funds, research, publications, conferences and seminars, student aid.
Limitations: Giving primarily in Guilford County, NC. No loans.
Publications: Application guidelines.
Application information: Application form required.
  Initial approach: Letter
  Copies of proposal: 1
  Deadline(s): None
  Board meeting date(s): Usually in March, June, December, and as required
  Final notification: 3 months
  Write: Robert O. Klepfer, Jr., Executive Director
Officers: Mrs. A.J. Tannenbaum,* President; Mrs. R. Mack Williams,* Vice-President; Sidney J. Stern, Jr.,* Secretary-Treasurer; Robert O. Klepfer, Jr., Executive Director.
Directors:* Howard E. Carr, Charles M. Reid, Jeanne Tannenbaum, Sigmund I. Tannenbaum, M.D., Rabbi Arnold S. Task.
Number of staff: 1 part-time professional.
Employer Identification Number: 566045483

3133
Stonecutter Foundation, Inc. ⋈
Spindale 28160   (704) 286-2341

Incorporated in 1944 in North Carolina.
Donor(s): Stonecutter Mills Corporation.
Financial data: (yr. ended 8/31/83): Assets, $3,040,363 (M); gifts received, $19,949; expenditures, $191,419, including $159,600 for 35 grants (high: $34,500; low: $50) and $13,500 for 19 loans.
Purpose and activities: Broad purposes; local giving, with emphasis on secondary and higher education, including student loans, youth agencies, and church support.
Types of support awarded: Student aid.
Limitations: Giving primarily in NC.
Application information: Student loans restricted to local area. Application form required.
  Deadline(s): None
  Write: J.T. Strickland, Treasurer
Officers: W.J. Stallings,* President; A.H. Rucker,* Vice-President; T.P. Walker, Secretary; J.T. Strickland, Treasurer.
Directors:* Ivy Cowan, H.W. Crenshaw, Z.E. Dobbins, Jr., K.S. Tanner, Jr.
Employer Identification Number: 566044820

3134
Stowe (Robert Lee), Jr. Foundation, Inc.
P.O. Box 351
100 North Main St.
Belmont 28012   (704) 825-5314

Incorporated in 1945 in North Carolina.
Donor(s): Robert Lee Stowe, Jr.,† Robert L. Stowe III.
Financial data: (yr. ended 12/31/83): Assets, $2,074,907 (M); expenditures, $280,599, including $267,038 for 73 grants (high: $58,629; low: $100).
Purpose and activities: Broad purposes; primarily local giving, with emphasis on church support, child welfare, and higher education.
Limitations: Giving primarily in NC.
Application information:
  Write: Robert L. Stowe III, Vice-President
Officers: R.L. Stowe, Jr., President; David M. McConnell, Vice-President and Secretary; Daniel Harding Stowe, Vice-President and Treasurer; Willis Smith, Robert L. Stowe III, Vice-Presidents.
Employer Identification Number: 566034773

3135
Thomasville Furniture Industries Foundation
c/o Wachovia Bank and Trust Company
P.O. Box 3099
Winston-Salem 27102   (919) 748-5991
Application address: c/o Carlyle Nance, Jr., Thomasville Furniture Industries, P.O. Box 339, Thomasville, NC 27360; Tel.: (919) 475-1361

Trust established in 1960 in North Carolina.
Donor(s): Thomasville Furniture Industries, Inc.
Financial data: (yr. ended 12/31/84): Assets, $2,618,724 (M); expenditures, $166,135, including $127,000 for 14 grants (high: $33,000; low: $500) and $39,135 for 54 grants to individuals.
Purpose and activities: Broad purposes; grants largely for higher and secondary education, including scholarships for children of employees of Thomasville Furniture Industries, and for hospitals, mainly in areas of company operations.
Types of support awarded: Employee related scholarships.
Limitations: Giving primarily in NC.
Application information:
  Initial approach: Letter
  Deadline(s): None
  Write: Warren C. Hodges
Administrative Committee: Frederick B. Starr, Chairman; Frank W. Burr, George W. Hofmann, Carlyle A. Nance, Jr., Charles G. O'Brien.
Trustee: Wachovia Bank and Trust Company.
Employer Identification Number: 566047870

3136
Whitener Academy ⋈
1941 English Rd., Box E
High Point 27260

Financial data: (yr. ended 12/31/82): Assets, $2,356,711 (M); expenditures, $214,293, including $165,530 for 34 grants (high: $50,000; low: $30).
Purpose and activities: Primarily local giving for higher education, social services and youth agencies, particularly orphanages; and Protestant church support.
Limitations: Giving primarily in NC.
Officers and Directors: Orin Whitener, President; Marshall Pittman, Vice-President; John H. Jenson, Secretary; Wayne C. Curry, Treasurer.
Employer Identification Number: 237335869

3137
Winston-Salem Foundation, The ▼
229 First Union National Bank Bldg.
Winston-Salem 27101   (919) 725-2382

Community foundation established in 1919 in North Carolina by declaration of trust.
Financial data: (yr. ended 12/31/83): Assets, $30,232,849 (M); gifts received, $1,818,722; expenditures, $3,373,031, including $2,985,596 for 253 grants.
Purpose and activities: Primarily local giving; student aid primarily to bona fide residents of Forsyth County; substantial portion of funds distributed to schools, colleges, and universities and for social services.
Types of support awarded: Seed money, emergency funds, student aid, special projects, matching funds, general purposes.
Limitations: Giving primarily in Winston-Salem and Forsyth County, NC. No grants to individuals, or for endowment or building funds, annual campaigns, equipment and materials, land acquisition, renovation projects, publications, or conferences.
Publications: Annual report, application guidelines.
Application information:
  Initial approach: Telephone
  Copies of proposal: 1
  Deadline(s): January 1, March 1, May 1, July 1, and September 1
  Board meeting date(s): Bimonthly beginning in February (applications not considered at December meeting)
  Final notification: 1 month
  Write: L. Andrew Bell III, Assistant Director
Officer: Henry M. Carter, Jr., Executive Director.
Foundation Committee: Ralph M. Stockton, Jr., Chairman; James A. Hancock, Vice-Chairman; Mrs. Albert Butler, Jr., F. Hudnall Christopher, Jr., James E. Humphreys, Jr., John F. McNair III, Douglas F. Peterson, Barbara K. Phillips, C. Edward Pleasants, Jr.
Trustees: First Union National Bank, North Carolina National Bank, The Northwestern Bank, Wachovia Bank and Trust Company.
Number of staff: 2 full-time professional; 2 full-time support.
Employer Identification Number: 566037615

3138
Woodson (Margaret C.) Foundation, Inc. ⌗
P.O. Box 829
Salisbury 28145

Incorporated in 1954 in North Carolina.
Donor(s): Margaret C. Woodson.†
Financial data: (yr. ended 12/31/83): Assets, $317,025 (M); gifts received, $309,485; expenditures, $327,342, including $301,515 for 33 grants (high: $54,000; low: $15).
Purpose and activities: Broad purposes; primarily local giving, with emphasis on higher education, cultural programs, and child welfare.
Limitations: Giving primarily in NC.
Officers: James L. Woodson,* President; Esther C. Shay,* Vice-President; Roy C. Hoffner, Secretary; Charles Cunningham,* Treasurer.
Directors:* Paul L. Bernhardt, Beulah Hillard, Elizabeth H. Taylor, Mary Holt W. Woodson, Paul B. Woodson.
Employer Identification Number: 566064938

NORTH DAKOTA

3139
Fargo-Moorhead Area Foundation
505 Second Ave. North
P.O. Box 1980
Fargo 58102   (701) 293-3313

Community foundation established in 1960 in North Dakota.
Financial data: (yr. ended 12/31/84): Assets, $2,155,633 (M); gifts received, $230,502; expenditures, $330,665, including $226,739 for 45 grants (high: $99,460; low: $100; average: $1,000-$10,000) and $86,974 for 46 grants to individuals.
Purpose and activities: Charitable and educational purposes; grants primarily to local community welfare agencies.
Types of support awarded: Continuing support, annual campaigns, seed money, emergency funds, building funds, equipment, matching funds, scholarship funds.
Limitations: Giving primarily in Cass County, ND, and Clay County, MN. No grants to individuals (except from restricted funds), or for operating budgets, deficit financing, land acquisition, endowment funds, research, special projects, publications or conferences; no loans.
Publications: Annual report, program policy statement, application guidelines.
Application information:
  Initial approach: Letter or proposal
  Copies of proposal: 4
  Deadline(s): Submit proposal preferably in February or March; deadline April 1
  Board meeting date(s): December and May
  Final notification: 3 months after board meeting

Write: Roger L. Sullivan, Secretary
Officers: Marsha Kierscht,* Chairperson; C. Nicholas Vogel,* Vice-Chairman; Roger L. Sullivan, Secretary.
Distribution Committee:* Charles Bailley, Edward Ellingson, Robert Feder, Alden Gjevre, C. Warner Litten.
Trustee Banks: American Bank & Trust Company, Dakota First Trust Company, Fargo National Bank and Trust Company, First Northwestern Trust Company, First Trust Company of North Dakota.
Number of staff: None.
Employer Identification Number: 456010377

3140
Leach (Tom & Frances) Foundation, Inc. ⌗
P.O. Box 1136
Bismark 58501

Trust established in 1955 in North Dakota.
Donor(s): Tom Leach,† Frances Leach.
Financial data: (yr. ended 12/31/83): Assets, $1,925,576 (M); expenditures, $496,743, including $66,950 for 38 grants (high: $8,000; low: $500).
Purpose and activities: Giving primarily in North Dakota and Tulsa, Oklahoma, to community development programs and social services.
Limitations: Giving primarily in ND, particularly in Bismark and Mandan, and in Tulsa, OK.
Officers and Directors: Ernest R. Fleck, President; James P. Wachter, Vice-President; Russel R. Mather, Secretary-Treasurer; Frank J. Bavendick, Julia B. Blakely, Robert P. Hendrickson, Paul D. Schliesman, Gilbert N. Olson.
Employer Identification Number: 456012703

3141
Myra Foundation
600 DeMers Ave.
P.O. Box 99
Grand Forks 58201   (701) 772-8111

Incorporated in 1941 in North Dakota.
Donor(s): John E. Myra.†
Financial data: (yr. ended 12/31/82): Assets, $2,633,412 (M); expenditures, $313,580, including $130,425 for 30 grants (high: $22,525; low: $100).
Purpose and activities: Broad purposes; local giving with emphasis on a historical museum, a hospital, higher and secondary education, social agencies, homes for the aged, and youth development.
Limitations: Giving limited to Grand Forks County, ND. No grants to individuals, or for endowment funds, research, or matching gifts; no loans.
Application information:
  Initial approach: Letter
  Copies of proposal: 1
  Deadline(s): Submit proposal preferably in October; deadline November 1
  Board meeting date(s): Quarterly
  Write: Edward C. Gillig, President

Officers: Edward C. Gillig, President; Hilda Stokes, Vice-President; Pauline Molvig, Secretary-Treasurer.
Employer Identification Number: 450215088

3142
North Dakota Community Foundation
2900 East Broadway
Bismarck 58501   (701) 222-8349

Established in 1977 in North Dakota.
Financial data: (yr. ended 12/31/84): Assets, $1,975,043 (M); gifts received, $277,153; expenditures, $197,173, including $171,765 for 102 grants (high: $21,310; low: $100; average: $1,000) and $9,150 for 19 grants to individuals.
Purpose and activities: Local giving, with unrestricted funds largely for aid to the elderly and disadvantaged; support also for health services, youth agencies, parks and recreation, arts and cultural programs, and mental health.
Types of support awarded: Operating budgets, continuing support, annual campaigns, seed money, building funds, equipment, matching funds, scholarship funds, special projects, research, publications, conferences and seminars.
Limitations: Giving primarily in ND. No support for lobbying or sectarian purposes; low priority given to national or out-of-state organizations, hospitals, organizations with substantial and professional fundraising programs, or organizations that raise money through gambling activities. No grants to individuals (except for scholarships), or for emergency or endowment funds, deficit financing, or land acquisition; no loans.
Publications: Annual report, program policy statement, application guidelines.
Application information: Application form available in December. Application form required.
  Initial approach: Letter
  Deadline(s): Submit application preferably between January 1 and March 15; deadline March 15
  Board meeting date(s): Annually in second quarter of year
  Final notification: 3 months
  Write: Richard H. Timmins, President
Officers and Directors: T.A. Roney, Chairman; A.L. Braaten, Vice-Chairman; Richard H. Timmins, President; Jim Davis, Secretary-Treasurer; Dale Anderson, Larry Atkins, Arden Burbidge, Warren DeKrey, Sarah Andrews Herman, Jo Jacobson, Karnes Johnson, Theodore F. Kessel, Sr., Gloria Legrid, Wayne Leiner, Daniel Lessard, J. Gerald Nilles, Dean R. Strinden, M.D.
Number of staff: 1 full-time professional; 1 full-time support.
Employer Identification Number: 450336015

3143
Stern (Alex) Family Foundation
Bill Stern Bldg., Suite 202
609 1/2 First Ave., North
Fargo 58102   (701) 237-0170

Established in 1964 in North Dakota.

Donor(s): William Stern,† Sam Stern,† Edward A. Stern.†
Financial data: (yr. ended 12/31/84): Assets, $5,307,155 (M); expenditures, $311,340, including $260,828 for 44 grants (high: $50,000; low: $1,000; average: $5,928).
Purpose and activities: Local giving, with emphasis on cultural programs, social agencies, and youth agencies; grants also for community organizations, temple support, and human interest and human services organizations.
Types of support awarded: Continuing support, annual campaigns, emergency funds, building funds, equipment, research, conferences and seminars, professorships, matching funds.
Limitations: Giving limited to the Fargo-Moorhead, ND, area. No grants to individuals, or for endowment funds; no loans.
Publications: Application guidelines.
Application information: Application form required.
  Initial approach: Letter, telephone, or full proposal
  Copies of proposal: 3
  Deadline(s): Submit application preferably between April and December; no set deadline
  Final notification: Within a few months
  Write: A.M. Eriksmoen, Executive Director
Officer and Trustees: A.M. Eriksmoen, Executive Director; W.R. Amundson, J.L. McCormick.
Number of staff: 1.
Employer Identification Number: 456013981

OHIO

3144
Acme Cleveland Foundation ⌶
30195 Chagrin Blvd., Suite 300
Pepper Pike 44124   (216) 292-2100

Incorporated in 1969 in Ohio.
Donor(s): Acme-Cleveland Corporation.
Financial data: (yr. ended 12/31/83): Assets, $521,626 (M); expenditures, $314,188, including $312,470 for 104 grants (high: $110,000; low: $120).
Purpose and activities: Giving limited to areas of company operations, mainly Cleveland and Detroit, with emphasis on community funds, higher education, hospitals, youth activities, and cultural organizations.
Types of support awarded: Operating budgets, continuing support, general purposes, annual campaigns, building funds, endowment funds, special projects, employee matching gifts.
Limitations: Giving primarily in Cleveland, OH, and Detroit, MI. No grants to individuals, or for research programs, scholarships or fellowships; no loans.
Application information:

Initial approach: Full proposal
Copies of proposal: 1
Deadline(s): Submit proposal preferably between December 1 and February 15
Board meeting date(s): Contribution committee meets at the end of February
Write: Mel A. Vogel
Officer and Trustee: W. Paul Cooper, President.
Employer Identification Number: 346527528

3145
Akron Community Foundation
One Cascade Plaza
Akron 44308   (216) 376-8522

Community foundation incorporated in 1955 in Ohio.
Financial data: (yr. ended 3/31/84): Assets, $7,783,724 (M); gifts received, $846,089; expenditures, $412,655, including $366,288 for 62 grants (high: $50,000; low: $50).
Purpose and activities: To promote charitable, benevolent, educational, recreational, health, esthetic, cultural, and public welfare activities, primarily but not exclusively in Summit County, Ohio; to support a program of research leading to the improvement of the health, education, and general well-being of all citizens of the Akron area; to give toward the support of experimental and demonstration programs, through established or new agencies; to test the validity of research findings in various fields of community planning directed toward the efficient and adequate coordination of public and private services organized to meet human needs.
Types of support awarded: Operating budgets, building funds, matching funds.
Limitations: Giving primarily in Summit County, OH. No support for community funds. No grants to individuals, or for continuing support, seed money, emergency or endowment funds, equipment, renovation, or scholarships and fellowships; no loans.
Publications: Annual report, application guidelines.
Application information:
  Initial approach: Full proposal, letter, or telephone
  Copies of proposal: 1
  Deadline(s): 30 days prior to board meeting
  Board meeting date(s): March, July, September, and December
  Final notification: 2 to 3 months
  Write: John L. Feudner, Jr., Executive Director
Officers: Melvin D. Sacks,* President; Robert W. Briggs,* Vice-President; Allan Johnson, Secretary; John F. Bennett,* Treasurer; John L. Feudner, Jr., Executive Director.
Trustees:* Tom H. Barrett, Randolph Baxter, Leon R. Brodeur, Richard B. Buchholzer, Ann Falor, James V. Gels, Ellen Hay, Karl S. Hay, Gerald L. Hill, David A. Lieberth, Stephen E. Myers, George T. Parry, Patrick C. Ross, C. David Shaffer, Robert A. Stefanko.
Trustee Banks: Bank One of Akron, First National Bank of Akron, National City Bank, Society National Bank.
Number of staff: 1 part-time professional; 1 full-time support.
Employer Identification Number: 237029875

3146
Albers (The William H.) Foundation, Inc. ⌶
c/o David Kallaher, Inc.
602 Main St., No. 801
Cincinnati 45202

Incorporated in 1982 in Ohio.
Financial data: (yr. ended 4/30/84): Assets, $1,160,509 (M); expenditures, $74,381, including $60,300 for 22 grants (high: $10,000; low: $300).
Purpose and activities: Primarily local giving, with emphasis on secondary and higher education, cultural programs, youth agencies, and hospitals.
Types of support awarded: General purposes, building funds, operating budgets.
Limitations: Giving primarily in Cincinnati, OH.
Officer and Trustees: Irene A. Dornheggen, President; John H. Dornheggen III, James L. Leonard, Luke J. Leonard.
Employer Identification Number: 316023881

3147
Allyn Foundation, The
2211 S. Dixie Ave.
Dayton 45409

Incorporated in 1955 in Ohio.
Donor(s): S.C. Allyn.†
Financial data: (yr. ended 12/31/84): Assets, $1,204,478 (M); expenditures, $84,448, including $68,000 for 43 grants (high: $7,000; low: $250).
Purpose and activities: Broad purposes; general giving, with emphasis on higher and secondary education; support also for hospitals, social services, aid to the handicapped, and a community fund, primarily in the southern Ohio area.
Limitations: Giving primarily in southern OH, with the exception of certain schools and universities. No grants to individuals, or for endowment funds.
Publications: 990-PF.
Application information:
  Write: Charles S. Allyn, Jr., President
Officers and Trustees: Charles S. Allyn, Jr., President; Mary Louise Sunderland, Vice-President; Compton Allyn, Secretary-Treasurer; Anne Reed Sunderland, Louise Allyn Sunderland.
Employer Identification Number: 316030791

3148
Alms (Eleanora C. U.) Trust
c/o The Fifth Third Bank
38 Fountain Square Plaza
Cincinnati 45202   (513) 579-5498
Mailing address: The Fifth Third Bank, Dept. 00850 Trust Division, Cincinnati, OH 45263

Trust established in 1939 in Ohio.
Donor(s): Eleanora C.U. Alms.†
Financial data: (yr. ended 9/30/84): Assets, $1,778,675 (M); expenditures, $124,139, including $119,800 for 4 grants (high: $25,000; low: $5,000; average: $5,000-$10,000).
Purpose and activities: Support for local charitable, educational, and artistic activities.

Types of support awarded: Building funds.
Limitations: Giving limited to the greater
Cincinnati, OH, area. No support for political
or religious purposes, or to other foundations.
No grants to individuals, or for operating
budgets; no loans.
Publications: Program policy statement,
application guidelines.
Application information:
  Initial approach: Letter
  Copies of proposal: 1
  Deadline(s): Early February, May, August, or
    November
  Board meeting date(s): March, June,
    September, and December
  Write: Carol A. Schneider, Trust Officer
Trustee: The Fifth Third Bank (Carol A.
Schneider, Trust Officer).
Employer Identification Number: 316019723

3149
Amcast Industrial Foundation
(formerly The Dayton Malleable Foundation)
3931 South Dixie Ave.
Kettering 45439   (513) 298-5251
Mailing address: P.O. Box 98, Dayton, OH
45401

Incorporated in 1952 in Ohio.
Donor(s): Amcast Industrial Corporation,
(formerly Dayton Malleable Inc.).
Financial data: (yr. ended 8/31/84): Assets,
$845,590 (M); expenditures, $110,090,
including $99,859 for 82 grants (high: $10,000;
low: $100) and $1,459 for 10 employee
matching gifts.
Purpose and activities: Grants mainly in areas
of company operations for community funds,
arts and cultural programs, and higher
education.
Types of support awarded: Continuing
support, annual campaigns, emergency funds,
building funds, employee matching gifts, special
projects, research.
Limitations: Giving primarily in areas of
company operations. No grants to individuals,
or for operating budgets, seed money, deficit
financing, equipment, land acquisition,
endowment funds, scholarships, fellowships,
publications, or conferences; no loans.
Application information:
  Board meeting date(s): November and August
  Write: Thomas G. Amato, Secretary-Treasurer
Officers and Trustees: Leo W. Ladehoff,
President; Timothy J. Keating, Vice-President;
Thomas G. Amato, Secretary-Treasurer.
Number of staff: None.
Employer Identification Number: 316016458

3150
American Financial Corporation
Foundation, The ▼
One East Fourth St.
Cincinnati 45202   (513) 579-2432

Established in 1971 in Ohio.
Donor(s): American Financial Corporation.

Financial data: (yr. ended 12/31/83): Assets,
$376,823 (M); gifts received, $1,453,750;
expenditures, $1,120,018, including
$1,119,965 for 77 grants (high: $250,000; low:
$50).
Purpose and activities: Primarily local giving,
with emphasis on organizations promoting
social change, economic study, and social
welfare, including hospitals, and public interest
organizations; grants also for education and the
arts.
Types of support awarded: Building funds,
endowment funds, operating budgets, special
projects.
Limitations: Giving primarily in the Cincinnati,
OH, area. No grants to individuals.
Application information:
  Initial approach: Letter
  Copies of proposal: 1
  Board meeting date(s): As required
  Final notification: 60 days
  Write: Sherwood W. McIntire, Treasurer
Officers and Directors:* Carl H. Lindner,*
President; Robert D. Lindner,* Vice-President;
Sandra W. Heimann, Secretary; Sherwood W.
McIntire, Treasurer.
Employer Identification Number: 237153009

3151
American Foundation Corporation,
The ▼ ⌀
720 National City Bank Bldg.
Cleveland 44114   (216) 241-6664

Incorporated in 1974 as successor to trust
established in 1944 in Ohio.
Donor(s): Members of the Corning, Murfey,
and Norweb families and others.
Financial data: (yr. ended 12/31/83): Assets,
$14,187,595 (M); gifts received, $77,052;
expenditures, $846,797, including $764,425
for 220 grants (high: $325,116; low: $50;
average: $50-$10,000).
Purpose and activities: General scientific,
educational, religious, and welfare activities,
with emphasis on an arboretum, museums,
higher and secondary education, child welfare,
and community funds, primarily in Ohio and
California.
Types of support awarded: Annual
campaigns, general purposes, continuing
support.
Limitations: Giving primarily in the Cleveland,
OH, area and CA. No grants to individuals,
capital or endowment funds, special projects,
research-related programs, scholarships and
fellowships, or matching gifts; no loans.
Application information: Funds presently
committed; applications for grants not invited.
  Deadline(s): None
  Board meeting date(s): March 14 (1984)
  Write: Maria G. Muth, Assistant Secretary
    and Treasurer
Officers: Claude F. Turben,* President; T.
Dixon Long,* Vice-President; Malvin E. Bank,
Secretary.
Trustees:* Henry H. Corning, Nathan E.
Corning, Spencer L. Murfey, Jr., William W.
Murfey.
Number of staff: None.
Employer Identification Number: 237348126

3152
Anderson Foundation ▼
P.O. Box 119
Maumee 43537   (419) 893-5050

Trust established in 1949 in Ohio.
Donor(s): Partners in The Andersons.
Financial data: (yr. ended 12/31/84): Assets,
$4,422,743 (M); expenditures, $744,937,
including $686,057 for 106 grants.
Purpose and activities: Broad purposes;
primarily local giving, including grants for
higher and secondary education, community
development, youth agencies, community
funds, religious organizations, and educational
and research associations.
Types of support awarded: Annual
campaigns, seed money, building funds,
equipment, research, special projects,
publications, scholarship funds, matching funds,
continuing support, general purposes,
emergency funds.
Limitations: Giving primarily in the greater
Toledo, OH, area, including Maumee and
Findlay. Grants also to organizations located
near plants in the following cities: Delphi,
Frankfort, and Dunkirk, IA; Champaign, IL; and
Albion, Webberville and White Pigeon, MI.
No grants to individuals, or for endowment
funds or travel.
Publications: Application guidelines.
Application information:
  Initial approach: Letter or telephone
  Copies of proposal: 1
  Deadline(s): First week of meeting month
  Board meeting date(s): Bimonthly beginning
    in February
  Final notification: Generally 2 months;
    depends on completeness of proposal
  Write: Tammy Smahaj, Secretary to the
    Chairman
Trustees: Thomas H. Anderson, Chairman;
Donald E. Anderson, John D. Anderson,
Michael J. Anderson, Robert J. Anderson,
Robert G. Bristow, Beverly J. McBride.
Number of staff: 1 full-time professional.
Employer Identification Number: 346528868

3153
Anderson (William P.) Foundation
c/o The Central Trust Company
Fourth and Vine Sts.
Cincinnati 45202

Incorporated in 1941 in Ohio.
Financial data: (yr. ended 10/31/83): Assets,
$2,590,027 (M); expenditures, $164,661,
including $135,100 for 35 grants (high:
$17,000; low: $500) and $17,844 for 7 grants
to individuals.
Purpose and activities: Broad purposes;
general giving, primarily in Cincinnati and
Boston, with emphasis on hospitals, community
funds, educational institutions, child welfare
and youth agencies, including problems of
juvenile delinquency, health agencies,
conservation, and the arts.
Limitations: Giving primarily in Cincinnati, OH
and Boston, MA.

Officers and Trustees: William G. Anderson, President and Treasurer; Vachael Anderson Coombe, C. Lawson Reed, Vice-Presidents; Paul D. Myers, Secretary; Grenville Anderson, William P. Anderson, Margot A. Claflin, Eva Jane Coombe, Paul D. Myers, Dorothy W. Reed, Katharine W. Taft, Henry W. Whittaker.
Employer Identification Number: 316034059

3154
Andrews Foundation, The
1127 Euclid Ave., Suite 210
Cleveland 44115   (216) 621-3215

Incorporated in 1951 in Ohio.
Donor(s): Mrs. Matthew Andrews.†
Financial data: (yr. ended 12/31/83): Assets, $3,247,469 (M); expenditures, $542,362, including $500,280 for grants.
Purpose and activities: Giving restricted to northeastern Ohio, primarily for higher and secondary education, the performing arts, and a child development center.
Limitations: Giving limited to northeastern OH. No grants to individuals.
Application information:
  Initial approach: Letter
  Copies of proposal: 1
  Board meeting date(s): Usually in November
  Write: Richard S. Tomer, President
Officers and Trustees: Richard S. Tomer, President and Treasurer; Barbara J. Baxter, Vice-President; James H. Dempsey, Jr., Secretary.
Employer Identification Number: 346515110

3155
Andrews (Mildred) Fund ¤
National City Bank
P.O. Box 5756
Cleveland 44101

Trust established in 1972 in Ohio.
Donor(s): Peter Putnam, and others.
Financial data: (yr. ended 12/31/83): Assets, $6,447,486 (M); gifts received, $238,175; expenditures, $134,226, including $114,171 for 25 grants (high: $77,350; low: $30).
Purpose and activities: A private operating foundation; primarily local giving for the arts and higher education.
Limitations: Giving primarily in the Cleveland, OH area.
Application information:
  Write: Peter Putnam
Trustees: Mrs. John Putnam, Peter Putnam.
Employer Identification Number: 237158695

3156
Armco Foundation ▼
703 Curtis St.
Middletown 45043   (513) 425-5280

Incorporated in 1951 in Ohio.
Donor(s): Armco Inc.
Financial data: (yr. ended 12/31/84): Assets, $9,997,947 (M); expenditures, $3,481,057, including $1,558,748 for 127 grants (high: $75,000; low: $50; average: $3,000), $229,298 for 122 grants to individuals and $661,722 for 878 employee matching gifts.

Purpose and activities: Broad purposes; capital and special program grants for civic welfare, educational, and medical institutions, primarily in areas of major production facilities of the Corporation; a matching grant program for higher educational and cultural institutions, and a volunteer support program for active employees.
Types of support awarded: Continuing support, annual campaigns, seed money, emergency funds, building funds, equipment, matching funds, consulting services, technical assistance, scholarship funds, employee related scholarships, exchange programs, research, conferences and seminars, employee matching gifts.
Limitations: Giving primarily in areas of company operations, with emphasis on OH. No support for religious organizations. No grants to individuals (except for company-employee scholarships), or for operating budgets, deficit financing, land acquisition, endowment funds, fellowships, demonstration projects, or publications; no loans.
Publications: Application guidelines, program policy statement.
Application information:
  Initial approach: Letter, telephone, or full proposal
  Copies of proposal: 1
  Deadline(s): None
  Board meeting date(s): January, April, July, and October
  Final notification: 8 weeks
  Write: Walter G. Smyth, Executive Director
Officers: Harry Holiday, Jr.,* President; John R. Holland, Executive Vice-President; Robert W. Kent, Vice-President and Secretary; W.L. Truebeck, Treasurer; Walter G. Smyth, Executive Director.
Trustees:* Frederick B. Dent, Chairman; R.E. Boni, Brage Golding, Juanita M. Kreps, John W. Ladish, C. William Verity, Jr.
Number of staff: 4 full-time professional; 2 full-time support.
Employer Identification Number: 316026565

3157
Armington (The Evenor) Fund
c/o Huntington Bank of Northeast Ohio
917 Euclid Ave.
Cleveland 44115

Established in 1954 in Ohio.
Donor(s): Everett Armington, and members of the Armington family.
Financial data: (yr. ended 12/31/82): Assets, $1,638,493 (M); expenditures, $161,260, including $151,000 for 33 grants (high: $15,000; low: $1,000; average: $1,000-$8,000).
Purpose and activities: Broad purposes; grants primarily for higher education, child welfare, health agencies, the arts, the environment, public policy organizations, including human rights, peace and justice, and the struggle against poverty.
Types of support awarded: Operating budgets, continuing support, annual campaigns, emergency funds, research, publications.

Limitations: No grants to individuals, or for seed money, deficit financing, capital, building or endowment funds, equipment, land acquisition, renovations, matching gifts, scholarships or fellowships, demonstration projects, or conferences.
Application information: Applications not encouraged; most grants are initiated by the advisors.
  Board meeting date(s): Annually in the summer
Advisors: Catherine Armington, David E. Armington, Paul S. Armington, Peter Armington, Rosemary Armington.
Trustee: Huntington Bank of Northeast Ohio.
Number of staff: None.
Employer Identification Number: 346522508

3158
Ashtabula Foundation, Inc., The
c/o Society Bank of Eastern Ohio
4717 Main Ave.
Ashtabula 44004   (216) 992-6818

Community foundation incorporated in 1922 in Ohio.
Financial data: (yr. ended 12/31/83): Assets, $5,319,806 (M); gifts received, $71,363; expenditures, $392,681, including $314,617 for 14 grants (high: $139,068; low: $103).
Purpose and activities: Broad purposes; to administer charitable trusts for the benefit of the Ashtabula area; support for health, welfare, and cultural programs, with emphasis on a community fund and church support.
Limitations: Giving limited to the Ashtabula, OH area.
Publications: Application guidelines.
Application information: Grant application guidelines for scholarship funds available. Application form required.
  Initial approach: Full proposal
  Copies of proposal: 4
  Deadline(s): February 15, May 15, August 15, and November 15
  Board meeting date(s): March, June, September, and December
  Write: Linda C. Henslee, Secretary-Treasurer
Officers and Trustees: Nelson Hague, President; Frank Koski, Vice-President; Linda C. Henslee, Secretary-Treasurer; Wilbur Anderson, David Felt, Eleanor Jammal, George A. Johnson, John Zaback, William C. Zweier.
Trustee Bank: Society Bank of Eastern Ohio.
Employer Identification Number: 346538130

3159
Austin Company Foundation, The
3650 Mayfield Rd.
Cleveland 44121

Trust established about 1952 in Ohio.
Donor(s): The Austin Company.
Financial data: (yr. ended 12/31/82): Assets, $2,614,379 (M); expenditures, $250,166, including $223,226 for 75 grants (high: $112,095; low: $25).
Purpose and activities: Charitable and educational purposes; general giving, with emphasis on community funds, higher education, and hospitals.

Application information:
Write: A.A. Wilhelm, Secretary
Officer and Trustees: A.A. Wilhelm, Secretary; George E. Beardsworth, Charles A. Shirk.
Employer Identification Number: 346551614

3160
Austin Memorial Foundation, The ⊭
3650 Mayfield Rd.
Cleveland Heights 44118

Incorporated in 1961 in Ohio.
Donor(s): Members of the Austin family.
Financial data: (yr. ended 12/31/83): Assets, $4,679,138 (M); gifts received, $10,000; expenditures, $412,158, including $331,833 for 33 grants (high: $50,000; low: $500).
Purpose and activities: Emphasis on higher and secondary education, hospitals, and Protestant church support.
Limitations: No grants to individuals.
Application information:
Initial approach: Letter
Copies of proposal: 1
Deadline(s): Submit proposal in December or September
Board meeting date(s): Semiannually
Write: Donald G. Austin, Jr., President
Officers: Donald G. Austin, Jr.,* President; Donald G. Austin,* Margaret A. Rodgers,* Vice-Presidents; Quentin Alexander, Secretary.
Trustees:* James W. Austin, Richard C. Austin, Stewart G. Austin, Thomas G. Austin, Winifred N. Austin, Sarah R. Cole, Ann R. Loeffler, David A. Rodgers.
Employer Identification Number: 346528879

3161
Baird Brothers Company Foundation ⊭
The Huntington National Bank
P.O. Box 1558
Columbus 43260
Application address: The Huntington National Bank, Trust Dept., 37 West Broad St., Columbus, OH 43215; Tel.: (614) 469-7626

Established in Ohio.
Financial data: (yr. ended 12/31/83): Assets, $3,010,317 (M); expenditures, $265,070, including $204,998 for 21 grants (high: $26,665; low: $200).
Purpose and activities: Grants only to organizations in Nelsonville, Ohio, primarily for a museum, civic affairs, a hearing center, and church support.
Limitations: Giving limited to Nelsonville, OH.
Application information:
Deadline(s): None
Write: Arlene B. Powell, Director
Trustee: Huntington National Bank.
Directors: Rev. J. Lloyd Evans, Arlene B. Powell, Wilbert W. Warren.
Employer Identification Number: 316194844

3162
Bates (The Georgine E.) Memorial Fund, Inc.
1221 Lippencott Rd.
P.O. Box 351
Urbana 43078

Established in 1979.
Financial data: (yr. ended 10/31/83): Assets, $1,051,104 (M); expenditures, $78,403, including $61,000 for 20 grants (high: $6,000; low: $1,000).
Purpose and activities: Local giving for higher and secondary education, youth agencies, health, and a center for senior citizens.
Limitations: Giving limited to Urbana, OH.
Officers: Marvin V. Humphrey, President; William Hoefer, James Wilson, Secretaries; Henry W. Houston, Treasurer.
Employer Identification Number: 341296531

3163
Beecher (Florence Simon) Foundation
c/o Mahoning National Bank of Youngstown, Trust Dept.
23 Federal Plaza
Youngstown 44501

Established in 1969.
Financial data: (yr. ended 12/31/84): Assets, $2,392,760 (M); gifts received, $242,970; expenditures, $114,332, including $89,100 for 17 grants (high: $14,000; low: $250).
Purpose and activities: Local giving, with emphasis on youth agencies and community development.
Types of support awarded: General purposes, equipment, building funds.
Limitations: Giving limited to Youngstown, OH.
Directors: Eleanor Beecher Flad, Erle L. Flad, Ward Beecher Flad, Arthur G. Young.
Trustee: Mahoning National Bank of Youngstown.
Employer Identification Number: 346613413

3164
Beecher (Ward) Foundation
Mahoning National Bank of Youngstown
23 Federal Plaza
Youngstown 44501   (216) 742-7000

Established in 1958 in Ohio.
Donor(s): Ward Beecher.†
Financial data: (yr. ended 12/31/84): Assets, $1,780,889 (M); expenditures, $136,813, including $122,000 for 3 grants (high: $120,000; low: $2,000).
Purpose and activities: Local giving, with emphasis on capital building drives for hospitals, community funds, and youth agencies.
Types of support awarded: Building funds, annual campaigns.
Limitations: Giving limited to the Youngstown, OH area. No grants to individuals, or for scholarships, fellowships, matching gifts, endowment funds, or research; no loans.
Application information:
Initial approach: Letter or full proposal
Copies of proposal: 1
Deadline(s): Submit proposal in the first quarter of the calendar year

Board meeting date(s): As required
Write: Gregory L. Ridler, Executive Vice-President and Trust Officer
Directors: Florence Simon Beecher, Eleanor Flad, Erle Flad, Ward Beecher Flad.
Trustee: Mahoning National Bank of Youngstown.
Number of staff: None.
Employer Identification Number: 346516441

3165
Beeghly (The Leon A.) Fund ▼
c/o Bank One of Eastern Ohio
Six Federal Plaza West
Youngstown 44503   (216) 743-3151
Mailing address: c/o James L. Beeghly, 808 Stambaugh Bldg., Youngstown, OH 44503

Trust established in 1940 in Ohio.
Donor(s): Leon A. Beeghly,† Mabel L. Beeghly.†
Financial data: (yr. ended 12/31/84): Assets, $4,737,017 (M); expenditures, $646,050, including $569,433 for 75 grants (high: $50,000; low: $200; average: $5,000-$10,000).
Purpose and activities: Broad purposes; local giving, with emphasis on Protestant church support and religious associations, higher education, hospitals, community funds, and aid to the handicapped.
Types of support awarded: General purposes, building funds, equipment, land acquisition, endowment funds, matching funds, professorships, scholarship funds.
Limitations: Giving primarily in the Youngstown, OH, metropolitan area; limited giving in western PA. No grants to individuals, or for research, special projects, publications, or conferences; no loans.
Publications: Program policy statement, application guidelines.
Application information:
Initial approach: Letter
Copies of proposal: 1
Deadline(s): None
Board meeting date(s): Quarterly
Final notification: 1 to 6 months
Write: James L. Beeghly, Executive Secretary
Appointing Committee: James L. Beeghly, Executive Secretary; John D. Beeghly, R.T. Beeghly.
Trustee: Bank One of Eastern Ohio.
Number of staff: 1 part-time support.
Employer Identification Number: 346514043

3166
Beerman Foundation, Inc., The ⊭
11 West Monument Bldg., 8th Fl.
Dayton 45402

Incorporated in 1945 in Ohio.
Donor(s): Arthur Beerman, Jessie Beerman, and others.
Financial data: (yr. ended 12/31/83): Assets, $6,987,163 (M); gifts received, $70,900; expenditures, $615,591, including $433,983 for 49 grants (high: $195,000; low: $25).
Purpose and activities: Charitable purposes; primarily local giving, with emphasis on a medical center, higher education, Jewish welfare funds, and social services.

Limitations: Giving primarily in Dayton, OH.
Officers and Trustees:* Barbara Beerman Weprin,* President; William S. Weprin,* Vice-President and Secretary; Val P. Hattemer, Richard J. Jacob.
Employer Identification Number: 316024369

3167
Bentz Foundation, The ☐
2569 Berwick Blvd.
Columbus 43209

Incorporated in 1948 in Ohio.
Donor(s): George B. Bentz, Agnes C. McConnell, Mary E. Bentz, and others.
Financial data: (yr. ended 10/31/83): Assets, $1,906,945 (M); gifts received, $26,000; expenditures, $315,169, including $314,918 for 6 grants (high: $295,506; low: $412) and $47,000 for 3 loans.
Purpose and activities: General purposes; grants and loans primarily for charitable purposes, with emphasis on Roman Catholic church support and missionary programs.
Limitations: No grants to individuals.
Application information:
Initial approach: Letter
Copies of proposal: 1
Board meeting date(s): As required
Write: George B. Bentz, President
Officers and Trustees: George B. Bentz, President; Edmund D. Doyle, Secretary and Treasurer; Robert Cull, Mrs. Edmund Doyle, Martin F. Shea, R. Patrick West.
Employer Identification Number: 316036015

3168
Benua Foundation, Inc., The ☐
17 South High St., Rm. 724
Columbus 43215

Incorporated in 1952 in Delaware.
Donor(s): A.R. Benua, Ebco Manufacturing Company.
Financial data: (yr. ended 12/31/83): Assets, $4,750,078 (M); expenditures, $179,609, including $168,548 for 94 grants (high: $25,000; low: $100).
Purpose and activities: Primarily local giving, with emphasis on conservation, higher education, and youth and health agencies.
Limitations: Giving primarily in OH.
Trustees: John M. Bowsher, Eleanor L. Craig, Mac Lee Henny.
Employer Identification Number: 316026443

3169
Berkman (The Louis and Sandra) Foundation ☐
(formerly The H. L. & Louis Berkman Foundation)
330 North Seventh St.
Steubenville 43952   (614) 283-3722
Application address: P.O. Box 576, Steubenville, OH 43952

Incorporated in 1952 in Ohio.
Donor(s): Louis Berkman,† Mrs. Louis Berkman, The Louis Berkman Company, Follansbee Steel Corporation, and others.

Financial data: (yr. ended 12/31/83): Assets, $1,734,625 (M); expenditures, $145,155, including $145,000 for 26 grants (high: $100,000; low: $50).
Purpose and activities: Broad purposes; grants primarily for Jewish welfare funds and higher education, primarily in Ohio, Pennsylvania, and Massachusetts.
Limitations: Giving primarily in OH, PA, and MA.
Application information:
Initial approach: Full proposal
Deadline(s): July 1 of year prior to year of grant
Write: Chester M. Anderson, Trustee
Officers and Trustees: Louis Berkman, President and Treasurer; Marshall L. Berkman, Robert A. Paul, Vice-Presidents; Francis D. O'Leary, Secretary; Sandra W. Berkman.
Employer Identification Number: 346526694

3170
Berry (Loren M.) Foundation ☐
P.O. Box 6000
3170 Kettering Blvd.
Dayton 45401   (513) 296-2224

Incorporated in 1960 in Ohio.
Donor(s): Loren M. Berry.†
Financial data: (yr. ended 12/31/83): Assets, $4,620,801 (M); gifts received, $61,500; expenditures, $421,931, including $420,206 for 91 grants (high: $165,000; low: $50).
Purpose and activities: Broad purposes; general giving, with emphasis on higher education, hospitals, youth agencies, medical research, and cultural programs.
Limitations: Giving primarily in OH. No grants to individuals or for operating budgets.
Application information: Funds presently committed; new applications not accepted.
Board meeting date(s): March, June, September, and December
Write: James O. Payne, Treasurer
Officers and Trustees: John W. Berry, Sr., President; John W. Berry, Jr., J. William Craig, Jr., Ray H. Eshelman, Martha B. Fraim, Leland Henry, Robert B. Womsley, Vice-Presidents; Hugh E. Wall, Jr., Secretary; James O. Payne, Treasurer.
Employer Identification Number: 316026144

3171
Bicknell Fund ☐
c/o Advisory Services, Inc.
1010 Hanna Bldg.
Cleveland 44115   (216) 696-1377

Incorporated in 1949 in Ohio.
Donor(s): Kate H. Bicknell, Warren Bicknell, Jr.,† Warren Bicknell, III, Kate B. Kirkham.
Financial data: (yr. ended 12/31/83): Assets, $2,207,686 (M); expenditures, $188,639, including $175,100 for 57 grants (high: $29,000; low: $1,000; average: $1,000-$5,000).
Purpose and activities: Broad purposes; primarily local giving for a community fund, health and social services, and higher and secondary educational institutions.

Limitations: Giving primarily in OH. No grants to individuals; no loans.
Publications: Application guidelines.
Application information:
Initial approach: Proposal
Copies of proposal: 1
Deadline(s): Submit proposal prior to May or November
Board meeting date(s): June and December
Write: Donald J. Hofman, Secretary
Officers: Kate H. Bicknell,* President; Warren Bicknell, III,* Vice-President; Donald J. Hofman, Secretary and Treasurer.
Trustees:* Guthrie Bicknell, Wendy H. Bicknell, George D. Kirkham, Kate B. Kirkham, Lyman Treadway III.
Employer Identification Number: 346513799

3172
Bingham (The William) Foundation ▼
1250 Leader Bldg.
Cleveland 44114   (216) 781-3270

Incorporated in 1955 in Ohio.
Donor(s): Elizabeth B. Blossom.†
Financial data: (yr. ended 12/31/83): Assets, $16,137,000 (M); expenditures, $947,000, including $640,244 for 27 grants (high: $115,294; low: $2,000; average: $5,000-$30,000) and $100,000 for 1 loan.
Purpose and activities: Charitable purposes; giving primarily for the arts, education, including higher education, health, and welfare.
Types of support awarded: General purposes, special projects, seed money, building funds, equipment, endowment funds, research, publications, conferences and seminars, scholarship funds, matching funds, program-related investments.
Limitations: Giving primarily in the eastern United States, with some emphasis on the Cleveland, OH area. No grants to individuals; no loans.
Publications: Annual report, program policy statement, application guidelines.
Application information:
Initial approach: Letter of 2 pages or less
Copies of proposal: 1
Deadline(s): Submit proposal preferably in February or July; deadline 2 months prior to board meeting dates
Board meeting date(s): Usually May and October
Final notification: 3 to 6 months
Write: Laura C. Hitchcox, Executive Director
Officers: Thomas H. Gale,* President; Mary E.G. Holweger,* Vice-President; Thomas F. Allen, Secretary; Dudley S. Blossom,* Treasurer; Laura C. Hitchcox, Executive Director.
Trustees:* C. Bingham Blossom, Laurel Blossom, Benjamin Gale, Elizabeth B. Heffernan.
Number of staff: 1 full-time professional; 1 full-time support.
Employer Identification Number: 346513791

3173
Bolton Foundation
c/o Advisory Services, Inc.
1010 Hanna Bldg.
Cleveland 44115 (216) 696-5245

Incorporated in 1952 in Ohio.
Donor(s): Fanny H. Bolton.†
Financial data: (yr. ended 12/31/83): Assets, $3,796,390 (M); expenditures, $251,218, including $249,000 for 35 grants (high: $58,000; low: $1,000).
Purpose and activities: General purposes; primarily local giving to institutions of particular interest to the trustees; grants largely for hospitals, health services, and secondary education.
Types of support awarded: Continuing support, building funds, endowment funds.
Limitations: Giving primarily in Cleveland, OH. No grants to individuals.
Application information:
Initial approach: Full proposal
Deadline(s): Submit proposal preferably in September; deadline September 30
Board meeting date(s): October and as required
Final notification: 3 months
Write: Paulette Kitko, Secretary-Treasurer
Officers: Richard H. Stewart,* President; Claire H.B. Jonklaas,* Betsy B. Schafer,* Vice-Presidents; Paulette Kitko, Secretary-Treasurer.
Trustees:* Charles P. Bolton, Anthony Jonklaas, Gertrude P. Oliva, Gilbert P. Schafer III.
Number of staff: None.
Employer Identification Number: 346513614

3174
Borden Foundation, Inc. ▼
180 East Broad St.
Columbus 43215 (614) 225-4340

Incorporated in 1944 in New York.
Donor(s): Borden, Inc.
Financial data: (yr. ended 12/31/83): Assets, $397,654 (M); gifts received, $1,070,686; expenditures, $1,104,026, including $908,321 for 385 grants (high: $95,700; low: $25; average: $1,000-$10,000) and $21,546 for employee matching gifts.
Purpose and activities: Broad purposes; general giving, with emphasis on health care services, higher education, community welfare funds, youth agencies, and cultural programs, with preference given to areas of company operations.
Types of support awarded: Operating budgets, continuing support, annual campaigns, seed money, emergency funds, equipment, matching funds, employee matching gifts, consulting services, technical assistance.
Limitations: Giving primarily in areas of company operations. No support for organizations receiving major government funding, or political lobbying organizations. No grants to individuals, or for deficit financing, building funds, land acquisition, renovation projects, endowment funds, scholarships, fellowships, advertisements, membership drives, research, special projects, publications, or conferences; no loans.

Publications: Program policy statement, application guidelines.
Application information:
Initial approach: Telephone or letter
Copies of proposal: 1
Deadline(s): First day of month preceding board meeting
Board meeting date(s): March, June, September, and December
Final notification: 2 to 4 weeks
Write: Judy Barker, President
Officers: Judy Barker, President; James T. McCrory, Vice-President; H. Cort Doughty, Secretary; George Crooks, Treasurer.
Directors: Bernard Nemtzow, R.J. Ventres.
Number of staff: 2 full-time professional; 1 full-time support.
Employer Identification Number: 136089941

3175
Bremer Foundation, The ⌘
708-9 Union National Bank Bldg.
Youngstown 44503

Incorporated in 1953 in Ohio.
Donor(s): Richard P. Bremer.†
Financial data: (yr. ended 12/31/83): Assets, $1,652,909 (M); expenditures, $152,433, including $141,358 for 25 grants (high: $63,000; low: $500).
Purpose and activities: Charitable purposes; primarily local giving, for higher education and social welfare.
Limitations: Giving primarily in OH.
Application information:
Write: James E. Mitchell, Secretary
Officers and Trustees: Gertrude I. Lewis, President; James E. Mitchell, Secretary; Jonas S. Bremer, Treasurer; Henry G. Gramblett, M.D., Lewis J. Qualman, W. Brooks Reed.
Employer Identification Number: 346514168

3176
Britton Fund ⌘
1010 Hanna Bldg.
Cleveland 44115 (216) 696-6836

Incorporated in 1952 in Ohio.
Donor(s): Gertrude H. Britton, Charles S. Britton, Brigham Britton.†
Financial data: (yr. ended 12/31/83): Assets, $3,654,645 (M); gifts received, $70,000; expenditures, $296,206, including $275,975 for 52 grants (high: $15,000; low: $1,000; average: $1,000-$20,000).
Purpose and activities: General purposes; primarily local giving to community funds and social agencies, higher and secondary education, hospitals and health services, and youth agencies.
Types of support awarded: General purposes, operating budgets, emergency funds.
Limitations: Giving primarily in OH. No grants to individuals.
Publications: Annual report.
Application information: Funds substantially committed.
Initial approach: Letter
Copies of proposal: 1
Deadline(s): Prior to board meetings
Board meeting date(s): May and November

Write: Betty J. Tuite, Secretary
Officers: Charles S. Britton, II,* President; Gertrude H. Britton,* Vice-President; Betty J. Tuite, Secretary; Donald Cook, Treasurer.
Trustees:* Lynda R. Britton.
Employer Identification Number: 346513616

3177
Browning (John N.) Family Fund, Inc. ⌘
First National Bank of Cincinnati
P.O. Box 1118
Cincinnati 45201

Incorporated in 1969 in Kentucky.
Donor(s): John N. Browning.†
Financial data: (yr. ended 4/30/83): Assets, $1,410,845 (M); expenditures, $53,957, including $49,400 for 15 grants (high: $10,000; low: $400).
Purpose and activities: Grants primarily for higher and secondary education; some support for youth agencies.
Officers and Directors: Laura B. Van Meter, President; Carlisle B. Van Meter, Secretary; George M. Van Meter, Jr., Treasurer; Isaac C. Van Meter, Jr.
Employer Identification Number: 237009543

3178
Brush Foundation, The
c/o AmeriTrust Company
900 Euclid Ave.
Cleveland 44101 (216) 771-8427

Trust established in 1928 in Ohio.
Donor(s): Charles F. Brush,† Maurice Perkins.
Financial data: (yr. ended 12/31/84): Assets, $1,996,700 (M); expenditures, $138,675, including $123,675 for 15 grants (high: $20,000; low: $4,500).
Purpose and activities: Grants for the control of population growth and betterment of the human race. The current major interests of the Foundation are adolescent sexuality and the control of adolescent pregnancy, preservation of the freedom of choice of women to have abortions, and how laws and regulations may control population growth.
Types of support awarded: General purposes, operating budgets, continuing support, annual campaigns, seed money, emergency funds, special projects, research, publications, conferences and seminars, matching funds.
Limitations: No grants to individuals, or for capital endowment funds, scholarships, or fellowships; no loans.
Application information:
Initial approach: Letter
Copies of proposal: 11
Deadline(s): Submit proposal preferably in March, August, or October; deadlines April 1, August 20, and November 7
Board meeting date(s): April, September, and December
Final notification: 1 week after board meeting
Write: David R. Weir, M.D., President

Officers and Managers: David R. Weir, M.D., President; Meacham Hitchcock, Vice-President; Doris B. Dingle, Secretary; Richard M. Donaldson, Treasurer; John J. Beeston, M.D., Charles F. Brush, Sally F. Burton, Virginia P. Carter, Jane Perkins Moffett, Edward A. Mortimer, M.D., William C. Weir, M.D.
Trustee: AmeriTrust Company.
Number of staff: None.
Employer Identification Number: 346000445

3179
Calhoun (Kenneth) Charitable Trust
c/o Society National Bank
127 Public Square
Cleveland 44114

Established in 1982 in Ohio.
Donor(s): Kenneth Calhoun.†
Financial data: (yr. ended 7/31/83): Assets, $2,575,523 (M); gifts received, $1,907,081; expenditures, $141,291, including $128,683 for 21 grants (high: $40,000; low: $20).
Purpose and activities: Local giving for hospitals, cultural programs, education, youth agencies, and social services.
Limitations: Giving limited to OH.
Trustee: Society National Bank.
Employer Identification Number: 341370330

3180
Casto (The Don M.) Foundation ⌑
209 E. State St.
Columbus 43215

Incorporated in 1962 in Ohio.
Donor(s): Members of the Casto family and family-related businesses.
Financial data: (yr. ended 5/31/84): Assets, $1,116,235 (M); gifts received, $45,000; expenditures, $58,626, including $56,250 for 30 grants (high: $10,000; low: $150).
Purpose and activities: Broad purposes; primarily local giving, with emphasis on cultural programs, community development, and higher and secondary education.
Limitations: Giving primarily in OH.
Trustees: Frank S. Benson, Jr., Frank S. Benson III, Don M. Casto III.
Employer Identification Number: 316049506

3181
Charities Foundation ⌑
One Sea Gate
Toledo 43666   (419) 247-1888

Trust established in 1937 in Ohio.
Donor(s): Owens-Illinois Inc., William E. Levis,† Harold Boeschenstein,† and others.
Financial data: (yr. ended 12/31/83): Assets, $3,300,566 (M); gifts received, $150,000; expenditures, $322,086, including $302,485 for 96 grants (high: $81,250; low: $100).
Purpose and activities: Contributions from the foundation are initiated internally, with emphasis on higher education, hospitals, church support, community funds, cultural programs, conservation, youth agencies and public affairs organizations.

Limitations: Giving primarily in OH; no grants outside the United States. No grants to individuals or for scholarships.
Application information: Applications not invited; funds largely committed.
Officer: John E. Price, Manager.
Trustees: Richard L. Berry, Jerome A. Bohland, Henry A. Page, Jr., Carter Smith.
Employer Identification Number: 346554560

3182
Cincinnati Foundation for the Aged, The ⌑
2000 Central Trust Tower
Cincinnati 45202

Established in 1891 in Ohio.
Donor(s): Oscar Cohrs,† Otto Luedeking,† and others.
Financial data: (yr. ended 3/31/83): Assets, $1,364,426 (M); gifts received, $66,397; expenditures, $189,990, including $179,113 for 9 grants (high: $64,012; low: $700).
Purpose and activities: To financially assist worthy, aged, and indigent men and women to enter as residents into homes established for aged and retired persons.
Officers: William Dock Meyer, President; Robert Porter, Jr., 1st Vice-President; Gordon T. Paine, Treasurer.
Employer Identification Number: 310536971

3183
Cincinnati Foundation, The Greater ▼
802 Carew Tower
Cincinnati 45202   (513) 241-2880

Community foundation established in 1963 in Ohio by bank resolution and declaration of trust.
Financial data: (yr. ended 12/31/84): Assets, $27,980,304 (M); gifts received, $4,823,872; expenditures, $2,050,260, including $1,928,486 for 550 grants (high: $50,000; low: $100).
Purpose and activities: Grants for a broad range of both new and existing activities in general categories of arts and culture, civic affairs, education, health, and social services, including youth agencies, for the benefit of inhabitants of Greater Cincinnati and vicinity.
Types of support awarded: Seed money, emergency funds, building funds, equipment, land acquisition, special projects, publications, conferences and seminars, matching funds, loans, technical assistance.
Limitations: Giving limited to the greater Cincinnati, OH, area. No grants to individuals, or for operating budgets, annual campaigns, deficit financing, endowment funds, scholarships, or fellowships.
Publications: Annual report, application guidelines, program policy statement.
Application information: Application form required.
  Initial approach: Letter or telephone, followed by interview with foundation staff
  Copies of proposal: 16
  Deadline(s): 30 days prior to board meetings
  Board meeting date(s): March, June, September, and December

  Final notification: 30 days
  Write: Carolyn F. McCoy, Executive Director
Officers: Carolyn F. McCoy, Executive Director; Jacob E. Davis, Volunteer Director; William D. Atteberry, Herbert R. Brown, Walter Lingle, Jr., Nelson Schwab, Jr., Robert Westheimer, Associate Directors.
Distribution Committee: Richard B. Buddle, M.D., Robert H. Castellini, William A. Friedlander, Mrs. William M. Ittmann, Robert O. Klausmeyer, Mrs. Kroger Pettengill, John L. Strubbe.
Trustee Banks: The Central Trust Company, The Fifth Third Bank, The First National Bank of Cincinnati, Lebanon-Citizens National Bank, The North Side Bank & Trust Company, The Provident Bank, The Southern Ohio Bank.
Number of staff: 2 full-time professional; 1 full-time support; 6 part-time support.
Employer Identification Number: 310669700

3184
Cincinnati Milacron Foundation
4701 Marburg Ave.
Cincinnati 45209

Incorporated in 1951 in Ohio.
Donor(s): Cincinnati Milacron Inc.
Financial data: (yr. ended 12/31/83): Assets, $543,579 (M); gifts received, $400,000; expenditures, $831,135, including $828,452 for 60 grants (high: $310,000; low: $250).
Purpose and activities: General purposes; primarily local giving, with emphasis on community funds and higher education; support also to youth agencies and cultural programs.
Limitations: Giving primarily in OH. No grants to individuals, or for endowment funds or special projects.
Application information:
  Initial approach: Full proposal
  Copies of proposal: 1
  Board meeting date(s): Quarterly
  Write: Jack J. Earl, Assistant Secretary-Treasurer
Officers and Trustees: James A.D. Geier, President and Treasurer; Clifford R. Meyer, Secretary; Gilbert G. McCurdy, C. Lawson Reed.
Employer Identification Number: 316030682

3185
Cleveland Electric Illuminating Foundation, The ▼
P.O. Box 5000
Cleveland 44101   (216) 622-9800

Incorporated in 1961 in Ohio.
Donor(s): The Cleveland Electric Illuminating Company.
Financial data: (yr. ended 12/31/82): Assets, $7,287,793 (M); expenditures, $770,978, including $719,550 for 82 grants (high: $348,300; low: $100) and $51,428 for 335 employee matching gifts.

Purpose and activities: General purposes; local giving, with emphasis on qualifying nonprofit organizations in charitable, health, welfare, civic, cultural or educational endeavors; support also for community funds and cultural programs.
Types of support awarded: Annual campaigns, building funds, equipment, general purposes, operating budgets, employee matching gifts.
Limitations: Giving limited to the northeast area of OH, particularly Cleveland. Generally, no grants to individuals, or for endowment funds, research, or scholarships and fellowships; no loans.
Application information:
Initial approach: Cover letter with full proposal
Copies of proposal: 1
Deadline(s): None
Board meeting date(s): Contributions Committee usually meets monthly
Final notification: 7 weeks
Write: Frank A. Kender, Chairman, Contributions Committee
Officers: Robert M. Ginn,* Chairman and Chief Executive Officer; Richard A. Miller,* President; Harold L. Williams,* Executive Vice-President; Edgar H. Maugans, Vice-President; Lyle E. Pepin, Jr., Secretary; Andrew R. Felmer, Treasurer.
Trustees:* Leigh Carter, Roy H. Holdt, Sister Mary Martha, S.N.D., Karl H. Rudolph, Craig R. Smith, Charles E. Spahr, Herbert E. Strawbridge, Allan J. Thomlinson, Richard B. Tullis, William J. Williams.
Number of staff: 2 part-time professional; 1 part-time support.
Employer Identification Number: 346514181

3186
Cleveland Foundation, The ▼
1400 Hanna Bldg.
Cleveland 44115   (216) 861-3810

Community foundation established in 1914 in Ohio by bank resolution and declaration of trust.
Financial data: (yr. ended 12/31/84): Assets, $305,000,000 (M); gifts received, $3,200,000; expenditures, $18,759,479, including $17,100,149 for 675 grants (high: $500,000; low: $250; average: $5,000-$50,000).

Purpose and activities: The pioneer community foundation which has served as a model for most community foundations in the United States; grants are made to private tax-exempt and governmental agencies and programs serving the greater Cleveland area in the fields of civic and cultural affairs, education and economic development, and health and social services. Current priorities are in economic development, neighborhood development, downtown revitalization, lakefront enhancement, programs dealing with the young, the aged and special constituencies, health care for the medically indigent and for underserved populations, and the professional performing and visual arts. Grants mainly as seed money for innovative projects or to developing institutions or services addressing unmet needs in the community. Very limited support for capital purposes for highly selective construction or equipment projects.
Types of support awarded: Seed money, special projects, matching funds, consulting services, technical assistance.
Limitations: Giving limited to the greater Cleveland area, with emphasis on Cleveland and Cuyahoga County, OH, unless specified by donor. No support for sectarian or religious activities, community services such as fire and police protection, and library and welfare services. No grants to individuals, or for endowment funds, operating costs, debt reduction, fundraising campaigns, publications, films and audiovisual materials (unless they are an integral part of a program already being supported), memberships, travel for bands, sports teams, classes and similar groups; capital support for planning, construction, renovation, or purchase of buildings; equipment and materials, land acquisition, or renovation of public space unless there is strong evidence that the program is of priority to the foundation.
Publications: Annual report, program policy statement, application guidelines.
Application information:
Initial approach: Letter, full proposal, or telephone
Copies of proposal: 2
Deadline(s): March 31, June 15, August 31, and December 15
Board meeting date(s): Distribution committee meets in March, June, September, and December
Final notification: 3 to 4 months
Write: Steven A. Minter, Director
Officers: Steven A. Minter, Director; Michael J. Hoffman, Secretary-Treasurer.
Distribution Committee: Richard W. Pogue, Chairman; Andrea Taylor Coaxum, John J. Dwyer, Henry J. Goodman, Mrs. Bruce Griswold, David G. Hill, Roy H. Holdt, Lindsay Jordan Morgenthaler, Harvey G. Oppmann, Thomas V.H. Vail.
Trustees: AmeriTrust Company, Bank One, Central National Bank of Cleveland, The Huntington Bank of Northeast Ohio, National City Bank, Society National Bank of Cleveland.
Number of staff: 11 full-time professional; 2 part-time professional; 16 full-time support; 1 part-time support.
Employer Identification Number: 340714588

3187
Cleveland-Cliffs Foundation, The ▼
Huntington Bldg., 14th Fl.
Cleveland 44115-1448   (216) 241-2356

Established in 1960 in Ohio.
Donor(s): The Cleveland-Cliffs Iron Company, and affiliated companies.
Financial data: (yr. ended 12/31/84): Assets, $307,513 (M); gifts received, $526,550; expenditures, $386,824, including $217,893 for 95 grants (high: $50,000; low: $50; average: $2,293) and $168,931 for 641 employee matching gifts.
Purpose and activities: General purposes; giving primarily in areas of company operations, for higher education, including an employee matching gifts program, community funds, hospitals, and social services, including youth agencies. Priority given to innovative educational projects.
Types of support awarded: General purposes, building funds, research, professorships, scholarship funds, employee matching gifts.
Limitations: Giving primarily in areas of company operations, with emphasis on Cleveland, OH and MI. No grants to individuals, or for endowment funds; no loans.
Publications: Application guidelines.
Application information:
Initial approach: Full proposal
Copies of proposal: 1
Deadline(s): None
Board meeting date(s): July, disbursement committee meets monthly
Final notification: 3 months
Write: R.P. Eide, Secretary-Treasurer
Officers and Trustees: S.K. Scovil, President; E.B. Johnson, Vice-President; R.P. Eide, Secretary-Treasurer; Harry J. Bolwell, James D. Ireland, Donald C. Platten, David V. Ragone, Richard S. Sheetz, Jeptha H. Wade, A.W. Whitehouse, Jr.
Number of staff: None.
Employer Identification Number: 346525124

3188
Codrington (The George W.) Charitable Foundation
1100 National City Bank Bldg.
Cleveland 44114   (216) 566-5500

Trust established in 1955 in Ohio.
Donor(s): George W. Codrington.†
Financial data: (yr. ended 12/30/84): Assets, $6,167,393 (M); expenditures, $411,698, including $375,800 for 74 grants (high: $45,000; low: $1,000).
Purpose and activities: Giving limited to Cuyahoga County and adjoining areas, with emphasis on higher education and hospitals; support also for community funds, museums, youth and health agencies, and music.
Limitations: Giving limited to Cuyahoga County, OH, and surrounding area. No grants to individuals or for endowment funds; no loans.
Publications: Annual report.
Application information:
Initial approach: Full proposal
Copies of proposal: 5

Deadline(s): Submit proposal preferably the month before board meetings
Board meeting date(s): March, June, September, and December
Write: Earl P. Schneider, Chairman, Supervisory Board
Officer: Raymond T. Sawyer, Secretary.
Supervisory Board: Earl P. Schneider, Chairman; W. Paul Cooper, Vice-Chairman; John J. Dwyer, William E. McDonald, Curtis E. Moll.
Trustee: AmeriTrust Company.
Number of staff: None.
Employer Identification Number: 346507457

3189
Columbus Foundation, The ▼
1265 Neil Ave.
Columbus 43201 (614) 294-7300

Community foundation established in 1943 in Ohio by resolution and declaration of trust.
Financial data: (yr. ended 12/31/83): Assets, $64,327,523 (M); gifts received, $6,105,748; expenditures, $6,658,659, including $5,854,271 for 1,113 grants (high: $1,025,665; low: $100; average: $10,000-$30,000).
Purpose and activities: A public charitable foundation for receiving funds for distribution to charitable organizations mainly in the central Ohio region. Grants made to strengthen existing agencies or to initiate new programs in the following categories: arts and humanities, civic affairs, conservation and environmental protection, education, hospitals and health, mental health and retardation, and social agencies.
Types of support awarded: Seed money, matching funds.
Limitations: Giving limited to central OH from unrestricted funds. No support for religious purposes, or for projects normally the responsibility of a public agency. No grants to individuals, or generally for budget deficits, conferences, scholarly research, or endowment funds.
Publications: Annual report, program policy statement, application guidelines, newsletter.
Application information: Grant requests to the Columbus Youth Foundation must be submitted by the first Friday in May and October for consideration at meetings held in July and December; requests to the Edgar W. Ingram Foundation must be submitted by the first Friday in February and September for consideration in April and November. Application form required.
Initial approach: Letter
Copies of proposal: 3
Deadline(s): 1st Friday in December, March, May, and August
Board meeting date(s): February, May, July, and October
Final notification: After quarterly meeting
Write: James I. Luck, President
Officers: James I. Luck, President; Tullia Brown Hamilton, Everett H. Krueger, Vice-Presidents.
Governing Committee: Robert S. Crane, Jr., Chairman; Thekla R. Shackelford, Mrs. William K. Westwater, Vice-Chairmen; John W. Kessler, Pat Ross, Eldon W. Ward, John Walton Wolfe.
Trustee Banks and Trustee Committee: BancOhio National Bank, (Andrew B. Craig III, President); Bank One Trust Company, (C. Thomas Rice, President); Huntington National Bank, (Frank Wobst, President).
Number of staff: 7 full-time professional; 6 full-time support.
Employer Identification Number: 316044264

3190
Commercial Shearing Foundation
1775 Logan Ave.
Youngstown 44501 (216) 746-8011

Trust established in 1953 in Ohio.
Donor(s): Commercial Shearing, Inc.
Financial data: (yr. ended 10/31/84): Assets, $299,064 (M); expenditures, $105,886, including $104,947 for 57 grants (high: $55,000; low: $25).
Purpose and activities: Broad purposes; general giving in areas of company operations, with emphasis on hospitals, higher education, youth agencies, and community funds; support also for economic education.
Types of support awarded: General purposes, annual campaigns, seed money, building funds.
Limitations: Giving primarily in areas of company operations. No grants to individuals, or for operating budgets, endowment funds, scholarships, fellowships, or matching gifts; no loans.
Application information:
Copies of proposal: 1
Deadline(s): Submit proposal preferably 60 days before meeting dates
Board meeting date(s): January, April, July and October
Write: Charles B. Cushwa III, Secretary
Officers and Trustees: John Nelson, Chairman and President; Don E. Tucker, Vice-President; Charles B. Cushwa III, Secretary; John S. Andrews, William W. Bresnahan, W.W. Cushwa, Marshall I. McMahon, Thomas J. Travers, Robert E. Williams.
Number of staff: None.
Employer Identification Number: 346517437

3191
Corbett Foundation, The ⌑
1501 Madison Rd., Suite 410
Cincinnati 45206 (513) 221-3330

Incorporated in 1958 in Ohio.
Donor(s): J. Ralph Corbett, Mrs. Patricia A. Corbett.
Financial data: (yr. ended 4/30/83): Assets, $5,791,556 (M); gifts received, $210,191; expenditures, $335,069, including $162,660 for 9 grants (high: $47,000; low: $1,000).
Purpose and activities: Charitable and scientific purposes; primarily local giving, with emphasis on music and musical education; support also for a local church. Presently in the process of phasing out; no new applications for grants invited.
Limitations: Giving primarily in OH.
Application information: No new applications invited.
Write: J. Ralph Corbett, President
Officers and Trustees: J. Ralph Corbett, President; Jean S. Reis, Vice-President and Secretary; Patricia A. Corbett, Vice-President and Treasurer; Alan J. Lehn, Perry B. Wydman.
Employer Identification Number: 316050360

3192
Coshocton Foundation
P.O. Box 15
Coshocton 43812

Community foundation established in 1966 in Ohio.
Financial data: (yr. ended 9/30/84): Assets, $1,511,223 (M); gifts received, $258,055; expenditures, $702,659, including $207,394 for 26 grants (high: $40,000; low: $125) and $11,525 for 5 foundation-administered programs.
Purpose and activities: Broad purposes; local giving, support largely for a park and a museum.
Limitations: Giving limited to Coshocton County, OH.
Publications: Annual report.
Application information:
Initial approach: Letter
Deadline(s): None
Board meeting date(s): Quarterly
Write: Orville Fuller, Treasurer, or Sam C. Clow, Chairman, Distribution Committee
Officers: Bruce Wallace, President; James Beach, Vice-President; Fred E. Johnston, Secretary; Orville Fuller,* Treasurer.
Trustees:* L.J. Burns, Edward E. Montgomery, Seward D. Schooler.
Distribution Committee: Sam C. Clow, Chairman; Robert B. Henderson, James A. Lee, M. Wilson McConnell, R. Leo Prindle.
Number of staff: None.
Employer Identification Number: 316064567

3193
Crandall (J. Ford) Memorial Foundation
1108 Mahoning Bank Bldg.
Youngstown 44503 (216) 744-2125

Trust established in 1975 in Ohio.
Donor(s): J. Ford Crandall.†
Financial data: (yr. ended 12/31/83): Assets, $3,203,619 (M); expenditures, $303,729, including $245,953 for 18 grants (high: $100,000; low: $500).
Purpose and activities: Giving limited to organizations in Mahoning County, including hospitals and social service agencies.
Types of support awarded: Building funds, equipment, endowment funds, scholarship funds.
Limitations: Giving limited to Mahoning County, OH. No grants to individuals, or for operating budgets or research; no loans.
Application information:
Initial approach: Letter
Copies of proposal: 3
Deadline(s): December 1
Board meeting date(s): Monthly
Write: R.M. Hammond, Secretary
Officers and Trustees: Horace G. Tetlow, Chairman; Arthur G. Young, Vice-Chairman; R.M. Hammond, Secretary.
Number of staff: None.
Employer Identification Number: 346513634

3194
Crosley Foundation, The ⋈
2100 DuBois Tower
511 Walnut St.
Cincinnati 45202

Incorporated in 1946 in Ohio.
Donor(s): Powel Crosley, Jr.†
Financial data: (yr. ended 4/30/83): Assets,
$1,845,129 (M); expenditures, $126,960,
including $116,200 for 15 grants (high:
$25,000; low: $800).
Purpose and activities: General purposes;
primarily local giving for cultural programs,
social services, higher education, and a
community fund.
Limitations: Giving primarily in OH. No grants
to individuals or for endowment funds or
operating budgets.
Application information:
  Initial approach: Letter
  Board meeting date(s): As required
Officers and Trustees: Mrs. Stanley E. Kess,
President and Treasurer; Wiley Dinsmore,
Secretary; Mrs. Albert C. Chatfield, Lewis M.
Crosley.
Employer Identification Number: 316028064

3195
Crosset Charitable Trust, The
205 Central Ave.
Cincinnati 45202

Trust established in 1943 in Ohio.
Donor(s): Richard B. Crosset, Robert J.
Crosset.†
Financial data: (yr. ended 12/31/84): Assets,
$2,645,900 (M); gifts received, $18,000;
expenditures, $169,645, including $156,086
for 220 grants (high: $10,000; low: $50) and
$7,725 for 14 grants to individuals.
Purpose and activities: Charitable purposes;
primarily local giving, with emphasis on church
support, youth agencies, higher education,
including scholarships for employees of The
Crosset Company, Inc., and social agencies.
Types of support awarded: Employee related
scholarships.
Limitations: Giving primarily in OH.
Application information: Application form
required for scholarship applicants.
  Initial approach: Full proposal
  Copies of proposal: 1
  Write: Richard B. Crosset, Trustee
Trustees: Richard B. Crosset, Richard B.
Crosset, Jr., Robert J. Crosset, Jr.
Number of staff: 1.
Employer Identification Number: 316037727

3196
Dana Corporation Foundation ▼
P.O. Box 1000
Toledo 43697   (419) 535-4500

Incorporated in 1956 in Ohio.
Donor(s): Dana Corporation.

Financial data: (yr. ended 12/31/83): Assets,
$4,732,909 (M); gifts received, $1,000,000;
expenditures, $1,418,144, including
$1,249,085 for 165 grants (high: $140,500;
low: $200; average: $500-$20,000) and
$142,342 for employee matching gifts.
Purpose and activities: Broad purposes; grants
primarily in areas of company operations, with
emphasis on community funds, higher
education including an employee matching gifts
program, social services, health services, civic
affairs, youth agencies, and cultural programs.
Also administers Dana Fund for International
and Comparative Legal Studies.
Types of support awarded: Employee
matching gifts, annual campaigns, building
funds, continuing support, deficit financing,
emergency funds, endowment funds,
equipment, land acquisition, operating budgets,
seed money.
Limitations: Giving primarily in areas of
company operations. No grants to individuals,
or for scholarships or fellowships; no loans.
Application information:
  Initial approach: Full proposal
  Copies of proposal: 1
  Deadline(s): Submit proposals by May 15 for
    Dana Fund grants; no other deadlines
  Board meeting date(s): April, August, and
    December
  Final notification: 60 to 90 days
  Write: Pauline Marzollini, Assistant Secretary
Officers and Directors: F.J. Voss, Acting
President; R.M. Leonardi, Secretary; R.A.
Habel, Treasurer; B.N. Cole, R.A. Cowie, T.J.
Fairhurst, C.H. Hirsch.
Number of staff: 1 full-time professional; 9
part-time professional.
Employer Identification Number: 346544909

3197
Dauby (Nathan L.) Charity Fund
720 Statler Office Tower
Cleveland 44115   (216) 861-1146

Trust established in 1944 in Ohio.
Donor(s): Nathan L. Dauby.†
Financial data: (yr. ended 12/31/84): Assets,
$2,243,950 (M); expenditures, $137,347,
including $109,225 for 32 grants (high:
$15,000; low: $500; average: $500-$15,000).
Purpose and activities: General charitable
purposes; primarily local giving in the
Cuyahoga County area.
Types of support awarded: Operating
budgets, continuing support, annual campaigns,
emergency funds, equipment, general purposes,
matching funds, scholarship funds, internships,
research.
Limitations: Giving primarily in Cuyahoga
County, OH, area. No grants to individuals, or
for seed money, deficit financing, building
funds, land acquisition, demonstration projects,
publications, or conferences; no loans.
Application information:
  Initial approach: Full proposal or letter
  Copies of proposal: 1
  Board meeting date(s): Usually in March,
    June, September, and December
  Write: Robert D. Gries, Committee Member

Distribution Committee: Richard Brezic, Ellen
G. Cole, Robert D. Gries.
Trustee: The National City Bank.
Number of staff: None.
Employer Identification Number: 346556349

3198
Dayco Charitable Foundation, Inc. ⋈
333 West First St.
Dayton 45402

Established in 1972.
Financial data: (yr. ended 12/31/83): Assets,
$89,234 (M); gifts received, $224,985;
expenditures, $161,316, including $161,257
for 36 grants (high: $73,625; low: $150).
Purpose and activities: Primarily local giving,
with emphasis on a community fund, the arts,
higher education, and hospitals.
Limitations: Giving primarily in OH.
Officers: N.G. Crnkovich, President; D.S.
Gutridge, Senior Vice-President; P.J. Neroni,
Executive Vice-President; P.W. Phillips, Vice-
President.
Employer Identification Number: 237223605

3199
Dayton Foundation, The
1395 Kettering Tower
Dayton 45423   (513) 222-0410

Community foundation established in 1921 in
Ohio by resolution and declaration of trust.
Financial data: (yr. ended 12/31/83): Assets,
$4,609,539 (L); gifts received, $332,645;
expenditures, $390,592, including $337,965
for 76 grants (high: $30,000; low: $200;
average: $4,000-$5,000).
Purpose and activities: To assist public
charitable, benevolent and educational
purposes which benefit citizens of Dayton and
Montgomery County, Ohio, and respond to a
wide variety of community needs, including
cultural programs, community development,
health and social services, and youth; "to help
launch new projects which represent a unique
and unduplicated opportunity for the
community," and to generate matching funds.
Types of support awarded: Seed money,
building funds, equipment, matching funds,
technical assistance, internships, special
projects.
Limitations: Giving limited to Dayton and
Montgomery County, OH. No grants to
individuals, or for continuing support, annual
campaigns, deficit financing, endowment funds,
or research.
Publications: Annual report, application
guidelines, program policy statement.
Application information:
  Initial approach: Full proposal, telephone, or
    letter
  Copies of proposal: 1
  Deadline(s): Submit proposal preferably 2
    weeks before board meeting
  Board meeting date(s): Bimonthly beginning
    in January
  Final notification: 4 to 6 weeks
  Write: Frederick Bartenstein, III, Director
Officer: Frederick Bartenstein, III, Director.

Distribution Committee: Frederick C. Smith, Chairman; John E. Moore, Vice-Chairman; Richard F. Glennon, Anne S. Greene, Jesse Philips.

Trustees and Bank Trustees: Douglas Hawthorne, Paul Hyde, Jerry L. Kirby, William A. Harrell, Frederick Schantz, Bank One, Dayton, The Central Trust Company, Citizens Federal Savings and Loan, The First National Bank, Third National Bank & Trust Company.

Number of staff: 1 full-time professional; 2 part-time professional; 2 part-time support.

Employer Identification Number: 316027287

3200
Deuble (George H.) Foundation
c/o AmeriTrust Company of Stark County
900 Euclid Ave.
Cleveland 44101
Mailing address: 1022 Ninth St., S.W., Canton, OH 44707; Tel.: (216) 455-0161

Trust established in 1947 in Ohio.
Donor(s): George H. Deuble.†
Financial data: (yr. ended 12/31/83): Assets, $8,303,001 (M); expenditures, $358,052, including $318,459 for grants (average: $5,000).
Purpose and activities: Broad purposes; almost all grants limited to the Stark County, Ohio, area for youth agencies, higher education, hospitals, cultural programs, and a community fund.
Types of support awarded: Continuing support, annual campaigns, emergency funds, building funds, equipment, endowment funds, matching funds, scholarship funds, loans, conferences and seminars.
Limitations: Giving primarily in the Stark County, OH, area. No grants to individuals, or for operating budgets, seed money, deficit financing, general endowments, land acquisition, research, or publications.
Application information:
 Initial approach: Letter
 Deadline(s): None
 Board meeting date(s): Monthly
 Final notification: 1 month
 Write: Andrew H. Deuble, Trustee
Officer and Trustees: Walter C. Deuble, President; Andrew H. Deuble, Stephen G. Deuble, Charles A. Morgan, AmeriTrust Company of Stark County.
Number of staff: None.
Employer Identification Number: 346500426

3201
Dively (Geo. S.) Foundation
55 Public Square
Cleveland 44113

Incorporated in 1956 in Ohio.
Donor(s): George S. Dively.
Financial data: (yr. ended 12/31/83): Assets, $1,231,178 (M); expenditures, $61,600, including $49,600 for 20 grants (high: $20,000; low: $100).
Purpose and activities: General purposes; grants mainly for higher education, Protestant church support, and awards for corporate leadership in civic and social areas.

Application information: Almost all grants initiated by the foundation and applications are generally not acknowledged.
 Initial approach: Letter
Officers and Trustees: George S. Dively, President; Michael A. Dively, Secretary and Vice-President; Thomas F. Allen, Treasurer; Juliette G. Dively, Richard B. Tullis.
Number of staff: None.
Employer Identification Number: 346526304

3202
Donnell (Lester F.) Memorial Fund
c/o Mahoning Natl. Bank of Youngstown
23 Federal Plaza, P.O. Box 479
Youngstown 44501

Established in 1981 in Ohio.
Donor(s): Lester F. Donnell.†
Financial data: (yr. ended 12/31/84): Assets, $1,516,729 (M); expenditures, $173,648, including $161,000 for 13 grants (high: $50,000; low: $1,600).
Purpose and activities: Local giving, with emphasis on hospitals, social services, and a youth organization.
Limitations: Giving limited to Youngstown, OH.
Directors: Betty Yaist Dill, Kenneth C. Schafer, Arthur G. Young.
Trustee: Mahoning National Bank of Youngstown.
Employer Identification Number: 346802575

3203
Eagle-Picher Foundation, The
580 Walnut St.
P.O. Box 779
Cincinnati 45201   (513) 721-7010

Incorporated in 1953 in Michigan; merged with The Union Steel Foundation in 1969.
Donor(s): Eagle-Picher Industries, Inc.
Financial data: (yr. ended 10/31/82): Assets, $37,515 (M); gifts received, $160,900; expenditures, $157,683, including $157,572 for 80 grants (high: $22,000; low: $50).
Purpose and activities: General purposes; grants largely for community funds, cultural programs, youth agencies, hospitals, and higher education in areas of company operations.
Limitations: Giving primarily in areas of company operations. No grants to individuals, or for endowment funds or matching gifts; no loans.
Application information:
 Initial approach: Letter
 Copies of proposal: 1
 Board meeting date(s): As required
 Write: Charles S. Dautel, President
Officers: Charles S. Dautel, President and Secretary; David N. Hall, Vice-President and Treasurer; Walter A. Suhre, Jr., Vice-President.
Employer Identification Number: 316029997

3204
Eaton Charitable Fund, The ▼
100 Erieview Plaza
Cleveland 44114   (216) 523-5000

Trust established in 1953 in Ohio.
Donor(s): Eaton Corporation.
Financial data: (yr. ended 12/31/82): Assets, $2,060,751 (M); gifts received, $2,000,000; expenditures, $2,576,200, including $2,193,228 for grants (high: $340,155) and $366,509 for employee matching gifts.
Purpose and activities: "To endeavor to improve the political, economic, and social environment so that the company may continue to grow and prosper and its employees may continue to enjoy the benefits of a free society." Contributions for eligible organizations which promote and provide effective charitable, civic, health, welfare, educational, youth, scientific, economic, and cultural programs and services. Grants largely to community funds and building programs for higher educational institutions, hospitals, youth agencies, and cultural programs in areas of company operations.
Types of support awarded: Operating budgets, building funds, employee matching gifts, annual campaigns, scholarship funds, fellowships, research.
Limitations: Giving primarily in areas of company operations. No support for religious denominations, fraternal organizations, and organizations which could be members of a United Fund or federated community fund but who choose not to participate. No grants to individuals, or for endowment funds, or fundraising events outside of specific company interests; no loans.
Publications: Company report, application guidelines.
Application information:
 Initial approach: Letter or full proposal
 Copies of proposal: 1
 Deadline(s): None
 Board meeting date(s): Quarterly
 Final notification: 60 to 90 days
 Write: Frederick B. Unger, Director, Community Affairs
Officer: Frederick B. Unger, Director, Community Affairs.
Trustee: Central National Bank of Cleveland.
Number of staff: 1 part-time professional; 2 part-time support.
Employer Identification Number: 346501856

3205
El-An Foundation ⌑
1800 Moler Rd.
Columbus 43207

Incorporated in 1957 in Ohio.
Donor(s): Schottenstein Trustees, Value City Furniture, Inc., W.M. Whitney & Co., Elyria City, Inc., and others.
Financial data: (yr. ended 12/31/83): Assets, $914,226 (M); gifts received, $400,000; expenditures, $342,861, including $341,438 for grants.
Purpose and activities: Primarily local giving, with emphasis on Jewish welfare funds and religious education.

Limitations: Giving primarily in OH.
Directors: Jerome Schottenstein, Chairman; Saul Schottenstein, Secretary; Alvin Schottenstein, Treasurer.
Employer Identification Number: 316050597

3206
Emery (The Thomas J.) Memorial ▼ ☐
c/o Frost and Jacobs
2500 Central Trust Center
Cincinnati 45202   (513) 621-3124

Incorporated in 1925 in Ohio.
Donor(s): Mrs. Mary Muhlenberg Emery.†
Financial data: (yr. ended 12/31/83): Assets, $11,917,491 (M); expenditures, $733,505, including $641,690 for 40 grants (high: $100,000; low: $1,000; average: $1,000-$25,000).
Purpose and activities: Educational and charitable purposes; primarily local giving, with emphasis on higher and secondary education, a community fund, cultural activities, youth agencies, and hospitals.
Limitations: Giving primarily in Cincinnati, OH.
Application information:
   Deadline(s): None
   Board meeting date(s): 4 times a year
   Final notification: 30 days to 3 months
Officers and Trustees: Henry W. Hobson, Jr., President; Stanley M. Rowe, Sr., Vice-President; Frank T. Hamilton, Secretary; Walter L. Lingle, Jr., Treasurer; Charles M. Barrett, M.D.
Number of staff: 2 part-time support.
Employer Identification Number: 310536711

3207
Ernst & Whinney Foundation ▼
2000 National City Center
Cleveland 44114   (216) 861-5000

Incorporated in 1937 in Ohio.
Donor(s): Ernst & Whinney Partnership.
Financial data: (yr. ended 12/31/82): Assets, $6,490,474 (M); gifts received, $200,000; expenditures, $990,758, including $432,521 for 68 grants (high: $29,500; low: $1,000; average: $1,000-$15,000), $100,139 for 25 grants to individuals and $427,974 for 3,076 employee matching gifts.
Purpose and activities: Grants for higher educational institutions in the field of accounting, including employee matching gifts, and to doctoral candidates in accounting.
Types of support awarded: Employee matching gifts, fellowships, professorships.
Limitations: No grants for capital or endowment funds, special projects, continuing support, or general purposes; no loans.
Publications: Application guidelines.
Application information:
   Deadline(s): None
   Board meeting date(s): Annually
   Write: L.J. Bruner, Chairman
Officers and Trustees: L.J. Bruner, Chairman and President; J.M. Saada, Secretary-Treasurer; P.C. Berry.
Number of staff: None.
Employer Identification Number: 346524211

3208
Ernsthausen (John F. and Doris E.) Charitable Foundation ☐
c/o Central National Bank of Cleveland
P.O. Box 6179
Cleveland 44101
Application address: Cornelius J. Ruffing, Citizens Bank Bldg., Norwalk, OH 44857

Trust established in 1956 in Ohio.
Donor(s): John F. Ernsthausen, Doris E. Ernsthausen.
Financial data: (yr. ended 12/31/83): Assets, $4,715,203 (M); expenditures, $311,496, including $280,000 for 13 grants (high: $70,000; low: $1,000).
Purpose and activities: Primarily local giving, with emphasis on Methodist church support, care of the aged, higher and secondary education, a community fund, and cultural programs.
Limitations: Giving primarily in OH.
Application information:
   Deadline(s): None
Managers: Paul L. Carpenter, Loyal L. Chaney, John F. Ernsthausen, Earle H. Lowe, Cornelius J. Ruffing.
Trustee: Central National Bank of Cleveland, (T.R. Becker, Trust Officer).
Employer Identification Number: 346501908

3209
Evans (The Thomas J.) Foundation ☐
1001 Newark Trust Bldg., 10th Fl.
32 North Second St.
Newark 43055   (614) 345-3431

Established in 1965 in Ohio.
Donor(s): Thomas J. Evans.†
Financial data: (yr. ended 10/31/83): Assets, $6,998,672 (M); gifts received, $10,000; expenditures, $274,224, including $246,652 for 4 grants (high: $142,000; low: $650).
Purpose and activities: To initiate seed capital projects, primarily in Licking County in the areas of public health, education, recreation, and protection of the environment.
Types of support awarded: Seed money, building funds.
Limitations: Giving primarily in Licking County, OH.
Application information:
   Initial approach: Letter
   Board meeting date(s): Quarterly
   Write: J. Gilbert Reese, President
Officers: John W. Alford,* Chairman and Treasurer; J. Gilbert Reese,* President; Sarah Wallace, Secretary.
Trustees:* Everett D. Reese.
Employer Identification Number: 316055767

3210
Eyman (Jesse) Trust ☐
c/o John S. Bath
132 1/2 Court St.
Washington Court House 43160

Trust established in 1924 in Ohio.
Donor(s): Jesse Eyman.†

Financial data: (yr. ended 12/31/83): Assets, $1,749,253 (M); expenditures, $152,449, including $130,687 for 149 grants (high: $15,000; low: $10).
Purpose and activities: Primarily local giving, with emphasis on payments for medical and dental care on behalf of needy persons; some support for social agencies.
Limitations: Giving primarily in Washington Court House, OH.
Trustees: John S. Bath, Jesse Persinger.
Employer Identification Number: 316040007

3211
Federated Department Stores Foundation ▼
7 W. Seventh St.
Cincinnati 45202
Application address for organizations outside company operations: One Allen Center, Suite 1330, Houston, TX 77002; for local organizations, apply directly to local divison of Federated Dep't. Stores

Originally incorporated in 1952 in Ohio and later dissolved; reestablished in 1980 in Ohio.
Donor(s): Federated Department Stores, Inc.
Financial data: (yr. ended 7/31/84): Assets, $30,342,619 (M); gifts received, $15,000,000; expenditures, $3,907,297, including $2,340,832 for 297 grants (high: $145,366; low: $100; average: $1,000-$50,000) and $421,717 for 68 employee matching gifts.
Purpose and activities: Giving nationally, but particularly in areas of company operations, with emphasis on higher edcuation and cultural programs; matching employee gifts to educational and cultural organizations and contributions of $500 or more to local organizations made by divisions of the company; support also for civic and urban affairs, hospitals, social services, especially population control and a community fund, and public policy organizations.
Types of support awarded: Employee matching gifts, general purposes, building funds, matching funds, special projects.
Limitations: Giving primarily in communities of company operations. No support for religious organizations for religious purposes. No grants to individuals.
Publications: Annual report.
Application information:
   Initial approach: Proposal
   Deadline(s): None
   Board meeting date(s): March and September
   Final notification: 6 to 8 weeks
   Write: Thomas G. Cody, Senior Vice-President, Law and Public Affairs
Officers and Trustees: Donald Stone, President; Stewart Orton, Executive Vice-President; Boris Auerbach, Secretary; James Leahy, Treasurer; Thomas G. Cody, Douglas Thomsen, John B. Utsey, James Zimmerman.
Number of staff: 1 full-time professional; 3 full-time support.
Employer Identification Number: 310996760

3212
Ferro Foundation ⌑
One Erieview Plaza
Cleveland 44114 (216) 641-8580

Incorporated in 1959 in Ohio.
Donor(s): Ferro Corporation.
Financial data: (yr. ended 4/30/83): Assets, $209,558 (M); expenditures, $114,021, including $113,000 for 28 grants (high: $60,000; low: $500).
Purpose and activities: Primarily local giving, with emphasis on a community fund, higher education, cultural programs, and hospitals.
Types of support awarded: Operating budgets, building funds.
Limitations: Giving primarily in OH.
Application information:
Write: A. Posnick, President
Officers and Directors:* A. Posnick,* President; A.C. Bersticker,* Vice-President; J.V. Goodger, Secretary-Treasurer; C.A. MacFie,* Treasurer .
Employer Identification Number: 346554832

3213
1525 Foundation, The ▼
1525 National City Bank Bldg.
Cleveland 44114 (216) 696-4200

Incorporated in 1971 in Ohio.
Donor(s): Kent H. Smith.†
Financial data: (yr. ended 12/31/83): Assets, $29,457,887 (M); gifts received, $1,129,079; expenditures, $1,039,851, including $945,161 for 22 grants (high: $315,000; low: $250).
Purpose and activities: Primarily local giving for charitable purposes, with emphasis on higher education, cultural programs, and social services.
Limitations: Giving primarily in OH, to charities of interest to founder during lifetime.
Application information:
Board meeting date(s): As required
Write: Phillip A. Ranney, Secretary-Treasurer
Officers: Hubert H. Schneider, President; Thelma G. Smith, Vice-President; Phillip A. Ranney, Secretary-Treasurer.
Employer Identification Number: 341089206

3214
Fifth Third Foundation, The
c/o The Fifth Third Bank
Dept. 00850
Cincinnati 45263 (513) 579-4264
Mailing address: P.O. Box 478, Cincinnati, OH 45201

Trust established in 1948 in Ohio.
Donor(s): The Fifth Third Bank.
Financial data: (yr. ended 12/31/83): Assets, $5,008,641 (M); expenditures, $390,116, including $371,195 for 57 grants (high: $136,000; low: $100).
Purpose and activities: General purposes; local giving only, with emphasis on higher education, hospitals, health agencies, youth agencies, and cultural programs.
Types of support awarded: Continuing support, annual campaigns, seed money, building funds, equipment, special projects, research, publications, conferences and seminars.
Limitations: Giving primarily in the Cincinnati, OH area. No grants to individuals, or for endowment funds, scholarships, or fellowships; no loans.
Publications: Application guidelines.
Application information:
Initial approach: Full proposal
Copies of proposal: 1
Deadline(s): Submit proposal in October through December; no set deadline
Board meeting date(s): Monthly
Write: Lois A. Fox, Administrative Officer
Trustee: The Fifth Third Bank.
Employer Identification Number: 316024135

3215
Finnegan (John D.) Foundation
c/o Mahoning National Bank of Youngstown
23 Federal Plaza
Youngstown 44501 (216) 742-7000

Trust established in 1957 in Ohio.
Donor(s): John D. Finnegan.†
Financial data: (yr. ended 12/31/84): Assets, $2,661,164 (M); expenditures, $209,583, including $189,000 for 12 grants (high: $137,500; low: $1,000).
Purpose and activities: Broad purposes; primarily local giving, with emphasis on care of the aged; support for Roman Catholic religious and welfare associations and for higher education.
Limitations: Giving primarily in Youngstown, OH. No grants to individuals, or for operating budgets, scholarships and fellowships, or matching gifts; no loans.
Application information:
Initial approach: Letter or proposal
Copies of proposal: 1
Deadline(s): Submit proposal preferably from January through March
Board meeting date(s): February, May, September, and December
Write: Gregory L. Ridler, Executive Vice-President
Directors: John M. Newman, Chairman; W.W. Bresnahan, Vice-Chairman; John F. Hynes II, Secretary; William J. Mullen, Arthur G. Young.
Trustee: The Mahoning National Bank of Youngstown, (Gregory L. Ridler, Executive Vice-President and Trust Officer).
Employer Identification Number: 346516439

3216
Firestone Trust Fund, The ▼
1200 Firestone Pkwy.
Akron 44317 (216) 379-6802

Trust established in 1952 in Ohio.
Donor(s): The Firestone Tire & Rubber Company.
Financial data: (yr. ended 10/31/83): Assets, $13,409,764 (M); expenditures, $1,331,138, including $960,579 for 128 grants (high: $105,000; low: $100; average: $1,000-$3,000) and $287,139 for 1,081 employee matching gifts.
Purpose and activities: Broad purposes; general giving in areas of company operations, with emphasis on higher education, including employee matching gifts, health, and welfare; also supports civic and community affairs, culture, and the arts.
Types of support awarded: Continuing support, annual campaigns, seed money, emergency funds, building funds, endowment funds, matching funds, employee matching gifts, research, special projects.
Limitations: Giving primarily in areas of company operations. No grants to individuals, or for operating budgets, deficit financing, equipment, land acquisition, scholarships and fellowships, demonstration projects, publications, or conferences; no loans.
Application information:
Initial approach: Letter
Copies of proposal: 1
Deadline(s): Submit proposal preferably by July; no set deadline
Board meeting date(s): As required
Final notification: 3 to 4 weeks
Write: Michael E. Fay, Manager, Community Responsibilities
Contributions Committee: M.J. Connor, Chairman; Michael E. Fay, Secretary.
Trustee: AmeriTrust Company, (Robert H. Case, Vice-President).
Number of staff: 1 full-time professional; 1 full-time support; 1 part-time support.
Employer Identification Number: 346505181

3217
Firman Fund ⌑
1010 Hanna Bldg.
Cleveland 44115 (216) 696-2757

Incorporated in 1951 in Ohio.
Donor(s): Pamela H. Firman.
Financial data: (yr. ended 12/31/83): Assets, $4,415,124 (M); expenditures, $257,215, including $237,725 for 86 grants (high: $50,000; low: $75; average: $100-$50,000).
Purpose and activities: Broad purposes; primarily local giving with grants largely for hospitals, higher and secondary education, cultural programs, youth agencies, and community funds.
Types of support awarded: Annual campaigns, general purposes, building funds.
Limitations: Giving primarily in OH. No grants to individuals or for research; no loans.
Application information:
Initial approach: Full proposal or letter
Copies of proposal: 1
Deadline(s): 6 weeks prior to meetings
Board meeting date(s): April and November
Write: Pamela H. Firman, President
Officers and Trustees: Pamela H. Firman,* President; Cynthia F. Webster,* Vice-President; Carol L. Colangelo, Secretary; M.G. Mikolaj, Treasurer.
Trustees:* Royal Firman, III.
Employer Identification Number: 346513655

3218
First Educational and Charitable Trust of Canton, Ohio
236 Third St., S.W.
Canton 44702 (216) 455-5281

Trust established in 1957 in Ohio.
Donor(s): Timken Foundation of Canton, W.J. Timken.
Financial data: (yr. ended 9/30/84): Assets, $2,973,672 (M); gifts received, $35,000; expenditures, $145,342, including $142,000 for 4 grants (high: $60,000; low: $5,000).
Purpose and activities: Broad purposes; grants largely for scholarship funds for local residents.
Types of support awarded: Scholarship funds.
Limitations: Giving primarily in Stark County, OH. No grants to individuals or for operating budgets.
Application information:
Deadline(s): None
Board meeting date(s): Quarterly
Write: D.H. Worth, Director
Trustees: W.J. Timken, W.J. Timken, Jr., D.H. Worth.
Employer Identification Number: 346519727

3219
First National Bank of Cincinnati Foundation, The
P.O. Box 1118
Cincinnati 45201

Trust established in 1967 in Ohio.
Financial data: (yr. ended 12/31/82): Assets, $920,654 (M); gifts received, $230,000; expenditures, $341,459, including $331,305 for 33 grants (high: $148,500; low: $500).
Purpose and activities: Broad purposes; grants only for local community funds and higher education.
Types of support awarded: General purposes, building funds, equipment, land acquisition.
Limitations: Giving limited to OH. No grants to individuals, or for endowment funds, research, scholarships and fellowships, or matching gifts; no loans.
Application information:
Initial approach: Letter
Board meeting date(s): Monthly
Officers and Trustees: John W. Gantt, President; Oliver W. Waddell, Vice-President; J. Rawson Collins, Secretary; James R. Bridgeland, Jr., V. Anderson Coombs, Herman J. Guckenberger, Jr., J.P. Hayden, Jr., Mark T. Johnson, Thomas J. Klinedinst, William N. Liggett, Philip M. Meyers, Jr., William W. Womack.
Number of staff: None.
Employer Identification Number: 316079013

3220
Fleischmann Foundation, The ⌑
4001 Carew Tower
Cincinnati 45202

Incorporated in 1931 in Ohio.
Donor(s): Julius Fleischmann.†
Financial data: (yr. ended 12/31/83): Assets, $2,394,620 (M); expenditures, $111,138, including $101,179 for 45 grants (high: $15,504; low: $50).
Purpose and activities: Broad purposes; primarily local giving, with emphasis on the humanities, including support for museums, especially for a museum of natural history, and the arts.
Limitations: Giving primarily in OH.
Application information:
Write: Charles Fleischmann III, President
Officers and Trustees: Charles Fleischmann, III, President and Treasurer; Eric B. Yeiser, Vice-President; Burd Blair S. Fleischmann, Secretary; Burd S. Schlessinger, Leonard A. Weakly.
Employer Identification Number: 316025516

3221
Flickinger Memorial Trust, Inc., The ⌑
115 West North St.
P.O. Box 1255
Lima 45802 (419) 222-5040

Trust established in 1965 in Ohio.
Donor(s): William J. Flickinger.†
Financial data: (yr. ended 12/31/83): Assets, $1,948,471 (M); gifts received, $28,500; expenditures, $149,820, including $23,600 for 22 grants (high: $2,500; low: $500) and $71,883 for 100 loans.
Purpose and activities: Broad purposes; primarily local giving, with emphasis on higher education, including student loans, and youth agencies.
Types of support awarded: Student aid.
Limitations: Giving primarily in OH.
Application information:
Initial approach: Full proposal
Deadline(s): None
Write: F. Miles Flickinger, M.D., Chairman
Officers and Trustees: F. Miles Flickinger, M.D., Chairman; Miriam Bandy, Secretary; Marhl P. Flickinger, Treasurer; Terrence Derck, Miss Irma L. Flickinger.
Employer Identification Number: 346527156

3222
Flowers (Albert W. and Edith V.) Charitable Trust ⌑
c/o Harter Bank and Trust Company
126 Central Plaza North
Canton 44702 (216) 489-5422
Application Address: Harter Bank and Trust Company, c/o Stephen C. Donatini, P.O. Box 500, Canton, OH 44701

Trust established in 1968 in Ohio.
Donor(s): Albert W. Flowers,† Edith V. Flowers.†
Financial data: (yr. ended 12/31/83): Assets, $1,210,630 (M); expenditures, $86,455, including $75,000 for 31 grants (high: $9,000; low: $200).
Purpose and activities: Primarily local giving, with emphasis on Protestant church support, a home for the aged, youth agencies, higher and secondary education, and cultural programs.
Limitations: Giving primarily in Stark County, OH.
Application information:
Initial approach: Letter
Deadline(s): November 15
Managers: F.E. McCullough, Albert C. Printz, Ronald B. Tynan, The Harter Bank & Trust Co.
Employer Identification Number: 346608643

3223
Flowers (H. Fort) Foundation, Inc. ⌑
Differential Ave.
P.O. Box 238
Findlay 45839

Incorporated in 1951 in Delaware.
Financial data: (yr. ended 12/31/83): Assets, $948,528 (M); gifts received, $129,180; expenditures, $352,718, including $352,500 for 5 grants (high: $250,000; low: $500).
Purpose and activities: Grants mainly for higher education and a recreation center.
Officers and Trustees:* D.F. Flowers,* President; E.M. Foster,* S.N.F. Georges,* J.R. Murray,* W.L. Woellert, Vice-Presidents; F.F. Flowers,* Secretary.
Employer Identification Number: 346513672

3224
Ford (The S. N.) and Ada Ford Fund
P.O. Box 849
Mansfield 44901 (419) 526-3493

Trust established in 1947 in Ohio.
Donor(s): Ada Ford, M.D.†
Financial data: (yr. ended 12/31/83): Assets, $4,439,192 (M); gifts received, $1,573,673; expenditures, $425,154, including $47,400 for 17 grants (high: $10,000; low: $300) and $312,228 for 321 grants to individuals.
Purpose and activities: Charitable and educational purposes; renders assistance to the aged and the sick, and provides scholarships for the youth of Richland County.
Types of support awarded: Building funds, student aid, grants to individuals.
Limitations: Giving primarily in Richland County, OH. No grants for endowment funds, or for operating budgets, special projects, general support, research, or matching gifts; no loans.
Publications: Annual report.
Application information: Application form required.
Initial approach: Telephone
Board meeting date(s): Monthly
Final notification: 2 months
Write: Ralph H. LeMunyon, President
Distribution Committee: Ralph H. LeMunyon, President; Frederick L. Tracy, Vice-President; Catherine A. Dorsey, Secretary and Investigator; David L. Upham, Secretary; Walter J. Kinkel, Burton Preston.
Trustee: First Buckeye Bank.
Employer Identification Number: 340842282

3225
Forest City Enterprises Charitable Foundation, Inc.
10800 Brookpark Rd.
Cleveland 44130

Trust established in 1976 in Ohio.

Donor(s): Forest City Enterprises, Inc.
Financial data: (yr. ended 1/31/84): Assets, $47,915 (M); expenditures, $305,350, including $304,893 for 249 grants (high: $68,343; low: $15).
Purpose and activities: Broad purposes; primarily local giving, with emphasis on Jewish welfare funds, a community fund, education, and cultural programs; support also for community development.
Limitations: Giving primarily in OH.
Application information:
  Write: Nathan Shafran
Officers and Trustees: Max Ratner, President; Sam Miller, Vice-President; Helen F. Morgan, Secretary; Albert Ratner, Charles Ratner, Nathan Shafran, J. Maurice Struchen.
Employer Identification Number: 341218895

3226
Fox (The Harry K. & Emma R.) Charitable Foundation
900 Bond Court Bldg.
Cleveland 44114   (216) 621-8400

Trust established in 1959 in Ohio.
Donor(s): Emma R. Fox.†
Financial data: (yr. ended 12/31/83): Assets, $3,250,000 (M); expenditures, $201,000, including $188,500 for 62 grants (high: $50,000; low: $600; average: $1,000-$10,000).
Purpose and activities: Primarily local giving to hospitals, education, cultural programs, youth agencies, and human services.
Limitations: Giving primarily in northeastern OH. No grants to individuals, or for endowment funds or matching gifts; no loans.
Publications: Application guidelines.
Application information:
  Initial approach: Full proposal
  Copies of proposal: 4
  Deadline(s): May 15 and November 15
  Board meeting date(s): June and December
  Final notification: 6 months
  Write: Harold E. Friedman, Secretary
Officer: Harold E. Friedman, Secretary.
Trustees: Marjorie S. Schweid, Chairman; George Rosenfeld, Vice-Chairman; National City Bank.
Number of staff: 1 part-time professional.
Employer Identification Number: 346511198

3227
France Stone Foundation
P.O. Box 1928
Toledo 43603   (419) 241-4101

Established in 1952 in Ohio.
Donor(s): George A. France,† The France Stone Company, and subsidiaries.
Financial data: (yr. ended 12/31/83): Assets, $2,859,159 (L); gifts received, $10,000; expenditures, $191,313, including $187,410 for 64 grants (high: $25,000; low: $100).
Purpose and activities: Giving primarily to hospitals, religious organizations, youth agencies, and higher and secondary education.
Types of support awarded: Continuing support, annual campaigns, building funds.

Limitations: Giving primarily in OH, MI, and IN. No grants to individuals, or for endowment funds, operating budgets, special projects, scholarships and fellowships, or matching gifts; no loans.
Application information: Application form required.
  Initial approach: Full proposal
  Copies of proposal: 1
  Deadline(s): October 1
  Board meeting date(s): October
  Final notification: 6 months
  Write: Clair F. Martig, President
Officers and Trustees: Charles E. Stimming, Chairman; Clair F. Martig, President; Ollie J. Risner, Vice-President; Clarence L. Mackey, Secretary-Treasurer.
Number of staff: None.
Employer Identification Number: 346523033

3228
Frohman (The Sidney) Foundation ¤
c/o Third National Bank
P.O. Box 1211
Sandusky 44870

Trust established in 1952 in Ohio.
Donor(s): Sidney Frohman,† Blanche P. Frohman.†
Financial data: (yr. ended 12/31/83): Assets, $4,221,167 (M); expenditures, $245,014, including $229,865 for 35 grants (high: $41,895; low: $500).
Purpose and activities: To promote the well-being of mankind; assistance to the sick, aged, and needy; guidance of youth; aid to higher and secondary education; support of public health and recreation; and the furtherance of research; primarily local giving.
Limitations: Giving primarily in OH, with emphasis on Erie County. No grants to individuals.
Trustees: Daniel C. Frohman, George T. Henderson, L.G. Parker, Max E. Stierwalt.
Employer Identification Number: 346517809

3229
Frohring (The William O. and Gertrude Lewis) Foundation, Inc.
3200 National City Center
Cleveland 44114   (216) 621-0200

Trust established in 1958 in Ohio; incorporated in 1963.
Donor(s): William O. Frohring,† Gertrude L. Frohring.
Financial data: (yr. ended 12/31/83): Assets, $2,404,612 (L); expenditures, $198,714, including $175,250 for 34 grants (high: $100,000; low: $250).
Purpose and activities: Local giving, primarily to establish charitable institutions concerned with health, education, and the arts.
Types of support awarded: Operating budgets, continuing support, annual campaigns, seed money, emergency funds, building funds, equipment, land acquisition.
Limitations: Giving primarily in Geauga County, OH. No grants to individuals, or for deficit financing, endowment funds, matching gifts, scholarships, or fellowships; no loans.

Application information:
  Initial approach: Letter or telephone
  Copies of proposal: 1
  Deadline(s): Submit proposal preferably in March and August; deadline 1 week before board meetings
  Board meeting date(s): May and October
  Final notification: 3 weeks after board meetings
  Write: William W. Falsgraf, Assistant Secretary
Officers and Trustees: Gertrude L. Frohring, Chairman; Glenn H. Frohring, Secretary; Lloyd W. Frohring, Treasurer; William W. Falsgraf, Elaine A. Szilagyi.
Employer Identification Number: 346516526

3230
Frost (Meshech) Testamentary Trust ¤
c/o BancOhio National Bank
155 E. Broad St.
Columbus 43251
Application address: Kenneth H. Myers, Secretary-Treasurer, 109 South Washington St., Tiffin, OH 44883

Trust established in 1922 in Ohio.
Donor(s): Meshech Frost.†
Financial data: (yr. ended 12/31/83): Assets, $1,909,928 (M); expenditures, $131,322, including $117,885 for 11 grants (high: $50,000; low: $35) and $651 for 4 grants to individuals.
Purpose and activities: Local giving only for civic improvement or beautification and for the needy poor and other charitable purposes, including support for a local college and hospital.
Limitations: Giving limited to Tiffin, OH.
Application information:
  Initial approach: Letter
  Write: Kenneth H. Myers, Secretary-Treasurer
Advisory Committee: Kenneth H. Myers, Secretary-Treasurer; Charles Hering, Jane Kalnow, Robert McDonald, Rev. David Kulp.
Trustee: The Ohio National Bank.
Employer Identification Number: 316019431

3231
Gallagher (The Lewis P.) Family Foundation ¤
Society National Bank, Trust Dept.
127 Public Square
Cleveland 44114

Established in 1980.
Donor(s): Lewis P. Gallagher Family Charitable Income Trust.
Financial data: (yr. ended 12/31/83): Assets, $1,886,845 (M); gifts received, $823,698; expenditures, $402,099, including $351,500 for 7 grants (high: $200,000; low: $2,500).
Purpose and activities: Primarily local giving for higher and secondary education, hospitals, and Protestant welfare organizations.
Types of support awarded: Matching funds, scholarship funds, building funds, operating budgets, general purposes.
Limitations: Giving primarily in OH.

Officers: Monford D. Custer, Jr., M.D., President; Gilbert V. Kelling, Jr., Secretary; Howard H. Fraser, Treasurer.
Employer Identification Number: 341325313

3232
GAR Foundation, The ▼
(formerly The Roush Foundation)
P.O. Box 1500
Akron 44309   (216) 376-5300

Trust established in 1967 in Ohio.
Donor(s): Ruth C. Roush,† Galen Roush.†
Financial data: (yr. ended 12/31/82): Assets, $103,505,531 (M); expenditures, $1,592,998, including $1,464,671 for 86 grants (high: $176,141; low: $1,200).
Purpose and activities: Broad purposes; primarily local giving, with emphasis on the arts, higher education, hospitals and social agencies.
Types of support awarded: Seed money, equipment, general purposes, endowment funds, research, matching funds.
Limitations: Giving primarily in northeastern OH, with emphasis on Akron. No grants to individuals, or for general operating expenses of the donee not directly related to its exempt purpose.
Application information:
Initial approach: Proposal
Copies of proposal: 1
Final notification: Varies
Write: Lisle M. Buckingham, Trustee
Distribution Committee: Lisle M. Buckingham,* Richard W. Hoss, George J. Roush, Thomas W. Roush, William F. Spitznagel, John L. Tormey, Charles F. Zodrow.
Trustees: BancOhio National Bank.
Number of staff: 1 full-time professional; 2 part-time professional.
Employer Identification Number: 346577710

3233
Gardner Foundation, The
P.O. Box 126
Middletown 45042

Incorporated in 1952 in Ohio.
Financial data: (yr. ended 5/31/83): Assets, $2,165,166 (M); gifts received, $1,454; expenditures, $193,094, including $118,140 for 12 grants (high: $9,332; low: $2,000) and $34,995 for 16 grants to individuals.
Purpose and activities: Broad purposes; support primarily for higher education, with emphasis on private colleges and universities in Ohio and a scholarship program for graduating seniors from schools in Middletown and Hamilton County.
Types of support awarded: Student aid.
Limitations: Giving primarily in OH, with emphasis on Middletown and Hamilton County.
Publications: Program policy statement, application guidelines.
Application information: Application form required.
Deadline(s): April 1 (for scholarships)

Officers and Trustees: Colin Gardner III, President; E.T. Gardner, Jr., Vice-President; Calvin F. Lloyd, Secretary and Treasurer; Ames Gardner, Jr., Colin Gardner IV, E. Ty Gardner III, Robert Q. Millan, Mary G. Neill.
Employer Identification Number: 316050604

3234
GenCorp Foundation Inc. ▼
(formerly General Tire Foundation, Inc.)
One General St.
Akron 44329   (216) 798-5050

Incorporated in 1961 in Ohio as successor to The General Tire Foundation, a trust established in 1950 in Ohio.
Donor(s): GenCorp, Inc., Aerojet General Corporation.
Financial data: (yr. ended 11/30/84): Assets, $18,000,000 (M); gifts received, $250,000; expenditures, $1,100,000, including $1,008,639 for 480 grants (high: $118,000; low: $25; average: $1,000-$10,000) and $60,000 for 100 employee matching gifts.
Purpose and activities: Charitable and educational purposes; general giving, with emphasis on higher education, community funds, and youth agencies in areas of company operations.
Types of support awarded: Employee matching gifts, annual campaigns, building funds, employee related scholarships, general purposes, continuing support.
Limitations: Giving limited to areas of company operations. No grants to individuals, or for endowment funds, or research; no loans.
Publications: Program policy statement.
Application information:
Initial approach: Letter
Copies of proposal: 1
Deadline(s): None
Board meeting date(s): As required
Final notification: 2 months
Write: Joseph M. Leyden, Secretary-Treasurer
Officers and Trustees: J.H. Miller,* President; J.D. Ritchie,* Vice-President; Joseph M. Leyden,* Secretary-Treasurer.
Number of staff: None.
Employer Identification Number: 346514223

3235
George Foundation, The ⌑
65 E. State St., Suite 2200
Columbus 43215

Established in 1982 in Ohio.
Donor(s): Kaplan Trucking Company.
Financial data: (yr. ended 12/31/83): Assets, $1,366,586 (M); expenditures, $79,238, including $77,965 for 49 grants (high: $40,000; low: $20).
Purpose and activities: Broad purposes; primarily local giving, with emphasis on higher education.
Limitations: Giving primarily in OH.
Official Trustees: Jack George, President; James George, Mildred George.
Employer Identification Number: 311030194

3236
Gerlach Foundation, Inc. ⌑
37 West Broad St., Rm. 835
Columbus 43215

Incorporated in 1953 in Ohio.
Donor(s): Pauline Gerlach,† John J. Gerlach, John B. Gerlach.
Financial data: (yr. ended 11/30/83): Assets, $3,814,139 (M); expenditures, $132,478, including $32,660 for 41 grants (high: $5,500; low: $25).
Purpose and activities: Broad purposes; primarily local giving, with emphasis on higher education and social services.
Types of support awarded: General purposes.
Limitations: Giving primarily in OH. No grants to individuals.
Application information:
Write: John J. Gerlach, President
Officers and Trustees: John J. Gerlach, President; Gretchen G. Ewing, Vice-President; John B. Gerlach, Secretary and Treasurer.
Employer Identification Number: 316023912

3237
Gerson (Benjamin S.) Family Foundation
2404 Derbyshire Rd.
Cleveland Heights 44106   (216) 229-1459

Trust established in 1958 in Ohio; foundation established in 1973.
Donor(s): Members of the Gerson family, Benjamin S. Gerson.†
Financial data: (yr. ended 12/31/83): Assets, $1,676,322 (M); expenditures, $116,669, including $109,650 for 29 grants (high: $17,000; low: $500; average: $500-$17,000).
Purpose and activities: Primarily local giving, with emphasis on community organizations, programs emphasizing access to education, alternative and innovative education, civil liberties, and children and family concerns; some support for national issue advocacy organizations.
Types of support awarded: Operating budgets, continuing support, seed money, emergency funds, building funds, equipment, matching funds, special projects, publications.
Limitations: Giving limited to the greater Cleveland, OH, community for operating programs. No grants to individuals, or for conferences.
Publications: Application guidelines.
Application information:
Initial approach: Telephone or letter requesting guidelines
Copies of proposal: 4
Deadline(s): Submit proposal preferably in September or October; deadline October 10
Board meeting date(s): November or later
Final notification: Suitable requests notified after board meets
Write: Eleanor R. Gerson, Chairperson
Trustees: Eleanor R. Gerson, Chairperson; Thomas E. Gerson, Richard Margolis, Rae Weil.
Number of staff: None.
Employer Identification Number: 346611446

3238
Goerlich Family Foundation, Inc. ☒
1200 National Bank Bldg.
Toledo 43604

Incorporated in 1965 in Ohio.
Financial data: (yr. ended 12/31/83): Assets,
$2,250,351 (M); expenditures, $114,225,
including $94,825 for 56 grants (high: $30,000;
low: $100).
Purpose and activities: Broad purposes;
primarily local giving, with emphasis on child
welfare, mental health, and community funds;
grants also for church support and religious
associations, the aged, handicapped, youth
agencies, and a population control organization.
Limitations: Giving primarily in Toledo, OH.
Officers: John Goerlich,* Chairman and
President; Paul Putnam,* Vice-President;
William F. Bates, Secretary and Treasurer.
Directors:* Edward H. Alexander, Sandrea Sue
Goerlich Alexander, Selma E. Goerlich, Robert
R. Hessler, William S. Miller, Selma Goerlich
Putnam.
Employer Identification Number: 340970919

3239
**Goodyear Tire & Rubber Company
Fund** ▼
1144 East Market St.
Akron 44316-0001   (216) 796-4028

Incorporated in 1945 in Delaware.
Donor(s): The Goodyear Tire & Rubber
Company.
Financial data: (yr. ended 12/31/83): Assets,
$13,059 (M); gifts received, $607,000;
expenditures, $597,402, including $497,300
for 85 grants (high: $50,000; low: $1,000;
average: $500-$5,250) and $100,091 for grants
to individuals.
Purpose and activities: Aid to colleges and
universities primarily but not exclusively in
states in which Goodyear plants are located.
Types of support awarded: Annual
campaigns, building funds, continuing support,
fellowships, operating budgets, research,
scholarship funds, employee related
scholarships, special projects, general purposes.
Limitations: Giving primarily in areas where
company plants and subsidiaries are located.
No grants to individuals (except for company-
employee scholarships), or for endowment
funds or matching gifts; no loans.
Application information:
  Initial approach: Letter or full proposal
  Copies of proposal: 1
  Deadline(s): Submit proposal preferably in
    July through December; no set deadline
  Board meeting date(s): May and as required
  Final notification: 3 to 4 months
  Write: John Davies, Assistant Secretary
Officers: Tom H. Barrett,* President; Frederick
S. Myers, Vice-President and Secretary; Donald
R. Kronenberger, Treasurer.

Trustees:* Robert E. Mercer, Chairman; Edwin
D. Dodd, W. Howard Fort, Lewis W. Foy,
Philip O. Geier, Jr., James R. Glass, Gertrude G.
Michelson, Charles J. Pilliod, Jr., Robert H.
Platt, F. Vincent Prus, Jacques R. Sardas, Lloyd
B. Smith, H. Guyford Stever, Ib Thomsen,
William C. Turner.
Number of staff: 2.
Employer Identification Number: 346522959

3240
**Greene (Helen Wade) Charitable
Trust** ☒
c/o The Ameritrust Co., Trust Tax
P.O. Box 5937
Cleveland 44101

Established in 1957.
Financial data: (yr. ended 12/31/82): Assets,
$5,384,177 (M); expenditures, $576,227,
including $533,998 for 35 grants (high:
$53,400; low: $4,866).
Purpose and activities: Giving in Cleveland
only, with emphasis on higher education,
especially a nursing school and a university,
museums, a social service organization, a
community fund, a hospital, and an arts
organization.
Limitations: Giving limited to Cleveland, OH.
Trustees: A. Dean Perry, Helen Green Perry,
Ellery Sedgwick, Jr., Ameritrust Company.
Employer Identification Number: 346527172

3241
**Gries (Lucile and Robert H.) Charity
Fund**
720 Statler Office Tower
Cleveland 44115   (216) 861-1146

Trust established in 1968 in Ohio.
Donor(s): Lucile D. Gries.
Financial data: (yr. ended 12/31/84): Assets,
$1,867,934 (M); expenditures, $181,394,
including $144,050 for 46 grants (high:
$22,500; low: $450; average: $500-$15,000).
Purpose and activities: General charitable
purposes; primarily local giving.
Types of support awarded: Operating
budgets, continuing support, annual campaigns,
emergency funds, equipment, endowment
funds, matching funds, internships, scholarship
funds, research.
Limitations: Giving primarily in Cuyahoga
County, OH. No grants to individuals, or for
seed money, deficit financing, building funds,
land acquisition, demonstration projects,
publications, or conferences; no loans.
Application information:
  Initial approach: Full proposal or letter
  Copies of proposal: 1
  Board meeting date(s): Usually in March,
    June, September, and December, and as
    required
  Write: Robert D. Gries
Distribution Committee: Ellen G. Cole,
Robert D. Gries.
Trustee: AmeriTrust Company.
Number of staff: None.
Employer Identification Number: 346507593

3242
Grimes Foundation, The ☒
200 South Main St.
Urbana 43078
Application address: Lewis B. Moore,
Chairman, 166 Tanglewood Dr., Urbana, IL
43708

Incorporated about 1951 in Ohio.
Donor(s): Warren G. Grimes.
Financial data: (yr. ended 12/31/83): Assets,
$2,020,657 (M); gifts received, $19,870;
expenditures, $185,575, including $167,300
for grants.
Purpose and activities: Giving primarily in
Ohio and Florida, with emphasis on higher
education and hospitals.
Types of support awarded: General purposes,
scholarship funds, building funds.
Limitations: Giving primarily in OH and FL.
No grants to individuals, or for endowment
funds, research, or matching gifts; no loans.
Application information:
  Initial approach: Letter or telephone
  Copies of proposal: 1
  Deadline(s): None
  Board meeting date(s): March and August
  Write: Lewis B. Moore, Chairman
Officers and Trustees: Lewis B. Moore,
Chairman and President; James S. Mihori,
Secretary-Treasurer; C.J. Brown, Jr., Frank J.
Lausche, Robert S. Oelman.
Number of staff: None.
Employer Identification Number: 346528288

3243
**Gross (Walter L. and Nell R.) Charitable
Trust**
105 East Fourth St., Rm. 710
Cincinnati 45202   (513) 721-5086

Established in 1955 in Ohio.
Donor(s): Members of the Gross family.
Financial data: (yr. ended 12/31/84): Assets,
$1,883,949 (M); expenditures, $161,447,
including $157,287 for 31 grants (high:
$100,300; low: $50).
Purpose and activities: Primarily local giving,
with emphasis on higher and secondary
education, youth agencies, cultural programs,
hospitals and health agencies, and Protestant
church support.
Limitations: Giving primarily in OH.
Application information:
  Write: Walter L. Gross, Jr. or Thomas R.
    Gross, Co-Trustees
Advisory Board: Walter L. Gross, Jr., Thomas
R. Gross.
Employer Identification Number: 316033247

3244
Gund (The George) Foundation ▼
One Erieview Plaza
Cleveland 44114   (216) 241-3114

Incorporated in 1951 in Ohio.
Donor(s): George Gund.†
Financial data: (yr. ended 12/31/84): Assets,
$128,675,000 (M); expenditures, $6,392,657,
including $5,469,723 for 360 grants (high:
$500,000; low: $600; average: $22,000).

Purpose and activities: Broad purposes; grants mainly to local institutions; priority to education projects, with emphasis on new concepts and methods of teaching and learning, and on increasing educational opportunities for the disadvantaged; to social programs, including improved services, employment opportunities, housing for minority and low-income groups, and meeting the special needs of women; support also for ecology, civic affairs, and the arts.

Types of support awarded: Operating budgets, continuing support, annual campaigns, seed money, emergency funds, land acquisition, matching funds, internships, scholarship funds, fellowships, loans, special projects, publications, conferences and seminars.

Limitations: Giving primarily in northeastern OH. Generally no grants to individuals, or for building or endowment funds, equipment, or research.

Publications: Annual report, program policy statement, application guidelines.

Application information:
Initial approach: Full proposal
Copies of proposal: 1
Deadline(s): January 15, April 15, August 15, and October 15
Board meeting date(s): March, June, October, and December
Final notification: 8 weeks
Write: James S. Lipscomb, Executive Director
Officers: Frederick K. Cox,* President and Treasurer; Geoffrey Gund,* Vice-President; William G. Caples,* Secretary; James S. Lipscomb, Executive Director.
Trustees:* Kathleen L. Barber, George Gund III, Llura Gund.
Number of staff: 4 full-time professional; 3 full-time support.
Employer Identification Number: 346519769

3245
Hamilton Community Foundation, Inc., The
319 North Third St.
Hamilton 45011   (513) 863-1389

Community foundation incorporated in 1951 in Ohio.
Financial data: (yr. ended 12/31/83): Assets, $3,707,938 (M); gifts received, $525,329; expenditures, $466,102, including $407,044 for 60 grants (high: $22,500; low: $25; average: $1,000-$20,000).
Purpose and activities: Established for the benefit of the inhabitants of the greater Hamilton-Fairfield area; grants for local institutions, with emphasis on youth and child welfare agencies and scholarships. Grants also for hospitals and health agencies, and cultural programs.
Types of support awarded: Seed money, emergency funds, scholarship funds, conferences and seminars.

Limitations: Giving limited to Butler County, OH. No grants to individuals, or for operating budgets, continuing support, annual campaigns, deficit financing, capital or endowment funds, matching gifts, program support, research, demonstration projects, or publications; no loans.
Publications: Annual report, application guidelines.
Application information:
Initial approach: Full proposal
Copies of proposal: 10
Deadline(s): Submit proposal 30 days prior to first Monday of months in which board meets
Board meeting date(s): February, April, June, October, and December
Final notification: 2 months
Write: Cynthia V. Parrish, Executive Director
Officers: Thomas J. Millikin,* President; Joseph Wolf,* Vice-President; Mrs. H.R. Grosvenor, Secretary; William Groth, Treasurer; Cynthia V. Parrish, Executive Director.
Trustees:* David L. Belew, Anne Carr, Gerald S. Hammond, William L. Hartford, Lamont Jacobs, Lee H. Parrish, Randy T. Rogers.
Trustee Banks: First National Bank and Trust Company, Second National Bank.
Number of staff: 1 part-time professional; 1 part-time support.
Employer Identification Number: 316038277

3246
Hankins Foundation, The
3835-4 Lander Rd.
Chagrin Falls 44022

Trust established in 1952 in Ohio.
Donor(s): Edward R. Hankins,† Ann H. Long,† Jane H. Lockwood,† Ruth L. Hankins.
Financial data: (yr. ended 12/31/83): Assets, $1,273,577 (M); expenditures, $250,578, including $231,220 for 75 grants (high: $27,500; low: $250).
Purpose and activities: To assist local public charitable and educational organizations, with emphasis on higher education, community funds, health agencies and hospitals, youth and social agencies, and cultural programs.
Limitations: Giving primarily in OH. No grants to individuals; no loans.
Application information:
Initial approach: Full proposal
Copies of proposal: 1
Board meeting date(s): As required
Write: Miss Ruth L. Hankins, Trustee
Trustees: Ruth L. Hankins, Richard R. Hollington, Edward G. Lockwood, Gordon G. Long, Janet L. Tarwater.
Employer Identification Number: 346565426

3247
Hartzell-Norris Charitable Trust ⌁
c/o Piqua National Bank & Trust Co.
131 West High St.
Piqua 45356

Trust established in 1943 in Ohio.
Donor(s): Hartzell Industries, Inc.

Financial data: (yr. ended 10/31/83): Assets, $2,790,910 (M); expenditures, $223,567, including $193,444 for 172 grants (high: $70,000; low: $10).
Purpose and activities: Primarily local giving, with emphasis on youth agencies, community funds, Protestant church support and religious associations, and higher education.
Limitations: Giving primarily in OH.
Distribution Committee: G.W. Hartzell, Chairman; Roy H. DePriest, Miriam H. Hartzell.
Trustee: Piqua National Bank & Trust Company.
Employer Identification Number: 316024521

3248
Haskell Fund
1010 Hanna Bldg.
Cleveland 44115   (216) 696-6836

Incorporated in 1955 in Ohio.
Donor(s): Melville H. Haskell, Coburn Haskell, Melville H. Haskell, Jr.
Financial data: (yr. ended 12/31/83): Assets, $1,292,094 (M); expenditures, $131,542, including $122,200 for 40 grants (high: $16,000; low: $400; average: $1,000-$6,000).
Purpose and activities: Broad purposes; general giving, primarily locally for community services and nationally for higher and secondary education, hospitals, and health agencies.
Limitations: Giving primarily in the Cleveland, OH, area for community service grants; other grants awarded nationally. No grants to individuals.
Publications: Annual report.
Application information:
Initial approach: Full proposal
Copies of proposal: 1
Board meeting date(s): Within the first 2 weeks of June
Write: Betty J. Tuite, Secretary
Officers: Melville H. Haskell,* President; Coburn Haskell,* Vice-President; Betty J. Tuite, Secretary; Donald C. Cook, Treasurer.
Trustees:* Mary H. Haywood.
Employer Identification Number: 346513797

3249
Hauss-Helms Foundation, Inc., The
Peoples National Bank Bldg.
P.O. Box 25
Wapakoneta 45895   (419) 738-4911

Incorporated in 1965 in Ohio.
Donor(s): Besse Hauss Helms,† W.B. Helms.†
Financial data: (yr. ended 12/31/83): Assets, $3,352,103 (M); expenditures, $227,729, including $185,470 for 121 grants to individuals.
Purpose and activities: Scholarships for graduating high school students who are residents of Auglaize and Allen counties.
Types of support awarded: Student aid.
Limitations: Giving limited to residents of Auglaize and Allen counties, OH.
Publications: Program policy statement, application guidelines.
Application information: Application form required.
Initial approach: Letter

Copies of proposal: 1
Deadline(s): January 15
Board meeting date(s): January, March,
April, May, June, December, and as
required
Write: James E. Weger, President
Officers: James E. Weger, President; Vincent
G. Hudson, Vice-President; Robert C. Lietz,
Secretary-Treasurer.
Trustee: N. Thomas Cornell.
Employer Identification Number: 340975903

3250
H.C.S. Foundation
1053 Huntington Bldg.
Cleveland 44115   (216) 781-3502

Trust established in 1959 in Ohio.
Donor(s): Harold C. Schott.†
Financial data: (yr. ended 12/31/83): Assets,
$4,613,643 (M); gifts received, $6,960;
expenditures, $172,895, including $138,785
for 7 grants (high: $41,390; low: $3,500).
Purpose and activities: Broad purposes; grants
primarily for Roman Catholic church support,
higher education, and social services.
Types of support awarded: Operating
budgets, scholarship funds, endowment funds,
building funds.
Limitations: Giving limited to OH.
Application information:
Copies of proposal: 1
Deadline(s): None
Trustees: Francie S. Hiltz, L. Thomas Hiltz, B.J.
Mulcahy, William Dunne Saal, Milton B.
Schott, Jr.
Employer Identification Number: 346514235

3251
Helping Hand Foundation, The
P.O. Box 295
Berlin 44610

Established in 1968.
Financial data: (yr. ended 12/31/83): Assets,
$997,733 (M); gifts received, $21,373;
expenditures, $210,564, including $117,703
for 7 grants (high: $57,233; low: $20).
Purpose and activities: Primarily local giving
for Mennonite church programs and
community development, especially
improvement of a park.
Limitations: Giving primarily in OH.
Officer: Ruby Hostetler, Secretary.
Employer Identification Number: 340996981

3252
Higbee Foundation, The
100 Public Square
Cleveland 44113   (216) 579-3363

Trust established in 1975 in Ohio as successor
to Higbee McKelvey Charitable Foundation.
Donor(s): The Higbee Company.
Financial data: (yr. ended 1/29/83): Assets,
$2,731 (M); gifts received, $141,916;
expenditures, $139,976, including $139,950
for 18 grants (high: $108,000; low: $250).

Purpose and activities: Primarily local giving,
with emphasis on community funds; support
also for higher education, hospitals, and
cultural organizations.
Limitations: Giving primarily in OH. No grants
to individuals.
Publications: 990-PF, application guidelines.
Application information:
Initial approach: Full proposal, letter, or
telephone
Copies of proposal: 1
Deadline(s): Submit proposal by January 1
Board meeting date(s): January
Write: Paul L. Volk, Trustee
Trustees: Herbert E. Strawbridge, Paul L. Volk,
Allan J. Zambie, R.B. Campbell, Raymond J.
Miller.
Number of staff: None.
Employer Identification Number: 510173783

3253
Hoover Foundation, The ▼
101 East Maple St.
North Canton 44720   (216) 499-9200

Trust established in 1945 in Ohio.
Donor(s): The Hoover Company, members of
the Hoover family.
Financial data: (yr. ended 12/31/84): Assets,
$31,247,759 (M); expenditures, $1,176,919,
including $1,116,055 for 88 grants (high:
$180,000; low: $150; average: $500-$50,000)
and $60,854 for 200 employee matching gifts.
Purpose and activities: To support projects in
areas in which company factories are located;
grants for youth agencies, hospital building
funds, community funds, and higher and
secondary education, including a matching gifts
program.
Types of support awarded: Building funds,
operating budgets, annual campaigns,
scholarship funds, general purposes, employee
matching gifts, matching funds.
Limitations: Giving limited to areas in which
company factories are located. No grants to
individuals or for endowment funds.
Application information:
Initial approach: Letter
Deadline(s): None
Board meeting date(s): Semiannually and as
required
Final notification: 1 week to 1 month
Write: J.S. Hoover, Chairman
Trust Committee: J.S. Hoover, Chairman;
Ronald K. Bennington, Secretary; Herbert W.
Hoover, Jr., Lawrence R. Hoover, W. Henry
Hoover.
Trustee: Society Bank of Eastern Ohio.
Number of staff: None.
Employer Identification Number: 346510994

3254
Hosler (Dr. R. S.) Memorial Educational
Fund ¤
50 Bortz St.
P.O. Box 5
Ashville 43103
Application address: 154 E. Main St., Ashville,
OH 43103; Tel.: (614) 983-2054

Financial data: (yr. ended 12/31/83): Assets,
$2,538,425 (M); expenditures, $177,958,
including $102,191 for 13 grants to individuals.
Purpose and activities: Giving for scholarships
to graduates of the Teays Valley and Amanda
Clearcreek, Ohio, school systems.
Types of support awarded: Student aid.
Limitations: Giving limited to Teays Valley and
Amanda Clearcreek, OH.
Application information: Application form
required.
Write: Vaundell White, Trustee
Trustee: Vaundell White.
Employer Identification Number: 311073939

3255
Huffy Foundation, Inc., The
P.O. Box 1204
Dayton 45401   (513) 866-6251

Incorporated in Ohio in 1959 as Huffman
Foundation; name changed in 1978.
Donor(s): Huffy Corporation.
Financial data: (yr. ended 6/30/84): Assets,
$275,218 (M); expenditures, $229,910,
including $218,260 for 116 grants (high:
$25,000; low: $100; average: $1,000) and
$8,419 for 27 employee matching gifts.
Purpose and activities: Giving primarily in
areas of company operations for higher
education, cultural programs, youth agencies,
community funds, civic affairs, and health.
Types of support awarded: Operating
budgets, continuing support, annual campaigns,
seed money, emergency funds, matching funds,
scholarship funds, special projects,
publications, employee matching gifts,
conferences and seminars.
Limitations: Giving primarily in areas of
company operations. No support for agencies
covered by the United Way. No grants to
individuals, or for deficit financing, endowment
funds, research, or fellowships; no loans.
Publications: Program policy statement,
application guidelines.
Application information:
Initial approach: Letter or full proposal
Deadline(s): None
Board meeting date(s): April, August, and
December
Final notification: Approximately 2 weeks
after board meetings
Write: R.R. Wieland, Secretary
Officers: S.J. Northrop,* President; R.R.
Wieland, Secretary.
Trustees:* F.C. Smith, Chairman; R.R.
Huffman, H.A. Shaw.
Number of staff: None.
Employer Identification Number: 316023716

3256
Humphrey (George M. and Pamela S.)
Fund
1010 Hanna Bldg.
Cleveland 44115   (216) 696-0320

Incorporated in 1951 in Ohio.
Donor(s): George M. Humphrey,† Pamela S.
Humphrey.†

Financial data: (yr. ended 12/31/84): Assets, $5,086,353 (M); expenditures, $370,912, including $286,550 for 60 grants (high: $31,000; low: $200).
Purpose and activities: Broad purposes; primarily local giving, with emphasis on hospitals, higher and secondary education, and community funds; support also for cultural programs and health agencies.
Types of support awarded: Operating budgets, continuing support, annual campaigns, emergency funds, building funds, equipment, endowment funds, matching funds, professorships, internships, research, technical assistance.
Limitations: Giving primarily in OH. No grants to individuals; no loans.
Publications: Annual report.
Application information:
  Initial approach: Letter or proposal
  Copies of proposal: 1
  Deadline(s): Submit proposal preferably in February or October; deadline October 15
  Board meeting date(s): April and November
  Final notification: 1 month
  Write: Carol H. Butler, President
Officers: Carol H. Butler,* President; John G. Butler,* Vice-President; H.N. Putnam, Treasurer.
Trustees:* Pamela B. Rutter.
Employer Identification Number: 346513798

3257
Humphrey (Gilbert W. & Louise Ireland) Foundation
1010 Hanna Bldg.
Cleveland 44115   (216) 696-3193

Incorporated in 1951 in Ohio.
Donor(s): Gilbert W. Humphrey,† Mrs. Louise Ireland Humphrey.
Financial data: (yr. ended 12/31/84): Assets, $1,252,081 (M); gifts received, $43,022; expenditures, $176,265, including $165,800 for 35 grants (high: $26,800; low: $200).
Purpose and activities: Broad purposes; primarily local giving, with emphasis on educational institutions, music, cultural programs, a community fund, hospitals, and social agencies.
Limitations: Giving primarily in OH. No grants to individuals.
Application information:
  Initial approach: Letter
  Copies of proposal: 1
  Deadline(s): Submit proposal preferably in first quarter of year; deadline September 1
  Board meeting date(s): First Tuesday of November
  Write: Mrs. Louise Ireland Humphrey, President
Officers: Louise Ireland Humphrey,* President; Margaret H. Bindhardt,* Vice-President; M.G. Mikolaj,* Secretary; Irene E. Manni, Treasurer.
Trustees:* George M. Humphrey, II.
Employer Identification Number: 346525832

3258
Huntington (The John) Fund for Education ▼
822 National City Bank Bldg.
Cleveland 44114   (216) 861-0777

Incorporated in 1954 in Ohio.
Donor(s): John Huntington.†
Financial data: (yr. ended 12/31/84): Assets, $14,381,000 (M); expenditures, $810,699, including $736,000 for 11 grants (high: $322,000; low: $9,500).
Purpose and activities: A limited number of tuition grants and grants-in-aid varying in amount are available to residents of Cuyahoga County, Ohio for study there in scientific and technological fields on full- or part-time, day or evening schedules. Grants are made to and administered by the educational institutions.
Types of support awarded: Scholarship funds.
Limitations: Giving limited to Cuyahoga County, OH. No grants to individuals.
Application information:
  Initial approach: Letter
  Copies of proposal: 1
  Deadline(s): April 30
  Board meeting date(s): Usually in June
  Write: Morris Everett, Treasurer
Officers: Peter W. Adams,* President; Oakley Andrews, Secretary; Morris Everett,* Treasurer; Earla Mae Inks, Executive Secretary.
Trustees:* Ralph M. Besse, Susan Murray, Peter R. Musselman, R. Henry Norweb, Jr., Leigh H. Perkins, Lewis Williams.
Employer Identification Number: 340714434

3259
Iddings Foundation
Kettering Tower, Suite 1620
Dayton 45423   (513) 224-1773

Trust established in 1973 in Ohio.
Donor(s): Roscoe C. Iddings,† Andrew S. Iddings.†
Financial data: (yr. ended 12/31/83): Assets, $5,705,700 (M); expenditures, $391,338, including $331,630 for 48 grants (high: $27,500; low: $500).
Purpose and activities: Local grants for higher education, health care, mental health, care of the aged and handicapped, youth agencies, cultural programs, the environment, welfare, and population control.
Types of support awarded: Operating budgets, continuing support, annual campaigns, seed money, emergency funds, building funds, equipment, land acquisition, matching funds, matching funds, scholarship funds, special projects, publications, consulting services.
Limitations: Giving limited to OH, with emphasis on the Dayton metropolitan area. No grants to individuals, or for endowment funds, deficit financing, research, or conferences; no loans.
Publications: Application guidelines.
Application information:
  Initial approach: Letter
  Copies of proposal: 8
  Deadline(s): March 1, June 1, September 1, or November 1
  Board meeting date(s): April, July, October, and December

Final notification: 1 1/2 to 2 months
  Write: Maribeth A. Eiken, Administrative Secretary
Trustee: Bank One, Dayton (L.W. Feldmann, III, Trust Officer).
Number of staff: 1 part-time support.
Employer Identification Number: 316135058

3260
Ingalls (The Louise H. and David S.) Foundation, Incorporated ▼
301 Tower East
20600 Chagrin Blvd.
Shaker Heights 44122   (216) 921-6000

Incorporated in 1953 in Ohio.
Donor(s): Louise H. Ingalls, Edith Ingalls Vignos, Louise Ingalls Brown, David S. Ingalls,† David S. Ingalls, Jr., Jane I. Davison, Anne I. Lawrence.
Financial data: (yr. ended 12/31/82): Assets, $7,264,366 (M); expenditures, $693,206, including $670,034 for 13 grants (high: $340,000; low: $2,000).
Purpose and activities: "The improvement of the physical, educational, mental, and moral condition of humanity throughout the world"; grants largely for higher and secondary education; support also for community funds and cultural programs, primarily in Ohio. Support mainly to organizations known to the trustees.
Types of support awarded: Annual campaigns, operating budgets, special projects.
Limitations: Giving primarily in Cleveland, OH.
Application information:
  Initial approach: Full proposal
  Deadline(s): None
  Board meeting date(s): As required
  Write: David S. Ingalls, Jr., President
Officers: David S. Ingalls, Jr.,* President and Treasurer; James H. Dempsey, Jr., Secretary.
Trustees:* Louise Ingalls Brown, Jane I. Davison, Anne I. Lawrence, Edith Ingalls Vignos.
Number of staff: 2 part-time support.
Employer Identification Number: 346516550

3261
Ingram (Edgar W.) Foundation ¤
P.O. Box 1498
555 West Goodale St.
Columbus 43216   (614) 228-5781

Incorporated in 1949 in Ohio.
Donor(s): Edgar W. Ingram,† White Castle System, Inc.
Financial data: (yr. ended 4/30/83): Assets, $8,078,032 (M); expenditures, $87,752, including $85,065 for 22 grants (high: $20,000; low: $500).
Purpose and activities: General purposes; primarily local giving, with emphasis on higher education, Columbus public schools, cultural programs, and hospitals.
Types of support awarded: General purposes, building funds, scholarship funds.
Limitations: Giving primarily in OH.
Application information: Application form required.
  Deadline(s): 6 weeks prior to the second week in November and April

Write: J.L. Trador, Assistant Secretary
Officers: Edgar W. Ingram III, President; James Petropoulos, Jr., Vice-President; Robert D. Hays, Secretary.
Trustees: Robert Crane, Nancy Jeffrey.
Employer Identification Number: 316051433

3262
Ireland Foundation, The
1010 Hanna Bldg.
Cleveland 44115   (216) 696-3193

Incorporated in 1951 in Ohio.
Donor(s): Margaret Allen Ireland,† R. Livingston Ireland,† Kate Ireland, and members of the Ireland family.
Financial data: (yr. ended 12/31/84): Assets, $5,630,458 (M); expenditures, $432,832, including $369,550 for 89 grants (high: $57,250; low: $100).
Purpose and activities: Broad purposes; grants largely for educational and charitable programs, with emphasis on nursing, higher and secondary education, and hospitals; grants also for music.
Types of support awarded: General purposes.
Limitations: No grants to individuals.
Application information:
Initial approach: Letter and brief proposal
Copies of proposal: 1
Deadline(s): Submit proposal preferably in first quarter of year
Board meeting date(s): First Tuesday of November
Write: Louise Ireland Humphrey, President
Officers: Louise Ireland Humphrey,* President and Treasurer; Kate Ireland,* Vice-President; M.G. Mikolaj, Secretary.
Trustees:* Melville H. Ireland, R.L. Ireland, III.
Employer Identification Number: 346525817

3263
Jarson (Isaac N. and Esther M.) Charitable Trust ⌺
105 East Fourth St., Suite 710
Cincinnati 45202

Trust established about 1953 in Ohio.
Donor(s): Isaac N. Jarson, G & J Pepsi-Cola Bottlers, Inc., Esther M. Jarson Trust.
Financial data: (yr. ended 12/31/83): Assets, $2,266,483 (M); expenditures, $108,053, including $103,920 for 36 grants (high: $30,000; low: $25).
Purpose and activities: Primarily local giving, with emphasis on Jewish welfare funds and temple support, education and cultural programs.
Limitations: Giving primarily in Cincinnati, OH.
Managers: Myran J. Kaplan, Stanley M. Kaplan.
Employer Identification Number: 316033453

3264
Jennings (The Martha Holden) Foundation ▼
1040 Huntington Bldg.
Cleveland 44115   (216) 589-5700
Business office: c/o Ann Pinkerton 4225 Mayfield Rd., Rm. 102A, South Euclid, OH 44121; Tel.: (216) 382-6278

Incorporated in 1959 in Ohio.
Donor(s): Martha Holden Jennings.†
Financial data: (yr. ended 12/31/83): Assets, $32,951,498 (M); expenditures, $1,712,100, including $888,841 for 107 grants (high: $96,684; low: $1,000) and $459,291 for 12 foundation-administered programs.
Purpose and activities: Local giving to foster development of the capabilities of young people through improving the quality of teaching in secular elementary and secondary schools; program includes awards in recognition of outstanding teaching; special educational programs for teachers in the fields of the humanities, the arts, and the sciences; awards to deserving students in furtherance of their recognized abilities; curriculum development projects; school evaluation studies; and educational television programs.
Types of support awarded: Continuing support, seed money, matching funds, professorships, scholarship funds, special projects, conferences and seminars.
Limitations: Giving limited to OH. No grants to individuals, or for operating budgets, annual campaigns, travel, emergency funds, deficit financing, capital or endowment funds, research, or publications; no loans.
Publications: Annual report, newsletter, program policy statement, application guidelines.
Application information: Application form required for Grants to Teachers Program.
Initial approach: 1-page project summary, cover letter, budget, and full proposal
Copies of proposal: 8
Deadline(s): 1st of each month
Board meeting date(s): Advisory and Distribution Committee meets monthly, except August and December
Final notification: 6 to 8 weeks
Write: Mrs. Joan M. Johnson, Program Director
Officers and Trustees: Arthur S. Holden, Jr., Chairman; George B. Chapman, Jr., President; William F. Hauserman, Frank W. Milbourn, Vice-Presidents; John H. Gherlein, Secretary; Allen H. Ford, Treasurer; Robert M. Ginn, Claire D. Holden.
Number of staff: 1 full-time professional; 1 part-time professional; 3 part-time support.
Employer Identification Number: 340934478

3265
Jergens (The Andrew) Foundation
c/o The Central Trust Company, N.A.
P.O. Box 1198
Cincinnati 45201   (513) 651-8377

Incorporated in 1962 in Ohio.
Donor(s): Andrew N. Jergens.†
Financial data: (yr. ended 8/31/84): Assets, $4,495,690 (M); gifts received, $80,788; expenditures, $357,781, including $354,228 for 42 grants (high: $45,000; low: $500).
Purpose and activities: To promote the health, education, social welfare, and cultural experiences of children from pre-school through high-school age; local giving; grants largely for secondary and elementary education, a community fund, cultural programs, community centers, and day care.

Types of support awarded: Operating budgets, seed money, special projects.
Limitations: Giving limited to the greater Cincinnati, OH, area. No grants to individuals, or for continuing support, annual campaigns, emergency or endowment funds, deficit financing, matching gifts, scholarships, fellowships, research, publications, or conferences; no loans.
Publications: Application guidelines, program policy statement.
Application information:
Initial approach: Letter or telephone
Copies of proposal: 8
Deadline(s): Submit proposal preferably in months when board does not meet; deadlines October 1, January 1, April 1, or July 1
Board meeting date(s): November, February, May, and August
Final notification: 6 months
Write: Nancy C. Gurney, Administrator
Officers and Trustees: Rev. Andrew N. Jergens, Jr., President; Thomas C. Hays, Vice-President; Leonard S. Meranus, Secretary and Treasurer; John W. Beatty, Mary Ann Hays, Linda Busken Jergens, Lavatus V. Powell, Jr.
Number of staff: 1 full-time professional.
Employer Identification Number: 316038702

3266
Jochum-Moll Foundation, The ⌺
5389 West 130th St.
Cleveland 44111

Incorporated in 1961 in Ohio.
Donor(s): M.T. & D. Company, and its subsidiaries.
Financial data: (yr. ended 7/31/83): Assets, $6,318,135 (M); gifts received, $211,222; expenditures, $322,980, including $257,970 for 33 grants (high: $30,000; low: $1,000).
Purpose and activities: Broad purposes; primarily local giving, with emphasis on higher and secondary education, and hospitals; grants also for a community fund, welfare and Protestant church support.
Limitations: Giving primarily in OH.
Officers and Trustees: Theo Moll, President; Emil Jochum, Vice-President; Curtis Moll, Treasurer; David J. Hessler.
Employer Identification Number: 346538304

3267
Juilfs Foundation, The ⌺
8485 Broadwell Rd.
Cincinnati 45244

Established in 1962 in Ohio.
Financial data: (yr. ended 12/31/83): Assets, $1,313,096 (M); expenditures, $66,793, including $64,075 for 52 grants (high: $15,000; low: $100).
Purpose and activities: Primarily local giving, with emphasis on higher education, hospitals, the arts, youth agencies and a community fund.
Limitations: Giving primarily in OH.
Trustees: George C. Juilfs, Howard W. Juilfs, Faye Kuluris.
Employer Identification Number: 316027571

3268
Kachelmacher Memorial, Inc. ⊐
Hocking Valley Community Hospital
P.O. Box 348
Logan 43138

Incorporated in 1969 in Ohio.
Financial data: (yr. ended 6/30/83): Assets, $2,475,482 (M); expenditures, $145,729, including $108,088 for 1 foundation-administered program.
Purpose and activities: A private operating foundation; local giving primarily for research and treatment of varicose veins.
Types of support awarded: Research.
Limitations: Giving primarily in Logan, OH.
Officers and Trustees: Dayton Schultheis, President; William Keynes, Vice-President; Earl D. Later, Secretary; John C. Owens, Treasurer; B.J. King.
Employer Identification Number: 310792046

3269
Kangesser (The Robert E., Harry A., and M. Sylvia) Foundation ⊐
1401 Lakeside Ave.
Cleveland 44114   (216) 621-7762

Incorporated in 1947 in Ohio.
Donor(s): Robert E. Kangesser,† Harry A. Kangesser,† M. Sylvia Kangesser.†
Financial data: (yr. ended 12/31/83): Assets, $3,387,837 (M); expenditures, $428,927, including $396,200 for 34 grants (high: $235,000; low: $100).
Purpose and activities: Broad purposes; primarily local giving, with emphasis on Jewish welfare funds and religious education.
Limitations: Giving primarily in the Cleveland, OH area.
Application information:
  Deadline(s): None
  Board meeting date(s): Usually in September or October
  Write: David G. Kangesser, President
Officers and Trustees: David G. Kangesser, President; H. Kangesser, Vice-President; Norman A. Sugarman, Secretary; H.L. Zucker, Treasurer.
Employer Identification Number: 346529478

3270
Kaplan-Halpert Foundation, Inc., The ⊐
65 E. State St., 22nd Fl.
Columbus 43215   (614) 228-1541

Incorporated about 1959 in Ohio.
Donor(s): Sadye M. Kaplan,† Jene Halpert, Kaplan Trucking Company, and others.
Financial data: (yr. ended 12/31/83): Assets, $1,693,436 (M); gifts received, $825,862; expenditures, $97,138, including $73,100 for 7 grants (high: $35,000; low: $100).
Purpose and activities: Primarily local giving, with emphasis on higher education.
Types of support awarded: General purposes.
Limitations: Giving primarily in OH.
Application information:
  Deadline(s): None
  Write: Noel F. George, President

Officer and Trustees: Noel F. George, President; Jack M. George, Secretary-Treasurer; A. Charles Tell.
Employer Identification Number: 237418063

3271
Kettering (Charles F.) Foundation
5335 Far Hills Ave., Suite 300
Dayton 45429   (513) 434-7300

Incorporated in 1927 in Ohio.
Donor(s): Charles F. Kettering.†
Financial data: (yr. ended 8/31/84): Assets, $87,039,040 (M); gifts received, $887,798; expenditures, $8,140,558, including $7,668,888 for 3 foundation-administered programs.
Purpose and activities: A private operating foundation concentrating in the areas of governing, educating, and science, particularly in how they interrelate on an international basis. Applies available funds to research efforts generally designed by Foundation staff, but welcomes partnerships with other institutions and individuals who are actively working on similar problems.
Publications: Annual report, newsletter.
Application information: Applications not accepted; the Foundation does not make grants.
  Board meeting date(s): May and November
  Write: Edwin H. Vause, Vice-President
Officers: David Mathews,* President and Chief Executive Officer; James P. Schwartzhoff, Vice-President and Treasurer; Robert F. Lehman, Vice-President and General Counsel; Edwin H. Vause, Vice-President.
Trustees:* Lisle C. Carter, Jr., Chairman; Nathaniel S. Colley, Sr., Norman Cousins, Lawrence A. Cremin, Clifford M. Hardin, Robert A. Kerr, Richard D. Lombard, Madeline H. McWhinney, Donna E. Shalala, James R. Thomas, Daniel Yankelovich.
Number of staff: 20 full-time professional; 3 part-time professional; 20 full-time support; 4 part-time support.
Employer Identification Number: 310549056

3272
Kettering Family Foundation, The
2400 Kettering Tower
Dayton 45423   (513) 228-1021

Incorporated in 1955 in Illinois; reincorporated in 1967 in Ohio.
Donor(s): E.W. Kettering,† V.W. Kettering, J.K. Lombard, S.K. Williamson, P.D. Williamson, M.D., Richard D. Lombard, B. Weiffenbach.†
Financial data: (yr. ended 12/31/84): Assets, $5,135,279 (M); gifts received, $327,962; expenditures, $267,734, including $204,900 for 11 grants (high: $50,000; low: $5,000; average: $5,000-$25,000).
Purpose and activities: Broad purposes; support largely for higher and secondary education, cultural programs, and health and medical research.

Types of support awarded: Operating budgets, annual campaigns, seed money, emergency funds, deficit financing, building funds, equipment, land acquisition, endowment funds, special projects, research, publications, conferences and seminars.
Limitations: Giving primarily in the U.S. No grants to individuals, or for scholarships or fellowships; no loans.
Publications: Annual report, application guidelines.
Application information:
  Initial approach: Letter stating amount requested
  Copies of proposal: 1
  Deadline(s): April 1 and October 1
  Board meeting date(s): May and November
  Final notification: 1 month after board meetings
  Write: Jack L. Fischer
Officers: Charles F. Kettering, III,* President; Susan K. Lipowicz,* Debra L. Williamson,* Vice-Presidents; W.V. Richards, Jr., Treasurer.
Trustees:* J.S. Kettering, Linda Kettering, Lisa S. Kettering, Mrs. V.W. Kettering, Richard A.F. Lipowicz, Jane K. Lombard, Richard D. Lombard, Douglas E. Williamson, Karen Williamson, Kyle Williamson, P.D. Williamson, M.D., Susan K. Williamson.
Number of staff: None.
Employer Identification Number: 310727384

3273
Kettering Fund, The ▼
c/o Bank One, Dayton
Kettering Tower
Dayton 45401   (513) 449-8884

Established in 1958 in Ohio.
Donor(s): Charles F. Kettering.†
Financial data: (yr. ended 6/30/84): Assets, $32,589,460 (M); expenditures, $2,198,258, including $2,125,000 for 34 grants (high: $500,000; low: $500; average: $1,000-$200,000).
Purpose and activities: Grants largely for medical research, with emphasis on cancer, and for higher education; support also for local social service and youth agencies, community funds, and museums.
Limitations: Giving primarily in OH. No grants to individuals.
Application information:
  Initial approach: Brief outline of proposal in letter form
  Deadline(s): April 1 and October 1
  Board meeting date(s): Usually in mid-May and mid-November
  Final notification: 10 days to 2 weeks after meeting date
Trustee: Bank One, Dayton.
Employer Identification Number: 316027115

3274
Kibble Foundation ⊐
P.O. Box 723
Pomeroy 45769

Established in 1976.

Financial data: (yr. ended 12/31/83): Assets, $1,483,104 (M); expenditures, $142,492, including $133,000 for grants.
Purpose and activities: Charitable purposes.
Trustee: Bernard V. Fultz.
Employer Identification Number: 316175971

3275
Kilburger (Charles) Scholarship Fund ☐
Equitable Bldg.
Lancaster 43130   (614) 653-0461

Established in 1968 in Ohio.
Donor(s): Charles Kilburger.†
Financial data: (yr. ended 5/31/83): Assets, $1,831,517 (M); expenditures, $185,843, including $122,361 for 84 grants to individuals.
Purpose and activities: Scholarship grants to students of Fairfield County for higher education.
Types of support awarded: Student aid.
Limitations: Giving limited to residents of Fairfield County, OH.
Application information: Students are recommended by guidance counselors at high schools and colleges.
  Write: Mr. and Mrs. Kermit Sitterly
Trustee: Kermit Sitterley.
Employer Identification Number: 316086870

3276
Knight Foundation ▼
One Cascade Plaza
Akron 44308   (216) 253-9301

Incorporated in 1950 in Ohio.
Donor(s): John S. Knight,† James L. Knight, their families and associates, and some of the original Knight Newspapers.
Financial data: (yr. ended 12/31/84): Assets, $33,510,484 (M); gifts received, $6,065,875; expenditures, $5,280,876, including $4,735,742 for 125 grants (high: $900,000; low: $1,000).
Purpose and activities: Grants primarily for education, health, social and cultural programs initiated by organizations in cities where original Knight newspapers are published, and journalism projects of national scope.
Types of support awarded: Special projects.
Limitations: Giving primarily in 11 cities where original Knight newspapers are published: Akron,OH; Detroit, MI; Charlotte, NC; Lexington, KY; Macon and Columbus, GA; Philadelphia, PA; and Boca Raton, Miami, Tallahassee, and Bradenton, FL. No grants to individuals, or for operating deficits, annual campaigns, land acquisition, equipment, or building funds; no loans.
Publications: Annual report, program policy statement, application guidelines.
Application information:
  Initial approach: Letter
  Deadline(s): February 1, May 1, August 1, and November 1
  Board meeting date(s): Late in March, June, September, and December
  Final notification: 2 weeks after meeting dates
  Write: C.C. Gibson, President

Officers and Trustees: James L. Knight, Chairman; C.C. Gibson, President; Charles E. Clark, Secretary and Treasurer; Alvah H. Chapman, Jr., Gordon E. Heffern, Lee Hills, Ben Maidenburg, Henry King Stanford, Edwin J. Thomas, Barbara K. Toomey.
Number of staff: 2 full-time professional; 1 part-time professional; 1 full-time support.
Employer Identification Number: 346519827

3277
Kramer (Louise) Foundation
Third National Bank Trust Dept.
Dayton 45402

Established in 1965 in Ohio.
Donor(s): Louise Kramer.†
Financial data: (yr. ended 12/31/84): Assets, $2,200,000 (M); expenditures, $162,000, including $150,000 for 25 grants (high: $50,000; low: $1,000).
Purpose and activities: Primarily local giving, with emphasis on higher education, health agencies, the handicapped, church support, community funds and youth agencies.
Limitations: Giving primarily in OH.
Officers and Trustees:* Norman L. Gebhart,* President; Joseph F. Connelly,* Vice-President; Hugh Wall III,* Secretary; C.R. Barnes, Treasurer.
Number of staff: None.
Employer Identification Number: 316055729

3278
Kulas Foundation ▼ ☐
1622 Hanna Bldg.
Cleveland 44115   (216) 621-1785

Incorporated in 1937 in Ohio.
Donor(s): Fynette H. Kulas,† E.J. Kulas.†
Financial data: (yr. ended 12/31/83): Assets, $13,210,116 (M); gifts received, $167,742; expenditures, $976,859, including $892,855 for 72 grants (high: $94,670; low: $172; average: $1,000-$10,000).
Purpose and activities: Broad purposes; grants largely to music institutions and for higher education in the greater Cleveland area; some support also for local performing arts and social services.
Limitations: Giving limited to the greater Cleveland, OH, area. No grants to individuals, or for endowment funds.
Application information:
  Initial approach: Letter
  Copies of proposal: 4
  Deadline(s): Submit proposal preferably a month or two before a meeting; no set deadline
  Board meeting date(s): February, May, August, and November
  Final notification: After board meetings
  Write: Frank E. Joseph, Secretary
Officers: Richard W. Pogue, President and Treasurer; Allen C. Holmes,* Vice-President; Frank E. Joseph, Secretary.
Trustees:* Herbert E. Strawbridge.
Employer Identification Number: 340770687

3279
Kuntz Foundation, The ☐
120 West Second St.
Dayton 45402

Incorporated in 1946 in Ohio.
Donor(s): The Peter Kuntz, Sr. family, The Peter Kuntz Company, and affiliated companies.
Financial data: (yr. ended 12/31/83): Assets, $2,122,892 (M); expenditures, $175,787, including $155,260 for 130 grants (high: $25,000; low: $50) and $8,237 for grants to individuals.
Purpose and activities: Broad purposes; primarily local giving, with emphasis on higher education, including scholarships to children of company employees, hospitals, Catholic church support, community funds, youth agencies, and an art museum.
Types of support awarded: Employee related scholarships.
Limitations: Giving primarily in OH.
Officers and Trustees: Peter H. Kuntz, President; Martin Kuntz, Secretary; Richard P. Kuntz, Treasurer; Richard Kuntz.
Employer Identification Number: 316016465

3280
Lancaster Lens Inc. ☐
37 W. Broad St., Rm. 530
Columbus 43215

Financial data: (yr. ended 7/31/83): Assets, $1,145,692 (M); expenditures, $52,459, including $4,150 for 4 grants (high: $1,400; low: $500).
Purpose and activities: Primarily local giving for higher education and community services.
Limitations: Giving primarily in OH. No grants to individuals.
Application information:
  Write: Clarence Clapham, Secretary
Officers: David R. Crater, President; Clarence Clapham, Secretary; Joseph E. Schmidhammer, Treasurer.
Employer Identification Number: 316023927

3281
Laub Foundation, The
19583 Coffinberry Blvd.
Fairview Park 44126   (216) 331-1499

Incorporated in 1958 in Ohio.
Donor(s): Herbert J. Laub,† Elsie K. Laub.†
Financial data: (yr. ended 10/31/83): Assets, $1,997,117 (M); expenditures, $160,164, including $130,050 for 42 grants (high: $25,000; low: $250).
Purpose and activities: Charitable purposes; primarily local giving, with emphasis on scholarship programs of colleges and private schools, cultural programs, and youth agencies.
Types of support awarded: Operating budgets, continuing support, annual campaigns, seed money, emergency funds, building funds, equipment, matching funds, scholarship funds, fellowships, publications, conferences and seminars.

Limitations: Giving primarily in Cuyahoga County, OH, and adjacent counties. No grants to individuals, or for deficit financing or endowment funds; no loans.
Publications: Annual report.
Application information: Final distribution of grants made at August meeting.
Initial approach: Letter followed by full proposal
Copies of proposal: 2
Deadline(s): None
Board meeting date(s): February, May, August, and November
Final notification: After August meeting
Write: Malcolm D. Campbell, Jr., President
Officers and Trustees: Malcolm D. Campbell, Jr., President and Treasurer; Amie Campbell, Vice-President; Robert B. Nelson, Secretary; Katherine C. Berry, Thomas C. Westropp.
Employer Identification Number: 346526087

3282
Lennon (Fred A.) Foundation ⌑
29500 Solon Rd.
Solon 44139

Established in 1965 in Ohio.
Financial data: (yr. ended 11/30/83): Assets, $5,211,001 (M); gifts received, $743,750; expenditures, $679,250, including $668,400 for 115 grants (high: $130,000; low: $100).
Purpose and activities: Primarily local giving, with emphasis on higher education and Roman Catholic church support; grants also for hospitals, public policy, and community funds.
Limitations: Giving primarily in OH.
Officers: Fred A. Lennon, President; John F. Fant, Jr., Secretary.
Employer Identification Number: 346572287

3283
Lincoln Electric Foundation, The ▼ ⌑
c/o Central National Bank of Cleveland
P.O. Box 6179
Cleveland 44101   (216) 481-8100
Application address: 22801 St. Clair Ave., Cleveland, OH 44117

Trust established in 1952 in Ohio.
Donor(s): Lincoln Electric Company.
Financial data: (yr. ended 12/31/83): Assets, $831,141 (M); gifts received, $50,000; expenditures, $495,251, including $491,800 for 39 grants (high: $108,000; low: $250; average: $500-$20,000).
Purpose and activities: Broad purposes; primarily local giving, with emphasis on higher education and a community fund; grants also for hospitals, social agencies, cultural programs, and civic institutions.
Limitations: Giving primarily in OH, with emphasis on Cleveland.
Application information:
Initial approach: Letter
Deadline(s): September 20
Board meeting date(s): November
Write: Ellis F. Smolik, Secretary
Officer and Trustee: Ellis F. Smolik, Secretary; Central National Bank of Cleveland (D.M. McDermott, Senior Trust Officer).
Number of staff: 1.
Employer Identification Number: 346518355

3284
Lorain County Community Foundation, Greater
6125 South Broadway
Lorain 44053   (216) 324-2822

Community foundation incorporated in 1980 in Ohio.
Financial data: (yr. ended 12/31/83): Assets, $2,550,241 (M); gifts received, $688,092; expenditures, $326,840, including $285,059 for 32 grants.
Purpose and activities: Local giving for social services, education, health, civic and cultural programs.
Types of support awarded: Program-related investments, research, seed money, emergency funds, scholarship funds.
Limitations: Giving limited to Lorain County, OH. No grants to individuals, or for annual campaigns, deficit financing, or special endowments; no loans.
Publications: Application guidelines, annual report.
Application information:
Copies of proposal: 1
Deadline(s): April 1 and November 1
Board meeting date(s): January, June, September, and December
Write: Jeptha J. Carrell, Executive Director
Officers: William E. Foster, President; John S. Corogin, Vice-President; Scribner L. Fauver, Treasurer.
Number of staff: 2 full-time professional; 2 full-time support.
Employer Identification Number: 341322781

3285
Lubrizol Foundation, The ▼
29400 Lakeland Blvd.
Wickliffe 44092   (216) 943-4200

Incorporated in 1952 in Ohio.
Donor(s): The Lubrizol Corporation.
Financial data: (yr. ended 12/31/83): Assets, $1,619,104 (M); gifts received, $500,000; expenditures, $724,505, including $600,232 for 223 grants (high: $46,000; low: $200; average: $2,000-$5,000) and $115,203 for 172 employee matching gifts.
Purpose and activities: General purposes; primarily local giving, with emphasis on higher education, social services, cultural programs, youth agencies, and hospitals.
Types of support awarded: Operating budgets, continuing support, annual campaigns, emergency funds, building funds, equipment, land acquisition, matching funds, professorships, internships, scholarship funds, fellowships, research, employee matching gifts.
Limitations: Giving primarily in OH, with emphasis on Cleveland. No grants to individuals, or for seed money, deficit financing, endowment funds, demonstration projects, publications, or conferences; no loans.
Publications: Annual report.
Application information:
Initial approach: Full proposal
Copies of proposal: 1
Deadline(s): None
Board meeting date(s): As required, usually three or four times a year

Final notification: 2 weeks after meeting
Write: Raymond W. Hussey, Secretary
Officers and Trustees: W.M. LeSuer, Chairman; Douglas W. Richardson, President; Raymond W. Hussey, Secretary; G.C. Obenauer, Treasurer; W.T. Beargie, Gordon B. Cameron, M. Roger Clapp, L.E. Coleman, Richard P. Eide, David K. Ford, T.W. Mastin, F. Alex Nason, M.J. O'Connor, Ralph S. Tyler, Jr.
Number of staff: 1 part-time professional; 1 part-time support.
Employer Identification Number: 346500595

3286
Mandel (Jack N. and Lilyan) Foundation
4500 Euclid Ave.
Cleveland 44103   (216) 391-8300

Established in 1963 in Ohio.
Donor(s): Jack N. Mandel, Lilyan Mandel.
Financial data: (yr. ended 12/31/83): Assets, $2,710,324 (M); gifts received, $34,400; expenditures, $109,127, including $92,246 for 43 grants (high: $40,000; low: $20).
Purpose and activities: Broad purposes; primarily local giving, with emphasis on Jewish welfare funds.
Limitations: Giving primarily in OH.
Application information:
Initial approach: Proposal
Deadline(s): None
Write: Jack N. Mandel, President
Officers and Trustees: Jack N. Mandel, President; Lilyan Mandel, Vice-President; Morton L. Mandel, Secretary and Treasurer.
Employer Identification Number: 346546418

3287
Mandel (Joseph and Florence) Foundation
4500 Euclid Ave.
Cleveland 44103   (216) 391-8300

Established in 1963 in Ohio.
Donor(s): Florence Mandel, Joseph Mandel.
Financial data: (yr. ended 12/31/83): Assets, $2,795,887 (M); gifts received, $34,400; expenditures, $71,704, including $61,389 for 35 grants (high: $16,666; low: $50).
Purpose and activities: Primarily local giving, with emphasis on Jewish welfare funds and education.
Limitations: Giving primarily in OH.
Application information:
Initial approach: Proposal
Deadline(s): None
Write: Joseph C. Mandel, Trustee
Officers: Joseph C. Mandel,* President; Florence Mandel,* Vice-President; Philip S. Sims, Secretary and Treasurer.
Trustees:* Michele Beyer, Penni Weinberg.
Employer Identification Number: 346546419

3288
Mandel (Morton and Barbara) Foundation
4500 Euclid Ave.
Cleveland 44103   (216) 391-8300

Established in 1963 in Ohio.

Donor(s): Morton L. Mandel, Barbara A. Mandel.
Financial data: (yr. ended 12/31/83): Assets, $2,935,496 (M); gifts received, $34,400; expenditures, $102,370, including $93,246 for 31 grants (high: $30,000; low: $30).
Purpose and activities: Support primarily for Jewish welfare funds and a community fund.
Application information:
  Initial approach: Proposal
  Deadline(s): None
  Write: Morton L. Mandel, President
Officers and Trustees: Morton L. Mandel, President; Barbara A. Mandel, Vice-President; Henry L. Zucker, Secretary-Treasurer.
Employer Identification Number: 346546420

3289
Marathon Oil Foundation, Inc. ▼
539 South Main St.
Findlay 45840   (419) 422-2121

Incorporated in 1952 in Ohio.
Donor(s): Marathon Oil Company.
Financial data: (yr. ended 6/30/83): Assets, $329,828 (M); gifts received, $1,750,000; expenditures, $2,568,574, including $1,789,407 for 368 grants (high: $200,000; low: $300), $197,778 for 50 grants to individuals and $579,335 for employee matching gifts.
Purpose and activities: Broad purposes; support of selected private higher educational institutions of direct interest to company operations and of an employee matching gift program and the Marathon Scholars Program for children of employees; giving also to community, youth, welfare, and civic programs in areas of company operations.
Types of support awarded: Seed money, building funds, research, conferences and seminars, scholarship funds, employee related scholarships, employee matching gifts, program-related investments.
Limitations: Giving limited to areas of company operations. No support for religious or fraternal groups, or local community organizations (except those located in communities where there are significant numbers of company employees). No grants to individuals (except for company-employee scholarships), or for endowment funds; no loans.
Publications: Annual report, application guidelines.
Application information:
  Initial approach: Full proposal
  Copies of proposal: 1
  Deadline(s): None
  Board meeting date(s): As required
  Final notification: 6 to 8 weeks
  Write: Jessica J. Moses, Assistant Secretary
Officers and Trustees:* G.N. Nicholson,* President; J.F. Brucklacher, Vice-President and Secretary; G.R. Jetton, Jr.,* C.E. Merzbacher,* R.E. White,* R.N. Yammine,* Vice-Presidents; C.K. Morgan, Treasurer.
Number of staff: 1.
Employer Identification Number: 346523012

3290
Markey (The John C.) Charitable Fund ⌑
P.O. Box 191
Bryan 43506

Established in 1966 in Ohio.
Donor(s): John C. Markey.†
Financial data: (yr. ended 6/30/83): Assets, $2,031,427 (M); expenditures, $94,579, including $92,260 for 69 grants (high: $20,910; low: $100).
Purpose and activities: Grants for higher education, Protestant church support, hospitals, libraries, and social agencies.
Officers and Trustees: John R. Markey, President and Treasurer; Catherine M. Anderson, Vice-President; Arthur S. Newcomer, Secretary; L.W. Lisle.
Employer Identification Number: 346572724

3291
Markus (Roy & Eva) Foundation, Inc. ⌑
c/o Board of Education, Rm. 152
1380 E. 6th St.
Cleveland 44114

Trust established in 1954 in Ohio; incorporated in 1967.
Donor(s): Roy C. Markus,† Eva Markus, Eli C. Markus,† Seymour H. Levy, Robert C. Coplan.
Financial data: (yr. ended 7/31/84): Assets, $1,930,961 (M); gifts received, $97,144; expenditures, $155,439, including $135,300 for 28 grants (high: $65,000; low: $50).
Purpose and activities: Broad purposes; giving largely for higher education, mainly through local scholarship funds; support also for health, cultural programs, and Jewish welfare funds, primarily in Ohio and California.
Types of support awarded: Scholarship funds, research.
Limitations: Giving primarily in OH and CA. No grants to individuals.
Publications: Annual report.
Application information: Funds committed for the forseeable future.
Officers and Trustees:* Eva Markus,* President; Robert C. Coplan,* Executive Vice-President and Secretary; Jack Borman,* Mark A. Levy,* Vice-Presidents; E.M. Glickman, Treasurer.
Employer Identification Number: 341018827

3292
Marx (Robert S.) Residuary Trust ⌑
1009 Tri-State Bldg.
Cincinnati 45202

Trust established in 1962 in Ohio.
Donor(s): Robert S. Marx.†
Financial data: (yr. ended 4/30/83): Assets, $1,174,617 (M); expenditures, $149,750, including $124,565 for 34 grants (high: $30,000; low: $15).
Purpose and activities: Charitable and educational purposes; grants principally for higher education and hospitals.
Trustees: Samuel Huttenbauer, John Kaichen, Hugh A. White.
Employer Identification Number: 316025640

3293
Massie (David Meade) Trust ⌑
P.O. Box 41
Chillicothe 45601

Financial data: (yr. ended 12/31/82): Assets, $2,827,444 (M); expenditures, $226,879, including $203,879 for 51 grants (high: $8,640; low: $800).
Purpose and activities: Giving limited to Chillicothe and Ross County, Ohio, with emphasis on community development, especially volunteer fire departments; and on youth, health and social agencies; support also for education and cultural programs.
Limitations: Giving limited to Chillicothe and Ross counties, OH.
Publications: Program policy statement, application guidelines.
Application information: Application form required.
  Deadline(s): March 1, June 1, September 1, and December 1
  Board meeting date(s): March 15, June 15, September 15, and December 15
Employer Identification Number: 316022292

3294
Mather (Elizabeth Ring) and William Gwinn Mather Fund ▼
1558 Huntington Bldg.
Cleveland 44115   (216) 861-5341

Incorporated in 1954 in Ohio.
Donor(s): Elizabeth Ring Mather.†
Financial data: (yr. ended 12/31/82): Assets, $3,847,094 (M); gifts received, $1,432,000; expenditures, $1,146,444, including $1,115,129 for 76 grants (high: $470,224; low: $250).
Purpose and activities: Broad purposes; generally for specific civic purposes in the Cleveland area, including the arts, hospitals and health agencies, higher and secondary education, conservation, and social welfare.
Types of support awarded: Annual campaigns, building funds, equipment, general purposes, publications, endowment funds.
Limitations: Giving primarily in OH, with emphasis on Cleveland. No grants to individuals, or for scholarships, fellowships, or matching gifts; no loans.
Application information: Applications for grants are not encouraged.
  Board meeting date(s): June and December
  Write: James D. Ireland, President
Officers and Trustees: James D. Ireland, President and Treasurer; Theodore R. Colborn, Secretary; Cornelia I. Hallinan, Cornelia W. Ireland, James D. Ireland, III, Lucy E. Ireland, R. Henry Norweb, Jr.
Number of staff: 1.
Employer Identification Number: 346519863

3295
Mather (The S. Livingston) Charitable Trust
1460 Huntington Bldg.
Cleveland 44115   (216) 942-6484

Trust established in 1953 in Ohio.

Donor(s): S. Livingston Mather.†
Financial data: (yr. ended 12/31/84): Assets, $2,313,800 (M); expenditures, $132,200, including $118,200 for 49 grants (high: $23,500; low: $150; average: $500-$5,000).
Purpose and activities: Broad purposes; primarily local giving, with emphasis on education, child welfare, youth programs, mental health, social services, cultural programs, and environment and natural resources. Support for both general operations and specific projects.
Types of support awarded: Operating budgets, continuing support, seed money, emergency funds, building funds, equipment, special projects.
Limitations: Giving primarily in northeast OH. No support for science and medical research programs; or in areas "appropriately supported by the government and United Way". No grants to individuals, or for annual campaigns, deficit financing, or mass mailing solicitation; no loans.
Publications: Annual report, program policy statement, application guidelines.
Application information: Mass mail solicitations not considered.
  Initial approach: Letter or telephone
  Copies of proposal: 1
  Deadline(s): None
  Board meeting date(s): Quarterly, and as required
  Final notification: 2 months
  Write: S. Sterling McMillan, Secretary
Distribution Committee: S. Sterling McMillan,* Secretary; Elizabeth M. McMillan, Madeleine M. Offutt.
Trustees:* AmeriTrust Company.
Number of staff: None.
Employer Identification Number: 346505619

3296
McAlonan (John A.) Trust
c/o Trust Division, BancOhio National Bank
P.O. Box 2009
Akron 44309   (216) 375-8704

Trust established in 1958 in Ohio.
Donor(s): John A. McAlonan.†
Financial data: (yr. ended 12/31/82): Assets, $2,633,901 (M); expenditures, $194,111, including $176,550 for 27 grants (high: $10,000; low: $1,500).
Purpose and activities: Giving to local charitable organizations, with emphasis on cultural programs and facilities, youth agencies, hospitals, the handicapped, and education.
Limitations: Giving limited to the Akron, OH, area. No grants to individuals.
Application information:
  Initial approach: Letter or full proposal
  Copies of proposal: 6
  Board meeting date(s): May and November
Trustee: BancOhio National Bank.
Employer Identification Number: 346513095

3297
McFawn (Lois Sisler) Trust No. 2
c/o AmeriTrust Company
P.O. Box 5937
Cleveland 44101   (216) 687-5632

Trust established in 1956 in Ohio.
Donor(s): Lois Sisler McFawn.
Financial data: (yr. ended 12/31/84): Assets, $5,581,428 (M); expenditures, $372,688, including $339,223 for 46 grants (high: $20,000; low: $1,000; average: $500-$10,000).
Purpose and activities: Giving primarily in the Akron, Ohio area, with emphasis on education, hospitals, minority group programs, cultural activities, and youth agencies.
Types of support awarded: General purposes, building funds, equipment, research, internships.
Limitations: Giving primarily in the Akron, OH, area. No grants to individuals, or for matching gifts, continuing support, seed money, emergency funds, deficit financing, land acquisition, publications, or conferences; no loans.
Application information:
  Initial approach: Proposal
  Copies of proposal: 1
  Deadline(s): None
  Board meeting date(s): Usually in June and December
  Write: Thomas B. Schneider, Vice-President
Distribution Committee: Ward Keener, Frank LePage, D. Bruce Mansfield, Fredrick Myers.
Trustee: AmeriTrust Company (Thomas B. Schneider, Vice-President).
Number of staff: None.
Employer Identification Number: 346508111

3298
McGregor (The A. M.) Home ▼
14900 Terrace Rd.
East Cleveland 44112   (216) 851-8200

Incorporated in 1904 in Ohio.
Financial data: (yr. ended 4/30/83): Assets, $41,387,723 (M); gifts received, $171,867; expenditures, $2,839,166, including $467,781 for 4 grants (high: $428,281; low: $10,000) and $854,643 for 1 foundation-administered program.
Purpose and activities: A private operating foundation; maintains a home for destitute aged men and women; grants awarded only to local agencies providing services directly to the elderly, primarily to the Benjamin Rose Institute.
Limitations: Giving limited to the greater Cleveland, OH, area.
Application information:
  Initial approach: Letter
  Deadline(s): None
  Board meeting date(s): 3rd Tuesday monthly, except in August and December
  Final notification: Within 60 days
  Write: Carol Ann Marks, Executive Director
Officers: Mrs. M.E. Mann,* President; C.K. Arter, Jr.,* O.F. Walker,* Vice-Presidents; Carol Ann Marks, Secretary and Executive Director; W.C. Young, Jr.,* Treasurer.

Trustees:* William G. Batcheller, G. Bicknell, Mrs. W. Birkhold, Mrs. William D. Buss II, David P. Handke, Jr., R.G. Harley, Frederick Heller, Mrs. F.S. Lamb, Charlotte B. Miller, M.D., Mary Willert.
Employer Identification Number: 340714356

3299
Mead Corporation Foundation, The ▼
Courthouse Plaza Northeast
Dayton 45463   (513) 222-6323

Trust established in 1957 in Ohio.
Donor(s): The Mead Corporation.
Financial data: (yr. ended 12/31/83): Assets, $10,989,393 (M); expenditures, $1,721,069, including $1,518,273 for 381 grants (high: $200,000; low: $50; average: $100-$25,000) and $151,971 for 230 employee matching gifts.
Purpose and activities: General giving to organizations in areas of Corporation operations, with emphasis on community funds, higher education, critical human services needs, and arts.
Types of support awarded: Annual campaigns, building funds, conferences and seminars, continuing support, emergency funds, employee matching gifts, equipment, fellowships, matching funds, operating budgets, research, scholarship funds, seed money, special projects, employee related scholarships.
Limitations: Giving primarily in areas of company operations. No support for national, fraternal, labor, or veterans organizations, or religious or denominational organizations. Grants rarely to tax supported institutions except for public colleges and universities. No grants to individuals, or for endowment funds; no loans; normally no operating support for organizations already receiving substantial support through United Way.
Publications: Informational brochure, program policy statement, application guidelines.
Application information: Applicants for grants in Mead operating communities should contact or apply to the local Mead unit manager. Application form required.
  Initial approach: Full proposal
  Deadline(s): None
  Board meeting date(s): February, April, July, October, and December
  Final notification: 2 months
  Write: Evelyn Stemen, Corporate Contributions Specialist
Officers: Ronald F. Budzik, Secretary and Executive Director; Robert E. Miller, Treasurer.
Trustee: First National Bank of Cincinnati.
Distribution Committee: C. Greene Garner, Chairman; Ronald P. Carzoli, S.G. Hawkes, Dudley P. Kircher, Steve C. Mason, James R. Samartini.
Number of staff: 1 full-time support; 3 part-time support.
Employer Identification Number: 316040645

3300
Mellen Foundation, The ⌑
3200 National City Center
Cleveland 44114
Address for nursing fellowship applications:
c/o Lillie R. Marquis, 9519 Arban Dr., St. Louis, MO 63216

Established in 1963 in Ohio.
Donor(s): Edward J. Mellen.
Financial data: (yr. ended 12/31/82): Assets, $2,455,960 (M); gifts received, $10,000; expenditures, $474,202, including $318,100 for 13 grants (high: $285,000; low: $100) and $79,175 for 20 grants to individuals.
Purpose and activities: Broad purposes; grants primarily for higher education, including fellowships for nursing education; some support also for churches and medical organizations.
Types of support awarded: Fellowships.
Application information: Application form required for fellowships. Application form required.
  Deadline(s): December 1 for requesting fellowship application form
  Write: Stephanie Keane, Treasurer
Officers: Edward J. Mellen,* President; James A. Cullen,* Vice-President and Executive Secretary; Alan G. Rorick,* Secretary; Stephanie Keane, Treasurer.
Trustees:* J. Raymond Barry, John Drinko, Douglas L. Newell.
Employer Identification Number: 346560874

3301
Melton (Samuel Mendel) Foundation ¤
88 East Broad St., Rm. 1425
Columbus 43215

Established in 1951 in Ohio.
Donor(s): Samuel Mendel Melton.
Financial data: (yr. ended 9/30/83): Assets, $1,062,362 (M); gifts received, $235,447; expenditures, $880,818, including $873,265 for 80 grants (high: $500,000; low: $25).
Purpose and activities: Giving primarily for higher education and youth agencies in Israel and Jewish religious educational organizations.
Application information:
  Deadline(s): None
Officers and Trustees: Samuel Mendel Melton, President and Treasurer; Mina Bess Melton Rehm, Vice-President; Donald Katz, Secretary; Stanley Katz.
Employer Identification Number: 316031944

3302
Midland-Ross Foundation ▼
20600 Chagrin Blvd.
Cleveland 44122   (216) 491-8400

Incorporated in 1957 in Ohio.
Donor(s): Midland-Ross Corporation.
Financial data: (yr. ended 12/31/83): Assets, $5,025 (M); gifts received, $367,000; expenditures, $407,360, including $373,220 for 102 grants (high: $75,000; low: $100; average: $500-$5,000) and $33,356 for 94 employee matching gifts.
Purpose and activities: Grants largely to advance education and health-care delivery in areas of company operations. The United Fund serves as principal conduit of social welfare grants. Some support also for cultural programs.
Types of support awarded: Annual campaigns, building funds, continuing support, employee matching gifts, equipment, general purposes, land acquisition, scholarship funds.

Limitations: Giving primarily in areas of company operations, with emphasis on Cleveland, OH, and including AZ, CA, MN, NJ, NY, and PA. No support for sectarian religious or political organizations. No grants to individuals, or for operating budgets for organizations supported by the United Way, good-will advertisements, purchase of tickets, or endowment funds; no loans.
Publications: Annual report, program policy statement, application guidelines.
Application information:
  Initial approach: Letter or full proposal
  Copies of proposal: 1
  Deadline(s): September 1
  Board meeting date(s): Quarterly
  Final notification: 1 month
  Write: Edward C. Gendron, Vice-Chairman
Officers: Harry J. Bolwell,* Chairman; E.C. Gendron,* Vice-Chairman; F.N. Fittipaldi, Secretary.
Trustees:* C.M. Blair.
Number of staff: 1 part-time professional; 1 part-time support.
Employer Identification Number: 346556087

3303
Miniger (Clement O.) Memorial Foundation ¤
Hillcrest Hotel, Rm. 229
Madison Ave. at 16th St.
Toledo 43624
Mailing address: P.O. Box 333, Toledo, OH 43691

Incorporated in 1952 in Ohio.
Donor(s): George M. Jones, Jr., Mrs. Eleanor Miniger Jones.
Financial data: (yr. ended 12/31/83): Assets, $3,762,804 (M); expenditures, $128,785, including $117,000 for 20 grants (high: $11,500; low: $500).
Purpose and activities: Broad purposes; primarily local giving, with emphasis on higher education, youth agencies, social services, and cultural programs.
Limitations: Giving primarily in OH.
Officers and Trustees: George M. Jones, Jr., President; Ford R. Weber, Vice-President; John C. Eberly, Executive Secretary and Treasurer; Richard Day, Thomas DeVilbiss, George M. Jones III, John A. Morse.
Employer Identification Number: 346523024

3304
MLM Charitable Foundation ¤
410 United Savings Bldg.
Toledo 43604

Established in 1967 in Ohio.
Donor(s): Mary L. McKenny.
Financial data: (yr. ended 12/31/83): Assets, $1,085,473 (M); expenditures, $74,947, including $71,900 for 25 grants (high: $17,750; low: $100).
Purpose and activities: Charitable purposes; grants primarily in Ohio and New York for higher education and Protestant church support.
Types of support awarded: Operating budgets.
Limitations: Giving primarily in OH and NY.

Officers: Mary L. McKenny, President; Anne E. McKenny, Vice-President; Charles A. McKenny, Treasurer.
Employer Identification Number: 341018519

3305
Monarch Machine Tool Company Foundation ¤
615 N. Oak St.
Sidney 45365

Trust established in 1952 in Ohio.
Donor(s): Monarch Machine Tool Company.
Financial data: (yr. ended 12/31/83): Assets, $1,035,456 (M); expenditures, $160,619, including $155,950 for 39 grants (high: $20,000; low: $150).
Purpose and activities: General purposes; primarily local giving for higher education, youth agencies, community funds, hospitals, community development, and a home for the aged.
Limitations: Giving primarily in OH.
Officers and Trustees: Kermit T. Kuck, President; Robert M. Peters, Secretary-Treasurer; N.V. Gusching.
Employer Identification Number: 346556088

3306
Montgomery Foundation ¤
Roscoe Village
Coshocton 43812

Established in 1972 in Ohio.
Donor(s): Edward E. Montgomery, Frances B. Montgomery.
Financial data: (yr. ended 6/30/83): Assets, $4,425,980 (M); gifts received, $742,244; expenditures, $316,741, including $272,685 for 5 grants (high: $271,000; low: $85).
Purpose and activities: Grants limited to the local area, with emphasis on an historic restoration project; limited support also for local charities.
Limitations: Giving primarily in Coshocton, OH.
Application information:
  Write: Edward E. Montgomery, President
Officer and Trustees: Edward E. Montgomery, President and Treasurer; R.W. Dunmire, R.J. Finnegan, F.E. Friedli, R.E. Hopkins, Jr., E.E. Montgomery, Jr., Frances B. Montgomery, J.S. Montgomery, R.L. Prindle, R.M. Thomas.
Employer Identification Number: 237165768

3307
Moore (Harry W. and Margaret) Foundation, Inc.
5051 Kitridge Rd.
Dayton 45424   (513) 233-0233

Incorporated in 1959 in Ohio.
Donor(s): Harry W. Moore.†
Financial data: (yr. ended 8/31/83): Assets, $1,227,364 (M); expenditures, $50,356, including $18,670 for 5 grants (high: $5,000; low: $1,170).

Purpose and activities: Primarily low-interest student loans to Dayton area students planning to attend local public, non-sectarian universities; loans currently granted on emergency basis only.

Limitations: Giving primarily in OH. No grants for operating budgets, scholarships and fellowships, deficit financing, or endowment funds.

Application information:
Initial approach: Telephone, letter, or full proposal
Copies of proposal: 1
Deadline(s): Submit proposal in April through September; no set deadline
Board meeting date(s): June and December
Write: Joe Tacinelli

Officers and Trustees: J.M. Biddison, President; J.N. Doyle, Vice-President; A.C. Reiger, Jr., Secretary-Treasurer; H.P. Jeffrey, E.R. Segee, N.F. Zimmers.

Employer Identification Number: 316040186

3308
Moores (The Harry C.) Foundation ▼
c/o Francis E. Caldwell
866 Clubview Blvd.
Worthington 43085   (614) 846-0389
Grant application office: 100 East Broad St., Columbus, OH 43215

Trust established in 1961 in Ohio.
Donor(s): Harry C. Moores.†
Financial data: (yr. ended 9/30/84): Assets, $8,624,152 (M); expenditures, $458,251, including $444,000 for 68 grants (high: $40,000; low: $1,000; average: $1,000-$15,000).
Purpose and activities: Local grants largely for rehabilitation of the handicapped, Protestant church support, hospitals, higher education, social service agencies concerned with the aged, child welfare, and the retarded, and cultural programs.
Types of support awarded: Seed money, emergency funds, building funds, research, scholarship funds.
Limitations: Giving primarily in the Columbus, OH, area. No grants to individuals, or for endowment funds, or matching gifts; no loans.
Application information:
Initial approach: Proposal in letter form
Copies of proposal: 1
Deadline(s): Submit proposal between October and July; deadline August 10
Board meeting date(s): April or May and August or September
Final notification: By October 15 (if affirmative)
Write: William H. Leighner, Secretary
Officers and Trustees: John J. Gerlach, Chairman; William H. Leighner, Secretary; Francis E. Caldwell, Treasurer; H.M. Clodfelter, M.D., William C. Jones.
Number of staff: None.
Employer Identification Number: 316035344

3309
Mount Vernon Community Trust, The
One South Main St.
P.O. Box 871
Mount Vernon 43050   (614) 397-6344
Mailing address: c/o First Knox National Bank, P.O. Box 871, Mount Vernon, OH 43050

Community foundation established in 1944 in Ohio by declaration of trust.
Financial data: (yr. ended 12/31/83): Assets, $2,981,937 (M); gifts received, $767,824; expenditures, $228,312, including $220,108 for 45 grants (high: $30,000; low: $17).
Purpose and activities: "To assist public, educational, charitable or benevolent enterprises" in Knox County. Grants, in accordance with the donors' wishes, for student loans and scholarship funds, Protestant church support, community funds, higher education, and youth agencies.
Limitations: Giving primarily in Knox County, OH. No grants to individuals, or for endowment funds or research; no loans.
Publications: Annual report.
Application information: Application form required.
Initial approach: Letter
Copies of proposal: 7
Board meeting date(s): Monthly
Write: Frederick N. Lorey, Chairman
Distribution Committee: Frederick N. Lorey, Chairman; James J. Cullers, Secretary; Dale E. Foster, J. Robert Purdy, Richard L. Smythe, M.D., Donald E. Steele.
Trustee: The First-Knox National Bank.
Number of staff: None.
Employer Identification Number: 316024796

3310
Murch Foundation, The ⌗
830 Hanna Bldg.
Cleveland 44115

Incorporated in 1956 in Ohio.
Donor(s): Maynard H. Murch.†
Financial data: (yr. ended 12/31/83): Assets, $7,810,165 (M); expenditures, $428,429, including $416,000 for 60 grants (high: $60,000; low: $1,000).
Purpose and activities: Primarily local giving, with emphasis on museums and cultural programs, higher and secondary education, hospitals, and community recreation.
Limitations: Giving primarily in OH.
Officers and Trustees: Maynard H. Murch IV, Vice-President; James H. Dempsey, Jr.
Employer Identification Number: 346520188

3311
Murphy (John P.) Foundation ⌗
100 Public Square, 10th Fl.
Cleveland 44113

Incorporated in 1960 in Ohio.
Donor(s): John P. Murphy.†
Financial data: (yr. ended 9/30/83): Assets, $17,909,192 (M); expenditures, $633,734, including $568,390 for 33 grants (high: $100,000; low: $1,000).

Purpose and activities: Broad purposes; primarily local giving, with emphasis on higher and secondary education; support also for hospitals, the arts, with emphasis on music, and a community fund.
Types of support awarded: Operating budgets, building funds, equipment, general purposes.
Limitations: Giving primarily in the greater Cleveland, OH, area. No grants to individuals or for endowment funds; no loans.
Application information:
Initial approach: Full proposal
Board meeting date(s): Monthly
Write: John Connell, Secretary
Officers and Trustees: Herbert E. Strawbridge, President; Claude M. Blair, Vice-President; John Connell, Secretary and Treasurer.
Employer Identification Number: 346528308

3312
National Machinery Foundation, Inc.
Greenfield St.
P.O. Box 747
Tiffin 44883   (419) 447-5211

Incorporated in 1948 in Ohio.
Donor(s): National Machinery Company.
Financial data: (yr. ended 12/31/83): Assets, $5,707,666 (M); expenditures, $243,979, including $175,641 for 175 grants (high: $50,000; low: $75) and $53,957 for 233 grants to individuals.
Purpose and activities: Grants to charitable, religious, and youth organizations, higher education, including scholarships, and aid to needy individuals, including former company employees.
Types of support awarded: Scholarship funds, grants to individuals.
Application information: Application form required.
Initial approach: Letter
Copies of proposal: 1
Board meeting date(s): Monthly
Write: Larry F. Baker, Secretary-Treasurer
Officers and Trustees: P. Aley, President; J.M. Permar, Vice-President; Larry F. Baker, Secretary-Treasurer; D.B. Bero, R.L. Callaghan, Jane F. Kalnow, D.E. King, Paul R. Martin, Jr., R.W. McDonald.
Employer Identification Number: 346520191

3313
Nationwide Foundation ▼
One Nationwide Plaza
Columbus 43216   (614) 227-4310

Incorporated in 1959 in Ohio.
Donor(s): Nationwide Mutual Insurance Company, and affiliates.
Financial data: (yr. ended 12/31/83): Assets, $16,857,246 (M); gifts received, $3,726,000; expenditures, $1,529,228, including $1,398,916 for 120 grants (high: $629,157; low: $300; average: $500-$25,000) and $127,212 for 611 employee matching gifts.

Purpose and activities: Broad purposes; primarily local giving with increased support for human services agencies; support also for cultural programs, community funds, and higher education, including employee matching gifts.

Types of support awarded: Operating budgets, continuing support, annual campaigns, seed money, emergency funds, special projects, research, scholarship funds, employee related scholarships, internships, employee matching gifts.

Limitations: Giving primarily in OH, particularly Columbus, and other communities where the company maintains offices. No support for public elementary and secondary schools, or fraternal or veterans' organizations. No grants to individuals or for building funds; no loans.

Publications: Informational brochure, program policy statement, application guidelines.

Application information:
  Initial approach: Letter
  Copies of proposal: 1
  Deadline(s): September 15
  Board meeting date(s): February, May, August, and November
  Write: J. Richard Bull, Vice-President

Officers: Paul A. Donald,* President; Peter F. Frenzer, Executive Vice-President; D.R. McFerson, Senior Vice-President, Finance; Gordon E. McCutchan, Senior Vice-President and General Counsel; Gerald W. Woodward, Vice-President and Treasurer; J. Richard Bull, Vice-President; Bert Price, Secretary.

Trustees:* John E. Fisher, Chairman; Charles L. Fuellgraf, James M. Lewis, John L. Marakas, Frank B. Sollars, Carl H. Stitzlein.

Contributions Committee: J. Richard Bull, Chairman; Paul A. Donald, W.E. Fitzpatrick, John L. Marakas, Robert H. Ourant.

Number of staff: 2 part-time support.

Employer Identification Number: 316022301

3314
NCR Foundation, The ▼
1700 South Patterson Blvd.
Dayton 45479   (513) 445-2577

Incorporated in 1953 in Ohio.

Donor(s): NCR Corporation.

Financial data: (yr. ended 12/31/83): Assets, $6,845,490 (M); gifts received, $4,000,000; expenditures, $2,261,739, including $2,011,589 for 173 grants (high: $634,853; low: $250; average: $1,000-$50,000) and $217,023 for employee matching gifts.

Purpose and activities: Broad purposes; primarily local giving, with emphasis on higher education, particularly computer science, an employee matching gifts program, and community funds; some support for cultural programs and urban affairs.

Types of support awarded: Operating budgets, annual campaigns, seed money, emergency funds, building funds, equipment, research, scholarship funds, employee related scholarships, employee matching gifts, continuing support.

Limitations: Giving primarily in areas of major company operations, with emphasis on Dayton, OH. No grants to individuals; no loans.

Application information:
  Initial approach: Letter or full proposal
  Copies of proposal: 1
  Deadline(s): None
  Board meeting date(s): March, June, September, and December
  Final notification: 3 to 6 months
  Write: R.F. Beach, Vice-President

Officers: W.S. Anderson,* Chairman; C.E. Exley, Jr., President; R.F. Beach, Vice-President; C.P. Russ III, Secretary; J.G. Keever, Treasurer.

Trustees:* Charles A. Anderson, G.A. Costanzo, Harry Holiday, Jr., Cathleen Synge Morawetz.

Number of staff: 2.

Employer Identification Number: 316030860

3315
Nippert (L & L) Charitable Foundation, The ¤
Fifth and Main Sts.
Cincinnati 45202

Established about 1981.

Donor(s): Louis Nippert, Louise Nippert.

Financial data: (yr. ended 12/31/83): Assets, $3,367,806 (M); expenditures, $175,508, including $157,500 for 23 grants (high: $50,000; low: $500).

Purpose and activities: Primarily local giving, with emphasis on education and conservation; support also for a zoological society.

Limitations: Giving primarily in OH.

Trustee: The Central Trust Company.

Employer Identification Number: 316219757

3316
Nordson Foundation ▼
6125 South Broadway
Elyria 44053   (216) 324-2822

Trust established in 1952 in Ohio.

Donor(s): Walter G. Nord,† Mrs. Walter G. Nord,† Nordson Corp., Evan Nord.

Financial data: (yr. ended 10/31/83): Assets, $18,206,250 (M); gifts received, $491,000; expenditures, $713,734, including $548,616 for 111 grants (high: $40,000; low: $25; average: $2,000-$5,000) and $105,000 for 1 loan.

Purpose and activities: Giving primarily in communities where there are large numbers of Nordson Corporation employees, including Lorain and Cuyahoga counties in Ohio and Atlanta, Georgia; emphasis on projects to assist the disadvantaged and minorities, including giving for secondary and higher education, social service, health service, cultural affairs, and civic activities.

Types of support awarded: Operating budgets, continuing support, annual campaigns, seed money, emergency funds, building funds, equipment, land acquisition, endowment funds, matching funds, consulting services, technical assistance, loans, special projects, publications.

Limitations: Giving limited to Lorain and Cuyahoga Counties, OH, and Atlanta, GA. No grants to individuals, or for deficit financing, research, scholarships and fellowships, or conferences.

Publications: Annual report, program policy statement, application guidelines.

Application information:
  Initial approach: Full proposal, letter, or telephone
  Copies of proposal: 1
  Deadline(s): Submit proposal at least one month before meetings; no set deadline
  Board meeting date(s): January, June, and October
  Final notification: 1 to 3 months
  Write: Jeptha J. Carrell, Executive Director

Officers and Trustees:* Evan W. Nord,* President; Eric T. Nord,* Vice-President; William D. Ginn,* Secretary; Jeptha J. Carrell, Executive Director.

Number of staff: 2 part-time professional; 2 part-time support.

Employer Identification Number: 346539234

3317
O'Bleness (Charles) Foundation No. 3 ¤
c/o Huntington National Bank, Trust Dept.
37 West Broad St.
Columbus 43215   (614) 469-7160

Established in 1963 in Ohio.

Donor(s): Charles O'Bleness,† Charles O'Bleness Foundation No. 1.

Financial data: (yr. ended 12/31/83): Assets, $1,267,435 (M); expenditures, $27,682, including $15,000 for 2 grants of $7,500 each.

Purpose and activities: Local giving to charitable organizations, with emphasis on education.

Limitations: Giving limited to Athens County, OH.

Application information:
  Deadline(s): October 15

Advisors: John Clark, John M. Jones.

Trustee: The Huntington National Bank.

Employer Identification Number: 316042978

3318
Oglebay Norton Foundation
1100 Superior Ave., 21st Fl.
Cleveland 44114   (216) 861-2814
Mailing address: P.O. Box 6508, Cleveland, OH 44101

Trust established in 1952 in Ohio; incorporated in 1959.

Donor(s): Oglebay Norton Company.

Financial data: (yr. ended 12/31/84): Assets, $254,413 (L); gifts received, $500,000; expenditures, $291,676, including $235,983 for 100 grants (high: $93,200; low: $200; average: $500-$1,000) and $54,940 for 64 employee matching gifts.

Purpose and activities: General purposes; primarily local giving, with emphasis on hospitals, social services, higher education, cultural programs, and conservation.

Types of support awarded: Operating budgets, continuing support, annual campaigns, emergency funds, employee matching gifts, research.
Limitations: Giving primarily in Cleveland, OH. No grants to individuals, or for seed money, deficit financing, equipment and materials, land acquisition, matching or challenge grants, scholarships, fellowships, publications, or conferences; no loans.
Application information:
 Initial approach: Full proposal
 Copies of proposal: 1
 Deadline(s): Submit proposal preferably in January or October
 Board meeting date(s): February, May, August, and November
 Final notification: 6 months
 Write: John Limbocker, Jr., Vice-President, Corporate Affairs, Oglebay Norton Company
Officers and Trustees*: Courtney Burton,* President; Fred R. White, Jr.,* Vice-President and Treasurer; Renold D. Thompson,* Vice-President; Kenneth R. Fair, Secretary.
Number of staff: 3 part-time support.
Employer Identification Number: 346513722

3319
Ohio Citizens Trust Company Foundation, The
405 Madison Ave.
P.O. Box 1688
Toledo 43603   (419) 259-7722

Trust established in 1953 in Ohio.
Donor(s): The Ohio Citizens Trust Company.
Financial data: (yr. ended 12/31/83): Assets, $30,092 (L); gifts received, $157,316; expenditures, $130,827, including $130,766 for 28 grants (high: $74,000; low: $100).
Purpose and activities: Broad purposes; primarily local giving, with emphasis on community funds, higher education, youth agencies, and hospitals.
Types of support awarded: Operating budgets, continuing support, annual campaigns, building funds.
Limitations: Giving primarily in northwest OH. No grants to individuals, or for endowment funds, scholarships, fellowships, or matching gifts; no loans.
Application information:
 Initial approach: Proposal
 Copies of proposal: 1
 Deadline(s): Submit proposal preferably in month prior to board meetings; deadlines March 1, June 1, September 1, and December 1
 Board meeting date(s): March, June, September, and December
 Final notification: 1 month
 Write: Mrs. Nancy L. Below, Vice-President
Trustees: Russell R. Berman, Dale L. Dietz, Willard I. Webb III.
Employer Identification Number: 346519189

3320
Ohio Valley Foundation, The
c/o The Fifth Third Bank
Dept. 00850
Cincinnati 45263   (513) 579-5498

Incorporated in 1946 in Ohio.
Donor(s): John J. Rowe.†
Financial data: (yr. ended 12/31/83): Assets, $1,725,314 (M); expenditures, $60,225, including $52,245 for 11 grants (high: $7,650; low: $1,595).
Purpose and activities: General purposes; primarily local giving, with emphasis on education, youth agencies, and cultural programs.
Limitations: Giving primarily in greater Cincinnati, OH. No grants to individuals, or for endowment funds, or operating budgets.
Application information:
 Initial approach: Proposal
 Copies of proposal: 1
 Deadline(s): November 15
 Board meeting date(s): December
 Final notification: Immediately after December meeting
 Write: Carol A. Schneider, Trustee
Trustees: Clement Buenger, Terence Lilly, William S. Rowe, Carol A. Schneider, John W. Warrington.
Number of staff: None.
Employer Identification Number: 316008508

3321
O'Neil (The M. G.) Foundation ¤
One General St.
Akron 44329

Incorporated in 1953 in Ohio.
Donor(s): M.G. O'Neil.
Financial data: (yr. ended 6/30/83): Assets, $1,557,270 (M); expenditures, $69,460, including $69,290 for 69 grants (high: $12,000; low: $10).
Purpose and activities: Primarily local giving, with emphasis on Roman Catholic organizations; some support for a community fund and social agencies.
Limitations: Giving primarily in OH.
Officers and Trustees: M.G. O'Neil, President and Treasurer; T.E. Pittenger, Vice-President and Secretary; J.S. Kearns.
Employer Identification Number: 346516968

3322
O'Neil (The W.) Foundation ▼
One General St.
Akron 44329

Incorporated in 1948 in Ohio.
Donor(s): W. O'Neil,† Grace O'Neil,† John O'Neil, Grace O'Neil Regan, and others.
Financial data: (yr. ended 12/31/82): Assets, $10,517,915 (M); expenditures, $639,673, including $626,238 for 31 grants (high: $297,238; low: $1,000).
Purpose and activities: Broad purposes; grants primarily for Roman Catholic church support and church-related institutions, particularly basic necessities programs (food, shelter, basic medical care, basic education).

Officers and Trustees:* John J. O'Neil,* President; Flora G. Flint, Vice-President, Secretary, and Treasurer; Elaine Brill, P.J. Moran,* Helene O'Neil, Helene Catherine O'Neil, Grace O'Neil Regan,* Vice-Presidents.
Employer Identification Number: 346516969

3323
Parker-Hannifin Foundation, The ¤
17325 Euclid Ave.
Cleveland 44112

Incorporated in 1953 in Ohio.
Donor(s): Parker-Hannifin Corporation.
Financial data: (yr. ended 6/30/83): Assets, $906 (M); gifts received, $460,964; expenditures, $463,652, including $394,506 for 297 grants (high: $24,500; low: $50) and $67,159 for employee matching gifts.
Purpose and activities: General purposes; grants largely for higher education, community funds, hospitals, and youth and health agencies.
Officers and Trustees:* D.S. Manning,* President; P.S. Parker,* P.G. Schloemer,* Vice-Presidents; J.D. Whiteman, Secretary; W.C. Young, Treasurer.
Employer Identification Number: 346555686

3324
Payne Fund, Inc. ¤
810 Hanna Bldg.
Cleveland 44115

Incorporated in 1929 in Ohio.
Donor(s): Frances P. Bolton.†
Financial data: (yr. ended 12/31/83): Assets, $2,398,131 (M); gifts received, $271,166; expenditures, $470,247, including $428,500 for 18 grants (high: $100,000; low: $1,000).
Purpose and activities: To initiate, assist, or conduct research and experiments in education and other activities in behalf of the welfare of mankind; support also for higher education, and cultural programs.
Officers: Thomas C. Bolton,* President; Charles P. Bolton,* Kenyon C. Bolton, III,* Vice-Presidents; Alfred M. Rankin,* Secretary; Charles E. Morgan, Treasurer.
Directors:* John B. Bolton, Phillip P. Bolton, William B. Bolton, David H. Carnahan, Barbara Bolton Gratry, Mary Bolton Hooper, Frederick B. Taylor.
Employer Identification Number: 135563006

3325
Perkins Charitable Foundation, The ¤
401 Euclid Ave., Rm. 480
Cleveland 44114

Trust established in 1950 in Ohio.
Donor(s): Members of the Perkins family.
Financial data: (yr. ended 12/31/83): Assets, $3,360,665 (M); expenditures, $165,452, including $153,000 for 44 grants (high: $17,000; low: $150).
Purpose and activities: Charitable purposes; primarily local giving, with emphasis on higher and secondary education, museums, hospitals, community funds, and conservation.

Limitations: Giving primarily in OH. No grants to individuals.
Trustees: Gertrude P. Oliva, Jacob B. Perkins, Leigh H. Perkins, Ralph Perkins, Jr., Sallie P. Sullivan.
Employer Identification Number: 346549753

3326
Peterloon Foundation ¤
1900 Carew Tower
Cincinnati 45202

Established in 1958.
Donor(s): John J. Emery.†
Financial data: (yr. ended 11/30/83): Assets, $3,433,716 (M); expenditures, $282,820, including $148,862 for grants.
Purpose and activities: Primarily local giving, with emphasis on arts and cultural programs, education, and social agencies.
Limitations: Giving primarily in OH.
Officers: Lela Emery Steele, President and Treasurer; Melissa Emery Lanier, Vice-President; Henry H. Chatfield, Secretary.
Trustees: Ethan Emery, Irene E. Goodale, Paul George Sittenfeld.
Employer Identification Number: 316037801

3327
Peterson (The Thomas F.) Foundation ¤
653 Huntington Bldg.
Cleveland 44115
Application address: 3200 National City Center, Cleveland, OH 44114; Tel.: (216) 621-0200

Established in 1953.
Financial data: (yr. ended 10/31/83): Assets, $1,271,973 (M); gifts received, $45,000; expenditures, $80,504, including $60,100 for 25 grants (high: $10,000; low: $100).
Purpose and activities: Broad purposes; primarily local giving for higher education, cultural programs, and youth agencies.
Types of support awarded: General purposes, scholarship funds.
Limitations: Giving primarily in OH. No grants to individuals.
Application information:
Deadline(s): None
Write: James E. Chapman, Secretary
Officers and Trustees:* Ethel B. Peterson,* President; Barbara P. Ruhlman,* Vice-President; James E. Chapman, Secretary; John D. Drinko,* Treasurer.
Employer Identification Number: 346524958

3328
Philips (Jesse) Foundation ¤
4801 Springfield St.
Dayton 45401

Incorporated in 1960 in Ohio.
Donor(s): Jesse Philips, Philips Industries, Inc., and subsidiaries.
Financial data: (yr. ended 2/28/83): Assets, $4,823,674 (M); gifts received, $701,000; expenditures, $294,790, including $279,831 for 82 grants (high: $65,000; low: $15).

Purpose and activities: Broad purposes; primarily local giving, with emphasis on Jewish welfare funds, hospitals, higher education, cultural programs, social services, and community development.
Limitations: Giving primarily in Dayton, OH.
Application information:
Write: Jesse Philips, President
Officers and Trustees: Jesse Philips, President; Irving Philips, Vice-President; Harold Croghan, Secretary; Milton Roisman, Treasurer.
Employer Identification Number: 316023380

3329
Polk Foundation, The ¤
P.O. Box 967
Dayton 45401

Incorporated in 1942 in Ohio.
Donor(s): Louis F. Polk, Sr., Louis F. Polk, Jr., Mrs. Paula Lillard.
Financial data: (yr. ended 12/31/82): Assets, $2,111,187 (M); expenditures, $112,085, including $87,395 for 60 grants (high: $10,000; low: $10).
Purpose and activities: Broad purposes; primarily local giving, with emphasis on higher and secondary education, military and technological associations, and cultural programs.
Limitations: Giving primarily in OH.
Officers and Trustees: Louis F. Polk, Sr., Chairman, President, and Treasurer; Paula Lillard, Vice-President; Louis F. Polk, Jr., Secretary.
Employer Identification Number: 316028725

3330
Pollock (The William B.) II and Kathryn Challiss Pollock Foundation
c/o Bank One of Eastern Ohio
Six Federal Plaza West
Youngstown 44503

Trust established in 1952 in Ohio.
Donor(s): William B. Pollock II, Kathryn Challiss Pollock.
Financial data: (yr. ended 12/31/84): Assets, $1,570,540 (M); expenditures, $101,538, including $86,353 for 50 grants (high: $20,000; low: $100).
Purpose and activities: Broad purposes; general local giving, with emphasis on hospitals, community funds, Protestant church support, cultural activities, education, youth and health agencies, and population control.
Types of support awarded: Operating budgets, continuing support, annual campaigns, seed money, emergency funds, deficit financing, building funds, equipment, land acquisition, endowment funds, research, special projects, publications, conferences and seminars.
Limitations: Giving limited to the Youngstown, OH area. No grants to individuals, or for matching gifts, or scholarships and fellowships; no loans.
Trustees: Franklin S. Bennett, Jr., Bank One of Eastern Ohio.
Number of staff: None.
Employer Identification Number: 346514079

3331
Premier Industrial Foundation
4500 Euclid Ave.
Cleveland 44103   (216) 391-8300

Trust established in 1953 in Ohio.
Donor(s): Jack N. Mandel, Joseph C. Mandel, Morton L. Mandel, Premier Industrial Corporation, and others.
Financial data: (yr. ended 12/31/83): Assets, $4,305,809 (M); expenditures, $923,002, including $864,679 for 100 grants (high: $125,000; low: $83).
Purpose and activities: To support charitable organizations operating in the health and welfare fields; to assist institutions of higher learning; grants largely for Jewish welfare funds, community funds, and higher education, including some scholarships to relatives of Premier Industrial Corporation employees only.
Types of support awarded: Employee related scholarships.
Application information:
Initial approach: Proposal
Write: Morton L. Mandel, Trustee
Trustees: Jack N. Mandel, Joseph C. Mandel, Morton L. Mandel, Philip S. Sims.
Employer Identification Number: 346522448

3332
Prentiss (The Elisabeth Severance) Foundation ▼
P.O. Box 5756
Cleveland 44101   (216) 575-2760

Trust established in 1944 in Ohio.
Donor(s): Mrs. Elisabeth Severance Prentiss,† Luther L. Miller, Kate W. Miller.
Financial data: (yr. ended 12/31/83): Assets, $30,350,195 (M); expenditures, $2,003,653, including $1,852,047 for 15 grants (high: $833,744; low: $1,000; average: $5,000-$32,000).
Purpose and activities: To promote medical and surgical research and to assist in the acquisition, advancement and dissemination of knowledge of medicine and surgery, and of means of maintaining health; to promote public health; to aid hospitals and health institutions in Cuyahoga County, Ohio, that are organized and operated exclusively for public charitable purposes by contributions for capital improvements or equipment, purchase of rare and expensive drugs, and expenses of operation or maintenence; to improve methods of hospital management and administration; to support programs to make hospital and medical care available to all, especially those of low income.
Types of support awarded: Research, operating budgets, continuing support, seed money, general purposes, building funds, equipment, endowment funds, special projects.
Limitations: Giving primarily in the greater Cleveland, OH, area. No support for national fundraising organizations and foundations. No grants to individuals, or for scholarships and fellowships, or matching gifts; no loans.
Publications: Annual report, application guidelines, program policy statement.
Application information:
Initial approach: Proposal

Copies of proposal: 1
Deadline(s): Submit proposal preferably in April or October; deadline prior to board meetings
Board meeting date(s): June and December
Final notification: 1 week to 10 days following board meetings
Write: Theodore W. Jones, Secretary
Officer: Theodore W. Jones, Secretary.
Managers:* Quentin Alexander, Harry J. Bolwell, William J. DeLancey, William A. Mattie.
Trustee: National City Bank.
Number of staff: None.
Employer Identification Number: 346512433

3333
Procter & Gamble Fund, The ▼ ¤
301 East Sixth St.
Cincinnati 45202   (513) 562-1100
Mailing address: P.O. Box 599, Cincinnati, OH 45201

Incorporated in 1952 in Ohio.
Donor(s): The Procter & Gamble Companies.
Financial data: (yr. ended 6/30/83): Assets, $14,934,852 (M); gifts received, $16,000,000; expenditures, $11,722,876, including $11,559,238 for 776 grants (high: $1,061,250; low: $50; average: $1,000-$60,000).
Purpose and activities: Broad purposes; grants nationally for private higher education and economic and public policy research organizations; support also for community funds, hospitals, youth agencies, cultural institutions, urban affairs, aid to the handicapped, and conservation; generally limited to areas of domestic company operations.
Types of support awarded: Annual campaigns, building funds, continuing support, emergency funds, equipment, land acquisition, matching funds, employee related scholarships, employee matching gifts.
Limitations: Giving limited to areas in the US where the company and its subsidiaries have large concentrations of employees; national giving for higher education and economic and public affairs. No grants to individuals.
Application information: Grant requests from colleges and universities are discouraged, as most grants are initiated by the trustees within specified programs.
Initial approach: Full proposal
Copies of proposal: 1
Deadline(s): None
Board meeting date(s): January, April, July, and October
Final notification: 1 month
Write: B.J. Nolan, Vice-President
Officers: W.W. Abbott,* President; T.C. Collins,* G.S. Gendell,* Vice-Presidents; B.J. Nolan, Vice-President and Secretary; E.H. Eaton, Treasurer.
Trustees:* J.W. Nethercott.
Number of staff: 5 full-time professional; 2 full-time support.
Employer Identification Number: 316019594

3334
Quatman (George B.) Foundation ¤
(also known as American Society of Ephesus, Inc.)
327 N. Elizabeth St.
Lima 45801

Incorporated in 1958.
Financial data: (yr. ended 12/31/82): Assets, $1,281,995 (M); expenditures, $99,215, including $81,525 for 2 grants (high: $47,275; low: $34,250).
Purpose and activities: Grants primarily for Roman Catholic church support and church-related institutions and programs, including restoration and maintenance of religious shrines and monuments, with emphasis on restoration of Christian shrines in and near Ephesus, Turkey; some local charitable giving.
Application information:
Write: George B. Quatman, III, Executive Secretary
Officers: George W. Quatman,* President; Joseph B. Quatman,* Vice-President; George B. Quatman, III, Executive Secretary.
Trustees:* Andrew Barone, Lucille Barone, Anthony J. Bowers.
Employer Identification Number: 346560998

3335
Ranney (P. K.) Foundation ¤
1525 National City Bank Bldg.
Cleveland 44114   (216) 696-4200

Incorporated in 1973 in Ohio.
Financial data: (yr. ended 12/31/83): Assets, $3,066,152 (M); expenditures, $138,365, including $117,000 for 5 grants (high: $90,000; low: $4,000).
Purpose and activities: Support primarily for a local community foundation.
Limitations: Giving primarily in OH.
Application information:
Write: Phillip A. Ranney, Secretary
Officers: Nancy R. Ranney, President; Peter K. Ranney, Vice-President and Treasurer; Phillip A. Ranney, Secretary.
Employer Identification Number: 237343201

3336
Record (George J.) School Foundation
P.O. Box 581
Conneaut 44030   (216) 599-8283

Incorporated in 1958 in Ohio.
Donor(s): George J. Record.†
Financial data: (yr. ended 12/31/83): Assets, $2,362,506 (M); expenditures, $180,393, including $132,097 for 112 grants to individuals.
Purpose and activities: Scholarships to qualified residents of Ashtabula County, Ohio.
Types of support awarded: Student aid.
Limitations: Giving limited to residents of Ashtabula County, OH.
Application information: Applicants must attend an approved private college and complete 6 quarter hours of religious study; formal interview at foundation is required. Application form required.

Deadline(s): May 20 for freshmen, June 20 for upperclassmen
Write: Charles N. Lafferty, President and Executive Director
Officers and Trustees: Charles N. Lafferty, President and Executive Director; Ralph E. Brokaw, Vice-President; Howard T. Glover, Secretary-Treasurer; William H. Gerdes, Harold M. Ladner.
Employer Identification Number: 340830818

3337
Reeves Foundation
232-4 West Third St.
P.O. Box 441
Dover 44622   (216) 364-4660

Trust established in 1966 in Ohio.
Donor(s): Margaret J. Reeves,† Helen F. Reeves,† Samuel J. Reeves.†
Financial data: (yr. ended 12/31/84): Assets, $9,393,585 (M); expenditures, $621,544, including $603,098 for 15 grants (high: $300,000; low: $500).
Purpose and activities: Primarily local giving, with emphasis on historical societies and hospitals; grants also for cultural activities, youth agencies, schools, and church support. Priority given to capital improvement projects.
Types of support awarded: Operating budgets, continuing support, building funds, equipment, matching funds.
Limitations: Giving primarily in OH, with emphasis on the Dover area. No grants to individuals, or for annual campaigns, seed money, emergency funds, deficit financing, land acquisition, renovation projects, endowment funds, scholarships, fellowships, special projects, research, publications, or conferences; no loans.
Application information:
Initial approach: Full proposal
Copies of proposal: 2
Deadline(s): 15th of months prior to those when board meets
Board meeting date(s): Bimonthly starting in February
Final notification: 2 to 7 weeks
Write: W.E. Zimmerman, Executive Director
Officers and Trustees:* Margaret H. Reeves,* President; Thomas R. Scheffer,* Vice-President; W.E. Lieser, Treasurer; W.E. Zimmerman,* Executive Director.
Number of staff: 1 full-time professional; 1 full-time support.
Employer Identification Number: 346575477

3338
Reinberger Foundation, The ▼
5183 Meadow Wood Blvd.
Lyndhurst 44124   (216) 473-5459

Established in 1968 in Ohio.
Donor(s): Clarence T. Reinberger.
Financial data: (yr. ended 12/31/83): Assets, $16,515,140 (M); expenditures, $891,996, including $720,172 for 39 grants (high: $100,000; low: $1,000; average: $1,000-$20,000).

Purpose and activities: Primarily local giving with emphasis on the arts, social welfare, Protestant church support, higher education, and medical research.
Types of support awarded: Operating budgets, continuing support, annual campaigns, building funds, equipment, endowment funds, matching funds, scholarship funds, research, publications, special projects.
Limitations: Giving primarily in OH. No grants to individuals, or for seed money, emergency funds, deficit financing, land acquisition, demonstration projects, or conferences; no loans.
Publications: 990-PF.
Application information:
  Initial approach: Full proposal
  Copies of proposal: 2
  Deadline(s): None
  Board meeting date(s): March, June, September, and December
  Final notification: 6 months
  Write: Robert N. Reinberger, Co-Director
Managers: Richard H. Oman, Secretary; Robert N. Reinberger, William C. Reinberger, Co-Directors; AmeriTrust Company.
Number of staff: 2 part-time professional.
Employer Identification Number: 346574879

3339
Reliance Electric Company Charitable, Scientific and Educational Trust ▼
c/o AmeriTrust Company
900 Euclid Ave.
Cleveland 44101   (216) 687-5713

Trust established in 1952 in Ohio.
Donor(s): Reliance Electric Company.
Financial data: (yr. ended 10/31/82): Assets, $331,198 (M); gifts received, $550,000; expenditures, $749,882, including $745,733 for 760 grants (high: $50,000; low: $50).
Purpose and activities: Broad purposes; grants largely for community funds, higher education, youth agencies, and hospitals; also funds an employee matching gifts program.
Types of support awarded: Employee matching gifts.
Limitations: Giving primarily in OH and IN.
Application information:
  Initial approach: Full proposal
  Copies of proposal: 1
  Board meeting date(s): Monthly
  Write: Ann Booms, Trust Officer
Trustee: AmeriTrust Company (Ann Booms, Trust Officer).
Employer Identification Number: 346505329

3340
Renner Foundation
13700 Shaker Blvd.
Cleveland 44120   (216) 751-2120

Incorporated in 1947 in Ohio as Renner Clinic Foundation.
Donor(s): R. Richard Renner, M.D.†
Financial data: (yr. ended 5/31/84): Assets, $1,765,740 (M); expenditures, $156,089, including $125,000 for 1 grant.

Purpose and activities: Broad purposes; grants for a college, a hospital, and a Christian religious organization.
Limitations: No grants to individuals.
Application information:
  Initial approach: Letter
  Deadline(s): Submit proposal preferably in January or February; deadline March
  Board meeting date(s): April
  Write: Robert R. Renner, President
Officers: Robert R. Renner,* President; John W. Renner,* Vice-President; Richard R. Renner,* Treasurer; Lillian M. Kozan, Secretary; Gary L. Slapnicker, Executive Director.
Trustees:* David F. Percy, Frank E. Percy, Ruth A. Percy, Daniel S. Renner, Jane Renner, Jennie S. Renner, Carlton B. Schnell.
Employer Identification Number: 340684303

3341
Republic Steel Corporation Educational and Charitable Trust ▼
c/o LTV Steel Company
LTV Steel Bldg., P.O. Box 6778
Cleveland 44101   (216) 687-5723

Trust established in 1950 in Ohio.
Donor(s): Republic Steel Corporation.
Financial data: (yr. ended 12/31/83): Assets, $8,934,815 (M); expenditures, $4,382,710, including $958,885 for 141 grants (high: $301,625; low: $25; average: $1,500) and $44,056 for 322 employee matching gifts.
Purpose and activities: Broad purposes; primarily local giving in areas of company operations, largely for community funds, hospitals, higher education, including establishment and maintenance of scholarships, fellowships, and professorships for the study of metallurgy, engineering, mining, and other arts and sciences; support for youth agencies, health agencies, urban renewal, and music.
Types of support awarded: Operating budgets, annual campaigns, building funds, equipment, endowment funds, special projects, research, professorships, fellowships, employee matching gifts, continuing support, scholarship funds.
Limitations: Giving limited to areas of company operations, with emphasis on OH. No support for religious purposes. No grants to individuals, or for seed money, emergency funds, deficit financing, land acquisition, publications, or conferences; no loans.
Publications: Company report, application guidelines, program policy statement.
Application information:
  Initial approach: Full proposal
  Copies of proposal: 1
  Deadline(s): None
  Board meeting date(s): Monthly except in August
  Final notification: 1 to 2 months
  Write: Karen H. Hornak, Corporate Contributions
Officer: Karen H. Hornak.
Trust Committee: E. Bradley Jones, John J. Loftus, William J. Williams.
Trustee: AmeriTrust Company.
Number of staff: 1 full-time professional.
Employer Identification Number: 346505330

3342
Richland County Foundation of Mansfield, Ohio, The
38 South Park St., Rm. 109
Mansfield 44902   (419) 525-3020

Community foundation incorporated in 1945 in Ohio.
Financial data: (yr. ended 12/31/82): Assets, $9,132,160 (M); gifts received, $1,119,285; expenditures, $1,314,638, including $1,259,537 for 195 grants (high: $574,923; low: $20).
Purpose and activities: To promote activities "of a charitable, educational, cultural, recreational and inspirational nature for the people of Richland County"; grants principally for local scholarships (paid directly to colleges), programs for the indigent aged, youth programs, hospital additions, a crippled children's center, and the local community fund.
Types of support awarded: Seed money, building funds, equipment, scholarship funds, operating budgets, emergency funds.
Limitations: Giving primarily in Richland County, OH. No support for sectarian religious purposes. No grants to individuals, or for endowment funds, annual campaigns, fellowships, highly technical or specialized research, operating or maintenance funds, or travel; no loans.
Publications: Annual report, application guidelines, program policy statement.
Application information:
  Initial approach: Full proposal
  Copies of proposal: 1
  Deadline(s): None
  Board meeting date(s): February, May, August, and November
  Final notification: At least 6 weeks
  Write: Mrs. Betty J. Crawford, Executive Director
Officers: Alex B. Curchin,* President; W.R. Cress,* James C. Gorman,* Ralph O. Wise,* Vice-Presidents; Miles Christian,* Secretary and Treasurer; Betty J. Crawford, Executive Director.
Trustees:* Walter C. Stevens, Chairman; Margaret Black, Roger A. Black, Donald Blasius, Samuel H. Campbell, James Curry, M.D., James H. Hoffman, George H. Keyser, Donn Kieft, Walter Kinkel, John A. Mintz, Charles E. Nail, Richard L. Phillips, John Robinson, John Roby, Pamela Siegenthaler, John Fern Yak.
Trustee Banks: Bank One of Mansfield, First Buckeye Bank, Richland Bank.
Number of staff: 1.
Employer Identification Number: 340872883

3343
Richman Brothers Foundation ⌑
1600 East 55th St.
Cleveland 44103   (216) 431-0200

Incorporated in 1932 in Ohio.
Donor(s): Nathan G. Richman, Charles L. Richman, Henry C. Richman.

Financial data: (yr. ended 12/31/83): Assets, $1,420,287 (M); expenditures, $165,082, including $77,670 for 49 grants (high: $29,000; low: $50) and $76,615 for 300 grants to individuals.
Purpose and activities: Primarily to aid the aged, sick, and needy employees and former employees of the Richman Brothers Company; scholarship aid to children of employees; limited giving to large national and local organizations, with emphasis on a community fund, and youth and health agencies.
Types of support awarded: Employee related scholarships, grants to individuals.
Limitations: Giving primarily in OH.
Application information: Application form required.
  Initial approach: Letter
  Deadline(s): November 15 for grants; January 1 for scholarships
Officers: Richard R. Moore, President; Ernest J. Marvar,* Lee R. Kolb, Vice-Presidents; Betty Bratovich, Secretary; Steven Antal, Treasurer.
Trustees:* D.J. Gerstenberger, Leonard G. Steuer.
Employer Identification Number: 346504927

3344
Ritchie (The Charles E. and Mabel M.) Memorial Foundation
c/o First National Bank of Akron
106 South Main St.
Akron 44308   (216) 384-7313

Trust established in 1954 in Ohio.
Donor(s): Mabel M. Ritchie.†
Financial data: (yr. ended 12/31/83): Assets, $3,048,000 (M); expenditures, $220,695, including $196,311 for 35 grants (high: $10,000; low: $500).
Purpose and activities: Broad purposes; grants to institutions within Summit County, including hospitals, youth agencies, and institutions of higher education, as directed by the Advisory Committee.
Limitations: Giving limited to Summit County, OH. No grants to individuals.
Application information:
  Initial approach: Full proposal
  Copies of proposal: 4
  Deadline(s): January 1, April 1, July 1, and October1
  Board meeting date(s): Distribution committee meets last week of January, April, July, and October
  Write: Gregory R. Bean, Trust Officer
Advisory Committee: Edward F. Carter, Kathryn M. Hunter, John D. Ong.
Trustee: First National Bank of Akron (Gregory R. Bean, Vice-President and Trust Officer).
Employer Identification Number: 346500802

3345
Robbins & Myers Foundation ☐
1400 Kettering Tower
Dayton 45423   (513) 222-2610

Incorporated in 1966 in Ohio.
Donor(s): Robbins & Myers, Inc.

Financial data: (yr. ended 8/31/83): Assets, $77,360 (M); expenditures, $110,805, including $109,650 for 45 grants (high: $36,500; low: $100).
Purpose and activities: Giving primarily for community funds, higher education, and cultural programs.
Types of support awarded: Employee matching gifts.
Limitations: Giving primarily in areas of company operations. No grants to individuals.
Application information:
  Initial approach: Letter
  Deadline(s): None
  Write: Fred G. Wall, President
Officers and Managers: Fred G. Wall, President; G.M. Walker, Vice-President; J.J. Mulligan, Secretary; H.O. Royer, Treasurer.
Employer Identification Number: 316064597

3346
Roscoe Village Foundation
381 Hill St.
Coshocton 43812   (614) 622-2218

Trust established in 1952 in Ohio.
Donor(s): The Montgomery family.
Financial data: (yr. ended 12/31/83): Assets, $3,897,761 (M); gifts received, $1,229,386; expenditures, $982,934, including $279,967 for 1 foundation-administered program.
Purpose and activities: A private operating foundation; all funds currently committed to the restoration of a historic canal town.
Limitations: Giving limited to the Roscoe Village, OH.
Publications: Newsletter.
Application information: Funds currently committed.
  Write: Joel L. Hampton, Executive Director
Officers: Samuel C. Clow,* President; John A. Beals,* Vice-President; Joel L. Hampton, Secretary and Executive Director; Wallace B. Saver,* Treasurer.
Trustees:* Edmund S. Bell, Jr., Robin Coffman, Steven L. Foster, Fred Johnston, Jean McConnell, Kay Metz, Edward Montgomery, Frances Montgomery, Daniel S. Moody, Leo Prindle, Robert B. Robinson, Wallace B. Sauer, Jerome Stenner, Lorena Sims, Richard Wolford.
Employer Identification Number: 316022295

3347
Rosenthal (The Samuel) Foundation ☐
c/o Leighton A. Rosenthal
1768 East 25th St.
Cleveland 44114   (216) 771-4040

Trust established in 1959 in Ohio.
Donor(s): Work Wear Corporation.
Financial data: (yr. ended 3/31/83): Assets, $4,118,822 (M); expenditures, $342,585, including $333,743 for 40 grants (high: $200,000; low: $25).

Purpose and activities: Broad purposes; grants for general, secular, Hebrew, and Jewish education; upgrading and increasing availability of vocational education; hospitals, medical research organizations, homes for the infirm and aged; health and welfare funds, including United Appeal and Jewish welfare funds; and cultural organizations.
Types of support awarded: Scholarship funds, general purposes, research.
Application information:
  Write: Charlotte R. Kramer, Trustee
Trustees: Cynthia R. Boardman, Jane R. Horvitz, Charlotte R. Kramer, Leighton A. Rosenthal.
Employer Identification Number: 346558832

3348
Ross (The James & Edith) Foundation ☐
P.O. Box 767
Conneaut 44030

Trust established in 1963 in Ohio.
Donor(s): James Ross,† Edith L. Ross.
Financial data: (yr. ended 12/31/82): Assets, $1,533,033 (M); expenditures, $138,027, including $128,000 for 7 grants (high: $100,000; low: $1,000).
Purpose and activities: Broad purposes; support largely for higher educational, medical, and charitable organizations in the United States and Israel; grants also for local Jewish welfare funds and intercultural relations.
Application information:
  Initial approach: Letter
  Copies of proposal: 1
  Board meeting date(s): Semiannually and as required
  Write: Michael Chait, President
Officers and Trustees: Michael Chait, President; Edith L. Ross, Vice-President and Treasurer; Arthur N.K. Friedman, Secretary; Deborah Bach, Robert Berns, Sulana Ross Chait.
Employer Identification Number: 346565430

3349
Rupp (Fran and Warren) Foundation ☐
1001 Bank One Bldg., Box 1288
Mansfield 44902   (419) 522-2345

Established in 1977.
Donor(s): Fran Rupp, Warren Rupp.
Financial data: (yr. ended 12/31/83): Assets, $1,680,971 (M); expenditures, $154,209, including $131,000 for 7 grants (high: $102,000; low: $1,000).
Purpose and activities: Primarily local giving, with emphasis on the arts and social agencies.
Types of support awarded: General purposes.
Limitations: Giving primarily in OH. No grants to individuals.
Application information:
  Initial approach: Letter
  Deadline(s): None
  Write: Donald Smith, Secretary
Officers and Trustees: Warren Rupp, President; Fran Rupp, Vice-President; Donald Smith, Secretary.
Employer Identification Number: 341230690

3350
Russell (Josephine S.) Charitable Trust
c/o Central Trust Company
P.O. Box 1198
Cincinnati 45201   (513) 651-8377

Trust established in 1976 in Ohio.
Donor(s): Josephine Schell Russell.†
Financial data: (yr. ended 6/30/84): Assets,
$3,317,373 (M); expenditures, $270,512,
including $270,068 for 32 grants (high:
$30,000; low: $1,000; average: $5,000-
$10,000).
Purpose and activities: Broad purposes; local
giving only, with emphasis on higher education
and aid to the handicapped; support also for
social agencies, cultural programs, and health.
Types of support awarded: Seed money,
equipment, land acquisition, matching funds,
special projects, publications.
Limitations: Giving limited to the greater
Cincinnati, OH, area. No grants to individuals,
or for endowment or emergency funds,
operating budgets, continuing support, annual
campaigns, deficit financing, scholarships, or
conferences; no loans.
Publications: Application guidelines.
Application information:
Initial approach: Letter, telephone, or
proposal
Copies of proposal: 7
Deadline(s): 1 month prior to board meetings
Board meeting date(s): Alternate months
beginning with January
Final notification: 3 months
Write: Mrs. Nancy C. Gurney, Exec. Assistant
Trustee: Central Trust Company.
Number of staff: 1 full-time professional.
Employer Identification Number: 316195446

3351
Saint Gerard Foundation ⌘
1220 Huntington Bldg.
Cleveland 44115

Donor(s): Mooney Chemicals, Inc.
Financial data: (yr. ended 12/31/83): Assets,
$879,716 (M); gifts received, $187,200;
expenditures, $230,775, including $226,605
for 204 grants (high: $33,039; low: $10).
Purpose and activities: Giving primarily for
conservative public policy organizations and
Roman Catholic church support, including
groups concerned with social isues; support
also for higher and secondary education.
Application information:
Write: William E. Reichard, Secretary
Officers: James B. Mooney, President and
Treasurer; Elizabeth C. Mooney, George Smith,
Vice-Presidents; William E. Reichard, Secretary.
Employer Identification Number: 346574667

3352
**Sapirstein (The Jacob) Foundation of
Cleveland** ⌘
10500 American Rd.
Cleveland 44144   (216) 252-7300

Incorporated in 1952 in Ohio.
Donor(s): Jacob Sapirstein.

Financial data: (yr. ended 5/31/84): Assets,
$14,281,325 (M); expenditures, $446,448,
including $400,950 for 69 grants (high:
$106,310; low: $100).
Purpose and activities: Broad purposes; giving
locally, nationally, and internationally for
Jewish welfare funds and secondary and higher
religious education.
Types of support awarded: General purposes.
Limitations: No grants to individuals, or for
scholarships or fellowships; no loans.
Application information:
Initial approach: Letter
Copies of proposal: 1
Deadline(s): Submit proposal in April
Board meeting date(s): Quarterly
Write: Irving I. Stone, President
Officers and Trustees: Irving I. Stone,
President; Morris S. Stone, Vice-President and
Secretary; Morry Weiss, Vice-President and
Treasurer.
Employer Identification Number: 346548007

3353
Schmidlapp (Charlotte R.) Fund
c/o The Fifth Third Bank
Dept. 00850, Fifth Third Center
Cincinnati 45263   (513) 579-5237
Mailing address: Fourth and Walnut Bldg.,
Cincinnati, OH 45202

Trust established in 1907 in Ohio.
Donor(s): Jacob G. Schmidlapp.†
Financial data: (yr. ended 12/31/83): Assets,
$9,880,000 (M); gifts received, $100,000;
expenditures, $648,000, including $377,000
for 228 grants to individuals.
Purpose and activities: "To aid young girls in
the preparation for womanhood, by bringing
their minds and hearts under the influence of
education, relieving their bodies from disease,
suffering or constraint and assisting them to
establish themselves in life." Grants for
scholarships for further education to assist
women preferably between 16 and 25 years of
age; preference given to residents of greater
Cincinnati who are recommended by high
school counselors; participants assume moral
obligation to return the money when able to do
so.
Types of support awarded: Student aid.
Limitations: Giving primarily in Cincinnati,
OH. No grants for building or endowment
funds, operating budgets, or special projects.
Publications: Application guidelines.
Application information:
Initial approach: Letter
Copies of proposal: 1
Deadline(s): March 1
Board meeting date(s): May
Write: Charles Kirby Bennett, Administrative
Officer
Trustee: The Fifth Third Bank (Charles Kirby
Bennett, Administrative Officer).
Employer Identification Number: 310532641

3354
Schmidlapp (Jacob G.) Trust No. 1 ▼
c/o The Fifth Third Bank
Dept. 00850, Fifth Third Center
Cincinnati 45263   (513) 579-5479
Mailing address: Fourth and Walnut Bldg.,
Cincinnati, OH 45202

Trust established in 1927 in Ohio.
Donor(s): Jacob G. Schmidlapp.†
Financial data: (yr. ended 9/30/84): Assets,
$18,593,168 (M); expenditures, $1,233,801,
including $1,159,759 for 29 grants (high:
$300,000; low: $5,000; average: $5,000-
$50,000).
Purpose and activities: Primarily local giving
for the relief of sickness, suffering, and distress,
and for care of young children or the helpless
and afflicted.
Types of support awarded: Seed money,
building funds, equipment, research, matching
funds, land acquisition, conferences and
seminars, endowment funds.
Limitations: Giving primarily in the greater
Cincinnati, OH, area, extending into KY and
possibly IN. No support for religious
purposes. No grants to individuals, or for
annual campaigns, emergency funds, deficit
financing, general support, scholarships,
fellowships, operating budgets, or continuing
support; no loans.
Publications: Annual report, program policy
statement, application guidelines.
Application information:
Initial approach: Letter, telephone, or
proposal
Copies of proposal: 2
Deadline(s): 10th of month preceeding board
meetings
Board meeting date(s): March, June,
September, and December
Final notification: Middle of months in
which board meets
Write: John W. Bales, Vice-President and
Trust Officer, The Fifth Third Bank
Trustee: The Fifth Third Bank (John W. Bales,
Vice-President and Trust Officer).
Number of staff: None.
Employer Identification Number: 316019680

3355
Schmidlapp (Jacob G.) Trust No. 2 ⌘
c/o The Fifth Third Bank
Dept. 00850, Fifth Third Center
Cincinnati 45263   (513) 579-4264
Mailing address: Fourth and Walnut Bldg.,
Cincinnati, OH 45202

Trust established in 1916 in Ohio.
Donor(s): Jacob G. Schmidlapp.†
Financial data: (yr. ended 12/31/83): Assets,
$1,518,871 (M); expenditures, $67,898,
including $60,244 for 14 grants (high: $6,770;
low: $500).
Purpose and activities: Grants for education,
with emphasis on capital programs for higher
educational institutions and cultural programs,
primarily in the greater Cincinnati area.
Limitations: Giving primarily in the greater
Cincinnati, OH, area. No grants to individuals,
or for endowment funds, operating budgets,
scholarships, or fellowships; no loans.

Publications: Program policy statement, application guidelines.
Application information:
Initial approach: Letter
Copies of proposal: 1
Board meeting date(s): March, June, September, and December
Write: Lois A. Fox, Administrative Officer
Trustee: The Fifth Third Bank.
Employer Identification Number: 316020109

3356
Scioto County Area Foundation, The
48 National Bank Bldg.
Portsmouth 45662   (614) 354-4612

Community foundation established in 1974 in Ohio.
Financial data: (yr. ended 12/31/82): Assets, $1,677,581 (M); gifts received, $44,672; expenditures, $195,816, including $172,657 for 29 grants.
Purpose and activities: Local giving for charitable purposes to benefit the citizens of Scioto County.
Types of support awarded: Seed money, equipment, matching funds, scholarship funds, special projects, publications, conferences and seminars.
Limitations: Giving limited to Scioto County, OH. No grants to individuals, or for operating budgets, continuing support, annual campaigns, emergency funds, deficit financing, building funds, land acquisition, endowments, consulting services, technical assistance, foundation-managed projects, professorships, internships, exchange programs, fellowships, program support, or research; no loans.
Publications: Application guidelines, annual report.
Application information: Application form required.
Write: Mr. Howard H. Harcha, Jr., Chairman
Officer: Howard H. Harcha, Jr., Chairman.
Number of staff: 1 part-time support.
Employer Identification Number: 237373780

3357
SCOA Foundation Inc. ⌗
33 North High St.
Columbus 43215   (614) 221-7262

Established in 1969 in Ohio.
Donor(s): SCOA Industries, Inc.
Financial data: (yr. ended 1/31/84): Assets, $5,735,134 (M); gifts received, $1,070,862; expenditures, $631,776, including $617,793 for 131 grants (high: $112,000; low: $26).
Purpose and activities: Grants primarily for Jewish welfare and community funds, support also for higher education, hospitals, and cultural activities.
Application information:
Deadline(s): None
Write: Larry Voelker, Vice-President
Officers: Larry Voelker, Vice-President and Treasurer; William K. Friend, Secretary.
Trustees: Herbert H. Schiff, Chairman; Gene E. Engleman, George R. Friese, Herbert H. Goldberger, Neil Papiano.
Employer Identification Number: 237002220

3358
Scott Fetzer Foundation, The ⌗
(formerly Scott and Fetzer Foundation)
28800 Clemens Rd.
Westlake 44145

Established in 1967 in Ohio.
Donor(s): The Scott Fetzer Company.
Financial data: (yr. ended 11/30/83): Assets, $1,181,863 (M); gifts received, $377,359; expenditures, $404,835, including $401,744 for 272 grants (high: $25,000; low: $50).
Purpose and activities: General giving, with emphasis on community funds, higher education, medical facilities, and social agencies in geographic areas where Scott Fetzer has facilities.
Types of support awarded:
Employee matching gifts.
Limitations: Giving primarily in areas of company operations. No support for organizations primarily supported by United Way funds, sectarian organizations, preschool, primary, or secondary schools. No grants to individuals, or for endowment or capital funds, travel, tickets, or advertising.
Publications: Program policy statement, application guidelines.
Officers: G.A. Childress, President; K.J. Semelsberger, Vice-President; Ralph C. Weber, Secretary; Kenneth D. Hughes, Treasurer.
Employer Identification Number: 346596076

3359
Scripps-Howard Foundation, The ▼
1100 Central Trust Tower
Cincinnati 45202   (513) 977-3037

Incorporated in 1962 in Ohio.
Donor(s): The E.W. Scripps Co., and Scripps Howard executives and employees.
Financial data: (yr. ended 7/31/83): Assets, $7,341,090 (M); gifts received, $1,462,249; expenditures, $1,097,763, including $618,260 for 132 grants (high: $375,000; low: $150; average: $1,000) and $308,885 for 240 grants to individuals.
Purpose and activities: The improvement and advancement of journalism through education and research, and to support the First Amendment; grants to colleges and universities for journalism-major scholarship programs; support also for journalism scholarship grants to individuals seeking through higher education to improve their fitness for careers in mass communications. Also grants for special journalism educational projects and National Journalism Awards.
Types of support awarded: Scholarship funds, student aid, special projects.
Limitations: Giving primarily in areas of company operations for scholarship and college grants and nationally for special grants and awards; national giving only for journalism and communications endeavors. No support for private foundations; generally no special grants to public causes, public radio and television, campus newspapers, governmental studies, or international projects. No grants for seminars, operating funds, capital campaigns, or annual campaigns.

Publications: Annual report, informational brochure, program policy statement, application guidelines.
Application information: Information on journalism award contests available from foundation. Application form required.
Initial approach: Letter or full proposal for journalism schools seeking scholarships; full proposal for any special grants
Deadline(s): Submit proposal in January for special grants; deadlines December 20 for individuals; April 15 for journalism schools
Board meeting date(s): Semiannually
Final notification: May 15 for scholarships; July or August for all other grants
Write: Jacques A. Caldwell, President
Officers: Jacques A. Caldwell,* President; Leo Hirtl,* Naoma Lowensohn,* David Stolberg,* James H. Wagner,* Vice-Presidents; D.J. Castellini, Secretary and Treasurer.
Trustees:* Matt Meyer, Chairman; Richard R. Campbell, Edward D. Cervenak, Jane D. Flatt, Mori E. Greiner, Jr., David Hendin, Banks Leonard, Robert R. Regalbuto, Albert J. Schottelkotte, Robert P. Scripps, M.C. Watters.
Number of staff: 1 full-time professional; 1 part-time professional; 1 full-time support.
Employer Identification Number: 316025114

3360
Sears Family Foundation, The
907 Park Bldg.
Cleveland 44114   (216) 241-6434

Trust established in 1949 in Ohio.
Donor(s): Anna L. Sears,† Lester M. Sears,† Ruth P. Sears,† Mary Ann Swetland.†
Financial data: (yr. ended 12/31/83): Assets, $1,996,333 (M); gifts received, $19,920; expenditures, $127,153, including $116,200 for 34 grants (high: $38,000; low: $100; average: $250-$30,000).
Purpose and activities: Local giving for health, education, welfare and environmental projects.
Types of support awarded: General purposes, operating budgets, continuing support, annual campaigns, seed money, emergency funds, deficit financing, building funds, equipment, land acquisition, matching funds, research.
Limitations: Giving limited to the Cleveland, OH area. No grants to individuals, or for scholarships or fellowships; no loans.
Publications: 990-PF.
Application information:
Initial approach: Letter
Copies of proposal: 1
Deadline(s): Submit proposal preferably before December
Board meeting date(s): As needed
Final notification: 60 days
Write: David W. Swetland, Trustee
Officer and Trustees: Ruth Swetland Eppig, Secretary; David Sears Swetland, David W. Swetland.
Number of staff: None.
Employer Identification Number: 346522143

3361
Semple (The Louise Taft) Foundation ▽

1800 First National Bank Center
Cincinnati 45202 (513) 381-2838
Grant application office: c/o Dudley S. Taft,
1718 Young St., Cincinnati, OH 45210

Incorporated in 1941 in Ohio.
Donor(s): Louise Taft Semple.†
Financial data: (yr. ended 12/31/82): Assets,
$7,766,683 (M); expenditures, $856,950,
including $780,711 for 31 grants (high:
$350,000; low: $2,000).
Purpose and activities: Broad purposes;
primarily local giving, with emphasis on the
arts, higher and secondary education, and a
community fund.
Types of support awarded: Building funds,
endowment funds, scholarship funds,
fellowships, professorships, matching funds.
Limitations: Giving primarily in Cincinnati,
OH. No grants to individuals, or for general
purposes, or research; no loans.
Application information:
  Initial approach: Letter
  Deadline(s): None
  Board meeting date(s): April, July, October,
    and December
  Final notification: 3 months
  Write: Dudley S. Taft, President
Officers: Dudley S. Taft,* President; Robert
Taft, Jr.,* Vice-President; James R. Bridgeland,
Jr.,* Secretary; Norma Gentzler, Treasurer.
Trustees:* Mrs. John T. Lawrence, Jr., Walter
L. Lingle, Jr., Lloyd B. Taft, Mrs. Robert A. Taft,
II.
Number of staff: None.
Employer Identification Number: 310653526

3362
Shafer (The Richard H. and Ann) Foundation ¤

Eight East Long St., Rm. 400
Columbus 43215 (614) 224-8111

Donor(s): Richard A. Shafer,† Ohio Road
Paving Company.
Financial data: (yr. ended 12/31/83): Assets,
$2,793,652 (M); gifts received, $5,000;
expenditures, $189,273, including $184,100
for 28 grants (high: $35,000; low: $100).
Purpose and activities: Primarily local giving,
with emphasis on hospitals and health
agencies, higher education, cultural programs,
and social agencies.
Limitations: Giving limited to OH.
Application information:
  Deadline(s): December 1
  Write: F.L. Shafer, Manager
Trustees: F.L. Shafer, Manager; Homer W. Lee,
John Reese.
Employer Identification Number: 316029095

3363
Sheadle (Jasper H.) Trust

c/o The Ameritrust Company, Box 5937
900 Euclid Ave.
Cleveland 44101 (216) 687-5360

Trust established in 1917 in Ohio.

Donor(s): Jasper H. Sheadle.†
Financial data: (yr. ended 12/31/82): Assets,
$1,621,391 (M); expenditures, $140,888,
including $128,051 for 37 grants to individuals
(high: $5,900; low: $900).
Purpose and activities: To provide pensions
for aged couples or aged women only, who are
residing in Cuyahoga or Mahoning counties.
Types of support awarded: Grants to
individuals.
Limitations: Giving limited to Cuyahoga and
Mahoning counties, OH.
Application information: Applicants usually
nominated by outside organizations.
Managers: Robert S. Kessler, Edward T.
Bartlett, Rt. Rev. James R. Moodey, Francis J.
Talty.
Trustee: The Ameritrust Company (Robert S.
Kessler, Vice-President).
Employer Identification Number: 346506457

3364
Sherman-Standard Register Foundation ¤

626 Albany St.
Dayton 45408

Incorporated in 1955 in Ohio.
Donor(s): Standard Register Company.
Financial data: (yr. ended 11/30/83): Assets,
$497,236 (M); gifts received, $100,000;
expenditures, $110,267, including $108,962
for 89 grants (high: $40,000; low: $25).
Purpose and activities: Primarily local giving,
with emphasis on community funds, higher
education, youth agencies, and health.
Limitations: Giving primarily in OH.
Officers: William P. Sherman, President; J.L.
Sherman, Vice-President; Otto F. Stock,
Secretary; W.J. Byrne, Treasurer.
Employer Identification Number: 316026027

3365
Sherwick Fund, The

c/o The Cleveland Foundation
1400 Hanna Bldg.
Cleveland 44115 (216) 861-3810

Incorporated in 1953 in Ohio.
Donor(s): John Sherwin, Frances Wick Sherwin.
Financial data: (yr. ended 12/31/82): Assets,
$5,326,788 (M); expenditures, $265,671,
including $232,451 for 40 grants (high:
$25,000; low: $400; average: $1,000-$5,000).
Purpose and activities: A supporting fund of
The Cleveland Foundation. Broad purposes;
primarily local giving, emphasis on youth
agencies, health, education, social services,
cultural programs, and community funds.
Types of support awarded: Seed money.
Limitations: Giving limited to the greater
Cleveland, OH area and Lake County. No
grants to individuals, or for endowment funds,
general operating budgets, or deficit financing;
no loans.
Publications: Annual report, application
guidelines, program policy statement.
Application information:
  Initial approach: Full proposal or letter of
    inquiry
  Copies of proposal: 2

Deadline(s): April 1 and October 1
Board meeting date(s): Usually in June and
  December
Final notification: 1 month after board meets
Write: Patricia Jansen Doyle, Secretary
Officers: Stanley C. Pace,* President; Steven
A. Minter, John Sherwin, Jr.,* Vice-Presidents;
Patricia Jansen Doyle, Secretary-Treasurer.
Trustees:* John Sherwin, Chairman; Harvey G.
Oppmann, Homer C. Wadsworth.
Employer Identification Number: 346526395

3366
Sherwin-Williams Foundation, The

101 Prospect Ave., N.W., 12th Fl.
Cleveland 44115 (216) 566-2511

Incorporated in 1964 in Ohio.
Donor(s): The Sherwin-Williams Company.
Financial data: (yr. ended 12/31/84): Assets,
$2,276 (L); gifts received, $476,000;
expenditures, $480,210, including $439,302
for 140 grants (high: $100,000; low: $250;
average: $1,000-$5,000) and $40,298 for 264
employee matching gifts.
Purpose and activities: Broad purposes;
support for higher education, community funds,
hospitals, youth agencies, and civic and cultural
organizations, mainly in areas of company
headquarters and plants.
Types of support awarded: Operating
budgets, continuing support, building funds,
equipment, matching funds, employee
matching gifts.
Limitations: Giving primarily in areas of
company headquarters and plants. No support
for institutions of higher education. No grants
to individuals, or for endowment funds, annual
campaigns, seed money, emergency funds,
deficit financing, land acquisition, special
projects, research, publications, scholarships,
fellowships, or conferences; no loans.
Application information:
  Initial approach: Telephone or letter
  Copies of proposal: 1
  Deadline(s): Submit proposal preferably in
    January, April, July, or October
  Board meeting date(s): March, June,
    September, and December
  Final notification: 6 months
  Write: Barbara Gadosik, Director, Corporate
    Contributions
Officers and Trustees:* John G. Breen,*
President and Chief Executive Officer; A.D.
Childs, F.T. Krotine, A.D. Maine, Vice-
Presidents; T.A. Commes,* Secretary and
Treasurer.
Number of staff: 1 full-time professional; 1
part-time support.
Employer Identification Number: 346555476

3367
Shinnick (William M.) Educational Fund ¤

534 Market St.
Zanesville 43701

Established in 1923 in Ohio.
Donor(s): William M. Shinnick, Eunice Hale
Buckingham.

Financial data: (yr. ended 6/30/83): Assets, $1,788,803 (M); gifts received, $75,396; expenditures, $176,617, including $426 for 1 grant, $59,600 for 23 grants to individuals and $206,000 for 175 loans.
Purpose and activities: Loans and scholarships to students for educational purposes and grants for higher education.
Types of support awarded: Student aid.
Limitations: Giving limited to Muskingum, OH.
Officers: Hazel L. Butterfield,* President; Annabelle Kinney, Secretary.
Trustees:* Ruth Galek, Harold Gottlieb, J. Lincoln Knapp, Norma Littud.
Employer Identification Number: 314394168

3368
Smith (The Emerson Sterling) Charitable Trust ⊐
101 E. Main St.
P.O. Box 167
Ravenna 44266

Established in 1980.
Financial data: (yr. ended 3/31/82): Assets, $448,300 (M); expenditures, $104,740, including $100,833 for 19 grants (high: $12,500; low: $100).
Purpose and activities: Primarily local giving, with emphasis on community development and civic affairs, and on Roman Catholic church support.
Limitations: Giving primarily in Ravenna, OH.
Trustee: Herbert W. Kane.
Employer Identification Number: 341304235

3369
Smith (Jack J.), Jr. Charitable Trust
c/o Central Trust Company, N.A.
P.O. Box 1198
Cincinnati 45201   (513) 651-8377

Established in 1972 in Ohio.
Donor(s): Jack J. Smith, Jr.†
Financial data: (yr. ended 9/30/84): Assets, $2,336,983 (M); gifts received, $7,779; expenditures, $207,154, including $206,011 for 26 grants (high: $25,000; low: $606; average: $5,000-$10,000).
Purpose and activities: Local giving for the benefit of needy or handicapped children.
Types of support awarded: Seed money, equipment, land acquisition, matching funds, special projects, publications.
Limitations: Giving limited to the greater Cincinnati, OH, area. No grants to individuals, or for operating budgets, continuing support, annual campaigns, emergency funds, deficit financing, endowment funds, scholarships, research, or conferences; no loans.
Publications: Application guidelines.
Application information:
   Initial approach: Letter, telephone, or full proposal
   Copies of proposal: 7
   Deadline(s): 1st of January, April, June, August, October, and December
   Board meeting date(s): Bimonthly beginning in January
   Final notification: 3 months
   Write: Nancy C. Gurney, Executive Assistant

Trustees: Thomas J. Reis, The Central Trust Company, N.A.
Number of staff: 1 full-time professional.
Employer Identification Number: 310912146

3370
Smith (The Kelvin and Eleanor) Foundation
1100 National City Bank Bldg.
Cleveland 44114   (216) 566-5612

Incorporated in 1955 in Ohio.
Donor(s): Kelvin Smith.†
Financial data: (yr. ended 10/31/83): Assets, $2,359,012 (M); expenditures, $190,441, including $182,750 for 50 grants (high: $20,000; low: $500; average: $500-$20,000).
Purpose and activities: Broad purposes; primarily local giving, with emphasis on education, cultural affairs, hospitals and conservation.
Types of support awarded: Operating budgets, continuing support, annual campaigns, seed money, building funds, equipment.
Limitations: Giving primarily in the greater Cleveland, OH area. No grants to individuals, or for endowment funds, scholarships or fellowships, or matching gifts; no loans.
Publications: Application guidelines.
Application information:
   Initial approach: Letter
   Copies of proposal: 2
   Deadline(s): Submit proposal in March or August; deadline April and September
   Board meeting date(s): May and October
   Final notification: 2 to 3 months
   Write: Donald F. Seaburn, Jr., Assistant Secretary
Officers and Trustees: Ralph S. Tyler, Jr., President; John L. Dampeer, Mrs. R. Preston Nash, Jr., Douglas W. Richardson, Ellen Stirn, Mrs. Howard F. Stirn.
Number of staff: None.
Employer Identification Number: 346555349

3371
South Waite Foundation, The
AmeriTrust Company
900 Euclid Ave.
Cleveland 44101

Incorporated in 1953 in Ohio.
Donor(s): Francis M. Sherwin,† Margaret H. Sherwin.
Financial data: (yr. ended 12/31/82): Assets, $1,442,968 (M); expenditures, $111,237, including $105,700 for 30 grants (high: $25,000; low: $800).
Purpose and activities: Broad purposes; grants usually to those local organizations foundation is familiar with; emphasis on community funds, the arts, secondary education, and medical research.
Limitations: Giving limited to the Cleveland, OH area. No grants to individuals, or for scholarships.
Officers and Trustees: Brian Sherwin, President; Margaret H. Sherwin, Vice-President; Donald W. Gruettner, Secretary and Treasurer; Sherman Dye, George Karch.
Employer Identification Number: 346526411

3372
Standard Products Foundation, The ⊐
2130 West 110th St.
Cleveland 44102

Incorporated in 1953 in Ohio.
Donor(s): Standard Products Company.
Financial data: (yr. ended 6/30/83): Assets, $3,381,526 (M); expenditures, $110,566, including $106,263 for 88 grants (high: $53,155; low: $10).
Purpose and activities: Broad purposes; emphasis on community funds, higher education, hospitals and cultural programs.
Application information:
   Write: James E. Chapman, Secretary
Officers and Trustees: James S. Reid, Jr., President; R.C. Jacob, Vice-President; James E. Chapman, Secretary; J.A. Robinson, Treasurer; E.B. Brandon, John T. Frieg, Werner D. Mueller.
Employer Identification Number: 346525047

3373
Stark County Foundation, The ▼
515 Third St., N.W.
Canton 44703   (216) 454-3426

Community foundation established in 1963 in Ohio by resolution and declaration of trust.
Financial data: (yr. ended 12/31/84): Assets, $10,779,000 (M); gifts received, $412,000; expenditures, $1,014,000, including $613,000 for 48 grants (high: $100,000; low: $200; average: $5,000-$25,000) and $53,500 for 61 loans.
Purpose and activities: To maintain the sound health and general welfare of the citizens of Canton and its immediate environs through support for civic improvement programs, including the Newmarket Project for redevelopment of downtown Canton; hospitals; and educational institutions.
Types of support awarded: Seed money, emergency funds, building funds, equipment, land acquisition, matching funds, scholarship funds, special projects, research, conferences and seminars, student aid, consulting services, technical assistance.
Limitations: Giving limited to Stark County, OH. No grants to individuals, or for endowment funds, operating budgets, continuing support, annual campaigns, publications, or deficit financing; no loans (except to Stock County college students).
Publications: Annual report, program policy statement, application guidelines.
Application information:
   Initial approach: Letter or full proposal
   Copies of proposal: 8
   Deadline(s): None
   Board meeting date(s): Monthly
   Final notification: 60 to 90 days
   Write: William K. Wilson, Executive Secretary
Officer: William K. Wilson, Executive Secretary.
Distribution Committee: Thomas A. Schauer, Chairman; Virginia A. Fellows, Donald A. Hart, Dr. Thomas H. Hoover, Harry Mestel.

Trustees: AmeriTrust Company of Stark County, The Central Trust Company of North Eastern Ohio, First National Bank in Massillon, First National City Bank of Alliance, The Harter Bank & Trust Company, The United National Bank & Trust Company.
Number of staff: 1 full-time professional; 1 part-time professional; 1 full-time support.
Employer Identification Number: 340943665

3374
Sterkel (Justine) Trust
c/o Bank One of Mansfield
28 Park Ave. West
Mansfield 44902

Trust established in 1966 in Ohio.
Donor(s): Justine Sterkel.†
Financial data: (yr. ended 12/31/83): Assets, $2,292,835 (M); expenditures, $118,280, including $95,797 for 5 grants (high: $46,250; low: $1,500).
Purpose and activities: Primarily local giving; support largely for health and social agencies.
Limitations: Giving primarily in OH.
Trustees: H. Eugene Ryan, Bank One of Mansfield.
Employer Identification Number: 346576810

3375
Stocker Foundation, The ▼
P.O. Box 2118
Lorain 44054   (216) 288-4581

Incorporated in 1979 in Ohio.
Donor(s): Beth K. Stocker.
Financial data: (yr. ended 9/30/84): Assets, $5,701,226 (M); gifts received, $600,000; expenditures, $595,436, including $567,892 for 71 grants (high: $50,000; low: $250; average: $1,000-$7,000).
Purpose and activities: Primarily local giving, with emphasis on short term youth development programs, social service agencies offering solutions to specific problems, education, including higher education, aid to the handicapped, and cultural programs.
Types of support awarded: Operating budgets, continuing support, seed money, emergency funds, building funds, equipment, endowment funds, matching funds, scholarship funds.
Limitations: Giving primarily in Lorain County, OH and southern AZ. No support for religious organizations for religious purposes. No grants to individuals, or for annual campaigns, or deficit financing; no loans.
Publications: Application guidelines.
Application information:
Initial approach: Telephone, letter, or full proposal
Copies of proposal: 4
Deadline(s): May 15 and December 1
Board meeting date(s): Summer and mid-winter
Final notification: 1 month after board meetings
Write: Sara Jane Norton, Secretary-Treasurer

Officers and Trustees: Beth K. Stocker, President; Sara Jane Norton, Secretary-Treasurer; Mary Ann Dobras, Nancy E. Woodling.
Corporate Trustee: The Ameritrust Company.
Number of staff: 1 part-time professional.
Employer Identification Number: 341293603

3376
Stouffer Corporation Fund, The
29800 Bainbridge Rd.
Solon 44139   (216) 248-3600

Incorporated in 1952 in Ohio.
Donor(s): Stouffer Foods Corporation.
Financial data: (yr. ended 6/30/83): Assets, $665,165 (M); gifts received, $225,000; expenditures, $183,669, including $180,124 for 205 grants (high: $43,750; low: $100; average: $200-$1,000).
Purpose and activities: Broad purposes; "to stabilize corporation giving"; grants primarily for community funds, higher education, cultural programs, and health.
Types of support awarded: Operating budgets, continuing support, annual campaigns, seed money, emergency funds, building funds, equipment, endowment funds, scholarship funds, special projects.
Limitations: No grants to individuals, or for matching gifts, research, publications, or conferences; no loans.
Application information:
Initial approach: Letter
Copies of proposal: 1
Deadline(s): Submit full proposal preferably in August through November
Board meeting date(s): September, December, February, and May
Write: Robert W. Loehr, Secretary-Treasurer
Officers: Donald Flagg, President; Thomas Stauffer, Vice-President; Robert W. Loehr, Secretary-Treasurer.
Trustees: Richard Atkinson, James Biggar, William Hulett, Anthony Martino, Robert McGuigan.
Number of staff: None.
Employer Identification Number: 346525245

3377
Stranahan Foundation ▼ ⌺
900 Upton Ave.
Toledo 43607   (419) 535-2567

Trust established in 1944 in Ohio.
Donor(s): Robert A. Stranahan,† Frank D. Stranahan,† and others.
Financial data: (yr. ended 12/31/83): Assets, $29,810,459 (M); gifts received, $2,500; expenditures, $1,387,121, including $1,259,540 for 35 grants (high: $500,000; low: $1,000; average: $1,000-$25,000).
Purpose and activities: Broad purposes; primarily local giving, largely for higher education; support also for a community fund, youth and social agencies, and health agencies.
Types of support awarded: Annual campaigns, building funds, equipment, land acquisition, endowment funds, general purposes.

Limitations: Giving primarily in Toledo, OH. No grants to individuals.
Application information:
Initial approach: Letter
Copies of proposal: 1
Deadline(s): October 1
Board meeting date(s): As required
Final notification: 4 months
Write: R.A. Stranahan, Jr., Trustee
Trustees: Francis G. Pletz, Duane Stranahan, Sr., R.A. Stranahan, Jr., Charles G. Yeager.
Number of staff: None.
Employer Identification Number: 346514375

3378
Tait (The Frank M.) Foundation
1840 Kettering Tower
Dayton 45423   (513) 222-2401

Incorporated in 1955 in Ohio.
Donor(s): Frank M. Tait,† Mrs. Frank M. Tait.†
Financial data: (yr. ended 12/31/84): Assets, $2,756,617 (M); expenditures, $235,000, including $186,640 for 37 grants (high: $15,840; low: $50; average: $500-$5,000).
Purpose and activities: Broad purposes; support for local youth agencies and cultural programs.
Types of support awarded: Annual campaigns, seed money, building funds, equipment, land acquisition, special projects.
Limitations: Giving limited to the Dayton, OH, area. No grants to individuals, or for endowment funds, operating budgets, continuing support, emergency funds, deficit financing, research, publications, conferences, or scholarships or fellowships; no loans.
Publications: Financial statement, program policy statement, application guidelines.
Application information:
Initial approach: Letter
Copies of proposal: 1
Deadline(s): March 15, June 15, September 15, and December 15
Board meeting date(s): April, July, October, and January
Final notification: 2 months
Write: Susan T. Rankin, Executive Director
Officers: Irvin G. Bieser,* President; Richard F. Beach,* Vice-President; Susan T. Rankin, Secretary-Treasurer and Executive Director.
Trustees:* Peter H. Forster, Frederick W. Schantz, Alexander J. Williams.
Number of staff: 1 part-time professional.
Employer Identification Number: 316037499

3379
Tamarkin Foundation ⌺
375 Victoria Rd.
Youngstown 44515

Established in 1968.
Donor(s): Tamarkin Company, Project Four, Inc., S&H Company, members of the Tamarkin family.
Financial data: (yr. ended 12/31/83): Assets, $238,297 (M); gifts received, $8,301; expenditures, $109,523, including $108,675 for 23 grants (high: $100,000; low: $50).
Purpose and activities: Primarily local giving for Jewish welfare agencies and temple support.

Limitations: Giving primarily in OH.
Officers and Trustees: Bertram Tamarkin, President; Jerry P. Tamarkin, Vice-President; Nathan H. Monus, Secretary; Jack P. Tamarkin, Treasurer; Michael I. Monus, Arthur N.K. Friedman.
Employer Identification Number: 341023645

3380
Tell (Paul P.) Foundation
2762 Mayfair Rd.
Akron 44312   (216) 733-6291

Incorporated in 1952 in Ohio.
Donor(s): The Tell family and their business interests.
Financial data: (yr. ended 12/31/83): Assets, $2,419,206 (M); gifts received, $7,725; expenditures, $201,088, including $182,626 for 112 grants (high: $25,200; low: $100).
Purpose and activities: For the furtherance of Evangelical Christianity; grants primarily for foreign missions and church-related educational institutions.
Types of support awarded: Operating budgets, continuing support, seed money.
Limitations: No grants to individuals, or for building or endowment funds, scholarships and fellowships, or matching gifts; no loans.
Application information: Applications for grants not invited.
  Board meeting date(s): June
  Write: Paul P. Tell, Jr., President
Officers: Paul P. Tell, Jr.,* President; David J. Schipper,* Vice-President; Anne Tell, Secretary and Treasurer.
Directors:* David Fair, Peter Keslar, Jean Ann Schipper, Michael Tell, Paul P. Tell, Sr.
Number of staff: None.
Employer Identification Number: 346537201

3381
Thompson (Joseph H.) Fund ☐
c/o C.E. Bartter, C.P.A.
503 Lyme Circle
Berea 44017

Incorporated in 1957 in Ohio.
Donor(s): Joseph H. Thompson.
Financial data: (yr. ended 12/31/83): Assets, $1,205,106 (M); expenditures, $99,806, including $80,000 for 27 grants (high: $10,000; low: $500).
Purpose and activities: Support primarily for hospitals, higher and secondary education, and social programs.
Officers: Elizabeth L. Thompson, President; William J. Clark, Vice-President and Treasurer; Lacey T. Neuhaus, Vice-President; Robert A. Toepfer, Secretary.
Employer Identification Number: 346520252

3382
Timken Company Charitable Trust, The ▼ ☐
1835 Dueber Ave., S.W.
Canton 44706   (216) 438-4005

Trust established in 1947 in Ohio.
Donor(s): The Timken Company.

Financial data: (yr. ended 12/31/83): Assets, $2,583,112 (M); expenditures, $1,253,120, including $1,219,330 for 74 grants (high: $400,000; low: $200; average: $200-$20,000).
Purpose and activities: Primarily local giving, with emphasis on higher education and community funds.
Limitations: Giving primarily in OH. No grants to individuals.
Application information:
  Write: Ward J. Timken, Advisor
Advisor: Ward J. Timken.
Trustee: The Central Trust Company of Northeastern Ohio.
Employer Identification Number: 346534265

3383
Timken Company Educational Fund, Inc., The ☐
1835 Dueber Ave., S.W.
Canton 44706

Established in 1957.
Donor(s): Timken Company Charitable Trust.
Financial data: (yr. ended 12/31/83): Assets, $745,944 (M); gifts received, $390,000; expenditures, $411,587, including $151,590 for 17 grants (high: $24,450; low: $2,640) and $248,524 for 31 grants to individuals.
Purpose and activities: Grants for higher education, including individual scholarships for children of company employees.
Types of support awarded: Employee related scholarships.
Application information: Application form required.
  Deadline(s): Application deadlines announced annually
Officers and Trustees: Ward J. Timken, President; J.H. Fellows, Vice-President; D.L. Hart, Secretary-Treasurer; A.B. Glassbrenner, R.W. Lang, M. Schober, C.H. West.
Employer Identification Number: 346520257

3384
Timken Foundation of Canton ▼
236 Third St., S.W.
Canton 44702   (216) 455-5281

Incorporated in 1934 in Ohio.
Donor(s): Members of the Timken family.
Financial data: (yr. ended 9/30/84): Assets, $101,261,030 (M); expenditures, $5,110,882, including $4,931,000 for 21 grants (high: $1,500,000; low: $10,000).
Purpose and activities: Giving primarily in areas where company domestic plants are located, in order to promote broad civic betterment by capital-fund grants; grants largely for schools, colleges, hospitals, cultural centers, conservation and recreation, and other charitable institutions.
Types of support awarded: Building funds, equipment.
Limitations: Giving primarily in areas of company domestic operations. No grants to individuals, or for operating budgets.
Application information:
  Deadline(s): None
  Board meeting date(s): As required
  Write: Douglas H. Worth, Secretary

Officers and Trustees: Ward J. Timken, President; W.R. Timken, W.R. Timken, Jr., Joseph F. Toot, Jr., Vice-Presidents; Douglas H. Worth, Secretary; H.E. Forrest, Treasurer.
Employer Identification Number: 346520254

3385
Timken International Fund, The ▼
236 Third St., S.W.
Canton 44702   (216) 455-5281

Incorporated in 1959 in Ohio.
Donor(s): H.H. Timken, Jr.,† W.R. Timken, J.M. Timken.
Financial data: (yr. ended 9/30/82): Assets, $9,880,122 (M); expenditures, $803,769, including $782,741 for 25 grants (high: $178,100; low: $1,812).
Purpose and activities: Broad purposes; grants primarily outside the United States to educational and charitable institutions in communities in which the company's plants are located. Support only for capital projects.
Types of support awarded: Building funds, equipment.
Limitations: Giving primarily in areas of company operations outside the United States. No grants to individuals.
Application information:
  Board meeting date(s): Quarterly
  Write: D.H. Worth, Director
Officers and Trustees: Ward J. Timken, President; W.R. Timken, W.R. Timken, Jr., Joseph F. Toot, Jr., Vice-Presidents; D.H. Worth, Secretary and Director; H.E. Forrest, Treasurer.
Employer Identification Number: 346520256

3386
Toledo Community Foundation
One Stranahan Square, Rm. 141
Toledo 43604   (419) 241-5049

Community foundation established in 1924 in Ohio by trust agreement; reactivated in 1973.
Financial data: (yr. ended 12/31/83): Assets, $6,978,236 (L); gifts received, $1,088,541; expenditures, $785,365, including $672,859 for 264 grants (high: $50,000; low: $100; average: $2,500-$10,000) and $130,000 for 2 loans.
Purpose and activities: To serve the people of the greater Toledo area, with emphasis on projects which promise to affect a broad segment of the citizens of northwestern Ohio or which tend to help those living in an area not being adequately served by local community resources. Areas of interest include arts and culture, conservation and environment, education and training, government and urban affairs, health, religion, social welfare, and united funds.
Types of support awarded: Seed money, emergency funds, matching funds.
Limitations: Giving primarily in greater Toledo, OH. No grants to individuals, or for operating budgets, or capital or endowment funds.
Publications: Annual report, application guidelines, program policy statement, informational brochure.
Application information:

Initial approach: Letter or telephone
Copies of proposal: 1
Deadline(s): Submit proposal preferably in months when board meets; deadline January, April, July, and October
Board meeting date(s): January, April, July, and October
Final notification: 2 months
Write: Miriam M. Bixler, Secretary
Distribution Committee: Robert J. Kirk, Chairman; Steven Timonere, Vice-Chairman; Lawrence T. Foster, Marvin S. Kobacker, Duane Stranahan, Jr.
Trustee Banks: First National Bank of Toledo, Huntington Bank of Toledo, Mid-American National Bank & Trust Company, Ohio Citizens Bank, Sylvania Savings Bank Company, Toledo Trust Company.
Number of staff: 1 full-time professional; 1 full-time support.
Employer Identification Number: 237284004

3387
Toledo Trust Foundation, The
c/o Toledo Trust Company
Three Seagate
Toledo 43603   (419) 259-8217

Trust established in 1953 in Ohio.
Donor(s): The Toledo Trust Company.
Financial data: (yr. ended 12/31/83): Assets, $291,394 (M); expenditures, $216,595, including $212,350 for 19 grants (high: $148,000; low: $100; average: $1,000-$10,000).
Purpose and activities: Charitable purposes; primarily local giving, with emphasis on community funds and higher and secondary education; grants also for cultural activities and youth agencies.
Types of support awarded: Operating budgets, continuing support, annual campaigns, emergency funds, building funds, equipment, land acquisition, consulting services, technical assistance, program-related investments.
Limitations: Giving primarily in OH. No grants to individuals, or for start-up funds, deficit financing, or matching gifts; no loans.
Publications: 990-PF.
Application information:
Initial approach: Letter
Deadline(s): None
Board meeting date(s): Monthly
Final notification: 2 months
Write: J.E. Lupe, Vice-President
Trustees: S.G. Carson, George W. Haigh, R.A. Stranahan, Jr., The Toledo Trust Company, Corporate Trustee.
Number of staff: None.
Employer Identification Number: 346504808

3388
Tremco Foundation ⌐
10701 Shaker Blvd.
Cleveland 44104

Trust established in 1950 in Ohio.
Donor(s): Tremco Manufacturing Company.

Financial data: (yr. ended 12/31/83): Assets, $886,323 (M); gifts received, $180,000; expenditures, $158,314, including $152,593 for 149 grants (high: $18,800; low: $20).
Purpose and activities: Charitable purposes; primarily local giving, with emphasis on community funds, higher education, and cultural programs.
Limitations: Giving primarily in Cleveland, OH.
Trustees: Leigh Carter, Gordon Harnett, Mark Steinbock.
Employer Identification Number: 346527566

3389
Treuhaft Foundation, The ▼
10701 Shaker Blvd.
Cleveland 44104   (216) 229-0166

Trust established in 1955 in Ohio.
Donor(s): Elizabeth M. Treuhaft, William C. Treuhaft.†
Financial data: (yr. ended 12/31/83): Assets, $13,549,061 (M); gifts received, $35,000; expenditures, $1,004,957, including $996,814 for 149 grants (high: $200,000; low: $100; average: $500-$200,000).
Purpose and activities: Broad purposes; primarily local giving, with emphasis on higher education, Jewish welfare funds, music and cultural programs, and health and welfare programs.
Types of support awarded: Operating budgets, continuing support, annual campaigns, seed money, emergency funds, building funds, endowment funds, professorships, scholarship funds, special projects, research, publications, conferences and seminars, general purposes.
Limitations: Giving primarily in the Cleveland, OH, area. No grants to individuals, or for matching gifts, or deficit financing; no loans.
Application information:
Initial approach: Letter
Deadline(s): None
Board meeting date(s): As required
Write: Mrs. William C. Treuhaft, Trustee
Trustees: Irwin M. Feldman, Arthur W. Treuhaft, Elizabeth M. Treuhaft.
Number of staff: None.
Employer Identification Number: 341206010

3390
Treu-Mart Fund, The
c/o The Cleveland Foundation
1400 Hanna Bldg.
Cleveland 44115   (216) 861-3810
Additional address: c/o The Jewish Community Federation of Cleveland, 1750 Euclid Ave., Cleveland, OH 44115. Tel.: (216) 566-9200

Established in 1980 in Ohio.
Donor(s): Elizabeth M. Treuhaft, William C. Treuhaft.†
Financial data: (yr. ended 12/31/84): Assets, $1,400,242 (M); expenditures, $85,973, including $75,300 for 14 grants (high: $20,000; low: $1,000).

Purpose and activities: Supporting organization of The Cleveland Foundation and The Jewish Community Federation of Cleveland; organization grants primarily for projects benefitting residents of the greater Cleveland area, especially those incorporating demonstration or research elements. Support largely for community development, cultural programs, health planning, and social service activities, including Jewish welfare agencies.
Types of support awarded: Research, special projects.
Limitations: Giving primarily in Cleveland, OH. No grants to individuals, or for operating budgets or annual campaigns.
Publications: Annual report, program policy statement, application guidelines.
Application information:
Initial approach: Full proposal
Copies of proposal: 1
Deadline(s): February 1, July 1, and October 1
Board meeting date(s): March, July and November
Final notification: 3 months
Write: Mrs. William C. Treuhaft, President
Officers: Elizabeth M. Treuhaft,* President and Chairman; Henry L. Zucker,* Vice-President; Howard R. Berger, Secretary; Mary Louise Hahn, Treasurer.
Trustees:* Frances M. King, Albert B. Ratner, Lloyd S. Schwenger, Arthur W. Treuhaft, Homer C. Wadsworth.
Employer Identification Number: 341323364

3391
Troy Foundation, The
c/o The First National Bank & Trust Company
910 West Main St.
Troy 45373   (513) 335-8351

Community foundation established in 1924 in Ohio by bank resolution and declaration of trust.
Donor(s): Nannie Kendall,† A.G. Stouder,† J.M. Spencer.†
Financial data: (yr. ended 12/31/84): Assets, $3,700,000 (M); gifts received, $440,000; expenditures, $325,000, including $280,000 for 22 grants (high: $75,000; low: $390).
Purpose and activities: To assist, encourage, and promote the well-being of mankind and primarily to the Troy City School District and its vicinity.
Types of support awarded: Seed money, building funds, equipment.
Limitations: Giving primarily in the Troy City, OH, School District. No grants to individuals, or for endowment funds, operating budgets, continuing support, annual campaigns, emergency funds, deficit financing, land acquisition, research, demonstration projects, publications, conferences, scholarships and fellowships, or matching gifts; no loans.
Publications: 990-PF, application guidelines.
Application information:
Initial approach: Full proposal
Copies of proposal: 5
Deadline(s): None
Board meeting date(s): As required
Final notification: 1 to 2 months
Write: Richard J. Fraas, Secretary

Officer and Trustees: Richard J. Fraas, Secretary; David L. Ault, Vernon T. Bowling, Thomas B. Hamler, Edward A. Hobart, William Hobart, Jr., Mark Knoop, Robert Koverman, Stewart I. Lipp, Robert B. Meeker, John M. Richardson, Wayne L. Roll, Jerrold R. Stammen.
Distribution Committee: Max Myers, Chairman; G. Joseph Reardon, Vice-Chairman; Doris Blackmore, Helen Meeker, R. Murray Dalton.
Number of staff: None.
Employer Identification Number: 316018703

3392
TRW Foundation ▼
23555 Euclid Ave.
Cleveland 44117   (216) 383-2412

Incorporated in 1953 in Ohio as the Thompson Products Foundation; became the Thompson Ramo Wooldridge Foundation in 1958, and adopted its present name in 1965.
Donor(s): TRW Inc.
Financial data: (yr. ended 12/31/84): Assets, $11,098,650 (M); gifts received, $420,000; expenditures, $5,207,556, including $4,059,135 for 408 grants (high: $450,000; low: $500; average: $2,500-$50,000) and $1,133,078 for 5,113 employee matching gifts.
Purpose and activities: Broad purposes; giving primarily in TRW plant communities; grants largely for higher education, particularly for engineering, technical, science, and/or business administration programs, and community funds; limited support for hospitals, welfare agencies, youth agencies, and civic and cultural organizations.
Types of support awarded: Employee matching gifts, scholarship funds, employee related scholarships, professorships, fellowships, research, building funds, operating budgets, deficit financing, equipment, general purposes, conferences and seminars, exchange programs, matching funds, special projects.
Limitations: Giving primarily in areas of company operations, with some emphasis on Cleveland, OH. No support for religious purposes, fraternal or labor organizations. No grants to individuals or for endowment funds.
Publications: Annual report, program policy statement, application guidelines, grants list.
Application information:
  Initial approach: Full proposal
  Copies of proposal: 1
  Deadline(s): Submit proposals preferably in August or September; deadline September 1 for organizations already receiving support from the foundation
  Board meeting date(s): December
  Final notification: 60 to 90 days
  Write: Donna L. Cummings, Manager
Officers: Thomas J. Fay,* President; Edward N. Button,* Alan F. Senger, Vice-Presidents; C. Thomas Harvie, Secretary.
Trustees:* Martin A. Coyle, Ruben F. Mettler, Stanley C. Pace.
Number of staff: 2 full-time professional; 2 full-time support.
Employer Identification Number: 346556217

3393
Tucker (Marcia Brady) Foundation, Inc.
106 Colonial Center Bldg.
Cincinnati 45227   (513) 561-3164

Incorporated in 1941 in New York.
Donor(s): Marcia Brady Tucker.†
Financial data: (yr. ended 12/31/82): Assets, $4,401,289 (M); expenditures, $216,008, including $166,250 for 15 grants (high: $30,000; low: $2,000).
Purpose and activities: Grants made only on the initiative of the foundation, mainly for education, conservation, and medical, religious or cultural institutions.
Limitations: No grants to individuals.
Application information: Grants made only on the initiative of the foundation.
Officers and Directors: Luther Tucker, President; Marcia T. Boogaard, Secretary; Carll Tucker III, Treasurer; Anne Draper, Elizabeth Sanders, Gay Tucker, Luther Tucker, Jr., Toinette Tucker.
Employer Identification Number: 136161561

3394
Tyler (Marion C.) Foundation ☐
c/o Central National Bank of Cleveland
P.O. Box 6179
Cleveland 44101   (216) 946-4100
Application address: 8200 Tyler Blvd., Mentor, OH 44060

Established in 1971.
Donor(s): W.S. Tyler, Inc.
Financial data: (yr. ended 12/31/82): Assets, $1,125,985 (M); expenditures, $258,886, including $247,377 for 178 grants to individuals.
Purpose and activities: Grants to retired employees of W.S. Tyler, Inc.
Types of support awarded: Grants to individuals.
Application information: Application form required.
  Deadline(s): None
  Write: Linda Wallingford
Trustee: Central National Bank of Cleveland.
Employer Identification Number: 346525274

3395
Van Huffel (The I. J.) Foundation ☐
The Union Savings & Trust Company
106 East Market St.
Warren 44481

Trust established in 1951 in Ohio.
Donor(s): Van Huffel Tube Corporation.
Financial data: (yr. ended 12/31/83): Assets, $1,365,518 (M); expenditures, $133,928, including $119,650 for 50 grants (high: $15,000; low: $200).
Purpose and activities: Charitable purposes; primarily local giving, with emphasis on higher education, Roman Catholic and Protestant church support, hospitals, and youth agencies.
Limitations: Giving primarily in OH.
Trustee: The Union Savings & Trust Company.
Employer Identification Number: 346516726

3396
Van Wert County Foundation, The
101-1/2 East Main St.
Van Wert 45891   (419) 238-1743

Incorporated in 1925 in Ohio.
Donor(s): Charles F. Wassenberg,† Gaylord Saltzgaber,† John D. Ault,† Kernan Wright,† Richard L. Klein,† Hazel Gleason,† Constance Eirich.†
Financial data: (yr. ended 12/31/84): Assets, $4,130,000 (M); expenditures, $257,510, including $153,160 for 24 grants (high: $41,760; low: $200) and $48,650 for 71 grants to individuals.
Purpose and activities: Local giving only, with emphasis on scholarships for residents of Van Wert County in art, music, agriculture, and home economics; support for youth agencies, an art center, and recreational facilities.
Types of support awarded: General purposes, equipment, research, student aid.
Limitations: Giving limited to Van Wert County, OH. No grants for endowment funds, or matching gifts; no loans.
Application information: Application forms and guidelines issued for scholarship program.
  Initial approach: Letter or full proposal
  Copies of proposal: 1
  Deadline(s): Submit proposal in May or November; deadlines May 25 and November 25
  Board meeting date(s): June and December
  Final notification: 1 week
  Write: Robert W. Games, Executive Secretary
Officer: Robert W. Games, Executive Secretary.
Trustees: D.L. Brumback, Jr., William S. Derry, A.C. Diller, Kenneth Koch, G.E. Leslie, Watson Ley, Paul W. Purmont, Jr., Charles Ross, C. Allan Runser, Donald C. Sutton, Roger Thompson, Sumner Walters, Larry Wendel, G. Dale Wilson, Fred Wollenhaupt.
Number of staff: 1 part-time professional; 1 part-time support.
Employer Identification Number: 340907558

3397
Wagnalls Memorial, The
150 E. Columbus St.
Lithopolis 43136   (614) 837-4765

Incorporated in 1924 in Ohio.
Donor(s): Mabel Wagnalls-Jones.†
Financial data: (yr. ended 8/31/84): Assets, $14,500,000 (M); expenditures, $648,803, including $13,655 for 4 grants (high: $2,700; low: $100) and $182,150 for 218 grants to individuals.
Purpose and activities: Local giving, primarily for scholarships and fellowships to graduates of Bloom Township high schools; support also for community development.
Types of support awarded: Student aid, fellowships.
Limitations: Giving limited to the Lithopolis, OH, area.
Application information: Application forms required for scholarships.
  Deadline(s): June 15
  Write: Jerry W. Neff, Executive Director
Officer: Jerry W. Neff, Executive Director.

Trustees: George W. Boving, Robert Faler, W.W. Haynes, Benjamin C. Humphrey, Robert Rager, Kermit C. Sitterley, Dwayne R. Spence.
Number of staff: 2 full-time professional; 9 full-time support; 6 part-time support.
Employer Identification Number: 314379589

3398
Warner (Marvin L.) Foundation ⌑
2727 Madison Rd.
Cincinnati 45209   (513) 871-3400

Established about 1959 in Ohio.
Donor(s): Marvin L. Warner, Warner National Corporation.
Financial data: (yr. ended 5/31/83): Assets, $89,744 (M); gifts received, $90,000; expenditures, $316,705, including $315,350 for 30 grants (high: $165,000; low: $100).
Purpose and activities: Giving primarily to Jewish welfare funds.
Trustees: Burton M. Bongard, Alyson W. Kuppin.
Employer Identification Number: 316061713

3399
Wasmer (The John C.) Foundation ⌑
13001 Athens Ave.
Lakewood 44107

Incorporated in 1959 in Ohio.
Financial data: (yr. ended 11/30/83): Assets, $425,760 (M); gifts received, $123,400; expenditures, $143,258, including $142,365 for 44 grants (high: $25,000; low: $25).
Purpose and activities: Primarily local giving, with emphasis on higher education, Roman Catholic organizations and church support.
Limitations: Giving primarily in Cleveland, OH.
Manager: Florence M. Wasmer.
Employer Identification Number: 346557408

3400
Watson (Walter E. and Caroline H.) Foundation ⌑
P.O. Box 450
Youngstown 44501   (216) 759-3100

Trust established in 1964 in Ohio.
Donor(s): Walter E. Watson.†
Financial data: (yr. ended 12/31/83): Assets, $3,175,915 (M); expenditures, $240,632, including $222,015 for 42 grants (high: $44,399; low: $500).
Purpose and activities: To support public institutions of learning in Ohio and public and charitable institutions in the Mahoning Valley; local giving, with emphasis on hospitals, youth agencies, community development, and cultural programs.
Limitations: Giving primarily in OH. No grants to individuals, or for endowment funds or operating budgets.
Application information:
   Initial approach: Proposal
   Copies of proposal: 4
   Deadline(s): Submit proposal between February and October

Board meeting date(s): Semiannually
Trustee: The Dollar Savings and Trust Company.
Employer Identification Number: 346547726

3401
Wean (The Raymond John) Foundation ▼
347 North Park Ave.
Warren 44482   (216) 841-7200

Trust established in 1949 in Ohio.
Donor(s): Raymond J. Wean.†
Financial data: (yr. ended 12/31/82): Assets, $16,255,927 (M); expenditures, $1,568,364, including $1,447,531 for 709 grants (high: $100,000; low: $50).
Purpose and activities: Broad purposes; grants largely for higher and secondary education, hospitals, health agencies, youth agencies, community funds, Protestant church support, and cultural programs.
Limitations: Giving primarily in OH, Palm Beach, FL, and Pittsburgh, PA.
Application information: Funds committed to selected organizations on an annual basis; applications are discouraged.
   Write: Raymond J. Wean, Jr., Chairman
Administrators: Raymond J. Wean, Jr., Chairman; Clara G. Petrosky, Raymond J. Wean III, Sara R. Wean.
Trustee: The Second National Bank of Warren.
Employer Identification Number: 346505038

3402
Weiss (The Clara) Fund ⌑
2225 Marks Rd.
Valley City 44280

Trust established in 1955 in Ohio.
Donor(s): L.C. Weiss, Mrs. L.C. Weiss.
Financial data: (yr. ended 12/31/83): Assets, $1,316,669 (M); expenditures, $91,893, including $86,600 for 98 grants (high: $5,000; low: $100).
Purpose and activities: Broad purposes; grants largely for higher and secondary education, health agencies, and welfare institutions in the Cleveland area.
Limitations: Giving primarily in the Cleveland, OH, area.
Trustees: David C. Weiss, Manager; Arthur D. Weiss, Robert L. Weiss.
Employer Identification Number: 346556158

3403
Wellman (S. K.) Foundation, The ⌑
1800 Union Commerce Bldg.
Cleveland 44115
Application address: R. Dugald Pearson, 548 Leader Bldg., Cleveland, OH 44114; tel: (216) 696-4640

Incorporated in 1951 in Ohio.
Donor(s): S.K. Wellman.†
Financial data: (yr. ended 12/31/82): Assets, $3,813,284 (M); expenditures, $272,633, including $236,000 for 55 grants (high: $15,000; low: $500).

Purpose and activities: Broad purposes; primarily local giving, with grants largely for education, cultural activities, health agencies, and social services.
Limitations: Giving primarily in OH. No grants to individuals.
Publications: Application guidelines.
Application information:
   Initial approach: Letter
   Deadline(s): December 31
Officers: John M. Wilson, Jr.,* President; R. Dugald Pearson, Executive Secretary.
Trustees:* Franklin B. Floyd, Mrs. Charles O'Gara, Mrs. John M. Wilson, Jr.
Employer Identification Number: 346520032

3404
Wexner Foundation ⌑
250 East Broad St., Rm. 1607
Columbus 43215

Established in 1973.
Donor(s): Leslie Wexner.
Financial data: (yr. ended 12/31/83): Assets, $23,637,420 (M); expenditures, $405,560, including $400,000 for 1 grant.
Purpose and activities: Primarily local giving, with emphasis on Jewish welfare funds.
Limitations: Giving primarily in OH.
Application information: Applications for grants not invited.
Officers: Leslie H. Wexner, President-Treasurer; Bella Wexner, Secretary.
Trustee: Gordon Schiffman.
Employer Identification Number: 237320631

3405
White Consolidated Industries, Inc. Foundation
c/o White Consolidated Industries, Inc.
11770 Berea Rd.
Cleveland 44111   (216) 252-3700

Established in 1951 in Ohio.
Donor(s): White Consolidated Industries, Inc., Franklin Manufacturing Company, Whitin Machine Works, Inc.
Financial data: (yr. ended 12/31/84): Assets, $963,413 (M); gifts received, $413,926; expenditures, $513,477, including $497,301 for 134 grants (high: $74,000; low: $100) and $14,585 for 43 employee matching gifts.
Purpose and activities: General giving in areas of company operations, with emphasis on community funds, higher education, hospitals, and cultural organizations.
Types of support awarded: General purposes, building funds, equipment, research, continuing support, operating budgets, employee matching gifts.
Limitations: Giving limited to areas of company operations.
Publications: 990-PF.
Application information:
   Initial approach: Proposal
   Copies of proposal: 1
   Board meeting date(s): As required
   Write: Ronald G. Fountain, Treasurer

Officers and Trustees:* Roy H. Holdt,*
President; Ward Smith,* Karl E. Ware,* Vice-
Presidents; W. Derald Hunt, Vice-President and
Controller; William G.E. Jacobs, Secretary;
Ronald G. Fountain,* Treasurer.
Employer Identification Number: 046032840

3406
White (Thomas H.) Charitable Trust
c/o AmeriTrust Company
P.O. Box 5937
Cleveland 44101   (216) 687-5632

Trust established in 1913 in Ohio.
Donor(s): Thomas H. White.†
Financial data: (yr. ended 12/31/84): Assets,
$9,973,625 (M); expenditures, $507,921,
including $464,768 for 75 grants (high:
$20,000; low: $500; average: $6,000).
Purpose and activities: Subject to numerous
life estates, the Trust first became active in
1939 when surplus income became available;
giving to support education and charitable
purposes in Cleveland, to provide scholarships,
to promote scientific research, to provide for
care of the sick, aged, or helpless, to improve
living conditions or provide recreation for all
classes in Cleveland only.
Types of support awarded: Continuing
support, seed money, emergency funds,
building funds, equipment, matching funds,
scholarship funds, special projects.
Limitations: Giving limited to Cleveland, OH.
No grants to individuals, or for annual
campaigns, deficit financing, land acquisition,
publications, or conferences; no loans.
Publications: Annual report, application
guidelines.
Application information: Mass mailings not
accepted.
  Initial approach: Letter
  Copies of proposal: 6
  Deadline(s): Submit proposal preferably in
    January, April, July, or September; deadline
    6 weeks prior to distribution committee
    meetings
  Board meeting date(s): Distribution
    committee meets in March, June,
    September, and December
  Final notification: 2 months
  Write: Thomas B. Schneider, Vice-President
Trustee: AmeriTrust Company (Thomas B.
Schneider, Vice-President).
Number of staff: 1 part-time professional.
Employer Identification Number: 346505722

3407
Whitewater Foundation ¤
P.O. Box 111
Cincinnati 45211

Established in 1957.
Financial data: (yr. ended 12/31/82): Assets,
$534,269 (M); expenditures, $211,861,
including $210,000 for 9 grants (high:
$100,000; low: $5,000).
Purpose and activities: Primarily local giving
for health and hospitals; support also for drug
rehabilitation and youth agencies.

Limitations: Giving primarily in Cincinnati, OH.
Trustees: John P. March, Perrin G. March III,
T.J. Noyes.
Employer Identification Number: 316048723

3408
Wildermuth (The E. F.) Foundation ¤
4770 Indianola Ave., Suite 140
Columbus 43214   (614) 846-5838

Established in 1962.
Financial data: (yr. ended 12/31/83): Assets,
$2,443,081 (M); expenditures, $121,751,
including $91,293 for 20 grants (high: $27,500;
low: $500).
Purpose and activities: Grants primarily for
higher education, particularly optometric
schools and research; support also for the arts
and a church.
Limitations: Giving primarily in OH.
Application information:
  Deadline(s): August 15
  Write: Homer W. Lee, Secretary
Trustees: Faurest Borton, Karl Borton, J. Patrick
Campbell, Genevieve Conable, W. Daniel
Driscoll, H. Ward Ewalt, Homer W. Lee, David
R. Patterson, David T. Patterson, Phillip N.
Phillipson, Roy E. Salzgaber.
Employer Identification Number: 316050202

3409
Wodecroft Foundation ¤
2100 DuBois Tower
Cincinnati 45202   (513) 621-6747

Trust established in 1958 in Ohio.
Donor(s): Roger Drackett.
Financial data: (yr. ended 12/31/83): Assets,
$2,939,664 (M); expenditures, $111,321,
including $106,850 for 25 grants (high:
$20,000; low: $200).
Purpose and activities: Broad purposes;
primarily local giving, with emphasis on cultural
programs, hospitals, and conservation.
Limitations: Giving primarily in OH. No grants
to individuals.
Application information:
  Initial approach: Letter
  Board meeting date(s): As required
  Write: H. Truxtun Emerson, Jr., Secretary
Officers and Trustees: Richard W. Barrett,
Chairman; H. Truxtun Emerson, Jr., Secretary;
Roger Drackett.
Employer Identification Number: 316047601

3410
Wolfe Associates Inc.
34 South Third St.
Columbus 43216   (614) 461-5220

Incorporated in 1973 in Ohio.
Donor(s): The Dispatch Printing Company, The
Ohio Company, WBNS TV Inc., RadiOhio Inc.
Financial data: (yr. ended 6/30/84): Assets,
$1,197,226 (M); gifts received, $1,197,226;
expenditures, $627,272, including $625,300
for 73 grants (high: $133,000; low: $150).

Purpose and activities: Broad purposes;
primarily local giving, with emphasis on a
community fund, higher and secondary
education, hospitals and medical research,
cultural activities, and youth and social
agencies.
Types of support awarded: Operating
budgets, continuing support, annual campaigns,
emergency funds, building funds, equipment,
matching funds, professorships.
Limitations: Giving primarily in central OH.
No grants to individuals, or for research,
demonstration projects, publications, or
conferences.
Publications: Program policy statement,
application guidelines.
Application information:
  Initial approach: Letter
  Deadline(s): None
  Board meeting date(s): January, April, July
    and September
  Final notification: After next board meeting
  Write: A.K. Pierce, Jr., Secretary-Treasurer
Officers: John Walton Wolfe, President; John
F. Wolfe, Nancy Wolfe Lane, William C.
Wolfe, Jr., Vice-Presidents; A. Kenneth Pierce,
Jr., Secretary-Treasurer.
Number of staff: None.
Employer Identification Number: 237303111

3411
Wright Foundation ¤
23555 Euclid Ave.
Cleveland 44117

Incorporated in 1953 in Ohio.
Donor(s): J.D. Wright.
Financial data: (yr. ended 12/31/83): Assets,
$1,470,400 (M); expenditures, $115,019,
including $108,312 for 72 grants (high:
$46,000; low: $37).
Purpose and activities: Broad purposes;
primarily local giving, with emphasis on
hospitals and higher education.
Limitations: Giving primarily in OH.
Application information:
  Write: J.D. Wright, President
Officers and Trustees: J.D. Wright, President;
Bernadine G. Wright, John D. Wright, Jr., Vice-
Presidents; Doris M. Toth, Secretary-Treasurer.
Employer Identification Number: 346520282

3412
Wuliger Foundation, Inc., The
Bond Court Bldg.
1300 East Ninth St.
Cleveland 44114

Incorporated in 1956 in Ohio.
Donor(s): Ernest M. Wuliger, Allan M. Unger,
Ohio-Sealy Mattress Mfg. Co.
Financial data: (yr. ended 12/31/82): Assets,
$1,107,892 (M); gifts received, $637,300;
expenditures, $318,836, including $310,870
for 69 grants (high: $100,000; low: $100).
Purpose and activities: Primarily local giving,
with emphasis on Jewish welfare funds; support
also for higher education, hospitals, and the
arts.
Limitations: Giving primarily in OH. No grants
to individuals.

Application information:
Initial approach: Full proposal
Officers: Ernest M. Wuliger, President and Treasurer; Maurice Saltzman, Vice-President; Timothy F. Wuliger, Secretary.
Employer Identification Number: 346527281

3413
XTEK Foundation ☐
211 Township Ave.
Cincinnati 45216   (513) 733-2957

Incorporated in 1962 in Ohio.
Donor(s): XTEK, Inc.
Financial data: (yr. ended 12/31/83): Assets, $514,017 (M); gifts received, $29,127; expenditures, $128,176, including $126,680 for 50 grants (high: $47,500; low: $100).
Purpose and activities: Primarily local giving, with emphasis on a community fund, cultural programs, and higher education; support also for health and youth agencies.
Limitations: Giving primarily in OH.
Application information:
Deadline(s): None
Write: John T. Metcalfe, Jr., Secretary-Treasurer
Officers: Sanford M. Brooks, President; John T. Metcalfe, Jr., Secretary-Treasurer.
Trustee: James D. Kiggen.
Employer Identification Number: 316029606

3414
Yassenoff (The Leo) Foundation ▼
37 North High St., Suite 304
Columbus 43215   (614) 221-4315

Incorporated in 1947 in Delaware.
Donor(s): Leo Yassenoff.†
Financial data: (yr. ended 12/31/83): Assets, $10,637,830 (M); expenditures, $1,833,376, including $722,960 for 98 grants (high: $200,000; low: $200; average: $1,000-$20,000).
Purpose and activities: Charitable purposes; local giving only.
Types of support awarded: Seed money, emergency funds, building funds, equipment, land acquisition, matching funds, consulting services, technical assistance, program-related investments, special projects, research, publications, conferences and seminars, professorships, internships, scholarship funds, fellowships, continuing support.
Limitations: Giving limited to the central OH area, with emphasis on Franklin County. No support for religious purposes, except to donor-designated recipients. No grants to individuals, or for operating support, annual campaigns, endowments, deficit financing, or debt reduction; no loans.
Publications: Annual report, program policy statement, application guidelines.
Application information:
Initial approach: Telephone, letter, or full proposal
Copies of proposal: 1
Deadline(s): 1st business day of every other month beginning in January
Board meeting date(s): Every other month beginning in January

Final notification: 2 months
Write: M. Ellen Gruber, Executive Director
Officer: M. Ellen Gruber, Executive Director.
Trustees: Melvin L. Schottenstein, Chairman; Frederick E. Dauterman, Jr., Vice-Chairman; Mary J. Hoover.
Number of staff: 2 full-time professional; 2 full-time support.
Employer Identification Number: 310829426

3415
Young (Hugo H. and Mabel B.) Foundation
416 North Wood St.
Loudonville 44842   (419) 994-4501

Incorporated in 1963 in Ohio.
Financial data: (yr. ended 4/30/84): Assets, $3,458,243 (M); gifts received, $22,200; expenditures, $305,438, including $294,854 for 11 grants (high: $100,000; low: $2,000).
Purpose and activities: Giving primarily to local charitable and civic organizations.
Types of support awarded: Building funds, equipment, scholarship funds.
Limitations: Giving primarily in Ashland County, OH. No grants to individuals, or for general purposes, or matching gifts; no loans.
Application information:
Initial approach: Letter
Copies of proposal: 5
Deadline(s): Submit proposal preferably in March
Board meeting date(s): May
Write: R.D. Mayer, Secretary-Treasurer
Officers and Trustees: Phillip Ranney, Chairman; R.H. Casner, President; Avery Hand, Vice-President; R.D. Mayer, Secretary-Treasurer, James Dudte, H.H. Schneider.
Number of staff: None.
Employer Identification Number: 346560664

3416
Youngstown Foundation, The ▼
c/o The Dollar Savings & Trust Company
P.O. Box 450
Youngstown 44501   (216) 744-9000

Community foundation established in 1918 in Ohio by bank resolution.
Financial data: (yr. ended 12/31/83): Assets, $6,338,686 (M); gifts received, $561,475; expenditures, $1,529,667, including $1,044,630 for 103 grants (high: $290,000; low: $500; average: $1,000-$10,000) and $5,500 for 11 loans.
Purpose and activities: To support local charitable and educational agencies for the betterment of the community; grants for capital purposes, with emphasis on the handicapped, community funds, youth agencies, music and cultural programs, and hospitals.
Types of support awarded: Student aid, building funds, equipment, annual campaigns.

Limitations: Giving limited to the Youngstown, OH, area. No grants to individuals, or for endowment funds, operating budgets, seed money, emergency funds, deficit financing, continuing support, land acquisition, demonstration projects, publications, conferences, research, scholarships, fellowships, or matching gifts.
Publications: 990-PF, application guidelines.
Application information:
Initial approach: Full proposal
Copies of proposal: 1
Deadline(s): None
Board meeting date(s): January, March, May, July, September, November, and December
Write: Herbert H. Pridham, Secretary
Officer: Herbert H. Pridham, Secretary.
Distribution Committee: D.W. McGowan, Chairman; William M. Cafaro, Vice-Chairman; Constance Rosselli, Fred Tod, Jr., John F. Tyler.
Trustee: The Dollar Savings and Trust Company (Herbert H. Pridham, Sr., Vice-President and Senior Trust Officer).
Number of staff: None.
Employer Identification Number: 346515788

OKLAHOMA

3417
Ashbrook (Mary K.) Foundation for El Reno, OK
P.O. Box 627
El Reno 73036   (405) 262-4684

Established in 1978 in Oklahoma.
Donor(s): Mary K. Ashbrook.†
Financial data: (yr. ended 6/30/83): Assets, $1,411,028 (M); expenditures, $95,804, including $82,060 for 16 grants (high: $18,110; low: $300).
Purpose and activities: Grants for education, cultural programs, civic affairs, community development, and welfare in El Reno .
Types of support awarded: Operating budgets, continuing support, annual campaigns, seed money, emergency funds, building funds, equipment, land acquisition, matching funds, scholarship funds, exchange programs, special projects.
Limitations: Giving limited to El Reno, OK. No grants to individuals, or for deficit financing, endowment funds, research, fellowships, demonstration projects, publications, or conferences; no loans.
Publications: Application guidelines.
Application information: Application form required.
Initial approach: Letter or telephone
Deadline(s): Submit proposal by first of each month
Board meeting date(s): Monthly
Final notification: 1 month

Trustees: Virginia Sue Douglas, Margery Fogg, Alleen Poole.
Number of staff: None.
Employer Identification Number: 731049531

3418
Bartlett (Edward E.) & Helen Turner Bartlett Foundation

c/o First National Bank and Trust Company of Tulsa
P.O. Box 1
Tulsa 74193 (918) 224-3400
Scholarship application address: c/o Antwine Pryor, Sapulpa High School, 1 South Mission, Sapulpa, OK 74066

Established in 1961.
Donor(s): Edward E. Bartlett.†
Financial data: (yr. ended 12/31/82): Assets, $2,603,254 (M); expenditures, $136,970, including $113,450 for 16 grants (high: $35,000; low: $500).
Purpose and activities: Local giving primarily for higher education, including scholarships for graduates of Sapulpa High School attending certain Oklahoma colleges and universities.
Types of support awarded: Student aid.
Limitations: Giving limited to OK.
Trustees: H.I. Bartlett, Harry Freeman, First National Bank and Trust Co. of Tulsa.
Employer Identification Number: 736092250

3419
Bovaird (The Mervin) Foundation ☐

320 South Boston, Suite 1300
Tulsa 74103

Established about 1956.
Donor(s): Mabel W. Bovaird.†
Financial data: (yr. ended 12/31/83): Assets, $18,874,832 (M); expenditures, $945,637, including $597,000 for 41 grants (high: $250,000; low: $500) and $226,655 for 62 grants to individuals.
Purpose and activities: Primarily local giving, with emphasis on scholarships to students attending the University of Tulsa, community development, social services, and hospitals.
Types of support awarded: Student aid.
Limitations: Giving primarily in Tulsa, OK.
Officers and Trustees: Fenelon Boesche, President; Tilford Eskridge, Thomas H. Trower, Vice-Presidents; Franklin D. Hettinger, Secretary and Treasurer.
Employer Identification Number: 736102163

3420
Broadhurst Foundation

320 South Boston, Suite 1111
Tulsa 74103 (918) 584-0661

Trust established in 1951 in Oklahoma.
Donor(s): William Broadhurst.†
Financial data: (yr. ended 12/31/83): Assets, $3,727,831 (L); expenditures, $478,402, including $354,076 for 140 grants (high: $33,804; low: $100; average: $2,000).

Purpose and activities: Broad purposes; giving mainly in the Midwest, largely for scholarship funds at institutions selected by the foundation, for students training for the Christian ministry; grants also to educational and religious institutions, and to medical research institutions, especially related to pediatric diseases.
Types of support awarded: Continuing support, seed money, building funds, equipment, scholarship funds.
Limitations: Giving primarily in the Midwest. No grants to individuals or for scholarship funds, except at 31 schools the foundation currently supports.
Application information:
 Initial approach: Letter or full proposal
 Copies of proposal: 1
 Deadline(s): None
 Board meeting date(s): Quarterly
 Final notification: 1 month
 Write: Ann Shannon Cassidy, Chairman
Trustees: Ann Shannon Cassidy, Chairman; John Cassidy, Jr., Ernestine Broadhurst Howard, Wishard Lemons.
Number of staff: 1 full-time professional; 1 part-time professional; 1 part-time support.
Employer Identification Number: 736061115

3421
Campbell (Max and Tookah) Foundation ☐

4107-A South Yale Ave.
Tulsa 74135

Trust established in 1964 in Oklahoma.
Donor(s): Max W. Campbell.†
Financial data: (yr. ended 12/31/83): Assets, $2,759,656 (M); expenditures, $1,807,783, including $138,812 for 37 grants (high: $30,000; low: $20).
Purpose and activities: Broad purposes; primarily local giving, with emphasis on Protestant church support and higher education; grants also for hospitals and health agencies, cultural programs, and youth agencies.
Limitations: Giving primarily in OK.
Trustees: Joe Francis, Iva R. Jones, Joan Lepley.
Employer Identification Number: 736111626

3422
Chapman (H. A. and Mary K.) Charitable Trust ▼ ☐

404 Cities Service Bldg.
Tulsa 74119

Trust established in 1976 in Oklahoma.
Donor(s): H.A. Chapman.†
Financial data: (yr. ended 12/31/83): Assets, $25,621,110 (M); gifts received, $2,207,633; expenditures, $1,065,709, including $848,037 for 20 grants (high: $333,000; low: $3,037).
Purpose and activities: Primarily local giving; grants largely for education, particularly higher education, and a hospital, social services and cultural programs.
Limitations: Giving primarily in Tulsa, OK.
Application information:
 Write: Ralph L. Abercrombie, Trustee
Trustees: Ralph L. Abercrombie, Donne W. Pitman.
Employer Identification Number: 736177739

3423
Cities Service Foundation ▼

110 West Seventh St.
P.O. Box 300
Tulsa 74102 (918) 561-8628

Incorporated in 1954 in Delaware.
Donor(s): Cities Service Company, Inc.
Financial data: (yr. ended 12/31/82): Assets, $8,503,792 (M); gifts received, $815,000; expenditures, $1,864,659, including $1,844,372 for 472 grants (high: $200,000; low: $50).
Purpose and activities: General purposes; general giving, with emphasis on higher education and community funds in areas of company operations.
Limitations: Giving primarily in areas of company operations. No grants to individuals, or for endowment funds or special projects; support rarely for building funds.
Application information:
 Initial approach: Letter
 Copies of proposal: 1
 Write: Ms. Janelle L. McCammon, Executive Secretary
Officers: D.A. Hentschel,* President; R.D. Dillsaver,* Vice-President; Janelle L. McCammon,* Executive Secretary; H.E. Bockelken, Secretary; F.O. Affeld,* Treasurer.
Trustees:* F. Bam, M.T. Edgerton, Jr., P.C. Hebner, S.F. Jones, G.O. Nolley, G.G. Zipf.
Number of staff: 1 full-time professional; 1 part-time professional; 1 full-time support.
Employer Identification Number: 136081799

3424
Collins (The George and Jennie) Foundation ☐

Collins Bldg.
317 East Lee St.
Sapulpa 74066

Trust established in 1943 in Oklahoma.
Donor(s): George F. Collins, Jr.,† Liberty Glass Company, and others.
Financial data: (yr. ended 12/31/82): Assets, $2,280,329 (M); expenditures, $43,497, including $40,675 for 15 grants (high: $10,000; low: $250).
Purpose and activities: Broad purposes; primarily local giving, with emphasis on higher and secondary education, community funds, and cultural programs.
Limitations: Giving primarily in OK.
Officers and Trustees: Loreine C. Dietrich, Chairman and Treasurer; Frank P. Collins, Secretary.
Employer Identification Number: 736093053

3425
Collins (George Fulton), Jr. Foundation

Collins Bldg.
317 East Lee St.
Sapulpa 74066 (918) 224-1440
Additional address: 2251 East Skelly Dr., Tulsa, OK 74105

Established in 1968 in Oklahoma.

Financial data: (yr. ended 12/31/83): Assets, $2,900,000 (M); expenditures, $75,424, including $71,650 for 11 grants (high: $60,000; low: $250).
Purpose and activities: Broad purposes; primarily local giving, with emphasis on higher education, health agencies, and Protestant church support.
Limitations: Giving primarily in OK.
Officers and Trustees: Fulton Collins, Chairman; Frank M. Engle, Secretary; Loreine C. Dietrich, Treasurer.
Employer Identification Number: 237008179

3426
Cuesta Foundation, Inc., The
One Williams Center, Suite 4400
Tulsa 74172

Incorporated in 1962 in Oklahoma.
Donor(s): Charles W. Oliphant, Allene O. Mayo, Allen G. Oliphant, Jr., Gertrude O. Sundgren.
Financial data: (yr. ended 4/30/84): Assets, $1,743,203 (M); gifts received, $102,000; expenditures, $231,731, including $220,883 for 62 grants (high: $30,000; low: $500).
Purpose and activities: Charitable purposes; primarily local giving, with emphasis on higher education; support also for the performing arts, social agencies, and a population control organization.
Limitations: Giving primarily in OK.
Officers and Directors: Charles W. Oliphant, Chairman; Eric B. Oliphant, President; Richard E. Wright, III, Secretary; Walter McAuley, Treasurer; Allene O. Mayo, Arline B. Oliphant, Gertrude O. Oliphant.
Employer Identification Number: 736091550

3427
Dobson (Nellie) Trust ⌂
c/o Bank of Oklahoma
P.O. Box 2300
Tulsa 74192

Trust established in 1968 in Oklahoma.
Donor(s): Nellie Dobson.†
Financial data: (yr. ended 1/31/82): Assets, $2,767,263 (M); expenditures, $566,923, including $348,102 for 1 grant.
Purpose and activities: Giving largely to a local junior college, including support for scholarships.
Types of support awarded: Scholarship funds.
Limitations: Giving primarily in OK.
Trustee: Bank of Oklahoma.
Employer Identification Number: 736131333

3428
Dolese Foundation, The ⌂
P.O. Box 677
Oklahoma City 73101

Established in 1979.
Financial data: (yr. ended 3/31/84): Assets, $19,139 (M); gifts received, $160,000; expenditures, $146,873, including $146,864 for 26 grants (high: $50,000; low: $300).

Purpose and activities: Primarily local giving for higher education, cultural programs, health organizations, and the environment.
Limitations: Giving primarily in OK.
Trustees: W. Bryan Arnn, Roger M. Dolese, Edmond E. Soule.
Employer Identification Number: 731074447

3429
Fields (Laura) Trust
P.O. Box 2394
Lawton 73502   (405) 355-3733

Trust established in 1950 in Oklahoma.
Donor(s): Laura Fields.†
Financial data: (yr. ended 6/30/84): Assets, $1,410,786 (M); gifts received, $52,919; expenditures, $94,525, including $17,000 for 12 grants (high: $3,391; low: $260), $11,000 for 17 grants to individuals and $53,140 for 40 loans.
Purpose and activities: Primarily local giving, with emphasis on student loans; grants also for higher education and youth agencies.
Types of support awarded: Lectureships, student aid, loans.
Limitations: Giving limited to Comanche County, OK, residents.
Application information: Application form required.
   Initial approach: Letter
   Copies of proposal: 1
   Deadline(s): None
   Board meeting date(s): Second Tuesday of each month
   Write: Jay Dee Fountain, Executive Secretary
Officer: T.D. Nicklas, Chairman; Jay Dee Fountain, Executive Secretary.
Trustees: George Bridges, Jack Brock, David Dennis, Jim Gordon, Clare Morford.
Number of staff: 2 part-time professional.
Employer Identification Number: 736095854

3430
First National Foundation, Inc. ⌂
120 North Robinson
P.O. Box 25189
Oklahoma City 73125   (405) 272-4193

Incorporated in 1954 in Oklahoma.
Donor(s): First National Bank and Trust Company.
Financial data: (yr. ended 12/31/83): Assets, $696,493 (M); expenditures, $266,372, including $263,357 for 63 grants (high: $49,483; low: $25).
Purpose and activities: Local giving, with emphasis on community funds, higher education, cultural programs, youth agencies, and hospitals.
Types of support awarded: Annual campaigns, seed money, building funds, equipment, consulting services, technical assistance, scholarship funds.
Limitations: Giving primarily in OK. No grants to individuals or for matching gifts; no loans.
Publications: Application guidelines.
Application information:
   Initial approach: Letter or proposal
   Copies of proposal: 1

Deadline(s): Submit proposal preferably in December, March, June, or September; deadline 15 days before board meetings
Board meeting date(s): January, April, July, and October
Final notification: 15 days after meetings
Write: John Sherry, Secretary
Officers: Charles A. Vose, Sr., Chairman; Charles A. Vose, Jr., Vice-Chairman; Charles Nelson, President; John Sherry, Secretary; William Dick, Treasurer.
Number of staff: 2.
Employer Identification Number: 736099287

3431
Gilcrease (Thomas) Foundation ⌂
2591 West Newton St.
Tulsa 74127

Incorporated in 1942 in Oklahoma.
Donor(s): Thomas Gilcrease.†
Financial data: (yr. ended 9/30/82): Assets, $1,262,690 (M); expenditures, $36,237.
Purpose and activities: Primarily local giving, with emphasis on a museum.
Limitations: Giving primarily in OK.
Officers and Trustees:* Barton Gilcrease,* President; Barta Gilcrease Busby,* Peter D. Denny,* Thomas G. Denny,* Eugene F. Gilcrease,* Grace Folsom Gilcrease,* Jana Gilcrease Moody,* Vice-Presidents; Mrs. E.C. Teenor, Secretary and Treasurer.
Employer Identification Number: 736009934

3432
Goddard (The Charles B.) Foundation
1000 Energy Center, Suite 102
P.O. Box 1485
Ardmore 73401   (405) 226-6040

Trust established in 1958 in Oklahoma.
Donor(s): Charles B. Goddard.†
Financial data: (yr. ended 6/30/83): Assets, $1,995,375 (M); expenditures, $199,929, including $193,464 for 52 grants (high: $25,000; low: $75).
Purpose and activities: Broad purposes; general giving, with emphasis on local community funds, youth agencies, and secondary and elementary education; grants limited to local organizations or programs of nationwide impact.
Types of support awarded: Operating budgets, continuing support, annual campaigns, seed money, emergency funds, building funds, equipment, land acquisition, research.
Limitations: Giving limited to southern OK and northern TX, and to programs of nationwide impact. No grants to individuals, or for endowment funds; no loans.
Publications: 990-PF.
Application information:
   Initial approach: Letter
   Copies of proposal: 1
   Deadline(s): Submit proposal preferably in March through September
   Board meeting date(s): April and October
   Write: William R. Goddard, Jr., Chairman

Officers and Trustees: William R. Goddard, Jr., Chairman; William M. Johns, Secretary-Treasurer; Elizabeth E. Cashman, Ann G. Corrigan, William R. Goddard.
Number of staff: None.
Employer Identification Number: 756005868

3433
Gussman (Herbert and Roseline) Foundation ⌑
3200 First National Tower
Tulsa 74103

Established in 1951 in Oklahoma.
Donor(s): Herbert Gussman, Roseline Gussman, Barbara Gussman, Ellen Jane Adelson.
Financial data: (yr. ended 12/31/83): Assets, $3,113,992 (M); expenditures, $106,869, including $99,313 for 61 grants (high: $25,000; low: $10).
Purpose and activities: Broad purposes; general giving, with emphasis on local Jewish welfare funds, cultural programs, and educational institutions.
Limitations: Giving primarily in OK.
Trustees: Herbert Gussman, Roseline Gussman.
Employer Identification Number: 736090063

3434
Harmon (Pearl M. and Julia J.) Foundation
P.O. Box 52568
Tulsa 74152   (918) 584-1778

Trust established in 1962 in Oklahoma.
Donor(s): Claude C. Harmon.†
Financial data: (yr. ended 5/31/84): Assets, $5,848,480 (M); expenditures, $567,968, including $337,393 for 5 grants.
Purpose and activities: Scholarship support to specified local universities and loans to charitable organizations in Oklahoma, Arkansas, New Mexico, Texas, and Kansas.
Types of support awarded: Scholarship funds, loans.
Limitations: Giving limited to organizations in OK, AR, KS, NM, and TX, with preference given to northeast OK. No grants to individuals.
Publications: Application guidelines.
Application information: Describe project, state amount requested, and enclose IRS exemption letter; scholarship applications should be directed to the financial aid offices of Oklahoma Baptist University, Oklahoma City University, or Tulsa University.
  Initial approach: Letter or telephone
  Copies of proposal: 1
  Board meeting date(s): Monthly
  Write: George L. Hangs, Jr., Secretary-Treasurer
Officers and Trustees: Julia J. Harmon, Chairman; George L. Hangs, Sr., Managing Trustee; George L. Hangs, Jr., Secretary-Treasurer; Hugh Conine, Naomi Hangs, George W. Lee, L.A. Leffler, First National Bank.
Employer Identification Number: 736095893

3435
Harris Foundation, Incorporated ⌑
6403 Northwest Grand Blvd.
Oklahoma City 73116   (405) 848-3371

Incorporated in 1938 in Oklahoma.
Donor(s): Vernon V. Harris.†
Financial data: (yr. ended 12/31/83): Assets, $2,235,711 (M); expenditures, $350,502, including $305,262 for 49 grants (high: $50,000; low: $150).
Purpose and activities: Broad purposes; primarily local giving with emphasis on higher education, youth and health agencies, Protestant church support, and cultural programs.
Types of support awarded: Building funds, equipment, fellowships.
Limitations: Giving primarily in OK, with emphasis on Oklahoma City.
Application information:
  Deadline(s): None
  Write: Margaret Harris Long, President
Officers and Directors: Margaret Harris Long, President; Pat J. Patterson, Secretary; Judith Harris Garrett, Jane C. Harris, William V. Harris, Robert F. Long.
Employer Identification Number: 736093072

3436
Helmerich Foundation, The
1579 East 21st St.
Tulsa 74114   (918) 742-5531

Established in 1965 in Oklahoma.
Donor(s): W.H. Helmerich.†
Financial data: (yr. ended 9/30/82): Assets, $1,452,192 (M); gifts received, $105,000; expenditures, $120,036, including $115,500 for 17 grants (high: $20,000; low: $500).
Purpose and activities: Local giving of large capital gifts, with emphasis on Protestant church support and religious organizations, and on cultural programs, youth and health agencies, and a community development project.
Types of support awarded: Building funds, equipment.
Limitations: Giving limited to the Tulsa, OK, area. No grants to individuals, or for general support, operating budgets, continuing support, annual campaigns, seed money, emergency funds, deficit financing, land acquisition, endowment funds, matching gifts, scholarships or fellowships, program support, research, demonstration projects, publications, or conferences; no loans.
Publications: Application guidelines, program policy statement.
Application information:
  Initial approach: Full proposal
  Copies of proposal: 1
  Deadline(s): None
  Board meeting date(s): As required
  Final notification: 4 weeks
  Write: Hans Helmerich, Assistant to the Director
Trustee: W.H. Helmerich, III.
Number of staff: None.
Employer Identification Number: 736105607

3437
Johnson (Dexter G.) Educational and Benevolent Trust ⌑
644 Avondale Dr.
Oklahoma City 73116

Trust established in 1971 in Oklahoma.
Financial data: (yr. ended 12/31/83): Assets, $3,689,839 (M); expenditures, $216,974, including $6,669 for 13 grants to individuals and $141,425 for 28 loans.
Purpose and activities: Local giving primarily for student loans; grants also to individuals for audiological evaluations, speech therapy, and medical equipment.
Types of support awarded: Student aid, equipment, grants to individuals.
Limitations: Giving limited to OK.
Trustee: Phil E. Daugherty.
Employer Identification Number: 237389204

3438
Jones (Montfort) and Allie Brown Jones Foundation ⌑
P.O. Box 567
Bristow 74010

Trust established in 1960 in Oklahoma.
Donor(s): Allie B. Jones.†
Financial data: (yr. ended 8/31/83): Assets, $2,449,655 (M); expenditures, $118,102, including $87,262 for 20 grants (high: $25,000; low: $40).
Purpose and activities: Charitable purposes; support for educational, civic, and charitable institutions in the local area only.
Limitations: Giving limited to OK. No grants for scholarships (except funds at Southern Methodist University and University of Mississippi).
Application information:
  Write: David H. Loeffler, Chairman
Officers and Trustees: David H. Loeffler, Chairman; David H. Loeffler, Jr., Rowland L. Collins, Velma J. Collins, Vice-Chairmen; Hazel S. Earnhardt, Secretary.
Employer Identification Number: 730721557

3439
Kerr Foundation, Inc., The ▼
6301 North Western, Suite 120
Oklahoma City 73118   (405) 842-1510
Mailing address: P.O. Box 13009, Oklahoma City, OK 73113

Incorporated in 1963 in Oklahoma.
Donor(s): Mrs. Grayce B. Kerr Flynn.†
Financial data: (yr. ended 12/31/84): Assets, $58,800,000 (M); expenditures, $3,560,800, including $1,537,500 for 82 grants (high: $200,000; low: $500; average: $18,750) and $610,950 for 1 foundation-administered program.
Purpose and activities: Challenge grants to organizations and institutions serving young people; agricultural program provides consultation and demonstration services to small farmers in eastern Oklahoma.

Types of support awarded: Continuing support, annual campaigns, seed money, emergency funds, building funds, equipment, land acquisition, matching funds, consulting services, professorships, internships, scholarship funds, fellowships, special projects, research, publications, conferences and seminars.
Limitations: Giving primarily in OK and the six adjoining states: AR, TX, NM, CO, KS, and MO. No grants to individuals.
Publications: Annual report, program policy statement, application guidelines.
Application information: Application form required.
  Initial approach: Letter
  Copies of proposal: 18
  Deadline(s): April 1 and October 1
  Board meeting date(s): June and December
  Final notification: Within 1 week of board meeting
  Write: Dr. Anne Hodges Morgan, Vice-President for Programs
Officers: Robert S. Kerr, Jr.,* President and Chairman; James E. Horne, Vice-President for Agriculture; Daniel P. Junkin, Administrative Vice-President; Anne H. Morgan, Vice-President for Programs; Gwendene Underwood, Secretary; Breene M. Kerr,* Treasurer.
Trustees:* Kay Kerr Adair, Vice-Chairman; Robert C. Adair, Sr., Joffa Kerr, Lou C. Kerr, Sheryl V. Kerr, William G. Kerr, Gerald R. Marshall, Elmer B. Staats, James E. Webb, Walter Woolley, Jr.
Number of staff: 12 full-time professional; 1 part-time professional; 18 full-time support; 3 part-time support.
Employer Identification Number: 736099312

3440
Kerr-McGee Foundation, Inc. ▼ ⌶
Kerr-McGee Center
Oklahoma City 73102   (405) 270-1313

Incorporated in 1963 in Oklahoma.
Donor(s): Kerr-McGee Corporation.
Financial data: (yr. ended 12/31/83): Assets, $1,029,042 (M); gifts received, $985,000; expenditures, $883,184, including $881,655 for 196 grants (high: $95,000; low: $10; average: $100-$20,000).
Purpose and activities: Charitable and educational purposes; primarily local giving, with emphasis on higher education; support also for cultural programs, health, social services, and a community fund.
Types of support awarded: Employee matching gifts.
Limitations: Giving primarily in OK. No grants to individuals; no loans.
Application information:
  Initial approach: Letter
  Deadline(s): None
  Board meeting date(s): Varies
  Write: R.D. Robins, Treasurer
Officers and Directors:* Dean A. McGee,* President; Marvin K. Hambrick,* Vice-President; William E. Heimann,* Secretary; R.D. Robins, Treasurer.
Number of staff: 1 full-time support.
Employer Identification Number: 510164960

3441
Kirkpatrick Foundation, Inc.
1300 North Broadway
Oklahoma City 73103   (405) 235-5621

Incorporated in 1955 in Oklahoma.
Donor(s): Eleanor B. Kirkpatrick, John E. Kirkpatrick, Kirkpatrick Oil Company, Joan E. Kirkpatrick, Kathryn T. Blake.†
Financial data: (yr. ended 12/31/82): Assets, $2,680,652 (L); expenditures, $789,162, including $673,882 for 178 grants (high: $420,000; low: $15).
Purpose and activities: Primarily local giving, with emphasis on community programs and cultural activities.
Types of support awarded: Operating budgets, continuing support, annual campaigns, emergency funds.
Limitations: Giving primarily in OK. No grants to individuals, or for building or endowment funds, or scholarships and fellowships; no loans.
Application information:
  Initial approach: Letter
  Copies of proposal: 1
  Deadline(s): None
  Board meeting date(s): March, June, September, and December
  Final notification: Up to 3 months
  Write: Joan E. Kirkpatrick, President
Officers and Directors: John E. Kirkpatrick, Chairman; Joan E. Kirkpatrick, President; Christian Kent Keesee, Vice-President; Eleanor J. Maurer, Secretary; Eleanor B. Kirkpatrick, Treasurer; Jack Abernathy, C.D. Ellison, Ed Joullian, Morrison G. Tucker.
Number of staff: None.
Employer Identification Number: 730701736

3442
Lyon (E. H.) and Melody Lyon Foundation, Inc. ⌶
c/o Union Bank and Trust Company
P.O. Box 939
Bartlesville 74003   (918) 336-0066

Established about 1975 in Oklahoma.
Donor(s): E.H. Lyon, Melody Lyon.†
Financial data: (yr. ended 12/31/83): Assets, $9,971,485 (M); gifts received, $54,421; expenditures, $574,099, including $509,278 for 9 grants (high: $411,665; low: $2,000).
Purpose and activities: Primarily local giving, with emphasis on civic projects, particularly parks and recreation, and on education and a medical foundation.
Limitations: Giving primarily in Bartlesville, OK.
Application information:
  Initial approach: Letter
  Deadline(s): None
  Write: Don Donaldson, President
Officers and Directors: Don Donaldson, President; Charles W. Selby, Vice-President; James W. Conner, Secretary and Treasurer; Walter W. Allison, John F. Kane.
Employer Identification Number: 237299980

3443
Mabee (The J. E. and L. E.) Foundation, Inc. ▼
420 Williams Center Tower I, One West Third St.
Tulsa 74103   (918) 584-4286

Incorporated in 1948 in Delaware.
Donor(s): J.E. Mabee,† L.E. Mabee.†
Financial data: (yr. ended 8/31/84): Assets, $341,450,443 (M); expenditures, $20,061,494, including $18,182,834 for 96 grants (high: $2,000,000; low: $300; average: $10,000-$400,000).
Purpose and activities: To aid Christian religious organizations, charitable organizations, vocational and technical schools, institutions of higher learning, and scientific research; to support hospitals and other agencies and institutions engaged in the discovery, treatment, and care of diseases.
Types of support awarded: Building funds, equipment, matching funds, continuing support, annual campaigns.
Limitations: Giving limited to OK, TX, KS, AR, MO, and NM. No support for secondary or elementary education, or tax-supported institutions. No grants to individuals, or for research, endowment funds, scholarships, fellowships, or operating expenses; no loans.
Publications: Program policy statement, application guidelines.
Application information:
  Initial approach: Full proposal
  Copies of proposal: 1
  Deadline(s): 15th of month preceding board meetings
  Board meeting date(s): January, April, July, and October
  Final notification: 1 week after board meetings
  Write: Guy R. Mabee, Chairman
Officers and Trustees: Guy R. Mabee, Chairman; John H. Conway, Jr., John W. Cox, Joe Mabee, Donald P. Moyers, Vice-Chairmen.
Number of staff: 5 part-time professional.
Employer Identification Number: 736090162

3444
MAPCO Educational Foundation, Inc.
P.O. Box 645
Tulsa 74101-0645   (918) 584-4471

Established in 1976 in Oklahoma.
Donor(s): MAPCO, Inc., and subsidiary companies.
Financial data: (yr. ended 12/31/82): Assets, $221,405 (M); gifts received, $186,545; expenditures, $423,240, including $397,200 for 24 grants (high: $135,000; low: $500) and $23,548 for 25 employee matching gifts.
Purpose and activities: Grants to private secondary schools, and to "junior colleges, colleges, universities, and similar institutions of higher learning."
Types of support awarded: Employee matching gifts.
Limitations: No grants to individuals; no loans.
Publications: Program policy statement, application guidelines.
Application information:
  Initial approach: Full proposal

Copies of proposal: 1
Write: W. Curtis Fossett, Assistant Treasurer
Officers and Trustees: Robert E. Thomas,* Chairman; James E. Barnes,* President; G. Dean Cosgrove, Vice-President and Treasurer; Joseph W. Craft III, James R. Grimm,* G.V. Rohleder, Vice-Presidents; Royse M. Parr, Secretary.
Employer Identification Number: 731025281

3445
McCasland Foundation ¤
P.O. Box 400
McCasland Bldg.
Duncan 73533   (405) 252-5580

Trust established in 1952 in Oklahoma.
Donor(s): Members of the McCasland family, Mack Oil Co., Jath Oil Co., and others.
Financial data: (yr. ended 12/31/83): Assets, $14,160,896 (M); gifts received, $1,777,768; expenditures, $615,727, including $580,925 for 49 grants (high: $115,000; low: $250).
Purpose and activities: Primarily local and regional giving, with emphasis on higher education, a hospital, a home for boys, and community welfare.
Types of support awarded: Scholarship funds, general purposes, building funds.
Limitations: Giving primarily in OK and the Southwest.
Application information:
Initial approach: Letter
Deadline(s): None
Write: W.H. Phelps, Trustee
Trustees: T.H. McCasland, Jr., Mary Frances Maurer, W.H. Phelps.
Employer Identification Number: 736096032

3446
McGee Foundation, Inc., The ¤
2900 McGee Tower
P.O. Box 25861
Oklahoma City 73125   (405) 270-1313

Incorporated in 1963 in Oklahoma.
Donor(s): Dean A. McGee.
Financial data: (yr. ended 6/30/83): Assets, $2,811,183 (M); gifts received, $30,000; expenditures, $122,665, including $119,231 for grants.
Purpose and activities: Charitable and educational purposes; primarily local and California giving for higher education and medical research.
Limitations: Giving primarily in OK and CA. No grants to individuals or for endowment funds.
Application information: Funds currently committed.
Initial approach: Full proposal
Copies of proposal: 1
Board meeting date(s): As required
Write: Dean A. McGee, President
Officers and Directors: Dean A. McGee, President; Dorothea S. McGee, Vice-President and Secretary; Marcia Ann Bieber, Patricia Dean Maino.
Employer Identification Number: 736099203

3447
McMahon Foundation, The ▼
714-716 C Ave.
P.O. Box 2156
Lawton 73502   (405) 355-4622

Incorporated in 1940 in Oklahoma.
Donor(s): Eugene D. McMahon,† Mrs. Louise D. McMahon.†
Financial data: (yr. ended 3/31/84): Assets, $19,116,107 (M); expenditures, $3,055,729, including $2,430,126 for 28 grants (high: $693,343; low: $260).
Purpose and activities: Primarily local giving for education, social welfare and youth agencies, and community projects.
Limitations: Giving primarily in Lawton and Comanche County, OK.
Application information:
Initial approach: Letter
Board meeting date(s): Monthly
Write: Charles S. Graybill, M.D., Chairman
Officers: Manville Redman,* Secretary-Treasurer; James F. Wood, Director.
Trustees: Charles S. Graybill, M.D., Chairman; Donald Angus, Vice-Chairman; Kenneth Bridges, Gale Sadler, Orban E. Sanders, Frank C. Steed.
Employer Identification Number: 730664314

3448
Merrick Foundation, The ¤
425 First Ave., Southwest
Ardmore 73401   (405) 223-1631

Trust established in 1947 in Oklahoma; incorporated in 1968.
Donor(s): Mrs. F.W. Merrick,† and others.
Financial data: (yr. ended 12/31/83): Assets, $4,449,946 (M); expenditures, $210,973, including $166,516 for 35 grants (high: $25,400; low: $98).
Purpose and activities: Primarily local giving, with emphasis on higher education and hospitals; grants also for medical research, youth agencies, and a community fund.
Limitations: Giving primarily in OK. No grants to individuals, or for endowment funds.
Application information:
Initial approach: Letter
Copies of proposal: 1
Deadline(s): Submit proposal in September or October
Board meeting date(s): Semiannually
Write: Ward S. Merrick, Jr., Vice-President
Officers and Trustees: Elizabeth Merrick Coe, President; Ward S. Merrick, Jr., Vice-President; Valda M. Buchanan, Secretary; Robert Batis, Michael A. Cawley, Charles R. Coe, Jr., Bill Goddard, Jack D. Wilkes.
Employer Identification Number: 736111622

3449
Noble (The Samuel Roberts) Foundation, Inc. ▼
P.O. Box 2180
Ardmore 73402   (405) 223-5810

Trust established in 1945 in Oklahoma; incorporated in 1952.
Donor(s): Lloyd Noble.†

Financial data: (yr. ended 10/31/84): Assets, $301,315,971 (M); expenditures, $16,002,833, including $9,609,110 for 104 grants (high: $1,000,000; low: $500; average: $100,000), $39,000 for 49 grants to individuals, $81,644 for 36 employee matching gifts and $5,287,031 for 2 foundation-administered programs.
Purpose and activities: Supports its own two operating programs: 1) basic biomedical research pertaining to cancer and degenerative diseases; and 2) agricultural research, consultation, and demonstration, along with wildlife management--primarily in south central Oklahoma--for the benefit of rural and urban people.Primarily, grants are for higher education capital funds and for health research pertaining to cancer and degenerative diseases.
Types of support awarded: Research, employee related scholarships, seed money, building funds, equipment, endowment funds, scholarship funds, matching funds.
Limitations: Giving primarily in the Southwest, with emphasis on OK. No grants to individuals (except through the scholarship program for children of employees of Noble organizations); no loans.
Publications: Annual report, program policy statement, application guidelines.
Application information: Application form required.
Initial approach: Letter
Copies of proposal: 1
Deadline(s): 6 weeks prior to board meeting dates
Board meeting date(s): Usually in January, April, July, and October
Final notification: 2 weeks after board meetings
Write: John F. Snodgrass, President
Officers: John F. Snodgrass,* President; M.K. Patterson, Jr., Gary D. Simmons, Vice-Presidents; Jackie N. Skidmore, Secretary; Larry Pulliam, Treasurer.
Trustees: Ann Noble Brown, David R. Brown, Ben D. Floyd, Jr., W.R. Goddard, John R. March, Edward E. Noble, Mary Jane Noble, Sam Noble, Joseph L. Parker.
Number of staff: 87 full-time professional.
Employer Identification Number: 730606209

3450
Noble (The Vivian Bilby) Foundation, Inc.
P.O. Box 817
Ardmore 73402   (405) 223-5810

Trust established in 1936 in Oklahoma; incorporated in 1959.
Donor(s): Lloyd Noble.†
Financial data: (yr. ended 12/31/84): Assets, $2,011,750 (M); expenditures, $86,390, including $86,300 for 9 grants (high: $50,000; low: $300; average: $9,500).
Purpose and activities: Broad purposes; giving primarily in the southwestern United States, with emphasis on education, church support, and youth agencies; some support also for cultural programs and community social service organizations.

Types of support awarded: Operating budgets, continuing support, annual campaigns, building funds, equipment, land acquisition, endowment funds.
Limitations: Giving primarily in the southwestern United States. No grants to individuals, or for seed money, emergency funds, deficit financing, matching gifts, scholarships, fellowships, special projects, research, publications, or conferences; no loans.
Publications: Application guidelines.
Application information: Application form required.
  Initial approach: Letter
  Copies of proposal: 1
  Deadline(s): Submit proposal preferably in June through August; deadline August 31
  Board meeting date(s): October and as needed
  Final notification: 2 months
  Write: Larry Pulliam, Assistant Secretary
Officers and Trustees: Edward E. Noble, President; Sam Noble, Vice-President; Ann Noble Brown, Secretary-Treasurer.
Number of staff: 1 part-time professional; 1 part-time support.
Employer Identification Number: 736090116

3451
Oklahoma City Community Foundation, Inc.
1300 North Broadway
Oklahoma City 73103   (405) 235-5603

Community foundation incorporated in 1969 in Oklahoma.
Financial data: (yr. ended 12/31/83): Assets, $21,137,785 (M); gifts received, $4,159,570; expenditures, $1,471,559, including $1,328,390 for 154 grants (high: $444,921; low: $47).
Purpose and activities: Primarily local giving to charitable, educational, health and cultural organizations.
Types of support awarded: Scholarship funds, fellowships, matching funds, operating budgets, continuing support, annual campaigns, seed money, emergency funds, building funds, equipment, research, special projects.
Limitations: Giving primarily in greater Oklahoma City, OK. No support for religious organizations. No grants to individuals, or for endowment funds, deficit financing, land acquisition, demonstration projects, publications, or conferences; no loans.
Publications: Annual report.
Application information:
  Initial approach: Telephone
  Copies of proposal: 1
  Deadline(s): October 1
  Board meeting date(s): January, April, July, and October
  Write: Robert Woolsey, Executive Director
Officers: Edward C. Joullian III,* President; Marilyn Meyers,* Vice-President; C. Don Ellison, Secretary; Eleanor J. Maurer, Treasurer; Robert Woolsey, Executive Director.
Trustees:* Jean I. Everest, Richard Harrison, Dan Hogan III, Gerald R. Marshall, F.M. Petree, Clayton Rich, Morrison G. Tucker.

Trustee Banks: Bank Oklahoma, Citizens National Bank, First National Bank and Trust Company, Liberty National Bank & Trust Company of Oklahoma City, Trust Company of Oklahoma.
Number of staff: 1 part-time professional; 1 full-time support; 1 part-time support.
Employer Identification Number: 237024262

3452
Oklahoma Gas and Electric Company Foundation, Inc.
321 North Harvey
P.O. Box 321
Oklahoma City 73101   (405) 272-3196

Incorporated in 1957 in Oklahoma.
Donor(s): Oklahoma Gas and Electric Company.
Financial data: (yr. ended 12/31/84): Assets, $1,157,862 (M); expenditures, $491,111, including $462,275 for 70 grants (high: $50,000; low: $200; average: $3,000-$10,000) and $20,412 for 83 employee matching gifts.
Purpose and activities: General purposes; giving in areas of Company operations, with emphasis on higher educational institutions, including building and scholarship funds, and on hospitals and youth agencies.
Types of support awarded: Operating budgets, continuing support, annual campaigns, seed money, building funds, equipment, employee matching gifts, professorships, scholarship funds.
Limitations: Giving limited to OK, in areas of company operations. No grants to individuals; no loans.
Application information:
  Initial approach: Letter or full proposal
  Copies of proposal: 1
  Deadline(s): None
  Board meeting date(s): As required
  Final notification: 1 month
  Write: James G. Harlow, Jr., President
Officers and Directors:* James G. Harlow, Jr., President; Patrick J. Ryan, A.M. Strecker, Vice-Presidents; Irma B. Elliott, Secretary-Treasurer.
Number of staff: None.
Employer Identification Number: 736093572

3453
Parker (The Robert L.) Foundation ☐
8 E. Third St.
Tulsa 74103

Established in 1973.
Donor(s): Robert L. Parker.
Financial data: (yr. ended 11/30/83): Assets, $537,348 (M); gifts received, $250,000; expenditures, $482,000, including $480,193 for grants.
Purpose and activities: Charitable purposes.
Trustees: Robert L. Parker, Jr., Jack E. Short.
Employer Identification Number: 510153008

3454
Parman (Robert A.) Foundation ☐
c/o First National Bank & Trust Co.
P.O. Box 25189
Oklahoma City 73125

Trust established in 1962 in Oklahoma.
Donor(s): Robert A. Parman.†
Financial data: (yr. ended 8/31/81): Assets, $1,194,941 (M); expenditures, $42,048, including $25,796 for 4 grants (high: $12,698; low: $200).
Purpose and activities: Primarily local giving, largely limited to a school, an organization for the blind, and two hospitals.
Limitations: Giving primarily in OK.
Trustees: Donald W. Burleson, Rev. J. Clyde Wheeler.
Employer Identification Number: 736098053

3455
Phillips (The Frank) Foundation, Inc.
P.O. Box 1647
Bartlesville 74005   (918) 336-0307

Incorporated in 1937 in Delaware.
Donor(s): Frank Phillips,† Mrs. Frank Phillips,† Phillips Petroleum.
Financial data: (yr. ended 12/31/83): Assets, $18,019,965 (M); gifts received, $621,216; expenditures, $1,109,966, including $32,083 for 12 grants (high: $8,000; low: $150; average: $2,000) and $981,271 for 1 foundation-administered program.
Purpose and activities: A private operating foundation established primarily to maintain and operate Woolaroc, a 3,500-acre wildlife preserve, Western-Indian museum, historic lodge, and the national Y-Indian guide center and its connecting nature trails, owned and operated by the foundation. Some grants to local eligible charitable agencies as funds are available, with emphasis on youth programs.
Limitations: Giving limited to OK. No grants to individuals, or for building or endowment funds, research programs, scholarships or fellowships; no loans.
Publications: Program policy statement, application guidelines.
Application information:
  Initial approach: Letter
  Copies of proposal: 1
  Board meeting date(s): Monthly
  Write: William R. Blakemore, General Manager
Officer: William R. Blakemore, Secretary-Treasurer and General Manager.
Trustees: Leo H. Johnstone, Vice-Chairman; William G. Creel, Donald Doty, Richard Kane, V.M. Lockard, Robert B. Phillips.
Number of staff: 31 full-time professional; 8 part-time professional.
Employer Identification Number: 730636562

3456
Phillips Petroleum Foundation, Inc. ▼ ☐
Phillips Bldg., 16th Fl.
Bartlesville 74004   (918) 661-6248

Incorporated in 1973 in Oklahoma.

Donor(s): Phillips Petroleum Company.
Financial data: (yr. ended 12/31/83): Assets,
$1,849,462 (M); gifts received, $5,296,108;
expenditures, $4,609,925, including
$3,595,030 for 712 grants (high: $520,801;
low: $60) and $980,935 for employee
matching gifts.
Purpose and activities: General giving, with
emphasis on higher education, community
funds, civic and youth organizations, and
cultural programs. Preference given to local
organizations at Phillips plant locations or
operating areas.
Types of support awarded: Employee
matching gifts, operating budgets, annual
campaigns, seed money, emergency funds,
building funds, equipment, land acquisition,
endowment funds, program-related
investments, research, conferences and
seminars, scholarship funds, fellowships,
professorships, internships, exchange programs,
matching funds, continuing support.
Limitations: Giving primarily in areas of
company operations. Generally no grants to
sectarian, religious, and specialized health
organizations. No grants to individuals or for
trips; no loans.
Publications: Application guidelines, 990-PF.
Application information:
 Initial approach: Proposal, letter, or
  telephone
 Copies of proposal: 1
 Deadline(s): None
 Board meeting date(s): January and as
  required
 Final notification: 6 to 8 weeks
 Write: John C. West, Executive Director
Officers: M.E. Kissell,* President; J.T. Boyd,*
C.B. Friley,* Vice-Presidents; G.C. Meese,
Secretary; R.E. Wahlgren, Treasurer;.
Directors:* D.J. Billam, E.R. Chandler, Colleen
Hutchison, Stanley R. Mueller.
Number of staff: 2 part-time professional; 2
part-time support.
Employer Identification Number: 237326611

3457
Price Foundation, Inc. ⌗
P.O. Box 1111
Bartlesville 74005

Incorporated in 1952 in Oklahoma.
Donor(s): Members of the Price family.
Financial data: (yr. ended 12/31/83): Assets,
$1,480,660 (M); expenditures, $49,153,
including $32,965 for 11 grants (high: $12,500;
low: $40).
Purpose and activities: Broad purposes;
primarily local giving, with emphasis on youth
agencies, cultural organizations, education, and
a local community fund.
Limitations: Giving primarily in Bartlesville, OK.
Application information:
 Write: Harold C. Price, President
Officers: Harold C. Price, President; Joe D.
Price, Vice-President; W.E. Yount, Secretary-
Treasurer.
Employer Identification Number: 736093113

3458
Puterbaugh Foundation ⌗
235 East Choctaw, First National Center, Suite
117
P.O. Box 729
McAlester 74501   (918) 426-1591

Trust established in 1949 in Oklahoma.
Donor(s): Jay Garfield Puterbaugh,† Leela
Oliver Puterbaugh.†
Financial data: (yr. ended 12/31/83): Assets,
$4,410,807 (M); gifts received, $145,722;
expenditures, $302,866, including $244,616
for 34 grants (high: $80,000; low: $30).
Purpose and activities: Broad purposes;
primarily local giving, with emphasis on
Unitarian religious associations, higher
education, a medical research foundation,
youth agencies, and social services.
Limitations: Giving primarily in OK.
Application information:
 Write: Don C. Phelps, Managing Trustee
Trustees: Don C. Phelps, Managing Trustee;
Tom E. Garrard, Alene Webb Puterbaugh.
Employer Identification Number: 736092193

3459
Rapp (Robert Glenn) Foundation ▼ ⌗
2301 N.W. 39th Expressway, Suite 206
Oklahoma City 73112   (405) 525-0057

Trust established about 1953 in Oklahoma.
Donor(s): Florence B. Clark.†
Financial data: (yr. ended 12/31/83): Assets,
$6,278,723 (M); expenditures, $2,328,650,
including $1,632,000 for 38 grants (high:
$300,000; low: $1,000; average: $10,000-
$50,000).
Purpose and activities: Primarily local giving,
with emphasis on higher education; support
also for medical research, hospitals, secondary
education, and cultural programs.
Limitations: Giving primarily in OK, with
emphasis on Oklahoma City.
Application information:
 Initial approach: Letter
 Board meeting date(s): Annually, usually in
  the latter part of the year
 Write: Leslie Harrison
Trustees: Stanley B. Catlett, James H. Milligan,
Lois Darlene Milligan.
Number of staff: None.
Employer Identification Number: 730616840

3460
Sand Springs Home ⌗
200 North Main St.
P.O. Box 278
Sand Springs 74063

Established in 1912.
Donor(s): Charles Page Family Care Charitable
Remainder Annuity Trust.
Financial data: (yr. ended 6/30/83): Assets,
$43,689,381 (M); gifts received, $74,675;
expenditures, $1,839,567, including $45,431
for grants and $1,416,574 for 1 foundation-
administered program.

Purpose and activities: A private operating
foundation; operates a local home for needy
and dependent children and a widows colony
for women who are widowed or legally
divorced and have two or more children to
support; limited grants to local organizations.
Limitations: Giving primarily in OK.
Trustees: Bill Brown, E.J. Doerner, J. Blan
Loflin, Buford A. McCuley, J.C. Warner, Joe A.
Williams.
Employer Identification Number: 730579278

3461
Sanditen (Edgar and Ira) Foundation
(formerly Otasco Foundation)
3314 E. 51st, Suite K
Tulsa 74135   (918) 742-2417

Incorporated in 1943 in Oklahoma.
Donor(s): Otasco, Inc., Edgar R. Sanditen.
Financial data: (yr. ended 12/31/83): Assets,
$55,785 (M); gifts received, $225,000;
expenditures, $225,370, including $225,000
for 1 grant.
Purpose and activities: To "engage in any and
all benevolent activities or acts which might be
calculated, reasoned or expected to bring
happiness, health or well-being to deserving
persons." Primarily local giving, with funds
presently committed to the Tulsa Jewish
Community Council.
Limitations: Giving primarily in the Tulsa, OK,
area.
Application information: Funds presently
committed.
Officers: Edgar Sanditen, President; Michael J.
Sanditen, Steven A. Sanditen, Vice-Presidents;
Don Mann, Secretary and Treasurer.
Number of staff: None.
Employer Identification Number: 736092466

3462
Sarkeys Foundation ▼
128 East Main, Suite 207
Norman 73069   (405) 364-3703

Established in 1962 in Oklahoma.
Donor(s): S.J. Sarkeys.
Financial data: (yr. ended 11/30/84): Assets,
$29,726,507 (M); expenditures, $1,475,544,
including $1,359,500 for 22 grants (high:
$505,000; low: $5,000).
Purpose and activities: Primarily local giving,
with emphasis on higher education; grants also
for community services, health and welfare,
and general charitable support. Preference
given to project-oriented grants over general
budgetary support.
Limitations: Giving primarily in OK. No
support for elementary or secondary
education. No grants to individuals.
Application information:
 Initial approach: Full proposal
 Deadline(s): Mid-March and mid-September
 Board meeting date(s): January, April, July,
  and October
 Write: R. Boyd Gunning, Managing Trustee

Trustees: R. Boyd Gunning, Managing Trustee; Richard Bell, Bishop Finis A. Crutchfield, Duane Draper, Philip C. Kidd, Robert Rennie, Robert S. Rizley, Frank Seay.
Number of staff: 2 full-time professional.
Employer Identification Number: 730736496

3463
Share (Charles Morton) Trust
Liberty National Bank and Trust Company
P.O. Box 25848, Trust Dept.
Oklahoma City 73125   (405) 231-6815

Trust established in 1959 in Oklahoma.
Donor(s): Charles Morton Share.†
Financial data: (yr. ended 6/30/83): Assets, $8,500,000 (M); expenditures, $848,000, including $581,000 for 33 grants (high: $100,000; low: $140; average: $15,000-$25,000).
Purpose and activities: Primarily local giving, with emphasis on higher education and hospitals; support also for community projects and a museum.
Types of support awarded: Scholarship funds.
Limitations: Giving primarily in OK. No grants to individuals, or for operating budgets, continuing support, annual campaigns, seed money, emergency, building, and endowment funds; deficit financing, equipment, land acquisition, renovations, matching gifts, special projects, research, publications, or conferences; no loans.
Application information:
  Initial approach: Full proposal
  Copies of proposal: 5
  Deadline(s): None
  Board meeting date(s): Quarterly and as required
  Final notification: 6 weeks
Trustees: J.R. Holder, C.E. Johnson, Gertrude Myers, The Liberty National Bank and Trust Company of Oklahoma City.
Number of staff: None.
Employer Identification Number: 736090984

3464
Taubman (Herman P. and Sophia) Foundation
1701 First National Bldg.
Tulsa 74103   (918) 585-9151

Trust established in 1955 in Oklahoma.
Donor(s): Herman P. Taubman,† Sophia Taubman.†
Financial data: (yr. ended 12/31/84): Assets, $2,525,650 (M); expenditures, $255,294, including $217,884 for 42 grants (high: $40,000; low: $50).
Purpose and activities: Broad purposes; grants largely for local Jewish welfare funds, hospitals, youth agencies and higher education.
Limitations: Giving primarily in OK. No grants to individuals or for building funds.
Application information:
  Initial approach: Letter
  Copies of proposal: 3
  Board meeting date(s): As required
  Write: Morris B. Taubman, Trustee

Trustees: David Fist, Louis Taubman, Morris B. Taubman.
Number of staff: None.
Employer Identification Number: 736092820

3465
Titus (C. W.) Foundation ⌑
1801 Philtower Bldg.
Tulsa 74103

Established in 1968 in Oklahoma.
Financial data: (yr. ended 12/31/82): Assets, $3,352,605 (M); expenditures, $332,729, including $295,700 for 55 grants (high: $100,000; low: $200).
Purpose and activities: Giving primarily in Oklahoma and Missouri, with emphasis on hospitals and health services, cultural programs, the handicapped, and social agencies.
Limitations: Giving primarily in OK and MO.
Trustee: Rosemary T. Reynolds.
Employer Identification Number: 237016981

3466
Tulsa Royalties Company
3229-A South Harvard Ave.
Tulsa 74135   (918) 747-5638

Incorporated in 1951 in Oklahoma.
Donor(s): William S. Bailey, Jr.
Financial data: (yr. ended 12/31/83): Assets, $2,300,153 (M); expenditures, $294,328, including $200,507 for 93 grants (high: $50,000; low: $50).
Purpose and activities: Primarily local giving, with emphasis on higher education, hospitals, social agencies, and Protestant church support.
Limitations: Giving primarily in OK. No grants to individuals or for matching gifts; no loans.
Application information: Funds largely committed.
  Board meeting date(s): January
Officers and Trustees: William S. Bailey, Jr., President; George H. Bowen, Vice-President; Lawrence A. Peitz, Secretary-Treasurer; Romayne W. Bailey, Leonard L. Jones.
Employer Identification Number: 736101744

3467
28:19, Inc. ⌑
P.O. Box 415
El Reno 73036   (405) 721-2797

Financial data: (yr. ended 11/30/82): Assets, $540,730 (M); gifts received, $98,150; expenditures, $265,466, including $212,445 for 445 grants (high: $10,000; low: $22).
Purpose and activities: Grants for Protestant religious organizations.
Officers and Directors: Gene Warr, President; John R. Repass, Irma Warr, Theopa Warr, Vice-Presidents; Nick D. Gramlich, Secretary-Treasurer.
Employer Identification Number: 736091732

3468
Warren Charite ⌑
P.O. Box 470372
Tulsa 74147-0372

Established in 1968 in Oklahoma.
Donor(s): William K. Warren.
Financial data: (yr. ended 11/30/82): Assets, $1,833,603 (M); gifts received, $160,000; expenditures, $136,383, including $132,160 for 25 grants (high: $95,000; low: $100) and $1,300 for 5 grants to individuals.
Purpose and activities: Primarily local giving; funds currently committed to a cancer research center and a hospital.
Limitations: Giving primarily in OK.
Application information: Applications not invited; funds currently committed.
Officers and Trustees: William K. Warren, President; Eleanor L. Corp, Vice-President; W.R. Lissau, Secretary.
Employer Identification Number: 730776064

3469
Warren (The William K.) Foundation ▼
P.O. Box 470372
Tulsa 74147-0372   (918) 492-8100

Incorporated in 1945 in Oklahoma.
Donor(s): William K. Warren, Mrs. William K. Warren.
Financial data: (yr. ended 12/31/83): Assets, $148,248,762 (M); gifts received, $1,448,104; expenditures, $7,212,327, including $6,103,050 for 30 grants (high: $5,615,000; low: $50).
Purpose and activities: Broad purposes; giving committed entirely to a medical research program and a local hospital that is currently expanding facilities.
Types of support awarded: Building funds, endowment funds, operating budgets, special projects.
Limitations: Giving primarily in OK. No grants to individuals.
Application information: Funds currently committed.
  Board meeting date(s): Semiannually
Officers: John A. Naughton, Vice-President and Treasurer; Dorothy Warren King,* Secretary.
Trustees:* Robert J. Stanton, Chairman; Natalie O. Warren, Vice-Chairman; Kenneth G. Miller, Patricia Warren Swindle, W.K. Warren, Jr.
Employer Identification Number: 730609599

3470
Wegener (The Herman and Mary) Foundation, Inc. ⌑
1711 First National Bldg.
Oklahoma City 73102   (405) 235-7200

Incorporated in 1954 in Oklahoma.
Donor(s): Herman H. Wegener.†
Financial data: (yr. ended 12/31/82): Assets, $2,416,026 (M); expenditures, $339,877, including $282,600 for 56 grants (high: $25,000; low: $100).

Purpose and activities: Charitable purposes; primarily local giving, with emphasis on hospitals and education; grants also for cultural programs, youth agencies, and social agencies.
Types of support awarded: Building funds, operating budgets, special projects.
Limitations: Giving primarily in OK. No grants to individuals or for endowment funds.
Application information:
Initial approach: Letter
Copies of proposal: 1
Board meeting date(s): Quarterly
Officers and Trustees: Willis B. Sherin, President; Wanda B. Burnett, C.D. Ellison, Vice-Presidents; Clenard Wegener, Secretary; Kenneth Wegener, Raymond Lee Wegener, Willis B. Wegener.
Employer Identification Number: 736095407

3471
Williams Companies Foundation, Incorporated, The ¤
One Williams Center
P.O. Box 2400
Tulsa 74172   (918) 588-2111

Incorporated in 1974 in Oklahoma.
Donor(s): The Williams Companies.
Financial data: (yr. ended 12/31/83): Assets, $3,991,175 (M); gifts received, $1,500,000; expenditures, $772,429, including $763,708 for 97 grants (high: $145,000; low: $132).
Purpose and activities: Primarily local giving, with emphasis on hospitals, higher, education, cultural programs, and youth.
Types of support awarded: General purposes, building funds, equipment, land acquisition, continuing support, seed money, annual campaigns, emergency funds, matching funds, employee matching gifts.
Limitations: Giving primarily in OK. No grants to individuals, or for endowment funds, research, scholarships, or fellowships; no loans.
Application information:
Initial approach: Proposal
Copies of proposal: 1
Board meeting date(s): June and December
Write: Hannah D. Robson, Manager
Officers: C.J. Head,* President; D.W. Calvert,* Robert W. Shower,* Vice-Presidents; Major O. Brunner, Secretary and Treasurer; Hannah D. Robson, Manager.
Directors: * Joseph H. Williams, Chairman; Vernon T. Jones, Charles P. Williams, John H. Williams.
Employer Identification Number: 237413843

3472
Wood (The W. P.) Charitable Trust ¤
P.O. Box 127
Shawnee 74801   (405) 273-2880

Established in 1973.
Financial data: (yr. ended 1/31/84): Assets, $2,125,397 (M); expenditures, $462,807, including $351,500 for 11 grants (high: $177,000; low: $250).
Purpose and activities: Primarily local giving, with support for higher education, programs to aid the handicapped, and social services.

Types of support awarded: Operating budgets, building funds, scholarship funds, research.
Limitations: Giving primarily in OK.
Application information:
Initial approach: Proposal
Deadline(s): None
Write: Steve Garner, Manager
Officer and Trustees: Steve Garner, Manager; Gerald D. McGehee, Lindsay Peters.
Employer Identification Number: 736152038

3473
Young (The R. A.) Foundation ¤
6401 North Pennsylvania Ave., Suite 209
Oklahoma City 73116

Incorporated in 1953 in Oklahoma.
Donor(s): Raymond A. Young.
Financial data: (yr. ended 11/30/83): Assets, $2,404,913 (M); expenditures, $94,692, including $86,250 for 35 grants (high: $29,745; low: $25).
Purpose and activities: Broad purposes; primarily local giving, with emphasis on Protestant church support and religious service associations, higher education, and arts and culture.
Limitations: Giving primarily in OK.
Officers and Trustees: Raymond A. Young, President; Carolyn Young Hodnett, Vice-President; Verna N. Young, Secretary-Treasurer.
Employer Identification Number: 736092654

3474
Zink (John Steele) Foundation ¤
1259 E. 26th St.
Tulsa 74114

Established in 1972.
Donor(s): John Steele Zink,† Jacqueline A. Zink.
Financial data: (yr. ended 10/31/82): Assets, $1,479,679 (M); gifts received, $1,120,000; expenditures, $1,158,693, including $1,129,500 for 14 grants (high: $1,000,000; low: $5,000).
Purpose and activities: Local giving, with emphasis on higher education and cultural programs.
Limitations: Giving primarily in Tulsa, OK.
Trustees: Horace Balling, Swannie Zink Tarbel, Jacqueline A. Zink, John Smith Zink.
Employer Identification Number: 237246964

OREGON

3475
Autzen Foundation, The
P.O. Box 3709
Portland 97208   (503) 226-6051

Incorporated in 1951 in Oregon.
Donor(s): Thomas J. Autzen.†
Financial data: (yr. ended 12/31/83): Assets, $3,596,208 (M); expenditures, $275,823, including $231,200 for 135 grants (high: $15,000; low: $25; average: $200-$10,000).
Purpose and activities: Broad purposes; primarily local giving, with emphasis on higher and secondary education, conservation, art, the performing arts, youth agencies, and rehabilitation.
Types of support awarded: Continuing support, seed money, building funds, research.
Limitations: Giving primarily in OR. No grants to individuals, or for scholarships and fellowships; no loans.
Application information:
Initial approach: Full proposal
Copies of proposal: 1
Deadline(s): April 15 and November 15
Board meeting date(s): May and December
Final notification: 3 to 4 months
Write: Vivienne B. Snow, Administrator
Officers and Trustees: Thomas E. Autzen, President; Duane Autzen, Vice-President; John B. Taylor, Secretary-Treasurer; Owen W. Bentley, Jr., Henry C. Houser.
Number of staff: 1 part-time professional.
Employer Identification Number: 936021333

3476
Barker (The Donald R.) Foundation ¤
P.O. Box 806
Eugene 97440

Established in 1977 in Oregon.
Donor(s): Donald R. Barker.
Financial data: (yr. ended 11/30/83): Assets, $3,291,556 (M); expenditures, $515,279, including $444,780 for 51 grants (high: $100,000; low: $500).
Purpose and activities: Primarily local giving, largely to higher education, the handicapped, and hospitals; support also for youth and health agencies, cultural programs, and high school athletic programs.
Types of support awarded: Operating budgets, scholarship funds, building funds, equipment, special projects.
Limitations: Giving primarily in OR.
Trustees: John R. Lamb, Coeta Barker McGowan, J.R. McGowan, Joseph A. Moore.
Employer Identification Number: 930698411

3477
Brown (The E. C.) Foundation/E. C. Brown Trust
300 S.W. Sixth Ave.
Portland 97204   (503) 295-0203

Trust established in 1939 in Oregon.
Donor(s): Ellis C. Brown, M.D.†
Financial data: (yr. ended 12/31/83): Assets, $2,632,576 (M); expenditures, $193,774, including $146,031 for foundation-administered programs.
Purpose and activities: To promote and carry on the program of the foundation in instruction and education with respect to sex and marriage; to facilitate growth in understanding and practice of positive human relationships, with emphasis on the family and health. Produces educational films relating to sex education, the family, and health.
Application information: Grants not ordinarily made, except in support of foundation-initiated projects.
Write: John A. Bruce, Executive Director
Officers: Paul Olum, Administrator; John A. Bruce, Executive Director.
Number of staff: 1 full-time professional; 1 part-time support.
Employer Identification Number: 930491026

3478
Carpenter Foundation, The
1005 East Main St., Suite 9
P.O. Box 816
Medford 97504   (503) 772-5851

Incorporated in 1957 in Oregon.
Donor(s): Helen Bundy Carpenter,† Alfred S.V. Carpenter,† Harlow Carpenter.
Financial data: (yr. ended 6/30/84): Assets, $5,020,277 (M); expenditures, $386,654, including $323,755 for 49 grants (high: $30,000; low: $500; average: $5,000-$10,000).
Purpose and activities: Broad purposes; primarily local giving, with emphasis on higher and secondary education, including scholarship funds; support also for human services, art and architecture, and the performing arts.
Types of support awarded: Operating budgets, seed money, emergency funds, building funds, equipment, matching funds, technical assistance, scholarship funds, fellowships, internships, loans, research, publications.
Limitations: Giving primarily in Jackson and Josephine counties, OR. No grants to individuals, or for deficit financing, endowment funds, or demonstration projects.
Application information:
Initial approach: Full proposal or letter
Copies of proposal: 1
Deadline(s): Submit proposal 3 weeks before board meeting
Board meeting date(s): Usually in March, June, September, and December
Final notification: 1 to 2 weeks
Write: Dunbar Carpenter, Treasurer
Officers and Directors: Jane H. Carpenter, President; Ann Daugherty Cheng, Vice-President; Dunbar Carpenter, Treasurer; Robertson Collins, Mrs. Robert Ogle.

Associate Trustees: Isobel Holt, Nancy Leonard, Mark Schiveley, James Sours.
Number of staff: 1 full-time support.
Employer Identification Number: 930491360

3479
Chiles Foundation ▼
900 S.W. Fifth Ave., Suite 2601
Portland 97204   (503) 222-2143

Incorporated in 1949 in Oregon.
Donor(s): Eva Chiles Meyer,† Earle A. Chiles,† Virginia H. Chiles.
Financial data: (yr. ended 12/31/82): Assets, $29,986,450 (M); expenditures, $2,655,382, including $2,248,026 for 81 grants (high: $149,000; low: $350).
Purpose and activities: Primarily local giving; grants traditionally to institutions of higher education for business schools, computer science education, scholarships and athletics; to selected grammar and secondary schools for special purposes; to structured youth organizations; and to organizations which provide residential care for emotionally disturbed youth; supports basic research in cancer and cardiopulmonary disease, and established community arts and cultural activities; assists elderly and indigent by making grants for food programs sponsored by locally operated non-profit agencies.
Types of support awarded: Building funds, equipment, research, matching funds.
Limitations: Giving primarily in OR, with emphasis on Portland, and the Pacific Northwest. No grants to individuals, or for deficit financing, mortgage retirement, projects involving litigation or projects and conferences already completed; no loans.
Application information:
Initial approach: Telephone or 1-page preliminary proposal
Deadline(s): March 1 and August 1
Board meeting date(s): Semiannually in spring and fall
Final notification: By December 31
Officers and Trustees: Earle M. Chiles, President; Virginia H. Chiles, Vice-President; Frank E. Nash, Secretary; Melvin E. Smith.
Number of staff: 3 full-time professional.
Employer Identification Number: 936031125

3480
Clark Foundation
255 Southwest Harrison St. GA 2
Portland 97201   (503) 223-5290

Established in 1968 in Oregon.
Donor(s): Maurie D. Clark.
Financial data: (yr. ended 12/31/82): Assets, $94,007 (M); gifts received, $127,645; expenditures, $301,030, including $273,200 for 141 grants (high: $20,000; low: $500).
Purpose and activities: Broad purposes; emphasis on building funds for higher education and for churches and religious associations; grants also for cultural programs, youth agencies, secondary education, the environment, and medical care.

Limitations: Giving primarily in the Portland, OR, area. No grants to individuals, or for endowment funds, research, or matching gifts; no loans.
Application information:
Initial approach: Letter
Copies of proposal: 1
Board meeting date(s): Bimonthly
Write: Maurie D. Clark, President
Officers: Maurie D. Clark, President and Treasurer; Donald J. Georgeson, Vice-President; Patrick E. Becker, Secretary.
Employer Identification Number: 237423789

3481
Clemens Foundation, The ⌖
P.O. Box 427
Philomath 97370   (503) 929-3541

Incorporated in 1959 in Oregon.
Donor(s): Rex Clemens, Ethel M. Clemens, Rex Veneer Company.
Financial data: (yr. ended 12/31/83): Assets, $3,133,003 (M); gifts received, $181,000; expenditures, $317,344, including $306,907 for 292 grants to individuals.
Purpose and activities: Broad purposes; local giving for scholarships for higher education.
Types of support awarded: Student aid.
Limitations: Giving limited to Philomath, Eddyville, Crane, and Alsea, OR.
Application information: Application form required for tuition grants.
Initial approach: Letter or telephone
Deadline(s): None
Officers and Trustees: Rex Clemens, President; Ethel M. Clemens, Vice-President, Secretary, and Treasurer; Elwood Berklund, Bernard C. Davis, Ron Edwards, Robert Hall, Wayne L. Howard, Homer Hull, Frank Kochis.
Employer Identification Number: 936023941

3482
Collins Foundation, The ▼
909 Terminal Sales Bldg.
Portland 97205   (503) 227-1219

Incorporated in 1947 in Oregon.
Donor(s): Members of the Collins family.
Financial data: (yr. ended 12/31/84): Assets, $45,349,137 (M); gifts received, $20,400; expenditures, $2,689,176, including $1,811,717 for 131 grants (high: $250,000; low: $725; average: $2,500-$15,000).
Purpose and activities: Broad purposes; local giving, with emphasis on higher and secondary education, particularly for science education; church support, youth and health agencies, social welfare, and the arts and cultural programs.
Types of support awarded: Building funds, equipment, research, conferences and seminars, matching funds, program-related investments, land acquisition, special projects.
Limitations: Giving limited to OR, with emphasis on Portland. No grants to individuals, or for deficit financing, legislative lobbying, endowment funds, general purposes, delayed projects, scholarships and fellowships, operating budgets, or annual campaigns.

Publications: Annual report, informational brochure, program policy statement, application guidelines.
Application information:
Initial approach: Letter
Copies of proposal: 1
Deadline(s): None
Board meeting date(s): Approximately 6 times a year
Final notification: 2 months
Write: William C. Pine, Executive Vice-President
Officers: Maribeth W. Collins,* President; William C. Pine, Executive Vice-President; Grace Collins Goudy,* Vice-President; Thomas B. Stoel, Secretary; Eugene E. Sharp, Treasurer.
Trustees:* Ralph Bolliger.
Number of staff: 1 part-time professional; 1 part-time support.
Employer Identification Number: 936021893

3483
Daly (Bernard) Educational Fund ¤
P.O. Box 309
Lakeview 97630   (503) 947-2196
Application address: P.O. Box 351, Lakeview, OR 97630

Established in 1922 in Oregon.
Donor(s): Bernard Daly.†
Financial data: (yr. ended 5/31/84): Assets, $1,204,331 (M); expenditures, $95,772, including $84,600 for 47 grants to individuals.
Purpose and activities: Financial aid to students of Lake County, Oregon, for study at Oregon technical schools and colleges.
Types of support awarded: Student aid.
Limitations: Giving limited to Lake County, OR.
Publications: Application guidelines.
Application information: Application form required.
Initial approach: Telephone
Copies of proposal: 2
Deadline(s): April 1
Board meeting date(s): June
Write: James C. Lynch, Secretary
Officers and Trustees: Alan Withers, Chairman; Carter Fetsch, Vice-Chairman; James C. Lynch, Secretary-Treasurer; Dorothy Howard.
Employer Identification Number: 936025466

3484
Fohs Foundation
P.O. Box 1001
Roseburg 97470   (503) 673-0141

Trust established in 1937 in New York.
Donor(s): F. Julius Fohs,† Mrs. Cora B. Fohs.†
Financial data: (yr. ended 12/31/82): Assets, $1,975,593 (M); expenditures, $197,289, including $177,500 for 7 grants (high: $100,000; low: $1,000).
Purpose and activities: To promote science, art, education, health, healthful recreation and good citizenship of children and adults; research in general, charitable, humanitarian, sociological and educational problems; support for Ella Fohs children's and senior citizens' camps in Connecticut; grants for Jewish-sponsored educational institutions.

Application information:
Initial approach: Letter
Copies of proposal: 1
Deadline(s): None
Board meeting date(s): April or May
Write: Mrs. Frances F. Sohn, Chairman
Officer: Charlotte Richards, Secretary-Treasurer.
Trustee: Frances F. Sohn, Chairman.
Number of staff: 1 part-time support.
Employer Identification Number: 746003165

3485
Ford (Kenneth W.) Foundation ¤
c/o Roseburg Lumber Company
P.O. Box 1088
Roseburg 97470

Incorporated in 1957 in Oregon.
Donor(s): Kenneth W. Ford, Hallie E. Ford, Roseburg Lumber Company.
Financial data: (yr. ended 4/30/83): Assets, $2,162,495 (M); gifts received, $86,000; expenditures, $87,419, including $87,400 for 14 grants (high: $25,000; low: $50).
Purpose and activities: Primarily local giving, with emphasis on community funds, youth agencies, and higher education.
Limitations: Giving primarily in OR.
Officers and Directors: Kenneth W. Ford, President; Hallie E. Ford, Vice-President; Frank H. Spears, Secretary.
Employer Identification Number: 936026156

3486
Frank (A. J.) Family Foundation ¤
P.O. Box 1467
Mill City 97360

Incorporated in 1959 in Oregon.
Donor(s): A.J. Frank, L.D. Frank, Frank Lumber Co., Inc., Frank Timber Products, Inc., and members of the Frank family.
Financial data: (yr. ended 9/30/83): Assets, $1,508,609 (M); gifts received, $31,228; expenditures, $140,975, including $136,989 for 22 grants (high: $52,000; low: $500).
Purpose and activities: Giving largely for Roman Catholic church support and welfare funds, and for secondary education.
Officers: A.J. Frank, President; J.T. Frank, Vice-President; D.D. Frank, Secretary; L.D. Frank, Treasurer.
Employer Identification Number: 930523395

3487
Friendly-Rosenthal Foundation, Inc., The
P.O. Box 562
Lake Oswego 97034   (503) 684-1810

Incorporated in 1946 in Oregon.
Donor(s): Jacob Rosenthal,† Seymour C. Friendly,† Julius C. Friendly.†
Financial data: (yr. ended 12/31/83): Assets, $1,525,032 (M); expenditures, $118,411, including $97,850 for 23 grants (high: $22,000; low: $500; average: $500-$30,000).

Purpose and activities: Broad purposes; grants only to existing local institutions concerned with social welfare programs, including Jewish welfare funds, and assistance to the aged, homeless, mentally retarded, and to new immigrants.
Types of support awarded: Continuing support, seed money, emergency funds.
Limitations: Giving primarily in Multnomah, Clackamas and Washington counties, OR, and organizations in Salem, OR, that serve these areas. No grants to individuals, or for building, capital, or endowment funds, scholarships, fellowships, or matching gifts; no loans.
Publications: 990-PF, application guidelines.
Application information:
Initial approach: Letter, full proposal, or telephone
Copies of proposal: 1
Deadline(s): Submit proposal preferably from September through November; deadline November 15
Board meeting date(s): January
Write: Mrs. Evelyn J. Harriman, Secretary
Officers: Milton Carl,* President and Chairman; Arthur Markewitz, Vice-President; Evelyn J. Harriman,* Secretary; Paul Akre,* Treasurer.
Trustees:* Stuart Durkheimer, Melvyn C. Friendly, James A. Meyer, A.B. Shields, M.D., Grant Stebner, Merritt S. Yoelin, U.S. National Bank of Oregon (Paul T. Akre, Trust Officer).
Number of staff: 1 part-time professional.
Employer Identification Number: 930395711

3488
Higgins (Lorene Sails) Charitable Trust
c/o The Bank of California
P.O. Box 3121
Portland 97208   (503) 225-2924

Trust established in 1968 in Oregon.
Donor(s): Lorene Sails Higgins.
Financial data: (yr. ended 12/31/83): Assets, $2,867,149 (M); expenditures, $195,304, including $145,649 for 22 grants (high: $25,000; low: $300).
Purpose and activities: Primarily local giving, with emphasis on cultural programs, the performing arts, higher education, and religious institutions with emphasis on Christian Science projects.
Types of support awarded: Building funds, equipment, matching funds.
Limitations: Giving primarily in the Portland, OR, metropolitan area. No grants to individuals, or for endowment funds, general support, or scholarships or fellowships; no loans.
Publications: Program policy statement, application guidelines.
Application information:
Initial approach: Letter or full proposal
Copies of proposal: 1
Deadline(s): None
Board meeting date(s): January, April, July, and October
Final notification: At most 3 months
Write: Marc Grignon, Trust Officer
Trustees: Lofton L. Tatum, The Bank of California.
Number of staff: None.
Employer Identification Number: 936050051

3489
Hunt (C. Giles) Charitable Trust ¤
c/o First Interstate Bank of Oregon
P.O. Box 10566
Eugene 97440 (503) 697-5952

Trust established in 1974 in Oregon.
Donor(s): C. Giles Hunt.†
Financial data: (yr. ended 12/31/83): Assets, $3,005,075 (M); expenditures, $247,404, including $223,246 for 44 grants (high: $19,700; low: $600).
Purpose and activities: Charitable purposes; giving primarily to benefit charities located in or serving the residents of Douglas County, Oregon with emphasis on social services, youth agencies, and education.
Limitations: Giving primarily in Douglas County, OR. No grants to individuals.
Publications: Application guidelines.
Application information: Application form required.
  Initial approach: Letter or full proposal
  Copies of proposal: 1
  Deadline(s): Submit proposal in January or February; deadline February 28
  Board meeting date(s): March or April
Trustee: First Interstate Bank of Oregon.
Employer Identification Number: 237428278

3490
Jackson Foundation, The ▼
c/o U.S. National Bank of Oregon
P.O. Box 3168
Portland 97208 (503) 225-4461

Trust established in 1960 in Oregon; Philip Ludwell Jackson Charitable and Residual Trusts were merged into The Jackson Foundation in 1981.
Donor(s): Maria C. Jackson.†
Financial data: (yr. ended 6/30/84): Assets, $6,593,542 (M); expenditures, $828,171, including $791,646 for 132 grants (high: $64,200; low: $300; average: $2,000-$10,000) and $764,330 for 18 loans.
Purpose and activities: Broad purposes; local giving, largely to aid needy persons through social agencies. Grants for higher and secondary education, including scholarship funds to selected colleges only; cultural programs, hospitals, scientific research and technology, the humanities, and youth agencies.
Types of support awarded: Seed money, emergency funds, building funds, equipment, research, scholarship funds, program-related investments, operating budgets, special projects, technical assistance.
Limitations: Giving limited to OR. No support for churches or temples. No grants to individuals, or for endowment funds, matching gifts, scholarships, fellowships, or building funds or equipment for religious organizations; no loans to individuals.
Publications: 990-PF.
Application information:
  Initial approach: Full proposal or telephone
  Copies of proposal: 1
  Deadline(s): None
  Board meeting date(s): September, December, April, and as required
  Final notification: 3 or 4 months

Write: Stephen W. Miller, Trust Officer
Trustees: Milo Ormseth, Gordon M. Tretheway, United States National Bank of Oregon (Stephen W. Miller, Trust Officer).
Number of staff: 3.
Employer Identification Number: 936020752

3491
Jeld-Wen, Wenco Foundation, The
3303 Lakeport Blvd.
P.O. Box 1329
Klamath Falls 97601 (503) 882-3451

Established in 1969.
Donor(s): Jeld-Wen Fiber Products, Inc. of Iowa, Jeld-Wen Co. of Arizona, Wenco, Inc. of North Carolina, Wenco, Inc. of Ohio, and other Jeld-Wen, Wenco companies.
Financial data: (yr. ended 12/31/83): Assets, $3,972,257 (M); gifts received, $750,177; expenditures, $194,833, including $176,238 for 70 grants (high: $26,137; low: $80).
Purpose and activities: Grants primarily to organizations in areas of company operations that benefit company employees and a large segment of the community; support largely for community funds, higher education, and health and youth agencies.
Types of support awarded: General purposes, seed money, building funds, equipment, land acquisition, special projects, scholarship funds, matching funds.
Limitations: Giving primarily in areas of company operations. No support for activities that are specifically religious or that duplicate services provided by other government or private agencies. No grants to individuals; no loans.
Publications: Program policy statement, application guidelines.
Application information:
  Initial approach: Full proposal or letter
  Copies of proposal: 1
  Deadline(s): Submit proposal preferably in March; no set deadline
  Board meeting date(s): March, May, September, and December
  Final notification: 3 months
  Write: R.C. Wendt, Secretary
Officer and Trustees: R.C. Wendt, Secretary; W.B. Early, T.H. Schnormeier, R.L. Wendt, L.V. Wetter.
Number of staff: None.
Employer Identification Number: 936054272

3492
Jenkins Student Loan Fund
c/o U.S. National Bank of Oregon
321 S.W. Sixth Ave., P.O. Box 3168
Portland 97208 (503) 225-4456

Established in 1960 in Oregon.
Donor(s): Hopkin Jenkins.†
Financial data: (yr. ended 6/30/83): Assets, $1,126,170 (M); expenditures, $167,890, including $146,078 for 200 loans.
Purpose and activities: Loans to students for college education costs; recipients must be Oregon residents.
Types of support awarded: Student aid.
Limitations: Giving limited to OR.

Publications: Program policy statement, application guidelines.
Application information: Application form required.
  Initial approach: Letter or telephone
  Copies of proposal: 1
  Deadline(s): Submit proposal preferably 30 days in advance of school terms
  Board meeting date(s): Usually in September, December, March, and June
  Write: Linda Babcock, Student Loan Administrator
Officer: Linda Babcock, Student Loan Administrator; United States National Bank of Oregon.
Distribution Committee: Grace Deierlein, Dorothy Flegel.
Trustee: United States National Bank of Oregon.
Number of staff: 2.
Employer Identification Number: 936020672

3493
John (B. P.) Foundation ¤
1404 Standard Plaza
Portland 97204

Financial data: (yr. ended 12/31/83): Assets, $1,270,979 (M); expenditures, $78,423, including $60,000 for 36 grants (high: $10,000; low: $400).
Purpose and activities: Support for Roman Catholic missionary and international relief organizations and for local church-sponsored and secular health and welfare agencies.
Officers: Lester M. John, President and Treasurer; Rudolph Ebner, Vice-President; Regina John, Secretary.
Employer Identification Number: 237110263

3494
John (Helen) Foundation ¤
1404 Standard Plaza
Portland 97204

Established in 1971.
Financial data: (yr. ended 12/31/83): Assets, $1,269,498 (M); expenditures, $79,802, including $58,570 for 22 grants (high: $8,214; low: $500).
Purpose and activities: Primarily local giving, with emphasis on Roman Catholic church support and welfare funds; support also for higher and secondary education and social services.
Limitations: Giving primarily in OR.
Officers and Directors: James G. Condon, President; Edwin G. Condon, Vice-President; Elizabeth C. Twilegar, Secretary and Treasurer; Mary Butler, Kenneth Condon.
Employer Identification Number: 237109040

3495
Johnson (The S. S.) Foundation
P.O. Box 356
Redmond 97756 (503) 548-8104

Incorporated in 1948 in California.
Donor(s): Samuel S. Johnson, Elizabeth Hill Johnson.

Financial data: (yr. ended 5/31/84): Assets, $1,555,347 (M); expenditures, $74,562, including $64,820 for 71 grants (high: $7,000; low: $100; average: $500-$1,000), $900 for 3 grants to individuals and $1,700 for 2 loans.
Purpose and activities: Broad purposes; support for educational, scientific, cultural, religious, health, and welfare organizations, primarily for limited emergency operational funds and limited emergency grants or loans to students through educational institutions located primarily in the Pacific Northwest and northern California.
Types of support awarded: Operating budgets, seed money, emergency funds, matching funds, scholarship funds, student aid, conferences and seminars.
Limitations: Giving primarily in the Pacific Northwest and northern CA. No grants for continuing support, annual campaigns, deficit financing, capital support, research, special projects, or publications.
Publications: 990-PF.
Application information: Application form required for scholarships.
  Initial approach: Letter
  Copies of proposal: 1
  Deadline(s): None
  Board meeting date(s): July and January
  Final notification: 2 to 3 weeks
  Write: Elizabeth Hill Johnson, President
Officers: Elizabeth Hill Johnson,* President and Treasurer; Shirley K. Comini, Secretary.
Directors:* Elizabeth K. Johnson, Patricia Johnson Nelson, Ralf H. Stinson, M.D.
Number of staff: 1 part-time support.
Employer Identification Number: 946062478

3496
Louisiana-Pacific Foundation
111 S.W. Fifth Ave.
Portland 97204

Established in 1973 in Oregon.
Donor(s): Louisiana-Pacific Corporation.
Financial data: (yr. ended 12/31/84): Assets, $1,489 (L); gifts received, $250,000; expenditures, $262,275, including $262,275 for 72 grants (high: $30,000; low: $100).
Purpose and activities: General giving, with emphasis on higher education and community funds; some support for health and youth agencies.
Types of support awarded: Employee related scholarships.
Officers: Harry A. Merlo,* Chairman and President; Gerald R. Griffin,* Vice-President; Donald R. Holman, Secretary; John C. Hart, Treasurer.
Trustees:* Robert E. Erickson.
Employer Identification Number: 237268660

3497
Macdonald (Maybelle Clark) Fund ¤
405 N.W. 18th Ave.
Portland 97209

Established about 1970.
Donor(s): Maybelle Clark Macdonald.

Financial data: (yr. ended 6/30/83): Assets, $0 (M); gifts received, $117,771; expenditures, $117,771, including $116,650 for 12 grants (high: $100,000; low: $25).
Purpose and activities: Giving largely for local cultural programs and Roman Catholic church support.
Limitations: Giving primarily in OR.
Officers: D. Ranney Munro, President; Sherman B. Kellar, Secretary; Daniel A. Callahan, Treasurer.
Employer Identification Number: 237108002

3498
Meyer (Fred) Charitable Trust ▼
1515 Southwest Fifth Ave., Suite 500
Portland 97201   (503) 228-5512

Trust established by will in 1978; obtained IRS status in Oregon in 1982.
Donor(s): Fred G. Meyer.†
Financial data: (yr. ended 3/31/85): Assets, $171,639,900 (M); gifts received, $5,998,159; expenditures, $9,621,500, including $6,365,583 for 94 grants (high: $555,000; low: $964; average: $20,000-$75,000), $292,000 for 1 foundation-administered program and $550,000 for 2 loans.
Purpose and activities: Trust began in late 1982 as a general purpose foundation; thus far, grantmaking programs in the fields of "Higher Education in an Information Society" and "Aging and Independence" have been conducted; also inaugurated a library information resources program for the Northwest. Initially, support primarily in Oregon, with occasional grants at the initiative of the Trust for programs in Washington, Idaho, Montana, and Alaska.
Types of support awarded: Seed money, building funds, equipment, matching funds, technical assistance, program-related investments, special projects, research.
Limitations: Giving primarily in OR. No support for sectarian or religious organizations for religious purposes. No grants to individuals, or for general support, endowment funds, annual campaigns, deficit financing, indirect or overhead costs, scholarships or fellowships, or matching gifts; occasional program-related loans only.
Publications: Annual report, informational brochure, program policy statement, application guidelines.
Application information: Special guidelines for aging program. Application form required.
  Initial approach: Full proposal or letter
  Copies of proposal: 1
  Deadline(s): No set deadline except for aging program
  Board meeting date(s): Monthly
  Final notification: 4 to 6 months for proposals that pass first screening; 2 to 3 months for those that don't
  Write: Charles S. Rooks, Executive Director
Officers: Charles S. Rooks, Secretary and Executive Director; Wayne G. Pierson, Treasurer.

Trustees: Travis Cross, Pauline Lawrence, Warne Nunn, G. Gerald Pratt, Oran B. Robertson.
Number of staff: 4 full-time professional; 6 full-time support; 2 part-time support.
Employer Identification Number: 930806316

3499
OCRI Foundation
P.O. Box 1682
Lake Oswego 97034   (503) 635-8010

Established in 1971 in Oregon.
Donor(s): Members of the Lamb family.
Financial data: (yr. ended 12/31/82): Assets, $2,512,893 (M); expenditures, $209,489, including $187,015 for 41 grants (high: $66,665; low: $300).
Purpose and activities: Local giving; supports Christian religious organizations, higher education, and youth programs.
Limitations: Giving limited to OR. No grants to individuals, or for building or endowment funds.
Application information:
  Initial approach: Letter
  Copies of proposal: 1
  Deadline(s): Submit proposal preferably during September and October
  Board meeting date(s): March, July, September, and December
  Write: Michele Leak, Office Manager
Officers and Directors: Dorothy J. Lamb, Chairman; Helen W. Lamb, Vice-Chairman; Anita Lamb Bailey, Secretary; Paula L. Lamb, Treasurer; Edna Lamb, F. Gilbert Lamb, Frank G. Lamb, Paul H. Lamb.
Number of staff: None.
Employer Identification Number: 237120564

3500
Oregon Community Foundation, The ▼
1110 Yeon Bldg.
522 S.W. Fifth Ave.
Portland 97204   (503) 227-6846

Community foundation established in 1973 in Oregon.
Financial data: (yr. ended 5/31/84): Assets, $27,329,882 (M); gifts received, $4,237,514; expenditures, $1,985,822, including $1,614,677 for 175 grants (high: $50,000; low: $500; average: $2,500-$50,000).
Purpose and activities: To "meet educational, cultural, medical, research, social and civic needs in all areas and at all levels of society throughout the state".
Types of support awarded: Operating budgets, continuing support, seed money, building funds, equipment, land acquisition, endowment funds, technical assistance, scholarship funds, special projects.
Limitations: Giving limited to OR. No support for films, or for religious organizations for religious purposes. No grants to individuals, or for emergency funding, matching gifts, annual campaigns, deficit financing, research, publications, or conferences; no loans.

Publications: Annual report, newsletter, program policy statement, application guidelines.
Application information: Application form required.
  Initial approach: Letter
  Copies of proposal: 12
  Deadline(s): Submit application preferably in March or August; deadline April 1 and September 1
  Board meeting date(s): January, June, September, and November
  Final notification: 3 months
  Write: Edward H. Look, Executive Director
Officers: Louis B. Perry,* President; Donald Frisbee,* Vice-President; Brian G. Booth,* Secretary; Virgil E. Solso,* Treasurer; Edward H. Look, Executive Director.
Directors:* Ted Baker, Kenneth W. Ford, Gwyneth Gamble, John Gray, Samuel S. Johnson, Kenneth Lewis, Sally McCragken, Walter C. Reynolds, M.D., William Swindell, Jr.
Participating Banks: The Bank of California, First Interstate Bank of Oregon, The Oregon Bank, United States National Bank of Oregon.
Number of staff: 3 full-time professional; 1 full-time support.
Employer Identification Number: 237315673

3501
Salem Foundation, The
c/o Pioneer Trust Co.
109 Commercial St., N.E.
Salem 97301   (503) 363-3136
Application address: The Salem Foundation, c/o Pioneer Trust Co., P.O. Box 2305, Salem, OR 97308

Community foundation established in 1930 in Oregon.
Financial data: (yr. ended 12/31/83): Assets, $466,307 (M); gifts received, $107,069; expenditures, $149,353, including $138,808 for 33 grants.
Purpose and activities: Local giving for charitable purposes to benefit the citizens of Salem.
Types of support awarded: Operating budgets, continuing support, seed money, emergency funds, building funds, equipment, land acquisition, matching funds, student aid, special projects, research, conferences and seminars.
Limitations: Giving limited to the Salem, OR, area. No grants for annual campaigns, deficit financing, endowments, or publications.
Publications: 990-PF, program policy statement, application guidelines.
Application information: Application form required.
  Board meeting date(s): Distribution committee meets in January
  Write: Michael S. Compton, Trust Officer
Trustee: Pioneer Trust Company (Michael S. Compton, Trust Officer).
Number of staff: None.
Employer Identification Number: 936018523

3502
Tektronix Foundation ▼
Y3-439
P.O. Box 500
Beaverton 97077   (503) 643-8146

Incorporated in 1952 in Oregon.
Donor(s): Tektronix, Inc.
Financial data: (yr. ended 12/31/83): Assets, $2,979,862 (M); gifts received, $673,843; expenditures, $1,772,777, including $1,533,923 for 88 grants (high: $125,000; low: $100), $34,164 for 24 grants to individuals and $187,350 for employee matching gifts.
Purpose and activities: Broad purposes; primarily local giving, with emphasis on education, especially physical sciences and employee gift matching, community funds and other social service programs, health agencies, and some limited arts grants; support also for scholarship programs for children of company employees.
Types of support awarded: Operating budgets, continuing support, annual campaigns, seed money, building funds, equipment, land acquisition, employee matching gifts, fellowships, employee related scholarships.
Limitations: Giving primarily in OR. No grants to individuals (except for company-employee scholarships), or for emergency or endowment funds, demonstration projects, matching or challenge gifts; deficit financing, research, publications, or conferences; no loans.
Application information:
  Initial approach: Proposal
  Copies of proposal: 1
  Deadline(s): 1 month before board meeting
  Board meeting date(s): February, May, August, and November
  Final notification: 4 months
  Write: William B. Webber, Secretary or Thomas O. Williams, Administrator
Officers and Trustees: Howard Vollum, Chairman; Charles H. Frost, Vice-Chairman; William B. Webber, Secretary; Richard Reisinger, Treasurer; Derrol Pennington, Jean E. Vollum, William D. Walker.
Number of staff: 1 part-time professional; 1 part-time support.
Employer Identification Number: 936021540

3503
Templeton (The Herbert A.) Foundation
1717 S.W. Park Ave.
Portland 97201   (503) 223-0036

Incorporated in 1955 in Oregon.
Donor(s): Herbert A. Templeton,† Members of the Templeton family.
Financial data: (yr. ended 12/31/83): Assets, $3,199,388 (M); gifts received, $487,000; expenditures, $231,678, including $200,300 for 112 grants (high: $15,000; low: $100; average: $500-$2,500).
Purpose and activities: Broad purposes; giving limited to educational, youth, cultural, religious (theological education), and social service organizations operating in Oregon or having programs significantly affecting Oregon residents.

Types of support awarded: Operating budgets, continuing support, seed money, emergency funds, scholarship funds, special projects.
Limitations: Giving limited to OR. No support for medical services, scientific research or technology, the aged, or parochial education. No grants to individuals, or for program-related investments, fellowships, building or endowment funds, or matching gifts; no loans.
Publications: Program policy statement, application guidelines.
Application information:
  Initial approach: Letter or full proposal
  Copies of proposal: 1
  Deadline(s): Submit proposal preferably in August or September; deadline October 1
  Board meeting date(s): February or March, July, October, and November
  Final notification: October or November
  Write: Mrs. Jane T. Bryson, President
Officers and Trustees: Jane T. Bryson, President; Ruth B. Richmond, Vice-President; Terrence R. Pancoast, Secretary-Treasurer; James E. Bryson, John R. Olsen, Hall Templeton, William B. Webber.
Number of staff: 1 part-time support.
Employer Identification Number: 930505586

3504
Tucker (Rose E.) Charitable Trust ▼
900 S.W. Fifth Ave., 24th Fl.
Portland 97204   (503) 224-3380

Trust established about 1976 in Oregon.
Donor(s): Rose E. Tucker,† Max and Rose Tucker Foundation.
Financial data: (yr. ended 6/30/84): Assets, $8,824,495 (M); expenditures, $714,598, including $664,250 for 184 grants (high: $25,000; low: $500; average: $1,000-$10,000).
Purpose and activities: Broad purposes; primarily local giving, with priority given to programs in fields of education, health and welfare, community development, social service, arts and culture, and care and education of underprivileged and handicapped.
Types of support awarded: Building funds, scholarship funds, general purposes, operating budgets, equipment, special projects.
Limitations: Giving primarily in OR, with emphasis on the Portland metropolitan area. No support for religion. No grants to individuals, or for fellowships or debt reduction.
Publications: Application guidelines.
Application information:
  Initial approach: Full proposal
  Copies of proposal: 1
  Deadline(s): None
  Board meeting date(s): Approximately every 2 months
  Final notification: Within 10 days of board meetings
  Write: Paul L. Boley or Thomas B. Stoel, Trustees
Trustees: Paul L. Boley, Thomas B. Stoel, United States National Bank of Oregon (Stephen W. Miller, Trust Officer).
Number of staff: None.
Employer Identification Number: 936119091

3505
Walton (William S.) Charitable Trust
c/o United States National Bank of Oregon
P.O. Box 3168
Portland 97208

Trust established in 1958 in Oregon.
Donor(s): William S. Walton.†
Financial data: (yr. ended 5/31/84): Assets,
$777,803 (M); expenditures, $174,521,
including $159,000 for 16 grants (high:
$25,000; low: $1,000; average: $2,000-
$8,000).
Purpose and activities: Local giving primarily
for youth agencies, higher education, cultural
programs, and Protestant welfare funds.
Support for capital improvements only,
including building funds, equipment and
materials and renovation projects.
Types of support awarded: Building funds,
equipment.
Limitations: Giving limited to the Salem, OR,
area. No grants to individuals, or for
endowment funds, general operating support,
scholarships, fellowships, or matching gifts; no
loans.
Application information:
Initial approach: Full proposal
Copies of proposal: 1
Deadline(s): Submit proposal preferably from
June through August; deadline September
15
Board meeting date(s): October
Final notification: October 30
Write: Floyd K. Bowers, Trustee
Trustees: Floyd K. Bowers, United States
National Bank of Oregon.
Number of staff: 2 part-time professional.
Employer Identification Number: 930432836

3506
Wessinger Foundation ¤
1133 W. Burnside
Portland 97209   (503) 222-4351

Established in 1979.
Financial data: (yr. ended 9/30/83): Assets,
$2,467,003 (M); gifts received, $229,572;
expenditures, $206,937, including $181,957
for 16 grants (high: $75,000; low: $500).
Purpose and activities: Primarily local giving
for cultural programs, youth agencies, social
services, and historic preservation organizations.
Limitations: Giving primarily in Portland, OR.
Officers and Directors: W.W. Wessinger,
President; Fred G. Wessinger, Vice-President
and Treasurer; Donald Frisbee, John C.
Hampton, Thomas B. Stoel.
Employer Identification Number: 930754224

3507
Wheeler Foundation
1211 S.W. Fifth Ave., Suite 2906
Portland 97204   (503) 228-0261

Established in 1965 in Oregon.
Donor(s): Coleman H. Wheeler,† Cornelia T.
Wheeler.

Financial data: (yr. ended 12/31/83): Assets,
$2,583,001 (M); gifts received, $1,218,250;
expenditures, $138,108, including $135,250
for 50 grants (high: $10,000; low: $750).
Purpose and activities: Broad purposes;
primarily local giving, with emphasis on higher
and secondary education, medical services and
research, cultural programs, and youth agencies.
Types of support awarded: General purposes.
Limitations: Giving primarily in OR. No grants
to individuals or for endowment funds.
Application information:
Initial approach: Letter along with copy of
IRS determination letter
Copies of proposal: 1
Board meeting date(s): March, June,
September, and December
Write: Samuel C. Wheeler, President
Officers and Directors: Samuel C. Wheeler,
President; John C. Wheeler, Vice-President;
David A. Kekel, Secretary-Treasurer; Lil M.
Hendrickson.
Number of staff: None.
Employer Identification Number: 930553801

PENNSYLVANIA

3508
Adams Foundation, Inc.
202 West Fourth St.
Bethlehem 18016

Incorporated in 1955 in Pennsylvania.
Donor(s): Rolland L. Adams,† South Jersey
Publishing Company, The Bethlehems' Globe
Publishing Company, Cleveland Coca-Cola
Bottling Company, Quaker State Coca-Cola
Bottling Company, and others.
Financial data: (yr. ended 12/31/82): Assets,
$1,019,742 (M); gifts received, $243,114;
expenditures, $178,069, including $177,085
for 58 grants (high: $52,500; low: $33).
Purpose and activities: Broad purposes; grants
largely for higher and secondary education,
hospitals, social services and Protestant church
support.
Application information:
Initial approach: Letter
Deadline(s): None
Write: Nancy A. Taylor, President
Officers and Trustees: Nancy A. Taylor,
President; Marcia A. Roehr, Vice-President;
Donald S. Taylor, Secretary and Treasurer; John
F. Bitzer, Jr., Mary A. Bitzer.
Employer Identification Number: 240866511

3509
Air Products Foundation, The ▼
Route 222
Trexlertown 18087   (215) 481-4986

Incorporated in 1979 in Pennsylvania.
Donor(s): Air Products and Chemicals, Inc.
Financial data: (yr. ended 9/30/84): Assets,
$1,439,634 (M); gifts received, $1,000,000;
expenditures, $875,852, including $873,578
for 290 grants (high: $93,000; low: $50).
Purpose and activities: Grants primarily for
higher education, educational associations, and
community funds; support also for health and
welfare organizations and cultural programs,
including public broadcasting.
Types of support awarded: Operating
budgets, continuing support, annual campaigns,
seed money, emergency funds, building funds,
equipment, endowment funds, special projects.
Limitations: No grants to individuals, or for
scholarships, fellowships, or matching gifts; no
loans.
Publications: 990-PF, annual report.
Application information:
Initial approach: Full proposal
Copies of proposal: 1
Deadline(s): None
Board meeting date(s): Bimonthly
Final notification: 6 weeks
Write: Greta Campbell, Contributions Officer
Officers: Leon C. Holt, Jr., Chairman; Richard
A. Gray, Jr., Secretary; Ronald D. Barclay,
Treasurer.
Trustees: P.L. Thibaut Brian, Ruth M. Davis,
Edward Donley, Walter F. Light, Harry D.
McNeeley, Cornelius P. Powell, Elmer B. Staats.
Number of staff: 1 full-time professional; 1
part-time support.
Employer Identification Number: 232130928

3510
Alco Standard Foundation
P.O. Box 834
Valley Forge 19482   (215) 296-8000

Established in 1974 in Pennsylvania.
Donor(s): Alco Standard Corporation.
Financial data: (yr. ended 12/31/82): Assets,
$789,611 (M); expenditures, $281,392,
including $206,543 for 277 grants (high:
$11,500; low: $13) and $71,358 for 463
employee matching gifts.
Purpose and activities: General giving,
primarily in areas of company operations, with
emphasis on community funds, education,
including an employee matching gift program,
hospitals, and health, youth, and cultural
programs.
Types of support awarded: Employee
matching gifts.
Limitations: Giving primarily in areas of
company operations.
Officers and Directors:* Tinkham Veale II,*
Chairman; Ray B. Mundt,* President; William
F. Drake, Jr.,* John H. Kennedy, Vice-
Presidents; Hugh G. Moulton, Secretary; O.
Gordon Brewer, Jr., Treasurer.
Employer Identification Number: 237378726

3511
Alcoa Foundation ▼
1501 Alcoa Bldg.
Pittsburgh 15219　　　　　(412) 553-4696

Trust established in 1952 in Pennsylvania; incorporated in 1964.
Donor(s): Aluminum Company of America.
Financial data: (yr. ended 12/31/84): Assets, $168,000,000 (M); expenditures, $10,566,000, including $7,970,717 for 1,468 grants (high: $100,000; low: $100), $481,200 for 239 grants to individuals and $956,710 for employee matching gifts.
Purpose and activities: General purposes; grants chiefly for higher education, and for cultural programs, health and welfare, civic and community development, and youth organizations, primarily in areas of company operations.
Types of support awarded: Annual campaigns, building funds, conferences and seminars, continuing support, emergency funds, employee matching gifts, equipment, fellowships, matching funds, operating budgets, research, scholarship funds, seed money, employee related scholarships.
Limitations: Giving primarily in areas of company operations. No support for religious organizations, or elementary or secondary schools. No grants to individuals (except for company-employee scholarships), or for endowment funds, trips or tours, or benefits; no loans.
Publications: Annual report, application guidelines, program policy statement.
Application information:
Initial approach: Full proposal
Copies of proposal: 1
Deadline(s): None
Board meeting date(s): Monthly
Final notification: 1 to 4 months
Write: Earl L. Gadbery, President
Officers: Earl L. Gadbery, President.
Directors:* Bruce R. Barstow, R.L. Fischer, J.E. Nettles, Vincent R. Scorsone, Robert F. Slagle, D.R. Whitlow.
Corporate Trustee: Mellon Bank.
Number of staff: 3 full-time professional; 4 full-time support.
Employer Identification Number: 251128857

3512
Allegheny Foundation ▼
P.O. Box 268
Pittsburgh 15230　　　　　(412) 392-2905

Incorporated in 1953 in Pennsylvania.
Donor(s): Richard M. Scaife.
Financial data: (yr. ended 12/31/83): Assets, $18,517,622 (M); gifts received, $228,850; expenditures, $1,812,622, including $1,660,910 for 46 grants (high: $125,000; low: $250; average: $2,000-$50,000).
Purpose and activities: Broad purposes; primarily local giving, with emphasis on organizations concerned with art and historic preservation, higher education, and animal welfare.
Types of support awarded: General purposes, equipment, publications, seed money, matching funds.

Limitations: Giving primarily in western PA, with emphasis on Pittsburgh. No grants to individuals, or for endowment funds, scholarships, or fellowships; no loans.
Publications: Annual report, program policy statement, application guidelines.
Application information:
Initial approach: Letter
Copies of proposal: 1
Deadline(s): None
Board meeting date(s): December
Write: Joanne B. Beyer, President
Officers: Joanne B. Beyer,* President; James M. Walton,* Vice-President; Gerald Walsh, Secretary-Treasurer.
Trustees:* Richard M. Scaife, Chairman; Peter B. Bell, Ralph H. Goettler, Doris O'Donnell, Nathan J. Stark, Arthur P. Ziegler, Jr.
Number of staff: 1 full-time professional.
Employer Identification Number: 256012303

3513
Allegheny International Foundation ⌑
Two Oliver Plaza
P.O. Box 456
Pittsburgh 15230

Incorporated in 1953 in Illinois as Chemetron Foundation.
Donor(s): Chemetron Corporation, Allegheny International Inc.
Financial data: (yr. ended 12/31/83): Assets, $128,524 (M); gifts received, $435,000; expenditures, $469,067, including $468,727 for 80 grants (high: $40,000).
Purpose and activities: Broad purposes; support largely for higher education, community funds, hospitals, cultural programs, and youth agencies.
Officers and Directors:* G.C. Oemhler,* President; T.P. Maletta, C.A. Sweeney,* Vice-Presidents; T.J. Dougherty,* Secretary; F.F. Babb,* Treasurer.
Employer Identification Number: 366058055

3514
American Bank and Trust Company of Pennsylvania Foundation
P.O. Box 1102
Reading 19603　　　　　(215) 320-2000

Trust established in 1956 in Pennsylvania.
Donor(s): American Bank and Trust Co. of Pennsylvania.
Financial data: (yr. ended 12/31/83): Assets, $45,370 (M); gifts received, $296,043; expenditures, $299,724, including $292,042 for 132 grants (high: $20,000; low: $50) and $7,370 for 65 employee matching gifts.
Purpose and activities: Broad purposes; primarily local giving, with emphasis on community funds, higher education, including employee matching gifts, and hospitals.
Types of support awarded: Employee matching gifts, annual campaigns, building funds, matching funds.
Limitations: Giving primarily in PA. No grants to individuals, or for endowment funds, scholarships, or fellowships; no loans.
Application information: Proposals are not solicited.

Board meeting date(s): Quarterly
Trustee: American Bank and Trust Company of Pennsylvania.
Employer Identification Number: 231976387

3515
Ames (Harriett) Charitable Trust ▼
P.O. Box 750
100 Matsonford Rd.
Radnor 19088　　　　　(215) 293-8902

Trust established in 1952 in New York.
Donor(s): Harriett Ames.
Financial data: (yr. ended 12/31/83): Assets, $10,086,482 (M); expenditures, $649,576, including $591,000 for 49 grants (high: $130,000; low: $1,000; average: $2,500-$20,000).
Purpose and activities: Grants to educational and charitable organizations, with emphasis on medical sciences, education, and health associations.
Limitations: Giving primarily in the New York, NY, metropolitan area. No grants to individuals.
Application information: Applications for grants not invited.
Trustee: Walter H. Annenberg.
Number of staff: None.
Employer Identification Number: 236286757

3516
AMP Foundation ▼
c/o H.A. Walfred, Principal Manager
P.O. Box 3608
Harrisburg 17105

Established in 1977 in Pennsylvania.
Donor(s): AMP Inc.
Financial data: (yr. ended 12/31/83): Assets, $7,935,495 (M); expenditures, $749,980, including $726,380 for 124 grants (high: $73,000; low: $100; average: $5,000-$15,000).
Purpose and activities: General giving, with emphasis on hospitals, higher education, community funds, and youth agencies.
Limitations: Giving primarily in PA, with some emphasis on the Harrisburg and Carlisle areas.
Foundation Managers: H.A. Walfred, Principal Manager; J.D. Brenner, C.J. Fredericksen, H.A. McInnes, W.F. Raab, Dauphin Bank and Trust Co.
Number of staff: 2 part-time professional; 1 part-time support.
Employer Identification Number: 232022928

3517
Anderson (The Mary) Trust ▼
c/o The Glenmede Trust Company
229 South 18th St.
Philadelphia 19103　　　　　(215) 875-3200

Trust established in 1957 in Pennsylvania.
Donor(s): Mary Ethel Pew,† Mabel Pew Myrin,† J. Howard Pew,† J.N. Pew, Jr.†
Financial data: (yr. ended 12/31/83): Assets, $19,591,449 (M); expenditures, $829,109, including $796,400 for 37 grants (high: $148,500; low: $2,000).

Purpose and activities: Broad purposes; primarily local giving, with emphasis on human services, including youth agencies; grants also for health.
Types of support awarded: Operating budgets, seed money, equipment, research, matching funds, special projects.
Limitations: Giving primarily in the greater Philadelphia, PA area. No support for the area of education, for deficit financing, general library acquisitions, or construction of non-academic facilities; in the area of health care for equipment, reimbursable programs, or disease-specific or clinical research; and in human services for research activities, publications, or conferences. No grants to individuals, or for endowment funds, scholarships, or fellowships; no loans.
Publications: 990-PF, application guidelines, program policy statement.
Application information:
   Initial approach: Letter, telephone, or full proposal
   Copies of proposal: 1
   Deadline(s): None
   Board meeting date(s): February, April, June, September, and December
   Write: Fred H. Billups, Jr., Vice-President
Trustee: The Glenmede Trust Company (Robert I. Smith, President).
Number of staff: None.
Employer Identification Number: 236234670

3518
Annenberg Fund, Inc., The ▼
100 Matsonford Rd.
P.O. Box 750
Radnor 19088   (215) 293-8902

Incorporated in 1951 in Delaware.
Donor(s): Walter H. Annenberg.
Financial data: (yr. ended 12/31/83): Assets, $41,790,071 (M); expenditures, $5,200,003, including $5,079,166 for 234 grants (high: $912,500; low: $100).
Purpose and activities: General giving, with emphasis on cultural institutions, higher education, Jewish welfare funds, and medical sciences, including medical education and research.
Limitations: No grants to individuals.
Application information: Applications for grants not invited.
Officers and Directors: Walter H. Annenberg, President; Leonore A. Annenberg, Vice-President; Harry C. Coles, Jr., Secretary; Albert V. Grifone, Treasurer.
Employer Identification Number: 236286756

3519
Annenberg (The M. L.) Foundation ▼
P.O. Box 750
100 Matsonford Rd.
Radnor 19088   (215) 293-8902

Incorporated in 1944 in Pennsylvania.
Donor(s): Triangle Publications, Inc.
Financial data: (yr. ended 12/31/83): Assets, $30,463 (M); gifts received, $835,000; expenditures, $838,730, including $832,616 for 64 grants (high: $133,000; low: $100).

Purpose and activities: Giving primarily for welfare and relief programs, higher education, Jewish welfare funds, and Christian church support.
Limitations: No grants to individuals.
Application information: Applications for grants not invited.
Officers and Directors: Walter H. Annenberg, President.
Employer Identification Number: 231401515

3520
Arcadia Foundation, The ▼
105 East Logan St.
Norristown 19401   (215) 275-8460

Incorporated in 1964 in Pennsylvania.
Donor(s): Edith C. Steinbright, Marilyn Lee Steinbright.
Financial data: (yr. ended 9/30/84): Assets, $8,093,732 (M); gifts received, $20,000; expenditures, $757,260, including $718,550 for 128 grants (high: $17,000; low: $150; average: $1,000-$10,000).
Purpose and activities: New grants limited to Pennsylvania, with emphasis on hospitals and health agencies, higher education, child welfare agencies, care of the handicapped, and cultural programs.
Types of support awarded: Operating budgets, annual campaigns, continuing support, emergency funds, building funds, equipment, endowment funds, research, special projects.
Limitations: Giving limited to PA. No grants to individuals, or for deficit financing, land acquisition, fellowships, demonstration projects, publications, or conferences; no loans.
Application information: Proposal must be in letter form and no more than 2 pages.
   Initial approach: Telephone, letter, or proposal
   Copies of proposal: 1
   Deadline(s): Submit proposal preferably in July or August; deadline August 15
   Board meeting date(s): September and November
   Final notification: 3 months
   Write: Marilyn Lee Steinbright, President
Officers and Directors: Marilyn Lee Steinbright, President; Tanya Hashorva, Vice-President; David Sandler, Secretary; Harvey S.S. Miller, Treasurer; Edward L. Jones, Jr., Kathleen Shellington.
Number of staff: 2.
Employer Identification Number: 236399772

3521
Asplundh Foundation ¤
Blair Mill Rd.
Willow Grove 19090

Incorporated in 1953 in Pennsylvania.
Donor(s): Carl Hj. Asplundh,† Lester Asplundh.
Financial data: (yr. ended 12/31/82): Assets, $1,395,273 (M); gifts received, $100,300; expenditures, $67,253, including $66,500 for 5 grants (high: $50,000; low: $1,000).
Purpose and activities: Primarily local giving, with emphasis on Protestant church support.
Limitations: Giving primarily in PA.

Officers and Directors: Lester Asplundh, President; E. Boyd Asplundh, Secretary; Edward K. Asplundh, Treasurer; Barr E. Asplundh.
Employer Identification Number: 236297246

3522
Barra Foundation, Inc. ▼
Wyndhill Professional Center, Suite 12A
8200 Flourtown Ave.
Wyndmoor 19118   (215) 242-1667

Incorporated in 1963 in Delaware.
Donor(s): Robert L. McNeil, Jr.
Financial data: (yr. ended 12/31/84): Assets, $15,443,811 (M); expenditures, $611,715, including $345,461 for grants (high: $24,000; low: $250).
Purpose and activities: Primarily local giving for the advancement and its effective application to human needs in certain fields, particularly in Eighteenth Century American art and material culture. Projects must be pilot studies or enterprises requiring foresight, not supported by other agencies or individuals; publication or studies required.
Types of support awarded: Matching funds.
Limitations: Giving primarily in the Philadelphia, PA area. No grants to individuals, or for annual campaigns, building or endowment funds, operating budgets, deficit drives, scholarships, fellowships, or ongoing programs; no loans.
Publications: Program policy statement.
Application information: Application form required.
   Initial approach: Letter
   Copies of proposal: 3
   Board meeting date(s): December and as appropriate
   Final notification: 3 to 6 months
   Write: Robert L. McNeil, Jr., President
Officers and Directors: Robert L. McNeil, Jr., President and Treasurer; William T. Tredennick, Vice-President; George M. Brodhead, Secretary; Herman R. Hutchinson, E. Marshall Nuckols, Jr.
Number of staff: 1 part-time support.
Employer Identification Number: 236277885

3523
Beatty (Helen D. Groome) Trust ¤
c/o Girard Trust Bank
One Girard Plaza
Philadelphia 19101   (215) 585-3208

Trust established in 1951 in Pennsylvania.
Donor(s): Helen D. Groome Beatty.†
Financial data: (yr. ended 9/30/83): Assets, $3,619,525 (M); gifts received, $3,593; expenditures, $420,344, including $390,659 for 110 grants (high: $20,000; low: $800).
Purpose and activities: To provide capital support for charitable and educational institutions within the Philadelphia metropolitan area, with emphasis on higher education, hospitals, and cultural programs.
Limitations: Giving primarily in the Philadelphia, PA, metropolitan area. No grants to individuals, or for endowment funds, or operating budgets.

Publications: Application guidelines.
Application information:
Initial approach: Full proposal, telephone, or letter
Copies of proposal: 1
Deadline(s): April 15 or October 15
Board meeting date(s): May 15 and November 15
Trustee: Girard Trust Bank.
Employer Identification Number: 236224798

3524
Benedum (Claude Worthington) Foundation ▼
223 Fourth Ave.
Pittsburgh 15222 (412) 288-0360

Incorporated in 1944 in Pennsylvania.
Donor(s): Michael Late Benedum,† Sarah N. Benedum.†
Financial data: (yr. ended 12/31/84): Assets, $108,939,234 (M); expenditures, $6,691,152, including $5,646,092 for 73 grants (high: $1,000,000; low: $2,500; average: $75,000).
Purpose and activities: Serves a broad variety of charitable purposes in West Virginia and in the greater Pittsburgh area. "Grants are made in areas of education, health, community development and social welfare, and the arts. Funds are provided for projects that address regional problems and needs, that establish demonstration projects with strong potential for replication in West Virginia, or that make outstanding contributions to the area. Local initiatives and voluntary support are encouraged by the Foundation."
Types of support awarded: Matching funds, consulting services, building funds, operating budgets, technical assistance, special projects, program-related investments, seed money.
Limitations: Giving limited to WV and to the greater Pittsburgh area. No support for national health and welfare campaigns, medical research, or religious activities. No grants to individuals.
Publications: Annual report, application guidelines.
Application information:
Initial approach: Letter
Copies of proposal: 1
Board meeting date(s): March, June, September, and December
Final notification: 6 months
Write: Paul R. Jenkins, Executive Vice-President
Officers: Henry A. Bergstrom,* President; Paul R. Jenkins,* Executive Vice-President; David L. Wagner, Vice-President and Treasurer; Betty Gardner Bailey, Secretary.
Trustees:* Paul G. Benedum, Jr., Harry C. Hamm, Jennings Randolph, Hulett C. Smith, George A. Stinson.
Number of staff: 5 full-time professional; 3 full-time support.
Employer Identification Number: 251086799

3525
Beneficia Foundation ☐
Jenkintown Plaza, Sixth Fl.
Jenkintown 19046

Incorporated in 1953 in Pennsylvania.
Donor(s): The Theodore Pitcairn family.
Financial data: (yr. ended 4/30/83): Assets, $8,184,085 (M); expenditures, $290,632, including $273,400 for 58 grants (high: $44,000; low: $400).
Purpose and activities: Broad purposes; primarily local giving, with emphasis on conservation, music, the arts, education, and church support.
Limitations: Giving primarily in PA.
Application information:
Write: Feodor U. Pitcairn, Executive Secretary
Officers and Directors: Laren Pitcairn, President; Miriam P. Mitchell, Vice-President; Feodor U. Pitcairn, Executive Secretary; John G.A. Pennink, Treasurer; Diene P. Cooper, Douglas J. Cooper, John D. Mitchell, Kirstin O. Pitcairn, Mary Eleanor Pitcairn.
Employer Identification Number: 246015630

3526
Bethlehem Area Foundation
430 E. Broad St.
Bethlehem 18018 (215) 867-7588

Community foundation established in 1967 in Pennsylvania.
Financial data: (yr. ended 6/30/83): Assets, $1,683,786 (M); gifts received, $142,907; expenditures, $252,536, including $114,907 for 28 grants.
Purpose and activities: Local giving for health, education, welfare, cultural programs, and civic needs.
Types of support awarded: Seed money, emergency funds, building funds, equipment, land acquisition, matching funds.
Limitations: Giving limited to the Bethlehem, PA, area. No grants to individuals, or for operating budgets, continuing support, annual campaigns, deficit financing, endowments, program support, research, demonstration projects, publications, or conferences and seminars; no loans.
Publications: Program policy statement, application guidelines, annual report.
Application information:
Write: Michael C. Schrader, Executive Director
Officers: Thomas E. Butterfield, Jr., Chairman; Mrs. John W. Leming, Jr., Vice-Chairman; Michael C. Schrader, Secretary and Executive Director.
Trustees: First Valley Bank, The First National Bank of Allentown, Union Bank and Trust Company of Eastern Pennsylvania.
Number of staff: 1 part-time professional.
Employer Identification Number: 231686634

3527
Blaisdell (Philo and Sarah) Foundation ☐
c/o Robert H. Wick
50 Boylston St.
Bradford 16701

Trust established in 1950 in Pennsylvania.
Donor(s): George G. Blaisdell, Zippo Manufacturing Company.
Financial data: (yr. ended 12/31/83): Assets, $1,899,474 (M); gifts received, $2,230; expenditures, $431,080, including $421,255 for 26 grants (high: $327,552).
Purpose and activities: Primarily local giving, with emphasis on youth and child welfare agencies, including a school for retarded children; support also for a university scholarship fund.
Limitations: Giving primarily in Bradford, PA.
Officer: Robert H. Wick, Executive Secretary.
Employer Identification Number: 256035748

3528
Brockway Glass Company Foundation
McCullough Ave.
Brockway 15824 (814) 261-6250

Trust established in 1957 in Pennsylvania.
Donor(s): Brockway, Inc.
Financial data: (yr. ended 12/31/83): Assets, $150,000 (L); gifts received, $240,000; expenditures, $241,000, including $210,800 for 160 grants (high: $20,000; low: $150), $20,200 for 13 grants to individuals and $10,000 for 45 employee matching gifts.
Purpose and activities: Grants for community funds, higher education, health and welfare, youth agencies, and church support.
Types of support awarded: Annual campaigns, emergency funds, building funds, scholarship funds, employee related scholarships, employee matching gifts.
Limitations: No grants to individuals (except for company-employee scholarships), or for endowment funds, research programs, special projects, conferences or publications; no loans.
Application information:
Initial approach: Letter
Copies of proposal: 1
Deadline(s): Submit proposal preferably in September
Board meeting date(s): As required
Write: William H. Weed, Treasurer
Officer: William H. Weed, Treasurer.
Trustees: G.H. Frieling, J.J. McMackin, R.D. Morison, J.A. Winfield.
Number of staff: None.
Employer Identification Number: 256067499

3529
Buhl Foundation, The ▼
Four Gateway Center, Rm. 1522
Pittsburgh 15222 (412) 566-2711

Trust established in 1927 in Pennsylvania.
Donor(s): Henry Buhl, Jr.†
Financial data: (yr. ended 6/30/84): Assets, $22,189,431 (M); expenditures, $1,314,642, including $999,097 for 42 grants (high: $100,000; low: $1,375; average: $24,000).

Purpose and activities: Emphasis on "developmental or innovative" grants to regional institutions, with special interest in education at all levels and in regional concerns, particularly those related to problems of children and youth.
Types of support awarded: Continuing support, seed money, special projects, research.
Limitations: Giving primarily in southwestern PA, particularly the Pittsburgh area. No support for religious activities or nationally funded organizations. No grants to individuals, or for building or endowment funds, operating budgets, scholarships, fellowships, equipment, land acquisition, annual campaigns, emergency funds, deficit financing, renovation projects, publications, conferences and seminars, or matching gifts; no loans.
Publications: Annual report, program policy statement, application guidelines.
Application information: Submit final proposal upon invitation only.
   Initial approach: Letter
   Copies of proposal: 1
   Board meeting date(s): Monthly
   Final notification: 2 to 3 months
   Write: Dr. Doreen E. Boyce, Executive Director
Officers and Managers:* John G. Frazer, Jr.,* President; Francis B. Nimick, Jr.,* William H. Rea,* Vice-Presidents; John M. Arthur,* Treasurer; J.G. Verwer, Jr., Secretary; Doreen E. Boyce, Executive Director.
Number of staff: 2 full-time professional; 2 full-time support.
Employer Identification Number: 250378910

3530
Cairncrest Foundation ▼
One Pitcairn Place
Jenkintown 19046   (215) 887-6700

Incorporated in 1953 in Pennsylvania.
Donor(s): The Harold F. Pitcairn family.
Financial data: (yr. ended 12/31/84): Assets, $9,184,993 (M); expenditures, $460,641, including $412,002 for 5 grants (high: $191,002; low: $3,000).
Purpose and activities: Broad purposes; primarily local giving, restricted to the General Church of the New Jerusalem and its related schools, societies, and organizations.
Limitations: Giving primarily in Bryn Athyn, PA. No grants to individuals.
Application information: Applications not accepted.
   Write: Stephen Pitcairn, Secretary
Officers and Directors: Joel Pitcairn, President; Judith P. Rhodes, Vice-President; Stephen Pitcairn, Secretary; Robert R. Pitcairn, Treasurer; Charis P. Cole, Louis S. Cole, Jr., Theodora C. Emery, Hilary P. Glenn, Beatrice S. Pitcairn, Cameron C. Pitcairn, Glenn P. Pitcairn, Jocelyn B. Pitcairn, John P. Pitcairn, M. Kate Pitcairn, Sue K. Pitcairn, Leon S. Rhodes.
Number of staff: None.
Employer Identification Number: 246015635

3531
Calhoun (Ernest N. and Cynthia S.) Foundation ⌱
504 Grant Bldg.
Pittsburgh 15219

Established in 1955 in Pennsylvania.
Donor(s): Ernest N. Calhoun.†
Financial data: (yr. ended 12/31/83): Assets, $800,304 (M); expenditures, $403,266, including $387,750 for 25 grants (high: $100,000; low: $500).
Purpose and activities: Charitable purposes; primarily local giving, with emphasis on the performing arts, education, family planning, and child development.
Limitations: Giving primarily in Pittsburgh, PA.
Trustees: Kenneth F. Dornbush, B. Timothy Stanny, Norbert F. Stanny.
Employer Identification Number: 256037408

3532
Cameron (Alpin J. and Alpin W.) Memorial Fund ⌱
c/o The First Pennsylvania Bank
Fifteenth and Chestnut Sts.
Philadelphia 19101

Trust established in 1957 in Pennsylvania.
Financial data: (yr. ended 9/30/82): Assets, $1,312,479 (M); gifts received, $4,976; expenditures, $142,339, including $124,450 for 74 grants (high: $10,000; low: $250).
Purpose and activities: Broad purposes; primarily local giving, with emphasis on higher education, cultural programs, and hospitals.
Limitations: Giving primarily in the Philadelphia, PA, area.
Application information:
   Write: Parke Hess, Trust Administrator
Overseers: Winston J. Churchill, Jr., Frederick A. Van Denbergh, Ross Van Denbergh, Thomas S. Weary.
Trustee: The First Pennsylvania Bank (Parke Hess, Trust Administrator).
Employer Identification Number: 236213225

3533
Campbell (Charles Talbot) Foundation ⌱
c/o The Union National Bank of Pittsburgh
P.O. Box 837
Pittsburgh 15230

Trust established in 1975 in Pennsylvania.
Donor(s): Charles Talbot Campbell.†
Financial data: (yr. ended 1/31/84): Assets, $4,336,594 (M); expenditures, $156,375, including $142,000 for 9 grants (high: $30,000; low: $5,000).
Purpose and activities: Primarily local giving, with emphasis on hospitals and ophthalmological research, agencies for the handicapped, and music.
Limitations: Giving primarily in PA.
Trustee: The Union National Bank of Pittsburgh.
Employer Identification Number: 251287221

3534
Caplan (Julius H.) Charity Foundation, Inc. ⌱
P.O. Box 208
Lebanon 17042

Incorporated in 1944 in New York.
Donor(s): Hyman S. Caplan, Keystone Weaving Mills, Inc.
Financial data: (yr. ended 12/31/83): Assets, $2,459,682 (M); gifts received, $60,000; expenditures, $113,268, including $110,342 for 27 grants (high: $63,000; low: $21).
Purpose and activities: Charitable purposes; giving primarily in Pennsylvania and New York, with emphasis on Jewish welfare funds; support also for higher education and hospitals.
Limitations: Giving primarily in PA and NY.
Officers: Hyman S. Caplan, President; Perry Caplan, Vice-President; Eli Caplan, Secretary.
Employer Identification Number: 136067379

3535
Carnegie Hero Fund Commission
606 Oliver Bldg.
Pittsburgh 15222   (412) 281-1302

Trust established in 1904 in Pennsylvania.
Donor(s): Andrew Carnegie.†
Financial data: (yr. ended 12/31/84): Assets, $12,953,219 (M); expenditures, $974,499, including $482,562 for grants to individuals.
Purpose and activities: A private operating foundation established to recognize, with the award of medals and sums of money, heroism voluntarily performed by civilians within the United States and Canada in saving or attempting to save the lives of others; and to grant monetary assistance to persons disabled in these efforts and to the dependents of those who have lost their lives in such heroic manner. No grants for any other purpose.
Types of support awarded: Grants to individuals.
Publications: Annual report, program policy statement, application guidelines.
Application information:
   Initial approach: Letter
   Copies of proposal: 1
   Board meeting date(s): January, April, July, and November
   Write: Robert W. Off, President
Officers and Members: Robert W. Off, President; Alfred M. Hunt, Vice-President; Walter F. Toerge, Vice-President and Secretary; James M. Walton, Treasurer; Henry H. Armstrong, F.J. Torrance Baker, J. Judson Brooks, E. Bayley Buchanan, George S. Ebbert, Jr., Benjamin R. Fisher, John G. Frazer, Jr., Lawrence Wm. Haywiser, T. Herbert Hamilton, Thomas J. Hilliard, Jr., David B. Oliver II, Frank Brooks Robinson, J. Evans Rose, Jr., Arthur M. Scully, Jr., Harton S. Semple, William P. Snyder III, George H. Taber, Alfred W. Wishart, Jr.
Employer Identification Number: 251062730

3536
Carpenter Technology Corporation Foundation ▼ ☐
101 West Bern St.
P.O. Box 662
Reading 19603   (215) 371-2214

Incorporated in 1953 in New Jersey; re-incorporated in 1981 in Delaware as the Carpenter Technology Corporation Foundation.
Donor(s): Carpenter Technology Corporation.
Financial data: (yr. ended 9/30/82): Assets, $1,212,144 (M); gifts received, $200,000; expenditures, $515,713, including $459,156 for 125 grants (high: $145,000; low: $25) and $51,933 for 56 employee matching gifts.
Purpose and activities: Broad purposes; giving primarily in areas of company operations, especially the Reading, Pennsylvania, area, with emphasis on community funds, higher education, hospitals, youth organizations, social agencies, and an employee matching gifts program to colleges and universities.
Types of support awarded: Employee matching gifts, scholarship funds, building funds, general purposes, fellowships, research, special projects.
Limitations: Giving primarily in areas of company operations, especially the Reading, PA, area. No grants to individuals.
Publications: Program policy statement, application guidelines.
Application information:
  Initial approach: Letter
  Board meeting date(s): Semiannually
  Write: W.J. Pendleton, Vice-President
Officers: P.R. Roedel,* President; W.J. Pendleton, Vice-President; D.K. Rothermel, Secretary; J.A. Schuler, Treasurer.
Directors:* H.O. Beaver, Jr., Chairman; T. Beaver, Jr., A.E. Bone, W.E.C. Dearden, W.W. Dixon, C.R. Garr, A.E. Humphrey, J.L. Jones, Jr., F.C. Langenberg, H.R. Sharbaugh, S. James Spitz, Jr., G.F. Verbeck, Jr., H.W. Walker II.
Employer Identification Number: 236235333

3537
Carthage Foundation, The ▼
P.O. Box 268
Pittsburgh 15230   (412) 392-2913

Incorporated in 1964 in Pennsylvania.
Donor(s): Richard M. Scaife.
Financial data: (yr. ended 12/31/83): Assets, $7,769,992 (M); gifts received, $1,079,032; expenditures, $3,073,265, including $2,986,000 for 42 grants (high: $535,000; low: $3,000).
Purpose and activities: Broad purposes; general giving, with emphasis on grants for public policy research, particularly in the areas of government and international affairs.
Types of support awarded: Conferences and seminars, general purposes, research.
Limitations: No grants to individuals, or for building or endowment funds.
Publications: 990-PF.
Application information:
  Initial approach: Letter
  Copies of proposal: 1
  Board meeting date(s): Spring and fall
  Write: Richard M. Larry, Treasurer

Officers and Trustees: Richard M. Scaife, Chairman; George R. McCullough, Vice-Chairman; R. Daniel McMichael, Secretary; Richard M. Larry, Treasurer; Clyde H. Slease III, Gerald Walsh.
Employer Identification Number: 256067979

3538
Cassett (Louis N.) Foundation
1500 Walnut St.
Philadelphia 19102   (215) 545-4100

Trust established in 1946 in Pennsylvania.
Donor(s): Louis N. Cassett.†
Financial data: (yr. ended 12/31/83): Assets, $3,551,609 (M); expenditures, $254,509, including $233,675 for 93 grants (high: $30,000; low: $200).
Purpose and activities: Broad purposes; emphasis on Jewish welfare funds, higher education, hospitals, medical research, and health agencies, including aid to the handicapped; some support also for cultural programs and Protestant church support.
Limitations: No grants to individuals or for endowment funds.
Application information:
  Initial approach: Full proposal
  Copies of proposal: 1
  Deadline(s): Submit proposal in second half of year
  Board meeting date(s): As required
  Write: William Gerstley II, Trustee
Trustees: Albert J. Elias, Carol Gerstley, Joseph Oberndorf.
Employer Identification Number: 236274038

3539
Central Valley Foundation, The ☐
c/o IVB
148 Garrett Rd.
Upper Darby 19082

Established in 1968 in Pennsylvania.
Donor(s): Industrial Valley Bank, Industrial Valley Title Insurance Company.
Financial data: (yr. ended 12/31/83): Assets, $10,105 (M); gifts received, $140,000; expenditures, $142,985, including $142,985 for 65 grants (high: $64,900; low: $100).
Purpose and activities: Broad purposes; primarily local giving, with emphasis on community funds; support also for education, cultural programs, and youth and social agencies.
Limitations: Giving primarily in PA.
Trustees: F. Robert Dieter, J.A. Gallagher, L. King, Patrick J. McGinley, J. Roger Williams, Jr.
Employer Identification Number: 236449300

3540
Charitable Fund, The
(formerly part of F. H. Buhl Trustees)
19 Vine Ave.
Sharon 16146   (412) 981-5522

Trust established in 1903 in Pennsylvania.
Donor(s): Frank H. Buhl.†

Financial data: (yr. ended 9/30/84): Assets, $1,718,929 (M); expenditures, $140,882, including $130,730 for 4 grants (high: $75,000; low: $400).
Purpose and activities: Charitable giving for the benefit of the citizens of Sharon and vicinity.
Limitations: Giving primarily in Sharon, PA and vicinity. No grants to individuals or for building funds.
Application information: Funds presently committed.
  Board meeting date(s): February, April, June, September, and December
  Write: H.H. Hanson, Treasurer
Officers and Trustees: Carlton E. Hutchison, President; Ray W. Rowney, Vice-President; George M. Lanier, Secretary; H.H. Hanson, Treasurer; A.E. Acker, Louis R. Epstein, J.E. Feeney, Leslie E. Spaulding, Mrs. William F. Whitla, G. Leo Winger.
Employer Identification Number: 237366997

3541
Charlestein (Julius and Ray) Foundation ☐
1710 Romano Dr.
Norristown 19401

Established in 1963.
Donor(s): Premier Dental Products Co., Premier Dental Import & Export Co., and related companies.
Financial data: (yr. ended 6/30/83): Assets, $815,125 (M); gifts received, $307,078; expenditures, $116,076, including $114,973 for 20 grants (high: $50,000).
Purpose and activities: Giving primarily to Jewish welfare funds.
Trustees: Morton Charlestein, Jerrold Frezel.
Employer Identification Number: 236398028

3542
CIGNA Foundation
(formerly INA Foundation)
One Logan Sq.
Philadelphia 19103   (215) 557-5422

Incorporated in 1962 in Pennsylvania; merged with Connecticut General Contributions and Civic Affairs Department in 1982.
Donor(s): CIGNA Corporation.
Financial data: (yr. ended 12/31/82): Assets, $4,096,144 (M); gifts received, $4,746,250; expenditures, $2,991,528, including $2,725,037 for 165 grants (high: $471,464; low: $250) and $209,671 for 1,000 employee matching gifts.
Purpose and activities: General purposes; giving to community welfare funds, health and handicapped, the arts, and youth agencies; support also for higher education, including a matching gifts program. Fiscal data for 1982 reflects only INA Foundation activities.
Types of support awarded: Employee matching gifts, general purposes, annual campaigns, seed money, emergency funds, endowment funds.

Limitations: No grants to individuals, or for building funds, research, operating expenses of United Way organizations, testimonial dinners or goodwill advertising; no loans.
Publications: Application guidelines, program policy statement, company report.
Application information:
Initial approach: Letter
Deadline(s): None
Board meeting date(s): January, April, July, and October
Final notification: 6 weeks
Write: Jeffrey P. Lindtner, Executive Director
Officers: Barry F. Wiksten, President; Jeffrey P. Lindtner, Vice-President and Executive Director; Robert L. Robinson, Secretary.
Directors: James W. Walker, Jr., Chairman; John K. Armstrong, Hartzel Z. Lebed, Andrew M. Rouse, George R. Trumbull, III.
Employer Identification Number: 236261726

3543
Claneil Foundation, Inc. ¤
1 Plymouth Meeting, Suite 511
Plymouth Meeting 19462

Incorporated in 1968 in Delaware.
Donor(s): Henry S. McNeil.
Financial data: (yr. ended 12/31/83): Assets, $5,091,643 (M); gifts received, $16,120; expenditures, $512,440, including $481,300 for 52 grants (high: $275,000; low: $500).
Purpose and activities: Broad purposes; primarily local giving with support largely for arts education, higher education and cultural programs.
Limitations: Giving primarily in PA.
Application information:
Write: George M. Brodhead, Secretary
Officers and Directors: Lois F. McNeil, President; Warrin C. Meyers, Vice-President; George M. Brodhead, Secretary; Langhorne B. Smith.
Employer Identification Number: 236445450

3544
Clapp (The Anne L. and George H.) Charitable and Educational Trust ¤
c/o Mellon Bank
Mellon Square
Pittsburgh 15230

Donor(s): George H. Clapp.†
Financial data: (yr. ended 9/30/82): Assets, $5,479,671 (M); expenditures, $365,090, including $338,500 for 21 grants (high: $30,500; low: $3,000).
Purpose and activities: Primarily local giving for education, hospitals, health and social services, cultural programs, a community fund, and youth agencies.
Limitations: Giving primarily in the Pittsburgh, PA, area.
Trustees: William E. Collin, Katherine Clapp Galbraith, Mellon Bank.
Employer Identification Number: 256018976

3545
Connelly Foundation ▼
9300 Ashton Rd.
Philadelphia 19136   (215) 698-5203

Incorporated in 1955 in Pennsylvania.
Donor(s): John F. Connelly, Josephine C. Connelly.
Financial data: (yr. ended 12/31/84): Assets, $75,442,247 (M); expenditures, $3,346,724, including $3,276,665 for 250 grants (high: $900,000; low: $50).
Purpose and activities: Primarily local giving to support educational and religious institutions and hospitals.
Limitations: Giving primarily in the Philadelphia, PA area. No grants to individuals or for endowment funds or research; no loans.
Publications: 990-PF.
Application information:
Initial approach: Letter
Copies of proposal: 1
Deadline(s): Submit proposal preferably early in the year
Board meeting date(s): February, June, September or October, and December
Write: John F. Connelly, President
Officers and Trustees: John F. Connelly, President; Joseph J. Donahue, Executive Vice-President, Secretary and Treasurer; Josephine C. Connelly, Josephine C. Mandeville, Vice-Presidents; Christine Connelly, Judith T. Connelly, Thomas S. Connelly, Chester C. Hilinski, Owen A. Mandeville, Jr., Emily Riley.
Employer Identification Number: 236296825

3546
Conston Foundation ¤
3250 South 76th St.
Philadelphia 19153

Established in 1959.
Donor(s): Conston, Inc.
Financial data: (yr. ended 12/31/83): Assets, $680,202 (M); gifts received, $100,000; expenditures, $119,015, including $118,825 for 38 grants (high: $60,000; low: $25).
Purpose and activities: Grants largely for Jewish welfare funds.
Manager: Charles Conston.
Employer Identification Number: 236297587

3547
Cook (Harry) Foundation ¤
1210 Ricewynne Rd.
Wyncote 19095

Financial data: (yr. ended 11/30/82): Assets, $1,060,821 (M); expenditures, $15,013, including $12,670 for 10 grants (high: $4,320).
Purpose and activities: Giving primarily for hospitals and Jewish welfare funds.
Limitations: Giving primarily in PA.
Officers: Herbert Cook, President; Rose Small, Secretary; D.W. Niesenbaum, Seymour Saslow, Treasurers.
Employer Identification Number: 236439332

3548
Copernicus Society of America
1950 Pennsylvania Ave.
P.O. Box 385
Fort Washington 19034   (215) 628-3632

Established in 1972 in Pennsylvania.
Donor(s): Edward J. Piszek, Sr.
Financial data: (yr. ended 6/30/84): Assets, $4,155,482 (M); gifts received, $11,808; expenditures, $250,854, including $179,553 for 12 grants (high: $30,000; low: $100; average: $1,000-$5,000).
Purpose and activities: Grants largely for cultural programs and historic preservation in the United States.
Types of support awarded: Continuing support, endowment funds, publications, conferences and seminars.
Limitations: No grants to individuals, or for special projects, operating budgets, annual campaigns, seed money, emergency funds, deficit financing, building funds, equipment and materials, land acquisition, matching gifts, scholarships and fellowships, or research; no loans.
Publications: Program policy statement, application guidelines.
Application information:
Initial approach: Full proposal
Copies of proposal: 1
Deadline(s): None
Board meeting date(s): Monthly
Final notification: 5 to 6 weeks
Write: P. Erik Nelson, Executive Director
Officers: Edward J. Piszek, Sr.,* Chairman and President; Helen P. Nelson,* Vice-President and Secretary; Francis Keenan, Edward J. Piszek, Jr.,* George Piszek,* Ann P. Reitenbaugh,* William P. Piszek,* Vice-Presidents; Olga P. Piszek,* Treasurer; P. Erik Nelson, Executive Director.
Directors: James Draper, Harold B. Montgomery, Bernard J. McLafferty.
Number of staff: 1 full-time professional; 3 part-time support.
Employer Identification Number: 237184731

3549
Craig (Earle M.) and Margaret Peters Craig Trust
c/o Mellon Bank
One Mellon Bank Center
Pittsburgh 15258   (412) 234-5248

Trust established in 1953 in Pennsylvania.
Donor(s): Earle M. Craig,† Margaret Peters Craig.†
Financial data: (yr. ended 12/31/83): Assets, $4,024,890 (M); expenditures, $937,203, including $904,750 for 200 grants (high: $55,000; low: $1,000).
Purpose and activities: Broad purposes; primarily local giving, largely for higher education, private secondary schools, hospitals, Protestant churches and religious organizations, the arts, public policy research, and social agencies.

Types of support awarded: Operating budgets, continuing support, annual campaigns, seed money, emergency funds, building funds, equipment, land acquisition, endowment funds, research, publications, conferences and seminars.
Limitations: Giving primarily in PA. No grants to individuals, or for deficit financing, matching gifts, scholarships, fellowships, or demonstration projects; no loans.
Application information: Applications not accepted; family directs distribution of funds.
  Board meeting date(s): As required
  Write: Edward S. McKenna, Assistant Vice-President
Trustee: Mellon Bank.
Number of staff: None.
Employer Identification Number: 256018660

3550
Crary Home, The ⌻
304 Warren National Bank Bldg.
Warren 16365

Established in 1965.
Financial data: (yr. ended 12/31/83): Assets, $663,254 (M); gifts received, $160,378; expenditures, $154,403, including $143,000 for 11 grants (high: $35,000; low: $5,000).
Purpose and activities: Giving primarily "in the fields of religion, education, care of the elderly, and medical services;" grants primarily for church support, hospitals, higher education, and homes for the elderly.
Application information:
  Initial approach: Proposal
  Write: Donald S. Mervine, Secretary-Treasurer
Officers and Directors: Gene Walker Crary, President; Alan H. Templeton, Vice-President; Donald S. Mervine, Secretary-Treasurer; A.L. Rasmussen, Rev. Jack E. Spencer.
Employer Identification Number: 256085744

3551
Crawford (E. R.) Estate
P.O. Box 487
McKeesport 15134

Trust established in 1936 in Pennsylvania.
Donor(s): E.R. Crawford.†
Financial data: (yr. ended 12/31/83): Assets, $4,784,362 (M); expenditures, $413,898, including $350,274 for 95 grants (high: $50,000; low: $100) and $29,347 for 38 grants to individuals.
Purpose and activities: Primarily local giving for hospitals, assistance to indigent families, a library, higher education, Protestant church support, youth agencies, and community funds.
Limitations: Giving primarily in PA.
Application information: Application form required.
  Deadline(s): None
  Write: Francis E. Neish, Trustee
Trustees: William O. Hunter, Frank J. Kelly, Francis E. Neish.
Employer Identification Number: 256031554

3552
Crels Foundation, The
P.O. Box 275
New Holland 17557   (717) 354-7901

Trust established in 1953 in Pennsylvania.
Donor(s): Edwin B. Nolt.
Financial data: (yr. ended 12/31/84): Assets, $3,036,376 (M); expenditures, $233,601, including $224,500 for 41 grants (high: $25,000; low: $1,000).
Purpose and activities: Primarily local giving for hospitals, nursing homes, Mennonite-related religious associations, and parochial elementary education.
Types of support awarded: General purposes, building funds, equipment, operating budgets.
Limitations: Giving primarily in PA, particularly the Lancaster County area. No grants to individuals, or for endowment funds, research programs, scholarships, fellowships, continuing support, annual campaigns, seed money, emergency funds, land acquisition, renovation projects, publications, conferences, matching gifts, or special projects; no loans.
Application information: Applications for grants not encouraged.
  Initial approach: Letter
  Copies of proposal: 1
  Deadline(s): Submit proposal preferably in September
  Board meeting date(s): October and as required
  Write: George C. Delp, Chairman
Officers and Trustees: George C. Delp, Chairman; Clarence J. Nelson, Secretary; John H. Frey, Edwin B. Nolt, Katie B. Nolt.
Number of staff: None.
Employer Identification Number: 236243577

3553
Cyclops Foundation
650 Washington Rd.
Pittsburgh 15228   (412) 343-4000

Trust established in 1953 in Pennsylvania.
Donor(s): Cyclops Corporation.
Financial data: (yr. ended 12/31/83): Assets, $262,641 (L); expenditures, $285,611, including $262,964 for 61 grants (high: $71,400; low: $200) and $20,697 for employee matching gifts.
Purpose and activities: General purposes; grants primarily for community funds, higher education, hospitals, and cultural organizations located in communities where the company is a significant employer.
Types of support awarded: Annual campaigns, seed money, building funds, equipment, land acquisition, employee matching gifts.
Limitations: Giving primarily in areas of company operations. No grants to individuals, or for endowment funds, research, scholarships, fellowships, challenge grants, special projects, deficit financing, operating budgets, continuing support, emergency funds, publications, or conferences; no loans.
Publications: Application guidelines.
Application information:
  Initial approach: Full proposal, letter, or telephone

Copies of proposal: 1
Deadline(s): None
Final notification: 1 to 2 months
Write: Susan J. Rutter, Manager-Cash & Banking
Trustees: W.D. Dickey, Chairman; W.H. Knoell, D.E. Mitchell, J.F. Will.
Number of staff: None.
Employer Identification Number: 256067354

3554
DeMoss (Arthur S.) Foundation ▼
150 Monument Rd.
Bala Cynwyd 19004   (215) 667-9010
Financial office where 990-PF is filed: Chattanooga, TN

Founded as the National Liberty Foundation.
Donor(s): Arthur S. DeMoss.†
Financial data: (yr. ended 12/31/84): Assets, $144,467,042 (M); gifts received, $44,052,500; expenditures, $22,188,580, including $4,487,245 for 40 grants (high: $851,984; low: $500) and $15,431,134 for 7 foundation-administered programs.
Purpose and activities: Support limited to Christian, evangelical projects which are evangelistic and discipling in nature in the United States and other countries.
Types of support awarded: Special projects, conferences and seminars.
Limitations: No support for local churches, denominational agencies or schools. No grants to individuals.
Application information:
  Initial approach: Brief proposal of not more than 2 pages
  Deadline(s): Submit proposal between January 1 and March 31, or between July 1 and September 30
  Board meeting date(s): Monthly
  Final notification: 90-120 days
Officers and Directors: Mrs. Arthur S. DeMoss, Chair and Chief Executive Officer; Robert G. DeMoss, President; Theodore G. DeMoss, Secretary and Treasurer; Charlotte A. DeMoss, Deborah L. DeMoss, Nancy L. DeMoss, R. Mark DeMoss.
Number of staff: 11 full-time professional; 1 part-time professional; 2 full-time support; 3 part-time support.
Employer Identification Number: 236404136

3555
Dietrich (The Daniel W.) Foundation, Inc. ▼ ⌻
1910 Rittenhouse Square
Philadelphia 19103   (215) 546-4312

Incorporated in 1953 in Delaware.
Donor(s): Members of the Dietrich family.
Financial data: (yr. ended 12/31/83): Assets, $3,439,373 (M); gifts received, $244,326; expenditures, $244,303, including $219,974 for 35 grants (high: $33,000; low: $100).
Purpose and activities: Broad purposes; grants primarily for local historic restoration programs and museums; support also for conservation, higher education, and the performing arts.
Limitations: Giving primarily in PA. No grants to individuals.

Application information:
Initial approach: Letter
Copies of proposal: 1
Board meeting date(s): Usually in January and July
Write: Daniel W. Dietrich II, President
Officers and Directors: Daniel W. Dietrich II,* President and Treasurer; Joseph G.J. Connolly, Secretary.
Employer Identification Number: 236255134

3556
Dietrich Foundation (Incorporated), The ¤
1910 Rittenhouse Square
Philadelphia 19103

Incorporated in 1936 in Delaware.
Donor(s): Daniel W. Dietrich Foundation, Inc., Henry D. Dietrich.†
Financial data: (yr. ended 12/31/83): Assets, $3,205,536 (M); gifts received, $3,068,647; expenditures, $80,890, including $76,100 for 84 grants (high: $18,000; low: $100).
Purpose and activities: Broad purposes; grants largely for conservation, higher and secondary education, museums, local historic restoration programs, and community funds.
Types of support awarded: Research, operating budgets, deficit financing, special projects.
Limitations: Giving primarily in PA.
Officers and Directors: William B. Dietrich, President and Treasurer; Sheldon M. Bonovitz, Secretary.
Employer Identification Number: 231515616

3557
Dolfinger-McMahon Foundation
(Comprised of four separate trusts)
One Franklin Plaza, 15th Fl.
Philadelphia 19102   (215) 854-6318

Trust established in 1957 in Pennsylvania, and comprised of four separate trusts: T/W of Henry Dolfinger, as modified by will of Mary McMahon; 1935 D/T of Henry Dolfinger; Trust under Item 6 of the will of Caroline D. McMahon; Maurice Heckscher and Sanford D. Beecher Trust.
Donor(s): Caroline D. McMahon,† Mary M. McMahon.†
Financial data: (yr. ended 9/30/84): Assets, $6,802,039 (M); expenditures, $521,990, including $426,526 for 76 grants (high: $19,240; low: $1,000).
Purpose and activities: Charitable and educational purposes; local giving, with emphasis on experimental, demonstration, or "seed money" projects in race relations, aid to the handicapped, higher and secondary education, social and urban programs, church programs, and health agencies. Beginning in 1981, the foundation has given increased consideration to true emergency situations. Grants limited to $20,000 in any one year to a single project or program.

Types of support awarded: Operating budgets, continuing support, seed money, emergency funds, matching funds, special projects, publications, conferences and seminars, deficit financing.
Limitations: Giving limited to the greater Philadelphia, PA, area. No support for medical or scientific research. No grants to individuals, or for endowment funds, physical facilities, building funds, scholarships, or fellowships.
Publications: Annual report, application guidelines.
Application information:
Initial approach: Full proposal
Copies of proposal: 2
Deadline(s): Submit proposal preferably in March or September; deadline April 1 and October 1
Board meeting date(s): April, October, and as required
Final notification: 1 week to 10 days following semiannual meeting
Write: Joyce E. Robbins, Executive Secretary
Officer: Joyce E. Robbins, Executive Secretary.
Trustees: Maurice Heckscher, Roland Morris.
Number of staff: None.
Employer Identification Number: 236207345

3558
Donnelly (Mary J.) Foundation
c/o Thomas J. Donnelly
2510 Centre City Tower
Pittsburgh 15222   (412) 471-5828

Trust established in 1951 in Pennsylvania.
Donor(s): Mary J. Donnelly.†
Financial data: (yr. ended 6/30/84): Assets, $1,809,287 (M); expenditures, $132,495, including $109,400 for 24 grants (high: $35,000; low: $1,000).
Purpose and activities: Primarily local giving, with emphasis on secondary and higher education, aid to the handicapped, and Roman Catholic associations and welfare funds.
Limitations: Giving primarily in PA. No grants to individuals, or for endowment funds, or matching gifts; no loans.
Application information:
Initial approach: Letter
Copies of proposal: 3
Deadline(s): None
Board meeting date(s): December and June
Write: Thomas J. Donnelly, Trustee
Trustees: Thomas J. Donnelly, Ruth D. Egler, C. Holmes Wolfe.
Number of staff: None.
Employer Identification Number: 256037469

3559
Douty (Alfred and Mary) Foundation
P.O. Box 317
Plymouth Meeting 19462   (215) 828-8145

Established in 1968 in Pennsylvania.
Donor(s): Alfred Douty,† Mary M. Douty.
Financial data: (yr. ended 12/31/83): Assets, $1,886,586 (M); gifts received, $2,000; expenditures, $103,629, including $77,580 for 42 grants (high: $5,000; low: $500; average: $3,000).

Purpose and activities: Primarily local giving, with emphasis on projects in the fields of education and community welfare, with special emphasis on services to disadvantaged people.
Types of support awarded: Operating budgets, conferences and seminars, general purposes, special projects.
Limitations: Giving primarily in the greater Philadelphia, PA, area, with preference given to Montgomery and Philadelphia counties, and including Bucks, Chester, and Delaware counties. No support for religious or political purposes. No grants to individuals, or for matching gifts; generally no support for capital projects or endowments; no loans.
Publications: Application guidelines, annual report.
Application information:
Initial approach: Proposal
Copies of proposal: 1
Deadline(s): Submit proposal preferably between December and May; no formal deadlines
Board meeting date(s): Monthly except July
Final notification: 4 months
Write: Mrs. Judith L. Bardes, Executive Secretary
Officers and Trustees: Mary M. Douty, Chairman; Judith L. Bardes, Executive Secretary; Richard G. Alexander, Norma Elias, Thomas B. Harvey, Frank M. Precopio, Paul William Putney.
Number of staff: 1 part-time professional.
Employer Identification Number: 236463709

3560
Dozor (Harry T. & Shirley W.) Foundation ¤
One Bala Cynwyd Plaza, Suite 317
Bala Cynwyd 19004

Established in 1955.
Donor(s): Harry Dozor.
Financial data: (yr. ended 5/31/83): Assets, $480,775 (M); expenditures, $114,593, including $112,568 for 64 grants (high: $20,000; low: $7).
Purpose and activities: Giving primarily for a university in Israel, and for Jewish welfare funds.
Trustees: Harry T. Dozor, Shirley W. Dozor, Allison Lit.
Employer Identification Number: 237033771

3561
Dravo Corporation & Subsidiaries Charitable Trust
One Oliver Plaza
Pittsburgh 15222   (412) 566-3842

Trust established in 1951 in Pennsylvania.
Donor(s): Dravo Corporation, and subsidiaries.
Financial data: (yr. ended 12/31/83): Assets, $1,081,896 (M); expenditures, $358,000, including $308,000 for 169 grants (high: $130,000; low: $25), $16,250 for 5 grants to individuals and $33,445 for 126 employee matching gifts.

Purpose and activities: General purposes; grants primarily for community funds, higher education institutions, including educational matching gifts for employees and scholarships to children of employees, health agencies, hospitals, and youth agencies.
Types of support awarded: Employee related scholarships, employee matching gifts.
Limitations: No support for labor or political organizations. No grants to individuals (except scholarships to children of company employees) or for endowment funds; no loans.
Application information:
Initial approach: Letter
Copies of proposal: 1
Deadline(s): Submit proposal in July or August; deadline September 1
Board meeting date(s): April and October
Write: Ms. Gail A. Gerono, Secretary, Contributions Committee
Trustee: Pittsburgh National Bank.
Number of staff: 1 part-time professional; 1 part-time support.
Employer Identification Number: 256025229

3562
Eccles (Ralph M. and Ella M.) Foundation
First Seneca Bank
Oil City 16301   (814) 676-8666

Trust established in 1972 in Pennsylvania.
Financial data: (yr. ended 12/31/84): Assets, $1,616,484 (M); expenditures, $95,321, including $78,790 for 6 grants (high: $35,000; low: $600).
Purpose and activities: Giving for operating expenses of Eccles-Lesher Memorial Library and for other community programs and projects in the Union School District of Clarion County.
Types of support awarded: General purposes, operating budgets, continuing support, annual campaigns, seed money, emergency funds, deficit financing, building funds, equipment, land acquisition.
Limitations: Giving limited to Union School District of Clarion County, PA. No grants to individuals, or for endowment funds, special projects, research, publications, conferences, scholarships, fellowships, or matching gifts; no loans.
Publications: Application guidelines.
Application information: Application form required.
Initial approach: Letter
Copies of proposal: 2
Deadline(s): Submit proposal preferably in April or November; no set deadline
Board meeting date(s): May and December
Final notification: 2 months
Write: R. Grant Carner, Trust Officer
Trustee: First Seneca Bank (R. Grant Carner, Trust Officer).
Number of staff: 1 full-time professional; 1 part-time support.
Employer Identification Number: 237261807

3563
Ellis (Charles E.) Grant and Scholarship Fund
c/o Provident National Bank
1632 Chestnut St.
Philadelphia 19103

Financial data: (yr. ended 2/28/84): Assets, $13,600,000 (M); expenditures, $1,200,000, including $1,000,000 for 1,500 grants to individuals.
Purpose and activities: Grants for high school scholarships given to functionally orphaned female high school students in Philadelphia County.
Types of support awarded: Student aid.
Limitations: Giving primarily in Philadelphia County.
Application information:
Write: Trust Administration Dept.
Employer Identification Number: 236725618

3564
Emporium Foundation, Inc., The ⌑
c/o Bucktail Bank and Trust Company
Fourth and Broad Sts.
Emporium 15834   (814) 483-3333

Community foundation incorporated in 1929 in Pennsylvania.
Financial data: (yr. ended 12/31/83): Assets, $1,810,598 (M); gifts received, $50,905; expenditures, $275,964, including $254,575 for 15 grants (high: $203,082; low: $100).
Purpose and activities: Established for the benefit of local residents for maintaining or assisting public schools, public libraries, recreation areas, community buildings, and other similar facilities.
Types of support awarded: Building funds, equipment.
Limitations: Giving limited to Cameron County, PA.
Application information:
Initial approach: Letter
Deadline(s): None
Write: Stephen P. Szemes, Treasurer
Officers and Directors: George B. Erskine, President; James A. Miller, Vice-President; Edwin W. Tomkins, II, Secretary; Stephen P. Szemes, Treasurer; Edward B. Lundberg, John Rogers.
Employer Identification Number: 250995760

3565
Erie Community Foundation, The ▼
419 G. Daniel Baldwin Bldg.
P.O. Box 1818
Erie 16507   (814) 454-0843

Community foundation established as Erie Endowment Foundation in 1935 in Pennsylvania; renamed in 1970.
Financial data: (yr. ended 12/31/84): Assets, $6,004,652 (M); gifts received, $516,092; expenditures, $873,977, including $801,322 for 87 grants (high: $105,000; low: $300; average: $1,000-$15,000) and $7,400 for 6 grants to individuals.

Purpose and activities: Primarily local giving to benefit all facets of Erie County life, with emphasis on education, the visual and performing arts, hospitals, health agencies, welfare, youth agencies, religious organizations, and recreation.
Types of support awarded: Seed money, emergency funds, building funds, equipment, matching funds, scholarship funds, research.
Limitations: Giving primarily in Erie County, PA. No grants to individuals (except for scholarships from restricted funds), operating budgets, continuing support, annual campaigns, deficit financing, land acquisition, endowment funds, special projects, publications, or conferences; no loans.
Publications: Application guidelines, informational brochure, grants list.
Application information: Application form required.
Initial approach: Letter or telephone
Copies of proposal: 4
Deadline(s): Submit proposal preferably in February, May, August, or November; deadlines 1st of the month of board meetings
Board meeting date(s): March, June, September, and December
Final notification: 3 to 4 weeks
Write: Edward C. Doll, President
Officers and Trustees: Edward C. Doll, President; William F. Grant, Vice-President; Charles H. Bracken, Secretary-Treasurer; David D. Dunn, M.D., Albert F. Duval, John R. Falcone, Susan H. Hagen, Fr. Steven P. Simon.
Trustee Banks: The First National Bank of Pennsylvania, Marine Bank, Mellon Bank, PennBank Erie.
Number of staff: 1 part-time support.
Employer Identification Number: 256032032

3566
Evans (D. A. & J. A.) Memorial Foundation ⌑
c/o Ellwood City Forge Corp.
Ellwood City 16117

Incorporated in 1953 in Pennsylvania.
Donor(s): Members of the Evans family.
Financial data: (yr. ended 12/31/83): Assets, $244,112 (M); gifts received, $92,000; expenditures, $120,243, including $92,700 for 26 grants (high: $50,000; low: $100) and $27,130 for grants to individuals.
Purpose and activities: Broad purposes; primarily local giving with emphasis on higher education, including scholarships for children of employees of Ellwood City Forge Corp.; grants also for a hospital and Protestant church support.
Types of support awarded: Employee related scholarships.
Limitations: Giving primarily in Ellwood City, PA.
Officers: Robert Barensfeld, President; Christina Evans, Vice-President; Geraldine Evans, Secretary and Treasurer.
Employer Identification Number: 256032325

3567
Falk (Leon) Family Trust
3315 Grant Bldg.
Pittsburgh 15219

Trust established in 1952 in Pennsylvania.
Financial data: (yr. ended 12/31/84): Assets,
$300,000 (M); gifts received, $90,000;
expenditures, $120,000, including $120,000
for 18 grants (high: $55,000; low: $500).
Purpose and activities: Broad purposes;
primarily local giving, with emphasis on the
performing arts, Jewish welfare funds, and a
community fund.
Types of support awarded: Special projects,
annual campaigns, operating budgets, building
funds.
Limitations: Giving primarily in Pittsburgh, PA.
Officer: Louis A. Devin, Jr., Secretary.
Trustees: Sholom Comay, Leon Falk, Jr., Loti
G. Falk, Marjorie L. Falk, Sigo Falk.
Employer Identification Number: 256065756

3568
Falk (Maurice) Medical Fund
3317 Grant Bldg.
Pittsburgh 15219   (412) 261-2485

Incorporated in 1960 in Pennsylvania.
Donor(s): Maurice and Laura Falk Foundation.
Financial data: (yr. ended 8/31/84): Assets,
$7,839,488 (M); expenditures, $495,468,
including $282,871 for 31 grants (high: $3,000;
low: $100; average: $1,000).
Purpose and activities: Grants program is
limited to long-term commitments and
endowments in the mental health field,
including racism and mental health, public
policy, and some manpower development
projects.
Types of support awarded: Continuing
support, seed money, emergency funds,
endowment funds, consulting services,
technical assistance, special projects,
publications, conferences and seminars.
Limitations: No grants to individuals, or for
operating budgets, annual campaigns, deficit
financing, capital funds, scholarships and
fellowships, or matching gifts; no loans.
Publications: Annual report, application
guidelines.
Application information:
  Initial approach: Letter or telephone
  Copies of proposal: 1
  Deadline(s): None
  Board meeting date(s): Quarterly
  Final notification: 2 to 3 weeks
  Write: Philip B. Hallen, President
Officers: Philip B. Hallen, President; Julian
Ruslander,* Secretary; George A. Stinson,*
Treasurer.
Trustees:* Sigo Falk, Chairman; John M.
Arthur, Vice-Chairman; Philip Baskin, Frank L.
Magee.
Number of staff: 2 full-time professional; 1 full-
time support.
Employer Identification Number: 251099658

3569
**Federation Foundation of Greater
Philadelphia**
226 S. 16th St.
Philadelphia 19102   (215) 893-5823

Established in 1971 in Pennsylvania.
Financial data: (yr. ended 11/30/84): Assets,
$6,076,793 (M); gifts received, $460,259;
expenditures, $1,437,824, including
$1,437,824 for 430 grants (high: $100,000;
low: $25).
Purpose and activities: Primarily giving to
Jewish welfare and educational organizations,
higher education, and Israel; support also for
social services.
Application information:
  Write: Robert S. Hass
Officers and Directors: George M. Ross,
President; Harry K. Madway, Frank Newburger,
Jr., Vice-Presidents; Stanley Ferst, Secretary;
Charles G. Sunstein, Treasurer; Michael R.
Belman, Richard J. Braemer, Robert Kassow,
Benjamin B. Levin.
Number of staff: 1 part-time professional; 1
part-time support.
Employer Identification Number: 237083735

3570
**Feinstein (Myer and Rosaline)
Foundation**
700 I.V.B. Bldg.
1700 Market St.
Philadelphia 19103

Trust established in 1945 in Pennsylvania;
incorporated in 1960 in Delaware.
Donor(s): Myer Feinstein,† Rosaline B.
Feinstein, and others.
Financial data: (yr. ended 12/31/83): Assets,
$3,442,564 (M); expenditures, $284,818,
including $257,658 for 19 grants (high:
$161,558; low: $100).
Purpose and activities: Primarily local giving,
with emphasis on Jewish welfare funds,
religious education, and a community fund.
Limitations: Giving primarily in PA. No grants
to individuals.
Application information:
  Board meeting date(s): July and as required
  Write: I. Jerome Stern, Executive Vice-
  President
Officers and Directors: Peggy Freedman,
President; I. Jerome Stern, Executive Vice-
President; Samuel Feinstein, Vice-President;
Bernice G. Spiegel, Secretary; Pauline Green.
Employer Identification Number: 236235232

3571
Fels (Samuel S.) Fund ▼
Two Penn Center Plaza
Philadelphia 19102   (215) 567-2808

Incorporated in 1935 in Pennsylvania.
Donor(s): Samuel S. Fels.†
Financial data: (yr. ended 12/31/83): Assets,
$20,674,763 (M); expenditures, $1,214,419,
including $947,943 for 124 grants (high:
$25,000; low: $250).

Purpose and activities: General purposes;
grants for continuing support of major projects
instituted by the fund itself, principally the Fels
Research Institute, Temple University Medical
School; the Fels Center of Government,
University of Pennsylvania; and the Fels
Institute for the Study of Human Development,
now part of the Wright State University School
of Medicine. Additional grants for short-term
assistance to projects and organizations that
help to demonstrate and evaluate ways to
prevent, lessen, or resolve contemporary social
problems, or that seek to provide permanent
improvements in the provision of services for
the improvement of daily life; to increase the
stability of arts organizations and enrich the
cultural life of the city of Philadelphia; limited
aid to locally based university presses.
Types of support awarded: Seed money,
emergency funds, matching funds, technical
assistance, fellowships, special projects,
research, conferences and seminars,
publications.
Limitations: Giving limited to the Philadelphia,
PA area. No grants to individuals, or for
capital or endowment funds, travel,
scholarships, or publications; no loans.
Publications: Annual report, program policy
statement, application guidelines.
Application information: Applications in the
field of arts and cultural services should be
submitted before January and June board
meetings. Application form required.
  Initial approach: Letter
  Copies of proposal: 9
  Deadline(s): None
  Board meeting date(s): Monthly except
  August
  Final notification: 1 month
  Write: Dennis J. Clark, Executive Director
Officers: Nochem S. Winnet,* President;
George H. Brown, Jr.,* Vice-President; Dennis
J. Clark, Secretary-Treasurer and Executive
Director.
Member-Directors:* John W. Bodine, Iso
Briselli, Brother Daniel Burke, F.S.C., Sandra
Featherman, David C. Melnicoff, David H.
Wice.
Number of staff: 1 full-time professional; 1 full-
time support.
Employer Identification Number: 231365325

3572
Female Association of Philadelphia ⌘
c/o Provident National Bank
1632 Chestnut St.
Philadelphia 19103

Established in 1881.
Financial data: (yr. ended 9/30/83): Assets,
$1,114,740 (M); expenditures, $67,979,
including $60,764 for grants.
Purpose and activities: Grants to "relieve
poverty and distress of women in reduced
circumstances".
Officers: Mrs. John E. Littleton, President; Mrs.
Richard Crampton, Vice-President; Mrs.
Harrison Therman, Secretary; Mrs. John P.
Bracken, Treasurer.
Employer Identification Number: 236214961

3573
Finley (J. B.) Charitable Trust ⌴
c/o Pittsburgh National Bank
P.O. Box 747
Pittsburgh 15230   (412) 355-3866

Trust established in 1919 in Pennsylvania.
Donor(s): J.B. Finley.†
Financial data: (yr. ended 9/30/83): Assets,
$2,145,668 (M); expenditures, $132,173,
including $124,500 for 27 grants (high:
$13,000; low: $500).
Purpose and activities: Primarily local giving,
with emphasis on Protestant church support
and religious organizations, higher and
secondary education, and cultural programs;
support also for a community fund and a
hospital.
Types of support awarded: Building funds,
general purposes, equipment.
Limitations: Giving primarily in PA.
Application information:
   Initial approach: Letter
   Deadline(s): None
   Write: Henry C. Flood, Jr.
Trustee: Pittsburgh National Bank.
Employer Identification Number: 256024443

3574
Foerderer (Percival E. and Ethel Brown) Foundation
P.O. Box 2368
Philadelphia 19103

Trust established in 1962 in Pennsylvania.
Donor(s): Ethel Brown Foerderer,† Percival E.
Foerderer.†
Financial data: (yr. ended 12/31/84): Assets,
$4,669,711 (M); expenditures, $343,271,
including $293,480 for 15 grants (high:
$200,000; low: $500).
Purpose and activities: Funds largely
committed to the Foerderer Fellowship
Program for students in the College of
Graduate Studies of Thomas Jefferson
University; remainder currently focused on a
research project concerning achondroplasia,
the failure of normal development of cartilage
resulting in dwarfism.
Types of support awarded: Fellowships.
Limitations: Giving primarily in the
Philadelphia, PA, area.
Publications: Biennial report.
Application information: Grant applications
not accepted.
   Board meeting date(s): April, September,
      and October
   Write: John M.K. Davis, Secretary
Officers and Trustees: Shirley Foerderer
Higginson, Chairman; John M.K. Davis,
Secretary; Spencer D. Wright III, Treasurer;
Mrs. John M.K. Davis, Edward C. Driscoll,
Thomas L. Higginson, Ethel D. Pendergrast,
Oliver W. Robbins.
Number of staff: 1 part-time support.
Employer Identification Number: 236296084

3575
Foster Charitable Trust
P.O. Box 67
Pittsburgh 15230

Trust established in 1962 in Pennsylvania.
Donor(s): Foster Industries, Inc.
Financial data: (yr. ended 12/31/83): Assets,
$885,373 (M); gifts received, $304,308;
expenditures, $250,468, including $244,886
for 16 grants (high: $190,000; low: $500).
Purpose and activities: Grants primarily to
Jewish welfare funds and hospitals.
Limitations: No grants to individuals,
endowment funds, or operating budgets.
Application information:
   Initial approach: Letter
   Copies of proposal: 1
   Board meeting date(s): As required
   Write: Jay L. Foster, Trustee
Trustees: J.R. Foster, Jay L. Foster, H. Roy
Gordon, B.S. Mars, Milton Porter.
Number of staff: None.
Employer Identification Number: 256064791

3576
Frick (The Helen Clay) Foundation ▼
1926 Frick Bldg.
Pittsburgh 15219   (412) 281-3328

Trust established in 1947 in Pennsylvania.
Donor(s): Miss Helen C. Frick.
Financial data: (yr. ended 12/31/84): Assets,
$23,496,397 (M); gifts received, $10,429,857;
expenditures, $2,667,358, including
$1,768,000 for 77 grants (high: $826,400; low:
$200).
Purpose and activities: General charitable
purposes; support of an art reference library in
New York City and operation of a museum of
art and a house museum in Pittsburgh; support
also for social services.
Limitations: Giving primarily in Pittsburgh, PA,
and NY. No grants to individuals.
Application information:
   Write: DeCourcy E. McIntosh, Executive
      Director
Trustees: Peter P. Blanchard III, I. Townsend
Burden III, Walter F. Cooley, Jr., Henry Clay
Frick II, Henry Clay Frick III, Edward R.
Weidlein, Jr., C. Holmes Wolfe, Jr., Mellon
Bank.
Number of staff: 1 full-time professional; 2 full-
time support.
Employer Identification Number: 256018983

3577
Frick (Henry C.) Educational Commission
7146 Horsman Dr.
Pittsburgh 15228   (412) 341-6560

Trust established in 1909 in Pennsylvania.
Donor(s): Henry C. Frick.†
Financial data: (yr. ended 12/31/83): Assets,
$3,114,541 (M); expenditures, $160,192,
including $103,802 for 26 grants (high:
$10,815; low: $300; average: $3,000-$5,000).

Purpose and activities: To improve or
enhance the quality of local public elementary
and secondary education. Invites and gives
preference to proposals that provide for or
encourage interaction among the various
community elements that make up and
contribute to public education.
Types of support awarded: Continuing
support, seed money, emergency funds,
matching funds, special projects, research,
publications, conferences and seminars.
Limitations: Giving limited to the city of
Pittsburgh and Allegheny, Fayette, Greene,
Washington, and Westmoreland counties in
southwestern PA. No grants to individuals, or
for operating budgets, annual campaigns, deficit
financing, capital or endowment funds,
scholarships, or fellowships; no loans.
Publications: Program policy statement,
application guidelines, informational brochure,
grants list.
Application information:
   Initial approach: Letter or telephone
   Copies of proposal: 1
   Deadline(s): Submit proposal preferably
      between July 1 and October 1; deadline
      October 1
   Board meeting date(s): May and December
   Final notification: 2 weeks after December
      meeting
   Write: Mrs. Margaret D. Wilson, Executive
      Director
Officers: Albert C. Van Dusen,* President;
Sandra J. McLaughlin,* Vice-President; Joseph
C. Swaim, Jr.,* Secretary-Treasurer; Margaret
D. Wilson, Executive Director.
Trustees:* Doreen E. Boyce, David
Henderson, George D. Lockhart, Rev. Donald
S. Nesti.
Number of staff: 1 full-time professional.
Employer Identification Number: 250965374

3578
Gibson (Addison H.) Foundation ▼ ⌴
1620 Investment Bldg.
239 Fourth Ave.
Pittsburgh 15222   (412) 261-1611

Trust established in 1936 in Pennsylvania.
Donor(s): Addison H. Gibson.†
Financial data: (yr. ended 12/31/83): Assets,
$10,798,400 (M); gifts received, $3,152;
expenditures, $1,465,388, including $562,500
for 58 grants (high: $15,000; low: $8,000;
average: $8,000-$15,000); $178,638 for 165
grants to individuals and $436,055 for 118
loans.
Purpose and activities: To provide (1) medical
and hospital care for local needy persons and
(2) loans to male students residing in western
Pennsylvania for college or university expenses
after at least one year's self-maintenance;
grants also to hospitals.
Types of support awarded: Student aid, grants
to individuals, loans.
Limitations: Giving limited to western PA. No
grants for building funds, endowments,
operating budgets, or special projects.
Application information: Application form
required.
   Initial approach: Letter or telephone to
      schedule personal interview

Deadline(s): None
Board meeting date(s): About 10 times a year
Final notification: Varies
Write: Miss Charlotte G. Kisseleff, Secretary
Officer: Charlotte G. Kisseleff, Secretary.
Trustees: Frank J. Gaffney, Earl F. Reed, Jr., The Union National Bank of Pittsburgh.
Number of staff: 1 full-time professional; 2 full-time support.
Employer Identification Number: 250965379

3579
Gillett (Elesabeth Ingalls) Foundation ⌑
c/o Girard Bank
One Girard Plaza, P.O. Box 7236
Philadelphia 19101

Established in 1980 in Pennsylvania.
Donor(s): The Ingalls Foundation, Robert Ingalls Testamentary Trust.
Financial data: (yr. ended 12/31/83): Assets, $3,893,568 (M); gifts received, $4,789; expenditures, $366,820, including $255,950 for 18 grants (high: $135,000; low: $100).
Purpose and activities: Broad purposes; grants largely for hospitals, social services, cultural programs, and a maritime college.
Officers: Elesabeth I. Gillett,* Chair, President, and Vice-President; F. Warrington Gillett, Jr., Secretary-Treasurer.
Directors:* Charles H. Norris, Jr.
Employer Identification Number: 232142065

3580
Girard Trust Bank Foundation ⌑
One Girard Plaza
Philadelphia 19101

Trust established in 1955 in Pennsylvania.
Donor(s): Girard Trust Bank.
Financial data: (yr. ended 11/30/83): Assets, $2,596,539 (M); expenditures, $207,119, including $183,021 for 288 grants (high: $10,000; low: $10) and $19,878 for 124 employee matching gifts.
Purpose and activities: Broad purposes; primarily local giving, with emphasis on higher education, cultural programs, and hospitals and a community fund.
Limitations: Giving primarily in PA.
Manager: Peter S. Anderson.
Trustees: Richard G. Gilmore, Girard Trust Bank, Corporate Trustee.
Board of Advisors: Thomas A. Cooper, William B. Eagleson, Jr., Robert G. Williams.
Employer Identification Number: 236227144

3581
Glencairn Foundation ⌑
Jenkintown Plaza, Sixth Fl.
Jenkintown 19046 (215) 887-6700

Incorporated in 1950 in Pennsylvania.
Donor(s): Raymond Pitcairn,† and members of the Pitcairn family.
Financial data: (yr. ended 12/31/83): Assets, $10,965,862 (M); expenditures, $224,416, including $202,000 for 3 grants (high: $97,000; low: $50,000).
Purpose and activities: Primarily local giving, with emphasis on Protestant church support and a church-related school.
Limitations: Giving primarily in Bryn Athyn, PA.
Application information:
Write: Lachlan Pitcairn, Secretary
Officers and Directors: Garthowen Pitcairn, President; Michael Pitcairn, Vice-President; Lachlan Pitcairn, Secretary; James F. Junge, Treasurer; Charles S. Cole, Jr., Kirk P. Pendleton.
Employer Identification Number: 231429828

3582
Glendorn Foundation
78 Main St.
Bradford 16701 (814) 368-7171

Trust established in 1953 in Texas.
Donor(s): Forest Oil Corporation, David F. Dorn, Ruth H. Dorn.
Financial data: (yr. ended 3/31/84): Assets, $3,526,516 (M); gifts received, $667,150; expenditures, $451,821, including $451,000 for 4 grants (high: $420,000; low: $1,000).
Purpose and activities: Broad purposes; funds currently committed.
Publications: 990-PF.
Application information: Grant applications currently not invited.
Write: William F. Higie, Foundation Manager
Manager and Trustees: William F. Higie, Foundation Manager; Clayton D. Chisum, David F. Dorn, John C. Dorn, Richard B. Dorn, Jay Bird Lawson, Roxanne M. Suffecool, Leslie D. Wilson.
Number of staff: None.
Employer Identification Number: 251024349

3583
Glosser (David A.) Foundation
72 Messenger St.
Johnstown 15902 (814) 535-7521

Incorporated in 1962 in Pennsylvania.
Donor(s): David A. Glosser.†
Financial data: (yr. ended 6/30/84): Assets, $1,764,664 (M); gifts received, $1,347,471; expenditures, $192,108, including $185,115 for 43 grants (high: $103,748; low: $30).
Purpose and activities: Broad purposes; primarily local giving, with emphasis on Jewish welfare funds and educational organizations.
Limitations: Giving primarily in Johnstown, PA. No grants to individuals, or for endowment funds.
Application information:
Initial approach: Letter
Copies of proposal: 1
Board meeting date(s): As required
Final notification: 2 months
Write: Lester Edelstein, President
Officers and Directors: Lester Edelstein, President; Lester Goldstein, Secretary; Robert Krantzler, Treasurer; Bennett Lyons.
Employer Identification Number: 256066913

3584
Goldman (William) Foundation
1700 Walnut St., Suite 800
Philadelphia 19103 (215) 546-2779

Trust established in 1952 in Pennsylvania.
Donor(s): William Goldman,† Helen L. Goldman.†
Financial data: (yr. ended 12/31/83): Assets, $2,353,283 (M); expenditures, $268,412, including $190,500 for grants.
Purpose and activities: Broad purposes; primarily local giving, with emphasis on graduate studies in the Philadelphia area, including medical education and/or graduate school scholarships, hospitals, child welfare, community funds, and Jewish welfare funds.
Types of support awarded: Operating budgets, annual campaigns, research, scholarship funds.
Limitations: Giving primarily in the Philadelphia, PA, area. No grants to individuals, or for endowment funds or matching gifts; no loans.
Application information: Application form required for scholarship funds.
Initial approach: Letter
Deadline(s): March 15 for scholarship funds only
Board meeting date(s): Quarterly
Write: Bessie Bartash, Executive Director
Officer: Bessie Bartash, Executive Director.
Trustees: William Goldman, Jr., Chairman and Treasurer; William R. Goldman, Vice-Chairman; Bernard M. Borish, Secretary; Lowell H. Dubrow, Alice S. Goldman, Randolph Louis Goldman, Anne G. Kravitz, Barbara G. Susman.
Number of staff: 1.
Employer Identification Number: 236266261

3585
Grass Family Foundation
4025 Crooked Hill Rd.
Harrisburg 17110

Established in 1972.
Donor(s): Alex Grass.
Financial data: (yr. ended 11/30/82): Assets, $1,988,714 (M); expenditures, $87,850, including $76,383 for 9 grants (high: $71,000; low: $50).
Purpose and activities: Grants largely for Jewish welfare funds, including those in Israel; some support also for higher education.
Manager: Alex Grass.
Employer Identification Number: 237218002

3586
Greenfield (The Albert M.) Foundation ⌑
2207 Oakwyn Rd.
Lafayette Hill 19444

Incorporated in 1953 in Pennsylvania.
Donor(s): Albert M. Greenfield.†
Financial data: (yr. ended 8/31/83): Assets, $2,589,131 (M); expenditures, $256,847, including $247,000 for 17 grants (high: $100,000; low: $1,000).

Purpose and activities: Broad purposes; grants largely to Philadelphia-area higher educational institutions, with emphasis on art and music education.
Limitations: Giving primarily in the Philadelphia, PA, area. No grants to individuals or for endowment funds.
Application information:
Initial approach: Letter
Copies of proposal: 1
Deadline(s): None
Board meeting date(s): As required
Write: Elizabeth G. Zeidman, Secretary
Officers and Trustees: Elizabeth M. Petrie, Chairman; Gordon K. Greenfield, President; Elizabeth G. Zeidman, Secretary; Gustave G. Amsterdam, Bruce H. Greenfield.
Employer Identification Number: 236050816

3587
Grumbacher (M. S.) Foundation ¤
c/o M.S. Grumbacher et al.
2801 E. Market St., P.O. Box 2821
York 17405

Established in 1958.
Donor(s): M.S. Grumbacher, Mailman Stores, Inc.
Financial data: (yr. ended 8/31/83): Assets, $2,026,011 (M); gifts received, $50,000; expenditures, $56,480, including $52,437 for 13 grants (high: $35,237; low: $100).
Purpose and activities: Grants largely for Jewish welfare funds and education.
Officers and Trustees: M.S. Grumbacher,* Chairman; M. Thomas Grumbacher,* Vice-Chairman; David J. Kaufman,* Secretary; Spurgeon E. Rohrbaugh, Treasurer.
Employer Identification Number: 236406993

3588
Grundy Foundation, The ▼
680 Radcliffe St.
P.O. Box 701
Bristol 19007   (215) 788-5460

Trust established in 1961 in Pennsylvania.
Donor(s): Joseph R. Grundy.†
Financial data: (yr. ended 12/31/83): Assets, $24,483,166 (M); expenditures, $1,652,141, including $913,298 for 77 grants (high: $204,886; low: $200; average: $1,000-$30,000).
Purpose and activities: General purposes; grants for higher education, libraries, hospitals, child welfare and youth agencies, community funds, recreation, and community planning; support also for the handicapped, historic preservation, and the aged. Restricted to Bucks County, Pennsylvania and activities in which the donor was interested during his lifetime.
Types of support awarded: Building funds, equipment, land acquisition, seed money, conferences and seminars, special projects.
Limitations: Giving limited to Bucks County, PA. No grants to individuals, or for endowment funds, research, scholarships, or fellowships; no loans.
Application information:
Initial approach: Letter
Copies of proposal: 1

Deadline(s): None
Board meeting date(s): Monthly except in August
Final notification: 1 week
Write: Leonard N. Snyder, Executive Director
Officer: Leonard N. Snyder, Executive Director.
Trustees: W. James MacIntosh, Chairman; Stanton C. Kelton, Jr., Edwin R. Rummler, William P. Wood, The Fidelity Bank.
Number of staff: 2 full-time professional.
Employer Identification Number: 231609243

3589
Gulf Oil Foundation of Delaware ▼
Gulf Bldg.
439 Seventh Ave., P.O. Box 1166
Pittsburgh 15230   (412) 263-5968

Incorporated in 1972 in Delaware.
Donor(s): Gulf Oil Corporation, Gulf Oil Foundation (Texas).
Financial data: (yr. ended 12/31/82): Assets, $2,784,277 (M); expenditures, $6,150,783, including $4,596,854 for 140 grants (high: $1,000,000; low: $100; average: $1,000-$50,000), $310,496 for grants to individuals and $1,504,120 for employee matching gifts.
Purpose and activities: General purposes; grants principally for higher education; some support for cultural programs, youth agencies, and health, welfare, and community service organizations.
Types of support awarded: Employee matching gifts, employee related scholarships, fellowships, endowment funds, special projects, research, matching funds, building funds.
Limitations: No support for religious groups or activities. No grants to individuals (except for company-employee scholarships).
Application information:
Initial approach: Letter
Deadline(s): None
Board meeting date(s): September
Write: Philo A. Hutcheson, Executive Director
Officers: William E. Moffett,* President; Philo A. Hutcheson,* Vice-President and Executive Director; Charles A. Boyce, Secretary; J.D. Mahaffey, Treasurer.
Directors: S.W. Murphy, R.E. Wainerdi.
Employer Identification Number: 237164363

3590
Hall (Evelyn A.) Charitable Trust ▼
100 Matsonford Rd.
P.O. Box 750
Radnor 19088   (215) 293-8902

Trust established in 1952 in New York.
Donor(s): Evelyn A. Hall.
Financial data: (yr. ended 12/31/82): Assets, $9,500,656 (M); expenditures, $1,061,879, including $960,430 for 69 grants (high: $505,800; low: $100).
Purpose and activities: Primarily local giving in New York City and Florida for museums, hospitals, medical research, higher education, and social services.
Limitations: Giving primarily in New York, NY, and FL. No grants to individuals.

Application information: Applications for grants not invited.
Trustee: Walter H. Annenberg.
Employer Identification Number: 236286760

3591
Hall Foundation, The ¤
2862 Russell Rd.
Camp Hill 17011

Trust established in 1952 in Pennsylvania.
Donor(s): John N. Hall, Hall's Motor Transit Company, and others.
Financial data: (yr. ended 9/30/82): Assets, $4,194,530 (M); gifts received, $46,164; expenditures, $348,427, including $71,252 for 57 grants (high: $31,525; low: $20) and $251,417 for 243 grants to individuals.
Purpose and activities: Primarily local giving, with emphasis on scholarship grants for children of employees and customers; support also for higher education, youth agencies, and sports and recreation.
Types of support awarded: Student aid.
Limitations: Giving primarily in PA.
Officers and Trustees: John N. Hall, President; W.L. Hall, Vice-President; Gerald N. Hall, Secretary; Robert E. Hall, Ronald L. Hall.
Employer Identification Number: 236243044

3592
Hallowell Foundation, The ¤
1022 Meetinghouse Rd.
Rydal 19406

Trust established in 1956 in Pennsylvania.
Financial data: (yr. ended 12/31/83): Assets, $1,642,501 (M); gifts received, $1,500; expenditures, $151,479, including $148,363 for 18 grants (high: $135,563; low: $100).
Purpose and activities: Charitable purposes; giving primarily in Pennsylvania and Maryland for hospitals and education.
Limitations: Giving primarily in PA and MD.
Trustees: Dorothy W. Hallowell, H. Thomas Hallowell, Jr., Howard T. Hallowell, III, Merritt W. Hallowell, Anne H. Miller.
Employer Identification Number: 236234545

3593
Hambay (James T.) Foundation
Dauphin Deposit Bank and Trust Company
P.O. Box 2961
Harrisburg 17105   (717) 255-2174

Trust established in 1941 in Pennsylvania.
Donor(s): J.T. Hambay.†
Financial data: (yr. ended 12/31/82): Assets, $1,699,265 (M); expenditures, $143,815, including $131,794 for grants.
Purpose and activities: To aid blind, crippled, and indigent children of Harrisburg and vicinity.
Limitations: Giving primarily in Harrisburg, PA, and vicinity. No grants for building funds, or for endowment funds, or operating budgets.
Application information:
Initial approach: Letter
Copies of proposal: 1
Board meeting date(s): Monthly
Write: Brenton M. Hake, Trust Officer

Officer: Joseph H. Desch, Secretary.
Trustees: Worthington C. Flowers, Dauphin Deposit Bank and Trust Company (Brenton M. Hake, Trust Officer).
Employer Identification Number: 236243877

3594
Hammermill Foundation, The ▼
P.O. Box 10050
Erie 16533   (814) 456-8811

Trust established in 1955 in Pennsylvania.
Donor(s): Hammermill Paper Company.
Financial data: (yr. ended 12/31/83): Assets, $3,463,493 (M); gifts received, $822,139; expenditures, $1,530,274, including $530,565 for 80 grants (high: $150,000; low: $210; average: $500-$10,000) and $35,732 for 156 employee matching gifts.
Purpose and activities: General purposes; grants largely for community funds and capital fund drives of colleges and universities; support also for educational associations, arts programs, and youth and social agencies.
Types of support awarded: Annual campaigns, emergency funds, equipment, employee matching gifts, building funds.
Limitations: Giving primarily in areas of company operations with emphasis on Erie, PA. No grants to individuals, or for endowment funds, operating funds, research, or scholarships and fellowships; no loans.
Publications: Program policy statement.
Application information:
  Initial approach: Letter
  Copies of proposal: 1
  Deadline(s): May 1
  Board meeting date(s): As required
  Final notification: 1 month
  Write: Robert J. Kilgore, Secretary
Officers and Trustees: Albert F. Duval, Chairman; Donald S. Leslie, Jr., Vice-Chairman; Robert J. Kilgore, Secretary; R.O. Smith, Treasurer; W. Craig McClelland, Donald C. Wright, Jr.
Number of staff: None.
Employer Identification Number: 256037066

3595
Harsco Corporation Fund ⊐
Camp Hill 17011-8888   (717) 763-7064

Trust established in 1956 in Pennsylvania.
Donor(s): Harsco Corporation.
Financial data: (yr. ended 12/31/83): Assets, $4,786,500 (M); gifts received, $25,000; expenditures, $382,529, including $368,520 for 203 grants (high: $133,385; low: $25).
Purpose and activities: Broad purposes; grants largely to community funds and health agencies in areas of corporation operations; educational and performing arts grants primarily for matching gifts. Requests for contributions originate with local operating management and are approved or disapproved at the fund's central office.
Types of support awarded: General purposes, operating budgets, continuing support, employee related scholarships, employee matching gifts.

Limitations: Giving primarily in areas of company operations. No grants to individuals, or for special projects, building or endowment funds, or research programs; no loans.
Publications: Program policy statement.
Application information: Applications not invited.
  Board meeting date(s): April and as required
  Write: Richard Y. Eby, Secretary
Officers: J.J. Burdge,* President; J.T. Simpson,* Vice-President; Richard Y. Eby, Secretary; George F. Rezich, Treasurer.
Trustees: L. Safier.
Employer Identification Number: 236278376

3596
Hassel Foundation, The
1845 Walnut St.
Philadelphia 19103   (215) 561-6400

Trust established in 1961 in Pennsylvania.
Donor(s): Morris Hassel,† Calvin Hassel.†
Financial data: (yr. ended 12/31/83): Assets, $2,696,994 (M); expenditures, $162,518, including $143,250 for 28 grants (high: $50,000; low: $500).
Purpose and activities: Broad purposes; primarily local giving, with emphasis on Jewish welfare funds, hospitals, temple support, and the aged.
Limitations: Giving primarily in PA. No grants to individuals.
Application information:
  Initial approach: Letter
  Board meeting date(s): June and as required
  Write: Herman H. Krekstein, Secretary
Officer and Trustees: Herman H. Krekstein, Secretary; Sarle H. Cohen, Jay L. Goldberg, George Khoury, Theodore Kobrin, Herman F. Kotzen, I.H. Krekstein, Lewis J. Laventhol, Morton M. Silton.
Employer Identification Number: 236251862

3597
Hazen (Lita) Charitable Trust ▼
100 Matsonford Rd.
P.O. Box 750
Radnor 19088   (215) 293-8902

Trust established in 1952 in New York.
Donor(s): Lita Hazen.
Financial data: (yr. ended 12/31/83): Assets, $7,068,737 (M); expenditures, $837,002, including $793,461 for 37 grants (high: $160,000; low: $250; average: $1,000-$50,000).
Purpose and activities: Grants largely in New York City for medical research, hospitals, medical education, and cultural programs.
Limitations: Giving primarily in New York, NY. No grants to individuals.
Application information: Applications for grants not invited.
Trustee: Walter H. Annenberg.
Number of staff: None.
Employer Identification Number: 236286759

3598
Heinz (H. J.) Company Foundation ▼
P.O. Box 57
Pittsburgh 15230   (412) 237-5436

Trust established in 1951 in Pennsylvania.
Donor(s): H.J. Heinz Company.
Financial data: (yr. ended 12/31/82): Assets, $3,682,553 (M); gifts received, $3,200,000; expenditures, $3,158,552, including $2,818,036 for 980 grants (high: $257,500; low: $20; average: $5,000-$10,000) and $314,478 for 279 employee matching gifts.
Purpose and activities: General giving, primarily in areas of company operations, with emphasis on community funds; grants also for higher education, including matching gifts, hospitals, youth and social agencies, cultural programs, and research in nutrition.
Types of support awarded: Annual campaigns, building funds, continuing support, employee matching gifts, operating budgets, seed money, technical assistance, emergency funds, equipment, internships, scholarship funds, fellowships, special projects, research, publications, conferences and seminars.
Limitations: Giving primarily in areas of company operations. No grants to individuals, or for endowment funds, deficit financing, or land acquisition; no loans.
Publications: Program policy statement, application guidelines.
Application information:
  Initial approach: Letter
  Copies of proposal: 1
  Deadline(s): None
  Board meeting date(s): January, April, July, and October
  Write: Mrs. Sandra B. Hemmings, Administrator
Officers and Trustees: Henry J. Heinz, II, Chairman; A.J.F. O'Reilly, Vice-Chairman; Howard R. Spicher, Secretary; R. Burt Gookin, S.D. Wiley, Mellon Bank, Corporate Trustee.
Number of staff: 1 full-time professional; 1 full-time support.
Employer Identification Number: 256018924

3599
Heinz (Howard) Endowment ▼
301 Fifth Ave., Suite 1417
Pittsburgh 15222   (412) 391-5122

Trust established in 1941 in Pennsylvania.
Donor(s): Howard Heinz,† Elizabeth Rust Heinz.†
Financial data: (yr. ended 12/31/83): Assets, $191,404,941 (M); expenditures, $5,361,723, including $4,637,323 for 108 grants (high: $500,000; low: $500; average: $5,000-$150,000).
Purpose and activities: Local giving; after gifts to certain agencies with which Mr. Heinz was associated during his life, the Endowment supports music and the arts, education, health, social services, and urban and international affairs, usually with one-time, non-renewable grants for new programs, seed money, and capital projects.

Types of support awarded: Seed money, building funds, annual campaigns, emergency funds, general purposes, equipment, endowment funds, research, scholarship funds, matching funds, program-related investments, operating budgets.
Limitations: Giving limited to PA, with emphasis on Pittsburgh and the Allegheny County area; educational grants limited to Pittsburgh and Allegheny County. No grants to individuals; no loans.
Publications: Annual report, program policy statement, application guidelines.
Application information: Application form required.
Initial approach: Letter, full proposal, or telephone
Copies of proposal: 1
Deadline(s): None
Board meeting date(s): Spring and fall
Final notification: 3 to 4 months
Write: Alfred W. Wishart, Jr., Executive Director
Officers: Alfred W. Wishart, Jr., Executive Director; William Lafe, Associate Director.
Trustees: Henry J. Heinz II, Chairman; Drue Heinz, Henry John Heinz III, Joseph W. Oliver, William H. Rea, Mellon Bank, Corporate Trustee.
Number of staff: 7 full-time professional; 5 full-time support.
Employer Identification Number: 251064784

3600
Heinz (Vira I.) Endowment
301 Fifth Ave., Suite 1417
Pittsburgh 15222-2494   (412) 391-5122

Trust established in 1983 in Pennsylvania.
Donor(s): Vira I. Heinz.†
Financial data: (yr. ended 12/31/84): Assets, $2,618,631 (M); expenditures, $243,201.
Purpose and activities: First year of operation 1984; "to benefit such charitable organizations and purposes as should be selected by the trustees".
Application information: In process of establishing guidelines.
Write: Alfred W. Wishart, Jr., Executive Director
Administrator: Alfred W. Wishart, Jr., Executive Director.
Trustees: James M. Walton, Chairman; William H. Rea, Helen P. Rush, John T. Ryan, Jr., S. Donald Wiley, Mellon Bank.
Employer Identification Number: 256235878

3601
Hershey Foods Corporation Fund, The
(formerly The Hershey Fund)
14 East Chocolate Ave.
Hershey 17033   (717) 534-7574

Trust established in 1960 in Pennsylvania.
Donor(s): Hershey Foods Corporation.
Financial data: (yr. ended 12/31/84): Assets, $178,164 (M); gifts received, $800,000; expenditures, $716,095, including $535,410 for 166 grants (high: $60,000; low: $150; average: $500-$5,000) and $180,005 for 525 employee matching gifts.

Purpose and activities: Primarily local giving, with emphasis on higher education, including employee matching gifts, and community funds; some support for health associations and a sports foundation.
Types of support awarded: Employee matching gifts, operating budgets, continuing support, annual campaigns, seed money, emergency funds, building funds, equipment, endowment funds, fellowships, research, publications, conferences and seminars.
Limitations: Giving primarily in PA. No grants to individuals, or for endowment funds that are not part of the higher education capital funds campaign; no loans.
Application information:
Initial approach: Letter
Copies of proposal: 1
Deadline(s): None
Board meeting date(s): Monthly
Final notification: 1 to 2 months
Write: L.W. Simmons, Chairman, Contributions Committee, Hershey Foods Corporation
Trustees: O.C. Johnson, Chairman; W.E. Dearden, K.L. Wolfe, R.A. Zimmerman.
Number of staff: None.
Employer Identification Number: 236239132

3602
Hilles (Allen) Fund ⌀
P.O. Box 8777
Philadelphia 19101-8777

Trust established in 1983 in Pennsylvania.
Donor(s): Edith Hilles Dewces.
Financial data: (yr. ended 12/31/83): Assets, $1,932,898 (M); gifts received, $1,762,271; expenditures, $129,239, including $121,750 for 14 grants (high: $50,000; low: $550).
Purpose and activities: "Support in the areas of education, health, counseling, and activities of the Religious Society of Friends." Giving primarily in the greater Philadelphia and Wilmington regions.
Limitations: Giving primarily in the greater Philadelphia, PA, and Wilmington, DE, areas.
Application information:
Deadline(s): None
Write: Judith L. Bardes, Manager
Manager: Judith L. Bardes.
Trustees: Doris H. Darnell, Robert L. Dewces, Jr., Polly Dewces Moffett, Bank of Delaware.
Employer Identification Number: 516154986

3603
Hillman Foundation, Inc., The ▼
2000 Grant Bldg.
Pittsburgh 15219   (412) 566-1480

Incorporated in 1951 in Delaware.
Donor(s): John Hartwell Hillman, Jr.,† J.H. Hillman & Sons Co., Hillman Land Company, and family-owned corporations.
Financial data: (yr. ended 12/31/84): Assets, $31,439,200 (M); expenditures, $1,896,855, including $1,555,030 for 63 grants (high: $100,000; low: $1,000; average: $20,000-$25,000).

Purpose and activities: Broad purposes; primarily local giving for cultural advancement in the arts, youth, conservation, health and medicine, civic affairs, community development, religion, social welfare, and education.
Types of support awarded: Continuing support, seed money, endowment funds, matching funds, professorships, scholarship funds, special projects, building funds, equipment, land acquisition.
Limitations: Giving primarily in Pittsburgh and southwestern PA. No grants to individuals, or for operating budgets, annual campaigns, deficit financing, travel, or conferences; no loans.
Publications: Annual report, program policy statement, application guidelines.
Application information:
Initial approach: Letter
Copies of proposal: 1
Deadline(s): None
Board meeting date(s): April, June, October, and December, and at annual meeting in May
Final notification: 3 to 4 months
Write: Ronald W. Wertz, Executive Director
Officers: Henry L. Hillman,* President; C.G. Grefenstette,* Vice-President; Ronald W. Wertz, Executive Director and Secretary; David H. Ross, Treasurer.
Directors:* H. Vaughan Blaxter III, Douglas G. Sisterson, Lawrence M. Wagner.
Number of staff: 2 full-time professional; 1 full-time support.
Employer Identification Number: 256011462

3604
Hillman (The Henry L.) Foundation
2000 Grant Bldg.
Pittsburgh 15219   (412) 566-1480

Established in 1964 in Pennsylvania.
Donor(s): Henry L. Hillman.
Financial data: (yr. ended 12/31/84): Assets, $4,896,000 (M); gifts received, $841,542; expenditures, $109,099, including $97,679 for 33 grants (high: $25,000; low: $250; average: $1,000-$5,000).
Purpose and activities: Broad purposes; primarily local giving, with emphasis on arts and cultural programs, youth, conservation, civic affairs, community development, social welfare, church support, secondary education, and hospitals.
Types of support awarded: Operating budgets, continuing support, annual campaigns, seed money, emergency funds, building funds, equipment, matching funds, scholarship funds, special projects.
Limitations: Giving primarily in Pittsburgh and southwestern PA. No grants to individuals, or for deficit financing, land acquisition, endowment funds, research, publications, or conferences; no loans.
Application information:
Initial approach: Letter
Copies of proposal: 1
Deadline(s): None
Board meeting date(s): March and December
Final notification: 3 to 4 months
Write: Ronald W. Wertz, Executive Director

Officers and Directors: Ronald W. Wertz, Executive Director and Secretary; David H. Ross, Treasurer; H. Vaughan Blaxter III, Henry L. Hillman.
Number of staff: 1 part-time professional.
Employer Identification Number: 256065959

3605
Hitchcock (The Margaret Mellon) Foundation ⌗
c/o Mellon Bank
P.O. Box 185
Pittsburgh 15230
Application address: Mellon Bank, One Mellon Bank Center, Pittsburgh, PA 15238; Tel.: (412) 234-5892

Trust established in 1961 in Pennsylvania.
Donor(s): Margaret Mellon Hitchcock.
Financial data: (yr. ended 12/31/83): Assets, $1,227,883 (M); expenditures, $102,057, including $91,000 for 23 grants (high: $25,000; low: $1,000).
Purpose and activities: Charitable purposes; grants largely for hospitals, music, aid to the handicapped, and secondary education, primarily in the New York City area.
Limitations: Giving primarily in the New York, NY, area. No grants to individuals, or for building or endowment funds, operating budgets, or special projects.
Application information: Grants made only to those charities in which trustees have an interest.
  Board meeting date(s): October or November
  Write: Leonard B. Richards III, Vice-President
Officer: A.A. Vestal, Secretary.
Trustees: Margaret Mellon Hitchcock, Thomas Hitchcock III, Alexander M. Laughlin, Mellon Bank (Leonard B. Richards, Vice-President).
Employer Identification Number: 256018992

3606
Hooker (Janet A.) Charitable Trust ▼
100 Matsonford Rd.
P.O. Box 750
Radnor 19088   (215) 293-8902

Trust established in 1952 in New York.
Donor(s): Mrs. Janet A. Neff Hooker.
Financial data: (yr. ended 12/31/83): Assets, $7,836,450 (M); expenditures, $838,504, including $790,800 for 78 grants (high: $70,000; low: $500; average: $1,000-$25,000).
Purpose and activities: Grants primarily in New York and Florida, largely for arts and culture, historic preservation, medical research and services, and social agencies; giving also for animal welfare, religion, and education.
Limitations: Giving primarily in NY and FL. No grants to individuals.
Application information: Applications for grants not invited.
  Write: Walter H. Annenberg, Trustee
Trustee: Walter H. Annenberg.
Number of staff: None.
Employer Identification Number: 236286762

3607
Hooper (Elizabeth S.) Foundation ▼ ⌗
Three Parkway, 13th Fl.
Philadelphia 19102

Established in 1967.
Donor(s): Interstate Marine Transport Co., Interstate Towing Co., Interstate Ocean Transport Co., Thomas Hooper, Adrian S. Hooper.
Financial data: (yr. ended 6/30/83): Assets, $1,145,066 (M); gifts received, $330,000; expenditures, $528,876, including $516,200 for 115 grants (high: $100,000; low: $100; average: $1,000-$20,000).
Purpose and activities: Giving largely for higher and secondary education; grants also for cultural programs, public policy organizations, health, and Protestant church support.
Types of support awarded: Building funds, special projects, general purposes, emergency funds, research, scholarship funds, operating budgets.
Officers: Adrian S. Hooper, President; Thomas Hooper, Vice-President; Bruce H. Hooper, Secretary; Ralph W. Hooper, Treasurer.
Employer Identification Number: 236434997

3608
Hopwood (John M.) Charitable Trust
c/o Pittsburgh National Bank
Trust Dept. - 965
Pittsburgh 15265

Trust established about 1948 in Pennsylvania.
Donor(s): John M. Hopwood.†
Financial data: (yr. ended 12/31/84): Assets, $6,850,689 (M); expenditures, $411,003, including $371,950 for 80 grants (high: $34,000; low: $300).
Purpose and activities: Primarily local giving and in Florida, with emphasis on hospitals, higher education, youth and social agencies, cultural programs, community funds, and church support.
Limitations: Giving primarily in PA and FL.
Trustees: William T. Hopwood, Pittsburgh National Bank.
Employer Identification Number: 256022634

3609
Hoyt Foundation, The
c/o First National Bank Bldg.
P.O. Box 1488
New Castle 16103

Incorporated in 1962 in Pennsylvania.
Donor(s): May Emma Hoyt,† Alex Crawford Hoyt.
Financial data: (yr. ended 10/31/84): Assets, $5,961,155 (M); gifts received, $615; expenditures, $509,428, including $386,760 for 32 grants (high: $200,000; low: $100) and $72,035 for 72 grants to individuals.
Purpose and activities: Broad purposes; primarily local giving, with emphasis on higher education, including scholarships, and a hospital; some support also for cultural programs.
Types of support awarded: Student aid.
Limitations: Giving primarily in PA.

Application information: Application form required.
  Initial approach: Proposal
  Deadline(s): July 15 and December 15 for scholarships
  Board meeting date(s): On or about July 15 and December 15
  Write: Dorothy A. Patton
Officers and Directors: Thomas V. Mansell, President and Secretary; Lauri G. Laurell, Treasurer; Paul H. Reed, Russell J. Schill.
Number of staff: 1 part-time support.
Employer Identification Number: 256064468

3610
Hulme (Milton G.) Charitable Foundation
720 Frick Bldg.
Pittsburgh 15219   (412) 281-2007

Established in 1960 in Pennsylvania.
Donor(s): Glover & MacGregor, Inc.
Financial data: (yr. ended 12/31/82): Assets, $1,633,512 (M); expenditures, $53,690, including $51,850 for 39 grants (high: $5,000; low: $200).
Purpose and activities: Primarily local giving, with emphasis on hospitals, higher education, and music; some support also for youth agencies.
Limitations: Giving primarily in PA. No grants to individuals.
Application information:
  Initial approach: Letter, full proposal, or telephone
  Copies of proposal: 1
  Deadline(s): Submit proposal preferably in early December; deadline December 15
  Board meeting date(s): December
  Final notification: 2 weeks after application deadline
  Write: Milton G. Hulme, Jr.
Trustees: Carol Gratton, Helen C. Hulme, Milton G. Hulme, Jr.
Number of staff: 2 part-time support.
Employer Identification Number: 256062896

3611
Hunt Foundation, The
600 Grant St., 57th Fl.
Pittsburgh 15219   (412) 562-8935
Additional address: L.B. Richards, 3rd, Mellon Bank, One Mellon Bank Center, Rm. 3845, Pittsburgh, PA 15258

Trust established in 1951 in Pennsylvania.
Donor(s): Roy A. Hunt,† and members of the Hunt family.
Financial data: (yr. ended 12/31/83): Assets, $10,646,735 (M); gifts received, $4,000; expenditures, $503,103, including $451,730 for 328 grants (high: $5,000; low: $250).
Purpose and activities: Broad purposes; grants, generally initiated by the trustees, primarily to local institutions, with emphasis on higher education, including major gifts to Hunt Institute for Botanical Documentation at Carnegie-Mellon University; smaller grants for secondary education, the Episcopal Church, and cultural and conservation programs.

Limitations: Giving primarily in PA. No grants to individuals.
Application information:
Initial approach: Letter
Copies of proposal: 1
Deadline(s): May 1 and October 1
Board meeting date(s): June and November
Write: Torrence M. Hunt, Jr., Admin. Trustee
Trustees: Andrew McQ. Hunt, Christopher M. Hunt, Helen M. Hunt, John B. Hunt, Marion McM. Hunt, Richard M. Hunt, Roy A. Hunt III, Susan M. Hunt, Torrence M. Hunt, Torrence M. Hunt, Jr., William E. Hunt, Daniel Kilner, Rachel McM. Hunt Scott, Mellon Bank.
Number of staff: 2 part-time professional; 1 part-time support.
Employer Identification Number: 256018925

3612
Hunt Manufacturing Co. Foundation
230 South Broad St.
Philadelphia 19102   (215) 732-7700

Established in 1955 in New Jersey.
Donor(s): Hunt Manufacturing Co.
Financial data: (yr. ended 11/27/83): Assets, $15,515 (M); gifts received, $229,500; expenditures, $225,950, including $217,700 for 93 grants (high: $25,000; low: $50) and $8,250 for 17 grants to individuals.
Purpose and activities: Primarily local giving and in Fresno, California; Florence, Kentucky; and Statesville, North Carolina; with grants largely for cultural programs, inner city revitalization, public policy research, civic groups, and higher education, including scholarships; some support also for youth and health agencies, and for community funds.
Types of support awarded: Operating budgets, continuing support, annual campaigns, seed money, building funds, equipment, scholarship funds, employee related scholarships.
Limitations: Giving primarily in Philadelphia, PA; Fresno, CA; Florence, KY; and Statesville, NC. No grants to individuals (except for company-employee scholarships), or for endowment funds or matching gifts; no loans.
Publications: 990-PF, application guidelines.
Application information:
Initial approach: Full proposal
Copies of proposal: 1
Deadline(s): 1 month prior to board meeting dates
Board meeting date(s): January, April, July, and October
Final notification: 3 months
Write: William E. Parshall, Secretary
Officers: George E. Bartol III,* President; William E. Parshall, Secretary; Rudolph M. Peins, Jr.,* Treasurer.
Trustees:* John Carney, Paula Cometto, Paul DeBacco, Ronald J. Naples.
Number of staff: 1 full-time professional; 1 part-time support.
Employer Identification Number: 226062897

3613
Hunt (The Roy A.) Foundation ▼
600 Grant St., 56th Fl.
Pittsburgh 15219   (412) 562-8935

Established in 1966 in Pennsylvania.
Donor(s): Roy A. Hunt.†
Financial data: (yr. ended 5/30/83): Assets, $20,407,223 (M); expenditures, $909,359, including $846,320 for 30 grants (high: $388,070; low: $7,000; average: $15,000).
Purpose and activities: Broad purposes; grants initiated by the trustees; primarily local giving to support the Hunt Institute for Botanical Documentation at Carnegie-Mellon University; smaller grants for higher and secondary education, Protestant church support, cultural and other local programs.
Limitations: Giving primarily in the Pittsburgh, PA, area.
Application information: Applications for grants not invited.
Deadline(s): April and September for solicited proposals only
Board meeting date(s): June and November
Write: Torrence M. Hunt, Jr., Administrative Trustee
Officers and Trustees: Torrence M. Hunt, Jr., Foundation Manager; Andrew McQ. Hunt, Christopher M. Hunt, Daniel Kilner Hunt, Helen McM. Hunt, John B. Hunt, Marion McM. Hunt, Richard McM. Hunt, Roy A. Hunt, III, Susan M. Hunt, Torrence M. Hunt, Rachel McM. Hunt Scott.
Number of staff: 2 part-time professional; 1 part-time support.
Employer Identification Number: 256105162

3614
Huston Foundation, The
c/o The Glenmede Trust Company
229 S. 18th St.
Philadelphia 19103   (215) 875-3200

Incorporated in 1957 in Pennsylvania.
Donor(s): Charles Lukens Huston, Jr.,† Mrs. Charles Lukens Huston, Jr., Miss Ruth Huston.†
Financial data: (yr. ended 12/31/83): Assets, $1,741,591 (M); gifts received, $18,250; expenditures, $159,753, including $142,670 for 48 grants (high: $7,500; low: $500).
Purpose and activities: Broad purposes; primarily local giving for community funds and Protestant missionary programs.
Types of support awarded: Operating budgets, special projects.
Limitations: Giving primarily in Chester County, PA. No grants to individuals, or for building or endowment funds, research programs, scholarships, fellowships, or matching gifts; no loans.
Application information:
Initial approach: Letter
Copies of proposal: 1
Deadline(s): Submit proposal preferably in March through April or September through October; deadlines April 1 and October 1
Board meeting date(s): May and November
Write: John Vangorder

Directors: George W. Connell, William M. Galt, III, Mrs. William M. Galt, III, Mrs. Richard L. Hansen, Charles L. Huston, III, Elinor H. Lashley, Andrew B. Young.
Number of staff: None.
Employer Identification Number: 236284125

3615
Hyman Family Foundation ¤
6315 Forbes Ave.
Pittsburgh 15217

Trust established in 1957 in Pennsylvania.
Donor(s): Samuel M. Hyman, and others.
Financial data: (yr. ended 8/31/83): Assets, $1,308,133 (M); gifts received, $463,736; expenditures, $199,883, including $186,348 for 29 grants (high: $70,000; low: $50).
Purpose and activities: General giving, with emphasis on Jewish welfare funds, higher education and temple support.
Manager: Yetta Elinoff.
Employer Identification Number: 256065761

3616
Independence Foundation ▼
2500 Philadelphia National Bank Bldg.
Philadelphia 19107-3493   (215) 563-8105

Established in 1932 as International Cancer Research Foundation; incorporated as Donner Foundation in 1945 in Delaware; divided in 1961 into Independence Foundation and a newly formed William H. Donner Foundation.
Donor(s): William H. Donner.†
Financial data: (yr. ended 12/31/84): Assets, $49,101,580 (M); expenditures, $2,678,347, including $2,310,802 for 105 grants (high: $125,000; low: $1,000).
Purpose and activities: Giving largely for independent secondary education, especially in the form of student loan funds; support for a limited number of educational and cultural organizations; support also for student aid in nursing education.
Types of support awarded: Endowment funds, scholarship funds, professorships, general purposes.
Limitations: No grants to individuals, or for building and development funds, travel, research, publications, operating budgets, college scholarships, graduate fellowships, or matching gifts.
Publications: Annual report, program policy statement, application guidelines.
Application information:
Initial approach: Letter
Copies of proposal: 5
Deadline(s): 3 weeks before meetings
Board meeting date(s): March, June, September, and December
Final notification: 3 to 6 weeks
Write: Robert A. Maes, President
Officers and Directors: Robert A. Maes, President; Alexander F. Barbieri, Secretary; Viola MacInnes, Treasurer; Frederick H. Donner, Andrew K. Marckwald, Robert M. Scott.
Number of staff: 3 full-time professional.
Employer Identification Number: 231352110

3617
Janssen (Henry) Foundation, Incorporated ⌗
1330 Penn Ave.
Wyomissing 19610   (215) 875-3200

Incorporated in 1931 in Delaware.
Donor(s): Members of the Janssen family.
Financial data: (yr. ended 12/31/82): Assets, $6,048,357 (M); gifts received, $52,477; expenditures, $371,258, including $329,225 for 34 grants (high: $100,000; low: $500).
Purpose and activities: Grants primarily to local organizations, with emphasis on hospitals, health, cultural programs, Protestant church support, higher education, and community funds.
Limitations: Giving primarily in PA, particularly Reading and Berks County.
Application information:
   Write: Mrs. Helene L. Master, President
Officers and Trustees: Helene L. Master, President; Elsa L. Bowman, Vice-President; John W. Bowman, Secretary; El Roy P. Master, Treasurer; F. Eugene Stapleton.
Employer Identification Number: 231476340

3618
Javitch Foundation, The ⌗
12 S. 12th St., 22nd Fl.
Philadelphia 19107

Incorporated in 1981 in Pennsylvania.
Donor(s): Lee H. Javitch.
Financial data: (yr. ended 8/31/83): Assets, $262,847 (M); gifts received, $139,000; expenditures, $1,004,045, including $1,000,865 for 37 grants (high: $715,000; low: $100).
Purpose and activities: Giving primarily to Jewish welfare funds and educational institutions.
Officers: Lee H. Javitch, President; Rona Javitch, Vice-President; Bennett Aaron, Secretary-Treasurer.
Employer Identification Number: 232185146

3619
J.D.B. Fund, The ▼
P.O. Box 157
Gwynedd 19436   (215) 699-2233

Trust established in 1966 in Pennsylvania.
Donor(s): John Drew Betz.
Financial data: (yr. ended 12/31/83): Assets, $7,514,924 (M); expenditures, $3,482,043, including $2,291,204 for 63 grants (high: $250,000; low: $5,000; average: $5,000-$75,000).
Purpose and activities: Foundation in transition. All grants now originate with the trustees.
Types of support awarded: Building funds, equipment, land acquisition, matching funds.

Limitations: Giving primarily in Philadelphia and the surrounding areas. No support for arts and sciences. No grants to individuals, or for endowment funds; for general support of established universities, charities, foundations, or hospitals; scholarships and fellowships; medical research, demonstration projects, publications, or conferences; no loans.
Application information: No applications currently accepted.
   Board meeting date(s): Monthly
   Write: John H. Shmidheiser, Manager
Manager: John H. Shmidheiser.
Trustees: Claire S. Betz, John Drew Betz.
Number of staff: 2.
Employer Identification Number: 236418867

3620
Jennings (The Mary Hillman) Foundation
1825 Pittsburgh National Bank
Pittsburgh 15222   (412) 566-2510

Incorporated in 1968 in Pennsylvania.
Donor(s): Mary Hillman Jennings.†
Financial data: (yr. ended 12/31/84): Assets, $16,000,000 (M); expenditures, $670,000, including $540,000 for 88 grants (high: $100,000; low: $500).
Purpose and activities: Broad purposes; primarily local giving, with emphasis on grants to schools, youth agencies, and hospitals and health associations.
Limitations: Giving primarily in the Pittsburgh, PA, area. No grants to individuals.
Application information:
   Initial approach: Letter
   Deadline(s): Submit proposal in February, May, or August; deadline September 15
   Board meeting date(s): March, June, September, and December, and as required
   Final notification: 3 to 6 months
   Write: Paul Euwer, Jr., Executive Director
Officers and Directors: Evan D. Jennings, II, President; Andrew L. Weil, Secretary; Irving A. Wechsler, Treasurer; Paul Euwer, Jr., Executive Director.
Number of staff: None.
Employer Identification Number: 237002091

3621
Justus (Edith C.) Trust
c/o First Seneca Bank and Trust Company
Oil City 16301   (814) 676-8666

Trust established in 1931 in Pennsylvania.
Donor(s): Edith C. Justus.†
Financial data: (yr. ended 12/31/84): Assets, $2,285,380 (M); expenditures, $152,652, including $129,337 for 11 grants (high: $33,333; low: $6,000; average: $5,000-$20,000).
Purpose and activities: Local giving largely for development of civic services, including a library and public parks, and for social agencies and health services.
Types of support awarded: General purposes, operating budgets, building funds, equipment, land acquisition, continuing support, annual campaigns, seed money, emergency funds, deficit financing.

Limitations: Giving limited to Venango County, PA, with emphasis on Oil City. No grants to individuals, or for endowment funds, matching gifts, scholarships, fellowships, special projects, research, publications, or conferences; no loans.
Publications: Application guidelines.
Application information: Application form required.
   Initial approach: Letter
   Copies of proposal: 2
   Deadline(s): Submit proposal in April, August, or November; no set deadline
   Board meeting date(s): May, September, and December
   Final notification: 2 months
   Write: R. Grant Carner, Trust Officer
Trustee: First Seneca Bank and Trust Company (R. Grant Carner, Trust Officer).
Number of staff: 1 full-time professional; 1 part-time support.
Employer Identification Number: 256031057

3622
Justus (Samuel) Charitable Trust
c/o First Seneca Bank
248 Seneca St.
Oil City 16301   (814) 676-8666

Trust established in 1967 in Pennsylvania.
Donor(s): Samuel Justus.†
Financial data: (yr. ended 12/31/84): Assets, $7,530,981 (M); expenditures, $428,263, including $365,705 for 30 grants (high: $49,789; low: $83; average: $5,000-$30,000).
Purpose and activities: Charitable purposes; local giving to benefit orphans, dependent, neglected, delinquent, disadvantaged, and disabled children and youth.
Types of support awarded: General purposes, operating budgets, building funds, land acquisition, equipment, continuing support, annual campaigns, seed money, emergency funds, deficit financing.
Limitations: Giving limited to Venango County, PA. No grants to individuals, or for endowment funds, matching gifts, scholarships, fellowships, special projects, research, publications, or conferences; no loans.
Publications: Annual report, application guidelines.
Application information: Application form required.
   Initial approach: Letter
   Copies of proposal: 2
   Deadline(s): Submit proposal preferably in April, August, or November; no set deadline
   Board meeting date(s): May, September, and December
   Final notification: 2 months
   Write: R. Grant Carner, Trust Officer
Trustee: First Seneca Bank (R. Grant Carner, Trust Officer).
Number of staff: 1 full-time professional; 1 part-time support.
Employer Identification Number: 256031058

3623
Kardon (Samuel and Rebecca) Foundation ⬡
c/o James M. Landsburg & Co.
1313 Architects Bldg.
Philadelphia 19103   (215) 567-0164

Trust established in 1952 in Pennsylvania.
Donor(s): Emanuel S. Kardon, American Bag & Paper Corp.
Financial data: (yr. ended 12/31/82): Assets, $2,373,531 (M); gifts received, $152,400; expenditures, $133,438, including $127,305 for 76 grants (high: $28,051; low: $50).
Purpose and activities: Primarily local giving, with emphasis on a music school and higher education; support also for hospitals, social agencies, and Jewish welfare funds.
Limitations: Giving primarily in PA.
Application information:
  Initial approach: Letter
  Deadline(s): None
Trustee: Emanuel S. Kardon.
Employer Identification Number: 236278123

3624
Kavanagh (T. James) Foundation, Inc.
(formerly T. J. Kavanagh Foundation)
57 Northwood Rd.
Newtown Square 19073   (215) 356-0743

Established in 1968 in Pennsylvania.
Donor(s): T. James Kavanagh.†
Financial data: (yr. ended 12/31/82): Assets, $3,002,552 (M); expenditures, $220,082, including $169,525 for 114 grants (high: $8,000; low: $100; average: $500-$1,000).
Purpose and activities: Broad purposes; primarily local giving; at least 51 percent of funding for Catholic church support and religious associations; support also for education.
Types of support awarded: Operating budgets, continuing support, annual campaigns, emergency funds, building funds, equipment, special projects, research.
Limitations: Giving primarily in PA. No support for other private foundations. No grants to individuals, or for endowment funds, seed money, deficit financing, land acquisition, publications, conferences, scholarships and fellowships, or matching gifts; no loans.
Publications: Application guidelines.
Application information: Submit proposal preferably in May, September, or Novembher.
  Initial approach: Full proposal
  Copies of proposal: 1
  Deadline(s): None
  Board meeting date(s): March, June, October, and December
  Final notification: 2 months
  Write: Brenda S. Brooks, Secretary
Officers and Trustees:* Frank J. Brooks,* President; Elaine A. Kavanagh, Thomas E. Kavanagh,* Vice-Presidents; Brenda S. Brooks,* Secretary and Treasurer.
Number of staff: 1 full-time professional; 1 part-time professional.
Employer Identification Number: 236442981

3625
Kelley (Kate M.) Foundation
341 West Penn Place
Pittsburgh 15224   (412) 661-0134

Foundation established in 1976 in Pennsylvania.
Donor(s): Edward J. Kelley.†
Financial data: (yr. ended 12/31/82): Assets, $2,970,786 (M); gifts received, $600,000; expenditures, $270,191, including $248,000 for 55 grants (high: $10,000; low: $1,000).
Purpose and activities: Giving largely for Roman Catholic church support and church-related education; some support also for other higher and secondary education, and for health education.
Application information:
  Write: Edward C. Ifft, Trustee
Trustees: Thomas R. Bartley, Roy G. Getty, Edward C. Ifft.
Employer Identification Number: 256090985

3626
Kennametal Foundation
P.O. Box 231
Latrobe 15650   (412) 539-5203

Trust established in 1955 in Pennsylvania.
Financial data: (yr. ended 6/30/84): Assets, $473,704 (M); gifts received, $150,000; expenditures, $130,914, including $129,283 for 100 grants (high: $33,198; low: $25).
Purpose and activities: General purposes; emphasis on higher education, hospitals, and community funds.
Types of support awarded: Continuing support, building funds, equipment, endowment funds, program-related investments, research, matching funds.
Limitations: No grants to individuals, or for scholarships and fellowships; no loans.
Application information:
  Initial approach: Letter
  Copies of proposal: 1
  Deadline(s): Submit proposal preferably in January
  Board meeting date(s): Monthly
  Write: Alex G. McKenna, Trustee
Trustees: Alex G. McKenna, Quentin C. McKenna, David B. Arnold, William C. Weaver.
Employer Identification Number: 256036009

3627
Kline (Charles and Figa) Foundation
P.O. Box 2687
Allentown 18001

Incorporated in 1957 in Pennsylvania.
Donor(s): Charles Kline,† Figa Cohen Kline.†
Financial data: (yr. ended 10/31/82): Assets, $2,221,956 (M); gifts received, $212,717; expenditures, $253,933, including $238,975 for 18 grants (high: $151,500; low: $25).
Purpose and activities: Broad purposes; primarily local giving, largely for Jewish welfare and community service agencies, temple support and a community fund.
Limitations: Giving primarily in Allentown, PA. No grants to individuals.
Application information:

Write: Leonard Rapoport, Director
Directors: Fabian I. Fraenkel, Henry R. Neimeyer, Leonard Rapoport.
Employer Identification Number: 236262315

3628
Kline (Josiah W. and Bessie H.) Foundation, Inc. ▼
42 Kline Village
Harrisburg 17104   (717) 232-0266

Incorporated in 1952 in Delaware.
Donor(s): Josiah W. Kline,† Bessie H. Kline.†
Financial data: (yr. ended 12/31/84): Assets, $8,722,493 (L); expenditures, $1,396,202, including $674,300 for grants (high: $100,000; low: $100).
Purpose and activities: Primarily local giving, with emphasis on higher education, hospitals, and the handicapped; support also for scientific or medical research and projects for the improvement of the law.
Types of support awarded: General purposes, continuing support, annual campaigns, emergency funds, building funds, equipment, scholarship funds, matching funds.
Limitations: Giving primarily in central PA. No grants to individuals, or for endowment funds, operating budgets, research, special projects, publications, conferences, or fellowships; no loans.
Publications: 990-PF.
Application information:
  Initial approach: Full proposal
  Copies of proposal: 2
  Board meeting date(s): Semiannually
  Final notification: 6 months
  Write: Harry R. Bughman, Secretary-Treasurer
Officers and Directors: Joseph T. Simpson, President; Richard E. Jordan, Vice-President; Harry R. Bughman, Secretary-Treasurer; William D. Boswell, Cleve J. Fredricksen, Homer L. Kreider, Wilson D. Lewis, William S. Masland, John C. Tuten.
Employer Identification Number: 236245783

3629
Knollbrook Trust, The
c/o The Glenmede Trust Company
229 South 18th St.
Philadelphia 19103   (215) 875-3200

Trust established in 1965 in Pennsylvania.
Donor(s): J. Howard Pew.†
Financial data: (yr. ended 12/31/83): Assets, $3,222,939 (M); expenditures, $203,128, including $197,500 for 11 grants (high: $31,000; low: $3,500).
Purpose and activities: Broad purposes; primarily local giving for health and social service organizations.
Types of support awarded: General purposes, operating budgets, continuing support, seed money, building funds, equipment, research, special projects, matching funds.
Limitations: Giving primarily in Philadelphia, PA. No support for individual church congregations. No grants to individuals, or for endowment funds, or scholarships and fellowships; no loans.

Publications: 990-PF, informational brochure, program policy statement, application guidelines.
Application information:
Initial approach: Letter, telephone, or full proposal
Copies of proposal: 1
Deadline(s): None
Board meeting date(s): February, April, June, September, and December
Write: Fred H. Billups, Jr., Vice-President
Trustee: The Glenmede Trust Company (Robert I. Smith, President).
Number of staff: None.
Employer Identification Number: 236407577

3630
Knudsen (Earl) Charitable Foundation
1337 Four Gateway Center, Suite 1337
Pittsburgh 15222   (412) 263-6716

Established about 1975.
Donor(s): Earl Knudsen.†
Financial data: (yr. ended 12/31/82): Assets, $2,532,887 (M); expenditures, $155,924, including $137,500 for 40 grants (high: $20,000; low: $500).
Purpose and activities: Primarily local giving with emphasis on higher education, hospitals, youth agencies, Protestant church support, and cultural programs.
Limitations: Giving primarily in PA. No grants to individuals, or for endowment funds, scholarships, fellowships, or matching gifts; no loans.
Application information:
Initial approach: Proposal
Copies of proposal: 1
Board meeting date(s): Quarterly and as required
Write: Frank R. Fleming III, Secretary to the Trustees
Trustees: Roy Thomas Clark, Edwin F. Rodenbaugh, The Union National Bank of Pittsburgh.
Employer Identification Number: 256062530

3631
Koppers Company Foundation, The ▼
1900 Koppers Bldg.
436 Seventh Ave.
Pittsburgh 15219   (412) 227-2755

Trust established in 1952 in Pennsylvania.
Donor(s): Koppers Company, Inc.
Financial data: (yr. ended 12/31/83): Assets, $843,181 (M); expenditures, $1,097,301, including $722,363 for 237 grants (high: $110,000; low: $25; average: $500-$25,000) and $359,234 for 577 employee matching gifts.
Purpose and activities: General purposes; grants primarily for higher education, arts, hospitals, and community funds in areas of company operations; support also for an employee matching gifts program and student aid programs at schools chosen by the foundation.

Types of support awarded: Operating budgets, continuing support, annual campaigns, seed money, building funds, equipment, employee matching gifts, scholarship funds, employee related scholarships, student aid, general purposes.
Limitations: Giving primarily in areas of company operations, with particular emphasis on the Pittsburgh, PA, area; no grants to foreign organizations. No support for sectarian, political, or military organizations. No grants to individuals, or for endowment funds, research, hospital operating funds, or program support.
Publications: Application guidelines.
Application information:
Initial approach: Telephone
Copies of proposal: 1
Deadline(s): None
Board meeting date(s): Monthly except in August and November
Final notification: 8 to 10 weeks
Write: Audrey Bonawitz, Administrator
Officers: Thomas C. Cochran, Jr., Vice-President and Secretary; Audrey Bonawitz, Administrator.
Trustees: Charles R. Pullin, Chairman; Fletcher L. Byrom, Douglas Grymes, Terrance Hanold, Andrew W. Mathieson, Mellon Bank.
Number of staff: 1 full-time professional.
Employer Identification Number: 256018910

3632
Korman (Hyman) Family Foundation
Two Neshaminy Interplex
P.O. Box 2000
Trevose 19047

Trust established in 1947 in Pennsylvania.
Donor(s): Members of the Korman family, Hyman Korman, Inc., and others.
Financial data: (yr. ended 12/31/82): Assets, $2,792,062 (M); gifts received, $14,544; expenditures, $243,556, including $207,073 for 11 grants (high: $101,000; low: $100).
Purpose and activities: Primarily local giving, with emphasis on Jewish welfare funds and religious organizations, and a hospital.
Limitations: Giving primarily in Philadelphia, PA. No grants to individuals.
Publications: 990-PF.
Trustees: Berton E. Korman, Leonard I. Korman, Samuel J. Korman, Steven H. Korman, I. Barney Moss.
Employer Identification Number: 236297326

3633
Kunkel (John Crain) Foundation ⌗
1400 Market St., Suite 203
Camp Hill 17011

Established in 1965 in Pennsylvania.
Financial data: (yr. ended 12/31/82): Assets, $4,083,083 (M); expenditures, $248,903, including $134,135 for 14 grants (high: $33,000; low: $2,500).
Purpose and activities: Primarily local giving, with emphasis on a hospital, higher and secondary education, cultural programs, and social agencies.
Limitations: Giving primarily in PA.
Application information:

Write: Hasbrouck S. Wright, Executive Trustee
Trustees: Hasbrouck S. Wright, Executive Trustee; W.M. Kunkel, K.R. Stark.
Employer Identification Number: 237026914

3634
Kynett (Edna G.) Memorial Foundation, Inc. ⌗
c/o Michael A. Walsh
1700 Market St., 10F
Philadelphia 19103

Incorporated in 1954 in Delaware.
Donor(s): Harold H. Kynett.†
Financial data: (yr. ended 12/31/83): Assets, $2,179,535 (M); expenditures, $134,458, including $119,000 for 3 grants (high: $64,000; low: $5,000).
Purpose and activities: Grants to hospitals for medical education and research, with emphasis on the study and treatment of heart and circulatory diseases.
Officers and Trustees: Joseph B. VanderVeer, M.D., President; F.W. Elliott Farr, Vice-President; Barclay Hallowell, Secretary; Michael A. Walsh, Treasurer; Dr. Elmer H. Funk, Jr., Davis W. Gregg, Norman B. Makous, M.D., James Shea, Edward S. Weyl, D. Straton Woodruff, Jr., M.D.
Employer Identification Number: 236296592

3635
Lancaster County Foundation, The
30 W. Orange St.
P.O. Box 1558
Lancaster 17603   (717) 394-3621

Community foundation established in 1924 in Pennsylvania.
Donor(s): Martin M. Harnish.†
Financial data: (yr. ended 12/31/83): Assets, $2,734,219 (M); gifts received, $50,000; expenditures, $234,901, including $231,033 for 40 grants (high: $102,834; low: $500) and $600 for 2 grants to individuals.
Purpose and activities: Local giving for welfare, social services, especially aid to the handicapped, youth agencies, cultural programs, and capital projects.
Types of support awarded: Building funds, equipment.
Limitations: Giving limited to Lancaster County, PA. No support for governmental agencies. No grants to individuals, or for operating budgets, continuing support, annual campaigns, deficit financing, land acquisition, endowment funds, matching gifts, scholarships, fellowships, research, or conferences and seminars; no loans.
Publications: Annual report, application guidelines.
Application information: Application form required.
Write: Gerald L. Molloy, Executive Director
Trustees: William D. Fisher, Chairman; Richard J. Ashby, Jr., and 12 trustee banks.

Distribution Committee: John B. Rengier, Chairman; Donald B. Hostetter, Vice-Chairman; Gerald L. Molloy, Executive Director; Kendig C. Bare, Robert Y. Garrett, Jr., Dawn K. Johnston, James W. Liddell, William J. Poorbaugh, Bruce P. Ryder, R. Wesley Shope.
Number of staff: 1 full-time support; 1 part-time support.
Employer Identification Number: 236419120

3636
Laros (The R. K.) Foundation ⌧
333 Spring St.
Bethlehem 18018   (215) 691-8535

Trust established in 1952 in Pennsylvania.
Donor(s): Russell K. Laros.†
Financial data: (yr. ended 12/31/83): Assets, $1,699,153 (M); expenditures, $115,050, including $103,750 for 10 grants (high: $35,000; low: $1,250).
Purpose and activities: Broad purposes; local giving with emphasis on higher education, community programs, and historic preservation.
Limitations: Giving limited to the Lehigh Valley area of eastern PA. No grants to individuals, or for endowment funds or operating budgets.
Application information:
Initial approach: Full proposal
Copies of proposal: 6
Deadline(s): Submit proposal preferably between January and June
Board meeting date(s): Annually between May and September
Write: Charlotte M. Fretz, Assistant Secretary
Officers: R.K. Laros, Jr., M.D., President; Talbot Shelton, Herman E. Collier, Jr., M.D., Vice-Presidents; Robert A. Spillman, Secretary; James G. Whilden, M.D., Treasurer.
Employer Identification Number: 236207353

3637
Laurel Foundation
Three Gateway Center, 6 North
Pittsburgh 15222   (412) 765-2400

Incorporated in 1951 in Pennsylvania.
Donor(s): Cordelia S. May.
Financial data: (yr. ended 12/31/83): Assets, $10,944,902 (M); expenditures, $662,350, including $530,900 for 35 grants (high: $50,000; low: $500).
Purpose and activities: Broad purposes; grants largely to organizations operating in the fields of higher and secondary education, conservation, health, cultural programs, and population planning, with concentration on projects originating in the Pittsburgh area; support also for immigration reform.
Types of support awarded: General purposes, building funds, special projects.
Limitations: Giving primarily in western PA. No grants to individuals.
Application information:
Initial approach: Letter
Copies of proposal: 1
Deadline(s): Submit proposal preferably between January and April or July and October; no set deadline
Board meeting date(s): June and December
Write: Gregory D. Curtis, President

Officers: Gregory D. Curtis, President and Secretary; Mrs. John F. Kraft, Jr.,* Vice-President; Roger F. Meyer, Vice-President and Treasurer.
Trustees:* Cordelia S. May, Chairman; Curtis S. Scaife, Robert E. Willison.
Number of staff: 2 part-time professional; 2 part-time support.
Employer Identification Number: 256008073

3638
Leeds & Northrup Foundation, The ⌧
Leeds & Northrup
Sumneytown Pike
North Wales 19454   (215) 643-2000

Trust established in 1952 in Pennsylvania.
Donor(s): Leeds & Northrup Company.
Financial data: (yr. ended 12/31/83): Assets, $228,082 (M); expenditures, $144,821, including $140,967 for 79 grants (high: $20,000; low: $100).
Purpose and activities: Broad purposes; local giving, with emphasis on human services, including community funds, and higher education, primarily scientific and engineering; support also for hospitals.
Limitations: Giving limited to PA. No grants to individuals.
Application information: Applications for grants are not invited.
Board meeting date(s): Semiannually
Write: R.W. Zelnick, Trustee
Trustees: D.H. Dresher, D.F. Fish, R.W. Zelnick, Philadelphia National Bank.
Employer Identification Number: 236233706

3639
Lesher (Margaret and Irvin) Foundation
c/o First Seneca Bank
Oil City 16301   (814) 676-8666

Trust established in 1963 in Pennsylvania.
Donor(s): Margaret W. Lesher.†
Financial data: (yr. ended 12/31/84): Assets, $1,129,810 (M); expenditures, $82,451, including $18,595 for 3 grants (high: $12,400; low: $500; average: $500-$20,000) and $49,925 for 71 grants to individuals.
Purpose and activities: Giving limited to scholarships for graduates of Union High School, Clarion County; support also for a rural medical center and a public library.
Types of support awarded: General purposes, operating budgets, building funds, equipment, land acquisition, matching funds, student aid, grants to individuals.
Limitations: Giving limited to Union School District of Clarion County, PA. No grants to individuals (except for scholarships), or for endowment funds; no loans.
Publications: Application guidelines.
Application information: Application form required.
Initial approach: Letter
Copies of proposal: 2
Deadline(s): Submit proposal preferably in April, August, or November
Board meeting date(s): May, September, and, if needed, December

Final notification: 2 months after board meeting
Write: R. Grant Carner, Trust Officer
Trustee: First Seneca Bank and Trust Company (R. Grant Carner, Trust Officer).
Number of staff: 1 full-time professional; 1 part-time support.
Employer Identification Number: 256067843

3640
Levee (Polly Annenberg) Charitable Trust ▼
100 Matsonford Rd.
P.O. Box 750
Radnor 19088   (215) 293-8902

Trust established in 1952 in New York.
Donor(s): Polly Annenberg Levee.†
Financial data: (yr. ended 12/31/83): Assets, $9,345,578 (M); expenditures, $1,203,867, including $1,148,000 for 23 grants (high: $200,000; low: $5,000; average: $10,000-$50,000).
Purpose and activities: Giving primarily in the Philadelphia and New York metropolitan areas; grants to hospitals, medical research institutes, social services, and educational institutions.
Limitations: Giving primarily in the Philadelphia, PA, and New York, NY, metropolitan areas. No grants to individuals.
Application information: Applications for grants not invited.
Trustee: Walter H. Annenberg.
Employer Identification Number: 236286761

3641
Levy (The Blanche P.) Foundation ⌧
c/o Alex Satinsky
2000 Market St., 10th Fl.
Philadelphia 19103

Established in 1967 in Pennsylvania.
Donor(s): Mrs. Blanche P. Levy.
Financial data: (yr. ended 9/30/83): Assets, $387,126 (M); expenditures, $327,457, including $326,225 for 37 grants (high: $50,000; low: $100).
Purpose and activities: Charitable and educational purposes; general giving, locally and in Palm Beach, Florida, with emphasis on higher and secondary education, community funds, and hospitals.
Limitations: Giving primarily in PA and Palm Beach, FL.
Trustees: Blanche P. Levy, Robert P. Levy, Alex Satinsky.
Employer Identification Number: 236435045

3642
Lindback (Mary F.) Trust
c/o The Fidelity Bank
Broad & Walnut Sts.
Philadelphia 19109

Trust established in 1955.
Donor(s): Mary F. Lindback.†

Financial data: (yr. ended 12/31/82): Assets, $2,173,675 (M); gifts received, $34,189; expenditures, $292,111, including $270,000 for 8 grants (high: $50,000; low: $5,000).
Purpose and activities: Educational purposes; grants to local higher educational and other charitable institutions.
Limitations: Giving limited to the Philadelphia area. No grants to individuals or for building or endowment funds.
Application information:
  Write: Morris Duane, Chairman
Trustees: Morris Duane, Chairman; Martin A. Heckscher, David J. Jones.
Employer Identification Number: 236290348

3643
Lord (The Thomas) Charitable Trust ⌗
c/o Security Peoples Trust Company
801 State St.
Erie 16538

Trust established in 1955.
Donor(s): Thomas Lord.
Financial data: (yr. ended 12/31/83): Assets, $1,604,579 (M); expenditures, $8,723.
Purpose and activities: Grants primarily for a Christian religious organization, a hospital, and a university.
Trustees: Thomas Lord, Edward P. Selden, Pennbank-Erie.
Employer Identification Number: 256028793

3644
Love (George H. and Margaret McClintic) Foundation ⌗
c/o Mellon Bank
Mellon Square
Pittsburgh 15230   (412) 232-4100

Trust established in 1952 in Pennsylvania.
Donor(s): George H. Love.
Financial data: (yr. ended 12/31/83): Assets, $3,405,191 (M); gifts received, $228,302; expenditures, $383,627, including $352,775 for 56 grants (high: $100,000; low: $100).
Purpose and activities: Charitable purposes; general giving, with emphasis on hospitals, higher and secondary education, and youth and social agencies.
Application information:
  Write: George H. Love, Director of Distributions
Officer: George H. Love, Director of Distributions.
Trustee: Mellon Bank.
Employer Identification Number: 256018655

3645
Lukens Foundation, The
(formerly The Lukens Steel Foundation)
50 South First Ave.
Coatesville 19320   (215) 383-2158

Trust established in 1966 in Pennsylvania.
Donor(s): Lukens, Inc.

Financial data: (yr. ended 12/31/84): Assets, $649,099 (L); expenditures, $115,417, including $97,115 for 44 grants (high: $50,000; low: $200; average: $1,000) and $15,110 for 70 employee matching gifts.
Purpose and activities: Broad purposes; grants primarily to organizations in areas of domestic company operations, with emphasis on community funds; conservation; cultural programs, including museums and performing arts; health and welfare efforts; human service projects; hospitals; and education, including an employee matching gift program supporting institutions of secondary and higher education.
Types of support awarded: Continuing support, annual campaigns, emergency funds, building funds, equipment, matching funds, employee matching gifts.
Limitations: No grants to individuals, or for endowment funds, or research; no loans.
Publications: Application guidelines, program policy statement.
Application information:
  Initial approach: Letter
  Copies of proposal: 1
  Deadline(s): Submit proposal preferably in October; deadline December 1
  Board meeting date(s): February, May, August, and November
  Final notification: 4 months
  Write: Charles Lukens Huston III, Secretary - Administrator
Officer: Charles Lukens Huston III, Secretary - Administrator.
Trustees: W.R. Wilson, Chairman; John R. Bartholdson, Robert J. Cain, P. Blaine Clemens, James F. Mulligan.
Employer Identification Number: 236424112

3646
Mack (The J. S.) Foundation ⌗
P.O. Box 34
Indiana 15701

Trust established in 1935 in Pennsylvania.
Financial data: (yr. ended 12/31/83): Assets, $5,424,458 (M); gifts received, $5,000; expenditures, $292,011, including $145,120 for 13 grants (high: $60,000; low: $100).
Purpose and activities: Primarily local giving, with emphasis on higher and secondary education; support also for youth agencies and welfare organizations.
Limitations: Giving primarily in IN. No grants to individuals.
Application information:
  Initial approach: Letter
  Copies of proposal: 1
  Board meeting date(s): January and as required
Officers and Trustees: L. Blaine Grube, President; Pete Stewart, Vice-President; Joseph N. Mack, Secretary and Treasurer; J. Merle Rife.
Employer Identification Number: 256002036

3647
Mandell (Samuel P.) Foundation
Two Mellon Bank Center, Suite 1104
Philadelphia 19102   (215) 569-3600

Trust established in 1955 in Pennsylvania.
Donor(s): Samuel P. Mandell.†
Financial data: (yr. ended 12/31/83): Assets, $5,710,945 (M); gifts received, $238,560; expenditures, $340,020, including $291,011 for grants.
Purpose and activities: Primarily local giving, with emphasis on Jewish welfare funds, hospitals, higher education, cultural programs, and community affairs.
Limitations: Giving primarily in PA.
Application information:
  Write: John L. Ricketts, Executive Secretary
Officer: John L. Ricketts, Executive Secretary.
Trustees: Judith Delfiner, Gerald Mandell, M.D., Morton Mandell, M.D., Ronald Mandell, Seymour Mandell.
Number of staff: 2 part-time support.
Employer Identification Number: 236274709

3648
Maneely Fund, Inc. ⌗
1529 Walnut St., Fifth Fl.
Philadelphia 19102

Incorporated in 1952 in Pennsylvania.
Donor(s): Edward F. Maneely.†
Financial data: (yr. ended 12/31/83): Assets, $2,101,091 (M); expenditures, $159,438, including $77,358 for 75 grants (high: $12,000; low: $14).
Purpose and activities: Broad purposes; grants largely for higher education, hospitals, and community funds.
Application information:
  Write: John J. O'Donnell, President
Officers: John J. O'Donnell, President; James E. O'Donnell, Vice-President and Treasurer.
Employer Identification Number: 231569917

3649
Massey Charitable Trust ⌗
2666 W. Liberty Ave.
Pittsburgh 15216

Established in 1968.
Donor(s): H.B. Massey, Doris J. Massey, Massey Rental.
Financial data: (yr. ended 12/31/83): Assets, $2,034,822 (M); gifts received, $204,000; expenditures, $66,482, including $66,035 for 34 grants (high: $20,000; low: $25).
Purpose and activities: Giving primarily for hospitals, health agencies, and Protestant church support.
Trustee: Walter J. Carroll.
Employer Identification Number: 237007897

3650
McCormick (Anne) Trust ⌗
c/o Dauphin Deposit Trust Company
213 Market St., P.O. Box 2961
Harrisburg 17105   (717) 255-2045

Trust established in Pennsylvania.

Donor(s): Anne McCormick.†
Financial data: (yr. ended 12/31/83): Assets, $3,454,273 (M); expenditures, $314,289, including $264,558 for 47 grants (high: $30,000; low: $100).
Purpose and activities: Local giving, with emphasis on hospitals, youth agencies, and higher education.
Limitations: Giving limited to Dauphin, Cumberland, and Perry counties, PA.
Application information:
Initial approach: Full proposal
Deadline(s): None
Write: Larry A. Hartman
Trustee: Dauphin Deposit Trust Company.
Employer Identification Number: 236471389

3651
McCune Foundation ▼
1104 Commonwealth Bldg.
316 Fourth Ave.
Pittsburgh 15222   (412) 644-8779

Trust established in 1956; McCune Foundation established in 1979; trust absorbed into McCune Foundation in 1980.
Donor(s): Charles L. McCune.†
Financial data: (yr. ended 9/30/84): Assets, $165,568,224 (M); gifts received, $90,608,234; expenditures, $4,509,526, including $3,857,300 for 49 grants (high: $250,000; low: $7,500; average: $25,000-$100,000).
Purpose and activities: Primarily local giving, including challenge grants, with emphasis on private higher education, hospitals, health care, social services, and youth. Preference is given to the organizations supported by the donor.
Types of support awarded: Equipment, endowment funds, special projects, matching funds.
Limitations: Giving primarily in western PA, especially in the Pittsburgh area. No grants to individuals, or for deficit financing, scholarships, or fellowships; no loans.
Publications: Program policy statement, application guidelines, multi-year report.
Application information:
Initial approach: Letter
Copies of proposal: 1
Deadline(s): November 1 and March 15
Board meeting date(s): January and June
Final notification: 3 months
Write: Earland I. Carlson, Executive Director
Distribution Committee: Richard D. Edwards, John R. McCune, Robert F. Patton.
Trustee: Union National Bank of Pittsburgh.
Number of staff: 1 full-time professional; 1 full-time support.
Employer Identification Number: 256210269

3652
McFeely-Rogers Foundation
Mellon Bank Bldg., Rm. 603
Main and Ligonier Sts.
Latrobe 15650   (412) 537-5588
Mailing address: P.O. Box 110, Latrobe, PA 15650

Incorporated in 1953 in Pennsylvania.

Donor(s): James H. Rogers,† Nancy K. McFeely,† Nancy M. Rogers.
Financial data: (yr. ended 12/31/84): Assets, $8,400,000 (M); expenditures, $228,600, including $145,619 for 70 grants (high: $20,000; low: $50; average: $1,000).
Purpose and activities: Broad purposes; support mainly to local educational and charitable institutions.
Types of support awarded: Operating budgets, continuing support, annual campaigns, seed money, emergency funds, deficit financing, building funds, equipment, matching funds, scholarship funds, general purposes.
Limitations: Giving primarily in the Latrobe and Pittsburgh, PA, areas. No grants to individuals, or for land acquisition, special projects, research, publications, or conferences; no loans.
Publications: Program policy statement, application guidelines.
Application information:
Initial approach: Letter or telephone
Copies of proposal: 2
Deadline(s): April 1 and November 1
Board meeting date(s): The end of April and November
Write: James R. Okonak, Executive Director
Officers and Trustees: Fred M. Rogers, President; Grant F. Neely, Vice-President and Treasurer; Nancy R. Crozier, Vice-President; James R. Okonak, Secretary and Executive Director; William P. Barker, Douglas R. Nowicki.
Number of staff: 3 part-time professional.
Employer Identification Number: 251120947

3653
McKee (Virginia A.) Poor Fund
c/o Pittsburgh National Bank
Trust Dept. - 970
Pittsburgh 15265   (412) 355-3787

Trust established in 1929 in Pennsylvania.
Donor(s): Virginia A. McKee.†
Financial data: (yr. ended 9/30/83): Assets, $1,495,006 (M); expenditures, $139,915, including $128,000 for 4 grants (high: $75,000; low: $5,000).
Purpose and activities: "For such deserving poor persons in the City of Pittsburgh" through grants to local welfare organizations, particularly for emergency funds.
Types of support awarded: Emergency funds.
Limitations: Giving limited to Pittsburgh, PA. No grants to individuals, or for building or endowment funds, research, scholarships and fellowships, or matching gifts; no loans.
Application information:
Initial approach: Letter
Copies of proposal: 1
Deadline(s): Submit proposal preferably in September
Board meeting date(s): March, June, September, and December
Final notification: 6 months
Write: Robert F. Milspaw, Administrative Vice-President
Trustee: Pittsburgh National Bank.
Employer Identification Number: 256023292

3654
McKelvy (B. T. & Eg. Morrison) Memorial Fund ¤
c/o Mellon Bank
Mellon Square
Pittsburgh 15230   (412) 234-5784

Trust established in 1982 in Pennsylvania.
Donor(s): Bessie Morrison McKelvy.†
Financial data: (yr. ended 12/31/82): Assets, $1,963,995 (M); gifts received, $2,039,293; expenditures, $217,953, including $209,154 for grants.
Purpose and activities: Charitable purposes.
Application information:
Write: Barbara Robinson
Trustee: Mellon Bank.
Employer Identification Number: 256220228

3655
McKenna (Katherine Mabis) Foundation, Inc.
P.O. Box 186
Latrobe 15650   (412) 539-5702

Incorporated in 1969 in Pennsylvania.
Donor(s): Katherine M. McKenna.
Financial data: (yr. ended 12/31/83): Assets, $12,448,838 (M); gifts received, $15,968; expenditures, $526,056, including $501,930 for 83 grants (high: $40,000; low: $500; average: $1,000-$10,000).
Purpose and activities: Primarily local giving, with emphasis on higher education, hospitals, welfare, and cultural programs.
Types of support awarded: General purposes, operating budgets, annual campaigns, seed money, building funds, equipment, endowment funds, special projects, scholarship funds.
Limitations: Giving primarily in western PA. No grants to individuals or for matching gifts; no loans.
Application information:
Initial approach: Letter
Copies of proposal: 1
Deadline(s): Submit proposal preferably in January through July; deadline November 1
Board meeting date(s): March, June, September, and December
Final notification: 3 to 6 months
Write: Norbert J. Pail, Secretary-Treasurer
Officers and Trustees: Alex G. McKenna, Chairman; Norbert J. Pail, Secretary-Treasurer; Linda McKenna Boxx, Wilma F. McKenna.
Number of staff: 2 full-time professional; 2 part-time professional; 3 full-time support.
Employer Identification Number: 237042752

3656
McKenna (Philip M.) Foundation, Inc. ▼
P.O. Box 186
Latrobe 15650   (412) 539-5702

Incorporated in 1967 in Pennsylvania.
Donor(s): Philip M. McKenna.†
Financial data: (yr. ended 12/31/83): Assets, $19,344,230 (M); expenditures, $1,046,362, including $1,016,617 for 77 grants (high: $225,000; low: $200; average: $1,000-$25,000).

Purpose and activities: Broad purposes; giving primarily in Pennsylvania for higher education, primarily for economic studies, general economic education, and public policy research; some support also for local programs.

Types of support awarded: Operating budgets, annual campaigns, seed money, building funds, equipment, research, scholarship funds.

Limitations: Giving limited to the U.S., with preference to programs in PA. No grants to individuals, or for endowment funds, or matching gifts; no loans; single-year grants only.

Application information:
Initial approach: Letter
Copies of proposal: 1
Deadline(s): Submit proposal preferably January through July; deadline November 1
Board meeting date(s): April, July, October, and December
Final notification: 3 to 6 months
Write: Norbert J. Pail, Secretary

Officers and Directors: Alex G. McKenna, Chairman; Donald C. McKenna, Vice-Chairman; Norbert J. Pail, Secretary-Treasurer.

Number of staff: 2 full-time professional; 2 part-time professional; 3 full-time support.

Employer Identification Number: 256082635

3657
McLean Contributionship, The
945 Haverford Rd.
Bryn Mawr 19010   (215) 527-6330

Trust established in 1951 in Pennsylvania.

Donor(s): William L. McLean, Jr.,† Robert McLean, Bulletin Company.

Financial data: (yr. ended 12/31/84): Assets, $8,116,155 (M); gifts received, $66,227; expenditures, $454,376, including $423,000 for 42 grants (high: $125,000; low: $500; average: $10,000-$15,000).

Purpose and activities: Broad purposes; primarily local giving, for educational, scientific and charitable programs, including hospitals, youth agencies, and conservation. Trustees prefer special projects rather than continuing programs.

Types of support awarded: Special projects.

Limitations: Giving primarily in the Philadelphia, PA, metropolitan area.

Publications: Application guidelines.

Application information:
Initial approach: Proposal
Copies of proposal: 2
Board meeting date(s): Quarterly
Write: John H. Buhsmer, Secretary

Officers: John H. Buhsmer, Secretary; Charles E. Catherwood, Treasurer.

Trustees: William L. McLean III, Chairman; R. Jean Brownlee, John H. Buhsmer, Joseph K. Gordon.

Employer Identification Number: 236396940

3658
McShain (John) Charities, Inc. ▼ ⌑
540 North Seventeenth St.
Philadelphia 19130   (215) 564-2322

Incorporated in 1949 in Pennsylvania.

Donor(s): John McShain, John McShain, Inc., and others.

Financial data: (yr. ended 3/31/84): Assets, $36,064,631 (M); gifts received, $132,065; expenditures, $2,078,586, including $1,608,908 for 290 grants (high: $350,000; low: $10; average: $100-$10,000).

Purpose and activities: Broad purposes; primarily local giving for higher and secondary education, Roman Catholic church support, and social welfare and cultural programs.

Limitations: Giving primarily in Philadelphia, PA. No grants to individuals.

Application information:
Initial approach: Letter
Write: John McShain, President

Officers and Directors: John McShain, President; Mary H. McShain, William L. Shinners, Vice-Presidents; C.A. McAvinue, Secretary-Treasurer.

Employer Identification Number: 236276091

3659
Measey (The Benjamin and Mary Siddons) Foundation ▼
c/o James C. Brennan
225 North Olive St., P.O. Box 1070
Media 19063   (215) 566-5800

Trust established in 1958 in Pennsylvania.

Donor(s): William Maul Measey.†

Financial data: (yr. ended 12/31/83): Assets, $12,452,975 (M); expenditures, $705,150, including $581,820 for 13 grants (high: $102,000; low: $5,000).

Purpose and activities: Broad purposes; grants to medical schools in Philadelphia for scholarships and fellowships.

Types of support awarded: Scholarship funds, fellowships.

Limitations: Giving limited to Philadelphia, PA. No grants to individuals.

Application information: Applications should be made to the dean of the particular medical school.
Deadline(s): 1 month prior to meeting
Board meeting date(s): March, June, September, and December
Final notification: 1 month following meeting

Officer: Matthew S. Donaldson, Jr., Secretary.

Board of Managers: Jonathan E. Rhoads, M.D., Chairman; James C. Brennan, Brooke Roberts, M.D., Willis J. Winn, Francis C. Wood, M.D.

Number of staff: 1 part-time support.

Employer Identification Number: 236298781

3660
Medical Trust, The ▼
c/o The Glenmede Trust Company
229 S. 18th St.
Philadelphia 19103   (215) 875-3200

Trust established in 1982 in Pennsylvania.

Donor(s): Mary Ethel Pew.†

Financial data: (yr. ended 12/31/83): Assets, $87,784,157 (M); gifts received, $4,830,000; expenditures, $4,454,360, including $4,216,008 for 26 grants (high: $1,000,000; low: $5,000; average: $5,000-$800,000).

Purpose and activities: Giving primarily in the five-county Philadelphia metropolitan area; focus on long-term community care for the frail elderly and chronically ill, physical rehabilitation, medical and scientific education, and mental health/mental retardation. Support annually for a hospital and a cancer research institute as specified in the will of the donor.

Types of support awarded: Operating budgets, seed money, equipment, special projects, research, matching funds.

Limitations: Giving primarily in the five-county, Philadelphia, PA, metropolitan area. No grants to individuals, or for annual campaigns, emergency funds, deficit financing, building or endowment funds, land acquisition, scholarships, fellowships, publications, or conferences and seminars; no loans.

Publications: Annual report, informational brochure, program policy statement, application guidelines.

Application information:
Initial approach: Letter, telephone, or proposal
Copies of proposal: 1
Deadline(s): None
Board meeting date(s): February, April, June, September, and December
Write: Fred H. Billups, Jr.

Trustees: Francis M. Richards, Jr., The Glenmede Trust Company (Robert I. Smith, President; Fred H. Billups, Jr., Vice-President).

Number of staff: 12 full-time professional; 6 full-time support.

Employer Identification Number: 232131641

3661
Mellon Bank Foundation ▼
One Mellon Bank Center, Rm. 368
Pittsburgh 15258   (412) 234-6266

Established in 1974 in Pennsylvania.

Donor(s): Mellon Bank.

Financial data: (yr. ended 12/31/84): Assets, $831,000 (M); gifts received, $1,366,000; expenditures, $1,217,000, including $1,217,000 for 126 grants (high: $450,000; low: $500; average: $500-$5,000).

Purpose and activities: Giving primarily to serve the overall vitality of several southwestern Pennsylvania communities, with emphasis on economic development, including employment and retraining initiatives, health and welfare, higher education, and cultural programs.

Types of support awarded: Operating budgets, continuing support, annual campaigns, building funds, endowment funds, matching funds, technical assistance, special projects.

Limitations: Giving primarily in southwestern PA. No support for fraternal or religious organizations, specialized health campaigns or other highly specialized projects with little or no positive impact on local communities, or United Way agencies (unless authorized to solicit corporations). No grants to individuals, or for seed money, emergency funds, deficit financing, equipment, land acquisition, scholarships and fellowships, research, demonstration projects, publications, or conferences; no loans.

Publications: Annual report, application guidelines.
Application information:
Initial approach: Full proposal
Copies of proposal: 1
Deadline(s): None
Board meeting date(s): Monthly
Final notification: 2 months
Write: Barbara K. Robinson, Assistant Vice-President (Mellon Bank, N.A.)
Officers: Charles H. Fletcher,* Chairman and President; Sylvia Clark, Vice-President and Secretary; James D. Roy, Treasurer.
Trustees:* J. David Barnes, George T. Farrell, G. Christian Lantzsch, C.G. Ford, N. Robertson.
Number of staff: None.
Employer Identification Number: 237423500

3662
Mellon (R. K.) Family Foundation
525 William Penn Place
Pittsburgh 15219   (412) 392-2800
Mailing address: P.O. Box 1138, Pittsburgh, PA 15230

Incorporated in Pennsylvania in 1978 through consolidation of Landfall, Loyalhanna, Rachelwood, and Cassandra Mellon Henderson Foundations.
Donor(s): Seward Prosser Mellon, Richard P. Mellon, Constance B. Mellon,† Cassandra M. Milbury.
Financial data: (yr. ended 12/31/84): Assets, $16,506,000 (M); expenditures, $789,604, including $657,800 for 63 grants (high: $85,000; low: $1,000; average: $1,000-$25,000).
Purpose and activities: Broad purposes; grants largely for education, social, medical, and conservation programs, with emphasis on local projects.
Types of support awarded: Annual campaigns, seed money, building funds, equipment, research, special projects.
Limitations: Giving primarily in western PA. No grants to individuals, or for endowment funds, scholarships and fellowships, or matching gifts; no loans.
Publications: Application guidelines, program policy statement, informational brochure.
Application information:
Initial approach: Full proposal
Copies of proposal: 1
Deadline(s): Submit proposal preferably between January and April or July and October; no set deadline
Board meeting date(s): June and November
Final notification: 1 to 6 months
Write: Robert B. Burr, Jr., Director
Officers: Robert B. Burr, Jr.,* Secretary and Director; Robert F. Gall, Treasurer.
Trustees:* George H. Taber, Chairman; Andrew W. Mathieson, Seward Prosser Mellon, Mason Walsh, Jr.
Number of staff: 8.
Employer Identification Number: 251356145

3663
Mellon (Richard King) Foundation ▼
525 William Penn Place
Pittsburgh 15219   (412) 392-2800

Trust established in 1947 in Pennsylvania; incorporated in 1971 in Pennsylvania.
Donor(s): Richard K. Mellon.†
Financial data: (yr. ended 12/31/84): Assets, $465,952,000 (M); expenditures, $28,236,000, including $24,520,772 for 107 grants (high: $9,000,000; low: $2,500; average: $10,000-$500,000).
Purpose and activities: Grant programs emphasize conservation, higher education, cultural and civic affairs, social services, medical research and health care, largely in Pittsburgh and western Pennsylvania. Also interested in conservation of natural areas and wildlife preservation elsewhere in the United States.
Types of support awarded: Seed money, building funds, equipment, land acquisition, endowment funds, research, matching funds, general purposes, continuing support.
Limitations: Giving primarily in Pittsburgh and western PA, except for nationwide conservation programs. No grants to individuals, or for fellowships or scholarships except through National Merit Scholarship Corporation.
Publications: Annual report, informational brochure, program policy statement, application guidelines.
Application information:
Initial approach: Full proposal
Copies of proposal: 1
Deadline(s): Submit proposal between January and April or July and September; deadline April 15 and October 15
Board meeting date(s): June and December
Write: George H. Taber, Vice-President
Officers: Seward Prosser Mellon,* President; George H. Taber,* Vice-President and Director; Robert B. Burr, Jr., Secretary; Andrew W. Mathieson,* Treasurer.
Trustees:* Richard P. Mellon, Chairman; Arthur M. Scully, Jr., Mason Walsh, Jr.
Number of staff: 5 part-time professional; 1 full-time support; 5 part-time support.
Employer Identification Number: 251127705

3664
Mengle (Glenn and Ruth) Foundation ⌑
c/o Deposit Bank
P.O. Box 607A
DuBois 15801

Trust established in 1956 in Pennsylvania.
Donor(s): G.A. Mengle, Ruth Mengle Blake.
Financial data: (yr. ended 12/31/83): Assets, $176,555 (M); gifts received, $173,000; expenditures, $175,813, including $173,000 for 28 grants (high: $25,000; low: $1,000).
Purpose and activities: Primarily local giving, with emphasis on youth agencies, hospitals, civic affairs, and community funds.
Limitations: Giving primarily in PA.
Trustees: Ruth E. Mengle Blake, Deposit Bank.
Employer Identification Number: 256067616

3665
Merchants Fund ⌑
Public Ledger Bldg., Rm. 266
Philadelphia 19106

Established prior to 1913.
Donor(s): Lewis Elkins Fund, Charles Fearon.†
Financial data: (yr. ended 12/31/82): Assets, $2,298,376 (M); gifts received, $449,783; expenditures, $264,610, including $224,733 for 61 grants to individuals.
Purpose and activities: Primarily local giving "to provide relief to indigent merchants or their widows and families".
Types of support awarded: Grants to individuals.
Limitations: Giving primarily in Philadelphia, PA.
Officer: Rev. Henry W. Kaufmann.
Employer Identification Number: 231980213

3666
Merit Gasoline Foundation, The
551 West Lancaster Ave.
Haverford 19041   (215) 527-7900

Trust established in 1956 in Pennsylvania.
Donor(s): Merit Oil Company, and affiliates.
Financial data: (yr. ended 8/31/84): Assets, $155,433 (M); expenditures, $145,181, including $125,706 for 115 grants (high: $50,000; low: $20; average: $3,000-$7,000), $12,000 for 9 grants to individuals and $6,606 for 55 employee matching gifts.
Purpose and activities: General giving, with emphasis on scholarship aid to children of employees of donor companies, civic affairs, higher education, social programs, and health agencies located in the urban areas of the Mid-Atlantic and New England states where Merit Oil Company has gasoline stations.
Types of support awarded: Continuing support, seed money, employee related scholarships, matching funds, employee matching gifts.
Limitations: Giving primarily in the New England and Mid-Atlantic states. No grants to individuals (except college scholarships for children of company employees), or for building or endowment funds, research, or special projects; no loans.
Publications: 990-PF, program policy statement, application guidelines.
Application information:
Initial approach: Proposal
Copies of proposal: 1
Deadline(s): Submit proposal preferably in January and July; no set deadline
Board meeting date(s): Usually in April and October
Write: Robert M. Harting, Executive Director
Officer: Robert M. Harting, Executive Director.
Trustees: Carl A. Levinson, Chairman; Samuel Bass, Ivan H. Gabel, Leonard Gilmar, Joseph M. Jerome, Morton Sand.
Number of staff: None.
Employer Identification Number: 236282846

3667
Miller (Edwill B.) Trust
c/o Dauphin Deposit Bank & Trust Co.
2055 South Queen St., P.O. Box 1544
York 17405

Established in 1977.
Donor(s): Edwill B. Miller.†
Financial data: (yr. ended 3/31/83): Assets,
$1,383,962 (M); expenditures, $119,869,
including $112,798 for 14 grants (high:
$16,965).
Purpose and activities: Primarily local giving
for hospitals, higher education, Protestant
church support, youth agencies, and a Masonic
home.
Limitations: Giving primarily in PA.
Trustee: Dauphin Deposit Bank & Trust Co.
Employer Identification Number: 236657558

3668
Millstein Charitable Foundation, The ☖
North Fourth St. & Gaskill Ave.
Jeanette 15644

Established in 1964.
Financial data: (yr. ended 9/30/83): Assets,
$1,227,018 (M); expenditures, $117,959,
including $104,911 for 153 grants (high:
$25,000; low: $10).
Purpose and activities: Grants primarily for
Jewish welfare funds and temple support.
Officer and Trustee: David J. Millstein,
Executive Secretary.
Employer Identification Number: 256064981

3669
Mine Safety Appliances Co. Charitable Trust
600 Penn Center Blvd.
Pittsburgh 15235   (412) 273-5045

Trust established in 1951 in Pennsylvania.
Donor(s): Mine Safety Appliances Co.
Financial data: (yr. ended 12/31/83): Assets,
$4,166,611 (M); gifts received, $755,000;
expenditures, $369,952, including $349,987
for 66 grants (high: $73,000; low: $100).
Purpose and activities: Largely local giving,
with emphasis on community funds, higher
education, hospitals, and health care; some
support for the performing arts.
Limitations: Giving primarily in PA. No grants
to individuals or for matching gifts; no loans.
Publications: Application guidelines.
Application information:
  Initial approach: Letter
  Copies of proposal: 1
  Board meeting date(s): Quarterly
  Write: J.W. Carville, Secretary
Trustee: Pittsburgh National Bank.
Number of staff: None.
Employer Identification Number: 256023104

3670
Moore (P. M.) Foundation ☖
112 Station St.
Aliquippa 15001

Incorporated in 1958 in Pennsylvania.
Donor(s): Paul M. Moore.†
Financial data: (yr. ended 12/31/83): Assets,
$1,727,540 (M); expenditures, $91,425,
including $87,100 for 31 grants (high: $25,000;
low: $100).
Purpose and activities: Primarily local giving,
with emphasis on higher education, Protestant
church support, and libraries.
Limitations: Giving primarily in Beaver County,
PA.
Officers: James S. Ruffner, President; Ruth Ann
Duff, Secretary; Dana L. Duff, Treasurer.
Employer Identification Number: 256066268

3671
Murphy (G. C.) Company Foundation
531 Fifth Ave.
McKeesport 15132   (412) 675-2000

Incorporated in 1952 in Pennsylvania.
Financial data: (yr. ended 12/31/83): Assets,
$1,957,590 (M); expenditures, $135,899,
including $117,800 for 79 grants (high:
$32,000; low: $50).
Purpose and activities: Broad purposes; giving
primarily in the eastern U.S., with emphasis on
education, a community fund, youth, and
social agencies.
Limitations: Giving primarily in the eastern U.S.
Application information:
  Initial approach: Letter
  Deadline(s): None
  Write: Philip W. Rogers
Officers and Directors: C.H. Lytle, President;
T.F. Hudak, Vice-President; J.K. Haggerty,
Secretary; L.J. Hufnagel, Treasurer; D. Malcolm
Anderson, R.T. Messner, Charles E. Palmer,
S.W. Robinson, P.W. Rogers.
Employer Identification Number: 256028651

3672
Musselman (Emma G.) Foundation ☖
c/o Philadelphia National Bank
Broad and Chestnut Sts.
Philadelphia 19101
Application address: c/o Franklin R. Bigham,
P.O. Box 338, Gettysburg, PA 17325; Tel.:
(717) 334-2159

Trust established in 1955 in Pennsylvania.
Donor(s): Emma G. Musselman.†
Financial data: (yr. ended 6/30/84): Assets,
$908,681 (M); expenditures, $117,218,
including $113,500 for 11 grants (high:
$25,000; low: $1,000).
Purpose and activities: Broad purposes;
primarily local giving, with emphasis on
community development, including a youth
agency, and higher education.
Limitations: Giving limited to Adams County,
PA.
Application information:
  Initial approach: Letter
  Deadline(s): None

Trustee: The Philadelphia National Bank.
Advisory Committee: Thomas E. Arnold,
Franklin R. Bigham, Nancy A. Oas.
Employer Identification Number: 236233856

3673
Myrin (The Mabel Pew) Trust ▼
The Glenmede Trust Company
229 South 18th St.
Philadelphia 19103   (215) 875-3200

Trust established in 1957 in Pennsylvania.
Donor(s): Mabel Pew Myrin.†
Financial data: (yr. ended 12/31/83): Assets,
$163,694,173 (M); expenditures, $6,137,653,
including $5,658,101 for 51 grants (high:
$950,000; low: $3,000; average: $5,000-
$75,000).
Purpose and activities: Primarily local giving,
with emphasis on education, local cultural
programs, and human services and health care.
Types of support awarded: Seed money,
building funds, equipment, matching funds,
special projects, continuing support.
Limitations: Giving primarily in the greater
Philadelphia, PA, area. No support for two-
year or community colleges, or individual
religious congregations. No grants to
individuals, or for endowment funds, or
scholarships and fellowships; no loans.
Publications: Annual report, program policy
statement, application guidelines.
Application information:
  Initial approach: Letter, telephone, or full
    proposal
  Copies of proposal: 1
  Deadline(s): None
  Board meeting date(s): February, April, June,
    September, and December
  Write: Fred H. Billups, Jr., Vice-President
Trustee: The Glenmede Trust Company
(Robert I. Smith, President).
Number of staff: None.
Employer Identification Number: 236234666

3674
National Central Foundation, The ☖
c/o National Central Bank
23 East King St.
Lancaster 17604

Incorporated in 1965 in Pennsylvania.
Donor(s): National Central Bank, Hamilton
Bank.
Financial data: (yr. ended 12/31/83): Assets,
$100,789 (M); gifts received, $250,990;
expenditures, $240,346, including $240,250
for grants.
Purpose and activities: Local giving, with
emphasis on community funds and higher
education, including employee matching gifts;
support also for hospitals, youth agencies, and
a performing arts center.
Limitations: Giving limited to six counties of
south central PA.
Trustees: National Central Bank, Hamilton
Bank.
Employer Identification Number: 236444555

3675
National Forge Foundation ⌐
c/o National Forge Company
Irvine 16329 (814) 563-7522

Incorporated in 1953 in Pennsylvania.
Donor(s): National Forge Company.
Financial data: (yr. ended 12/31/83): Assets,
$1,038,278 (M); gifts received, $5,046;
expenditures, $283,970, including $261,542
for 23 grants (high: $80,000; low: $250).
Purpose and activities: Charitable purposes;
grants primarily for recreation, higher education
in areas of Company operations, and
community funds.
Limitations: No grants to individuals, or for
building or endowment funds or operating
budgets.
Application information:
Initial approach: Proposal
Copies of proposal: 1
Board meeting date(s): Quarterly
Write: J.G. Koedel, Jr., Secretary
Officers: Robert O. Wilder, President; J.H.
Morse, Vice-President; J.G. Koedel, Jr.,
Secretary; M.J. Cashman, Treasurer.
Employer Identification Number: 256067621

3676
1957 Charity Trust, The ⌐
c/o Girard Trust Bank
One Girard Plaza
Philadelphia 19101

Trust established in 1957 in Pennsylvania.
Donor(s): Elizabeth R. Moran.
Financial data: (yr. ended 6/30/83): Assets,
$7,756,092 (M); expenditures, $361,813,
including $325,500 for 39 grants (high:
$30,000; low: $500).
Purpose and activities: Primarily local giving,
with emphasis on education, hospitals, health
associations, youth agencies, and community
funds.
Limitations: Giving primarily in PA.
Application information:
Write: John M. Register
Committee Members: Elizabeth R. Moran,
James M. Moran, Jr., John M. Register.
Trustee: Girard Trust Bank.
Employer Identification Number: 236227603

3677
Oberlaender (Gustav) Foundation, Inc.
P.O. Box 896
Reading 19603

Incorporated in 1934 in Delaware.
Donor(s): Gustav Oberlander.†
Financial data: (yr. ended 12/31/83): Assets,
$1,474,579 (M); expenditures, $93,217,
including $82,700 for 82 grants (high: $7,000;
low: $100).
Purpose and activities: Primarily local giving,
with emphasis on cultural programs, hospitals,
community funds, social services, higher
education, and youth agencies.
Limitations: Giving primarily in PA.
Application information:
Initial approach: Letter or full proposal
Deadline(s): None

Write: Harold O. Leinbach, President
Officers and Trustees: Harold O. Leinbach,
President; Henry B. Seleiss, Secretary and
Treasurer; Jean Breitinger, Harold E. Bright,
Gustav O. Leinbach, Richard O. Leinbach,
Greta Smith.
Employer Identification Number: 236282493

3678
Oxford Foundation, Inc.
55 South Third St.
Oxford 19363

Incorporated in 1947 in Delaware.
Donor(s): John H. Ware, 3rd, Marian S. Ware.
Financial data: (yr. ended 12/31/82): Assets,
$2,256,813 (M); gifts received, $10,000;
expenditures, $305,422, including $299,615
for 103 grants (high: $50,000; low: $15).
Purpose and activities: Broad purposes;
primarily local giving, with emphasis on higher
education and church support; support also for
health agencies, hospitals, and social welfare
agencies.
Limitations: Giving primarily in PA. No grants
for scholarships; no loans.
Application information:
Initial approach: Letter
Write: John H. Ware, 3rd, Trustee
Trustees: Carol W. Gates, Marilyn W. Lewis,
John H. Ware, 3rd, John H. Ware, 4th, Marian
S. Ware, Paul W. Ware.
Employer Identification Number: 236278067

3679
Packer (Horace B.) Foundation, Inc. ⌐
61 Main St.
Wellsboro 16901 (717) 724-1406

Incorporated in 1951 in Pennsylvania.
Donor(s): Horace B. Packer.†
Financial data: (yr. ended 12/31/83): Assets,
$1,097,294 (M); gifts received, $2,050;
expenditures, $100,669, including $73,048 for
10 grants (high: $25,000; low: $1,000) and
$17,163 for 44 grants to individuals.
Purpose and activities: To provide relief
assistance or to furnish services to benefit the
youth of Tioga County; grants to educational
institutions for scholarships for students residing
in the county; awards to students attending
medical institutions who intend to work in
Tioga County.
Types of support awarded: Scholarship funds,
student aid.
Limitations: Giving limited to Tioga County,
PA.
Application information:
Initial approach: Letter
Deadline(s): None
Board meeting date(s): Annually
Write: Charles G. Webb, President
Officer: Charles G. Webb, President.
Trustees: Carl Carson, Don Gill, Harold
Hershberger, Jr., Elwyn Lewis, Rev. George
Lineker, William Nichols, Northern Central
Bank and Trust Company.
Employer Identification Number: 236390932

3680
Paley (The Goldie) Foundation ⌐
c/o Alex Satinsky
2000 Market St., 10th Fl.
Philadelphia 19103

Established in 1964 in Pennsylvania.
Donor(s): Mrs. Goldie Paley.†
Financial data: (yr. ended 10/31/83): Assets,
$2,033,583 (M); expenditures, $354,331,
including $350,000 for 2 grants (high:
$250,000; low: $100,000).
Purpose and activities: Broad purposes; grants
to local universities.
Limitations: Giving limited to Philadelphia, PA.
Trustees: Blanche P. Levy, William S. Paley,
Alex Satinsky.
Employer Identification Number: 236392054

3681
Parklands Foundation ⌐
One Franklin Plaza, 15th Fl.
Philadelphia 19102

Established in 1977.
Donor(s): Charles H. Woodward.
Financial data: (yr. ended 2/29/84): Assets,
$635,225 (M); expenditures, $524,184,
including $518,472 for 4 grants (high:
$500,000; low: $3,800).
Purpose and activities: Primarily local giving
for the improvement and maintenance of parks.
Limitations: Giving primarily in Philadelphia,
PA.
Officers and Directors: Martin A. Heckscher,
President; Sheldon M. Bonavitz, Secretary-
Treasurer; Donald Auten.
Employer Identification Number: 232026438

3682
Patterson (W. I.) Charitable Fund
407 Oliver Bldg.
Pittsburgh 15222 (412) 281-5580

Trust established in 1955 in Pennsylvania.
Donor(s): W.I. Patterson.†
Financial data: (yr. ended 7/31/84): Assets,
$1,587,654 (M); expenditures, $118,042,
including $96,312 for 35 grants (high: $19,262;
low: $500).
Purpose and activities: Primarily local giving,
with emphasis on higher education, a library,
hospitals, and health and welfare funds.
Types of support awarded: Operating
budgets, continuing support, annual campaigns,
seed money, emergency funds, deficit
financing, building funds, equipment, land
acquisition, research, publications, conferences
and seminars.
Limitations: Giving primarily in PA. No grants
to individuals, or for endowment funds, special
projects, scholarships or fellowships, or
matching gifts; no loans.
Application information:
Initial approach: Full proposal
Copies of proposal: 1
Deadline(s): Submit proposal preferably in
May or June; deadline July 15
Board meeting date(s): At least 6 times a
year, including February, May, July,
September, and November

Write: Robert B. Shust, Trustee
Trustees: Ross I. Pontius, Robert B. Shust, Lester K. Wolf.
Number of staff: None.
Employer Identification Number: 256028639

3683
Penn (The William) Foundation ▼
1630 Locust St.
Philadelphia 19103   (215) 732-5114

Incorporated in 1945 in Delaware.
Donor(s): Otto Haas,† Phoebe W. Haas,† Otto Haas and Phoebe W. Haas Charitable Trusts.
Financial data: (yr. ended 12/31/84): Assets, $278,836,985 (M); gifts received, $5,779,833; expenditures, $13,179,921, including $11,978,564 for 408 grants (high: $1,000,000; low: $1,000) and $68,476 for 190 employee matching gifts.
Purpose and activities: Broad purposes; general local giving, principally for educational, cultural, health, conservation, and human service projects; matching gift program for board members, former board members, and employees.
Types of support awarded: Seed money, equipment, matching funds, employee matching gifts, special projects.
Limitations: Giving limited to the Philadelphia, PA area. No grants to individuals, or for operating budgets, continuing support, annual campaigns, emergency funds, deficit financing, building funds, land acquisition, endowment funds, scholarships and fellowships, research, publications, or conferences; no loans.
Publications: Annual report, application guidelines.
Application information:
  Initial approach: Full proposal
  Copies of proposal: 1
  Deadline(s): None
  Board meeting date(s): January, April, July, October, and December
  Final notification: 2 to 3 months
  Write: Bernard C. Watson, President
Officers: Bernard C. Watson,* President; C. Stewart Hebden, Vice-President for Finance and Treasurer; Harry E. Cerino, Vice-President for Programs; Roland H. Johnson, Secretary and Senior Program Officer.
Directors:* John C. Haas, Chairman; Dorothy W. Haas, Vice-Chairman; Frederick W. Anton, Richard K. Bennett, Nelson A. Diaz, Chara C. Haas, Frederick R. Haas, Janet Haas, M.D., Thomas W. Haas, William D. Haas, Barbara Hanrahan, Philip C. Herr, II, Paul M. Ingersoll, James H. Robinson, Grace B. Sullivan.
Number of staff: 8 full-time professional; 1 part-time professional; 6 full-time support; 1 part-time support.
Employer Identification Number: 231503488

3684
Pennwalt Foundation ▼
Pennwalt Bldg.
Three Benjamin Franklin Pkwy.
Philadelphia 19102   (215) 587-7653

Trust established in 1957 in Pennsylvania.
Donor(s): Pennwalt Corporation.

Financial data: (yr. ended 12/31/83): Assets, $275,729 (M); gifts received, $915,000; expenditures, $866,796, including $633,675 for 181 grants (high: $100,000; low: $50; average: $500-$20,000), $83,850 for 51 grants to individuals and $146,532 for 431 employee matching gifts.
Purpose and activities: Broad purposes; giving primarily for community funds, higher education, including scholarships for children of company employees and matching gifts, hospitals, and cultural programs.
Types of support awarded: Operating budgets, general purposes, continuing support, annual campaigns, seed money, emergency funds, deficit financing, building funds, equipment, land acquisition, matching funds, employee matching gifts, employee related scholarships.
Limitations: Giving primarily in areas of company operations. No support for public education; veterans, fraternal, or labor organizations; or sectarian religious organizations. No grants to individuals (except for scholarships to children of company employees), or for endowment funds, special projects, research, publications, conferences, courtesy advertising, or entertainment promotions; no loans.
Application information:
  Initial approach: Full proposal
  Copies of proposal: 1
  Deadline(s): None
  Board meeting date(s): March, June, September, and December
  Final notification: 1 to 3 months
  Write: George L. Hagar, Executive Secretary
Trustees: J. Gordon Logue, Chairman; A.P. Fortino, Seymour S. Preston III.
Number of staff: 1 part-time professional; 1 full-time support.
Employer Identification Number: 236256818

3685
Peters (Charles F.) Foundation, The ☒
2008 Duquesne Ave.
McKeesport 15132

Trust established in 1965 in Pennsylvania.
Donor(s): Charles F. Peters.†
Financial data: (yr. ended 12/31/83): Assets, $1,640,734 (M); expenditures, $126,671, including $105,000 for 149 grants (high: $5,000; low: $250).
Purpose and activities: Local giving for Protestant church support, youth agencies, and community services.
Limitations: Giving limited to the McKeesport, PA, area. No grants to individuals.
Application information:
  Initial approach: Proposal or letter
  Copies of proposal: 1
  Deadline(s): None
  Board meeting date(s): Monthly
  Write: J. Charles Peterson, Administrator
Administrators: William H. Balter, J. Charles Peterson, Kathryn Peters Schoeller.
Trustee: Equibank.
Employer Identification Number: 256070765

3686
Pew (The J. Howard) Freedom Trust ▼
c/o The Glenmede Trust Company
229 South 18th St.
Philadelphia 19103   (215) 875-3200

Trust established in 1957 in Pennsylvania.
Donor(s): J. Howard Pew.†
Financial data: (yr. ended 12/31/83): Assets, $259,978,450 (M); expenditures, $8,023,731, including $7,296,000 for grants (high: $2,000,000; low: $5,000; average: $10,000-$500,000).
Purpose and activities: Broad purposes; grants primarily for religious organizations and theological seminaries; colleges, universities, and educational associations; and programs dealing with the study of foreign policy, economic, and defense policy issues; support also for local youth agencies, human services, and international relief.
Types of support awarded: Operating budgets, seed money, equipment, research, conferences and seminars, matching funds, continuing support.
Limitations: No grants to individuals, or for endowment funds, scholarships, or fellowships; no loans.
Publications: Annual report, informational brochure, program policy statement, application guidelines.
Application information:
  Initial approach: Letter, telephone, or full proposal
  Copies of proposal: 1
  Deadline(s): None
  Board meeting date(s): February, April, June, September, and December
  Write: Fred H. Billups, Jr., Vice-President
Trustee: The Glenmede Trust Company (Robert I. Smith, President; Fred H. Billups, Jr., Vice-President).
Number of staff: None.
Employer Identification Number: 236234671

3687
Pew (J. N.), Jr. Charitable Trust, The ▼
c/o The Glenmede Trust Company
229 South 18th St.
Philadelphia 19103   (215) 875-3200

Trust established in 1963 in Pennsylvania.
Donor(s): J.N. Pew, Jr.†
Financial data: (yr. ended 12/31/83): Assets, $116,566,386 (M); expenditures, $4,270,275, including $4,067,635 for 24 grants (high: $1,000,000; low: $15,000; average: $40,000-$350,000).
Purpose and activities: Broad purposes; grants for community health care, higher education, human service projects, and conservation.
Types of support awarded: Operating budgets, seed money, equipment, building funds, research, matching funds, continuing support, conferences and seminars, special projects.
Limitations: No grants to individuals, or for endowment funds, or scholarships and fellowships; no loans.
Publications: Program policy statement, application guidelines, annual report.
Application information:

Initial approach: Letter, telephone, or full proposal
Copies of proposal: 1
Deadline(s): None
Board meeting date(s): February, April, June, September, and December
Write: Fred H. Billups, Jr., Vice-President
Trustee: The Glenmede Trust Company (Robert I. Smith, President).
Number of staff: None.
Employer Identification Number: 236299309

3688
Pew Memorial Trust, The ▼
c/o The Glenmede Trust Company
229 South 18th St.
Philadelphia 19103   (215) 875-3200

Trust established in 1957 in Pennsylvania as successor to The Pew Memorial Foundation, incorporated in 1948.
Donor(s): Mary Ethel Pew,† Mabel Pew Myrin,† J. Howard Pew,† Joseph N. Pew, Jr.†
Financial data: (yr. ended 12/31/83): Assets, $1,171,419,665 (M); expenditures, $49,025,021, including $45,617,847 for 256 grants (high: $3,020,000; low: $2,000).
Purpose and activities: Broad purposes; general giving, with primary emphasis in the area of health, particularly health policy and health care managment; education, with emphasis on independent colleges and universities; and support for human services and cultural activities.
Types of support awarded: Seed money, matching funds, continuing support, emergency funds, building funds, equipment, research.
Limitations: No support for religious congregations, except for historic preservation projects. No grants to individuals, or for endowment funds, deficit financing, scholarships or fellowships; no loans.
Publications: Annual report, application guidelines, program policy statement.
Application information:
Initial approach: Letter, telephone, or full proposal
Copies of proposal: 1
Deadline(s): None
Board meeting date(s): February, April, June, September, and December
Write: Fred H. Billups, Jr., Vice-President
Trustee: The Glenmede Trust Company (Robert I. Smith, President).
Number of staff: None.
Employer Identification Number: 236234669

3689
Philadelphia Foundation, The ▼
Two Mellon Bank Center, Suite 2017
Philadelphia 19102   (215) 563-6417

Community foundation established in 1918 in Pennsylvania by bank resolution.
Financial data: (yr. ended 4/30/84): Assets, $43,000,000 (M); gifts received, $310,000; expenditures, $3,575,452, including $3,265,542 for 370 grants (high: $81,601; low: $183; average: $500-$15,000).

Purpose and activities: For the purpose of promoting local charitable, educational, and civic activities; most of the funds have specific purposes or named beneficiary institutions, with emphasis on health and welfare, including hospitals and community activities; grants also for education and cultural programs.
Types of support awarded: Operating budgets, continuing support, seed money, emergency funds, equipment, matching funds, special projects, consulting services, technical assistance.
Limitations: Giving limited to Philadelphia and to Bucks, Chester, Delaware, and Montgomery counties in southeastern PA, except for designated funds. No support for national organizations, government agencies, private schools, religious organizations, umbrella-funding organizations. No grants to individuals, or for annual campaigns, building funds, land acquisition, endowment funds, scholarships and fellowships, research, publications, conferences, or deficit financing; no loans.
Publications: Annual report, application guidelines, program policy statement.
Application information:
Initial approach: Full proposal
Copies of proposal: 1
Deadline(s): Submit proposal preferably during May and June or November and December; deadlines July 31 and January 31
Board meeting date(s): April and November
Final notification: 3 to 4 months
Write: John E. Ruthrauff, Director
Officer: John E. Ruthrauff, Director.
Distribution Committee: Ione D. Vargus, Chairman; Ernesta Drinker Ballard, Peter Hearn, Walter R. Livingston, Jr., Mary MacGregor Mather, Don Jose Stovall, Leon C. Sunstein, Jr.
Trustees: Central-Penn National Bank, Continental Bank and Trust Company, The Fidelity Bank, The First Pennsylvania Banking and Trust Company, Industrial Valley Bank and Trust Company, Mellon Bank, The Philadelphia National Bank, Provident National Bank.
Number of staff: 3 full-time professional; 1 part-time professional; 2 full-time support; 1 part-time support.
Employer Identification Number: 231581832

3690
Phillips (Dr. & Mrs. Arthur William) Charitable Trust ⌑
c/o William J. McFate, Trustee
229 Elm St., P.O. Box 316
Oil City 16301

Trust established in 1978 in Pennsylvania.
Donor(s): Arthur William Phillips.†
Financial data: (yr. ended 9/30/83): Assets, $7,151,453 (M); expenditures, $498,472, including $442,409 for 21 grants (high: $75,000; low: $3,000).
Purpose and activities: Primarily local giving, with emphasis on health agencies; support also for Protestant churches and welfare funds, youth agencies, and higher education.
Limitations: Giving primarily in PA.
Trustees: Hugh R. Gilmore, Jr., William J. McFate.
Employer Identification Number: 256201015

3691
Pitcairn-Crabbe Foundation
301 Fifth Ave., Suite 1417
Pittsburgh 15222-2494   (412) 391-5122

Incorporated in 1940 in Pennsylvania.
Donor(s): Susan Lee Hunt.†
Financial data: (yr. ended 12/31/84): Assets, $4,421,220 (M); expenditures, $380,006, including $321,988 for 23 grants (high: $30,768; low: $750; average: $10,000-$25,000).
Purpose and activities: Primarily local giving for Christian education, primary and higher education, Protestant religious and church work, youth agencies, community welfare, and relief.
Types of support awarded: General purposes, seed money, emergency funds, building funds, equipment, endowment funds, matching funds.
Limitations: Giving primarily in western PA. No support for the arts, or the medical needs of hospitals and scientific causes. No grants to individuals, or for operating budgets, scholarships and fellowships, annual campaigns of national organizations, or research; no loans.
Publications: Multi-year report, program policy statement, application guidelines.
Application information: Application form required.
Initial approach: Letter, full proposal, or telephone
Copies of proposal: 1
Deadline(s): None
Board meeting date(s): January, May, and October
Final notification: 2 months
Write: Alfred W. Wishart, Jr., Executive Secretary
Officers: John G. Frazer, Jr.,* President; George M. Heiner,* Vice-President; Thomas J. Gillespie III,* Secretary-Treasurer; Alfred W. Wishart, Jr., Executive Secretary.
Directors:* William H. Genge, Thomas C. Graham, Benson G. Henderson, Ralph B. Martin, L. Colvin McCrady, Jr., Samuel K. McCune, Robert G. Runnette, Arthur M. Scully, Jr., G. Dixon Shrum, Jr., Dorothy R. Williams.
Number of staff: 2 full-time professional; 1 full-time support.
Employer Identification Number: 250965459

3692
Pittsburgh Forgings Foundation ⌑
c/o Mellon Bank
P.O. Box 185
Pittsburgh 15230   (412) 234-5784

Trust established in 1951 in Pennsylvania.
Donor(s): Pittsburgh Forgings Company, Greenville Steel Car Company, and others.
Financial data: (yr. ended 12/31/83): Assets, $2,104,563 (M); expenditures, $112,793, including $89,150 for 16 grants (high: $30,000; low: $25) and $6,000 for 4 grants to individuals.
Purpose and activities: Primarily local giving, with emphasis on community funds and higher education.
Limitations: Giving primarily in PA.
Application information:

Write: Barbara Robinson, Assistant Vice-President

Trustees: Irving J. Berkman, Louis Berkman, Marshall L. Berkman, Edward H. Moore, Robert A. Paul, Mellon Bank.

Employer Identification Number: 256018926

3693
Pittsburgh Foundation, The ▼
301 Fifth Ave., Suite 1417
Pittsburgh 15222-2494   (412) 391-5122

Community foundation established in 1945 in Pennsylvania by bank resolution and declaration of trust.

Financial data: (yr. ended 12/31/84): Assets, $70,021,080 (M); gifts received, $1,377,260; expenditures, $5,188,151, including $4,289,491 for 664 grants (high: $150,000; low: $37; average: $5,000-$50,000).

Purpose and activities: Organized for the permanent administration of funds placed in trust for public charitable and educational purposes; funds used largely locally, for programs to support special projects of regularly established agencies, capital and equipment needs, research of a non-technical nature, and demonstration projects. Grants primarily for human services, health, education, urban affairs, and the arts. Unless specified by the donor, grants are generally nonrecurring.

Types of support awarded: Special projects, seed money, building funds, equipment, research.

Limitations: Giving limited to Pittsburgh and Allegheny County, PA. No support for churches, private schools, or hospitals. No grants to individuals, or for annual campaigns, endowment funds, travel, operating budgets, scholarships or fellowships, or research of a highly technical or specialized nature; no loans.

Publications: Annual report, program policy statement, application guidelines, newsletter.

Application information: Application form required.

  Initial approach: Letter, full proposal, or telephone
  Copies of proposal: 1
  Deadline(s): 60 days prior to board meeting; deadline for higher education proposals March 31 or September 30 for consideration in June or December
  Board meeting date(s): March, June, September, and December
  Final notification: 4 to 6 weeks
  Write: Alfred W. Wishart, Jr., Executive Director

Officers: Alfred W. Wishart, Jr., Executive Director; William Lafe, Associate Director and Chief Program Officer.

Distribution Committee:* John L. Propst, Chairman; John M. Arthur, Vice-Chairman; Dorothy R. Williams, Treasurer; Roger S. Ahlbrandt, Mrs. Richard S. Caliguiri, Sholom D. Comay, Robert Dickey, III, Benjamin R. Fisher, John G. Frazer, Jr., Phyllis Moorman Goode, Frieda G. Shapira.

Trustees: Equibank, Mellon Bank, Pittsburgh National Bank, The Union National Bank of Pittsburgh.

Number of staff: 7 full-time professional; 1 part-time professional; 7 full-time support.

Employer Identification Number: 250965466

3694
Pittsburgh National Foundation ▼
Fifth Ave. and Wood St.
Pittsburgh 15222   (412) 355-0904

Established in 1970 in Pennsylvania.

Donor(s): Pittsburgh National Bank.

Financial data: (yr. ended 12/31/83): Assets, $3,000,000 (M); expenditures, $783,209, including $758,734 for 188 grants (high: $240,000; low: $75; average: $250-$75,000) and $19,900 for employee matching gifts.

Purpose and activities: Primarily local giving, with emphasis on community funds; some support for hospitals and health agencies, cultural programs, youth agencies, and higher education.

Types of support awarded: Operating budgets, continuing support, annual campaigns, seed money, emergency funds, deficit financing, general purposes, building funds, equipment, land acquisition, endowment funds, matching funds, employee matching gifts, professorships, technical assistance, program-related investments, research, special projects, publications, conferences and seminars.

Limitations: Giving limited to southwestern PA. No support for religious purposes. No grants to individuals; no loans.

Application information:

  Initial approach: Full proposal
  Copies of proposal: 1
  Deadline(s): None
  Board meeting date(s): Monthly
  Final notification: 6 weeks
  Write: Robert C. Milsom, Chairman, Pittsburgh National Bank (for written requests); William Boyd, Jr. (telephone contact)

Trustee: Pittsburgh National Bank (Robert C. Milsom, Chairman).

Officer: Marlyn E. Carle, Secretary.

Number of staff: None.

Employer Identification Number: 251202255

3695
Plankenhorn (The Harry) Foundation, Inc. ⌘
c/o Abram M. Snyder
R.D. 2
Cogan Station 17728

Incorporated in 1959 in Pennsylvania.

Donor(s): Harry Plankenhorn.†

Financial data: (yr. ended 12/31/83): Assets, $2,172,717 (M); gifts received, $48,790; expenditures, $120,800, including $113,995 for 36 grants (high: $13,499; low: $250).

Purpose and activities: Primarily local giving for youth agencies and child welfare, including handicapped children; some support also for health and social agencies.

Limitations: Giving primarily in PA.

Officers and Directors: Lester L. Greevy, President; E. Earl Miller, 1st Vice-President; A. William Gehron, 2nd Vice-President; Carl H. Sump, Secretary; Abram M. Snyder, Treasurer; John H. Archer, Phyllis Feese, Fred A. Foulkrod, Rev. Willard S. Rabert, Jr., Lucinda A. Wagner, Eleanor W. Whiting.

Employer Identification Number: 246023579

3696
Polk Foundation, Inc., The
2000 Grant Bldg.
Pittsburgh 15219   (412) 566-1480

Incorporated in 1957 in Pennsylvania.

Donor(s): Mrs. Patricia Hillman Miller.†

Financial data: (yr. ended 12/31/84): Assets, $2,118,972 (M); expenditures, $111,330, including $90,000 for 2 grants (high: $85,000; low: $5,000).

Purpose and activities: Broad purposes; local giving, with emphasis on a school for exceptional children.

Types of support awarded: Seed money, building funds, equipment.

Limitations: Giving limited to Pittsburgh and southwestern PA. No grants to individuals, or for operating budgets, continuing support, annual campaigns, emergency funds, deficit financing, land acquisition, endowment funds, matching gifts, scholarships, fellowships, research, special projects, publications, or conferences; no loans.

Application information:

  Initial approach: Letter
  Copies of proposal: 1
  Deadline(s): None
  Board meeting date(s): May and December
  Final notification: 4 to 6 months
  Write: Ronald W. Wertz, Executive Director

Officers: Henry L. Hillman,* President; Douglas G. Sisterson,* Vice-President; H. Vaughan Blaxter, III,* Secretary; Lawrence M. Wagner, Treasurer; Ronald W. Wertz, Executive Director.

Directors:* Patricia M. Duggan, C.G. Grefenstette.

Number of staff: 1 part-time professional.

Employer Identification Number: 251113733

3697
PPG Industries Foundation ▼
One PPG Place
Pittsburgh 15272   (412) 434-2970

Incorporated in 1951 in Pennsylvania.

Donor(s): PPG Industries, Inc.

Financial data: (yr. ended 12/31/84): Assets, $15,648,446 (M); gifts received, $2,630,325; expenditures, $3,840,529, including $3,464,012 for 1,500 grants (high: $320,000; low: $100; average: $5,000-$20,000) and $376,517 for 2,720 employee matching gifts.

Purpose and activities: Broad purposes; giving primarily locally and in other areas of company operations, with emphasis on community funds, higher education, hospitals and health organizations, cultural programs, and social and urban problems.

Types of support awarded: Annual campaigns, operating budgets, seed money, emergency funds, building funds, equipment, research, publications, conferences and seminars, scholarship funds, employee related scholarships, employee matching gifts, general purposes, continuing support.

Limitations: Giving primarily in areas of company operations, with emphasis on the Pittsburgh, PA, region. No support for religious groups for religious purposes. No grants to individuals, or for endowment funds, advertising, benefits, grants (other than matching gifts) of less than $100, or operating support of United Way member agencies; no loans.
Publications: Annual report, program policy statement, application guidelines.
Application information: No grant applications for less than $100 accepted; grant decisions made by the Screening Committee.
  Initial approach: Letter
  Copies of proposal: 1
  Deadline(s): September 1
  Board meeting date(s): Usually in March, June, September, and December
  Final notification: Following board meetings
  Write: David C. Green, Executive Director, or Roslyn Rosenblatt, Program Officer
Officers and Directors:* Vincent S. Sarni,* Chairman; E.J. Slack,* President; Frank V. Breeze, Russell A. Eberly,* Robert H. Mitchel,* Vice-Presidents; Edward Mazeski, Jr., Secretary; Raymond W. LeBoeuf, Treasurer; David C. Green,* Executive Director.
Number of staff: 2 full-time professional; 1 full-time support.
Employer Identification Number: 256037790

3698
Presser Foundation, The ⌷
Presser Place
Bryn Mawr 19010   (215) 525-4797

Founded in 1916; incorporated in 1939 in Pennsylvania.
Donor(s): Theodore Presser.†
Financial data: (yr. ended 6/30/83): Assets, $7,001,375 (M); gifts received, $681,042; expenditures, $957,621, including $300,570 for 161 grants (high: $50,000; low: $500) and $9,100 for 73 grants to individuals.
Purpose and activities: To maintain a retirement home for teachers of music; to provide scholarship aid grants to accredited colleges and universities for worthy undergraduate students of music; to increase music education in institutions of learning and to popularize the teaching of music as a profession; to administer emergency aid through small grants to worthy music teachers in need.
Types of support awarded: Grants to individuals, scholarship funds.
Application information: Application forms available for financial aid to needy music teachers and for scholarship aid grants to educational institutions. Application form required.
  Deadline(s): None
  Write: Morris Duane, President
Officers and Trustees: Morris Duane, President; John W. York, Vice-President; Thomas M. Hyndman, Jr., Secretary; Charles F. Nagel, Treasurer; Boyd T. Barnard, Edwin E. Heidakka, Natalie Hinderas, Edith A. Reinhardt, Felix C. Robb, Henderson Supplee III, William E. Vauclain, James D. Winsor III.
Employer Identification Number: 232164013

3699
Quaker Chemical Foundation, The
Elm and Lee Sts.
Conshohocken 19428   (215) 828-4250

Trust established in 1959 in Pennsylvania.
Donor(s): Quaker Chemical Corporation.
Financial data: (yr. ended 6/30/84): Assets, $491,064 (M); gifts received, $247,500; expenditures, $338,245, including $204,267 for 146 grants (high: $25,000; low: $14), $86,977 for 29 grants to individuals and $47,001 for 168 employee matching gifts.
Purpose and activities: Broad purposes; grants largely for higher education, including scholarships and matching gifts, and for local community funds, hospitals, and cultural programs.
Types of support awarded: Scholarship funds, employee matching gifts, employee related scholarships.
Limitations: Giving primarily in PA. No grants to individuals (except company-employee scholarships), or for building or endowment funds; no loans.
Publications: Application guidelines.
Application information:
  Initial approach: Full proposal
  Copies of proposal: 1
  Deadline(s): April 30
  Board meeting date(s): Quarterly
  Final notification: 2 weeks
  Write: Karl H. Spaeth, Chairman
Trustees: Karl H. Spaeth, Chairman; Mercedes Alexander, Alan G. Keyser, Ellen B. Morrow, D. Robert Yarnall, Jr.
Number of staff: 5.
Employer Identification Number: 236245803

3700
Redmond (John Charles & Kathryn S.) Foundation ⌷
1700 Market St.
Philadelphia 19103

Financial data: (yr. ended 12/31/83): Assets, $1,140,607 (M); expenditures, $94,910, including $89,100 for 8 grants (high: $50,000).
Purpose and activities: Giving primarily for higher and secondary education, and church support.
Officers: John C. Redmond, President; John C. Redmond III, Secretary; Dorothy Roche, Treasurer.
Employer Identification Number: 236279089

3701
Rehmeyer (Herbert M.) Trust ⌷
c/o The York Bank & Trust Company
21 East Market St.
York 17401

Established in 1981.
Financial data: (yr. ended 4/30/83): Assets, $1,292,633 (M); expenditures, $156,409, including $140,700 for 35 grants (high: $10,000; low: $1,000).
Purpose and activities: Primarily local giving; grants largely for arts and cultural programs, including historical societies; youth and social agencies; and hospitals and health agencies.

Limitations: Giving primarily in York, PA.
Trustees: Henry Leader, Lester Naylor, The York Bank & Trust Company.
Employer Identification Number: 236708035

3702
Reidler Foundation ⌷
Hazleton National Bank Bldg.
Broad and Laurel Sts.
Hazleton 18201   (717) 459-4242

Incorporated in 1944 in Pennsylvania.
Donor(s): John W. Reidler.
Financial data: (yr. ended 10/31/82): Assets, $2,431,016 (M); gifts received, $16,000; expenditures, $170,500, including $140,000 for 52 grants (high: $20,000; low: $500).
Purpose and activities: Broad purposes; primarily local giving, with emphasis on Protestant church support, higher education, hospitals, and youth agencies.
Limitations: Giving primarily in the Ashland and Hazleton, PA, areas. No grants to individuals.
Application information:
  Initial approach: Letter
  Deadline(s): Submit proposal preferably between October and March
  Board meeting date(s): April, June, and October
  Write: John P. Brew, Secretary-Treasurer
Officer: John P. Brew, Secretary-Treasurer.
Employer Identification Number: 246022888

3703
Reliance Insurance Companies Foundation
c/o Corporate Tax Dept.
Four Penn Center Plaza
Philadelphia 19103

Trust established in 1967 in Pennsylvania.
Donor(s): Reliance Insurance Companies.
Financial data: (yr. ended 12/31/83): Assets, $12,586 (M); gifts received, $200,000; expenditures, $220,720, including $206,727 for 44 grants (high: $72,000; low: $100) and $13,993 for 111 employee matching gifts.
Purpose and activities: Primarily local giving, with emphasis on community funds, cultural programs, including music, and higher education, including an employee matching gift program; support also for community development.
Types of support awarded: Employee matching gifts.
Limitations: Giving primarily in PA.
Trustees: Harry L. Richter, Robert M. Steinberg, Saul P. Steinberg.
Employer Identification Number: 236420936

3704
Rittenhouse Foundation
225 S. 15th St.
Philadelphia 19102   (215) 735-3863

Incorporated in 1952 in Pennsylvania.
Donor(s): Philip Klein.

Financial data: (yr. ended 12/31/84): Assets, $1,851,604 (M); expenditures, $179,000, including $150,800 for grants (high: $10,000; low: $100).

Purpose and activities: To assist charitable and educational institutions; primarily local giving, with emphasis on higher education, music and the arts, Jewish welfare funds, and youth agencies.

Types of support awarded: Continuing support, seed money, equipment, publications, scholarship funds.

Limitations: Giving primarily in the Philadelphia, PA area. No grants to individuals, or for endowment funds, operating budgets, or matching gifts; no loans.

Publications: Annual report, application guidelines.

Application information:
  Initial approach: Letter
  Copies of proposal: 1
  Deadline(s): None
  Board meeting date(s): January, April, July, and September
  Final notification: 30 days
  Write: Arthur Klein, President

Officers and Directors:* Arthur Klein,* President; Esther Klein,* Executive Vice-President; Michael Temin, Secretary; Karen Mannes,* Treasurer.

Number of staff: 1 part-time professional; 2 part-time support.

Employer Identification Number: 236005622

3705
Robinson (Donald & Sylvia) Family Foundation
6507 Wilkins Ave.
Pittsburgh 15217   (412) 661-1200

Financial data: (yr. ended 10/31/83): Assets, $1,177,569 (M); gifts received, $25,000; expenditures, $74,157, including $69,383 for 50 grants (high: $25,000; low: $100).

Purpose and activities: Primarily local giving, with emphasis on Jewish welfare funds and the performing arts.

Limitations: Giving primarily in PA.

Trustees: Donald Robinson, Sylvia Robinson.

Employer Identification Number: 237062017

3706
Robinson Foundation, The
c/o Provident National Bank
1632 Chestnut St.
Philadelphia 19103

Trust established in 1952 in Pennsylvania.

Donor(s): Members of the William M.M. Robinson family.

Financial data: (yr. ended 12/31/84): Assets, $1,445,466 (M); expenditures, $99,722, including $88,500 for 10 grants (high: $30,000; low: $500).

Purpose and activities: Grants for Protestant church support and social agencies, higher and secondary education, and family planning.

Application information:
  Initial approach: Letter
  Deadline(s): September 1
  Board meeting date(s): October or November

Write: James E. Blount, Jr., Vice-President

Trustees: Margaret Bailey, Samuel S. Robinson, Mrs. Samuel S. Robinson, Timothy R. Talbot, Mrs. Timothy R. Talbot, Provident National Bank.

Number of staff: None.

Employer Identification Number: 236207354

3707
Rockwell Foundation, The
500 North Lexington Ave.
Pittsburgh 15208   (412) 765-3990

Trust established in 1956 in Pennsylvania.

Donor(s): Willard F. Rockwell,† and family.

Financial data: (yr. ended 12/31/84): Assets, $7,602,146 (M); expenditures, $353,525, including $325,500 for 100 grants (high: $28,000; low: $100) and $2,100,000 for 1 loan.

Purpose and activities: Broad purposes; primarily local giving, with emphasis on higher and secondary education; support also for music, conservation, health agencies, and historic preservation.

Limitations: Giving primarily in PA. No grants to individuals, or for scholarships and fellowships; no loans.

Application information:
  Initial approach: Letter or telephone
  Copies of proposal: 1
  Board meeting date(s): As required
  Write: H. Campbell Stuckeman, Secretary

Officer and Trustees: H. Campbell Stuckeman, Secretary; George Peter Rockwell, Russell A. Rockwell, Willard F. Rockwell, Jr.

Employer Identification Number: 256035975

3708
Rockwell International Corporation Trust ▼
600 Grant St.
Pittsburgh 15219   (412) 565-7436

Trust established in 1959 in Pennsylvania.

Donor(s): Rockwell International Corporation.

Financial data: (yr. ended 9/30/84): Assets, $26,000,000 (M); gifts received, $20,000,000; expenditures, $7,908,000, including $7,310,440 for grants (high: $700,000; low: $25; average: $1,000-$50,000) and $489,560 for 3,243 employee matching gifts.

Purpose and activities: Broad purposes; general giving in areas of corporate operations, with emphasis on higher education, community funds, youth agencies, cultural programs, social services, and civic and public affairs.

Types of support awarded: Operating budgets, continuing support, building funds, employee matching gifts, scholarship funds, employee related scholarships, fellowships, professorships.

Limitations: Giving primarily in areas of corporate operations, except for national organizations and universities which are sources of recruits. No grants to individuals, or for hospital capital campaigns or general endowments; no loans.

Application information:
  Initial approach: Proposal
  Copies of proposal: 1

Deadline(s): None
Board meeting date(s): Monthly
Final notification: 30 to 60 days
Write: J.J. Christin, Secretary, Trust Committee, or W.R. Fitz, Assistant Secretary

Trust Committee: J.J. Christin, Secretary; Robert Anderson, Donald R. Beall, Robert A. DePalma, Martin D. Walker.

Trustee: Pittsburgh National Bank.

Number of staff: 3.

Employer Identification Number: 251072431

3709
Rust Foundation, The
1801 Commonwealth Bldg.
316 4th Ave.
Pittsburgh 15222   (412) 566-2233

Trust established in 1950 in Pennsylvania.

Donor(s): The Rust family.

Financial data: (yr. ended 12/31/83): Assets, $3,036,323 (M); expenditures, $152,204, including $118,600 for 120 grants (high: $11,200; low: $100).

Purpose and activities: Broad purposes; giving limited to interests of individual trustees, including grants for health care, education, environmental conservancy, church support, and community funds.

Application information:
  Initial approach: Letter
  Copies of proposal: 1
  Board meeting date(s): Irregularly
  Write: D.A Nimick, Secretary

Officer: D.A. Nimick, Secretary.

Trustees: Mary Rust Gillies, William B. Gillies III, George M. Rust, S.M. Rust, Jr., S.M. Rust III, Alice Rust Scheetz, J. Paul Scheetz.

Employer Identification Number: 256049037

3710
S 'n S Foundation, The ⌘
Two Girard Plaza, Suite 1916
Philadelphia 19102

Trust established in 1952 in Pennsylvania.

Donor(s): William Netzky, John Netzky, Frank Netzky, Jacob Stiffel, Mannie Mitchell, Ship 'n Shore, Inc.

Financial data: (yr. ended 12/31/82): Assets, $149,480 (M); gifts received, $500; expenditures, $124,368, including $123,005 for 37 grants (high: $100,000; low: $100).

Purpose and activities: Primarily local giving for Jewish welfare funds.

Limitations: Giving primarily in PA.

Trustees: Mannie Mitchell, Frank W. Netzky, John Netzky, William Netzky, Jacob Stiffel.

Employer Identification Number: 236270414

3711
Scaife (Sarah) Foundation, Inc. ▼
P.O. Box 268
Pittsburgh 15230   (412) 392-2900

Trust established in 1941; incorporated in 1959 in Pennsylvania; present name adopted in 1974.

Donor(s): Mrs. Sarah Mellon Scaife.†

Financial data: (yr. ended 12/31/83): Assets, $141,336,647 (M); expenditures, $8,299,115, including $6,937,305 for 66 grants (high: $830,000; low: $1,000; average: $25,000-$75,000).

Purpose and activities: Broad purposes; grants primarily directed toward public policy programs that address major international and domestic issues; also supports Pittsburgh area organizations in the fields of education, culture, health and medicine, recreation, and youth activities.

Types of support awarded: Operating budgets, continuing support, annual campaigns, seed money, building funds, equipment, matching funds, fellowships, research, special projects, publications, conferences and seminars.

Limitations: Giving primarily in western PA for education, culture, health, and recreation; giving nationally for public affairs. No support for national organizations for general fundraising campaigns. No grants to individuals, or for deficit financing or scholarships; no loans.

Publications: Annual report, application guidelines.

Application information:
Initial approach: Letter or full proposal
Copies of proposal: 1
Deadline(s): None
Board meeting date(s): February, May, September, and November
Final notification: 2 to 4 weeks
Write: Richard M. Larry, President

Officers: Richard M. Larry,* President; Donald C. Sipp, Vice-President, Investments; Barbara L. Slaney, Vice-President; R. Daniel McMichael, Secretary; Gerald Walsh, Treasurer.

Trustees:* Richard M. Scaife, Chairman; James L. Winokur, Vice-Chairman; Robert L. Becker, Jr., Anthony J.A. Bryan, Peter Denby, Arch S. Jeffery, W. McMichael Jones, Matthew B. Ridgway, Clyde H. Slease, III.

Number of staff: 3 full-time professional; 3 part-time professional; 3 part-time support.

Employer Identification Number: 251113452

3712
Schautz (The Walter L.) Foundation ⌑
150 East Grove St.
Dunmore 18512

Incorporated in 1948 in Pennsylvania.
Donor(s): Walter L. Schautz, Madalene L. Schautz, Grove Silk Company.
Financial data: (yr. ended 1/31/83): Assets, $1,586,593 (M); gifts received, $10,000; expenditures, $101,368, including $57,081 for 70 grants (high: $5,000).
Purpose and activities: Primarily local giving, with grants for welfare programs, youth agencies, church support, higher education, including theological seminars, and a community fund.
Limitations: Giving primarily in PA.
Application information:
Write: Madalene L. Schautz, President
Officers: Madalene L. Schautz, President; Nancy L. Miles, Secretary; Walter L. Schautz, Jr., Treasurer.
Employer Identification Number: 246018362

3713
Scholler Foundation, The
2000 Two Penn Center Plaza
Philadelphia 19102   (215) 568-7500

Trust established in 1939 in Pennsylvania.
Donor(s): F.C. Scholler.†
Financial data: (yr. ended 12/31/83): Assets, $6,096,585 (M); expenditures, $325,067, including $251,930 for 24 grants (high: $28,475; low: $4,400; average: $5,000-$10,000).
Purpose and activities: Local giving for the alleviation of poverty and destitution, for the promotion of scientific research, including the branches of chemistry, and other literary, educational, and public purposes; support largely for hospitals and higher education, with emphasis on grants for small community hospitals to purchase medical equipment.
Types of support awarded: Equipment, research.
Limitations: Giving limited to the Delaware Valley, PA. No grants to individuals, or for general support, endowment funds, scholarships and fellowships, or matching gifts; no loans.
Application information:
Initial approach: Full proposal
Copies of proposal: 1
Deadline(s): February 1, May 1, August 1, and November 1
Board meeting date(s): February, May, August, and November
Write: Frederick L. Fuges, Executive Director
Officers and Trustees: Ernest E. Rettberg, Jr., Chairman and President; Frederick L. Fuges, Secretary-Treasurer and Executive Director; E.C. Dreby III, A. Winston Edwards, E. Brooks Keffer, Jr.
Number of staff: None.
Employer Identification Number: 236245158

3714
Schoonmaker (Lucy Kay) Foundation
c/o Mellon Bank, Rm. 2816
Mellon Square, P.O. Box 185
Pittsburgh 15230   (412) 232-5784

Trust established in 1957.
Donor(s): Mrs. Lucy K. Schoonmaker.†
Financial data: (yr. ended 12/31/82): Assets, $751,160 (M); expenditures, $111,038, including $101,900 for 28 grants (high: $30,000; low: $250).
Purpose and activities: Primarily local giving, with emphasis on social services, hosptials, education, and church support; support also for community funds.
Types of support awarded: Continuing support, annual campaigns, building funds, general purposes, matching funds.
Limitations: Giving primarily in PA. No grants to individuals, or for research, or scholarships and fellowships; no loans.
Application information:
Initial approach: Letter
Copies of proposal: 1
Deadline(s): Submit proposal preferably in the early fall
Board meeting date(s): Monthly
Write: Barbara Robinson, Trust Officer

Officer: G. Donald Gerlach, Director of Distributions.
Trustee: Mellon Bank.
Employer Identification Number: 256018687

3715
Scott Paper Company Foundation ▼
One Scott Plaza
Philadelphia 19113   (215) 522-5398

Trust established in 1953 in Pennsylvania.
Donor(s): Scott Paper Company.
Financial data: (yr. ended 12/31/83): Assets, $3,885 (M); gifts received, $885,000; expenditures, $910,555, including $683,211 for 140 grants (high: $25,000; low: $350), $100,000 for 64 grants to individuals and $78,144 for 750 employee matching gifts.
Purpose and activities: General giving, primarily to communities with major company operations, with emphasis on higher education, community funds, health associations, community programs and minority development; supports an employee matching-gift program to qualified educational institutions, and a company-employee scholarship program.
Types of support awarded: Seed money, employee related scholarships, employee matching gifts, publications, consulting services, continuing support, emergency funds, equipment, matching funds, special projects, technical assistance.
Limitations: Giving primarily in areas of major company operations. No grants to individuals (except for company-employee scholarships), or for endowment funds, operating budgets, deficit financing, land acquisition, or research; no loans.
Publications: Annual report, program policy statement, application guidelines.
Application information:
Initial approach: Letter
Copies of proposal: 1
Deadline(s): None
Board meeting date(s): January, April, July, and October
Final notification: 3 months
Write: Cynthia D. Giroud, Manager of Social Investment
Trustees: Philip J. Webster, Chairman; Clemens S. Andes, Edward B. Betz, Frank W. Bubb, 3rd, James A. Morril, James E. O'Neill, Nelson P. Wainman, Jr.
Number of staff: 1 full-time professional; 1 full-time support; 1 part-time support.
Employer Identification Number: 236231564

3716
Scranton Area Foundation, The ⌑
419 Bank Towers
Scranton 18503   (717) 347-6203

Community foundation established in 1954 in Pennsylvania by resolution and declaration of trust.
Financial data: (yr. ended 12/31/83): Assets, $4,131,929 (M); gifts received, $272,664; expenditures, $319,131, including $280,606 for grants (high: $55,000).

Purpose and activities: Broad purposes; grants only within the greater Scranton area, principally for the local community fund, churches, mental health, and higher education.
Types of support awarded: Seed money, general purposes, research, special projects, publications, conferences and seminars, matching funds.
Limitations: Giving limited to the Scranton, PA, area. No grants to individuals, or for building or endowment funds, or operating budgets.
Publications: Application guidelines.
Application information: Application form required.
Initial approach: Telephone
Copies of proposal: 8
Deadline(s): Submit proposal preferably in month preceding board meeting; no set deadline
Board meeting date(s): January, April, July, and October
Write: George Joel, Executive Director
Officers: George Joel, Executive Director; William J. Calpin, Jr., Secretary.
Governors: Marion M. Isaacs, Chairman; C. Welles Belin, Vice-Chairman; Francis E. Crowley, William M. Dawson, William J. Garvey, Edwin Kosik, H. Myron Wetzel.
Trustee: Northeastern Bank.
Employer Identification Number: 246022055

3717
Seybert (Adam and Maria Sarah) Institution for Poor Boys and Girls
(also known as Seybert Institution)
1500 Walnut St., 15th Fl.
Philadelphia 19102   (215) 893-8228

Incorporated in 1914 in Pennsylvania.
Donor(s): Adam Seybert,† Maria Sarah Seybert.†
Financial data: (yr. ended 12/31/84): Assets, $2,970,800 (M); expenditures, $259,548, including $172,400 for 47 grants (high: $20,000; low: $500).
Purpose and activities: Limited to the assistance of needy children in Philadelphia through support for educational programs, including a scholarship program, aimed at helping the nonconforming child; innovative teaching methods; counseling services in the areas of child abuse, drugs, dropouts, and runaways; cultural, artistic, and craft programs bringing out the best qualities of youth and giving to each individual a sense of dignity.
Types of support awarded: Scholarship funds, seed money, emergency funds, research, matching funds.
Limitations: Giving limited to Philadelphia, PA. No grants to individuals, or for building or endowment funds.
Publications: Application guidelines.
Application information:
Initial approach: Telephone or letter
Copies of proposal: 10
Deadline(s): One month before board meets
Board meeting date(s): Last Friday in January, April, July, and October; grants awarded in October are for following year
Write: Mrs. Helen R. Green, Executive Secretary

Officers and Trustees: H. Gates Lloyd III, President; Hon. Lois G. Forer, Vice-President; William C. Bullitt, Secretary; Steven R. Garfinkel, Treasurer; Susan C. Day, M.D., Graham S. Finney, Rev. Barbara C. Harris, Carver A. Portlock, J. Peter Williams.
Number of staff: 1 part-time professional.
Employer Identification Number: 236260105

3718
Sheppard (Lawrence B.) Foundation, Inc. ⌑
c/o Hanover Shoe Farms, Inc.
P.O. Box 339
Hanover 17331

Incorporated in 1946 in Pennsylvania.
Donor(s): Lawrence B. Sheppard.
Financial data: (yr. ended 11/30/83): Assets, $1,071,007 (M); expenditures, $102,031, including $93,853 for 23 grants (high: $25,000; low: $353).
Purpose and activities: Primarily local giving, with emphasis on secondary education, health agencies, Protestant church support, youth agencies, and community development.
Types of support awarded: General purposes, building funds, land acquisition.
Limitations: Giving primarily in the Hanover, PA, area.
Officers: Paul E. Spears, President; Charlotte S. Devan, Vice-President; Horace E. Smith, Secretary; Betty J. Nolt, Treasurer.
Directors: Charlotte N. Sheppard, Chairman; Lawrence S. Devan, W. Todd Devan, A.C. Mudge, Patricia S. Winder.
Employer Identification Number: 236251690

3719
Shoemaker (The Thomas H. and Mary Williams) Fund
c/o The First Pennsylvania Banking and Trust Company
Fifteenth and Chestnut Sts.
Philadelphia 19101   (215) 569-3436

Trust established in 1953 in Pennsylvania.
Donor(s): Mary Williams Shoemaker,† Thomas H. Shoemaker,† Thomas H. and Mary Williams Shoemaker Trust.
Financial data: (yr. ended 9/30/83): Assets, $3,527,199 (M); expenditures, $245,249, including $243,100 for 57 grants (high: $14,000; low: $500).
Purpose and activities: Primarily local giving, with emphasis on religious, charitable, and educational institutions of the Religious Society of Friends.
Types of support awarded: General purposes, continuing support, seed money, building funds, endowment funds, scholarship funds, operating budgets.
Limitations: Giving primarily in PA. No grants to individuals, or for matching gifts; no loans.
Application information:
Initial approach: Full proposal
Copies of proposal: 6
Deadline(s): April 15 and October 15
Board meeting date(s): May and November
Final notification: 3 weeks after meetings
Write: Eleanor Stabler Clarke, Secretary

Managers: William P. Camp, Eleanor Stabler Clarke, Alan Reeve Hunt, H. Mather Lippincott, Jr., Barbara S. Sprogell.
Trustee: The First Pennsylvania Banking and Trust Company (Frederick T. Seving, Jr., Senior Trust Officer).
Number of staff: 1 full-time support.
Employer Identification Number: 236209783

3720
SICO Foundation, The ▼ ⌑
15 Mount Joy St.
Mount Joy 17552   (717) 653-1411

Incorporated in 1941 in Delaware.
Donor(s): Clarence Schock.†
Financial data: (yr. ended 5/31/83): Assets, $8,016,847 (M); expenditures, $492,965, including $400,000 for 9 grants (high: $163,875; low: $9,000).
Purpose and activities: Support for public higher education and scholarship funds for education of elementary school teachers.
Types of support awarded: Scholarship funds.
Limitations: Giving limited to PA, DE, and MD.
Publications: Informational brochure, application guidelines.
Application information: Application form required.
Copies of proposal: 3
Deadline(s): Must be postmarked on or before February 15
Officer and Directors: Harry K. Gerlach, President; B.L. Biemesderfer, William H. Duncan, Franklin R. Eichler, Fred S. Engle, S. Harold Hacker, Arthur A. Hackman, Carl R. Hallgren, Robert P. McGinley, Joseph D. Moore, John N. Weidman.
Number of staff: 5 part-time support.
Employer Identification Number: 236298332

3721
Silverstein (Louis) No. 4 Charitable Trust ⌑
c/o Provident National Bank
1632 Chestnut St.
Philadelphia 19103

Established in 1976.
Donor(s): Louis J. Silverstein.†
Financial data: (yr. ended 1/31/82): Assets, $880,342 (M); expenditures, $198,896, including $150,000 for 3 grants (high: $75,000; low: $25,000).
Purpose and activities: Support primarily for a local university.
Limitations: Giving primarily in PA.
Trustee: Provident National Bank.
Employer Identification Number: 236620071

3722
Simon (Esther) Charitable Trust ▼
100 Matsonford Rd.
P.O. Box 750
Radnor 19088   (215) 293-8902

Trust established in 1952 in New York.
Donor(s): Mrs. Esther Simon.

Financial data: (yr. ended 12/31/83): Assets, $8,165,743 (M); expenditures, $848,184, including $800,000 for 37 grants (high: $250,000; low: $1,000).
Purpose and activities: Grants to charitable, cultural, and educational institutions.
Limitations: No grants to individuals.
Application information: Applications for grants not invited.
Trustee: Walter H. Annenberg.
Employer Identification Number: 236286763

3723
Smith (Ethel Sergeant Clark) Memorial Fund ▼
c/o The Philadelphia National Bank
P.O. Box 7618
Philadelphia 19101   (215) 629-3798

Trust established in 1977 in Pennsylvania.
Donor(s): Ethel Sergeant Clark Smith.†
Financial data: (yr. ended 5/31/84): Assets, $6,694,955 (M); expenditures, $670,430, including $614,921 for 24 grants (high: $125,000; low: $4,000; average: $4,000-$50,000).
Purpose and activities: Charitable purposes; local giving to hospitals, social service organizations, libraries, colleges, and cultural organizations, including museums, historical buildings, and recreation, music and drama facilities.
Types of support awarded: Building funds, continuing support, emergency funds, equipment, general purposes, land acquisition, operating budgets, research, special projects.
Limitations: Giving limited to Delaware County, PA. No grants to individuals, or for funds on a long-term basis, deficit financing, endowment funds, or scholarships and fellowships; no loans.
Publications: Biennial report, program policy statement, application guidelines.
Application information:
Initial approach: Letter
Copies of proposal: 1
Deadline(s): March 1 and September 1
Board meeting date(s): May and November
Final notification: 2 months
Write: Charles A. Fritz, III, Senior Trust Officer
Trustee: The Philadelphia National Bank (Charles A. Fritz III, Senior Trust Officer).
Number of staff: None.
Employer Identification Number: 236648857

3724
Smith Foundation
E-105 Cathedral Village
600 East Cathedral Rd.
Philadelphia 19128

Incorporated in 1920 in Pennsylvania.
Donor(s): W. Hinckle Smith,† H. Harrison Smith.†
Financial data: (yr. ended 12/31/82): Assets, $3,657,882 (M); expenditures, $348,686, including $309,750 for 68 grants (high: $25,000; low: $500).

Purpose and activities: To aid the sick, aged, and poor, as well as to aid in the education of needy boys and girls through local organizations engaged in such work; grants for hospitals, child welfare, the aged, and the handicapped.
Types of support awarded: Building funds, operating budgets, special projects.
Limitations: Giving limited to southeastern PA. No grants to individuals or for endowment funds.
Publications: Annual report.
Application information: Application form required.
Initial approach: Letter
Copies of proposal: 1
Deadline(s): October 31
Board meeting date(s): Semiannually
Write: Robert F. Brown, Treasurer
Officers and Directors: Richer M. Goodwin, President; Roger P. Hollingsworth, Vice-President; Robert F. Brown, Secretary-Treasurer; Joseph H. Barber, Robert L. Strayer.
Employer Identification Number: 236238148

3725
Smith (W. W.) Charitable Trust ▼
100 Chetwynd Dr., Suite 200
Rosemont 19010   (215) 525-9667

Trust established in 1977 in Pennsylvania.
Donor(s): William Wikoff Smith.†
Financial data: (yr. ended 6/30/84): Assets, $59,304,413 (M); gifts received, $261,064; expenditures, $3,855,555, including $3,464,066 for 170 grants (high: $80,000; low: $5,000; average: $5,000-$40,000).
Purpose and activities: Primarily local giving with emphasis on financial aid programs for qualified needy undergraduate students at accredited universities and colleges, hospital programs for the medical care of the poor and needy, scientific medical research programs with particular emphasis on those dealing with cancer and heart diseases, and programs of organizations providing shelter, food, and clothing for children and the aged.
Types of support awarded: Scholarship funds, research, operating budgets, seed money, emergency funds, building funds, equipment, land acquisition, special projects, publications, matching funds, general purposes, continuing support.
Limitations: Giving primarily in the Philadelphia, PA, area. No grants to individuals, or for deficit financing or endowment funds; no loans; no long-term grants.
Publications: Biennial report, application guidelines, program policy statement.
Application information: Applications for medical research grants must be submitted in triplicate.
Initial approach: Full proposal or letter
Copies of proposal: 1
Deadline(s): For financial aid programs March 1; for hospital programs December 1; for cancer research April 15; for heart research July 15; for social service programs December 1 and June 1
Board meeting date(s): January, April, July, and October

Final notification: 4 months
Write: Charles A. Fritz III, Vice-President
Trustees: Mary L. Smith, The Philadelphia National Bank (Charles A. Fritz III, Vice-President).
Number of staff: 4.
Employer Identification Number: 236648841

3726
SmithKline Beckman Foundation ¤
One Franklin Plaza
P.O. Box 7929
Philadelphia 19101   (215) 751-5149

Trust established in 1952 in Pennsylvania.
Donor(s): SmithKline Beckman Corporation.
Financial data: (yr. ended 12/31/83): Assets, $4,619,060 (M); expenditures, $938,035, including $336,110 for 1 grant, $63,130 for 15 grants to individuals and $420,971 for 693 employee matching gifts.
Purpose and activities: Foundation maintains an employee matching gift program for qualifying educational institutions and hospitals; support also for community funds and the C. Mahlon Kline Memorial Scholarship program for children of disabled or deceased employees of the Corporation.
Types of support awarded: Employee related scholarships, employee matching gifts.
Limitations: Giving primarily in PA. No grants to individuals (except for scholarships for children of deceased or disabled company employees), or for operating budgets or building or endowment funds; no loans.
Publications: Annual report.
Application information: Grant applications not accepted. Application form required.
Board meeting date(s): May
Write: William L. Grala, President
Officers and Directors: William L. Grala, President; Richard V. Holmes, Secretary; Kurt W. Reiss, Treasurer; Alan J. Dalby, Thomas G. Davis, M.D., Stanley E. Jacke.
Employer Identification Number: 232120418

3727
Snayberger (Harry E. and Florence W.) Memorial Foundation ¤
c/o Pennsylvania National Bank and Trust Company
One South Centre St.
Pottsville 17901   (717) 622-4200

Established in 1976 in Pennsylvania.
Donor(s): Harry E. Snayberger.†
Financial data: (yr. ended 3/31/83): Assets, $3,022,043 (M); expenditures, $173,943, including $23,124 for 47 grants (high: $10,000; low: $34) and $117,028 for 839 grants to individuals.
Purpose and activities: Giving limited to Schuylkill County, with emphasis on scholarships, church support, and community affairs.
Types of support awarded: Student aid, operating budgets, special projects.
Limitations: Giving primarily in Schuylkill County, PA.
Application information: Application form required.

Initial approach: Letter
Copies of proposal: 1
Deadline(s): February and March
Board meeting date(s): Weekly as required
Write: Pennsylvania National Bank and Trust Company

Trustee: Pennsylvania National Bank and Trust Company.
Employer Identification Number: 232056361

3728
Snyder (W. P.) Charitable Fund ¤
One Oliver Plaza, Suite 3550
Pittsburgh 15222

Trust established in 1950 in Pennsylvania.
Donor(s): W.P. Snyder, Jr.,† W.P. Snyder III, The Shenango Furnace Company.
Financial data: (yr. ended 12/31/82): Assets, $6,416,636 (M); expenditures, $387,450, including $353,966 for 45 grants (high: $70,000; low: $500).
Purpose and activities: Broad purposes; primarily local giving, with emphasis on community funds, higher and secondary education, and hospitals; support also for cultural programs, including historic preservation, and social agencies.
Limitations: Giving primarily in PA.
Trustees: John K. Foster, G. Whitney Snyder, W.P. Snyder III.
Employer Identification Number: 256034967

3729
Sordoni Foundation, Inc.
c/o Warren E. Myers
R. D. 5, Box 148, Elmcrest Dr.
Dallas 18612 (717) 675-5730

Incorporated in 1946 in Pennsylvania.
Donor(s): Andrew J. Sordoni, Sr.,† Andrew J. Sordoni, Jr.,† Ruth A. Sordoni,† and others.
Financial data: (yr. ended 7/31/83): Assets, $3,342,569 (M); gifts received, $8,250; expenditures, $337,302, including $153,862 for 29 grants (high: $30,000; low: $100) and $43,800 for 48 grants to individuals.
Purpose and activities: Broad purposes; primarily local giving, with emphasis on medical and higher education, including a scholarship program restricted to residents of Luzerne County, Pennsylvania; support also for libraries.
Types of support awarded: Building funds, equipment, student aid.
Limitations: Giving primarily in PA.
Application information: Application form required.
Deadline(s): May 1
Board meeting date(s): As required
Write: Warren E. Myers, Secretary-Treasurer

Officers and Directors: Andrew J. Sordoni, III, President; Helen Mary Sekera, Vice-President; Warren E. Myers, Secretary-Treasurer, and Executive Director; Jule Ayers, Benjamin Badman, Jr., Margaret B. English, Thomas H. Kiley, Roy E. Morgan.
Employer Identification Number: 246017505

3730
Spang & Company Charitable Trust ¤
P.O. Box 751
Butler 16001

Established in 1972.
Donor(s): Spang & Company, Magnetics, Inc.
Financial data: (yr. ended 12/31/83): Assets, $643,416 (M); gifts received, $27,100; expenditures, $131,253, including $124,089 for 49 grants (high: $40,000; low: $40).
Purpose and activities: Primarily local giving to hospitals and community funds, and for community development.
Limitations: Giving primarily in the Butler, PA, area.
Trustee: Union National Bank of Pittsburgh.
Employer Identification Number: 256020192

3731
SPS Foundation
Highland Ave.
Jenkintown 19046

Trust established in 1953 in Pennsylvania.
Donor(s): SPS Technologies, Inc.
Financial data: (yr. ended 12/31/84): Assets, $444,095 (M); gifts received, $140,000; expenditures, $126,908, including $111,035 for 117 grants (high: $45,000; low: $25; average: $100-$500) and $15,208 for 82 employee matching gifts.
Purpose and activities: Broad purposes; primarily local giving for community funds, higher education, hospitals, youth activities, and the arts.
Types of support awarded: Operating budgets, continuing support, annual campaigns, emergency funds, building funds, equipment, employee matching gifts, special projects, research.
Limitations: Giving primarily in PA, Cleveland, OH, and Santa Ana, CA. No grants to individuals, or for seed money, land acquisition, matching funds, scholarships, fellowships, demonstration projects, publications, or conferences and seminars; no loans.
Application information:
Final notification: 1 month
Write: Rockwell M. Groves, Chairman, Gifts Committee

Manager: Rockwell M. Groves, Chairman, Gifts Committee.
Trustees: H. Thomas Hallowell, Joseph Rhein, John R. Selby.
Number of staff: None.
Employer Identification Number: 236294553

3732
St. Marys Catholic Foundation
1935 State St.
St. Marys 15857 (814) 781-1591

Incorporated in 1960 in Pennsylvania.
Donor(s): Benedict R. Reuscher, Alfred A. Gleixner, Richard J. Reuscher, R.B. Reuscher, E.H. Gleixner, W.E. Reuscher, EB & Associates, Keystone Carbon Co.
Financial data: (yr. ended 1/31/85): Assets, $2,438,569 (L); gifts received, $793,572; expenditures, $632,513, including $627,550 for 18 grants (high: $104,500; low: $5,000).
Purpose and activities: Broad purposes; support for local Roman Catholic-sponsored elementary and secondary schools and colleges to supplement teachers' salaries and for school equipment; support also for Roman Catholic religious associations and organizations of interest to the donor.
Types of support awarded: Equipment, operating budgets, general purposes, continuing support, seed money, research, publications, conferences and seminars, matching funds.
Limitations: Giving primarily in PA, with emphasis on St. Marys area. No grants to individuals, or for endowment funds, scholarships, or fellowships; no loans.
Application information:
Initial approach: Letter
Board meeting date(s): Quarterly
Write: Richard J. Reuscher, Secretary-Treasurer

Officers and Trustees: E.H. Gleixner, President; William E. Reuscher, Vice-President; Richard J. Reuscher, Secretary-Treasurer; Benedict R. Reuscher, R.B. Reuscher.
Number of staff: None.
Employer Identification Number: 256036961

3733
Stabler (The Donald B. and Dorothy L.) Foundation
c/o Dauphin Deposit Bank and Trust Company
Box 2961
Harrisburg 17105 (717) 255-2044

Established in 1966 in Pennsylvania.
Donor(s): Stabler Companies, Inc.
Financial data: (yr. ended 12/31/84): Assets, $1,916,622 (L); gifts received, $179,614; expenditures, $209,379, including $186,700 for 63 grants (high: $100,000; low: $250; average: $1,400).
Purpose and activities: Primarily local giving, with emphasis on higher education, hospitals, and religious purposes.
Types of support awarded: Operating budgets, continuing support, annual campaigns, building funds, equipment, endowment funds, matching funds, scholarship funds, professorships.
Limitations: Giving primarily in PA. No grants to individuals, or for seed money, research programs, land acquisition, special projects, publications, conferences, deficit financing, or emergency funds; no loans.
Application information:
Initial approach: Letter
Copies of proposal: 1
Deadline(s): 1 month prior to board meetings
Board meeting date(s): Usually in May, September, and October
Final notification: 1 month after board meetings
Write: Wilson D. Lewis, Chairman

Officers and Trustees: Wilson D. Lewis, Chairman; Frank A. Sinon, Secretary; Richard E. Jordan, Harold S. Mohler, W. Stewart Taylor.
Number of staff: None.
Employer Identification Number: 236422944

3734
Stackpole-Hall Foundation ▼
19 North St. Marys St.
St. Marys 15857   (814) 781-1167

Trust established in 1951 in Pennsylvania.
Donor(s): Lyle G. Hall,† J. Hall Stackpole,†
Harrison C. Stackpole, Adelaide Stackpole,†
L.C. Jamieson, Mary Reeves.
Financial data: (yr. ended 12/31/83): Assets,
$11,300,530 (M); expenditures, $792,563,
including $693,369 for 36 grants (high:
$133,333; low: $175; average: $1,500-
$15,000).
Purpose and activities: Broad purposes;
primarily local giving, with emphasis on health
care, education, youth agencies, and civic
affairs.
Types of support awarded: Building funds,
annual campaigns, seed money, equipment,
matching funds.
Limitations: Giving primarily in Elk County,
PA. No grants to individuals, or for
scholarships and fellowships; generally, no
grants for operating budgets, or endowment
funds; no loans.
Publications: Informational brochure, program
policy statement, application guidelines.
Application information:
Initial approach: Letter
Copies of proposal: 1
Deadline(s): None
Board meeting date(s): February, May,
August, and December
Final notification: 3 months
Write: William C. Conrad, Executive
Secretary
Officer: William C. Conrad, Executive
Secretary.
Trustees: Benn F. Goodrich, Chairman;
Harrison C. Stackpole, Vice-Chairman; Douglas
R. Dobson, Alexander G. Hall, Lyle G. Hall, Jr.,
J.M. Hamlin Johnson, R. Dauer Stackpole.
Number of staff: 2.
Employer Identification Number: 256006650

3735
Staunton Farm Foundation ▼
c/o Mellon Bank
One Mellon Bank Ctr., 40th Fl.
Pittsburgh 15230
Application address: Philip B. Hallen, 3317
Grant Bldg., Pittsburgh, PA 15219; Tel.: (412)
261-2485

Incorporated in 1937 in Pennsylvania.
Donor(s): Mathilda Craig Staunton.
Financial data: (yr. ended 12/31/84): Assets,
$15,560,765 (M); expenditures, $399,131,
including $311,000 for 14 grants (high:
$71,250; low: $3,000; average: $1,000-
$50,000).
Purpose and activities: Grants limited to
hospitals or local organizations concerned with
mental health, the emotionally handicapped
and child welfare.
Limitations: Giving limited to Allegheny
County, PA.
Application information:
Initial approach: Letter
Deadline(s): None
Board meeting date(s): Quarterly

Write: Philip B. Hallen
Officers and Directors: John P. Davis, Jr.,
President; John G. Maloney, Secretary-
Treasurer; Albert B. Craig, Jr., Mrs. George L.
Craig, Jr., Joseph D. Dury, Jr., Joseph Craig
Ferree, Elizabeth C. Griffiths, Kathleen C.
Knight, George D. Lockhart, Mrs. David
McCargo, Charles J. Ramsburg, Jr., William L.
Standish.
Manager: Mellon Bank.
Number of staff: 1 part-time professional; 1
part-time support.
Employer Identification Number: 250965573

3736
Stein (Louis) Foundation ☐
1700 Walnut St., Suite 925
Philadelphia 19111   (215) 546-8100

Established in 1953 in New Jersey.
Donor(s): Louis Stein, Walter Liventhal, Stanley
Merves, Stein, Stein & Engel, and others.
Financial data: (yr. ended 12/31/83): Assets,
$579,719 (M); gifts received, $380,338;
expenditures, $396,899, including $394,360
for 47 grants (high: $82,000; low: $10).
Purpose and activities: Giving primarily to
Jewish welfare funds and universities; some
support also to health agencies.
Application information:
Initial approach: Letter
Deadline(s): None
Write: Louis Stein, Trustee
Trustees: Marilyn Bellet, Louis Stein.
Employer Identification Number: 236395253

3737
Steinman (James Hale) Foundation
Eight West King St.
Lancaster 17603

Trust established in 1952 in Pennsylvania.
Donor(s): James Hale Steinman,† Louise
Steinman von Hess,† Lancaster Newspapers,
Inc., and others.
Financial data: (yr. ended 12/31/83): Assets,
$5,216,035 (M); gifts received, $200,000;
expenditures, $586,775, including $559,637
for 36 grants (high: $450,720; low: $250).
Purpose and activities: Broad purposes;
primarily local giving, with emphasis on historic
preservation, education, including scholarships
to children of company employees and
newspaper carriers, social services, and a
community fund.
Types of support awarded: Employee related
scholarships.
Limitations: Giving primarily in Lancaster, PA.
Application information: Application form
available for scholarships (children of
employees only). Application form required.
Deadline(s): February 28 of senior year of
high school, for scholarships (for children
of employees only)
Write: Willis W. Shenk, Treasurer; Larry
Baumann for scholarships
Officers and Trustees: Caroline S. Nunan,
Chairman; Clair R. McCollough, Beverly R.
Steinman, Vice-Chairmen; Jack S. Gerhart,
Secretary; Willis W. Shenk, Treasurer; I.Z.
Buckwalter, John M. Buckwalter.
Employer Identification Number: 236266377

3738
Steinman (John Frederick) Foundation
Eight West King St.
Lancaster 17603

Trust established in 1952 in Pennsylvania.
Donor(s): John Frederick Steinman,† Shirley
W. Steinman,† Lancaster Newspapers, Inc.,
and others.
Financial data: (yr. ended 12/31/83): Assets,
$7,309,621 (M); gifts received, $200,000;
expenditures, $488,847, including $434,200
for 66 grants (high: $77,000; low: $100) and
$15,000 for grants to individuals.
Purpose and activities: Broad purposes;
primarily local giving, with emphasis on higher
and secondary education, community funds,
hospitals, and the handicapped; also funds a
fellowship program limited to graduate study in
mental health or a related field.
Types of support awarded: Fellowships.
Limitations: Giving primarily in PA.
Application information: Application for
fellowship program available upon request.
Deadline(s): February 1 for fellowships
Write: Willis W. Shenk, Treasurer; for
fellowships, Jay H. Wenrich, Fellowship
Program Secretary
Officers and Trustees: Shirley S. Katzenbach,
Chairman; Jack S. Gerhart, Secretary; Willis W.
Shenk, Treasurer; I.Z. Buckwalter, J.M.
Buckwalter, Clair R. McCollough, Henry
Pildner, Jr.
Employer Identification Number: 236266378

3739
Steinsapir (Julius L. and Libbie B.) Family Foundation ☐
900 Lawyers Bldg.
Pittsburgh 15219   (412) 391-2920

Established in 1969 in Pennsylvania.
Donor(s): I.H. Steinsapir,† Standard Emblem
Jewelers.
Financial data: (yr. ended 1/31/84): Assets,
$1,619,180 (M); expenditures, $158,031,
including $123,946 for 62 grants (high:
$22,500; low: $10).
Purpose and activities: Primarily local giving,
with emphasis on temple support, Jewish
welfare funds, and secondary education.
Limitations: Giving primarily in PA.
Application information:
Deadline(s): None
Write: Samuel Horovitz
Trustees: Samuel Horovitz, Melvin L. Mallit,
Albert C. Shapira, Lewis Silverboard, Julius
Steinsapir.
Employer Identification Number: 256104248

3740
Stokes (Lydia B.) Foundation
3400 Centre Square West
1500 Market St.
Philadelphia 19102   (215) 972-3594

Trust established in 1959 in New Jersey.
Donor(s): Lydia B. Stokes.

Financial data: (yr. ended 6/30/84): Assets, $1,542,106 (M); expenditures, $146,736, including $134,500 for 10 grants (high: $30,000; low: $2,000).
Purpose and activities: Broad purposes; primarily local giving, with emphasis on social services and educational institutions affiliated with the Religious Society of Friends, a hospital, and a community fund.
Limitations: Giving primarily in PA. No grants to individuals.
Application information:
  Initial approach: Letter
  Copies of proposal: 1
  Deadline(s): None
  Board meeting date(s): As required
  Final notification: 1 month
  Write: Kenneth W. Gemmill, Trustee
Trustees: Kenneth W. Gemmill, Lydia B. Stokes, Samuel Emlen Stokes, Jr., First Fidelity Bank.
Number of staff: None.
Employer Identification Number: 216016107

3741
Stott (The Louis L.) Foundation
2000 One Logan Square
Philadelphia 19103   (215) 963-5281
Mailing address: c/o Mill Tract Farm, R.D. No.2, Douglassville, PA 19518

Trust established in 1968 in Pennsylvania.
Donor(s): Mrs. Martha Stott Diener.
Financial data: (yr. ended 9/30/84): Assets, $1,582,575 (M); expenditures, $103,668, including $83,900 for 44 grants (high: $20,000; low: $200; average: $1,000).
Purpose and activities: Broad purposes, including support of scientific and technological research, education, medical research, encouragement of art, or preservation of wildlife; primarily local giving, with emphasis on elementary and secondary education, and population and environmental control.
Types of support awarded: Operating budgets, continuing support, annual campaigns, seed money, emergency funds, building funds, equipment, land acquisition, special projects, research.
Limitations: Giving primarily in Berks County, PA. No grants to individuals, or for endowment funds, scholarships and fellowships, publications, conferences, or matching gifts; no loans.
Publications: Application guidelines, program policy statement.
Application information:
  Initial approach: Full proposal or letter
  Copies of proposal: 1
  Deadline(s): Submit proposal preferably between January and August; no set deadline
  Board meeting date(s): July and August
  Final notification: 2 to 3 months
  Write: William P. Wood, Secretary
Officers and Trustees: Martha Stott Diener, Chairman; William P. Wood, Secretary; Brady O. Bryson, Benjamin W. Stott, Edward Barrington Stott, Jonathan D. Stott.
Number of staff: 1 part-time professional; 1 part-time support.
Employer Identification Number: 237009027

3742
Strauss Foundation
c/o The Fidelity Bank
135 South Broad St.
Philadelphia 19109

Trust established in 1951 in Pennsylvania.
Donor(s): Maurice L. Strauss.
Financial data: (yr. ended 12/31/83): Assets, $15,851,072 (M); expenditures, $297,912, including $281,275 for 196 grants (high: $12,000; low: $75).
Purpose and activities: General giving, primarily in Pennsylvania, with emphasis on Jewish welfare funds in the United States and Israel, education, hospitals, and cultural programs.
Limitations: Giving primarily in PA.
Application information: Grant applications are not invited.
Trustees: Henry A. Gladstone, Sandra S. Krause, Elaine Strauss Kaufman, Benjamin Strauss, Robert Perry Strauss, The Fidelity Bank, Corporate Trustee.
Employer Identification Number: 236219939

3743
Strawbridge (Margaret Dorrance) Foundation ▼
125 Strafford Ave.
Bldg. 3, Suite 108
Wayne 19087   (215) 688-9262

Incorporated in 1958 in Delaware.
Donor(s): Diana Strawbridge Norris, George Strawbridge, Jr.
Financial data: (yr. ended 12/31/83): Assets, $4,191,394 (M); gifts received, $634,959; expenditures, $480,327, including $445,600 for 45 grants (high: $100,000; low: $500; average: $1,000-$25,000).
Purpose and activities: Emphasis on higher and secondary education, hospitals and medical research, and community funds and programs.
Types of support awarded: Seed money, operating budgets, continuing support.
Limitations: No grants to individuals, or for capital or endowment funds, scholarships, or fellowships; no loans.
Application information: Solicitations for grants are not invited.
  Write: George Strawbridge, Vice-President
Officers and Directors: George Strawbridge, Jr., President; Diana Strawbridge Norris, George Strawbridge, Vice-Presidents; Charles H. Norris, Jr., Nina S. Strawbridge.
Number of staff: None.
Employer Identification Number: 232339257

3744
Stroud Foundation, The
c/o Girard Trust Bank
One Girard Plaza
Philadelphia 19101
Application address: Landhope R.D. 2, West Grove, PA 19390

Trust established in 1961 in Pennsylvania.
Donor(s): Mrs. Joan M. Stroud.

Financial data: (yr. ended 12/31/82): Assets, $575,168 (M); gifts received, $437,045; expenditures, $342,918, including $339,950 for 62 grants (high: $50,000; low: $100).
Purpose and activities: Support largely for higher and secondary education and a natural science museum; some support also for cultural programs and environment.
Types of support awarded: General purposes, continuing support, annual campaigns, seed money, emergency funds, building funds, equipment, land acquisition, endowment funds, research, scholarship funds.
Limitations: No grants to individuals or for matching gifts; no loans.
Application information:
  Initial approach: Letter
  Copies of proposal: 1
  Deadline(s): None
  Board meeting date(s): Quarterly
  Write: W.B. Dixon Stroud, Manager
Managers: Joan S. Blaine, T. Sam Means, Joan M. Stroud, Morris W. Stroud, W.B. Dixon Stroud, Truman Welling.
Number of staff: None.
Employer Identification Number: 236255701

3745
Superior-Pacific Fund ☒
Seven Wynnewood Rd.
Wynnewood 19096
Scholarship application address: Superior Tube Company Scholarship Committee, P.O. Box 191, Norristown, PA 19404

Trust established in 1952 in Pennsylvania.
Donor(s): Superior Tube Company, Pacific Tube Company.
Financial data: (yr. ended 12/31/82): Assets, $2,846,621 (M); expenditures, $253,406, including $233,586 for 65 grants (high: $75,000; low: $20) and $8,750 for 17 grants to individuals.
Purpose and activities: Broad purposes; grants primarily for higher and secondary education, including scholarships for children of company employees, community funds, hospitals, health agencies, and music.
Types of support awarded: Employee related scholarships.
Application information: Application form required for scholarships. Application form required.
  Deadline(s): January 9
Officers and Directors: Clarence A. Warden, Jr., Chairman and President; Paul E. Kelly, Secretary-Treasurer; Richard H. Gabel.
Employer Identification Number: 236298237

3746
Tabas (Samuel) Family Foundation
915 North Delaware Ave.
Philadelphia 19123

Trust established in 1951 in Pennsylvania.
Donor(s): Members of the Tabas family.
Financial data: (yr. ended 5/31/83): Assets, $1,473,718 (M); gifts received, $36,040; expenditures, $73,069, including $68,846 for 125 grants (high: $10,500; low: $10).

Purpose and activities: Broad purposes; general giving, with emphasis on Jewish welfare funds, health services, and higher education.
Trustees: Charles L. Tabas, Daniel M. Tabas.
Employer Identification Number: 236254348

3747
Thomson (The John Edgar) Foundation
The Rittenhouse Claridge, Suite 318
Philadelphia 19103   (215) 545-6083

Endowment established in 1882 in Pennsylvania.
Donor(s): John Edgar Thomson.†
Financial data: (yr. ended 12/31/83): Assets, $3,607,107 (M); expenditures, $222,399, including $191,453 for foundation-administered programs.
Purpose and activities: A private operating foundation; active in the education and maintenance of daughters of deceased railroad employees.
Application information:
  Write: Gilda Verstein, Director
Officers: Gilda Verstein, Director; Richard A. Hanlon, Treasurer.
Trustees: H. William Brady, John J. Maher, Carl L. Rugart, Jr.
Number of staff: 1 full-time professional; 1 full-time support.
Employer Identification Number: 231382746

3748
Trexler (Harry C.) Trust ▼
1227 Hamilton St.
P.O. Box 303
Allentown 18105   (215) 434-9645

Trust established in 1934 in Pennsylvania.
Donor(s): Harry C. Trexler,† Mary M. Trexler.†
Financial data: (yr. ended 3/31/84): Assets, $30,971,473 (M); gifts received, $8,211; expenditures, $2,138,506, including $1,537,073 for 37 grants (high: $491,018; low: $1,000; average: $5,000-$50,000).
Purpose and activities: The will provides that one-fourth of the income shall be added to the corpus, one-fourth paid to the City of Allentown for park purposes, and the remainder distributed to such charitable organizations and objects as shall be "of the most benefit to humanity," but limited to Allentown and Lehigh County, particularly for hospitals, churches, institutions for the care of the crippled and orphans, youth agencies, social services, cultural programs, and support of ministerial students at two named Pennsylvania institutions.
Types of support awarded: Building funds, matching funds, general purposes, operating budgets, continuing support, land acquisition.
Limitations: Giving primarily in Allentown and Lehigh County, PA. No grants to individuals, or for endowment funds, research, scholarships, or fellowships; no loans.
Publications: Annual report, application guidelines.
Application information:
  Initial approach: Letter
  Copies of proposal: 5

Deadline(s): January 31 for consideration at annual fund distribution
Board meeting date(s): Monthly; however, grant distribution takes place annually after March 31
Final notification: May 1
Write: Thomas H. Christman, Secretary to the Trustees
Trustees: Dexter F. Baker, Chairman; William B. Butz, Carl J.W. Hessinger, Richard K. White, M.D., Joseph S. Young.
Staff: Thomas H. Christman, Secretary to the Trustees.
Number of staff: 2 full-time professional; 1 full-time support; 1 part-time support.
Employer Identification Number: 231162215

3749
Union Benevolent Association
c/o Nettie W. Taylor
One Parkway, 9th Fl.
Philadelphia 19101   (215) 466-4365

Incorporated in 1830 in Pennsylvania.
Financial data: (yr. ended 12/31/83): Assets, $1,292,092 (M); gifts received, $1,245; expenditures, $88,153, including $74,529 for 38 grants (high: $45,000; low: $995).
Purpose and activities: Local giving, for the encouragement of industry, suppression of pauperism, and relief of suffering among the worthy poor.
Limitations: Giving limited to the greater Philadelphia, PA, area. No support for national organizations or government agencies. No grants to individuals, or for capital funds, or deficit financing.
Publications: Program policy statement, application guidelines.
Application information:
  Initial approach: Letter
  Copies of proposal: 1
  Deadline(s): February 1, May 1, and December 1
  Board meeting date(s): February, May, and December
  Final notification: 3 months
  Write: Floyd W. Alston, Allocations Chairman
Board of Managers: Theodore T. Newbold, President; Martin A. Heckscher, G. Malcolm Laws, Jr., Vice-Presidents; John M. Register, Secretary; Lloyd M. Coates, Jr., Treasurer; Floyd W. Alston, Alan J. Davis, Mrs. Raymond K. Denworth, William L. Elkins, M.D., William J. Lee, Roberta G. Mason, Mrs. Samuel L. Taylor.
Number of staff: 1 part-time support.
Employer Identification Number: 231360861

3750
United States Steel Foundation, Inc. ▼
600 Grant St., Rm. 6284
Pittsburgh 15230   (412) 433-5237

Incorporated in 1953 in Delaware.
Donor(s): United States Steel Corporation, and certain subsidiaries.

Financial data: (yr. ended 11/30/84): Assets, $30,029,330 (M); expenditures, $6,943,546, including $6,811,090 for 387 grants (high: $860,000; low: $50) and $121,793 for 190 employee matching gifts.
Purpose and activities: Support to higher education, primarily the private sector, including college and university development grants, special purpose grants, project assistance, matching gifts, manpower development grants, and support to educational associations; scientific and research grants, including capital, operating, project, and research support; civic and cultural grants for capital and operating needs; medicine and health grants for research, capital, and operating purposes; and national and community social services support, including united funds, American Red Cross and other voluntary agencies.
Types of support awarded: General purposes, operating budgets, continuing support, annual campaigns, seed money, emergency funds, building funds, equipment, land acquisition, endowment funds, special projects, research, employee matching gifts.
Limitations: No support for publicly supported colleges and universities. No grants to individuals, or for conferences, seminars, travel, scholarships or fellowships, publications, or films; no loans.
Publications: Annual report, application guidelines.
Application information:
  Initial approach: Full proposal
  Copies of proposal: 1
  Deadline(s): Public, cultural, and scientific affairs - January 15; aid to education - April 15; medical, health, hospitals and national and community social services - July 15
  Board meeting date(s): As required
  Write: William A. Gregory, Jr., Manager
Officers: Peter B. Mulloney,* President; William E. Lewellen, Vice-President and Treasurer; G.O. Harrison, Vice-President - Investments; Charles A. Corry, Vice-President and Comptroller; Richard M. Hays, Secretary; William A. Gregory, Jr., Manager.
Trustees:* David M. Roderick, Chairman; W. Bruce Thomas, Vice-Chairman; Neil A. Armstrong, William O. Beers, John D. deButts, John H. Filer, David C. Garrett, Jr., James A.D. Geier, Thomas C. Graham, Raymond H. Herzog, Harold D. Hoopman, David C. Jones, John McGillicuddy, Walter H. Page, Robert C. Scrivener, Mark Shepherd, Jr., Donald B. Smiley, Cyrus R. Vance, T.A. Wilson.
Number of staff: 2 full-time professional; 2 full-time support.
Employer Identification Number: 136093185

3751
Vincent (Anna M.) Trust ⌐
c/o Girard Trust Bank
One Girard Plaza
Philadelphia 19101   (215) 585-3208
Application address: R. McKernan, Girard Bank, Three Girard Plaza, Philadelphia, PA 19101

Trust established in 1967 in Pennsylvania.

Donor(s): Anna M. Vincent.†
Financial data: (yr. ended 6/30/83): Assets, $2,378,425 (M); expenditures, $168,261, including $143,174 for 116 grants to individuals.
Purpose and activities: Scholarships for residents of Philadelphia and environs for graduate or undergraduate study at any recognized college, university, or other institution of higher learning.
Types of support awarded: Student aid.
Limitations: Giving limited to the Delaware Valley, PA, area. No grants for building or endowment funds, operating budgets, or special projects.
Application information: Application form required.
  Initial approach: Letter
  Copies of proposal: 1
  Deadline(s): Submit proposal preferably between January 15 and March 1; deadline March 1
  Board meeting date(s): March and April
Trustees: Robert I. Whitelaw, Girard Trust Bank.
Employer Identification Number: 236422666

3752
Walker (Alex C.) Educational and Charitable Foundation ⋈

c/o Pittsburgh National Bank
P.O. Box 747
Pittsburgh 15230   (412) 355-3628

Trust established in 1967 in Pennsylvania.
Donor(s): Alex C. Walker.†
Financial data: (yr. ended 12/31/81): Assets, $2,396,289 (M); expenditures, $166,273, including $140,290 for 18 grants (high: $35,000; low: $500).
Purpose and activities: Grants largely for research in the field of economics.
Types of support awarded: Research.
Limitations: No grants to individuals, or for building or endowment funds.
Publications: Program policy statement.
Application information:
  Initial approach: Proposal
  Copies of proposal: 1
  Board meeting date(s): Quarterly
  Write: Watson C. Marshall, Vice-President
Trustees: Barrett C. Walker, T. Urling Walker, Pittsburgh National Bank (Watson C. Marshall, Vice-President).
Employer Identification Number: 256109746

3753
Warren Foundation, The ⋈

P.O. Drawer 69
Warren 16365

Community foundation established in 1949 in Pennsylvania by declaration of trust.
Financial data: (yr. ended 12/31/81): Assets, $2,161,614 (M); gifts received, $77,722; expenditures, $172,724, including $100,163 for 35 grants (high: $23,373; low: $89) and $60,075 for 105 grants to individuals.

Purpose and activities: To promote the well-being of the local inhabitants; the bulk of funds has been designated as to use by the donors, with distributions for child welfare, church building maintenance, community funds, scholarships, and delinquency and crime prevention.
Types of support awarded: Student aid.
Limitations: Giving limited to Warren County, PA.
Application information:
  Write: Holger N. Elmquist, Director
Officers: Holger N. Elmquist, Director and Secretary; Gerald A. Huber, Assistant Director and Secretary.
Distribution Committee: W. Scott Calderwood, Chairman; Clare J. Crary, Mrs. Paul E. Harrington, Harry A. Logan, William R. Walker.
Trustees: Pennsylvania Bank and Trust Company, Warren National Bank.
Employer Identification Number: 256020340

3754
Waters (Robert S.) Charitable Trust ⋈

Mellon Bank, Rm. 2608
Mellon Square, P.O. Box 185
Pittsburgh 15230   (412) 234-5784

Trust established in 1952 in Pennsylvania.
Donor(s): Robert S. Waters.†
Financial data: (yr. ended 12/31/82): Assets, $1,410,230 (M); expenditures, $135,634, including $121,500 for 36 grants (high: $25,000; low: $500).
Purpose and activities: Primarily local giving, with emphasis on cultural programs, conservation, secondary education, social services, and historic preservation.
Limitations: Giving primarily in PA. No grants to individuals, or for scholarships and fellowships; no loans.
Application information: Application form required.
  Initial approach: Letter
  Copies of proposal: 2
  Deadline(s): September 1
  Board meeting date(s): September
  Write: Mrs. Barbara K. Robinson, Trust Officer
Trustees: John P. Davis, Jr., Mellon Bank (Barbara K. Robinson, Trust Officer).
Employer Identification Number: 256018986

3755
Weisbrod (Robert and Mary) Foundation ⋈

c/o The Union National Bank of Pittsburgh
P.O. Box 837
Pittsburgh 15230

Established in 1968 in Pennsylvania.
Donor(s): Mary E. Weisbrod.†
Financial data: (yr. ended 12/31/83): Assets, $5,251,350 (M); expenditures, $367,668, including $332,180 for 23 grants (high: $75,000; low: $1,000).
Purpose and activities: Broad purposes; primarily local giving, with emphasis on hospitals, social agencies, and a planetarium.

Limitations: Giving primarily in the Pittsburgh, PA, area.
Application information:
  Deadline(s): None
  Write: The Distribution Committee
Trustee: The Union National Bank of Pittsburgh (William R. Watkins, Vice-President).
Employer Identification Number: 256105924

3756
Westinghouse Educational Foundation ▼

Westinghouse Electric Company
Westinghouse Bldg., Rm. 806
Pittsburgh 15222   (412) 642-2419

Trust established in 1944 in Pennsylvania.
Donor(s): Westinghouse Electric Corporation.
Financial data: (yr. ended 12/31/84): Assets, $9,547,443 (M); gifts received, $2,000,000; expenditures, $3,578,008, including $2,621,465 for 94 grants (high: $50,000; low: $500; average: $10,000), $352,750 for 163 grants to individuals and $602,263 for 3,036 employee matching gifts.
Purpose and activities: Grants to colleges and universities for academic and development programs, almost exclusively in the fields of engineering and associated physical sciences, with maximum support of $50,000 per year for no more than a three-year period for any one institution; scholarships for children of employees; matching employee gifts; supports the annual Science Talent Search for high school seniors. Eligible colleges and universities must be four-year institutions with emphasis on engineering education and related science.
Types of support awarded: Continuing support, seed money, employee matching gifts, employee related scholarships, exchange programs, special projects.
Limitations: No support for medical education, humanities, graduate or pre-college education. No grants to individuals (except for scholarships for company employees), or for operating budgets, annual campaigns, emergency, capital, or endowment funds, deficit financing, professorships, research, publications, or conferences; no loans.
Publications: Annual report, informational brochure.
Application information:
  Initial approach: Letter
  Copies of proposal: 2
  Deadline(s): Submit proposal preferably from January through March, or June through August; deadline March 15 and September 15
  Board meeting date(s): May and November
  Final notification: 1 week after board meetings
  Write: Walter A. Schratz, Secretary
Officers: Walter A. Schratz, Secretary; Donald C. Korb, Treasurer.
Trustees: R.L. Reinhart, Chairman; W.O. Carlsen, E.J. Cattabiani, Merle E. Gilliand, Donald J. Povejsil, R.F. Pugliese, Chester A. Sadlow, M.C. Sardi, D.D. Stark, Leo W. Yochum.
Number of staff: None.
Employer Identification Number: 256037105

3757
Westinghouse Electric Fund ▼
Westinghouse Bldg.
Gateway Center
Pittsburgh 15222   (412) 642-3017

Trust established in 1952 in Pennsylvania.
Donor(s): Westinghouse Electric Corporation.
Financial data: (yr. ended 12/31/83): Assets,
$7,656,032 (M); expenditures, $2,373,911,
including $2,055,102 for 272 grants (high:
$65,000; low: $2,000; average: $5,000-
$15,000) and $251,658 for 3,474 employee
matching gifts.
Purpose and activities: General charitable
purposes; grants primarily for United Ways and
United Funds; some support for plant-
community hospitals, youth agencies, the
elderly, and the handicapped; selected cultural
grants in plant cities.
Types of support awarded: Special projects,
publications, employee matching gifts, building
funds.
Limitations: Giving primarily in areas of
company operations. No support for religious
organizations or specialized health campaigns.
No grants to individuals, or for general support,
equipment, operating budgets, annual
campaigns, continuing support, seed money,
land acquisition, renovation projects, deficit
financing, conferences, research, emergency or
endowment funds, or scholarships and
fellowships; no loans.
Publications: Annual report, application
guidelines.
Application information:
  Initial approach: Telephone or proposal
  Copies of proposal: 1
  Deadline(s): None
  Final notification: 2 months
  Write: C.M. Springer, Executive Director
Officer: C.M. Springer, Executive Director.
Trustees: M.C. Sardi, Chairman; W.O. Carlsen,
E.J. Cattabiani, M.E. Gilliand, D.J. Povejsil, R.F.
Pugliese, R.L. Reinhart, C.A. Sadlow, D.D.
Stark, Leo W. Yochum.
Number of staff: 4 full-time professional; 1
part-time support.
Employer Identification Number: 256029688

3758
**Westmoreland Coal Company and
  Penn Virginia Corporation
  Foundation** ⌑
2500 Fidelity Bldg.
Philadelphia 19109   (215) 545-2500

Trust established in 1974 in Pennsylvania.
Donor(s): Westmoreland Coal Company, Penn
Virginia Corporation.
Financial data: (yr. ended 12/31/82): Assets,
$1,752,906 (M); gifts received, $4,648;
expenditures, $213,898, including $18,500 for
5 grants and $175,495 for 206 grants to
individuals.
Purpose and activities: Grants primarily for
college scholarships to children of company
employees; some support for community
development in areas of company operations.
Types of support awarded: Employee related
scholarships.

Limitations: Giving primarily in areas of
company operations.
Application information: Application form
required for scholarships.
  Board meeting date(s): Annually
  Write: Philip D. Weinstock, Manager
Manager: Philip D. Weinstock.
Trustees: John L. Kemmerer, III, M.J.
McDonnell, H. Kenneth Nelson.
Employer Identification Number: 237398163

3759
Whalley Charitable Trust ⌑
1210 Graham Ave.
Windber 15963

Trust established in 1961 in Pennsylvania.
Donor(s): John J. Whalley, John Whalley, Jr.,
Mary Whalley.
Financial data: (yr. ended 12/31/83): Assets,
$1,817,918 (M); expenditures, $119,900,
including $105,909 for 38 grants (high:
$21,666; low: $25).
Purpose and activities: Primarily local giving,
with support for health, civic affairs, education,
religious organizations, and cultural programs.
Limitations: Giving primarily in PA.
Trustees: David Klementik, G. Lesko.
Employer Identification Number: 237128436

3760
**Wheeling-Pittsburgh Steel Foundation,
  Inc.**
c/o Thomas F. Frankart
P.O. Box 118
Pittsburgh 15230   (412) 288-3560

Incorporated in 1963 in West Virginia.
Donor(s): Wheeling-Pittsburgh Steel
Corporation.
Financial data: (yr. ended 12/31/84): Assets,
$156 (M); gifts received, $159,470;
expenditures, $159,470, including $159,470
for 23 grants (high: $50,000; low: $100).
Purpose and activities: Primarily local giving,
with emphasis on community funds; support
also for higher education and youth agencies.
Limitations: Giving primarily in PA.
Application information:
  Board meeting date(s): January
Officers: Dennis J. Carney,* President; George
Raynovich, Jr.,* Executive Vice-President;
Thomas F. Frankart, Secretary; John W. Testa,*
Treasurer.
Directors:* Robert F. Good, Roger C. McLean,
Manfred Rose.
Employer Identification Number: 556021213

3761
Whitaker Foundation, The ▼
875 Poplar Church Rd.
Camp Hill 17011   (717) 763-1391

Trust established in 1975 in New York.
Donor(s): U.A. Whitaker,† Helen F. Whitaker.†
Financial data: (yr. ended 2/29/84): Assets,
$157,893,494 (M); gifts received, $6,282,290;
expenditures, $5,119,385, including
$4,580,667 for 109 grants (high: $950,000;
low: $200).

Purpose and activities: Support for projects
which integrate engineering with biomedical
research at institutions in the United States,
including Puerto Rico; grants also to
community service agencies, educational
institutions, and cultural organizations in
Harrisburg, Pennsylvania and vicinity.
Types of support awarded: Seed money,
building funds, equipment, land acquisition,
matching funds, research, special projects.
Limitations: Giving primarily in the U.S.,
including Puerto Rico, for biomedical
engineering research programs; and in the
Harrisburg, PA, area for community service,
educational, and cultural organizations. No
support for sectarian religious purposes. No
grants to individuals, or for operating budgets
or established programs, deficit financing, or
endowment funds; no loans.
Publications: Program policy statement,
application guidelines.
Application information: Application
procedures are outlined in separate guidelines
for medical research grants and regional
program.
  Initial approach: Letter or telephone for
    regional program; preliminary application
    for medical research program
  Copies of proposal: 1
  Deadline(s): April 1, August 1, and
    December 1 for regional program
    proposals, and February 1, June 1 and
    October 1 for biomedical research and
    engineering program
  Board meeting date(s): February, June, and
    October
  Final notification: 5 months
  Write: Miles J. Gibbons, Jr., Executive
    Director
Officer: Miles J. Gibbons, Jr., Executive
Director.
Committee Members: C.J. Fredricksen,
Chairman; Allan W. Cowley, M.D., Eckley B.
Coxe, IV, G. Burtt Holmes, Ruth W. Holmes.
Trustee: Chemical Bank.
Number of staff: 1 full-time professional; 1
part-time professional; 1 full-time support; 1
part-time support.
Employer Identification Number: 222096948

3762
**Widener Memorial Foundation in Aid
  of Handicapped Children** ▼
665 Thomas Rd.
P.O. Box 178
Lafayette Hill 19444   (215) 836-7500

Incorporated in 1912 in Pennsylvania.
Donor(s): Peter A.B. Widener.†
Financial data: (yr. ended 12/31/83): Assets,
$2,315,230 (M); gifts received, $485,980;
expenditures, $441,884, including $433,833
for 12 grants (high: $130,000; low: $3,000;
average: $25,000-$50,000).
Purpose and activities: Local giving to support
research into the causes, treatment, and
prevention of diseases and conditions which
handicap children orthopedically; to aid and
assist public and private charitable institutions
and associations in the care, education, and
rehabilitation of children so handicapped.

Types of support awarded: Seed money, building funds, equipment, special projects, research.
Limitations: Giving limited to Delaware Valley, PA. No grants to individuals, or for endowment funds, scholarships and fellowships, or matching gifts; no loans.
Publications: Application guidelines.
Application information:
Initial approach: Letter
Copies of proposal: 1
Deadline(s): April 30
Board meeting date(s): May and November
Final notification: Immediately after board meetings
Write: F. Eugene Dixon, Jr., President
Officers: F. Eugene Dixon, Jr.,* President; Peter M. Mattoon,* Vice-President; John E. Albrecht, Jr., Secretary and Treasurer.
Trustees:* Bruce L. Castor, Edith Robb Dixon, George Widener Dixon, John H. Wolf, Sr., M.D.
Number of staff: None.
Employer Identification Number: 236267223

3763
Williams (John C.) Charitable Trust ⌐
c/o Pittsburgh National Bank
Trust Division, 29th Fl.
Pittsburgh 15265   (412) 355-2000

Trust established in 1936 in Pennsylvania.
Donor(s): John C. Williams.†
Financial data: (yr. ended 12/31/82): Assets, $2,925,219 (M); expenditures, $299,890, including $275,000 for 8 grants (high: $105,000; low: $10,000).
Purpose and activities: For the benefit of the communities of Steubenville, Ohio, and Weirton, West Virginia, with emphasis on higher education, hospitals, a community center, and youth agencies.
Limitations: Giving limited to Steubenville, OH, and Weirton, WV. No grants to individuals, or for fellowships or matching gifts; no loans.
Publications: Application guidelines.
Application information: Application form required.
Initial approach: Letter
Copies of proposal: 3
Deadline(s): None
Board meeting date(s): March and September
Write: R. Steven Bonnett, Vice-President
Trustee: Pittsburgh National Bank (R. Steven Bonnett, Vice-President).
Employer Identification Number: 256024153

3764
Williamsport Foundation ▼ ⌐
102 West Fourth St.
Williamsport 17701   (717) 326-2611

Community foundation established in 1916 in Pennsylvania by bank resolution.
Financial data: (yr. ended 12/31/83): Assets, $16,821,254 (M); expenditures, $1,095,562, including $899,945 for 84 grants (high: $115,000; low: $24; average: $1,000-$30,000) and $130,409 for 4 loans.

Purpose and activities: Charitable purposes; distribution of funds to serve the needs of Williamsport and vicinity, particularly in educational, social service, or recreational projects; giving for higher education, civic affairs, cultural programs, health and hospitals, and youth agencies.
Types of support awarded: Building funds, emergency funds, equipment, general purposes, matching funds, program-related investments, research, seed money, special projects, loans.
Limitations: Giving limited to organizations located in the greater Williamsport, PA, area. No grants to individuals, or for endowment funds or operating budgets.
Publications: Annual report.
Application information:
Initial approach: Letter
Copies of proposal: 5
Deadline(s): None
Board meeting date(s): At least 4 times a year
Final notification: 2 months
Write: Harold D. Hershberger, Jr., Secretary
Officer: Harold D. Hershberger, Jr.,* Secretary.
Administrative Committee:* John E. Person, Jr., Chairman; Ralph R. Cranmer, William E. Nichols, Jr., Mary Elizabeth Stockwell.
Trustees: Bank of Central Pennsylvania, Commonwealth Bank & Trust Company, Northern Central Bank, Williamsport National Bank.
Employer Identification Number: 246013117

3765
Wolf (Benjamin & Fredora) Foundation
Park Towne Place - North Bldg. 1205
Philadelphia 19130   (215) 787-6079

Incorporated in 1955 in Pennsylvania.
Donor(s): Fredora K. Wolf.†
Financial data: (yr. ended 5/31/84): Assets, $1,137,527 (M); expenditures, $109,097, including $94,250 for 108 grants to individuals.
Purpose and activities: Local giving to individuals for college scholarships.
Types of support awarded: Student aid.
Limitations: Giving primarily in the Philadelphia, PA, area. No grants for any purposes except scholarships; no loans.
Application information: Application form required.
Copies of proposal: 1
Deadline(s): June 1
Board meeting date(s): June and December
Write: Dr. David A. Horowitz, Administrator
Officers: Max Kohn, President; Mrs. Howard Hurtig, Vice-President; Mrs. Herbert Fogel, Secretary; Richard I. Abrahams, Treasurer.
Trustees: Mrs. John Briscoe, Mrs. J. Ronald Gray, John Tuton, Clarence Wolf, Mrs. Edwin Wolf.
Number of staff: 1 part-time support.
Employer Identification Number: 236207344

3766
Wurts (Henrietta Tower) Memorial
c/o Fidelity Bank
135 South Broad St.
Philadelphia 19109   (215) 985-7320

Incorporated in 1934 in Pennsylvania.

Donor(s): Henrietta Tower Wurts.†
Financial data: (yr. ended 12/31/83): Assets, $1,738,742 (M); expenditures, $118,988, including $113,170 for 47 grants (high: $5,000; low: $1,000; average: $1,000-$5,000).
Purpose and activities: To contribute to nonsectarian corporate institutions in the Philadelphia area only, which are engaged in helping or caring for people in need or alleviating the conditions under which they live.
Types of support awarded: General purposes, building funds, equipment, operating budgets, continuing support, annual campaigns, seed money, emergency funds.
Limitations: Giving limited to Philadelphia, PA. No grants to individuals, or for endowment funds, scholarships or fellowships, or matching gifts; no loans.
Publications: Application guidelines.
Application information: Application form required.
Initial approach: Letter
Copies of proposal: 1
Deadline(s): Submit proposal preferably before January 1, May 1, or September 1
Board meeting date(s): February, June, and October
Final notification: 2 weeks after meeting
Write: Paul B. Kurtz, Secretary
Officers and Directors: S. Stoney Simons, President; Mrs. Henry T. Reath, Vice-President; Paul B. Kurtz, Secretary; The Fidelity Bank, Treasurer; Mrs. M. Carton Dittmann, Jr., Lillian Gest, Howard Kellogg, Edith A. Reinhardt, Sidney N. Repplier, Richard Ferree Smith.
Number of staff: None.
Employer Identification Number: 236297977

3767
Wyomissing Foundation, Inc. ▼
1015 Penn Ave.
Wyomissing 19610   (215) 376-7496

Incorporated in 1929 in Delaware.
Donor(s): Ferdinand Thun,† and family.
Financial data: (yr. ended 12/31/84): Assets, $8,958,759 (M); expenditures, $714,924, including $613,250 for 55 grants (high: $250,000; low: $500; average: $1,000-$10,000).
Purpose and activities: Charitable purposes; primarily local giving with emphasis on hospitals, higher education, civic affairs, youth and social service agencies, and a community fund; support also for conservation and music.
Types of support awarded: Operating budgets, continuing support, annual campaigns, seed money, emergency funds, building funds, equipment, matching funds.
Limitations: Giving primarily in Berks County, PA and contiguous counties. No grants to individuals, or for endowment funds, deficit financing, land acquisition, demonstration projects, publications, conferences, scholarships, or fellowships; no loans.
Publications: Program policy statement, application guidelines.
Application information:
Initial approach: Proposal letter not exceeding 2 pages (excluding supporting materials)
Copies of proposal: 1

Deadline(s): Submit proposal preferably in February, May, August, or October; deadline 25th of month preceding board meeting

Board meeting date(s): March, June, September, and November

Final notification: 3 months

Write: Lawrence A. Walsky, Secretary

Officers: Louis R. Thun,* President; Ferdinand K. Thun,* Vice-President; Lawrence A. Walsky, Secretary and Treasurer.

Trustees:* Thomas A. Beaver, Mrs. Harvey M. Buckman, Anna M. Cherney, Mrs. Herbert Karasin, Sidney D. Kline, Jr., John G. Williams.

Number of staff: 1 part-time professional; 2 part-time support.

Employer Identification Number: 231980570

3768
Yarway Foundation ⌀
Norristown and Narcissa Rd.s
Blue Bell 19422   (215) 825-2100

Trust established in 1959 in Pennsylvania.
Donor(s): Yarway Corporation.
Financial data: (yr. ended 12/31/83): Assets, $356,782 (M); expenditures, $104,882, including $89,850 for 39 grants (high: $39,600; low: $200) and $14,000 for 5 grants to individuals.
Purpose and activities: Broad purposes; primarily local giving, with emphasis on higher education, including the D. Robert Yarnell-Bernard G. Waring Scholarship Award Program for children of company employees, and a community fund.
Types of support awarded: Employee related scholarships.
Limitations: Giving primarily in PA.
Application information: Application form required.
 Deadline(s): November 15
 Write: Jean Harland, Personnel Department
Trustees: Theodore B. Palmer, 3rd, George I. Tyndall, D. Robert Yarnall, Jr.
Employer Identification Number: 236265621

PUERTO RICO

3769
Harvey Foundation, Inc. ⌀
507 First Federal Bldg.
1519 Ponce de Leon Ave.
Santurce 00909

Incorporated in 1963 in Puerto Rico.
Financial data: (yr. ended 12/31/83): Assets, $1,108,440 (M); expenditures, $99,531, including $71,500 for 9 grants (high: $25,000; low: $500) and $12,039 for 5 grants to individuals.

Purpose and activities: Primarily local giving, with emphasis on higher education, including scholarships.
Types of support awarded: Scholarship funds, general purposes, student aid.
Limitations: Giving primarily in PR.
Officers: Arthur J. Harvey, Jr., President; Gertrude Harvey, Vice-President; Alfonso Miranda, Secretary; Charles M. Hitt, Treasurer.
Employer Identification Number: 660271454

RHODE ISLAND

3770
Alperin Foundation, The ⌀
160 Taunton Ave.
East Providence 02914

Established in 1956 in Rhode Island.
Donor(s): Members of the Alperin family.
Financial data: (yr. ended 4/30/83): Assets, $2,523,178 (M); gifts received, $259,449; expenditures, $327,436, including $81,284 for 138 grants (high: $16,850; low: $10).
Purpose and activities: Broad purposes; giving largely for Jewish welfare funds, higher and secondary education, including religious education, and temple support.
Trustees: Barry Alperin, Max Alperin, Melvin G. Alperin, Ruth Alperin, David Hirsch.
Employer Identification Number: 056008387

3771
Armbrust Foundation ⌀
735 Allens Ave.
Providence 02905

Trust established about 1951 in Rhode Island.
Donor(s): Armbrust Chain Company.
Financial data: (yr. ended 12/31/83): Assets, $1,124,686 (M); expenditures, $54,810, including $53,760 for 43 grants (high: $11,500; low: $35).
Purpose and activities: Primarily local giving, with emphasis on a community fund, Protestant church support, and hospitals; support also for higher education, cultural programs, and youth agencies.
Limitations: Giving primarily in RI.
Trustees: Adelaide P. Armbrust, Howard W. Armbrust.
Employer Identification Number: 056088332

3772
Champlin Foundations ▼
P.O. Box 637
Providence 02901   (401) 421-3719

Trusts established in 1932, 1947, and 1975 in Delaware.

Donor(s): George S. Champlin,† Florence C. Hamilton,† Hope C. Neaves.
Financial data: (yr. ended 12/31/84): Assets, $110,979,215 (M); gifts received, $500,000; expenditures, $8,094,187, including $7,296,539 for 98 grants (high: $510,000; low: $3,000; average: $25,000-$50,000).
Purpose and activities: Primarily local giving for education, health, historic preservation, libraries, scientific and cultural activities, youth, elderly, and social services.
Types of support awarded: Building funds, equipment, land acquisition, endowment funds.
Limitations: Giving primarily in RI. No grants to individuals, or for general support, program or operating budgets, matching gifts, special projects, research, publications, or conferences; no loans.
Publications: Informational brochure, program policy statement, application guidelines.
Application information:
 Initial approach: Letter
 Copies of proposal: 1
 Deadline(s): Submit proposal preferably between April 1 and August 31; deadline August 31
 Board meeting date(s): Distribution Committee meets in November
 Final notification: After November meeting
 Write: David A. King, Executive Director
Distribution Committee: Francis C. Carter, John Gorham, Louis R. Hampton, Robert W. Kenyon, David A. King, Norma B. LaFreniere, John W. Linnell, Mario F. Veltri.
Trustee: Bank of Delaware.
Number of staff: 3 part-time professional; 1 part-time support.
Employer Identification Number: 516010168

3773
Citizens Charitable Foundation
c/o Citizens Trust Company
870 Westminster St.
Providence 02903   (401) 456-7285

Established in 1967 in Rhode Island.
Donor(s): Citizens Savings Bank, FSB; Citizens Trust Company.
Financial data: (yr. ended 12/31/84): Assets, $638,626 (M); gifts received, $225,000; expenditures, $233,389, including $228,173 for 54 grants (high: $115,500; low: $300).
Purpose and activities: Local giving, with emphasis on community funds, higher education, hospitals, arts and culture, and youth and civic agencies.
Types of support awarded: Building funds, equipment, land acquisition, special projects, technical assistance, employee related scholarships.
Limitations: Giving primarily in RI. No support for United Way member agencies except for capital funds. No grants to individuals, or for endowment funds, general support, research programs, or matching gifts; no loans.
Publications: Program policy statement, application guidelines.
Application information:
 Initial approach: Letter
 Copies of proposal: 6
 Deadline(s): Submit proposal preferably in June; no set deadline

Board meeting date(s): January, April, July, and October
Final notification: 3 to 6 months
Write: D. Faye Sanders, Principal Manager
Trustees: Jonathan A. Barnes, Flordeliza G. Inonog, D. Faye Sanders, James H. Sweet.
Number of staff: None.
Employer Identification Number: 056022653

3774
Cranston Foundation, The ⋈
c/o Administrator
1381 Cranston St.
Cranston 02920   (401) 943-4800

Trust established in 1960 in Rhode Island.
Donor(s): Cranston Print Works Company.
Financial data: (yr. ended 6/30/83): Assets, $668,228 (M); gifts received, $119,572; expenditures, $207,988, including $103,994 for 102 grants (high: $10,000; low: $49) and $99,878 for 47 grants to individuals.
Purpose and activities: Broad purposes; grants largely for higher education, including a scholarship program for children of Cranston Corporation employees. Support also for community funds, hospitals, and cultural programs, primarily in Massachusetts and Rhode Island.
Types of support awarded: Employee related scholarships.
Limitations: Giving primarily in RI and MA.
Application information:
Initial approach: Full proposal
Deadline(s): April 15
Board meeting date(s): At least quarterly
Trustees: Leo G. Hutchings, Frederic L. Rockefeller, Richard Schein, George W. Shuster.
Employer Identification Number: 056015348

3775
Fleet Charitable Trust
111 Westminster St.
Providence 02903   (401) 278-6449

Trust established in 1955 in Rhode Island.
Donor(s): Fleet National Bank.
Financial data: (yr. ended 12/31/82): Assets, $4,038,265 (M); expenditures, $64,921, including $59,148 for 98 grants (high: $20,000; low: $15) and $4,265 for 22 employee matching gifts.
Purpose and activities: Restricted to Rhode Island-based organizations. Grants generally for capital purposes of major charities, including United Way, higher education, including an employee matching gift program, and hospitals. Support also for work/study scholarships paid to colleges on behalf of Rhode Island high school seniors from minority groups.
Types of support awarded: Operating budgets, continuing support, annual campaigns, seed money, emergency funds, building funds, equipment, land acquisition, special projects, scholarship funds, employee matching gifts.
Limitations: Giving limited to RI-based organizations. No grants to individuals or for endowment funds; no loans.
Publications: Application guidelines.
Application information:

Initial approach: Proposal
Copies of proposal: 1
Deadline(s): None
Board meeting date(s): As required
Final notification: 2 months after board meeting
Write: Ms. Georgina Macdonald, Vice-President
Trustee: Fleet National Bank.
Number of staff: None.
Employer Identification Number: 056007619

3776
Galkin (Ira S. and Anna) Charitable Trust ⋈
36 Freeman St.
Pawtucket 02862

Trust established in 1947 in Rhode Island.
Donor(s): Ira S. Galkin.
Financial data: (yr. ended 12/31/82): Assets, $1,768,007 (M); gifts received, $100,000; expenditures, $124,466, including $120,278 for 156 grants (high: $35,000; low: $10).
Purpose and activities: Broad purposes; primarily local giving, with emphasis on hospitals, Jewish and community welfare funds, temple support, and higher education, including medical education.
Limitations: Giving primarily in RI.
Application information:
Write: Ira S. Galkin, Trustee
Trustees: Anna Galkin, Arnold T. Galkin, Ira S. Galkin.
Employer Identification Number: 056006231

3777
Genesis Foundation
173 Waterman St.
Providence 02906   (401) 861-4323

Established in 1981 in Rhode Island.
Donor(s): Solon Foundation.
Financial data: (yr. ended 12/31/82): Assets, $46,725 (M); gifts received, $265,000; expenditures, $228,999, including $129,148 for 8 grants (high: $32,000; low: $25; average: $10-$50,000).
Purpose and activities: Emphasis on pre-school, primary, secondary and adult basic educational needs in rural areas of southern Africa through financial assistance to schools and other educational resources; some support for adult basic educational needs of selected refugee populations in a few urban areas of the northeastern United States in cases where government support is not available.
Types of support awarded: Scholarship funds, special projects, seed money, equipment, matching funds, consulting services, technical assistance.

Limitations: Giving limited to rural areas of Botswana, Lesotho, South Africa, Swaziland, Zimbabwe, and for minorities in the northeastern U.S. No support for non-educational programs, education in urban areas, or sectarian education. No grants to individuals, or for operating budgets, building funds, continuing support, annual campaigns, emergency funds, deficit financing, land acquisition, renovation projects, endowments, employee-matching gifts, research, publications, or conferences and seminars; no loans.
Publications: Program policy statement, application guidelines.
Application information:
Initial approach: Letter or telephone
Copies of proposal: 1
Deadline(s): March 31 and June 30
Board meeting date(s): Annually
Final notification: 4 months
Write: John K. Harwood, President
Officer and Directors: John K. Harwood, President, Treasurer and Secretary; Charlynn W. Goins, John W. Mattern.
Number of staff: 1 full-time professional; 1 full-time support.
Employer Identification Number: 050391649

3778
Haffenreffer Family Fund ⋈
c/o Fleet National Bank
100 Westminster St.
Providence 02903

Trust established in 1943 in Rhode Island.
Donor(s): Members of the Haffenreffer family.
Financial data: (yr. ended 12/31/82): Assets, $2,826,338 (M); gifts received, $2,742; expenditures, $209,912, including $183,694 for 128 grants (high: $8,197; low: $100).
Purpose and activities: Assistance to charitable and educational institutions in which members of the family are actively interested, with emphasis on higher and secondary education, community funds, church support, cultural programs, and hospitals, largely in Rhode Island and southeastern New England.
Limitations: Giving primarily in RI and southeastern New England.
Trustees: Jean H. Baker, Carl W. Haffenreffer, Carolyn B. Haffenreffer, David H. Haffenreffer, Karl Haffenreffer, Rudolph F. Haffenreffer III, R.F. Haffenreffer IV, Virginie P. Haffenreffer, Fleet National Bank.
Employer Identification Number: 056012787

3779
Hassenfeld Foundation, The
1027 Newport Ave.
Pawtucket 02861   (401) 726-4100

Established in 1944 in Rhode Island.
Donor(s): Hastor Industries Inc., and other members of the Hassenfeld family.
Financial data: (yr. ended 12/31/82): Assets, $129,249 (M); gifts received, $344,500; expenditures, $473,672, including $469,357 for 9 grants (high: $311,757; low: $100).

Purpose and activities: Giving primarily for Jewish welfare funds; grants also for higher education, including religious education.
Officers and Directors: Sylvia Hassenfeld, Vice-President; Stephen Hassenfeld, Secretary and Treasurer; Carmel Joan Engle, Alan Hassenfeld, Leon S. Mann, Frank Supnick.
Employer Identification Number: 056015373

3780
Johnstone (Phyllis Kimball) and H. Earle Kimball Foundation ⊭
c/o Rhode Island Hospital Trust National Bank
One Hospital Trust Plaza
Providence 02903

Established in 1957 in Delaware.
Donor(s): Phyllis Kimball Johnstone.†
Financial data: (yr. ended 11/30/82): Assets, $2,670,563 (M); expenditures, $233,138, including $209,932 for 36 grants (high: $34,000; low: $300).
Purpose and activities: Broad purposes; primarily local giving, with emphasis on hospitals, and youth agencies; grants also for a community fund.
Limitations: Giving primarily in RI.
Trustees: John R. Fales, Jr., Gordon A. Feiner, Avery Seaman, Jr.
Employer Identification Number: 056015723

3781
Kimball (Horace A.) and S. Ella Kimball Foundation ⊭
c/o Rhode Island Hospital Trust National Bank
One Hospital Trust Plaza
Providence 02903

Incorporated in 1956 in Delaware.
Donor(s): H. Earle Kimball.†
Financial data: (yr. ended 9/30/82): Assets, $2,319,017 (M); expenditures, $246,943, including $227,450 for 24 grants (high: $40,000; low: $500).
Purpose and activities: Broad purposes; primarily local giving, with emphasis on health services, secondary education, community funds, youth agencies, and cultural programs.
Limitations: Giving primarily in RI.
Trustees: Thomas F. Black, Jr., Thomas F. Black, III, Dexter Clarke.
Employer Identification Number: 056006130

3782
Koffler Family Foundation, The ⊭
c/o The Koffler Corporation
170 Westminster St., Suite 640
Providence 02903

Established in 1978 in Rhode Island.
Donor(s): The Koffler Corporation.
Financial data: (yr. ended 7/31/83): Assets, $2,284,359 (M); expenditures, $246,463, including $234,758 for 108 grants (high: $158,452; low: $5).
Purpose and activities: Primarily local giving to Jewish welfare funds and religious organizations, and higher education.

Limitations: Giving primarily in RI.
Trustees: Leonard Granoff, Lillian Koffler, Sol Koffler.
Employer Identification Number: 050376269

3783
Little Family Foundation
c/o Fleet National Bank
100 Westminster St.
Providence 02903

Trust established in 1946 in Rhode Island.
Donor(s): Royal Little.
Financial data: (yr. ended 12/31/83): Assets, $9,200,000 (M); expenditures, $300,000, including $235,000 for 62 grants (high: $40,000; low: $100) and $65,000 for 29 grants to individuals.
Purpose and activities: Giving primarily for higher and secondary education including scholarship funds, a science museum, youth development agencies, cultural programs, and hospitals.
Types of support awarded: Operating budgets, continuing support, annual campaigns, emergency funds, building funds, equipment, endowment funds, matching funds, scholarship funds, fellowships.
Limitations: No grants for seed money, deficit financing, or land acquisition; no loans.
Publications: Application guidelines.
Application information:
Initial approach: Letter
Write: Deborah DiNardo, Trust Representative
Trustees: Augusta Willoughby Little Bishop, E. Janice Leeming, Arthur D. Little, Royal Little, Fleet National Bank (Deborah DiNardo, Trust Representative).
Employer Identification Number: 056016740

3784
Morgan (The Roy T.) Foundation
115 South Main St.
Providence 02903   (401) 751-1500

Trust established in Rhode Island.
Donor(s): Roy T. Morgan.†
Financial data: (yr. ended 3/31/83): Assets, $1,611,900 (M); expenditures, $121,293, including $100,000 for 5 grants (high: $35,000; low: $15,000).
Purpose and activities: Grants in New England for the care and treatment of handicapped children and adults; support also for hospitals.
Limitations: Giving primarily in New England. No grants for endowment funds, scholarships, fellowships, or matching gifts; no loans.
Application information:
Initial approach: Letter
Copies of proposal: 3
Deadline(s): March 1
Board meeting date(s): March, June, September, and December
Write: Walter F. Gibbons, Trustee
Trustees: Russell S. Boles, Jr., M.D., Walter F. Gibbons, Vaughn G. Gooding.
Employer Identification Number: 050368103

3785
Newport Restoration Foundation
2 Marlborough St.
Newport 02840

Established in 1968 in Rhode Island.
Donor(s): Doris Duke.
Financial data: (yr. ended 12/31/82): Assets, $14,133,628 (M); expenditures, $682,242, including $194,782 for 1 foundation-administered program.
Purpose and activities: A private operating foundation. Broad purposes; operating programs and grants for restoration and preservation of architecturally or historically significant buildings primarily in the county of Newport; collection and exhibition to the public of articles having historic or geographic interest; establishment and maintenance of craft centers for teaching and display of handicrafts characteristic of the area during the colonial period.
Limitations: Giving primarily in Newport County, RI.
Officers: Doris Duke,* President and Treasurer; Marion Charles,* Jacqueline K. Onassis,* Vice-Presidents; Benjamin Reed, Manager.
Trustees:* J. Carter Brown.
Number of staff: 3 full-time professional; 15 full-time support; 10 part-time support.
Employer Identification Number: 050317816

3786
Old Stone Bank Charitable Foundation
180 South Main St.
Providence 02903   (401) 278-2213

Established in 1969 in Rhode Island.
Donor(s): Old Stone Bank.
Financial data: (yr. ended 12/31/84): Assets, $518,089 (M); gifts received, $590,000; expenditures, $251,653, including $238,798 for 24 grants (high: $140,000; low: $150) and $12,855 for 124 employee matching gifts.
Purpose and activities: Broad purposes; local giving, with emphasis on community funds, education, cultural activities, and social services.
Types of support awarded: Seed money, building funds, land acquisition, program-related investments, employee matching gifts, special projects.
Limitations: Giving limited to RI. No grants to individuals, or for endowment funds, scholarships and fellowships, or general operating support; no loans.
Publications: Annual report, program policy statement, application guidelines.
Application information:
Initial approach: Letter or telephone
Copies of proposal: 1
Deadline(s): First day of months when board meets
Board meeting date(s): Bimonthly beginning in January
Final notification: 4 to 6 weeks
Write: Kay H. Low, Coordinator

Distribution Committee: Allen H. Howland, Chairman; Kay H. Low, Coordinator; Theodore W. Barnes, Ernest Corner, Thomas P. Dimeo, Bayard Ewing, Beverly E. Ledbetter, Winfield W. Major, Thomas F. Schutte.
Number of staff: 1 part-time professional.
Employer Identification Number: 237029175

3787
Providence Journal Charitable Foundation ☼
75 Fountain St.
Providence 02902   (401) 277-7205

Trust established in 1956 in Rhode Island.
Donor(s): Providence Journal Co.
Financial data: (yr. ended 12/31/82): Assets, $26,399 (M); gifts received, $200,000; expenditures, $193,145, including $192,416 for 33 grants (high: $73,000; low: $250).
Purpose and activities: Primarily local giving, with emphasis on higher education and a community fund; support also for youth agencies, cultural programs, and hospitals.
Limitations: Giving primarily in RI. No grants to individuals.
Application information:
  Initial approach: Letter or proposal
  Copies of proposal: 1
  Deadline(s): None
  Board meeting date(s): Monthly
  Write: William G. Chafee, Trustee
Trustees: William G. Chafee, Benjamin L. Cook, Jr., Norman M. Fain, Paul C. Nicholson, Jr., John C.A. Watkins.
Employer Identification Number: 056015372

3788
Rapaporte (The Samuel), Jr. Foundation ☼
395 Rochambeau Ave.
Providence 02906

Trust established in 1946 in Rhode Island.
Financial data: (yr. ended 11/30/83): Assets, $1,059,573 (M); expenditures, $86,045, including $83,842 for 43 grants (high: $47,000; low: $10).
Purpose and activities: Primarily local giving for social services, education, and health, with emphasis on Jewish organizations.
Limitations: Giving primarily in RI.
Trustees: Riepa Rapaporte, Samuel Rapaporte, Jr.
Employer Identification Number: 056006254

3789
Ress Family Foundation ☼
c/o Joseph W. Ress, Trustee
P.O. Box 6485
Providence 02940

Trust established in 1955 in Rhode Island.
Donor(s): Joseph W. Ress, Anne Ress.
Financial data: (yr. ended 12/31/82): Assets, $1,032,304 (M); gifts received, $10,400; expenditures, $114,637, including $96,551 for 67 grants (high: $34,350; low: $10).

Purpose and activities: Broad purposes; primarily local giving, with emphasis on Jewish welfare funds and temple support, higher education, and health.
Limitations: Giving primarily in RI.
Trustee: Ivan Ress Reeves, Joseph W. Ress.
Employer Identification Number: 056006308

3790
Rhode Island Foundation, The ▼
957 North Main St.
Providence 02904   (401) 274-4564

Community foundation incorporated in 1916 in Rhode Island.
Financial data: (yr. ended 12/31/82): Assets, $33,071,397 (M); gifts received, $1,185,604; expenditures, $2,863,191, including $2,609,502 for 200 grants (high: $125,000; low: $500).
Purpose and activities: To promote educational and charitable activities which will tend to improve the living conditions and well-being of the inhabitants of Rhode Island; grants for capital and operating purposes principally to Rhode Island agencies working in the fields of education, health care, the arts and cultural affairs, youth, the aged, social services, urban affairs, historic preservation, and the environment. Some restricted grants for scholarships and medical research.
Types of support awarded:
Operating budgets, seed money, emergency funds, building funds, equipment, land acquisition, matching funds, consulting services, technical assistance, special projects, scholarship funds, research, publications, conferences and seminars.
Limitations: Giving limited to RI. No support for sectarian organizations or medical research except as specified by donors. No grants to individuals, or for endowment funds or operating deficits; no loans.
Publications: Annual report, program policy statement, application guidelines.
Application information: Priority given to first 25 applications received prior to each board meeting.
  Initial approach: Telephone, meeting, letter, or full proposal
  Copies of proposal: 8
  Board meeting date(s): January, March, May, July, September, and November
  Final notification: 3 months
  Write: Douglas M. Jansson, Executive Director
Officer: Douglas M. Jansson, Secretary and Executive Director.
Distribution Committee: Robert H.I. Goddard, Chairman; Mrs. F. Steele Blackall, III, Norman M. Fain, Andrew M. Hunt, Frank Licht, Bancroft Littlefield, Erskine N. White, Jr.
Trustee: The Rhode Island Hospital Trust National Bank.
Number of staff: 1 full-time professional; 2 part-time professional; 1 full-time support; 1 part-time support.
Employer Identification Number: 050208270

3791
Roddy (Fred M.) Foundation, Inc. ☼
Rhode Island Hospital Trust Nat'l Bank
One Hospital Trust Plaza
Providence 02903

Trust established in 1969.
Donor(s): Fred M. Roddy.†
Financial data: (yr. ended 12/31/82): Assets, $5,485,326 (M); expenditures, $414,367, including $355,720 for 22 grants (high: $100,000; low: $2,500).
Purpose and activities: General purposes; giving primarily in Rhode Island and Massachusetts, with grants for higher education and medical research; support also for hospitals.
Limitations: Giving primarily in RI and MA.
Directors: Lee Kintzel, John W. McIntyre.
Employer Identification Number: 056037528

3792
Textron Charitable Trust, The ▼
P.O. Box 878
Providence 02901   (401) 421-2800

Trust established in 1953 in Vermont.
Donor(s): Textron Inc.
Financial data: (yr. ended 12/31/83): Assets, $11,882,543 (M); expenditures, $1,373,438, including $1,038,121 for 265 grants (high: $110,000; low: $100; average: $500-$50,000) and $291,998 for 522 employee matching gifts.
Purpose and activities: General charitable purposes; giving primarily for community funds, higher education, including National Merit Scholarships; hospitals, and youth agencies; support also for urban programs, minorities, health agencies, and cultural programs.
Types of support awarded: Building funds, equipment, matching funds, employee matching gifts, technical assistance, employee related scholarships.
Limitations: Giving primarily in areas of company operations nationwide, with emphasis on the Providence, RI, area. No grants to individuals, or for endowment funds, land acquisition, deficit financing, research, demonstration projects, publications, or conferences; no loans.
Publications: Application guidelines.
Application information:
  Initial approach: Full proposal
  Copies of proposal: 1
  Deadline(s): None
  Board meeting date(s): Monthly
  Final notification: 8 weeks
  Write: Delores A. Francis, Manager - Corporate Contributions
Contributions Committee: Raymond W. Caine, Jr., Chairman.
Trustee: Rhode Island Hospital Trust National Bank.
Number of staff: 1 full-time professional.
Employer Identification Number: 256115832

3793
Watson (The Thomas J.) Foundation ▼
217 Angell St.
Providence 02906   (401) 274-1952

Trust established in 1961 in New York.
Donor(s): Jeannette K. Watson,† Arthur K.
Watson,† Thomas J. Watson, Jr.
Financial data: (yr. ended 5/31/84): Assets,
$32,937,984 (M); gifts received, $809,080;
expenditures, $2,064,087, including
$1,705,660 for 47 grants (high: $1,000,000;
low: $1,500; average: $10,000-$30,000).
Purpose and activities: Sponsors fellowship
program for independent study and travel
abroad through 50 colleges and universities;
occasional other foundation-initiated grants.
Types of support awarded: Fellowships.
Publications: Informational brochure.
Application information: Applicant must be
nominated by her/his college and must be a
graduating senior. Application form required.
Deadline(s): Nomination deadline November
5
Final notification: March 15
Write: Joseph V. Long III, Executive Director
Officers: Joseph V. Long III, Executive
Director; David McKinney,* Executive
Secretary.
Advisory Committee:* Helen Watson
Buckner, Thomas J. Watson, Jr., Thomas J.
Watson III.
Trustee: Morgan Guaranty Trust Company of
New York.
Number of staff: 2 full-time professional.
Employer Identification Number: 136038151

SOUTH CAROLINA

3794
Abney Foundation, The ▼
P.O. Box 1138
Greenwood 29648   (803) 229-5777

Trust established in 1957 in South Carolina.
Donor(s): John S. Abney,† Mrs. Susie M.
Abney,† and others.
Financial data: (yr. ended 12/31/84): Assets,
$17,324,787 (M); expenditures, $817,764,
including $727,275 for 23 grants (high:
$500,000; low: $250; average: $250-$12,000).
Purpose and activities: Primarily local giving,
with emphasis on higher education.
Types of support awarded: Annual
campaigns, seed money, emergency funds,
building funds, land acquisition, general
purposes, endowment funds, research,
scholarship funds, fellowships, professorships,
internships, continuing support.
Limitations: Giving primarily in SC. No grants
to individuals, or for matching gifts; no loans.
Application information:
Initial approach: Letter

Copies of proposal: 1
Deadline(s): Submit proposal preferably
during the first half of the year; no set
deadline
Board meeting date(s): January, April, July,
and October
Write: William N. Bobo, Secretary
Officers and Trustees: J.R. Fulp, Jr., Chairman;
D.W. Johnson, Vice-Chairman; William N.
Bobo, Secretary-Treasurer; Carlette F. Holmes,
John R. Fulp III, Sally A. Rose.
Number of staff: 2.
Employer Identification Number: 576019445

3795
Aiken Foundation, Inc., The ☐
Drawer F-12
Florence 29501

Incorporated in 1947 in South Carolina.
Donor(s): The Aiken family.
Financial data: (yr. ended 12/31/83): Assets,
$1,524,460 (M); expenditures, $106,138,
including $64,600 for 10 grants (high: $20,000;
low: $500).
Purpose and activities: Primarily local giving,
with emphasis on higher education.
Limitations: Giving primarily in SC.
Officers: O.S. Aiken, President; J.B. Aiken, Jr.,
John D. Aiken, P.S. Knox, Jr., David H.
McLeod, Vice-Presidents; O.S. Aiken, Jr.,
Secretary.
Employer Identification Number: 576019769

3796
Arkwright Foundation, The ☐
P.O. Box 1086
Spartanburg 29301   (803) 585-9213

Incorporated in 1945 in South Carolina.
Donor(s): The M.L. Cates and W.S.
Montgomery families.
Financial data: (yr. ended 12/31/82): Assets,
$3,704,907 (M); expenditures, $154,286,
including $122,240 for 79 grants (high:
$20,000; low: $25).
Purpose and activities: Broad purposes;
primarily local giving, with emphasis on a
community fund, higher and secondary
education, youth agencies, and Protestant
church support.
Limitations: Giving primarily in SC.
Application information:
Initial approach: Letter, personal visit, or
telephone
Write: Joe W. Smith, Secretary
Officers and Trustees: MacFarlane L. Cates,
Sr., Chairman; Walter S. Montgomery, Vice-
Chairman; Joe W. Smith, Secretary and
Treasurer; M.L. Cates, Jr., R.Z. Cates, W.S.
Montgomery, Jr.
Employer Identification Number: 576000066

3797
Bailey Foundation, The ☐
P.O. Drawer 1215
Clinton 29325   (803) 833-5500

Trust established in 1951 in South Carolina.

Donor(s): Lydia Cotton Mills, Clinton Cotton
Mills, Elastic Fabrics of America, and others.
Financial data: (yr. ended 8/31/83): Assets,
$3,621,188 (M); gifts received, $82,158;
expenditures, $441,478, including $377,959
for 21 grants (high: $250,000; low: $453),
$21,182 for 15 grants to individuals, $23,047
for 25 employee matching gifts and $177,547
for 49 loans.
Purpose and activities: Charitable purposes;
support primarily for higher education,
including a student loan and scholarship
program for children of employees of Clinton
Mills or M.S. Bailey and Son; support also for
churches.
Types of support awarded: Student aid,
employee related scholarships.
Limitations: No grants to individuals (except
scholarships for children of company
employees).
Application information: Application form
required.
Deadline(s): April 15 of applicant's senior
year in high school
Write: Claude Crocker
Directors: Emily F. Bailey, George H.
Cornelson, C. Bailey Dixon, G. Thaddeus
Williams, Mercer V. Wise.
Trustee: M.S. Bailey & Son, Bankers.
Advisory Committee: Clarice W. Johnson,
W.E. Little, James MacDonald, Joseph O.
Nixon, Donny Ross, Donny Wilder.
Employer Identification Number: 576018387

3798
Baruch (The Belle W.) Foundation ☐
Bellefield Plantation
Georgetown 29440

Trust established in 1964 in New York.
Donor(s): Belle W. Baruch.†
Financial data: (yr. ended 12/31/82): Assets,
$40,430,549 (M); expenditures, $744,519,
including $607,330 for foundation-administered
programs.
Purpose and activities: A private operating
foundation promoting education and research
in the conservation of natural resources, with
special emphasis on forestry, marine biology,
the care and propagation of wildlife and flora
and fauna; grants to be implemented only
through South Carolina universities and
colleges; to develop Hobcaw Center in
Georgetown, South Carolina, for research
and education in ecology.
Limitations: Giving primarily in SC.
Application information:
Write: Miss Ella A. Severin, Trustee
Trustees: H.M. Arthur, Nelson A. Buhler, Leon
I. Cohen, Leonard T. Scully, Ella A. Severin, E.
Craig Wall.
Employer Identification Number: 570564080

3799
Belk-Simpson Foundation ☐
P.O. Box 1449
Greenville 29602
Grant application office: P.O. Box 528,
Greenville, SC 29602

Trust established in 1944 in South Carolina.

Donor(s): Belk's Stores.
Financial data: (yr. ended 12/31/83): Assets, $2,219,070 (M); gifts received, $60,631; expenditures, $178,743, including $164,800 for 78 grants (high: $25,000; low: $100).
Purpose and activities: Broad purposes; local giving, with emphasis on Protestant church support and higher education; grants also to social agencies.
Limitations: Giving primarily in SC. No grants to individuals.
Application information:
 Initial approach: Letter
 Copies of proposal: 1
 Board meeting date(s): May and November
 Write: Willou Bichel
Directors: Willou Bichel, C.L. Efrid, Jr., Sarah Belk Gambrell, J.A. Kuhne, Nell M. Rice, Kate M. Simpson, W.H.B. Simpson, Charles W. White.
Trustee: South Carolina National Bank.
Employer Identification Number: 576020261

3800
Byrnes (James F.) Foundation
P.O. Box 9596
Columbia 29290   (803) 776-1211

Trust established in 1947 in South Carolina.
Donor(s): James F. Byrnes,† and others.
Financial data: (yr. ended 6/30/83): Assets, $1,897,164 (M); gifts received, $6,130; expenditures, $168,800, including $128,150 for 104 grants to individuals (average: $1,500).
Purpose and activities: A private operating foundation; college scholarship assistance to orphans or part-orphans resident in South Carolina.
Types of support awarded: Student aid.
Limitations: Giving primarily in SC.
Publications: Application guidelines.
Application information: Application form required.
 Initial approach: Letter or telephone
 Copies of proposal: 1
 Deadline(s): Submit proposal preferably in January or February; deadline March 1
 Board meeting date(s): June and December
 Write: Margaret Courtney, Executive Secretary
Officers and Directors: W.D. Workman, Jr., President; W.J. Hunsucker, Vice-President and Treasurer; Lois H. Anderson, R.R. Mallard, Hal Norton, G.R. Shafto, W.C. Westmoreland.
Number of staff: 1 part-time professional.
Employer Identification Number: 576024756

3801
Citizens and Southern National Bank of South Carolina Foundation
1801 Main St.
Columbia 29222   (803) 765-8251

Trust established in 1960 in South Carolina.
Donor(s): Citizens and Southern National Bank of South Carolina, C & S Systems.

Financial data: (yr. ended 12/31/84): Assets, $409,134 (M); gifts received, $574,671; expenditures, $504,165, including $488,923 for 77 grants (high: $50,000; low: $500; average: $1,000-$25,000) and $14,784 for 169 employee matching gifts.
Purpose and activities: Primarily local giving for community funds and higher education, support also for hospitals and youth agencies.
Types of support awarded: Continuing support, annual campaigns, building funds, matching funds, employee matching gifts.
Limitations: Giving primarily in SC. No grants to individuals, or for operating budgets, scholarships, fellowships, research, special projects, publications, or conferences; no loans.
Publications: Application guidelines.
Application information:
 Initial approach: Letter or full proposal
 Copies of proposal: 1
 Deadline(s): None
 Board meeting date(s): March, June, September, and December
 Final notification: 3 months
 Write: Hugh M. Chapman, Trustee
Trustees: Gayle O. Averyt, Chairman; Hugh M. Chapman, Hugh C. Lane, Jr., Ben R. Morris, Robert V. Royall, Jr.
Number of staff: 1 part-time support.
Employer Identification Number: 576024906

3802
Daniel Foundation of South Carolina, The
The Daniel Bldg., Fifth Fl.
Greenville 29602

Established in 1978 in South Carolina as partial successor to The Daniel Foundation.
Donor(s): Daniel International Corporation.
Financial data: (yr. ended 12/31/83): Assets, $7,688,731 (M); gifts received, $45,000; expenditures, $682,262, including $622,645 for grants.
Purpose and activities: Grants largely for higher education, including scholarships; some support for youth agencies.
Officers: H.M. Daniel, Chairman; Buck Mickel, President; Jean G. Bissell, James F. Daniel, III, Vice-Presidents; Barbara C. Lewis, Secretary and Treasurer.
Employer Identification Number: 570673409

3803
Fairey (Kittie M.) Educational Fund
c/o The South Carolina National Bank
P.O. Box 168
Columbia 29202   (803) 765-3576
Street address: 1241 Main St., Columbia, SC 29226

Trust established in 1967 in South Carolina.
Donor(s): Kittie Moss Fairey.†
Financial data: (yr. ended 9/30/82): Assets, $1,644,321 (M); expenditures, $186,000, including $184,586 for 49 grants to individuals.
Purpose and activities: To provide scholarships for South Carolinians attending a college or university within the state.

Types of support awarded: Student aid.
Limitations: Giving limited to SC.
Trustee: The South Carolina National Bank.
Employer Identification Number: 576037140

3804
Fuller (C. G.) Foundation
P.O. Box 2307
Columbia 29202   (803) 771-2990

Established in 1972 in South Carolina.
Donor(s): Cornell G. Fuller.†
Financial data: (yr. ended 12/31/83): Assets, $1,579,029 (M); gifts received, $2,400; expenditures, $143,923, including $64,100 for 13 grants (high: $10,000; low: $1,500; average: $5,000) and $65,500 for 33 grants to individuals.
Purpose and activities: Scholarships only for residents of South Carolina attending colleges or universities in the State; support also for charitable, humanitarian, and religious organizations in South Carolina.
Types of support awarded: Annual campaigns, seed money, building funds, equipment, student aid.
Limitations: Giving limited to SC. No grants for endowment funds or matching gifts; no loans.
Publications: 990-PF.
Application information: Application form required.
 Initial approach: Letter
 Board meeting date(s): Quarterly
 Final notification: 6 to 9 months
 Write: Victor B. John, Trustee, or Calhoun Lemon, Trustee
Trustees: Victor B. John, Calhoun Lemon, Bankers Trust of South Carolina.
Number of staff: None.
Employer Identification Number: 576050492

3805
Greenville, Inc., Community Foundation of Greater
825 E. Washington St.
Greenville 29601   (803) 233-5925

Community foundation established in 1956 in South Carolina; incorporated in 1970.
Financial data: (yr. ended 12/31/83): Assets, $3,109,080 (L); gifts received, $347,040; expenditures, $116,549, including $30,683 for 10 grants (high: $5,000; low: $144).
Purpose and activities: "For such charitable purposes as...will make for the mental, moral, intellectual and physical improvement, assistance and relief of the people of Greenville County, South Carolina."
Limitations: Giving limited to Greenville County, SC.
Application information:
 Initial approach: Telephone or letter
 Deadline(s): Submit proposal preferably in March, June, or September; deadline 30 days before board meetings
 Board meeting date(s): January, March, May, September, and November

Officers and Directors: Max M. Heller, President; G. Franklin Mims, Vice-President; Ruth A. Nicholson, Secretary; Robert R. Christie, Jr., Treasurer; Clarence B. Bauknight, Mamie J. Bruce, David L. Freeman, Yancey S. Gilkerson, Dexter N. Hagy, Mrs. Minor H. Mickel, Paul W. Nipper, Jr., William H. Orders, Mary P. Sterling, Lewis N. Terry, Jr., M.D., Leonard M. Todd, N. Barton Tuck, Wilson C. Wearn, Harriet S. Wyche.
Employer Identification Number: 576019318

3806
Gregg-Graniteville Foundation, Inc.
P.O. Box 418
Graniteville 29829   (803) 663-7552

Incorporated in 1949 in South Carolina.
Donor(s): Graniteville Company.
Financial data: (yr. ended 12/31/83): Assets, $10,580,721 (M); gifts received, $629,196; expenditures, $470,016, including $113,543 for 37 grants (high: $47,485; low: $50; average: $1,500) and $40,971 for 38 grants to individuals.
Purpose and activities: Broad purposes; giving primarily in Richmond County, Georgia, and locally; emphasis on health and youth agencies and community funds.
Types of support awarded: Continuing support, annual campaigns, seed money, emergency funds, building funds, endowment funds, matching funds, employee related scholarships, research, special projects.
Limitations: Giving primarily in Aiken County, SC, and Richmond County, GA. No grants to individuals (except for company-employee scholarships), or for operating budgets, deficit financing, equipment, land acquisition, demonstration projects, publications, or conferences; no loans.
Publications: Annual report.
Application information:
  Initial approach: Letter
  Copies of proposal: 1
  Deadline(s): None
  Board meeting date(s): Quarterly and as required
  Final notification: 3 months
  Write: Joan F. Phibbs, Secretary
Officers: Robert P. Timmerman,* President; John W. Cunningham,* Jerry R. Johnson,* Vice-Presidents; Joan F. Phibbs, Secretary; Carl W. Littlejohn, Jr.,* Treasurer.
Directors: Robert M. Bell, William C. Lott, James A. Randall, Clyde F. Strom.
Number of staff: 1 full-time professional.
Employer Identification Number: 570314400

3807
Inman-Riverdale Foundation
Inman 29349   (803) 472-2121

Incorporated in 1946 in South Carolina.
Donor(s): Inman Mills.
Financial data: (yr. ended 11/30/83): Assets, $2,553,435 (M); gifts received, $150,829; expenditures, $273,198, including $190,300 for 38 grants (high: $36,000; low: $150) and $32,525 for 14 grants to individuals.

Purpose and activities: Broad purposes; primarily local giving, with emphasis on higher education, including a company-employee scholarship fund, Protestant church support, youth agencies, and community funds.
Types of support awarded: Employee related scholarships.
Limitations: Giving primarily in SC.
Application information:
  Initial approach: Letter
  Copies of proposal: 1
  Board meeting date(s): Quarterly
  Write: W. Marshall Chapman, Chairman
Officers: W. Marshall Chapman,* Chairman; Robert H. Chapman, Jr.,* Vice-Chairman; Dorothy D. Maxwell, Secretary; John F. Renfro, Jr.,* Treasurer.
Trustees: W. Marshall Chapman, Robert C. Martin.
Employer Identification Number: 576019736

3808
Kennedy (Francis Nathaniel and Kathryn Padgett) Foundation
P.O. Box 49
Laurens 29360   (803) 984-4551

Established in 1973 in South Carolina.
Donor(s): Kathryn Padgett Kennedy.†
Financial data: (yr. ended 6/30/83): Assets, $1,220,260 (M); expenditures, $106,488, including $60,463 for 15 grants (high: $17,611; low: $100) and $28,200 for 50 grants to individuals.
Purpose and activities: Grants largely to local higher educational institutions, including scholarship funds, and for missionary programs; support also for youth agencies and a church.
Types of support awarded: Scholarship funds, grants to individuals.
Limitations: Giving primarily in SC.
Application information:
  Write: D.F. Patterson, Secretary
Officer and Trustees: D.F. Patterson, Secretary and Treasurer; John P. Faris, J. Hewlette Wasson, G.D. Sherer, Sam M. Smith.
Employer Identification Number: 237347655

3809
Liberty Corporation Foundation, The ⌗
P.O. Box 789
Greenville 29602

Established in 1965 in South Carolina.
Donor(s): Liberty Corporation.
Financial data: (yr. ended 8/31/83): Assets, $228,654 (M); gifts received, $472,500; expenditures, $381,225, including $381,131 for grants.
Purpose and activities: Broad purposes; support primarily for higher education, including an employee matching gifts program, and for a community fund; some grants also to youth agencies and cultural institutions.
Types of support awarded: Employee matching gifts.
Limitations: No grants to individuals.
Application information:
  Deadline(s): None
  Write: Herman N. Hipp, President

Officers: H.N. Hipp,* President; M.A. Bunton, R.G. Hilliard, Vice-Presidents; R.T. Coleman, Secretary; B.L. Edwards, Treasurer.
Directors: F.M. Hipp, Chairman; W.H. Hipp, M.G. Patton, R.E. Williams.
Employer Identification Number: 570468195

3810
Merck Family Fund
Five Exchange St.
Charleston 29401   (803) 722-8375

Incorporated in 1954 in New Jersey.
Donor(s): Members of the Merck family.
Financial data: (yr. ended 11/30/83): Assets, $8,371,263 (M); gifts received, $5,000; expenditures, $325,189, including $324,000 for 26 grants (high: $20,000; low: $3,000).
Purpose and activities: Broad purposes; grants in areas of major company operations, largely for conservation, education, and mental health; support also for medical research, and rehabilitation of the handicapped. Grants limited to organizations of direct interest to the trustees.
Types of support awarded: Seed money, building funds, equipment, fellowships, employee matching gifts.
Limitations: Giving primarily in areas with major company operations. No grants to individuals (except The Merck Sharp & Dohme International Fellowships for Clinical Pharmacology), or for endowment funds, or matching gifts; no loans.
Application information:
  Initial approach: Letter
  Copies of proposal: 1
  Deadline(s): None
  Board meeting date(s): Semiannually and as required
  Write: Antony M. Merck, President
Officers and Trustees: Antony M. Merck, President; Judith M. Buechner, Vice-President; Patience M. Chamberlin, Secretary; George Wall Merck, Treasurer; Anne M. Abeles, Josephine M. Coy, Francis W. Hatch III.
Number of staff: 6.
Employer Identification Number: 226063382

3811
Moore (Alfred) Foundation ⌗
c/o C.L. Page Enterprises, Inc.
P.O. Box 18426
Spartanburg 29318   (803) 582-6844

Incorporated in 1949 in South Carolina.
Donor(s): Jackson Mills.
Financial data: (yr. ended 12/31/83): Assets, $1,421,861 (L); gifts received, $20,657; expenditures, $73,266, including $43,750 for 35 grants (high: $5,000; low: $75) and $16,350 for 15 grants to individuals.
Purpose and activities: General purposes; local giving, with emphasis on higher education, including scholarships, and on youth and social agencies.
Types of support awarded: Student aid.
Limitations: Giving limited to Anderson and Spartanburg counties, SC.
Application information:
  Initial approach: Letter

Deadline(s): Scholarships, April 15; loans, June 15
Write: Cary L. Page, Jr., Chairman
Officers: Cary L. Page, Jr., Chairman; Bernell Demo, Vice-Chairman; Thomas P. Young, Jr., Secretary and Treasurer.
Employer Identification Number: 576018424

3812
Post and Courier Foundation ⌥
134 Columbus St.
Charleston 29402
Application address: P.O. Box 758, Charleston, SC 29402

Incorporated in 1951 in South Carolina.
Donor(s): The News and Courier Company, Evening Post Publishing Company, Packet Motor Express.
Financial data: (yr. ended 12/31/83): Assets, $1,036,145 (M); gifts received, $316,628; expenditures, $234,989, including $233,514 for grants.
Purpose and activities: Broad purposes; emphasis on higher education, including scholarships for news carriers in South Carolina, and Christian religious organizations; support also for cultural programs.
Types of support awarded: Employee related scholarships.
Application information:
Initial approach: Proposal
Deadline(s): None
Write: J.F. Smoak, Treasurer
Officers: Peter Manigault, President; H.T. McGee, Jr., Vice-President; Dewey B. Nettles, Secretary; J.F. Smoak, Treasurer.
Employer Identification Number: 576020356

3813
Riegel Textile Corporation Foundation
Green Gate Park
25 Woods Lake Rd.
Greenville 29607   (803) 242-6050

Trust established in 1956 in New York.
Donor(s): Riegel Textile Corporation.
Financial data: (yr. ended 9/30/83): Assets, $618,971 (M); gifts received, $350,000; expenditures, $372,520, including $272,656 for 74 grants (high: $70,000; low: $100) and $99,864 for 242 employee matching gifts.
Purpose and activities: Broad purposes; general giving, with emphasis on higher and secondary education; some support for community funds and youth agencies.
Types of support awarded: General purposes, seed money, building funds, equipment, research, conferences and seminars, scholarship funds, employee related scholarships, employee matching gifts.
Limitations: No grants to individuals or for endowment funds; no loans.
Application information:
Initial approach: Full proposal
Copies of proposal: 1
Deadline(s): None
Board meeting date(s): February, May, August, and November
Final notification: 1 month
Write: Jane H. Greer, Trustee

Trustees: Joseph T. Allmon, Robert E. Coleman, Jane H. Greer, Henry B. Leonard, Clayteen Lewis, Colin Sayer.
Number of staff: None.
Employer Identification Number: 136113570

3814
Roe Foundation, The
712 Crescent Ave.
Greenville 29601   (803) 235-8955

Incorporated in 1968 in South Carolina.
Donor(s): Thomas A. Roe.
Financial data: (yr. ended 12/31/83): Assets, $3,416,840 (M); expenditures, $157,117, including $132,000 for 43 grants (high: $33,515; low: $50; average: $1,000-$10,000).
Purpose and activities: Giving primarily for public policy organizations promoting free enterprise and limited government.
Types of support awarded: Operating budgets, continuing support, annual campaigns, seed money, emergency funds, building funds, equipment, land acquisition, fellowships.
Limitations: No grants to individuals or for matching gifts; no loans.
Publications: Program policy statement.
Application information:
Initial approach: Letter
Deadline(s): None
Board meeting date(s): Semiannually
Final notification: 6 months
Write: Thomas A. Roe, Chairman
Officers and Trustees: Thomas A. Roe, Chairman and Treasurer; Alfred F. Burgess, Vice-Chairman; Shirley W. Roe, Secretary; Edwin Feulner, Jr.
Number of staff: None.
Employer Identification Number: 237011541

3815
Sargent Foundation ⌥
P.O. Box 3714 Park Place
Greenville 29608

Established in 1954.
Financial data: (yr. ended 4/30/84): Assets, $1,213,790 (M); expenditures, $146,337, including $136,250 for grants.
Purpose and activities: Primarily local giving for community funds, Protestant religious groups, and a hospital.
Limitations: Giving primarily in SC.
Application information:
Initial approach: Proposal
Write: Ruth Nicholson, Vice-President
Officers: Eleanor Sargent, President; Ruth Nicholson, Vice-President; John McAdams, Treasurer.
Trustee: Thomas Parker.
Employer Identification Number: 576019317

3816
Scurry (D. L.) Foundation
P.O. Box 10885, Federal Station
Greenville 29603   (803) 271-4290

Trust established in 1968 in South Carolina.
Donor(s): D.L. Scurry.†

Financial data: (yr. ended 6/30/83): Assets, $2,221,199 (M); expenditures, $169,506, including $157,250 for 52 grants (high: $4,000; low: $250).
Purpose and activities: Local giving, with emphasis on higher education; support also for child welfare.
Types of support awarded: Endowment funds, scholarship funds.
Limitations: Giving limited to SC. No grants to individuals, or for building funds or matching gifts; no loans.
Application information:
Initial approach: Full proposal
Copies of proposal: 1
Deadline(s): Submit proposal preferably in December; deadline December 31
Write: James F. Burgess, Trustee
Trustee: James F. Burgess.
Employer Identification Number: 576036622

3817
Self Foundation, The ▼
P.O. Drawer 1017
Greenwood 29648   (803) 229-2571

Incorporated in 1942 in South Carolina.
Donor(s): James C. Self.†
Financial data: (yr. ended 12/31/84): Assets, $16,813,795 (M); expenditures, $850,612, including $665,435 for 24 grants (high: $150,000; low: $1,500; average: $1,500-$50,000).
Purpose and activities: Broad purposes; grants almost exclusively in South Carolina with primary interest in health care and higher education; support mainly in Greenwood, South Carolina for cultural programs and activities for youth and the elderly; grants mainly for capital or special purposes.
Types of support awarded: Seed money, emergency funds, building funds, equipment, matching funds, technical assistance, special projects.
Limitations: Giving limited to SC. No grants to individuals, or for endowment funds, land acquisition, operating budgets, continuing support, annual campaigns, deficit financing, publications, conferences, scholarships and fellowships, or research-related programs; no loans.
Publications: Annual report, program policy statement, application guidelines.
Application information:
Initial approach: Letter
Copies of proposal: 1
Deadline(s): Submit proposal preferably in the 2 months prior to board meetings; deadlines first day of months in which board meets
Board meeting date(s): March, June, September, and December
Final notification: 10 days after board meeting
Write: Frank J. Wideman, Jr., Executive Vice-President
Officers: James C. Self,* President; Frank J. Wideman, Jr., Executive Vice-President; Bruce R. Sigmon,* Vice-President; W.M. Self,* Secretary; Kenneth E. Young,* Treasurer.

Trustees:* Virginia S. Brennan, John E. Eck, Rev. Dr. Theodore R. Morton, William B. Patrick, Jr., James C. Self, Jr.
Number of staff: 1 full-time professional.
Employer Identification Number: 570400594

3818
Simpson Foundation, The ☒
c/o C & S National Bank of South Carolina
P.O. Box 1449
Greenville 29602

Trust established in 1956 in South Carolina.
Donor(s): W.H.B. Simpson.
Financial data: (yr. ended 12/31/83): Assets, $1,470,972 (M); gifts received, $285,424; expenditures, $152,392, including $144,330 for 46 grants (high: $26,350; low: $100).
Purpose and activities: Broad purposes; primarily local giving, with emphasis on Protestant church support and religious organizations; support also for higher and secondary education.
Limitations: Giving primarily in NC and SC.
Directors: Willou R. Bichel, Gloria Bond, Francis Dudley, C.L. Efrid, Sr., Sarah Belk Gambrell, Nell M. Rice, Charles W. White.
Employer Identification Number: 576017451

3819
South Carolina National Charitable & Educational Foundation ☒
1241 Main St.
Columbia 29226

Established in 1961.
Donor(s): South Carolina National Bank.
Financial data: (yr. ended 12/31/82): Assets, $900,377 (M); gifts received, $161,366; expenditures, $261,881, including $254,491 for 100 grants (high: $66,443).
Purpose and activities: Primarily local giving for higher education, youth agencies, cultural programs, and a community fund.
Limitations: Giving primarily in SC.
Officer and Trustee: Joan Gallaway Bissell, Secretary.
Employer Identification Number: 576019497

3820
Spartanburg County Foundation, The
805 Montgomery Bldg.
Spartanburg 29301   (803) 582-0138

Community foundation incorporated in 1943 in South Carolina.
Donor(s): Leland L. Larrabee,† Nell B. Larrabee,† Robert B. Olney.†
Financial data: (yr. ended 12/31/84): Assets, $9,490,580 (M); gifts received, $3,266,603; expenditures, $557,166, including $359,200 for 80 grants (high: $50,000; low: $250; average: $500-$40,000).
Purpose and activities: To provide "for the mental, moral, intellectual and physical improvement, assistance and relief of the inhabitants of Spartanburg County." Support for local projects in education, arts, humanities, recreation, health, and welfare.

Types of support awarded: Continuing support, seed money, emergency funds, building funds, equipment, matching funds, conferences and seminars, consulting services.
Limitations: Giving limited to Spartanburg County, SC. No grants to individuals, or for operating budgets, annual campaigns, deficit financing, land acquisition, or endowment funds; no loans.
Publications: Annual report, program policy statement, application guidelines.
Application information:
Initial approach: Telephone
Copies of proposal: 1
Deadline(s): Submit proposal preferably in first 6 months of year, and at least 1 week before board meetings
Board meeting date(s): Monthly
Final notification: 1 month
Write: Frank H. Cunningham, Executive Director
Officers: John T. Wardlaw,* Secretary; Edward P. Perrin,* Treasurer; Frank H. Cunningham, Executive Director.
Trustees:* Martha C. Chapman, Chairman; W.D. Bain, Jr., Vice-Chairman; MacFarlane L. Cates, Jr., Everett Clarkson, Harry Phillips, Jr.
Number of staff: 1 part-time professional; 2 part-time support.
Employer Identification Number: 570351398

3821
Springs (Elliott White) Foundation, Inc. ▼
P.O. Drawer 460
Lancaster 29720   (803) 286-2196

Incorporated in 1942 in Delaware.
Donor(s): Elliott W. Springs,† Anne Springs Close, Frances Ley Springs.†
Financial data: (yr. ended 12/31/84): Assets, $17,835,064 (M); expenditures, $1,882,181, including $1,546,984 for 61 grants (high: $309,006; low: $175), $20,000 for grants to individuals and $171,704 for 132 loans.
Purpose and activities: Broad purposes; primarily local giving for the benefit of residents of Lancaster County and/or the townships of Fort Mill and Chester; support largely for hospitals, recreation, student loans, medical scholarships, public schools, and higher education, including vocational training; some assistance for community funds.
Types of support awarded: Student aid, building funds, equipment, endowment funds, publications, professorships, matching funds, general purposes, special projects.
Limitations: Giving primarily in Lancaster County and Fort Mill and Chester townships, SC. No grants to individuals (except through the Springs Medical Scholarship Program).
Publications: Annual report, program policy statement, application guidelines.
Application information: Application form required for student loans.
Initial approach: Telephone or brief letter
Copies of proposal: 1
Deadline(s): None
Board meeting date(s): February, May, August, and November
Final notification: 3 months
Write: Charles A. Bundy, President

Officers and Directors: Anne Springs Close, Chairman; Charles A. Bundy, President; R.C. Hubbard, Vice-President and Secretary; Crandall C. Bowles, Vice-President and Treasurer; James Bradley, Derick S. Close, Elliott Springs Close, H.W. Close, Jr., Katherine Anne Close, Leroy Springs Close, Frances Close Hart, J.W. Medford.
Number of staff: 1 full-time professional; 2 full-time support.
Employer Identification Number: 570426344

3822
Springs (Frances Ley) Foundation, Inc.
P.O. Drawer 460
Lancaster 29720   (803) 286-2196

Incorporated in 1969 in South Carolina.
Donor(s): Members of the Springs and Close families.
Financial data: (yr. ended 12/31/84): Assets, $6,520,029 (M); gifts received, $45,000; expenditures, $330,198, including $279,048 for 22 grants (high: $95,748; low: $300) and $6,840 for 4 loans.
Purpose and activities: Broad purposes; primarily local giving, with emphasis on recreation, higher education, including student loans, health care, and community services.
Limitations: Giving primarily in SC and NC. No grants to individuals.
Application information: Application form for student loans.
Initial approach: Proposal
Copies of proposal: 1
Board meeting date(s): April, September, and December
Write: Charles A. Bundy, President
Officers and Directors: Anne Springs Close, Chairman; Charles A. Bundy, President; R.C. Hubbard, Vice-President and Secretary; Crandall Close Bowles, Vice-President and Treasurer; James Bradley, Derick S. Close, Elliott Springs Close, H.W. Close, Jr., Katherine A. Close, Leroy Springs Close, Frances Close Hart, Pat C. Hastings.
Employer Identification Number: 237013986

3823
State-Record Company Foundation, The ☒
P.O. Box 1333
Columbia 29202   (803) 799-9209
Application address: 923 Calhoun St., Columbia, SC 29201

Trust established in 1963 in South Carolina.
Donor(s): Columbia Newspapers, Inc.
Financial data: (yr. ended 6/30/83): Assets, $395,544 (M); gifts received, $220,000; expenditures, $137,668, including $134,900 for 42 grants (high: $51,200; low: $150).
Purpose and activities: Charitable purposes; local giving, with emphasis on higher and secondary education, a community fund, and hospitals; support also for cultural programs and historic preservation.
Limitations: Giving limited to SC.
Application information:
Initial approach: Letter
Deadline(s): January 1

Write: Augustus T. Graydon, Chairman
Trustees: Augustus T. Graydon, Chairman; Mary Fleming Finlay, Ben R. Morris, South Carolina National Bank.
Employer Identification Number: 576025621

3824
Stevens (John T.) Foundation ♯
P.O. Box 158
Kershaw 29067

Established in 1948 in South Carolina.
Donor(s): John T. Stevens.
Financial data: (yr. ended 5/31/83): Assets, $2,141,231 (M); expenditures, $124,593, including $102,450 for 30 grants (high: $23,500; low: $250).
Purpose and activities: Primarily local giving, with emphasis on Protestant church support, medical and secondary education, and youth agencies.
Limitations: Giving primarily in SC.
Officers and Directors: John S. Davidson, President; O.W. Knight, Vice-President; Steve L. Williams, Secretary and Treasurer; Mattie Seegars, Douglas H. Williams.
Employer Identification Number: 576005554

3825
Symmes (F. W.) Foundation
c/o South Carolina National Bank
P.O. Box 969
Greenville 29602   (803) 239-6838

Trust established in 1954 in South Carolina.
Donor(s): F.W. Symmes.†
Financial data: (yr. ended 3/31/84): Assets, $5,879,616 (M); expenditures, $389,333, including $349,804 for 16 grants (high: $100,000; low: $500).
Purpose and activities: Broad purposes; primarily local giving, with emphasis on church support, child welfare, hospitals, youth agencies, music, and recreation.
Limitations: Giving primarily in SC. No grants to individuals.
Publications: Application guidelines.
Application information:
    Initial approach: Letter or telephone
    Copies of proposal: 5
    Deadline(s): 4 weeks before board meetings
    Board meeting date(s): Semiannually
    Final notification: 2 weeks following meeting
    Write: Douglas G. Holman, Jr., Trust Officer
Trustees: William H. Orders, Wilson C. Wearn, Katherine McK. Wilkinson, The South Carolina National Bank, Corporate Trustee (Douglas G. Holman, Jr., Vice-President and Trust Officer).
Number of staff: None.
Employer Identification Number: 576017472

SOUTH DAKOTA

3826
Hatterscheidt Foundation, Inc., The
c/o First Bank-Aberdeen
320 South First St.
Aberdeen 57401   (605) 225-9400

Incorporated in 1947 in Delaware.
Donor(s): Ruth K. Hatterscheidt, F.W. Hatterscheidt Trusts.
Financial data: (yr. ended 12/31/84): Assets, $3,403,809 (M); gifts received, $11,975; expenditures, $193,343, including $35,750 for 34 grants (high: $5,000; low: $150; average: $1,000) and $100,000 for 100 grants to individuals.
Purpose and activities: Giving primarily in North and South Dakota to assist graduating high school seniors in the top quarter of their class in their first year of college; North Dakota graduates limited to residents within 100-mile radius of Jamestown; support also for local charitable organizations.
Types of support awarded: Student aid.
Limitations: Giving primarily in SD and ND. No grants for endowment funds or matching gifts; no loans.
Application information:
    Initial approach: Letter
    Copies of proposal: 1
    Deadline(s): Submit proposal preferably in February
    Board meeting date(s): March and October
    Write: Kenneth P. Johnson, Vice-President and Trust Officer, First Bank-Aberdeen
Officers and Trustees: Margaret M. Meyers, President; Arthur J. Eagleson, Vice-President; Terrance A. O'Keefe, Francis Rinke.
Employer Identification Number: 466012543

TENNESSEE

3827
Ansley (Dantzler Bond) Foundation ♯
c/o Third National Bank
Nashville 37244

Incorporated in 1980 in Tennessee.
Donor(s): Mildred B. Ansley.†
Financial data: (yr. ended 4/30/83): Assets, $4,012,549 (M); expenditures, $228,692, including $215,000 for 20 grants (high: $50,000; low: $2,000).

Purpose and activities: Support primarily for health and medical research, higher and secondary education, and cultural programs.
Trustees: John O. Ellis, Thomas M. Evans, Thomas F. Frist.
Employer Identification Number: 592111990

3828
Belz Foundation ♯
P.O. Box 171199
Memphis 38187-1199

Incorporated in 1952 in Tennessee.
Donor(s): Jack A. Belz, Philip Belz, and others.
Financial data: (yr. ended 12/31/83): Assets, $2,809,082 (M); gifts received, $418,315; expenditures, $112,836, including $106,809 for 163 grants (high: $8,500; low: $10).
Purpose and activities: Primarily local giving, with emphasis on Jewish welfare funds and temple support.
Limitations: Giving primarily in Memphis, TN. No grants to individuals.
Managers: Jack A. Belz, Martin S. Belz, Philip Belz, Raymond Shainberg, Jack Weil, Jimmie D. Williams.
Employer Identification Number: 626046715

3829
Benwood Foundation, Inc. ▼
1600 American National Bank Bldg.
Chattanooga 37402   (615) 267-4311

Incorporated in 1944 in Delaware; in 1945 in Tennessee.
Donor(s): George Thomas Hunter.†
Financial data: (yr. ended 12/31/83): Assets, $46,358,225 (M); expenditures, $2,757,005, including $2,477,159 for 89 grants (high: $400,000; low: $250; average: $1,000-$50,000).
Purpose and activities: Primarily local giving, with support for higher and secondary education, health agencies and hospitals, cultural programs including the performing arts, beautification, welfare agencies, and Christian religious organizations.
Types of support awarded: Research, annual campaigns, seed money, emergency funds, deficit financing, building funds, equipment, land acquisition, conferences and seminars, endowment funds, professorships, scholarship funds, matching funds, general purposes, continuing support.
Limitations: Giving primarily in the Chattanooga, TN area. No grants to individuals or for building or operating funds of churches; no loans.
Publications: Application guidelines.
Application information: Application form required.
    Initial approach: Letter
    Copies of proposal: 6
    Deadline(s): End of each month preceding board meetings
    Board meeting date(s): January, April, July, and October
    Final notification: 3 days after board meeting
    Write: William A. Walter, Executive Director

Officers and Trustees:* E.Y. Chapin III,*
Chairman; W.R. Randolph, Jr.,* President;
Joseph H. Davenport, Jr.,* Vice-President;
Sebert Brewer, Jr.,* Secretary; Scott L.
Probasco, Jr.,* Treasurer; William A. Walter,
Executive Director.
Number of staff: 1 full-time professional; 2 full-time support.
Employer Identification Number: 620476283

3830
Briggs (T. W.) Welcome Wagon Foundation, Inc. ⊠
6055 Primacy Pkwy., Suite 242
Memphis 38119

Established in 1957.
Financial data: (yr. ended 9/30/83): Assets,
$2,476,405 (M); gifts received, $123,626;
expenditures, $219,940, including $177,244
for 29 grants (high: $100,000; low: $400).
Purpose and activities: Primarily local giving,
with emphasis on higher education, an arts
council, a community fund, and youth agencies.
Limitations: Giving primarily in TN.
Officers and Directors: Hubert A. McBride,
President; Elsie Helwig, William T. Morris, S.
Herbert Rhea, Vice-Presidents; Mary K. Boone,
Secretary-Treasurer.
Employer Identification Number: 626039986

3831
Brinkley Foundation, The ⊠
c/o National Bank of Commerce
Nine Commerce Square
Memphis 38150

Trust established in 1968 in Tennessee.
Donor(s): Hugh M. Brinkley.†
Financial data: (yr. ended 12/31/83): Assets,
$1,477,802 (M); expenditures, $116,327,
including $108,000 for 12 grants (high:
$35,000; low: $5,000).
Purpose and activities: Broad purposes; to
support educational or charitable programs in
Tennessee and Arkansas. Giving primarily for
hospitals, health services, and secondary
education.
Limitations: Giving primarily in TN and AR.
Application information:
   Deadline(s): None
Distribution Committee: Barbara H. Sprunt.
Trustee: National Bank of Commerce.
Employer Identification Number: 626079631

3832
Brown (The Dora Maclellan) Charitable Trust ▼
1101 Maclellan Bldg.
Chattanooga 37402   (615) 266-5257

Trust established in 1965 in Tennessee;
incorporated in 1976 in Tennessee.
Donor(s): Dora Maclellan Brown.†
Financial data: (yr. ended 12/31/84): Assets,
$8,832,935 (M); expenditures, $667,865,
including $640,302 for 111 grants (high:
$36,000; low: $250; average: $1,000-$10,000).

Purpose and activities: Primarily local giving
for Christian evangelical organizations through
scholarships for persons planning to be trained
for the ministry, serve as missionaries, and
Bible teachers; also giving for higher and
secondary education.
Types of support awarded: Operating
budgets, continuing support, annual campaigns,
scholarship funds, conferences and seminars,
fellowships.
Limitations: Giving primarily in Chattanooga,
TN. No grants to individuals, or for seed
money, emergency funds, graduate education,
deficit financing, capital funds, endowment
funds, equipment and materials, land
acquisition, renovation projects, special
programs, research, publications, or generally
for matching gifts; no loans.
Publications: Application guidelines.
Application information: Application form
required.
   Copies of proposal: 1
   Deadline(s): Submit proposal prior to third
      week of any month
   Board meeting date(s): Monthly
   Final notification: Immediately after board
      meets
   Write: W. Henry Trotter, President
Officers and Directors: W. Henry Trotter,
President and Treasurer; Llewellyn Boyd,
Robert F. Huffaker, Vice-Presidents; Raymond
R. Murphy, Jr., Secretary; Henry A. Henegar,
Hugh D. Huffaker, John E. Steffner.
Custodian and Fiscal Agent: American
National Bank and Trust Company.
Number of staff: 1 part-time support.
Employer Identification Number: 510200174

3833
Buckman (John Dustin) Charitable Trust ⊠
165 Madison Ave.
P.O. Box 84
Memphis 38101
Application address: Advisory Panel, John D.
Buckman Foundation, c/o Burch Porter and
Johnson, 130 N. Court Ave., Memphis, TN
38103

Established in 1980.
Donor(s): John Dustin Buckman.†
Financial data: (yr. ended 9/30/83): Assets,
$5,299,107 (M); gifts received, $4,665,062;
expenditures, $425,413, including $399,000
for 9 grants (high: $110,000; low: $5,000).
Purpose and activities: Primarily local giving,
with emphasis on education and child health
and welfare.
Limitations: Giving primarily in Memphis, TN.
Application information:
   Initial approach: Full proposal
   Deadline(s): None
   Board meeting date(s): May and October
   Write: Joe Duncan, Secretary
Officer: Joe Duncan, Secretary.
Trustee: First Tennessee Bank.
Employer Identification Number: 626155483

3834
Bullard (George Newton) Foundation ⊠
c/o Kraft Brothers, Esstman, Patton, and Harrell
404 James Robertson Pkwy.
Nashville 37219

Established in 1967 in Tennessee.
Financial data: (yr. ended 12/31/83): Assets,
$4,665,412 (M); gifts received, $777,689;
expenditures, $275,360, including $226,276
for 80 grants (high: $20,000; low: $150).
Purpose and activities: Primarily local giving;
with emphasis on social agencies; support for
churches and religious associations, higher and
secondary education, and cultural programs.
Limitations: Giving primarily in TN.
Trustees: George N. Bullard, Jr., Elizabeth B.
Stadler.
Employer Identification Number: 626077171

3835
Chattanooga, Inc., The Community Foundation of Greater
1600 American National Bank Bldg.
Chattanooga 37402   (615) 267-4311

Community foundation incorporated in 1963 in
Tennessee.
Financial data: (yr. ended 12/31/83): Assets,
$7,054,226 (M); gifts received, $150,000;
expenditures, $497,096, including $442,366
for 55 grants (high: $40,000; low: $100) and
$11,602 for 15 grants to individuals.
Purpose and activities: Broad purposes; to
promote and enhance the well-being of the
inhabitants of the greater Chattanooga area.
Types of support awarded: Student aid,
continuing support, seed money, emergency
funds, building funds, equipment, conferences
and seminars.
Limitations: Giving primarily in the greater
Chattanooga, TN, area. No grants for matching
gifts; no loans.
Application information:
   Initial approach: Brief letter
   Copies of proposal: 6
   Deadline(s): End of month preceding Grants
      Committee meeting
   Board meeting date(s): Annually; Grants
      Committee meets in February, May,
      August, and November
   Write: William A. Walter, Executive Director
Officers: E.Y. Chapin, III,* President; James
Robinson,* 1st Vice-President; Llewellyn
Boyd,* 2nd Vice-President; J. Guy Beatty, Jr.,
Secretary; Richard H. Houck,* Treasurer;
William A. Walter, Executive Director.
Directors:* Frank A. Brock, Hardwick
Caldwell, Jr., Joseph Decosimo, John P.
Franklin, Daniel K. Frierson, John P. Guerry,
Jane W. Harbaugh, H. James Hitching, William
Holmberg, N.C. Hughes, Jr., Willliam S. Hunt,
III, James W. Lail, Carl D. Long, T.A. Lupton,
Jr., David McCallie, Olan Mills, II, Frederick W.
Obear, William G. Raoul, James Robinson,
Robert J. Sudderth, Jr., William D. Wellbrock,
Lynn Woodworth, Sam I. Yarnell.
Employer Identification Number: 626045999

3836
Church of Christ Foundation, Inc. ▼
224 Second Ave. North
P.O. Box 1301
Nashville 37202   (615) 244-0600

Incorporated in 1946 in Tennessee.
Donor(s): G.L. Comer.
Financial data: (yr. ended 12/31/83): Assets, $13,177,053 (M); expenditures, $616,384, including $591,850 for 149 grants (high: $85,000; low: $100; average: $1,000-$5,000).
Purpose and activities: Support mainly for Church of Christ-related organizations, including churches, schools and colleges, throughout the United States; grants for health and welfare primarily in the Nashville, Tennessee area.
Types of support awarded: Operating budgets.
Limitations: Giving limited to U.S. for Church of Christ-related organizations; support primarily in the Nashville, TN area for health and welfare.
Application information: Applications for grants currently not invited.
    Board meeting date(s): Quarterly
    Write: Paul A. Hargis, President
Officers and Trustees: Paul A. Hargis, President; E.M. Shepherd, Vice-President; R. Hix Clark, Secretary; Paschall H. Young, Treasurer; Howard R. Amacher, Andrew Benedict, James M. Denton III, Richard P. Howard, Neal L. Jennings, Athens Clay Pullias, Robert C. Taylor.
Number of staff: 1.
Employer Identification Number: 620649477

3837
Cole (The Robert H. and Monica M.) Foundation
First American National Bank, Trust Dept.
505 South Gay St.
Knoxville 37902

Established in 1976.
Financial data: (yr. ended 9/30/82): Assets, $1,456,187 (M); expenditures, $91,302, including $84,750 for 24 grants (high: $10,000; low: $250).
Purpose and activities: Grants primarily for medical research on Parkinson's disease, higher education, and church support; support also for cultural programs and health.
Application information:
    Write: James P. Weller, Vice-President
Trustees: Monica M. Cole, William W. Davis, Park National Bank.
Employer Identification Number: 626137973

3838
Currey (Brownlee) Foundation
c/o Commerce Union Bank, Trust Dept.
One Commerce Place
Nashville 37219   (615) 749-3164

Established in 1967.
Financial data: (yr. ended 12/31/83): Assets, $1,498,962 (M); expenditures, $87,534, including $84,250 for 13 grants (high: $50,000; low: $50).

Purpose and activities: Giving primarily for cultural programs, education, health, and a community fund.
Types of support awarded: Annual campaigns, research.
Application information:
    Initial approach: Letter
    Deadline(s): None
    Write: M. Kirk Scobey, Senior Vice-President
Trustee: Commerce Union Bank, (M. Kirk Scobey, Senior Vice-President and Trust Officer).
Employer Identification Number: 626077710

3839
Day Foundation, The
3475 Central Ave.
P.O. Box 11409
Memphis 38111   (901) 452-6800

Established in 1960 in Mississippi.
Donor(s): Clarence C. Day, Day Companies, Inc.
Financial data: (yr. ended 12/31/84): Assets, $180,000 (M); gifts received, $1,000; expenditures, $183,000, including $172,000 for 40 grants (high: $25,000; low: $25).
Purpose and activities: Primarily local giving, with emphasis on community projects in the arts and social services.
Types of support awarded: Seed money, matching funds.
Limitations: Giving primarily in the Memphis, TN, area and Cuthbert, GA. No grants to individuals, or for endowment funds, scholarships and fellowships, capital funds, or operating budgets; no loans.
Publications: Application guidelines, annual report, informational brochure.
Application information:
    Initial approach: Full proposal
    Copies of proposal: 1
    Deadline(s): None
    Board meeting date(s): Monthly
    Final notification: 2 to 3 months
    Write: Rita S. Allen, Coordinator
Trustees: Clarence Day, Chairman; Michael B. Brewer, S. Herbert Rhea, Sally Thomason.
Coordinator: Rita S. Allen.
Number of staff: 1 part-time support.
Employer Identification Number: 646025122

3840
Evans Foundation, Inc., The ⌑
450 Maclellan Bldg.
Chattanooga 37402   (615) 756-5880
Application address: 428 McCallie Ave., Chattanooga, TN 37402

Incorporated in 1952 in Delaware.
Donor(s): Nell Evans Johnson,† Joseph W. Johnson, Jr., M.D., H. Clay Evans Johnson, David F.S. Johnson.
Financial data: (yr. ended 12/31/83): Assets, $2,753,024 (M); expenditures, $144,402, including $138,550 for 29 grants (high: $25,000; low: $300).

Purpose and activities: Broad purposes; primarily local giving, with emphasis on higher and secondary education, including awards to high school teachers and scholarship funds, and on youth agencies and a community fund.
Limitations: Giving primarily in TN.
Publications: Application guidelines.
Application information:
    Deadline(s): None
    Write: Carl J. Arnold, President
Officers and Trustees: Carl J. Arnold, President and Treasurer; H. Clay Evans Johnson, Vice-President; Douglas A. Nelson, Secretary; Margaret J. Curtis, Mrs. L. Wayne Farmer, Mrs. William B. Hamilton, Joseph W. Johnson, Jr., M.D., Barbara J. Prickett, Sally J. Shy.
Employer Identification Number: 626040820

3841
Goldsmith Foundation, Inc. ⌑
123 South Main St.
P.O. Box 449
Memphis 38143

Incorporated in 1944 in Tennessee.
Donor(s): Members of the Goldsmith family.
Financial data: (yr. ended 12/31/83): Assets, $2,934,037 (M); gifts received, $1,400; expenditures, $242,064, including $218,018 for 250 grants (high: $45,750; low: $15).
Purpose and activities: General purposes; primarily local giving, with emphasis on Jewish welfare funds, health, education, and social services.
Limitations: Giving primarily in TN.
Officers and Trustees: Jack L. Goldsmith, President; Edwin M. Marks, Fred Goldsmith, Jr., Vice-Presidents; Elias J. Goldsmith, Jr., Secretary-Treasurer.
Employer Identification Number: 626039604

3842
Hamico, Inc. ⌑
1715 West 38th St.
Chattanooga 37409

Incorporated in 1956 in Tennessee.
Financial data: (yr. ended 12/31/83): Assets, $3,177,379 (M); gifts received, $43,150; expenditures, $142,145, including $137,625 for 34 grants (high: $30,400; low: $150).
Purpose and activities: Broad purposes; primarily local giving, with emphasis on higher and secondary education, and cultural programs.
Limitations: Giving primarily in Chattanooga, TN.
Officers and Trustees: Alex Guerry, President; John P. Guerry, Vice-President; Durwood C. Harvey, Secretary-Treasurer; Ray W. Evans, James M. Holbert.
Employer Identification Number: 627040782

3843

Hutcheson (Hazel Montague) Foundation ¤

American National Bank & Trust Company
736 Market St.
Chattanooga 37402

Established in 1962 in Tennessee.
Donor(s): Hazel G.M. Montague.†
Financial data: (yr. ended 6/30/83): Assets, $1,794,925 (M); expenditures, $83,437, including $73,069 for 32 grants (high: $12,500; low: $100).
Purpose and activities: Broad purposes; giving largely in Tennessee and Florida, with emphasis on private secondary schools, Protestant church support, health agencies, and cultural programs.
Limitations: Giving primarily in TN and FL.
Trustees: Betty R. Hutcheson, Theodore M. Hutcheson, W. Frank Hutcheson, Hazel Hutcheson Meadow.
Employer Identification Number: 626045925

3844

Hyde (J. R.) Foundation, Inc.

1991 Corporate Ave.
Memphis 38132

Incorporated in 1961 in Tennessee.
Donor(s): J.R. Hyde.†
Financial data: (yr. ended 8/31/82): Assets, $6,406,803 (M); gifts received, $169,786; expenditures, $466,928, including $444,360 for 71 grants (high: $100,000; low: $200).
Purpose and activities: Broad purposes; grants in the Mid-South for higher education, including scholarship funds, secondary education, and Protestant church support.
Limitations: Giving primarily in the Mid-South. No grants to individuals, or for general support, capital or endowment funds, research programs, or matching grants; no loans.
Application information:
Board meeting date(s): September and as required
Write: Ms. Margaret R. Hyde, President
Officers: Margaret R. Hyde, President; J.R. Hyde, III, Vice-President; Jane Hyde Scott, Secretary.
Trustee: First Tennessee Bank.
Employer Identification Number: 620677725

3845

Jewell (The Daniel Ashley and Irene Houston) Memorial Foundation ¤
(formerly Crystal Foundation)
c/o American National Bank & Trust Company
P.O. Box 1638
Chattanooga 37402

Trust established in 1951 in Georgia.
Donor(s): The Crystal Springs Textiles Corporation.
Financial data: (yr. ended 6/30/81): Assets, $1,444,002 (M); expenditures, $147,308, including $128,108 for 36 grants (high: $25,000; low: $100) and $4,000 for 4 grants to individuals.

Purpose and activities: Broad purposes; general giving, primarily in Tennessee and Georgia, with emphasis on a hospital, church support, public schools and higher education, including scholarships, and community funds.
Limitations: Giving primarily in TN.
Application information:
Write: C. Callaway, Jr., Treasurer
Officers and Trustees: D.A. Jewell IV, Chairman; John L. Hutcheson, Jr., Vice-Chairman; W. Henry Trotter, Secretary; C. Callaway, Jr., Treasurer; Malcolm A. Cross, Stanley C. Cunningham, Mrs. D.A. Jewell, Jr., E. Dunbar Jewell, J. Ralston Wells.
Employer Identification Number: 626086062

3846

Lowenstein (William P. and Marie R.) Foundation

100 North Main Bldg., Rm. 3020
Memphis 38103   (901) 525-5744

Incorporated about 1959 in Tennessee.
Donor(s): Marie R. Lowenstein.†
Financial data: (yr. ended 12/31/83): Assets, $2,500,000 (M); expenditures, $185,000, including $150,000 for 30 grants (high: $25,000; low: $300).
Purpose and activities: Giving locally and in Israel, primarily for Jewish welfare funds, higher education, hospitals, and health agencies.
Types of support awarded: Operating budgets, seed money, equipment, scholarship funds, fellowships.
Limitations: Giving limited to TN and Israel. No grants to individuals, or for endowment funds, or matching gifts; no loans.
Application information: Application form required.
Initial approach: Letter or full proposal
Copies of proposal: 1
Deadline(s): April 15 and October 15
Board meeting date(s): May and December
Final notification: 10 months
Write: Alvin A. Gordon, Executive Director
Officers and Directors: Alvin A. Gordon, President and Executive Director; Gordon I. Gordon, Vice-President; Russell J. Perel, Secretary-Treasurer; Elaine K. Gordon, Marshall D. Gordon, Ed Marlowe, Ted M. Winestone.
Number of staff: 1 full-time professional; 1 full-time support.
Employer Identification Number: 626037976

3847

Lyndhurst Foundation ▼

701 Tallan Bldg.
Chattanooga 37402   (615) 756-0767

Incorporated in 1938 in Delaware.
Donor(s): Cartter Lupton,† Central Shares Corporation.
Financial data: (yr. ended 12/31/84): Assets, $91,695,737 (M); expenditures, $4,102,814, including $2,827,077 for 50 grants (high: $350,000; low: $2,000; average: $30,000-$150,000) and $305,000 for 13 grants to individuals.

Purpose and activities: Grants generally limited to the Southeast, with emphasis on health, education, and the arts. Health-related grants mainly support activities surrounding primary care, particularly for areas which are poorly served. Grants for education usually directed at secondary education. Grants to arts organizations to help increase or diversify audiences, improve management, or strengthen potential for earnings.
Types of support awarded: General purposes, seed money, scholarship funds, matching funds, operating budgets, program-related investments, special projects.
Limitations: Giving limited to the southeastern United States. No support for arts and social service organizations in metropolitan areas. No grants to individuals (except at initiative of foundation), or for building or endowment funds, general support for hospitals, colleges or universities, or religious organizations; equipment, deficit financing, medical or university-based research, publications, or conferences; no loans.
Publications: Annual report, application guidelines, program policy statement.
Application information: Application form required for grants to individuals; awards made only at the initiative of the foundation.
Initial approach: Letter
Copies of proposal: 1
Deadline(s): 4 weeks before board meetings; February 1 for Lyndhurst Teachers, Awards
Board meeting date(s): February, May, August, and November
Final notification: 3 months
Write: Deaderick C. Montague, President
Officers: Deaderick C. Montague,* President; Rodolph B. Davenport, III,* Vice-President; Joel W. Richardson, Jr., Secretary; Charles B. Chitty, Treasurer; Jack E. Murrah, Executive Director.
Trustees:* John T. Lupton, Chairman; Robert Coles, J. Burton Frierson.
Number of staff: 4 full-time professional; 3 full-time support.
Employer Identification Number: 626044177

3848

Maclellan Foundation, Inc., The ▼
Provident Bldg.
Chattanooga 37402   (615) 755-1291

Incorporated in 1945 in Delaware.
Donor(s): Robert J. Maclellan,† and members of the Maclellan family.
Financial data: (yr. ended 12/31/83): Assets, $78,545,339 (M); gifts received, $1,493,235; expenditures, $4,894,651, including $4,735,992 for 68 grants (high: $650,000; low: $1,000; average: $50,000-$150,000).
Purpose and activities: Charitable purposes; grants largely for local higher education, Protestant church support and religious associations, youth agencies and social services.
Types of support awarded: Continuing support, annual campaigns, seed money, building funds, equipment, matching funds, scholarship funds.

Limitations: Giving primarily in the Chattanooga, TN, area. No grants to individuals, or for operating budgets, emergency funds, deficit financing, land acquisition, renovations, endowment funds, research, demonstration projects, publications, or conferences; no loans.

Application information:
Initial approach: Letter
Copies of proposal: 1
Deadline(s): 3 weeks prior to board meetings
Board meeting date(s): 10 times a year
Write: Hugh O. Maclellan, Sr., President

Officers and Trustees: Hugh O. Maclellan, Sr., President; Dudley Porter, Jr., Vice-President; Hugh O. Maclellan, Jr., Secretary and Treasurer; Frank A. Brock, G. Richard Hostetter, Kathrina H. Maclellan.

Number of staff: 1 full-time professional; 1 full-time support.

Employer Identification Number: 626041468

3849
Maclellan (R. J.) Charitable Trust ▼
Provident Bldg.
Chattanooga 37402   (615) 755-1291

Trust established in 1954 in Tennessee.
Donor(s): Robert J. Maclellan.†
Financial data: (yr. ended 12/31/83): Assets, $31,144,696 (M); expenditures, $1,823,393, including $1,752,482 for 56 grants (high: $400,000; low: $1,000; average: $10,000-$30,000).

Purpose and activities: Primarily local giving for higher education, youth agencies, a theological seminary, Protestant religious associations, and cultural programs.

Types of support awarded: Continuing support, annual campaigns, seed money, building funds, equipment, matching funds, scholarship funds.

Limitations: Giving primarily in the Chattanooga, TN, area. No grants to individuals, or for operating budgets, emergency funds, deficit financing, land acquisition, renovations, endowment funds, special projects, research, publications, or conferences; no loans.

Application information:
Initial approach: Letter
Copies of proposal: 1
Deadline(s): 3 weeks before board meetings
Board meeting date(s): 10 times annually
Write: Hugh O. Maclellan, Sr., Chairman

Trustees: Hugh O. Maclellan, Sr., Chairman; Dudley Porter, Jr., American National Bank and Trust Company of Chattanooga (John Wright).

Number of staff: 1 full-time professional; 2 full-time support.

Employer Identification Number: 626037023

3850
Maclellan (Robert L. and Kathrina H.) Foundation
Tallan Bldg., Suite 1100
Two Union Square
Chattanooga 37402   (615) 756-7100

Established in 1972 in Tennessee.
Donor(s): Kathrina H. Maclellan.

Financial data: (yr. ended 12/31/84): Assets, $2,091,978 (M); gifts received, $230,000; expenditures, $113,643, including $100,000 for 1 grant.

Purpose and activities: Giving primarily to evangelistic Christian educational programs.

Types of support awarded: General purposes.

Application information:
Initial approach: Letter
Deadline(s): May
Board meeting date(s): May
Write: Joseph F. Decosimo, Secretary

Officers and Directors: Kathrina H. Maclellan, President and Treasurer; Joseph F. Decosimo, Secretary; Lee S. Anderson, Robert H. Maclellan.

Number of staff: None.

Employer Identification Number: 237159802

3851
Massengill-DeFriece Foundation, Inc.
Holston Plaza, Suite 208
516 Holston Ave.
Bristol 37620   (615) 764-3833

Incorporated in 1949 in Tennessee.
Donor(s): Frank W. DeFriece,† Pauline M. DeFriece.†

Financial data: (yr. ended 12/31/83): Assets, $3,197,094 (M); expenditures, $310,684, including $287,329 for 20 grants (high: $64,356; low: $465).

Purpose and activities: Giving locally and in Virginia for private higher education and health.

Types of support awarded: Continuing support, annual campaigns, emergency funds, equipment.

Limitations: Giving primarily in Bristol, TN, and VA. No grants to individuals, or for endowment funds, special projects, research, matching gifts, publications, or conferences; no loans.

Application information:
Initial approach: Letter
Copies of proposal: 1
Board meeting date(s): Usually in June and December, and as required
Final notification: 3 months
Write: Frank W. DeFriece, Jr., Vice-President

Officers and Directors: Josephine D. Wilson, President; Frank W. DeFriece, Jr., Albert S. Kelly, Jr., Vice-Presidents; John C. Paty, Jr., Secretary-Treasurer; Paul E. DeFriece, Polly D. Wills.

Number of staff: 1 part-time support.

Employer Identification Number: 626044873

3852
Massey (Jack C.) Foundation ⌑
One Park Plaza
P.O. Box 3
Nashville 37203

Trust established in 1966 in Tennessee.
Donor(s): Jack C. Massey.
Financial data: (yr. ended 12/31/83): Assets, $8,229,817 (M); expenditures, $651,348, including $521,612 for 127 grants (high: $75,000; low: $50).

Purpose and activities: Broad purposes; primarily local giving, with emphasis on higher and secondary education and medical research; grants also for cultural programs.

Types of support awarded: Research.

Limitations: Giving primarily in TN.

Application information:
Write: Jack C. Massey, Trustee

Officers: Omega C. Sattler, Secretary; Clarence Edmonds,* Treasurer.

Trustees:* Barbara M. Clark, Jack C. Massey, J. Brad Reed.

Employer Identification Number: 626065672

3853
Meade Haven Charitable Trust ⌑
c/o Third National Bank
P.O. Box 76
Nashville 37244

Trust established in 1961 in Tennessee.
Donor(s): Jesse E. Wills.
Financial data: (yr. ended 12/31/83): Assets, $2,073,497 (M); expenditures, $186,687, including $156,700 for 11 grants (high: $62,680; low: $1,000).

Purpose and activities: Broad purposes; primarily local giving, with emphasis on higher and secondary education, Protestant church support, and a children's museum.

Limitations: Giving primarily in TN.

Trustees: Walter Robinson, Vernon Sharp, Robert W. Sturdivant, Ellen Buchner Wills, Jesse W. Wills, Matthew Buchner Wills, William Ridley Wills, Third National Bank.

Employer Identification Number: 626032780

3854
Memphis-Plough Community Foundation, The
1755 Lynnfield, Suite 249
Memphis 38119   (901) 761-3806

Community foundation established in 1974 in Tennessee.

Financial data: (yr. ended 4/30/84): Assets, $9,508,654 (M); gifts received, $4,772,903; expenditures, $1,232,677, including $1,031,610 for 226 grants (high: $150,619; low: $25; average: $25-$10,000).

Purpose and activities: Broad purposes; support from unrestricted funds primarily for the benefit of western Tennessee, especially Memphis and Shelby County, and northern Mississippi.

Types of support awarded: Seed money.

Limitations: Giving limited to western TN, especially Memphis and Shelby County; northern Mississippi; and surrounding area. No grants to individuals, or for operating budgets, continuing support, annual campaigns, emergency funds, deficit financing, capital or endowment funds, matching gifts, scholarships, fellowships, special projects, research, publications, or conferences; no loans.

Publications: Annual report, application guidelines, program policy statement, newsletter.

Application information: Application form required.
Initial approach: Letter or telephone

Copies of proposal: 10
Deadline(s): May 15 and November 15
Board meeting date(s): March, June, September, and December
Final notification: 1 month after deadline
Write: Lisa Bell Shouse, Program Officer
Officers: John K. Fockler,* President; Lisa Bell Shouse, Secretary and Program Officer; Donald F. Schuppe,* Treasurer.
Governors:* Dunbar Abston, Jr., Chairman; Mrs. Harry J. Phillips, Vice-Chairman; Walter P. Armstrong, Jr., Roy E. Bell, Jr., Gary Ross Betz, Milton S. Binswanger, Jr., L. Palmer Brown III, Bruce E. Campbell, Edmond Cicala, Warren G. Creighton, Fred L. Davis, Nancy Fulmer, James S. Gilliland, Olin Morris, Charles A. Scruggs, Janet Sheahan, Joseph S. Sims, Thomas H. Todd, Jr., Sonia Walker, Willis H. Willey III, Joseph R. Williams, James D. Witherington, Ben H. Woodson.
Agency Banks: Commerce Union Bank, Commercial and Industrial Bank, First Tennessee Bank, Memphis Bank and Trust, National Bank of Commerce, Union Planters National Bank.
Number of staff: 2 full-time professional; 1 part-time professional; 1 full-time support.
Employer Identification Number: 237047899

3855
Plough Foundation ▼
4646 Poplar Ave., Suite 417
Memphis 38117   (901) 761-9180
Application address: c/o B.R. Haltom, Chief Operating Officer, P.O. Box 11087, Memphis, TN 38111

Trust established in 1972 in Tennessee.
Donor(s): Abe Plough.†
Financial data: (yr. ended 12/31/83): Assets, $35,121,700 (M); gifts received, $2,000,000; expenditures, $1,666,550, including $1,380,888 for 136 grants (high: $300,000; low: $25; average: $100-$250,000).
Purpose and activities: General giving, primarily in the Memphis and Shelby County, Tennessee, areas for community projects, including a community fund, social agencies, and civic affairs; support also for schools of pharmacy within major universities.
Types of support awarded: Operating budgets, continuing support, annual campaigns, seed money, emergency funds, deficit financing, equipment, matching funds, scholarship funds, general purposes.
Limitations: Giving primarily in Memphis and Shelby Counties, TN. No grants to individuals, or for building or endowment funds, land acquisition, renovation projects, research, special projects, publications, or conferences; no loans.
Application information:
Initial approach: Full proposal
Copies of proposal: 1
Deadline(s): None
Board meeting date(s): February, May, August, and November
Final notification: 2 weeks
Write: B.R. Haltom, Chief Operating Officer

Officer and Trustees: B.R. Haltom, Chief Operating Officer; Eugene J. Callahan, Noris R. Haynes, Jr., Cecil C. Humphreys, R.N. Lloyd, Jr., Jocelyn P. Rudner, Steve Wishnia, Union Planters National Bank.
Number of staff: None.
Employer Identification Number: 237175983

3856
Potter (The Justin and Valere) Foundation ▼ ¤
c/o Commerce Union Bank
One Commerce Place
Nashville 37239   (615) 244-6380

Trust established in 1951 in Tennessee.
Donor(s): Justin Potter,† Mrs. Valere Blair Potter.
Financial data: (yr. ended 12/31/83): Assets, $14,414,273 (M); expenditures, $719,445, including $665,000 for 17 grants (high: $165,000; low: $5,000; average: $5,000-$35,000).
Purpose and activities: Local giving, primarily for higher education, including scholarship funds and medical education; support also for cultural programs and medical research.
Types of support awarded: Scholarship funds, operating budgets, special projects, research.
Limitations: Giving primarily in Nashville, TN.
Application information:
Initial approach: Letter
Deadline(s): None
Board meeting date(s): As needed
Write: M. Kirk Scobey, Senior V.P. & Trust Officer
Distribution Committee: Albert Menefee, Jr., David K. Wilson, Justin Wilson.
Trustee: Commerce Union Bank (M. Kirk Scobey, Senior Vice-President and Trust Officer).
Number of staff: None.
Employer Identification Number: 626033081

3857
Schadt Foundation, Inc., The ¤
One Commerce Square, Rm. 1550
Memphis 38103   (901) 526-8637

Incorporated in 1958 in Tennessee.
Donor(s): Charles F. Schadt, Sr., Harry E. Schadt, Sr.,† Harry E. Schadt, Jr.
Financial data: (yr. ended 12/31/83): Assets, $2,083,500 (M); expenditures, $119,312, including $115,900 for 21 grants (high: $21,000; low: $200).
Purpose and activities: Broad purposes; local giving, with emphasis on secondary education and youth agencies.
Limitations: Giving limited to Shelby County, TN. No grants to individuals.
Application information: Applications for grants not invited.
Board meeting date(s): Annually
Write: Charles F. Schadt, Sr., President
Officers and Directors: Charles F. Schadt, Sr., President; Robert N. Lloyd, Jr., Charles F. Schadt, Jr., Harry E. Schadt, Jr., Stephen C. Schadt, Vice-Presidents.
Employer Identification Number: 626040050

3858
Speech Foundation of America
P.O. Box 11749
Memphis 38111   (901) 452-0995
Application address: Jane Fraser Gruss, President, 5139 Klingle St., Washington, DC 20016; Tel.:(202) 362-6116

Established in 1947 in Tennessee.
Donor(s): Members of the Fraser family.
Financial data: (yr. ended 12/31/83): Assets, $3,270,464 (M); gifts received, $44,413; expenditures, $181,582, including $9,500 for grants and $118,599 for foundation-administered programs.
Purpose and activities: A private operating foundation; support for foundation-initiated programs in therapy and prevention of stuttering.
Limitations: No grants to individuals, or for building or endowment funds, general purposes, scholarships, or fellowships.
Application information: Funds largely committed to support of operating programs; few grants awarded.
Initial approach: Letter
Board meeting date(s): December
Write: Jane Fraser Gruss, President
Officers and Directors: Jane Fraser Gruss, President; Malcolm H. Fraser, Vice-President; Hubert A. McBride, Secretary; Donald Edwards, Treasurer; John Doggett, James W. Garrison, Donald Lineback, William Parker, W.E. White.
Number of staff: 4.
Employer Identification Number: 626047678

3859
Toms Foundation, The
Valley Fidelity Bank Bldg., Ninth Fl.
P.O. Box 2466
Knoxville 37901   (615) 544-3000

Trust established in 1954 in Tennessee.
Donor(s): W.P. Toms.†
Financial data: (yr. ended 6/30/84): Assets, $2,406,000 (M); expenditures, $70,825, including $10,250 for 16 grants (high: $4,000; low: $100; average: $650).
Purpose and activities: Broad purposes; primarily local giving, with emphasis on higher education and youth agencies.
Types of support awarded: Seed money, emergency funds, building funds, equipment, land acquisition, professorships, research.
Limitations: Giving primarily in eastern TN. No grants to individuals, or for endowment funds, operating budgets, continuing support, annual campaigns, publications, demonstration projects, conferences, deficit financing, matching gifts, scholarships or fellowships; no loans.
Publications: Annual report.
Application information:
Initial approach: Letter of inquiry followed by full proposal
Copies of proposal: 1
Deadline(s): Submit proposal preferably in June; deadline June 30
Board meeting date(s): August and as required

Final notification: 1 month after annual meeting
Write: William C. Wilson, President
Officers and Trustees: William C. Wilson, President; Eleanor C. Krug, Vice-President; Ronald L. Grimm, Secretary; George C. Krug, Treasurer; Mary Mayne Perry, Dorothy B. Wilson.
Employer Identification Number: 626037668

3860
Tonya Memorial Foundation ▼
1033 Volunteer State Life Bldg.
Chattanooga 37402   (615) 757-3401
Application address: Maurice H. Martin, Trust Dept., American National Bank and Trust Company, 736 Market St., Chattanooga, TN 37402

Incorporated in 1949 in Delaware.
Donor(s): Burkett Miller.†
Financial data: (yr. ended 12/31/82): Assets, $11,823,834 (M); expenditures, $579,136, including $457,997 for 11 grants (high: $350,000; low: $350).
Purpose and activities: Grants to new donees limited to capital projects of a nonsectarian nature in the Chattanooga, Tennessee, area; emphasis on downtown rehabilitation, parks, hospitals, and community educational projects; continuing support for a few existing projects approved during the founder's lifetime.
Types of support awarded: Building funds, land acquisition, equipment.
Limitations: Giving primarily in Chattanooga, TN, for new grants recipients. No grants to individuals, or for endowment funds, or operating budgets.
Application information:
  Initial approach: Letter
  Copies of proposal: 1
  Deadline(s): None
  Board meeting date(s): January, April, July, and October
  Final notification: 6 months
  Write: Maurice H. Martin, President
Officers and Directors: H. James Hitching, Chairman; Maurice H. Martin, President and Treasurer; James F. Waterhouse, Vice-President and Secretary; James R. Hedges, III, Vice-President.
Number of staff: 1 part-time professional.
Employer Identification Number: 626042269

3861
Washington Foundation, The ⌑
224 Second Ave. North
Nashville 37201

Trust established in 1962 in Tennessee.
Financial data: (yr. ended 12/31/83): Assets, $2,466,651 (M); expenditures, $136,543, including $133,200 for 49 grants (high: $10,000; low: $100).
Purpose and activities: Broad purposes; primarily local giving for higher and secondary education, church support, community funds, and cultural programs.
Limitations: Giving primarily in TN.
Trustees: Parkes Armistead, William W. Berry, R. Hix Clark, Paul A. Hargis.
Employer Identification Number: 626047266

3862
Werthan Foundation
P.O. Box 1310
Nashville 37202   (615) 259-9331

Trust established in 1945 in Tennessee.
Donor(s): Werthan Bag Corporation, Bernard Werthan, Albert Werthan, Werthan Industries, Inc.
Financial data: (yr. ended 11/30/83): Assets, $4,242,780 (M); gifts received, $116,574; expenditures, $346,036, including $276,619 for 13 grants (high: $117,894; low: $50; average: $5,000).
Purpose and activities: Broad purposes; primarily local giving, with emphasis on Jewish welfare funds, higher education, and a community fund; support also for cultural programs.
Limitations: Giving primarily in TN.
Application information:
  Initial approach: Letter
  Deadline(s): None
  Write: Albert Werthan
Officers and Trustees: Bernard Werthan, Chairman; Bernard Werthan, Jr., Secretary; Albert Werthan, Treasurer; Herbert M. Shayne, Morris Werthan II, Werthan Industries, Inc.
Number of staff: None.
Employer Identification Number: 626036283

3863
Westend Foundation, Inc.
1100 American National Bank Bldg.
736 Market St.
Chattanooga 37402   (615) 265-8881

Incorporated in 1956 in Delaware.
Donor(s): George West.†
Financial data: (yr. ended 12/31/82): Assets, $2,384,579 (M); expenditures, $161,490, including $83,500 for 28 grants (high: $10,000; low: $500) and $59,871 for 34 grants to individuals.
Purpose and activities: Primarily local giving, with emphasis on scholarships, higher education, a university medical research laboratory in Arizona and Protestant church support.
Types of support awarded: General purposes, student aid.
Limitations: Giving primarily in the Chattanooga, TN, area.
Application information:
  Write: Raymond B. Witt, Jr., Secretary
Officers and Trustees: Lewis W. Oehmig, President; J. Burton Frierson, Jr., Vice-President; Raymond B. Witt, Jr., Secretary and Treasurer; Daniel W. Oehmig.
Employer Identification Number: 626041060

3864
Woods-Greer Foundation
c/o American National Bank and Trust Company, Trust Dept.
736 Market St., P.O. Box 1638
Chattanooga 37401   (615) 757-3203

Established in 1976.

Financial data: (yr. ended 5/31/83): Assets, $1,313,652 (M); expenditures, $112,841, including $103,333 for 16 grants (high: $45,000; low: $500).
Purpose and activities: Giving mainly for higher education, Christian religious organizations, and the arts.
Types of support awarded: Operating budgets, continuing support, annual campaigns, seed money, building funds, equipment, publications, scholarship funds, matching funds.
Limitations: Giving primarily in the southeastern United States. No grants to individuals; no loans.
Application information:
  Initial approach: Letter
  Copies of proposal: 1
  Deadline(s): Submit proposal preferably in April or May; no set deadline
  Board meeting date(s): July
  Write: The Very Rev. C. Cecil Woods, Jr., Chairman
Officers: The Very Rev. C. Cecil Woods, Jr., Chairman; Marie Cartinhour Woods, Vice-Chairman; Kathleen Woods Van Devender, Secretary.
Trustees: William G. Brown, Ellen Woods Polansky, Margaret C. Woods-Denkler.
Number of staff: None.
Employer Identification Number: 626126272

3865
Zimmerman Foundation, The ⌑
c/o Byrd, Land & Proctor
3818 Cleghorn Ave., Suite 200
Nashville 37215-2514

Established in 1979.
Donor(s): Jack Byrd Trust.
Financial data: (yr. ended 11/30/83): Assets, $362,893 (M); gifts received, $186,000; expenditures, $199,719, including $194,617 for 36 grants (high: $50,000; low: $100).
Purpose and activities: Primarily local giving for Jewish welfare funds and hospitals.
Limitations: Giving primarily in TN.
Application information:
  Write: Raymond Zimmerman, Manager
Officers and Directors: Raymond Zimmerman, President; Peggy Steine, Secretary; Rabbi Randall Falk, Sue Kresge, Doris Tenenbaum.
Employer Identification Number: 621058309

TEXAS

3866
Abell-Hanger Foundation ▼
First National Bank Bldg., Rm. 615
Midland 79701 (915) 684-6655
Mailing address: P.O. Box 430, Midland, TX
79702

Incorporated in 1954 in Texas.
Donor(s): George T. Abell,† Gladys H. Abell.
Financial data: (yr. ended 6/30/83): Assets,
$49,224,386 (M); gifts received, $4,997,065;
expenditures, $4,964,344, including
$4,476,797 for 88 grants (high: $500,000; low:
$600; average: $5,000-$100,000).
Purpose and activities: Broad purposes;
primarily local giving, with emphasis on higher
education, youth activities, cultural programs,
health services, the handicapped, and social
welfare agencies.
Types of support awarded: General purposes,
operating budgets, continuing support, annual
campaigns, seed money, emergency funds,
deficit financing, building funds, endowment
funds, matching funds, professorships,
scholarship funds, research, equipment.
Limitations: Giving limited to TX, preferably
within the Permian Basin. No grants to
individuals, including for individual scholarships
or fellowships; no loans.
Publications: 990-PF, program policy
statement, application guidelines.
Application information: Application form
required.
   Initial approach: Letter
   Copies of proposal: 3
   Deadline(s): Varies
   Board meeting date(s): June 1 and as
      required
   Final notification: 6 months
   Write: David L. Smith, Manager
Officers: Gladys H. Abell,* President; James T.
Trott,* Vice-President; Lester Van Pelt, Jr.,
Secretary-Treasurer.
Trustees:* John P. Butler, Robert L. Leibrock,
John F. Younger.
Number of staff: 1 full-time professional; 2
part-time professional; 1 part-time support.
Employer Identification Number: 756020781

3867
Abercrombie (The J. S.) Foundation ▼
P.O. Box 27339
Houston 77027 (713) 627-9440

Trust established in 1950 in Texas.
Donor(s): J.S. Abercrombie.†
Financial data: (yr. ended 12/31/82): Assets,
$8,831,341 (M); expenditures, $1,926,817,
including $1,731,224 for 58 grants (high:
$150,000; low: $500).
Purpose and activities: Primarily local giving
for higher education and health; support also
for social welfare and cultural programs.
Limitations: Giving primarily in TX. No grants
to individuals.

Application information:
   Initial approach: Full proposal
   Copies of proposal: 1
   Deadline(s): Submit proposal preferably in
      April or October; deadlines May 15 and
      November 15
   Board meeting date(s): June and December
   Write: Thomas M. Weaver, Manager
Officers: Josephine E. Abercrombie,*
President; Seth A. McMeans, Secretary; John B.
Howenstine,* Treasurer.
Trustees:* Edwina Gregg, George A. Robinson,
Jamie A. Robinson.
Employer Identification Number: 746048281

3868
Adams (The Moody) Foundation ☒
5002 Happy Hollow
Houston 77018

Established in 1981.
Donor(s): James M. Adams.
Financial data: (yr. ended 1/31/82): Assets,
$768,550 (M); gifts received, $992,000;
expenditures, $297,260, including $297,048
for 11 grants (high: $100,000; low: $3,000).
Purpose and activities: Giving primarily in
Texas and Mississippi, with emphasis on
education and Protestant church support.
Limitations: Giving primarily in TX and MS.
Officers and Trustees: James M. Adams,
President; Marcene Hazel Adams, Vice-
President, Secretary and Treasurer; George T.
Flott, Carl Schulse.
Employer Identification Number: 760024365

3869
Akin Foundation, The ☒
P.O. Box 19429
Houston 77024

Incorporated in 1948 in Texas.
Donor(s): J.W. Akin.
Financial data: (yr. ended 4/30/82): Assets,
$930,490 (M); expenditures, $410,271,
including $370,429 for grants.
Purpose and activities: Aid to various
Churches of Christ.
Officers and Trustees: Harry Pickup, Jr.,
President; James D. Yates, Secretary; Fred A.
Hutson, Treasurer.
Employer Identification Number: 756036487

3870
Allbritton Foundation, The
(formerly The Joe L. and Barbara B. Allbritton
Foundation)
5615 Kirby Dr., Suite 310
Houston 77005

Established in 1958 in Texas.
Donor(s): Joe L. Allbritton, Perpetual
Corporation, and others.
Financial data: (yr. ended 11/30/84): Assets,
$61,525 (M); gifts received, $350,000;
expenditures, $504,388, including $490,975
for 40 grants (high: $100,000; low: $100).
Purpose and activities: Grants mainly for
Christian religious organizations, education, and
cultural programs.

Officers: Joe Allbritton,* President; Barbara B.
Allbritton,* Vice-President; Virginia L. White,
Secretary and Treasurer.
Trustees:* Lawrence I. Hebert, Stephen A.
Massey, Thomas W. Wren.
Number of staff: 1 part-time support.
Employer Identification Number: 746051876

3871
Allied Endowment, Inc. ☒
815 Walker
P.O. Box 1515
Houston 77001

Incorporated in 1979 in Texas.
Donor(s): Allied Bank of Texas.
Financial data: (yr. ended 12/31/82): Assets,
$10,025 (M); expenditures, $329,292,
including $328,601 for 105 grants (high:
$82,100; low: $50).
Purpose and activities: Primarily local giving,
with emphasis on cultural programs, including
the performing arts, community funds, and
social agencies; support also for civic affairs,
youth agencies, health, and education.
Limitations: Giving primarily in TX.
Officers: Gerald H. Smith, President; Jay C.
Crager, Jr.,* Vice-President; William C.
Hatfield,* Secretary; Jules C. Pollard, Treasurer.
Directors:* Thomas C. Clausen, Walter E.
Johnson, Bob D. Ward.
Employer Identification Number: 742066478

3872
Amarillo Area Foundation, Inc.
1000 Polk St.
P.O. Box 2569
Amarillo 79105 (806) 376-4521

Community foundation established as a trust in
1957 in Texas.
Financial data: (yr. ended 12/31/84): Assets,
$9,025,954 (M); gifts received, $2,194,051;
expenditures, $1,361,082, including $957,064
for 33 grants (high: $371,177; low: $500;
average: $10,000-$20,000) and $11,800 for 32
grants to individuals.
Purpose and activities: Primarily local giving;
broad purposes with emphasis on community
development, including education, arts and
cultural programs, and a medical center.
Types of support awarded: Seed money,
emergency funds, building funds, equipment,
land acquisition, matching funds, consulting
services, technical assistance, scholarship
funds, special projects, research.
Limitations: Giving primarily in 26 most
northern counties of TX Panhandle. No grants
to individuals (except for limited scholarships
from designated funds), or for operating
budgets, continuing support, annual campaigns,
deficit financing, endowment funds,
publications, or conferences; no loans.
Publications: Annual report, application
guidelines.
Application information:
   Initial approach: Letter or telephone
   Copies of proposal: 8
   Deadline(s): October 1
   Board meeting date(s): Quarterly; executive
      committee meets monthly

Write: Jack Cromartie, Executive Director
Officers: David Warren, President; R.C. Neely, Jr., First Vice-President; Jose Rael, Second Vice-President; Betty Howell, Secretary; Morris Morelano, Treasurer; Jack Cromartie, Executive Director.
Number of staff: 2 full-time professional; 1 full-time support.
Employer Identification Number: 750978220

3873
American Petrofina Foundation

c/o Fred Stitzell
8350 North Central Expressway
Dallas 75206   (214) 750-2838
Mailing address: P.O. Box 2159, Dallas, TX 75221

Incorporated in 1974 in Texas.
Donor(s): American Petrofina, Inc.
Financial data: (yr. ended 6/30/83): Assets, $2,474,021 (M); expenditures, $279,645, including $273,835 for 100 grants (high: $53,020; low: $50).
Purpose and activities: Primarily local giving, with emphasis on community funds, cultural programs, education, and civic affairs.
Types of support awarded: Continuing support, annual campaigns, seed money, emergency funds, building funds, equipment, research, scholarship funds, employee matching gifts, matching funds.
Limitations: Giving primarily in TX. No grants to individuals.
Application information:
Initial approach: Full proposal
Copies of proposal: 1
Board meeting date(s): Approximately every 6 weeks
Final notification: 90 days
Officers and Director:* Verne H. Maxwell,* President; John R. Sears, Jr., Vice-President and Secretary; J.F. Stitzell, Vice-President and Treasurer.
Employer Identification Number: 237391423

3874
Anderson (Josephine) Charitable Trust ⌑

P.O. Box 8
Amarillo 79105

Trust established in Texas.
Donor(s): Josephine Anderson.†
Financial data: (yr. ended 2/29/84): Assets, $3,751,218 (M); expenditures, $296,243, including $147,350 for 27 grants (high: $15,000; low: $350).
Purpose and activities: Primarily local giving, with emphasis on health and social services, community development, cultural programs, and churches.
Limitations: Giving primarily in Amarillo, TX.
Officers and Trustees: L.A. White, Managing Trustee; Imadell Carter, Secretary.
Employer Identification Number: 751469596

3875
Anderson (M. D.) Foundation ▼

1301 Fannin St., 21st Fl.
P.O. Box 809
Houston 77001   (713) 658-6998

Trust established in 1936 in Texas.
Donor(s): M.D. Anderson.†
Financial data: (yr. ended 12/31/84): Assets, $65,368,593 (M); expenditures, $5,079,832, including $4,656,700 for 87 grants (high: $400,000; low: $300).
Purpose and activities: "The improvement of working conditions among workers generally...; the establishment, support and maintenance of hospitals, homes, and institutions for the care of the sick, the young, the aged, the incompetent and the helpless among the people; the improvement of living conditions among people generally." Support for a large local medical center and for educational and related projects, mainly in the Houston area .
Types of support awarded: Building funds, equipment, matching funds, research, seed money.
Limitations: Giving primarily in the Houston, TX, area. No support for institutions outside of Texas. No grants to individuals, or for endowment funds or operating budgets.
Publications: Multi-year report, application guidelines.
Application information:
Initial approach: Letter
Copies of proposal: 5
Deadline(s): None
Board meeting date(s): Monthly
Final notification: 1 month
Write: Carroll Sunseri, Secretary-Treasurer
Officers and Trustees:* Hugh Q. Buck,* President; Kraft W. Eidman,* Gibson Gayle, Jr.,* A.G. McNeese, Jr.,* Vice-Presidents; Carroll Sunseri, Secretary-Treasurer.
Number of staff: None.
Employer Identification Number: 746035669

3876
Andress Foundation, The ⌑

P.O. Box 5198
3130 Antilley Rd.
Abilene 79608

Established in 1977.
Donor(s): Tony D. Andress, Sr.
Financial data: (yr. ended 11/30/82): Assets, $931,432 (M); gifts received, $215,000; expenditures, $127,466, including $125,000 for 11 grants (high: $50,000; low: $1,000).
Purpose and activities: Primarily local giving for higher education and social services, including a rehabilitation center.
Limitations: Giving primarily in Abilene, TX.
Officers: Tony D. Andress, Sr.,* President; Tony D. Andress, Jr.,* Vice-President; John Allen Chalk, Vice-President and Secretary; Jerry L. Howard, Treasurer.
Directors:* Diana Dawn Andress, Kellie E. Andress.
Employer Identification Number: 751577382

3877
Bank of the Southwest National Association Houston Foundation ⌑

910 Travis St.
P.O. Box 2629
Houston 77001   (713) 751-6100

Trust established in 1952 in Texas.
Donor(s): Bank of the Southwest National Association.
Financial data: (yr. ended 12/31/83): Assets, $171,397 (M); gifts received, $60,000; expenditures, $240,927, including $240,000 for 30 grants (high: $120,000; low: $500).
Purpose and activities: Charitable purposes; primarily local giving, with emphasis on community funds; support also for hospitals, cultural activities, and higher education.
Limitations: Giving primarily in TX.
Application information:
Deadline(s): None
Write: Lamont R. Richie
Trustee: Bank of the Southwest.
Employer Identification Number: 746037985

3878
Bass Foundation, The ⌑

4224 Thanksgiving Tower
Dallas 75201

Trust established in 1945 in Texas; in 1983, foundation split up into Bass Foundation and Harry Bass Foundation.
Donor(s): Harry W. Bass, Sr., Mrs. Harry W. Bass, Sr.
Financial data: (yr. ended 12/31/83): Assets, $5,147,031 (M); expenditures, $254,697, including $233,333 for 59 grants (high: $55,000; low: $100; average: $200-$10,000).
Purpose and activities: Educational and charitable purposes; primarily local giving, with emphasis on cultural programs, education, and hospitals.
Types of support awarded: Building funds, general purposes.
Limitations: Giving primarily in the Dallas, TX, metropolitan area.
Application information:
Initial approach: Proposal
Deadline(s): None
Board meeting date(s): As required
Write: Steve Bossart
Trustees: Richard D. Bass, Thurman R. Taylor, Harry M. Wittingdon.
Number of staff: None.
Employer Identification Number: 756013540

3879
Bass Foundation

309 Main St.
Fort Worth 76102   (817) 336-0494

Established in 1945 in Texas.
Donor(s): Perry R. Bass, Lee Bass, Edward Bass, Sid Richardson Carbon and Gasoline Company.
Financial data: (yr. ended 12/31/84): Assets, $2,240,446 (M); gifts received, $301,000; expenditures, $22,370, including $10,000 for 2 grants of $5,000 each.

Purpose and activities: Giving primarily for arts and cultural institutions; some support for conservation.

Application information:

Initial approach: Letter

Deadline(s): None

Write: Valleau Wilkie, Jr.

Officers and Directors: Perry R. Bass, President; Nancy Lee Bass, Vice-President; Dora Neely, Secretary-Treasurer.

Number of staff: None.

Employer Identification Number: 756033983

3880
Baumberger (Charles) Testamentary Trust ⌑

325 North Saint Mary's St.

P.O. Box 300

San Antonio 78291

Trust established in 1972 in Texas.

Donor(s): Charles Baumberger, Jr.†

Financial data: (yr. ended 12/31/83): Assets, $17,441,209 (M); expenditures, $1,852,518, including $1,741,938 for grants.

Purpose and activities: All grants paid for college scholarships through the Baumberger Endowment.

Limitations: Giving limited to Bexar County, TX.

Trustees: Travis M. Moursund, Republic Bank.

Employer Identification Number: 746180005

3881
Baumberger Endowment ⌑

7701 Broadway, Dijon Plaza

P.O. Box 6067

San Antonio 78209 (512) 822-8915

Trust established in 1972 in Texas.

Donor(s): Charles Baumberger, Jr.†

Financial data: (yr. ended 12/31/82): Assets, $275,059 (M); gifts received, $1,832,978; expenditures, $1,949,174, including $1,791,608 for 496 grants to individuals.

Purpose and activities: Scholarships to Bexar County students attending Texas colleges and universities who would be unable to attend college without financial assistance.

Types of support awarded: Student aid.

Limitations: Giving limited to Bexar County, TX.

Publications: Program policy statement, application guidelines.

Application information: Application form required.

Deadline(s): January 31 for financial aid forms; February 15 for high school transcript

Final notification: May

Officers: Travis M. Moursund,* Secretary-Treasurer; Jerome F. Weynand, Executive Director.

Trustees:* S.H. Schmidt, Chairman; James F. Bartlett, Ronald Schmidt, A.J. Wetzel.

Employer Identification Number: 237225925

3882
Beal Foundation

First National Bank of Midland, Trust Dept.

P.O. Box 270

Midland 79702 (915) 682-3753

Incorporated in 1962 in Texas.

Donor(s): Carlton Beal, W.R. Davis.

Financial data: (yr. ended 12/31/82): Assets, $1,130,678 (M); expenditures, $358,103, including $205,000 for 22 grants (high: $63,000; low: $1,000).

Purpose and activities: Broad purposes; primarily local giving, with emphasis on secondary education, agencies for youth and the needy, health associations and hospitals, and a community fund.

Limitations: Giving primarily in TX.

Application information:

Write: Carlton Beal, Chairman

Officers and Trustees: Carlton Beal, Chairman; Keleen Beal, Vice-Chairman; John Bates, Secretary-Treasurer; Barry A. Beal, Carlton Beal, Jr., Spencer Beal, Mitchell A. Cappadonna, Robert J. Cowan, Jane B. Ramsland, Pomeroy Smith, Allen K. Trobaugh, Tom Welch.

Employer Identification Number: 756034480

3883
Beasley (Theodore and Beulah) Foundation, Inc. ▼

Two Turtle Creek Village, Suite 422

Dallas 75219 (214) 522-8790

Incorporated in 1957 in Texas.

Donor(s): Theodore P. Beasley.

Financial data: (yr. ended 12/31/82): Assets, $1,171,076 (M); expenditures, $5,744,327, including $5,575,921 for 30 grants (high: $2,027,956).

Purpose and activities: Primarily local giving, with emphasis on higher education, youth agencies, hospitals, and Protestant church support.

Limitations: Giving primarily in the Dallas, TX, area.

Application information:

Write: Theodore P. Beasley, President

Officers: Theodore P. Beasley, President; Samuel Dashefsky, Vice-President and Treasurer; Linda Montgomery, Secretary.

Employer Identification Number: 756035806

3884
Behmann Brothers Foundation ⌑

5250 Weber, Suite C

Corpus Christi 78411

Established in 1979.

Donor(s): Herman W. Behmann.†

Financial data: (yr. ended 6/30/83): Assets, $2,969,935 (M); expenditures, $157,747, including $133,800 for 30 grants (high: $57,000; low: $250).

Purpose and activities: Primarily local giving for agricultural research programs; support also for Christian church support and youth agencies.

Limitations: Giving primarily in TX.

Officers and Directors: Charles L. Kosarek, President; John Lloyd Bluntzer, Vice-President; Ross Mitchon, Secretary; Willie J. Kosarek, Treasurer; Ted M. Anderson.

Employer Identification Number: 742146739

3885
Bell Trust ⌑

10726 Plano Rd.

Dallas 75238 (214) 349-0060

Trust established in 1957 in Texas.

Donor(s): R.S. Bell, Katherine Bell.

Financial data: (yr. ended 12/31/83): Assets, $1,853,458 (M); expenditures, $260,285, including $236,864 for 91 grants (high: $6,000; low: $404).

Purpose and activities: Grants to Churches of Christ.

Limitations: No grants to individuals, or for building or endowment funds, scholarships, fellowships, or matching gifts; no loans.

Application information:

Initial approach: Full proposal

Copies of proposal: 1

Deadline(s): None

Board meeting date(s): March, June, September, and December

Write: H.L. Packer, Trustee

Trustees: Hulen L. Jackson, James N. Muns, Mrs. James N. Muns, H.L. Packer, Mrs. H.L. Packer.

Number of staff: None.

Employer Identification Number: 756020180

3886
Biological Humanics Foundation ⌑

3808 Euclid Ave.

Dallas 75205 (214) 521-2924

Trust established in 1950 in Texas.

Donor(s): Eugene McDermott.†

Financial data: (yr. ended 12/31/83): Assets, $4,819,580 (M); expenditures, $192,488, including $170,000 for 3 grants (high: $80,000; low: $10,000).

Purpose and activities: To advance knowledge in the field of human growth and development with emphasis on medical aspects of symmetry and asymmetry.

Types of support awarded: Research, scholarship funds.

Limitations: No grants to individuals or for endowment funds.

Application information:

Initial approach: Letter

Copies of proposal: 1

Board meeting date(s): Quarterly

Write: Miss Mary McDermott, President

Officers and Trustees: Mary McDermott, President; Philip O'B. Montgomery, Jr., Vice-President; Patricia Brown, Secretary; Kevin McBride, Treasurer; Charles A. LeMaistre, Philip O'B. Montgomery III.

Employer Identification Number: 756009766

3887
Bivins (Mary E.) Foundation ▼ ¤
414 Polk St.
P.O. Box 708
Amarillo 79105

Incorporated in 1949 in Texas.
Donor(s): Mary E. Bivins Trust, and others.
Financial data: (yr. ended 8/31/82): Assets,
$17,798,657 (M); gifts received, $4,884,177;
expenditures, $3,112,488, including $521,172
for 19 grants (high: $200,000; low: $390).
Purpose and activities: A private operating
foundation; operates a home and nursing
facility for the aged; also local giving, with
emphasis on social service agencies and
Christian colleges, including scholarship funds.
Limitations: Giving primarily in TX.
Officers: E.T. Evans,* President; L.L. Ward,*
Vice-President; Bob Churchill,* Secretary; Terry
Odom, Executive Director.
Directors: * Tom Bivins, Betty B. Childer, Don
McFarland, Forrest Stockdale.
Employer Identification Number: 750842370

3888
Blaffer (Sarah Campbell) Foundation ¤
913 River Oaks Bank & Trust Bldg.
2001 Kirby Dr.
Houston 77019   (713) 528-5279

Incorporated in 1964 in Texas.
Donor(s): Sarah C. Blaffer.†
Financial data: (yr. ended 12/31/82): Assets,
$14,301,178 (M); gifts received, $1,650,000;
expenditures, $751,760, including $383,628
for 37 grants (high: $100,000; low: $500) and
$169,140 for foundation-administered
programs.
Purpose and activities: A private operating
foundation; primarily local giving, with
emphasis on cultural programs, church support,
and secondary and higher education; also
operates a program of art exhibits.
Limitations: Giving primarily in TX. No grants
to individuals, or for endowment funds,
scholarships, or fellowships; no loans.
Application information:
  Initial approach: Letter
  Copies of proposal: 1
  Deadline(s): Submit proposal from January
    through August; deadline August 31
  Board meeting date(s): March and October
  Write: Edward Joseph Hudson, Jr., Secretary
Officers and Trustees: Charles W. Hall,
President; Jane Blaffer Owen, Vice-President
and Treasurer; Cecil Blaffer von Furstenberg,
Vice-President; Edward Joseph Hudson, Jr.,
Secretary; Gilbert M. Denman, Jr.
Employer Identification Number: 746065234

3889
Brackenridge (George W.)
  Foundation ▼
535 Travis Park Plaza
711 Navarro St.
San Antonio 78205   (512) 224-1011

Trust established in 1920 in Texas.
Donor(s): George W. Brackenridge.†

Financial data: (yr. ended 12/31/84): Assets,
$8,727,023 (M); expenditures, $557,969,
including $467,575 for 20 grants (high:
$100,000; low: $1,000; average: $3,000-
$50,000).
Purpose and activities: Giving limited to
support of accredited educational institutions in
Texas.
Types of support awarded: Equipment,
endowment funds, research, special projects,
publications, conferences and seminars,
scholarship funds, professorships, internships,
fellowships.
Limitations: Giving limited to TX. No grants to
individuals, or for general purposes, continuing
support, seed money, emergency funds, land
acquisition, renovation projects, building funds,
operating budgets, annual campaigns, deficit
financing, or matching gifts; no loans.
Application information: Applications for
grants not invited; all grants made on the
foundation's own initiative.
  Board meeting date(s): March, June,
    September, and December
  Final notification: Given quarterly
  Write: Gilbert M. Denman, Jr., Trustee
Trustees: Gilbert M. Denman, Jr., Leroy G.
Denman, Jr., Charles W. Harper, John B.
McDaniel, Jr.
Number of staff: None.
Employer Identification Number: 746034977

3890
Bridwell (The J. S.) Foundation ▼
500 City National Bldg.
Wichita Falls 76301   (817) 322-4436

Incorporated in 1949 in Texas.
Donor(s): J.S. Bridwell,† Margaret B. Bowdle.
Financial data: (yr. ended 12/31/83): Assets,
$18,441,963 (M); expenditures, $841,583,
including $733,454 for 53 grants (high:
$220,000; low: $100; average: $100-$12,500).
Purpose and activities: Broad purposes; giving
only to local organizations, with emphasis on
higher education, social services, and youth
agencies.
Types of support awarded: Building funds,
special projects.
Limitations: Giving limited to TX. No grants to
individuals, or for endowment funds or
operating budgets.
Officers and Directors: Herbert B. Story,
President; Clifford G. Tinsley, Secretary-
Treasurer; Ralph S. Bridwell, Garrett Oliver.
Employer Identification Number: 756032988

3891
Brinker (Maureen Connolly) Girls'
  Tennis Foundation, Inc. ¤
5419 Wateka Dr.
Dallas 75209   (214) 357-1604

Financial data: (yr. ended 4/30/83): Assets,
$1,256,466 (M); gifts received, $227,200;
expenditures, $253,809, including $84,543 for
44 grants (high: $18,850; low: $10) and
$18,610 for 26 grants to individuals.
Purpose and activities: Grants to individuals
and organizations for the "furtherance of
women's tennis".

Types of support awarded: Grants to
individuals.
Application information:
  Initial approach: Letter
  Deadline(s): None
  Write: Mrs. Frank Jeffett, President
Officer: Mrs. Frank A. Jeffett, President.
Trustees: Norman Brinker, Robert C. Taylor.
Employer Identification Number: 237040481

3892
Brookshire (B. C. & Addie) Kleberg
  County Charitable Foundation ¤
c/o Guaranty Nat'l. Bank & Trust
P.O. Drawer 749
Corpus Christi 78403

Established in 1958.
Financial data: (yr. ended 6/30/83): Assets,
$1,020,203 (M); expenditures, $58,907,
including $46,145 for 9 grants (high: $10,745;
low: $1,000).
Purpose and activities: Primarily local giving
for youth recreation agencies, community
centers, education, and cultural programs.
Limitations: Giving primarily in Kleberg
County, TX.
Trustee: Texas Commerce Bank.
Employer Identification Number: 746108397

3893
Brown Foundation, Inc., The ▼
2118 Welch Ave.
P.O. Box 13646
Houston 77219   (713) 523-6867

Incorporated in 1951 in Texas.
Donor(s): Herman Brown,† Mrs. Herman
Brown,† George R. Brown, Alice Pratt Brown.†
Financial data: (yr. ended 6/30/84): Assets,
$241,534,223 (M); expenditures, $16,378,888,
including $14,753,281 for 116 grants (high:
$2,547,250; low: $100) and $80,021 for
employee matching gifts.
Purpose and activities: Charitable purposes;
primarily local giving, with emphasis on higher
education, including medical education and
employee matching gifts; support also for
secondary education, the performing arts,
museums, social service and youth agencies,
hospitals, medical research, health
organizations, Protestant church support, and
public policy organizations.
Types of support awarded: Operating
budgets, continuing support, annual campaigns,
seed money, building funds, equipment, land
acquisition, endowment funds, matching funds,
professorships, fellowships, special projects,
research, publications, conferences and
seminars, employee matching gifts.
Limitations: Giving primarily in TX, with
emphasis on Houston. No grants to
individuals; no loans.
Publications: Application guidelines.
Application information:
  Initial approach: Full proposal
  Copies of proposal: 1
  Deadline(s): None
  Board meeting date(s): February, May,
    August, and November
  Final notification: 3 months

Write: Katherine B. Dobelman, Executive Director

Officers: Nancy Brown Negley,* President; C.M. Hudspeth,* Vice-President; Louisa Stude Sarofim,* Secretary; Katherine B. Dobelman, Treasurer and Executive Director.

Trustees:* Lesley Negley Crosthwaite, Alice Pratt Negley Dorn, George R. O'Connor, Maconda Brown O'Connor, James R. Paden, M.S. Stude, Isabel Brown Wilson.

Number of staff: 1 full-time professional; 6 full-time support.

Employer Identification Number: 746036466

3894
Brown (M. K.) Foundation, Inc. ¤
P.O. Box 662
Pampa 79066-0662   (806) 669-6851

Established in 1960 in Texas.

Donor(s): M.K. Brown.†

Financial data: (yr. ended 12/31/83): Assets, $1,823,654 (M); expenditures, $401,968, including $381,752 for 29 grants (high: $132,000; low: $250).

Purpose and activities: Primarily local giving, with emphasis on Protestant church support, youth agencies, community projects, and social agencies.

Limitations: Giving primarily in Pampa, TX. No grants to individuals.

Application information:
Initial approach: Full proposal
Deadline(s): July 1 and December 1
Write: Bill Waters, Chairman

Officers and Trustees: Bill W. Waters, Chairman; David E. Holt, Secretary-Treasurer; Alice T. Smith.

Employer Identification Number: 756034058

3895
Brown (T. J.) and C. A. Lupton Foundation, Inc. ▼ ¤
209 West Hattie St.
P.O. Box 1378
Fort Worth 76101

Incorporated in 1942 in Texas.

Donor(s): T.J. Brown,† C.A. Lupton,† V.J. Earnhart, J.A. Gooch.

Financial data: (yr. ended 12/31/83): Assets, $17,320,795 (M); expenditures, $1,042,780, including $960,831 for 17 grants (high: $710,000; low: $1,000; average: $1,000-$12,500).

Purpose and activities: Broad purposes; primarily local giving, with emphasis on higher education; some support for medical research and hospitals.

Limitations: Giving primarily in TX, with emphasis on Fort Worth.

Officer and Directors: Sam P. Woodson, III, President and Managing Director; V.J. Earnhart, Vice-President and Treasurer; J.A. Gooch, Secretary; Whitfield J. Collins, Gloria Lupton Tennison.

Employer Identification Number: 750992690

3896
Bryce (William and Catherine) Memorial Fund
c/o Texas American Bank/Fort Worth
P.O. Box 2050
Fort Worth 76113   (817) 338-8457

Trust established in 1944 in Texas.

Financial data: (yr. ended 9/30/83): Assets, $7,728,724 (M); expenditures, $528,472, including $468,500 for 50 grants (high: $30,500; low: $2,500).

Purpose and activities: Primarily local giving, with emphasis on child welfare, higher education, the aged, cultural programs, youth agencies, hospitals, and a community fund.

Limitations: Giving primarily in TX, particularly in the Fort Worth area. No grants to individuals.

Application information:
Initial approach: Letter
Copies of proposal: 1
Deadline(s): August 31
Board meeting date(s): October
Write: Robert M. Lansford

Trustee: Texas American Bank-Fort Worth.

Employer Identification Number: 756013845

3897
Burkitt Foundation, The
2000 West Loop South, Suite 1485
Houston 77027   (713) 439-0149

Incorporated in 1962 in Texas.

Donor(s): Elizabeth B. Crane.†

Financial data: (yr. ended 9/30/83): Assets, $8,500,000 (M); expenditures, $507,085, including $306,800 for 52 grants (high: $25,000; low: $500; average: $2,000-$5,000).

Purpose and activities: Broad purposes; giving limited primarily to the southwestern United States, with emphasis on Roman Catholic church-sponsored programs.

Types of support awarded: Operating budgets, continuing support, annual campaigns, seed money, endowment funds, matching funds, scholarship funds, fellowships, professorships, internships, exchange programs, special projects, research, publications, conferences and seminars.

Limitations: Giving limited to the southwestern United States. No grants to individuals or for deficit financing; no loans.

Publications: Annual report, application guidelines.

Application information:
Initial approach: Letter
Copies of proposal: 1
Deadline(s): February 15 and August 15
Board meeting date(s): March and September; screening committee meets monthly for initial review
Final notification: 30 days after board meetings
Write: Joseph W. Ryan, Vice-President

Officers and Trustees: Cornelius O. Ryan, President; Joseph W. Ryan, Vice-President and Secretary-Treasurer; William E. Ryan, Vice-President; Mary Lou Ryan Ray, Carl E. Ryan, Robert C. Ryan, Rev. James F. Wilson, C.S.B.

Number of staff: None.

Employer Identification Number: 746053270

3898
Butler (The George and Anne) Foundation ¤
1000 Louisiana, Suite 2220
Houston 77002

Incorporated in 1956 in Texas.

Donor(s): George A. Butler, Anne G. Butler,† Houston Corporation, McEvoy Company.

Financial data: (yr. ended 12/31/83): Assets, $2,062,309 (M); gifts received, $455,708; expenditures, $199,154, including $199,135 for 66 grants (high: $35,000; low: $25).

Purpose and activities: Broad purposes; primarily local giving for higher and secondary education, arts and cultural programs, health, youth, and Protestant church support.

Limitations: Giving primarily in TX.

Officers and Trustees:* George A. Butler,* President; Anne B. Leonard,* Ida Jo B. Moran,* Vice-Presidents; J. Hardy Windham, Treasurer.

Employer Identification Number: 746063429

3899
Butt (H. E.) Foundation
P.O. Box 670
Kerrville 78029   (512) 896-2505

Incorporated in 1933 in Texas.

Donor(s): H.E. Butt, Howard E. Butt, Jr., H.E. Butt Grocery Company, and others.

Financial data: (yr. ended 12/31/83): Assets, $4,165,122 (M); gifts received, $1,232,670; expenditures, $914,459.

Purpose and activities: A private operating foundation supporting the operation of camps in Texas used by qualifying groups and programs related to church renewal, lay theological education, and mental health.

Types of support awarded: Operating budgets.

Limitations: Giving limited to TX. No grants to individuals, or for building or endowment funds.

Application information:
Deadline(s): None
Board meeting date(s): December
Write: Howard E. Butt, Jr., President

Officers and Trustees: Howard E. Butt, Jr., President; Charles C. Butt, Vice-President; Barbara Dan Butt, Secretary-Treasurer; H.E. Butt, Sr., Mrs. H.E. Butt, Sr.

Number of staff: 7 full-time professional; 10 full-time support.

Employer Identification Number: 741239819

3900
Cain (Effie and Wofford) Foundation
6116 North Central Expressway, Suite 909
Dallas 75206   (214) 361-4201

Incorporated in 1952 in Texas.

Donor(s): Effie Marie Cain, R. Wofford Cain.†

Financial data: (yr. ended 10/31/84): Assets, $38,883,537 (M); gifts received, $150; expenditures, $1,069,628, including $820,098 for 38 grants (high: $542,748; low: $500; average: $7,000).

Purpose and activities: Broad purposes; primarily local giving, with emphasis on civic affairs, higher education, and hospitals; support also for cultural programs, youth agencies, and a community center.

Limitations: Giving limited to TX. No grants to individuals or for operating budgets.
Publications: Application guidelines.
Application information:
Copies of proposal: 1
Deadline(s): August 31
Board meeting date(s): October
Write: Harvey L. Walker, Executive Director
Officers: Effie Marie Cain,* President; Frank W. Denius,* Vice-President; R.J. Smith,* Secretary and Treasurer; Harvey L. Walker, Executive Director.
Trustees:* James B. Cain.
Number of staff: 1 full-time professional; 1 full-time support; 1 part-time support.
Employer Identification Number: 756030774

3901
Cameron (Harry S. and Isabel C.) Foundation ▼
P.O. Box 2555
Houston 77252-2555   (713) 652-6526

Established in 1966 in Texas.
Donor(s): Isabel C. Cameron.†
Financial data: (yr. ended 6/30/83): Assets, $13,452,087 (M); expenditures, $952,264, including $848,530 for 110 grants (high: $127,800; low: $100; average: $1,000-$10,000).
Purpose and activities: Primarily local giving, with emphasis on higher, elementary, and secondary education, Roman Catholic church support, and health.
Types of support awarded: Building funds, research, equipment, scholarship funds, general purposes.
Limitations: Giving primarily in TX, especially Houston. No grants to individuals, or for operating support, endowment funds, or matching gifts; no loans.
Application information:
Initial approach: Letter
Copies of proposal: 5
Deadline(s): Prior to board meetings
Board meeting date(s): April, August, and December
Final notification: 2 weeks after board meetings when action is favorable
Write: Carl W. Schumacher, Jr.
Directors: Charlotte Cameron, David W. Cameron, V.M. Cameron, Estelle Cameron Maloney, Frances Cameron Miller.
Trustee: InterFirst Bank Houston.
Number of staff: None.
Employer Identification Number: 746073312

3902
Carter (Amon G.) Foundation ▼ ¤
1212 InterFirst Bank Bldg.
P.O. Box 1036
Fort Worth 76101   (817) 332-2783

Incorporated in 1945 in Texas.
Donor(s): Amon G. Carter,† N.B. Carter,† Star-Telegram Employees Fund, Carter Foundation Production Company.

Financial data: (yr. ended 12/31/83): Assets, $146,553,828 (M); expenditures, $7,946,033, including $5,796,737 for 89 grants (high: $2,243,560; low: $100; average: $50,000-$500,000).
Purpose and activities: Broad purposes; primarily local giving, principally for higher education, youth agencies, the arts, hospitals, and child welfare; sponsors and largely supports an art museum and a youth camp; grants also for aid to the handicapped, and health agencies.
Types of support awarded: Continuing support, annual campaigns, seed money, emergency funds, building funds, equipment, land acquisition, matching funds, professorships, research.
Limitations: Giving primarily in Fort Worth and Tarrant County, TX. No grants to individuals, or for operating budgets, deficit financing, endowment funds, demonstration projects, publications, or conferences; no loans.
Application information:
Initial approach: Letter
Copies of proposal: 1
Deadline(s): None
Board meeting date(s): March, June, September, and December
Final notification: Within 10 days of board meeting
Write: Bob J. Crow, Executive Director
Officers: Ruth Carter Stevenson,* President; Robert W. Brown, M.D.,* Vice-President; Katrine Deakins,* Secretary-Treasurer; Bob J. Crow, Executive Director.
Directors:* Paul W. Mason.
Number of staff: 1 full-time professional; 2 part-time professional; 1 part-time support.
Employer Identification Number: 756000331

3903
Central and South West Foundation ¤
2700 One Main Place
Dallas 75250

Trust established in 1962 in Illinois.
Donor(s): Central and South West Corporation, Central Power and Light Company, Public Service Company of Oklahoma, Southwestern Electric Power Company, West Texas Utilities Company.
Financial data: (yr. ended 10/31/83): Assets, $1,742,339 (M); gifts received, $45,000; expenditures, $83,603, including $71,645 for 112 grants (high: $5,000; low: $10).
Purpose and activities: Grants largely for higher education, hospitals, studies in economics and agriculture, youth agencies, cultural programs, and community funds, primarily in areas of company operations.
Limitations: Giving primarily in areas of company operations.
Advisors: Durwood Chalker, Chairman; M.L. Borchelt, Glen D. Churchill, Jerry C. Edmondson, Martin E. Fate, Jr., John W. Turk.
Trustee: Harris Trust & Savings Bank.
Employer Identification Number: 366031631

3904
Chilton Foundation Trust, The
InterFirst Bank in Dallas
P.O. Box 83791
Dallas 75283

Trust established in 1945 in Texas.
Donor(s): Arthur L. Chilton,† Leonore Chilton.†
Financial data: (yr. ended 12/31/83): Assets, $6,500,000 (M); expenditures, $400,000, including $360,000 for 25 grants (high: $200,000; low: $1,000).
Purpose and activities: Giving primarily for youth, hospitals, health, education, social agencies and church support.
Limitations: Giving primarily in TX.
Trustee: InterFirst Bank in Dallas.
Employer Identification Number: 756006996

3905
C.I.O.S., Inc.
500 South Fifth
Waco 76706   (817) 757-2787

Incorporated about 1952 in Tennessee.
Donor(s): Paul P. Piper, Piper Industries, Inc., and others.
Financial data: (yr. ended 6/30/84): Assets, $4,908,384 (M); gifts received, $1,688,697; expenditures, $8,648, including $1,000 for 1 grant.
Purpose and activities: Religious and humanitarian purposes; grants for Protestant church support and religious programs, including support for foreign missions.
Publications: Program policy statement, application guidelines.
Application information:
Initial approach: Proposal
Board meeting date(s): Monthly
Write: Paul P. Piper, Trustee
Trustees: Paul P. Piper, Paul P. Piper, Jr., Mrs. Paul P. Piper, Ronald K. Piper.
Number of staff: 1 full-time professional.
Employer Identification Number: 626041388

3906
Clark Foundation, The ▼
6116 North Central Expressway, Suite 906
Dallas 75206   (214) 361-7498

Trust established in 1951 in Texas.
Donor(s): Anson L. Clark, M.D.†
Financial data: (yr. ended 12/31/83): Assets, $2,142,205 (M); expenditures, $691,889, including $506,875 for 31 grants (high: $50,000; low: $1,000; average: $1,000-$50,000).
Purpose and activities: Grants largely for education, including scholarships and research solely within Texas, with emphasis on the Dallas-Ft. Worth metropolitan area, and primarily at the initiative of the trustees.
Types of support awarded: Seed money, equipment, endowment funds, matching funds, scholarship funds, fellowships, research.

Limitations: Giving limited to TX, with emphasis on the Dallas-Ft. Worth metropolitan area. No grants to individuals, or for operating budgets, continuing support, annual campaigns, emergency or building funds, deficit financing, land acquisition, special projects, publications, or conferences; no loans.

Application information: Scholarship applications accepted only through the Dallas Independent School District and the Texas Interscholastic League.

Initial approach: Letter, telephone, or full proposal
Copies of proposal: 1
Deadline(s): November 15
Board meeting date(s): February, April, August, October, and December
Final notification: 45 days
Write: Walter Kerbel, Executive Secretary

Officer and Trustees: Walter Kerbel, Executive Secretary; Robert H. Middleton, DeWitt T. Weaver.

Number of staff: 1 full-time professional; 1 part-time support.

Employer Identification Number: 756015614

3907
Clayton Fund, The ▼ ⌺
P.O. Box 2538
Houston 77001

Trust established in 1952 in Texas.
Donor(s): William L. Clayton,† Susan V. Clayton.†
Financial data: (yr. ended 12/31/82): Assets, $16,254,955 (M); gifts received, $25,000; expenditures, $1,370,643, including $1,364,976 for 57 grants (high: $252,835; low: $100).
Purpose and activities: Educational and charitable purposes; support largely for higher education, including medical education and scholarships; grants also for hospitals, medical research, social services, aid to the handicapped, population control, and cultural programs.
Limitations: Giving primarily in TX.
Application information:
Write: S.M. McAshan, Jr., Trustee
Trustees: T.J. Barlow, W. St. John Garwood, Jr., S.M. McAshan, Jr.
Employer Identification Number: 746042331

3908
Cockrell Foundation ▼
999 Main Bldg.
Houston 77002   (713) 651-1271

Trust established in 1957 in Texas; incorporated in 1966.
Donor(s): Mrs. Dula Cockrell,† E. Cockrell, Jr.†
Financial data: (yr. ended 12/31/83): Assets, $22,594,915 (M); expenditures, $1,320,933, including $908,634 for 27 grants (high: $800,000; low: $500; average: $33,653).
Purpose and activities: Broad purposes; local giving for higher education; support also for hospitals, community funds, and youth agencies.
Limitations: Giving primarily in TX. No grants to individuals.
Publications: 990-PF.

Application information:
Initial approach: Full proposal
Copies of proposal: 1
Board meeting date(s): March and October
Write: Mary Horger, Executive Director
Officers: Alf Roark,* President; Ernest H. Cockrell,* Vice-President; W.F. Wright, Jr., Secretary-Treasurer.
Directors:* Janet S. Cockrell, Carol Cockrell Curran, Richard B. Curran.
Employer Identification Number: 746076993

3909
Collins (Carr P.) Foundation, Inc. ▼
P.O. Box 1330
Lewisville 75067   (214) 221-6202

Incorporated in 1962 in Texas.
Donor(s): Carr P. Collins.
Financial data: (yr. ended 12/31/84): Assets, $17,305,318 (M); expenditures, $1,077,970, including $883,500 for 15 grants (high: $250,000; low: $2,500; average: $5,000-$10,000).
Purpose and activities: Broad purposes; support for higher education, youth agencies, religious organizations, and medical facilities.
Limitations: Giving primarily in TX. No grants to individuals.
Application information: Funds committed through 1988; applications currently not accepted.
Initial approach: Letter
Deadline(s): None
Board meeting date(s): Annually
Write: Connie G. Romans, Treasurer
Officers: Ruth Collins Sharp,* President; Michael J. Collins,* Vice-President; R. Hubbard Hardy, Secretary; Connie G. Romans, Treasurer.
Directors:* J.C. Cantrell, Calvert Collins, Carr P. Collins, Jr., James M. Collins, Lynn Craft, W. Dewey Presley, Robert H. Stewart, III.
Number of staff: 1.
Employer Identification Number: 756011615

3910
Collins (The James M.) Foundation ⌺
10311 Gaywood Rd.
Dallas 75229

Established in 1964 in Texas.
Donor(s): James M. Collins.
Financial data: (yr. ended 12/31/83): Assets, $4,316,577 (M); expenditures, $174,054, including $165,425 for 31 grants (high: $50,000; low: $100).
Purpose and activities: Primarily local giving, with emphasis on higher education, church support and religious associations, hospitals, and youth agencies.
Limitations: Giving primarily in TX.
Trustees: Dorothy Dann Collins, James M. Collins, Beverly Kishpaugh.
Employer Identification Number: 756040743

3911
Communities Foundation of Texas, Inc. ▼
4605 Live Oak St.
Dallas 75204   (214) 826-5231

Community foundation established in 1953 in Texas; incorporated in 1960.
Financial data: (yr. ended 6/30/84): Assets, $89,520,522 (M); gifts received, $9,084,043; expenditures, $11,310,838, including $11,310,838 for 925 grants (high: $1,050,923; low: $15; average: $10,000-$25,000).
Purpose and activities: Broad purposes; to promote the well-being of the inhabitants of Texas, primarily in the Dallas area; grants from unrestricted funds are generally for education, health and hospitals, social services, youth, and cultural programs.
Types of support awarded: Operating budgets, annual campaigns, seed money, emergency funds, building funds, equipment, land acquisition, matching funds, consulting services, technical assistance, special projects, program-related investments, research, publications, conferences and seminars.
Limitations: Giving primarily in the Dallas, TX, area. No support for religious purposes from general fund, media projects, or organizations which redistribute funds to other organizations. No grants to individuals, or for continuing support, deficit financing, endowment funds, scholarships or fellowships.
Publications: Program policy statement, application guidelines, financial statement.
Application information:
Initial approach: Letter
Copies of proposal: 1
Deadline(s): 30 days before Committee meetings
Board meeting date(s): Distribution Committee for unrestricted funds meets in March, August, and November
Final notification: 1 week after Distribution Committee meeting
Write: Edward M. Fjordbak, Executive Vice-President
Officers: Russell H. Perry,* Chairman and President; Edward M. Fjordbak, Executive Vice-President and Secretary; Dana Ann Holton, Vice-President-Grant Administration; Harmon Schepps,* Treasurer; Pamela Dees, Financial Officer.
Trustees:* John F. Stephens, Vice-Chairman; Ebby Halliday Acers, William E. Cooper, Jack B. Jackson, Ruth Collins Sharp.
Number of staff: 3 full-time professional; 1 part-time professional; 6 full-time support; 1 part-time support.
Employer Identification Number: 750964565

3912
Constantin Foundation, The ▼
2510 Mercantile Bank Bldg.
Dallas 75201   (214) 741-1248

Trust established in 1947 in Texas.
Donor(s): E. Constantin, Jr.,† Mrs. E. Constantin, Jr.†

Financial data: (yr. ended 12/31/84): Assets, $23,900,000 (M); expenditures, $2,295,000, including $2,176,000 for 31 grants (high: $1,048,900; low: $1,000; average: $50,000).
Purpose and activities: Educational and charitable purposes; primarily local giving, with emphasis on higher education; some support for youth agencies and hospitals.
Types of support awarded: Building funds, endowment funds, scholarship funds, matching funds, general purposes, land acquisition, equipment.
Limitations: Giving primarily in the Dallas, TX, metropolitan area. No support for state schools. No grants to individuals, or for research-related programs; no loans.
Application information:
   Initial approach: Full proposal
   Copies of proposal: 6
   Deadline(s): November 1; grants considered only at December meeting
   Board meeting date(s): March, June, September, and December
   Final notification: January
   Write: Trustees
Trustees: Henry C. Beck, Jr., Gene H. Bishop, Walter L. Fleming, Jr., Joel T. Williams.
Number of staff: 1 part-time professional; 2 part-time support.
Employer Identification Number: 756011289

3913
Cook (Loring) Foundation
P.O. Box 1060
McAllen 78501

Incorporated in 1953 in Texas.
Financial data: (yr. ended 3/31/83): Assets, $1,235,389 (M); expenditures, $100,632, including $94,770 for 56 grants (high: $15,300; low: $100).
Purpose and activities: Broad purposes; primarily local giving, with emphasis on Protestant church support, cancer and heart disease research, higher education, youth and social agencies, and cultural programs.
Limitations: Giving primarily in TX.
Officers: Vannie E. Cook, Jr., President; Charles E. Thompson, Vice-President; Mrs. Loring T. Cook, Secretary.
Employer Identification Number: 746050063

3914
Cooley (The Denton A.) Foundation
6655 Travis, Suite 900
Houston 77030
Mailing address: P.O. Box 20660, Houston, TX 77225

Incorporated in 1960 in Texas.
Donor(s): Denton A. Cooley, M.D., Mrs. Denton A. Cooley.
Financial data: (yr. ended 11/30/83): Assets, $834,430 (M); gifts received, $226,025; expenditures, $543,189, including $532,050 for 64 grants (high: $150,000; low: $100).
Purpose and activities: Broad purposes; primarily local giving, with emphasis on medical education and research, higher education, and health agencies.

Types of support awarded: Operating budgets, building funds, endowment funds, special projects, research.
Limitations: Giving primarily in the Houston, TX, area. No grants to individuals, or for scholarships, fellowships, publications, or conferences; no loans.
Publications: 990-PF.
Application information:
   Initial approach: Full proposal
   Copies of proposal: 1
   Deadline(s): None
   Board meeting date(s): Quarterly
   Final notification: 4 to 6 months
Officers and Trustees: Denton A. Cooley, M.D., President; Louise T. Cooley, Vice-President; Gerald A. Maley, Secretary-Treasurer; Richard C. Hudson.
Number of staff: None.
Employer Identification Number: 746053213

3915
Cooper Foundation
(also known as The Madison Alexander Cooper and Martha Roane Cooper Foundation)
1801 Austin Ave.
Waco 76701   (817) 754-0315

Trust established in 1943 in Texas.
Donor(s): Madison Alexander Cooper, Jr.†
Financial data: (yr. ended 3/31/82): Assets, $5,000,000 (M); expenditures, $664,918, including $605,517 for 14 grants (high: $283,000; low: $10,000).
Purpose and activities: Broad purposes; to make Waco "a better or more desirable city in which to live"; assumes the entire first-year budgets of new enterprises, which, upon proving their worth, will be supported subsequently as agencies of the community fund or by other public organizations.
Limitations: Giving primarily in the city of Waco, TX. No grants to individuals, or for campaigns, endowment funds, or causes for which funds are available from other sources; no loans.
Publications: Multi-year report.
Application information:
   Initial approach: Telephone
   Copies of proposal: 8
   Deadline(s): 1 week before monthly meeting
   Board meeting date(s): 2nd Tuesday of every month
   Write: Jerome Cartwright, Executive Director
Officers: R.D. Pattillo,* Secretary-Treasurer; Jerome Cartwright, Executive Director.
Trustees:* Raymond B. Goddard, Sr., Chairman; Franklin Smith, Vice-Chairman; J.W. Bush, Hilton H. Howell, Abner V. McCall, Joe L. Ward, Jr.
Employer Identification Number: 741272389

3916
Cooper Industries Foundation ▼
First City Tower, Suite 4000
P.O. Box 4446
Houston 77210   (713) 739-5632

Incorporated in 1964; absorbed Crouse-Hinds Foundation in 1982.
Donor(s): Cooper Industries, Inc.

Financial data: (yr. ended 12/31/83): Assets, $8,110,837 (M); gifts received, $53,950; expenditures, $2,014,895, including $1,753,535 for grants (high: $300,000; average: $1,000-$5,000), $12,015 for grants to individuals and $223,316 for employee matching gifts.
Purpose and activities: General purposes; functions solely as a conduit through which Cooper Industries, Inc. and its operating units throughout the country make contributions to local charities, community funds, higher education, and the visual and performing arts.
Types of support awarded: Operating budgets, continuing support, annual campaigns, seed money, emergency funds, matching funds, employee matching gifts, consulting services, technical assistance, employee related scholarships, research, special projects.
Limitations: Giving primarily in Houston, TX, and other communities of company operations. No grants to individuals (except for scholarships to children of company employees), or for endowment funds, publications, or conferences; no loans.
Application information:
   Initial approach: Letter
   Copies of proposal: 1
   Deadline(s): None
   Board meeting date(s): February; distribution committee meets quarterly
   Final notification: 1 month
   Write: Patricia B. Mottram, Secretary
Officers and Trustees:* Robert Cizik,* Chairman; Thomas W. Campbell,* President; Alan E. Riedel,* Vice-President; Patricia Mottram, Secretary; D.K. Cross,* Treasurer.
Number of staff: 1 full-time professional; 1 full-time support.
Employer Identification Number: 316060698

3917
Costa (Aubrey M.) Foundation
5580 LBJ Freeway, Suite 530
Dallas 75240   (214) 239-8133

Established in 1968 in Texas.
Donor(s): Aubrey M. Costa.†
Financial data: (yr. ended 12/31/83): Assets, $1,325,925 (M); expenditures, $139,603, including $112,916 for 21 grants (high: $25,000; low: $250).
Purpose and activities: Broad purposes; primarily local giving, with emphasis on a university education program on mortgage banking; support also for health agencies and community funds.
Limitations: Giving primarily in TX. No grants to individuals.
Application information:
   Initial approach: Letter
   Copies of proposal: 1
   Deadline(s): None
   Board meeting date(s): As required
   Final notification: 2 weeks
   Write: Edward C. Greene, Trustee
Trustees: Edward C. Greene, M.J. Greene.
Number of staff: None.
Employer Identification Number: 756085394

3918
Craig (J. Paul) Foundation
c/o Amarillo National Bank, Trust Dept.
Box 1611
Amarillo 79181   (806) 378-8331

Financial data: (yr. ended 9/30/83): Assets, $1,217,716 (M); expenditures, $149,372, including $136,000 for 18 grants (high: $27,000; low: $2,000).
Purpose and activities: Primarily local giving for youth and child welfare, and the aged.
Limitations: Giving primarily in the Panhandle area of TX.
Trustee: Amarillo National Bank.
Employer Identification Number: 751689765

3919
Crow (Trammell) Family Foundation ¤
2001 Bryan St., Suite 3200
Dallas 75201

Established in 1979.
Donor(s): Margaret D. Crow, Trammell S. Crow, Harlan Crow, Lucy Crow Billingsley, Dallas Market Center Company.
Financial data: (yr. ended 12/31/83): Assets, $17,133 (M); gifts received, $534,351; expenditures, $550,573, including $550,452 for 59 grants (high: $301,000; low: $100).
Purpose and activities: Primarily local giving for higher and secondary education, social services, cultural programs, community development, and a linguistic center.
Types of support awarded: General purposes, research, special projects, building funds.
Limitations: Giving primarily in Dallas, TX.
Officers: Trammell S. Crow,* President; Howard Crow,* Vice-President; H.D. Johnson III, Secretary; Harlan Crow,* Treasurer.
Directors:* Lucy Crow Billingsley, Ashley H. Priddy, Howard Putoff, Mrs. Harry Ransom, Jack W. Robinson, George Schreder.
Employer Identification Number: 751685708

3920
Crump (Joe and Jessie) Fund ▼
Texas American Bank/Fort Worth
P.O. Box 2050
Fort Worth 76113   (817) 338-8151

Trust established in 1965 in Texas.
Donor(s): Joe L. Crump.†
Financial data: (yr. ended 9/30/82): Assets, $6,090,216 (M); expenditures, $1,470,949, including $718,498 for 12 grants (high: $156,493; low: $10,000) and $325,000 for 3 loans.
Purpose and activities: Broad purposes; local giving for an Episcopal theological seminary for scholarships, cultural research, and lectureships; support also for cancer research, aid to handicapped children, and Episcopal church building funds.
Types of support awarded: Research, scholarship funds, loans.
Limitations: Giving limited to TX. No grants to individuals, or for building or endowment funds, matching gifts, or general purposes.
Application information:
  Initial approach: Letter

Copies of proposal: 1
Board meeting date(s): As required
Write: Robert M. Lansford, Senior Vice-President
Trustees: David C. Blevins, III, Mrs. Jessie B. Crump, Texas American Bank-Fort Worth (Robert M. Lansford, Senior Vice-President).
Employer Identification Number: 756045044

3921
Cullen Foundation, The ▼
601 Jefferson, 40th Fl.
Houston 77002   (713) 651-8837
Mailing address: P.O. Box 1600, Houston, TX 77251

Trust established in 1947 in Texas.
Donor(s): Hugh Roy Cullen,† Lillie Cullen.†
Financial data: (yr. ended 12/31/83): Assets, $110,423,136 (M); expenditures, $12,499,841, including $4,545,593 for 28 grants (high: $1,900,000; low: $5,000; average: $10,000-$70,000).
Purpose and activities: Primarily local giving for charitable, educational, medical, and other eleemosynary purposes; grants for hospitals, eye research, and higher education; support also for music, the performing arts, social services, drug abuse prevention, and community funds.
Types of support awarded: Annual campaigns, deficit financing, building funds, equipment, land acquisition, general purposes, matching funds, professorships, research.
Limitations: Giving limited to TX, with emphasis on Houston. No grants to individuals; no loans.
Publications: 990-PF, application guidelines.
Application information:
  Initial approach: Proposal, letter, or telephone
  Copies of proposal: 1
  Deadline(s): None
  Board meeting date(s): Usually in January, April, July, October, and as required
  Final notification: Varies
  Write: Joseph C. Graf, Executive Secretary
Officers: Wilhelmina Cullen Robertson,* President; Roy Henry Cullen,* Vice-President; Isaac Arnold, Jr.,* Secretary-Treasurer; Joseph C. Graf, Executive Secretary.
Trustees:* Douglas B. Marshall, Jr., A. Frank Smith, Jr.
Number of staff: 1 full-time professional; 1 full-time support.
Employer Identification Number: 746048769

3922
Curtis Mathes Foundation
c/o Curtis Mathes Corporation
1411 Greenway Dr.
Irving 75062   (214) 659-1122

Established in 1982 in Texas.
Donor(s): Curtis Mathes Corporation.
Financial data: (yr. ended 8/31/83): Assets, $30,706 (M); gifts received, $163,328; expenditures, $133,004, including $132,993 for 12 grants (high: $129,870; low: $100).

Purpose and activities: First year of operation 1982-83; giving primarily for education, particularly to an innovative school in Toronto, Canada; remaining grants to charitable organizations in Texas.
Types of support awarded: Operating budgets.
Limitations: Giving primarily in TX.
Application information:
  Deadline(s): October 1
  Board meeting date(s): October 30
  Final notification: November 30
  Write: Bill Park, Chairman
Directors: Bill Park, Chairman; Jack Sheedy, Secretary; Bill Nieman, Treasurer; Ralph Campbell, Barry Goldberg, Melinda Mathes.
Employer Identification Number: 751869223

3923
Dallas Foundation, The ▼
3300 Republic Bank Tower
Dallas 75201   (214) 969-5515

Community foundation established in 1929 in Texas.
Financial data: (yr. ended 12/31/84): Assets, $8,906,366 (M); gifts received, $193,468; expenditures, $656,366, including $564,888 for 20 grants (high: $119,450; low: $3,800).
Purpose and activities: Local giving to promote charitable, educational, cultural, recreational, and health programs through grants to community organizations and agencies, principally for capital purposes.
Types of support awarded: Building funds, equipment, land acquisition.
Limitations: Giving limited to the City and County of Dallas, TX. No grants to individuals, or for endowment funds, operating budgets, research, general support, scholarships or fellowships; no loans.
Publications: Newsletter, program policy statement, application guidelines, informational brochure.
Application information:
  Initial approach: One page proposal
  Copies of proposal: 11
  Deadline(s): None
  Board meeting date(s): Usually in February, May, and October
  Final notification: 4 months
  Write: Miss Nelle Johnston, Executive Secretary
Officer: Nelle Johnston, Executive Secretary.
Governors: Carl J. Thomsen, Chairman; Charles G. Cullum, Joe M. Dealey, Gerald W. Fronterhouse, Richard M. Hart, Jerry Lastelick, George Schrader, John Field Scovell, Jon B. White.
Trustee Banks: Allied Lakewood Bank, BancTexas Dallas, First City Bank of Dallas, InterFirst Bank Dallas, North Dallas Bank & Trust Company, Preston State Bank, RepublicBank Dallas, RepublicBank Greenville Avenue, RepublicBank Oak Cliff, Texas American Bank.
Number of staff: 1 part-time professional; 3 part-time support.
Employer Identification Number: 756038529

3924
Dallas Morning News - WFAA Foundation, The
(formerly The G. B. Dealey Foundation)
A.H. Belo Corporation
Young and Houston Sts.
Dallas 75265   (214) 977-6600

Trust established in 1952 in Texas.
Donor(s): A.H. Belo Corporation.
Financial data: (yr. ended 12/31/84): Assets, $3,200,000 (M); expenditures, $270,500, including $268,500 for 17 grants (high: $25,000; low: $2,000; average: $15,800).
Purpose and activities: Charitable purposes; primarily local giving, with emphasis on hospitals, higher education, private secondary schools, cultural programs, youth agencies, and health and social service organizations.
Types of support awarded: Building funds, endowment funds.
Limitations: Giving primarily in TX. No grants to individuals.
Application information: Application form required.
    Copies of proposal: 1
    Board meeting date(s): June and December
    Write: W.G. Mullins
Trustees: Joe M. Dealey, Robert W. Decherd, James M. Moroney, Jr., Reece A. Overcash, Jr., William H. Seay, Thomas B. Walker, Jr.
Number of staff: None.
Employer Identification Number: 756012569

3925
Dallas Rehabilitation Foundation
P.O. Box 202503
Dallas 75220   (214) 920-8011

Established in 1981 in Texas.
Donor(s): National Medical Enterprises, Inc.
Financial data: (yr. ended 10/31/84): Assets, $3,058,302 (M); gifts received, $29,000; expenditures, $255,819, including $150,236 for 5 grants (high: $60,000; low: $6,000; average: $30,000-$50,000) and $105,583 for 6 foundation-administered programs.
Purpose and activities: Primarily local giving for projects that advance the science and art of rehabilitation of severely physically handicapped individuals, primarily through research activities; some support also for educational projects.
Types of support awarded: Equipment, special projects, research, seed money, matching funds, scholarship funds, professorships, internships, fellowships, publications, conferences and seminars.
Limitations: Giving primarily in TX. No grants to individuals, or for indirect costs, operating budgets, continuing support, annual campaigns, emergency funds, deficit financing, building funds, land acquisition, renovation projects, endowments, program-related investments, or exchange programs; no loans.
Publications: Program policy statement, application guidelines.
Application information: Application form required.
    Initial approach: Proposal or letter
    Copies of proposal: 1
    Deadline(s): September 15

Board meeting date(s): February, May, August, and November or December
Final notification: December
Write: Raymond L. Dabney, President
Officers and Trustees: Randolph B. Marston, Chairman; Raymond L. Dabney, President; George W. Works III, Vice-President; Thomas W. Wassell, Secretary; Larry Edwards, Treasurer; Manuel Avila, Tom J. Dean, Jack W. Hawkins, Robert O. Helberg, Frank J. Morris, Mrs. Paul W. Phy, Paul Stanley, Francis W. Thayer, George W. Wharton, Robert J. Wright.
Number of staff: 2 full-time professional.
Employer Identification Number: 751783741

3926
Davidson Family Charitable Foundation ▼
Texas American Bank, Fort Worth
P.O. Box 2050
Fort Worth 76113

Trust established in 1961 in Texas.
Donor(s): C.J. Davidson.†
Financial data: (yr. ended 6/30/84): Assets, $13,636,796 (M); expenditures, $2,096,062, including $1,799,425 for 80 grants (high: $200,000; low: $400).
Purpose and activities: Primarily local giving, with emphasis on education, particularly higher education, welfare, hospitals, health services, and youth.
Types of support awarded: Building funds, equipment, scholarship funds, endowment funds, general purposes.
Limitations: Giving primarily in TX.
Application information:
    Initial approach: Letter
    Deadline(s): None
    Board meeting date(s): Quarterly
    Write: Robert M. Lansford, Senior Vice-President
Advisory Board: H.W. Davidson, Chairman; John T. Bean, T.C. Blasingame, R.S. Davidson, Hilton Ray, John J. Wilson.
Trustee: Texas American Bank, Fort Worth.
Number of staff: 2.
Employer Identification Number: 756014529

3927
Davis (Ken W.) Foundation ⌑
610 Main St.
Fort Worth 76101

Incorporated in 1954 in Texas.
Donor(s): Ken W. Davis,† Ken W. Davis, Jr., T.C. Davis, W.S. Davis, Mid-Continent Supply Co.
Financial data: (yr. ended 10/31/82): Assets, $3,757,818 (M); expenditures, $302,559, including $290,000 for 115 grants (high: $52,525; low: $50).
Purpose and activities: To assist various charitable and religious organizations; general giving, primarily in Texas and Oklahoma, with emphasis on community funds, youth agencies, health, and higher education; support also for the handicapped.
Limitations: Giving primarily in TX and OK.
Application information:
    Write: W.E. Strittmatter, Secretary

Officers and Directors: Ken W. Davis, Jr., President; Kay Davis, T.C. Davis, Vice-Presidents; W.E. Strittmatter, Secretary and Treasurer.
Employer Identification Number: 756012722

3928
DeBakey Medical Foundation, The
One Shell Plaza, Suite 4300
Houston 77002   (713) 224-4262

Incorporated in 1961 in Texas.
Donor(s): Michael E. DeBakey, M.D., James F. Breuil, Eugene C. Pulliam, Rosa Taub Kahn, and others.
Financial data: (yr. ended 4/30/82): Assets, $6,102,643 (M); gifts received, $777,668; expenditures, $559,995, including $504,041 for 6 grants (high: $379,041; low: $15,000).
Purpose and activities: To encourage education and research in medicine; support primarily for a private medical school in Texas.
Limitations: Giving primarily in TX. No grants to individuals.
Application information:
    Initial approach: Letter
    Board meeting date(s): December
    Write: Michael E. DeBakey, M.D., President
Officers and Trustees: Michael E. DeBakey, M.D., President; Albert B. Altek, Mrs. Lloyd H. Smith, Vice-Presidents; Henry J.N. Taub, Secretary-Treasurer.
Employer Identification Number: 746053822

3929
Diamond M Foundation, Inc., The
911 Twenty-fifth St.
P.O. Box 1149
Snyder 79549   (915) 573-6311

Trust established in 1950; incorporated in 1957 in Texas.
Donor(s): C.T. McLaughlin.†
Financial data: (yr. ended 12/31/82): Assets, $2,717,161 (M); expenditures, $179,864, including $3,126 for 5 grants (high: $1,000; low: $200) and $142,641 for 1 foundation-administered program.
Purpose and activities: A private operating foundation; primarily local giving. General education through art displays in a museum; some giving for charitable activities, including community funds, community services, and higher education.
Limitations: Giving primarily in TX.
Officers and Directors: Evelyn McLaughlin Knox-Davies, President; George Killam, Vice-President; J. Mark McLaughlin, Treasurer; W.G. Holt, Jay Huckabee, Jean McLaughlin Kahle, Ruth McLaughlin Riddle.
Employer Identification Number: 756015426

3930
Dickson (The Raymond) Foundation ⌑
P.O. Box 406
Hallettsville 77964   (512) 798-2531

Trust established in 1958 in Texas.
Donor(s): Raymond Dickson.†

Financial data: (yr. ended 12/31/83): Assets, $1,180,487 (M); expenditures, $67,211, including $58,600 for 29 grants (high: $10,000; low: $100).
Purpose and activities: Broad purposes; giving limited to Texas, with emphasis on youth agencies, higher education, and health.
Limitations: Giving limited to TX. No grants to individuals or for building funds.
Publications: Program policy statement, application guidelines.
Application information:
  Initial approach: Proposal
  Copies of proposal: 1
  Board meeting date(s): November or December
  Write: Robert K. Jewett, Chairman
Officers and Trustees: Robert K. Jewett, Chairman; Wilbur H. Baber, Jr., G. Cameron Duncan, Vaughan B. Meyer.
Employer Identification Number: 746052983

3931
Dodge Jones Foundation ▼ ⌗
P.O. Box 176
Abilene 79604

Incorporated in 1954 in Texas.
Donor(s): Ruth Leggett Jones,† and others.
Financial data: (yr. ended 12/31/82): Assets, $26,187,715 (M); gifts received, $7,890,019; expenditures, $3,672,291, including $1,129,800 for 32 grants (high: $650,000; low: $100; average: $1,000-$15,000) and $473,943 for 1 foundation-administered program.
Purpose and activities: Broad purposes; primarily local support for general charitable and educational activities. Grants largely for higher education, hospitals, and operation of a job training and placement service for minorities; support also for cultural programs and youth and social agencies.
Types of support awarded: General purposes.
Limitations: Giving primarily in Abilene, TX. No grants to individuals, or for scholarships or capital funds; no loans.
Application information:
  Initial approach: Letter
  Deadline(s): None
  Final notification: Varies; rejections are immediate
  Write: Joseph E. Cannon, Vice-President
Officers: Julia Jones Matthews,* President; Joseph E. Cannon,* Melvin W. Holt,* Kade L. Matthews, Vice-Presidents; Eugene Allen, Secretary-Treasurer.
Directors:* Joe B. Matthews, John A. Matthews, Jr.
Number of staff: 1 full-time professional; 3 part-time professional; 1 part-time support.
Employer Identification Number: 756006386

3932
Dorset Foundation, The ⌗
412 Merchants & Planters National Bank Bldg.
Sherman 75090   (214) 893-6103

Incorporated about 1957 in Texas.
Donor(s): W.S. Dorset.†

Financial data: (yr. ended 12/31/83): Assets, $1,741,949 (M); expenditures, $84,554, including $73,700 for grants.
Purpose and activities: Primarily local giving, with emphasis on community projects and medicine.
Limitations: Giving primarily in TX.
Application information:
  Initial approach: Letter
  Write: Roy C. Sewell
Officers: Roy C. Sewell, President and Treasurer; Ben G. Sewell, Vice-President; Carolyn Nail Sewell, Secretary.
Employer Identification Number: 756013384

3933
Doss (The M. S.) Foundation
Community Chapel Center, SW 11th St. Extension
P.O. Box 1338
Seminole 79360   (915) 758-2770

Trust established in 1959 in Texas.
Donor(s): M.S. Doss,† Mrs. M.S. Doss.†
Financial data: (yr. ended 12/31/83): Assets, $6,592,752 (M); expenditures, $373,727, including $201,961 for 7 grants (high: $54,928; low: $2,266).
Purpose and activities: Primarily local giving; grants largely to a chapel building fund and youth agencies.
Limitations: Giving primarily in west TX, particularly Gaines County. No grants to individuals.
Application information:
  Initial approach: Letter
  Copies of proposal: 1
  Deadline(s): None
  Board meeting date(s): October and as required
  Write: James W. Satterwhite, Executive Director
Officers: A.E. Brooks,* Chairman; Joe K. McGill,* Vice-Chairman; Fannie J. Smith,* Secretary; Stuart Robertson,* Treasurer; James W. Satterwhite, Executive Director.
Directors:* Richard Spaaberry.
Number of staff: 1.
Employer Identification Number: 756022292

3934
Dougherty (The James R.), Jr. Foundation ▼
P.O. Box 640
Beeville 78104-0640   (512) 358-3560

Trust established in 1950 in Texas.
Donor(s): James R. Dougherty,† Mrs. James R. Dougherty.†
Financial data: (yr. ended 11/30/83): Assets, $7,626,293 (M); expenditures, $2,505,646, including $1,905,165 for 138 grants (high: $150,000; low: $400).
Purpose and activities: Broad purposes; primarily local giving, with emphasis on Roman Catholic church-related institutions, including higher, secondary, and other education; cultural programs; health and hospitals; and youth and social agencies.

Types of support awarded: Operating budgets, land acquisition, research, endowment funds, building funds, scholarship funds, equipment, annual campaigns.
Limitations: Giving primarily in TX. No grants to individuals; no loans.
Application information:
  Initial approach: Proposal
  Copies of proposal: 1
  Deadline(s): None
  Board meeting date(s): Semiannually
  Final notification: 6 months or less
  Write: Hugh Grove, Jr., Assistant Secretary
Officers and Trustees: May Dougherty King, Chairman; Mary Patricia Dougherty, Secretary-Treasurer; F. William Carr, Jr., Stephen T. Dougherty, Ben F. Vaughan III, Genevieve Vaughan.
Employer Identification Number: 746039858

3935
Dresser Foundation, Inc. ▼
P.O. Box 718
Dallas 75221   (214) 746-6744

Trust established in 1953 in Texas.
Donor(s): Dresser Industries, Inc.
Financial data: (yr. ended 10/31/84): Assets, $12,499,449 (M); expenditures, $2,508,262, including $2,220,418 for 378 grants (high: $143,198; low: $100) and $225,181 for 281 employee matching gifts.
Purpose and activities: Broad purposes; general giving, primarily local, with emphasis on community funds and higher education; support also for hospitals, youth agencies, and cultural programs.
Types of support awarded: General purposes, employee matching gifts, building funds, matching funds.
Limitations: Giving primarily in areas of company operations, particularly Austin, Houston, and Dallas, TX. No grants to individuals or for endowment funds; no loans.
Publications: 990-PF.
Application information:
  Initial approach: Full proposal
  Copies of proposal: 1
  Deadline(s): None
  Board meeting date(s): As required
  Final notification: 2 months
  Write: Paul W. Willey, Treasurer
Officers and Directors:* J.J. Murphy,* Chairman; E.R. Luter,* President; G.E. Leeson,* B.D. St. John,* Vice-Presidents; Lillian Edwards, Secretary; Paul W. Willey, Treasurer.
Trustees: RepublicBank Dallas, Merrill Lynch Asset Management, Inc.
Number of staff: 1 full-time professional; 1 full-time support.
Employer Identification Number: 237309548

3936
Dresser-Harbison Foundation, Inc.
P.O. Box 718
Dallas 75202

Incorporated in 1940 in Pennsylvania.
Donor(s): Lee J. Morganroth.†

Financial data: (yr. ended 10/31/83): Assets, $206,000 (M); gifts received, $190,000; expenditures, $286,033, including $70,000 for 14 grants (high: $32,000; low: $1,000) and $216,033 for 214 grants to individuals.
Purpose and activities: Giving primarily in areas of company operations, with emphasis on community funds, scholarships for children of employees, youth agencies, hospitals, health, higher education, and loans to elderly former company employees.
Types of support awarded: Building funds, scholarship funds, employee related scholarships.
Limitations: Giving primarily in areas of company operations. No grants to individuals (except for scholarships for children of employees), or for general support, operating budgets, endowment funds, or matching gifts; no loans.
Publications: 990-PF.
Application information:
  Initial approach: Full proposal
  Copies of proposal: 1
  Deadline(s): None
  Board meeting date(s): As required
  Final notification: 2 months
  Write: Paul W. Willey, Treasurer
Officers and Directors:* J.J. Murphy,* President; E.R. Luter,* G.E. Leeson, B.D. St. John,* Vice-Presidents; Lillian Edwards, Secretary; Paul W. Willey, Treasurer.
Trustee: RepublicBank Dallas.
Number of staff: None.
Employer Identification Number: 251113416

3937
Duncan (A. J. and Jessie) Foundation ⌑
1200 Oil and Gas Bldg.
Fort Worth 76102   (817) 335-6261

Incorporated in 1955 in Texas.
Donor(s): A.J. Duncan,† Jessie Duncan.†
Financial data: (yr. ended 2/29/84): Assets, $4,936,355 (M); expenditures, $272,372, including $253,179 for 17 grants (high: $85,500; low: $1,000).
Purpose and activities: Broad purposes; primarily local giving to social welfare institutions and for Protestant religious support; some support for higher education.
Types of support awarded: Operating budgets, equipment, endowment funds, building funds.
Limitations: Giving primarily in TX. No grants to individuals.
Application information: Applications for grants not invited.
  Board meeting date(s): May and as required
  Write: C. Harold Brown, President
Officers and Directors: C. Harold Brown, President; James C. Pollard, Vice-President; Carol Brown, Secretary and Treasurer.
Employer Identification Number: 756018425

3938
Duncan (The Lillian H. and C. W.) Foundation
7 TCT 37
P.O. Box 2558
Houston 77252-8037

Established in 1964 in Texas.
Donor(s): C.W. Duncan.†
Financial data: (yr. ended 9/30/82): Assets, $2,817,629 (M); expenditures, $167,501, including $145,919 for 24 grants (high: $60,000; low: $45).
Purpose and activities: Primarily local giving, with emphasis on medical research; grants also for education, Protestant religious organizations, and youth agencies.
Limitations: Giving primarily in TX.
Officers and Directors: John W. Duncan, President; C.W. Smith, Jr., Secretary-Treasurer; Charles W. Duncan, Jr., John W. Duncan, Jr.
Employer Identification Number: 746064215

3939
Edwards (J. E. S.) Foundation ⌑
4424 Westridge Ave.
Fort Worth 76116   (817) 737-6924

Foundation established about 1975.
Donor(s): Jareen E. Schmidt.
Financial data: (yr. ended 7/31/83): Assets, $1,051,510 (M); gifts received, $40,000; expenditures, $192,245, including $157,000 for 19 grants (high: $22,500; low: $1,000).
Purpose and activities: Primarily local giving; grants largely for social, health and youth agencies and Protestant church support.
Limitations: Giving primarily in TX.
Application information:
  Initial approach: Letter
  Write: Jareen E. Schmidt
Officers: Jareen E. Schmidt, President; Loyd L. Edwards, Vice-President; Helen Fraser Edwards, Secretary.
Employer Identification Number: 510173260

3940
El Paso Community Foundation, The
El Paso National Bank Bldg., Suite 1616
El Paso 79901   (915) 533-4020

Community foundation incorporated in 1977 in Texas.
Financial data: (yr. ended 12/31/83): Assets, $2,648,835 (M); gifts received, $1,056,076; expenditures, $625,695, including $505,542 for 155 grants.
Purpose and activities: Local giving for charitable purposes, including scholarships.
Types of support awarded: Operating budgets, continuing support, annual campaigns, seed money, emergency funds, building funds, land acquisition, endowment funds, matching funds, special projects, fellowships, loans, publications, conferences and seminars, student aid.
Limitations: Giving limited to the El Paso, TX, area. No grants to individuals (except for scholarships), or for deficit financing or research.

Publications: Annual report, application guidelines.
Application information:
  Write: Mrs. Janice Windle, Executive Director
Officers: Richard H. Feville, President; Betty Moore MacGuire,* Vice-President; Walter Dean Hester,* Treasurer; Janice W. Windle, Executive Director.
Trustees:* Frances R. Bagwell, H.M. Daughtery, Jr., Hugh K. Frederick, Jr., Eleanor Gardea, Joseph P. Hammond, Paul Harvey, Sr., Stanley J. Jarmiolowski, Carroll S. Jones, Cheryl A. McCown, Laurance N. Nickey.
Number of staff: 2 full-time professional.
Employer Identification Number: 741839536

3941
Elkins (J. A. and Isabel M.) Foundation ⌑
1007 First City National Bank Bldg.
Houston 77002

Trust established in 1956 in Texas.
Financial data: (yr. ended 8/31/82): Assets, $1,880,939 (M); gifts received, $332,760; expenditures, $416,230, including $405,000 for 33 grants (high: $250,000; low: $1,000).
Purpose and activities: Broad purposes; primarily local giving, with emphasis on child welfare and hospitals and health agencies; grants also for church support and religious associations.
Limitations: Giving primarily in TX.
Trustees: J.A. Elkins, Jr., J.A. Elkins, III, W.S. Elkins.
Employer Identification Number: 746047894

3942
Ellwood Foundation, The ▼ ⌑
P.O. Box 52482
Houston 77052   (713) 651-2168

Trust established in 1958 in Texas.
Donor(s): D.C. Ellwood,† Irene L. Ellwood.†
Financial data: (yr. ended 9/30/83): Assets, $8,065,603 (M); expenditures, $773,290, including $674,500 for 14 grants (high: $150,000; low: $2,500).
Purpose and activities: Primarily local giving, with emphasis on medical institutions, including medical education, health agencies, a mental health center, and social welfare agencies.
Limitations: Giving primarily in the Houston, TX, area.
Application information:
  Initial approach: Letter
  Deadline(s): None
  Write: Raybourne Thompson, Trustee
Trustees: C'Marie Groves, Louis E. Scherck, Raybourne Thompson.
Employer Identification Number: 746039237

3943
ENSERCH Foundation ⌑
300 S. St. Paul
Dallas 75201

Established in 1982 in Texas.
Donor(s): ENSERCH Corporation.

Financial data: (yr. ended 12/31/82): Assets, $597,462 (M); gifts received, $800,000; expenditures, $264,775, including $244,650 for 82 grants (high: $45,500; low: $50) and $6,750 for 37 employee matching gifts.
Purpose and activities: Initial year of operation 1982; grants for higher education, including employee matching gifts, and for community funds, cultural programs, and youth agencies; some emphasis on giving in Texas.
Types of support awarded: Employee matching gifts.
Officers: W.C. McCord,* President; W.T. Satterwhite,* S.R. Singer,* R.B. Williams,* Vice-Presidents; M.G. Fortado, Secretary; A.E. Gallatin, Treasurer.
Directors:* R.G. Fowler, C.V. Helm, J.A. Scarola.
Employer Identification Number: 751816069

3944
Fain Foundation ⌷
500 City National Bldg.
Wichita Falls 76301

Established in 1942 in Texas.
Donor(s): Minnie Rhea Wood.
Financial data: (yr. ended 12/31/83): Assets, $1,203,787 (M); expenditures, $98,815, including $87,800 for 27 grants (high: $26,450; low: $100).
Purpose and activities: Primarily local giving for health and social services, youth agencies, and Protestant organizations.
Types of support awarded: Operating budgets, special projects.
Limitations: Giving primarily in TX.
Application information: Application form required.
Officers and Directors: Minnie Rhea Wood, President; Martha Fain White, Vice-President; Jerry C. Helfenstine, Herbert B. Story.
Employer Identification Number: 756016679

3945
Fair (The R. W.) Foundation ▼
P.O. Box 689
Tyler 75710   (214) 592-3811

Trust established in 1936; incorporated in 1959 in Texas.
Donor(s): R.W. Fair,† Mattie Allen Fair.†
Financial data: (yr. ended 12/31/83): Assets, $14,911,664 (M); expenditures, $1,664,589, including $1,059,393 for 100 grants (high: $181,500; low: $200; average: $1,000-$25,000).
Purpose and activities: Broad purposes; grants largely for Protestant church support and church-related programs and for higher and secondary education; some support for hospitals, youth and social agencies, and cultural activities mainly in Texas and the Southwest.
Types of support awarded: Seed money, building funds, equipment, general purposes, endowment funds, research, special projects, scholarship funds, matching funds.
Limitations: Giving primarily in the Southwest, with emphasis on TX. No grants to individuals or for operating budgets.

Publications: Application guidelines.
Application information: Application form required.
   Initial approach: Letter
   Copies of proposal: 1
   Deadline(s): None
   Board meeting date(s): March, June, September, and December
   Final notification: 3 months
   Write: Wilton H. Fair, President
Officers and Directors: Wilton H. Fair, President; James W. Fair, Senior Vice-President; Sam Bright, Vice-President; Marvin N. Wilson, Secretary-Treasurer; Calvin N. Clyde, Sr., Will Knight, Nancy Lake, B.B. Palmore, C.E. Peeples, Richard L. Ray, Robert J. Ray, Eugene Talbert.
Number of staff: 3.
Employer Identification Number: 756015270

3946
Faith Foundation
5650 Kirby Dr.
Houston 77005   (713) 524-7411
Mailing address: P.O. Box 7, Houston, TX 77001

Trust established in 1956 in Texas.
Donor(s): Wesley West,† Mrs. Wesley West.
Financial data: (yr. ended 12/31/84): Assets, $4,900,000 (M); expenditures, $470,000, including $356,500 for 21 grants (high: $100,000; low: $2,000).
Purpose and activities: Broad purposes; primarily local giving, with emphasis on medical and educational purposes.
Types of support awarded: General purposes, building funds, equipment, land acquisition, matching funds, research.
Limitations: Giving primarily in TX. No grants to individuals, or for endowment funds, scholarships, fellowships, or operating budgets; no loans.
Publications: Annual report.
Application information:
   Initial approach: Letter
   Copies of proposal: 1
   Deadline(s): Submit proposal in November; deadline December 1
   Board meeting date(s): December
   Write: William E. Watson, Jr., Trustee
Trustees: W.H. Hodges, Betty West Stedman, Stuart West Stedman, William E. Watson, Jr., Wesley West.
Number of staff: None.
Employer Identification Number: 746039393

3947
Farish (The William Stamps) Fund ▼
1100 Louisiana, Suite 4500
Houston 77002   (713) 757-7313

Incorporated in 1951 in Texas.
Donor(s): Mrs. Libbie Rice Farish.
Financial data: (yr. ended 6/30/82): Assets, $14,222,781 (M); gifts received, $1,348,228; expenditures, $1,402,342, including $1,303,670 for 92 grants (high: $250,000; low: $200; average: $1,000-$25,000).

Purpose and activities: Primarily local giving, with emphasis on elementary, higher, and secondary education, including theological education; the humanities, including fine arts, music, and the performing arts; hospitals, social welfare, and medical research.
Types of support awarded: Research, general purposes.
Limitations: Giving primarily in TX. No grants to individuals.
Publications: Application guidelines, annual report.
Application information:
   Initial approach: Proposal
   Copies of proposal: 1
   Deadline(s): June 30
   Board meeting date(s): Annually
   Write: W.S. Farish III, President
Officers: W.S. Farish III,* President; Martha Farish Gerry,* J.O. Winston, Jr.,* Vice-Presidents; Jere Scrinopskie, Secretary and Treasurer.
Trustees:* Myrtle M. Camp, Dan R. Japhet.
Employer Identification Number: 746043019

3948
Fasken Foundation, The ▼
500 West Texas Ave., Suite 1160
Midland 79701   (915) 683-5401

Incorporated in 1955 in Texas.
Donor(s): Andrew A. Fasken,† Helen Fasken House.†
Financial data: (yr. ended 12/31/83): Assets, $3,702,261 (M); gifts received, $45,000; expenditures, $564,943, including $382,472 for 254 grants (high: $100,000; low: $1,000; average: $5,000-$15,000).
Purpose and activities: Broad purposes; local giving, with emphasis on higher education, including scholarship funds to Texas institutions for local residents, and youth agencies.
Types of support awarded: Annual campaigns, building funds, emergency funds, professorships, scholarship funds, endowment funds, operating budgets.
Limitations: Giving limited to TX. No grants to individuals; no loans.
Publications: Application guidelines.
Application information: Application form required.
   Initial approach: Letter
   Copies of proposal: 1
   Deadline(s): Submit proposal in April or October; no set deadline
   Board meeting date(s): May or December
   Final notification: 6 months
   Write: Murray Fasken, President
Officers and Trustees: Murray Fasken, President; Mary White, Secretary-Treasurer; F. Andrew Fasken, Steven P. Fasken, William P. Franklin, Durwood M. Goolsby.
Number of staff: 1 full-time professional.
Employer Identification Number: 756023680

3949
Favrot Fund, The
8383-B Westview
Houston 77055   (713) 467-1310

Incorporated in 1952 in Texas.
Donor(s): Laurence H. Favrot,† Johanna A. Favrot, George B. Strong.
Financial data: (yr. ended 12/31/83): Assets, $4,303,332 (M); expenditures, $241,898, including $195,315 for 15 grants (high: $25,000; low: $3,000).
Purpose and activities: Giving primarily in San Diego, Houston, New York, or Washington, D.C., with emphasis on community-based programs directed toward health, support of the needy, and the arts; support for education, the performing arts, and social agencies, including youth agencies, population control, and a program for the aged.
Types of support awarded: Operating budgets, building funds, equipment.
Limitations: Giving primarily in TX, CA, NY, and DC.
Application information:
 Initial approach: Letter
 Copies of proposal: 1
 Deadline(s): September 30
 Board meeting date(s): October or November
Officers and Trustees: Johanna A. Favrot, President; Lenoir M. Josey, Vice-President and Manager; Celestine Favrot Arndt, Laurence de Kanter Favrot, Marcia Favrot, Jeanette Favrot Peterson, Romelia Favrot Stephens.
Employer Identification Number: 746045648

3950
Feldman Foundation, The ▼
7800 Stemmons Freeway
P.O. Box 1046
Dallas 75221   (214) 689-4337

Trust established in 1946 in Texas.
Donor(s): Commercial Metals Company subsidiaries.
Financial data: (yr. ended 12/31/83): Assets, $8,829,598 (M); gifts received, $377,354; expenditures, $1,162,127, including $1,043,450 for 37 grants (high: $200,000; low: $200; average: $500-$20,000).
Purpose and activities: Giving primarily in Texas and New York for Jewish welfare funds; some support for medical research, hospitals, higher education and social service agencies.
Types of support awarded: Research, building funds, general purposes.
Limitations: Giving primarily in TX and NY.
Application information:
 Initial approach: Proposal
 Deadline(s): None
 Write: Jacob Feldman, Trustee
Trustees: Daniel E. Feldman, Jacob Feldman, Moses Feldman, Robert L. Feldman, M.B. Zale.
Employer Identification Number: 756011578

3951
Ferguson (Arch L.) Foundation, Inc. ⊭
601 East Abram St.
Arlington 76101

Established in 1970.
Donor(s): Mr. and Mrs. Edwin V. Bonneau.
Financial data: (yr. ended 12/31/83): Assets, $2,297,096 (M); gifts received, $34,487; expenditures, $155,240, including $71,843 for 93 grants (high: $1,000; low: $213) and $19,748 for 51 grants to individuals.
Purpose and activities: Giving primarily for Protestant church support, religious welfare funds, and missionary activities.
Officers and Directors: Arch L. Ferguson, President; Delos V. Johnson, Manager; Edwin V. Bonneau, Ralph Gage, Wayne Hood.
Employer Identification Number: 237103241

3952
Fikes (Leland) Foundation, Inc. ▼ ⊭
3206 Republic National Bank Tower
Dallas 75201   (214) 754-0144

Incorporated in 1952 in Delaware.
Donor(s): Leland Fikes,† Catherine W. Fikes.
Financial data: (yr. ended 12/31/83): Assets, $38,003,424 (M); expenditures, $8,125,564, including $3,242,675 for 117 grants (high: $500,000; low: $250; average: $500-$250,000).
Purpose and activities: Giving primarily for local health, medical research, education, and cultural programs; grants also for youth and social services, public interest organizations, population research and control, and Protestant church support.
Types of support awarded: Annual campaigns, seed money, emergency funds, building funds, equipment, land acquisition, endowment funds, research, scholarship funds, matching funds, continuing support.
Limitations: Giving primarily in the Dallas, TX, area. No grants to individuals; no loans.
Publications: Application guidelines.
Application information: Submit proposal upon request.
 Initial approach: Letter
 Copies of proposal: 1
 Deadline(s): None
 Board meeting date(s): Monthly
 Write: Nancy Solana, Research and Grant Administration
Officers and Trustees: Catherine W. Fikes, Chairman; Lee Fikes, President and Treasurer; John N. Jackson, Vice-President and Secretary; Amy L. Fikes.
Number of staff: 2 full-time professional.
Employer Identification Number: 756035984

3953
Fish (Ray C.) Foundation ▼ ⊭
2001 Kirby Dr., Suite 605
Houston 77019   (713) 522-0741

Incorporated in 1957 in Texas.
Donor(s): Raymond Clinton Fish,† Mirtha G. Fish.†

Financial data: (yr. ended 6/30/83): Assets, $14,015,174 (M); gifts received, $46,623; expenditures, $1,375,889, including $1,251,500 for 81 grants (high: $300,000; low: $500; average: $1,000-$25,000).
Purpose and activities: General purposes; primarily local giving, with emphasis on educational institutions, hospitals, medical research, youth and social service agencies, and cultural organizations, including the performing arts.
Types of support awarded: General purposes.
Limitations: Giving primarily in TX, with emphasis on Houston.
Application information:
 Write: Barbara F. Daniel, President
Officers: Barbara F. Daniel,* President; James L. Daniel, Jr.,* Vice-President and Treasurer; Thad T. Hutcheson,* Vice-President; Maxine Costello, Secretary.
Trustees: Christopher J. Daniel.
Number of staff: 1.
Employer Identification Number: 746043047

3954
Fleming Foundation, The ▼
1007 Interfirst Fort Worth Bldg.
Fort Worth 76102   (817) 335-3741

Incorporated in 1936 in Texas.
Donor(s): William Fleming.†
Financial data: (yr. ended 12/31/83): Assets, $10,640,881 (M); expenditures, $1,411,607, including $1,175,055 for 53 grants (high: $338,705; low: $100; average: $500-$30,000).
Purpose and activities: Broad purposes; primarily local giving, with emphasis on Protestant church support and church-related activities, including radio and television programs, and music; support also for cultural programs and higher education.
Types of support awarded: Operating budgets, continuing support, annual campaigns, seed money, emergency funds, equipment, professorships, internships, research, special projects.
Limitations: Giving primarily in TX, with emphasis on Forth Worth. No grants to individuals, or for deficit financing, building or endowment funds, land acquisition, matching gifts, scholarships or fellowships, demonstration projects, publications, or conferences; single-year grants only; no loans.
Application information:
 Initial approach: Full proposal
 Copies of proposal: 1
 Deadline(s): None
 Board meeting date(s): January, April, July, and September
 Final notification: 2 months
 Write: G. Malcolm Louden, Assistant Secretary
Officers and Directors: Mary D. Walsh,* President; F. Howard Walsh,* Vice-President; G. Malcolm Louden, Secretary; F. Howard Walsh, Jr.,* Treasurer.
Number of staff: 1 full-time professional; 1 full-time support.
Employer Identification Number: 756022736

3955
Florence Foundation, The ⌘
P.O. Box 241
Dallas 75221

Established in 1956.
Financial data: (yr. ended 11/30/82): Assets, $820,946 (M); expenditures, $137,014, including $127,450 for 31 grants (high: $15,000; low: $250).
Purpose and activities: Primarily local giving for social services, hospitals, higher education, and cultural programs.
Types of support awarded: General purposes, matching funds, equipment, building funds, special projects.
Limitations: Giving primarily in TX.
Trustee: RepublicBank Dallas.
Employer Identification Number: 756008029

3956
Fondren Foundation, The ▼
7 TCT 37
P.O. Box 2558
Houston 77252-8037   (713) 236-4410

Trust established in 1948 in Texas.
Donor(s): Mrs. W.W. Fondren, Sr.,† and others.
Financial data: (yr. ended 10/31/83): Assets, $36,706,581 (M); gifts received, $442,910; expenditures, $3,261,915, including $3,146,500 for grants (average: $5,000-$25,000).
Purpose and activities: Broad purposes; grants primarily to specific projects in the Houston area, with emphasis on higher and secondary education, hospitals, social agencies, and cultural organizations.
Limitations: Giving primarily in TX, with emphasis on Houston. No grants to individuals, or for annual fund drives.
Officers and Trustees: David M. Underwood, Chairman; Doris Fondren Berton, Vice-Chairman; W. Bryan Trammell, Jr., Secretary-Treasurer; Ellanor Ann Fondren, Walter W. Fondren III, Wash Bryan Trammell, Lynda Knapp Underwood, Sue Trammell Whitfield.
Employer Identification Number: 746042565

3957
Frees Foundation, The ⌘
5373 W. Alabama, Suite 404
Houston 77056

Established in 1983 in Texas.
Donor(s): C. Norman Frees, Cumamex, S.A.
Financial data: (yr. ended 12/31/83): Assets, $3,494,014 (M); gifts received, $4,030,000; expenditures, $634,501, including $625,739 for 2 grants (high: $624,739; low: $1,000).
Purpose and activities: First year of operation in 1983; nearly all support to the Salvation Army to establish a children's home in Mexico City.
Directors: C. Norman Frees, Shirley B. Frees, Thomas J. Rosser.
Employer Identification Number: 760053200

3958
Fuller Foundation, Inc., The ⌘
2020 Texas American Bank Bldg.
Fort Worth 76102   (817) 336-2020

Incorporated in 1951 in Texas and in Delaware.
Financial data: (yr. ended 12/31/83): Assets, $3,195,414 (M); expenditures, $146,582, including $128,600 for 44 grants (high: $10,000; low: $250).
Purpose and activities: Broad purposes; general giving, with emphasis on hospitals, secondary and higher education, art, and music; grants also for Protestant church support, and youth agencies.
Application information:
  Initial approach: Full proposal
  Deadline(s): December 31
  Write: William M. Fuller, President
Officers and Directors: William M. Fuller, President; Andrew P. Fuller, Vice-President and Secretary; R.L. Bowen, Treasurer.
Employer Identification Number: 756015942

3959
Garvey Texas Foundation, Inc. ⌘
P.O. Box 9600
Fort Worth 76107

Incorporated in 1962 in Texas.
Donor(s): James S. Garvey, Shirley F. Garvey, Garvey Foundation.
Financial data: (yr. ended 12/31/82): Assets, $2,831,566 (M); gifts received, $104,033; expenditures, $53,583, including $53,057 for 64 grants (high: $6,082; low: $10).
Purpose and activities: Broad purposes; largely local support primarily for youth agencies, education, cultural activities, community funds, and hospitals.
Limitations: Giving primarily in TX.
Officers: Shirley F. Garvey,* President; James S. Garvey,* Vice-President; Jeffrey L. Ault, Secretary; C.B. Felts, Jr., Treasurer.
Trustees:* Richard F. Garvey, Janet G. Sawyer, Carol G. Sweat.
Employer Identification Number: 756031547

3960
George Foundation, The ▼
207 South Third St.
P.O. Drawer C
Richmond 77469   (713) 342-6109

Trust established in 1945 in Texas.
Donor(s): A.P. George,† Mamie E. George.†
Financial data: (yr. ended 12/31/82): Assets, $92,484,372 (M); expenditures, $5,432,420, including $437,590 for 14 grants (high: $182,510; low: $500) and $1,282,780 for 1 foundation-administered program.
Purpose and activities: Broad purposes; local giving, with emphasis on hospitals, libraries, Christian church support, education, recreation, and historial restorations.
Limitations: Giving limited to Fort Bend County, TX. No grants to individuals.
Publications: 990-PF.
Application information:
  Initial approach: Letter
  Copies of proposal: 1

Board meeting date(s): 12 times a year
Write: John G. Heard, Trustee
Trustees: J.A. Elkins, Jr., John G. Heard.
Employer Identification Number: 746043368

3961
Gifford (Kenneth P.) Foundation
c/o MBank of El Paso, Trust Division
One MBank Plaza
El Paso 79901   (915) 532-9922

Established in 1977.
Financial data: (yr. ended 12/31/83): Assets, $1,679,105 (M); expenditures, $120,072, including $97,000 for grants (high: $36,800; low: $800).
Purpose and activities: Primarily local giving, with emphasis on two local foundations concerned with care for the aged and youth; supports scholarship program sponsored by El Paso Community Foundation for students of local high schools, for undergraduate study at University of Texas-El Paso.
Types of support awarded: Scholarship funds.
Limitations: Giving primarily in El Paso County, TX. No grants to individuals.
Application information:
  Initial approach: Letter
  Copies of proposal: 1
  Deadline(s): March 1
  Board meeting date(s): March
  Write: Doris Ryan
Board of Managers: Henry Ellis, W.A. Thurmond, Robert Young.
Employer Identification Number: 741977400

3962
Gill (A. Smith) Trust ⌘
c/o Interfirst Bank Fort Worth
P.O. Box 1317
Fort Worth 76101

Established in 1979.
Financial data: (yr. ended 3/31/84): Assets, $664,824 (M); expenditures, $147,422, including $136,880 for 9 grants (high: $106,880; low: $1,000).
Purpose and activities: Primarily local giving; support for agencies and homes for needy children.
Limitations: Giving primarily in Fort Worth, TX.
Trustee: Interfirst Bank Fort Worth.
Employer Identification Number: 751641579

3963
Gordon (Meyer and Ida) Foundation ⌘
820 Fannin St.
Houston 77002

Incorporated in 1950 in Texas.
Donor(s): Members of the Gordon family, Gordon's Jewelry Company, and others.
Financial data: (yr. ended 12/31/83): Assets, $5,057,753 (M); expenditures, $18,380, including $15,261 for 14 grants (high: $2,000; low: $25).
Purpose and activities: Broad purposes; grants largely for Jewish welfare funds.
Application information:
  Deadline(s): None

Write: Harry B. Gordon, President

Officers and Trustees: Harry B. Gordon, President; Aron S. Gordon, Vice-President and Treasurer; I.L. Miller, Secretary.

Employer Identification Number: 746046795

3964
Green Foundation, The ⌷

3525 Turtle Creek Blvd., Suite 20A
Dallas 75219

Trust established in 1958 in Texas.
Donor(s): Cecil H. Green, Ida M. Green.
Financial data: (yr. ended 12/31/82): Assets, $889,912 (M); expenditures, $126,506, including $124,600 for 18 grants (high: $25,000; low: $100).
Purpose and activities: General purposes; primarily local giving, with emphasis on cultural programs, higher education, a secondary school and a community fund.
Limitations: Giving primarily in the Dallas, TX, area.
Application information:
Write: Cecil H. Green, President
Officers and Trustees: Cecil H. Green, President; William E. Collins, Ida M. Green.
Employer Identification Number: 756015446

3965
Griffin (Rosa May) Foundation

P.O. Box 1775
Kilgore 75662   (214) 984-2187

Incorporated in 1960 in Texas.
Donor(s): Rosa May Griffin.†
Financial data: (yr. ended 12/31/84): Assets, $2,800,000 (M); expenditures, $223,496, including $181,591 for 16 grants (high: $50,000; low: $500).
Purpose and activities: Broad purposes; local giving for Presbyterian church support, higher education, and hospitals.
Types of support awarded: General purposes, operating budgets, continuing support, annual campaigns, emergency funds, building funds, equipment, matching funds.
Limitations: Giving limited to TX. No grants to individuals, or for endowment funds, or scholarships and fellowships; no loans.
Publications: Program policy statement.
Application information:
Initial approach: Letter or proposal
Copies of proposal: 1
Deadline(s): Submit proposal in October
Board meeting date(s): Monthly
Final notification: 1 month
Write: Byron G. Bronstad, Secretary
Officers and Trustees: O.N. Pederson, President; E.B. Mobley, Vice-President; Byron G. Bronstad, Secretary-Treasurer.
Number of staff: None.
Employer Identification Number: 756011866

3966
Haas (Paul and Mary) Foundation

P.O. Box 2928
Corpus Christi 78403

Trust established in 1954 in Texas.
Donor(s): Mary Haas, Paul R. Haas.
Financial data: (yr. ended 12/31/84): Assets, $903,475 (M); gifts received, $1,000,000; expenditures, $457,456, including $401,987 for 59 grants (high: $100,000; low: $75) and $16,691 for 34 grants to individuals.
Purpose and activities: Broad purposes; primarily local giving with emphasis on social agencies, youth agencies, church support, higher education, hospitals and medical research, and cultural programs.
Types of support awarded: Student aid.
Limitations: Giving primarily in TX. No grants to individuals (except for student aid).
Publications: Multi-year report.
Application information:
Initial approach: Letter
Copies of proposal: 1
Deadline(s): None
Board meeting date(s): As needed
Write: Paul R. Haas, Trustee
Trustees: Mary F. Haas, Paul R. Haas, Raymond P. Haas, Rene Haas, Rheta Haas Page.
Number of staff: 1 part-time professional; 1 part-time support.
Employer Identification Number: 746031614

3967
Haggar Foundation, The ▼ ⌷

6113 Lemmon Ave.
Dallas 75209   (214) 352-8481

Trust established in 1950 in Texas.
Donor(s): Joseph M. Haggar, Rose M. Haggar, Haggar Company, and others.
Financial data: (yr. ended 6/30/83): Assets, $15,195,343 (M); gifts received, $118,000; expenditures, $942,826, including $879,971 for 77 grants (high: $300,000; low: $60; average: $1,000-$10,000).
Purpose and activities: Primarily local giving in areas of company operations, with emphasis on higher and secondary education, including a scholarship program for children of company employees, and hospitals; support also for youth agencies.
Types of support awarded: Employee related scholarships, building funds.
Limitations: Giving primarily in south TX and OK.
Publications: Application guidelines.
Application information: Application guidelines available for company-employee scholarship program. Application form required.
Deadline(s): Submit scholarship application in January or February; deadline March 31
Write: Bob Qualls
Trustees: Edmond R. Haggar, Joseph M. Haggar, Joseph M. Haggar, Jr., Rosemary Haggar Vaughan.
Employer Identification Number: 756019237

3968
Haggerty Foundation ⌷

5455 Northbrook Dr.
Dallas 75220

Established in 1950 in Texas.
Donor(s): Patrick E. Haggerty.†
Financial data: (yr. ended 12/31/82): Assets, $4,558,944 (M); gifts received, $133,542; expenditures, $22,466, including $21,100 for 5 grants (high: $5,600; low: $2,500).
Purpose and activities: Primarily local giving for social services and education.
Types of support awarded: General purposes.
Limitations: Giving primarily in TX.
Officers: Patrick F. Haggerty, Jr., Vice-President; Teresa H. Parravano, Secretary-Treasurer.
Trustees: Beatrice M. Haggerty, Chairman; Michael G. Haggerty, Kathleen H. Moossy, Sheila H. Turner.
Employer Identification Number: 237011735

3969
Halff (G. A. C.) Foundation ⌷

3355 Cherry Ridge Dr., Suite 201
San Antonio 78230
Mailing address: c/o Conroy, Inc., P.O. Box 4-GG, San Antonio, TX 78201

Incorporated in 1951 in Texas.
Donor(s): G.A.C. Halff.†
Financial data: (yr. ended 2/28/83): Assets, $3,646,553 (M); expenditures, $203,052, including $170,000 for 18 grants (high: $30,000; low: $1,000).
Purpose and activities: General purposes; primarily local giving, with emphasis on social agencies, aid to the handicapped, youth agencies, population control, and a community fund.
Limitations: Giving primarily in TX.
Application information:
Write: Roland R. Arnold, Vice-President
Officers and Trustees: Hugh Halff, Jr., President; Roland R. Arnold, Vice-President and Treasurer; Catherine H. Edson, Secretary; Thomas H. Edson, Marie M. Halff, Catherine H. Luhn, George M. Luhn.
Employer Identification Number: 746042432

3970
Halliburton Foundation, Inc. ▼

2600 Southland Center
400 North Olive, Lock Box 263
Dallas 75201   (214) 748-7261

Incorporated in 1965 in Texas.
Donor(s): Halliburton Company, Brown & Root, Inc., and other subsidiaries.
Financial data: (yr. ended 12/31/83): Assets, $11,357,020 (M); gifts received, $712,756; expenditures, $1,374,773, including $1,013,500 for 107 grants (high: $100,000; low: $500; average: $2,500-$10,000) and $327,640 for 762 employee matching gifts.

Purpose and activities: Giving for higher education primarily in the Southwest, restricted to faculty support in engineering schools; also supports a program for matching employee gifts to higher education; some limited support for select charitable organizations.

Types of support awarded: Operating budgets, continuing support, annual campaigns, employee matching gifts, research, conferences and seminars, special projects.

Limitations: Giving primarily in the Southwest, with emphasis on TX. No grants to individuals, or for seed money, emergency funds, deficit financing, building funds, equipment and materials, land acquisition, renovation projects, endowment funds, scholarships, fellowships, demonstration projects, or publications; no loans.

Application information:
  Initial approach: Proposal
  Copies of proposal: 1
  Deadline(s): None
  Board meeting date(s): February and September
  Final notification: Within 3 months
  Write: Hayden L. Hankins, Vice-President

Officers: Thomas H. Cruikshank,* President; Hayden L. Hankins, Vice-President and Secretary; C. Robert Fielder, Vice-President and Treasurer; Robert M. Kennedy, Vice-President-Legal.

Trustees:* Thomas J. Feehan, B.G. Taylor.
Number of staff: None.
Employer Identification Number: 751212458

3971
Halsell (The Ewing) Foundation ▼
San Antonio Bank and Trust Bldg., Suite 537
San Antonio 78205   (512) 223-2640

Trust established in 1957 in Texas.
Donor(s): Ewing Halsell,† Mrs. Ewing Halsell,† Mrs. Grace F. Rider.†
Financial data: (yr. ended 6/30/84): Assets, $30,221,144 (M); expenditures, $3,717,575, including $3,180,981 for 53 grants (high: $1,640,000; low: $50; average: $100-$60,000).
Purpose and activities: Grants for educational and charitable purposes; local giving for cultural programs, health organizations and youth agencies.

Types of support awarded: Operating budgets, continuing support, annual campaigns, building funds, equipment, land acquisition, research, publications, technical assistance, seed money.

Limitations: Giving limited to TX, with emphasis on southwestern TX and particularly San Antonio. No grants to individuals, or for deficit financing, emergency funds, general endowments, matching gifts, scholarships and fellowships, demonstration projects, or conferences; no loans.

Publications: Biennial report, application guidelines, program policy statement.

Application information:
  Initial approach: Letter or full proposal
  Copies of proposal: 1
  Deadline(s): None
  Board meeting date(s): Quarterly
  Final notification: 3 months

Write: Robert L. Washington, Grant Coordinator

Officers and Trustees: Gilbert M. Denman, Jr., Chairman; Helen Campbell, Secretary-Treasurer; Leroy G. Denman, Jr., William H. George, Jean McDonald.

Number of staff: 1 full-time professional; 2 part-time support.

Employer Identification Number: 746063016

3972
Hamman (George and Mary Josephine) Foundation ▼
1000 Louisiana, Suite 820
Houston 77002   (713) 658-8345

Incorporated in 1954 in Texas.
Donor(s): Mrs. Mary Josephine Hamman,† George Hamman.
Financial data: (yr. ended 4/30/84): Assets, $13,220,055 (M); expenditures, $681,859, including $239,050 for 120 grants (high: $15,000; low: $500; average: $1,000-$10,000) and $116,250 for 97 grants to individuals.

Purpose and activities: Broad purposes; local giving for construction and operation of hospitals, and medical treatment and research organizations and programs; grants to churches and affiliated religious organizations (nondenominational); individual scholarship program for local high school students; grants to building programs or special educational projects at colleges and universities, mostly local; contributions also to cultural programs, social services, and youth agencies.

Types of support awarded: Annual campaigns, emergency funds, building funds, equipment, research, professorships, scholarship funds, continuing support.

Limitations: Giving limited to TX, primarily in the Houston area. No support for post-graduate education. No grants to individuals (except for scholarships), or for deficit financing, maintenance of buildings, or endowment funds.

Publications: Application guidelines.
Application information:
  Initial approach: Letter
  Copies of proposal: 1
  Deadline(s): None
  Board meeting date(s): Monthly
  Final notification: 60 days
  Write: Thomas P. Stone, Operating Manager

Officers and Directors: Charles D. Milby, President; Patrick B. Feagin, Vice-President; Henry R. Hamman, Secretary; Louise Milby Feagin.

Employer Identification Number: 746061447

3973
Harding Foundation, The
Harding Foundation Bldg.
Fifth and Hidalgo, P.O. Box 130
Raymondville 78580   (512) 689-2706

Incorporated in 1947 in Texas.
Donor(s): W.A. Harding,† Laura V. Harding.†

Financial data: (yr. ended 12/31/84): Assets, $1,438,923 (M); expenditures, $146,000, including $76,056 for 80 grants (high: $3,600; low: $100) and $21,420 for 10 grants to individuals.

Purpose and activities: For the furthering of Christian education in homes, schools, and churches; primarily local giving with emphasis on Christian church support and religious associations, evangelical programs, and child welfare.

Limitations: Giving primarily in TX. No grants for scholarships (except for theological students).

Application information:
  Initial approach: Letter
  Deadline(s): None
  Board meeting date(s): 2nd Tuesday in February
  Write: Glenn W. Harding, Vice-President

Officers and Directors: John A. Fambrough, President; Glenn W. Harding, Vice-President and Treasurer; Dorothy J. Parr, Secretary.

Number of staff: 1 full-time professional.
Employer Identification Number: 746025883

3974
Harrington (The Don and Sybil) Foundation ▼
801 South Fillmore St.
Amarillo 79101   (806) 373-8353

Trust established in 1951 in Texas; incorporated in 1971.
Donor(s): D.D. Harrington,† Mrs. Sybil B. Harrington.
Financial data: (yr. ended 12/31/83): Assets, $59,091,433 (M); expenditures, $5,139,442, including $4,193,957 for 66 grants (high: $1,000,000; low: $1,000).

Purpose and activities: Broad purposes; interests include hospitals and health agencies, cultural programs, higher education, including scholarship funds, youth agencies, social services, and civic affairs, with preference to local and state area.

Limitations: Giving primarily in TX, with emphasis on Amarillo. No grants to individuals, or for operating budgets.

Application information:
  Initial approach: Letter
  Copies of proposal: 1
  Deadline(s): Submit proposal 1 month prior to board meetings
  Board meeting date(s): April, August, December, and as required
  Final notification: 4 to 6 weeks
  Write: Mrs. Lynn Singleton, Executive Vice-President

Officers: Lynn Singleton, Executive Vice-President; T.L. Roach, Jr.,* Vice-President; Gene Edwards,* Secretary.

Directors:* Sybil Harrington, Wales H. Madden, Jr., Avery Rush, Jr., Katherine Seewald.
Number of staff: 3 full-time professional.
Employer Identification Number: 751336604

3975
Hawn Foundation, Inc. ▼ ¤
1540 Republic Bank Bldg.
Dallas 75201 (214) 741-1814

Incorporated in 1962 in Texas.
Donor(s): Mildred Hawn.†
Financial data: (yr. ended 8/31/83): Assets,
$9,736,270 (M); expenditures, $558,792,
including $471,610 for 44 grants (high:
$110,000; low: $100).
Purpose and activities: Largely local giving,
with emphasis on medical research, hospitals,
higher education, and social services.
Limitations: Giving primarily in TX.
Application information:
 Initial approach: Letter
 Write: E.S. Blythe, Director
Directors: E.S. Blythe, W.R. Hawn, R.S.
Strauss, I.N. Taylor.
Employer Identification Number: 756036761

3976
Heath (Ed and Mary) Foundation ¤
P.O. Box 338
Tyler 75710 (214) 597-7435

Established in 1954 in Texas.
Donor(s): J.E. Heath,† Mary M. Heath.†
Financial data: (yr. ended 12/31/82): Assets,
$1,979,229 (M); expenditures, $237,864,
including $117,482 for 116 grants (high:
$20,000; low: $15) and $1,000 for grants to
individuals.
Purpose and activities: Primarily local giving
for Protestant church support, youth agencies,
recreation, and health services.
Limitations: Giving primarily in TX, particularly
Smith County. No grants to individuals or for
endowment funds.
Application information:
 Initial approach: Letter
 Copies of proposal: 1
 Board meeting date(s): March, June,
 September, and December
 Write: W.R. Smith, Chairman
Directors: W.R. Smith, Chairman; Thomas W.
Hathaway, Vice-Chairman; L.H. Reese,
Secretary-Treasurer; Ben Goodwin, James
Oliver, Wendell Pool, W.M. Shamburger.
Employer Identification Number: 756021506

3977
Hemphill-Wells Foundation ¤
1212 Ave. J
P.O. Box 981
Lubbock 79408

Trust established in 1963 in Texas.
Donor(s): Spencer A. Wells.†
Financial data: (yr. ended 9/30/82): Assets,
$1,104,739 (M); expenditures, $59,982,
including $56,950 for 41 grants (high: $11,000;
low: $50).
Purpose and activities: Broad purposes;
primarily local giving for higher education,
community funds, cultural programs, youth
agencies, and a hospital.
Limitations: Giving primarily in Lubbock, TX.
Trustees: B.E. Collins, Scottie R. Johnson, B.E.
Rushing, Jr.
Employer Identification Number: 756013279

3978
**Henck (August J. and Sadie L.)
Memorial Fund** ¤
400 West 15th St.; Suite 1610
Austin 78701 (512) 477-9831
Mailing address: P.O. Box 1237, Austin, TX
78767

Trust established in 1960 in Texas.
Donor(s): Sadie L. Henck.†
Financial data: (yr. ended 12/31/82): Assets,
$1,636,816 (M); expenditures, $153,340,
including $130,212 for 14 grants (high:
$25,000; low: $2,462).
Purpose and activities: Primarily local giving
to Roman Catholic educational institutions,
hospitals, and churches.
Limitations: Giving primarily in TX.
Application information:
 Initial approach: Full proposal
 Deadline(s): None
Trustees: Ronald J. Byers, Ruben H. Johnson,
James H. Johnston, Jr., Adolph A. Kremel, Jr.,
Albert J. Maloney.
Employer Identification Number: 237397187

3979
**Henderson (Simon and Louise)
Foundation** ¤
P.O. Box 1365
Lufkin 75901 (713) 634-3448

Established in 1958 in Texas.
Donor(s): Louise Henderson.†
Financial data: (yr. ended 12/31/83): Assets,
$2,606,972 (M); expenditures, $177,781,
including $157,874 for 13 grants (high:
$150,000; low: $25).
Purpose and activities: General purposes;
primarily local giving, with emphasis on a
hospital.
Limitations: Giving primarily in east TX.
Application information:
 Deadline(s): None
 Board meeting date(s): December and as
 required
 Write: Simon W. Henderson, Jr., President
Officers: Simon W. Henderson, Jr., President;
Loucile J. Henderson, Vice-President; Simon W.
Henderson, III, Secretary-Treasurer.
Employer Identification Number: 756022769

3980
Hightower (Walter) Foundation
c/o El Paso National Bank
P.O. Drawer 140
El Paso 79980 (915) 546-6515

Established in 1980.
Donor(s): Walter Hightower.†
Financial data: (yr. ended 9/30/84): Assets,
$5,150,058 (M); expenditures, $293,934,
including $233,574 for grants (high: $40,000).
Purpose and activities: Giving in west Texas
and southern New Mexico for health care for
crippled children under the age of 21.
Types of support awarded: General purposes,
operating budgets, continuing support, annual
campaigns, seed money, building funds,
equipment, program-related investments, grants
to individuals.

Limitations: Giving limited to west TX and
southern NM. No grants for endowment funds,
scholarships, fellowships, or matching gifts; no
loans.
Publications: Program policy statement,
application guidelines.
Application information: Application form
required.
 Initial approach: Letter
 Copies of proposal: 2
 Deadline(s): July 1
 Board meeting date(s): Annually
 Final notification: 2 months
 Write: Terry Crenshaw, Charitable Services
 Officer
Trustee: El Paso National Bank (Terry
Crenshaw, Trust Administrative Officer).
Number of staff: 1 full-time professional; 1
part-time professional.
Employer Identification Number: 746293379

3981
Hillcrest Foundation ▼
c/o InterFirst Bank Dallas
Interfirst Two, Fifth Fl., P.O. Box 83791
Dallas 75283 (214) 573-4642

Trust established in 1959 in Texas.
Donor(s): Mrs. W.W. Caruth, Sr.†
Financial data: (yr. ended 5/31/83): Assets,
$37,814,750 (M); expenditures, $2,465,369,
including $2,340,385 for 49 grants (high:
$151,502; low: $2,000; average: $10,000-
$150,000).
Purpose and activities: To relieve poverty,
advance education, and promote health; local
giving, with emphasis on higher education,
hospitals, rehabilitation, and free enterprise.
Types of support awarded: Building funds,
equipment, land acquisition, seed money,
research, matching funds.
Limitations: Giving limited to TX, with
emphasis on Dallas. No grants to individuals,
or for endowment funds, operating budgets, or
scholarships and fellowships; no loans.
Application information:
 Initial approach: Telephone
 Copies of proposal: 1
 Deadline(s): None
 Board meeting date(s): As required, usually 3
 or 4 times annually
 Write: Cave L. Johnson, Jr.
Trustees: D. Harold Byrd, Jr., W.W. Caruth,
Jr., Donald Case, Harry A. Shuford, InterFirst
Bank Dallas (Cave L. Johnson, Jr., Vice-
President).
Number of staff: 1 part-time professional.
Employer Identification Number: 756007565

3982
HNG Foundation ▼
1200 Travis
P.O. Box 1188
Houston 77001 (713) 654-6484

Established in 1980 in Texas.
Donor(s): Houston Natural Gas Corporation.

Financial data: (yr. ended 7/31/83): Assets, $2,572,751 (M); gifts received, $1,013,070; expenditures, $904,329, including $789,012 for 107 grants (high: $300,000; low: $200) and $112,511 for 152 employee matching gifts.
Purpose and activities: Broad purposes; emphasis on health and welfare, education, community funds, civic affairs, and arts and culture.
Types of support awarded: Operating budgets, continuing support, annual campaigns, seed money, emergency funds, deficit financing, building funds, equipment, land acquisition, research, professorships, internships, scholarship funds, exchange programs, fellowships, matching funds, endowment funds, employee matching gifts.
Limitations: Giving limited to areas where the company or its employees are located, with emphasis on the Houston, TX, area. No support for sectarian purposes. No grants to individuals (including direct student scholarships), or for advertisements for benefit purposes; no loans.
Publications: Program policy statement, application guidelines.
Application information:
Initial approach: Proposal, including a financial statement or letter
Copies of proposal: 1
Deadline(s): Submit proposal preferably in September or October; deadline October 1
Board meeting date(s): April, July, October, and January, but awards grants only in November
Final notification: Within a few weeks
Write: Joyce A. Gandy, Administrator, Corporate Contributions
Officers: James A. Harrison,* President; Raymond E. Denny,* Vice-President and Treasurer; Joyce A. Gandy, Secretary and Administrator.
Trustees:* Peggy B. Menchaca.
Number of staff: 1 part-time support.
Employer Identification Number: 742124032

3983
Hobby Foundation ⌑
P.O. Box 272389
Houston 77277

Incorporated in 1945 in Texas.
Donor(s): W.P. Hobby,† Mrs. Oveta Culp Hobby, The Houston Post Company.
Financial data: (yr. ended 12/31/83): Assets, $9,196,250 (M); gifts received, $225,000; expenditures, $410,746, including $339,940 for 107 grants (high: $100,000; low: $25).
Purpose and activities: Broad purposes; primarily local giving, with emphasis on higher and secondary education, museums, cultural programs, and hospitals.
Limitations: Giving primarily in TX.
Officers: Oveta Culp Hobby,* President; William P. Hobby, Jr.,* Vice-President; Audrey Horn, Secretary; Peggy C. Buchanan, Treasurer.
Trustees:* George A. Butler, Jessica Hobby Catto, Diana P. Hobby.
Employer Identification Number: 746026606

3984
Hoblitzelle Foundation ▼
1410 Republic Bank Bldg.
Dallas 75201   (214) 979-0321

Trust established in 1942 in Texas; incorporated in 1953.
Donor(s): Karl St. John Hoblitzelle,† Esther T. Hoblitzelle.†
Financial data: (yr. ended 4/30/84): Assets, $73,479,819 (M); expenditures, $3,017,853, including $3,015,228 for 53 grants (high: $250,000; low: $1,000; average: $10,000-$100,000).
Purpose and activities: Local giving, with emphasis on higher and secondary education, hospitals and health services, medical research, youth agencies, cultural programs, social services, and community development; also lends paintings and objects of art to charitable and educational institutions.
Types of support awarded: Seed money, building funds, equipment, land acquisition, matching funds, general purposes.
Limitations: Giving limited to TX, primarily in Dallas. No support for religious organizations for sectarian purposes. No grants to individuals; only occasional board-initiated support for operating budgets, debt reduction, research, scholarships, or endowments; no loans.
Publications: Annual report, program policy statement, application guidelines.
Application information:
Initial approach: Letter
Copies of proposal: 1
Deadline(s): April 15, August 15, and December 15
Board meeting date(s): Latter part of May, September, and January
Final notification: After next board meeting
Write: Robert Lynn Harris, Grant Coordinator
Officers: James W. Aston,* Chief Executive Officer and Chairman; James W. Keay,* President; Robert Lynn Harris,* Executive Vice-President and Grant Coordinator; Catherine Ragsdale, Executive Secretary; John M. Stemmons,* Treasurer.
Directors:* Lillian M. Bradshaw, Van Alen Hollomon, Sarah T. Hughes, Sara Hulsey, George L. MacGregor, Charles C. Sprague, M.D.
Number of staff: 1 full-time professional; 1 full-time support.
Employer Identification Number: 756003984

3985
Hofheinz (Roy M.) Charitable Foundation ⌑
P.O. Box 2555
Houston 77001

Established in 1965 in Texas.
Donor(s): Irene C. Hofheinz,† Roy M. Hofheinz.†
Financial data: (yr. ended 12/31/83): Assets, $7,034,783 (M); expenditures, $360,846, including $278,600 for 30 grants (high: $75,000; low: $500).
Purpose and activities: Local support primarily for higher education, a museum, and medical research.

Types of support awarded: Research.
Limitations: Giving primarily in TX.
Trustee: Dene Hofheinz Antone, Fred Hofheinz, Roy Hofheinz, Jr., Inter-First Bank.
Employer Identification Number: 746069482

3986
Hofstetter (Bessie I.) Trust ⌑
c/o Interfirst Bank Corsicana
P.O. Box 613
Corsicana 75110

Trust established in 1934 in Texas.
Donor(s): Bessie I. Hofstetter.
Financial data: (yr. ended 6/30/83): Assets, $2,217,780 (M); expenditures, $161,732, including $147,010 for 19 grants (high: $35,000; low: $99).
Purpose and activities: Primarily local giving; grants largely for social agencies, health agencies, and a Protestant church; support also for a community fund.
Limitations: Giving primarily in the Corsicana, TX, area. No grants to individuals.
Trustee: Interfirst Bank Corsicana, N.A.
Employer Identification Number: 756006485

3987
HOR Foundation ⌑
11221 Katy Freeway
Houston 77079   (713) 464-4900

Donor(s): John J. Ryan, Christa M. Ryan, HOR Energy Company.
Financial data: (yr. ended 11/30/82): Assets, $334,758 (M); gifts received, $105,000; expenditures, $158,921, including $1,000 for 1 grant (average: $5,000-$50,000) and $155,000 for 3 grants to individuals.
Purpose and activities: Direct research grants for younger medical research scientists having five or fewer years active experience; grants only to physicians or Ph.D.s who are members of the teaching or research faculties of publicly supported medical schools or research hospitals.
Types of support awarded: Research, fellowships.
Application information:
Initial approach: Proposal
Deadline(s): Submit proposal from September to March of academic year; deadline March 31
Final notification: About May 15
Write: Joseph A. Imparato, Director
Trustees: Joseph A. Imparato,* Director; James E. Babcock, Vincent Boemio.
Grant Committee:* Robert W. McConnell, M.D., Joseph M. Merrill, M.D.
Employer Identification Number: 742171639

3988
Houston Endowment Inc. ▼
P.O. Box 52338
Houston 77052   (713) 223-4043

Incorporated in 1937 in Texas.
Donor(s): Jesse H. Jones,† Mrs. Jesse H. Jones.†

Financial data: (yr. ended 12/31/83): Assets, $303,416,058 (M); expenditures, $21,319,341, including $18,164,325 for 308 grants (high: $1,000,000; low: $1,000; average: $5,000-$50,000).

Purpose and activities: Primarily local giving for "the support of any charitable, educational, or religious undertaking." Grants largely for higher education (scholarships, buildings, and equipment) and health care facilities (construction and equipping of hospitals) but also including some cultural and religious activities, with highest priority placed on local and state needs. Scholarships granted directly to educational institutions which select recipients and administer the funds.

Types of support awarded: Building funds, equipment, scholarship funds, special projects, fellowships, professorships, matching funds.

Limitations: Giving primarily in TX; no grants outside the continental U.S. No grants to individuals, or for permanent endowment funds, or operating budgets; no loans.

Publications: Biennial report, program policy statement, application guidelines.

Application information:
  Initial approach: Letter
  Copies of proposal: 1
  Deadline(s): None
  Board meeting date(s): Monthly
  Final notification: 1 to 2 months
  Write: Marshall F. Wells, Grants Coordinator

Officers and Trustees: J.H. Creekmore, President and Treasurer; Jo Murphy, Vice-President; Alvin R. Thigpen, Secretary; Audrey Jones Beck, H.J. Nelson III, Philip G. Warner, H.F. Warren.

Number of staff: 3 full-time professional; 4 part-time professional.

Employer Identification Number: 746013920

3989
Hugg (Leola W. and Charles H.) Trust
c/o Carroll Sunseri, First City National Bank
P.O. Box 809
Houston 77001

Established in 1979.

Financial data: (yr. ended 12/31/84): Assets, $1,702,289 (M); expenditures, $170,334, including $110,125 for 181 grants to individuals.

Purpose and activities: Grants for scholarships to students from Williamson County to attend colleges and universities in Texas.

Types of support awarded: Student aid.

Limitations: Giving limited to Williamson County, TX.

Publications: Application guidelines.

Application information: Application forms and guidelines available upon request from participating high schools, or from the director of the Texas Baptist Children's Home in Round Rock, Texas, or the Office of Student Financial Aid at Southwestern University, in Georgetown, Texas. Application form required.
  Deadline(s): May 1
  Board meeting date(s): Annually
  Final notification: May

Trustees: William D. Swift, Kirk Treible, First City National Bank.

Employer Identification Number: 741907673

3990
Humphreys Foundation, The
1915 Trinity St.
Box 1139
Liberty 77575   (409) 336-3321

Incorporated in 1957 in Texas.

Donor(s): Geraldine Davis Humphreys.†

Financial data: (yr. ended 9/30/83): Assets, $3,173,666 (M); expenditures, $329,609, including $247,900 for 16 grants (high: $100,000; low: $2,000; average: $2,000-$10,000).

Purpose and activities: Local giving largely for local theater and opera programs and performing arts college scholarships.

Types of support awarded: Scholarship funds, special projects.

Limitations: Giving limited to TX. No grants to individuals or for building funds; no loans.

Publications: Application guidelines.

Application information: Application form required.
  Initial approach: Letter or full proposal
  Copies of proposal: 4
  Deadline(s): Submit proposal preferably in August; deadline August 15
  Board meeting date(s): September and as required
  Write: L.Q. Van Deventer, Jr., Manager

Officers and Trustees: John S. Boles, President; Claude C. Roberts, Vice-President and Secretary; Mrs. J.G. Bertman, Vice-President and Treasurer.

Manager: L.Q. Van Deventer, Jr.

Number of staff: 1 part-time professional; 1 full-time support.

Employer Identification Number: 746061381

3991
Hunt (The Ruth Ray) Foundation ⌗
2900 InterFirst One Bldg.
Dallas 75202

Established in 1981.

Financial data: (yr. ended 6/30/83): Assets, $25,093 (M); expenditures, $140,175, including $140,000 for 4 grants (high: $80,000; low: $5,000).

Purpose and activities: Broad purposes; primarily local giving, with emphasis on education.

Limitations: Giving primarily in TX.

Officers and Directors: Ruth Ray Hunt, Chairman; Ray L. Hunt, President; Walter J. Humann, Vice-President; George Cunyus, Secretary; E.T. Moffatt, Treasurer.

Employer Identification Number: 751726227

3992
Huthsteiner Fine Arts Trust
c/o El Paso National Bank
P.O. Drawer 140
El Paso 79980   (915) 546-6515

Established in 1980.

Donor(s): Robert and Pauline Huthsteiner Trust.

Financial data: (yr. ended 7/31/84): Assets, $1,240,619 (M); expenditures, $56,439, including $44,050 for 10 grants (high: $12,000; low: $300).

Purpose and activities: Primarily local giving, with emphasis on the arts, especially music.

Limitations: Giving primarily in TX.

Trustees: El Paso National Bank (Terry Crenshaw, Charitable Trust Administrative Officer).

Number of staff: 1 full-time professional; 1 part-time professional.

Employer Identification Number: 746308412

3993
Interferon Foundation, The ⌗
2660 South Tower
Pennzoil Place
Houston 77002   (713) 224-8224

Established in 1979 in Texas.

Donor(s): Atlantic Richfield Foundation, Shell Oil Foundation, ARCO, Dresser Foundation, Halliburton Company, Noble Foundation, Pennzoil Company, and others.

Financial data: (yr. ended 7/31/83): Assets, $2,054,600 (M); gifts received, $1,210,019; expenditures, $2,665,760, including $2,657,460 for 4 grants (high: $2,448,443; low: $23,650).

Purpose and activities: Grants for medical and scientific research, specifically for purchase of interferon for cancer research.

Application information:
  Initial approach: Full proposal
  Deadline(s): None
  Final notification: 3 months
  Write: Leon Davis, Chairman

Officers: Leon Davis, Chairman; Roy M. Huffington, Vice-Chairman; Barry A. Brown, Secretary; Richard Green, Treasurer.

Employer Identification Number: 742077812

3994
Johnson (The Burdine) Foundation ⌗
503 River Oaks Bank Bldg.
2001 Kirby
Houston 77019   (713) 528-6778

Trust established in 1960 in Texas.

Donor(s): Burdine C. Johnson, J.M. Johnson.

Financial data: (yr. ended 12/31/83): Assets, $141,479 (M); gifts received, $237,421; expenditures, $265,149, including $264,950 for 11 grants (high: $171,450; low: $500).

Purpose and activities: Broad purposes; primarily local giving, with emphasis on cultural programs, including a performing arts organization, education, and social services.

Limitations: Giving primarily in TX.

Application information:
  Initial approach: Full proposal
  Deadline(s): None

Trustees: Thomas James Barlow, Burdine C. Johnson, William T. Johnson.

Employer Identification Number: 746036669

3995
Johnson (M. G. and Lillie A.) Foundation, Inc. ▼
P.O. Box 508
Wharton 77488   (409) 532-3851

Incorporated in 1958 in Texas.

Donor(s): M.G. Johnson,† Lillie A. Johnson.
Financial data: (yr. ended 11/30/83): Assets, $8,245,874 (M); gifts received, $1,594,728; expenditures, $2,387,326, including $2,317,524 for 11 grants (high: $600,000; low: $2,000).
Purpose and activities: Primarily local giving, with emphasis on building funds for hospitals, medical research centers, higher educational institutions, social services, civic affairs, and religious organizations.
Types of support awarded: Building funds, equipment, land acquisition, matching funds.
Limitations: Giving primarily in TX. No grants to individuals, or for general support, operating budgets, endowment funds, scholarships and fellowships, research (except medical research), special projects, publications or conferences; no loans.
Application information:
 Initial approach: Full proposal
 Copies of proposal: 2
 Deadline(s): Submit proposal one month before meetings; no set deadline
 Board meeting date(s): February and October
 Write: Arnold Koop, President
Officers: Arnold Koop,* President; Lillie A. Johnson, Jack R. Morrison,* Vice-Presidents; Rev. M.H. Lehnhardt,* Secretary; Irving Moore, Jr., Treasurer.
Trustees:* M.H. Brock, Lloyd Rust.
Number of staff: None.
Employer Identification Number: 746076961

3996
Johnston (Ralph A.) Foundation, Inc. ⌧
9 Greenway Plaza, No.2112
Houston 77046

Trust established in 1959 in Texas; incorporated in 1963.
Donor(s): Ralph A. Johnston.
Financial data: (yr. ended 5/31/83): Assets, $847,775 (M); expenditures, $165,586, including $159,000 for 19 grants (high: $35,000; low: $100).
Purpose and activities: Primarily local grants for hospitals and medical research, higher education, and social services, including child welfare.
Limitations: Giving primarily in TX.
Officers: James J. Johnston, President; Jerry J. Andrew, Lyle E. Carbaugh, Vice-Presidents; Gladys Watford, Secretary-Treasurer.
Employer Identification Number: 746051797

3997
Jonsson Foundation, The
3300 Republic Bank Tower
Dallas 75201 (214) 969-5535

Incorporated in 1954 in Texas.
Donor(s): J.E. Jonsson,† Mrs. Margaret E. Jonsson.†
Financial data: (yr. ended 12/31/83): Assets, $2,583,997 (M); expenditures, $139,946, including $120,100 for 13 grants (high: $40,000; low: $1,000).

Purpose and activities: Charitable purposes; primarily local giving in areas of health, education, culture, and general community interests.
Types of support awarded: General purposes, building funds, equipment, land acquisition, matching funds.
Limitations: Giving primarily in TX, with some emphasis on the Dallas area. No grants to individuals, or for endowment funds, scholarships, or fellowships; no loans.
Publications: Application guidelines.
Application information: Funds largely committed.
 Initial approach: Letter
 Copies of proposal: 1
 Deadline(s): None
 Board meeting date(s): February, May, and September
 Final notification: At next meeting
 Write: Nelle C. Johnston, Secretary
Officers: Mrs. George V. Charlton,* President; Kenneth A. Jonsson,* Vice-President and Treasurer; Philip R. Jonsson,* Vice-President; Nelle C. Johnston, Secretary.
Trustees:* J.E. Jonsson.
Number of staff: 3.
Employer Identification Number: 756012565

3998
Kay (Mary) Foundation ⌧
8787 Stemmons Freeway
Dallas 75247

Incorporated in 1969 in Texas.
Donor(s): Mary Kay Ash.
Financial data: (yr. ended 6/30/83): Assets, $3,321,673 (M); expenditures, $80,443, including $79,685 for 44 grants (high: $22,450; low: $100).
Purpose and activities: Primarily local giving for medical research, health agencies, social services, and public policy organizations.
Types of support awarded: Research.
Limitations: Giving primarily in TX.
Application information:
 Deadline(s): None
Trustees: Gerald M. Allen, Mary Kay Ash, Monty C. Barber, Richard R. Rogers.
Employer Identification Number: 756081602

3999
Kayser Foundation, The ⌧
806 Main St., Suite 1030
Houston 77002

Incorporated in 1961 in Texas.
Donor(s): Paul Kayser, Mrs. Paul Kayser.
Financial data: (yr. ended 12/31/83): Assets, $2,412,082 (M); expenditures, $132,949, including $85,729 for 22 grants (high: $70,000; low: $100).
Purpose and activities: Broad purposes; primarily local giving, with emphasis on medical research, education, and social services.
Limitations: Giving primarily in TX.
Officer and Trustees: Henry O. Weaver, President; John Dawson, Charles Sapp, Vice-Presidents; Juanita B. Stanley, Secretary-Treasurer.
Employer Identification Number: 746050591

4000
Keith (Ben E.) Foundation Trust
c/o Texas American Bank/Fort Worth
P.O. Box 2050
Fort Worth 76113

Trust established in 1951 in Texas.
Financial data: (yr. ended 6/30/82): Assets, $1,743,497 (M); gifts received, $14,336; expenditures, $151,887, including $136,735 for 60 grants (high: $5,000; low: $200).
Purpose and activities: Charitable purposes; local giving, with emphasis on higher education and social agencies; some support also for cultural programs and hospitals.
Types of support awarded: General purposes, operating budgets, continuing support, annual campaigns, seed money, emergency funds, deficit financing, building funds, equipment, land acquisition, endowment funds, matching funds.
Limitations: Giving limited to TX. No grants to individuals, or for scholarships and fellowships; no loans.
Application information:
 Board meeting date(s): March and September
Officers and Directors: John Beauchamp, Chairman; R.L. Mitchell, Secretary; Howard Hallam, Robert Hallam, Troy LaGrone, Ronnie Wallace, Hugh Watson.
Trustee: Texas American Bank, Fort Worth.
Number of staff: None.
Employer Identification Number: 756013955

4001
Kempner (Harris and Eliza) Fund ▼
P.O. Box 119
Galveston 77553 (409) 765-6671

Trust established in 1946 in Texas.
Donor(s): Various Kempner interests and members of the Kempner family.
Financial data: (yr. ended 12/31/83): Assets, $12,784,000 (M); gifts received, $280,500; expenditures, $699,101, including $519,356 for 92 grants (high: $60,000; low: $100; average: $2,000-$5,000), $22,745 for 78 employee matching gifts and $120,000 for loans.
Purpose and activities: Broad purposes; primarily local giving, with emphasis on higher education, including scholarship funds, student loans, a matching gifts program, community funds, welfare funds, community projects, and cultural programs, including historic preservation.
Types of support awarded: General purposes, operating budgets, continuing support, annual campaigns, seed money, emergency funds, deficit financing, building funds, equipment, land acquisition, endowment funds, scholarship funds, professorships, student aid, special projects, research, publications, conferences and seminars, employee matching gifts.
Limitations: Giving primarily in TX. No grants to individuals.
Application information:
 Initial approach: Letter or full proposal
 Copies of proposal: 1
 Deadline(s): Submit proposal preferably no later than 1 month prior to board meetings; no set deadline

Board meeting date(s): Usually in May and December and as required
Final notification: 2 weeks
Write: Harris L. Kempner, Chairman
Officers and Trustees: Harris L. Kempner, Chairman; Harris K. Weston, Vice-Chairman; Leonora K. Thompson, Secretary-Treasurer; Arthur M. Alpert, Jack Currie, Mrs. Harris L. Kempner, Jr., Lyda Ann Thomas.
Number of staff: 1 part-time professional; 1 part-time support.
Employer Identification Number: 746042458

4002
Kenedy (The John G. and Marie Stella) Memorial Foundation ▼ ⌑
1020 First City Tower II
Corpus Christi 78478

Incorporated in 1960 in Texas.
Donor(s): Mrs. Sarita Kenedy East.†
Financial data: (yr. ended 12/31/83): Assets, $98,340,219 (M); expenditures, $5,403,949, including $3,329,659 for 27 grants (high: $1,088,659; low: $5,000).
Purpose and activities: Local giving for sectarian purposes, primarily Roman Catholic, and social service agencies; ten percent of income annually is disbursed to the Bishop of the Diocese of Corpus Christi for distribution to charity.
Limitations: Giving limited to TX.
Application information: Application form required.
Write: James R. McCown, Director
Officers and Directors: Elena S. Kenedy, President; Bishop Thomas Drury, Vice-President; Kenneth Oden, Secretary-Treasurer; B.R. Goldapp, Lee H. Lytton, Jr.
Employer Identification Number: 746040701

4003
King (Carl B. and Florence E.) Foundation ▼
One Preston Centre
8222 Douglas Ave., Suite 370
Dallas 75225   (214) 750-1884

Incorporated in 1966 in Texas.
Donor(s): Carl B. King,† Florence E. King,† Dorothy E. King.
Financial data: (yr. ended 12/31/83): Assets, $16,701,345 (M); gifts received, $70,100; expenditures, $1,181,799, including $732,050 for 64 grants (high: $150,000; low: $500; average: $5,000-$20,000) and $73,000 for 74 grants to individuals.
Purpose and activities: Primarily local giving, with emphasis on higher and secondary education, youth agencies, and hospitals and health agencies; scholarships limited to Texas high school students; some support for welfare agencies and cultural programs.
Types of support awarded: Scholarship funds, special projects, student aid.
Limitations: Giving primarily in the Dallas, TX, area. No support for religious purposes.
Publications: Program policy statement, application guidelines.

Application information: Application forms required for scholarships only, and limited to Texas high school students; no direct requests accepted. Application form required.
Initial approach: Letter
Copies of proposal: 1
Deadline(s): None
Board meeting date(s): Quarterly
Final notification: 6 weeks
Write: Carl Yeckel, Vice-President
Officers: Dorothy E. King,* President; Carl Yeckel,* Vice-President; Thomas W. Vett, Secretary-Treasurer.
Directors:* M.E. Childs, Jack Phipps, Sam G. Winstead.
Number of staff: 4 full-time professional.
Employer Identification Number: 756052203

4004
King Ranch Family Trust
P.O. Box 1418
Kingsville 78363   (512) 592-6411

Trust established in 1946 in Texas.
Donor(s): King Ranch, Inc.
Financial data: (yr. ended 12/31/84): Assets, $4,816,541 (M); expenditures, $166,767, including $151,800 for 23 grants (high: $77,400; low: $50).
Purpose and activities: Local giving, with emphasis on higher education; grants also for a hospital, youth activities, and religious organizations.
Types of support awarded: Research, scholarship funds, matching funds.
Limitations: Giving primarily in TX, with emphasis on south TX. No grants to individuals or for endowment funds; no loans.
Publications: Application guidelines.
Application information:
Initial approach: Cover letter with full proposal
Copies of proposal: 1
Deadline(s): May and December
Board meeting date(s): June and December
Final notification: 30 days after board meeting
Write: Richard M. Kleberg, III, Chairman
Gift Committee: Richard M. Kleberg, III,* Chairman; Nelva Lou Shelton, Secretary; Henrietta Armstrong, Ida L. Clement, Leslie C. Finger,* Helen K. Groves, Mary Lewis Kleberg, Michael Reynolds, Richard G. Sugden.
Trustees:* James H. Clement.
Employer Identification Number: 746044809

4005
Kleberg (Caesar) Foundation for Wildlife Conservation ▼
711 Navarro St., Suite 535
San Antonio 78205   (512) 224-1011

Trust established about 1951 in Texas.
Donor(s): Caesar Kleberg.†
Financial data: (yr. ended 12/31/83): Assets, $13,924,118 (M); expenditures, $902,311, including $415,194 for 5 grants (high: $300,000; low: $6,750).
Purpose and activities: Primarily local giving to aid in the conservation of game and other wildlife.

Limitations: Giving primarily in southwest TX. No grants to individuals, or for building or endowment funds, scholarships and fellowships, or matching gifts; no loans.
Application information:
Initial approach: Letter
Copies of proposal: 3
Deadline(s): None
Board meeting date(s): Semiannually and as required
Final notification: 3 months
Write: Leroy G. Denman, Jr., Trustee
Trustees: Leroy G. Denman, Jr., Stephen J. Kleberg, Duane M. Leach.
Number of staff: None.
Employer Identification Number: 746038766

4006
Kleberg (Robert J.), Jr. and Helen C. Kleberg Foundation ▼
700 North St. Mary's St., Suite 1200
San Antonio 78205   (512) 223-2640

Incorporated in 1950 in Texas.
Donor(s): Helen C. Kleberg,† Robert J. Kleberg, Jr.†
Financial data: (yr. ended 12/31/83): Assets, $51,772,737 (M); gifts received, $18,542,454; expenditures, $2,506,695, including $1,170,929 for 35 grants (high: $400,000; low: $1,000; average: $5,000-$150,000).
Purpose and activities: Broad purposes; giving on a national basis for medical research, veterinary science, wildlife, and related activities; grants for community organizations limited to Texas.
Types of support awarded: Building funds, equipment, research, conferences and seminars, matching funds.
Limitations: No support for community organizations outside Texas, for non-tax-exempt organizations, or for organizations limited by race or religion. No grants to individuals, or for general purposes, endowments, deficit financing, ongoing operating expenses, overhead or indirect costs, scholarships, or fellowships; no loans.
Publications: Annual report, application guidelines.
Application information:
Initial approach: Letter
Copies of proposal: 1
Deadline(s): None
Board meeting date(s): Usually in June and December
Final notification: 6 months
Write: Robert Washington, Grants Coordinator
Officers and Directors: Helen K. Groves, President; Helen C. Alexander, Vice-President; John D. Alexander, Jr., Vice-President and Secretary; Emory G. Alexander, Vice-President and Treasurer; Caroline Alexander, Henrietta Alexander.
Number of staff: 1 full-time professional.
Employer Identification Number: 746044810

4007
Klein (Nathan J.) Fund
P.O. Box 20446
Houston 77025

Trust established in 1953 in Texas.
Donor(s): Nathan J. Klein, Almeda Harold
Corporation, and others.
Financial data: (yr. ended 12/31/83): Assets,
$1,509,549 (M); gifts received, $76,500;
expenditures, $114,366, including $106,984
for 66 grants (high: $25,285; low: $500).
Purpose and activities: Broad purposes; grants
largely for Jewish welfare funds and religious
organizations, social and cultural organizations,
and higher education including support for
institutions in Israel.
Trustees: Amelia Klein, Nathan J. Klein, Martha
K. Lottman, Shirley K. Markey.
Employer Identification Number: 746060543

4008
Knapp Foundation ⌑
331 S. Kansas Ave.
Weslaco 78596

Donor(s): F.E. Knapp, J.A. Knapp.
Financial data: (yr. ended 12/31/83): Assets,
$1,125,267 (M); gifts received, $50,000;
expenditures, $96,622, including $94,000 for
21 grants (high: $25,000; low: $2,000).
Purpose and activities: Primarily local giving
for Protestant church support, religious
organizations, and a hospital.
Limitations: Giving primarily in TX.
Officer: Gilson Knapp, President.
Employer Identification Number: 746060544

4009
**Knox (Robert W.), Sr. and Pearl Wallis
Knox Charitable Foundation**
c/o InterFirst Bank Houston
P.O. Box 2555
Houston 77252-2555

Established in 1964 in Texas.
Donor(s): Robert W. Knox, Jr.†
Financial data: (yr. ended 8/31/84): Assets,
$2,501,996 (M); gifts received, $11,118;
expenditures, $85,590, including $59,968 for 7
grants (high: $45,592; low: $50).
Purpose and activities: Primarily local giving,
with emphasis on cultural programs, youth
activities, parks, and a college.
Limitations: Giving primarily in Houston, TX.
Trustee: InterFirst Bank Houston.
Employer Identification Number: 746064974

4010
Lard (Mary Potishman) Trust ▼ ⌑
P.O. Box 2050
Fort Worth 76113

Trust established in 1968 in Texas.
Donor(s): Mary P. Lard.†
Financial data: (yr. ended 12/31/83): Assets,
$7,504,977 (M); expenditures, $1,038,711,
including $485,000 for 68 grants (high:
$75,000; low: $500).

Purpose and activities: Primarily local giving,
with emphasis on education, including higher
education; support also for social services,
youth agencies, hospitals, medical research,
and cultural organizations.
Limitations: Giving primarily in TX, with
emphasis on Fort Worth.
Trustees: Bayard Friedman, Mayme Friedman.
Employer Identification Number: 756210697

4011
LBJ Family Foundation
Tenth and Brazos Sts.
P.O. Box 1209
Austin 78767   (512) 472-4993

Trust established in 1957 in Texas.
Donor(s): Lyndon B. Johnson,† Mrs. Lyndon B.
Johnson, Texas Broadcasting Corporation.
Financial data: (yr. ended 12/31/82): Assets,
$1,488,661 (M); expenditures, $203,639,
including $194,203 for 134 grants (high:
$25,000; low: $16).
Purpose and activities: Broad purposes;
primarily local giving, with emphasis on
conservation and recreation; some support for
higher and secondary education, educational
television, hospitals, and cultural programs,
including support of presidential libraries.
Limitations: Giving primarily in Austin, TX. No
grants to individuals or for endowment funds;
no loans.
Application information:
  Initial approach: Letter
  Copies of proposal: 1
  Write: John M. Barr, Manager
Trustees: Claudia T. Johnson, Luci B. Johnson,
Charles S. Robb, Lynda J. Robb.
Employer Identification Number: 746045768

4012
Lennox Foundation
7920 Belt Line
P.O. Box 809000
Dallas 75380-9000   (214) 980-6000

Incorporated in 1951 in Iowa.
Donor(s): Lennox Industries Inc.
Financial data: (yr. ended 11/30/84): Assets,
$6,000,000 (M); expenditures, $375,000,
including $375,000 for 20 grants (high:
$100,000; low: $1,000).
Purpose and activities: General purposes;
grants primarily for private colleges and
universities, and community development in
areas in which the company operates.
Limitations: Giving limited to areas of
company operations. No grants to individuals.
Application information:
  Initial approach: Full proposal
  Copies of proposal: 1
  Deadline(s): January 30
  Board meeting date(s): February
  Write: Richard W. Booth, Chairman
Officers and Trustees: Richard W. Booth,
Chairman and Treasurer; David H. Anderson,
Vice-Chairman; David V. Brown, Secretary.
Employer Identification Number: 426053380

4013
Leppard (J. A.) Foundation Trust ⌑
1949 Donaldson
San Antonio 78228

Trust established in 1980 in Texas.
Donor(s): J.A. Leppard.†
Financial data: (yr. ended 12/31/83): Assets,
$1,212,200 (M); expenditures, $122,612,
including $94,100 for 14 grants (high: $18,400;
low: $1,500).
Purpose and activities: Primarily local giving;
grants exclusively for Christian education,
church support, and missionary work.
Limitations: Giving primarily in San Antonio,
TX. No grants to individuals.
Officer and Trustees: Dorothy C. Mackey,
Administrator; Harry James Fraser, Jr., J.A.
Leppard, Jr., George Poppas, Jr.
Employer Identification Number: 742044159

4014
LeTourneau Foundation, The ⌑
P.O. Box 736
Rockwall 75087   (214) 722-8325

Incorporated in 1935 in California.
Donor(s): Robert G. LeTourneau,† Mrs. Robert
G. LeTourneau.
Financial data: (yr. ended 12/31/83): Assets,
$7,720,796 (M); expenditures, $718,152,
including $89,384 for 8 grants (high: $48,284;
low: $500).
Purpose and activities: Religious and
charitable purposes; grants limited to
evangelical Christian activities in foreign
missions, evangelism, and education.
Application information:
  Board meeting date(s): Quarterly
Officers and Directors: Roy S. LeTourneau,
President; James Stjernstrom, Vice-President;
Brenda J. LeTourneau, Secretary and Treasurer;
Mike LeTourneau, Mrs. Robert G. LeTourneau.
Employer Identification Number: 756001947

4015
Lewis (Lillian Kaiser) Foundation
P.O. Box 809
Houston 77001   (713) 658-6486

Trust established in 1966 in Texas.
Donor(s): Lillian Kaiser Lewis.†
Financial data: (yr. ended 9/30/84): Assets,
$1,139,839 (M); expenditures, $108,625,
including $105,025 for 45 grants (high:
$20,000; low: $500).
Purpose and activities: Primarily local giving,
with emphasis on programs relating to children,
including grants to hospitals, health agencies,
and educational activities.
Types of support awarded: Operating
budgets, continuing support, annual campaigns,
emergency funds, deficit financing, building
funds, equipment, endowment funds.
Limitations: Giving primarily in TX. No grants
to individuals, or for scholarships and
fellowships, or matching gifts; no loans.
Application information:
  Initial approach: Full proposal
  Copies of proposal: 3

Board meeting date(s): March, June, September, and December
Write: Carroll G. Sunseri, V.P., First City National Bank of Houston
Trustees: G. Sidney Buchanan, Hyman Judah Schachtel, First City National Bank of Houston (Carroll G. Sunseri, Vice-President).
Employer Identification Number: 746076511

4016
Lightner Sams Foundation ⌘
11811 Preston Rd., Suite 200
Dallas 75230

Established in 1980.
Financial data: (yr. ended 12/31/82): Assets, $13,323,944 (M); expenditures, $600,674, including $458,000 for 37 grants (high: $100,000; low: $200).
Purpose and activities: Giving for cultural programs, including a zoo and a playhouse, and education; some support also for hospitals, youth organizations, Protestant religious organizations, and social services.
Trustees: Earl Sams Lightner, Larry Lightner, Robin Lightner.
Employer Identification Number: 742139849

4017
Lindsay (Franklin) Student Aid Fund ▼
Texas Commerce Bank of Austin
P.O. Box 550
Austin 78789   (512) 476-6611

Trust established in 1957 in Texas.
Donor(s): Franklin Lindsay.†
Financial data: (yr. ended 12/31/83): Assets, $7,127,408 (M); expenditures, $206,609, including $871,871 for loans.
Purpose and activities: Student loans limited to students attending colleges or universities in Texas.
Types of support awarded: Student aid.
Limitations: Giving limited to students at institutions of higher learning in TX.
Publications: Program policy statement, application guidelines, informational brochure.
Application information: Address application to appropriate Loan Committee member (depending on area of Texas where student resides). Application form required.
  Initial approach: Application form
  Copies of proposal: 1
  Deadline(s): Varies according to each committee member
  Board meeting date(s): January and July
  Final notification: 1 month
  Write: Rebecca McClary, Trust Department
Loan Committee: Alvin P. Bormann, Jr., M.H. Connelly, Lawrence L. Crum, John B. Hubbard, Mrs. Sherwood Inkley, James R. Kay, George C. Miller, B.G. Montgomery, H. Hart Nance, Mrs. Murray Nance, Robert F. Parker, V.P. Patterson, Mrs. Joseph M. Ray, James W. Stegall, John Stuart, Jim Valentine.
Trustee: The Texas Commerce Bank of Austin.
Number of staff: 2.
Employer Identification Number: 746031753

4018
Lone Star Gas Foundation ⌘
300 S. St. Paul
Dallas 75201

Established in 1982 in Texas.
Donor(s): ENSERCH Corporation.
Financial data: (yr. ended 12/31/82): Assets, $693,324 (M); gifts received, $1,200,000; expenditures, $579,977, including $579,977 for 107 grants (high: $161,945; low: $25).
Purpose and activities: Initial year of operation 1982; primarily local giving, with emphasis on community funds, hospitals, cultural programs, youth organizations, and higher education.
Limitations: Giving primarily in TX.
Officers and Directors:* W.C. McCord,* Chairman; C.L. Neaves,* President; W.T. Satterwhite,* S.R. Singer,* R.B. Williams,* Vice-Presidents; M.G. Fortado, Secretary; E.E. McAlister, Jr.,Treasurer.
Employer Identification Number: 751816053

4019
Luling Foundation, The
523 South Mulberry Ave.
P.O. Drawer 31
Luling 78648   (512) 875-2438

Trust established in 1927 in Texas.
Donor(s): Edgar B. Davis.†
Financial data: (yr. ended 12/31/83): Assets, $1,824,579 (M); expenditures, $263,189, including $9,470 for 7 grants (high: $3,150; low: $20; average: $1,000), $3,000 for 3 grants to individuals, $43,858 for 18 foundation-administered programs and $21,065 for 57 loans.
Purpose and activities: Local giving to help the farmer through demonstrations of farming techniques and to help the 4-H and F.F.A. students of Caldwell, Gonzales, and Guadalupe Counties for a period of two years with marketing show animals; principal activity is the operation of an agricultural demonstration farm.
Types of support awarded: Loans, special projects.
Limitations: Giving limited to Caldwell, Gonzales, and Guadalupe counties, TX. No grants for building or endowment funds, land acquisition, operating budgets, or matching gifts; no loans.
Publications: 990-PF, application guidelines, informational brochure.
Application information: Application form required.
  Deadline(s): April 30
  Board meeting date(s): January, April, July, and October, and as required
  Write: Archie Abrameit, Manager
Officers: Marylou Rogas, Secretary-Treasurer; Archie Abrameit, Manager.
Trustees: Cleburne Siltmann, Chairman; Stan Reese, Vice-Chairman; Calvin Baker, Tony Breitschopf, Lewis Freeman, Tom Wehe, Kermit Westerholm.
Number of staff: 2 full-time professional; 5 full-time support; 1 part-time support.
Employer Identification Number: 741143102

4020
MacDonald (Mrs. Zoe Blunt) Trust ⌘
c/o Bank of the Southwest Trust Dept.
P.O. Box 2629
Houston 77001

Established in 1954.
Financial data: (yr. ended 12/31/83): Assets, $896,713 (M); expenditures, $175,042, including $100,872 for 11 grants (high: $91,872; low: $500).
Purpose and activities: Support primarily for a local hospital.
Limitations: Giving primarily in Houston, TX.
Trustee: Bank of the Southwest.
Employer Identification Number: 746038356

4021
Mays Foundation ⌘
914 Tyler St.
Amarillo 79101

Established in 1965.
Donor(s): W.A. Mays and Agnes Mays Trust.
Financial data: (yr. ended 7/31/83): Assets, $1,322,212 (M); gifts received, $12,818; expenditures, $158,281, including $116,996 for 36 grants (high: $23,200; low: $25).
Purpose and activities: Primarily local giving, with emphasis on Baptist church organizations and higher education.
Limitations: Giving primarily in TX.
Trustees: Troy M. Mays, W.A. Mays.
Employer Identification Number: 751213346

4022
McAshan Educational and Charitable Trust ▼ ⌘
P.O. Box 2538
Houston 77001

Trust established in 1952 in Texas.
Donor(s): Susan C. McAshan.
Financial data: (yr. ended 12/31/83): Assets, $1,106,646 (M); gifts received, $719,565; expenditures, $705,204, including $702,812 for 74 grants (high: $71,802; low: $100).
Purpose and activities: Primarily local giving, with emphasis on education, including the handicapped, population control, conservation, cultural programs, and the arts.
Limitations: Giving primarily in TX, with emphasis on Houston.
Trustees: W. St. John Garwood, Jr., Lucy I. Hadac, Susan C. McAshan.
Employer Identification Number: 746042210

4023
McCreless (Sollie & Lilla) Foundation for Christian Evangelism, Christian Missions, and Christian Education
P.O. Box 2341
San Antonio 78298   (512) 227-1281

Foundation established in 1958 in Texas.
Donor(s): Sollie E. McCreless.†
Financial data: (yr. ended 12/31/84): Assets, $3,929,511 (M); expenditures, $228,679, including $189,315 for 33 grants (high: $25,000; low: $600).

Purpose and activities: Support for Protestant churches, theological education, and evangelical organizations, with some emphasis on the local area.

Types of support awarded: Special projects, general purposes.

Application information:
Initial approach: Letter
Deadline(s): None
Write: Marjorie Gerfen, Secretary

Officers: Frances Jean Sunderland,* President; Robert B. Sunderland,* Vice-President; Marjorie Gerfen, Secretary and Treasurer.

Directors:* G.R. Ferdenanatsen, Dennis A. Kinlaw.

Number of staff: None.

Employer Identification Number: 741485541

4024
McDermott (The Eugene) Foundation ▼

3803 Euclid
Dallas 75205   (214) 521-2924

Incorporated in 1972 in Texas; The McDermott Foundation merged into above in 1977.

Donor(s): Eugene McDermott,† Mrs. Eugene McDermott.

Financial data: (yr. ended 8/31/82): Assets, $31,408,183 (M); expenditures, $1,826,765, including $1,715,000 for 19 grants (high: $300,000; low: $10,300).

Purpose and activities: Charitable purposes; primarily local giving, including support for building funds, in areas of higher and secondary education, health, culture, including museums, and general community interests.

Types of support awarded: Building funds, equipment.

Limitations: Giving primarily in Dallas, TX. No grants to individuals.

Application information:
Initial approach: Letter
Copies of proposal: 1
Board meeting date(s): Quarterly
Write: Mrs. Eugene McDermott, President

Officers and Trustees: Mrs. Eugene McDermott, President; J.E. Jonsson, Vice-President; Mary McDermott, Secretary-Treasurer; C.J. Thomsen.

Employer Identification Number: 237237919

4025
McGovern (John P.) Foundation ▼

6969 Brompton
Houston 77025   (713) 661-4808

Established in 1961 in Texas.

Donor(s): John P. McGovern, M.D.

Financial data: (yr. ended 8/31/83): Assets, $13,061,840 (M); gifts received, $1,578,173; expenditures, $953,915, including $870,650 for 148 grants (high: $302,550; low: $50) and $3,300 for 1 grant to an individual.

Purpose and activities: To provide assistance to organizations engaged in medical research, particularly relating to allergies, and to provide scholarships for deserving students to study the causes of allergies; support also hospitals, health agencies, and other higher and medical education.

Limitations: Giving primarily in the Houston, TX, area. No grants to individuals (except for research grants and honorariums).

Application information: Grants usually initiated by the foundation; applications for grants not invited.
Deadline(s): Usually on or before August 31

Officers: John P. McGovern, M.D., President; Richard B. Davies, Vice-President; Katherine McGovern, Secretary and Treasurer.

Number of staff: 2 part-time professional; 4 part-time support.

Employer Identification Number: 746053075

4026
McKee (Robert E. and Evelyn) Foundation

P.O. Box 13348
6006 North Mesa, Suite 906
El Paso 79913   (915) 581-4025

Incorporated in 1952 in Texas.

Donor(s): Robert E. McKee,† Evelyn McKee,† Robert E. McKee, Inc., The Zia Company.

Financial data: (yr. ended 12/31/83): Assets, $3,241,692 (M); expenditures, $302,038, including $239,500 for 85 grants (high: $30,450; low: $100).

Purpose and activities: General giving; emphasis on local hospitals, community funds, and the handicapped; grants also for higher education, youth agencies, child welfare, and medical research.

Types of support awarded: Operating budgets, continuing support, annual campaigns, seed money, emergency funds, building funds, equipment, scholarship funds, research.

Limitations: Giving primarily in TX, with emphasis on El Paso. No support for organizations limited by race or ethnic origin; to other private foundations except for a local community foundation; or to religious organizations except local Episcopal churches. No grants to individuals, or for endowment funds, or deficit financing; no loans.

Publications: Annual report, program policy statement, application guidelines.

Application information:
Initial approach: Full proposal
Copies of proposal: 1
Deadline(s): Submit proposal preferably in November; deadline December 10
Board meeting date(s): May
Final notification: 1 week after board meeting
Write: John S. McKee, President

Officers and Trustees: John S. McKee, President and Treasurer; C.D. McKee, Louis B. McKee, Philip S. McKee, Robert E. McKee, Jr., Vice-Presidents; R.L. Hazelton, Secretary; Frances McKee Hays, Margaret McKee Lund, Tad R. Smith.

Number of staff: 1 full-time professional; 1 full-time support.

Employer Identification Number: 746036675

4027
McMillan (Bruce), Jr. Foundation, Inc. ▼

P.O. Box 9
Overton 75684   (214) 834-3148

Trust established in 1951 in Texas.

Donor(s): V. Bruce McMillan, M.D.,† Mary Moore McMillan.†

Financial data: (yr. ended 6/30/83): Assets, $10,603,053 (M); expenditures, $1,124,192, including $819,625 for 65 grants (high: $75,000; low: $100; average: $1,000-$20,000) and $72,948 for 114 grants to individuals.

Purpose and activities: Broad purposes, to benefit the people of east Texas; grants largely for higher education, including a scholarship program for graduates of specific high schools within the immediate Overton area; support also for health agencies, church support, social services and youth agencies, agricultural conservation, and medical research.

Types of support awarded: Student aid.

Limitations: Giving limited to east TX.

Publications: Application guidelines.

Application information: Application form required.
Deadline(s): June 5 (for scholarships)
Write: Ralph Ward, President

Officers and Directors:* Reginald H. Field,* Chairman; Ralph Ward,* President and Treasurer; Ralph B. Shank,* Vice-President; Ralph Ward, Jr., Secretary; Donald B. Leverett, John L. Pope.

Employer Identification Number: 750945924

4028
McQueen (Adeline and George) Foundation of 1960

c/o Texas American Bank
P.O. Box 2050
Fort Worth 76113

Trust established in 1960 in Texas.

Financial data: (yr. ended 12/31/83): Assets, $7,864,464 (M); expenditures, $565,919, including $402,000 for 35 grants (high: $35,000; low: $3,000).

Purpose and activities: Primarily local giving, with emphasis on hospitals and youth agencies; support also for social agencies, medical research, and a Protestant theological seminary.

Limitations: Giving primarily in TX.

Application information:
Initial approach: Full proposal
Copies of proposal: 1
Deadline(s): Submit proposal preferably in August; deadline September 15
Board meeting date(s): October
Write: Robert M. Landsford, Senior Vice-President

Trustee: Texas American Bank (Robert M. Landsford, Senior Vice-President and Trust Officer).

Employer Identification Number: 756014459

4029
Meadows Foundation, Inc. ▼
Wilson Historic Block
2922 Swiss Ave.
Dallas 75204   (214) 826-9431

Incorporated in 1948 in Texas.
Donor(s): Algur Hurtle Meadows,† Mrs.
Virginia Meadows.†
Financial data: (yr. ended 12/31/83): Assets,
$324,123,001 (M); gifts received, $174,700;
expenditures, $10,399,481, including
$7,500,859 for 164 grants (high: $1,000,000;
low: $607; average: $25,000-$50,000).
Purpose and activities: Broad purposes; local
giving, with emphasis on the arts, social
services, health, education and civic programs.
Operates a historic preservation investment-
related program using a cluster of Victorian
homes as offices for non-profit agencies.
Types of support awarded: Operating
budgets, continuing support, seed money,
emergency funds, deficit financing, building
funds, equipment, land acquisition, matching
funds, scholarship funds, professorships,
internships, fellowships, special projects,
research, publications, conferences and
seminars, program-related investments,
technical assistance, consulting services.
Limitations: Giving limited to TX, with
emphasis on Dallas. No grants to individuals,
or for general endowment funds, or annual
campaigns; no loans. Generally no grants for
church construction or media projects in
planning stages.
Publications: Annual report, application
guidelines, program policy statement.
Application information:
  Initial approach: Full proposal
  Copies of proposal: 1
  Deadline(s): None
  Board meeting date(s): April and November
    on major grants; Grants Review
    Committee meets monthly
  Final notification: 3 to 4 months
  Write: Dr. Sally R. Lancaster, Executive Vice-
    President
Officers: Curtis W. Meadows, Jr.,* President;
Sally R. Lancaster,* Executive Vice-President;
G. Thomas Rhodus, Vice-President and
Secretary; Judy Culbertson, Robert A.
Meadows,* Linda S. Perryman,* Eloise Rouse,*
Robert E. Wise, Vice-Presidents.
Directors:* Evelyn Meadows Acton, James D.
Berry, John Broadfoot, Vela Broadfoot, J.W.
Bullion, Eudine Meadows Cheney, John A.
Hammack, J.H. Murrell, Evy Kay Ritzen,
Dorothy C. Wilson.
Number of staff: 8 full-time professional; 1
part-time professional; 11 full-time support; 1
part-time support.
Employer Identification Number: 756015322

4030
Menil Foundation, Inc.
1427 Branard St.
Houston 77006   (713) 524-9028

Incorporated in 1953 in Texas.
Donor(s): John de Menil,† Dominique de
Menil.

Financial data: (yr. ended 12/31/83): Assets,
$92,540,521 (M); gifts received, $528,036;
expenditures, $2,999,436, including $343,312
for 19 grants (high: $103,648; low: $200;
average: $15,000) and $1,510,341 for 7
foundation-administered programs.
Purpose and activities: A private operating
foundation primarily exhibiting its art collection
at Rice University in Houston and museums
throughout the world; currently building
museum at Houston to permanently house and
exhibit its collection; supports art centers at
Rice University; conducts research projects on
black iconography, Magritte and Max Ernst,
and colloquiums at The Rothko Chapel.
Application information: No applications
considered.
  Board meeting date(s): Annually
Officers: Dominique de Menil,* President;
Miles Glaser,* Vice-President; P.M.
Schlumberger, Secretary.
Directors:* Miles Glaser, Walter Hopps,
Christophe de Menil, Dominique de Menil,
Francois de Menil, Philippa de Menil,
Francesco Pellizzi, Paul Winkler, Peter Wood.
Employer Identification Number: 746045327

4031
Menil Fund
3363 San Felipe
Houston 77019

Established in 1980 in Texas.
Donor(s): Dominique de Menil.
Financial data: (yr. ended 9/30/83): Assets,
$6,202,146 (M); expenditures, $265,396,
including $264,050 for 32 grants (high:
$160,000; low: $100; average: $1,000-$5,000).
Purpose and activities: Giving largely for
higher education and Roman Catholic church
support and religious associations.
Types of support awarded: Operating
budgets, continuing support, annual campaigns,
seed money, emergency funds, deficit
financing, general purposes.
Limitations: No grants to individuals, or for
scholarships or fellowships; no loans.
Application information:
  Initial approach: Full proposal
  Board meeting date(s): As required
  Write: Dominique de Menil, President
Officers: Dominique de Menil, President; P.M.
Schlumberger, Secretary; Jody Blazek, Treasurer.
Number of staff: None.
Employer Identification Number: 742095103

4032
Meredith Foundation ⌑
Chamber of Commerce Bldg.
Mineola 75773

Trust established in 1958 in Texas.
Donor(s): Harry W. Meredith.†
Financial data: (yr. ended 12/31/81): Assets,
$1,828,931 (M); expenditures, $599,649,
including $280,033 for 8 grants (high: $90,511;
low: $1,350).
Purpose and activities: Broad purposes; grants
solely for the benefit of residents of Mineola
and its environs.

Limitations: Giving limited to Mineola, TX,
residents.
Publications: Program policy statement.
Application information:
  Initial approach: Proposal
  Copies of proposal: 2
  Board meeting date(s): Monthly
Trustees: R.C. Lukenbill, Chairman; T.W.
Benham, Sid Cox, James O. Dear, Harry Jones.
Employer Identification Number: 756024469

4033
Millhollon (Nettie) Educational Trust ⌑
P.O. Box 32
Stanton 79782

Trust established in 1963 in Texas.
Donor(s): Nettie Milhollon.†
Financial data: (yr. ended 6/30/83): Assets,
$1,958,553 (M); expenditures, $33,998,
including $195,259 for loans.
Purpose and activities: Educational loans to
deserving students who are residents of Texas
only.
Types of support awarded: Student aid.
Limitations: Giving limited to TX.
Officers and Trustees: Ed Lawson, Chairman;
R.O. Anderson, Gordon Stone, Vice-Chairmen;
Paul Crosthwait, Secretary-Treasurer; H.S.
Blocker, O.B. Bryon, Gerald Hanson, W.C.
Houston, Jr., Bruce Key, John Zant.
Employer Identification Number: 756024639

4034
Moncrief (William A. and Elizabeth B.)
Foundation ⌑
Ninth at Commerce
Fort Worth 76102   (817) 336-7232

Established in 1954.
Donor(s): W.A. Moncrief, Deep Water, Inc.
Financial data: (yr. ended 9/30/83): Assets,
$2,199,637 (M); expenditures, $644,510,
including $625,439 for 6 grants (high:
$586,439; low: $800).
Purpose and activities: Primarily local giving
for a hospital and higher education.
Types of support awarded: General purposes,
operating budgets.
Limitations: Giving primarily in TX.
Manager: William A. Moncrief, Jr.
Employer Identification Number: 756036329

4035
Moody Foundation, The ▼
704 Moody National Bank Bldg.
Galveston 77550   (409) 763-5333

Trust established in 1942 in Texas.
Donor(s): William Lewis Moody, Jr.,† Libbie
Shearn Moody.†
Financial data: (yr. ended 12/31/83): Assets,
$270,000,000 (M); expenditures, $14,060,000,
including $9,452,399 for 142 grants (high:
$515,000; low: $600), $350,495 for 518
grants to individuals and $3,887,000 for 3
foundation-administered programs.

Purpose and activities: Funds to be used locally for historic restoration projects, performing arts organizations, cultural programs; for promotion of health, science, and education; for community and social services; and in the field of religion.

Types of support awarded: Seed money, emergency funds, building funds, equipment, consulting services, technical assistance, matching funds, professorships, fellowships, special projects, research, publications, conferences and seminars, student aid.

Limitations: Giving limited to TX. No grants to individuals (except for students covered by two scholarship funds in Galveston County), or for operating budgets, except for start-up purposes; continuing support, annual campaigns, deficit financing, or land acquisition; no loans.

Publications: Annual report, application guidelines.

Application information:
Initial approach: Letter or telephone
Copies of proposal: 1
Deadline(s): 4 weeks prior to board meetings
Board meeting date(s): Quarterly
Final notification: 2 weeks after board meetings
Write: Robert E. Baker, Executive Administrator

Officer: Robert E. Baker, Executive Administrator and Secretary-Treasurer.

Trustees: Mary Moody Northen, Chairman; Robert L. Moody, Vice-Chairman; Shearn Moody, Jr.

Number of staff: 13.

Employer Identification Number: 741403105

4036
Mosle (Rotan) Foundation
P.O. Box 3226
Houston 77253

Established in 1972.

Donor(s): Rotan Mosle, Inc.

Financial data: (yr. ended 9/30/82): Assets, $165,681 (M); gifts received, $200,000; expenditures, $141,343, including $140,600 for 128 grants (high: $25,000; low: $100).

Purpose and activities: Primarily local giving for community funds, higher education, cultural programs, hospitals, and social services, to organizations in which company employees are actively involved.

Limitations: Giving primarily in TX.

Application information:
Write: Stuart Hellmann, Trustee

Officer: Gary Wood, Secretary.

Trustees: Stuart Hellmann, Philip Plant.

Employer Identification Number: 237300336

4037
Moss (Harry S.) Foundation ⌘
2641 First International Bldg.
Dallas 75270

Incorporated in 1952 in Texas.

Donor(s): Harry S. Moss, Florence M. Moss, Moss Petroleum Company.

Financial data: (yr. ended 11/30/83): Assets, $2,010,552 (M); expenditures, $120,928, including $108,585 for 25 grants (high: $30,000; low: $500).

Purpose and activities: Broad purposes; primarily local giving, with emphasis on arts and cultural programs, youth agencies, and education.

Limitations: Giving primarily in TX.

Officers: Frank S. Ryburn, President; John M. Little, Jr., Frank M. Ryburn, Jr., Vice-Presidents; Anna Fae McGee, Treasurer.

Employer Identification Number: 756036333

4038
Moss (Harry S.) Heart Trust ▼
P.O. Box 83791
Dallas 75283   (214) 573-4642

Trust established in 1973 in Texas.

Donor(s): Harry S. Moss, Florence M. Moss.

Financial data: (yr. ended 9/30/83): Assets, $13,000,000 (M); expenditures, $1,980,000, including $1,850,000 for 6 grants (high: $750,000; low: $15,000).

Purpose and activities: Local giving for the prevention and cure of heart disease.

Types of support awarded: Research.

Limitations: Giving limited to TX, with emphasis on Dallas County.

Application information:
Initial approach: Full proposal
Copies of proposal: 1
Deadline(s): None
Board meeting date(s): As required
Write: Cave L. Johnson, Jr., Trust Officer

Trustees: Frank M. Ryburn, Jr., InterFirst Bank Dallas (Cave L. Johnson, Jr., Trust Officer).

Employer Identification Number: 756147501

4039
Munson (W. B.) Foundation ⌘
c/o Texas American Bank
P.O. Box 341
Denison 75020   (214) 465-3030

Trust established in 1943 in Texas.

Financial data: (yr. ended 12/31/83): Assets, $3,188,704 (M); expenditures, $126,349, including $92,444 for 11 grants (high: $50,000; low: $200) and $9,619 for 20 grants to individuals.

Purpose and activities: Funds limited to local organizations; support for a hospital, an agricultural project, the arts, and scholarships for local high school graduates.

Types of support awarded: Student aid.

Limitations: Giving limited to Grayson County, TX.

Application information:
Initial approach: Letter
Deadline(s): None
Write: Roy Poe

Officer and Governors: Joseph W. Gay, President; Roy McKinney III, W.B. Munson III.

Trustee: Texas American Bank of Denison (Roy Poe, Senior Vice-President and Trust Officer).

Employer Identification Number: 756015068

4040
Navarro Community Foundation ▼
531 First National Bank Bldg.
P.O. Box 1035
Corsicana 75110   (214) 874-9301

Community foundation established in 1938 in Texas.

Financial data: (yr. ended 12/31/83): Assets, $5,177,194 (M); expenditures, $645,683, including $548,818 for 16 grants (high: $300,000; low: $800).

Purpose and activities: Local giving, with support largely for public schools, higher education, community development, and a community fund; grants also for Protestant church support, child welfare, youth agencies, a hospital, a library, and cultural programs.

Types of support awarded: Annual campaigns, seed money, building funds, scholarship funds, matching funds, general purposes.

Limitations: Giving limited to Navarro County, TX. No grants to individuals, or for research, conferences, endowment funds, publications, or special projects; no loans.

Application information:
Initial approach: Full proposal
Copies of proposal: 2
Deadline(s): January 1, April 1, July 1, or October 1
Board meeting date(s): January, April, July, and October
Write: David M. Brown, Executive Secretary

Officers and Trustees: Ralph R. Brown, Chairman; C.E. Middleton, 2nd Vice-Chairman; David M. Brown, Executive Secretary-Treasurer; O.L. Albritton, Jr., C. David Campbell, M.D., William Clarkson, III, J.M. Dyer, Tom Eady, Embry Ferguson, Mrs. Jack McFerran, H.R. Stroube, Jr.

Trustee Banks: The Corsicana National Bank, The First National Bank, The State National Bank.

Number of staff: 1 full-time professional; 1 part-time professional.

Employer Identification Number: 750800663

4041
Northen (Mary Moody), Inc. ⌘
7348 Lakehurst Ave.
Dallas 75230   (214) 692-7973

Established in 1964.

Donor(s): Mary Moody Northen.

Financial data: (yr. ended 6/30/83): Assets, $3,406,852 (M); gifts received, $1,000,000; expenditures, $165,219, including $116,200 for 4 grants (high: $90,000; low: $1,200).

Purpose and activities: Grants for "educational institutions and programs outside of Texas".

Limitations: Giving limited to organizations outside of TX.

Application information: Grants are usually made in the second quarter of each year.
Initial approach: Letter
Deadline(s): None
Write: G.F. Orcutt, Treasurer

Officers and Directors: Mary Moody Northen, President; Edward L. Protz, Vice-President; G.F. Orcutt, Treasurer.

Employer Identification Number: 751171741

4042
O'Connor (The Kathryn) Foundation ▼
400 Victoria Bank and Trust Bldg.
Victoria 77901   (512) 578-6271

Incorporated in 1951 in Texas.
Donor(s): Mrs. Kathryn S. O'Connor, Tom O'Connor, Jr., Dennis O'Connor.
Financial data: (yr. ended 12/31/82): Assets, $4,778,648 (M); expenditures, $1,725,924, including $1,218,885 for 14 grants (high: $750,000; low: $300).
Purpose and activities: Broad purposes; support for institutions for the advancement of religion, education, and the relief of poverty within Refugio County; grants also for hospitals.
Types of support awarded: Operating budgets, continuing support, annual campaigns, seed money, emergency funds, deficit financing, building funds, equipment, land acquisition, endowment funds, professorships, general purposes.
Limitations: Giving limited to Refugio County in south TX. No grants to individuals or for matching gifts; no loans.
Application information:
  Initial approach: Letter or full proposal
  Deadline(s): Submit proposal preferably in November or December
  Board meeting date(s): As required
Officer: Dennis O'Connor, President; Tom O'Connor, Jr., Vice-President; Venable B. Proctor, Secretary; Mary O'Connor Braman, Treasurer.
Number of staff: None.
Employer Identification Number: 746039415

4043
O'Donnell Foundation ▼
3388 InterFirst One
Dallas 75202   (214) 698-9915

Incorporated in 1957 in Texas.
Donor(s): Peter O'Donnell, Jr., Mrs. Peter O'Donnell, Jr.
Financial data: (yr. ended 11/30/83): Assets, $40,720,609 (M); gifts received, $2,792,100; expenditures, $7,390,232, including $5,697,331 for 71 grants (high: $1,000,000; low: $500; average: $5,000-$150,000).
Purpose and activities: Charitable and educational purposes; primarily local giving, with emphasis on private education, drug abuse programs, public interest organizations and foreign policy research, and health.
Limitations: Giving primarily in Dallas, TX. No grants to individuals or for scholarships.
Application information:
  Initial approach: Letter with brief proposal
  Deadline(s): None
  Board meeting date(s): As required
  Write: Carolyn R. Bacon, Executive Director
Officers: Peter O'Donnell, Jr.,* President; Rita C. Clements,* Vice-President; Edith Jones O'Donnell,* Secretary and Treasurer; Carolyn R. Bacon, Executive Director.
Directors:* Duncan Boeckman.
Number of staff: 1 full-time support.
Employer Identification Number: 756023326

4044
Oldham Little Church Foundation ▼ ¤
2200 South Post Oak Blvd., Suite 405
Houston 77056   (713) 621-4190

Trust established in 1949 in Texas.
Donor(s): Morris C. Oldham.†
Financial data: (yr. ended 12/31/83): Assets, $12,923,346 (M); gifts received, $6,200; expenditures, $652,791, including $573,322 for 278 grants (high: $5,000; low: $123; average: $1,000-$4,000).
Purpose and activities: To aid small Protestant churches and religious educational institutions.
Types of support awarded: Special projects.
Limitations: No grants to individuals, or for operating budgets, building funds, or endowments.
Application information: Application form required.
  Initial approach: Letter
  Copies of proposal: 1
  Board meeting date(s): Monthly
  Final notification: 60 days
  Write: Harry A. Kinney, Executive Vice-President
Officers and Trustees: Harry A. Kinney, Executive Vice-President; Stewart Morris, Secretary; W. Carloss Morris, Jr., Treasurer; Ross E. Dillon, Raymond E. Hankamer, John F. McIntyre, James S. Riley.
Number of staff: 1 full-time professional; 1 full-time support; 1 part-time support.
Employer Identification Number: 741240696

4045
Orleans (Carrie S.) Trust
c/o Interfirst Bank Dallas
P.O. Box 83791
Dallas 75283   (214) 573-4609

Financial data: (yr. ended 6/30/83): Assets, $1,192,448 (M); expenditures, $110,177, including $102,400 for 25 grants (high: $20,000; low: $500).
Purpose and activities: To provide food and clothing for the poor and needy of Dallas County through public and private welfare agencies.
Limitations: Giving limited to Dallas County, TX.
Application information:
  Initial approach: Letter
  Deadline(s): None
  Write: Ed Dendooven
Trustee: InterFirst Bank in Dallas, N.A.
Employer Identification Number: 756006730

4046
Overlake Foundation, Inc. ¤
8333 Douglas Ave., Suite 1313
Dallas 75225

Incorporated in 1981 in Texas.
Donor(s): Mary Alice Fitzpatrick.
Financial data: (yr. ended 11/30/82): Assets, $2,130,896 (M); gifts received, $2,000,000.
Purpose and activities: First year of operation 1981/82; no grants awarded.

Officers: Mary Alice Fitzpatrick, President; Donald J. Malouf, Vice-President and Secretary; Rayford L. Keller, Vice-President and Treasurer.
Employer Identification Number: 751793068

4047
Owen (B. B.) Trust ¤
905 Custer Rd.
P.O. Box 68
Richardson 75080

Trust established in 1974 in Texas.
Donor(s): B.B. Owen.†
Financial data: (yr. ended 9/30/82): Assets, $12,123,226 (M); expenditures, $581,003, including $304,500 for 8 grants (high: $100,000; low: $1,000).
Purpose and activities: Primarily local giving, with emphasis on hospitals, youth agencies, and social agencies.
Limitations: Giving primarily in TX.
Trustees: Spencer Carver, Monty J. Jackson, Wendell W. Judd.
Employer Identification Number: 751385809

4048
Owsley (Alvin and Lucy) Foundation
3000 One Shell Plaza
Houston 77002   (713) 229-1271

Trust established in 1950 in Texas.
Donor(s): Alvin M. Owsley,† Lucy B. Owsley.
Financial data: (yr. ended 12/31/83): Assets, $2,804,980 (M); expenditures, $212,000, including $160,095 for 60 grants (high: $25,000; low: $100; average: $1,000-$2,000).
Purpose and activities: Local giving only, with emphasis on education, medicine, cultural activities, and civic and social services.
Types of support awarded: Operating budgets, continuing support, annual campaigns, seed money, emergency funds, building funds, endowment funds, matching funds, scholarship funds.
Limitations: Giving limited to TX. No grants to individuals, or for endowment funds; no loans.
Application information:
  Initial approach: Letter
  Copies of proposal: 1
  Deadline(s): Submit proposal preferably in months when board meets; no set deadline
  Board meeting date(s): March, June, September, and December
  Final notification: 2 months
  Write: Alvin M. Owsley, Jr., General Manager
Trustees: Constance Owsley Garrett, Alvin M. Owsley, Jr., David T. Owsley, Lucy B. Owsley.
Number of staff: None.
Employer Identification Number: 756047221

4049
Pangburn Foundation, The
c/o Texas American Bank/Fort Worth
500 Throckmorton St., P.O. Box 2050
Fort Worth 76113   (817) 338-8151

Established in 1962 in Texas.

Financial data: (yr. ended 3/31/84): Assets, $3,646,863 (M); expenditures, $142,500, including $142,500 for 19 grants (high: $25,000; low: $1,000).
Purpose and activities: Local giving, with emphasis on cultural programs, especially music and the performing arts; grants also for higher education, youth agencies, child development, and the handicapped.
Limitations: Giving limited to the Fort Worth, TX. No grants to individuals.
Application information:
  Initial approach: Letter
  Copies of proposal: 1
  Deadline(s): Submit proposal preferably in July or August
  Board meeting date(s): October or November
  Write: Robert M. Lansford, Senior Vice-President
Trustee: Texas American Bank, Fort Worth (Robert M. Lansford, Senior Vice-President).
Employer Identification Number: 756042630

4050
Parker Foundation, The ¤
1111 Alamo National Bldg.
San Antonio 78205

Incorporated in 1957 in Texas.
Donor(s): Members of the Parker family.
Financial data: (yr. ended 3/31/84): Assets, $1,388,691 (M); expenditures, $107,564, including $97,318 for 53 grants (high: $5,790; low: $97).
Purpose and activities: Broad purposes; primarily local giving, with emphasis on secondary and higher education, social agencies, cultural programs, and Christian religious associations.
Limitations: Giving primarily in the San Antonio, TX, area.
Officers and Directors: George Parker, Jr., President; Camilla M. Parker, Joseph B. Parker, Mary H. Parker, Vice-Presidents; John M. Parker, Secretary-Treasurer; Patricia H. Parker, William A. Parker.
Employer Identification Number: 746040454

4051
Parry Foundation ¤
c/o William W. Vann
P.O. Box 2538
Houston 77001   (713) 651-0641

Established in 1952.
Financial data: (yr. ended 12/31/82): Assets, $2,408,645 (M); expenditures, $152,985, including $137,091 for 10 grants (high: $35,000; low: $1,200; average: $500-$1,500).
Purpose and activities: Grants primarily for higher education, including scholarship funds, with emphasis on training nurses for practice in Texas and the Southwest.
Types of support awarded: Scholarship funds.
Limitations: Giving primarily in TX and the Southwest, including OK.
Trustees: Lyle E. Bethune, Milton K. Eckert, Robert W. Sumners, William W. Vann.
Employer Identification Number: 746057587

4052
Perkins (The Joe and Lois) Foundation ▼ ¤
1212 City National Bldg.
P.O. Box 1470
Wichita Falls 76307   (817) 723-7163

Incorporated in 1941 in Texas.
Donor(s): J.J. Perkins.†
Financial data: (yr. ended 12/31/83): Assets, $8,254,243 (M); expenditures, $532,992, including $355,549 for 25 grants (high: $107,525; low: $100).
Purpose and activities: Broad purposes; primarily local giving, with emphasis on social services, education, hospitals, and church support.
Types of support awarded: Operating budgets.
Limitations: Giving primarily in TX.
Application information:
  Deadline(s): None
  Write: Charles N. Prothro, Vice-President
Officers: Elizabeth P. Protho,* President; Charles N. Protho,* Vice-President; Glynn D. Huff, Secretary-Treasurer.
Directors:* Charles V. Prothro, James E. Prothro, Joe N. Prothro, Mark H. Prothro, Herbert B. Story, Kathryn P. Yeager.
Employer Identification Number: 756012450

4053
Perkins-Prothro Foundation ¤
P.O. Box 2099
Wichita Falls 76307

Established in 1967.
Donor(s): Lois Perkins, Charles N. Prothro.
Financial data: (yr. ended 6/30/83): Assets, $628,324 (M); gifts received, $518,000; expenditures, $250,013, including $250,000 for 1 grant.
Purpose and activities: Primarily local giving, with emphasis on higher education; support also for health.
Limitations: Giving primarily in TX.
Officers and Trustees: Charles N. Prothro, President; Elizabeth P. Prothro, Kathryn Prothro Yeager, Vice-Presidents; Glynn D. Huff, Secretary; Joe N. Prothro, Treasurer; Mark H. Prothro.
Employer Identification Number: 751247407

4054
Perry (The M. G. and Johnnye D.) Foundation
P.O. Box 466
Robstown 78380   (512) 387-2911

Trust established in 1946 in Texas.
Donor(s): M.G. Perry,† Mrs. M.G. Perry.
Financial data: (yr. ended 12/31/84): Assets, $2,279,600 (M); expenditures, $731,100, including $8,650 for 5 grants (high: $5,107; low: $95) and $375,000 for 1 foundation-administered program.
Purpose and activities: A private operating foundation; agricultural and economic research, including an experimental farm for benefit of farmers, stockmen, ranchers, and oil and gas producers of south Texas.
Limitations: Giving limited to south TX.

Publications: Application guidelines.
Application information:
  Initial approach: Letter
  Copies of proposal: 1
  Deadline(s): Submit proposal in September; no set deadline
  Board meeting date(s): As required
  Write: Thomas F. Priestly, Trustee
Officer: V.M. Harris, Director of Agricultural Research.
Trustees: James M. Perry, Richard H. Perry, Thomas E. Perry, Thomas F. Priestly.
Employer Identification Number: 741093218

4055
Peyton (The Mary L.) Foundation
1706 El Paso National Bank Bldg.
El Paso 79901   (915) 533-9698

Incorporated in 1937 in Texas.
Donor(s): Joe C. Peyton.†
Financial data: (yr. ended 5/31/84): Assets, $2,209,983 (M); expenditures, $189,597, including $118,096 for grants to individuals (high: $85; low: $60; average: $75).
Purpose and activities: To provide health, welfare, and vocational educational benefits for legal residents of El Paso County unable to obtain assistance elsewhere; preference given to children of needy present or former employees of the Peyton Packing Company or its predecessors.
Types of support awarded: Grants to individuals.
Limitations: Giving limited to legal residents of El Paso County, TX. No support for groups or organizations. No grants for building or endowment funds, scholarships, fellowships, or matching gifts; no loans.
Application information: Application form required.
  Initial approach: Letter
  Board meeting date(s): Third Thursday of each month
  Write: Mrs. Nadine Prestwood, Executive Director
Officers and Trustees: Francis S. Ainsa, Chairman; Mrs. Alfred Blumenthal, Vice-Chairman; Mrs. R.F. Boverie, Freeman Harris, Mrs. William L. Massey, Nadine Prestwood, MBank El Paso.
Number of staff: 1 full-time professional; 1 full-time support; 1 part-time support.
Employer Identification Number: 741276102

4056
Piper (Minnie Stevens) Foundation ▼
201 North St. Mary's St., Suite 100
San Antonio 78205   (512) 227-8119

Incorporated in 1950 in Texas.
Donor(s): Randall G. Piper,† Minnie Stevens Piper.†
Financial data: (yr. ended 12/31/82): Assets, $13,737,830 (M); expenditures, $1,771,269, including $418,202 for 33 grants (high: $335,316; low: $30), $238,378 for grants to individuals, $155,730 for 2 foundation-administered programs and $300,369 for loans.

Purpose and activities: To support charitable and educational undertakings in Texas, especially to contribute toward the education of worthy students and to support community funds and other organizations or activities dedicated to the furtherance of the general welfare; administers a student loan fund, annual Piper Professor awards to recognize teaching excellence at the college level, Piper Scholar awards of four-year college scholarships to outstanding high school graduates in Texas, a Piper Fellows Program for former Piper Scholars, a student aid library and information center, and a scholarship clearinghouse. Grants to individuals as educational loans, scholarships, and teaching awards are made only through the programs operated by the foundation.
Types of support awarded: Scholarship funds, fellowships, student aid.
Limitations: Giving limited to TX. No grants for building or endowment funds.
Publications: Multi-year report, program policy statement, newsletter, application guidelines.
Application information: Recipients of scholarship and professorship award programs must be nominated; nomination not necessary for student loans.
  Deadline(s): February and July 1
  Board meeting date(s): March, June, September, and December
  Write: Michael J. Balint, Executive Director
Officers and Directors: Bruce Thomas, President; Leatrice F. Cleveland, Vice-President; William C. Wiederhold, Secretary-Treasurer; A.C. Bowman, Martin R. Harris, George A. Musselman, Frank Slavik, J. Burleson Smith.
Employer Identification Number: 741292695

4057
Polemanakos Foundation, The ⌑
c/o First City National Bank
P.O. Box 809
Houston 77001

Established in 1964.
Financial data: (yr. ended 12/31/83): Assets, $1,164,111 (M); expenditures, $77,695, including $67,695 for 16 grants (high: $35,195; low: $1,000).
Purpose and activities: Primarily local giving for higher education, social services, and a Greek Orthodox church.
Limitations: Giving primarily in TX.
Trustee: First City National Bank.
Employer Identification Number: 746064811

4058
Potts and Sibley Foundation ⌑
c/o First National Bank of Midland
P.O. Box 270
Midland 79701

Established in 1967.
Donor(s): Effie Potts Sibley Irrevocable Trust.
Financial data: (yr. ended 7/31/83): Assets, $1,792,645 (M); expenditures, $177,449, including $109,250 for 19 grants (high: $50,000; low: $2,000).

Purpose and activities: Primarily local giving, with emphasis on higher education, cultural programs, and ecology programs.
Limitations: Giving primarily in TX.
Trustees: Robert W. Bechtel, M.R. Bullock, D.J. Sibley, Jr., First National Bank of Midland.
Employer Identification Number: 756081070

4059
Pryor (Myra Stafford) Charitable Trust ⌑
P.O. Box 1600
San Antonio 78296   (512) 220-4449

Trust established in 1943 in Texas.
Donor(s): Mrs. Myra Stafford Pryor.†
Financial data: (yr. ended 6/30/82): Assets, $5,806,566 (M); expenditures, $372,476, including $324,170 for 29 grants (high: $50,000; low: $161).
Purpose and activities: Support locally for general charitable organizations.
Limitations: Giving limited to TX.
Application information:
  Initial approach: Proposal
  Copies of proposal: 1
  Board meeting date(s): March, July, and October
  Write: William Clyborne, Vice-President
Trust Committee: Frost National Bank (William Clyborne, Vice-President).
Employer Identification Number: 746032020

4060
Quanex Foundation, The ⌑
(formerly LaSalle Steel Foundation)
1900 West Loop South, Suite 1500
Houston 77027

Incorporated in 1951 in Illinois.
Donor(s): La Salle Steel Company.
Financial data: (yr. ended 12/31/83): Assets, $1,252,229 (M); expenditures, $50,385, including $38,632 for 29 grants (high: $10,000; low: $100).
Purpose and activities: General giving, with emphasis on community funds and community development.
Limitations: No grants to individuals.
Officers: F. James Farquhar,* President; James W. Collier, Secretary; Gary L Hellner,* Treasurer.
Directors:* Goeffrey D. Fallon, D. James Staas.
Employer Identification Number: 366065490

4061
R G K Foundation
2815 San Gabriel
Austin 78705   (512) 474-9298

Incorporated in 1966 in Texas.
Donor(s): George Kozmetsky, Ronya Kozmetsky.
Financial data: (yr. ended 12/31/83): Assets, $17,951,592 (M); gifts received, $865,045; expenditures, $1,030,497, including $603,278 for 29 grants (high: $200,000; low: $2,000) and $134,295 for 7 foundation-administered programs.

Purpose and activities: Broad purposes; primarily local grants to higher educational institutions, with emphasis on medical and educational research.
Types of support awarded: Matching funds, professorships, research, publications, conferences and seminars.
Limitations: Giving primarily in TX. No grants to individuals, or for building or endowment funds, operating budgets, or fellowships; no loans.
Publications: Program policy statement, annual report.
Application information:
  Initial approach: Letter or proposal
  Copies of proposal: 1
  Deadline(s): Submit proposal before December; no set deadline
  Board meeting date(s): Annually
  Final notification: 2 to 3 months
  Write: Ronya Kozmetsky, President
Officers and Trustees: Ronya Kozmetsky, President and Treasurer; Gregory Kozmetsky, Vice-President and Secretary; Daniel Fogel, Charles Hurwitz, George Kozmetsky, Nadya Kozmetsky Scott.
Number of staff: 3 full-time support; 2 part-time support.
Employer Identification Number: 746077587

4062
Redman Foundation ⌑
c/o Mercantile National Bank of Dallas
P.O. Box 225415
Dallas 75206
Application address: Mary Redman, Manager, 6021 Llano, Dallas, TX 75206

Trust established in 1951 in Michigan.
Donor(s): Harold F. Redman,† Clara M. Redman.†
Financial data: (yr. ended 12/31/83): Assets, $8,387,779 (M); expenditures, $404,230, including $386,790 for 30 grants (high: $51,000; low: $5,000).
Purpose and activities: Primarily local giving for higher education, Protestant church support, and social and health programs.
Limitations: Giving primarily in TX.
Application information:
  Deadline(s): None
Officer: Mary Redman, Manager.
Trustees: James Redman, Chairman; William E. Collins, Mrs. James Redman, Comerica Bank, Mercantile National Bank of Dallas.
Employer Identification Number: 386045047

4063
Richardson (Sid) Memorial Fund
309 Main St.
Fort Worth 76102   (817) 336-0494

Incorporated in 1965 in Texas.
Donor(s): Sid W. Richardson.†
Financial data: (yr. ended 12/31/84): Assets, $2,900,000 (M); expenditures, $374,891, including $130,000 for 5 grants (high: $75,000; low: $5,000; average: $20,000) and $172,718 for 70 grants to individuals.

Purpose and activities: Broad purposes; limited to scholarships for spouses and direct descendants of donor's employees and support for scholarship programs at two specific institutions.

Types of support awarded: Scholarship funds, student aid.

Limitations: No grants for capital or endowment funds, operating budgets, general support, special projects, research, or matching gifts; no loans.

Publications: Application guidelines.

Application information: Application form required.

Initial approach: Letter
Copies of proposal: 1
Deadline(s): Submit application between January and March; deadline March 31
Board meeting date(s): July; selection committee meets annually in June
Final notification: 3 months
Write: Jo Helen Dean, Administrator

Officers: C.T. Floyd,* President; Valleau Wilkie, Jr.,* Executive Vice-President; Jo Helen Dean, Administrator; Cynthia Kesey, Treasurer.

Directors:* William A. Landreth.

Number of staff: 1 part-time professional.

Employer Identification Number: 751220266

4064
Richardson (Sid W.) Foundation ▼
309 Main St.
Fort Worth 76102   (817) 336-0494

Established in 1947 in Texas.

Donor(s): Sid W. Richardson,† and associated companies.

Financial data: (yr. ended 12/31/84): Assets, $138,247,000 (M); expenditures, $5,394,800, including $4,015,100 for 79 grants (high: $2,000,000; low: $1,060; average: $1,000-$250,000).

Purpose and activities: Broad purposes; general local giving only, with emphasis on education, health, the arts, and human service programs.

Types of support awarded: Operating budgets, seed money, building funds, equipment, land acquisition, endowment funds, research, publications, conferences and seminars, matching funds, special projects.

Limitations: Giving limited to TX, with emphasis on the Fort Worth area. No grants to individuals, or for scholarships and fellowships; no loans.

Publications: Annual report, application guidelines, program policy statement.

Application information: Application form required.

Initial approach: Letter
Copies of proposal: 1
Deadline(s): February 15, May 15, and September 15
Board meeting date(s): Spring, summer, and fall
Final notification: Varies
Write: Valleau Wilkie, Jr., Executive Vice-President

Officers and Directors:* Perry R. Bass,* President; Valleau Wilkie, Jr., Executive Vice-President; M.E. Chappell,* Vice-President and Treasurer; Nancy Lee Bass,* Sid R. Bass,* Vice-Presidents; Jo Helen Dean, Secretary.

Number of staff: 1 full-time professional; 3 full-time support.

Employer Identification Number: 756015828

4065
Roberts (Dora) Foundation ▼
715 Edwards Blvd.
Big Spring 79720   (817) 338-8442
Application address: c/o Texas American Bank, Ft. Worth, P.O. Box 2050, Fort Worth, TX 76113

Trust established in 1948 in Texas.

Donor(s): Mrs. Dora Roberts.†

Financial data: (yr. ended 12/31/83): Assets, $10,720,817 (M); expenditures, $1,467,726, including $985,000 for 24 grants (high: $150,000; low: $5,000; average: $5,000-$100,000).

Purpose and activities: Broad purposes; local giving, with emphasis on Protestant church support, higher education, social service, youth agencies, hospitals, and rehabilitation.

Types of support awarded: General purposes.

Limitations: Giving primarily in Big Spring, TX.

Application information:

Initial approach: Proposal
Deadline(s): September 31
Board meeting date(s): Annually in October or November
Write: Rick Piersall, Vice-President and Trust Officer (Texas American Bank, Ft. Worth)

Advisory Board: Ralph W. Caton, Chairman; Roger Canter, Mrs. Horace Garrett, Sue Garrett Partee, J.P. Taylor, Ann Garrett Turner, R.H. Weaver.

Trustee: Texas American Bank.

Employer Identification Number: 756013899

4066
Rockwell Fund, Inc. ▼
910 Travis St., Suite 1921
Houston 77002   (713) 659-7204

Trust established in 1931; incorporated in 1949 in Texas; absorbed Rockwell Brothers Endowment, Inc. in 1981.

Donor(s): Members of the James M. Rockwell family, Rockwell Bros. & Co., Rockwell Lumber Company.

Financial data: (yr. ended 12/31/83): Assets, $35,049,390 (M); expenditures, $1,642,011, including $1,450,750 for 202 grants (high: $50,000; low: $250).

Purpose and activities: Broad purposes; primarily local giving to organizations of interest to the founders and donors, with emphasis on higher education, religious programs, medical education, hospitals, rehabilitation, cultural programs, municipalities, and general welfare.

Types of support awarded: Annual campaigns, seed money, emergency funds, deficit financing, general purposes, building funds, equipment, land acquisition, internships, scholarship funds.

Limitations: Giving primarily in TX, with emphasis on Houston. No support for organizations or projects attempting to influence legislation or elections. No grants to individuals, or for endowment funds, research or matching gifts; no loans; grants awarded on a one-time basis only; no future commitments.

Publications: Annual report, program policy statement, application guidelines.

Application information:

Initial approach: Letter
Board meeting date(s): March and October
Final notification: December 15
Write: Joe M. Green, Jr., President

Officers and Trustees: Joe M. Green, Jr., President; R. Terry Bell, Vice-President; Helen N. Sterling, Secretary-Treasurer; Elizabeth A. Rockwell.

Number of staff: 1 full-time professional; 2 full-time support.

Employer Identification Number: 746040258

4067
Rogers Bros. Foundation, Inc. ▼ ¤
595 Orleans St.
P.O. Box 1310
Beaumont 77704   (409) 838-6681

Incorporated in 1961 in Texas.

Donor(s): Members of the Rogers family.

Financial data: (yr. ended 11/30/82): Assets, $4,358,565 (M); expenditures, $420,412, including $409,153 for 165 grants (high: $100,000; low: $25).

Purpose and activities: Funding largely for Jewish welfare funds; support also for higher education, hospitals, youth agencies, and cultural programs.

Limitations: Giving primarily in TX. No grants to individuals.

Application information:

Board meeting date(s): As required

Officers and Directors: Ben J. Rogers, President; Sol J. Rogers, Victor J. Rogers, Vice-Presidents; N. Jay Rogers, Secretary and Treasurer; Fred L. Brown.

Employer Identification Number: 746063588

4068
Rogers (Ralph B.) Foundation
8100 Carpenter Freeway
Dallas 75247   (214) 637-3100

Trust established in 1953 in Texas.

Donor(s): Ralph B. Rogers.

Financial data: (yr. ended 12/31/83): Assets, $1,401,978 (M); expenditures, $692,888, including $677,621 for 32 grants (high: $165,300; low: $10).

Purpose and activities: Primarily local giving, with emphasis on cultural programs, health education, medical research, and an independent school.

Limitations: Giving primarily in TX.

Application information:

Initial approach: Letter
Deadline(s): None
Board meeting date(s): December
Write: Ralph B. Rogers, Trustee

Managers: Robert Alpert, Ralph B. Rogers, Robert D. Rogers.
Number of staff: 1.
Employer Identification Number: 136153567

4069
Rowan (The Arch and Stella) Foundation, Inc. ✶
1515 Oil and Gas Bldg.
Fort Worth 76102   (817) 336-2679

Established in 1963.
Donor(s): Stella S. Rowan.
Financial data: (yr. ended 8/31/83): Assets, $2,063,521 (M); expenditures, $122,073, including $119,500 for 22 grants (high: $50,000; low: $500).
Purpose and activities: Primarily local giving, with grants for arts and cultural programs, higher education, and hospitals.
Limitations: Giving primarily in TX. No grants to individuals.
Application information:
  Initial approach: Letter
Officers: Hamilton Rogers, President; Stella S. Rowan, Vice-President; B.S. Brants, Secretary-Treasurer.
Employer Identification Number: 756030348

4070
Rudman Foundation, The ✶
711 Mercantile Dallas Bldg.
Dallas 75201

Trust established in 1946 in Texas.
Donor(s): I. Rudman,† Rose Rudman.
Financial data: (yr. ended 12/31/83): Assets, $667,066 (M); expenditures, $314,690, including $270,951 for 73 grants (high: $50,000; low: $25).
Purpose and activities: Broad purposes; grants largely for local Jewish welfare funds, a health agency in Israel, and medical research.
Limitations: Giving primarily in TX.
Managers and Trustees: M.B. Rudman, R.E. Sater.
Employer Identification Number: 756020439

4071
Sams (Earl C.) Foundation, Inc. ✶
101 North Shoreline Dr., Suite 435
Corpus Christi 78401   (512) 888-6485

Incorporated in 1946 in New York.
Donor(s): Earl C. Sams.†
Financial data: (yr. ended 12/31/83): Assets, $14,494,946 (M); expenditures, $614,393, including $494,703 for 30 grants (high: $250,000; low: $946).
Purpose and activities: Broad purposes; grants primarily for a zoological society, higher and secondary education, and medical purposes; support also for social and youth agencies, community funds, and churches, primarily in south Texas.
Limitations: Giving primarily in south TX.
Application information:
  Initial approach: Proposal
  Deadline(s): None
  Write: Dorothy P. Hawn, President

Officers and Directors: Dorothy P. Hawn, President; Jack M. Roney, Vice-President; John D. Hawn, Vice-President and Treasurer; Thomas R. LeViness, Secretary.
Employer Identification Number: 741463151

4072
San Antonio Area Foundation
808 Travis Bldg.
405 North St. Mary's
San Antonio 78205   (512) 225-2243

Community foundation incorporated in 1964 in Texas.
Financial data: (yr. ended 12/31/83): Assets, $7,799,838 (M); gifts received, $1,833,115; expenditures, $2,406,260, including $1,676,437 for 174 grants (high: $116,000; low: $61) and $27,300 for 37 grants to individuals.
Purpose and activities: To provide an effective channel for private giving by and for the people in the San Antonio area to meet educational, cultural, medical, research, social, religious, and civic needs at all levels of society.
Types of support awarded: Operating budgets, continuing support, annual campaigns, seed money, emergency funds, building funds, equipment, land acquisition, endowment funds, matching funds, scholarship funds, special projects, research, publications, conferences and seminars, student aid.
Limitations: Giving limited to the San Antonio, TX, area, except when specified otherwise by donor. No support for lobbying programs. No grants for deficit financing; no loans.
Publications: Annual report, program policy statement, application guidelines.
Application information: Application form required.
  Initial approach: Letter
  Copies of proposal: 1
  Deadline(s): Submit proposal in February; deadline February 15
  Board meeting date(s): April and November, and as required
  Final notification: 8 weeks
  Write: Katherine Netting Folbre, Executive Director
Officer: Katherine Netting Folbre, Secretary-Treasurer and Executive Director.
Distribution Committee: William Reddell, Chairman; John E. Banks, Sr., John H. Foster, Pat Legan, Edith McAllister, Al Notzon, John Streiber, Dale A. Wood, M.D.
Trustee Banks: Broadway National Bank, First City Bank-Central Park, Frost National Bank, Groos National Bank, Interfirst Bank in San Antonio, Kelly Field National Bank, MBank Alamo, MBank Travis Park, National Bank of Commerce, RepublicBank San Antonio.
Number of staff: 1 part-time professional; 1 part-time support.
Employer Identification Number: 746065414

4073
Scaler Foundation, Inc. ▼
2200 Post Oak Blvd., Suite 707
Houston 77056   (713) 627-2440

Incorporated in 1954 in Texas.
Financial data: (yr. ended 12/31/83): Assets, $15,218,289 (M); expenditures, $1,791,827, including $1,751,357 for 13 grants (high: $1,523,795; low: $40).
Purpose and activities: Grants for art museums and cultural programs; support for organizations both in the United States and France.
Types of support awarded: Operating budgets, seed money, special projects, general purposes, continuing support.
Limitations: Giving primarily in the U.S. and France. No grants to individuals, or for building and endowment funds, research, scholarships, fellowships, or matching gifts; no loans.
Application information: Funds presently committed.
  Board meeting date(s): Annually and as required
  Write: Elliott A. Johnson, Secretary
Officers and Directors: Eric Boissonnas, President; Sylvie Boissonnas, Vice-President; Elliott A. Johnson, Secretary and Treasurer.
Number of staff: None.
Employer Identification Number: 746036684

4074
Scarborough (W. F.) Educational Trust ▼ ✶
P.O. Box 1536
Midland 79701

Trust established in 1966 in Texas.
Donor(s): W.F. Scarborough.†
Financial data: (yr. ended 12/31/83): Assets, $1,977,505 (M); expenditures, $640,605, including $619,035 for 42 grants (high: $267,788; low: $180; average: $1,000-$15,000) and $14,218 for 7 grants to individuals.
Purpose and activities: Charitable purposes; primarily local giving, with emphasis on higher education, Protestant religious associations, a hospital, and child welfare.
Limitations: Giving primarily in TX.
Trustee: Evelyn Linebery.
Employer Identification Number: 756054021

4075
Scott (William E.) Foundation
3200 Continental Plaza
Fort Worth 76102   (817) 336-0361

Incorporated in 1960 in Texas.
Donor(s): William E. Scott.†
Financial data: (yr. ended 5/31/84): Assets, $2,260,047 (M); expenditures, $219,639, including $123,595 for 25 grants (high: $25,000; low: $1,000; average: $5,000).
Purpose and activities: Broad purposes; local giving primarily for programs in the arts; some grants for elementary and higher education, youth agencies, and community funds.

Limitations: Giving primarily in the Fort Worth-Tarrant County, TX area. No grants to individuals.
Application information: Application form required.
  Initial approach: Letter
  Copies of proposal: 1
  Board meeting date(s): As required
  Write: Robert W. Decker, President
Officers and Directors: Robert W. Decker, President; Margaret Fenelon, Vice-President and Secretary; Raymond B. Kelly, III, Vice-President.
Number of staff: 1 part-time support.
Employer Identification Number: 756024661

4076
Scurlock Foundation ▼
P.O. Box 4648
Houston 77210   (713) 739-4100

Incorporated in 1954 in Texas.
Donor(s): E.C. Scurlock, Scurlock Oil Company, D.E. Farnsworth, W.C. Scurlock, J.S. Blanton, and other members of the Blanton family.
Financial data: (yr. ended 12/31/83): Assets, $8,840,354 (M); gifts received, $69,262; expenditures, $514,872, including $494,739 for 121 grants (high: $66,664; low: $25; average: $100-$10,000).
Purpose and activities: Broad purposes; primarily local giving, with emphasis on hospitals and secondary and higher education; support also for health agencies, youth agencies, Protestant churches, social service agencies, cultural programs, and public interest groups.
Types of support awarded: Building funds, general purposes, annual campaigns, emergency funds, land acquisition, endowment funds, research, matching funds, continuing support.
Limitations: Giving primarily in TX. No grants to individuals, or for scholarships or fellowships; no loans.
Application information: Funds committed for approximately the next two years.
  Initial approach: Letter
  Copies of proposal: 1
  Deadline(s): None
  Board meeting date(s): December and as required
  Write: J.S. Blanton, President
Officers and Directors: J.S. Blanton, President; Kenneth Fisher, Secretary-Treasurer.
Number of staff: None.
Employer Identification Number: 741488953

4077
Seibel (The Abe and Annie) Foundation
c/o The United States National Bank
P.O. Box 179
Galveston 77550   (409) 763-1211

Trust established in 1960 in Texas.
Donor(s): Abe Seibel.
Financial data: (yr. ended 7/31/83): Assets, $8,570,033 (M); expenditures, $757,510, including $655,500 for 359 loans.

Purpose and activities: Interest-free loans to needy and worthy students enrolled in higher educational institutions in Texas.
Types of support awarded: Student aid.
Limitations: Giving primarily in TX.
Application information: Application form required.
  Deadline(s): July 31
  Write: Judith T. Whelton, Trust Director
Trustee: United States National Bank (Judith T. Whelton, Trust Officer).
Employer Identification Number: 746035556

4078
Semmes Foundation, Inc.
5307 Broadway
San Antonio 78209   (512) 822-5221

Incorporated in 1952 in Texas.
Donor(s): Douglas R. Semmes.†
Financial data: (yr. ended 12/31/83): Assets, $4,513,378 (M); gifts received, $225,057; expenditures, $189,282, including $157,517 for 24 grants (high: $112,500; low: $10).
Purpose and activities: Broad purposes; primarily local giving to youth agencies, a family planning organization, a local university, and an art institute.
Types of support awarded: Operating budgets, continuing support, annual campaigns, seed money, emergency funds, deficit financing, building funds, equipment, land acquisition, matching funds, professorships, special projects, research, publications, conferences and seminars, general purposes.
Limitations: Giving primarily in TX. No grants to individuals, or for endowment funds; no loans.
Application information:
  Initial approach: Letter
  Deadline(s): None
  Board meeting date(s): February
  Final notification: 6 months
  Write: Thomas R. Semmes, President
Officers and Directors: Thomas R. Semmes, President; Julia Y. Semmes, Vice-President; E.L. LaMoy, L.I. Morrison, D.R. Semmes, Jr.
Number of staff: 1 part-time professional; 1 part-time support.
Employer Identification Number: 746062264

4079
Shanor (The M. L.) Foundation ⌷
P.O. Box 7522
Wichita Falls 76307   (817) 761-2401

Donor(s): N.T.P. Company.
Financial data: (yr. ended 12/31/83): Assets, $1,860,479 (M); gifts received, $33,828; expenditures, $105,654, including $42,750 for 20 grants (high: $7,500; low: $200) and $45,140 for 37 grants to individuals.
Purpose and activities: Primarily local giving, with emphasis on scholarships to individuals; grants also to local charitable organizations, especially a hospital.
Types of support awarded: General purposes, student aid.
Limitations: Giving primarily in TX.
Application information: Application form required.

  Deadline(s): August 1 for scholarships
  Write: J.B. Jarratt, President
Officer and Directors: J.B. Jarratt, President; Alvin Barnes, L.C. Henderson.
Employer Identification Number: 756012834

4080
Sharp (Charles S. and Ruth C.) Foundation, Inc. ⌷
P.O. Box 38665
Dallas 75238

Incorporated in 1965 in Texas.
Donor(s): Charles S. Sharp, Ruth Collins Sharp.
Financial data: (yr. ended 12/31/83): Assets, $2,631,429 (M); expenditures, $208,905, including $183,333 for 5 grants (high: $50,000; low: $25,000).
Purpose and activities: Primarily local giving, with emphasis on Protestant church support, higher education, hospitals, and youth agencies.
Types of support awarded: Operating budgets, general purposes.
Limitations: Giving primarily in Dallas, TX.
Officers: Charles S. Sharp,* President; Ruth Collins Sharp,* Vice-President; Ruth M. Pierce, Secretary; Margot Cryer, Treasurer.
Directors:* Herschel V. Forester, H. Barbara Hardy, Miles Woodall.
Employer Identification Number: 756045366

4081
Shell Companies Foundation, Incorporated ▼
Two Shell Plaza
P.O. Box 2099
Houston 77002   (713) 241-3616

Incorporated in 1953 in New York.
Donor(s): Shell Oil Company, and other participating companies.
Financial data: (yr. ended 12/31/83): Assets, $47,609,735 (M); gifts received, $10,088,700; expenditures, $14,338,992, including $12,272,746 for 986 grants (high: $583,150; low: $500; average: $1,000-$25,000) and $1,622,213 for 4,320 employee matching gifts.
Purpose and activities: Preferred areas of giving are education and community funds. About 61 percent of the budget channeled through a number of planned programs that provide student aid, faculty development, basic research grants, and departmental grants to some 532 colleges and universities, 140 private, independent secondary schools, and to a few national educational organizations. Approximately 22 percent of the budget directed to United Way organizations in cities or towns where Shell employees reside. The remaining funds paid to a number of national organizations concerned with a broad range of needs and to local organizations in communities where significant numbers of Shell employees reside.
Types of support awarded: Building funds, conferences and seminars, continuing support, employee matching gifts, equipment, fellowships, general purposes, operating budgets, professorships, publications, research, scholarship funds, special projects, employee related scholarships.

Limitations: Giving primarily in areas of company operations. No support for special requests of colleges and universities, college fundraising associations, or hospital operating expenses. No grants to individuals, or for endowment funds, capital campaigns of national organizations, or development funds; no loans.
Publications: Annual report.
Application information: Scholarship programs administered through National Merit Scholarship Corporation.
  Initial approach: Letter
  Copies of proposal: 1
  Deadline(s): Submit proposal January through September; deadline September 30
  Board meeting date(s): December and March
  Final notification: 1 month
  Write: Mrs. Doris J. O'Connor, Senior Vice-President
Officers: J.F. Bookout,* President; Doris J. O'Connor,* Senior Vice-President; J.C. Jacobsen,* V.G. Whittington,* Vice-Presidents; Ron L. Kuhns, Secretary; D.E. Cannon, Treasurer.
Directors:* C.L. Blackburn, P.J. Carroll, J.B. Henderson, K.L. Mai, F.H. Richardson.
Number of staff: 4 full-time professional; 4 full-time support; 2 part-time support.
Employer Identification Number: 136066583

4082
Smith (Bob and Vivian) Foundation ☐
2000 West Loop South, Suite 1900
Houston 77027

Established about 1969.
Donor(s): R.E. Smith, Vivian L. Smith.
Financial data: (yr. ended 12/31/83): Assets, $5,576,998 (M); gifts received, $50,000; expenditures, $334,787, including $317,000 for 8 grants (high: $50,000; low: $2,000).
Purpose and activities: Primarily local giving, with emphasis on medical research and education.
Limitations: Giving primarily in Houston, TX.
Officers: Vivian L. Smith,* President; Neva Goree, Secretary.
Trustees:* Bobby Smith Cohn, Sandra Smith Dompier, W.N. Finnegan III, E.H. Suhr.
Employer Identification Number: 237029052

4083
South Texas Charitable Foundation ☐
101 S. Main St.
P.O. Box 2549
Victoria 77902

Established in 1981 in Texas.
Donor(s): Maude O'Connor Williams.
Financial data: (yr. ended 11/30/82): Assets, $5,637,425 (M); gifts received, $3,800,000; expenditures, $80,007, including $80,000 for 1 grant.
Purpose and activities: First year of operation was 1982, with one grant for a local hospital.
Limitations: Giving primarily in TX.
Officers: Maude O'Connor Williams, President; Roger P. Williams, Vice-President; Rayford L. Keller, Secretary-Treasurer.
Employer Identification Number: 742148107

4084
Southland Foundation ☐
P.O. Box 610208
Irving 75061-0208   (214) 556-0500

Established in 1974 in Texas.
Donor(s): Southland Life Insurance Company, Southland Financial Corporation, Las Colinas Corporation, Southland Corporate Services, Inc., Southland Investment Properties.
Financial data: (yr. ended 12/31/83): Assets, $2,180 (M); gifts received, $705,500; expenditures, $706,704, including $706,675 for 52 grants (high: $293,550; low: $75).
Purpose and activities: Primarily local giving, with emphasis on health, community funds, higher education, youth, social agencies, and cultural programs.
Types of support awarded: Building funds, operating budgets, general purposes.
Limitations: Giving primarily in TX. No grants to individuals.
Application information:
  Initial approach: Letter
  Copies of proposal: 1
  Board meeting date(s): Monthly
  Write: J. Michael Lewis, Secretary
Officers: Ben H. Carpenter, President; Dan C. Williams, Vice-President; J. Michael Lewis, Secretary.
Employer Identification Number: 237337606

4085
Stark (Nelda C. and H. J. Lutcher) Foundation
602 West Main St.
P.O. Box 909
Orange 77630   (713) 883-3513

Incorporated in 1961 in Texas.
Donor(s): H.J. Lutcher Stark,† Nelda C. Stark.
Financial data: (yr. ended 2/28/83): Assets, $53,304,001 (M); gifts received, $609,050; expenditures, $1,229,867, including $52,208 for 4 grants (high: $27,208; low: $5,000), $1,670 for 4 grants to individuals and $1,025,346 for 2 foundation-administered programs.
Purpose and activities: Broad purposes; with emphasis upon education, historical restoration and the performing arts; projects include the construction, operation, and maintenance of a museum to house and exhibit an extensive art collection owned by the Foundation and to underwrite performances of a Theater for the Performing Arts to be donated to the City of Orange, Texas.
Limitations: Giving limited to TX and southwest LA. No grants to individuals, or for endowment funds, or operating budgets.
Application information:
  Initial approach: Brief proposal
  Board meeting date(s): Monthly
  Write: Clyde V. McKee, Jr., Secretary-Treasurer
Officers and Trustees: Nelda C. Stark, Chairman; Eunice R. Benckenstein, Vice-Chairman; Clyde V. McKee, Jr., Secretary-Treasurer; William J. Butler, Sidney H. Phillips, Homer B.H. Stark.
Employer Identification Number: 746047440

4086
Starling (Dorothy Richard) Foundation ☐
P.O. Box 66527
Houston 77006

Foundation established in 1969 in Texas.
Donor(s): Frank M. Starling.†
Financial data: (yr. ended 12/31/83): Assets, $7,268,567 (M); expenditures, $345,090, including $270,000 for 8 grants (high: $75,000; low: $10,000).
Purpose and activities: Support for institutions offering instruction in classical violin performance and study arts.
Application information:
  Initial approach: Letter
Trustees: Robert K. Jewett, A.C. Speyer, Jr., H. Allen Weatherby.
Employer Identification Number: 746121656

4087
Steinhagen (B. A. and Elinor) Benevolent Trust
P.O. Box 3391
Beaumont 77704   (713) 838-9281

Trust established in 1939 in Texas.
Donor(s): B.A. Steinhagen,† Elinor Steinhagen.†
Financial data: (yr. ended 8/31/84): Assets, $1,617,005 (M); expenditures, $213,885, including $196,525 for 12 grants (high: $37,000; low: $3,000; average: $10,000-$20,000).
Purpose and activities: Local giving only for the housing and general assistance of the elderly and the helpless and afflicted of any age.
Types of support awarded: Seed money, building funds, equipment, land acquisition, matching funds, research, publications, endowment funds.
Limitations: Giving limited to Jefferson County, TX. No grants to individuals, or for operating budgets, continuing support, annual campaigns, emergency funds, deficit financing, special projects, conferences, or scholarships and fellowships; no loans.
Publications: Application guidelines.
Application information: Application form required.
  Initial approach: Letter
  Copies of proposal: 1
  Deadline(s): May 31
  Board meeting date(s): Annually
  Final notification: End of August
  Write: Ann Knupple, Trust Officer
Trustee: First City Bank of Beaumont.
Number of staff: None.
Employer Identification Number: 746039544

4088
Stemmons Foundation ☐
1200 Tower East
2700 Stemmons Freeway
Dallas 75207   (214) 631-7910

Established in 1963 in Texas.
Financial data: (yr. ended 12/31/83): Assets, $1,410,743 (M); expenditures, $102,470, including $94,733 for 52 grants (high: $20,000; low: $100).

Purpose and activities: Primarily local giving for cultural programs, youth agencies, social services, health agencies, and education.
Limitations: Giving primarily in Dallas, TX.
Application information:
Initial approach: Proposal
Write: Ann M. Roberts, Vice-President
Officers: John M. Stemmons, Jr., President; Ann M. Roberts, Allison S. Simon, Vice-Presidents; John M. Stemmons, Ruth T. Stemmons, Secretary-Treasurers.
Employer Identification Number: 756039966

4089
Strake Foundation ▼
3300 Texas Commerce Bank Bldg.
712 Main St.
Houston 77002   (713) 227-2065

Trust established in 1952 in Texas; incorporated in 1983.
Donor(s): George W. Strake,† Mrs. Susan K. Strake,† George W. Strake, Jr., Susan S. Dilworth, Georganna S. Parsley.
Financial data: (yr. ended 12/31/84): Assets, $13,589,000 (M); expenditures, $811,922, including $706,300 for 182 grants (high: $20,000; low: $500; average: $1,000-$10,000).
Purpose and activities: Broad purposes; giving primarily in Texas and largely for Roman Catholic-affiliated associations, including hospitals and higher and secondary educational institutions.
Types of support awarded: Building funds, operating budgets, continuing support, annual campaigns, seed money, emergency funds, equipment, endowment funds, matching funds, special projects, research, conferences and seminars.
Limitations: Giving primarily in TX; no grants outside the U.S. No support for elementary schools. No grants to individuals, or for deficit financing, employee matching gifts, consulting services, technical assistance, demonstration projects, or publications; no loans.
Publications: Application guidelines, annual report.
Application information:
Initial approach: Brief proposal
Copies of proposal: 1
Deadline(s): Submit proposal preferably in March or September; deadline 1 month prior to board meetings
Board meeting date(s): May or June, and November or December
Final notification: 1 month after board meetings
Write: George W. Strake, Jr., President
Officers and Trustees: George W. Strake, Jr., President and Treasurer; Georganna S. Parsley, Vice-President and Secretary; Susan S. Dilworth, Vice-President; Diana D. Hoover, Robert S. Parsley, Joseph A. Reich, Jr., Weldon H. Smith, George W. Strake III, Chester H. Taylor.
Number of staff: 1 part-time professional; 1 part-time support.
Employer Identification Number: 760041524

4090
Straus (Eugene) Charitable Trust
Interfirst Bank Dallas
P.O. Box 83791
Dallas 75283   (214) 977-4622

Trust established in 1975 in Texas.
Donor(s): Eugene Straus.†
Financial data: (yr. ended 8/31/84): Assets, $1,287,486 (M); expenditures, $118,422, including $108,000 for 5 grants (high: $28,000; low: $10,000; average: $20,000).
Purpose and activities: For building or maintenance of capital improvements for local charitable organizations.
Types of support awarded: Building funds.
Limitations: Giving limited to Dallas County, TX. No grants to individuals, or for operating budgets, continuing support, annual campaigns, seed money, emergency funds, deficit financing, equipment, land acquisition, special projects, publications, conferences, endowment funds, research, scholarships and fellowships, or matching gifts; no loans.
Application information:
Initial approach: Letter
Copies of proposal: 1
Deadline(s): Submit proposal preferably in April; deadline May 30
Board meeting date(s): June
Final notification: August 31
Write: Patrice Hurst, Assistant Vice-President-Trust
Trustee: Interfirst Bank Dallas.
Number of staff: None.
Employer Identification Number: 756229249

4091
Sumners (Hatton W.) Foundation ⌑
4500 Republic National Bank Tower
Dallas 75201

Trust established in 1949 in Texas.
Financial data: (yr. ended 12/31/83): Assets, $14,375,991 (M); gifts received, $7,895; expenditures, $165,975, including $114,617 for 6 grants (high: $30,000).
Purpose and activities: Local giving largely for youth organizations and higher education for the study and teaching of the science of self government.
Limitations: Giving limited to TX.
Application information:
Initial approach: Letter
Deadline(s): None
Write: J. Cleo Thompson, Jr., Chairman
Officers and Trustees: J. Cleo Thompson, Jr., Chairman; Edwin C. Pannell, Vice-Chairman; Elmore Whitehurst, Secretary; Charles E. Long, Jr., Treasurer; Gordon R. Carpenter, Alfred P. Murrah, Jr., William C. Pannell, Thomas S. Walker.
Employer Identification Number: 756003490

4092
Tandy (Anne Burnett and Charles D.) Foundation ▼
1577 InterFirst Tower
801 Cherry St.
Fort Worth 76102   (817) 877-3344

Established in 1978 in Texas.
Donor(s): Anne Burnett Tandy,† Charles D. Tandy,† Ben Bird.
Financial data: (yr. ended 12/31/83): Assets, $196,634,794 (M); expenditures, $9,147,113, including $8,437,454 for 24 grants (high: $1,000,000; low: $2,500).
Purpose and activities: Broad purposes; primarily local giving, with emphasis on higher education, health care, cultural organizations, including major museum projects; some support also for social and youth agencies.
Types of support awarded: General purposes, building funds, equipment, special projects, technical assistance.
Limitations: Giving primarily in TX. No grants to individuals, or for scholarships or fellowships.
Publications: Program policy statement, application guidelines.
Application information: Application form required.
Initial approach: Letter or telephone
Copies of proposal: 1
Deadline(s): None
Board meeting date(s): Generally in February, June, and October
Final notification: 90 days
Write: Thomas F. Beech, Executive Vice-President
Officers: Anne W. Sowell,* President; Edward R. Hudson, Jr.,* Vice-President and Secretary-Treasurer; Perry R. Bass,* Vice-President; Thomas F. Beech, Executive Vice-President.
Trustees:* James R. Sowell.
Number of staff: 2.
Employer Identification Number: 751638517

4093
Tandy (David L.) Foundation
1700 One Tandy Center
Fort Worth 76102

Established in 1968 in Texas.
Financial data: (yr. ended 5/31/84): Assets, $1,915,381 (M); expenditures, $165,770, including $164,900 for 21 grants (high: $40,000; low: $1,000).
Purpose and activities: Primarily local giving for educational and cultural programs.
Limitations: Giving primarily in TX.
Application information:
Initial approach: Letter
Deadline(s): None
Board meeting date(s): Second Monday in July
Write: William H. Michero, Secretary
Officers and Directors:* Emmett Duemke,* President; A.R. Tandy, Jr., Vice-President; William H. Michero,* Secretary; B.R. Roland,* Treasurer.
Number of staff: None.
Employer Identification Number: 756083140

4094
Tarrant County, The Community Trust of Metropolitan
210 E. Ninth St.
Fort Worth 76102   (817) 335-3473

Community foundation established in 1980 in Texas.

Financial data: (yr. ended 12/31/83): Assets, $6,000,000 (M); expenditures, $81,098 for 6 grants (high: $42,372; low: $1,000; average: $10,000).
Purpose and activities: Primarily local giving for charitable purposes to benefit the community; support for community development, social services, education, communications, health, cultural programs, religion, and science and technology.
Types of support awarded: Equipment, general purposes, internships, lectureships, seed money, matching funds.
Limitations: Giving primarily in Tarrant County, TX. No grants to individuals.
Publications: Application guidelines.
Application information:
  Initial approach: Letter to request guidelines
  Deadline(s): None
  Board meeting date(s): Quarterly
  Write: Matthew E. Brown, Manager

4095
Tartt (Hope Pierce) Scholarship Fund
P.O. Box 1964
Marshall 75670   (214) 938-6622

Trust established in 1978 in Texas.
Donor(s): Hope Pierce Tartt.†
Financial data: (yr. ended 5/31/83): Assets, $5,930,069 (M); expenditures, $454,151, including $443,103 for 26 grants (high: $89,000; low: $750).
Purpose and activities: To assist in providing education for East Texas students at private institutions, principally in Texas.
Types of support awarded: Student aid.
Limitations: Giving primarily in Harrison, Gregg, Marion, Upshur, and Panola counties, TX.
Publications: Program policy statement, application guidelines.
Application information: Application form required.
  Initial approach: Letter
  Copies of proposal: 1
  Deadline(s): Submit proposal in March; deadline July 31
  Board meeting date(s): February and as required
Officers: E.N. Smith, Jr., Chairman; Rev. Frank Boutwell, Rev. L.B. Broach, William L. Gaw, Vice-Chairmen; Robert L. Duvall, Secretary-Treasurer.
Employer Identification Number: 756263272

4096
Taub Foundation, The ⌗
333 West Loop North, Fourth Fl.
Houston 77024

Incorporated in 1953 in Texas.
Donor(s): Henry J.N. Taub, Ben Taub.
Financial data: (yr. ended 6/30/83): Assets, $1,786,192 (M); gifts received, $5,838; expenditures, $154,605, including $127,387 for 23 grants (high: $15,567; low: $100).

Purpose and activities: Broad purposes; primarily local giving, with emphasis on education, including a college of medicine, a preparatory school, and a research and rehabilitation institute.
Limitations: Giving primarily in TX.
Trustees: Gail Hendryx, H. Ben Taub, Henry J.N. Taub, Henry J.N. Taub II, John B. Taub, Marcy E. Taub, I. Mark Westheimer.
Employer Identification Number: 746060216

4097
Technical Foundation of America
P.O. Box 1622
San Marcos 78666

Chartered in 1898 in Massachusetts as American Technical Society; incorporated in 1980 in Illinois under current name.
Financial data: (yr. ended 6/30/83): Assets, $4,120,691 (M); expenditures, $416,451, including $126,353 for 19 grants (high: $15,000; low: $200; average: $5,000-$10,000).
Purpose and activities: Grants, technical assistance, and programs to the industrial education community at the national, state, and local levels, interests include evaluating and establishing priorities for critical industrial issues, improving leadership, upgrading industrial education, increasing effectiveness of industrial pilot programs, and raising the public perception of industrial education. In future years, giving will rotate on an annual basis to national and state organizations, local school systems, and colleges and universities.
Types of support awarded: Seed money, matching funds, consulting services, technical assistance, special projects, research, publications, conferences and seminars.
Limitations: No support for cultural, artistic, or religious groups. No grants to individuals, or for general support, operating programs, capital or endowment funds, scholarships, fellowships, continuing support, annual campaigns, emergency funds, or deficit financing; no loans.
Publications: Multi-year report, informational brochure, program policy statement, application guidelines.
Application information:
  Initial approach: Letter or full proposal
  Copies of proposal: 2
  Deadline(s): February 1 and April 1
  Board meeting date(s): Quarterly
  Final notification: 3 months
  Write: Dean A. Wertz, Executive Director
Officers and Trustees: David E. Hall, President; G. Eugene Martin, Vice-President; Dean A. Wertz, Secretary and Executive Director; John Eames, Treasurer.
Number of staff: 2 full-time support.
Employer Identification Number: 360730670

4098
Temple (T. L. L.) Foundation ▼
109 Temple Blvd.
Lufkin 75901   (409) 639-5197

Trust established in 1962 in Texas.
Donor(s): Georgie T. Munz.†

Financial data: (yr. ended 11/30/83): Assets, $23,436,828 (M); expenditures, $1,772,209, including $1,676,362 for 78 grants (high: $400,000; low: $288; average: $1,000-$50,000).
Purpose and activities: Primarily local giving, with emphasis on education, hospitals, and social services; support also for civic affairs and cultural programs.
Types of support awarded: Operating budgets, seed money, emergency funds, building funds, equipment, land acquisition, matching funds, scholarship funds, special projects, research, conferences and seminars.
Limitations: Giving limited to counties in TX constituting the East Texas Pine Timber Belt. No support for private foundations, or churches or organizations that teach religion. No grants to individuals, or for continuing support, annual campaigns, deficit financing, or endowment funds; no loans.
Publications: Application guidelines, program policy statement, annual report.
Application information:
  Initial approach: Letter
  Deadline(s): None
  Board meeting date(s): Monthly
  Final notification: 2 months
  Write: Ward R. Burke, Executive Secretary
Officers and Trustees: Arthur Temple, Chairman; Ward R. Burke, Executive Secretary; W. Temple Webber, Jr.
Number of staff: 1 full-time professional.
Employer Identification Number: 756037406

4099
Texas Commerce Bank Foundation, Inc. ▼
P.O. Box 2558
Houston 77252   (713) 236-4004

Incorporated in 1952 in Texas.
Donor(s): Texas Commerce Bank, Houston.
Financial data: (yr. ended 12/31/83): Assets, $1,365,645 (M); gifts received, $496,500; expenditures, $650,729, including $650,618 for 121 grants (high: $303,500; low: $25; average: $50-$10,000).
Purpose and activities: Giving limited to the Houston area, with emphasis on a community fund, higher education, civic and cultural affairs, and medical research organizations.
Types of support awarded: Annual campaigns, building funds, continuing support, employee matching gifts, research.
Limitations: Giving primarily in the Houston, TX, area. No grants to individuals or for endowment funds; no loans.
Application information: Applications not invited; funds presently committed.
  Board meeting date(s): As required
  Write: Carol Bohannon, Corporate Contributions Administrator
Officers: Charles C. Beall, Jr., President; Timothy Irvine, Secretary; Marc J. Shapiro, Treasurer.
Number of staff: 1 full-time professional; 1 part-time professional.
Employer Identification Number: 746036696

4100
Texas Educational Association, The ▼
7201 W. Vickery Blvd., Suite 106
Fort Worth 76116   (817) 763-5557

Incorporated in 1949 in Texas.
Donor(s): George W. Armstrong, Sr.†
Financial data: (yr. ended 12/31/83): Assets,
$7,665,116 (M); expenditures, $1,040,919,
including $874,375 for 137 grants (high:
$40,000; low: $100).
Purpose and activities: To support educational
undertakings "through financial assistance to
schools, colleges, universities and other
educational mediums advocating the
perpetuation of constitutional government."
Grants only for educational programs on
American ideals and traditional values; support
also for cultural programs and religious
activities.
Types of support awarded: Conferences and
seminars, internships, publications, research,
general purposes.
Limitations: Giving primarily in TX. No grants
to individuals, or for capital or endowment
funds, operating budgets, or matching gifts; no
loans.
Publications: Application guidelines.
Application information:
Initial approach: Full proposal
Copies of proposal: 1
Deadline(s): None
Board meeting date(s): February and October
Final notification: 2 months
Write: Beverley V. Thompson, Jr., President
Officers and Trustees: Beverley V. Thompson,
Jr., President and Treasurer; John H. James,
Vice-President and Secretary; Thomas K.
Armstrong, Vice-President.
Number of staff: 3 part-time professional; 1
full-time support.
Employer Identification Number: 756003209

4101
Texas Industries Foundation
8100 Carpenter Freeway
Dallas 75247   (214) 637-3100

Incorporated in 1965 in Texas.
Donor(s): Texas Industries, Inc.
Financial data: (yr. ended 12/31/84): Assets,
$472 (M); gifts received, $254,010;
expenditures, $254,010, including $237,535
for 64 grants (high: $25,000; low: $250) and
$16,475 for 5 grants to individuals.
Purpose and activities: Broad purposes;
primarily local giving with emphasis on higher
education, including scholarships for
dependents of Company employees, and
community funds.
Types of support awarded: Employee related
scholarships, building funds, research,
scholarship funds.
Limitations: Giving primarily in TX. No grants
for operating funds.
Application information:
Deadline(s): January 15
Officers: Robert D. Rogers,* President; Fergus
J. Walker, Jr., Vice-President; Joseph C. Nelson,
Secretary; Kenneth Darden, Treasurer.
Directors: Ralph B. Rogers, Chairman; Peter F.
Carleton.
Employer Identification Number: 756043179

4102
Texas Instruments Foundation ▼
13500 North Central Expressway
P.O. Box 225474, Mail Station 232
Dallas 75265   (214) 995-4848

Trust established in 1951 in Texas;
incorporated in 1964.
Donor(s): Texas Instruments Incorporated, and
wholly-owned subsidiaries.
Financial data: (yr. ended 12/31/82): Assets,
$9,995,540 (M); gifts received, $600,000;
expenditures, $1,009,110, including $800,390
for 78 grants (high: $243,000; low: $200;
average: $500-$20,000) and $103,427 for 875
employee matching gifts.
Purpose and activities: General giving, largely
for community funds; grants also for higher and
secondary education, including employee
matching gifts, hospitals, youth agencies, and
cultural programs.
Types of support awarded: Employee
matching gifts, operating budgets, building
funds, scholarship funds.
Limitations: No grants to individuals, or for
company products or advertising; no loans.
Application information:
Initial approach: Letter
Deadline(s): 1 month before board meeting
    dates
Board meeting date(s): February, May,
    August, and December
Final notification: Within 1 month
Write: C.J. Thomsen, President
Officers: C.J. Thomsen,* President; S.T.
Harris,* Vice-President; James H. Johnson,
Secretary; William A. Aylesworth, Treasurer.
Directors:* J. Fred Bucy, J.E. Jonsson, Mark
Shepherd, Jr.
Number of staff: 1 full-time support.
Employer Identification Number: 756038519

4103
Tobin Foundation, The
P.O. Box 2101
San Antonio 78297   (512) 223-6203

Incorporated in 1951 in Texas.
Donor(s): Edgar G. Tobin,† Mrs. Margaret
Batts Tobin.
Financial data: (yr. ended 12/31/83): Assets,
$1,324,362 (M); expenditures, $114,321,
including $101,845 for 23 grants (high:
$25,000; low: $100).
Purpose and activities: Primarily local giving
to cultural programs, community funds, and
education; support also for a church.
Limitations: Giving primarily in TX.
Application information:
Write: Arnold Swartz
Officers: Margaret Batts Tobin, President;
R.L.B. Tobin, Vice-President and Treasurer;
Harold Gasnell, Secretary.
Trustee: James T. Hart.
Employer Identification Number: 746035718

4104
Trull Foundation, The ▼
404 Fourth St.
P.O. Box 1050
Palacios 77465   (512) 972-5241

Trust established in 1967 in Texas.
Donor(s): R.B. Trull, Florence M. Trull,†
Gladys T. Brooking, Jean T. Herlin, Laura
Shiflett, and others.
Financial data: (yr. ended 12/31/83): Assets,
$9,215,075 (M); expenditures, $595,661,
including $464,810 for 114 grants (high:
$60,000; low: $50; average: $5,000).
Purpose and activities: Broad purposes; local
giving for Protestant church support, higher and
secondary education, and welfare and youth
agencies.
Types of support awarded: Operating
budgets, continuing support, annual campaigns,
seed money, emergency funds, deficit
financing, equipment, land acquisition,
matching funds, professorships, internships,
scholarship funds, special projects, research,
publications, conferences and seminars,
exchange programs, fellowships.
Limitations: Giving primarily in south TX. No
grants to individuals, and rarely for building or
endowment funds; no loans.
Publications: Biennial report, application
guidelines.
Application information:
Initial approach: Letter
Copies of proposal: 2
Deadline(s): None
Board meeting date(s): Usually 3 to 5 times
    a year; contributions committee meets
    monthly and as required
Final notification: 6 weeks
Write: Colleen Claybourn, Trustee
Officers and Trustees: R.B. Trull, Chairman; J.
Fred Huitt, Vice-Chairman; Colleen Claybourn,
Secretary-Treasurer and Executive Director;
Jean T. Herlin, Rose C. Lancaster.
Number of staff: 1 full-time professional; 1 full-
time support.
Employer Identification Number: 237423943

4105
Turner Charitable Foundation ¤
950 Houston Club Bldg.
Houston 77002

Incorporated in 1960 in Texas.
Donor(s): Mrs. Isla Carroll Turner, P.E. Turner.†
Financial data: (yr. ended 2/28/83): Assets,
$5,214,255 (M); expenditures, $401,842,
including $378,233 for 31 grants (high:
$42,500; low: $500).
Purpose and activities: Broad purposes;
primarily local giving, with emphasis on higher
and secondary education, youth agencies,
cultural institutions, and Protestant church
support and religious programs.
Limitations: Giving primarily in Houston, TX.
No grants to individuals.
Officers: T.R. Reckling III, President; Bert F.
Winston, Jr., Vice-President; Clyde J.
Verheyden, Secretary; E.C. Scurlock, Treasurer.
Employer Identification Number: 741460482

4106
Tyler Foundation, The
3200 San Jacinto Tower
Dallas 75201 (214) 754-7800

Established in 1971 in Texas.
Donor(s): Tyler Corporation.
Financial data: (yr. ended 12/31/83): Assets,
$1,843,717 (M); expenditures, $149,514,
including $146,550 for 75 grants (high:
$45,000; low: $100).
Purpose and activities: Primarily local giving,
with emphasis on welfare, the arts, youth
agencies, and recreation.
Limitations: Giving primarily in TX. No grants
to individuals, or for scholarships and
fellowships, or matching gifts; no loans.
Application information:
 Initial approach: Full proposal
 Copies of proposal: 1
 Board meeting date(s): As required
 Final notification: 3 to 4 weeks
 Write: Ben R. Murphy, President
Officers: Ben R. Murphy,* President; W.
Michael Kipphut, Secretary; D.L. Smart,*
Treasurer.
Trustees:* Joseph F. McKinney, Chairman.
Number of staff: None.
Employer Identification Number: 237140526

4107
Vale-Asche Foundation, The ⌑
1300 Main St., Suite 603
Houston 77002

Incorporated in 1956 in Delaware.
Donor(s): Ruby Vale,† Mrs. Ruby Vale,† Fred
B. Asche.
Financial data: (yr. ended 11/30/82): Assets,
$1,765,217 (M); expenditures, $158,107,
including $148,300 for 15 grants (high:
$30,000; low: $300).
Purpose and activities: Grants for local
charitable and educational purposes, with
emphasis on medical research, health care, and
aid to the handicapped; support also for
secondary education and cultural programs.
Limitations: Giving primarily in TX.
Officers and Trustees: Mrs. Vale Asche
Ackerman, President; Bettyann Asche
McCullough, Vice-President; Herbert E. Holm,
Secretary-Treasurer.
Employer Identification Number: 516015320

4108
Vaughn Foundation, The ⌑
c/o Allied Bank of Texas, Trust Dept.
P.O. Box 3326
Houston 77001

Trust established in 1952 in Texas.
Donor(s): Edgar H. Vaughn,† Mrs. Lillie Mae
Vaughn.
Financial data: (yr. ended 12/31/82): Assets,
$3,744,787 (M); expenditures, $421,673,
including $376,043 for 165 grants (high:
$116,500; low: $10).
Purpose and activities: Broad purposes;
interests include higher education, hospitals,
health agencies, Protestant church support, and
a related foundation.

Limitations: Giving primarily in the Southwest,
with emphasis on TX.
Trustees: James M. Vaughn, James M. Vaughn,
Jr., Allied Bank of Texas, Corporate Trustee.
Employer Identification Number: 756008953

4109
Waggoner (Crystelle) Charitable Trust
c/o InterFirst Bank
P.O. Box 1317
Fort Worth 76101 (817) 390-6925

Established in 1982 in Texas.
Donor(s): Crystelle Waggoner.†
Financial data: (yr. ended 6/30/84): Assets,
$2,635,245 (M); expenditures, $339,922,
including $339,922 for 33 grants (high:
$50,000; low: $2,000; average: $10,000).
Purpose and activities: General purposes;
giving to charitable organizations in Texas.
Types of support awarded: General purposes,
annual campaigns, building funds, conferences
and seminars, emergency funds, endowment
funds, equipment, fellowships, internships, land
acquisition, lectureships, operating budgets,
professorships, program-related investments,
publications, research, scholarship funds, seed
money, special projects, technical assistance,
general purposes.
Limitations: Giving limited to TX, especially
Fort Worth and Decatur. No grants to
individuals, or for challenge grants, consulting
services, deficit financing, or matching gifts; no
loans.
Publications: Application guidelines.
Application information:
 Initial approach: Letter
 Copies of proposal: 1
 Deadline(s): End of each quarter
 Board meeting date(s): January, April, July,
 and October
 Final notification: 6 months, only if request
 is granted
 Write: Jayne Lipe, Vice-President
Trustee: InterFirst Bank Fort Worth (Jayne Lipe,
Vice-President and Trust Officer).
Employer Identification Number: 751881219

4110
**Waggoner (The E. Paul and Helen
 Buck) Foundation, Inc.** ⌑
P.O. Box 2130
Vernon 76384 (817) 552-2521

Incorporated in 1966 in Texas.
Donor(s): E. Paul Waggoner,† Helen Buck
Waggoner.†
Financial data: (yr. ended 4/30/83): Assets,
$7,382,215 (M); expenditures, $353,606,
including $343,000 for 17 grants (high:
$200,000; low: $1,000).
Purpose and activities: Primarily local giving,
with emphasis on higher and secondary
education, including agricultural research and
scholarship funds; grants also for medical
research and youth agencies.
Limitations: Giving primarily in TX.
Application information:
 Initial approach: Full proposal
 Write: Gene Willingham

Officers and Directors: Electra Waggoner
Biggs, President; Electra Biggs Winston, 1st Vice-
President; Helen Biggs Willingham, Secretary
and Treasurer; Gene W. Willingham, Charles F.
Winston.
Employer Identification Number: 751243683

4111
**Walthall (Marjorie T.) Perpetual
 Charitable Trust** ⌑
110 E. Crockett St.
San Antonio 78205 (512) 223-9223

Trust established in 1976 in Texas.
Donor(s): Marjorie T. Walthall.
Financial data: (yr. ended 12/31/83): Assets,
$1,491,159 (M); expenditures, $99,637,
including $87,800 for 15 grants (high: $27,300;
low: $500).
Purpose and activities: Primarily local giving;
emphasis on health, medical education,
scientific research and similar activities
conducted primarily in south Texas. Support
also for a nursing school and cultural programs.
Limitations: Giving primarily in south Texas.
Application information:
 Initial approach: Letter
 Deadline(s): October 1
 Write: John W. Pancoast, Trustee
Trustees: John W. Pancoast, Thomas W.
Folbre, Marjorie T. Walthall.
Employer Identification Number: 510170313

4112
Warren Foundation, The
c/o Thomas L. Goad
6300 Ocean Dr.
Corpus Christi 78412 (512) 991-8481

Incorporated in 1955 in Texas.
Donor(s): Guy I. Warren,† Mrs. Guy I. Warren.
Financial data: (yr. ended 9/30/84): Assets,
$1,029,164 (M); expenditures, $119,492,
including $109,819 for 16 grants (high:
$61,452; low: $1,000).
Purpose and activities: Broad purposes;
primarily local giving, with emphasis on higher
education.
Limitations: Giving primarily in TX.
Application information:
 Write: Thomas L. Goad, Secretary-Treasurer
Officers and Trustees: B. Alan Sugg,
President; Thomas L. Goad, Secretary-
Treasurer; Harvie Branscomb, Jr., Mrs. John
Allen King.
Employer Identification Number: 741262852

4113
Weaver (The Gil and Dody) Foundation
200 Interfirst Tower
801 Cherry St.
Fort Worth 76102

Established in 1980 in Texas.
Donor(s): Galbraith McF. Weaver.
Financial data: (yr. ended 9/30/82): Assets,
$2,731,698 (M); expenditures, $256,256,
including $180,077 for 28 grants (high:
$25,000; low: $100).

Purpose and activities: Support largely for youth agencies, organizations aiding the aged, and education, in the Southwest only.
Types of support awarded: Operating budgets, continuing support, building funds, equipment, special projects, research.
Limitations: Giving limited to the southwestern U.S. No grants to individuals, or for seed money, emergency funds, deficit financing, land acquisition, renovation projects, endowment funds, matching gifts, scholarships and fellowships, publications, or conferences; no loans.
Application information:
  Initial approach: Letter or full proposal
  Deadline(s): Submit proposal preferably in June; deadline July 31
  Board meeting date(s): September
  Write: Galbraith McF. Weaver, Trustee
Trustees: Eudora J. Weaver, Galbraith McF. Weaver, William R. Weaver, M.D.
Number of staff: 1.
Employer Identification Number: 751729449

4114
Weiner Foundation, Inc., The ☐
P.O. Box 2612
Houston 77001

Incorporated in 1958 in Texas.
Donor(s): Weiner's Stores, and others.
Financial data: (yr. ended 12/31/82): Assets, $2,351,958 (M); gifts received, $587,476; expenditures, $90,632, including $64,111 for 95 grants (high: $10,000; low: $25).
Purpose and activities: Primarily local giving, with emphasis on Jewish welfare funds and temple support; some support for social services.
Limitations: Giving primarily in TX.
Officers and Directors: Sol B. Weiner, Vice-President; Leon Weiner, Secretary-Treasurer.
Employer Identification Number: 746060381

4115
Welch (The Robert A.) Foundation ▼
4605 Post Oak Place, Suite 200
Houston 77027   (713) 961-9884

Trust established in 1954 in Texas.
Donor(s): Robert A. Welch.†
Financial data: (yr. ended 8/31/84): Assets, $180,571,000 (M); expenditures, $14,126,000, including $9,693,907 for 400 grants to individuals (high: $60,000; low: $20,000; average: $20,000-$30,000).
Purpose and activities: A private operating foundation; giving limited to the state of Texas. Grants for chemistry research, for which applicants must be full-time tenured or tenure-track faculty at educational institutions; for scholarships in chemistry; for the Welch Award in Chemistry; and for professorships in the field of chemistry research.
Types of support awarded: Research, professorships, scholarship funds, grants to individuals.
Limitations: Giving limited to TX. No support for any purpose other than basic chemistry research.

Publications: Annual report, application guidelines, newsletter.
Application information: Application form required.
  Initial approach: Telephone or personal interview
  Copies of proposal: 1
  Deadline(s): February 1 for regular research grant program; March 1 for Robert A. Welch Award in Chemistry
  Board meeting date(s): Monthly
  Final notification: Approximately 2 months
  Write: Norbert Dittrich, Executive Manager
Officers and Trustees: Jack S. Josey, President; E.L. Wehner, Vice-President; Marvin K. Collie, Secretary; R.P. Doherty, Jr., Treasurer; Richard J.V. Johnson.
Number of staff: 3 full-time professional; 8 full-time support.
Employer Identification Number: 741216248

4116
Welder (Rob and Bessie) Wildlife Foundation
P.O. Box 1400
Sinton 78387   (512) 364-2643

Trust established in 1954 in Texas.
Donor(s): R.H. Welder,† Mrs. R.H. Welder.†
Financial data: (yr. ended 12/31/83): Assets, $8,462,945 (M); expenditures, $819,188, including $127,248 for 16 grants to individuals.
Purpose and activities: A private operating foundation established to further the education of people in wildlife conservation, to support research into wildlife problems, and to develop scientific methods for increasing wildlife populations; operates a wildlife refuge.
Types of support awarded: Fellowships, internships.
Limitations: Giving limited to the U.S. No grants for building or endowment funds, or operating budgets.
Publications: Program policy statement, application guidelines.
Application information: Application form required.
  Initial approach: Letter
  Copies of proposal: 2
  Deadline(s): Submit application preferably in spring; deadline April 1
  Board meeting date(s): Usually in December and June
  Write: James G. Teer, Director
Officer: James G. Teer, Director.
Trustees: M. Harvey Weil, John J. Welder, Patrick H. Welder.
Employer Identification Number: 741381321

4117
West Foundation, The ☐
P.O. Box 491
Houston 77001

Trust established in 1938 in Texas.
Donor(s): J.M. West,† Jessie Dudley West,† Wesley W. West, Leslie L. Appelt.
Financial data: (yr. ended 12/31/83): Assets, $6,407,656 (M); expenditures, $347,203, including $211,000 for 10 grants (high: $120,000; low: $500).

Purpose and activities: Broad purposes; primarily local giving, largely for higher education, health agencies, and a religious organization.
Limitations: Giving primarily in TX.
Application information:
  Initial approach: Letter
  Deadline(s): None
  Write: Coordinator of Grants
Trustees: William B. Blakemore III, Margene West Lloyd, William R. Lloyd, Jr., Robert H. Parsley, James A. Reichert.
Employer Identification Number: 746040396

4118
West (J. M.) Texas Corporation ☐
P.O. Box 491
Houston 77001

Incorporated in 1957 in Texas.
Financial data: (yr. ended 2/29/84): Assets, $3,638,343 (M); expenditures, $307,799, including $148,000 for 10 grants (high: $55,000; low: $1,000).
Purpose and activities: Broad purposes; primarily local giving, with emphasis on higher education and medical research; support also for youth agencies and cultural programs.
Limitations: Giving primarily in TX.
Application information:
  Initial approach: Letter
Officers: William R. Lloyd, Jr.,* President; William B. Blakemore II,* James A. Reichert, Jack T. Trotter,* Vice-Presidents; Robert H. Parsley,* Secretary; Merle D. Wauson, Treasurer.
Trustees:* Margene West Lloyd.
Employer Identification Number: 746040389

4119
West (James L. and Eunice) Charitable Trust ☐
c/o Billy R. Roland, Managing Trustee
1700 Tandy Center
Fort Worth 76102

Established in 1980.
Financial data: (yr. ended 12/31/83): Assets, $22,308,799 (M); expenditures, $913,862, including $907,500 for 13 grants (high: $265,000; low: $1,000).
Purpose and activities: Primarily local giving for youth and child welfare organizations, cultural programs, hospitals, higher education, church support, and a community fund.
Types of support awarded: General purposes, operating budgets.
Limitations: Giving primarily in Fort Worth, TX.
Trustees: Billy R. Roland, Managing Trustee; Loren Q. Hanson, Dean Lawrence, Eunice West, Herschel Winn.
Employer Identification Number: 751724903

4120
White (G. R.) Trust ▼ ☐
c/o Joe T. Lenamon
P.O. Box 2050
Fort Worth 76113

Trust established in Texas.

Donor(s): G.R. White.†
Financial data: (yr. ended 9/30/83): Assets, $11,057,465 (M); expenditures, $689,939, including $522,777 for 50 grants (high: $131,452; low: $500).
Purpose and activities: Primarily local giving, with emphasis on hospitals, youth agencies, higher education and church support.
Limitations: Giving primarily in TX.
Committee Members: Charles Darley, Joe T. Lenamon, Fred Wulff.
Trustee: Texas American Bank & Trust.
Employer Identification Number: 756094930

4121
White (Tom C.) Foundation
900 Hamilton Bldg.
Wichita Falls 76301   (817) 723-1660

Established in 1959.
Donor(s): Tommie O. White.
Financial data: (yr. ended 12/31/83): Assets, $1,099,526 (M); gifts received, $5,543; expenditures, $81,197, including $80,200 for 22 grants (high: $10,000; low: $500; average: $500-$10,000).
Purpose and activities: Primarily local giving, with emphasis on Protestant church support and a theological seminary, social and youth agencies, higher education, and health.
Types of support awarded: General purposes, continuing support, annual campaigns, seed money, emergency funds, building funds, equipment, land acquisition, endowment funds, research, scholarship funds.
Limitations: Giving limited to TX. No grants to individuals or for matching gifts; no loans.
Publications: 990-PF.
Application information:
 Initial approach: Letter
 Copies of proposal: 1
 Deadline(s): Submit proposal preferably in December; deadline December 31
 Board meeting date(s): Monthly
 Final notification: 6 months
 Write: Mrs. Tommie O. White, Director
Trustees: Evelyn C.W. Parkhurst, David H. White, Tommie O. White.
Number of staff: None.
Employer Identification Number: 756037052

4122
Wilson (John & Nevils) Foundation
P.O. Drawer S & P
Wichita Falls 76307-7511   (817) 322-3145

Established in 1968 in Texas.
Donor(s): J.H. Wilson.†
Financial data: (yr. ended 11/30/83): Assets, $2,473,044 (M); gifts received, $100,000; expenditures, $202,230, including $166,982 for 11 grants (high: $102,100; low: $1,000).
Purpose and activities: Grants primarily for a local Protestant church and health care delivery.
Limitations: Giving primarily in Wichita County, TX. No grants to individuals or for scholarships or fellowships; no loans.
Application information:
 Initial approach: Letter
 Copies of proposal: 5

Deadline(s): Submit proposal in August through October; deadline November 1
Board meeting date(s): February and November
Write: Joseph N. Sherrill, Jr., Vice-President
Officers and Trustees: Evelyn Wilson Egan, President; Virginia Wilson Ewing, Joseph N. Sherrill, Jr., Vice-Presidents; Earle W. Crawford, David A. Kimbell.
Employer Identification Number: 756080151

4123
Wilson (Ralph) Public Trust ⊭
c/o Don Keen
600 South General Bruce Dr.
Temple 76501

Established in 1974.
Donor(s): Ralph Wilson.†
Financial data: (yr. ended 12/31/81): Assets, $2,545,623 (M); expenditures, $251,419, including $250,000 for 7 grants (high: $140,000; low: $5,000).
Purpose and activities: Primarily local giving, with support mainly for the Ralph Wilson Youth Clubs; support also for cultural programs and child welfare.
Limitations: Giving primarily in TX.
Officers: Jim Bowmer, President; Ralph Wilson, Jr., Vice-President; Betty Prescott, Secretary; Don Keen, Treasurer.
Employer Identification Number: 237351606

4124
Wiseda Foundation, The ⊭
P.O. Box 12507
Fort Worth 76116

Established in 1976 in Texas.
Donor(s): William S. Davis, Davoil, Inc.
Financial data: (yr. ended 9/30/82): Assets, $52,438 (M); gifts received, $50,000; expenditures, $108,767, including $108,400 for 11 grants (high: $50,000; low: $500).
Purpose and activities: Primarily local giving, with emphasis on social agencies, health, and museums and cultural programs.
Limitations: Giving primarily in TX.
Trustee: William S. Davis.
Employer Identification Number: 751533548

4125
Wolff (The Pauline Sterne) Memorial Foundation ▼ ⊭
333 West Loop North, Fourth Fl.
Houston 77024   (713) 688-2426

Incorporated in 1922 in Texas.
Financial data: (yr. ended 12/31/82): Assets, $9,207,079 (M); expenditures, $791,867, including $692,015 for 26 grants (high: $250,000; low: $1,000).
Purpose and activities: Primarily local giving largely for medical education and research, and Jewish welfare organizations; support also for hospitals.
Limitations: Giving primarily in Harris County, TX.
Application information:
 Initial approach: Letter

Deadline(s): December 1
Write: Henry J.N. Taub, Vice-President
Officers and Trustees:* Henry J.N. Taub, I. Mark Westheimer,* Vice-Presidents and Treasurers; Aaron J. Farfel,* Vice-President.
Employer Identification Number: 741110698

4126
Woltman (B. M.) Foundation ⊭
2200 West Loop South, Suite 225
Houston 77027
Application address: Lutheran Church-Synod, 7900 U.S. 290 East, Austin, TX 78724

Trust established in 1948 in Texas.
Donor(s): B.M. Woltman,† Woltman Furniture Company, and others.
Financial data: (yr. ended 12/31/82): Assets, $3,551,616 (M); gifts received, $2,700; expenditures, $311,507, including $205,671 for 63 grants (high: $94,000; low: $50) and $51,750 for 46 grants to individuals.
Purpose and activities: Broad purposes; local giving only for Lutheran church support, local church-related secondary schools, hospitals, and higher education; scholarships for Texas Lutheran ministerial students only.
Types of support awarded: Student aid.
Limitations: Giving limited to TX.
Application information: Scholarship applications must be received before the school term begins in order to allow sufficient time for processing. Application form required.
 Write: Frederick Boden, Executive Director
Officers and Trustees: W.J. Woltman, President; W. Carloss Morris, Secretary-Treasurer; Richard D. Chandler, Jr., Rev. Hobart Meyer, Rev. Glenn O'Shoney.
Employer Identification Number: 741402184

4127
Wortham Foundation, The ▼
2777 Allen Pkwy., Suite 984
Houston 77019   (713) 526-8849

Trust established in 1958 in Texas.
Donor(s): Gus S. Wortham,† Lyndall F. Wortham.
Financial data: (yr. ended 9/30/83): Assets, $95,422,613 (M); expenditures, $3,819,083, including $2,757,955 for 21 grants (high: $877,500; low: $100).
Purpose and activities: Broad purposes; local giving with emphasis on community improvement and cultural programs.
Types of support awarded: Annual campaigns, seed money, emergency funds, deficit financing, general purposes, matching funds, continuing support.
Limitations: Giving primarily in Houston and Harris County, TX. Generally no grants to colleges, universities, or hospitals. No grants to individuals or for building funds.
Application information:
 Initial approach: Letter
 Copies of proposal: 1
 Deadline(s): Submit proposal preferably in October, January, April, or July; no set deadline
 Board meeting date(s): November, February, May, and August

Final notification: 1 month
 Write: Allen H. Carruth, President
Officer and Trustees: Allen H. Carruth, President; H. Charles Boswell, Brady F. Carruth, E.A. Stumpf, III, R.W. Wortham, III.
Number of staff: 2 full-time support.
Employer Identification Number: 741334356

4128
Wright (Lola) Foundation, Inc.
P.O. Box 1138
Georgetown 78627-1138   (512) 255-3067

Incorporated in 1954 in Texas.
Donor(s): Miss Johnie E. Wright.†
Financial data: (yr. ended 12/31/82): Assets, $5,689,362 (M); expenditures, $1,107,009, including $607,936 for 52 grants (high: $58,333; low: $50).
Purpose and activities: Charitable and educational purposes; local giving with emphasis on higher education, including medical education, hospitals, health and social agencies, youth development, mental health programs, and cultural programs.
Types of support awarded: Matching funds, building funds, equipment, endowment funds, continuing support, scholarship funds.
Limitations: Giving limited to TX. No grants to individuals or for operating budgets.
Publications: Application guidelines.
Application information:
 Initial approach: Letter
 Copies of proposal: 6
 Deadline(s): April 1 and October 1
 Board meeting date(s): Semiannually
 Write: Patrick H. O'Donnell, President
Officers and Directors: Patrick H. O'Donnell, President; William Hilgers, Vice-President; Vivian Todd, Secretary-Treasurer.
Employer Identification Number: 746054717

4129
Zale Foundation, The ▼
P.O. Box 152777
Irving 75015   (214) 257-4789

Incorporated in 1951 in Texas.
Donor(s): Zale Corporation, and members of the Zale and Lipshy families.
Financial data: (yr. ended 12/31/83): Assets, $9,113,321 (M); gifts received, $240,000; expenditures, $676,135, including $664,102 for 24 grants (high: $279,500; low: $500).
Purpose and activities: Program policies currently under revision; giving in the past to strengthen the independent family unit by supporting programs which set up family-to-family support systems, with emphasis on care of children and the aged; grants for Jewish welfare agencies, hospitals, and social services.
Types of support awarded: Operating budgets, seed money, building funds, professorships, internships, consulting services, technical assistance, scholarship funds.

Limitations: No grants to individuals, or for continuing support, annual campaigns, emergency funds, deficit financing, equipment, renovation projects, special projects, research, endowment funds, conferences, study, films, publications, scholarships, fellowships, land acquisition, or matching gifts; no loans. No grants for periods of more than 3 to 5 years.
Publications: Annual report, program policy statement, application guidelines.
Application information:
 Initial approach: Letter and brief proposal of not more than 2 or 3 pages
 Copies of proposal: 1
 Deadline(s): None
 Board meeting date(s): Semiannually
 Final notification: 3 months
 Write: Michael F. Romaine, President
Officers: Michael F. Romaine, President; George Tobolowsky, Secretary-Treasurer.
Trustees: Bruce A. Lipshy, Chairman; Leo Fields, Donald Zale, Marvin Zale.
Number of staff: 1 full-time professional; 1 full-time support.
Employer Identification Number: 756037429

UTAH

4130
Bamberger (Ruth Eleanor) and John Ernest Bamberger Memorial Foundation
175 South Main St., No. 1407
Salt Lake City 84111   (801) 364-2045

Incorporated in 1947 in Utah.
Donor(s): Ernest Bamberger,† Eleanor F. Bamberger.†
Financial data: (yr. ended 12/31/82): Assets, $3,709,937 (M); expenditures, $170,831, including $109,496 for 82 grants (high: $25,000; low: $100; average: $500), $21,965 for 29 grants to individuals and $9,041 for 4 loans.
Purpose and activities: Primarily local giving for charitable or educational purposes; support for higher education, especially undergraduate scholarships for student nurses, and for schools, hospitals and health agencies, and youth and child welfare agencies.
Types of support awarded: Operating budgets, continuing support, scholarship funds, loans, equipment, student aid.
Limitations: Giving primarily in UT. No grants to individuals (except for scholarships to local students), or for endowment or building funds, research, or matching gifts; occasional loans for medical education.
Application information:
 Initial approach: Letter
 Copies of proposal: 1

Deadline(s): Submit proposal preferably in the month preceding the next board meeting
 Board meeting date(s): Bimonthly beginning in February
 Final notification: Two months
 Write: William H. Olwell, Secretary-Treasurer
Officers and Directors: F. Henri Henriod, Chairman; William H. Olwell, Secretary-Treasurer; Clifford L. Ashton, Clarence Bamberger, Jr., Joseph E. Bernolfo, Jr.
Number of staff: 1 part-time support.
Employer Identification Number: 876116540

4131
Caine (Marie Eccles) Charitable Foundation ¤
324 North 500 East
Brigham City 84302   (801) 723-2770

Established in 1981 in Utah.
Donor(s): Marie Eccles Caine.†
Financial data: (yr. ended 5/31/82): Assets, $1,566,926 (M); gifts received, $1,527,530; expenditures, $793.
Purpose and activities: Primarily local giving for the advancement of the fine arts in the Logan, Utah, community, particularly at Utah State University, and for other programs at that university which were of interest to the donor.
Limitations: Giving primarily in Logan County, UT.
Application information:
 Initial approach: Proposal
 Write: Manon Russell or Dan C. Russell
Trustee: First Security Bank of Utah.
Committee members: Dan C. Russell, Manon C. Russell, George R. Wanlass, Kathryn C. Wanlass.
Employer Identification Number: 942764258

4132
Callister (Louise E.) Foundation ¤
2005 South 300 West
Salt Lake City 84115

Incorporated in 1958 in Utah.
Donor(s): Paul Q. Callister, Mary B. Callister.
Financial data: (yr. ended 6/30/83): Assets, $1,852,597 (M); expenditures, $158,351, including $141,000 for 15 grants (high: $107,000; low: $100).
Purpose and activities: Primarily local giving, with emphasis on the Mormon church and higher education.
Limitations: Giving primarily in UT. No grants to individuals.
Application information:
 Board meeting date(s): Quarterly and as required
Officers and Directors: Mary B. Callister, President; Paul S. Callister, Secretary; Jane C. Thorne, Treasurer; Jan E. Callister, Marna C. Fryer.
Employer Identification Number: 876118299

4133
Castle Foundation ¤
c/o Continental Bank & Trust Company
P.O. Box 30177
Salt Lake City 84130

Established in 1953.
Financial data: (yr. ended 6/30/83): Assets, $1,336,101 (M); expenditures, $107,377, including $94,000 for 53 grants (high: $5,000; low: $500).
Purpose and activities: Primarily local giving, with emphasis on the arts, youth and social agencies, higher and secondary education, and hospitals.
Limitations: Giving primarily in UT.
Application information:
Initial approach: Letter
Deadline(s): None
Advisory Committee: Fred S. Ball, Francis W. Douglas, G. Richard Lee, M.D.
Trustee: Continental Bank & Trust Company.
Employer Identification Number: 876117177

4134
Christensen (A. Lee) Family Foundation ¤
Crandall Bldg., Suite 600
Salt Lake City 84101
Application address: 50 South Main, Suite 1700, Salt Lake City, UT 84144; Application address for Jerusalem Study-Abroad Program: Dan Horne, Administrator, Brigham Young University, Provo, UT 84602; Tel.: (801) 378-3946

Established in 1971.
Financial data: (yr. ended 12/31/83): Assets, $582,636 (M); expenditures, $127,153, including $121,000 for 5 grants (high: $70,000; low: $1,000).
Purpose and activities: Giving primarily to a local university for study-abroad program; support also for a hospital.
Limitations: Giving primarily in UT.
Publications: Application guidelines.
Application information:
Initial approach: Letter
Deadline(s): None
Write: Max B. Lewis, Foundation Manager
Officers: A. Lee Christensen, President; Richard L. Christensen, Vice-President; Max B. Lewis, Secretary and Manager; Susan R. Christensen, Treasurer.
Trustees: M. Craig Johns, Suzanne H. Christensen.
Employer Identification Number: 237119127

4135
Dee (Annie Taylor) Foundation
1212 First Security Bldg.
2404 Washington Blvd.
Ogden 84401   (801) 621-0700

Trust established in 1961 in Utah.
Donor(s): Maude Dee Porter.†
Financial data: (yr. ended 12/31/83): Assets, $1,196,727 (M); expenditures, $100,016, including $92,185 for 8 grants (high: $48,000; low: $1,000).

Purpose and activities: Primarily local giving to assist the McKay-Dee Hospital; some support for higher education, cultural programs, and other local charities.
Limitations: Giving primarily in UT. No grants to individuals; no loans.
Application information:
Initial approach: Letter
Copies of proposal: 1
Deadline(s): Submit proposal preferably in September
Board meeting date(s): April and October
Write: Thomas D. Dee II, Chairman
Distribution Committee: Thomas D. Dee II, Chairman; Thomas D. Dee III, Vice-Chairman; Jack D. Lampros, Secretary; Geary Pehrson.
Trustee: First Security Bank of Utah.
Employer Identification Number: 876116380

4136
Dee (Lawrence T. and Janet T.) Foundation
1212 First Security Bldg.
2404 Washington Blvd.
Ogden 84401   (801) 621-4863

Established in 1971 in Utah.
Donor(s): L.T. Dee,† Janet T. Dee.†
Financial data: (yr. ended 12/31/83): Assets, $3,389,146 (M); expenditures, $174,755, including $160,885 for 21 grants (high: $92,000; low: $1,000).
Purpose and activities: Primarily local giving, with emphasis on hospitals, particularly the McKay-Dee Hospital; support also for higher education, cultural programs, and social agencies.
Types of support awarded: Annual campaigns, emergency funds, building funds, equipment, endowment funds, research, scholarship funds, matching funds.
Limitations: Giving primarily in UT. No grants to individuals; no loans.
Application information:
Initial approach: Letter
Copies of proposal: 1
Deadline(s): Submit proposal preferably in September
Board meeting date(s): March and September
Write: Thomas D. Dee II, Chairman
Managers: Thomas D. Dee II, Chairman; Thomas D. Dee III, Vice-Chairman; Jack D. Lampros, Secretary; David L. Dee.
Trustee: First Security Bank of Utah.
Employer Identification Number: 876150803

4137
Dumke (Dr. Ezekiel R. and Edna Wattis) Foundation ¤
450 S. 900 E., Suite 210
Salt Lake City 84102

Incorporated in 1959 in Utah.
Financial data: (yr. ended 12/31/83): Assets, $3,553,283 (M); expenditures, $166,983, including $128,102 for 50 grants (high: $15,000; low: $250).
Purpose and activities: Broad purposes; grants largely for higher education, cultural programs, medical and hospital services, and youth agencies in Idaho and Utah.

Limitations: Giving primarily in UT and ID.
Officers and Trustees: Ezekiel R. Dumke, Jr., President; Martha Ann Dumke Healy, Vice-President; Max B. Lewis, Secretary and Manager; Edmund W. Dumke, Treasurer; Edmund E. Dumke, Claire Dumke Mitchener, Nancy Healy Schwanfelder.
Employer Identification Number: 876119783

4138
Eccles (The George S.) and Dolores Dore Eccles Foundation ¤
79 South Main St., Rm. 201
P.O. Box 30006
Salt Lake City 84111

Incorporated in 1958 in Utah; absorbed Lillian Ethel Dufton Charitable Trust in 1981.
Donor(s): George S. Eccles.†
Financial data: (yr. ended 12/31/82): Assets, $4,839,450 (M); gifts received, $100,000; expenditures, $532,249, including $481,070 for 26 grants (high: $50,000; low: $500).
Purpose and activities: Charitable purposes; primarily local giving, with emphasis on higher education, hospitals and medical research, and the performing arts.
Limitations: Giving primarily in UT.
Officer and Directors: David P. Gardner, President; Dolores Dore Eccles, Spencer F. Eccles, Alonzo W. Watson.
Employer Identification Number: 876118245

4139
Eccles (Marriner S.) Foundation ▼ ¤
c/o First Security Bank of Utah
P.O. Box 30007
Salt Lake City 84130
Grant application office: 701 Desert Bldg., 79 South Main St., Salt Lake City, UT 84111; Tel.: (801) 322-0116

Established in 1973.
Financial data: (yr. ended 3/31/83): Assets, $13,464,180 (M); expenditures, $1,259,949, including $1,187,211 for 65 grants (high: $110,000; low: $1,000).
Purpose and activities: Local giving, with emphasis on art museums, hospitals, higher education, the performing arts, and family services; support also for social services and cultural programs.
Types of support awarded: Equipment, seed money, operating budgets, general purposes, building funds, scholarship funds, research.
Limitations: Giving limited to UT. No grants to individuals.
Application information:
Initial approach: Proposal
Copies of proposal: 7
Deadline(s): None
Officers: Sara M. Eccles, Chairman; Alonzo W. Watson, Jr., Secretary.
Trustee: First Security Bank of Utah, N.A.
Employer Identification Number: 237185855

4140

Green (Edith Dee) Foundation
4245 Skyline Dr.
Ogden 84403   (801) 621-1485

Financial data: (yr. ended 12/31/83): Assets,
$1,089,039 (M); expenditures, $115,307,
including $108,875 for 18 grants (high:
$52,500; low: $60).
Purpose and activities: Primarily local giving,
with emphasis on a university and a hospital;
grants also for social services and health
agencies.
Limitations: Giving primarily in UT.
Application information:
    Write: Harold J. Mack, Co-Chairman
Trustees: D. Wade Mack, Chairman; Harold J.
Mack, Co-Chairman; Elizabeth D.S. Stewart,
First Security Bank of Utah.
Employer Identification Number: 876149837

4141

**Harris (The William H. and Mattie
    Wattis) Foundation**
Crandall Bldg., Suite 600
10 West 1st South St.
Salt Lake City 84101   (801) 363-7863

Trust established in 1960 in Utah.
Donor(s): Mattie Wattis Harris,† William H.
Harris.
Financial data: (yr. ended 12/31/83): Assets,
$3,682,577 (M); expenditures, $201,527,
including $140,500 for 59 grants (high:
$25,000; low: $500).
Purpose and activities: Charitable purposes;
primarily giving in western U.S.; emphasis on
arts, education, social programs, conservation,
and science.
Limitations: Giving primarily in the western
U.S. No support for religious or tax-supported
organizations. No grants to individuals or for
scholarships; no loans.
Publications: Program policy statement,
application guidelines.
Application information: Application form
required.
    Initial approach: Letter or proposal
    Copies of proposal: 9
    Deadline(s): March 1 and September 1
    Board meeting date(s): April and October
    Write: Max B. Lewis, President
Officer and Trustees: Max B. Lewis, President
and Foundation Manager; Marguerite Heydt,
Vice-President; Marilyn H. Hite, Secretary; C.
Don Brown, Treasurer; James W. Hite.
Employer Identification Number: 870405724

4142

Masonic Foundation of Utah ⌑
650 East South Temple St.
Salt Lake City 84102   (801) 363-2936

Established in 1929.
Donor(s): Roy Craddock.†
Financial data: (yr. ended 12/31/83): Assets,
$2,176,347 (M); gifts received, $58,281;
expenditures, $129,969, including $106,917
for 47 grants (high: $10,000; low: $500).

Purpose and activities: Primarily local giving,
with emphasis on health, higher education,
including student loan funds, youth agencies,
and social agencies.
Types of support awarded: Research, student
aid, equipment, general purposes.
Limitations: Giving primarily in UT.
Application information:
    Deadline(s): None
    Write: Murray G. Stowe, Secretary-Treasurer
Officers and Trustees: Francis W. Douglas,
Chairman; Murray G. Stowe, Secretary-
Treasurer; LeRoy S. Axland, Marven H.
Clayton, Newell B. Dayton, Curtis N. Lancaster.
Employer Identification Number: 870261722

4143

**Michael (Herbert I. and Elsa B.)
    Foundation** ⌑
c/o Continental Bank and Trust Company
200 South Main St.
Salt Lake City 84101
Application address: The Continental Bank and
Trust Company, Trust Dept., P.O. Box 30177,
Salt Lake City, UT 84130

Established in 1950 in Utah.
Donor(s): Elsa B. Michael.†
Financial data: (yr. ended 9/30/83): Assets,
$3,262,941 (M); gifts received, $5,192;
expenditures, $246,736, including $198,855
for 32 grants (high: $20,000; low: $1,000).
Purpose and activities: Primarily local giving,
with emphasis on cultural programs and higher
and secondary education; support also for
hospitals and social agencies.
Limitations: Giving primarily in UT. No
support for sectarian religious activities.
Trustees: Albert J. Colton, K. Jay Holdsworth,
Continental Bank and Trust Company,.
Advisory Committee: David P. Gardner,
Gordon Hall, Francis W. Douglas.
Employer Identification Number: 876122556

4144

**Shaw (The Mary Elizabeth Dee)
    Charitable Trust**
First Security Bank of Utah
P.O. Box 9936
Ogden 84409   (801) 626-9533

Trust established in 1959 in Utah.
Donor(s): Mary Elizabeth Dee Shaw.†
Financial data: (yr. ended 12/31/83): Assets,
$1,708,992 (M); expenditures, $135,537,
including $125,003 for 1 grant.
Purpose and activities: Primarily to assist
Weber State College and McKay-Dee Hospital;
some support for local charities.
Limitations: Giving limited to UT. No grants
to individuals.
Application information:
    Initial approach: Letter
    Copies of proposal: 1
    Deadline(s): Submit proposal in September
    Board meeting date(s): March and September
    Write: Jack D. Lampros, Secretary

Distribution Committee: Elizabeth S. Stewart,
Chairman; Donnell B. Stewart, Vice-Chairman;
Jack D. Lampros, Secretary; Dean W. Hurst,
C.W. Stromberg.
Trustee: First Security Bank of Utah.
Employer Identification Number: 876116370

4145

Thrasher Research Fund ▼
50 East North Temple St., Seventh Fl.
Salt Lake City 84150   (801) 531-3386

Established in 1977 in Utah.
Donor(s): E.W. (Al) Thrasher, Mrs. E.W.
Thrasher.
Financial data: (yr. ended 12/31/84): Assets,
$20,470,050 (M); expenditures, $1,136,023,
including $967,210 for grants (average: $1,000-
$30,000).
Purpose and activities: To promote child
health research and related projects with a
particular interest in international child health
research. Current priorities include health
promotion, infectious diseases, and nutrition
studies.
Types of support awarded: Special projects,
research, conferences and seminars, fellowships.
Limitations: No support for cancer or cancer-
related studies, or for reproductive physiology,
including contraception technology, in vitro
fertilization, and abortions. No grants to
individuals, or for building funds, salaries of
principal investigators or professional study
directors, general support, renovation projects,
or continuing operations.
Publications: Annual report, informational
brochure, program policy statement,
application guidelines.
Application information: Application form
required.
    Initial approach: Letter, including a
        prospectus, or by telephone
    Deadline(s): None
    Board meeting date(s): February, May,
        August, and November
    Final notification: 6 months
    Write: Robert M. Briem, Associate Director
Executive Committee: Richard P. Lindsay,
Chairman; E.W. (Al) Thrasher, Vice-Chairman;
Dan S. Bushnell, Janath R. Cannon, Reed L.
Clegg, Isaac C. Ferguson, Harvey S. Glade,
David M. Kennedy, James O. Mason, M.D.,
Val D. MacMurray, Alexander B. Morrison,
Glenn L. Pace.
Number of staff: 1 full-time professional; 1
part-time professional; 1 full-time support; 1
part-time support.

4146

Treadwell (Nora Eccles) Foundation ⌑
Ray, Quinne & Nebeker
P.O. Box 3850
Salt Lake City 84110-3850

Established in 1962 in California.
Donor(s): Nora Eccles Treadwell Harrison.†
Financial data: (yr. ended 12/31/83): Assets,
$513,481 (M); gifts received, $2,466,278;
expenditures, $2,516,239, including
$2,437,017 for 28 grants (high: $475,000; low:
$500).

Purpose and activities: Grants largely in Utah and California, with emphasis on health and on cardiovascular, diabetes, and arthritis research.
Types of support awarded: Professorships, research, general purposes, equipment.
Limitations: Giving limited to UT and CA.
Application information:
  Deadline(s): None
  Write: Richard A. Harrison, President
Officers: Richard A. Harrison, President and Treasurer; Alonzo W. Watson, Jr., Secretary.
Directors: Patricia Canepa, Nicholas T. Prepouses, S.J. Quinney.
Employer Identification Number: 237425351

VERMONT

4147
Edwards (O. P. and W. E.) Foundation, Inc.
Hearthstone Village
South Londonderry 05155   (802) 824-6255

Incorporated in 1962 in New York.
Donor(s): William E. Edwards,† J.N. Edwards,† Harriet E. Gamper.
Financial data: (yr. ended 8/31/84): Assets, $2,177,892 (M); gifts received, $7,000; expenditures, $452,977, including $431,334 for 45 grants (high: $50,000; low: $500; average: $5,000-$10,000).
Purpose and activities: Major interest in programs helping disadvantaged young people become able to survive and thrive on their own, with preference to smaller, comprehensive programs that are integral parts of their communities' networks of services.
Types of support awarded: Operating budgets, continuing support, seed money, emergency funds, deficit financing, matching funds, program-related investments, scholarship funds, loans.
Limitations: No support for organizations with national affiliations or operating budgets above $250,000. No grants to individuals, or for capital or endowment funds.
Publications: Program policy statement, application guidelines.
Application information:
  Initial approach: Letter
  Copies of proposal: 1
  Deadline(s): None
  Board meeting date(s): As required
  Final notification: 1 to 2 months
  Write: David E. Gamper, President
Officers and Directors: David E. Gamper, President and Treasurer; Jo Ann Eder, Vice-President; Harriet E. Gamper, Secretary.
Number of staff: None.
Employer Identification Number: 136100965

4148
General Educational Fund, Inc. ¤
c/o The Merchants Trust Company
P.O. Box 1009
Burlington 05402

Incorporated in 1918 in Vermont.
Donor(s): Emma Eliza Curtis,† Lorenzo E. Woodhouse.†
Financial data: (yr. ended 7/31/83): Assets, $5,083,610 (M); gifts received, $74,914; expenditures, $279,321, including $232,850 for 352 grants to individuals.
Purpose and activities: Educational purposes; aid to students from Vermont.
Types of support awarded: Student aid.
Limitations: Giving primarily in VT. No grants for building or endowment funds, operating budgets, or special projects.
Application information: Application form required.
  Initial approach: Full proposal
  Copies of proposal: 1
  Deadline(s): Submit proposal in May
  Write: David W. Webster, President
Officers and Trustees: David W. Webster, President and Treasurer; Fred G. Smith, Vice-President; F.R. McGibney, Secretary; S.P. Mitchelides.
Employer Identification Number: 036009912

4149
Lintilhac Foundation ¤
c/o Thomas Amidon
P.O. Box 1016
Stowe 05672

Established in 1975.
Donor(s): Claire D. Lintilhac.
Financial data: (yr. ended 12/31/82): Assets, $1,309,989 (M); gifts received, $37,750; expenditures, $276,581, including $260,500 for 11 grants (high: $219,125; low: $750).
Purpose and activities: Primarily local giving with emphasis on a medical education program; support also for health services and community development.
Limitations: Giving primarily in VT.
Officers and Trustees: Claire Lintilhac, President; Thomas Amidon, Secretary; George Sharrow, Treasurer; Philip Lintilhac, Manager.
Employer Identification Number: 510176851

4150
Scott (Olin) Fund, Inc.
100 South St.
P.O. Box 1208
Bennington 05201   (802) 447-1096

Incorporated in 1920 in Vermont.
Donor(s): Olin Scott.†
Financial data: (yr. ended 6/30/83): Assets, $2,072,204 (M); expenditures, $204,961, including $75,000 for 3 grants of $25,000 each and $73,294 for 64 loans.
Purpose and activities: Student loans for young men in Bennington County.
Types of support awarded: Student aid.

Limitations: Giving limited to Bennington County, VT. No grants for building or endowment funds, operating budgets, or special projects.
Application information: Application form required.
  Initial approach: Letter or telephone
  Copies of proposal: 1
  Board meeting date(s): As required
  Write: Melvin A. Dyson, Secretary-Treasurer
Officers: Frank Hogel, President; Frederick H. Welling, Vice-President; Melvin A. Dyson, Secretary-Treasurer.
Employer Identification Number: 036005697

4151
Windham Foundation, Inc., The ▼
P.O. Box 68
Grafton 05146   (802) 843-2211

Incorporated in 1963 in Vermont.
Donor(s): The Bunbury Company, Inc., Dean Mathey.†
Financial data: (yr. ended 10/31/83): Assets, $25,520,995 (M); expenditures, $1,223,621, including $230,641 for 57 grants (high: $30,000; low: $100) and $116,590 for 357 grants to individuals.
Purpose and activities: A private operating foundation; eighty-five percent of adjusted net income applied to operating programs of foundation, including civic improvement and historic preservation; primary activity is preservation of properties in rural areas of Vermont to maintain their charm and historic, native, or unusual features, with emphasis on restoration of houses in Grafton; remaining fifteen percent of income for general charitable giving, primarily confined to the disadvantaged, youth activities, aid to students and to educational institutions, and organizations assisting the disabled.
Types of support awarded: Operating budgets, seed money, building funds, matching funds, continuing support, student aid, special projects.
Limitations: Giving limited to VT, with emphasis on Windham County. No grants to individuals (except for college scholarship program), or for endowment funds; no loans.
Publications: Annual report, program policy statement, application guidelines.
Application information:
  Initial approach: Letter
  Copies of proposal: 1
  Deadline(s): None
  Board meeting date(s): February, May, July, and October
  Final notification: Following the board meeting
  Write: Stephan A. Morse, Executive Director
Officers and Trustees: Howard W. Stepp, Chairman; James R. Cogan, President; William B. Wright, Vice-President and Treasurer; Frank H. Dickison, Jr., Secretary; Stephan A. Morse, Executive Director; Charles B. Atwater, Samuel W. Lambert III, Edward J. Toohey.
Number of staff: 3 full-time professional; 1 part-time professional.
Employer Identification Number: 136142024

VIRGINIA

4152
Armour (George & Frances) Foundation, Inc.
7342 Ruthven Rd.
Norfolk 23505

Incorporated in 1957 in New York.
Donor(s): George L. Armour, Frances Armour.†
Financial data: (yr. ended 3/31/83): Assets, $1,433,465 (M); expenditures, $273,823, including $127,547 for 50 grants (high: $14,485; low: $50).
Purpose and activities: Grants primarily for hospitals, health agencies, education, and Jewish welfare funds.
Limitations: No grants to individuals.
Officers: Elizabeth Wainger, President; Stephen Wainger, Vice-President and Secretary-Treasurer; Nan Van Etsen, Vice-President.
Employer Identification Number: 136155619

4153
Beazley Foundation, Inc. ☒
3720 Brighton St.
Portsmouth 23707-1788

Incorporated in 1948 in Virginia.
Donor(s): F.W. Beazley,† Marie C. Beazley,† F.W. Beazley, Jr.†
Financial data: (yr. ended 12/31/83): Assets, $12,608,603 (M); gifts received, $26,000; expenditures, $833,002, including $278,021 for 20 grants (high: $100,245) and $64,743 for 4 foundation-administered programs.
Purpose and activities: "To further the cause of charity, education and religion." Grants for operation of community and senior citizens centers and a dental clinic for the indigent. Support also for secondary and medical education, community funds, the aged, youth agencies, and other endeavors, generally within the state of Virginia. Major outside grants to be curtailed during the next few years.
Limitations: Giving primarily in VA. No grants to individuals.
Publications: 990-PF.
Application information:
Initial approach: Proposal
Copies of proposal: 1
Board meeting date(s): March; operating committee meets monthly
Write: Joseph J. Quadros, Jr., Vice-President
Officers and Trustees: Lawrence W. I'Anson, President; Joseph J. Quadros, Jr., Vice-President and Treasurer; John T. Kavanaugh, Vice-President; Malcolm F. Beazley, Jr., Secretary; Mrs. Jewel A. Bush, Mills E. Godwin, Jr., Eugene C. Lipscomb.
Employer Identification Number: 540550100

4154
Best Products Foundation ☒
P.O. Box 26303
Richmond 23260
Office address: 2000 P St., N.W., Washington, DC 20036; Tel.: (202) 331-1714

Established in 1967 in Virginia.
Donor(s): Best Products Company.
Financial data: (yr. ended 6/30/83): Assets, $3,697,654 (M); gifts received, $1,287,618; expenditures, $1,264,853, including $1,161,240 for 833 grants (high: $60,000; low: $25).
Purpose and activities: Broad purposes; support primarily in areas of company operations for museums and cultural programs, a vocational-technical study scholarship program, community and social welfare organizations, including youth agencies, higher education, hospitals, community funds, an employee matching gifts program, and projects concerning reproductive rights.
Types of support awarded: Matching funds, special projects, employee matching gifts, student aid, seed money, emergency funds.
Limitations: Giving primarily in areas of company operations. No support for religious institutions, government-supported organizations, or secondary or elementary schools. No grants to individuals (except through scholarship program administered by Citizens' Scholarship Program), or for operating funds, or building or endowment funds; no loans.
Publications: Application guidelines, program policy statement, 990-PF.
Application information: Information brochures available for general policies, scholarship program, and employee matching gifts program.
Initial approach: Letter
Copies of proposal: 1
Deadline(s): 2 months before board meetings
Board meeting date(s): Usually in January, March, June, September, and November
Write: Susan L. Butler, Executive Director
Officers: Sydney Lewis, President; Robert L. Burrus, Jr., Secretary; Susan L. Butler, Treasurer and Executive Director.
Directors: Frances Lewis, Chair; Robert E.R. Huntley, Andrew M. Lewis.
Employer Identification Number: 237139981

4155
Blount (David S.) Educational Foundation ☒
c/o Colonial American National Bank
P.O. Box 13888
Roanoke 24038

Established in 1973 in Virginia.
Financial data: (yr. ended 3/31/83): Assets, $1,251,840 (M); expenditures, $106,911, including $99,181 for grants to individuals.
Purpose and activities: Scholarships for Virginia residents to obtain a college education at colleges located in Virginia.
Types of support awarded: Student aid.
Limitations: Giving limited to VA.
Application information:
Initial approach: Letter

Deadline(s): None
Trustee: Colonial American National Bank (Colin C. Murchison, Trust Officer).
Employer Identification Number: 546111717

4156
Bryant Foundation ☒
P.O. Box 275
Alexandria 22314

Established about 1949.
Donor(s): J.C. Herbert Bryant.
Financial data: (yr. ended 12/31/83): Assets, $2,228,232 (M); expenditures, $32,558, including $26,434 for 33 grants (high: $10,000; low: $10).
Purpose and activities: Primarily local giving for education, with some support for social services and health.
Limitations: Giving primarily in VA.
Officers: Arthur H. Bryant II, President and Treasurer; Howard W. Smith, Jr., Secretary.
Employer Identification Number: 546032840

4157
Cabell (The Robert G.) III and Maude Morgan Cabell Foundation
P.O. Box 1377
Richmond 23211   (804) 780-2050

Incorporated in 1957 in Virginia.
Donor(s): Robert G. Cabell III,† Maude Morgan Cabell.†
Financial data: (yr. ended 12/31/84): Assets, $10,646,465 (M); expenditures, $681,557, including $600,000 for 13 grants (high: $150,000; low: $15,000; average: $25,000-$50,000).
Purpose and activities: Broad purposes; primarily local giving with emphasis on education, health care, historic preservation, the arts, and cultural projects.
Limitations: Giving primarily in VA. No support for political organizations or special interest groups. No grants to individuals, or for endowment funds, or operating budgets.
Application information:
Initial approach: Letter
Copies of proposal: 1
Deadline(s): Submit proposal in April or October; deadline May 1 and November 1
Board meeting date(s): March, May, and November
Final notification: Before end of calendar year
Write: B. Walton Turnbull, Executive Director
Officers: J. Read Branch,* President; Royal E. Cabell, Jr.,* Secretary; B. Walton Turnbull, Executive Director.
Directors:* Joseph L. Antrim III, Patteson Branch, Jr., Charles Cabell, Robert G. Cabell, Edmund A. Rennolds, Jr., John K.B. Rennolds.
Number of staff: 1 part-time professional; 2 part-time support.
Employer Identification Number: 546039157

4158
Camp (Carrie S.) Foundation, Inc. ⌐
P.O. Box 557
Franklin 23851

Incorporated about 1949 in Virginia.
Donor(s): Edith Clay Camp.
Financial data: (yr. ended 12/31/83): Assets,
$1,333,915 (M); expenditures, $107,459,
including $101,500 for 10 grants (high:
$52,500; low: $250).
Purpose and activities: Primarily local giving
with emphasis on a local recreation
organization; support also for youth agencies
and education.
Types of support awarded: General purposes,
building funds.
Limitations: Giving primarily in VA.
Officers: William M. Camp, Jr.,* President;
Leon Clay Camp,* Vice-President; Mildred M.
Branche, Secretary and Treasurer.
Directors:* Barbara P. Camp, Shirlie S. Camp.
Employer Identification Number: 546052446

4159
Camp Foundation ▼
P.O. Box 813
Franklin 23851   (804) 562-3439

Incorporated in 1942 in Virginia.
Donor(s): James L. Camp, P.D. Camp, and
their families.
Financial data: (yr. ended 12/31/83): Assets,
$5,032,269 (M); expenditures, $458,019,
including $399,700 for 86 grants (high:
$25,000; low: $500; average: $1,000-$20,000)
and $52,000 for 26 grants to individuals.
Purpose and activities: "To provide or aid in
providing in or near the town of Franklin,
Virginia, ... parks, playgrounds, recreational
facilities, libraries, hospitals, clinics, homes for
the aged or needy, refuges for delinquent,
dependent or neglected children, training
schools, or other like institutions or activities."
Grants limited primarily to Franklin,
Southampton County, Isle of Wight County,
and Tidewater, Virginia and northeastern North
Carolina. Grants also to select organizations in
other areas of Virginia, with emphasis on youth
agencies, hospitals, higher and secondary
education, including scholarships filed through
high school principals, recreation, historic
preservation, and cultural programs.
Types of support awarded: Annual
campaigns, seed money, emergency funds,
building funds, equipment, land acquisition,
matching funds, scholarship funds, student aid.
Limitations: Giving primarily in Franklin,
Southampton County, Isle of Wight County,
and Tidewater, VA, and northeastern NC.
Publications: Informational brochure, 990-PF.
Application information:
   Initial approach: Letter
   Copies of proposal: 1
   Deadline(s): Submit proposal between June
   and August; deadline September 1;
   scholarship application deadlines February
   26 for filing with high school principals;
   March 15 for principals to file with
   foundation
   Board meeting date(s): May and December
   Final notification: 3 months

Write: Harold S. Atkinson, Executive
   Secretary
Officers and Directors: Robert C. Ray,
Chairman; Sol W. Rawls, Jr., President; James
L. Camp, Vice-President; John C. Parker,
Secretary; John M. Camp, Jr., Treasurer; John
M. Camp III, W.M. Camp, Jr., Clifford A.
Cutchins, III, William W. Cutchins, Mills E.
Godwin, Jr., Paul Camp Marks, John D.
Munford, S. Waite Rawls, Jr., J.E. Ray III,
Richard E. Ray, Toy D. Savage, Jr., W.H. Story.
Number of staff: 1 part-time professional; 2
part-time support.
Employer Identification Number: 546052488

4160
Camp (J. L.) Foundation, Inc. ⌐
Franklin 23851
Application address: James L. Camp III,
President, P.O. Box 3816, University Station,
Charlottesville, VA 22903; Tel.: (604) 293-7004

Incorporated in 1946 in Virginia.
Donor(s): J.L. Camp, Jr.,† Mrs. J.L. Camp, Jr.,
James L. Camp III.
Financial data: (yr. ended 12/31/83): Assets,
$2,185,743 (M); gifts received, $76,609;
expenditures, $102,811, including $96,927 for
16 grants (high: $37,575; low: $750).
Purpose and activities: Broad purposes;
primarily local giving, with emphasis on higher
and secondary education, a student aid fund,
the arts, youth agencies, and religion.
Types of support awarded: Continuing
support.
Limitations: Giving primarily in VA. No
support for private foundations. No grants for
scholarships, propaganda, or voter registration
drives.
Application information:
   Initial approach: Full proposal
   Deadline(s): None
Officer and Directors: James L. Camp III,
President; Jane G. Camp, Vice-President and
Treasurer; Toy D. Savage, Jr., Vice-President;
Douglas B. Ellis, Secretary.
Employer Identification Number: 540742940

4161
Campbell (Ruth and Henry) Foundation ⌐
c/o Trust Tax Division, Souvran Bank
P.O. Box 26903
Richmond 23261

Established in 1957.
Financial data: (yr. ended 12/31/83): Assets,
$6,104,940 (M); expenditures, $200,609,
including $171,500 for 15 grants (high:
$50,000; low: $1,000).
Purpose and activities: Grants primarily for
higher and secondary education, hospitals, and
youth agencies.
Directors: Paul Camp Marks, Charles R.
Younts, Willie Camp Younts.
Trustee: Souvran Bank.
Employer Identification Number: 546031023

4162
Campbell (Ruth Camp) Charitable Trust ⌐
c/o Souvran Bank, Trust Tax Division
P.O. Box 26903
Richmond 29261

Trust established in 1976 in Virginia.
Donor(s): Ruth Camp McDougall.†
Financial data: (yr. ended 12/31/83): Assets,
$5,297,671 (M); expenditures, $184,194,
including $158,500 for 16 grants (high:
$32,000; low: $1,500).
Purpose and activities: Broad purposes; giving
primarily for higher and secondary education;
support also for youth agencies, and cultural
programs.
Trustee: Souvran Bank.
Employer Identification Number: 546162697

4163
Central Fidelity Banks Inc. Foundation ⌐
c/o Central Fidelity Bank
P.O. Box 27602
Richmond 23261

Established in 1980.
Financial data: (yr. ended 12/31/83): Assets,
$31,740 (M); gifts received, $399,014;
expenditures, $410,900, including $410,628
for 252 grants (high: $50,000; low: $50).
Purpose and activities: Primarily local giving
for higher education, community funds, and
cultural programs; support also for health and
hospitals, youth agencies, and social services.
Limitations: Giving primarily in VA.
Application information:
   Initial approach: Letter
   Deadline(s): None
   Write: Donald F. Delaney, Trustee
Trustees: Donald F. Delaney, Lewis B. Goode,
Jr., Carroll L. Saine.
Employer Identification Number: 546173939

4164
Cole (Quincy) Trust ⌐
c/o First & Merchants National Bank
P.O. Box 26903
Richmond 23261

Donor(s): Quincy Cole.†
Financial data: (yr. ended 6/30/83): Assets,
$3,559,058 (M); expenditures, $266,790,
including $246,795 for 13 grants (high:
$53,895; low: $5,000).
Purpose and activities: Primarily local giving,
with emphasis on cultural programs, including
the performing arts, museums, and historic
preservation, and for higher education.
Limitations: Giving primarily in VA.
Trustee: First & Merchants National Bank.
Employer Identification Number: 546086247

4165
Dalis Foundation ☐
c/o Goodman and Company
500 Plume St. East
Norfolk 23514

Established in 1956.
Donor(s): M. Dan Dalis.†
Financial data: (yr. ended 5/31/83): Assets,
$3,319,070 (M); expenditures, $241,551,
including $220,020 for 3 grants (high:
$140,820; low: $10,000).
Purpose and activities: Primarily local giving,
with emphasis on a Jewish welfare fund,
hospitals, and a television station.
Limitations: Giving primarily in Norfolk, VA.
Officers: Joan Dalis Martone, President;
William P. Oberndorfer, Vice-President;
Alexander L. Martone, Secretary.
Employer Identification Number: 546046229

4166
Dan River Foundation ☐
P.O. Box 261
Danville 24541
Scholarship application address: Chairman,
Scholarship Committee, P.O. Box 2178,
Danville, VA 24541; Tel.: (804) 799-7384

Incorporated in 1957 in Virginia.
Donor(s): Dan River Inc.
Financial data: (yr. ended 12/31/83): Assets,
$2,158,973 (M); expenditures, $306,348,
including $291,937 for 126 grants (high:
$50,000; low: $25) and $3,250 for 4 grants to
individuals.
Purpose and activities: General purposes;
grants in areas of company operations, largely
for community funds, higher education,
including educational associations, scholarships
to company employees and their children, and
welfare organizations; some support for cultural
programs, youth agencies, health agencies and
hospitals.
Types of support awarded: Employee related
scholarships.
Application information: Application form
required.
Initial approach: Letter
Copies of proposal: 1
Deadline(s): February 28
Board meeting date(s): April and December
Write: Grover S. Elliot, President
Officers: Grover S. Elliot,* President; David E.
Cromwell,* Gerard A. Sager,* Vice-Presidents;
G.J. Fluri, Secretary and Treasurer.
Directors:* L.A. Hudson, Jr., D.W. Johnston,
Jr., W.J. Mika, Robert S. Small, James F.
Sutherland.
Employer Identification Number: 546036112

4167
Easley (Andrew H. & Anne O.) Trust
(also known as The Easley Foundation)
c/o Trust Dept., Central Fidelity Bank
P.O. Box 700
Lynchburg 24505

Established in 1968 in Virginia.
Donor(s): Andrew H. Easley.†

Financial data: (yr. ended 6/30/83): Assets,
$3,628,851 (M); gifts received, $10,169;
expenditures, $107,954, including $87,500 for
6 grants (high: $25,000; low: $500).
Purpose and activities: Primarily local giving
to youth organizations, education, health care,
social services, and cultural programs, including
historic preservation.
Limitations: Giving limited to the Lynchburg,
VA, area. No support for religious
organizations. No grants to individuals, or for
research, deficit financing, seed money, annual
campaigns, or conferences and seminars; no
loans.
Publications: Application guidelines.
Application information:
Initial approach: Proposal not exceeding 2
pages
Copies of proposal: 6
Deadline(s): April 1 and October 1
Board meeting date(s): June and December
Write: Secretary, The Easley Foundation
Trustee: Central Fidelity Bank.
Number of staff: None.
Employer Identification Number: 546074720

4168
English Foundation-Trust, The ☐
1522 Main St.
Altavista 24517   (804) 369-4771

Established in 1956 in Virginia.
Financial data: (yr. ended 12/31/83): Assets,
$1,282,742 (M); gifts received, $50,000;
expenditures, $94,623, including $65,285 for
55 grants (high: $10,500; low: $25).
Purpose and activities: Primarily local giving,
with emphasis on civic affairs and community
development; Protestant religious organizations
and church support, and higher education,
including scholarships; support also for health.
Limitations: Giving primarily in the Campbell
County, VA, area.
Application information: Application form
required.
Write: E.R. English, Trustee
Trustees: E.R. English, E.R. English, Jr., W.C.
English, Sarah F. Simpson.
Employer Identification Number: 546036409

4169
English (W. C.) Foundation ☐
Altavista 24517   (804) 324-7241

Trust established in 1954 in Virginia.
Donor(s): Members of the English family.
Financial data: (yr. ended 5/31/83): Assets,
$3,392,680 (M); gifts received, $415,447;
expenditures, $376,240, including $354,219
for 21 grants (high: $120,000; low: $144).
Purpose and activities: Broad purposes;
primarily local giving, with emphasis on
independent secondary schools and Protestant
church activities, including missionary work.
Limitations: Giving primarily in VA.
Application information:
Initial approach: Letter
Deadline(s): None
Write: W.C. English, Chairman

Officers and Trustees: W.C. English,
Chairman; Joan E. Allen, Richard R. Allen,
Louise T. English, Margaret Lester, Morton
Lester.
Employer Identification Number: 546061817

4170
Flagler Foundation, The ▼ ☐
c/o H. William Kuehl, Jr., CPA
1001 East Main St., Suite 601
Richmond 23219   (804) 648-5033

Incorporated in 1963 in Virginia.
Donor(s): Jessie Kenan Wise.†
Financial data: (yr. ended 10/31/83): Assets,
$16,082,712 (M); expenditures, $4,120,759,
including $4,018,861 for 61 grants (high:
$2,470,138; low: $1,000; average: $1,000-
$10,000).
Purpose and activities: Charitable purposes;
support largely for higher and secondary
education, historic restoration and preservation,
and a performing arts center; primarily in
Virginia and Florida.
Limitations: Giving primarily in VA, with
emphasis on Richmond, and in FL, with
emphasis on St. Augustine.
Application information:
Initial approach: Proposal
Deadline(s): October 1
Write: Lawrence Lewis, Jr., President
Officers and Directors: Lawrence Lewis, Jr.,
President and Treasurer; Mary L.F. Wiley, Vice-
President; Janet P. Lewis, Secretary.
Employer Identification Number: 546051282

4171
Gottwald Foundation ☐
c/o F.D. Gottwald, Sr.
P.O. Box 2189
Richmond 23217

Established in 1957.
Donor(s): F.D. Gottwald, Sr.
Financial data: (yr. ended 12/31/83): Assets,
$1,213,077 (M); expenditures, $71,611,
including $69,400 for grants.
Purpose and activities: Primarily local giving,
with emphasis on education, hospitals, cultural
programs, and youth agencies.
Limitations: Giving primarily in VA.
Officers: F.D. Gottwald, Jr., President; Anne C.
Gottwald, Vice-President; Bruce C. Gottwald,
Secretary-Treasurer.
Employer Identification Number: 546040560

4172
Gray (Garland) Foundation
P.O. Box 82
Waverly 23890

Established in Virginia.
Donor(s): Garland Gray.†
Financial data: (yr. ended 12/31/82): Assets,
$7,793,057 (M); expenditures, $506,992,
including $458,583 for 14 grants (high:
$402,500; low: $1,000).
Purpose and activities: Primarily local giving,
with emphasis on education and community
development.

Types of support awarded: Operating budgets, continuing support, annual campaigns, seed money, building funds, equipment, land acquisition, endowment funds, scholarship funds, matching funds.
Limitations: Giving limited to VA, with emphasis on Waverly. No grants to individuals, or for emergency funds, deficit financing, research, special projects, publications or conferences; no loans.
Application information:
  Initial approach: Letter
  Board meeting date(s): As required
Officers and Directors:* Elmon T. Gray,* President-Treasurer; Charles F. Duff,* Wallace Stettinius,* Thomas H. Tullidge,* Vice-Presidents; Carle E. Davis, Secretary.
Number of staff: None.
Employer Identification Number: 546071867

4173
Harris (Holbert L.) Testamentary Trust "B" ⌑
c/o United Virginia Bank
P.O. Box 179
Richmond 23261   (703) 838-3267

Established in 1955 in Virginia.
Financial data: (yr. ended 12/31/82): Assets, $992,205 (M); expenditures, $220,851, including $199,333 for 5 grants (high: $133,333; low: $1,000).
Purpose and activities: Primarily local giving for higher education and social services.
Limitations: Giving primarily in VA.
Application information:
  Initial approach: Letter
  Deadline(s): None
  Write: Henrietta O. Hutchinson, Trust Officer
Trustee: United Virginia Bank.
Employer Identification Number: 546060823

4174
Hastings Trust, The ⌑
c/o Robert C. Hastings
544 Settlers Landing Rd.
Hampton 23669

Established in 1964.
Donor(s): Charles E. Hastings,† Mary C. Hastings.†
Financial data: (yr. ended 12/31/83): Assets, $1,270,003 (M); expenditures, $75,506, including $70,684 for 19 grants (high: $31,714; low: $10).
Purpose and activities: Grants primarily for a private school; support also for higher education.
Trustees: John A. Hastings, Robert C. Hastings, Carol H. Sanders.
Employer Identification Number: 546040247

4175
Hopeman Memorial Fund, Inc. ⌑
435 Essex Ave.
P.O. Box 1345
Waynesboro 22980

Incorporated in 1980 in Virginia.

Donor(s): Hopeman Brothers, Inc., Royston Manufacturing Corporation.
Financial data: (yr. ended 12/31/83): Assets, $1,915,077 (M); expenditures, $560,346, including $560,100 for 12 grants (high: $250,000; low: $100).
Purpose and activities: Giving primarily to conservative public policy institutes; support also for higher education and a foster home.
Types of support awarded: General purposes.
Officers and Trustees: A.A. Hopeman, Jr., President; H.W. Hopeman, Vice-President; Bertram C. Hopeman, Secretary; A.A. Hopeman III, Treasurer.
Employer Identification Number: 541156930

4176
Hopkins (The John Jay) Foundation
1199 North Fairfax St.
P.O. Box 1101
Alexandria 22313

Trust established in 1954 in the District of Columbia.
Donor(s): John J. Hopkins.†
Financial data: (yr. ended 12/31/83): Assets, $1,300,000 (M); expenditures, $150,300, including $100,300 for 34 grants (high: $15,000; low: $250; average: $2,500).
Purpose and activities: Giving to pre-selected charitable organizations, primarily locally and in Washington, D.C., for Protestant church support and church-related schools, and higher education; support also for cultural programs.
Types of support awarded: Continuing support, annual campaigns, building funds, fellowships.
Limitations: Giving primarily in VA and the Washington, DC, metropolitan area. No grants to individuals, or for endowment funds, operating budgets, seed money, emergency funds, deficit financing, land acquisition, matching gifts, special projects, research, publications, or conferences; no loans.
Application information: Proposals not accepted.
  Board meeting date(s): October or November and as required
  Write: Lianne H. Conger, President, or Philip Tierney, Secretary
Officers and Trustees: Lianne H. Conger, President; Philip Tierney, Secretary; Clement E. Conger, Treasurer; Dorothy Young, Jay A. Conger.
Number of staff: None.
Employer Identification Number: 526036649

4177
Jeffress (Thomas F. and Kate Miller) Memorial Trust ▼
c/o Sovran Bank, Trust Division
P.O. Box 26903
Richmond 23261   (804) 788-2964

Established in 1981 in Virginia.
Donor(s): Robert M. Jeffress.†
Financial data: (yr. ended 6/30/84): Assets, $10,243,502 (M); expenditures, $841,399, including $759,648 for 10 grants (high: $200,934; low: $6,650; average: $6,650-$64,000).

Purpose and activities: Primarily local giving, with emphasis on grants to colleges and universities for research activities.
Types of support awarded: Research.
Limitations: Giving primarily in VA. No support for clinical research. No grants to individuals.
Publications: Program policy statement, application guidelines.
Application information:
  Deadline(s): None
  Board meeting date(s): October, February, and May
  Final notification: After meeting at which proposal has been considered
  Write: J. Samuel Gillespie, Jr., Advisor
Trustee: Sovran Bank.
Number of staff: 1 part-time professional; 1 part-time support.
Employer Identification Number: 546094925

4178
Jones (W. Alton) Foundation, Inc. ▼
433 Park St.
Charlottesville 22901   (804) 295-2134

Incorporated in 1944 in New York.
Donor(s): W. Alton Jones.†
Financial data: (yr. ended 12/31/83): Assets, $127,100,917 (M); expenditures, $9,885,747, including $7,288,717 for 92 grants (high: $2,708,333; low: $3,000; average: $4,000-$100,000).
Purpose and activities: Broad purposes; the foundation's energies are currently focused on building a sustainable society and preventing nuclear war, and include grants for promoting renewable natural resources and the encouragement of international accord through disarmament and alternative methods of conflict resolution; some continuing support for institutions previously receiving grants, particularly a biological research institute.
Types of support awarded: General purposes, special projects, research, conferences and seminars, seed money, matching funds.
Limitations: No grants to individuals, or for building or endowment funds, deficit financing, or scholarships and fellowships; no loans.
Publications: Annual report, informational brochure, program policy statement, application guidelines.
Application information:
  Initial approach: Proposal
  Copies of proposal: 1
  Deadline(s): January 15, April 15, July 15, October 15
  Board meeting date(s): March, June, September, and December
  Final notification: 3 months
  Write: R. Jeffrey Kelleher, Director
Officers: Mrs. W. Alton Jones,* Chairman; Patricia Jones Edgerton,* Vice-President and Treasurer; William A. Edgerton,* Secretary; R. Jeffrey Kelleher, Director.
Trustees: James S. Bennett, Bernard F. Curry, Bradford W. Edgerton, Elizabeth Marie Jones, Scott McVay, Diane Edgerton Miller, Francis D. Murnaghan, Jr.
Number of staff: 2 full-time professional; 1 full-time support.
Employer Identification Number: 136034219

4179
Landmark Charitable Foundation
150 West Brambleton Ave.
Norfolk 23510   (804) 446-2018

Incorporated in 1953 in Virginia.
Donor(s): The Virginian - Pilot and Ledger - Star, Greensboro Daily News and Greensboro Record, The Roanoke Times and The World - News, WTAR-AM and FM, WLTY-FM, KLAS-TV, KNTV-TV.
Financial data: (yr. ended 12/31/83): Assets, $5,440,047 (M); gifts received, $925,000; expenditures, $534,235, including $518,665 for 178 grants (high: $71,000; low: $100).
Purpose and activities: Broad purposes; grants largely for higher education, cultural organizations, hospitals, and community funds in areas served by the donor newspapers and radio-TV stations; support also for local and national journalism associations.
Limitations: Giving primarily in VA and NC.
Officers: Richard F. Barry III,* President; J. William Diederich,* Vice-President; Louis F. Ryan,* Secretary; James D. Wagner, Treasurer.
Directors:* Frank Batten, Chairman; Robert D. Benson, Carl W. Mangum, Perry Morgan, Walter Rugaber, John O. Wynne.
Employer Identification Number: 546038902

4180
Lane (The Edward H.) Foundation ¤
E. Franklin Ave.
Altavista 24517

Established in 1956.
Financial data: (yr. ended 11/30/83): Assets, $835,037 (M); gifts received, $65,026; expenditures, $317,381, including $312,276 for 22 grants (high: $50,776; low: $1,000).
Purpose and activities: Primarily local giving for Protestant organizations and church support, education, hospitals and medical research, and a youth agency.
Limitations: Giving primarily in VA.
Officer: John F. Richards, Manager.
Trustees: B.B. Lane, E.H. Lane, L.B. Lane.
Employer Identification Number: 546040095

4181
Lincoln-Lane Foundation, The
One Main Plaza East, Suite 1102
Norfolk 23510   (804) 622-2557

Incorporated in 1928 in Virginia.
Donor(s): John H. Rogers.†
Financial data: (yr. ended 7/31/84): Assets, $3,509,108 (M); expenditures, $220,869, including $181,590 for 132 grants to individuals.
Purpose and activities: Charitable purposes; provides only college scholarship aid for the benefit of students who are permanent local residents of the Tidewater, Virginia area.
Types of support awarded: Student aid.
Limitations: Giving limited to the Tidewater, VA, area. No grants for endowment or building programs, operating budgets, or special projects; no loans.
Publications: Application guidelines, program policy statement.

Application information: New applications available starting October 1. Application form required.
   Initial approach: Letter or telephone
   Board meeting date(s): April, May, July, and December
   Final notification: Scholarship recipients notified in April
   Write: Arthur W. Dennis, Executive Director
Officers and Directors: M. Lee Payne, President; Edward H. Burgess, Vice-President; Arthur W. Dennis, Secretary, Treasurer, and Executive Director; Margery Loomis Krome, Charles E. Jenkins II.
Employer Identification Number: 540601700

4182
Mars Foundation, The
1651 Old Meadow Rd.
McLean 22102   (703) 821-4900

Incorporated in 1956 in Illinois.
Donor(s): Forrest E. Mars.
Financial data: (yr. ended 12/31/82): Assets, $3,345,795 (M); expenditures, $269,519, including $250,000 for 67 grants (high: $15,000; low: $1,000).
Purpose and activities: Broad purposes; support for higher and secondary education, health agencies, the arts, and medical research. Scholarship program discontinued.
Types of support awarded: Continuing support, annual campaigns, building funds, equipment, endowment funds, research, matching funds.
Limitations: No grants to individuals or for scholarships; no loans.
Publications: Application guidelines.
Application information:
   Initial approach: Telephone, letter, or full proposal
   Copies of proposal: 1
   Deadline(s): Submit proposal in September, October, or November; no set deadline
   Board meeting date(s): June and December
   Write: William C. Turnbull, Secretary-Treasurer
Officers and Directors: Forrest E. Mars, Jr., President; John F. Mars, David H. Badger, Vice-Presidents; William C. Turnbull, Secretary-Treasurer; Jacqueline M. Badger, Adrienne B. Mars, Virginia C. Mars.
Number of staff: 2.
Employer Identification Number: 546037592

4183
Massey Foundation ▼ ¤
Massey Bldg.
P.O. Box 26765
Richmond 23261

Established in 1958 in Virginia.
Donor(s): A.T. Massey Coal Co., Inc.
Financial data: (yr. ended 11/30/83): Assets, $21,160,539 (M); expenditures, $1,394,388, including $1,266,883 for 76 grants (high: $303,000; low: $100; average: $1,000-$100,000).

Purpose and activities: Broad purposes; local giving, primarily for higher and secondary education; some support for health services and cultural programs.
Limitations: Giving primarily in VA, particularly Richmond.
Application information:
   Initial approach: Letter
   Write: William E. Massey, President
Officers: William E. Massey, President; William Blair Massey, Vice-President; William E. Massey, Jr., Secretary; E. Morgan Massey, Treasurer.
Employer Identification Number: 546049049

4184
McCrea Foundation ¤
c/o Carle E. Davis
1000 Ross Bldg.
Richmond 23219

Established in 1960 in Virginia.
Donor(s): Mary Corling McCrea.†
Financial data: (yr. ended 2/29/84): Assets, $1,801,620 (M); expenditures, $77,436, including $57,500 for 7 grants (high: $10,000; low: $2,500).
Purpose and activities: Grants for medical research and education.
Officers and Trustees: John L. Welsh, Jr., President; Carle E. Davis, Vice-President; John L. Welsh III, Secretary-Treasurer; George C. Baron.
Employer Identification Number: 546052010

4185
Memorial Foundation for Children, The
c/o United Virginia Bank
P.O. Box 26665
Richmond 23261

Established about 1934 in Virginia.
Donor(s): Alexander S. George,† Elizabeth Strother Scott.†
Financial data: (yr. ended 12/31/83): Assets, $216,899 (M); expenditures, $229,304, including $156,450 for 23 grants (high: $12,000; low: $3,000; average: $10,000).
Purpose and activities: Aid to nonprofit groups in the local area for the care and education of children.
Types of support awarded: Operating budgets, continuing support, seed money, special projects.
Limitations: Giving limited to the Richmond, VA, area. No grants to individuals, or for capital or endowment funds, annual campaigns, emergency funds, deficit financing, matching gifts, publications, conferences, or scholarships and fellowships; no loans.
Publications: Program policy statement, application guidelines.
Application information: Application form required.
   Initial approach: Letter or full proposal
   Copies of proposal: 1
   Deadline(s): Submit proposal preferably in January through June; deadline July 1
   Board meeting date(s): March, June, October, and December
   Final notification: By December

Write: Mrs. Herbert E. Fitzgerald, Jr.
Officers: Mrs. Robert Carter, President; Mrs. Perkins Wilson, Vice-President; Mrs. Paul Sutro, Recording Secretary; Mrs. Armistead Talman, Corresponding Secretary; Mrs. John Oakey, Treasurer.
Number of staff: None.
Employer Identification Number: 540536103

4186
Morgan (Marietta M. & Samuel T.), Jr. Foundation ▼

c/o Sovran Bank, Trust Dept.
P.O. Box 26903
Richmond 23261   (804) 788-2963

Trust established in 1967 in Virginia.
Donor(s): Marietta McNeill Morgan,† Samuel T. Morgan, Jr.†
Financial data: (yr. ended 6/30/83): Assets, $8,172,694 (M); expenditures, $689,813, including $618,700 for 28 grants (high: $60,000; low: $4,000; average: $5,000-$45,000).
Purpose and activities: Broad purposes; capital grants to local organizations only, with emphasis on promoting the cause of the church, fostering Christian education, and supporting agencies concerned with less fortunate local residents.
Types of support awarded: Building funds, equipment, matching funds.
Limitations: Giving limited to VA. No grants to individuals, or for any purposes save capital expenses; no loans.
Publications: Program policy statement, application guidelines.
Application information:
  Initial approach: Letter
  Copies of proposal: 1
  Deadline(s): Submit proposal preferably in February, March, September or October; deadlines May 1 and November 1
  Board meeting date(s): June and December
  Final notification: 3 weeks after board meeting
  Write: Mrs. Elizabeth D. Seaman, Consultant
Trustee: Sovran Bank (Mrs. Elizabeth D. Seaman, Consultant).
Number of staff: 1 part-time professional; 1 part-time support.
Employer Identification Number: 546069447

4187
Norfolk Foundation, The

201 Granby Mall Bldg., Suite 406
Norfolk 23510   (804) 622-7951

Community foundation established in 1950 in Virginia by resolution and declaration of trust.
Financial data: (yr. ended 12/31/84): Assets, $15,336,405 (M); gifts received, $1,024,564; expenditures, $1,011,982, including $728,757 for 42 grants (high: $54,550; low: $653) and $186,271 for 150 grants to individuals.

Purpose and activities: General purposes; support for local hospitals, educational institutions, family and child welfare agencies, a community fund, and cultural and civic programs; certain donor-designated scholarships restricted by residence in nearby localities and/or area colleges, and payable directly to the school.
Types of support awarded: Seed money, building funds, equipment, land acquisition, research, special projects.
Limitations: Giving primarily in the city of Norfolk, VA, and a 50-mile area from its boundaries. No grants to individuals (except for donor-designated scholarships), or for operating budgets, or matching gifts; no loans.
Publications: Annual report, application guidelines, program policy statement.
Application information:
  Initial approach: Letter or telephone
  Copies of proposal: 1
  Deadline(s): For scholarships only, December 1 to March 1
  Board meeting date(s): As required
  Final notification: 3 to 4 months
  Write: R.L. Sheetz, Executive Director
Officer: R.L. Sheetz, Executive Director and Secretary.
Distribution Committee: Charles F. Burroughs, Jr., Chairman; Toy D. Savage, Jr., Vice-Chairman; Pretlow Darden, Raymond L. Gottlieb, Charles L. Kaufman, H.P. McNeal, H.B. Price, III, Bank of Virginia Trust Company, First Virginia Bank of Tidewater, Souran Bank, United Bank-Seaboard.
Number of staff: 2 part-time professional; 1 part-time support.
Employer Identification Number: 540722169

4188
Ohrstrom Foundation, Inc., The

c/o Whitewood
The Plains 22117
Mailing address: c/o George L. Ohrstrom, Jr., 540 Madison Ave., New York, NY 10022

Incorporated in 1953 in Delaware.
Donor(s): Members of the Ohrstrom family.
Financial data: (yr. ended 5/31/83): Assets, $11,067,259 (M); gifts received, $3,000; expenditures, $506,914, including $471,000 for 98 grants (high: $75,000; low: $1,000; average: $1,000-$75,000).
Purpose and activities: Broad purposes; primarily local giving, with emphasis on elementary, secondary and higher education; support also for civic affairs, conservation, hospitals, and museums.
Types of support awarded: Operating budgets, continuing support, annual campaigns, seed money, emergency funds, building funds, equipment, land acquisition, endowment funds, matching funds.
Limitations: Giving primarily in VA and NY. No grants to individuals, or for deficit financing, scholarships and fellowships, research, special projects, publications, or conferences; no loans.
Application information:
  Initial approach: Letter
  Deadline(s): Submit proposal preferably from September to March; deadline March 31
  Final notification: 3 to 6 months

Officers and Trustees: Ricard R. Ohrstrom, George L. Ohrstrom, Jr., Vice-Presidents; Eriberto Scocimara, Treasurer; Magalen O. Bryant, Kenneth N. LaVine.
Number of staff: 1 part-time support.
Employer Identification Number: 546039966

4189
Olmsted (The George) Foundation ⌑

1515 North Courthouse Rd., Suite 305
Arlington 22201   (703) 527-9070

Incorporated in 1960 in Virginia.
Donor(s): George Olmsted.
Financial data: (yr. ended 12/31/83): Assets, $6,165,037 (M); expenditures, $367,802, including $223,810 for 18 grants (high: $50,000; low: $15) and $66,342 for 48 grants to individuals.
Purpose and activities: Grants for higher education and charitable purposes, with emphasis on scholarships for a few career military officers nominated by their branches of the Armed Forces only; scholarships not awarded to non-military students.
Types of support awarded: Scholarship funds.
Limitations: No grants to individuals (except for Olmstead Scholars).
Publications: Annual report, application guidelines, program policy statement.
Application information: Applications handled through Military Services; funds largely committed.
  Board meeting date(s): January, April, July, and October
Officers: B. Frank Taylor,* President; Barbara S. Schimpff, Executive Vice-President; Jerauld L. Olmsted, Secretary and Treasurer.
Directors:* David S. Smith, Chairman; Clyde D. Dean, James L. Holloway III, Darrell K. Koerner, Carol S. Olmsted, George Olmsted, Ben Sternberg, Jr.
Employer Identification Number: 546049005

4190
Olsson (Elis) Memorial Foundation ⌑

c/o Carle E. Davis
1400 Ross Bldg.
Richmond 23219

Established in 1966 in Virginia.
Donor(s): Inga Olsson Nylander,† Signe Maria Olsson.†
Financial data: (yr. ended 12/31/83): Assets, $5,915,730 (M); gifts received, $389,453; expenditures, $303,682, including $276,580 for 43 grants (high: $35,000; low: $250).
Purpose and activities: General purposes; primarily local giving, with emphasis on higher and secondary education and Protestant church support.
Limitations: Giving primarily in VA.
Officers and Trustees: Sture G. Olsson, President; Shirley C. Olsson, Vice-President and Treasurer; Carle E. Davis, Secretary.
Employer Identification Number: 546062436

4191

Perry Foundation, Incorporated ⌺

Court Square
Charlottesville 22901   (804) 977-8590

Incorporated in 1946 in Virginia.
Donor(s): Hunter Perry, Lillian Perry Edwards.
Financial data: (yr. ended 12/31/83): Assets,
$7,364,779 (M); expenditures, $349,892,
including $326,319 for 16 grants (high:
$139,469; low: $1,000).
Purpose and activities: Broad purposes;
primarily local giving, with emphasis on higher
and secondary education; grants also for a
community fund, hospitals and aid to the
handicapped.
Types of support awarded: General purposes,
building funds.
Limitations: Giving primarily in VA. No grants
to individuals, or for operating budgets.
Application information:
  Initial approach: Letter
  Copies of proposal: 5
  Deadline(s): Submit proposal in September or
    October; no set deadline
  Board meeting date(s): Annually
  Write: Junius R. Fishburne, President
Officers and Trustees: Junius R. Fishburne,
President; William A. Perkins, Secretary; Francis
H. Fife, Treasurer; W. Wright Harrison, George
C. Palmer II.
Employer Identification Number: 546036446

4192

Reinsch (Emerson G. & Dolores G.) Foundation ⌺

2040 Columbia Pike
Arlington 22204   (703) 920-3600

Established in 1964.
Financial data: (yr. ended 12/31/83): Assets,
$1,361,442 (M); expenditures, $74,923,
including $68,865 for 34 grants (high: $41,300;
low: $20).
Purpose and activities: Giving primarily in
northern Virginia for health services, with
emphasis on alcoholic rehabilitation; support
also for education.
Types of support awarded: Continuing
support.
Limitations: Giving primarily in northern VA.
Application information:
  Initial approach: Letter, except for
    continuing support
  Write: Emerson G. Reinsch
Trustees: Paul F. Neff, Lola C. Pierre, Emerson
G. Reinsch.
Employer Identification Number: 546055396

4193

Reynolds Metals Company Foundation ▼ ⌺

P.O. Box 27003
Richmond 23261   (804) 281-2222

Foundation established around 1978.
Donor(s): Reynolds Metals Company.

Financial data: (yr. ended 12/31/83): Assets,
$56,307 (M); expenditures, $587,754,
including $507,311 for 153 grants (high:
$100,000; low: $100) and $78,166 for
employee matching gifts.
Purpose and activities: Broad purposes;
support primarily in areas of company
operations with emphasis on higher education,
including an employee matching gifts program,
community funds, hospitals and health
associations, youth agencies, and civic affairs.
Types of support awarded: Employee
matching gifts, building funds, scholarship
funds, special projects.
Limitations: Giving primarily in areas of
company operations, with some emphasis on
Richmond, VA.
Application information:
  Write: Janice Bailey
Officers: Thomas A. Graves, Jr.,* President; R.
Bern Crowl,* Executive Vice-President; Joseph
F. Awad,* John H. Galea,* John R. McGill, D.
Brickford Rider,* Vice-Presidents; Richard I.
Dawes, Secretary; Julian H. Taylor, Treasurer.
Directors:* David P. Reynolds, Chairman;
William S. Leonhardt, Vice-Chairman; William
O. Bourke, Randolph N. Reynolds, William G.
Reynolds, Jr.
Employer Identification Number: 541084698

4194

Reynolds (Richard S.) Foundation

Reynolds Metals Bldg.
Richmond 23261
Application address: David P. Reynolds, 6601
W. Broad St., Richmond, VA 23261; Tel.: (804)
281-4801

Incorporated in 1965 in Virginia.
Donor(s): Julia L. Reynolds.†
Financial data: (yr. ended 6/30/84): Assets,
$2,208,420 (M); gifts received, $18,981;
expenditures, $143,095, including $120,500
for 8 grants (high: $50,000; low: $1,000).
Purpose and activities: Broad purposes;
primarily local giving, with emphasis on higher
and secondary education, health, hospitals, and
museums.
Limitations: Giving primarily in VA.
Application information:
  Initial approach: Letter
  Deadline(s): None
Officers and Directors: David P. Reynolds,
President; Mrs. Glenn R. Martin, Vice-
President; Richard S. Reynolds, III, Secretary;
William G. Reynolds, Jr., Treasurer.
Number of staff: None.
Employer Identification Number: 546037003

4195

Richardson (C. E.) Benevolent Foundation ⌺

74 Main St., Rm. 211
P.O. Box 1120
Pulaski 24301   (703) 980-6628
Additional telephone number: (703) 980-1704

Established in 1979.

Financial data: (yr. ended 5/31/83): Assets,
$2,099,632 (M); expenditures, $181,838,
including $158,700 for 23 grants (high:
$10,000; low: $2,000).
Purpose and activities: Local giving, with
support for programs for needy children, aged
people, and indigent or handicapped persons,
and for private colleges and universities;
support also for cultural programs.
Limitations: Giving limited to VA.
Publications: Program policy statement,
application guidelines.
Application information: Application form
required.
  Initial approach: Letter or telephone
  Deadline(s): 1 month after published public
    notice stating date, usually September 15
  Write: Betty S. King, Secretary
Officer: Betty S. King, Secretary.
Trustees: James D. Miller, Annie S. Muire,
James C. Turk.
Employer Identification Number: 510227549

4196

Richmond Community Foundation, Greater ⌺

c/o R.J. Lechner
311 Forest Plaza Bldg., 7201 Glen Forest Dr.
Richmond 23226

Established in 1918 in Virginia.
Financial data: (yr. ended 12/31/83): Assets,
$1,012,004 (L); gifts received, $123,347;
expenditures, $46,869, including $23,000 for
11 grants (high: $5,000; low: $500).
Purpose and activities: Local giving for
charitable purposes.
Types of support awarded: Continuing
support, endowment funds, research, operating
budgets, annual campaigns, employee matching
gifts, consulting services, technical assistance.
Limitations: Giving limited to Richmond, VA.
No grants to individuals, or for scholarships,
fellowships, seed money, emergency funds,
deficit financing, building funds, equipment,
land acquisition, publications, or conferences
and seminars; no loans.
Publications: Annual report, application
guidelines.
Application information:
  Initial approach: Telephone or proposal
  Copies of proposal: 1
  Deadline(s): December 1
  Board meeting date(s): As needed
    (approximately 10 times a year)
  Final notification: 60 days
Officers: William H. Higgins, Jr., M.D.,
Chairman; Anne Marie Whittemore, Vice-
Chairman; John A. Mapp, Secretary and
Executive Director; S. Buford Scott, Treasurer.
Number of staff: 1 part-time professional; 1
part-time support.
Employer Identification Number: 237009135

4197

Robertshaw Controls Company Charitable and Educational Foundation ⌺

1701 Byrd Ave.
P.O. Box 26544
Richmond 23261   (804) 281-0702

Trust established in 1958 in Virginia.
Donor(s): Robertshaw Controls Company.
Financial data: (yr. ended 12/31/83): Assets,
$202,159 (M); gifts received, $80,000;
expenditures, $163,036, including $162,211
for 147 grants (high: $15,000; low: $25).
Purpose and activities: General giving, with
emphasis on community funds, higher
education, youth agencies, hospitals, and
health agencies.
Limitations: No grants to individuals.
Application information:
 Initial approach: Proposal
 Copies of proposal: 1
 Deadline(s): November 1
 Board meeting date(s): Semimonthly
 Write: Robert W. Pendergast, Vice-President
Officer: Robert W. Pendergast, Vice-President.
Trustee: Central Fidelity Bank.
Employer Identification Number: 546033124

4198
Scott (The William H., John G., and Emma) Foundation
Davenport & Company
Ross Bldg., Eighth and Main Sts.
Richmond 23219   (804) 780-2035

Incorporated in 1956 in Virginia.
Donor(s): Rev. John G. Scott,† Emma Scott
Taylor.
Financial data: (yr. ended 9/30/84): Assets,
$3,850,000 (M); expenditures, $3,135,977,
including $3,121,356 for 80 grants (high:
$100,000; low: $2,000).
Purpose and activities: Broad purposes;
emphasis on higher and secondary education.
Limitations: Giving primarily in VA. No grants
for endowment funds, scholarships, or
operating budgets.
Application information:
 Initial approach: Letter
 Copies of proposal: 2
 Deadline(s): Submit proposal preferably in
  November; deadline December 1
 Board meeting date(s): November,
  December, January, and June, and as
  required
 Final notification: 1 year
 Write: Clinton Webb, Treasurer
Officers: Thomas W. Murrell, Jr., M.D.,*
President; John W. Riely,* Vice-President; R.E.
Cabell, Jr.,* Secretary; Clinton Webb, Treasurer
and Assistant to President.
Trustees:* Reverend Don Raby Edwards,
Charles M. Guthridge, Frank W. Heindl, T.
Justin Moore, Jr., Edwin P. Munson, Elizabeth
Copeland Norfleet, C. Cotesworth Pinckney.
Number of staff: 1 full-time professional.
Employer Identification Number: 540648772

4199
Seay (George and Effie) Memorial Trust
c/o Sovran Bank, Trust Dept.
P.O. Box 26903
Richmond 23261   (804) 788-2963

Trust established in 1957 in Virginia.
Donor(s): George J. Seay,† Effie L. Seay.†

Financial data: (yr. ended 6/30/83): Assets,
$1,719,790 (M); expenditures, $119,143,
including $109,158 for 23 grants (high:
$10,500; low: $109).
Purpose and activities: Broad purposes; local
giving, with emphasis on higher and secondary
education, youth agencies, and assistance for
the handicapped.
Types of support awarded: General purposes,
operating budgets, building funds, equipment,
special projects, publications, scholarship
funds, matching funds.
Limitations: Giving limited to VA. No grants
to individuals, or for endowment funds; no
loans.
Publications: Program policy statement,
application guidelines.
Application information:
 Initial approach: Letter
 Copies of proposal: 1
 Deadline(s): Submit proposal preferably in
  February or March, and September or
  October; deadlines May 1 and November 1
 Board meeting date(s): June and December
 Final notification: 3 weeks after board
  meetings
 Write: Mrs. Elizabeth D. Seaman, Consultant
Trustee: Sovran Bank (Elizabeth D. Seaman,
Consultant).
Number of staff: 1.
Employer Identification Number: 546030604

4200
Slemp Foundation, The ¤
c/o W. C. Edmonds
Big Stone Gap 24219
Mailing address: c/o The First National Bank
of Cincinnati, P.O. Box 1118, Cincinnati, OH
45201; Tel.: (513) 852-4585

Trust established in 1943 in Virginia.
Donor(s): C. Bascom Slemp.†
Financial data: (yr. ended 6/30/83): Assets,
$4,347,182 (M); expenditures, $360,019,
including $125,375 for 31 grants (high:
$31,529; low: $50) and $166,900 for 209
grants to individuals.
Purpose and activities: Charitable and
educational purposes; maintenance of three
named institutions; improvement of health of
residents of Lee and Wise counties, Virginia, or
their descendants wherever located; primarily
local giving, with emphasis on scholarships, a
museum, higher and secondary education,
libraries, and hospitals.
Types of support awarded: Student aid.
Limitations: Giving limited to Lee and Wise
counties, VA, for scholarship grants.
Application information: Application form
required.
 Initial approach: Letter
 Copies of proposal: 1
 Deadline(s): October 1
 Board meeting date(s): April, July, and
  November
Trustees: Campbell S. Edmonds, W. Campbell
Edmonds, John A. Reid, Nancy E. Smith.
Employer Identification Number: 316025080

4201
Sovran Foundation, Inc.
(formerly First and Merchants Foundation, Inc.)
c/o Trust Dept., Sovran Bank, N.A.
P.O. Box 26903
Richmond 23219

Incorporated in 1966 in Virginia.
Donor(s): Sovran Financial Corporation.
Financial data: (yr. ended 12/31/82): Assets,
$24,410 (M); gifts received, $330,633;
expenditures, $374,849, including $356,462
for 153 grants (high: $25,000; low: $150) and
$17,894 for 134 employee matching gifts.
Purpose and activities: Primarily local giving,
in areas where Sovran offices are located, with
emphasis on higher education, community
funds, health, and the arts.
Types of support awarded: Employee
matching gifts, continuing support, annual
campaigns, building funds, equipment, land
acquisition, endowment funds, matching funds,
publications.
Limitations: Giving limited to communities in
which the company has facilities. No grants to
individuals, or for scholarships or fellowships;
no loans.
Publications: Program policy statement,
application guidelines.
Application information:
 Initial approach: Letter
 Copies of proposal: 1
 Deadline(s): May 15 and October 15
 Board meeting date(s): July and January
 Write: Mrs. Elizabeth D. Seaman, Secretary-
  Treasurer
Officer: Elizabeth D. Seaman, Secretary-
Treasurer.
Trustee: Sovran Financial Corporation.
Employer Identification Number: 546066961

4202
Taylor Foundation, The ¤
6969 Tidewater Dr.
P.O. Box 2556
Norfolk 23501

Trust established in 1951 in Virginia.
Donor(s): West India Fruit and Steamship
Company, Inc., members of the Taylor family,
and others.
Financial data: (yr. ended 12/31/83): Assets,
$1,436,580 (M); expenditures, $159,074,
including $148,670 for 34 grants (high:
$75,000; low: $250).
Purpose and activities: General giving,
primarily in Virginia and the Southeast, with
emphasis on hospitals, higher education,
Protestant church support, social agencies, and
a sailors' retirement home.
Limitations: Giving primarily in VA. No grants
to individuals.
Officers and Trustees: William R. Taylor,
President; J. Lewis Rahls, Jr., Secretary.
Employer Identification Number: 540555235

4203
Thalhimer Brothers Foundation ☒
615 East Broad St.
Richmond 23219   (804) 643-4211

Incorporated in 1950 in Virginia.
Donor(s): Thalhimer Brothers, Inc., and its subsidiaries.
Financial data: (yr. ended 11/30/83): Assets, $778 (M); gifts received, $195,366; expenditures, $194,654, including $192,555 for 65 grants (high: $40,000; low: $100).
Purpose and activities: Primarily local giving, with emphasis on community funds, higher education, environmental activities, Jewish welfare funds, and cultural programs, especially in the performing arts.
Limitations: Giving primarily in Richmond, VA. No grants to individuals.
Application information:
 Initial approach: Letter
 Copies of proposal: 1
 Deadline(s): None
 Write: James E. Branson
Officers and Directors: William B. Thalhimer, Jr., President; Charles G. Thalhimer, Vice-President; James E. Branson, Secretary and Treasurer;.
Employer Identification Number: 546047107

4204
Thalhimer (William B.), Jr. and Family Foundation ☒
615 East Broad St.
Richmond 23219   (804) 643-4211

Incorporated in 1953 in Virginia.
Donor(s): William B. Thalhimer, Jr., Barbara J. Thalhimer.
Financial data: (yr. ended 10/31/83): Assets, $1,308,823 (M); expenditures, $113,302, including $105,680 for 51 grants (high: $27,000; low: $10).
Purpose and activities: Primarily local giving, with emphasis on Jewish welfare funds and temple support; grants also for cultural progams and higher education.
Limitations: Giving primarily in VA.
Application information:
 Initial approach: Letter
 Deadline(s): None
 Write: William B. Thalhimer, Jr., President
Officers and Directors: William B. Thalhimer, Jr., President; Charles G. Thalhimer, Robert L. Thalhimer, William B. Thalhimer III, Vice-Presidents; Barbara J. Thalhimer, Secretary-Treasurer; Rhoda R. Thalhimer.
Employer Identification Number: 546047110

4205
Thomas (Theresa A.) Memorial Foundation ☒
Sovran Center
1111 E. Main St., 23rd Fl.
Richmond 23219

Established in 1975.
Financial data: (yr. ended 8/31/83): Assets, $5,242,308 (M); gifts received, $3,139,031; expenditures, $105,744, including $93,134 for 12 grants (high: $30,000; low: $1,000).
Purpose and activities: Primarily local giving for hospitals and health services, particularly for emergency rescue squads; support also for a college.
Types of support awarded: Operating budgets.
Limitations: Giving primarily in VA.
Officers and Directors: Charles L. Reed, President and Treasurer; Thomas P. Carr, Secretary; James C. Roberts.
Employer Identification Number: 510146629

4206
Three Swallows Foundation ☒
1300 N. 17th St., Suite 1400
Rosslyn 22209

Established in 1981 in Virginia.
Financial data: (yr. ended 10/31/82): Assets, $32,652,116 (M); expenditures, $251,496, including $232,061 for 29 grants (high: $133,811; low: $50).
Purpose and activities: First year of operation in 1981/82; support mainly for the construction of a school; grants also for higher education and religious organizations.
Officers: Paul N. Temple, President; Diane E. Temple, Secretary; D. Barry Abell, Treasurer.
Employer Identification Number: 521234546

4207
Thurman (The Edgar A.) Charitable Foundation for Children
P.O. Box 13888
Roanoke 24034   (703) 344-8851

Trust established in 1953 in Virginia.
Donor(s): Edgar A. Thurman.†
Financial data: (yr. ended 6/30/84): Assets, $3,500,000 (M); expenditures, $230,000, including $175,000 for 35 grants (high: $10,000; low: $1,000).
Purpose and activities: To provide maintenance, care, and education for needy children, preferably in Roanoke City and Roanoke County; primarily local giving, with emphasis on child welfare, orphanages, youth agencies, preschool education, and social agencies.
Limitations: Giving primarily in Roanoke City and Roanoke County, VA. No grants to individuals, or for building or endowment funds, salaries, or deficit financing.
Publications: Program policy statement, application guidelines.
Application information: Application form required.
 Initial approach: Letter
 Copies of proposal: 2
 Deadline(s): Submit proposal in first quarter of year; deadline June 15
 Board meeting date(s): Annually
 Final notification: August 15
 Write: Harry L. Shinn, Jr., Foundation Manager
Distribution Committee: G. Chapman Duffy, Kenneth L. Neathery, Jr., Charles W. Walker.
Trustee: Colonial American National Bank (Colin C. Murchison, Trust Officer).
Employer Identification Number: 546113281

4208
Titmus Foundation, Inc., The
P.O. Box 10
Sutherland 23885   (804) 265-5834

Incorporated in 1945 in Virginia.
Donor(s): Edward Hutson Titmus, Sr.†
Financial data: (yr. ended 1/31/83): Assets, $5,839,737 (M); expenditures, $254,559, including $190,321 for 72 grants (high: $43,800; low: $100) and $52,694 for 100 employee matching gifts.
Purpose and activities: Broad purposes; primarily local giving, with emphasis on Baptist church support and religious organizations, higher education, health, and child welfare.
Limitations: Giving primarily in VA.
Officers: Edward B. Titmus, President; George M. Modlin, John J. Whitt, Vice-Presidents; Margaret V. Pamplin, Secretary-Treasurer.
Employer Identification Number: 546051332

4209
Treakle (The J. Edwin) Foundation, Inc.
P.O. Box 1157
Gloucester 23061   (804) 693-3101

Incorporated in 1963 in Virginia.
Donor(s): J. Edwin Treakle.†
Financial data: (yr. ended 4/30/84): Assets, $2,318,552 (L); expenditures, $149,593, including $95,200 for 50 grants (high: $8,400; low: $200).
Purpose and activities: Broad purposes; primarily local giving, with emphasis on Protestant church support, community development, youth agencies, higher education, hospitals, and cultural organizations.
Limitations: Giving primarily in VA. No grants to individuals.
Application information: Application form required.
 Copies of proposal: 1
 Deadline(s): Submit proposal between January 1 and April 30
 Board meeting date(s): Thursday after second Monday in February, April, June, August, October, and December
 Write: John W. Cooke, Treasurer
Officers and Directors: James B. Martin, President; Harry E. Dunn, Vice-President; J. Kirkland Jarvis, Secretary; John W. Cooke, Treasurer.
Number of staff: 2 full-time support.
Employer Identification Number: 546051620

4210
Truland Foundation, The ☒
1511 North 22nd St.
Arlington 22209

Trust established in 1954 in Virginia.
Donor(s): Truland of Florida, Inc., and members of the Truland family.
Financial data: (yr. ended 3/31/84): Assets, $1,936,100 (M); gifts received, $50,000; expenditures, $92,634, including $87,437 for 78 grants (high: $50,000; low: $5).

Purpose and activities: Broad purposes; primarily local giving, with emphasis on conservation; some support also for community welfare, higher education, and the arts.
Limitations: Giving primarily in VA.
Trustees: Alice O. Truland, Robert W. Truland, Walter R. Truland.
Employer Identification Number: 546037172

4211
United Virginia Charitable Trust
c/o United Virginia Bank
P.O. Box 26665
Richmond 23261 (804) 782-5074

Established in 1964.
Financial data: (yr. ended 12/31/82): Assets, $1,293,621 (M); expenditures, $300,220, including $276,850 for 22 grants (high: $50,000; low: $600).
Purpose and activities: Primarily local giving for higher education, hospitals, and cultural programs.
Types of support awarded: General purposes, continuing support, annual campaigns, building funds, equipment, land acquisition, endowment funds, matching funds.
Limitations: Giving primarily in VA. No support for government-supported organizations, or for religious or national health agencies. No grants to individuals, or for scholarships and fellowships; no loans.
Publications: Informational brochure, program policy statement, application guidelines.
Application information:
  Initial approach: Letter, telephone, or full proposal in 1 copy
  Copies of proposal: 1
  Deadline(s): September 30
  Board meeting date(s): Semiannually and as required
  Final notification: 1 to 6 months
  Write: Horace W. Harrison, Executive Vice-President
Trustee: United Virginia Bank (Horace H. Harrison, Executive Vice-President - Trusts).
Number of staff: 3.
Employer Identification Number: 546054608

4212
Universal Leaf Foundation ¤
Hamilton St. at Broad
P.O. Box 25099
Richmond 23260

Established in 1975 in Virginia.
Donor(s): Universal Leaf Tobacco Co., Inc.
Financial data: (yr. ended 6/30/84): Assets, $316,346 (M); expenditures, $320,907, including $318,199 for grants.
Purpose and activities: Primarily local giving, with emphasis on higher education, community funds, museums, and youth agencies.
Limitations: Giving primarily in VA.
Officers: T.R. Towers,* President; W.L. Chandler,* Vice-President; L.D. Owen, Secretary; O.K. Dozier, Treasurer.
Directors: S.G. Christian, Jr., J.M. White.
Employer Identification Number: 510162337

4213
UVB Foundation
919 East Main St.
Richmond 23219 (804) 782-5074

Established in 1973 in Virginia.
Donor(s): United Virginia Bank, and other affiliates of United Virginia Bankshares.
Financial data: (yr. ended 12/31/82): Assets, $2,128 (M); gifts received, $460,000; expenditures, $390,743, including $337,048 for 198 grants (high: $67,500; low: $10) and $53,405 for 249 employee matching gifts.
Purpose and activities: Priority given to community funds and established educational and cultural organizations in the communities served by bank affiliates; support also for capital campaigns of private colleges and universities located in Virginia.
Types of support awarded: Building funds, employee matching gifts.
Limitations: Giving limited to VA and communities served by bank affiliates. No support for government-supported, religious, or national health agencies. No grants to individuals, or for research, or scholarships and fellowships; no loans.
Publications: Informational brochure, program policy statement, application guidelines.
Application information:
  Initial approach: Letter, telephone, or full proposal
  Copies of proposal: 1
  Deadline(s): Submit proposal before October
  Board meeting date(s): Semiannually as required
  Write: Horace H. Harrison, President
Officers: Horace H. Harrison, President; Lewis B. Flinn, Jr., Secretary-Treasurer.
Employer Identification Number: 237336418

4214
Virginia Environmental Endowment ▼
P.O. Box 790
Richmond 23206 (804) 644-5000

Incorporated in 1977 in Virginia.
Donor(s): Allied Chemical Corporation, FMC Corporation.
Financial data: (yr. ended 3/31/84): Assets, $12,830,143 (M); expenditures, $1,003,867, including $729,559 for 18 grants (high: $250,000; low: $2,875; average: $52,605).
Purpose and activities: Grants in Virginia are limited to support of activities to improve the quality of the environment. Grants for Water Quality Program limited to projects related to water quality in the Ohio River and Kanawha River valley regions.
Types of support awarded: Operating budgets, continuing support, seed money, matching funds, scholarship funds, loans, special projects, research.
Limitations: Giving limited to VA and the Ohio River and Kanawha River valley regions. No grants to individuals, or for capital or endowment funds, annual campaigns, emergency funds, or deficit financing.
Publications: Annual report, program policy statement, application guidelines.
Application information:
  Initial approach: Full proposal

Copies of proposal: 4
Deadline(s): April 15, July 15, October 15, and January 15
Board meeting date(s): Usually in June, September, December, and March
Final notification: 3 months
Write: Gerald P. McCarthy, Executive Director
Officers: William B. Cummings,* President; Henry W. MacKenzie, Jr.,* Senior Vice-President; Ross P. Bullard,* Vice-President; Gerald P. McCarthy, Secretary and Executive Director; George L. Yowell,* Treasurer.
Directors:* Dixon M. Butler, Virginia R. Holton, Thomas K. Wolfe, Jr.
Number of staff: 2 full-time professional; 1 full-time support.
Employer Identification Number: 541041973

4215
Washington Forrest Foundation
2300 Ninth St. South
Arlington 22204 (703) 920-3688

Incorporated in 1968 in Virginia.
Donor(s): Benjamin M. Smith.†
Financial data: (yr. ended 6/30/83): Assets, $4,544,454 (M); expenditures, $352,673, including $166,673 for 56 grants (high: $16,701; low: $500).
Purpose and activities: Primarily local giving, with emphasis on the arts and humanities, education, health, religion, science, and welfare.
Types of support awarded: General purposes, operating budgets, continuing support, annual campaigns, seed money, emergency funds, building funds, equipment, matching funds.
Limitations: Giving primarily in northern VA. No grants to individuals, or for endowment funds, or scholarships and fellowships; no loans.
Publications: Program policy statement, application guidelines.
Application information:
  Initial approach: Letter
  Copies of proposal: 1
  Deadline(s): 1 month before meeting month
  Board meeting date(s): July, October, January, and May
  Final notification: 1 week
  Write: Berryman Davis, Executive Director
Officers and Directors: Benjamin M. Smith, Jr., President; Mrs. David S. Peete, Vice-President; Carolyn V. Dameron, Secretary; Edward M. Smith, Treasurer.
Number of staff: None.
Employer Identification Number: 237002944

4216
Wheat Foundation ¤
707 E. Main St.
Richmond 23219 (804) 649-2311

Established in 1959.
Financial data: (yr. ended 3/31/84): Assets, $498,259 (M); expenditures, $171,742, including $165,484 for 44 grants (high: $15,000; low: $500).
Purpose and activities: Giving primarily in Virginia, West Virginia, and North Carolina, for higher and secondary education, hospitals, and health services.

Types of support awarded: Building funds, professorships, operating budgets, endowment funds.
Limitations: Giving primarily in VA, WV, and NC. No grants to individuals.
Application information:
  Deadline(s): None
  Write: William V. Daniel, Vice-President
Officers: James C. Wheat, Jr.,* President; William V. Daniel,* Vice-President and Treasurer; F. Carlyle Tiller,* Vice-President; A. Jack Brent II, Secretary and Treasurer.
Trustees:* William B. Lucas.
Employer Identification Number: 546047119

4217
Wilfred Fund, The
c/o Yount, Hyde & Barbour
P.O. Box 467
Middleburg 22117   (703) 687-6381

Incorporated in 1956 in New York.
Donor(s): Frederick M. Warburg.†
Financial data: (yr. ended 6/30/83): Assets, $1,391,707 (M); expenditures, $124,535, including $115,125 for 56 grants (high: $20,250; low: $50).
Purpose and activities: Broad purposes, with emphasis on secondary education, hospitals, and social agencies.
Limitations: Giving primarily in New York City, NY, and VA. No grants to individuals.
Application information:
  Initial approach: Letter
  Copies of proposal: 1
  Deadline(s): Submit proposal preferably between January and May or September and December
  Board meeting date(s): Monthly
  Write: Mrs. Wilma S. Warburg, President
Officers and Directors: Wilma S. Warburg, President; Tom Slaughter, Vice-President; Jerome A. Manning, Secretary; Marc Keller, Treasurer.
Employer Identification Number: 136088216

WASHINGTON

4218
Anderson Foundation
P.O. Box 24304
Seattle 98124   (206) 762-0600

Established in 1952.
Donor(s): Charles M. Anderson.
Financial data: (yr. ended 6/30/83): Assets, $1,429,235 (M); gifts received, $50,000; expenditures, $72,409, including $61,350 for 30 grants (high: $10,000; low: $150).

Purpose and activities: Primarily local giving, with emphasis on Protestant church support, higher education, and health agencies; support also for hospitals and a medical research center.
Types of support awarded: Building funds, equipment, land acquisition, program-related investments, research, scholarship funds, professorships.
Limitations: Giving primarily in the Pacific Northwest, particularly WA. No grants to individuals, or for endowment funds or matching gifts; no loans.
Application information:
  Copies of proposal: 1
  Board meeting date(s): Semiannually
Officers: Charles M. Anderson, President; Gordon D. Lawrence, Vice-President; Dorothy I. Anderson, Secretary and Treasurer.
Employer Identification Number: 916031724

4219
Archibald (Norman) Charitable Foundation
c/o First Interstate Bank of Washington
P.O. Box 21927
Seattle 98111   (206) 292-3540

Established in 1976 in Washington.
Donor(s): Norman Archibald.†
Financial data: (yr. ended 9/30/84): Assets, $4,236,945 (M); expenditures, $243,647, including $221,400 for 58 grants (high: $25,000; low: $1,000; average: $4,900).
Purpose and activities: Giving primarily in the Puget Sound region, with emphasis on cultural programs, youth and child welfare agencies, higher and secondary education, health, Christian organizations, social agencies, conservation, and community funds.
Types of support awarded: General purposes, operating budgets, seed money, building funds, equipment, land acquisition.
Limitations: Giving primarily in the Puget Sound region of WA. No support for government entities. No grants to individuals, or for endowment funds, scholarships, fellowships, research, special projects, publications, or matching gifts; no loans.
Publications: Annual report, application guidelines.
Application information:
  Initial approach: Proposal
  Copies of proposal: 3
  Deadline(s): Submit proposal preferably between September and May
  Board meeting date(s): About 6 times a year, between October and June
  Write: Stuart H. Prestrud, Secretary
Managers: Lowell P. Mickelwait, Chairman; Stuart H. Prestrud, Secretary; Durwood Alkire.
Trustee: First Interstate Bank of Washington.
Employer Identification Number: 916215419

4220
Bishop (E. K. and Lillian F.) Foundation ▼
c/o Rainier National Bank, Charitable Services Dept.
P.O. Box 3966
Seattle 98124   (206) 621-4445

Trust established in 1971 in Washington.
Donor(s): E.K. Bishop,† Lillian F. Bishop.†
Financial data: (yr. ended 4/30/83): Assets, $12,709,245 (M); expenditures, $653,845, including $568,821 for 30 grants (high: $115,000; low: $1,000).
Purpose and activities: To promote the welfare of young people through grants to educational, cultural, and welfare organizations, preferably in Grays Harbor County or the state of Washington.
Types of support awarded: Seed money, building funds, equipment, matching funds, general purposes.
Limitations: Giving primarily in Grays Harbor County or state of WA. No grants to individuals, or for endowment funds, research, scholarships, or fellowships; no loans.
Publications: Program policy statement, application guidelines.
Application information: Application form required.
  Initial approach: Letter
  Deadline(s): January 1, April 1, July 1, and October 1
  Board meeting date(s): January, April, July, and October
  Final notification: 2 to 3 months
Directors: Maxwell Carlson, Gladys Phillips, Janet Skadon.
Trustee: Rainier National Bank.
Employer Identification Number: 916116724

4221
Bishop Foundation
Rainier National Bank, Trust Div.
P.O. Box 3966
Seattle 98124   (206) 621-4445

Trust established in 1962 in Washington.
Donor(s): E.K. Bishop,† Lillian F. Bishop.†
Financial data: (yr. ended 7/31/83): Assets, $1,558,362 (M); expenditures, $98,040, including $78,160 for 2 grants (high: $75,660; low: $2,500).
Purpose and activities: Cure of diseases of the eye, the correction of faulty vision, the relief of needy sufferers from eye afflictions, and for use in related fields.
Limitations: Giving primarily in WA. No grants to individuals.
Application information: Funds presently committed.
  Board meeting date(s): Semiannually
  Write: c/o Charitable Services Department
Directors: Charles H. Badgley, Winston Brown, John Hall, Carl D.J. Jensen, M.D., Walter Petersen, M.D.
Trustee: Rainier National Bank.
Employer Identification Number: 916027252

4222
Bloedel Foundation, Inc., The ⌘
7501 Northeast Dolphin Dr.
Bainbridge Island 98110

Incorporated in 1952 in Delaware.
Donor(s): Prentice Bloedel, J.H. Bloedel,† Eulalie Bloedel Schneider, Virginia Merrill Bloedel.

Financial data: (yr. ended 6/30/83): Assets, $2,790,451 (M); gifts received, $500,000; expenditures, $168,974, including $143,500 for 66 grants (high: $25,000; low: $50).
Purpose and activities: Charitable and educational purposes; primarily local giving, with emphasis on museums, the performing arts, and Protestant church support; some support for secondary education, social agencies and conservation.
Limitations: Giving primarily in WA.
Officers and Trustees: Prentice Bloedel, President; Virginia Bloedel Wright, Vice-President; John E. Gordon, Secretary-Treasurer; Virginia Merrill Bloedel, Eulalie Bloedel Schneider.
Employer Identification Number: 916035027

4223
Boeing Company Charitable Trust, The ▼ ⌑
c/o First Interstate Bank of Washington
P.O. Box 21927
Seattle 98111

Trust established in 1964 in Washington as successor to the Boeing Airplane Company Charitable Trust, established in 1952.
Donor(s): The Boeing Company.
Financial data: (yr. ended 12/31/83): Assets, $11,551,800 (M); expenditures, $1,520,091, including $1,457,500 for 7 grants (high: $899,500; low: $40,000; average: $40,000-$175,000).
Purpose and activities: Charitable purposes; primarily local giving, with emphasis on community funds and cultural programs.
Types of support awarded: Employee matching gifts.
Limitations: Giving primarily in WA.
Trustee: First Interstate Bank of Washington.
Employer Identification Number: 916056738

4224
Brechemin Family Foundation, The ⌑
3036 Cascadia Ave. South
Seattle 98144

Established in 1963.
Donor(s): Charlotte B. Brechemin.
Financial data: (yr. ended 6/30/83): Assets, $661,526 (M); gifts received, $165,000; expenditures, $214,628, including $207,504 for 12 grants (high: $47,500; low: $2,000).
Purpose and activities: Primarily local giving, with emphasis on cultural programs, including music and other performing arts; some support also for higher education and a secondary school.
Limitations: Giving primarily in Seattle, WA.
Officers and Trustees: Charlotte B. Brechemin, President; Gordon Harper, Mina B. Person, Vice-Presidents; John F. Hall, Secretary; Stuart H. Prestrud, Treasurer.
Employer Identification Number: 916050290

4225
Bullitt Foundation, Inc., The
333 Dexter Ave. North
Seattle 98109 (206) 343-3997

Incorporated in 1952 in Washington.
Donor(s): Members of the Bullitt family.
Financial data: (yr. ended 2/28/85): Assets, $1,600,000 (M); expenditures, $205,000, including $173,000 for 27 grants (high: $25,000; low: $1,000).
Purpose and activities: Broad purposes; primarily local giving, with emphasis on conservation and environmental programs, and organizations to promote world peace.
Limitations: Giving primarily in the Pacific Northwest. No grants to individuals.
Publications: Application guidelines.
Application information:
 Initial approach: Letter
 Deadline(s): 3 weeks prior to board meetings
 Board meeting date(s): Quarterly
 Write: Emory Bundy, Director
Officers and Trustees: Priscilla Bullitt Collins, President; Dorothy S. Bullitt, Vice-President; Stimson Bullitt, Secretary and Treasurer; Harriett Bullitt, Katherine M. Bullitt.
Number of staff: 1 part-time professional.
Employer Identification Number: 916027795

4226
Burlington Northern Foundation ▼
999 Third Ave.
Seattle 98104-4097 (206) 467-3895

Incorporated in 1953 in Minnesota; renamed in 1970.
Donor(s): Burlington Northern Inc.
Financial data: (yr. ended 12/31/83): Assets, $9,882,749 (M); gifts received, $9,596,387; expenditures, $5,533,024, including $5,043,024 for 514 grants (high: $300,000; low: $50) and $455,000 for 530 employee matching gifts.
Purpose and activities: Grants primarily to organizations and institutions that are located in or serve areas where Burlington Northern, Inc. operates and where its employees live and work. Grants devoted to assisting youth, human and civic services, higher education, cultural programs, health, and community funds.
Types of support awarded: Employee matching gifts, annual campaigns, building funds, equipment, general purposes.
Limitations: Giving primarily in areas of company operations. No support for religious organizations, war veterans and fraternal service organizations, national health organizations and programs, chambers of commerce, taxpayer associations, state railroad associations, and other bodies whose activities might benefit the company, or political organizations, campaigns, or candidates. No grants to individuals, or for operating budgets of hospitals, fundraising events, corporate memberships, endowment funds, scholarships, or fellowships; no loans.
Publications: Annual report, program policy statement, application guidelines.
Application information: Application form required.
 Initial approach: Letter

Copies of proposal: 1
Deadline(s): None
Board meeting date(s): As required
Final notification: 4 to 5 months
Write: Donald K. North, President
Officers: Donald K. North,* President; Donald R. Wood,* Vice-President; Ralph S. Nelson, Secretary; Francis J. Boyle, Treasurer.
Directors:* Allan R. Boyce, Chairman; Christopher T. Bayley.
Number of staff: 1 full-time professional.
Employer Identification Number: 416022304

4227
Carman (Nellie Martin) Scholarship Trust
c/o Seattle Trust & Savings Bank
P.O. Box 12907
Seattle 98111 (206) 223-2220

Trust established in 1943 in Washington.
Donor(s): Nellie M. Carman.†
Financial data: (yr. ended 12/31/83): Assets, $1,432,141 (M); expenditures, $89,980, including $1,200 for 9 grants (high: $200; low: $100) and $84,425 for 86 grants to individuals.
Purpose and activities: To provide scholarships to graduating public high school students in King, Snohomish, and Pierce counties who attend Washington colleges or universities; smaller grants paid annually to specified charitable organizations.
Types of support awarded: Student aid.
Limitations: Giving primarily in WA, with emphasis on King, Snohomish, and Pierce counties.
Publications: Multi-year report.
Application information: Application form required for scholarships only. Application form required.
 Deadline(s): Submit applications in April
 Board meeting date(s): May and December
 Write: Barbara Scott, Secretary to Scholarship Committee
Trustee: Seattle Trust and Savings Bank.
Scholarship Committee: Judge Francis E. Holman, Chairman.
Number of staff: 1 full-time professional; 1 part-time support.
Employer Identification Number: 916023774

4228
Cawsey Trust, Inc. ⌑
700 Wall Street Bldg.
Everett 98201

Incorporated in 1960 in Washington.
Donor(s): Mrs. Hugh R. Cawsey.†
Financial data: (yr. ended 12/31/83): Assets, $1,303,804 (M); expenditures, $52,638, including $40,250 for 8 grants (high: $24,000; low: $500).
Purpose and activities: Primarily local giving, with emphasis on youth and social agencies.
Limitations: Giving primarily in WA.
Officers and Trustees: Anson B. Moody, President; J.P. Hunter, Secretary; Murray Campbell, Treasurer; D.A. Duryee.
Employer Identification Number: 916053815

4229
Cheney (Ben B.) Foundation ▼
First Interstate Plaza, Suite 1550
Tacoma 98402 (206) 572-2442

Incorporated in 1955 in Washington.
Donor(s): Ben B. Cheney,† Marian Cheney Olrogg.†
Financial data: (yr. ended 12/31/84): Assets, $11,099,264 (M); gifts received, $558,702; expenditures, $1,037,732, including $783,553 for 78 grants (high: $50,000; low: $500; average: $5,000-$50,000).
Purpose and activities: Broad purposes; giving in the states of Washington and Oregon, primarily for education, health, social services, youth, community development, and cultural programs.
Types of support awarded: Seed money, building funds, equipment, general purposes, scholarship funds, special projects, emergency funds.
Limitations: Giving limited to WA and OR. No support for religious organizations for sectarian purposes or programs for which government funds are available. No grants to individuals, or for endowment funds, basic research, or operating budgets; no loans.
Publications: Application guidelines, program policy statement, informational brochure.
Application information: Application form required.
  Initial approach: Letter
  Copies of proposal: 5
  Deadline(s): 4 weeks prior to board meetings
  Board meeting date(s): April, July, October, and December
  Final notification: Within 3 months
  Write: Elgin E. Olrogg, Treasurer
Officers and Trustees: Francis I. Cheney, President; R. Gene Grant, Vice-President; John F. Hansler, Secretary; Elgin E. Olrogg, Treasurer and Executive Director.
Number of staff: 1 full-time professional; 1 full-time support.
Employer Identification Number: 916053760

4230
Comstock Foundation ▼
1200 Washington Trust Financial Center
Spokane 99204 (509) 455-6000

Trust established in 1950 in Washington.
Donor(s): Mrs. E.A. Shadle.†
Financial data: (yr. ended 12/31/83): Assets, $8,553,463 (M); expenditures, $825,649, including $761,218 for 69 grants (high: $125,000; low: $70; average: $300-$35,000).
Purpose and activities: Charitable purposes; giving in Spokane County, with emphasis on capital grants to recreational facilities and other community development projects, social agencies, aid to the handicapped, child welfare, and youth agencies. Giving also for arts, civic affairs, and higher education.
Types of support awarded: Building funds, equipment, land acquisition, scholarship funds, research.

Limitations: Giving limited to Spokane County, WA. No grants to individuals, or for endowment funds or operating budgets; no loans. In general, no grants payable for reserve purposes, deficit financing, publications, films, emergency funds, conferences, or travel.
Publications: Informational brochure, program policy statement, application guidelines.
Application information: Application form required.
  Initial approach: Proposal
  Copies of proposal: 1
  Deadline(s): None
  Board meeting date(s): Weekly
  Final notification: 10 days
  Write: Horton Herman, Trustee
Trustees: Harold W. Coffin, Horton Herman, Luke G. Williams.
Number of staff: 1.
Employer Identification Number: 916028504

4231
Cowles (Harriet Cheney) Foundation, Inc. ♯
P.O. Box 2160
Spokane 99210

Incorporated in 1944 in Washington.
Donor(s): Spokane Chronicle Company, Cowles Publishing Company, Inland Empire Paper Company.
Financial data: (yr. ended 12/31/83): Assets, $3,630,586 (M); gifts received, $312,000; expenditures, $324,041, including $307,933 for 2 grants (high: $292,933; low: $15,000).
Purpose and activities: Broad purposes; local giving for a symphony orchestra and a museum.
Limitations: Giving primarily in Spokane, WA.
Officers and Trustees: William H. Cowles 3rd, President; James P. Cowles, Vice-President; M.K. Nielsen, Secretary-Treasurer.
Employer Identification Number: 910689268

4232
Cowles (William H.) Foundation, Inc. ♯
P.O. Box 2160
Spokane 99210

Incorporated in 1952 in Washington.
Donor(s): William H. Cowles.†
Financial data: (yr. ended 12/31/83): Assets, $1,778,153 (M); expenditures, $21,635, including $10,000 for 1 grant.
Purpose and activities: Broad purposes; giving for higher education.
Officers and Trustees: William H. Cowles 3rd, President; James P. Cowles, Vice-President; M.K. Nielsen, Secretary-Treasurer.
Employer Identification Number: 916020496

4233
Dupar Foundation
(formerly Dupar Charitable Foundation)
10604 N.E. 38th Place, Suite 223
Quad One North
Kirkland 98033 (206) 827-9997

Incorporated in 1954 in Washington.
Donor(s): Frank A. Dupar, Ethel L. Dupar, Palmer Supply Company.

Financial data: (yr. ended 1/31/84): Assets, $1,313,325 (M); expenditures, $100,868, including $93,900 for 53 grants (high: $10,000; low: $500).
Purpose and activities: Broad purposes; primarily local giving, with emphasis on higher education, youth agencies, and community funds; grants limited to institutions located in Washington.
Limitations: Giving limited to WA.
Publications: Program policy statement, application guidelines.
Application information: Application form required.
  Initial approach: Letter
  Copies of proposal: 2
  Deadline(s): Submit proposal preferably between October or November or April and May; deadlines May 31 and November 30
  Board meeting date(s): January, and June or July
  Write: Frank A. Dupar, Jr., President
Officers and Trustees: Frank A. Dupar, Jr., President; James W. Dupar, Jr., Vice-President; Dorothy D. Lynch, Secretary-Treasurer; E.L. Dupar, R.W. Dupar, T.E. Dupar, Marilyn McIntosh.
Employer Identification Number: 916027389

4234
Forest Foundation ♯
820 A St., Suite 545
Tacoma 98402 (206) 627-1634

Incorporated in 1957 in Washington.
Donor(s): C. Davis Weyerhaeuser, William T. Weyerhaeuser.
Financial data: (yr. ended 10/31/83): Assets, $10,925,361 (M); gifts received, $50,000; expenditures, $658,840, including $451,699 for 54 grants (high: $65,000; low: $500).
Purpose and activities: Giving primarily for social services, religious associations, medical research, performing arts, and museums.
Types of support awarded: Building funds, equipment, general purposes, operating budgets, continuing support, emergency funds, land acquisition, matching funds.
Limitations: Giving primarily in WA and the Northwest. No grants to individuals, or for endowment funds, research, scholarships, or fellowships; no loans.
Publications: Program policy statement, application guidelines.
Application information:
  Initial approach: Full proposal
  Copies of proposal: 4
  Deadline(s): Submit proposal preferably in January, April, July, or October; no set deadline
  Board meeting date(s): Quarterly
  Final notification: 60 to 90 days
  Write: Frank D. Underwood, Executive Director
Officers: Gail T. Weyerhaeuser,* President and Treasurer; Annette B. Weyerhaeuser,* Vice-President; J. Thomas McCully, Secretary; Frank D. Underwood, Executive Director.
Directors:* C. Davis Weyerhaeuser, William T. Weyerhaeuser.
Number of staff: None.
Employer Identification Number: 916020514

4235
Fuchs (Gottfried & Mary) Foundation
c/o The Bank of California
P.O. Box 1917
Tacoma 98401   (206) 591-2549

Trust established in 1960 in Washington.
Donor(s): Gottfried Fuchs,† Mary Fuchs.†
Financial data: (yr. ended 12/31/83): Assets, $5,543,130 (M); expenditures, $271,641, including $246,301 for 35 grants (high: $21,000; low: $1,000; average: $7,000).
Purpose and activities: Priority of support for local charitable, educational, scientific, literary or religious purposes not normally financed by tax funds; emphasis on child welfare and youth agencies, higher and secondary education, cultural programs, and hospitals. Prefers funding special capital or services projects rather than operating budgets.
Types of support awarded: Continuing support, annual campaigns, emergency funds, building funds, equipment, land acquisition, scholarship funds, research.
Limitations: Giving primarily in Tacoma, Pierce County, and the lower Puget Sound area of WA. No grants to individuals, or for operating budgets, seed money, deficit financing, matching gifts, publications, or conferences; no loans.
Publications: Application guidelines, program policy statement.
Application information: Application form required.
  Initial approach: Letter
  Copies of proposal: 5
  Deadline(s): 3 weeks prior to board meetings
  Board meeting date(s): November, April, and August
  Write: Richard L. Graham, Board Member
Trustee: The Bank of California.
Number of staff: None.
Employer Identification Number: 916022284

4236
Glaser Foundation, Inc.
P.O. Box N
Edmonds 98020   (206) 525-5050

Incorporated in 1952 in Washington.
Donor(s): Paul F. Glaser.†
Financial data: (yr. ended 11/30/84): Assets, $4,000,000 (M); expenditures, $222,056, including $188,871 for 41 grants (high: $18,000; low: $800; average: $3,000-$5,400).
Purpose and activities: Broad purposes; local giving with emphasis on hospitals and health agencies, child welfare, youth agencies, the handicapped, and some arts organizations.
Types of support awarded: Emergency funds, matching funds, special projects, research.
Limitations: Giving limited to WA. No grants to individuals, or for general support, building or endowment funds, scholarships, fellowships, publications, or conferences; no loans.
Publications: Program policy statement, application guidelines.
Application information:
  Initial approach: Letter
  Copies of proposal: 2
  Deadline(s): 3 weeks prior to next board meeting

Board meeting date(s): February, May, August, and November
Final notification: 2 weeks after meeting
Write: R.W. Carlstrom, Executive Director
Officers and Directors: R. Thomas Olson, President; R.N. Brandenburg, Vice-President; R.W. Carlstrom, Secretary-Treasurer and Executive Director; P.F. Patrick, Janet L. Politeo.
Number of staff: None.
Employer Identification Number: 916028694

4237
Green (Joshua) Foundation, Inc.
1414 Fourth Ave.
P.O. Box 720
Seattle 98111   (206) 344-2285

Trust established in 1956 in Washington.
Donor(s): Joshua Green, Mrs. Joshua Green.
Financial data: (yr. ended 12/31/84): Assets, $2,100,000 (M); gifts received, $15,000; expenditures, $130,000, including $125,000 for 71 grants (high: $50,000; low: $250; average: $1,000-$3,000).
Purpose and activities: Broad purposes; largely local giving, with emphasis on higher and secondary education, community funds, cultural programs, hospitals, and church support.
Limitations: Giving primarily in the Seattle, WA, area. No grants to individuals, or for scholarships or fellowships; no loans.
Application information:
  Initial approach: Full proposal
  Copies of proposal: 1
  Board meeting date(s): March, July, September, and December
  Write: Joshua Green, Jr., President
Officers: Joshua Green, Jr.,* President; Joshua Green, III,* Vice-President; Victoria C. Lemke, Secretary; Steven E. Carlson,* Treasurer.
Trustees:* Elmer M. Anderson.
Employer Identification Number: 916050748

4238
Haas (Saul and Dayee G.) Foundation, Inc.
2000 IBM Bldg.
Seattle 98101   (206) 623-7580

Incorporated in 1971 in Washington.
Donor(s): Saul Haas,† Dayee G. Haas.
Financial data: (yr. ended 6/30/83): Assets, $2,447,982 (M); expenditures, $276,539, including $236,129 for 230 grants (average: $50-$2,000).
Purpose and activities: Broad purposes; primarily local giving, with emphasis on a school-administered fund to aid indigent high school students to complete their education, and merit awards to university students in communications schools. Also sponsors a local university lecture series on broadcasting.
Types of support awarded: Emergency funds.
Limitations: Giving primarily in WA state. No grants to individuals, or for equipment, land acquisition, renovation projects, endowment funds, or matching gifts.
Application information: Applications for grants not encouraged.
  Initial approach: Telephone

Board meeting date(s): July
Write: Charles E. Kincaid, Executive Director
Officers and Directors: Charles Horowitz, Vice-President and Secretary; Charles E. Kincaid, Treasurer and Executive Director; Jon Bowman, Gerald Grinstein, Fred Haley, Solomon Katz, Duff Kennedy, Warren G. Magnuson, Robert A. Nathane, Richard Roddis, Janet Tourtellotte.
Employer Identification Number: 237189670

4239
Hubbard Family Foundation ¤
c/o Seattle-First National Bank
P.O. Box 3586
Seattle 98124

Established in 1983 in Washington.
Donor(s): Lawrence E. Hubbard.†
Financial data: (yr. ended 7/31/83): Assets, $1,005,310 (M); gifts received, $1,000,000; expenditures, $2,492, including $1,000 for 1 grant.
Purpose and activities: First year of operation in 1983; only one grant for civic upkeep in a local city.
Limitations: Giving primarily in Edmonds, WA.
Trustee: Seattle-First National Bank.
Employer Identification Number: 916253897

4240
Johnston Foundation, The
E. 627 17th Ave.
Spokane 99203   (509) 838-2108

Trust established in 1948 in Washington.
Donor(s): Eric Johnston.†
Financial data: (yr. ended 12/31/84): Assets, $3,235,365 (M); expenditures, $162,382, including $141,900 for 40 grants (high: $21,000; low: $250).
Purpose and activities: Broad purposes; local giving only, with the exception of independent education; emphasis on private higher and secondary education, youth agencies, and cultural programs.
Limitations: Giving limited to Spokane, WA. No support for publicly supported educational institutions. No grants to individuals, or for scholarships or fellowships; no loans.
Application information:
  Initial approach: Telephone or letter
  Copies of proposal: 1
  Deadline(s): None
  Board meeting date(s): Usually in April, June, September, and December
  Final notification: 3 months
  Write: Mrs. William C. Fix, Treasurer
Officers and Trustees: Mrs. Eric Johnston, President; Mrs. Fred Hanson, Secretary; Mrs. William C. Fix, Treasurer; William C. Fix, Fred Hanson, Maage LaCounte, Scott B. Lukins.
Number of staff: 2 part-time professional.
Employer Identification Number: 910749593

4241
Kawabe Memorial Fund
(also known as Harry S. Kawabe Trust)
c/o Seattle First National Bank, Charitable Trust
Administration
P.O. Box 3586
Seattle 98124   (206) 583-3160

Trust established in 1972 in Washington.
Donor(s): Tomo Kawabe,† Harry Kawabe.†
Financial data: (yr. ended 12/31/82): Assets,
$1,351,475 (M); expenditures, $129,407,
including $105,000 for 15 grants (high:
$53,000; low: $1,000; average: $3,700) and
$4,000 for 2 grants to individuals.
Purpose and activities: Giving primarily
locally and in Alaska for Buddhist and
Protestant church support, including training
teachers and clergy and improving facilities;
support also for colleges and universities,
including scholarship funds; research
foundations, and institutions devoted to care
for the indigent, children, and the aged.
Preference given to Alaskan citizens and
institutions for scholarships and research.
Types of support awarded: Operating
budgets, continuing support, seed money,
emergency funds, building funds, equipment,
land acquisition, scholarship funds, research,
publications.
Limitations: Giving primarily in the Seattle,
WA, area and AK.
Application information:
   Initial approach: Full proposal
   Copies of proposal: 1
   Deadline(s): None
   Board meeting date(s): Approximately 4
   times a year with no set schedule
Allocation Committee: Yasue Brevig, Yoshito
Fujii, Tsuyoshi Horike, Harry H. Iwata, Frank Y.
Kinomoto, Jeanette Y. Otsuka, Toru Sakahara,
Terrance M. Toda, Chiyoko Yasutake, W.T.
Yasutake.
Trustee: Seattle First National Bank (William C.
Blanchard, Trust Officer).
Number of staff: None.
Employer Identification Number: 916116549

4242
Keyes (Bernice A. B.) Trust ⊠
c/o Puget Sound National Bank, Trust
P.O. Box 1258
Tacoma 98401   (206) 593-3832

Established in 1978.
Financial data: (yr. ended 12/31/83): Assets,
$1,357,026 (M); expenditures, $133,304,
including $46,000 for 2 grants (high: $36,000;
low: $10,000) and $60,666 for 29 grants to
individuals.
Purpose and activities: Local giving to high
schools and to individuals for scholarships.
Types of support awarded: Scholarship funds,
student aid.
Limitations: Giving limited to the Tacoma,
WA, area.
Application information: Scholarship
application forms available through college
counselors at local high schools. Application
form required.
   Deadline(s): None

Write: John A. Cunningham
Trustees: Robert Ellison, Dean Mullin, Puget
Sound National Bank, Trust.
Employer Identification Number: 916111944

4243
**Kilworth (Florence B.) Charitable
Foundation**
c/o Puget Sound National Bank, Trust
P.O. Box 1258
Tacoma 98401   (206) 593-3832

Established in 1977.
Financial data: (yr. ended 12/31/83): Assets,
$2,147,971 (M); expenditures, $173,584,
including $150,100 for 31 grants (high:
$10,000; low: $800).
Purpose and activities: Broad purposes;
primarily local giving for cultural programs,
higher education, hospitals, youth agencies,
and Protestant church support.
Limitations: Giving primarily in the Tacoma,
WA, area.
Application information:
   Deadline(s): None
   Write: John A. Cunningham
Trustees: Florence Morris, Puget Sound
National Bank, Trust.
Employer Identification Number: 916221495

4244
Kilworth (William) Charitable Trust
c/o Puget Sound National Bank Trust
P.O. Box 1258
Tacoma 98401

Trust established in 1968 in Washington.
Financial data: (yr. ended 12/31/84): Assets,
$2,078,436 (M); expenditures, $185,676,
including $167,000 for 44 grants (high:
$35,000; low: $1,000).
Purpose and activities: Local giving, with
emphasis on higher education, including
college scholarships to students from Pierce
County; support also for youth agencies and
child welfare.
Types of support awarded: Scholarship funds.
Limitations: Giving limited to the Tacoma,
WA, area. No grants to individuals.
Application information: Scholarship program
administered by colleges; standard forms
available from each school.
Trustee: Puget Sound National Bank (Carl A.
Peterson, Trust Officer).
Employer Identification Number: 916072527

4245
Kreielsheimer Foundation Trust ⊠
c/o Seattle First National Bank
P.O. Box 3586
Seattle 98124
Additional application address: send 1 copy of
proposal to Charles F. Osborn, c/o Bogle &
Gates, Bank of California Center, Seattle, WA
98164

Established in 1979 in Washington.
Donor(s): Leo T. Kreielsheimer,† Greye M.
Kreielsheimer.†

Financial data: (yr. ended 5/31/84): Assets,
$6,693,506 (M); expenditures, $403,851,
including $327,161 for 7 grants (high:
$269,161; low: $2,500).
Purpose and activities: Giving in the Pacific
Northwest, with emphasis on cultural
programs, higher education, and hospitals.
Limitations: Giving limited to the Pacific
Northwest, including western AK, and with
emphasis on WA. No grants to individuals.
Publications: Application guidelines.
Application information:
   Initial approach: Proposal
   Board meeting date(s): Quarterly
   Final notification: Grants made within 30
   days of the end of each calendar quarter
   Write: Eugene A. Brown, Vice-President
Trustees: Charles Osborn, Seattle First National
Bank.
Employer Identification Number: 916232127

4246
Laird, Norton Foundation ▼
1300 Norton Bldg.
Seattle 98104   (206) 464-5292

Incorporated in 1940 in Minnesota.
Donor(s): Many individuals members of the
founding family and family-related businesses.
Financial data: (yr. ended 12/31/83): Assets,
$367,954 (M); gifts received, $466,816;
expenditures, $385,799, including $362,312
for 362 grants (high: $25,000; low: $25;
average: $25-$5,000).
Purpose and activities: Funds devoted to
distinctive programs of creative philanthropy
that reflect the family's forest industry heritage
and are directed generally to forestry,
conservation and economic education; grants
also for continued support of designated
recipients in other fields.
Types of support awarded: Building funds,
special projects, publications, internships,
scholarship funds, matching funds, equipment,
land acquisition.
Limitations: No grants to individuals, or for
endowment funds, operating budgets, or
general purposes; no loans.
Publications: 990-PF, program policy
statement, application guidelines, annual report.
Application information: Application form
required.
   Initial approach: Letter
   Copies of proposal: 1
   Deadline(s): 2 weeks prior to board meetings
   Board meeting date(s): October, February,
   and June
   Final notification: 2 weeks after board
   meeting
   Write: Christina B. Wilson, President
Officers: Christina B. Wilson,* President;
Rebecca S. Richardson,* Vice-President;
Margaret F. Berger, Secretary; Henry P.
Brown,* Treasurer.
Trustees:* Elizabeth Clapp, Norton Clapp,
Tamsin O. Clapp, Elizabeth Helmoholz, Marie
Pampush, Joan Ueland.
Number of staff: 2 part-time support.
Employer Identification Number: 916048373

4247
Leuthold Foundation, Inc.
1006 Old National Bank Bldg.
Spokane 99201   (509) 624-3944

Incorporated in 1948 in Washington.
Donor(s): Members of the Leuthold family.
Financial data: (yr. ended 6/30/83): Assets,
$5,038,475 (M); expenditures, $305,104,
including $250,550 for 68 grants (high:
$25,000; low: $50).
Purpose and activities: Local giving, primarily
for youth agencies, hospitals, secondary and
higher education, Protestant church support,
community funds, and music.
Types of support awarded: Operating
budgets, continuing support, annual campaigns,
building funds, matching funds, employee
related scholarships.
Limitations: Giving limited to Spokane County,
WA. No grants to individuals; no loans.
Publications: Application guidelines, program
policy statement.
Application information: Application form
required.
    Initial approach: Letter
    Copies of proposal: 1
    Deadline(s): Submit proposal preferably in
        May or November; deadlines May 31 and
        November 15
    Board meeting date(s): July and December
    Final notification: 1 week after board meets
    Write: John H. Leuthold, President
Officers and Trustees: John H. Leuthold,
President; Betty B. Leuthold, Vice-President;
O.M. Kimmel, Jr., Secretary-Treasurer; Conrad
Gotzian, Caroline E. Leuthold, Allan H. Toole.
Employer Identification Number: 916028589

4248
Matlock Foundation
900 Fourth Ave.
Seattle 98164   (206) 292-5000

Incorporated in 1954 in Washington.
Donor(s): Simpson Timber Company, Simpson
Paper Company.
Financial data: (yr. ended 12/31/84): Assets,
$494,970 (M); expenditures, $479,808,
including $475,100 for 236 grants (high:
$45,410; low: $25).
Purpose and activities: Broad purposes;
allocates funds for giving by Simpson Timber
Company Fund, Simpson Paper Company
Fund, and Simpson Reed Fund to community
funds and hospitals, and for scholarships and
internships, for graduate work at forestry or
forest products management schools of
universities; giving also for cultural programs,
education, youth agencies, and religious
purposes.
Types of support awarded: Seed money,
general purposes, emergency funds, building
funds, equipment, land acquisition, conferences
and seminars, scholarship funds, internships,
employee matching gifts.
Limitations: No grants to individuals, or for
endowments or operating budgets; no loans.
Application information: Application form
required.
    Initial approach: Letter
    Copies of proposal: 1

Deadline(s): Submit application preferably
    one month before board meetings
Board meeting date(s): March, June, and
    November
Final notification: 1 week following board
    meeting
Write: Betty Y. Dykstra, Secretary
Officers: Joseph L. Leitzinger,* President; Betty
Y. Dykstra, Secretary; J. Thurston Roach,
Treasurer.
Directors:* John J. Fannon, Robert B.
Hutchinson, Furman C. Moseley, Susan R.
Moseley, Eleanor H. Reed, William G. Reed, Jr.
Number of staff: 1.
Employer Identification Number: 916029303

4249
McEachern (Ida J.) Charitable Trust
c/o The Bank of California
P.O. Box 3123
Seattle 98114   (206) 587-3623

Trust established in 1966 in Washington.
Donor(s): Ida J. McEachern,† D.V.
McEachern.†
Financial data: (yr. ended 8/31/84): Assets,
$5,815,039 (M); expenditures, $466,302,
including $416,193 for 38 grants (high:
$50,000; low: $1,000).
Purpose and activities: Local giving only,
almost exclusively for capital funding of youth
agencies serving children under the age of 18,
where purpose is to give a better start in life to
all children, both physically and mentally.
Prefers organizations in existence at least 5 •
years and whose operational funding comes
generally from a non-tax based source.
Types of support awarded: Emergency funds,
building funds, equipment, land acquisition.
Limitations: Giving limited to Seattle, WA, and
the Puget Sound area. No grants to individuals,
or for endowment funds, scholarships or
fellowships, operating budgets, continuing
support, annual campaigns, seed money, deficit
financing, special projects, publications,
conferences, research programs, or matching
gifts; no loans.
Publications: Program policy statement.
Application information:
    Initial approach: Letter
    Copies of proposal: 1
    Deadline(s): None
    Board meeting date(s): Usually in February,
        May, August, and November
    Final notification: 3 to 6 months
    Write: J.W. Grubbs, Jr., Trust Officer
Trustees: L.L. Allison, Robert B. McEachern,
The Bank of California (J.W. Grubbs, Jr., Trust
Officer).
Number of staff: None.
Employer Identification Number: 916063710

4250
Medina Foundation ▼
Norton Bldg., 13th Fl.
Seattle 98104   (206) 464-5231

Incorporated in 1948 in Washington.

Financial data: (yr. ended 12/31/83): Assets,
$21,088,340 (M); expenditures, $856,462,
including $657,702 for 63 grants (high:
$56,500; low: $500).
Purpose and activities: Broad purposes; local
giving only for direct service delivery programs
for emergency food and shelter, to aid the
handicapped, improve the effectiveness of
eleemosynary and/or governmental
organization; support also for cultural
programs, youth and child welfare, community
development, and for education.
Types of support awarded: Emergency funds,
building funds, equipment, technical assistance,
operating budgets, seed money.
Limitations: Giving limited to the greater Puget
Sound, WA, area, with emphasis on Seattle.
No support for public institutions. No grants to
individuals, or for endowment funds, research,
scholarships and fellowships, or matching gifts;
no loans.
Publications: Informational brochure, program
policy statement, application guidelines.
Application information: Application form
required.
    Initial approach: Letter
    Deadline(s): None
    Board meeting date(s): Monthly
    Final notification: 30 to 60 days
    Write: Gregory P. Barlow, Executive Director
Officers: Norton Clapp,* President; Samuel H.
Brown,* Linda J. Henry,* Vice-Presidents;
Margaret Ames, Secretary; Gary MacLeod,*
Treasurer; Gregory P. Barlow, Executive
Director.
Trustees:* James N. Clapp II, Kristina H.
Clapp, K. Elizabeth Clapp, Matthew N. Clapp,
Jr., Marion Hand, Patricia M. Henry, Anne M.
Simons.
Number of staff: 1 full-time professional; 1 full-
time support.
Employer Identification Number: 910745225

4251
Merrill (The R. D.) Foundation ⊐
1411 Fourth Ave. Bldg., Suite 1415
Seattle 98101   (206) 682-3939

Incorporated in 1953 in Washington.
Donor(s): R.D. Merrill, R.D. Merrill Company.
Financial data: (yr. ended 6/30/83): Assets,
$3,598,096 (M); expenditures, $204,474,
including $167,630 for 60 grants (high:
$50,000; low: $100).
Purpose and activities: Local giving to
institutions and charities to which contributions
have heretofore been made; interests include
art museums, the performing arts, secondary
education, hospitals, and the handicapped.
Limitations: Giving limited to WA.
Application information:
    Write: Lois Hawkins, Assistant Secretary
Officers and Directors: Virginia Merrill
Bloedel, Chairman; Corydon Wagner, Jr.,
President; Virginia Bloedel Wright, Vice-
President and Treasurer; Justin M. Martin,
Wendy Wagner Wyerhaeuser, Vice-Presidents;
W.J. Wright, Secretary; Eulalie Merrill Wagner.
Employer Identification Number: 916029949

4252

Murdock (M. J.) Charitable Trust ▼
915 Broadway
Vancouver 98660   (206) 694-8415
Mailing address: P.O. Box 1618, Vancouver,
WA 98668

Trust established in 1975 in Washington.
Donor(s): Melvin Jack Murdock.†
Financial data: (yr. ended 12/31/83): Assets,
$151,794,533 (M); expenditures, $7,680,464,
including $7,297,707 for 103 grants (high:
$545,000; low: $2,500; average: $5,000-
$75,000).
Purpose and activities: Primarily supports
special projects or programs of private, nonprofit Pacific Northwest (Washington, Oregon,
Idaho, Montana and Alaska) charitable
organizations aimed at the solution or
prevention of significant problems with
implications beyond the immediate
geographical area and which are able to thrive
after initial funding. Willing to assume a local
responsibility by assisting projects which
address critical problems for the Portland,
Oregon/Vancouver, Washington area.
Desirable characteristics include self-help, free
enterprise concepts leading to greater self-
sufficiency and capability for organizations and
the people they serve, a strategy for using up-
front money including assistance from other
supporters, and evidence that the problem
solving effort will make an important
difference. Also provides seed money for
selected natural-science research programs
which have been identified as major priorities.
Grants usually for a limited time, one or two
years.
Types of support awarded: Seed money,
building funds, equipment, research, special
projects.
Limitations: Giving primarily in the Pacific
Northwest. No support for government
programs; projects common to many
organizations without distinguishing merit;
community-based projects outside the Portland,
OR/Vancouver, WA, area; propagandizing or
influencing legislation or elections; sectarian or
religious organizations whose principal activities
are for the benefit of their own members;
agencies served by United Way of Columbia-
Willamette; or institutes which unfairly
discriminate against race, ethnic origin, sex, or
creed. No grants to individuals, or for annual
campaigns, general support, continuing support,
deficit financing, endowment funds,
scholarships, fellowships, or matching gifts; no
loans.
Publications: Annual report, application
guidelines, program policy statement.
Application information: Submit 4 copies of
non-research proposal, 9 copies of research or
technical proposal.
  Initial approach: Letter or telephone
  Deadline(s): None
  Board meeting date(s): Monthly
  Final notification: 3 to 6 months
  Write: Sam C. Smith, Executive Director

Officers: Sam C. Smith, Executive Director;
Larry R. Fies, Director of Finance; Ford A.
Anderson, II, Senior Program Officer; Ray W.
Honerlah, Program Officer.
Trustees: Paul L. Boley, James B. Castles,
Walter P. Dyke.
Number of staff: 4 full-time professional; 3 full-
time support.
Employer Identification Number: 237456468

4253

Murray Foundation ⌑
First Interstate Plaza, Suite 1750
Tacoma 98402   (206) 383-4911

Trust established in 1952 in Washington.
Donor(s): L.T. Murray Trust.
Financial data: (yr. ended 12/31/83): Assets,
$2,373,213 (M); expenditures, $124,083,
including $107,059 for 9 grants (high: $20,659;
low: $500).
Purpose and activities: Primarily local giving,
with emphasis on higher and secondary
education, hospitals, cultural programs, and
community funds. Priority given to capital
programs in the Puget Sound area.
Types of support awarded: Building funds.
Limitations: Giving primarily in Tacoma, WA.
No grants to individuals, or for endowment
funds, research, or scholarships and
fellowships; no loans.
Publications: 990-PF.
Application information:
  Initial approach: Letter
  Copies of proposal: 1
  Board meeting date(s): December and as
  required (3 to 4 times a year)
Officers and Directors: L.T. Murray, Jr., Ann
Murray Barbey, Vice-Presidents; Charles F.
Osborn, Secretary; Amy Lou Eckstrom,
Treasurer; Lowell Butson.
Employer Identification Number: 510163345

4254

Norcliffe Fund, The ▼
First Interstate Center, Suite 1515
999 Third Ave.
Seattle 98104   (206) 682-4820

Incorporated in 1952 in Washington.
Donor(s): Mrs. Theiline M. McCone.
Financial data: (yr. ended 11/30/84): Assets,
$8,864,851 (M); gifts received, $181,873;
expenditures, $549,925, including $539,225
for 152 grants (high: $98,847; low: $25;
average: $1,000-$2,500).
Purpose and activities: Broad purposes; local
giving, with emphasis on cultural programs,
Roman Catholic church support and religious
associations, hospitals, higher and secondary
education, and historic preservation; support
also for medical research, youth agencies, the
aged, and conservation.
Types of support awarded: Operating
budgets, continuing support, annual campaigns,
seed money, emergency funds, building funds,
equipment, land acquisition, research, special
projects.

Limitations: Giving limited to the Pacific
Northwest, especially Seattle, WA. No grants
to individuals, or for deficit financing, matching
gifts, scholarships, or fellowships; no loans.
Publications: Program policy statement,
application guidelines.
Application information:
  Initial approach: Full proposal or letter
  Copies of proposal: 1
  Deadline(s): None
  Board meeting date(s): As required
  Final notification: 6 to 8 weeks
  Write: Mary Ellen Hughes, President
Officers and Trustees*: Theiline M. McCone,*
Chairman; Mary Ellen Hughes,* President;
Carol R. Peterson, Secretary; Ann P. Wyckoff,*
Treasurer; Virginia S. Helsell, Charles M. Pigott,
James C. Pigott, Theiline Scheumann.
Number of staff: 1 part-time support.
Employer Identification Number: 916029352

4255

PACCAR Foundation ▼
P.O. Box 1518
Bellevue 98009   (206) 455-7400

Incorporated in 1951 in Washington.
Donor(s): PACCAR Inc.
Financial data: (yr. ended 11/30/83): Assets,
$1,989,822 (M); gifts received, $500,000;
expenditures, $921,258, including $894,854
for 101 grants (high: $177,594; low: $320).
Purpose and activities: Primarily local giving
with emphasis on non-tax-supported higher
educational institutions, community funds,
cultural programs, hospitals, and youth agencies.
Types of support awarded: Employee
matching gifts, endowment funds, operating
budgets, continuing support, annual campaigns,
building funds.
Limitations: Giving primarily in areas of
company operations, particularly Seattle, WA.
No grants to individuals or for scholarships or
fellowships.
Application information:
  Initial approach: Full proposal
  Copies of proposal: 1
  Deadline(s): None
  Board meeting date(s): Quarterly
  Final notification: 2 to 3 months
  Write: E.A. Carpenter, Vice-President
Officers: Charles M. Pigott,* President; E.A.
Carpenter, Vice-President and Treasurer.
Trustees:* Harold J. Haynes, W.J. Pennington,
J.C. Pigott, John W. Pitts, James H. Wiborg,
T.A. Wilson.
Number of staff: None.
Employer Identification Number: 916030638

4256

Poncin Scholarship Fund
c/o Seattle-First National Bank, Charitable Trust
Administration
1001 Fourth Ave., P.O. Box 3586
Seattle 98124   (206) 583-3160

Trust established in 1966 in Washington.
Donor(s): Cora May Poncin.†

Financial data: (yr. ended 12/31/82): Assets, $1,306,891 (M); expenditures, $91,655, including $10,200 for 2 grants (high: $7,200; low: $3,000; average: $3,600) and $65,700 for 29 grants to individuals.
Purpose and activities: Grants limited to individuals in the state of Washington for medical research.
Types of support awarded: Research, grants to individuals.
Limitations: Giving limited to the state of WA. No grants for operating budgets, continuing support, annual campaigns, seed money, emergency funds, deficit financing, building or endowment funds, scholarships and fellowships, matching gifts, special projects, publications, or conferences; no loans.
Application information:
 Deadline(s): None
 Board meeting date(s): Trust officers committee meets weekly
 Final notification: 2 weeks
Trustee: Seattle-First National Bank.
Number of staff: None.
Employer Identification Number: 916069573

4257
Rainier Bancorporation Foundation ⌑
One Rainier Square
1301 5th Ave.
Seattle 98101

Established in 1980.
Donor(s): Rainier Bancorporation.
Financial data: (yr. ended 12/31/83): Assets, $96,078 (M); gifts received, $560,040; expenditures, $524,321, including $521,578 for 86 grants (high: $38,500; low: $26).
Purpose and activities: Primarily local giving for community funds, higher education, and the arts.
Limitations: Giving primarily in WA.
Trustee: Rainier National Bank.
Employer Identification Number: 911121274

4258
Robertson Charitable & Educational Trust
c/o First Interstate Bank of Washington
P.O. Box 21927
Seattle 98111   (509) 575-7425

Established in 1972 in Washington.
Donor(s): W.H. Robertson, Ruth Robertson, Dorothy Robertson.
Financial data: (yr. ended 12/31/83): Assets, $1,400,860 (M); expenditures, $108,876, including $74,637 for 14 grants (high: $20,000; low: $100).
Purpose and activities: Local giving, with emphasis on youth agencies and cultural programs.
Types of support awarded: Operating budgets, continuing support, annual campaigns, seed money, emergency funds, building funds, equipment, land acquisition, endowment funds, matching funds, professorships, internships, scholarship funds, exchange programs, fellowships.

Limitations: Giving limited to the Yakima, WA, area. No grants to individuals, or for deficit financing or employee matching gifts.
Application information:
 Board meeting date(s): As needed
Trustee: First Interstate Bank of Washington.
Employer Identification Number: 916159252

4259
Seattle Foundation, The ▼
1411 Fourth Ave. Bldg., Suite 1522
Seattle 98112   (206) 622-2294

Community foundation incorporated in 1946 in Washington.
Financial data: (yr. ended 6/30/84): Assets, $18,889,707 (M); gifts received, $1,206,236; expenditures, $1,605,310 for 209 grants.
Purpose and activities: To administer gifts and bequests for the benefit of the charitable, cultural, educational, health, and welfare organizations within the state of Washington, with preference to organizations in Greater Seattle, unless otherwise designated by the donor at the time of his gift or bequest.
Types of support awarded: Building funds, equipment.
Limitations: Giving limited to the Seattle, WA area. No grants to individuals, or for scholarships, fellowships, endowment funds, research, operating budgets, general purposes, matching gifts, conferences, exhibits, film production, or publications; no loans.
Publications: Annual report, informational brochure, program policy statement, application guidelines.
Application information:
 Initial approach: Telephone, followed by full proposal
 Copies of proposal: 1
 Deadline(s): February 1, May 1, August 1, and November 1
 Board meeting date(s): March, June, September, and December
 Final notification: 6 weeks to 2 months
 Write: Mrs. Anne V. Farrell, President
Officers: Anne V. Farrell, President; Kimbrough Street, Secretary; Walter H. Crim,* Treasurer.
Trustees:* Mrs. Holt W. Webster, Chairman; P. Cameron DeVore, Samuel Stroum, Vice-Chairmen; Joseph C. Baillargeon, Bruce Baker, Christopher T. Bayley, John A. Blethen, Mrs. Robert F. Buck, Charles J. Devine, Frank A. Dupar, Jr., David Ederer, Marli Janssen Iverson, Jane M. Lang, Elaine R. Monsen, M.D., Furman C. Moseley, J. Shan Mullin, Donald G. Phelps, Constance Rice, Walter Schoenfeld, E. Gene Treneer, John H. Walker, Jane Williams, Howard S. Wright.
Trustee Banks: The Bank of California, Old National Bank of Washington, First Interstate Bank, Peoples National Bank of Washington, Rainier National Bank, Seattle-First National Bank, Seattle Trust and Savings Bank, Washington Mutual Savings Bank.
Number of staff: 2 full-time professional; 1 full-time support.
Employer Identification Number: 916013536

4260
Sequoia Foundation
820 A St., Suite 545
Tacoma 98402   (206) 627-1634

Established in 1982 in Washington.
Donor(s): WBW Trust No. 1, W. John Driscoll, C. Davis Weyerhaeuser, F.T. Weyerhaeuser, William T. Weyerhaeuser.
Financial data: (yr. ended 8/31/83): Assets, $4,803,715 (M); gifts received, $3,825,644; expenditures, $1,090,763, including $1,030,585 for 15 grants (high: $550,000; low: $5,000).
Purpose and activities: Giving primarily to further "the growth of individual personhood"; fields of interest include "Aesthetics, Education and Training, Social Welfare, Religion and Religious training and Christian Psychological endeavors"; giving in 1983 primarily for higher education, including theological education; Protestant social service agencies, community development, and conservation.
Types of support awarded: Special projects, building funds, general purposes, operating budgets, scholarship funds, fellowships, research.
Limitations: Giving primarily in western WA, with special emphasis on Seattle and Tacoma. No grants to individuals, or for long-time commitments, lobbying or political propaganda, voter registration drives, conferences, travel, publications, film projects; grants rarely made in conjunction with other donors, or to recipients of tax money.
Publications: Annual report, program policy statement, application guidelines.
Application information:
 Initial approach: Letter or proposal
 Copies of proposal: 2
 Deadline(s): None
 Write: Frank D. Underwood, Executive Director
Officers and Directors:* William T. Weyerhaeuser,* President and Treasurer; Gail T. Weyerhaeuser,* Vice-President; J. Thomas McCully, Secretary; Frank D. Underwood, Executive Director.
Employer Identification Number: 911178052

4261
Shemanski (Tillie and Alfred) Testamentary Trust ⌑
c/o Seattle First National Bank
P.O. Box 3586
Seattle 98124

Trust established in 1974 in Washington.
Donor(s): Alfred Shemanski, Tillie Shemanski.†
Financial data: (yr. ended 12/31/83): Assets, $2,426,007 (M); expenditures, $204,097, including $178,571 for 28 grants (high: $32,334; low: $1,786).
Purpose and activities: Primarily local giving, with emphasis on Jewish welfare funds, temple support, higher education, health associations and hospitals, and youth and child welfare agencies.
Limitations: Giving primarily in WA.
Application information:
 Initial approach: Letter

Deadline(s): November 30
Write: William C. Blanchard, Asst. V.P.
Trustee: Seattle-First National Bank.
Employer Identification Number: 916196855

4262
Skinner Foundation
Skinner Bldg., Seventh Fl.
Seattle 98101 (206) 623-6480

Trust established in 1956 in Washington.
Donor(s): Skinner Corporation, Alpac
Corporation, NC Machinery.
Financial data: (yr. ended 3/31/84): Assets,
$1,939,862 (M); gifts received, $503,000;
expenditures, $336,010, including $324,998
for 106 grants (high: $20,000; low: $500;
average: $3,000) and $6,780 for 31 employee
matching gifts.
Purpose and activities: Broad purposes; grants
in areas of company operations in Alaska,
Hawaii, and western Washington for civic
betterment, cultural enhancement, education,
health and welfare, social services, and youth
betterment.
Types of support awarded: Operating
budgets, annual campaigns, seed money,
emergency funds, building funds, equipment,
endowment funds, matching funds, technical
assistance, professorships, publications,
fellowships, scholarship funds.
Limitations: Giving limited to areas of
company operations in western WA, AK, and
HI. No support for religious organizations for
religious purposes. No grants to individuals, or
for continuing support, United Ways for
operating funds, deficit financing, research,
demonstration projects, or conferences; no
loans.
Publications: Annual report, application
guidelines, program policy statement.
Application information: Application form
required.
Initial approach: Letter
Copies of proposal: 7
Deadline(s): Submit application in June,
September, December, or March; deadline
21 days before board meetings
Board meeting date(s): April, July, October,
and January
Final notification: 2 weeks
Write: Sally Skinner Behnke, Chairman
Trustees: Sally Skinner Behnke, Chairman;
Cathy W. Behnke, Shari D. Behnke, A.E.
Nordhoff, D.E. Skinner.
Number of staff: 1 full-time professional.
Employer Identification Number: 916025144

4263
Snyder (Frost and Margaret) Foundation ⌗
c/o Puget Sound National Bank, Trust Dept.
P.O. Box 1258
Tacoma 98401-1258

Trust established in 1957 in Washington.
Donor(s): Frost Snyder,† Margaret Snyder.†
Financial data: (yr. ended 12/31/83): Assets,
$5,009,109 (M); expenditures, $384,517,
including $346,000 for 15 grants (high:
$100,000; low: $2,500).

Purpose and activities: Primarily local giving,
for the benefit of Roman Catholic educational
and religious associations only.
Limitations: Giving primarily in WA.
Trustees: Catherine S. Brockert, Margaret S.
Cunningham, August Von Boecklin, Puget
Sound National Bank.
Employer Identification Number: 916030549

4264
Spokane Inland Empire Foundation
926 Paulsen Bldg.
Spokane 99201 (509) 624-2606

Community foundation incorporated in 1974 in
Washington.
Financial data: (yr. ended 6/30/84): Assets,
$1,250,916 (M); gifts received, $192,894;
expenditures, $249,561, including $169,024
for 157 grants (high: $3,500; low: $242;
average: $1,000), $18,550 for 53 grants to
individuals and $50 for 1 employee matching
gift.
Purpose and activities: Local giving in the
inland Northwest for charitable and
philanthropic purposes in the fields of music,
the arts, the elderly, education and youth, civic
improvement, historical restoration,
rehabilitation, and social and health services.
Types of support awarded: Operating
budgets, continuing support, annual campaigns,
equipment, land acquisition, endowment funds,
matching funds, special projects, publications,
seed money, building funds, consulting
services, technical assistance, student aid.
Limitations: Giving limited to the inland
Northwest. No grants to individuals (except for
scholarships), or for deficit financing, building
funds, conferences and seminars, emergency
funds, research, or matching grants; no loans.
Publications: Annual report, program policy
statement, application guidelines, 990-PF.
Application information: Application form
required.
Initial approach: Letter
Copies of proposal: 11
Deadline(s): October 1 (Spokane, WA);
November 1 (Pullman and Dayton, WA)
Board meeting date(s): September through
June
Final notification: 3 months
Write: Jeanne L. Ager, Executive Director
Officers: Marvin F. Soehren, President; John C.
Hilsen, Vice-President; Allan H. Toole,
Secretary; Edwin Jolicoeur, Treasurer; Jeanne L.
Ager, Executive Director.
Number of staff: 1 full-time professional; 1
part-time professional; 1 part-time support.
Employer Identification Number: 910941053

4265
Stewardship Foundation, The ▼
Tacoma Financial Center, Suite 1500
1145 Broadway Plaza
Tacoma 98402 (206) 272-8336
Application address: P.O. Box 1278, Tacoma,
WA 98401

Trust established in 1962 in Washington.
Donor(s): C. Davis Weyerhaeuser Irrevocable
Trust.

Financial data: (yr. ended 10/31/84): Assets,
$47,112,121 (M); expenditures, $4,201,737,
including $3,523,031 for 147 grants (high:
$1,374,668; low: $110).
Purpose and activities: At least 80 percent of
funds paid for evangelical religious
organizations whose ministries reach beyond
the local community.
Types of support awarded: Annual
campaigns, building funds, equipment, general
purposes.
Limitations: No grants to individuals, or for
endowment funds, research, scholarships,
fellowships, or matching gifts; no loans.
Application information:
Initial approach: Letter
Copies of proposal: 1
Deadline(s): Submit proposal preferably in
September or October
Board meeting date(s): March, June,
September, and December
Final notification: 90 days
Write: C. Davis Weyerhaeuser, Trustee
Trustees: Annette B. Weyerhaeuser, C. Davis
Weyerhaeuser, William T. Weyerhaeuser.
Employer Identification Number: 916020515

4266
Stubblefield, Estate of Joseph L.
249 West Alder St.
P.O. Box 1757
Walla Walla 99362 (509) 525-5800

Trust established in 1902 in Washington.
Donor(s): Joseph L. Stubblefield.†
Financial data: (yr. ended 12/31/82): Assets,
$2,079,530 (M); gifts received, $2,000;
expenditures, $146,984, including $112,500
for 2 grants (high: $110,000; low: $2,500) and
$15,921 for 40 grants to individuals.
Purpose and activities: Grants for indigent and
elderly widows and orphans and organizations
that assist such persons.
Types of support awarded: Grants to
individuals.
Limitations: Giving limited to WA and OR.
Application information: Applications not
invited.
Write: H.H. Hayner, Trustee
Trustees: H.H. Hayner, James K. Hayner,
Robert O. Kenyon.
Employer Identification Number: 916031350

4267
Tacoma Community Foundation, Greater
P.O. Box 1121
Tacoma 98401 (206) 383-5622

Community foundation incorporated in 1977 in
Washington.
Financial data: (yr. ended 5/31/84): Assets,
$572,856 (M); gifts received, $682,004;
expenditures, $1,062,436, including $827,995
for grants.
Purpose and activities: Primarily local giving,
for charitable, educational, cultural, health,
social, and civic purposes to benefit the citizens
of Pierce County.

Types of support awarded: Consulting services, technical assistance, emergency funds, seed money, building funds, equipment, matching funds.
Limitations: Giving limited to Pierce County, WA, especially Tacoma. No support for religious activities. No grants to individuals, or for annual campaigns, scholarships, fellowships, publications, operating budgets, continuing support, deficit financing, land acquisition, endowments, or conferences and seminars.
Publications: Annual report, program policy statement, application guidelines.
Application information:
  Initial approach: Letter or telephone
  Copies of proposal: 1
  Deadline(s): March 1 and September 1
  Board meeting date(s): Quarterly
  Final notification: Within 3 months
  Write: Margy McGroarty, Associate Director
Number of staff: 1 full-time professional; 1 part-time professional; 1 full-time support.
Employer Identification Number: 911007459

4268
Univar Foundation ⊭
1600 Norton Bldg.
Seattle 98104

Established in 1967.
Donor(s): Univar Corporation.
Financial data: (yr. ended 2/28/82): Assets, $382,181 (M); gifts received, $112,276; expenditures, $127,919, including $127,905 for 36 grants.
Purpose and activities: Primarily local giving to community funds, cultural programs, higher education, and youth agencies.
Types of support awarded: General purposes, building funds, operating budgets, research.
Limitations: Giving primarily in the Seattle, WA, area.
Officers: Robert D. O'Brien,* President; Harry Speiser, Secretary; N. Stewart Rogers,* Treasurer.
Trustees:* M.M. Harris, James Wiborg.
Employer Identification Number: 910826180

4269
Washington Mutual Savings Bank Foundation ⊭
1101 Second Ave.
Seattle 98101
Grant application address: c/o Foundation Secretary, WA Mutual Savings Bank, P.O. Box 834, Seattle, WA 98101

Established in 1979 in Washington.
Donor(s): Washington Mutual Savings Bank.
Financial data: (yr. ended 12/31/83): Assets, $129,550 (M); gifts received, $1,319; expenditures, $226,787, including $225,871 for 36 grants (high: $100,000; low: $200) and $375 for 6 employee matching gifts.
Purpose and activities: Primarily local giving in areas of company operations "to provide assistance and encouragement to local communities through non-profit organizations in the areas of health and welfare, cultural enhancement, and civic betterment," including support for higher education.

Types of support awarded: Operating budgets, scholarship funds, matching funds, special projects, employee matching gifts.
Limitations: Giving primarily in WA. No support for religious organizations for religious purposes, elementary or secondary schools, or veterans or labor organizations. No grants to individuals.
Publications: Program policy statement, application guidelines.
Application information: Application form required.
Officers and Directors: Sally S. Behnke, President; Robert Flowers, Vice-President; Deloria J. McWashington, Secretary; Ernest Jurdana, Treasurer; Herbert M. Bridge, Lawrence Connell, Rev. Samuel B. McKinney, Lou Pepper, Andrew V. Smith, Holt Webster.
Employer Identification Number: 911070920

4270
Welch (Carrie) Trust
P.O. Box 244
Walla Walla 99362

Trust established in 1946 in Washington.
Donor(s): Carrie Welch.†
Financial data: (yr. ended 10/31/83): Assets, $1,129,972 (M); expenditures, $192,436, including $137,339 for 9 grants (high: $30,000; low: $339) and $17,245 for 25 grants to individuals.
Purpose and activities: Local giving, with emphasis on higher education and aid to needy individuals.
Limitations: Giving limited to WA state, with preference to the Walla Walla area.
Application information: Funds fully committed.
Trustee: Vera Conkey.
Employer Identification Number: 916030361

4271
Welch (George T.) Testamentary Trust
c/o Baker-Boyer National Bank
P.O. Box 1796
Walla Walla 99362   (509) 525-2000

Established in 1938.
Financial data: (yr. ended 9/30/84): Assets, $1,863,547 (M); expenditures, $289,730, including $194,000 for 150 grants (high: $2,000; low: $300) and $95,730 for 60 grants to individuals.
Purpose and activities: Giving to local residents only; grants to the needy, including medical assistance, and for scholarships; some support also for youth agencies and cultural programs.
Types of support awarded: Special projects, scholarship funds, student aid, grants to individuals.
Limitations: Giving limited to Walla Walla County, WA. No grants for capital or endowment funds, general support, or matching gifts; no loans.
Publications: Program policy statement, application guidelines.
Application information: Application form required.
  Initial approach: Full proposal

Copies of proposal: 1
Deadline(s): May 1 for scholarships, July 1 for community projects, and February 20, May 20, August 20, and November 20 for health and welfare for the needy
Board meeting date(s): February, May, August, and November
Final notification: 30 days
Write: Bettie Loiacono, Trust Officer
Trustee: Baker-Boyer National Bank.
Number of staff: None.
Employer Identification Number: 916024318

4272
Wells (A. Z.) Foundation ⊭
c/o Seattle-First National Bank
P.O. Box 3586
Seattle 98124

Trust established in 1950 in Washington.
Donor(s): A.Z. Wells.
Financial data: (yr. ended 12/31/83): Assets, $8,973,768 (M); expenditures, $416,629, including $355,348 for 19 grants (high: $80,829; low: $5,000).
Purpose and activities: Primarily local giving within city of Wenatchee and north central Washington for hospitals, youth agencies, health agencies and a social service agency.
Limitations: Giving limited to north central WA, with emphasis on Wenatchee.
Trustee: Seattle-First National Bank (William C. Blanchard, Trust Officer).
Employer Identification Number: 916026580

4273
West (W. F. & Blanche E.) Educational Fund
c/o First Interstate Bank of Washington, Trust Dept.
473 N. Market Blvd., P.O. Box 180
Chehalis 98532

Established in 1969.
Financial data: (yr. ended 12/31/83): Assets, $1,602,864 (M); expenditures, $104,422, including $89,013 for grants to individuals.
Purpose and activities: Scholarships to local residents.
Types of support awarded: Student aid.
Limitations: Giving limited to graduates of a Chehalis, WA, high school, who have also been residents of Lewis County, WA, for at least 2 years.
Application information: Scholarships to graduates of W.F. West High School only; application forms available at school.
  Deadline(s): April 15
Trustee: First Interstate Bank of Washington.
Employer Identification Number: 916101769

4274
Weyerhaeuser Company Foundation ▼
Tacoma 98477   (206) 924-3159

Incorporated in 1948 in Washington.
Donor(s): Weyerhaeuser Company.

Financial data: (yr. ended 12/31/84): Assets, $31,310,987 (M); expenditures, $6,901,219, including $3,670,271 for 527 grants (high: $187,000; low: $150; average: $1,000-$5,000) and $186,629 for 115 grants to individuals.

Purpose and activities: Grants awarded for two purposes: community giving to enhance the quality of life in areas of company activity, and grants to increase understanding of and leadership for issues related to the forest products industry.

Types of support awarded: Seed money, emergency funds, building funds, equipment, land acquisition, scholarship funds, employee related scholarships, fellowships, publications, conferences and seminars, employee matching gifts.

Limitations: Giving limited to areas of company operations for community services; giving to national organizations in industry-related fields. No support for religious organizations for religious purposes, or for political bodies. No grants to individuals (except for company-employee scholarships), or for endowments or memorials.

Publications: Annual report, application guidelines.

Application information: Application form required.

  Initial approach: Letter
  Copies of proposal: 1
  Deadline(s): None
  Board meeting date(s): February; executive committee meets in March, June, September, and December
  Final notification: 90 to 120 days
  Write: Mary Stewart Hall, Vice-President

Officers: A.M. Fisken,* President; Mary Stewart Hall,* Vice-President and Executive Director; Kenneth Miller, Secretary; William C. Stivers, Treasurer.

Trustees:* R.B. Wilson, Chairman; Charles W. Bingham, D.R. Edwards, D.L. McInnes, W. Howarth Meadowcroft, Harry E. Morgan, Jr., William H. Oliver, Robert L. Schuyler, George H. Weyerhaeuser, Chuck H. Wiggins, John H. Wilkinson, F.L. Wyatt.

Number of staff: 4 full-time professional; 3 full-time support.

Employer Identification Number: 916024225

4275
Wharton Foundation, Inc., The
12168 S.E. 17th Place
Bellevue 98005   (206) 643-4699

Established in 1954 in Maryland.
Donor(s): Sara P. Wharton.
Financial data: (yr. ended 12/31/83): Assets, $1,204,588 (M); gifts received, $45,000; expenditures, $87,743, including $84,537 for 136 grants (high: $10,000; low: $25; average: $200-$2,000).

Purpose and activities: Giving primarily for higher and secondary education, civic affairs and community development, cultural programs, and youth agencies.

Types of support awarded: Operating budgets, continuing support, annual campaigns, seed money, emergency funds, deficit financing, building funds, equipment, endowment funds, land acquisition.

Limitations: No grants to individuals, or for scholarships, fellowships, program support, research, demonstration projects, publications, conferences and seminars, or matching gifts; no loans.

Publications: Application guidelines.

Application information:

  Initial approach: Proposal
  Copies of proposal: 1
  Deadline(s): None
  Final notification: 3 months
  Write: Joseph B. Wharton III, Vice-President

Officers: S.P. Wharton, President; J.B. Wharton, Vice-President and Secretary; J.W. Pettitt, W.R. Wharton, Vice-Presidents.

Number of staff: None.

Employer Identification Number: 366130748

4276
Wyman Youth Trust ⋈
701 Skinner Bldg.
1326 Fifth Ave.
Seattle 98101

Trust established in 1951 in Washington.
Donor(s): Members of the Wyman family.
Financial data: (yr. ended 12/31/83): Assets, $1,957,513 (M); expenditures, $110,014, including $85,559 for 75 grants (high: $6,000; low: $50).

Purpose and activities: Giving locally and in York County, Nebraska, with emphasis on "youth-oriented projects, civic and cultural development, and special community endeavors"; support also for schools and health services.

Limitations: Giving limited to King County, WA, and York County, NE. No grants to individuals or for capital funds.

Publications: Program policy statement, application guidelines.

Application information:

  Initial approach: Proposal
  Copies of proposal: 1
  Deadline(s): March 1, June 1, September 1, and December 1
  Board meeting date(s): March, June, September, and December
  Final notification: 4 to 6 months
  Write: Deehan M. Wyman, Trustee

Trustees: David C. Wyman, Deehan M. Wyman, Virginia D. Wyman.

Number of staff: None.

Employer Identification Number: 916031590

WEST VIRGINIA

4277
Bowen (Ethel N.) Foundation
c/o First National Bank of Bluefield
500 Federal St.
Bluefield 24701   (304) 325-8181

Established about 1968 in West Virginia.
Donor(s): Ethel N. Bowen.†
Financial data: (yr. ended 12/31/83): Assets, $1,825,522 (M); expenditures, $150,471, including $134,617 for 80 grants to individuals (average: $2,000).

Purpose and activities: Furthering the education of students in the southern West Virginia and southwestern Virginia coalfields; support for scholarships only.

Types of support awarded: Student aid.

Limitations: Giving limited to southern WV and southwestern VA. No loans.

Application information:

  Initial approach: Letter
  Copies of proposal: 1
  Board meeting date(s): Monthly
  Write: R.W. Wilkinson, Secretary-Treasurer

Officers: Virginia M. Bowen, President; B.L. Jackson, Director; R.W. Wilkinson, Secretary-Treasurer.

Trustee: The First National Bank of Bluefield.

Employer Identification Number: 237010740

4278
Carbon Fuel Foundation, Inc.
511 Kanawha Valley Bldg.
Charleston 25301

Incorporated in 1953 in West Virginia.
Donor(s): Carbon Fuel Company, Kentucky Carbon Corporation.
Financial data: (yr. ended 12/31/83): Assets, $1,464,813 (M); expenditures, $126,819, including $119,630 for 31 grants (high: $30,000; low: $80).

Purpose and activities: Primarily local giving to educational and charitable organizations, with emphasis on higher education, youth and child welfare agencies, and health agencies.

Types of support awarded: Operating budgets, building funds, research, scholarship funds.

Limitations: Giving primarily in WV.

Officers and Trustees: L.N. Thomas, President; James R. Thomas II, Vice-President; Sherman E. Witt, Jr., Secretary and Treasurer; Robert F. Barroner, David M. Giltinan, Jr., David S. Long, Quin Morton, John M. Wells, Sr.

Employer Identification Number: 556015917

4279
Carter Family Foundation ⌘
c/o Raleigh County National Bank
129 Main St.
Beckley 25801   (304) 252-6581

Established in 1981 in West Virginia.
Donor(s): Bernard E. Carter.†
Financial data: (yr. ended 6/30/83): Assets,
$1,119,576 (M); expenditures, $61,169,
including $54,500 for 43 grants (high: $5,000;
low: $500).
Purpose and activities: Primarily local giving,
with emphasis on higher education, church
support, social services, and health.
Limitations: Giving limited to WV.
Application information:
Initial approach: Letter and resume
Deadline(s): None
Write: W. David Mullins, Trust Officer
Trustee: Raleigh County National Bank.
Employer Identification Number: 550606479

4280
Chambers (James B.) Memorial ⌘
2207 National Rd.
Wheeling 26003

Established in 1924 in West Virginia.
Financial data: (yr. ended 12/31/83): Assets,
$2,265,031 (M); expenditures, $144,158,
including $124,066 for 21 grants (high:
$25,000; low: $507).
Purpose and activities: Local giving, with
emphasis on education, including higher
education, social services, youth agencies, and
community development.
Limitations: Giving limited to Wheeling, WV.
Officer: Stephen E. Hannig, Executive Director.
Employer Identification Number: 550360517

4281
Daywood Foundation, Inc., The
1200 Charleston National Plaza
Charleston 25301   (304) 343-4841

Incorporated in 1958 in West Virginia.
Donor(s): Ruth Woods Dayton.
Financial data: (yr. ended 12/31/83): Assets,
$5,124,523 (M); expenditures, $432,384,
including $384,748 for 43 grants (high:
$40,000; low: $1,000).
Purpose and activities: Broad purposes; grants
restricted to local organizations (except for a
few out-of-state training institutions), with
emphasis on higher education; some support
for welfare agencies, youth agencies, and
community funds.
Limitations: Giving limited to WV. No grants
to individuals, or for endowment funds,
research, scholarships, or fellowships; no loans.
Publications: Application guidelines.
Application information:
Initial approach: Letter
Copies of proposal: 1
Deadline(s): Submit proposal preferably in
January through May; deadline May 31
Board meeting date(s): July and December
Write: Ernest H. Gilbert, Secretary-Treasurer

Officers and Directors: George H. Vick,
President; R.K. Talbott, Vice-President; Ernest
H. Gilbert, Secretary-Treasurer; L. Newton
Thomas.
Employer Identification Number: 556018107

4282
Fenton Foundation, Inc.
c/o Frank M. Fenton
310 Fourth St.
Williamstown 26187

Established in 1955.
Financial data: (yr. ended 12/31/82): Assets,
$1,485,894 (M); gifts received, $69,031;
expenditures, $100,366, including $90,175 for
51 grants (high: $25,000; low: $25).
Purpose and activities: Giving locally and in
Marietta, Ohio, largely for higher education,
church support, and community funds.
Limitations: Giving primarily in Williamstown,
WV, and Marietta, OH.
Officers and Directors: Wilmer C. Fenton,
President; Thomas K. Fenton, Vice-President;
Elinor P. Fenton, Secretary; Frank M. Fenton,
Treasurer.
Employer Identification Number: 556017260

4283
Harless (James) Foundation,
Incorporated ⌘
Drawer D
Gilbert 25621   (304) 664-3227

Established in 1967.
Donor(s): James H. Harless, Gilbert Imported
Hardwoods, and others.
Financial data: (yr. ended 12/31/83): Assets,
$1,497,031 (M); gifts received, $540,250;
expenditures, $513,342, including $489,430
for 45 grants (high: $300,000; low: $25),
$5,131 for 13 grants to individuals and
$18,875 for 11 loans.
Purpose and activities: Primarily local giving
to higher and secondary education, and
Protestant religious organizations.
Limitations: Giving primarily in WV.
Application information: Application form
required.
Deadline(s): None
Write: Ruth Phipps, Secretary
Officers: James M. Harless, President; Larry J.
Harless, Vice-President; Ruth Phipps, Secretary.
Employer Identification Number: 237093387

4284
Jacobson (Bernard H. and Blanche E.)
Foundation ⌘
c/o Kanawha Valley Bank Trust Dept.
P.O. Box 1793
Charleston 25326

Established in 1954 in West Virginia.
Donor(s): Bernard H. Jacobson, Balche E.
Jacobson.
Financial data: (yr. ended 12/31/83): Assets,
$1,196,736 (M); expenditures, $86,760,
including $79,550 for 29 grants (high: $30,000;
low: $100).

Purpose and activities: Primarily local giving
to education, social services (including local
chapters of national associations), Jewish
welfare funds, and a community fund.
Limitations: Giving primarily in WV,
particularly Kanawha Valley and Charleston.
Trustees: Charles W. Loeb, John L. Ray, L.N.
Thomas, Jr., Kanawha Valley Bank.
Employer Identification Number: 556014902

4285
Kanawha Valley Foundation, The
Greater
P.O. Box 3041
Charleston 25331   (304) 346-3620

Community foundation established in 1962 in
West Virginia.
Financial data: (yr. ended 12/31/83): Assets,
$12,906,620 (M); gifts received, $861,172;
expenditures, $639,757, including $406,559
for 91 grants (high: $25,000; low: $89;
average: $500-$5,000) and $200,371 for 200
grants to individuals.
Purpose and activities: Giving to benefit
residents of the Kanawha Valley area; support
for education, social services, health, the arts,
and recreation.
Types of support awarded: Operating
budgets, continuing support, seed money,
emergency funds, building funds, equipment,
land acquisition, student aid, special projects,
research, publications, conferences and
seminars, consulting services, technical
assistance.
Limitations: Giving limited to the Greater
Kanawha Valley, WV, area, except scholarships
which are limited to residents of WV. No
grants for annual campaigns, deficit financing,
general endowments, or matching gifts; no
loans.
Publications: Annual report, application
guidelines.
Application information:
Initial approach: Full proposal
Copies of proposal: 1
Deadline(s): 1st of April, July, October and
December
Board meeting date(s): Usually in April, July,
October, and December
Final notification: Immediately after Board
action
Write: Stanley Loewenstein, Executive
Director
Officers and Trustees: Olivia R. Singleton,*
Chairman; Thomas N. McJunkin,* Vice-
Chairman; Charles W. Loeb,* Secretary;
Stanley Loewenstein, Executive Director; G.
Thomas Battle, Frederick H. Belden, Jr., David
C. Hardesty, Jr., James H. Nix, Mark H. Schaul,
Adeline J. Voorhees.
Advisory Committee:* Paul N. Bowles, Bert
A. Bradford, Jr., W.G. Caperton, Elizabeth E.
Chilton, William M. Davis, Willard H. Erwin,
Jr., Brent B. Galyean, J.W. Hubbard, Jr., Harry
Moore, R.F. Randolph, Dolly Sherwood,
Charles B. Stacy, L. Newton Thomas, Jr.

Trustee Banks: Bank of West Virginia, Charleston National Bank, City National Bank of Charleston, Kanawha Banking & Trust Company, Kanawha Valley Bank, National Bank of Commerce of Charleston.
Number of staff: 1 full-time professional; 1 full-time support.
Employer Identification Number: 556024430

4286
McDonough (Bernard) Foundation, Inc.
1000 Grand Central Mall
P.O. Box 1825
Parkersburg 26102 (304) 485-4494

Incorporated in 1961 in West Virginia.
Donor(s): Bernard P. McDonough.
Financial data: (yr. ended 12/31/83): Assets, $2,724,087 (M); expenditures, $268,059, including $208,600 for 15 grants (high: $100,000; low: $1,000).
Purpose and activities: General purposes; with priority given to local programs with no other source of funding; higher education, civic affairs, health, and social agencies, including the handicapped.
Limitations: Giving primarily in WV. No support for religious organizations, or national health or welfare campaigns. No grants to individuals, or for personnel or operating expenses, or publications.
Application information:
 Initial approach: Letter
 Copies of proposal: 1
 Deadline(s): Submit full proposal preferably in October; no deadline
 Board meeting date(s): December
 Final notification: 1 to 2 weeks
 Write: James T. Wakley, President
Officers: James T. Wakley,* President; Alma McDonough,* Vice-President; D.E. Fidler, Secretary and Treasurer.
Directors:* Carl Broughton, Mark C. Kury, F.C. McCusker, Bernard P. McDonough.
Number of staff: 2 part-time professional.
Employer Identification Number: 556023693

4287
Minor (The Berkeley) and Susan Fontaine Minor Foundation
c/o John L. Ray
1210 One Valley Square
Charleston 25301

Trust established in 1957 in West Virginia.
Donor(s): Berkeley Minor, Jr.†
Financial data: (yr. ended 12/31/83): Assets, $1,247,664 (M); expenditures, $80,593, including $500 for 1 grant and $68,000 for 18 grants to individuals.
Purpose and activities: Scholarships for West Virginia residents admitted to the University of Charleston, the University of Virginia, the Protestant Episcopal Theological Seminary of Virginia, Marshall University, or West Virginia University.
Types of support awarded: Student aid.
Limitations: Giving limited to residents of WV attending colleges and universities in WV and VA.

Application information: Only students attending West Virginia universities and colleges, or Marshall University, should apply directly to the Foundation.
 Initial approach: Letter
 Deadline(s): August 1
 Board meeting date(s): August and as required
Trustees: Charles W. Loeb, John L. Ray, William E. Thayer, Jr., Kanawha Valley Bank.
Employer Identification Number: 556014946

4288
Price (Herschel C.) Educational Foundation
P.O. Box 412
Huntington 25708 (304) 529-3852

Trust established in 1975 in West Virginia.
Donor(s): Herschel C. Price.†
Financial data: (yr. ended 4/30/84): Assets, $1,890,832 (M); expenditures, $170,324, including $145,375 for 229 grants to individuals (high: $1,500; low: $175; average: $650).
Purpose and activities: Scholarships awarded directly to deserving students for attendance at accredited local educational institutions, with preference given to undergraduates residing in West Virginia, or attending West Virginia colleges and universities. Interviews generally required with selection based on financial need as well as scholastic standing.
Types of support awarded: Student aid, grants to individuals.
Limitations: Giving primarily in WV.
Application information: Application form required.
 Initial approach: Letter
 Deadline(s): Submit application from February to March or August to September; deadlines April 1 and October 1
 Board meeting date(s): May and November
 Final notification: Directly after board meeting dates
 Write: E. Joann Price, Trustee
Trustees: Chandos H. Peak, E. Joann Price, The First Huntington National Bank.
Number of staff: 2 full-time professional.
Employer Identification Number: 556076719

4289
Prichard School, Board of Trustees of the ⌑
c/o Trust Dept. FHNB
P.O. Box 179
Huntington 25707
Application address: Willowvale Square, Rte. 2, South Point, OH 45680; Tel.: (614) 894-4704

Established in 1923.
Financial data: (yr. ended 12/31/83): Assets, $4,544,544 (M); expenditures, $311,634, including $293,000 for 11 grants (high: $88,000; low: $1,000).
Purpose and activities: Primarily local giving to higher and secondary education and youth organizations.
Application information:

 Write: Dr. Robert M. Wild
Officers: Paul W. McCreight, Secretary; William F. Agee, Treasurer.
Employer Identification Number: 550435910

4290
Vecellio (The Enrico) Family Foundation, Inc. ⌑
c/o Raleigh County National Bank
129 Main St.
Beckley 25801

Established in 1972.
Financial data: (yr. ended 12/31/83): Assets, $1,441,239 (M); gifts received, $9,250; expenditures, $157,979, including $99,500 for 33 grants (high: $10,000; low: $500) and $39,256 for 19 grants to individuals.
Purpose and activities: Grants for higher education, including scholarships to students from local high schools, youth and social agencies, and church support.
Types of support awarded: Student aid.
Limitations: Giving primarily in WV. No grants to individuals (except scholarships for graduates of local high schools).
Application information: Application form required.
 Write: W. David Mullins, Treasurer
Officers and Trustees:* Leo A. Vecellio,* President; Leo A. Vecellio, Jr.,* Vice-President; John L. Taylor, Secretary; W. David Mullins, Treasurer.
Employer Identification Number: 550538242

WISCONSIN

4291
Alexander Charitable Foundation, Inc. ⌑
c/o Samuel A. Casey
100 Wisconsin River Dr.
Port Edwards 54469 (715) 887-5111

Incorporated in 1955 in Wisconsin.
Donor(s): John E. Alexander.†
Financial data: (yr. ended 12/31/83): Assets, $3,950,232 (M); expenditures, $161,161, including $145,722 for 4 grants (high: $126,520; low: $1,000).
Purpose and activities: Broad purposes; primarily local giving, with emphasis on a youth agency, Protestant church support, and hospitals.
Limitations: Giving primarily in WI. No grants to individuals.
Application information:
 Initial approach: Letter
 Copies of proposal: 1
 Board meeting date(s): Quarterly
 Write: Samuel A. Casey, Secretary

Officers and Directors: Gerard E. Veneman, President; Charles Lester, Vice-President; Margaret Boyarski, Secretary; Samuel A. Casey, Treasurer.
Employer Identification Number: 396045140

4292
Alexander (Judd S.) Foundation, Inc.
500 Third St., Suite 509
P.O. Box 418
Wausau 54401 (715) 845-4556

Incorporated in 1973 in Wisconsin.
Donor(s): Anne M. Alexander.†
Financial data: (yr. ended 6/30/84): Assets, $8,937,425 (M); expenditures, $392,587, including $270,472 for 56 grants (high: $29,000; low: $175) and $157,723 for 3 loans.
Purpose and activities: Primarily local giving, with emphasis on civic affairs, youth agencies, higher education, cultural programs, and social agencies.
Types of support awarded: Seed money, emergency funds, building funds, equipment, land acquisition, matching funds, technical assistance, program-related investments.
Limitations: Giving primarily in WI. No grants to individuals, or for endowment funds, scholarships or fellowships, special projects, research, publications, or conferences.
Publications: Application guidelines.
Application information:
 Initial approach: Letter, full proposal, or telephone
 Copies of proposal: None
 Deadline(s): None
 Board meeting date(s): Monthly
 Final notification: 60 days
 Write: Stanley F. Staples, Jr., President
Officers and Directors: Stanley F. Staples, Jr., President; Harry N. Heinemann, Jr., Vice-President; John F. Michler, Secretary; Richard D. Dudley, Treasurer.
Number of staff: None.
Employer Identification Number: 237323721

4293
Alexander (Walter) Foundation, Inc.
502 Third St.
P.O. Box 418
Wausau 54401 (715) 845-4556

Incorporated in 1952 in Wisconsin.
Donor(s): Ruth Alexander,† Anne M. Alexander.†
Financial data: (yr. ended 11/30/83): Assets, $1,937,941 (M); expenditures, $102,090, including $73,118 for 30 grants (high: $9,000; low: $600).
Purpose and activities: Charitable purposes; primarily local giving, with emphasis on higher and secondary education, cultural programs and social agencies.
Types of support awarded: Operating budgets, seed money, emergency funds, building funds, equipment, land acquisition, matching funds.
Limitations: Giving primarily in WI. No grants to individuals, or for endowment funds, scholarships or fellowships, special projects, research, or conferences; no loans.

Publications: Program policy statement, application guidelines.
Application information:
 Initial approach: Letter, full proposal, or telephone
 Copies of proposal: 1
 Deadline(s): None, but preferably before June
 Board meeting date(s): 3 times a year or as required
 Final notification: 4 months
 Write: Stanley F. Staples, Jr., Secretary
Officers and Directors: Jean A. Koskinen, President; Nancy Anne Cordaro, Vice-President; Stanley F. Staples, Jr., Secretary; John F. Michler, Treasurer; Robert C. Altman.
Number of staff: None.
Employer Identification Number: 396044635

4294
Allis-Chalmers Foundation, Inc. ▼
1205 South 70th St.
West Allis 53214 (414) 475-2995

Incorporated in 1951 in Wisconsin.
Donor(s): Allis-Chalmers Corporation.
Financial data: (yr. ended 12/31/82): Assets, $30,039 (M); gifts received, $655,000; expenditures, $658,308, including $656,323 for 275 grants (high: $176,000).
Purpose and activities: All contributions activities are suspended for an indeterminate period. Normally, broad purposes; primarily local giving in plant communities, particularly the Milwaukee area, with emphasis on higher education, community funds, and cultural programs.
Types of support awarded: General purposes, operating budgets, continuing support, annual campaigns, seed money, emergency funds, deficit financing, building funds, equipment, land acquisition, consulting services, technical assistance, professorships, scholarship funds, fellowships, special projects, research, publications, conferences and seminars.
Limitations: Giving primarily in areas of company operations, with emphasis on the Milwaukee, WI area. No support for religious organizations. No grants to individuals, or for endowment funds, or matching gifts; no loans.
Application information: All contributions activities as well as board meetings suspended for an undetermined period.
 Initial approach: Letter
 Deadline(s): None
 Final notification: 2 to 3 months
 Write: R.P. Buchman, Secretary
Officers: W.F. Bueche,* President; R.M. FitzSimmons,* C.W. Parker, Jr.,* Vice-Presidents; R.P. Buchman, Secretary; P.B. Oldam, Treasurer.
Directors:* David C. Scott, Chairman; Joseph J. Laferty, Mary D. Scott, J.L. Platner.
Number of staff: None.
Employer Identification Number: 390846355

4295
Amundson (Alvin R.) Charitable Remainder Trust
c/o Marshall and Ilsley Bank, Madison Trust Office
P.O. Box 830
Madison 53701

Financial data: (yr. ended 3/31/82): Assets, $1,083,756 (M); expenditures, $77,504, including $68,225 for 12 grants (high: $38,225; low: $1,000).
Purpose and activities: Local giving for community development, including a Fire Commission, and youth agencies.
Limitations: Giving limited to the Village of Cambridge and surrounding municipalities.
Trustee: Marshall & Ilsley Bank, Madison Trust Office.
Employer Identification Number: 396274739

4296
Andres (Frank G.) Charitable Trust ⌑
c/o Farmers & Merchants' Bank
1001 Superior Ave., P.O. Box 753
Tomah 54660

Trust established in Wisconsin.
Financial data: (yr. ended 6/30/83): Assets, $1,276,400 (M); expenditures, $133,335, including $116,675 for 17 grants (high: $30,000; low: $400).
Purpose and activities: Primarily local giving, with emphasis on civic affairs, a hospital, education, social agencies, and cultural programs.
Limitations: Giving primarily in Tomah, WI.
Application information:
 Deadline(s): May 15
Officer and Trustees: Richard Baumgarten, Treasurer; John W. Drew, Earl Fisher, Donald Kortbein, David Myer, Roxann O'Connor.
Employer Identification Number: 510172405

4297
Apollo Fund Limited ⌑
c/o Orin Purintun
777 East Wisconsin Ave.
Milwaukee 53202

Established in 1948.
Financial data: (yr. ended 7/31/83): Assets, $1,447,894 (M); expenditures, $78,657, including $68,500 for 39 grants (high: $10,000; low: $500).
Purpose and activities: Primarily local giving, with emphasis on higher education, youth agencies, cultural programs, health agencies, and hospitals.
Limitations: Giving primarily in Milwaukee, WI.
Officers and Directors: F.H. Roby, President; R.B. Bradley, Vice-President; O. Purintun, Secretary; R.J. Maier, Treasurer; James F. McKenna.
Employer Identification Number: 396044029

4298
ARMCO Insurance Group Foundation
c/o Armco Insurance Group, Inc.
731 North Jackson St.
Milwaukee 53202 (414) 765-8500

Established in 1967 in Wisconsin.
Donor(s): Armco Insurance Group, Inc.

Financial data: (yr. ended 12/31/84): Assets, $1,712,065 (M); expenditures, $291,932, including $239,032 for 49 grants (high: $52,750; low: $100) and $45,000 for 183 employee matching gifts.
Purpose and activities: General giving, with emphasis on community funds, higher education, including employee matching gifts, cultural programs, health, and youth agencies.
Types of support awarded: Employee matching gifts.
Application information:
Write: Robert C. Whitaker, Secretary
Officers and Trustees: D.H. Daehling, Vice-President and Treasurer; Robert C. Whitaker, Secretary; George E. Doty, Loren L. Fligg.
Employer Identification Number: 396102416

4299
Badger Meter Foundation, Inc.
4545 West Brown Deer Rd.
Milwaukee 53223   (414) 355-0400

Incorporated in 1952 in Wisconsin.
Donor(s): Badger Meter, Inc.
Financial data: (yr. ended 12/31/84): Assets, $1,877,483 (M); expenditures, $133,272, including $117,700 for 60 grants (high: $20,000; low: $100; average: $100-$10,000).
Purpose and activities: Giving exclusively in Wisconsin and primarily in the greater Milwaukee area, with grants largely for community funds, higher education, the arts, health care, and programs for the disabled.
Types of support awarded: Operating budgets, continuing support, annual campaigns, seed money, emergency funds, deficit financing, building funds, equipment, land acquisition, endowment funds, research, special projects.
Limitations: Giving limited to WI, with emphasis on the greater Milwaukee area. No grants to individuals, or for matching gifts, scholarships, fellowships, publications, or conferences; no loans.
Application information:
Initial approach: Letter
Copies of proposal: 1
Deadline(s): Submit proposal preferably in November
Board meeting date(s): Usually in March, June, September, and December
Final notification: 30 to 60 days
Write: Teresa Kelley, Manager
Officers: James O. Wright,* President; E.G. Smith,* Vice-President; R. Robert Howard, Treasurer.
Directors:* Ronald H. Dix, Richard S. Gallagher, Barbara M. Wiley.
Number of staff: 1 part-time professional.
Employer Identification Number: 396043635

4300
Banta Company Foundation, Inc.
Curtis Reed Plaza
Menasha 54952   (414) 722-7771

Incorporated in 1953 in Wisconsin.
Donor(s): George Banta Company, Inc.

Financial data: (yr. ended 12/31/82): Assets, $5,004 (M); gifts received, $150,000; expenditures, $149,001, including $136,200 for 46 grants (high: $30,000; low: $100) and $12,780 for 18 employee matching gifts.
Purpose and activities: Broad purposes; local giving, with emphasis on higher education and youth agencies; support also for cultural programs, including a historical society, and hospitals.
Types of support awarded: Operating budgets, continuing support, annual campaigns, seed money, emergency funds, deficit financing, building funds, equipment, land acquisition, employee matching gifts.
Limitations: Giving limited to WI. No grants to individuals, or for scholarships or fellowhips, or endowments; no loans.
Application information:
Initial approach: Letter
Copies of proposal: 1
Deadline(s): Submit proposal preferably from September through December for the following year
Board meeting date(s): April, June, September, and December
Write: Dean E. Bergstrom, Vice-President
Officers: Harry W. Earle, President; Dean E. Bergstrom, Vice-President and Secretary-Treasurer; Margaret B. Humleker, Donald S. Koskinen, Anton G. Stepanek, Vice-Presidents.
Number of staff: None.
Employer Identification Number: 396050779

4301
Beloit Foundation, Inc. ▼
Beloit Corporation
One St. Lawrence Ave.
Beloit 53511   (608) 364-7014

Incorporated in 1959 in Wisconsin.
Donor(s): Elbert H. Neese.†
Financial data: (yr. ended 12/31/83): Assets, $12,949,556 (M); gifts received, $81,286; expenditures, $954,371, including $767,368 for 43 grants (high: $200,000; low: $500; average: $500-$25,000).
Purpose and activities: Broad purposes; local giving, for education, with emphasis on a local college; social and youth agencies, and a community fund.
Types of support awarded: Building funds, matching funds, seed money.
Limitations: Giving limited to Beloit, WI. No grants to individuals, or for endowment funds, research, or scholarships and fellowships; no loans.
Application information: Application form required.
Initial approach: Letter
Copies of proposal: 1
Deadline(s): Submit proposal in December or June; no set deadline
Board meeting date(s): February and August
Write: Gary G. Grabowski, Secretary
Officers and Directors: E.H. Neese, Chairman; J.H. Franz, President; R.H. Neese, Vice-President and Treasurer; Gary G. Grabowski, Secretary; A.B. Adams, Harry C. Moore.
Employer Identification Number: 396068763

4302
Bradley Family Foundation, Inc., The ⌑
c/o Irene Braeger
1201 South Second St.
Milwaukee 53204

Incorporated in 1967 in Wisconsin.
Donor(s): Margaret B. Bradley,† Jane Bradley Pettit.
Financial data: (yr. ended 9/30/83): Assets, $3,345,910 (M); gifts received, $347,500; expenditures, $172,405, including $107,618 for 1 foundation-administered program.
Purpose and activities: General giving, primarily in Milwaukee, Wisconsin, and Florida, with emphasis on a sculpture garden operated by the foundation.
Limitations: Giving primarily in WI and FL. No grants to individuals, or for building or endowment funds, or operating budgets.
Application information:
Board meeting date(s): Annually
Officers and Directors: Jane Bradley Pettit, President; Lloyd H. Pettit, Vice-President; Lynde V. Olson, Secretary; David V. Uihlein, Jr., Treasurer.
Employer Identification Number: 396105450

4303
Bradley (The Lynde and Harry) Foundation, Inc. ▼
(formerly Allen-Bradley Foundation, Inc.)
1201 South Second St.
Milwaukee 53204   (414) 671-2000

Incorporated in 1942 in Wisconsin.
Donor(s): Harry L. Bradley,† Caroline D. Bradley,† Margaret B. Bradley, Margaret Loock Trust, Allen-Bradley Company.
Financial data: (yr. ended 7/31/83): Assets, $14,332,897 (M); gifts received, $749,504; expenditures, $1,529,220, including $1,395,185 for 166 grants (high: $255,000; low: $75; average: $1,000-$25,000).
Purpose and activities: General purposes; support for higher education, community funds, social services, community development, health agencies, hospitals, the performing arts, cultural programs, public policy, and youth agencies, with some emphasis on the Milwaukee area.
Limitations: No support for strictly denominational organizations. No grants to individuals.
Application information:
Initial approach: Full proposal
Deadline(s): 6 weeks before board meetings
Board meeting date(s): February, May, and September
Final notification: 2 weeks
Write: I. Andrew Rader, President
Officers and Directors: I. Andrew Rader, President; William H. Brady, Jr., Vice-President; Wayne J. Roper, Secretary; James D. Ericson, Treasurer; Julie T. Carpenter, Program Director; Sarah Louise Barder, Richard H. Lillie, John W. Matheus, David V. Uihlein, Jr.
Number of staff: None.
Employer Identification Number: 396037928

4304
Brady (W. H.) Foundation, Inc.
727 West Glendale Ave.
Milwaukee 53209

Incorporated in 1956 in Wisconsin.
Donor(s): W.H. Brady Co.
Financial data: (yr. ended 7/31/84): Assets, $3,144,834 (M); gifts received, $105,000; expenditures, $109,607, including $83,737 for 41 grants (high: $13,334; low: $100).
Purpose and activities: General giving, about one-third to organizations in Wisconsin with an emphasis on higher education, cultural programs, and welfare; giving to national organizations with emphasis on public policy and education in economics and the social sciences; grants also for general higher education.
Officers and Directors: William H. Brady, Jr., President and Treasurer; Irene J. Brady, Vice-President; Elizabeth A. Brady, William H. Brady, III, Peter J. Lettenberger, Elizabeth B. Lurie, James E. Larson.
Employer Identification Number: 396064733

4305
Braun (Victor F.) Foundation, Incorporated
c/o Quarles and Brady
780 N. Water St.
Milwaukee 53202

Established in 1956.
Financial data: (yr. ended 11/30/83): Assets, $4,967,783 (M); expenditures, $335,815, including $327,500 for 85 grants (high: $15,000; low: $1,000).
Purpose and activities: Broad purposes; local giving, including chapters of national organizations, with emphasis on medical research, hospitals, higher, secondary, and vocational education, social services and agencies, cultural programs, and youth agencies.
Limitations: Giving primarily in WI, with emphasis on Milwaukee; also in KY, MI, AR, and CT.
Officers and Directors:* James V. Braun,* President; Victor F. Braun,* Vice-President; Roger Myers, Secretary; John H. Ladish,* Treasurer.
Employer Identification Number: 396043604

4306
Briggs & Stratton Corporation Foundation, Inc. ▼
12301 W. Wirth St.
P.O. Box 702
Wauwatosa 53201   (414) 259-5333

Incorporated in 1954 in Wisconsin.
Donor(s): Briggs & Stratton Corporation.
Financial data: (yr. ended 11/30/84): Assets, $4,622,480 (M); gifts received, $384,000; expenditures, $687,846, including $641,172 for 54 grants (high: $190,000; low: $100; average: $500-$10,000) and $39,500 for 40 grants to individuals.

Purpose and activities: Primarily local giving, with emphasis on higher education, community funds, youth agencies, hospitals, and cultural programs.
Types of support awarded: Operating budgets, special projects, employee related scholarships.
Limitations: Giving primarily in WI, with emphasis on Milwaukee. No support for religious organizations. No grants to individuals (except company employee scholarships).
Application information:
  Initial approach: Proposal
  Copies of proposal: 1
  Deadline(s): January 31 for employee scholarship program; none for public charity grants
  Board meeting date(s): June and November
  Final notification: 4 months
  Write: K.K. Preston, Secretary-Treasurer
Officers and Directors: F.P. Stratton, Jr., President; L.G. Regner, Vice-President; K.K. Preston, Secretary-Treasurer.
Number of staff: 1.
Employer Identification Number: 396040377

4307
Brotz (Frank G.) Family Foundation, Inc. ⊠
3518 Lakeshore Rd.
Sheboygan 53081

Incorporated in 1953 in Wisconsin.
Donor(s): Plastics Engineering Company.
Financial data: (yr. ended 9/30/82): Assets, $4,750,081 (M); gifts received, $300,000; expenditures, $387,855, including $381,400 for 90 grants (high: $50,000; low: $150).
Purpose and activities: Broad purposes; primarily local giving, including support for building funds, with emphasis on hospitals, higher education, youth agencies, cultural programs, and a retirement home.
Types of support awarded: Building funds.
Limitations: Giving primarily in WI.
Officers and Members: Ralph T. Brotz, President; Frank M. Brotz, Secretary-Treasurer; William A. Jackson, Roland M. Neumann, Joseph H. Schilder.
Employer Identification Number: 396060552

4308
Bucyrus-Erie Foundation, Inc. ▼
1100 Milwaukee Ave.
P.O. Box 56
South Milwaukee 53172   (414) 768-5005

Incorporated in 1951 in Wisconsin.
Donor(s): Bucyrus-Erie Company.
Financial data: (yr. ended 12/31/83): Assets, $8,147,146 (M); expenditures, $493,755, including $455,056 for 167 grants (high: $58,713; low: $25; average: $100-$10,000).
Purpose and activities: Broad purposes; primarily local giving in metropolitan Milwaukee and other areas of company operations, with emphasis on higher education, the arts, hospitals, and community funds; support also for social services and youth agencies.

Types of support awarded: Operating budgets, continuing support, annual campaigns, building funds, equipment, endowment funds, employee matching gifts, employee related scholarships.
Limitations: Giving primarily in metropolitan Milwaukee, WI, and other areas of company operations, including CA, ID, and PA. No grants to individuals, or for research, special projects, seed money, emergency funds, deficit financing, land acquisition, matching gifts, publications, or conferences; no loans.
Application information:
  Initial approach: Letter
  Deadline(s): Submit request preferably in December or August; no set deadline
  Board meeting date(s): February and October
  Final notification: At the latest, after next board meeting
  Write: D.L. Strawderman, Manager
Officers and Directors: N.K. Ekstrom, President; D.M. Goelzer, Secretary; G.M. Decker, Treasurer; D.L. Strawderman, Manager; P.W. Cotter, J.F. Heil, Jr., D.E. Porter, B.H. Rupple.
Number of staff: 2 part-time support.
Employer Identification Number: 396075537

4309
Clark (Emory T.) Family Foundation
2300 N. Mayfair Rd., Suite 805
Milwaukee 53226

Established in 1982 in Wisconsin.
Donor(s): Emory T. Clark.
Financial data: (yr. ended 3/31/84): Assets, $2,194,331 (M); gifts received, $900,050; expenditures, $148,421, including $137,500 for 1 grant.
Purpose and activities: First year of grant-making in 1984; one gift to a local university; foundation will not be fully operational until 1986.
Limitations: Giving primarily in WI.
Application information:
  Initial approach: Proposal
  Write: William J. Labadie, Director
Director: William J. Labadie.
Trustee: First Wisconsin Trust Company.
Employer Identification Number: 391410324

4310
Consolidated Papers Foundation, Inc.
231 First Ave. North
P.O. Box 50
Wisconsin Rapids 54494   (715) 422-3368

Incorporated in 1951 in Wisconsin.
Donor(s): Consolidated Papers, Inc., Hotel Mead Corporation, Consoweld Corporation.
Financial data: (yr. ended 12/31/83): Assets, $4,290,736 (M); gifts received, $403,100; expenditures, $568,519, including $546,942 for 57 grants (high: $70,000; low: $100; average: $8,000-$9,000) and $7,391 for 34 employee matching gifts.

Purpose and activities: Broad purposes; primarily local giving, with emphasis on higher education, including technological education, community funds, and youth and social agencies; educational grants generally limited to independent accredited four-year colleges and universities in Wisconsin.
Types of support awarded: Operating budgets, continuing support, annual campaigns, seed money, emergency funds, building funds, equipment, land acquisition, endowment funds, professorships, employee matching gifts, internships, scholarship funds, employee related scholarships, exchange programs, fellowships.
Limitations: Giving primarily in WI, usually near areas of company operations. No grants to individuals, deficit financing, special projects, research, publications, or conferences; no loans.
Application information:
 Initial approach: Full proposal
 Copies of proposal: 1
 Deadline(s): Submit proposal in January or July; deadlines March 31 and September 30
 Board meeting date(s): May or June, and November or December
 Final notification: 3 months
 Write: Daniel P. Meyer, President
Officers: Daniel P. Meyer,* President; Mrs. Howard J. Bell,* Vice-President; Carl R. Lemke, Secretary; Lamont O. Jaeger, Treasurer.
Directors:* L.H. Boling, I.F. Boyce, Groff Collett, L.A. Engelhardt, George W. Mead, Stanton W. Mead.
Number of staff: None.
Employer Identification Number: 396040071

4311
Cudahy (Patrick and Anna M.) Fund ▼
P.O. Box 11978
Milwaukee 53211   (414) 962-6820

Incorporated in 1949 in Wisconsin.
Donor(s): Michael F. Cudahy.†
Financial data: (yr. ended 12/31/83): Assets, $14,233,056 (M); expenditures, $1,042,812, including $876,660 for 116 grants (high: $50,000; low: $400; average: $1,000-$10,000).
Purpose and activities: Broad purposes; some emphasis on local projects including social service and youth agencies; support also for national programs concerned with environmental and social issues; and education.
Types of support awarded: General purposes, operating budgets, continuing support, annual campaigns, seed money, emergency funds, deficit financing, building funds, equipment, land acquisition, matching funds, consulting services, technical assistance, scholarship funds, special projects, research, publications, conferences and seminars, fellowships.
Limitations: Giving primarily in WI and Chicago, IL, and for national programs. No grants to individuals or for endowments; no loans.
Publications: Application guidelines.
Application information:
 Initial approach: Letter
 Copies of proposal: 1
 Deadline(s): 1 month prior to board meetings
 Board meeting date(s): Usually in March, June, September, and December
 Final notification: 1 week after meeting

 Write: Richard W. Yeo, Administrator
Officers: Janet S. Cudahy,* President; Raleigh Woolf,* Vice-President; Louise A. McMenamin, Secretary-Treasurer; Richard W. Yeo, Administrator.
Directors:* Richard D. Cudahy, Chairman; James Bailey, Joan Feitler, Dudley J. Godfrey, Jr., Jean Holtz, Thomas Plein, Wesley Scott.
Number of staff: 1 part-time professional.
Employer Identification Number: 390991972

4312
CUNA Mutual Insurance Group Charitable Foundation, Inc.
5910 Mineral Point Rd.
Madison 53705   (608) 238-5851

Incorporated in 1967 in Wisconsin.
Financial data: (yr. ended 12/31/83): Assets, $193,738 (M); gifts received, $123,420; expenditures, $190,985, including $189,950 for 87 grants (high: $50,000; low: $25; average: $500) and $1,020 for 17 employee matching gifts.
Purpose and activities: Broad purposes; primarily local and parochial giving, with emphasis on community funds, youth agencies, higher and secondary education, and cultural programs.
Types of support awarded: Operating budgets, continuing support, annual campaigns, seed money, emergency funds, employee matching gifts, scholarship funds, fellowships, special projects, research, conferences and seminars.
Limitations: Giving primarily in WI. No grants to individuals, or for deficit financing, land acquisition, endowment funds, challenge grants, or publications; no loans.
Application information: Application form required for requests of over $500.
 Initial approach: Full proposal, letter or telephone
 Copies of proposal: 1
 Board meeting date(s): February, May, August, and November
 Final notification: 1 month to 6 weeks
 Write: George V. Whitford, Assistant Secretary-Treasurer
Officers and Directors: Richard C. Robertson, President; James C. Barbre, Vice-President; Robert L. Curry, Secretary-Treasurer and Executive Officer.
Number of staff: None.
Employer Identification Number: 396105418

4313
Demmer (Edward U.) Foundation ¤
c/o The Marine Trust Company
P.O. Box 1308
Milwaukee 53201

Trust established in 1963 in Wisconsin.
Donor(s): Edward U. Demmer.†
Financial data: (yr. ended 12/31/83): Assets, $2,246,342 (M); expenditures, $254,885, including $235,250 for 32 grants (high: $38,750; low: $1,000).

Purpose and activities: Funds to be expended for the public use and benefit of the people of the State of Wisconsin, with emphasis on cultural programs, higher education, hospitals, and youth agencies.
Limitations: Giving primarily in WI. No grants to individuals.
Application information:
 Initial approach: Full proposal
 Copies of proposal: 4
 Deadline(s): March 1, June 1, September 1, and December 1
 Board meeting date(s): March, June, September, and December
Trustees: Harrold J. McComas, Carl N. Otien, The Marine Trust Company.
Employer Identification Number: 396064898

4314
DeRance, Inc. ▼
7700 West Blue Mound Rd.
Milwaukee 53213   (414) 475-7700

Incorporated in 1946 in Wisconsin.
Donor(s): Harry G. John.
Financial data: (yr. ended 12/31/83): Assets, $185,151,134 (M); expenditures, $12,935,739, including $9,204,105 for 371 grants (high: $250,000; low: $500; average: $1,000-$100,000).
Purpose and activities: Broad purposes; charitable and religious giving, with emphasis on Roman Catholic church support, religious associations, missionary work, and welfare funds in the United States and abroad; support for higher education; support for educational and other programs for the Native American peoples, and for Latin American, African, and Asian educational and social development programs.
Types of support awarded: Operating budgets, scholarship funds, matching funds, general purposes, continuing support, building funds, research, publications, conferences and seminars, equipment.
Limitations: No grants to individuals, or for endowment funds; no loans.
Publications: Program policy statement, application guidelines.
Application information: All applications should be in English; applications from foreign countries should come from a diocese or religious order with the request from the bishop, archbishop, or the superior, as is appropriate.
 Initial approach: Full proposal
 Copies of proposal: 2
 Deadline(s): None
 Board meeting date(s): Monthly
 Final notification: 6 to 12 months
 Write: Idella J. Gallagher, Senior Vice-President
Officers and Directors: Donald A. Gallagher, President; Erica P. John, Executive Vice-President; Idella J. Gallagher, Senior Vice-President; Harry G. John.
Number of staff: 3 full-time professional; 15 full-time support.
Employer Identification Number: 391053272

4315
Evinrude (Ralph) Foundation, Inc.
c/o Quarles and Brady
780 North Water St.
Milwaukee 53202   (414) 277-5000

Incorporated in 1959 in Wisconsin.
Donor(s): Ralph Evinrude.
Financial data: (yr. ended 7/31/84): Assets, $887,062 (M); gifts received, $16,250; expenditures, $683,650, including $654,200 for 57 grants (high: $200,000; low: $100).
Purpose and activities: Broad purposes; giving largely in Milwaukee, Wisconsin, and Stuart, Florida, with emphasis on education, hospitals, health agencies, cultural programs, youth agencies, and community funds.
Limitations: Giving primarily in Milwaukee, WI, and Stuart, FL. No grants to individuals; no loans.
Application information:
   Initial approach: Proposal or letter
   Copies of proposal: 1
   Deadline(s): Submit proposal preferably in February or July
   Board meeting date(s): Spring and early fall
   Write: Patrick W. Cotter, Secretary
Officers and Directors: Ralph Evinrude, President; Frances Evinrude, Vice-President; Patrick W. Cotter, Secretary-Treasurer; Thomas J. Donnelly.
Employer Identification Number: 396040256

4316
Evjue Foundation, Inc., The
1901 Fish Hatchery Rd.
P.O. Box 8060
Madison 53708   (608) 252-6401

Incorporated in 1958 in Wisconsin.
Donor(s): William T. Evjue.†
Financial data: (yr. ended 2/29/84): Assets, $1,050,397 (M); gifts received, $911,314; expenditures, $597,732, including $561,315 for 142 grants (high: $130,000; low: $170; average: $1,000-$5,000).
Purpose and activities: Broad purposes; primarily local giving, with emphasis on mental health, higher education, cultural programs, youth agencies, and social agencies.
Types of support awarded: Continuing support, annual campaigns, seed money, emergency funds, special projects, scholarship funds, professorships, internships, publications, conferences and seminars, endowment funds.
Limitations: Giving primarily in Dane County, WI. No support for medical or scientific research. No grants to individuals, or for building funds, equipment, land acquisition, renovation projects, or operating expenses; no loans.
Publications: Program policy statement, application guidelines.
Application information:
   Initial approach: Letter
   Copies of proposal: 1
   Deadline(s): Submit proposal preferably in October or November
   Board meeting date(s): January, March, June, and September, and as required
   Final notification: 3 months
   Write: Frederick W. Miller, Treasurer

Officers and Directors: John Lussier, President; Mrs. Frederick W. Miller, Vice-President; Frederick H. Gage, Secretary; Frederick W. Miller, Treasurer; Frederick K. Gage, Nancy Brooke Gage, James D. Lussier.
Number of staff: 1 part-time support.
Employer Identification Number: 396073981

4317
Falk (Herman W.) Memorial Foundation, Inc.
3001 West Canal St.
P.O. Box 492
Milwaukee 53201   (414) 342-3131

Incorporated in 1953 in Wisconsin.
Donor(s): The Falk Corporation.
Financial data: (yr. ended 12/31/83): Assets, $779,048 (M); expenditures, $189,266, including $179,500 for 55 grants (high: $60,000; low: $100; average: $2,200).
Purpose and activities: Primarily local giving, with emphasis on community funds, youth agencies, hospitals, and higher education.
Types of support awarded: Operating budgets, continuing support, annual campaigns, building funds, research.
Limitations: Giving primarily in Milwaukee, WI. No grants to individuals, or for seed money, emergency funds, deficit financing, equipment, land acquisition, endowments, matching gifts, special projects, publications, conferences, scholarships, or fellowships; no loans.
Application information:
   Initial approach: Letter
   Copies of proposal: 1
   Deadline(s): Submit proposal preferably from November through January; deadline January 31
   Board meeting date(s): March
   Final notification: 2 to 4 months
   Write: William L. Bardeen, President
Officer: William L. Bardeen, President.
Number of staff: None.
Employer Identification Number: 396078001

4318
First Wisconsin Foundation, Inc. ▼ ¤
777 East Wisconsin Ave.
Milwaukee 53202   (414) 765-4145

Incorporated in 1954 in Wisconsin.
Donor(s): First Wisconsin Bankshares Corporation affiliates.
Financial data: (yr. ended 12/31/83): Assets, $4,794,149 (M); gifts received, $25,000; expenditures, $652,451, including $641,997 for 149 grants (high: $185,000; low: $25; average: $100-$20,000).
Purpose and activities: Broad purposes; local giving, with emphasis on a community fund, cultural programs, secondary and higher education, youth agencies, social service agencies, and health.
Types of support awarded: Annual campaigns, building funds, continuing support, deficit financing, equipment, general purposes.

Limitations: Giving primarily in the Milwaukee, WI, area. No grants to individuals, or for endowment funds, research, or matching gifts; no loans.
Publications: Program policy statement, application guidelines.
Application information:
   Initial approach: Letter
   Copies of proposal: 1
   Deadline(s): None
   Board meeting date(s): Monthly
   Final notification: 60 days
   Write: Walter J. Fiorentini, Secretary
Officers and Directors:* Hal C. Kuehl,* Chairman; John H. Hendee, Jr.,* President; L.G. Milunovich, William H. Risch, Vice-Presidents; Walter J. Fiorentini, Secretary-Treasurer.
Number of staff: 3.
Employer Identification Number: 396042050

4319
Fort Howard Paper Foundation, Inc. ▼
1919 South Broadway
P.O. Box 91325
Green Bay 54305   (414) 435-8821

Incorporated in 1953 in Wisconsin.
Donor(s): Fort Howard Paper Company.
Financial data: (yr. ended 9/30/84): Assets, $9,909,005 (M); expenditures, $602,553, including $394,117 for 23 grants (high: $91,400; low: $1,000).
Purpose and activities: Broad purposes; emphasis on health-care facilities, primary and secondary education, cultural programs, and social services; support also for scholarships for graduates of high schools in Brown County, Wisconsin.
Limitations: Giving primarily in Green Bay, WI; Muskogee, OK, and limited surrounding areas.
Application information: Application form required.
   Deadline(s): November 1 for scholarship program
   Write: J.A. Prindiville
Officers: Paul J. Schierl,* President; Kathleen J. Hempel,* Robert E. Manger,* Michael J. Schierl,* James J. Schoshinski,* Thomas L. Shaffer,* Carol A. Twomey,* Vice-Presidents; Cheryl A. Thomson, Secretary; Susan M. Van Schyndle, Treasurer.
Directors:* John W. Hickey.
Employer Identification Number: 362761910

4320
Frankenthal Family Foundation, Inc. ¤
120 South Quincy St.
P.O. Box 1462
Green Bay 54301   (414) 432-9347

Incorporated in 1967 in Wisconsin.
Donor(s): Members of the Frankenthal family.
Financial data: (yr. ended 8/31/83): Assets, $2,170,864 (M); gifts received, $35,000; expenditures, $165,699, including $127,846 for 38 grants (high: $30,000; low: $30).

Purpose and activities: Broad purposes; primarily local giving, with emphasis on hospitals, higher education, and Jewish welfare funds; some support for the aged, community funds, and youth agencies.
Types of support awarded: General purposes, building funds, equipment, land acquisition, endowment funds, professorships, scholarship funds, matching funds.
Limitations: Giving primarily in WI. No grants to individuals; no loans.
Application information:
  Initial approach: Proposal
  Copies of proposal: 1
  Deadline(s): Submit proposal preferably in July; deadline July 31
  Board meeting date(s): August
  Write: Betty J. Frankenthal, President
Officer: Betty J. Frankenthal, President.
Number of staff: 2.
Employer Identification Number: 396106541

4321
Fromm (Walter and Mabel) Scholarship Trust
c/o First Wisconsin Trust Company
P.O. Box 2054
Milwaukee 53201

Established in 1975.
Donor(s): Mabel Fromm,† Walter Fromm.†
Financial data: (yr. ended 2/28/82): Assets, $1,120,202 (M); expenditures, $106,196, including $96,700 for 31 grants to individuals.
Purpose and activities: Support primarily for college and nursing school scholarships for graduates of the Maple Grove (elementary) School in Hamburg, Wisconsin and/or Merrill Senior Public High School in Merrill, Wisconsin.
Types of support awarded: Student aid.
Limitations: Giving primarily in Hamburg and Merrill, WI.
Publications: Application guidelines.
Application information: Scholarship application guidelines available.
  Write: G. Lindemann
Committee Members: Leonard Hamann, Richard Monka, Lanny Tibaldo, Gary Woller.
Trustee: First Wisconsin Trust Company.
Employer Identification Number: 396250027

4322
G. P. Foundation, Ltd. ⌖
7123 North Barnett Ln.
Milwaukee 53217

Established in 1977.
Donor(s): Gilbert Palay, J. Dorothy Palay.
Financial data: (yr. ended 6/30/83): Assets, $15 (M); gifts received, $3,900; expenditures, $178,348, including $175,000 for 2 grants (high: $160,000; low: $15,000).
Purpose and activities: Local giving primarily for Jewish welfare funds; support also for cultural programs.
Limitations: Giving primarily in Milwaukee, WI.
Officers: Gilbert Palay, President and Treasurer; J. Dorothy Palay, Vice-President and Secretary.
Employer Identification Number: 391287503

4323
Gelatt Foundation, Inc., The
P.O. Box 1087
La Crosse 54601   (608) 784-6000

Incorporated in 1954 in Wisconsin.
Donor(s): Charles D. Gelatt, Northern Engraving and Manufacturing Company.
Financial data: (yr. ended 6/30/84): Assets, $1,615,057 (M); expenditures, $140,761, including $135,953 for 70 grants (high: $15,000; low: $100).
Purpose and activities: Educational and charitable purposes; primarily local giving, with emphasis on youth agencies, hospitals, community funds, and higher education.
Types of support awarded: Operating budgets, continuing support, annual campaigns, building funds, matching funds.
Limitations: Giving primarily in WI. No grants to individuals, or for seed money, emergency or endowment funds, deficit financing, equipment, land acquisition, scholarships or fellowships, research, special projects, publications, or conferences; no loans.
Application information:
  Initial approach: Letter
  Copies of proposal: 1
  Deadline(s): Submit proposal in April or May; deadline June 1
  Board meeting date(s): As required
  Final notification: 1 month
  Write: Donald B. Lee, Secretary-Treasurer
Officers: Charles D. Gelatt, President; Robert P. Smyth, Vice-President; Donald B. Lee, Secretary-Treasurer.
Number of staff: None.
Employer Identification Number: 396044165

4324
Giddings and Lewis Foundation, Inc. ⌖
142 Doty St.
Fond du Lac 54935

Incorporated in 1952 in Wisconsin.
Donor(s): Giddings and Lewis Machine Tool Company.
Financial data: (yr. ended 12/31/83): Assets, $2,092,327 (M); expenditures, $118,957, including $113,575 for 67 grants (high: $31,000; low: $25).
Purpose and activities: General purposes; giving primarily in Wisconsin, with emphasis on education, community funds and community development, and to local chapters of national social service organizations.
Types of support awarded: Building funds, scholarship funds, matching funds, research.
Limitations: Giving primarily in Fond du Lac, WI.
Officers and Directors: Charles A. Zwerg, President; Frank W. Jones, Vice-President; Richard C. Kleinfeldt, Secretary-Treasurer.
Trustees: John K. Draeger, Harry A. Hall, Robert A. Lewis, Myron A. Lindgren, John MacIntyre, Robert J. Siewert, Edward F. Woytych.
Employer Identification Number: 396061306

4325
Harnischfeger Foundation, Inc.
P.O. Box 554
Milwaukee 53201   (414) 671-4400

Incorporated in 1929 in Wisconsin.
Donor(s): Walter Harnischfeger,† Harnischfeger Corporation.
Financial data: (yr. ended 12/31/82): Assets, $1,486,931 (M); expenditures, $129,592, including $110,048 for 39 grants (high: $40,000; low: $100).
Purpose and activities: Broad purposes; general giving, with emphasis on hospitals, a community fund, higher education, cultural activities, and youth agencies.
Limitations: No grants to individuals, or for endowment funds, research, scholarships, fellowships, or matching gifts; no loans.
Application information:
  Initial approach: Letter
  Copies of proposal: 1
  Board meeting date(s): May and November
  Write: Henry Harnischfeger, President
Officers and Directors: Henry Harnischfeger,* President; Elizabeth Ogden,* Vice-President; George B. Knight,* Secretary; Norman R. Rieboldt, Treasurer.
Employer Identification Number: 396040450

4326
Heileman Old Style Foundation, Inc.
100 Harborview Plaza
P.O. Box 459
La Crosse 54601   (608) 785-1000

Incorporated in 1966 in Wisconsin.
Donor(s): G. Heileman Brewing Company, Inc., Heileman Baking Company, Inc.
Financial data: (yr. ended 12/31/83): Assets, $141,749 (M); gifts received, $159,700; expenditures, $198,407, including $197,794 for 140 grants (high: $25,000; low: $25).
Purpose and activities: Broad purposes; grants mainly in areas of company operations for community funds; support also for higher education and hospitals.
Limitations: Giving primarily in areas of company operations. No grants to individuals or for endowment funds; no loans.
Publications: 990-PF.
Application information:
  Initial approach: Telephone or full proposal
  Copies of proposal: 1
  Deadline(s): Submit proposal preferably in month preceding board meeting
  Board meeting date(s): Quarterly
  Write: George E. Smith
Officers and Trustees: Russell G. Cleary, Manager; John S. Pedace, William G. Roth, Arthur N. Trausch, Jr.
Number of staff: None.
Employer Identification Number: 396094334

4327
Helfaer (Evan and Marion) Foundation ▼ ⌖
735 North Water St.
Milwaukee 53202   (414) 276-3600

Established in 1971 in Wisconsin.

Donor(s): Evan P. Helfaer.†
Financial data: (yr. ended 7/31/83): Assets, $10,236,896 (M); gifts received, $662,317; expenditures, $717,212, including $668,050 for 118 grants (high: $50,000; low: $50; average: $1,000-$20,000).
Purpose and activities: Broad purposes; local giving, with emphasis on higher education, cultural programs, youth and social service agencies, and health.
Types of support awarded: Lectureships, professorships, building funds, research.
Limitations: Giving limited to WI. No grants to individuals.
Application information: Application form available, but not required or preferred. Application form required.
  Initial approach: Letter
  Deadline(s): None
  Board meeting date(s): Periodically
  Final notification: Within 90 days after end of fiscal year
  Write: Thomas L. Smallwood, Trustee
Trustees: Thomas L. Smallwood, Administrator; Jack F. Hellner, Marshall & Ilsley Bank.
Number of staff: 1.
Employer Identification Number: 396238856

4328
Hobbs Foundation ☐
131 South Barstow St., Rm. 309
Eau Claire 54701   (715) 832-6645

Trust established in 1958 in Wisconsin.
Donor(s): Roswell H. Hobbs,† Jessie M. Hobbs.†
Financial data: (yr. ended 12/31/83): Assets, $2,380,503 (M); expenditures, $366,779, including $332,338 for 29 grants (high: $96,476; low: $60) and $20,000 for 10 grants to individuals.
Purpose and activities: Charitable purposes, especially helping the young people of the community; primarily local giving for youth and recreation programs, social services and a library.
Limitations: Giving primarily in Eau Claire, WI. No grants to individuals (except for limited special scholarships), or for endowment funds or operating budgets.
Application information: Scholarship program for special purposes only, and not open to any new applicants.
  Initial approach: Letter
  Copies of proposal: 3
  Deadline(s): None
  Board meeting date(s): March, June, September, and December
  Write: Francis J. Wilcox, Trustee
Trustees: Kempton L. German, Ray E. Wachs, Francis J. Wilcox.
Employer Identification Number: 396068746

4329
Jacobus/Heritage Foundation, Inc.
2323 North Mayfair Rd.
Wauwatosa 53226   (414) 475-6660

Incorporated in 1956 in Wisconsin.

Donor(s): The Jacobus Company, Jacobus Quickflash, Heritage Bank, Heritage Wisconsin Corporation, The Olson Companies, and others.
Financial data: (yr. ended 4/30/84): Assets, $1,857,915 (M); gifts received, $229,939; expenditures, $147,796, including $107,640 for 84 grants (high: $20,037; low: $100) and $15,000 for 10 grants to individuals.
Purpose and activities: Primarily local giving, with emphasis on higher education, including scholarships for children of company employees, and youth agencies; support also for cultural programs, community funds, and hospitals.
Types of support awarded: Employee related scholarships, operating budgets, building funds, equipment, general purposes.
Limitations: Giving primarily in southeastern WI. No grants for endowment funds, or matching gifts; no loans.
Application information:
  Initial approach: Letter, full proposal, or telephone
  Copies of proposal: 1
  Deadline(s): None
  Board meeting date(s): Monthly
  Final notification: 6 weeks
  Write: A.P.N. McArthur, Secretary
Officers and Directors: D.C. Jacobus, Chairman; C.D. Jacobus, President; J.T. Jacobus, Vice-President; A.P.N. McArthur, Secretary; R.G. Jacobus, Treasurer.
Number of staff: 2.
Employer Identification Number: 396043029

4330
Janesville Foundation, Inc.
121 North Parker Dr.
Janesville 53545   (608) 752-1032
Mailing address: P.O. Box 1492, Janesville, WI 53547

Incorporated in 1944 in Wisconsin.
Donor(s): Parker Pen Company, Merchants and Savings Bank, and others.
Financial data: (yr. ended 12/31/84): Assets, $6,005,729 (M); gifts received, $16,550; expenditures, $626,777, including $551,813 for 37 grants (high: $120,000; low: $100; average: $5,000-$10,000) and $24,500 for 27 grants to individuals.
Purpose and activities: Broad purposes; local giving, largely for the purpose of equipping individuals to help themselves and to aid the community; emphasis on higher and secondary education, scholarships for local high school graduates, youth and child welfare agencies, community funds, and historic restoration.
Types of support awarded: Continuing support, seed money, building funds, equipment, land acquisition, matching funds, student aid, special projects, conferences and seminars.
Limitations: Giving limited to Janesville, WI. No support for political projects. No grants to individuals (except for scholarships), or for operating budgets, or endowment funds; no loans.
Publications: Application guidelines, program policy statement.
Application information:

Initial approach: Letter with brief outline of proposal, or by telephone
Deadline(s): March 1, June 1, September 1, and December 1
Board meeting date(s): March, June, September, and December
Final notification: 1 week after board meeting
Write: Alan W. Dunwiddie, Jr., Executive Director
Officers: Alan W. Dunwiddie, Jr.,* President and Executive Director; Roger E. Axtell, Alfred P. Diotte,* Vice-Presidents; Phyllis Saevre, Secretary-Treasurer.
Directors:* George S. Parker, Chairman; Rowland J. McClellan, James R. Peterson.
Number of staff: 1 full-time professional; 2 part-time support.
Employer Identification Number: 396034645

4331
Johnson Controls Foundation ▼
5757 North Green Bay Ave.
P.O. Box 591
Milwaukee 53201   (414) 228-2219

Trust established in 1952 in Wisconsin.
Donor(s): Johnson Controls, Inc.
Financial data: (yr. ended 12/31/83): Assets, $8,258,330 (M); gifts received, $2,000,000; expenditures, $1,321,341, including $665,525 for 232 grants (high: $232,000; low: $25; average: $100-$5,000), $43,110 for 29 grants to individuals and $571,583 for employee matching gifts.
Purpose and activities: Grants for higher education, hospitals, community funds, aid to the handicapped, care of children and the aged, and civic and arts organizations.
Types of support awarded: Operating budgets, continuing support, annual campaigns, seed money, emergency funds, building funds, endowment funds, matching funds, employee related scholarships, employee matching gifts.
Limitations: No grants to individuals (except for company-employee scholarships), or for deficit financing, equipment, land acquisition, special projects, research, publications, and conferences; no loans.
Publications: Program policy statement, application guidelines.
Application information:
  Initial approach: Letter
  Deadline(s): None
  Board meeting date(s): March, June, and September
  Final notification: 60 days
  Write: Florence R. Klatt, Secretary
Advisory Board: Florence R. Klatt, Secretary; Robert N. Bell, Fred L. Brengel, Robert T. Foote, H.D. Thomas.
Trustee: First Wisconsin Trust Company.
Number of staff: 5 part-time support.
Employer Identification Number: 396036639

4332
Johnson Foundation, Inc., The
P.O. Box 547
Racine 53401   (414) 639-3211

Incorporated in 1958 in New York.

Donor(s): S.C. Johnson & Son, Inc., and descendants of H.J. Johnson.†
Financial data: (yr. ended 6/30/84): Assets, $9,532,563 (M); gifts received, $1,805,035; expenditures, $2,178,502, including $23,875 for 7 grants (high: $7,700; low: $175; average: $1,000-$3,000) and $2,154,627 for 113 foundation-administered programs.
Purpose and activities: A private operating foundation; supports four broad areas of activity: international understanding, educational excellence, intellectual and cultural growth, and improvement of the human environment. An operating foundation whose principal activity is planning and carrying out conferences at Wingspread, its educational conference center in Racine. Grants limited to activities directly related to Wingspread programs. Publications based on Wingspread conferences available on request.
Types of support awarded: Conferences and seminars, publications.
Limitations: No grants to individuals.
Publications: Annual report, application guidelines, program policy statement.
Application information:
　Initial approach: Letter
　Copies of proposal: 1
　Board meeting date(s): June and December
　Final notification: Approximately 8 weeks
　Write: Lovice M. Becker, Assistant Secretary
Officers: Samuel C. Johnson,* Chairman; William B. Boyd,* President; Catherine B. Cleary,* Vice-President and Secretary; B.H. Regenburg, Administrative Vice-President and Treasurer.
Trustees:* James L. Allen, Robben W. Fleming, Patricia Albjerg Graham, Jerome H. Holland, Robert M. O'Neil, Donald S. Perkins.
Number of staff: 6 full-time professional; 11 full-time support.
Employer Identification Number: 390958255

4333
Johnson Foundation Trust ¤
c/o American Bank and Trust Company
441 Main St.
Racine 53403

Established in 1937.
Financial data: (yr. ended 6/30/84): Assets, $1,030,521 (M); gifts received, $50,000; expenditures, $115,021, including $105,798 for 16 grants (high: $30,000; low: $500).
Purpose and activities: General purposes; grants primarily for higher education, cultural programs, conservation, and recreation programs.
Officers: Samuel C. Johnson, Chairman; Robert C. Hart, Secretary.
Trustees: John M. Schroeder, M & I Marshall and Ilsley Bank.
Employer Identification Number: 396052073

4334
Johnson (John A.) Foundation ¤
P.O. Box 8100
Madison 53708
Application address: 27 Bayside Dr., Madison, WI 53704; Tel.: (608) 249-2313

Incorporated in 1951 in Wisconsin.
Donor(s): Gisholt Machine Company.
Financial data: (yr. ended 12/31/83): Assets, $1,503,216 (M); expenditures, $84,399, including $72,834 for 21 grants (high: $29,604; low: $500).
Purpose and activities: General purposes; primarily local giving, with emphasis on scholarships, higher education, youth agencies, cultural programs and a community fund.
Types of support awarded: Scholarship funds.
Limitations: Giving primarily in WI.
Application information:
　Deadline(s): None
　Write: John C. Weston, President
Officers and Directors: John C. Weston, President; Gordon G. Volz, Secretary-Treasurer; John A. Bolz, Richmond Johnson, Stanley A. Johnson, John R. Pike, Toby F. Sherry, Thomas O. Zilavy.
Employer Identification Number: 396078592

4335
Johnson (Viola) Charitable Trust ¤
c/o Marshall & Ilsley Bank
P.O. Box 2035
Milwaukee 53201　　　　　(414) 765-8173

Trust established in 1979 in Wisconsin.
Donor(s): Viola A. Johnson.†
Financial data: (yr. ended 2/29/84): Assets, $1,069,132 (M); expenditures, $196,597, including $179,473 for 11 grants (high: $60,000; low: $2,947).
Purpose and activities: Primarily local giving with emphasis on youth agencies, the handicapped, and higher education; support also for Christian Science organizations.
Limitations: Giving primarily in WI.
Application information:
　Initial approach: Letter
　Deadline(s): None
　Write: K. M. Ryan
Trustees: Nancy Johnson, Roy Labudde, Bob Templin, George Watts, Marshall & Ilsley Bank.
Employer Identification Number: 396307918

4336
Johnson's Wax Fund, Inc., The ▼
1525 Howe St.
Racine 53403　　　　　(414) 631-2551

Incorporated in 1959 in Wisconsin.
Donor(s): S.C. Johnson & Son, Inc.
Financial data: (yr. ended 6/30/84): Assets, $1,507,016 (M); gifts received, $1,751,673; expenditures, $1,784,868, including $755,943 for 108 grants (high: $10,000; low: $1,000), $315,202 for 169 grants to individuals and $609,816 for 801 employee matching gifts.
Purpose and activities: Scholarship program for children of company employees; scholarships and fellowships in specific areas of interest, i.e., chemistry, biology, marketing, and business; grants to colleges, primarily in Wisconsin and the Midwest; support for local welfare, cultural, and civic organizations; grants also for environmental protection.

Types of support awarded: Seed money, building funds, equipment, land acquisition, matching funds, scholarship funds, exchange programs, fellowships, research, publications, employee matching gifts, employee related scholarships.
Limitations: Giving primarily in WI and the Midwest in areas of company operations. No support for national health organizations, or for religious or social groups. No grants to individuals (except for scholarships for children of company employees), or for operating budgets, emergency funds, deficit financing, demonstration projects, or conferences; no loans.
Publications: Application guidelines, program policy statement.
Application information:
　Initial approach: Letter and full proposal
　Copies of proposal: 1
　Deadline(s): None
　Board meeting date(s): Bimonthly
　Final notification: 3 to 4 months
　Write: Serge E. Logan, Vice-President
Officers: Samuel C. Johnson,* Chairman and President; David H. Cool,* Vice-Chairman; Serge E. Logan, Vice-President; Reva A. Holmes, Secretary; John M. Schroeder, Treasurer.
Trustees:* Raymond F. Farley, James R. Fiene, Sandra Y. McClaron, Jack C. Moll, M. Garvin Shankster, Richard M. Spinks.
Number of staff: 1 full-time professional; 1 part-time professional; 1 part-time support.
Employer Identification Number: 396052089

4337
Kearney and Trecker Foundation, Inc.
11000 Theodore Trecker Way
West Allis 53214　　　　　(414) 476-8300

Incorporated in 1945 in Wisconsin.
Donor(s): Kearney and Trecker Corporation.
Financial data: (yr. ended 9/30/84): Assets, $1,349,306 (L); expenditures, $205,936, including $202,991 for 81 grants (high: $58,000; low: $100) and $2,945 for employee matching gifts.
Purpose and activities: General purposes; primarily local giving, with emphasis on higher education and on community funds, youth agencies, hospitals and medical organizations, and cultural programs.
Limitations: Giving primarily in WI. No grants to individuals or for endowment funds; no loans.
Application information: No written guidelines, but details upon request.
　Initial approach: Full proposal
　Copies of proposal: 1
　Board meeting date(s): March and September
　Write: Donald E. Porter, Secretary
Officers: Richard T. Lindgreen,* President; Donald P. Muench, Vice-President and Treasurer; Donald E. Porter, Secretary.
Directors:* Francis J. Trecker,* Chairman; Patrick W. Cotter, Michael J. Garland, Russell A. Heddon, H.W. Pohle, M.D., Brenton H. Rupple, R.R. Spitzer.
Employer Identification Number: 396044253

4338
Kimberly-Clark Foundation, Inc. ▼
North Lake St.
Neenah 54956 (414) 721-2000

Incorporated in 1952 in Wisconsin.
Donor(s): Kimberly-Clark Corporation.
Financial data: (yr. ended 12/31/82): Assets, $478,815 (M); gifts received, $1,748,214; expenditures, $1,983,353, including $1,730,191 for 255 grants (high: $240,000; low: $200; average: $1,000-$20,000) and $251,103 for 544 employee matching gifts.
Purpose and activities: General giving in areas of company operations; emphasis on higher education. National Merit and achievement scholarship funds, community funds, hospitals, community development, social services, and cultural programs.
Types of support awarded: Annual campaigns, building funds, continuing support, deficit financing, emergency funds, employee matching gifts, equipment, land acquisition, matching funds, operating budgets, seed money, scholarship funds, general purposes.
Limitations: Giving primarily in communities where the company has operations. No support for preschool, elementary, or secondary education (except employee matching gifts), state-supported institutions, denominational religious organizations, or sports or athletics. No grants to individuals or for endowment funds; no loans.
Publications: Annual report.
Application information:
Initial approach: Full proposal
Copies of proposal: 1
Deadline(s): None
Board meeting date(s): April; contributions committee meets monthly
Final notification: 6 to 8 weeks
Write: John S. Sensenbrenner, Jr., President
Officers: John S. Sensenbrenner, Jr.,* President; Darlene Petersen, Vice-President and Secretary; Sumner Parker, Treasurer.
Directors:* Bruce P. Nolop, Edmund W. Sanderson, Darwin E. Smith, William W. Wicks.
Contributions Committee: John S. Sensenbrenner, Jr., Chairman; James D. Bernd, David W. Dusendschon, Archie H. Johnson, Darlene Petersen, William W. Wicks.
Number of staff: 3.
Employer Identification Number: 396044304

4339
Koehring Foundation
200 Executive Dr.
Brookfield 53005

Incorporated in 1952 in Wisconsin.
Donor(s): Koehring Company.
Financial data: (yr. ended 12/31/83): Assets, $555,026 (M); expenditures, $108,477, including $105,245 for 58 grants (high: $21,000; low: $10) and $3,146 for 29 employee matching gifts.
Purpose and activities: Grants primarily for community funds, higher education, including matching gifts, hospitals, and youth agencies in the nine states where the Company has plants.
Limitations: Giving primarily in in areas of company operations.

Officers and Directors:* Vincent L. Martin,* President; James R. Moore,* Gary Noel,* Vice-Presidents; Peter Stange,* Secretary; Shirley Klenke, Treasurer.
Employer Identification Number: 396044275

4340
Kohl (Allen D.) Charitable Foundation, Inc. ⊭
4300 W. Brown Deer Rd., Suite 120
Milwaukee 53223

Incorporated in 1972 in Wisconsin.
Donor(s): Allen D. Kohl.
Financial data: (yr. ended 12/31/83): Assets, $5,225,215 (M); expenditures, $357,338, including $315,700 for 25 grants (high: $200,000; low: $100).
Purpose and activities: Grants for charitable causes of interest to the directors; support primarily for a local Jewish welfare agency.
Limitations: No grants to individuals.
Officers and Directors: Allen D. Kohl, President; Ralph Bultman, Secretary and Treasurer; Mary Kohl.
Employer Identification Number: 237211587

4341
Kohl (H. H.) Charities, Inc. ⊭
825 N. Jefferson, Suite 250
Milwaukee 53202

Incorporated in 1979 in Wisconsin.
Donor(s): Max Kohl,† Wisconsin Center for Public Policy, Inc.
Financial data: (yr. ended 6/30/84): Assets, $2,633,488 (M); gifts received, $832,271; expenditures, $12.091.
Purpose and activities: Grants largely for local Jewish welfare funds.
Limitations: Giving primarily in Milwaukee, WI.
Officers and Directors: Herbert H. Kohl, President and Treasurer; Marvin E. Klitsner, Vice-President and Secretary; Mary Kohl.
Employer Identification Number: 391341364

4342
Kohler Foundation, Inc.
501 Highland Dr.
Kohler 53044 (414) 458-1972

Incorporated in 1940 in Wisconsin.
Donor(s): Herbert V. Kohler,† Marie C. Kohler,† Evangeline Kohler,† Lillie B. Kohler,† O.A. Kroos.†
Financial data: (yr. ended 12/31/83): Assets, $2,429,322 (M); expenditures, $607,173, including $501,185 for 99 grants (high: $125,000; low: $333).
Purpose and activities: Distributes funds solely within Wisconsin to colleges and universities, only for scholarships and capital improvement programs; scholarships to local graduating high school students; grants to local nonprofit institutions for cultural improvement programs.
Types of support awarded: General purposes, seed money, building funds, equipment, land acquisition, endowment funds, publications, conferences and seminars, scholarship funds, fellowships, matching funds.

Limitations: Giving limited to WI. No support for health care, or medical programs. No grants to individuals (except for scholarships in Sheboygan County), or for operating budgets; no loans.
Publications: Application guidelines.
Application information:
Initial approach: Letter
Copies of proposal: 1
Deadline(s): Submit proposal preferably between September and November or January and April; deadlines April 15 and November 15
Board meeting date(s): May and December and as required
Final notification: 1 week after contributions meetings
Write: Eleanor A. Jung, Executive Director
Officers: Herbert V. Kohler, Jr.,* President; Linda Karger Kohler, Vice-President; Frank C. Jacobson,* Secretary; Eugene P. Seifert, Treasurer; Eleanor A. Jung, Executive Director.
Directors:* Sam H. Davis, Ruth DeYoung Kohler II.
Number of staff: 2 part-time professional; 1 part-time support.
Employer Identification Number: 390810536

4343
Krause (Charles A.) Foundation
4300 West Brown Deer Rd.
Milwaukee 53223 (414) 355-7500
Mailing address: P.O. Box 1156, Milwaukee, WI 53201

Incorporated in 1952 in Wisconsin.
Financial data: (yr. ended 12/31/83): Assets, $1,608,916 (M); expenditures, $132,543, including $127,150 for 29 grants (high: $20,000; low: $100).
Purpose and activities: General purposes; primarily local giving, with emphasis on higher and secondary education, conservation, museums, and cultural programs.
Limitations: Giving primarily in WI.
Application information:
Write: W.G. Sullivan, President
Officers and Directors: W.G. Sullivan, President; E.A. Longenecker, Vice-President; Charles A. Krause III, Secretary-Treasurer; Carol K. Wythes.
Employer Identification Number: 396044820

4344
Kress (The George) Foundation, Inc. ⊭
c/o Kellogg Trust
1700 North Webster Ave., P.O. Box 1107
Green Bay 54305

Incorporated in 1953 in Wisconsin.
Financial data: (yr. ended 12/31/83): Assets, $1,298,628 (M); expenditures, $246,251, including $232,297 for 160 grants (high: $25,500; low: $50).
Purpose and activities: Broad purposes; general giving, with emphasis on youth agencies, community funds, higher education, including scholarship funds, health agencies, the environment, community development, and church support.

Officers and Directors: George F. Kress, President; James F. Kress, Vice-President; S. Lawrence Mayer, Secretary-Treasurer; Donald Kress, Max Sielaff, Marilyn Kress Swanson.
Employer Identification Number: 396050768

4345
Kurth Religious Trust ¤
11514 N. Port Washington Rd., 13-W, Suite 106
Mequon 53092

Trust established in 1946 in Wisconsin.
Donor(s): Kurth Malting Corporation.
Financial data: (yr. ended 12/31/83): Assets, $3,880,220 (M); gifts received, $53,193; expenditures, $165,471, including $144,920 for 34 grants (high: $36,150; low: $20).
Purpose and activities: Religious and charitable purposes; grants largely for Lutheran church support, religious associations and welfare funds; some support for higher education.
Trustees: Herbert Kurth, Katherine Kurth, Thomas Kurth, Tineka Kurth Messinger, Elisabeth Kurth Wrean.
Employer Identification Number: 396048744

4346
La Crosse Foundation
P.O. Box 489
La Crosse 54602-0489   (608) 782-1148

Community foundation established in 1929 in Wisconsin.
Financial data: (yr. ended 12/31/84): Assets, $3,037,083 (M); gifts received, $175,778; expenditures, $172,400, including $142,059 for 45 grants (high: $30,000; low: $100; average: $2,300) and $9,816 for 20 grants to individuals.
Purpose and activities: Local giving for charitable purposes to benefit the citizens of La Crosse County; support also for higher education.
Types of support awarded: Operating budgets, continuing support, annual campaigns, seed money, emergency funds, building funds, equipment, matching funds, scholarship funds, professorships, internships, exchange programs, fellowships, research, conferences and seminars, grants to individuals, program-related investments, publications, employee matching gifts.
Limitations: Giving limited to La Crosse County, WI. No grants for deficit financing, land acquisition, consulting services, or technical assistance; grants to individuals from restricted funds or from discretionary funds only in extraordinary circumstances; no loans.
Publications: 990-PF, application guidelines, annual report.
Application information: Application form required.
   Initial approach: Letter
   Copies of proposal: 1
   Deadline(s): Submit proposal preferably one month before committee meetings
   Board meeting date(s): April, June, September, and December

Final notification: Within 1 month of committee meeting
   Write: Carol B. Popelka, Progam Director
Officer: E.J. Albrecht, Executive Secretary.
Number of staff: 1 part-time professional.
Employer Identification Number: 396037996

4347
Ladish Company Foundation ¤
5481 South Packard Ave.
Cudahy 53110

Trust established in 1952 in Wisconsin.
Donor(s): Ladish Company.
Financial data: (yr. ended 11/30/83): Assets, $5,740,542 (M); expenditures, $422,274, including $409,000 for 74 grants (high: $35,000; low: $100).
Purpose and activities: Primarily local giving, with emphasis on community funds, youth agencies, hospitals and medical research, and higher education including scholarship funds and building funds.
Types of support awarded: General purposes, research, scholarship funds, endowment funds, building funds, annual campaigns.
Limitations: Giving primarily in WI.
Trustees: Victor F. Braun, Richard Harder, John H. Ladish.
Employer Identification Number: 396040489

4348
Ladish (Herman W.) Family Foundation, Inc. ▼ ¤
790 North Jackson St.
Milwaukee 53202   (414) 271-4763

Incorporated in 1956 in Wisconsin.
Donor(s): Herman W. Ladish.†
Financial data: (yr. ended 6/30/84): Assets, $26,140,044 (M); expenditures, $1,389,380, including $1,339,000 for 61 grants (high: $105,000; low: $1,000; average: $5,000-$75,000).
Purpose and activities: Primarily local giving, with emphasis on higher and secondary education, health and youth organizations, hospitals, medical research, and cultural programs.
Limitations: Giving primarily in WI.
Officers: John H. Ladish,* President; Victor F. Braun,* Vice-President; Robert T. Stollenwerk, Secretary and Treasurer.
Directors:* Elwin J. Zarwell.
Employer Identification Number: 396063602

4349
Ladish (The Herman W.) Foundation, Inc. ¤
790 North Jackson St.
Milwaukee 53202

Incorporated in 1949 in Wisconsin.
Donor(s): Herman W. Ladish.†
Financial data: (yr. ended 6/30/81): Assets, $3,674,427 (M); expenditures, $356,293, including $338,500 for 20 grants (high: $120,000; low: $1,000).

Purpose and activities: Broad purposes; local giving with emphasis on higher education, hospitals and youth agencies.
Limitations: Giving primarily in WI.
Officers: John H. Ladish,* President; Victor F. Braun,* Vice-President; Robert T. Stollenwerk, Secretary-Treasurer.
Directors:* Elwin J. Zarwell.
Employer Identification Number: 396063604

4350
Ladish Malting Company Foundation, Inc. ¤
790 North Jackson St.
Milwaukee 53202

Incorporated in 1957 in Wisconsin.
Donor(s): Ladish Malting Company.
Financial data: (yr. ended 6/30/83): Assets, $1,737,989 (M); expenditures, $121,494, including $118,050 for 11 grants (high: $45,000; low: $100).
Purpose and activities: Broad purposes; giving primarily to hospitals; grants also for youth and social agencies, including a community fund.
Officers and Directors: John H. Ladish, President and Treasurer; Victor F. Braun, Vice-President; Robert T. Stollenwerk, Secretary.
Employer Identification Number: 396045284

4351
Lindsay Foundation, Inc.
31982 W. Treasure Isle Dr.
Hartland 53029

Established in 1963.
Donor(s): Walter Lindsay.†
Financial data: (yr. ended 12/31/83): Assets, $1,188,963 (M); expenditures, $105,106, including $95,000 for 13 grants (high: $15,000; low: $5,000).
Purpose and activities: Primarily local giving, with emphasis on hospitals and health agencies.
Limitations: Giving primarily in WI.
Application information:
   Write: Lorna L. Mayer, President
Officer: Lorna L. Mayer, President.
Number of staff: None.
Employer Identification Number: 396086904

4352
Loock (Margaret & Fred) Foundation, Inc. ¤
622 North Water St.
Milwaukee 53202

Incorporated in 1967 in Wisconsin.
Donor(s): Fred F. Loock,† Margaret Loock.
Financial data: (yr. ended 12/31/83): Assets, $116,729 (M); expenditures, $208,181, including $187,050 for 31 grants (high: $35,000; low: $300).
Purpose and activities: Broad purposes; largely local giving in Milwaukee and Colorado, with emphasis on higher and secondary education and youth agencies. Support also for hospitals, cultural and religious organizations, and a community fund.
Limitations: Giving primarily in Milwaukee, WI, and CO.

Application information:
Write: William F. Fox, Secretary
Officers and Directors: Fitzhugh Scott, President; Eileen Scott, Vice-President; William F. Fox, Secretary and Treasurer.
Employer Identification Number: 391193117

4353
Marine Foundation, Inc., The
111 East Wisconsin Ave.
P.O. Box 481
Milwaukee 53201   (414) 765-2624

Incorporated in 1958 in Wisconsin.
Donor(s): Marine Bank, National Association, and other Marine banks in Wisconsin.
Financial data: (yr. ended 12/31/84): Assets, $2,539 (M); gifts received, $276,430; expenditures, $280,436, including $259,148 for 81 grants (high: $100,000; low: $100; average: $3,200) and $21,199 for 244 employee matching gifts.
Purpose and activities: Broad purposes; local giving, with emphasis on a community fund, cultural programs, higher education, and youth agencies.
Types of support awarded: General purposes, operating budgets, continuing support, annual campaigns, seed money, emergency funds, deficit financing, building funds, equipment, employee matching gifts, special projects, research, conferences and seminars.
Limitations: Giving limited to WI. No grants to individuals, or for land acquisition, endowment funds, scholarships, fellowships, or publications; no loans.
Application information:
Initial approach: Full proposal
Copies of proposal: 1
Deadline(s): None
Board meeting date(s): January, May, August, and December
Final notification: 2 to 3 months
Write: Frances G. Cole, Secretary
Officers and Directors:* George R. Slater,* President; Leila Fraser,* Daniel J. Gannon,* Norman A. Jacobs,* James C. LaVelle,* Jon R. Schumacher,* Otto H. Wirth,* Vice-Presidents; Frances G. Cole, Secretary; Timothy L. King, Treasurer.
Number of staff: None.
Employer Identification Number: 396050680

4354
Marshall & Ilsley Bank Foundation, Inc. ¤
770 North Water St.
Milwaukee 53202

Incorporated in 1958 in Wisconsin.
Donor(s): Marshall & Ilsley Bank.
Financial data: (yr. ended 12/31/83): Assets, $899,036 (M); gifts received, $410,077; expenditures, $455,991, including $443,100 for 54 grants (high: $62,500; low: $250) and $11,999 for 10 grants to individuals.
Purpose and activities: Broad purposes; primarily local giving, with emphasis on higher education, community funds, the arts, hospitals, and youth agencies.
Limitations: Giving primarily in WI.

Publications: Application guidelines.
Officers: John A. Puelicher,* President; James A. Wigdale,* Vice-President; Diane L. Sebion, Secretary.
Directors:* Robert M. Hoffer, Burleigh E. Jacobs, Jack Kellner, Herbert Kurth, James O. Wright.
Employer Identification Number: 396043185

4355
Mason (B. A.) Trust ¤
1251 First Ave.
Chippewa Falls 54729

Trust established about 1953.
Donor(s): Mason Shoe Manufacturing Company.
Financial data: (yr. ended 12/31/83): Assets, $617,874 (M); expenditures, $117,338, including $111,450 for 14 grants (high: $40,000; low: $1,000).
Purpose and activities: Local giving, with emphasis on youth agencies; support also for a secondary school, a community fund, and two Roman Catholic church parishes.
Limitations: Giving primarily in WI.
Foundation Managers: Victor T. Mason, Rosemary Mason Scobie, William M. Scobie.
Employer Identification Number: 396075816

4356
McBeath (Faye) Foundation ▼
1020 North Broadway
Milwaukee 53202   (414) 272-5805

Trust established in 1964 in Wisconsin.
Donor(s): Miss Faye McBeath.†
Financial data: (yr. ended 12/31/83): Assets, $10,514,900 (M); expenditures, $1,061,670, including $949,506 for 35 grants (high: $116,755; low: $10,000; average: $10,000-$50,000).
Purpose and activities: To benefit the people of Wisconsin by providing homes and care for elderly persons; promoting education and research in medical science and public health; providing medical, nursing, and hospital care for the sick and disabled; promoting the welfare of children; promoting research in civics and government directed towards improvement in the efficiency of local government; and by supporting the arts and cultural programs.
Types of support awarded: Seed money, building funds, equipment, special projects, matching funds.
Limitations: Giving limited to WI, with emphasis on the greater Milwaukee area. No support for specific medical or scientific research projects. No grants to individuals, or for annual campaigns, endowment funds, or scholarships and fellowships; rarely for emergency funds; no loans.
Publications: Annual report, program policy statement, application guidelines.
Application information:
Initial approach: Brief letter, telephone, or full proposal
Copies of proposal: 1
Deadline(s): 1 month prior to board meetings

Board meeting date(s): At least bimonthly, beginning in January
Final notification: 2 weeks after meetings
Write: David M.G. Huntington, Secretary
Officer: David M.G. Huntington, Secretary.
Trustees: William L. Randall, Chairman; Charles A. Krause, Vice-Chairman; Catherine B. Cleary, Thomas J. McCollow, Bonnie R. Weigell, First Wisconsin Trust Company.
Number of staff: 2 full-time professional; 2 full-time support.
Employer Identification Number: 396074450

4357
Miller (The Steve J.) Foundation ¤
(formerly The Miller Foundation)
15 North Central Ave.
Marshfield 54449

Trust established about 1946 in Wisconsin.
Donor(s): Central Cheese Company, Inc., Steve J. Miller.†
Financial data: (yr. ended 12/31/83): Assets, $2,483,602 (M); expenditures, $219,008, including $199,300 for 37 grants (high: $27,100; low: $200).
Purpose and activities: Grants largely for higher education, health agencies, community development, and cultural programs, locally and in Tucson, Arizona.
Limitations: Giving primarily in WI and Tucson, AZ.
Officers: E. Black Miller, Chairman; Norman C. Miller, President; Isabelle E. Black, Vice-President; H.D. Te Stroke, Secretary and Manager; William T. Gous, Treasurer.
Employer Identification Number: 396051879

4358
Milwaukee Foundation ▼
1020 North Broadway
Milwaukee 53202   (414) 272-5805

Community foundation established in 1915 in Wisconsin by declaration of trust.
Financial data: (yr. ended 12/31/83): Assets, $30,042,659 (M); gifts received, $3,380,743; expenditures, $2,459,569, including $1,607,423 for 332 grants (high: $115,000; low: $39; average: $1,000-$3,000).
Purpose and activities: Broad charitable purposes for the benefit of local residents; present funds include some unrestricted and many funds designated by the donors to benefit specific institutions or for special purposes, including scholarship funds, health facilities and programs, care of the aged, welfare of children and youth, mental health, the arts and cultural projects, social services and community development.
Types of support awarded: Seed money, building funds, equipment, matching funds, scholarship funds, special projects.

Limitations: Giving limited to the Milwaukee, WI, area. No support for the general use of churches or for sectarian religious purposes, or for specific medical or scientific projects; all except from components of the foundation established for such purposes. No grants to individuals (except for established awards), or for operating budgets, continuing support, annual campaigns, emergency funds, deficit financing, land acquisition, endowment funds, research, publications, or conferences; no loans.
Publications: Annual report, program policy statement, application guidelines.
Application information: Application form required.
  Initial approach: Full proposal, telephone, or letter
  Copies of proposal: 1
  Deadline(s): Submit proposal preferably 8 weeks before board meetings; deadlines January 1, April 1, July 1, and October 1
  Board meeting date(s): March, June, September, December, and as needed
  Final notification: 2 weeks after board meetings
  Write: David M.G. Huntington, Executive Director
Officer: David M.G. Huntington, Secretary and Executive Director.
Foundation Board: John C. Geilfuss, Chairman; John Galanis, Vice-Chairman; Orren J. Bradley, Doris H. Chortek, Gwen T. Jackson, Charles W. Parker, Jr., J. Patrick Ronan.
Trustees: First Bank Milwaukee, First Wisconsin Trust Company, Heritage Trust Company, Marine Trust Company, M & I Marshall & Ilsley Bank.
Number of staff: 2 full-time professional; 2 part-time professional; 3 full-time support.
Employer Identification Number: 396036407

4359
Neenah Foundry Foundation, Inc. ☐
2121 Brooks Ave.
Neenah 54956

Incorporated in 1953 in Wisconsin.
Donor(s): Neenah Foundry Company.
Financial data: (yr. ended 12/31/83): Assets, $2,669,652 (M); expenditures, $186,216, including $181,159 for 59 grants (high: $25,000; low: $25).
Purpose and activities: Broad purposes; primarily local giving, with emphasis on higher and secondary education, youth agencies, and a community fund.
Limitations: Giving primarily in WI.
Officers: E.W. Aylward, President; E.B. Aylward, Vice-President; F.C. Hathaway, Secretary-Treasurer.
Employer Identification Number: 396042143

4360
Nekoosa Papers Foundation Incorporated
100 Wisconsin River Dr.
Port Edwards 54469   (715) 887-5590

Incorporated in 1947 in Wisconsin.
Donor(s): Nekoosa Papers Inc.

Financial data: (yr. ended 12/31/84): Assets, $906,883 (L); gifts received, $200,000; expenditures, $169,141, including $162,265 for 24 grants (high: $47,600; low: $25).
Purpose and activities: Broad purposes; grants limited to Wisconsin and primarily to areas of Company operations, particularly within the South Wood County area and Ashdown, Arkansas. Grants for scholarships through Wisconsin educational institutions for employees and their children; support for state and national charities, community funds, and hospitals that benefit Wisconsin and Arkansas residents or Company employees and their families.
Types of support awarded: Employee related scholarships.
Limitations: Giving primarily in the South Wood County, WI, area, and Ashdown, AR. No grants to individuals (except for company-employee scholarships).
Application information:
  Initial approach: Proposal
  Copies of proposal: 1
  Board meeting date(s): June and December or January
  Write: Franklin E. Robinson, Secretary
Officers and Directors: Gerard E. Veneman, President; Arthur A. Bernhardt, James G. Crump, Jr., Vice-Presidents; Franklin E. Robinson, Secretary; John P. Melsen, Treasurer; Harry G. Brown, Jr., Phyllis Huffman, Terry O. Norris, Francis J. Podvin, Raymond H. Taylor, Germaine Thompson.
Employer Identification Number: 396022264

4361
Oshkosh Foundation
c/o First Wisconsin National Bank of Oshkosh
P.O. Box 2448
Oshkosh 54903   (414) 424-4283
Street address: 111 North Main St., Oshkosh, WI 54901

Community foundation established in 1928 in Wisconsin by declaration of trust.
Financial data: (yr. ended 2/28/84): Assets, $3,759,560 (M); expenditures, $336,223, including $141,039 for 20 grants (high: $55,000; low: $300) and $92,000 for grants to individuals.
Purpose and activities: For the benefit of local residents only; emphasis on scholarships, hospitals, medical care of the indigent, community funds, and cultural programs. Scholarships awarded for graduating Oshkosh high school seniors for a 4-year term only.
Types of support awarded: Continuing support, annual campaigns, emergency funds, building funds, equipment, student aid.
Limitations: Giving limited to Oshkosh, WI. No grants for endowments, operating support, matching gifts, seed money, deficit financing, special projects, research, publications, or conferences; no loans.
Publications: Annual report, application guidelines.
Application information: Applications not accepted unless residency requirements are met.
  Initial approach: Full proposal
  Copies of proposal: 1

Deadline(s): Submit proposal preferably in April; no set deadline
  Board meeting date(s): Usually in April and as required
  Final notification: 6 weeks
  Write: Sandra A. Noe, Trust Administrator
Officers: Carl E. Steiger,* President; Marie Hoyer,* Vice-President; Virginia Nelson,* Secretary.
Foundation Committee:* Edith Collins, Fred Leist, Edward Leyhe, Lewis Magnusen.
Trustee: First Wisconsin National Bank of Oshkosh (Sandea A. Noe, Trust Administrator).
Number of staff: 1 full-time professional; 1 full-time support.
Employer Identification Number: 396041638

4362
Oshkosh Truck Foundation, Inc.
2307 Oregon St.
P.O. Box 2566
Oshkosh 54903   (414) 235-9150

Incorporated in 1960 in Wisconsin.
Donor(s): Oshkosh Truck Corporation.
Financial data: (yr. ended 12/31/83): Assets, $183,525 (M); gifts received, $250,000; expenditures, $199,945, including $194,365 for 50 grants (high: $30,000; low: $20; average: $3,900) and $5,500 for 11 grants to individuals.
Purpose and activities: Primarily local giving for youth agencies and higher and secondary education; support also for a hospital and a community fund. Scholarships to children of Oshkosh Truck Corporation employees who attend local high schools.
Types of support awarded: Operating budgets, continuing support, annual campaigns, emergency funds, building funds, equipment, employee related scholarships.
Limitations: Giving primarily in WI. No grants for seed money, deficit financing, land acquisition, special projects, research, publications, conferences, general endowments, or matching gifts; no loans.
Publications: Application guidelines.
Application information: Application guidelines for scholarships for children of company employees only.
  Initial approach: Letter
  Deadline(s): Submit proposals in February
  Board meeting date(s): March, June, September, and December
  Final notification: 1 to 3 months
  Write: Peter Mosling
Officers: J.P. Mosling, President; E.H. Rudov, Vice-President; John E. Dempsey, Secretary; Carl Biederman, Treasurer.
Number of staff: None.
Employer Identification Number: 396062129

4363
Pabst Breweries Foundation ☐
917 W. Juneau Ave.
P.O. Box 766
Milwaukee 53201   (414) 347-7863

Incorporated in 1945 in Illinois.
Donor(s): Pabst Brewing Company.

Financial data: (yr. ended 12/31/83): Assets, $32,574 (M); expenditures, $178,738, including $177,950 for 42 grants (high: $70,000; low: $100).
Purpose and activities: Giving primarily in areas of company operations, with emphasis on community funds, higher and medical education, and the arts.
Limitations: Giving primarily in areas of company operations in WI and IL.
Application information:
Initial approach: Letter
Deadline(s): None
Write: Charles L. Wallace
Officers and Directors: W.F. Smith, President; A.J. Dooley, S.B. Lubar, Vice-Presidents; C.L. Wallace, Secretary and Treasurer.
Employer Identification Number: 396048295

4364
Peck (Milton) Family Foundation, Inc. ⌷

c/o Irving Lowe
200 South Limmcer Ln.
Milwaukee 53233

Established in 1958.
Donor(s): Peck Meat Packing Corporation, Emmber Brands, Inc., Gibbon Packing, Inc., Moo-Battue, Inc.
Financial data: (yr. ended 12/31/83): Assets, $1,641,462 (M); gifts received, $300,000; expenditures, $78,257, including $78,257 for 46 grants (high: $18,234; low: $25).
Purpose and activities: Grants primarily for a war memorial fund, hospitals, and Jewish welfare funds and temple support.
Application information:
Deadline(s): None
Officers: Milton Peck, President; Irving Lowe, Secretary.
Employer Identification Number: 396051782

4365
Peters (R. D. and Linda) Foundation, Inc. ⌷

c/o The Marine Trust Company
P.O. Box 1308
Milwaukee 53201

Established in 1965.
Donor(s): R.D. Peters.†
Financial data: (yr. ended 12/31/83): Assets, $999,717 (M); gifts received, $392,000; expenditures, $550,446, including $536,600 for 13 grants (high: $185,400; low: $6,000).
Purpose and activities: Primarily local giving, with emphasis on higher education, conservation, and Protestant church support.
Limitations: Giving primarily in WI.
Trustee: The Marine Trust Company.
Employer Identification Number: 396097994

4366
Peterson (Fred J.) Foundation, Inc. ⌷

75 Utopia Circle
Sturgeon Bay 54235

Incorporated in 1962 in Wisconsin.

Donor(s): Peterson Builders, Inc., Mary Jo Peterson.
Financial data: (yr. ended 9/30/83): Assets, $1,264,535 (M); expenditures, $127,416, including $125,086 for 72 grants (high: $12,300; low: $95).
Purpose and activities: Primarily local giving to organizations working to improve the quality of life for Wisconsin citizens; grants for higher education, including scholarships through Rotary International, cultural programs, health agencies, and community development.
Limitations: Giving primarily in WI.
Application information: All scholarship decisions made by Rotary International.
Write: Marsha Kerley, Treasurer
Officers: Fred J. Peterson, President; Marsha Kerley, Treasurer.
Employer Identification Number: 396075901

4367
Phillips (The L. E.) Family Foundation, Inc. ▼ ⌷

(formerly The L.E. Phillips Charities, Inc.)
c/o National Presto Industries, Inc.
Eau Claire 54701

Incorporated in 1943 in Wisconsin.
Donor(s): Members of the Phillips family and a family-related company.
Financial data: (yr. ended 2/28/83): Assets, $22,966,702 (M); expenditures, $1,886,629, including $1,748,730 for 47 grants (high: $1,650,000; low: $10; average: $100-$10,000).
Purpose and activities: General purposes; primarily local giving, with emphasis on a Jewish welfare fund.
Limitations: Giving primarily in WI.
Officers and Directors: Melvin S. Cohen, President; Maryjo Cohen, Edith Phillips, Vice-Presidents; Louis R. Weinberg, Secretary-Treasurer; Eileen Phillips Cohen.
Employer Identification Number: 396046126

4368
Pick (Melitta S.) Charitable Trust

777 East Wisconsin Ave., Suite 3800
Milwaukee 53202   (414) 271-2400

Trust established in 1972 in Wisconsin.
Donor(s): Melitta S. Pick.†
Financial data: (yr. ended 1/31/82): Assets, $7,390,703 (M); expenditures, $433,918, including $386,000 for 27 grants (high: $100,000; low: $1,000).
Purpose and activities: Giving primarily to local charities of interest to the trustees, with emphasis on the arts, youth agencies, and a community development fund.
Limitations: Giving primarily in southeastern WI. No grants to individuals.
Application information:
Initial approach: Letter
Board meeting date(s): As required, usually quarterly
Write: Harrold J. McComas, Trustee
Trustees: Harrold J. McComas, Joan M. Pick.
Employer Identification Number: 237243490

4369
Polybill Foundation, Inc. ⌷

735 North Water St., Suite 1328
Milwaukee 53202

Incorporated in 1960 in Wisconsin.
Donor(s): William D. Van Dyke, Polly H. Van Dyke.
Financial data: (yr. ended 12/31/83): Assets, $325,989 (M); gifts received, $397,875; expenditures, $443,914, including $437,000 for 16 grants (high: $186,000; low: $1,000).
Purpose and activities: Broad purposes; primarily local giving, with emphasis on private secondary education, the arts, conservation, and a population control organization.
Limitations: Giving primarily in WI.
Officers and Directors: Polly H. Van Dyke, President and Treasurer; William D. Van Dyke III, Secretary; Leonard G. Campbell, Jr., Paul F. Meissner.
Employer Identification Number: 396078550

4370
Racine Environmental Committee Educational Fund

310 Fifth St., Rm. 101
Racine 53403   (414) 631-5600

Trust established in 1967 in Wisconsin.
Donor(s): S.C. Johnson and Son, Inc., and others.
Financial data: (yr. ended 12/31/83): Assets, $15,550 (M); gifts received, $190,000; expenditures, $213,964, including $113,931 for 150 grants to individuals (average: $797).
Purpose and activities: College scholarships and tuition payments for students residing in the Racine area.
Types of support awarded: Continuing support, student aid.
Limitations: Giving limited to the Racine, WI, area. No grants to individuals directly, or for building or endowment funds, matching gifts, special projects, research, publications, or conferences; no loans.
Publications: Program policy statement, application guidelines, annual report.
Application information: Application form required.
Initial approach: Telephone
Deadline(s): June 30 and October 30
Board meeting date(s): July and November
Final notification: August and December
Write: Mary Day, Executive Director
Officers: M. Michael Connolly,* President; Laurence Schwartz,* Secretary; Larry Mecha, Treasurer; Mary Day, Executive Director.
Trustees: Robert Slade, Trust Officer; Drue S. Guy, Julian Thomas, Grice Williams.
Directors:* Robert Gunnerson, James P. May, Steve McKeel, Charles Raine, Robert Simpson, Ralph Wagner.
Number of staff: 4 full-time professional.
Employer Identification Number: 396123892

4371
Rahr Foundation ¤
P.O. Box 130
Manitowoc 54220   (414) 684-5515

Incorporated in 1942 in Wisconsin.
Donor(s): Rahr Malting Co.
Financial data: (yr. ended 12/31/82): Assets,
$2,204,492 (M); expenditures, $589,436,
including $557,721 for 84 grants (high:
$436,330; low: $32) and $12,665 for grants to
individuals.
Purpose and activities: Support for charitable
and educational institutions and public welfare,
higher and secondary education, youth
agencies, social services, cultural programs, and
a scholarship program for children of company
employees.
Types of support awarded: Employee related
scholarships.
Limitations: No grants for endowment funds or
research programs; no loans.
Application information: Application form
required.
  Initial approach: Letter
  Copies of proposal: 1
  Deadline(s): March 15
  Board meeting date(s): Annually
  Write: Mrs. JoAnn Weyenberg
Officers: Guido R. Rahr, Jr., President;
Frederick W. Rahr, Vice-President; John P.
Nash, Secretary; George D. Gackle, Treasurer.
Directors: Elizabeth B. Rahr, G.R. Rahr, Sr.
Employer Identification Number: 396046046

4372
**Rennebohm (The Oscar) Foundation,
Inc.** ▼ ¤
P.O. Box 5187
Madison 53705   (608) 271-0297

Incorporated in 1949 in Wisconsin.
Donor(s): Oscar Rennebohm.†
Financial data: (yr. ended 12/31/83): Assets,
$13,354,695 (M); gifts received, $2,098,238;
expenditures, $713,855, including $658,000
for 13 grants (high: $426,000; low: $1,000;
average: $1,000-$50,000).
Purpose and activities: Broad purposes;
primarily local giving, with emphasis on higher
education, especially the University of
Wisconsin, and social welfare agencies,
including homes for the aged and for children.
Limitations: Giving primarily in WI.
Application information:
  Write: John L. Sonderegger, Secretary
Officers and Directors: William L. Jackman,
President and Treasurer; Mary F. Rennebohm,
Vice-President; John L. Sonderegger, Secretary;
Leona A. Sonderegger, William H. Young,
Lenor Zeeh.
Employer Identification Number: 396039252

4373
Rexnord Foundation Inc. ▼
350 N. Sunny Slope
Brookfield 53005   (414) 797-5678
*Company-employee scholarship application
address:* Ms. Pat Utrecht, Human Resources
Dept., Rexnord Inc., P.O. Box 2022,
Milwaukee, WI 53201

Incorporated in 1953 in Wisconsin.
Donor(s): Rexnord Inc.
Financial data: (yr. ended 10/31/84): Assets,
$2,292,500 (M); gifts received, $1,004,949;
expenditures, $1,141,929, including $768,415
for 139 grants (high: $105,000; low: $200;
average: $1,000-$10,000), $36,750 for 49
grants to individuals and $326,738 for
employee matching gifts.
Purpose and activities: Charitable purposes;
grants primarily for community funds, higher
education, including an employee matching
gifts program, hospitals, cultural programs, and
youth agencies.
Types of support awarded: Building funds,
special projects, employee related scholarships,
employee matching gifts.
Limitations: Giving primarily in areas of
company facilities, with some emphasis on
Milwaukee, WI. No support for political or
religious organizations. No grants to individuals
(except for company-employee scholarships),
or for endowment funds.
Application information:
  Initial approach: Letter or proposal
  Deadline(s): Submit grant proposals
    preferably in February/March or June/July;
    deadline May 11 for scholarship
    applications only
  Board meeting date(s): 3 or 4 times a year
  Final notification: 3 months
  Write: Virginia A. Klecka, Administrator
Officers: R.V. Krikorian, President; D. Taylor,*
Vice-President; D.L. Shanks, Secretary; W.E.
Schauer,* Treasurer.
Directors:* E.W. Mentzer, W.C. Messinger,
G.H. Moede, Jr.
Number of staff: 2.
Employer Identification Number: 396042029

4374
**Rochlin (Abraham and Sonia)
Foundation** ▼ ¤
c/o Pluswood, Inc.
P.O. Box 2248
Oshkosh 54903

Established in 1969 in California.
Donor(s): Abraham Rochlin,† Sonia Rochlin.
Financial data: (yr. ended 12/31/83): Assets,
$15,292,704 (M); gifts received, $307,000;
expenditures, $854,116, including $703,860
for 46 grants (high: $125,000; low: $100;
average: $100-$26,000).
Purpose and activities: Grants primarily for
Jewish welfare funds and higher education.
Officers: Larry Rochlin, President; Franz L.
Boschwitz, Secretary; Anne Boschwitz,
Treasurer.
Employer Identification Number: 941696244

4375
Roddis (Hamilton) Foundation, Inc. ¤
c/o Augusta D. Roddis
1108 East Fourth St.
Marshfield 54449

Incorporated in 1953 in Wisconsin.
Donor(s): Hamilton Roddis,† Augusta D.
Roddis, Catherine P. Roddis, Roddis Plywood
Corporation.

Financial data: (yr. ended 12/31/83): Assets,
$2,143,057 (M); gifts received, $21,500;
expenditures, $143,170, including $134,400
for 45 grants (high: $17,500; low: $100).
Purpose and activities: Broad purposes;
general giving, with emphasis on Episcopal
church support and religious education,
medical research, educational organizations,
historic preservation and local associations.
Limitations: No grants to individuals.
Officers and Directors: William H. Roddis, II,
President; Mrs. Gordon R. Connor, Vice-
President; Augusta D. Roddis, Secretary and
Treasurer.
Employer Identification Number: 396077001

4376
Rutledge (Edward) Charity
404 North Bridge St.
P.O. Box 369
Chippewa Falls 54729   (715) 723-6618

Incorporated in 1911 in Wisconsin.
Donor(s): Edward Rutledge.†
Financial data: (yr. ended 5/31/84): Assets,
$1,478,000 (M); expenditures, $88,137,
including $19,625 for 115 grants (high: $6,000;
low: $10; average: $170) and $29,217 for 34
grants to individuals.
Purpose and activities: To furnish relief and
charity for worthy poor and to aid charitable
associations or institutions only in Chippewa
County; grants for scholarships, youth agencies,
and a community fund.
Types of support awarded: Grants to
individuals, student aid, special projects,
operating budgets.
Limitations: Giving limited to Chippewa
County, WI. No grants for endowment funds.
Application information:
  Initial approach: Telephone
  Copies of proposal: 1
  Deadline(s): None
  Board meeting date(s): Twice a week
  Write: John Frampton, President
Officers and Directors:* John Frampton,*
President; Richard H. Stafford,* Vice-President;
Gerald Naiberg, Secretary-Treasurer.
Number of staff: 1 full-time professional; 1 full-
time support.
Employer Identification Number: 390806178

4377
Schroeder (Walter) Foundation, Inc. ▼
741 North Milwaukee St., Rm. 300
Milwaukee 53202   (414) 276-5494

Incorporated in 1963 in Wisconsin.
Donor(s): Walter Schroeder Trust.
Financial data: (yr. ended 6/30/83): Assets,
$10,639,632 (M); expenditures, $1,752,644,
including $1,623,809 for 76 grants (high:
$700,000; low: $50; average: $200-$25,000).
Purpose and activities: Primarily local giving,
with emphasis on higher education, including
medical education; aid for the aged, hospitals,
welfare, and youth agencies.
Limitations: Giving primarily in Milwaukee
County, WI.
Application information:
  Deadline(s): None

Board meeting date(s): February, May, August, and November
Write: Miss Hope H. Anderson, President
Officers and Directors: Hope H. Anderson, President; William T. Gaus, Vice-President and Treasurer; Robert M. Hoffer, J.A. Puelicher.
Number of staff: 1 full-time professional; 1 full-time support; 1 part-time support.
Employer Identification Number: 396065789

4378
Sentry Foundation, Inc.
1800 North Point Dr.
Stevens Point 54481

Incorporated in 1963 in Wisconsin.
Donor(s): The Sentry Corporation.
Financial data: (yr. ended 12/31/83): Assets, $1,002,976 (M); gifts received, $25,050; expenditures, $124,747, including $122,150 for 27 grants (high: $50,000; low: $250).
Purpose and activities: Broad purposes; primarily local giving, with emphasis on higher education and a community fund.
Limitations: Giving primarily in WI.
Application information:
Write: Lillian Hanson, Executive Director
Officers: Vernon H. Holmes,* President; Lillian Hanson,* Vice-President and Executive Director; Caroline E. Fribance,* Secretary; David L. Stephenson, Treasurer.
Directors:* Bernard C. Hlavac, John W. Joanis, Philip Marshall, Jane Staples.
Employer Identification Number: 391037370

4379
Siebert Lutheran Foundation, Inc. ▼
2600 North Mayfair Rd., Suite 390
Wauwatosa 53226   (414) 257-2656

Incorporated in 1952 in Wisconsin.
Donor(s): A.F. Siebert,† Reginald L. Siebert,† Milwaukee Electric Tool Corporation.
Financial data: (yr. ended 12/31/83): Assets, $34,768,883 (M); expenditures, $1,388,075, including $1,308,487 for 210 grants (high: $200,000; low: $100; average: $5,000-$10,000).
Purpose and activities: Broad purposes; primarily local giving, with support limited to Lutheran churches and other Lutheran institutions, including hospitals, colleges and schools, youth agencies, and other religious welfare agencies.
Types of support awarded: Operating budgets, seed money, emergency funds, building funds, equipment, special projects, conferences and seminars, matching funds, consulting services.
Limitations: Giving primarily in WI; no grants outside the U.S. No grants to individuals, or for endowment funds, or scholarships and fellowships; no loans.
Publications: Program policy statement, application guidelines.
Application information:
Initial approach: Letter
Copies of proposal: 1
Deadline(s): March 15, June 15, September 15, and December 15

Board meeting date(s): April, July, October, and January
Final notification: 1 week after board meeting
Write: Jack S. Harris, President
Officers: Jack S. Harris, President; Glenn W. Buzzard,* Secretary; Neil A. Turnbull,* Treasurer.
Directors:* Edward A. Grede, Chairman; Richard C. Barkow, Vice-Chairman; Jack R. Jaeger, Merton E. Knisely, John E. Koenitzer, Russell M. Rutter.
Number of staff: 1 full-time professional; 1 full-time support.
Employer Identification Number: 396050046

4380
Smith (A. O.) Foundation, Inc.
P.O. Box 584
Milwaukee 53201   (414) 447-4438

Incorporated in 1951 in Wisconsin.
Donor(s): A.O. Smith Corporation.
Financial data: (yr. ended 6/30/83): Assets, $346,355 (M); expenditures, $299,622, including $298,443 for 70 grants (high: $130,000; low: $400).
Purpose and activities: Giving primarily for civic, cultural, and social welfare; for higher education; and for medical research and local health services in areas of company operations.
Types of support awarded: Continuing support, annual campaigns, building funds, scholarship funds.
Limitations: Giving primarily in WI and in areas of company operations. No grants to individuals.
Publications: Annual report, application guidelines.
Application information:
Initial approach: Letter, telephone, or full proposal
Copies of proposal: 1
Deadline(s): March 30 for consideration in the following year's budget
Board meeting date(s): June and as required
Final notification: 3 months
Write: Jack M. Birchhill, Secretary
Officers and Directors: L.B. Smith,* President; A.O. Smith,* Vice-President; Jack M. Birchhill,* Secretary; Robert A. Rietz, Treasurer.
Employer Identification Number: 396076924

4381
Stackner Family Foundation, Inc. ▼
780 North Water St.
Milwaukee 53202   (414) 277-5000

Incorporated in 1966 in Wisconsin.
Donor(s): John S. Stackner,† Irene M. Stackner.†
Financial data: (yr. ended 8/31/84): Assets, $9,624,850 (M); gifts received, $34,755; expenditures, $968,943, including $845,589 for 172 grants (high: $30,000; low: $300).
Purpose and activities: Local giving only; grants largely for higher education, youth agencies, elementary and secondary education, community funds, the handicapped, and mental health.

Types of support awarded: Operating budgets, continuing support, annual campaigns, seed money, emergency funds, building funds, equipment, land acquisition, endowment funds, matching funds, special projects, research, publications, conferences and seminars.
Limitations: Giving limited to the greater Milwaukee, WI area. No grants to individuals, or for deficit financing, or scholarships and fellowships; no loans.
Application information:
Initial approach: Full proposal or letter
Copies of proposal: 1
Deadline(s): Submit proposal preferably in March or August
Board meeting date(s): April and September
Final notification: 3 weeks after board meetings
Write: Patrick W. Cotter, Secretary
Officers and Directors: Patricia S. Treiber, President; Phillip A. Treiber, Vice-President; Patrick W. Cotter, Secretary and Treasurer.
Number of staff: None.
Employer Identification Number: 396097597

4382
Stolper-Wensink Foundation, Inc. ¤
P.O. Box 190
Menomonee Falls 53051

Established in 1969.
Financial data: (yr. ended 12/31/83): Assets, $9,227 (M); gifts received, $100,000; expenditures, $109,519, including $109,425 for 33 grants (high: $75,000; low: $50).
Purpose and activities: Primarily local giving, with emphasis on community funds and higher education.
Limitations: Giving primarily in WI.
Officers and Directors: Mary Ann Gerlach, President; Rev. Norman Ream, Vice-President; Lloyd A. Gerlach, Secretary-Treasurer.
Employer Identification Number: 391140442

4383
Trane Company Foundation, Inc., The ¤
3600 Pammel Creek Rd.
La Crosse 54601   (608) 787-2000

Incorporated in 1964 in Wisconsin.
Donor(s): The Trane Company.
Financial data: (yr. ended 12/31/83): Assets, $699,896 (M); gifts received, $450,000; expenditures, $412,781, including $377,934 for 102 grants (high: $67,000; low: $100) and $34,253 for employee matching gifts.
Purpose and activities: General giving, with emphasis on community funds, the performing arts, hospitals, and youth agencies within areas of Company operations and for higher education in business and engineering.
Limitations: Giving primarily in in areas of company operations.
Publications: Application guidelines.
Application information:
Initial approach: Letter
Deadline(s): Submit proposal in August or September; deadline October 15
Board meeting date(s): As required

Officers: Alan A. Sachs, Secretary; John Shuey, Treasurer.
Directors: William H. Bast, William G. Roth.
Employer Identification Number: 396084804

4384
Universal Foods Foundation, Inc.
433 East Michigan St.
Milwaukee 53202

Incorporated in 1958 in Wisconsin.
Donor(s): Universal Foods Corporation.
Financial data: (yr. ended 9/30/84): Assets, $2,959,000 (M); gifts received, $500,000; expenditures, $392,000, including $375,000 for 140 grants and $4,500 for employee matching gifts.
Purpose and activities: Broad purposes; giving largely for community funds, hospitals, and higher education.
Limitations: No grants to individuals.
Officers: J.L. Murray, President; G.A. Osborn, D.E. Wilde, Vice-Presidents; Dan McMullen, Secretary-Treasurer.
Number of staff: 1 part-time professional; 1 part-time support.
Employer Identification Number: 396044488

4385
Vilter Foundation, Inc. ⌀
2217 South First St.
Milwaukee 53207

Incorporated in 1961 in Wisconsin.
Donor(s): Vilter Manufacturing Company.
Financial data: (yr. ended 7/31/83): Assets, $2,383,094 (M); expenditures, $160,478, including $132,169 for 102 grants (high: $15,000; low: $100).
Purpose and activities: Broad purposes; primarily local giving, with emphasis on community funds, hospitals, religious welfare funds, and higher and secondary education.
Limitations: Giving primarily in WI.
Officers and Directors: A.A. Silverman, President; E.J. Kocher, Vice-President; W.I. Grant, Treasurer.
Employer Identification Number: 390678640

4386
Walter (Byron L.) Family Trust
c/o The Marine Trust Company
P.O. Box 19029
Green Bay 54307-9029   (414) 437-0421

Trust established in 1981 in Wisconsin.
Donor(s): Arlene B. Walter.†
Financial data: (yr. ended 4/30/84): Assets, $5,884,517 (M); expenditures, $125,300, including $82,000 for 10 grants (high: $25,000; low: $8,200).
Purpose and activities: Broad purposes; local giving only.
Limitations: Giving limited to Brown County, WI. No grants to individuals or for matching gifts; no loans.
Publications: Application guidelines.
Application information:
Initial approach: Letter
Copies of proposal: 1

Deadline(s): Submit proposal preferably from January through March; no set deadline
Board meeting date(s): January, April, July, September, and December
Final notification: 6 months
Trustees: Fred Will, Marine Trust Company (Richard J. Blahnik).
Number of staff: None.
Employer Identification Number: 396346563

4387
Wehr (The Todd) Foundation, Inc. ⌀
2100 Marine Plaza
Milwaukee 53202   (414) 271-8210

Incorporated in 1953 in Wisconsin.
Donor(s): C. Frederic Wehr.†
Financial data: (yr. ended 12/31/83): Assets, $6,859,263 (M); expenditures, $449,927, including $365,000 for 12 grants (high: $75,000; low: $1,000).
Purpose and activities: Broad purposes; primarily local giving, with emphasis on higher education.
Limitations: Giving primarily in WI. No grants to individuals.
Application information:
Initial approach: Letter
Copies of proposal: 1
Board meeting date(s): Quarterly
Write: Robert P. Harland, President
Officers and Directors: Robert P. Harland, President; William J. Hardy, Vice-President and Treasurer; Ralph G. Schulz, Secretary; M. James Termondt, Winfred W. Wuesthoff.
Employer Identification Number: 396043962

4388
Wisconsin Electric System Foundation, Inc. ⌀
231 W. Michigan St.
Milwaukee 53203

Incorporated in 1982 in Wisconsin.
Donor(s): Wisconsin Electric Power Company, Wisconsin Natural Gas Company.
Financial data: (yr. ended 12/31/83): Assets, $3,341,185 (M); gifts received, $2,000,000; expenditures, $755,869, including $755,864 for 280 grants (high: $300,000; low: $20).
Purpose and activities: First year of grant-making in 1983; primarily local giving for community funds, hospitals, higher education, community development and civic affairs, and cultural programs.
Limitations: Giving primarily in WI.
Officers: Charles S. McNeer, President; Russell W. Britt, Vice-President; John H. Goetsch, Secretary; Jerry C. Remmel, Treasurer.
Employer Identification Number: 391433726

4389
Wisconsin Public Service Foundation, Inc. ⌀
700 North Adams St.
P.O. Box 700
Green Bay 54305   (414) 433-1465

Scholarship application address: Wisconsin Public Service Foundation, Inc. Scholarship Program, College Scholarship Service/ Sponsored Scholarships Program, P.O. Box 176, Princeton, NJ 08541

Incorporated in 1964 in Wisconsin.
Donor(s): Wisconsin Public Service Corporation.
Financial data: (yr. ended 12/31/83): Assets, $2,787,514 (M); gifts received, $500,000; expenditures, $324,286, including $252,850 for grants (high: $60,000) and $54,050 for grants to individuals.
Purpose and activities: General purposes; grants largely for higher education, including a scholarship program and buildings and equipment; support also for community funds.
Types of support awarded: Operating budgets, building funds, equipment, student aid.
Limitations: Giving limited to WI and upper MI. No grants for endowment funds.
Application information: Application form required.
Initial approach: Letter
Copies of proposal: 1
Deadline(s): Submit proposal preferably in January; no set deadline
Board meeting date(s): May and as required
Write: Mr. P.D. Ziemer, President
Officers and Directors: P.D. Ziemer, President; L.M. Stoll, Vice-President; J.H. Liethen, Secretary and Treasurer.
Employer Identification Number: 396075016

4390
Woodson (The Aytchmonde) Foundation, Inc. ⌀
602 First American Center
Wausau 54401   (715) 845-9201

Incorporated in 1947 in Wisconsin.
Donor(s): Members of the Woodson family.
Financial data: (yr. ended 6/30/83): Assets, $6,363,806 (M); expenditures, $240,965, including $175,865 for 13 grants (high: $50,000; low: $128).
Purpose and activities: Support almost exclusively for a museum in Wausau, Wisconsin.
Limitations: Giving primarily in Wausau, WI. No grants to individuals or for endowment funds.
Application information:
Initial approach: Letter
Copies of proposal: 1
Board meeting date(s): September
Write: Nancy Woodson Spire, President
Officers and Directors: Nancy Woodson Spire, President; Alice Woodson Forester, Vice-President; John E. Forester, Secretary; San W. Orr, Jr., Treasurer; John M. Coates, Frederick W. Fisher, Lyman J. Spire.
Employer Identification Number: 391017853

4391
Young (Irvin L.) Foundation, Inc. ▼
Snow Valley Ranch
Palmyra 53156   (414) 495-2485

Incorporated in 1949 in Wisconsin.
Donor(s): Irvin L. Young.†

Financial data: (yr. ended 12/31/83): Assets, $8,358,333 (M); expenditures, $672,430, including $645,143 for 48 grants (high: $65,000; low: $237).
Purpose and activities: Broad purposes; grants largely for Protestant medical missionary programs in Africa, including the training of African medical workers.
Types of support awarded: Building funds, equipment, general purposes, operating budgets, scholarship funds, matching funds.
Limitations: No grants to individuals.
Application information:
  Initial approach: Letter
  Copies of proposal: 1
  Deadline(s): Submit proposal in October or November
  Board meeting date(s): As required
  Write: Mrs. Fern D. Young, President
Officers and Directors: Fern D. Young, President; Mary Longbrake, Vice-President; James Vance, Secretary; Ruth Williams, Treasurer; Arden Almquist, Gwilyn Davies, David S. Fisher, Robert Reminger.
Number of staff: None.
Employer Identification Number: 396077858

4392
Youth Foundation, Inc.
4314 West Forest Home Ave.
Milwaukee 53219   (414) 327-6700

Incorporated about 1956 in Wisconsin.
Donor(s): Arthur L. Richards.†
Financial data: (yr. ended 12/31/83): Assets, $1,160,000 (M); expenditures, $124,400, including $70,000 for 40 grants (high: $20,000; low: $200; average: $2,000), $12,000 for 1 employee matching gift and $40,000 for 15 foundation-administered programs.
Purpose and activities: Giving primarily in Milwaukee to assist needy youth and support youth organizations.
Types of support awarded: Seed money, emergency funds, matching funds, scholarship funds, special projects, research.
Limitations: Giving primarily in WI. No grants to individuals, or for operating budgets, continuing support, annual campaigns, building funds, equipment, publications, or conferences; no loans.
Application information:
  Initial approach: Letter
  Deadline(s): None
  Board meeting date(s): As required
  Final notification: 2 months
  Write: Henry J. Wojcik, President
Officers: Henry J. Wojcik,* President; Martin A. Jordan,* Vice-President; Dennis McGuire,* Secretary; Lyle Larcheid, Treasurer.
Directors:* Marjorie Coyne, Jaren E. Hiller, John Ogden, Gerald Sobczak.
Number of staff: 1 part-time support.
Employer Identification Number: 390945311

4393
Ziegler Foundation, Inc., The ⌺
215 North Main St.
West Bend 53095

Incorporated in 1944 in Wisconsin.
Donor(s): Members of the Ziegler family, The West Bend Company.
Financial data: (yr. ended 12/31/83): Assets, $3,431,014 (M); expenditures, $159,586, including $146,150 for 49 grants (high: $50,000; low: $150).
Purpose and activities: General purposes; grants for educational and charitable activities in the state; support primarily for higher education, including a scholarship fund, church support, and youth agencies; support also for hospitals.
Limitations: Giving primarily in the West Bend, WI, area. No grants to individuals.
Application information:
  Deadline(s): None
  Write: Bernard C. Ziegler, President
Officers and Directors: Bernard C. Ziegler, President; Harrold J. McComas, R.D. Ziegler, Vice-Presidents; C.J. Schucht, Secretary-Treasurer.
Employer Identification Number: 396044762

4394
Ziemann Foundation, Inc. ⌺
10930 West Potter Rd.
Milwaukee 53226

Established in 1963.
Donor(s): Lillian Ziemann.
Financial data: (yr. ended 12/31/83): Assets, $1,032,391 (M); expenditures, $505,186, including $500,000 for 1 grant.
Purpose and activities: Primarily local giving, with emphasis on social agencies, aid to the handicapped, an independent secondary school, and a home for the aged.
Limitations: Giving primarily in WI.
Officers and Directors: Carolyn Wright, President and Treasurer; Robert Veenendaal, Vice-President; Cynthia Linnan, Secretary; Louis J. Selzer, Glen O. Starke.
Employer Identification Number: 396069677

WYOMING

4395
Bryan (Dodd and Dorothy L.) Foundation
P.O. Box 6287
Sheridan 82801   (307) 672-3535

Established in 1965 in Wyoming.
Donor(s): Dorothy L. Bryan.†

Financial data: (yr. ended 12/31/82): Assets, $1,977,736 (M); expenditures, $161,736, including $116,525 for 65 loans.
Purpose and activities: Provides educational loans for students from Sheridan, Campbell and Johnson Counties in Wyoming and from Powder River, Big Horn, and Rosebud Counties in Montana.
Types of support awarded: Student aid.
Limitations: Giving limited to Sheridan, Campbell and Johnson Counties, WY, and Powder River, Rosebud and Big Horn Counties, MT. No grants for general support, capital funds, endowment funds, matching gifts, scholarships, or fellowships.
Publications: Application guidelines.
Application information: Application form required.
  Initial approach: Letter
  Deadline(s): Submit application preferably in May or June; deadline July 15
  Board meeting date(s): Monthly
  Final notification: 2 months after board meeting
  Write: J.E. Goar, Manager
Officers: W.D. Redle, President; J. Leonard Graham, Vice-President; Jack E. Pellisier, Secretary; Don Brayton, Treasurer; J.E. Goar, Manager.
Director: Jack Mullinax.
Number of staff: 1 full-time professional.
Employer Identification Number: 836006533

4396
Goodstein Foundation, The ⌺
P.O. Box 1699
Casper 82602

Incorporated in 1952 in Colorado.
Donor(s): J.M. Goodstein.
Financial data: (yr. ended 6/30/83): Assets, $4,267,616 (M); expenditures, $512,046, including $509,650 for 27 grants (high: $100,000; low: $50).
Purpose and activities: Charitable purposes; grants, primarily in Colorado and Wyoming, for higher education, Jewish welfare funds, and hospitals.
Limitations: Giving primarily in CO and WY.
Officers: Fred Goodstein, President; J.M. Goodstein, Vice-President.
Employer Identification Number: 836003815

4397
Kamps (Gertrude) Memorial
Foundation ⌺
c/o First Interstate Bank of Casper
P.O. Box 40
Casper 82602

Established in 1976.
Donor(s): Gertrude Kamps.†
Financial data: (yr. ended 7/31/83): Assets, $1,498,994 (M); expenditures, $254,837, including $207,362 for 14 grants (high: $125,580; low: $1,039).
Purpose and activities: Primarily local giving, with emphasis on youth, child welfare, and social agencies.
Limitations: Giving primarily in Casper, WY.
Trustee: First Interstate Bank of Casper.
Employer Identification Number: 836024918

4398
Stock (Paul) Foundation ⌷
1130 Rumsey Ave.
P.O. Box 2020
Cody 82414   (307) 587-5275

Incorporated in 1958 in Wyoming.
Donor(s): Paul Stock,† Eloise J. Stock.
Financial data: (yr. ended 12/31/83): Assets, $7,012,749 (M); gifts received, $65,067; expenditures, $421,925, including $254,217 for 14 grants (high: $85,000; low: $154) and $97,179 for 96 grants to individuals.
Purpose and activities: Primarily local giving, with emphasis on higher education, including student aid; grants also for hospitals, child welfare, and youth agencies.
Types of support awarded: Student aid.
Limitations: Giving primarily in WY.
Application information: Application form and instructions for educational grants only.
  Initial approach: Letter
  Deadline(s): June 30 and November 30 for educational grants
  Board meeting date(s): July and December
  Write: Kenneth S. Bailey, Secretary-Treasurer
Officers: Charles G. Kepler, President; Eloise J. Stock, Vice-President; Kenneth S. Bailey, Secretary-Treasurer.
Employer Identification Number: 830185157

4399
Surrena (Harry and Thelma) Memorial Fund ⌷
101 W. Brundage
P.O. Box 728
Sheridan 82801

Established in 1973 in Wyoming.
Financial data: (yr. ended 10/31/81): Assets, $2,394,373 (M); expenditures, $211,119, including $180,200 for 6 grants (high: $102,700; low: $10,000).
Purpose and activities: Primarily local giving for youth agencies and social service agencies.
Limitations: Giving primarily in WY.
Trustees: Henry A. Burgess, Clair Robinson.
Employer Identification Number: 237435554

4400
Tonkin (Tom and Helen) Foundation
c/o The Wyoming National Bank of Casper
P.O. Box 2799
Casper 82602   (307) 266-1100

Trust established in 1956 in Wyoming.
Donor(s): Helen B. Tonkin,† T.C. Tonkin.†
Financial data: (yr. ended 7/31/84): Assets, $1,416,469 (M); expenditures, $120,657, including $96,900 for 30 grants (high: $12,000; low: $83; average: $2,000-$10,000).
Purpose and activities: To aid local youth, particularly those handicapped by illness, injury, or poverty, from ages 6-21.
Types of support awarded: Operating budgets, seed money, emergency funds, deficit financing, matching funds, scholarship funds, publications, conferences and seminars.

Limitations: Giving limited to WY, with emphasis on the Casper area. No grants to individuals, or for continuing support, annual campaigns, building or endowment funds, land acquisition, special projects, or research; no loans.
Publications: 990-PF, application guidelines.
Application information:
  Initial approach: Letter
  Copies of proposal: 7
  Deadline(s): None
  Board meeting date(s): As required
  Final notification: 60 days
  Write: Elona Anderson
Members: A.F. Haskey, Chairman; James A. Barlow, Jr., Sheri Carlisle, Warren A. Morton, R.M. Robertson.
Trustee Bank: Wyoming National Bank (Dan W. Guerttman, Trust Officer).
Number of staff: 1 part-time professional.
Employer Identification Number: 836002200

4401
Weiss (William E.) Foundation, Inc.
1501 Stampede Ave., Suite 3040
P.O. Box 2930
Cody 82414

Incorporated in 1955 in New York.
Donor(s): William E. Weiss, Jr., Helene K. Brown.†
Financial data: (yr. ended 3/31/84): Assets, $3,141,506 (M); expenditures, $93,326, including $19,000 for 22 grants (high: $5,000; low: $100).
Purpose and activities: Broad purposes; grants largely for higher and secondary education, historic preservation, hospitals, and Protestant church support.
Limitations: No grants to individuals.
Application information:
  Initial approach: Full proposal
  Deadline(s): Submit proposal preferably in November
  Board meeting date(s): January and July
Officers: William E. Weiss, Jr.,* President and Treasurer; Ann E. Zatkos, Secretary.
Directors:* P. Tate Brown, W.D. Weiss.
Employer Identification Number: 556016633

4402
Whitney Benefits, Inc.
P.O. Box 691
Sheridan 82801   (307) 674-7303

Incorporated in 1927 in Wyoming.
Donor(s): Edward A. Whitney.†
Financial data: (yr. ended 12/31/84): Assets, $6,852,076 (M); expenditures, $165,154, including $105,800 for 1 grant and $193,438 for 61 loans.
Purpose and activities: To provide interest-free student loans to graduates of Sheridan County, Wyoming, high schools; loans for baccalaureate degrees only. Support also for a local youth agency.
Types of support awarded: Student aid.
Limitations: Giving limited to Sheridan County, WY.
Publications: Annual report.

Application information: Applications accepted for loan program only. Foundation does not fund grants. Application form required.
  Initial approach: Telephone, letter, or full proposal
  Copies of proposal: 1
  Deadline(s): Submit application preferably between May and July; deadline 5 days before first Monday of each month
  Board meeting date(s): Monthly
  Write: Jack R. Hufford, Secretary
Officers and Trustees: Peter E. Madsen, President; Henry A. Burgess, Vice-President; Jack R. Hufford, Secretary-Treasurer; John P. Chase, William E. Cook, George E. Ewan, George R. Gligorea, Burton C. Kerns, Dorothy King, C.B. Metz, Nels A. Nelson, Jr., Jane S. Schroeder, Homer Scott, David Withrow.
Number of staff: 2.
Employer Identification Number: 830168511

APPENDIX A

Foundation Information Received After Press Deadlines

The following foundations with assets in excess of $1 million or grants of over $100,000 were identified after the closing of Edition 10 computer files.

C.S. Fund
469 Bohemian Hwy.
Freestone, California 95472   (707) 829-5444

Established in 1981 in California as "pass through" fund for annual gifts of donors.
Donor(s): Maryanne Mott, Herman E. Warsh.
Financial Data (yr. ended 12/31/84): Assets, $0; expenditures, $1,529,083, including $1,329,638 for 98 grants (high: $50,000; low: $2,000).
Purpose and Activities: Giving for programs with national or international impact, in the areas of peace, especially arms control; toxics in the environment; civil liberties; and genetic diversity.
Limitations: No grants to individuals, or for endowment funds, capital ventures, or emergency requests.
Publications: grants list, informational brochure, which includes application guidelines and a program policy statement.
Application Information:
Initial approach: proposal
Copies of proposal: 2
Deadlines: January 15, May 15, and September 15, or next business day
Final notification: approximately 10 weeks after each deadline
Administrative Officer: Marty Teitel, Executive Director.
Directors: Maryanne Mott, Herman E. Warsh.
Employer Identification No.: 953607882

Kroc (Joan B.) Foundation
8939 Villa La Jolla Dr., Suite 201
La Jolla, California 92037   (619) 453-3737

Established in 1984 in California.
Donor(s): Joan B. Kroc.
Financial Data (yr. ended 12/31/84): Assets, $35,072,934 (M); gifts received, $33,017,733; expenditures, $6,887,380, including $5,984,388 for 57 grants (high: $2,455,306; low: $50).
Purpose and Activities: To initiate and sustain programs and activities that help people to accept and overcome conditions that may undermine individual worth and family love; supports communication and educational programs in the areas of alcoholism and chemical dependence, child abuse, world hunger, and the prevention of nuclear war.
Types of Support Awarded: operating budgets, continuing support, seed money, emergency funds, building funds, equipment, land acquisition, matching funds, consulting services, technical assistance, research, conferences and seminars, special projects.
Limitations: Programs serving a particular community generally limited to the San Diego region. No support for religious events; generally does not fund traditional medical research. No grants to individuals, or for annual campaigns, fundraisers, deficit financing, renovation projects, endowment funds, program-related investments, scholarships, or fellowships; no loans.
Publications: annual report, program policy statement.
Application Information: Most programs initiated by the foundation; applications generally not invited.
Initial approach: letter
Deadlines: none
Board meeting dates: annually
Final notification: 3 weeks
Write: Elizabeth E. Benes, General Counsel
Officers: Joan B. Kroc,* President and Secretary; Ballard F. Smith,* Chief Financial Officer and Vice-President.
Directors: Linda A. Smith
Number of Staff: 1 full-time professional, 2 part-time professional, 2 full-time support
Employer Identification No.: 330001724.

Pollock-Krasner Foundation, Inc., The
460 Park Ave.
New York, New York 10022   (212) 838-4600
Application address: P.O. Box 4957, New York, NY 10185

Incorporated in 1984 in Delaware.
Donor(s): Lee Krasner.†
Financial Data (yr. beginning 4/1/85): Assets, approximately $20,000,000 (M)
Purpose and Activities: Grants to worthy and needy individual artists—painters, sculptors, and graphic and mixed media artists; grants may be used for professional or personal requirements.
Types of Support Awarded: emergency funds, grants to individuals.
Limitations: No support for organizations or institutions; grants only to individual artists.
Publications: program policy statement, application guidelines, informational brochure.
Application Information: Application form required.
Initial approach: letter
Deadlines: none
Board meeting dates: quarterly
Final notification: 4 months, except for emergency grants
Write: Charles C. Bergman, Executive Vice-President
Officers and Directors: Gerald Dickler,* Chairman; Eugene Victor Thaw,* President; Charles C. Bergman, Executive Vice-President.
Number of Staff: 1 full-time professional, 1 part-time professional, 1 full-time support, 1 part-time support
Employer Identification No.: 133255693

APPENDIX B

The following foundations appeared in *Edition 9* of *The Foundation Directory* but are not included in *Edition 10* for the reasons stated. For those foundations which no longer qualify for inclusion on the basis of size, the current assets and grants figures are supplied for the year of record as well as the current address.

Aga Khan Awards, The
741 North 25th Street, Philadelphia, PA 19130
  No recent data available; presumed terminated

AHS Foundation
W555, First National Bank Building, St. Paul, MN 55101
  Yr. ended 6/30/84: Assets, $957,831 (M); grants, $47,490

Alpert & Alpert Foundation, The
1820 South Soto Street, Los Angeles, CA 90023
  Yr. ended 6/30/83: Assets, $269,645 (M); grants, $66,081

Ames Foundation, Inc.
2418 Main Street, Rocky Hill, CT 06067
  Yr. ended 1/31/83: Assets, $6,931 (M); grants, $79,013

AMF Foundation
White Plains, NY
  Terminated; acts as pass through for corporation

Amway Charitable Trust
Grand Rapids, MI
  Terminated; assets have been distributed to specified beneficiaries

Arabel Foundation, Inc.
400 Park Avenue, New York, NY 10022
  Yr. ended 12/31/82: Assets, $82,404 (M); grants, $45,013

Auerbach (Herman) Memorial Trust, Fund No. 2
c/o Bankers Trust Company, P.O. Box 1297, Church St. Station, New York, NY 10015
  Yr. ended 9/30/83: Assets, $76,042 (M); grants, $4,982

Avery International Foundation
150 North Orange Grove Boulevard, Pasadena, CA 91103
  No longer active

Bay Branch Foundation, The
Boca Raton, FL
  Liquidating corpus

Bendit (Leo H.) Charitable Foundation
c/o Seidman & Seidman, 15 Columbus Circle, New York, NY 10023
  Yr. ended 12/31/83: Assets, $892,670 (M); grants, $375

Bendix Foundation, The
Cleveland, OH
  Merged with Allied Foundation; formerly The Warner & Swasey Foundation

Blodgett (Margaret Kendrick) Foundation
c/o Fiduciary Trust Company of New York, Two World Trade Center, New York, NY 10048
  Yr. ended 12/31/84: Assets, $792,000 (M); grants, $44,600

Boys Incorporated of America
Dallas, TX
  Terminated

Brenner Foundation, Inc.
P.O. Box 76, Winston-Salem, NC 27102
  Yr. ended 4/30/83: Assets, $683,631 (M); grants, $54,050

Bretzfelder (Helen) Foundation, Inc.
New York, NY
  Specified beneficiaries

Brookline Fund
43 Garrison Road, Brookline, MA 02146
  Yr. ended 12/30/82: Assets, $386,541 (M); grants, $22,593

Brown (Alice and Harry) Foundation
c/o Cleary, Gottlieb, Steen & Hamilton, One State Street Plaza, 27th Fl., New York, NY 10004
  Yr. ended 12/31/82: Assets, $719,970 (M); grants, $36,058

Butterworth (William) Memorial Trust
Moline, IL
  Operating funds and specified beneficiaries only

Carmichael Foundation, Inc.
c/o First Source Bank, One First Source Center, South Bend, IN 46601
  Yr. ended 12/31/83: Assets, $887,523 (M); grants, $87,550

Carrier Corporation Foundation, Inc.
Syracuse, NY
  Carrier Corporation is now a wholly-owned subsidiary of United Technologies; no longer uses the Foundation as its vehicle for corporate philanthropy

Castle & Cook International Charitable Fund, Inc.
50 California Street, San Francisco, CA 94111
  Yr. ended 12/31/83: Assets, $8,901 (M)

Coates (Mr. and Mrs. George H.) Foundation
San Antonio, TX
  Terminated

Cohen (The William and Rosalie) Family Foundation, Inc.
6000 Executive Boulevard, Rockville, MD 20852
  Yr. ended 11/30/83: Assets, $31,965 (M); grants, $46,820

Continental Group Foundation, Inc.
Stamford, CT
  Terminated; company will make grants through corporate contributions only

Conwed Foundation
P.O. Box 64237, St. Paul, MN 55164
  Yr. ended 11/30/84: Assets, $518,900 (M); grants, $16,350; scholarships, $23,690; matching gifts, $13,490

Coon (Owen L.) Foundation
Glenview, IL
  Specified beneficiaries

Coughlin-Saunders Foundation, Inc.
934 Third Street, Suite 703, Alexandria, LA 71301
  Yr. ended 11/30/84: Assets, $170,000 (M); grants, $36,817

Cultural Society, Inc., The
P.O. Box 27459, Indianapolis, IN 46227
  Yr. ended 6/30/83: Assets, $22,982 (M); grants, $35,170; scholarships, $27,800; programs, $28,506

Daily News Foundation Inc.
220 East 42nd Street, New York, NY 10017
Yr. ended 12/31/82: Assets, $926,777 (M); grants, $45,000

Djerassi Foundation, The
Woodside, CA
Operating foundation

Eastmet Foundation, Inc.
P.O. Box 507, Cockeysville, MD 21030
Yr. ended 5/31/83: Assets, $123,618 (M); grants, $97,725

Eaton Foundation, Inc., The
Boston, MA
Terminated; assets transferred to Amelia Peabody Foundation, also in Massachusetts

Envirotech Foundation
Menlo Park, CA
Terminated; final return filed 3/31/83

Everett (David) Foundation, Inc.
150 East 69th Street, New York, NY 10021
Yr. ended 12/31/83: Assets, $921,092 (M); grants, $21,953

Fabick Charitable Trust, Inc.
One Fabick Drive, Fenton, MO 63026
Yr. ended 12/31/83: Assets, $10,554 (M); grants, $44,100

Farber Charitable Trust
10 Institute Road, Worcester, MA 01608
Yr. ended 12/31/82: Assets, $46,428 (M); grants, $700

Felix (The Sylvanus G.) Foundation
P.O. Box 20609, Oklahoma City, OK 73156
Yr. ended 10/31/83: Assets, $243,744 (M); grants, $11,220

Ferguson (Elizabeth) Trust
c/o The First National Bank of Chicago, One First National Plaza, Chicago, IL 60670
Yr. ended 10/31/83: Assets, $652,598 (M); grants, $50,000

Ferndale Foundation, Inc.
c/o First Trust Company of St. Paul, W-555 First National Bank Building, St. Paul, MN 55101
Yr. ended 10/31/83: Assets, $17,276 (M); grants, $76,200

Ferre (The Luis A.) Foundation, Inc.
Hato Rey, PR
Operating foundation

Field Enterprises Charitable Corporation
Chicago, IL
Terminated

Financial Foundation
185 South State Street, Suite 202, Salt Lake City, UT 84111
Yr. ended 12/31/83: Assets, $155 (M); grants, $99,159

First Federal Savings and Loan Association of Chicago Foundation
Chicago, IL
Terminated; FFS & L Assoc. of Chicago has been acquired by Citicorp; corporate contributions will be administered by Citicorp's Community Development Department

Fisher Fund
Pittsburgh, PA
Merged with Pittsburgh Foundation

Fleet (Reuben H.) Foundation
San Diego, CA
Terminated; assets transferred to the San Diego Community Foundation

Friedlaender (Eugen) Foundation, Inc.
c/o Bernard E. Brandes, 61 Broadway, New York, NY 10006
Yr. ended 12/31/82: Assets, $783,652 (M); grants, $76,706

Genshaft Family Foundation
4718 Greenbriar, N.E., Canton, OH 44714
Year ended 12/31/83: Assets, $417,538 (M); grants, $97,050

GK Technologies Foundation, Inc.
Greenwich, CT
Terminated

Goldome Foundation
One Fountain Plaza, Buffalo, NY 14203
Yr. ended 12/31/82: Assets, $97,585 (M); grants, $9,940; formerly N.Y.B.F.S. Foundation

Goldstein (The Samuel and Abraham) Foundation
7600 Jericho Turnpike, Woodbury, NY 11797
Yr. ended 6/30/83: Assets, $327,502 (M); grants, $97,850

Goodhill Foundation, Inc.
New York, NY
Terminated

Grant (Alexander) and Company Foundation
Prudential Plaza, 39th Floor, Chicago, IL 60601
Yr. ended 7/31/83: Assets, $50 (M); grants, $95,067

Grede Foundation, Inc.
P.O. Box 26499, Milwaukee, WI 53226
Yr. ended 12/31/83: Assets, $189,477 (M); grants, $51,589

Halper (The Louis M. and Birdie) Foundation
Los Angeles, CA
Terminating by end of 1985; all assets to be distributed as medical scholarships in July

Hamilton (The J & C) Foundation
132 South Rodeo Drive, Suite 600, Beverly Hills, CA 90212
Yr. ended 11/30/82: Assets, $850,816 (M); grants, $31,429

Hanes Foundation, The
460 Park Avenue, New York, NY 10022
Yr. ended 12/31/82: Assets, $377,645 (M); grants, $58,700

Hansen (Fred J.) Foundation
San Diego, CA
Specified beneficiaries

Herndon Foundation
c/o F.D. Gottwald, Jr., 300 Herndon Road, Richmond, VA 23229
Yr. ended 12/31/83: Assets, $812,636 (M); grants, $23,720

Hill (The Nelson P.) Foundation
Birmingham, AL
Terminated

Honey (William E.) Foundation, Inc.
3100 Equitable Building, Atlanta, GA 30303
Yr. ended 12/31/83: Assets, $852,776 (M); grants, $92,000

Huntsinger Foundation
250 West Stanley Avenue, Ventura, CA 93001
Yr. ended 12/31/83: Assets, $264,614 (M); grants, $51,275

Huyck (Edmund Niles) Foundation
New York, NY
Specified beneficiaries

Insurance Medical Scientist Scholarship Fund, The
Washington, DC
Terminated; the Fund is now part of the Life and Health Insurance Medical Research Fund, also in Washington, DC

International Harvester Foundation
401 North Michigan Avenue, Chicago, IL 60611
Yr. ended 10/31/84: Assets, $48,500 (M)

Jacobs (Joseph B. and Lena B.) Foundation, Inc.
3236 East Wood Valley Road, N.W., Atlanta, GA 30327
Yr. ended 10/31/83: Assets, $872,506 (M); grants, $34,750

Janss Foundation
301 E. Wilbur Road, Thousand Oaks, CA 91360-5442
Yr. ended 12/31/83: Assets, $844,654 (M); grants, $77,538

Joseph Foundation, The
777 Grain Exchange Building, Minneapolis, MN 55415
Yr. ended 7/31/83: Assets, $4 (M); grants, $600

K-Products Foundation
Industrial Air Park, Orange City, IA 51041
Yr. ended 5/31/83: Assets, $422 (M); grants, $82,630

Kaelber Private Foundation
3808 Locarno Drive, Anchorage, AK 99508
Yr. ended 12/31/83: Assets, $7,045 (M); grants, $2,745

Kauffman (Ewing M. and Muriel I.) Foundation
1100 Commerce Bank Building, 922 Walnut, Kansas City, MO
64106
Yr. ended 6/30/83: Assets, $1,962 (M); grants, $37,800

Kay (A. S.) Foundation, Inc.
5454 Wisconsin Avenue, Suite 1300, Chevy Chase, MD 20815
Yr. ended 12/31/83: Assets, $927,536 (M); grants, $91,385

Kaye Foundation
c/o Fred N. Fishman, 425 Park Avenue, New York, NY 10022
Yr. ended 11/30/82: Assets, $266,367 (M); grants, $57,700

Kellogg (John L. and Helen) Foundation
Chicago, IL
Terminated

Kennedy (William M.) Charitable Trust
Delray Beach, FL
Specified beneficiaries

Kimerling Foundation, Inc., The
2020 Vanderbilt Road, Birmingham, AL 35234
Yr. ended 7/31/83: Assets, $130,573 (M); grants, $29,417

King's Foundation, The
390 Main Street, Worcester, MA 01608
Yr. ended 1/31/83: Assets, $9,619 (M); grants, $9,355

Kirschner (E. P. & Roberta L.) Foundation
409 Commercial Bank Bldg., Muscogee, OK 74401
Yr. ended 5/31/84: Assets, $964,263 (M); grants, $15,000

Kroger Companies Charitable Trust, The
1014 Vine Street, Cincinnati, OH 45201
Terminated; grants awarded directly by company

Lamson and Sessions Foundation, The
c/o Central National Bank of Cleveland, P.O. Box 6179, Cleveland,
OH 44114
Yr. ended 12/31/83: Assets, $606 (M); grants, $52,260

Lazear (Martha Edwards) Foundation
Pittsburgh, PA
Merged into the Pittsburgh Foundation

Leavitt (N. R.) Foundation
Watchung, NJ
Specified beneficiaries

Lehman (Orin) Foundation, Inc.
c/o Albert Heit, 424 Madison Avenue, New York, NY 10017
Yr. ended 12/31/82: Assets, $44,242 (M); grants, $89,718

Levine (Joseph M.) Foundation
55 West Monroe, No. 2727, Chicago, IL 60603
Yr. ended 10/31/83: Assets, $715,413 (M); grants, $86,700

Levy (The Leon) Foundation
c/o Alex Satinsky, 2000 Market Street, Tenth Floor, Philadelphia, PA
19102
Yr. ended 11/30/83: Assets, $267,233 (M); grants, $100

Lindner (Carl H.) Foundation
3955 Montgomery Road, Norwood, OH 45212
Yr. ended 12/31/83: Assets, $300,353 (M)

Lowy Family Foundation
8200 Wilshire Boulevard, Beverly Hills, CA 90211-2394
Yr. ended 6/30/83: Assets, $21,956 (M); grants, $66,435

Lyons Memorial Fund
Cincinnati, OH
Terminated; final distribution of assets was made in November,
1983

Mann (Frederick R.) Foundation
1617 John F. Kennedy Boulevard, Philadelphia, PA 19103
Yr. ended 12/31/83: Assets, $5,042 (M); grants, $95,650

Manville Fund, Inc.
P.O. Box 17086, Denver, CO 80217
Grantmaking suspended for at least 3 years due to company's
bankruptcy

McFadden (Ella C.) Charitable Trust
Fort Worth, TX
Terminated as of January 12, 1985

McKee (Arthur G.) & Company Charitable Trust
Cleveland, OH
Terminated

McNutt (V. H.) Memorial Foundation
San Antonio, TX
Specified beneficiaries

McQuay-Perfex Foundation of Minnesota, Inc.
Minneapolis, MN
In the process of terminating

McRoberts (Flossie J.) Trust
St. Louis, MO
Terminating in 1984-1985

McWilliams Memorial Hospital Trust
Kansas City, MO
Specified beneficiaries

Menasha Corporation Foundation
P.O. Box 367, Neenah, WI 54956
Yr. ended 12/31/83: Assets, $346,514 (M); grants, $53,752

Mericos Foundation, The
1600 Huntington Drive, South Pasadena, CA 91030
Yr. ended 12/31/83: Assets, $348,170 (M)

Merkin (Leib and Hermann) Foundation, Inc.
One Whitehall Street, 10th Floor, New York, NY 10004
Yr. ended 6/30/83: Assets, $786 (M); grants, $54,592

Metcalf (Arthur G. B.) Foundation
One Memorial Drive, Cambridge, MA 02142
Yr. ended 12/31/83: Assets, $293 (M); grants, $12,780

Miller (I. L. and Bertha G.) Foundation
820 Fannin Street, Houston, TX 77002
    Yr. ended 12/31/83: Assets, $180,485 (M); grants, $48,545

Miller (Lila J.) Trust
c/o Rainier National Bank, P.O. Box 136, Yakima, WA 98907
    Yr. ended 12/31/83: Assets, $861,260 (M); grants, $90,855

Mix (Charles L.) Memorial Fund, Inc.
Americus, GA
    Specified beneficiaries

Mohasco Memorial Fund, Inc.
57 Lyon Street, Amsterdam, NY 12010
    Yr. ended 12/31/83: Assets, $851,834 (M); grants, $58,354;
matching gifts, $8,030

Mohawk-Hudson Community Foundation, Inc.
877 Madison Avenue, Albany, NY 12208
    Yr. ended 12/31/82: Assets, $497,390 (M); grants, $96,193

Morgan (Urban) Educational Fund
New York, NY
    Specified beneficiaries

Morrison Charitable Trust
Winston-Salem, NC
    Specified beneficiaries

Murphey (John and Helen) Foundation
4445 N. Campbell Avenue, Tucson, AZ 85718
    Yr. ended 12/31/83: Assets, $164,021 (M); grants, $20,001

Nashua Corporation Fund, Inc.
Nashua, NH
    Inactive as of December, 1982

Newhouse Foundation, Incorporated
San Francisco, CA
    Funds merged into Jewish Community Endowment Fund, a
component of the Jewish Community Federation

Nielson Foundation, The
Cody, WY
    Terminated in 1985

Nord (E. A.) Foundation
P.O. Box 1187, Everett, WA 98206
    Yr. ended 11/30/83: Assets, $59,956 (M); grants, $95,930

Norwest Financial Foundation
Des Moines, IA
    Terminating in 1985 or 1986

O'Neil (The Tom and Claire) Foundation, Inc.
107 West Lyon Farm Drive, Greenwich, CT 06830
    Yr. ended 12/31/82: Assets, $880,170 (M); grants, $79,875

O'Neill Brothers Foundation, The
23200 Chagrin Boulevard, Cleveland, OH 44122
    Yr. ended 12/31/83: Assets, $126,976 (M); grants, $9,000

Oishei (John R.) Appreciation Charitable Trust
Buffalo, NY
    Specified beneficiaries

Orleans (Arnold and Ruth) Charitable Foundation
5272 River Road, Suite 760, Bethesda, MD 20816
    Yr. ended 3/31/83: Assets, $1,579 (M); grants, $250

Overseas Foundation, Inc.
511 Fifth Avenue, New York, NY 10017
    Yr. ended 6/30/83: Assets, $899,655 (M); grants, $44,960

Owen Foundation, The
3535 Harney Street, Omaha, NE 68131
    Yr. ended 11/30/83: Assets, $691,088 (M); grants, $80,234

Parten Foundation, The
2100 Travis, Suite 810, Houston, TX 77002
    Yr. ended 3/31/84: Assets, $632,361 (M); grants, $66,085

Pebble Hill Foundation, Inc.
Thomasville, GA
    Specified beneficiaries

Penta Corporation
c/o E. E. van Bronkhorst, 3000 Hanover Street, Palo Alto, CA 94304
    Yr. ended 12/31/83: Assets, $787,606 (M); grants, $50,000

Pentland (Robert), Jr. Charitable Trust
Jacksonville, FL
    Specified beneficiaries

Petersen (The Murray) Foundation
2900 Las Vegas Boulevard South, Las Vegas, NV 89109
    Yr. ended 12/31/83: Assets, $94,170 (M); grants, $56,898

Pfleger (George T.) Foundation
Newport Beach, CA
    Specified beneficiaries

Pine Level Foundation, Incorporated
c/o Charles P. Stetson, 368 Center Street, Southport, CT 06490
    Yr. ended 12/31/82: Assets, $742,291 (M); grants, $78,000

Ralston (Ella Kate and Wallace) Medical and Nursing Students Loan Fund
Houston, TX
    Terminated

Rapids-Standard Foundation, The
Grand Rapids, MI
    Terminated as of November 1, 1983

Rasmuson Foundation, The
c/o National Bank of Alaska, P.O. Box 600, Anchorage, AK 99510
    Yr. ended 12/31/83: Assets, $931,506 (M); grants, $54,723

Reflection Riding
Chattanooga, TN
    Operating funds and specified beneficiaries only

Resources for the Future
Washington, DC
    Granted public charity status as of February 1, 1984 by IRS

Rockmeadow Foundation, Inc.
575 Madison Avenue, New York, NY 10022
    Terminated

Rockwell Foundation, The
Corning, NY
    Operating foundation; not grantmaking

Rose (Edward and Bertha) Revocable Charitable Trust
c/o Shawmut Bank of Boston, P.O. Box 4276, Boston, MA 02211
    Yr. ended 6/30/83: Assets, $29,058 (M); grants, $0

Rosenthal (David) Foundation, Inc.
New York, NY
    Terminated

Russell (Tom) Charitable Foundation, Inc.
341 W. Superior Street, Chicago, IL 60610
    Yr. ended 8/31/82: Assets, $713,592 (L); grants, $6,200

Sackler (Arthur M.) Foundation
Washington, DC
    Operating foundation only

Salmanson Family Foundation
75 Sabin Street, Pawtucket, RI 02860
Yr. ended 11/30/82: Assets, $322,970 (M); grants, $7,259

Salvatori (Henry and Grace) Foundation
Los Angeles, CA
Terminated as of December 19, 1984

Schack Family Trust Fund
1130 Norton Avenue, Everett, WA 98201
Yr. ended 12/31/83: Assets, $91,556 (M); grants, $5,485

Schenley Fund, Inc., The
595 Madison Avenue, 37th Floor, New York, NY 10022
Yr. ended 12/31/84: Assets, $60,000 (M); grants, $9,000

Schlitz Foundation, Inc.
Milwaukee, WI
Terminated as of June 10, 1982

Schneier (Saul) Charitable Trust
Syracuse, NY
Specified beneficiaries

Schwartz Foundation
910 Grand Avenue, P.O. Box 10363, Des Moines, IA 50309
Yr. ended 12/31/83: Assets, $525,802 (M); grants, $63,011

Shapell (David and Fela) Foundation
9401 Wilshire Boulevard, Suite 1200, Beverly Hills, CA 90212
Yr. ended 7/31/83: Assets, $472,293 (M); grants, $98,114

Short (Robert E.) Foundation, Inc.
803 Degree of Honor Building, St. Paul, MN 55101
Yr. ended 6/30/83: Assets, $266,464 (M); grants, $1,000

Sigall (Marie Stauffer) Foundation
520 South Fourth Street, Las Vegas, NV 89101
Yr. ended 12/31/82: Assets, $732,423 (M); grants, $36,900

Smoller (Seymour and Clara) Foundation
2150 Sans Souci Boulevard, North Miami, FL 33181
Yr. ended 12/31/83: Assets, $2,344 (M); grants, $50,000

Society Foundation
Cleveland, OH
Terminated as of December 31, 1984

Southern Pacific Foundation
Chicago, IL
Merged with Santa Fe Industries Foundation to become Santa Fe-Southern Pacific Foundation

Southland Paper Mills Foundation
Houston, TX
Terminated

St. Joseph Foundation, Inc.
82 Kennedy Drive, P.O. Box 587, Forest Park, GA 30050
Yr. ended 12/31/83: Assets, $17,504 (M); grants, $56,100

Stark (Virgil and Judith) Foundation, Inc.
660 Madison Avenue, New York, NY 10021
Yr. ended 12/31/82: Assets, $426,366 (M); grants, $62,690

Stein (Jules and Doris) Foundation
Universal City, CA
Terminated

Steinberg Charitable Trust, The
St. Louis, MO
Terminated

Stephens Charitable Trust, The
114 East Capitol, Little Rock, AR 72201
Yr. ended 12/31/83: Assets, $153,543 (M); grants, $11,750

Steuart (Guy T.) Foundation, Inc.
4646 Fortieth Street, N.W., Washington, DC 20016
Yr. ended 7/31/83: Assets, $874,229 (M); grants $48,500

Stiemke (Walter & Olive) Foundation
Milwaukee, WI
Terminated as of December, 1984; assets distributed to the Milwaukee Foundation to establish the Walter and Olive Stiemke Fund as a permanent component of the community

Straub Foundation
1922 Ingersoll Avenue, Des Moines, IA 50309
Yr. ended 12/31/84: Assets, $935,227 (M); grants, $52,958

Strichman Foundation, Inc., The
c/o Colt Industries, Inc., 430 Park Avenue, New York, NY 10022
Yr. ended 12/31/82: Assets, $156 (M); grants, $0

Stuart (C. H.) Foundation
105 Pine Ridge Drive, Newark, NY 14513
Yr. ended 12/31/82: Assets, $491,549 (M); grants, $30,110; scholarships, $43,839

Swanson (Gilbert C.) Foundation, Inc.
3335 No. 93 Street, Suite 1000, Omaha, NE 68134
Yr. ended 12/31/83: Assets, $52,321 (M); grants, $65,516; scholarships, $13,136

Sybron Community Fund
c/o Sybron Corp., 1100 Midtown Tower, Rochester, NY 14604
Yr. ended 12/31/84: Assets, $32,000 (M); grants, $12,000

Tananbaum (The Alfred) Foundation, Inc.
c/o Arnold S. Alperstein, 261 Madison Avenue, New York, NY 10016
Yr. ended 12/31/82: Assets, $556,438 (M); grants, $41,340

Tanner (Obert C. and Grace A.) Foundation
1930 South State Street, Salt Lake City, UT 84115
Yr. ended 12/31/83: Assets, $12,240 (L); grants, $76,404

Toyota Twenty-Fifth Anniversary Celebration Fund
Torrance, CA
Terminated in 1982; all future giving will be through Toyota Motor Sales, U.S.A. Inc.

Trinity Foundation, The
P.O. Box 10025, Birmingham, AL 35202
Yr. ended 8/31/83: Assets, $103,346 (M); grants, $53,896

Turner (D. A. and Elizabeth B.) Foundation, Inc.
Columbus, GA
Merged with the Bradley (W. C. and Sarah H.) Foundation, also in Georgia, to form the Bradley-Turner Foundation

Turner (Robert Lee) Foundation, Inc.
300 South Ocean Boulevard, P.O. Box 2273, Palm Beach, FL 33480
Yr. ended 9/30/83: Assets, $92,669 (M); grants, $76,446

Uhrig (Edward A.) Foundation
Milwaukee, WI
Terminated; assets have been transferred to the Milwaukee Foundation to establish the Edward A. Uhrig Fund as a component of the community trust

Uihlein (Marie and Erwin) Foundation
777 East Wisconsin Avenue, Suite 2395, Milwaukee, WI 53202
Yr. ended 12/31/83: Assets, $944,498 (M); grants, $88,500

United Charitable Trust
Boston, MA
   Terminated

Wacker Foundation
10848 Strait Lane, Dallas, TX 75229
   Yr. ended 6/30/83: Assets, $256,627 (M); grants, $21,118

Wallace-Murray Foundation
Prospect Heights, IL
   Terminated in 1983

Walton Avenue Foundation
P.O. Box 85285, San Diego, CA 92138
   Yr. ended 11/30/83: Assets, $94,504 (M); grants, $60,916

Warren Family Foundation
P.O. Box 915, Rancho Santa Fe, CA 92067
   Yr. ended 6/30/83: Assets, $269,552 (M); grants, $63,914

Webber (Eloise and Richard) Foundation
Detroit, MI
   Merged as of December, 1983, into Hudson-Webber Foundation, Detroit, MI

Webber (The Richard H. and Eloise Jenks) Charitable Fund, Inc.
Detroit, MI
   Merged as of December, 1983, into Hudson-Webber Foundation, Detroit, MI

Weinberg (Judd A. & Marjorie) Family Foundation
55 West Monroe Street, Room 3580, Chicago, IL 60603
   Yr. ended 12/31/83: Assets, $517,629 (M); grants, $31,039

Weir (Ernest and Mary Hayward) Foundation
300 Park Avenue, Room 2100, New York, NY 10022
   Yr. ended 12/31/84: Assets, $50,000 (M)

Western Electric Fund
New York, NY
   Terminated as of December, 1984; assets transferred to AT&T Foundation, also of New York

Weyerhaeuser (C. Davis) Trust
Tacoma, WA
   Terminated; merged into Stewardship Foundation as of June 11, 1984

Weyerhaeuser (F. K. and Vivian O'Gara) Foundation
2100 First National Bank Building, St. Paul, MN 55010
   Yr. ended 12/31/83: Assets, $97,031 (M); grants, $97,031

Wheelabrator Foundation, Inc.
Hampton, NH
   Merged into Signal Companies Charitable Foundation

Wheeler (Robert C.) Foundation
82 Second Street, San Francisco, CA 94105
   Yr. ended 12/31/84: Assets, $390,000 (M); grants, $41,000

Whitehead (The John C.) Foundation
New York, NY
   Terminated; assets were transferred to Whitehead Foundation, New York, NY, as of July 1, 1982

Winchester Foundation, Inc.
Baltimore, MD
   Terminated as of December 31, 1982

Wood (The Frank and Bea) Foundation
2304 Midwestern Parkway, Suite 204, Wichita Falls, TX 76308
   Yr. ended 12/31/82: Assets, $50,007 (M); grants, $42,316; scholarships, $15,900

Woodheath Foundation, Inc.
c/o Lehman Brothers, Kuhn, Loeb, Inc., 55 Water Street, New York, NY 10041
   Yr. ended 6/30/82: Assets, $371,595 (M); grants, $83,237

Wurzweiler (The Gustav) Foundation, Inc.
New York, NY
   Liquidating

York County, Society for the Preservation of Historic Landmarks in York, ME
   Merged with Old Gaol Museum and Old York Historical and Improvement Society as of January 1, 1984

Zellerbach (Harold and Doris) Fund
150 California Street, Suite 302, San Francisco, CA 94111
   Yr. ended 12/31/83: Assets, $448,940 (M); grants, $76,850

APPENDIX C

The following organizations are classified as private operating foundations under the IRS tax code. Their primary purpose is to conduct research, social welfare, or other programs determined by their individual governing bodies or establishment charters. Although they recently met the asset criteria set for *The Foundation Directory* (assets of $1 million or more), they are excluded from this volume because they do not maintain active grantmaking programs.

STATE	EMPLOYEE I.D. NUMBER
Arizona	
DeGrazia Art and Cultural Foundation, Inc.	860339837
National Historical Fire Foundation	366111510
Arkansas	
HAR-BER Village Foundation	710541295
California	
American Physical Fitness Research Institute, Inc.	952287919
Arms (Thelma), Inc.	946236765
Chaparral Foundation	237146893
Del Monte Forest Foundation, Inc.	946061665
Eden Housing	231716750
Friendly Hills Foundation	237393087
Hon Foundation	953335452
Mechanics Institute	941254644
Meditation Groups, Inc.	066054153
Monterey Bay Aquarium Foundation	942487469
Ormsby Hill Trust	951866004
Paloheimo Charitable Trust	953643948
Reid (Lucile) Cancer Institute—Trust D	956392310
Rest Haven Preventorium for Children	952128344
Santa Catalina Island Conservancy	237228407
Sherman Foundation	952672431
Simon (Norton) Inc. Museum of Art	956038921
Spring Valley Nursing Home, Inc.	586045561
Wrigley Memorial Garden Foundation	952574307
Colorado	
Colorado Masons Benevolent Fund Association	840406813
McClelland Children's Foundation	840411087
Myron Stratton Home	840404260
Connecticut	
Colony Foundation	060261454
Newinton-Cropsey Foundation	060972155
Old Lyme-Phoebe Griffin Noyes Library Association	237209074
Promisek Inc.	060964701
Stone Trust Corporation, The	060552923
Stowe Beecher Hooker Seymour Day Memorial Library and Historical Foundation	066042822
Delaware	
Charitable Research Foundation, Inc.	510077267
Delaware Museum of Natural History	510083535
Longwood Gardens, Inc.	510110625
Palmer Home, Inc.	510066737
Second Champlin Foundation Trust	516010449

STATE	EMPLOYEE I.D. NUMBER
District of Columbia	
Accokeek Foundation, Inc.	526037288
Dickson (John) Home	530204688
Howe (Dr. O. E.) Home for Unfortunate Girls	526040762
Lisner (Abraham and Laura) Home for Aged Women	530228120
Logistics Management Institute	520741393
Louise Home, Trustees of the	530196601
Phillips Collection	530204620
Sackler (Arthur M.) Foundation	521074954
Shoemaker (Elizabeth R.) Home	530211708
Florida	
Archbold Expeditions	236400408
Cummer (Deetee Holden) Museum Foundation	590870278
Dali (Salvador) Foundation	346527073
DuPont (Alfred I.) Awards Foundation	596122735
Harbor Branch Foundation	591542017
Hearn (Lydia and Sam B.) Foundation	596153323
Lannan Foundation	366062451
Martin County Historical Society	590913326
Morse Charitable Trust	341331872
Naples Institute for Advanced Studies in Medicine and the Humanities	232012011
Ocala Leases Housing Corp.	237245119
Georgia	
Lockerly Arboretum Foundation	581078686
Tuttle (Newton) Home	580566249
Hawaii	
Kukuiolono Park Endowment Fund	997003335
Lunalio Home	990075244
Illinois	
Centralia Foundation	376029269
Everly Home for the Aged Trust	376047799
King—Bruwaert House	362167769
Morton Arboretum	361505770
Smith (Washington and Jane) Home	362167948
Tatman Village, Inc.	371075972
Indiana	
Bethesda Elderly Housing Corp.	351401887
Blaffer (Robert Lee) Trust	746060871
Caldwell (Jennie E.) Memorial Home Trust	350907305
Compton Oriental Arts Foundation	510183635
Ford (Charles) Trust D/B/A Charles Ford Memorial Home	350985961
Sabin (Ruth C.) Home	350886845

Iowa

Cooks (Clarissa C.) Home for the Friendless	420723017
Home for Aged Women	420681101
Shadle (Webb) Memorial Fund	420746005

Kansas

Cato Institute	237432162
Reno County Child Care Association, Inc.	480840803

Kentucky

Home of the Innocents	610445834
Lincoln Foundation, Inc., The	610449631
Louisville Protestant Altenheim	610449634
Moorman (Charles P.) Home for Women	610665366

Louisiana

Milne Asylum for Destitute Orphan Girls	720261790
Noel Foundation Inc.	237177629
O'Brien (Kathleen) Register Foundation	726025708
Poydras Home Female Orphan Society	720451616
San Francisco Plantation	720789586
Society for the Relief of Destitute Orphan Boys	720408986
Webb (Del E.) Foundation	720451616

Maine

Bangor Children's Home	010211481
Farmington Home for Aged People	010217212
Good Samaritan Home Association	010211507
Home for Aged Women—Portland, Maine	010200791
Old Folks Home in Bath	010131540
Owl's Head Foundation Trust	237307367
Pine Tree Conservation Society, Inc.	237158781
Redington Memorial Home	010211547
Wardwell Home for Old Ladies of Saco and Biddeford	010213987

Maryland

Chase Home, Inc.	520613676
Episcopal Ministries to the Aging, Inc.	237405177
Ferguson (Alice) Foundation	520694646
Home for the Aged of Frederick City	526036221
Maryland Anti-Vivisection Society	526001538

Massachusetts

Ames Free Library of Easton	237245953
Anagnos (Michael) Schools	046012768
Archimedes Foundation	042680893
Art Complex Inc.	046155696
Barnard (Frances Merry) Home	042137224
Battles Home	042134817
Berkeley Retirement Home	042104374
Berkshire County Home for Aged Women	042103875
Bertram Home for Aged Men	042103743
Business Fund for the Arts Inc.	042637112
Cambridge Home for Aged People	042103958
Carleton (Elizabeth) House	042105924
Chestnut Knoll Springfield Home for Aged Women	042105937
Concords Home for the Aged	042103762
Colonial Society of Massachusetts	046110988

Massachusetts

Cumberland Farms Conservation Trust	042616919
Dana Home of Lexington	042111392

Fitch Home, Inc.	042111388
Gardner (Isabella Stewart) Museum	042104334
Griffin-White Home for Aged Men and Aged Couples, Inc.	042148009
Hayden (Josiah Willard) Recreation Centre	042203700
Home for Aged Men in Worcester	042121348
Home for Aged People in Fall River	042104315
Home for Aged Women in Salem	042104318
Home for Aged Women	042108367
Hopedale Community House, Inc.	042133252
Kendall Whaling Museum Trust	042294937
Koch (William) Foundation	510179280
Lathrop Home	042104372
Leland Home	042400385
Loomis House Inc.	042108366
Lynn Historical Society Inc.	042269520
Lynn Home for Elderly Persons	042400070
Managers of Boston Port and Seamen's Aid Society	042104688
Merrimack Valley Textile Museum Inc.	042276089
Mount Pleasant Home, The	
Nantucket Historical Trust	042303741
Nantucket Ornithological Association	136176966
New England Home for the Deaf	042104760
Newburyport Society for the Relief of Aged Men	042111219
Orleans Conservation Trust	237418072
Park (Francis William) Trust	046092035
Raptelis (Demosthenis) Foundation	046233953
Rowland Institute for Science, Inc.	042704639
Roxbury Home for Aged Women	042104858
Springfield Home for the Elderly	042105936
Stanley Park of Westfield Inc.	042131404
Taunton Female Charitable Association	042105743
Union of Concerned Scientists, Inc.	042535767
Wadleigh (George C.) Home for Aged Men	042720087
Wales Home for Aged Women	041940730
Widows Society in Boston	042306840
Willard House and Clock Museum, Inc.	042671799
World Peace Foundation	042105854

Michigan

Detroit Neurosurgical Foundation	382127946
Ford (Edsel and Eleanor) House	382218274
Gilmore (Genevieve and Donald) Foundation	386154163
Hannan (Luella) Memorial Home	381358386
Kalamazoo Aviation History Museum	382144402
McFarlan Home	381390531
Old Ladies Home Association of Ann Arbor	381381276
Thompson (Mary) Foundation	381359097

Minnesota

Babbage (Charles) Foundation	382127946
Bakken Library of Electricity in Life	510175508
Belwin Foundation	410967891
Burke (Mary & Jackson) Foundation	237275337
Carpenter (Thomas E. & Edna D.) Foundation	237275337
Charlson Research Foundation	411313302
Dodge (Thomas Divine) Foundation	416081794
South Washington County Senior and Handi-capped Housing, Inc.	411349989

Mississippi

Hand (James) Foundation	646024146

STATE	EMPLOYEE I.D. NUMBER	STATE	EMPLOYEE I.D. NUMBER

Missouri

Blind Girls Home, Inc.	430662450
Centre for International Understanding	430922802
Charless Home	430666753
Drumm (Andrew) Institute	440569643
Hall (Linda A.) Library Trusts	440527122
Hughes (Charles and Ethel) Foundation	646024146
Memorial Home, Inc.	430657946
Newman (Eric P.) Numismatic Education Society	436048614
St. Louis Mercantile Library Association	440694564

Nebraska

Internorth Art Foundation	470615942
Swanson Center for Nutrition, Inc.	237175802

New Hampshire

Chase Home for Children in Portsmouth, New Hampshire	022229190
Dover Children's Home	022233230
Gafney Home for the Aged	020222132
Gale Home	020223444
Home for Aged Women	020223603
Hunt (John M.) Home	020222143
Hunt (Mary E.) Home	020222144
New Hampshire Centennial Home for the Aged	020224596
Norwell Home	020225753
Prospect Hill Home	020222146
Scott-Farrar Home	020241739
Sweeney (Mary A.) Home	020312307
Taylor Home	020222149
Webster (Rannie) Foundation	020331198
Wentworth Home for Chronic Invalids	020222243
Wentworth Home for the Aged	020223354
Women's Aid Home	020222249
Woodward Home, Inc.	020220400

New Jersey

Campbell Museum	226080478
Eckert (Fred and Clara) Foundation for Children	456016766
Elizabethtown Historical Foundation	226055641
Fellowship in Prayer, Inc.	135562408
Gund Collection of Western Art	346623289
Industry-Community Center, Inc.	237097421
Institute for Advanced Studies of World Religion	237085108
Jonas (Louis Albert) Foundation	141387863
Mannheimer Primatological Foundation	221851590
Memorial Home of Upper Montclair for Aged People	221487239
Noyes (Mr. & Mrs. Fred Winslow) Historical and Cultural Foundation	237247632
Ward Home for Aged and Respectable Bachelors and Widowers	221574538
Wheaton Historical Foundation	221849118

New Mexico

San Felipe Del Rio, Inc.	237276447

New York

Adirondack Historical Association	135635801
Aeroflex Museum	226103961
Africa Fund	136202430

Agricultural Development Council, Inc.	131771777
Albany Guardian Society	141363010
Boscobel Restoration, Inc.	141458845
Branch-Wilbur Fund, Inc.	166093008
Brooklyn Section Community Senior Citizen Center	237389126
Camargo Foundation	132622714
Canajoharie Library and Art Gallery	141398373
Cantor (B. G.) Art Gallery	136227347
Chenango Valley Home for Aged People	150543650
Clark Manor House	160755755
Comunita Giovanile San Michele, Inc.	136102743
Corning Museum of Glass	160764349
Culinarians Home Foundation, Inc.	131635296
Davis (Westmoreland) Memorial Foundation	136170029
Dia Art Foundation, Inc.	237397946
Dreyfus Medical Foundation	136086089
Fish (Alice and Hamilton) Library	132933774
Freedman (Andrew) Home	131739915
Glens Falls Home	141340067
Home for the Aged	160766337
Hudson New York Home for the Aged	141436628
Ingersoll Memorial for Aged Men, Inc.	141364550
Lehrman Institute	237218534
Marien-Heim Tower, Inc.	112355029
Miner (Alice T.) Colonial Collection	141405827
Myrin Institute	111857581
New York Friends Group Inc.	135680254
Norcross Wildlife Foundation, Inc.	132041622
Old Westbury Gardens, Inc.	111902968

New York

Orentreich Foundation for the Advancement of Science, Inc.	136154215
Pack Foundation for Medical Research	132971722
Palisades Geophysical Institute, Inc.	237069955
Public Art Fund, Inc.	132898805
Regional Arts Foundation, Inc.	132914346
Rock Foundation	060944728
Rockwell Foundation	166052043
Saint Georges Society of New York	237426425
Schweinfurth Memorial Art Center	161097876
Seabury Memorial Home	131740038
Sleepy Hollow Restoration, Inc.	131692606
Special Olympics, Inc.	520889518
Strong (Margaret Woodbury) Museum	160954168
Syracuse Home Association	150533582
Trotting Horse Museum, Inc.	141368198
Two Hundred Seventy-two to Two Hundred Eighty Linwood Avenue, Inc. (also known as Baptist Manor, Inc.)	237372052
Welch (Clara) Thanksgiving Home	150543655
Young (Morse) Historic Site	141619998

North Carolina

Reynolds House, Inc.	560810676
Walthour-Moss Foundation	237380583

North Dakota

Oppen Family Guidance Institute, Inc.	237186904

Ohio

Abbott Home	314379421
Bell (Samuel W.) Home for Sightless, Inc.	310537120
Blackburn Home for Aged People Association	340714543

STATE	EMPLOYEE I.D. NUMBER
Bluechner (Lucy R.) Corporation	346000449
Clark Memorial Home Association	310585915
Columbus Home for the Aged	314380044
Lincoln (James F.) Arc Welding Foundation	346553433
Oberlin (Shansi) Memorial Association	340768350
Palmer (Judson) Home	344436480
Philada Home Fund	310677810
Rex Foundation	341320874
Sauder Museum Inc.	237042835
Sea Research Foundation Inc.	341222723
Toledo Community Foundation Donor Directed Pooled Fund	341243271

Oklahoma
Goddard Youth Foundation	730749570

Pennsylvania
Andalusia Foundation	232115258
Coxe (Sophia G.) Charitable Trust Fund	236001974
Dorflinger Suydam Wildlife Sanctuary Inc.	232137456
Easton Home for Aged Women	240801265
Forrest (Edwin) Home	231351240
Gibbons Home	231381979
Hahn Home	231425032
Heinz (Sarah) House Association	250965390
Henry Foundation for Botanical Research	231365145
Kirby (Fred M. and Jessie A.) Episcopal House	240826175
Long (Henry C.) Asylum	231352360
Hershey (M. S.) Foundation	236242734
Lycoming House	231365326
Morris Animal Refuge	231352237
Nugent (George) Home for Baptists	231365377
Park Home Inc.	240522575
Pennsylvania Society of Sons of the Revolution	231353372
Polk (Charles P. and Margaret E.) Foundation	236296772
Ressler Mill Foundation	236430663
Watson Memorial Home	250965602

Rhode Island
Ballou Home for the Aged at Woonsocket	050260671

South Carolina
Arnold (Ben) Memorial Foundation	576034371

Tennessee
Christian Home	620511452
Dixon Gallery and Gardens	620943809
Memphis Sunshine Home for Aged Men	620202745
Street (Gordon) Foundation	620634450

Texas
Brownson Home, Inc.	741237326
Collins (Ben & Jane) Home for Women	750939908
Davis (T. W.) Memorial Park	746026891
Gihon Foundation	751612234
Hall (David Graham) Trust	750868395
Haly (Nita Stewart) Memorial Library	237327454
Heights Towers Services Co.	237437989
Kimbell Art Foundation	756036226
Pate Foundation	756036779
Read Youth Charities	237048642
Smith (Vivian L.) Foundation for Restorative Neurology	742139770
Stehlin Foundation for Cancer Research	741622404
Valley Zoological Society	741604409

Vermont
Converse Home, Inc.	030179406
Fisher (O. M.) Home, Inc.	030184240
Homestead, Inc.	030195636

Virginia
Agecroft Association	540805729
Ballentine (Mary F.) Home for the Aged	540538201
Brookfield, Inc.	540638415
Chastain Home for Gentlewomen	546044813
Human Resources Research Organization	237029310
Jones (George M.) Library Association	540505921
Kaufman Americana Foundation	510217081
Lewis (Sydney and Frances) Foundation	546061170
Miller Home of Lynchburg, Va.	540505999
Petersburg Home for Ladies	540515720
Williams Home, Inc.	540524517

Washington
Franke (Todey Jones) Home	910575957
Frye (Charles & Emma) Free Public Art Museum Inc., Testamentary Trust of Charles H. Frye	910659435
Whatcom Foundation Incorporated	910905571

West Virginia
Alten Heim Board of Trustees	550371584

Wisconsin
HHK Foundation for Contemporary Art, Inc.	391300476
Milwaukee Home for the Friendless	390837518
Paine Art Center and Arboretum	390785483
Rutledge (Hannah M.) Home for the Aged	390806179
Woodson (Leigh Yawkey) Art Museum, Inc.	237281913

Wyoming
Whedon (Earl & Bessie) Cancer Detection Foundation	830176313

The following organizations are classified as private nonoperating foundations under the IRS tax code. On the basis of statements from the organizations or an analysis of their most recent fiscal statements, it appears that these foundations contribute only to a few specified beneficiaries or to the support of a single organization or institution. Therefore, they are not included in this volume. Without further information, grantseekers are advised NOT to apply to these foundations for grant support.

STATE	EMPLOYER I.D. NUMBER
Alabama	
Marinos (George) Trust	636018531
California	
Bachrach (Marguerite) Charitable Trust	946465724
Hansen (Fred J.) Foundation	953247772
Morbio (Adolph) Trust	946486955
Pfleger (George T.) Foundation	952561117
Portola Foundation	237079734
Sicular (Henry & Geraldyn) Foundation	946104509
Singleton (Edward C.) Trust	946465282
Singleton (Edward C.) Trust for Shriners Hospital for Crippled Children	946466283
Steiner (Lionel) Trust	946445242
Colorado	
Wann (The Ralph J.) Foundation	846022561
Connecticut	
Bradley Home for the Aged, The	060646552
Fisher (Stanley D.) Trust	066223974
Swebilius (C. G.) Trust	066021035
Delaware	
Kelly (Eugene V.) Trust for Initial/Teaching Alphabet	237277016
District of Columbia	
Plummer (George P.) Trust	526181726
Reid (Helen Dwight) Educational Foundation, Inc.	526039144
Scholz (Robert O.) Foundation	521104075
Florida	
Bickel (Karl A.) Charitable Trust	596515937
Kennedy (William) Memorial Trust	596692270
Laufer (Charles A.) Trust	596121126
Pentland (Robert), Jr. Charitable Trust	596686559
Williams (Charles J.) Foundation	596159052
Georgia	
Mix (Charles L.) Memorial Fund, Inc.	580699008
Illinois	
Buehler (Christian) Memorial	370661194
Butterworth (William) Charitable Trust	596692270
Coon (Owen L.) Foundation	366066907
Manaster (Abe and Esther)—Dr. Charles H. Solomon Scholarship Fund	366729062
Mather (Alonzo Clark) Trust 0930675	366010112
Indiana	
Golay Foundation, Inc.	310929865
Newland (Helen Gregory) Testamentary Trust	310967188

STATE	EMPLOYER I.D. NUMBER
Iowa	
Aliber (Robert) Charitable Trust	426273581
King (Edith) Pearson Trust	426069932
Knoxville Medical Center Foundation	421084522
Maine	
McArthur Home for Aged People Association	010212437
Massachusetts	
Ashton (Elisha V.) Trust	046016303
Babson (Isabel) Memorial Inc.	046031813
Davenport Memorial Foundation	042104142
Duebener-Juenemann Foundation	416010762
Elliot (John & Sarah) Charitable Trust	046282546
Heritage Plantation of Sandwich Fund	237259864
Newburyport Society for the Relief of Aged Women	042121771
Peters (G. Gorham) Testamentary Trust	046111827
River Road Charitable Corporation	046169258
Salem Young Women's Association	042103847
U.S.S. Massachusetts Development Corporation	042379775
Michigan	
Kiwanis of Michigan Foundation	381723513
Krasl (George) Charitable Trust	386370529
Minnesota	
Anderson (Arthur H.) Foundation	416021773
Hallett Charitable Trust	
Hormel Foundation, The	410694716
Hull Educational Foundation	416019516
Missouri	
Dunn (Thomas) Memorial Trust	436020367
Hedrick (Minnie B.) Trust	446008725
Loose (Jacob L.) Million Dollar Charity Fund Trust #55	446009244
Loose (Ella C.) Trust 4316	446009265
McWilliams Memorial Hospital Trust	436062691
Seay Foundation	436055549
Montana	
Copulos Family Hospital Trust	816043540
New Jersey	
Leavitt (N. R.) Foundation	226034106
New York	
American Electric Power Systems Educational Trust Fund	237418083
Bolton Fund, Inc.	136069816
Dixon (The Hugo) Foundation	136037692
Duffy (George) Foundation	146016445
Ferncliff Cemetery Association—4th Fund	136062036
Bretzfelder (Helen) Foundation, The	133010479

STATE	EMPLOYER I.D. NUMBER
Gleason Fund, Inc. Life Benefit Plan 411230210	166024331
Huntington (A. M.) Trust for the Benefit of Brookgreen Gardens	136035523
Huyck (Edmund Niles) Foundation	136047631
Jacobs (Harry & Rose) Foundation	136161740
Kissam/Fordham Law Trust	136806139
Leir (Henry J. & Erna D.) Foundation	237176054
Linsky (Jack and Belle) Foundation, Inc.	133006623
Morgan (Urban) Educational Fund	136750433
Oishei (John R.) Appreciation Charitable Trust	166093037
Peckham (Mary M.) Trust for the Benefit of Chenago Valley Home	156017709
Phipps (John S.) Foundation	136021639
Rare Breeds Survival Foundation of America	
Tinker (Edward R.) 1957 Charitable Trust	136772877
Wolf (Charles F.) Medical Scholarship Fund	141580597

North Carolina

Bryan (The Kathleen Price and Joseph M.) Family Foundation	566046952
Morrison Charitable Trust	566093800

Ohio

DeGenhart Paperweight and Glass Museum	310957101
Green (Helen Wade) Charitable Trust	346527172
Hipple Foundation	316063133
Kulas (Elroy J.) Trust #1	346747424
True (Henry A.) Trust	310679235
University Suburban Health Center Foundation	340153052
Weatherhead (Albert J.) Estate Trust u/w Item IV	346580925

Oklahoma

Charitable Trust for the Benefit of St. George's Greek Orthodox Church	736174509

Oregon

Failing (Henry) Fund	936120362

Pennsylvania

American Historical Truck Museum and Library	237240758
Baumeister Reichard Trust Fund	232137301
Coulter (William A.) Trust	256018848
Countess Detrampe Home for Unwanted Dogs	232020935
Elkins (Lewis) Fund	236214962
England (Elizabeth R.) Trust	236606334
Ephrata Recreation Center	231392955
Erdman (Florence Waring) Trust	236225822
Jenkins (Est. H. Lawrence) Residuary T/W	236491966

STATE	EMPLOYEE I.D. NUMBER
Lowengrad (Leon) Scholarship Foundation	236236909
Mercer Fonthill Museum, Trustees of the	236213940
Woods-Marchland (Mary M.) Foundation	256018836

South Carolina

Milliken (Seth M.) Foundation	236213940

South Dakota

McCrossan Foundation	460241590

Tennessee

Carrier (Robert M. & Lenore W.) Foundation	626035575
Potter (Valere B.) Trust	581309898
Reflection Riding, Inc.	620670240

Texas

Auxiliaries to the Devotion of the Holy Infant	746109704
Baldus (Charles B. & Ida H.) Memorial Trust	746266785
Bryce (William) Trust #417	751682810
Cartmell Home for the Aged & Orphans	750869320
Chandler Memorial Home	741143117
Excellence in Education Foundation	751075163
Gething (Margaret Allan) Memorial Trust	136600238
McNutt (V. H.) Memorial Foundation	746035044
Miller (Rudolph C.) Community Fund	741983753
Moor (Lee) Children's Home	746033972
North Texas Higher Education Authority	237133739
Ripley (Daniel & Edith) Foundation	746049474
Slaughter (Dick) Trust	756007584
Slick (Tom) Memorial Trust for the Mind Science Foundation	

Virginia

Brooks (The Thomas M.) Charitable Foundation	510232357

Washington

Cheney (Ben B.) Foundation, Trust for	237215379
Egtvedt (The Clairmont L. & Evelyn S.) Charitable Trust	
Trimble (George W.)	916026531

Wisconsin

Brown-Wilcox Trustees Company Inc., Brown-Wilcox Home for Aged	390806176
Frank Family Memorial Scholarship Fund	396270979
Layton School of Art	390806164
Wisconsin Electric Utilities Research Foundation	396076905

Wyoming

Cody Medical Foundation	836006491
Ivinson Memorial Home for Aged Ladies	830179773
White (Ted & Marie) Memorial Foundation	836018510

INDEXES

INDEX TO DONORS, OFFICERS, TRUSTEES

Aall, Sally Sample, 2047
Aaron, Bennett, 3618
Aaron, Charles, 1035
Aarons, Stuart, 551
Abbiati, Lawrence B., 1398
Abbott, Ann B., 1656
Abbott, Catherine, 2881
Abbott, Herbert A., Jr., 1197
Abbott Laboratories, 918
Abbott, Lysle I., 1208
Abbott, W.W., 3333
Abboud, A. Robert, 302
Abegg, Edward, 487
Abel, Alice, 2049, 2063
Abel, Clinton, 2212
Abel Construction Company, 2049
Abel, Elizabeth, 2049
Abel, George, 2049
Abeles, Anne M., 3810
Abeles, Charles C., 662
Abell (A.S.) Company, 1399
Abell, D. Barry, 4206
Abell, George T., 3866
Abell, Gladys H., 3866
Abell, P.G., 1291
Abell, Williams S., Jr., 1399
Abely, Joseph F., Jr., 3105
Abercrombie, J.S., 3867
Abercrombie, Josephine E., 3867
Abercrombie, Ralph L., 3422
Abernathy, Jack, 3441
Abernathy, Taylor S., 1981
Abess, Leonard C., 697
Abex Corporation, 488
Abma, JoAnn, 2230
Abney, John S., 3794
Abney, Susie M., 3794
Abnot, Selma C., 197
Aboodi, Oded, 2929
Abraham, Alexander, 2288
Abraham, Henry L., 1456
Abrahams, Richard I., 3765
Abram, Morris B., 2995
Abrameit, Archie, 4019
Abramovitz, Charles, 2911
Abrams, Benjamin, 2214
Abrams, C.W., 53
Abrams, Robert H., 3003
Abrams, Roberta, 2768
Abrons, Anne S., 2215
Abrons, Herbert, 2215
Abrons, Herbert L., 2931
Abrons, Louis, 2215
Abrons, Richard, 2215
Abston, Dunbar, Jr., 3854
Acers, Ebby Halliday, 3911
ACF Industries, 2217
Achelis, Elizabeth, 2218
Acheson, George H., 1538
Acker, A.E., 3540
Ackerman, Herb, 2477
Ackerman, Jack, 2583
Ackerman, James H., 937

Ackerman, Lee James, 937
Ackerman, Loraine E., 937
Ackerman, Page, 646
Ackerman, Roger G., 2368
Ackerman, Simona, 2716
Ackerman, Thomas C., Jr., 194
Ackerman, Mrs. Vale Asche, 4107
Acmaro Securities Corporation, 876
Acme Spinning Company, 3112
Acme-Cleveland Corporation, 3144
Acton, Evelyn Meadows, 4029
Acushnet Company, 1466
Adair, Kay Kerr, 3439
Adair, Robert C., Sr., 3439
Adam, John, Jr., 1659
Adams, A.B., 4301
Adams, Albert E., 416
Adams, Boyd, 2
Adams, Caroline J., 1467
Adams, Charles E., 1467
Adams, Charles F., 1560
Adams, D. Nelson, 3029
Adams, Derek F.C., 389
Adams, Dinsmore, 2596
Adams, Edward, Jr., 1673
Adams, Elizabeth Helms, 214
Adams, Emma J., 2219
Adams, Eugene H., 454, 455
Adams, Eula, 873
Adams Fabricated Steel Corporation, 2696
Adams, Frederick G., 533
Adams, James M., 3868
Adams, Janet Noyes, 1246
Adams, Leland C., 928
Adams, Louise B., 496, 689
Adams, Marcene Hazel, 3868
Adams, Marsha H., 209
Adams, Paul W., 579
Adams, Peter W., 3258
Adams, R.M., 1890
Adams, Rex D., 2743
Adams, Robert M., 2162
Adams, Robert McCormick, 2902
Adams, Rolland L., 3508
Adams, Roy M., 1153
Adams, S. Kent, 1101
Adams, Stewart E., 433
Adams, Warren S., II, 791
Addington, Keene H., 925
Addington, Leonard M., 1830, 1916
Addison, Johnny B., 1378
Ade, James L., 731
Adel, Catherine, 43
Adelberg, Edward A., 2446
Adelson, Ellen Jane, 3433
Ades, Albert, 2220
Ades, Isaac, 2220
Ades, Joseph, 2220
Ades, Robert, 2220
Adess, Melvin S., 1063
Adler, Frederick, 44
Adler, Helen R., 2221

Adler, John, 2221
Adler, Louis, 2222
Adler (Louis) Realty Company, 2222
Adler, Morton M., 2221
Adler, Robert L., 1070
Adler, Shane, 356
Admire, Jack G., 763
Adolph's Food Products Mfg. Co., 64, 256
Adolph's Ltd., 64, 256
Advance Carter Co., 1859
Advertising Checking Bureau, 2603
Aeroflex Corporation, 2223
Aerojet General Corporation, 3234
Aeroquip Corporation, 1662
Aetna Freight Lines, 652
Aetna Life and Casualty Company, 489
Affeld, F.O., 3423
Affiliated Publications, 1483
Agan, Robert E., 2239
Agee, Eloise R., 2070
Agee, Richard R., 2070
Agee, Richard W., 2070
Agee, William F., 4289
Ageno, Tak, 69
Ager, Jeanne L., 4264
Ager, Mrs. John C., Jr., 3116
Ager, John Curtis, 3116
Agway, Inc., 2224
Ahlberg, Wayne H., 1032
Ahlbrandt, Roger S., 3693
Ahmanson, Caroline L., 114
Ahmanson, Howard F., 65
Ahmanson, Howard F., Jr., 65
Ahmanson, Robert H., 65
Ahmanson, William H., 65
Ahuja, Elias, 610
Aicher, Joyce, 582
Aicher, Paul J., 582
Aicher, Peter, 582
Aicher, Susan, 582
Aidinoff, M. Bernard, 2468
Aidner, Sandye Berger, 2103
Aigner, Fred, 919
Aigner (G.J.) Company, 919
Aigner, George J., 919
Aigner, Henrietta, 919
Aijian, Richard, 323
Aiken, J.B., Jr., 3795
Aiken, John D., 3795
Aiken, Linda H., 2140
Aiken, O.S., 3795
Aiken, O.S., Jr., 3795
Ailes, Garry, 2071
Ainsa, Francis S., 4055
Ainsworth, Laine, 212
Air Products and Chemicals, 3509
Aitken, Roy L., 799
Akamine, Robert N., 905
Akers, C. Scott, 3072
Akers, Charles W., 3072
Akers, John M., 3072
Akin, J.W., 3869

Akre, Charles T., 673
Akre, Paul, 3487
Alandt, Lynn F., 1699
Albers, Anni, 490
Albers, Josef, 490
Albert, R.B., 2160
Alberts, Thomas, 1207
Albertson, Hazel H., 67
Albrecht, E.J., 4346
Albrecht, John E., Jr., 3762
Albrecht, Paul A., 211
Albright, Adam M., 675
Albright, Blandina, 675
Albright, Cynthia, 1899
Albright, Harry W., Jr., 2294
Albright, Joseph P., 675
Albright, Josephine P., 675
Albright, Martina L., 1486
Albritton, O.L., Jr., 4040
Alco Standard Corporation, 3510
Alcock, Nancy W., 537
Alcock, Thomas H., 949
Alcorn, Robert R., 49
Alcott, James A., 1888
Aldeen (G.W.) Charitable Trust, 536
Alden, George I., 1468
Aldrich, Hope, 2578, 2876
Aldrich, Hulbert S., 2889
Aldridge, Francis, 692
Aldridge, Francis C., 696
Alexander, Anne M., 4292, 4293
Alexander, Arthur W., 2919
Alexander, Bruce J., 233
Alexander, Caroline, 4006
Alexander, Edward H., 3238
Alexander, Elaine B., 873
Alexander, Emory G., 4006
Alexander, Frank L., 2415
Alexander, George H., 935
Alexander, Gordon L., 1825
Alexander, Helen C., 4006
Alexander, Henrietta, 4006
Alexander, James E., 2735
Alexander, John D., Jr., 4006
Alexander, John E., 4291
Alexander, Joseph, 2227
Alexander, Judith T., 1783
Alexander, Mercedes, 3699
Alexander, Norman E., 2971
Alexander, Mrs. Paule R., 2667
Alexander, Quentin, 3160, 3332
Alexander, Richard G., 3559
Alexander, Ruth, 4293
Alexander, Sander P., 2857
Alexander, Sandrea Sue Goerlich, 3238
Alexander, W.R., 455
Alexander, Willard A., 816
Alexy, R.J., 626
Aley, P., 3312
Alfert, Arthur, 2227
Alfond, Dorothy, 1391
Alfond, Harold, 1391
Alfond, Theodore, 1391

Alford, Albert L., Jr., 326
Alford, John W., 3209
Alford, Kenneth M., 2376
Alford, L.E., 207
Aliber (M.M.) Trust, 1259
Alkire, Durwood, 4219
Allain, Emery E., 529
Allaire, P., 594
Allbright, Bruce G., 1834
Allbritton, Barbara B., 3870
Allbritton, Joe, 3870
Allbritton, Joe L., 3870
Allegheny International, 3513
Allen & Company, 2228
Allen, Arthur H., 1949
Allen, Brandt R., 2493
Allen, C. Robert, III, 2228
Allen, Charles, Jr., 2228
Allen, Charles C., Jr., 1987
Allen, Christine, 2273, 2399
Allen, D.K., 173
Allen, Douglas, 1397
Allen, Douglas E., 2273
Allen, Edna M., 914
Allen, Eugene, 3931
Allen, Gerald M., 3998
Allen, Herbert, 2228
Allen, Herbert Anthony, 2228
Allen, Ivan, Jr., 876
Allen, James L., 4332
Allen, Joan E., 4169
Allen, Joseph K., 124
Allen, Kenton L., 1284
Allen, Mrs. Lee Barclay Patterson, 863
Allen, Marjorie P., 1323
Allen, Marjorie Powell, 1752
Allen, Peter T., 2593
Allen, Philip D., 2273, 2399
Allen, Richard C., 2823
Allen, Richard R., 4169
Allen, Rita S., 3839
Allen, Robert L., 1569
Allen, Thomas F., 3172, 3201
Allen, W. James, 1757
Allen, William H., Jr., 706
Allen, William W., 1757
Allen-Bradley Company, 4303
Allex, Kenneth R., 2301
Allied Bank of Texas, 3871, 4108
Allied Chemical Corporation, 4214
Allied Corporation, 2098
Allied Lakewood Bank, 3923
Allied Stores Corporation, 2230
Allied Tube & Conduit Corporation, 921
Allinson, A. Edward, 2337
Allis-Chalmers Corporation, 4294
Allison, D. Clifford, 1307
Allison, Dwight L., Jr., 1482
Allison, L.L., 4249
Allison, Walter W., 3442
Allison, William C., IV, 1495
Alliss, Charles C., 1805
Alliss, Ellora Martha, 1805
Allmon, Joseph T., 3813
Alloway, Lawrence, 2492
Allstate Insurance Company, 922
Allyn, Charles S., Jr., 3147
Allyn, Compton, 3147
Allyn, Dawn, 2231
Allyn, Janet, 2231
Allyn, Lou F., 2231
Allyn, S.C., 3147
Allyn, Sonya, 2231
Allyn, William F., 2231
Allyn, William G., 2231
Alma Piston Company, 1784
Almaney, Kathleen M., 1108
Almeda Harold Corporation, 4007
Almog, Z., 2708
Almquist, Arden, 4391
Alms, Eleanora C.U., 3148
Alpac Corporation, 4262
Alper, Hortense, 1717
Alperin, Barry, 3770

Alperin, Max, 3770
Alperin, Melvin G., 3770
Alperin, Ruth, 3770
Alperstein, Arnold, 2977
Alperstein, Eileen, 2977
Alpert, Arthur M., 4001
Alpert, Benjamin, 2126
Alpert, Charles, 2508
Alpert, Joseph, 2508
Alpert, Robert, 4068
Alsaker, E.C., 1862
Alschuler, Anne S., 935
Alsdorf, James W., 923
Alsdorf, Marilynn, 923
Alston, Floyd W., 3749
Alta Mortgage Company, 223
Altek, Albert B., 3928
Althaus, Charles T., 1384
Altheimer, Alan J., 1119
Altier, Betty J., 2464
Altman, Benjamin, 2232
Altman, Lawrence K., 2689
Altman, Norman, 1079
Altman, Robert C., 4293
Altobello, Daniel J., 670
Alton, David, 2200
Altschul, Arthur G., 2652, 2774, 2807, 3032, 3041
Altschul, Diana L., 2807
Altschul, Frank, 2807
Altschul, Helen G., 2807
Altschul, Jeanette Cohen, 2233
Altschul, Louis, 2233
Aluminum Company of America, 3511
Alvord, Ellsworth C., 634
Alvord, Ellsworth C., Jr., 634
Alvord, Robert W., 634
Alworth, Marshall W., 1806
Alyea, Ethan D., 2345
Amacher, Fritz, 340
Amacher, Howard R., 3836
Amado, Maurice, 68
Amado, Milton S., 68
Amado, Richard J., 68
Amarillo National Bank, 3918
Amato, Thomas G., 3149
Amax Foundation, 2741
AMAX Inc., 491
Ambler, John D., 2981
Ambrose, Katharine Schultz, 2179, 2180
Amcast Industrial Corporation, 3149
Amendt, Anne, 1664
American and Efird Mills, 3092
American Bag & Paper Corp., 3623
American Bank and Trust Company, 1354, 3139
American Bank and Trust Company of Pennsylvania, 3514
American Can Company, 492
American Decal and Manufacturing Company, 996
American Enka Corporation, 3073
American Express Company, 2235
American Financial Corporation, 3150
American Flange & Manufacturing Co., 2168
American Fletcher National Bank and Trust Company, 1226
American Hoist & Derrick Company, 1807
American Honda Motor Co., 69
American Information Technologies, 926
American Insulated Wire Corporation, 2659
American Manufacturers Mutual Insurance Company, 1060
American Motorists Insurance Company, 1060
American National Bank and Trust Company, 927, 1713, 1912, 3832
American National Bank and Trust Company of Chattanooga, 3849
American National Bank and Trust Company of Chicago, 925, 961, 968

American National Bank and Trust Company of Michigan, 1728
American Petrofina, 3873
American Saw and Manufacturing Company, 1511
American Security and Trust Company, 642
American Security Bank, 669
American Telephone & Telegraph Co., 2249
American Trading and Production Corporation, 1405, 1458
American-Standard, Inc., 2237
AmeriFirst Florida Trust Company, 706
AmeriTrust Company, 3178, 3186, 3188, 3216, 3240, 3241, 3295, 3297, 3338, 3339, 3341, 3363, 3375, 3406
AmeriTrust Company of Stark County, 3200, 3373
Amerock Corporation, 927
Ames, Aubin Z., 2181
Ames, C.G., Jr., 1227
Ames, Edward A., 2327
Ames, George J., 2734
Ames, Harriett, 3515
Ames, James B., 1621
Ames, Margaret, 4250
Ames, Morgan P., 567
AMETEK, Inc., 2238
Amfac, Inc., 888
Amidon, Thomas, 4149
Ammon, James E., 1368
Amoco Corp., 928
Amory, Elizabeth H.G., 2507
Amory, Walter, 1621
Amos, Harold, 2689
Amoskeag National Bank and Trust Company, 2091, 2097
AMP, Inc., 3516
AmSouth Bank, 14, 24
Amsted Industries Incorporated, 929
Amsterdam, Gustave G., 3586
Amsterdam, Jack, 2659
Amundson, W.R., 3143
Anaconda Company, 2741
Anastasio, Carol, 2535
Anchorage Times Publishing Company, 26
Andberg, Ernest W., 1836
Anders, Steven M., 236, 413
Andersen Corporation, 1815
Andersen, Anthony L., 1928
Andersen, Arthur A., 930
Andersen, Arthur E., III, 930
Andersen, Carol F., 1810
Andersen, Christine E., 1810
Andersen, Eleanor J., 1808
Andersen, Elmer L., 1808
Andersen, F.N., 1798
Andersen, Fred, 1865
Andersen, Fred C., 1809
Andersen, Harold W., 2066
Andersen, Hugh J., 1810
Andersen, Jane K., 1810
Andersen, Joan N., 930
Andersen, Julian, 1808
Andersen, Katherine B., 1809, 1815, 1865
Andersen, Sarah J., 1810
Anderson, Alice C., 506
Anderson, Angela, 1074
Anderson, Barbara P., 516
Anderson, Barton P., 536
Anderson, Bradley S., 536
Anderson, Bruce, 1955
Anderson, Calvin J., 1825
Anderson, Catherine M., 3290
Anderson, Charles A., 3314
Anderson, Charles M., 4218
Anderson, D. Malcolm, 3671
Anderson, Dale, 3142
Anderson, David H., 4012

Anderson, Donald E., 3152
Anderson, Dorothy, 1962
Anderson, Dorothy I., 4218
Anderson, Douglas G., 2240
Anderson, E.B., 2131
Anderson, E.W., 1696
Anderson, Elizabeth Milbank, 2737
Anderson, Elmer L., 1805
Anderson, Elmer M., 4237
Anderson, Erland, 1836
Anderson, Ford A., II, 4252
Anderson, Frederic D., 1246
Anderson, George M., 81
Anderson, George W., 2246
Anderson, Grenville, 3153
Anderson, Herbert T., 2731
Anderson, Hope H., 4377
Anderson, Irene, 1261
Anderson, Jack, 2741
Anderson, James D., 710
Anderson, James W., 2803
Anderson, Jane G., 2240
Anderson, Jean M., 2940
Anderson, John, Jr., 1322
Anderson, John D., 2239, 2240, 3152
Anderson, John T., 1052
Anderson, John W., 1195
Anderson, John W., II, 1677
Anderson, Joseph A., 1752
Anderson, Josephine, 3874
Anderson, June C.A., 536
Anderson, Kenneth G., 780
Anderson, Laura, 1910
Anderson, Lee S., 3850
Anderson, Lois H., 3800
Anderson, M.D., 3875
Anderson, Marcia F., 1303
Anderson, Michael J., 3152
Anderson, Nancy, 2876
Anderson, Patricia, 2852
Anderson, Paul G., Jr., 1166
Anderson, Paul H., 536
Anderson, Peter S., 3580
Anderson, R.E. Olds, 1761
Anderson, R.O., 78, 4033
Anderson, R.T., 1049
Anderson, Robert, 3708
Anderson, Robert C., 3074
Anderson, Robert E., 275
Anderson, Robert J., 3152
Anderson, Roger E., 1011
Anderson, Roger L., 2063
Anderson, S. Wyndham, 2823
Anderson, Sadie Gaither, 3074
Anderson, Shirley S., 2052
Anderson, Ted M., 3884
Anderson, Thomas H., 3152
Anderson, Thomas R., 1060
Anderson, Timothy J., 536
Anderson, Veda, 1671
Anderson, W.S., 3314
Anderson, Warren H., 1821
Anderson, Wendell W., Jr., 1677
Anderson, Wilbur, 3158
Anderson, William G., 3153
Anderson, William P., 3153
Andes, Clemens S., 3715
Andras, Stephan J., 935
Andras, Walter E., 2473
Andreas, Dorothy Inez, 1811
Andreas, Dwayne O., 1811
Andreas, Glenn A., 1811
Andreas, L.W., 932
Andreas, Lowell W., 1811
Andreas, Michael D., 1811
Andreason, Ralph A., 935
Andreini, Alan J., 122
Andreoli, James M., 237
Andres, F. William, 1495
Andres, William A., 1834
Andress, Diana Dawn, 3876
Andress, Kellie E., 3876
Andress, Tony D., Jr., 3876
Andress, Tony D., Sr., 3876

Beidler, Francis, 941
Beidler, Francis, II, 941
Beihl, William J., 3062
Beilfuss, Bruce, 1073
Beilin, Ronald A., 502
Beim, David O., 2700
Beim, N.C., 1816
Beim, R.N., 1816
Beim, Raymond N., 1816
Beim, William H., 1816
Beim, William H., Jr., 1816
Beimfohr, Edward G., 2121
Beinecke, Edwin J., 2275
Beinecke, Elizabeth G., 2842
Beinecke, Frederick W., 2842
Beinecke, John B., 2842
Beinecke (Katherine Sperry) Trust, 2804
Beinecke, Walter, Jr., 2804
Beinecke, William S., 2842
Beir, Joan S., 2276
Beir, Robert L., 2276
Beiser, Gerald J., 505
Beito, G., 1856
Bekins Company, 90
Bekins, Mary Louise, 90
Bekins, Milo W., 90, 278
Bekins, Milo W., Jr., 90
Belasco, Edna R., 2101
Belden Corporation, 942
Belden, Frederick H., Jr., 4285
Belden, J.C., Jr., 942
Belding, Annie K., 2445
Belding Heminway Company, 2532
Belding, Milo M., 2445
Belew, David L., 3245
Belfer, Arthur B., 2277
Belfer Corporation, 2277
Belfer, Robert A., 2277
Belfint, Charles I., 601
Belin, C. Welles, 3716
Belin, Daniel N., 65
Belin, Harriet B., 2362
Belin, J.C., 713
Belin, Oscar F., 1309
Belk, Irwin, 3077
Belk, John M., 3077
Belk, Katherine M., 3074
Belk, L.W., 806
Belk mercantile corporations, 3077
Belk, Thomas M., 3077
Belkin, Richard, 1274
Belk's Stores, 3799
Bell, A.C., 1050
Bell & Howell Company, 943
Bell, Charles H., 1817
Bell, Deborah Hodges, 873
Bell, Drummond C., 2365
Bell, Edmund S., Jr., 3346
Bell, Ford W., 1817
Bell, Mrs. Howard J., 4310
Bell, Ida M., 750
Bell, James F., Jr., 750
Bell, James Ford, 1817
Bell, Julius A., 2250
Bell, Katherine, 3885
Bell, Malcolm, 847
Bell, Peter B., 3512
Bell, R.F., 2901
Bell, R.S., 3885
Bell, R. Terry, 4066
Bell, Richard, 3462
Bell, Robert D., 1333
Bell, Robert M., 3806
Bell, Robert N., 4331
Bell, Roy E., Jr., 3854
Bell, Samuel H., 1817
Bellairs, Mrs. Robert H., 1674
Bellamah, Dale J., 2206
Belleau, Charles, 1354
Bellet, Marilyn, 3736
Bellinger, Geraldine G., 2465
Bellinger, John D., 897
Bellor, Mary M., 660
Belman, Michael R., 3569

Belo (A.H.) Corporation, 3924
Belsom, Walter J., Jr., 1389
Beltz, H.A., 1854
Beltzer, Herman M., 2998
Belz, Jack A., 3828
Belz, Martin S., 3828
Belz, Philip, 3828
Belzer, Alan, 2098
Belzer, Ruth K., 1030
Beman, C.E., 3117
Bemis Company, 1818
Bemis, F. Gregg, 1546
Benckenstein, Eunice R., 4085
Bender, Dorothy G., 639
Bender, Howard M., 639
Bender, Jack I., 639
Bender, Jefferson Radin, 331
Bender, Sondra D., 639
Bender, Stanley S., 639
Bendetsen, Karl R., 505
Bendheim, Charles H., 2278
Bendheim, John M., 2680
Bendheim, Nannette, 2278
Bendheim, Robert, 2680
Benedict, Andrew, 3836
Benedict, Francis W., 168, 169
Benedict, Peter B., 2972
Benedum, Michael Late, 3524
Benedum, Paul G., Jr., 3524
Benedum, Sarah N., 3524
Beneficial Corporation, 596
Benham, T.W., 4032
Benincasa, Mary Ann, 3030
Benison, John E., 2767
Benjamin, Adelaide W., 1380
Benjamin, Florence M., 284
Benjamin, Norman L., 266
Bennack, Frank A., Jr., 2537, 2538
Benner, Richard F., 901
Bennett, Bruce, 499
Bennett, Carl, 499
Bennett, Dorothy, 499
Bennett, Edward F., 2702
Bennett, Franklin S., Jr., 3330
Bennett, James Gordon, 2279
Bennett, James S., 4178
Bennett, Jay I., 2857
Bennett, John F., 3145
Bennett, Leslie W., 942
Bennett, M.B., 2149
Bennett, Marc, 499
Bennett, Nina B., 628
Bennett, Richard K., 3683
Bennett, Robert E., 865
Bennett, Susan, 771
Bennett, Thompson, 1681
Bennington, Ronald K., 3253
Bennion, Adam Y., 86
Benson, Alvin G., 1727
Benson, E.M., Jr., 78
Benson, Frank S., III, 3180
Benson, Frank S., Jr., 3180
Benson, Lucy Wilson, 2938
Benson, Marvin A., 866
Benson, Robert D., 4179
Bent, John P., 1161
Bentele, Raymond F., 1988
Bentley, Alvin M., 1671
Bentley, Alvin M., IV, 1671
Bentley, Ann, 1671
Bentley, Antoinette C., 2114
Bentley, Arvella D., 1671
Bentley, Barbara Factor, 162
Bentley, Clark H., 1671
Bentley, Michael D., 1671
Bentley, Owen W., Jr., 3475
Bentley, Peter, 537
Benton, Adrianne, 640
Benton, Charles, 640
Benton, Helen, 640
Benton, Marjorie Craig, 644
Benton, William, 640
Bentz, George B., 3167
Bentz, Mary E., 3167

Bentzen, Michael P., 655
Benua, A.R., 3168
Benziger, Adelrick, Jr., 3029
Berchtold, Don, 1298
Berde, Botond, 2174
Bere, James F., 968
Berelson, Irving P., 2267
Berenblum, Marvin B., 2366
Berens, Sheldon L., 2453
Beresford, R.H., 2426
Berg, Gordon, 3102
Berg, Harold E., 187
Berg, Warren S., 1623
Bergbauer, Urban C., Jr., 2039
Bergeman, Richard P., 2113
Bergen, Charlotte V., 2102
Berger, Frances C., 91
Berger, Frank M., 2132
Berger, George V., 785
Berger, H.N., 91
Berger, Howard R., 3390
Berger, John N., 91
Berger, Margaret, 2103
Berger, Margaret F., 4246
Berger, Paul S., 661
Berger, Sol, 2103
Berger, T.E., 1186
Bergin, Robert P., 2514
Bergman, Edwin A., 1120
Bergreen, B., 2470
Bergstein, Bernard, 2786
Bergstrom, Dean E., 4300
Bergstrom, Henry A., 3524
Berk, Tony B., 2813
Berkey, Andrew D., II, 92
Berkey, Anne S., 92
Berkey, Peter, 92
Berkley, E.B., 2031
Berkley, Eliot S., 2031
Berkley, Richard L., 2031
Berkman, Irving J., 3692
Berkman, Lillian, 2230
Berkman, Louis, 3169, 3692
Berkman, Mrs. Louis, 3169
Berkman (The Louis) Company, 3169
Berkman, Marshall L., 3169, 3692
Berkman, Sandra W., 3169
Berkovitch, Boris S., 2750
Berkowitz, Bernard S., 2161
Berkowitz, Linda M., 2710
Berkshire Hathaway, Inc., 2052
Berle, Peter A.A., 2995
Berlin, Arnold M., 944
Berlin, Charles, 2675
Berlin, Ellin, 2280
Berlin, Irving, 2280
Berlin, M.H., 944
Berlinger, George F., 2281
Berlinger, Rhonie H., 2281
Berman, Alfred, 2252
Berman, Edgar F., 679
Berman, L., 2991
Berman, Mandell L., 1773
Berman, Russell R., 3319
Bermont, Peter L., 706
Bernard, Eugene L., 680
Bernard, James H., 1980
Bernard, Robert G., 282
Bernd, James D., 4338
Berner, T.R., 2901
Bernhard, Adele, 2570
Bernhard Foundation, 2282, 2570
Bernhard, Joan M., 2570
Bernhard, John T., 1787
Bernhard, Michael, 63
Bernhard, Michael R., 2570
Bernhard, Nancy, 63
Bernhard, Robert A., 2570, 2653
Bernhard, Sheryl, 63
Bernhard, Steven, 63
Bernhard, Steven G., 2570
Bernhard, William L., 2282
Bernhardt, Arthur A., 4360

Bernhardt, Paul L., 3138
Bernheim, Mrs. Leonard H., 2644
Bernolfo, Joseph E., Jr., 4130
Berns, Robert, 3348
Bernstein, Barney, 2220
Bernstein, Caryl S., 651
Bernstein, Daniel L., 2684
Bernstein, Edward M., 2684
Bernstein, George L., 2684
Bernstein, Haim, 2716
Bernstein, James D., 58
Bernstein, Marvin, 1598
Bernstein, Morton J., 2905
Bernstein, Nate, 1259
Bernstein, Paula, 1903
Bernstein, R.L., 355
Bernstein, William, 175, 1903
Bero, D.B., 3312
Berohin, G.J., 1382
Berra, Robert E., 1999
Berresford, Susan V., 2444
Berry, Donald C., Jr., 2718
Berry, Heidi, 668
Berry, Ilona M., 1002
Berry, James D., 4029
Berry, John W., Jr., 3170
Berry, John W., Sr., 3170
Berry, Katherine C., 3281
Berry, Loren M., 3170
Berry, Lowell W., 93
Berry, P.C., 3207
Berry, Ray, 333
Berry, Richard L., 3181
Berry, Mrs. Robert, 79
Berry, Robert V., 2192
Berry, William W., 3861
Berryman, Robert L., 1385
Berson, Joel I., 2221
Bersted, Alfred, 945, 1094
Bersticker, A.C., 3212
Berthold, James P., 2027
Bertini, Catherine, 976
Bertman, Mrs. J.G., 3990
Bertolli, Eugene E., 2767
Berton, Doris Fondren, 3956
Bertrand, Patricia M., 518
Berylson, Amy S., 1628
Bescherer, Edwin A., Jr., 2415
Besecker, Horace, Jr., 1559
Bess, Douglas R., 1
Besse, Ralph M., 3258
Bessemer Trust Company of Florida, 706
Besser, Albert G., 2202
Besser Company, 1672, 1673
Besser, J.H., 1672
Bessey, Richard B., 2368
Best Fertilizer Company of Texas, 93
Best Products Company, 4154
Besthoff, Walda, 1384
Betanzos, Amalia V., 2460
Bethke, William M., 2167
Bethlehems' Globe Publishing Company, 3508
Bethune, Lyle E., 4051
Bettingen, Burton G., 199
Bettis, Harry Little, 911
Bettis, Mary Yale, 566
Bettke, Edward W., 1660
Betz, Bill B., 235
Betz, Claire S., 3619
Betz, Edward B., 3715
Betz, Gary Ross, 3854
Betz, John Drew, 3619
Beuscher, Frank J., 1368
Beusing, Charles J., 1572
Bevan, D.C., Jr., 2991
Bevan, William, 1077, 2499
Beveridge, Frank Stanley, 1475
Bevis, J. Wayne, 1280
Bevis, Terry Lynn, 1811
Beyer, Herbert A., 1685
Beyer, Joanne B., 3512
Beyer, Michele, 3287
Beynon, Kathryne, 94

Boettcher, Mrs. Charles, II, 436
Boettcher, Fannie, 436
Boettiger, John R., 2859
Bogart, Max, 2573
Bogert, Mrs. H. Lawrence, 2584
Bogert, Jeremiah M., 3058
Bogert, Margot C., 3058
Boggs, Roderic V.O., 637
Bogue, Mary W., 1192
Bohen, Mildred M., 1261
Bohen (Mildred M.) Charitable Trust, 1261
Bohland, Jerome A., 3181
Bohlig, Paul, 1279
Bohn, Reese R., 731
Bohne, P.W., 1362
Bohnett, F. Newell, 891
Bohnett, James N., 891
Bohnett, Joe, III, 891
Bohnett, Thomas D., 891
Bohnett, William C., III, 891
Boice, John E., Jr., 641
Boillot, Mrs. Claude, 2637
Boillot, Lynn H., 2553
Boise, Spencer C., 275
Boisselle, Mary S., 704
Boissevain, Jean Dreyfus, 2411
Boissonnas, Eric, 4073
Boissonnas, Sylvie, 4073
Boit, Charles S., 1486
Bok, Anthony S., 689
Bok, Edward W., 689
Boknecht, R.K., 928
Boland, E.W., 254
Boland, John J., 2728
Boland, Laura Hill, 846
Boland, Maurice J., 2979
Bold, John, 360
Boles, John S., 3990
Boles, Russell S., Jr., 3784
Boley, Paul L., 3504, 4252
Bolin, Joan I., 83
Boling, L.H., 4310
Bolliger, Ralph, 3482
Bolling, Landrum R., 654
Bolling, Robert H., Jr., 632
Bollinger, Ben A., 799
Bolster, Marshall G., 1644
Bolt, John F., 736
Bolton, Archer L., Jr., 1614
Bolton, Charles P., 3173, 3324
Bolton, Fanny H., 3173
Bolton, Frances P., 3324
Bolton, John B., 3324
Bolton, Kenyon C., III, 3324
Bolton, Marjorie, 318
Bolton, Phillip P., 3324
Bolton, Thomas C., 3324
Bolton, William B., 3324
Bolwell, Harry J., 3187, 3302, 3332
Bolz, John A., 4334
Boman, John H., Jr., 866
Bomar, Thomas R., 706
Bomberger, Arthur B., 734
Bomberger, Carolyn L., 734
Bomberger, Dorothy C., 734
Bomberger, William A., 734
Bommer, William, 1466
Bonaparte, T.H., 2911
Bonavia, Emily Garvey, 1308
Bonavitz, Sheldon M., 3681
Bonawitz, Audrey, 3631
Bond, Christopher S., 1967
Bond, Elaine R., 2337
Bond, Elizabeth G., 1967
Bond, Gloria, 3818
Bond, Harry I., 657
Bond, Sally K., 226
Bondurant, William L., 3075
Bone, A.E., 3536
Boney, Bess R., 3127
Boney, Betsy R., 3107
Boney, Sion A., 3107
Bonfield, Robert E., 1664

Bongard, Burton M., 3398
Bongi, Robert T., 2311
Bongiovi, Albert R., 2828
Bonham, Robert G., 450
Boni, R.E., 3156
Bonifield, William C., 1238
Bonneau, Edwin V., 3951
Bonneau, Mrs. Edwin V., 3951
Bonner, Cleve B., 154
Bonner, James, 116
Bonner, Sarah L., 715
Bonnewyn, Patrick, 2310
Bonney, Flora MacDonald, 2685
Bonomo, Victor A., 2820
Bonovitz, Sheldon M., 3556
Bonsey, Elisabeth K., 51
Bonsey, Steven Keller, 51
Bonter, Louise, 1212
Boogaard, Marcia T., 3393
Booher, Edward E., 2535
Bookout, J.F., 4081
Bookshester, Dennis S., 964
Boone, Clara Seabury, 1143
Boone County National Bank, 1943
Boone, Daniel J., 1143
Boone, Elisa, 423
Boone, Mary K., 3830
Boone, Philip S., 433
Boone, Richard W., 2432
Boone, Sylvia A., 2881
Boos, Mary C., 1916
Booth, Beatrice C., 1827
Booth, Brian G., 3500
Booth, Chancie Ferris, 2296
Booth, Harry F., Jr., 91
Booth, I.M., 1602
Booth, Melissa Sage, 1764
Booth, Richard W., 4012
Booth, Theodore H., 2396
Booth, Willis H., 2296
Borchelt, M.L., 3903
Borchers, John F., 310
Borden, Ann R., 628
Borden, Benjamin J., 2679
Borden, Bertram H., 2104
Borden, Inc., 3174
Borden, John C., Jr., 2104
Borden, William H., 2104
Borel Bank and Trust Company, 318
Borger, Robert, 1207
Borg-Warner Corporation, 950
Borish, Bernard M., 3584
Borisoff, Richard, 2173
Borman, Jack, 3291
Borman, Marvin, 1859, 1887
Bormann, Alvin P., Jr., 4017
Bornholdt, Laura, 646
Bornholm, Howard W., 576
Bornhorst, Joseph F., 1197
Borsilli, Edward, 551
Bortle, Laura J., 1413
Borton, Faurest, 3408
Borton, Karl, 3408
Borun, Anna, 97
Borun, Harry, 97
Bosche, John H., 375
Boschwitz, Anne, 4374
Boschwitz, Franz L., 4374
Bossier Bank & Trust Company, 1383
Boston Gas Company, 1518
Boston Safe Deposit and Trust
    Company, 1480, 1482, 1498, 1502,
    1561, 1608, 1647
Bostwick, Albert C., 2297
Bostwick, Albert C., Jr., 2297
Bostwick, Eleanor P., 2297
Boswell, C.A., 777
Boswell, H. Charles, 4127
Boswell, James C., 321
Boswell, James G., 98
Boswell, James G., II, 98
Boswell, Rosalind M., 98
Boswell, W.W., 134
Boswell, Mrs. W.W., 134

Boswell, Mrs. W.W., Sr., 134
Boswell, William D., 3628
Bosworth, Mary Ellen, 2071
Botero, Rodrigo, 2444
Bothin, Ellen Chabot, 99
Bothin, Henry E., 99
Bothmen, Annette Friedman, 175
Bott, Wilma, 1397
Bottomley, John T., 1532
Bottomley, Lydia Fuller, 1532
Bottomley, Pamela, 1532
Botts, Guy W., 689
Botwinick, Benjamin, 2298
Botwinick, Bessie, 2298
Botwinick, Edward, 2298
Botwinick, David, 2388
Boudreau, Edward, 2495
Boughton, Jerry, 1359
Bouick, James B., III, 117
Boulpaep, Emile L., 498
Bourke, William O., 4193
Bourne, D.J., 834
Boutault, E.C., 377
Boutell, Arnold, 1675
Boutell, Gertrude, 1675
Boutwell, Frank, 4095
Boutwell, Roswell M., 3rd, 1553
Bovaird, Mabel W., 3419
Boverie, Mrs. R.F., 4055
Boveroux, George L., Jr., 2968
Boving, George W., 3397
Bowditch, Helen A., 1659
Bowdle, Margaret B., 3890
Bowen, Arthur H., Jr., 1952
Bowen, Arthur L., 2363
Bowen, Ethel N., 4277
Bowen, George H., 3466
Bowen, Lem W., 1744
Bowen, Otis R., 1238
Bowen, R.L., 3958
Bowen, Taylor L., 2006
Bowen, Virginia M., 4277
Bower, Marvin, 2315
Bower, Roger N., 1614
Bowers, Anthony J., 3334
Bowers, Floyd K., 3505
Bowersock, Justin Dewitt, 682
Bowland, Ruth R., 1198
Bowles, Crandall C., 3821
Bowles, Crandall Close, 3822
Bowles, Ethel W., 100
Bowles, Margaret C., 1206
Bowles, Paul N., 4285
Bowling, Doris C., 55
Bowling, Vernon T., 3391
Bowman, A.C., 4056
Bowman, Ann F., 1707
Bowman, Elsa L., 3617
Bowman, John W., 992, 3617
Bowman, Jon, 4238
Bowman, Roger M., 1899
Bowmer, Jim, 4123
Bowne & Co., 2299
Bowsher, John M., 3168
Bowyer, Ambrose, 951
Bowyer, Gladys, 951
Boxx, Linda McKenna, 3655
Boyarski, Margaret, 4291
Boyce, Allan R., 4226
Boyce, Charles A., 3589
Boyce, Doreen E., 3529, 3577
Boyce, I.F., 4310
Boyd, Barbara, 2475
Boyd, Edward B., 1314
Boyd, J.A., 726
Boyd, J.T., 3456
Boyd, John W., 216
Boyd, Llewellyn, 3832, 3835
Boyd, McDill, 1309
Boyd, William, 1985
Boyd, William B., 4332
Boyd, William W., 1985
Boyer, Ernest L., 2109
Boyett, Barrie, 134

Boyle, Dennis, 1789
Boyle, Fosten A., 1861
Boyle, Francis J., 4226
Boyle, Richard J., 1861, 2337
Boylston, A.D., 841
Boylston, A.D., Jr., 860, 876
Boyne, William C., 1910
Boynton, Bertha Gillespie, 952
Boynton, Charles Otis, 952
Boynton, Cynthia, 1880
Boynton, Dora C., 1484
Bozeman, Bruce L., 3015
Braaten, A.L., 3142
Brabston, Donald, 3
Bracey, Hilton, 1997
Brach, Helen, 954
Bracken, Alexander M., 1199, 1200
Bracken, Charles H., 3565
Bracken, Mrs. John P., 3572
Bracken, Rosemary B., 1200
Brackenridge, George W., 3889
Bradbeer, Ann, 2049
Bradbury, Elizabeth W., 2041
Brademas, John, 640, 2877
Braden, Robert G., 1296
Braden, Thomas W., 644
Bradford, Bert A., Jr., 4285
Bradford Exchange AG, 1076
Bradford, Standish, Jr., 1578
Bradlee, Dudley, II, 1556
Bradlee, Dudley H., II, 1495
Bradley, Betsy Forbes, 593
Bradley, Caroline D., 4303
Bradley, Frank W., 685
Bradley, Gaytha L., 36
Bradley, Harry L., 4303
Bradley, J. Greg, 449
Bradley, James, 3821, 3822
Bradley, Margaret B., 4302, 4303
Bradley, Orren J., 4358
Bradley, R.B., 4297
Bradley, Robert F., 2221
Bradley, W.C., 807
Bradley, William, 719
Bradshaw, Eugene B., 2495
Bradshaw, Lillian M., 3984
Bradshaw, T.F., 78
Bradshaw, Thornton F., 2875
Bradt, Samuel E., 917
Brady, Elizabeth A., 4304
Brady, H. William, 3747
Brady, Irene J., 4304
Brady, James C., Jr., 2105
Brady, Nicholas, 2105
Brady (W.H.) Co., 4304
Brady, William H., III, 4304
Brady, William H., Jr., 4303, 4304
Braemer, Richard J., 3569
Braga, George A., 2218
Braga, Mary B., 2294
Bragin, D.H., 794
Braislin, Gordon S., 2294
Braitmayer, John W., 1485
Braitmayer, Karen L., 1485
Braitmayer, Marian S., 1485
Braje, Thomas, 888
Brakensiek, W.N., 119
Braley, Francis, 1271
Braly, Hugh C., 435
Braman, Mary O'Connor, 4042
Bramlett, Norris, 187
Branagh, John C., 93
Branch, J. Read, 4157
Branch, Patteson, Jr., 4157
Branche, Mildred M., 4158
Brand, Martha, 2300
Brandegee, Mary B., 1486
Brandenburg, R.N., 4236
Brandes, B.E., 2238
Brandman, Saul, 155
Brandon, Christopher, 840
Brandon, E.B., 3372
Brandt, E. Ned, 1712, 1748
Brandt, Lloyd L., 1842

Branham, William T., 1142
Brann, Helen, 2706
Brannon, Ben W., 854
Branscomb, Harvie, Jr., 4112
Branson, James E., 4203
Branton, W. Coleman, 1306
Branton, Wiley A., 58
Branton, William Coleman, 1324
Brants, B.S., 4069
Bratnober, Patricia, 1868
Bratovich, Betty, 3343
Brattle Company Corp., 1617
Braun, C. Allan, 102
Braun, Carl F., 101
Braun, H.E., Jr., 1798
Braun, Henry A., 102
Braun, James V., 4305
Braun, Japnell D., 1999
Braun, John G., 101, 102
Braun, S.D., 2708
Braun, Mrs. Stanley D., 1070
Braun, Victor F., 4305, 4347, 4348,
   4349, 4350
Brauner, David A., 2481
Brauntuch, Jack, 2584
Brawer, Catherine Coleman, 2888
Bray, Viola E., 1676
Brayton, Don, 4395
Breazeale, Robert P., 1354
Brechemin, Charlotte B., 4224
Breckenridge, Franklin E., 1243
Brecknock, M.R., 1142
Breech, E. Robert, Jr., 103
Breech, Ernest R., 103
Breech, Thelma K., 103
Breech, William H., 103
Breed, William C., III, 2282, 2963
Breen, John G., 3366
Breen, Marion I., 2954
Breeze, Frank V., 3697
Bregar, H.H., 946, 948
Breidenthal, George Gray, 1295
Breidenthal, Mary G., 1295
Breidenthal, Mary P., 1295
Breidenthal, Willard J., 1295
Breitbard, Robert, 336
Breitinger, Jean, 3677
Breitmeyer, Julie F., 1371
Breitschopf, Tony, 4019
Bremer, James S., 3175
Bremer, Otto, 1822
Bremer, Patsy R., 628
Bremer, Richard P., 3175
Bremer, William S., 627
Breneman, David, 1787
Brengel, Fred L., 4331
Brennan, C.M., III, 1020
Brennan, Edward A., 1145
Brennan, Herbert J., 2174
Brennan, James C., 3659
Brennan, Thomas P., 1866
Brennan, Virginia S., 3817
Brenneman, Howard L., 1311
Brenner, Charles S., 2521
Brenner, Edgar H., 2521
Brenner, Henry R., 2769
Brenner, J.D., 3516
Brenner, Mervyn L., 104
Brenninkmeyer, Anthony, 2301
Brenninkmeyer, Derick, 2301
Brenninkmeyer, Felix G.M., 2301
Brenninkmeyer, Johannes A.P., 2301
Brenninkmeyer, Michael L.M., 2301
Brenninkmeyer, Roland M., 2301
Brent, A. Jack, II, 4216
Brent, Allan R., 1354
Breslav, Walter, Jr., 502
Breslin, Nancy K., 2784
Bresnahan, William W., 3190, 3215
Bressler, Alfred W., 2758
Breuil, James F., 3928
Brevig, Yasue, 4241
Brew, John P., 3702
Brewer, Ann Fraser, 3012

Brewer, Michael B., 3839
Brewer, Michael F., 1210
Brewer, O. Gordon, Jr., 3510
Brewer, Sebert, Jr., 3829
Brewster, Kingman, 644
Brewton, Kenneth L., Jr., 2174
Brezic, Richard, 3197
Brezicka, D.R., 1862
Brian, P.L. Thibaut, 3509
Brice, Deborah L., 2676
Bricker, Eugene H., 1987
Brickner, Mary E., 479
Bridge, Herbert M., 4269
Bridgeland, James R., Jr., 3219, 3361
Bridges, Alice M., 105
Bridges, David M., 105
Bridges, Edson L., 2073
Bridges, George, 3429
Bridges, James R., 105
Bridges, Kathryn, 875
Bridges, Kenneth, 3447
Bridges, Robert, 357
Bridges, Robert L., 105
Bridgewater, B.A., Jr., 1944, 1945
Bridgforth, W.R., 1933
Bridgwood, John B., 2649
Bridwell, J.S., 3890
Bridwell, Ralph S., 3890
Briganti, A.N., 547
Briggs & Stratton Corporation, 4306
Briggs, Beatrice E., 698
Briggs, Donald C., 117
Briggs, James L., 698
Briggs, John N., 698
Briggs, Robert G., 1909
Briggs, Robert W., 3145
Briggs, Stephen F., 698
Brigham, Dana P., 737
Brigham, Jack, 218
Brigham, Margaret Hoover, 226
Bright, Barbara, 2088
Bright, Harold E., 3677
Bright, Horace O., 1487
Bright, Sam, 3945
Brignola, Paul J., 2533
Brill, Arthur W., 590
Brill, Elaine, 3322
Brim, Orville G., Jr., 2445
Brinberg, Simeon, 3053
Brindisi, P. Arthur, 3005
Bring, Robert L., 1783
Brink, Gail E., 1712, 1757
Brinker, Norman, 3891
Brinkerhoff, J. Donald, 2217
Brinkley, Hugh M., 3831
Brinkman, Earl W., 2382
Brinkman, Robert J., 2382
Brinkman, Sue E., 113
Brinn, Lawrence E., 2259, 2261, 2371,
   2633
Brinton, S. Jervis, Jr., 2161, 2171
Briscoe, Mrs. John, 3765
Briselli, Iso, 3571
Bristol, Barbara F., 1707
Bristol Door and Lumber Company, 2338
Bristol-Myers Company, 2302
Bristow, Aurelia B., 496
Bristow, Robert G., 3152
Britt, David V.B., 2773
Britt, Jerry, 1711
Britt, Russell W., 4388
Brittain, Warner L., 1431
Brittenham, Raymond L., 2986
Britton, Brigham, 3176
Britton, Charles S., 3176
Britton, Charles S., II, 3176
Britton, Gertrude H., 3176
Britton, Lynda R., 3176
Broach, L.B., 4095
Broad, John W., 408
Broad, Morris N., 699
Broad, Ruth K., 699
Broad, Shepard, 699
Broad, William L., 2703

Broadfoot, John, 4029
Broadfoot, Vela, 4029
Broadhurst, William, 3420
Broadway National Bank, 4072
Brock, Frank A., 3835, 3848
Brock, Harry B., Jr., 7
Brock, Jack, 3429
Brock, M.H., 3995
Brockert, Catherine S., 4263
Brockett, Mrs. E.D., 1354
Brockey, Harold, 870
Brockie, A.H., 2098
Brockton Public Market, 1394
Brockway, Inc., 3528
Broder, Mrs. Marvin, 2104
Brodeur, Leon R., 3145
Brodhead, George M., 3522, 3543
Brodhead, William M., 1773
Brodie, Bertram Z., 953
Brodie, David H., 389
Brodie, Hazel S., 953
Brodie, Melvin, 2839
Brodsky, Elbert, 2977
Brody, Bernard B., 2463
Brody, Christopher, 2640
Brody, Christopher W., 106
Brody, Frances L., 106
Brody, Marjorie E., 2272
Brody, Sidney F., 106
Brody, Susan L., 106
Brokaw, Dennis, 206
Brokaw, Meredith A., 674
Brokaw, Ralph E., 3336
Brolin, G.E., 358
Brom, Paul A., 301
Bronfman, Ann L., 2303, 2676
Bronfman, Edgar M., 2304
Bronson, Eleanor D., 1509
Bronstad, Byron G., 3965
Bronstein, Herbert, 1070
Bronstein, Lenore, 2430
Bronstein, Robert, 2430
Bronstein, Sol, 1203
Brooking, Gladys T., 4104
Brookman, Nancy, 2383
Brooks, A.E., 3933
Brooks, Brenda S., 3624
Brooks, Chandler McC., 2135
Brooks, Christopher A., 588
Brooks, Conley, 1819, 1878, 1887
Brooks, Conley, Jr., 1819, 1878
Brooks, David A., 138
Brooks, Edward, 1878
Brooks, Edwin J., 2318
Brooks, Ernest, Jr., 2863
Brooks, Frank J., 3624
Brooks, Harry W., Jr., 2463
Brooks, Harvey, 646, 659
Brooks, Helen M., 791
Brooks, J. Judson, 3535
Brooks, Markell C., 1878
Brooks (Markell C.) Charitable Trust,
   1878
Brooks, Owen E., 2427
Brooks, Robert A., 35
Brooks, Sanford M., 3413
Brooks, Virginia D., 1912
Brooksher, K. Dane, 2817
Brookshire, Stamford R., 3104
Brooks-Scanlon, Inc., 1819
Brophy, Theodore F., 531
Brosnan, Mary, 588
Broste, John, 1828
Brothers, Benton H., 583
Brotz, Frank M., 4307
Brotz, Ralph T., 4307
Brouard, Patricia M., 236, 413
Broughton, Carl, 4286
Brown, Alice Pratt, 3893
Brown & Root, 3970
Brown, Ann Noble, 3449, 3450
Brown, Arthur W., Jr., 1119
Brown, Barbara E., 1044
Brown, Barry A., 3993

Brown, Ben B., 3
Brown, Bennett A., 812, 816
Brown, Bill, 3460
Brown Brothers Harriman Trust Co.,
   2774
Brown, Bruce E., 949
Brown, C. Don, 4141
Brown, C. Harold, 3937
Brown, C.J., Jr., 3242
Brown, Carol, 3937
Brown, Charles E., 1861
Brown, Charles S., 917, 918
Brown, David M., 4040
Brown, David R., 3449
Brown, David V., 4012
Brown, Donald E., 781
Brown, Dora Maclellan, 3832
Brown, Dorothy A., 1586
Brown, Dorothy Dorsett, 1355
Brown, Dyke, 202
Brown, Edwin L., Jr., 981
Brown, Elizabeth K., 1044
Brown, Ellis C., 3477
Brown, Frances Carroll, 1432
Brown, Fred L., 4067
Brown, George H., Jr., 3571
Brown, George R., 3893
Brown, George Warren, 1944
Brown, Gilbert L., Jr., 206
Brown, Gordon M., 2427
Brown Group, 1945
Brown, Harold, 2877
Brown, Harry G., Jr., 4360
Brown, Helen M., 2329
Brown, Helene K., 4401
Brown, Henry N., 845
Brown, Henry P., 4246
Brown, Herbert R., 3183
Brown, Herman, 3893
Brown, Mrs. Herman, 3893
Brown, Howard J., 1044
Brown, J. Carter, 3785
Brown, J. Graham, 1336
Brown, James W., 766
Brown, James W., Jr., 18
Brown, Mrs. Joe W., 1355
Brown, John A., 567
Brown, John E., 1346, 1348
Brown, Kathryn, 1656
Brown, Kiyoko O., 2404
Brown, L. Palmer, III, 3854
Brown, L.J., 2426
Brown, Linda L., 628
Brown, Louise Ingalls, 3260
Brown, M.K., 3894
Brown, Marion, 1525
Brown, Martin S., 1337
Brown, Mary Lynn, 2033
Brown, Meredith M., 2956
Brown, Morgan C., III, 2435
Brown, Ned M., 1314
Brown, Noma S., 1943
Brown, Oliver S., 1293
Brown, Owsley, II, 1337
Brown, P. Tate, 4401
Brown, Patricia, 3886
Brown, Paul, 1671
Brown, Paul W., 1804
Brown, R. Manning, Jr., 2938
Brown, R.C., 3101
Brown, Ralph R., 4040
Brown, Ralph S., 2939
Brown, Richard, 1377
Brown, Richard P., 442
Brown, Robert F., 3724
Brown, Robert M., 217
Brown, Robert W., 3902
Brown, Roger O., 1044
Brown, Ronald H., 685
Brown, Roscoe, Jr., 2460
Brown, S.M., 1296
Brown, Samuel H., 4250
Brown, T.J., 3895
Brown, Virginia, 2038

Brown, Virginia S., 1955
Brown, W.L. Lyons, 1337
Brown, Mrs. W.L. Lyons, 1337
Brown, W.L. Lyons, Jr., 1337
Brown, Walter R., 2404
Brown, Willard R., 2927
Brown, Mrs. William, 2667
Brown, William, Jr., 521
Brown, William G., 3864
Brown, William L., 1473
Brown, Winston, 4221
Brown, Zadoc, 894
Brownell, C.R., Jr., 1375
Browning, John N., 3177
Browning, Laurance L., Jr., 1959, 2020
Browning, Robert R., 984
Brownlee, Helen, 2566
Brownlee, R. Jean, 3657
Broyhill Furniture Industries, 3081
Broyhill, James E., 3081
Broyhill, M. Hunt, 3081
Broyhill, Paul H., 3081
Bruce, Ailsa Mellon, 2722
Bruce, John A., 3477
Bruce, Mamie J., 3805
Brucker, Mary, 2020
Brucklacher, J.F., 3289
Bruderman, John M., 2310
Bruderman, John M., Jr., 2310
Brudney, Victor, 3070
Bruen, Edward F.L., 3063
Brumback, Charles T., 972, 1089, 1090
Brumback, D.L., Jr., 3396
Brumley, Charles K., 2621
Brummett, Paul E., 1390
Brundage, Howard D., 2181
Brundige, Winston T., 1420
Brunelli, Donald E., 1510
Bruner, James D., 29
Bruner, Joshua E., 2309
Bruner, L.J., 3207
Bruner, Martha, 2309
Bruner, R. Simeon, 2309
Bruner, Rudy, 2309
Brunini, Edmund L., 1939
Brunner, Fred J., 700
Brunner, Major O., 3471
Brunner, Robert, 2310
Brunner, Ruth, 700
Bruno, Eli T., 3023
Brunot, R.L., 966
Bruns, Carl H., 707, 766
Bruns, Nicholaus, Jr., 1046
Brunson, E.T., 9
Brunson, J.B., 9
Brunswick Corporation, 955
Brusati, Peter J., 183
Brush, Charles F., 3178
Brush, David M., 2467
Brust, R.W., 1890
Bryan, Anthony J.A., 644, 3711
Bryan, Byron E., 3082
Bryan, Dorothy L., 4395
Bryan, James E., 3082
Bryan, John H., Jr., 928, 1139
Bryan, Joseph M., 3083
Bryan, Joseph M., Jr., 3083
Bryan, Kathleen Price, 3083
Bryan, Mary Ann, 689
Bryan, Mary Z., 3082
Bryan, Pauline, 849
Bryan, Robert F., 827
Bryant, Arthur H., II, 4156
Bryant, Farris, 689
Bryant, Frances V., 3102
Bryant, J.C. Herbert, 4156
Bryant, Magalen O., 4188
Bryant, Oscar S., Jr., 1340
Bryant, Robert P., 964
Bryce, Hugh G., 1904
Bryon, O.B., 4033
Bryson, Brady O., 3741
Bryson, James E., 3503

Bryson, Jane T., 3503
Bryson, V.D., 1237
Bubb, Frank W., 3rd, 3715
Buchalter, Irwin R., 108
Buchalter, Nemer, Fields, Chrystie & Younger, 108
Buchanan, C.J., 3111
Buchanan, D.W., Jr., 956
Buchanan, D.W., Sr., 956
Buchanan, E. Bayley, 3535
Buchanan, G. Sidney, 4015
Buchanan, J. Robert, 2344, 3068
Buchanan, Kenneth H., 956
Buchanan, Peggy C., 3983
Buchanan, Valda M., 3448
Bucher, Theresa Von Hagen, 264
Buchholzer, Richard B., 3145
Buchman, R.P., 4294
Bucholz, Frederick S., 2073
Buck, Hugh Q., 3875
Buck, Junior C., 2158
Buck, Kristen Wells, 63
Buck, Randal, 63
Buck, Mrs. Robert F., 4259
Buckbee, John A., 2506
Buckingham, Eunice Hale, 3367
Buckingham, Lisle M., 3232
Buckland, William H., 1414
Buckler, Sheldon A., 1602
Buckles, Jane S., 1264
Buckles, Jane Stanley, 1284
Buckley, Robert, 220
Buckley, Thomas D., 2051
Buckman, Mrs. Harvey M., 3767
Buckman, John Dustin, 3833
Bucknam, Elizabeth M., 2082
Bucknam, Gilbert, 2082
Buckner, Elizabeth B., 2447
Buckner, Helen W., 2447
Buckner, Helen Watson, 3793
Buckner, Thomas W., 2447
Buckner, Walker G., 2447
Buckner, Walker G., Jr., 2447
Buckwalter, I.Z., 3737, 3738
Buckwalter, J.M., 3738
Buckwalter, John M., 3737
Bucy, J. Fred, 4102
Bucyrus-Erie Company, 4308
Buddenhagen, Kathleen B., 2454
Buddle, Richard B.,, 3183
Buden, Clare P., 2876
Budge, William W., 99
Budnick, Theodora Stillman, 2560
Budzik, Ronald F., 3299
Bueche, W.F., 4294
Buechner, Judith M., 3810
Buechner, Thomas, 2985
Buechner, Thomas S., 2368
Buehler, A.C., Jr., 957
Buehler, Albert C., 957
Buehler, Carl, III, 957
Buehler, Mrs. Fern D., 957
Buell, Temple Hoyne, 437
Buelow, Raymond A., 152
Buenger, Clement, 3320
Buesing, Ann, 1572
Buesing, Gregory P., 1572
Buesing, Guy K., 1572
Buffett, Susan T., 2052
Buffett, Warren E., 2052
Buffington, Marilyn A., 1476
Buffmire, Donald K., 35
Bughman, Harry R., 3628
Bugliarello, George, 2505, 2979
Buhl, Frank H., 3540
Buhl, Henry, Jr., 3529
Buhler, Nelson A., 3798
Buhsmer, John H., 3657
Buice, William T., III, 2957
Bulkeley, Christy C., 2463
Bull, J. Richard, 3313
Bull, Maud L., 109
Bull, Sharen R., 1999
Bullard, George N., Jr., 3834

Bullard, Robert L., 1821, 1889
Bullard, Ross P., 4214
Bullen, Wilbur W., 1576
Bulletin Company, 3657
Bullion, J.W., 4029
Bullis, William, 419
Bullitt, Dorothy S., 4225
Bullitt, Harriett, 4225
Bullitt, Katherine M., 4225
Bullitt, Stimson, 4225
Bullitt, William C., 3717
Bullock, Brent, 2574
Bullock, Ellis F., Jr., 1870
Bullock, H. Ridgely, 583
Bullock, M.R., 4058
Bullock, Maree G., 1170
Bullock, Mary Brown, 2344
Bullock, Richard, 1660
Bultman, Ralph, 4340
Bulzacchelli, John, 547
Bunbury Company, 4151
Bundschuh, George A.W., 2776
Bundy, Charles A., 3821, 3822
Bundy Corporation, 1677
Bundy, Mary, 2535
Bunnen, Lucinda W., 856, 2787
Bunnen, Melissa, 2787
Bunnen, Robert L., 856
Bunnen, Robert L., Jr., 856, 2787
Bunting, G. Lloyd, 1444
Bunting, George L., Jr., 1399, 1444
Bunton, Howard E., 37
Bunton, M.A., 3809
Burbidge, Arden, 3142
Burch, Robert D., 95, 2076, 2077
Burchfield, C. Arthur, 2314
Burchfield, Charles E., 2314
Burden, Amanda, 2985
Burden, Carter, 2315
Burden, Florence V., 2315
Burden, I. Townsend, III, 3576
Burden, Margaret L., 2315
Burden, Ordway P., 2315
Burden, Shirley C., 2315
Burden, Susan L., 2315
Burdette, Warren A., 1424
Burdge, J.J., 3595
Burdick, C. Lalor, 617
Burdick, Douglas L., 1726
Burdick, Henry C., III, 593
Burdick, Lalor, 617
Burdon, Mrs. Paul F., 1586
Buresh, E.J., 1269
Burford, A.L., Jr., 319
Burg, Helen R., 1347
Burge, W.L., 831
Burger, Van Vetchen, 791
Burgess, Alfred F., 3814
Burgess, Edward H., 4181
Burgess, H.D., 370
Burgess, Henry A., 4399, 4402
Burgess, James E., 1274
Burgess, James F., 3816
Burk, Swen, 1322
Burke, Coleman, 2137
Burke, Daniel, 3571
Burke, Daniel B., 2322
Burke, Doris L., 1651
Burke, F. William, 669
Burke, Gilman S., 2175
Burke, J.W., 793
Burke, J.W., Jr., 793
Burke, James B., 2175
Burke, John S., Jr., 2232
Burke, Marion O'Shaughnessy, 1900
Burke, Mary Griggs, 1852
Burke, Thomas C., 808, 2232
Burke, Thomas G., 2567
Burke, Thomas R., 2057
Burke, Vincent E., Jr., 1407
Burke, Walter, 522
Burke, Walter F., III, 522
Burke, Ward R., 4098
Burket, Richard E., 932

Burkholder, Betsy B., 807
Burkly, John J., 2347
Burleson, Donald W., 3454
Burlington Industries, 3084
Burlington Northern, 4226
Burmeister, Richard F., 1795
Burnand, Alphonse A., III, 110, 382
Burnand, Audrey Steele, 382
Burnap, Bartlett, 419
Burnett, Mrs. Horace, 1255
Burnett, Nancy Packard, 308
Burnett, Wanda B., 3470
Burnette, Ty W., 3097
Burney, Harvey G., 3058
Burney, Leroy E., 2737
Burnham, Alfred G., 2316
Burnham, Duane L., 918
Burnham, Rae O., 2316
Burns, Antoinette, 2821
Burns, Donald S., 959
Burns, Florence C., 1474
Burns, Fritz B., 111
Burns, Ingrid Lilly, 2454
Burns, Ivan A., 2217
Burns, Jacob, 2317
Burns, John L., 583
Burns, Julie Ann, 959
Burns, Katharine S., 75
Burns, L.J., 3192
Burns, Lucy Keating, 959
Burns, Phillip, 1259
Burns, Thomas R., 2454
Burns, Ward, 2962
Burpos, Althea M., 1488
Burr, Francis H., 1560, 1646
Burr, Frank W., 3135
Burr, Robert B., Jr., 3662, 3663
Burr, Willie O., 550
Burrell, Craig D., 2174
Burrill, W. Gregory, 1555
Burroughs, Charles F., Jr., 4187
Burroughs Wellcome Co., 3085
Burrus, Clark, 1002
Burrus, Robert L., Jr., 4154
Burstein, Herbert, 2156
Burt, Barbara, 1214
Burton, Courtney, 3318
Burton, Donald E., 463
Burton, Marion, 58
Burton, Sally F., 3178
Burton, William T., 1356
Burton (Wm. T.) Industries, 1356
Burtt, John, 1664
Busby, A. Jay, 36
Busby, Barta Gilcrease, 3431
Busch, Alice, 1940
Busch, Alice K., 2367
Busch (August A.) & Co. of Massachusetts, 1940
Busch, August A., III, 1940
Busch, August A., Jr., 1940
Busche, Eugene M., 1230
Bush, Archibald, 1823
Bush, Mrs. Archibald, 1823
Bush, Edyth, 701
Bush, Francis M., 1321
Bush, J.W., 3915
Bush, Mrs. Jewel A., 4153
Bush, John, 2274
Bush, Julia Howard, 539
Bush, W.G., 1005
Bushee, Florence Evans, 1525
Bushnell, Dan S., 4145
Buske, John, 1812
Buss, Mrs. William D., II, 3298
Butare, Joseph J., Jr., 1659
Butcher, Willard C., 2337
Butler, Mrs. Albert, Jr., 3137
Butler, Anne G., 3898
Butler, C.C., 807
Butler, Carol H., 3256
Butler, Cecil C., 1189
Butler, Dean, 240
Butler, Dixon M., 4214

Butler, George A., 3898, 3983
Butler, Ira, 2270
Butler, J. Homer, 2318
Butler, John, 1698
Butler, John G., 3256
Butler, John P., 3866
Butler, John W., 1678
Butler, Lewis, 1052
Butler, Lewis H., 63, 334
Butler Manufacturing Company, 1946
Butler, Mary, 3494
Butler, Mary D., 2975
Butler, Miriam S., 871
Butler, Patrick, 1824
Butler, Patrick, Jr., 1824
Butler, Peter M., 1824
Butler, Sandra, 1753
Butler, Sandra K., 1824
Butler, Stephen T., 807
Butler, Susan L., 4154
Butler, Susan Storz, 2072
Butler, William G., 1770
Butler, William J., 2864, 4085
Butler, William M., 3089
Butner, Ray, 1180
Butson, Lowell, 4253
Butt, Barbara Dan, 3899
Butt, Charles C., 3899
Butt, H.E., 3899
Butt (H.E.) Grocery Company, 3899
Butt, H.E., Sr., 3899
Butt, Mrs. H.E., Sr., 3899
Butt, Howard E., Jr., 3899
Butt, Martha G., 1894
Buttenwieser, Benjamin J., 2858
Buttenwieser, Lawrence B., 2519, 2764
Butterfield, Hazel L., 3367
Butterfield, Linda, 84
Butterfield, Thomas E., Jr., 3526
Butterworth, Arnold, 1748
Butterworth, George, 1545
Buttinger, Joseph, 2779
Buttinger, Muriel M., 2779
Button, A. Dwight, 1305
Button, Edward N., 3392
Butts, Charles A., 2416
Butz, Barbara T., 30
Butz, Theodore C., 30
Butz, Theodore H., 30
Butz, William B., 3748
Buzzard, Glenn W., 4379
Byard, Spencer, 2968
Bye, James E., 444, 473
Byeda, C. Richard, 1462
Byers, Donald C., 1276
Byers, Ronald J., 3978
Byington, Alicia, 2316
Bynner, Witter, 2207
Bynum, Joe, 9
Byrd, D. Harold, Jr., 3981
Byrd (Jack) Trust, 3865
Byrne, W.J., 3364
Byrnes, James F., 3800
Byrns, Priscilla U., 1181
Byrom, Fletcher L., 3631
Byuarm, S. Walter, 3102

C & S National Bank, 814
C & S Systems, 3801
Cabell, Charles, 4157
Cabell, Maude Morgan, 4157
Cabell, R.E., Jr., 4198
Cabell, Robert G., 4157
Cabell, Robert G., III, 4157
Cabell, Royal E., Jr., 4157
Cabot, Anne P., 2821
Cabot, Charles C., 1490
Cabot Corporation, 1488
Cabot, Godfrey L., 1489
Cabot, Lewis, 2790
Cabot, Louis W., 1488, 1489
Cabot, Maryellen, 1488
Cabot, Paul C., 1490

Cabot, Paul C., Jr., 1490
Cabot, Thomas D., 1488, 1489
Cabot, Virginia C., 1490
Cabranes, Jose A., 2995
Caccia, Alexander L., 2692
Caceres, Ann R., 18
Caddock, Anne M., 113
Caddock, Richard E., 113
Caddock, Richard E., Jr., 113
Cades, J. Russell, 906
Cades, Milton, 906
Cadman, Wilson, 1305
Cadman, Wilson K., 1315
Cadmus, Joan B., 2404
Cady, John L., 2720, 2721
Caestecker, Charles E., 960
Caestecker, Thomas F., 960
Cafaro, William M., 3416
Cafritz, Gwendolyn D., 643
Cafritz, Morris, 643
Cagwin, Douglas, 2331
Cahalan, Patrick, 245
Cahill, Catherine G., 2282
Cahill, Francis, 1004
Cahill, George F., Jr., 2221
Cahn, Emile L., 1357
Cahn, Jules L., 1357
Cahn, Steven, 2398
Cahners, Mrs. Norman L., 1589
Cahouet, Frank V., 274
Cahr, Michael, 1070
Cain, Effie Marie, 3900
Cain, James B., 3900
Cain, R. Wofford, 3900
Cain, Robert J., 3645
Caine, Marie Eccles, 4131
Caine, Raymond W., Jr., 3792
Calabresi, Guido, 1827
Calder, Alexander, Jr., 2194
Calder, Louis, 2320
Calderini, J.J., 127
Calderwood, W. Scott, 3753
Caldor, Inc., 499
Caldwell, Francis E., 3308
Caldwell, Hardwick, Jr., 3835
Caldwell, Jacques A., 3359
Caldwell, R.P., 3121
Caldwell, Will M., 1702
Calhoun, David T., 2063
Calhoun, Eric R., 3127
Calhoun, Ernest N., 3531
Calhoun, Jose M., 512
Calhoun, Ken, 1313
Calhoun, Kenneth, 3179
Califano, Joseph A., Jr., 242
California Canadian Bank, 318
California First Bank, 328
Caliguiri, Mrs. Richard S., 3693
Calkins (Ina) Trust, 1947
Call, Richard W., 350
Callaghan, R.L., 3312
Callahan, Daniel A., 3497
Callahan, Eugene J., 3855
Callahan, Richard J., 453
Callaway, C., Jr., 3845
Callaway Foundation, 812
Callaway, Fuller E., Sr., 811
Callaway Institute, 810
Callaway, Mark Clayton, 810, 811
Callaway Mills, 810
Callison, Fred W., 118
Callison, James W., 825
Callison, Kay Nichols, 2000
Callister, Jan E., 4132
Callister, Mary B., 4132
Callister, Paul Q., 4132
Callister, Paul S., 4132
Callow, N. Bruce, 977
Calloway, D. Wayne, 2820
Calpin, William J., Jr., 3716
Calvert, D.W., 3471
Calvert, Dan, 472
Calvert, Roger, 472
Calvin, Peter DeMille, 146

Cambridge Trust Company, 1491
Cameron, C.C., 3102
Cameron, Charlotte, 3901
Cameron, David W., 3901
Cameron, George B., 2564
Cameron, Gordon B., 3285
Cameron, Isabel C., 3901
Cameron, Steele C., 2416
Cameron, V.M., 3901
Cameron, William A., 3043
Camp, Barbara P., 4158
Camp, Clifton D., Jr., 757
Camp, Edith Clay, 4158
Camp, Hugh D., 2194
Camp, J.L., Jr., 4160
Camp, James L., 4159
Camp, James L., III, 4160
Camp, Jane G., 4160
Camp, John M., III, 4159
Camp, John M., Jr., 4159
Camp, Leon Clay, 4158
Camp, Lindley M., 721
Camp, Myrtle M., 3947
Camp, P.D., 4159
Camp, Shirlie S., 4158
Camp, W.M., Jr., 4159
Camp, William M., Jr., 4158
Camp, William P., 3719
Campbell, Albert M., 1245
Campbell, Amie, 3281
Campbell, Beatrice, 3058
Campbell, Bruce E., 3854
Campbell, Bushrod H., 1492
Campbell, C. David, 4040
Campbell, Charles Talbot, 3533
Campbell, Chuck, 1182
Campbell, Colin G., 2374
Campbell, Douglas, 2422
Campbell, Hazard K., 2622
Campbell, Helen, 3971
Campbell, J. Bulow, 813
Campbell, J. Fred, Jr., 756
Campbell, J. Patrick, 3408
Campbell, Jack, 2054
Campbell, John P., 608, 612
Campbell, Joseph, 2613
Campbell, Laura Berry, 813
Campbell, Leonard G., Jr., 4369
Campbell, Malcolm D., Jr., 3281
Campbell, Marion D., 988
Campbell, Max W., 3421
Campbell, Murray, 4228
Campbell, Murray C., 1758
Campbell, R.B., 3252
Campbell, Ralph, 3922
Campbell, Richard R., 3359
Campbell, Ruth Taylor, 482
Campbell, Samuel H., 3342
Campbell, Sara, 365, 366
Campbell Soup Company, 2107
Campbell, Stewart F., 2938
Campbell, Thomas H., 2195
Campbell, Thomas W., 3916
Campbell, Van C., 2368
Campbell, W.R., 760
Campbell, William Durant, 3058
Campe, Ed Lee, 2321
Campe, Jean, 2321
Campion, Lynn H., 458
Campion, Robert T., 253
Campion, Thomas B., 458
Canaday, Mariam C., 1493
Canaday, Ward M., 1493
Canavan, Gregory H., 216
Cane, Myles A., 2918
Cane, Paul W., 87, 88
Canepa, Patricia, 4146
Canning, J.B., 542
Cannon, Brown W., Jr., 450
Cannon, C.N., 173
Cannon, Charles A., 3086
Cannon, D.E., 4081
Cannon, J.W., 2249

Cannon, Janath R., 4145
Cannon, Joseph E., 3931
Cannon Manufacturing Company, 1538
Cannon Mills Company, 3086
Cannon, Ted, 2068
Cannon, W.C., 3086
Cannon, William B., 2432
Cannon, William R., 866
Cantacuzene, Rodion, 678
Canter, Roger, 4065
Cantor, Arthur, 2882
Cantor, Sanford, 1070
Cantrell, Barbara B., 683
Cantrell, G.W., 1319
Cantrell, J.C., 3909
Capell, Odette, 804
Caperton, W.G., 4285
Capital Bank and Trust Company, 1354
Capital Cities Communications, 2322
Capital Research & Management Company, 340
Capitano, Nick, 782
Caplan, Eli, 3534
Caplan, Hyman S., 3534
Caplan, Perry, 3534
Caples, William G., 3244
Cappadonna, Mitchell A., 3882
Capps, George H., 1955
Capranica, Ruth M., 1426, 1427
Capron, Jeffrey P., 655
Capuzzo, Sal, 3034
Carbaugh, Lyle E., 3996
Carbon Fuel Company, 4278
Cardin, Shoshana, 1419
Cardoza, K.H., 979, 980
Carew, Martin J., 1556
Carey, James, 2588
Carey, James H., 2337
Carey, Kathryn A., 69
Carey, Margaret H., 470
Cargill Charitable Trust, 1825
Cargill Incorporated, 1825
Cargill, J.R., 1825
Carhuff, John R., 2435
Carl, Milton, 3487
Carle, Marlyn E., 3694
Carleton, Peter F., 4101
Carley, James P., Jr., 577
Carley, Joan Davidson, 911
Carlin, Celia, 963
Carlin, Jerome E., 963
Carlin, Leo J., 946, 963, 1133
Carlisle, Robert D.B., 2181
Carlisle, Sheri, 4400
Carlsen, W.O., 3756, 3757
Carlson, Arleen E., 1826
Carlson, C. Dean, 1279
Carlson, Carl, 269
Carlson, Curtis L., 1826
Carlson, Edward E., 242
Carlson, Eric O., 497
Carlson, Herbert E., Sr., 577
Carlson, Maxwell, 4220
Carlson, Steven E., 4237
Carlstrom, R.W., 4236
Carlton, Jerry W., 144
Carlton, P.E., 188
Carman, Nellie M., 4227
Carmichael, Daniel P., 1237
Carmichael, Le Roy, 2774
Carmichael, William D., 2444
Carmichael, William P., 939
Carmody, Guerin B., 548
Carmouche, Edward M., 1364
Carnahan, David H., 2324, 3324
Carnahan, Katharine J., 2324
Carnation Company, 119, 120
Carnegie, Andrew, 644, 2109, 2325, 3535
Carnes, Mrs. Paul, 1573
Carney, Arlo E., 942
Carney, Dennis J., 3760
Carney, Grace, 543
Carney, Helen M., 543

Carney, John, 3612
Carnival Cruise Lines, 691
Caro, Herman, 2771
Carolan, D.M., 1950
Carolina Steel Corporation, 3087
Carothers, Lucille K., 2615
Carousel Snack Bars of Minnesota, 1875
Carpenter, Alfred S.V., 3478
Carpenter, Ben H., 4084
Carpenter, Clifford J., 1105
Carpenter, Dennis E., 959
Carpenter, Dow W., Jr., 400
Carpenter, Dunbar, 3478
Carpenter, E.A., 4255
Carpenter, E.N., II, 610
Carpenter, Gordon R., 4091
Carpenter, Harlow, 3478
Carpenter, Helen Bundy, 3478
Carpenter, James W., 1715
Carpenter, Jane H., 3478
Carpenter, Julie T., 4303
Carpenter, Paul L., 3208
Carpenter, R.R.M., Jr., 599
Carpenter Technology Corporation, 3536
Carpenter, Thomas W., 1273
Carpenter, William K., 599
Carr, Anne, 3245
Carr, F. William, Jr., 3934
Carr, Frank E., 2123
Carr, Howard E., 3132
Carr, Thomas P., 4205
Carraway, Gertrude, 3109
Carrell, Jeptha J., 3316
Carrera, J.A., 83
Carrico, John D., 2135
Carrington, Janet A., 1246
Carrithers, Ashley K., 233
Carrithers, Catherine M., 233
Carroad, Gunhilde, 2796
Carroll, Barry J., 1159
Carroll, Donald C., 210
Carroll, Gieriet S., 1172
Carroll, Jane, 2554
Carroll, John J., 2112
Carroll, Martin C., 1172
Carroll, Michael A., 1238
Carroll, P.J., 4081
Carroll, Peggy L., 1670
Carroll, Wallace, 3075
Carroll, Wallace E., 1159
Carroll, Wallace E., Jr., 438
Carroll, Walter J., 3649
Carruth, Allen H., 4127
Carruth, Brady F., 4127
Carse, James P., 2881
Carskadden, Ralph R., 206
Carson, C.M., 1324
Carson, Carl, 3679
Carson, Edward M., 29
Carson International, 964
Carson, Mrs. John C., 336
Carson Pirie Scott & Company, 964
Carson, S.G., 3387
Carsons, Morris, 2953
Carstarphen, J.M., 3115
Carswell, Bruce, 531
Carswell, Gale Fisher, 908, 909
Carter, Amon G., 3902
Carter, Bernard E., 4279
Carter, Donnel E., 2117
Carter, Edward F., 3344
Carter, Edward W., 230
Carter, Edwin L., 898, 903, 908
Carter, Fay S., 439
Carter Foundation Production Company, 3902
Carter, Frances P., 3027
Carter, Francis C., 3772
Carter, Frederic D., Jr., 2810
Carter, Henry M., Jr., 3137
Carter, Hodding, III, 2995
Carter, Imadell, 3874
Carter, James W., 2326
Carter, Joseph R., 1660

Carter, Leigh, 3185, 3388
Carter, Lisle, 873
Carter, Lisle C., Jr., 3271
Carter, Margaret W., 2326
Carter, Marjorie Sells, 503
Carter, Matthew G., 2197
Carter, N.B., 3902
Carter, Mrs. Robert, 4185
Carter, Robert T., 1048
Carter, Victor, 165
Carter, Virginia P., 3178
Cartmell, Carvel H., 2912
Cartmill, George E., 1734
Cartwright, Jerome, 3915
Caruth, W.W., Jr., 3981
Caruth, Mrs. W.W., Sr., 3981
Caruthers, John D., Jr., 1383
Carver, Lillian Ahrens, 3038
Carver, Spencer, 4047
Carwile, Charles W., 1356
Cary, Frank T., 2155
Cary, Mary Flagler, 2327
Carzoli, Ronald P., 3299
Casale, Maria, 675
Casassa, Charles S., 111, 246
Case, Donald, 3981
Casey, A. Michael, 99
Casey, Annie E., 504
Casey, E.P., 1694
Casey, Louie C., Jr., 731
Casey, Lyman H., 99
Casey, Samuel A., 4291
Casher, Clare, 559
Cashman, Elizabeth E., 3432
Cashman, M.J., 3675
Caslin, Mary E., 2218, 2294
Casner, R.H., 3415
Caspar, George J., 538
Caspersen, Barbara M., 2111
Caspersen, Finn M.W., 2111
Caspersen, Freda R., 596, 2111
Caspersen, O.W., 2111
Cassans, Robert A., 2629
Cassel, Milton E., 2229
Cassel, Rita Allen, 2229
Cassell, Ray E., 1270
Casselman, William A., 2279
Cassett, Louis N., 3538
Cassidy, Ann Shannon, 3420
Cassidy, Anna M., 1960
Cassidy, Mrs. Henry F., 1412
Cassidy, John, Jr., 3420
Cassidy, L.J., 1960
Cassidy, Sandra M., 756
Cassity, Dean A., 1312
Cassullo, Joanne L., 2656
Castagnola, George, 309
Castaybert, Patricia, 2290
Castellini, D.J., 3359
Castellini, Robert H., 3183
Castenskiold, Christian, 246
Castiglia, James, 1443
Castino, Jack W., 1936
Castle, Harold K.L., 893
Castle, Mrs. Harold K.L., 893
Castle, James C., 893, 894
Castle, James C., Jr., 893
Castle, Mary, 894
Castle, W. Donald, 894
Castleman, Riva, 2345
Castles, James B., 4252
Casto, Don M., III, 3180
Castor, Bruce L., 3762
Castro, Nash, 2234, 2577
Caswell, Philip, 1475
Catalina Associates, 212
Catan, Mary P., 816
Catanese, J.M., 1359
Catanzaro, Michael J., 2672
Cater, William B., 2196
Catera, Joseph P., 2312
Cates, M.L., Jr., 3796
Cates, MacFarlane L., Jr., 3820
Cates, MacFarlane L., Sr., 3796

Cates, R.Z., 3796
Cathcart, Silas S., 1045
Catherwood, Charles E., 3657
Catlett, Stanley B., 3459
Catlin, Loring, 2344
Catlin, Sara H., 539
Caton, Ralph W., 4065
Catron, Linda, 209
Catron, Thomas B., III, 2207
Catsman, David P., 722
Cattabiani, E.J., 3756, 3757
Cattarulla, E.R., 2426
Cattell, James McKeen, 2328
Catterall, Elaine, 2121
Catto, Jessica Hobby, 3983
Cauldwell, Charles M., 2724
Cavaliere, Anthony L., 2743
Cavanaugh, Teddi, 772
Cave, John B., 2721
Cavell, Walter E., 2459
Cavicke, David C., 581
Cavins, John, 1290
Cawley, Michael A., 3448
Cawley, William V., 2924
Cawsey, Mrs. Hugh R., 4228
Cay, Andrew R., 1568
Cay, John E., III, 847
CBS, 2329
Ceco Steel Products Corporation, 1097
Cena, L., 1138
Center, Hugh Stuart, 121
Center, Raymond H., 756
Centerre Bank, 1948
Centerre Bank of Kansas City, 1971
Centerre Trust Company, 1945, 1959, 2008, 2012
Centerre Trust Company of St. Louis, 561, 1940, 1948, 2010, 2016, 2020, 2034, 2041
Central and South West Corporation, 3903
Central Bank of Denver, 442
Central Bank of the South, 3
Central Cheese Company, 4357
Central Exchange Agency, 1828
Central Fidelity Bank, 4167, 4197
Central Manufacturing Distributors, 1123
Central National Bank of Cleveland, 3186, 3204, 3208, 3283, 3394
Central National Bank of Mattoon, 1171
Central Newspapers, 1204
Central Power and Light Company, 3903
Central Shares Corporation, 3847
Central Soya Company, 1205
Central Trust Company, 3183, 3199, 3315, 3350
Central Trust Company of Northeastern Ohio, 3373, 3382
Central Trust Company, N.A., 3369
Central-Penn National Bank, 3689
Cerino, Harry E., 3683
Cernak, Frank J., 1697
Cerny, Howard F., 2534
Cerulli, Robert F., 1991
Cerutti, E.V., 2628
Cervenak, Edward D., 3359
Cessna Aircraft Company, 1297
Chadwick, Dorothy J., 2332
Chafee, William G., 3787
Chaffin, Lawrence, 411
Chaiken, Frank, 615
Chait, Abraham, 2333
Chait, Burton D., 2333
Chait, Marilyn, 2333
Chait, Michael, 3348
Chait, Sulana Ross, 3348
Chalfant, William Y., 1300
Chalk, John Allen, 3876
Chalker, Durwood, 3903
Chalmers, Kenneth K., 977
Chalsty, John S., 2979
Chamberlain, J. Boatner, 389
Chamberlain, Philetus M., 2891
Chamberlain, Thomas M., 706

Chamberlin, Donald F., 1678
Chamberlin, Gerald W., 1678
Chamberlin, Joanne M., 1678
Chamberlin, Myrtle F., 1678
Chamberlin, Patience M., 3810
Chamberlin Products, 1678
Chambers, Anne Cox, 801, 822
Chambers, David L., Jr., 1246
Chambers, James Cox, 801
Champion, Hale, 242
Champion International Corporation, 505
Champion Pneumatic Machinery Co., 438
Champlin, George S., 3772
Chan, Miriam, 2611
Chan, Stephen, 2611
Chance (A.B.) Company, 1949
Chance, F. Gano, 1949
Chance, John H., 1949
Chance, Phillip G., 1949
Chandler, Alice, 2858
Chandler, Charles H., Jr., 841
Chandler, Clarissa H., 1024
Chandler, E.R., 3456
Chandler, Floyd J., 3027
Chandler, Otis, 321, 400
Chandler, Ralph B., 5
Chandler, Richard D., Jr., 4126
Chandler, W.L., 4212
Chaney, Aaron, 899
Chaney, Loyal L., 3208
Chaney, William R., 2251
Chang, Caroline, 1589
Chanin, Henry I., 2334
Chanin, Irwin S., 2334
Chanin, Marcy, 2334
Chanin, Paul R., 2334
Channing, Susan Stockard, 2044
Chapin, E.Y., III, 3829, 3835
Chapin, John R., 1616
Chapin, Melville, 1491
Chapin, Monroe, 725
Chapin, Richard, 1551
Chapin, S.B., 3088
Chaplow, B.A., 1765
Chaplow, Thomas J., 1765
Chapman, Alvah H., Jr., 3276
Chapman, Austin, 1860
Chapman, George B., Jr., 3264
Chapman, H.A., 3422
Chapman, Hugh M., 3095, 3801
Chapman, Irving, 79
Chapman, James C., 997
Chapman, James E., 3327, 3372
Chapman, John S., 1022
Chapman, John S., Jr., 2188
Chapman, Kenneth, 1248
Chapman, Lise P., 322
Chapman, Martha C., 3820
Chapman, Richard P., 1476
Chapman, Robert H., Jr., 3807
Chapman, W. Marshall, 3807
Chappell, M.E., 4064
Chapple, Thomas L., 2463
Charles, Marion, 3785
Charlestein, Morton, 3541
Charleston National Bank, 4285
Charlesworth, Richard K., 2478
Charlton, Earle P., Jr., 1496
Charlton, Mrs. George V., 3997
Charlton, Helena M., 3050
Charpie, Robert A., 1488
Charsky, Albert W., 1656
CharterBank of Carthage, 2022
Chase, Alfred E., 1497, 1498
Chase, Alice P., 1498
Chase, Edith, 588
Chase, John P., 1649, 4402
Chase, Kathy, 29
Chase, Leon O., 28
Chase Lincoln First Bank, 2565, 2774
Chase Manhattan Bank, 2337, 2393, 2441, 2526, 2580, 2581, 2774, 2802, 2947

Chasin, Gail, 2387
Chasin, Laura R., 2875
Chasin, Richard M., 2876
Chason, Stanley, 1846
Chastain, Robert Lee, 702
Chastain, Thomas M., 702
Chatfield, Mrs. Albert C., 3194
Chatfield, Charles H., Jr., 2572
Chatfield, Henry H., 3326
Chatfield, Terry R., 559
Chatham, Hugh G., 3106, 3118
Chatham, Hugh Gwyn, II, 3089
Chatham, Lucy Hanes, 3106
Chatham, Richard T., 3089
Chatkis, Jacob, 1530
Chatlos, Alice E., 2338
Chatlos, William F., 2338
Chatlos, William J., 2338
Chaudet, S.E., 266
Chauncey, Tom, II, 29
Cheatham, Celeste W., 2340
Cheatham, Harvey M., 858
Cheatham, Owen Robertson, 2340
Cheek, C.W., 3126
Cheek, Charles W., 3128
Cheek, George C., 326
Cheit, Earl F., 2902
Chell, Beverly C., 2688
Chemetron Corporation, 3513
Chemical Bank, 2242, 2619, 2625, 2760, 2767, 2774, 2863, 2927, 3761
Chemical Bank and Trust Company, 1668
Cheney, Ben B., 4229
Cheney, Eudine Meadows, 4029
Cheney, Francis I., 4229
Cheng, Ann Daugherty, 3478
Chenoweth, B.M., Jr., 848
Chenoweth, Maynard B., 1757
Cherney, Anna M., 3767
Cherniss, Charles, 314
Chernoff, Patricia, 2806
Chernofsky, Morris I., 2341, 2342
Cherokee State Bank, 1283
Cherry, Earl R., 2068
Cherry, James R., 2882
Cherry, Wendell, 1344
Chertkof, David W., 1406
Chertkof, Howard L., 1406
Chester, Annetta Rosenhaus, 2172
Chester, Gila Rosenhaus, 2172
Chester, J. Chapman, 637
Chevron USA, 115
Chew, Hon, 159
Chicago Bridge & Iron Company, 966
Chicago Title and Trust Company, 968, 971, 1070
Chicago Tribune Company, 972
Chiesa, Robert L., 1576
Chilcote, Hazel S., 1414
Child, William K., 1555
Childer, Betty B., 3887
Childers, James A., 1308
Childress, Francis B., 703
Childress, G.A., 3358
Childress, Miranda Y., 703
Childress, Owen F., 49
Childs, A.D., 3366
Childs, Anne Carmichael, 506
Childs, Daniel H., 2950
Childs, Daniel R., 2315
Childs, David M., 1154
Childs, Edward C., 2225
Childs, Mrs. Frederick, 2950
Childs, Hope S., 506
Childs, John W., 506, 2225
Childs, M.E., 4003
Childs, Margaret B., 2315
Childs, Richard S., 2225
Childs, Richard S., Jr., 2225
Childs, Roberta M., 1499
Childs, Starling W., 506
Childs, Starling W., II, 506
Childs, Timothy W., 2225

Chiles, Earle A., 3479
Chiles, Earle M., 3479
Chiles, Virginia H., 3479
Chilson, Hatfield, 436
Chilton, Arthur L., 3904
Chilton, Elizabeth E., 4285
Chilton, Leonore, 3904
Ching, Philip H., 897
Chinitz, J.S., 3026
Chino, Tetsuo, 69
Chinski, Arthur, 108
Chisholm, A.F., 1931
Chisholm, Donald H., 1982, 1983
Chisholm, Margaret A., 1931
Chisholm, William H., 2499, 2825
Chisolm, William A., 2810
Chisum, Clayton D., 3582
Chittenden, William S., 2565
Chitty, Charles B., 3847
Choate, Arthur B., 2762
Choate, Donald H., 1108
Chookaszian, Dennis H., 1008
Choromanski, J.J., 1922
Chortek, Doris H., 4358
Chrisman, Roswell H., 1091
Christ, Chris T., 1732
Christensen, A. Lee, 4134
Christensen, Allen D., 124
Christensen, Carmen M., 124
Christensen, David C., 488
Christensen, Leslie N., 1059
Christensen, M.D., 1259
Christensen, Neil H., 47
Christensen, Richard L., 4134
Christensen, Susan R., 4134
Christensen, Suzanne H., 4134
Christenson, Neil O., 987
Christian, Carolyn McKnight, 1827
Christian, Charles L., 3043
Christian Heritage School, 536
Christian, Michael W., 1562
Christian, Miles, 3342
Christian, S.G., Jr., 4212
Christiansen, Paul J., 2119, 2193
Christianson, Laura C., 2524
Christie, Ann S., 1118
Christie, Francis J., 706
Christie, Robert R., Jr., 3805
Christin, J.J., 3708
Christman, Thomas H., 3748
Christopher, F. Hudnall, Jr., 3137
Christopher, Glenn A., 2021
Christopherson, Weston R., 926, 1077
Christovich, Mary Lou M., 1386
Chrysler Corporation, 1679
Chubb, Corinne A., 2197
Chubb, Hendon, 2197
Chubb, Percy, III, 2197
Chubb, Sally, 2197
Chudy, Raymond F., 1501
Churchill, Bob, 3887
Churchill, Glen D., 3903
Churchill, Winston J., Jr., 3532
Churchwell, Charles D., 646
Churn, Margaret, 2077
Chute, Richard S., 1573
Ciarleglio, Nancy, 559
Cicala, Edmond, 3854
Cicero, Frank, Jr., 1063
CIGNA Corporation, 3542
Cincinnati Milacron, 3184
Cintas, Oscar B., 2345
Circle K Corporation, 31
Cisneros, Henry G., 676
C.I.T. Financial Corporation, 2112
Citibank, 2262, 2326, 2381, 2409, 2596, 2701, 2740, 2774, 2922
Cities Service Company, 3423
Citizens and Southern National Bank, 802, 808, 812, 816, 838
Citizens and Southern National Bank of South Carolina, 3801
Citizens Commercial Trust and Savings Bank, 314

Citizens Federal Savings and Loan, 3199
Citizens Fidelity Bank and Trust Company, 1338
Citizens National Bank, 1249, 3451
Citizens National Bank of Decatur, 1163
Citizens Savings Bank, FSB, 3773
Citizens Trust Company, 3773
City Bank & Trust Company, 1772
City Investing Company, 125
City National Bank, 114, 1354
City National Bank of Charleston, 4285
City National Bank of Miami, 706
City of Hartford, 592
Citytrust, 502, 588
Ciulla, Elsa, 2307
Ciulla, Robert W., 2307
Cizik, Robert, 3916
Claeyssens, Ailene B., 431
Claeyssens, Pierre P., 431
Claflin, Margot A., 3153
Claiborne, Herbert A., Jr., 885
Claire, Ralph H., 224
Clancy, John G., 2422
Clancy, Mary Alyce, 2589
Clancy, Thomas G., 972
Clapham, Clarence, 3280
Clapp, Alfred C., 2161
Clapp, Elizabeth, 4246
Clapp, George H., 3544
Clapp, James N., II, 4250
Clapp, K. Elizabeth, 4250
Clapp, Kristina H., 4250
Clapp, M. Roger, 3285
Clapp, Matthew N., Jr., 4250
Clapp, Mrs. John S., 1481
Clapp, Norton, 4246, 4250
Clapp, Tamsin O., 4246
Clardy, Harold C., 3088
Clareman, Jack, 2859
Clark, A. James, 664
Clark, Aaron, 276
Clark, Alfred C., 2347
Clark, Alton, 1641
Clark, Anson L., 3906
Clark, Barbara M., 3852
Clark, Charles E., 3276
Clark, Charles F., Jr., 1161
Clark, Dennis J., 3571
Clark, Dick, 638, 640
Clark, Donald C., 1162
Clark, Donald R., 1060
Clark, Duncan W., 2135, 2774
Clark, Edna McConnell, 625, 2346
Clark, Elizabeth G., 1407
Clark, Emory T., 4309
Clark, Eugene V., 2560
Clark, Florence B., 3459
Clark Foundation, 2585
Clark, Frank E., 2348
Clark, Frank W., Jr., 190
Clark, Frank, Jr., 405
Clark, George W., 2563
Clark, Hays, 625, 2346
Clark, Henry B., Jr., 903
Clark, Horace P., 2305
Clark, Irving, 1853, 1868, 1894
Clark (J.L.) Manufacturing Co., 974
Clark, James A., 1012
Clark, James M., 625, 2346
Clark, James McConnell, 625
Clark, Jane F., II, 2347
Clark, John, 3317
Clark, Kim, 1224
Clark, Mariana L., 2272
Clark, Mary Chichester du Pont, 600
Clark, Mary H., 1539, 1604
Clark, Maurie D., 3480
Clark, Meredith, 1789
Clark, Nolan P., 3130
Clark, O. James, 1748
Clark, Peggy, 59
Clark, Peter B., 1691
Clark, R. Hix, 3836, 3861
Clark, Robert, 2490

Clark, Robert Sterling, 2349
Clark, Roger A., 643
Clark, Roseanne, 2985
Clark, Roy Thomas, 3630
Clark, Royal, 149
Clark, Shirley M., 1894
Clark, Stephen, Jr., 2585
Clark, Stephen C., Jr., 2347
Clark, Sylvia, 3661
Clark, W. Van Alan, 2346
Clark, W. Van Alan, Jr., 1539, 1604
Clark, William J., 3381
Clark, William N., 1089
Clarke, Amy P., 2833
Clarke, Dexter, 3781
Clarke, Eleanor Stabler, 3719
Clarke, Glenn S., 2251
Clarke, Howard P., 1899
Clarke, Jack G., 2325
Clarke, James McClure, 3116
Clarke, Kay Knight, 2223
Clarke, Owen T., Jr., 2416
Clarke, Paul, 1214
Clarkson, Everett, 3820
Clarkson, William, III, 4040
Clausen, Thomas C., 3871
Clauson, Bronwyn Baird, 2258
Clay, J.C., 2160
Claybourn, Colleen, 4104
Claypool, James H., 1806
Clayton, Marven H., 4142
Clayton, Susan V., 3907
Clayton, Susan Vaughan, 1400
Clayton, William L., 3907
Cleary, Catherine B., 4332, 4356
Cleary, Russell G., 4326
Cleaveland, J. Philip, 810, 811
Clebsch, William A., 261
Clegg, Reed L., 4145
Cleland, Alan E., 1826
Clem, George M., 1325
Clemens, Ethel M., 3481
Clemens, P. Blaine, 3645
Clemens, Rex, 3481
Clement, Ida L., 4004
Clement, James H., 4004
Clements, Glenn, 2063
Clements, Keith R., 1809
Clements, Rita C., 4043
Clemins, C.F., 991
Clendenin, John, 952
Cleveland Coca-Cola Bottling Company, 3508
Cleveland Electric Illuminating Company, 3185
Cleveland, Harlan, 2730
Cleveland, Harland, 1848
Cleveland, Leatrice F., 4056
Cleveland-Cliffs Iron Company, 3187
Clifford, Cornelia W., 3059
Clifford, Robert, 2075
Clifford, Stewart B., 3059
Clifford, Thomas J., 1823
Cline, Robert T., 2849
Clinton, Mrs. C. Kenneth, 3063
Clinton Cotton Mills, 3797
Clinton, Hillary Rodham, 2773
Clinton, John L., 3063
Clodfelter, Daniel G., 3124
Clodfelter, H.M., 3308
Clonan, J., 508
Cloninger, Kermit, 3100
Clorox Company, 127
Close, Anne Springs, 3821, 3822
Close, David P., 678
Close, Derick S., 3821, 3822
Close, Elliott Springs, 3821, 3822
Close, H.W., Jr., 3821, 3822
Close, Katherine Anne, 3821, 3822
Close, Leroy Springs, 3821, 3822
Close, William F., 565
Cloud, Joe C., 1328
Cloudt, H.J.H., 2301
Clougherty, Coleman, 2672

Connell, Lawrence, 4269
Connell, Michael J., 131
Connell, William F., 2575
Connelly, Christine, 3545
Connelly, John E., Jr., 612
Connelly, John F., 3545
Connelly, Joseph F., 3277
Connelly, Josephine C., 3545
Connelly, Judith T., 3545
Connelly, M.H., 4017
Connelly, Thomas S., 3545
Connelly, William H., 533
Conner, James W., 3442
Connick, Harris R., 269
Connolly, Arthur G., Jr., 616
Connolly, Arthur G., Sr., 616
Connolly, James F., 3127
Connolly, Joseph G.J., 3555
Connolly, M. Michael, 4370
Connolly, Ruth E., 1256
Connolly, Stephen, 2285
Connolly, Walter J., Jr., 512, 532
Connor, Frank J., 492
Connor, Mrs. Gordon R., 4375
Connor, John T., 2155
Connor, M.J., 3216
Connor, Robert P., 2264
Connors, David M., 570
Connors, R.J., 2030
Conrad, Austin G., 103
Conrad, Carol, 893
Conrad, Donald G., 489
Conrad, Gene R., 1786
Conrad, William C., 3734
Conron, John J., 1960
Consolidated Papers, 4310
Consolini, Michael G., 2767
Consortium of Universities, 662
Consoweld Corporation, 4310
Constable, Mrs. William G., 1621
Constance, James C., 2063
Constantin, E., Jr., 3912
Constantin, Mrs. E., Jr., 3912
Conston, Charles, 3546
Conston, Inc., 3546
Consumers Rock and Cement Company, 210
Container Corporation of America, 976
Contee Sand & Gravel Company, 661
Continental Bank and Trust Company, 3689, 4133, 4143
Continental Corporation, 2365
Continental Equities, 759
Continental Grain Company, 2366, 2453
Continental Group, Inc., 508
Continental Illinois Corporation, 977
Continental Illinois National Bank and Trust Company of Chicago, 945, 968, 981, 1113, 1184
Continental Ore Corporation, 2865
Converse, Philip E., 2902
Convisser, Helen Coe, 2664
Conway, E. Virgil, 2689
Conway, J.C., 915
Conway, Jill K., 2405
Conway, John H., Jr., 3443
Conway, John P., 992
Conway, S.S., Jr., 488
Conway, William G., 2234, 2507
Cony, Edward R., 2117
Cook, Benjamin L., Jr., 3787
Cook, Bruce L., 978
Cook, Charles W., 2188
Cook, D. Charles, III, 978
Cook, Donald, 3176
Cook, Donald C., 3248
Cook, Edward D., Jr., 1621
Cook, Emajean, 1680
Cook (Frances Kerr) Trust, 978
Cook, Franklin C., 132
Cook, George, 2827
Cook, Gregory M., 1502
Cook, Herbert, 3547
Cook, Howard F., 132

Cook, J.B., 1709, 1710
Cook, James, 446
Cook, Jane B., 2410
Cook, Joe, 717
Cook, John Brown, 1502
Cook, Kathleen M., 132
Cook, L.M., 78
Cook, Mrs. Loring T., 3913
Cook, Marian Miner, 1502
Cook, Paul W., 2657
Cook, Peter C., 1680
Cook, Phyllis, 334
Cook, R.E., 1135
Cook, Samuel DuBois, 646
Cook, Stanton R., 1089, 1090
Cook, Susan V., 132
Cook, Thomas P., 1903
Cook, Vannie E., Jr., 3913
Cook, W.S., 2997
Cook, Wallace L., 1502, 2379
Cook, Wayne S., 2891
Cook, William E., 4402
Cook, William H., 132
Cooke, Anna C., 895
Cooke Chevrolet Company, 1339
Cooke, Elva, 1339
Cooke, John W., 4209
Cooke, Lori, 1339
Cooke Pontiac Company, 1339
Cooke, Richard A., Jr., 895
Cooke, Samuel A., 895, 899
Cooke, V.V., 1339
Cooke, V.V., Jr., 1339
Cookson, John S., 2090
Cool, David H., 4336
Coolbrith, Alison G., 489
Cooley, Denton A., 3914
Cooley, Mrs. Denton A., 3914
Cooley, Louise T., 3914
Cooley, Walter F., Jr., 3576
Coolidge, Amory, 1646
Coolidge, Gloria, 1646
Coolidge, Lawrence, 1651
Coolidge, T. Jefferson, 1646
Coolidge, T. Jefferson, Jr., 1546
Coolidge, Thomas R., 2248
Coolidge, William A., 1646
Coombe, Eva Jane, 3153
Coombe, Vachael Anderson, 3153
Coombes, William R., 497
Coombs, John W., 1392
Coombs, V. Anderson, 3219
Cooney, Eleanor S., 2767
Cooper Industries, 3916
Cooper, Bernard, 663
Cooper, Diene P., 3525
Cooper, Douglas J., 3525
Cooper, E., 933
Cooper, Joseph H., 2054
Cooper, Madison Alexander, Jr., 3915
Cooper, Marsh A., 243
Cooper, N.K., 1409
Cooper, Owen, 1936
Cooper, R. John, 3062
Cooper, Thomas A., 3580
Cooper, W. Paul, 3144, 3188
Cooper, Warren S., 2096
Cooper, William E., 3911
Coor, Lattie F., 1956
Coors, Adolph, Jr., 441
Coors, Gertrude, 441
Coors, Jeffrey H., 441
Coors, Joseph, 441
Coors, Peter H., 441
Coors, William K., 441, 455
Cope, James B., 1220
Copeland, Clyde, Jr., 2149
Copeland, Gerret van S., 604, 618
Copeland, Lammot du Pont, 604, 629
Copeland, Mrs. Lammot du Pont, 629
Copeland, Lammot du Pont, Jr., 629
Coplan, Alfred I., 1456
Coplan, Robert C., 3291
Copland, Milton, 3003

Copley, David C., 133
Copley, Helen K., 133
Copley Press, Inc., 133
Copley, R.D., Jr., 188
Coppersmith, J., 624
Coppersmith, Jack, 768
Coquillette, James E., 1269
Corash, Paul, 2719
Corbally, John E., 1077
Corbally, Richard V., 2712
Corbett, Adelaide T., 3029
Corbett, J. Ralph, 3191
Corbett, Patricia A., 693, 3191
Corbin, Hunter W., 2134
Corbus, William, 2528
Corcoran, Helena S., 627
Corcoran, Hugh J., 1632
Corcoran, Mrs. Leslie S., 134
Corcoran, Nancy P., 2165
Corcoran, Walter G., 2379
Corcoran, William J., 2527
Cord, Steven B., 2911
Cordaro, Nancy Anne, 4293
Cordell, J.B., 788
Cordero, Mrs. Walter G., 340
Cordner, Warren C., 274
Cordova, Donald E., 442
Corey, William G., 299
Cori, Tom, 1987
Corlew, John G., 1930
Corley, Mary Jo, 1762
Corman, Robert P., 2125, 2161
Cormier, Margaret, 1390
Corn, Elizabeth T., 807
Corn, Lovick P., 807
Corneille, Barbara Berry, 93
Cornelius, James M., 1237
Cornelius, William E., 2034
Cornell, Peter C., 2367
Cornell (Peter C.) Trust, 2593
Cornell, N. Thomas, 3249
Cornell, S. Douglas, 2367
Cornelson, George H., 3797
Corner, Ernest, 3786
Cornerstone Farm & Gin Company, 61
Corning Glass Works, 2368
Corning, Henry H., 3151
Corning, Nathan E., 3151
Corning, Ursula, 3012
Cornish, John G., 1543
Corno, Walter J., 2600
Cornwall, Barbara W., 2125
Cornwall, Jos. C., 2125
Corogin, John S., 3284
Corp, Eleanor L., 3468
Corrigan, Ann G., 3432
Corrou, Vincent R., Jr., 3005
Corry, Charles A., 3750
Cors, Allan D., 685
Corsicana National Bank, 4040
Corvin, Mrs. Robert, 389
Corvin, Mrs. William, 389
Cosgrove, G. Dean, 3444
Cossman, Jerome, 2172
Cost, David, 1895
Costa, Aubrey M., 3917
Costanzo, G.A., 3314
Costello, Cyril J., 2039
Costello, John J., 2560
Costello, Maxine, 3953
Coster, Nancy L., 2295
Costley, Gary E., 1749
Cote, Samuel A., 1916
Cotham, Ralph, 53
Cotter, Harvey S., 2463
Cotter, Joseph F., 1625
Cotter, P.W., 4308
Cotter, Patrick W., 997, 4315, 4337, 4381
Cotton, Harold N., 1659
Cotton, Robert L., 1902
Cottrell, Frederick Gardner, 44
Couch, William C., 3027
Coudrai, Marcelle, 2638

Coughenour, Willda, 1320
Coughlin, Virginia B., 2469
Coulson, Helen McMaster, 675
Coulson, Robert, 2493
Coulter, George S., 780
Coulter, William, 1501
County Bank of Tower Grove, 2040
Couper, Richard W., 742, 2514, 2824
Courts, Malon C., 820
Courts, Richard W., 820
Courts, Richard W., II, 813, 820, 839
Courts, Virginia Campbell, 820
Cousins, Ann D., 821
Cousins, Norman, 1753, 3271
Cousins, Thomas G., 821
Covert, Robert E., 710
Covey, Moody, 188
Covington, John R., 1191
Covington, Olive W., 683
Cowan, Harry A., 1504
Cowan, Ivy, 3133
Cowan, J.C., Jr., 3084
Cowan, Martha A., 1659
Cowan, Robert J., 3882
Cowden, Louetta M., 1952
Cowdrey, Ruth F., 1648
Cowell, S.H., 136
Cowie, R.A., 3196
Cowles, Charles, 2369
Cowles, Florence C., 1262
Cowles, Gardner, 2369
Cowles, Gardner, III, 2369
Cowles, Gardner, Jr., 1262
Cowles, James P., 4231, 4232
Cowles, Jan S., 2369
Cowles, John, 1832
Cowles, John, Jr., 1832
Cowles Publishing Company, 4231
Cowles, Russell, II, 1832
Cowles, Sage Fuller, 1832
Cowles, William H., 4232
Cowles, William H., 3rd, 4231, 4232
Cowley, Allan W., 3761
Cowley, James M., 106
Cox, Andrew, 1642
Cox, C. Russell, 931
Cox, David C., 1888
Cox Enterprises, 822
Cox, Frederick K., 3244
Cox, James M., 889
Cox, Jessie B., 1506
Cox, John F., 538, 2251
Cox, John W., 3443
Cox, Lawrence, 327
Cox, Margaret J., 818
Cox, Martha W., 1505
Cox, R.F., 78
Cox, Sid, 4032
Cox, William C., Jr., 1505, 1506
Coxe, Eckley B., IV, 3761
Coy, John F., 987
Coy, Josephine M., 3810
Coyer, Frank P., Jr., 1706
Coyle, John J., 2187
Coyle, Martin A., 3392
Coyne, Marjorie, 4392
Coyne, Mary V., 910
Coyne, Richard L., 2059
Cozad, James W., 928
Cozzolino, Salvatore J., 2360
Crabtree, Lotta M., 1507
Craddock, Roy, 4142
Craft, Ira Q., 824
Craft, Joseph W., III, 3444
Craft, Lynn, 3909
Crager, Jay C., Jr., 3871
Crahan, Brian D., 278
Craib, Donald F., Jr., 922
Craig, Albert B., Jr., 3735
Craig, Albert M., 1546
Craig, David M., 1912
Craig, Earle M., 3549
Craig, Edith C., 2606

Daghlian, Nazar, 323
Dahill, Thomas H., 1573
Dahl, C.R., 139
Dahling, Louis F., 1720
Dahne, Frank M., 1426
Dahowski, John F., 1656
Dahrendorf, Ralf, 2444
Dailey, Judy B., 1333
Daily, Mary Ann, 1573
Dain, Kalman and Quail, Incorporated, 1867
Dains, Orth I., 626
Dakota First Trust Company, 3139
Dalbey, Joan W., 3048
Dalbey, Marie O., 3048
Dalby, Alan J., 3726
Dale, Berteline Baier, 2257
Dale, K., 81
Dalianes, Art, 228
Dalis, M. Dan, 4165
Dall'Armi, Lorenzo, Jr., 403
Dallas Market Center Company, 3919
Dalrymple, Jean, 2479
Dalsemer, Leonard, 2528
Dalton, A.T., 1050
Dalton, Ann V., 715
Dalton, Dorothy U., 1681
Dalton, Matt, 1207
Dalton, R. Murray, 3391
Daly, Bernard, 3483
Daly, Charles U., 1052
Daly, Charles W., 525
Daly, Evelyn F., 541
Daly, James J., 2308
Daly, Richard L., 2055
Daly, Robert P., 541
Dalziel, R.D., 2249
D'Amato, D. Donald, 3016
D'Amato, Donald P., 3016
D'Amato, Lawrence L., 3016
D'Ambrosio, A. Daniel, 2102
Dame, Mrs. W. Page, Jr., 1461
Dameron, Carolyn V., 4215
Dammann, Richard W., 2378
Dammerman, Dennis D., 527
Damon, Mrs. John L., 1586
Damon, Peter S., 1495
Dampeer, John L., 3370
Dan River Inc., 4166
Dana Corporation, 3196
Dana, Charles A., 2379
Dana, Charles A., Jr., 2379
Dana, Eleanor N., 2379
Dana, Herman, 1508
Dana, Lester Harold, 1508
D'Andrade, Hugh A., 2178
Dane, Edward N., 1571
Danelian, Mrs. Richard, 323
Danforth, Donald, Jr., 1955
Danforth, Mrs. William H., 1955
Danforth, William H., 1955
Daniel International Corporation, 3802
Daniel W. Dietrich Foundation, 3556
Daniel, Barbara F., 3953
Daniel, Charles W., 7
Daniel, Christopher J., 3953
Daniel, D. Ronald, 2700
Daniel, Gerard, 2380
Daniel (Gerard) & Company, 2380
Daniel, H.M., 3802
Daniel, James F., III, 3802
Daniel, James L., Jr., 3953
Daniel, M.C., 7
Daniel, Mary P., 1777
Daniel, R. Hugh, 7
Daniel, Ray L., Jr., 2059
Daniel, Ruth, 2380
Daniel, William V., 4216
Danielewski, Walter E., 504
Daniels, Bruce G., 1509
Daniels, Clarence W., Jr., 1509
Daniels, Emma A., 2869
Daniels, F.H., 1509
Daniels, Frank A., 3091

Daniels, Frank A., Jr., 3091
Daniels, Gordon, 1789
Daniels, Lillian I., 2724
Danielson, Barbara D., 988
Danielson, James Deering, 988
Danielson, Ray, 420
Danielson, Richard E., Jr., 988
Dann, Mrs. Tyler, 2416
D'Anneo, Paul, 123
Danner, Douglas, 1608
Dansby, Stewart, 24, 1753
Danson, Evan R., 1806
Dantzler, Alf F., Jr., 1930
Danzig, Charles, 2127
Danziger, Richard M., 2255
Danziger, Robert F., 2145
D'Arata, Joy E., 2338
Darby (Harry) Foundation, 1299
Darby, Harry, 1299
d'Arcambal, T.R., 888
D'Arcy, June B., 92
Darden, Kenneth, 4101
Darden, Pretlow, 4187
Dargene, Carl J., 927
Darland, Raymond W., 403, 1806
Darley, Charles, 4120
Darling, Jeannette C., 1642
Darling, Morris F., 1642
Darling, Nelson J., Jr., 1615, 1642
Darling, Robert E., Jr., 520
Darling, Ruth A., 1642
Darling, Ruth L., 1642
Darling, Ruth LaCroix, 1615
Darling, Thomas W., 1642
Darling, William H., 1642
Darnell, Doris H., 3602
Darney, Elizabeth L., 2417
Darrah, Jessie S., 2381
Darrow, Anita S., 1189
Darrow, Jill C., 1189
Dashefsky, Samuel, 3883
D'Atri, Alexander C., 3014
Dauby, Nathan L., 3197
Daugherty, Phil E., 3437
Daugherty, R.B., 2053
Daugherty, Robert B., 2074
Daughtery, H.M., Jr., 3940
Daum, Paul L., 2478
Daum, Richard, 278
Daum, Virginia, 90
Dauphin Bank and Trust Co., 3516
Dauphin Deposit Bank and Trust
  Company, 3593, 3650, 3667
Dautel, Charles S., 3203
Dauterman, Frederick E., Jr., 3414
Davee, Adeline B., 986
Davee, Ken M., 986
Davenport, Alice M., 1510
Davenport, Edith F., 795
Davenport, George P., 1392
Davenport, Joseph H., Jr., 3829
Davenport, Palmer, 1567
Davenport, Rodolph B., III, 3847
David, Edward E., Jr., 2514
Davidowitz, Rosalind, 2755
Davidson Pipe Company, 2383
Davidson, Betsy, 2598
Davidson, Bradford, 2598
Davidson, C.J., 3926
Davidson, Dorothy, 924
Davidson, H. Peter, 2383
Davidson, H.W., 3926
Davidson, Harry R., 1669
Davidson, James E., 1879
Davidson, Joan K., 2598
Davidson, John Matthew, 2598
Davidson, John S., 3824
Davidson, Mrs. Joseph L., 1097
Davidson, Marjorie Moore, 911
Davidson, Park R., 3084
Davidson, Peter, 2598
Davidson, Philip, 2383
Davidson, R.S., 3926

Davidson, Robert T.H., 1982, 2286, 2957
Davidson, Suzette M., 1103
Davidson, Virginia G., 1879
Davidson, William P., 2911
Davie, Robert N., 588
Davies, Alan, 2387
Davies, Alicia C., 143
Davies, Barbara B., 251
Davies, Gwilyn, 4391
Davies, Mrs. J. Clarence, Jr., 2540
Davies, John R., 1666
Davies, Michael B., 2512
Davies, Nicholas E., 802
Davies, Mrs. Paul, 341
Davies, Mrs. Paul L., Jr., 251
Davies, Paul L., Jr., 251
Davies, Paul Lewis, III, 251
Davies, Ralph K., 143
Davies, Richard B., 4025
Davies, Robert N., 2481
Davis, A. Dano, 794
Davis, A. Stephen, 356
Davis, Abraham M., 2386
Davis, Alan, 356
Davis, Alan J., 3749
Davis, Alfred A., 823
Davis, Allan V., 806
Davis, Archie K., 3078, 3095
Davis, Arthur Vining, 707
Davis, Bernard C., 3481
Davis, Brian, 1397
Davis, Carle E., 4172, 4184, 4190
Davis, Carolyn P., 1932
Davis, Clyde R., 1196
Davis, Corwith, Jr., 51
Davis, Cynthia K., 51
Davis, Donald W., 507, 512, 577
Davis, Dudley G., 1446
Davis, Edgar B., 1600, 4019
Davis, Edgar G., 1237
Davis, Edwin W., 1833
Davis, Ellen Scripps, 349
Davis, Evan A., 2460
Davis, Evelyn Green, 2500
Davis, F. Elwood, 641
Davis, Fred L., 3854
Davis, Frederick W., 1833
Davis, G. Gordon, 2373
Davis, Gale E., 2055
Davis, Harold T., 1603
Davis, Holbrook R., 707
Davis, Irene E., 1511
Davis, J. Morton, 2755
Davis, J.R., 22
Davis, Jacob E., 3183
Davis, James E., 794, 1511
Davis, James H., 1338
Davis, Jay M., 823
Davis, Jean M., 689
Davis, Jim, 3142
Davis, Joel P., 707
Davis, John H., 1511
Davis, John M.K., 3574
Davis, John P., Jr., 3735, 3754
Davis, K.R., 163
Davis, Kay, 3927
Davis, Ken W., 3927
Davis, Ken W., Jr., 3927
Davis, Laura A., 1732
Davis, Laurianne T., 1782
Davis, Leon, 3993
Davis, Leonard, 2384
Davis, LeVan, 721
Davis, Lincoln K., 1600
Davis, Mary, 1740
Davis, Mary E., 1833
Davis, Meyer, 2386
Davis, Milton Austin, 708
Davis, Mrs. John M.K., 3574
Davis, Nathanael V., 707
Davis, Peter, 277
Davis, Philip J., 2251
Davis, Preston W., 584

Davis, Robert D., 794
Davis, Robert S., 1889, 1917
Davis, Roger, 2641
Davis, Ruth, 2386
Davis, Ruth M., 646, 3509
Davis, Sam H., 4342
Davis, Samuel S., 1833
Davis, Shelby Cullom, 2385
Davis, Shelby M. Cullom, 2385
Davis, Sophie, 2384
Davis, Suzanne, 2598
Davis, T.C., 3927
Davis, Thomas G., 3726
Davis, Tine W., 709
Davis, Tine W., Jr., 709
Davis, W.R., 3882
Davis, W.S., 3927
Davis, William M., 4285
Davis, William S., 4124
Davis, William W., 3837
Davison, Jane I., 3260
Davito, William J., 1053
Davoil, Inc., 4124
Davy, George E., 1243
Davy, Louise W., 1920
Dawes, Richard I., 4193
Dawson, John, 3999
Dawson, Judith, 890
Dawson, William M., 3716
Day, C. Burke, Jr., 824
Day, Carl, 1933
Day, Cecil B., 824
Day, Clarence, 3839
Day, Clarence C., 3839
Day, Clinton W., 824
Day Companies, 3839
Day, Howard M., 144, 243
Day, John F., 3095
Day, Laurence W., 144
Day, Lon L., Jr., 824
Day, Lynn W., 1925
Day, Mary, 4370
Day, Nancy Sayles, 509
Day, Richard, 3303
Day, Robert A., Jr., 144, 243
Day, Susan C., 3717
Day, Tammis M., 144, 243
Day, Theodore J., 144, 243
Day, Willametta K., 144, 243
Dayton Hudson Corporation, 1834
Dayton, Alida, 2876
Dayton, Alida Rockefeller, 2578
Dayton, Anne S., 1929
Dayton, Brandt W., 1929
Dayton, Bruce B., 1929
Dayton, Bruce Bliss, 2325
Dayton, Bruce C., 1883
Dayton, David D., 1883
Dayton, Donald C., 1829
Dayton, Douglas J., 1883
Dayton, Edward N., 1929
Dayton, John W., 1829
Dayton, Kenneth N., 2877
Dayton, Lucy B., 1929
Dayton, Lucy J., 1829
Dayton, Mark B., 1929, 2875
Dayton, Mary Lee, 1887
Dayton, Newell B., 4142
Dayton, Robert J., 1829
Dayton, Ruth Woods, 4281
Dayton, Shirley D., 1883
Dayton, Virginia Y., 1929
de Armas, Raul, 1154
De Bakcsy, Alex, 133
De Bardeleben, John, 2776
de Brye, Barbara, 372
De Felippo, Olga, 2702
De Graaf, Norman, 1715
de Groote, Jacques, 498
de Hirsch, Baron Maurice, 2387
de Hirsch, Baroness Clara, 2387
de Hoffmann, Frederic, 2221
de Janosi, Peter E., 2902
De Jong, Hubert, 1203

De Jur, Harry, 2388
De Jur, Marian, 2388
de Kay, Helen M., 2389
de Limur, Genevieve Bothin, 99
de Neergaard, William F., 2427
de Rham, Casimir, 1525
de Rham, Casimir, Jr., 1492
de Rothschild, Bethsabee, 2390
de Rothschild, Edmond, 2391
de Vegh, Diana, 2271
de Vegh, Pierre J., 2271
De Yong, R.G., 984
Deagon, John, 915
Deakins, Katrine, 3902
Dealey, Joe M., 3923, 3924
Dean, Arthur H., 2973
Dean, C. Rees, 1698
Dean, Clyde D., 4189
Dean, Gillian, 1410
Dean, Gretchen, 1410
Dean, Howard B., 1145
Dean, J. Simpson, Jr., 632
Dean, Jo Helen, 4063, 4064
Dean, Joel, 1410
Dean, Joel, Jr., 1410
Dean, Jurrien, 1410
Dean, Paul R., 670
Dean, Thomas A., 1172
Dean, Tom J., 3925
Dean, Yvonne, 126
Dear, James O., 4032
Dearden, W.E., 3601
Dearden, W.E.C., 3536
Deason, Larry, 2579
Deats, Paul, Jr., 1494
Deaver, John Q., 2366, 2453
DeBacco, Paul, 3612
DeBakey, Michael E., 3928
Debevoise, Dickinson R., 2125
Debs, Barbara Knowles, 2116
Debs, Richard A., 644
deButts, John D., 3095, 3750
Dechert, Robert W., 3924
Decio, Arthur J., 1211
Decio, Patricia C., 1211
Deck, Raymond H., 534
Deckenbach, E.A., 2989
Decker, Alonzo G., Jr., 1403
Decker, G.M., 4308
Decker, Robert W., 4075
Decosimo, Joseph, 3835
Decosimo, Joseph F., 3850
DeCosta, Alyce H., 1036
DeCosta, Edwin J., 1036
DeDeyn, Anthony, 766
Dee, David L., 4136
Dee, Janet T., 4136
Dee, L.T., 4136
Dee, Thomas D., II, 4135, 4136
Dee, Thomas D., III, 4135, 4136
Deems, Richard E., 2537, 2538
Deen, R.B., Jr., 1937
Deeney, Gerald D., 1864
Deep Water, Inc., 4034
Deere & Company, 987
Deering, L. Patrick, 1454
Dees, Eleanor Lloyd, 264
Dees, Pamela, 3911
DeFriece, Frank W., 3851
DeFriece, Frank W., Jr., 3851
DeFriece, Paul E., 3851
DeFriece, Pauline M., 3851
DeGaetano, Peter F., 2318
Degen, Sylvia W., 797
DeGeorge, Barbara Tananbaum, 2977
Degheri, Chris, 2805
DeGroot, Shirley A., 74
DeHaan, B., 965
DeHart, Donald M., 1514
Dehavenon, Anna Lou, 2800
Deibel, Thomas G., 1727
Deicke, Edwin F., 710
Deicke, Lois L., 710
Deierlein, Grace, 3492

Deikel, Beverly, 1841
Deisher, William C., 935
DeKalb AgResearch, 989
DeKan, Madeleine, 2310
DeKrey, Warren, 3142
DeKruif, Robert M., 65
DeKryger, Maynard, 1705
del Campo, Philip, 336
del Mar, Elizabeth Adams, 647
Del Monte Foods, 115
Delacorte, Albert P., 711
Delacorte, George T., Jr., 711
Delacorte, Valerie, 711
DeLana, W.G., 500
DeLancey, William J., 3332
Deland, F. Stanton, 1586
Deland, F. Stanton, Jr., 1503
Delaney, Donald F., 4163
Delaney, Philip A., 1028
Delano, Georgia, 2683
Delano, Winifred G., 1100
Delany, Beatrice P., 2393
Deleray, Penny, 159
Delfiner, Judith, 3647
deLima, Richard F., 1602
Deliyanne, Gregory, 1735
Delmar, Charles, 647
Delmas, Gladys Krieble, 2394
Deloria, Vine, Jr., 2432
Delp, George C., 3552
Delta Air Lines, 825
DeLuxe Check Printers, 1835
DeMallie, Bayard T., 1659
DeMaria, Joseph A., 239
DeMars, Richard B., 1230
Demetrion, Dorothea L., 2656
Deming, Bertie Murphy, 54
Deming, John W., 54
Demmer, Edward U., 4313
Demo, Bernell, 3811
Demos, Nicholas, 990
DeMoss, Arthur S., 3554
DeMoss, Mrs. Arthur S., 3554
DeMoss, Charlotte A., 3554
DeMoss, Deborah L., 3554
DeMoss, Nancy L., 3554
DeMoss, R. Mark, 3554
DeMoss, Robert G., 3554
DeMoss, Theodore G., 3554
Demoulas, Telemachus A., 1513
Demouth, R.M., 1168
Dempsey, James H., Jr., 3154, 3260, 3310
Dempsey, John E., 4362
Dempsey, John N., 1892
Denbrow, Victor D., 783
Denby, Peter, 3711
Denegre, George, 1370
Denison, Margaret S., 2015
Denius, Frank W., 3900
Denker, H.F., 1918
Denman, Gilbert M., Jr., 3888, 3889, 3971
Denman, Leroy G., Jr., 3889, 3971, 4005
Dennett, Marie G., 511
Dennis, Arthur W., 4181
Dennis, David, 3429
Dennis, Edwin W., 1575
Dennis, Lloyd B., 170
Dennis, Richard, 969
Dennis, Richard J., 969
Dennis, Thomas, 969
Dennis, Thomas A., 969
Dennison, Stanley S., 837
Denny, Brewster, 2995
Denny, Brewster C., 2995
Denny, James M., 1144
Denny, Peter D., 3431
Denny, Raymond E., 3982
Denny, Thomas G., 3431
Densmore, Morris A., 421
Dent, Frederick B., 3156
Dent, Gloria G., 2396

Dent, Harry M., 2396
Dent, Harry M., Jr., 2396
Dent, Lucy, 2396
Denton, James M., III, 3836
Denton, W.R., 1138
Denver National Bank, 442
Denworth, Mrs. Raymond K., 3749
DePalma, Robert A., 3708
DePew, Thomas N., 2020
Deposit Bank, 3664
Deposit Guaranty National Bank, 1934
DePriest, Roy H., 3247
Derby, Dora C., 895
Derck, Terrence, 3221
Derderian, H.S., 1741
Dermody, William H., 2464
Dern, James R., 2243
deRoulet, Sandra, 3043
DeRoy, Helen, 1683
DeRoy, Helen L., 1682
Derr, Melvin H., 1431
Derry, William S., 3396
Des Jardins, Jerry L., 1671
Desch, Joseph H., 3593
DeShetler, Sally, 1705
DeSipio, George, 2604, 2652, 2933
DeSoto, Inc., 991
DeStefano, James R., 1154
Detar, Rex R., 1225
Deter, Robert N., 117
Detroit Bank and Trust Company, 1684
Dettman, Douglas R., 712
Dettman, Gregory L., 712
Dettman, Leroy E., 712
Dettman, Sophie B., 712
Detweiler, Frank H., 2443, 2774
Deuble, Andrew H., 3200
Deuble, George H., 3200
Deuble, Stephen G., 3200
Deuble, Walter C., 3200
Deurinck, Gaston, 498
Deutsch, Alex, 147
Deutsch, Carl, 147
Deutsch Company, 147
Deutsch, Donald A., 1145
Deutsch, Lawrence E., 256
Deutsch, Lester, 147
Devan, Charlotte S., 3718
Devan, Lawrence S., 3718
Devan, W. Todd, 3718
Devecchi, Betsy, 2389
Devens, Charles, 1560
Devereaux, N.P., 119
Devereaux, Zilph P., 2188
DeVilbiss, Thomas, 3303
Devin, Louis A., Jr., 3567
Devine, Charles J., 4259
DeVlieg, Charles B., 1685
DeVlieg, Charles R., 1685
DeVlieg Machine Company, 1685
DeVore, Floyd, 1301
DeVore, P. Cameron, 4259
DeVore, Richard A., 1301
DeVore, William D., 1301
DeVos, Helen J., 1686
deVos, Marius, 1554
DeVos, Richard M., 1686
DeVries, Donald L., 1403
Dewar, Jessie Smith, 2397
DeWaters, Enos A., 1687
Dewces, Edith Hilles, 3602
Dewces, Robert L., Jr., 3602
Dewey, Barbara Stokes, 311
Dewey, Francis H., III, 1468
Dewey, Mrs. John, 2398
DeWind, Adrian, 2432
DeWind, Adrian W., 2858
DeWoody, Beth, 2899
Dexter Corporation, 512
Dexter, Henrietta F., 1515
Dexter Shoe Company, 1391
di San Faustino, Genevieve Lyman, 99
Diamond, Henry L., 2577
Diamond, Richard E., 2778

Diana, Joseph A., 1077
Diaz, Nelson A., 3683
Dibner, Barbara, 513
Dibner, Bern, 513
Dibner, David, 513
Dick, Mrs. Vernon S., 1481
Dick, William, 3430
Dickason, John H., 745
Dicke, Richard M., 2430
Dickey, Robert, III, 3693
Dickey, W.D., 3553
Dickinson, Betty J., 1276
Dickinson, Dallas P., 449
Dickinson, H. Tyndall, 61
Dickison, Frank H., 2106
Dickison, Frank H., Jr., 4151
Dickler, Gerald, 2322
Dickson, Alan L., 3092, 3093
Dickson, Alan Thomas, 3118
Dickson, D.N., 119
Dickson, R. Stuart, 3092, 3093
Dickson, Raymond, 3930
Dickson, Rush S., 3093
Dickson, Rush S., III, 3092, 3093
Dickson, Thomas W., 3092, 3093
DiCristina, Vito G., 2693, 2694
Diederich, J. William, 4179
Diehl, John, 1853
Diener, Martha Stott, 3741
Dietel, William M., 2875
Dieter, Audrey J., 1850
Dieter, F. Robert, 3539
Dietrich, Daniel W., II, 3555
Dietrich, Henry D., 3556
Dietrich, Loreine C., 3424, 3425
Dietrich, William B., 3556
Dietz, Charlton, 1890
Dietz, Dale L., 3319
Dietz, F.H., 775
Dietz, John S., 2331
Dietz, Milton S., 1602
Dietz, Philip E.L., Jr., 1459
DiGirolamo, Joseph, 1209
Dileo, Victor, 2182
Dill, Betty Yaist, 3202
Dill, William R., 2109
Dille, John F., Jr., 1201
Diller, A.C., 3396
Diller, William J., 2115
Dillivan, Marilyn, 1278
Dillon, C. Douglas, 2399, 2400
Dillon, Clarence, 2399, 2400
Dillon, Douglas K., 2478
Dillon, Francis B., 71
Dillon, George C., 1946
Dillon, Mary L., 1157
Dillon, Peter W., 992
Dillon, Robert D., Jr., 2945
Dillon, Ross E., 4044
Dillon, Susan S., 2400
Dillon, Terrance J., 1157
Dillon, W. Martin, 992
Dillsaver, R.D., 3423
Dilworth, Susan S., 4089
Dimatteo, John R., 1393
Dimeo, Thomas P., 3786
Dimick, Marion Tully, 637
Dingle, Doris B., 3178
Dingman, Michael D., 2528
Dinneen, Gerald P., 1861
Dinner, Richard S., 391, 392
DiNome, Anthony J., 2987
Dinse, Ann G., 2193
Dinsmore, Wiley, 3194
Dinunzio, Mark A., 34
Dinwoody, Mrs. David T., 1481
Diotte, Alfred P., 4330
Dircks, Robert J., 2200
Discher, C. Dale, 1686, 1788
Disipio, George, 2980
Dismore, George B., 731
Disney, Abigail E., 150
Disney, Edna F., 150

Disney, Lillian B., 149
Disney, Patricia Ann, 150
Disney, Roy E., 150
Disney, Roy O., 150
Disney, Roy Patrick, 150
Disney, Timothy J., 150
Disney (Walt) Productions, 148
Dispatch Printing Company, 3410
Dittmann, Mrs. M. Carton, Jr., 3766
Dittrich, Raymond J., 1884
Dittus, Jay E., 1048
Dively, George S., 3201
Dively, Juliette G., 3201
Dively, Michael A., 3201
Diver, Joan M., 1561, 1562
Dix, Ronald H., 4299
Dixie Mill Supply Co., 1357
Dixon, C. Bailey, 3797
Dixon, Edith Robb, 3762
Dixon, F. Eugene, Jr., 3762
Dixon, George H., 1842
Dixon, George Widener, 3762
Dixon, Ruth B., 1668
Dixon, Stewart S., 1161
Dixon, W.W., 3536
Dixon, Wendell L., 1208
Dixson, Robert J., 2140
Djordjevich, Michael, 168
Doan, Glenda, 134
Doan, H.D., 1688
Doan, Herbert D., 1690
Doan, Leslie J., 134
Doane, Lawrence S., 1154
Dobbins, Charles G., 674
Dobbins, Hugh Trowbridge, 123
Dobbins, Leslie E., 123
Dobbins, Roberta Lloyd, 123
Dobbins, Z.E., Jr., 3133
Dobbs, Josephine A., 826
Dobbs, R. Howard, Jr., 826
Dobbs, W.L., 867
Dobelman, Katherine B., 3893
Dobras, Mary Ann, 3375
Dobson, Douglas R., 3734
Dobson, John S., 1733
Dobson, Nellie, 3427
Dobson, Robert, 2054
Dobson, Stephen, 1664
Dockson, Robert R., 211
Dodd, Edwin D., 3239
Dodd, Glenn W., 1138
Dodds, R. Harcourt, 505
Doder Trust Limited, 2268
Dodge, Cleveland E., Jr., 2402, 2825
Dodge, Cleveland H., 2402
Dodge, David S., 2402
Dodge, George W., 1368
Dodge, Geraldine R., 2116
Dodge, Warren A., 1616
Dods, Walter A., Jr., 897
Dodson, Charles, 1659
Dodson, Clara May, 827
Dodson, David L., 1210
Doehla, Harry, 1516
Doehrman, Druscilla S., 1254
Doelger, Henry, 153
Doering, Sarah Cowles, 1832
Doermann, Elisabeth W., 1928
Doermann, Humphrey, 1823
Doerner, E.J., 3460
Doerr, Henry, 1821, 1891
Doft, Alan, 2403
Doft, Avrom, 2403
Doft, Emanuel, 2403
Doft, Pauline, 2403
Doggett, John, 3858
Doheny (Carrie Estelle) Foundation
  Corporation, 154
Doheny, Mrs. Edward L., 154
Doheny, William H., 407
Doherty, David, 1698
Doherty, Mrs. Henry L., 2404
Doherty, James P., Jr., 1134
Doherty, R.P., Jr., 4115

Dolan, James F., 2744, 3029
Dolan, Myles, 474
Dolan, Roger M., 2119
Doldo, John, Jr., 3027
Dole, Burton A., Jr., 1306, 1324
Dolese, Roger M., 3428
Doll, Edward C., 3565
Doll, Richard C., 1603
Dollar Savings and Trust Company,
  3400, 3416
Dollar, JoAnn F., 824
Dolley, Kenneth, 1397
Dombowsky, David, 834
Dominick, Frank, 3
Dominion Steel Export Co., Ltd., 2988
Domino of California, Incorporated, 155
Dompier, Sandra Smith, 4082
Donahoo, John W., Jr., 731
Donahue, John A., 1141
Donahue, Joseph J., 3545
Donahue, Richard K., 1052
Donald, Barbara, 159
Donald, Paul A., 3313
Donaldson Company, 1836
Donaldson, Don, 3442
Donaldson, F.A., 1836
Donaldson, Forrest, 487
Donaldson, Matthew S., Jr., 3659
Donaldson, Oliver S., 1517
Donaldson, Richard M., 3178
Donaldson, William H., 489
Donley, Edward, 3509
Donley, Robert D., 1555
Donnan, Brian, 185
Donnell, Lester F., 3202
Donnelley, Dorothy Ranney, 994
Donnelley, Elliott, 993
Donnelley, Gaylord, 994
Donnelley, James R., 2265
Donnelley, Thomas E., II, 993
Donnelly, Jane, 2102
Donnelly, John L., 1267
Donnelly, Mary J., 3558
Donnelly, Thomas J., 3558, 4315
Donner, Frederick H., 3616
Donner, Joseph W., 2405
Donner, Robert, Jr., 2405
Donner, William H., 2405, 3616
Donohue, Bernadine Murphy, 295
Donohue, Daniel J., 295
Donohue, Elise R., 1924
Donohue, Rosemary E., 295
Donohue, Thomas F., 1507
Donovan, Ann Fuller, 1532
Donovan, Hedley, 644
Donovan, John M., 1806
Donovan Leisure Newton & Irvine, 2406
Donovan, Warren, 1554
Doody, J. Robert, 21
Doolen, Paul D., 1077, 1132
Dooley, A.J., 4363
Dor, Barbara, 2430
Dorf, Alfred R., 2145
Dorian, Harry A., 2600
Dorian, Richard M., 2600
Dorman, Gerald D., 2836
Dorman, L.C., 1748
Dorminy, John H., III, 828
Dorminy, John Henry, Jr., 828
Dorminy, Mrs. John Henry, Jr., 828
Dorminy, W.J., 828
Dorn, Alice Pratt Negley, 3893
Dorn, David F., 3582
Dorn, John C., 3582
Dorn, Richard B., 3582
Dorn, Ruth H., 3582
Dornbush, Kenneth F., 3531
Dorney, Dic L., 1745
Dorney, Dil L., 1746
Dornheggen, Irene A., 3146
Dornheggen, John H., III, 3146
Dornsife, David, 212
Dornsife, Ester M., 212
Dornsife, H.W., 212

Doroshow, Carol A., 1574
Doroshow, Helen L., 1574
Doroshow, James E., 1574
Doroshow, William, 1574
Dorr, John, 2408
Dorrance, John T., Jr., 2107
Dorris, Thomas B., 941
Dorset, W.S., 3932
Dorsett, Burt N., 44
Dorsett, C. Powers, 883
Dorsey, Bob Rawls, 243
Dorsey, Catherine A., 3224
Dorsey, Earl L., 1337
Dorsey, Eugene C., 2463, 2464
Dorsey, Gerard E., 583
Dorsey, Peter, 1825
Dorskind, Albert A., 311
Doshan, Diana L., 1905
Doskocil, Jacquelin, 1302
Doskocil, Larry D., 1302
Doskocil, Lawrence D., 1302
Doss, Lawrence P., 1722
Doss, M.S., 3933
Doss, Mrs. M.S., 3933
Doty, Donald, 3455
Doty, George E., 4298
Doty, Marjorie P., 502
Doubleday, Janet, 2409
Dougan, Francis L., 2975
Dougherty, Alfred F., Jr., 1991
Dougherty, Edward J., 1818
Dougherty, James R., 3934
Dougherty, Mrs. James R., 3934
Dougherty, M.J., 32
Dougherty, Mrs. M.J., 32
Dougherty, Mary Patricia, 3934
Dougherty, Robert B., 2059
Dougherty, Stephen T., 3934
Dougherty, T.J., 3513
Doughty, H. Cort, 3174
Douglas, Francis W., 4133, 4142, 4143
Douglas, George W., 2368
Douglas, Gerald E., 2473
Douglas, Jean W., 3020
Douglas, John A., 2114
Douglas, John W., 644
Douglas, Mary St. John, 3042
Douglas, Mrs. Philip C., 1469
Douglas, R.D., Jr., 3109
Douglas, Virginia Sue, 3417
Douglas, William A., 436
Douglass, Arthur R., 2526
Douglass, Katheryn Cowles, 1084
Douglass, Kingman Scott, 1084
Douglass, Louise J., 1084
Douglass, Robert Dun, 1084
Douglass, Robert R., 2337
Douglass, Timothy P., 1084
Dousman, Cynthia C., 2264
Douthat, Anne S., 2015
Douty, Alfred, 3559
Douty, Mary M., 3559
Dove, Roger, 534
Dover, Charles I., 3094
Dover Mill Company, 3094
Dow, Barbara B., 2792
Dow, Barbara C., 1689
Dow Chemical Company, 1688
Dow, G. Lincoln, Jr., 1616
Dow, Grace A., 1690
Dow, H.H., 1688
Dow, Herbert H., 1689, 1690
Dow, Herbert H., II, 1689
Dow, Mrs. James R., 340
Dow Jones & Company, 2117, 2410
Dow, Michael L., 1690
Dow, Willard H., III, 1689
Dowd, Hector G., 2452
Dowen, Thomas, 977
Dowling, M.G., 726
Downer, J.P., 78
Downer, Susan Q., 825
Downey, Anne Cunningham, 1247
Downey, Joe, 834

Downey, Judith Y., 637
Downing, Peter E., 1120
Downs, Harry S., 817
Doyle, Christopher E., 2912
Doyle, Donald W., 1340, 1376
Doyle, Mrs. Edmund, 3167
Doyle, Edmund D., 3167
Doyle, Frank P., 527
Doyle, George, 1229
Doyle, J.N., 3307
Doyle, John H., 634, 647
Doyle, Morris M., 230
Doyle, Patricia Jansen, 3365
Doyle, T.N., 1824
Doyle, Thomas M., 2496, 2906
Dozier, O.K., 4212
Dozor, Harry, 3560
Dozor, Harry T., 3560
Dozor, Shirley W., 3560
Drackett, Roger, 3409
Draeger, John K., 4324
Drake, Carl B., Jr., 1820
Drake, Francis E., Jr., 742
Drake, Harrington, 2415
Drake, Judy, 439
Drake, Philip M., 2374
Drake, William F., Jr., 3510
Drangel, M., 1613
Draper Corporation, 1555
Draper, Anne, 3393
Draper, C. Stark, 216
Draper, Dana, 2512
Draper, Duane, 3462
Draper, J. Avery, 599
Draper, James, 3548
Draper, Renee C., 599
Draper, Wickliffe P., 2831
Dravo Corporation, 3561
Dreblow, Donald G., 1845
Dreby, E.C., III, 3713
Dreher, Reinhold, 2320
Dreicer, N.J., 2249
Dreier, Geraldine I., 995
Drell, William, 116
Drennan, Altie Don, 1360
Drennan, Dorothea F., 2085
Drennan, Joseph A., 2085
Drennan, Rudith A., 1360
Dresdner, K. Philip, 2165
Dresher, D.H., 3638
Dresser Foundation, 3993
Dresser Industries, 3935
Drew, John W., 4296
Drew, Roy M., 310
Drew, William F., Jr., 3102
Drewry, Judson H., 1046
Dreyer's Ice Cream, 404
Dreyfus, Alice L., 985
Dreyfus, Camille, 2411
Dreyfus, Carolyn S., 985
Dreyfus, Louis, 2412
Dreyfus, Victoria, 2413
Driesen, Anson I., 160
Driggers, Nathan B., 1716
Drinko, John, 3300
Drinko, John D., 3327
Driscoll, Edward C., 3574
Driscoll, Elizabeth S., 1837, 1925
Driscoll, George E., 1153
Driscoll, Margot H., 1837
Driscoll, Rudolph W., 1837
Driscoll, W. Daniel, 3408
Driscoll, W. John, 1837, 1894, 4260
Drost, Charles M., 1356
Drought, Richard M., 1412
Droulia, Virginia Helis, 1365
Droz, F., 185
Druliner, Kathryn, 2054
Drum, Frank G., 156
Drummond, Burke W. W., 2451
Drumwright, Elenita M., 2724
Drury, Charles F., 1726
Drury, Thomas, 4002
du Bois, Alan, 33

du Bois, E. Blois, 33
du Pont, A. Felix, Jr., 600
du Pont, Allaire C., 600
du Pont, Caroline J., 600
du Pont, Edward B., 605, 618, 629, 632
du Pont, Elizabeth Lee, 610
du Pont, Henry B., 605, 629
du Pont, Mrs. Henry B., 629
du Pont, Irenee, 606
du Pont, Irenee, Jr., 606
du Pont, Jessie Ball, 713
du Pont, Joan, 502
du Pont, Lydia Chichester, 600
du Pont, Marka T., 600
du Pont (Margaret F.) Trust, 621
du Pont, Miren deA., 621
du Pont, Pierre S., 618, 632
du Pont, Richard C., Jr., 600
du Pont, Willis H., 621
Duane, Morris, 3642, 3698
DuBain, Myron, 230
Duberg, H.P.J., 514
DuBois, J.S., 9
DuBois, Jennifer Land, 1611
DuBois, Philip, 1611
Dubrow, Eli B., 158
Dubrow, Lowell H., 3584
DuBrul, Stephen M., 1691
Dubuque Packing Co., 1288
Duclos, David L., 1884
Ducournau, Jackson P., 1372
Duda (A.) and Sons, Inc., 714
Duda, Andrew, Jr., 714
Duda, Andrew L., 714
Duda, Ferdinand, 714
Duda, Ferdinand S., 714
Duda, John, 714
Duda, John L., 714
Dudley, Francis, 3818
Dudley, Henry A., 677
Dudley, Richard D., 4292
Dudley, Spottswood P., 677
Dudley, William, 1443
Dudman, Richard, 2088
Dudte, James, 3415
Duemke, Emmett, 4093
Duesenberg, Richard W., 1999
Duff, Charles F., 4172
Duff, Dana L., 3670
Duff, Ruth Ann, 3670
Duffy, G. Chapman, 4207
Duffy, John, 2256
Duffy, John J., 351, 2649
Duffy, Mrs. Bernard J., Jr., 1995
Duffy, Michael G., 628
Duffy, Robert A., 216
Duffy, William, Jr., 620
Dufour, Edith Libby, 1372
Dufrene, Phillip A., 1864
Dufresne, Walter, 913
Dugan, John L., Jr., 2505
Dugdale, J.W., 986
Duggan, Agnes B., 1336
Duggan, Jerry T., 1983
Duggan, Patricia M., 3696
Duhme, Carol M., 2012
Duke, Angier Biddle, 3001
Duke, Barbara Foshay, 2736
Duke, Doris, 2118, 3095, 3785
Duke, James Buchanan, 3095
Dula, Julia W., 2414
Dulaney, Douglas A., 1102
Dulany, Peggy, 2875, 2876
Dulin, Eugenia B., 653
Dulin, William R., 3119
Dullea, Charles, 207
Dulude, Richard, 2368
Dumke, Edmund E., 4137
Dumke, Edmund W., 4137
Dumke, Ezekiel R., Jr., 4137
Dumpson, James R., 2774
Dumser, Robert W., 2711
Dun & Bradstreet Group, 2415
Dunbar, C. Wendell, 1783

Dunbar, Mrs. Wallace H., 1341
Dunbar, Wallace H., 1341
Duncan, A.J., 3937
Duncan, Anneliese H., 1411
Duncan, Brooke H., 1376
Duncan, C.W., 3938
Duncan, Charles W., Jr., 3938
Duncan, G. Cameron, 3930
Duncan, George T., 835
Duncan, Harry F., 1411
Duncan, J.H., 1787
Duncan, Jessie, 3937
Duncan, Joe, 3833
Duncan, John G., 443
Duncan, John W., 3938
Duncan, John W., Jr., 3938
Duncan, Susan M., 477
Duncan, Virginia B., 230
Duncan, William H., 3720
Duncombe, Harmon, 2746, 3006, 3011
Dunfey, Walter J., 2092
Dunford, Betty P., 895
Dunker, Robert H., 2102
Dunkerton, Nathan, 3129
Dunlop, Joy S., 510
Dunmire, R.W., 3306
Dunn, David D., 3565
Dunn, Edward, 2751
Dunn, Edward C., 1464
Dunn, Harry E., 4209
Dunn, Milo, 1850
Dunn, T. Sterling, 1381
Dunn, Thomas D., 2194
Dunne, Dennis W., 1899
Dunnigan, Frank J., 2838
Dunnigan, Joseph J., 1728
Dunning, Richard, 1711
Dunnington, Carl E., 655
Dunnington, Walter G., Jr., 2188, 2949, 2951
Dunphy, Dean R., 336
Dunsire, P. Kenneth, 1239
Dunwiddie, Alan W., Jr., 4330
Dunwody, Atwood, 707, 787
Dunwody, W.E., Jr., 707
Dupar, E.L., 4233
Dupar, Ethel L., 4233
Dupar, Frank A., 4233
Dupar, Frank A., Jr., 4233, 4259
Dupar, James W., Jr., 4233
Dupar, R.W., 4233
Dupar, T.E., 4233
DuPont, Allaire C., 633
duPont, Jessie Ball, 716
DuPont, Richard C., Jr., 633
DuPont, Rip, 770
Dupuis, Sylvio, 2092
Duquette, Arthur L., 1511
Durben, Irwin, 2992
Durfee Attleboro Bank, 1517
Durfee, Louis, 1208
Durgin, Eugene J., 1566
Durgin, Katherine B., 258
Durkheimer, Stuart, 3487
Durot, Marcel, 1144
Dury, Joseph D., Jr., 3735
Duryee, D.A., 4228
Duryee, Sacket R., 1533, 1660
Dusenberry, G.R., 806
Dusendschon, David W., 4338
Dusick, Ellen A., 228
Dustan, Jane, 2445
Dusto, F.R., 540
Dutcher, Phillip, 1687
Duval Spirits, 1387
Duval, Albert F., 3565, 3594
Duval, Betty, 2117
Duvall, Robert L., 4095
Dweck, Ralph, 650
Dweck, Rena, 650
Dweck, Samuel R., 650
Dwight, Thomas J., 1898
Dworsky, Alan J., 2976
Dwyer, John J., 3186, 3188

Dybala, Richard L., 931
Dyck, Harold P., 1311
Dye, Glen M., 1838
Dye, Harry M., 1838
Dye, Sherman, 3371
Dyer, J.M., 4040
Dyer, William A., Jr., 1204
Dyke, Walter P., 4252
Dykstra, Betty Y., 4248
Dysard, Elsie, 1332
Dyson, Anne E., 2417
Dyson, Charles H., 2417
Dyson, John S., 2417
Dyson, Margaret M., 2417
Dyson, Melvin A., 4150
Dyson, Peter L., 2417
Dyson, Robert R., 2417
Dyson-Kissner-Moran Corporation, 2417

Eadie, Ronald E., 423
Eady, Tom, 4040
Eagan, Emmett E., 1718, 1764
Eagan, Emmett E., Jr., 1764
Eagle-Picher Industries, 3203
Eagleson, Arthur J., 3826
Eagleson, William B., Jr., 3580
Eagle-Tribune Publishing Company, 1610
Eaglin, Joseph, Jr., 684
Eames, John, 4097
Earhart, Harry Boyd, 1691
Earl, Orrin K., Jr., 314
Earle, Mrs. Edgar, 1469
Earle, Harry W., 4300
Earle, Mary, 2248
Early, Jack, 1170
Early, Rexford C., 1226
Early, W.B., 3491
Earnhardt, Hazel S., 3438
Earnhart, Don B., 1233
Earnhart, V.J., 3895
Easley, Andrew H., 4167
East, Sarita Kenedy, 4002
Eastern Associated Coal Corp., 1518
Eastern Cold Storage Insulation Company, 2816
Eastern Gas and Fuel Associates, 1518
Eastman Kodak Company, 2418
Eastman, Lee V., 490
Eaton Corporation, 3204
Eaton, Charles F., Jr., 1586
Eaton, E.H., 3333
Eaton, H.C., 1101
Eaton, Harry C., 1102
Eaton (Hubert) Estate Trust, 174
Eaton, John S., 927
Eaton, Joseph E., 1616
Eaton, Richard, 1979
EB & Associates, 3732
Ebbert, George S., Jr., 3535
Ebbott, R.D., 1890
Ebco Manufacturing Company, 3168
Eberhart, Guy F., 1145
Eberle, Edward R., 2140
Eberle, William D., 3001
Eberly, John C., 3303
Eberly, Russell A., 3697
Ebert, Carroll E., 964
Ebert, Robert H., 2737
Eberts, K. Marvin, Jr., 1255
Eble, Charles E., 2221
Ebner, Rudolph, 3493
Ebright, Mitchell, 237
Ebsary (F.G.), Inc., 2419
Ebsary, Frederick G., 2419
Ebsary, Margaret E., 2419
Eby, Richard Y., 3595
Eccles, Dolores Dore, 4138
Eccles, George S., 4138
Eccles, Sara M., 4139
Eccles, Spencer F., 4138
Echaveste, Maria, 2773
Echlin, Beryl G., 718
Echlin, John E., 718

Echlin, John E., Jr., 718
Eck, John E., 3817
Eckels, Rolland M., 1242
Eckerd (Jack) Corporation, 719
Eckert, Milton K., 4051
Eckley, Robert S., 1166
Eckstrom, Amy Lou, 4253
Ector, Howard, 802
Eddie, Charles P., 239
Eddie, Gloria, 239
Eddy, Arthur D., 1693
Eddy, C. Russell, 1616
Eddy, Charles R., Jr., 1616
Eddy, Edwin H., 1839
Eddy, Jane Lee J., 2976
Eddy, Latimer B., 1475
Edelman, Dorothy, 2816
Edelman, Ethel M., 2707
Edelman, Marian W., 489
Edelman, Peter B., 2773
Edelman, Richard, 2707
Edelman, Stanley, 2781
Edelstein, Lester, 3583
Eden, William J., 32
Eder Bros., 515
Eder, Andrew J., 515
Eder, Arthur, 515
Eder, Jo Ann, 4147
Eder, Sidney, 515
Ederer, David, 4259
Edey, Helen, 2913
Edge, Robert G., 855
Edgerton, Bradford W., 4178
Edgerton, M.T., Jr., 3423
Edgerton, Malcolm J., Jr., 63, 2493
Edgerton, Patricia Jones, 4178
Edgerton, William A., 4178
Edison Brothers Stores, 1957
Edison, Bernard, 1957
Edison, Charles, 2119
Edison, Harry, 1958
Edison, Irving, 1958
Edison, Julian, 1957
Edison, Patricia H., 1715
Edman, J.R., 1709, 1710
Edmonds, Campbell S., 4200
Edmonds, Clarence, 3852
Edmonds, E.H., 806
Edmonds, W. Campbell, 4200
Edmondson, J. Richard, 2302
Edmondson, Jerry C., 3903
Edson, Catherine H., 3969
Edson, Thomas H., 3969
Edwards, A. Winston, 3713
Edwards, B.L., 3809
Edwards, Charles C., Jr., 1262
Edwards, D.R., 1297, 4274
Edwards, Don Raby, 4198
Edwards, Donald, 3858
Edwards, Edith W., 797
Edwards, Gene, 3974
Edwards, Grace M., 1520
Edwards, Helen Fraser, 3939
Edwards, J.N., 4147
Edwards, James B., 2513
Edwards, James C., 2620
Edwards, Kathleen Bryan, 3083
Edwards, Larry, 3925
Edwards, Lillian, 3935, 3936
Edwards, Lillian Perry, 4191
Edwards, Loyd L., 3939
Edwards, Morris D., 797
Edwards, Patrick, 2230
Edwards, Ray, 1840
Edwards, Richard D., 3651
Edwards, Robert, 2109
Edwards, Rodney J., 1839
Edwards, Ron, 3481
Edwards, William E., 4147
Edwards, William H., 962
Edwards, William J., 1671
Eells, Richard, 3028
Efrid, C.L., Jr., 3799
Efrid, C.L., Sr., 3818

Efroymson, Clarence W., 1216
Efroymson, Robert A., 1216, 1226
EG&G, 1521
Egan, Eugene L., 2187
Egan, Evelyn Wilson, 4122
Egan, John V., Jr., 977
Egan, Leo A., 2711
Eggleston, Gloria E., 1020
Eggum, John, 1130
Egler, Ruth D., 3558
Egli, Herbert, 2924
Ehlers, Fred G., 1850
Ehlers, Walter G., 2344
Ehre, Victor T., 3005
Ehrenkranz, Joel S., 3038
Ehrhardt, Thomas H., 1971
Ehrlich, Delia F., 172
Ehrlich, John Stephen, Jr., 172
Ehrlich, P.S., Jr., 433
Ehrlich, Richard M., 2468
Ehrmann, Amelia S., 2918
Eichenbaum, Inez, 160
Eichenbaum, J.K., 160
Eichenbaum, Sidney C., 160
Eichenberg, Joyce N., 2486
Eichler, Franklin R., 3720
Eichman, Thelma L., 683
Eide, R.P., 3187
Eide, Richard P., 3285
Eidman, Kraft W., 3875
Einan, Michael J., 1835
Einbender, Alvin, 2747
Eirich, Constance, 3396
EIS Automotive, 517
Eiseman, Marion, 1491
Eiseman, Paul, 1142
Eisen, Herman N., 2446
Eisen, M.J., 2249
Eisenberg, Barbara K., 563
Eisenberg, Fillmore B., 832
Eisenberg, George M., 996
Eisenberg, Joseph, 2850
Eisenberg, Saul, 2850
Eisenhardt, Elizabeth Haas, 202
Eisner, Margaret D., 2378
Eisner, Morton, 494
Eitel, Karl E., 445
Eklund, Dariel Ann, 1016
Eklund, Dariel P., 1016
Eklund, Kent, 1877
Eklund, Roger P., 1016, 1962
Eklund, Sally S., 1016
Ekman, E.V., 3037
Ekstrom, N.K., 4308
El Paso National Bank, 3980, 3992
Elam, Lloyd C., 2155, 2938
Elastic Fabrics of America, 3797
Elbaum, Ruth, 1070
Elberson, Robert E., 1139
Elden, A.D., 2939
Elden, Vera, 2939
Eldred, Robert, 2849
Eldridge, Huntington, 956
Eldridge, Huntington, Jr., 956
Elfers, William, 522
Elgin, Vera M., 1910
Elias, Albert J., 3538
Elias, Clifford E., 1614, 1630
Elias, Norma, 3559
Elicker, Paul, 2924
Eliel, S.E., 2247
Elinoff, Yetta, 3615
Eliot, Allen E., 1157
Elish, Herbert, 2574
Elkins, J.A., III, 3941
Elkins, J.A., Jr., 3941, 3960
Elkins (Lewis) Fund, 3665
Elkins, W.S., 3941
Elkins, William L., 3749
Ellingson, Edward, 3139
Ellington, Charles P., 834
Elliot, Grover S., 4166
Elliot, Osborn, 644
Elliott, A. Wright, 2337

Elliott, Carol K., 139
Elliott, Eleanor T., 2346, 2445
Elliott, Frank G., Jr., 502
Elliott, George B., 1233
Elliott, Irma B., 3452
Elliott, J.A., 1294
Elliott, John J., 2156
Elliott, Lloyd H., 680
Elliott, Thomas, 3129
Elliott, Thomas L., Jr., 575
Ellis, Belle L., 396
Ellis, Douglas B., 4160
Ellis, Elizabeth W., 2120
Ellis, Hayne, III, 1980
Ellis, Henry, 3961
Ellis, Herbert O., 1664
Ellis, Jim, 359
Ellis, John B., 813, 820
Ellis, John O., 3827
Ellis, Lucille T., 396
Ellis, Peter S., 1555
Ellis, R.A.L., 1980
Ellis, Raymond G., 2120
Ellis, Sally Long, 1980
Ellis, Willard L., 130, 202, 203, 204
Ellis, William D., Jr., 861
Ellis, William S., 2533
Ellison, C.D., 3441, 3470
Ellison, C. Don, 3451
Ellison, Eben H., 1522
Ellison, Edward, 1850
Ellison, Robert, 4242
Ellison, Spearl, 220
Ellison, William P., 1522
Ellsam, Anna, 2854
Ellsworth, David H., 1523
Ellsworth, John E., 520
Ellsworth, Robert, 659
Ellsworth, Ruth H., 1523
Ellwood, D.C., 3942
Ellwood, Irene L., 3942
Elmhurst National Bank, 1178
Elmore, Dale, 1390
Elmquist, Holger N., 3753
Eloise and Richard Webber Foundation, 1722
Elrod, Donald S., 1094
Elrod, Maxine, 1094
Elrod, Scott M., 1094
Elston, Frances Beinecke, 2842
Elston, Lloyd W., 548
Elston, Mrs. Lloyd W., 548
Elston, Richard L., 548
Elwell, Joanne, 1830
Elworth, James E., 1068, 1110
Ely, Hiram B., Jr., 2188
Ely, J. Wallace, 2382
Ely, Leonard, 341
Ely, Richard, 1520
Ely, William L., 2382
Elyria City, 3205
Eman, John, 1664
Emerson, David L., 2421
Emerson Electric Company, 1959
Emerson, Fred L., 2421
Emerson, H. Truxtun, Jr., 3409
Emerson, Lee, 191
Emerson, Peter J., 2421
Emerson, Tilly-Jo B., 2161
Emerson, William V., 2421
Emery Air Freight Corporation, 518
Emery, Ethan, 3326
Emery, John C., Jr., 518
Emery, John C., Sr., 518
Emery, Mrs. John C., Sr., 518
Emery, John J., 3326
Emery, John M., 625, 2346
Emery, Mary Muhlenberg, 3206
Emery, Theodora C., 3530
Emery, Walter C., 442
Emery, William K., 1793
Emke, Robert W., Jr., 1770
Emmanuel, Michael G., 765
Emmber Brands, 4364

Emmert, John C., 2290
Emmet, M., 560
Emory, Katherine R., 2908
Empsall, Frank A., 3027
Endo Laboratories, 2617
Enemark, Fred, 79
Engel, Edward G., 2127, 2195
Engel, Joseph G., 2127, 2134, 2195
Engel, William V., 2127, 2195
Engelhard, Charlene B., 2121
Engelhard, Charles, 2121
Engelhard Hanovia, Inc., 2121
Engelhard, Jane B., 2121
Engelhard, Sophie, 2121
Engelhardt, L.A., 4310
Engelhardt, Rebecca A., 1749
Engelhardt, Sara L., 2325
Engelman, Donald M., 3037
Engels, Robert H., 1845
Engeman, Frances, 2145
England, Joseph W., 987
England, Lois H., 1421
England, Richard, 1421
Engle, Carmel Joan, 3779
Engle, Frank M., 3425
Engle, Fred S., 3720
Englehardt, E.A., 1021
Engleman, Ephraim P., 207
Engleman, Gene E., 3357
Engleman, Thomas E., 2117
Engler, R.E., 1183
Englert, Herbert C., 2171
Englert, Joseph F., 822
Engles, Earl F., Jr., 1688
English, E.R., 4168
English, E.R., Jr., 4168
English, Florence Cruft, 830
English, John W., 2444
English, Louise T., 4169
English, Margaret B., 3729
English, Mary Tower, 1212
English, W.C., 4168, 4169
Enlow, Mary, 185
Enlund, E. Stanley, 971
Ennis, Charles W., 434
Eno, William Phelps, 519
Enright, Joseph J., 1960
ENSERCH Corporation, 3943, 4018
Ensign, Chester O., Jr., 491
Ensign, Elizabeth, 483
Ensign-Bickford Industries, 520
Ensworth, Antoinette L., 521
Entmacher, Paul S., 2732
Entrikin, Ronald H., 927
Enyart, J.C., 1276
Epperson, George A., 485
Eppig, Ruth Swetland, 3360
Eppinga, Augusta, 1767
Epps, Claude M., Jr., 3088
Epps, Edgar G., 873
Epstein, Bennett N., 615
Epstein, E. Allan, 1167
Epstein, E.A., 933
Epstein, Florence, 963
Epstein, Jeffrey, 1167
Epstein, Louis R., 3540
Epstein, Paul H., 2391
Epstein, Rae W., 1167
Epstein, Stanley, 2305
Epstein, Stuart, 1167
Equibank, 3685, 3693
Equifax Inc., 831
Equitable Bank, 1413
Equitable Trust Co., 1416
Equitable Trust Company, 1419
Erburu, Robert, 154, 217
Erburu, Robert F., 240, 321, 400
Erdman, Christian P., 2081
Erdman, Frank, 692
Erdmann, Jack, 1904
Ericksen, George W., 704
Erickson, Betty, 2339
Erickson, J.D., 136
Erickson, John R., 309

Erickson, M.A., 944
Erickson, Marti, 341
Erickson, R.L., 932
Erickson, Robert E., 3496
Ericson, James D., 4303
Eriksen, Rolf F., 615
Eriksmoen, A.M., 3143
Erikson, Karl H., 927
Erker, William H., 2035
Ernst & Whinney Partnership, 3207
Ernst, Katherine R., 2263
Ernst, Richard C., 2290
Ernst, Robert, 2263
Ernst, Susan B., 2290
Ernsthausen, Doris E., 3208
Ernsthausen, John F., 3208
Erpf, Armand G., 2422
Erskine, George B., 3564
Ervin, John B., 1955
Erving Paper Mills, 1558
Erwin, Willard H., Jr., 4285
Esbenshade, Richard D., 292
Escalera, Yasha, 521
Escherich, William W., 246
Escola, A.R., 87
Escott, Barry, 2403
Eshelman, Ray H., 3170
Eshleman, Jon W., 1738
Eskew, W.T., 1138
Eskridge, Tilford, 3419
Esmark, Inc., 939
Esmiol, Morris A., 476
Esmiol, Morris A., Jr., 476
Ess, Henry N., III, 2248
Essick, Bryant, 161
Essick Investment Company, 161
Essick, James H., 161
Essick, Jeanette Marie, 161
Essick, Robert N., 161
Estes, Carroll, 684
Estes, Clementine Z., 2912
Estey Charitable Income Trust, 1550
Estill, Barbara Tweed, 2912
Estrin, Mary, 1848
Estrin, Robert L., 1848
Etsen, Nan Van, 4152
Ettelson, Jerome L., 216
Ettinger, Barbara, 516
Ettinger, Elsie, 516
Ettinger, Elsie A., 2423
Ettinger, Richard P., 516
Ettinger, Richard P., Jr., 516, 2423
Ettinger, Virgil P., 516
Etzwiler, Marion, 1887
Etzwiler, Marion G., 1845
Eulau, Milton B., 2663, 2936
Eure, Dexter D., 1483
Eurich, Nell P., 2109
Euwer, Paul, Jr., 3620
Evans, Barbara W., 2204
Evans, Betty B., 2424
Evans, Christina, 3566
Evans, Daniel F., 1197
Evans, Daniel J., 2109, 2995
Evans, David W., Jr., 1313
Evans, Dennis E., 1842
Evans, Dennis L., 1315
Evans, E. Hervey, Jr., 3117
Evans, E.T., 3887
Evans, Edward P., 2424, 2688
Evans, Eli N., 2858
Evans, Geraldine, 3566
Evans, H.G., 768
Evans, H.L., 1194
Evans, Hugh McC., 1368
Evans, J. Lloyd, 3161
Evans, James H., 2875, 2997
Evans, John C., 2682
Evans, John H., 2204
Evans, John R., 2877
Evans, Kay J., 398
Evans, L.K., 1196
Evans, Lettie Pate, 832
Evans, McNair, 3117

Evans, N. Earle, 2331
Evans, Ray W., 3842
Evans, Thomas J., 3209
Evans, Thomas M., 3827
Evans, Thomas M., Jr., 2424
Evans, Thomas Mellon, 2424
Evarts, William M., Jr., 2347, 2774
Evelt, Sibylle, 2541
Evening Post Publishing Company, 3812
Everest, Jean I., 3451
Everets, Pamela, 1475
Everett, Fred M., 2425
Everett, Herbert E., 1774
Everett, Morris, 3258
Everett, Ora H., 2425
Everitt, S.A., 542
Evers, William L., 2411
Eversole, Mrs. Urban H., 1481
Evey, S.W., 188
Evinrude, Frances, 4315
Evinrude, Ralph, 4315
Evinrude, Ralph S., 997
Evjue, William T., 4316
Ewald, Russell V., 1880
Ewalt, H. Ward, 3408
Ewan, George E., 4402
Eweson, Dorothy Dillon, 2273, 2399
Ewing, Bayard, 3786
Ewing, Dan C., 1336
Ewing, Gretchen G., 3236
Ewing, Robert P., 1077, 1132
Ewing, Rumsey, 1985
Ewing, Virginia Wilson, 4122
Ex-cell-o Corporation, 1694
Exley, C.E., Jr., 3314
Exxon Corporation, 2426
Eyman, Jesse, 3210
Eyre, Stephen C., 2769

Faber, Herbert A., 1331
Faber, Mrs. Herbert A., 1331
Faber, Herbert H., 2392
Faber, Mrs. Stuart L., 1331
Faber, Stuart L., 1331
Faberson, Paul, 1046
Fabian, Larry L., 644
Factor, David Jack, Jr., 162
Fad, Otto C., 605
Fads, Pauline, 2008
Fafian, Joseph, Jr., 492
Fagan, Helene Irwin, 231
Faggioli, R.E., 2426
Fahey, Donald E., 1965
Fahey, J. James, 2416
Fahrney, Helen, 1265
Faigle, Ida M., 1695
Faile, David Hall, Jr., 514
Faile, John B., 514
Fain, Mary J., 1374
Fain, Norman M., 3787, 3790
Fair, David, 3380
Fair, James W., 3945
Fair, Kenneth R., 3318
Fair, Mattie Allen, 3945
Fair, R.W., 3945
Fair, Wilton H., 3945
Fairchild Industries, 1414
Fairchild, May, 522
Fairchild, Sherman, 522
Faircloth, Nancy Bryan, 3083
Fairey, Kittie Moss, 3803
Fairfield, Freeman E., 163, 446
Fairhurst, T.J., 3196
Fairman, Endsley P., 621
Falcone, John R., 3565
Falcone, Lynn R., 2735
Falcone, Michael J., 2331
Faldet, Marion M., 1160
Falencki, Karin, 2595
Faler, Robert, 3397
Fales, Haliburton, II, 2197
Fales, John R., Jr., 3780
Fales, Judith S., 1146

Falk Corporation, 4317
Falk, David A., 720
Falk, Isidore, 2428
Falk, Karl, 2911
Falk, Leon, Jr., 3567
Falk, Loti G., 3567
Falk, Marian, 998
Falk, Marian C., 998
Falk, Marjorie L., 3567
Falk, Mary Irene McKay, 720
Falk, Maurice, 2428
Falk (Maurice and Laura) Foundation, 3568
Falk, Myron, 1354
Falk, Myron S., Jr., 2775
Falk, Pauline, 2643
Falk, Randall, 3865
Falk, Sigo, 3567, 3568
Fall, John, 3047
Fallon, Gail A., 510
Fallon, Goeffrey D., 4060
Fallon, James P., 2455
Falor, Ann, 3145
Falsgraf, William W., 3229
Fambrough, John A., 3973
Familian, Elizabeth, 164
Familian, Gary, 164
Familian, Isadore, 164
Familian, Zalec, 165
Fancher, Edwin, 1248
Fannon, John J., 4248
Fant, John F., Jr., 3282
Fant, W.F., 794
Farb, W.L., 1003
Farber, Denise L., 1759
Farfel, Aaron J., 4125
Fargo National Bank and Trust Company, 3139
Faris, John P., 3808
Farish, Libbie Rice, 3947
Farish, W.S., III, 3947
Farley, J. Michael, 442
Farley, James D., 2528
Farley, Raymond E., 1060
Farley, Raymond F., 4336
Farm Service Company, 93
Farmer, Bill J., 31, 38
Farmer, Mrs. L. Wayne, 3840
Farmers and Merchants State Bank, 1292
Farmers State Bank, 459, 471
Farnsworth, Charles H., 1526
Farnsworth, D.E., 4076
Farquhar, F. James, 4060
Farr, C. Sims, 2362
Farr, F.W. Elliott, 3634
Farrar, Marjorie M., 2724
Farrell, Anne V., 4259
Farrell, David C., 1991
Farrell, George T., 3661
Farrell, Gregory R., 2460
Farrell, James P., 2455
Farrell, Neal J., 1996
Farris, Mrs. W. Clayton, Jr., 2164
Farver, Mary Joan, 1273, 1280
Fashion Bar, 462
Fasken, Andrew A., 3948
Fasken, F. Andrew, 3948
Fasken, Murray, 3948
Fasken, Steven P., 3948
Fast, Eric C., 2688
Fate, Martin E., Jr., 3903
Fatzinger, Walter R., Jr., 669
Faude, C. Frederick, 166
Faulkner, E.J., 2054
Faulkner, Marianne Gaillard, 2429
Faulkner, William B., 1807
Faulstich, George L., 1095
Fauntleroy, Gaylord, 1966
Fauver, Scribner L., 3284
Favrot, C. Allen, 1358
Favrot, Clifford F., 1358
Favrot, Clifford F., Jr., 1358
Favrot, D. Blair, 1358
Favrot, Johanna A., 3949

Favrot, Laurence de Kanter, 3949
Favrot, Laurence H., 3949
Favrot, Marcia, 3949
Favrot, Thomas B., 1358
Fawcett, Daniel W., 1500, 1643
Fay, Michael E., 3216
Fay, Paul B., Jr., 303
Fay, Thomas J., 3392
Fay, William E., Jr., 2940
FDL Foods, 1288
Feagin, Louise Milby, 3972
Feagin, Patrick B., 3972
Feaker, Darrell L., 1046
Fearn, George B., 65
Fearnley, John, 2272
Fearon, Charles, 3665
Fearon, Janet A., 2162
Featherman, Sandra, 3571
Fechter, John, 2009
Feder, Robert, 3139
Federal, Joseph L., 567
Federal National Mortgage Association, 651
Federal Republic of Germany, 659
Federal-Mogul Corporation, 1696
Federated Department Stores, 3211
Federer, Gloria B., 1726
Feehan, Thomas J., 3970
Feehily, Walter P., 103
Feeney, J.E., 3540
Feeney, Thomas E., 118, 338
Feese, Phyllis, 3695
Fehr, Robert O., 2541
Fehsenfeld, David T., 1449
Feil, Francis A., 2469
Feinberg, Herbert D., 3033
Feinberg, Midge, 1070
Feiner, Gordon A., 3780
Feinstein, Myer, 3570
Feinstein, Rosaline B., 3570
Feinstein, Samuel, 3570
Feit, Susan, 1070
Feitelson, Helen L., 167
Feitelson, Lorser, 167
Feitler, Joan, 4311
Feitler, Robert, 2939
Fel-Pro Incorporated, 1000, 1107
Fel-Pro International, 1000
Fel-Pro Realty, 1000
Felburn, J. Phil, 652
Feld, Selma S., 1961
Feldberg, Max, 1527
Feldberg, Morris, 1527
Feldberg, Stanley H., 1527, 1661
Feldberg, Sumner, 1527, 1661
Feldman, Daniel E., 3950
Feldman, Irwin M., 3389
Feldman, Jacob, 3950
Feldman, Moses, 3950
Feldman, Robert L., 3950
Feldstein, Judy, 2631
Feldstein, Richard, 2631
Felheim, Lasalle, 2583
Feliciotti, E., 2150
Felix, Patricia Berry, 93
Felker, Jean, 2197
Fellows, J.H., 3383
Fellows, Virginia A., 3373
Fellows-Williamson, Earle W., 721
Felmer, Andrew R., 3185
Felmeth, William H., 2204
Feloney, Lawrence F., 1491
Fels, Samuel S., 3571
Felt, David, 3158
Felt Products Manufacturing Co., 1000, 1131
Felts, C.B., Jr., 3959
Felts, James R., Jr., 3095
Fenelon, Margaret, 4075
Fenlon, Thomas, 2915
Fennell, Doris, 2902
Fenniman, W.C., 500
Fenno, J. Brooks, 1547
Fenstermacher, H.R., 31

Fenton, Elinor P., 4282
Fenton, Frank M., 4282
Fenton, John L., 3063
Fenton, Thomas K., 4282
Fenton, Wilmer C., 4282
Fenzi, Warren E., 340, 2825
Ferald (Cyrus F.) Trust, 795
Ferdenanatsen, G.R., 4023
Ferebee, Percy, 3097
Ferga, Garland P., 1431
Ferguson, A. Barlow, 88, 251
Ferguson, Alfred, 2625
Ferguson, Ann, 1910
Ferguson, Arch L., 3951
Ferguson, C. Clyde, Jr., 644
Ferguson, David G., 2134
Ferguson, Embry, 4040
Ferguson, Isaac C., 4145
Ferguson, Mrs. Robert G., 340
Ferguson, Robert H.M., 3042
Ferkauf, Estelle, 2430
Ferkauf, Eugene, 2430
Fernald, David G., 2578, 2875, 2876
Fernandes, Alvin C., Jr., 1197
Fernandez, Louis, 1999
Fero, Franklin L., 2243
Ferree, Joseph Craig, 3735
Ferris, Dakin B., 2728
Ferris, Richard J., 928, 1179
Ferris, Sally, 2314
Ferro Corporation, 3212
Ferst, Stanley, 3569
Festivale Maritime, 691
Fetsch, Carter, 3483
Feudner, John L., Jr., 3145
Feulner, Edwin, Jr., 3814
Feville, Richard H., 3940
Fewin, H.R., 966
Fey, Eugene C., 2245, 2830
Fey, John T., 187
ffolliot, Sheila, 1894
Ficke, Carl H., 2257
Fiddler, T. Robert, 1368
Fidelity Bank, 3588, 3689, 3742, 3766
Fidelity File Box, 1844
Fidelity Management & Research Co., 1528
Fidelity National Bank, 1354
Fidelity Union Bank, 2122
Fidler, D.E., 4286
Fiduciary Trust Company of New York, 2774
Field, Arthur Norman, 2305, 2846
Field, Benjamin R., 1818
Field, Edward J., 368
Field, Evelyn B., 3050
Field Foundation, 1001
Field, Frances K., 2493
Field, Irwin S., 368
Field, John W., 587
Field, Lyman, 1954, 2629
Field, Marshall, 970, 1001
Field, Marshall, III, 2432
Field, Marshall, IV, 1001
Field, Reginald H., 4027
Field, Ruth P., 2432
Fieldcrest Mills, 3098
Fielder, C. Robert, 3970
Fields, D. Wallace, 734
Fields, Gregory F., 600
Fields, Joyce M., 321
Fields, Laura, 3429
Fields, Laura Kemper, 1974
Fields, Leo, 4129
Fields, Murray M., 108
Fields, Richard B., 873
Fields, Samuel, 2655
Fiene, James R., 4336
Fies, Larry R., 4252
Fife, Arlene, 2433
Fife, Bernard, 2433
Fife, Francis H., 4191
Fifer, Albert C., 942

Fifth Third Bank, 3148, 3183, 3214, 3353, 3354, 3355
Fikes, Catherine W., 3952
Fikes, Lee, 3952
Fikes, Leland, 3952
Filene, Edward A., 2995
Filene, Lincoln, 1529
Filer, John H., 3750
Finberg, Barbara D., 2325, 2775
Finch, Charles B., 2689
Finch, David, 3100
Finch, Doak, 3099
Finch, Edward R., Jr., 425, 2219
Finch, Edward Ridley, Jr., 2866
Finch, Elizabeth Lathrop, 2866
Finch, Mrs. Herman, 1070
Finch, John, 3100
Finch, Meredith Slane, 3100
Finch, Nathan C., 308
Finch, Pauline Swayze, 2219
Finch, Sumner, 3100
Finch, Thomas Austin, Jr., 3100
Findlay, Duncan M., 2792
Findley, Barry, 60
Finger, Gregory, 1494
Finger, Leslie C., 4004
Fingerhut, Manny, 1841
Fingerhut, Ronald, 1841
Fingerhut, Rose, 1841
Fink, David, 2434
Fink, Elise M., 1697
Fink, George R., 1697
Fink, H. Bernerd, 1303
Fink, Herbert, 2985
Fink, Nathan, 2434
Fink, Peter M., 1697
Fink, Ruth G., 1303, 1307
Fink, Vivian R., 2434
Finkbeiner, J.V., 1798
Finlay, John David, Jr., 12
Finlay, Louis M., Jr., 20
Finlay, Mary Fleming, 3823
Finley, A.E., 3101
Finley, J.B., 3573
Finley, John H., 1560
Finley, Raymond, 1698
Finn, Richard L., 2011
Finnegan, Catherine E., 2765
Finnegan, James J., 2058
Finnegan, John D., 3215
Finnegan, Neal F., 1624
Finnegan, Patrick T., 2279
Finnegan, R.J., 3306
Finnegan, W.N., III, 4082
Finney, Graham S., 3717
Fioratti, Helen, 2864
Fiorentini, Walter J., 4318
FIP Corporation, 523
Fireman's Fund Insurance Company, 169
Firestone Tire & Rubber Company, 3216
Firestone, Bernard, 1109
Firestone, Richard, 1726
Firestone, S. Edward, 656
Firman, Pamela H., 3217
First Alabama Bank, 3
First American Bank of Washington, 680, 682
First & Merchants National Bank, 4164
First Atlanta Corporation, 833
First Bank & Trust Company, 1226
First Bank Duluth, 1927
First Bank Milwaukee, 4358
First Bank of Minneapolis, 1842
First Bank of Saint Paul, 1842
First Boston Corporation, 2435
First Buckeye Bank, 3224, 3342
First Citizens Bank and Trust, 3096
First City Bank of Beaumont, 4087
First City Bank of Dallas, 3923
First City Bank-Central Park, 4072
First City National Bank, 3989, 4057
First City National Bank of Houston, 2919, 4015
First Fidelity Bank, 2102, 3740

First Franklin Parking Corp., 1617
First Hawaiian Bank, 902
First Huntington National Bank, 4288
First Interstate Bank, 114, 159, 228, 4259
First Interstate Bank of Arizona, 34
First Interstate Bank of California, 170, 318
First Interstate Bank of California Foundation, 115
First Interstate Bank of Casper, 4397
First Interstate Bank of Denver, 442, 443, 447, 452, 454
First Interstate Bank of Oregon, 3489, 3500
First Interstate Bank of Utah, 1919
First Interstate Bank of Washington, 4219, 4223, 4258, 4273
First Mississippi Corporation, 1936
First Missouri Bank and Trust Company of Creve Coeur, 2020
First National Bank, 958, 1289, 1296, 2033, 3199, 3434, 4040
First National Bank and Trust Company, 1730, 3245, 3430, 3451
First National Bank and Trust Co. of Tulsa, 3418
First National Bank and Trust Company of Rockford, 936, 1003
First National Bank in Massillon, 3373
First National Bank in Wabash, 1244
First National Bank in Wichita, 1304
First National Bank of Akron, 3344
First National Bank of Allentown, 3526
First National Bank of Atlanta, 802, 803, 839, 861, 862, 868
First National Bank of Birmingham, 3
First National Bank of Bluefield, 4277
First National Bank of Bossier, 1383
First National Bank of Boston, 1467, 1496, 1557, 1563, 1589
First National Bank of Chicago, 968, 1002, 1034, 1181
First National Bank of Cincinnati, 3183, 3299
First National Bank of Clearwater, 727, 756
First National Bank of Colorado Springs, 460
First National Bank of Denver, 481
First National Bank of Florida, 756
First National Bank of Glens Falls, 2476
First National Bank of Kansas City, 1952, 1963, 2015, 2017, 2018
First National Bank of Malden, 1577
First National Bank of Maryland, 1415, 1447
First National Bank of Midland, 4058
First National Bank of Minneapolis, 1838, 1843, 1887
First National Bank of Mobile, 2, 20
First National Bank of Ohio, 3145
First National Bank of Pennsylvania, 3565
First National Bank of Shreveport, 1359, 1369, 1383
First National Bank of Toledo, 3386
First National Bank of Topeka, 1312
First National Bank of Tuscaloosa, 23
First National City Bank of Alliance, 3373
First National State Bank of New Jersey, 2163
First Northwestern Trust Company, 3139
First of America Bank, 1754
First of America Bank - Michigan, 1728
First of America Bank-Central, 1735
First Pennsylvania Bank, 3532
First Pennsylvania Banking and Trust Company, 3689, 3719
First Security Bank of Utah, 4131, 4135, 4136, 4139, 4140, 4144
First Seneca Bank, 3562, 3622
First Seneca Bank and Trust Company, 3621, 3639

First State Bank and Trust Company, 842
First State Bank and Trust Co. of Larned, 1314
First Tennessee Bank, 3833, 3844, 3854
First Trust Company of Montana, 2043
First Trust Company of North Dakota, 3139
First Trust Company of St. Paul, 1805, 1840, 1872, 1873, 1898, 1912, 1923
First Trust Corporation, 442
First Union National Bank, 3096, 3137
First Valley Bank, 3526
First Virginia Bank of Tidewater, 4187
First Wisconsin Bankshares Corporation, 4318
First Wisconsin National Bank of Oshkosh, 4361
First Wisconsin Trust Company, 4309, 4321, 4331, 4356, 4358
Firstbank of Westland, 442
First-City Division of Lincoln First Bank, 2795
First-Knox National Bank, 3309
Firth, Nicholas L.D., 2412
Firth, Valli V. Dreyfus, 2412
Fisch, Charles, 1233
Fischbach, Jerome, 2436
Fischel, Harry, 2437
Fischer, Aaron, 1956
Fischer, M. Peter, 1956
Fischer, Malinda B., 2873
Fischer, Miles P., 2301
Fischer, R.L., 3511
Fischer, Robert M., 1899
Fischer, Teresa M., 1956
Fischman, Bernard D., 2295
Fish, D.F., 3638
Fish, Frederick L., 1510
Fish, Harry, 2438
Fish, James B., 3027
Fish, L.M., 200
Fish, Lawrence K., 1589
Fish, Mirtha G., 3953
Fish, Raymond Clinton, 3953
Fish, Vain B., 2438
Fishback, Harmes C., 448
Fishberg, Arthur M., 2758
Fishburne, Junius R., 4191
Fishel, Grace J., 1988
Fisher, Allan H., 1430
Fisher, Arthur M., 1003
Fisher, Arthur M., Jr., 1003
Fisher, Benjamin R., 3535, 3693
Fisher, Mrs. Bruce C., 1531
Fisher, David S., 4391
Fisher, Earl, 4296
Fisher, Eugene, 1754
Fisher, Frederick W., 4390
Fisher, Hinda, 523
Fisher, J. William, 1266
Fisher, James W., 1083
Fisher, John E., 3313
Fisher, John W., 1199
Fisher, Kenneth, 4076
Fisher, L.N., 173
Fisher, Max M., 1771, 2998
Fisher, Orville E., Jr., 1870
Fisher, Richard B., 2325
Fisher, Roy, 640
Fisher (Stanley D.) Trust, 523
Fisher, Vera Maureen, 1003
Fisher, W.S., 3086
Fisher, William D., 3635
Fishman, Felix A., 2758
Fisk, Charles B., 1143
Fisk, Mary A., 2527
Fiske, Mrs. George F., Jr., 3029
Fisken, A.M., 4274
Fist, David, 3464
Fister, Richard E., 1962, 2037
Fister, Virginia M., 2037
Fitchburg Foundry, 2090
Fiterman, Ben, 1844
Fiterman, Michael, 1844

Fittipaldi, F.N., 3302
Fitzer, Isabel, 1768
Fitzgerald, Dennis, 1094
Fitzgerald, Dennis M., 3010
Fitz-Gerald, F. Gregory, 2235
Fitzgerald, James M., 1004
Fitzpatrick, Jean R., 1638
Fitzpatrick, Jerry, 359
Fitzpatrick, Marjorie, 228
Fitzpatrick, Mary Alice, 4046
Fitzpatrick, Nancy, 2982
Fitzpatrick, Thomas C., 83
Fitzpatrick, W.E., 3313
Fitzpatrick, William J., 399
FitzSimmons, R.M., 4294
Fix, Mrs. William C., 4240
Fix, William C., 4240
Fizer, Don, 2704
Fjellman, Carl, 2193
Fjordbak, Edward M., 3911
Flack, Eleanor, 8
Flack, J. Hunter, 8
Flad, Eleanor, 3164
Flad, Eleanor Beecher, 3163
Flad, Erle, 3164
Flad, Erle L., 3163
Flad, Ward Beecher, 3163, 3164
Flagg, Donald, 3376
Flagship National Bank of Miami, 706
Flamm, Alec, 2365
Flamson, Richard J., III, 351
Flanagan, Edward P., 567
Flanagin, Neil, 1142
Flanders, Graeme L., 1466
Flarsheim, Louis, 1963
Flather, Newell, 1506, 1592
Flatt, Jane D., 3359
Flechtner, Richard O., 3027
Fleck, Ernest R., 3140
Fleck, G. Peter, 2390
Fleet National Bank, 3775, 3778, 3783
Flegel, Dorothy, 3492
Fleischer, Charles H., 683
Fleischman, Charles D., 2781
Fleischman, Henry L., 2781
Fleischmann, Burd Blair S., 3220
Fleischmann, Charles, III, 3220
Fleischmann, Julius, 3220
Fleischmann, Ruth H., 3048
Fleisher, Hilda W., 2083
Fleishhacker, David, 171
Fleishhacker, Janet C., 171
Fleishhacker, Leslie, 172
Fleishhacker, Mortimer, III, 172
Fleishhacker, Mortimer, Jr., 171
Fleishhacker, Mortimer, Sr., 172
Fleishman, Joel L., 2700
Fleming, Barbara Jane, 712
Fleming, Cres, 440
Fleming, David D., 1096
Fleming, Dean, 2075
Fleming, Harold C., 2773, 2976
Fleming, R.J., 1279
Fleming, Robben W., 4332
Fleming, Robert J., 1270
Fleming, Walter L., Jr., 3912
Fleming, William, 3954
Flemm, John J., 2439
Flemming, Arthur, 684
Flemming, Arthur S., 685
Fletcher, Charles H., 3661
Fletcher, Denise K., 2777
Fletcher, Henry C., 935
Fletcher, James C., 928
Fletcher, Marion S., 1635
Fletcher, Paris, 1468, 1533, 1635
Fletcher, Warner S., 1635
Flettrich, Albert J., 1362, 1368
Flexman, Ralph E., 742
Flick, John E., 400
Flickinger, F. Miles, 3221
Flickinger, Irma L., 3221
Flickinger, Marhl P., 3221
Flickinger, William J., 3221

Fligg, Loren L., 4298
Flinn, Irene, 35
Flinn, Lewis B., Jr., 4213
Flinn, Robert S., 35
Flint, Flora G., 3322
Flint, Mrs. Lucile E. d.P., 606
Flood, James C., 423
Florida National Bank, 716, 756
Florida National Bank of Miami, 706
Florio, Margaret, 2400
Florman, Marvin S., 697
Flory, Lee J., 1022
Flott, George T., 3868
Flournoy, Houston, 240
Flowers, Albert W., 3222
Flowers, D.F., 3223
Flowers, Edith V., 3222
Flowers, F.F., 3223
Flowers, Langdon S., 813
Flowers, Robert, 4269
Flowers, Walter C., III, 1362
Flowers, Worthington C., 3593
Floyd, Ben D., Jr., 3449
Floyd, C.T., 4063
Floyd, Franklin B., 3403
Floyd, Maynard, 717
Flug, Laura Gurwin, 2518
Fluharty, Orland, 2086
Fluor Corporation, 173
Fluor, J.R., II, 173
Fluornoy, H.I., 266
Fluri, G.J., 4166
Flynn, E. Paul, 2421
Flynn, Edward J., 274
Flynn, Grayce B. Kerr, 3439
Flynn, James L., 2368
Flynn, Richard J., 1588
Flynn, Thomas J., 1344
FMB Lumbermans' Bank, 1754
FMC Corporation, 1005, 4214
Focht, James L., 327
Fockler, John K., 3854
Foellinger, Esther A., 1213
Foellinger, Helene R., 1213
Foerderer, Ethel Brown, 3574
Foerderer, Percival E., 3574
Foerstner, George C., 1269
Fogarty, W. Philip, 1431
Fogel, Daniel, 4061
Fogel, Mrs. Herbert, 3765
Fogelson, David, 743
Fogerty, Arthur J., 2224
Fogg, Margery, 3417
Fohs, Cora B., 3484
Fohs, F. Julius, 3484
Folbre, Katherine Netting, 4072
Folbre, Thomas W., 4111
Foley, Adrian M., Jr., 2161, 2167
Foley, Frank M., 2908
Foley, P.A., 1227
Folger, John Dulin, 653
Folger, Kathrine Dulin, 653
Folger, Lee M., 685
Folger, Lee Merritt, 653
Folger, Neil Clifford, 653
Folkert, R.A., 249
Follansbee Steel Corporation, 3169
Follis, R. Gwen, 281
Folsom, Charles Stuart, 524
Fomon, Robert, 2569
Fondren, Ellanor Ann, 3956
Fondren, Mrs. W.W., Sr., 3956
Fondren, Walter W., III, 3956
Fonseca, Elizabeth K., 2598
Fonseca, Isabel, 2598
Fonseca, Quina, 2598
Fontaine, Douglass L., 1930
Fontaine, John C., 2629
Foorman, Mrs. Sidney, 364
Foote, A.M., Jr., 762
Foote, Cone & Belding Communications, 1006
Foote, Emerson, 2926
Foote, Mrs. Robert, 968

Foote, Robert L., 1041
Foote, Robert T., 4331
Foote, William D., 1434
Forbes, F. Murray, Jr., 1619, 1622
Forbes, Herman, 2441
Forbes, Inc., 2440
Forbes, J.I., 2045
Forbes, Malcolm S., 2440
Forbes, Malcolm S., Jr., 2440
Forbes, William A., 548
Forchheimer, Julia, 2442
Forchheimer, Leo, 2442
Forchheimer, Rudolph, 2442
Ford, Ada, 3224
Ford, Allen H., 3264
Ford, Benson, 1699
Ford, C.G., 3661
Ford, David K., 3285
Ford, Edsel, 2444
Ford, Edward E., 2443
Ford, Eleanor Clay, 1700
Ford, F. Richards, III, 2692
Ford Foundation, 646, 676, 2460
Ford, Frank I., Jr., 72
Ford, Hallie E., 3485
Ford, Harry, 2727
Ford, Henry, 2444
Ford, Henry, II, 1700, 1701
Ford, Jefferson L., Jr., 722
Ford, Josephine F., 1700, 1703
Ford, Kenneth W., 3485, 3500
Ford, Martha F., 1704
Ford Motor Company, 1702
Ford, Natasha B., III, 2692
Ford, Thomas P., 243, 2340, 2607
Ford, Walter B., II, 1703
Ford, William Clay, 1700, 1702, 1704
Ford, William D., 2360
Fordyce, Alice, 2640
Fordyce, Anne B., 2640
Fordyce, James W., 2640
Foreman, Charles W.L., 584
Foreman, Eugene, 1452, 1453
Foreman, Robert L., Jr., 861
Foremost-McKesson, 283
Forer, Lois G., 3717
Forest City Enterprises, 3225
Forest City Realty, 517
Forest Lawn Co., 174
Forest Oil Corporation, 3582
Forester, Alice Woodson, 4390
Forester, Herschel V., 4080
Forester, John E., 4390
Forger, Alexander D., 2656
Forkner, Joanne S., 2138
Forlini, Rina, 2689
Forman, Roxanne P., 1901
Forman, Willis M., 1901
Formo, Peter L., 27
Formon, Willis M., 1912
Forrest, H.E., 3384, 3385
Forrow, Brian D., 2098
Forsham, Peter H., 369
Forster, Peter H., 3378
Forsyth, James G., 1985
Forsythe, Peter W., 2346
Fort Howard Paper Company, 4319
Fort Wayne National Bank, 1205, 1212
Fort, Daniel M., 964
Fort, W. Howard, 3239
Fortado, M.G., 3943, 4018
Forte, Edward A., 2279
Fortin, Dorothy, 2044
Fortin, Mary Alice, 2044
Fortin, Philip N., 2044
Fortino, A.P., 3684
Fortner, J.G., 1709
Foshay, William Ward, 2736
Foster Industries, 3575
Foster, Dale E., 3309
Foster, Daniel H., 1118
Foster, E.M., 3223
Foster, Esther, 1530
Foster, Esther J., 1530

Foster, J. Galen, 79
Foster, J.R., 3575
Foster, Jay L., 3575
Foster, John B., 1048
Foster, John H., 4072
Foster, John K., 3728
Foster, Lawrence T., 3386
Foster, Margery S., 2167
Foster, Steven L., 3346
Foster, T. Jack, 318
Foster, William E., 3284
Foulke, Roy A., Jr., 2911
Foulkrod, Fred A., 3695
Fountain, Jay Dee, 3429
Fountain, June S., 1554
Fountain, N. Jean, 1905
Fountain, Ronald G., 3405
Fountaine, George J., 2513
Four Wheels, Inc., 1009
Fourth National Bank and Trust Company, 1305
Fowle, William C., 2443
Fowler, Anderson, 2105
Fowler, F. David, 2817
Fowler, Pearl Gunn, 655
Fowler, R.G., 3943
Fox, Emma R., 3226
Fox, Fred, Jr., 409
Fox, Julius I., 1462
Fox, Lewis, 525
Fox, Mary P., 1331, 1351
Fox, P. Fred, 2521
Fox, Renee, 2902
Fox, Richard, 1695
Fox, Robert P., 1807
Fox, William F., 4352
Foy, Douglas J., 1199, 1200
Foy, Lewis W., 3239
Fraas, Richard J., 3391
Fraenkel, Fabian I., 3627
Frager, Albert F., 1639
Frahm, Donald R., 534
Fraim, Martha B., 3170
Frampton, John, 4376
France Stone Company, 3227
France, Annita A., 1416
France, George A., 3227
France, Jacob, 1416
France, Phyllis B., 1823
Francis, Dorothy E., 2249
Francis, Gaylord E., 1208
Francis, Joe, 3421
Francis, John B., 1324
Francis, John R., 1671
Francis, Mary B., 1324
Francis, Norman, 2109
Francis, Parker B., 1324
Francis, Parker B., III, 1306
Francis, Richard H., 2237
Francisco, Leon A., 524
Francqe, Albert, III, 2926
Frank, A.J., 3486
Frank, Barney, 684
Frank, Curtiss E., 2217
Frank, D.D., 3486
Frank, Elaine S., 1009
Frank, J.T., 3486
Frank, James S., 1009
Frank, L.D., 3486
Frank Lumber Co., 3486
Frank, Roxanne Harris, 1030
Frank, Sam, 175
Frank, Seth E., 2684
Frank, Thomas, 2387
Frank Timber Products, 3486
Frank (Z.), Inc., 1009
Frank, Zollie S., 1009
Frank, Mrs. Zollie S., 1070
Frankart, Thomas F., 3760
Frankel, Elizabeth F., 2449
Frankel, G. David, 2449
Frankel, George, 2449
Frankel, Joan Murtaugh, 2494
Frankenbach, Charles H., Jr., 2201

Frankenhoff, Mary Ann, 379
Frankenhoff, William P., 512
Frankenthal, Betty J., 4320
Franklin, Alice, 829
Franklin, Andrew D., 829, 2787
Franklin, Barbara Hackman, 489
Franklin, Calvin, 685
Franklin, Carl M., 380, 418
Franklin, Haswell, 1412
Franklin, James R., 2962
Franklin, John, 835
Franklin, John P., 3835
Franklin, M.B., 3098
Franklin Manufacturing Company, 3405
Franklin, Mary O., 835
Franklin, Shirley C., 803
Franklin, William P., 3948
Frankos, P.E., 11
Franks, George V., 2167
Franks, Mrs. M.B., 2324
Franks, Myron B., 2465
Frantz, Curtis J., 609
Franz, J.H., 4301
Frasch, Elizabeth Blee, 2450
Fraser, Douglas A., 242, 684
Fraser, Harry James, Jr., 4013
Fraser, Howard H., 3231
Fraser, James H., 2424
Fraser, K.W., Jr., 3098
Fraser, Leila, 4353
Fraser, Malcolm H., 3858
Fraser, Marilee, 1237
Fratus, Ruth, 2476
Frauenthal, Harold, 1754
Frawley, F. Joseph, 428
Fray, J., 1544
Frazel, Jerome V., 973
Frazel, Jerome, Jr., 973
Frazel, Joanne K., 973
Frazer, David R., 35
Frazer, John B., Jr., 326
Frazer, John G., Jr., 3529, 3535, 3691, 3693
Frazier, Betty Mikal, 1360
Frazier, Elizabeth B., 1434
Frazier, J. Walter, 1360
Frazier, James Walter, Jr., 1360
Frear, Mary D., 898
Frear, Walter F., 898
Freas, Arnold O., 520
Freccero, M., 84
Frechette, Priscilla K., 2090
Frederichs, Doris, 1200
Frederick, Hugh K., Jr., 3940
Fredericksen, C.J., 3516
Fredricks, Shirley, 422
Fredricksen, C.J., 3761
Fredricksen, Cleve J., 3628
Fredrickson, Robert R., 290
Free, James L., Jr., 340
Freeauf, Gilbert C., 2523
Freed, Elizabeth Ann, 656
Freed, Frances W., 656
Freed, Gerald A., 656
Freedman, Joseph, 1720
Freedman, Peggy, 3570
Freeland, Alfred B., 1361
Freeman, Betty, 424
Freeman, Carl M., 1417
Freeman, Charles, 652
Freeman, David F., 2125, 2913
Freeman, David L., 3805
Freeman, Gaylord, 1077
Freeman, Harry, 3418
Freeman, Houghton, 2954
Freeman, Jean H., 1910
Freeman, Lewis, 4019
Freeman, Louis M., 1361, 1380
Freeman, Mrs. Montine McD., 1361
Freeman, Orville L., 3001
Freeman, R.H., 1518
Freeman, Richard F., 502
Freeman, Richard W., 1361
Freeman, Richard W., Jr., 1361, 1380

Freeman, Virginia, 1417
Freeman, Wendell R., 1522
Freer, Lester, 2416
Frees, C. Norman, 3957
Frees, Shirley B., 3957
Frehse, Robert M., Jr., 2537, 2538
Frei, Gilbert, 2596
Freidenrich, John, 361
Freidman, Sydney N., 439
Freiert, Don, Jr., 1446
Frelinghuysen, Barratt, 2123
Frelinghuysen, Frederick, 2123
Frelinghuysen, George, 2824
Frelinghuysen, George L.K., 2123
Frelinghuysen, H.O.H., 2123
Frelinghuysen, Mrs. H.O.H., 2123
Frelinghuysen, Peter, 2123, 2218
Frelinghuysen, Mrs. Peter H.B., 2123
Frelinghuysen, Rodney P., 2123
Fremer, Geraldine, 2318
Fremont-Smith, Marion R., 644
French, Clara M., 2451
French, D.E., 2451
French, H. Louis, 1401
French, J. Edward, 1723
French, J. Fred, 2095
French, James H., 2379
Frenkel, Barbara P., 1759
Frenkel, Dale P., 1759
Frenkel, Marvin A., 1759
Frenza, James, 1664
Frenzer, Peter F., 3313
Frese, Arnold D., 2452
Frese, Ines, 2452
Freund, Erwin O., 1010
Freund, Janet W., 1010
Frew, B.L., 1997
Frey, Albert J., 2174
Frey, Donald N., 943
Frey, John H., 2063, 3552
Freygang, Dale G., 2085
Freygang, Dorothy B., 2085
Freygang, Gustav G., Jr., 2085
Freygang, Katherine A., 2085
Freygang, Marie A., 2085
Freygang, W. Nicholas, 2085
Freygang, Walter Henry, 2085
Frezel, Jerrold, 3541
Fribance, Caroline E., 4378
Fribourg, Lucienne, 2453
Fribourg, Mary Ann, 2453
Fribourg, Michel, 2366, 2453
Frick, Helen C., 3576
Frick, Henry C., 3577
Frick, Henry Clay, II, 3576
Frick, Henry Clay, III, 3576
Frick, James W., 2496
Frick, Robert W., 84
Fried, Emil A., 2044
Friedersdorf, Max L., 2820
Friedlaender, H.N., 2238
Friedlander, Lillian, 815
Friedlander, William A., 3183
Friedli, F.E., 3306
Friedman, Albert, 175
Friedman, Art, 404
Friedman, Arthur N.K., 3348, 3379
Friedman Bag Co., 175
Friedman, Bayard, 4010
Friedman, Cheryl S., 2963
Friedman, Edgar L., 117
Friedman, Erwin B., 873
Friedman, Freda F., 162
Friedman, Harold E., 3226
Friedman, Harvey, 175
Friedman, Judith M., 2819
Friedman, Mayme, 4010
Friedman, Phyllis K., 258
Friedman, R., 2708
Friedman, Rivka, 2708
Friedman, Robert S., 2896
Friedman, Saul, 345
Friedman, Sidney, 442
Friedman, Sidney O., 2684

Friedman, Wilbur H., 2291, 3056
Friedman, Wilbur M., 2466
Friedman, William, Jr., 1270
Friedman, William E., 2918
Friedman, William K., 2304
Friedsam, Michael, 2232
Frieg, John T., 3372
Frieling, G.H., 3528
Frieling, Gerald H., Jr., 1723
Friend, Eugene L., 248
Friend, William K., 3357
Friendly, Julius C., 3487
Friendly, Melvyn C., 3487
Friendly, Seymour C., 3487
Frierson, Daniel K., 3835
Frierson, J. Burton, 3847
Frierson, J. Burton, Jr., 3863
Friese, George R., 3357
Friesen, William L., 1311, 1327
Friley, C.B., 3456
Frindel, Estelle, 2351
Frisbee, Donald, 3500, 3506
Frisch, Alfred M., 2124
Frisch, Ethel, 2124
Frisina, D. Robert, 2464
Frist, Thomas F., 3827
Frito-Lay, 2820
Fritz, Bertha G., 1537
Frizen, Edwin L., Jr., 981, 1178
Froderman, Carl M., 1215
Froderman, Harvey, 1215
Froelich, Edwin F., 340
Froelich, Kathleen, 1768
Froelich, Mary S., 2605
Froelicher, F. Charles, 450
Frohlich, Ludwig W., 2454
Frohm (Carl) Insurance Trust, 2056
Frohman, Blanche P., 3228
Frohman, Daniel C., 3228
Frohman, Sidney, 3228
Frohring, Gertrude L., 3229
Frohring, Glenn H., 3229
Frohring, Lloyd W., 3229
Frohring, William O., 3229
Froio, Anthony, 1552
Fromm, Mabel, 4321
Fromm, Walter, 4321
Frommel, Robert A., 2568
Frommelt, Andrew E.R., Jr., 2176
Fronske, M.G., 43
Fronterhouse, Gerald W., 3923
Frost National Bank, 4059, 4072
Frost, Camela, 114
Frost, Camilla C., 230
Frost, Charles H., 3502
Frost, E.D., Jr., 2741
Frost, Edwin D., Jr., 2825
Frost, Gordon T., 353
Frost, H.G., 52
Frost, Meshech, 3230
Frost, Virginia C., 449
Frost, William Lee, 2675
Fruchtman, Joann C., 1429
Frueauff, Charles A., 2455
Frueauff, Harry D., 2455
Fruehauf, Angela, 1707
Fruehauf Corporation, 1706
Fruehauf, Harvey C., Jr., 1707, 2078
Frumkes, Alana Martin, 2152
Fry, Caroline M., 526
Fry, J.C., 3121
Fry, Lloyd A., 1011
Fry, Lloyd A., Jr., 1011
Fry, William Henry, 526
Fryar, Kenneth, 2265
Fryberger, Buchanan, Smith & Frederick, 1927
Frye, Clayton W., Jr., 2577
Frye, David B., 704
Fryer, Marna C., 4132
Fuchs, Gottfried, 4235
Fuchs, Mary, 4235
Fuchsberg & Fuchsberg, 2456, 2457
Fuchsberg, Abraham, 2456, 2457

Fuchsberg Family Foundation, 2456
Fuchsberg, Jacob D., 2457
Fuchsberg, Meyer, 2456, 2457
Fuchsberg, Seymour, 2456
Fuchsberg, Shirley, 2457
Fuellgraf, Charles L., 3313
Fuges, Frederick L., 3713
Fuglestad, J.T., 1050
Fuhrman, R.A., 266
Fujii, Yoshito, 4241
Fuld, Florentine M., 2458
Fuld, Leonhard Felix, 2458
Fulham, Gerard A., 1601
Fuller, Alfred W., 1478
Fuller, Alvan T., Sr., 1532
Fuller, Andrew P., 3958
Fuller, C.B., 2150
Fuller, Charles N., 1600
Fuller, Cornell G., 3804
Fuller, Ernest M., 1533
Fuller, Frederic J., 2711
Fuller, Gay, 2023
Fuller, George F., 1533
Fuller, George M., Jr., 134
Fuller, H. Laurance, 928
Fuller, James E., 1717
Fuller, Orville, 3192
Fuller, Peter, 1532
Fuller, Peter D., Jr., 1532
Fuller, Russell E., 1533
Fuller, William M., 3958
Fullerton, Alma H., 2459
Fullerton, Robert, III, 313
Fullinwider, Carol C., 998
Fulljames, W. Richard, 527
Fulmer, Nancy, 3854
Fulp, J.R., Jr., 3794
Fulp, John R., III, 3794
Fulrath, Logan, Jr., 2625
Fulton, Maurice, 1120
Fulton, Rose H., 27
Fulton, William Duncan, 27
Fulton, William Shirley, 27
Fultz, Bernard V., 3274
Fund for New Jersey, 2120
Funderburk, James O., 3102
Funk, Alvin, 1327
Funk, Elmer H., Jr., 3634
Funk, Herbert, 93
Fuqua, Dorothy C., 836
Fuqua, J. Rex, 836
Fuqua, J.B., 836
Furlaud, Richard M., 2799
Furlong, James W., 1781
Furlong, R. Michael, 975
Furman, James M., 1077
Furnas, Leto M., 1012
Furnas, W.C., 1012
Furst, Gerald, 2461
Furst, Hilda, 2461
Furst, Sol, 2461
Furst, Violet, 2461
Fusco, Richard A., 1376
Fusenot, Germaine, 176
Fuson, Esten P., 1215
Futcher, John F., 170
Futter, Ellen V., 2737

G & J Pepsi-Cola Bottlers, 3263
Gabel, Ivan H., 3666
Gabel, Richard H., 3745
Gaberman, Barry D., 2444
Gabriel, Linda, 2583
Gabriel, Mrs. Robert, 1510
Gackle, George D., 4371
Gadbery, Earl L., 3511
Gaddes, Richard, 2968
Gaffney, Charles J., 2149
Gaffney, Frank J., 3578
Gaffney, Owen, 1602
Gage, Frederick H., 4316
Gage, Frederick K., 4316
Gage, Nancy Brooke, 4316

Gage, Ralph, 3951
Gagliardi, Lee P., 522
Gahagan, Katharine du Pont, 600
Gailey, Jane E., 2396
Gaillard, Elizabeth N., 2912
Gaillard, Henry E., 2912
Gaines, Alex P., 855, 887
Gaines, John, 90
Gaines, Tyler B., 2057
Gaines, Weaver H., Jr., 2572
Gaiser, Mary Jewett, 238
Gaisman, Catherine V., 2462
Gaisman, Henry J., 2462
Gaither, A.C., 389
Gaither, James C., 202, 334, 644
Galanis, John, 4358
Galbraith, Katherine Clapp, 3544
Galbraith, Robert L., 2474
Gale, Benjamin, 3172
Gale, Edward, 2312, 2313
Gale, Elizabeth S., 2692
Gale, Joan G., 2312
Gale, Thomas H., 3172
Galea, John H., 4193
Galek, Ruth, 3367
Galkin, Anna, 3776
Galkin, Arnold T., 3776
Galkin, Ira S., 3776
Gall, Robert F., 3662
Gallagher, Donald A., 4314
Gallagher, Gerald R., 1834
Gallagher, Idella J., 4314
Gallagher, J.A., 3539
Gallagher, J. Peter, 3107
Gallagher (Lewis P.) Family Charitable Income Trust, 3231
Gallagher, Lloyd E., 321
Gallagher, Richard S., 4299
Gallagher, Terence J., 2823
Gallaher, Art, Jr., 2207
Gallatin, A.E., 3943
Gallef, Myron S., 2539
Gallegos, Herman E., 2877
Gallen, Irene, 2092
Galler, Gerald H., 1056
Galler, Ida E., 2954
Gallick, Joseph J., 1867
Galligan, Richard P., 1274
Gallo, David E., 178, 179
Gallo (E. & J.) Winery, 178
Gallo, Ernest, 178, 179
Gallo, Joseph E., 178, 179
Gallo, Julio R., 180
Gallo, Robert J., 180
Gallon, Stanley J., 332
Galloway, Herbert R., 1858
Galloway, Janice T., 1858
Galloway, M.O., 825
Galloway, Richard B., 1858
Galloway, Robert F., 1310
Galster, E.S., 181
Galt, Mrs. William M., III, 3614
Galt, William M., III, 3614
Galter, Dollie, 1013
Galter, Jack, 1013
Galvin, Christopher B., 1015
Galvin, Mary Barnes, 1015
Galvin, Paul V., 1014
Galvin, Robert W., 1015, 1104
Galyean, Brent B., 4285
Gamble, B.C., 1845
Gamble, Bertin C., 1845
Gamble, Gwyneth, 3500
Gamble, James N., 313, 314
Gamble, Robert W., 326
Gambrell, Sarah Belk, 3799, 3818
Games, Robert W., 3396
Gamper, David E., 4147
Gamper, Harriet E., 4147
Gandy, Joyce A., 3982
Gann, Ronald W., 853
Gannett Foundation, 2464
Gannett, Frank E., 2463
Gannett (Guy) Publishing Co., 1393

Gannett, John D., 1555
Gannett, John H., 1393
Gannett, William B., 1555
Gannon, Daniel J., 4353
Gantt, John W., 3219
Garabedian, Mike, 70
Garabedian, Mitchell, 1501
Garb, Melvin, 1708
Garbe, F. James, 935
Garber, Eugene B., 1375
Garcetti, Gilbert, 335
Garcetti, Susan, 335
Garcia, Joseph, 782
Gardea, Eleanor, 3940
Gardner, Ames, Jr., 3233
Gardner, Colin, III, 3233
Gardner, Colin, IV, 3233
Gardner, David L., 1977
Gardner, David P., 4138, 4143
Gardner, Delbert R., 962
Gardner, E. Ty, III, 3233
Gardner, E.T., Jr., 3233
Gardner, George P., Jr., 1560
Gardner, James C., 1383
Gardner, Michael R., 674
Gardner, Stephen D., 2183
Gardner, William L., Jr., 2712
Garey, Gerard S., 627, 628
Garey, Patricia M., 627
Garfield Trust, 649
Garfinkel, Barry, 2774
Garfinkel, Steven R., 3717
Garland, Louise Grant, 182
Garland, Michael J., 4337
Garlotte, Helen W., 1236, 1256
Garner, C. Greene, 3299
Garner, Steve, 3472
Garr, C.R., 3536
Garran, Frank W., Jr., 1567
Garrard, Tom E., 3458
Garretson, D.E., 1890
Garrett, Constance Owsley, 4048
Garrett, David C., Jr., 825, 3750
Garrett, Dorothy Salant, 177
Garrett, Mrs. Horace, 4065
Garrett, J. Richard, 534
Garrett, Judith Harris, 3435
Garrett, Margaret Dodge, 2402
Garrett, Richard, 1465
Garrett, Robert, 1399, 2402
Garrett, Robert Y., Jr., 3635
Garrett, Sylvia H., 1465
Garrettson, Mrs. John A., 2265
Garrison, James W., 3858
Garrison, Lloyd K., 2976
Garry, Fred W., 527
Garsoian, Nina G., 2444
Gartland, John J., Jr., 2712
Gartner, Barbara M., 464
Garton, Deidre W., 3048
Garver, Stuart, 1432
Garvey, Edward C., 1964
Garvey Foundation, 3959
Garvey, James S., 1307, 3959
Garvey, Jean K., 1308
Garvey, John K., 1308
Garvey, Olive W., 1307
Garvey, Richard F., 3959
Garvey, Shirley F., 3959
Garvey, Willard W., 1307, 1308
Garvey, William J., 3716
Garvin, T.M., 1057
Garwood, W. St. John, Jr., 3907, 4022
Gary, Nancy, 444, 473
Gary, Samuel, 444, 473
Gasnell, Harold, 4103
Gasser, Kurt, 964
Gassman, Robert S., 2521
Gast, Aaron E., 2162
Gates, Agnes M., 1863
Gates, Carol W., 3678
Gates, Charles, 450
Gates, Charles C., 450
Gates, Hazel, 450

Gates, John, 450
Gates, Moore, Jr., 2229
Gates, Peter P. McN., 2248
Gath, Marie C., 378
Gathany, Van R., 1161
Gatlin, Lila L., 1318
Gaudi, Arthur R., 236, 413
Gaunt, Joseph A., 2105
Gaus, William T., 4377
Gautier, Agnes, 2541
Gauvreau, Paul R., 1120
Gavan, Gordon S., 3050
Gavin, Austin F., 154
Gavin, J.J., Jr., 950
Gaw, William L., 4095
Gay, Joseph W., 4039
Gay, L., 1696
Gayle, Gibson, Jr., 3875
Gaylin, Willard, 2432
Gaylord, Catherine M., 1965
Gaylord, Clayton D., 1047
Gaylord, Clifford W., 1966
Gaylord, Edson I., 1047
Gaylord, Robert M., Jr., 1047
Gaynor, Mary Catherine, 2136
Gazette Company, 1267
Gearen, John J., 1141
Geary, J.D., 1518
Gebbie, Marion B., 2465
Gebhard, Katherine, 1962
Gebhard, Mrs. Paul, 990
Gebhart, Norman L., 3277
Geddes, William W., 621
Gee, Edwin A., 2574
Geehern, Joseph J., 1475
Geer, John F., 2237
Gehrig, Cynthia, 1868
Gehron, A. William, 3695
Geier, James A.D., 3184, 3750
Geier, Philip O., Jr., 3239
Geilfuss, John C., 4358
Geils, Edwin J., 2158
Geisel, Audrey, 355
Geisel, Theodor S., 355
Geiselman, Lucy Ann, 433
Geisler, William F., 99
Geist, Irving, 2126
Geitner, Rudy, 166
Gelatt, Charles D., 4323
Gelb, Bruce S., 2302, 2466
Gelb, John T., 2466
Gelb, Lawrence M., 2466
Gelb, Lawrence N., 2466
Gelb, Richard L., 2302, 2466, 2777
Gelco Corporation, 1846
Gelder, John W., 1764
Gell, Carl L., 669
Gellert, Annette, 184
Gellert, Mrs. Arthur, 2416
Gellert, Carl, 183
Gellert, Celia Berta, 183
Gellert, Fred, Jr., 184
Gellert, Fred, Sr., 184
Gellert, Gertrude E., 183
Gellert, Gisela, 184
Gellhorn, Alfred, 2773
Gellis, Sidney, 798
Gell-Mann, Murray, 1077
Gelman, Estelle S., 658
Gelman, Melvin, 658
Gels, James V., 3145
Gemmill, Kenneth W., 3740
GenCorp, 3234
Gendell, G.S., 3333
Gendron, E.C., 3302
General Circuits, 2834
General Electric Company, 527
General Foods Corporation, 2467
General Mills, 1847
General Motors Corporation, 1709, 1710
General Telephone & Electronics Corporation, 531
Genesee Merchants Bank & Trust Co., 1674, 1676

Genest, Jacques, 2155
Genge, William H., 3691
GenRad, 1534
Genssler, Rolf, 491
Gentleman, Alexander W., 2438
Gentleman, Vivian F., 2438
Gentry, John R., 104
Gentzler, Norma, 3361
George and Frances Armour Foundation, 2099
George Banta Company, 4300
George C. Shaw Company, 1394
George, A.P., 3960
George, Alexander S., 4185
George, Jack, 3235
George, Jack M., 3270
George, James, 3235
George, Mamie E., 3960
George, Mildred, 3235
George, Noel F., 3270
George, Raymond E., Jr., 30
George, William H., 3971
Georges, John A., 2574
Georges, S.N.F., 3223
Georgeson, Donald J., 3480
Georgia-Pacific Corporation, 837
Gepson, Mrs. John M., 1481
Gerace, Frank, 1748
Gerard, C.H. Coster, 608
Gerard, James W., 608, 3063
Gerard, Mrs. James W., 3063
Gerard, Sumner, 608
Gerber Products Company, 1711
Gerber, Oscar L., 1017
Gerber, Virginia, 1705
Gerbode, Frank A., 186
Gerbode, Frank L.A., 186
Gerdes, William H., 3336
Gerdine, Leigh, 1965
Gerfen, Marjorie, 4023
Gerhart, Jack S., 3737, 3738
Gerhart, John D., 2444
Gerhart, Paul, 2200
Gerken, Walter B., 114, 230, 243
Gerlach, G. Donald, 3714
Gerlach, Harry K., 3720
Gerlach, John B., 3236
Gerlach, John J., 3236, 3308
Gerlach, Lloyd A., 4382
Gerlach, Mary Ann, 4382
Gerlach, Pauline, 3236
German, Kempton L., 4328
Gerrish, Elliot, 1510
Gerry, Elbridge T., Jr., 2689
Gerry, Elbridge T., Sr., 2527
Gerry, Martha Farish, 3947
Gerschel, Laurent, 2734
Gerschel, Marianne, 2734
Gerschel, Patrick, 2734
Gerson, Benjamin S., 3237
Gerson, Eleanor R., 3237
Gerson, Thomas E., 3237
Gerst, C.A., 1351
Gerstacker, Carl A., 1712, 1757
Gerstacker, Eda U., 1712
Gerstacker, Lisa J., 1712, 1757
Gerstein, David, 2839
Gerstenberger, D.J., 3343
Gerstley, Carol, 3538
Gerstner, L.V., 2235
Gerstung, Sandra L., 1422
Gertz, Herman F., 1736
Gessula, Benjamin, 3003
Gest, Lillian, 3766
Getchell, C.W., 111
Getman, Frank, 2397
Getsch, Marjorie D., 1838
Getsch, William C., 1838
Getty, Gordon P., 187
Getty, J. Paul, 187
Getty, Ronald, 187
Getty, Roy G., 3625
Getz, Bert A., 29, 48
Getzels, Jacob W., 1160

Geuting, Pat, 627
Gheens, C. Edwin, 1340
Gherlein, John H., 3264
Gholston, J. Knox, 838
Giamatti, A. Bartlett, 2444
Giannini, A.P., 83
Giannini, Allan V., 99
Giant Food, 1418
Gibb, Margaret K., 560
Gibbon Packing, 4364
Gibbons, C.C., 1787
Gibbons, John J., 2125
Gibbons, Miles J., Jr., 3761
Gibbons, Walter F., 3784
Gibbs & Cox, 2468
Gibbs, Daniel M., 1777
Gibbs Die Casting Aluminum, Corp., 1232
Gibbs, Elizabeth, 1777
Gibbs, J. Ronald, 371
Gibbs, James Lowell, Jr., 2325
Gibbs, James R., 372
Gibbs, John C., 1703
Giberga, Ulises, 2345
Gibney, Paul B., Jr., 2386
Gibson, Addison H., 3578
Gibson, G.C., 3276
Gibson, E. Martin, 2239, 2368
Gibson, E.L., 9
Gibson, Floyd R., 1983
Gibson, G.C., 455
Gibson, H.D., 9
Gibson, Harvey D., 2762
Gibson, Mrs. Harvey D., 2762
Gibson, James O., 672
Gibson, Malcolm L., 2239
Gibson, Paul, 2460
Gibson, Robert L., 1187
Gibson, Robert W., 1254
Gibson, Thomas R., 2187
Giclas, Henry L., 43
Giddings and Lewis Machine Tool Company, 4324
Giddings, Jane R., 890, 894, 899
Giesecke, Raymond H., 1094
Giesen, Richard A., 970
Giffey, Donald F., 1850
Giffin, William M., 534
Gifford, Rosamond, 2469
Gigray, Margaret, 916
Gilbert, Ernest H., 4281
Gilbert Imported Hardwoods, 4283
Gilbert, Marion Moore, 2748
Gilbert, Price, Jr., 839
Gilbert, S. Parker, 2689
Gilcrease, Barton, 3431
Gilcrease, Eugene F., 3431
Gilcrease, Grace Folsom, 3431
Gilcrease, Thomas, 3431
Gilcrest, Kathleen A., 65
Gildea, John R., 1243
Gilder, Richard, 3049
Gildred, Stuart C., 66
Gildred, Theodore E., 189
Gilfix, Joseph W., 517
Gilkerson, Yancey S., 3805
Gilkey, Charles, 134
Gill, Daniel E., 2269
Gill, Don, 3679
Gill, George N., 1335
Gill, Juliann, 2415
Gill, Patricia Hogan, 453
Gill, R. Wayne, 1099
Gilleran, James E., 2817
Gillespie, Alexander J., Jr., 2246
Gillespie, George J., III, 2245, 2799, 2830
Gillespie, Mrs. Lee Day, 509
Gillespie, S. Hazard, 1317
Gillespie, Thomas J., III, 3691
Gillespie, Tyrone W., 1763
Gillett, Elesabeth I., 3579
Gillett, F. Warrington, Jr., 3579
Gillette Company, 1535

Gillette, Edmond S., Jr., 219, 268, 375, 429
Gillette, Howard E., 935
Gillhouse, Robert F., 1066
Gilliand, M.E., 3757
Gilliand, Merle E., 3756
Gillies, Linda L., 2248
Gillies, Mary Rust, 3709
Gillies, William B., III, 3709
Gillig, Edward C., 3141
Gilliland, Caroline K., 51
Gilliland, James S., 3854
Gilliland, Jason B., 826
Gilliland, Robertson L., 51
Gillin, Alelia, 79
Gillis, Harvey, 84
Gilliss, Sister Columba, 1347
Gilman Foundation, 2470
Gilman, Howard, 2470
Gilman, John S., 3030
Gilman, Leighton C., 926
Gilman, Sylvia, 2470
Gilmar, Leonard, 3666
Gilmore (A.F.) Co., 190
Gilmore, Elizabeth Burke, 2730
Gilmore, Genevieve U., 1787
Gilmore, Hugh R., Jr., 3690
Gilmore, Irving S., 1713
Gilmore, Joyce Mertz, 2730
Gilmore, Kenneth O., 2851
Gilmore, Marie Dent, 190
Gilmore, R.E., 965
Gilmore, Richard G., 3580
Gilmore, Robert W., 2683, 2730
Gilmore, Voit, 3074
Gilmore, William G., 191
Gilmore, Mrs. William G., 191
Gilmour, A.D., 1702
Gilmour, Lloyd S., 2292
Gilmour, Lloyd S., Jr., 2292
Gilmour, Margery B., 2292
Gilmour, Monroe T., 3102
Gilsdorf, Frank, 1752
Giltinan, David M., Jr., 4278
Gimbel, Alva B., 528
Gimbel, Bernard F., 528
Gimbel Brothers, 2903
Gimbel Brothers Foundation, 2471
Gimbel, Helen C., 1406
Gimbel, Peter R., 528
Gimbel, Robert B., 528
Gimon, Eleanor H., 217
Ginger, Lyman V., 1351
Ginn, Betty N., 599
Ginn, Edwin, 1495
Ginn, Robert M., 3185, 3264
Ginn, William D., 3316
Ginsberg, Calmon J., 2472
Ginsberg, Morris, 2472
Ginsberg, Moses, 2472
Ginsburg, Marianne L., 659
Ginter (Karl) Trust, 3104
Ginzburg, Leon, 2462
Girard Trust Bank, 3523, 3580, 3676, 3751
Gire, Leroy M., 96
Gisel, William G., 2376
Gisholt Machine Company, 4334
Giuffre, Salvatore V., 159
Giuggio, John, 1483
Giusti, G.P., 834
Given, Davis, 707
Given, Sam Perry, 22
Given, Mrs. William B., Jr., 707
Gjevre, Alden, 3139
Glade, Fred M., Jr., 2069
Glade, Harvey S., 4145
Gladfelter, Millard E., 2162
Gladson, J. Glen, 117
Gladston, B. Paul, 2989
Gladstone, Henry A., 3742
Glancy, A.R., III, 840
Glancy, Alfred R., Sr., 840
Glarner, Gaylord W., 1868

Glaser, Miles, 4030
Glaser, Paul F., 4236
Glaser, Robert, 308
Glaser, Robert J., 745, 2362
Glass, James R., 3239
Glass, Margaret, 745
Glassbrenner, A.B., 3383
Glasser, James, 985
Glasser, Louise R., 985
Glassmoyer, Thomas P., 2162
Glavach, Victor C., 750
Glazar, R.A., 127
Glazer, Donald, 1504
Glazer, Edward, 1268
Glazer, Ellen, 1504
Glazer, Madelyn L., 1268
Gleason, Hazel, 3396
Gleason, James, 2473
Gleason, James E., 994
Gleason, James S., 2474
Gleason, Miriam B., 2474
Gleason, Ruth M., 192
Gleason, Walter M., 112, 192, 193
Gleason, William F., Jr., 2365
Gleason, William J., 112, 192, 193
Gleixner, Alfred A., 3732
Gleixner, E.H., 3732
Glenmede Trust Company, 3517, 3629, 3660, 3673, 3686, 3687, 3688
Glenn, Alston, 802
Glenn, Beverly M., 1108
Glenn, Hilary P., 3530
Glenn, Jack, 841
Glenn, Paul F., 2475
Glenn, Tyler B., 122
Glenn, Wadley R., 841
Glenn, Wilbur F., 841
Glenn, Wilbur H., 865
Glennon, Richard F., 3199
Glickenhaus & Company, 2477
Glickenhaus, James, 2477
Glickenhaus, Seth, 2432
Glickman, E.M., 3291
Gligorea, George R., 4402
Globe Oil and Refining Companies, 1900
Globe Valve Corporation, 1017
Gloeckner, Frederick C., 2478
Gloin, James A., 1197
Glosser, David A., 3583
Gloster, John G., 2325
Glover & MacGregor, 3610
Glover, Charles C., III, 672
Glover, Howard T., 3336
Glowatz, Benjamin, 2407, 2491, 2829, 3021
Gloyd, Lawrence E., 927
Glusac, M.M., 1679
Glynn, Edward, 2158
Goad, Thomas L., 4112
Goar, J.E., 4395
Goddard, Bill, 3448
Goddard, Charles B., 3432
Goddard, Raymond B., Sr., 3915
Goddard, Robert H.I., 3790
Goddard, W.R., 3449
Goddard, William R., 3432
Goddard, William R., Jr., 3432
Godfrey, Dudley J., Jr., 4311
Godfrey, W.K., 2150
Godkin, Paul, 359
Godshall, Clara May, 827
Godshall, Ellis, 827
Godwin, Mills E., Jr., 4153, 4159
Goebel, Paul G., Jr., 1671
Goeke, Clayton, 2075
Goelet, Robert G., 2784
Goeltz, Richard Karl, 2304
Goelzer, D.M., 4308
Goerlich, John, 3238
Goerlich, Selma E., 3238
Goethe, Roy M., 1748
Goetsch, John H., 4388
Goetschel, Arthur W., 929
Goett, Edward J., 616

Goettler, Ralph H., 3512
Goggin, Joseph P., 1908
Gogolak, Erin McHugh, 465
Gogolin, Calvin A., 2691, 2728
Goheen, Robert F., 644, 2125
Goins, Charlynn W., 3777
Gold, Walter, 626
Goldapp, B.R., 4002
Goldberg, Albert S., 1536
Goldberg, Arthur J., 312
Goldberg, Arthur H., 1620
Goldberg, Avram J., 1639
Goldberg, Barbara, 462
Goldberg, Barry, 3922
Goldberg, Carol R., 1482, 1639
Goldberg, Dena J., 283
Goldberg, Elizabeth, 2511
Goldberg, Herbert A., 1536
Goldberg, Israel, 1536
Goldberg, Jay L., 3596
Goldberg, Joel, 803, 870
Goldberg, Matilda, 1536
Goldberg, Peter, 492
Goldberg, Rosalie A., 2317
Goldberger, Herbert H., 3357
Golden, Barbara, 871
Golden, John, 2479
Golden, Morley R., 194
Golden, Muriel A., 3028
Golden Nugget, 2079
Golden, Robert M., 194
Golden, Sibyl L., 2480
Golden, Sibyl R., 2480
Golden, Sol I., 854
Golden, William T., 2480, 2605, 2800
Goldenberg, Blanche, 571
Goldenberg, Max, 1018
Goldin, William T., 2890
Golding, Brage, 3156
Goldman (William P.) & Bros., 2482
Goldman, Alice S., 3584
Goldman, Byron, 2482
Goldman, Guido, 659, 2790
Goldman, Helen L., 3584
Goldman, Herman, 2481
Goldman, Justin, 2482
Goldman, Morris, 1019
Goldman, Randolph Louis, 3584
Goldman, Rhoda H., 195, 204, 258
Goldman, Richard N., 195
Goldman, Richard W., 195
Goldman, Roger A., 3038
Goldman, Rose, 1019
Goldman, William, 3584
Goldman, William, Jr., 3584
Goldman, William P., 2482
Goldman, William R., 3584
Goldmann, Robert B., 2387
Goldmark, Mrs. Carl, Jr., 2583
Goldmark, Peter C., Jr., 2875
Goldmuntz, Lawrence, 216
Goldring (N.) Corp., 1363
Goldring, Sidney, 1538
Goldring, Stephen, 1363
Goldschmidt, Walter M., 2366
Goldseker, Morris, 1419
Goldseker, Samuel, 1419
Goldseker, Sheldon, 1403, 1419
Goldseker, Simon, 1419
Goldsmith, Barbara, 2681
Goldsmith, Elias J., Jr., 3841
Goldsmith, Fred, Jr., 3841
Goldsmith, Grace R., 2483
Goldsmith, Helen P., 888
Goldsmith, Horace, 2483
Goldsmith, Jack L., 3841
Goldsmith, Robert, 44
Goldsmith, Mrs. Warren R., 2583
Goldstein, Alfred G., 492
Goldstein, Alfred R., 2681
Goldstein, Ann L., 2681
Goldstein, Donald M., 867
Goldstein, Elliott, 815
Goldstein, Emanuel, 2481

Goldstein, Frederic S., 2437
Goldstein, Gabriel F., 2437
Goldstein, Harriet, 815
Goldstein, Israel, 2233
Goldstein, Lester, 3583
Goldstein, Marc E., 1154
Goldstein, Michael L., 2481
Goldstein, Seth M., 2437
Goldstein, Simeon H.F., 2437
Goldstick, Ida, 2977
Goldware, June, 333
Goldwyn, Frances H., 196
Goldwyn, Francis, 196
Goldwyn, John, 196
Goldwyn, Peggy E., 196
Goldwyn, Samuel, 196
Goldwyn, Samuel, Jr., 196
Golieb, Abner J., 2603
Golly, Jeanne M., 2237
Golub Corporation, 2484
Golub, Lewis, 2484
Gonnerman, Mary F., 1997
Gonzalez, Fausto, 2318
Gonzalez, Michael Ibs, 336
Gonzalez, Xavier, 2985
Gooch, J.A., 3895
Good, Daniel J., 940
Good, Robert F., 3760
Good, W.R., 508
Goodale, Irene E., 3326
Goodall, Gene, 487
Goodall, John C., Jr., 1033
Goodban, J. Nicholas, 972
Goode, Lewis B., Jr., 4163
Goode, Phyllis Moorman, 3693
Goode, Robert B., Jr., 534
Goodes, Melvin R., 2200
Goodfellow, R., 1867
Goodger, J.V., 3212
Gooding, Vaughn G., 3784
Goodman, Barbara N., 983
Goodman, Clare F., 2486
Goodman, D.L., 127
Goodman, Henry J., 3186
Goodman, Jack, 2176
Goodman, Jane, 800
Goodman, Jerrold F., 800
Goodman, Leonard C., 983
Goodman, Marian, 1018
Goodman, Richard Crown, 983
Goodman, Roy M., 2485
Goodman, Suzanne C., 983
Goodman, Mrs. Zmira, 2384
Goodnow, Charles, 1754
Goodpaster, Andrew, 659
Goodrich, Benn F., 3734
Goodrich, Calvin, 414
Goodrich, Enid, 1236, 1256
Goodrich, Jean S., 414
Goodrich, John B., 1236
Goodrich, Pierre F., 1236
Goodson, Suzanne, 2494
Goodson, W. Kenneth, 3095
Goodstein, Albert, 2487
Goodstein, Fred, 4396
Goodstein, Irving, 2760
Goodstein, J.M., 4396
Goodstein, Jacob I., 2749
Goodstein, Robert, 2487
Goodstein, William, 2487
Goodwin, Ben, 3976
Goodwin, David P., 2084
Goodwin, Richer M., 3724
Goodwin, William M., 1238
Goodyear, Frank H., 2488
Goodyear, Josephine L., 2488
Goodyear, R., 1679
Goodyear, Robert M., 2488
Goodyear Tire & Rubber Company, 3239
Googins, Robert R., 507
Gookin, R. Burt, 3598
Goolsby, Durwood M., 3948
Goppert, Clarence H., 37
Goppert, Richard D., 37

Griffin, Bobby I., 1884
Griffin, Dale G., 1749
Griffin, Donald R., 2513
Griffin, Frederick W., 2083
Griffin, Gerald R., 3496
Griffin, John C., 21
Griffin, Rosa May, 3965
Griffin, T. McLean, 1473
Griffin, W.L. Hadley, 1944, 1945
Griffin, William M., 2551
Griffis, Hughes, 530, 2507
Griffis, Nixon, 2507
Griffis, Stanton, 2507
Griffith, C. Perry, Jr., 1217
Griffith, David H., 1920
Griffith, Katherine W., 1920
Griffith, Lawrence S.C., 2972
Griffith, Richard L., 888
Griffith, Ruth Perry, 1217
Griffith, Theodore B., 1197
Griffith, Mrs. Theodore B., 1197
Griffith, W.C., Jr., 1217
Griffith, Walter Stuhr, 1217
Griffith, William C., 1217
Griffith, William C., III, 1217
Griffiths, Elizabeth C., 3735
Grifone, Albert V., 3518
Griggs, C.F. Bayliss, 1852
Griggs, Eleanor, 1852
Griggs, Mary L., 1852
Grimes, Warren G., 3242
Grimm, James R., 3444
Grimm, Roland D., 1573
Grimm, Ronald L., 3859
Grinnell, C.W., 488
Grinstein, Gerald, 4238
Grisanti, E.P., 2571
Griswold, Mrs. Bruce, 3186
Groh, Lorraine E., 250
Groman, Arthur, 302, 1026
Grompeter, R. Peter, 935
Groos National Bank, 4072
Grosberg, Julius, 1712, 1748
Grose, Mrs. William E., 1461
Groseclose, Everett, 2117
Gross, Carl R., 822
Gross, R.M., 542
Gross, Ronald N., 1883, 1929
Gross, Stella B., 201
Gross, Thomas R., 3243
Gross, Walter L., Jr., 3243
Grossberg, Louis C., 1462
Grossberg, Solomon, 1462
Grosse, Rose B., 957
Grossman, A., 933
Grossman, Allen, 921
Grossman, Andrew, 1846
Grossman, Bernard, 2599
Grossman, Bernard D., 1540
Grossman, Everett P., 1540
Grossman, F.N., 1138
Grossman, Harry, 2437
Grossman, Joseph B., 1540
Grossman, Joseph B., II, 1540
Grossman, Maurice, 1540
Grossman, Morton S., 1540
Grossman, N. Bud, 1846
Grossman, Nathan, 938
Grossman, Nissie, 1540
Grosvenor, Gilbert, 2405
Grosvenor, Mrs. H.R., 3245
Groth, William, 3245
Grotz, Lester, 505
Grove Silk Company, 3712
Groves, C.T., 1854
Groves, C'Marie, 3942
Groves, F.N., 1854
Groves, Frank M., 1854
Groves, Helen K., 4004, 4006
Groves, Robert A., 220
Groves, Rockwell M., 3731
Groves (S.J.) & Sons Company, 1854
Growald, Eileen R., 2876
Grube, F.W., 1251

Grube, Karl P., 935
Grube, L. Blaine, 3646
Gruber, Barry, 2509
Gruber, Carl E., 2260
Gruber, Daryl, 2509
Gruber, M. Ellen, 3414
Gruber, Marilyn L., 2302
Gruber, Murray, 2509
Gruber, Warren W., 1736
Grublesky, Anthony B., 1055
Gruel, Marilyn, 2339
Gruettner, Donald W., 3371
Gruld, Alice F., 899
Grumbacher, M. Thomas, 3587
Grumbacher, M.S., 3587
Grumman, Carol B., 1494
Grumman, David L., 2093
Grumman, Elizabeth S., 1494
Grumman, G. Sterling, 1494
Grumman, Helen Burr, 1494
Grumman, Paul Martin, 1494
Grumman, Sandra Martin, 1494
Grund, Benjamin, 2649
Grundman, Eileen L., 1906
Grundy, Joseph R., 3588
Grune, George V., 2851
Grupe, William F., 2128
Gruson, Sydney, 2777
Gruss, Emanuel, 2511
Gruss, Jane Fraser, 3858
Gruss, Oscar, 2511
Gruss, Regina, 2511
Gruss, Riane, 2511
Grymes, Douglas, 3631
Guaranty Bank and Trust Company,
    442, 1659
Guaranty Trust Company of Missouri,
    2020
Guardia, E.J., 2467
Guarino, Donald J., 2310
Guckenberger, Herman J., Jr., 3219
Gudelsky, Homer, 1420
Gudelsky, John, 1420
Gudelsky, Martha, 1420
Gudger, Robert H., 594
Guernsey, George T., 2039
Guerrera, S., 1918
Guerrero, Manuel R., 2535
Guerri, William, 2009
Guerry, Alex, 3842
Guerry, John P., 3835, 3842
Guggenheim, Charles, 1955
Guggenheim, Daniel, 2512
Guggenheim, Florence, 2512
Guggenheim, Harry Frank, 2513
Guggenheim, Robert, Jr., 2512
Guggenheim, Simon, 2514
Guggenheim, Mrs. Simon, 2514
Guggenheimer, Charles H., 2608
Guidice, Sal J., 492
Guidone, Rosemary L., 2839
Guild, Henry R., Jr., 1548
Guilden, Ira, 2313
Guilden, Louise B., 2312
Guilden, Paul, 2313
Guilden, Paul B., 2312
Guinzburg, Harold K., 2515
Guinzburg, Thomas H., 2515
Gulf + Western Industries, 2516
Gulf Oil Corporation, 3589
Gulf Oil Foundation (Texas), 3589
Gulf States Paper Corporation, 23
Gulton, Edith, 2517
Gulton, Leslie K., 2517
Gund, Geoffrey, 3244
Gund, George, 3244
Gund, George, III, 3244
Gund, Llura, 3244
Gunderson, Charles H., 1006
Gunderson, Richard L., 1805, 1820
Gunn, Colin, 2838
Gunn, Harold A., 2252
Gunnerson, Robert, 4370
Gunning, R. Boyd, 3462

Gunnon, Judy, 459
Gunterman, Anthony, 152
Gunther, Arthur G., 2820
Gunther, William E., Jr., 329
Gurash, John T., 421
Gurwin, Eric, 2518
Gurwin, Joseph, 2518
Gurwin, Rosalind, 2518
Gusack, Milton, 664
Gusching, N.V., 3305
Gushee, Richard B., 1718, 1785
Gussman, Barbara, 3433
Gussman, Herbert, 3433
Gussman, Roseline, 3433
Gustafsen, Bruce A., 2217
Gustafson, E.W., 456
Gutfreund, John H., 2519
Guth, Paul C., 2653
Guthridge, Charles M., 4198
Guthrie, Elizabeth, 2411
Guthrie, Henry B., 2411
Guthrie, Randolph H., 583
Gutman, Edna C., 2520
Gutman, Monroe C., 2520
Gutridge, D.S., 3198
Guttman, Charles, 2521
Guttman, Stella, 2521
Guttowsky, Lois K., 1751
Guy, Drue S., 4370
Guy, Martha, 3116
Guyer, Alissa C., 2819
Guyer, Carol P., 2819
Guyer, Gordon E., 1663
Guyer, Shelly D., 2819
Guyton, Robert P., 1936
Gwaltney, Nancy R., 18
Gwartney, J. Ted, 2911
Gwin, Hugh F., 1904
Gwyn, John E., 2616

H & R Block, Inc., 1941
Haag, Robert, 2063
Haake, Donald B., 86
Haake, Richard H., 86
Haaland, John E., 1892
Haan, Elsie F., 942
Haas, Chara C., 3683
Haas, David R., 3023
Haas, Dayee G., 4238
Haas, Dorothy W., 3683
Haas, Elise, 204
Haas, Elise S., 204
Haas, Evelyn D., 202
Haas, Flora Oppenheimer, 2802
Haas, Frederick R., 3683
Haas, Janet, 3683
Haas, John C., 3683
Haas, Mary, 3966
Haas, Mary F., 3966
Haas, Miriam L., 203
Haas, Otto, 3683
Haas (Otto) and Phoebe W. Haas
    Charitable Trusts, 3683
Haas, Paul R., 3966
Haas, Peter E., 138, 203, 204, 258, 337
Haas, Phoebe W., 3683
Haas, Raymond P., 3966
Haas, Rene, 3966
Haas, Robert D., 202
Haas, Saul, 4238
Haas, Thomas W., 3683
Haas, Walter A., 204
Haas, Walter A., Jr., 202, 204, 258
Haas, Walter J., 202
Haas, Warren J., 646
Haas, William D., 3683
Haase, Vernon H., 935
Haayen, Richard J., 922
Habel, R.A., 3196
Habig, Anthony P., 1219
Habig, Arnold F., 1218, 1219
Habig, Douglas, 1218
Habig, Douglas A., 1219

Habig, John B., 1218, 1219
Habig, Thomas L., 1218, 1219
Hachmann, Hans G., 2597
Hacker, Harold S., 3030
Hacker, Joanne, 1735
Hacker, S. Harold, 3720
Hackett, Denis, 2129
Hackett, Denis P., 2129
Hackett, John T., 1210
Hackett, R. Kevin, 2129
Hackett, Sister Patricia Mary, 2129
Hackett, William J., 2129
Hackman, Arthur A., 3720
Hadac, Lucy I., 4022
Haddad, Abraham, 1659
Hadden, Alexander M., 3063
Hadden, Mrs. Alexander M., 3063
Haddock, H., Jr., 2840
Hadler, Richard A., 1664
Hadley, Monica W., 228
Hadley, Stanton T., 1182
Hadsell, Philip A., Jr., 1723
Haefner, B.A., 1731
Haegele, John E., 2572
Hafey, Joan, 3062
Haff, Theodore L., Jr., 2940
Haffenreffer, Carl W., 3778
Haffenreffer, Carolyn B., 3778
Haffenreffer, David H., 3778
Haffenreffer, Karl, 3778
Haffenreffer, R.F., IV, 3778
Haffenreffer, Rudolph F., III, 3778
Haffenreffer, Virginie P., 3778
Haffner, Charles C., III, 1024, 1103,
    1161
Haffner, Charles C., Jr., 1024
Haffner, Mrs. Charles C., Jr., 1024
Hagedorn, Ruth Marie, 2523
Hagedorn, William, 2523
Hagen, Arthur E., 1729
Hagen, Arthur E., Jr., 1729
Hagen, Susan H., 3565
Hagey, Harry H., 985
Haggar Company, 3967
Haggar, Edmond R., 3967
Haggar, Joseph M., 3967
Haggar, Joseph M., Jr., 3967
Haggar, Rose M., 3967
Haggerty, Beatrice M., 3968
Haggerty, J.K., 3968
Haggerty, Michael G., 3968
Haggerty, Patrick E., 3968
Haggerty, Patrick F., Jr., 3968
Haggerty, Robert Johns, 2686
Haggin, Margaret Voorhies, 2524
Hague, Nelson, 3158
Hague, R.W., 1696
Hagy, Dexter N., 3805
Hahn, Anne D., 2525
Hahn, Anne S., 2525
Hahn, Charles J., 2343, 2525
Hahn, Charles O., 2525
Hahn, Eric S., 2525
Hahn, Ernest W., 205
Hahn, Jean E., 205
Hahn, K. Robert, 253
Hahn, Mary Louise, 3390
Hahn, Philip Y., 206
Hahn, Ronald L., 336
Hahn, Saul T., 1536
Hahn, T. Marshall, Jr., 837
Haigh, George W., 3387
Haigler, Theodore E., Jr., 3085
Haigney, John E., 541
Haines, C. Gordon, 1444
Haines, Charles Davis, 679
Haines, Jordan, 1305
Haines, Robert H., 2780
Hair, Charles M., 263
Hakanson, Joseph G., 1398
Hakim, Joseph E., 666, 2812
Halas, George, 1443
Halby, Christian G., 1848
Haldeman, Harry J., Jr., 428

Haldeman, Lowell, 1318
Hale, Elfreda, 207
Hale, Elywn C., 207
Hale, James T., 1834
Hale, M. Eugenie, 207
Hale, Roger L., 1915
Hale, Thomas, 2373
Hales, Burton W., 1025
Hales, Burton W., Jr., 1025
Hales, G. Willard, 1025
Hales, Marion J., 1025
Hales, Mary C., 1025
Hales, William M., 1025
Haley, Alex, 311
Haley, Eloise, 842
Haley, Fred, 4238
Haley, John C., 2337
Haley, W.B., Jr., 842
Halff, G.A.C., 3969
Halff, Hugh, Jr., 3969
Halff, Marie M., 3969
Halkin, Abraham S., 2708
Halkyard, Edwin M., 2098
Hall, Adah F., 1492
Hall, Alexander G., 3734
Hall, Bennett A., 836
Hall, Charles T., 2465
Hall, Charles W., 3888
Hall, Clarence, 1183
Hall, David E., 4097
Hall, David N., 3203
Hall, Donald J., 1968
Hall, E.A., 1968
Hall, Elizabeth, 1012
Hall, Esta J., 176
Hall, Euphemia V., 2373
Hall, Evelyn A., 3590
Hall, George E., 2924
Hall, Gerald N., 3591
Hall, Giles S., 319
Hall, Gordon, 4143
Hall, Harry A., 4324
Hall, Howard, Sr., 176
Hall, Jackson O., 2979
Hall, Jesse S., 830, 857
Hall, John, 4221
Hall, John F., 350, 4224
Hall, John N., 3591
Hall, Joyce C., 1968
Hall, Kenneth, 1915
Hall, Mrs. Lawrence B., 906
Hall, Lowell K., 1272
Hall, Lyle G., 3734
Hall, Lyle G., Jr., 3734
Hall, M. Lewis, Jr., 689
Hall, Marion T., 1052
Hall, Mary Stewart, 4274
Hall, Mortimer W., 2832
Hall, R.B., 1968
Hall, Robert, 3481
Hall, Robert E., 3591
Hall, Ronald L., 3591
Hall, Ross F., 134
Hall, Thomas, 1259
Hall, W.L., 3591
Hall, Mrs. Wendell G., 592
Hall, William A., 1968
Hallagan, Kevin J., 977
Hallam, Howard, 4000
Hallam, Robert, 4000
Hallaran, Iris, 902
Hallen, Philip B., 3568
Haller, Calvin J., 2343
Haller, J. Gary, 1362
Haller, T. Frank, 1362
Hallett, John V., 2476
Hallett, Stanley J., 1189
Hallgren, Carl R., 3720
Halliburton Company, 3970, 3993
Halliday, William J., Jr., 1686, 1788
Hallinan, Cornelia I., 3294
Hallmark Cards, 1968
Hallock, Richard W., 2621
Hallock, Robert P., Jr., 1533

Hallowell, Barclay, 3634
Hallowell, Dorothy W., 3592
Hallowell, H. Thomas, 3731
Hallowell, H. Thomas, Jr., 3592
Hallowell, Howard T., III, 3592
Hallowell, Merritt W., 3592
Hall's Motor Transit Company, 3591
Halperin, James R., 2948
Halpern, Anne, 2794
Halpern, Susan, 3003
Halpert, Jene, 3270
Halsell, Ewing, 3971
Halsell, Mrs. Ewing, 3971
Halsell, Oliver L., 208
Halsey, James L., 1997
Halsey, Stephen S., 2235
Halsted, Robert E., 2465
Haltom, B.R., 3855
Halvorson, Harlyn C., 2446
Halvorson, Newman T., Jr., 672
Hamamoto, Howard, 898
Hamann, Leonard, 4321
Hamaty, Edward C., 1507
Hambay, J.T., 3593
Hamblin, Lynn T., 1783
Hambrick, Marvin K., 3440
Hamburg, Beatrix A., 2499
Hamburg, David A., 2325
Hamburger, Lewis, 1456
Hamcke, William R., 2575
Hamilburg, Daniel M., 1541
Hamilton, A. Scott, 1341
Hamilton, Mrs. A. Scott, 1341
Hamilton Bank, 3674
Hamilton, Charles V., 2775, 2995
Hamilton, Edward K., 489
Hamilton, Florence C., 3772
Hamilton, Florence P., 75
Hamilton, Fowler, 522
Hamilton, Frank T., 3206
Hamilton, George E., Jr., 682
Hamilton, Jack H., 395, 1303
Hamilton, John D., 2324, 2465
Hamilton, Owen M., 1208
Hamilton, R.P., 1032
Hamilton, Ruth Simms, 2325
Hamilton, T. Herbert, 3535
Hamilton, Tullia Brown, 3189
Hamilton, Mrs. William B., 3840
Hamler, Thomas B., 3391
Hamm, Candace S., 1893
Hamm, Edward H., 1855, 1860, 1893
Hamm, Harry C., 3524
Hamm, William H., 1893
Hamm, William H., III, 1855
Hamm, William, Jr., 1860
Hammack, John A., 4029
Hamman, George, 3972
Hamman, Henry R., 3972
Hamman, Marilyn P., 45
Hamman, Mary Josephine, 3972
Hammel, J. Carter, 2135
Hammer, Armand, 302, 1026
Hammer, Frederick S., 2337
Hammer, Roy A., 1506
Hammer, Victor, 1026
Hammerman, Harry, 1998
Hammermill Paper Company, 3594
Hammond, Carleton E., 503
Hammond, Frank, 1805, 1889, 1928
Hammond, Franklin T., Jr., 1651
Hammond, Gerald S., 3245
Hammond, Harold F., 519
Hammond, J. David, 2421
Hammond, Joseph P., 3940
Hammond, R.M., 3193
Hampton, Colin C., 1397
Hampton, Joel L., 3346
Hampton, John C., 3506
Hampton, Louis R., 3772
Hamrick, Charles F., 2459
Hamrick, John, 2459
Hamrick, William J., 793
Hamrick, Wylie L., 2459

Hanavan, Claire F., 541
Hanavan, Taylor W., 541
Hance, William A., 2252
Hancock, Carol E., 209
Hancock, Denise J., 209
Hancock, James A., 3137
Hancock, Jane, 209
Hancock, John S., 2703
Hancock, Loni, 356
Hancock, Lorraine A., 209
Hancock, Luke B., 209
Hancock, Marian, 209
Hancock, Noble, 209
Hancock, Wesley, 209
Hancock, William, 209
Hand, Avery, 3415
Hand, J.T., 1613
Hand, Marion, 4250
Hand, W. Brevard, 16
Handelman, Blanche B., 2685
Handelman, Donald E., 2336, 2704
Handelman, Joseph W., 2704
Handelman, Walter J., 2685
Handelman, William R., 2336, 2704
Handke, David P., Jr., 3298
Handler, J., 2657
Handler, Leslie, 668
Handley, Harold J., 939
Handsky, Milton, 3070
Handy, Ed, 46
Hanemann, Bettie Conley, 1365
Hanes, Eldridge C., 3105
Hanes, Frank Borden, 3106, 3118
Hanes, Frank Borden, Jr., 3106
Hanes, Gordon, 3105, 3106
Hanes, James G., 3106
Hanes, James G., III, 3105
Hanes, James Gordon, 3105
Hanes, John W., 3106
Hanes, Mary Ruffin, 3105
Hanes, R. Philip, Jr., 3106
Hanes, Ralph P., 3106
Hanes, Robert M., 3106
Hangs, George L., Jr., 3434
Hangs, George L., Sr., 3434
Hangs, Naomi, 3434
Hankamer, Raymond E., 4044
Hankins, Edward R., 3246
Hankins, Hayden L., 3970
Hankins, Ruth L., 3246
Hanks, George R., 2145
Hanley, Charles E., 1123
Hanley, Ellen, 1754
Hanley, James R., 918
Hanley, William Lee, Jr., 2584
Hanlon, Richard A., 3747
Hanlon, Robert W., 1582
Hanly, Joan K., 1172
Hannig, Stephen E., 4280
Hannon, W. Herbert, 111
Hannum, Hildegarde, 530
Hannum, Hunter G., 530
Hanold, Terrance, 3631
Hanrahan, Barbara, 3683
Hanrahan, Barbara B., 3027
Hanrahan, Charles J., 2090
Hans, Patricia, 2891
Hans, Robert L., 2063
Hansel, Lincoln B., 1616
Hansen, C.W., 2049
Hansen, Dane G., 1309
Hansen, Duane G., 3122
Hansen, Mrs. Edward A., 2265
Hansen, Frederick, 1317
Hansen, James B., 134
Hansen, Joanne B., 1012
Hansen, Julie A., 1145
Hansen, Kenneth, 626
Hansen, L.C., 1949
Hansen, Mrs. Richard L., 3614
Hansen, Richard W., 516, 1012
Hansen, Robert, 134
Hansen, Robert U., 471
Hanseth, Winifred W., 50

Hansler, John F., 4229
Hansmann, Ralph E., 2480, 3070
Hanson, Allen D., 1850
Hanson, Fred, 4240
Hanson, Gerald, 4033
Hanson, H.H., 3540
Hanson, Lillian, 4378
Hanson, Loren Q., 4119
Hanson, Mrs. Fred, 4240
Hanson, T.E., 2817
Hanson, T.J., 1050
Hanson, W.N., 1863
Hapeman, Lloyd W., 2416
Hapgood, Cyrus, 516
Hapgood, David, 2088
Hapgood, Elaine, 2423
Hapgood, Elaine P., 516
Harbaugh, Jane W., 3835
Harbeck, Eugene O., Jr., 1738
Harcha, Howard H., Jr., 3356
Harcharik, David, 1934
Harcus, Sinclair J., 1663
Hard, Michael, 27
Hardart, Thomas R., 2711
Hardegree, William B., 865
Harder, C.S., 127
Harder, Delmar S., 1716
Harder, Elizabeth, 1716
Harder, Henry U., 2116
Harder, Richard, 4347
Harder, William E., 1834
Hardesty, David C., Jr., 4285
Hardie, Eben, 1372
Hardin, Clifford M., 3271
Hardin, Edward P., 2743
Hardin, Philip Bernard, 1937
Harding, Glenn W., 3973
Harding, Henry J., 2526
Harding, Laura V., 3973
Harding, Louis, 2182
Harding, Robert L., 2526
Harding, Robert L., Jr., 2526
Harding, W.A., 3973
Hardinge Brothers, Inc., 2239
Hardin's Bakeries Corp., 1937
Hardon, Allen, 2408
Hardon, Roger, 2408
Hardwick, A.H., Jr., 2164
Hardwick Knitted Fabrics, 1597
Hardy, Ann S., 993
Hardy, Coleman J., 3108
Hardy, David J., 1123
Hardy, Donna, 1726
Hardy, Gene M., 1736
Hardy, H. Barbara, 4080
Hardy, R. Hubbard, 3909
Hardy, William J., 4387
Haresign, W. Gordon, 1114
Harff, Charles H., 2587
Hargis, Paul A., 3836, 3861
Hargrave, Louis W., 1461
Hargrave, Sarah Q., 1145
Harkins, Joseph J., 2337
Harkness, Edward S., 2362
Harkness, Mrs. Edward S., 2362
Harkness, Elaine H., 1524
Harkness, Mrs. Stephen V., 2362
Harl, Sidney W., 2808
Harlan, Stephen D., 685
Harland, John H., 843
Harland (John H.) Company, 844
Harland, Robert P., 4387
Harless, James H., 4283
Harless, James M., 4283
Harless, Larry J., 4283
Harleston, Bernard W., 2689
Harley, R.G., 3298
Harley, Richard M., 1524
Harlor, John, 1602
Harlow, I. Frank, 1690, 1712, 1757
Harlow, James G., Jr., 3452
Harman, John R., 1201
Harmon, Claude C., 3434
Harmon, Gail McGreevy, 687

Harmon, Gene, 1145
Harmon, Julia J., 3434
Harmon, Margaret Weyerhaeuser, 1926
Harmon, R.L., 1993
Harnedy, Edmund, 2776
Harner, G. William, 1099
Harnett, Gordon, 3388
Harney, Charles L., 210
Harney (Charles L.), Inc., 210
Harney, Michael J., 1507
Harney, Mrs. P.E., 210
Harnischfeger Corporation, 4325
Harnischfeger, Henry, 4325
Harnischfeger, Walter, 4325
Harnish, Martin M., 3635
Harnois, T.P., 974
Harp, Steve, 446
Harper, C.M., 2053
Harper, Cecilia DeMille, 146
Harper, Charles W., 3889
Harper, Gordon, 4224
Harper, John W., 1114
Harper, Marianne S., 1007
Harper, Owen H., 138
Harper, Philip S., 1027
Harper, Philip S., Jr., 1027
Harper, Ralph E., 2473, 2474
Harper-Wyman Company, 1027
Harpole, Myron E., 350
Harrell, William A., 3199
Harren, Michael, 3030
Harriman, Evelyn J., 3487
Harriman, Mary W., 2527
Harriman, Pamela C., 2527
Harriman, W. Averell, 2527
Harrington (Charles A.) Foundation, 1542
Harrington, D.D., 3974
Harrington, Deborah Weil, 2548, 2787
Harrington, Francis A., 1542
Harrington, Francis A., Jr., 1542
Harrington, George, 1543
Harrington, George S., 621
Harrington, Hollis E., Jr., 2092
Harrington, Jacquelyn H., 1542
Harrington, James H., 1542
Harrington, Katherine, 2947
Harrington, Patricia J., 442
Harrington, Mrs. Paul E., 3753
Harrington, Sybil, 3974
Harrington, Sybil B., 3974
Harris, Avery, 2439
Harris, Barbara, 2130
Harris, Barbara C., 3717
Harris, Bette D., 1029
Harris, Charles E., 1259
Harris, Charles R., 1331
Harris Corporation, 726
Harris, Daniel, 2439
Harris, Edward M., Jr., 2035, 2535
Harris, Frederick G., 2410
Harris, Freeman, 4055
Harris, George W., 2130
Harris, H.W., 1135
Harris, Helen, 1698
Harris, Henry U., Jr., 1652
Harris, Herman Mark, 2542
Harris, Howard C., 803
Harris, Irving B., 1030, 1120
Harris, J. Ira, 968, 1031
Harris, Jack S., 4379
Harris, Jane C., 3435
Harris, Janette H., 2881
Harris, Jay, 2117
Harris, Joan W., 1030
Harris, John B., 2127
Harris, Judah J., 2439
Harris, Judith C., 1578
Harris, Katherine, 1029
Harris, King, 1029
Harris, Lee B., 2675
Harris, Lewis R., 1901
Harris, M.M., 4268
Harris, Martin R., 4056
Harris, Mattie Wattis, 4141

Harris, Michael, 2439
Harris, Mrs. Richard, 2729
Harris, Myrtle W., 77
Harris, Neison, 1029, 1030, 1120
Harris, Nicki, 1031
Harris, Philip B., 1845, 1892
Harris, R.B., 1933
Harris, Robert C., 191, 337
Harris, Robert Lynn, 3984
Harris, Ron, 2063
Harris, Rose, 2439
Harris, S.T., 4102
Harris, Thomas E., 258
Harris Trust and Savings Bank, 947, 968, 1014, 1018, 1028, 1072, 1080, 3903, 1129
Harris, V.M., 4054
Harris, Vernon V., 3435
Harris, Walter I., 2130
Harris, William C., 962
Harris, William H., 4141
Harris, William V., 3435
Harris, William W., 1030, 1120
Harrisburg Grocery Company, 668
Harrison, Carter H., 1623
Harrison, David B., 2773
Harrison, Edward E., 502, 516
Harrison, Frances M., 2344
Harrison, G.O., 3750
Harrison, Horace H., 4213
Harrison, James A., 3982
Harrison, Jean, 2213
Harrison, Lois Cowles, 2369
Harrison, Louise C., 434
Harrison, Nora Eccles Treadwell, 4146
Harrison, Richard, 3451
Harrison, Richard A., 4146
Harrison, W. Wright, 4191
Harriss, C. Lowell, 2911
Harsco Corporation, 3595
Harshman, Deroy, 2071
Hart, Barbara O., 732
Hart, D.L., 3383
Hart, Donald A., 3373
Hart, Frances Close, 3821, 3822
Hart, George D., 215
Hart, James T., 4103
Hart, John C., 3496
Hart, Kenneth N., 2406
Hart, Marcia Cook, 1502
Hart, Mrs. Max A., 2512
Hart, Nelson P., 588
Hart, Richard M., 3923
Hart, Robert C., 4333
Hart Schaffner & Marx, 1032
Hart, William B., Jr., 2092
Hart, William D., Jr., 2540
Hart, William G., 1096
Harte, Richard, Jr., 1652
Harter Bank & Trust Co., 3222, 3373
Hartford Courant Company, 532
Hartford Fire Insurance Company, 534
Hartford, George L., 2528
Hartford, John A., 2528
Hartford, Robert D., 107
Hartford, William L., 3245
Hartigan, James J., 1179
Harting, Robert M., 3666
Hartley, Fred L., 407, 676
Hartley, J.T., 726
Hartley, Mrs. James R., 458
Hartley, Richard O., 1763
Hartloff, Paul W., Jr., 403
Hartman, Betty R., 1130
Hartman, Clinton W., 1209
Hartman, Francis M., 2711
Hartman, Jesse, 535
Hartman, M.B., 190
Hartmann, Roy, 351
Hartmann, Virginia L., 2138
Hartnack, Carl E., 351
Hartstein, Raymond E., 955
Hartung, Richard K., 1145
Hartz, L.B., 1856

Hartz, Onealee, 1856
Hartzell Corporation, 1857
Hartzell, G.W., 3247
Hartzell Industries, 3247
Hartzell, James R., 1857
Hartzell, Miriam H., 3247
Hartzell, Robert, 1857
Harvey, Arthur J., Jr., 3769
Harvey, Constance, 2779
Harvey, Durwood C., 3842
Harvey, Edward J., 2365
Harvey, F. Barton, Jr., 1408
Harvey, Gertrude, 3769
Harvey, Hal, 2779
Harvey, Joan, 2779
Harvey, L.A., 950
Harvey, Paul, 1077
Harvey, Paul, Sr., 3940
Harvey, Robert D.H., 1436
Harvey, Robert P., 463
Harvey, Thomas B., 3559
Harvie, C. Thomas, 3392
Harwick, H.J., 1910
Harwood, John K., 3777
Hasenauer, John F., 2474
Hasenfeld, Alexander, 2529
Hasenfeld, Zissy, 2529
Hashorva, Tanya, 3520
Haskell, Antoinette M., 679
Haskell, Coburn, 3248
Haskell, John H.F., Jr., 498
Haskell, Mary D.F., 2219
Haskell, Melville H., 3248
Haskell, Melville H., Jr., 3248
Haskey, A.F., 4400
Haskin, Kenneth W., 2773
Haskins & Sells, 2395
Haskins, Caryl P., 646, 2325
Haskins, Ralph, 1656
Hasler, Joseph W., 1187
Hassee, Edward F., 1242
Hassel, Calvin, 3596
Hassel, Morris, 3596
Hasselquist, Maynard B., 1849
Hassenfeld, Alan, 3779
Hassenfeld, Stephen, 3779
Hassenfeld, Sylvia, 3779
Hassler, Howard E., 2230
Hastings, Alfred B., Jr., 294
Hastings, Barry M., 706
Hastings, Charles E., 4174
Hastings, David R., II, 1396
Hastings, Emita E., 2530
Hastings, J. Neil, 324
Hastings, John A., 4174
Hastings, John N., 1397
Hastings, Mary C., 4174
Hastings, Pat C., 3822
Hastings, Peter G., 1396
Hastings, Robert C., 4174
Hastings, Ruth, 324
Hastor Industries, 3779
Hatch, Augustus, 2382
Hatch, Francis W., 2726
Hatch, Francis W., III, 3810
Hatch, Harold A., 2350
Hatch, John W., 2773
Hatch, Margaret Milliken, 2350, 2531
Hatch, Mrs. Rakia I., 2531
Hatch, Richard L., 2531
Hatch, Serena M., 2726
Hatcher, Claud A., 865
Hatcher, William K., 731, 865
Hatfield, William C., 3871
Hathaway, E. Phillips, 1440
Hathaway, F.C., 4359
Hathaway, H. Grant, 1413
Hathaway, Thomas W., 3976
Hattemer, Val P., 3166
Hatterscheidt (F.W.) Trusts, 3826
Hatterscheidt, Ruth K., 3826
Hattier, Robert L., 1362
Hattler, Andrea M., 670
Hattler, Denise M., 670

Hauben, Helen G., 743
Hauer, Richard, 1106
Haugabrook, J.R., 1050
Haugo, Olaf, 1850
Haupert, Ruth C., 2234, 2577
Hauptfuhrer, Barbara, 2700
Haury, Emil W., 27
Hauser, Russell L., 670
Hauserman, William F., 3264
Havana National Bank, 1092
Havemeyer, Harry W., 3042
Havens, Charles G., 2533
Havens, Susan S., 2904
Haverty, Harold V., 1835
Hawaiian Trust Company, Limited, 890, 894, 895, 899, 904, 910
Hawk, E.J., 1999
Hawkes, Benjamin G., 295
Hawkes, S.G., 3299
Hawkins, Harman, 2308
Hawkins, Harold E., 1336
Hawkins, Jack W., 3925
Hawkins, Kathryn A., 2080
Hawkins, Margaret C., 349
Hawkins, Prince A., 2080
Hawkins, Robert M., 2080
Hawkins, Thomas L., Jr., 2226
Hawkins, William L., 502
Hawkinson, John, 583
Hawkinson, Robert W., 942
Hawley, Henry B., 1270
Hawley, Mrs. Henry B., 1270
Hawley, Jean Gannett, 1393
Hawley, Jess, 913
Hawley, John T., 913
Hawley, Philip M., 114, 211
Hawley, Samuel W., 502
Hawley, Wendell C., 1178
Hawn, Dorothy P., 4071
Hawn, John D., 4071
Hawn, Mildred, 3975
Hawn, W.R., 3975
Hawthorne, Betty E., 2377
Hawthorne, Douglas, 3199
Haxter, Chouttie, 1359
Hay, Bonita, 1074
Hay, Ellen, 3145
Hay, John, 2704
Hay (John I.) Trust, 1033
Hay, Karl S., 3145
Haycraft, Howard, 3047
Hayden, Charles, 2534
Hayden, Ida, 1383
Hayden, J.P., Jr., 3219
Haydock, Mrs. Francis B., 1586
Hayeck, Ernest S., 1659
Hayes, Betty Frost, 665
Hayes, Edmund B., 1220
Hayes, Mariam C., 3086
Hayes, Merrick C., 1151
Hayes, N.P., Jr., 3087
Hayes, Ralph W., 603
Hayes, Stanley W., 1220
Hayes, Stephen H., 1220
Hayes, Synnova B., 2270, 2814
Hayes, Waldo, 1397
Haykin, Howard, 2358
Haykin, Marilyn, 2358
Hayner, H.H., 4266
Hayner, James K., 4266
Hayner, John F., 1221
Haynes, Harold J., 4255
Haynes, I.M., 2045
Haynes, J.E., 2045
Haynes, John Randolph, 211
Haynes, Mrs. John Randolph, 211
Haynes, Noris R., Jr., 3855
Haynes, Thelma G., 1922
Haynes, W.W., 3397
Hays, Frances McKee, 4026
Hays, Mary Ann, 3265
Hays, Richard M., 3750
Hays, Robert D., 3261
Hays, Thomas C., 3265

Hays, Mrs. William H., III, 3029
Hayward, John T., 216, 727
Hayward, Pierre Dupont, 609
Hayward, Winifred M., 727
Haywiser, Lawrence Wm., 3535
Haywood, Alice V., 865
Haywood, Mary H., 3248
Haywood, T.C., 3086
Hazard, Mrs. Vincent H., 1573
Hazel, Lewis F., 2343
Hazeltine, Herbert S., 222
Hazelton, R.L., 4026
Hazen, Edward Warriner, 2535
Hazen, Helen Russell, 2535
Hazen, Joseph H., 2536
Hazen, Lita, 3597
Hazen, Lita A., 2536
Hazen, Lucy Abigail, 2535
Hazzard, George W., 1468
Hazzard, Jean F., 1659
Head, C.J., 3471
Head, Floyd, 1711
Healey, Judith K., 1894
Healy, J.F., 2249
Healy, James T., 402
Healy, John D., Jr., 1912
Healy, Martha Ann Dumke, 4137
Healy, Thomas B., Jr., 2343
Heaney, Cornelius, 2306
Heaney, Cornelius A., 2306
Heard, Alexander, 2444
Heard, Anita C., 2361
Heard, John G., 3960
Heard, S. Berton, 1382
Heard, Thomas H., 2361
Hearin, William J., 5
Hearn, Peter, 3689
Hearn, Ruby P., 2140
Hearst, David W., 2537, 2538
Hearst, George R., Jr., 2538
Hearst, George, Jr., 2537
Hearst, John R., Jr., 2537
Hearst, Randolph A., 2537, 2538
Hearst, William R., 2537, 2538
Hearst, William Randolph, 2537, 2538
Heath, Charles K., 920
Heath, Harriet A., 920
Heath, J.E., 3976
Heath, John E.S., 920
Heath, Karen, 2806
Heath, Mary M., 3976
Heaton, Mary Alice J., 1796
Heavenrich, M.P., Jr., 1798
Heaviside, Robert C., 2231
Heazel, Francis J., Jr., 820
Hebden, C. Stewart, 3683
Hebert, Lawrence I., 3870
Hebner, P.C., 3423
Hebner, Paul C., 302
Hebrew Union Jewish Institute of
  Religion, 1203
Hechinger Company, 1421
Hechinger, Fred M., 2325, 2777
Hechinger, John W., 1421
Hechinger, John W., Jr., 672, 685
Hechinger, June R., 1421
Hecht, Alexander, 1422
Hecht, Selma H., 1422
Heckman, A.A., 1853, 1868
Heckscher, August, 2540, 2995
Heckscher, Martin A., 3642, 3681, 3749
Heckscher, Maurice, 3557
Hecktman, Mrs. Melvin, 1070
Hector, Louis J., 706, 745
Hed, Gordon E., 1837, 1911, 1926
Hedberg, Victor, 741
Heddon, Russell A., 4337
Hedges, James R., III, 3860
Hedges, James S., II, 2416
Hedien, Wayne E., 922
Hedley, R.O., 407
Hedling, Susan, 439
Hedrick, Frank E., 1294

Hedrick, Thomas H., 1412
Hee, Harold S.Y., 892
Heed, Thomas D., 1034
Heed, Mrs. Thomas D., 1034
Heegaard, Peter, 1881
Heegaard, Peter A., 1821
Heely, James A., 2783
Heenan, D.A., 896
Heenan, Earl I., 1691
Heffern, Gordon E., 3276
Heffernan, Elizabeth B., 3172
Heft, Frederick J.W., 2339
Heft, Harold, 1000
Heftler, Pierre V., 1699, 1700, 1701,
  1703, 1704, 1800
Hegel, Richard, 593
Heginbotham, Will E., 451
Hehl, D.K., 1736
Heiberg, Kenneth, 2427
Heidakka, Edwin E., 3698
Heide, Robert D., 782
Heidt, John M., 411
Heil, J.F., Jr., 4308
Heileman Baking Company, 4326
Heileman (G.) Brewing Company, 4326
Heilicher, Amos, 1859
Heilicher, Daniel, 1859
Heiligman, Richard I., 2331
Heimann, John G., 940
Heimann, Sandra W., 3150
Heimann, William E., 3440
Heimlich, Donald, 2898
Heimlich, Lydia, 2898
Hein, Edward H., 2149
Heindl, Frank W., 4198
Heineman, Andrew D., 63
Heineman, Ben W., 1109
Heineman, Dannie N., 2541
Heineman, James H., 2541
Heineman, Melvin L., 2878
Heineman, William W., 2387
Heinemann, Harry N., Jr., 4292
Heiner, George M., 3691
Heinke, W.R., 2741
Heinlein, Charles H., 2427
Heinsheimer, Alfred M., 2775
Heinsheimer, Louis A., 2775
Heinz, Drue, 3599
Heinz, Elizabeth Rust, 3599
Heinz (H.J.) Company, 3598
Heinz, Henry J., II, 3598, 3599
Heinz, Henry John, III, 3599
Heinz, Howard, 3599
Heinz, Martha H., 848
Heinz, Vira I., 3600
Heisey, Charles E., 2046
Heiskell, Marian S., 2155, 2777, 2969
Heit, Joe, 478
Hekemian, James S., 1590, 1591
Helberg, Robert O., 3925
Held, Huyler C., 2726, 2727
Heldrich, John J., 2139, 2148
Helfaer, Evan P., 4327
Helfenstine, Jerry C., 3944
Helies, Anthony, 2624
Helies, Brenda, 2623
Helies, Brenda Christy, 2624
Helis, Cassandra Marie, 1365
Helis, William G., Jr., 1365
Hellendale, Robert, 529
Heller, Alfred E., 213
Heller, Ann McGreevy, 687
Heller, Anne C., 3068
Heller, Anne E., 213
Heller, Bernard, 2542
Heller, Clarence E., 213
Heller, Elinor R., 213
Heller, Florence G., 1035
Heller, Frederick, 3298
Heller, Helen H., 2382
Heller, Janet F., 213
Heller, Katherine, 213
Heller, Max M., 3805

Heller, Peter E., 1035
Heller, Robert, 1902
Heller, Ruth B., 213
Heller, Walter, 659
Heller, Walter E., 1036
Hellmann, Stuart, 4036
Hellmuth, Paul F., 2496
Hellner, Gary L, 4060
Hellner, Jack F., 4327
Helm, C.V., 3943
Helm, George T., 1575
Helm, Harold H., 2161
Helm, Joy, 476
Helmer, Marilyn T., 2377
Helmerich, W.H., 3436
Helmerich, W.H., III, 3436
Helmick, Maureen Stans, 378
Helmick, Walter, 378
Helming, Carlton T., 2798
Helmke, Walter P., 1213
Helmoholz, Elizabeth, 4246
Helms Bakeries, 214
Helms, Besse Hauss, 3249
Helms, F.B., 3092, 3093
Helms, J.R., 3121
Helms, W.B., 3249
Helmsley, Harry B., 2543
Helmsley, Leona M., 2543
Helsell, Virginia S., 4254
Helton, Richard E., 1258
Helvering, Elsa, 1310
Helvering, R. L., 1310
Helwig, Bernardine, 421
Helwig, Elsie, 3830
Hemann, Charles W., 34
Heming, Henry L., 2420
Heming, Kate S., 2420
Hempel, Kathleen J., 4319
Henck, Sadie L., 3978
Hendee, John H., Jr., 4318
Henderson, Barclay G.S., 1547
Henderson, Benson G., 3691
Henderson, David, 3577
Henderson, Ernest, 1547
Henderson, Ernest, III, 1547, 1548
Henderson, George B., 1547, 1548
Henderson, George T., 3228
Henderson, Gerard C., 1548
Henderson, Harriet W., 414
Henderson, J.B., 4081
Henderson, James A., 1210
Henderson, James D., 1532
Henderson, John, 952
Henderson, John W., 881
Henderson, L.C., 4079
Henderson, Loucile J., 3979
Henderson, Louise, 3979
Henderson, Mary Fuller, 1532
Henderson, Robert B., 3192
Henderson, Rutson R., 2397
Henderson, Simon W., III, 3979
Henderson, Simon W., Jr., 3979
Henderson, Thomas J., 76
Hendin, Clara H., 637
Hendin, David, 3359
Hendricks, Donald R., 1220
Hendricks, Richard L., 1196
Hendrickson, Arthur J., 2545
Hendrickson Bros., 2545
Hendrickson, John C., 2545
Hendrickson, Lil M., 3507
Hendrickson, Milton A., 2545
Hendrickson, Robert P., 3140
Hendrickson, William G., 44
Hendryx, Gail, 4096
Henegar, Henry A., 3832
Hengesbaugh, Bernard L., 1008
Henikoff, Leo M., 1161
Heningburg, Gustav, 2125
Henley, Benjamin J., Jr., 99
Henley, John C., III, 10
Henley, Walter E., 10
Henn, Catherine E.C., 1483
Hennebach, Ralph L., 2246, 2741

Hennessey, Frank M., 1722
Hennessey, John W., Jr., 507, 2737
Hennessy, Edward L., Jr., 2098
Henning, Barbara H., 935
Henny, Mac Lee, 3168
Henrichs, Milton J., 917, 918
Henriod, F. Henri, 4130
Henry, Dorothy J., 1566
Henry, Esther Helis, 1365
Henry, Frederick B., 1261
Henry, H.W., 1688
Henry, J. Campbell, 3063
Henry, J.D., 78
Henry, Leland, 3170
Henry, Linda J., 4250
Henry, Patricia M., 4250
Henry, Peggy Maitland, 2101
Henshel, Henry, 2313
Henshel, Joy, 2313
Henske, John M., 561
Henslee, Linda C., 3158
Hensleigh, Inez M., 1096
Hensley, Louis S., Jr., 1226
Hensley, Robert T., Jr., 1972
Henson, James M., 859
Hentschel, D.A., 3423
Heppen, Henry C., 2888
Heraty, Laurette, 745
Herberger, G.R., 29
Herberich, E. Alfred, 2201
Herbert, Peter A., 2521
Herbert, Thomas W., 1734
Herbst, Herman H., 215
Herbst, Jay A., 1716
Herbst, Maurice H., 215
Herd, J. Victor, 2364
Herd, Pauline Hoffmann, 2364
Herd, Pauline May, 2364
Herd, Victoria Prescott, 2364
Herenton, Willie W., 873
Hergenhan, Joyce, 527
Hering, Charles, 3230
Heritage Bank, 4329
Heritage Trust Company, 4358
Heritage Wisconsin Corporation, 4329
Heritage-Pullman Bank, 968
Herlihy, E. Herbert, 176
Herlihy, Elizabeth, 176
Herlihy, F. George, 75
Herlihy, Richard G., 176
Herlin, Jean T., 4104
Herman, Donald, 1717
Herman, Horton, 4230
Herman, Karen M., 2003
Herman, Rose, 1717
Herman, Sarah Andrews, 3142
Hermann, Grover M., 1037
Hermann, Sarah T., 1037
Hernandez-Colon, Rafael, 644
Herndon, Norris B., 845
Herndon, Vernon, 220
Herod, J.W., 9
Herold, H. Robert, II, 322
Herold, Matthew G., Jr., 322
Heron, Harriet W., 1920
Herr, Earl B., Jr., 1237
Herr, Kenneth J., 2722
Herr, Philip C., II, 3683
Herr, Stephen F., 1064
Herrick Corporation, 212
Herrick, Hazel M., 1718
Herrick, Kenneth C., 1718
Herrick, Ray W., 1718
Herrick, S.G., 212
Herrick, Todd W., 1718
Herrigel, Fred, III, 2850
Herrigel, Fred, Jr., 2850
Herring, Mabel B., 262
Herron, John E., 1008
Hershberger, Harold D., Jr., 3764
Hershberger, Harold, Jr., 3679
Hershey Foods Corporation, 3601
Herson, Marjorie, 1504
Herson, Richard J.L., 2309

Hertz, Fannie K., 216
Hertz, John D., 216
Hertz, Willard J., 1752
Hertzog, George B., 677
Hervey Foundation, 31
Hervey, Fred, 31, 38
Herz, John W., 2966
Herzog, Raymond H., 3750
Heselden, John E., 2463
Hess, C. Curtis, 756
Hess, Glen E., 1063
Hess, Helen, 2960
Hess, John B., 2546
Hess, Leon, 2546
Hess, Norma, 2546
Hess, Robert G., 1468
Hess, Susan, 2960
Hess, Walter W., Jr., 2387, 2420
Hess, William D., 2960
Hessberg, Albert, II, 2226
Hessinger, Carl J.W., 3748
Hessler, David J., 3266
Hessler, Robert R., 3238
Hesston Corporation, 1311
Hester, James M., 2513, 2653
Hester, Walter Dean, 3940
Hetherington, E. Mavis, 2445
Hetherman, Roger W., 2090
Hettinger, Albert J., III, 2547
Hettinger, Albert J., Jr., 2547
Hettinger, Franklin D., 3419
Hettinger, William R., 2547
Heublein, Inc., 538
Heuchling, Theodore P., 1578
Heuser, Charlotte B., 701
Heuser, Henry V., 1353
Heuser, Henry V., Jr., 1353
Heuser, Marshall V., 1353
Heuser, William B., 701
Hewitt, John H., 1586
Hewitt, Louis R., 2100
Hewitt, Patricia, 2282
Hewitt, Richard G., 2706
Hewlett, Walter B., 217
Hewlett, William R., 217
Hewlett, Mrs. William R., 217
Hewlett-Packard Company, 218
Hexter, Maurice B., 2605
Hexter, Paul L., 216
Heydt, Marguerite, 4141
Heydt, Matilda L., 1549
Heyler, David B., Jr., 280
Heyman, Carl K., 1040
Heyman, George H., Jr., 2914
Heyman, Joseph K., 870
Heyman, Stephen D., 2775
Heymann, Jerry, 1366, 1367
Heymann, Jimmy, 1366, 1367
Heymann, Mrs. Jimmy, 1366, 1367
Heymann, Leon, 1367
Heymann, Mrs. Leon, 1367
Heyns, Roger W., 217, 230
Heywood, Eastman F., 1554
Heyworth, John, 990
Hezzelwood, Ruth, 1848
Hiam, Edwin W., 1652
Hiatt, Arnold, 1640
Hiatt, Frances L., 1550
Hiatt, Howard, 1753
Hiatt, Jacob, 1550
Hibbel, Celien, 2646
Hibben, Joseph W., 336
Hibberd, William F., 2318, 2527
Hibernia Bank, 318
Hickey, Edward J., 1684
Hickey, John T., 1104
Hickey, John W., 4319
Hickox, Charles C., 2265
Hickox, Mrs. Charles C., 2265
Hickox, Mrs. Charles V., 2265
Hickox, John B., 2265
Hicks, John E., 930
Hicks, Patricia F., 1988
Hicks, Paul B., Jr., 2981

Hicks, Romayne E., 1795
Hidalgo, Hilda, 2161
Hidary, Abraham, 2549
Hidary, Isaac, 2549
Hidary (M.) Company, 2549
Hidary, Moses, 2549
Hiersteiner, Walter, 2031
Higbee Company, 3252
Higbie, Carlton M., Jr., 1744
Higgins, Austin D., 1395
Higgins, Carol W., 1189
Higgins, Eunice Olin, 2002
Higgins, James G., 892
Higgins, James W., 3027
Higgins, Laurence, 782
Higgins, Lorene Sails, 3488
Higgins (Mary S.) Trust No. 2, 1551
Higgins, Milton P., 1551
Higgins, Richard C., 1636
Higgins, Robert F., 2315
Higgins, Trumbull, 2219
Higgins Trust No. 13, 1551
Higgins, William H., Jr., 4196
Higginson, Corina, 662
Higginson, Shirley Foerderer, 3574
Higginson, Thomas L., 3574
Hightower, George H., 819
Hightower, Julian T., 819
Hightower, Neil H., 819
Hightower, Walter, 3980
Hightower, William H., Jr., 819
Higie, William F., 3582
Hilbert, Robert J., 444, 473
Hildebrandt, A. Thomas, 2382
Hildebrandt, Austin E., 2382
Hildebrandt, Elizabeth H., 2382
Hildreth, R.J., 999
Hilen, Frances Gilmore, 190
Hilgers, William, 4128
Hilinski, Chester C., 3545
Hill, B. Harvey, Jr., 855
Hill, Charlotte B., 2795
Hill, David G., 3186
Hill, E. Eldred, 2667
Hill, Gerald L., 3145
Hill, Harold M., 1594
Hill, Harriet, 74
Hill, J. Jerome, 1868
Hill, James Scott, 762
Hill, Jesse, Jr., 845
Hill, Julian W., 617
Hill, Leonard F., 2140, 2148
Hill, Louis W., Jr., 1853, 1894
Hill, Louis W., Sr., 1894
Hill, Luther L., Jr., 1262
Hill, Norman A., 573
Hill, R.J., 1109
Hill, Rebecca Travers, 846
Hill, Richard D., 1473
Hill, Robert E., 2308, 3068
Hill, Virginia W., 452
Hill, W.W., Jr., 1236
Hill, Walter Clay, 846
Hillard, Beulah, 3138
Hilleary, Robert, 1754
Hillenbrand, Daniel A., 1223
Hillenbrand, George C., 1223
Hillenbrand, George M., 1223
Hillenbrand Industries, 1223
Hillenbrand, John A., II, 1223
Hillenbrand, Ray J., 1223
Hillenbrand, W. August, 1223
Hillenbrand, William A., 1223
Hiller, Jaren E., 4392
Hilliard, David C., 1189
Hilliard, R.G., 3809
Hilliard, Thomas J., Jr., 3535
Hillman, Alex L., 2551
Hillman, Henry L., 3603, 3604, 3696
Hillman (J.H.) & Sons Co., 3603
Hillman, John Hartwell, Jr., 3603
Hillman Land Company, 3603
Hillman, Rita K., 2551
Hills, Edward E., 219

Hills, Lee, 3276
Hills, Reuben W., III, 219
Hillstrom-Masi, Susan, 209
Hillyard, Gerald R., Jr., 458
Hilsen, John C., 4264
Hilsman, Joseph H., 861
Hilson, John S., 2959
Hilton, Andrew C., 2360
Hilton, Conrad N., 220
Hilton, Eric M., 220
Hilton, William Barron, 220
Hiltz, Francie S., 3250
Hiltz, L. Thomas, 3250
Himelhoch, Charles S., 1684
Himmel, Clarence, 1719
Himmelman, Bonnie, 522
Hinderas, Natalie, 3698
Hindley, George, 269
Hineline, Mrs. Thomas G., 3005
Hines, Donald, 1735
Hines, Kimberly, 1804
Hinkle, Harry H., 2743
Hinman, Robert W., 1535
Hinson, J.A., 754
Hinson, Robin L., 3102
Hipp, F.M., 3809
Hipp, R.H., 3809
Hipp, W.H., 3809
Hirsch, C.H., 3196
Hirsch, David, 3770
Hirsch, Herbert, 2431
Hirsch, James G., 2689
Hirsch, John F., 3rd, 2568
Hirsch, Philip J., 2739
Hirsch, Sanford, 2492
Hirschberg, William S., 2379
Hirschey, Lee, 2837
Hirschfield, Ira, 202
Hirschhorn, Barbara B., 1404
Hirschhorn, David, 1404, 1405
Hirschl, Irma T., 2552
Hirschman, F.F., 1227
Hirshon, Dorothy, 2976
Hirtl, Leo, 3359
Hiser, Harold R., Jr., 2178
Hitch, Thomas K., 903
Hitchcock, Ethan A., 3057
Hitchcock, Margaret Mellon, 3605
Hitchcock, Martha H., 2057
Hitchcock, Meacham, 3178
Hitchcock, Thomas, III, 3605
Hitchcox, Laura C., 3172
Hitching, H. James, 3835, 3860
Hitchings, George H., 3085
Hite, James W., 4141
Hite, Marilyn H., 4141
Hitt, Charles M., 3769
Hladky, J.F., III, 1267
Hladky, J.F., Jr., 1267
Hlavac, Bernard C., 4378
Hlavacek, Lawrence L., 2443
Ho, Chinn, 900
Ho, Dean T.W., 900
Ho, Stuart, 900
Hoag, George Grant, 221
Hoag, George Grant, II, 221
Hoag, Grace E., 221
Hoag, John A., 897
Hoag, Merritt E., 817
Hoag, Patty, 221
Hoagland, Karl K., Jr., 1100
Hoar, Fred W., 176
Hobart, Edward A., 3391
Hobart, William, Jr., 3391
Hobbs, Jessie M., 4328
Hobbs, John H., 2445
Hobbs, Roswell H., 4328
Hobby, Diana P., 3983
Hobby, Oveta Culp, 3983
Hobby, W.P., 3983
Hobby, William P., Jr., 3983
Hoblitzell, Allan P., 1464
Hoblitzelle, Esther T., 3984
Hoblitzelle, Karl St. John, 3984

Hobson, Charles M., III, 122
Hobson, Henry W., Jr., 3206
Hochschild, Adam, 2553, 2554, 2637
Hochschild, Arlie R., 2553
Hochschild, Harold K., 2554
Hochschild, Kathrin S., 2553
Hochschild, Richard, 2475
Hochstein, Bernard, 2555
Hock, Bernice, 2037
Hockaday, Irvine O., 1968
Hockenberg, Harlan D., 1259
Hockenjos, G. Frederick, 2171
Hockstader, Leonard A., II, 2643
Hodell, Lisle D., 1253
Hodes, Richard S., 782
Hodge, Sarah Mills, 847
Hodges, Charles E., 2912
Hodges, W.H., 3946
Hodgkin, John P., 2763
Hodgkins, H. Follett, Jr., 2331
Hodgson, Daniel B., 855
Hodgson, Morton S., Jr., 859
Hodnett, Carolyn Young, 3473
Hodsdon, Louise, 3010
Hoefer, William, 3162
Hoellen, John J., 1173
Hoenemeyer, Frank J., 2193
Hoerner, John L., 1197
Hoernle, Adolph W., 2556
Hoffberger, Charles H., 1423
Hoffberger, Jerold C., 1423
Hoffberger, Judith R., 1450
Hoffberger, LeRoy E., 1423
Hoffenberg, Betty, 383
Hoffenberg, Marvin, 383
Hoffenberg, Peter H., 383
Hoffer, Helen C., 1039
Hoffer, Mary, 592
Hoffer Plastics Corporation, 1039
Hoffer, Robert A., 1039
Hoffer, Robert A., Jr., 1039
Hoffer, Robert M., 4354, 4377
Hoffman, Alfred, 1997
Hoffman, Anna R., 2640
Hoffman, Arnold J., 739
Hoffman, Arthur S., 2865
Hoffman, Burton, 580
Hoffman, C.L., 1601
Hoffman, Claire Giannini, 83
Hoffman, Dan H., 1354
Hoffman, E.R., 580
Hoffman, Edna M., 2355
Hoffman, Elaine S., 222
Hoffman, Gene Knudsen, 246
Hoffman, H. Leslie, 222
Hoffman, James H., 3342
Hoffman, Laurence K., 580
Hoffman, Michael J., 3186
Hoffman, Robert S., 1471
Hoffman, Samuel, 2238, 2889
Hoffman, Sidney, 580
Hoffman, Stanley, 654
Hoffman, Stephen J., 580
Hoffman, Walter H., 259
Hoffman, Walter W., 263
Hoffmann-La Roche, Inc., 2131
Hoffner, Roy C., 3138
Hofheinz, Fred, 3985
Hofheinz, Irene C., 3985
Hofheinz, Roy M., 3985
Hofheinz, Roy, Jr., 3985
Hofman, Donald J., 3171
Hofmann Company, 223
Hofmann, George W., 3135
Hofmann Homes Realty, 223
Hofmann, J. Michael, 1735
Hofmann, Kenneth H., 223
Hofmann, Martha J., 223
Hofmann, Philip B., 2140
Hofstetter, Bessie I., 3986
Hogan, C. Lester, 341
Hogan, Claude H., 410
Hogan, Dan, III, 3451
Hogan, Jack D., 453

Hubbard, R.C., 3821, 3822
Hubbard, Robert V., Sr., 314
Hubbard, Stanley E., 1864
Hubbard, Stanley S., 1864
Hubbard, Thomas J., 2412
Hubbard, William N., Jr., 1732
Hubbel (Harvey) Incorporated, 540
Hubbell, Fred, 1290
Hubbell, James W., Jr., 1270
Hubbs, Donald H., 220
Hubbs, Ronald M., 1820, 1912
Huber, Catherine G., 2133
Huber, David G., 2133
Huber, Gerald A., 3753
Huber, Hans A., 2133
Huber, Hans W., 2133
Huber, Joseph, 2611
Huber, Marion, 2133
Huber, Michael W., 2133
Huck, John L., 2155
Huck, Leonard W., 47
Huckabee, Jay, 3929
Hudak, T.F., 3671
Huddleson, Edwin E., Jr., 393
Hudner, Philip, 156
Hudson, Charles D., 810, 811
Hudson, Edward Joseph, Jr., 3888
Hudson, Edward R., Jr., 4092
Hudson, Gilbert, 1722
Hudson, Ida Callaway, 810, 811
Hudson, J.K., 943
Hudson (J.L.) Company, 1722
Hudson, Joseph L., Jr., 1722, 1755
Hudson, L.A., Jr., 4166
Hudson, Michael H., 1045
Hudson, O.W., 726
Hudson, Remy L., 241
Hudson, Richard C., 3914
Hudson, Vincent G., 3249
Hudson, William H., 2368
Hudspeth, C.M., 3893
Huebner, Edward C., 1573
Huebner, Robert W., 502
Hueg, William F., Jr., 834
Huegli, Richard F., 1781
Hueston, R.E., 2149
Huetteman, Raymond T., Jr., 1665
Huff, Glynn D., 4052, 4053
Huff, Peg, 2054
Huff, Robert B., 943
Huff, W.C., 263
Huff, William E., 1251
Huffaker, Hugh D., 3832
Huffaker, Robert F., 3832
Huffington, Roy M., 3993
Huffman, Phyllis, 4360
Huffman, R.R., 3255
Huffman, Robert R., 313
Hufford, Jack R., 4402
Huffy Corporation, 3255
Hufnagel, L.J., 3671
Hufstedler, Shirley Mount, 1077
Hugenberg, Stanley F., Jr., 1336
Hugenberger, Paul W., 1586
Huger, Eugenie Jones, 1370
Huger, Killian L., 1370
Hughes, Al E., 1288
Hughes, Bill M., 2051
Hughes, David Emery, 1397
Hughes, David H., 1968
Hughes, Harriette, 379
Hughes, John E., 975
Hughes, Katharine W., 1474, 1510
Hughes, Kenneth D., 3358
Hughes, Lois J., 586
Hughes, Mabel Y., 454
Hughes, Mareen D., 647
Hughes, Mark F., 2359
Hughes, Mary Ellen, 4254
Hughes, N.C., Jr., 3835
Hughes, Mrs. O.P., 249
Hughes, Sarah T., 3984
Hughes, Thomas L., 644
Hugonnet, Barbara M., 3043

Huisking, Edward P., 541
Huisking, Frank R., 541
Huisking, Richard V., 541
Huisking, William W., 541
Huitt, J. Fred, 4104
Hulett, William, 3376
Hulings, A.D., 1815
Hulings, Albert D., 1865
Hulings, Mary A., 1815
Hulings, Mary Andersen, 1865
Hull, Addis E., 1036
Hull, C.W., 87
Hull, Gerry, 840
Hull, Homer, 3481
Hull, R.L., 966
Hullin, Tod, 1144
Hulme, Helen C., 3610
Hulme, Milton G., Jr., 3610
Hulseman, J.F., 1158
Hulseman, L.J., 1158
Hulseman, R.L., 1158
Hulsen, Robert B., 1101, 1102
Hulsey, Sara, 3984
Hultz, Helen L., 573
Hulz, Margaret T., 2962
Humana Inc., 1344
Humann, Walter J., 3991
Humiston, P.A., 1731
Humleker, Margaret B., 4300
Humm, Cletus, 734
Humphrey, A.E., 3536
Humphrey, Benjamin C., 3397
Humphrey, Dean, 1297
Humphrey, George M., 3256
Humphrey, George M., II, 3257
Humphrey, Gilbert W., 3257
Humphrey, Hubert, 3124
Humphrey, James, III, 3047
Humphrey, Louise Ireland, 3257, 3262
Humphrey, Marvin V., 3162
Humphrey, Pamela S., 3256
Humphrey, William R., Jr., 1878
Humphreys, Cecil C., 3855
Humphreys, Ethel Mae Craig, 1953
Humphreys, Geraldine Davis, 3990
Humphreys, Henry J., 2711
Humphreys, J.P., 1953
Humphreys, James E., Jr., 3137
Humphreys, Ruth Boettcher, 436
Humphry, John A., 646
Hundred Club of Detroit, 1781
Hundt, P.R., 979, 980
Hungerpiller, James E., 847
Hunnicutt, Leland J., 270
Hunsicker, J. Quincy, III, 2320
Hunsinger, J.J., 1232
Hunsucker, W.J., 3800
Hunt, Alan Reeve, 3719
Hunt, Alfred M., 3535
Hunt, Andrew M., 3790
Hunt, Andrew McQ., 3611, 3613
Hunt, C. Giles, 3489
Hunt, Charles A., 1574
Hunt, Christopher M., 3611, 3613
Hunt, Daniel Kilner, 3613
Hunt, Donald M., 2837
Hunt, Donald S., 1028
Hunt, Gerald E., 2465
Hunt, Helen McM., 3611, 3613
Hunt, John B., 3611, 3613
Hunt, John D., 1624
Hunt Manufacturing Co., 3612
Hunt, Marion McM., 3611, 3613
Hunt, Ray L., 3991
Hunt, Richard McM., 3611, 3613
Hunt, Robert M., 1089, 1090
Hunt, Roy A., 3611, 3613
Hunt, Roy A., III, 3611, 3613
Hunt, Ruth Ray, 3991
Hunt, Samuel P., 2087
Hunt, Samuel W., Jr., 1035
Hunt, Susan Lee, 3691
Hunt, Susan M., 3611, 3613
Hunt, Susan R., 1108

Hunt, Torrence M., 3611, 3613
Hunt, Torrence M., Jr., 3611, 3613
Hunt, V. William, 1196
Hunt, W. Derald, 3405
Hunt, William E., 3611
Hunt, Willliam S., III, 3835
Hunter, A.V., 455
Hunter, Allan B., 216
Hunter, Andrew A., 1621
Hunter, Christine F., 1266
Hunter, David R., 2806, 2960
Hunter, E.K., 1355
Hunter, Edward, 1723
Hunter, George, 141
Hunter, George Thomas, 3829
Hunter, Graham, 2567
Hunter, Howard W., 416
Hunter, Irma, 1723
Hunter, J.P., 4228
Hunter, Jack, 1099
Hunter, Kathryn M., 3344
Hunter, Raymond P., 678
Hunter, Robert P., Jr., 821
Hunter, Thelma, 1868
Hunter, William O., 3551
Hunter, William T., 1266
Hunter-Gault, Charlayne, 2445
Hunting, David D., Jr., 1775
Hunting, David D., Sr., 1775
Huntington Bank of Northeast Ohio,
    3157, 3186
Huntington Bank of Toledo, 3386
Huntington, David M.G., 4356, 4358
Huntington, John, 3258
Huntington, Lawrence S., 2689
Huntington National Bank, 3161, 3189,
    3317
Huntley, Robert E.R., 4154
Huntting, J.G., Jr., 1862
Hupp, L.D., 780
Hurd, George A., Sr., 1113
Hurd, Priscilla Payne, 1113
Hurlbut, Sally D., 1586
Hurley, Ed E., 1369
Hurley, James G., 2809
Hurley, James H., Jr., 431
Hurley, Joseph G., 311
Hurley, Robert J., 2783
Hurst, Anthony P., 1724
Hurst, Dean W., 4144
Hurst, Elizabeth S., 1724
Hurst, Peter F., 1724
Hurst, Ronald F., 1724
Hurt, Mrs. J.S., 848
Hurtig, Mrs. Howard, 3765
Hurtig, Peggy Helms, 214
Hurwitz, Charles, 4061
Hurwitz, Roger, 2003
Husband, Elizabeth F., 27
Hussey, Jerry, 771
Hussey, Neil, 2223
Hussey, Raymond W., 3285
Husted, Ralph W., 1236, 1256
Huston, Beatrice L., 1812
Huston, Charles L., III, 3614
Huston, Charles Lukens, III, 3645
Huston, Charles Lukens, Jr., 3614
Huston, Mrs. Charles Lukens, Jr., 3614
Huston, John A., 2374
Huston, Ruth, 3614
Huston, William T., 416
Hutchens, Barbara Baker, 693
Hutcheson, Betty R., 3843
Hutcheson, John L., Jr., 3845
Hutcheson, Philo A., 3589
Hutcheson, Susanne Lilly, 1876
Hutcheson, Thad T., 3953
Hutcheson, Theodore M., 3843
Hutcheson, W. Frank, 3843
Hutchings, John A., 1184
Hutchings, Leo G., 3774
Hutchins, Francis S., 1351
Hutchins, Mary J., 2568
Hutchins, Robert A., 1154

Hutchins, Waldo, III, 2568
Hutchins, Waldo, Jr., 2568
Hutchinson, H.D., 1101
Hutchinson, Herman R., 3522
Hutchinson, Peter C., 1834
Hutchinson, Robert B., 4248
Hutchinson, Robert E., 31, 38
Hutchinson, Virginia L., 77
Hutchison, Carlton E., 3540
Hutchison, Colleen, 3456
Hutchison, D.T., 951
Huthsteiner (Robert and Pauline) Trust,
    3992
Hutson, Fred A., 3869
Huttenbauer, Samuel, 3292
Hutton (E.F.) and Company, 2569
Hyams, Godfrey M., 1561
Hyams (Godfrey M.) Trust, 1562
Hybl, William J., 445
Hyde, Henry, 2557
Hyde, Henry B., 2422
Hyde, J.R., 3844
Hyde, J.R., III, 3844
Hyde, Lester, 1803
Hyde, Lillia Babbitt, 2134
Hyde, M.L., 2030
Hyde, Margaret R., 3844
Hyde, Paul, 3199
Hydeman, A.L., Jr., 2911
Hyman, George, 664
Hyman Korman, Inc., 3632
Hyman, Marjorie, 2214
Hyman, Sadie, 664
Hyman, Samuel M., 3615
Hyndman, Thomas M., Jr., 3698
Hynes, John F., II, 3215
Hyun, Bong Hak, 1546

Iakovos, Bishop, 990
Ianco-Starrels, Josine, 167
Iandoli, Louis C., 1659
I'Anson, Lawrence W., 4153
Ibarguen, Alberto, 532
Idaho First National Bank, 912
Iddings, Andrew S., 3259
Iddings, Roscoe C., 3259
Idema, Jane H., 1715
Ifft, Edward C., 3625
Ihrig, Charles Glenn, 679
Ikeda, Charleen K., 888
Ikenberry, Stanley, 2109
Ilchman, Alice S., 2700
Illges, A., Jr., 848
Illges, Custis G., 849
Illges, Emmy Lou P., 849
Illges, John P., 849
Illges, John P., III, 848, 849
Illingworth, G.E., 1180
Illinois Cereal Mills, 1187
Illinois Consolidated Telephone
    Company, 1075
Illinois Tool Works, 1045
Imboden, Mary Ellen, 1401, 1403
Imerman, Stanley, 1725
Imparato, Joseph A., 3987
Indian Head, 2572
Indiana Gas & Chemical Corporation,
    1225
Indiana National Bank, 1216, 1226,
    1233, 1258
Indianapolis Newspapers, 1204
Industrial Valley Bank, 3539
Industrial Valley Bank and Trust
    Company, 3689
Industrial Valley Title Insurance
    Company, 3539
Infanger, Marie, 2231
Ingalls, Daniel H.H., 1546
Ingalls, David S., 3260
Ingalls, David S., Jr., 3260
Ingalls Foundation, 3579
Ingalls, Louise H., 3260
Ingalls (Robert) Testamentary Trust, 3579

Ingalls, Robert U., 1599
Ingersoll, James H., 1134
Ingersoll Milling Machine Company, 1047
Ingersoll, Paul M., 3683
Ingersoll, Ward, 118
Ingham, Linda Bridges, 105
Ingraham, Christopher, 1602
Ingram, Edgar W., 3261
Ingram, Edgar W., III, 3261
Ingram, Fred G., 282
Ingram, G. Conley, 887
Ingram, Joe, 1971
Ingwersen, James C., 76
Inkley, Mrs. Sherwood, 4017
Inks, Earla Mae, 3258
Inland Container Corporation, 1227
Inland Empire Paper Company, 4231
Inland Steel Company, 1048
Inman, Charles E., 2836
Inman Mills, 3807
Innes, Martha M., 2493
Inonog, Flordeliza G., 3773
Interco, 1972
Intercon Overseas, Inc., 691
Inter-First Bank, 3985
InterFirst Bank Corsicana, 3986
InterFirst Bank Dallas, 3904, 3923, 3981, 4038, 4045, 4090
InterFirst Bank Fort Worth, 3962, 4109
InterFirst Bank Houston, 3901, 4009
InterFirst Bank in San Antonio, 4072
Interlake, 1049
International Flavors & Fragrances, 2571
International Metals & Machines, 438
International Minerals & Chemical Corporation, 1046
International Minerals and Metals Corporation, 2794
International Multifoods, 1866
International Ore and Fertilizer Corporation, 2865
International Paper Company, 2574
InterNorth, 2058
Inter-Regional Financial Group, 1867
Interstate Bank, 314
Interstate Marine Transport Co., 3607
Interstate Ocean Transport Co., 3607
Interstate Towing Co., 3607
Intra-West Bank of Boulder, 472
Intra-West Bank of Denver, 442, 446
Irby Construction Company, 1938
Irby, Margaret L., 1938
Irby, Stuart C., Jr., 1938
Irby (Stuart C.) Company, 1938
Irby, Stuart M., 1938
Ireland, Cornelia W., 3294
Ireland, James D., 3187, 3294
Ireland, James D., III, 3294
Ireland, Kate, 3262
Ireland, Lucy E., 3294
Ireland, Margaret Allen, 3262
Ireland, Melville H., 3262
Ireland, R. Livingston, 3262
Ireland, R.L., III, 2362, 3262
Irish, Ann K., 1733
Irish, Dorothy R., 2331
Irvin, C. Alan, 1338
Irvine, James, 230
Irvine, Janet M., 1685
Irvine, Timothy, 4099
Irving Trust Company, 2350, 2375, 2531, 2575, 2774, 2855, 2943, 3040
Irwin, Charles J., 493
Irwin, Fannie M., 231
Irwin, James, 1664
Irwin, John N., II, 2986
Irwin, Philip D., 270
Irwin, Robert J.A., 2376
Irwin, Robert J.A., Jr., 2260
Isaacs, Bertram, 2603
Isaacs, Marion M., 3716
Isaacs, Myron S., 2387, 3015
Isakower, Gloria, 2599

Iselin, Lewis, 2985
Iseman, Joseph S., 2173, 2380, 2913
Ishikawa, Tadao, 3001
Ishiyama, George S., 232
Ishiyama, Setsuko, 232
Islami, Abdol H., 2128
Isles, Philip H., 2653
Israel, A.C., 611
Israel, Edmond, 2654
Israel, George, 867
Israel, Myer, 1537
Israel, Thomas C., 611
Itami, Hiroyuki, 3001
ITT Rayonier, Incorporated, 542
Ittleson, Blanche F., 2576
Ittleson, H.A., 2112
Ittleson, H. Anthony, 2576
Ittleson, Mrs. H. Anthony, 2576
Ittleson, Henry, 2576
Ittleson, Henry, Jr., 2576
Ittleson, Mrs. Henry, Jr., 2576
Ittleson, Lee F., 2576
Ittleson, Nancy S., 2576
Ittmann, Mrs. William M., 3183
Iverson, Marli Jannsen, 4259
Ives, Dermod, 2580, 2581
Iwamoto, Karen H., 888
Iwata, Harry H., 4241
Ix, Alexander E., Jr., 2136
Ix, Douglas E., 2136
Ix (Franklin) and Sons, 2136
Izzo, A.J., 2249

Jacangelo, Nicholas, 2792
Jack, N.R., 1020
Jacke, Stanley E., 3726
Jackier, Joseph H., 1667, 1725
Jackier, Lawrence S., 1667, 1725
Jackman, William L., 4372
Jackson, Alexander, 2748
Jackson (Ann) Family Charitable Trust, 234
Jackson, Ann G., 234
Jackson, B.L., 4277
Jackson, Edgar R., 311
Jackson, F.H., 1736
Jackson, Geraldine, 1510
Jackson, Gwen T., 4358
Jackson, Herrick, 3090
Jackson, Hulen L., 3885
Jackson, J.D., 1138
Jackson, Jack B., 3911
Jackson, Mrs. James H., 1573
Jackson, John N., 3952
Jackson, Katherine, 2892
Jackson, Maria C., 3490
Jackson, Mary R., 3090
Jackson Mills, 3811
Jackson, Monty J., 4047
Jackson, Palmer G., 234
Jackson, Peter, 234
Jackson, Robert W., 3090
Jackson, Stephen K., 837
Jackson, Ted M., 1409
Jackson, Thad R., 1555
Jackson, Theodora, 2775
Jackson, Thomas A., 876
Jackson, William A., 4307
Jacob, John E., 2775
Jacob, R.C., 3372
Jacob, Richard J., 3166
Jacobi, Herbert J., 2327
Jacobs, Burleigh E., 4354
Jacobs, Edna L., 2980
Jacobs, J.G., 1731
Jacobs, James P., 2051
Jacobs, Jennifer L., 2648
Jacobs, Lamont, 3245
Jacobs, N., 997
Jacobs, Norman A., 4353
Jacobs, Robert, 1049
Jacobs, William G.E., 3405
Jacobs, William K., Jr., 2980

Jacobsen, J.C., 4081
Jacobsen, Leslie A., 2431
Jacobson, A.F., 1890
Jacobson, Balche E., 4284
Jacobson, Bernard H., 4284
Jacobson, Frank C., 4342
Jacobson, Howard, 1659
Jacobson, Jo, 3142
Jacobson, Leon O., 1161
Jacobson, Leslie A., 2797
Jacobson, Sibyl C., 2732
Jacobus, C.D., 4329
Jacobus, Catherine H., 2284
Jacobus Company, 4329
Jacobus, D.C., 4329
Jacobus, J.T., 4329
Jacobus Quickflash, 4329
Jacobus, R.G., 4329
Jacott, William E., 1806
Jacques, Andre, 498
Jaeger, Jack R., 4379
Jaeger, Lamont O., 4310
Jaeger, Marilyn R., 2153
Jaeger, Robert, 1831
Jaeger, Ursula, 1831
Jaffe, Donna, 1564
Jaffe, Edwin A., 1564
Jaffe, Lola, 1564
Jaffe, Meyer, 1564
Jaffe, Miles, 1774, 1792
Jaffe, Robert, 1564
Jaffe, Samuel S., 2472
Jaffin, Charles L., 2154
Jagels, George D., 313
Jaicks, Frederick G., 1048
Jallow, Raymond, 350
Jalovec, Richard S., 1021
James, Donald E., 892
James, F.L., 794
James, H. Thomas, 1160
James, Howard P., 1625
James, Jean Butz, 30
James, John H., 4100
James, Patrick J., 2316
Jameson (J.W.) Corporation, 235
Jamieson, L.C., 3734
Jammal, Eleanor, 3158
Janes, Walter C., 2000
Janicki, Robert, 918
Janjigian, Edward, 2600
Janklow, Linda, 3013
Jannopoulo, Jerome A., 766
Jansen, Miriam Victor, 2006
Janssen, Daniel, 498
Jansson, Douglas M., 3790
Janzen, Curtis, 1412
Japan Shipbuilding Industry Foundation, 3001
Japhet, Dan R., 3947
Jaquith, Richard D., 1126
Jarmiolowski, Stanley J., 3940
Jarratt, J.B., 4079
Jarson (Esther M.) Trust, 3263
Jarson, Isaac N., 3263
Jarvis, David, 1895
Jarvis, J. Kirkland, 4209
Jaspan, Michael, 2437
Jaspan, Norman, 2437
Jaspan, Ronald, 2437
Jath Oil Co., 3445
Javitch, Lee H., 3618
Javitch, Rona, 3618
Jay, Byron, 2528
Jeanes, Anna T., 873
Jeanes Teachers of the Southern States, 873
Jeannero, Douglas M., 1705
Jedele, Paul W., 1723
Jeffers, John, 1727
Jeffers, Lottie L., 2361
Jefferson Bank and Trust, 442
Jefferson, Mary C., 236
Jefferson National Bank of Miami Beach, 706

Jeffery, Arch S., 3711
Jeffery, Clara L.D., 2137
Jeffery, William, 336
Jeffett, Mrs. Frank A., 3891
Jeffords, George V. McL., 2401
Jeffords, Kathleen McL., 2401
Jeffords, Walter M., Jr., 2401
Jeffress, Robert M., 4177
Jeffrey, H.P., 3307
Jeffrey, Nancy, 3261
Jeffries, McChesney H., 803
Jeffries, Porter C., 37
Jeld-Wen Co. of Arizona, 3491
Jeld-Wen Fiber Products, 3491
Jelinek, Fran, 1664
Jelley, Philip M., 369
Jenkins, A.H., 1688
Jenkins, Carol, 732
Jenkins, Charles E., II, 4181
Jenkins, Charles H., Sr., 732
Jenkins, Elizabeth C., 3108
Jenkins, George W., 732
Jenkins, Hopkin, 3492
Jenkins, Howard, 732
Jenkins, John T., Jr., 3108
Jenkins, Lee B., 3108
Jenkins, Paul R., 3524
Jenkins, R. Lee, 2178
Jenkins, Robert, 1476
Jenkins, Rockwood, 2419
Jenks, Margaret B., 1989
Jenn, Gerald R., 1229
Jenn, Louis J., 1229
Jenner, Albert E., Jr., 1036
Jenner, Edward, 2331
Jennings, Evan D., II, 3620
Jennings, Frank G., 2573
Jennings, Madelyn P., 2463
Jennings, Martha Holden, 3264
Jennings, Mary, 2057
Jennings, Mary Hillman, 3620
Jennings, Neal L., 3836
Jennings, Richard G., Jr., 3116
Jensen, Carl D.J., 4221
Jensen, Eric F., 2217
Jenson, John H., 3136
Jenson, Thor, 1272
Jentes, William R., 1063
Jephson, Lucretia Davis, 2580, 2581
Jepsen, Grace, 342
Jepson, Hans P., 2244
Jergens, Andrew N., 3265
Jergens, Andrew N., Jr., 3265
Jergens, Linda Busken, 3265
Jernstedt, Dorothy, 212
Jerome, Franklin D., 1576
Jerome, Joseph M., 3666
Jerry, John L., 1820, 1831
Jess, Mary Jo, 1821
Jesselson, Erica, 2582
Jesselson, Ludwig, 2442, 2582
Jesselson, Michael, 2582
Jessup, John B., 2983
Jessup, Philip S., II, 2405
Jetton, G.R., Jr., 3289
Jewel Companies, 1050
Jewell, D.A., IV, 3845
Jewell, Mrs. D.A., Jr., 3845
Jewell, E. Dunbar, 3845
Jewell, G.H., 2919
Jewell, Robert, 1754
Jewell, Robert H., 1618
Jewett, George F., Jr., 326, 1925
Jewett, George Frederick, 238
Jewett, George Frederick, Jr., 238
Jewett, Lucille McIntyre, 238
Jewett, Robert K., 3930, 4086
Jewitt, David W.P., 493
Jinishian, Vartan H., 2600
Jinks, G.C., 850
Jinks, G.C., Sr., 850
Jinks, Ruth T., 850
Joan Carol Corp., 545
Joanis, John W., 4378

Kennedy, Augustus H., 1872
Kennedy, Chester, 1735
Kennedy, David B., 1691
Kennedy, David M., 4145
Kennedy, Duff, 4238
Kennedy, Edward M., 666
Kennedy, Elizabeth E., 1733
Kennedy, George D., 1046, 1060
Kennedy, James Cox, 822, 889
Kennedy, John H., 3510
Kennedy, John R., Sr., 2141
Kennedy, Joseph P., 666
Kennedy, Mrs. Joseph P., 666
Kennedy, Kathryn Padgett, 3808
Kennedy, R. Craig, 1052
Kennedy, Robert M., 3970
Kennedy, Roger G., 275
Kennedy, Rosalind Freund, 1010
Kennedy, Thomas J., 1328
Kennedy, William J., III, 1126
Kenney, William, 1145
Kenniston, Phyllis, 1397
Kennon, Lawrence E., 1189
Kent, A. Atwater, Jr., 613
Kent (Atwater) Foundation, 613
Kent, Fred I., III, 2234
Kent, Helene D., 1425
Kent, Jack, 437
Kent, Otis Beall, 1425
Kent, Robert W., 3156
Kent, Wendel, 766
Kentucky Carbon Corporation, 4278
Kenworthy, Walter, 2426
Kenyon, Robert O., 4266
Kenyon, Robert W., 3772
Keough, Richard W., 2732
Kepler, Charles G., 4398
Kerbel, Walter, 3906
Kerekes, Gabriel, 2911
Kerley, Marsha, 4366
Kerlin, Gilbert, 2330, 2402
Kern, George C., Jr., 2230
Kern, John C., 1062
Kernan, James S., Jr., 3005
Kerney, James C., 2142
Kerns, Burton C., 4402
Kerr (A.H.) Corporation, 244
Kerr, Alexander H., 244
Kerr, Breene M., 3439
Kerr, David C.G., 720
Kerr Glass Corporation, 244
Kerr, Joffa, 3439
Kerr, Lou C., 3439
Kerr, Louise H., 2402
Kerr, Robert A., 3271
Kerr, Robert S., Jr., 3439
Kerr, Ruth, 244
Kerr, Sheryl V., 3439
Kerr, William A., 244
Kerr, William G., 3439
Kerr-McGee Corporation, 3440
Kerschbaum, Robert B., 1664
Kerst, Richard N., 2540
Kerstein, David A., 1365
Kerth, Alfred H., III, 1948
Kesey, Cynthia, 4063
Keslar, Peter, 3380
Kess, Mrs. Stanley E., 3194
Kessel, Theodore F., Sr., 3142
Kessel, William, 1798
Kessler, Barbara, 1131
Kessler, Dennis, 1000
Kessler, John W., 3189
Kessler, Ralph K., 575
Kessler, Robert S., 3363
Ketcham, Roy C., 2416
Kettering, Charles F., 3271, 3273
Kettering, Charles F., III, 3272
Kettering, E.W., 3272
Kettering, J.S., 3272
Kettering, Linda, 3272
Kettering, Lisa S., 3272
Kettering, Mrs. V.W., 3272
Kettering, V.W., 3272

Kettler, James R., 1753
Keusch, Suzanne, 2583
Kevorkian, Hagop, 2611
Kevorkian, Marjorie, 2611
Key Biscayne Bank and Trust Company, 706
Key, Bruce, 4033
Key, James W., 865
Key Trust Co., 2311, 2860
Keydel, Frederick R., 1707
Keynes, William, 3268
Keyser, Alan G., 3699
Keyser, George H., 3342
Keystone Carbon Co., 3732
Keystone Weaving Mills, 3534
Kezar, Charles, 1510
Kezer, C. Henry, 1474
KFC Corporation, 538
Khoury, George, 3596
Kibler, Burke, III, 689
Kick, Frank J., 2319
Kidd, Philip C., 3462
Kidd, Mrs. Wilmot H., 2587
Kidde, John L., 2534
Kidder, Dorothy R., 2332
Kidder, George H., 1646
Kidder, Peabody & Co., 2612
Kieckhefer, John I., 39
Kieckhefer, John W., 39
Kieckhefer, Robert H., 39
Kieckhefer, Virginia O., 39
Kieft, Donn, 3342
Kiermaier, John W., 2329
Kiernat, Elizabeth M., 1928
Kierscht, Marsha, 3139
Kies, Mabel B., 560
Kies, W.S., 560
Kies, William S., III, 560
Kieschnick, W.F., Jr., 78
Kiewit, Marjorie H., 2059
Kiewit, Peter, 2059
Kiewit, Peter, Jr., 2059
Kiggen, James D., 3413
Kilbourne, Edgar, 1231
Kilbride, R.S., 1101
Kilburger, Charles, 3275
Kilcarr, Andrew J., 2406
Kiley, Thomas H., 3729
Kilgore, John E., Jr., 659
Kilgore, Robert J., 3594
Kilgore, Ronald N., 1681
Kilkeary, Nan, 1185
Killam, George, 3929
Killip, Wilfred, 43
Killough, Walter H.D., 2613
Kilmartin, J.F., 1834
Kilner, Daniel, 3611
Kilpatrick, Marjorie K., 612
Kilpatrick, Samuel M., 2495
Kimball, H. Earle, 3781
Kimball International, 1219
Kimball, Richard A., Jr., 2726
Kimball, W.R., Jr., 417
Kimball, William R., 334
Kimbell, David A., 4122
Kimberly, John R., 1465
Kimberly-Clark Corporation, 4338
Kimble, Gregory, 2328
Kimbrell, Charles H., 706
Kimbrough, A. Richard, 82, 380
Kimmel, Caesar P., 2361
Kimmel, O.M., Jr., 4247
Kimmel, Philip, 2520
Kimmelman, Helen, 2614
Kimmelman, Milton, 2614
Kimmerer, Richard G., 2243
Kincaid, Charles E., 4238
Kincannon, Louis E., 1251
Kind, Patricia van A., 3006
Kindermac Partnership, 465
King, B.J., 3268
King, Betty S., 4195
King, Calvin A., 1476
King, Carl B., 4003

King, Charles A., 1571
King, D.E., 3312
King, David A., 3772
King, Dennis B., 215
King, Doris, 722
King, Dorothy, 4402
King, Dorothy E., 4003
King, Dorothy Warren, 3469
King, Edward H., 1183
King, Edward M., 153
King, Florence E., 4003
King, Frances M., 3390
King, Hazel H., 520
King, Mrs. John Allen, 4112
King, John F., 170
King, John T., III, 1401
King, Judith S., 1635
King, L., 3539
King, Louis, 1432
King, Louise Straus, 2965
King, Mary E., 638
King, May Dougherty, 3934
King, Patricia A., 2902
King Ranch, 4004
King, Reatha Clark, 1912
King, Richard C., 1975
King, Richard H., 532, 1866
King, Robert E., 1162, 1385
King, Roger J., 2965
King, Susan E., 2368
King, Thomas E., 1960
King, Thomas L., 2096
King, Timothy L., 4353
King, Verne L., 587
Kingman, Alton H., Jr., 170
Kings Point Industries, 2518
Kingsbury Machine Tool Corporation, 2090
Kingsbury Manufacturing Company, 2090
Kingsbury-Smith, J., 2537, 2538
Kingsland, James A., 2643
Kingsley, F.G., 614, 2740
Kingsley, Frederick W., 489
Kingsley, Ora Rimes, 614
Kingsmore, Harold D., 1
Kinkade, Maurice E., 2416
Kinkel, Walter, 3342
Kinkel, Walter J., 3224
Kinlaw, Dennis A., 4023
Kinnaird, Charles R., 1776
Kinne, Frances B., 731
Kinney, Annabelle, 3367
Kinney, Harry A., 4044
Kinney, Henry E., 738
Kinney, Ida Lindstrom, 1272
Kinney, Martha Hodsdon, 3010
Kinney, Richard J., 2178
Kinney, Samuel M., Jr., 2158
Kinneyman, Nellie S., 2567
Kinnisten, D.E., 1731
Kinomoto, Frank Y., 4241
Kinseila, Deborah, 2804
Kinsey, Margaret W., 1383
Kintzel, Lee, 3791
Kinzel, Augustus B., 393
Kiplinger, Austin H., 667
Kiplinger, LaVerne C., 667
Kiplinger, Willard M., 667
Kippen, Christina M., 1881
Kipphut, W. Michael, 4106
Kirby, Allan P., Jr., 2143
Kirby, Allan P., Sr., 2143
Kirby, Ann K., 2143
Kirby, Ann Pfohl, 2705
Kirby, F.M., 2143
Kirby, Fred M., II, 2143
Kirby, Jerry L., 3199
Kirby, Robert, 3102
Kirby, W.J., 1005
Kirby, William T., 1077, 1132
Kircher, Dudley P., 3299
Kircher, Kenneth J., 596

Kirchmeyer, Frederick J., 917
Kirgan, Mary, 1447
Kirk, Arthur W., 235
Kirk, Edward, 1520
Kirk, Grayson, 2986
Kirk, Mrs. Harris C., 79
Kirk, Leland L., 148
Kirk, Richard A., 436
Kirk, Robert J., 3386
Kirk, Russell, 428
Kirkham, George D., 3171
Kirkham, Kate B., 3171
Kirkpatrick, Clayton, 1089, 1090
Kirkpatrick, Eleanor B., 3441
Kirkpatrick, Frederick S., 1789
Kirkpatrick, Isabel, 771
Kirkpatrick, Joan E., 3441
Kirkpatrick, John E., 3441
Kirkpatrick Oil Company, 3441
Kirkpatrick, Roderick J., 2435
Kirkpatrick, William A., 1786
Kirsch, C. John, 1827
Kirtland, Dorance L., 1134
Kiser, Anthony C.M., 2506
Kiser, John W., III, 2506
Kish, Stephen A., 2231
Kishpaugh, Beverly, 3910
Kisseleff, Charlotte G., 3578
Kissell, M.E., 3456
Kissinger, Henry A., 2875
Kistler, William H., 458
Kitko, Paulette, 3173
Kitrosner, Mary S., 2939
KixMiller, Richard W., 2134
Kjorlien, Clarence J., 883
Klapp, William D., 1909
KLAS-TV, 4179
Klatt, Florence R., 4331
Klau, David W., 2615
Klau, James D., 2615
Klau, Sadie K., 2615
Klausmeyer, Robert O., 3183
Kleberg, Caesar, 4005
Kleberg, Helen C., 4006
Kleberg, Mary Lewis, 4004
Kleberg, Richard M., III, 4004
Kleberg, Robert J., Jr., 4006
Kleberg, Stephen J., 4005
Klee, Conrad C., 2616
Klee, Virginia, 2616
Kleefeld, Carolyn Mary, 394
Kleier, George O., 56
Klein, Amelia, 4007
Klein, Anne L., 1906
Klein, Arthur, 3704
Klein, Bertram W., 1334
Klein, Charles T., 2455
Klein, David L., 2617
Klein, Edith Miller, 914
Klein, Edward C., Jr., 2128
Klein, Esther, 3704
Klein, Hannah, 2752
Klein, Henry D., 151
Klein, Miriam, 2617
Klein, Nathan J., 4007
Klein, Nora R., 151
Klein, Paul R., 151
Klein, Philip, 3704
Klein, Richard A., 1906
Klein, Richard L., 3396
Klein, Robert H., 151
Klein, Russel R., 79
Klein, Ruth, 2222
Klein, Samuel H., 1334
Klein, Seymour M., 2222, 2590
Klein, Stanley M., 2481
Kleinfeldt, Richard C., 4324
Klementik, David, 3759
Klemeyer, J.A., 700
Klenke, Shirley, 4339
Klepfer, Robert O., Jr., 3132
Klesener, Shirley B., 2941
Klich, Bill, 770
Kligler, Seymour H., 2481

Kline, Bessie H., 3628
Kline, Charles, 3627
Kline, Figa Cohen, 3627
Kline, Gary H., 1001
Kline, Hess, 1823
Kline, John R., 2045
Kline, Josiah W., 3628
Kline, Lowell L., 981
Kline, Platt C., 43
Kline, Sidney D., Jr., 3767
Klinedinst, Thomas J., 3219
Klingen, Richard A., 1912
Klingener, Ellen L., 2984
Klingenstein, Esther A., 2618
Klingenstein, Frederick A., 2618, 2959
Klingenstein, John, 2618, 2959
Klingenstein, Joseph, 2618
Klingenstein, Patricia D., 2618
Klingenstein, Sharon L., 2618
Klitsner, Marvin E., 769, 4341
Klopp, Marjorie K.C., 2622
Klosk, Laurence, 2619
Klosk, Louis, 2619
Kloska, Ronald F., 1211
Kluge, John W., 2930
Knabusch, C.T., 1736
Knabusch, E.M., 1736
Knapp, David W., 1176
Knapp, Donald F., 1224
Knapp, F.E., 4008
Knapp Foundation, 1426
Knapp, George O., 2620
Knapp, George O., II, 2620
Knapp, George O., III, 2620
Knapp, Gilson, 4008
Knapp, J. Lincoln, 3367
Knapp, J.A., 4008
Knapp, Joseph Palmer, 1427
Knapp, Russell S., 622
Knapper, Judson A., 1728
Knauss, D.L., 1162
Knieter, Gerald L., 2573
Knight, Donna, 1867
Knight, Elliot P., 1657
Knight, Frank M., 2495
Knight, George B., 4325
Knight, George W., 3058
Knight, H. Stuart, 676
Knight, James L., 3276
Knight, John S., 3276
Knight, Kathleen C., 3735
Knight, O.W., 3824
Knight, Robert V., Jr., 3076
Knight, Roger D., Jr., 458
Knight, Townsend J., 2263
Knight, Will, 3945
Knirko, L.J., 1142
Knisely, Merton E., 4379
Knistrom, Fanny, 1572
Knistrom, Svante, 1572
Knoell, W.H., 3553
Knoop, Mark, 3391
Knopf, Amy D., 1838
Knopf, Elmer, 1687
Knopf, Kenneth M., 1838
Knott, Francis X., 1428
Knott, Henry J., 1428
Knott, Henry J., Jr., 1428
Knott, James F., 1428
Knott, Marion I., 1428
Knott, Martin G., 1428
Knower, John L., 3005
Knowles, Charles P., 1570
Knowles, James T., 1570
Knowles, Jean L., 1570
Knowles, John H., Jr., 1570
Knowlton, R.L., 1862
Knox, Bernard M.W., 674
Knox, Eleanor E., 2621
Knox Gelatine, 2621
Knox, John B., 2621
Knox, Northrup R., 2622
Knox, P.S., Jr., 3795
Knox, Philip M., Jr., 1145

Knox, Robert K., 2386
Knox, Robert W., Jr., 4009
Knox, Seymour H., 2622
Knox, Seymour H., III, 2622
Knox, W. Graham, 2359
Knox-Davies, Evelyn McLaughlin, 3929
KNTV-TV, 4179
Knudsen, Earl, 3630
Knudsen, Richard, 2054
Knudsen, Th. R., 246
Knudsen, Valley M., 246
Knutson, Darrell G., 1842
Kobacker, Marvin S., 3386
Kobrin, Theodore, 3596
Koch, Carl E., 734
Koch, Carl G., 926
Koch, Charles, 1316
Koch, Charles G., 1316
Koch, David A., 1849
Koch, David H., 1317
Koch, Elizabeth, 1316
Koch, Fred C., 1317
Koch (Fred C.) Foundation, 1316
Koch (Fred C.) Trusts for Charity, 1316
Koch, Fred J., 185
Koch (George) Sons, 1232
Koch Industries, 1317
Koch, John J., 734
Koch, Kenneth, 3396
Koch, L.J., Jr., 1232
Koch, Mary R., 1317
Koch, Morton, 921
Koch, Paula, 734
Koch, Robert L., 1232
Koch, Robert L., II, 1232
Koch, Shari, 734
Koch, Sumner S., 2213
Koch, W.A., 1232
Koch, Walter K., 436
Koch, William I., 1317
Koch-Weser, Reimer, 2597, 2854
Kocher, E.J., 4385
Kochis, Frank, 3481
Kociba, Richard J., 1757
Kock, E. James, Jr., 1372
Kockritz, Frank, 355, 401
Kocur, John A., 1812
Koedel, J.G., Jr., 3675
Koehler, Clair, 1064
Koehler, Robert, 1064
Koehring Company, 4339
Koelbel, Gene N., 469
Koenig, Fred, 1997
Koenig, Harry C., 984
Koenig, James F., 259
Koenig, Wirth H., 2316
Koenitzer, John E., 4379
Koerner, Darrell K., 4189
Koerner, James D., 2938
Koffler Corporation, 3782
Koffler, Lillian, 3782
Koffler, Sol, 3782
Kogan, Nathan B., 2300
Kogan, Richard J., 2178
Kohl, Allen D., 4340
Kohl, Dorothy, 735
Kohl, Herbert H., 4341
Kohl, Mary, 735, 4340, 4341
Kohl, Max, 4341
Kohl, Nicole, 998
Kohl, Sidney, 735
Kohlenbrener, Robert M., 1008
Kohler, Evangeline, 4342
Kohler, Herbert V., 4342
Kohler, Herbert V., Jr., 4342
Kohler, Lillie B., 4342
Kohler, Linda Karger, 4342
Kohler, Marie C., 4342
Kohler, Mary Conway, 1170
Kohler, Ruth DeYoung, II, 4342
Kohlruss, Fred S., 1208
Kohn, Anne F., 2321
Kohn, Bernhard L., Jr., 545
Kohn, Bernhard L., Sr., 545

Kohn, Henry, 1958, 2321, 2644
Kohn, Janet S., 1771
Kohn, Joan J., 545
Kohn, Max, 3765
Kohn, Robert I., Jr., 1771
Kokenes, Tom, 11
Kokomo Sanitary Pottery Corporation, 1017
Kolb, Jerry W., 2395
Kolb, Lee R., 3343
Kolin, Oscar, 2896
Koltai, Leslie, 2109
Kolvig, Ann B., 2264
Komar (Charles) and Sons, 2144
Komes, Flora, 247
Komes, Jerome W., 247
Koning, Owen, 1743
Kontopoulos, Perry, 11
Kooken, John F., 351
Kooker, J.L., 1005
Koons, Robert W., 50
Koontz, James L., 2090
Koop, Arnold, 3995
Koopman, Georgette A., 494, 549, 572
Koopman, Richard, 494, 549
Koory, Susan K., 1740
Kopelman, Frank, 1612
Kopf, R.C., 2274, 2623, 2624
Kopidlansky, Victor R., 1104
Koppers Company, 3631
Kopperud, Roy, 1828
Koprowski, John, 2444
Korb, Donald C., 3756
Koren, M. Robert, 2955
Koret, Joseph, 248
Koret, Stephanie, 248
Koret, Susan, 248
Korman, Berton E., 3632
Korman, Leonard I., 3632
Korman, Rochelle, 356
Korman, Samuel J., 3632
Korman, Steven H., 3632
Korn, Charles, 2449
Korn, William C., 2820
Kortbein, Donald, 4296
Kory, Geraldine, 2214
Kosarek, Charles L., 3884
Kosarek, Willie J., 3884
Koscielack, Frank A., 1882, 1921
Koshland, Robert J., 318
Kosik, Edwin, 3716
Koski, Frank, 3158
Koskinen, Donald S., 4300
Koskinen, Jean A., 4293
Koslan, Spencer L., 2797
Kostishack, John, 1822
Kott, Mrs. H. Stephen, 1481
Kotzen, Herman F., 3596
Koulaieff, B.J., 249
Koulaieff, Ivan V., 249
Koulogeorge, Emily, 1183
Kountze, Charles, 2057
Kountze, Denman, 2057
Kountze, Neely, 2057
Kovacs, Stephen, 2420
Kovan, Samuel C., 1773
Kovar, Margaret W., 159
Koverman, Robert, 3391
Kovler, Everett, 948
Kovler, H. Jonathan, 946, 948
Kovler, Peter, 946, 948
Kowaloff, Arthur D., 2815
Kozan, Lillian M., 3340
Kozmetsky, George, 4061
Kozmetsky, Gregory, 4061
Kozmetsky, Ronya, 4061
Kraft, Mrs. John F., Jr., 3637
Kraft, Myra H., 1550
Kraft, Robert K., 1550
Kraines, Sidney, 2482
Krakower, Victor, 671
Kramarsky, Sarah Ann, 2832
Kramer, Catherine, 2626
Kramer, Charlotte R., 3347

Kramer, Elizabeth Abrams, 2214
Kramer, John R., 2432
Kramer, Karl, 245
Kramer, Karl, Jr., 245
Kramer, Lawrence I., Jr., 268, 429
Kramer, Louise, 3277
Kramer, Nina, 245
Kramer, Saul, 2627
Krane, Howard G., 1063
Krane, Samuel, 286
Krannert, Ellnora D., 1233
Krannert, Herman C., 1233
Kranson, Bernice S., 298
Krantzler, Robert, 3583
Kranzow, Glenn, 756
Krasnansky, Marvin L., 283
Krasow, Herbert, 523
Krassner, Albert, 2342
Krassner, Martin P., 2341, 2342
Kratz, C. Ruth, 1399
Krause, Charles A., 4356
Krause, Charles A., III, 4343
Krause, Kathryn, 2467
Krause, Norman L., 1318
Krause Plow Corporation, 1318
Krause, R.A., 760
Krause, Sandra S., 3742
Krauss, Bernard, 2939
Krauss Company, Ltd., 1367
Kravitz, Anne G., 3584
Kreamer, Janice C., 1981, 1983, 2029
Krehbiel, P.W., 2754
Kreid, Mrs. Leland F., Jr., 1100
Kreider, Esther S., 2027
Kreider, Homer L., 3628
Kreidler, Robert N., 2379
Kreielsheimer, Greye M., 4245
Kreielsheimer, Leo T., 4245
Kreiger, Donald, 2231
Krekstein, Herman H., 3596
Krekstein, I.H., 3596
Krell, Walter E., 1695
Kremel, Adolph A., Jr., 3978
Kreps, Juanita M., 3095, 3156
Kresge, Bruce A., 1734
Kresge, Sebastian S., 1734
Kresge, Stanley S., 6, 1734
Kresge, Sue, 3865
Kress, Claude W., 2629
Kress, Donald, 4344
Kress, George F., 4344
Kress, James F., 4344
Kress, Rush H., 2629
Kress, Samuel H., 2629
Kresse, Robert J., 3036
Kreulen, Grace, 74
Kreuzberger, Donald, 1572
Kreuzberger, Virginia, 1572
Krevans, Julius R., 2211
Kriedmann, Arthur M., 2552
Krieger, Abraham, 1429
Krieger, John J., 657
Krikorian, L., 70
Krikorian, R.V., 4373
Krim, Arthur B., 2630
Krimendahl, H. Frederick, II, 2699
Kring, Gary S., 478
Kring, Lesley E., 478
Krinsky, Josephine B., 2813
Krinsky, Robert D., 2813
Kriser, David, 2631
Kriser, Leonard, 2631
Kriser, Sidney, 2631
Kriser, Sidney P., 2631
Kristina Tara Fondaras Charitable Lead Trust, 142
Kroc, Joan B., 250
Kroc, Ray A., 250
Kroc, Robert L., 250
Krock, Barry L., 1659
Kroeger, R.F., 2019
Kroenlein, David F., 2292
Kroft, F.C., Jr., 2741
Krome, Margery Loomis, 4181

Kronenberger, Donald R., 3239
Kronstadt, Lillian, 663
Kroos, O.A., 4342
Krotine, F.T., 3366
Krueger, Everett H., 3189
Krueger, Stuart, 2383
Krug, Eleanor C., 3859
Krug, George C., 3859
Kruidenier, David, 1262, 1888
Kruidenier, Elizabeth S., 1262
Krultz, Mike, Jr., 1073
Krumm, Daniel J., 1276
Krupsky, J.F., 1950
KSTP, 1864
Kubiak, Jon S., 1081
Kubie, Mrs. David, 2729
Kuck, Kermit T., 3305
Kuehl, Hal C., 4318
Kugle, J. Alan, 892
Kuhlin, Michael E., 926
Kuhne, J.A., 3799
Kuhns, Ron L., 4081
Kuhns, William G., 2221
Kuhrts, G.J., III, 110
Kulas, E.J., 3278
Kulas, Fynette H., 3278
Kulenkamp, William, 1664
Kully, Robert I., 2064
Kulp, David, 3230
Kuluris, Faye, 3267
Kummel, R.D., 119, 120
Kunkel, W.M., 3633
Kunstadter, Christopher, 2632
Kunstadter, Elizabeth, 2632
Kunstadter, Geraldine S., 2632
Kunstadter, John W., 2632
Kunstadter, John W., Jr., 2632
Kunstadter, Lisa, 2632
Kunstadter, Peter, 2632
Kunstadter, Sally Lennington, 2632
Kuntz, Martin, 3279
Kuntz (The Peter) Company, 3279
Kuntz, Peter H., 3279
Kuntz, Richard, 3279
Kuntz, Richard P., 3279
Kuntzman, R.G., 2131
Kunzel, Herbert, 327
Kunzman, Edwin D., 2182
Kunzman, Steven, 2182
Kuper, Charles A., 1414
Kuper, Maurice R., 1219
Kupferberg, Max L., 3016
Kuppin, Alyson W., 3398
Kurland, Philip B., 1956
Kurlich, Phillip J., 2478
Kuroda, Linda K., 896
Kurras, Herbert L., 722
Kurrelmeier, Herman M., 1187
Kurth, Herbert, 4345, 4354
Kurth, Katherine, 4345
Kurth Malting Corporation, 4345
Kurth, Thomas, 4345
Kurtis, Virginia Cowles, 2369
Kurtz, Bernard D., 1270
Kurtz, Paul B., 3766
Kurtz, Renee Berger, 2103
Kurtz, Richard, 2103
Kury, Mark C., 4286
Kurzman, H. Michael, 267
Kusche, William R., Jr., 3129
Kushen, Allan S., 2178
Kusnetzky, Leon G., 37
Kuster, Gerald, 1850
Kutz, Hattie, 615
Kutz, Milton, 615
Kuyper, E. Lucille Gaass, 1273
Kuyper, Peter H., 1273
Kvamme, J.N., 119, 120
Kyd, George H., 2010
Kyle, John E., 692
Kyle, Richard E., 1924
Kyle, Richard H., Jr., 1912
Kynes, J.W., 788
Kynett, Harold H., 3634

La Claire, David B., 1715
La Fond, Laura Jane V.E., 1919
La Sala, A. Stephen, 2634
La Sala, Andrew J., 2634
La Sala, Anthony, 2634
La Sala Contracting Company, 2634
La Sala, Frank, 2634
La Salle Steel Company, 4060
La Ware, John P., 1623
Labadie, William J., 4309
Labalme, George, Jr., 2553, 2637
Labalme, Patricia, 2394
Labouisse, Henry R., 2347
Labrecque, Thomas G., 2337
Labudde, Roy, 4335
Lachman, Lawrence, 2868
Lachman, M. Leanne, 971
Lackland, David, 2182
Laclede Gas Company, 1977
LaCounte, Maage, 4240
Lacy, Bill, 2985
Lacy, Dan, 2721
Ladd, George E., III, 1529
Ladd, George E., Jr., 1529
Ladd, George M., 1529
Ladd, Kate Macy, 2689
Ladd, Lincoln F., 1529
Ladd, Robert M., 1529
Ladehoff, Leo W., 3149
Ladish Company, 4347
Ladish, Herman M., 4348, 4349
Ladish, John H., 4305, 4347, 4348, 4349, 4350
Ladish, John W., 3156
Ladish Malting Company, 4350
Ladner, Harold M., 3336
Lafayette Bank & Trust Co., 502
Lafe, William, 3599, 3693
Lafer, Fred S., 2146, 2189, 2190
Laferty, Joseph J., 4294
Lafferty, Charles N., 3336
Lafley, Alan F., 2337
LaFreniere, Norma B., 3772
Lagerlof, Stanley C., 380
LaGrone, Troy, 4000
Lahanas, Constantine J., 1534
Lahiff, Alice M., 1906
Lahiff, Mary Elizabeth, 1906
Laidig, William R., 529
Lail, James W., 3835
Laing, Charles B., 2138
Laird, E. Cody, Jr., 826
Lakari, David, 1395
Lake, John B., 757
Lake, Nancy, 3945
Lake, Thomas H., 1238
Laketon Asphalt Refining Co., 1203
Lallemand, Jean, 2744
Lally, Francis J., 1482
Lalor, Willard A., 617
Lamar, Charles C., 1027
Lamb, Dorothy J., 3499
Lamb, Edna, 3499
Lamb, F. Gilbert, 3499
Lamb, Mrs. F.S., 3298
Lamb, Frank G., 3499
Lamb, George C., Jr., 504, 584
Lamb, George R., 2234, 2577
Lamb, Helen W., 3499
Lamb, John R., 3476
Lamb, Kirkland S., 3110
Lamb, Marguerite B., 2043
Lamb, Paul H., 3499
Lamb, Paula L., 3499
Lamb, Rena B., 3110
Lamb, Teri M., 1920
Lambert Brake Corporation, 1782
Lambert, Clement T., 1658
Lambert, Harry W., 719
Lambert, Samuel W., III, 2106, 2154, 4151
Lambeth, Thomas W., 3124
Lamey, W.L., Jr., 991
Lamkin, J.C., 1933

Lamm, Harvey H., 2187
Lamond, Alice, 1600
Lamont, Tara, 142
LaMoy, E.L., 4078
LaMoy, Raymond, 588
Lampen, J. Oliver, 2446
Lamphere, Robert G., 1021
Lampros, Jack D., 4135, 4136, 4144
Lanahan, W. Wallace, Jr., 1403
Lancashire, B.J., 1227
Lancaster, Curtis N., 4142
Lancaster Newspapers, 3737, 3738
Lancaster, Rose C., 4104
Lancaster, Ruth, 1320
Lancaster, Sally R., 4029
Lance, Inc., 3111
Lance, L.H., 3098
Land, Edwin H., 1611
Land, Helen M., 1611
Landegger, Carl, 736
Landegger, George, 736
Landegger, Lena, 736
Landes, Robert N., 2721
Landesman, Frederic Rocco, 516
Landesman, Heidi P., 516
Landfather, Samuel G., 2027
Landgraf, Theodore R., 935
Landis, Dennis, 582
Landmark Union Trust Bank of St. Petersburg, 756
Landolt, Rudolph F., 1060
Landon, S. Whitney, 2193
Landreth, William A., 4063
Landrum, Baylor, 1346
Lane, B.B., 4180
Lane, E.H., 4180
Lane, Fleetwood T., 777
Lane, H. Merritt, Jr., 1370
Lane, Hugh C., Jr., 3801
Lane, Joan F., 337
Lane, L.B., 4180
Lane, Michael J., 1021
Lane, Nancy Wolfe, 3410
Lane, Nelle Kennedy Stuart, 777
Lane, Susan Jones, 1370
Lane, Thomas M., 851
Lane, Mrs. Warren W., 2311
Lane, William A., Jr., 715
Laney, James T., 812
Lang, David A., 2636
Lang, Eugene M., 2636
Lang, Helen, 1873
Lang, Jane M., 4259
Lang, Margaret A., 2807
Lang, R.W., 3383
Lang, Sarah F., 1855
Lang, Stephen, 2636
Lang, Theodora, 1855
Lang, Theresa, 2636
Langbauer, Del N., 1716
Langbauer, Lucille E., 1716
Lange, J.B., 1936
Langeley, Lydia B., 1532
Langeloth, Jacob, 2637
Langenberg, E. L., 2014
Langenberg, F.C., 3536
Langenberg, Oliver M., 1987
Langerhans, Robert H., 1066, 1102
Langevin, Beda A., 1656
Langford, J. Beverly, 1762
Langford, Robert D., 1915
Langhaug, Woodrow P., 1877
Langie, Louis A., Jr., 2474
Langner, Jay B., 2693
Langrock, Karl F., 1276
Lanier, Bruce N., Jr., 881
Lanier, Bruce N., Sr., 881
Lanier, George M., 3540
Lanier, Helen S., 852
Lanier, John Reese, 852
Lanier, Joseph L., Jr., 883
Lanier, Lawrence L., 2667
Lanier, Melissa Emery, 3326
Lanier, S., 2951

Lanier, Sartain, 852
Lanier, Susan I., 849
Lanigan, James S., 2512
Lanman, Ben Marr, 516
Lanning, William D., 1714
Lansing, Livingston, 2837
Lanterman, Joseph B., 1060
Lantzsch, G. Christian, 3661
Lapham Hickey Steel Company, 973
Lapidos, Morris, 615
LaPierre, Donald J., 1656
Lappin, W.R., 1309
Larcheid, Lyle, 4392
Lard, Mary P., 4010
Large, Edwin K., Jr., 2145
Large, George K., 2145
Lario Oil and Gas Company, 1900
Larkin, F.X., 3098
Larkin, Frank Y., 2784
Larkin, Jean M., 3118
Larkin, June Noble, 2784
Larkin, Thomas A., 2911
Larned, P.F., 127
LaRoche, R.E., 950
Laros, R.K., Jr., 3636
Laros, Russell K., 3636
LaRosa, William R., 727
Larrabee Fund, 550
Larrabee, Leland L., 3820
Larrabee, Nell B., 3820
Larrieu, Marie-Josette, 2826
Larry, Richard M., 3537, 3711
Larsen, Christopher, 2638
Larsen, Jonathan Z., 2638
Larsen, Randolph C., 2649
Larsen, Robert R., 2638
Larsen, Roy E., 2638
Larsen, Susan M., 1180
Larson, Bradley, 1073
Larson, Carl E., 2593
Larson, D.W., 1890
Larson, Dorothy R., 502
Larson, Elwin S., 2427
Larson, George, 1556
Larson, Gordon, 1874
Larson, Harold, 1874
Larson, James E., 4304
Larson, Joseph, 1828
Larson, Lester G., 1850
Larson, Marie, 1110
Larson, Roy, 2478
Lartique, H.J., Jr., 2426
LaRue, Dolly F., 1978
LaRue, George A., 1978
LaRue, Susan M., 150
LaRue, W., 84
Las Colinas Corporation, 4084
LaSalle, Nancy N., 2788
LaSalle National Bank, 968
Lasater, Donald E., 1996
Lascor, Leon A., 467, 484
Lascor, Patricia J., 484
Lasdon, J.S., 2639
Lasdon, M.S., 2639
Lasdon, Stanley S., 2639
Lasdon, W.S., 2639
Lasdon, William S., 2639
Lasell, Chester K., 987
Lash, Earl, 37
Lash, Wendy, 2652
Lash, Wiley, 3131
Lashley, Elinor H., 3614
Lashly, John F., 2020
Laske, A.C., Jr., 2754
Laske, Arthur C., 2754
Lasker, Albert D., 2640
Lasker, Joel M., 1242
Lasker, Mary W., 2640
Laskin, Barbara, 1069
Lasky, Harry, 1065
Lasky, Sadie, 1065
Lassalle, Diana, 2787
Lassalle, Honor, 2787
Lassalle, Nancy N., 2787

Lassalle, Philip, 2787
Lassen, Helen Lee, 2404
Lasser, Miles L., 2339
Lassiter, Daisy Hanes, 3106
Lastavica, John, 1646
Lastelick, Jerry, 3923
Lastfogel, Abe, 2641
Lastfogel, Frances, 2641
Lasurdo, I. Jerry, 3016
Later, Earl D., 3268
Lathorn, Alex A., 1065
Latimer, Thomas H., 505
Laub, Elsie K., 3281
Laub, Herbert J., 3281
Laubach, Robert S., 978
Lauby, Paul T., 1546
Lauder, Estee, 2642
Lauder, Joseph H., 2642
Lauder, Leonard A., 2642
Lauder, Ronald S., 2642
Laudone, Anita H., 2825
Lauer, Robert L., 1139
Laughlin, Alexander M., 3605
Laurell, Lauri G., 3609
Laurence, Joyce Aigner, 919
Laurie, M., 2249
Laurie, William D., 1691
Lausche, Frank J., 3242
Lautenberg, Frank R., 2146
Lautenberg (Frank R.) Charitable Trusts, 2146
Lautenberg, Lois, 2146
Lauver, R.C., 2840
Lavanburg, Fred L., 2643, 2644
LaVelle, James C., 4353
Laventhol, David, 532
Laventhol, Lewis J., 3596
Laverge, Hendrik J., 2366, 2453
Laversin, Robert W., 117
Lavezzo, Janette, 71
Lavezzo, Nellie, 71
Lavezzorio, Leonard M., 1087
Lavezzorio, Tina, 1087
LaViers, Barbara P., 1345
LaViers, Harry, 1345
LaViers, Harry, Jr., 1338, 1345
Lavine, Henry W., 685
LaVine, Kenneth N., 4188
Law Enforcement Assistance Administration, 676
Law, Mary Jane, 738
Law, Mary K., 738
Law, Robert O., 738
Law, Robert O., III, 738
Lawford, Patricia Kennedy, 666
Lawing, A.P., Jr., 1347
Lawler, John A., 2359
Lawler, Kieran J., 2774
Lawler, Oscar T., 295
Lawler, T. Newman, 2280, 2478
Lawrence, A. Charles, 937, 1115
Lawrence, Anne I., 3260
Lawrence, Barbara Childs, 2225
Lawrence, Charles M., 269
Lawrence, Dean, 4119
Lawrence, Elizabeth A., 1517
Lawrence, Emily D., 2204
Lawrence, Frederick V., 1567
Lawrence, Gordon D., 4218
Lawrence, J. Vinton, 506
Lawrence, James J., 937
Lawrence, James Vinton, 2225
Lawrence, John E., 1560
Lawrence, Mrs. John T., Jr., 3361
Lawrence, Kent, 937, 1115
Lawrence, Larry E., 1294
Lawrence, Pauline, 3498
Lawrence, Richard W., Jr., 2373
Lawrence, Robert J., 1115
Lawrence, Sull, 325
Lawrence, Sylvan, 2351
Lawrence, William J., Jr., 1728
Laws, G. Malcolm, Jr., 3749
Lawson, Ed, 4033

Lawson, Jay Bird, 3582
Lawson-Johnston, Peter O., 2513, 2643
Lawson-Johnston, Peter, II, 2513
Lawton, Jack E., 1356
Lawton, Virginia, 2851
Lawton, William B., 1356
Lay, Henry A., 1991
Laybourne, Everett B., 311
Layton, Thomas C., 186
Lazar, Mrs. Buryl, 1070
Lazar, Helen B., 2646
Lazar, Jack, 2646
Lazard Freres & Co., 2734
Lazarof, Janice A., 394
Lazarus, Monte, 1179
La-Z-Boy Chair Company, 1736
Leach, Duane M., 4005
Leach, Frances, 3140
Leach, James A., 2995
Leach, Tom, 3140
Leach, Willis R., 377
Leader, Henry, 3701
Leaf, Hayim, 2708
Leahy, Charles E., 1664
Leahy, James, 3211
Leahy, Michael S., 1757
Leamon, Joyce, 43
Leander, Henry A., 1224
Lear Siegler, 253
Lear, William S., 1002
Leary, Eleen P., 1445
Leary, Thomas S., 1356
Leather, Richard B., 2454
Leatherman, Laramie L., 1340
Leavens, Marvin, 2563
Leaver, Jack, 1711
Leavey, Dorothy, 254
Leavey, Joseph James, 254
Leavey, Thomas E., 254
Leavis, Gordon W., 1656
Lebanon-Citizens National Bank, 3183
Lebed, Hartzel Z., 533, 3542
Lebensfeld, Harry, 2647
Lebherz, Sybil H., 20
LeBlanc, William H., 1354
LeBoeuf, Raymond W., 3697
Lebsack, Chester W., 153
LeBuhn, Robert, 2116
Lebworth, Caral G., 528
Leckart, Ida G., 1537
Ledbetter, Beverly E., 3786
Lederberg, Joshua, 2325, 2411
Lederer, Anne P., 1067
Lederer, Francis L., II, 1067
Leduc, Robert F., 435
Lee, Aubrey, 318
Lee, Charles R., 531
Lee, Donald B., 4323
Lee, Doris Shoong, 359
Lee, Dwight E., 2264
Lee, Essie, 2583
Lee, Francis Childress, 703
Lee, G. Richard, 4133
Lee, George W., 3434
Lee, H. Clifford, 701
Lee, Homer W., 3362, 3408
Lee, Mrs. J. Philip, 2833
Lee, James A., 3192
Lee, James T., 2649
Lee, Jonathan C., 1354
Lee, Joseph A., 289
Lee, L. Max, 1705
Lee, Laurence R., 918
Lee, Mary Elizabeth, 853
Lee, Ray M., 853
Lee, Richard H., 655
Lee, Sidney S., 2737
Lee, Ted, 359
Lee, William J., 3749
Lee, Yvonne, 1711
Leeds & Northrup Company, 3638
Leegant, Bernard, 2438
Leemhuis, Andrew J., 1922
Leeming, E. Janice, 3783

Leenhouts, Norman, 2873
Leeson, G.E., 3935, 3936
Leet, Mildred Robbins, 2592
Leet, R.H., 928
Leetz, Paul A., 1178
Leff, Carl, 2650
Leff, Eleanor, 2650
Leff, Joseph, 2650
Leff, Lilian, 2650
Leff, Phillip, 2650
Leffler, L.A., 3434
Lefkowitz, Elise G., 658
Lefkowitz, Sidney M., 797
Lefkowitz, Stephen, 2460
Lefrak, Simon J., 2651
Legan, Pat, 4072
Leganza, Leonard F., 574
Leggat, John E., 1648
Leggat, Thomas E., 1592
Legge, Alexander, 999
LeGrange, U.J., 2426
Legrid, Gloria, 3142
Lehman, Brenda L., 2583
Lehman, Edith A., 2652
Lehman, Elliot, 1107
Lehman, Frances, 1000, 1107
Lehman, Herbert, 2652
Lehman, Jane B., 681
Lehman, Jane Bagley, 638
Lehman, John R., 2652
Lehman, Kenneth, 1107
Lehman, Lucy, 1107
Lehman, Paul, 1000, 1107
Lehman, Robert, 2653
Lehman, Robert F., 3271
Lehman, Ronna Stamm, 1107
Lehmann, Marguerite S., 1068
Lehmann, Otto W., 1068
Lehmann, Robert O., 1068
Lehn, Alan J., 3191
Lehnhardt, M.H., 3995
Lehr, L.W., 1890
Lehrman, Charlotte, 1418
Lehrman, Charlotte F., 668
Lehrman, Fredrica, 668
Lehrman, Jacob J., 668
Lehrman, Samuel, 668
Leibensberger, D.W., 888
Leibowitz, J.S., 2665
Leibowitz, Joyce R., 2167
Leibrock, Robert L., 3866
Leidesdorf, Arthur D., 739
Leidesdorf, Samuel D., 739
Leidesdorf, Tova D., 739
Leidy, John J., 1430
Leighner, William H., 3308
Leighton, Judd, 1235
Leighton, Mary Morris, 1235
Leighton, Richard T., 936
Lein, Don C., 1870
Leinbach, Gustav O., 3677
Leinbach, Harold O., 3677
Leinbach, Jill L., 2824
Leinbach, Richard O., 3677
Leineimann, Paul F., 2074
Leiner, Wayne, 3142
Leinsdorf, Gregor, 2794
Leir, Erna D., 2865
Leir, Henry J., 2654, 2865
Leis, Barbara E., 2136
Leist, Fred, 4361
Leisure, George S., Jr., 2406
Leitzinger, Joseph L., 4248
Lejins, Peter, 689
Leland, Katherine A., 1567
Leland, Marc E., 659
LeMaistre, Charles A., 3886
Lemann, Thomas B., 1389
Lemberg, Samuel, 2655
Leming, Mrs. John W., Jr., 3526
Lemke, Carl R., 4310
Lemke, Victoria C., 4237
Lemkemeier, Ned O., 1969
Lemle, Louis G., 1381

Lemmel, David, 774
Lemon, Calhoun, 3804
Lemons, Wishard, 3420
Lemos, Gloria, 685
LeMunyon, Ralph H., 3224
Lenahan, Helen Dent, 2396
Lenamon, Joe T., 4120
Lenart, Yvonne Ramus, 277
Lennartz, David C., 1273
Lennon, Fred A., 3282
Lennon, Theodore, 422
Lennox Industries, 4012
Lenoir, James S., 1934
Lents, Max R., 243
Lentz, Hover T., 436
Leonard, Anne B., 3898
Leonard, Banks, 3359
Leonard, Henry B., 3813
Leonard, James L., 3146
Leonard, Judith, 2273
Leonard, Luke J., 3146
Leonard, Nancy, 3478
Leonard, Patricia A., 1670
Leonard, Reid, 3131
Leonard, W.O., 3071
Leonard, Walter, 2109
Leonard, William F., 738
Leonardi, R.M., 3196
Leonhardt, Frederick, 2656
Leonhardt, Frederick H., 2656
Leonhardt, William S., 4193
LePage, Frank, 3297
Lepak, Robert R., 1511
Lepley, Joan, 3421
Leppard, J.A., 4013
Leppard, J.A., Jr., 4013
Lerchen, Edward H., 1734
Lerer, Carol Dugger, 137
Lerner, I., 2131
Lerner, Ralph E., 2671
Leroy, Warner, 3013
Lesher, Margaret W., 3639
Lesinski, Dean A., 2469
Lesko, G., 3759
Leslie, Donald S., Jr., 3594
Leslie, G.E., 3396
Leslie, James W., 1069
Leslie, John E., 2254
Leslie, John H., 1069, 1152
Leslie, Robert, 1870
Leslie, Virginia A., 1069
Lessard, Daniel, 3142
Lessing, Fred W., 2556
Lessler, Edith, 383
Lester, Charles, 4291
Lester, Margaret, 4169
Lester, Morton, 4169
LeSuer, W.M., 3285
LeTourneau, Brenda J., 4014
LeTourneau, Mike, 4014
LeTourneau, Mrs. Robert G., 4014
LeTourneau, Robert G., 4014
LeTourneau, Roy S., 4014
Lettenberger, Peter J., 4304
Leu, Harry P., 740
Leu, Mary Jane, 740
Leuthold, Betty B., 4247
Leuthold, Caroline E., 4247
Leuthold, John H., 4247
LeVan, John A., 449
Levantine, Rose B., 3069
Levavy, Zvi, 2599
Levee, Polly Annenberg, 3640
Leven, Ann R., 2325
Leventon, Aileen R., 2868
Leventritt, David, 2154
Lever Brothers Company, 2657
Lever, Martha O., 1954
Leverett, Donald B., 4027
Levering, Walter B., 560
Levett, Edith, 2505
Levey, N. James, 1771
Levey, Richard, 1771
Levi, Alexander H., 1422

THE FOUNDATION DIRECTORY

Mawby, Russell G., 1732
Maxey, Tom, 759
Maxey, Wirt, 759
Maxfield, Naomi, 967
Maxfield, Robert Gary, 967
Maxfield, Thomas O., III, 967
Maxon, Frank C., Jr., 2836
Maxwell, David O., 651
Maxwell, Dorothy D., 3807
Maxwell, Douglas W., 731
Maxwell, Verne H., 3873
Maxwell, Virginia, 2408
May, Cordelia S., 3637
May, David, II, 276
May Department Stores Company, 1991
May, Harold E., 615
May, Irenee du Pont, 618
May, Isabel, 724
May, James P., 4370
May, John L., 2032
May, Morton J., 1990
May, Peter, 724
May, Richard, 2333
May, Samuel D., 724
May, Thomas J., 117
May, Walter W., 1362
May, Wilbur D., 276
May, William F., 2777
Mayeda, Cynthia, 1834
Mayer, Allan C., 1086
Mayer, Anthony R., 457
Mayer, C.L., 2030
Mayer, Charles B., 1362
Mayer, Elsa S., 1086
Mayer, Frederick M., 457
Mayer, Frederick R., 457
Mayer, George J., 1362
Mayer, Harold F., 1086
Mayer, Harold M., 1086
Mayer, Jan Perry, 457
Mayer, Jean, 2865
Mayer, Julia R., 362, 363, 365, 366
Mayer, Lorna L., 4351
Mayer, Louis B., 277
Mayer, Oscar G., 1086
Mayer, Oscar G., Sr., 1086
Mayer, Patricia A., 1220
Mayer, R.D., 3415
Mayer, Richard P., 538
Mayer, S. Lawrence, 4344
Mayer, William E., 2435
Mayers, Paul-Henri, 2654
Mayerson, Joy G., 2407
Mayerson, Philip, 2407, 2491
Mayher, John W., Jr., 849
Mayhew, Bruce R., 1667
Maynard, Frederick C., Jr., 539
Maynard, Olivia, 1687
Maynard, Robert C., 2877
Mayne, Calvin, 2463
Mayo, Allene O., 3426
Mayo, James O., 667
Mayr, George Henry, 278
Mays, J.W., 3034
Mays, Troy M., 4021
Mays, W.A., 4021
Mays (W.A) and Agnes Mays Trust, 4021
Maytag Company, 1276
Maytag, Fred, II, 1277
Maytag, Frederick L., III, 1277
Maytag, Kenneth P., 1277
Mayworm, Daniel E., 1141
Mazer (Abraham) Family Fund, 2710
Mazer (Abraham) Foundation, 556
Mazer, David, 556
Mazer, Frank B., 2710
Mazer, Helen, 2710
Mazer, Joseph M., 2709
Mazer, Richard, 556
Mazer, Robert C., 2710
Mazer, Ruth, 556
Mazer, William, 2709, 2710
Mazeski, Edward, Jr., 3697
Mazza (Louise T.) Trust, 1087

MBank Alamo, 4072
MBank El Paso, 4055
MBank Travis Park, 4072
MCA, 279
McAdam, Sally Gannett, 2463
McAdam, Terry W., 220
McAdams, John, 3815
McAfee, Ethel, 902
McAfee, Horace J., 2950
McAlister, Consuela Cuneo, 984
McAlister, E.E., Jr., 4018
McAlister, Fern Smith, 280
McAlister, Harold, 280
McAlister, Hobart S., 280
McAlister, Soni, 280
McAllister, Edith, 4072
McAllister, Francis R., 2246
McAlonan, John A., 3296
McAlpin, David Hunter, 2116
McArthur, A.P.N., 4329
McArthur, Bruce E., 1177
McArthur, Charlotte A., 1177
McArthur, Daniel E., 284
McArthur, David M., 1177
McAshan, S.M., Jr., 3907
McAshan, Susan C., 4022
McAuley, C.M., 1936
McAuley, Walter, 3426
McAvinue, C.A., 3658
McBean, Atholl, 281
McBean, Edith, 281, 296
McBean, Mrs. Peter, 281
McBean, Peter, 281, 296
McBeath, Faye, 4356
McBratney, Audrey C., 2161
McBride, Beverly J., 3152
McBride, Hubert A., 3830, 3858
McBride, John H., 564
McBride, Kevin, 3886
McBride, Rex L., 269
McCabe, Edward, 685
McCabe, Eleonora W., 586
McCahill, Eugene P., 1906
McCaig, Nancy C., 1100
McCall, Abner V., 3915
McCall, Billy G., 3095
McCall, Dorothy R., 2404
McCall, Helen, 491
McCallie, David, 3835
McCammon, David N., 1702
McCammon, Janelle L., 3423
McCandless, Jack E., 450
McCandless, Stephen P., 2246
McCann Foundation, 2416
McCann, Frank P., 153
McCann, Franklin W., 3050
McCann, Frasier W., 3050
McCann, James J., 2712
McCann, John J., 2406
McCannel, Laurie H., 1920
McCannel, Louise Walker, 1920
McCargo, Mrs. David, 3735
McCarrick, Theodore E., 670
McCarthy, A. Gregory, IV, 670
McCarthy, Albert G., III, 670
McCarthy, Denis M., 518
McCarthy, Gerald P., 4214
McCarthy, J. Thomas, 254
McCarthy, James A., 2713
McCarthy, John Peters, 1948
McCarthy, Kathleen Leavey, 254
McCarthy, Louise Roblee, 2012
McCarthy, Lucy A., 2713
McCarthy, Lucy R., 1924
McCarthy, Margaret E., 2714
McCarthy, Marion P., 2713
McCarthy, Mary E., 3023
McCarthy, Michael A., 1154
McCarthy, Michael W., 2714
McCarthy, Peter F., 2713
McCarthy, Robert H., 2713
McCue, Maclyn, 3043
McCarty, Marilu H., 835
McCarty, Stuart, 742, 2565

McCarville, Mark J., 1139
McCashin, Helen B., 2272
McCasland, T.H., Jr., 3445
McCauley, Daniel J., 518
McClain, Terry J., 2074
McClaran, Eve, 228
McClarity, Harry C., 510
McClaron, Sandra Y., 4336
McClellan, C.E., 1050
McClellan, Rowland J., 4330
McClelland, R.K., 1101
McClelland, W. Craig, 3594
McClintic, William E., 1108
McClintock, John R.D., 1499
McCloskey, John J., 330
McCloy, John J., 2799
McClure, Nathan D., Jr., 936
McClure, R.W., 1325
McClure, Robert E., 1220
McClurkin, Werdna, 1932
McClymond, J.J., 2058
McCollough, Clair R., 3737, 3738
McCollow, Thomas J., 4356
McCollum, H.W., 2546
McColough, C. Peter, 594
McComas, Harrold J., 4313, 4368, 4393
McCone, Theiline M., 4254
McConkey, Carl W., 1790
McConnell, Agnes C., 3167
McConnell, B. Scott, 2715
McConnell, David M., 3134
McConnell, Jean, 3346
McConnell, M. Wilson, 3192
McConnell, Neil A., 2715
McConnell, R.L., 827
McConnell, Robert W., 3987
McCooey, Robert H., 2221
McCord, W.C., 3943, 4018
McCorkindale, Douglas H., 2463
McCorkle, Clark G., 1947
McCormack, Elizabeth J., 2578
McCormack, Robert C., 1125
McCormack, William J., 2749
McCormick, Anne, 3650
McCormick, Brooks, 968, 1088
McCormick (Brooks) Trust, 1088
McCormick, Charles Deering, 1088
McCormick (Charles Deering) Trust, 1088
McCormick, Donald F., 2161
McCormick, J.L., 3143
McCormick, James, 1088
McCormick, Richard B., 2311
McCormick, Robert R., 1089, 1090
McCormick (Robert R.) Charitable Trust, 1090
McCormick (Roger) Trust, 1088
McCormick, William H., 1412
McCormick, William W., 169
McCortney, John H., 1188
McCown, Cheryl A., 3940
McCoy, Albert D., 935
McCoy, Arthur H., 464
McCoy, Carolyn F., 3183
McCoy, Craig W., 464
McCoy, Gregory L., 159
McCoy, R.F., 3117
McCoy, Robert C., 607
McCoy, Virginia G., 464
McCracken, Frank H., 2026
McCracken, G., 768
McCracken, Paul, 659
McCrady, Howard C., 47
McCrady, L. Colvin, Jr., 3691
McCragken, Sally, 3500
McCrea, Mary Corling, 4184
McCreight, Paul W., 4289
McCreless, Sollie E., 4023
McCrory Corporation, 2716
McCrory, James T., 3174
McCue, Howard M., III, 1011
McCuley, Buford A., 3460
McCullough, Betty, 631

McCullough, Bettyann Asche, 4107
McCullough, F.E., 3222
McCullough, G.B., 2426
McCullough, George R., 3537
McCully, J. Thomas, 4234, 4260
McCune, Charles L., 3651
McCune, John R., 3651
McCune, Samuel K., 3691
McCune, William J., Jr., 1602
McCurdy, Gilbert G., 3184
McCusker, F.C., 4286
McCutchan, Gordon E., 3313
McCutchen, Brunson S., 2153
McCutchen, Charles W., 2153
McCutchen, Margaret W., 2153
McDaniel, Ivan, 229
McDaniel, John B., Jr., 3889
McDaniel, Marshall L., 229
McDermott, Eugene, 3886, 4024
McDermott, Mrs. Eugene, 4024
McDermott, Mary, 3886, 4024
McDermott, Thomas C., 2269
McDonagh, T.S., 2426
McDonald, David L., 1337
McDonald, Donald D., 2037
McDonald, Edwin P., 799
McDonald, Ellice, Jr., 609
McDonald, Evelyn M., 2037
McDonald, F.J., 1710
McDonald, Future H., 2718
McDonald, Helen, 2686
McDonald, James M., III, 2718
McDonald, James M., Sr., 2718
McDonald, Jean, 3971
McDonald, John A., 1968
McDonald, John F., Jr., 609
McDonald, Judy, 310
McDonald, Kevin, 2686
McDonald, Lee, 2686
McDonald, Lewis, 43
McDonald, Malcolm, 1853
McDonald, Malcolm W., 1820, 1928
McDonald, R.W., 3312
McDonald, Robert, 3230
McDonald, Rosa H., 609
McDonald, Thomas J., 2252
McDonald, Thomas R., 1348
McDonald, Mrs. William C., Jr., 3
McDonald, William E., 3188
McDonnell, Archie R., 1937
McDonnell Douglas Corporation, 1993
McDonnell, Everett N., 1091
McDonnell, Florence L., 1091
McDonnell, James S., 1994
McDonnell, James S., III, 1993, 1994
McDonnell, John F., 1993, 1994
McDonnell, M.J., 3758
McDonnell, Sanford N., 1993
McDonough, Alma, 4286
McDonough, Bernard P., 4286
McDonough, William J., 1002
McDougal, C. Bouton, 994
McDougall, A.B., 2426
McDougall, Ruth Camp, 4162
McDowell, Boyd, 2239
McEachern, D.V., 4249
McEachern, Ida J., 4249
McEachern, John H., Jr., 935
McEachern, Robert B., 4249
McElroy, William, 327
McElvenny, Ralph T., 1755
McEvoy, Charles L., 984
McEvoy Company, 3898
McEvoy, George A., 1581
McEvoy, George H., 1581
McEvoy, Mildred H., 1581
McEvoy, Rosemary, 984
McFadden, Robert F., 1411
McFarland, Alan R., 2735
McFarland, Don, 3887
McFarland, Ellen Michel, 2735
McFarland, Stuart A., 651
McFate, William J., 3690
McFawn, Lois Sisler, 3297

McFeely, Nancy K., 3652
McFerran, Mrs. Jack, 4040
McFerran, Richard, 1846
McFerson, D.R., 3313
McGarry, James, 2765
McGaugh, James L., 1170
McGaw, Foster G., 1093
McGee, Anna Fae, 4037
McGee, Dean A., 3440, 3446
McGee, Dorothea S., 3446
McGee, Edward F., 2972
McGee, Frank, 1995
McGee, Mrs. Frank, 1995
McGee, H.T., Jr., 3812
McGee, Joseph J., 1995
McGee, Mrs. Joseph J., 1995
McGee, Joseph J., Jr., 1995
McGee, Louis B., 1995
McGee, Robert W., 48
McGee (Thomas) and Sons, 1995
McGee, Thomas F., Jr., 1995
McGee, Thomas R., 1995
McGehee, C. Collier, Jr., 730, 731
McGehee, Gerald D., 3472
McGehee, Hobson C., 1935
McGehee, Hobson C., Jr., 1935
McGehee, Thomas R., 731
McGeorge Contracting Company, 61
McGeorge, Harvey W., 61
McGeorge, W. Scott, 61
McGeorge, Wallace P., Jr., 61
McGibney, F.R., 4148
McGill, Joe K., 3933
McGill, John R., 4193
McGill, Robert E., III, 512
McGill, William J., 421, 2679
McGillicuddy, John, 3750
McGinley, Patrick J., 3539
McGinley, Robert P., 3720
McGinnis, Barbara J., 257
McGinnis, Carl L., 257
McGinnis, Clara L., 257
McGinnis, Felix S., Jr., 257
McGinnis, J. Frank, 257
McGlade, Keith L., 532
McGonagle, Dextra Baldwin, 2719
McGough, George, 2253
McGovern, John P., 4025
McGovern, Joseph W., 2279
McGovern, Katherine, 4025
McGowan, Coeta Barker, 3476
McGowan, D.W., 3416
McGowan, J.R., 3476
McGrath, George W., 2792
McGrath, Helen B., 246
McGrath, M.E., 955
McGrath, W.J., 1135
McGraw, Donald C., 2720
McGraw, Donald C., Jr., 2720
McGraw, Harold W., Jr., 2154
McGraw, James D., 1625
McGraw, John L., 2154, 2720
McGraw, Max, 1094
McGraw, Richard F., 1094
McGraw-Edison Co., 1094
McGraw-Hill, 2721
McGreevy, Barbara James, 687
McGreevy, Milton, 687
McGreevy, Thomas J., 687
McGregor Fund, 1781
McGregor, James L., 2395
McGregor Printing Corporation, 671
McGregor, Thomas W., 671
McGregor, Tilda R., 630
McGregor, Tracy W., 1744
McGregor, Mrs. Tracy W., 1744
McGrew, Jane Lang, 2636
McGriff, Thomas J., 717
McGuigan, E. Gayle, Jr., 2810
McGuigan, Robert, 3376
McGuire, Dennis, 4392
McGuire, Florence Carney, 543
McGuire, Francis X., 543
McGuire, James, 581

McGuire, William B., 3095
McHenry, Alan F., 2679
McHenry, Barnabas, 2550, 2635, 2645, 3019
McHenry, Donald F., 2444
McHenry, James F., 1967
McHenry, Merl, 231
McHenry, W. Barnabas, 2234, 2851
McHugh, Alice L., 616
McHugh, Anabel C., 465
McHugh, Frank A., Jr., 616
McHugh, Godfrey T., 677
McHugh, Jerome P., 465
McHugh, Jerome P., Jr., 465
McHugh, John J., 125
McHugh, Marie Louise, 616
McInerny, Elizabeth DeCamp, 2392
McInerny, Ella, 903
McInerny, James D., 903
McInerny, James H., 2392
McInerny, William H., 903
McIninch, Ralph A., 2087
McInnes, D. Joseph, 4
McInnes, D.L., 4274
McInnes, H.A., 3516
McIntire, Sherwood W., 3150
McIntosh, Joan H., 746
McIntosh, Josephine H., 746
McIntosh, Marilyn, 4233
McIntosh, Michael A., 746
McIntosh, Peter H., 746
McIntosh, Winsome D., 746
McIntyre, David L., 1746
McIntyre, Jane E., 1745
McIntyre, John F., 4044
McIntyre, John W., 816, 3791
McIntyre, Robert C., 1376
McIsaac, George W., 539
McJunkin, Eleanor F., 2718
McJunkin, Reed L., 2718
McJunkin, Thomas N., 4285
McKay, Herbert G., 720, 765
McKay, James C., 1434
McKay, Robert B., 2858, 3066
McKean, Hugh, 2985
McKean, Hugh F., 701
McKean, Mrs. Q.A.S., 2104
McKee, C.D., 4026
McKee, Clyde V., Jr., 4085
McKee, Evelyn, 4026
McKee, John F., II, 935
McKee, John S., 4026
McKee, Louis B., 4026
McKee, Philip S., 4026
McKee, Robert E., 4026
McKee, Robert E., Jr., 4026
McKee, Stephen J., 369
McKee, Virginia A., 3653
McKeel, Steve, 4370
McKelvey, Patricia E., 1780
McKelvy, Bessie Morrison, 3654
McKenna, Alex G., 3626, 3655, 3656
McKenna, Andrew, 1211
McKenna, Donald C., 3656
McKenna, James F., 4297
McKenna, Katherine M., 3655
McKenna, L.W., 1999
McKenna, Leo C., 1502
McKenna, Philip M., 3656
McKenna, Quentin C., 3626
McKenna, Wilma F., 3655
McKenney, W. Foster, 1255
McKenny, Albert M., 657
McKenny, Anne E., 3304
McKenny, Charles A., 3304
McKenny, Mary L., 3304
McKenzie, Rosalind B., 1354
McKeown, Edward C., 1245
McKesson Corporation, 115
McKim, Judith, 1816
McKinley, John K., 2155
McKinley, William L., 1711
McKinney, David, 3793
McKinney, Dean B., 964

McKinney, F.H., 3092, 3093
McKinney, Joseph F., 4106
McKinney, Luther C., 1126
McKinney, Mary, 1313
McKinney, Roy, III, 4039
McKinney, Samuel B., 4269
McKinney, Walker, 1791
McKirahan, Robert, 266
McKissock, David L., 2168
McKissock, Diana, 2168
McKnew, Robert O., 977
McKnight, H. Turney, 1881
McKnight, Maude L., 1880
McKnight, Sumner T., 1881
McKnight, William L., 1880
McLafferty, Bernard J., 3548
McLanahan, Mrs. Duer, 2667
McLane, John R., Jr., 1553, 2083
McLane, Malcolm, 2089
McLane-Bradley, Elizabeth, 1531, 2092
McLaughlin, C.T., 3929
McLaughlin, J. Mark, 3929
McLaughlin, James P., 504, 584
McLaughlin, Megan E., 2493
McLaughlin, Sandra J., 3577
McLaughlin, W. Earle, 2951
McLean, Justina W., 1939
McLean, Robert, 3657
McLean, Roger C., 3760
McLean, William L., III, 3657
McLean, William L., Jr., 3657
McLearn, Michael B., 583
McLendon, Barbara, 2912
McLendon, Charles A., Jr., 3084
McLeod, A. Neil, 1236, 1256
McLeod, David H., 3795
McLeod, Marilyn P., 1323
McMackin, J.J., 3528
McMahon, Caroline D., 3557
McMahon, Eugene D., 3447
McMahon, John, 13
McMahon, Louise D., 3447
McMahon, Marshall I., 3190
McMahon, Mary M., 3557
McMannis, Haskell, 747
McManus, Paul A., 2345
McMeans, Seth A., 3867
McMenamin, Mrs. Edward B., 2347
McMenamin, Louise A., 4311
McMichael, R. Daniel, 3537, 3711
McMillan (D.W.) Trust, 12
McMillan, E.C., 867
McMillan, Ed Leigh, II, 12
McMillan, Elizabeth M., 3295
McMillan, Elridge W., 873
McMillan, H.W., 59
McMillan, Hugh, 2408
McMillan, James M., 1684
McMillan, Mary Bigelow, 1928
McMillan, Mary Moore, 4027
McMillan, S. Sterling, 3295
McMillan, S. Sterling, III, 2703
McMillan, V. Bruce, 4027
McMillen, Barry W., 1241
McMillen, Dale W., 1241
McMillen, Dale W., Jr., 1241
McMillen, Harold L., 1241
McMillen, John F., 1241
McMonigle, James B., 326
McMorris, Donald L., 2042
McMorrow, William J., 1535
McMullen, Dan, 4384
McMullen, Thomas, 1663
McMurtrie, Sandra Andreas, 1811
McNair, C.A., 877
McNair, John F., III, 3137
McNamara, Francis J., Jr., 2374
McNamara, Robert S., 2444, 3001
McNary, Gordon E., 353
McNeal, H.P., 4187
McNealy, Thomas W., 2912
McNeeley, Harry D., 3509
McNeely, Adelaide F., 1921
McNeely, Donald G., 1921

McNeely, Gregory, 1882
McNeely, Harry G., 1882
McNeer, Charles S., 4388
McNeese, A.G., Jr., 3875
McNeil, Henry S., 3543
McNeil, Lois F., 3543
McNeil, Robert L., Jr., 3522
McNeill, William H., 990
McNichols, Betty, 1990
McPeak, J., 2150
McPhail, D.W., 78
McPhail, Ian, 342
McPhee, Sharon, 898
McPherson, Mary Patterson, 2109, 2689
McQuary, Kip, 326
McQuillan, Jeremiah E., 497
McQuirk, John, 2711
McQuiston, W. James, 1749
McRae, Thomas C., 58
McRoberts, R.A., 540
McRoberts, Robert H., 2008
McShain, John, 3658
McShain (John), Inc., 3658
McShain, Mary H., 3658
McSpadden, Jack D., 3
McTier, Charles H., 832, 876, 884, 885
McVay, Scott, 2116, 4178
McVean, James E., 3027
McVie, A. Malcolm, 1246
McWane, J.R., 13
McWashington, Deloria J., 4269
McWhinney, Madeline H., 3271
McWilliams, Josephine, 451
Mead Corporation, 3299
Mead, Elise G., 284
Mead, George W., 4310
Mead, Giles W., Jr., 284
Mead, Jane W., 284
Mead Johnson & Company, 1242
Mead, Stanton W., 4310
Meade, Caroline, 306
Meade, N. Mitchell, 1351
Meader, Edwin E., 1786
Meadow, Hazel Hutcheson, 3843
Meadow, Stephen, 286
Meadowcroft, Elizabeth W., 1925
Meadowcroft, W. Howarth, 4274
Meadows, Algur Hurtle, 4029
Meadows, Curtis W., Jr., 4029
Meadows, Jack E., 400
Meadows, Robert A., 4029
Meadows, Virginia, 4029
Meagher, John B., 2113
Meaher, Augustine, III, 16
Meaher, Augustine, Jr., 16
Meanley, Edward S., 349
Means, Harvey H., 72
Means, T. Sam, 3744
Measelle, Richard L., 1722
Measey, William Maul, 3659
Meathe, Philip J., 1722
Mecha, Larry, 4370
Mechanics Bank, 1641, 1659
Meckauer, Ilse C., 2340
Mecke, Theodore H., Jr., 1722
Medal Distilled Products Company, 1078
Medberry, C.J., 83
Medberry, Chauncey J., III, 240
Medford, J.W., 3821
Medica, Alfred A., 1153
Medicine Bow Ranch Company, 435
Meditch, Boris E., 1230
Medtronic, 1884
Meehan, John J., 2496, 2906
Meehan, P.M., 127
Meek, Patricia Ann Shea, 357
Meeker, David B., 1162
Meeker, Helen, 3391
Meeker, Robert B., 3391
Meekin, John R., 2337
Meenaghan, James, 168, 169
Meese, G.C., 3456
Mefferd, G.W., 173
Meier, Anne R., 2263

Meier, Stephen C., 400
Meier, Walter C., 2263
Meikle, Thomas H., Jr., 3068
Meinert, Herman J., 2205
Meinert, J.R., 1032
Meinert, Marion, 2205
Meisel, Seymour L., 2743
Meissner, Frederick G., Jr., 2161
Meissner, Harold C., 1815
Meissner, Paul F., 4369
Melamed, Arthur C., 1885
Melamed, Arthur D., 1885
Melamed, Robert L., 1885
Melamed, Ruth H., 1885
Melander, Dorothy E., 1313
Melander-Dayton, Steven J., 1883
Melby, Edward J., 1828
Melchior, Louis, 1957
Melet, Michael D., 1687
Melfe, Thomas A., 3043
Mellen, Edward J., 3300
Mellon Bank, 707, 3511, 3544, 3549,
   3565, 3576, 3598, 3599, 3600,
   3605, 3611, 3631, 3644, 3654,
   3661, 3689, 3692, 3693, 3714,
   3735, 3754
Mellon, Constance B., 3662
Mellon, Paul, 2722
Mellon, Richard K., 3663
Mellon, Richard P., 3662, 3663
Mellon, Seward Prosser, 3662, 3663
Mellon, Susan, 570
Mellon, Timothy, 570, 2722
Mellor, M.L., 357
Mellor, Michael L., 105, 247
Melnicoff, David C., 3571
Melohn, Alfons, 2723
Melsen, John P., 4360
Melting, Robert Alan, 1228
Melton, Rollan D., 2943
Melton, Samuel Mendel, 3301
Meltzer, Robert, 2985
Melville, David B., 1582
Melville, Donald R., 1588
Melville, L. Scott, 502
Melvin, Richard S., 1195
Melvin, Thomas S., 539
Melvoin, Hugo J., 1146
Membership Department Stores, 185
Memphis Bank and Trust, 3854
Menard, Edward F., 2443
Menard, Julia F., 2443
Menchaca, Peggy B., 3982
Mendel, Edwin J., 1747
Mendel, Herbert D., 1747
Mendelsohn, Leslie, 175
Mendelsohn, Walter, 2605
Mendelson, Ida, 1437
Mendelson, Murry, 1437
Mendelsund, Judith G., 528
Mendenhall, J.R., 2997
Menefee, Albert, Jr., 3856
Mengle, G.A., 3664
Menil, Christophe de, 4030
Menil, Dominique de, 4030, 4031
Menil, Francois de, 4030
Menil, John de, 4030
Menil, Philippa de, 4030
Menlo, Judith, 285
Menlo, Sam, 285
Menlo, Vera, 285
Menninger, Karl A., 1170
Menschel Foundation, 2335
Menschel, Joyce F., 2725
Menschel, Richard, 2483
Menschel, Richard L., 41, 2335
Menschel, Robert B., 2483, 2725
Menschel, Ronay, 2335
Mensel, Robert C., 2094
Mentzer, E.W., 4373
Meoni, Ronald J., 2767
Meranus, Leonard S., 3265
Mercantile National Bank of Dallas, 4062

Mercantile Trust Company, 1972, 1973,
   1992, 1996, 2009, 2020, 2028, 2032
Mercantile-Safe Deposit and Trust
   Company, 1401, 1402, 1403
Mercer, Henry D., Jr., 2452
Mercer, Robert E., 3239
Merchants and Savings Bank, 4330
Merchants National Bank, 15, 2087
Merchants National Bank & Trust
   Company, 1217, 1226
Merchants National Bank of Terre
   Haute, 1225
Merck, Albert W., 2155
Merck & Co., 2155
Merck, Antony M., 3810
Merck, George Wall, 3810
Merck, Serena S., 2726
Meredith (Edna E.) Charitable Trust, 1261
Meredith, Charles, 812
Meredith, E.T., III, 1278
Meredith, Harry W., 4032
Meredith, Katherine C., 1278
Meredith Publishing Company, 1278
Meresman, Harry, 2858
Merit Oil Company, 3666
Merkel, Alfred W., 321
Merkert Enterprises, 1583
Merkert, Eugene F., 1583
Merkling, E. Jeanne, 2499
Merksamer, Geraldine F., 2449
Merlo, Harry A., 3496
Merlotti, Frank H., 1775
Merrell, John B., 2743
Merrell, Stanley W., 2269
Merrick, Anne M., 1438
Merrick, Mrs. F.W., 3448
Merrick, G. Clinton, 2158
Merrick, Robert G., Jr., 1438
Merrick, Robert G., Sr., 1416, 1438
Merrick, Ward S., Jr., 3448
Merrill, Charles E., 2691
Merrill, James I., 2727
Merrill, Joseph M., 3987
Merrill Lynch Asset Management, 3935
Merrill Lynch, Pierce, Fenner & Smith,
   2728
Merrill, Newton P.S., 2493
Merrill, R.D., 4251
Merrill (R.D.) Company, 4251
Merriman, Hemingway, 862
Merriman, Jack C., 1420
Merritt, Mrs. John F., 340
Merritt, Raymond W., 670
Merry, Ellis B., 1755
Merry Mary Fabrics, 286
Merryman, Sam B., Jr., 228
Merszei, Zoltan, 302
Mertens, Gertrude H., 2133
Mertens, Robert E., 2133
Mertz, DeWitt W., 2729
Mertz, LuEsther T., 2683, 2730
Mertz, Richard J., 2730
Merves, Stanley, 3736
Mervine, Donald S., 3550
Merwin, Irene Crown, 983
Merzbacher, C.E., 3289
Meschke, John A., 145
Meserve, Albert W., 557
Meserve, Helen C., 557
Meserve, J. Robert, 374
Meslow, John A., 1884
Messing, Morris M., 2156
Messing, Robert H., 2156
Messing, Roswell, Jr., 125
Messinger, Ruth, 2583
Messinger, Tineka Kurth, 4345
Messinger, W.C., 4373
Messinger, William C., 1162
Messler, Joseph D., 313
Messner, R.T., 3671
Mestel, Harry, 3373
Mestre, Barbara B., 2968
Metcalf, Karen, 2774
Metcalf, Pamela H., 2512

Metcalf, Stanley W., 2731
Metcalf, Susan S., 337
Metcalfe, John M., 1830
Metcalfe, John T., Jr., 3413
Metropolitan Life Insurance Company,
   2732
Metsch, Guenter F., 2257
Mettler, Ruben F., 2155, 3392
Metz, C.B., 4402
Metz, Kay, 3346
Metzger, Estelle, 2733
Metzger, William H., 2606
Meyer, Adolph H., 1663
Meyer, Agnes E., 672
Meyer, Alex, 1269
Meyer, Andre, 2734
Meyer, Baron de Hirsch, 748
Meyer, Bertram, 2157
Meyer, Betty, 74
Meyer, C. Louis, 1097
Meyer, Charles G., Jr., 2349
Meyer, Clifford J., 108
Meyer, Clifford R., 3184
Meyer, Daniel, 1030
Meyer, Daniel P., 4310
Meyer, Eugene, 672
Meyer, Eva Chiles, 3479
Meyer, Fred G., 3498
Meyer, Hobart, 4126
Meyer (Ida M.) Charitable Remainder
   Annuity Trust, 1663
Meyer, Jack R., 2877
Meyer, James A., 3487
Meyer, John E., 14
Meyer, Larry K., 756
Meyer, Matt, 3359
Meyer, Milton, 287
Meyer, Philippe, 2734
Meyer, Polly de Hirsch, 748
Meyer, Robert R., 14
Meyer, Roger F., 3637
Meyer, Russell W., Jr., 1297
Meyer, Schuyler M., Jr., 2493
Meyer, Vaughan B., 3930
Meyer, Virginia A.W., 563
Meyer, W. Fred, 1196
Meyer, William Dock, 3182
Meyerhoff, Harvey M., 1439
Meyerhoff, Joseph, 1403, 1439
Meyerhoff, Mrs. Joseph, 1439
Meyers, David R., 1082
Meyers, Gail, 2540
Meyers, Leon, 2914
Meyers, Margaret M., 3826
Meyers, Marilyn, 3451
Meyers, Philip M., Jr., 3219
Meyers, Robert M., 2767
Meyers, Warrin C., 3543
MFA Incorporated, 1997
MFA Oil Company, 1997
Miami Corporation, 988
Micallef, Joseph S., 1833, 1837, 1911,
   1924, 1925, 1926
Michael, Elsa B., 4143
Michaels, William, 776
Michalis, Clarence F., 2689
Michel, Barbara R., 2735
Michel, Bernice, 1682, 1683
Michel, Betsy S., 2138
Michel, Clifford L., 2138, 2735
Michel, Clifford W., 2735
Michel, Gilbert, 1683
Michelson, Gertrude G., 1126, 2700,
   2896, 3239
Michero, William H., 4093
Michigan National Bank, 1687, 1715,
   1740
Michler, John F., 4292, 4293
Mick, Priscilla J., 196
Mickel, B., 173
Mickel, Buck, 3802
Mickel, Mrs. Minor H., 3805
Mickelwait, Lowell P., 4219

Mid-American National Bank & Trust
   Company, 3386
Midas-International Corporation, 1150
Midas-International Corporation
   Foundation, 1150
Mid-Continent Supply Co., 3927
Middendorf, Alice C., 1440
Middendorf, Henry S., Jr., 3063
Middendorf, J. William, Jr., 1440
Middendorf, Peter B., 1440
Middlebrook, Stephen B., 489
Middlebrooks, E.A., Jr., 780
Middleman, Denise L., 2187
Middleton, C.J., 4040
Middleton, Mrs. Henry B., 3043
Middleton, Robert H., 3906
Midgley, Elizabeth, 659
Midkiff, Robert R., 890, 894
Midland Affiliated Co., 1518
Midland-Ross Corporation, 3302
Midlantic National Bank, 2177
Midonick, Millard L., 2644
Mihori, James S., 3242
Mika, Ernest A., 1715
Mika, W.J., 4166
Mike-Mayer, Maria, 2981
Mikolaj, M.G., 3217, 3257, 3262
Milam, Elizabeth J., 1938
Milam, Mrs. J.L., 1938
Milas, Lawrence W., 2798
Milbank, Albert G., 2724
Milbank, David L., 2724
Milbank, Dunlevy, 2736
Milbank, Jeremiah, 2584
Milbank, Jeremiah, Jr., 2584, 2926
Milbank, Katharine S., 2584
Milbank, Samuel L., 2724, 2737
Milbourn, Frank W., 3264
Milbury, Cassandra M., 3662
Milby, Charles D., 3972
Milco Industries, 2742
Miles, Jean H., 200
Miles Laboratories, 1243
Miles, Mary L., 2104
Miles, Nancy L., 3712
Miles, William, 200
Miles, William, Jr., 200
Milhollon, Nettie, 4033
Mill, Jean, 241
Millan, Jacqueline R., 2820
Millan, Robert Q., 3233
Millar, Richard R., 2616
Millard, Adah K., 1098
Millborne, Nancy, 1544
Miller, Anne H., 3592
Miller, Arjay, 217, 2722
Miller, Barbara B., 1808
Miller, Beatrice R., 1054
Miller, Bobby L., 1388
Miller, Burkett, 3860
Miller, C. Richard, Jr., 1431
Miller, Calvin A., 2474
Miller, Catherine G., 1228
Miller, Charles J., 2469
Miller, Charles W., 2496
Miller, Charlotte B., 3298
Miller, Mrs. Dale, 685
Miller, Dale, Jr., 799
Miller, Darrel L., 17
Miller, Diane D., 149
Miller, Diane Edgerton, 4178
Miller, Dolores E., 2700
Miller, Donald R., 1301
Miller, E. Black, 4357
Miller, E. Earl, 3695
Miller, Edward S., 2973
Miller, Edwill B., 3667
Miller, Elaine G., 658
Miller, Eleanor Bingham, 1335
Miller, Elizabeth G., 1228
Miller, Eugene, 1182
Miller Felpar Corp., 1886
Miller, Florence Lowden, 1125
Miller, Francena L., 3030

Miller, Frances Cameron, 3901
Miller, Francis C., 1276, 1277
Miller, Frederick W., 4316
Miller, Mrs. Frederick W., 4316
Miller, George C., 4017
Miller, H. Prentice, 817
Miller, Harold L., 1054
Miller, Harvey S.S., 3520
Miller, Hugh Thomas, 1228
Miller, I.L., 3963
Miller, J.H., 3234
Miller, J. Irwin, 1210, 1228
Miller, James A., 3564
Miller, James D., 4195
Miller, Joe, 916
Miller, John R., 2827
Miller, Joyce D., 659
Miller, Kate W., 3332
Miller, Kathryn B., 2739
Miller, Kenneth, 4274
Miller, Kenneth G., 3469
Miller, Louise B., 1749
Miller, Luther L., 3332
Miller, M.I., 1020
Miller, Margaret Carnegie, 2325
Miller, Margaret I., 1228
Miller, Mavis S., 758
Miller, Middleton, 994
Miller, Milton J., 1771
Miller, Norman C., 4357
Miller, Norvell E., III, 1412
Miller, Olive T., 1749
Miller, Orvin, 1302
Miller, Patricia Hillman, 3696
Miller, Paul A., 114
Miller, Paul F., Jr., 2444
Miller, Pearl, 2351
Miller, Phillip Lowden, 1125
Miller, Polly C., 807
Miller, R.N., 188
Miller, R.S., Jr., 1679
Miller, R.W., 1886
Miller, Raymond J., 3252
Miller, Richard, 335
Miller, Richard A., 3185
Miller, Richard J., 927
Miller, Richard K., 156
Miller, Robert B., 1749
Miller, Robert B., Jr., 1749
Miller, Robert C., 1782
Miller, Robert E., 3299
Miller, Robert F., 1054
Miller, Robert N., 673
Miller, Rudolph, 3030
Miller, S.M., 2432
Miller, Sam, 3225
Miller, Samuel M., 3033
Miller, Sandra Stream, 1364
Miller, Simon, 64, 256
Miller, Stephen R., 756
Miller, Steve J., 4357
Miller, T. Wainwright, Jr., 758
Miller, Warren Pullman, 1125
Miller, William D., 2831
Miller, William H., 2921
Miller, William I., 1228
Miller, William R., 2302
Miller, William S., 3238
Miller, William T., 865
Miller, Willodyne, 1349
Miller, Xenia S., 1228
Milhouse, Barbara B., 3075
Milligan, A.A., 259
Milligan, James H., 3459
Milligan, Lois Darlene, 3459
Milligan, Robert B., 579
Milligan, Robert S., 2063
Milliken & Company, 2740
Milliken, Gerrish H., 2880
Milliken, Helen, 1753
Milliken, Justine V.R., 2880
Milliken, Minot K., 614, 623, 2740, 2880
Milliken, Phoebe, 623

Milliken, Roger, 623, 2740, 2880
Milliken, W. Dickerson, 221
Milliken, William G., 2444
Millikin, James, 1099
Millikin National Bank of Decatur, 1023
Millikin, Thomas J., 3245
Millington, G.P., Jr., 1020
Millman, Herbert, 2644
Mills, Alice du Pont, 600
Mills, Amelia Louise, 245
Mills, Edward, 274
Mills, Frances Goll, 1750
Mills, James Paul, 600
Mills, John, 2208
Mills, Olan, II, 3835
Mills, P. Gerald, 1834
Mills, Ralph E., 1348
Mills, William B., 716
Millspaugh, Gordon A., Jr., 2197
Millstein, David J., 3668
Millstone, David S., 1998
Millstone, Goldie G., 1998
Millstone, I.E., 1998
Milne, Carolyn W., 796
Milne, Hodge & Milne, 774
Milnor, M. Ryrie, 1100
Milstein, Paul, 2998
Milstein, Seymour, 2931, 2998
Milunovich, L.G., 4318
Milwaukee Electric Tool Corporation, 4379
Milwaukee Golf Development Corporation, 984
Mims, G. Franklin, 3805
Minary, John S., 2808
Minasian, Ralph D., 2611
Mine Safety Appliances Co., 3669
Miner, Earl H., 1691
Miner, Phebe S., 1633, 1634
Mingenback, E.C., 1320
Mingst, Caryll S., 376
Minis, Abram, Jr., 847
Mink, John R., 1347
Minkin, Isadore, 2742
Minneapolis Star and Tribune Company, 1888
Minnesota Mining & Manufacturing Company, 1890
Minnesota Trust Company, 1871
Minnick, Gates, 2063
Minnix, George, 1201
Minnow, Newton N., 2329
Minor, Berkeley, Jr., 4287
Minor, C. Venable, 1985
Minow, Martha L., 2499
Minow, Newton, 1031
Minter, Steven A., 3186, 3365
Mintz, John A., 3342
Mirabella, Richard J., 2568
Miranda, Alfonso, 3769
Mirich, Beatriz, 2864
Mische, Joseph, 2553, 2554
Mischler, Harland L., 2269
Miscoll, James P., 84
Missar, R.R., 991
Mission Linen Companies, 309
Mitchel, Robert H., 3697
Mitchelides, S.P., 4148
Mitchell, A.S., 16
Mitchell, Mrs. A.S., 16
Mitchell, Braxton D., 1461
Mitchell, D.E., 3553
Mitchell, David W., 341
Mitchell, Edward D., 288
Mitchell, Elizabeth Seabury, 1143
Mitchell, H. Maurice, 55
Mitchell, James E., 3175
Mitchell, John, 1544
Mitchell, John C., II, 436
Mitchell, John D., 3525
Mitchell, Joseph C., 2905
Mitchell, Joseph N., 288
Mitchell, Joseph S., Jr., 1589
Mitchell, Kayla, 288

Mitchell, Kevin, 1846
Mitchell, Lee, 970
Mitchell, Lucy C., 1827, 1913
Mitchell, Mannie, 3710
Mitchell, Mary E., 1212
Mitchell, Mrs. Mayer, 17
Mitchell, Miriam P., 3525
Mitchell, R.L., 4000
Mitchell, Robert L., 2411
Mitchell, Wade T., 877
Mitchener, Claire Dumke, 4137
Mithun, Raymond O., 1845
Mitrani, Marco, 2742
Mittell, Sherman F., 674
Mittenthal, Richard, 2774
Mittenthal, Stephen D., 29
Mitterwager, Sylvia F., 2606
Mitton, Robert L., 458
Mix, Mrs. Kendall A., 1855
Mix, Phoebe A., 1855
Mize, E.M., 1321
Mnookin, I.J., 1941
Moates, Homer, 9
Mobil Oil Corporation, 2743
Mobley, E.B., 3965
Mobley, Ernestine L. Finch, 3100
Mobley, Robert L., 259
Model, Alan L., 2685
Model, Alice H., 2685
Model, Leo, 2745
Modlin, George M., 4208
Moe, John P., 1408
Moecker, Herman E., 2396
Moede, G.H., Jr., 4373
Moede, Gustave H., Jr., 1162
Moeller, Charles, Jr., 2528
Moelter, Helen, 1909
Moffatt, E.T., 3991
Moffett, George M., 791
Moffett, George M., II, 791
Moffett, James A., 791
Moffett, Jane Perkins, 3178
Moffett, Kenworth, 2790
Moffett, Polly Dewces, 3602
Moffett, William E., 3589
Mohler, Harold S., 3733
Mohn, Christian J., 3011
Mohorovic, Jesse R., 1518
Mojo, Mrs. Arthur O., 2950
Molinari, Joseph P., Jr., 3024
Moline, Jill, 31
Moline, Kenneth A., 248
Moline, Ray, 420
Molineaux, Charles B., Jr., 1595
Moll, Curtis, 3266
Moll, Curtis E., 3188
Moll, Jack C., 4336
Moll, Theo, 3266
Molla, Sarah R., 1753
Molloy, Gerald L., 3635
Molloy, John F., 40
Moloney, Thomas W., 2362
Molvig, Pauline, 3141
Momjian, Albert, 323
Monahan, Sherwood, 656
Monarch Machine Tool Company, 3305
Moncrief, W.A., 4034
Moncrief, William A., Jr., 4034
Monfort, Kenneth W., 466
Monheimer, Marc H., 104, 430
Monka, Richard, 4321
Monks, Millicent S., 1395
Monks, Robert A.G., 1395
Monrad, Ernest E., 1486
Monroe, Laura, 684
Monsanto Company, 1999
Monsen, Elaine R., 4259
Montague, Deaderick C., 3847
Montague, Hazel G.M., 3843
Montague, Robert M., Jr., 666
Montague, Sidney, 437
Monte, Constance, 3066
Montebello Trust, 2846

Montecto Mfg. Co., 309
Montera, Kaye C., 466
Montgomery, Albert C., 978
Montgomery, B.G., 4017
Montgomery, Charles H., 1002
Montgomery, E.E., Jr., 3306
Montgomery, Edward, 3346
Montgomery, Edward E., 3192, 3306
Montgomery, Frances, 3346
Montgomery, Frances S., 3306
Montgomery, Harold B., 3548
Montgomery, J.S., 3306
Montgomery, John L., Jr., 560
Montgomery, Linda, 3883
Montgomery, Philip O'B., III, 3886
Montgomery, Philip O'B., Jr., 3886
Montgomery, W.S., Jr., 3796
Montgomery, Walter S., 3796
Montgomery Ward & Co., 1185
Montminy, Mrs. Raymond J., 1621
Montoya, Dolores, 2213
Monumental Corporation, 1445
Monus, Michael I., 3379
Monus, Nathan H., 3379
Moo-Battue, Inc., 4364
Moodey, James R., 3363
Moody, Anson B., 4228
Moody, Daniel S., 3346
Moody, Frank M., 23
Moody, G.W., 1662
Moody, George F., 114, 351
Moody, Hiram F., Jr., 3037
Moody, Jana Gilcrease, 3431
Moody, Libbie Shearn, 4035
Moody, N., 2470
Moody, Robert L., 4035
Moody, Shearn, Jr., 4035
Moody, W.H., 2817
Moody, William, 498
Moody, William Lewis, Jr., 4035
Moog, Hubert C., 2020
Moon, Julia A., 2972
Mooney Chemicals, 3351
Mooney, Elizabeth C., 3351
Mooney, James B., 3351
Mooney, Michael, 2881
Moor, Walter E., 1441
Moore, Albert W., 2473
Moore, Brenda B., 1245
Moore, Carolyn N., 2748
Moore, Dorothy M., 2030
Moore, E.H., 954
Moore, Edward H., 3692
Moore, Edward S., Jr., 2748
Moore, Evelyn N., 2748
Moore, Frank G., 2107
Moore, Frank M., 1245
Moore, Harold J., 3005
Moore, Harry, 4285
Moore, Harry C., 4301
Moore, Harry W., 3307
Moore, Irving, Jr., 3995
Moore, James R., 4339
Moore, James W., 1099
Moore, John E., 1297, 3199
Moore, Joseph A., 3476
Moore, Joseph D., 2170, 3720
Moore, Lewis B., 3242
Moore, Maria M., 2968
Moore, Marjorie, 558
Moore, Mark B., 1245
Moore, Martha G., 530
Moore, Martin J., 1245
Moore, Mrs. Maurice T., 2682
Moore, Meta, 235
Moore, Michael L., 2783
Moore, Paul M., 3670
Moore, Peter C., 772
Moore, Richard A., 1852, 1912
Moore, Richard R., 3343
Moore, Sara Giles, 859
Moore, Starr, 859
Moore, T. Justin, Jr., 4198
Moore, Thomas F., Jr., 2232

Moore, Virlyn B., Jr., 804, 835
Moore, Winston C., 1083
Moorer, T.H., 1414
Moores, Harry C., 3308
Moorman, Albert J., 1833
Moorman, Bette D., 1833, 1925
Moorman, C.A., 1102
Moorman, Mrs. C.A., 1102
Moorman, Edgar V., 1066
Moorman, Jessie, 1066
Moorman Manufacturing Company, 1066, 1101, 1102
Moossy, Kathleen H., 3968
Moot, John R., 3039
Moot, Richard, 3039
Moot, Welles V., 3039
Moot, Welles V., Jr., 3039
Morales, Josephine, 2775
Moran, Edward P., Jr., 2082
Moran, Elizabeth R., 3676
Moran, Ida Jo B., 3898
Moran, James M., Jr., 3676
Moran, John A., 2417
Moran, John R., Jr., 452
Moran, Lee J., 2700
Moran, P.J., 3322
Moran, Susan B., 2082
Morawetz, Cathleen S., 2938
Morawetz, Cathleen Synge, 3314
Morehead, John Motley, 3118
Morehouse, Dean H., 1705
Moreland, Donald W., 1573, 1651
Morelano, Morris, 3872
Moret, Marc, 2174
Moreton, Charles, 1936
Morey, Joseph H., Jr., 2367
Morey, Loren, 1997
Morf, Claudia, 2820
Morf, Darrel A., 1269
Morford, Clare, 3429
Morgan, Anne H., 3439
Morgan, C.K., 3289
Morgan, Charles A., 3200
Morgan, Charles E., 3324
Morgan, Charles O., 2338
Morgan Construction Company, 1584
Morgan, Daniel M., 1584
Morgan, Edwin, 3119
Morgan, Eleanor, 749
Morgan, Elise McK., 3119
Morgan, Elizabeth E., 3119
Morgan, Francis S., 896
Morgan, Frank J., 1126
Morgan Guaranty Trust Company, 2774
Morgan Guaranty Trust Company of New York, 2194, 2296, 2389, 2468, 2498, 2559, 2609, 2687, 2750, 2921, 2928, 2944, 2957, 3029, 3793
Morgan, Harry E., Jr., 4274
Morgan, Helen F., 3225
Morgan, James F., Jr., 890, 899
Morgan, James L., 3119
Morgan, John, 2003
Morgan, John A., 574, 1946
Morgan, Louie R., 749
Morgan, M. Morrison, 3119
Morgan, Marietta McNeill, 4186
Morgan, Mildred, 749
Morgan Mills, Inc., 3119
Morgan, Paul B., Jr., 1584
Morgan, Paul S., 1584
Morgan, Perry, 4179
Morgan, Peter S., 1584
Morgan, Philip R., 1584
Morgan, Priscilla, 2786
Morgan, Roy E., 3729
Morgan, Roy T., 3784
Morgan, Russell H., 2211
Morgan, Samuel H., 1808
Morgan, Samuel T., Jr., 4186
Morgan Stanley & Co., 2751
Morgan, Walter L., 619
Morganroth, Lee J., 3936

Morgens, Edwin H., 242
Morgenstern, Frank N., 2752
Morgenstern, Morris, 2752
Morgenthaler, Lindsay Jordan, 3186
Morgenthau, Joan E., 242
Morgenthau, Robert, 2387
Moriano, Hugo J., 1179
Moriarty, Donald P., 2315
Morison, R.D., 3528
Morita, Akio, 2945
Moritz, Charles W., 2415
Morley, Burrows, 1751
Morley, Burrows, Jr., 1751
Morley, E.B., Jr., 1727
Morley, Edward B., Jr., 1751
Morley, George B., 1751
Morley, Peter B., 1751
Morley, Ralph Chase, Sr., 1751
Morley, Mrs. Ralph Chase, Sr., 1751
Morley, Robert S., 1751
Moroney, James M., Jr., 3924
Morrell (John) and Company, 2998
Morril, James A., 3715
Morrill, Thomas C., 1166
Morrill, Mrs. Vaughan, 1100
Morris, Adele G., 2753
Morris, Albert J., 633
Morris, Andrew J., 2205
Morris, Ben R., 3801, 3823
Morris, Benjamin H., 1337
Morris, Byon, 730, 731
Morris, Diane Y., 750
Morris, Donna T., 1780
Morris, E.A., 3120
Morris, Mrs. E.A., 3120
Morris, Edward L., 2753
Morris, Florence, 4243
Morris, Frank J., 3925
Morris, Ida A., 750
Morris, Irving, 615
Morris, James T., 1238
Morris, Jewell P., 1759
Morris, Jonathan B., 2302
Morris, Joseph E., 3120
Morris, L. Allen, 750
Morris, Lester J., 1759
Morris, Louis Fisk, 1143
Morris (Margaret T.) Trust, 41
Morris, Mary Lou, 3120
Morris, Max, 707
Morris, Norman M., 2753
Morris, Olin, 3854
Morris, R.A., 950
Morris, Richard I., 2496
Morris, Robert, 1000
Morris, Robert E., 2753
Morris, Robert P., 1759
Morris, Roland, 3557
Morris, S.B., 2467
Morris, Stewart, 4044
Morris, Thornton B., 520
Morris, Mrs. Victor O., 2416
Morris, W. Allen, 750
Morris, W. Carloss, 4126
Morris, W. Carloss, Jr., 4044
Morris, William T., 2754, 3830
Morrisett, Lloyd N., 393, 2700
Morrison, Alexander B., 4145
Morrison, Clinton, 1825, 1887
Morrison, Donald K., 1913
Morrison, Harry W., 914
Morrison, Howard Jackson, Jr., 851
Morrison, J.C., 1168
Morrison, Jack R., 3995
Morrison, Jacqueline A., 2244
Morrison, James K., 269
Morrison, John J., 2823
Morrison, L.I., 4078
Morrison, Madeline B., 761
Morrison, Mills Lane, 851
Morrison, Robert, 782
Morrison, Velma V., 914
Morrissey, Edmund J., 156
Morrissey, Thomas L., 2196

Morrow, Ellen B., 3699
Morrow, G.E., 182
Morrow, Richard M., 928
Morrow, Richard T., 150
Morrow, Winston V., 399, 676
Morse, Alan R., Jr., 1605
Morse, David, 2640
Morse, Earl, 2917
Morse, Enid W., 3044
Morse, Eric Robert, 1605
Morse, J. Robert, 1605
Morse, J.H., 3675
Morse, John A., 3303
Morse, John, Jr., 1605
Morse, John, Sr., 1605
Morse, Lester S., Jr., 3044
Morse, Robert W., 44
Morse, Sarah D., 1509
Morse, Stephan A., 2106, 4151
Morse, Theresa J., 1561, 1562, 1605
Morss, Everett, Jr., 1616
Mortenson, Doane, 1828
Mortenson, Robert S., 2157
Mortimer, Edward A., 3178
Mortimer, John, 2279
Mortimer, Robert J., 2590
Morton, David H., 2033
Morton, Dean, 218
Morton Fund, 1103
Morton, Quin, 4278
Morton, S. Sidney, 301
Morton, Sterling, 1103
Morton, Theodore R., 3817
Morton, Vincent P., Jr., 1630
Morton, Warren A., 4400
Mosbacher, Barbara, 2757
Mosbacher, Emil, 2757
Mosbacher, Emil, III, 2756
Mosbacher, Emil, Jr., 2452, 2756, 2757
Mosbacher, Gertrude, 2757
Mosbacher, John D., 2756
Mosbacher, Patricia, 2756
Mosbacher, R. Bruce, 2756
Mosbacher, Robert, 2757
Moscoso, Jose T., 2968
Moseley, Carlos D., 2905
Moseley, Elaine R., 1136
Moseley, Frederick S., III, 1560
Moseley, Furman C., 4248, 4259
Moseley, Jack, 1403, 1460
Moseley, James B., 2585
Moseley, Robert D., Jr., 2211
Moseley, Susan R., 4248
Moser, George P., 2128
Moses, Billy, 1356
Moses, Henry L., 2758
Moses, Lucy G., 2758
Moseson, Darrell, 1828
Mosher, Margaret C., 290
Mosher, Samuel B., 290
Moskin, Morton, 2287
Mosler, Edwin H., Jr., 2759
Mosley, W. Kelly, 835
Mosling, J.P., 4362
Moss, Diane, 2896
Moss, Florence M., 4037, 4038
Moss, Harry S., 4037, 4038
Moss, I. Barney, 3632
Moss, Morrie A., 302
Moss Petroleum Company, 4037
Moss, Robert D., 2798
Mosser, Norman, 2048
Mossler, Candace, 792
Mossler, Jacques, 792
Mosteller, Frederick, 2902
Mosteller, Richard G., 1743
Mote, William R., 751
Motorola Inc., 1104
Mott, C.S. Harding, 787, 1752, 1753
Mott, C.S. Harding, II, 1752
Mott, Charles Stewart, 1752
Mott, Hanno D., 2673
Mott, Lowell C., 723
Mott, Maryanne, 1752, 1753

Mott, Paul B., Jr., 2143, 2842
Mott, Ruth R., 1753, 2763
Mott, Stewart R., 1753, 2763
Mottaz, Judith, 924
Mottaz, Rolla J., 2002
Motto, Vincent J., 2979
Mottram, Patricia, 3916
Moulding, Mary B., 790
Moulton, Donald W., 411
Moulton, Hugh G., 3510
Mounger, William H., 1936
Mountcastle, Katharine B., 681, 3075, 3124
Mountcastle, Kenneth F., III, 3075
Mountcastle, Kenneth F., Jr., 3075
Mountcastle, Mary, 3124
Moursund, Travis M., 3880, 3881
Moxley, Lucina B., 1199
Moyers, Donald P., 3443
M.T. & D. Company, 3266
Muchnic, H.E., 1321
Muchnic, Helen Q., 1321
Muchnic, William H., 1321
Mudd, Henry T., 114
Mudd, Merle W., 1553
Mudd, Sidney P., 1053
Mudge, A.C., 3718
Muehl, William, 559
Muehlstein, Caryl B., 2764
Muehlstein, Herman, 2764
Muelbauer, J.H., 1232
Mueller (C.F.) Company, 2158
Mueller, Carl M., 2514
Mueller, Charles S., 2274, 2624
Mueller, J.R., 1862
Mueller, James R., 1980
Mueller, Nancy Sue, 2623, 2624
Mueller, Stanley R., 3456
Mueller, Werner D., 3372
Muench, Donald P., 4337
Muhlfelder, Mrs. Lewis, 2226
Muire, Annie S., 4195
Mulcahy, B.J., 3250
Mulcahy, John A., 42
Mulcahy Lumber Co., 42
Mulford, Clarence E., 1396
Mulford, Donald L., 1441
Mulford, Edith, 1441
Mulford, Vincent S., 1441
Mulford, Vincent S., Jr., 1441
Mulholland, B., 185
Mulitz, Shelley G., 661
Mullan, C. Louise, 1442
Mullan, Charles A., 1442
Mullan, Joseph, 1442
Mullan, Thomas F., Jr., 1442
Mullan, Thomas F., Sr., 1442
Mullen, Arnold, 735
Mullen, Catherine S., 467
Mullen, Frank, 2427
Mullen, Hugh M., 199
Mullen (The J.K.) Company, 467
Mullen, John K., 467
Mullen, William J., 3215
Muller, Frank, 291
Muller, Helen A., 554
Muller, James, 291
Muller, John, 291
Muller, Steven, 659, 1419
Muller, T., 291
Muller, Walter, 291
Mullett, Heather M., 2098
Mulligan, J.J., 3345
Mulligan, James F., 3645
Mulligan, Luke A., 2141
Mullin, Dean, 4242
Mullin, J. Shan, 4259
Mullin, Leo F., 1002
Mullinax, Jack, 4395
Mullins, W. David, 4290
Mullins, William B., 2181
Mulloney, Peter B., 3750
Mulnix, Frances, 1666
Mulreany, Robert H., 2201, 2528, 3128

Mulroy, Esther D., 1642
Mulshine, R.A., 2840
Muma, Dorothy E., 2792
Muma, Edith N., 2792
Mumma, Richard M., 2711
Mund, Richard G., 2743
Mundt, Ray B., 3510
Munford, Dillard, 2463
Munford, John D., 4159
Munger, Charles T., 292, 376
Munger, Charlotte K., 519
Munger, Edwin S., 2088
Munger, John H., 1125
Munger, Nancy B., 292
Muniz, Hilary Hattler de, 670
Munnelly, Kevin V., 336
Munro, D. Ranney, 3497
Munro, Walter J., Jr., 3129
Munro, Walter J., Sr., 3129
Munroe, George B., 2825
Muns, James N., 3885
Muns, Mrs. James N., 3885
Munsinger, Gary M., 44
Munson, Betty, 2048
Munson, Edwin P., 4198
Munson, Thomas L., 1762
Munson, W.B., III, 4039
Munyan, Winthrop R., 2349
Munz, Georgie T., 4098
Munzer, Rudy J., 240
Murakami, Edward S., 237
Murch, Maynard H., 3310
Murch, Maynard H., IV, 3310
Murdoch, David M., 1077
Murdock, Melvin Jack, 4252
Murdy, John A., III, 293
Murdy, John A., Jr., 293
Murdy (Norma) Trust B, 293
Murfey, Spencer L., Jr., 3151
Murfey, William W., 3151
Murnaghan, Francis D., Jr., 4178
Murphey, Lluella Morey, 294
Murphy, Annette Cross, 1954
Murphy, Ben R., 4106
Murphy, C.H., Jr., 54
Murphy, Charles C., 704
Murphy, Charles E., Jr., 2528
Murphy, Charles F., 1849
Murphy, Darrell L., 1346
Murphy, David Clark, 557
Murphy, David R., 458
Murphy, Diana E., 1823
Murphy, Evelyn, 684
Murphy, F., 185
Murphy, Franklin D., 65, 187, 400, 2629
Murphy, George E., 1954
Murphy, George H., 2140
Murphy, Grayson M-P., 2411
Murphy, Henry L., Jr., 1567
Murphy, J.J., 3935, 3936
Murphy, James E., 2728
Murphy, Jane, 2009
Murphy, Mrs. Jo, 3988
Murphy, Johanna, 521
Murphy, John P., 3311
Murphy, John T., 922
Murphy, John W., 35
Murphy, Johnie W., 54
Murphy, K. Mark, 532
Murphy, Michael E., 1139
Murphy, Norbert R., 2202
Murphy, Patrick V., 676
Murphy, Raymond R., Jr., 3832
Murphy, Richard F., 1521
Murphy, Robert F., Jr., 1648
Murphy, Robert L., 1021
Murphy, S.W., 3589
Murphy, Samuel W., Jr., 2406
Murphy, T.A., 173
Murphy, Thomas A., 2938
Murphy, Thomas S., 2322
Murphy, Walter Y., 866
Murphy, William J., 2795
Murphy, William R., 1502

Murrah, Alfred P., Jr., 4091
Murrah, Jack E., 3847
Murray, Archibald R., 2775, 2913
Murray, Arthur W., II, 1096
Murray, Fred D., 144
Murray, Haydn H., 2127, 2195
Murray, J. Ralph, 2239
Murray, J.L., 4384
Murray, J.R., 3223
Murray, L.T., Jr., 4253
Murray (L.T.) Trust, 4253
Murray, Margaret M., 2149
Murray, Susan, 3258
Murray, W.F., 1168
Murray, William E., 1517
Murray, William P., Jr., 136
Murrell, J.H., 4029
Murrell, Thomas W., Jr., 4198
Murrill, Paul W., 1936
Murry's Steaks, 1437
Murtagh, Robert J., 2296
Murtha, John S., 533
Musarra, Arthur F., 2955
Muse, J.H., 3117
Muse, Martha T., 2217, 2986
Musil, James, 1073
Muskal, Joseph, 1147
Muskopf, Wayne, 1948
Musselman, Emma G., 3672
Musselman, Francis H., 2724, 2737
Musselman, George A., 4056
Musselman, Peter R., 3258
Musser, Clifton R., 1848
Musser, Elizabeth W., 1848
Musser, John M., 1848
Musser, Marcie J., 1848
Musser, Margaret K., 1848
Musser, Robert C., 2743
Musser, Robert W., 1848
Musser, William L., Jr., 2315
Mustain, Robert, 2314
Muth, Robert J., 2246
Myer, David, 4296
Myers, A.G., Jr., 3121
Myers, Charles F., Jr., 3095
Myers, Frederick S., 3239
Myers, Fredrick, 3297
Myers, Gertrude, 3463
Myers, John, 2727
Myers, Kenneth H., 3230
Myers, Max, 3391
Myers, Paul D., 3153
Myers, Robert C., 2950
Myers, Robert H., 2140
Myers, Roger, 4305
Myers, Stephen E., 3145
Myers, Warren E., 3729
Myers, Wyckoff, 728
Myhers, Richard, 626
Mylod, Robert J., 651
Myra, John E., 3141
Myrin, Mabel Pew, 3517, 3673, 3688

Nabisco, 2159
Nabors, James D., 18
Nadel, Benjamin, 2742, 2854
Naftalin, Frances, 1887
Nagel, Charles F., 3698
Nagel, Ernest, 2398
Nagel, Frederick E., 1904
Nagle, Patricia Herold, 322
Nagy, Julia Ann, 2133
Naiberg, Gerald, 4376
Nail, Charles E., 3342
Naiman, Ada, 663
Nairne, Doris, 269
Nakagawa, Cressey H., 112, 192, 193
Nakauchi, Isao, 3001
Nalbach, Kay C., 1032
Nalco Chemical Company, 1105
Nally, Joseph T., 307
Nalty, Donald J., 1368, 1381
Nance, Carlyle A., Jr., 3135

Nance, H. Hart, 4017
Nance, Mrs. Murray, 4017
Nanon, Patricia, 2780
Napier Company, 2767
Naples, Ronald J., 3612
Napoletano, Ricci, 404
Narcavage, G.A., 78
Nardi, Nicholas J., 2374
Narkis, Robert J., 588
Nary, Gilbert R., 1012
Nash, Frank E., 3479
Nash, Frederick C., 1800
Nash, John F., 1823
Nash, John P., 4371
Nash, Mrs. R. Preston, Jr., 3370
Nash, Robert J., 2616
Nason, F. Alex, 3285
Nason, John W., 2373
Nastro, Joan C., 29
Nathan, Edward A., 410, 433
Nathan, Margaret S., 2520
Nathane, Robert A., 4238
National Bank & Trust Company, 1202
National Bank and Trust Company of South Bend, 1247
National Bank of Commerce, 3831, 3854, 4072
National Bank of Commerce of Charleston, 4285
National Bank of Detroit, 1696, 1715, 1739, 1745, 1746, 1755, 1756, 1799
National Bank of Georgia, 802
National Bank of North Carolina, 3087, 3113
National Bank of Washington, 636
National Boulevard Bank of Chicago, 968
National By-Products, 1279
National Central Bank, 3674
National City Bank, 3145, 3186, 3197, 3226, 3332
National City Bank of Evansville, 1203
National Distributing Company, 823
National Dollar Stores, Ltd., 359
National Endowment for the Humanities, 646
National Forge Company, 3675
National Machinery Company, 3312
National Medical Enterprises, 3925
National Presto Industries, 626
National Savings and Trust Company, 635
National Spinning Co., 2650
National Starch & Chemical Corporation, 2160
National Vulcanized Fibre Company, 624
National Westminster Bank, 2774
Nationwide Mutual Insurance Company, 3313
Naughton, John, 2376
Naughton, John A., 3469
Naumburg, George W., Jr., 2387
Naurison, James Z., 1585
Navin, Louis E., 1861
Naylor, Lester, 3701
Naylor, William B., 1793
NC Machinery, 4262
NCNB National Bank of Florida, 756
NCR Corporation, 3314
Neal, Stephen C., 1063
Neal, Stephen L., 3124
Neale, Gail Potter, 2362
Neathery, Kenneth L., Jr., 4207
Neaves, C.L., 4018
Neaves, Hope C., 3772
Nebraska Furniture Mart, 2050
Nechemie, Abraham H., 2190
Nee, David M., 2315
Needham, George A., 2435
Neely, Dora, 3879
Neely, Grant F., 3652
Neely, Mark E., Jr., 1239
Neely, Mary M., 1748
Neely, R.C., Jr., 3872
Neenah Foundry Company, 4359

Nees, Kenneth L., 2945
Neese, E.H., 4301
Neese, Elbert H., 4301
Neese, R.H., 4301
Neff, Jerry W., 3397
Neff, Paul F., 4192
Neff, W. Perry, 2287
Negley, Nancy Brown, 3893
Neill, Mary G., 3233
Neill, Robert, 1973
Neilson, George W., 1891
Neilson, Phillipa C., 2822
Neimeyer, Henry R., 3627
Neish, Francis E., 3551
Neisner, Fred, 3030
Neisser, Edward, 938, 1119
Nekoosa Papers, 4360
Nelco Sewing Machine Sales Corp., 2770
Nelli, Clara D., 280
Nelson, C.A., 119
Nelson, Carol, 390
Nelson, Catherine, 1094
Nelson, Charles, 3430
Nelson, Cholmondeley, 313
Nelson, Clarence J., 3552
Nelson, Clarke A., 385
Nelson, Donald O., 333
Nelson, Douglas A., 3840
Nelson, H.J., III, 3988
Nelson, H. Kenneth, 3758
Nelson, Helen P., 3548
Nelson, Helene D., 942
Nelson, Herbert T., 2139
Nelson, Mrs. Herman, 340
Nelson, J.A., 2495
Nelson, James A., 891
Nelson, James G., 1465
Nelson, John, 3190
Nelson, John H., 2071
Nelson, John M., III, 1436
Nelson, Joseph C., 4101
Nelson, Mrs. Karl H., 2071
Nelson, Ludvig, 1322
Nelson, Lyle M., 217
Nelson, Maurice O., 487
Nelson, Nels A., Jr., 4402
Nelson, Norma E., 262
Nelson, P. Erik, 3548
Nelson, Patricia Johnson, 3495
Nelson, Ralph S., 4226
Nelson, Raymond, 390
Nelson, Richard A., 3058
Nelson, Robert, 685
Nelson, Robert B., 3281
Nelson, S. James, 1812
Nelson, Selma, 1322
Nelson, Virginia, 4361
Nelson, W.L., 834
Nelson, W.O., 974
Nemer, James J., Jr., 977
Nemer, Stanley, 1841
Nemtzow, Bernard, 3174
Neppl, Walter J., 2116
Neroni, P.J., 3198
Nesbeda, Lucy, 2346
Nesti, Donald S., 3577
Nestor, Alexander, 546
Nestor, Alexander R., 544
Nethercott, J.W., 3333
Netter, R.J., 614, 623, 2740, 2880
Netterville, Jake L., 1354
Nettles, Dewey B., 3812
Nettles, J.E., 3511
Netzer, Dick, 2492
Netzky, Frank, 3710
Netzky, Frank W., 3710
Netzky, John, 3710
Netzky, William, 3710
Neu, Doris, 2771
Neu, Hugo, 2771
Neu (Hugo) & Sons, 2771
Neu, John, 2771
Neu, Richard, 2771
Neuberger, James A., 2772

Neuberger, Marie S., 2772
Neuberger, Roy R., 2772
Neufeld, Adele, 63
Neufeld, Peter, 63
Neuharth, Allen H., 2463
Neuhaus, Lacey T., 3381
Neuhauser, Raymond, 1850
Neuhoff, Louise H., 637
Neumann, Roland M., 4307
Neumann, Waldemar J., 2427
Neustadt, Richard, 640
Neuwirth, Benjamin, 2388
Neville, R.J., 980
Nevins, Blake R., 348
Nevins, John A., 2745
Nevius, John A., 683
New Britain Bank and Trust Company, 558
New Castle Corporation, 2938
New York Life Insurance Company, 2776
New York Post Corporation, 2832
New York Racing Association, 2585
New York Times Company, 2777
Newberger, Mrs. Arnold, 1070
Newbery, Charles C., 2762
Newbold, Theodore T., 3749
Newburg, Andre W.G., 498
Newburg, Elsie V., 2493
Newburger, Frank, Jr., 3569
Newbury, Nathan, III, 1609
Newcombe, Charlotte W., 2162
Newcombe, Margaret P., 1427
Newcomer, Arthur S., 3290
Newell, Barbara W., 644
Newell, David E., 2421
Newell, Douglas L., 3300
Newell, Frank K., 1034
Newhall, George, 296
Newhall, Henry Kleiser, 296
Newhall, Jane, 296
Newhall, John B., 1609
Newhall Land and Farming Company, 296
Newhall, Scott, 296
Newhall, Walter Scott, Jr., 296
Newhouse, Donald E., 2778
Newhouse, Mitzi E., 2778
Newhouse, Norman N., 2778
Newhouse, Samuel I., 2778
Newhouse, Samuel I., Jr., 2778
Newhouse, Theodore, 2778
Newkirk, Judith A., 157
Newlin, George W., 1228
Newman, Andrew, 1957
Newman, Bruce L., 968
Newman, Dean G., 1812
Newman, Elizabeth L., 2780
Newman, Eric P., 1957, 1958
Newman, Frank, 2109
Newman, Gordon H., 1139
Newman, Howard A., 2780
Newman, Jerome A., 2780
Newman, John M., 3215
Newman, John V., 230
Newman, Jule M., 2064
Newman, Lawrence, 798
Newman, Lucile F., 2773
Newman, Martha S., 532
Newman, Murray H., 2064
Newman, Racquel H., 297
Newman, Ralph, 1170
Newman, Stephanie K., 2775
Newman, William C., 2780
Newmont Mining Corporation, 2741
News and Courier Company, 3812
News and Observer Publishing Company, 3091
News Publishing Company, 1213
Newsweek, 660
Newton, Alice F., 1344
Newton, Blake T., III, 2881
Newton, Charles, 348
Newton, H.H., 3098
Neylon Freight Lines, 52

NFL Alumni Association, 1443
NFL Charities, 1443
Nias, Henry, 2781
Nibco Inc., 1240
Nicasho, Francis, 575
Nicholas, Diane, 1074
Nicholls, John C., Jr., 1743
Nichols, Carlton E., 1636
Nichols, Carlton E., Jr., 1636
Nichols, Charles W., III, 2782
Nichols, Charles W., Jr., 2782
Nichols, James R., 1470
Nichols, Jeannette, 2000
Nichols, John D., 1045
Nichols, Kate Cowles, 2369
Nichols, Marguerite S., 2294
Nichols, Marguerite Sykes, 2782
Nichols, Miller, 2000
Nichols, R.G., 2840
Nichols, Richard M., 1470, 1599
Nichols, Vivian, 348
Nichols, William, 3679
Nichols, William E., Jr., 3764
Nicholson, G.N., 3289
Nicholson, James J., 2113
Nicholson, Nellie Jo, 2048
Nicholson, Norman C., Jr., 1586, 1621
Nicholson, Paul C., Jr., 3787
Nicholson, Ruth, 3815
Nicholson, Ruth A., 3805
Nicholson, William S., 1509
Nickels, R.E., 1135
Nickelson, Donald E., 240
Nickelson, John R., 1285
Nickerson, E. Carlton, 1567
Nickerson, Elizabeth H., 573
Nickerson, Frank L., 1567
Nickerson, Hazel P., 573
Nickerson, Thorpe A., 573
Nickey, Laurance N., 3940
Nicklas, T.D., 3429
Nicks, Jess, 583
Nicolais, Michael A., 2347
Nida, Richard H., 252
Nielsen, M.K., 4231, 4232
Nielsen, W.A., 78
Nieman, Bill, 3922
Niemann, W.L., 955
Niesenbaum, D.W., 3547
Nilles, J. Gerald, 3142
Nilsen, Edward L., 228
Nimick, D.A., 3709
Nimick, Francis B., Jr., 3529
Nipper, Paul W., Jr., 3805
Nippert, Louis, 3315
Nippert, Louise, 3315
Nisen, Charles M., 1113
Nishkian, Queenie, 70
Nissen, James F., 2063
Nitz, Mike, 69
Niven, James G., 2715
Niven, W. John, 80
Nix, James H., 4285
Nixon, Joseph H., 1224
Nixon, Joseph O., 3797
NL Industries, 2783
Noble, Edward E., 3449, 3450
Noble, Edward John, 2784
Noble, Ethel G., 2785
Noble Foundation, 3993
Noble, Lloyd, 3449, 3450
Noble, Mary Jane, 3449
Noble, Sam, 3449, 3450
Nocas, Andrew I., 117
Noel, Elizabeth B., 525
Noel, Gary, 4339
Noguchi, Isamu, 2786
Nolan, Arthur A., Jr., 1134
Nolan, B.J., 3333
Nolan, Eleanor, 1813
Nolan, John S., 673
Nolan, Joseph T., 1999
Noland, John B., 1354
Noland, Mariam C., 1889

Noland, Robert L., 2238
Nolley, G.O., 3423
Nolop, Bruce P., 4338
Nolt, Betty J., 3718
Nolt, Edwin B., 3552
Nolt, Katie B., 3552
Nolte, Henry R., Jr., 1702
Nolte, Richard H., 2088
Noonan, Frank M., 1587
Noonan, James W., 1575
Noonan, John T., 1566
Noonan, Patrick F., 2234
Nord, Eric T., 3316
Nord, Evan, 3316
Nord, Evan W., 3316
Nord, Mrs. Walter G., 3316
Nord, Walter G., 3316
Nord, Wesley H., 2381
Norden, William B., 2798
Nordhoff, A.E., 4262
Nordman, Ben E., 259, 263
Nordson Corp., 3316
Norfleet, Elizabeth Copeland, 4198
Norgren (C.A.) Company, 469
Norgren, C. Neil, 469
Norgren, Carl A., 469
Norgren, Donald K., 469
Norgren, Juliet E., 469
Norgren, Leigh H., 469
Norman, Aaron E., 2787, 2788
Norman, Abigail, 2787
Norman, Andrew, 298
Norman, Andrew E., 2787, 2788
Norman, Don H., 652
Norman Foundation, 2548
Norman, Fred, 914
Norman, Helen D., 2788
Norman, Margaret, 2787
Norman, Myra, 2046
Norman, Rebecca, 2787
Norman, Richard A., 2252
Norman, Sarah, 2787
Norman, Theodore, 2387
Normine, Barbara, 1554
Norris, Charles H., Jr., 3579, 3743
Norris, Diana Strawbridge, 3743
Norris, Eileen L., 299
Norris, Harlyne J., 299
Norris, Kenneth T., 299
Norris, Kenneth T., Jr., 299
Norris, Sue, 1910
Norris, Terry O., 4360
Norry, Neil S., 3030
Norstar Bank of Upstate New York, 2789, 3045
North Carolina National Bank, 3071, 3074, 3088, 3099, 3104, 3109, 3111, 3137
North Dallas Bank & Trust Company, 3923
North Side Bank & Trust Company, 3183
North, Donald K., 4226
North, Ernest D., 2193
Northam, Hazel, 2837
Northeastern Bank, 3716
Northen, Mary Moody, 4035, 4041
Northern Central Bank, 3764
Northern Central Bank and Trust Company, 3679
Northern Engraving and Manufacturing Company, 4323
Northern Trust Bank of Florida, 706
Northern Trust Company, 968, 1062, 1073, 1093, 1098, 1103, 1108, 1127, 1144, 1164
Northrop, Edward H., 2527
Northrop, S.J., 3255
Northrup, Martha H., 2331
Northwest Industries, 1109
Northwestern Bank, 3137
Northwestern National Bank of Minneapolis, 1887
Northwestern Steel and Wire Company, 992

Northwood Finance and Realty Corporation, 2916
Norton Company, 1588
Norton, Eleanor Holmes, 685, 2877
Norton, Mrs. George W., 1349
Norton, Grace Geraldi, 1016
Norton, Hal, 3800
Norton, Jane Morton, 1349
Norton, Patrick H., 1736
Norton, Sara Jane, 3375
Norweb, R. Henry, Jr., 3258, 3294
Norwest Bank Duluth, 1839
Norwest Bank Minneapolis, 1874
Norwest Bank Saint Paul, 1912
Norwest Capital Management and Trust Co. Nebraska, 2066
Norwest Corporation, 1895
Noss, Stanley, 495
Nostitz, Drewry Hanes, 3105
Nottelmann, O. Robert, 1048
Notzon, Al, 4072
Novak, Barbara, 1446
Novatny, D.A., 1977
Nowicki, Douglas R., 3652
Noxell Corporation, 1444
Noyes, Carol R., 2323
Noyes, Charles F., 2792
Noyes, Evan L., Jr., 1246
Noyes, Jansen, Jr., 2979
Noyes, Marguerite Lilly, 1246
Noyes, Nicholas H., 1246
Noyes, Richard, 2911
Noyes, T.J., 3407
Noyle, Linda J., 1152
N.T.P. Company, 4079
Nuckols, E. Marshall, Jr., 3522
Nuernberger, W.W., 2054
Nunan, Caroline S., 3737
Nunn, Warne, 3498
Nusbaum, Beryl, 2490
Nutt, William D., 1938
Nutter McClennen and Fish, 1609
Nutter, W.L., 542
Nuveen, Grace B., 752
Nuveen, John, V, 752
Nye, Jane, 3003
Nye, William R., 3015
Nygren, Karl F., 1063
Nylander, Inga Olsson, 4190
Nystrom, Robert V., 1015

Oak Park Trust and Savings Bank, 1165
Oakes, John B., 2775
Oakey, Mrs. John, 4185
Oas, Nancy A., 3672
Oatman, Mrs. Jack L., 336
Obear, Frederick W., 3835
Obenauer, G.C., 3285
Ober, Agnes E., 1879
Ober, Stephen S., 1879
Oberdorfer, Lala H., 874
Oberkotter, Paul, 504, 584
Oberlander, Gustav, 3677
Oberndorf, Joseph, 3538
Oberndorfer, William P., 4165
O'Bleness, Charles, 3317
O'Bleness (Charles) Foundation No. 1, 3317
Obolensky, Ivan, 2561
O'Brien, Alice M., 1896
O'Brien, Catherine L., 369
O'Brien, Charles G., 3135
O'Brien, Donal C., Jr., 2578
O'Brien, Eleanor M., 1896
O'Brien, Fred K., 913
O'Brien, J.F., 979, 980, 2107
O'Brien, James F., 2284
O'Brien, Kevin P., 685
O'Brien, R.C., 1518
O'Brien, Robert B., Jr., 2161
O'Brien, Robert D., 4268
O'Brien, Terance G., 1896
O'Brien, Thomond R., 1896

O'Brien, William J., 1896
Obrow, Norman C., 126
O'Callaghan, Mike, 2079
Ocampo, Ralph R., 336
Occidental Petroleum Corporation, 302
Ochiltree, Ned A., Jr., 1097
O'Connell, Jane B., 2232
O'Connell, Philip R., 505
O'Connor, Dennis, 4042
O'Connor, Doris J., 4081
O'Connor, George R., 3893
O'Connor, Havourneen, 126
O'Connor, John M., 467, 657
O'Connor, Kathryn S., 4042
O'Connor, M.J., 3285
O'Connor, Maconda Brown, 3893
O'Connor, Maureen F., 330
O'Connor, Olive B., 2795
O'Connor, Richard L., 396
O'Connor, Roxann, 4296
O'Connor, Sally, 496
O'Connor, Susan, 2121
O'Connor, Tom, Jr., 4042
Odahowski, David A., 1922
O'Day, Patricia, 1793
Oddo, Nancy E., 2413
Oddou, Brenda K., 75
Odear, R.M., 3079
Odell, Donald A., 2732
Odell, Helen Pfeiffer, 303
Odell, Robert Stewart, 303
O'Dell, Ruth K., 244
Oden, Kenneth, 4002
Odom, Terry, 3887
O'Donnell, Doris, 3512
O'Donnell, Edith Jones, 4043
O'Donnell, J.P., 2053
O'Donnell, James E., 3648
O'Donnell, John J., 3648
O'Donnell, Patrick H., 4128
O'Donnell, Paul J., 2116
O'Donnell, Peter, Jr., 4043
O'Donnell, Mrs. Peter, Jr., 4043
Oehmig, Daniel W., 3863
Oehmig, Lewis W., 3863
Oelman, Robert S., 3242
Oemhler, G.C., 3513
Oenslager, Mary P., 2177
Oestreicher, Ann, 2796
Oestreicher, Irvin, 3131
Oestreicher, Sylvan, 2796
O'Fallon, Martin J., 470
Off, Robert W., 3535
Offield, Dorothy Wrigley, 1110
Offield, Edna Jean, 1110
Offield, James S., 1110
Offield, Paxson H., 1110
Offield, Wrigley, 1110
Offutt, Madeleine M., 3295
Ofner, David, 1006
O'Gara, Mrs. Charles, 3403
Ogawa, George, 420
Ogden, Alfred, 2512
Ogden, Elizabeth, 4325
Ogden, John, 4392
Ogden, Margaret, 2912
Ogden, Margaret H., 2797
Ogden, Ralph E., 2797
Ogie, Elizabeth C., 807
Ogilvie, Richard B., 2140
Ogle, Mrs. Robert, 3478
Oglebay Norton Company, 3318
O'Halloran, Michael, 534
O'Hara, Jack B., 1980
O'Hara, John A., 2550, 2635, 3019
O'Hare, Don R., 1174
O'Hare, Michael V., 644
O'Hearn, John, 757
Ohga, Norio, 2945
Ohio Citizens Bank, 3386
Ohio Citizens Trust Company, 3319
Ohio Company, 3410
Ohio National Bank, 3230
Ohio Road Paving Company, 3362

Ohio-Sealy Mattress Mfg. Co., 3412
Ohrstrom, George L., Jr., 4188
Ohrstrom, Ricard R., 4188
Oishei, John R., 2593
O'Kane, C.P., 1194
O'Keefe, Bernard J., 1521
O'Keefe, Daniel F., 2476
O'Keefe, Raymond T., 2649
O'Keefe, Terrance A., 3826
Oishei, Julian R., 2593
Okinow, Harold, 1875
Okinow, Sandra, 1875
Oklahoma Gas and Electric Company, 3452
Okonak, James R., 3652
Olbrycht, Alfred A., 83
Old American Insurance Co., 1995
Old Kent Bank and Trust Company, 1666, 1715, 1775
Old National Bank of Washington, 4259
Old Stone Bank, 3786
Oldam, P.B., 4294
Oldham, Morris C., 4044
Oldham, Theodore, 1692
Olds, Astrida M., 507
Olds, Jane Fagan, 231
Olds, Ransom E., 1761
Olds, William Lee, Jr., 231
O'Leary, Francis D., 3169
Oleck, Estelle, 3066
Olin, Ann W., 2002
Olin Corporation, 561
Olin, Franklin W., 2798
Olin, John M., 2001, 2799
Olin, Kent, 440
Olin, Spencer T., 2002
Olincy, Dan, 298
Olincy, Virginia G., 298
Oliphant, Allen G., Jr., 3426
Oliphant, Arline B., 3426
Oliphant, Charles W., 3426
Oliphant, Eric B., 3426
Oliphant, Gertrude O., 3426
Oliva, Gertrude P., 3173, 3325
Olive, Jack, 171
Oliver, Ann, 2804
Oliver, Bartley P., 402
Oliver, Christine Bireley, 96
Oliver, Daniel, 2357
Oliver, David, 1954
Oliver, David B., II, 3535
Oliver, Garrett, 3890
Oliver, Gertrude F., 1954
Oliver, Harry M., Jr., 1125
Oliver, James, 3976
Oliver, Joseph W., 3599
Oliver, Louise, 2357
Oliver, Roberta M., 1311
Oliver, William H., 4274
Oliver, William J., 1835
Ollen, Richard A., 657
Olmsted, Carol S., 4189
Olmsted, George, 4189
Olmsted, Jerauld L., 4189
Olney, Robert B., 3820
O'Loughlin, John K., 922
Olrogg, Elgin E., 4229
Olrogg, Marian Cheney, 4229
Olsen, Charles N., 2997
Olsen, Eugene R., 1835
Olsen, George, 2307
Olsen, John R., 3503
Olson Companies, 4329
Olson, Gerald L., 1905
Olson, Gilbert N., 3140
Olson, H.E., 385, 386, 387
Olson, Lynde V., 4302
Olson, Paul M., 1821
Olson, R. Thomas, 4236
Olson, Robert A., 1983
Olson, W.G., 1194
Olsson, John, 2054
Olsson, Shirley C., 4190
Olsson, Signe Maria, 4190

Olsson, Sture G., 4190
Olum, Paul, 3477
Olwell, William H., 4130
Omaha National Bank, 2055, 2056, 2059, 2060, 2061, 2065
Omaha World-Herald Company, 2066
Oman, Richard H., 3338
O'Malley, Edward V., Jr., 35
O'Malley, Peter, 246
O'Mara, John M., 2540
O'Meara, Alfred, Jr., 470
O'Meara, Brian, 470
Onan, David W., II, 1897
Onan, David W., III, 1897
Onan, Elizabeth H., 1897
Onan, Lois C., 1897
Onasch, Donald C., 888
Onassis, Jacqueline K., 3785
Onderdonk, Kay S., 67
100 Church Street Management Corporation, 3056
Oneal, Louis, 121
O'Neal, Solon F., Jr., 765
O'Neal, Thelma K., 1461
Oneida National Bank & Trust Company of Central New York, 3005
O'Neil, Albert T., 1898
O'Neil, Casey A. T., 1898
O'Neil, Cyril F., 2801
O'Neil, Grace, 3322
O'Neil, Helene, 3322
O'Neil, Helene Catherine, 3322
O'Neil, John, 2088, 3322
O'Neil, John J., 3322
O'Neil, M.G., 3321
O'Neil, Ralph M., 2801
O'Neil, Robert M., 2109, 4332
O'Neil, Steven, 1425
O'Neil, W., 3322
O'Neill, Abby M., 2875
O'Neill, Brendan M., 1109
O'Neill, Cynthia K., 1855
O'Neill, D., 488
O'Neill, Edward L., 1944
O'Neill, Gail, 2876
O'Neill, James E., 3715
O'Neill, Kelley M., 1855
O'Neill, Robert F., 67
O'Neill, William J., Jr., 1602
Onello, Deborah M., 2916
Ong, John D., 3344
Ongley, Patrick A., 2344
Oppenheim, David J., 2413
Oppenheim, Paula K., 2615
Oppenheimer, Edward, 1111
Oppenheimer, Harry D., 1111
Oppenheimer, James, 1111
Oppenheimer, James R., 1821
Oppenheimer, James W., 1917
Oppenheimer, Seymour, 1111
Oppenlander, R., 825
Oppenstein, Michael, 2003
Oppikofer, Ulrich H., 2174
Oppmann, Harvey G., 3186, 3365
Ora Mill Company, 3094
Orb, John A., 2940
Orcutt, G.F., 4041
Ordean, Albert, 1899
Ordean, Louise, 1899
Orders, William H., 3805, 3825
Ordman, Howard F., 2912
Oreffice, P.F., 1688
Oreffice, Paul F., 1712
Oregon Bank, 3500
O'Reilly, A.J.F., 3598
Orendorf, Jo Tilden, 1350
Orick, Millard, 31
Orick, Rick, 38
Oriel, Patrick J., 1757
Ormond, Mary Clark, 935
Ormond, Neil, 935
Ormsby, R.B., 266
Ormseth, Milo, 3490

O'Rourke, L.D., 269
Orr, Dudley W., 2089
Orr, James H., 1652
Orr, San W., Jr., 4390
Orr, Susan Packard, 308
Orscheln, D.W., 2004
Orscheln, G.A., 2004
Orscheln Industries, 2004
Orscheln, Phillip A., 2004
Orscheln, W.L., 2004
Orth, T.M., 1138
Orton, Stewart, 3211
Osborn, Charles, 4245
Osborn, Charles F., 4253
Osborn, Donald R., 2736
Osborn, Edward B., 2803
Osborn, Mrs. Edward B., 2803
Osborn, G.A., 4384
Osborn, Judy, 421
Osborne, Charles M., 1835
Osborne, Richard deJ., 2246
Osborne, Robert E., 246
Osborne, T.C., 2246
Osgood, Edward H., 1575
O'Shaughnessy, Donald E., 1900
O'Shaughnessy, Eileen, 1900
O'Shaughnessy, I.A., 1900
O'Shaughnessy, John F., 1900
O'Shea, John P., 2416
Oshei, R. John, 2593
Osheowitz, Michael W., 2493
Oshkosh Truck Corporation, 4362
Oshman, M. Kenneth, 341
O'Shoney, Glenn, 4126
Osmon, D.R., 1890
Osmond, Russell, 802
Osmun, Jeffrey T., 2102
Osmundsen, Lita, 3037
Ostergard, Paul M., 527
Ostrow, Laurie, 305
Ostrow, Seniel, 305
Oswald, Warren W., 1327
Oswalt, William, 1789
Otasco, Inc., 3461
Otien, Carl N., 4313
Otis, James C., 1879
O'Toole, John E., 1006
O'Toole, Theresa, 2805
Otsuka, Jeanette Y., 4241
Otten, Mrs. Louis, 2729
Ottinger, Betty Ann, 2806
Ottinger, Lawrence, 2806
Ottinger, Louise L., 2806
Ottinger, Randy, 2806
Ottinger, Richard L., 2806
Ottinger, Ronald, 2806
Ottinger, Sharon, 2806
Ottley, Marian W., 861, 862
Otto, Jack L., 1744
Otwell, Raymond C., 872
Ouellette, Roland A., 519
Ouimet, Mark, 1664
Ourant, Robert H., 3313
Outboard Marine Corporation, 997
Overby, Andrew N., 2435
Overcash, Reece A., Jr., 3924
Ovitz, J.D., 1194
Ovrom, Arthur P., 1285
Owen, B.B., 4047
Owen, Elizabeth LaViers, 1345
Owen, George A., 705
Owen, Harry V., 1213
Owen, J. Churchill, 458
Owen, Jane Blaffer, 3888
Owen, L.D., 4212
Owens, Alice, 2307
Owens, Augusta L., 703
Owens, John, 2175
Owens, John C., 3268
Owens, Samuel H., 2563
Owens-Illinois, Inc., 3181
Owsley, Alvin M., 4048
Owsley, Alvin M., Jr., 4048
Owsley, David T., 4048

Owsley, Lucy B., 4048
Oxler, Ann Bixby, 2011
Oxman, Phyllis S., 2833
Oxnard, Thomas Thornton, 306
Oyler, Robert B., 1325

Pabst Brewing Company, 4363
PACCAR, 4255
Pace, Glenn L., 4145
Pace, Stanley C., 3365, 3392
Pacific Coast Construction Company, 183
Pacific Tube Company, 3745
Pacific Union Bank & Trust Company, 318
Packard, David, 308
Packard, David Woodley, 308
Packard, Julie E., 308
Packard, Lucile, 308
Packer, Augusta L., 2359
Packer, H.L., 3885
Packer, Mrs. H.L., 3885
Packer, Horace B., 3679
Packet Motor Express, 3812
Packs, Carol S., 1617
Paddock, David S., 1156
Paddock, James W., 1325
Paden, James R., 3893
Padilla, Wilfred, 2212
Paganucci, Paul D., 2496
Page, Beatrice H., 595
Page, Cary L., Jr., 3811
Page (Charles) Family Care Charitable Remainder Annuity Trust, 3460
Page, George B., 309
Page, George C., 229
Page, Henry A., Jr., 3181
Page, Raymond S., Jr., 2107
Page, Rheta Haas, 3966
Page, Roger M., 1343
Page, Ruth, 1112
Page, Seaver T., 397
Page, Shelby H., 498
Page, Walter H., 3750
Pagen, William R., 316
Paige, Sidney A., 1045
Paight, A.S., 560
Pail, Norbert J., 3655, 3656
Paine, B.L., 1319
Paine, Gordon T., 3182
Paine, Peter S., 2248, 2294
Paine, Mrs. Stephen D., 1586
Paine, W.K., 1932
Painter, Alan S., 2098
Paisley, Beverly M., 1670
Pake, George E., 1955
Pako Corporation, 1838
Palay, Gilbert, 4322
Palay, J. Dorothy, 4322
Palenske, Victor C., 1782
Palermo, Alfonsine, 722
Palermo, Anthony, 722
Palermo, Anthony R., 3030
Paley, Goldie, 3680
Paley, Martin A., 337
Paley, William S., 2808, 3680
Palisano, Charles J., 2809
Palisano, Harriet A., 2809
Palisano, Joseph S., 2809
Pallotti, Marianne, 217
Palmer, Bernard, 1178
Palmer, Charles E., 3671
Palmer, E. Christopher, 1582
Palmer, Edward L., 2825
Palmer, Francis Asbury, 2810
Palmer, George C., II, 4191
Palmer, James D., 845
Palmer, Joseph B., 1475
Palmer, Lloyd J., 1105
Palmer Supply Company, 4233
Palmer, Theodore B., 3rd, 3768
Palmer, Victor D., 2265
Palmer, Virginia, 562

Palmieri, Victor H., 2877
Palmiter, Marilyn W., 2849
Palmore, B.B., 3945
Palzkill, Mary T., 949
Pamplin, Margaret V., 4208
Pampush, Marie, 4246
Pan American Bank, 706
Pancoast, John W., 4111
Pancoast, Terrence R., 3503
Panelli, John, 1443
Pannell, Edwin C., 4091
Pannell, William C., 4091
Pansing, Lu, 2063
Pansini, Francis D., 154
Pantages, Lloyd A., 2118
Pantasote Inc., 563
Panzarella, Marian, 2339
Papadeas, C.D., 11
Papageorge, Antigone, 11
Papas, James, 11
Papas, Philip, 11
Papas, Sam, 11
Pape, Lutz, 1867
Paper, Calmenson and Company, 1901
Paper, Lewis, 1901
Papiano, Neil, 3357
Pappas, A.R., 9
Pappas, Betsy Z., 1590, 1591
Pappas, Charles A., 1590, 1591
Pappas, Helen K., 1590, 1591
Pappas, Theodore J., 706
Pappas, Thomas A., 1591
Pappas (Thomas Anthony) Charitable Foundation, 1590
Paradis, Daisy, 2271
Pardee, Arthur P., 2446
Pardee, Elsa U., 1757
Pardee (Sarah Norton) Trust, 576
Parenti, Renato R., 71
Parfet, Martha G., 1728
Parfet, Mrs. Ray T., Jr., 1787
Parish, P.S., 1787
Parish, Richard L., 2168
Parish, Richard L., III, 2168
Parish, Richard L., Jr., 2168
Parish, Suzanne D., 1681
Park, Alvin L., 1818
Park, Bill, 3922
Park, Dale, Jr., 957, 1059
Park, Jane M., 2565
Park Lane Associates, 2651
Park National Bank, 3837
Parker Pen Company, 4330
Parker, C.W., Jr., 4294
Parker, Camilla M., 4050
Parker, Catherine, 2314
Parker, Charles W., Jr., 4358
Parker, David R., 492
Parker, Franklin E., 2234, 2577
Parker, George, Jr., 2981, 4050
Parker, George E., III, 1785
Parker, George S., 4330
Parker, Gerald T., 310
Parker, Geraldine, 2465
Parker, H.L., 1168
Parker, Inez Grant, 310
Parker, John, 2869
Parker, John C., 4159
Parker, John M., 4050
Parker, John O., 1553
Parker, Joseph B., 4050
Parker, Joseph L., 3449
Parker, L.G., 3228
Parker, Maclyn T., 1207
Parker, Margaret H., 2197
Parker, Mary E., 598
Parker, Mary H., 4050
Parker, P.S., 3323
Parker, Patricia H., 4050
Parker, Paul L., 1847
Parker, Robert F., 4017
Parker, Robert L., 3453
Parker, Robert L., Jr., 3453
Parker, Sumner, 4338

Parker, Theodore Edson, 1592
Parker, Thomas, 3815
Parker, William, 3858
Parker, William A., 4050
Parker, William A., Jr., 813, 820
Parker, William I., 2465
Parker-Hannifin Corporation, 3323
Parkhurst, Evelyn C.W., 4121
Parkhurst, William D., 691
Parkhurst, William M., 2257
Parkin, J. Stanley, 2580
Parkin, Joe L., 1132
Parkins, J. Stanley, 2581
Parkinson, Elizabeth B., 2289
Parkinson, J. David, 2192
Parkinson, John, 2289
Parkinson, Roger, 1888
Parkinson, Thomas I., Jr., 2737
Parkman, Rosalie M., 628
Parks, Floyd L., 1713, 1786
Parks, Lewis H., 1514
Parks, R.J., Jr., 1933
Parma, Leon W., 282
Parman, Robert A., 3454
Parmelee, David W., 525
Parmelee, Jean D., 230, 242
Parr, Dorothy J., 3973
Parr, Royse M., 3444
Parravano, Teresa H., 3968
Parris, John, 3097
Parrish, Cynthia V., 3245
Parrish, Eugene M., 1373
Parrish, Lee H., 3245
Parrott, Marion A., 2831
Parrott, William G., 2005
Parrott, William G., Jr., 2005
Parry, George T., 3145
Parry, Gwyn, 221
Parry-Okeden, Blair, 889
Parsegian, Vasken L., 2600
Parshall, Daryl, 2738
Parshall, William E., 3612
Parshelsky, Moses L., 2813
Parshootto, C., 249
Parsley, Georganna S., 4089
Parsley, Robert H., 4117, 4118
Parsley, Robert S., 4089
Parsons, Henry K., 2202
Parsons, Mary Stone, 579
Parsons, R.J., 950
Parsons, Ralph M., 311
Parsons, Robert W., Jr., 2134
Parsons, Roger B., 2134
Parsons, Thomas, III, 3068
Parsons, Vinson A., 3073
Parsons, William, 2774
Parsons, William, Jr., 579
Partain, June P., 809
Partee, Sue Garrett, 4065
Parvin, Albert B., 312
Parvin, Phyllis, 312
Pascal, D.D., 2160
Pascal, Donald, 2505
Pascal, Nancy W., 789
Pasculano, Lynne, 2647
Pastor, Kensington Congregational Church, 558
Pastor, Kensington Methodist Church, 558
Pate, A., 119
Pate, Mrs. Glenn, 1935
Patek, Patrick J., 597
Patek, Rose B., 597
Patel, Blyth G., 2292
Patel, C.K.N., 2294
Patenaude, Dean J., 507
Paton, Leland, 2253
Paton, Richard G., 2769
Patrick, Charles F., 133
Patrick, Mary B., 597
Patrick, P.F., 4236
Patrick, Ueal E., 1726
Patrick, William B., Jr., 3817
Patterson, Alicia, 675

Patterson, Charles J., 337
Patterson, Clara Guthrie, 564
Patterson, D.F., 3808
Patterson, David K., 2616
Patterson, David R., 3408
Patterson, David T., 3408
Patterson, Donald H., 1399
Patterson, E.H., 56
Patterson, Ellmore C., 2938, 2951
Patterson, Eugene C., 757
Patterson, Frederick W., 863
Patterson, Ida Brittain, 863
Patterson, Mrs. James T., 617
Patterson, Jane S., 3124
Patterson, M.K., Jr., 3449
Patterson, Pat J., 3435
Patterson, Remington P., 2252
Patterson, Robert Leet, 564
Patterson, Robert P., Jr., 2499, 2810
Patterson (Robert) Trust No. 2, 564
Patterson, V.P., 4017
Patterson, W.I., 3682
Pattillo, D.B., 864
Pattillo, H.G., 864
Pattillo, R.D., 3915
Pattiz, Cathy Lee, 315
Pattiz, Henry A., 315
Pattiz, Leona, 315
Pattiz, Oscar S., 315
Patton, Henry, 2512
Patton, Leland R., 1392
Patton, M.G., 3809
Patton, Robert F., 3651
Patty, F.M., Jr., 1933
Paty, John C., Jr., 3851
Paul, John H., 491
Paul, Josephine Bay, 2814
Paul, Lee G., 313
Paul, Raymonde I., 2270, 2814
Paul, Robert A., 3169, 3692
Paul, Toni H., 1029
Pauley, Edwin W., 316
Paulucci, Gina J., 1902
Paulucci, Jeno F., 1902
Paulucci, Lois M., 1902
Paulucci, Michael J., 1902
Paulus, David J., 1002
Paulus, Firmin A., 1748
Pauly, Robert L., 183
Pawson, Katherine R., 2455
Paxson, Howard H., 1782
Paxton, Joe, 309
Payne, Frederick B., 2372
Payne, James O., 3170
Payne, M. Lee, 4181
Payne, Seba B., 1113
Payne, W. Anderson, 1985
Payne, W.C., Jr., 721
Paynter, John W., 1722
Payson, Mrs. Charles S., 3043
Payton, Robert L., 2426
Pazol, James L., 345
Peabody, Amelia, 1593
Peabody, George, 873
Peach, Harry A., 451
Peacock, C.W., 542
Peacock, John E.D., 1197
Peak, Chandos H., 4288
Pear, Henry E., 1430
Pearce, R. Jack, 1046
Pearl, Judson W., 2361
Pearlman, Alex W., 2816
Pearlman, Henry, 2816
Pearlman, Rose, 2816
Pearlstone, Peggy Meyerhoff, 1445
Pearlstone, Richard L., 1445
Pearsall, Amos C., Jr., 1270
Pearson, Alvin W., 2520, 2653
Pearson, Andrall E., 2820
Pearson, D.J., 1863
Pearson, Ferne L., 1114
Pearson, Mrs. G. Burton, Jr., 607
Pearson, George, 1316
Pearson, George H., 1317

Phillips, Elliott, 2210
Phillips, Ellis L., 2093
Phillips, Ellis L., III, 2093
Phillips, Ellis L., Jr., 2093
Phillips, Frank, 3455
Phillips, Mrs. Frank, 3455
Phillips, Genevieve E., 2210
Phillips, George R., 74
Phillips, Gladys, 4220
Phillips, Harry, Jr., 3820
Phillips, Mrs. Harry J., 3854
Phillips, Howard, 754
Phillips, Jay, 1903
Phillips, John G., 1373
Phillips, Lawrence S., 2828
Phillips, Marion G., 2093
Phillips, Mary, 1506
Phillips, Mary Bird, 1476
Phillips, Morton B., 1903
Phillips, P.W., 3198
Phillips, Pauline, 1903
Phillips Petroleum Company, 3455, 3456
Phillips, Richard F., 2155
Phillips, Richard L., 3342
Phillips, Robert B., 3455
Phillips, Rose, 1903
Phillips, Russell A., Jr., 2671, 2875
Phillips, Seymour J., 2828
Phillips, Sidney H., 4085
Phillips, Virginia, 2210
Phillips, W. Thomas, 1126
Phillips, Warren H., 2117, 2410
Phillips, William, 2408
Phillips, William G., 1866
Phillipson, Phillip N., 3408
Phillips-Van Heusen Corporation, 2828
Philpott, Harry M., 883
Philpott, Helen, 1698
Phippen, Richard D., 1570, 1615, 1642
Phippen, Susanne LaCroix, 1615
Phipps, Benjamin K., 755
Phipps, Colin S., 755
Phipps, Helen Clark, 1904
Phipps, Howard, 2577
Phipps, Howard, Jr., 565, 2248, 2784
Phipps, Jack, 4003
Phipps, John E., 755
Phipps, Mary S., 2218
Phipps, Robert L., 2432
Phipps, Ruth, 4283
Phipps, Stephen C., 1904
Phleger, Atherton, 231
Phleger, Herman, 231
Phoenix Newspapers, 1204
Phy, Mrs. Paul W., 3925
Piasecki, Grzegorz, 2586
Piatigorsky, Joram, 2390
Piatoff, Mary, 2772
Picard, William, 212
Pichon, John N., Jr., 1207
Pick, Albert, III, 1119
Pick, Albert, Jr., 1119
Pick, Corinne F., 1119
Pick, Joan M., 4368
Pick, Melitta S., 4368
Pickens, Marshall I., 3095
Pickens, William, III, 3001
Picker, Harvey, 2211
Picker, James, 2211
Picker, Jean, 2211
Pickett, Lynda M., 2499
Pickup, Harry, Jr., 3869
Piel, Gerard, 242, 2445
Pier, Nancy G., 2477
Pierce, A. Kenneth, Jr., 3410
Pierce, Harold Whitworth, 1599
Pierce, Ruth M., 4080
Piercy, George T., 2979
Pierpont, Henry B., 2071
Pierpont, Wilbur K., 1734
Pierre, Lola C., 4192
Pierrepont, John, 2248
Pierson, Edward, 1430
Pierson, W. Michel, 1430

Pierson, Wayne G., 3498
Pietrafesa, Richard C., Sr., 2331
Pietrini, Andrew G., 2647
Pifer, Alan, 2109
Pifer, Erica, 516
Pigott, Charles M., 4254, 4255
Pigott, J.C., 4255
Pigott, James C., 4254
Pike, John R., 4334
Pildner, Henry, Jr., 3738
Pilhashy, Milton, 1773
Pilliod, Charles J., Jr., 3239
Pillsbury Company, 1830, 1905
Pillsbury, Edwin S., 2007
Pillsbury, Fred H., 2007
Pillsbury, George S., 1913
Pillsbury, Harriette Brown, 2007
Pillsbury, John S., 1913
Pillsbury, Mrs. John S., 1913
Pillsbury, John S., III, 1913
Pillsbury, John S., Jr., 1913
Pillsbury, Joyce S., 2007
Pillsbury, William E., 2007
Pinckney, C. Cotesworth, 4198
Pincus, Lionel, 659
Pincus, Lionel L., 2576
Pine Bluff Sand & Gravel Company, 61
Pine, Barbara, 1019
Pine, William C., 3482
Pineo, Charles C., III, 1814
Pineo, Linda Baker, 1814
Pinet, Herve M., 940
Pingree, Hugh, 897
Pingree, Mary Weld, 1653
Pingree, Sally E., 2121
Pinkerton, Robert A., 2245, 2830
Pinnick, Joseph, 1711
Pioneer Bank & Trust Company, 1383
Pioneer Federal, 756
Pioneer Insurance Company, 710
Pioneer Trust Company, 3501
Pioneer Village, 223
Piper Industries, 3905
Piper, Minnie Stevens, 4056
Piper, Paul P., 3905
Piper, Mrs. Paul P., 3905
Piper, Paul P., Jr., 3905
Piper, Randall G., 4056
Piper, Ronald K., 3905
Piqua National Bank & Trust Company, 3247
Pirovano, John, 1117
Piskor, Frank P., 2784
Piszek, Edward J., Jr., 3548
Piszek, Edward J., Sr., 3548
Piszek, George, 3548
Piszek, Olga P., 3548
Piszek, William P., 3548
Pitcairn, Beatrice S., 3530
Pitcairn, Cameron C., 3530
Pitcairn, Feodor U., 3525
Pitcairn, Garthowen, 3581
Pitcairn, Glenn P., 3530
Pitcairn, Jocelyn B., 3530
Pitcairn, Joel, 3530
Pitcairn, John P., 3530
Pitcairn, Kirstin O., 3525
Pitcairn, Lachlan, 3581
Pitcairn, Laren, 3525
Pitcairn, M. Kate, 3530
Pitcairn, Mary Eleanor, 3525
Pitcairn, Michael, 3581
Pitcairn, Raymond, 3581
Pitcairn, Robert R., 3530
Pitcairn, Stephen, 3530
Pitcairn, Sue K., 3530
Pite, C.R., 2299
Pitfield, P. Michael, 2995
Pitman, Donne W., 3422
Pittel, Joseph A., 1806
Pittenger, T.E., 3321
Pittinger, Vernon T., 1416
Pittman, J.E., 9
Pittman, Marshall, 3136

Pitts, C.L., 810, 811
Pitts, John W., 4255
Pitts, Margaret A., 866
Pitts, William I.H., 866
Pittsburgh Forgings Company, 3692
Pittsburgh National Bank, 3561, 3573, 3608, 3653, 3669, 3693, 3694, 3708, 3752, 3763
Pius, Charles, 359
Pivik, Robert W., 2395
Pivnick, Isadore, 389
Plaggemeyer, Mary, 1438
Planchon, Gerard C., 1884
Plankenhorn, Harry, 3695
Plant, Philip, 4036
Plastics Engineering Company, 4307
Platner, J.L., 4294
Platt, Abraham S., 2420
Platt, Robert H., 3239
Platten, Donald C., 2109, 2379, 2887, 3187
Player, Willa B., 1752
Pleasants, C. Edward, Jr., 3137
Plein, Thomas, 4311
Plekenpol, L.W., 2249
Pletsch, George B., 1037
Pletz, Francis G., 3377
Plimpton, Anne G., 1569
Plimpton, Francis T.P., 2956
Plinio, Alex J., 2167
Plough, Abe, 3855
Plough Foundation, 2178
Plourde, Robert J., 82, 226
Plummer, John A., 1474, 1510
Plummer, Robert, 1208
Plunkett, Lamar R., 872
Plunkett, Michael S., 987
Plunkett, Paul M., 1188
Plunkett, Warren F., 1871
Pluta, Andrew, 2834
Pluta, Helen, 2834
Pluta, James, 2834
Pluta, John, 2834
Pluta Manufacturing Corp., 2834
Pluta, Peter, 2834
Pluta, Mrs. Peter, 2834
Plym, Mrs. Francis J., 1758
Plym, Lawrence J., 1758
Poboisk, D.P., 932
Podvin, Francis J., 4360
Poelker, John S., 816
Poesch, Gustav H., 2478
Pogue, Richard W., 3186, 3278
Pohle, H.W., 4337
Poindexter, R.D., 1378
Poindexter, T.C., 1378
Poitras, James, 1649
Pokorny, Gene, 640
Pokross, David R., Sr., 1482
Polansky, Ellen Woods, 3864
Polaroid Corporation, 1602
Polgreen, Philip W., 1174
Polier, Justine W., 2432
Poling, Harold, 1702
Polinger, Geraldine, 1448
Polinger, Howard, 1448
Politeo, Janet L., 4236
Polk Brothers, Inc., 1121
Polk, Eugene P., 39, 41, 2335
Polk, Louis F., Jr., 3329
Polk, Louis F., Sr., 3329
Polk, Morris G., 1121
Polk, Samuel S., 2724
Polk, Sol, 1121
Pollack, G.J., 542
Pollack, Lester, 3066
Pollack, Ronald F., 684
Pollak, Ruth S., 1140
Pollak, Stephen J., 1140
Pollard, Carl F., 1344
Pollard, James C., 3937
Pollard, Jules C., 3871
Pollitt, John V., 340
Pollock, Davis E., 1285

Pollock, John P., 240
Pollock, John V., 685
Pollock, Kathryn Challiss, 3330
Pollock, William B., II, 3330
Polokoff, Edwin, 2311
Polsky, Cynthia H., 2536
Polsky, Virginia Harris, 1030
Pomeranz, Lee, 2917
Pomeroy, Grace E., 36
Pomeroy, Katherine, 588
Pomplun, Herbert, 1828
Poncin, Cora May, 4256
Pond, Byron O., 1081
Ponder, Henry, 2962
Pontius, Ross I., 3682
Pool, Wendell, 3976
Poole, Alleen, 3417
Poole, Cecil F., 202
Poole, Richard G., 2637
Poole, Stewart E., 605
Poorbaugh, William J., 3635
Pope, Anthony, 2835
Pope, Catherine, 2835
Pope, Fortune, 2835
Pope, Generoso, 2835
Pope, John L., 4027
Pope, K.A., 997
Popkin, Alice B., 674
Popovich, Jane H., 222
Poppas, George, Jr., 4013
Poppensick, George C., 2202
Popper, Joe E., 867
Popper, Robert L., 2644
Popvic, Deyan M., 2185
Port Sutton, 784
Portaro, Sam A., Jr., 1125
Portenoy, Norman S., 2413
Portenoy, Winifred Riggs, 685, 2413
Porter, Donald E., 4308, 4337
Porter, Dudley, Jr., 3848, 3849
Porter, James Hyde, 867
Porter, John W., 1752
Porter, Kay, 336
Porter, Mark M., 1937
Porter, Maude Dee, 4135
Porter, Milton, 3575
Porter, Oliver E., 2416
Porter, Robert, Jr., 3182
Porter, Rose Marie K., 1428
Porter, T.L., 2249
Portlock, Carver A., 3717
Portnoy, Fern C., 444, 473
Posner, Roy, 2677
Posner, S., 624, 768
Posner, V., 624
Posner, Victor, 768
Posnick, A., 3212
Posnick, Ethel C., 1406
Post, Allen, 868
Post, Judith, 2439
Post, Leona, 2439
Post, Marjorie Merriweather, 677, 678
Post, Robert, 2439
Post-Newsweek Stations, 660
Poston, Met R., 3073
Posvar, Wesley W., 644
Potash Corporation of Saskatchewan, 834
Poteat, Janis T., 1783
Potenziani, A.F., 2206
Potenziani, Frank A., 2206
Potenziani, Martha M., 2206
Potenziani, William, 2206
Potlatch Corporation, 326
Pott, Phenie, 2009
Potter, Alton W., 1114
Potter, Charles S., 1122
Potter, Edward H., 2221
Potter, Harriet, 2063
Potter, Helen A., 2221
Potter, Justin, 3856
Potter, Peter N., 109
Potter, R.G., 1999
Potter, Mrs. Valere Blair, 3856

Rand-Whitney Packaging Corporation, 1550
Randall, B. Carter, 1464
Randall, Blanchard, 1464
Randall, Dean B., 1861
Randall, James A., 3806
Randall, Kennedy, Jr., 897
Randall, Kenneth A., 1060
Randall, L.A., 1299
Randall, William B., 1853
Randall, William L., 4356
Randazzo, C.L., 2532
Randle, Kathryn A., 2338
Randol, Margaret Neustadt, 2859
Randolph, Jennings, 3524
Randolph, Linda A., 2773
Randolph, R.F., 4285
Randolph, W.R., Jr., 3829
Rands, Dale G., 1725
Ranger, Thomas F., 1663
Rankin, Alfred M., 3324
Rankin, C. Kenneth, 166
Rankin, Sarrah W., 21
Rankin, Susan T., 3378
Rankin, William J., 916
Ranney, George A., 1048
Ranney, George A., Jr., 1001, 1048, 1125, 1160
Ranney, Nancy R., 3335
Ranney, Peter K., 3335
Ranney, Phillip, 3415
Ranney, Phillip A., 3213, 3335
Ransom, Mrs. Harry, 3919
Raoul, William G., 3835
Rapaporte, Riepa, 3788
Rapaporte, Samuel, Jr., 3788
Rapoport, Bernard R., 2680
Rapoport, Leonard, 3627
Rapp, G.W., Jr., 78
Rappaporte, Samuel, Jr., 1530
Rappleye, Richard K., 1752
Raschke, K.O., 2249
Raskin, A.H., 2279
Raskin, Braine, 2847
Raskin, Hirsch, 2847
Raskin, Rose, 2847
Raskob, Anthony W., 628
Raskob, Benjamin G., 628
Raskob, John J., 627, 628
Raskob, Richard G., 628
Raskob, William F., III, 627, 628
Rasmussen, A.L., 3550
Rasmussen, Arthur E., 928, 1001
Rason Asphalt, 2545
Rassas, Nicholas, 1157
Rast, L. Edmund, 835
Ratcliffe, G.J., 540
Rathbone, John S., 340
Ratliff, Eugene F., 1238
Ratliff, Floyd, 2513
Ratner, Albert, 3225
Ratner, Albert B., 3390
Ratner, Charles, 3225
Ratner, Mark, 1070
Ratner, Max, 3225
Ratner (Milton M.) Trust, 1762
Ratshesky, A.C., 1605
Ratti, Marlene, 2589
Rauch, John G., Jr., 1248
Rauch, Louis, 2848
Rauch, Philip, 2848
Rauch, Stephen, 2765
Rauch, William T., 34
Rauchenberger, Louis J., 2329
Rauenhorst Corporation, 1907
Rauenhorst, Gerald A., 1907
Rauenhorst, Henrietta, 1907
Rauenhorst, Mark, 1907
Ravenscroft, Marguerite Doe, 152
Ravitch, Donald N., 630
Ravitch, Richard, 2995
Ravitz, Robert J., 2502
Rawlinson, Joseph E., 111
Rawls, Sol Waite, Jr., 4159

Rawson, William R., 1095
Ray, Adele Richardson, 3127
Ray, Donald, 1979
Ray, Hilton, 3926
Ray, J.E., III, 4159
Ray, James C., 475
Ray, Joan L., 475
Ray, John L., 4284, 4287
Ray, Mrs. Joseph M., 4017
Ray, Mary Lou Ryan, 3897
Ray, Richard E., 4159
Ray, Richard L., 3945
Ray, Robert C., 4159
Ray, Robert J., 3945
Ray, William F., 2310
Ray, William I., Jr., 822
Rayfield, Allan L., 531
Raymond, George, 2849
Raymond, George G., Jr., 2849
Raymond, Jean C., 2849
Raymond, Pete, 2849
Raymond, R.O., 43
Raymond, Stephen S., 2849
Raynovich, George, Jr., 3760
R.C.M. Corporation, 2266
Rea, Cleveland D., 2402
Rea, William H., 3529, 3599, 3600
Read, Charles L., 2850
Read, H.T., 2741
Read, John R., 1066
Read, Robert, 1271
Reade, Edith M., 1129
Reader's Digest Association, 2851
Reading, Richard F., 2381
Reagan, James W., 1912
Reagan, John C., 533
Realty Leasing Corporation of Georgia, 750
Ream, Norman, 4382
Reames, Timothy P., 275
Reardon, Edward J., 567, 1995
Reardon, G. Joseph, 3391
Reardon, Robert J., 1822
Rearwin, Kenneth R., 310
Reath, Mrs. Henry T., 3766
Rebsamen Companies, 55
Reckling, T.R., III, 4105
Record, George J., 3336
Red Wing Shoe Company, 1908
Reddell, William, 4072
Redle, W.D., 4395
Redlin, Gerald G., 1850
Redman, Clara M., 4062
Redman, Harold F., 4062
Redman, James, 4062
Redman, Mrs. James, 4062
Redman, Manville, 3447
Redman, Mary, 4062
Redmond, Charles R., 321, 400, 532
Redmond, John C., 3700
Redmond, John C., III, 3700
Redmond, W.T., 1731
Redna Incorporated, 150
Redpath, Frederick L., 2188
Reed, A. Lachlan, 1914
Reed, Anne E., 2121
Reed, Benjamin, 3785
Reed, C. Lawson, 3153, 3184
Reed, Charles L., 4205
Reed, Dorothy W., 3153
Reed, Earl F., Jr., 3578
Reed, Eleanor H., 4248
Reed, Glenda C., 532
Reed, Homer E., 450
Reed, Ina N., 1922
Reed, J. Brad, 3852
Reed, John J., 2026
Reed, John S., 2902
Reed, Martha S., 1914
Reed, Maurice T., Jr., 1936
Reed, Paul H., 3609
Reed, Philip D., 2852
Reed, Philip D., Jr., 2852
Reed, Thomas A., 1306, 1324

Reed, Vincent, 685
Reed, Vincent E., 660
Reed, W. Brooks, 3175
Reed, William G., Jr., 4248
Reed, William S., 1914
Reeder, Jack A., 3076
Reekie, Robert B., 978
Rees, Albert, 2938
Rees, Charles, 327
Rees, William M., 2700
Reese, C.M., 456
Reese, Charles Lee, Jr., 617
Reese, Eleanor Steele, 2957
Reese, Emmet P., 2957
Reese, Everett D., 679, 3209
Reese, J. Gilbert, 3209
Reese, John, 3362
Reese, L.H., 3976
Reese, Stan, 4019
Reeves Brothers, Inc., 2170
Reeves Brothers Mills, 2170
Reeves, Charles B., Jr., 1461
Reeves, Charles H., 329
Reeves, Ferrell, 9
Reeves, Helen F., 3337
Reeves, Ivan Ress, 3789
Reeves, J.E., 2170
Reeves (J.M.) Brothers, 2170
Reeves, John E., 2170
Reeves, John E., Jr., 2170
Reeves, Margaret H., 3337
Reeves, Margaret J., 3337
Reeves, Mary, 3734
Reeves, Samuel J., 3337
Regalbuto, Robert R., 3359
Regan, Grace O'Neil, 3322
Regan, James P., 37
Regan, Joseph J., 1083
Regenburg, B.H., 4332
Regenstein, Helen, 1130
Regenstein, Joseph, 1130
Regenstein, Joseph, Jr., 1130
Reghanti, Thomas J., 1706
Register, John M., 3676, 3749
Regner, L.G., 4306
Regnery, Henry, 1082
Regnery, William H., II, 1082
Rehm, Mina Bess Melton, 3301
Reice, Charles T., 964
Reich, Ann Sheffer, 2994
Reich, Joseph A., Jr., 4089
Reich, Robert L., 2187
Reichard, William E., 3351
Reichel, Aaron I., 2437
Reichel & Drews, 1152
Reichel, John, 2046
Reichel, O. Asher, 2437
Reicher, Harry J., 2853
Reichert, James A., 4117, 4118
Reichman, Vivian, 2233
Reicin, Ronald I., 1112
Reid, Ala H., 1506
Reid, Charles M., 3132
Reid, Fergus, III, 2248
Reid, James S., Jr., 3372
Reid, John A., 4200
Reid, Richard, 952
Reidler, John W., 3702
Reidman, Barbara J., 1397
Reifsnyder, C. Frank, 654
Reiger, A.C., Jr., 3307
Reighley, H. Ward, 2443
Reilly, Elizabeth B., 1250
Reilly, Frank J., 1990
Reilly, Jonathan, 2729
Reilly, Jonathan B., 2729
Reilly, Peter C., 1250
Reilly, Robert F., 2828
Reilly Tar & Chemical Corporation, 1250
Reilly, William F., 2688
Reily, H.E., 1379
Reily, R.D., 1379
Reily, William B., III, 1379
Reily (Wm. B.) & Co., 1379

Reiman, Thomas J., 926
Reimann, Auguste, 2854
Reimann, Kurt P., 2854
Reimann, Mrs. Kurt P., 2854
Reimel, Gretchen R., 1139
Reimers, A.J., 2010
Reimers, Arthur H., 84
Reinberger, Clarence T., 3338
Reinberger, Robert N., 3338
Reinberger, William C., 3338
Reinhard, Martin, 717
Reinhardt, Edith A., 3698, 3766
Reinhardt, Hazel, 1888
Reinhart, R.L., 3756, 3757
Reinhold, Peter E., 1651
Reinsch, Emerson G., 4192
Reis, Jean S., 3191
Reis, Thomas J., 3369
Reis, Vanessa, 277
Reisenbach, Marvin S., 2187
Reisinger, Richard, 3502
Reiss, Irwin H., 1236
Reiss, Jacob L., 2855
Reiss, Kurt W., 3726
Reiss, Raymond H., 2855
Reiss, Robert R., 2855
Reister, Russell W., 1664
Reitenbaugh, Ann P., 3548
Reiter, Robin, 770
Reitz, Carl F., 1672, 1673
Reitz, Ralph E., 1309
Reliable Electric Company, 1502
Reliance Electric Company, 3339
Reliance Insurance Companies, 3703
Reller, William H., 1220
Rembar, Charles, 688
Rembe, Toni, 410
Reminger, Robert, 4391
Remmel, Jerry C., 4388
Remmert, J.E., 2426
Renard, Henry P., 612
Renault-Morgan, Suzanne, 1501
Renfro, John F., Jr., 3807
Rengier, John B., 3635
Rennebohm, Mary F., 4372
Rennebohm, Oscar, 4372
Renner, Daniel S., 3340
Renner, Jane, 3340
Renner, Jennie S., 3340
Renner, John W., 3340
Renner, R. Richard, 3340
Renner, Richard R., 3340
Renner, Robert R., 3340
Rennert, William J., 2683
Rennie, Robert, 3462
Rennolds, Edmund A., Jr., 4157
Rennolds, John K.B., 4157
Reno, Robert H., 2089, 2092
Renov, Ruki, 2755
Rentrop, Gary, 1663
Renzel, Ernest, 341
Repass, John R., 3467
Repplier, Sidney N., 3766
Republic Bank, 3880
Republic National Bank, 2774
Republic Steel Corporation, 3341
RepublicBank Dallas, 3923, 3935, 3936, 3955
RepublicBank Greenville Avenue, 3923
RepublicBank Oak Cliff, 3923
RepublicBank San Antonio, 4072
Resnick, Lauren, 2109
Resnick, Louis, 2856
Resnick, Mildred, 2856
Resnik, Harold, 2305, 2846
Resor, Story Clark, 2234
Ress, Anne, 3789
Ress, Joseph W., 3789
Resseguier, Olga, 563
Rettberg, Ernest E., Jr., 3713
Retter, Betty, 2885
Retter, Marcus, 2885
Rettig, Alice J., 701
Reusch, Belinda Bunnen, 2787

Robinson, Horace B.B., 3063
Robinson, I. Christopher, 628
Robinson, J. William, 843, 844
Robinson, J.A., 3372
Robinson, Jack W., 3919
Robinson, James, 3835
Robinson, James D., III, 2235, 2938
Robinson, James H., 3683
Robinson, Jamie A., 3867
Robinson, John, 3342
Robinson, John R., 981, 2275, 2610
Robinson, Josephine R., 620
Robinson, Marshall, 498
Robinson, Marshall A., 2902
Robinson, Michael J., 619
Robinson, Nan S., 2877
Robinson, Peter S., 2301
Robinson, Ralph S., Jr., 3074
Robinson, Robert B., 3346
Robinson, Robert L., 3542
Robinson, S.W., 3671
Robinson, Samuel S., 3706
Robinson, Mrs. Samuel S., 3706
Robinson, Sylvia, 3705
Robinson, Sylvia B., 2275, 2610
Robinson, Violet E., 1550
Robinson, Walter, 3853
Robinson, Walter G., 1567
Robison, Doris B., 2871
Robison, Ellis, 2871
Robison, James A., 2871
Robison, Richard G., 2871
Roblee (Florence) Trust, 2012
Roblewsky, Jerry, 445
Robock, Stefan, 2088
Robson, Hannah D., 3471
Robson, John E., 1144
Roby, F.H., 4297
Roby, John, 3342
Roby, Katherine W., 3048
Roche, Dorothy, 3700
Roche, Edward, 2872
Rochlin, Abraham, 4374
Rochlin, Larry, 4374
Rochlin, Sonia, 4374
Rockefeller Brothers Fund, 2234, 2577
Rockefeller, David, 2875
Rockefeller, David, Jr., 2875
Rockefeller, Diana N., 2876
Rockefeller Foundation, 2344
Rockefeller, Frederic L., 3774
Rockefeller, Godfrey S., 2690
Rockefeller, John D., Jr., 2577, 2875
Rockefeller, John D., Sr., 2877
Rockefeller, John D., 3rd, 2578, 2875
Rockefeller, Mrs. John D., 3rd, 2578
Rockefeller, L.S., 1709
Rockefeller, Laurance, 2234, 2577,
    2875, 2876
Rockefeller, Laurance S., 2234, 2550,
    2577, 2645, 2875
Rockefeller, Mrs. Laurance S., 2774
Rockefeller, Martha Baird, 2875
Rockefeller, Mary, 2293
Rockefeller, Nelson A., 2875
Rockefeller, Richard G., 2876
Rockefeller, Rodman C., 2875
Rockefeller, Wendy, 2876
Rockefeller, William, 2116
Rockefeller, Winthrop, 58, 2875
Rockefeller, Winthrop Paul, 58
Rockwell Bros. & Co., 4066
Rockwell, D.M., 500
Rockwell, Elizabeth A., 4066
Rockwell, George Peter, 3707
Rockwell, Hays, 2389
Rockwell International Corporation, 3708
Rockwell Lumber Company, 4066
Rockwell, Russell A., 3707
Rockwell, Virginia, 442
Rockwell, Willard F., 3707
Rockwell, Willard F., Jr., 3707
Roddis, Augusta D., 4375
Roddis, Catherine P., 4375

Roddis, Hamilton, 4375
Roddis Plywood Corporation, 4375
Roddis, Richard, 4238
Roddis, William H., II, 4375
Roddy, Fred M., 3791
Rodecker, Arthur, 1682, 1683
Rodenbaugh, Edwin F., 3630
Rodeno, Raymond A., 399
Roderick, David M., 3750
Rodes, Harold P., 1752
Rodes, Joe W., 1336
Rodgers, David A., 3160
Rodgers, John A., 1386
Rodgers, Margaret A., 3160
Rodgers, Melinda A., 435
Rodgers, Melissa A., 435
Rodgers, Sue A., 435
Rodriguez, Eddie, Jr., 502
Roe, Benson B., 268
Roe, J. Woodward, 1761
Roe, Shirley W., 3814
Roe, Thomas A., 3814
Roedel, P.R., 3536
Roehner, Henry J., 1398
Roehr, Marcia A., 3508
Roesch, Frederick A., 2769
Roesler, Max A., 1239
Roetger, Russell R., 2972
Rogas, Marylou, 4019
Roge, Paul, 918
Rogers, Alexander H., II, 1610
Rogers, Ben J., 4067
Rogers, Catherine, 577
Rogers, Charles B., 325
Rogers, Charles E., 2827
Rogers, Christopher W., 1633, 1634
Rogers, David E., 2140
Rogers, Dorothy K.G., 2622
Rogers, Elizabeth Davis, 264
Rogers, Ellery W., 1522
Rogers, Emery H., 218
Rogers, F. Patrick, 2318
Rogers, Florence L., 3130
Rogers, Fred M., 3652
Rogers, Hamilton, 4069
Rogers, Harriet E., 1522
Rogers, Howard G., 1602
Rogers, Irving E., 1610
Rogers, Irving E., Jr., 1610
Rogers, James H., 3652
Rogers, John, 3564
Rogers, John H., 4181
Rogers, John W., 584
Rogers, Lorene L., 2981
Rogers, Marie M., 2070
Rogers, Mary Pickford, 325
Rogers, N. Jay, 4067
Rogers, N. Stewart, 4268
Rogers, Nancy M., 3652
Rogers, P.W., 3671
Rogers, Paul G., 2155
Rogers, Ralph B., 4068, 4101
Rogers, Randy T., 3245
Rogers, Richard H., 2070
Rogers, Richard R., 3998
Rogers, Robert D., 4068, 4101
Rogers, Rutherford D., 3047
Rogers, Samuel S., 1633, 1634
Rogers, Sol J., 4067
Rogers, Theodore C., 2783
Rogers, Thomas P., 1132
Rogers, Victor J., 4067
Rogers, William L., 1302
Rogers, William P., 643
Rogerson, Charles E., II, 1616
Rohan, Helen, 2869
Rohan, Vincent, 2869
Rohatyn, Elizabeth, 2878
Rohatyn, Felix, 2248
Rohatyn, Felix G., 2878
Rohleder, G.V., 3444
Rohlfing, Joan H., 890
Rohm, John M., 1245
Rohrbach, Beth, 976

Rohrbaugh, Spurgeon E., 3587
Roiko, Leo J., 1558
Roisman, Milton, 3328
Roland, B.R., 4093
Roland, Billy R., 4119
Roland, Jack J., 2510
Rolfing, William A., 1194
Rolfson, Carl, 1213
Roll, Wayne L., 3391
Rolland, Ian M., 1239
Rolscreen Company, 1280
Romaine, Michael F., 4129
Romans, Connie G., 3909
Romanucci, L., 560
Romasanta, Antonio R., 152
Rome, Benjamin T., 664
Romerovski Brothers, Inc., 2879
Romerovski, Martin, 2879
Romerovski, Rose, 2879
Ronan, J. Patrick, 4358
Rones, Louis, 2126
Rones, Steven, 2126
Roney, Jack M., 4071
Roney, T.A., 3142
Ronnow, H. Kris, 1028
Roodhouse, Linda C., 159
Rooke, D.L., 1688
Rooks, Charles S., 3498
Roon, Donald R., 512
Rooney, Arthur, 1443
Roosevelt, William D., 2405
Root, Carol Jean, 1094
Roothbert, Albert, 2881
Roothbert, Toni, 2881
Roper Corporation, 1135
Roper, Richard W., 2161
Roper, Wayne J., 4303
Rorick, Alan G., 3300
Rosato, Angelo, 2471, 2903
Rosborough, George S., Jr., 2020
Rose, Billy, 2882
Rose, Eugene, 2384
Rose, J. Evans, Jr., 3535
Rose, Leo, Jr., 748
Rose, Manfred, 3760
Rose, Marian, 2541
Rose, Milton C., 322, 2293, 3075
Rose, S.J., 910
Rose, Sally A., 3794
Roseburg Lumber Company, 3485
Rosen, Abraham A., 2883
Rosen, Irving, 2811
Rosen, Jonathan P., 2883
Rosen, Leonard, 3066
Rosen, Miriam, 2883
Rosenbaum, Francis, Jr., 2387
Rosenbaum, S.A., 1937
Rosenberg, Abraham, 2521, 2884
Rosenberg, Albert J., 2781
Rosenberg, Allen L., 29
Rosenberg, David, 2583
Rosenberg, Henry A., Jr., 1404, 1405,
    1450, 1458
Rosenberg, Max L., 334
Rosenberg, Norman, 2140
Rosenberg, Ruth B., 1404, 1405, 1458
Rosenberg, Ruth Blaustein, 1450
Rosenberg, Sonia, 2521, 2884
Rosenberg, Tina, 763
Rosenberg, William F., 2781
Rosenberry, Walter S., III, 1924, 1925
Rosenblatt, Bruce, 331
Rosenblatt, C., 2885
Rosenblatt, Joseph, 2295
Rosenblatt, Melvin M., 1659
Rosenfeld, Donald T., 415
Rosenfeld, George, 3226
Rosenfeld, Mark, 1726
Rosenhaus, Albert, 2172
Rosenhaus, Irving, 2172
Rosenhaus, Lawrence, 2172
Rosenhaus, Matthew B., 2172
Rosenhaus, Sarah, 2172
Rosenheim, Margaret K., 2325

Rosenstiel, Blanka A., 2886
Rosenstiel, Lewis S., 2886
Rosenstreich, Judy P., 2325
Rosenthal, Babette, 985
Rosenthal, Benjamin, 2887
Rosenthal, Benjamin J., 1136
Rosenthal, Edmund A., 2887
Rosenthal, Harry, 2221
Rosenthal, Hinda Gould, 569
Rosenthal, Ida, 2888
Rosenthal, Jacob, 3487
Rosenthal, Jane S., 2887
Rosenthal, Leighton A., 3347
Rosenthal, Marie-Louise, 985
Rosenthal, Richard L., 569
Rosenthal, Richard L., Jr., 569
Rosenthal, Samuel R., 985
Rosenthal, William, 2888
Rosenwald, Mary K., 2889
Rosenwald, Nina, 2889
Rosenwald, William, 2889
Rosenzweig, Elias, 2481
Rosett, Richard N., 1060
Rosin, Axel G., 2913
Rosin, Katharine S., 2913
Rosloff, Joseph H., 1243
Rosner, Bernat, 2691
Rosovsky, Henry, 1546, 3028
Ross, Arthur, 2890
Ross, Barbara B., 957
Ross, Charles, 3396
Ross, Clifford A., 2890
Ross, Daniel, 2709
Ross, Daniel G., 2658, 2923
Ross, David H., 3603, 3604
Ross, David P., 1947
Ross, David W., 177
Ross, Dickinson C., 240
Ross, Donald K., 2776, 2876
Ross, Donny, 3797
Ross, Dorothea Haus, 2891
Ross, Edith L., 3348
Ross, Elmer, 301
Ross, Elmer E., 301
Ross, Emrys J., 80, 100
Ross, Esther C., 59
Ross, George M., 3569
Ross, Hugh, 2968
Ross, J.G., 212
Ross, James, 3348
Ross, Jane, 59
Ross, John W., 2382
Ross, Loren D., 2902
Ross, Norman A., 1002
Ross, Pat, 3189
Ross, Patrick C., 3145
Ross, Paul, 1948
Ross, Richard M., 917
Ross, Robert T., 2318
Ross, T.L., 3086
Ross, Ted L., 1174
Ross, Mrs. Walter L., II, 2265
Ross, William W., 2014
Rossant, M.J., 2995
Rossbach, Richard M., 2643
Rosselli, Constance, 3416
Rosser, Pearl, 672
Rosser, Thomas J., 3957
Rossi, Anthony T., 692, 696
Rossman, George A., 1821
Rostad, Lyle, 626
Rosuck, Donald, 939
Roswell, Elizabeth B., 1404
Rotan Mosle, Inc., 4036
Roth, Elsie, 2173
Roth, Gerald, 499
Roth, Michael, 335
Roth, Patricia, 335
Roth, Robert, 2173
Roth, Stanley, Jr., 2173
Roth, Stanley, Sr., 2173
Roth, Susan, 335
Roth, William G., 4326, 4383

Schreiber, Mary, 2885
Schreiber, Rita B., 347
Schreiber, Taft B., 347
Schreiber, Toby I., 347
Schreier, Andrew M., 2846
Schreier, William, 2846
Schreyer, William A., 2728
Schroder (J. Henry) Bank and Trust Co., 2774
Schroeder, Charles E., 988, 1088
Schroeder, Diane, 510
Schroeder, Jane S., 4402
Schroeder, John M., 4333, 4336
Schroeder, John P., 2825
Schroeder, Lorraine D., 1250
Schroeder (Walter) Trust, 4377
Schroeder, William A., 493
Schroedter, Edward J., 997
Schroeter, Donald G., 928
Schroll, Maud Hill, 1894
Schuchardt, D.N., 1005
Schuchinski, Luis, 2113
Schucht, C.J., 4393
Schuette, William D., 1712
Schuler, J.A., 3536
Schuler, Jack W., 918
Schulman, Alvin, 2358
Schulse, Carl, 3868
Schulte, Anthony M., 2913
Schultheis, Dayton, 3268
Schultz, George L., 2179, 2180
Schultz, Gerald, 3051
Schultz, Mabel L., 2179
Schultz, Margaret F., 2179, 2180
Schultz, Roger, 2172
Schulz, Ralph G., 4387
Schumacher, Jon R., 4353
Schumann, Florence F., 2181
Schumann, John J., Jr., 2181
Schumann, Robert F., 2181
Schumann, W. Ford, 2181
Schuppe, Donald F., 3854
Schurz Communications, 1252
Schutrum, Robert J., Sr., 2314
Schutte, Thomas F., 3786
Schuyler, Robert L., 4274
Schwab, Martin J., 2999
Schwab, Nelson, Jr., 3183
Schwabacher, Christopher C., 2387
Schwaibold, Edgar, 2597
Schwake, Henry, 2071
Schwanfelder, Nancy Healy, 4137
Schwartz, Alan E., 1769, 1801
Schwartz, Mrs. Alan E., 1722
Schwartz (Arnold) Charitable Trust, 2920
Schwartz, Arnold A., 2182
Schwartz, Arthur Jay, 815
Schwartz, Bernard L., 630
Schwartz, Bernard W., 2576
Schwartz, Carol List, 551
Schwartz, David, 2183
Schwartz, Douglas W., 2207
Schwartz, Eric A., 630
Schwartz, Eugene J., 1624
Schwartz, Henry L., 2305, 2846
Schwartz, Horace J., 943
Schwartz, Irene, 2183
Schwartz, Laurence, 4370
Schwartz, Leonard, 2386
Schwartz, Marianne S., 1769
Schwartz, Marie D., 2920
Schwartz, Michael L., 630
Schwartz, Rebecca, 2305
Schwartz, Renee G., 2779
Schwartz, Richard J., 2183
Schwartz, Robert C., 815
Schwartz, Rosalyn R., 630
Schwartz, Sonia, 815
Schwartz, Stephen L., 2305, 2846
Schwartz, Steven G., 2873
Schwartz, Suzanne, 2252
Schwartz, W.B., 815
Schwartz, W.B., III, 815
Schwartz, W.B., Jr., 815

Schwartzhoff, James P., 3271
Schwarz, Bernard M., 517
Schwarz, H. Marshall, 2411
Schwarz, Kurt, 2921
Schwarz, Maurice L., 517
Schwarz, Theresa R., 517
Schwecherl, Robert, 3029
Schweckendieck, Edith M., 2922
Schwegel, A.J., 700
Schweid, Marjorie S., 3226
Schweitzer, Louis, 2923
Schweitzer, Lucille, 2923
Schweitzer, M. Peter, 2923
Schweitzer, Robert, 1836
Schwenger, Lloyd S., 3390
Schweppe, Harry N., Jr., 1100
Schwerdlin, Alfred I., 1147
Schwilck, Gene L., 1955
Schwing, Rose J., 2246
Schwob Company of Florida, 871
Schwob, Henry, 871
Schwob, Joyce, 871
Schwob Manufacturing Company, 871
Schwob Realty Company, 871
SCM Corporation, 2924
SCOA Industries, 3357
Scobie, Rosemary Mason, 4355
Scobie, William M., 4355
Scocimara, Eriberto, 4188
Scoon, D.S., 1050
Scorsone, Vincent R., 3511
Scott and Fetzer Company, 3358
Scott, Andrew, 1873
Scott, David C., 4294
Scott, Eileen, 4352
Scott, Elizabeth Strother, 4185
Scott, Fitzhugh, 4352
Scott, Frank L., 81
Scott, Homer, 4402
Scott, Jane Hyde, 3844
Scott, John A., 2463, 2464
Scott, John G., 2711, 4198
Scott, Mary D., 4294
Scott, Mayme P., 1382
Scott, Nadya Kozmetsky, 4061
Scott, Olin, 4150
Scott Paper Company, 3715
Scott, Rachel McM. Hunt, 3611, 3613
Scott, Robert M., 3616
Scott, Roderic M., 565
Scott, Ross G., 1705
Scott, Rupert R., 1382
Scott, S. Buford, 4196
Scott, T.H., 1382
Scott, T.H., Jr., 1382
Scott, Virginia Steele, 348
Scott, Walter C., 814
Scott, Wesley, 4311
Scott, Will, 1702
Scott, William C., 2780
Scott, William E., 4075
Scovell, John Field, 3923
Scovil, S.K., 3187
Scovill Manufacturing Company, 574
Scoville, Herbert, Jr., 679
Scranton, William W., 2777
Screven, M.L., Jr., 16
Scribner, Howard A., Jr., 2481
Scrinopskie, Jere, 3947
Scripps (The E.W.) Co., 3359
Scripps, Ellen Browning, 349
Scripps, John P., 349
Scripps, Paul K., 349
Scripps, Robert P., 3359
Scripps, Robert Paine, 349
Scrivener, Robert C., 3750
Scruggs, Charles A., 3854
Scudder, John Haas, 346
Scudder, Mark F., 346
Scudder, Valerie Schmidt, 346
Scully, Arthur M., Jr., 3535, 3663, 3691
Scully, Leonard T., 2697, 3798
Scully, Richard E., 2149
Scurlock, E.C., 4076, 4105

Scurlock Oil Company, 4076
Scurlock, W.C., 4076
Scurry, D.L., 3816
Seabury, Charlene B., 1143
Seabury, Charles Ward, 1143
Seabury, John Ward, 1143
Seabury, Louise Lovett, 1143
Seacrest, Kent, 2063
Seagram (Joseph E.) and Sons, 2304
Sealy Mattress Company of Illinois, 1055
Sealy of Eastern New York, 3064
Sealy of Minnesota, 3064
Seaman, Avery, Jr., 3780
Seaman, Elizabeth D., 4201
Searle (G.D.) & Co., 1144
Sears, Anna L., 3360
Sears, C. Alex, 865
Sears, Clara Endicott, 1619
Sears, John R., Jr., 3873
Sears, Lester M., 3360
Sears, Richard K., 168, 169
Sears, Roebuck and Co., 1145
Sears, Ruth P., 3360
Seattle First National Bank, 120, 388, 4239, 4241, 4245, 4256, 4259, 4261, 4272
Seattle Trust and Savings Bank, 4227, 4259
Seaver, Blanche Ebert, 350
Seaver, Christopher, 350
Seaver, Frank R., 350
Seaver, Richard C., 350, 397
Seaver, Victoria, 350
Seay, Effie L., 4199
Seay, Frank, 3462
Seay, George J., 4199
Seay, William H., 3924
Sebastian, Audrey M., 1766
Sebastian, James R., 1766
Sebastian, John O., 1766
Sebastian, Raymond F., 122
Sebion, Diane L., 4354
Second National Bank, 3245
Second National Bank of Saginaw, 1675, 1693, 1727, 1750
Second National Bank of Warren, 3401
Secor, Rita J., 1105
Secrest, James Richard B., 2421
Security Bank & Trust Company, 3131
Security Bank of Nevada, 2080
Security Pacific, 115
Security Pacific Bank, 228
Security Pacific Corporation, 351
Security Pacific Investment Managers, 340
Security Pacific National Bank, 81, 114, 134, 271, 314, 333, 345, 385, 397
Security Trust Company, 2495
Seder, Harold, 1606
Sedgwick, Ellery, Jr., 3240
Sedgwick, Walter C., 233
See, Charles B., 352
See, Harry A., 352
Seed, Harris W., 403
Seegars, Mattie, 3824
Seeley, Donald L., 1144
Seeley, Halsted H., 1146
Seeley, Jane P., 1146
Seeley, John G., 2478
Seeley, Laurel H., 1146
Seeley, Miles G., 1146
Seeley, Miles P., 1146
Seelig, G.L., 2098
Seesel, H. James, Jr., 1928
Seewald, Katherine, 3974
Seftenberg, Stephen L., 920
Sefton, Donna K., 353
Sefton, J.W., Jr., 353
Sefton, Thomas W., 353
Segal, Marilyn M., 2693
Segal, Martin E., 2460, 2896
Segal, Richard D., 2693
Segal, S.A., 2160
Segall, Maurice, 1661

Segee, E.R., 3307
Segesta, S.T., 1685
Segnar, S.F., 2058
Seibel, Abe, 4077
Seidel, Samuel, 2742
Seidler, Lee J., 2930
Seidler, Lynn L., 2930
Seidman, Esther L., 1767
Seidman, Frank E., 1767
Seidman, L. William, 1767
Seidman, Oliver G., 2999
Seidman, Philip K., 1767
Seidner, Bette Lou, 1150
Seifert, Eugene P., 4342
Seifert, Lynn M., 1905
Seigle, John T., 104, 215
Seitel, Fraser P., 2337
Seitz, Collins, 615
Seitz, Collins J., 616
Seitz, Frederick, 742, 2679
Sejima, Ryuzo, 3001
Sekera, Helen Mary, 3729
Selber, Irving S., 1961
Selby, Charles W., 3442
Selby, John D., 1726
Selby, John R., 3731
Selby, Marie M., 766
Selby, William G., 766
Selden, Edward P., 3643
Seleiss, Henry B., 3677
Selesko, Barrie W., 3033
Self, James C., 3095, 3817
Self, James C., Jr., 3817
Self, W.M., 3817
Seligson, Aaron, 2599
Selinger, Maurice A., Jr., 2232
Sellars, Richard B., 2140
Sellers, Edna E., 163
Sellers, Mary, 52
Sellers, Merl F., 1300
Sellmeyer, Regina, 62
Sellner, James J., Jr., 1870
Sells, Boake A., 1834
Sells, Carol B., 2081
Sells, John E., 2081
Sells, Richard E., 1446
Selzer, Louis J., 4394
Selznick, Daniel Mayer, 277
Selznick, Irene Mayer, 277
Semans, Harold L., 252
Semans, James H., 3078
Semans, Mary D.B.T., 3078, 3095
Semelsberger, K.J., 3358
Semler, Bernard, 921
Semler, Bernard H., 917
Semmes, D.R., Jr., 4078
Semmes, Douglas R., 4078
Semmes, Julia Y., 4078
Semmes, Thomas R., 4078
Semple, Cecil S., 502
Semple, Harton S., 3535
Semple, Louise Taft, 3361
Senger, Alan F., 3392
Senn, Milton J.E., 2432
Sensenbrenner, John S., Jr., 4338
Senter, Roger C., 1625
Sentman, David K., 1209
Sentry Corporation, 4378
Senturia, Brenda Baird, 2258
Sergievsky, Kira, 2553
Serra-Badue, Daniel, 2345
Sessions, Lee, 802
Sessions, Lee M., Jr., 816
Sessums, T. Terrell, 782
Setter, Marjorie I., 1315
Setterstrom, William N., 1108
Setzer, G. Cal, 354
Setzer, Gene W., 2234, 2577
Setzer, Hardie C., 354
Seuffert, Charles F., 2419
Seven-Up Bottling Company, 1053
Severin, Ella A., 2697, 3798
Sewall, Charles, 3005
Seward, George C., 2493

Sewell, Ben G., 3932
Sewell, Carolyn Nail, 3932
Sewell, Roy C., 3932
Sewell, Warren P., 872
Sexauer, James M., 2925
Sexauer, John A., 2925
Sexauer, Mae M., 2925
Sexton, Richard, 2924
Seybert, Adam, 3717
Seybert, Maria Sarah, 3717
Seydel, John R., 887
Seydel, Paul V., 887
Seyferth, Donald, 1754
Seymour, B.A., Jr., 1768
Seymour, Mrs. B.A., Sr., 1768
Seymour, H. Randolph, 2451, 2731
Seymour, J.M., 593
Shack, Ruth, 706
Shackelford, Thekla R., 3189
Shade, T.L., 1101
Shadle, Mrs. E.A., 4230
Shaefler, Leon, 2559
Shafer, F.L., 3362
Shafer, Richard A., 3362
Shaffer, Arthur H., 2542
Shaffer, C. David, 3145
Shaffer, G. Rives, 2188
Shaffer, Thomas L., 4319
Shafran, Nathan, 3225
Shafto, G.R., 3800
Shainberg, Raymond, 3828
Shakely, Jack, 114
Shakespeare, Frank J., 2584
Shalala, Donna E., 2460, 3271
Shalom, Henry, 2793
Shalom, Joseph, 2793
Shalom, Stephen, 2793
Shalowitz, Mervin, 1008
Shamburger, W.M., 3976
Shamrock Industries, 1844
Shanahan, James A., Jr., 2083
Shands, Bliss, 1964
Shands, Mary Norton, 1346
Shane, Sidney, 1203
Shaner, Wayne, 1435
Shank, Ralph B., 4027
Shankin, Simon, 305
Shanks, D.L., 4373
Shankster, M. Garvin, 4336
Shanley, Bernard M., 2197
Shanley, Kevin, 2197
Shannahan, William P., 66, 189
Shannon, Foster, 685
Shannon, James P., 1823, 1847
Shannon, Robert L., 1510
Shapero, J.E., 1769
Shapero, Nate S., 1769
Shapero, Ray A., 1769
Shapero, Ruth B., 1769
Shapira, Albert C., 3739
Shapira, Amy, 2430
Shapira, Frieda G., 3693
Shapiro, Abraham, 1620
Shapiro, Albert, 1452, 1453
Shapiro, Arthur H., 1148
Shapiro, Carl, 767
Shapiro, Charles, 1147
Shapiro, Earl, 1148
Shapiro, George, 1620
Shapiro, George M., 2391
Shapiro, Harold T., 2938
Shapiro, Henry, 1148
Shapiro, Irving S., 2444
Shapiro, Jacob M., 1136
Shapiro, Joseph, 1452
Shapiro, Marc J., 4099
Shapiro, Mary, 1147
Shapiro, Milton, 1081
Shapiro, Morris R., 1147
Shapiro, Norman, 301
Shapiro, Robert, 1144, 2182
Shapiro, Ruth, 767
Shapleigh, Warren McK., 1944
Sharan, S., 2708

Sharbaugh, H.R., 3536
Share, Charles Morton, 3463
Sharf, S., 1679
Sharon Steel Corporation, 768
Sharp, Billy B., 1170
Sharp, Charles S., 4080
Sharp, Eugene E., 3482
Sharp, Evelyn, 2926
Sharp, H. Rodney, III, 618
Sharp, Hugh R., Jr., 604
Sharp, Peter, 2926
Sharp, Ruth Collins, 3909, 3911, 4080
Sharp, Vernon, 3853
Sharpe, Vera E., 2838
Sharpnack, Richard L., 1259
Sharrow, George, 4149
Shastid, Jon B., 180
Shattuck, Mrs. Clinton H., 1481
Shattuck, Sarah D., 1291
Shattuck, W.A., 1291
Shaw, Francis G., 1621
Shaw, Frank, 1298
Shaw, Gardiner Howland, 1622
Shaw, George, 343
Shaw, George T., 1506
Shaw, H.A., 3255
Shaw, Harold, 1178
Shaw, Jerome, 2389
Shaw, John I., 1149
Shaw, Jonathan A., 689
Shaw, Joseph A., 1915
Shaw, L., 266
Shaw, Marguerite G., 1621
Shaw, Mary Elizabeth Dee, 4144
Shaw, Maryanna G., 186
Shaw, Morgan L., 1381
Shaw, Robert Gould, 1621
Shaw, Roger D., 1149
Shaw, S. Parkman, III, 1621
Shaw, Will, 289
Shawmut Bank, 1482
Shawmut Bank of Boston, 1512, 1623, 1654, 1655
Shawmut Worcester County Bank, 1624, 1659
Shawmut Worcester County Trust, 1607
Shay, Esther C., 3138
Shayne, Herbert M., 3862
Shea, Edmund H., Jr., 358
Shea, Felice K., 2615
Shea, Isabelle C., 552
Shea (J.F.) Company, 358
Shea, James, 3634
Shea, John B., 1501
Shea, John F., 357, 358
Shea, Martin F., 2232, 2744, 3167
Shea, Mary B., 2447
Shea, Peter O., 358
Sheadle, Jasper H., 3363
Sheafer, Emma A., 2928
Sheahan, Janet, 3854
Sheedy, Jack, 3922
Sheehy, W.J., 1862
Sheetz, D.P., 1688
Sheetz, R.L., 4187
Sheetz, Richard S., 3187
Sheffer, Ralph, 2994
Shehee, Virginia K., 1383
Sheinbaum, Moshe, 2599
Sheinbein, Stanley J., 1993, 1994
Sheinberg, Sidney J., 279
Shelby, Jerome, 2865
Shelden, Allan, III, 1770
Shelden, Elizabeth Warren, 1770
Shelden, Frances W., 1770
Shelden, W. Warren, 1770
Shelden, William W., Jr., 1770
Sheldon, Edith S., 2169
Sheldon, Eleanor B., 2877
Sheldon, W. Warren, 1744
Shell Oil Company, 4081
Shell Oil Foundation, 3993
Shelley, Brenda K., 1408
Shelley, Roger, 2857

Shellington, Kathleen, 3520
Shelstad, Terrance G., 1908
Shelter Insurance Companies, 1997
Shelton, Nelva Lou, 4004
Shelton, Talbot, 3636
Shemanski, Alfred, 4261
Shemanski, Tillie, 4261
Shenango Furnace Company, 3728
Shenk, Willis W., 3737, 3738
Shepard, Frank S., 423
Shepard, Gordon, 1822
Shepard, Henry B., Jr., 1647
Shepard, Roger B., Jr., 1820
Shephard, Richard G., 139
Shepherd, E.M., 3836
Shepherd, Mark, Jr., 3750, 4102
Sheppard, Charlotte N., 3718
Sheppard, Lawrence B., 3718
Sheppard, Thomas B., 274
Shepperd, A.J., 3085
Sheraton Corporation, 1625
Sherbrooke, Ross E., 1528
Sherbunt, Judith M., 3025
Sherbunt, Norbert J., 3025
Sherburne, Philip S., 1832
Sherer, G.D., 3808
Sheridan, Beatrice Rice, 1134
Sheridan, Elizabeth M., 1454
Sheridan, Jack R., 379
Sheridan, Jack R., II, 379
Sheridan, Thomas B., 1454
Sherin, Willis B., 3470
Sherman, Beatrice B., 1626
Sherman, David C., 1814
Sherman, George, 1626
Sherman, J.L., 3364
Sherman, Jonathan G., 2613
Sherman, Kenneth, 351
Sherman, L.G., Jr., 874
Sherman, Michael B., 107
Sherman, Nate H., 1150
Sherman, Norton L., 1626
Sherman, Robert A., 489
Sherman, Roger H., 977
Sherman, Sandra B., 1814
Sherman, William P., 3364
Sherratt, J.D., 1568
Sherrill, Henry Knox, 610
Sherrill, Joseph N., Jr., 4122
Sherrill, W.A., 3131
Sherry, John, 3430
Sherry, Toby F., 4334
Sherwin, Brian, 3371
Sherwin, Frances Wick, 3365
Sherwin, Francis M., 3371
Sherwin, John, 3365
Sherwin, John, Jr., 3365
Sherwin, Margaret H., 3371
Sherwin-Williams Company, 3366
Sherwood, Dolly, 4285
Sherwood, John G., 213
Sherwood, Mrs. John R., 1461
Shibuya, Hironobu, 3001
Shideler, Shirley A., 1204
Shields, A.B., 3487
Shields, Elizabeth B., 2271
Shields, L. Donald, 44
Shields, Richard, 2271
Shiffman, Abraham, 1771
Shiflett, Laura, 4104
Shifrin, Edwin, 1979
Shih, Daphne B., 2271
Shilensky, Morris, 2882
Shineman, Edward W., Jr., 2243
Shinn, George L., 44, 2777
Shinners, William L., 3658
Shinnick, William M., 3367
Ship 'n Shore, 3710
Shipley, Charles, 1627
Shipley, Charles B., 1627
Shipley, Lucia, 1627
Shipley, Lucia H., 1627
Shipley, Richard C., 1627
Shir, Phillip, 1620

Shircliff, Robert T., 731
Shirk, Charles A., 3159
Shirk, James A., 1151
Shirk, Russell O., 1151
Shirley, Aaron, 2432
Shirley, Betsy B., 2138
Shirley, Carl, 2138
Shirley, Mrs. Carl, 2138
Shirley, M.J., 915
Shmidheiser, John H., 3619
Shoch, David, 1034
Shockley, Julia G., 18
Shoemaker, E.J., 1736
Shoemaker, George Franklin, 1115
Shoemaker, Mary Williams, 3719
Shoemaker, Ome C., 1115
Shoemaker, Thomas H., 3719
Shoemaker (Thomas H. and Mary Williams) Trust, 3719
Shoemaker, William, 1115
Shoenberg, Robert H., 2014
Shoenberg, Sydney M., 2014
Shoenberg, Sydney M., Jr., 2014
Shomaker, Richard W., 1945
Shook, Barbara I., 19
Shook, Robert P., 19
Shoong, Corinne, 359
Shoong, Joe, 359
Shoong, Milton W., 359
Shoong, Rose, 359
Shope, R. Wesley, 3635
Shore Haven Apartments, 2992
Shore, Mrs. William, 2950
Short, Harry S., 607
Short, Jack E., 3453
Shourd, R., 2919
Shouse, Catherine F., 1529
Shouse, Lisa Bell, 3854
Shower, Robert W., 3471
Shrier, Ben F., 2050
Shriver, Eunice Kennedy, 666
Shropshire, Ogden, 19
Shrum, G. Dixon, Jr., 3691
Shub, Anatole, 2088
Shubert, J.J., 2930
Shubert, Kerttu H., 2930
Shubert, Lee, 2930
Shubin, Harry A., 656
Shuck, V. DeWitt, 310
Shuey, John, 1378, 4383
Shuford, Harry A., 3981
Shuler, E.H., 188
Shulga, John A., 2767
Shull, Willard C., III, 1834
Shulman, Alan, 312
Shulman, Lloyd J., 3034
Shulman, Max L., 3034
Shulman, Sylvia W., 3034
Shults, Robert, 58
Shur, Walter, 2776
Shurtleff, W.R., 953
Shust, Robert B., 3682
Shuster, George W., 3774
Shute, Benjamin R., Jr., 2875
Shutz, Byron T., 1983
Shwartz, Cary, 2236
Shwartzstein, Avigdor, 2716
Shy, Sally J., 3840
Si, Francis A., 1999
Sibert, Robert, 190
Sibley, D.J., Jr., 4058
Sibley (Effie Potts) Irrevocable Trust, 4058
Sibley, James M., 832, 861, 876, 884
Siciliano, Rocco C., 187, 399
Sieber, Edward, 2837
Sieber, Fred B., 747
Siebert, A.F., 4379
Siebert, E.W., 965
Siebert, Reginald L., 4379
Siegel, A., 2840
Siegel, Adele, 2330
Siegel, Arthur, 2988
Siegel, Bernard, 615

Smith, Geraldine O., 1897
Smith, Gilbert W., 713
Smith, Glee S., 1314
Smith, Gordon, 3085
Smith, Mrs. Gordon H., 968
Smith, Graham Wood, 2396
Smith, Greta, 3677
Smith, H. Harrison, 3724
Smith, Harold Byron, 1045
Smith, Harold Byron, Jr., 1045
Smith, Harold N., 721
Smith, Harold W., 780
Smith, Harriet T., 2015
Smith, Helen Gilman, 2307
Smith, Herbert J., 1350
Smith, Horace E., 3718
Smith, Howard W., Jr., 4156
Smith, Hulett C., 3524
Smith, J. Burleson, 4056
Smith, J. Henry, 2193
Smith, J. Kellum, Jr., 2722
Smith, Jack J., Jr., 3369
Smith, James C., 588
Smith, James H., 2086
Smith, James S., 2452
Smith, Jane Prouty, 1603
Smith, Jean K., 2812
Smith, Jean Kennedy, 644, 666
Smith, Jeremy T., 2784
Smith, Joe W., 3796
Smith, John M., 1340
Smith, Kathleen D., 627, 628
Smith, Kelvin, 3370
Smith, Kenneth B., 968
Smith, Kent H., 3213
Smith, L.B., 4380
Smith, Langhorne B., 3543
Smith, Lawrence L., 1338
Smith, Leonard W., 1773
Smith, Leslie Stockard, 2044
Smith, Lewis W., 749
Smith, Lloyd B., 3239
Smith, Mrs. Lloyd H., 3928
Smith, M.W., Jr., 20
Smith, Malcolm B., 2514, 2775
Smith, Margaret Chase, 1238
Smith, Marion, 1628
Smith, Mary L., 3725
Smith, May, 371, 372
Smith, Melvin E., 3479
Smith, Menlo F., 2026
Smith, Miles J., Sr., 3131
Smith, Molly R., 3107
Smith, Myron, 174
Smith, Nancy E., 4200
Smith, Newland V., Jr., 1656
Smith, Norvel L., 334
Smith, Numa L., Jr., 673
Smith Oil Corporation, 1156
Smith, Ora K., 614
Smith, Paul J., 2985
Smith, Peter G., 21
Smith, Philip L., 678
Smith, Pomeroy, 3882
Smith, R.B., 1709, 1710
Smith, R.E., 4082
Smith, R.J., 3900
Smith, R.O., 3594
Smith, Ralph L., 2015
Smith, Ralph L., Jr., 2015
Smith, Raymond T., 1059
Smith, Richard A., 1628, 1991, 2284
Smith, Richard Ferree, 3766
Smith, Richard G., III, 3107
Smith, Robert, 154
Smith, Robert A., 1628
Smith, Robert E., 584
Smith, Robert F., 2235
Smith, Robert H., 351
Smith, Roger D., 2409
Smith, Rosemarie, 941
Smith, Royden J., 2473
Smith, S. Garry, 7
Smith, Sam C., 4252

Smith, Sam M., 3808
Smith, Samuel H., Jr., 3102
Smith, Sherwood H., Jr., 3124
Smith, Sidney O., Jr., 855
Smith, Mrs. Stanley, 372
Smith, Stephen B., 1045
Smith, Stephen E., 2812
Smith, Susan M., 1628
Smith, Tad R., 4026
Smith, Thelma G., 3213
Smith, Thomas R., 599
Smith, Vivian L., 4082
Smith, W. Hinckle, 3724
Smith, W.F., 4363
Smith, W.R., 3976
Smith, Walker, Jr., 414
Smith, Ward, 3405
Smith, Weldon H., 4089
Smith, Wilbur S., 519
Smith, William C., 206, 2063
Smith, William E., 2170
Smith, William French, 114
Smith, William L., 1819
Smith, William T., 865, 2284
Smith, William Wikoff, 3725
Smith, Willis, 3134
Smith, Zachary T., 3075, 3124
Smithburg, William D., 1126
Smithers, Adele C., 2941
Smithers, Charles F., 2941
Smithers, Christopher D., 2941
Smithers, Mabel B., 2941
Smithers, R. Brinkley, 2941
SmithKline Beckman Corporation, 3726
Smoak, J.F., 3812
Smock, Laura L., 1253
Smoliar, Burton, 1432
Smolik, Ellis F., 3283
Smoot, J. Tom, Jr., 771
Smyth, Herbert C., 2567
Smyth, Marion C., 2095
Smyth, Patricia K., 1428
Smyth, Robert P., 4323
Smyth, Walter G., 3156
Smythe, Richard L., 3309
Snavely, Guy E., Jr., 865
Snayberger, Harry E., 3727
Snell, D., 1185
Snell, Thaddeus S., 1182
Snider, Eliot, 1010
Snider, Ruth F., 1010
Snite, Fred B., 1157
Snodgrass, John F., 3449
Snow, Ann, 2083
Snow, John Ben, 2942, 2943
Snow Manufacturing Company, 1784
Snow, Ralph W., 2942
Snow, Vernon F., 2942, 2943
Snowden, Muriel S., 1482
Snowden, Richard, 685
Snowdon, Richard W., 637
Snyder, Abram M., 3695
Snyder, D.C., 542
Snyder, David T., 1696
Snyder, Donn A., 2201
Snyder, Franklin C., 2537, 2538
Snyder, Frost, 4263
Snyder, G. Whitney, 3728
Snyder, Leonard N., 3588
Snyder, Margaret, 4263
Snyder, Mary Ann, 969
Snyder, Patricia H., 1219
Snyder, Ruth B., 1295
Snyder, Sheda T., 2944
Snyder, W.P., III, 3728
Snyder, W.P., Jr., 3728
Snyder, W.R., 1409
Snyder, William B., 657
Snyder, William P., III, 3535
Sobczak, Gerald, 4392
Sobel, Ronald B., 2733
Sobel, Seymour, 2333
Soble, Morris, 921
Social Research Foundation, 3057

Society Bank of Eastern Ohio, 3158, 3253
Society National Bank, 3145, 3179
Society National Bank of Cleveland, 3186
Sode, Lizabeth, 939
Soderberg, Elsa A., 2231
Soderberg, Peter, 2231
Soderberg, Robert C., 2231
Soderstrom, Cynthia Paulucci, 1902
Soehren, Marvin F., 4264
Sohn, Frances F., 3484
Sohn, John P., 1196
Soiland, Albert, 374
Sola, Dorothy, 118
Solberg, Carl, 2881
Soldwedel, Donald N., 29
Solem, Bill, 2048
Solem, Ellen, 2048
Solem, William M., 2048
Solender, Sanford, 2644, 2764
Soley, Judith, 3026
Soley, Robert, 3026
Solinger, Hope G., 528
Sollars, Frank B., 3313
Sollenne, Peter, 1446
Sollins, Karen R., 2913
Solnit, Albert, 2779
Solo Cup Company, 1158
Solomon, Isadore, 1065
Solomon, Milton, 2594
Solomon, Milton D., 2319
Solomon, Peter J., 2675
Solon Foundation, 3777
Solovy, Jerold S., 1112
Solovy, Mrs. Jerold S., 1070
Solso, Virgil E., 3500
Somerville, Bill, 318
Sommer, Linda, 426
Sommers, Davidson, 685
Sonat Inc., 21
Sondeen, Frank, 1711
Sonderegger, John F., 1046
Sonderegger, John L., 4372
Sonderegger, Leona A., 4372
Sondheim, Walter, Jr., 1401
Sonne, Christian R., 1441
Sonneborn, Clara L., 2283
Sonneborn, Henry, III, 2283
Sonneborn, Richard F., 2226
Sonneborn, Rudolf G., 2283
Sonnenberg, Benjamin, 2497
Sonntag, Alfred, 1159
Sonntag, Christine, 1159
Sono, Ayako, 3001
Sony Corporation of America, 2945
Soos, George C., 2666
Sopranos, O.J., 929
Sordoni, Andrew J., III, 3729
Sordoni, Andrew J., Jr., 3729
Sordoni, Andrew J., Sr., 3729
Sordoni, Ruth A., 3729
Soref, Helene K., 769
Soref, Samuel M., 769
Sorensen, Arlo G., 426
Sorensen, Harvey L., 375
Sorensen, J. William, 436
Sorensen, Maud C., 375
Sorensen, Nancy M., 1028
Sorenson, Ingvold B., 1874
Soriero, Frances, 2911
Sorkin, Sylvia, 1844
Soros, George, 2946
Fisher (Stanley D.) Trust, 523
Sosland, Estelle, 2003
Sosland, H.J., 1329
Sosland, Morton I., 1329, 1941, 1968
Sosland, Neil, 1329
Soublet, R.C., 127
Souers, Sylvia N., 2016
Soule, Edmond E., 3428
Souran Bank, 4187
Sours, James, 3478
Soutar, Douglas H., 2246

South Bend Tribune, 1252
South Carolina National Bank, 3799, 3803, 3819, 3823, 3825
South Jersey Publishing Company, 3508
South Sea Imports, 286
South Trust Bank, 3
Southeast Bank, 695, 706, 763
Southeast Banking Corporation, 770
Southeast Banks Trust Co., 756, 766
Southeast First National Bank of Miami, 707
Southern California Protective Society, 244
Southern Ohio Bank, 3183
Southland Corporate Services, 4084
Southland Financial Corporation, 4084
Southland Investment Properties, 4084
Southland Life Insurance Company, 4084
SouthTrust Bank of Alabama, 10
Southwestern Electric Power Company, 3903
Southwestern Operating Company, 56
Southwestern Publishing Company, 56
Souvran Bank, 4161, 4162
Sovern, Michael I., 2930
Sovran Bank, 4177, 4186, 4199
Sovran Financial Corporation, 4201
Sowell, Anne W., 4092
Sowell, James R., 4092
Sowell, Sam C., 55
Sowers, Wesley H., 1298
Spaaberry, Richard, 3933
Spaeth, Carl F., Jr., 1726
Spaeth, Karl H., 3699
Spahr, Charles E., 3185
Spaidal, Donald R., 2972
Spalding, Charles C., 895
Spalding, Hughes, Jr., 832, 885
Spalding, Philip F., 268
Spanbock, Marion, 2583
Spanbock, Maurice S., 2573
Spang & Company, 3730
Spangler, P.A., 2042
Spanier, David B., 2719
Spanier, Helen G., 2719
Spanier, Maury L., 2719
Sparber, Byron L., 706
Sparber, Norman, 2481
Sparks, Herschel E., Jr., 2493
Sparks, Robert A., Jr., 1351
Sparks, Robert D., 1732
Sparks, W. Alvon, Jr., 657
Sparrow, Marvin, 1626
Spartus Corporation, 1013
Spaulding, Leslie E., 3540
Spaulding, Richard C., 1201
Spear, R.D., 824
Spears, Frank H., 3485
Spears, Paul E., 3718
Speas Company, 2017, 2018
Speas, Effie E., 2017, 2018
Speas, Victor E., 2017, 2018
Speed, Leland R., 1936
Speed, Ronald K., 1861
Speer, Katie, 60
Speight, Randolph L., 2831
Speir, Kenneth G., 1311
Speiser, Harry, 4268
Spence, A. Michael, 1546
Spence, Dwayne R., 3397
Spence, Janet, 2328
Spence, Lewis H., 1561, 1562
Spencer, B.P., 1355
Spencer, Catherine M., 1160
Spencer, Eben S., 1839
Spencer, Edson W., 2444
Spencer, Harry I., Jr., 1624
Spencer, J.M., 3391
Spencer, Jack E., 3550
Spencer, James B., 847
Spencer, John R., 360
Spencer, Lyle M., 1160
Spencer, Lyle M., Jr., 1160
Spencer, William I., 2769

Spencer, William M., III, 3, 14
Sperry Corporation, 2947
Spevak, Charles J., 88
Speyer, A.C., Jr., 4086
Spicher, Howard R., 3598
Spiecker, John S., 423
Spiegal, Pat, 615
Spiegel, Bernice G., 3570
Spiegel, James I., 547
Spillman, Robert A., 3636
Spingold, Frances, 2948
Spingold, Nathan B., 2948
Spinks, Richard M., 4336
Spinola, Raymond, 2395
Spire, Lyman J., 4390
Spire, Nancy Woodson, 4390
Spitz, S. James, Jr., 3536
Spitz, S.J., Jr., 2571
Spitzer, Doreen, 1493
Spitzer, Lyman, Jr., 1493
Spitzer, N.C., 1493
Spitzer, R.R., 4337
Spitznagel, William F., 3232
Spivak, Gloria H., 2344
Spliedt, William F., 1460
Spoehrer, Charles H., 1969
Spoehrer, Harriet B., 1969
Spofford, Margaret Walker, 1791
Spokane Chronicle Company, 4231
Sponsel, Clifford W., 340
Spoor, William H., 1905
Sporck, Barbara R., 2871
Sporn, Arthur, 2387
Sposato, C.G., Jr., 2677
Sprague, Caryll M., 376
Sprague, Charles C., 3984
Sprague, Harley, 717
Sprague, Norman F., III, 376
Sprague, Norman F., Jr., 376
Sprague, Seth, 2949
Sprague, W.W., Jr., 814
Sprague,, Norman F., Jr., 376
Spraker, Edward, 2243
Spring, Richard G., 2502
Springer, C.M., 3757
Springer, D.H., 2107
Springfield Marine Bank, 1043
Springmeier, Clara G., 2019
Springs, Elliott W., 3821
Springs, Frances Ley, 3821
Sprinkle, Betty, 2048
Sprogell, Barbara S., 3719
Sprole, Frank A., 2620
Sprole, Frank Jared, 2620
Sproull, Robert L., 742, 2362
Sprunt, Barbara H., 3831
SPS Technologies, 3731
Spugnardi, Mary, 1397
Square D Company, 1162
Squires, Anna Pearl, 1375
Squires, James D., 972
St. Botolph Holding Company, 1617
St. Clair, D.W., 2150
St. Clair, James, 1593
St. John, B.D., 3935, 3936
St. Louis - San Francisco Railroad, 886
St. Louis Union Trust Company, 2001
St. Onge, Paul J., 581
St. Pe, Jerry, 1930
Staas, D. James, 4060
Staats, Elmer B., 3439, 3509
Staats, Richard J., 2416
Stabins, Samuel J., 2463
Stabler Companies, 3733
Stabler, Mrs. W. Laird, Jr., 632
Stack, Edward W., 2347
Stackner, Irene M., 4381
Stackner, John S., 4381
Stackpole, Adelaide, 3734
Stackpole, Harrison C., 3734
Stackpole, J. Hall, 3734
Stackpole, R. Dauer, 3734
Stacy, Charles B., 4285
Stadler, Elizabeth B., 3834

Stadler, George M., 44
Stadler, M.F., 2131
Stadtman, Verne A., 2109
Stafford, Richard H., 4376
Staheli, Donald L., 2366
Staley, Augustus Eugene, Jr., 1163
Staley, Catherine H., 772
Staley, Emma L., 1164
Staley, Martha G., 1967
Staley, Shirley H., 772
Staley, Thomas F., 772
Staley, Thomas F., Jr., 772
Staley, Walter G., 1967
Staley, Walter G., Jr., 1967
Stallings, W.J., 3133
Stalnaker, Armand C., 1944
Stam, David H., 2394
Stamas, S., 2426
Stamas, Stephen, 2405, 2979
Stammen, Jerrold R., 3391
Stammer, Mrs. Norbert F., 1331
Stammer, Norbert F., 1331
Stamps, James L., 377
Stanadyne, Inc., 1165
Stanback, Fred J., Jr., 3131
Stanback, W.C., 3131
Stancell, A.F., 2743
Standard Brands, 2951
Standard Emblem Jewelers, 3739
Standard Investment Company, 61, 494
Standard Motor Products, Incorporated, 2433
Standard Products Company, 3372
Standard Register Company, 3364
Standex International Corporation, 2096
Standish, William L., 3735
Stanford, Dwight E., 336
Stanford, Henry King, 3276
Stange, Peter, 4339
Stanhome, Inc., 1475
Stankard, Francis X., 2337
Stanley, Alix W., 577
Stanley, Alma Timolat, 2952
Stanley, C. Maxwell, 1264
Stanley, David M., 1264, 1284
Stanley, Edmund A., Jr., 1459, 2299
Stanley, Elizabeth M., 1264, 1284
Stanley, Emily, 2299
Stanley, Esther, 2755
Stanley, Jennifer, 1459, 2299
Stanley, Juanita B., 3999
Stanley, Lisa A., 1459
Stanley, Mary Jo, 1284
Stanley, Paul, 3925
Stanley, Richard H., 1264, 1284
Stanley, Robert C., III, 2952
Stanley, Robert Crooks, Jr., 2952
Stanley, Talcott, 577
Stanley, Thomas O., 2299
Stanley Works, 578
Stanny, B. Timothy, 3531
Stanny, N. Callaghan, 2078
Stanny, Norbert F., 2078, 3531
Stans, Diane, 378
Stans, Kathleen C., 378
Stans, Maurice H., 89, 378
Stans, Steven H., 378
Stans, Susan, 378
Stans, Theodore M., 378
Stanton, Anne M., 627
Stanton, Helen LaFetra, 2327
Stanton, J. Michael, Jr., 627
Stanton, Robert J., 3469
Stanton, Susan Y., 628
Staples, Emily Anne, 1889
Staples, Jane, 4378
Staples, Stanley F., Jr., 4292, 4293
Stapleton, Benjamin F., 448
Stapleton, F. Eugene, 3617
Stark, D.C., 1135
Stark, D.D., 3756, 3757
Stark, H.J. Lutcher, 4085
Stark, Homer B.H., 4085
Stark, Jane C., 773

Stark, K.R., 3633
Stark, Nathan J., 3512
Stark, Nelda C., 4085
Stark, Richard A., 2656
Stark, William B., 853
Starke, Glen O., 4394
Starling, Frank M., 4086
Starr, Cornelius V., 2954
Starr, Frederick B., 3135
Starr, Harry, 2675
Starr, Jacob, 2953
Starr, Lita, 2953
Starr, Melvin, 2953
Starr, S. Frederick, 2875
Starrett, Clifford W., 2171
Star-Telegram Employees Fund, 3902
State Bank of Albany, 2717
State Farm Insurance Companies, 1166
State National Bank, 1061, 4040
State National Bank of Connecticut, 526
State Street Bank and Trust Company, 1482, 1484, 1526, 1629, 2574
Statland, Suzanne, 2003
Statler, Ellsworth Milton, 2955
Statter, Amy P., 2833
Staub, Kay A., 131
Staub, William H., 1757
Stauder, Lloyd P., 587
Stauffacher, Charles B., 1060
Stauffer, John, 379, 380
Stauffer, Thomas, 3376
Staunton, Mathilda Craig, 3735
Stavrakis, Nick, 11
Steadman, Richard C., 659
Stearns, Andree B., 1631
Stearns, Artemas W., 1630
Stearns, Russell B., 1631
Stebbins, James F., 2956
Stebbins, Mary Emma, 2956
Stebbins, Rowland, III, 1465, 2562
Stebbins, Theodore E., 2956
Stebman, Betty J., 2566
Stebner, Grant, 3487
Stec, Cynthia M., 262
Steckler, Philip H., Jr., 1516
Stedman, Betty West, 3946
Stedman, Stuart West, 3946
Steed, Frank C., 3447
Steel, Alison, 381
Steel, Arthur J., 3022
Steel, Eric, 381
Steel, Gordon, 381
Steel, Jane, 381
Steel, Lauri, 381
Steel, Lewis M., 3022
Steel, Marshall, Jr., 381
Steel, Ruth M., 3022
Steelcase, Inc., 1775
Steele, Charles G., 2395
Steele, Donald E., 3309
Steele, Elizabeth R., 382
Steele, Grace C., 348, 382
Steele, Howard E., 1239
Steele, John L., Jr., 1534
Steele, Lela Emery, 3326
Steele, Richard, 382
Steele, Richard A., 1230
Steen, Raymond L., 2142
Steenburg, Walter C., 1247
Stefanko, Robert A., 3145
Steffen, E. Andrew, 926
Steffner, John E., 3832
Stegall, James W., 4017
Steiber, Richard I., 502
Steiger (Albert), Inc., 1632
Steiger, Albert A., Jr., 1632
Steiger, Allen, 1632
Steiger, Carl E., 4361
Steiger, Chauncey A., 1632
Steiger, Philip C., Jr., 1632
Steiger, Ralph A., 1632
Steiger, Ralph A., II, 1632
Steiger, Robert R., 1632
Steigerwaldt, Donna W., 1192

Stein, Allen A., 2958
Stein, Doris, 224
Stein, Helene, 2358
Stein, Joseph F., 2958
Stein, Joyce, 323
Stein, Louis, 3736
Stein, Marilyn A., 2463
Stein, Melvin, 17
Stein, Melvin M., 2958
Stein, Morris, 588
Stein, Ronald J., 2244, 2303
Stein, Sidney, 2358
Stein, Stein & Engel, 3736
Stein, Suzanne, 688
Stein, William S., 175
Steinbach, Milton, 2959
Steinbach, Ruth A., 2959
Steinberg, Ann, 32
Steinberg, Robert M., 3703
Steinberg, Saul P., 3703
Steinbock, Mark, 3388
Steinbright, Edith C., 3520
Steinbright, Marilyn Lee, 3520
Steine, Peggy, 3865
Steiner, Albert, 874
Steiner, Daniel F., 2800
Steiner, Gilbert Y., 2445
Steiner, L., 500
Steiner, Lisa A., 3043
Steiner, Prudence L., 2800
Steinhacker, Monroe, 2759
Steinhagen, B.A., 4087
Steinhagen, Elinor, 4087
Steinhart, Ella S., 2071
Steinhart, Morton, 2071
Steinhauer, W.R., 814
Steinkraus, Helen Z., 595
Steinman, Beverly R., 3737
Steinman, James Hale, 3737
Steinman, John Frederick, 3738
Steinman, Lewis, 2898
Steinman, Shirley W., 3738
Steinmetz, Jack, 1729
Steinsapir, I.H., 3739
Steinsapir, Julius, 3739
Steinschneider, Jean M., 541
Steinschneider, Richard, Jr., 541
Steinway, Henry Z., 2889
Steinweg, Bernard, 2453
Steiss, Albert J., 402
Stella D'Oro Biscuit Co., 2628
Stellner, Herbert M., Jr., 1910
Stemlar, John S., 1274
Stemmons, John M., 3984, 4088
Stemmons, John M., Jr., 4088
Stemmons, Ruth T., 4088
Stempel, Ernest E., 2954
Stemski, Conrad, 2368
Stender, Bruce, 1821
Stenner, Jerome, 3346
Stenson, Glen E., 451
Step, Eugene L., 1237
Stepanek, Anton G., 4300
Stepanian, Tania W., 137
Stephan, Edmund A., 1141
Stephan, J.S., 84
Stephen, Edmund A., 1011
Stephen, Mrs. John, 314
Stephens, Ann C., 2363
Stephens, David, 1659
Stephens, Dianne, 34
Stephens, John F., 3911
Stephens, John L., 1028
Stephens, Louis C., Jr., 3095
Stephens, Martha Roby, 2369
Stephens, Phyllis, 261
Stephens, Romelia Favrot, 3949
Stephenson, David L., 4378
Stephenson, Donald E., 1625
Stephenson, Donald G., 867
Stephenson, Edward C., 1776
Stephenson, Hazel, 1776
Stephenson, Horace C., 2984
Stephenson, John D., 2046

Stephenson, John W., 813
Stephenson, Mary L., 2067
Stepp, Howard W., 2106, 4151
Sterkel, Justine, 3374
Sterling, Helen N., 4066
Sterling, Mary P., 3805
Sterling, Sonja, 987
Stern, Alfred R., 2362
Stern, Bernard, 743
Stern, David, 2960
Stern, Edward A., 3143
Stern, Eve, 2960
Stern, Fritz, 659
Stern, Ghity, 2186
Stern, H. Peter, 2797
Stern, Henriette J., 2961
Stern, Henry, 2960
Stern, I. Jerome, 3570
Stern, Irvin, 1167
Stern, Jane M., 2961
Stern, Jerome L., 2961
Stern, Leonard N., 2186
Stern, M.M., 1185
Stern, Max, 2186
Stern, Paula, 2960
Stern, Philip M., 2960
Stern, S. Sidney, 383
Stern, Sam, 3143
Stern, Sidney J., Jr., 3132
Stern, Stanley, 2186
Stern, William, 3143
Sternberg, Ben, Jr., 4189
Sternberger, Sigmund, 3132
Sterne, Charles S., 480
Sterne, Dorothy Elder, 480
Sterne, Edwin L., 827
Stetson, Barbara, 555
Stetson, Charles P., 555
Stetson, Charles P., Jr., 555
Stetson, J.C., 1168
Stetson, John C., 1060
Stetson, Kathleen P., 2206
Stettinius, Wallace, 4172
Steuer, Leonard G., 3343
Stevens, Abbot, 1633
Stevens, Charles F., 1538
Stevens, E.W. Dann, 2488
Stevens, Edith, 2169
Stevens, Edith S., 2169
Stevens, H. Allen, 1474
Stevens, Harold A., 2496
Stevens, Harry L., Jr., 299
Stevens, Howard B., 351
Stevens, J.E., 1138
Stevens (J.P.) & Co., 2962
Stevens, John Belk, 3077
Stevens, John E., 80
Stevens, John P., III, 2169
Stevens, John P., Jr., 2169
Stevens, John T., 3824
Stevens, L.G., 1736
Stevens, Lee, 2641
Stevens, Lowell F., 1934
Stevens, Mark C., 1671
Stevens, Nathaniel, 1634
Stevens, Robert E., 525
Stevens, Virgil A., 774
Stevens, W.E., 1950
Stevens, Walter C., 3342
Stevens, Whitney, 2962
Stevenson, Alice F., 2119
Stevenson, Janet S., 2093
Stevenson, John R., 2722
Stevenson, Lawrence C., 1096
Stevenson, Lloyd C., 1096
Stevenson, Marion H., 528
Stevenson, Ruth Carter, 3902
Stevenson, W.H., 1291
Stever, H. Guyford, 3239
Stewart, Anna L., 1455
Stewart, C.L., 1032
Stewart, Donnell B., 4144
Stewart, Dorothy I., 314
Stewart, Elizabeth D.S., 4140

Stewart, Elizabeth S., 4144
Stewart, H.T., 1910
Stewart, Mrs. J.B., 2950
Stewart, J. Benham, 808
Stewart, J. Benton, 782
Stewart, J.M., 1731
Stewart, James P., 2142
Stewart, Jefferson D., Jr., 1338
Stewart, Jeffrey O., 1884
Stewart, Laura May, 384
Stewart, Margaret, 1698
Stewart, Mary E., 682
Stewart, Max, Jr., 1313
Stewart, Patricia Carry, 2346, 2365
Stewart, Pete, 3646
Stewart, R., 488
Stewart, Raymond A., Jr., 2042
Stewart, Rebecca W., 2573
Stewart, Richard E., 2700
Stewart, Richard H., 3173
Stewart, Robert A., 1705
Stewart, Robert H., III, 3909
Stewart-Warner Corporation, 1168
Stich, Jac, 1384
Stickel, Richard W., 1572
Stickelber, Merlin C., 775
Stickelber, Merlin C., Jr., 775
Stiefel, Lothar, 2598
Stierwalt, Max E., 3228
Stifel, Laurence D., 2877
Stiff, Robert M., 757
Stiffel, Jacob, 3710
Stifler, Jean, 1464
Stiles, Meredith N., Jr., 2561
Stilley, John, 43
Stillman, Charles L., 2682
Stillman, Chauncey, 2560
Stillman, Ellen, 1645
Stilwell, Lois J., 2130
Stimans, Mary, 2084
Stimming, Charles E., 3227
Stimpson, John H., 2776
Stinchcomb, Lawrence S., 685
Stinchfield, Frank, 2550
Stine, Charles E., 139
Stine, Jo, 740
Stine, Joseph P., 740
Stinnett, William, 1332
Stinson, George A., 3524, 3568
Stinson, Ira, 1272
Stinson, Ralf H., 3495
Stirn, Ellen, 3370
Stirn, Mrs. Howard F., 3370
Stitzell, J.F., 3873
Stitzlein, Carl H., 3313
Stivers, William C., 4274
Stjernstrom, James, 4014
Stock, Eloise J., 4398
Stock, Otto F., 3364
Stock, Paul, 4398
Stockard, Hubert, 732
Stockdale, Forrest, 3887
Stocker, Beth K., 3375
Stockert, Lois M., 205
Stockham, Richard J., Jr., 22
Stockham Valves and Fittings, 22
Stockholm, Charles M., 138, 186
Stockman, Herbert, 22
Stockton, Ralph M., Jr., 3137
Stockwell, Florence, 1316, 1317
Stockwell, Mary Elizabeth, 3764
Stoddard, Gerard F., 2924
Stoddard, Harry G., 1635
Stoddard, Helen E., 1635
Stoddard, Robert W., 1635
Stoddard, William, 93
Stoel, Thomas B., 3482, 3504, 3506
Stoessel, Walter, 659
Stokely, Alfred J., 1255
Stokely, Kay H., 1255
Stokely, W.B., Jr., 1255
Stokely, William B., III, 1255
Stokes, Hilda, 3141
Stokes, Lydia B., 3740

Stokes, Samuel Emlen, Jr., 3740
Stolberg, David, 3359
Stoll, L.M., 4389
Stoll, Reiner G., 2411
Stollenwerk, Robert T., 4348, 4349, 4350
Stoller, Morris, 2641
Stollings, Juanita, 1351
Stollman, Bernard, 1778
Stollman, Gerald, 1778
Stollman, Max, 1778
Stollman, Phillip, 1778
Stoltz, Jean, 1288
Stone, Barbara, 1170
Stone, Charles Lynn, 579
Stone, Charles Lynn, Jr., 579
Stone, Clement, 1170
Stone Container Corporation, 1169
Stone, David B., 2534
Stone, David L., 1508
Stone, Dewey D., 1637
Stone, Donald, 3211
Stone, Donna J., 1170
Stone, Doris Z., 1389
Stone, Edward E., 579
Stone, Elmer L., 307
Stone, Gordon, 4033
Stone, Irving I., 3352
Stone, Jerome H., 1169
Stone, Jessie V., 1170
Stone, John K.P., III, 1529
Stone, Judith N., 579
Stone, Marion H., 579
Stone, Marion R., 2690
Stone, Marvin H., 1169
Stone, Morris S., 3352
Stone, Norman C., 1170
Stone, Norman H., 1169
Stone, Norman J., 2479
Stone, Peggie, 1705
Stone, Robert W., 2575
Stone, Roger D., 2345, 2422
Stone, Roger T., 1389
Stone, Roger W., 1169
Stone, Sara S., 579
Stone, Stephen A., 1637
Stone, Thomas D., 825
Stone, Troy E., 176
Stone, W. Clement, 1170
Stonecutter Mills Corporation, 3133
Stoneman, Anne, 1638
Stoneman, Miriam H., 1638
Stoner, Richard B., 1210, 1228
Stoops, Dale I., 301
Stop & Shop Companies, 1639
Stopfel, Virginia, 1524
Stopher, Joseph E., 1340
Storer, James P., 776
Storer, Peter, 776
Storms, Clifford B., 2113
Story, Herbert B., 3890, 3944, 4052
Story, W.H., 4159
Storz, Mildred T., 2072
Storz, Robert Herman, 2072
Stotsenberg, Edward G., 325
Stott, Benjamin W., 3741
Stott, Donald B., 2964
Stott, Edward Barrington, 3741
Stott, Gilmore, 2881
Stott, Jonathan D., 3741
Stott, Robert L., 2964
Stott, Robert L., Jr., 2964
Stottlemyer, Charles E., 766
Stouder, A.G., 3391
Stouffer Foods Corporation, 3376
Stouse, James A., 1372
Stout, Charles L., 1464
Stout, Frank D., 1059
Stout, William J., 1197
Stoutenburgh, Eric K., 2416
Stovall, Don Jose, 3689
Stowe, Daniel Harding, 3134
Stowe, Daniel J., 3115
Stowe, Murray G., 4142

Stowe, R.L., Jr., 3134
Stowe, Robert L., III, 3134
Stowe, Robert Lee, Jr., 3134
Straight, Candace L., 2445
Strait, Rex, 1285
Strake, George W., 4089
Strake, George W., III, 4089
Strake, George W., Jr., 4089
Strake, Susan K., 4089
Stranahan, Ann, 468
Stranahan, Duane, 468
Stranahan, Duane, Jr., 468, 3386
Stranahan, Duane, Sr., 3377
Stranahan, Eileen B., 468
Stranahan, Frances, 468
Stranahan, Frank D., 3377
Stranahan, George S., 468
Stranahan, Josh, 468
Stranahan, Mary C., 468
Stranahan, Michael, 468
Stranahan, Molly, 468
Stranahan, Patricia Q., 468
Stranahan, Patrick J., 468
Stranahan, R.A., Jr., 3377, 3387
Stranahan, Robert A., 3377
Stranahan, Stephen, 468
Stranahan, Virginia, 468
Strang, Steven B., 446
Strasbourger, Samuel, 2948
Strassler, David H., 2266
Strassler, Gary M., 2266
Strassler, Robert B., 2266
Strassler, Samuel A., 2266
Stratton, F.P., Jr., 4306
Stratton, William G., 1059
Straub, Gertrude S., 904
Straub, Joan E., 1189
Straub, John W., 1189
Straughn, A. Pinckney, 880
Straus, Aaron, 1456
Straus, Betty B., 2965
Straus, Donald B., 644, 2843
Straus, Eugene, 4090
Straus, Harry H., III, 2965
Straus, Harry H., Sr., 2965
Straus, Lillie, 1456
Straus, Lynn, 2966
Straus, Oscar S., II, 2512, 2643
Straus, Oscar S., III, 2512, 2643
Straus, Philip, 1516
Straus, Philip A., 2966
Straus, Ralph I., 2843
Straus, Rebecca S., 2775
Straus, Roger W., Jr., 2513, 2514
Strauss, Barbara Bachmann, 2255
Strauss, Benjamin, 3742
Strauss, Donald A., 89
Strauss, Maurice L., 3742
Strauss, Peter, 216
Strauss, R.S., 3975
Strauss, Robert Perry, 3742
Strauss, Sara Lavanburg, 2644
Strauss, Thomas W., 2255
Strauss, W.A., 2058
Strausse, Donald, 1288
Strawbridge, George, 3743
Strawbridge, George, Jr., 3743
Strawbridge, Herbert E., 3185, 3252, 3278, 3311
Strawbridge, Nina S., 3743
Strawderman, D.L., 4308
Strayer, Robert L., 3724
Stream, Harold H., II, 1364
Stream, Harold H., III, 1364
Stream, Matilda Gray, 1364
Strecker, A.M., 3452
Street, Kimbrough, 4259
Streeter, Frank, 3043
Streeter, Wendell E., 1656
Streiber, John, 4072
Streim, Lynn A., 2341
Strichman, George A., 2360
Strickland, Carol A., 3000
Strickland, J.T., 3133

Taper, S. Mark, 394
Tappan, D.S., Jr., 173
Tarbel, Swannie Zink, 3474
Tarleton, Toni, 2213
Tarlov, Alvin R., 242
Tarnow, Robert L., 2495
Tartiere, Gladys R., 1136
Tartt, Hope Pierce, 4095
Tarwater, Janet L., 3246
Task, Arnold S., 3132
Tate, R.E., 1315
Tatum, Donn B., 148
Tatum, Lofton L., 3488
Taub, Arlene, 2190
Taub, Ben, 4096
Taub, H. Ben, 4096
Taub, Henry, 2146, 2189
Taub, Henry J.N., 3928, 4096, 4125
Taub, Henry J.N., II, 4096
Taub, John B., 4096
Taub, Joseph, 2146, 2190
Taub, Marcy E., 4096
Taub, Marilyn, 2189
Taub, Robert A., 1702
Taube, Thaddeus N., 248
Tauber, Alfred I., 1457
Tauber, Hans, 2541
Tauber, Ingrid D., 1457
Tauber, Laszlo N., 1457
Taubman, Herman P., 3464
Taubman, Louis, 3464
Taubman, Morris B., 3464
Taubman, Sophia, 3464
Taufer, Carol E., 351
Taylor Development Corp., 783
Taylor, Alfred H., Jr., 1734
Taylor, B. Frank, 4189
Taylor, B.G., 3970
Taylor, Barbara Olin, 2002
Taylor, Billy, 2877
Taylor, Chester H., 4089
Taylor, Curt, 1910
Taylor, D., 4373
Taylor, David, 3102
Taylor, David G., 977
Taylor, David H., 2382
Taylor, Donald S., 3508
Taylor, Douglas F., 2382
Taylor, Elizabeth H., 3138
Taylor, Elly, 783
Taylor, Emma Scott, 4198
Taylor, Fred C., 2978
Taylor, Frederick, 2117
Taylor, Frederick B., 3324
Taylor, Mrs. H.J., 6
Taylor, Mrs. H.M., 902
Taylor, Hart, 2382
Taylor, Herbert J., 6
Taylor, I.N., 3975
Taylor, J.P., 4065
Taylor, Jack, 783
Taylor, James S., 1209
Taylor, James W.Z., 109
Taylor, John B., 3475
Taylor, John I., 1483
Taylor, John L., 4290
Taylor, Julian H., 4193
Taylor, Kenneth N., 1178
Taylor, Lydia K., 3014
Taylor, Margaret C., 2414
Taylor, Margaret W., 1178
Taylor, Mark D., 1178
Taylor, Mitchell, 783
Taylor, Nancy A., 3508
Taylor, Orley R., 1852
Taylor, Paul E., Jr., 2890
Taylor, Raymond H., 4360
Taylor, Robert C., 3836, 3891
Taylor, Robert H., 2972
Taylor, Robert P., 1189
Taylor, Mrs. Samuel L., 3749
Taylor, Thurman R., 3878
Taylor, Vernon, Jr., 482
Taylor, W. Stewart, 3733

Taylor, William Davis, 1483
Taylor, William O., 1483
Taylor, William R., 4202
te Groen, John, 224
Te Stroke, H.D., 4357
te Velde, Harm, 74
te Velde, John, 74
te Velde, Marvin, 74
te Velde, Ralph, 74
te Velde, Zwaantina, 74
Teagle, Rowena Lee, 2979
Teagle, Walter C., 2979
Teagle, Walter C., III, 2979
Teagle, Walter C., Jr., 2979
Teal, Norwood, 1285
Tech, William A., 1008
Teddi of California, 286
Teenor, Mrs. E.C., 3431
Teer, James G., 4116
Teichgraeber, James, 1313
Tektronix, 3502
Teledyne Inc., 395
Teleklen Productions, 422
Tell, A. Charles, 3270
Tell, Andrew P., 45
Tell, Anne, 3380
Tell, Mary J., 45
Tell, Michael, 3380
Tell, Paul P., Jr., 3380
Tell, Paul P., Sr., 3380
Tellalian, Aram H., Jr., 544, 546
Tellalian, Robert S., 502, 544, 546
Teller, Edward, 216
Telling, Edward R., 1145
Temin, Michael, 3704
Temme-Keating, Lynne E., 1056
Temple, Alvis, 1350
Temple, Arthur, 4098
Temple, Diane E., 4206
Temple, Paul N., 4206
Temple-Inland, 1227
Templer, Charles E., 1951
Templeton, Alan H., 3550
Templeton, Hall, 3503
Templeton, Herbert A., 3503
Templin, Bob, 4335
Tenenbaum, Doris, 3865
Tengi, Frank R., 2954
Tennant Company, 1915
Tennent, Val L., 906
Tenney, Daniel G., Jr., 2584
Tenney, Delbert, 535
Tenney, Margot H., 535
Tenney, S. Marsh, 1324
Tennison, Gloria Lupton, 3895
Tenny, Barron M., 2444
Tension Envelope Corporations, 2031
Teplow, Theodore, 1637
Tepperman, Marvin T., 104
Terminal Agency, 1850
Termondt, James M., 957
Termondt, M. James, 1011, 1036, 4387
Termondt, M.J., 998
Terner, Emmanuel M., 2191
Terra, D.J., 1168
Terraciano, Anthony P., 2337
Terre Haute Gas Corporation, 1225
Terrill, Mildred K., 1059
Terry, Frederick A., Jr., 746, 2554
Terry, Lewis N., Jr., 3805
Terry, Sally A., 100
Teruya, Albert T., 905
Teruya, Raymond T., 905
Teruya, Wallace T., 905
Testa, John W., 3760
Testerman, Philip, 1850
Tetlow, Horace G., 3193
Tettemer, Frank L., 467
Texaco, 2981
Texas American Bank, 3923, 4028, 4065, 4120
Texas American Bank of Denison, 4039
Texas American Bank, Fort Worth, 3896, 3920, 3926, 4000, 4049

Texas Broadcasting Corporation, 4011
Texas Commerce Bank, 3892
Texas Commerce Bank of Austin, 4017
Texas Commerce Bank, Houston, 4099
Texas Industries, 4101
Texas Instruments Incorporated, 4102
Texasgulf Inc., 834
Textile Benefit Association, 810
Textiles, Incorporated, 3121
Textron, 3792
Thacher, Carter P., 427
Thacher, Thomas, 2533
Thacher, William A., 738
Thagard, George F., Jr., 396
Thagard, Raymond G., 396
Thal, Helen M., 1877
Thaler, Decisive, 729
Thaler, Manley, 729
Thaler, Rachael, 729
Thalheimer, Louis B., 1404, 1405, 1458
Thalhimer Brothers, 4203
Thalhimer, Barbara J., 4204
Thalhimer, Charles G., 4203, 4204
Thalhimer, Rhoda R., 4204
Thalhimer, Robert L., 4204
Thalhimer, William B., III, 4204
Thalhimer, William B., Jr., 4203, 4204
Thatcher, Elizabeth N., 2177
Thayer, Francis W., 3925
Thayer, Gladys Brooks, 2308
Thayer, Harvey H., 1602
Thayer, James N., 253
Thayer, John A., 1174
Thayer, William E., Jr., 4287
Theiss, Louis J., Jr., 3016
Thelen, Max, Jr., 136
Therman, Mrs. Harrison, 3572
Thesaurus Foundation, 6
Theus, Caroline G., 51
Theus, James G., 51
Thiele, S.W., 1890
Thien, William, 1183
Thieriot, Charles H., 306, 2585, 3029
Thigpen, Alvin R., 3988
Thill, Daniel, 1754
Thimann, Kenneth V., 2446
Third National Bank, 1970, 3853
Third National Bank & Trust Company, 3199
Thoma, David D., 893
Thomas & Betts Corporation, 2192
Thomas, Ann D., 3102
Thomas, Ann Freda, 2583
Thomas, Bruce, 4056
Thomas, C. Dean, 1101
Thomas, Don, 1290
Thomas, Edward D., 2192
Thomas, Edwin J., 3276
Thomas, Ewart V., 2200
Thomas, Franklin A., 2329, 2444
Thomas, Georgia Seaver, 397
Thomas, H. Emerson, 2201
Thomas, H. Seely, Jr., 2145
Thomas, H.D., 4331
Thomas, James R., 3271
Thomas, James R., II, 4278
Thomas, Jimmy L., 2463
Thomas, John S., 3120
Thomas, Julian, 4370
Thomas, Kenneth B., 1313
Thomas, L. Newton, 4281
Thomas, L. Newton, Jr., 4285
Thomas, L.N., 4278
Thomas, L.N., Jr., 4284
Thomas, Lee B., Jr., 1341
Thomas, Mrs. Lee B., Jr., 1341
Thomas, Lee B., Sr., 1341
Thomas, Lewis, 2514, 2679
Thomas, Lillian, 525
Thomas, Lyda Ann, 4001
Thomas, Michael, 784, 2653
Thomas, R.M., 3306
Thomas, Richard L., 914, 1002
Thomas, Robert, 784

Thomas, Robert E., 3444
Thomas, Roy E., 397
Thomas, W. Bruce, 3750
Thomas, Walter J., 878
Thomas, Wayne, 784
Thomas, William F., 321
Thomason, Sally, 3839
Thomaston Cotton Mills, 819
Thomasville Furniture Industries, 3135
Thomlinson, Allan J., 3185
Thompson, Ann J., 1980
Thompson, Betty E., 2573
Thompson, Beverley V., Jr., 4100
Thompson, Charles E., 3913
Thompson, Charles N., 1226
Thompson, Curtis B., 1861
Thompson, Dean A., 1257
Thompson, E. Arthur, 2054
Thompson, Edward, 862
Thompson, Edward T., 2635, 2645, 2851, 3019
Thompson, Elizabeth L., 3381
Thompson, Elwood N., 2054
Thompson, Eric G., 1997
Thompson, George C., 2093
Thompson, George S., 1971
Thompson, Germaine, 4360
Thompson, J. Cleo, Jr., 4091
Thompson, J.E., 2741
Thompson (J. Walter) Company, 2982
Thompson, James, 1338
Thompson, James C., Jr., 2039
Thompson, Jerry T., 1257
Thompson, Joe, 770
Thompson, John Larkin, 1482
Thompson, Joseph H., 3381
Thompson, Kenneth W., 2363
Thompson, Leonora K., 4001
Thompson, M.B., 1862
Thompson, M.O., 806
Thompson, Marcia, 2913
Thompson, Margaret S., 1910
Thompson, Mary Agnes, 646
Thompson, N.M., 291
Thompson, P.B., 3079
Thompson, Paul F., 1257
Thompson, Pauline Thrush, 1257
Thompson, Raybourne, 3942
Thompson, Renold D., 3318
Thompson, Robert D., 962
Thompson, Robert L., 1257
Thompson, Roger, 3396
Thompson, T.S., 508
Thompson, Thomas, 1643
Thompson, Thomas C., Jr., 1407
Thompson, Verneice, 433
Thompson, W.P., 1355
Thompson, Walter A.L., 2595
Thompson, Winifred H., 1575
Thomsen, C.J., 4024, 4102
Thomsen, Carl J., 3923
Thomsen, Douglas, 3211
Thomsen, Ib, 3239
Thomson, Andrew, 2393
Thomson, Cheryl A., 4319
Thomson, Eleanor C., 3010
Thomson, John Edgar, 3747
Thomson, Lucy M., 1751
Thomson, Robert C., Jr., 3010
Thomson, Teresa, 2952
Thoreen, John F., 1917
Thoresen, Catherine E., 785
Thoresen, William E., 785
Thorn, Laura, 2876
Thorn, Therese M., 1745
Thornburg, James F., 1235
Thorndike, Robert L., 2328
Thorne, David H., 2983
Thorne, Jane C., 4132
Thorne, Jane W., 2125
Thorne, Jean D., 975
Thorne, Julia L., 2983
Thorne, Landon K., 2983
Thorne, Miriam, 2983

Thorne, Mrs. Oakleigh B., 2738
Thorne, Oakleigh B., 2738, 2984
Thorne, Samuel, Jr., 2912
Thorne, Thomas H., 975
Thornton, Charles B., 398
Thornton, Charles B., Jr., 398
Thornton, Flora L., 398
Thornton, Gerald, 1278
Thornton, R.R., 965
Thornton, William Laney, 398
Thorpe, Edith D., 1916
Thorpe, James R., 1916
Thorpe, Merle, Jr., 654
Thorpe, Samuel S., III, 1916
Thostesen, Byrl, 2071
Thrasher, E.W. (Al), 4145
Thrasher, Mrs. E.W., 4145
Threads, Incorporated, 3121
Throdahl, Josephine, 2020
Thrune, Charles J., 1780
Thrush, Homer A., 1257
Thulin, Walter W., 1988
Thun, Ferdinand, 3767
Thun, Ferdinand K., 3767
Thun, Louis R., 3767
Thunack, Maurice F., 1059
Thunell, Arthur E., 154
Thurber, Cleveland, 1684, 1785
Thurber, Peter P., 1744, 1785
Thurman, Charles, 3030
Thurman, Edgar A., 4207
Thurmond, Harriet R., 1037
Thurmond, W.A., 3961
Thurston, Ann, 1649
Thurston, Lester R., Jr., 2158
Thwaits, J.A., 1890
Thyen, H.E., 1219
Thyen, James C., 1219
Thyen, Ronald J., 1219
Tiano, Joseph A., 2970
Tibaldo, Lanny, 4321
Tibbetts, Carol, 1559
Tibbetts, H.M., 2150
Tibbs, R.F., 753
Ticktin, Richard M., 2504
Ticor, 399
Tiede, Charles R., 1224
Tiede, Milton G., 987
Tieken, Elizabeth, 990
Tierney, Evangeline, 1659
Tierney, Philip, 4176
Tietje, Marion R., 2855
Tietze, Arnold, 478
Tiffany, Francis B., 1894
Tiffany, Louis Comfort, 2985
Tifft, Bela C., 2239, 2240
Tiller, F. Carlyle, 4216
Tillery, Homer, 782
Tilles, Cap Andrew, 2032
Tillinghast, Charles C., Jr., 2682
Tilton, Sumner B., Jr., 1523, 1542, 1581, 1659
Times Mirror Company, 400
Timken Company, 3382
Timken Company Charitable Trust, 3383
Timken Foundation of Canton, 3218
Timken, H.H., Jr., 3385
Timken, J.M., 3385
Timken, W.J., 3218
Timken, W.J., Jr., 3218
Timken, W.R., 3384, 3385
Timken, W.R., Jr., 3384, 3385
Timken, Ward J., 3382, 3383, 3384, 3385
Timmerman, Robert P., 3806
Timmins, Richard H., 3142
Timmons, Kathryn K., 51
Timmons, R. Randall, 51
Timonere, Steven, 3386
Timoshuk, Walter W., 362, 365
Timothy, Robert K., 450
Tinker, Edward Larocque, 2986
Tinsley, Clifford G., 3890
Tippett, Henry H., 1782

Tipton, Gwendlyn I., 1207
Tisch Hotels, 2987
Tisch, Joan H., 2987
Tisch, Laurence A., 2677, 2987
Tisch, Mrs. Laurence, 2387
Tisch, Preston R., 2987
Tisch, Wilma S., 2764, 2987
Tiscornia, James W., 1782
Tiscornia, Lester, 1782
Tiscornia, Waldo V., 1782
Tishman, Alan V., 2870
Tishman, David, 2870
Tishman, Robert V., 2870
Titan Industrial Corporation, 2988
Titchell, Haskell, 215
Titcomb, E. Rodman, Jr., 1911
Titcomb, Edward R., 1911
Titcomb, Julie C., 1911, 1925
Titmus, Edward B., 4208
Titmus, Edward Hutson, Sr., 4208
Titus, Mrs. Roy V., 2896
Titus, Roy V., 2896
Toalson, Nathan A., 1949
Toben, B.T., 3079
Tobias, Harold S., 1717
Tobin, Edgar G., 4103
Tobin, James, 2995
Tobin, John E., 2406
Tobin, Margaret Batts, 4103
Tobin, Michael S., 925
Tobin, R.L.B., 4103
Tobolowsky, George, 4129
Tod, Fred, Jr., 3416
Tod, Mabel A., 2318
Toda, Terrance M., 4241
Todd, George E., 1189
Todd, H.T., 2989
Todd, Leonard M., 3805
Todd, Paul H., 1787
Todd, Rucker, 1349
Todd, Thomas H., Jr., 3854
Todd, Vivian, 4128
Todd, W. Parsons, 2989
Todt, Mrs. Malcolm S., 588
Toepfer, Robert A., 3381
Toerge, Walter F., 3535
Toft, Richard, 971
Toland, Henry, 784
Toledo Trust Company, 468, 3386, 3387
Toler, John L., 1368
Toll, Daniel R., 1944
Toll, Maynard J., 144, 211
Tolley, J.L., 1679
Tomberlin, M.C., 797
Tomchik, James F., 502
Tomer, Richard S., 3154
Tomkins, Edwin W., II, 3564
Tomlinson, Alexander C., 2435
Tomlinson, Charles C., III, 539
Tomlinson, Lillian, 181
Tomlinson, Mark P., 875
Tommaney, John J., 2506
Tompkins, Joseph, 2751
Toms, W.P., 3859
Tone, F. Jerome, IV, 213
Tone, Miranda H., 213
Tonkin, Helen B., 4400
Tonkin, T.C., 4400
Tonnessen, Trygve H., 2979
Toohey, Edward J., 2106, 4151
Toole, Allan H., 4247, 4264
Toomey, Barbara K., 3276
Toomey, John D., 2476
Toor, Harold O., 786
Toor, Harriet R., 786
Toot, Joseph F., Jr., 3384, 3385
Topal, Dee, 2235
Topping, Brian, 638
Toran, Richard, 1268
Toran, William, 1268
Tormey, John L., 3232
Torres-Gil, Fernando, 684
Tostenrud, Don B., 28, 48
Toth, Doris M., 3411

Totino, Rose, 1830
Toumarkine, Sadie C., 601
Toupin, Arthur V., 83, 84
Toups, Roland M., 1354
Tourtellotte, Janet, 4238
Towbin, Belmont, 2990
Tower, H.L., 1475
Tower, John C., 936
Tower, R.C., 1005
Towers, Inc., 658
Towers, John, 2741
Towers, T.R., 4212
Towey, James F., 561
Towler, Stephen, 1342
Townes, C.H., 1709
Townsend, Mark, 405
Townsend, R.E., 2033
Towse, Thomas C., 379
Towsley, Harry A., 1783
Towsley, Margaret D., 1783
Tozer, David, 1917
Trabosh, Susan, 2815
Tracht, Melvin T., 1153
Tracy, Emmet E., 1784
Tracy, Emmet E., Jr., 1784
Tracy, Frances A., 1784
Tracy, Frederick L., 3224
Trafford, Perry D., 2408
Train, Russell E., 659, 2234, 2875
Trammell, W. Bryan, Jr., 3956
Trammell, Wash Bryan, 3956
Trane Company, 4383
Transway International Corporation, 2991
Traub, Marjorie, 2617
Traubner, Edward, 300
Trausch, Arthur N., Jr., 4326
Travassos, Nathan J., 762
Travelli, Charles I., 1644
Travelli, Emma R., 1644
Traveras, Juan, 1987
Travers, Thomas J., 3190
Travis, G. Emerson, 750
Traylor, Mrs. Robert H., 1481
Traynor, Michael, 142
Treadway, Lyman, III, 3171
Treakle, J. Edwin, 4209
Treckelo, Richard M., 1211
Trecker, Francis J., 4337
Treckman, Howard, 1203
Tredennick, William T., 3522
Tree, Marietta, 2329
Treeger, Clarence R., 2970
Trefts, John C., Jr., 2396
Treiber, Patricia S., 4381
Treiber, Phillip A., 4381
Treible, Kirk, 3989
Treloar, Donald N., 2167
Tremayne, William H., 2167
Tremco Manufacturing Company, 3388
Treneer, E. Gene, 4259
Tressler, Charles E., 1431
Tretheway, Gordon M., 3490
Treuhaft, Arthur W., 3389, 3390
Treuhaft, Elizabeth M., 3389, 3390
Treuhaft, William C., 3389, 3390
Trevor, John B., 2831
Trexler, Harry C., 3748
Trexler, Mary M., 3748
Triangle Publications, 3519
Tribune-Star Publishing Company, 1225
Trigg, Paul Jr., Jr., 1784
Trimble, Margaret Brown, 1432
Trimble, William C., 1461
Trimble, William C., Jr., 1464
Triolo, James S., 336
Tripp, William V., III, 1586
Trobaugh, Allen K., 3882
Troester, Charles E., 1768
Trogdon, Dewey L., 3071
Troiano, John G., 3014
Trost, William B., 2019
Trott, James T., 3866

Trotter, George A., Jr., 293
Trotter, J.M., 3074
Trotter, Jack T., 4118
Trotter, Maxine, 293
Trotter, W. Henry, 3832, 3845
Trowbridge, C. Robertson, 2092
Trower, Dorothy H., 1600
Trower, Thomas H., 3419
Troxell, D. Chase, 3050
Troyer, Thomas A., 2325, 2960
Trucklease Corporation, 1606
Truebeck, W.L., 3156
Truitt, Evelyn, 360
Truland, Alice O., 4210
Truland of Florida, 4210
Truland, Robert W., 4210
Truland, Walter R., 4210
Trull, Florence M., 4104
Trull, R.B., 4104
Truman, David B., 2995
Trumble, Eugene, 1881
Trumbull, George R., III, 3542
Trump, Donald, 2992
Trump, Fred C., 2992
Trump Village Construction Corporation, 2992
Truschke, E.F., 84
Trust Committee of United Missouri Bank of Kansas City, 1976
Trust Company Bank, 802, 817, 827, 830, 841, 846, 852, 857, 860, 866, 877, 880
Trust Company Bank of Georgia, 813
Trust Company Bank of Middle Georgia, 867
Trust Company of Oklahoma, 3451
Trust Services of America, 114, 255
Trustman, Benjamin A., 1529
Truyens, Lillian D., 149
Truzinski, Charles G., 1807
TRW, 3392
Tschudy, Jane S., 1969
Tuch, Michael, 2993
Tuck, Deborah, 468
Tuck, Edward H., 498
Tuck, Elizabeth, 2993
Tuck, Eugene, 2993
Tuck, Katherine, 1785
Tuck, N. Barton, 3805
Tucker (Max and Rose) Foundation, 3504
Tucker, Carll, III, 3393
Tucker, David S., Sr., 301
Tucker, Don E., 3190
Tucker, Gay, 3393
Tucker, Helen, 2497
Tucker, Helen Sonnenberg, 2497
Tucker, Luther, 3393
Tucker, Luther, Jr., 3393
Tucker, Marcia Brady, 3393
Tucker, Morrison G., 3441, 3451
Tucker, Robert A., 596
Tucker, Rose E., 3504
Tucker, Ruth H., 1551
Tucker, Steven, 2497
Tucker, Toinette, 3393
Tucker, William P., 2427
Tuite, Betty J., 3176, 3248
Tulcin, Doris F., 2449
Tull, J.M., 878
Tull (J.M.) Metal and Supply Company, 878
Tullidge, Thomas H., 4172
Tullis, R.B., 726
Tullis, Richard B., 3185, 3201
Tullis, Robert Wood, 993
Tully, Alice, 2765
Tully, Herbert A., 427
Tully, Paul, 3129
Tuohy, Alice Tweed, 403
Turben, Claude F., 3151
Turino, Alfred C., 2702
Turk, James C., 4195
Turk, John W., 3903
Turletes, Vincent N., 2738

White, B. Wade, 773
White, Benjamin T., 855, 887
White, Carter H., 2767
White Castle System, 3261
White, Charles W., 3799, 3818
White Consolidated Industries, 3405
White, Daphne M., 2724
White, David H., 4121
White, Donald G., 1353
White, Edward L., Jr., 824
White, Erskine N., Jr., 3790
White, Fred R., Jr., 3318
White, G.E., 1679
White, G.R., 4120
White, Gilbert F., 1848
White, H. Blair, 1128
White, Hazel B., 1188
White, Helen T., 483
White, Hugh A., 1794, 3292
White, J. Robert, 47
White, J.M., 4212
White, John F., 1465
White, Jon B., 3923
White, Jonathan R., 1795
White, L.A., 3874
White, Larry L., 333
White, Mahlon T., 483
White, Margaret R., 3107
White, Martha Fain, 3944
White, Mary, 3948
White, R.E., 3289
White, Richard K., 3748
White, Robert, 770
White, Robert A., 706
White, Robert P., 1188
White, Roger B., 1188
White, Steven R., 1188
White, Thomas H., 3406
White, Tommie O., 4121
White, Vaundell, 3254
White, Virginia L., 3870
White, W.E., 3858
White, Wayne A., 989
White, William A., 2711
White, William Bew, Jr., 19, 24
White, William P., 1188
White, William R., 2279
White, William S., 1723, 1752
Whitebeck, Carl G., 2836
Whited, Edwin F., 449
Whitehead, A. Pennington, 2347
Whitehead, Conkey Pate, 885
Whitehead, Edwin C., 590
Whitehead, Jaan W., 3041
Whitehead, John, 590
Whitehead, John C., 2109, 2181, 3032, 3041
Whitehead (John C.) Foundation, 3041
Whitehead, Joseph B., Jr., 884
Whitehead, Peter, 590
Whitehead, Susan, 590
Whitehill, Clifford L., 1847
Whitehouse, A.W., Jr., 3187
Whitehurst, Elmore, 4091
Whitelaw, Robert I., 3751
Whiteman, J.D., 3323
Whitener, Orin, 3136
Whiteside, Thomas, 1621
Whitfield, Sue Trammell, 3956
Whitin Machine Works, 3405
Whiting, Eleanor W., 3695
Whiting, Mrs. Giles, 3042
Whiting, Helen Dow, 1797
Whiting, Macauley, 1797
Whiting, Mary Macauley, 1797
Whitla, Mrs. William F., 3540
Whitley, H.B., 576
Whitley, R.K., 979
Whitlock, Foster B., 2140
Whitlock, John B., 1711
Whitlow, D.R., 3511
Whitman, Christine T., 2161
Whitman, Frederick C., 137
Whitmore, Susan H., 2561

Whitney Blake Company, 1502
Whitney, Edward A., 4402
Whitney, Helen G., 2591
Whitney, Lewis, 245
Whitney, Maurice P., 2239
Whitney, Richard, 29
Whitney, Thomas P., 591
Whitney, Valerie T., 401
Whitney (W.M.) & Co., 3205
Whitney, Wheelock, 1881
Whitridge, Frederick W., 137
Whitridge, William C., 1464
Whitsett, Elizabeth A., 77
Whitsett, John F., 77
Whitsitt, William L., 1145
Whitt, John J., 4208
Whittaker, Ethel A., 2240
Whittaker, Henry W., 3153
Whittell, Elia, 425
Whittemore, Anne Marie, 4196
Whittemore, Clark M., Jr., 2379
Whittemore, Donald L., Jr., 782
Whittenberger, Ethel B., 916
Whittier, Leland K., 265, 426
Whittington, Robert B., 2463
Whittington, V.G., 4081
Whittle, Carolyn, 3015
Whitton, J.G., 3131
Whitwam, David R., 1793
Whyel, George L., 1752
Whyte, Joseph L., 669
Whyte, William H., Jr., 2234
Wiborg, James, 4268
Wiborg, James H., 4255
Wice, David H., 3571
Wick, Robert H., 3527
Wick, Warner A., 1125
Wickes, Harvey Randall, 1798
Wickham, Don, 2377
Wicks, William W., 4338
Wideman, Frank J., Jr., 3817
Widener, Peter A.B., 3762
Widmer, Michael J., 1488
Widnall, Sheila E., 2325
Wieboldt, Anna Krueger, 1189
Wieboldt, Nancy A., 1189
Wieboldt, William A., 1189
Wiedemann, Gladys H.G., 1330
Wiedemann (K.T.) Trust, 1330
Wiedenman, Jeanne M., 3009
Wiederhold, William C., 4056
Wiegand, Ann K., 2078
Wiegand, Edwin L., 2078
Wiehoff, Dale, 2960
Wieland, R.R., 3255
Wien, Lawrence A., 3044
Wien, Mae L., 3044
Wiener, Ann F., 2792
Wies, Catherine K., 1428
Wiesel, Torsten N., 1538
Wigdale, James A., 4354
Wiggins, Chuck H., 4274
Wiggins, Donald D., 1318
Wiggins, W. Frank, 1187
Wightman, Julia P., 2414
Wightman, Orrin S., III, 2414
Wiig, Paul O., 2080
Wiksten, Barry F., 3542
Wikstrom, A.S., 3045
Wilbur, Brayton, Jr., 427
Wilbur, Colburn S., 308
Wilbur, Marguerite Eyer, 428
Wilbur, Ray L., 341
Wilbur-Ellis Company, 427
Wilcher, Denny, 25
Wilcox, Francis J., 4328
Wilcox, George N., 908
Wilcox, Julia O'Brien, 1896
Wilcox, Phillip S., 340
Wilcox, Richard S., Jr., 1896
Wilcox, Samuel Whitney, 909
Wilcox, Thomas R., 220, 243
Wild, Michael M., 1695
Wilde, D.E., 4384

Wilder, Amherst H., 1928
Wilder, Mrs. Amherst H., 1928
Wilder, Billy, 365, 366
Wilder, Donny, 3797
Wilder, Gary, 792
Wilder, Mrs. George H., 2164
Wilder, Michael S., 534
Wilder, Rita, 792
Wilder, Robert O., 3675
Wilderson, Frank B., Jr., 1823
Wildman, Paul W., 332
Wiley, Barbara M., 4299
Wiley, Mary L.F., 4170
Wiley, Robert, 93
Wiley, S. Donald, 3598, 3600
Wilf, Elizabeth, 2203
Wilf, Harry, 2203
Wilf, Joseph, 2203
Wilf, Judith, 2203
Wilfley, George M., 436
Wilhelm, A.A., 3159
Wilhite, Marion J., 181
Wilhoit, Ray B., 860, 880
Wilkening, Leonard H., 1889, 1928
Wilkes, Jack D., 3448
Wilkie, James W., 1190
Wilkie, Leighton A., 1190
Wilkie, Robert J., 1190
Wilkie, Valleau, Jr., 4063, 4064
Wilking, Virginia N., 2493
Wilkins, M.P., 1999
Wilkins, Wilfred G., 1195
Wilkinson, Herbert S., 917
Wilkinson, Herbert S., Sr., 918
Wilkinson, John H., 4274
Wilkinson, Katherine McK., 3825
Wilkinson, Peter, 960
Wilkinson, R.W., 4277
Will, Albert A., Jr., 799
Will, Fred, 4386
Will, J.F., 3553
Willaman, P. Owen, 3027
Willard, Eugenia B., 2912
Willard, L.S., 1408
Willcox, Dale F., 1012
Wille, Robert H., 2243
Willemetz, J. Lester, 2002
Willens, Joan G., 367
Willert, Mary, 3298
Willes, Mark H., 1847
Willett, Howard L., 1191
Willett, Howard L., Jr., 1191
Willey, Paul W., 3935, 3936
Willey, Willis H., III, 3854
Willi, Edward J., 2468
Williams, A.F., 485
Williams, Mrs. A.F., 485
Williams, Alexander J., 3378
Williams, Anita S., 648
Williams, Arthur A., 1658
Williams, Arthur A., Jr., 1658
Williams, B.E., 188
Williams, Barbara Steele, 382
Williams, C.W., 2426
Williams, Charles J., III, 793
Williams, Charles P., 3471
Williams, Clarence E., 2164
Williams Companies, 3471
Williams, Dan C., 4084
Williams, David S., 1658
Williams, Dorothy R., 3691, 3693
Williams, Douglas S., 3824
Williams, E. Belvin, 2193
Williams, Edith K., 1570
Williams, Edna Sproull, 793
Williams, Edward J., 1028, 1049, 1095
Williams, Emory, 1058
Williams, Ernest E., 1213
Williams, Ernest G., 23
Williams, Eugene F., Jr., 2799
Williams, Frank D., 2889
Williams, Franklin H., 1160
Williams, G. Thaddeus, 3797
Williams, Gray, Jr., 2188

Williams, Grice, 4370
Williams, Harold B., 336
Williams, Harold L., 3185
Williams, Harold M., 187, 365, 367
Williams, Harold S., 2643
Williams, Hazel O., 713, 716
Williams, J. Harold, 552
Williams, J. Kelley, 1936
Williams, J. Peter, 3717
Williams, J. Roger, Jr., 3539
Williams, James B., 876
Williams, Jane, 4259
Williams, Jimmie D., 3828
Williams, Joe A., 3460
Williams, Joel T., 3912
Williams, John, 1705
Williams, John C., 3763
Williams, John G., 3767
Williams, John H., 3471
Williams, John O., 596
Williams, Joseph H., 3471
Williams, Joseph R., 3854
Williams, Katherine B., 1157
Williams, L. Kemper, 1386
Williams, L. Neil, Jr., 887
Williams, Lamar Harper, 1027
Williams, Leila M., 1386
Williams, Lewis, 3258
Williams, Lillian L., 3110
Williams, Luke G., 4230
Williams, Marie, 748
Williams, Marvin S., 1439
Williams, Mary Louise, 1449
Williams, Mary R., 2979
Williams, Maude O'Connor, 4083
Williams, Michael, 40
Williams, Murat W., 679
Williams, Nick B., 382
Williams, Norris S.L., 1368
Williams, Patrick M., 793
Williams, Phillip L., 400, 532
Williams, R.B., 3943, 4018
Williams, R.E., 3809
Williams, R.L., III, 1020
Williams, Mrs. R. Mack, 3132
Williams, Ralph B., 1616
Williams, Mrs. Rhys, 1573
Williams, Richard, 970
Williams, Richard A., 3110
Williams, Robert A., 434
Williams, Robert E., 3190
Williams, Robert G., 3580
Williams, Robert I., 2683
Williams, Roger P., 4083
Williams, Ronald D., 502
Williams, Ronald W., 444, 473
Williams, Ruth, 4391
Williams, Samuel C., Jr., 2196
Williams, Sarah P., 635, 636
Williams, Shirley, 2995
Williams, Stanley E., 1894
Williams, Steve L., 3824
Williams, Thomas B., 1573
Williams, Thomas B., Jr., 1616
Williams, Thomas M., 1570
Williams, Thomas R., 833
Williams, William, 1658
Williams, William J., 3185, 3341
Williamson, Debra L., 3272
Williamson, Douglas E., 3272
Williamson, Douglas F., Jr., 2715
Williamson, E.L., 1373
Williamson, Jeanette L., 2849
Williamson, Karen, 3272
Williamson, Kyle, 3272
Williamson, P.D., 3272
Williamson, S.K., 3272
Williamson, Sheila C., 2161
Williamson, Susan K., 3272
Williamson, William H., III, 3102
Williamsport National Bank, 3764
Williford, Lawrence H., 922, 1145
Willingham, Frank F., 3105
Willingham, Gene W., 4110

Willingham, Helen Biggs, 4110
Willis, Ralph N., 1464
Willison, Charles H., 1757
Willison, Robert E., 3637
Willits, Harris L., 2204
Willits, Itto A., 2204
Willits, John F., 2204
Willits, Patricia P., 2005
Willits, Robert W., 2005
Willmott, Peter S., 964
Wills, Ellen Buchner, 3853
Wills, Jesse E., 3853
Wills, Jesse W., 3853
Wills, Kenneth, 1935
Wills, Matthew Buchner, 3853
Wills, Polly D., 3851
Wills, William Ridley, 3853
Willson, George C., III, 1967
Wilmans, Carol Wattis, 417
Wilmington Trust Company, 598
Wilsen, Laura, 693
Wilsen, Oscar, 693
Wilson, Alfred G., 1800
Wilson, Amanda, 50
Wilson, Barbara, 888
Wilson, Blenda J., 2362
Wilson, Bruce P., 1401
Wilson, C.J., 446
Wilson, Charles B., 43
Wilson, Christina B., 4246
Wilson, David K., 3856
Wilson, Diane Wenger, 1792
Wilson, Donald, 2764
Wilson, Donald E., 1162
Wilson, Dorothy B., 3859
Wilson, Dorothy C., 4029
Wilson, Edwin, 2479
Wilson, Elmer H., 1102
Wilson, Eugene, 93
Wilson, Eugene R., 78
Wilson, Frances W., 886
Wilson, Frank S., 520
Wilson, Fred B., 886
Wilson, G. Dale, 3396
Wilson, G.L., 1319
Wilson, Mrs. H. Clifton, 2416
Wilson, H.W., 3047
Wilson, Mrs. H.W., 3047
Wilson (The H.W.) Company, 3047
Wilson, Herbert J., 1720
Wilson, Howard O., 319, 383
Wilson, Huey J., 1354
Wilson, Isabel Brown, 3893
Wilson, J. Christine, 3048
Wilson, J. Richard, 3048
Wilson, J.H., 4122
Wilson, J.R., 1672
Wilson, Jack, 867
Wilson, James, 3162
Wilson, James B., 1153
Wilson, James F., 3897
Wilson, James Q., 676
Wilson, Jean H., 50
Wilson, Jess C., Jr., 240
Wilson, John, 2751
Wilson, John J., 3926
Wilson, John M., Jr., 3403
Wilson, Mrs. John M., Jr., 3403
Wilson, Joseph C., 3048
Wilson, Josephine D., 3851
Wilson, Justin, 3856
Wilson, Katherine M., 3046, 3048
Wilson, Kendrick R., Jr., 883
Wilson, Kenneth Pat, 55
Wilson, Kirke, 334
Wilson, Leslie D., 3582
Wilson, Lula C., 1799
Wilson, Margaret Bush, 676
Wilson, Margaret D., 3577
Wilson, Marie C., 3048
Wilson, Marillyn B., 3049
Wilson, Marvin N., 3945
Wilson, Mary, 1348
Wilson, Matilda R., 1800

Wilson, O. Meredith, 2346
Wilson, Penelope P., 2821
Wilson, Mrs. Perkins, 4185
Wilson, R.B., 4274
Wilson, Ralph, 4123
Wilson, Ralph, Jr., 4123
Wilson, Richard A., 131
Wilson, Richard F., 50
Wilson, Robert, 50
Wilson, Robert A., 2823
Wilson, Robert W., 3049
Wilson, Sandra H., 782
Wilson, Soonya, 50
Wilson, T.A., 3750, 4255
Wilson, Thomas, 1464
Wilson, W.R., 3645
Wilson, William C., 3859
Wilson, William K., 3373
Wimsett, Marian, 1334
Winandy, J.P., 2571
Winant, Rivington R., 2499
Winchcole, Dorothy C., 1407
Winder, Patricia S., 3718
Windham, J. Hardy, 3898
Winding, Charles A., 2240
Windle, Janice W., 3940
Windon, Bernard, 1144
Windsor, Robert G., 441
Winegarden, Joel, 1463
Winestone, Ted M., 3846
Winfield, J.A., 3528
Winger, G. Leo, 3540
Wingfield, C.L., 2112
Wingfield, W.T., 886
Winkelman, Stanley J., 1801
Winkelman Stores, 1801
Winkler, Paul, 4030
Winn, Arlene, 174
Winn, Herschel, 4119
Winn, Willis J., 3659
Winn-Dixie Stores, 794
Winnet, Nochem S., 3571
Winnick, Louis, 2444
Winokur, James L., 3711
Winslow, Edna M., 2419
Winslow, Enid, 2594
Winsor, Curtin, Jr., 2405
Winsor, James D., III, 3698
Winstead, Sam G., 4003
Winston, Bert F., Jr., 4105
Winston, Charles F., 4110
Winston, Electra Biggs, 4110
Winston, Harry, 3051
Winston, J.O., Jr., 3947
Winston (The N.K.) Foundation, 3052
Winston, Norman K., 3052
Winston, Ronald, 3051
Winter, Arthur, 1167
Winter, Dorothy G., 1167
Winter, Richard, 1167
Winter, Stanley, 1167
Winters, Lucille, 1294
Winters, Robert C., 2167
Winthrop, John, 2305
Wirt, Stanley S., 940
Wirtanen, Donald G., 1899
Wirth, Charles, III, 1362
Wirth, Conrad L., 2234, 2577
Wirth, Lawrence R., 2774
Wirth, Otto H., 4353
Wirth, Willard R., Jr., 1006
Wisconsin Center for Public Policy, 4341
Wisconsin Electric Power Company, 4388
Wisconsin Natural Gas Company, 4388
Wisconsin Public Service Corporation, 4389
Wisdom, Mary Elizabeth, 1380
Wise, Charles G., III, 1446
Wise, Daniel P., 1651
Wise, George S., 706
Wise, Jessie Kenan, 4170
Wise, Mercer V., 3797
Wise, Ralph O., 3342

Wise, Robert E., 4029
Wise, Robert W., 1322
Wise, Stephanie, 2652
Wiseheart, Dorothy A., 796
Wiseheart, Malcolm B., 796
Wiseheart, Malcolm B., Jr., 796
Wishart, Alfred W., Jr., 3535, 3599, 3600, 3691, 3693
Wishnia, Steve, 3855
Wishnick, William, 3053
Wisnom, David, Jr., 268
Witco Chemical Corporation, 3053
Witherington, James D., 3854
Withers, Alan, 3483
Withers, Barbara B., 1910
Withington, Nathan, 1556
Withrow, David, 4402
Withrow, J.D., Jr., 1679
Witt, Raymond B., Jr., 3863
Witt, Sherman E., Jr., 4278
Witte, John H., Jr., 1289
Wittenborn, John R., 2108
Witter, Dean, 429
Witter, Mrs. Dean, 429
Witter, Dean, III, 429
Witter (Dean) & Company, 429
Witter, William D., 429
Witting, Chris J., 2331
Wittingdon, Harry M., 3878
Wittlich, Jae L., 1008
Wittmann, Otto, 187
Witunski, Michael, 1993, 1994
Witz, Herbert E., 1424
WLTY-FM, 4179
Woehrle, Charles B., 1838
Woellert, W.L., 3223
Wohlgemuth, Alexander, 3054
Wohlgemuth, Esther, 3054
Wohlgemuth, Morton, 3054
Wohlgemuth, Robert, 3054
Wohlstetter, Charles, 2882
Wojcik, Henry J., 4392
Wolaham, E.W., 2981
Wolbach, William W., 1482, 1543
Wolcott, J.W., 2991
Wolcott, Samuel H., Jr., 1616, 1653
Woldenberg, Malcolm, 1387
Wolf, Austin K., 502
Wolf, Clarence, 3765
Wolf, Daniel A., 1248
Wolf, Mrs. Edwin, 3765
Wolf, Estelle, 486
Wolf, Frances, 663
Wolf, Fredora K., 3765
Wolf, Harry H., Jr., 1192
Wolf, Jamie G.R., 569
Wolf, John H., Sr., 3762
Wolf, Joseph, 3245
Wolf, Lawrence, 486
Wolf, Lee J., 2849
Wolf, Leon M., 1367
Wolf, Lester K., 3682
Wolf, Martha R., 2887
Wolf, Marvin, 486
Wolf, May H., 1366, 1367
Wolf, Robert, 2779
Wolf, Rosalie J., 2574
Wolf, Wendy, 486
Wolfe, C. Holmes, 3558
Wolfe, C. Holmes, Jr., 3576
Wolfe, Joan M., 2694
Wolfe, John F., 3410
Wolfe, John M., 2605
Wolfe, John Walton, 3189, 3410
Wolfe, K.L., 3601
Wolfe, Laurence A., 421
Wolfe, Thomas K., Jr., 4214
Wolfe, William C., Jr., 3410
Wolfensohn, James D., 2298, 2877
Wolfensperger, Diana Potter, 268
Wolff, Benno F., 1030
Wolff, Edith D., 2040
Wolff, Herbert E., 897
Wolff, John M., III, 2040

Wolff, John M., Jr., 2040
Wolff, Sidney A., 2486
Wolfman, Paul I., 1008
Wolford, Richard, 3346
Wolfson, Cecil, 797
Wolfson, Dennis M., 797
Wolfson, Donald M., 797
Wolfson, Erwin S., 3056
Wolfson, Florence M., 797
Wolfson, Gary L., 797
Wolfson, John, 3056
Wolfson, Louis E., 797, 798
Wolfson Management Corporation, 3056
Wolfson, Nathan, 797
Wolfson, Richard J., 797
Wolfson, Rose F., 3056
Wolfson, Sam W., 797
Wolfson, Saul, 797
Wolfson, Stephen P., 797
Wolfson, Zev W., 3055
Wolgemuth, Robert, 3054
Wolgemuth, Sam, 1178
Wollenberg, H.L., 430
Wollenberg, J. Roger, 430
Wollenberg, Richard P., 430
Wollenhaupt, Fred, 3396
Woller, Gary, 4321
Woltman, B.M., 4126
Woltman Furniture Company, 4126
Woltman, W.J., 4126
Wolverine Shoe and Tanning Corporation, 1803
Womack, L.T., 2063
Womack, Milton, 1354
Womack, William W., 3219
Womsley, Robert B., 3170
Wong, Donald M., 900
Wong, James, 166
Wong, Theodore F.K., 899
Wood, Alma W., 2952
Wood, Barbara M.J., 1134
Wood, Charles F., 1336
Wood, Cynthia S., 431
Wood, Dale A., 4072
Wood, David E., 1464
Wood, Donald R., 4226
Wood, Francis C., 3659
Wood, Gary, 4036
Wood, Hayden R., 1658
Wood, Howell R., Jr., 1621
Wood, J. Warren, III, 2140
Wood, James, 2583
Wood, James A., 1601
Wood, James F., 3447
Wood, John M., Jr., 1618
Wood, Kate B., 2175
Wood, Lawrence, 472
Wood, Lowell L., 216
Wood, Minnie Rhea, 3944
Wood, Peter, 4030
Wood, R.L., 1135
Wood, Richard D., 1237, 1238
Wood, Robert A., 1967
Wood, William P., 3588, 3741
Woodall, Miles, 4080
Woodard, Frances M., 701
Woodard, Milton P., 701
Woodcock, Julian A., Jr., 3116
Woodhead, R.K., 915
Woodhouse, Lorenzo E., 4148
Woodling, Nancy E., 3375
Woodruff, C.E., 883
Woodruff, D. Straton, Jr., 3634
Woodruff, J. Barnett, 848
Woodruff, Robert W., 876
Woods, C. Cecil, Jr., 3864
Woods, David L., 2041
Woods, Edwin Newhall, 296
Woods, Frank H., 1193
Woods, James H., 2041
Woods, James H., Jr., 2041
Woods, John R., 2041
Woods, John W., III, 1342
Woods, Laura Lee Whittier, 265

Woods, Marie Cartinhour, 3864
Woods, Nelle C., 1193
Woods, Thomas C., III, 1193, 2063
Woods, Thomas C., Jr., 1193
Woods-Denkler, Margaret C., 3864
Woodside, William S., 492
Woodson, Ben H., 3854
Woodson, James L., 3138
Woodson, Margaret C., 3138
Woodson, Mary Holt W., 3138
Woodson, Paul B., 3138
Woodson, Sam P., III, 3895
Woodward, Catherine M., 485
Woodward, Charles H., 3681
Woodward, Gerald W., 3313
Woodward Governor Company, 487
Woodward, Paul E., 485
Woodward, Richmond B., 1538
Woodwell, George, 1753
Woodworth, David A., 977
Woodworth, Lynn, 3835
Wooldridge, James A., 1066
Woolf, Geraldine H., 1388
Woolf, Harry, 2877
Woolf, Raleigh, 4311
Woolf, William C., 1388
Woolfe, Walter L., 762
Woollam, Tina F., 1361
Woolley, Samuel H., 522
Woolley, Vasser, 887
Woolley, Walter, Jr., 3439
Woolsey, Robert, 3451
Woosley, Anne I., 27
Work Wear Corporation, 3347
Workman, W.D., Jr., 3800
Works, George W., III, 3925
World Color Press, 125
Worley, Bland W., 3076
Worley, Jack, 872
Worrell, Glen A., 117
Worth, D.H., 3218, 3385
Worth, Douglas H., 3384
Worth, Robert R., 2554
Wortham, Gus S., 4127
Wortham, Lyndall F., 4127
Wortham, R.W., III, 4127
Worthen Bank and Trust Company, 57
Worthington, Charles D., 2161
Wortis, Ethel, 3015
Wouk, Betty Sarah, 688
Wouk, Herman, 688
Wouk, Joseph, 688
Wouk, Nathanial, 688
Woytych, Edward F., 4324
Wrape, A.J., Jr., 62
Wrape, A.M., 62
Wray, Jane L., 799
Wrean, Elisabeth Kurth, 4345
Wren, Thomas W., 3870
Wrenn, Peter J., 1141
Wright, Arthur M., 1045
Wright, Bernadine G., 3411
Wright, Bernard, 1099
Wright, Carolyn, 4394
Wright, Charles, III, 1722
Wright, Donald C., Jr., 3594
Wright, Donald R., 311
Wright, Elizabeth J., 693
Wright, Emmett, Jr., 2188
Wright, G. Burke, 2998
Wright, Hasbrouck S., 3633
Wright, Helena DuPont, 633
Wright, Howard S., 4259
Wright, J.A., 173
Wright, J.D., 3411
Wright, James O., 4299, 4354
Wright, John D., Jr., 3411
Wright, Johnie E., 4128
Wright, Katherine Deane, 1010
Wright, Kathryn, 582
Wright, Kernan, 3396
Wright, Marjorie, 577
Wright, Paul G., Jr., 731
Wright, Peter C., 128

Wright, Richard E., III, 3426
Wright, Robert J., 3925
Wright, Robert W., 1069
Wright, Spencer D., III, 3574
Wright, Thomas H., 646
Wright, Virginia Bloedel, 4222, 4251
Wright, W.F., Jr., 3908
Wright, W.J., 4251
Wright, W.R., 707
Wright, William B., 2106, 4151
Wrightson, J. Wallace, 694
Wrigley, Elizabeth S., 80
Wriston, Walter B., 2769
Wrzesinski, Susan, 1726
WTAR-AM and FM, 4179
Wu, Kinglui, 490
Wu, M., 1731
Wuester, William O., 2195
Wuesthoff, Winfred W., 4387
Wugalter, Harry, 2535
Wulff, Fred, 4120
Wuliger, Ernest M., 3412
Wuliger, Timothy F., 3412
Wunsch, Eric M., 3061
Wunsch, Ethel, 3061
Wunsch, Joseph W., 3061
Wunsch, Samuel, 3061
Wurlitzer, Farny R., 1194
Wurlitzer, Grace K., 1194
Wurlitzer, Mrs. Howard E., 2213
Wurtele, C.A., 1918
Wurts, Henrietta Tower, 3766
Wyatt, Douglas W., 2711
Wyatt, F.L., 4274
Wyatt, Jerry H., 2170
Wyatt, Wilson W., Sr., 1346
Wyche, Harriet S., 3805
Wyckoff, Ann P., 4254
Wyckoff, Clinton R., Jr., 2488
Wyckoff, Dorothy G., 2488
Wyckoff, Kevin M., 2488
Wycoff, R.E., 78
Wydman, Perry B., 3191
Wyerhaeuser, Wendy Wagner, 4251
Wyeth, Phyllis Mills, 600
Wyland, Susan T., 1783
Wyman, David C., 4276
Wyman, Deehan M., 4276
Wyman, Henry W., 563
Wyman, Maria, 563
Wyman, Ralph M., 563
Wyman, Richard M., 1610
Wyman, Thomas H., 2444
Wyman, Timothy E., 2864
Wyman, Virginia D., 4276
Wyman-Gordon Co., 1660
Wymer, Harold D., 333
Wynn, Elaine, 2079
Wynn, Stephen A., 2079
Wynne, John O., 4179
Wynne, Marjorie West, 882
Wynne, Robert, 882
Wyoming National Bank, 4400
Wytana Inc., 2060
Wythes, Carol K., 4343

Xavier, Deanna M., 275
Xerox Corporation, 594
XTEK, Inc., 3413

Yablick, Herman, 800
Yablon, Leonard H., 2440
Yacavone, Peter F., 529
Yaeger, Peter E., 2605
Yaggy, Michael E., 1461
Yak, John Fern, 3342
Yammine, R.N., 3289
Yamont, P.E., 495
Yancey, Benjamin W., 1386
Yancey, James D., 809
Yanitelli, Victor R., 670
Yankelovich, Daniel, 3271
Yarborough, N. Patricia, 588

Yarnall, D. Robert, Jr., 3699, 3768
Yarnell, Kenneth A., Jr., 492
Yarnell, Sam I., 3835
Yarowsky, Medda, 1420
Yarrington, Blaine J., 968
Yarway Corporation, 3768
Yassenoff, Leo, 3414
Yasutake, Chiyoko, 4241
Yasutake, W.T., 4241
Yates, A.P., 87
Yates, Burnham, 2054
Yates, James D., 3869
Yde, Nancy, 1095
Yeager, Charles G., 3377
Yeager, Kathryn Prothro, 4052, 4053
Yeates, Jean W., 414
Yeckel, Carl, 4003
Yee, Clifford H.N., 899
Yee, Edward B.H., 117
Yehle, E.C., 1688
Yehle, Eugene C., 1780
Yeiser, Eric B., 3220
Yellow Freight System, 2042
Yeo, L.J., 1798
Yeo, Richard W., 4311
Ylvisaker, Paul N., 1482, 2535, 3075
Ylvisaker, William T., 1020
Yochum, Leo W., 3756, 3757
Yoder, Mrs. L.W., 1224
Yoe, Robert, 3
Yoelin, Merritt S., 3487
Yoho, Bill L., 1455
Yontz, Merle R., 1096
York Bank & Trust Company, 3701
York, E.T., Jr., 834
York, John W., 3698
York, Wallace E., 301
Yorkin, Bud, 432
Yorkin, Peg, 432
Yorston, Carolyn, 1923
Yost, Charles W., 654
Yost, Lyle E., 1311
Young, Alan, 2063
Young, Alice H., 2464
Young & Rubicam, 3062
Young, Andrew B., 619, 3614
Young, Arthur G., 3163, 3193, 3202, 3215
Young, Augustus J., 2830
Young, Byrnes M., 1375
Young, Crawford, 2307
Young, Dorothy, 4176
Young, Fern D., 4391
Young, Gertrude, 2307
Young, Irvin L., 4391
Young, J.G., 1252
Young, John, 218
Young, John R., 1625, 2336, 2494, 2496, 2704, 2822
Young, Joseph S., 3748
Young, Kenneth E., 910, 3817
Young, Madeleine K., 2849
Young, Mathilda, 2163
Young, P. Woodrow, 598
Young, Paschall H., 3836
Young, R.A., 1997
Young, R.S., 78
Young, Raymond A., 3473
Young, Richard B., 1466
Young, Robert, 3961
Young, Stuart A., Jr., 2104
Young, Thomas P., Jr., 3811
Young, Verna N., 3473
Young, W.C., 3323
Young, W.C., Jr., 3298
Young, William H., 4372
Younger, Evelle J., 108
Younger, John F., 3866
Younglove, Eileen M., 1179
Youngs, Gerald A., 734
Younkers, Inc., 1290
Yount, W.E., 3457
Younts, Charles R., 4161
Younts, Willie Camp, 4161

Youtsey, Karl J., 1180
Yowell, George L., 4214
Yoxall, James R., 1293
Yulman, Helen, 3064
Yulman, Morton, 3064
Yunich, David L., 2167

Zaback, John, 3158
Zabel, R.L., 1850
Zabelle, Robert, 2626
Zacharia, Isaac H., 3065
Zachos, Kimon S., 2092
Zadok, Charles, 2653
Zaesch, Jacques, 2654
Zafris, James G., Jr., 1657
Zagat, Nina S., 2586
Zagorac, Michael, Jr., 719
Zahn, J. Hillman, 680
Zahnow, Melvin J., 1798
Zale Corporation, 4129
Zale, Donald, 4129
Zale, M.B., 3950
Zale, Marvin, 4129
Zalk, Morton, 1846
Zambetti, Felice, 2628
Zambie, Allan J., 3252
Zane, E.R., 3113
Zant, John, 4033
Zapapas, J. Richard, 1237
Zarkin, Fay, 3066
Zarlengo, Anthony F., 481
Zarlengo, Richard A., 474
Zaroff, Carolyn R., 3030
Zarwell, Elwin J., 4348, 4349
Zatkos, Ann E., 4401
Zayre Corporation, 1661
Zbornik, Frances I., 1282
Zbornik, Jim J., 1282
Zealy, James M., 3082
Zecher, J. Richard, 2337
Zeeh, Lenor, 4372
Zeftel, Leo, 615
Zeidman, Elizabeth G., 3586
Zeimer, C.O., 966
Zell, Herman, 2184
Zell, Jacob, 2184
Zell, Marsha, 2184
Zeller, Julia L., 2568
Zellerbach, Jennie B., 433
Zellerbach, William J., 433
Zelnick, R.W., 3638
Zemurray, Sarah W., 1389
Zenge, Earl, 1102
Zenkel, Bruce, 2183
Zenkel, Lois R., 2183
Zenorini, Henry J., 2318
Zeri, Frederico, 187
Zervigon, Mary K., 1371
Zerwekh, Charles E., Jr., 1602
Zetterberg, Anne, 2273
Zia Company, 4026
Zick, J.W., 2840
Ziegler, Arthur P., Jr., 3512
Ziegler, Bernard C., 4393
Ziegler, Henry S., 2941
Ziegler, R.D., 4393
Ziegler, Mrs. William, 595
Ziegler, William, III, 595
Ziegler, William A., 3047
Ziemann, Lillian, 4394
Ziemer, P.D., 4389
Zier, Ronald E., 2200
Zieselman, Jerold, 2739
Zifkin, Walter, 2641
Zigler, Fred B., 1390
Zigler, Ruth B., 1390
Zigmund, Harold F., 1821
Zilavy, Thomas O., 4334
Zilkha & Sons, 3067
Zilkha, Cecile E., 3067
Zilkha, Ezra K., 3067
Zilkha, Selim K., 3067
Zimet, Erwin, 2416

GEOGRAPHIC INDEX

Foundations in bold face type make grants on a national or regional basis; the others generally limit giving to the city or state in which they are located.

ALABAMA
Alexander City Russell 18
Birmingham Birmingham 3, Daniel 7, Linn-Henley 10, McWane 13, Meyer 14, **Sonat 21,** Stockham 22, Webb 24
Brewton McMillan 12
Daphne **Malbis 11,** Smith 20
Enterprise Gibson 9
Mobile Bedsole 2, Chandler 5, Middleton 15, Mitchell 16, Mobile 17
Montgomery Blount 4, **Christian 6,** Flack 8
Mountain Brook Shook 19
Sylacauga Avondale 1
Tuscaloosa Warner 23

see also 775, 813, 865, 1775

ALASKA
Anchorage Alaska 25, Atwood 26

see also 1853, 4241, 4245, 4252, 4262

ARIZONA
Dragoon **Amerind 27**
Flagstaff Raymond 43, Wilson 50
Paradise Valley Waddell 48
Phoenix Arizona 28, Arizona 29, Circle K 31, Dougherty 32, du Bois 33, First 34, Flinn 35, Hervey 38, **Tell 45, Van Schaik 46,** VNB 47, Webb 49
Prescott Butz 30, **Kieckhefer 39,** Morris 41
Scottsdale Goppert 37
Sierra Vista Fry 36
Tucson Marshall 40, Mulcahy 42, **Research 44**

see also 98, 290, 377, 449, 701, 1104, 1204, 1813, 1989, 2483, 3375, 4357

ARKANSAS
Arkadelphia Ross 59
El Dorado Murphy 54
Fort Smith **Reynolds 56**
Little Rock **Inglewood 51,** Lyon 53, Rebsamen 55, Riggs 57, Rockefeller 58, **Wrape 62**
Malvern Sturgis 60
Pine Bluff Trinity 61
Springdale Jones 52

see also 326, 449, 1369, 1374, 3434, 3439, 3443, 3831, 4305, 4360

CALIFORNIA
Aptos Santa Cruz 342
Arcadia Berger 91
Badger G.A.G. 177
Bakersfield Arkelian 72
Beverly Hills Brotman 107, **City 125, Crummer 140, Eichenbaum 160,** Factor 162, Familian 164, Green 199, **Litton 262,** Lloyd 264, Mayer 277, Mead 284, **Ostrow 305,** Pattiz 315, Schreiber 347, Simon 367, Taper 394
Borrego Springs Burnand 110
Buena Park **Gemco 185**
Burbank Adolph's 64, Disney 148, Disney 149, Disney 150, **Ledler 256, Lockheed 266**
Burlingame Peninsula 318
Carmel Valley Upjohn 408
Claremont Bacon 80
Concord **Hofmann 223**
Corcoran Corcoran 134
Corona del Mar Beckman 89
Covelo Island 233
Covina Galster 181
Daly City Doelger 153, Gellert 184
Downey Pacific 307, Stamps 377
El Segundo Incentive 229
Encino **Kerr 244**
Eureka Humboldt 228
Ferndale Lytel 269
Fresno Corti 135, Peters 320
Fullerton Thagard 396
Glendale Bireley 96, Forest 174
Hawthorne Mattel 275
Hollywood Gospel 197, Muller 291
Indian Wells **Philibosian 323**
Irvine **Fluor 173,** Schmidt 346
La Canada **Atkinson 77**
La Habra Marshburn 273
La Jolla California 116, Copley 133, Gildred 189, Parker 310, Pratt 328, Seuss 355, **Signal 360**
Lafayette Turn 404
Livermore **Hertz 216**
Long Beach Fairfield 163, Norris 299, Van Camp 409
Los Altos Packard 308
Los Altos Hills **Newman 297**
Los Angeles Ahmanson 65, Albertson 67, **Amado 68, Artevel 74,** Associated 75, **Atlantic 78,** Baker 82, Baxter 86, **Bekins 90,** Beynon 94, Bing 95, Borun 97, Boswell 98, Bowles 100, Braun 101, Braun 102, **Breech 103, Brody 106,** Buchalter 108, Burns 111, California 114, **Carnation 119, Carnation 120,** Civitas 126, **Cook 132,** Crocker 138, Day 144, DeMille 146, Deutsch 147, Doheny 154, Domino 155, Early 158, Essick 161, Familian 165, Feitelson 167, First 170, **Friedman 175,** Fusenot 176, **Getty 187, Getty 188,** Gilmore 190, Goldwyn 196, Grancell 198, Haynes 211, **Hilton 220,** Hoag 221, Hoffman 222, **Hollywood 224,** Hoover 226, Jerome 237, Jones 240, **Keck 243,** Kirchgessner 245, Knudsen 246, Leavey 254, **Lebus 255, Leonardt 257, Levy 260, Mahony 271,** Martin 274, May 276, McAlister 280, **Menlo 285, Merry 286, Mitchell 288, Munger 292,** Murphey 294, Murphy 295, Norman 298, **Nosutch 300, Occidental 302, Parsons 311, Parvin 312,** Pauley 316, Pfaffinger 321, **R & R 329,** Richards 332, Roth 335, **Sassoon 343,** Schermer 345, Seaver 350, Security 351, See 352, **Simon 361,** Simon 364, Sprague 376, Stauffer 379, Stauffer 380, Stuart 385, Stuart 386, Stuart 387, Stuart 388, **Teledyne 395,** Thomas 397, Thornton 398, Ticor 399, Times 400, Tyler 405, Union 406, **Union 407,** Van Nuys 411, Wasserman 415, Watson 416, Webb 418, Weingart 421, **Whitelight 424,** Yorkin 432
Menlo Park Distribution 151, **Hewlett 217,** Johnson 239, **Kaiser 242**
Modesto Gallo 178, Gallo 179, Gallo 180
Monterey Monterey 289
Newport Beach Layne 252, **Soiland 374,** Steele 382
North Fork Arakelian 70
North Hollywood Von der Ahe 412
Norwalk **Sinaiko 368, Weinberg 420**
Novato **Fire 168,** Fireman's 169
Oakland Berry 93, Clorox 127, East Bay 159, Hedco 212, Oakland 301, **Skaggs 369**
Orange **Baker 81**
Oxnard Levy 259, Livingston 263
Pacific Palisades Greenville 200, Stern 383
Palm Desert **Phillips 324**
Palm Springs McCallum 282
Palo Alto Charis 123, **Christensen 124,** Hancock 209, **Hewlett-Packard 218, System 393,** Weiler 419
Pasadena Connell 131, Garland 182, **Howe 227,** MacKenzie 270, **Pasadena 313,** Pasadena 314, Peppers 319, Scott 348, Simon 362, **Simon 363,** Simon 365, **Simon 366, Stans 378**
Pebble Beach Coburn 128, Steel 381
Rancho Santa Fe Scripps 349
Redwood Valley Helms 214
Riverside **Caddock 113,** Riverside 333, Stewart 384
Sacramento Arata 71, Setzer 354
San Diego Golden 194, Hahn 205, **Hahn 206,** Joslyn 241, Mosher 290, Powell 327, R. P. 330, San Diego 336, Sefton 353, Timken-Sturgis 401
San Francisco Abelard 63, Bank 83, **BankAmerica 84, Bechtel 87,** Bechtel 88, Bothin 99, Brenner 104, Bridges 105, **Bull 109, Burns-Dunphy 112,** California 115, California 117, Callison 118, **CFS 122,** Columbia 130, Cowell 136, Crocker 137, **Crown 139,** Damien 142, Davies 143, de Guigne

145, Drum 156, Fleishhacker 171, Fleishhacker 172, Gellert 183, Gerbode 186, Gilmore 191, **Gleason 192, Gleason 193,** Goldman 195, Haas 202, Haas 203, Haas 204, Hale 207, Harney 210, Heller 213, Herbst 215, Hills 219, Holt 225, Irvine 230, Irwin 231, **Ishiyama 232, Jewett 238,** Komes 247, Koret 248, **Koulaieff 249,** Lakeside 251, **Levi 258,** Lurie 267, Lux 268, Marini 272, Mayr 278, McBean 281, McKesson 283, **Meyer 287,** Newhall 296, Odell 303, Oxnard 306, **Potlatch 326,** Radin 331, Rosenberg 334, San Francisco 337, Sandy 338, Sanguinetti 339, **Saturno 344, Shalan 356,** Shoong 359, Smith 370, Smith 371, **Smith 372,** Snelling 373, Sorensen 375, Stulsaft 389, **Swig 391, Swig 392,** Trust 402, van Loben Sels 410, Walker 414, Wattis 417, Wells 423, **Whittell 425,** Wilbur 427, Witter 429, **Wollenberg 430,** Zellerbach 433

San Jose Crummey 141, Gross 201, Santa Clara 341
San Leandro **Coleman 129**
San Mateo Orleton 304
San Rafael Babcock 79
Santa Ana **Halsell 208,** Murdy 293
Santa Barbara Battistone 85, **Berkey 92, Doe 152,** Jackson 234, Jefferson 236, **Kroc 250, Page 309,** Santa Barbara 340, Tuohy 403, **Wade 413, Wilbur 428,** Wood-Claeyssens 431
Santa Clara Arrillaga 73, Center 121
Santa Cruz **Sundean 390**
Santa Monica Durfee 157, Lear 253, **Pfeiffer 322,** Pickford 325, Welk 422
Sausalito Faude 166
Sierra Madre Jameson 235
Solvang A.I.D. 66
South Pasadena L.L.W.W. 265, Whittier 426
South San Francisco **Atkinson 76**
Stanford Lewis 261
Sunnyvale **Peery 317**
Torrance **American 69**
Universal City **MCA 279**
Walnut Shea 357, Shea 358

see also 49, 701, 715, 818, 995, 1083, 1103, 1118, 1167, 1660, 1775, 1777, 1813, 1837, 1893, 1923, 2059, 2118, 2251, 2557, 2641, 2691, 2719, 2839, 2974, 3151, 3248, 3291, 3446, 3495, 3612, 3731, 3949, 4146, 4308

COLORADO
Aurora Levy 462
Boulder Carter 439, **Needmor 468,** Pilot 472
Brush Joslin-Needham 459, Petteys 471
Colorado Springs Colorado 440, El Pomar 445, Joslyn 460, **McCoy 464,** Sachs 476
Denver Animal 434, Anschutz 435, Boettcher 436, Buell 437, Coors 441, Denver 442, Duncan 443, 8 South 444, Fairfield 446, First 447, Fishback 448, **Frost 449,** Gates 450, Hill 452, Hogan 453, Hughes 454, Hunter 455, Jenkins 456, **JFM 457,** Johnson 458, Lowe 463, McHugh 465, Mullen 467, Norgren 469, O'Fallon 470, Piton 473, **Ray 475, Schlessman 477,** Silver 479, Sterne-Elder 480, Swan 481, **Taylor 482,** Weckbaugh 484, Wolf 486
Englewood Rabb 474
Fort Collins **Woodward 487**
Fort Morgan Williams 485
Franktown Carroll 438
Greeley Monfort 466
Holyoke Heginbotham 451
Lakewood Schramm 478
Pueblo Thatcher 483
Woodrow **Kejr 461**

see also 233, 308, 407, 822, 2051, 2154, 3439, 4352, 4396

CONNECTICUT
Bridgeport American 493, Bridgeport 502, **Duberg 514,** Jones 544, Jost 546, **Stratfield 580, Warnaco 587**
Bristol Barnes 496, **Barnes 497**
Danbury Barden 495
Fairfield **General 527**
Farmington Heublein 538
Greenwich **Amax 491, American 492,** Casey 504, **Dennett 511, Fairchild 522,** Fry 526, Gimbel 528, **Huisking 541,** List 551, **Mazer 556, Panwy 563, UPS 584, Whitehead 590**
Hartford Aetna 489, **Bissell 500,** Connecticut 507, Ensworth 521, Fox 525, Hartford 532, Hartford 534, Howard 539, **Larrabee 550,** Long 552, Preston 566, Robinson 568, **Society 576, Stanley 578,** Sullivan 581, Widow's 592
Harwinton **Folsom 524**
Manchester **Price 567**
New Britain Moore 558, Stanley 577
New Canaan **Perkin 565**
New Haven **Belgian 498, Childs 506,** Eder 515, **Meserve 557,** New Haven 559, **Sachem 570,** Woman's 593
New London Bodenwein 501, Palmer 562
Newington Savin 571
Newtown Scott 573
Norwalk **Dell 510, Dibner 513,** Vanderbilt 585
Old Lyme **Grubb 530,** MacCurdy-Salisbury 553
Old Saybrook EIS 517
Orange **Albers 490, Hubbell 540**
Pomfret **Topsfield 582**
Simsbury Ensign-Bickford 520
Southport Main 555, **Stone 579,** Wahlstrom-Johnson 586, Wheeler 589
Stamford **Abex 488,** Bennett 499, **Carter 503, Champion 505, Conway 508,** Day 509, **Great 529,** GTE 531, **Hartman 535, Herzog 537, ITT 542, Kayser-Roth 547,** Maguire 554, **Olin 561,** Patterson 564, **Rosenthal 569, Singer 575, UMC 583, Xerox 594, Ziegler 595**
Trumbull Heritage 536
Washington **Whitney 591**
Waterbury **Kazanjian 548, Scovill 574,** Waterbury 588
West Hartford Auerbach 494, Fisher 523, Hartford 533, J.J.C. 543, Joseloff 545, Koopman 549, Schiro 572
Weston **Oaklawn 560**
Westport **Educational 516, Eno 519**
Wilton Emery 518
Windsor Locks **Dexter 512**

see also 573, 605, 660, 1441, 1585, 1639, 1827, 2225, 2272, 2275, 2389, 2452, 2531, 2656, 2692, 2695, 2748, 2754, 2767, 2807, 2863, 2872, 2908, 4305

DELAWARE
Claymont Lovett 619
Dover **Birch 597, Israel 611,** Marshall 622
Greenville Carpenter 599, **Glencoe 609**
Milford **Vale 631**
Wilmington **Beneficial 596,** Bishop 598, Chichester 600, Cohen 601, Cohen 602, Common 603, Copeland 604, Crestlea 605, Crystal 606, Ederic 607, **Gerard 608, Good 610, Kent 612,** Kent-Lucas 613, **Kingsley 614, Kutz 615,** Laffey-McHugh 616, **Lalor 617,** Longwood 618, Lynch 620, Marmot 621, **Milliken 623,** National 624, **Penzance 625, Presto 626, Raskob 627, Raskob 628,** Red Clay 629, **Schwartz 630,** Welfare 632, Woodstock 633

see also 716, 2251, 3720

DISTRICT OF COLUMBIA
Washington **Alvord 634,** Appleby 635, Appleby 636, April 637, **Arca 638, Bender 639, Benton 640,** Bloedorn 641, Brownley 642, Cafritz 643, **Carnegie 644,** Cohen-Solomon 645, **Council 646, Delmar 647,** Dimick 648, **Discount 649, Dweck 650,** Federal 651, Felburn 652, Folger 653, **Foundation 654,** Fowler 655, **Freed 656, GEICO 657,** Gelman 658, **German 659, Graham 660,** Gudelsky 661, Higginson 662, Himmelfarb 663, Hyman 664, Johnston 665, **Kennedy 666,** Kiplinger 667, Lehrman 668, Loughran 669, **Loyola 670,** McGregor 671, Meyer 672, Miller 673, **National 674, Patterson 675, Police 677, Post 678, Public 679,** Ross 680, Sapelo 681, Stewart 682, Strong 683, **Villers 684,** Washington 685, **Weir 686, Westport 687, Wouk 688**

see also 1407, 1411, 1417, 1418, 1434, 1437, 1448, 1459, 2016, 2332, 2431, 2584, 2812, 3949, 4176

FLORIDA
Arcadia Morgan 749
Bal Harbour **Ford 722**
Bartow **Stuart 777**
Bay Harbor Islands Broad 699
Boca Raton **Echlin 718,** Lynn 744, Ritter 761
Bradenton **Aurora 692, Bible 696, Eagles 717, Nuveen 752**
Clearwater **Eckerd 719, Hayward 727,** Pinellas 756
Clewiston United 787
Coral Gables Rainforth 759, Rosenberg 763, **Ware 789**
Deerfield Beach **Brunner 700**
Delray Beach **Staley 772**
Destin Stickelber 775
Fort Lauderdale **Bastien 694, Dettman 712,** Gore 723, Law 738, Soref 769, **Wells 790, Wray 799**
Fort Myers Southwest 771
Fort Pierce **Link 742,** Sample 764
Gainesville **Koch 734**
Jacksonville Childress 703, **Davis 707, Davis 708, Davis 709,** du Pont 713, **duPont 716,** Jacksonville 730, Jacksonville 731, River 762, Stevens 774, Swisher 780, Williams 793, **Winn-Dixie 794,** Wolfson 797, **Wolfson 798**
Key Biscayne Wilder 792
Lake Wales American 689
Lakeland Jenkins 732
Lighthouse Point Howell 729
Long Boat Key Mote 751
Melbourne **Harris 726**
Miami Arison 691, Blank 697, Dade 706, Dunspaugh-Dalton 715, Larsh 737, **Markey 745, Morris 750,** Southeast 770, **Storer 776,** Taylor 783, Wiseheart 796
Miami Beach **Applebaum 690, Greenburg 724,** Greene 725, Meyer 748, **Sharonsteel 768,** Yablick 800
Naples Briggs 698, **Swensrud 779**
New Smyrna Beach **Landegger 736**
North Fort Myers Price 758
North Palm Beach **Delacorte 711**
Orlando Leu 740, Phillips 753, Phillips 754, Sylvester 781
Oviedo **Duda 714**
Palm Beach Chastain 702, **Hollingsworth 728,** Johnson 733, **Kohl 735,** Leidesdorf 739, Lowe 743, **Shapiro 767, Toor 786, Whitehall 791**
Pensacola Fellows 721
Plantation Deicke 710
Riviera Beach **Lewis 741**
Sarasota Beattie 695, Selby 766, **Stark 773, Sudakoff 778**
Seminole Thoresen 785
St. Petersburg **McMannis 747, Poynter 757**
Surfside Baker 693
Tallahassee Phipps 755
Tamarac **Crane 705**

GEORGIA

HAWAII

IDAHO

ILLINOIS

INDIANA

IOWA

MICHIGAN

Alpena Besser 1672, Besser 1673
Ann Arbor Ann Arbor 1664, **Earhart 1691,** Kennedy 1733, Towsley 1783
Battle Creek Battle Creek 1669, Kellogg 1731, **Kellogg 1732,** Miller 1749, Winship 1802
Bay City Kantzler 1729
Benton Harbor Michigan 1747, **Whirlpool 1793**
Birmingham Americana 1663, Lyon 1739, **Mardigian 1742,** Prentis 1759, **Slaughter 1774,** Vollbrecht 1790
Bloomfield Hills White 1794, Wilson 1799
Dearborn **Ford 1702**
Detroit Avery 1665, **Bundy 1677, Chrysler 1679,** DeRoy 1682, DeRoy 1683, Detroit 1684, Faigle 1695, **Federal-Mogul 1696, Ford 1699,** Ford 1700, Ford 1701, Ford 1703, **Ford 1704, Fruehauf 1706,** Fruehauf 1707, **Garb 1708, General 1709, General 1710,** Herrick 1718, Holden 1720, Honigman 1721, Hudson-Webber 1722, **Levy 1737,** Masco 1743, McGregor 1744, McIntyre 1745, McIntyre 1746, National 1755, Pagel 1756, Ratner 1762, Sage 1764, Shapero 1769, Shelden 1770, Shiffman 1771, Skillman 1773, Stroh 1779, Tracy 1784, Tuck 1785, Wilson 1800, Winkelman 1801
East Detroit Chamberlin 1678, **Harder 1716**
Flint Bishop 1674, Bray 1676, DeWaters 1687, Flint 1698, **Mott 1752, Mott 1753,** Whiting 1796
Fremont Fremont 1705, **Gerber 1711**
Grand Rapids Baldwin 1666, Cook 1680, **DeVos 1686, Gordon 1714,** Grand 1715, Loutit 1738, Mallery 1740, Sebastian 1766, Seidman 1767, Steelcase 1775, VanAndel 1788, **Wolverine 1803**
Grosse Ile Student 1781
Grosse Pointe Farms Earl-Beth 1692
Grosse Pointe Woods Stephenson 1776, Stewart 1777
Harper Woods Fink 1697
Holland Prince 1760
Jackson **Aeroquip 1662,** Hurst 1724, Jackson 1726, Simpson 1772
Kalamazoo Dalton 1681, Gilmore 1713, Kalamazoo 1728, Upjohn 1786, **Upjohn 1787,** Vicksburg 1789
Lansing Lansing 1735, Ransom 1761, Whiteley 1795
Marquette Kaufman 1730
Midland Barstow 1668, **Dow 1688,** Dow 1689, Dow 1690, Gerstacker 1712, Midland 1748, **Pardee 1757,** Royal 1763, Strosacker 1780, Whiting 1797
Monroe La-Z-Boy 1736
Muskegon Muskegon 1754, **Walker 1791**
Niles Hunter 1723, Plym 1758
Owosso Bentley 1671
Petoskey Youth 1804
Pontiac **Wenger 1792**
Royal Oak DeVlieg 1685
Saginaw Boutell 1675, Eddy 1693, Jeffers 1727, Mills 1750, Morley 1751, Wickes 1798
Southfield **Bargman 1667,** Himmel 1719, Imerman 1725
St. Clair Shores **Seymour 1768**
St. Joseph Tiscornia 1782
Taylor **Manoogian 1741**
Troy Bauervic 1670, **Ex-cell-o 1694, Herman 1717, Kresge 1734,** Stollman 1778
Utica Scott 1765

see also 253, 660, 840, 926, 1181, 1660, 1923, 2989, 3144, 3152, 3187, 3227, 4305, 4324, 4389

MINNESOTA

Austin Hormel 1862, **Kasal 1871**
Bayport **Andersen 1809,** Andersen 1810, Bayport 1815, Hulings 1865
Duluth Alworth 1806, Eddy 1839, J.N.M. 1869, Ordean 1899, **Paulucci 1902,** Whiteside 1927
Eden Prairie Gelco 1846
Grand Rapids Blandin 1821
Inver Grove Heights **Cenex 1828**
Mahtomedi O'Brien 1896
Mankato **Andreas 1811**
Minneapolis Apache 1812, Athwin 1813, Baker 1814, Beim 1816, Bell 1817, **Bemis 1818,** Bend 1819, Cargill 1825, Carlson 1826, Carolyn 1827, Chadwick 1829, Charity 1830, Cowles 1832, **Dayton 1834, Donaldson 1836,** Dye 1838, Fingerhut 1841, First 1842, First 1843, **Fiterman 1844,** Gamble 1845, **General 1847,** Graco 1849, Greystone 1851, Groves 1854, Heilicher 1859, Honeywell 1861, Hubbard 1864, International 1866, Inter-Regional 1867, Jostens 1870, Larson 1874, Lieberman-Okinow 1875, **Lutheran 1877,** Marbrook 1878, McKnight 1880, McKnight 1881, Meadowood 1883, **Medtronic 1884, Melamed 1885, Miller 1886,** Minneapolis 1887, Minneapolis 1888, Neilson 1891, North 1892, **Norwest 1895,** Onan 1897, Phillips 1903, **Pillsbury 1905,** Quinlan 1906, Rauenhorst 1907, Southways 1913, Tennant 1915, Thorpe 1916, Valspar 1918, Walker 1920, Wasie 1922, Wood-Rill 1929
Red Wing Red Wing 1908
Rochester Rochester 1910
St. Joseph Van Evera 1919
St. Paul Alliss 1805, **American 1807,** Andersen 1808, Bigelow 1820, Bremer 1822, Bush 1823, Butler 1824, Circle 1831, **Davis 1833, DeLuxe 1835,** Driscoll 1837, Edwards 1840, **General 1848, Grain 1850,** Griggs 1852, Grotto 1853, Hamm 1855, Hartzell 1857, Hersey 1860, Hotchkiss 1863, Jerome 1868, Kennedy 1872, Lang 1873, Lilly 1876, Mardag 1879, McNeely 1882, Minnesota 1889, **Minnesota 1890,** Northern 1893, **Northwest 1894,** O'Neil 1898, **O'Shaughnessy 1900,** Paper 1901, **Phipps 1904,** Rodman 1911, Saint Paul 1912, Warner 1921, **Weyand 1923,** Weyerhaeuser 1924, **Weyerhaeuser 1925,** Weyerhaeuser 1926, Wilder 1928
Stillwater Rivers 1909, Tozer 1917
Thief River Falls Hartz 1856
Wayzata **Sweatt 1914**
White Bear Lake Hawthorne 1858

see also 326, 3139

MISSISSIPPI

Jackson Community 1932, Deposit 1934, Feild 1935, First 1936, **Irby 1938,** Walker 1939
Laurel Chisholm 1931
Meridian Hardin 1937
Pascagoula Bacot 1930
Yazoo City Day 1933

see also 865, 3854, 3868

MISSOURI

Carthage Steadley 2022
Centralia **Chance 1949**
Chesterfield Sachs 2013
Clayton Fischer-Bauer-Knirps 1962, Garvey 1964, Love 1985, **Olin 2001,** Sycamore 2030
Columbia Boone 1943, MFA 1997
Dutzow **Voelkerding 2036**
Joplin Craig 1953
Kansas City Block 1941, **Butler 1946,** Calkins 1947, Commerce 1951, Cowden 1952, **Cross 1954,** Enright 1960, Feld 1961, Flarsheim 1963, Hall 1968, Ingram 1971, Kemper 1974, Kemper 1975, Kemper 1976, LaRue 1978, Long 1980, Loose 1981, Loose 1982, Loose 1983, Lowenstein 1986, McGee 1995, Nichols 2000, Oppenstein 2003, Parrott 2005, Pendergast-Weyer 2006, Reynolds 2011, **Smith 2015,** Speas 2017, Speas 2018, Sunderland 2025, Swinney 2029, **Tension 2031,** Yellow 2042
Mexico Green 1967
Moberly Orscheln 2004
Saint Louis **Emerson 1959**

Sedalia Ilgenfritz 1970
St. Ann **Vatterott 2035**
St. Joseph Townsend 2033
St. Louis **Anheuser-Busch 1940,** Boatmen's 1942, Brown 1944, Brown 1945, Centerre 1948, Chromalloy 1950, **Danforth 1955, Deer 1956,** Edison 1957, Edison 1958, Gaylord 1965, Gaylord 1966, H.B.S. 1969, Interco 1972, Jordan 1973, Laclede 1977, Leader 1979, **Lopata 1984, Mallinckrodt 1987, Mallinckrodt 1988,** Mathews 1989, May 1990, **May 1991,** McDavid 1992, **McDonnell 1993, McDonnell 1994,** Mercantile 1996, Millstone 1998, **Monsanto 1999,** Olin 2002, Pillsbury 2007, Pitzman 2008, Pott 2009, **Ralston 2010,** Roblee 2012, Shoenberg 2014, Souers 2016, Springmeier 2019, St. Louis 2020, St. Louis 2021, Stupp 2023, Stupp 2024, Sunmark 2026, **Sunnen 2027, Swift 2028,** Tilles 2032, Union 2034, **Webb 2037,** Westlake 2038, Whitaker 2039, Wolff 2040, **Woods 2041**

see also 37, 1299, 1411, 1980, 2217, 2414, 3439, 3443, 3465

MONTANA

Billings Bair 2043, Fortin 2044, **Sample 2047**
Bozeman Haynes 2045
Chinook Sweet 2048
Great Falls Heisey 2046

see also 482, 1828, 1842, 1850, 4252, 4395

NEBRASKA

Atkinson Weller 2075
Chappell Buckley 2051
Grand Island Reynolds 2069
Holdrege Phelps 2067
Lincoln Abel 2049, Cooper 2054, Lincoln 2062, Lincoln 2063, Rogers 2070
Nebraska City Steinhart 2071
Omaha Blumkin 2050, **Buffett 2052,** ConAgra 2053, Criss 2055, Frohm 2056, Hitchcock 2057, **InterNorth 2058,** Kiewit 2059, **Kiewit 2060,** Lane 2061, Livingston 2064, Omaha 2065, Omaha 2066, Storz 2072, Swanson 2073
Scottsbluff Quivey 2068
Valley Valmont 2074

see also 1098, 1193, 2025, 4276

NEVADA

Incline Village **Sells 2081**
Las Vegas **Bing 2076,** Golden 2079
Reno Bing 2077, ELW 2078, Hawkins 2080

see also 49, 239, 276, 401

NEW HAMPSHIRE

Concord Bean 2083, Jameson 2089, New Hampshire 2092
Hanover **Institute 2088**
Keene Kingsbury 2090, Putnam 2094
Lyme **Phillips 2093**
Manchester Cogswell 2084, Hunt 2087, Lord 2091, Smyth 2095, Wagner 2097
Nashua Barker 2082
Salem **Standex 2096**
Walpole **Hubbard 2086**

Wolfeboro **Freygang 2085**

see also 1532, 1576

NEW JERSEY

Andover **Caspersen 2111**
Avenel **Mamiye 2151**
Bay Head Orange 2164
Bernardsville Jockey 2138
Bridgewater **National 2160**
Butler **International 2135**
Camden Campbell 2107
Cedar Grove **Penick 2165**
Chatham Township Hyde 2134
Clifton Berger 2103, Schultz 2179, Schultz 2180
Convent Station Lindberg 2149
Cranbury Hoyt 2132
Dayton Cape 2108
E. Hanover **Sandoz 2174**
East Hanover **Nabisco 2159**
East Orange **Edison 2119**, Fund 2125, **Taub 2190,** Turrell 2193
Edison **Hackett 2129**, Schenck 2177, Visceglia-Summit 2198
Englewood **CPC 2113**
Englewood Cliffs Ix 2136, **Lipton 2150**
Far Hills **Engelhard 2121,** Frelinghuysen 2123
Flemington Large 2145
Fords Borden 2104
Fort Lee **Frisch 2124**
Franklin Lakes **Roth 2173**
Gladstone Brady 2105
Hackensack Perkins 2166
Harrison **Stern 2186**
Hoboken **Vollmer 2199**
Jersey City **Mueller 2158**
Lebanon Harris 2130
Linden **Psychists 2168**
Livingston **C.I.T. 2112**, Grupe 2128, Taub 2189
Madison **Rippel 2171, Schering-Plough 2178**
Margate **Simon 2184**
Montclair **Schumann 2181,** Victoria 2197
Montvale **Kennedy 2141**
Morris Plains **Warner-Lambert 2200**
Morristown **Allied 2098, Bergen 2102, Crum 2114,** Dodge 2116, **Kirby 2143,** Rosenhaus 2172, **Sullivan 2188**
Mount Holly Belasco 2101
Murray Hill Willits 2204, Youths' 2205
New Brunswick **Johnson 2139**
Newark Elizabeth 2120, Fidelity 2122, Geist 2126, Ohl 2163, Prudential 2167, Upton 2196, **Wetterberg 2202**
North Haledon Schamach 2176
North Plainfield Levin 2147
Nutley **Hoffmann-La Roche 2131**
Orange New Jersey 2161
Paramus **Martin 2152**
Paterson **Armour 2099**
Pennsauken **Subaru 2187**
Piscataway **Terner 2191**
Plainfield McCutchen 2153, **Quaker 2169**
Princeton Atlantic 2100, Bunbury 2106, **Carnegie 2109, Dow 2117, Johnson 2140,** L'Hommedieu 2148, McGraw 2154, **Newcombe 2162**
Rahway **Merck 2155**
Raritan Thomas 2192
Roseland Lautenberg 2146
Rumson **Huber 2133**
Secaucus **Carroll 2110**, Schwartz 2183
Somerville Duke 2118, **South 2185**
South Amboy **Komar 2144**
South Plainfield **Messing 2156**
Stone Harbor Diller 2115
Summit **Jeffery 2137, Reeves 2170,** Sawtelle 2175
Trenton Kerney 2142
Union **Wilf 2203**
Warren Schwartz 2182
Watchung Grassmann 2127, Union 2195
Wayne **Union 2194**

West Orange Meyer 2157
Westfield Westfield 2201

see also 743, 1441, 2079, 2389, 2399, 2720, 2846, 2850, 2855, 2872, 2952, 2973, 2989, 3041

NEW MEXICO

Albuquerque **Bellamah 2206, Picker 2211,** Sizemore 2212
Carlsbad Carlsbad 2208
Hobbs Maddox 2209
Santa Fe **Bynner 2207, Phillips 2210**
Taos Wurlitzer 2213

see also 35, 306, 407, 449, 3434, 3439, 3443, 3980

NEW YORK

Albany Albany's 2226, McDonald 2717, Norstar 2789, Reynolds 2860, Wikstrom 3045
Amsterdam Wasserman 3025
Ardsley-on-Hudson St. Faith's 2950
Auburn Emerson 2421, Everett 2425, French 2451, Metcalf 2731
Ballston Lake **Jehovah 2579**
Bayside Vogler 3016
Bedford **Dorr 2408**
Binghamton Hoyt 2565, Klee 2616
Bridgehampton Warner 3022
Brockport **Ross 2891**
Bronx **Kresevich 2628, Wilson 3047**
Bronxville McGraw 2720, **Ryan 2901**
Brooklyn Brooklyn 2306, **Brooklyn 2307,** Davidson-Krueger 2383, Faith 2427, **House 2563,** Parshelsky 2813, **Ritter 2869,** Vinmont 3015, Wunsch 3061
Buffalo Baird 2260, Buffalo 2311, **Burchfield 2314,** Children's 2343, Cornell 2367, Cummings 2376, Dent 2396, Goodyear 2488, **Hackett 2522,** Hahn 2525, Julia 2593, Knox 2622, **LeBrun 2648,** Palisano 2809, Rich 2862, **Statler 2955,** Wendt 3036, Western 3039
Callicoon Kautz 2606
Canajoharie Arkell 2243
Carle Place Furst 2461
Carmel Weinstein 3034
Corning **Corning 2368,** Houghton 2562
Cortland **McDonald 2718**
Eden Baird 2258
Elizabethtown Crary 2373
Ellenville **Resnick 2856**
Elmira Anderson 2239, Anderson 2240
Garden City Trump 2992, Zimtbaum 3069
Glen Cove **Li 2664**
Glen Head **Schaefer 2910**
Glens Falls Glens 2476
Great Neck Gruber 2509, Gurwin 2518, Ushkow 3004, **Waldbaum 3017**
Greene Raymond 2849
Greenvale **Levitt 2660**
Hartsdale Gaisman 2462
Hobart O'Connor 2795
Hudson **Potts 2836**
Jamestown Carnahan-Jackson 2324, Chautauqua 2339, Gebbie 2465
Johnstown **Knox 2621**
Larchmont **Bezalel 2283,** Bulova 2312
Lawrence **Doft 2403**
Little Neck Leviton 2659
Long Island City **Fife 2433, Mathis-Pfohl 2705,** Noguchi 2786
Mamaroneck Nias 2781, Straus 2966
Manhasset **Glenn 2475**
Mill Neck **Smithers 2941**
Millbrook Millbrook 2738
Mineola LILCO 2666
Monroe Wohlgemuth 3054
Mountainville Ogden 2797

New Rochelle **Daniel 2380,** La Sala 2634, **Lubin 2681**
New York Abrams 2214, Abrons 2215, Abrons 2216, **ACF 2217,** Achelis 2218, Adams 2219, **Ades 2220,** Adler 2222, **Aeroflex 2223, AKC 2225,** Alexander 2227, Allen 2228, **Allen 2229, Allied 2230,** Altman 2232, Altschul 2233, **American 2234, American 2235,** American 2236, **American-Standard 2237, AMETEK 2238,** Appleman 2241, **Archbold 2242,** Aron 2244, **ARW 2245, ASARCO 2246,** Associated 2247, Astor 2248, **AT&T 2249, Atran 2250, Avon 2251, Axe-Houghton 2252, Bache 2253,** Bache 2254, Bachmann 2255, Badgeley 2256, **Baier 2257, Baird 2259,** Baird 2261, Baker 2262, Banbury 2263, Barker 2264, Barker 2265, **Barrington 2266, Barth 2267,** Bat Hanadiv 2268, **Bay 2270,** Bayne 2271, **Bedminster 2273, Beefeater 2274,** Beir 2276, Belfer 2277, **Bendheim 2278, Bennett 2279,** Berlin 2280, **Berlinger 2281,** Bernhill 2282, **Biddle 2284,** Bieber 2285, **Bingham's 2286, Blackmer 2287,** Bleibtreu 2288, Bliss 2289, Bloomingdale 2290, Blum 2291, **Blythmour 2292, Bobst 2293,** Bodman 2294, Boehm 2295, **Booth 2296,** Botwinick-Wolfensohn 2298, Bowne 2299, Brand 2300, **Brencanda 2301, Bristol-Myers 2302,** Bronfman 2303, Bronfman 2304, Brookdale 2305, **Brooks 2308,** Bruner 2309, **Brunner 2310,** Bulova 2313, **Burden 2315, Burnham 2316,** Burns 2317, **Butler 2318, Bydale 2319,** Calder 2320, Campe 2321, **Capital 2322, Caritas 2323, Carnegie 2325,** Carter 2326, Cary 2327, **Cattell 2328, CBS 2329,** Centennial 2330, Chadwick 2332, **Chait 2333,** Chanin 2334, **Charina 2335,** Charlpeg 2336, **Chase 2337, Chatlos 2338, Cheatham 2340, Chernow 2341,** Chernow 2342, **China 2344, Cintas 2345, Clark 2346,** Clark 2347, Clark 2348, Clark 2349, Cobble 2350, Cohen 2351, **Cohen 2352,** Cohen 2353, Cohn 2355, Coleman 2356, **Coleman 2357, Coles 2358, Collins 2359, Colt 2360,** Colt 2361, **Commonwealth 2362, Compton 2363,** Constans-Culver 2364, **Continental 2365, Continental 2366,** Cowles 2369, **Craigmyle 2370,** Crane 2371, Cranshaw 2372, **Culpeper 2374,** Cummings 2375, **Dammann 2378, Dana 2379,** Darrah 2381, **Davis 2384,** Davis 2385, Davis 2386, **de Hirsch 2387,** De Jur 2388, de Kay 2389, **de Rothschild 2390, de Rothschild 2391, DeCamp 2392, Delany 2393, Delmas 2394, Deloitte 2395, Dewey 2398,** Dillon 2399, **Dillon 2400,** Dobson 2401, **Doherty 2404, Donner 2405,** Donovan 2406, **Dorot 2407,** Doubleday 2409, **Dow 2410, Dreyfus 2411, Dreyfus 2412,** Dreyfus 2413, Dula 2414, **Dun 2415,** Dyson 2417, Elsmere 2420, Erpf 2422, **Ettinger 2423,** Evans 2424, **Exxon 2426, Falk 2428,** Faulkner 2429, **Ferkauf 2430,** FFHS & J 2431, **Field 2432, Fink 2434, First 2435, Fischel 2437,** Fish 2438, **Flemm 2439, Forbes 2440, Forbes 2441,** Forchheimer 2442, **Ford 2443, Ford 2444, Foundation 2445, Foundation 2446,** Foundation 2447, Frank 2448, Frankel 2449, **Frasch 2450,** Frese 2452, Fribourg 2453, Frohlich 2454, **Frueauff 2455, Fuchsberg 2456, Fuchsberg 2457, Fuld 2458, Fullerton 2459,** Fund 2460, **Gelb 2466, Gibbs 2468,** Gilman 2470, **Gimbel-Saks 2471,** Ginsberg 2472, **Gloeckner 2478, Golden 2479, Golden 2480,** Goldman 2481, Goldman 2482, Goldsmith 2483, Goodman 2485, Goodman 2486, Goodstein 2487, **Gordon 2489,** Gottesman 2491, **Gottlieb 2492,** Gould 2493, **Gould 2494, Grace 2496,** Gramercy 2497, Grant 2498, **Grant 2499,** Green 2500, Greenberg 2501, Greene 2502, **Greene 2503,** Greenebaum 2504, Greenwall 2505, **Greve 2506, Griffis 2507,** Grossinger 2508, **Grumbacher 2510, Gruss 2511, Guggenheim 2512, Guggenheim 2513, Guggenheim 2514,** Guinzburg 2515, **Gulf 2516,** Gutfreund 2519, **Gutman 2520, Guttman 2521,** Hagedorn 2523, Haggin 2524, Harding 2526, Harriman 2527, **Hartford 2528, Hasenfeld 2529,** Hastings 2530, Hatch 2531, **Hausman 2532,** Havens 2533, Hayden 2534, **Hazen 2535,** Hazen 2536, **Hearst 2537, Hearst 2538,** Hebrew 2539,

Heckscher 2540, **Heineman 2541,** Heller 2542, **Helmsley 2543, HEM 2544, Hess 2546, Hettinger 2547, Hickrill 2548, Hidary 2549,** High 2550, Hillman 2551, Hirschl 2552, Hochschild 2553, Hochschild 2554, **Hochstein 2555,** Holmes 2557, Holtzmann 2558, Homan 2559, **Homeland 2560,** Hopkins 2561, Howard 2564, **Hughes 2566, Hunter 2567,** Hutchins 2568, **Hutton 2569,** Hycliff 2570, **IFF 2571, Indian 2572, International 2574,** Irving 2575, **Ittleson 2576, Jackson 2577, JDR 2578, Jephson 2580, Jephson 2581, Jesselson 2582,** Jewish 2583, **J.M. 2584, Jockey 2585,** Johnson 2586, **Johnson 2587, Johnson 2588, Johnson 2589, Johnson 2590, Joselow 2592,** Jurodin 2594, **Jurzykowski 2595, Kade 2596, Kade 2597,** Kaplan 2598, **Kaplun 2599,** Karagheusian 2600, Karpas 2601, **Kassin 2602, Katzenberger 2603, Kaufman 2604,** Kaufmann 2605, **Keck 2607, Kempner 2608, Kenan 2609, Kevorkian 2611, Kidder 2612, Killough 2613,** Kimmelman 2614, Klau 2615, Klein 2617, **Klingenstein 2618,** Klosk 2619, **Knapp 2620,** Kopf 2623, **Kopf 2624,** Kraft 2625, Kramer 2626, Kramer 2627, **Kress 2629,** Krim 2630, Kriser 2631, **Kunstadter 2632,** L and L 2633, **Lakeview 2635,** Lang 2636, Langeloth 2637, Larsen 2638, **Lasdon 2639, Lasker 2640,** Lastfogel 2641, Lauder 2642, **Lavanburg 2643,** Lavanburg-Corner 2644, L.A.W. 2645, Lazar 2646, **Lebensfeld 2647,** Lee 2649, **Leff 2650, Lehman 2652,** Lehman 2653, **Leir 2654,** Lemberg 2655, **Leonhardt 2656,** Lever 2657, Levinson 2658, **Levy 2661, Levy 2662,** Lewis 2663, **Liebowitz 2665,** Lincoln 2667, **Lindemann 2668,** Linder 2669, **Lingnan 2671, Link 2672, Lipchitz 2673,** Lippman 2674, **Littauer 2675, Loeb 2676, Loews 2677,** Lopin 2678, **Lounsbery 2679,** Lowenstein 2680, **Luce 2682, Lurcy 2684,** MacDonald 2686, **MacKall 2687,** Macmillan 2688, **Macy 2689, Mad 2690,** Magowan 2691, Maguire 2692, **Mailman 2694,** Mandeville 2695, **Manealoff 2696, Manning 2697, Manufacturers 2698,** Marcus 2699, **Markle 2700, Martinson 2701, Mastronardi 2702, Mathers 2704,** Matthews 2706, Matz 2707, **Matz 2708, Mazer 2709, Mazer 2710, McCaddin-McQuirk 2711, McCarthy 2714,** McConnell 2715, **McCrory 2716,** McGonagle 2719, **McGraw-Hill 2721, Mellon 2722,** Melohn 2723, **Memton 2724, Menschel 2725, Merck 2726, Merrill 2727, Merrill 2728,** Mertz 2729, **Mertz-Gilmore 2730,** Metropolitan 2732, Metzger-Price 2733, **Meyer 2734, Michel 2735,** Milbank 2736, **Milbank 2737, Miller 2739, Milliken 2740, Minerals 2741,** Mitrani 2742, **Mobil 2743, Mocquereau 2744, Model 2745, Monell 2746, Monterey 2747,** Moore 2748, **Morania 2749,** Morgan 2750, Morgan 2751, Morris 2754, Morton 2755, **Mosbacher 2756, Mosbacher 2757,** Moses 2758, **Mosler 2759,** Mossman 2760, **Mostazafan 2761, Mostyn 2762, Mott 2763,** Muehlstein 2764, Musica 2765, **Muskiwinni 2766,** Napier 2767, **Nathanson-Abrams 2768, National 2769,** Nelco 2770, Neu 2771, **Neuberger 2772, New World 2773,** New York 2774, New York 2775, **New York 2776,** New York 2777, **Newhouse 2778, New-Land 2779,** Newman 2780, Nichols 2782, **NL 2783, Noble 2784,** Noble 2785, **Norman 2787, Normandie 2788, Northeastern 2790, Norwood 2791, Noyes 2792,** N've Shalom 2793, O.C.F. 2794, **Oestreicher 2796, Olin 2798, Olin 2799, Olive 2800,** O'Neil 2801, Oppenheimer 2802, Osborn 2803, **Osceola 2804, O'Toole 2805, Ottinger 2806,** Overbrook 2807, Paley 2808, **Palmer 2810, Parapsychology 2811,** Park 2812, **Paul 2814, PBP 2815,** Pearlman 2816, **Peat 2817,** Peierls 2818, **Penney 2819, Perkins 2821, Pettus-Crowe 2822, Pfizer 2823, Pforzheimer 2824, Phelps 2825, Philippe 2826, Phillips 2827, Phillips-Van Heusen 2828,** Pinewood 2829, Pinkerton 2830, **Pioneer 2831,** Pisces 2832, Plant 2833, Pope 2835, **Pren-Hall 2838,** Price 2839, **Price 2840, Propp 2841, Prospect 2842, R and D 2843, Raisler 2844,** Raisler 2845, Ramapo 2846, **Raskin 2847,** Read 2850, **Reed 2852, Reicher**

2853, **Reimann 2854,** Reiss 2855, **Revlon 2857, Revson 2858, Reynolds 2859, Rice 2861,** Richardson 2863, **Richmond 2864, Ridgefield 2865, Ridley 2866, Ritter 2867,** Ritter 2868, Robert 2870, Roche 2872, **Rockefeller 2875, Rockefeller 2876, Rockefeller 2877,** Rohatyn 2878, **Romerovski 2879,** Romill 2880, **Roothbert 2881,** Rose 2882, **Rosen 2883, Rosenberg 2884, Rosenblatt 2885,** Rosenstiel 2886, **Rosenthal 2887, Rosenthal 2888,** Rosenwald 2889, Ross 2890, **Rothschild 2892, Ruben 2893, Rubenstein 2894, Rubin 2895,** Rubinstein 2896, Rudin 2897, Rudin 2898, Rudin 2899, **Russ 2900, Sage 2902, Saks 2903,** Salomon 2904, Samuels 2905, Santa Maria 2906, Sarne 2907, Sasco 2908, **Sayour 2909, Schalkenbach 2911, Schepp 2912, Scherman 2913,** Scheuer 2914, Schieffelin 2915, Schiff 2916, **Schimmel 2917, Schimper 2918, Schlumberger 2919,** Schwartz 2920, **Schwarz 2921,** Schweckendieck 2922, **Schweitzer 2923, SCM 2924,** Sharp 2926, Shatford 2927, Sheafer 2928, **Shiah 2929, Shubert 2930, Silberman 2931, Silbermann 2932,** Simon 2933, **Sinsheimer 2935,** Slade 2936, **Slifka 2937, Sloan 2938, Smart 2939, Smith 2940,** Snyder 2944, **Sony 2945,** Soros 2946, **Sperry 2947,** Spingold 2948, Sprague 2949, **Standard 2951,** Stanley-Timolat 2952, **Starr 2953, Starr 2954, Steele-Reese 2957,** Steinbach 2959, **Stern 2960,** Stern 2961, **Stevens 2962,** Stony 2963, Stott 2964, **Stuart 2967, Sullivan 2968,** Sulzberger 2969, **Summerfield 2970,** Sun 2971, **Surdna 2972,** Sussman 2973, Swanson 2974, Switzer 2975, Taconic 2976, **Tananbaum 2977, Teagle 2979,** Tebil 2980, **Thompson 2982,** Thorne 2983, **Thorne 2984, Tiffany 2985, Tinker 2986, Tisch 2987,** Titan 2988, Todd 2989, **Towbin 2990,** Tuch 2993, **Tudor 2994, Twentieth 2995,** Ungar 2996, **Union 2997, United 2998,** United 2999, United 3000, **United 3001, Unterberg 3002,** Uris 3003, van Ameringen 3006, van Ameringen 3007, van Ameringen 3008, **Vanneck-Bailey 3009, Vetlesen 3011,** Vidda 3012, Vidor 3013, **Walker 3018, Wallace 3019,** Wallach 3021, Warner 3023, Wasserman 3026, **Weatherhead 3028, Weezie 3029,** Weiler 3031, **Weinberg 3032, Weinstein 3033, Wellington 3035, Wenner-Gren 3037,** Werblow 3038, **Westvaco 3040,** Whitehead 3041, **Whiting 3042, Whitney 3043, Wien 3044,** Wilson 3049, Winfield 3050, Winston 3051, Winston 3052, **Witco 3053, Wolfowski 3055, Wolfson 3056, Wood 3057, Woodland 3058,** Wooley-Clifford 3059, **Wrightson-Ramsing 3060, Young 3062, Youth 3063,** Zacharia 3065, Zarkin 3066, **Zilkha 3067, Zimmermann 3068, Zlinkoff 3070**

North Merrick Lindner 2670
North Tarrytown **Vernon 3010**
Old Brookville **Villa 3014**
Old Westbury Bostwick 2297
Oneonta Dewar 2397, Warren 3024
Pearl River **Gulton 2517**
Pleasantville **Reader's 2851, Simon 2934**
Port Chester **Straus 2965**
Port Washington **Lucerna 2683,** Rauch 2848
Poughkeepsie Dutchess 2416, McCann 2712
Pulaski Snow 2942, Snow 2943
Purchase PepsiCo 2820
Rego Park Lefrak 2651
Riverdale **Dodge 2402**
Rochester Bausch 2269, Cohn 2354, Curtice-Burns 2377, Davenport-Hatch 2382, Eastman 2418, Ebsary 2419, **Gannett 2463, Gannett 2464,** Gleason 2473, Gleason 2474, Gordon 2490, Jones 2591, Pluta 2834, **Rochester 2873,** Rochester 2874, Taylor 2978, Wegman 3030, Wilson 3046, Wilson 3048
Rockville Centre Morgenstern 2752
Roslyn Heights **Initial 2573**
Rye **Adler 2221,** Beinecke 2275, Fischbach 2436, **Kerry 2610**
Scarsdale Bedford 2272, **Glickenhaus 2477,** Stein 2958
Schenectady **Golub 2484,** Yulman 3064
Seneca Falls Goulds 2495
Skaneateles Allyn 2231

South Salem **Wallace 3020**
Syosset **Stebbins 2956**
Syracuse **Agway 2224,** Central 2331, Gifford 2469, Mather 2703, Pratt-Northam 2837
Troy McCarthy 2713, Robison 2871
Utica Utica 3005
Valley Stream Hendrickson 2545
Watertown Watertown 3027
White Plains **General 2467,** Macdonald 2685, **Mailman 2693,** Morris 2753, **Sexauer 2925, Texaco 2981, Transway 2991**
Yonkers Hoernle 2556

see also 155, 177, 306, 330, 493, 517, 526, 528, 539, 551, 585, 625, 660, 711, 725, 739, 743, 818, 862, 1053, 1167, 1404, 1406, 1439, 1441, 1613, 1643, 1778, 1832, 1852, 1868, 2103, 2118, 2123, 2126, 2129, 2132, 2134, 2138, 2143, 2146, 2147, 2171, 2172, 2205, 3078, 3304, 3515, 3534, 3576, 3590, 3597, 3605, 3606, 3640, 3949, 3950, 4188, 4217

NORTH CAROLINA

Asheville McClure 3116
Belmont Lineberger 3112, Stowe 3134
Chapel Hill Morehead 3118
Charlotte ABC 3071, Anderson 3074, **BarclaysAmerican 3076,** Belk 3077, Blumenthal 3080, Carolina 3087, Chapin 3088, Dickson 3092, Dickson 3093, Duke 3095, Finch 3099, Foundation 3102, Ginter 3104, Kellenberger 3109, **Lamb 3110,** Lance 3111, Love 3113, P & B 3122
Concord Cannon 3086
Durham Biddle 3078, **Morris 3120**
Eden **Fieldcrest 3098**
Elizabeth City Elizabeth 3096
Elkin Chatham 3089
Enka Akzona 3073
Fayetteville Rogers 3130
Gastonia Akers 3072, Garrison 3103, **Myers-Ti-Caro 3121**
Greensboro **Blue Bell 3079,** Bryan 3083, Burlington 3084, **Connemara 3090,** Hillsdale 3107, Richardson 3125, **Richardson 3126, Richardson 3127, Richardson 3128,** Sternberger 3132
High Point Whitener 3136
Kinston Jenkins-Tapp 3108
Laurel Hill Morgan 3119
Laurinburg Memorial 3117
Lenoir Broyhill 3081
McAdenville McAdenville 3115
Raleigh Bryan 3082, Daniels 3091, Finley 3101
Research Triangle Park **Burroughs 3085**
Salisbury Salisbury 3131, Woodson 3138
Shelby Dover 3094
Spindale Stonecutter 3133
Statesville **Rixson 3129**
Winston-Salem **Babcock 3075,** Ferebee 3097, Finch 3100, Hanes 3105, Hanes 3106, **Martin 3114,** Reynolds 3123, Reynolds 3124, **Thomasville 3135,** Winston-Salem 3137

see also 665, 693, 813, 865, 1775, 2376, 2459, 2962, 3612, 3818, 3822, 4159, 4179, 4202, 4216

NORTH DAKOTA

Bismarck North Dakota 3142
Bismark Leach 3140
Fargo Fargo-Moorhead 3139, Stern 3143
Grand Forks Myra 3141

see also 1822, 1823, 1828, 1842, 1850, 1853, 3826

OHIO

Akron Akron 3145, **Firestone 3216**, GAR 3232, **GenCorp 3234, Goodyear 3239, Knight 3276**, McAlonan 3296, O'Neil 3321, **O'Neil 3322**, Ritchie 3344, **Tell 3380**
Ashtabula Ashtabula 3158
Ashville Hosler 3254
Berea **Thompson 3381**
Berlin Helping 3251
Bryan **Markey 3290**
Canton First 3218, Flowers 3222, Stark 3373, Timken 3382, **Timken 3383, Timken 3384, Timken 3385**
Chagrin Falls Hankins 3246
Chillicothe Massie 3293
Cincinnati Albers 3146, Alms 3148, American 3150, Anderson 3153, **Browning 3177, Cincinnati 3182**, Cincinnati 3183, Cincinnati 3184, Corbett 3191, Crosley 3194, Crosset 3195, **Eagle-Picher 3203**, Emery 3206, **Federated 3211**, Fifth 3214, First 3219, Fleischmann 3220, Gross 3243, Jarson 3263, Jergens 3265, Juilfs 3267, **Marx 3292**, Nippert 3315, Ohio 3320, Peterloon 3326, **Procter 3333**, Russell 3350, Schmidlapp 3353, Schmidlapp 3354, Schmidlapp 3355, **Scripps-Howard 3359**, Semple 3361, Smith 3369, **Tucker 3393, Warner 3398**, Whitewater 3407, Wodecroft 3409, XTEK 3413
Cleveland American 3151, Andrews 3154, Andrews 3155, **Armington 3157, Austin 3159**, Bicknell 3171, **Bingham 3172**, Bolton 3173, Britton 3176, **Brush 3178**, Calhoun 3179, Cleveland 3185, Cleveland 3186, Cleveland-Cliffs 3187, Codrington 3188, Dauby 3197, Deuble 3200, **Dively 3201, Eaton 3204, Ernst 3207**, Ernsthausen 3208, Ferro 3212, 1525 3213, Firman 3217, Forest 3225, Fox 3226, Frohring 3229, Gallagher 3231, Greene 3240, Gries 3241, Gund 3244, **Haskell 3248**, H.C.S. 3250, Higbee 3252, Humphrey 3256, Humphrey 3257, Huntington 3258, **Ireland 3262**, Jennings 3264, Jochum-Moll 3266, Kangesser 3269, Kulas 3278, Lincoln 3283, Mandel 3286, Mandel 3287, **Mandel 3288**, Markus 3291, Mather 3294, Mather 3295, McFawn 3297, **Mellen 3300, Midland-Ross 3302**, Murch 3310, Murphy 3311, Oglebay 3318, **Parker-Hannifin 3323, Payne 3324**, Perkins 3325, Peterson 3327, **Premier 3331**, Prentiss 3332, Ranney 3335, **Reliance 3339, Renner 3340, Republic 3341**, Richman 3343, **Rosenthal 3347, Saint Gerard 3351, Sapirstein 3352**, Sears 3360, Sheadle 3363, Sherwick 3365, **Sherwin-Williams 3366**, Smith 3370, South 3371, **Standard 3372**, Tremco 3388, Treuhaft 3389, Treu-Mart 3390, **TRW 3392, Tyler 3394**, Wellman 3403, **White 3405**, White 3406, Wright 3411, Wuliger 3412
Cleveland Heights **Austin 3160**, Gerson 3237
Columbus Baird 3161, **Bentz 3167**, Benua 3168, **Borden 3174**, Casto 3180, Columbus 3189, El-An 3205, Frost 3230, George 3235, Gerlach 3236, Ingram 3261, Kaplan-Halpert 3270, Lancaster 3280, **Melton 3301**, Nationwide 3313, O'Bleness 3317, **SCOA 3357**, Shafer 3362, Wexner 3404, Wildermuth 3408, Wolfe 3410, Yassenoff 3414
Conneaut Record 3336, **Ross 3348**
Coshocton Coshocton 3192, Montgomery 3306, Roscoe 3346
Dayton **Allyn 3147**, Beerman 3166, Berry 3170, Dayco 3198, Dayton 3199, **Huffy 3255**, Iddings 3259, **Kettering 3271, Kettering 3272**, Kettering 3273, Kramer 3277, Kuntz 3279, **Mead 3299**, Moore 3307, NCR 3314, Philips 3328, Polk 3329, **Robbins 3345**, Sherman-Standard 3364, Tait 3378
Dover Reeves 3337
East Cleveland McGregor 3298
Elyria Nordson 3316
Fairview Park Laub 3281
Findlay **Flowers 3223, Marathon 3289**
Hamilton Hamilton 3245
Kettering **Amcast 3149**
Lakewood Wasmer 3399
Lancaster Kilburger 3275
Lima Flickinger 3221, **Quatman 3334**
Lithopolis Wagnalls 3397

Logan Kachelmacher 3268
Lorain Lorain 3284, Stocker 3375
Loudonville Young 3415
Lyndhurst Reinberger 3338
Mansfield Ford 3224, Richland 3342, Rupp 3349, Sterkel 3374
Maumee Anderson 3152
Middletown **Armco 3156**, Gardner 3233
Mount Vernon Mount 3309
Newark Evans 3209
North Canton **Hoover 3253**
Pepper Pike Acme 3144
Piqua Hartzell-Norris 3247
Pomeroy **Kibble 3274**
Portsmouth Scioto 3356
Ravenna Smith 3368
Sandusky Frohman 3228
Shaker Heights Ingalls 3260
Sidney Monarch 3305
Solon Lennon 3282, **Stouffer 3376**
Steubenville Berkman 3169
Tiffin **National 3312**
Toledo Charities 3181, **Dana 3196**, France 3227, Goerlich 3238, Miniger 3303, MLM 3304, Ohio 3319, Stranahan 3377, Toledo 3386, Toledo 3387
Troy Troy 3391
Urbana Bates 3162, Grimes 3242
Valley City Weiss 3402
Van Wert Van Wert 3396
Wapakoneta Hauss-Helms 3249
Warren Van Huffel 3395, Wean 3401
Washington Court House Eyman 3210
Westlake **Scott 3358**
Wickliffe Lubrizol 3285
Worthington Moores 3308
Youngstown Beecher 3163, Beecher 3164, Beeghly 3165, Bremer 3175, **Commercial 3190**, Crandall 3193, Donnell 3202, Finnegan 3215, Pollock 3330, Tamarkin 3379, Watson 3400, Youngstown 3416
Zanesville Shinnick 3367

see also 304, 345, 926, 1083, 1332, 1712, 1744, 1776, 2251, 2801, 3731, 3763, 4282

OKLAHOMA

Ardmore Goddard 3432, Merrick 3448, **Noble 3449, Noble 3450**
Bartlesville Lyon 3442, Phillips 3455, **Phillips 3456**, Price 3457
Bristow Jones 3438
Duncan **McCasland 3445**
El Reno Ashbrook 3417, **28:19 3467**
Lawton Fields 3429, McMahon 3447
McAlester Puterbaugh 3458
Norman Sarkeys 3462
Oklahoma City Dolese 3428, First 3430, Harris 3435, Johnson 3437, **Kerr 3439**, Kerr-McGee 3440, Kirkpatrick 3441, McGee 3446, Oklahoma 3451, Oklahoma 3452, Parman 3454, Rapp 3459, Share 3463, Wegener 3470, Young 3473
Sand Springs Sand 3460
Sapulpa Collins 3424, Collins 3425
Shawnee Wood 3472
Tulsa Bartlett 3418, Bovaird 3419, **Broadhurst 3420**, Campbell 3421, Chapman 3422, **Cities 3423**, Cuesta 3426, Dobson 3427, Gilcrease 3431, Gussman 3433, Harmon 3434, Helmerich 3436, **Mabee 3443, MAPCO 3444, Parker 3453**, Sanditen 3461, Taubman 3464, Titus 3465, Tulsa 3466, Warren 3468, Warren 3469, Williams 3471, Zink 3474

see also 449, 2973, 3140, 3927, 3967, 4051, 4319

OREGON

Beaverton Tektronix 3502

Eugene Barker 3476, Hunt 3489
Klamath Falls **Jeld-Wen 3491**
Lake Oswego Friendly-Rosenthal 3487, OCRI 3499
Lakeview Daly 3483
Medford Carpenter 3478
Mill City **Frank 3486**
Philomath Clemens 3481
Portland Autzen 3475, **Brown 3477**, Chiles 3479, Clark 3480, Collins 3482, Higgins 3488, Jackson 3490, Jenkins 3492, **John 3493**, John 3494, **Louisiana-Pacific 3496**, Macdonald 3497, Meyer 3498, Oregon 3500, Templeton 3503, Tucker 3504, Walton 3505, Wessinger 3506, Wheeler 3507
Redmond Johnson 3495
Roseburg **Fohs 3484**, Ford 3485
Salem Salem 3501

see also 123, 191, 264, 1819, 1828, 4229, 4245, 4252, 4266

PENNSYLVANIA

Aliquippa Moore 3670
Allentown Kline 3627, Trexler 3748
Bala Cynwyd **DeMoss 3554, Dozor 3560**
Bethlehem **Adams 3508**, Bethlehem 3526, Laros 3636
Blue Bell Yarway 3768
Bradford Blaisdell 3527, **Glendorn 3582**
Bristol Grundy 3588
Brockway **Brockway 3528**
Bryn Mawr McLean 3657, **Presser 3698**
Butler Spang 3730
Camp Hill Hall 3591, **Harsco 3595**, Kunkel 3633, **Whitaker 3761**
Coatesville **Lukens 3645**
Cogan Station Plankenhorn 3695
Conshohocken Quaker 3699
Dallas Sordoni 3729
DuBois Mengle 3664
Dunmore Schautz 3712
Ellwood City Evans 3566
Emporium Emporium 3564
Erie Erie 3565, Hammermill 3594, **Lord 3643**
Fort Washington **Copernicus 3548**
Gwynedd J.D.B. 3619
Hanover Sheppard 3718
Harrisburg AMP 3516, **Grass 3585**, Hambay 3593, Kline 3628, McCormick 3650, Stabler 3733
Haverford **Merit 3666**
Hazleton Reidler 3702
Hershey Hershey 3601
Indiana Mack 3646
Irvine **National 3675**
Jeanette **Millstein 3668**
Jenkintown Beneficia 3525, Cairncrest 3530, Glencairn 3581, SPS 3731
Johnstown Glosser 3583
Lafayette Hill Greenfield 3586, Widener 3762
Lancaster Lancaster 3635, National 3674, Steinman 3737, Steinman 3738
Latrobe **Kennametal 3626**, McFeely-Rogers 3652, McKenna 3655, **McKenna 3656**
Lebanon Caplan 3534
McKeesport Crawford 3551, **Murphy 3671**, Peters 3685
Media Measey 3659
Mount Joy SICO 3720
New Castle Hoyt 3609
New Holland Crels 3552
Newtown Square Kavanagh 3624
Norristown Arcadia 3520, **Charlestein 3541**
North Wales Leeds 3638
Oil City Eccles 3562, Justus 3621, Justus 3622, Lesher 3639, Phillips 3690
Oxford Oxford 3678
Philadelphia Anderson 3517, Beatty 3523, Cameron 3532, **Cassett 3538, CIGNA 3542**, Connelly 3545, **Conston 3546**, Dietrich 3555, Dietrich 3556, Dolfinger-McMahon 3557, Ellis 3563, **Federation**

3569, Feinstein 3570, Fels 3571, **Female 3572,** Foerderer 3574, **Gillett 3579,** Girard 3580, Goldman 3584, Hassel 3596, Hilles 3602, **Hooper 3607,** Hunt 3612, Huston 3614, **Independence 3616, Javitch 3618,** Kardon 3623, Knollbrook 3629, **Kynett 3634,** Levy 3641, Lindback 3642, Mandell 3647, **Maneely 3648,** McShain 3658, Medical 3660, Merchants 3665, Musselman 3672, Myrin 3673, 1957 3676, Paley 3680, Parklands 3681, Penn 3683, **Pennwalt 3684, Pew 3686, Pew 3687, Pew 3688,** Philadelphia 3689, **Redmond 3700,** Reliance 3703, Rittenhouse 3704, **Robinson 3706,** S 'n S 3710, Scholler 3713, **Scott 3715,** Seybert 3717, Shoemaker 3719, Silverstein 3721, Smith 3723, Smith 3724, SmithKline 3726, **Stein 3736,** Stokes 3740, Stott 3741, Strauss 3742, **Stroud 3744, Tabas 3746, Thomson 3747,** Union 3749, Vincent 3751, **Westmoreland 3758,** Wolf 3765, Wurts 3766

Pittsburgh **Alcoa 3511,** Allegheny 3512, **Allegheny 3513,** Benedum 3524, Buhl 3529, Calhoun 3531, Campbell 3533, **Carnegie 3535, Carthage 3537,** Clapp 3544, Craig 3549, **Cyclops 3553,** Donnelly 3558, **Dravo 3561,** Falk 3567, **Falk 3568,** Finley 3573, **Foster 3575,** Frick 3576, Frick 3577, Gibson 3578, **Gulf 3589, Heinz 3598,** Heinz 3599, **Heinz 3600,** Hillman 3603, Hillman 3604, Hitchcock 3605, Hopwood 3608, Hulme 3610, Hunt 3611, Hunt 3613, **Hyman 3615,** Jennings 3620, **Kelley 3625,** Knudsen 3630, **Koppers 3631,** Laurel 3637, **Love 3644, Massey 3649,** McCune 3651, McKee 3653, **McKelvy 3654,** Mellon 3661, Mellon 3662, Mellon 3663, Mine 3669, Patterson 3682, Pitcairn-Crabbe 3691, Pittsburgh 3692, Pittsburgh 3693, Pittsburgh 3694, Polk 3696, PPG 3697, Robinson 3705, Rockwell 3707, **Rockwell 3708, Rust 3709,** Scaife 3711, Schoonmaker 3714, Snyder 3728, Staunton 3739, Steinsapir 3739, **United 3750, Walker 3752,** Waters 3754, Weisbrod 3755, **Westinghouse 3756, Westinghouse 3757,** Wheeling-Pittsburgh 3760, Williams 3763

Plymouth Meeting Claneil 3543, Douty 3559
Pottsville Snayberger 3727
Radnor Ames 3515, **Annenberg 3518, Annenberg 3519, Hall 3590,** Hazen 3597, Hooker 3606, Levee 3640, **Simon 3722**
Reading American 3514, **Carpenter 3536,** Oberlaender 3677
Rosemont Smith 3725
Rydal Hallowell 3592
Scranton Scranton 3716
Sharon Charitable 3540
St. Marys St. Marys 3732, Stackpole-Hall 3734
Trevose Korman 3632
Trexlertown **Air 3509**
Upper Darby Central 3539
Valley Forge **Alco 3510**
Warren **Crary 3550,** Warren 3753
Wayne **Strawbridge 3743**
Wellsboro Packer 3679
Williamsport Williamsport 3764
Willow Grove Asplundh 3521
Windber Whalley 3759
Wyncote Cook 3547
Wyndmoor Barra 3522
Wynnewood **Superior-Pacific 3745**
Wyomissing Janssen 3617, Wyomissing 3767
York **Grumbacher 3587,** Miller 3667, Rehmeyer 3701

see also 600, 613, 618, 619, 761, 789, 1113, 1463, 1831, 2101, 2107, 2129, 2143, 2217, 2605, 2669, 2903, 2973, 3165, 3169, 3401, 4308

PUERTO RICO
Santurce Harvey 3769

RHODE ISLAND
Cranston Cranston 3774
East Providence **Alperin 3770**
Newport Newport 3785
Pawtucket Galkin 3776, **Hassenfeld 3779**
Providence Armbrust 3771, Champlin 3772, Citizens 3773, Fleet 3775, **Genesis 3777,** Haffenreffer 3778, Johnstone 3780, Kimball 3781, Koffler 3782, **Little 3783, Morgan 3784,** Old 3786, Providence 3787, Rapaporte 3788, Ress 3789, Rhode 3790, Roddy 3791, **Textron 3792, Watson 3793**

see also 1575, 1639, 2659

SOUTH CAROLINA
Charleston **Merck 3810, Post 3812**
Clinton **Bailey 3797**
Columbia Byrnes 3800, Citizens 3801, Fairey 3803, Fuller 3804, South Carolina 3819, State-Record 3823
Florence Aiken 3795
Georgetown Baruch 3798
Graniteville Gregg-Graniteville 3806
Greenville Belk-Simpson 3799, **Daniel 3802,** Greenville 3805, **Liberty 3809, Riegel 3813, Roe 3814,** Sargent 3815, Scurry 3816, Simpson 3818, Symmes 3825
Greenwood Abney 3794, Self 3817
Inman Inman-Riverdale 3807
Kershaw Stevens 3824
Lancaster Springs 3821, Springs 3822
Laurens Kennedy 3808
Spartanburg Arkwright 3796, Moore 3811, Spartanburg 3820

see also 813, 827, 865, 994, 1655, 2120, 2459, 2880, 2962, 3077, 3084, 3095, 3102, 3111

SOUTH DAKOTA
Aberdeen Hatterscheidt 3826

see also 1823, 1828, 1842, 1850, 1853

TENNESSEE
Bristol Massengill-DeFriece 3851
Chattanooga Benwood 3829, Brown 3832, Chattanooga 3835, Evans 3840, Hamico 3842, Hutcheson 3843, Jewell 3845, **Lyndhurst 3847,** Maclellan 3848, Maclellan 3849, **Maclellan 3850,** Tonya 3860, Westend 3863, **Woods-Greer 3864**
Knoxville **Cole 3837,** Toms 3859
Memphis Belz 3828, Briggs 3830, Brinkley 3831, Buckman 3833, Day 3839, Goldsmith 3841, **Hyde 3844,** Lowenstein 3846, Memphis-Plough 3854, Plough 3855, Schadt 3857, **Speech 3858**
Nashville Ansley 3827, Bullard 3834, Church 3836, **Currey 3838,** Massey 3852, Meade 3853, Potter 3856, Washington 3861, Werthan 3862, Zimmerman 3865

see also 653, 813, 865, 1369, 2969

TEXAS
Abilene Andress 3876, Dodge 3931
Amarillo Amarillo 3872, Anderson 3874, Bivins 3887, Craig 3918, Harrington 3974, Mays 4021
Arlington **Ferguson 3951**

Austin Henck 3978, LBJ 4011, Lindsay 4017, **R G K 4061**
Beaumont Rogers 4067, Steinhagen 4087
Beeville Dougherty 3934
Big Spring Roberts 4065
Corpus Christi Behmann 3884, Brookshire 3892, Haas 3966, Kenedy 4002, Sams 4071, Warren 4112
Corsicana Hofstetter 3986, Navarro 4040
Dallas American 3873, Bass 3878, Beasley 3883, **Bell 3885, Biological 3886, Brinker 3891,** Cain 3900, **Central 3903,** Chilton 3904, Clark 3906, Collins 3910, Communities 3911, Constantin 3912, Costa 3917, Crow 3919, Dallas 3923, Dallas 3924, Dallas 3925, **Dresser 3935, Dresser-Harbison 3936, ENSERCH 3943,** Feldman 3950, Fikes 3952, Florence 3955, Green 3964, Haggar 3967, Haggerty 3968, **Halliburton 3970,** Hawn 3975, Hillcrest 3981, Hoblitzelle 3984, Hunt 3991, Jonsson 3997, Kay 3998, King 4003, Lennox 4012, **Lightner 4016,** Lone 4018, McDermott 4024, Meadows 4029, Moss 4037, Moss 4038, **Northen 4041,** O'Donnell 4043, Orleans 4045, **Overlake 4046,** Redman 4062, Rogers 4068, Rudman 4070, Sharp 4080, Stemmons 4088, Straus 4090, Sumners 4091, Texas 4101, **Texas 4102,** Tyler 4106
Denison Munson 4039
El Paso El Paso 3940, Gifford 3961, Hightower 3980, Huthsteiner 3992, McKee 4026, Peyton 4055
Fort Worth **Bass 3879,** Brown 3895, Bryce 3896, Carter 3902, Crump 3920, Davidson 3926, Davis 3927, Duncan 3937, Edwards 3939, Fleming 3954, **Fuller 3958,** Garvey 3959, Gill 3962, Keith 4000, Lard 4010, McQueen 4028, Moncrief 4034, Pangburn 4049, **Richardson 4063,** Richardson 4064, Rowan 4069, Scott 4075, Tandy 4092, Tandy 4093, Tarrant 4094, Texas 4100, Waggoner 4109, **Weaver 4113,** West 4119, White 4120, Wiseda 4124
Galveston Kempner 4001, Moody 4035, Seibel 4077
Georgetown Wright 4128
Hallettsville Dickson 3930
Houston Abercrombie 3867, Adams 3868, **Akin 3869, Allbritton 3870,** Allied 3871, Anderson 3875, Bank 3877, Blaffer 3888, Brown 3893, **Burkitt 3897,** Butler 3898, Cameron 3901, Clayton 3907, Cockrell 3908, Cooley 3914, Cooper 3916, Cullen 3921, DeBakey 3928, Duncan 3938, Elkins 3941, Ellwood 3942, Faith 3946, Farish 3947, Favrot 3949, Fish 3953, Fondren 3956, **Frees 3957, Gordon 3963,** Hamman 3972, **HNG 3982,** Hobby 3983, Hofheinz 3985, **HOR 3987,** Houston 3988, Hugg 3989, **Interferon 3993,** Johnson 3994, Johnston 3996, Kayser 3999, **Klein 4007,** Knox 4009, Lewis 4015, MacDonald 4020, McAshan 4022, **McGovern 4025, Menil 4030, Menil 4031,** Mosle 4036, **Oldham 4044,** Owsley 4048, Parry 4051, Polemanakos 4057, **Quanex 4060,** Rockwell 4066, **Scaler 4073,** Scurlock 4076, **Shell 4081,** Smith 4082, **Starling 4086,** Strake 4089, Taub 4096, Texas 4099, Turner 4105, Vale-Asche 4107, Vaughn 4108, Weiner 4114, Welch 4115, West 4117, West 4118, Wolff 4125, Woltman 4126, Wortham 4127
Irving Curtis 3922, Southland 4084, **Zale 4129**
Kerrville Butt 3899
Kilgore Griffin 3965
Kingsville King 4004
Lewisville Collins 3909
Liberty Humphreys 3990
Lubbock Hemphill-Wells 3977
Lufkin Henderson 3979, Temple 4098
Luling Luling 4019
Marshall Tartt 4095
McAllen Cook 3913
Midland Abell-Hanger 3866, Beal 3882, Fasken 3948, Potts 4058, Scarborough 4074
Mineola Meredith 4032
Orange Stark 4085
Overton McMillan 4027
Palacios Trull 4104
Pampa Brown 3894
Raymondville Harding 3973
Richardson Owen 4047

Richmond George 3960
Robstown Perry 4054
Rockwall **LeTourneau 4014**
San Antonio Baumberger 3880, Baumberger 3881, Brackenridge 3889, Halff 3969, Halsell 3971, Kleberg 4005, **Kleberg 4006, Leppard** 4013, **McCreless 4023,** Parker 4050, Piper 4056, Pryor 4059, San Antonio 4072, Semmes 4078, Tobin 4103, Walthall 4111
San Marcos **Technical 4097**
Seminole Doss 3933
Sherman Dorset 3932
Sinton **Welder 4116**
Snyder Diamond 3929
Stanton Millhollon 4033
Temple Wilson 4123
Tyler Fair 3945, Heath 3976
Vernon Waggoner 4110
Victoria O'Connor 4042, South Texas 4083
Waco **C.I.O.S. 3905,** Cooper 3915
Weslaco Knapp 4008
Wharton Johnson 3995
Wichita Falls Bridwell 3890, Fain 3944, Perkins 4052, Perkins-Prothro 4053, Shanor 4079, White 4121, Wilson 4122

see also 31, 225, 306, 407, 449, 482, 818, 1369, 1374, 1409, 1660, 1900, 2209, 2217, 3432, 3434, 3439, 3443

UTAH
Brigham City Caine 4131
Ogden Dee 4135, Dee 4136, Green 4140, Shaw 4144
Salt Lake City Bamberger 4130, Callister 4132, Castle 4133, Christensen 4134, Dumke 4137, Eccles 4138, Eccles 4139, Harris 4141, Masonic 4142, Michael 4143, **Thrasher 4145,** Treadwell 4146

see also 370, 479

VERMONT
Bennington Scott 4150
Burlington General 4148
Grafton Windham 4151
South Londonderry **Edwards 4147**
Stowe Lintilhac 4149

see also 1576, 1643, 2193, 2564, 4324

VIRGINIA
Alexandria Bryant 4156, Hopkins 4176
Altavista English 4168, English 4169, Lane 4180
Arlington **Olmsted 4189,** Reinsch 4192, Truland 4210, Washington 4215
Big Stone Gap Slemp 4200
Charlottesville **Jones 4178,** Perry 4191
Danville **Dan 4166**
Franklin Camp 4158, Camp 4159, Camp 4160
Gloucester Treakle 4209
Hampton **Hastings 4174**
Lynchburg Easley 4167
McLean **Mars 4182**
Middleburg Wilfred 4217
Norfolk **Armour 4152,** Dalis 4165, Landmark 4179, Lincoln-Lane 4181, Norfolk 4187, Taylor 4202

Portsmouth Beazley 4153
Pulaski Richardson 4195
Richmond **Best 4154,** Cabell 4157, **Campbell 4161, Campbell 4162,** Central 4163, Cole 4164, Flagler 4170, Gottwald 4171, Harris 4173, Jeffress 4177, Massey 4183, **McCrea 4184,** Memorial 4185, Morgan 4186, Olsson 4190, **Reynolds 4193,** Reynolds 4194, Richmond 4196, **Robertshaw 4197,** Scott 4198, Seay 4199, Sovran 4201, Thalhimer 4203, Thalhimer 4204, Thomas 4205, United 4211, Universal 4212, UVB 4213, Virginia 4214, Wheat 4216
Roanoke Blount 4155, Thurman 4207
Rosslyn **Three 4206**
Sutherland Titmus 4208
The Plains Ohrstrom 4188
Waverly Gray 4172
Waynesboro **Hopeman 4175**

see also 669, 716, 865, 1237, 1434, 2143, 2251, 3084, 3851, 4277, 4287

WASHINGTON
Bainbridge Island Bloedel 4222
Bellevue PACCAR 4255, **Wharton 4275**
Chehalis West 4273
Edmonds Glaser 4236
Everett Cawsey 4228
Kirkland Dupar 4233
Seattle **Anderson 4218,** Archibald 4219, Bishop 4220, Bishop 4221, Boeing 4223, Brechemin 4224, Bullitt 4225, **Burlington 4226,** Carman 4227, Green 4237, Haas 4238, Hubbard 4239, Kawabe 4241, Kreielsheimer 4245, **Laird 4246, Matlock 4248,** McEachern 4249, Medina 4250, Merrill 4251, Norcliffe 4254, Poncin 4256, Rainier 4257, Robertson 4258, Seattle 4259, Shemanski 4261, Skinner 4262, Univar 4268, Washington 4269, Wells 4272, Wyman 4276
Spokane Comstock 4230, Cowles 4231, **Cowles 4232,** Johnston 4240, Leuthold 4247, Spokane 4264
Tacoma Cheney 4229, **Forest 4234,** Fuchs 4235, Keyes 4242, Kilworth 4243, Kilworth 4244, Murray 4253, Sequoia 4260, Snyder 4263, **Stewardship 4265,** Tacoma 4267, **Weyerhaeuser 4274**
Vancouver Murdock 4252
Walla Walla Stubblefield 4266, Welch 4270, Welch 4271

see also 123, 191, 238, 373, 388, 504, 660, 1828, 1850, 3495

WEST VIRGINIA
Beckley Carter 4279, Vecellio 4290
Bluefield Bowen 4277
Charleston Carbon 4278, Daywood 4281, Jacobson 4284, Kanawha 4285, Minor 4287
Gilbert Harless 4283
Huntington Price 4288, **Prichard 4289**
Parkersburg McDonough 4286
Wheeling Chambers 4280
Williamstown Fenton 4282

see also 1332, 2217, 3524, 3763, 4216

WISCONSIN
Beloit Beloit 4301
Brookfield **Koehring 4339, Rexnord 4373**
Chippewa Falls Mason 4355, Rutledge 4376
Cudahy Ladish 4347
Eau Claire Hobbs 4328, Phillips 4367
Fond du Lac Giddings 4324
Green Bay Fort 4319, Frankenthal 4320, **Kress 4344,** Walter 4386, Wisconsin 4389
Hartland Lindsay 4351
Janesville Janesville 4330
Kohler Kohler 4342
La Crosse Gelatt 4323, **Heileman 4326,** La Crosse 4346, **Trane 4383**
Madison Amundson 4295, CUNA 4312, Evjue 4316, Johnson 4334, Rennebohm 4372
Manitowoc **Rahr 4371**
Marshfield Miller 4357, **Roddis 4375**
Menasha Banta 4300
Menomonee Falls Stolper-Wensink 4382
Mequon **Kurth 4345**
Milwaukee Apollo 4297, **ARMCO 4298,** Badger 4299, Bradley 4302, **Bradley 4303, Brady 4304,** Braun 4305, Clark 4309, **Cudahy 4311,** Demmer 4313, **DeRance 4314,** Evinrude 4315, Falk 4317, First 4318, Fromm 4321, G.P. 4322, **Harnischfeger 4325,** Helfaer 4327, **Johnson 4331,** Johnson 4335, **Kohl 4340,** Kohl 4341, Krause 4343, Ladish 4348, Ladish 4349, **Ladish 4350,** Loock 4352, Marine 4353, Marshall 4354, McBeath 4356, Milwaukee 4358, Pabst 4363, **Peck 4364,** Peters 4365, Pick 4368, Polybill 4369, Schroeder 4377, **Smith 4380,** Stackner 4381, **Universal 4384,** Vilter 4385, Wehr 4387, Wisconsin 4388, Youth 4392, Ziemann 4394
Neenah **Kimberly-Clark 4338,** Neenah 4359
Oshkosh Oshkosh 4361, Oshkosh 4362, **Rochlin 4374**
Palmyra **Young 4391**
Port Edwards Alexander 4291, Nekoosa 4360
Racine **Johnson 4332, Johnson 4333, Johnson's 4336,** Racine 4370
Sheboygan Brotz 4307
South Milwaukee Bucyrus-Erie 4308
Stevens Point Sentry 4378
Sturgeon Bay Peterson 4366
Tomah Andres 4296
Wausau Alexander 4292, Alexander 4293, Woodson 4390
Wauwatosa Briggs 4306, Jacobus/Heritage 4329, Siebert 4379
West Allis Allis-Chalmers 4294, Kearney 4337
West Bend Ziegler 4393
Wisconsin Rapids Consolidated 4310

see also 926, 960, 1048, 1086, 1140, 1822, 1828, 1838, 1853, 1904, 1919, 2855, 2903

WYOMING
Casper Goodstein 4396, Kamps 4397, Tonkin 4400
Cody Stock 4398, **Weiss 4401**
Sheridan Bryan 4395, Surrena 4399, Whitney 4402

see also 407, 452, 482, 1828, 2059

TYPES OF SUPPORT INDEX

Foundations in bold face type make grants on a national or regional basis; the others generally limit giving to the city or state in which they are located.

Annual campaigns: any organized effort by a nonprofit to secure gifts on an annual basis; also called annual appeals.

Building funds: money raised for construction and/or renovation of buildings; may be part of an organization's capital campaign.

Capital support: SEE Building funds; Equipment.

Conferences and seminars: a grant to cover the expenses of holding a conference.

Consulting services: professional staff support provided by the foundation to a nonprofit to consult on a project of mutual interest or to evaluate services (not a cash grant).

Continuing support: a grant that is renewed on a regular basis.

Deficit financing: also known as debt reduction. A grant to reduce the recipient organization's indebtedness; frequently refers to mortgage payments.

Emergency funds: a one-time grant to cover immediate short-term funding needs on an emergency basis.

Employee matching gifts: a contribution to a charitable organization by a corporate employee which is matched by a similar contribution from the employer. Many corporations support employee matching gift programs in higher education to stimulate their employees to give to the college or university of their choice.

Employee-related scholarships: a scholarship program funded by a company-sponsored foundation usually for children of employees; programs are frequently administered by the National Merit Scholarship Corporation which is responsible for selection of scholars.

Endowment funds: a bequest or gift intended to be kept permanently and invested to provide income for continued support of an organization.

Equipment: a grant to purchase equipment, furnishings, or other materials.

Exchange programs: usually refers to funds for educational exchange programs for foreign students.

Fellowships: usually indicates funds awarded to educational institutions to support fellowship programs. A few foundations award fellowships directly to individuals.

General purposes: a grant made to further the general purpose or work of an organization, rather than for a specific purpose or project; also called unrestricted grants.

Grants to individuals: awards such as scholarships, fellowships, or aid to the needy made directly by the foundation to individuals rather than to a nonprofit organization. (See also "Student aid.")

Internships: usually indicates funds awarded to an institution or organization to support an internship program rather than to an individual.

Land acquisition: a grant to purchase real estate property.

Lectureships: usually indicates a grant to an educational institution to support a lectureship program rather than a grant to an individual.

Loans: temporary award of funds which usually must be repaid. (See also "Program-related investments"; for student loans, see "Student aid.")

Matching funds: a grant which is made to match funds provided by another donor. (See also "Employee matching gifts.")

Operating budgets: a grant to cover the day-to-day personnel, administrative, and other expenses for an existing program or organization.

Professorships: usually indicates a grant to an educational institution to endow a professorship or chair.

Program-related investments: a loan made by a private foundation to profit-making or nonprofit organizations for a project related to the foundation's stated purpose and interests. Program-related investments are often made from a revolving fund; the foundation generally expects to receive its money back with interest which will then provide additional funds for loans to other organizations. Program-related investments are made by relatively few foundations.

Publications: a grant to fund reports or other publications issued by a nonprofit resulting from research or projects of interest to the foundation.

Research: usually indicates funds awarded to institutions to cover costs of investigations and clinical trials. Research grants for individuals are usually referred to as fellowships.

Scholarship funds (to institutions): indicates a grant paid only to an educational institution or organization (not to an individual) to support a scholarship program, mainly for students at the undergraduate level. (See also "Employee-related scholarships"; for scholarships paid to individuals, see "Student aid.")

Seed money: a grant or contribution used to start a new project or organization. Seed grants may cover salaries and other operating expenses of a new project. Also known as "start-up funds."

Special projects: grants to support specific projects or programs as opposed to general purpose grants.

Student aid: assistance awarded directly to individuals in the form of educational loans, grants, or scholarships. (See also "Employee-related scholarships.")

Technical assistance: operational or management assistance given to nonprofit organizations; may include fundraising assistance, budgeting and financial planning, program planning, legal advice, marketing, and other aids to management. Assistance may be offered directly by a foundation staff member or in the form of a grant to pay for the services of an outside consultant.

Annual campaigns

Alabama: Smith 20

Arizona: Arizona 29, Circle K 31, First 34, Hervey 38, **Kieckhefer 39,** Mulcahy 42

California: A.I.D. 66, Albertson 67, **American 69, BankAmerica 84,** Beckman 89, Copley 133, Corcoran 134, Crocker 138, Disney 148, Distribution 151, Drum 156, Fireman's 169, Fleishhacker 171, **Fluor 173,** Fusenot 176, Gellert 183, Gildred 189, Gilmore 191, Goldwyn 196, Haas 204, **Kerr 244,** Knudsen 246, Koret 248, Lear 253, Levy 259, **Litton 262,** Lurie 267, Orleton 304, **Page 309,** Parker 310, **Philibosian 323,** Pratt 328, Schreiber 347, Security 351, Simon 362, **Simon 363,** Simon 365, **Simon 366,** Stamps 377, **Stans 378,** Stauffer 379, Stern 383, Thornton 398, Ticor 399, Union 406, **Union 407,** Walker 414, Welk 422, **Wilbur 428,** Yorkin 432

Colorado: Anschutz 435, Buell 437, Colorado 440, Duncan 443, El Pomar 445, Hughes 454, Hunter 455, Johnson 458, Joslyn 460, Norgren 469, **Woodward 487**

Connecticut: **Abex 488,** Bridgeport 502, Connecticut 507, Eder 515, Ensign-Bickford 520, **General 527,** Hartford 532, **ITT 542,** Oaklawn 560, **Olin 561, Panwy 563,** Scott 573, Stanley 577, **Stanley 578, UMC 583,** Xerox 594, **Ziegler 595**

Delaware: **Beneficial 596,** Laffey-McHugh 616, Longwood 618, Welfare 632

District of Columbia: Bloedorn 641, Cafritz 643, **Freed 656,** Higginson 662, Kiplinger 667, Sapelo 681

Florida: Briggs 698, **Brunner 700, Dettman 712,** duPont 716, **Eckerd 719, Harris 726, Koch 734,** Phipps 755, Price 758, Southeast 770, **Winn-Dixie 794**

Georgia: Callaway 810, Callaway 811, **Coca-Cola 818, Day 824,** EMSA 829, Equifax 831, Glancy 840, Harland 843, Hill 846, Livingston 854, Lubo 856, Rich 870, **Wilson 886**

Hawaii: **Amfac 888,** Castle 893, Cooke 895

Illinois: **Abbott 918,** American 925, **Amoco 928, Amsted 929,** Barber-Colman 936, **Becker 940, CBI 966, Clark 974,** Coleman 975, Crown 982, **Deere 987, DeKalb 989,** Dillon 992, **Evinrude 997,** First 1002, Furnas 1012, **Gould 1020,** Haffner 1024, Hales 1025, Harris 1028, **Harris 1030, Illinois 1045,** IMC 1046, Ingersoll 1047, Kaplan 1055, McCormick 1090, **McGraw 1094, Nalco 1105,** Northern 1108, **Northwest 1109,** Peterborough 1117, **Quaker 1126,** R. F. 1128, Sara 1139, **Sears-Roebuck 1145,** United 1179, UOP 1180, USG 1182, **Walgreen 1183,** Ward 1185, White 1188, Wurlitzer 1194

Indiana: **Credithrift 1208,** CTS 1209, Cummins 1210, Indianapolis 1226, Jordan 1230, Krannert 1233, **Lilly 1238,** Oliver 1247

Iowa: Des Moines 1263, Hall 1269, Maytag 1277, National 1279, Pella 1280, Vermeer 1287, Wahlert 1288

Kansas: Coleman 1298, Garvey 1307, **Hesston 1311, Marley 1319,** Powell 1323, Sosland 1329, Wiedemann 1330

Kentucky: Bingham 1335, Cooke 1339, Vogt 1353

Louisiana: Jones 1370

Maryland: **Fairchild 1414,** Hoffberger 1423, Kelly 1424, Meyerhoff 1439, Middendorf 1440, Noxell 1444, Pearlstone 1445, **PHH 1446,** Sheridan 1454, U.S.F. & G. 1460

Massachusetts: Acushnet 1466, **Alden 1468,** Bank 1473, Bayrd 1474, Brandegee 1486, **Cabot 1488,** Cabot 1489, Cove 1503, Daniels 1509, Davis 1511, **Eastern 1518,** Ellsworth 1523, Fuller 1532, Fuller 1533, Hyams 1561, **Little 1578,** Morgan-Worcester 1584, Pappas 1591, Russell 1614, Schrafft 1618, **Sheraton 1625,** Stoddard 1635, Thompson 1643, Wallace 1647, **Webster 1652, Wyman-Gordon 1660**

Michigan: **Aeroquip 1662,** Americana 1663, **Bargman 1667,** Barstow 1668, Besser 1673, Bishop 1674, Bray 1676, **Chrysler 1679,** DeRoy 1682, Dow 1690, **Federal-Mogul 1696, Ford 1702, General 1710, Gerber 1711,** Gerstacker

1712, **Harder 1716,** Holden 1720, Hudson-Webber 1722, Hunter 1723, Imerman 1725, Kaufman 1730, Loutit 1738, McGregor 1744, Miller 1749, Morley 1751, **Mott 1752,** Muskegon 1754, Seidman 1767, Shelden 1770, Skillman 1773, Tiscornia 1782, Towsley 1783, **Whirlpool 1793,** Wilson 1799

Minnesota: **American 1807,** Apache 1812, **Bemis 1818,** Bend 1819, Bremer 1822, Butler 1824, **Davis 1833, Dayton 1834,** First 1842, First 1843, Graco 1849, Greystone 1851, Groves 1854, Honeywell 1861, Hormel 1862, International 1866, Inter-Regional 1867, Lilly 1876, Marbrook 1878, McNeely 1882, **Medtronic 1884, Minnesota 1890,** O'Brien 1896, O'Neil 1898, **O'Shaughnessy 1900,** Paper 1901, **Pillsbury 1905,** Quinlan 1906, Thorpe 1916

Mississippi: First 1936

Missouri: **Anheuser-Busch 1940,** Block 1941, Brown 1944, Brown 1945, **Butler 1946,** Centerre 1948, Commerce 1951, Edison 1958, Gaylord 1965, McGee 1995, Millstone 1998, **Monsanto 1999,** Olin 2002, Reynolds 2011, Sunderland 2025, Union 2034, **Webb 2037**

Nebraska: Cooper 2054, Hitchcock 2057, **InterNorth 2058**

Nevada: **Sells 2081**

New Hampshire: Hunt 2087, **Phillips 2093**

New Jersey: **Allied 2098,** Caspersen 2111, **Hackett 2129, Huber 2133, Johnson 2139,** Ohl 2163, Prudential 2167, **Schering-Plough 2178, Subaru 2187,** Union 2194, **Vollmer 2199, Warner-Lambert 2200,** Westfield 2201

New York: Abrons 2215, **ACF 2217,** Agway 2224, **Allied 2230, American-Standard 2237, AMETEK 2238,** Atran 2250, Barker 2264, Barker 2265, **Bristol-Myers 2302, Chase 2337, Chatlos 2338,** Clark 2347, **Coles 2358, Compton 2363,** Cornell 2367, Cowles 2369, Curtice-Burns 2377, **Dammann 2378,** Dillon 2399, **Dillon 2400, Dow 2410, Dun 2415,** Eastman 2418, Emerson 2421, **Ford 2443,** Frueauff 2455, Gebbie 2465, **General 2467,** Gifford 2469, Goodstein 2487, **Grace 2496, Guggenheim 2512, International 2574,** Irving 2575, **Jurzykowski 2595, Knapp 2620,** Lang 2636, **Lasdon 2639,** Lee 2649, Macdonald 2685, Macmillan 2688, **Manufacturers 2698,** McCann 2712, **McDonald 2718,** McGonagle 2719, **McGraw-Hill 2721, Memton 2724, Merrill 2728, Michel 2735,** Moore 2748, Morgan 2750, Morgan 2751, New York 2777, **New-Land 2779,** Nichols 2782, **NL 2783,** Norwood 2791, O'Connor 2795, **O'Toole 2805, PBP 2815,** Pfizer 2823, **Phelps 2825, Phillips-Van Heusen 2828, Prospect 2842, Rosenthal 2888,** Samuels 2905, **Sony 2945, Standard 2951, Starr 2954, Thorne 2984,** Union 2997, United 3000, **Vinmont 3015,** Watertown 3027, Wikstrom 3045, Wilson 3048, **Witco 3053**

North Carolina: **BarclaysAmerican 3076,** Burlington 3084, Cannon 3086, Chatham 3089, **Connemara 3090,** Ferebee 3097, Finch 3100, Hanes 3105, Hanes 3106, Morgan 3119, Reynolds 3123, Reynolds 3124

North Dakota: Fargo-Moorhead 3139, North Dakota 3142, Stern 3143

Ohio: Acme 3144, **Amcast 3149,** American 3151, Anderson 3152, **Armco 3156, Armington 3157,** Beecher 3164, **Borden 3174, Brush 3178,** Cleveland 3185, **Commercial 3190, Dana 3196,** Dauby 3197, Double 3200, **Eaton 3204,** Fifth 3214, **Firestone 3216,** Firman 3217, France 3227, Frohring 3229, **GenCorp 3234, Goodyear 3239,** Gries 3241, Gund 3244, **Hoover 3253, Huffy 3255,** Humphrey 3256, Iddings 3259, Ingalls 3260, **Kettering 3272,** Laub 3281, Lubrizol 3285, Mather 3294, **Mead 3299, Midland-Ross 3302,** Nationwide 3313, NCR 3314, Nordson 3316, Oglebay 3318, Ohio 3319, Pollock 3330, **Procter 3333,** Reinberger 3338, **Republic 3341,** Sears 3360, Smith 3370, **Stouffer 3376,** Stranahan 3377, Tait 3378, Toledo 3381, Treuhaft 3389, Wolfe 3410, Youngstown 3416

Oklahoma: Ashbrook 3417, First 3430, Goddard 3432, **Kerr 3439,** Kirkpatrick 3441, **Mabee 3443,**

Noble 3450, Oklahoma 3451, Oklahoma 3452, **Phillips 3456,** Williams 3471

Oregon: Tektronix 3502

Pennsylvania: **Air 3509, Alcoa 3511,** American 3514, Arcadia 3520, **Brockway 3528, CIGNA 3542,** Craig 3549, **Cyclops 3553,** Eccles 3562, Falk 3567, Goldman 3584, Hammermill 3594, **Heinz 3598,** Heinz 3599, Hershey 3601, Hillman 3604, Hunt 3612, Justus 3621, Justus 3622, Kavanagh 3624, Kline 3628, **Koppers 3631, Lukens 3645,** McFeely-Rogers 3652, McKenna 3655, **McKenna 3656,** Mellon 3661, Mellon 3662, Patterson 3682, **Pennwalt 3691,** Pittsburgh 3694, PPG 3697, Scaife 3711, Schoonmaker 3714, SPS 3731, Stabler 3733, Stackpole-Hall 3734, Stott 3741, **Stroud 3744, United 3750,** Wurts 3766, Wyomissing 3767

Rhode Island: Fleet 3775, **Little 3783**

South Carolina: Abney 3794, Citizens 3801, Fuller 3804, Gregg-Graniteville 3806, **Roe 3814**

Tennessee: Benwood 3829, Brown 3832, **Currey 3838,** Maclellan 3848, Maclellan 3849, Massengill-DeFriece 3851, Plough 3855, **Woods-Greer 3864**

Texas: Abell-Hanger 3866, American 3873, Brown 3893, **Burkitt 3897,** Carter 3902, Communities 3911, Cooper 3916, Cullen 3921, Dougherty 3934, El Paso 3940, Fasken 3948, Fikes 3952, Fleming 3954, Griffin 3965, **Halliburton 3970,** Halsell 3971, Hamman 3972, Hightower 3980, **HNG 3982,** Keith 4000, Kempner 4001, Lewis 4015, McKee 4026, **Menil 4031,** Navarro 4040, O'Connor 4042, Owsley 4048, Rockwell 4066, San Antonio 4072, Scurlock 4076, Semmes 4078, Strake 4089, Texas 4099, Trull 4104, Waggoner 4109, White 4121, Wortham 4127

Utah: Dee 4136

Virginia: Camp 4159, Gray 4172, Hopkins 4176, **Mars 4182,** Ohrstrom 4188, Richmond 4196, Sovran 4201, United 4211, Washington 4215

Washington: **Burlington 4226,** Fuchs 4235, Leuthold 4247, Norcliffe 4254, PACCAR 4255, Robertson 4258, Skinner 4262, Spokane 4264, **Stewardship 4265, Wharton 4275**

Wisconsin: Allis-Chalmers 4294, Badger 4299, Banta 4300, Bucyrus-Erie 4308, Consolidated 4310, **Cudahy 4311,** CUNA 4312, Evjue 4316, Falk 4317, First 4318, Gelatt 4323, **Johnson 4331, Kimberly-Clark 4338,** La Crosse 4346, Ladish 4347, Marine 4353, Oshkosh 4361, Oshkosh 4362, **Smith 4380,** Stackner 4381

Building funds

Alabama: Blount 4, Meyer 14, Smith 20, **Sonat 21,** Webb 24

Arizona: Arizona 29, Circle K 31, First 34, Hervey 38, **Kieckhefer 39,** Morris 41, Mulcahy 42

Arkansas: Ross 59

California: Adolph's 64, Ahmanson 65, A.I.D. 66, Albertson 67, **American 69, Artevel 74, Atkinson 76, Atkinson 77, Atlantic 78,** Baker 81, **BankAmerica 84,** Baxter 86, Beckman 89, Beynon 94, Bothin 99, Clorox 127, Coburn 128, Copley 133, Corcoran 134, Cowell 136, Crocker 138, **Doe 152,** Drum 156, Fireman's 169, First 170, Fleishhacker 171, Fleishhacker 172, **Fluor 173,** Fusenot 176, Gellert 183, Gellert 184, Gildred 189, Haas 203, Haas 204, Hedco 212, Herbst 215, Holt 225, Irvine 230, Irwin 231, **Jewett 238,** Jones 240, **Keck 243, Kerr 244,** Lakeside 251, Lear 253, **Levi 258,** Levy 259, Lloyd 264, Lytel 269, Mayer 277, Monterey 289, Mosher 290, Murphey 294, Norris 299, Orleton 304, Packard 308, Parker 310, Pasadena 314, Pauley 316, Pickford 325, Pratt 328, Riverside 333, San Francisco 337, Santa Barbara 340, Schreiber 347, Security 351, Shoong 359, Smith 371, **Smith 372, Stans 378,** Stauffer 380, Steele 382, Stern 383, Stulsaft 389, Thornton 398, Ticor 399, Tuohy 403, Union 406, **Union 407,** Weingart 421, Welk 422, Witter 429

Conferences and seminars

Consulting services

Semmes 4078, **Shell 4081,** Strake 4089, Texas
4099, Trull 4104, **Weaver 4113,** White 4121,
Wortham 4127, Wright 4128
Utah: Bamberger 4130
Vermont: **Edwards 4147,** Windham 4151
Virginia: Camp 4160, Gray 4172, Hopkins 4176,
Mars 4182, Memorial 4185, Ohrstrom 4188,
Reinsch 4192, Richmond 4196, Sovran 4201,
United 4211, Virginia 4214, Washington 4215
Washington: **Forest 4234,** Fuchs 4235, Kawabe
4241, Leuthold 4247, Norcliffe 4254, PACCAR
4255, Robertson 4258, Spokane 4264, **Wharton
4275**
West Virginia: Kanawha 4285
Wisconsin: Allis-Chalmers 4294, Badger 4299, Banta
4300, Bucyrus-Erie 4308, Consolidated 4310,
Cudahy 4311, CUNA 4312, **DeRance 4314,** Evjue
4316, Falk 4317, First 4318, Gelatt 4323, Janesville
4330, **Johnson 4331, Kimberly-Clark 4338,** La
Crosse 4346, Marine 4353, Oshkosh 4361,
Oshkosh 4362, Racine 4370, **Smith 4380,** Stackner
4381

Deficit financing

Alabama: Smith 20
Arizona: Morris 41, Mulcahy 42
California: **Baker 81,** Drum 156, Fleishhacker 171,
Gellert 183, Haas 203, **Page 309,** Stern 383,
Stulsaft 389
Connecticut: **ITT 542,** Xerox 594
District of Columbia: Higginson 662
Florida: Conn 704, **duPont 716**
Georgia: Glancy 840, Hill 846, Lubo 856
Hawaii: **Amfac 888,** Hawaiian 899
Illinois: **DeKalb 989,** Sara 1139, **Sears-Roebuck
1145,** Wurlitzer 1194
Indiana: Heritage 1222
Kansas: Sosland 1329
Kentucky: Bingham 1335
Maryland: Knott 1428, Meyerhoff 1439, Pearlstone
1445
Massachusetts: Ellsworth †523, Fuller 1532, Lindsay
1576, **Little 1578,** Rowland 1611, **Wyman-
Gordon 1660**
Michigan: Bishop 1674, Dalton 1681, Loutit 1738,
Mott 1752
Minnesota: Bremer 1822, Greystone 1851, Mardag
1879, Paper 1901, Quinlan 1906
Missouri: **Anheuser-Busch 1940,** Block 1941, Brown
1944, Brown 1945, Gaylord 1965, McGee 1995,
Millstone 1998, Sunderland 2025
Nebraska: **InterNorth 2058**
New Jersey: **Allied 2098, Hackett 2129,** Prudential
2167, Victoria 2197
New York: Anderson 2240, Brookdale 2305, **Gannett
2463, Griffis 2507,** Lee 2649, **Memton 2724,
Prospect 2842, Rosenthal 2887,** Sheafer 2928,
Sony 2945, Stony 2963, **Thorne 2984,** Wilson
3048
North Carolina: Sternberger 3132
Ohio: **Dana 3196, Kettering 3272,** Pollock 3330,
Sears 3360, **TRW 3392**
Pennsylvania: Dietrich 3556, Dolfinger-McMahon
3557, Eccles 3562, Justus 3621, Justus 3622,
McFeely-Rogers 3652, Patterson 3682, **Pennwalt
3684,** Pittsburgh 3694
Tennessee: Benwood 3829, Plough 3855
Texas: Abell-Hanger 3866, Cullen 3921, **HNG 3982,**
Keith 4000, Kempner 4001, Lewis 4015, Meadows
4029, **Menil 4031,** O'Connor 4042, Rockwell
4066, Semmes 4078, Trull 4104, Wortham 4127
Vermont: **Edwards 4147**
Washington: **Wharton 4275**
Wisconsin: Allis-Chalmers 4294, Badger 4299, Banta
4300, **Cudahy 4311,** First 4318, **Kimberly-Clark
4338,** Marine 4353
Wyoming: Tonkin 4400

Emergency funds

Alabama: Smith 20
Alaska: Alaska 25
Arizona: Arizona 29, First 34, **Kieckhefer 39,**
Mulcahy 42, Wilson 50
Arkansas: **Inglewood 51,** Ross 59
California: **Atkinson 76, Baker 81,** Beckman 89,
Bothin 99, Copley 133, Corcoran 134, Cowell 136,
Crocker 137, Crocker 138, Drum 156, Fleishhacker
171, **Fluor 173,** Gilmore 191, Haas 204, Hancock
209, **Hewlett 217,** Hoover 226, Johnson 239, **Kerr
244,** Lear 251, Levi 258, Levy 259, **Litton 262,**
Lurie 267, McKesson 283, Monterey 289, **Page
309,** Parker 310, Peninsula 318, Pratt 328,
Riverside 333, Santa Barbara 340, Santa Clara 341,
Santa Cruz 342, Schreiber 347, Stamps 377, Stern
383, Trust 402, Union 406, van Loben Sels 410,
Wilbur 428, Yorkin 432
Colorado: Anschutz 435, Colorado 440, Duncan 443,
8 South 444, El Pomar 445, Hughes 454, Norgren
469, Piton 473, **Ray 475, Woodward 487**
Connecticut: **Abex 488,** Aetna 489, **American 492,**
Bridgeport 502, Eder 515, Ensworth 521, Hartford
533, **ITT 542,** New Haven 559, **Olin 561, Panwy
563,** Scott 573, **Stanley 578,** Waterbury 588, erox
594
Delaware: **Glencoe 609,** Laffey-McHugh 616,
Marmot 621, **Raskob 628**
District of Columbia: **Graham 660,** Higginson 662,
Meyer 672, Washington 685
Florida: Bush 701, Dade 706, **duPont 716, Eckerd
719,** Falk 720, Phipps 755
Georgia: Atlanta 802, Atlanta 803, **Day 824,** EMSA
829, Equifax 831, Glancy 840, Hill 846, Loridans
855, Lubo 856, Ottley 861, **Wilson 886,** Woolley
887
Hawaii: Brewer 892, Castle 893
Idaho: Whittenberger 916
Illinois: Abbott 918, Amoco 928, Amsted 929, **CBI
966,** Chicago 968, **Chicago 969, Clark 974,
Crowell 981, DeKalb 989,** Dillon 992, Field 1001,
Haffner 1024, Hales 1025, IMC 1046, **Joyce 1052,**
Joyce 1053, **MacArthur 1076,** McCormick 1089,
McCormick 1090, **Nalco 1105,** New Prospect
1107, Northern 1108, Pick 1119, Sara 1139, **Sears-
Roebuck 1145,** Stern 1167, **Walgreen 1183,** Ward
1185, White 1188, Wurlitzer 1194
Indiana: Anderson 1195, Cummins 1210, Fort 1214,
Heritage 1222, Honeywell 1224
Iowa: Des Moines 1263, Hall 1269, Wahlert 1288
Kansas: Powell 1323, Sosland 1329, Wiedemann 1330
Kentucky: Ashland 1332, Bingham 1335, Cooke
1339, Louisville 1346
Louisiana: Baton Rouge 1354, New Orleans 1376
Maine: Davenport 1392
Maryland: Baker 1401, **Fairchild 1414,** Goldseker
1419, Knott 1428, Meyerhoff 1439, Noxell 1444,
Pearlstone 1445, **PHH 1446**
Massachusetts: Acushnet 1466, **Alden 1468,** Bank
1473, Bayrd 1474, **Beveridge 1475,** Blanchard
1480, Boston 1482, Codman 1500, Daniels 1509,
Davis 1511, **Eastern 1518,** Ellsworth 1523, **Filene
1529,** Fuller 1532, Fuller 1533, Kelley 1567,
Kendall 1569, Little 1578, Morgan-Worcester
1584, Polaroid 1602, Ratshesky 1605, Rowland
1611, Russell 1614, Shaw 1622, Stevens 1634,
Stoddard 1635, Thompson 1643, Worcester 1659,
Wyman-Gordon 1660
Michigan: Ann Arbor 1664, Barstow 1668, Battle
Creek 1669, Besser 1673, Bishop 1674, Bray 1676,
Chrysler 1679, Dalton 1681, DeRoy 1682,
Fremont 1705, **General 1710,** Gerstacker 1712,
Grand 1715, **Harder 1716,** Hunter 1723,
Kalamazoo 1728, Kaufman 1730, Loutit 1738,
Manoogian 1741, McGregor 1744, Midland 1748,
Miller 1749, Mills 1750, Morley 1751, **Mott 1752,**
Simpson 1772, Skillman 1773, Tiscornia 1782,
Whirlpool 1793, Wilson 1799
Minnesota: Bigelow 1820, Blandin 1821, Bremer
1822, First 1842, **General 1847,** Greystone 1851,
Grotto 1853, Hormel 1862, International 1866,
Marbrook 1878, Mardag 1879, McKnight 1880,
McNeely 1882, Minneapolis 1887, **Minnesota**

1890, O'Neil 1898, Paper 1901, Quinlan 1906,
Rochester 1910, Saint Paul 1912, Wasie 1922
Mississippi: First 1936
Missouri: **Anheuser-Busch 1940,** Block 1941, Boone
1943, Brown 1944, Brown 1945, **Butler 1946,**
Cowden 1952, Gaylord 1965, Green 1967, Hall
1968, Laclede 1977, McGee 1995, Millstone 1998,
Oppenstein 2003, Pendergast-Weyer 2006,
Reynolds 2011, Speas 2018, St. Louis 2020,
Sunderland 2025, **Sunnen 2027,** Swinney 2029,
Union 2034
Nebraska: Cooper 2054, **InterNorth 2058,** Lincoln
2063, Phelps 2067
New Hampshire: Bean 2083, Hunt 2087, **Phillips
2093**
New Jersey: **Allied 2098,** Belasco 2101, **Caspersen
2111, Hackett 2129,** Hyde 2134, **Johnson 2139,**
Prudential 2167, Schultz 2179, Schultz 2180,
Schumann 2181, Subaru 2187, Turrell 2193,
Victoria 2197, **Warner-Lambert 2200**
New Mexico: Carlsbad 2208
New York: Adams 2219, **Agway 2224, Atran 2250,**
Boehm 2295, Brookdale 2305, Buffalo 2311,
Carnegie 2325, Central 2331, **Chase 2337,
Chatlos 2338,** Chautauqua 2339, Clark 2347,
Cornell 2367, Cowles 2369, **de Hirsch 2387, Dorr
2408,** Dutchess 2416, Emerson 2421, **Frueauff
2455, Gannett 2463,** Gifford 2469, Glens 2476,
Goodstein 2487, Goodyear 2488, Greenwall 2505,
Heckscher 2540, Hoyt 2565, Irving 2575, Jones
2591, Kaplan 2598, Lang 2636, Lee 2649,
Lounsbery 2679, Macdonald 2685, **McGraw-Hill
2721, Memton 2724,** Moore 2748, New York
2777, **NL 2783,** O'Connor 2795, **O'Toole 2805,
Ottinger 2806, Pfizer 2823, Phillips-Van Heusen
2828, Prospect 2842,** Ramapo 2846, Robert 2870,
Rochester 2873, Rosenthal 2887, Samuels 2905,
Scherman 2913, Snyder 2944, **Sony 2945,** St.
Faith's 2950, **Surdna 2972, Thorne 2984,
Vinmont 3015,** Vogler 3016, Watertown 3027,
Wegman 3030, **Wenner-Gren 3037,** Wilson 3048
North Carolina: **Babcock 3075,** Biddle 3078,
Burroughs 3085, Connemara 3090, Duke 3095,
Ferebee 3097, Foundation 3102, Garrison 3103,
Hanes 3105, Hanes 3106, Reynolds 3123,
Reynolds 3124, Sternberger 3132, Winston-Salem
3137
North Dakota: Fargo-Moorhead 3139, Stern 3143
Ohio: **Amcast 3149,** Anderson 3152, **Armco 3156,
Armington 3157, Borden 3174,** Britton 3176,
Brush 3178, Cincinnati 3183, **Dana 3196,** Dauby
3197, Deuble 3200, **Firestone 3216,** Frohring
3229, Gerson 3237, Gries 3241, Gund 3244,
Hamilton 3245, **Huffy 3255,** Humphrey 3256,
Iddings 3259, **Kettering 3272,** Laub 3281, Lorain
3284, Lubrizol 3285, Mather 3295, **Mead 3299,**
Moores 3308, Nationwide 3313, NCR 3314,
Nordson 3316, Oglebay 3318, Pollock 3330,
Procter 3333, Richland 3342, Sears 3360, Stark
3373, Stocker 3375, **Stouffer 3376,** Toledo 3386,
Toledo 3387, Treuhaft 3389, White 3406, Wolfe
3410, Yassenoff 3414
Oklahoma: Ashbrook 3417, Goddard 3432, **Kerr
3439,** Kirkpatrick 3441, Oklahoma 3451, **Phillips
3456,** Williams 3471
Oregon: Carpenter 3478, Friendly-Rosenthal 3487,
Jackson 3490, Johnson 3495, Salem 3501,
Templeton 3503
Pennsylvania: **Air 3509, Alcoa 3511,** Arcadia 3520,
Bethlehem 3526, **Brockway 3528, CIGNA 3542,**
Craig 3549, Dolfinger-McMahon 3557, Eccles
3562, Erie 3565, **Falk 3568,** Fels 3571, Frick 3577,
Hammermill 3594, **Heinz 3598,** Heinz 3599,
Hershey 3601, Hillman 3604, **Hooper 3607,** Justus
3621, Justus 3622, Kavanagh 3624, Kline 3628,
Lukens 3645, McFeely-Rogers 3652, McKee 3653,
Patterson 3682, **Pennwalt 3684, Pew 3688,**
Philadelphia 3689, Pitcairn-Crabbe 3691, Pittsburgh
3694, PPG 3694, **Scott 3715,** Seybert 3717, Smith
3723, Smith 3725, SPS 3731, Stott 3741, **Stroud
3744, United 3750,** Williamsport 3764, Wurts
3766, Wyomissing 3767
Rhode Island: Fleet 3775, **Little 3783,** Rhode 3790

South Carolina: Abney 3794, Gregg-Graniteville 3806, **Roe 3814,** Self 3817, Spartanburg 3820

Tennessee: Benwood 3829, Chattanooga 3835, Massengill-DeFriece 3851, Plough 3855, Toms 3859

Texas: Abell-Hanger 3866, Amarillo 3872, American 3873, Carter 3902, Communities 3911, Cooper 3916, El Paso 3940, Fasken 3948, Fikes 3952, Fleming 3954, Griffin 3965, Hamman 3972, **HNG 3982,** Keith 4000, Kempner 4001, Lewis 4015, McKee 4026, Meadows 4029, **Menil 4031,** Moody 4035, O'Connor 4042, Owsley 4048, Rockwell 4066, San Antonio 4072, Scurlock 4076, Semmes 4078, Strake 4089, Temple 4098, Trull 4104, Waggoner 4109, White 4121, Wortham 4127

Utah: Dee 4136

Vermont: **Edwards 4147**

Virginia: **Best 4154,** Camp 4159, Ohrstrom 4188, Washington 4215

Washington: Cheney 4229, **Forest 4234,** Fuchs 4235, Glaser 4236, Haas 4238, Kawabe 4241, **Matlock 4248,** McEachern 4249, Medina 4250, Norcliffe 4254, Robertson 4258, Skinner 4262, Tacoma 4267, **Weyerhaeuser 4274, Wharton 4275**

West Virginia: Kanawha 4285

Wisconsin: Alexander 4292, Alexander 4293, Allis-Chalmers 4294, Badger 4299, Banta 4300, Consolidated 4310, **Cudahy 4311,** CUNA 4312, Evjue 4316, **Johnson 4331, Kimberly-Clark 4338,** La Crosse 4346, Marine 4353, Oshkosh 4361, Oshkosh 4362, Siebert 4379, Stackner 4381, Youth 4392

Wyoming: Tonkin 4400

Employee matching gifts

California: **Atlantic 78, BankAmerica 84,** California 114, Clorox 127, Copley 133, Crocker 138, Fireman's 169, First 170, **Fluor 173, Kaiser 242,** Lear 253, Levy 259, Mattel 275, McKesson 283, **Occidental 302,** Pratt 328, Santa Clara 341, Security 351, **Teledyne 395,** Ticor 399, Union 406, **Union 407,** Wells 423

Connecticut: **Abex 488,** Aetna 489, **Amax 491, American 492, Champion 505,** Connecticut 507, **Dexter 512,** Ensign-Bickford 520, **General 527, GTE 531,** Hartford 534, Heublein 538, **Hubbell 540, Olin 561, Scovill 574, Singer 575, Stanley 578, UPS 584, Warnaco 587, Xerox 594**

District of Columbia: **German 659,** Kiplinger 667

Florida: Beattie 695, **Eckerd 719, Harris 726,** Stickelber 775, **Winn-Dixie 794**

Georgia: **Citizens 816, Coca-Cola 818,** Lane 851

Hawaii: **Amfac 888**

Illinois: **Abbott 918, Allstate 922,** American 925, **Ameritech 926,** Barber-Colman 936, **Becker 940,** Borg-Warner 950, **Brunswick 955, Caterpillar 965, CBI 966,** Chicago 971, Chicago 972, **Clark 974,** Deere 987, **DeKalb 989,** Fel-Pro 1000, First 1002, **FMC 1005, Gould 1020,** Harris 1028, **Illinois 1045, Interlake 1049,** Jewel 1050, **Joyce 1052,** Kaplan 1055, **Keebler 1057,** Motorola 1104, Northern 1108, **Northwest 1109, Quaker 1126, Santa Fe 1138,** Sara 1139, **Signode 1152, Square D 1162, United 1179,** UOP 1180, USG 1182, Ward 1185

Indiana: Mead 1242

Iowa: Maytag 1276

Kansas: **Cessna 1297, Hesston 1311, Marley 1319**

Kentucky: **Ashland 1333,** Bingham 1335

Maine: Unionmutual 1397

Maryland: Abell 1399, Commercial 1408, **Fairchild 1414,** Noxell 1444, **PHH 1446**

Massachusetts: Boston 1483, **Cabot 1488, Eastern 1518, EG&G 1521,** GenRad 1534, **Kendall 1568,** Morgan-Worcester 1584, Polaroid 1602, **Wyman-Gordon 1660**

Michigan: **Chrysler 1679, Federal-Mogul 1696, Ford 1702,** Hudson-Webber 1722, Morley 1751, **Mott 1752,** National 1755, **Whirlpool 1793**

Minnesota: **Bemis 1818,** Bremer 1822, **DeLuxe 1835,** First 1842, First 1843, **General 1847,** Graco 1849, Honeywell 1861, International 1866, Inter-Regional 1867, Jostens 1870, McNeely 1882, **Medtronic 1884, Minnesota 1890, Pillsbury 1905,** Tennant 1915

Mississippi: First 1936

Missouri: **Anheuser-Busch 1940,** Block 1941, Brown 1945, Centerre 1948, **Danforth 1955, Emerson 1959,** McDonnell 1993, **Monsanto 1999, Ralston 2010,** Union 2034

Nebraska: **InterNorth 2058**

New Jersey: **Allied 2098,** Campbell 2107, **Johnson 2139,** Lipton 2150, **Merck 2155, Nabisco 2159, National 2160,** Prudential 2167, **Schering-Plough 2178, Subaru 2187, Union 2194**

New Mexico: Carlsbad 2208

New York: **ACF 2217, American 2235, American-Standard 2237, ASARCO 2246, AT&T 2249, Bristol-Myers 2302,** Central 2331, **Continental 2365, Corning 2368, Deloitte 2395, Donovan 2406,** Dun 2415, **Exxon 2426, First 2435, Gannett 2463, General 2467,** Goodyear 2488, **Grace 2496, Gulf 2516, Hartford 2528, IFF 2571, International 2574,** Irving 2575, **J.M. 2584,** Kaplan 2598, **Loews 2677, Luce 2682, Macy 2689, Manufacturers 2698, McGraw-Hill 2721, Metropolitan 2732, Mobil 2743,** Morgan 2750, Morgan 2751, New York 2774, New York 2777, **NL 2783,** Peat 2817, **PepsiCo 2820,** Phelps 2825, **Pren-Hall 2838,** Price 2840, Reader's 2851, Revlon 2857, Rockefeller 2875, SCM 2924, **Sony 2945,** Stevens 2962, **Texaco 2981, Thompson 2982, Transway 2991,** United 3000, **Westvaco 3040, Young 3062**

North Carolina: Akzona 3073, **Blue Bell 3079,** Burlington 3084, Garrison 3103

Ohio: Acme 3144, **Amcast 3149, Armco 3156, Borden 3174,** Cleveland 3185, Cleveland-Cliffs 3187, **Dana 3196, Eaton 3204, Ernst 3207, Federated 3211, Firestone 3216, GenCorp 3234, Hoover 3253, Huffy 3255,** Lubrizol 3285, **Marathon 3289, Mead 3299, Midland-Ross 3302,** Nationwide 3313, NCR 3314, Oglebay 3318, **Procter 3333, Reliance 3339, Republic 3341, Robbins 3345,** Scott 3358, **Sherwin-Williams 3366, TRW 3392, White 3405**

Oklahoma: Kerr-McGee 3440, **MAPCO 3444,** Oklahoma 3452, **Phillips 3456,** Williams 3471

Oregon: Tektronix 3502

Pennsylvania: **Alco 3510, Alcoa 3511,** American 3514, **Brockway 3528, Carpenter 3536, CIGNA 3542, Cyclops 3553, Dravo 3561, Gulf 3589,** Hammermill 3594, **Harsco 3595, Heinz 3598,** Hershey 3601, **Koppers 3631, Lukens 3645, Merit 3666,** Penn 3683, **Pennwalt 3684,** Pittsburgh 3694, PPG 3697, Quaker 3699, Reliance 3703, **Rockwell 3708, Scott 3715,** SmithKline 3726, SPS 3731, **United 3750, Westinghouse 3756,** Westinghouse 3757

Rhode Island: Fleet 3775, Old 3786, **Textron 3792**

South Carolina: Citizens 3801, **Liberty 3809, Merck 3810,** Riegel 3813

Texas: American 3873, Brown 3893, Cooper 3916, **Dresser 3935, ENSERCH 3943, Halliburton 3970, HNG 3982,** Kempner 4001, **Shell 4081,** Texas 4099, **Texas 4102**

Virginia: **Best 4154, Reynolds 4193,** Richmond 4196, Sovran 4201, UVB 4213

Washington: Boeing 4223, **Burlington 4226, Matlock 4248,** PACCAR 4255, Washington 4269, **Weyerhaeuser 4274**

Wisconsin: **ARMCO 4298,** Banta 4300, Bucyrus-Erie 4308, Consolidated 4310, CUNA 4312, **Johnson 4331, Johnson's 4336, Kimberly-Clark 4338,** La Crosse 4346, Marine 4353, **Rexnord 4373**

Employee related scholarships

Alabama: **Sonat 21,** Stockham 22

California: **Atlantic 78, BankAmerica 84, Carnation 120, City 125,** Crocker 138, Disney 148, Fireman's 169, First 170, **Fluor 173,** Lear 253, Leavey 254, **Levi 258, Lockheed 266,** McKesson 283, Security 351, **Union 407**

Connecticut: **Abex 488, Amax 491, American 492, Barnes 497,** Eder 515, Emery 518, Ensign-Bickford 520, Heublein 538, **ITT 542, Olin 561, Singer 575, UPS 584,** Xerox 594

Delaware: **Beneficial 596, Presto 626**

Florida: **Dettman 712**

Georgia: Bibb 806, Rich 870

Hawaii: **Amfac 888**

Illinois: Aigner 919, Andrew 931, Belden 942, **Brunswick 955, Evinrude 997, FMC 1005, Gould 1020,** Harris 1028, **Illinois 1045,** Inland 1048, Jewel 1050, Kaplan 1055, Maremont 1081, **McGraw 1094, Quaker 1126, Roper 1135, Santa Fe 1138,** Sara 1139, Scholl 1142, **Signode 1152, Square D 1162, State 1166, Sundstrand 1174, United 1179,** UOP 1180

Indiana: Anderson 1195, Central 1204, **Credithrift 1208,** Cummins 1210, Habig 1219, Mead 1242, **Reilly 1250**

Iowa: Maytag 1276, Pella 1280, **Salsbury 1282**

Kansas: **Koch 1317, Marley 1319**

Kentucky: **Ashland 1333**

Maryland: Abell 1399, **Fairchild 1414, Knapp 1426, Martin 1435**

Massachusetts: Fuller 1532, Housen 1558, Polaroid 1602, **Wyman-Gordon 1660**

Michigan: **Chrysler 1679,** DeVlieg 1685, **Gerber 1711,** Tiscornia 1782, **Whirlpool 1793**

Minnesota: **American 1807, Bemis 1818,** Bremer 1822, First 1842, **General 1847,** Graco 1849, Groves 1854, Hotchkiss 1863, **Pillsbury 1905,** Saint Paul 1912, Tennant 1915, Valspar 1918

Missouri: **Anheuser-Busch 1940,** Block 1941, **Butler 1946, Emerson 1959,** Hall 1968, **Ralston 2010,** Union 2034

New Hampshire: Kingsbury 2090

New Jersey: **Allied 2098, Mueller 2158, National 2160,** Prudential 2167, Schultz 2180, **Union 2194**

New York: **ACF 2217, American 2235, AMETEK 2238, ARW 2245,** Avon 2251, Bristol-Myers 2302, Brookdale 2305, **Chase 2337, Continental 2365, Dow 2410, Dun 2415, Gannett 2463, Gannett 2464, General 2467, Grace 2496, Gulf 2516, Loews 2677, McGraw-Hill 2721, Mobil 2743,** New York 2777, **NL 2783, Sony 2945, Teagle 2979, Texaco 2981, Witco 3053**

North Carolina: Chatham 3089, **Fieldcrest 3098, Myers-Ti-Caro 3121, Thomasville 3135**

Ohio: **Armco 3156,** Crosset 3195, **GenCorp 3234, Goodyear 3239,** Kuntz 3279, **Marathon 3289, Mead 3299,** Nationwide 3313, NCR 3314, **Premier 3331, Procter 3333,** Richman 3343, **Timken 3383, TRW 3392**

Oklahoma: Noble 3449

Oregon: **Louisiana-Pacific 3496,** Tektronix 3502

Pennsylvania: **Alcoa 3511, Brockway 3528, Dravo 3561,** Evans 3566, **Gulf 3589, Harsco 3595,** Hunt 3612, **Koppers 3631, Merit 3666, Pennwalt 3684,** PPG 3697, Quaker 3699, **Rockwell 3708, Scott 3715,** SmithKline 3726, Steinman 3737, **Superior-Pacific 3745, Westinghouse 3756, Westmoreland 3758,** Yarway 3768

Rhode Island: Citizens 3773, Cranston 3774, **Textron 3792**

South Carolina: **Bailey 3797,** Gregg-Graniteville 3806, Inman-Riverdale 3807, **Post 3812, Riegel 3813**

Texas: Cooper 3916, **Dresser-Harbison 3936,** Haggar 3967, **Shell 4081,** Texas 4101

Virginia: **Dan 4166**

Washington: Leuthold 4247, **Weyerhaeuser 4274**

Wisconsin: Briggs 4306, Bucyrus-Erie 4308, Consolidated 4310, Jacobus/Heritage 4329, **Johnson 4331, Johnson's 4336,** Nekoosa 4360, Oshkosh 4362, **Rahr 4371, Rexnord 4373**

Endowment funds

Alabama: Blount 4, Smith 20
Arizona: **Kieckhefer 39,** Morris 41, Mulcahy 42
Arkansas: Ross 59
California: Adolph's 64, Ahmanson 65, **Atkinson 77,** Beckman 89, Clorox 127, Corcoran 134, Cowell 136, Fireman's 169, First 170, Fleishhacker 171, Gellert 183, Haas 204, Jones 240, **Keck 243, Litton 262,** Martin 274, Mead 284, **Philibosian 323,** Pickford 325, Santa Cruz 342, Schreiber 347, Stauffer 380, Steele 382, Stern 383, Thornton 398, **Wollenberg 430**
Colorado: Buell 437, **Frost 449,** Hughes 454, **Taylor 482**
Connecticut: Auerbach 494, **ITT 542,** Moore 558, **Oaklawn 560, Panwy 563,** Scott 573, **Stone 579,** Vanderbilt 585
Delaware: Longwood 618, **Schwartz 630**
District of Columbia: Bloedorn 641, **Freed 656, Graham 660,** Kiplinger 667, Ross 680
Florida: **Davis 707, Dettman 712,** Wilder 792
Georgia: Atlanta 803, Baker 804, Campbell 813, EMSA 829, Equifax 831, Glancy 840, Harland 843, Hill 846, Lane 851, Loridans 855, Ottley 861, **Tull 878**
Hawaii: **Amfac 888,** Watumull 907
Illinois: Aurora 935, Borg-Warner 950, Crown 982, **Crown 983, DeKalb 989, Donnelley 994,** First 1002, **Gould 1020,** Grainger 1022, **Griswold 1023,** Haffner 1024, Hales 1025, Kaplan 1055, McCormick 1089, **Peterborough 1117,** Regenstein 1130, Schmitt 1141, Wurlitzer 1194
Indiana: Clowes 1206, Cummins 1210, Honeywell 1224, Jordan 1230, Krannert 1233, Noyes 1246, Oliver 1247
Iowa: Cowles 1262, **Lee 1274,** Vermeer 1287
Kansas: Baughman 1293, Fourth 1305, Sosland 1329, Wiedemann 1330
Kentucky: Cooke 1339
Louisiana: Jones 1370
Maryland: Abell 1399, Baker 1401, **Fairchild 1414,** Hoffberger 1423, Kelly 1424, Knott 1428, Meyerhoff 1439, Middendorf 1440, Pearlstone 1445, Sheridan 1454, U.S.F. & G. 1460
Massachusetts: Bayrd 1474, Cabot 1489, Daniels 1509, Fidelity 1528, Fuller 1532, Fuller 1533, Merkert 1583, Pappas 1591, Riley 1608, Schrafft 1618, Stevens 1634, Stone 1637, Wallace 1647, **Webster 1652**
Michigan: Barstow 1668, Battle Creek 1669, Dow 1690, Gerstacker 1712, **Harder 1716,** Loutit 1738, **Manoogian 1741,** Miller 1749, Muskegon 1754, Seidman 1767, Shelden 1770, Strosacker 1780, Towsley 1783, Wilson 1800
Minnesota: Bush 1823, Butler 1824, Lilly 1876, Marbrook 1878, McNeely 1882, **O'Shaughnessy 1900,** Paper 1901, Quinlan 1906, Thorpe 1916, Van Evera 1919, Wasie 1922
Mississippi: First 1936, Hardin 1937
Missouri: **Anheuser-Busch 1940,** Commerce 1951, **Cross 1954,** Gaylord 1965, Green 1967, Roblee 2012, Sunderland 2025
Nebraska: Hitchcock 2057
Nevada: **Sells 2081**
New Hampshire: **Phillips 2093**
New Jersey: Grassmann 2127, **Kirby 2143,** Union 2195
New Mexico: Carlsbad 2208
New York: **American-Standard 2237,** Astor 2248, **Atran 2250,** Baird 2260, Barker 2264, Beinecke 2275, Brookdale 2305, Campe 2321, **Coles 2358, Compton 2363, Corning 2368,** Cowles 2369, Curtice-Burns 2377, **Dammann 2378,** Dillon 2399, **Dillon 2400, Dodge 2402,** Emerson 2421, **Forbes 2440, Ford 2443, Frueauff 2455, Greve 2506, Hearst 2537, Hearst 2538, Jephson 2581, Kenan 2609, Kunstadter 2632,** L.A.W. 2645, Lemberg 2655, **Link 2672, Littauer 2675,** Macdonald 2685, Macmillan 2688, **Manufacturers 2698, Mellon 2722, Memton 2724, Michel 2735,** Moore 2748, Moses 2758, New York 2777, Nichols 2782, **Noble 2784, Norwood 2791,** O'Connor 2795, **Phelps 2825, Phillips 2827,** Price 2839, **Prospect**

2842, Ritter 2868, Robert 2870, Romill 2880, **Rosenthal 2888, Rubin 2895,** Schweckendieck 2922, Sheafer 2928, Snyder 2944, **Sony 2945, Starr 2954, Statler 2955, Steele-Reese 2957, Thorne 2984,** Tuch 2993, **Tudor 2994,** United 3000, Vidda 3012, **Weatherhead 3028,** Western 3039, Wikstrom 3045, Wilson 3048, **Witco 3053**
North Carolina: **Connemara 3090,** Duke 3095, Garrison 3103, Hanes 3105, Hanes 3106, Morgan 3119, Reynolds 3124
Ohio: Acme 3144, American 3150, Beeghly 3165, **Bingham 3172,** Bolton 3173, Crandall 3193, **Dana 3196,** Deuble 3200, **Firestone 3216,** GAR 3232, Gries 3241, H.C.S. 3250, Humphrey 3256, **Kettering 3272,** Mather 3294, Nordson 3316, Pollock 3330, Prentiss 3332, Reinberger 3338, **Republic 3341,** Schmidlapp 3354, Semple 3361, Stocker 3375, **Stouffer 3376,** Stranahan 3377, Treuhaft 3389
Oklahoma: **Noble 3449, Noble 3450, Phillips 3456,** Warren 3469
Oregon: Oregon 3500
Pennsylvania: **Air 3509,** Arcadia 3520, **CIGNA 3542, Copernicus 3548,** Craig 3549, **Falk 3568, Gulf 3589,** Heinz 3599, Hershey 3601, Hillman 3603, **Independence 3616, Kennametal 3626,** McCune 3651, McKenna 3655, Mellon 3661, Mellon 3663, Pitcairn-Crabbe 3691, Pittsburgh 3694, Shoemaker 3719, Stabler 3733, **Stroud 3744, United 3750**
Rhode Island: Champlin 3772, **Little 3783**
South Carolina: Abney 3794, Gregg-Graniteville 3806, Scurry 3816, Springs 3821
Tennessee: Benwood 3829
Texas: Abell-Hanger 3866, Brackenridge 3889, Brown 3893, **Burkitt 3897,** Clark 3906, Constantin 3912, Cooley 3914, Dallas 3924, Davidson 3926, Dougherty 3934, Duncan 3937, El Paso 3940, Fair 3945, Fasken 3948, Fikes 3952, **HNG 3982,** Keith 4000, Kempner 4001, Lewis 4015, O'Connor 4042, Owsley 4048, Richardson 4064, San Antonio 4072, Scurlock 4076, Steinhagen 4087, Strake 4089, Waggoner 4109, White 4121, Wright 4128
Utah: Dee 4136
Virginia: Gray 4172, **Mars 4182,** Ohrstrom 4188, Richmond 4196, Sovran 4201, United 4211, Wheat 4216
Washington: PACCAR 4255, Robertson 4258, Skinner 4262, Spokane 4264, **Wharton 4275**
Wisconsin: Badger 4299, Bucyrus-Erie 4308, Consolidated 4310, Evjue 4316, Frankenthal 4320, **Johnson 4331,** Kohler 4342, Ladish 4347, Stackner 4381

Equipment

Alabama: Blount 4, Meyer 14, Smith 20, Webb 24
Alaska: Alaska 25
Arizona: Arizona 29, Butz 30, Circle K 31, First 34, Hervey 38, **Kieckhefer 39,** Mulcahy 42
Arkansas: Ross 59
California: Adolph's 64, Ahmanson 65, A.I.D. 66, Albertson 67, **American 69,** Associated 75, **Atlantic 78, Baker 81,** Beckman 89, Bothin 99, Copley 133, Corcoran 134, Cowell 136, Crocker 137, Distribution 151, Drum 156, East Bay 159, Fireman's 169, Fleishhacker 171, Fleishhacker 172, Fusenot 176, Gellert 183, Gellert 184, Gildred 189, Goldwyn 196, Haas 202, Haas 203, Haas 204, Hedco 212, Hoover 226, Humboldt 228, Irvine 230, Irwin 231, **Jewett 238,** Jones 240, **Keck 243, Kerr 244,** Lear 253, **Levi 258,** Levy 259, Lloyd 264, Lux 268, Lytel 269, Mayer 277, Monterey 289, Murphey 294, Norris 299, Packard 308, Parker 310, **Parsons 311,** Pasadena 314, Peninsula 318, Pickford 325, Powell 327, Pratt 328, Riverside 333, San Diego 336, San Francisco 337, Santa Barbara 340, Santa Cruz 342, Shoong 359, **Stans 378,** Stauffer 379, Stauffer 380, Steele 382, Stern 383, Stulsaft 389, Tuohy 403, Union 406, Weingart 421, Welk 422, Witter 429

Colorado: Boettcher 436, Buell 437, Colorado 440, Duncan 443, El Pomar 445, **Frost 449,** Heginbotham 451, Hill 452, Hughes 454, Johnson 458, Joslyn 460, Norgren 469, **Ray 475,** Schramm 478, **Woodward 487**
Connecticut: Barnes 496, Bridgeport 502, Ensign-Bickford 520, Hartford 533, Howard 539, **ITT 542,** Moore 558, New Haven 559, **Olin 561, Panwy 563,** Patterson 564, Scott 573, **UPS 584,** Wahlstrom-Johnson 586, Waterbury 588
Delaware: **Beneficial 596,** Crystal 606, **Glencoe 609,** Laffey-McHugh 616, Longwood 618, Marmot 621, **Raskob 628,** Schwartz 630, Welfare 632
District of Columbia: **Graham 660,** Higginson 662, **Loyola 670,** Stewart 682
Florida: Beattie 695, Briggs 698, **Brunner 700,** Bush 701, Conn 704, Dade 706, **Davis 707, Dettman 712,** duPont 716, Falk 720, **Koch 734,** Phipps 755, Selby 766, Southwest 771, Stickelber 775, **Whitehall 791, Winn-Dixie 794**
Georgia: Atlanta 802, Atlanta 803, Callaway 810, Callaway 811, Campbell 813, **Day 824,** Equifax 831, Evans 832, Glancy 840, Harland 843, Hill 846, Lane 851, Loridans 855, Lubo 856, Ottley 861, Rich 870, Trust 877, Whitehead 884, **Wilson 886,** Woolley 887
Hawaii: **Amfac 888,** Brewer 892, Castle 893, Castle 894, Cooke 895, Frear 898, Hawaiian 899, McInerny 903, Wilcox 908
Idaho: Whittenberger 916
Illinois: **Abbott 918, Amoco 928, Amsted 929,** Aurora 935, Barber-Colman 936, Borg-Warner 950, Camp 962, Carson 964, Chicago 968, **Chicago 969, Clark 974,** Coleman 975, **Crowell 981,** Crown 982, **Crown 983,** Cuneo 984, **Deere 987, DeKalb 989, Evinrude 997,** Field 1001, First 1002, **FMC 1005,** Fry 1011, Furnas 1012, **Gould 1020,** Grainger 1022, Haffner 1024, Harris 1028, **Harris 1030, MacArthur 1076,** McCormick 1089, **McGraw 1094,** Millard 1098, **Moorman 1101,** Moorman 1102, **Nalco 1105,** Northern 1108, Payne 1113, **Quaker 1126,** R. F. 1128, Regenstein 1130, Sara 1139, Scholl 1142, Siragusa 1153, **Square D 1162, Sundstrand 1174,** UOP 1180, USG 1182, White 1188, Wurlitzer 1194
Indiana: **Arvin 1196,** Cole 1207, Fort 1214, Froderman 1215, Hayner 1221, Heritage 1222, Honeywell 1224, Indianapolis 1226, Krannert 1233, Lilly 1237
Iowa: Hall 1269, Maytag 1277, Wahlert 1288
Kansas: **Cessna 1297,** Fourth 1305, Garvey 1307, Hansen 1309, **Hesston 1311,** Jordaan 1314, **Marley 1319,** Powell 1323, Sosland 1329, Wiedemann 1330
Kentucky: Appalachian 1331, Bingham 1335, Cooke 1339, Ogden 1350, Vogt 1353
Louisiana: Baton Rouge 1354, Brown 1355, German 1362, Jones 1370, Physicians 1377, Shreveport-Bossier 1383, Zigler 1390
Maryland: Baker 1401, **Fairchild 1414,** Hoffberger 1423, Kelly 1424, Knott 1428, Noxell 1444, **PHH 1446,** Sheridan 1454, U.S.F. & G. 1460
Massachusetts: **Alden 1468,** Bacon 1472, Bayrd 1474, **Beveridge 1475,** Blanchard 1480, Boston 1482, Boynton 1484, **Cabot 1488,** Cabot 1489, Cambridge 1491, Campbell 1492, Codman 1500, Daniels 1509, Dexter 1515, **Eastern 1518,** Ellsworth 1523, **Filene 1529, Friendship 1531,** Fuller 1532, Hyams 1561, Kelley 1567, Lindsay 1576, Morgan-Worcester 1584, Old 1589, Parker 1592, Ratshesky 1605, Riley 1608, Russell 1614, Stevens 1634, Stoddard 1635, Stone 1637, Thompson 1643, Vingo 1646, Wallace 1647, **Walsh 1648, Webster 1652,** Worcester 1659, **Wyman-Gordon 1660**
Michigan: **Aeroquip 1662,** Americana 1663, Ann Arbor 1664, Barstow 1668, Battle Creek 1669, Besser 1673, Bishop 1674, Bray 1676, Dalton 1681, DeWaters 1687, Dow 1689, Dow 1690, **Ford 1702, General 1710,** Gerstacker 1712, Grand 1715, Herrick 1718, Holden 1720, Hunter 1723, Hurst 1724, Jackson 1726, Kantzler 1729, **Kresge 1734,** Lansing 1735, Loutit 1738, **Manoogian**

Exchange programs

Fellowships

General purposes

Oregon: Collins 3482, **Jeld-Wen 3491,** Oregon 3500, Salem 3501, Tektronix 3502
Pennsylvania: Bethlehem 3526, Craig 3549, **Cyclops 3553,** Eccles 3562, Grundy 3588, Hillman 3603, J.D.B. 3619, Justus 3621, Justus 3622, Lesher 3639, Mellon 3663, Patterson 3682, **Pennwalt 3684,** Pittsburgh 3694, Sheppard 3718, Smith 3723, Smith 3725, Stott 3741, **Stroud 3744,** Trexler 3748, **United 3750, Whitaker 3761**
Rhode Island: Champlin 3772, Citizens 3773, Fleet 3775, Old 3786, Rhode 3790
South Carolina: Abney 3794, **Roe 3814**
Tennessee: Benwood 3829, Toms 3859, Tonya 3860
Texas: Amarillo 3872, Brown 3893, Carter 3902, Communities 3911, Constantin 3912, Cullen 3921, Dallas 3923, Dougherty 3934, El Paso 3940, Faith 3946, Fikes 3952, Halsell 3971, Hillcrest 3981, **HNG 3982,** Hoblitzelle 3984, Johnson 3995, Jonsson 3997, Keith 4000, Kempner 4001, Meadows 4029, O'Connor 4042, Richardson 4064, Rockwell 4066, San Antonio 4072, Scurlock 4076, Semmes 4078, Steinhagen 4087, Temple 4098, Trull 4104, Waggoner 4109, White 4121
Virginia: Camp 4159, Gray 4172, Norfolk 4187, Ohrstrom 4188, Sovran 4201, United 4211
Washington: **Anderson 4218,** Archibald 4219, Comstock 4230, **Forest 4234,** Fuchs 4235, Kawabe 4241, **Laird 4246, Matlock 4248,** McEachern 4249, Norcliffe 4254, Robertson 4258, Spokane 4264, **Weyerhaeuser 4274, Wharton 4275**
West Virginia: Kanawha 4285
Wisconsin: Alexander 4292, Alexander 4293, Allis-Chalmers 4294, Badger 4299, Banta 4300, Consolidated 4310, **Cudahy 4311,** Frankenthal 4320, Janesville 4330, **Johnson's 4336, Kimberly-Clark 4338,** Kohler 4342, Stackner 4381

Lectureships
Massachusetts: **Grass 1538,** Lowell 1579
New York: **Homeland 2560, Peat 2817**
Oklahoma: Fields 3429
Texas: Tarrant 4094, Waggoner 4109
Wisconsin: Helfaer 4327

Loans
Arizona: Mulcahy 42
California: Adolph's 64, Babcock 79, Corcoran 134, Gerbode 186, **Koulaieff 249,** Layne 252, Monterey 289, Norman 298, Packard 308, Peninsula 318, San Francisco 337
Colorado: 8 South 444
Connecticut: Hartford 533, New Haven 559
District of Columbia: Washington 685
Florida: Bush 701, Fellows 721
Georgia: Equifax 831
Illinois: Chicago 968, **Joyce 1052**
Kentucky: Houchens 1343
Maryland: Goldseker 1419
Massachusetts: Hopedale 1555, **Kendall 1569,** Riley 1608, Shaw 1622
Michigan: Grand 1715, Jackson 1726, Miller 1749, **Mott 1752,** Muskegon 1754
Minnesota: Blandin 1821, Minneapolis 1887, North 1892, Ordean 1899
New Hampshire: Bean 2083, New Hampshire 2092
New Mexico: Carlsbad 2208
New York: Albany's 2226, Bruner 2309, **Carnegie 2325,** Clark 2349, **de Hirsch 2387,** Fund 2460, Gebbie 2465, **Hartford 2528,** New York 2774, O'Connor 2795, **Richmond 2864,** Ritter 2868, **Scherman 2913, Stern 2960,** Western 3039, Wilson 3049
Ohio: Cincinnati 3183, Deuble 3200, Gund 3244, Nordson 3316
Oklahoma: Fields 3429, Harmon 3434

Oregon: Carpenter 3478
Pennsylvania: Gibson 3578, Williamsport 3764
Texas: Crump 3920, El Paso 3940, Luling 4019
Utah: Bamberger 4130
Vermont: **Edwards 4147**
Virginia: Virginia 4214

Matching funds
Alabama: Blount 4, Smith 20, **Sonat 21**
Alaska: Alaska 25
Arizona: Arizona 29, First 34, **Kieckhefer 39,** Mulcahy 42, Wilson 50
Arkansas: **Inglewood 51,** Rockefeller 58, Ross 59
California: **Abelard 63,** Adolph's 64, Ahmanson 65, A.I.D. 66, **American 69, Atlantic 78,** Bacon 80, **BankAmerica 84,** Beckman 89, Bothin 99, California 114, Corcoran 134, Cowell 136, Crocker 137, Crocker 138, Distribution 151, Drum 156, East Bay 159, First 170, Gallo 178, **Getty 187,** Gildred 189, Haas 204, Hancock 209, Hedco 212, **Hewlett 217, Hilton 220,** Holt 225, Hoover 226, Irvine 230, **Jewett 238, Kaiser 242,** Koret 248, **Levi 258,** Lurie 267, Lux 268, Mayer 277, McKesson 283, Mead 284, Monterey 289, Norman 298, Orleton 304, Oxnard 306, Packard 308, Parker 310, **Parsons 311,** Pasadena 314, Peninsula 318, **Pfeiffer 322,** Pratt 328, Riverside 333, San Diego 336, Santa Barbara 340, Santa Clara 341, Seaver 350, **Shalan 356,** Shoong 359, **Skaggs 369,** Stamps 377, Stauffer 380, Steele 382, Stern 383, Stulsaft 389, Tuohy 403, van Loben Sels 410, Weingart 421, Welk 422, **Wilbur 428**
Colorado: Boettcher 436, **Frost 449,** Johnson 458, Norgren 469, **Ray 475**
Connecticut: Aetna 489, **Amax 491, American 492,** Connecticut 507, **Educational 516,** Ensworth 521, Hartford 533, Howard 539, **ITT 542,** Moore 558, New Haven 559, **Oaklawn 560, Olin 561,** Patterson 564, **Stanley 578, Topsfield 582, UPS 584,** Wahlstrom-Johnson 586, Waterbury 588, Woman's 593
Delaware: Laffey-McHugh 616, Marmot 621, **Raskob 628,** Schwartz 630, Welfare 632
District of Columbia: **Benton 640,** Cafritz 643, **Graham 660,** Higginson 662, **Loyola 670,** Meyer 672, **Public 679,** Ross 680, Stewart 682
Florida: Beattie 695, **Brunner 700,** Bush 701, Conn 704, **Davis 707,** duPont 716, Falk 720, **Koch 734,** Phipps 755, Price 758, Saunders 766, Selby 766, Southwest 771, Stickelber 775, **Storer 776, Stuart 777,** Wilder 792, **Winn-Dixie 794**
Georgia: Atlanta 803, Callaway 810, Callaway 811, Campbell 813, **Coca-Cola 818, Day 824,** Lane 851, Loridans 855, Lubo 856, **Southern 873,** Woolley 887
Hawaii: Cooke 895, Frear 898, Hawaiian 899, McInerny 903, Wilcox 908
Illinois: **Abbott 918, Amoco 928, Amsted 929,** Aurora 935, Borg-Warner 950, Chicago 968, **Chicago 969,** Coleman 975, **Crowell 981,** Crown 982, **Crown 983,** Cuneo 984, **DeKalb 989,** Fel-Pro 1000, First 1002, Fry 1011, Furnas 1012, Harris 1028, **Joyce 1052,** Joyce 1053, **MacArthur 1077,** McCormick 1089, **McGraw 1094,** New Prospect 1107, **Quaker 1126,** Retirement 1132, Sara 1139, Siragusa 1153, Stern 1167, USG 1182, Woods 1193
Indiana: Anderson 1195, Ball 1199, Cole 1207, Cummins 1210, Fort 1214, Hayner 1221, Heritage 1222, Honeywell 1224, Indianapolis 1226, Jordan 1230, Lilly 1237, **Lilly 1238,** Moore 1245, Noyes 1246, Oliver 1247
Iowa: Cowles 1262, Des Moines 1263, Maytag 1277, **Salsbury 1282**
Kansas: Coleman 1298, Garvey 1307, **Hesston 1311,** Jordaan 1314, Powell 1323, Sosland 1329, Wiedemann 1330
Kentucky: Bingham 1335
Louisiana: Baton Rouge 1354, Jones 1370, **Louisiana 1373,** Physicians 1377

Maine: Davenport 1392
Maryland: **Fairchild 1414,** Goldseker 1419, Hoffberger 1423, Kelly 1424, Knott 1428, Meyerhoff 1439, Middendorf 1440, Pearlstone 1445
Massachusetts: **Alden 1468,** Bacon 1472, Bank 1473, **Beveridge 1475,** Blanchard 1480, Boston 1482, **Cabot 1488,** Codman 1500, Cove 1503, Daniels 1509, Dexter 1515, **Filene 1529,** Fuller 1532, Hyams 1561, Kelley 1567, Lindsay 1576, Polaroid 1602, Ratshesky 1605, Shaw 1622, Shawmut 1623, Stevens 1634, Stoddard 1635, Thompson 1643, Wallace 1647, **Webster 1652,** Worcester 1659
Michigan: Ann Arbor 1664, Barstow 1668, Besser 1672, Besser 1673, Bray 1676, **Bundy 1677,** Dalton 1681, DeWaters 1687, **Federal-Mogul 1696,** Flint 1698, **Ford 1702,** Fremont 1705, **Gerber 1711,** Gerstacker 1712, Grand 1715, **Harder 1716,** Holden 1720, Hudson-Webber 1722, Hunter 1723, Jackson 1726, Kalamazoo 1728, Kantzler 1729, **Kresge 1734,** Loutit 1738, **Manoogian 1741,** Midland 1748, Miller 1749, Mills 1750, Morley 1751, **Mott 1752, Mott 1753,** Muskegon 1754, Simpson 1772, Towsley 1783, **Whirlpool 1793,** Wilson 1800
Minnesota: Apache 1812, Bend 1819, Bigelow 1820, Blandin 1821, Bremer 1822, Bush 1823, Butler 1824, Carolyn 1827, **Dayton 1834, General 1847,** Graco 1849, Hormel 1862, **Kasal 1871,** Lilly 1876, Marbrook 1878, Mardag 1879, McKnight 1880, **Medtronic 1884, Minnesota 1890,** Neilson 1891, Ordean 1899, Phillips 1903, **Pillsbury 1905,** Quinlan 1906, Rochester 1910, Saint Paul 1912
Mississippi: First 1936, Hardin 1937
Missouri: Block 1941, **Butler 1946,** Gaylord 1965, Hall 1968, Laclede 1977, Oppenstein 2003, **Sunnen 2027**
Nebraska: Cooper 2054, Hitchcock 2057, **InterNorth 2058,** Kiewit 2059, Lincoln 2063, Omaha 2066, Phelps 2067
Nevada: **Sells 2081**
New Hampshire: Bean 2083, Hunt 2087, Kingsbury 2090
New Jersey: Belasco 2101, **Bergen 2102,** Borden 2104, Campbell 2107, Dodge 2116, Fund 2125, **Huber 2133,** Hyde 2134, **Johnson 2139,** New Jersey 2161, Ohl 2163, Prudential 2167, Schultz 2179, Schultz 2180, **Schumann 2181,** Turrell 2193, Victoria 2197, **Warner-Lambert 2200,** Westfield 2201
New Mexico: **Bynner 2207,** Carlsbad 2208
New York: Abrons 2215, Achelis 2218, Albany's 2226, Astor 2248, **AT&T 2249, Atran 2250,** Avon 2251, Baird 2260, Baker 2262, Barker 2265, **Bay 2270,** Beinecke 2275, **Bingham's 2286,** Boehm 2295, Brookdale 2305, Buffalo 2311, **Burchfield 2314, Bydale 2319,** Cary 2327, Central 2331, **Chatlos 2338, China 2344, Compton 2363,** Cornell 2367, Cowles 2369, Cummings 2376, **Dana 2379, DeCamp 2392, Dodge 2402, Donner 2405, Dorr 2408,** Emerson 2421, **Exxon 2426,** Faulkner 2429, **Ford 2443, Ford 2444, Frueauff 2455,** Gebbie 2465, Glens 2476, Goodyear 2488, **Grace 2496,** Greenwall 2505, **Greve 2506, Guggenheim 2512,** Hayden 2534, **Hazen 2535, Hearst 2537, Hearst 2538,** Hochschild 2553, Howard 2564, Hoyt 2565, **International 2574,** Irving 2575, **Ittleson 2576, Jackson 2577, J.M. 2584,** Johnson 2587, Jones 2591, **Jurzykowski 2595,** Kaplan 2598, **Kenan 2609, Kress 2629,** Lakeview 2635, **Lasdon 2639, Lavanburg 2643,** Lavanburg-Corner 2644, Lincoln 2667, **Littauer 2675, Lounsbery 2679, Mailman 2693,** Matthews 2706, **McGraw-Hill 2721, Mellon 2722,** Moore 2748, Morgan 2750, Moses 2758, New York 2774, New York 2775, Nichols 2782, **Noble 2784, Norman 2787,** O'Connor 2795, **O'Toole 2805,** Pfizer 2823, Ramapo 2846, Ritter 2868, **Rockefeller 2875, Rockefeller 2877, Ross 2891, Rubin 2895,** Rubinstein 2896, Samuels 2905, **Schalkenbach 2911, Scherman 2913, Sloan 2938,** Snow 2943, Spingold 2948, St. Faith's 2950, **Steele-Reese 2957, Stern 2960, Surdna 2972, Tinker 2986, Tudor 2994, Union 2997,** United 3000, **United 3001,** Utica 3005, **van Ameringen 3006,**

Wallace 3019, Watertown 3027, Western 3039, Wikstrom 3045, Wilson 3048, Wilson 3049
North Carolina: **BarclaysAmerican 3076,** Biddle 3078, Burlington 3084, Cannon 3086, Duke 3095, Foundation 3102, Garrison 3103, Hanes 3105, Hanes 3106, Morgan 3119, Reynolds 3123, Reynolds 3124, Rogers 3130, Sternberger 3132, Winston-Salem 3137
North Dakota: Fargo-Moorhead 3139, North Dakota 3142, Stern 3143
Ohio: Akron 3145, Anderson 3152, **Armco 3156,** Beeghly 3165, **Bingham 3172, Borden 3174, Brush 3178,** Cincinnati 3183, Cleveland 3186, Columbus 3189, Dauby 3197, Dayton 3199, Deuble 3200, **Federated 3211, Firestone 3216,** Gallagher 3231, GAR 3232, Gerson 3237, Gries 3241, Gund 3244, **Hoover 3253, Huffy 3255,** Humphrey 3256, Iddings 3259, Jennings 3264, Laub 3281, Lubrizol 3285, **Mead 3299,** Nordson 3316, **Procter 3333,** Reeves 3337, Reinberger 3338, Russell 3350, Schmidlapp 3354, Scioto 3356, Sears 3360, Semple 3361, **Sherwin-Williams 3366,** Smith 3369, Stark 3373, Stocker 3375, Toledo 3386, **TRW 3392,** White 3406, Wolfe 3410, Yassenoff 3414
Oklahoma: Ashbrook 3417, **Kerr 3439, Mabee 3443, Noble 3449,** Oklahoma 3451, **Phillips 3456,** Williams 3471
Oregon: Carpenter 3478, Chiles 3479, Collins 3482, Higgins 3488, **Jeld-Wen 3491,** Johnson 3495, Meyer 3498, Salem 3501
Pennsylvania: **Alcoa 3511,** Allegheny 3512, American 3514, Anderson 3517, Barra 3522, Benedum 3524, Bethlehem 3526, Dolfinger-McMahon 3557, Erie 3565, Fels 3571, Frick 3577, **Gulf 3589,** Heinz 3599, Hillman 3603, Hillman 3604, J.D.B. 3619, **Kennametal 3626,** Kline 3628, Knollbrook 3629, Lesher 3639, **Lukens 3645,** McCune 3651, McFeely-Rogers 3652, Medical 3660, Mellon 3661, Mellon 3663, **Merit 3666,** Myrin 3673, Penn 3683, **Pennwalt 3684, Pew 3686, Pew 3687, Pew 3688,** Philadelphia 3689, Pitcairn-Crabbe 3691, Pittsburgh 3694, Scaife 3711, Schoonmaker 3714, **Scott 3715,** Scranton 3716, Seybert 3717, Smith 3725, St. Marys 3732, Stabler 3733, Stackpole-Hall 3734, Trexler 3748, **Whitaker 3761,** Williamsport 3764, Wyomissing 3767
Rhode Island: **Genesis 3777, Little 3783,** Rhode 3790, **Textron 3792**
South Carolina: Citizens 3801, Gregg-Graniteville 3806, Self 3817, Spartanburg 3820, Springs 3821
Tennessee: Benwood 3829, Day 3839, **Lyndhurst 3847,** Maclellan 3848, Maclellan 3849, Plough 3855, **Woods-Greer 3864**
Texas: Abell-Hanger 3866, Amarillo 3872, American 3873, Anderson 3875, Brown 3893, **Burkitt 3897,** Carter 3902, Clark 3906, Communities 3911, Constantin 3912, Cooper 3916, Cullen 3921, Dallas 3925, **Dresser 3935,** El Paso 3940, Fair 3945, Faith 3946, Fikes 3952, Florence 3955, Griffin 3965, Hillcrest 3981, **HNG 3982,** Hoblitzelle 3984, Houston 3988, Johnson 3995, Jonsson 3997, Keith 4000, King 4004, **Kleberg 4006,** Meadows 4029, Moody 4035, Navarro 4040, Owsley 4048, **R G K 4061,** Richardson 4064, San Antonio 4072, Scurlock 4076, Semmes 4078, Steinhagen 4087, Strake 4089, Tarrant 4094, **Technical 4097,** Temple 4098, Trull 4104, Wortham 4127, Wright 4128
Utah: Dee 4136
Vermont: **Edwards 4147,** Windham 4151
Virginia: **Best 4154,** Camp 4159, Gray 4172, **Jones 4178, Mars 4182,** Morgan 4186, Ohrstrom 4188, Seay 4199, Sovran 4201, United 4211, Virginia 4214, Washington 4215
Washington: Bishop 4220, **Forest 4234,** Glaser 4236, **Laird 4246,** Leuthold 4247, Robertson 4258, Skinner 4262, Spokane 4264, Tacoma 4267, Washington 4269
Wisconsin: Alexander 4292, Alexander 4293, Beloit 4301, **Cudahy 4311, DeRance 4314,** Frankenthal 4320, Gelatt 4323, Giddings 4324, Janesville 4330, **Johnson 4331, Johnson's 4336,** Kimberly-Clark 4338, Kohler 4342, La Crosse 4346, McBeath

4356, Milwaukee 4358, Siebert 4379, Stackner 4381, **Young 4391,** Youth 4392
Wyoming: Tonkin 4400

Operating budgets
Alabama: Smith 20, **Sonat 21**
Arizona: Arizona 29, Butz 30, Circle K 31, du Bois 33, Hervey 38, **Kieckhefer 39,** Morris 41, Mulcahy 42
Arkansas: Murphy 54
California: **Abelard 63,** Ahmanson 65, **American 69,** Associated 75, **Atkinson 76, Atlantic 78, Carnation 119,** Clorox 127, Connell 131, Corcoran 134, Disney 148, Drum 156, East Bay 159, Fireman's 169, Fleishhacker 171, Fleishhacker 172, **Fluor 173,** Fusenot 176, Gellert 183, Gellert 184, Gilmore 191, Goldwyn 196, Haas 203, Haas 204, Hancock 209, **Hewlett 217, Jewett 238,** Johnson 239, **Keck 243, Kerr 244,** Kreoter 248, Lakeside 251, Lear 253, Levy 259, **Litton 262,** Lloyd 264, Lux 268, Lytel 269, Mattel 275, Mayer 277, McKesson 283, Monterey 289, Packard 308, **Page 309,** Parker 310, Peninsula 318, Pratt 328, San Francisco 337, Sandy 338, Santa Cruz 342, Security 351, **Shalan 356,** Shoong 359, Smith 371, **Smith 372,** Stamps 377, Stern 383, Stulsaft 389, Thornton 398, Union 406, **Wilbur 428, Wollenberg 430,** Yorkin 432
Colorado: Anschutz 435, Boettcher 436, Buell 437, Duncan 443, 8 South 444, El Pomar 445, Hughes 454, Hunter 455, Johnson 458, Joslyn 460, O'Fallon 470, Piton 473, **Ray 475,** Schramm 478, Wolf 486
Connecticut: **Abex 488,** Aetna 489, **American 492,** Connecticut 507, Eder 515, **Educational 516, ITT 542,** Jost 546, Main 555, Moore 558, New Haven 559, **Olin 561, Panwy 563,** Scott 573, **Scovill 574, Stanley 578, Topsfield 582, UPS 584,** Vanderbilt 585, erox 594
Delaware: Cohen 602, **Glencoe 609, Good 610,** Kent-Lucas 613, Longwood 618, **Raskob 628, Schwartz 630**
District of Columbia: **Arca 638,** Cafritz 643, Higginson 662, Kiplinger 667, **Public 679,** Sapelo 681
Florida: Conn 704, **Eckerd 719,** Falk 720, **Greenburg 724, Harris 726,** Jenkins 732, **Koch 734,** Phillips 754, Phipps 755, Southeast 770
Georgia: Callaway 811, EMSA 829, Equifax 831, Glancy 840, Harland 843, Hill 846, Livingston 854, Lubo 856, Ottley 861, Rich 870, **Wilson 886**
Hawaii: **Amfac 888,** Atherton 890, Castle 894, First 897, Frear 898, Hawaiian 899, McInerny 903
Illinois: **Abbott 918, Allstate 922,** American 925, **Amoco 928, Amsted 929,** Barber-Colman 936, **Becker 940,** Bersted 945, Camp 962, Chicago 968, **Chicago 969,** Coleman 975, **Crowell 981, Deere 987, Donnelley 994,** Fel-Pro 1000, First 1002, **Griswold 1023,** Haffner 1024, Hales 1025, Harris 1028, **Illinois 1045,** IMC 1046, Ingersoll 1047, Inland 1048, **Joyce 1052,** Kaplan 1055, **MacArthur 1076, MacArthur 1077,** McCormick 1090, **McGraw 1094,** Millikin 1099, **Moorman 1101,** Moorman 1102, Motorola 1104, **Nalco 1105,** New Prospect 1107, Northern 1108, **Northwest 1109,** Payne 1113, **Peterborough 1117,** Pick 1119, **Quaker 1126,** R. F. 1128, Sara 1139, Shirk 1151, Siragusa 1153, Stern 1167, **United 1179,** UOP 1180, White 1188, Woods 1193, Wurlitzer 1194
Indiana: Anderson 1195, **Arvin 1196,** Clowes 1206, **Credithrift 1208,** Cummins 1210, Foellinger 1213, Froderman 1215, Hayner 1221, Heritage 1222, Honeywell 1224, Irwin-Sweeney-Miller 1228, Jordan 1230, Krannert 1233, **Liberty 1236,** Lilly 1237, Moore 1245, Noyes 1246, **Thirty 1256**
Iowa: Cowles 1262, Des Moines 1263, Hall 1269, Maytag 1277, National 1279

Kansas: Baughman 1293, Coleman 1298, Fink 1303, Garvey 1307, Hansen 1309, **Hesston 1311,** Jordaan 1314, **Marley 1319,** Powell 1323, Sosland 1329
Kentucky: Appalachian 1331, Ashland 1332, Bingham 1335
Louisiana: Brown 1355, German 1362, Zigler 1390
Maine: Davenport 1392
Maryland: Baker 1401, **Fairchild 1414,** Freeman 1417, Knott 1428, Pearlstone 1445, **PHH 1446,** Town 1459, U.S.F. & G. 1460
Massachusetts: Adams 1467, Bank 1473, Bayrd 1474, **Beveridge 1475,** Boston 1483, Boynton 1484, Brandegee 1486, Cambridge 1491, Campbell 1492, **CarEth 1494,** Codman 1500, Cove 1503, Daniels 1509, Davis 1511, Ellsworth 1523, Fidelity 1528, **Filene 1529,** Fuller 1532, Hyams 1561, Hyams 1562, Kelley 1567, **Kendall 1569,** Lindsay 1576, Morgan-Worcester 1584, Old 1589, Ratshesky 1605, Schrafft 1618, Shaw 1622, Shawmut 1623, Vingo 1646, **Walsh 1648, Webster 1652, Wyman-Gordon 1660**
Michigan: Barstow 1668, Besser 1673, Bishop 1674, **Bundy 1677, Chrysler 1679,** Dalton 1681, DeRoy 1682, Dow 1690, Fremont 1705, **General 1710, Gerber 1711, Harder 1716,** Holden 1720, Hudson-Webber 1722, Hurst 1724, Kaufman 1730, La-Z-Boy 1736, Loutit 1738, Lyon 1739, **Manoogian 1741,** McGregor 1744, Mills 1750, Morley 1751, **Mott 1752, Mott 1753,** Skillman 1773, Stephenson 1776, Strosacker 1780, Tuck 1785, Vicksburg 1789, **Whirlpool 1793,** Wickes 1798, Wilson 1799, Wilson 1800
Minnesota: **American 1807,** Andersen 1808, Andersen 1810, Apache 1812, Athwin 1813, Bremer 1822, Cargill 1825, Carolyn 1827, **Davis 1833, Dayton 1834, DeLuxe 1835,** First 1842, Gamble 1845, **General 1847,** Graco 1849, Greystone 1851, Honeywell 1861, Hormel 1862, Hulings 1865, International 1866, Maronite 1878, McKnight 1880, McNeely 1882, **Medtronic 1884, Minnesota 1890,** O'Brien 1896, O'Neil 1898, Ordean 1899, Paper 1901, Quinlan 1906, Rodman 1911, Thorpe 1916, Wasie 1922
Mississippi: First 1936, Hardin 1937
Missouri: Block 1941, Brown 1944, Brown 1945, Centerre 1948, **Cross 1954,** Gaylord 1965, Hall 1968, Jordan 1973, Laclede 1977, McGee 1995, Millstone 1998, **Monsanto 1999,** Oppenstein 2003, Pendergast-Weyer 2006, Speas 2017, Speas 2018, St. Louis 2020, Sunderland 2025, Swinney 2029, Union 2034, **Webb 2037**
Nebraska: **InterNorth 2058**
Nevada: **Sells 2081**
New Hampshire: **Phillips 2093**
New Jersey: **Allied 2098, Caspersen 2111, Edison 2119, Hackett 2129, Huber 2133, Johnson 2139, Kirby 2143,** Prudential 2167, Schenck 2177, **Schering-Plough 2178,** Schultz 2179, Schultz 2180, **Schumann 2181, Subaru 2187,** Turrell 2193, **Union 2194,** Victoria 2197, **Warner-Lambert 2200**
New Mexico: Carlsbad 2208
New York: Abrons 2215, Achelis 2218, Alexander 2227, Anderson 2240, Astor 2248, **Avon 2251,** Barker 2264, Barker 2265, Bat Hanadiv 2268, **Bay 2270,** Beinecke 2275, Bernhill 2282, **Bingham's 2286,** Bowne 2299, Buffalo 2311, **Burchfield 2314, Bydale 2319,** Calder 2320, **Carnegie 2325,** Cary 2327, Central 2331, **Chase 2337, Chatlos 2338,** Chautauqua 2339, Clark 2347, **Coles 2358, Colt 2360, Compton 2363,** Cornell 2367, **Corning 2368,** Cowles 2369, Curtice-Burns 2377, **de Hirsch 2387,** Dillon 2399, **Dillon 2400, Dun 2415, Exxon 2426,** Faulkner 2429, **Frueauff 2455, Gannett 2463, Gibbs 2468,** Gifford 2469, Gould 2493, **Grace 2496,** Grant 2498, **Griffis 2507, Gulf 2516,** Gutfreund 2519, Hagedorn 2523, **Hartford 2528, Hearst 2537, Hearst 2538,** High 2550, **Hochstein 2555, Homeland 2560,** Hoyt 2565, Hycliff 2570, Irving 2575, **Ittleson 2576, Johnson 2587,** Jones 2591, **Jurzykowski 2595, Kunstadter 2632, Lakeview 2635,** Lang 2636, L.A.W. 2645, Lever 2657, **Lingnan 2671,** Macdonald 2685, Macmillan

2688, **McGraw-Hill 2721, Memton 2724, Mertz-Gilmore 2730, Metropolitan 2732, Michel 2735,** Moore 2748, Morgan 2750, Morgan 2751, New York 2775, **New York 2776,** New York 2777, **NL 2783,** Norwood 2791, **PBP 2815, Pfizer 2823, Phillips 2827, Phillips-Van Heusen 2828,** Price 2839, **Rockefeller 2876,** Rubinstein 2896, Samuels 2905, **Scherman 2913, Schwarz 2921, Shubert 2930, Smithers 2941,** Snyder 2944, **Sony 2945,** Sprague 2949, **Steele-Reese 2957, Thorne 2984, Union 2997,** United 3000, **van Ameringen 3006, Vinmont 3015, Wallace 3019,** Watertown 3027, Wikstrom 3045, Wilson 3048

North Carolina: **Babcock 3075, BarclaysAmerican 3076,** Chatham 3089, Duke 3095, Finch 3100, Foundation 3102, Garrison 3103, Reynolds 3123, Reynolds 3124

North Dakota: North Dakota 3142

Ohio: Acme 3144, Akron 3145, Albers 3146, American 3150, **Armington 3157, Borden 3174,** Britton 3176, **Brush 3178,** Cleveland 3185, **Dana 3196,** Dauby 3197, **Eaton 3204,** Ferro 3212, Frohring 3229, Gallagher 3231, Gerson 3237, **Goodyear 3239,** Gries 3241, Gund 3244, H.C.S. 3250, **Hoover 3253, Huffy 3255,** Humphrey 3256, Iddings 3259, Ingalls 3260, Jergens 3265, **Kettering 3272,** Laub 3281, Lubrizol 3285, Mather 3295, **Mead 3299,** MLM 3304, Murphy 3311, Nationwide 3313, NCR 3314, Nordson 3316, Oglebay 3318, Ohio 3319, Pollock 3330, Prentiss 3332, Reeves 3337, Reinberger 3338, **Republic 3341,** Richland 3342, Sears 3360, **Sherwin-Williams 3366,** Smith 3370, Stocker 3375, **Stouffer 3376, Tell 3380,** Toledo 3387, Treuhaft 3389, **TRW 3392, White 3405,** Wolfe 3410

Oklahoma: Ashbrook 3417, Goddard 3432, Kirkpatrick 3441, **Noble 3450,** Oklahoma 3451, Oklahoma 3452, **Phillips 3456,** Warren 3469, Wegener 3470, Wood 3472

Oregon: Barker 3476, Carpenter 3478, Jackson 3490, Johnson 3495, Oregon 3500, Salem 3501, Tektronix 3502, Templeton 3503, Tucker 3504

Pennsylvania: **Air 3509, Alcoa 3511,** Anderson 3517, Arcadia 3520, Benedum 3524, Craig 3549, Crels 3552, Dietrich 3556, Dolfinger-McMahon 3557, Douty 3559, Eccles 3562, Falk 3567, Goldman 3584, **Harsco 3595, Heinz 3598,** Heinz 3599, Hershey 3601, Hillman 3604, **Hooper 3607,** Hunt 3612, Huston 3614, Justus 3621, Justus 3622, Kavanagh 3624, Knollbrook 3629, **Koppers 3631,** Lesher 3639, McFeely-Rogers 3652, McKenna 3655, **McKenna 3656,** Medical 3660, Mellon 3661, Patterson 3682, **Pennwalt 3684, Pew 3686, Pew 3687,** Philadelphia 3689, Pittsburgh 3694, PPG 3697, **Rockwell 3708,** Scaife 3711, Shoemaker 3719, Smith 3723, Smith 3724, Smith 3725, Snayberger 3727, SPS 3731, St. Marys 3732, Stabler 3733, Stott 3741, **Strawbridge 3743,** Trexler 3748, **United 3750,** Wurts 3766, Wyomissing 3767

Rhode Island: Fleet 3775, **Little 3783,** Rhode 3790

South Carolina: **Roe 3814**

Tennessee: Brown 3832, Church 3836, Lowenstein 3846, **Lyndhurst 3847,** Plough 3855, Potter 3856, **Woods-Greer 3864**

Texas: Abell-Hanger 3866, Brown 3893, **Burkitt 3897,** Butt 3899, Communities 3911, Cooley 3914, Cooper 3916, Curtis 3922, Dougherty 3934, Duncan 3937, El Paso 3940, Fain 3944, Fasken 3948, Favrot 3949, Fleming 3954, Griffin 3965, **Halliburton 3970,** Halsell 3971, Hightower 3980, **HNG 3982,** Keith 4000, Kempner 4001, Lewis 4015, McKee 4026, Meadows 4029, **Menil 4031,** Moncrief 4034, O'Connor 4042, Owsley 4048, Perkins 4052, Richardson 4064, San Antonio 4072, **Scaler 4073,** Semmes 4078, Sharp 4080, **Shell 4081,** Southland 4084, Strake 4089, Temple 4098, **Texas 4102,** Trull 4104, Waggoner 4109, **Weaver 4113,** West 4119, **Zale 4129**

Utah: Bamberger 4130, Eccles 4139

Vermont: **Edwards 4147,** Windham 4151

Virginia: Gray 4172, Memorial 4185, Ohrstrom 4188, Richmond 4196, Seay 4199, Thomas 4205, Virginia 4214, Washington 4215, Wheat 4216

Washington: Archibald 4219, **Forest 4234,** Kawabe 4241, Leuthold 4247, Medina 4250, Norcliffe 4254, PACCAR 4255, Robertson 4258, Sequoia 4260, Skinner 4262, Spokane 4264, Univar 4268, Washington 4269, **Wharton 4275**

West Virginia: Carbon 4278, Kanawha 4285

Wisconsin: Alexander 4293, Allis-Chalmers 4294, Badger 4299, Banta 4300, Briggs 4306, Bucyrus-Erie 4308, Consolidated 4310, **Cudahy 4311,** CUNA 4312, **DeRance 4314,** Falk 4317, Gelatt 4323, Jacobus/Heritage 4329, **Johnson 4331, Kimberly-Clark 4338,** La Crosse 4346, Marine 4353, Oshkosh 4362, Rutledge 4376, Siebert 4379, Stackner 4381, Wisconsin 4389, **Young 4391**

Wyoming: Tonkin 4400

Professorships

Arizona: Mulcahy 42

California: **American 69,** Bacon 80, Baxter 86, Beckman 89, Drum 156, Haas 204, Jones 240, **Kaiser 242,** Koret 248, Oxnard 306, **Parsons 311,** Powell 327, Stauffer 380, Timken-Sturgis 401, **Union 407**

Colorado: Buell 437, **Frost 449**

Connecticut: **Amax 491, Educational 516,** Patterson 564, **UPS 584, Xerox 594**

Florida: **Davis 707, duPont 716, Harris 726**

Georgia: Callaway 812, **Coca-Cola 818,** Equifax 831, Harland 843, Lane 851, Loridans 855, Woolley 887

Illinois: **Abbott 918,** Borg-Warner 950, Coleman 975, Crown 982, Grainger 1022, Hales 1025, Harris 1028, Kaplan 1055, White 1188

Indiana: Ball 1199, Lilly 1237

Kentucky: **Ashland 1333,** Cooke 1339

Louisiana: Jones 1370

Maryland: **Fairchild 1414,** Meyerhoff 1439, Middendorf 1440

Massachusetts: Acushnet 1466, **Alden 1468,** Daniels 1509, Fuller 1532, Harrington 1543, Kelley 1567, Pappas 1591, Rowland 1611, Stoddard 1635, **Webster 1652**

Michigan: **Earhart 1691, Ex-cell-o 1694,** La-Z-Boy 1736, Skillman 1773

Minnesota: Marbrook 1878, **Minnesota 1890,** Phillips 1903, Wasie 1922

Mississippi: Hardin 1937

Missouri: **Anheuser-Busch 1940,** Boone 1943, Commerce 1951, Edison 1958, Loose 1982

New Jersey: **Allied 2098,** Belasco 2101, **Schering-Plough 2178, Warner-Lambert 2200**

New York: Astor 2248, **Atran 2250,** Brookdale 2305, **Coles 2358, Culpeper 2374,** Curtice-Burns 2377, **Dana 2379, DeCamp 2392, Exxon 2426, Ford 2443, Ford 2444, Foundation 2446, General 2467,** Greenwall 2505, **Griffis 2507,** Ittleson 2576, **Johnson 2587, Kenan 2609, Kress 2629,** Lang 2636, **Lingnan 2671, Luce 2682, Mellon 2722,** Moses 2758, **Olin 2799, Peat 2817, Pfizer 2823, Phelps 2825, Potts 2836, Price 2840,** Ramapo 2846, Robert 2870, **Rubin 2895,** Rubinstein 2896, **Schlumberger 2919,** Spingold 2948, **Starr 2954, Statler 2955, Steele-Reese 2957,** Utica 3005

North Carolina: Biddle 3078, Burlington 3084, **Burroughs 3085,** Duke 3095

North Dakota: Stern 3143

Ohio: Beeghly 3165, Cleveland-Cliffs 3187, **Ernst 3207,** Humphrey 3256, Jennings 3264, Lubrizol 3285, **Republic 3341,** Semple 3361, Treuhaft 3389, **TRW 3392,** Wolfe 3410, Yassenoff 3414

Oklahoma: **Kerr 3439,** Oklahoma 3452, **Phillips 3456**

Pennsylvania: Hillman 3603, **Independence 3616,** Pittsburgh 3694, **Rockwell 3708,** Stabler 3733

South Carolina: Abney 3794, Springs 3821

Tennessee: Benwood 3829, Toms 3859

Texas: Abell-Hanger 3866, Brackenridge 3889, Brown 3893, **Burkitt 3897,** Carter 3902, Cullen 3921, Dallas 3925, Fasken 3948, Fleming 3954, Hamman 3972, **HNG 3982,** Houston 3988, Kempner 4001,

Meadows 4029, Moody 4035, O'Connor 4042, **R G K 4061,** Semmes 4078, **Shell 4081,** Trull 4104, Waggoner 4109, Welch 4115, **Zale 4129**

Utah: Treadwell 4146

Virginia: Wheat 4216

Washington: **Anderson 4218,** Robertson 4258, Skinner 4262

Wisconsin: Allis-Chalmers 4294, Consolidated 4310, Evjue 4316, Frankenthal 4320, Helfaer 4327, La Crosse 4346

Program-related investments

California: Corcoran 134, Gerbode 186, Hancock 209, Monterey 289, Packard 308, Parker 310, Rosenberg 334, San Francisco 337, **Shalan 356**

Colorado: Coors 441, 8 South 444, Piton 473

Connecticut: Connecticut 507, New Haven 559, erox 594

Delaware: Crystal 606

District of Columbia: Washington 685

Florida: Bush 701

Georgia: Atlanta 802

Illinois: **FMC 1005, Joyce 1052**

Indiana: Cole 1207, Cummins 1210, Heritage 1222, Indianapolis 1226

Kansas: Powell 1323

Massachusetts: **Levinson 1574,** Stevens 1634

Michigan: Ann Arbor 1664, Battle Creek 1669, Hudson-Webber 1722, Miller 1749, **Mott 1752**

Minnesota: Blandin 1821, Hulings 1865, McKnight 1880, McNeely 1882, North 1892, **Northwest 1894,** Ordean 1899, Saint Paul 1912

Mississippi: Hardin 1937

Missouri: Block 1941, **Butler 1946**

New Hampshire: Bean 2083

New Jersey: **Vollmer 2199**

New Mexico: Carlsbad 2208

New York: **Archbold 2242, Carnegie 2325,** Cary 2327, **Ford 2444, Hartford 2528,** Howard 2564, **New World 2773,** O'Connor 2795, **Scherman 2913, Statler 2955,** Taconic 2976

North Carolina: **Babcock 3075,** Bryan 3083, Hanes 3105

Ohio: **Bingham 3172,** Lorain 3284, **Marathon 3289,** Toledo 3387, Yassenoff 3414

Oklahoma: **Phillips 3456**

Oregon: Collins 3482, Jackson 3490, Meyer 3498

Pennsylvania: Benedum 3524, Heinz 3599, **Kennametal 3626,** Pittsburgh 3694, Williamsport 3764

Rhode Island: Old 3786

Tennessee: **Lyndhurst 3847**

Texas: Communities 3911, Hightower 3980, Meadows 4029, Waggoner 4109

Vermont: **Edwards 4147**

Washington: **Anderson 4218**

Wisconsin: Alexander 4292, La Crosse 4346

Publications

Alabama: Blount 4, Smith 20

Alaska: Alaska 25

Arizona: **Kieckhefer 39**

Arkansas: Ross 59

California: **Abelard 63,** Bacon 80, **Baker 81,** Columbia 130, Corcoran 134, Crocker 137, Crocker 138, Drum 156, First 170, Fleishhacker 172, Gellert 183, **Getty 187, Kaiser 242, Kerr 244,** Koret 248, Norman 298, Parker 310, Peninsula 318, Pratt 328, Santa Cruz 342, Stulsaft 389, **System 393,** Trust 402, van Loben Sels 410, **Wilbur 428,** Witter 429, Yorkin 432

Colorado: Anschutz 435, **Frost 449,** Ray 475

Connecticut: Albers 490, American 492, **Educational 516,** Ensign-Bickford 520, **General 527, Kazanjian 548, Olin 561,** Waterbury 588

Delaware: **Glencoe 609**
District of Columbia: **Arca 638, Benton 640,** Cafritz 643, **Freed 656, German 659,** Higginson 662, Washington 685
Florida: Beattie 695, **duPont 716,** Falk 720, **Koch 734,** Phipps 755, Southeast 770, **Whitehall 791**
Georgia: Atlanta 802, Harland 843, Lubo 856
Hawaii: Cooke 895, Hawaiian 899
Idaho: Whittenberger 916
Illinois: Borg-Warner 950, Coleman 975, **Crown 983, DeKalb 989, Donnelley 994, Farm 999, FMC 1005,** Fry 1011, **Graham 1021, Harris 1030,** Ingersoll 1047, **Joyce 1052, MacArthur 1076, Quaker 1126, Tyndale 1178**
Indiana: Ball 1199, Cummins 1210, Froderman 1215, Heritage 1222, Honeywell 1224
Kansas: Hansen 1309, Jordaan 1314
Maryland: Knott 1428, Meyerhoff 1439, Pearlstone 1445, Town 1459
Massachusetts: **Alden 1468, Beveridge 1475, Cook 1502,** Dexter 1515, **Endowment 1524, Friendship 1531, Kendall 1569, Little 1578,** Russell 1614, **Walsh 1648**
Michigan: Ann Arbor 1664, Battle Creek 1669, **Earhart 1691, Ford 1702, General 1710,** Kalamazoo 1728, Miller 1749, **Mott 1752, Mott 1753,** Muskegon 1754
Minnesota: Andersen 1808, **Dayton 1834,** Greystone 1851, Lilly 1876, Wasie 1922
Mississippi: Hardin 1937
Missouri: Boone 1943, **Butler 1946,** Gaylord 1965, Green 1967, Loose 1983, Reynolds 2011, **Sunnen 2027,** Swinney 2029
New Hampshire: Hunt 2087
New Jersey: Dodge 2116, Fund 2125, **International 2135,** New Jersey 2161, Ohl 2163, Schultz 2179, Schultz 2180
New Mexico: Carlsbad 2208
New York: **Archbold 2242, Atran 2250,** Barker 2265, Boehm 2295, Brookdale 2305, Buffalo 2311, **Burden 2315, Bydale 2319, Carnegie 2325,** Central 2331, **Chatlos 2338,** Chautauqua 2339, Clark 2349, **Corning 2368, Dillon 2400, Donner 2405, Dorr 2408,** Dutchess 2416, **Exxon 2426, Field 2432, Ford 2443, Ford 2444, Foundation 2445, Foundation 2446, Fuld 2458, Gannett 2463,** Glens 2476, Grant 2498, **Griffis 2507, Hartford 2528,** Initial 2573, **International 2574, Ittleson 2576, Jackson 2577, J.M. 2584,** Jones 2591, **Jurzykowski 2595,** Kaplan 2598, **Klingenstein 2618, Kress 2629, Lavanburg 2643, L.A.W. 2645, Lingnan 2671, Littauer 2675, Lounsbery 2679, Mailman 2693, Matz 2708,** McCann 2712, **McGraw-Hill 2721,** New York 2774, New York 2775, New York 2777, O'Connor 2795, **Olin 2799,** Pfizer 2823, Potts 2836, Ramapo 2846, Ritter 2868, **Rockefeller 2877, Ross 2891,** Rubinstein 2896, **Sage 2902, Schalkenbach 2911, Schimper 2918, Smart 2939,** Snow 2943, **Stern 2960, Thorne 2984, United 3001, van Ameringen 3006,** Watertown 3027, **Wenner-Gren 3037,** Western 3039
North Carolina: Duke 3095, Garrison 3103, Hanes 3105, Hanes 3106, Reynolds 3124, **Richardson 3128,** Sternberger 3132
North Dakota: North Dakota 3142
Ohio: Anderson 3152, **Armington 3157, Bingham 3172, Brush 3178,** Cincinnati 3183, Fifth 3214, Gerson 3237, Gund 3244, **Huffy 3255,** Iddings 3259, **Kettering 3272,** Laub 3281, Mather 3294, Nordson 3316, Pollock 3330, Reinberger 3338, Russell 3350, Scioto 3356, Smith 3369, Treuhaft 3389, Yassenoff 3414
Oklahoma: **Kerr 3439**
Oregon: Carpenter 3478
Pennsylvania: Allegheny 3512, **Copernicus 3548,** Craig 3549, Dolfinger-McMahon 3557, **Falk 3568,** Fels 3571, Frick 3577, **Heinz 3598,** Hershey 3601, Patterson 3682, Pittsburgh 3694, PPG 3697, Rittenhouse 3704, Scaife 3711, **Scott 3715,** Scranton 3716, Smith 3725, St. Marys 3732, **Westinghouse 3757**
Rhode Island: Rhode 3790
South Carolina: Springs 3821

Tennessee: **Woods-Greer 3864**
Texas: Brackenridge 3889, Brown 3893, **Burkitt 3897,** Communities 3911, Dallas 3925, El Paso 3940, Halsell 3971, Kempner 4001, Meadows 4029, Moody 4035, **R G K 4061,** Richardson 4064, San Antonio 4072, Semmes 4078, **Shell 4081,** Steinhagen 4087, **Technical 4097,** Texas 4100, Trull 4104, Waggoner 4109
Virginia: Seay 4199, Sovran 4201
Washington: Kawabe 4241, **Laird 4246,** Skinner 4262, Spokane 4264, **Weyerhaeuser 4274**
West Virginia: Kanawha 4285
Wisconsin: Allis-Chalmers 4294, **Cudahy 4311, DeRance 4314,** Evjue 4316, **Johnson 4332, Johnson's 4336,** Kohler 4342, La Crosse 4346, Stackner 4381
Wyoming: Tonkin 4400

Research

Alabama: Blount 4, Meyer 14, Smith 20, **Sonat 21**
Alaska: Alaska 25
Arizona: Butz 30, First 34, Flinn 35, Hervey 38, **Kieckhefer 39,** Mulcahy 42, **Research 44**
Arkansas: Ross 59
California: A.I.D. 66, Albertson 67, **American 69, Baker 81,** Bank 83, Baxter 86, Beckman 89, California 116, Columbia 130, Corcoran 134, Crocker 138, Distribution 151, Drum 156, Early 158, Factor 162, Fleishhacker 171, Fusenot 176, Gellert 183, Gellert 184, Gildred 189, Goldwyn 196, Haas 204, Haynes 211, Hoag 221, Holt 225, Hoover 226, Irwin 231, Jameson 235, **Jewett 238,** Johnson 239, Jones 240, **Kaiser 242, Keck 243,** Kirchgessner 245, **Kroc 250,** Lewis 261, Lurie 267, Martin 274, Mayer 277, Mead 284, Monterey 289, Norman 298, Norris 299, Oxnard 306, Packard 308, Parker 310, Peninsula 318, **Pfeiffer 322,** Pratt 328, Rosenberg 334, San Diego 336, Schreiber 347, Seaver 350, Shoong 359, **Smith 372,** Stern 383, Stulsaft 389, **System 393,** Thornton 398, Timken-Sturgis 401, Trust 402, **Union 407,** van Loben Sels 410, Walker 414, Weingart 421, Welk 422, **Wilbur 428,** Witter 429, Yorkin 432
Colorado: Animal 434, Anschutz 435, Duncan 443, **Frost 449,** Hughes 454, Johnson 458, **Needmor 468,** Ray 475, Taylor 482, Wolf 486
Connecticut: **Albers 490, Amax 491, American 492, Childs 506,** Connecticut 507, **Educational 516,** Ensign-Bickford 520, **General 527,** Hartford 532, **Kazanjian 548,** Olin 561, **Panwy 563,** Patterson 564, **Rosenthal 569,** Scott 573, **Stanley 578, UPS 584,** Wahlstrom-Johnson 586, Waterbury 588, **Whitehead 590,** Woman's 593, erox 594
Delaware: **Beneficial 596, Lalor 617,** Longwood 618, Marmot 621, **Schwartz 630**
District of Columbia: **Benton 640, Foundation 654, Freed 656,** Higginson 662, **Kennedy 666,** Lehrman 668, Ross 680, Sapelo 681, Washington 685
Florida: Briggs 698, **Brunner 700,** Dade 706, **Davis 707, duPont 716, Greenburg 724, Harris 726, Hayward 727, Koch 734, Markey 745,** Phipps 755, Price 758, **Storer 776, Whitehall 791,** Wilder 792, **Winn-Dixie 794**
Georgia: Atlanta 803, EMSA 829, Equifax 831, **Foundation 834,** Steiner 874, Trust 877
Hawaii: Castle 893, Cooke 895, Hawaiian 899
Illinois: **Abbott 918, Ameritech 926, Amsted 929, Aronberg 933,** Borg-Warner 950, Chicago 968, Coleman 975, **Crown 982, Crown 983, Donnelley 994, Evinrude 997, Farm 999, FMC 1005,** Fry 1011, **Gould 1020, Graham 1021,** Grainger 1022, Hales 1025, **Harris 1030,** Johnson 1051, **MacArthur 1076, MacArthur 1077,** McCormick 1089, **McGraw 1094, Northwest 1109, Peterborough 1117,** Petersen 1118, Regenstein 1130, **Retirement 1132,** Scholl 1142, Siragusa 1153, **Spencer 1160,** Sprague 1161, **United 1179,** UOP 1180, USG 1182, White 1188, Wieboldt 1189, Woods 1193, Wurlitzer 1194

Indiana: Anderson 1195, Ball 1199, Clowes 1206, Heritage 1222, Honeywell 1224, Krannert 1233, **Lilly 1238,** Oliver 1247
Iowa: Hall 1269, Maytag 1277, **Salsbury 1282**
Kansas: Garvey 1307, **Hesston 1311,** Jordaan 1314, Sosland 1329, Wiedemann 1330
Kentucky: Bingham 1335, Vogt 1353
Louisiana: Baton Rouge 1354, Brown 1355, Physicians 1377, Schlieder 1381
Maryland: Knott 1428, Meyerhoff 1439, Straus 1456, Town 1459
Massachusetts: **Alden 1468,** Bayrd 1474, Blanchard 1480, Boston 1482, Brandegee 1486, Campbell 1492, **CarEth 1494, Cox 1506, Endowment 1524,** Fuller 1532, Fuller 1533, **Grass 1538, Harvard-Yenching 1546, Hood 1553,** Kelley 1567, **Kendall 1569, King 1571, Little 1578,** Merkert 1583, Pappas 1591, Rowland 1611, Shaw 1622, **Sheraton 1625,** Stevens 1634, Stoddard 1635, Stone 1637, **Webster 1652**
Michigan: Americana 1663, Ann Arbor 1664, Bishop 1674, Dalton 1681, DeRoy 1682, Dow 1690, **Earhart 1691, Ex-cell-o 1694, Federal-Mogul 1696, Ford 1702, General 1710,** Gerstacker 1712, Herrick 1718, Holden 1720, Hudson-Webber 1722, Jackson 1726, Kalamazoo 1728, Lyon 1739, **Manoogian 1741,** Morley 1751, **Mott 1753,** Muskegon 1754, **Pardee 1757,** Shelden 1770, **Upjohn 1787, Whirlpool 1793,** Wilson 1800
Minnesota: Andersen 1810, Chadwick 1829, **General 1848,** Graco 1849, Greystone 1851, Grotto 1853, Hulings 1865, Lilly 1876, Marbrook 1878, Mardag 1879, McKnight 1880, **Minnesota 1890,** Neilson 1891, Northwest 1892, **Northwest 1894,** O'Brien 1896, **O'Shaughnessy 1900,** Phillips 1903, Quinlan 1906, Saint Paul 1912, Walker 1920, Wasie 1922
Mississippi: First 1936, Hardin 1937
Missouri: **Anheuser-Busch 1940,** Boone 1943, **Butler 1946, Cross 1954,** Green 1967, Loose 1981, Loose 1982, Loose 1983, **Mallinckrodt 1987,** Millstone 1998, Olin 2002, Reynolds 2011, Speas 2017, Speas 2018, St. Louis 2020, Swinney 2029, **Webb 2037**
Nebraska: Cooper 2054, Lane 2061, Lincoln 2063
New Hampshire: **Phillips 2093**
New Jersey: **Allied 2098,** Atlantic 2100, Belasco 2101, Cape 2108, **Carnegie 2109, Caspersen 2111, Edison 2119,** Fund 2125, **Hoffmann-La Roche 2131,** Hyde 2134, **Johnson 2139, Johnson 2140, Lipton 2150,** New Jersey 2161, Ohl 2163, Prudential 2167, **Rippel 2171, Schering-Plough 2178,** Schultz 2179, Schultz 2180, **South 2185, Union 2194,** Upton 2196, Victoria 2197, **Vollmer 2199, Warner-Lambert 2200,** Wetterberg 2202
New Mexico: **Bynner 2207,** Picker 2211
New York: Abrons 2216, **Adler 2221,** Alexander 2227, **Allied 2230, AMETEK 2238, Archbold 2242, AT&T 2249, Atran 2250, Axe-Houghton 2252,** Baird 2260, Barker 2264, **Bay 2270,** Beinecke 2275, **Bingham's 2286, Bristol-Myers 2302,** Brookdale 2305, Buffalo 2311, **Burden 2315, Bydale 2319,** Calder 2320, **Carnegie 2325, China 2344,** Clark 2346, Clark 2349, **Coles 2358, Commonwealth 2362, Culpeper 2374,** Cummings 2375, Cummings 2376, Curtice-Burns 2377, **Dana 2379, de Hirsch 2387, DeCamp 2392, Delmas 2394, Deloitte 2395,** Dillon 2399, **Doherty 2404, Donner 2405, Dorr 2408, Dreyfus 2411, Dreyfus 2413,** Dutchess 2416, **Dyson 2417,** Eastman 2418, Ebsary 2419, Emerson 2421, **Field 2432, Ford 2443, Ford 2444, Foundation 2445, Frasch 2450, Gibbs 2468,** Gifford 2469, **Glenn 2475,** Glens 2476, **Grant 2499,** Greenwall 2505, **Greve 2506, Griffis 2507, Guggenheim 2512,** Guggenheim 2513, **Hartford 2528, Hearst 2537, Hearst 2538,** Hirschl 2552, **House 2563, IFF 2571,** Initial 2573, **International 2574, Ittleson 2576, J.M. 2584,** Julia 2593, **Jurzykowski 2595,** Kevorkian 2611, **Klingenstein 2618, Knapp 2620, Kress 2629, Lasdon 2639,** Lee 2649, Lemberg 2655, **Lingnan 2671, Littauer 2675, Lounsbery 2679, Luce 2682,** Macdonald 2685, **Mailman 2693, Manning 2697, Markle 2700,** McDonald 2718, **McGraw-Hill**

2721, Mellon 2722, Merck 2726, Merrill 2728, Metropolitan 2732, Milbank 2737, Mobil 2743, Moore 2748, Moses 2758, New York 2774, New York 2777, **New-Land 2779,** Nichols 2782, **NL 2783,** Norstar 2789, O'Connor 2795, **Olin 2799, O'Toole 2805, Ottinger 2806, Parapsychology 2811, Peat 2817, Pfizer 2823, Philippe 2826, Phillips-Van Heusen 2828, Potts 2836, Price 2840,** Prospect 2842, Ramapo 2846, **Revson 2858,** Ritter 2868, **Rockefeller 2877,** Rose 2882, **Ross 2891, Rubin 2895,** Rubinstein 2896, Rudin 2899, **Sage 2902,** Samuels 2905, **Schalkenbach 2911, Schimper 2934, Simon 2934, Sloan 2938, Smart 2939,** Smithers 2941, Snow 2943, Spingold 2948, **Standard 2951, Starr 2954, Statler 2955,** Stein 2958, **Stern 2960,** Stony 2963, **Surdna 2972, Teagle 2979,** Texaco 2981, **Thorne 2984, Tinker 2986, Tisch 2987,** United 3000, **United 3001,** Uris 3003, **van Ameringen 3006, Vanneck-Bailey 3009,** Vidda 3012, Vogler 3016, Watertown 3027, **Weatherhead 3028, Wenner-Gren 3037, Wilson 3047,** Wilson 3048, Winston 3051, **Witco 3053, Wunsch 3061**

North Carolina: Biddle 3078, **Burroughs 3085, Connemara 3090,** Duke 3095, **Foundation 3102,** Hanes 3105, Hanes 3106, **Richardson 3128,** Rogers 3130, Sternberger 3132

North Dakota: North Dakota 3142, Stern 3143

Ohio: **Amcast 3149,** Anderson 3152, **Armco 3156, Armington 3157, Bingham 3172, Brush 3178,** Cleveland-Cliffs 3187, Dauby 3197, **Eaton 3204,** Fifth 3214, **Firestone 3216,** GAR 3232, **Goodyear 3239,** Gries 3241, Humphrey 3256, Kachelmacher 3268, **Kettering 3272,** Lorain 3284, Lubrizol 3285, **Marathon 3289,** Markus 3291, McFawn 3297, **Mead 3299,** Moores 3308, Nationwide 3313, NCR 3314, Oglebay 3318, Pollock 3330, Prentiss 3332, Reinberger 3338, **Republic 3341, Rosenthal 3347,** Schmidlapp 3354, Sears 3360, Stark 3373, Treuhaft 3389, Treu-Mart 3390, **TRW 3392,** Van Wert 3396, **White 3405,** Yassenoff 3414

Oklahoma: Goddard 3432, **Kerr 3439, Noble 3449,** Oklahoma 3451, **Phillips 3456,** Wood 3472

Oregon: Autzen 3475, Carpenter 3478, Chiles 3479, Collins 3482, Jackson 3490, Meyer 3498, Salem 3501

Pennsylvania: **Alcoa 3511,** Anderson 3517, Arcadia 3520, Buhl 3529, **Carpenter 3536, Carthage 3537,** Craig 3549, Dietrich 3556, Erie 3565, Fels 3571, Frick 3577, Goldman 3584, **Gulf 3589, Heinz 3598,** Heinz 3599, Hershey 3601, **Hooper 3607,** Kavanagh 3624, **Kennametal 3626,** Knollbrook 3629, **McKenna 3656,** Medical 3660, Mellon 3662, Mellon 3663, Patterson 3682, **Pew 3686, Pew 3687, Pew 3688,** Pittsburgh 3693, Pittsburgh 3694, PPG 3697, Scaife 3713, Scholler 3713, Scranton 3716, Seybert 3717, Smith 3723, Smith 3725, SPS 3731, St. Marys 3732, Stott 3741, **Stroud 3744, United 3750, Walker 3752, Whitaker 3761,** Widener 3762, Williamsport 3764

Rhode Island: Rhode 3790

South Carolina: Abney 3794, Gregg-Graniteville 3806, **Riegel 3813**

Tennessee: Benwood 3829, **Currey 3838,** Massey 3852, Potter 3856, Toms 3859

Texas: Abell-Hanger 3866, Amarillo 3872, American 3873, Anderson 3875, **Biological 3886, Brackenridge 3889,** Brown 3893, **Burkitt 3897,** Cameron 3901, Carter 3902, Clark 3906, Communities 3911, Cooley 3914, Cooper 3916, Crow 3919, Crump 3920, Cullen 3921, Dallas 3925, Dougherty 3934, Fair 3945, Faith 3946, Farish 3947, Feldman 3950, Fikes 3952, Fleming 3954, **Halliburton 3970,** Halsell 3971, Hamman 3972, Hillcrest 3981, **HNG 3982,** Hofheinz 3985, **HOR 3987,** Kay 3998, Kempner 4001, King 4004, **Kleberg 4006,** McKee 4026, Meadows 4029, Moody 4035, Moss 4038, **R G K 4061,** Richardson 4064, San Antonio 4072, Scurlock 4076, Semmes 4078, **Shell 4081,** Steinhagen 4087, Strake 4089, **Technical 4097,** Temple 4098, Texas 4099, Texas 4100, Texas 4101, Trull 4104, Waggoner 4109, **Weaver 4113,** Welch 4115, White 4121

Utah: Dee 4136, Eccles 4139, Masonic 4142, **Thrasher 4145,** Treadwell 4146

Virginia: Jeffress 4177, **Jones 4178, Mars 4182,** Norfolk 4187, Richmond 4196, Virginia 4214

Washington: **Anderson 4218,** Comstock 4230, Fuchs 4235, Glaser 4236, Kawabe 4241, Murdock 4252, Norcliffe 4254, Poncin 4256, Sequoia 4260, Univar 4268

West Virginia: Carbon 4278, Kanawha 4285

Wisconsin: Allis-Chalmers 4294, Badger 4299, **Cudahy 4311,** CUNA 4312, **DeRance 4314,** Falk 4317, Giddings 4324, Helfaer 4327, **Johnson's 4336,** La Crosse 4346, Ladish 4347, Marine 4353, Stackner 4381, Youth 4392

Scholarship funds

Alabama: Blount 4, Meyer 14, Smith 20

Arizona: Arizona 29, du Bois 33, First 34, Hervey 38, Morris 41, Mulcahy 42, Raymond 43, **Van Schaik 46,** Wilson 50

California: Ahmanson 65, **American 69,** Associated 75, **Atkinson 76, Atkinson 77, Atlantic 78, Baker 81, BankAmerica 84,** Copley 133, Corcoran 134, Cowell 136, Crocker 138, Disney 148, Drum 156, East Bay 159, Factor 162, Fireman's 169, First 170, Gellert 183, Goldwyn 196, Haas 204, Haynes 211, Holt 225, Jameson 235, Jones 240, **Kaiser 242, Keck 243,** Koret 248, **Koulaieff 249,** Lear 253, **Levi 258,** Levy 259, **Lockheed 266,** Lurie 267, Lux 268, Lytel 269, Mayer 277, Mayr 278, Mead 284, Norris 299, Orleton 304, Packard 308, **Parsons 311,** Peninsula 318, **Philibosian 323,** Pickford 325, Powell 327, Richards 332, Riverside 333, Shoong 359, Stauffer 379, Stauffer 380, Steele 382, Stern 383, Stulsaft 389, Trust 402, Tuohy 403, **Union 407,** Watson 416, **Wilbur 428**

Colorado: Boettcher 436, Buell 437, El Pomar 445, **Frost 449,** Hill 452, Johnson 458, Petteys 471, Schramm 478, Wolf 486

Connecticut: **Abex 488, Amax 491, American 492,** Barden 495, **Bissell 500,** Connecticut 507, **Educational 516,** Ensign-Bickford 520, **General 527, Grubb 530, GTE 531,** Hartford 532, Hartford 533, **ITT 542,** Long 552, Main 555, **Oaklawn 560, Olin 561, Panwy 563,** Patterson 564, **Rosenthal 569,** Sullivan 581, **UMC 583, UPS 584,** Woman's 593, erox 594

Delaware: Cohen 602

District of Columbia: Cafritz 643, **Delmar 647, Freed 656,** Johnston 665, Lehrman 668, Miller 673, Sapelo 681

Florida: **Bastien 694,** Beattie 695, Briggs 698, Conn 704, **Davis 707, duPont 716,** Eckerd 719, **Harris 726, McMannis 747,** Price 758, Saunders 765, Selby 766, Southeast 770, **Stuart 777,** Wilder 792, **Winn-Dixie 794**

Georgia: Baker 804, **Coca-Cola 818,** Equifax 831, Franklin 835, Harland 843, Hodge 847, Lane 851, Loridans 855, **Whitehead 885, Wilson 886,** Woolley 887

Hawaii: Brewer 892, Frear 898, Hawaiian 899, McInerny 903, Watumull 907, Wilcox 908

Illinois: **Abbott 918, Allstate 922, Amoco 928,** Aurora 935, Carson 964, **CBI 966,** Coleman 975, **Crowell 981, Crown 983, Deere 987,** Dillon 992, **Evinrude 997, Farm 999,** First 1002, **FMC 1005,** Hales 1025, Harris 1028, Inland 1048, **Joyce 1052,** Kaplan 1055, Kemper 1060, McCormick 1089, **McGraw 1094, Monticello 1100, Moorman 1101,** Motorola 1104, **Northwest 1109, Quaker 1126, Santa Fe 1138,** Schmitt 1141, Shirk 1151, **State 1166, Sundstrand 1174, United 1179,** UOP 1180, White 1188

Indiana: Clowes 1206, Froderman 1215, Heritage 1222, Lincoln 1239, Mead 1242, Noyes 1246, **Pott 1249**

Iowa: Des Moines 1263, Maytag 1276, Pella 1280

Kansas: Baughman 1293, Coleman 1298, Fink 1303, Fourth 1305, Garvey 1307, Hansen 1309, Jordaan

1314, Powell 1323, **Schowalter 1327,** Sosland 1329, Wiedemann 1330

Kentucky: Appalachian 1331, **Ashland 1333, Margaret 1347,** Robinson 1351

Louisiana: Jones 1370, **Louisiana 1373,** Physicians 1377

Maryland: **Fairchild 1414,** Hoffberger 1423, Kelly 1424, Marriott 1433, Meyerhoff 1439, **PHH 1446,** Ryan 1451, Sheridan 1454, U.S.F. & G. 1460

Massachusetts: Acushnet 1466, Adams 1467, **Alden 1468,** Cabot 1488, Campbell 1492, Daniels 1509, DeLoura 1512, Fuller 1532, Harvard 1545, **Harvard-Yenching 1546,** Kelley 1567, Lindsay 1576, Pappas 1591, Polaroid 1602, Ratshesky 1605, Riley 1608, Russell 1614, Schrafft 1618, **Sheraton 1625,** Stoddard 1635, Stone 1637, Travelli 1644, **Walsh 1648, Webster 1652,** Worcester 1659, **Wyman-Gordon 1660**

Michigan: Ann Arbor 1664, Battle Creek 1669, Besser 1672, DeRoy 1682, DeVlieg 1685, DeWaters 1687, Ford 1700, **Gerber 1711,** Grand 1715, Herrick 1718, Holden 1720, Kaufman 1730, Loutit 1738, **Manoogian 1741,** Midland 1748, Miller 1749, Morley 1751, Muskegon 1754, Skillman 1773, Stephenson 1776, Tuck 1785, Wickes 1798, Wilson 1800

Minnesota: Alliss 1805, **American 1807,** Bigelow 1820, Blandin 1821, Bremer 1822, Carolyn 1827, **Cenex 1828, Davis 1833, DeLuxe 1835, General 1847, Grain 1850,** Grotto 1853, Honeywell 1861, **Kasal 1871, Medtronic 1884, Minnesota 1890,** O'Neil 1898, Ordean 1899, Phillips 1903, **Pillsbury 1905,** Quinlan 1906, Rodman 1911, Saint Paul 1912, Thorpe 1916, Van Evera 1919, Wasie 1922

Mississippi: First 1936, Hardin 1937

Missouri: **Anheuser-Busch 1940,** Boone 1943, Brown 1944, Brown 1945, **Butler 1946,** Gaylord 1965, Green 1967, Laclede 1977, **McDonnell 1993,** Roblee 2012, Speas 2017, St. Louis 2020, Union 2034, **Webb 2037**

Montana: Haynes 2045, Heisey 2046

Nebraska: Cooper 2054, Hitchcock 2057, Lincoln 2063, Omaha 2066, Phelps 2067

New Hampshire: Barker 2082, **Hubbard 2086,** New Hampshire 2092, Smyth 2095

New Jersey: **Allied 2098,** Belasco 2101, **Bergen 2102,** Grassmann 2127, Jockey 2138, Kerney 2142, **Lipton 2150, Nabisco 2159, Newcombe 2162,** Ohl 2163, **Schering-Plough 2178,** Schultz 2179, Schultz 2180, **South 2185, Sullivan 2188,** Turrell 2193, Victoria 2197, Westfield 2201, Willits 2204

New Mexico: **Bellamah 2206,** Carlsbad 2208

New York: Abrons 2215, **Allied 2230,** Anderson 2240, Arkell 2243, **ASARCO 2246,** Astor 2248, **Atran 2250,** Baird 2260, **Bay 2270,** Beinecke 2275, Boehm 2295, **Bristol-Myers 2302,** Brookdale 2305, Buffalo 2311, Calder 2320, Campe 2321, **Chatlos 2338, China 2344, Coles 2358, Compton 2363, Continental 2365, Corning 2368,** Curtice-Burns 2377, **Dana 2379, de Hirsch 2387, Deloitte 2395, Dreyfus 2411,** Dutchess 2416, Ebsary 2419, Emerson 2421, **Ford 2443, Frueauff 2455, Gannett 2463, General 2467,** Glens 2476, **Golden 2479,** Goodstein 2487, Gould 2493, **Grace 2496,** Greenwall 2505, **Hearst 2537, Hearst 2538, Hettinger 2547,** Hirschl 2552, **Homeland 2560,** Hoyt 2565, **International 2574, Jephson 2580, Jephson 2581, J.M. 2584, Johnson 2587,** Knapp 2620, Lakeview 2635, Lang 2636, Lavanburg-Corner 2644, Lee 2649, Lemberg 2655, Lincoln 2667, **Link 2672, Lounsbery 2679,** Macdonald 2685, McCann 2712, **McGraw-Hill 2721, Memton 2724,** Moore 2748, Moses 2758, Muehlstein 2764, **New York 2776,** New York 2777, Nichols 2782, **NL 2783, Noble 2784, Norwood 2791,** Noyes 2792, O'Connor 2795, Palisano 2809, **Peat 2817, Pfizer 2823, Phelps 2825, Potts 2836,** Price 2839, **Price 2840,** Ramapo 2846, **Ridley 2866,** Ritter 2868, **Rosenthal 2888, Rubin 2895,** Rubinstein 2896, Rudin 2899, **Schlumberger 2919,** Simon 2933, Snow 2943, Spingold 2948, **Starr 2954, Statler**

2955, Steele-Reese 2957, Stein 2958, **Surdna 2972,** Switzer 2975, **Teagle 2979,** Tuch 2993, Uris 3003, Vogler 3016, **Wallace 3019,** Wegman 3030, **Wilson 3047,** Wilson 3048, **Witco 3053, Wunsch 3061**

North Carolina: Akzona 3073, Biddle 3078, Broyhill 3081, Bryan 3082, Burlington 3084, **Burroughs 3085, Connemara 3090,** Duke 3095, Foundation 3102, Garrison 3103, McClure 3116, Morehead 3118, Reynolds 3123, Reynolds 3124, **Richardson 3127,** Sternberger 3132

North Dakota: Fargo-Moorhead 3139, North Dakota 3142

Ohio: Anderson 3152, **Armco 3156,** Beeghly 3165, **Bingham 3172,** Cleveland-Cliffs 3187, Crandall 3193, Dauby 3197, Deuble 3200, **Eaton 3204,** First 3218, Gallagher 3231, **Goodyear 3239,** Gries 3241, Grimes 3242, Gund 3244, Hamilton 3245, H.C.S. 3250, **Hoover 3253, Huffy 3255,** Huntington 3258, Iddings 3259, Ingram 3261, Jennings 3264, Laub 3281, Lorain 3284, Lubrizol 3285, **Marathon 3289,** Markus 3291, **Mead 3299, Midland-Ross 3302,** Moores 3308, **National 3312,** Nationwide 3313, NCR 3314, Peterson 3327, Reinberger 3338, **Republic 3341,** Richland 3342, **Rosenthal 3347,** Scioto 3356, **Scripps-Howard 3359,** Semple 3361, Stark 3373, Stocker 3375, **Stouffer 3376,** Treuhaft 3389, **TRW 3392,** White 3406, Yassenoff 3414, Young 3415

Oklahoma: Ashbrook 3417, **Broadhurst 3420,** Dobson 3427, First 3430, Harmon 3434, **Kerr 3439, McCasland 3445, Noble 3449,** Oklahoma 3451, Oklahoma 3452, **Phillips 3456,** Share 3463, Wood 3472

Oregon: Barker 3476, Carpenter 3478, Jackson 3490, **Jeld-Wen 3491,** Johnson 3495, Oregon 3500, Templeton 3503, Tucker 3504

Pennsylvania: **Alcoa 3511, Brockway 3528, Carpenter 3536,** Erie 3565, Goldman 3584, **Heinz 3598,** Heinz 3599, Hillman 3603, Hillman 3604, **Hooper 3607,** Hunt 3612, **Independence 3616,** Kline 3628, **Koppers 3631,** McFeely-Rogers 3652, McKenna 3655, **McKenna 3656,** Measey 3659, Packer 3679, PPG 3697, **Presser 3698,** Quaker 3699, Rittenhouse 3704, **Rockwell 3708,** Seybert 3717, Shoemaker 3719, SICO 3720, Smith 3725, Stabler 3733, **Stroud 3744**

Puerto Rico: Harvey 3769

Rhode Island: Fleet 3775, **Genesis 3777, Little 3783,** Rhode 3790

South Carolina: Abney 3794, Kennedy 3808, **Riegel 3813,** Scurry 3816

Tennessee: Benwood 3829, Brown 3832, Lowenstein 3846, **Lyndhurst 3847,** Maclellan 3848, Maclellan 3849, Plough 3855, Potter 3856, **Woods-Greer 3864**

Texas: Abell-Hanger 3866, Amarillo 3872, American 3873, **Biological 3886,** Brackenridge 3889, **Burkitt 3897,** Cameron 3901, Clark 3906, Constantin 3912, Crump 3920, Dallas 3925, Davidson 3926, Dougherty 3934, **Dresser-Harbison 3936,** Fair 3945, Fasken 3948, Fikes 3952, Gifford 3961, Hamman 3972, **HNG 3982,** Houston 3988, Humphreys 3990, Kempner 4001, King 4003, King 4004, McKee 4026, Meadows 4029, Navarro 4040, Owsley 4048, Parry 4051, Piper 4056, **Richardson 4063,** Rockwell 4066, San Antonio 4072, **Shell 4081,** Temple 4098, Texas 4101, **Texas 4102,** Trull 4104, Waggoner 4109, Welch 4115, White 4121, Wright 4128, **Zale 4129**

Utah: Bamberger 4130, Dee 4136, Eccles 4139

Vermont: **Edwards 4147**

Virginia: Camp 4159, Gray 4172, **Olmsted 4189, Reynolds 4193,** Seay 4199, Virginia 4214

Washington: **Anderson 4218,** Cheney 4229, Comstock 4230, Fuchs 4235, Kawabe 4241, Keyes 4242, Kilworth 4244, **Laird 4246, Matlock 4248,** Robertson 4258, Sequoia 4260, Skinner 4262, Washington 4269, Welch 4271, **Weyerhaeuser 4274**

West Virginia: Carbon 4278

Wisconsin: Allis-Chalmers 4294, Consolidated 4310, **Cudahy 4311,** CUNA 4312, **DeRance 4314,** Evjue 4316, Frankenthal 4320, Giddings 4324, Johnson

4334, **Johnson's 4336, Kimberly-Clark 4338,** Kohler 4342, La Crosse 4346, Ladish 4347, Milwaukee 4358, **Smith 4380, Young 4391,** Youth 4392

Wyoming: Tonkin 4400

Seed money

Alabama: Smith 20
Alaska: Alaska 25
Arizona: Arizona 29, Circle K 31, First 34, Mulcahy 42, Wilson 50
Arkansas: **Inglewood 51,** Rockefeller 58, Ross 59
California: **Abelard 63,** Adolph's 64, Ahmanson 65, A.I.D. 66, **American 69, Atkinson 76, Atlantic 78, Baker 81,** Beckman 89, Columbia 130, Copley 133, Corcoran 134, Cowell 136, Crocker 137, Crocker 138, Distribution 151, Drum 156, East Bay 159, Fleishhacker 172, **Fluor 173,** Fusenot 176, Gildred 189, Goldman 195, Goldwyn 196, Haas 202, Haas 204, Hancock 209, **Hewlett 217, Hilton 220,** Hoover 226, Irvine 230, Johnson 239, Jones 240, **Kaiser 242, Keck 243,** Koret 248, Lear 253, **Levi 258, Litton 262,** Lux 268, Lytel 269, Mattel 275, McKesson 283, Mead 284, Monterey 289, Norman 298, Orleton 304, **Page 309,** Parker 310, **Parsons 311,** Peninsula 318, Riverside 333, San Diego 336, San Francisco 337, Santa Clara 341, Santa Cruz 342, Seaver 350, Shoong 359, **Skaggs 369,** Stamps 377, Stern 383, Stulsaft 389, Trust 402, Tuohy 403, **Union 407,** van Loben Sels 410, Weingart 421, Welk 422, **Wilbur 428,** Yorkin 432

Colorado: Anschutz 435, Boettcher 436, Buell 437, Colorado 440, Coors 441, Duncan 443, 8 South 444, **Frost 449,** Hughes 454, Johnson 458, **Needmor 468,** Piton 473, **Ray 475, Woodward 487**

Connecticut: Aetna 489, **Albers 490, American 492,** Bridgeport 502, Connecticut 507, Eder 515, **Educational 516,** Ensign-Bickford 520, Ensworth 521, **General 527,** Hartford 533, **ITT 542, Kazanjian 548,** Moore 558, New Haven 559, **Olin 561,** Palmer 562, **Panwy 563,** Patterson 564, Scott 573, **Scovill 574, Stanley 578, Stone 579, Topsfield 582, UPS 584,** Wahlstrom-Johnson 586, Waterbury 588, Woman's 593, erox 594

Delaware: **Beneficial 596,** Crystal 606, **Glencoe 609,** Laffey-McHugh 616, **Raskob 628**

District of Columbia: April 637, **Arca 638,** Cafritz 643, **German 659, Graham 660,** Higginson 662, **Kennedy 666,** Meyer 672, **Public 679,** Sapelo 681, Stewart 682, Washington 685

Florida: Briggs 698, **Brunner 700,** Bush 701, Conn 704, Dade 706, **duPont 716, Eckerd 719,** Falk 720, **Koch 734,** Phipps 755, Southeast 770, Southwest 771, **Stuart 777, Whitehall 791**

Georgia: Atlanta 802, Atlanta 803, **Day 824,** EMSA 829, Equifax 831, Evans 832, Glancy 840, Hill 846, Lane 851, Loridans 855, Lubo 856, **Southern 873, Tull 878,** Whitehead 884, **Wilson 886,** Woolley 887

Hawaii: **Amfac 888,** Castle 893, Frear 898, Hawaiian 899, McInerny 903, Wilcox 908, Wilcox 909

Illinois: **Abbott 918,** Aigner 919, **Allstate 922, Amoco 928,** Barber-Colman 936, Borg-Warner 950, Chicago 968, **Chicago 969,** Coleman 975, **Deere 987, DeKalb 989,** Dillon 992, **Evinrude 997,** Fel-Pro 1000, **FMC 1005,** Fry 1011, Haffner 1024, Harris 1028, **Harris 1030,** Illinois 1045, IMC 1046, Ingersoll 1047, **Joyce 1052, MacArthur 1076, McGraw 1094,** Millard 1098, Motorola 1104, **Nalco 1106,** New Prospect 1107, Northern 1108, **Peterborough 1117,** Pick 1119, **Retirement 1132,** Sara 1139, **Sears-Roebuck 1145,** Stern 1167, Ward 1185, White 1188, Woods 1193

Indiana: Cole 1207, Cummins 1210, Fort 1214, Hayner 1221, Heritage 1222, Honeywell 1224, Indianapolis 1226, Irwin-Sweeney-Miller 1228, **Lilly 1238**

Iowa: Cowles 1262, Des Moines 1263, Hall 1269, Maytag 1277, Vermeer 1286, Vermeer 1287, Wahlert 1288

Kansas: Garvey 1307, **Hesston 1311,** Powell 1323, Sosland 1329, Wiedemann 1330

Kentucky: Ashland 1332, Bingham 1335, Louisville 1346

Louisiana: Baton Rouge 1354, New Orleans 1376

Maine: Davenport 1392

Maryland: Baker 1401, **Fairchild 1414,** Goldseker 1419, Hoffberger 1423, Knott 1428, Meyerhoff 1439, Noxell 1444, Pearlstone 1445, **PHH 1446,** Ryan 1451, Straus 1456, Town 1459

Massachusetts: Acushnet 1466, **Alden 1468,** Bacon 1472, **Beveridge 1475,** Bird 1476, Blanchard 1480, Boston 1482, Boynton 1484, **Cabot 1488,** Cabot 1489, Cambridge 1491, Campbell 1492, **Cook 1502, Cove 1503, Cox 1506,** Davis 1511, **Eastern 1518,** Ellsworth 1523, **Friendship 1531,** Fuller 1533, Hyams 1561, Kelley 1567, **Kendall 1569, Levinson 1574, Little 1578,** Morgan-Worcester 1584, Old 1589, Parker 1592, Polaroid 1602, Riley 1608, Shaw 1622, Stevens 1634, Stoddard 1635, Wallace 1647, **Walsh 1648,** Worcester 1659, **Wyman-Gordon 1660**

Michigan: Ann Arbor 1664, Barstow 1668, Battle Creek 1669, Besser 1672, Besser 1673, Bishop 1674, Bray 1676, Dalton 1681, DeWaters 1687, Flint 1698, Fremont 1705, **General 1710,** Gerstacker 1712, Grand 1715, **Harder 1716,** Hudson-Webber 1722, Hurst 1724, Jackson 1726, Kalamazoo 1728, Kantzler 1729, Kaufman 1730, **Kellogg 1732,** Kennedy 1733, Loutit 1738, **Manoogian 1741,** McGregor 1744, Midland 1748, Miller 1749, Mills 1750, Morley 1751, **Mott 1752, Mott 1753,** Muskegon 1776, Simpson 1772, Tiscornia 1782, Upjohn 1786, Wilson 1799

Minnesota: Andersen 1810, Beim 1816, Bend 1819, Bigelow 1820, Blandin 1821, Bremer 1822, Bush 1823, Carolyn 1827, **General 1847,** Greystone 1851, Grotto 1853, Honeywell 1861, Hormel 1862, Hulings 1865, Inter-Regional 1867, Lilly 1876, **Lutheran 1877,** Marbrook 1878, Mardag 1879, McKnight 1880, McNeely 1882, **Medtronic 1884,** Minneapolis 1887, North 1892, O'Brien 1896, O'Neil 1898, Paper 1901, Quinlan 1906, Rochester 1910, Saint Paul 1911, Thorpe 1916, Wasie 1922, **Weyerhaeuser 1925**

Mississippi: Hardin 1937

Missouri: **Anheuser-Busch 1940,** Block 1941, Boone 1943, Brown 1944, Brown 1945, **Butler 1946,** Commerce 1951, Cowden 1952, Gaylord 1965, Green 1967, Hall 1968, McGee 1995, **Monsanto 1999,** Oppenstein 2003, Reynolds 2011, Roblee 2012, Speas 2018, St. Louis 2020, Sunderland 2025, **Sunnen 2027,** Swinney 2029, Webb 2037

Nebraska: Cooper 2054, **InterNorth 2058,** Lincoln 2063, Omaha 2066, Phelps 2067

Nevada: **Sells 2081**

New Hampshire: Bean 2083, Hunt 2087, New Hampshire 2092, **Phillips 2093**

New Jersey: **Allied 2098,** Belasco 2101, **Bergen 2102,** Borden 2104, Dodge 2116, **Edison 2119,** Fund 2125, **Hackett 2129, Huber 2133,** Hyde 2134, **International 2135, Johnson 2140, Merck 2155,** New Jersey 2161, Ohl 2163, Prudential 2167, **Schering-Plough 2178,** Schultz 2179, Schultz 2180, **Schumann 2181, Subaru 2187,** Turrell 2193, Victoria 2197, **Vollmer 2199, Warner-Lambert 2200**

New Mexico: **Bynner 2207,** Carlsbad 2208

New York: Abrons 2215, **Agway 2224,** Astor 2248, **Atran 2250, Axe-Houghton 2252,** Barker 2264, **Bay 2270,** Bernhill 2282, **Bingham's 2286,** Boehm 2295, Bowne 2299, Brookdale 2305, Buffalo 2311, **Burden 2315, Bydale 2319, Carnegie 2325,** Central 2331, **Chase 2337,** Chautauqua 2343, **Clark 2346,** Clark 2347, **Coles 2358, Compton 2363,** Cornell 2367, **Corning 2368,** Cowles 2369, Cummings 2376, **Dammann 2378, Dana 2379, de Hirsch 2387,** DeCamp 2389, **Donner 2408, Dorr 2408,** Dreyfus 2411, Dutchess 2416, **Field 2432, Ford 2443, Ford 2444, Gannett 2463,** Gebbie 2465, **General 2467,** Gifford 2469, Glens 2476,

Goodyear 2488, Gould 2493, Grant 2498, **Grant 2499,** Greenwall 2505, **Greve 2506, Griffis 2507, Guggenheim 2512, Guggenheim 2513,** Gutfreund 2519, **Hazen 2535,** Heckscher 2540, Howard 2564, Hoyt 2565, Hycliff 2570, **International 2574, Ittleson 2576, Johnson 2587,** Jones 2591, Kaplan 2598, Lang 2636, **Lavanburg 2643,** Lavanburg-Corner 2644, Lincoln 2667, **Lingnan 2671, Lounsbery 2679, Luce 2682,** Macdonald 2685, **Mailman 2693,** McCann 2712, McGonagle 2719, **McGraw-Hill 2721, Memton 2724, Metropolitan 2732,** Moore 2748, Morgan 2750, Morgan 2751, New York 2774, New York 2775, New York 2777, **New-Land 2779, NL 2783,** Noble 2784, **Norman 2787,** Norwood 2791, O'Connor 2795, **Olin 2799, Ottinger 2806, Pfizer 2823, Potts 2836, Prospect 2842,** Ramapo 2846, **Richmond 2864, Rochester 2873, Rockefeller 2875, Rockefeller 2876, Rosenthal 2888, Ross 2891,** Rubinstein 2896, **Sage 2902,** Samuels 2905, **Scherman 2913, Schimper 2918, Schwarz 2921,** Sheafer 2928, **Sloan 2938,** Snow 2943, Snyder 2944, **Sony 2945,** Sprague 2949, St. Faith's 2950, **Stern 2960, Surdna 2972,** Taconic 2976, **Teagle 2979, Thorne 2984,** United 3000, Utica 3005, **van Ameringen 3006, Vinmont 3015,** Vogler 3016, Watertown 3027, Wegman 3030, **Wenner-Gren 3037, Wilson 3047,** Wilson 3048

North Carolina: **Babcock 3075,** Biddle 3078, Bryan 3083, **Burroughs 3085,** Duke 3095, Ferebee 3097, Finch 3100, Foundation 3102, Garrison 3103, Hanes 3105, Hanes 3106, Morgan 3119, Reynolds 3123, Reynolds 3124, **Richardson 3128,** Rogers 3130, Salisbury 3131, Sternberger 3132, Winston-Salem 3137

North Dakota: Fargo-Moorhead 3139, North Dakota 3142

Ohio: Anderson 3152, **Armco 3156, Bingham 3172, Borden 3174, Brush 3178,** Cincinnati 3183, Cleveland 3186, Columbus 3189, **Commercial 3190, Dana 3196,** Dayton 3199, Evans 3209, Fifth 3214, **Firestone 3216,** Frohring 3229, GAR 3232, Gerson 3237, Gund 3244, Hamilton 3245, **Huffy 3255,** Iddings 3259, Jennings 3264, Jergens 3265, **Kettering 3272,** Laub 3281, Lorain 3284, **Marathon 3289,** Mather 3295, **Mead 3299,** Moores 3308, Nationwide 3313, NCR 3314, Nordson 3316, Pollock 3330, Prentiss 3332, Richland 3342, Russell 3350, Schmidlapp 3354, Scioto 3356, Sears 3360, Sherwick 3365, Smith 3369, Smith 3370, Stark 3373, Stocker 3375, **Stouffer 3376,** Tait 3378, **Tell 3380,** Toledo 3386, Treuhaft 3389, Troy 3391, White 3406, Yassenoff 3414

Oklahoma: Ashbrook 3417, **Broadhurst 3420,** First 3430, Goddard 3432, **Kerr 3439, Noble 3449,** Oklahoma 3451, Oklahoma 3452, **Phillips 3456,** Williams 3471

Oregon: Autzen 3475, Carpenter 3478, Friendly-Rosenthal 3487, Jackson 3490, **Jeld-Wen 3491,** Johnson 3495, Meyer 3498, Oregon 3500, Salem 3501, Tektronix 3502, Templeton 3503

Pennsylvania: **Air 3509, Alcoa 3511,** Allegheny 3512, Anderson 3517, Benedum 3524, Bethlehem 3526, Buhl 3529, **CIGNA 3542,** Craig 3549, **Cyclops 3553,** Dolfinger-McMahon 3557, Eccles 3562, Erie 3565, **Falk 3568,** Fels 3571, Frick 3577, Grundy 3588, **Heinz 3598,** Heinz 3599, Hershey 3601, Hillman 3603, Hillman 3604, Hunt 3612, Justus 3621, Justus 3622, Knollbrook 3629, **Koppers 3631,** McFeely-Rogers 3652, McKenna 3655, **McKenna 3656,** Medical 3660, Mellon 3662, Mellon 3663, **Merit 3666,** Myrin 3673, Patterson 3682, Penn 3683, **Pennwalt 3684, Pew 3686, Pew 3687, Pew 3688,** Philadelphia 3689, Pitcairn-Crabbe 3691, Pittsburgh 3693, Pittsburgh 3694, Polk 3696, PPG 3697, Rittenhouse 3704, Scaife 3711, **Scott 3715,** Scranton 3716, Seybert 3717, Shoemaker 3719, Smith 3725, St. Marys 3732, Stackpole-Hall 3734, Stott 3741, **Strawbridge 3743, Stroud 3744, United 3750, Westinghouse 3756, Whitaker 3761,** Widener 3762, Williamsport 3764, Wurts 3766, Wyomissing 3767

Rhode Island: Fleet 3775, **Genesis 3777,** Old 3786, Rhode 3790

South Carolina: Abney 3794, Fuller 3804, Gregg-Graniteville 3806, **Merck 3810, Riegel 3813, Roe 3814,** Self 3817, Spartanburg 3820

Tennessee: Benwood 3829, Chattanooga 3835, Day 3839, Lowenstein 3846, **Lyndhurst 3847,** Maclellan 3848, Maclellan 3849, Memphis-Plough 3854, Plough 3855, Toms 3859, **Woods-Greer 3864**

Texas: Abell-Hanger 3866, Amarillo 3872, American 3873, Anderson 3875, Brown 3893, **Burkitt 3897,** Carter 3902, Clark 3906, Communities 3911, Cooper 3916, Dallas 3925, El Paso 3940, Fair 3945, Fikes 3952, Fleming 3954, Halsell 3971, Hightower 3980, Hillcrest 3981, **HNG 3982,** Hoblitzelle 3984, Keith 4000, Kempner 4001, McKee 4026, Meadows 4029, **Menil 4031,** Moody 4035, Navarro 4040, O'Connor 4042, Owsley 4048, Richardson 4064, Rockwell 4066, San Antonio 4072, **Scaler 4073,** Semmes 4078, Steinhagen 4087, Strake 4089, Tarrant 4094, **Technical 4097,** Temple 4098, Trull 4104, Waggoner 4109, White 4121, Wortham 4127, **Zale 4129**

Utah: Eccles 4139

Vermont: **Edwards 4147,** Windham 4151

Virginia: **Best 4154,** Camp 4159, Gray 4172, **Jones 4178,** Memorial 4185, Norfolk 4187, Ohrstrom 4188, Virginia 4214, Washington 4215

Washington: Archibald 4219, Bishop 4220, Cheney 4229, Kawabe 4241, **Matlock 4248,** Medina 4250, Murdock 4252, Norcliffe 4254, Robertson 4258, Skinner 4262, Spokane 4264, Tacoma 4267, **Weyerhaeuser 4274, Wharton 4275**

West Virginia: Kanawha 4285

Wisconsin: Alexander 4292, Alexander 4293, Allis-Chalmers 4294, Badger 4299, Banta 4300, Beloit 4301, Consolidated 4310, **Cudahy 4311,** CUNA 4312, Evjue 4316, Janesville 4330, **Johnson 4331, Johnson's 4336, Kimberly-Clark 4338,** Kohler 4342, La Crosse 4346, Marine 4353, McBeath 4356, Milwaukee 4358, Siebert 4379, Stackner 4381, Youth 4392

Wyoming: Tonkin 4400

Special projects

Alabama: Smith 20, Webb 24
Alaska: Alaska 25
Arizona: Arizona 29, Circle K 31, Flinn 35, Hervey 38, **Kieckhefer 39,** Mulcahy 42, Wilson 50
Arkansas: **Inglewood 51,** Rockefeller 58, Ross 59
California: **Abelard 63,** Adolph's 64, Ahmanson 65, A.I.D. 66, **American 69, Atlantic 78, BankAmerica 84,** California 114, California 115, Coburn 128, Columbia 130, Connell 131, Corcoran 134, Crocker 137, Damien 142, Disney 148, Distribution 151, Drum 156, East Bay 159, First 170, Fleishhacker 171, Fleishhacker 172, Gellert 183, Gellert 184, Gerbode 186, **Getty 187,** Gildred 189, Goldman 195, Goldwyn 196, Haas 202, Haas 203, Haas 204, **Hewlett 217, Hilton 220,** Holt 225, Humboldt 228, Irvine 230, **Jewett 238,** Johnson 239, Jones 240, **Kaiser 242, Keck 243, Kerr 244,** Koret 248, Lloyd 264, Lurie 267, Lux 268, Mattel 275, Monterey 289, Murphy 295, Norman 298, **Page 309,** Parker 310, Peninsula 318, Richards 332, Riverside 333, Rosenberg 334, San Francisco 337, Santa Cruz 342, Seaver 350, **Skaggs 369, Smith 372,** Stamps 377, Steele 382, Stern 383, Stulsaft 389, **Union 407,** van Loben Sels 410, Walker 414, Weingart 421, Welk 422, Wells 423, **Wilbur 428,** Witter 429, **Wollenberg 430,** Yorkin 432
Colorado: Anschutz 435, Duncan 443, 8 South 444, **Frost 449,** Hughes 454, Johnson 458, Joslyn 460, **Ray 475**
Connecticut: **Albers 490, American 492,** Bridgeport 502, Connecticut 507, **Educational 516,** Ensign-Bickford 520, **General 527,** Hartford 533, Howard 539, **ITT 542, Kazanjian 548,** Long 552, Moore 558, **Olin 561,** Palmer 562, Patterson 564, **Stanley 578, UPS 584,** Vanderbilt 585, Wahlstrom-Johnson 586, Waterbury 588, Woman's 593
Delaware: **Beneficial 596, Glencoe 609, Good 610,** Marmot 621
District of Columbia: **Arca 638, Benton 640, Council 646, German 659,** Higginson 662, Meyer 672, **Public 679,** Sapelo 681, Washington 685
Florida: Briggs 698, **duPont 716,** Jenkins 732, **Koch 734,** Phillips 754, **Whitehall 791, Winn-Dixie 794**
Georgia: Atlanta 802, EMSA 829, Equifax 831, Hill 846, Lubo 856, Ottley 861, Trust 877, Whitehead 884
Hawaii: Castle 894, Cooke 895, Frear 898, Hawaiian 899, McInerny 903, Watumull 907
Illinois: **Abbott 918,** Aigner 919, American 925, **Ameritech 926, Amoco 928,** Borg-Warner 950, Chicago 968, Chicago 971, Coleman 975, Crown 982, **Crown 983, DeKalb 989, Evinrude 997,** Fel-Pro 1000, Field 1001, **FMC 1005,** Fry 1011, **Graham 1021,** Harris 1028, **Harris 1030,** IMC 1046, Ingersoll 1047, **Joyce 1052, MacArthur 1077, Monticello 1100,** Moorman 1102, New Prospect 1107, Northern 1108, **Northwest 1109, Peterborough 1117,** Pick 1119, **Quaker 1126,** Regenstein 1130, **Retirement 1132,** Sara 1139, Scholl 1142, **Sears-Roebuck 1145,** Siragusa 1153, Sprague 1161, **Tyndale 1178,** White 1188, Woods 1193, Wurlitzer 1194
Indiana: Anderson 1195, **Arvin 1196,** Ball 1199, Clowes 1206, Cummins 1210, Foellinger 1213, Fort 1214, Heritage 1221, Honeywell 1224, Indianapolis 1226, Irwin-Sweeney-Miller 1228, **Liberty 1236,** Moore 1245, **Thirty 1256**
Iowa: Des Moines 1263, Hall 1269, Maytag 1277, Van Buren 1285
Kansas: Baughman 1293, Coleman 1298, **Hesston 1311,** Jordaan 1314, Sosland 1329
Kentucky: Bingham 1335, Louisville 1346, **Margaret 1347**
Louisiana: New Orleans 1376, Physicians 1377, Shreveport-Bossier 1383
Maryland: Goldseker 1419, Kelly 1424, Knott 1428, Pearlstone 1445, Ryan 1451, Town 1459, U.S.F. & G. 1460
Massachusetts: Bank 1473, Bayrd 1474, Blanchard 1480, Boston 1482, Boston 1483, Brandegee 1486, **Cabot 1488,** Cambridge 1491, Campbell 1492, **CarEth 1494,** Cove 1503, **Cox 1506,** Daniels 1509, Dexter 1515, Fidelity 1528, **Filene 1529, Friendship 1531,** Fuller 1532, Kelley 1567, **Kendall 1569, Levinson 1574,** Lindsay 1576, **Little 1578,** Parker 1592, Riley 1608, Shawmut 1623, Steiger 1632, Stevens 1634, Thompson 1643, Vingo 1646, **Webster 1652**
Michigan: Ann Arbor 1664, Barstow 1668, Battle Creek 1669, **Chrysler 1679,** Dalton 1681, Dow 1690, Flint 1698, **General 1710,** Herrick 1718, Hudson-Webber 1722, Hurst 1724, Jackson 1726, Kaufman 1730, Loutit 1738, McGregor 1744, Morley 1751, **Mott 1752, Mott 1753,** Muskegon 1754, Simpson 1772, Strosacker 1780, Towsley 1783, Upjohn 1786, Vicksburg 1789, Wilson 1800
Minnesota: Andersen 1810, Athwin 1813, Bigelow 1820, Blandin 1821, Bremer 1822, Bush 1823, Butler 1824, Cargill 1825, Carolyn 1827, **Dayton 1834, DeLuxe 1835,** First 1842, Gamble 1845, **General 1847, General 1848,** Graco 1849, Greystone 1851, Grotto 1853, Honeywell 1861, Jerome 1868, Lilly 1876, Marbrook 1878, Mardag 1879, **Medtronic 1884,** Minneapolis 1887, **Minnesota 1890, Northwest 1894,** Quinlan 1906, Saint Paul 1912, Walker 1920, Wasie 1922, **Weyerhaeuser 1925**
Mississippi: First 1936, Hardin 1937
Missouri: Boone 1943, **Butler 1946,** Commerce 1951, Gaylord 1965, Green 1967, Hall 1968, Jordan 1973, Laclede 1977, Loose 1981, Loose 1982, Loose 1983, **McDonnell 1993,** Millstone 1998, **Monsanto 1999,** Oppenstein 2003, Speas 2017, Speas 2018, **Sunnen 2027,** Swinney 2029
Nebraska: **InterNorth 2058,** Lincoln 2063

New Hampshire: Bean 2083, Cogswell 2084, New Hampshire 2092
New Jersey: **Allied 2098,** Belasco 2101, Borden 2104, Dodge 2116, **Dow 2117, Edison 2119,** Fund 2125, **Hackett 2129, Huber 2133,** Johnson **2139, Johnson 2140, Kirby 2143,** New Jersey 2161, Prudential 2167, Sawtelle 2175, Schenck 2177, Schultz 2179, **South 2185, Subaru 2187, Union 2194,** Victoria 2197
New Mexico: **Bynner 2207,** Carlsbad 2208
New York: Abrons 2215, **American 2235, AT&T 2249, Avon 2251,** Axe-Houghton **2252,** Barker 2264, Barker 2265, Bat Hanadiv 2268, Bernhill 2282, **Bingham's 2286,** Bowne 2299, Brookdale 2305, Bruner 2309, Buffalo 2311, **Burden 2315, Bydale 2319,** Calder 2320, Campe 2321, **Carnegie 2325,** Cary 2327, Central 2331, **Chase 2337, Chatlos 2338,** Clark 2347, Clark 2349, **Coles 2358, Commonwealth 2362, Compton 2363, Corning 2368,** Curtice-Burns 2377, **Dammann 2378,** de Hirsch 2387, **DeCamp 2392,** Dillon 2399, **Dorr 2408, Dreyfus 2411, Dreyfus 2413,** Dutchess 2416, Emerson 2421, **Exxon 2426, Field 2432, Ford 2443, Ford 2444, Foundation 2445, Foundation 2446, Fuld 2458, Gannett 2463, General 2467,** Glens 2476, Gould 2493, Grant 2498, **Grant 2499,** Greenwall 2505, **Gulf 2516, Hartford 2528, Hazen 2535,** Howard 2564, Hoyt 2565, **Initial 2573, International 2574, Ittleson 2576, J.M. 2584,** Jones 2591, **Jurzykowski 2595,** Kaplan 2598, **Klingenstein 2618, Knapp 2620, Kunstadter 2632, Lakeview 2635,** Lang 2636, **Lavanburg 2643,** Lavanburg-Corner 2644, L.A.W. 2645, Lee 2649, Lemberg 2655, Lincoln 2667, **Lounsbery 2679, Luce 2682,** Macdonald 2685, **Macy 2689, Mailman 2693, Markle 2700,** McConnell 2715, **McGraw-Hill 2721,** Moore 2748, Morgan 2750, **New World 2773,** New York 2774, **New York 2776, Norman 2787,** O'Connor 2795, **Olin 2799, O'Toole 2805, Ottinger 2806, PBP 2815,** Peat 2817, **Pfizer 2823, Phillips-Van Heusen 2828,** Potts 2836, Price 2839, Ramapo 2846, **Revson 2858, Richmond 2864, Rockefeller 2875, Rockefeller 2876, Rockefeller 2877,** Rose 2882, **Rosenthal 2887, Ross 2891,** Rubinstein 2896, **Sage 2902, Scherman 2921, Schwarz 2921, Smart 2939, Smithers 2941,** Snyder 2944, Spingold 2948, St. Faith's 2950, **Stern 2960,** Stony 2963, **Sullivan 2968, Surdna 2972, Thorne 2984, Tinker 2986,** United 3000, **United 3001,** van Ameringen **3006, Vetlesen 3011,** Vidda 3012, Vogler 3016, Watertown 3027, **Weatherhead 3028,** Wegman 3030, Western 3039, Wilson 3048
North Carolina: **Babcock 3075,** Broyhill 3081, **Burroughs 3085,** Duke 3095, Foundation 3102, Garrison 3103, Hanes 3105, Hanes 3106, Kellenberger 3109, Morehead 3118, Reynolds 3124, Salisbury 3131, Sternberger 3132, Winston-Salem 3137
North Dakota: North Dakota 3142
Ohio: Acme 3144, **Amcast 3149,** American 3150, Anderson 3152, **Bingham 3172, Brush 3178,** Cincinnati 3183, Cleveland 3186, Dayton 3199, **Federated 3211,** Fifth 3214, **Firestone 3216,** Gerson 3232, **Goodyear 3239,** Gund 3244, **Huffy 3255,** Iddings 3259, Ingalls 3260, Jennings 3264, Jergens 3265, **Kettering 3272, Knight 3276,** Mather 3295, **Mead 3299,** Nationwide 3313, Nordson 3316, Pollock 3330, Prentiss 3332, Reinberger 3338, **Republic 3341,** Russell 3350, Scioto 3356, **Scripps-Howard 3359,** Smith 3369, Stark 3373, **Stouffer 3376,** Tait 3378, Treuhaft 3389, Treu-Mart 3390, **TRW 3392,** White 3406, Yassenoff 3414
Oklahoma: Ashbrook 3417, **Kerr 3439,** Oklahoma 3451, Warren 3469, Wegener 3470
Oregon: Barker 3476, Collins 3482, Jackson 3490, **Jeld-Wen 3491,** Meyer 3498, Oregon 3500, Salem 3501, Templeton 3503, Tucker 3504
Pennsylvania: **Air 3509,** Anderson 3517, Arcadia 3520, Benedum 3524, Buhl 3529, **Carpenter 3536, DeMoss 3554,** Dietrich 3556, Dolfinger-McMahon 3557, Douty 3559, Falk 3567, **Falk 3568,** Fels 3571, Frick 3577, Grundy 3588, **Gulf**

3589, Heinz 3598, Hillman 3603, Hillman 3604, **Hooper 3607,** Huston 3614, Kavanagh 3624, Knollbrook 3629, Laurel 3637, McCune 3651, McKenna 3655, McLean 3657, Medical 3660, Mellon 3661, Mellon 3662, Myrin 3673, Penn 3683, **Pew 3687,** Philadelphia 3689, Pittsburgh 3693, Pittsburgh 3694, Scaife 3711, **Scott 3715,** Scranton 3716, Smith 3723, Smith 3724, Smith 3725, Snayberger 3727, SPS 3731, Stott 3741, **United 3750, Westinghouse 3756, Westinghouse 3757, Whitaker 3761,** Widener 3762, Williamsport 3764
Rhode Island: Citizens 3773, Fleet 3775, **Genesis 3777,** Old 3786, Rhode 3790
South Carolina: Gregg-Graniteville 3806, Self 3817, Springs 3821
Tennessee: **Lyndhurst 3847,** Potter 3856
Texas: Amarillo 3872, Brackenridge 3889, Bridwell 3890, Brown 3893, **Burkitt 3897,** Communities 3911, Cooley 3914, Cooper 3916, Crow 3919, Dallas 3925, El Paso 3940, Fain 3944, Fair 3945, Fleming 3954, Florence 3955, **Halliburton 3970,** Houston 3988, Humphreys 3990, Kempner 4001, King 4003, Luling 4019, **McCreless 4023,** Meadows 4029, Moody 4035, **Oldham 4044,** Richardson 4064, San Antonio 4072, **Scaler 4073,** Semmes 4078, **Shell 4081,** Strake 4089, Tandy 4092, **Technical 4097,** Temple 4098, Trull 4104, Waggoner 4109, **Weaver 4113**
Utah: **Thrasher 4145**
Vermont: Windham 4151
Virginia: **Best 4154, Jones 4178,** Memorial 4185, Norfolk 4187, **Reynolds 4193,** Seay 4199, Virginia 4214
Washington: Cheney 4229, Glaser 4236, **Laird 4246,** Murdock 4252, Norcliffe 4254, Sequoia 4260, Spokane 4264, Washington 4269, Welch 4271
West Virginia: Kanawha 4285
Wisconsin: Allis-Chalmers 4294, Badger 4299, Briggs 4306, **Cudahy 4311,** CUNA 4312, Evjue 4316, Janesville 4330, Marine 4353, McBeath 4356, Milwaukee 4358, **Rexnord 4373,** Rutledge 4376, Siebert 4379, Stackner 4381, Youth 4392

Student aid

Arizona: Dougherty 32, Fry 36
Arkansas: Murphy 54, Trinity 61
California: California 117, Corti 135, **Fluor 173, Gemco 185, Hertz 216,** Monterey 289, Oakland 301, **Potlatch 326,** Richards 332, Santa Barbara 340, Santa Clara 341
Colorado: Fairfield 446, Piton 473, Sachs 476, Thatcher 483
Connecticut: **Carter 503, Conway 508, Folsom 524,** Fox 525, MacCurdy-Salisbury 553, **Panwy 563, Society 576**
Delaware: **Kutz 615,** Lynch 620, **Raskob 627**
District of Columbia: Sapelo 681, Strong 683
Florida: **Aurora 692, Eagles 717,** Fellows 721, Gore 723, Phillips 754, **Poynter 757,** Rinker 760, Sample 764, Southwest 771, **Stark 773,** Winter 795
Georgia: Baker 804, Bibb 806, Callaway 811, Cobb 817, **Georgia-Pacific 837, Pickett 865**
Hawaii: Atherton 890, **Bohnett 891,** Hawaiian 899, Straub 904, Zimmerman 910
Illinois: **Abbott 917,** Andrew 931, Aurora 935, Boynton 952, Burgess 958, Caestecker 960, Fel-Pro 1000, Fitzgerald 1004, Furnas 1012, **Griswold 1023,** Koehler 1064, Levie 1070, McFarland 1092, **Mellinger 1096, National 1106,** Petersen 1118, Pick 1119, Pullman 1125, Stump 1171
Indiana: Baber 1198, Cole 1207, CTS 1209, Cummins 1210, Kilbourne 1231, Minear 1244
Iowa: Fahrney 1265, Jay 1271, Maytag 1276, Sherman 1283, Van Buren 1285
Kansas: Abell 1291, **Baker 1292,** Davis 1300, Jones 1313, Jordaan 1314
Kentucky: Appalachian 1331, **Hope 1342,** Louisville 1346, Ogden 1350

Louisiana: Brown 1355, Burton 1356, Hurley 1369, Zigler 1390
Maine: Davenport 1392
Maryland: Loats 1431, Stewart 1455
Massachusetts: Colgan 1501, Edwards 1520, Evans 1525, **Hood 1554,** Hopedale 1555, Kelley 1567, Naurison 1585, Pilgrim 1600, Stone 1636, Sudbury 1641, Urann 1645, Warren 1649, Wells 1656, Wheelwright 1657, **Williams 1658**
Michigan: Bentley 1671, Fremont 1705, Grand 1715, Jeffers 1727, Midland 1748, Muskegon 1754, Student 1781, Whiteley 1795, Winship 1802
Minnesota: Alworth 1806, Bend 1819, Eddy 1839, Jostens 1870, Phillips 1903, Tozer 1917, Whiteside 1927
Mississippi: Day 1933, Feild 1935, Hardin 1937, Walker 1939
Missouri: Hall 1968, Ilgenfritz 1970, Ingram 1971, McDavid 1992, MFA 1997, Orscheln 2004, Speas 2018, Tilles 2032, Westlake 2038
Montana: Bair 2043, Sweet 2048
Nebraska: Kiewit 2059, Lane 2061, Phelps 2067, Weller 2075
Nevada: Golden 2079
New Hampshire: Cogswell 2084, Lord 2091, New Hampshire 2092, Wagner 2097
New Jersey: **CPC 2113, Dow 2117,** Grupe 2128, **Reeves 2170,** Sawtelle 2175
New York: **Barth 2267, Bennett 2279,** Chautauqua 2339, Clark 2347, **Coles 2358,** Crary 2373, **de Hirsch 2387,** Glens 2476, **Golub 2484, Jehovah 2579, Li 2664,** Kautz 2606, **Mostazafan 2761, National 2769,** Pratt-Northam 2837, Reynolds 2860, **Roothbert 2881, Schepp 2912, Starr 2954,** Stony 2963, Sussman 2973, Utica 3005, Watertown 3027, **Youth 3063**
North Carolina: Elizabeth 3096, Ferebee 3097, Foundation 3102, Sternberger 3132, Stonecutter 3133, Winston-Salem 3137
Ohio: Flickinger 3221, Ford 3224, Gardner 3233, Hauss-Helms 3249, Hosler 3254, Kilburger 3275, Record 3336, Schmidlapp 3353, **Scripps-Howard 3359,** Shinnick 3367, Stark 3373, Van Wert 3396, Wagnalls 3397, Youngstown 3416
Oklahoma: Bartlett 3418, Bovaird 3419, Fields 3429, Johnson 3437
Oregon: Clemens 3481, Daly 3483, Jenkins 3492, Johnson 3495, Salem 3501
Pennsylvania: Ellis 3563, Gibson 3578, Hall 3591, Hoyt 3609, **Koppers 3631,** Lesher 3639, Packer 3679, Snayberger 3727, Sordoni 3729, Vincent 3751, Warren 3753, Wolf 3765
Puerto Rico: Harvey 3769
South Carolina: **Bailey 3797,** Byrnes 3800, Fairey 3803, Fuller 3804, Moore 3811, Springs 3821
South Dakota: Hatterscheidt 3826
Tennessee: Chattanooga 3835, Westend 3863
Texas: Baumberger 3881, El Paso 3940, Haas 3966, Hugg 3989, Kempner 4001, King 4003, Lindsay 4017, McMillan 4027, Millhollon 4033, Moody 4035, Munson 4039, Piper 4056, **Richardson 4063,** San Antonio 4072, Seibel 4077, Shanor 4079, Tartt 4095, Woltman 4126
Utah: Bamberger 4130, Masonic 4142
Vermont: General 4148, Scott 4150, Windham 4151
Virginia: **Best 4154,** Blount 4155, Camp 4159, Lincoln-Lane 4181, Slemp 4200
Washington: Carman 4227, Keyes 4242, Spokane 4264, Welch 4271, West 4273
West Virginia: Bowen 4277, Kanawha 4285, Minor 4287, Price 4288, Vecellio 4290
Wisconsin: Fromm 4321, Janesville 4330, Oshkosh 4361, Racine 4370, Rutledge 4376, Wisconsin 4389
Wyoming: Bryan 4395, Stock 4398, Whitney 4402

Technical assistance

Alaska: Alaska 25
Arizona: Arizona 29

Arkansas: Rockefeller 58

California: **Abelard 63,** Adolph's 64, Bothin 99, California 114, Corcoran 134, Fireman's 169, First 170, **Fluor 173,** Gerbode 186, Haas 202, Hancock 209, Koret 248, Monterey 289, Packard 308, Peninsula 318, San Diego 336, San Francisco 337, Santa Clara 341, Santa Cruz 342, **Skaggs 369,** Zellerbach 433

Colorado: Anschutz 435, 8 South 444, **Frost 449,** Johnson 458, **Needmor 468,** Piton 473, **Ray 475**

Connecticut: Aetna 489, Bridgeport 502, Connecticut 507, New Haven 559

District of Columbia: **Arca 638, Benton 640,** Sapelo 681, Washington 685

Florida: Bush 701, Southeast 770, **Whitehall 791**

Georgia: Atlanta 802, Rich 870

Hawaii: Hawaiian 899

Illinois: Bersted 945, Harris 1028, Inland 1048, **Joyce 1052,** Northern 1108, **Stone 1170,** USG 1182

Indiana: Cummins 1210, Heritage 1222, Honeywell 1224, Irwin-Sweeney-Miller 1228

Kansas: **Schowalter 1327,** Sosland 1329

Kentucky: Ashland 1332, Louisville 1346

Louisiana: New Orleans 1376

Maryland: Goldseker 1419

Massachusetts: **Little 1578,** Ratshesky 1605, Shaw 1622

Michigan: Jackson 1726, Simpson 1772

Minnesota: Blandin 1821, **Dayton 1834,** Minneapolis 1887, **Northwest 1894,** Rochester 1910

Missouri: **Danforth 1955,** Loose 1983, Swinney 2029

New Jersey: **Allied 2098, Carnegie 2109, Johnson 2139,** New Jersey 2161, Prudential 2167, Victoria 2197

New Mexico: Carlsbad 2208

New York: **Avon 2251,** Buffalo 2311, **Clark 2346, Field 2432, Ford 2444,** Fund 2460, Glens 2476, Hoyt 2565, **Initial 2573, J.M. 2584,** Jones 2591, Kaplan 2598, Morgan 2750, **New World 2773,** New York 2774, New York 2775, O'Connor 2795, Rubinstein 2896

North Carolina: Duke 3095, Foundation 3102

Ohio: **Armco 3156, Borden 3174,** Cincinnati 3183, Cleveland 3186, Dayton 3199, Humphrey 3256, Nordson 3316, Stark 3373, Toledo 3387, Yassenoff 3414

Oklahoma: First 3430

Oregon: Carpenter 3478, Jackson 3490, Meyer 3498, Oregon 3500

Pennsylvania: Benedum 3524, **Falk 3568,** Fels 3571, **Heinz 3598,** Mellon 3661, Philadelphia 3689, Pittsburgh 3694, **Scott 3715**

Rhode Island: Citizens 3773, **Genesis 3777,** Rhode 3790, **Textron 3792**

South Carolina: Self 3817

Texas: Amarillo 3872, Communities 3911, Cooper 3916, Halsell 3971, Meadows 4029, Moody 4035, Tandy 4092, **Technical 4097,** Waggoner 4109,• **Zale 4129**

Virginia: Richmond 4196

Washington: Medina 4250, Skinner 4262, Spokane 4264, Tacoma 4267

West Virginia: Kanawha 4285

Wisconsin: Alexander 4292, Allis-Chalmers 4294, **Cudahy 4311**

SUBJECT INDEX

Foundations in bold face type make grants on a national or regional basis; the others generally limit giving to the city or state in which they are located.

Accounting
Adult education
Africa
Aged
Agriculture
Alcoholism
Animal welfare
Anthropology
Archaeology
Architecture
Arms control
  see also **International affairs; Peace**
Arts
  see also **Cultural programs; Fine arts; Music; Performing arts**
Asia
Australia

Belgium
Biochemistry
Biological sciences
  see also **Agriculture; Ecology; Marine sciences; Medical sciences; Science and technology**
British Commonwealth
  SEE United Kingdom
Business administration
  see also **Accounting; Hotel administration; Insurance education**

Canada
Cancer
  see also **Health; Medical research**
Caribbean
Catholic giving
  SEE Religion, Roman Catholic
Chemistry
Children
  SEE Child development; Child welfare; Youth
Child development
Child welfare
Citizenship
Civic affairs
Civil rights
  see also **Minorities**
Colleges and universities
  SEE Higher education

Communications
  see also **Journalism**
Community colleges
  SEE Higher education
Community development
  see also **Housing; Leadership development; Rural development; Urban affairs**
Community funds
Conservation
  see also **Ecology; Environment; Wildlife**
Crime and law enforcement
  see also **Law and justice**
Cultural programs
  see also **Arts; Historic preservation; Libraries; Museums; Music; Performing arts**

Day care
  SEE Child welfare
Demography
  SEE Population studies
Dentistry
  see also **Medical education**
Dermatology
Drug abuse

Earth sciences
  SEE Physical sciences
Ecology
  see also **Conservation; Environment**
Economics
Education
  see also **Adult education; Elementary education; Higher education; Insurance education; Legal education; Medical education; Secondary education; Theological education; Vocational education**
Education—building funds
Education—minorities
Education, early childhood
Educational associations
Educational research
Educational television
  SEE Communications
Elementary education
Energy

Engineering
England
  SEE United Kingdom
Environment
  see also **Conservation; Ecology**
Europe
  see also **Belgium; France; Greece; Italy; Poland; Scotland; United Kingdom**

Family planning
  SEE Population control
Family services
Fine arts
France
Freedom

Government
  see also **Law and justice; Political science**
Greece

Handicapped
  see also **Rehabilitation; Speech pathology**
Health
Health services
Heart disease
Heroism
Higher education
Historic preservation
History
Horticulture
  SEE Agriculture
Hospitals
  see also **Medical research**
Hospitals—building funds
Hotel administration
Housing
Human rights
  SEE Civil rights
Humanities
  see also **Arts; History; Language and literature; Museums; Music**

Immigration
Insurance education
Intercultural relations

International affairs
  see also **Arms control; Peace**
International development
International law
International studies
Israel
Italy

Japan
Jewish giving
  SEE **Religion, Jewish**
Journalism
  see also **Communications**

Labor
Land management
  SEE **Conservation; Environment**
Language and literature
Latin America
  see also **Caribbean; Mexico; Venezuela**
Law and justice
  see also **Civil rights; Crime and law enforcement; International law; Legal education**
Leadership development
Legal education
Leprosy
Libraries
Life sciences
  SEE **Biological sciences; Medical sciences**

Marine sciences
Medical education
  see also **Dentistry; Nursing**
Medical research
  see also **Cancer; Heart disease; Leprosy; Schistosomiasis**
Medical sciences
  see also **Dentistry; Dermatology; Nursing; Ophthalmology; Pharmacy; Psychiatry**
Mental health
  see also **Psychiatry; Psychology**
Mexico
Middle East
  see also **Israel**
Military personnel
Minorities
  see also **Civil rights; Education— minorities; Native Americans; Race relations; Women**

Museums
Music

Native Americans
Nursing
  see also **Health services; Medical education**
Nutrition

Oceanography
  SEE **Marine sciences**
Ophthalmology

Parapsychology
Peace
  see also **Arms control; International affairs**
Performing arts
  see also **Cultural programs; Music**
Pharmacy
Philippines
Physical sciences
  see also **Biochemistry; Chemistry; Engineering; Science and technology**
Poland
Police services
  SEE **Crime and law enforcement**
Political science
  see also **Government; Law and justice**
Population control
Population studies
Primary education
  SEE **Elementary education**
Protestant giving
  SEE **Religion, Protestant**
Psychiatry
Psychology
Public administration
  see also **Government**
Public policy

Race relations
  see also **Civil rights; Intercultural relations; Minorities**
Recreation
Rehabilitation
  see also **Alcoholism; Drug abuse; Handicapped**
Religion
  see also **Theological education**
Religion—missionary programs
Religion, Christian
Religion, Jewish

Religion, Protestant
Religion, Roman Catholic
Rural development

Safety
Schistosomiasis
Science and technology
  see also **Biological sciences; Physical sciences**
Scotland
Seamen
Secondary education
Social sciences
  see also **Anthropology; Economics; History; Political science; Sociology**
Social services
  see also **Aged; Child welfare; Family services; Handicapped; Welfare; Youth**
Sociology
South Pacific
Special education
  SEE **Handicapped**
Speech pathology

Television
  SEE **Communications**
Theological education
Transportation
  see also **Urban affairs**

United Kingdom
Urban affairs
  see also **Community development**

Venezuela
Veterans
  SEE **Military personnel**
Vocational education

Welfare
  see also **Aged; Child welfare; Family services; Handicapped; Social services**
Wildlife
Women

Youth
  see also **Child development; Child welfare**

Accounting
New York: **Deloitte 2395, Price 2840**
Ohio: **Ernst 3207**

Adult education
California: **American 69**
Michigan: Faigle 1695, **Kellogg 1732, Mott 1752**
New Jersey: **Newcombe 2162**
Rhode Island: **Genesis 3777**

Africa
Rhode Island: **Genesis 3777**
Wisconsin: **DeRance 4314, Young 4391**

Aged
California: Arakelian 70, California 114, Callison 118, East Bay 159, Factor 162, Garland 182, Goldman 195, Haas 202, Hancock 209, Joslyn 241, Kirchgessner 245, **Levi 258,** Lytel 269, **Parsons 311,** Pasadena 314, Peninsula 318, San Diego 336, Smith 371
Colorado: Anschutz 435, Hill 452, Hunter 455, Joslyn 460, Rabb 474
Connecticut: **Bissell 500, Educational 516,** EIS 517, Hartford 533, List 551, Robinson 568
District of Columbia: Lehrman 668, **Villers 684**
Florida: Bush 701, **du Pont 713, Eagles 717,** Falk 720, Howell 729, Selby 766
Georgia: Callaway 810, Courts 820, English 830, Pitts 866, **Whitehead 885**
Hawaii: Cooke 895, King's 902, Wilcox 908
Illinois: **Abbott 917,** Alton 924, Beidler 941, Camp 962, Eisenberg 996, Field 1001, **Retirement 1132,** Siragusa 1153, Stern 1167, Willett 1191
Indiana: Smock 1253
Iowa: Van Buren 1285
Maryland: Warfield 1461
Massachusetts: Bacon 1472, Boynton 1484, Campbell 1492, Chase 1498, Farnsworth 1526, Home 1552, Old 1589, Sailors' 1616
Michigan: Gerstacker 1712, Kalamazoo 1728, Strosacker 1780, Whiting 1796
Minnesota: Gamble 1845, Mardag 1879, **Medtronic 1884,** Rivers 1909
Missouri: Hall 1968, Oppenstein 2003, Speas 2018, St. Louis 2020
New Jersey: **Allied 2098,** Duke 2118, Elizabeth 2120, **Rippel 2171**
New York: Albany's 2226, Astor 2248, Brookdale 2305, **Brooklyn 2307,** Bruner 2309, **Burden 2315, Commonwealth 2362,** Cummings 2376, de Kay 2389, **Dorr 2408, Dreyfus 2413,** Faith 2427, **General 2467,** Gifford 2469, **Glenn 2475,** Green 2500, Hagedorn 2523, **Hartford 2528,** Hatch 2531, Jones 2591, **Killough 2613,** Klosk 2619, Lincoln 2667, **McDonald 2718,** New York 2775, Nias 2781, Parshelsky 2813, Ramapo 2846, Reiss 2855, **Richmond 2864, Russ 2900, Schimper 2918,** Schweckendieck 2922, Wegman 3030, Wikstrom 3045
North Carolina: Foundation 3102, Winston-Salem 3137
North Dakota: Myra 3141, North Dakota 3142
Ohio: **Cincinnati 3182,** Cleveland 3186, Ernsthausen 3208, Finnegan 3215, Ford 3224, Frohman 3228, Goerlich 3238, Iddings 3259, McGregor 3298, Moores 3308, Richland 3342, **Rosenthal 3347,** Sheadle 3363, White 3406
Oregon: Chiles 3479, **Fohs 3484,** Friendly-Rosenthal 3487, Meyer 3498

Pennsylvania: **Crary 3550,** Crels 3552, Grundy 3588, Hassel 3596, Medical 3660, Smith 3724, Smith 3725, **Westinghouse 3757**
Rhode Island: Champlin 3772, Rhode 3790
South Carolina: Self 3817
Tennessee: Church 3836
Texas: Bivins 3887, Bryce 3896, Craig 3918, Gifford 3961, Steinhagen 4087, **Weaver 4113**
Virginia: Beazley 4153, Camp 4159
Washington: Kawabe 4241, Norcliffe 4254, Spokane 4264
Wisconsin: Frankenthal 4320, **Johnson 4331,** McBeath 4356, Milwaukee 4358, Schroeder 4377, Siebert 4379

Agriculture
Arkansas: Rockefeller 58
California: Corti 135, Lytel 269, Newhall 296
Florida: **Whitehall 791**
Georgia: **Foundation 834**
Illinois: **Farm 999,** Moorman 1101
Kansas: Breidenthal 1295
Louisiana: Gray 1364
Massachusetts: Wells 1656
Michigan: Americana 1663, **Gerber 1711,** Kellogg 1732
Minnesota: **Grain 1850**
Mississippi: First 1936
Missouri: **Butler 1946**
New York: **Agway 2224, Ford 2444, Frasch 2450, Gloeckner 2478,** Hahn 2525, **Rockefeller 2877, Wallace 3020**
Ohio: Van Wert 3396
Oklahoma: **Kerr 3439, Noble 3449**
Texas: Behmann 3884, **Central 3903,** Luling 4019, McMillan 4027, Perry 4054, Waggoner 4110

Alcoholism
California: **Kroc 250**
Hawaii: Frear 898
Massachusetts: **Webster 1652**
Minnesota: Walker 1920
New York: **Carnegie 2325,** Gifford 2469, **J.M. 2584, Metropolitan 2732,** Smithers 2941
North Carolina: Chatham 3089
Virginia: Reinsch 4192

Anthropology
Arizona: **Amerind 27**
Indiana: **Plumsock 1248**

New York: **Guggenheim 2513,** Wenner-Gren 3037

Archaeology
Arizona: **Amerind 27**
California: Packard 308
New York: **Bingham's 2286, Kress 2629**

Architecture
Colorado: Buell 437
Illinois: **Graham 1021, Skidmore 1154**
New York: Kaplan 2598
Oregon: Carpenter 3478

Arms control
California: Damien 142
Connecticut: **Topsfield 582**
District of Columbia: **Carnegie 644**
Iowa: **Stanley 1284**
Maryland: **Baker 1400**
Massachusetts: **Kendall 1569, Levinson 1574**
Michigan: **Mott 1753**
New York: Boehm 2295, **Compton 2363, Field 2432, Ford 2444, Mott 2763, New World 2773, New-Land 2779,** Reynolds 2859, **Rockefeller 2875, Rockefeller 2876, Scherman 2913**
Virginia: **Jones 4178**

Arts
Alabama: Blount 4
Arizona: Arizona 28
California: Adolph's 64, Ahmanson 65, **Atlantic 78, BankAmerica 84,** California 114, **Christensen 124,** Columbia 130, Disney 149, Fleishhacker 171, Fleishhacker 172, **Fluor 173,** Gerbode 186, **Getty 188,** Haas 204, **Keck 243, Ledler 256,** L.L.W.W. 265, Mayer 277, Mead 284, Monterey 289, Norman 298, San Francisco 337, Seaver 350, Security 351, Seuss 355, **Signal 360,** Simon 362, **Skaggs 369,** Walker 414, Wells 423, Wilbur 427, Yorkin 432, Zellerbach 433
Colorado: El Pomar 445, Gates 450
Connecticut: Aetna 489, **Albers 490,** Day 509, Ensworth 521, **Fairchild 522, General 527, Great 529,** Hartford 532, New Haven 559, **Rosenthal 569,** Waterbury 588
District of Columbia: **Graham 660,** Meyer 672, **Weir 686, Wouk 688**
Florida: Arison 691, Dade 706, Jacksonville 730, Lowe 743, River 762
Georgia: Atlanta 802, **Coca-Cola 818,** Cox 822, First 833, Haley 842, Hill 846, Lee 853, Lubo 856, Rich 870, Tomlinson 875, Trebor 876, Whitehead 884, Woolley 887
Hawaii: Atherton 890, Brewer 892, Cooke 895, McInerny 903, Watumull 907
Illinois: American 925, Atwood 934, Buchanan 956, **Carlin 963,** Carson 964, **Container 976,** Davee 986, **Hammer 1026,** House 1043, Lederer 1067, **MacArthur 1077,** McCormick 1088, **Quaker 1126,** Regenstein 1130, Sara 1139, Ward 1185
Indiana: Clowes 1206, Griffith 1217, Honeywell 1224, Irwin-Sweeney-Miller 1228, Leighton-Oare 1235
Iowa: Maytag 1277
Kansas: Sosland 1329
Kentucky: Bank 1334, Brown 1337, Louisville 1346
Louisiana: Helis 1365

Animal welfare
Arizona: du Bois 33
California: Baker 82, **Crummer 140, Doe 152,** Doelger 153, Green 199, Humboldt 228
Colorado: Animal 434, Jenkins 456
Delaware: Bishop 598
Florida: Baker 693, Ritter 761
Georgia: Anncox 801
Illinois: **Brach 954, Donnelley 994**
Iowa: **Salsbury 1282**
Massachusetts: Crabtree 1507, Johnson 1565
Minnesota: Greystone 1851
New Jersey: Dodge 2116, **Jeffery 2137, South 2185**
New York: **Bay 2270,** Hopkins 2561, **Mertz-Gilmore 2730**
Pennsylvania: Allegheny 3512, Hooker 3606

Asia

Australia

Belgium

Biochemistry

Biological sciences

Business administration

Canada

Cancer

Caribbean

Chemistry

Child development

Child welfare

Colorado: Anschutz 435, Colorado 440, Hogan 453, Hunter 455, Piton 473, **Ray 475,** Swan 481
Connecticut: Casey 504, Palmer 562, Scott 573
Delaware: **Kutz 615,** Laffey-McHugh 616, **Milliken 623,** National 624
District of Columbia: Appleby 636, **GEICO 657,** Loughran 669
Florida: du Pont 713, Falk 720, Lowe 743, Meyer 748, Phillips 753, **Ware 789,** Wolfson 797
Georgia: Dodson 827, Evans 832, Harland 843, Murphy 860, **Tull 878,** Whitehead 884
Hawaii: Wilcox 908
Idaho: Cunningham 911
Illinois: Alton 924, Beidler 941, Brach 953, Galvin 1015, **Harper 1027,** Keating 1056, Kendall 1061, Lehmann 1068, Manilow 1079, **Marquette 1082,** McCormick 1088, **McGraw 1094,** Pittway 1120, Seabury 1143, Smith 1156, Upton 1181
Indiana: Indianapolis 1226, Koch 1232
Iowa: Hawley 1270, Ruan 1281
Kansas: Breidenthal 1295, Davis 1300
Maryland: Leidy 1430, Loats 1431, Marshall 1434, Wilson 1464
Massachusetts: Chase 1497, Chase 1498, Childs 1499, Dexter 1515, **Donaldson 1517,** Heydt 1549, **Hood 1553,** Lindsay 1576, **Phillips 1598,** Pilgrim 1600, Riley 1608, Stride 1640, Weber 1651
Michigan: DeRoy 1682, Earl-Beth 1692, **Ford 1699, Ford 1704,** Himmel 1719, Holden 1720, Kalamazoo 1728, Pagel 1756, Sage 1764, Scott 1765, Skillman 1773, Youth 1804
Minnesota: Carolyn 1827, O'Neil 1898
Missouri: Calkins 1947, Enright 1960, Gaylord 1965, Gaylord 1966, Long 1980, Loose 1983, Oppenstein 2003, Speas 2018, Springmeier 2019, St. Louis 2020, **Sunnen 2027, Webb 2037,** Whitaker 2039
Nebraska: Quivey 2068
Nevada: Hawkins 2080
New Jersey: Duke 2118, Grassmann 2127, Orange 2164, Schwartz 2182, Youths' 2205
New York: Altman 2232, Astor 2248, Bachmann 2255, Buffalo 2311, **Carnegie 2325, Chatlos 2338,** Children's 2343, **Clark 2346,** Clark 2349, Cummings 2376, Darrah 2381, Dewar 2397, Dula 2414, Faith 2427, **Field 2432, Foundation 2445, Frueauff 2455,** Goodyear 2488, Gould 2493, **Hazen 2535,** Heckscher 2540, **Hess 2546,** Julia 2593, **Karagheusian 2600,** L and L 2633, Lauder 2642, Lavanburg-Corner 2644, Lee 2649, **Mailman 2693, Mastronardi 2702, Mathers 2704, McCrory 2716, McDonald 2718, Memton 2724,** Metzger-Price 2733, Millbrook 2738, Nichols 2782, Oppenheimer 2802, Park 2812, **Phillips-Van Heusen 2828,** Roche 2872, Rochester 2874, **Rosen 2883, Ross 2891,** Rubinstein 2896, Schweckendieck 2922, Snyder 2944, Sprague 2949, St. Faith's 2950, Straus 2966, **Summerfield 2970,** Tuch 2993, Wegman 3030, Wendt 3036
North Carolina: ABC 3071, Broyhill 3081, **Connemara 3090,** Duke 3095, Hanes 3106, Rogers 3130, Stowe 3134, Whitener 3136, Woodson 3138
Ohio: American 3151, Anderson 3153, **Armington 3157, Borden 3174,** Cleveland 3186, Gerson 3237, Goerlich 3238, Hamilton 3245, Mather 3295, Moores 3308, Schmidlapp 3354, Smith 3369, Yassenoff 3414
Pennsylvania: Arcadia 3520, Blaisdell 3527, Buhl 3529, Douty 3559, Goldman 3584, Grundy 3588, Hambay 3593, Justus 3622, Plankenhorn 3695, Seybert 3717, Smith 3724, Smith 3725, Warren 3753, Widener 3762
South Carolina: Fuller 3804, Scurry 3816, Symmes 3825
Tennessee: Buckman 3833
Texas: Bryce 3896, Carter 3902, Craig 3918, Elkins 3941, Ellwood 3942, Gill 3962, Harding 3973, Hightower 3980, Johnston 3996, McKee 4026, Navarro 4040, Scarborough 4074, West 4119, Wilson 4123
Utah: Bamberger 4130, **Thrasher 4145**
Virginia: Camp 4159, Memorial 4185, Thurman 4207, Titmus 4208

Washington: Archibald 4219, Bishop 4220, Fuchs 4235, Glaser 4236, Kawabe 4241, Kilworth 4244, McEachern 4249, Medina 4250, Shemanski 4261, Wyman 4276
West Virginia: Carbon 4278
Wisconsin: Janesville 4330, **Johnson 4331,** McBeath 4356, Milwaukee 4358, Youth 4392
Wyoming: Kamps 4397, Stock 4398, Tonkin 4400

Citizenship
California: Haas 202
Illinois: Ingersoll 1047
Michigan: **Mott 1752**
Missouri: **Deer 1956**
New York: **Norman 2787**

Civic affairs
Alabama: Blount 4, Chandler 5, Gibson 9
Alaska: Atwood 26
Arkansas: **Reynolds 56**
California: **City 125,** Clorox 127, Crocker 138, Fireman's 169, First 170, **Fluor 173,** Goldman 195, Herbst 215, **Keck 243, Levi 258,** Lurie 267, McKesson 283, **Ostrow 305, Parsons 311,** San Diego 336, Seaver 350, Security 351, **Signal 360,** Stewart 384, Wells 423
Colorado: Coors 441, Fairfield 446, Johnson 458, **Needmor 468,** Petteys 471, Piton 473
Connecticut: **Amax 491, American 492,** Bodenwein 501, Hartford 532, Hartford 533, Hartford 534, Palmer 562, Preston 566
Delaware: Lovett 619
District of Columbia: **Discount 649**
Florida: **Sharonsteel 768, Winn-Dixie 794**
Georgia: Atlanta 802, **Coca-Cola 818,** Evans 832, Porter 867, Trebor 876, Whitehead 884
Hawaii: Frear 898
Illinois: **Allstate 922,** Andrew 931, Blum-Kovler 948, Borg-Warner 950, **Brunswick 955, Carlin 963,** Chicago 968, Chicago 970, Chicago 972, Coleman 975, **Container 976, DeKalb 989,** Dillon 992, First 1002, **FMC 1005, Gould 1020, Hart 1032,** Inland 1048, Lingle 1072, Meyer-Ceco 1097, New Prospect 1107, **Northwest 1109, Quaker 1126,** Sara 1139, Smith 1156, USG 1182, **Walgreen 1183,** Warner 1185, Wurlitzer 1194
Indiana: Cole 1207, Foellinger 1213, Habig 1219, Heritage 1222, Hillenbrand 1223, Indianapolis 1226, Krannert 1233, Lilly 1237, **Lilly 1238**
Kansas: Fourth 1305, Hansen 1309, Helvering 1310, Jordaan 1314, **Marley 1319,** Sosland 1329
Kentucky: Bank 1334, Bingham 1335, Brown 1336
Louisiana: Freeman 1361, Helis 1365, Reily 1379, RosaMary 1380
Maryland: Duncan 1411, **Fairchild 1414**
Massachusetts: **Levinson 1574,** Morgan-Worcester 1584, Worcester 1659
Michigan: **Chrysler 1679,** Dow 1690, **Ford 1702,** Fremont 1705, **General 1710,** Gerstacker 1712, National 1755, Wickes 1798
Minnesota: **Bemis 1818,** Bremer 1822, Cargill 1825, **DeLuxe 1835, General 1847,** Inter-Regional 1867, Minneapolis 1888, **Phipps 1904, Pillsbury 1905,** Wood-Rill 1929
Missouri: Block 1941, Gaylord 1965, Ingram 1971, Loose 1982, Nichols 2000, Sunmark 2026
Nebraska: Cooper 2054, **InterNorth 2058,** Kiewit 2059, **Kiewit 2060,** Lincoln 2063, Omaha 2066, Rogers 2070, Steinhart 2071
New Hampshire: Putnam 2094
New Jersey: **Crum 2114,** Fund 2125, **Johnson 2139, Merck 2155,** Prudential 2167, **Subaru 2187, Union 2194**
New York: Abrons 2215, **American-Standard 2237, Avon 2251, Barth 2267, Bristol-Myers 2302, CBS**

2329, Constans-Culver 2364, **Corning 2368,** Fund 2460, **Gannett 2463, Gimbel-Saks 2471, Grace 2496,** Harriman 2527, Kaplan 2598, Lever 2657, McCann 2712, **McGraw-Hill 2721, Mellon 2722, Mertz-Gilmore 2730, Metropolitan 2732, Mobil 2743,** Morgan 2750, **PepsiCo 2820, Pfizer 2823, Phelps 2825, Resnick 2856,** Rubinstein 2896, **Stevens 2962,** United 3000, Vidor 3013, Warren 3024, Whitehead 3041
North Carolina: Belk 3077, Burlington 3084, Elizabeth 3096, Ferebee 3097, Jenkins-Tapp 3108
Ohio: Anderson 3152, **Armco 3156,** Baird 3161, **Borden 3174,** Cincinnati 3183, Cleveland 3186, Columbus 3189, **Dana 3196,** Dayton 3199, **Dively 3201, Eaton 3204, Federated 3211, Firestone 3216,** Frost 3230, Gund 3244, **Huffy 3255,** Mather 3294, **Mead 3299,** Nordson 3316, **Procter 3333, Sherwin-Williams 3366,** Smith 3368, Stark 3373, **TRW 3392,** Yassenoff 3414, Young 3415
Oklahoma: Ashbrook 3417, Jones 3438, Lyon 3442, **Phillips 3456**
Oregon: Oregon 3500
Pennsylvania: **Alcoa 3511,** Benedum 3524, Fels 3571, Hillman 3603, Hillman 3604, Hunt 3612, Justus 3621, Mandell 3647, Mellon 3661, Mellon 3663, Mengle 3664, **Merit 3666,** Philadelphia 3689, **Rockwell 3708,** Stackpole-Hall 3734, Trexler 3748, Whalley 3759, Williamsport 3764, Wyomissing 3767
Rhode Island: Citizens 3773
Tennessee: Plough 3855
Texas: Allied 3871, American 3873, Anderson 3875, Brookshire 3892, Cain 3900, Harrington 3974, **HNG 3982,** Johnson 3995, Knox 4009, Meadows 4029, O'Donnell 4043, Owen 4047, Owsley 4048, Rockwell 4066, San Antonio 4072, Temple 4098
Virginia: English 4168, Norfolk 4187, Ohrstrom 4188, **Reynolds 4193**
Washington: **Burlington 4226,** Comstock 4230, Skinner 4262, Spokane 4264, **Wharton 4275**
West Virginia: McDonough 4286
Wisconsin: Alexander 4292, Andres 4296, **Cudahy 4311,** Fort 4319, **Johnson 4331, Johnson's 4336,** McBeath 4356, Wisconsin 4388

Civil rights
California: **Abelard 63,** Damien 142
Connecticut: Aetna 489
District of Columbia: **Discount 649**
Illinois: **Chicago 969,** Davee 986, **MacArthur 1076**
Indiana: Cummins 1210, Irwin-Sweeney-Miller 1228
Massachusetts: **Levinson 1574**
Minnesota: **Andreas 1811**
Missouri: **Deer 1956**
New Jersey: **South 2185, Warner-Lambert 2200**
New York: Boehm 2295, **Bydale 2319, Donovan 2406,** FFHS & J 2431, **Field 2432, Ford 2444,** Gutfreund 2519, **Hughes 2566,** Hycliff 2570, Kaplan 2598, Krim 2630, Lever 2657, **Mertz-Gilmore 2730, Muskiwinni 2766, New World 2773,** New-Land 2779, **Norman 2787, Normandie 2788,** Ottinger 2806, **PBP 2815, Rockefeller 2877, Rubin 2895, Stern 2960,** Straus 2966, Warner 3022

Communications
California: Mayer 277, **MCA 279,** Smith 370
Delaware: **Presto 626**
District of Columbia: **Benton 640, National 674**
Florida: **Davis 707**
Illinois: **Ameritech 926,** Harris 1030, MacArthur 1077, **Mason 1084**
Massachusetts: Boston 1483, GenRad 1534
Michigan: Masco 1743

Community development

Community funds

Myers 2302, Campe 2321, Cohen 2353, Cohn 2354, **Colt 2360, Continental 2365, Corning 2368,** Cowles 2369, Curtice-Burns 2377, Dent 2396, **Dow 2410, Dun 2415,** Emerson 2421, **Ettinger 2423, First 2435,** Fribourg 2453, Gebbie 2465, **Gimbel-Saks 2471,** Gleason 2474, Goodyear 2488, **Grace 2496,** Harriman 2527, Hutchins 2568, **Hutton 2569, Indian 2572,** Irving 2575, Klee 2616, Knox 2622, Leviton 2659, LILCO 2666, Linder 2669, Macdonald 2685, Maguire 2692, McCarthy 2713, **Memton 2724,** Metropolitan 2732, **Milliken 2740, Mobil 2743, New York 2776, Newhouse 2778, NL 2783,** Norstar 2789, **PepsiCo 2820, Pfizer 2823, Phelps 2825, Phillips-Van Heusen 2828, Pren-Hall 2838,** Price 2839, Raymond 2849, **Reed 2852, Revlon 2857,** Rich 2862, **Rosenthal 2888, Ryan 2901, Saks 2903, Smith 2940, Sony 2945, Sperry 2947, Standard 2951, Stevens 2962, Straus 2965,** Sulzberger 2969, **Thorne 2984, Tisch 2987, Transway 2991, United 2998,** United 2999, Watertown 3027, Wendt 3036, **Westvaco 3040, Witco 3053, Young 3062**
North Carolina: ABC 3071, Akzona 3073, **BarclaysAmerican 3076,** Belk 3077, **Blue Bell 3079,** Broyhill 3081, Burlington 3084, Carolina 3087, Dickson 3092, Dickson 3093, Dover 3094, **Fieldcrest 3098,** Finch 3100, **Martin 3114,** Richardson 3125
North Dakota: Stern 3143
Ohio: Acme 3144, **Amcast 3149,** American 3151, Anderson 3152, Anderson 3153, **Austin 3159,** Beecher 3164, Beeghly 3165, **Borden 3174,** Britton 3176, Charities 3181, Cincinnati 3184, Cleveland 3185, Cleveland-Cliffs 3187, Codrington 3188, **Commercial 3190, Dana 3196, Eagle-Picher 3203, Eaton 3204, Firestone 3216,** Firman 3217, First 3219, France 3227, **GenCorp 3234,** Goerlich 3238, Hankins 3246, Hartzell-Norris 3247, Higbee 3252, **Hoover 3253, Huffy 3255,** Humphrey 3256, Ingalls 3260, Jergens 3265, Kramer 3277, Kuntz 3279, Lennon 3282, **Marathon 3289, Mead 3299, Midland-Ross 3302,** Monarch 3305, Mount 3309, Nationwide 3313, NCR 3314, Ohio 3319, **Parker-Hannifin 3323,** Perkins 3325, Pollock 3330, **Premier 3331, Procter 3333, Reliance 3339, Republic 3341, Robbins 3345, SCOA 3357,** Scott 3358, Sherman-Standard 3364, Sherwick 3365, **Sherwin-Williams 3366,** South 3371, **Standard 3372, Stouffer 3376,** Timken 3382, Toledo 3386, Toledo 3387, Tremco 3388, **TRW 3392,** Wean 3401, **White 3405,** Youngstown 3416
Oklahoma: **Cities 3423,** Collins 3424, Cuesta 3426, First 3430, Goddard 3432, Kirkpatrick 3441, **Phillips 3456**
Oregon: Ford 3485, **Jeld-Wen 3491, Louisiana-Pacific 3496,** Tektronix 3502
Pennsylvania: **Air 3509, Alco 3510, Allegheny 3513,** American 3514, AMP 3516, **Annenberg 3519, Brockway 3528, Carpenter 3536,** Central 3539, **CIGNA 3542,** Crawford 3551, **Cyclops 3553,** Dietrich 3556, **Dravo 3561,** Goldman 3584, **Gulf 3589,** Hammermill 3594, **Harsco 3595, Heinz 3598,** Hershey 3601, Hopwood 3608, Hunt 3612, Huston 3614, Janssen 3617, **Kennametal 3626,** Kline 3627, **Koppers 3631,** Leeds 3638, Levy 3641, **Lukens 3645, Maneely 3648,** Mellon 3661, Mengle 3664, Mine 3669, National 3674, **National 3675,** 1957 3676, Oberlaender 3677, **Pennwalt 3684,** Pitcairn-Crabbe 3691, Pittsburgh 3692, Pittsburgh 3694, PPG 3697, Quaker 3699, Reliance 3703, **Rockwell 3708, Rust 3709,** Schoonmaker 3714, **Scott 3715,** SmithKline 3726, Snyder 3728, Spang 3730, SPS 3731, Steinman 3738, **Strawbridge 3743, Superior-Pacific 3745, United 3750,** Warren 3753, **Westinghouse 3757,** Wheeling-Pittsburgh 3760, **Whitaker 3761**
Rhode Island: Citizens 3773, Cranston 3774, Fleet 3775, Galkin 3776, Haffenreffer 3778, Kimball 3781, Old 3786, **Textron 3792**
South Carolina: Citizens 3801, Gregg-Graniteville 3806, Inman-Riverdale 3807, **Riegel 3813,** Sargent 3815, Springs 3821, State-Record 3823

Tennessee: Church 3836, Goldsmith 3841, Jewell 3845, Tonya 3860, Washington 3861
Texas: Allied 3871, American 3873, Bank 3877, **Central 3903,** Cockrell 3908, Cooper 3916, Costa 3917, Cullen 3921, Davis 3927, **Dresser 3935, Dresser-Harbison 3936, ENSERCH 3943,** Fasken 3948, Hemphill-Wells 3977, **HNG 3982,** Kempner 4001, Lone 4018, McKee 4026, Mosle 4036, **Quanex 4060,** Sams 4071, Scott 4075, **Shell 4081,** Southland 4084, Texas 4101, **Texas 4102,** Tobin 4103, Turner 4105
Virginia: Beazley 4153, **Best 4154,** Central 4163, **Dan 4166,** Landmark 4179, Perry 4191, **Reynolds 4193, Robertshaw 4197,** Sovran 4201, Thalhimer 4203, Universal 4212, UVB 4213
Washington: Archibald 4219, Boeing 4223, **Burlington 4226,** Dupar 4233, Green 4237, Leuthold 4247, **Matlock 4248,** Murray 4253, PACCAR 4255, Rainier 4257, Univar 4268
West Virginia: Daywood 4281, Fenton 4282
Wisconsin: Allis-Chalmers 4294, **ARMCO 4298,** Badger 4299, **Bradley 4303,** Briggs 4306, Bucyrus-Erie 4308, Consolidated 4310, CUNA 4312, Evinrude 4315, Falk 4317, Frankenthal 4320, Gelatt 4323, Giddings 4324, **Heileman 4326,** Jacobus/Heritage 4329, Janesville 4330, **Johnson 4331,** Kearney 4337, **Kimberly-Clark 4338, Koehring 4339, Kress 4344,** Ladish 4347, Marshall 4354, Nekoosa 4360, Oshkosh 4361, Pabst 4363, **Rexnord 4373,** Stackner 4381, Stolper-Wensink 4382, **Trane 4383, Universal 4384,** Vilter 4385, Wisconsin 4388, Wisconsin 4389

Conservation
Alaska: Alaska 25
Arizona: Morris 41
Arkansas: Rockefeller 58, Ross 59
California: Damien 142, Heller 213, Island 233, McCallum 282, Murdy 293, Packard 308, Santa Cruz 342, Scripps 349, See 352, Steel 381, Witter 429
Colorado: Piton 473
Connecticut: **Dennett 511, Sachem 570,** Vanderbilt 585
Delaware: Chichester 600, Copeland 604, Crestlea 605, Ederic 607, Marmot 621, Red Clay 629
District of Columbia: **Wouk 688**
Florida: Briggs 698, Phipps 755, **Stark 773, Storer 776**
Hawaii: Anthony 889
Illinois: **Amoco 928,** Bersted 945, Burns 959, Camp 962, Deering 988, **Donnelley 994, Joyce 1052,** Leslie 1069, McCormick 1088, **TYF 1177**
Indiana: Hayes 1220
Iowa: **Bohen 1261, Meredith 1278**
Kansas: Beech 1294
Kentucky: Brown 1337
Maryland: **Baker 1400, Knapp 1427,** Middendorf 1440, Town 1459
Massachusetts: Cabot 1489, **Green 1539, Kendall 1569,** Peabody 1593, Pierce 1599, Rodgers 1609, Stevens 1633, Stevens 1634
Michigan: Dow 1690, Kennedy 1733, **Kresge 1734, Mott 1752**
Minnesota: Baker 1814, Bell 1817, Chadwick 1829, Driscoll 1837, **General 1848,** Griggs 1852, Marbrook 1878, Mardag 1879, McKnight 1881, Neilson 1891, Rivers 1909, **Weyerhaeuser 1925**
Missouri: Green 1967, LaRue 1978, **Smith 2015, Woods 2041**
New Hampshire: **Phillips 2093,** Putnam 2094
New Jersey: Cape 2108, **Engelhard 2121,** Jockey 2138, New Jersey 2161, Prudential 2167, **South 2185,** Union 2195
New York: AKC 2225, **American 2234,** Baird 2258, Baker 2262, **Barth 2267, Bayne 2271,** Bedford 2272, Cary 2327, Charlpeg 2336, **Coleman 2357,** Dobson 2401, **Donner 2405, Dorr 2408,** Erpf 2422, Foundation 2447, Gilman 2470, **Griffis 2507,** Hahn 2525, Hastings 2530, High 2550,

Jackson 2577, Kaplan 2598, **Kerry 2610,** Larsen 2638, L.A.W. 2645, **Mad 2690, Mellon 2722, Mertz-Gilmore 2730,** Nichols 2782, **Noble 2784, Perkins 2821, Prospect 2842,** Richardson 2863, **Rockefeller 2875, Rockefeller 2876,** Sasco 2908, **Scherman 2913,** Schieffelin 2915, **Steele-Reese 2957, Thorne 2984,** van Ameringen 3007, Vidda 3012, **Wallace 3020,** Wilson 3049
North Carolina: Hanes 3105, Hillsdale 3107
Ohio: Anderson 3153, **Armington 3157,** Benua 3168, Charities 3181, Columbus 3189, Dayton 3199, Evans 3209, Mather 3294, Nippert 3315, Oglebay 3318, Perkins 3325, **Procter 3333,** Smith 3370, **Timken 3384,** Toledo 3386, **Tucker 3393,** Wodecroft 3409
Oregon: Autzen 3475
Pennsylvania: Beneficia 3525, Dietrich 3555, Dietrich 3556, Hillman 3603, Hillman 3604, Hunt 3611, Laurel 3637, **Lukens 3645,** McLean 3657, Mellon 3662, Mellon 3663, Penn 3683, **Pew 3687,** Rockwell 3707, Waters 3754, Wyomissing 3767
South Carolina: Baruch 3798, **Merck 3810**
Texas: **Bass 3879,** LBJ 4011, McAshan 4022, **Welder 4116**
Virginia: **Jones 4178,** Ohrstrom 4188, Truland 4210
Washington: Archibald 4219, Bloedel 4222, Bullitt 4225, **Laird 4246,** Norcliffe 4254, Sequoia 4260
Wisconsin: **Cudahy 4311, Johnson 4333,** Krause 4343, Peters 4365, Polybill 4369

Crime and law enforcement
California: Sefton 353
District of Columbia: **Police 676**
Georgia: Woolley 887
Hawaii: Wilcox 908
Illinois: **Chicago 969**
Massachusetts: Shaw 1622
Michigan: Hudson-Webber 1722
New York: **Burden 2315, Clark 2346, Ford 2444, McDonald 2718,** Pisces 2832, **Richmond 2864**
Ohio: Anderson 3153
Pennsylvania: Warren 3753

Cultural programs
Alabama: Avondale 1, Birmingham 3, Blount 4, Daniel 7, Linn-Henley 10, Shook 19, **Sonat 21**
Alaska: Atwood 26
Arizona: Arizona 29, First 34, Raymond 43, VNB 47, Waddell 48
Arkansas: Rebsamen 55, **Reynolds 56**
California: **Baker 81, BankAmerica 84, Bechtel 87,** Bechtel 88, Berger 91, Berry 93, Bing 95, Bothin 99, Braun 102, Brenner 104, **Brody 106,** Callison 118, Center 121, **CFS 122,** CN, Clorox 127, **Coleman 129,** Connell 131, Copley 133, Cowell 136, Crocker 137, Crocker 138, **Crown 139,** Crummey 141, Damien 142, Davies 143, Day 144, DeMille 146, Disney 148, Durfee 157, East Bay 159, Familian 164, Familian 165, **Fire 168,** Fireman's 169, First 170, Fleishhacker 171, Fleishhacker 172, **Fluor 173,** Garland 182, Gellert 184, **Getty 188,** Golden 194, Goldwyn 196, Haas 203, Hancock 209, Heller 213, **Hewlett-Packard 218,** Hoag 221, Humboldt 228, Incentive 229, Irvine 230, Irwin 231, Johnson 239, **Keck 243,** Knudsen 246, Komes 247, Lakeside 251, Lear 253, Levy 259, Lloyd 264, Lurie 267, Lytel 269, **MCA 279,** McBean 281, McKesson 283, Muller 291, Murdy 293, Murphey 294, Norris 299, **Ostrow 305, Parker 310, Parsons 311,** Pauley 316, Peters 320, **R & R 329,** R. P. 330, Roth 335, San Diego 336, Santa Barbara 340, Santa Cruz 342, **Sassoon 343,** Security 351, See 352, Setzer 354, Seuss 355, **Signal 360,** Steel 381, Steele 382, Stern 383, Stewart 384, Stuart 388, Stulsaft 389, **Swig 391,**

Tandy 4092, Tarrant 4094, Taub 4096, Temple 4098, Texas 4100, Tobin 4103, **Weaver 4113**
Virginia: **Armour 4152,** Beazley 4153, Bryant 4156, Camp 4158, Easley 4167, Gottwald 4171, Gray 4172, Lane 4180, **McCrea 4184,** Memorial 4185, Norfolk 4187, Reinsch 4192, Washington 4215
Washington: Bishop 4220, Cheney 4229, Haas 4238, **Matlock 4248,** Medina 4250, Seattle 4259, Skinner 4262, Spokane 4264, Wyman 4276
West Virginia: Chambers 4280, Jacobson 4284, Kanawha 4285
Wisconsin: Andres 4296, Beloit 4301, **Cudahy 4311,** Evinrude 4315, Helfaer 4327, **Johnson 4332, Johnson's 4336, Kimberly-Clark 4338,** Oshkosh 4362, Rutledge 4376
Wyoming: Bryan 4395

Education--building funds
New York: **Olin 2798**
Ohio: **Eaton 3204**
Texas: Johnson 3995
Wisconsin: Ladish 4347

Education--minorities
California: **Jewett 238,** McKesson 283
Colorado: Sachs 476
Connecticut: **General 527, Xerox 594**
Georgia: **Southern 873**
Illinois: Borg-Warner 950
Minnesota: **Pillsbury 1905, Weyerhaeuser 1925**
Missouri: **Danforth 1955**
New York: **Caritas 2323, Compton 2363, Ford 2444, International 2574, Macy 2689, New-Land 2779, PepsiCo 2820**
Rhode Island: **Genesis 3777**

Education, early childhood
California: Johnson 239, Rosenberg 334
Hawaii: Castle 894
Illinois: Borg-Warner 950
Michigan: Towsley 1783
Missouri: Green 1967
New York: **Carnegie 2325,** Goldman 2481
Ohio: Jergens 3265
Virginia: Thurman 4207

Educational associations
California: **American 69**
Connecticut: **General 527, ITT 542**
Georgia: Anncox 801, **Delta 825**
Massachusetts: **Cook 1502**
Minnesota: **Donaldson 1836**
Missouri: Stupp 2023
New Jersey: **Vollmer 2199**
New York: **Allied 2230,** Crary 2373, **Exxon 2426, General 2467, Mobil 2743,** Neu 2771, New York 2777, Romill 2880
North Carolina: **Richardson 3126**
Ohio: **Borden 3174,** Jennings 3264, **Procter 3333**
Pennsylvania: **Air 3509, Alcoa 3511,** Hammermill 3594, **Pew 3686, United 3750, Westinghouse 3756**
Virginia: **Dan 4166**
Wisconsin: **Roddis 4375**

Educational research
Arkansas: Rockefeller 58
California: Haynes 211
Connecticut: **General 527**
Delaware: **Lalor 617**
Illinois: **Spencer 1160**
Maryland: Wilson 1464
Mississippi: Hardin 1937
New York: **Exxon 2426, Ford 2444**
Ohio: Jennings 3264
Texas: Clark 3906, **R G K 4061,** Texas 4100

Elementary education
Arizona: Marshall 40
California: Braun 102, Cowell 136, Johnson 239
Connecticut: **Educational 516**
Delaware: Ederic 607
Georgia: Callaway 810, Sewell 872
Illinois: Chicago 968
Indiana: Moore 1245
Kentucky: Honey 1341
Maryland: Kelly 1424
New Jersey: Schwartz 2182
New York: Beir 2276, **Bingham's 2286, Gordon 2489, Initial 2573**
Ohio: Cleveland 3186, Gund 3244, Jennings 3264, Jergens 3265
Oklahoma: Goddard 3432
Oregon: **Brown 3477**
Pennsylvania: Benedum 3524, Crels 3552, Frick 3577, Pitcairn-Crabbe 3691, SmithKline 3726, Stott 3741
South Carolina: Springs 3821
Texas: Cameron 3901, Fikes 3952, Scott 4075
Virginia: Ohrstrom 4188
Wisconsin: Fort 4319, Stackner 4381

Energy
California: Orleton 304
Florida: **Link 742**
Illinois: **Amoco 928**
Massachusetts: Hyams 1561, **Kendall 1569, Levinson 1574**
New Jersey: Dodge 2116
New York: **Glickenhaus 2477,** Hahn 2525
Virginia: **Jones 4178**

Engineering
California: **Atlantic 78, Keck 243,** Mayr 278, Powell 327
Connecticut: **Amax 491, General 527**
Illinois: **Amoco 928,** Inland 1048
New York: **ASARCO 2246, Dreyfus 2411, Gibbs 2468, International 2574, Schlumberger 2919, Wunsch 3061**
Ohio: **Republic 3341, TRW 3392**
Pennsylvania: Leeds 3638, **Westinghouse 3756, Whitaker 3761**
Texas: **Halliburton 3970**
Wisconsin: **Trane 4383**

Environment
Alaska: Alaska 25
Arizona: Wilson 50
California: **Abelard 63, Atlantic 78,** Boswell 98, California 114, Columbia 130, Damien 142, Gerbode 186, Goldman 195, Haas 204, Heller 213, **Hewlett 217,** Island 233, Monterey 289,

Norman 298, Peninsula 318, San Francisco 337, Santa Cruz 342, **Shalan 356,** van Loben Sels 410
Colorado: **Needmor 468,** Pilot 472
Connecticut: **Barnes 497,** Ensworth 521
District of Columbia: **Arca 638**
Florida: Chastain 702, **McIntosh 746**
Georgia: EMSA 829
Hawaii: Atherton 890, Cooke 895, Hawaiian 899
Illinois: Buchanan 956, Fel-Pro 1000, IMC 1046, **Joyce 1052**
Kentucky: Louisville 1346
Maryland: **Baker 1400**
Massachusetts: Bird 1476, **Bright 1487, Cox 1506, Friendship 1531, Kendall 1569, Levinson 1574**
Michigan: Americana 1663, **Harder 1716, Mott 1753**
Minnesota: Bush 1823, Carolyn 1827, **Davis 1833, Donaldson 1836,** First 1843, **General 1848, Northwest 1894,** Red Wing 1908
Missouri: St. Louis 2020
New Hampshire: New Hampshire 2092
New Jersey: Dodge 2116, Fund 2125, New Jersey 2161, Victoria 2197
New York: Abrons 2215, **Bydale 2319, Dorr 2408,** Erpf 2422, **Ford 2444,** Kaplan 2598, **Mellon 2722,** Morgan 2750, Moses 2758, New York 2777, **New-Land 2779, Noyes 2792,** O'Connor 2795, **Penney 2819,** Plant 2833, **Prospect 2842, Rockefeller 2875, Wallace 3020**
North Carolina: **Babcock 3075,** Reynolds 3124
Ohio: **Armington 3157,** Columbus 3189, Dayton 3199, Iddings 3259, Mather 3295, **Rosenthal 3347,** Sears 3360, Toledo 3386
Oklahoma: Dolese 3428
Oregon: Clark 3480
Pennsylvania: Mellon 3663, **Rust 3709,** Stott 3741, **Stroud 3744**
Rhode Island: Rhode 3790
Virginia: Thalhimer 4203, Virginia 4214
Washington: Bullitt 4225, **Laird 4246, Weyerhaeuser 4274**
Wisconsin: **Cudahy 4311, Johnson 4332, Kress 4344**

Europe
District of Columbia: **German 659**
New York: **Kade 2597, Mocquereau 2744**

Family services
California: Haas 202, Johnson 239, **Levi 258**
Colorado: Piton 473
Connecticut: Palmer 562, Stanley 577
District of Columbia: **Kennedy 666**
Georgia: Hodge 847
Hawaii: Hawaiian 899
Illinois: **Chicago 969,** Freund 1010, Woods 1193
Indiana: Indianapolis 1226, Irwin-Sweeney-Miller 1228
Louisiana: German 1362
Massachusetts: Boston 1483, Cabot 1489, Perini 1594, Weber 1651
Michigan: Himmel 1719, **Mott 1752**
Minnesota: Grotto 1853
New Jersey: Borden 2104
New York: Buffalo 2311, **Clark 2346,** Clark 2349, Cohn 2354, **Foundation 2445, Lavanburg 2643, Penney 2819**
Ohio: Gerson 3237
Oregon: **Brown 3477**
Texas: **Zale 4129**
Utah: Eccles 4139

Oppenstein 2003, St. Louis 2020, Swinney 2029, **Webb 2037**
Nebraska: Lincoln 2063
Nevada: ELW 2078
New Hampshire: Bean 2083, New Hampshire 2092
New Jersey: **Allied 2098,** Belasco 2101, Borden 2104, **Johnson 2140, Kirby 2143,** New Jersey 2161, Prudential 2167, **Schumann 2181, Union 2194, Vollmer 2199,** Youths' 2205
New Mexico: **Bellamah 2206**
New York: Achelis 2218, Adams 2219, **American 2235, American-Standard 2237, Archbold 2242,** Badgeley 2256, Barker 2265, Belfer 2277, **Berlinger 2281, Bobst 2293,** Bruner 2309, Burns 2317, Calder 2320, Centennial 2330, **Chatlos 2338, Chernow 2341,** Clark 2347, Clark 2348, **Commonwealth 2362,** Continental 2365, Cornell 2367, **Corning 2368, Culpeper 2374, Dana 2379,** DeCamp 2392, **Delany 2393, Donner 2405, Dun 2415, Ettinger 2423,** Forchheimer 2442, **Frueauff 2455, Fullerton 2459, Gannett 2463, General 2467,** Glens 2476, Goldman 2481, Goulds 2495, **Griffis 2507, Guggenheim 2512,** Hoernle 2556, Hoyt 2565, **Ittleson 2576,** Jones 2591, **Kimmelman 2614, Klingenstein 2618,** Krim 2630, Kriser 2631, Lang 2636, **Lasker 2640,** Lastfogel 2641, Lever 2657, **Liebowitz 2665,** Lindner 2670, **Lubin 2681,** MacKall 2687, **Macy 2689,** Marcus 2699, **McGraw-Hill 2721, Mellon 2722,** Mertz 2729, **Metropolitan 2732,** Morgan 2750, Mossman 2760, New York 2774, **Noyes 2792, Pfizer 2823,** Phelps 2825, **Phillips-Van Heusen 2828, Revlon 2857, Rockefeller 2877,** Rosenstiel 2886, Rubinstein 2896, Schieffelin 2915, Snow 2943, **Summerfield 2970,** Tebil 2980, **Union 2997,** Uris 3003, Watertown 3027, Wegman 3030, Wilson 3048, Wohlgemuth 3054
North Carolina: Broyhill 3081, Foundation 3102, Hanes 3105, Winston-Salem 3137
Ohio: Akron 3145, Ashtabula 3158, Bates 3162, Bicknell 3171, **Bingham 3172,** Cleveland 3185, Cleveland 3186, Columbus 3189, **Dana 3196,** Evans 3209, Frohring 3229, Gross 3243, **Huffy 3255,** Iddings 3259, Markus 3291, **Mead 3299,** Moores 3308, Nordson 3316, **Rosenthal 3347, Ross 3348,** Russell 3350, Sears 3360, Sherman-Standard 3364, Sherwick 3365, **Stouffer 3376,** Stranahan 3377, Toledo 3386, Treuhaft 3389, Treu-Mart 3390, XTEK 3413
Oklahoma: Dolese 3428, Kerr-McGee 3440, Oklahoma 3451, Sarkeys 3462, Warren 3468
Oregon: Barker 3476, **Brown 3477,** Oregon 3500, Tucker 3504
Pennsylvania: **Air 3509, Alco 3510, Alcoa 3511,** Anderson 3517, **CIGNA 3542,** Heinz 3599, Hillman 3603, **Hooper 3607,** Jennings 3620, Justus 3621, Knollbrook 3629, Laurel 3637, **Massey 3649,** Mellon 3661, Mellon 3663, 1957 3676, Patterson 3682, Penn 3683, **Pew 3686, Pew 3687, Pew 3688,** Philadelphia 3689, Pittsburgh 3693, Sheppard 3718, **Stein 3736, United 3750,** Whalley 3759, Williamsport 3764
Rhode Island: Champlin 3772, Rapaporte 3788, Ress 3789
South Carolina: Gregg-Graniteville 3806, Spartanburg 3820
Tennessee: **Ansley 3827,** Benwood 3829, **Cole 3837, Currey 3838,** Goldsmith 3841, Massengill-DeFriece 3851
Texas: Abell-Hanger 3866, Abercrombie 3867, Allied 3871, Anderson 3875, Beal 3882, Brown 3893, Butler 3898, Cameron 3901, Chilton 3904, Collins 3909, Communities 3911, Cullen 3921, Dallas 3923, Dallas 3924, Davis 3927, Dickson 3930, **Dresser-Harbison 3936,** Ellwood 3942, Faith 3946, Hightower 3980, Jonsson 3997, Kay 3998, **Kleberg 4006,** McDermott 4024, Meadows 4029, O'Donnell 4043, Perkins-Prothro 4053, Peyton 4055, Redman 4062, Richardson 4067, Rogers 4067, Rogers 4068, San Antonio 4072, Scurlock 4076, Shanor 4079, Southland 4084, Stemmons 4088, Tandy 4092, Tarrant 4094, Walthall 4111, White 4121, Wiseda 4124

Utah: Green 4140, Masonic 4142, **Thrasher 4145,** Treadwell 4146
Virginia: Central 4163, Easley 4167, English 4168, Reynolds 4194, Sovran 4201, Titmus 4208, Washington 4215
Washington: Archibald 4219, **Burlington 4226,** Cheney 4229, Seattle 4259, Skinner 4262
West Virginia: Carter 4279, Kanawha 4285, McDonough 4286
Wisconsin: **ARMCO 4298,** First 4318, Helfaer 4327, Kearney 4337, **Kimberly-Clark 4338,** Ladish 4348, McBeath 4356, **Smith 4380**

Health services

Alabama: Birmingham 3, Blount 4, Gibson 9, McMillan 12, Russell 18
Arizona: Arizona 28, Circle K 31, Flinn 35
Arkansas: **Reynolds 56**
California: Arakelian 70, Babcock 79, **Baker 81, BankAmerica 84, Berkey 92,** Berry 93, Bireley 96, **Breech 103,** Brenner 104, California 114, **Coleman 129,** de Guigne 145, Distribution 151, Domino 155, Fairfield 163, Fireman's 169, **Fluor 173,** Gilmore 190, Goldman 195, Goldwyn 196, Hedco 212, Helms 214, **Hofmann 223,** Jameson 235, Jefferson 236, Jerome 237, **Jewett 238, Kaiser 242, Kerr 244,** Komes 247, Lear 253, **Leonardt 257,** Levy 259, Livingston 263, Lurie 267, May 276, **Munger 282,** Norris 299, **Pfeiffer 322,** Pickford 325, **R & R 329,** Schermer 345, Schmidt 346, Simon 364, **Soiland 374,** Stuart 386, Stuart 387, Stuart 388, Timken-Sturgis 401, Van Nuys 411, Von der Ahe 412, Webb 418, Wood-Claeyssens 431
Colorado: Hill 452, Johnson 458, Weckbaugh 484
Connecticut: **Abex 488, American 492,** Fisher 523, Howard 539, **Hubbell 540, ITT 542,** J.J.C. 543, **Kayser-Roth 547,** New Haven 559, **Olin 561,** Waterbury 588
Delaware: **Birch 597,** Carpenter 599, Crestlea 605, Ederic 607
District of Columbia: **Bender 639,** McGregor 671, **Post 677,** Ross 680, Stewart 682
Florida: Baker 693, Broad 699, **Brunner 700,** Bush 701, Conn 704, Dade 706, **Davis 709,** duPont 716, **Eckerd 719,** Ford 722, Greene 725, **Hollingsworth 728,** Law 738, Meyer 748, Price 758, **Ware 789**
Georgia: **Citizens 816,** Evans 832, Lee 853, Moore 859, Murphy 860, Patterson-Barclay 863, Porter 867, Rich 870, Sewell 872, Tomlinson 875, Trust 877, **West Point 883**
Illinois: Atwood 934, Barber-Colman 936, Blum 946, Blum 947, Blum-Kovler 948, Borg-Warner 950, Brach 953, Buehler 957, Callner 961, Chicago 970, Christiana 973, Coleman 975, Dreier-Penrith 995, Field 1001, First 1002, **Forest 1007,** Furnas 1012, Haffner 1024, Hales 1025, **Harper 1027,** Heller 1036, IMC 1046, Keating 1056, Lehmann 1068, Lizzadro 1074, **Lumpkin 1075, Maltz 1078, Martin 1083,** Material 1085, McCormick 1090, McDonnell 1091, **Moorman 1101, Nalco 1105,** Northern 1108, Pittway 1120, Polk 1121, **Retirement 1132,** Shaw 1149, Sprague 1161, **Square D 1162,** Staley 1163, **Stanadyne 1165,** UOP 1180, Willett 1191
Indiana: **Central 1205,** Indianapolis 1226, Leighton-Oare 1235, Mead 1242, **Plumsock 1248,** Stokely 1255, Thrush 1257
Iowa: Hall 1269, **Meredith 1278,** Ruan 1281
Kansas: **Hesston 1311, Marley 1319**
Kentucky: Bingham 1335, Brown 1336, Gheens 1340, Robinson 1351
Louisiana: Goldring 1363, Heymann 1366, Poindexter 1378, Shreveport-Bossier 1383
Maine: Unionmutual 1397
Maryland: Clark-Winchcole 1407, Goldseker 1419, Hoffberger 1423, Mullan 1442

Massachusetts: Chase 1498, Dexter 1515, **Donaldson 1517,** Gorin 1537, Hamilburg 1541, Hopedale 1555, Jackson 1563, Johnson 1565, Knistrom 1572, Lindsay 1576, **Little 1578, Persky 1597, Pneumo 1601, Sawyer 1617, Sheraton 1625,** Wellman 1655, Wells 1656
Michigan: Avery 1665, Bishop 1674, DeWaters 1687, Faigle 1695, Fruehauf 1707, Herrick 1718, Himmel 1719, Holden 1720, Imerman 1725, **Kresge 1734,** La-Z-Boy 1736, Skillman 1773, Vollbrecht 1790
Minnesota: Blandin 1821, Bush 1823, Carolyn 1827, **Donaldson 1836,** Edwards 1840, Fingerhut 1841, Greystone 1851, Marbrook 1878, **Medtronic 1884,** Minneapolis 1887, O'Neil 1898, Paper 1901, Saint Paul 1912, Thorpe 1916
Mississippi: Walker 1939
Missouri: Chromalloy 1950, **Emerson 1959,** Fischer-Bauer-Knirps 1962, Gaylord 1966, McGee 1995, Olin 2002, Oppenstein 2003, Pott 2009, Speas 2017, Speas 2018, Springmeier 2019, Stupp 2023
Nebraska: Buckley 2051, Kiewit 2059, Omaha 2066, Rogers 2070
New Hampshire: **Standex 2096**
New Jersey: Berger 2103, **Crum 2114,** Duke 2118, Hoyt 2132, **Johnson 2139, Johnson 2140,** Large 2145, L'Hommedieu 2148, Lindberg 2149, **Merck 2155,** Ohl 2163, **Psychists 2168,** Rosenhaus 2172, Schamach 2176, **Schering-Plough 2178,** Schwartz 2183, **Subaru 2187,** Thomas 2192
New York: **ACF 2217,** Albany's 2226, **Allied 2230,** Altschul 2233, Arkell 2243, Aron 2244, **AT&T 2249, Baird 2259, Barth 2267, Beefeater 2274, Biddle 2284,** Bostwick 2297, **Bristol-Myers 2302,** Bruner 2309, Buffalo 2311, **Capital 2322,** Central 2331, **China 2344,** Clark 2347, Colt 2361, **Dammann 2378, Dreyfus 2413,** Emerson 2421, **Fife 2433,** Frankel 2449, **Frueauff 2455,** Greenebaum 2504, **Guttman 2521,** Hagedorn 2523, Harriman 2527, **Hartford 2528, Hausman 2532, Hearst 2537, Hearst 2538,** Hendrickson 2545, Hirschl 2552, Hochschild 2553, **Hutton 2569,** Irving 2575, Julia 2593, **Karagheusian 2600,** Kramer 2626, Langeloth 2637, Lavanburg-Corner 2644, **Lehman 2652,** LILCO 2666, Lincoln 2667, **Manufacturers 2698,** McDonald 2717, **McDonald 2718, Memton 2724, Merrill 2728,** Metzger-Price 2733, **Mobil 2743, Monell 2746,** Morris 2754, **Mostyn 2762, New World 2773, NL 2783,** Norstar 2789, Paley 2808, **PepsiCo 2820,** Plant 2833, Potts 2836, **Raisler 2845,** Rauch 2848, **Ritter 2869, Rosenthal 2887,** Rubinstein 2896, Schiff 2916, **Sperry 2947,** Sprague 2949, Stanley-Timolat 2952, **Stevens 2962, Straus 2965, Surdna 2972, Tananbaum 2977, Texaco 2981, Thorne 2984,** Titan 2988, **Transway 2991,** Trump 2992, Ungar 2996, United 3000, Utica 3005, van Ameringen 3008, Vogler 3016, **Wallace 3020,** Warner 3022, Wendt 3036
North Carolina: Reynolds 3123, Reynolds 3124
North Dakota: North Dakota 3142
Ohio: Anderson 3153, **Armington 3157,** Benua 3168, Bolton 3173, **Borden 3174,** Cincinnati 3183, Codrington 3188, Dayton 3199, **Eaton 3204,** Eyman 3210, Fifth 3214, Ford 3224, Hankins 3246, **Haskell 3248,** Humphrey 3256, Kramer 3277, Massie 3293, Mather 3294, **Midland-Ross 3302,** Moore 3307, **Parker-Hannifin 3323,** Pollock 3330, **Republic 3341,** Richman 3343, Shafer 3362, Sterkel 3374, Wean 3401, Weiss 3402, Wellman 3403, White 3406, Whitewater 3407, Yassenoff 3414
Oklahoma: Campbell 3421, Collins 3425, Harris 3435, Helmerich 3436, Johnson 3437, **Noble 3449,** Titus 3465
Oregon: Clark 3480, Collins 3482, **Jeld-Wen 3491, John 3493, Louisiana-Pacific 3496,** Tektronix 3502, Wheeler 3507
Pennsylvania: Ames 3515, Arcadia 3520, Benedum 3524, **Brockway 3528, Cassett 3538,** Clapp 3544, **Crary 3550,** Dolfinger-McMahon 3557, **Dravo 3561,** Erie 3565, **Gulf 3589, Harsco 3595,** Hershey 3601, Hunt 3612, Janssen 3617, **Kelley 3625, Lukens 3645,** McCune 3651, Medical 3660, **Merit 3666,** Mine 3669, Myrin 3673, Oxford

Heart disease

Heroism

Higher education

South Carolina: Citizens 3801, Springs 3821, State-Record 3823, Symmes 3825
Tennessee: Benwood 3829, Brinkley 3831, Lowenstein 3846, Tonya 3860, Zimmerman 3865
Texas: Bank 3877, Bass 3878, Beasley 3883, Brown 3893, Brown 3895, Bryce 3896, Cain 3900, Carter 3902, **Central 3903,** Chilton 3904, Clayton 3907, Cockrell 3908, Collins 3910, Communities 3911, Constantin 3912, Cullen 3921, Dallas 3924, Davidson 3926, Dodge 3931, **Dresser 3935, Dresser-Harbison 3936,** Elkins 3941, Fair 3945, Farish 3947, Feldman 3950, Fikes 3952, Fish 3953, Florence 3955, Fondren 3956, **Fuller 3958,** Garvey 3959, George 3960, Griffin 3965, Haas 3966, Haggar 3967, Halsell 3971, Hamman 3972, Harrington 3974, Hawn 3975, Henck 3978, Hillcrest 3981, Hobby 3983, Hoblitzelle 3984, Houston 3988, Johnston 3996, Keith 4000, King 4003, LBJ 4011, Lewis 4015, **Lightner 4016,** Lone 4018, **McGovern 4025,** McKee 4026, McQueen 4028, Mosle 4036, O'Connor 4042, Owen 4047, Perkins 4052, Roberts 4065, Rockwell 4066, Rogers 4067, Rowan 4069, Scurlock 4076, Sharp 4080, Strake 4089, Temple 4098, **Texas 4102,** Turner 4105, Vaughn 4108, West 4119, White 4120, Wolff 4125, Woltman 4126, Wright 4128, **Zale 4129**
Utah: Bamberger 4130, Castle 4133, Dee 4136, Eccles 4138, Eccles 4139, Michael 4143
Vermont: Windham 4151
Virginia: **Armour 4152, Best 4154,** Camp 4159, **Campbell 4161,** Dalis 4165, **Dan 4166,** Gottwald 4171, Landmark 4179, Lane 4180, Morgan 4186, Norfolk 4187, Ohrstrom 4188, Perry 4191, **Reynolds 4193,** Reynolds 4194, **Robertshaw 4197,** Slemp 4200, Taylor 4202, Thomas 4205, Treakle 4209, United 4211, Wheat 4216, Wilfred 4217
Washington: **Anderson 4218,** Fuchs 4235, Glaser 4236, Green 4237, Kilworth 4243, Kreielsheimer 4245, Leuthold 4247, **Matlock 4248,** Murray 4253, Norcliffe 4254, PACCAR 4255, Shemanski 4261, Wells 4272
Wisconsin: Alexander 4291, Apollo 4297, Banta 4300, **Bradley 4303,** Braun 4305, Briggs 4306, Brotz 4307, Bucyrus-Erie 4308, **Cudahy 4311,** Demmer 4313, Evinrude 4315, Falk 4317, Fort 4319, Frankenthal 4320, Gelatt 4323, **Harnischfeger 4325, Heileman 4326,** Jacobus/Heritage 4329, **Johnson 4331,** Kearney 4337, **Kimberly-Clark 4338, Koehring 4339,** Ladish 4347, Ladish 4348, Ladish 4349, **Ladish 4350,** Lindsay 4351, Loock 4352, Marshall 4354, Nekoosa 4360, Oshkosh 4361, **Peck 4364, Rexnord 4373,** Schroeder 4377, Siebert 4379, **Trane 4383, Universal 4384,** Vilter 4385, Wisconsin 4388
Wyoming: Goodstein 4396, Stock 4398, **Weiss 4401**

Hospitals--building funds
Connecticut: **ITT 542**
Illinois: Jewel 1050
Ohio: **Eaton 3204, Hoover 3253**
Texas: Johnson 3995

Hotel administration
New York: **Statler 2955**

Housing
California: Battistone 85
Colorado: Piton 473

Connecticut: Connecticut 507
Delaware: Crestlea 605
Illinois: New Prospect 1107, Scheinfeld 1140
Maryland: **Baker 1400,** Goldseker 1419
Massachusetts: Charlesbank 1495, Parker 1592
Michigan: Kalamazoo 1728
Minnesota: First 1843
New York: **Ford 2444, Lavanburg 2643, Penney 2819,** Taconic 2976, Wilson 3048
Ohio: Cleveland 3186, Gund 3244

Humanities
California: Adolph's 64, Ahmanson 65, Bacon 80, California 114, Haas 204, Lewis 261, Norman 298, San Francisco 337, Simon 365, Stern 383, van Loben Sels 410
Colorado: El Pomar 445, Gates 450
Connecticut: **General 527,** New Haven 559
Delaware: Common 603
Florida: Chastain 702
Illinois: Ingersoll 1047, Woods 1193
Kentucky: Louisville 1346
Maryland: Giant 1418
Massachusetts: Adams 1467, **Braitmayer 1485,** Dexter 1515, Heydt 1549
Michigan: **Kresge 1734**
Minnesota: Bush 1823, Jerome 1868, **Northwest 1894**
New Hampshire: New Hampshire 2092
New Jersey: **Newcombe 2162,** Union 2195
New Mexico: Wurlitzer 2213
New York: **Dewey 2398, Ford 2444, Griffis 2507,** Hoyt 2565, **Littauer 2675, Luce 2682, Mellon 2722, Rockefeller 2877, Whiting 3042**
North Carolina: Blumenthal 3080, Hillsdale 3107
Ohio: Columbus 3189, Dayton 3199, Fleischmann 3220
Oregon: Jackson 3490
Pennsylvania: Barra 3522
South Carolina: Spartanburg 3820
Texas: Farish 3947
Virginia: Washington 4215

Immigration
California: **Koulaieff 249,** Rosenberg 334
Maryland: Meyerhoff 1439
New York: **Biddle 2284, de Hirsch 2387**

Insurance education
Illinois: **State 1166**
Indiana: Lincoln 1239
New York: **New York 2776**

Intercultural relations
Delaware: **Glencoe 609**
District of Columbia: **German 659**
Massachusetts: **Henderson 1547, Levinson 1574**
Minnesota: Carlson 1826
New York: Bache 2254, **Baier 2257,** Bruner 2309, Centennial 2330, **Continental 2366, Corning 2368, Donner 2405, First 2435,** Fribourg 2453, **Sony 2945, Tudor 2994, United 3001, Vetlesen 3011, Zilkha 3067**
Ohio: **Ross 3348**

International affairs
California: **Crown 139,** Gildred 189, **Jewett 238**
Connecticut: **Amax 491, American 492, General 527,** Maguire 554, erox 594
District of Columbia: **Carnegie 644, German 659, Post 677**
Illinois: Borg-Warner 950, **MacArthur 1076**
Iowa: **Stanley 1284**
Massachusetts: **Friendship 1531**
Minnesota: J.N.M. 1869, **Weyerhaeuser 1925**
Missouri: Sycamore 2030
New Hampshire: **Institute 2088**
New Jersey: **South 2185**
New York: **American 2235, Bronfman 2303, Bydale 2319, Carnegie 2325,** Centennial 2330, Cobble 2350, **Corning 2368, First 2435, Ford 2444,** Harriman 2527, **IFF 2571, Mertz-Gilmore 2730, Olin 2799,** Overbrook 2807, **PepsiCo 2820, Pfizer 2823, Phillips-Van Heusen 2828, R and D 2843, Reed 2852, Reynolds 2859, Rockefeller 2875, Rockefeller 2877,** Rohatyn 2878, **Starr 2954,** Straus 2966, **Twentieth 2995, United 3001,** Wallach 3021
Ohio: **Kettering 3271**
Pennsylvania: **Carthage 3537,** Heinz 3599, **Pew 3686**
Wisconsin: **Johnson 4332**

International development
Arizona: Wilson 50
California: **Levi 258, Saturno 344**
District of Columbia: **Public 679**
Indiana: **Lilly 1238**
Kansas: **Schowalter 1327**
New Jersey: **International 2135, Vollmer 2199**
New York: **Burchfield 2314, Carnegie 2325, Chase 2337, Ford 2444,** Hatch 2531, **Homeland 2560, Joselow 2592, Karagheusian 2600, LeBrun 2648, Littauer 2675, Loeb 2676, Rockefeller 2875, Rockefeller 2877, Rubin 2895**
Ohio: **Kettering 3271, Timken 3385**

International law
New York: **Ford 2444**
Ohio: **Dana 3196**

International studies
California: Lakeside 251
Connecticut: **Belgian 498**
District of Columbia: **Delmar 647, German 659**
Iowa: **Stanley 1284**
Michigan: **Earhart 1691, Kellogg 1732**
New York: **Compton 2363, Continental 2366, Ford 2444, Lingnan 2671, Lounsbery 2679, Luce 2682, Mosbacher 2757, Reed 2852**

Israel
California: **Eichenbaum 160, Levy 260, Merry 286, Simon 361, Swig 391**
Florida: Yablick 800
Illinois: **Aronberg 933,** Crown 982, **Crown 983,** Stern 1167
Indiana: **Gershon 1216**
Maryland: Blaustein 1404, Meyerhoff 1439
Massachusetts: **Foster 1530**
Michigan: **Bargman 1667,** Honigman 1721, Shiffman 1771, Stollman 1778

New Jersey: **Frisch 2124,** Lautenberg 2146, **Stern 2186**

New York: American 2236, Bat Hanadiv 2268, **Bezalel 2283,** Davidson-Krueger 2383, Davis 2386, **de Hirsch 2387,** De Jur 2388, **de Rothschild 2390, de Rothschild 2391, Dorot 2407,** Fischbach 2436, **Flemm 2439,** Forchheimer 2442, Fribourg 2453, Greenberg 2501, **Gulton 2517,** Hazen 2536, **Jesselson 2582, Lindemann 2668, Mazer 2709, Mitrani 2742, Model 2745, Phillips-Van Heusen 2828, Raskin 2847, Ridgefield 2865,** Ritter 2868, **Romerovski 2879, Rosenblatt 2885, Schwarz 2921,** Slade 2936, Spingold 2948, Stern 2961, **Tisch 2987,** Titan 2988, Weinstein 3034, **Wolfowski 3055**

Ohio: Melton 3301, Ross 3348

Pennsylvania: **Dozor 3560, Federation 3569, Grass 3585, Hyman 3615**

Tennessee: Lowenstein 3846

Texas: Rudman 4070

Italy

California: **Saturno 344**
Minnesota: **Paulucci 1902**
New Jersey: Perkins 2166

Japan

New York: **United 3001**

Journalism

District of Columbia: **Graham 660,** Kiplinger 667, **Patterson 675**
Florida: **Poynter 757**
Illinois: Chicago 972
Iowa: **Lee 1274**
Minnesota: Minneapolis 1888
New Jersey: **Dow 2117**
New York: Bennett 2279, Gannett 2463, Hearst 2538, Markle 2700, New York 2777, **Reader's 2851**
Ohio: **Knight 3276, Scripps-Howard 3359**

Labor

Illinois: **Retirement 1132**
New York: Atran 2250, United 3001

Language and literature

Connecticut: **Whitney 591**
New Mexico: Bynner 2207
New York: Atran 2250, Axe-Houghton 2252, **Beefeater 2274, Cintas 2345,** Gould 2494, **Jurzykowski 2595, Kade 2597, Littauer 2675, Matz 2708, Merrill 2727, Pforzheimer 2824**

Latin America

California: **Sundean 390**
District of Columbia: Delmar 647
Indiana: **Plumsock 1248**
Michigan: **Kellogg 1732**

Minnesota: **General 1848**
New Jersey: Vollmer 2199
New York: **Guggenheim 2514, Tinker 2986, United 2998**
Wisconsin: **DeRance 4314**

Law and justice

California: **Abelard 63,** Durfee 157
Connecticut: Aetna 489
District of Columbia: Meyer 672
Illinois: **Bauer 937, Chicago 969, MacArthur 1076, MacArthur 1077**
Kansas: Garvey 1308
Massachusetts: Shaw 1622
Missouri: **Deer 1956, Sunnen 2027**
New Jersey: Borden 2104
New York: Blum 2291, Boehm 2295, **Burden 2315,** Burns 2317, **Bydale 2319,** Clark 2346, **Culpeper 2374,** Donovan 2406, FFHS & J 2431, **Field 2432, Ford 2444, Fuchsberg 2457, Gibbs 2468, Guggenheim 2512, Hazen 2535,** Hughes 2566, Hycliff 2570, Jones 2591, **LeBrun 2648, Olin 2799, Ottinger 2806, Revson 2858, Rubin 2895, Stern 2960**
North Carolina: Reynolds 3124
Pennsylvania: **Carthage 3537,** Kline 3628

Leadership development

Colorado: Gates 450
Indiana: **Lilly 1238**
Michigan: **Kellogg 1732, Mott 1752**
Minnesota: **Lutheran 1877**
Missouri: Roblee 2012
New York: **Lakeview 2635, Wallace 3019**
North Carolina: **Richardson 3128**

Legal education

Nebraska: Lane 2061
New York: Blum 2291, Boehm 2295, FFHS & J 2431
Ohio: **Dana 3196**

Leprosy

New York: Butler 2318

Libraries

California: **Atlantic 78**
Connecticut: **Dibner 513**
District of Columbia: **Council 646, National 674**
Florida: **Eagles 717**
Georgia: Callaway 810
Idaho: Whittenberger 916
Illinois: **Lumpkin 1075**
Iowa: Kinney-Lindstrom 1272
Maine: Mulford 1396
Maryland: **Knapp 1427**
Massachusetts: Kelley 1567
New York: **Brooks 2308, China 2344,** Dula 2414, Gebbie 2465, Gramercy 2497, **Heineman 2541,** Macmillan 2688, O'Connor 2795, **Olin 2798, Osceola 2804, Pforzheimer 2824, Vetlesen 3011, Wilson 3047**
North Carolina: Chapin 3088
Ohio: **Markey 3290**

Oregon: Meyer 3498
Pennsylvania: Emporium 3564, Moore 3670, Sordoni 3729
Rhode Island: Champlin 3772, Rhode 3790
Texas: George 3960
Virginia: Slemp 4200

Marine sciences

California: Scripps 349
Connecticut: Woman's 593
District of Columbia: Sapelo 681
Florida: Larsh 737, **Link 742,** Mote 751
Hawaii: Castle 893
Indiana: Clowes 1206
Massachusetts: **Grass 1538**
New Jersey: Atlantic 2100
New York: **Doherty 2404, Donner 2405, Griffis 2507**
South Carolina: Baruch 3798

Medical education

Arizona: Flinn 35, Marshall 40, Mulcahy 42, **Van Schaik 46**
California: Gellert 184, **Kaiser 242,** MacKenzie 270, Mayer 277, **Pfeiffer 322,** Sprague 376
Colorado: **Frost 449**
Connecticut: **Duberg 514, Educational 516, Grubb 530, Stone 579**
Delaware: **Kingsley 614**
Florida: Lowe 743, **Wolfson 798**
Georgia: Trebor 876, **Whitehead 885**
Hawaii: Zimmerman 910
Illinois: **Abbott 918, Bauer 937,** Boothroyd 949, Buehler 957, Lederer 1067, **Pritzker 1124,** Rice 1134, Scholl 1142
Indiana: Froderman 1215, Lilly 1237
Kentucky: Appalachian 1331
Massachusetts: Dana 1508, Fuller 1532, **Harvard 1544,** Humane 1560, Kelley 1567, Rubenstein 1612, Rubin 1613
Michigan: **Gerber 1711,** Holden 1720, Towsley 1783
Minnesota: Bayport 1815, O'Brien 1896, Phillips 1903
Missouri: **Cross 1954,** Loose 1983, **Mallinckrodt 1987,** Olin 2002, Speas 2017, Speas 2018
Nevada: Bing 2077
New Jersey: Berger 2103, Grupe 2128, Hoyt 2132, **Johnson 2140, Merck 2155, Sandoz 2174, Schering-Plough 2178, Warner-Lambert 2200**
New Mexico: **Picker 2211**
New York: Abrams 2214, **Adler 2221,** Albany's 2226, Allyn 2231, Aron 2244, Bache 2254, **Bronfman 2304,** Bruner 2309, **Chait 2333,** Chernow 2342, **China 2344, Collins 2359,** Colt 2361, Cummings 2376, **DeCamp 2392,** Forchheimer 2442, Frankel 2449, Goodstein 2487, Greenwall 2505, Hirschl 2552, Homan 2559, **Hunter 2567, IFF 2571,** Kramer 2627, Lazar 2646, Lee 2649, **Macy 2689, Mazer 2710, Mellon 2722, Merck 2726, Metropolitan 2732,** Metzger-Price 2733, Muehlstein 2764, **New York 2776, New-Land 2779,** Nias 2781, **Potts 2836, Ritter 2867,** Rosenwald 2889, Rudin 2898, **Ruben 2893,** Sinsheimer 2935, Spingold 2948, Stony 2963, **Straus 2965, Surdna 2972, Teagle 2979,** Winston 3052, **Zimmermann 3068, Zlinkoff 3070**
North Carolina: **Burroughs 3085**
Oklahoma: Share 3463
Pennsylvania: **Annenberg 3518,** Goldman 3584, Hazen 3597, **Kynett 3634,** Measey 3659, Smith 3723, Sordoni 3729
Rhode Island: Galkin 3776
South Carolina: Springs 3821, Stevens 3824
Tennessee: Potter 3856

Texas: Brown 3893, Clayton 3907, Cooley 3914, DeBakey 3928, Ellwood 3942, **McGovern 4025,** Rockwell 4066, Walthall 4111, Wolff 4125
Vermont: Lintilhac 4149
Wisconsin: **Johnson's 4336,** Pabst 4363, Schroeder 4377

Medical research

Alabama: Shook 19, Stockham 22
Arizona: Butz 30, Flinn 35, **Kieckhefer 39,** Waddell 48, Webb 49
California: A.I.D. 66, Albertson 67, Baker 82, Bank 83, Baxter 86, Beckman 89, Bireley 96, Bowles 100, Doelger 153, Factor 162, Gildred 189, Haas 204, Hoag 221, Hoover 226, Jameson 235, Jerome 237, **Jewett 238, Keck 243,** Kirchgessner 245, **Kroc 250,** Leavey 254, May 276, Mayer 277, **MCA 279,** Norris 299, Oxnard 306, Pacific 307, Parker 310, **Parvin 312, Pfeiffer 322,** Scripps 349, **Soiland 374,** Stamps 377, Stauffer 379, Stuart 385, Stuart 387, Timken-Sturgis 401, Tyler 405, Wasserman 415, Weiler 419, Welk 422
Colorado: Fishback 448, Lowe 463, Swan 481, **Taylor 482**
Connecticut: **Childs 506, Educational 516, Fairchild 522, Herzog 537,** Patterson 564, **Whitehead 590**
Delaware: **Beneficial 596, Schwartz 630**
District of Columbia: **Freed 656,** Himmelfarb 663, Lehrman 668, Ross 680, Stewart 682
Florida: **Applebaum 690, Davis 709, du Pont 713, Ford 722, Greenburg 724, Hayward 727,** Lowe 743, **Markey 745, Sharonsteel 768, Toor 786**
Georgia: Glancy 840
Hawaii: Zimmerman 910
Idaho: Morrison 914, **Morrison-Knudsen 915**
Illinois: **Abbott 918, Amoco 928, Andersen 930,** Berlin 944, Blum-Kovler 948, Boothroyd 949, **Carlin 963, CBI 966,** Coleman 975, Eisenberg 996, **Falk 998,** Fry 1011, Goldenberg 1018, Grainger 1022, **Hammer 1026, Harper 1027,** Harris 1029, **Hokin 1040,** Johnson 1051, Lederer 1067, McCormick 1089, **McGraw 1094,** Oppenheimer 1111, **Perkins 1115,** Regenstein 1130, **Retirement 1132,** Siragusa 1153, Sprague 1161, Svenson 1176, **Walgreen 1183**
Indiana: Krannert 1233
Kansas: **Francis 1306, Puritan-Bennett 1324**
Kentucky: LaViers 1345, Vogt 1353
Louisiana: Schlieder 1381
Maryland: Straus 1456, Wilson 1464
Massachusetts: Campbell 1492, **Donaldson 1517,** Ellison 1522, **Grass 1538,** Harrington 1542, **Hood 1553,** Humane 1560, King 1571, Levy 1575, McEvoy 1581, Merkert 1583, New England 1586, Rubenstein 1612, **Webster 1652**
Michigan: Avery 1665, Ford 1703, **Ford 1704, General 1710,** Holden 1720, **Pardee 1757,** Prentis 1759, Ratner 1762, **Slaughter 1774,** Towsley 1783, Wilson 1800
Minnesota: **Andersen 1809,** Andersen 1810, Baker 1814, Bayport 1815, Chadwick 1829, Eddy 1839, Greystone 1851, Marbrook 1878, McKnight 1880, O'Brien 1896, Onan 1897, **Paulucci 1902**
Missouri: **Cross 1954,** Love 1985, **Mallinckrodt 1987, Olin 2001,** Reynolds 2011, **Smith 2015,** Speas 2018, **Sunnen 2027,** Whitaker 2039
Nevada: ELW 2078
New Hampshire: **Phillips 2093**
New Jersey: **Armour 2099, Edison 2119,** Geist 2126, **Hoffmann-La Roche 2131,** Hoyt 2132, **Messing 2156, Sandoz 2174,** Schultz 2180, **Warner-Lambert 2200**
New Mexico: **Phillips 2210**
New York: **Adler 2221,** Alexander 2227, Allen 2228, **Allen 2229, AMETEK 2238,** Badgeley 2256, **Biddle 2284,** Bieber 2285, **Blythmour 2292, Bobst 2293,** Bostwick 2297, **Bristol-Myers 2302, Burnham 2316, Chait 2333, Cheatham 2340,**

Chernow 2341, Chernow 2342, **China 2344, Clark 2346,** Cohn 2354, **Culpeper 2374,** Cummings 2375, Cummings 2376, **DeCamp 2392,** Dent 2396, **Dreyfus 2412, Dreyfus 2413, Dyson 2417, Evans 2424, Ferkauf 2430,** Frankel 2449, Frohlich 2454, **Fullerton 2459,** Gebbie 2465, Gifford 2469, **Glenn 2475,** Goldman 2482, Greenwall 2505, Gruber 2509, **Guttman 2521, Hartford 2528, Hearst 2537, Hearst 2538, Helmsley 2543,** Hirschl 2552, Hopkins 2561, **J.M. 2584,** Julia 2593, **Jurzykowski 2595,** Klein 2617, **Klingenstein 2618, Lasker 2640,** Lauder 2642, **Levitt 2660, Link 2672, Lounsbery 2679, Manning 2697,** McGraw 2720, **Merck 2726, Meyer 2734, Miller 2739, Monell 2746,** Osborn 2803, **Peierls 2818,** Price 2839, Ramapo 2846, Rauch 2848, **Revson 2858,** Ritter 2868, Rose 2882, **Ross 2891,** Rubinstein 2896, Schwartz 2920, Schweckendieck 2922, Sharp 2926, **Simon 2934, Sinsheimer 2935,** Sprague 2949, **Starr 2954,** Stein 2958, Stony 2963, **Straus 2965, Surdna 2972,** Swanson 2974, **Vernon 3010, Vetlesen 3011, Wallace 3020, Wellington 3035, Whitney 3043,** Wilson 3048, Winston 3051, **Wolfson 3056, Wood 3057, Zlinkoff 3070**
North Carolina: **Burroughs 3085,** Foundation 3102, Lance 3111
Ohio: Berry 3170, Cleveland 3186, Kachelmacher 3268, **Kettering 3272,** Kettering 3273, Prentiss 3332, Reinberger 3338, **Rosenthal 3347,** South 3371, Wolfe 3410
Oklahoma: **Broadhurst 3420, Mabee 3443,** McGee 3446, Merrick 3448, **Noble 3449,** Rapp 3459, Warren 3469
Oregon: Wheeler 3507
Pennsylvania: Ames 3515, **Annenberg 3518, Cassett 3538,** Fels 3571, **Hall 3590,** Hazen 3597, Hooker 3606, Kline 3628, Levee 3640, Mellon 3663, Smith 3725, **Strawbridge 3743**
Rhode Island: Roddy 3791
South Carolina: **Merck 3810**
Tennessee: **Ansley 3827, Cole 3837,** Massey 3852, Potter 3856
Texas: Anderson 3875, Brown 3893, Brown 3895, Clayton 3907, Cooley 3914, Crump 3920, Dallas 3925, DeBakey 3928, Duncan 3938, Farish 3947, Feldman 3950, Fikes 3952, Fish 3953, Haas 3966, Halsell 3971, Hamman 3972, Hawn 3975, Hoblitzelle 3984, Hofheinz 3985, **HOR 3987, Interferon 3993,** Johnson 3995, Johnston 3996, Kay 3998, Kayser 3999, **Kleberg 4006,** Lard 4010, **McGovern 4025,** McKee 4026, McMillan 4027, McQueen 4028, **R G K 4061,** Rogers 4068, Rudman 4070, Smith 4082, Texas 4099, Vale-Asche 4107, Waggoner 4110, Walthall 4111, West 4118, Wolff 4125
Utah: Eccles 4138, **Thrasher 4145,** Treadwell 4146
Virginia: Lane 4180, **Mars 4182, McCrea 4184**
Washington: Murdock 4252, Norcliffe 4254, Poncin 4256
Wisconsin: Braun 4305, Ladish 4347, Ladish 4348, **Roddis 4375, Smith 4380**

Medical sciences

California: Ahmanson 65, Connell 131, **Kaiser 242,** Mead 284
Connecticut: **Perkin 565, Rosenthal 569, Stone 579, UPS 584**
Florida: **Davis 707**
Massachusetts: Harrington 1543
Minnesota: **Northwest 1894**
New Jersey: **Engelhard 2121,** Hyde 2134, **International 2135, Johnson 2139**
New York: **Bay 2270, Commonwealth 2362,** Cummings 2376, Gebbie 2465, **Heineman 2541, Jurzykowski 2595, Kade 2597, Lasdon 2639, Macy 2689, Metropolitan 2732, Milbank 2737,** Nichols 2782, **Pforzheimer 2824**

North Carolina: **BarclaysAmerican 3076, Burroughs 3085**
Oregon: Chiles 3479
Pennsylvania: **Annenberg 3518,** Mellon 3662, Mellon 3663, **United 3750**
Texas: Fikes 3952, Owsley 4048
Utah: **Thrasher 4145**
Wisconsin: McBeath 4356

Mental health

Arkansas: Ross 59
California: Martin 274, Sanguinetti 339, See 352, Seuss 355, **Simon 363,** Simon 367, Zellerbach 433
Colorado: Lowe 463
District of Columbia: **Kennedy 666,** Meyer 672
Hawaii: Frear 898
Illinois: Keating 1056, **MacArthur 1077, Seeley 1146,** Stern 1167, **Stone 1170**
Kentucky: Gheens 1340
Maryland: Giant 1418
Massachusetts: Dexter 1515, **Doehla 1516,** Harrington 1543, Hyams 1561
Michigan: Dalton 1681, DeWaters 1687
Minnesota: Circle 1831, **Davis 1833,** McKnight 1880
Missouri: Loose 1983, Olin 2002, Roblee 2012, Swinney 2029
New York: **Frueauff 2455,** Goldman 2481, **Grant 2499, Gulton 2517, Ittleson 2576, Monell 2746, New-Land 2779,** Oppenheimer 2802, Parshelsky 2813, **Rosenthal 2887, van Ameringen 3006,** van Ameringen 3007, van Ameringen 3008
North Dakota: North Dakota 3142
Ohio: Columbus 3189, Goerlich 3238, Mather 3295
Oregon: Friendly-Rosenthal 3487
Pennsylvania: **Falk 3568,** Medical 3660, Scranton 3716, Staunton 3735, Steinman 3738
South Carolina: **Merck 3810**
Texas: Butt 3899, Wright 4128
Washington: Medina 4250
Wisconsin: Evjue 4316, Stackner 4381

Mexico

Arizona: **Amerind 27**

Middle East

California: **Philibosian 323**
District of Columbia: **Foundation 654**
New York: **Dodge 2402, Karagheusian 2600, Kevorkian 2611, Mostazafan 2761**

Military personnel

California: **Hollywood 224**
Virginia: **Olmsted 4189**

Minorities

California: **Abelard 63,** Gildred 189, **Levi 258,** Norman 298, Packard 308, Peninsula 318, San Diego 336, Shoong 359
Colorado: Sachs 476
Connecticut: Aetna 489
Georgia: Hodge 847

Illinois: **Archer-Daniels-Midland 932, Brunswick 955,** Fel-Pro 1000, **FMC 1005,** Harris 1028, **Keebler 1057,** Scheinfeld 1140
Indiana: Cummins 1210, **Lilly 1238,** Lincoln 1239
Massachusetts: Dexter 1515, **Webster 1652**
Michigan: **Ford 1701, Manoogian 1741, Mardigian 1742,** Strosacker 1780
Minnesota: **Andreas 1811,** Grotto 1853
Missouri: **Butler 1946, Deer 1956**
New Jersey: **Dow 2117,** Elizabeth 2120, Fund 2125, **Johnson 2140, Newcombe 2162,** Prudential 2167
New York: **American 2235, Avon 2251, Bristol-Myers 2302, Capital 2322, Commonwealth 2362, Field 2432, Ford 2444, General 2467, Grace 2496, Hearst 2537, Hearst 2538,** Krim 2630, Morgan 2751, **Muskiwinni 2766, New World 2773,** New York 2775, New York 2777, **Normandie 2788, Peierls 2818, Revlon 2857, Revson 2858, Shiah 2929, Tinker 2986, Vinmont 3015**
Ohio: Gund 3244, McFawn 3297, Nordson 3316
Rhode Island: **Textron 3792**
Texas: Dodge 3931

Museums

Arizona: VNB 47, Waddell 48
California: Ahmanson 65, **Atlantic 78,** Braun 102, **Christensen 124,** Holt 225, Incentive 229, **Jewett 238,** Mead 284, Security 351, Sefton 353, Simon 365, **Simon 366,** Sprague 376, Steel 381, Wells 423
Colorado: Hughes 454, **JFM 457**
Connecticut: **Albers 490,** American 493, Gimbel 528
Delaware: **Glencoe 609,** Marmot 621
District of Columbia: Cafritz 643
Florida: Thoresen 785
Georgia: Anncox 801, Hill 846
Hawaii: Watumull 907
Illinois: **Allen-Heath 920,** Chicago 972, Deering 988, Grainger 1022, **Hammer 1026,** Heller 1036, Mayer 1086, Morton 1103, **Nalco 1105, Skidmore 1154, Wilkie 1190**
Indiana: Koch 1232, Noyes 1246
Kansas: **Cessna 1297,** Muchnic 1321
Maryland: Blaustein 1405, Middendorf 1440
Massachusetts: Blake 1478, Boston 1483, Daniels 1509, **Johnson 1566,** McEvoy 1581, Prouty 1603, Sagamore 1615, Weld 1653
Michigan: **Ford 1699,** Ford 1700, Ford 1703, Masco 1743
Minnesota: Griggs 1852, **Pillsbury 1905**
Missouri: Kemper 1975, **Olin 2001, Swift 2028**
Montana: **Sample 2047**
Nevada: **Bing 2076**
New Jersey: Brady 2105, Cape 2108
New York: Adler 2222, Barker 2265, **Bay 2270, Bezalel 2283,** Bieber 2285, Blum 2291, Clark 2347, Cowles 2369, **Daniel 2380,** Dobson 2401, **Evans 2424, Forbes 2440,** Forchheimer 2442, **Gibbs 2468,** Goldsmith 2483, Hastings 2530, Hayden 2534, Hazen 2536, High 2550, Hillman 2551, Hochschild 2553, **Kress 2629,** Lauder 2642, L.A.W. 2645, Lehman 2653, **Loeb 2676, Martinson 2701, Mellon 2722, Monell 2746,** Moore 2748, **Mosbacher 2757, Nathanson-Abrams 2768,** New York 2777, **Noguchi 2786,** Pearlman 2816, **Prospect 2842,** Rose 2882, Ross 2890, **Rothschild 2892,** Rudin 2899, Scheuer 2914, Schiff 2916, **Schimmel 2917,** Sharp 2926, Simon 2933, Sprague 2949, Stern 2961, Tebil 2980, Thorne 2983, **Tiffany 2985, Tisch 2987, Transway 2991, Vetlesen 3011,** Warner 3023, Wilson 3046, **Wrightson-Ramsing 3060**
Ohio: American 3151, Codrington 3188, Fleischmann 3220, Greene 3240, Murch 3310, Perkins 3325
Pennsylvania: Dietrich 3555, Dietrich 3556, **Hall 3590,** Smith 3723
Texas: Brown 3893, Hobby 3983, McDermott 4024, **Scaler 4073,** Tandy 4092, Wiseda 4124
Utah: Eccles 4139

Virginia: **Best 4154,** Cabell 4157, Cole 4164, Ohrstrom 4188, Reynolds 4194, Universal 4212
Washington: Bloedel 4222, **Forest 4234,** Merrill 4251
Wisconsin: Krause 4343

Music

California: **Ledler 256,** Packard 308, **Whitelight 424**
Colorado: **McCoy 464**
Connecticut: Day 509, New Haven 559, Preston 566
District of Columbia: Appleby 635, Cafritz 643, Dimick 648
Florida: Beattie 695, **Sharonsteel 768**
Georgia: Schwob 871
Hawaii: Frear 898
Illinois: Mayer 1086, McCormick 1090, Regenstein 1130, Wurlitzer 1194
Indiana: Clowes 1206
Iowa: **Fisher 1266**
Kansas: Brown 1296, Fourth 1305, **Hesston 1311**
Louisiana: Helis 1365, Holmes 1368
Maryland: Blaustein 1405, First 1415, **Hechinger 1421,** Hecht-Levi 1422, Kelly 1424, Maryland 1436, Rosenberg 1450
Massachusetts: **Filene 1529,** Harvard 1545, Kenwood 1570, Prouty 1603, Sagamore 1615, Tamarack 1642
Michigan: **DeVos 1686,** Earl-Beth 1692, Eddy 1693, Ford 1700, Kalamazoo 1728, Shapero 1769, Tuck 1785
Minnesota: Baker 1814, Carlson 1826, **Davis 1833,** Jerome 1868, McKnight 1881, **O'Shaughnessy 1900,** Tozer 1917, Weyerhaeuser 1924
Missouri: Commerce 1951, Gaylord 1965, May 1990, St. Louis 2021, Whitaker 2039
Nevada: **Sells 2081**
New Hampshire: Smyth 2095
New Jersey: **Bergen 2102,** Borden 2104, Hoyt 2132, Visceglia-Summit 2198, Youths' 2205
New York: Baird 2258, **Bayne 2271,** Berlin 2280, **Bezalel 2283,** Botwinick-Wolfensohn 2298, Campe 2321, Cary 2327, **Cintas 2345,** Crane 2371, **Evans 2424,** Gilman 2470, Goodman 2485, Gramercy 2497, **Guggenheim 2514,** Heckscher 2540, **Heineman 2541,** Hochschild 2553, Holmes 2557, Marcus 2699, **Mathers 2704, Mocquereau 2744,** Musica 2765, **Newhouse 2778, Noble 2784, Osceola 2804, Paul 2814, Reimann 2854,** Ritter 2868, **Ryan 2901,** Scheuer 2914, Schwartz 2920, **Sullivan 2968,** Vidda 3012, Wilson 3049, Winfield 3050
North Carolina: Biddle 3078
Ohio: Codrington 3188, Corbett 3191, Humphrey 3257, **Ireland 3262,** Kulas 3278, Murphy 3311, **Republic 3341,** Treuhaft 3389, Van Wert 3396, Youngstown 3416
Pennsylvania: Beneficia 3525, Campbell 3533, Greenfield 3586, Hitchcock 3605, Hulme 3610, Kardon 3623, **Presser 3698,** Reliance 3703, Rittenhouse 3704, Rockwell 3707, Smith 3723, **Superior-Pacific 3745,** Wyomissing 3767
South Carolina: Symmes 3825
Texas: Cullen 3921, Farish 3947, Fikes 3952, Fleming 3954, **Fuller 3958,** Huthsteiner 3992, Pangburn 4049, **Starling 4086**
Washington: Brechemin 4224, Leuthold 4247, Spokane 4264

Native Americans

California: **Hahn 206**
Connecticut: **Educational 516**
Massachusetts: Knistrom 1572
Minnesota: Grotto 1853
New York: **Ford 2444**
Oklahoma: Phillips 3455
Wisconsin: **DeRance 4314**

Nursing

California: Coburn 128, Lytel 269
District of Columbia: Johnston 665
Florida: Stevens 774
Georgia: Trebor 876, **Whitehead 885**
Hawaii: Zimmerman 910
Illinois: **Abbott 918, Allstate 922, Kemper 1060,** McFarland 1092
Indiana: Indianapolis 1226
Michigan: **Gerber 1711,** Tuck 1785
New Jersey: Grupe 2128, **Johnson 2140**
New York: **China 2344, Fuld 2458,** Lincoln 2667, O'Connor 2795, Rudin 2898, Switzer 2975, **Teagle 2979**
Ohio: **Ireland 3262, Mellen 3300**
Texas: Parry 4051
Wisconsin: Fromm 4321

Nutrition

Florida: **Eagles 717**
Kansas: Garvey 1307
Michigan: **Mott 1753**
Minnesota: **Pillsbury 1905**
Nebraska: Swanson 2073
New Jersey: **Lipton 2150**
New York: **Donner 2405, General 2467, Glenn 2475, Standard 2951, Statler 2955, United 2998, Wallace 3020**
Oregon: Chiles 3479
Pennsylvania: **Heinz 3598**
Utah: **Thrasher 4145**

Ophthalmology

California: Doheny 154, Gellert 184
Connecticut: **Ziegler 595**
Illinois: **Heed 1034**
Michigan: Royal 1763
New York: **Adler 2221,** Gaisman 2462, Lippman 2674
Ohio: Wildermuth 3408
Pennsylvania: Campbell 3533
Washington: Bishop 4221

Parapsychology

Missouri: **McDonnell 1994**
New York: **Parapsychology 2811**

Peace

California: Columbia 130, Greenville 200, **Parvin 312**
Connecticut: **Topsfield 582**
District of Columbia: **Foundation 654**
Hawaii: Straub 904
Iowa: **Stanley 1284**
Kansas: Schowalter 1327
Massachusetts: **CarEth 1494, Levinson 1574**
Michigan: **Mott 1753**
Minnesota: **General 1848**
New Jersey: Rosenhaus 2172
New York: **Carnegie 2325, Compton 2363, Field 2432, Glickenhaus 2477, Mertz-Gilmore 2730, New World 2773, Penney 2819, Reynolds 2859, Rubin 2895, Scherman 2913,** Wallach 3021
Ohio: **Armington 3157**
Virginia: **Jones 4178**
Washington: Bullitt 4225

Performing arts

Alabama: Blount 4
Arizona: Arizona 29, Morris 41
California: Adolph's 64, **Atlantic 78**, Bridges 105, Davies 143, Deutsch 147, First 170, Gellert 184, **Hewlett 217, Jewett 238, MCA 279**, Mead 284, **Nosutch 300, Skaggs 369**, Taper 394, Wasserman 415, Wattis 417, **Whitelight 424**
Colorado: **JFM 457**, Sterne-Elder 480, Weckbaugh 484
Connecticut: Gimbel 528, **UMC 583**
District of Columbia: **Alvord 634**, Federal 651, **Freed 656**
Florida: Meyer 748
Georgia: Lubo 856
Illinois: **Ameritech 926**, IMC 1046, Levy 1071, **Page 1112**
Indiana: Krannert 1233
Iowa: **Bohen 1261, Fisher 1266**
Louisiana: Magale 1374
Maryland: Pearlstone 1445, Rosenberg 1450
Massachusetts: **Filene 1529**, Hamilburg 1541
Minnesota: Bush 1823, Jerome 1868, Marbrook 1878, **Miller 1886, O'Shaughnessy 1900, Pillsbury 1905**, Thorpe 1916, Wood-Rill 1929
Missouri: Commerce 1951, Flarsheim 1963, Garvey 1964, Hall 1968, Kemper 1975, LaRue 1978, Parrott 2005
Nevada: **Sells 2081**
New Jersey: Dodge 2116, Rosenhaus 2172
New York: Anderson 2239, Baird 2261, Barker 2265, Bieber 2285, Blum 2291, **CBS 2329**, Centennial 2330, Chadwick 2332, Fribourg 2453, **Golden 2479**, Goldman 2481, Goldsmith 2483, **Grace 2496**, Gramercy 2497, Green 2500, **HEM 2544**, Hopkins 2561, **JDR 2578, Johnson 2587, Katzenberger 2603**, L and L 2633, **Lasdon 2639**, L.A.W. 2645, Lemberg 2655, **Loeb 2676**, Macmillan 2688, **Martinson 2701, Mathers 2704**, Matthews 2706, **Mazer 2710, Mellon 2722, Merrill 2727, Merrill 2728, Monell 2746**, Morgan 2750, New York 2777, Newman 2780, **Osceola 2804, Prospect 2842, Reimann 2854, Richmond 2864**, Ritter 2868, Rohatyn 2878, Rose 2882, **Rosen 2883**, Rosenstiel 2886, **Rosenthal 2888**, Rudin 2899, Samuels 2905, **Scherman 2913**, Schiff 2916, Sharp 2926, Sheafer 2928, **Shiah 2929, Shubert 2930, Simon 2934, Sony 2945**, Tuch 2993, Western 3039, **Young 3062, Zilkha 3067**
North Carolina: Foundation 3102
Ohio: Andrews 3154, **Federated 3211**, Kulas 3278, **Tucker 3393**
Oklahoma: Cuesta 3426
Oregon: Autzen 3475, Carpenter 3478, Higgins 3488
Pennsylvania: Calhoun 3531, Craig 3549, Dietrich 3555, Erie 3565, Falk 3567, **Harsco 3595**, Mine 3669, Robinson 3705, Smith 3723
Rhode Island: Rhode 3790
Tennessee: Benwood 3829
Texas: Allied 3871, Brown 3893, Cooper 3916, Cullen 3921, Farish 3947, Favrot 3949, Fikes 3952, Fish 3953, Humphreys 3990, Moody 4035, Pangburn 4049, Richardson 4064, Wright 4128
Utah: Eccles 4138, Eccles 4139
Virginia: Cole 4164, Thalhimer 4203
Washington: Bloedel 4222, Brechemin 4224, **Forest 4234**, Merrill 4251
Wisconsin: **Bradley 4303**, Bucyrus-Erie 4308, **Johnson 4331, Trane 4383**

Pharmacy

California: Pfeiffer 322
Florida: **Eckerd 719**
Illinois: **Abbott 918, Walgreen 1183**
Indiana: Lilly 1237
New Jersey: **Warner-Lambert 2200**
North Carolina: **Burroughs 3085**

Philippines

Arizona: **Van Schaik 46**
New York: China 2344, Guggenheim 2514

Physical sciences

Arizona: **Research 44**
California: Hertz 216, Smith 372
Connecticut: **Amax 491, General 527, Perkin 565**
Minnesota: **Northwest 1894**
New York: Biddle 2284, Gloeckner 2478, Kade 2597, Minerals 2741, Mobil 2743, Monell 2746, Vetlesen 3011
Ohio: **Republic 3341**
Oregon: Tektronix 3502
Pennsylvania: **Westinghouse 3756, Whitaker 3761**

Poland

New York: **Jurzykowski 2595**, Rosenstiel 2886

Political science

Florida: **Poynter 757**
Michigan: **Earhart 1691**
New York: **Bydale 2319, Littauer 2675, Monell 2746, PBP 2815, Tinker 2986**
Pennsylvania: **Carthage 3537**

Population control

California: Bing 95, Cowell 136, **Jewett 238**, Orleton 304, Steele 382, Walker 414, Webb 418
Colorado: **Needmor 468**
Connecticut: **Educational 516**
District of Columbia: **Public 679**
Florida: **Swensrud 779**
Maryland: **Baker 1400**
Massachusetts: Cabot 1489, Campbell 1492
Michigan: Kennedy 1733, Upjohn 1786
Minnesota: **General 1848, Weyerhaeuser 1925**
Missouri: Kemper 1974, **Sunnen 2027**
Nevada: **Bing 2076**
New Jersey: Dodge 2116, **Huber 2133, Kirby 2143**
New York: Baird 2258, **Burnham 2316, Caritas 2323**, Clark 2349, **Compton 2363**, Doubleday 2409, **Ford 2444, Mott 2763, Noble 2784, Noyes 2792, Peierls 2818, Pettus-Crowe 2822**, Plant 2833, **Scherman 2913**, Sharp 2926, Wilson 3049
Ohio: **Brush 3178**, Iddings 3259, Pollock 3330
Oklahoma: Cuesta 3426
Pennsylvania: Calhoun 3531, Laurel 3637, **Robinson 3706**, Stott 3741
Texas: Clayton 3907, Fikes 3952, Halff 3969, McAshan 4022
Virginia: **Best 4154**

Population studies

California: **Hewlett 217**, Packard 308
Colorado: **Needmor 468**
Minnesota: **General 1848**
New York: **Mellon 2722, Rockefeller 2877**
Texas: Fikes 3952

Psychiatry

Illinois: **Harris 1030**
New York: **Ittleson 2576**

Psychology

Illinois: **Harris 1030**
New York: **Bingham's 2286, Cattell 2328, Grant 2499, Guggenheim 2513, IFF 2571**

Public administration

California: **Getty 188**
New York: Clark 2349
Pennsylvania: **Pew 3686**

Public policy

California: **Atlantic 78**, Damien 142, **Hewlett 217**, Lear 253, **Ostrow 305, R & R 329, Shalan 356**, Wasserman 415, Weingart 421
Colorado: Anschutz 435, Coors 441, Gates 450
Connecticut: **Amax 491, American 492, Dexter 512, General 527, Xerox 594**
District of Columbia: **Arca 638**, Federal 651, **Villers 684**, Washington 685
Florida: **Swensrud 779**
Illinois: **Ameritech 926**, Blum-Kovler 948, **MacArthur 1076, MacArthur 1077, Marquette 1082**, McGaw 1093, **Retirement 1132**, Scheinfeld 1140, Woods 1193
Indiana: **Lilly 1238**
Iowa: Maytag 1277
Louisiana: First 1359, Keller 1371
Maryland: Town 1459
Massachusetts: **Cabot 1488, CarEth 1494, Cook 1502, Filene 1529, Kendall 1569, Levinson 1574**
Michigan: **Kresge 1734, Mott 1753**
Minnesota: **Andreas 1811**, Apache 1812
Missouri: **Emerson 1959**, Sunmark 2026
Nevada: **ELW 2078**
New Jersey: Campbell 2107, Fund 2125, **Johnson 2139**
New York: Blum 2291, **Bydale 2319**, Centennial 2330, **Davis 2385, Field 2432, Ford 2444, Foundation 2445**, Fund 2460, **Golden 2480**, Harriman 2527, Krim 2630, **Luce 2682, Manufacturers 2698, Milliken 2740, Monell 2746, Mott 2763, New World 2773, Olin 2799, PBP 2815**, Reed 2852, Revson 2858, **Rockefeller 2876**, Rohatyn 2878, **Sloan 2938, Stern 2960, United 3001, Wilson 3047**
North Carolina: **Babcock 3075**, Broyhill 3081, **Morris 3120**, Reynolds 3124, **Richardson 3126, Richardson 3128**
Ohio: American 3150, **Armington 3157, Borden 3174**, Charities 3181, **Federated 3211**, Gerson 3237, Lennon 3282, **Procter 3333, Saint Gerard 3351**
Pennsylvania: **Carthage 3537**, Craig 3549, **Hooper 3607**, Hunt 3612, **McKenna 3656, Pew 3686, Rockwell 3708**, Scaife 3711, **Walker 3752**
South Carolina: **Roe 3814**
Texas: Anderson 3875, Brown 3893, Kay 3998, Scurlock 4076
Virginia: **Hopeman 4175**
Wisconsin: **Bradley 4303, Brady 4304, Cudahy 4311**

Race relations

Illinois: Field 1001, Scheinfeld 1140

Tennessee: Benwood 3829, **Cole 3837, Woods-Greer 3864**

Texas: **Akin 3869, Allbritton 3870,** Behmann 3884, **Bell 3885,** Bivins 3887, Blaffer 3888, Chilton 3904, George 3960, Haas 3966, Harding 3973, Leppard 4013, **LeTourneau 4014,** McMillan 4027, O'Connor 4042, Parker 4050, Perkins 4052, Rockwell 4066, West 4119, White 4120

Virginia: Morgan 4186, **Three 4206**

Washington: Archibald 4219, Green 4237

West Virginia: Carter 4279, Fenton 4282, Vecellio 4290

Wisconsin: Johnson 4335

Religion, Jewish

California: **Amado 68,** Baker 82, Borun 97, Brenner 104, **Brody 106,** Buchalter 108, **Coleman 129,** Deutsch 147, Domino 155, **Eichenbaum 160,** Factor 162, Familian 164, Fleishhacker 171, **Friedman 175,** G.A.G. 177, Grancell 198, Koret 248, **Levy 260,** Lurie 267, **Menlo 285, Merry 286, Meyer 287, Mitchell 288, Newman 297,** Pattiz 315, **Sassoon 343,** Schermer 345, Schreiber 347, **Simon 361,** Simon 364, **Sinaiko 368, Swig 391, Swig 392,** Wasserman 415, **Weinberg 420,** Yorkin 432

Colorado: Levy 462, Rabb 474

Connecticut: Auerbach 494, Bennett 499, **Dibner 513,** Eder 515, EIS 517, Fisher 523, Gimbel 528, Joseloff 545, **Kayser-Roth 547,** Koopman 549, List 551, **Mazer 556,** Savin 571, Schiro 572, **Stratfield 580**

Delaware: Cohen 601, Cohen 602, **Kutz 615**

District of Columbia: **Bender 639,** Cohen-Solomon 645, **Dweck 650,** Gelman 658, Gudelsky 661, Himmelfarb 663, Lehrman 668, **Wouk 688**

Florida: **Applebaum 690,** Arison 691, Blank 697, Broad 699, **Greenburg 724,** Greene 725, **Kohl 735,** Leidesdorf 739, Lowe 743, **Shapiro 767, Sharonsteel 768,** Soref 769, **Sudakoff 778,** Taylor 783, **Toor 786,** Wolfson 797, **Wolfson 798**

Georgia: Chatham 815, **Davis 823,** Schwob 871

Hawaii: **Holy 901**

Illinois: **Allied 921, Baum 938,** Berlin 944, Blum 946, Blum 947, Blum-Kovler 948, Callner 961, **Carlin 963,** Crown 982, **Crown 983, D and R 985,** Frank 1009, **Galter 1013,** Gerber 1017, **Goldman 1019,** Harris 1029, **Harris 1030, Harris 1031, Heller 1035, Hokin 1040,** I and G 1044, **JSR 1054,** Kaplan 1055, Keating 1056, **Lasky 1065,** Lederer 1067, Levy 1071, **Maltz 1078,** Manilow 1079, Perlman 1116, Polk 1121, **Pritzker 1124, Relations 1131, Sang 1137, Shapiro 1147, Shapiro 1148,** Sherman 1150, Stern 1167, **Stone 1169, Susman 1175**

Indiana: Bronstein 1203

Iowa: Aliber 1259, Blank 1260, Glazer 1268, Younkers 1290

Kansas: Sosland 1329

Louisiana: Cahn 1357, Goldring 1363, Physicians 1377, **Woldenberg 1387**

Maryland: Blaustein 1404, Blaustein 1405, Chertkof 1406, Freeman 1417, **Gudelsky 1420, Hechinger 1421,** Hecht-Levi 1422, Hoffberger 1423, Krieger 1429, Mendelson 1437, Meyerhoff 1439, Pearlstone 1445, Polinger 1448, Rosenberg 1450, Shapiro 1452, **Shapiro 1453,** Straus 1456, **Tauber 1457,** Thalheimer 1458, **Wasserman 1462,** Weinberg 1463

Massachusetts: Dana 1508, Feldberg 1527, **Foster 1530,** Goldberg 1536, Gorin 1537, **Grossman 1540,** Hiatt 1550, Housen 1558, **Levinson 1574,** Lipsky 1577, **Persky 1597,** Ribakoff 1606, Rubin 1613, **Sawyer 1617,** Shapiro 1620, Sherman 1626, **Smith 1628,** Stone 1637, **Stoneman 1638, Zayre 1661**

Michigan: **Bargman 1667,** DeRoy 1682, DeRoy 1683, **Ford 1701, Garb 1708, Herman 1717,** Himmel 1719, Honigman 1721, Imerman 1725,

Michigan 1747, Prentis 1759, Shapero 1769, Shiffman 1771, Stollman 1778

Minnesota: Fingerhut 1841, **Fiterman 1844,** Heilicher 1859, Lieberman-Okinow 1875, **Melamed 1885, Miller 1886,** Paper 1901, Phillips 1903

Missouri: Edison 1957, Edison 1958, Feld 1961, **Lopata 1984,** Lowenstein 1986, May 1990, Sachs 2013, Shoenberg 2014, **Tension 2031**

Nebraska: Blumkin 2050, Frohm 2056, Livingston 2064

New Jersey: **Armour 2099,** Berger 2103, **Frisch 2124,** Geist 2126, **Komar 2144,** Lautenberg 2146, Levin 2147, **Mamiye 2151, Messing 2156, Reeves 2170,** Rosenhaus 2172, **Roth 2173,** Schamach 2176, Schwartz 2183, **Simon 2184, Stern 2186,** Taub 2189, **Taub 2190, Terner 2191, Wilf 2203**

New York: Abrams 2214, Abrons 2215, **Ades 2220,** Adler 2222, Alexander 2227, Allen 2228, Altschul 2233, Appleman 2241, Associated 2247, **Bache 2253,** Bachmann 2255, **Barrington 2266,** Beir 2276, Belfer 2277, **Bendheim 2278,** Berlin 2280, **Berlinger 2281, Bezalel 2283,** Bieber 2285, Bleibtreu 2288, Bloomingdale 2290, Botwinick-Wolfensohn 2298, Brand 2300, **Bronfman 2304, Burnham 2316,** Burns 2317, Campe 2321, Chanin 2334, **Chernow 2341,** Chernow 2342, Cohen 2351, **Cohen 2352,** Cohen 2353, Cohn 2355, Coleman 2356, **Coles 2358,** Colt 2361, **Daniel 2380,** Davidson-Krueger 2383, **Davis 2384,** Davis 2386, De Jur 2388, **de Rothschild 2391, Doft 2403, Dorot 2407,** Elsmere 2420, **Falk 2428,** FFHS & J 2431, **Fife 2433, Fink 2434,** Fischbach 2436, **Fischel 2437, Flemm 2439, Forbes 2441,** Forchheimer 2442, Frankel 2449, Fribourg 2453, **Fuchsberg 2456, Fuchsberg 2457,** Furst 2461, Ginsberg 2472, Goldman 2482, Goldsmith 2483, Goodman 2485, Goodstein 2487, Gordon 2490, Gottesman 2491, Green 2500, Greenberg 2501, Greene 2502, **Greene 2503,** Greenebaum 2504, Grossinger 2508, Gruber 2509, **Grumbacher 2510, Gruss 2511,** Gurwin 2518, **Hasenfeld 2529, Hausman 2532,** Hazen 2536, **Heineman 2541,** Heller 2542, **Hess 2546, Hidary 2549,** Hochstein 2555, Holtzmann 2558, **Jesselson 2582, Joselow 2592,** Jurodin 2594, **Kaplun 2599,** Karpas 2601, **Kassin 2602,** Kaufman 2604, **Kempner 2608, Kimmelman 2614,** Klau 2615, Klein 2617, Klosk 2619, Kramer 2627, Krim 2630, Kriser 2631, **Lasdon 2639,** Lastfogel 2641, **Lebensfeld 2647,** LeBrun 2648, **Leff 2650,** Lefrak 2651, Lemberg 2655, Levinson 2658, Leviton 2659, **Levy 2661, Levy 2662,** Lewis 2663, **Liebowitz 2665, Lindemann 2668,** Linder 2669, Lippman 2674, **Loeb 2676, Loews 2677,** Lopin 2678, **Lubin 2681, Mailman 2694, Manealoff 2696,** Matz 2707, **Matz 2708, Mazer 2709, Mazer 2710, McCrory 2716,** Melohn 2723, **Mitrani 2742, Model 2745, Monterey 2747,** Morgenstern 2752, Morris 2753, Morton 2755, Moses 2758, **Mosler 2759,** Muehlstein 2764, Nelco 2770, Neu 2771, **Newhouse 2778,** Newman 2780, Nias 2781, N've Shalom 2793, O.C.F. 2794, **Olive 2800,** Oppenheimer 2802, Overbrook 2807, Parshelsky 2813, **Phillips-Van Heusen 2828,** Price 2839, **Propp 2841, Raisler 2844, Raisler 2845, Raskin 2847, Reicher 2853, Resnick 2856, Revson 2858, Ridgefield 2865, Ritter 2867,** Ritter 2868, Robert 2870, **Romerovski 2879,** Rose 2883, **Rosenberg 2884, Rosenblatt 2885, Rosenthal 2888,** Rosenwald 2889, **Ruben 2893, Rubenstein 2894, Russ 2900,** Salomon 2904, Sarne 2907, Scheuer 2914, **Schwarz 2921, Silbermann 2932, Simon 2934,** Slade 2936, **Slifka 2937,** Spingold 2948, **Starr 2953,** Stein 2958, Steinbach 2959, Stern 2961, Straus 2966, Sun 2971, **Tananbaum 2977, Tisch 2987,** Titan 2988, Trump 2992, Tuch 2993, **Tudor 2994,** Ungar 2996, United 2999, **Unterberg 3002,** Ushkow 3004, **Waldbaum 3017,** Wallach 3021, Wasserman 3024, Weiler 3031, **Weinberg 3032,** Weinstein 3034, Werblow 3038, **Wien 3044,** Winston 3052, Wohlgemuth 3054, **Wolfowski 3055, Wolfson 3056, Wunsch 3061,** Yulman 3064, Zacharia 3065, Zarkin 3066, **Zilkha 3067**

North Dakota: Stern 3143

Ohio: Beerman 3166, Berkman 3169, El-An 3205, Forest 3225, Gerson 3237, Jarson 3263, Kangesser 3269, Mandel 3286, Mandel 3287, **Mandel 3288,** Markus 3291, **Melton 3301,** Philips 3328, **Premier 3331, Rosenthal 3347, Ross 3348, Sapirstein 3352, SCOA 3357,** Tamarkin 3379, Treuhaft 3389, Treu-Mart 3390, **Warner 3398,** Wuliger 3412

Oklahoma: Gussman 3433, Sanditen 3461, Taubman 3464

Oregon: **Fohs 3484,** Friendly-Rosenthal 3487

Pennsylvania: **Annenberg 3519,** Caplan 3534, **Cassett 3538, Charlestein 3541, Conston 3546,** Cook 3547, **Dozor 3560,** Falk 3567, **Federation 3569,** Feinstein 3570, **Foster 3575,** Glosser 3583, Goldman 3584, **Grass 3585, Grumbacher 3587,** Hassel 3596, **Hyman 3615, Javitch 3618,** Kardon 3623, Kline 3627, Korman 3632, Mandell 3647, **Millstein 3668,** Rittenhouse 3704, Robinson 3705, S 'n S 3710, **Stein 3736,** Steinsapir 3739, Strauss 3742, **Tabas 3746**

Rhode Island: **Alperin 3770,** Galkin 3776, **Hassenfeld 3779,** Koffler 3782, Rapaporte 3788, Ress 3789

Tennessee: Belz 3828, Goldsmith 3841, Lowenstein 3846, Werthan 3862, Zimmerman 3865

Texas: Feldman 3950, **Gordon 3963, Klein 4007,** Rogers 4067, Rudman 4070, Weiner 4114, Wolff 4125, **Zale 4129**

Virginia: **Armour 4152,** Thalhimer 4203, Thalhimer 4204

Washington: Shemanski 4261

West Virginia: Jacobson 4284

Wisconsin: Frankenthal 4320, G.P. 4322, **Kohl 4340,** Kohl 4341, **Peck 4364,** Phillips 4367, **Rochlin 4374**

Wyoming: Goodstein 4396

Religion, Protestant

Alabama: Flack 8, Mitchell 16, Smith 20

Arizona: **Tell 45**

Arkansas: Jones 52, Lyon 53, Murphy 54, Riggs 57

California: **Artevel 74, Atkinson 76,** Berry 93, **Caddock 113,** Charis 123, Crummey 141, Gilmore 190, Greenville 200, Helms 214, Jameson 235, Lloyd 264, Marshburn 273, **Munger 292,** Murdy 293, Orleton 304, **Peery 317,** Stamps 377, **Sundean 390**

Connecticut: **Bissell 500,** Fry 526, Main 555, **Society 576,** Wheeler 589

Delaware: **Milliken 623**

District of Columbia: Appleby 635, **Delmar 647, Weir 686**

Florida: Childress 703, **Crane 705, Duda 714,** Larsh 737, Lynn 744, Morgan 749, **Morris 750,** Rainforth 759, Rinker 760, Sample 764, **Staley 772, Stuart 777,** Williams 793, Wiseheart 796, **Wray 799**

Georgia: Baker 804, Campbell 813, Cousins 821, **Day 824,** Dobbs 826, Gholston 838, Hill 846, Lee 853, Moore 859, Pattillo 864, Pitts 866, Ragan 868, **Rainbow 869,** Sewell 872, **West 882, Wilson 886**

Hawaii: Atherton 890, **Bohnett 891,** Wilcox 908

Illinois: Hales 1025, **Harper 1027,** Hoover 1041, **Layman 1066,** McCormick 1088, McGaw 1093, **TYF 1177, Tyndale 1178,** Werner 1187

Indiana: Kilbourne 1231, Smock 1253, Thrush 1257

Iowa: **E & M 1264,** Vermeer 1287

Kansas: DeVore 1301, Garvey 1308, Hansen 1309, Nelson 1322, Rouback 1326, **Schowalter 1327,** Wiedemann 1330

Kentucky: Cooke 1339, Houchens 1343, LaViers 1345

Louisiana: Favrot 1358

Maryland: Baldwin 1402, Clark-Winchcole 1407, **M. E. 1432,** Middendorf 1440, Mulford 1441

Massachusetts: Wellman 1655

Michigan: Chamberlin 1678, Cook 1680, Fink 1697, Ford 1703, Herrick 1718, McIntyre 1745, Pagel 1756, Ransom 1761, **Slaughter 1774,** Whiteley 1795

Delaware: Crestlea 605, Crystal 606, Ederic 607, **Gerard 608, Israel 611,** Laffey-McHugh 616, Marmot 621, **Milliken 623**

District of Columbia: **Alvord 634,** Fowler 655, Johnston 665, McGregor 671, **Post 677**

Florida: Childress 703, Conn 704, **Crane 705,** duPont **716, Echlin 718,** Wilder 792, Wiseheart 796, **Wray 799**

Georgia: Callaway 810, Community 819, Franklin 835, **Fuqua 836,** Gilbert 839, Glancy 840, Lane 851, Ottley 861, **Ottley 862,** Patterson-Barclay 863, Sewell 872, Tomlinson 875, **Tull 878, West Point 883**

Hawaii: Anthony 889, Castle 894, Ho 900, Teruya 905

Idaho: Whittenberger 916

Illinois: **Andersen 930,** Barber-Colman 936, Burns 959, Chapin 967, Chicago 968, Christiana 973, Crown 982, Fry 1011, Galvin 1015, Haffner 1024, Harris 1029, **Heller 1035,** House 1043, I and G 1044, Joyce 1053, Lederer 1067, **Lumpkin 1075, Marquette 1082,** McCormick 1088, **Prince 1122,** Scholl 1142, Seabury 1143, **Solo 1158,** Sulzer 1173, Willett 1191

Indiana: Griffith 1217, Kuehn 1234, Moore 1245, Noyes 1246, **Plumsock 1248**

Iowa: **Bohen 1261**

Kansas: Sosland 1329

Kentucky: Brown 1336, Honey 1341, **Margaret 1347**

Louisiana: Favrot 1358, First 1359, Morgan 1375, RosaMary 1380, **Woldenberg 1387,** Zigler 1390

Maine: Alfond 1391, Monks 1395, Unionmutual 1397, Warren 1398

Maryland: Abell 1399, Baldwin 1402, Blaustein 1405, Egenton 1412, France 1416, Kelly 1424, Knott 1428, Krieger 1429, Middendorf 1440, Mulford 1441, Mullan 1442, Price 1449, Sheridan 1454

Massachusetts: Birmingham 1477, Cox 1505, **Demoulas 1513, Donaldson 1517,** GenRad 1534, Harrington 1542, Higgins 1551, Hornblower 1556, **Johnson 1566,** Kenwood 1570, Levy 1575, Lipsky 1577, Pappas 1590, Peabody 1593, Pierce 1599, Prouty 1603, Rogers 1610, Rubin 1613, Schrafft 1618, Shipley 1627, Stearns 1630, Sudbury 1641, **Webster 1652,** Weld 1653, Wellman 1655

Michigan: Bauervic 1670, Chamberlin 1678, Earl-Beth 1692, Fink 1697, Ford 1700, Herrick 1718, Honigman 1721, Hurst 1724, Kaufman 1730, Lyon 1739, **Manoogian 1741,** Morley 1751, **Mott 1752,** Ransom 1761, Sage 1764, **Seymour 1768,** Shelden 1770, Tracy 1784, VanAndel 1788, **Walker 1791,** Wenger 1792, Wilson 1799

Mississippi: Walker 1939

Missouri: **Danforth 1955,** Fischer-Bauer-Knirps 1962, Garvey 1964, Hall 1968, Jordan 1973, Kemper 1974, Kemper 1975, Laclede 1977, Lowenstein 1986, Mathews 1989, **McDonnell 1994,** Parrott 2005, **Swift 2028,** Tilles 2032, **Webb 2037, Woods 2041**

Nebraska: Hitchcock 2057

Nevada: **Bing 2076**

New Jersey: **Armour 2099,** Bunbury 2106, Cape 2108, **Caspersen 2111, Crum 2114,** Dodge 2116, **Engelhard 2121,** Frelinghuysen 2123, Hoyt 2132, Ix 2136, Jockey 2138, Ohl 2163, **Penick 2165, Psychists 2168, Quaker 2169,** Schwartz 2182, **Stern 2186, Terner 2191,** Union 2195, Youths' 2205

New York: Adler 2222, Altman 2232, Bachmann 2255, **Baier 2257,** Baird 2258, Baker 2262, Banbury 2263, Bedford 2272, Beinecke 2275, Beir 2276, **Bingham's 2286,** Bliss 2289, **Booth 2296,** Botwinick-Wolfensohn 2298, **Brooks 2308,** Charlpeg 2336, **Coleman 2357, Corning 2368,** Cowles 2369, Craigmyle 2370, **Dodge 2402,** Dula

2414, Emerson 2421, **Ettinger 2423, Forbes 2440, Ford 2443,** Foundation 2447, Fribourg 2453, **Gelb 2466,** Gifford 2469, **Gordon 2489,** Gordon 2490, Green 2500, Greene 2502, Greenebaum 2504, **Gutman 2520,** Hagedorn 2523, Harriman 2527, **Hettinger 2547,** Hochschild 2553, **Initial 2573, International 2574, Jephson 2581, Johnson 2589,** Julia 2593, **Katzenberger 2603, Keck 2607, Kenan 2609, Kerry 2610, Kidder 2612, Klingenstein 2618, Knapp 2620, Knox 2621,** Knox 2622, Kraft 2625, **Kresevich 2628,** La Sala 2634, **Lakeview 2635, Lebensfeld 2647, Leonhardt 2656,** Lewis 2663, **Link 2672, Lounsbery 2679,** Macdonald 2685, MacDonald 2686, Magowan 2691, Mandeville 2695, **Mathis-Pfohl 2705,** McCann 2712, Metzger-Price 2733, **Michel 2735,** Millbrook 2738, **Miller 2739, Milliken 2740, Monterey 2747,** Morgan 2750, Mossman 2760, Napier 2767, Neu 2771, New York 2777, **Newhouse 2778,** Nichols 2782, **Norwood 2791,** O'Neil 2801, Osborn 2803, Overbrook 2807, Palisano 2809, Park 2812, Parshelsky 2813, **Perkins 2821, Phillips 2827,** Pope 2835, **Prospect 2842,** Rauch 2848, Sasco 2908, Shatford 2927, **Shiah 2929,** Snow 2942, Sprague 2949, Stein 2958, Steinbach 2959, Stern 2961, **Stevens 2962,** Stott 2964, **Thorne 2984, Tisch 2987,** Uris 3003, **Vanneck-Bailey 3009,** Vidor 3013, **Walker 3018, Wallace 3019,** Warren 3024, Wasserman 3026, **Weinberg 3032,** Wilson 3046, Winston 3052, **Woodland 3058**

North Carolina: Akzona 3073, Biddle 3078, **Blue Bell 3079,** Bryan 3082, Cannon 3086, Chatham 3089, Dickson 3093, Dover 3094, Finch 3099, Finch 3100, Hanes 3105, Jenkins-Tapp 3108, Lineberger 3112, **Myers-Ti-Caro 3121,** Stonecutter 3133, **Thomasville 3135**

North Dakota: Myra 3141

Ohio: Albers 3146, **Allyn 3147,** American 3151, Anderson 3152, Andrews 3154, **Austin 3160,** Bates 3162, Bicknell 3171, Bolton 3173, Britton 3176, **Browning 3177,** Casto 3180, Cleveland 3185, Cleveland 3186, Emery 3206, Ernsthausen 3208, Firman 3217, Flowers 3222, France 3227, Frohman 3228, Gallagher 3231, Gerson 3237, Gund 3244, **Haskell 3248, Hoover 3253,** Humphrey 3256, Ingalls 3260, Ingram 3261, **Ireland 3262,** Jennings 3264, Jergens 3265, Jochum-Moll 3266, **Kettering 3272,** Laub 3281, Mather 3294, Murch 3310, Murphy 3311, Nordson 3316, Perkins 3325, Polk 3329, Reeves 3337, **Saint Gerard 3351,** Semple 3361, South 3371, **Thompson 3381,** Toledo 3387, **Warner 3398,** Wean 3401, Weiss 3402, Wolfe 3410

Oklahoma: Collins 3424, Cuesta 3426, Goddard 3432, **MAPCO 3444,** Rapp 3459, Wegener 3470

Oregon: Autzen 3475, Barker 3476, **Brown 3477,** Carpenter 3478, Chiles 3479, Clark 3480, Collins 3482, **Frank 3486,** Jackson 3490, John 3494, Wheeler 3507

Pennsylvania: **Adams 3508,** Benedum 3524, Craig 3549, Dietrich 3556, Dolfinger-McMahon 3557, Donnelly 3558, Ellis 3563, Finley 3573, Frick 3577, Hillman 3604, Hitchcock 3605, **Hooper 3607,** Hunt 3611, Hunt 3613, **Independence 3616, Kelley 3625,** Kunkel 3633, Laurel 3637, Levy 3641, **Love 3644,** Lukens 3645, Mack 3646, McShain 3658, **Redmond 3700, Robinson 3706,** Rockwell 3707, Sheppard 3718, Smith 3723, SmithKline 3726, Snyder 3728, Steinman 3738, Steinsapir 3739, Stott 3741, **Strawbridge 3743, Stroud 3744, Superior-Pacific 3745,** Waters 3754

Rhode Island: **Alperin 3770, Genesis 3777,** Haffenreffer 3778, Kimball 3781, **Little 3783**

South Carolina: Arkwright 3796, **Merck 3810, Riegel 3813,** State-Record 3823, Stevens 3824

Tennessee: **Ansley 3827,** Benwood 3829, Brinkley 3831, Brown 3832, Bullard 3834, Church 3836, Evans 3840, Hamico 3842, Hutcheson 3843, **Hyde 3844, Lyndhurst 3847,** Massey 3852, Meade 3853, Schadt 3857, Washington 3861

Texas: Beal 3882, Blaffer 3888, Brown 3893, Butler 3898, Cameron 3901, Crow 3919, Cullen 3921, Dallas 3924, Fair 3945, Farish 3947, Fikes 3952,

Fondren 3956, **Fuller 3958,** Haggar 3967, Hobby 3983, Hoblitzelle 3984, King 4003, LBJ 4011, McDermott 4024, O'Connor 4042, Parker 4050, Sams 4071, Scurlock 4076, **Shell 4081,** Strake 4089, **Texas 4102,** Trull 4104, Turner 4105, Vale-Asche 4107, Waggoner 4110, Woltman 4126

Utah: Bamberger 4130, Castle 4133, Harris 4141, Michael 4143

Virginia: Cabell 4157, Camp 4159, Camp 4160, **Campbell 4161, Campbell 4162,** English 4169, Flagler 4170, **Mars 4182,** Massey 4183, Morgan 4186, Ohrstrom 4188, Olsson 4190, Perry 4191, Reynolds 4194, Scott 4198, Seay 4199, Slemp 4200, Wheat 4216, Wilfred 4217

Washington: Archibald 4219, Bloedel 4222, Fuchs 4235, Green 4237, Johnston 4240, Leuthold 4247, Merrill 4251, Murray 4253, Norcliffe 4254, Snyder 4263, **Wharton 4275**

West Virginia: Harless 4283, **Prichard 4289**

Wisconsin: Alexander 4293, Braun 4305, CUNA 4312, First 4318, Fort 4319, Janesville 4330, Kohler 4342, Krause 4343, Ladish 4348, Loock 4352, Neenah 4359, Polybill 4369, **Rahr 4371,** Siebert 4379, Stackner 4381, Vilter 4385

Wyoming: **Weiss 4401**

Social sciences

California: Haynes 211
Connecticut: **Rosenthal 569**
Kansas: **Koch 1317**
New York: Boehm 2295, **Littauer 2675, Luce 2682, Northeastern 2790,** Sage 2902, Tinker 2986
Wisconsin: **Brady 4304**

Social services

Alabama: Bedsole 2, Birmingham 3, Chandler 5, Daniel 7, McWane 13, Mitchell 16, Webb 24
Arizona: First 34, **Kieckhefer 39,** Webb 49
Arkansas: **Inglewood 51,** Reynolds 56, Sturgis 60
California: **Abelard 63,** Ahmanson 65, Arrillaga 73, **Atkinson 76, Atkinson 77, Atlantic 78, Baker 81, BankAmerica 84, Bechtel 87, Bekins 90,** Bothin 99, Braun 102, California 114, **CFS 122,** Charis 123, Clorox 127, Connell 131, Cowell 136, **Crown 139, Crummer 140,** Crummey 141, Damien 142, DeMille 146, Deutsch 147, Domino 155, Drum 156, Familian 165, Faude 166, Fireman's 169, **Fluor 173,** Gellert 183, Gellert 184, **Gemco 185,** Gilmore 190, Goldwyn 196, Haas 204, Hahn 205, Hancock 209, Heller 213, **Hilton 220, Hofmann 223, Hollywood 224,** Humboldt 228, Irwin 231, **Jewett 238,** Johnson 239, **Kerr 244,** Koret 248, Lear 253, Levy 259, Lurie 267, Lytel 269, Marini 272, McAlister 280, Monterey 289, Muller 291, Murdy 293, Norris 299, **Nosutch 300,** Odell 303, **Ostrow 305, Parsons 311,** Peninsula 318, Pfaffinger 321, **R & R 329,** San Diego 336, Sanguinetti 339, Santa Cruz 342, **Sassoon 343,** Schermer 345, Schmidt 346, Seaver 350, Setzer 354, **Signal 360,** Simon 364, Simon 367, **Skaggs 369,** Smith 371, Steel 381, Stuart 386, Stulsaft 389, Trust 402, Turn 404, Van Nuys 411, Walker 414, Weingart 421, Welk 422, Wells 423, **Whitelight 424**
Colorado: Anschutz 435, Coors 441, Denver 442, First 447, **Frost 449,** Hill 452, Johnson 458, McHugh 465, O'Fallon 470, Piton 473, Schramm 478, Swan 481, **Taylor 482**
Connecticut: **Amax 491, American 492,** Bodenwein 501, **Duberg 514,** Fry 526, Hartford 532, Hartford 533, Hartford 534, **Hubbell 540,** Long 552, Maguire 554, **Sachem 570,** Waterbury 588, erox 594
Delaware: Chichester 600, Crystal 606, **Kent 612, Kingsley 614, Kutz 615,** Laffey-McHugh 616,

Longwood 618, Lovett 619, Marmot 621, **Presto 626,** Welfare 632
District of Columbia: April 637, Cafritz 643, Dimick 648, **Freed 656, GEICO 657,** Loughran 669, Meyer 672, **Post 677, Public 679,** Washington 685, **Weir 686, Westport 687**
Florida: Applebaum 690, **Aurora 692, Brunner 700,** Bush 701, Dade 706, **Davis 709,** Dunspaugh-Dalton 715, **duPont 716,** Falk 720, Howell 729, Jenkins 732, Leidesdorf 739, **Morris 750,** Rosenberg 763, Selby 766, Soref 769, Stickelber 775, **Sudakoff 778,** Swisher 780, Sylvester 781, Thoresen 785, **Walter 788,** Williams 793, **Winn-Dixie 794,** Winter 795
Georgia: Atlanta 802, Bradley-Turner 807, EMSA 829, **Harland 844,** Herndon 845, Jinks 850, **Ottley 862,** Patterson-Barclay 863, Porter 867, Rich 870, **Tull 878,** Wehadkee 881
Hawaii: Brewer 892, Cooke 895, First 897
Illinois: Aigner 919, Alton 924, **Amoco 928,** Aurora 935, **Bell 943,** Bersted 945, Blum 946, Blum 947, Blum-Kovler 948, Borg-Warner 950, Buchanan 956, Chapin 967, Chicago 968, **Chicago 969,** Chicago 970, Chicago 971, Coleman 975, **Container 976, DeKalb 989,** Dillon 992, Eisenberg 996, Fel-Pro 1000, Field 1001, First 1002, Fisher 1003, Fry 1011, Goldenberg 1018, **Goldman 1019, Griswold 1023,** Haffner 1024, Hales 1025, **Harper 1027,** Harris 1029, **Hermann 1037,** Hoover 1041, IMC 1046, Ingersoll 1047, Jewel 1050, Johnson 1051, **JSR 1054,** Kendall 1061, Lehmann 1068, Leslie 1069, **Mason 1084,** Mazza 1087, McCormick 1089, McCormick 1090, McGaw 1093, **McGraw-Edison 1095,** Moorman 1102, New Prospect 1107, Northern 1108, **Northwest 1109,** Pittway 1120, Polk 1121, **Prince 1122, Relations 1131,** Rosenthal 1136, **Santa Fe 1138,** Sara 1139, Scheinfeld 1140, Schmitt 1141, Scholl 1142, Smail 1155, **Sundstrand 1174, TYF 1177, Walgreen 1183,** Ward 1184, Ward 1185, Warner 1186
Indiana: Ball 1199, Beardsley 1201, Bowsher-Booher 1202, **Central 1205,** Clowes 1206, English-Bonter-Mitchell 1212, Foellinger 1213, Heritage 1222, Honeywell 1224, Indianapolis 1226, Krannert 1233, **Lilly 1238,** Martin 1240, **Reilly 1250**
Iowa: Hall 1269, Hawley 1270, Maytag 1277, Pella 1280, Wahlert 1288, Witte 1289
Kansas: Coleman 1298, DeVore 1301, First 1304, Kansas 1315, Rice 1325, Sosland 1329, Wiedemann 1330
Kentucky: Appalachian 1331, Bingham 1335, Citizens 1338, Louisville 1346, Mills 1348, Norton 1349
Louisiana: German 1362, **Louisiana 1373,** Magale 1374, Physicians 1377, Woolf 1388
Maine: Gannett 1393
Maryland: Clark-Winchcole 1407, France 1416, Giant 1418, **Hechinger 1421,** Hoffberger 1423, Kelly 1424, Leidy 1430, Marriott 1433, Mendelson 1437, Mulford 1441, Price 1449, Stewart 1455, Straus 1456, Wilson 1464
Massachusetts: Bank 1473, Blanchard 1480, Boston 1483, Boynton 1484, **Cabot 1488,** Charlesbank 1495, Chase 1497, Cove 1503, Davis 1511, Dexter 1515, **Friendship 1531,** Fuller 1533, GenRad 1534, Hyams 1561, Hyams 1562, Jackson 1563, **Kendall 1568,** Massachusetts 1580, Merkert 1583, Old 1589, Parker 1592, Polaroid 1602, Ratshesky 1605, Riley 1608, Rowland 1611, Rubin 1613, Shawmut 1623, Steiger 1632, Stevens 1634, Sudbury 1641, Thompson 1643, **Williams 1658**
Michigan: Avery 1665, Baldwin 1666, Barstow 1668, Besser 1673, Bishop 1674, DeRoy 1683, **DeVos 1686,** DeWaters 1687, Dow 1690, Faigle 1695, Ford 1703, Fremont 1705, **General 1710, Gerber 1711,** Grand 1715, Herrick 1718, Hunter 1723, Hurst 1724, **Kresge 1734,** McGregor 1744, Sage 1764, Seidman 1767, **Slaughter 1774,** Steelcase 1775, Stroh 1779, Towsley 1783, Tuck 1785, Upjohn 1786, Vollbrecht 1790, Wickes 1798, Wilson 1800, **Wolverine 1803**
Minnesota: Andersen 1808, Andersen 1810, Bigelow 1820, Blandin 1821, Bremer 1822, Bush 1823, Butler 1824, Cargill 1825, Carolyn 1827, Circle

1831, **Davis 1833, Dayton 1834, DeLuxe 1835,** Edwards 1840, Fingerhut 1841, First 1842, First 1843, Gelco 1846, **General 1847,** Groves 1854, Hartzell 1857, Hotchkiss 1863, Hulings 1865, Inter-Regional 1867, Jostens 1870, Marbrook 1878, Mardag 1879, McKnight 1880, **Northwest 1894,** Norwest 1895, O'Brien 1896, Ordean 1899, **O'Shaughnessy 1900,** Tennant 1915, Thorpe 1916, Wilder 1928
Mississippi: Community 1932, Deposit 1934, Feild 1935
Missouri: Boatmen's 1942, Boone 1943, Enright 1960, Feld 1961, Gaylord 1965, Gaylord 1966, Hall 1968, H.B.S. 1969, Interco 1972, Jordan 1973, Loose 1983, Mathews 1989, May 1990, **May 1991, Monsanto 1999,** Olin 2002, Pillsbury 2007, Pitzman 2008, Pott 2009, Reynolds 2011, Speas 2018, St. Louis 2020, Stupp 2024, Sunmark 2026, **Webb 2037,** Wolff 2040, Yellow 2042
Nebraska: Criss 2055, Hitchcock 2057, **InterNorth 2058,** Kiewit 2059
New Hampshire: **Hubbard 2086,** Jameson 2089, Kingsbury 2090, New Hampshire 2092, **Phillips 2093**
New Jersey: **Allied 2098, Armour 2099,** Belasco 2101, Borden 2104, Campbell 2107, Duke 2118, Elizabeth 2120, Grassmann 2127, Hyde 2134, **Kennedy 2141,** Large 2145, **Mamiye 2151,** New Jersey 2161, Rosenhaus 2172, Schenck 2177, **Subaru 2187,** Taub 2189, **Union 2194,** Union 2195, **Vollmer 2199,** Willits 2204
New Mexico: **Phillips 2210**
New York: Abrons 2215, Achelis 2218, Adams 2219, Altschul 2233, Anderson 2240, Appleman 2241, **Archbold 2242,** Arkell 2243, **Avon 2251, Bache 2253,** Bache 2254, Badgeley 2256, Baird 2258, **Barth 2267,** Bat Hanadiv 2268, **Beefeater 2274,** Beinecke 2275, Beir 2276, Bieber 2285, Bodman 2294, **Booth 2296,** Bowne 2299, Bruner 2309, **Bydale 2319,** Campe 2321, **Caritas 2323,** Coleman 2356, Corning 2368, Crary 2373, De Jur 2388, **de Rothschild 2391, Dreyfus 2413,** Dula 2414, Dutchess 2416, Ebsary 2419, Elsmere 2420, Emerson 2421, **Field 2432, Forbes 2441,** Forchheimer 2442, Foundation 2447, Frank 2448, Frohlich 2454, Gilman 2470, **Glickenhaus 2477,** Goldman 2481, **Grace 2496, Guggenheim 2512, Gulf 2516,** Guttman 2521, Harriman 2527, Hatch 2531, Hayden 2534, **Hazen 2535,** Heckscher 2540, Hirschl 2552, Hochschild 2553, Hoernle 2556, Hoyt 2565, **Johnson 2589, Johnson 2590,** Kraft 2625, Krim 2630, La Sala 2634, Lastfogel 2641, Lauder 2642, Lefrak 2651, **Leir 2654, Leonhardt 2656, Levitt 2660,** Lindner 2670, Lopin 2678, **Mad 2690,** Maguire 2692, Mandeville 2695, Marcus 2699, **Mathers 2704, Mathis-Pfohl 2705,** McCann 2712, McCarthy 2713, McGonagle 2719, McGraw 2720, **Menschel 2725,** Mertz 2729, Metzger-Price 2733, **Mitrani 2742, Monell 2746, Monterey 2747,** Morgan 2750, Moses 2758, Mossman 2760, **Mostyn 2762,** Napier 2767, **New World 2773,** New York 2774, **New York 2776,** New York 2777, **New-Land 2779,** Nichols 2782, **Peierls 2818, Penney 2819, Phillips-Van Heusen 2828, Prospect 2842,** Rauch 2848, **Richmond 2864, Ridgefield 2865,** Roche 2872, Rochester 2874, Rubinstein 2896, Rudin 2899, **Scherman 2913,** Scheuer 2914, Slade 2936, Snyder 2944, Sprague 2949, **Starr 2954, Stevens 2962, Summerfield 2970,** Sun 2971, **Teagle 2979,** Tebil 2980, **Texaco 2981, Union 2997,** Uris 3003, Utica 3005, van Ameringen 3007, van Ameringen 3008, Vidor 3013, **Vinmont 3015,** Wasserman 3026, Wendt 3036, Werblow 3038, Western 3039, Wilson 3048, Wilson 3049, **Wood 3057,** Wooley-Clifford 3059, Yulman 3064
North Carolina: Akers 3072, **Babcock 3075,** Cannon 3086, **Connemara 3090,** Dover 3094, Finch 3099, Foundation 3102, Hanes 3105, Hanes 3106, Reynolds 3124, Sternberger 3132, Whitener 3136, Winston-Salem 3137
North Dakota: Leach 3140, Myra 3141, Stern 3143
Ohio: **Allyn 3147,** American 3150, **Armington 3157,** Beerman 3166, Bicknell 3171, Britton 3176,

Calhoun 3179, Cincinnati 3183, Cleveland 3186, Cleveland-Cliffs 3187, Columbus 3189, Crandall 3193, Crosley 3194, Crosset 3195, **Dana 3196,** Dayton 3199, Donnell 3202, Emery 3206, Eyman 3210, **Federated 3211,** 1525 3213, Fox 3226, GAR 3232, Gerlach 3236, Gund 3244, Hankins 3246, **Haskell 3248,** H.C.S. 3250, Humphrey 3257, Jergens 3265, Kettering 3273, Kulas 3278, Lancaster 3280, Lincoln 3283, Lubrizol 3285, **Markey 3290,** Massie 3293, Mather 3294, Mather 3295, **Mead 3299,** Miniger 3303, Moores 3308, Nationwide 3313, Nordson 3316, Oglebay 3318, O'Neil 3321, Peterloon 3326, Philips 3328, **Procter 3333,** Reinberger 3338, Rupp 3349, Russell 3351, Schmidlapp 3354, **Scott 3358,** Shafer 3362, Sherwick 3365, Sterkel 3374, Stocker 3375, **Thompson 3381,** Treu-Mart 3390, Wellman 3403, Wolfe 3410, Yassenoff 3414
Oklahoma: Bovaird 3419, Chapman 3422, Cuesta 3426, Kerr-McGee 3440, McMahon 3447, **Noble 3450,** Oklahoma 3451, Puterbaugh 3458, Sarkeys 3462, Titus 3465, Tulsa 3466, Wegener 3470, Wood 3472
Oregon: Carpenter 3478, Collins 3482, Friendly-Rosenthal 3487, Hunt 3489, Jackson 3490, **John 3493,** John 3494, Tektronix 3502, Templeton 3503, Wessinger 3506
Pennsylvania: **Adams 3508,** Anderson 3517, Arcadia 3520, **Carpenter 3536,** Central 3539, Clapp 3544, Craig 3549, Douty 3559, Erie 3565, **Federation 3569,** Fels 3571, Frick 3576, **Gillett 3579,** Grundy 3588, **Hall 3590,** Hammermill 3594, **Heinz 3598,** Heinz 3599, Hillman 3603, Hillman 3604, Hooker 3606, Hopwood 3608, Justus 3621, Kardon 3623, Knollbrook 3629, Kunkel 3633, Laros 3636, Leeds 3638, Levee 3640, **Love 3644, Lukens 3645,** McCune 3651, Mellon 3662, Mellon 3663, **Merit 3666, Murphy 3671,** Myrin 3673, Oberlaender 3677, Oxford 3678, Penn 3683, Peters 3685, **Pew 3686, Pew 3687, Pew 3688,** Pittsburgh 3693, Plankenhorn 3695, Rehmeyer 3701, **Robinson 3706, Rockwell 3708,** Schoonmaker 3714, Snyder 3728, Staunton 3735, Steinman 3737, Stokes 3740, Trexler 3748, **United 3750,** Waters 3754, Weisbrod 3755, **Westinghouse 3757, Whitaker 3761,** Williamsport 3764, Wurts 3766, Wyomissing 3767
Rhode Island: Champlin 3772, Old 3786, Rapaporte 3788, Rhode 3790
South Carolina: Belk-Simpson 3799, Moore 3811
Tennessee: Benwood 3829, Brown 3832, Bullard 3834, Church 3836, Goldsmith 3841, Maclellan 3848, Plough 3855
Texas: Abell-Hanger 3866, Abercrombie 3867, Allied 3871, Anderson 3874, Anderson 3875, Andress 3876, Beal 3882, Bivins 3887, Bridwell 3890, Brown 3893, Brown 3894, Chilton 3904, Clayton 3907, Communities 3911, Cook 3913, Crow 3919, Cullen 3921, Dallas 3924, Dodge 3931, Edwards 3939, Ellwood 3942, Fain 3944, Fair 3945, Farish 3947, Fasken 3948, Favrot 3949, Feldman 3950, Fikes 3952, Fish 3953, Florence 3955, Fondren 3956, Haas 3966, Haggerty 3968, Halff 3969, Halsell 3971, Hamman 3972, Harrington 3974, Hawn 3975, **HNG 3982,** Hoblitzelle 3984, Hofstetter 3986, Johnson 3994, Johnson 3995, Johnston 3996, Kay 3998, Kayser 3999, Keith 4000, Kenedy 4002, **Klein 4007,** Lard 4010, **Lightner 4016,** McAshan 4022, McMillan 4027, McQueen 4028, Meadows 4029, Moody 4035, Mosle 4036, Owsley 4048, Parker 4050, Perkins 4052, Polemanakos 4057, Redman 4062, Richardson 4064, Roberts 4065, Sams 4071, San Antonio 4072, Scurlock 4076, Southland 4084, Stemmons 4088, Tandy 4092, Tarrant 4094, Temple 4098, Weiner 4114, White 4121, Wiseda 4124, Wright 4128, **Zale 4129**
Utah: Castle 4133, Dee 4136, Eccles 4139, Green 4140, Masonic 4142, Michael 4143, Treadwell 4146
- *Virginia:* Central 4163, Easley 4167, Harris 4173, Morgan 4186, Richardson 4195, Taylor 4202, Thurman 4207, Wilfred 4217

Sociology

South Pacific

Speech pathology

Theological education

Transportation

United Kingdom

Urban affairs

Venezuela

Vocational education

Welfare

Ohio: Akron 3145, American 3150, **Armco 3156,** Ashtabula 3158, **Bingham 3172, Borden 3174,** Bremer 3175, Cleveland 3185, Eyman 3210, Finnegan 3215, **Firestone 3216,** Frohman 3228, Frost 3230, Iddings 3259, Jochum-Moll 3266, **Knight 3276, Marathon 3289, National 3312, O'Neil 3322,** Richman 3343, **Rosenthal 3347, Ross 3348,** Schmidlapp 3354, Sears 3360, Stark 3373, Toledo 3386, Treuhaft 3389, **TRW 3392,** Weiss 3402
Oklahoma: Ashbrook 3417, Sarkeys 3462
Oregon: Friendly-Rosenthal 3487, Jackson 3490, Tucker 3504
Pennsylvania: **Air 3509, Alcoa 3511, Annenberg 3519, Brockway 3528,** Crawford 3551, **Female 3572,** Gibson 3578, **Gulf 3589,** Mack 3646, McKee 3653, McKenna 3655, McShain 3658, Merchants 3665, Patterson 3682, Philadelphia 3689, Pitcairn-Crabbe 3691, **Rockwell 3708,** Schautz 3712, Union 3749, Wurts 3766
South Carolina: Spartanburg 3820
Tennessee: Day 3839
Texas: Davidson 3926, Duncan 3937, Johnson 3995, Kempner 4001, King 4003, Orleans 4045, Peyton 4055, Steinhagen 4087, Trull 4104, Tyler 4106
Virginia: **Best 4154, Dan 4166,** Richardson 4195, Truland 4210, Washington 4215
Washington: **Burlington 4226,** Kawabe 4241, Seattle 4259, Skinner 4262, Stubblefield 4266, Washington 4269, Welch 4270, Welch 4271
West Virginia: Daywood 4281
Wisconsin: **Brady 4304, DeRance 4314,** Oshkosh 4361, Rutledge 4376, Schroeder 4377

Wildlife

California: Whittier 426
Colorado: Jenkins 456
Delaware: **Milliken 623,** Red Clay 629
Maryland: **Knapp 1427**
Minnesota: Bell 1817
New Jersey: **Engelhard 2121**
New York: **Dorr 2408, Mad 2690, Prospect 2842,** Schieffelin 2915
Oklahoma: Phillips 3455
Pennsylvania: Mellon 3663
South Carolina: Baruch 3798
Texas: Kleberg 4005, **Kleberg 4006, Welder 4116**

Women

California: East Bay 159, **Levi 258, Parsons 311,** Richards 332
Connecticut: **Larrabee 550**
Florida: Lowe 743
Georgia: **Whitehead 885**
Illinois: Alton 924, **Chicago 969, Monticello 1100,** Scheinfeld 1140
Maryland: Warfield 1461
Massachusetts: Association 1469, Bacon 1472
Minnesota: Butler 1824
New Jersey: **Frisch 2124, Newcombe 2162**
New York: **Avon 2251, Bristol-Myers 2302, Ford 2444,** Goodyear 2488, **International 2574,** Jewish 2583, Jones 2591, Mertz 2729, **Muskiwinni 2766,** New York 2775, **Pettus-Crowe 2822, Revlon 2857, Revson 2858,** Roche 2872, **Rockefeller 2876,** Rubinstein 2896, Switzer 2975
Ohio: Gund 3244, Schmidlapp 3353
Pennsylvania: **Female 3572**
Texas: **Brinker 3891**

Youth

Alabama: Blount 4, Daniel 7, Mitchell 16, Russell 18, **Sonat 21,** Warner 23
Arizona: Arizona 29, Circle K 31, First 34, Hervey 38, **Kieckhefer 39,** Marshall 40, Mulcahy 42, VNB 47, Waddell 48
Arkansas: **Inglewood 51,** Murphy 54, **Reynolds 56,** Riggs 57, Ross 59, Sturgis 60
California: **American 69,** Arakelian 70, Arkelian 72, **Atkinson 76, Atlantic 78, Baker 81, BankAmerica 84, Bekins 90, Berkey 92,** Berry 93, Beynon 94, Bothin 99, Brenner 104, Bridges 105, Burnand 110, California 114, Callison 118, **City 125,** Clorox 127, Cowell 136, **Crown 139,** Disney 148, Distribution 151, East Bay 159, Fairfield 163, Fireman's 169, First 170, **Fluor 173,** Forest 174, Galster 181, Garland 182, **Gemco 185, Getty 188,** Gildred 189, Gilmore 190, Gilmore 191, Goldwyn 196, Gospel 197, Gross 201, Hahn 205, **Halsell 208,** Hancock 209, Helms 214, **Hilton 220,** Hoag 221, Hoffman 222, Hoover 226, **Howe 227,** Irvine 230, Jameson 235, Jerome 237, **Keck 243,** Kirchgessner 245, Lakeside 251, Lear 253, **Levi 258,** Levy 259, Lloyd 264, May 276, **MCA 279,** McCallum 282, Mosher 290, Murphey 294, Odell 303, Packard 308, **Page 309,** Parker 310, **Parsons 311, Pasadena 313,** Pasadena 314, **Peery 317,** Peninsula 318, Peters 320, Pratt 328, Radin 331, Rosenberg 334, San Diego 336, Sanguinetti 339, **Sassoon 343,** Scripps 349, Security 351, Setzer 354, Seuss 355, **Signal 360,** Simon 367, Stamps 377, Steele 382, Stuart 385, Stuart 386, Stuart 387, Stuart 388, Taper 394, **Teledyne 395,** Ticor 399, Tuohy 403, Van Camp 409, Van Nuys 411, **Wade 413,** Walker 414, Wood-Claeyssens 431
Colorado: Anschutz 435, Colorado 440, Coors 441, Duncan 443, First 447, Fishback 448, **Frost 449,** Gates 450, Hogan 453, Johnson 458, Joslyn 460, Norgren 469, Piton 473, **Schlessman 477,** Silver 479, **Taylor 482,** Thatcher 483, **Woodward 487**
Connecticut: **Abex 488,** Aetna 489, **American 492,** Auerbach 494, **Bissell 500,** Bodenwein 501, Day 509, **Dexter 512,** Ensworth 521, Fry 526, **Great 529,** Hartford 533, Heublein 538, Howard 539, **Hubbell 540, Kayser-Roth 547,** New Haven 559, **Oaklawn 560, Olin 561,** Palmer 562, Robinson 568, **Scovill 574,** Stanley 577, **Stanley 578, UMC 583,** Wahlstrom-Johnson 586, Waterbury 588
Delaware: **Birch 597,** Ederic 607, Laffey-McHugh 616, Longwood 618, Marmot 621
District of Columbia: Appleby 635, Bloedorn 641, Cafritz 643, **Delmar 647,** Fowler 655, **GEICO 657, Graham 660,** Gudelsky 661, **Kennedy 666,** Kiplinger 667, Loughran 669, **Public 679,** Washington 685
Florida: Baker 693, **Bastien 694, Brunner 700,** Bush 701, Childress 703, Conn 704, Dade 706, **Davis 709,** Deicke 710, **Delacorte 711,** Dunspaugh-Dalton 715, **duPont 716,** Falk 720, **Harris 726,** Jenkins 732, Law 738, Leu 740, Phillips 753, Price 758, Rainforth 759, Ritter 761, River 762, Rosenberg 763, Saunders 765, Selby 766, **Sharonsteel 768, Stark 773, Sudakoff 778,** Swisher 780, Tampa 782, Thomas 784, **Ware 789,** Williams 793, **Winn-Dixie 794**
Georgia: Atlanta 803, Bradley-Turner 807, C B & T 809, **Citizens 816,** Courts 820, English 830, Evans 832, First 833, Franklin 835, **Georgia-Pacific 837,** Gilbert 839, Harland 843, **Harland 844,** Hodge 847, Illges 849, Lanier 852, Murphy 860, **Ottley 862,** Patterson-Barclay 863, Trebor 876, Trust 877, **Tull 878,** Wardlaw 880, Wehadkee 881, **West Point 883,** Whitehead 884, Woolley 887
Hawaii: **Amfac 888, Bohnett 891,** Brewer 892, Castle 893, Castle 894, Cooke 895, Davies 896, Frear 898, Hawaiian 899, McInerny 903
Illinois: **Allstate 922,** American 925, Amerock 927, **Amoco 928, Amsted 929, Archer-Daniels-Midland 932,** Atwood 934, Aurora 935, Barber-Colman 936, **Bauer 937, Becker 940,** Beidler 941, **Bell 943,** Bersted 945, **Brunswick 955,** Burns 959, Chapin 967, Chicago 968, Chicago 970, Christiana 973, **Clark 974,** Cuneo 984, **Deere 987, DeKalb 989,** DeSoto 991, Dillon 992, Donnelley 993, Eisenberg 996, Field 1001, First 1002, Fisher 1003, **FMC 1005, Foote 1006,** Frank 1009, Furnas 1012, Geraldi-Norton 1016, **Gould 1020, Griswold 1023, Harper 1027,** Hoffer 1039, Hoover 1041, Hopper 1042, **Illinois 1045,** IMC 1046, **Interlake 1049,** Jewel 1050, Johnson 1051, Lehmann 1068, Leslie 1069, **Marquette 1082,** Material 1085, McCormick 1089, McCormick 1090, **McGraw 1094, McGraw-Edison 1095,** Meyer-Ceco 1097, Millard 1098, Millikin 1099, **Moorman 1101,** Moorman 1102, **Nalco 1105, Northwest 1109, Prince 1122, Quaker 1126,** Rice 1134, **Roper 1135,** Rosenthal 1136, Sara 1139, Seabury 1143, Shirk 1151, **Signode 1152,** Smith 1156, **Square D 1162, Stanadyne 1165,** Stewart-Warner 1168, **Stone 1170,** Sulzer 1173, **Sundstrand 1174,** UOP 1180, Upton 1181, USG 1182, Ward 1184, Warner 1186, **Wolf 1192**
Indiana: Anderson 1195, **Arvin 1196, Central 1205,** Cole 1207, Cummins 1210, English-Bonter-Mitchell 1212, Froderman 1215, Hayes 1220, Hillenbrand 1223, Indianapolis 1226, Inland 1227, **Jenn 1229,** Kilbourne 1231, Koch 1232, **Lilly 1238,** McMillen 1241, Mead 1242, Noyes 1246, Oliver 1247, **Plumsock 1248,** Rock Island 1251, Somers 1254, Thrush 1257
Iowa: Gazette 1267, Hall 1269, Hawley 1270, Kinney-Lindstrom 1272, **Lee 1274, Meredith 1278,** National 1279, Ruan 1281, Witte 1289
Kansas: Baughman 1293, Beech 1294, Breidenthal 1295, **Cessna 1297,** Coleman 1298, DeVore 1301, First 1304, Fourth 1305, Hansen 1309, **Hesston 1311,** Kansas 1315, Powell 1323, Rice 1325, Rouback 1326, Smoot 1328, Wiedemann 1330
Kentucky: Brown 1336, Houchens 1343, Norton 1349, Schneider 1352
Louisiana: German 1362, Helis 1365, Poindexter 1378, Scott 1382, Shreveport-Bossier 1383, Wheless 1385, Woolf 1388, Zigler 1390
Maine: Alfond 1391, **Market 1394,** Mulford 1396
Maryland: Commercial 1408, Duncan 1411, Equitable 1413, First 1415, **Hechinger 1421,** Kelly 1424, Loats 1431, Noxell 1444, Pearlstone 1445
Massachusetts: Acushnet 1466, **Alden 1468,** Babson 1470, Bank 1473, **Beveridge 1475,** Boston 1482, Boston 1483, **Cabot 1488,** Cabot 1489, Charlesbank 1495, Chase 1497, Chase 1498, Cove 1503, **Demoulas 1513,** Devonshire 1514, Dexter 1515, **Donaldson 1517, Eastern 1518,** Ellsworth 1523, Fuller 1533, **Gillette 1535,** Harrington 1543, **Henderson 1547,** Heydt 1549, Hopedale 1555, Hyams 1561, Hyams 1562, Jackson 1563, Kelley 1567, Knistrom 1572, Levy 1575, Lipsky 1577, Norton 1588, Old 1589, Pappas 1591, Peabody 1593, Perini 1594, Pierce 1599, Pilgrim 1600, **Pneumo 1601,** Polaroid 1602, Ratshesky 1605, Riley 1608, Schrafft 1618, Shawmut 1624, **Sheraton 1625,** Stevens 1633, Stoddard 1635, Warren 1649, Weber 1651, **Webster 1652, Williams 1658, Wyman-Gordon 1660**
Michigan: **Aeroquip 1662,** Bauervic 1670, Bishop 1674, Chamberlin 1678, Cook 1680, Dalton 1681, DeRoy 1683, Detroit 1684, DeVlieg 1685, DeWaters 1687, Earl-Beth 1692, Faigle 1695, **Ford 1699, Ford 1701,** Ford 1703, **Ford 1704,** Fremont 1705, **Fruehauf 1706,** Fruehauf 1707, Gerstacker 1712, Grand 1715, Herrick 1718, Himmel 1719, Holden 1720, Hurst 1724, Kalamazoo 1728, Kaufman 1730, La-Z-Boy 1736, Loutit 1738, Lyon 1739, McGregor 1744, Morley 1751, **Mott 1753,** Ransom 1761, Sage 1764, Scott 1765, Shelden 1770, Skillman 1773, **Slaughter 1774,** Steelcase 1775, Tiscornia 1782, Tuck 1785, Upjohn 1786, Vollbrecht 1790, **Whirlpool 1793,** Whiting 1796, Wickes 1798, Wilson 1799, Wilson 1800, **Wolverine 1803**
Minnesota: **Andersen 1809,** Andersen 1810, **Andreas 1811,** Apache 1812, Baker 1814, Bayport 1815, Beim 1816, Bell 1817, Cargill 1825, Carolyn 1827, **Cenex 1828, Davis 1833, DeLuxe 1835, Donaldson 1836,** Dye 1838, Edwards 1840, First 1842, First 1843, Gamble 1845, Graco 1849, **Grain 1850,** Hawthorne 1858, Hersey 1860,

Honeywell 1861, Hormel 1862, Hotchkiss 1863, Hubbard 1864, Hulings 1865, International 1866, Jostens 1870, Mardag 1879, **Medtronic 1884,** Minneapolis 1887, **Minnesota 1890,** Northern 1893, **Northwest 1894,** Ordean 1899, Paper 1901, **Pillsbury 1905,** Red Wing 1908, Rivers 1909, Rodman 1911, Tennant 1915, Thorpe 1916, Van Evera 1919

Mississippi: Chisholm 1931, Deposit 1934, First 1936, Walker 1939

Missouri: **Anheuser-Busch 1940,** Brown 1944, Brown 1945, Calkins 1947, Centerre 1948, **Chance 1949,** Commerce 1951, Craig 1953, **Cross 1954, Emerson 1959,** Garvey 1964, Gaylord 1965, Gaylord 1966, H.B.S. 1969, Kemper 1974, Kemper 1976, Laclede 1977, Long 1980, **Mallinckrodt 1988,** Mercantile 1996, MFA 1997, **Monsanto 1999, Olin 2001,** Parrott 2005, Pitzman 2008, Pott 2009, **Ralston 2010,** Reynolds 2011, **Smith 2015,** Speas 2018, Springmeier 2019, Stupp 2024, Sunderland 2025, **Sunnen 2027,** Townsend 2033, Whitaker 2039, **Woods 2041**

Montana: Fortin 2044, **Sample 2047**

Nebraska: ConAgra 2053, Cooper 2054, Criss 2055, Hitchcock 2057, **InterNorth 2058,** Kiewit 2059, **Kiewit 2060,** Omaha 2065, Quivey 2068, Reynolds 2069, Rogers 2070, Valmont 2074

Nevada: Bing 2077, Hawkins 2080

New Hampshire: Barker 2082, Cogswell 2084, **Hubbard 2086,** Hunt 2087, Kingsbury 2090, Putnam 2094, **Standex 2096**

New Jersey: **Allied 2098,** Belasco 2101, Berger 2103, Borden 2104, Brady 2105, Bunbury 2106, Campbell 2107, **Crum 2114,** Elizabeth 2120, Fidelity 2122, Kerney 2142, Large 2145, L'Hommedieu 2148, Lindberg 2149, **Lipton 2150,** Meyer 2157, **National 2160,** Orange 2164, **Reeves 2170,** Sawtelle 2175, Schenck 2177, Schwartz 2182, Thomas 2192, Turrell 2193, **Union 2194,** Union 2195, Visceglia-Summit 2198, **Vollmer 2199, Warner-Lambert 2200,** Youths' 2205

New Mexico: **Bellamah 2206,** Maddox 2209

New York: **ACF 2217,** Achelis 2218, Adler 2222, **Agway 2224,** Allen 2228, Allyn 2231, Altman 2232, Altschul 2233, **American 2235, American-Standard 2237, Archbold 2242,** Arkell 2243, Badgeley 2256, **Baier 2257, Baird 2259,** Baird 2261, Baker 2262, Barker 2265, **Beefeater 2274,** Beinecke 2275, **Berlinger 2281,** Bleibtreu 2288, **Blythmour 2292, Bobst 2293,** Bodman 2294, Bostwick 2297, Bowne 2299, **Bristol-Myers 2302,** Bruner 2309, Calder 2320, Campe 2321, **Capital 2322,** Carnahan-Jackson 2324, Charlpeg 2336, Children's 2343, **Clark 2346,** Clark 2347, **Colt 2360,** Craigmyle 2370, **Culpeper 2374,** Cummings 2376, Curtice-Burns 2377, Darrah 2381, Davenport-Hatch 2382, De Jur 2388, Dewar 2397, **Dodge 2402, Dorr 2408,** Doubleday 2409, **Dreyfus 2413, Dun 2415,** Ebsary 2419, Emerson 2421, **Ettinger 2423,** Everett 2425, **Field 2432,** Fish 2438, French 2451, Frohlich 2454, Gebbie 2465, **General 2467,** Gifford 2469, **Gimbel-Saks 2471,** Goodyear 2488, **Gordon 2489, Grant 2499,** Green 2500, **Hackett 2522,** Hagedorn 2523, Harriman 2527, Hayden 2534, **Hazen 2535,** Heckscher 2540, Hendrickson 2545, **Hess 2546,** Hochschild 2553, Holmes 2557, Hopkins 2561, **Hutton 2569, Indian 2572, J.M. 2584,** Jones 2591, Julia 2593, **Katzenberger 2603, Kempner 2608,** L and L 2633, Lavanburg-Corner 2644, **Leir 2654,** Macdonald 2685, **Mailman 2693, Manufacturers 2698, Mathers 2704,** McDonald 2717, **McDonald 2718, Memton 2724,** Metcalf 2731, **Milliken 2740,** Moore 2748, Morgenstern 2752, Morris 2754, Moses 2758, **Mosler 2759,** Mossman 2760, **Mostyn 2762,** Muehlstein 2764, Napier 2767, New York 2775, **Newhouse 2778,** Nias 2781, Nichols 2782, Norstar 2789, O'Connor 2795, **Oestreicher 2796,** Osborn 2803, Parshelsky 2813, **Peierls 2818, PepsiCo 2820,** Pinkerton 2830, Price 2839, **Prospect 2842,** Raymond 2849, **Reader's 2851,** Ritter 2868, Roche 2872, Rochester 2874, **Rosenthal 2888, Russ 2900,** Sasco 2908, Schiff

2916, Simon 2933, **Smith 2940,** Snow 2942, Sprague 2949, St. Faith's 2950, **Stevens 2962,** Taconic 2976, Taylor 2978, **Teagle 2979, Thorne 2984, Transway 2991,** Trump 2992, **United 2998, Vanneck-Bailey 3009, Vernon 3010,** Vogler 3016, **Wallace 3019, Weezie 3029,** Wegman 3030, Western 3039, Wilson 3048, **Wood 3057, Woodland 3058, Young 3062,** Zarkin 3066

North Carolina: Akzona 3073, **Babcock 3075, BarclaysAmerican 3076,** Belk 3077, Cannon 3086, Chatham 3089, Dickson 3092, Dickson 3093, **Fieldcrest 3098,** Finley 3101, Foundation 3102, Hanes 3106, **Martin 3114,** Memorial 3117, Reynolds 3124, Stonecutter 3133, Whitener 3136, Winston-Salem 3137

North Dakota: Myra 3141, North Dakota 3142, Stern 3143

Ohio: Acme 3144, Albers 3146, Anderson 3152, Anderson 3153, Bates 3162, Beecher 3163, Beecher 3164, Benua 3168, Berry 3170, **Borden 3174,** Britton 3176, **Browning 3177,** Calhoun 3179, Charities 3181, Cincinnati 3183, Cincinnati 3184, Cleveland-Cliffs 3187, Codrington 3188, **Commercial 3190,** Crosset 3195, **Dana 3196,** Dayton 3199, Deuble 3200, **Eagle-Picher 3203, Eaton 3204,** Emery 3206, Fifth 3214, **Firestone 3216,** Firman 3217, Flickinger 3221, Flowers 3222, Fox 3226, France 3227, Frohman 3228, **GenCorp 3234,** Goerlich 3238, Gross 3243, Gund 3244, Hamilton 3245, Hartzell-Norris 3247, **Hoover 3253, Huffy 3255,** Iddings 3259, Jergens 3265, Juilfs 3267, Kettering 3273, Kramer 3277, Kuntz 3279, Laub 3281, Lubrizol 3285, **Marathon 3289,** Massie 3293, Mather 3295, McAlonan 3296, McFawn 3297, **Melton 3301,** Miniger 3303, Monarch 3305, Mount 3309, **National 3312,** Ohio 3319, Ohio 3320, **Parker-Hannifin 3323,** Peterson 3327, Pollock 3330, **Procter 3333,** Reeves 3337, **Reliance 3339, Republic 3341,** Richland 3342, Richman 3343, Ritchie 3344, Sherman-Standard 3364, Sherwick 3365, **Sherwin-Williams 3366,** Smith 3369, Stocker 3375, Stranahan 3377, Tait 3378, Toledo 3387, **TRW 3392,** Van Huffel 3395, Van Wert 3396, **Warner 3398,** Watson 3400, Wean 3401, White 3406, Whitewater 3407, Wolfe 3410, XTEK 3413, Yassenoff 3414, Youngstown 3416

Oklahoma: Campbell 3421, Fields 3429, First 3430, Goddard 3432, Harris 3435, Helmerich 3436, **Kerr 3439, Mabee 3443,** McMahon 3447, Merrick 3448, **Noble 3450,** Oklahoma 3452, Phillips 3455, **Phillips 3456,** Price 3457, Puterbaugh 3458, Taubman 3464, Wegener 3470, Williams 3471

Oregon: Autzen 3475, Barker 3476, Chiles 3479, Clark 3480, Collins 3482, **Fohs 3484,** Ford 3485, Hunt 3489, Jackson 3490, **Jeld-Wen 3491, Louisiana-Pacific 3496,** OCRI 3499, Templeton 3503, Walton 3505, Wessinger 3506, Wheeler 3507

Pennsylvania: **Alco 3510, Alcoa 3511, Allegheny 3513,** AMP 3516, Anderson 3517, Blaisdell 3527, **Brockway 3528,** Buhl 3529, **Carpenter 3536,** Central 3539, **CIGNA 3542,** Clapp 3544, Crawford 3551, **Dravo 3561,** Erie 3565, Grundy 3588, **Gulf 3589,** Hall 3591, Hammermill 3594, Hillman 3603, Hillman 3604, Hopwood 3608, Hulme 3610, Hunt 3612, Jennings 3620, Justus 3622, Knudsen 3630, Leeds 3638, **Love 3644,** Mack 3646, McCormick 3650, McCune 3651, McLean 3657, Mellon 3661, Mengle 3664, Miller 3667, **Murphy 3671,** National 3674, 1957 3676, Oberlaender 3677, Packer 3679, Peters 3685, **Pew 3686,** Phillips 3690, Pitcairn-Crabbe 3691, Pittsburgh 3694, Plankenhorn 3695, Rehmeyer 3701, Reidler 3702, Rittenhouse 3704, Schautz 3712, Seybert 3717, Sheppard 3718, SPS 3731, Stackpole-Hall 3734, Trexler 3748, Union 3749, **Westinghouse 3757,** Whalley 3759, Wheeling-Pittsburgh 3760, Williams 3763, Williamsport 3764, Wyomissing 3767

Rhode Island: Armbrust 3771, Champlin 3772, Citizens 3773, **Genesis 3777,** Johnstone 3780, Kimball 3781, **Little 3783,** Providence 3787, Rhode 3790, **Textron 3792**

South Carolina: Arkwright 3796, Citizens 3801, **Daniel 3802,** Gregg-Graniteville 3806, Inman-Riverdale 3807, Kennedy 3808, Moore 3811, **Riegel 3813,** Self 3817, South Carolina 3819, Stevens 3824, Symmes 3825

Tennessee: Briggs 3830, Evans 3840, Hutcheson 3843, Maclellan 3848, Maclellan 3849, Schadt 3857, Toms 3859

Texas: Abell-Hanger 3866, Allied 3871, Anderson 3875, Beal 3882, Beasley 3883, Behmann 3884, Bridwell 3890, Brookshire 3892, Brown 3893, Brown 3894, Bryce 3896, Butler 3898, Cain 3900, Carter 3902, **Central 3903,** Chilton 3904, Cockrell 3908, Collins 3909, Collins 3910, Communities 3911, Constantin 3912, Cook 3913, Craig 3918, Dallas 3924, Davidson 3926, Davis 3927, Dickson 3930, Dodge 3931, Doss 3933, **Dresser 3935, Dresser-Harbison 3936,** Duncan 3938, Edwards 3939, **ENSERCH 3943,** Fain 3944, Fair 3945, Fasken 3948, Fikes 3952, Fish 3953, **Fuller 3958,** Garvey 3959, Gifford 3961, Gill 3962, Haas 3966, Haggar 3967, Halff 3969, Halsell 3971, Hamman 3972, Heath 3976, Hemphill-Wells 3977, Hoblitzelle 3984, King 4003, King 4004, Knox 4009, Lard 4010, **Lightner 4016,** Lone 4018, Luling 4019, McKee 4026, McMillan 4027, McQueen 4028, Moss 4037, Navarro 4040, Owen 4047, Pangburn 4049, Richardson 4064, Roberts 4065, Rogers 4067, Sams 4071, Scott 4075, Scurlock 4076, Semmes 4078, Sharp 4080, Southland 4084, Stemmons 4088, Sumners 4091, **Texas 4102,** Trull 4104, Turner 4105, Tyler 4106, Waggoner 4110, **Weaver 4113,** West 4118, West 4119, White 4120, White 4121, Wright 4128

Utah: Bamberger 4130, Castle 4133, Dumke 4137, Masonic 4142

Vermont: **Edwards 4147,** Windham 4151

Virginia: Beazley 4153, **Best 4154,** Camp 4158, Camp 4159, Camp 4160, **Campbell 4161, Campbell 4162,** Central 4163, **Dan 4166,** Easley 4167, Gottwald 4171, Norfolk 4187, **Reynolds 4193, Robertshaw 4197,** Seay 4199, Thurman 4207, Treakle 4209, Universal 4212

Washington: Archibald 4219, Bishop 4220, **Burlington 4226,** Cawsey 4228, Cheney 4229, Comstock 4230, Dupar 4233, Fuchs 4235, Glaser 4236, Johnston 4240, Kilworth 4243, Kilworth 4244, Leuthold 4247, **Matlock 4248,** McEachern 4249, Medina 4250, Norcliffe 4254, PACCAR 4255, Robertson 4258, Shemanski 4261, Skinner 4262, Spokane 4264, Univar 4268, Welch 4271, Wells 4272, **Wharton 4275,** Wyman 4276

West Virginia: Carbon 4278, Chambers 4280, Daywood 4281, **Prichard 4289,** Vecellio 4290

Wisconsin: Alexander 4292, Amundson 4295, Apollo 4297, **ARMCO 4298,** Banta 4300, Beloit 4301, **Bradley 4303,** Braun 4305, Briggs 4306, Brotz 4307, Bucyrus-Erie 4308, Consolidated 4310, **Cudahy 4311,** CUNA 4312, Demmer 4313, Evinrude 4315, Evjue 4316, Falk 4317, First 4318, Frankenthal 4320, Gelatt 4323, **Harnischfeger 4325,** Helfaer 4327, Hobbs 4328, Jacobus/Heritage 4329, Janesville 4330, **Johnson 4331,** Johnson 4334, Johnson 4335, **Johnson's 4336,** Kearney 4337, **Koehring 4339, Kress 4344,** Ladish 4347, Ladish 4348, Ladish 4349, Loock 4352, Marine 4353, Marshall 4354, Mason 4355, Neenah 4359, Oshkosh 4362, Pick 4368, **Rahr 4371, Rexnord 4373,** Rutledge 4376, Schroeder 4377, Siebert 4379, Stackner 4381, **Trane 4383,** Youth 4392, Ziegler 4393

Wyoming: Kamps 4397, Stock 4398, Surrena 4399, Tonkin 4400

FOUNDATION NAME INDEX

Abbott (The Clara) Foundation, IL, 917
Abbott Laboratories Fund, IL, 918
ABC Foundation, NC, 3071
Abel Foundation, The, NE, 2049
Abelard Foundation, Inc., The, CA, 63
Abell (The A. S.) Company Foundation, Inc., MD, 1399
Abell (Jennie G. and Pearl) Education Trust, KS, 1291
Abell-Hanger Foundation, TX, 3866
Abercrombie (The J. S.) Foundation, TX, 3867
Abex Foundation, Inc., CT, 488
Abney Foundation, The, SC, 3794
Abrams (Benjamin and Elizabeth) Foundation, Inc., NY, 2214
Abrons (Louis and Anne) Foundation, Inc., NY, 2215
Abrons (Richard & Mimi) Foundation, Inc., NY, 2216
ACF Foundation, Inc., NY, 2217
Achelis Foundation, The, NY, 2218
Acme Cleveland Foundation, OH, 3144
Acushnet Foundation, The, MA, 1466
Adams (Emma J.) Memorial Fund, Inc., NY, 2219
Adams Foundation, Inc., PA, 3508
Adams (Frank W. and Carl S.) Memorial Fund, MA, 1467
Adams (The Moody) Foundation, TX, 3868
Ades Foundation, Inc., NY, 2220
Adler Foundation, Inc., NY, 2221
Adler (Louis and Bessie) Foundation, Inc., NY, 2222
Adolph's Foundation, The, CA, 64
Aeroflex Foundation, The, NY, 2223
Aeroquip Foundation, MI, 1662
Aetna Life & Casualty Foundation, Inc., CT, 489
Agway Foundation, NY, 2224
Ahmanson Foundation, The, CA, 65
A.I.D. Foundation, CA, 66
Aigner (G. J.) Foundation, Inc., IL, 919
Aiken Foundation, Inc., The, SC, 3795
Air Products Foundation, The, PA, 3509
AKC Fund, Inc., NY, 2225
Akers Foundation, Inc., NC, 3072
Akin Foundation, The, TX, 3869
Akron Community Foundation, OH, 3145
Akzona Foundation, The, NC, 3073
Alaska Conservation Foundation, AK, 25
Albany's Hospital for Incurables, NY, 2226
Albers (Josef) Foundation, Inc., CT, 490
Albers (The William H.) Foundation, Inc., OH, 3146
Albertson Foundation, The, CA, 67
Alco Standard Foundation, PA, 3510
Alcoa Foundation, PA, 3511
Alden (George I.) Trust, MA, 1468
Alexander Charitable Foundation, Inc., WI, 4291
Alexander (Joseph) Foundation, NY, 2227
Alexander (Judd S.) Foundation, Inc., WI, 4292
Alexander (Walter) Foundation, Inc., WI, 4293
Alfond (The Harold) Trust, ME, 1391
Aliber Foundation, IA, 1259
Allbritton Foundation, The, TX, 3870
Allbritton (The Joe L. and Barbara B.) Foundation, *see* 3870
Allegheny Foundation, PA, 3512
Allegheny International Foundation, PA, 3513
Allen (Frances) Foundation, NY, 2228

Allen (Rita) Foundation, Inc., NY, 2229
Allen-Bradley Foundation, Inc., *see* 4303
Allen-Heath Memorial Foundation, IL, 920
Allied Corporation Foundation, NJ, 2098
Allied Endowment, Inc., TX, 3871
Allied Stores Foundation, Inc., NY, 2230
Allied Tube & Conduit Foundation, IL, 921
Allis-Chalmers Foundation, Inc., WI, 4294
Alliss (Charles and Ellora) Educational Foundation, MN, 1805
Allstate Foundation, The, IL, 922
Allyn Foundation, Inc., NY, 2231
Allyn Foundation, The, OH, 3147
Alms (Eleanora C. U.) Trust, OH, 3148
Alperin Foundation, The, RI, 3770
Alsdorf Foundation, IL, 923
Altman Foundation, NY, 2232
Alton Women's Home Association, IL, 924
Altschul Foundation, The, NY, 2233
Alvord Foundation, The, DC, 634
Alworth (Marshall H. and Nellie) Memorial Fund, MN, 1806
Amado (Maurice) Foundation, CA, 68
Amarillo Area Foundation, Inc., TX, 3872
Amax Foundation, Inc., CT, 491
Amcast Industrial Foundation, OH, 3149
American Bank and Trust Company of Pennsylvania Foundation, PA, 3514
American Can Company Foundation, CT, 492
American Conservation Association, Inc., NY, 2234
American Express Foundation, NY, 2235
American Financial Corporation Foundation, The, OH, 3150
American Foundation Corporation, The, OH, 3151
American Foundation, Incorporated, The, FL, 689
American Friends of Israel, NY, 2236
American Hoist and Derrick Foundation, MN, 1807
American Honda Foundation, CA, 69
American National Bank and Trust Company of Chicago Foundation, IL, 925
American Petrofina Foundation, TX, 3873
American Seamen's Friend Society, The, CT, 493
American Society of Ephesus, Inc., *see* 3334
Americana Foundation, MI, 1663
American-Standard Foundation, NY, 2237
Amerind Foundation, Inc., The, AZ, 27
Ameritech Foundation, IL, 926
Amerock Charities Trust, IL, 927
Ames (Harriett) Charitable Trust, PA, 3515
AMETEK Foundation, Inc., NY, 2238
Amfac Foundation, HI, 888
Amoco Foundation, Inc., IL, 928
AMP Foundation, PA, 3516
Amsted Industries Foundation, IL, 929
Amundson (Alvin R.) Charitable Remainder Trust, WI, 4295
Andersen (Arthur) Foundation, IL, 930
Andersen (Elmer L. & Eleanor J.) Foundation, MN, 1808
Andersen Foundation, MN, 1809
Andersen (Hugh J.) Foundation, MN, 1810
Anderson (Douglas G.) - Leigh R. Evans Foundation, NY, 2239

Anderson Foundation, Inc., The, NY, 2240
Anderson Foundation, OH, 3152
Anderson Foundation, WA, 4218
Anderson (John W.) Foundation, IN, 1195
Anderson (Josephine) Charitable Trust, TX, 3874
Anderson (M. D.) Foundation, TX, 3875
Anderson (The Mary) Trust, PA, 3517
Anderson (Robert C. and Sadie G.) Foundation, NC, 3074
Anderson (William P.) Foundation, OH, 3153
Andreas Foundation, The, MN, 1811
Andres (Frank G.) Charitable Trust, WI, 4296
Andress Foundation, The, TX, 3876
Andrew (Aileen S.) Foundation, IL, 931
Andrews Foundation, The, OH, 3154
Andrews (Mildred) Fund, OH, 3155
Anheuser-Busch Charitable Trust, MO, 1940
Animal Assistance Foundation, CO, 434
Ann Arbor Area Foundation, MI, 1664
Anncox Foundation, Inc., GA, 801
Annenberg Fund, Inc., The, PA, 3518
Annenberg (The M. L.) Foundation, PA, 3519
Anschutz Family Foundation, The, CO, 435
Ansley (Dantzler Bond) Foundation, TN, 3827
Anthony (The Barbara Cox) Foundation, HI, 889
Apache Foundation, MN, 1812
Apollo Fund Limited, WI, 4297
Appalachian Fund, Inc., KY, 1331
Applebaum Foundation, Inc., The, FL, 690
Appleby Foundation, The, DC, 635
Appleby (Scott B. and Annie P.) Trust, DC, 636
Appleman Foundation, Inc., The, NY, 2241
April Trust, The, DC, 637
Arakelian (K.) Foundation, CA, 70
Arata Brothers Trust, CA, 71
Arca Foundation, The, DC, 638
Arcadia Foundation, The, PA, 3520
Archbold (Adrian & Jessie) Charitable Trust, NY, 2242
Archer-Daniels-Midland Foundation, IL, 932
Archibald (Norman) Charitable Foundation, WA, 4219
Arison Foundation, Inc., FL, 691
Arizona Bank Charitable Foundation, AZ, 28
Arizona Community Foundation, AZ, 29
Arkelian (Ben H. and Gladys) Foundation, CA, 72
Arkell Hall Foundation Incorporated, NY, 2243
Arkwright Foundation, The, SC, 3796
Armbrust Foundation, RI, 3771
Armco Foundation, OH, 3156
ARMCO Insurance Group Foundation, WI, 4298
Armington (The Evenor) Fund, OH, 3157
Armour Family Foundation, The, NJ, 2099
Armour (George & Frances) Foundation, Inc., VA, 4152
Aron (J.) Charitable Foundation, Inc., NY, 2244
Aronberg (Lester) Foundation, IL, 933
Arrillaga (John) Foundation, CA, 73
Artevel Foundation, CA, 74
Arvin Foundation, Inc., The, IN, 1196
ARW Foundation, The, NY, 2245
ASARCO Foundation, NY, 2246
Ashbrook (Mary K.) Foundation for El Reno, OK, OK, 3417
Ashland Foundation, Inc., Greater, KY, 1332

Ashland Oil Foundation, Inc., The, KY, 1333
Ashtabula Foundation, Inc., The, OH, 3158
Asplundh Foundation, PA, 3521
Associated Foundations Incorporated, CA, 75
Associated Metals and Minerals Foundation, Inc., NY, 2247
Association for the Relief of Aged Women of New Bedford, MA, 1469
Astor (The Vincent) Foundation, NY, 2248
AT&T Foundation, NY, 2249
Atherton Family Foundation, HI, 890
Athwin Foundation, MN, 1813
Atkinson Foundation, CA, 76
Atkinson (Myrtle L.) Foundation, CA, 77
Atlanta Community Foundation, Inc., Metropolitan, GA, 802
Atlanta Foundation, GA, 803
Atlantic Foundation, The, NJ, 2100
Atlantic Richfield Foundation, The, CA, 78
Atran Foundation, Inc., NY, 2250
Atwood Foundation Incorporated, AK, 26
Atwood Foundation, IL, 934
Auerbach (The Beatrice Fox) Foundation, CT, 494
Aurora Foundation, The, FL, 692
Aurora Foundation, The, IL, 935
Austin Company Foundation, The, OH, 3159
Austin Memorial Foundation, The, OH, 3160
Autzen Foundation, The, OR, 3475
Avery (Charles Shirley) Foundation, MI, 1665
Avon Products Foundation, Inc., NY, 2251
Avondale Educational & Charitable Foundation, Inc., The, AL, 1
Axe-Houghton Foundation, NY, 2252
Ayres Foundation, Inc., IN, 1197

Babcock (Mary Reynolds) Foundation, Incorporated, NC, 3075
Babcock (William) Memorial Endowment, CA, 79
Baber (Weisell) Foundation, Inc., IN, 1198
Babson (The Paul and Edith) Foundation, MA, 1470
Babson-Webber-Mustard Fund, MA, 1471
Bache Corporation Foundation, NY, 2253
Bache (H. L.) Foundation, NY, 2254
Bache Halsey Stuart Shields Foundation, see 2253
Bachmann Foundation, Inc., The, NY, 2255
Bacon (Charles F.) Trust, MA, 1472
Bacon (The Francis) Foundation, Inc., CA, 80
Bacot Foundation, Inc., MS, 1930
Badgeley (Rose M.) Residuary Charitable Trust, NY, 2256
Badger Meter Foundation, Inc., WI, 4299
Baier (Marie) Foundation, Inc., NY, 2257
Bailey Foundation, The, SC, 3797
Bair (Charles M.) Memorial Trust, MT, 2043
Baird Brothers Company Foundation, OH, 3161
Baird (The Cameron) Foundation, NY, 2258
Baird (David, Josephine, & Winfield) Foundation, Inc., NY, 2259
Baird Foundation, The, NY, 2260
Baird (Winfield) Foundation, NY, 2261
Baker (Clark and Ruby) Foundation, GA, 804
Baker (Clayton) Trust, MD, 1400
Baker Foundation, MN, 1814
Baker (The George F.) Trust, NY, 2262
Baker (The George T.) Foundation, Inc., FL, 693
Baker (J. H.) Trust, KS, 1292
Baker (The R. C.) Foundation, CA, 81
Baker (The Solomon R. and Rebecca D.) Foundation, Inc., CA, 82
Baker (The William G.), Jr. Memorial Fund, MD, 1401
Baldwin Foundation, MI, 1666
Baldwin (Summerfield), Jr. Foundation, MD, 1402
Ball Brothers Foundation, IN, 1199
Ball (George and Frances) Foundation, IN, 1200
Baltimore Area, Inc., The Community Foundation of the Greater, MD, 1403
Bamberger (Ruth Eleanor) and John Ernest Bamberger Memorial Foundation, UT, 4130
Banbury Fund, Inc., NY, 2263
Bank of America - Giannini Foundation, CA, 83
Bank of Boston Corporation Charitable Foundation, MA, 1473
Bank of Louisville Charities, Inc., KY, 1334

Bank of the Southwest National Association Houston Foundation, TX, 3877
Bank South Charitable Trust, GA, 805
BankAmerica Foundation, CA, 84
Banta Company Foundation, Inc., WI, 4300
Barber-Colman Foundation, IL, 936
BarclaysAmerican/Foundation, Inc., NC, 3076
Barden Foundation, Inc., The, CT, 495
Bargman (Theodore and Mina) Foundation, MI, 1667
Barker (The Donald R.) Foundation, OR, 3476
Barker Foundation Inc., The, NH, 2082
Barker (J. M. R.) Foundation, NY, 2264
Barker Welfare Foundation, The, NY, 2265
Barnes Foundation, Incorporated, The, CT, 496
Barnes Group Foundation, Inc., CT, 497
Barra Foundation, Inc., PA, 3522
Barrington Foundation, Inc., The, NY, 2266
Barstow Foundation, The, MI, 1668
Barth (The Theodore H.) Foundation, Inc., NY, 2267
Bartlett (Edward E.) & Helen Turner Bartlett Foundation, OK, 3418
Baruch (The Belle W.) Foundation, SC, 3798
Bass Foundation, The, TX, 3878
Bass Foundation, TX, 3879
Bastien Foundation, see 694
Bastien (John E. and Nellie J.) Foundation, FL, 694
Bat Hanadiv Foundation, No. 3, NY, 2268
Bates (The Georgine E.) Memorial Fund, Inc., OH, 3162
Baton Rouge Area Foundation, LA, 1354
Battistone Foundation, CA, 85
Battle Creek Foundation, Greater, MI, 1669
Bauer (M. R.) Foundation, IL, 937
Bauervic (Charles M.) Foundation, Inc., MI, 1670
Baughman Foundation, KS, 1293
Baum (The Alvin H.) Family Fund, IL, 938
Baumberger (Charles) Testamentary Trust, TX, 3880
Baumberger Endowment, TX, 3881
Bausch & Lomb Foundation, Inc., NY, 2269
Baxter (The Donald E.) Foundation, CA, 86
Bay (Charles Ulrick and Josephine) Foundation, Inc., NY, 2270
Bayne (The Howard) Fund, NY, 2271
Bayport Foundation, Inc., MN, 1815
Bayrd (Adelaide Breed) Foundation, MA, 1474
Beal Foundation, TX, 3882
Bean (Norwin S. and Elizabeth N.) Foundation, NH, 2083
Beardsley (Andrew Hubble) and Walter Raper Beardsley Foundation, see 1201
Beardsley Foundation, The, IN, 1201
Beasley (Theodore and Beulah) Foundation, Inc., TX, 3883
Beatrice Foundation, The, IL, 939
Beattie (Cordelia Lee) Foundation Trust, FL, 695
Beatty (Helen D. Groome) Trust, PA, 3523
Beazley Foundation, Inc., VA, 4153
Bechtel Foundation, CA, 87
Bechtel (S. D.), Jr. Foundation, CA, 88
Becker (A. G.) Paribas Foundation, IL, 940
Beckman (Arnold and Mabel) Foundation, CA, 89
Bedford Fund, Inc., The, NY, 2272
Bedminster Fund, Inc., The, NY, 2273
Bedsole (J. L.) Public Welfare Trust, AL, 2
Beech Aircraft Foundation, KS, 1294
Beecher (Florence Simon) Foundation, OH, 3163
Beecher (Ward) Foundation, OH, 3164
Beefeater Foundation, NY, 2274
Beeghly (The Leon A.) Fund, OH, 3165
Beerman Foundation, Inc., The, OH, 3166
Behmann Brothers Foundation, TX, 3884
Beidler (Francis) Charitable Trust, IL, 941
Beim Foundation, The, MN, 1816
Beinecke (Edwin J.) Trust, NY, 2275
Beir Foundation, The, NY, 2276
Bekins (Milo W.) Foundation, CA, 90
Belasco (The Edna & Jack) Foundation, NJ, 2101
Belden (Joseph C.) Foundation, IL, 942
Belding Hausman Foundation, Inc., see 2532
Belfer Foundation, Inc., The, NY, 2277
Belgian American Educational Foundation, Inc., CT, 498
Belk Foundation, The, NC, 3077
Belk-Simpson Foundation, SC, 3799

Bell & Howell Foundation, IL, 943
Bell (James F.) Foundation, MN, 1817
Bell Trust, TX, 3885
Bellamah (Dale J.) Foundation, NM, 2206
Beloit Foundation, Inc., WI, 4301
Belz Foundation, TN, 3828
Bemis Company Foundation, MN, 1818
Bend Foundation, MN, 1819
Bender Foundation, Inc., DC, 639
Bendheim (Charles and Els) Foundation, NY, 2278
Benedum (Claude Worthington) Foundation, PA, 3524
Beneficia Foundation, PA, 3525
Beneficial Foundation, Inc., DE, 596
Bennett (Carl and Dorothy) Foundation, Inc., CT, 499
Bennett (The James Gordon) Memorial Corporation, NY, 2279
Bentley (Alvin M.) Foundation, MI, 1671
Benton Foundation, The, DC, 640
Bentz Foundation, The, OH, 3167
Benua Foundation, Inc., The, OH, 3168
Benwood Foundation, Inc., TN, 3829
Bergen (Frank and Lydia) Foundation, NJ, 2102
Berger (H. N. and Frances C.) Foundation, CA, 91
Berger (Sol and Margaret) Foundation, NJ, 2103
Berkey (Peter) Foundation, CA, 92
Berkman (The H. L. & Louis) Foundation, see 3169
Berkman (The Louis and Sandra) Foundation, OH, 3169
Berlin (Irving) Charitable Fund, Incorporated, NY, 2280
Berlin (M. H.) Foundation, IL, 944
Berlinger (Rhonie & George) Foundation, Incorporated, NY, 2281
Bernhill Fund, The, NY, 2282
Berry (Loren M.) Foundation, OH, 3170
Berry (The Lowell) Foundation, CA, 93
Bersted Foundation, The, IL, 945
Besser Foundation, MI, 1672
Besser (Jesse) Fund, Inc., MI, 1673
Best Products Foundation, VA, 4154
Bethlehem Area Foundation, PA, 3526
Beveridge (The Frank Stanley) Foundation, Inc., MA, 1475
Beynon (The Kathryne) Foundation, CA, 94
Bezalel Foundation, Inc., NY, 2283
Bibb Foundation, Inc., The, GA, 806
Bible Alliance, FL, 696
Bicknell Fund, OH, 3171
Biddle (Margaret T.) Foundation, NY, 2284
Biddle (The Mary Duke) Foundation, NC, 3078
Bieber (The Siegfried & Josephine) Foundation, Inc., NY, 2285
Bigelow (F. R.) Foundation, MN, 1820
Bing Fund, CA, 95
Bing Fund Corporation, NV, 2076
Bing Fund Inc., NV, 2077
Bingham Enterprises Foundation of Kentucky, Inc., KY, 1335
Bingham (The William) Foundation, OH, 3172
Bingham's (Mr.) Trust for Charity, NY, 2286
Biological Humanics Foundation, TX, 3886
Birch (Stephen and Mary) Foundation, Inc., DE, 597
Bird Companies Charitable Foundation, Inc., MA, 1476
Bireley Foundation, The, CA, 96
Birmingham Foundation, MA, 1477
Birmingham Foundation, The Greater, AL, 3
Bishop (A. G.) Charitable Trust, MI, 1674
Bishop (E. K. and Lillian F.) Foundation, WA, 4220
Bishop (Edward E. and Lillian H.) Foundation, DE, 598
Bishop Foundation, WA, 4221
Bissell (J. Walton) Foundation, CT, 500
Bivins (Mary E.) Foundation, TX, 3887
Blackmer (Henry M.) Foundation, Inc., NY, 2287
Blaffer (Sarah Campbell) Foundation, TX, 3888
Blaisdell (Philo and Sarah) Foundation, PA, 3527
Blake (Curtis) Foundation, MA, 1478
Blake (S. P.) Foundation, MA, 1479
Blanchard Foundation, The, MA, 1480
Blandin (Charles K.) Foundation, MN, 1821
Blank (The Myron and Jacqueline) Charity Fund, IA, 1260
Blank (Samuel) and Family Foundation, FL, 697
Blaustein (The Jacob and Hilda) Foundation, Inc., MD, 1404

Blaustein (The Louis and Henrietta) Foundation, Inc., MD, 1405
Bleibtreu (Jacob) Foundation, Incorporated, NY, 2288
Bliss (Cornelius N.) Memorial Fund, NY, 2289
Block (The H & R) Foundation, MO, 1941
Bloedel Foundation, Inc., The, WA, 4222
Bloedorn (Walter A.) Foundation, DC, 641
Bloomingdale (Samuel J.) Foundation, NY, 2290
Blount (David S.) Educational Foundation, VA, 4155
Blount Foundation, Inc., The, AL, 4
Blue Bell Foundation, NC, 3079
Blum (Edith C.) Foundation, NY, 2291
Blum (Harry and Maribel G.) Foundation, IL, 946
Blum (The Nathan and Emily S.) Fund, IL, 947
Blumenthal Foundation, The, NC, 3080
Blumkin Foundation, Incorporated, NE, 2050
Blum-Kovler Foundation, IL, 948
Blythmour Corporation, NY, 2292
Boatmen's National Bank of St. Louis Irrevocable Charitable Trust, MO, 1942
Bobst (The Elmer and Mamdouha) Foundation, Inc., NY, 2293
Bodenwein Public Benevolent Foundation, CT, 501
Bodman Foundation, The, NY, 2294
Boehm Foundation, The, NY, 2295
Boeing Company Charitable Trust, The, WA, 4223
Boettcher Foundation, CO, 436
Bohen Foundation, The, IA, 1261
Bohnett (Vi) Memorial Foundation, HI, 891
Bolton Foundation, OH, 3173
Boone County Community Trust, MO, 1943
Booth Ferris Foundation, NY, 2296
Boothroyd (Charles H. and Bertha L.) Foundation, IL, 949
Borden Foundation, Inc., OH, 3174
Borden (The Mary Owen) Memorial Foundation, NJ, 2104
Borg-Warner Foundation, Inc., IL, 950
Borun (Anna and Harry Borun Foundation, CA, 97
Boston Fatherless & Widows Society, MA, 1481
Boston Foundation, MA, 1482
Boston Globe Foundation, The, MA, 1483
Bostwick (The Albert C.) Foundation, NY, 2297
Boswell (The James G.) Foundation, CA, 98
Bothin Foundation, The, CA, 99
Bothin Helping Fund, The, see 99
Botwinick-Wolfensohn Foundation, Incorporated, NY, 2298
Boutell (Arnold and Gertrude) Memorial Fund, MI, 1675
Bovaird (The Mervin) Foundation, OK, 3419
Bowen (Ethel N.) Foundation, WV, 4277
Bowles (The Ethel Wilson) and Robert Bowles Memorial Fund, CA, 100
Bowne (Robert) Foundation, Inc., The, NY, 2299
Bowsher-Booher Foundation, The, IN, 1202
Bowyer (The Ambrose and Gladys) Foundation, IL, 951
Boynton Gillespie Memorial Fund, IL, 952
Boynton (John W.) Fund, MA, 1484
Brach (Edwin J.) Foundation, IL, 953
Brach (Helen) Foundation, IL, 954
Brackenridge (George W.) Foundation, TX, 3889
Bradley Family Foundation, Inc., The, WI, 4302
Bradley (The Lynde and Harry) Foundation, Inc., WI, 4303
Bradley (W. C. and Sarah H.) Foundation, see 807
Bradley-Turner Foundation, GA, 807
Brady Foundation, NJ, 2105
Brady (W. H.) Foundation, Inc., WI, 4304
Braitmayer Foundation, The, MA, 1485
Brand (The Martha and Regina) Foundation, Inc., NY, 2300
Brandegee Charitable Foundation, MA, 1486
Braun (Carl F.) Trust, CA, 101
Braun Foundation, CA, 102
Braun (Victor F.) Foundation, Incorporated, WI, 4305
Bray (Viola E.) Charitable Trust, MI, 1676
Brechemin Family Foundation, The, WA, 4224
Breech Foundation, The, CA, 103
Breidenthal (Willard J. and Mary G.) Foundation, KS, 1295
Bremer Foundation, The, OH, 3175
Bremer (Otto) Foundation, MN, 1822
Brencanda Foundation, NY, 2301

Brenner (The Mervyn L.) Foundation, Inc., CA, 104
Brewer (C.) Charitable Foundation, HI, 892
Bridgeport Area Foundation, Inc., The, CT, 502
Bridges (Robert and Alice) Foundation, CA, 105
Bridwell (The J. S.) Foundation, TX, 3890
Briggs & Stratton Corporation Foundation, Inc., WI, 4306
Briggs Family Foundation, The, FL, 698
Briggs (T. W.) Welcome Wagon Foundation, Inc., TN, 3830
Bright (Horace O.) Charitable Fund, MA, 1487
Brinker (Maureen Connolly) Girls' Tennis Foundation, Inc., TX, 3891
Brinkley Foundation, The, TN, 3831
Bristol-Myers Fund, Inc., The, NY, 2302
Britton Fund, OH, 3176
Broad (The Shepard) Foundation, Inc., FL, 699
Broadhurst Foundation, OK, 3420
Brockway Glass Company Foundation, PA, 3528
Brody (Frances and Sidney) Charitable Fund, Inc., CA, 106
Bronfman (Ann L.) Foundation, NY, 2303
Bronfman (The Samuel) Foundation, Inc., NY, 2304
Bronstein (The Sol and Arlene) Foundation, IN, 1203
Brookdale Foundation, The, NY, 2305
Brooklyn Benevolent Society, NY, 2306
Brooklyn Home for Aged Men, NY, 2307
Brooks (Gladys) Foundation, NY, 2308
Brookshire (B. C. & Addie) Kleberg County Charitable Foundation, TX, 3892
Brotman Foundation of California, CA, 107
Brotz (Frank G.) Family Foundation, Inc., WI, 4307
Brown (The Dora Maclellan) Charitable Trust, TN, 3832
Brown (The E. C.) Foundation/E. C. Brown Trust, OR, 3477
Brown Foundation, Inc., The, TX, 3893
Brown (George Warren) Foundation, MO, 1944
Brown Group, Inc. Charitable Trust, MO, 1945
Brown (James Graham) Foundation, Inc., KY, 1336
Brown (Joe W. & Dorothy Dorsett) Foundation, LA, 1355
Brown (M. K.) Foundation, Inc., TX, 3894
Brown (Samuel M. and Laura H.) Charitable Trust, KS, 1296
Brown (T. J.) and C. A. Lupton Foundation, Inc., TX, 3895
Brown (W. L. Lyons) Foundation, KY, 1337
Browning (John N.) Family Fund, Inc., OH, 3177
Brownley (Walter) Trust, DC, 642
Broyhill Foundation, Inc., NC, 3081
Bruner Foundation, Inc., NY, 2309
Brunner (Fred J.) Foundation, FL, 700
Brunner (The Robert) Foundation, NY, 2310
Brunswick Foundation, Inc., The, IL, 955
Brush Foundation, The, OH, 3178
Bryan (Dodd and Dorothy L.) Foundation, WY, 4395
Bryan (James E. and Mary Z.) Foundation, Inc., NC, 3082
Bryan (The Kathleen Price and Joseph M.) Family Foundation, Inc., NC, 3083
Bryant Foundation, VA, 4156
Bryce (William and Catherine) Memorial Fund, TX, 3896
Buchalter, Nemer, Fields, Chrystie & Younger Charitable Foundation, CA, 108
Buchanan Family Foundation, The, IL, 956
Buckley (Thomas D.) Trust, NE, 2051
Buckman (John Dustin) Charitable Trust, TN, 3833
Bucyrus-Erie Foundation, Inc., WI, 4308
Buehler (A. C.) Foundation, IL, 957
Buell (Temple Hoyne) Foundation, CO, 437
Buffalo Foundation, The, NY, 2311
Buffett Foundation, The, NE, 2052
Buhl (F.H.) Trustees, see 3540
Buhl Foundation, The, PA, 3529
Bull (The Henry W.) Foundation, CA, 109
Bullard (George Newton) Foundation, TN, 3834
Bullitt Foundation, Inc., The, WA, 4225
Bulova (The Arde) Memorial Fund, Inc., NY, 2312
Bulova Fund, Inc., NY, 2313
Bunbury Company, Inc., The, NJ, 2106
Bundy Foundation, The, MI, 1677
Burchfield (Charles E.) Foundation, Inc., NY, 2314

Burden (Florence V.) Foundation, NY, 2315
Burgess (The William, Agnes & Elizabeth) Memorial Scholarship Fund, IL, 958
Burke (Thomas C.) Foundation, GA, 808
Burkitt Foundation, The, TX, 3897
Burlington Industries Foundation, NC, 3084
Burlington Northern Foundation, WA, 4226
Burnand (The Alphonse A.) Medical and Educational Foundation, CA, 110
Burnham (Alfred G.) Donor Fund, Inc., NY, 2316
Burns Family Foundation, IL, 959
Burns Foundation, Inc., see 2317
Burns (Fritz B.) Foundation, CA, 111
Burns (Jacob) Foundation, Inc., NY, 2317
Burns-Dunphy Foundation, CA, 112
Burroughs Wellcome Fund, The, NC, 3085
Burton (The William T. and Ethel Lewis) Foundation, LA, 1356
Bush (Edyth) Charitable Foundation, Inc., FL, 701
Bush Foundation, The, MN, 1823
Butler (The George and Anne) Foundation, TX, 3898
Butler (J. Homer) Foundation, NY, 2318
Butler Manufacturing Company Foundation, MO, 1946
Butler (Patrick and Aimee) Family Foundation, MN, 1824
Butt (H. E.) Foundation, TX, 3899
Butz Foundation, The, AZ, 30
Bydale Foundation, The, NY, 2319
Bynner (The Witter) Foundation for Poetry, Inc., NM, 2207
Byrnes (James F.) Foundation, SC, 3800

C B & T Charitable Trust, GA, 809
Cabell (The Robert G.) III and Maude Morgan Cabell Foundation, VA, 4157
Cabot Corporation Foundation, Inc., MA, 1488
Cabot Family Charitable Trust, MA, 1489
Cabot-Saltonstall Charitable Trust, MA, 1490
Caddock Foundation, Inc., CA, 113
Caestecker (The Charles and Marie) Foundation, IL, 960
Cafritz (The Morris and Gwendolyn) Foundation, DC, 643
Cahn Family Foundation, LA, 1357
Cain (Effie and Wofford) Foundation, TX, 3900
Caine (Marie Eccles) Charitable Foundation, UT, 4131
Cairncrest Foundation, PA, 3530
Calder (The Louis) Foundation, NY, 2320
Calhoun (Ernest N. and Cynthia S.) Foundation, PA, 3531
Calhoun (Kenneth) Charitable Trust, OH, 3179
California Community Foundation, CA, 114
California Educational Initiatives Fund, CA, 115
California Foundation for Biochemical Research, CA, 116
California Masonic Foundation, CA, 117
Calkins (Ina) Board, MO, 1947
Callaway Foundation, Inc., GA, 810
Callaway (Fuller E.) Foundation, GA, 811
Callaway (Fuller E.) Professorial Chairs, The Trust for, GA, 812
Callison Foundation, The, CA, 118
Callister (Louise E.) Foundation, UT, 4132
Callner (Milton H.) Foundation, IL, 961
Cambridge Foundation, The, MA, 1491
Cameron (Alpin J. and Alpin W.) Memorial Fund, PA, 3532
Cameron (Harry S. and Isabel C.) Foundation, TX, 3901
Camp (Apollos) and Bennet Humiston Trust, IL, 962
Camp (Carrie S.) Foundation, Inc., VA, 4158
Camp Foundation, VA, 4159
Camp (J. L.) Foundation, Inc., VA, 4160
Campbell (Bushrod H.) and Adah F. Hall Charity Fund, MA, 1492
Campbell (Charles Talbot) Foundation, PA, 3533
Campbell (J. Bulow) Foundation, GA, 813
Campbell (Max and Tookah) Foundation, OK, 3421
Campbell (Ruth and Henry) Foundation, VA, 4161
Campbell (Ruth Camp) Charitable Trust, VA, 4162
Campbell Soup Fund, NJ, 2107
Campe (The Ed Lee and Jean) Foundation, Inc., NY, 2321

Canaday (Ward M. & Mariam C.) Educational and Charitable Trust, MA, 1493
Cannon Foundation, Inc., The, NC, 3086
Cape Branch Foundation, NJ, 2108
Capital Cities Foundation, Inc., NY, 2322
Caplan (Julius H.) Charity Foundation, Inc., PA, 3534
Carbon Fuel Foundation, Inc., WV, 4278
CarEth Foundation, MA, 1494
Cargill Foundation, The, MN, 1825
Caritas Fund, NY, 2323
Carlin Fund, IL, 963
Carlsbad Foundation, Inc., NM, 2208
Carlson (The Curtis L.) Foundation, MN, 1826
Carman (Nellie Martin) Scholarship Trust, WA, 4227
Carnahan-Jackson Foundation, NY, 2324
Carnation Company Foundation, CA, 119
Carnation Company Scholarship Foundation, CA, 120
Carnegie Corporation of New York, NY, 2325
Carnegie Endowment for International Peace, DC, 644
Carnegie Foundation for the Advancement of Teaching, The, NJ, 2109
Carnegie Hero Fund Commission, PA, 3535
Carolina Steel Foundation, NC, 3087
Carolyn Foundation, MN, 1827
Carpenter Foundation, Inc., The, DE, 599
Carpenter Foundation, The, OR, 3478
Carpenter Technology Corporation Foundation, PA, 3536
Carroll Foundation, The, CO, 438
Carroll Foundation, NJ, 2110
Carson Pirie Scott Foundation, IL, 964
Carter (Amon G.) Foundation, TX, 3902
Carter Family Foundation, WV, 4279
Carter (Fay S.) Foundation, CO, 439
Carter Fund, The, NY, 2326
Carter (Marjorie Sells) Boy Scout Scholarship Fund, CT, 503
Carthage Foundation, The, PA, 3537
Cary (Mary Flagler) Charitable Trust, NY, 2327
Casey (The Annie E.) Foundation, CT, 504
Caspersen (O. W.) Foundation for Aid to Health and Education, Inc., NJ, 2111
Cassett (Louis N.) Foundation, PA, 3538
Castle Foundation, UT, 4133
Castle (Harold K. L.) Foundation, HI, 893
Castle (Samuel N. and Mary) Foundation, HI, 894
Casto (The Don M.) Foundation, OH, 3180
Caterpillar Foundation, IL, 965
Cattell (James McKeen) Fund, NY, 2328
Cawsey Trust, Inc., WA, 4228
CBI Foundation, IL, 966
CBS Foundation Inc., NY, 2329
Cenex Foundation, MN, 1828
Centennial Foundation, NY, 2330
Center (Hugh Stuart) Charitable Trust, CA, 121
Centerre Bank N.A. Charitable Trust, MO, 1948
Central and South West Foundation, TX, 3903
Central Fidelity Banks Inc. Foundation, VA, 4163
Central New York Community Foundation, Inc., NY, 2331
Central Newspapers Foundation, IN, 1204
Central Soya Foundation, IN, 1205
Central Valley Foundation, The, PA, 3539
Cessna Foundation, Inc., KS, 1297
CFS Foundation, CA, 122
Chadwick (Dorothy Jordan) Fund, NY, 2332
Chadwick Foundation, MN, 1829
Chait (The Sara) Memorial Foundation, Inc., NY, 2333
Chamberlin (Gerald W.) Foundation, Inc., MI, 1678
Chambers (James B.) Memorial, WV, 4280
Champion International Foundation, The, CT, 505
Chance Foundation, The, MO, 1949
Chandler Foundation, The, AL, 5
Chanin Family Foundation, Inc., NY, 2334
Chapin Foundation of Myrtle Beach, S.C., NC, 3088
Chapin (Frances) Foundation, IL, 967
Chapman (H. A. and Mary K.) Charitable Trust, OK, 3422
Charina Foundation, Inc., NY, 2335
Charis Fund, CA, 123
Charitable Fund, The, PA, 3540
Charities Foundation, OH, 3181
Charity, Inc., MN, 1830

Charlesbank Homes, MA, 1495
Charlestein (Julius and Ray) Foundation, PA, 3541
Charlotte Foundation, Inc., The Greater, see 3102
Charlpeg Foundation, Inc., The, NY, 2336
Charlton (Earle P.), Jr. Charitable Trust, MA, 1496
Chase (The Alfred E.) Charity Foundation, MA, 1497
Chase (Alice P.) Trust, MA, 1498
Chase Manhattan International Foundation, The, NY, 2337
Chastain (Robert Lee) and Thomas M. Chastain Charitable Foundation, FL, 702
Chatham Foundation, The, GA, 814
Chatham Foundation, Inc., NC, 3089
Chatham Valley Foundation, Inc., The, GA, 815
Chatlos Foundation, Inc., The, NY, 2338
Chattanooga, Inc., The Community Foundation of Greater, TN, 3835
Chautauqua Region Community Foundation, Inc., NY, 2339
Cheatham (Owen) Foundation, NY, 2340
Cheney (Ben B.) Foundation, WA, 4229
Chernow (Michael) Trust for the Benefit of Charity Dated 03/13/75, NY, 2341
Chernow (Michael) Trust for the Benefit of Charity Dated 4/16/68, NY, 2342
Chertkof (David W. and Annie) Mitzvah Fund, Inc., MD, 1406
Chicago Community Trust, The, IL, 968
Chicago Resource Center, IL, 969
Chicago Sun-Times Charity Trust, IL, 970
Chicago Title and Trust Company Foundation, IL, 971
Chicago Tribune Foundation, IL, 972
Chichester du Pont Foundation, Inc., DE, 600
Children's Foundation of Erie County, Inc., NY, 2343
Childress (The Francis and Miranda) Foundation, Inc., FL, 703
Childs (The Jane Coffin) Memorial Fund for Medical Research, CT, 506
Childs (Roberta M.) Charitable Foundation, MA, 1499
Chiles Foundation, OR, 3479
Chilton Foundation Trust, The, TX, 3904
China Medical Board of New York, Inc., NY, 2344
Chisholm Foundation, The, MS, 1931
Christensen (A. Lee) Family Foundation, UT, 4134
Christensen Fund, The, CA, 124
Christian Workers Foundation, The, AL, 6
Christiana Foundation, Inc., IL, 973
Chromalloy American Foundation, MO, 1950
Chrysler Corporation Fund, MI, 1679
Church of Christ Foundation, Inc., TN, 3836
CIGNA Foundation, PA, 3542
Cincinnati Foundation for the Aged, The, OH, 3182
Cincinnati Foundation, The Greater, OH, 3183
Cincinnati Milacron Foundation, OH, 3184
Cintas Foundation, Inc., NY, 2345
C.I.O.S., Inc., TX, 3905
Circle Foundation, The, MN, 1831
Circle K/Sun World Foundation, AZ, 31
C.I.T. Foundation, Inc., The, NJ, 2112
Cities Service Foundation, OK, 3423
Citizens and Southern Fund, The, GA, 816
Citizens and Southern National Bank of South Carolina Foundation, SC, 3801
Citizens Charitable Foundation, RI, 3773
Citizens Fidelity Foundation, Inc., KY, 1338
City Investing Company Foundation, CA, 125
Civitas Fund, CA, 126
Claneil Foundation, Inc., PA, 3543
Clapp (The Anne L. and George H.) Charitable and Educational Trust, PA, 3544
Clark (The Edna McConnell) Foundation, NY, 2346
Clark (Emory T.) Family Foundation, WI, 4309
Clark Foundation, IL, 974
Clark Foundation, The, NY, 2347
Clark Foundation, OR, 3480
Clark Foundation, The, TX, 3906
Clark (Frank E.) Charitable Trust, NY, 2348
Clark (Robert Sterling) Foundation, Inc., NY, 2349
Clark-Winchcole Foundation, MD, 1407
Clayton Fund, The, TX, 3907
Clemens Foundation, The, OR, 3481
Cleveland Electric Illuminating Foundation, The, OH, 3185
Cleveland Foundation, The, OH, 3186

Cleveland-Cliffs Foundation, The, OH, 3187
Clorox Company Foundation, The, CA, 127
Clowes Fund, Inc., The, IN, 1206
Cobb (Ty) Educational Fund, GA, 817
Cobble Pond Foundation, NY, 2350
Coburn (The Maurine Church) Charitable Trust, CA, 128
Coca-Cola Foundation, The, GA, 818
Cockrell Foundation, TX, 3908
Codman (The Ogden) Trust, MA, 1500
Codrington (The George W.) Charitable Foundation, OH, 3188
Cogswell Benevolent Trust, NH, 2084
Cohen (Elias A.) Foundation, Inc., NY, 2351
Cohen (The Harry) Foundation, Inc., DE, 601
Cohen (Melvin S.) Foundation, Inc., DE, 602
Cohen (Sherman & Edward Baron) Foundation, Inc., NY, 2352
Cohen (Wilfred P.) Foundation, Inc., NY, 2353
Cohen-Solomon Family Foundation, Inc., DC, 645
Cohn (Herman & Terese) Foundation, NY, 2354
Cohn (Peter A. and Elizabeth S.) Foundation, Inc., NY, 2355
Cole (Olive B.) Foundation, Inc., IN, 1207
Cole (Quincy) Trust, VA, 4164
Cole (The Robert H. and Monica M.) Foundation, TN, 3837
Coleman Charitable Trust, Inc., KS, 1298
Coleman Foundation, Inc., The, IL, 975
Coleman Foundation, The, NY, 2356
Coleman (George E.), Jr. Foundation, NY, 2357
Coleman (Sylvan C.) Foundation, CA, 129
Coles Foundation, The, NY, 2358
Colgan (The James W.) Fund, MA, 1501
Colgan (The James W.) Trust, see 1501
Collins (Carr P.) Foundation, Inc., TX, 3909
Collins Foundation, The, OR, 3482
Collins (The George and Jennie) Foundation, OK, 3424
Collins (George Fulton), Jr. Foundation, OK, 3425
Collins (The James M.) Foundation, TX, 3910
Collins (Joseph) Foundation, NY, 2359
Colorado Springs Community Trust Fund, CO, 440
Colt Industries Charitable Foundation, Inc., NY, 2360
Colt (James J.) Foundation, Inc., NY, 2361
Columbia Foundation, CA, 130
Columbus Foundation, The, OH, 3189
Commerce Foundation, The, MO, 1951
Commercial Credit Companies Foundation, Inc., MD, 1408
Commercial Shearing Foundation, OH, 3190
Common Wealth Trust, The, DE, 603
Commonwealth Fund, The, NY, 2362
Communities Foundation of Texas, Inc., TX, 3911
Community Enterprises, Inc., GA, 819
Community Foundation, Inc., The, MS, 1932
Compton Foundation, Inc., NY, 2363
Comstock Foundation, WA, 4230
ConAgra Charitable Foundation, Inc., NE, 2053
Conn Memorial Foundation, Inc., FL, 704
Connecticut Mutual Life Foundation, CT, 507
Connell (Michael J.) Foundation, CA, 131
Connelly Foundation, PA, 3545
Connemara Fund, NC, 3090
Consolidated Foods Foundation, The, see 1139
Consolidated Papers Foundation, Inc., WI, 4310
Constans-Culver Foundation, NY, 2364
Constantin Foundation, The, TX, 3912
Conston Foundation, PA, 3546
Container Corporation of America Foundation, IL, 976
Continental Bank Foundation, IL, 977
Continental Corporation Foundation, The, NY, 2365
Continental Grain Foundation, NY, 2366
Conway (Carle C.) Scholarship Foundation, CT, 508
Cook Brothers Educational Fund, CA, 132
Cook (David C.) Foundation, IL, 978
Cook (Harry) Foundation, PA, 3547
Cook (John Brown) Foundation Inc., MA, 1502
Cook (Loring) Foundation, TX, 3913
Cook (Peter C. and Emajean) Charitable Trust, MI, 1680
Cooke Foundation, Limited, HI, 895
Cooke (V. V.) Foundation Corporation, KY, 1339
Cooley (The Denton A.) Foundation, TX, 3914
Cooper Foundation, NE, 2054

Cooper Foundation, TX, 3915
Cooper Industries Foundation, TX, 3916
Cooper (The Madison Alexander) and Martha Roane
   Cooper Foundation, *see* 3915
Coors (Adolph) Foundation, CO, 441
Copeland Andelot Foundation, Inc., DE, 604
Copernicus Society of America, PA, 3548
Copley (James S.) Foundation, CA, 133
Corbett Foundation, The, OH, 3191
Corcoran Community Foundation, The, CA, 134
Cornell (Peter C.) Trust, NY, 2367
Corning Glass Works Foundation, NY, 2368
Corti Family Agricultural Fund, CA, 135
Coshocton Foundation, OH, 3192
Costa (Aubrey M.) Foundation, TX, 3917
Council on Library Resources, Inc., DC, 646
Courts Foundation, Inc., GA, 820
Cousins Foundation, Inc., The, GA, 821
Cove Charitable Trust, The, MA, 1503
Cowan (The Lillian L. and Harry A.) Foundation
   Corporation, MA, 1504
Cowden (Louetta M.) Foundation, MO, 1952
Cowell (S. H.) Foundation, CA, 136
Cowles Charitable Trust, The, NY, 2369
Cowles (Gardner and Florence Call) Foundation, Inc.,
   IA, 1262
Cowles (Harriet Cheney) Foundation, Inc., WA, 4231
Cowles (John and Elizabeth Bates) Foundation, MN,
   1832
Cowles (William H.) Foundation, Inc., WA, 4232
Cox Foundation, Inc., MA, 1505
Cox (The James M.) Foundation of Georgia, Inc., GA,
   822
Cox (Jessie B.) Charitable Trust, MA, 1506
CPC Educational Foundation, NJ, 2113
Crabtree, Trustees under the Will of Lotta M., MA,
   1507
Craig (The E. L.) Foundation, Inc., MO, 1953
Craig (Earle M.) and Margaret Peters Craig Trust, PA,
   3549
Craig (J. Paul) Foundation, TX, 3918
Craigmyle Foundation, The, NY, 2370
Crandall (J. Ford) Memorial Foundation, OH, 3193
Crane Fund, The, IL, 979
Crane Fund for Widows and Children, IL, 980
Crane (Josephine B.) Foundation, NY, 2371
Crane (The Raymond E. and Ellen F.) Foundation, FL,
   705
Crane-Rogers Foundation, The, *see* 2088
Cranshaw Corporation, NY, 2372
Cranston Foundation, The, RI, 3774
Crary (Bruce L.) Foundation, Inc., NY, 2373
Crary Home, The, PA, 3550
Crawford (E. R.) Estate, PA, 3551
Credithrift Financial - Richard E. Meier Foundation,
   Inc., IN, 1208
Crels Foundation, The, PA, 3552
Crestlea Foundation, Inc., DE, 605
Criss (Dr. C. C. and Mabel L.) Memorial Foundation,
   NE, 2055
Crocker (The Mary A.) Trust, CA, 137
Crocker National Bank Foundation, CA, 138
Crosley Foundation, The, OH, 3194
Cross Foundation, Inc., The, MO, 1954
Crosset Charitable Trust, The, OH, 3195
Crow (Trammell) Family Foundation, TX, 3919
Crowell (Henry P.) and Susan C. Crowell Trust, IL, 981
Crown (Arie and Ida) Memorial, IL, 982
Crown Central Petroleum Foundation, Inc., MD, 1409
Crown (Edward A.) Charitable Fund, IL, 983
Crown Zellerbach Foundation, CA, 139
Crum and Forster Foundation, NJ, 2114
Crummer (Roy E.) Foundation, CA, 140
Crummey (Vivan G.) Benevolent Trust, CA, 141
Crump (Joe and Jessie) Fund, TX, 3920
Crystal Foundation, *see* 3845
Crystal Trust, DE, 606
CTS Foundation, IN, 1209
Cudahy (Patrick and Anna M.) Fund, WI, 4311
Cuesta Foundation, Inc., The, OK, 3426
Cullen Foundation, The, TX, 3921
Culpeper (Charles E.) Foundation, Inc., NY, 2374
Cummings (Frances & Edwin) Memorial Fund, NY,
   2375

Cummings (James H.) Foundation, Inc., NY, 2376
Cummins Engine Foundation, IN, 1210
CUNA Mutual Insurance Group Charitable
   Foundation, Inc., WI, 4312
Cuneo Foundation, The, IL, 984
Cunningham (Laura Moore) Foundation, Inc., ID, 911
Currey (Brownlee) Foundation, TN, 3838
Curtice-Burns/Pro-Fac Foundation, NY, 2377
Curtis Mathes Foundation, TX, 3922
Cyclops Foundation, PA, 3553

D and R Fund, IL, 985
Dade Foundation, FL, 706
Dalis Foundation, VA, 4165
Dallas Foundation, The, TX, 3923
Dallas Morning News - WFAA Foundation, The, TX,
   3924
Dallas Rehabilitation Foundation, TX, 3925
Dalton (Dorothy U.) Foundation, Inc., MI, 1681
Daly (Bernard) Educational Fund, OR, 3483
Damien Foundation, CA, 142
Dammann Fund, Inc., The, NY, 2378
Dan River Foundation, VA, 4166
Dana (The Charles A.) Foundation, Incorporated, NY,
   2379
Dana Corporation Foundation, OH, 3196
Dana (Herman) Charitable Trust, MA, 1508
Danforth Foundation, The, MO, 1955
Daniel Foundation of Alabama, The, AL, 7
Daniel Foundation of South Carolina, The, SC, 3802
Daniel (Gerard & Ruth) Foundation, Inc., NY, 2380
Daniels (Fred Harris) Foundation, Inc., MA, 1509
Daniels (The Josephus) Charitable Foundation, NC,
   3091
Darby (Edith and Harry) Foundation, KS, 1299
Darrah (Jessie S.) Charitable Trust, NY, 2381
Dauby (Nathan L.) Charity Fund, OH, 3197
Daugherty Foundation, ID, 912
Davee Foundation, The, IL, 986
Davenport (George P.) Trust Fund, ME, 1392
Davenport Memorial Foundation, MA, 1510
Davenport-Hatch Foundation, Inc., The, NY, 2382
Davidson Family Charitable Foundation, TX, 3926
Davidson (The Philip) Foundation, Inc., *see* 2383
Davidson-Krueger Foundation Inc., The, NY, 2383
Davies Charitable Trust, CA, 143
Davies Foundation, The, HI, 896
Davis (The Arthur Vining) Foundations, FL, 707
Davis (Edwin W. and Catherine M.) Foundation, MN,
   1833
Davis Foundation, Inc., The, GA, 823
Davis (Irene E. and George A.) Foundation, MA, 1511
Davis (James A. and Juliet L.) Foundation, Inc., KS,
   1300
Davis (Ken W.) Foundation, TX, 3927
Davis (The Leonard and Sophie) Foundation, Inc., NY,
   2384
Davis (M. Austin) Family-WD Charities, Inc., FL, 708
Davis (Shelby Cullom) Foundation, NY, 2385
Davis (Simon and Annie) Foundation, NY, 2386
Davis (The Tine W.) Family - W.D. Charities, Inc., FL,
   709
Davis (The Tine Wayne) Foundation, Inc., *see* 709
Day (Carl and Virginia Johnson) Trust, MS, 1933
Day (Cecil B.) Foundation, Inc., GA, 824
Day Companies Foundation, Inc., *see* 824
Day Foundation, The, TN, 3839
Day (Nancy Sayles) Foundation, CT, 509
Day (Willametta K.) Foundation, CA, 144
Dayco Charitable Foundation, Inc., OH, 3198
Dayton Foundation, The, OH, 3199
Dayton Hudson Foundation, MN, 1834
Dayton Malleable Foundation, The, *see* 3149
Daywood Foundation, Inc., The, WV, 4281
de Guigne (Christian) Memorial Foundation, CA, 145
de Hirsch (The Baron) Fund, NY, 2387
De Jur (Harry) Foundation, Inc., NY, 2388
de Kay Foundation, The, NY, 2389
de Rothschild (B.) Foundation for the Advancement of
   Science in Israel, NY, 2390
de Rothschild (The Edmond) Foundation, NY, 2391
Dealey (The G. B.) Foundation, *see* 3924
Dean (Joel) Foundation, Inc., MD, 1410

DeBakey Medical Foundation, The, TX, 3928
DeCamp (The Ira W.) Foundation, NY, 2392
Decio (Arthur J.) Foundation, IN, 1211
Dee (Annie Taylor) Foundation, UT, 4135
Dee (Lawrence T. and Janet T.) Foundation, UT, 4136
Deer Creek Foundation, MO, 1956
Deere (John) Foundation, IL, 987
Deering Foundation, IL, 988
Deicke (Edwin F.) Foundation, FL, 710
DeKalb AgResearch Foundation, The, IL, 989
Delacorte (George) Fund, FL, 711
Delany (Beatrice P.) Charitable Trust, NY, 2393
Dell (The Hazel) Foundation, CT, 510
Delmar (The Charles) Foundation, DC, 647
Delmas (The Gladys Krieble) Foundation, NY, 2394
Deloitte Haskins & Sells Foundation, NY, 2395
DeLoura Family Trust, The, MA, 1512
Delta Air Lines Foundation, GA, 825
DeLuxe Check Printers Foundation, MN, 1835
DeMille (Cecil B.) Trust, CA, 146
Demmer (Edward U.) Foundation, WI, 4313
Demos (N.) Foundation, Inc., IL, 990
DeMoss (Arthur S.) Foundation, PA, 3554
Demoulas Foundation, MA, 1513
Dennett (Marie G.) Foundation, CT, 511
Dent (Harry) Family Foundation, Inc., NY, 2396
Denver Foundation, The, CO, 442
Deposit Guaranty Foundation, MS, 1934
DeRance, Inc., WI, 4314
DeRoy (The Helen L.) Foundation, MI, 1682
DeRoy Testamentary Foundation, MI, 1683
Des Moines Community Foundation, Greater, IA, 1263
DeSoto Foundation, IL, 991
Detroit Community Trust, The, MI, 1684
Dettman (Leroy E.) Foundation, Inc., FL, 712
Deuble (George H.) Foundation, OH, 3200
Deutsch Foundation, The, CA, 147
DeVlieg (The Charles B. and Charles R.) Foundation,
   MI, 1685
Devonshire Associates, MA, 1514
DeVore Foundation, Inc., KS, 1301
DeVos (The Richard and Helen) Foundation, MI, 1686
Dewar (James A. and Jessie Smith) Foundation, Inc.,
   NY, 2397
DeWaters Charitable Trust, MI, 1687
Dewey (John) Foundation, NY, 2398
Dexter Corporation Foundation, Inc., CT, 512
Dexter (Eugene A.) Charitable Fund, MA, 1515
Diamond M Foundation, Inc., The, TX, 3929
Dibner Fund, Inc., The, CT, 513
Dickson Foundation, Inc., The, NC, 3092
Dickson (The Raymond) Foundation, TX, 3930
Dickson (Rush S.) Family Foundation, Inc., NC, 3093
Dietrich (The Daniel W.) Foundation, Inc., PA, 3555
Dietrich Foundation (Incorporated), The, PA, 3556
Diller (The William & Helen) Charitable Foundation,
   NJ, 2115
Dillon (Clarence and Anne) Dunwalke Trust, NY, 2399
Dillon Foundation, IL, 992
Dillon Fund, The, NY, 2400
Dimick Foundation, The, DC, 648
Discount Foundation, The, DC, 649
Disney Foundation, CA, 148
Disney (The Lillian B.) Foundation, CA, 149
Disney (Roy) Family Foundation, CA, 150
Distribution Fund, The, CA, 151
Dively (Geo. S.) Foundation, OH, 3201
Dobbs (Helen and Howard) Foundation, GA, 826
Dobson Foundation, Inc., The, NY, 2401
Dobson (Nellie) Trust, OK, 3427
Dodge (Cleveland H.) Foundation, Inc., NY, 2402
Dodge (Geraldine R.) Foundation, Incorporated, NJ,
   2116
Dodge Jones Foundation, TX, 3931
Dodson (The James Glenwell and Clara May)
   Foundation, GA, 827
Doe (The Marguerite) Foundation, CA, 152
Doehla (Harry) Foundation, Inc., MA, 1516
Doelger Charitable Trust, CA, 153
Doft (Beryl H.) Foundation, Inc., NY, 2403
Doheny (Carrie Estelle) Foundation, CA, 154
Doherty (The Henry L. and Grace) Charitable
   Foundation, Inc., NY, 2404
Dolese Foundation, The, OK, 3428

Dolfinger-McMahon Foundation, PA, 3557
Domino Foundation, CA, 155
Donaldson Foundation, The, MN, 1836
Donaldson (Oliver S. and Jennie R.) Charitable Trust, MA, 1517
Donnell (Lester F.) Memorial Fund, OH, 3202
Donnelley (Elliott and Ann) Foundation, IL, 993
Donnelley (Gaylord and Dorothy) Foundation, IL, 994
Donnelley (Gaylord) Foundation, see 994
Donnelly (Mary J.) Foundation, PA, 3558
Donner (The William H.) Foundation, Inc., NY, 2405
Donovan Leisure Newton & Irvine Foundation, Inc., NY, 2406
Dorminy (John Henry) Foundation, Inc., GA, 828
Dorot Foundation, NY, 2407
Dorr Foundation, NY, 2408
Dorset Foundation, The, TX, 3932
Doskocil Family Foundation, Inc., The, KS, 1302
Doss (The M. S.) Foundation, TX, 3933
Doubleday (Russell and Janet) Fund, NY, 2409
Dougherty Foundation, Inc., AZ, 32
Dougherty (The James R.), Jr. Foundation, TX, 3934
Douty (Alfred and Mary) Foundation, PA, 3559
Dover Foundation, Inc., The, NC, 3094
Dow Chemical Company Foundation, The, MI, 1688
Dow (Herbert H. and Barbara C.) Foundation, MI, 1689
Dow (The Herbert H. and Grace A.) Foundation, MI, 1690
Dow Jones Foundation, NY, 2410
Dow Jones Newspaper Fund, Inc., The, NJ, 2117
Dozor (Harry T. & Shirley W.) Foundation, PA, 3560
Dravo Corporation & Subsidiaries Charitable Trust, PA, 3561
Dreier-Penrith Family Foundation, IL, 995
Dresser Foundation, Inc., TX, 3935
Dresser-Harbison Foundation, Inc., TX, 3936
Dreyfus (The Camille and Henry) Foundation, Inc., NY, 2411
Dreyfus (Jean and Louis) Foundation, Inc., NY, 2412
Dreyfus (The Max and Victoria) Foundation, Inc., NY, 2413
Driscoll Foundation, MN, 1837
Drum Foundation, The, CA, 156
du Bois (E. Blois) Foundation, Inc., AZ, 33
du Pont (Alfred I.) Foundation, FL, 713
Duberg (Dorys McConnell) Charitable Trust, CT, 514
Duda Foundation, The, FL, 714
Dufresne (The Walter and Leona) Foundation, Inc., ID, 913
Duke (The Doris) Foundation, Inc., NJ, 2118
Duke Endowment, The, NC, 3095
Dula (The Caleb C. and Julia W.) Educational and Charitable Foundation, NY, 2414
Dumke (Dr. Ezekiel R. and Edna Wattis) Foundation, UT, 4137
Dun & Bradstreet Corporation Foundation, The, NY, 2415
Duncan (A. J. and Jessie) Foundation, TX, 3937
Duncan (Harry F.) Foundation, Inc., MD, 1411
Duncan (John G.) Trust, CO, 443
Duncan (The Lillian H. and C. W.) Foundation, TX, 3938
Dunspaugh-Dalton Foundation, Inc., The, FL, 715
Dupar Charitable Foundation, see 4233
Dupar Foundation, WA, 4233
duPont (Jessie Ball) Religious, Charitable and Educational Fund, FL, 716
Durfee Foundation, The, CA, 157
Dutchess County, The Area Fund of, NY, 2416
Dweck (Samuel K.) Foundation, DC, 650
Dye (The Glen M.) - Pako Foundation, MN, 1838
Dyson Foundation, NY, 2417

E & M Charities, IA, 1264
Eagle-Picher Foundation, The, OH, 3203
Eagles Memorial Foundation, Inc., FL, 717
Earhart Foundation, MI, 1691
Earl-Beth Foundation, MI, 1692
Early (Margaret E.) Medical Research Trust, CA, 158
Easley (Andrew H. & Anne O.) Trust, VA, 4167
Easley Foundation, The, see 4167
East Bay Community Foundation, The, CA, 159

Eastern Associated Foundation, The, MA, 1518
Eastman Kodak Charitable Trust, NY, 2418
Eaton Charitable Fund, The, OH, 3204
Eaton (Georgina Goddard) Memorial Fund, MA, 1519
Ebsary Charitable Foundation, The, NY, 2419
Eccles (The George S.) and Dolores Dore Eccles Foundation, UT, 4138
Eccles (Marriner S.) Foundation, UT, 4139
Eccles (Ralph M. and Ella M.) Foundation, PA, 3562
Echlin Foundation, FL, 718
Eckerd (Jack) Corporation Foundation, FL, 719
Eddy (C. K.) Family Memorial Fund, MI, 1693
Eddy Foundation, MN, 1839
Eder (The Sidney and Arthur) Foundation, Inc., CT, 515
Ederic Foundation, Inc., DE, 607
Edison Brothers Stores Foundation, MO, 1957
Edison (Charles) Fund, NJ, 2119
Edison (Harry) Foundation, MO, 1958
Educational Foundation of America, The, CT, 516
Edwards (J. E. S.) Foundation, TX, 3939
Edwards Memorial Trust, MN, 1840
Edwards (O. P. and W. E.) Foundation, Inc., VT, 4147
Edwards Scholarship Fund, MA, 1520
EG&G Foundation, MA, 1521
Egenton Home, MD, 1412
Eichenbaum (J. K. and Inez) Foundation, CA, 160
8 South 54 East, Inc., CO, 444
EIS Foundation, Inc., CT, 517
Eisenberg (The George M.) Foundation, IL, 996
El Paso Community Foundation, The, TX, 3940
El Pomar Foundation, CO, 445
El-An Foundation, OH, 3205
Elizabeth City Foundation, NC, 3096
Elizabeth Foundation, The, NJ, 2120
Elkins (J. A. and Isabel M.) Foundation, TX, 3941
Ellis (Charles E.) Grant and Scholarship Fund, PA, 3563
Ellison Foundation, The, MA, 1522
Ellsworth (Ruth H. and Warren A.) Foundation, MA, 1523
Ellwood Foundation, The, TX, 3942
Elsmere Foundation, Inc., NY, 2420
ELW Foundation, The, NV, 2078
Emerson Charitable Trust, MO, 1959
Emerson (Fred L.) Foundation, Inc., NY, 2421
Emery Air Freight Educational Foundation, Inc., CT, 518
Emery (The Thomas J.) Memorial, OH, 3206
Emporium Foundation, Inc., The, PA, 3564
EMSA Fund, Inc., GA, 829
Endowment for Biblical Research, Boston, MA, 1524
Engelhard (The Charles) Foundation, NJ, 2121
English (The Florence C. and Harry L.) Memorial Fund, GA, 830
English Foundation-Trust, The, VA, 4168
English (W. C.) Foundation, VA, 4169
English-Bonter-Mitchell Foundation, IN, 1212
Eno Foundation for Transportation, Inc., CT, 519
Enright Foundation, Inc., MO, 1960
ENSERCH Foundation, TX, 3943
Ensign-Bickford Foundation, Inc., The, CT, 520
Ensworth Charitable Foundation, The, CT, 521
Equifax Foundation, GA, 831
Equitable Bank Foundation, Inc., The, MD, 1413
Equitable Trust Company Foundation, Inc., see 1413
Erie Community Foundation, The, PA, 3565
Ernst & Whinney Foundation, OH, 3207
Ernsthausen (John F. and Doris E.) Charitable Foundation, OH, 3208
Erpf (The Armand G.) Fund, Inc., NY, 2422
Esmark, Inc. Foundation, see 939
Essick Foundation, Inc., The, CA, 161
Ettinger Foundation, Inc., The, NY, 2423
Evans (D. A. & J. A.) Memorial Foundation, PA, 3566
Evans Foundation, Inc., The, TN, 3840
Evans (Lettie Pate) Foundation, Inc., GA, 832
Evans (The T. M.) Foundation, Inc., NY, 2424
Evans (The Thomas J.) Foundation, OH, 3209
Evans (Wilmot Roby) Corporation, MA, 1525
Everett (Fred M. and Ora H.) Charitable Trust, NY, 2425
Evinrude (The Ole) Foundation, IL, 997
Evinrude (Ralph) Foundation, Inc., WI, 4315
Evjue Foundation, Inc., The, WI, 4316
Ex-cell-o Corporation Foundation, MI, 1694

Exxon Education Foundation, NY, 2426
Eyman (Jesse) Trust, OH, 3210

Factor (Max) Family Foundation, CA, 162
Fahrney Education Foundation, IA, 1265
Faigle (Ida M.) Charitable Foundation, MI, 1695
Fain Foundation, TX, 3944
Fair (The R. W.) Foundation, TX, 3945
Fairchild Industries Foundation, Inc., MD, 1414
Fairchild (The Sherman) Foundation, Inc., CT, 522
Fairey (Kittie M.) Educational Fund, SC, 3803
Fairfield (Freeman E.) - Meeker Charitable Trust, CO, 446
Fairfield (Freeman E.) Foundation, CA, 163
Faith Foundation, TX, 3946
Faith Home Foundation, NY, 2427
Falk (The David) Foundation, Inc., FL, 720
Falk (Dr. Ralph and Marian) Medical Research Foundation, IL, 998
Falk (Herman W.) Memorial Foundation, Inc., WI, 4317
Falk (Leon) Family Trust, PA, 3567
Falk (Maurice) Medical Fund, PA, 3568
Falk (Michael David) Foundation, Inc., NY, 2428
Familian (Isadore and Sunny) Family Foundation, CA, 164
Familian (Zalec) Foundation, CA, 165
Fargo-Moorhead Area Foundation, ND, 3139
Farish (The William Stamps) Fund, TX, 3947
Farm Foundation, IL, 999
Farnsworth (Charles H.) Trust, MA, 1526
Fasken Foundation, The, TX, 3948
Faude (C. Frederick) Foundation, CA, 166
Faulkner (Marianne Gaillard) Trust, NY, 2429
Favrot (Clifford F.) Family Fund, LA, 1358
Favrot Fund, The, TX, 3949
Federal National Mortgage Association Foundation, DC, 651
Federal-Mogul Corporation Charitable Trust, MI, 1696
Federated Department Stores Foundation, OH, 3211
Federation Foundation of Greater Philadelphia, PA, 3569
Feild Co-Operative Association, Inc., MS, 1935
Feinstein (Myer and Rosaline) Foundation, PA, 3570
Feitelson (Lorser and Helen Lundeberg) Arts Foundation, CA, 167
Felburn Foundation, DC, 652
Feld (Milton W.) Charitable Trust, MO, 1961
Feldberg Family Foundation, The, MA, 1527
Feldman Foundation, The, TX, 3950
Fellows (J. Hugh and Earle W.) Memorial Fund, FL, 721
Fel-Pro/Mecklenburger Foundation, IL, 1000
Fels (Samuel S.) Fund, PA, 3571
Female Association of Philadelphia, PA, 3572
Fenton Foundation, Inc., WV, 4282
Ferebee (Percy B.) Endowment, NC, 3097
Ferguson (Arch L.) Foundation, Inc., TX, 3951
Ferkauf (The Eugene and Estelle) Foundation, NY, 2430
Ferro Foundation, OH, 3212
FFHS & J Fund, Inc., NY, 2431
Fidelity Foundation, MA, 1528
Fidelity Union Foundation, NJ, 2122
Field Foundation, Inc., The, NY, 2432
Field Foundation of Illinois, Inc., The, IL, 1001
Fieldcrest Foundation, NC, 3098
Fields (Laura) Trust, OK, 3429
Fife (Elias and Bertha) Foundation, Inc., NY, 2433
1525 Foundation, The, OH, 3213
Fifth Third Foundation, The, OH, 3214
Fikes (Leland) Foundation, Inc., TX, 3952
Filene (Lincoln and Therese) Foundation, Inc., MA, 1529
Finch (The Doak) Foundation, NC, 3099
Finch (Thomas Austin) Foundation, NC, 3100
Fingerhut Family Foundation, The, MN, 1841
Fink Foundation, KS, 1303
Fink Foundation, Inc., NY, 2434
Fink (George R. and Elise M.) Foundation, MI, 1697
Finley (A. E.) Foundation, Inc., NC, 3101
Finley (J. B.) Charitable Trust, PA, 3573
Finnegan (John D.) Foundation, OH, 3215
Fire Fund Endowment, CA, 168

Fireman's Fund Insurance Company Foundation, CA, 169
Firestone Trust Fund, The, OH, 3216
Firman Fund, OH, 3217
First and Merchants Foundation, Inc., see 4201
First Atlanta Foundation, Inc., GA, 833
First Bank System Foundation, MN, 1842
First Boston Foundation Trust, The, NY, 2435
First Educational and Charitable Trust of Canton, Ohio, OH, 3218
First Hawaiian Foundation, HI, 897
First Interstate Bank Foundation, CO, 447
First Interstate Bank of Arizona, N.A. Charitable Foundation, AZ, 34
First Interstate Bank of California Foundation, CA, 170
First Maryland Foundation, Inc., MD, 1415
First Mississippi Corporation Foundation, Inc., MS, 1936
First National Bank in Wichita Charitable Trust, KS, 1304
First National Bank of Arizona Charitable Foundation, see 34
First National Bank of Chicago Foundation, IL, 1002
First National Bank of Cincinnati Foundation, The, OH, 3219
First National Bank of Minneapolis Foundation, MN, 1843
First National Boston Corporation Foundation, see 1473
First National Family Foundation, Inc., LA, 1359
First National Foundation, Inc., OK, 3430
First Wisconsin Foundation, Inc., WI, 4318
Fischbach Foundation Incorporated, NY, 2436
Fischel (Harry and Jane) Foundation, NY, 2437
Fischer-Bauer-Knirps Foundation, MO, 1962
Fish (Ray C.) Foundation, TX, 3953
Fish (Vain and Harry) Foundation, Inc., NY, 2438
Fishback (Harmes C.) Foundation Trust, CO, 448
Fisher Charitable Trust, IL, 1003
Fisher Foundation, Inc., CT, 523
Fisher (Gramma) Foundation, IA, 1266
Fiterman (The Jack and Bessie) Foundation, MN, 1844
Fitzgerald (Father James M.) Scholarship Trust, IL, 1004
Flack (J. Hunter) Foundation, Inc., AL, 8
Flagler Foundation, The, VA, 4170
Flarsheim (Louis and Elizabeth) Charitable Foundation, MO, 1963
Fleet Charitable Trust, RI, 3775
Fleischmann Foundation, The, OH, 3220
Fleishhacker (Janet and Mortimer) Foundation, CA, 171
Fleishhacker (Mortimer) Foundation, CA, 172
Fleming Foundation, The, TX, 3954
Flemm (John J.) Foundation, Inc., NY, 2439
Flickinger Memorial Trust, Inc., The, OH, 3221
Flinn Foundation, The, AZ, 35
Flint Public Trust, The, MI, 1698
Florence Foundation, The, TX, 3955
Flowers (Albert W. and Edith V.) Charitable Trust, OH, 3222
Flowers (H. Fort) Foundation, Inc., OH, 3223
Fluor Foundation, The, CA, 173
FMC Foundation, IL, 1005
Foellinger Foundation, Inc., IN, 1213
Foerderer (Percival E. and Ethel Brown) Foundation, PA, 3574
Fohs Foundation, OR, 3484
Folger Fund, The, DC, 653
Folsom (Maud Glover) Foundation, Inc., CT, 524
Fondren Foundation, The, TX, 3956
Foote, Cone & Belding Foundation, IL, 1006
Forbes Foundation, NY, 2440
Forbes (Herman) Charitable Trust, NY, 2441
Forchheimer Foundation, Inc., NY, 2442
Ford (Benson and Edith) Fund, MI, 1699
Ford (The Edward E.) Foundation, NY, 2443
Ford (Eleanor and Edsel) Fund, MI, 1700
Ford Foundation, The, NY, 2444
Ford (The Henry) II Fund, MI, 1701
Ford (Jefferson Lee) III Memorial Foundation, Inc., FL, 722
Ford (Kenneth W.) Foundation, OR, 3485
Ford Motor Company Fund, MI, 1702
Ford (The S. N.) and Ada Ford Fund, OH, 3224
Ford (Walter and Josephine) Fund, MI, 1703

Ford (William and Martha) Fund, MI, 1704
Forest City Enterprises Charitable Foundation, Inc., OH, 3225
Forest Foundation, WA, 4234
Forest Fund, The, IL, 1007
Forest Lawn Foundation, CA, 174
Fort Howard Paper Foundation, Inc., WI, 4319
Fort Wayne Foundation, Inc., The, IN, 1214
Fortin Foundation of Montana, MT, 2044
Foster Charitable Trust, PA, 3575
Foster (Joseph C. and Esther) Foundation, Inc., MA, 1530
Foundation for Agronomic Research, Inc., GA, 834
Foundation for Child Development, NY, 2445
Foundation for Health Enhancement, IL, 1008
Foundation for Microbiology, NY, 2446
Foundation for Middle East Peace, DC, 654
Foundation for the Carolinas, NC, 3102
Foundation for the Needs of Others, Inc., NY, 2447
Fourth National Bank in Wichita Charitable Trust, KS, 1305
Fowler (John Edward) Memorial Foundation, DC, 655
Fox (The Harry K. & Emma R.) Charitable Foundation, OH, 3226
Fox (Jacob L. & Lewis) Foundation Trust, CT, 525
France (The Jacob and Annita) Foundation, Inc., MD, 1416
France Stone Foundation, OH, 3227
Francis (The Parker B.) Foundation, see 1324
Francis (Parker B.) III Foundation, KS, 1306
Frank (A. J.) Family Foundation, OR, 3486
Frank (Ernst & Elfriede) Foundation, NY, 2448
Frank (Zollie and Elaine) Fund, IL, 1009
Frankel (George and Elizabeth F.) Foundation, Inc., NY, 2449
Frankenthal Family Foundation, Inc., WI, 4320
Franklin (John and Mary) Foundation, Inc., GA, 835
Frasch (Herman) Foundation for Chemical Research, NY, 2450
Frazier Foundation, Inc., LA, 1360
Frear (Mary D. and Walter F.) Eleemosynary Trust, HI, 898
Freed (The Allie S. and Frances W.) Foundation, Inc., see 656
Freed Foundation, Inc., The, DC, 656
Freeman (Carl M.) Foundation, Inc., MD, 1417
Freeman (The Ella West) Foundation, LA, 1361
Frees Foundation, The, TX, 3957
Frelinghuysen Foundation, The, NJ, 2123
Fremont Area Foundation, The, MI, 1705
French (D. E.) Foundation, Inc., NY, 2451
Frese (Arnold D.) Foundation, Inc., NY, 2452
Freund (The Erwin O. and Rosalind H.) Foundation, IL, 1010
Freygang (Walter Henry) Foundation, NH, 2085
Fribourg Foundation, Inc., NY, 2453
Frick (The Helen Clay) Foundation, PA, 3576
Frick (Henry C.) Educational Commission, PA, 3577
Friedman Brothers Foundation, CA, 175
Friendly-Rosenthal Foundation, Inc., The, OR, 3487
Friendship Fund, Inc., MA, 1531
Frisch Foundation, Inc., The, NJ, 2124
Froderman Foundation, Inc., The, IN, 1215
Frohlich (Ludwig W.) Charitable Trust, NY, 2454
Frohm (Carl) Memorial Foundation, NE, 2056
Frohman (The Sidney) Foundation, OH, 3228
Frohring (The William O. and Gertrude Lewis) Foundation, Inc., OH, 3229
Fromm (Walter and Mabel) Scholarship Trust, WI, 4321
Frost Foundation, Ltd., The, CO, 449
Frost (Meshech) Testamentary Trust, OH, 3230
Frueauff (Charles A.) Foundation, Inc., NY, 2455
Fruehauf Corporation Charitable Fund, Inc., MI, 1706
Fruehauf Foundation, The, MI, 1707
Fry (Erwin) Foundation, AZ, 36
Fry (Lily Palmer) Memorial Trust, CT, 526
Fry (Lloyd A.) Foundation, IL, 1011
Fuchs (Gottfried & Mary) Foundation, WA, 4235
Fuchsberg (Abraham) Family Foundation, Inc., NY, 2456
Fuchsberg Family Foundation, Inc., NY, 2457
Fuld (Helene) Health Trust, NY, 2458
Fuller (C. G.) Foundation, SC, 3804

Fuller Foundation, Inc., The, MA, 1532
Fuller Foundation, Inc., The, TX, 3958
Fuller (George F. and Sybil H.) Foundation, MA, 1533
Fullerton Foundation, The, NY, 2459
Fulton Charitable Trust, see 805
Fund for New Jersey, The, NJ, 2125
Fund for the City of New York, Inc., NY, 2460
Fuqua (J. B.) Foundation, Inc., GA, 836
Furnas Foundation, Inc., IL, 1012
Furst (Sol and Hilda) Foundation, NY, 2461
Fusenot (Georges and Germaine) Charity Foundation, CA, 176

G. P. Foundation, Ltd., WI, 4322
G.A.G. Charitable Corporation, CA, 177
Gaisman (The Catherine and Henry J.) Foundation, NY, 2462
Galkin (Ira S. and Anna) Charitable Trust, RI, 3776
Gallagher (The Lewis P.) Family Foundation, OH, 3231
Gallo (The Ernest) Foundation, CA, 178
Gallo Foundation, CA, 179
Gallo (The Julio R.) Foundation, CA, 180
Galster Foundation, The, CA, 181
Galter Foundation, The, IL, 1013
Galvin (Paul V.) Trust, IL, 1014
Galvin (Robert W.) Foundation, IL, 1015
Gamble (The B. C.) and P. W. Skogmo Foundation, MN, 1845
Gamble (B. C.) Foundation, see 1845
Gannett Foundation, Inc., NY, 2463
Gannett (Frank) Newspapercarrier Scholarships, Inc., NY, 2464
Gannett (Guy) Foundation, ME, 1393
GAR Foundation, The, OH, 3232
Garb Foundation, The, MI, 1708
Gardner Foundation, The, OH, 3233
Garland (John Jewett & H. Chandler) Foundation, CA, 182
Garrison Community Foundation of Gaston County, Inc., NC, 3103
Garvey (Edward Chase) Memorial Foundation, MO, 1964
Garvey Foundation, KS, 1307
Garvey Kansas Foundation, KS, 1308
Garvey Texas Foundation, Inc., TX, 3959
Gates Foundation, CO, 450
Gaylord (The Catherine Manley) Foundation, MO, 1965
Gaylord (Clifford Willard) Foundation, MO, 1966
Gazette Foundation, IA, 1267
Gebbie Foundation, Inc., NY, 2465
GEICO Philanthropic Foundation, DC, 657
Geist Foundation, The, NJ, 2126
Gelatt Foundation, Inc., The, WI, 4323
Gelb (Lawrence M.) Foundation, Inc., NY, 2466
Gelco Foundation, The, MN, 1846
Gellert (The Carl) Foundation, CA, 183
Gellert (The Fred) Foundation, CA, 184
Gelman (Melvin and Estelle) Foundation, DC, 658
Gemco Charitable and Scholarship Fund, CA, 185
GenCorp Foundation Inc., OH, 3234
General Educational Fund, Inc., VT, 4148
General Electric Foundation, CT, 527
General Foods Fund, Inc., The, NY, 2467
General Mills Foundation, MN, 1847
General Motors Cancer Research Foundation, Inc., MI, 1709
General Motors Foundation, MI, 1710
General Service Foundation, MN, 1848
General Telephone & Electronics Foundation, see 531
General Tire Foundation, Inc., see 3234
Genesis Foundation, RI, 3777
GenRad Foundation, MA, 1534
George Foundation, The, OH, 3235
George Foundation, The, TX, 3960
Georgia-Pacific Foundation, Inc., GA, 837
Geraldi-Norton Memorial Corporation, IL, 1016
Gerard (Sumner) Foundation, DE, 608
Gerber Baby Foods Fund, MI, 1711
Gerber (The Max and Lottie) Foundation, Inc., IL, 1017
Gerbode (Wallace Alexander) Foundation, CA, 186
Gerlach Foundation, Inc., OH, 3236
German Marshall Fund of the United States, DC, 659

German Protestant Orphan Asylum Association, LA, 1362
Gershon Ben-Ephraim Fund, IN, 1216
Gerson (Benjamin S.) Family Foundation, OH, 3237
Gerstacker (The Rollin M.) Foundation, MI, 1712
Getty (J. Paul) Museum, see 187
Getty (J. Paul) Trust, CA, 187
Getty Oil Company Foundation, CA, 188
Gheens Foundation, Inc., The, KY, 1340
Gholston (J. K.) Trust, GA, 838
Giant Food Foundation, Inc., MD, 1418
Gibbs Brothers Foundation, NY, 2468
Gibson (Addison H.) Foundation, PA, 3578
Gibson (E. L.) Foundation, AL, 9
Giddings and Lewis Foundation, Inc., WI, 4324
Gifford (Kenneth P.) Foundation, TX, 3961
Gifford (The Rosamond) Charitable Corporation, NY, 2469
Gilbert (Price), Jr. Charitable Trust, GA, 839
Gilcrease (Thomas) Foundation, OK, 3431
Gildred Foundation, CA, 189
Gill (A. Smith) Trust, TX, 3962
Gillett (Elesabeth Ingalls) Foundation, PA, 3579
Gillette Charitable and Educational Foundation, The, MA, 1535
Gilman (The Howard) Foundation, Inc., NY, 2470
Gilmore (Earl B.) Foundation, CA, 190
Gilmore Foundation, MI, 1713
Gilmore (The William G.) Foundation, CA, 191
Gimbel (Bernard F. and Alva B.) Foundation, Inc., CT, 528
Gimbel-Saks Trust Fund, NY, 2471
Ginsberg (Moses) Family Foundation, Inc., NY, 2472
Ginter (Karl and Anna) Foundation, NC, 3104
Girard Trust Bank Foundation, PA, 3580
Glancy (Lenora and Alfred) Foundation, Inc., GA, 840
Glaser Foundation, Inc., WA, 4236
Glazer (Madelyn L.) Foundation, IA, 1268
Gleason Fund, Inc., NY, 2473
Gleason (James) Foundation, CA, 192
Gleason (Katherine) Foundation, CA, 193
Gleason Memorial Fund, Inc., NY, 2474
Glencairn Foundation, PA, 3581
Glencoe Foundation, Inc., DE, 609
Glendorn Foundation, PA, 3582
Glenn (Paul F.) Foundation for Medical Research, Inc., NY, 2475
Glenn (The Wilbur Fisk) Memorial Foundation, Inc., GA, 841
Glens Falls Foundation, The, NY, 2476
Glickenhaus Foundation, The, NY, 2477
Gloeckner (The Fred C.) Foundation, Inc., NY, 2478
Glosser (David A.) Foundation, PA, 3583
Goddard (The Charles B.) Foundation, OK, 3432
Goerlich Family Foundation, OH, 3238
Goldberg (Israel and Matilda) Family Foundation, MA, 1536
Golden (John) Fund, Inc., NY, 2479
Golden Nugget Scholarship Fund, Inc., NV, 2079
Golden (Robert M.) Foundation, CA, 194
Golden (Sibyl and William T.) Foundation, NY, 2480
Goldenberg (Max) Foundation, IL, 1018
Goldman (Herman) Foundation, NY, 2481
Goldman (Morris and Rose) Foundation, IL, 1019
Goldman (Richard and Rhoda) Fund, CA, 195
Goldman (William) Foundation, PA, 3584
Goldman (The William P.) and Brothers Foundation, Inc., NY, 2482
Goldring Family Foundation, LA, 1363
Goldseker (Morris) Foundation of Maryland, Inc., MD, 1419
Goldsmith Foundation, Inc., TN, 3841
Goldsmith (Horace W.) Foundation, NY, 2483
Goldwyn (The Samuel) Foundation, CA, 196
Golub Foundation, The, NY, 2484
Good Samaritan, Inc., DE, 610
Goodman Family Foundation, The, NY, 2485
Goodman (Joseph C. and Clare F.) Memorial Foundation, Inc., NY, 2486
Goodstein (David) Family Foundation, Inc., NY, 2487
Goodstein Foundation, The, WY, 4396
Goodyear (Josephine) Foundation, NY, 2488
Goodyear Tire & Rubber Company Fund, OH, 3239
Goppert Foundation, The, AZ, 37

Gordon Christian Foundation, MI, 1714
Gordon Fund, NY, 2489
Gordon (Isaac) Foundation, Inc., NY, 2490
Gordon (Meyer and Ida) Foundation, TX, 3963
Gore Family Memorial Foundation Trust, FL, 723
Gorin (The Nehemias) Foundation, MA, 1537
Gospel Foundation of California, 197
Gottesman (D. S. and R. H.) Foundation, NY, 2491
Gottlieb (Adolph and Esther) Foundation, Inc., NY, 2492
Gottwald Foundation, VA, 4171
Gould (Edwin) Foundation for Children, NY, 2493
Gould (Florence) Arts Foundation, Inc., NY, 2494
Gould Inc. Foundation, IL, 1020
Goulds Pumps Foundation, NY, 2495
Grace Foundation Inc., NY, 2496
Graco Foundation, The, MN, 1849
Graham Foundation for Advanced Studies in the Fine Arts, IL, 1021
Graham (The Philip L.) Fund, DC, 660
Grain Terminal Foundation, MN, 1850
Grainger Foundation Inc., The, IL, 1022
Gramercy Park Foundation, see 2497
Gramercy Park Foundation Incorporated, The, NY, 2497
Grancell (I. H. and Anna) Foundation, CA, 198
Grand Rapids Foundation, MI, 1715
Grant (Charles M. & Mary D.) Foundation, NY, 2498
Grant (William T.) Foundation, NY, 2499
Grass Family Foundation, PA, 3585
Grass Foundation, The, MA, 1538
Grassmann (E. J.) Trust, NJ, 2127
Gray (Garland) Foundation, VA, 4172
Gray (The Matilda Geddings) Foundation, LA, 1364
Great Northern Nekoosa Foundation, Inc., CT, 529
Green (Allen P. & Josephine B.) Foundation, MO, 1967
Green (Burton E.) Foundation, CA, 199
Green (Edith Dee) Foundation, UT, 4140
Green Foundation, The, TX, 3964
Green Fund, Inc., The, NY, 2500
Green Island, Inc., MA, 1539
Green (Joshua) Foundation, Inc., WA, 4237
Greenberg (The Alan C.) Foundation, Inc., NY, 2501
Greenburg (The Harry) Foundation, Inc., FL, 724
Greene (The David J.) Foundation, Inc., NY, 2502
Greene (Helen Wade) Charitable Trust, OH, 3240
Greene (The Jerome L.) Foundation, Inc., NY, 2503
Greene (Robert Z.) Foundation, FL, 725
Greenebaum (The Charles and Estelle) Foundation, Inc., NY, 2504
Greenfield (The Albert M.) Foundation, PA, 3586
Greenville, Inc., Community Foundation of Greater, SC, 3805
Greenville Foundation, The, CA, 200
Greenwall Foundation, The, NY, 2505
Gregg-Graniteville Foundation, Inc., SC, 3806
Greve (The William and Mary) Foundation, Inc., NY, 2506
Greystone Foundation, The, MN, 1851
Gries (Lucile and Robert H.) Charity Fund, OH, 3241
Griffin (Rosa May) Foundation, TX, 3965
Griffis Foundation, Inc., The, NY, 2507
Griffith (The W. C.) Foundation, IN, 1217
Griggs (Mary Livingston) and Mary Griggs Burke Foundation, MN, 1852
Grimes Foundation, The, OH, 3242
Griswold (Harry E.) Trust, IL, 1023
Gross (Stella B.) Charitable Trust, CA, 201
Gross (Walter L. and Nell R.) Charitable Trust, OH, 3243
Grossinger (Jennie) Foundation, Inc., NY, 2508
Grossman Family Trust, MA, 1540
Grotto Foundation, Inc., MN, 1853
Groves Foundation, MN, 1854
Groves Fund, see 1854
Grubb (Hunter) Foundation, Inc., CT, 530
Gruber (Lila) Research Foundation, NY, 2509
Grumbacher (M. S.) Foundation, PA, 3587
Grumbacher (Stanley and Kathleen) Foundation, Inc., NY, 2510
Grundy Foundation, The, PA, 3588
Grupe (William F.) Foundation, Inc., NJ, 2128
Gruss (Oscar and Regina) Charitable and Educational Foundation, Inc., NY, 2511

GTE Foundation, CT, 531
Gudelsky (The Homer and Martha) Family Foundation, Inc., MD, 1420
Gudelsky (The Isadore and Bertha) Family Foundation, Inc., DC, 661
Guggenheim (The Daniel and Florence) Foundation, NY, 2512
Guggenheim (The Harry Frank) Foundation, NY, 2513
Guggenheim (John Simon) Memorial Foundation, NY, 2514
Guinzburg Fund, The, NY, 2515
Gulf + Western Foundation, Inc., NY, 2516
Gulf Oil Foundation of Delaware, PA, 3589
Gulton Foundation, Inc., NY, 2517
Gund (The George) Foundation, OH, 3244
Gurwin (J.) Foundation, Inc., NY, 2518
Gussman (Herbert and Roseline) Foundation, OK, 3433
Gutfreund Foundation, Inc., The, NY, 2519
Gutman (Edna and Monroe C.) Foundation, Inc., NY, 2520
Guttman (Stella and Charles) Foundation, Inc., NY, 2521

Haas (Evelyn and Walter), Jr. Fund, CA, 202
Haas (Miriam and Peter) Fund, CA, 203
Haas (Paul and Mary) Foundation, TX, 3966
Haas (Saul and Dayee G.) Foundation, Inc., WA, 4238
Haas (Walter and Elise) Fund, CA, 204
Habig (Arnold F.) Foundation, Inc., IN, 1218
Habig Foundation Inc., The, IN, 1219
Hackett (Charlotte Cuneen) Charitable Trust, NY, 2522
Hackett Foundation, Inc., The, NJ, 2129
Haffenreffer Family Fund, RI, 3778
Haffner Foundation, IL, 1024
Hagedorn Fund, The, NY, 2523
Haggar Foundation, The, TX, 3967
Haggerty Foundation, TX, 3968
Haggin (Margaret Voorhies) Trust in Memory of her late husband, James Ben Ali Haggin, NY, 2524
Hahn (Ernest W. and Jean E.) Foundation, CA, 205
Hahn Family Foundation, NY, 2525
Hahn (Philip Y.) Foundation, CA, 206
Hale (The Crescent Porter) Foundation, CA, 207
Hales Charitable Fund, Inc., IL, 1025
Haley (W. B.) Foundation, GA, 842
Halff (G. A. C.) Foundation, TX, 3969
Hall (Evelyn A.) Charitable Trust, PA, 3590
Hall Family Foundations, MO, 1968
Hall Foundation, Inc., The, IA, 1269
Hall Foundation, The, PA, 3591
Halliburton Foundation, Inc., TX, 3970
Hallmark Educational Foundations, see 1968
Hallowell Foundation, The, PA, 3592
Halsell (The Ewing) Foundation, TX, 3971
Halsell (O. L.) Foundation, CA, 208
Hambay (James T.) Foundation, PA, 3593
Hamico, Inc., TN, 3842
Hamilburg (Joseph M.) Foundation, MA, 1541
Hamilton Community Foundation, Inc., The, OH, 3245
Hamm Foundation, MN, 1855
Hamman (George and Mary Josephine) Foundation, TX, 3972
Hammer (Armand) Foundation, IL, 1026
Hammermill Foundation, The, PA, 3594
Hancock (The Luke B.) Foundation, CA, 209
Hanes (James G.) Memorial Fund/Foundation, NC, 3105
Hanes (The John W. and Anna H.) Foundation, NC, 3106
Hankins Foundation, The, OH, 3246
Hansen (Dane G.) Foundation, KS, 1309
Harder Foundation, MI, 1716
Hardin (Phil) Foundation, MS, 1937
Harding Educational and Charitable Foundation, The, NY, 2526
Harding Foundation, The, TX, 3973
Harland (John H. and Wilhelmina D.) Charitable Foundation, Inc., GA, 843
Harland (John H.) Company Foundation, GA, 844
Harless (James) Foundation, Incorporated, WV, 4283
Harmon (Pearl M. and Julia J.) Foundation, OK, 3434
Harney Foundation, The, CA, 210
Harnischfeger Foundation, Inc., WI, 4325

Harper (Philip S.) Foundation, IL, 1027
Harriman (Mary W.) Foundation, NY, 2527
Harrington (The Don and Sybil) Foundation, TX, 3974
Harrington (Francis A. & Jacquelyn H.) Foundation, MA, 1542
Harrington (George) Trust, MA, 1543
Harris Bank Foundation, IL, 1028
Harris Brothers Foundation, NJ, 2130
Harris Family Foundation, IL, 1029
Harris Foundation, FL, 726
Harris Foundation, The, IL, 1030
Harris Foundation, Incorporated, OK, 3435
Harris (Holbert L.) Testamentary Trust "B", VA, 4173
Harris (J. Ira and Nicki) Foundation, IL, 1031
Harris (The William H. and Mattie Wattis) Foundation, UT, 4141
Harsco Corporation Fund, PA, 3595
Hart Schaffner & Marx Charitable Foundation, IL, 1032
Hartford Courant Foundation, Incorporated, The, CT, 532
Hartford Foundation for Public Giving, CT, 533
Hartford Insurance Group Foundation, Inc., The, CT, 534
Hartford (The John A.) Foundation, Inc., NY, 2528
Hartman (Jesse and Dorothy) Foundation, CT, 535
Hartz Foundation, MN, 1856
Hartzell Foundation, MN, 1857
Hartzell-Norris Charitable Trust, OH, 3247
Harvard Apparatus Foundation, Inc., MA, 1544
Harvard Musical Association, MA, 1545
Harvard-Yenching Institute, MA, 1546
Harvey Foundation, Inc., PR, 3769
Hasenfeld (A. & Z.) Foundation, Inc., NY, 2529
Haskell Fund, OH, 3248
Hassel Foundation, The, PA, 3596
Hassenfeld Foundation, The, RI, 3779
Hastings (Merrill G. and Emita E.) Foundation, NY, 2530
Hastings Trust, The, VA, 4174
Hatch (Margaret Milliken) Charitable Trust, NY, 2531
Hatterscheidt Foundation, Inc., The, SD, 3826
Hausman Belding Foundation, Inc., NY, 2532
Hauss-Helms Foundation, Inc., The, OH, 3249
Havens Relief Fund Society, The, NY, 2533
Hawaiian Foundation, The, HI, 899
Hawkins (Robert Z.) Foundation, NV, 2080
Hawley Foundation, IA, 1270
Hawn Foundation, Inc., TX, 3975
Hawthorne Foundation Incorporated, MN, 1858
Hay (John I.) Foundation, IL, 1033
Hayden (Charles) Foundation, NY, 2534
Hayes (Stanley W.) Research Foundation, Inc., IN, 1220
Hayner Foundation, IN, 1221
Haynes Foundation, MT, 2045
Haynes (The John Randolph) and Dora Haynes Foundation, CA, 211
Hayward (The John T. and Winifred) Foundation Charitable Trust, FL, 727
Hazen (The Edward W.) Foundation, Inc., NY, 2535
Hazen (Joseph H.) Foundation, NY, 2536
Hazen (Lita) Charitable Trust, PA, 3597
H.B.S. Fund, MO, 1969
H.C.S. Foundation, OH, 3250
Hearst Foundation, Inc., The, NY, 2537
Hearst (William Randolph) Foundation, NY, 2538
Heath (Ed and Mary) Foundation, TX, 3976
Hebrew Technical Institute, NY, 2539
Hechinger (Sidney L.) Foundation, MD, 1421
Hecht-Levi Foundation, Inc., The, MD, 1422
Heckscher Foundation for Children, The, NY, 2540
Hedco Foundation, CA, 212
Heed Ophthalmic Foundation, IL, 1034
Heginbotham (Will E.) Trust, CO, 451
Heileman Old Style Foundation, Inc., WI, 4326
Heilicher (Menaham) Charitable Foundation, MN, 1859
Heineman Foundation for Research, Educational, Charitable and Scientific Purposes, Inc., NY, 2541
Heinz (H. J.) Company Foundation, PA, 3598
Heinz (Howard) Endowment, PA, 3599
Heinz (Vira I.) Endowment, PA, 3600
Heisey Foundation, The, MT, 2046
Helfaer (Evan and Marion) Foundation, WI, 4327

Helis Foundation, The, LA, 1365
Heller Charitable and Educational Fund, CA, 213
Heller (Dr. Bernard) Foundation, NY, 2542
Heller (Florence G.) Foundation, IL, 1035
Heller (Walter E.) Foundation, IL, 1036
Helmerich Foundation, The, OK, 3436
Helms Foundation, Inc., CA, 214
Helmsley (The Harry B.) Foundation, Inc., NY, 2543
Helping Hand Foundation, The, OH, 3251
Helvering (R. L. and Elsa) Trust, KS, 1310
HEM Charitable Trust, The, NY, 2544
Hemphill-Wells Foundation, TX, 3977
Henck (August J. and Sadie L.) Memorial Fund, TX, 3978
Henderson Foundation, MA, 1547
Henderson (The George B.) Foundation, MA, 1548
Henderson (Simon and Louise) Foundation, TX, 3979
Hendrickson Bros. Foundation, Inc., NY, 2545
Herbst Foundation, Inc., The, CA, 215
Heritage Foundation, Inc., The, CT, 536
Heritage Fund of Bartholomew County, Inc., IN, 1222
Herman (John and Rose) Foundation, MI, 1717
Hermann (The Grover) Foundation, IL, 1037
Herndon (Alonzo F.) and Norris B. Herndon Foundation, Inc., GA, 845
Herrick Foundation, MI, 1718
Hersey Foundation, MN, 1860
Hershey Foods Corporation Fund, The, PA, 3601
Hershey Fund, The, see 3601
Hertz (Fannie and John) Foundation, CA, 216
Hervey Foundation, AZ, 38
Herzog (The Carl J.) Foundation, Inc., CT, 537
Hess Foundation, Inc., NY, 2546
Hesston Foundation, Inc., KS, 1311
Hettinger Foundation, NY, 2547
Heublein Foundation, Inc., CT, 538
Hewlett (The William and Flora) Foundation, CA, 217
Hewlett-Packard Company Foundation, CA, 218
Heydt (Nan and Matilda) Fund, MA, 1549
Heymann (Mr. and Mrs. Jimmy) Special Account, LA, 1366
Heymann-Wolf Foundation, LA, 1367
Hiatt (Jacob and Frances) Foundation, Inc., MA, 1550
Hickrill Foundation, Inc., NY, 2548
Hidary (Jacob) Foundation, Inc., NY, 2549
Higbee Foundation, The, OH, 3252
Higgins (Aldus C.) Foundation, MA, 1551
Higgins (Lorene Sails) Charitable Trust, OR, 3488
Higginson (Corina) Trust, DC, 662
High Winds Fund, Inc., NY, 2550
Hightower Charitable Foundation, IL, 1038
Hightower (Walter) Foundation, TX, 3980
Hill Foundation, CO, 452
Hill (Walter Clay) and Family Foundation, GA, 846
Hillcrest Foundation, TX, 3981
Hillenbrand (John A.) Foundation, Inc., IN, 1223
Hilles (Allen) Fund, PA, 3602
Hillman (The Alex) Family Foundation, NY, 2551
Hillman Foundation, Inc., The, PA, 3603
Hillman (The Henry L.) Foundation, PA, 3604
Hills (The Edward E.) Fund, CA, 219
Hillsdale Fund, Inc., NC, 3107
Hilton (Conrad N.) Foundation, CA, 220
Himmel (The Clarence and Jack) Foundation, MI, 1719
Himmelfarb (Paul and Annetta) Foundation, Inc., DC, 663
Hirschl (Irma T.) Trust for Charitable Purposes, NY, 2552
Hitchcock (Gilbert M. and Martha H.) Foundation, NE, 2057
Hitchcock (The Margaret Mellon) Foundation, PA, 3605
H.K.H. Foundation, see 2554
HNG Foundation, TX, 3982
Ho (Chinn) Foundation, HI, 900
Hoag Foundation, CA, 221
Hobbs Foundation, WI, 4328
Hobby Foundation, TX, 3983
Hoblitzelle Foundation, TX, 3984
Hochschild Fund, Inc., NY, 2553
Hochschild (Harold K.) Foundation, NY, 2554
Hochstein Foundation, Inc., NY, 2555
Hodge Foundation, Inc., The, GA, 847
Hoernle (A. W.) Foundation, NY, 2556

Hoffberger Foundation, Inc., MD, 1423
Hoffer Foundation, IL, 1039
Hoffman (The H. Leslie) and Elaine S. Hoffman Foundation, CA, 222
Hoffmann-La Roche Foundation, The, NJ, 2131
Hofheinz (Roy M.) Charitable Foundation, TX, 3985
Hofmann (K. H.) Foundation, CA, 223
Hofstetter (Bessie I.) Trust, TX, 3986
Hogan (Jack) Charitable Foundation, CO, 453
Hokin (The Dave) Foundation, IL, 1040
Holden (James and Lynelle) Fund, MI, 1720
Hollingsworth (J. E. & Mildred) Foundation, Inc., FL, 728
Hollywood Canteen Foundation, The, CA, 224
Holmes (D. H.) Foundation, LA, 1368
Holmes Foundation, Inc., NY, 2557
Holt (William Knox) Foundation, CA, 225
Holtzmann (Jacob L. and Lillian) Foundation, NY, 2558
Holy Land Charitable Trust, HI, 901
Homan (B. H.), Jr. Trust, NY, 2559
Home for Aged Men in the City of Brockton, MA, 1552
Homeland Foundation, Inc., NY, 2560
Honey Locust Foundation, KY, 1341
Honeywell Foundation, Inc., The, IN, 1224
Honeywell Foundation, MN, 1861
Honeywell Fund, see 1861
Honigman Foundation, Inc., MI, 1721
Hood (Charles H.) Foundation, MA, 1553
Hood (Charles H.) Fund, MA, 1554
Hooker (Janet A.) Charitable Trust, PA, 3606
Hooper (Elizabeth S.) Foundation, PA, 3607
Hoover Foundation, The, OH, 3253
Hoover (The H. Earl) Foundation, IL, 1041
Hoover (The Margaret W. and Herbert), Jr. Foundation, CA, 226
Hope (Blanche and Thomas) Fund, KY, 1342
Hopedale Foundation, The, MA, 1555
Hopeman Memorial Fund, Inc., VA, 4175
Hopkins (The John Jay) Foundation, VA, 4176
Hopkins (Josephine Lawrence) Foundation, NY, 2561
Hopper (Bertrand) Memorial Foundation, IL, 1042
Hopwood (John M.) Charitable Trust, PA, 3608
HOR Foundation, TX, 3987
Hormel (George A.) Testamentary Trust, MN, 1862
Hornblower (Henry) Fund, Inc., MA, 1556
Horne (Mabel A.) Trust, MA, 1557
Hosler (Dr. R. S.) Memorial Educational Fund, OH, 3254
Hotchkiss (W. R.) Foundation, MN, 1863
Houchens Foundation, Inc., KY, 1343
Houghton Foundation, The, NY, 2562
House of St. Giles the Cripple, The, NY, 2563
House (Susan Cook) Educational Trust, IL, 1043
Housen Foundation, Inc., MA, 1558
Houston Endowment Inc., TX, 3988
Howard and Bush Foundation, Inc., The, CT, 539
Howard Benevolent Society, MA, 1559
Howard (Cecil) Charitable Trust, NY, 2564
Howe (Lucile Horton) and Mitchell B. Howe Foundation, CA, 227
Howell (Eric and Jessie) Foundation, Inc., FL, 729
Hoyt Foundation, The, NJ, 2132
Hoyt Foundation, The, PA, 3609
Hoyt (Stewart W. & Willma C.) Foundation, NY, 2565
Hubbard Family Foundation, WA, 4239
Hubbard Farms Charitable Foundation, NH, 2086
Hubbard Foundation, The, MN, 1864
Hubbell (The Harvey) Foundation, CT, 540
Huber Foundation, The, NJ, 2133
Hudson-Webber Foundation, MI, 1722
Huffy Foundation, Inc., The, OH, 3255
Hugg (Leola W. and Charles H.) Trust, TX, 3989
Hughes (The Charles Evans) Memorial Foundation, Inc., NY, 2566
Hughes (Mabel Y.) Charitable Trust, CO, 454
Huisking Foundation, Inc., The, CT, 541
Hulings (Mary Andersen) Foundation, MN, 1865
Hulme (Milton G.) Charitable Foundation, PA, 3610
Humana Foundation, Inc., The, KY, 1344
Humane Society of the Commonwealth of Massachusetts, MA, 1560
Humboldt Area Foundation, The, CA, 228

Humphrey (George M. and Pamela S.) Fund, OH, 3256

Humphrey (Gilbert W. & Louise Ireland) Foundation, OH, 3257

Humphreys Foundation, The, TX, 3990

Hunt (C. Giles) Charitable Trust, OR, 3489

Hunt Foundation, The, PA, 3611

Hunt Manufacturing Co. Foundation, PA, 3612

Hunt (The Roy A.) Foundation, PA, 3613

Hunt (The Ruth Ray) Foundation, TX, 3991

Hunt (Samuel P.) Foundation, NH, 2087

Hunter (A. V.) Trust, Incorporated, CO, 455

Hunter (Edward and Irma) Foundation, MI, 1723

Hunter (Graham) Foundation, NY, 2567

Huntington (The John) Fund for Education, OH, 3258

Hurley (Ed E. and Gladys) Foundation, LA, 1369

Hurst Foundation, The, MI, 1724

Huston Foundation, The, PA, 3614

Hutcheson (Hazel Montague) Foundation, TN, 3843

Hutchins (Mary J.) Foundation, Inc., NY, 2568

Huthsteiner Fine Arts Trust, TX, 3992

Hutton (Edward F.) Foundation, NY, 2569

Hyams (Godfrey M.) Trust, MA, 1561

Hyams (Sarah A.) Fund, Inc., MA, 1562

Hycliff Foundation, Inc., The, NY, 2570

Hyde and Watson Foundation, The, NJ, 2134

Hyde (J. R.) Foundation, Inc., TN, 3844

Hyde (The Lillia Babbitt) Foundation, see 2134

Hyman Family Foundation, PA, 3615

Hyman (The George and Sadie) Foundation, DC, 664

I and G Charitable Foundation, IL, 1044

Iddings Foundation, OH, 3259

IFF Foundation, Inc., The, NY, 2571

Ilgenfritz (May H.) Testamentary Trust, MO, 1970

Illges (A. and M. L.) Memorial Foundation, Inc., GA, 848

Illges (John P. and Dorothy S.) Foundation, Inc., GA, 849

Illinois Tool Works Foundation, IL, 1045

IMC Foundation, IL, 1046

Imerman (Stanley) Memorial Foundation, MI, 1725

INA Foundation, see 3542

Incentive Aid Foundation, CA, 229

Independence Foundation, PA, 3616

Indian Head Foundation, NY, 2572

Indiana Chemical Trust, IN, 1225

Indianapolis Foundation, The, IN, 1226

Ingalls (The Louise H. and David S.) Foundation, Incorporated, OH, 3260

Ingersoll Foundation, Inc., The, IL, 1047

Ingersoll Foundation, The, see 1047

Ingersoll Foundation, Inc., The, IL, 1047

Ingersoll Foundation, The, see 1047

Inglewood Foundation, The, AR, 51

Ingram (Edgar W.) Foundation, OH, 3261

Ingram (Joe) Trust, MO, 1971

Initial Teaching Alphabet Foundation, Inc., NY, 2573

Inland Container Corporation Foundation, Inc., IN, 1227

Inland Steel-Ryerson Foundation, Inc., IL, 1048

Inman-Riverdale Foundation, SC, 3807

Institute of Current World Affairs, Inc., NH, 2088

Interco, Inc. Charitable Trust, MO, 1972

Interferon Foundation, The, TX, 3993

Interlake Foundation, IL, 1049

International Foundation, The, NJ, 2135

International Multifoods Charitable Foundation, MN, 1866

International Paper Company Foundation, NY, 2574

InterNorth Foundation, The, NE, 2058

Inter-Regional Financial Group, Inc., Foundation, MN, 1867

Intrawest Foundation, see 447

Irby (Elizabeth M.) Foundation, MS, 1938

Ireland Foundation, The, OH, 3262

Irvine (The James) Foundation, CA, 230

Irving One Wall Street Foundation, Inc., NY, 2575

Irwin (The William G.) Charity Foundation, CA, 231

Irwin-Sweeney-Miller Foundation, IN, 1228

Ishiyama Foundation, The, CA, 232

Island Foundation, CA, 233

Israel (A. Cremieux) Foundation, Inc., DE, 611

ITT Rayonier Foundation, The, CT, 542

Ittleson Foundation, Inc., NY, 2576

Ix Foundation, The, NJ, 2136

Jackson (Ann) Family Foundation, CA, 234

Jackson Foundation, The, MI, 1726

Jackson Foundation, The, OR, 3490

Jackson Hole Preserve, Incorporated, NY, 2577

Jackson (Marion Gardner) Charitable Trust, MA, 1563

Jacksonville Community Foundation (Donor-Directed Fund), Greater, FL, 730

Jacksonville Community Foundation, Greater, FL, 731

Jacobson (Bernard H. and Blanche E.) Foundation, WV, 4284

Jacobus/Heritage Foundation, Inc., WI, 4329

Jaffe Foundation, The, MA, 1564

Jameson (J. W. and Ida M.) Foundation, CA, 235

Jameson (Oleonda) Trust, NH, 2089

Janesville Foundation, Inc., WI, 4330

Janssen (Henry) Foundation, Incorporated, PA, 3617

Jarson (Isaac N. and Esther M.) Charitable Trust, OH, 3263

Javitch Foundation, The, PA, 3618

Jay (George S. & Grace A.) Memorial Trust, IA, 1271

J.D.B. Fund, The, PA, 3619

JDR 3rd Fund, Inc., The, NY, 2578

Jeffers (Michael) Memorial Foundation, MI, 1727

Jefferson (John Percival and Mary C.) Endowment Fund, CA, 236

Jeffery (Clara L. D.) Charitable Residuary Trust, NJ, 2137

Jeffress (Thomas F. and Kate Miller) Memorial Trust, VA, 4177

Jehovah Jireh, Inc., NY, 2579

Jeld-Wen, Wenco Foundation, The, OR, 3491

Jellison (Arthur D. and Maude S.) Charitable Trust, KS, 1312

Jenkins (Alice N.) Foundation, CO, 456

Jenkins (George W.) Foundation, Inc., FL, 732

Jenkins Student Loan Fund, OR, 3492

Jenkins-Tapp Foundation, Inc., NC, 3108

Jenn Foundation, IN, 1229

Jennings (The Martha Holden) Foundation, OH, 3264

Jennings (The Mary Hillman) Foundation, PA, 3620

Jephson Educational Trust No. 1, NY, 2580

Jephson Educational Trust No. 2, NY, 2581

Jergens (The Andrew) Foundation, OH, 3265

Jerome Foundation, CA, 237

Jerome Foundation, MN, 1868

Jesselson Foundation, NY, 2582

Jewel Foundation, IL, 1050

Jewell (The Daniel Ashley and Irene Houston) Memorial Foundation, TN, 3845

Jewett (George Frederick) Foundation, CA, 238

Jewish Foundation for Education of Women, NY, 2583

JFM Foundation, The, CO, 457

Jinks (Ruth T.) Foundation, GA, 850

J.J.C. Foundation, Inc., CT, 543

J.M. Foundation, The, NY, 2584

J.N.M. 1966 Gift Trust, MN, 1869

Jochum-Moll Foundation, The, OH, 3266

Jockey Club Foundation, NY, 2585

Jockey Hollow Foundation, Inc., The, NJ, 2138

John (B. P.) Foundation, OR, 3493

John (Helen) Foundation, OR, 3494

Johnson (A. D.) Foundation, IL, 1051

Johnson & Johnson Family of Companies Contribution Fund, NJ, 2139

Johnson (Barbara Piasecka) Foundation, NY, 2586

Johnson (The Burdine) Foundation, TX, 3994

Johnson (Christian A.) Endeavor Foundation, NY, 2587

Johnson Controls Foundation, WI, 4331

Johnson (The D. Mead) Foundation, Inc., FL, 733

Johnson (Dexter G.) Educational and Benevolent Trust, OK, 3437

Johnson (Edward C.) Fund, MA, 1565

Johnson Foundation, Inc., The, WI, 4332

Johnson Foundation Trust, WI, 4333

Johnson (Helen K. and Arthur E.) Foundation, CO, 458

Johnson (The Howard) Foundation, MA, 1566

Johnson (The J. S.) & Barbara Piasecka Johnson Charitable Trust, NY, 2588

Johnson (John A.) Foundation, WI, 4334

Johnson (M. G. and Lillie A.) Foundation, Inc., TX, 3995

Johnson (R. B.) Foundation, Inc., NY, 2589

Johnson (The Robert Wood) Foundation, NJ, 2140

Johnson (The S. S.) Foundation, OR, 3495

Johnson (Viola) Charitable Trust, WI, 4335

Johnson (Walter S.) Foundation, CA, 239

Johnson (Willard T. C.) Foundation, Inc., NY, 2590

Johnson's Wax Fund, Inc., The, WI, 4336

Johnston Foundation, The, WA, 4240

Johnston (The James M.) Trust for Charitable and Educational Purposes, DC, 665

Johnstone (Ralph A.) Foundation, Inc., TX, 3996

Johnstone (Phyllis Kimball) and H. Earle Kimball Foundation, RI, 3780

Jones (The Cyrus W. & Amy F.) & Bessie D. Phelps Foundation, Inc., CT, 544

Jones (Daisy Marquis) Foundation, NY, 2591

Jones (Eugenie and Joseph) Family Foundation, LA, 1370

Jones Foundation, The, CA, 240

Jones (The Harvey and Bernice) Foundation, AR, 52

Jones (Montfort) and Allie Brown Jones Foundation, OK, 3438

Jones (W. Alton) Foundation, Inc., VA, 4178

Jones (Walter S. and Evan C.) Foundation, KS, 1313

Jonsson Foundation, The, TX, 3997

Jordaan Foundation Trust, KS, 1314

Jordan (Arthur) Foundation, IN, 1230

Jordan (Mary Ranken) and Ettie A. Jordan Charitable Foundation, MO, 1973

Joseloff (Morris) Foundation, Inc., CT, 545

Joselow Foundation, NY, 2592

Joselow Foundation, The, see 2592

Joselow Foundation, NY, 2592

Joselow Foundation, The, see 2592

Joslin-Needham Family Foundation, CO, 459

Joslyn (The Carl W. and Carrie Mae) Charitable Trust, CO, 460

Joslyn (The Marcellus L.) Foundation, CA, 241

Jost (Charles & Mabel P.) Foundation, Incorporated, CT, 546

Jostens Foundation, Inc., The, MN, 1870

Joyce Foundation, The, IL, 1052

Joyce (The John M. and Mary A.) Foundation, IL, 1053

JSR Foundation, IL, 1054

Juilfs Foundation, The, OH, 3267

Julia R. and Estelle L. Foundation, Inc., NY, 2593

Jurodin Fund, Inc., NY, 2594

Jurzykowski (Alfred) Foundation, Inc., NY, 2595

Justus (Edith C.) Trust, PA, 3621

Justus (Samuel) Charitable Trust, PA, 3622

Kachelmacher Memorial, Inc., OH, 3268

Kade (Annette) Fund, NY, 2596

Kade (Max) Foundation, Inc., NY, 2597

Kaiser (The Henry J.) Family Foundation, CA, 242

Kalamazoo Foundation, MI, 1728

Kamps (Gertrude) Memorial Foundation, WY, 4397

Kanawha Valley Foundation, The Greater, WV, 4285

Kangesser (The Robert E., Harry A., and M. Sylvia) Foundation, OH, 3269

Kansas Gas and Electric Charitable Foundation, KS, 1315

Kantzler Foundation, The, MI, 1729

Kaplan (The J. M.) Fund, Inc., NY, 2598

Kaplan (Mayer and Morris) Foundation, IL, 1055

Kaplan-Halpert Foundation, Inc., The, OH, 3270

Kaplun (Morris J. and Betty) Foundation, NY, 2599

Karagheusian (The Howard) Commemorative Corporation, NY, 2600

Kardon (Samuel and Rebecca) Foundation, PA, 3623

Karpas Family Foundation, Inc., NY, 2601

Kasal (Father) Charitable Trust, MN, 1871

Kassin (Otsar) Foundation, Inc., NY, 2602

Katzenberger Foundation, Inc., The, NY, 2603

Kaufman (Henry & Elaine) Foundation, Inc., NY, 2604

Kaufman (Louis G.) Endowment Fund, MI, 1730

Kaufmann (Henry) Foundation, NY, 2605

Kautz (Charles P. and Pauline M.) Foundation, NY, 2606

Kavanagh (T. J.) Foundation, see 3624

Kavanagh (T. James) Foundation, Inc., PA, 3624

Kawabe (Harry S.) Trust, *see* 4241
Kawabe Memorial Fund, WA, 4241
Kay (Mary) Foundation, TX, 3998
Kayser Foundation, The, TX, 3999
Kayser-Roth Foundation, CT, 547
Kazanjian (The Calvin K.) Economics Foundation, Inc., CT, 548
Kearney and Trecker Foundation, Inc., WI, 4337
Keating Family Foundation, Inc., IL, 1056
Keck (W. M.) Foundation, CA, 243
Keck (William M.), Jr. Foundation, NY, 2607
Keebler Company Foundation, IL, 1057
Keith (Ben E.) Foundation Trust, TX, 4000
Kejr Foundation, Inc., CO, 461
Kellenberger (May Gordon Latham) Historical Foundation, NC, 3109
Keller Family Foundation, LA, 1371
Kelley (Edward Bangs) and Elza Kelley Foundation, Inc., MA, 1567
Kelley (Kate M.) Foundation, PA, 3625
Kellogg Company 25-Year Employees Fund, Inc., MI, 1731
Kellogg (W. K.) Foundation, MI, 1732
Kellstadt Foundation, IL, 1058
Kelly (Ensign C. Markland), Jr. Memorial Foundation, Inc., MD, 1424
Kemper (The David Woods) Memorial Foundation, MO, 1974
Kemper Educational and Charitable Fund, IL, 1059
Kemper (Enid and Crosby) Foundation, MO, 1975
Kemper (The James S.) Foundation, IL, 1060
Kemper (R. C.) Charitable Trust & Foundation, MO, 1976
Kempner Foundation, Inc., The, NY, 2608
Kempner (Harris and Eliza) Fund, TX, 4001
Kenan (William R.), Jr. Charitable Trust, NY, 2609
Kendall Company Foundation, MA, 1568
Kendall (The George R.) Foundation, IL, 1061
Kendall (The Henry P.) Foundation, MA, 1569
Kenedy (The John G. and Marie Stella) Memorial Foundation, TX, 4002
Kennametal Foundation, PA, 3626
Kennedy (Augustus H.) Memorial Fund Trust, MN, 1872
Kennedy (Elizabeth E.) Fund, MI, 1733
Kennedy (Francis Nathaniel and Kathryn Padgett) Foundation, SC, 3808
Kennedy (The John R.) Foundation, Inc., NJ, 2141
Kennedy (The Joseph P.), Jr. Foundation, DC, 666
Kent (The Ada Howe) Foundation, DE, 612
Kentland Foundation, Inc., MD, 1425
Kent-Lucas Foundation, Inc., DE, 613
Kenwood Foundation, MA, 1570
Kern Foundation Trust, IL, 1062
Kerney (The James) Foundation, NJ, 2142
Kerr (A. H.) Foundation, CA, 244
Kerr (Alexander H.) Benevolent Association, *see* 244
Kerr Foundation, Inc., The, OK, 3439
Kerr-McGee Foundation, Inc., OK, 3440
Kerry Foundation, Inc., The, NY, 2610
Kettering (Charles F.) Foundation, OH, 3271
Kettering Family Foundation, The, OH, 3272
Kettering Fund, The, OH, 3273
Kevorkian (Hagop) Fund, NY, 2611
Keyes (Bernice A. B.) Trust, WA, 4242
Kibble Foundation, OH, 3274
Kidder Peabody Foundation, The, NY, 2612
Kieckhefer (J. W.) Foundation, AZ, 39
Kiewit (Peter) Foundation, NE, 2059
Kiewit (The Peter) Sons Company Foundation, NE, 2060
Kilbourne (E. H.) Residuary Charitable Trust, IN, 1231
Kilburger (Charles) Scholarship Fund, OH, 3275
Killough (Walter H. D.) Trust, NY, 2613
Kilworth (Florence B.) Charitable Foundation, WA, 4243
Kilworth (William) Charitable Trust, WA, 4244
Kimball (Horace A.) and S. Ella Kimball Foundation, RI, 3781
Kimberly-Clark Foundation, Inc., WI, 4338
Kimmelman Foundation, NY, 2614
King (Carl B. and Florence E.) Foundation, TX, 4003
King (Charles A.) Trust, MA, 1571
King Ranch Family Trust, TX, 4004

King's Daughters' Foundation, HI, 902
Kingsbury Fund, NH, 2090
Kingsley Foundation, The, DE, 614
Kinney-Lindstrom Foundation, Inc., IA, 1272
Kiplinger Foundation, Inc., The, DC, 667
Kirby (F. M.) Foundation, Inc., NJ, 2143
Kirchgessner (The Karl) Foundation, CA, 245
Kirkland & Ellis Foundation, IL, 1063
Kirkpatrick Foundation, Inc., OK, 3441
Klau (The David and Sadie) Foundation, NY, 2615
Kleberg (Caesar) Foundation for Wildlife Conservation, TX, 4005
Kleberg (Robert J.), Jr. and Helen C. Kleberg Foundation, TX, 4006
Klee (The Conrad and Virginia) Foundation, Inc., NY, 2616
Klein (David L.), Jr. Memorial Foundation, Inc., NY, 2617
Klein (Nathan J.) Fund, TX, 4007
Kline (Charles and Figa) Foundation, PA, 3627
Kline (Josiah W. and Bessie H.) Foundation, Inc., PA, 3628
Klingenstein (The Esther A. and Joseph) Fund, Inc., NY, 2618
Klosk (Louis & Rose) Fund, NY, 2619
Knapp Educational Fund, Inc., MD, 1426
Knapp Foundation, Inc., The, MD, 1427
Knapp Foundation, TX, 4008
Knapp Fund, The, NY, 2620
Knight Foundation, OH, 3276
Knistrom (Fanny and Svante) Foundation, MA, 1572
Knollbrook Trust, The, PA, 3629
Knott (The Marion I. and Henry J.) Foundation, Inc., MD, 1428
Knox Gelatine Foundation, NY, 2621
Knox (Robert W.), Sr. and Pearl Wallis Knox Charitable Foundation, TX, 4009
Knox (The Seymour H.) Foundation, Inc., NY, 2622
Knudsen (Earl) Charitable Foundation, PA, 3630
Knudsen (The Tom and Valley) Foundation, CA, 246
Koch (Charles G.) Charitable Foundation, KS, 1316
Koch Foundation, Inc., FL, 734
Koch (The Fred C.) Foundation, Inc., KS, 1317
Koch (George) Sons Foundation, Inc., IN, 1232
Koehler (John G.) Fund, IL, 1064
Koehring Foundation, WI, 4339
Koffler Family Foundation, The, RI, 3782
Kohl (Allen D.) Charitable Foundation, Inc., WI, 4340
Kohl (H. H.) Charities, Inc., WI, 4341
Kohl (Sidney) Foundation, Inc., FL, 735
Kohler Foundation, Inc., WI, 4342
Komar (Charles & Esther) Foundation, NJ, 2144
Komes Foundation, CA, 247
Koopman Fund, Inc., The, CT, 549
Kopf (Elizabeth Christy) Foundation, NY, 2623
Kopf Foundation, Inc., NY, 2624
Koppers Company Foundation, The, PA, 3631
Koret Foundation, CA, 248
Korman (Hyman) Family Foundation, PA, 3632
Koulaieff (The Trustees of Ivan V.) Educational Fund, CA, 249
Kraft (E. A.) Charitable Trust, NY, 2625
Kramer (C. L. C.) Foundation, NY, 2626
Kramer Foundation, NY, 2627
Kramer (Louise) Foundation, OH, 3277
Krannert Charitable Trust, IN, 1233
Krause (Charles A.) Foundation, WI, 4343
Krause (Henry) Charitable Foundation, KS, 1318
Kreielsheimer Foundation Trust, WA, 4245
Kresevich Foundation, Inc., The, NY, 2628
Kresge Foundation, The, MI, 1734
Kress (The George) Foundation, Inc., WI, 4344
Kress (Samuel H.) Foundation, NY, 2629
Krieger Fund, Inc., The, MD, 1429
Krim (The Mathilde and Arthur B.) Foundation, Inc., NY, 2630
Kriser (Charles and Bertha) Foundation, Inc., NY, 2631
Kroc Foundation, The, CA, 250
Kuehn Foundation, IN, 1234
Kulas Foundation, OH, 3278
Kunkel (John Crain) Foundation, PA, 3633
Kunstadter (The Albert) Family Foundation, NY, 2632
Kuntz Foundation, The, OH, 3279
Kurth Religious Trust, WI, 4345

Kutz (Milton and Hattie) Foundation, DE, 615
Kuyper (Peter H.) and E. Lucille Gaass Foundation, IA, 1273
Kynett (Edna G.) Memorial Foundation, Inc., PA, 3634

L and L Foundation, NY, 2633
La Crosse Foundation, WI, 4346
La Sala (The Stefano) Foundation, Inc., NY, 2634
Laclede Gas Charitable Trust, MO, 1977
Ladish Company Foundation, WI, 4347
Ladish (Herman W.) Family Foundation, Inc., WI, 4348
Ladish (The Herman W.) Foundation, Inc., WI, 4349
Ladish Malting Company Foundation, Inc., WI, 4350
Laffey-McHugh Foundation, DE, 616
Laird, Norton Foundation, WA, 4246
Lakeside Foundation, CA, 251
Lakeview Fund, Inc., NY, 2635
Lalor Foundation, The, DE, 617
Lamb (Kirkland S. and Rena B.) Foundation, Inc., NC, 3110
Lancaster County Foundation, The, PA, 3635
Lancaster Lens Inc., OH, 3280
Lance Foundation, NC, 3111
Landegger Charitable Foundation, Inc., The, FL, 736
Landmark Charitable Foundation, VA, 4179
Lane (The Edward H.) Foundation, VA, 4180
Lane (Mills Bee) Memorial Foundation, Inc., GA, 851
Lane (Winthrop and Frances) Foundation, NE, 2061
Lang (Eugene M.) Foundation, NY, 2636
Lang (Helen) Charitable Trust, MN, 1873
Langeloth (The Jacob and Valeria) Foundation, NY, 2637
Lanier Brothers Foundation, GA, 852
Lansing Foundation, The Greater, MI, 1735
Lard (Mary Potishman) Trust, TX, 4010
Large Foundation, The, NJ, 2145
Laros (The R. K.) Foundation, PA, 3636
Larrabee Fund Association, CT, 550
Larsen Fund, Inc., NY, 2638
Larsh Foundation Charitable Trust, FL, 737
Larson (Joseph N.) Foundation, MN, 1874
LaRue (George A. and Dolly F.) Trust, MO, 1978
LaSalle Steel Foundation, *see* 4060
Lasdon Foundation, Inc., NY, 2639
Lasker (Albert and Mary) Foundation, Inc., NY, 2640
Lasky (Harry and Sadie) Foundation, IL, 1065
Lastfogel (Abe and Frances) Foundation, NY, 2641
Laub Foundation, The, OH, 3281
Lauder Foundation, The, NY, 2642
Laurel Foundation, PA, 3637
Lautenberg Foundation, The, NJ, 2146
Lavanburg (Fred L.) Foundation, NY, 2643
Lavanburg-Corner House, Inc., The, NY, 2644
LaViers (Harry and Maxie) Foundation, Inc., KY, 1345
L.A.W. Fund, Inc., NY, 2645
Law (Robert O.) Foundation, FL, 738
Layman Trust for Evangelism, IL, 1066
Layne Foundation, CA, 252
Lazar Foundation, The, NY, 2646
La-Z-Boy Chair Foundation, MI, 1736
LBJ Family Foundation, TX, 4011
Leach (Tom & Frances) Foundation, Inc., ND, 3140
Leader Foundation, The, MO, 1979
Lear Siegler Foundation, CA, 253
Leavey (Thomas and Dorothy) Foundation, CA, 254
Lebensfeld Foundation, The, NY, 2647
LeBrun Foundation, NY, 2648
Lebus (Bertha) Trust, CA, 255
Lederer (The Francis L.) Foundation, IL, 1067
Ledler Foundation, The, CA, 256
Lee Foundation, IA, 1274
Lee (James T.) Foundation, Inc., NY, 2649
Lee (The Ray M. and Mary Elizabeth) Foundation, Inc., GA, 853
Leeds & Northrup Foundation, The, PA, 3638
Leff Foundation, Inc., NY, 2650
Lefrak (Samuel J. & Ethel) Foundation, Inc., NY, 2651
Lehman (Edith and Herbert) Foundation, Inc., NY, 2652
Lehman (Robert) Foundation, Inc., NY, 2653
Lehmann (Otto W.) Foundation, IL, 1068
Lehrman (Jacob and Charlotte) Foundation, Inc., DC, 668

Leidesdorf Foundation, Inc., FL, 739
Leidy (John J.) Foundation, Inc., MD, 1430
Leighton-Oare Foundation, Inc., IN, 1235
Leir (Henry J. and Erna D.) Foundation, Inc., NY, 2654
Lemberg Foundation, Inc., NY, 2655
Lend A Hand Society, MA, 1573
Lennon (Fred A.) Foundation, OH, 3282
Lennox Foundation, TX, 4012
Leonardt Foundation, CA, 257
Leonhardt Foundation, Inc., The, NY, 2656
Leppard (J. A.) Foundation Trust, TX, 4013
Lesher (Margaret and Irvin) Foundation, PA, 3639
Leslie Fund, Inc., IL, 1069
LeTourneau Foundation, The, TX, 4014
Leu (Harry P.) Foundation, FL, 740
Leuthold Foundation, Inc., WA, 4247
Levee (Polly Annenberg) Charitable Trust, PA, 3640
Lever Brothers Company Foundation, Inc., NY, 2657
Levi Strauss Foundation, CA, 258
Levie (Marcus and Theresa) Educational Fund, IL, 1070
Levin (The Philip & Janice) Foundation, NJ, 2147
Levinson (Max and Anna) Foundation, MA, 1574
Levinson (Morris L.) Foundation, Inc., NY, 2658
Leviton Foundation, Inc. - New York, NY, 2659
Levitt Foundation, The, NY, 2660
Levitt (Richard S.) Foundation, IA, 1275
Levy (Achille) Foundation, CA, 259
Levy (The Blanche P.) Foundation, PA, 3641
Levy (Chas. and Ruth) Foundation, IL, 1071
Levy Foundation, The, MI, 1737
Levy (Hyman Jebb) Foundation, CA, 260
Levy (Isaac Youssef) Family Foundation, NY, 2661
Levy (The Jerome) Foundation, NY, 2662
Levy (June Rockwell) Foundation Incorporated, MA, 1575
Levy (The Raphael) Memorial Foundation, Inc., CO, 462
Lewis Foundation, Inc., The, NY, 2663
Lewis (Frank J.) Foundation, FL, 741
Lewis (Lillian Kaiser) Foundation, TX, 4015
Lewis (Mabelle McLeod) Memorial Fund, CA, 261
L'Hommedieu (Frances B. and Paige D.) Trust, NJ, 2148
Li Foundation, Inc., The, NY, 2664
Libby-Dufour Fund, LA, 1372
Liberty Corporation Foundation, The, SC, 3809
Liberty Fund, Inc., IN, 1236
Lieberman-Okinow Foundation, The, MN, 1875
Liebowitz (J. S.) Foundation, Inc., NY, 2665
Lightner Sams Foundation, TX, 4016
LILCO Charitable Trust, NY, 2666
Lilly (Eli) and Company Foundation, IN, 1237
Lilly Endowment, Inc., IN, 1238
Lilly (Richard Coyle) Foundation, MN, 1876
Lincoln Electric Foundation, The, OH, 3283
Lincoln Family Foundation, NE, 2062
Lincoln Foundation Inc., NE, 2063
Lincoln Fund, The, NY, 2667
Lincoln National Life Foundation, Inc., The, IN, 1239
Lincoln-Lane Foundation, The, VA, 4181
Lindback (Mary F.) Trust, PA, 3642
Lindberg Foundation, The, NJ, 2149
Lindemann Foundation, Inc., The, NY, 2668
Linder (Albert A. & Bertram N.) Foundation, Inc., NY, 2669
Lindner (Fay J.) Foundation, NY, 2670
Lindsay (Agnes M.) Trust, MA, 1576
Lindsay Foundation, Inc., WI, 4351
Lindsay (Franklin) Student Aid Fund, TX, 4017
Lineberger Foundation, Inc., NC, 3112
Lingle (Bowman C.) Trust, IL, 1072
Lingnan University, Trustees of, NY, 2671
Link Foundation, The, FL, 742
Link (George), Jr. Foundation, Inc., NY, 2672
Linn-Henley Charitable Trust, AL, 10
Lintilhac Foundation, VT, 4149
Lipchitz (Jacques and Yulla) Foundation, Inc., NY, 2673
Lippman Rose Schnurmacher Fund, Inc., NY, 2674
Lipsky (Fred & Sarah) Charitable Foundation, MA, 1577
Lipton (Thomas J.) Foundation, Inc., NJ, 2150
List (Albert A.) Foundation, Inc., CT, 551
Listeman (Marguerite) Foundation, IL, 1073
Littauer (The Lucius N.) Foundation, Inc., NY, 2675

Little (The Arthur D.) Foundation, MA, 1578
Little Family Foundation, RI, 3783
Litton Industries, Foundation of the, CA, 262
Livingston Foundation, Inc., GA, 854
Livingston Memorial Foundation, CA, 263
Livingston (The Milton S. and Corinne N.) Foundation, Inc., NE, 2064
Lizzadro (Joseph) Family Foundation, IL, 1074
Lloyd (The Ralph B.) Foundation, CA, 264
L.L.W.W. Foundation, CA, 265
Loats Foundation, Inc., MD, 1431
Lockheed Leadership Fund, CA, 266
Loeb (Frances and John L.) Foundation, NY, 2676
Loews Foundation, NY, 2677
Lone Star Gas Foundation, TX, 4018
Long (George A. and Grace L.) Foundation, CT, 552
Long (R. A.) Foundation, MO, 1980
Longwood Foundation, Inc., DE, 618
Loock (Margaret & Fred) Foundation, Inc., WI, 4352
Loose (Carrie J.) Fund, see 1981
Loose (Carrie J.) Trust, MO, 1981
Loose (Harry Wilson) Trust, MO, 1982
Loose (Jacob L. and Ella C.) Foundation, MO, 1983
Lopata (Stanley and Lucy) Foundation, MO, 1984
Lopin (The Sam and Anna) Foundation, Inc., NY, 2678
Lorain County Community Foundation, Greater, OH, 3284
Lord (Henry C.) Scholarship Fund Trust, NH, 2091
Lord (The Thomas) Charitable Trust, PA, 3643
Loridans (Charles) Foundation, Inc., GA, 855
Loughran (Mary and Daniel) Foundation, Inc., DC, 669
Louisiana Land and Exploration Company Foundation, The, LA, 1373
Louisiana-Pacific Foundation, OR, 3496
Louisville Community Foundation, Inc., The, KY, 1346
Louisville Foundation, Inc., The, see 1346
Lounsbery (Richard) Foundation, Inc., NY, 2679
Loutit Foundation, The, MI, 1738
Love (George H. and Margaret McClintic) Foundation, PA, 3644
Love (John Allan) Charitable Foundation, MO, 1985
Love (Martha and Spencer) Foundation, NC, 3113
Lovett Foundation, Inc., The, DE, 619
Lowe Foundation, CO, 463
Lowe (The Joe and Emily) Foundation, Inc., FL, 743
Lowell Institute, Trustees of the, MA, 1579
Lowenstein Brothers Foundation, MO, 1986
Lowenstein (Leon) Foundation, Inc., NY, 2680
Lowenstein (William P. and Marie R.) Foundation, TN, 3846
Loyola Foundation, Inc., The, DC, 670
Lubin (Joseph I. and Evelyn J.) Foundation, Inc., NY, 2681
Lubo Fund, Inc., GA, 856
Lubrizol Foundation, The, OH, 3285
Luce (The Henry) Foundation, Inc., NY, 2682
Lucerna Fund, NY, 2683
Lukens Foundation, The, PA, 3645
Lukens Steel Foundation, The, see 3645
Luling Foundation, The, TX, 4019
Lumpkin Foundation, The, IL, 1075
Lurcy (Georges) Charitable and Educational Trust, NY, 2684
Lurie (Louis R.) Foundation, CA, 267
Lutheran Brotherhood Foundation, MN, 1877
Lux (Miranda) Foundation, CA, 268
Lynch (John B.) Scholarship Foundation, DE, 620
Lyndhurst Foundation, TN, 3847
Lynn (E. M.) Foundation, FL, 744
Lyon (E. H.) and Melody Lyon Foundation, Inc., OK, 3442
Lyon Foundation, Inc., AR, 53
Lyon Foundation, Inc., MI, 1739
Lytel (Bertha Russ) Foundation, CA, 269

M. E. Foundation, The, MD, 1432
Mabee (The J. E. and L. E.) Foundation, Inc., OK, 3443
MacArthur (J. Roderick) Foundation, IL, 1076
MacArthur (John D. and Catherine T.) Foundation, IL, 1077
MacCurdy-Salisbury Educational Foundation, Inc., The, CT, 553
Macdonald (James A.) Foundation, NY, 2685

MacDonald (Marquis George) Foundation, Inc., NY, 2686
Macdonald (Maybelle Clark) Fund, OR, 3497
MacDonald (Mrs. Zoe Blunt) Trust, TX, 4020
Mack (The J. S.) Foundation, PA, 3646
MacKall (The Paul) & Evanina Evans Bell MacKall Trust, NY, 2687
MacKenzie Foundation, The, CA, 270
Maclellan Foundation, Inc., The, TN, 3848
Maclellan (R. J.) Charitable Trust, TN, 3849
Maclellan (Robert L. and Kathrina H.) Foundation, TN, 3850
Macmillan Foundation, The, NY, 2688
Macy (Josiah), Jr. Foundation, NY, 2689
Mad River Foundation, NY, 2690
Maddox (J. F.) Foundation, NM, 2209
Magale Foundation, The, LA, 1374
Magowan Family Foundation, Inc., The, NY, 2691
Maguire Foundation, Inc., The, CT, 554
Maguire (The Russell) Foundation, Inc., NY, 2692
Mahony (Patrick) Charitable Trust, CA, 271
Mailman (A. L.) Family Foundation, Inc., NY, 2693
Mailman Foundation, Inc., The, NY, 2694
Main Street Foundation, Inc., CT, 555
Malbis Memorial Foundation, AL, 11
Mallery Charitable Trust, see 1740
Mallery (J. Harvey) Trust, MI, 1740
Mallinckrodt (Edward), Jr. Foundation, MO, 1987
Mallinckrodt Fund, Inc., The, MO, 1988
Maltz (B. N.) Foundation, IL, 1078
Mamiye Foundation, Inc., NJ, 2151
Mandel (Jack N. and Lilyan) Foundation, OH, 3286
Mandel (Joseph and Florence) Foundation, OH, 3287
Mandel (Morton and Barbara) Foundation, OH, 3288
Mandell (Samuel P.) Foundation, PA, 3647
Mandeville Foundation, Inc., The, NY, 2695
Manealoff Foundation, Inc., NY, 2696
Maneely Fund, Inc., PA, 3648
Manilow (Nathan) Foundation, IL, 1079
Manning (The James Hilton) and Emma Austin Manning Foundation, NY, 2697
Manoogian (Alex and Marie) Foundation, MI, 1741
Mansfield (Albert & Anne) Foundation, IL, 1080
Manufacturers Hanover Foundation, NY, 2698
MAPCO Educational Foundation, Inc., OK, 3444
Marathon Oil Foundation, Inc., OH, 3289
Marbrook Foundation, MN, 1878
Marcus (James S.) Foundation, NY, 2699
Mardag Foundation, MN, 1879
Mardigian Foundation, MI, 1742
Maremont Corporation Foundation, IL, 1081
Margaret Hall Foundation, Inc., KY, 1347
Marine Foundation, Inc., The, WI, 4353
Marini Family Trust, CA, 272
Market Trust, ME, 1394
Markey (The John C.) Charitable Fund, OH, 3290
Markey (Lucille P.) Charitable Trust, FL, 745
Markle (The John and Mary R.) Foundation, NY, 2700
Markus (Roy & Eva) Foundation, Inc., OH, 3291
Marley Fund, The, KS, 1319
Marmot Foundation, The, DE, 621
Marquette Charitable Organization, IL, 1082
Marriott (The J. Willard) Family Foundation, see 1433
Marriott (The J. Willard) Foundation, MD, 1433
Mars Foundation, The, VA, 4182
Marshall & Ilsley Bank Foundation, Inc., WI, 4354
Marshall Foundation, AZ, 40
Marshall (George Preston) Foundation, MD, 1434
Marshall (Harriet McDaniel) Trust in Memory of Sanders McDaniel, GA, 857
Marshall (Silver) Foundation, Inc., DE, 622
Marshburn Foundation, The, CA, 273
Martin (Bert William) Foundation, IL, 1083
Martin (Della) Foundation, CA, 274
Martin Foundation Inc., The, IN, 1240
Martin Marietta Corporation Foundation, MD, 1435
Martin Marietta Philanthropic Trust, NC, 3114
Martin (The Sylvia) Foundation, Inc., NJ, 2152
Martinson (Joseph) Memorial Foundation, NY, 2701
Martinson (Joseph) Memorial Fund, see 2701
Marx (Robert S.) Residuary Trust, OH, 3292
Maryland National Foundation, Inc., The, MD, 1436
Masco Screw Products Company Charitable Trust, MI, 1743

Mason (B. A.) Trust, WI, 4355
Mason Charitable Foundation, IL, 1084
Masonic Foundation of Utah, UT, 4142
Massachusetts Charitable Mechanic Association, MA, 1580
Massengill-DeFriece Foundation, Inc., TN, 3851
Massey Charitable Trust, PA, 3649
Massey Foundation, VA, 4183
Massey (Jack C.) Foundation, TN, 3852
Massie (David Meade) Trust, OH, 3293
Mastronardi (The Charles A.) Foundation, NY, 2702
Material Service Foundation, IL, 1085
Mather (Elizabeth Ring) and William Gwinn Mather Fund, OH, 3294
Mather (The Richard) Fund, NY, 2703
Mather (The S. Livingston) Charitable Trust, OH, 3295
Mathers (G. Harold & Leila) Charitable Foundation, NY, 2704
Mathews Foundation, The, MO, 1989
Mathis (The Alice K.) Memorial Foundation, GA, 858
Mathis-Pfohl Foundation, NY, 2705
Matlock Foundation, WA, 4248
Mattel Foundation, CA, 275
Matthews (Hale) Foundation, NY, 2706
Matz Foundation (Edelman Division), NY, 2707
Matz (Israel) Foundation, NY, 2708
May (The Morton J.) Foundation, MO, 1990
May Stores Foundation, Inc., The, MO, 1991
May (Wilbur D.) Foundation, CA, 276
Mayer (The Louis B.) Foundation, CA, 277
Mayer (Oscar G. and Elsa S.) Charitable Trust, IL, 1086
Mayr (George Henry) Trust, CA, 278
Mays Foundation, TX, 4021
Maytag Company Foundation, Inc., The, IA, 1276
Maytag (The Fred) Family Foundation, IA, 1277
Mazer (The Jacob & Ruth) Foundation, CT, 556
Mazer (Joseph & Ceil) Foundation, Inc., NY, 2709
Mazer (William and Helen) Foundation, Inc., NY, 2710
Mazza Foundation, IL, 1087
MCA Foundation Ltd., CA, 279
McAdenville Foundation, Inc., The, NC, 3115
McAlister (The Harold) Charitable Foundation, CA, 280
McAlonan (John A.) Trust, OH, 3296
McAshan Educational and Charitable Trust, TX, 4022
McBean (The Atholl) Foundation, CA, 281
McBeath (Faye) Foundation, WI, 4356
McCaddin-McQuirk Foundation, Inc., The, NY, 2711
McCallum Desert Foundation, CA, 282
McCann (James J.) Charitable Trust, NY, 2712
McCarthy Charities, Inc., The, NY, 2713
McCarthy (The Michael W.) Foundation, NY, 2714
McCasland Foundation, OK, 3445
McClure (James G. K.) Educational and Development Fund, Inc., NC, 3116
McConnell (Neil A.) Foundation, Inc., NY, 2715
McCormick (Anne) Trust, PA, 3650
McCormick (Chauncey and Marion Deering) Foundation, IL, 1088
McCormick (Robert R.) Charitable Trust, IL, 1089
McCormick (Robert R.) Foundation, IL, 1090
McCoy Foundation, The, CO, 464
McCrea Foundation, VA, 4184
McCreless (Sollie & Lilla) Foundation for Christian Evangelism, Christian Missions, and Christian Education, TX, 4023
McCrory Foundation, Inc., The, NY, 2716
McCune Foundation, PA, 3651
McCutchen Foundation, The, NJ, 2153
McDavid (G. N. and Edna) Dental Education Trust, MO, 1992
McDermott (The Eugene) Foundation, TX, 4024
McDonald (Frederick) Trust, NY, 2717
McDonald (J. M.) Foundation, Inc., NY, 2718
McDonnell Douglas Foundation, MO, 1993
McDonnell (Everett N.) Foundation, IL, 1091
McDonnell Foundation, Inc., see 1994
McDonnell (James S.) Foundation, MO, 1994
McDonough (Bernard) Foundation, Inc., WV, 4286
McEachern (Ida J.) Charitable Trust, WA, 4249
McEvoy (Mildred H.) Foundation, MA, 1581
McFarland Charitable Foundation, IL, 1092
McFawn (Lois Sisler) Trust No. 2, OH, 3297
McFeely-Rogers Foundation, PA, 3652
McGaw (Foster G.) Foundation, IL, 1093

McGee Foundation, The, MO, 1995
McGee Foundation, Inc., The, OK, 3446
McGonagle (Dextra Baldwin) Foundation, Inc., NY, 2719
McGovern (John P.) Foundation, TX, 4025
McGraw (The Curtis W.) Foundation, NJ, 2154
McGraw (The Donald C.) Foundation, Inc., NY, 2720
McGraw Foundation, IL, 1094
McGraw-Edison Foundation, IL, 1095
McGraw-Hill Foundation, Inc., The, NY, 2721
McGregor (The A. M.) Home, OH, 3298
McGregor Fund, MI, 1744
McGregor (Thomas and Frances) Foundation, DC, 671
McHugh Family Foundation, The, CO, 465
McInerny Foundation, HI, 903
McIntosh Foundation, The, FL, 746
McIntyre (B. D. and Jane E.) Foundation, MI, 1745
McIntyre (C. S. and Marion F.) Foundation, MI, 1746
McKee (Robert E. and Evelyn) Foundation, TX, 4026
McKee (Virginia A.) Poor Fund, PA, 3653
McKelvy (B. T. & Eg. Morrison) Memorial Fund, PA, 3654
McKenna (Katherine Mabis) Foundation, Inc., PA, 3655
McKenna (Philip M.) Foundation, Inc., PA, 3656
McKesson Foundation, Inc., CA, 283
McKnight Foundation, The, MN, 1880
McKnight (The Sumner T.) Foundation, MN, 1881
McLean Contributionship, The, PA, 3657
McMahon Foundation, The, OK, 3447
McMannis (William J.) and A. Haskell McMannis Educational Fund, FL, 747
McMillan (Bruce), Jr. Foundation, Inc., TX, 4027
McMillan (D. W.) Foundation, AL, 12
McMillen Foundation, Inc., IN, 1241
McNeely Foundation, The, MN, 1882
McQueen (Adeline and George) Foundation of 1960, TX, 4028
McShain (John) Charities, Inc., PA, 3658
McWane Foundation, AL, 13
Mead Corporation Foundation, The, OH, 3299
Mead (Giles W. and Elise G.) Foundation, CA, 284
Mead Johnson & Company Foundation, Inc., IN, 1242
Meade Haven Charitable Trust, TN, 3853
Meadowood Foundation, MN, 1883
Meadows Foundation, Inc., TX, 4029
Measey (The Benjamin and Mary Siddons) Foundation, PA, 3659
Medical Trust, The, PA, 3660
Medina Foundation, WA, 4250
Medtronic Foundation, The, MN, 1884
Melamed Foundation, The, MN, 1885
Mellen Foundation, The, OH, 3300
Mellinger (Edward Arthur) Educational Foundation, Inc., IL, 1096
Mellon (The Andrew W.) Foundation, NY, 2722
Mellon Bank Foundation, PA, 3661
Mellon (R. K.) Family Foundation, PA, 3662
Mellon (Richard King) Foundation, PA, 3663
Melohn Foundation, Inc., The, NY, 2723
Melton (Samuel Mendel) Foundation, OH, 3301
Melville (The David B.) Foundation, MA, 1582
Memorial Foundation for Children, The, VA, 4185
Memorial Fund, Inc., The, NC, 3117
Memphis-Plough Community Foundation, The, TN, 3854
Memton Fund, Inc., The, NY, 2724
Mendelson (Alfred G. and Ida) Family Foundation, Inc., MD, 1437
Mengle (Glenn and Ruth) Foundation, PA, 3664
Menil Foundation, Inc., TX, 4030
Menil Fund, TX, 4031
Menlo Foundation, CA, 285
Menschel (The Robert B.) Foundation, NY, 2725
Mercantile Trust Company Charitable Trust, MO, 1996
Merchants Fund, PA, 3665
Merck Company Foundation, The, NJ, 2155
Merck Family Fund, SC, 3810
Merck (John) Fund, NY, 2726
Meredith (Edwin T.) Foundation, IA, 1278
Meredith Foundation, TX, 4032
Merit Gasoline Foundation, The, PA, 3666
Merkert (E. F.) Foundation, MA, 1583
Merrick Foundation, The, OK, 3448

Merrick (Robert G. and Anne M.) Foundation, Inc., MD, 1438
Merrill (The Ingram) Foundation, NY, 2727
Merrill Lynch & Co. Foundation, Inc., NY, 2728
Merrill (The R. D.) Foundation, WA, 4251
Merry Mary Charitable Foundation, Inc., CA, 286
Mertz (Martha) Foundation, Inc., NY, 2729
Mertz-Gilmore (Joyce) Foundation, NY, 2730
Meserve (Albert & Helen) Memorial Fund, CT, 557
Messing (The Morris M. and Helen F.) Foundation, NJ, 2156
Metcalf (Stanley W.) Foundation, Inc., NY, 2731
Metropolitan Life Foundation, NY, 2732
Metzger-Price Fund, NY, 2733
Meyer (Aaron and Rachel) Memorial Foundation, Inc., NJ, 2157
Meyer (The Andre and Bella) Foundation, Inc., NY, 2734
Meyer (The Baron de Hirsch) Foundation, FL, 748
Meyer (Eugene and Agnes E.) Foundation, DC, 672
Meyer (Fred) Charitable Trust, OR, 3498
Meyer (Milton and Sophie) Fund, CA, 287
Meyer (Robert R.) Foundation, AL, 14
Meyer-Ceco Foundation, The, IL, 1097
Meyerhoff (The Joseph) Fund, Inc., MD, 1439
MFA Foundation, MO, 1997
Michael (Herbert I. and Elsa B.) Foundation, UT, 4143
Michel (Barbara and Clifford) Foundation, Inc., NY, 2735
Michigan Standard Alloys - Arthur S. Mendel Foundation, MI, 1747
Middendorf Foundation, Inc., MD, 1440
Middleton (Kate Kinloch) Fund, AL, 15
Midland Foundation, MI, 1748
Midland-Ross Foundation, OH, 3302
Milbank (The Dunlevy) Foundation, Inc., NY, 2736
Milbank Memorial Fund, NY, 2737
Miles Laboratories Foundation, IN, 1243
Millard (Adah K.) Charitable Trust, IL, 1098
Millbrook Tribute Garden, Inc., NY, 2738
Miller (Albert L. and Louise B.) Foundation, Inc., MI, 1749
Miller & Chevalier Charitable Foundation, The, DC, 673
Miller (Edwill B.) Trust, PA, 3667
Miller Foundation, The, see 4357
Miller (The Gladys and Rudolph) Foundation, MN, 1886
Miller (Kathryn & Gilbert) Fund, Inc., NY, 2739
Miller (The Steve J.) Foundation, WI, 4357
Millhollon (Nettie) Educational Trust, TX, 4033
Milliken Foundation, NY, 2740
Milliken (Gerrish H.) Foundation, DE, 623
Millikin (James) Trust, IL, 1099
Mills (Frances Goll) Fund, MI, 1750
Mills (Ralph E.) Foundation, KY, 1348
Millstein Charitable Foundation, The, PA, 3668
Millstone Foundation, MO, 1998
Milwaukee Foundation, WI, 4358
Mine Safety Appliances Co. Charitable Trust, PA, 3669
Minear (Ruth M.) Educational Trust, IN, 1244
Minerals Industry Educational Foundation, The, NY, 2741
Mingenback (The Julia J.) Foundation, Inc., KS, 1320
Miniger (Clement O.) Memorial Foundation, OH, 3303
Minneapolis Foundation, The, MN, 1887
Minneapolis Star and Tribune Foundation, MN, 1888
Minnesota Foundation, MN, 1889
Minnesota Mining and Manufacturing Foundation, Inc., MN, 1890
Minor (The Berkeley) and Susan Fontaine Minor Foundation, WV, 4287
Mission Linen Foundation, see 309
Mitchell (Edward D. and Anna) Family Foundation, CA, 288
Mitchell Foundation, The, AL, 16
Mitrani Family Foundation, Inc., NY, 2742
MLM Charitable Foundation, OH, 3304
Mobil Foundation, Inc., NY, 2743
Mobile Community Foundation, The, AL, 17
Mocquereau (The Dom) Foundation, Inc., NY, 2744
Model (Jane & Leo) Foundation, Inc., NY, 2745
Monarch Machine Tool Company Foundation, OH, 3305

Moncrief (William A. and Elizabeth B.) Foundation, TX, 4034
Monell (The Ambrose) Foundation, NY, 2746
Monfort Charitable Foundation, CO, 466
Monks (G. G.) Foundation, ME, 1395
Monsanto Fund, MO, 1999
Monterey County, Community Foundation for, CA, 289
Monterey Fund, Inc., NY, 2747
Monterey Peninsula Foundation, see 289
Montgomery Foundation, OH, 3306
Monticello College Foundation, The, IL, 1100
Moody Foundation, The, TX, 4035
Moore (Alfred) Foundation, SC, 3811
Moore (Edward S.) Foundation, Inc., NY, 2748
Moore Foundation, IN, 1245
Moore (Harry W. and Margaret) Foundation, Inc., OH, 3307
Moore (James Starr) Memorial Foundation, Inc., GA, 859
Moore (Marjorie) Charitable Foundation, CT, 558
Moore (P. M.) Foundation, PA, 3670
Moores (The Harry C.) Foundation, OH, 3308
Moorman Company Fund, IL, 1101
Moorman Foundation, The, IL, 1102
Morania Foundation, Inc., NY, 2749
Morehead (The John Motley) Foundation, NC, 3118
Morgan City Fund, The, LA, 1375
Morgan Guaranty Trust Company of New York Charitable Trust, NY, 2750
Morgan (Louie R. and Gertrude) Foundation, FL, 749
Morgan (Marietta M. & Samuel T.), Jr. Foundation, VA, 4186
Morgan (The Roy T.) Foundation, RI, 3784
Morgan Stanley Foundation, NY, 2751
Morgan Trust for Charity, Religion, and Education, The, NC, 3119
Morgan-Worcester, Inc., MA, 1584
Morgenstern (Morris) Foundation, NY, 2752
Morley Brothers Foundation, MI, 1751
Morris (The Allen) Foundation, FL, 750
Morris (E. A.) Charitable Foundation, NC, 3120
Morris (Margaret T.) Foundation, AZ, 41
Morris (Norman M.) Foundation, Inc., NY, 2753
Morris (The William T.) Foundation, Inc., NY, 2754
Morrison (Harry W.) Family Foundation, Inc., see 914
Morrison (Harry W.) Foundation, Inc., ID, 914
Morrison-Knudsen Employees Foundation, Inc., ID, 915
Morton Foundation, Inc., NY, 2755
Morton (The Sterling) Charitable Trust, IL, 1103
Mosbacher (Emil), Jr. Foundation, Inc., NY, 2756
Mosbacher Foundation, Inc., NY, 2757
Moses (Henry and Lucy) Fund, Inc., NY, 2758
Mosher (Samuel B.) Foundation, CA, 290
Mosle (Rotan) Foundation, TX, 4036
Mosler (Edwin H.), Jr. Foundation, NY, 2759
Moss (Harry S.) Foundation, TX, 4037
Moss (Harry S.) Heart Trust, TX, 4038
Mossman (J. Malcolm) Charitable Trust, NY, 2760
Mostazafan Foundation of New York, The, NY, 2761
Mostyn Foundation Inc., NY, 2762
Mote Scientific Foundation, Inc., FL, 751
Motorola Foundation, IL, 1104
Mott (Charles Stewart) Foundation, MI, 1752
Mott (Ruth) Fund, MI, 1753
Mott (Stewart R.) Charitable Trust, NY, 2763
Mount Vernon Community Trust, The, OH, 3309
Muchnic Foundation, KS, 1321
Muehlstein (The Herman) Foundation, Inc., NY, 2764
Mueller (C. F.) Company Scholarship Foundation, NJ, 2158
Mulcahy Foundation, The, AZ, 42
Mulford (The Clarence E.) Trust, ME, 1396
Mulford (Vincent) Foundation, MD, 1441
Mullan (The Thomas F. and Clementine L.) Foundation, Inc., MD, 1442
Mullen (The John K. and Catherine S.) Benevolent Corporation, CO, 467
Muller (Frank), Sr. Foundation, CA, 291
Munger (Alfred C.) Foundation, CA, 292
Munson (W. B.) Foundation, TX, 4039
Murch Foundation, The, OH, 3310
Murdock (M. J.) Charitable Trust, WA, 4252

Murdy Foundation, CA, 293
Murphey (Lluella Morey) Foundation, CA, 294
Murphy (Dan) Foundation, CA, 295
Murphy Foundation, The, AR, 54
Murphy (G. C.) Company Foundation, PA, 3671
Murphy (John P.) Foundation, OH, 3311
Murphy (Katherine and John) Foundation, GA, 860
Murray Foundation, WA, 4253
Musica Aeterna, Inc., NY, 2765
Muskegon County Community Foundation, Inc., MI, 1754
Muskiwinni Foundation, The, NY, 2766
Musselman (Emma G.) Foundation, PA, 3672
Myers-Ti-Caro Foundation, Inc., NC, 3121
Myra Foundation, ND, 3141
Myrin (The Mabel Pew) Trust, PA, 3673

Nabisco Foundation, NJ, 2159
Nalco Foundation, The, IL, 1105
Napier Foundation, The, NY, 2767
Nathanson-Abrams Family Foundation, NY, 2768
National Bank of Detroit Charitable Trust, MI, 1755
National By-Products Foundation, Inc., IA, 1279
National Central Foundation, The, PA, 3674
National City Foundation, The, NY, 2769
National Forge Foundation, PA, 3675
National Home Library Foundation, DC, 674
National Institute for the Food Service Industry, IL, 1106
National Machinery Foundation, Inc., OH, 3312
National Starch & Chemical Foundation, Inc., NJ, 2160
National Vulcanized Fibre Company Community Services Trust Fund, DE, 624
Nationwide Foundation, OH, 3313
Naurison (James Z.) Scholarship Fund, MA, 1585
Navarro Community Foundation, TX, 4040
NCR Foundation, The, OH, 3314
Needmor Fund, The, CO, 468
Neenah Foundry Foundation, Inc., WI, 4359
Neilson (George W.) Foundation, MN, 1891
Nekoosa Papers Foundation Incorporated, WI, 4360
Nelco Foundation, Inc., NY, 2770
Nelson (The Ludvig and Selma) Religious, Educational and Charitable Trust, KS, 1322
Neu (Hugo and Doris) Foundation, Inc., NY, 2771
Neuberger (Roy R. and Marie S.) Foundation, Inc., NY, 2772
New England Peabody Home for Crippled Children, MA, 1586
New Hampshire Charitable Fund, The, NH, 2092
New Haven Foundation, The, CT, 559
New Jersey, Community Foundation of, NJ, 2161
New Orleans Regional Foundation, The Greater, LA, 1376
New Prospect Foundation, IL, 1107
New World Foundation, The, NY, 2773
New York Community Trust, The, NY, 2774
New York Foundation, NY, 2775
New York Life Foundation, NY, 2776
New York Times Company Foundation, Inc., The, NY, 2777
Newcombe (The Charlotte W.) Foundation, NJ, 2162
Newhall (The Henry Mayo) Foundation, CA, 296
Newhouse (Samuel I.) Foundation, Inc., NY, 2778
New-Land Foundation, Inc., The, NY, 2779
Newman (Calvin M. and Racquel H.) Charitable Trust, CA, 297
Newman (Jerome A. and Estelle R.) Assistance Fund, Inc., NY, 2780
Newport Restoration Foundation, RI, 3785
NFL Alumni Foundation Fund, MD, 1443
Nias (Henry) Foundation, Inc., NY, 2781
Nichols Foundation, Inc., NY, 2782
Nichols (Miller) Foundation, MO, 2000
1957 Charity Trust, The, PA, 3676
Nippert (L & L) Charitable Foundation, The, OH, 3315
NL Industries Foundation, Inc., The, NY, 2783
Noble (Edward John) Foundation, Inc., NY, 2784
Noble (John H. and Ethel G.) Charitable Trust, NY, 2785
Noble (The Samuel Roberts) Foundation, Inc., OK, 3449
Noble (The Vivian Bilby) Foundation, Inc., OK, 3450

Noguchi (Isamu) Foundation, Inc., NY, 2786
Noonan (Deborah Munroe) Memorial Fund, MA, 1587
Norcliffe Fund, The, WA, 4254
Nordson Foundation, OH, 3316
Norfolk Foundation, The, VA, 4187
Norgren (Carl A.) Foundation, CO, 469
Norman (Andrew) Foundation, CA, 298
Norman Foundation, Inc., NY, 2787
Normandie Foundation, Inc., NY, 2788
Norris (The Kenneth T. and Eileen L.) Foundation, CA, 299
Norstar Bank of Upstate NY Foundation, NY, 2789
North Dakota Community Foundation, ND, 3142
North Star Research Foundation, MN, 1892
Northeastern Pooled Common Fund for Education in the Social Sciences and the Arts, NY, 2790
Northen (Mary Moody), Inc., TX, 4041
Northern Star Foundation, MN, 1893
Northern Trust Company Charitable Trust, The, IL, 1108
Northwest Area Foundation, MN, 1894
Northwest Industries Foundation, Inc., IL, 1109
Norton Company Foundation, MA, 1588
Norton (The George W.) Foundation, Inc., KY, 1349
Norwest Foundation, MN, 1895
Norwood Foundation, Inc., NY, 2791
Nosutch Foundation of California, CA, 300
Noxell Foundation, Inc., The, MD, 1444
Noyes (Jessie Smith) Foundation, Inc., NY, 2792
Noyes (Nicholas H.), Jr. Memorial Foundation, Inc., IN, 1246
Nuveen Benevolent Trust, FL, 752
N've Shalom Foundation, Inc., NY, 2793

Oakland Scottish Rite Scaife and Oakland Scottish Rite Scholarship Foundations, CA, 301
Oaklawn Foundation, The, CT, 560
Oberlaender (Gustav) Foundation, Inc., PA, 3677
O'Bleness (Charles) Foundation No. 3, OH, 3317
O'Brien (Alice M.) Foundation, MN, 1896
Occidental Petroleum Charitable Foundation, Inc., CA, 302
O.C.F. Foundation, Inc., NY, 2794
O'Connor (A. Lindsay and Olive B.) Foundation, NY, 2795
O'Connor (The Kathryn) Foundation, TX, 4042
OCRI Foundation, OR, 3499
Odell (Robert Stewart) and Helen Pfeiffer Odell Fund, CA, 303
O'Donnell Foundation, TX, 4043
Oestreicher (Sylvan and Ann) Foundation, Inc., NY, 2796
O'Fallon (Martin J. and Mary Anne) Trust, CO, 470
Offield (Dorothy Wrigley) Charity Fund, Inc., see 1110
Offield Family Foundation, The, IL, 1110
Ogden College Fund, The, KY, 1350
Ogden (Ralph E.) Foundation, Inc., NY, 2797
Oglebay Norton Foundation, OH, 3318
Ohio Citizens Trust Company Foundation, The, OH, 3319
Ohio Valley Foundation, The, OH, 3320
Ohl (George A.), Jr. Trust, NJ, 2163
Ohrstrom Foundation, Inc., The, VA, 4188
Oklahoma City Community Foundation, Inc., OK, 3451
Oklahoma Gas and Electric Company Foundation, Inc., OK, 3452
Old Colony Charitable Foundation, MA, 1589
Old Stone Bank Charitable Foundation, RI, 3786
Oldham Little Church Foundation, TX, 4044
Olin Corporation Charitable Trust, CT, 561
Olin Foundation, Inc., NY, 2798
Olin (John M.) Charitable Trust, MO, 2001
Olin (John M.) Foundation, Inc., NY, 2799
Olin (Spencer T. and Ann W.) Foundation, MO, 2002
Olive Bridge Fund, Inc., NY, 2800
Oliver Memorial Trust Foundation, IN, 1247
Olmsted (The George) Foundation, VA, 4189
Olsson (Elis) Memorial Foundation, VA, 4190
Omaha National Bank Charitable Trust, NE, 2065
Omaha World-Herald Foundation, The, NE, 2066
Onan Family Foundation, MN, 1897
O'Neil (The Albert T.) Foundation, see 1898

O'Neil (The Casey Albert T.) Foundation, MN, 1898
O'Neil (Cyril F. and Marie E.) Foundation, NY, 2801
O'Neil (The M. G.) Foundation, OH, 3321
O'Neil (The W.) Foundation, OH, 3322
Oppenheimer Family Foundation, The, IL, 1111
Oppenheimer (Leo) and Flora Oppenheimer Haas Trust, NY, 2802
Oppenstein Brothers Foundation, MO, 2003
Orange Orphan Society, The, NJ, 2164
Ordean Foundation, MN, 1899
Oregon Community Foundation, The, OR, 3500
Orleans (Carrie S.) Trust, TX, 4045
Orleton Trust Fund, CA, 304
Orscheln Industries Foundation, Inc., MO, 2004
Osborn (Edward B.) Charitable Trust, NY, 2803
Osceola Foundation, Inc., NY, 2804
O'Shaughnessy (I. A.) Foundation, Inc., MN, 1900
Oshkosh Foundation, WI, 4361
Oshkosh Truck Foundation, Inc., WI, 4362
Ostrow (Seniel and Dorothy) Foundation, CA, 305
Otasco Foundation, see 3461
O'Toole (Theresa and Edward) Foundation, NY, 2805
Ottinger Foundation, Inc., The, NY, 2806
Ottley (Marian W.) Trust - Atlanta, GA, 861
Ottley (Marian W.) Trust - Watertown, GA, 862
Overbrook Foundation, The, NY, 2807
Overlake Foundation, Inc., TX, 4046
Owen (B. B.) Trust, TX, 4047
Owsley (Alvin and Lucy) Foundation, TX, 4048
Oxford Foundation, Inc., PA, 3678
Oxnard Foundation, CA, 306

P & B Foundation, NC, 3122
Pabst Breweries Foundation, WI, 4363
PACCAR Foundation, WA, 4255
Pacific Western Foundation, CA, 307
Packard (The David and Lucile) Foundation, CA, 308
Packer (Horace B.) Foundation, Inc., PA, 3679
Page (George B.) Foundation, CA, 309
Page (The Ruth) Foundation, IL, 1112
Pagel (William M. and Mary E.) Trust, MI, 1756
Paley (The Goldie) Foundation, PA, 3680
Paley (William S.) Foundation, Inc., NY, 2808
Palisano (The Vincent H. "Jim") Foundation, NY, 2809
Palmer (Francis Asbury) Fund, NY, 2810
Palmer (The Frank Loomis) Fund, CT, 562
Pangburn Foundation, The, TX, 4049
Panwy Foundation, CT, 563
Paper (Lewis and Annie F.) Foundation, MN, 1901
Pappas (Bessie) Charitable Foundation, Inc., MA, 1590
Pappas Family Foundation, see 1590
Pappas (Thomas Anthony) Charitable Foundation, Inc., MA, 1591
Parapsychology Foundation, Inc., NY, 2811
Pardee (Elsa U.) Foundation, MI, 1757
Park Foundation, The, NY, 2812
Parker Foundation, The, CA, 310
Parker Foundation, The, TX, 4050
Parker (The Robert L.) Foundation, OK, 3453
Parker (The Theodore Edson) Foundation, MA, 1592
Parker-Hannifin Foundation, The, OH, 3323
Parklands Foundation, PA, 3681
Parman (Robert A.) Foundation, OK, 3454
Parrott (William G.) Foundation, MO, 2005
Parry Foundation, TX, 4051
Parshelsky (Moses L.) Foundation, NY, 2813
Parsons (The Ralph M.) Foundation, CA, 311
Parvin (The Albert) Foundation, CA, 312
Pasadena Area Residential Aid A Corp., CA, 313
Pasadena Foundation, CA, 314
Patterson (Alicia) Foundation, DC, 675
Patterson (Robert Leet) & Clara Guthrie Patterson Trust, CT, 564
Patterson (W. I.) Charitable Fund, PA, 3682
Patterson-Barclay Memorial Foundation, Inc., GA, 863
Pattillo Foundation, The, GA, 864
Pattiz Family Foundation, CA, 315
Paul (Josephine Bay and C. Michael) Foundation, Inc., NY, 2814
Pauley (The Edwin W.) Foundation, CA, 316
Paulucci Family Foundation, The, MN, 1902
Payne (Frank E.) and Seba B. Payne Foundation, IL, 1113

Payne Fund, Inc., OH, 3324
PBP Foundation of New York, Inc., NY, 2815
Peabody (Amelia) Foundation, MA, 1593
Pearlman (Henry and Rose) Foundation, Inc., NY, 2816
Pearlstone (The Peggy Meyerhoff) Foundation, Inc., MD, 1445
Pearson (The Patsy) Memorial Fund, IL, 1114
Peat, Marwick, Mitchell Foundation, The, NY, 2817
Peck (Milton) Family Foundation, Inc., WI, 4364
Peery (Richard T.) Foundation, CA, 317
Peierls Foundation, Inc., The, NY, 2818
Pella Rolscreen Foundation, IA, 1280
Pendergast-Weyer Foundation, The, MO, 2006
Penick (Albert) Fund, NJ, 2165
Peninsula Community Foundation, CA, 318
Penn (The William) Foundation, PA, 3683
Penney (James C.) Foundation, Inc., NY, 2819
Pennwalt Foundation, PA, 3684
Penzance Foundation, DE, 625
Peppers (The Ann) Foundation, CA, 319
PepsiCo Foundation, Inc., NY, 2820
Perini (Joseph) Memorial Foundation, MA, 1594
Perini Memorial Foundation, Inc., MA, 1595
Perkin Fund, The, CT, 565
Perkins Charitable Foundation, The, OH, 3325
Perkins (F. Mason) Trust, NJ, 2166
Perkins (The George W.) Memorial Foundation, NY, 2821
Perkins (The Joe and Lois) Foundation, TX, 4052
Perkins (Kitty M.) Foundation, IL, 1115
Perkins-Prothro Foundation, TX, 4053
Perlman (Louis & Anita) Family Foundation, IL, 1116
Permanent Charity Fund of Boston, see 1482
Perpetual Benevolent Fund, The, MA, 1596
Perry Foundation, Incorporated, VA, 4191
Perry (The M. G. and Johnnye D.) Foundation, TX, 4054
Persky (Joseph) Foundation, MA, 1597
Peterborough Foundation, IL, 1117
Peterloon Foundation, OH, 3326
Peters (Charles F.) Foundation, The, PA, 3685
Peters (Leon S.) Foundation, CA, 320
Peters (R. D. and Linda) Foundation, Inc., WI, 4365
Petersen (Esper A.) Foundation, IL, 1118
Peterson (Fred J.) Foundation, Inc., WI, 4366
Peterson (The Thomas F.) Foundation, OH, 3327
Petteys (The Jack) Memorial Foundation, CO, 471
Pettus-Crowe Foundation, Inc., NY, 2822
Pew (The J. Howard) Freedom Trust, PA, 3686
Pew (J. N.), Jr. Charitable Trust, The, PA, 3687
Pew Memorial Trust, The, PA, 3688
Peyton (The Mary L.) Foundation, TX, 4055
Pfaffinger Foundation, CA, 321
Pfeiffer (Gustavus and Louise) Research Foundation, CA, 322
Pfizer Foundation, Inc., The, NY, 2823
Pforzheimer (The Carl and Lily) Foundation, Inc., NY, 2824
Phelps County Community Foundation, Inc., NE, 2067
Phelps Dodge Foundation, NY, 2825
PHH Group Foundation Incorporated, MD, 1446
Philadelphia Foundation, The, PA, 3689
Philibosian (Stephen) Foundation, CA, 323
Philippe Foundation, Inc., NY, 2826
Philips (Jesse) Foundation, OH, 3328
Phillips (A. P.) Foundation, Inc., FL, 753
Phillips (Charlotte Palmer) Foundation, Inc., NY, 2827
Phillips (Dr. & Mrs. Arthur William) Charitable Trust, PA, 3690
Phillips (The Dr. P.) Foundation, FL, 754
Phillips (Edwin) Trust, MA, 1598
Phillips (Ellis L.) Foundation, NH, 2093
Phillips Foundation, The, CA, 324
Phillips Foundation, The, MN, 1903
Phillips (The Frank) Foundation, Inc., OK, 3455
Phillips (The L. E.) Family Foundation, Inc., WI, 4367
Phillips (The L.E.) Charities, Inc., see 4367
Phillips Petroleum Foundation, Inc., OK, 3456
Phillips (Waite and Genevieve) Charitable Trust, NM, 2210
Phillips-Van Heusen Foundation, Inc., NY, 2828
Phipps Florida Foundation, FL, 755
Phipps (William H.) Foundation, MN, 1904

Physicians New Orleans Foundation, LA, 1377
Pick (The Albert), Jr. Fund, IL, 1119
Pick (Melitta S.) Charitable Trust, WI, 4368
Picker (James) Foundation, NM, 2211
Pickett & Hatcher Educational Fund, Inc., GA, 865
Pickford (Mary) Foundation, CA, 325
Pierce (Harold Whitworth) Charitable Trust, MA, 1599
Pilgrim Foundation, The, MA, 1600
Pillsbury Company Foundation, The, MN, 1905
Pillsbury Foundation, The, MO, 2007
Pilot Trust, CO, 472
Pinellas County Community Foundation, FL, 756
Pinewood Foundation, NY, 2829
Pinkerton Foundation, The, NY, 2830
Pioneer Fund, Inc., The, NY, 2831
Piper (Minnie Stevens) Foundation, TX, 4056
Pisces Foundation, The, NY, 2832
Pitcairn-Crabbe Foundation, PA, 3691
Piton Foundation, The, CO, 473
Pitts (William I. H. and Lula E.) Foundation, GA, 866
Pittsburgh Forgings Foundation, PA, 3692
Pittsburgh Foundation, The, PA, 3693
Pittsburgh National Foundation, PA, 3694
Pittway Corporation Charitable Foundation, IL, 1120
Pitzman Fund, MO, 2008
Plankenhorn (The Harry) Foundation, Inc., PA, 3695
Plant (Henry B.) Memorial Fund, Inc., NY, 2833
Plitt (Clarence Manger & Audrey Cordero) Trust, MD, 1447
Plough Foundation, TN, 3855
Plumsock Fund, The, IN, 1248
Pluta Family Foundation, Inc., NY, 2834
Plym Foundation, MI, 1758
Pneumo Foundation, MA, 1601
Poindexter Foundation, Inc., LA, 1378
Polaroid Foundation, Inc., MA, 1602
Polemanakos Foundation, The, TX, 4057
Police Foundation, DC, 676
Polinger (Howard and Geraldine) Foundation, Inc., MD, 1448
Polk Brothers Foundation, Inc., IL, 1121
Polk Foundation, The, OH, 3329
Polk Foundation, Inc., The, PA, 3696
Pollock (The William B.) II and Kathryn Challiss Pollock Foundation, OH, 3330
Polybill Foundation, Inc., WI, 4369
Poncin Scholarship Fund, WA, 4256
Pope Foundation, The, NY, 2835
Porter (James Hyde) Testamentary Trust, GA, 867
Post and Courier Foundation, SC, 3812
Post (The Marjorie Merriweather) Foundation, DC, 677
Post (Marjorie Merriweather) Foundation of D.C., DC, 678
Potlatch Foundation for Higher Education, CA, 326
Pott (Phenie R. & Herman T.) Foundation, MO, 2009
Pott (Robert and Elaine) Foundation, IN, 1249
Potter (The Justin and Valere) Foundation, TN, 3856
Potts and Sibley Foundation, TX, 4058
Potts Memorial Foundation, The, NY, 2836
Powell (The Charles Lee) Foundation, CA, 327
Powell Family Foundation, The, KS, 1323
Poynter Fund, The, FL, 757
PPG Industries Foundation, PA, 3697
Pratt (Arthur P.) and Jeanette Gladys Pratt Memorial Fund, CA, 328
Pratt-Northam Foundation, The, NY, 2837
Premier Industrial Foundation, OH, 3331
Pren-Hall Foundation, Inc., The, NY, 2838
Prentis (The Meyer and Anna) Family Foundation, Inc., MI, 1759
Prentiss (The Elisabeth Severance) Foundation, OH, 3332
Presser Foundation, The, PA, 3698
Presto Foundation, DE, 626
Preston (Evelyn) Trust, CT, 566
Price Foundation, Inc., OK, 3457
Price (Herschel C.) Educational Foundation, WV, 4288
Price (The John E. & Aliese) Foundation, Inc., FL, 758
Price (The Louis and Harold) Foundation, Inc., NY, 2839
Price (Lucien B. and Katherine E.) Foundation, Incorporated, CT, 567
Price (T. Rowe) Associates Foundation, MD, 1449
Price Waterhouse Foundation, NY, 2840

Prichard School, Board of Trustees of the, WV, 4289
Prince (Abbie Norman) Trust, IL, 1122
Prince Foundation, IL, 1123
Prince Foundation, MI, 1760
Pritzker Foundation, IL, 1124
Procter & Gamble Fund, The, OH, 3333
Propp (Morris and Anna) Sons Fund, Inc., NY, 2841
Prospect Hill Foundation, Inc., The, NY, 2842
Prouty (Olive Higgins) Foundation, Inc., MA, 1603
Providence Journal Charitable Foundation, RI, 3787
Prudential Foundation, The, NJ, 2167
Pryor (Myra Stafford) Charitable Trust, TX, 4059
Psychists, Inc., NJ, 2168
Public Welfare Foundation, Inc., DC, 679
Pullman (George M.) Educational Foundation, IL, 1125
Puritan-Bennett Foundation, KS, 1324
Puterbaugh Foundation, OK, 3458
Putnam Foundation, NH, 2094

Quaker Chemical Foundation, The, PA, 3699
Quaker Hill Foundation, The, NJ, 2169
Quaker Oats Foundation, The, IL, 1126
Quanex Foundation, The, TX, 4060
Quarrie (William F., Mabel E., and Margaret K.) Charitable Trust No. 2, IL, 1127
Quatman (George B.) Foundation, OH, 3334
Quinlan (The Elizabeth C.) Foundation, Inc., MN, 1906
Quivey--Bay State Foundation, NE, 2068

R and D Fund, Inc., The, NY, 2843
R & R Foundation, The, CA, 329
R. F. Foundation, IL, 1128
R G K Foundation, TX, 4061
R. P. Foundation, Inc., CA, 330
Rabb (Harry W.) Foundation, CO, 474
Racine Environmental Committee Educational Fund, WI, 4370
Radin Foundation, CA, 331
Ragan and King Charitable Foundation, GA, 868
Rahr Foundation, WI, 4371
Rainbow Fund, GA, 869
Rainforth Foundation, FL, 759
Rainier Bancorporation Foundation, WA, 4257
Raisler (The Harold K.) Foundation, Inc., NY, 2844
Raisler (The Robert K.) Foundation, Inc., NY, 2845
Ralston Purina Trust Fund, MO, 2010
Ram Island, Inc., MA, 1604
Ramapo Trust, NY, 2846
Ranney (P. K.) Foundation, OH, 3335
Ransom Fidelity Company, MI, 1761
Rapaporte (The Samuel), Jr. Foundation, RI, 3788
Rapp (Robert Glenn) Foundation, OK, 3459
Raskin (Hirsch and Braine) Foundation, Inc., NY, 2847
Raskob (The Bill) Foundation, Inc., DE, 627
Raskob Foundation for Catholic Activities, Inc., DE, 628
Ratner (Milton M.) Foundation, MI, 1762
Ratshesky (A. C.) Foundation, MA, 1605
Rauch Foundation, Inc., NY, 2848
Rauenhorst (Gerald) Family Foundation, MN, 1907
Ray Foundation, CO, 475
Raymond Educational Foundation, Inc., AZ, 43
Raymond Foundation, NY, 2849
Read (The Charles L.) Foundation, NY, 2850
Reade Industrial Fund, IL, 1129
Reader's Digest Foundation, NY, 2851
Rebsamen Fund, AR, 55
Record (George J.) School Foundation, OH, 3336
Red Clay Reservation, Inc., DE, 629
Red Wing Shoe Company Foundation, MN, 1908
Redman Foundation, TX, 4062
Redmond (John Charles & Kathryn S.) Foundation, PA, 3700
Redskin Foundation, Inc., see 1434
Reed (Philip D.) Foundation, Inc., NY, 2852
Reeves Brothers Foundation, Inc., The, NJ, 2170
Reeves Foundation, OH, 3337
Regenstein Foundation, The, IL, 1130
Rehmeyer (Herbert M.) Trust, PA, 3701
Reicher (Anne & Harry J.) Foundation, NY, 2853
Reidler Foundation, PA, 3702
Reilly Foundation, IN, 1250
Reily Foundation, LA, 1379

Reimann (Kurt P.) Foundation, Inc., NY, 2854
Reinberger Foundation, The, OH, 3338
Reinsch (Emerson G. & Dolores G.) Foundation, VA, 4192
Reiss (Jacob L.) Foundation, NY, 2855
Relations Foundation, IL, 1131
Reliance Electric Company Charitable, Scientific and Educational Trust, OH, 3339
Reliance Insurance Companies Foundation, PA, 3703
Rennebohm (The Oscar) Foundation, Inc., WI, 4372
Renner Foundation, OH, 3340
Republic Steel Corporation Educational and Charitable Trust, OH, 3341
Research Corporation, AZ, 44
Resnick (Louis and Mildred) Foundation, NY, 2856
Ress Family Foundation, RI, 3789
Retirement Research Foundation, The, IL, 1132
Revlon Foundation, Inc., NY, 2857
Revson (Charles H.) Foundation, Inc., NY, 2858
Rexnord Foundation Inc., WI, 4373
Reynolds (The Christopher) Foundation, Inc., NY, 2859
Reynolds (The Donald W.) Foundation, Inc., AR, 56
Reynolds (Edgar) Foundation, Inc., NE, 2069
Reynolds (Edith Grace) Estate Residuary Trust, NY, 2860
Reynolds (The J. B.) Foundation, MO, 2011
Reynolds (Kate B.) Charitable Trust, NC, 3123
Reynolds Metals Company Foundation, VA, 4193
Reynolds (Richard S.) Foundation, VA, 4194
Reynolds (Z. Smith) Foundation, Inc., NC, 3124
Rhoades (Otto L. and Hazel T.) Fund, IL, 1133
Rhode Island Foundation, The, RI, 3790
Ribakoff (Eugene J. and Corinne A.) Charitable Foundation, MA, 1606
Rice (The Albert W.) Charitable Foundation, MA, 1607
Rice (Ethel and Raymond F.) Foundation, KS, 1325
Rice Foundation, IL, 1134
Rice (Jacob & Sophie) Family Foundation, Inc., NY, 2861
Rich Foundation, Inc., The, GA, 870
Rich Foundation, Inc., NY, 2862
Richards (The Mabel Wilson) Scholarship Fund, CA, 332
Richardson (Anne S.) Fund, NY, 2863
Richardson (C. E.) Benevolent Foundation, VA, 4195
Richardson (Grace Jones) Trust, NC, 3125
Richardson (H. Smith) Charitable Trust, NC, 3126
Richardson (The Mary Lynn) Fund, NC, 3127
Richardson (Sid) Memorial Fund, TX, 4063
Richardson (Sid W.) Foundation, TX, 4064
Richardson (Smith) Foundation, Inc., NC, 3128
Richland County Foundation of Mansfield, Ohio, The, OH, 3342
Richman Brothers Foundation, OH, 3343
Richmond Community Foundation, Greater, VA, 4196
Richmond (The Frederick W.) Foundation, Inc., NY, 2864
Ridgefield Foundation, The, NY, 2865
Ridley (Jessie) Foundation, Inc., NY, 2866
Riegel Textile Corporation Foundation, SC, 3813
Riggs Benevolent Fund, AR, 57
Riley Foundation, The, MA, 1608
Rinker Companies Foundation, Inc., FL, 760
Rippel (Fannie E.) Foundation, NJ, 2171
Ritchie (The Charles E. and Mabel M.) Memorial Foundation, OH, 3344
Rittenhouse Foundation, PA, 3704
Ritter Foundation, Inc., The, NY, 2867
Ritter (The Gerald & May Ellen) Memorial Fund, NY, 2868
Ritter (May Ellen and Gerald) Foundation, NY, 2869
Ritter (R. A.) Foundation, FL, 761
River Branch Foundation, FL, 762
Rivers (Margaret) Fund, MN, 1909
Rixson (Oscar C.) Foundation, Inc., NC, 3129
Robbins & Myers Foundation, OH, 3345
Robert Alan Foundation, Inc., The, NY, 2870
Roberts (Dora) Foundation, TX, 4065
Robertshaw Controls Company Charitable and Educational Foundation, VA, 4197
Robertson Charitable & Educational Trust, WA, 4258
Robinson (Charles Nelson) Fund, CT, 568

Robinson (Donald & Sylvia) Family Foundation, PA, 3705
Robinson (E. O.) Mountain Fund, KY, 1351
Robinson Foundation, The, PA, 3706
Robison (The Ellis H. and Doris B.) Foundation, NY, 2871
Roblee (Joseph H. and Florence A.) Foundation, MO, 2012
Roche (Edward & Ellen) Relief Foundation, NY, 2872
Rochester Area Foundation, MN, 1910
Rochester Area Foundation, NY, 2873
Rochester Female Charitable Society, NY, 2874
Rochlin (Abraham and Sonia) Foundation, WI, 4374
Rock Island Refining Foundation, IN, 1251
Rockefeller Brothers Fund, NY, 2875
Rockefeller Family Fund, Inc., NY, 2876
Rockefeller Foundation, The, NY, 2877
Rockefeller (Winthrop) Foundation, AR, 58
Rockwell Foundation, The, PA, 3707
Rockwell Fund, Inc., TX, 4066
Rockwell International Corporation Trust, PA, 3708
Roddis (Hamilton) Foundation, Inc., WI, 4375
Roddy (Fred M.) Foundation, Inc., RI, 3791
Rodgers (Elizabeth Killam) Trust, MA, 1609
Rodman Foundation, The, MN, 1911
Roe Foundation, The, SC, 3814
Rogers Bros. Foundation, Inc., TX, 4067
Rogers Family Foundation, The, MA, 1610
Rogers (The Florence) Charitable Trust, NC, 3130
Rogers Foundation, NE, 2070
Rogers (Ralph B.) Foundation, TX, 4068
Rohatyn (Felix G.) Foundation, Inc., NY, 2878
Romerovski (Martin) Foundation, Inc., NY, 2879
Romill Foundation, NY, 2880
Roothbert Fund, Inc., The, NY, 2881
Roper Foundation, IL, 1135
RosaMary Foundation, The, LA, 1380
Roscoe Village Foundation, OH, 3346
Rose (Billy) Foundation, Inc., NY, 2882
Rosen (Joseph) Foundation, Inc., NY, 2883
Rosenberg Foundation, CA, 334
Rosenberg (The Henry and Ruth Blaustein) Foundation, Inc., MD, 1450
Rosenberg (Sunny and Abe) Foundation, Inc., NY, 2884
Rosenberg (William J. & Tina) Foundation, FL, 763
Rosenblatt Family Foundation, Inc., NY, 2885
Rosenhaus (The Sarah and Matthew) Peace Foundation, Inc., NJ, 2172
Rosenstiel Foundation, The, NY, 2886
Rosenthal (Benj.) Foundation, Inc., NY, 2887
Rosenthal (Benjamin J.) Foundation, IL, 1136
Rosenthal (The Ida and William) Foundation, Inc., NY, 2888
Rosenthal (The Richard and Hinda) Foundation, CT, 569
Rosenthal (The Samuel) Foundation, OH, 3347
Rosenwald (The William) Family Fund, Inc., NY, 2889
Ross (Arthur) Foundation, Inc., NY, 2890
Ross (The Dorothea Haus) Foundation, NY, 2891
Ross Foundation, The, AR, 59
Ross (The James & Edith) Foundation, OH, 3348
Ross (Walter G.) Foundation, DC, 680
Roth Family Foundation, CA, 335
Roth (Stanley & Elsie) Foundation, Inc., NJ, 2173
Rothschild (Robert and Maurine) Fund, Inc., NY, 2892
Rouback Family Foundation, KS, 1326
Roush Foundation, The, see 3232
Rowan (The Arch and Stella) Foundation, Inc., TX, 4069
Rowland Foundation, Inc., MA, 1611
Royal (May Mitchell) Foundation, MI, 1763
Ruan (John) Foundation Trust, IA, 1281
Ruben Family Foundation, NY, 2893
Rubenstein (Frank) Foundation, Inc., NY, 2894
Rubenstein (Lawrence J. and Anne) Charitable Foundation, MA, 1612
Rubin (Cele H. and William B.) Family Fund, Inc., MA, 1613
Rubin (Samuel) Foundation, Inc., NY, 2895
Rubinstein (Helena) Foundation, Inc., NY, 2896
Rudin Foundation, Inc., NY, 2897
Rudin (The Louis and Rachel) Foundation, Inc., NY, 2898

Simon (The Lucille Ellis) Foundation, CA, 364
Simon (Norton) Art Foundation, CA, 365
Simon (The Norton) Foundation, CA, 366
Simon (Norton), Inc. Foundation for Education, *see* 363
Simon (Norton), Inc. Museum of Art, *see* 365
Simon (Richard and Betty) Foundation, NJ, 2184
Simon (The Robert Ellis) Foundation, CA, 367
Simon (Sidney, Milton and Leoma) Foundation, NY, 2934
Simpson Foundation, The, MI, 1772
Simpson Foundation, The, SC, 3818
Sinaiko (Isaac D. and Ruth G.) Foundation, CA, 368
Singer Company Foundation, The, CT, 575
Sinsheimer (The Alexandrine and Alexander L.) Fund, NY, 2935
Siragusa Foundation, The, IL, 1153
Sizemore (Luther A.) Foundation, NM, 2212
Skaggs (L. J.) and Mary C. Skaggs Foundation, CA, 369
Skidmore, Owings & Merrill Foundation, IL, 1154
Skillman Foundation, The, MI, 1773
Skinner Foundation, WA, 4262
Skogmo (P. W.) Foundation, *see* 1845
Slade Foundation, Inc., The, NY, 2936
Slaughter (William E.), Jr. Foundation, Inc., MI, 1774
Slemp Foundation, The, VA, 4200
Slifka (Joseph & Sylvia) Foundation, NY, 2937
Sloan (Alfred P.) Foundation, NY, 2938
Smail Family Foundation, IL, 1155
Smart Family Foundation, NY, 2939
Smith (A. O.) Foundation, Inc., WI, 4380
Smith, Barney Foundation, The, NY, 2940
Smith (Bob and Vivian) Foundation, TX, 4082
Smith Charitable Trust, IL, 1156
Smith (The Emerson Sterling) Charitable Trust, OH, 3368
Smith (Ethel Sergeant Clark) Memorial Fund, PA, 3723
Smith Foundation, PA, 3724
Smith (George D.) Fund, Inc., CA, 370
Smith (Jack J.), Jr. Charitable Trust, OH, 3369
Smith (The Kelvin and Eleanor) Foundation, OH, 3370
Smith (M. W.), Jr. Foundation, AL, 20
Smith (The May and Stanley) Trust, CA, 371
Smith (Ralph L.) Foundation, MO, 2015
Smith (Richard and Susan) Foundation, MA, 1628
Smith (The Stanley) Horticultural Trust, CA, 372
Smith (W. W.) Charitable Trust, PA, 3725
Smithers (The Christopher D.) Foundation, Inc., NY, 2941
SmithKline Beckman Foundation, PA, 3726
Smock (Frank L. and Laura L.) Foundation, IN, 1253
Smoot Charitable Foundation, KS, 1328
Smyth (Marion C.) Trust, NH, 2095
Snayberger (Harry E. and Florence W.) Memorial Foundation, PA, 3727
Snelling (The Gustavus J. & Helen Crowe) Foundation, CA, 373
Snite (Fred B.) Foundation, IL, 1157
Snow (The John Ben) Foundation, Inc., NY, 2942
Snow (John Ben) Memorial Trust, NY, 2943
Snyder (Frost and Margaret) Foundation, WA, 4263
Snyder (The Valentine Perry) Fund, NY, 2944
Snyder (W. P.) Charitable Fund, PA, 3728
Society for the Increase of the Ministry, The, CT, 576
Soiland (Albert) Cancer Foundation, CA, 374
Solo Cup Foundation, IL, 1158
Somers (Byron H.) Foundation, IN, 1254
Sonat Foundation, Inc., The, AL, 21
Sonntag (Christine and Alfred) Foundation for Cancer Research, IL, 1159
Sony Corporation of America Foundation, Inc., NY, 2945
Sordoni Foundation, Inc., PA, 3729
Soref (Samuel M.) Charitable Trust, FL, 769
Sorensen (The Harvey L.) and Maud C. Sorensen Foundation, CA, 375
Soros (George) Charitable Trust, NY, 2946
Sosland Foundation, The, KS, 1329
Souers (Sidney W. and Sylvia N.) Charitable Trust, MO, 2016
South Branch Foundation, The, NJ, 2185

South Carolina National Charitable & Educational Foundation, SC, 3819
South Texas Charitable Foundation, TX, 4083
South Waite Foundation, The, OH, 3371
Southeast Banking Corporation Foundation, FL, 770
Southern Education Foundation, Inc., GA, 873
Southern Pacific Foundation, *see* 1138
Southland Foundation, TX, 4084
Southways Foundation, The, MN, 1913
Southwest Florida Community Foundation, Inc., The, FL, 771
Sovran Foundation, Inc., VA, 4201
Spang & Company Charitable Trust, PA, 3730
Spartanburg County Foundation, The, SC, 3820
Speas (John W. and Effie E.) Memorial, MO, 2017
Speas (Victor E.) Foundation, MO, 2018
Speech Foundation of America, TN, 3858
Spencer Foundation, The, IL, 1160
Sperry Corporation Foundation, NY, 2947
Spingold (Nate B. and Frances) Foundation, Inc., NY, 2948
Spokane Inland Empire Foundation, WA, 4264
Sprague (Caryll M. and Norman F.) Foundation, CA, 376
Sprague (The Otho S. A.) Memorial Institute, IL, 1161
Sprague (The Seth) Educational and Charitable Foundation, NY, 2949
Springmeier Foundation, MO, 2019
Springs (Elliott White) Foundation, Inc., SC, 3821
Springs (Frances Ley) Foundation, Inc., SC, 3822
SPS Foundation, PA, 3731
Square D Foundation, IL, 1162
St. Faith's House Foundation, NY, 2950
St. Louis Community Foundation, MO, 2020
St. Louis Post - Dispatch Foundation, MO, 2021
St. Marys Catholic Foundation, PA, 3732
Stabler (The Donald B. and Dorothy L.) Foundation, PA, 3733
Stackner Family Foundation, Inc., WI, 4381
Stackpole-Hall Foundation, PA, 3734
Staley (A. E.), Jr. Foundation, IL, 1163
Staley (Emma L.) Foundation, IL, 1164
Staley (Thomas F.) Foundation, FL, 772
Stamps (James L.) Foundation, Inc., CA, 377
Stanadyne Foundation, IL, 1165
Standard Brands Charitable, Scientific and Educational Foundation, The, NY, 2951
Standard Products Foundation, The, OH, 3372
Standex Foundation of New York, Inc., NH, 2096
Stanley (The Alix W.) Charitable Foundation, Inc., CT, 577
Stanley Foundation, The, IA, 1284
Stanley Works Foundation, The, CT, 578
Stanley-Timolat Foundation, Inc., The, NY, 2952
Stans Foundation, The, CA, 378
Stark County Foundation, The, OH, 3373
Stark (Donald A. and Jane C.) Charitable Trust, FL, 773
Stark (Nelda C. and H. J. Lutcher) Foundation, TX, 4085
Starling (Dorothy Richard) Foundation, TX, 4086
Starr (Anne and Jacob) Foundation, NY, 2953
Starr Foundation, The, NY, 2954
State Bank of Albany Foundation, *see* 2789
State Farm Companies Foundation, IL, 1166
State Street Boston Charitable Fund, MA, 1629
State-Record Company Foundation, The, SC, 3823
Statler Foundation, The, NY, 2955
Stauffer (John and Beverly) Foundation, CA, 379
Stauffer (John) Charitable Trust, CA, 380
Staunton Farm Foundation, PA, 3735
Steadley (Kent D. & Mary L.) Memorial Trust, MO, 2022
Stearns (Artemas W.) Trust, MA, 1630
Stearns Charitable Trust, MA, 1631
Stebbins Fund, Inc., The, NY, 2956
Steel (Marshall), Sr. Foundation, CA, 381
Steelcase Foundation, MI, 1775
Steele (Harry G.) Foundation, CA, 382
Steele-Reese Foundation, The, NY, 2957
Steiger (Albert) Memorial Fund, Inc., MA, 1632
Stein (Joseph F.) Foundation, Inc., NY, 2958
Stein (Louis) Foundation, PA, 3736
Steinbach (Ruth and Milton) Fund, Inc., NY, 2959
Steiner (Albert) Charitable Fund, GA, 874

Steinhagen (B. A. and Elinor) Benevolent Trust, TX, 4087
Steinhart Foundation, Inc., The, NE, 2071
Steinman (James Hale) Foundation, PA, 3737
Steinman (John Frederick) Foundation, PA, 3738
Steinsapir (Julius L. and Libbie B.) Family Foundation, PA, 3739
Stemmons Foundation, TX, 4088
Stephenson (The Edward C. and Hazel L.) Foundation, MI, 1776
Sterkel (Justine) Trust, OH, 3374
Stern (Alex) Family Foundation, ND, 3143
Stern Fund, NY, 2960
Stern (Irvin) Foundation, IL, 1167
Stern (Jerome L. and Jane) Foundation, Inc., NY, 2961
Stern (Max) Foundation, Inc., NJ, 2186
Stern (Sidney) Memorial Trust, CA, 383
Sternberger (Sigmund) Foundation, Inc., NC, 3132
Sterne-Elder Memorial Trust, CO, 480
Stevens (The Abbot and Dorothy H.) Foundation, MA, 1633
Stevens (Ida M.) Foundation, Inc., FL, 774
Stevens (J. P.) & Co., Inc. Foundation, NY, 2962
Stevens (John T.) Foundation, SC, 3824
Stevens (The Nathaniel and Elizabeth P.) Foundation, MA, 1634
Stewardship Foundation, The, WA, 4265
Stewart (Alexander and Margaret) Trust, DC, 682
Stewart (J. C.) Memorial Trust, MD, 1455
Stewart (Laura May) Trust, CA, 384
Stewart (Sarah A.) Foundation, MI, 1777
Stewart-Warner Foundation, IL, 1168
Stickelber Charitable Foundation, FL, 775
Stock (Paul) Foundation, WY, 4398
Stocker Foundation, The, OH, 3375
Stockham (The William H. and Kate F.) Foundation, Inc., AL, 22
Stoddard Charitable Trust, The, MA, 1635
Stokely (The William B.), Jr. Foundation, IN, 1255
Stokes (Lydia B.) Foundation, PA, 3740
Stollman Foundation, The, MI, 1778
Stolper-Wensink Foundation, Inc., WI, 4382
Stone (Albert H. & Reuben S.) Fund, MA, 1636
Stone Charitable Foundation, Inc., The, MA, 1637
Stone Foundation, Inc., The, CT, 579
Stone Foundation, Inc., IL, 1169
Stone (W. Clement and Jessie V.) Foundation, IL, 1170
Stonecutter Foundation, Inc., NC, 3133
Stoneman (Anne and David) Charitable Foundation, Inc., MA, 1638
Stony Wold - Herbert Fund, Inc., NY, 2963
Stop & Shop Charitable Foundation, The, MA, 1639
Storer (The George B.) Foundation, Inc., FL, 776
Storz (Robert Herman) Foundation, NE, 2072
Stott (The Louis L.) Foundation, PA, 3741
Stott (Robert L.) Foundation, Inc., NY, 2964
Stouffer Corporation Fund, The, OH, 3376
Stowe (Robert Lee), Jr. Foundation, Inc., NC, 3134
Strake Foundation, TX, 4089
Stranahan Foundation, OH, 3377
Stratfield Fund, CT, 580
Straub (Gertrude S.) Trust Estate, HI, 904
Straus (The Aaron) and Lillie Straus Foundation, Inc., MD, 1456
Straus (Eugene) Charitable Trust, TX, 4090
Straus (Martha Washington) - Harry H. Straus Foundation, Inc., NY, 2965
Straus (The Philip A. and Lynn) Foundation, Inc., NY, 2966
Strauss Foundation, PA, 3742
Strawbridge (Margaret Dorrance) Foundation, PA, 3743
Stride Rite Charitable Foundation, Inc., The, MA, 1640
Stroh Brewery Foundation, MI, 1779
Strong (Hattie M.) Foundation, DC, 683
Strosacker (The Charles J.) Foundation, MI, 1780
Stroud Foundation, The, PA, 3744
Stuart (The Edward C.) Foundation Incorporated, FL, 777
Stuart (Elbridge and Evelyn) Foundation, CA, 385
Stuart (Elbridge and Mary) Foundation, CA, 386
Stuart (Elbridge) Foundation, CA, 387
Stuart Foundation, Inc., The, NY, 2967
Stuart (Mary Horner) Foundation, CA, 388
Stubblefield, Estate of Joseph L., WA, 4266

Van Wert County Foundation, The, OH, 3396
VanAndel (Jay and Betty) Foundation, MI, 1788
Vanderbilt (R. T.) Trust, CT, 585
Vanneck-Bailey Foundation, The, NY, 3009
Vatterott Foundation, MO, 2035
Vaughn Foundation, The, TX, 4108
Vecellio (The Enrico) Family Foundation, Inc., WV, 4290
Vermeer Charitable Foundation, Inc., IA, 1286
Vermeer Foundation, The, see 1287
Vermeer Foundation Co., IA, 1287
Vernon (Miles Hodsdon) Fund, Inc., NY, 3010
Vetlesen (G. Unger) Foundation, NY, 3011
Vicksburg Foundation, MI, 1789
Victoria Foundation, Inc., NJ, 2197
Vidda Foundation, The, NY, 3012
Vidor (Doris Warner) Foundation, Inc., NY, 3013
Villa Banfi Foundation, The, NY, 3014
Villers Foundation, Inc., The, DC, 684
Vilter Foundation, Inc., WI, 4385
Vincent (Anna M.) Trust, PA, 3751
Vingo Trust II, MA, 1646
Vinmont Foundation, Inc., NY, 3015
Virginia Environmental Endowment, VA, 4214
Virlane Foundation, LA, 1384
Visceglia (Vincent and Anna) Foundation, see 2198
Visceglia-Summit Associates Foundation, NJ, 2198
VNB Foundation, Inc., AZ, 47
Voelkerding (Walter and Jean) Charitable Trust, MO, 2036
Vogler (The Laura B.) Foundation, Inc., NY, 3016
Vogt (The Henry) Foundation, Inc., KY, 1353
Vollbrecht (Frederick A.) Foundation, MI, 1790
Vollmer Foundation, Inc., NJ, 2199
Von der Ahe Foundation, CA, 412

Waddell (Donald Ware) Foundation, AZ, 48
Wade (The Elizabeth Firth) Endowment Fund, CA, 413
Waggoner (Crystelle) Charitable Trust, TX, 4109
Waggoner (The E. Paul and Helen Buck) Foundation, Inc., TX, 4110
Wagnalls Memorial, The, OH, 3397
Wagner (Edward) and George Hosser Scholarship Fund Trust, NH, 2097
Wahlert Foundation, IA, 1288
Wahlstrom Foundation, Inc., The, see 586
Wahlstrom-Johnson Foundation, Inc., The, CT, 586
Waldbaum (The I.) Family Foundation, Incorporated, NY, 3017
Walgreen Benefit Fund, IL, 1183
Walker (Alex C.) Educational and Charitable Foundation, PA, 3752
Walker (Archie D. and Bertha H.) Foundation, MN, 1920
Walker (The George Herbert) Foundation, NY, 3018
Walker (L. C. and Margaret) Foundation, MI, 1791
Walker (T. B.) Foundation, CA, 414
Walker (W. E.) Foundation, MS, 1939
Wallace (DeWitt) Fund, Inc., NY, 3019
Wallace Genetic Foundation, Inc., NY, 3020
Wallace (The George R.) Foundation, MA, 1647
Wallach (Miriam and Ira D.) Foundation, NY, 3021
Walsh (Blanche M.) Charity Trust, MA, 1648
Walter (Byron L.) Family Trust, WI, 4386
Walter (Jim) Corporation Foundation, FL, 788
Walthall (Marjorie T.) Perpetual Charitable Trust, TX, 4111
Walton (William S.) Charitable Trust, OR, 3505
Ward (The A. Montgomery) Foundation, IL, 1184
Ward (Harry E.) Foundation, GA, 879
Ward (Montgomery) Foundation, IL, 1185
Wardlaw (Gertrude and William C.) Fund, Inc., GA, 880
Ware Foundation, The, FL, 789
Warfield (Anna Emory) Memorial Fund, Inc., MD, 1461
Warnaco Fund, Inc., CT, 587
Warner (Albert and Bessie) Fund, NY, 3022
Warner Communications Foundation, Inc., NY, 3023
Warner (David) Foundation Trust, AL, 23
Warner Electric Foundation, IL, 1186
Warner (Lee and Rose) Foundation, MN, 1921
Warner (Marvin L.) Foundation, OH, 3398

Warner-Lambert Foundation, The, NJ, 2200
Warren Benevolent Fund, Inc., MA, 1649
Warren Charitable Trust, see 1623
Warren Charite, OK, 3468
Warren Foundation, The, PA, 3753
Warren Foundation, The, TX, 4112
Warren Memorial Foundation, ME, 1398
Warren (Riley J. and Lillian N.) and Beatrice W. Blanding Foundation, NY, 3024
Warren (The William K.) Foundation, OK, 3469
Washington, Inc., The Community Foundation of Greater, DC, 685
Washington Forrest Foundation, VA, 4215
Washington Foundation, The, TN, 3861
Washington Mutual Savings Bank Foundation, WA, 4269
Wasie Foundation, The, MN, 1922
Wasmer (The John C.) Foundation, OH, 3399
Wasserman (The David) Foundation, Inc., NY, 3025
Wasserman Foundation, CA, 415
Wasserman (George) Foundation, Inc., MD, 1462
Wasserman (Lucius P.) Foundation, Inc., NY, 3026
Waterbury Foundation, CT, 588
Waters Foundation, The, MA, 1650
Waters (Robert S.) Charitable Trust, PA, 3754
Watertown Foundation, Inc., NY, 3027
Watson (The John Jay and Eliza Jane) Foundation, see 2134
Watson (Louisa P.) Residuary Trust-Fund D, CA, 416
Watson (The Thomas J.) Foundation, RI, 3793
Watson (Walter E. and Caroline H.) Foundation, OH, 3400
Wattis (The Paul L. and Phyllis) Foundation, CA, 417
Watumull Foundation, HI, 906
Watumull (J.) Estate, Inc., HI, 907
Wean (The Raymond John) Foundation, OH, 3401
Weatherhead Foundation, The, NY, 3028
Weaver (The Gil and Dody) Foundation, TX, 4113
Webb (Del E.) Foundation, AZ, 49
Webb Foundation, MO, 2037
Webb (Susan Mott) Charitable Trust, AL, 24
Webb (Torrey H. and Dorothy K.) Educational and Charitable Trust, CA, 418
Webber (Richard H. and Eloise Jenks) Charitable Fund, see 1722
Weber (The Frederick E.) Charities Corporation, MA, 1651
Webster (Edwin S.) Foundation, MA, 1652
Weckbaugh (Eleanore Mullen) Foundation, CO, 484
Weezie Foundation, The, NY, 3029
Wegener (The Herman and Mary) Foundation, Inc., OK, 3470
Wegman (John F.) Foundation, Inc., NY, 3030
Wehadkee Foundation, Inc., GA, 881
Wehr (The Todd) Foundation, Inc., WI, 4387
Weiler (F.) Charity Fund, NY, 3031
Weiler Foundation, The, CA, 419
Weiler (Ralph J.) Foundation, see 419
Weinberg (Adolph and Etta) Foundation, CA, 420
Weinberg (The Harry and Jeanette) Foundation, Incorporated, MD, 1463
Weinberg (The John L.) Foundation, NY, 3032
Weiner Foundation, Inc., The, TX, 4114
Weingart Foundation, CA, 421
Weinstein (The Alex J.) Foundation, Inc., NY, 3033
Weinstein (J.) Foundation, Inc., NY, 3034
Weir Foundation Trust, DC, 686
Weisbrod (Robert and Mary) Foundation, PA, 3755
Weiss (The Clara) Fund, OH, 3402
Weiss (William E.) Foundation, Inc., WY, 4401
Welch (Carrie) Trust, WA, 4270
Welch (George T.) Testamentary Trust, WA, 4271
Welch (The Robert A.) Foundation, TX, 4115
Weld Foundation, MA, 1653
Welder (Rob and Bessie) Wildlife Foundation, TX, 4116
Welfare Foundation, Inc., DE, 632
Welk (Lawrence) Foundation, CA, 422
Weller Foundation, Inc., NE, 2075
Wellington Foundation, Inc., NY, 3035
Wellman (Arthur O. & Gullan M.) Foundation, MA, 1654
Wellman Foundation, The, MA, 1655

Wellman (S. K.) Foundation, The, OH, 3403
Wells (A. Z.) Foundation, WA, 4272
Wells Fargo Foundation, CA, 423
Wells (Fred W.) Trust Fund, MA, 1656
Wells (Lillian S.) Foundation, Inc., FL, 790
Wendt (The Margaret L.) Foundation, NY, 3036
Wenger (Henry E. and Consuelo S.) Foundation, Inc., MI, 1792
Wenner-Gren Foundation for Anthropological Research, Incorporated, NY, 3037
Werblow (Nina W.) Charitable Trust, NY, 3038
Werner (Clara and Spencer) Foundation, Inc., IL, 1187
Werthan Foundation, TN, 3862
Wessinger Foundation, OR, 3506
West Foundation, GA, 882
West Foundation, The, TX, 4117
West (J. M.) Texas Corporation, TX, 4118
West (James L. and Eunice) Charitable Trust, TX, 4119
West Point - Pepperell Foundation, Inc., GA, 883
West (W. F. & Blanche E.) Educational Fund, WA, 4273
Westend Foundation, Inc., TN, 3863
Western New York Foundation, The, NY, 3039
Westfield Foundation, The, NJ, 2201
Westinghouse Educational Foundation, PA, 3756
Westinghouse Electric Fund, PA, 3757
Westlake (James L. & Nellie M.) Scholarship Fund, MO, 2038
Westmoreland Coal Company and Penn Virginia Corporation Foundation, PA, 3758
Westport Fund, The, DC, 687
Westvaco Foundation Trust, NY, 3040
Wetterberg (The Harold) Foundation, NJ, 2202
Wexner Foundation, OH, 3404
Weyand (Louis F. and Florence H.) Charitable Trust, see 1923
Weyand (Louis F. and Florence H.) 1977 Charitable Trust, MN, 1923
Weyerhaeuser (The Charles A.) Memorial Foundation, MN, 1924
Weyerhaeuser Company Foundation, WA, 4274
Weyerhaeuser Foundation, Inc., MN, 1925
Weyerhaeuser (The Frederick and Margaret L.) Foundation, MN, 1926
Whalley Charitable Trust, PA, 3759
Wharton Foundation, Inc., The, WA, 4275
Wheat Foundation, VA, 4216
Wheeler Foundation, OR, 3507
Wheeler (Wilmot) Foundation, Inc., CT, 589
Wheeling-Pittsburgh Steel Foundation, Inc., PA, 3760
Wheelwright Scientific School, MA, 1657
Wheless Foundation, The, LA, 1385
Whirlpool Foundation, MI, 1793
Whitaker Foundation, The, PA, 3761
Whitaker (Mr. and Mrs. Lyndon C.) Charitable Foundation, MO, 2039
White Consolidated Industries, Inc. Foundation, OH, 3405
White Foundation, The, MI, 1794
White (G. R.) Trust, TX, 4120
White (Thomas H.) Charitable Trust, OH, 3406
White (Tom C.) Foundation, TX, 4121
White (W. P. and H. B.) Foundation, IL, 1188
Whitehall Foundation, Inc., FL, 791
Whitehead Charitable Foundation, The, CT, 590
Whitehead Foundation, The, NY, 3041
Whitehead (Joseph B.) Foundation, GA, 884
Whitehead (Lettie Pate) Foundation, Inc., GA, 885
Whiteley (The John and Elizabeth) Foundation, MI, 1795
Whitelight Foundation, The, CA, 424
Whitener Academy, NC, 3136
Whiteside (Robert B. and Sophia) Scholarship Fund, MN, 1927
Whitewater Foundation, OH, 3407
Whiting Foundation, The, MI, 1796
Whiting (Macauley and Helen Dow) Foundation, MI, 1797
Whiting (Mrs. Giles) Foundation, NY, 3042
Whitney Benefits, Inc., WY, 4402
Whitney (The Helen Hay) Foundation, NY, 3043
Whitney (Julia A.) Foundation, CT, 591
Whittell (Elia) Trust for Disabled Veterans of Foreign Wars, CA, 425

Whittenberger (Claude R. and Ethel B.) Foundation, ID, 916

Whittier Foundation, CA, 426

Wickes (Harvey Randall) Foundation, MI, 1798

Widener Memorial Foundation in Aid of Handicapped Children, PA, 3762

Widow's Society, CT, 592

Wieboldt Foundation, IL, 1189

Wiedemann (K. T.) Foundation, Inc., KS, 1330

Wien (Lawrence A.) Foundation, Inc., NY, 3044

Wikstrom Foundation, NY, 3045

Wilbur (Brayton) Foundation, CA, 427

Wilbur (Marguerite Eyer) Foundation, CA, 428

Wilcox (G. N.) Trust, HI, 908

Wilcox (S. W.) Trust, HI, 909

Wilder (Amherst H.) Foundation, MN, 1928

Wilder Foundation, The, FL, 792

Wildermuth (The E. F.) Foundation, OH, 3408

Wilf Family Foundation, NJ, 2203

Wilfred Fund, The, VA, 4217

Wilkie Brothers Foundation, IL, 1190

Willett (Howard L.) Foundation, Inc., IL, 1191

Williams (Arthur Ashley) Foundation, MA, 1658

Williams Companies Foundation, Incorporated, The, OK, 3471

Williams (Edna Sproull) Foundation, FL, 793

Williams Family Foundation, The, CO, 485

Williams (John C.) Charitable Trust, PA, 3763

Williams (Kemper and Leila) Foundation, LA, 1386

Williamsport Foundation, PA, 3764

Willits Foundation, The, NJ, 2204

Wilson (Elaine P. and Richard U.) Foundation, NY, 3046

Wilson (The Frances Wood) Foundation, Inc., GA, 886

Wilson (The H. W.) Foundation, Inc., NY, 3047

Wilson (John & Nevils) Foundation, TX, 4122

Wilson (Lula C.) Trust, MI, 1799

Wilson (Marie C. and Joseph C.) Foundation, NY, 3048

Wilson (Matilda R.) Fund, MI, 1800

Wilson (Ralph) Public Trust, TX, 4123

Wilson (Robert and Marillyn) Foundation, NY, 3049

Wilson (Robert T.) Foundation, AZ, 50

Wilson (Thomas) Sanitarium for Children of Baltimore City, MD, 1464

Windham Foundation, Inc., The, VT, 4151

Winfield Foundation, NY, 3050

Winkelman Brothers Apparel Foundation, MI, 1801

Winn-Dixie Stores Foundation, FL, 794

Winship Memorial Scholarship Foundation, MI, 1802

Winston (Harry) Research Foundation, Inc., NY, 3051

Winston (The Norman and Rosita) Foundation, Inc., NY, 3052

Winston-Salem Foundation, The, NC, 3137

Winter Park Community Trust Fund, FL, 795

Wisconsin Electric System Foundation, Inc., WI, 4388

Wisconsin Public Service Foundation, Inc., WI, 4389

Wiseda Foundation, The, TX, 4124

Wiseheart Foundation, Inc., FL, 796

Witco Chemical Corporation Foundation, see 3053

Witco Foundation, The, NY, 3053

Witte (John H.), Jr. Foundation, IA, 1289

Witter (Dean) Foundation, CA, 429

Wodecroft Foundation, OH, 3409

Wohlgemuth (Esther & Martin) Foundation, Inc., NY, 3054

Woldenberg (Dorothy & Malcolm) Foundation, LA, 1387

Wolf (Benjamin & Fredora) Foundation, PA, 3765

Wolf (Harry H.), Sr. & Jr. Foundation, IL, 1192

Wolf (Marvin and Estelle) Foundation, CO, 486

Wolfe Associates Inc., OH, 3410

Wolff (The John M.) Foundation, MO, 2040

Wolff (The Pauline Sterne) Memorial Foundation, TX, 4125

Wolfowski Foundation, Inc., NY, 3055

Wolfson (Erwin S. and Rose F.) Foundation, Inc., NY, 3056

Wolfson Family Foundation, Inc., The, FL, 797

Wolfson (Louis E.) Foundation, FL, 798

Wollenberg Foundation, The, CA, 430

Woltman (B. M.) Foundation, TX, 4126

Wolverine Charitable Foundation, MI, 1803

Woman's Seamen's Friend Society of Connecticut, CT, 593

Wood Kalb Foundation, NY, 3057

Wood (The W. P.) Charitable Trust, OK, 3472

Wood-Claeyssens Foundation, CA, 431

Woodland Foundation, Inc., NY, 3058

Wood-Rill Foundation, MN, 1929

Woods Charitable Fund, Inc., IL, 1193

Woods (James H.) Foundation, MO, 2041

Woods-Greer Foundation, TN, 3864

Woodson (The Aytchmonde) Foundation, Inc., WI, 4390

Woodson (Margaret C.) Foundation, Inc., NC, 3138

Woodstock Foundation, Inc., DE, 633

Woodward Governor Company Charitable Trust, CO, 487

Wooley-Clifford Foundation, The, NY, 3059

Woolf (William C.) Foundation, LA, 1388

Woolley (The Vasser) Foundation, Inc., GA, 887

Worcester Community Foundation, Inc., Greater, MA, 1659

Wortham Foundation, The, TX, 4127

Wouk (Abe) Foundation, Inc., DC, 688

Wrape Family Charitable Trust, The, AR, 62

Wray (The Floyd L.) Memorial Foundation, Inc., FL, 799

Wright Foundation, OH, 3411

Wright (Lola) Foundation, Inc., TX, 4128

Wrightson-Ramsing Foundation, Inc., NY, 3060

Wuliger Foundation, Inc., The, OH, 3412

Wunsch Foundation, Inc., NY, 3061

Wurlitzer (The Farny R.) Foundation, IL, 1194

Wurlitzer (The Helene) Foundation of New Mexico, NM, 2213

Wurts (Henrietta Tower) Memorial, PA, 3766

Wye Institute, Inc., MD, 1465

Wyman Youth Trust, WA, 4276

Wyman-Gordon Foundation, MA, 1660

Wyomissing Foundation, Inc., PA, 3767

Xerox Foundation, The, CT, 594

XTEK Foundation, OH, 3413

Yablick Charities, Inc., FL, 800

Yarway Foundation, PA, 3768

Yassenoff (The Leo) Foundation, OH, 3414

Yellow Freight System Foundation, MO, 2042

Yorkin Foundation, The, CA, 432

Young & Rubicam Foundation, The, NY, 3062

Young (Hugo H. and Mabel B.) Foundation, OH, 3415

Young (Irvin L.) Foundation, Inc., WI, 4391

Young (The R. A.) Foundation, OK, 3473

Youngstown Foundation, The, OH, 3416

Younkers Foundation, Inc., IA, 1290

Youth Foundation, Inc., NY, 3063

Youth Foundation, Inc., WI, 4392

Youth Foundation of America, The, MI, 1804

Youths' Friends Association, Inc., NJ, 2205

Yulman (Morton & Helen) Trust, NY, 3064

Zacharia (Isaac Herman) Foundation, Inc., NY, 3065

Zale Foundation, The, TX, 4129

Zarkin (Charles) Memorial Foundation, Inc., NY, 3066

Zayre Foundation, Inc., MA, 1661

Zellerbach Family Fund, The, CA, 433

Zemurray Foundation, LA, 1389

Ziegler (The E. Matilda) Foundation for the Blind, Inc., CT, 595

Ziegler Foundation, Inc., The, WI, 4393

Ziemann Foundation, Inc., WI, 4394

Zigler (Fred B. and Ruth B.) Foundation, LA, 1390

Zilkha Foundation, Inc., The, NY, 3067

Zimmerman Foundation, The, TN, 3865

Zimmerman (Hans and Clara Davis) Foundation, HI, 910

Zimmermann (Marie and John) Fund, Inc., NY, 3068

Zimtbaum (Arthur) Foundation, Inc., NY, 3069

Zink (John Steele) Foundation, OK, 3474

Zion Research Foundation, see 1524

Zlinkoff (Sergei S.) Fund for Medical Research and Education, Inc., NY, 3070